A Word About Cumulative Indexes in

Contemporary Authors

The cumulative index that would have appeared in this volume under the usual schedule will appear instead in the next volume, 97-100, which is scheduled to be published late in 1980.

Until the cumulative index appears in volume 97-100, users should consult the cumulative index bound into CA 85-88.

Contemporary Authors

Contemporary Authors

A Bio-Bibliographical Guide to
Current Writers in Fiction, General Nonfiction,
Poetry, Journalism, Drama, Motion Pictures,
Television, and Other Fields

FRANCES C. LOCHER
Editor

volumes 93-96

GALE RESEARCH COMPANY • THE BOOK TOWER • DETROIT, MICHIGAN 48226

CONTEMPORARY AUTHORS

Published by
Gale Research Company, Book Tower, Detroit, Michigan 48226
Each Year's Volumes Are Revised About Five Years Later

Frederick G. Ruffner, *Publisher*   James M. Ethridge, *Editorial Director*

Christine Nasso, *General Editor, Contemporary Authors*

Frances C. Locher, *Editor, Original Volumes*

Ann F. Ponikvar, *Associate Editor*
Anne M. Guerrini, B. Hal May, Kathleen Ceton Newman,
Nancy M. Rusin, Les Stone, David Versical,
and Martha G. Winkel, *Assistant Editors*
Denise M. Cloutier, Marie Evans, Kim Jakubiak,
Michaelene F. Pepera, Norma Sawaya, Shirley Seip,
and Laurie M. Serwatowski, *Editorial Assistants*

Alan E. Abrams and Adele Sarkissian, *Contributing Editors*
Martha J. Abele, Andrea Geffner, Arlene True,
and Benjamin True, *Sketchwriters*
John F. Baker, Peter Benjaminson, Jean W. Ross,
and Richard E. Ziegfeld, *Interviewers*

Eunice Bergin, *Copy Editor*
Michaeline Nowinski, *Production Director*

Special recognition is given to the staffs of
Journalist Biographies Master Index
and
Young People's Literature Department

Copyright © 1980 by
GALE RESEARCH COMPANY

ISBN 0-8103-0049-4

Preface

The more than 1,300 entries in *Contemporary Authors,* Volumes 93-96, bring to more than 60,000 the number of authors, either living or deceased since 1960, now represented in the *Contemporary Authors* series. *CA* includes nontechnical writers in all genres—fiction, nonfiction, poetry, drama, etc.—whose books are issued by commercial, risk publishers or by university presses. Authors of books published only by known vanity or author-subsidized firms are ordinarily not included. Since native language and nationality have no bearing on inclusion in *CA,* authors who write in languages other than English are included in *CA* if their works have been published in the United States or translated into English.

Although *CA* focuses primarily on authors of published books, the series also encompasses prominent persons in communications: newspaper and television reporters and correspondents, columnists, newspaper and periodical editors, photojournalists, syndicated cartoonists, screenwriters, television scriptwriters, and other media people.

No charge or obligation is attached to a *CA* listing. Authors are included in the series solely on the basis of the above criteria and their interest to *CA* users.

Compilation Methods

The editors make every effort to secure information directly from the authors through questionnaires and personal correspondence. If authors of special interest to *CA* users are deceased or fail to reply to requests for information, material is gathered from other reliable sources. Biographical dictionaries are checked (a task made easier through the use of Gale's *Biographical Dictionaries Master Index, Author Biographies Master Index,* and other volumes in the "Gale Biographical Index Series"), as are bibliographical sources, such as *Cumulative Book Index* and *The National Union Catalog.* Published interviews, feature stories, and book reviews are examined, and often material is supplied by the authors' publishers. All sketches, whether prepared from questionnaires or through extensive research, are sent to the authors for review prior to publication.

The value of such cooperation by the individual authors listed in *CA* is very great. Not only do most authors check manuscripts of their entries, but some often work even more closely with *CA*'s editors, both to ensure the completeness of their listings and to provide incisive sidelights—comments on their lives and writings, personal philosophies, etc. Among the authors in this volume who have amplified their sketches with lengthy sidelights are Judith Gwyn Brown, artist and juvenile author, who reveals her thoughts about art and book illustrating; and Burne Hogarth, illustrator of the famed "Tarzan" comic strip for more than a decade, who describes his vision of our technological society.

Equally extensive efforts go into the compilation of full-length entries on deceased authors of current interest to *CA* readers. This volume contains listings on, among others, H.E. Bates, Marvella Bayh, Pablo Casals, Yasunari Kawabata, Freda Kirchwey, Charles A. Lindbergh, Charles Mingus, Laszlo Nemeth, Edwin O'Connor, and Pier Paolo Pasolini.

In addition to the individuals mentioned above, numerous other authors and media people of particular interest are sketched in this volume, such as Lauren Bacall, Frank Blair, Kenneth Clark, Rainer Werner Fassbinder, Jean-Luc Godard, Chaim Grade, William X. Kienzle, Harry Kullman, Richard E. Leakey, Margaret Leech, William K. Marimow, Johnny Miller, Stan Musial, Hans Erich Nossack, Margaret Osmer, Reginald Leslie Ottley, Morley Safer, Patti Smith, Hans-Juergen Syberberg, Strobe Talbott, Margaret Trudeau, Orson Welles, and Wim Wenders.

New Feature: Exclusive Interviews

Beginning with Volumes 89-92, *Contemporary Authors* is including exclusive new primary information. The new section of the sketch headed *CA INTERVIEWS THE AUTHOR* presents a never-before-published conversation with the author, prepared specifically for *CA.* Previously, authors' remarks to *CA*'s editors were reserved for the Sidelights section of their sketches. While no limitations are placed on the length of such material, the editors believed that readers might want even more comment from some of *CA*'s authors.

The new interview feature, with its give-and-take format, provides such additional commentary. Through *CA*'s interviewers, the user is given the opportunity to learn the authors' thoughts, in depth, about their craft. Subjects chosen for interviews are authors who the editors feel hold special interest for *CA*'s readers, and their remarks are a further source of useful primary material.

Authors and journalists in this volume whose sketches include interviews are Vicki Baum, Edward Dorn, David Gerrold, Charles Gordone, John Shively Knight, William Loeb, Peter Maas, W.H. Manville, William Maxwell, Richard B. Sewall, and William Wharton.

Obituary Notices Make *CA* Timely and Comprehensive

To be as timely and comprehensive as possible, *CA* publishes obituary notices on deceased authors within the scope of the series. These notices provide date and place of birth and death, highlight the author's career and writings, and list other sources where additional biographical information and obituaries may be found. To distinguish them from full-length sketches, obituaries are identified with the heading *OBITUARY NOTICE*.

CA includes obituary notices both for authors who already have full-length sketches in earlier *CA* volumes, thus effectively completing the sketches, and for authors not yet sketched in the series. Eighteen percent of the obituary notices contained in this volume are for authors with listings already in *CA*. Deceased authors of special interest presently represented in the series only by obituary notices are scheduled for full-length sketch treatment in forthcoming *CA* volumes.

Cumulative Index Should Always Be Consulted

Since *CA* is a multi-volume series that does not repeat author entries from volume to volume, the most recent *CA* cumulative index should always be consulted to locate an individual author's listing. Each new volume contains authors not previously included in the series and is revised approximately five years after its original publication. The cumulative index indicates the original or revised volume in which an author appears. Authors removed from the revision cycle and placed in the *CA Permanent Series* are listed in the index as having appeared in specific original volumes of *CA* (for the benefit of those who do not hold *Permanent Series* volumes), *and* as having their finally revised sketches in a specific *Permanent Series* volume.

For the convenience of *CA* users, the *CA* cumulative index also includes references to all entries in three related Gale series—*Contemporary Literary Criticism,* which is devoted entirely to current criticism of major authors, poets, and playwrights, *Something About the Author,* a series of heavily illustrated sketches on juvenile authors and illustrators, and *Authors in the News,* a compilation of news stories and feature articles from American newspapers and magazines covering writers and other members of the communications media.

As always, suggestions from users about any aspect of *CA* will be welcomed.

The cumulative index that would have appeared in this volume under the usual schedule will appear instead in the next volume, 97-100, which is scheduled to be published late in 1980.

CONTEMPORARY
AUTHORS

Indicates that a listing has been compiled from secondary sources believed to be reliable, but has not been personally verified for this edition by the author sketched.

A

AARONS, Edward S(idney) 1916-1975
(Paul Ayres, Edward Ronns)

PERSONAL: Born in 1916, in Philadelphia, Pa.; died June 16, 1975, in New Milford, Conn.; married Ruth Ives (deceased); married Grace Dyer. *Education:* Earned degree at Columbia University. *Residence:* Washington, Conn.

CAREER: Mystery and short story writer. Worked variously as newspaper reporter, millhand, salesman, and fisherman. *Military service:* U.S. Coast Guard, beginning in 1941; became chief petty officer. *Member:* Mystery Writers of America.

WRITINGS—"Assignment" series; published by Fawcett, except as noted: *Assignment to Disaster,* 1955; *Assignment: Suicide,* 1956; . . . *Budapest,* 1957; . . . *Angelina,* 1958; . . . *Madeleine,* 1958; . . . *Karachi,* 1962; . . . *The Girl in the Gondola,* 1964; . . . *Palermo,* c. 1966; . . . *Zoraya,* Jenkins, 1967, Fawcett, 1972; . . . *Cairo Dancers,* 1970; . . . *School for Spys,* 1970; . . . *Mara Tirana,* 1971; . . . *Bangkok,* 1972; . . . *Carlotta Cortez,* 1972; . . . *Golden Girl,* 1972; . . . *Star Stealers,* 1972; . . . *Cong Hai Kill,* 1973; . . . *Maltese Maiden,* 1973; . . . *Nuclear Nude,* 1973; . . . *Silver Scorpion,* 1973; . . . *Sorrento Siren,* 1973; . . . *Tokyo,* 1973; . . . *Treason,* 1973; . . . *Ceylon,* 1974; . . . *Stella Marni,* 1974; . . . *Sumatra,* 1974; . . . *White Rajah,* 1974; . . . *Ankara,* 1975; . . . *Black Gold,* 1975; . . . *Black Viking,* 1975; . . . *Helene,* 1975; . . . *Lili Lamris,* 1975; . . . *Lowlands,* 1975; . . . *Peking,* 1975; . . . *Quayle Question,* 1975; . . . *Afghan Dragon,* 1976; . . . *Manchurian Doll,* 1976; . . . *Amazon Queen,* 1977; . . . *Moon Girl,* 1977; . . . *Sulu Sea,* 1977; . . . *Unicorn,* 1978.

Other: *Terror in the Town,* McKay, 1947; *Nightmare,* McKay, 1948; (under pseudonym Paul Ayres) *Dead Heat: A Crime Photographer Mystery,* Bell Publishing, 1950; *Girl on the Run,* Fawcett, 1954; *Hell to Eternity,* Fawcett, c. 1960; *Say it With Murder,* 3rd edition, Manor, 1971; *The Decoy,* Fawcett, 1972; *Don't Cry Beloved,* Fawcett, 1972; *The Net,* Manor, 1972; *Escape to Love,* Fawcett, 1973; *The Glass Cage,* Manor, 1973; *Passage to Terror,* Fawcett, 1973; *The Art Studio Murders,* Manor, 1975. Also author of *Dark Destiny,* published by Manor.

Under pseudonym Edward Ronns: *Death in a Lighthouse,* Phoenix Press, c. 1938; *Murder Money,* Phoenix Press, c. 1938; *The Corpse Hangs High,* Phoenix Press, c. 1939; *No Place to Live,* McKay, 1947; *Gift of Death: A Jerry Benedict Novel,* McKay, 1948; *Catspaw Ordeal,* Fawcett, 1950; *Dark Memory,* Quinn, 1950; *Million Dollar Murder,* Fawcett, 1950; *State Department Murders,* Fawcett, 1950; *I Can't Stop Running,* Fawcett, 1951; *Point of Peril,* Bouregy, 1956; *Death Is My Shadow,* Mystery House, 1957, 2nd edition, Manor, 1975.

SIDELIGHTS: Edward Aarons's "Assignment" spy novels have sold over 23 million copies, and have been translated into seventeen languages. Sam Durell, a fictional agent for the Central Intelligence Agency (CIA), is the main character.

OBITUARIES: New York Times, June 20, 1975; *Washington Post,* June 21, 1975.*

*   *   *

ABBOTT, George 1887-

PERSONAL: Born June 25, 1887, in Forestville, N.Y.; son of George Burwell (a businessman) and Mary (McLaury) Abbott; married Ednah Levis, 1914 (died, 1930); married Mary Sinclair, 1946 (divorced, 1951); children: (first marriage) Judith Ann. *Education:* University of Rochester, B.A., 1911; graduate study at Harvard University, 1911-12. *Address:* c/o Playboy Press, 747 Third Ave., New York, N.Y. 10017.

CAREER: Actor, playwright, director, producer. Actor in plays, including "The Misleading Lady," 1913, "Daddies," 1918, and "Hellbent for Heaven," 1924, and in television productions, including "The Skin of Our Teeth," 1955; director of plays, including "Chicago," 1926, "Twentieth Century," 1932, "Brown Sugar," 1937, "Pal Joey," 1940, "Sweet Charity," 1942, "On the Town," 1944, "Call Me Madam," 1950, "A Funny Thing Happened on the Way to the Forum," 1962, and "The Education of H*Y*M*A*N K*A*P*L*A*N," 1968. Director of several films, including "All Quiet on the Western Front," 1930. Founder with Philip Dunning of Abbott-Dunning, Inc., 1931-34.

AWARDS, HONORS: Award from *Boston Globe,* 1912, for "Man in the Manhole"; Donaldson Award, 1946, for direction of "Billion Dollar Baby," and 1948, for "High Button Shoes"; New York Drama Critics Circle award for best musical, Antoinette Perry (Tony) Award, and Donaldson Award, all 1953, all for "Wonderful Town"; Antoinette Perry Award and Donaldson Award, both 1955, both for "The Pajama Game"; Antoinette Perry Award, 1956, for "Damn Yankees"; Pulitzer Prize in drama, 1960, Antoinette Perry Award, 1960, and New York Drama Critics Circle award, 1961, all for "Fiorello!"; honorary doctorate from University of Rochester, 1961; Outer Circle award for "most effective individual contribution," 1962, and Antoinette Perry Award for best director, 1963, both for "A Funny Thing Happened on the Way to the Forum"; Society of Stage Directors award of merit, 1968; elected to Theater Hall of Fame and Museum, New York City, 1972.

WRITINGS—Plays: "Head of the Family" (one-act), first produced in Cambridge, Mass., 1912; "Man in the Manhole" (one-act), first produced in Boston, Mass., at Bijou Art Theatre, 1912; (with James Gleason) *The Fall Guy* (three-act; first produced in New York City at Eltinge Theatre, March 10, 1925), Samuel French, 1928; (with Winchell Smith) *A Holy Terror: A None-Too-Serious Drama* (first produced in New York City at George M. Cohan Theatre, September 28, 1925), Samuel French, 1926; (with John V. A. Weaver; and director) *Love 'Em and Leave 'Em* (three-act; first produced in New York City at Harris Theatre, February 3, 1926), Samuel French, 1926; (with Pearl Franklin) "Cowboy Crazy," first produced in New York City, 1926.

Other plays; all as director: (With Philip Dunning) *Broadway* (first produced on Broadway at Broadhurst Theatre, September 16, 1926), Doran, 1927; (with Dana Burnett) *Four Walls* (first produced on Broadway at John Golden Theatre, September 19, 1927), Samuel French, 1928; (with Ann Preston Bridgers) *Coquette* (three-act; first produced in New York City at Maxine Elliott's Theatre, November 8, 1927), Longmans, Green, 1928; (with Edward A. Paramore, Jr., and Hyatt Daab) "Ringside," first produced on Broadway at Broadhurst Theatre, August 29, 1928.

(With S. K. Lauren) "Those We Love," first produced on Broadway at John Golden Theatre, February 19, 1930; (with Dunning) "Lilly Turner," first produced on Broadway at Morosco Theatre, September 19, 1932; (with Leon Abrams) "Heat Lightning," first produced on Broadway at Booth Theatre, September 15, 1933; "Ladies' Money," first produced on Broadway at Ethel Barrymore Theatre, November 1, 1934; "Page Miss Glory," first produced in New York City at Mansfield Theatre, November 27, 1934; (with John Cecil Holm) *Three Men on a Horse* (first produced on Broadway at the Playhouse, January 30, 1935), Samuel French, 1935; "On Your Toes," first produced on Broadway at Imperial Theatre, April 11, 1936; "Sweet River" (adapted from the novel, *Uncle Tom's Cabin*, by Harriet Beecher Stowe), first produced in New York City at Fifty-First Street Theatre, October 28, 1936; *The Boys From Syracuse* (adapted from the play, *A Comedy of Errors*, by William Shakespeare; first produced on Broadway at Alvin Theatre, November 23, 1938), Chappell, 1965.

(With Holm) "Best Foot Forward," first produced on Broadway at Ethel Barrymore Theatre, October 1, 1941; (with George Marion, Jr.) "Beat the Band," first produced on Broadway at Forty-Sixth Street Theatre, October 14, 1942; *Where's Charley?* (adapted from the play, *Charley's Aunt*, by Brandon Thomas; first produced on Broadway at St. James Theatre, October 11, 1948), Samuel French, 1965; (with Betty Smith) "A Tree Grows in Brooklyn" (adapted from the novel by Betty Smith), first produced on Broadway at Alvin Theatre, April 19, 1951; (with Richard Bissell) *The Pajama Game* (adapted from the novel, *7½ Cents*, by Bissell; first produced on Broadway at St. James Theatre, May 13, 1954), Random House, 1954; (with Douglass Wallop) *Damn Yankees* (adapted from the novel, *The Year the Yankees Lost the Pennant*, by Wallop; first produced on Broadway at Forty-Sixth Street Theatre, May 5, 1955), Random

House, 1956; *New Girl in Town* (adapted from the play, *Anna Christie*, by Eugene O'Neill; first produced on Broadway at Forty-Sixth Street Theatre, May 14, 1957), Random House, 1958; (with Jerome Weidman) *Fiorello!* (first produced on Broadway at Broadhurst Theatre, November 23, 1959), Random House, 1960.

(With Weidman) *Tenderloin* (adapted from the work of Samuel Hopkins Adams; first produced on Broadway at Forty-Sixth Street Theatre, October 17, 1960), Random House, 1961; (with Robert Russell) "Flora, the Red Menace," first produced on Broadway at Alvin Theatre, May 11, 1965; (with Guy Bolton) "Anya" (adapted from the play, *Anastasia*, by Marcelle Maurette and Bolton), first produced on Broadway at Ziegfield Theatre, November 29, 1965; "Music Is" (adapted from the play, *Twelfth Night*, by Shakespeare), first produced in Seattle, Wash., 1976.

Other: *Mister Abbott* (autobiography), Random House, 1963; *Tryout* (novel), Playboy Press, 1979.

Screenplays; and director: "The Pajama Game," Warner Brothers, 1957; "Damn Yankees," Warner Brothers, 1958.

SIDELIGHTS: George Abbott has been so successful as a Broadway producer and director that he has often been described as "the sole possessor of a superhuman faculty called 'the Abbott Touch.'" In a 1970 interview for *Cue* magazine, however, he denied such miraculous theatrical power. "I never knew what they were talking about when people wrote about the Abbott Touch," he insisted. "I direct for economy. I strip a show to its essentials and then do it, that's all." Then he added, "I have not been infallible, you know."

In his autobiography, *Mister Abbott,* he freely discussed not only his triumphs but his failures, professional as well as personal. The book, which many critics described as "candid," is a detailed account of the author's childhood, his education in a Nebraskan military school and at the University of Rochester, and his participation in Professor Baker's famous theatre workshop at Harvard University. Some critics objected to the frankness with which he portrayed his adult personal life. Lenore Philbin, for example, accused him of "shocking his reader by revealing too much and reporting in detail the unfortunate results of his personal promiscuity."

Still, critics generally agreed on the merit of Abbott's account of the theatrical world. Claire McGlinchee wrote that "the worthwhile parts of the book—and they are excellent—are those that define for present-day aspirants to theater fame, or the sidelines devotees of this art, such things as the nature of stage-fright or the types of directors who may be met at auditions." Calling Abbott the personification of the term "man of the theater," George Oppenheimer concluded that in his autobiography the author added to his "prodigious record with an extremely well-written, honest, and absorbing book."

Abbott's *Tryout* began as a play but evolved into a novel. In an article in *Library Journal*, Abbott discussed his first and only novel: "My novel has no message, nor do I have any message. *Tryout* is about people and situations. It is, I think what is called a well-made story, with a beginning, a middle and an end. It attempts to deal truthfully with situations in the theater and in Palm Beach."

In addition to Abbott's other honors, the Fifty-Fourth Street Theatre in New York City was renamed the George Abbott Theatre in 1965.

BIOGRAPHICAL/CRITICAL SOURCES: Theatre Arts,

February, 1936; *Literary Digest,* August 15, 1936; *Newsweek,* November 1, 1937; *Time,* November 1, 1937; September 26, 1938; *Fortune,* February, 1938; *Life,* January 18, 1960, December 13, 1963; *New York Post Magazine,* May 20, 1962; *New York Times,* June 25, 1962; *New York Herald Tribune,* July 1, 1962, July 5, 1964; *Saturday Review,* November 23, 1963; *New York Times Book Review,* November 24, 1963; *Best Sellers,* December 15, 1963; *America,* January 11, 1964; *Cue,* January 10, 1970; *Library Journal,* June 15, 1979.*

*   *   *

ABBS, Peter 1942-

PERSONAL: Born February 22, 1942, in Norfolk, England; son of Eric (a coach driver) and Mary (a shop assistant; maiden name, Bullock) Abbs; married Barbara Beazeley, June 29, 1963; children: Annabel, Miranda, Theodore. *Education:* University of Bristol, B.A. (with honors), 1965. *Home:* 38 Prince Edward Rd., Lewes, Sussex, England. *Office:* Education Development Building, University of Sussex, Falmer, Brighton, Sussex BN1 9RG, England.

CAREER: Teacher of English at high schools in Bristol, England, 1966-70; free-lance writer, 1970-76; University of Sussex, Brighton, England, lecturer in education, 1976—.

WRITINGS: English for Diversity, Heinemann, 1969; *Autobiography in Education,* Heinemann, 1974; *The Black Rainbow* (essays), Heinemann, 1975; *Root and Blossom* (essays), Heinemann, 1976; (with Graham Carey) *Proposal for a New College,* Heinemann, 1977; *For Man and Islands* (poems), Tern Press, 1978; *Reclamations* (on the arts in education), Heinemann, 1979; *Songs of a New Taliesin* (poems), Tern Press, 1979. Editor of *Tract.*

WORK IN PROGRESS: A book defending the place of English as one of the arts in education, publication by Heinemann expected in 1980; poems.

SIDELIGHTS: Abbs comments: "I edit a quarterly journal which is unsupported by government grants or advertising. Its aim is to draw into a living unity the best ideas of our times. My books on education and culture are attempts to defend the crucial place of feeling and imagination in human life. My poems, I hope, define at a more intimate level many of the themes tackled in my work on culture and society."

*   *   *

ABDULLAHI, Guda 1946-

PERSONAL: Born April 7, 1946, in Garko, Nigeria; son of Abubakar and Uwami Abdullahi; married Saadatu Mohammed, June 11, 1978. *Education:* Abdullahi Bayero College (now Bayero University), B.A., 1972; University of London, M.A., 1975. *Religion:* Islam. *Office:* Ministry of Education, Kano, Nigeria.

CAREER: Ministry of Education, Kano, Nigeria, teacher, 1972-73, planner, 1973-74, 1975—, school principal, 1975-77, administrator, 1977—.

WRITINGS: (With Michael Crowder) *Nigeria: An Introduction to Its History,* Longman, 1979. Also author of *A History of West Africa, 1000 A.D. to the Present* (with Crowder), and *The Golden Voice of Africa: A Biography of the Life and Times of Nigeria's Abubakar Tafawa Balewa.*

AVOCATIONAL INTERESTS: Travel (Europe, Africa, the Middle East).

ABELLA, Alex 1950-

PERSONAL: Surname is pronounced Ah-*beh*-ya; born November 8, 1950, in Havana, Cuba; came to the United States in 1961, naturalized citizen, 1972; son of Lorenzo P. (a poet) and Elvira (Alvarez) Abella; married, 1976. *Education:* Columbia University, B.A., 1972. *Residence:* San Francisco, Calif. *Agent:* Michael Larsen, Michael Larsen/Elizabeth Pomada, 1029 Jones St., San Francisco, Calif. 94109. *Office:* KTVU-TV, 1 Jack London Sq., Oakland, Calif.

CAREER: Ticketron Entertainment, New York City, general manager, assistant editor, restaurant reviewer, and feature writer, 1972-74; Gurtman, Murtha & Associates, New York City, public relations writer, 1974-75; Sullivan Associates, Menlo Park, Calif., educational writer (in Spanish), 1975-76; KPOO-FM radio, San Francisco, Calif., newscaster (in Spanish), 1976—; KEMO-TV, San Francisco, Calif., newswriter for Spanish language newscast and traffic assistant, 1975; Berlitz School of Languages, San Francisco, Calif., Spanish interpreter and translator, 1975-77; *San Francisco Chronicle,* San Francisco, Calif., general assignment reporter, 1977-78; KTVU-TV, Oakland, Calif., writer for daily newscast and foreign affairs reporter, 1979—. *Member:* San Francisco Press Club, San Francisco Media Alliance, World Affairs Council of Northern California.

WRITINGS: The Total Banana (nonfiction), Harcourt, 1979. Contributor to *People's Almanac.* Contributor to magazines, including *Oui,* and newspapers. Translator of *Saddleman's Review.*

WORK IN PROGRESS: A novel, *The White Rose.*

*   *   *

ABERNATHY, William J(ackson) 1933-

PERSONAL: Born November 21, 1933, in Columbia, Tenn.; son of Sidney Guy (an editor) and Estha (a teacher; maiden name, Jackson) Abernathy; married Claire St. Arnand, March 7, 1961; children: Evelyn Claire, William J., Jr., Janine Suzanne. *Education:* University of Tennessee, B.S., 1955; Harvard University, M.B.A., 1964, D.B.A., 1967. *Home:* 10 Wingate Rd., Lexington, Mass. 02173. *Office:* Business School, Harvard University, Boston, Mass. 02163.

CAREER: E. I. DuPont, Columbia, Tenn., engineer in Film Division, 1955-56; General Dynamics/Electronics, Rochester, N.Y., project engineer in Electronic Systems Division, 1959-62; University of California, Los Angeles, assistant professor of business, 1967-68; Stanford University, Stanford, Calif., assistant professor of business, 1968-72; Harvard University, Business School, Boston, Mass., associate professor, 1972-77, professor of business, 1977—. Consultant to government and business.

WRITINGS: (With Alan Sheldon and C. K. Prahalad) *The Management of Health Care: A Technology Perspective,* Ballinger, 1974; (with Paul W. Marshall and others) *Operations Management: Text and Cases,* Irwin, 1975; *The Productivity Dilemma,* Johns Hopkins Press, 1978; (editor with Douglas Ginsburg) *Government, Technology, and the Future of the Automobile,* McGraw, 1979. Contributor to academic journals.

SIDELIGHTS: Abernathy comments: "The management of technology and innovation within firms and the government is a special focus of my work at Harvard Business School. The contribution of science and technology in management decision and in economic planning both in the United States and abroad has been a common theme of my research and publications, and the automobile industry has been a special subject in recent work. Recent research in Europe is expected to lead to future work on international competition in technology.

"The U.S. automobile industry is in turmoil as a result of high gasoline prices and shortages, government regulation, and the legacy of past decisions. Many problems call for resolution. The book, *Government, Technology and the Future of the Automobile,* is the result of a series of conferences and meetings between automotive executives from the United States and abroad, government administrators, consumer advocates, suppliers, labor, and other concerned parties. Held at the Harvard Business School during 1977 and 1978, the purpose was to bring adversarial groups together to better understand one another's points of view and vital concerns with the hope of making a first step toward a resolution of current problems facing the industry, the government, and the public as regards the automobile. The book presents papers written by these participants and comments from the symposium as discussed in the October, 1978, symposium at Harvard."

* * *

ABERNETHY, Virginia 1934-

PERSONAL: Born October 4, 1934, in Havana, Cuba; American citizen born abroad; daughter of Bernard Charles (an executive) and Helen (Arnold) Deane; married George L. Abernethy (a physician; deceased); children: Hugh Kendrick, Jack Kendrick, Helen Kendrick, Diana Kendrick. *Education:* Wellesley College, B.A., 1955; Harvard University, M.A., 1969, Ph.D., 1970. *Politics:* Republican. *Home:* 159 Charleston Park, Nashville, Tenn. 37205. *Office:* Department of Psychiatry, Vanderbilt University Medical School, Nashville, Tenn. 37232.

CAREER: Harvard University, Medical School, Cambridge, Mass., postdoctoral research fellow, 1969-71, research associate, 1971-72, associate in psychiatry (anthropology), 1972-75, co-director of Family Planning Services in Psychiatric Hospital, 1972-73, director of Studies in Population and the Family, 1972-75; Vanderbilt University, Medical School, Nashville, Tenn., assistant professor, 1975-76, associate professor of psychiatry (anthropology) and director of Division of Human Behavior, 1976—, senior research associate of Vanderbilt Institute for Public Policy Studies, 1978—, special consultant of Women's Center, 1979—. Member of Advisory Board of Murphy School for Pregnant Teenagers, 1976-78, chairman, 1978-79; member of Medical Advisory Committee, Planned Parenthood Association, 1976—; investigator for research organizations. *Member:* World Population Society (charter member), American Anthropological Association (fellow), American Association for the Advancement of Science, Society for Medical Anthropology, Sigma Xi. *Awards, honors:* Co-recipient of commendation from American Psychiatric Association, 1975, for development of Reproduction Counseling Service and Clinic at Massachusetts Mental Health Center.

WRITINGS: Population Pressure and Cultural Adjustment, Human Sciences Press, 1979; (editor) *Frontiers in Medical Ethics: Applications in a Medical Setting,* Ballinger, 1980. Contributor of more than thirty articles to professional journals.

* * *

ABLE, James A(ugustus), Jr. 1928-

PERSONAL: Born December 30, 1928, in Decatur, Ill.; son of James A. (an electrician) and Florence E. (Gerhardt)

Able; married Martha Collins, February 15, 1952 (divorced April 27, 1972); married Mary Mathews (a registered nurse), April 28, 1972; children: (first marriage) James B., Cynthia Able Hotz, Robert G., Cheryl A. *Education:* Atlanta Law School, LL.B., 1953, LL.M., 1954. *Politics:* Independent. *Religion:* "No particular religion." *Home:* 4408 Harbor View Ave., Tampa, Fla. 33611.

CAREER: Materials Handling Equipment Co., Atlanta, Ga., office manager, 1951-53; R. S. Kerr & Co., Atlanta, office manager, 1953-55; Associates Investment Co., Atlanta, staff attorney, 1955-61; self-employed attorney, Atlanta, 1961-69; State of Georgia, Department of Human Resources, security officer, 1970-73; Advance Industrial Security, Atlanta, security manager and licensed private investigator, 1973-74; Wells, Fargo & Co., Atlanta, security manager and licensed private investigator, 1974-75; writer, 1975—. *Military service:* U.S. Army, 1946-49, 1950-51; served in Korea; became sergeant first class.

WRITINGS: Victims: Story of a Teenage Hooker (novel), Ashley Books, 1979.

WORK IN PROGRESS: The Ends of Justice, a novel about the politically motivated murder trial of a black militant; a historical novel about the cattle industry in Florida, 1835-1873, completion expected in 1980.

SIDELIGHTS: Able writes: "Thirty years ago I planned to pursue journalism. Two hitches in the Army sidetracked me, and I went into law instead. Twenty-five years later I said, 'To heck with it!,' moved to Florida, and settled down to write. I'm quite happy with it and glad to be 'back home again.' But the time wasn't wasted. Both of my novels are based upon events I experienced and persons I met in fourteen years of law practice and five years of security and investigation.

"I have been asked why I choose to write fiction when the current trend in publishing is overwhelmingly toward nonfiction. One reason, I guess, is that, as a former trial lawyer, I'm better at telling things like I would have you *believe* them to be than like they *are.* The other is best expressed in a quotation—taped to the wall over my desk—from Ray Bradbury's short story, 'The Man in the Rohrschacht Shirt,' in *I Sing the Body Electric!:* 'Intuited novels are far more "true" than all your scribbled data-fact reportage in the history of the world!' "

BIOGRAPHICAL/CRITICAL SOURCES: Decatur Daily Review, Decatur, Ill., August 6, 1979.

* * *

ABRAMS, Harry N(athan) 1904-1979

OBITUARY NOTICE: Born December 8, 1904, in London, England; died November 25, 1979, in New York, N.Y. Publisher, advertising executive, and art collector. Dissatisfied with the printing and marketing of art books by major companies, Abrams founded his own publishing house in 1949, which later became known for producing high quality art books. He was chairman of the board of the Harry N. Abrams Company until 1977, when he left to found Abbeville Press, also publishers of art books. From 1936 until 1950, he was an executive with the Book-of-the-Month Club. Obituaries and other sources: *Current Biography,* Wilson, 1958, January, 1980; *Who's Who in World Jewry,* Pitman, 1972; *Washington Post,* November 27, 1979; *New York Times,* November 27, 1979.

ADAMS, Franklin P(ierce)   1881-1960
(F.P.A.)

OBITUARY NOTICE: Born November 15, 1881, in Chicago, Ill.; died March 23, 1960. Journalist, editor, translator, lyricist, and author of several volumes of poetry and humorous verse. Best known for his writings under his initials F.P.A., Adams's first column appeared in the *Chicago Journal* in 1903, and he later wrote for the *New York Evening Mail*, *New York Herald Tribune*, and *New York Post*. He is credited with increasing the popularity of writer Samuel Pepys, through his Saturday diary column which imitated Pepys's language and style. Adams collaborated with O. Henry on the lyrics for the musical comedy "Lo" in 1909. He also translated Latin classics into English. Among his books are *Tobogganing on Parnassus*, *Nods and Becks*, and *Half a Loaf*. Obituaries and other sources: *Current Biography*, Wilson, 1941, May, 1960; *New York Times*, March 24, 1960; *The Oxford Companion to American Literature*, 4th edition, Oxford University Press, 1965; *The Reader's Encyclopedia*, 2nd edition, Crowell, 1965.

*   *   *

ADAMS, George Matthew   1878-1962

OBITUARY NOTICE: Born August 23, 1878, in Saline, Mich.; died October 28, 1962. Columnist, publisher, and author. In 1916, Adams became president of his own syndicated feature company, George Matthew Adams Service, which was the syndicator of Edgar A. Guest, among others. For more than twenty years, Adams was author of the column "Today's Talk." His books include *You Can*, 1913, *Take It*, 1917, *Just Among Friends*, 1928, and *The Great Little Things*, 1953. Obituaries and other sources: *The Reader's Encyclopedia of American Literature*, Crowell, 1962; *Who Was Who in America*, 4th edition, Marquis, 1968.

*   *   *

ADAMS, Rachel Leona White   1905(?)-1979

OBITUARY NOTICE: Born c. 1905; died December 16, 1979, in Lincoln, N.H. Artist and author. Adams served on the New Hampshire Commission of the Arts from 1965 until 1971. Her autobiography is entitled *On the Other Hand*. Obituaries and other sources: *New York Times*, December 17, 1979; *Chicago Tribune*, December 18, 1979.

*   *   *

ADAMSON, Joy(-Friederike Victoria)   1910-1980

OBITUARY NOTICE—See index for *CA* sketch: Born January 20, 1910, in Troppau, Silesia (now Opava, Czechoslovakia); died January 3, 1980, in Kenya. Painter, conservationist, and writer. While on a vacation trip to Kenya, Austrian-born Joy Adamson fell in love with that East African nation, and moved there permanently in 1937. For several years she devoted herself to painting pictures of the native flowers, animals, and people, many of which are displayed in Kenya's National Museum in Nairobi. In 1956, she and her husband, game warden George Adamson, adopted a motherless lion cub named Elsa. Their efforts to train Elsa to fend for herself in the wild are chronicled in Adamson's *Born Free*, a best-selling book that spawned a movie and television series. Two subsequent books, *Living Free* and *Forever Free*, continue Elsa's story. Among Adamson's other works are *The Spotted Sphinx*, *Pippa's Challenge*, and an autobiography, *The Searching Spirit*. Proceeds from her books and movies are turned over to the Elsa Wild Animal Appeal, an organization that Adamson founded to preserve threatened wildlife species. During the last five years of her life she was working on a study of leopards at a camp near the Samburu game preserve. When her body was discovered near that camp, officials at first speculated that Adamson had been mauled to death by a lion, but later reports said that she had been murdered. Obituaries and other sources: Roy Newquist, *Counterpoint*, Simon & Schuster, 1964; *Current Biography*, Wilson, 1972; *Who's Who in America*, 40th edition, Marquis, 1978; Joy Adamson, *The Searching Spirit*, Harcourt, 1979; *New York Times*, January 5, 1980; *Washington Post*, January 5, 1980; *Publishers Weekly*, January 18, 1980; *Time*, January 21, 1980.

*   *   *

AIKEN, Irene (Nixon)

PERSONAL: Born in Cash, Tex.; daughter of Albert W. (a carpenter) and Louella (Voss) Nixon; married Jack K. Aiken (a truck driver), April 3, 1948; children: Charles, Doris, Carl, Lloyd, Janet. *Education:* Attended high school in Greenville, Tex. *Office:* 2910 Anderson St., Greenville, Tex. 75401.

CAREER: Writer, 1969—.

WRITINGS—Children's books: *Mom's Musing*, Nazarene Publishing, 1972; *Teen Tempo*, Nazarene Publishing, 1974; *Daddy, Come Home*, Victor, 1978. Contributor of nearly a thousand juvenile stories to religious periodicals.

WORK IN PROGRESS: *Jeffrey's Last Hope*, a juvenile book.

SIDELIGHTS: Irene Aiken writes: "I never stop writing, day or night. My mind swirls in words and events and characters and plots, I'd say almost constantly. In each story I try to put a nucleus of some concrete truth, then weave my story around this core, making two stories in one."

*   *   *

AISLIN
See MOSHER, (Christopher) Terry
*   *   *

AITKIN, Don(ald Alexander)   1937-

PERSONAL: Born August 4, 1937, in Sydney, Australia; son of Alexander George (a teacher) and Edna Irene (a teacher; maiden name, Taylor) Aitkin; married Janice Wood, December 20, 1958 (divorced, May, 1977); married Susan Tracy Elderton (a lecturer), May 20, 1977. *Education:* University of New England, B.A. (with honors), 1959, M.A. (with honors), 1961; Australian National University, Ph.D., 1964. *Religion:* None. *Agent:* Curtis Brown Ltd., 86 William St., Paddington, New South Wales 2021, Australia. *Office:* Department of Political Science, 1AS, Australian National University, Canberra, Australian Capital Territory 2600, Australia.

CAREER: Australian National University, Canberra, research fellow, 1965-67, senior research fellow, 1968-71; Macquarie University, North Ryde, Australia, professor of politics, 1971-79; Australian National University, professor of political science, 1980—. Consultant to Australian business corporations. *Member:* Australian Political Studies Association (president, 1979-80), Australian Society of Authors, Academy of Social Sciences in Australia (fellow), American Political Science Association. *Awards, honors:* Australian National University post-doctoral traveling fellowship, 1964.

WRITINGS: The Colonel (biography), Australian National University Press, 1969; *The Country Party in New South Wales,* Australian National University Press, 1972; *The Second Chair* (novel), Angus & Robertson, 1977; *Stability and Change in Australian Politics,* St. Martin's, 1977, 2nd edition, 1980; (with Brian E. Jinks) *Australian Political Institutions,* Pitman, 1980. Author of "Between the Lines," a column in *Canberra Times,* 1968-71, and "Perspective," in *National Times,* 1971—. Contributor to magazines and newspapers. Contributing editor of *Newsweek International,* 1977.

WORK IN PROGRESS: A novel, *Turning Point,* completion expected in 1980.

SIDELIGHTS: Aitkin commented: "I have an abiding interest in what is characteristic of Australian politics, especially in comparison with politics in the United States and England. Constant production of books, articles, and newspaper pieces has made writing a craft—the side of academic life I enjoy the most.

"My novel sat around in my head for ten years or so, and more or less wrote itself."

BIOGRAPHICAL/CRITICAL SOURCES: American Political Science Review, March, 1979.

*   *   *

ALBA de GAMEZ, Cielo Cayetana   1920-
(Tana de Gamez)

PERSONAL: Born September 9, 1920, in Malaga, Spain; came to the United States in 1936, naturalized citizen, 1941; daughter of Jose (a cultural attache) and Teresa (a chess master; maiden name, Taracido) Alba de Gamez; married Jorge A. Losada (a journalist), 1945 (divorced, 1951). *Education:* University of California, Los Angeles, B.A., 1942. *Politics:* "European socialist." *Religion:* Roman Catholic. *Home address:* P.O. Box 4223, Key West, Fla. 33040.

CAREER: Free-lance musician, writer, translator, and broadcaster, 1939-55; Gres Gallery, Washington, D.C., owner and director, 1956-60; commentator on WBAI-Radio, 1967-69; editor-in-chief of International Division of Simon & Schuster, 1968-76. *Awards, honors: The International* was named best reference book of the year by American Library Association and *Choice,* 1973, selected as most complete and exhaustive dictionary by Autonomous University of Madrid, 1975.

WRITINGS—Under name Tana de Gamez: (With Arthur R. Pastore) *Mexico and Cuba on Your Own,* R. D. Cortina, 1954; *Like a River of Lions* (novel), New York Graphic Society, 1962; *The Yoke and the Star* (novel), Bobbs-Merrill, 1966; *Alicia Alonso at Home and Abroad,* Citadel, 1971; (editor-in-chief) *The International* (Spanish/English dictionary), Simon & Schuster, 1973, revised edition, 1975. Also author of a bilingual (Spanish/English) dictionary, Warner Books, 1980.

Also translator into Spanish of John Steinbeck's *The Pearl* in 1944, Ernest Hemingway's *Old Man and the Sea* for W. M. Jackson in the 1950's, and an autobiography of Andres Segovia for Macmillan in 1976 into English. Author of radio scripts for networks in New York and Los Angeles, and for Voice of America. Contributor to magazines, including *Art News* and *Musical America.*

WORK IN PROGRESS: A Sheep in Wolf's Clothing (tentative title), an autobiography, completion expected in 1981; translating poems of Garcia Lorca.

SIDELIGHTS: De Gamez writes: "I studied theatre arts with Max Reinhardt and William Dieterle, music with Nina Koshetz and Boris Morros, and European literature with, among others, Erich Maria Remarque, Vicki Baum, and Thomas Mann.

"I have been a free-lancer most of my life, first as a musician. I was a guitarist (at one time a pupil of Andres Segovia), playing halls, clubs, night spots, and local radio stations in Los Angeles, San Francisco, Tucson, and Phoenix, and eventually fine supper clubs in New York. Later I free-lanced as a writer, translator, journalist, radio newscaster and commentator, and eventually as an editor and lexicographer.

"My life, first as a very young displaced person and refugee of the Spanish civil war, and later as a conscientious world citizen, gave me the experience and the themes for my two novels: *Like a River of Lions,* about the Spanish civil war; and *The Yoke and the Star,* about the Cuban revolution.

"As for my work in lexicography: reading, living, and traveling were my mentors, more than academic training. Perhaps my love of foreign languages and cultures and the ear of a musician also helped. By the age of four I could read three languages and write and compose in two. I place personal experience above academic training as the best breeding ground for a writer. The 'form' can be learned, but the content must be *lived*—or faithfully extracted from reading, dreaming, and observing—in order to ring true."

*   *   *

ALDERMAN, Geoffrey   1944-

PERSONAL: Born February 10, 1944, in Hampton Court, England; son of Samuel (a manufacturer's agent) and Lily (Landau) Alderman; married Marion Joan Freed (a graphic designer), September 9, 1973; children: Naomi Alicia, Eliot Daniel. *Education:* Lincoln College, Oxford, B.A. (with honors), 1965, M.A. and D.Phil., both 1969. *Religion:* Jewish. *Home:* 172 Colindeep Lane, London NW9 6EA, England. *Agent:* Murray Pollinger, 4 Garrick St., London WC2E 9BH, England. *Office:* Department of History, Royal Holloway College, University of London, Egham Hill, Egham, Surrey TW20 OEX, England.

CAREER: University of London, University College, London, England, research assistant in history, 1968-69; University of Wales, University College of Swansea, Swansea, temporary lecturer in politics, 1969-70; University of Reading, Reading, England, research fellow, 1970-72; University of London, Royal Holloway College, Egham, England, lecturer in history and politics, 1972—. Election analyst for Independent Television, 1979; broadcaster in England, the Netherlands, and Israel. Member of Social Science Research Council shipping committee, 1975. Honorary academic adviser to Hillel Foundation, 1974; member of research committee of Board of Deputies of British Jews, 1976—. *Member:* Political Studies Association of the United Kingdom, Jewish Historical Society of England, British Association for Jewish Studies, Royal Historical Society (fellow), Economic History Society, Society for the Study of Labour History, Historical Association, Association of University Teachers. *Awards, honors:* Grant from British Academy, 1978-79.

WRITINGS: The History of Hackney Downs School, Clove Club, 1972; *The Railway Interest,* Leicester University Press, 1973; (contributor) A. Newman, editor, *Provincial Jewry in Victorian Britain,* Jewish Historical Society of England, 1975; *The History of the Hendon Synagogue, 1928-1978,* privately printed, 1978; *British Elections: Myth and*

Reality, Batsford, 1978. Contributor of more than fifteen articles and reviews to history and religious journals and newspapers.

WORK IN PROGRESS: A book on the history of the Jewish vote in England.

SIDELIGHTS: Alderman commented to *CA:* "My current interests revolve around the development of the British political system in the late nineteenth and twentieth centuries and, in particular, the processes of political socialization and integration. I am also much interested in the phenomenon of class in politics and society, and the factors which bear upon its salience in British political life.

"In recent years I have developed a special interest in the politics and political activities of ethnic minorities, and I am at present engaged in research for study of the development and impact of the Jewish vote in the United Kingdom over the past one hundred and fifty years, the changing political attitudes of the Anglo-Jewish community, and the part played by Jews in British party politics. This research is being carried out by conventional methods of historical research, by the use of computer-based data, and by personal interview and social survey methods.

"I am interested in teaching all aspects of British history and politics since 1830, and would particularly welcome the opportunity to develop courses which emphasize the social and economic factors influencing political action and attitudes, both historically and in contemporary British society.

"At first sight my writings appear to be devoid of any common theme. My present work is on the history of how British Jews have voted. No book on the Jewish vote in the United Kingdom has ever been written before, and the news that I was writing one has caused misgivings in Anglo-Jewish establishment circles. I am totally unrepentant about my work. It is precisely because the subject is taboo that it has to be investigated.

"In fact, here is the thread linking all my writings: I want to illuminate the dark corners of recent British history and politics, and overturn widely held misconceptions. Too many political scientists simply write for their fellow academics. I believe I have a message for the general public, and if those with a vested interest in the perpetuation of false assumptions don't like what I write in my books, or say on radio and television, then I know I'm doing a good job."

BIOGRAPHICAL/CRITICAL SOURCES: British Book News, January, 1979.

*   *   *

ALDYNE, Nathan
    See McDOWELL, Michael

*   *   *

ALEXANDER, Robert
    See GROSS, Michael (Robert)

*   *   *

ALITTO, Guy S(alvatore)   1942-

PERSONAL: Born June 12, 1942, in Harrisburg, Pa.; son of Samuel P. (a clerk) and Rose (Buela) Alitto; married Susan Biele (a teacher), November 23, 1968; children: Emily Rose. *Education:* King's College, Wilkes-Barre, Pa., B.A., 1964; University of Chicago, M.A., 1966; Harvard University, Ph.D., 1975. *Religion:* Roman Catholic. *Office:* Department of History, Harvard University, Cambridge, Mass. 02138.

CAREER: University of California, Berkeley, research associate at Center for Chinese Studies, 1973-75; Oberlin College, Oberlin, Ohio, director of Inter-Institutional Language and Area Studies Program in Taiwan, 1975-76; University of Akron, Akron, Ohio, assistant professor of history, 1976-80; Harvard University, Cambridge, Mass., associate professor of history, 1980—. Research associate at Center for Far Eastern Studies, University of Chicago, 1977-78. *Member:* Association for Asian Studies.

WRITINGS: The Last Confucian: Liang Shu-ming and the Chinese Dilemma of Modernity, University of California Press, 1979. Contributor to Asian studies and history journals.

WORK IN PROGRESS: A social history of "a remote three-county in Honan Province, China, called Wan-hsi."

SIDELIGHTS: Alitto's special interest is modern Chinese history. He spent several years studying in Asia, and speaks Chinese, Japanese, Italian, and French.

The Last Confucian is a biography of Liang Shu-ming, a Confucian radical whose well-known 1921 book, *Eastern and Western Cultures,* studied the problem of Westernization in China. Jonathan Spence commented: "Liang is lucky to have found in Mr. Alitto a biographer who takes him seriously: Liang emerges from this study as a dour but rather commanding figure, a man of fierce integrity and considerable imagination, who managed forcefully to restate many of the basic tenets of Confucianism even as he anticipated a number of the radical facets of Maoism." Spence also praised the book as "an absorbing perspective on China's revolution—and on the idea of sacrifice and duty."

BIOGRAPHICAL/CRITICAL SOURCES: New York Times Book Review, August 12, 1979.

*   *   *

ALLEN, Alex B.
    See HEIDE, Florence Parry

*   *   *

ALLEN, Gerald   1942-

PERSONAL: Born January 15, 1942, in Lumberton, N.C.; son of Henry Pitman (a farmer) Elliot (McLean) Allen. *Education:* Yale University, B.A. (with honors), 1964, M.Phil., 1968, M.Arch., 1972; Corpus Christi College, Cambridge, M.A., 1966. *Politics:* Democrat. *Religion:* Episcopal. *Office: Architectural Record,* 1221 Avenue of the Americas, New York, N.Y. 10020.

CAREER: Philip Johnson & John Burgee (architects), New York City, architect, 1972-73; *Architectural Record,* New York City, editor, 1973—. Architect with Peter L. Gluck & Associates, 1976—; graphic designer for Santa Fe Opera, 1976—. Has had group exhibitions in New York and Los Angeles. *Member:* Society of Architectural Historians, Association of Collegiate Schools of Architecture (patron member), Architectural League of New York.

WRITINGS: (With Charles Moore and Donlyn Lyndon) *The Place of Houses: Three Architects Suggest Ways to Build and Inhabit Houses,* Holt, 1974; (with Moore) *Dimensions: Space, Shape, and Scale in Architecture,* Architectural Record Books, 1977; (contributor) Sam Davis, editor, *The Form of Housing,* Rinehold, 1977. Contributor of articles and designs to architecture journals and popular magazines, including *New York, Glamour,* and *Cosmopolitan.*

SIDELIGHTS: Allen's books have been published in Spanish and Japanese.

ALLEN, Marcus
   See DONICHT, Mark Allen

* * *

ALLEN, Mark
   See DONICHT, Mark Allen

* * *

ALLEN, Ruth Finney   1898-1979

PERSONAL: Born in 1898 in Chicago, Ill.; died March 20, 1979, in Washington, D.C.; daughter of John and Mary (Morrison) Finney; married Robert S. Allen (a journalist), 1929. *Residence:* Washington, D.C.

CAREER/WRITINGS: Worked for Scripps-Howard Newspaper Alliance as reporter, city editor, and Washington correspondent for newspapers, including *Sacramento Star, San Francisco News,* and *Albuquerque Tribune,* 1918-1968. Author of column, "Washington Calling," published in numerous Scripps-Howard newspapers; and two collections of poetry, in addition to an autobiographical account of her career as a newspaper woman.

SIDELIGHTS: Ruth Finney Allen, one of the first women ever to achieve the position of city editor of a newspaper, was once known as "Poison Ivy Finney" for her coverage of political events. Her notable assignments include the death of President Harding, the investigations and executions of Sacco and Vanzetti, and every presidential nomination convention from the 1920's to the 1960's.

OBITUARIES: New York Times, March 21, 1979; *Washington Post,* March 21, 1979.*

* * *

ALLISON, Rosemary   1953-

PERSONAL: Born June 18, 1953, in Jamaica; daughter of Stanley George and Ruth (a decorator and consultant; maiden name, deRoux) Allison. *Education:* Ontario College of Art, A.O.C.A., 1974. *Politics:* "Prefer anarchy; am slightly left of center." *Religion:* "Pantheist." *Home address:* P.O. Box 6704, Station A, Toronto, Ontario, Canada.

CAREER: Founding member of staff of Kids-Can-Press, 1972-75; writer, 1975—. Coordinator of Rhino Books, 1979—. *Member:* Writers Union of Canada, Canscaip. *Awards, honors:* Canada Council grant, 1978.

WRITINGS: The Travels of Ms. Beaver (juvenile), Canadian Women's Educational Press, 1973; *I Never Saw a Monster I Didn't Like* (juvenile), Flying Rabbit, 1973; *The Green Harpy at the Corner Store* (juvenile), Kids-Can-Press, 1976; (author of adaptation) Christine Duchesne, *Lazarus Laughs and the Lonely Dragon* (juvenile), James Lorimer, 1978; *Ms. Beaver Travels East* (juvenile), Canadian Women's Educational Press, 1979; *The Pillow,* James Lorimer, 1979.

WORK IN PROGRESS: A collection of stories about male-female relationships; short stories; self-made folk tale.

SIDELIGHTS: Rosemary Allison writes: "Generally I write to please myself, but find writing more difficult than painting or drawing, which I do well. I enjoy traveling, and yearn for the guts to give everything up and be a gypsy. I love Guatemala and London, England." *Avocational interests:* Photography.

BIOGRAPHICAL/CRITICAL SOURCES: In Review, August, 1979.

ALLMAN, T. D.   1944-

PERSONAL: Born October 16, 1944, in Tampa, Fla.; son of Paul Joseph (a naval officer and ship captain) and Felicia (a businesswoman; maiden name, Edmonds) Allman. *Education:* Harvard University, B.A. (cum laude), 1966; graduate study at St. Antony's College, Oxford, 1971-75. *Politics:* Independent. *Religion:* None. *Agent:* Peter Skolnik, Sanford J. Greenburger Associates, 825 Third Ave., New York, N.Y. 10022. *Office: Harper's* Magazine, Two Park Ave., New York, N.Y. 10016; and Pacific News Service, 604 Mission St., San Francisco, Calif. 94105.

CAREER: Journalist. Associated with *Anchorage Daily News,* Anchorage, Alaska, 1964; *Philadelphia Bulletin,* Philadelphia, Pa., reporter on police beat, 1965; Peace Corps volunteer, Nepal, 1966-68; free-lance foreign correspondent, Southeast Asia, 1968-71; *Guardian,* London, England, foreign correspondent, 1971-75; Third Century America Project, Berkeley, Calif., director of urban research, 1976—; Pacific News Service, San Francisco, Calif., senior editor, 1977—; *Harper's* magazine, New York, N.Y., contributing editor, 1977—. Notable assignments include investigative and analytical reporting on the war in Indochina and the outbreak of the Cambodian war. *Awards, honors:* Edward R. Murrow fellowship from Council on Foreign Relations, 1975-76.

WRITINGS: Global City, U.S.A.: The American Future Moves Downtown, Harcourt, 1980. Contributor to periodicals, including *GEO, New Republic, Far Eastern Economic Review, New Statesman,* and *New Times,* and to newspapers, including *Washington Post, New York Times, Los Angeles Times, Le Monde diplomatique,* and *Bangkok Post.*

WORK IN PROGRESS: Studies of Iran and Turkey.

SIDELIGHTS: Allman's journalistic assignments have ranged from an iconoclastic analysis of the urban crisis to a critique of the sociology of the nouvelle cuisine. He has interviewed Governor Jerry Brown of California and the Ayatollah Khomeini of Iran.

Allman told *CA:* "Free-lance journalists are probably the most underpaid and overcompensated people in the world. It's a wonderful career if you love work, new challenges, human beings, and the English language. But it's an absolute disaster if what you want is either security or a life style. Writing is a vocation, something that chooses you, not the other way around. Now that I am no longer a child in the profession, I tell newcomers: 'Forget Lou Grant and the Woodstein Twins. If you don't have something original to say, in an original way, go to law school.'"

* * *

ALVAREZ, Alejandro Rodriguez   1903-1965
   (Alejandro Casona)

OBITUARY NOTICE: Born March 23, 1903, in Besullo, Asturias, Spain; died September 17, 1965, in Madrid, Spain. Educator, director, poet, playwright, and screenwriter. Casona wrote and directed plays in Spain until 1939, when his popular play "Nuestra Natacha" offended the ruling Falangist government. He then fled to Buenos Aires, Argentina, and continued to work in the theatre until 1962. Some of his best known plays, including "Prohibido suicidarse en primavera" ("Suicide Prohibited in the Springtime") and "La barca sin pescador" ("The Boat Without a Fisherman"), were translated into English. Casona also wrote film scripts for several of his plays. He received the national prize for literature in 1932 for his juvenile adaptations of great myths and the Lope de Vega Prize in 1933 for "La Sirena Varada." Obituaries and other sources: *Hispania,* March, 1960, March, 1966; *Modern Language Journal,* April, 1960; *Encyclopedia of World Literature in the Twentieth Century,* updated edition, Ungar, 1967; *Modern World Drama: An Encyclopedia,* Dutton, 1972; *Cassell's Encyclopaedia of World Literature,* revised edition, Morrow, 1973.

* * *

ANDERSCH, Alfred 1914-1980

OBITUARY NOTICE—See index for *CA* sketch: Born February 4, 1914, in Munich, Germany; died February 21, 1980, in Berzona, Switzerland. Editor, radio broadcaster, and writer of novels, essays, short stories, radio scripts, and travel books. Because of Andersch's involvement with a Communist youth organization, in 1933 he spent six months in the Dachau concentration camp. Despite his continuing opposition to the Nazi regime, he was drafted into the German Army. In 1944 he deserted and became an American prisoner-of-war, an experience that is recounted in one of his books, *Die Kirschen der Freiheit.* After the war, Andersch's position as an editor for two periodicals, *Der Ruf* and *Texte und Zeichen,* made him one of the most influential spokesmen of his generation. His books include *Sansibar; Oder, Der letze Grund,* translated into English as *Flight to Afar,* and *Mein Verschwinden in Providence,* translated into English as *My Disappearance in Providence and Other Stories.* A common thread that runs through all his works is the moral responsibility that each individual has for his own actions. Obituaries and other sources: *Encyclopedia of World Literature in the Twentieth Century,* updated edition, Ungar, 1967; *The Penguin Companion to European Literature,* McGraw, 1969; *Cassell's Encyclopaedia of World Literature,* revised edition, Morrow, 1973; *Who's Who in the World,* 2nd edition, Marquis, 1973; *The Oxford Companion to German Literature,* Clarendon Press, 1976; *The International Who's Who,* Europa, 1979; *New York Times,* February 23, 1980; *London Times,* March 10, 1980.

* * *

ANDERSON, Barbara 1948-

PERSONAL: Born August 10, 1948, in Ames, Iowa; daughter of A. I. (a physical chemist) and Carolyn (a teacher; maiden name, Barnes) Snow; married Michael Peter Anderson (a mathematician), June 14, 1969. *Education:* University of Chicago, B.A., 1970; Princeton University, Ph.D., 1974. *Office:* Department of Sociology, Brown University, Providence, R.I. 02912.

CAREER: Yale University, New Haven, Conn., research associate at Economic Growth Center, 1974-76, assistant professor of sociology, 1975-76; Brown University, Providence, R.I., associate professor of sociology, 1976—. *Member:* American Sociological Association, American Historical Association, Population Association of America, Council on Foreign Relations. *Awards, honors:* M.A. from Brown University, 1977.

WRITINGS:(With Ansley J. Coale) *Human Fertility in Russia Since the Nineteenth Century,* Princeton University Press, 1979; *Internal Migration During the Modernization of Russia,* Princeton University Press, 1980; *Migration and Modernization,* Free Press, 1980. Contributor to economic and social science journals.

* * *

ANDERSON, E. Ruth 1907-

PERSONAL: Born June 23, 1907, in Newport, R.I.; daugh-

ter of Cameron Bishop and Almina Alice (Dale) Anderson. *Education:* Attended Boston University, 1924-25, and New England Conservatory of Music, 1931. *Home address:* P.O. Box 194, Marshfield Hills, Mass. 02051.

CAREER: Violinist and private teacher of violin, 1931-43; U.S. Department of Defense, Washington, D.C., employed in classified positions, 1946-53; American Meteorological Society, Boston, Mass., news editor of *Bulletin,* 1954-70. *Military service:* U.S. Naval Reserve, Women Accepted for Volunteer Emergency Service (WAVES), 1943-45; became aerographer first class. *Awards, honors:* First prize from Music Library Association, 1976, for *Contemporary American Composers.*

WRITINGS: Contemporary American Composers: A Biographical Dictionary, G. K. Hall, 1976.

WORK IN PROGRESS: A revision of *Contemporary American Composers.*

* * *

ANDERSON, Elliott 1944-

PERSONAL: Born January 23, 1944, in Iowa City, Iowa; son of Keith E. (an engineer) and Marion (Cochran) Anderson; married Mary Jasper, September 27, 1966 (divorced September, 1971); married Cynthia Shanahan (a designer), April 21, 1972; children: Claire Beth, Erin Shanahan. *Education:* Beloit College, B.A., 1966; University of Aix-Marseille, certificate, 1965; University of Iowa, M.F.A., 1971. *Home:* 809 Michigan Ave., Evanston, Ill. 60202. *Office:* Triquarterly, Northwestern University, 1735 Benson Ave., Evanston, Ill. 60201.

CAREER: Northwestern University, Evanston, Ill., lecturer, 1972—, editor of *Triquarterly,* 1975—.

WRITINGS: (Editor) *Contemporary Israeli Literature,* Jewish Publication Society, 1977; (editor with David Hayman) *In the Wake of the Wake,* University of Wisconsin Press, 1979; (editor with Mary Kinzie) *The Little Magazine in America: A Modern Documentary History,* Pushcart Book Press, 1979; (contributor) *Literary Publishing,* Pushcart Book Press, 1979.

Translator: *Otherwise and Other Poems,* Writers Workshop Press (Bombay, India), 1972; (with Anselm Hollo) *Nile* (poems), Windhover Press, 1973; *Snow* (poems), Toothpaste Press, 1973; *Turbines* (poems), Toothpaste Press, 1974.

Screenplays: "Trooper Hudson," for Artichoke Productions; "Humboldt's Gift," for WTTW-TV.

Work represented in anthologies, including *Extreme Unctions,* Latitudes Press, 1974. Contributor of articles and reviews to magazines, including *National Observer* and *Partisan Review,* and newspapers. Book reviewer for *Chicago Tribune* and *Chicago Sun-Times,* 1973—.

WORK IN PROGRESS: Dead Is Forever, a novel.

* * *

ANDERSON, Patrick (John MacAllister) 1915-1979

PERSONAL: Born August 4, 1915, in Ashted, Surrey, England; died in 1979, in Halstead, Essex, England; married Peggy Doernbach (divorced). *Education:* Earned B.A. and M.A. from Oxford University; earned M.A. from Columbia University. *Address:* Field House, Gosfield Lake, Halstead, Essex, England.

CAREER: Poet and writer. Selwyn House School, Montreal, Quebec, teacher, 1940-46; McGill University, Montreal, assistant professor, 1948-50; Trent Park College, Barnet, Hertfordshire, England, member of faculty, 1957-79, principal lecturer and head of English department, 1968-79. Lecturer, University of Malaya, 1950-52, and Dudley Training College, 1954-57. *Awards, honors:* Commonwealth fellowship, 1938; Harriet Monroe Memorial Prize, 1946.

WRITINGS: A Tent for April (poems), First Statement, 1945; *The White Centre* (poems), Ryerson Press, 1946; *The Color as Naked* (poems), McLelland & Stewart, 1953; *Snake Wine: A Singapore Episode*, Chatto & Windus, 1955; *First Steps in Greece*, Chatto & Windus, 1958; *Search Me: Autobiography; The Black Country, Canada, and Spain*, British Book Centre, 1958; (editor with Alistair Sutherland) *Eros: An Anthology of Friendship*, Blond, 1961, published as *Eros: An Anthology of Male Friendship*, Citadel Press, 1963; *Finding Out About the Athenians*, F. Muller, 1961; *The Character Ball: Chapters of Autobiography*, Chatto & Windus, 1963; *Dolphin Days: A Writer's Notebook of Mediterranean Pleasures*, V. Gollancz, 1963; *The Smile of Apollo: A Literary Companion to Greek Travel*, Chatto & Windus, 1964; *Over the Alps: Reflections on Travel and Travel Writing With Special Reference on the Grand Tours of Boswell, Beckford and Byron*, Hart-Davis, 1969; *Foxed!; or, Life in the Country*, Chatto & Windus, 1972; *A Visiting Distance* (poems), Borealis Press, 1976; *Return to Canada: Selected Poems*, McLelland & Stewart, c. 1977. Member of editorial boards, including *Preview, En Masse,* and *Northern Review.* Co-founder of *Preview.*

BIOGRAPHICAL/CRITICAL SOURCES: Patrick Anderson, *Search Me: Autobiography; The Black Country, Canada, and Spain*, British Book Centre, 1958; Anderson, *The Character Ball: Chapters of Autobiography*, Chatto & Windus, 1963; *Observer*, June 25, 1972.

OBITUARIES: AB Bookman's Weekly, April 16, 1979.*

* * *

ANDERSON, Peggy 1938-

PERSONAL: Born in 1938; daughter of Kay McMillan (a nurse). *Home:* 1642 Lombard St., Philadelphia, Pa. 19146. *Agent:* Jay Acton, Edward J. Acton, Inc., 17 Grove St., New York, N.Y. 10014.

CAREER: Former reporter for *Philadelphia Inquirer*, Philadelphia, Pa.; free-lance writer. Contributor to magazines, including *Ms., Redbook,* and *Glamor.*

WRITINGS: The Daughters: An Unconventional Look at America's Fan Club–The D.A.R., St. Martin's, 1974; *Nurse*, St. Martin's, 1978.

WORK IN PROGRESS: A book about a children's hospital in Philadelphia; a book on her personal experience following her father's murder.

SIDELIGHTS: In order to research her first book, *The Daughters*, Peggy Anderson spent a year interviewing various members of the Daughters of the American Revolution. Her investigation of that organization earned kudos from Elaine Kendall. "Miss Anderson puts the D.A.R. into perspective, and she does so with considerable grace and style," Kendall wrote in the *New York Times Book Review.* "It's clear from the tone of her book that she revised some of her own preconceptions in the process of writing it, cheerfully relinquishing some handy and amusing stereotypes that a lesser reporter might have preserved to the end."

Anderson also exercised her reportorial skills in her bestselling book, *Nurse.* The daughter of a nurse, Anderson was disturbed by the stereotypical nurses presented in books, movies, and television. She resolved to write a book that would dispel the image of nurses as either cruel, silly, or saintly, and launched a search for a real nurse who would give a straightforward account of the profession. Once Anderson found an R.N. who consented to be interviewed, she spent long hours recording the nurse's recollections. The woman stipulated that her identity not be revealed to the public, so she adopted a pseudonym in the book, Mary Benjamin.

The account of Mary Benjamin's daily life as a nurse in a large general hospital received mixed reviews. Rosellen Meighan Garrett objected to *Nurse:* "The author aimed to portray the image of a nurse who is not the stereotypical Florence Nightingale or Cherry Ames. What she succeeded in doing was to give us today's stereotype of a nurse. For whom this book is intended, I do not know. The young may react with fear, hesitation or disillusionment; the not-so-young may react with cynicism." Other reviewers were more complimentary. "This work is of primary importance," B. J. Kalisch declared, "because it reveals the vital role a nurse plays in the curative, preventive, and rehabilitative aspects of health care and because it sheds light on a profession which is almost always overshadowed by medicine."

BIOGRAPHICAL/CRITICAL SOURCES: New York Times Book Review, August 4, 1974, April 22, 1979; *Booklist*, September 1, 1974; *Choice*, February, 1975; *Library Journal*, September 15, 1978; *Washington Monthly*, October, 1978; *Best Sellers*, February, 1979.*

* * *

ANDREWS, E(ric) M(ontgomery) 1933-

PERSONAL: Born May 8, 1933, in London, England; son of John Charles (a gardener) and Alice (Hanmore) Andrews; married Shirley Mason (a nurse), August 20, 1955; children: Steven (deceased), Katie. *Education:* Exeter College, Oxford, B.A., 1957, diploma in education, 1958; Australian National University, Ph.D., 1966. *Politics:* "Parliamentary socialist." *Religion:* None. *Home:* 4 Pryors Lane, Warners Bay, New South Wales 2282, Australia. *Office:* Department of History, University of Newcastle, Newcastle, New South Wales 2308, Australia.

CAREER: Teacher at private grammar school in Lancaster, England, 1957-63; History teacher and department head at girls' high school in London, England, 1966-67; University of Newcastle, Newcastle, Australia, lecturer, 1967-72, senior lecturer in history, 1972—. Radio and television broadcaster. *Military service:* British Army, Royal Army Educational Corps, 1952-54. *Member:* Society for the Study of the History of Australian Defence and Foreign Policy, Federation of Australian University Staff Associations.

WRITINGS: Isolationism and Appeasement in Australia: Reactions to the European Crises, 1935-1939, Australian National University Press, 1970; *Australia in the Modern World* (textbook), Longman, 1974; *A History of Australian Foreign Policy* (high school textbook), Longman, 1979. Contributor to learned journals.

WORK IN PROGRESS: The British Commonwealth and the Manchurian Crisis, 1931-35, on reactions in England, Australia, New Zealand, and Canada, and the impact of the crisis on the development of the commonwealth; research on Australian relations with China, 1850-1970.

SIDELIGHTS: Andrews comments: "I was brought up in a poor area of London, went to the local grammar school, and won a free place to Oxford University. This was the result of the educational policy introduced by the Atlee Labour government in England. I wanted to do historical research, but got married instead and went into teaching. The chance of a scholarship led me to Australia in 1963. I finally settled there, teaching in the university. I continue to work in the field of Australian foreign policy history, especially the 1930 period, and am particularly interested in the tendency of the Australian government to look for powerful allies—Britain in the 1930's, America in the 1960's and 1970's. I hope Australian government from now on will adopt a more *independent* foreign policy."

*   *   *

ANDREWS, Henry N(athaniel), Jr.   1910-

PERSONAL: Born June 15, 1910, in Melrose, Mass.; son of Henry Nathaniel (a lawyer) and Florence (Hollings) Andrews; married Elisabeth C. Ham, 1939; children: Hollings Torrey, Henry Nathaniel III, Nancy Robnett. *Education:* Massachusetts Institute of Technology, B.S., 1934; graduate study at University of Massachusetts, 1934-35, and Cambridge University, 1937-38; Washington University, St. Louis, Mo., M.S., 1937, Ph.D., 1939. *Home address:* R.F.D. 1, Laconia, N.H. 03246.

CAREER: Washington University, St. Louis, Mo., instructor, 1938-39, assistant professor, 1939-42, associate professor, 1942-45, professor of botany, 1945-64, dean of School of Botany, 1947-64; University of Connecticut, Storrs, professor of biology, 1964-75, professor emeritus, 1975—, head of department, 1964-70. Paleobotanist at Missouri Botanical Garden, 1941-61; botanist with U.S. Geological Survey, 1950-54, 1959—. *Member:* National Academy of Sciences, Botanical Society of America, American Geological Society, Torrey Botany Club. *Awards, honors:* Guggenheim fellow, 1950-51, 1958-59; Fulbright fellow at University of Poona, 1960-61; National Science Foundation senior fellow in Sweden, 1964; certificate of merit from Botanical Society of America, 1966.

WRITINGS: Ancient Plants and the World They Live In, Cornell University Press, 1947; *Studies in Paleobotany,* Wiley, 1961; *The Fossil Hunters,* Cornell University Press, 1980. Contributor to scientific journals.

SIDELIGHTS: Andrews told *CA:* "I have several books on fossil plants, all quite different. They were written partly because I enjoyed doing so and partly because I thought they all fitted a particular need. As an example, my first book, written in 1947, was a semi-popular one called *Ancient Plants* intended for the layman with an interest in the plants of past ages. It is still selling after more than thirty years and thus seems to have been justified. I feel strongly that we need more and better books that bring scientific developments to the people. And I believe that these books should be written by the scientists who have done the original research, or participated in it, and not just 'science writers.'"

*   *   *

ANKER, Charlotte   1934-

PERSONAL: Born July 13, 1934, in Wilmington, Del.; daughter of Neil (a gambler) and Helen (a bookkeeper; maiden name, Price) Lubin; married Jerry David Anker (an attorney), April 12, 1959; children: Deborah, Daniel. *Education:* Temple University, A.B., 1955; graduate study at Columbia University, 1955-56. *Residence:* Potomac, Md. *Agent:* Harold Freedman, Brandt & Brandt, 1501 Broadway, New York, N.Y.

CAREER: International Union of Electrical, Radio & Machine Workers, Washington, D.C., assistant education director, 1957-60; *Washington World,* Washington, D.C., assistant book review editor, 1961-62; George Washington University, Washington, D.C., assistant professorial lecturer in sociology, 1965-70. Poet, playwright, and author. *Member:* Authors Guild of America, Society of Children's Book Writers, Dramatists Guild (associate member), District of Columbia Sociological Society, Washington Independent Writers. *Awards, honors:* First prize for children's literature from Philadelphia Writers Conference, 1974, for *Last Night I Saw Andromeda.*

WRITINGS: Last Night I Saw Andromeda (juvenile), Walck, 1975; (with Irene Rosenberg) "Onward Victoria" (two-act musical play), first produced in New York, N.Y., at Greenwich Mews Theatre, February 22, 1979. Also author of "Stroke Three" (two-act play). Contributor of poems and articles to magazines.

WORK IN PROGRESS: Ding Dong the Witch Is Dead, a novel for young adults; "Boardwalk Action," a play; a revision of "Onward Victoria" for production on Broadway.

SIDELIGHTS: Anker told *CA:* "I wrote my first poem at the age of six and the adventure of it was enough to hook me for life. One form of writing often led to another: a poem begging to be more fully developed in a short story; research for a story leading to nonfiction. I wrote a magazine article on the discovery of prehistoric fossils in back yards and building sites and that led to my novel for children. Writing for the theatre was totally unexpected. It happened as a result of reading biographical material on the life of Victoria Woodhull, a flamboyant nineteenth-century spiritualist and the first woman stockbroker. In 1872, when women could not vote, she ran for president on a platform of free thought, free speech, and free love. The woman seemed to cry out to me: 'Put me on the stage!' Without considering that it was a turning point in my life, I plunged into the project with co-author Irene Rosenberg. The result was 'Onward Victoria,' first as a straight comedy, then turned into a musical. Now I find theatre the most satisfying outlet of all. I'm intrigued with the paradoxes of human emotion—ambivalence, tragedy as farce. I enjoy setting up larger-than-life characters, letting them rub against one another, and watching the sparks fly."

BIOGRAPHICAL/CRITICAL SOURCES: Washington Star, March 9, 1979; *Washington Post,* April 8, 1979.

*   *   *

APPLETON, Arthur   1913-

PERSONAL: Born December 7, 1913, in Sunderland, England; son of Arthur (a fitter and turner) and Violet Owen (Welsh) Appleton; married Mary Germain, December 5, 1942; children: Germaine (Mrs. Nigel Stanger). *Education:* Attended school in Sunderland, England. *Home:* Washington, Tyne & Wear, 78 Biddick Lane, London NE38 8AA, England.

CAREER: British Broadcasting Corp., radio news and sports reporter in Newcastle, England, 1948-60, general program producer and senior news assistant in Newcastle, England, 1960-70, outside broadcasts producer in Manchester, England, 1971-75. Tutor for Durham County Council, 1976—. *Military service:* British Army, Royal Engineers, 1945-48; became staff sergeant. *Member:* Northern Playwrights' Society.

WRITINGS: Hotbed of Soccer, Hart-Davis, 1960; *Mary Ann Cotton: Her Story and Trial,* Transatlantic, 1974; *Sunder-*

land and the Cup, Frank Graham, 1974; *Sunderland A.F.C. Centenary History,* Sunderland Association Football Club, 1979.

Author of "Farewell, Jobling," a television film for British Broadcasting Corp., 1976. Author of twenty radio features. Contributor of short stories and hundreds of articles to newspapers and magazines.

WORK IN PROGRESS: A novel; an autobiography.

SIDELIGHTS: Mary Ann Cotton was made into a three-part series by British Broadcasting Corp. in 1976, entitled "A Slight Case of Poison."

Appleton writes: "I was smitten chronically, when in my teens, to find the ideal free life away from the imprisonment of doing uncongenial work for other people. I imagined I would be a great novelist. Not so, not even a little minor one, but I have done a great deal of writing, mainly for radio talks, because that was where the opportunity came—first in army broadcasting, then in short stories and articles and nonfiction books. Radio writing, for a network in which time is precious, has made my writing spare, progressive, unrepetitive. And I pick my way clear of cliches, when I see them.

"In nonfiction writing and journalism quite a lot of writers repeat statements and observations unnecessarily, quite often more than twice—in other words, of course. Also, they often continue to add superfluous, obvious detail. Some published writers are really bad writers, by that I mean turgid and repetitive. Unfortunately, some editors and producers do not know good and bad writing when they see it. In short stories many writers begin before they have thought their storyline through. The thinking time to do this could be only a few minutes."

*　　*　　*

ARDREY, Robert　1908-1980

OBITUARY NOTICE—See index for *CA* sketch: Born October 16, 1908, in Chicago, Ill.; died of cancer, January 14, 1980, in Kalk Bay, South Africa. Playwright, screenwriter, novelist, and author of books on anthropology. Although Ardrey studied the natural and social sciences at the University of Chicago, he fell under the influence of Thornton Wilder and decided to become a dramatist. His first three plays—"Star Spangled," "How to Get Tough About It," and "Casey Jones"—had brief runs but led to his being offered a job as a Hollywood screenwriter in 1938. For the next several years he alternately turned out film scripts, novels, and plays. One of his plays, "Thunder Rock," was a wartime hit in London, and a film version was released by MGM. As a dramatist, Ardrey had always been fascinated by the question of human motivation, and in 1955 he decided to take a more scientific approach to this problem. His research into the fields of anthropology and ethology led to his writing four nonfiction books: *African Genesis, The Territorial Imperative, The Social Contract,* and *The Hunting Hypothesis.* In these books Ardrey sets forth his controversial theory that man is an innately aggressive creature, driven by a desire to protect his property and to hold sway over others. Although some scientists scorned Ardrey as an amateur, others praised him for helping to popularize a complex field of study. Despite his new-found interest in anthropology, Ardrey continued to write for the screen, including such films as "The Four Horsemen of the Apocalpyse" and "Khartoum." Shortly before he died he had finished an autobiography. Obituaries and other sources: *Modern World Drama: An Encyclopedia,* Dutton, 1972; *Celebrity Register,* 3rd edition, Simon & Schuster, 1973; *Current Biography,*

Wilson, 1973; *Biography News,* Volume I, Gale, 1974; *Contemporary Dramatists,* 2nd edition, St. Martin's, 1977; *Who's Who in America,* 40th edition, Marquis, 1978; *New York Times,* January 16, 1980; *Chicago Tribune,* January 16, 1980; *Time,* January 28, 1980; *Newsweek,* January 28, 1980.

*　　*　　*

ARMSTRONG, Benjamin Leighton　1923-

PERSONAL: Born October 18, 1923, in Newark, N.J., son of Benjamin Leighton and Margaret Smith (a poet; maiden name, Denison) Armstrong; married Ruth Freed (a teacher), April 11, 1946; children: Robert Leighton, Bonnie Mildred, Debbie Margaret Armstrong Vacchiano. *Education:* Attended Houghton College, 1941-43, and Nyack College, 1943-45; New York University, B.S., 1948, M.A., 1950, Ph.D., 1967; postdoctoral study at Princeton Theological Seminary, 1950-51; Union Theological Seminary, M.Div., 1955. *Home:* 675 Woodland Ave., Madison, N.J. 07940. *Office:* National Religious Broadcasters, P.O. Box 2254-R, Morristown, N.J. 07960.

CAREER: Ordained United Presbyterian minister, 1949; pastor of Presbyterian churches in Paterson, N.J., 1950-55, and Ringwood, N.J., 1955-57; Trans World Radio, Chatham, N.J., director in Chatham and Monte Carlo, Monaco, 1957-66; National Religious Broadcasters, Morristown, N.J., executive director, 1967—. Workshop director; film producer. Member of board of directors of Telemissions International and advisory board of Intercristo; member of New York City Council for Cooperation in Communication, 1971—. *Member:* National Association of Evangelicals (member of board of directors), Royal Geographical Society (fellow), Kappa Delta Pi (Beta Pi chapter), Nyack College Honor Society.

WRITINGS: The Electric Church, Thomas Nelson, 1979; *1979 Directory of Religious Broadcasting,* National Religious Broadcasters, 1979. Contributor to professional journals. Editor of *Religious Broadcasting,* 1968—.

WORK IN PROGRESS: Battle for the Airwaves, for Christian Herald Publishers.

*　　*　　*

ARMSTRONG, Hamilton Fish　1893-1973

PERSONAL: Born April 7, 1893, in New York, N.Y.; died April 24, 1973, in New York, N.Y.; son of David Maitland (an artist and foreign diplomat) and Helen (Neilson) Armstrong; married Helen Macgregor Byrne, December 31, 1918 (divorced, 1938); married Carmen Barnes (an author), December 27, 1945 (divorced); married Christa von Tippelskrich, July 11, 1951; children: (first marriage) Gregor. *Education:* Princeton University, A.B., 1916. *Residence:* New York, N.Y.

CAREER: New York Evening Post, New York City, member of editorial staff, 1919-21, special correspondent in Eastern Europe, 1921-22; *Foreign Affairs* (quarterly review), New York City, managing editor, 1922-28, editor, 1928-72. Member of advisory committee of post-war foreign affairs for U.S. State Department, 1942-44; special adviser to Secretary of State, 1945; adviser to U.S. delegation at San Francisco Conference, 1945; member of President's Advisory Committee on Political Refugees. Special assistant to U.S. ambassador in London, England, 1944. Director of Council on Foreign Relations. Trustee of Woodrow Wilson Foundation (vice-president, 1928-30, president, 1935-37). *Military service:* U.S. Army, 1917-18; served in infantry, and as military attache to Serbian war mission in United States and American legation in Belgrade, Yugoslavia; became second lieutenant. *Member:* American Philosophical Society, School of Slavonic Studies (corresponding member). *Awards, honors:* Serbian Decorated Order of St. Sava, 1918; Serbian Order of the White Eagle (with swords), 1919; Romanian Order of the Crown, 1924; Czechoslovakian Order of the White Lion, 1937; created Officer of the French Legion of Honor, 1937, Commander, 1947; LL.D. from Brown University, 1942, and Columbia University, 1963; Litt.D. from Yale University, 1957, Princeton University, 1961, and Harvard University, 1963; Dr.Hon.Causa from University of Basel, 1960; created Commander of the Order of the British Empire, 1972.

WRITINGS—Politics: *Hitler's Reich: The First Phase,* Macmillan, 1933; *Europe Between Wars?,* Macmillan, 1934; *"We or They?": Two Worlds in Conflict,* Macmillan, 1936; (with Allen W. Dulles) *Can We Be Neutral?,* Council on Foreign Relations, 1936, reprinted, Books for Libraries Press, 1971; *When There Is No Peace,* Macmillan, 1939; *The Calculated Risk,* Macmillan, 1947; (editor with James Chace, Carol Kahn, and Jennifer Whittaker) *Fifty Years of Foreign Affairs,* Praeger, 1972. Also author with Dulles of *Can America Stay Neutral?,* 1939.

History: *The New Balkans,* Harper, 1926; *Where the East Begins,* Harper, 1929; *Chronology of Failure: The Last Days of the French Empire,* Macmillan, 1940.

Other: (Editor) *The Book of New York Verse,* Putnam, 1917; *Tito and Goliath,* Macmillan, 1951; *Those Days* (autobiographical), Harper, 1963; *Peace and Counterpeace: From Wilson to Hitler* (memoirs), Harper, 1971. Also editor with William L. Langer of *Foreign Affairs Bibliography,* 1933.

Contributor to periodicals, including *Foreign Affairs.*

SIDELIGHTS: Hamilton Fish Armstrong was associated with the quarterly review, *Foreign Affairs,* for fifty years, including forty-four as editor. Under Armstrong's leadership, the periodical came to be regarded worldwide as the "quasi-official voice of the U.S. Department of State," related a writer for *Newsweek.* The reputation of *Foreign Affairs* stemmed, in part, from an impressive list of contributors: Leon Trotsky, Nikita Khrushchev, Franklin D. Roosevelt, John F. Kennedy, and Marshal Tito, to name a few.

In 1933, Armstrong became the first American to be granted an interview with Adolf Hitler. The German, however, "ignored all Armstrong's questions," reported a *Newsweek* reviewer, "indulged in a monologue disclaiming any desire for war, followed by a menacing harangue about Poland." Though considered by some at the time to be relatively harmless, Armstrong saw the danger in this man who had just come to power. *Hitler's Reich: The First Phase* was the result of Armstrong's assessment of the dictator. In his next book, *Europe Between Wars,* Armstrong voiced his concerns over the state of world affairs and predicted World War II five years before the outbreak of battle.

Upon hearing of Armstrong's death in 1973, former Secretary of State Henry A. Kissinger reflected: "Hamilton Fish Armstrong was a friend and an inspiration. Urbane, concerned, wise, open to different opinions, he always knew that our common values were greater than our differences and that America could be true to herself and be relevant morally and politically to the rest of the world. This was the spirit of *Foreign Affairs,* with which his name grew synonymous over half a century. The country will miss him and his friends' lives will be emptier without him."

BIOGRAPHICAL/CRITICAL SOURCES: Hamilton Fish

Armstrong, *Those Days,* Harper, 1963; Armstrong, *Peace and Counterpeace: From Wilson to Hitler,* Harper, 1971; *Publishers Weekly,* March 22, 1971; *Newsweek,* June 28, 1971, October 2, 1972; *New Yorker,* July 10, 1971; *New York Times Book Review,* July 11, 1971, December 5, 1971; *Time,* October 4, 1971; *Saturday Review,* October 9, 1971; *America,* November 20, 1971; *Washington Post Book World,* February 4, 1973; *New Republic,* February 17, 1973; *Times Literary Supplement,* April 27, 1973.

OBITUARIES: New York Times, April 25, 1973; *Newsweek,* May 7, 1973; *Time,* May 7, 1973; *AB Bookman's Weekly,* June 25, 1973; *Foreign Affairs,* July, 1973.*

*   *   *

ARMSTRONG, O(rland) K(ay)   1893-

PERSONAL: Born October 2, 1893, in Willow Springs, Mo.; son of William Calvin (a minister) and Agnes (Brockus) Armstrong; married Louise McCool, May 21, 1922 (died October 21, 1947); married Marjorie Moore (a free-lance writer and editor), December 11, 1949; children: Milton McCool, O.K., Jr., Louise Armstrong Cattan (deceased), Stanley A., Charles L. *Education:* Drury College, B.S., 1916; Cumberland University, Lebanon, Tenn., B.LL., 1922; University of Missouri, B.S. and M.A., both 1925. *Religion:* Baptist. *Home and office address:* Highlands, Route 2, Box 75-A, Republic, Mo. 65738. *Agent:* James Brown Associates, Inc., 25 West 43rd St., New York, N.Y. 10032.

CAREER: Southwest Baptist College, Bolivar, Mo., teacher of English and public speaking, 1916-17; Baptist Young People's Union, Jacksonville, Fla., director, 1920-21; University of Florida, Gainesville, professor of journalism and founder of department, 1925-28; executive secretary for Missouri Century of Progress Commission, 1931-32; Missouri House of Representatives, Jefferson City, Republican representative, 1933-44; staff writer for *Reader's Digest,* 1944-51; U.S. House of Representatives, Washington, D.C., Republican Representative, 1951-53; editorial staff writer for *Reader's Digest,* 1953-77. Chairman of Citizens' Council Against Pornography, 1957—. Presidential elector from Missouri, 1972. *Military service:* U.S. Army, Aviation Section, 1917-19; became 2nd lieutenant.

WRITINGS: Old Massa's People: The Old Slaves Tell Their Story, Bobbs-Merrill, 1931; *This Is the West,* Rand McNally, 1949; *The Fifteen Decisive Battles of the United States,* Longmans, Green, 1961; (with wife, Marjorie Moore Armstrong) *Religion Can Conquer Communism,* Thomas Nelson, 1964; (with Armstrong) *The Indomitable Baptists,* Doubleday, 1967; (with Armstrong) *Baptists Who Shaped a Nation,* Broadman, 1975; (with Armstrong) *The Baptists in America,* Doubleday, 1979. Also author of *Gambling: You Cannot Win,* 1980, and an as yet unpublished manuscript, *The Trail of Tears.*

WORK IN PROGRESS: It Might Have Been, "historical facts, fictionalized," completion expected in 1980.

SIDELIGHTS: Armstrong writes that his specialties as a writer have included government, foreign affairs, American Indians, the U.S. bicentennial celebration, and exposes of pornography and obscenity.

*   *   *

ARNOLD, Alvin L(incoln)   1929-

PERSONAL: Born February 12, 1929, in Brooklyn, N.Y.; son of Irving (a merchant) and Mary (Spielholz) Arnold; married Nancy Oshrin (a teacher), August 7, 1960; children:

Melissa Beth, Laurence Ira. *Education:* Cornell University, A.B., 1949; Harvard University, LL.B., 1952. *Home:* 25 Longfellow Rd., Great Neck, N.Y. 11023. *Office:* Warren, Gorham & Lamont, Inc., 390 Plandome Rd., Manhasset, N.Y. 11030.

CAREER: Institute for Business Planning (publisher), Greenvale, N.Y., real estate editor, 1962-65; Strasser, Spiegelberg, Fried & Frank (attorneys), New York, N.Y., associate, 1965-69; Warren, Gorham & Lamont, Inc. (publisher), Manhasset, N.Y., vice-president and general counsel, 1969—. Adjunct professor at New York University. Acting village justice of Saddle Rock, N.Y. *Military service:* U.S. Air Force, 1953-55; became first lieutenant. *Member:* National Association of Real Estate Editors.

WRITINGS: (With Victor Sparrow) *Modern Corporation Checklists,* Warren, Gorham & Lamont, 1972; *Analyzing a Real Estate Investment,* Warren, Gorham & Lamont, 1974; *Real Estate Financing Techniques,* Warren, Gorham & Lamont, 1974; *Modern Real Estate and Mortgage Forms,* Warren, Gorham & Lamont, Volume I, 1970, revised edition, 1978, Volume III (with Owen T. Smith), 1974, revised edition, 1976, Volume II (with Donald Benton and Robert Lopatin), 1979; *How to Evaluate Apartment Building Investments,* Warren, Gorham & Lamont, 1978; (with Jack Kusnet) *Arnold Encyclopedia of Real Estate,* Warren, Gorham & Lamont, 1978; (with Charles H. Wurzebach and Mike E. Miles) *Modern Real Estate, 1980,* Warren, Gorham & Lamont, 1980. Editor of *Real Estate Review* and *Mortgage and Real Estate Executives Report.*

SIDELIGHTS: Arnold told *CA:* "Real estate has undergone a dynamic transformation in the past twenty years. At the beginning of that period, it was a local investment medium for upper-income investors. Today, the real estate market is national and even international, with investors ranging from large pension funds and public syndicates to the small investor. During these two decades, an enormous demand for information and instruction in real estate has developed and I was fortunate to have chosen this field to specialize in. Writing a twice-monthly newsletter is challenging because it requires me to keep current in the field. At the other extreme, putting together a project as large as the *Encyclopedia of Real Estate,* which runs over one thousand pages, enabled me to pull together in one place a comprehensive collection of material on the subject.

"Although real estate values are not likely to grow for the balance of the century at the rate of the past ten years, real estate investment will never revert to its earlier pattern of domination by a small group of sophisticated investors. Instead, it will remain a strong competitor with the stock market for the investment capital of both institutions and individuals. At the same time, the public increasingly recognizes the important social and economic role of the 'built-environment.' Witness recent trends toward historic preservation, limits on new development (particularly residential), and energy conservation in buildings. All this means that participation in real estate—whether as investor, critic, author, or otherwise—should be exciting in the years ahead."

* * *

ARNOLD, Bruce 1936-

PERSONAL: Born September 6, 1936, in London, England; son of George (in military) and Margaret (Shaw) Arnold; married Ysabel Maeve Cleave (a writer); children: Hugo George Jacob, Samuel Joshua, Polly Maeve. *Education:* Trinity College, M.A., 1961. *Home:* Rosney House, Albert Rd., Glenageary, County Dublin, Ireland. *Agent:* Curtis Brown, 1 Craven Hill, London W2 3EW, England.

CAREER: Writer. *Irish Times,* Dublin, Ireland, staff writer, 1961-64; free-lance journalist, 1964-71; *Irish Independent,* Dublin, parliamentary correspondent, 1971-79. Also worked as teacher and director of gallery. *Military service:* British Army, 1954-56; became 2nd lieutenant. *Awards, honors:* Outstanding Journalist Award from Benson & Hedges, 1976, 1977.

WRITINGS: A Concise History of Irish Art, Thames & Hudson, 1969; *A Singer at the Wedding* (novel), Hamish Hamilton, 1978; *The Nightingale* (novel), Hamish Hamilton, 1980; *Orpen* (biography of William Orpen), J. Cape, 1980. Author of columns for *Irish Independent* and *Magill.* Contributor to *Hibernia, Manchester Guardian,* and *Sunday Independent.*

WORK IN PROGRESS: The Spanish Captive and *The Diary of a Naval Man,* the final volumes in a tetralogy which includes *A Singer at the Wedding* and *The Nightingale.*

SIDELIGHTS: Arnold told *CA:* "*A Singer at the Wedding* is about the attempt which a child, grown up, makes to untangle the unhappiness of a parent. *The Nightingale* deals with a more tragic and far-reaching set of events. *The Spanish Captive* continues the story into the early manhood of the son and the further disintegration of the father. The final volume, *The Diary of a Naval Man,* goes back in time to a brief set of episodes in which a measure of happiness was attained. The overall title for the four novels is 'The Coppinger Redemption.'

"I have always been a journalist writing on many subjects, but principally on art and politics. I published the first comprehensive history of Irish art, and also wrote a biography of the Irish painter William Orpen, the leading World War I artist."

In his review of *A Singer at the Wedding,* Auberon Waugh decribed Arnold as "a writer who shows promise." He also noted that the book had "some good moments," and advised Arnold to "show a little more wit, a little less solemnity."

BIOGRAPHICAL/CRITICAL SOURCES: Evening Standard, January 31, 1978.

* * *

ARNOLD, Janet 1932-

PERSONAL: Born October 6, 1932, in Bristol, England; daughter of Frederick Charles and Adeline (Jacob) Arnold. *Education:* West of England College of Art, intermediate certificate in arts and crafts, 1951, N.D.D., 1953, art teacher's diploma, 1954; University of Bristol, certificate in education, 1954. *Office:* Department of Drama and Theatre Studies, Royal Holloway College, University of London, Egham Hill, Egham, Surrey TW20 OEX, England.

CAREER: Part-time theatrical experience in cutting period costumes and working in wardrobes of Theatre Royal, Bristol, England, and Mermaid Theatre, London, 1952-62; industrial experience of couture methods of cutting and sewing at Frederick Starke Ltd. and Victor Stiebel Ltd., 1954-55; Hammersmith Day College, London, England, lecturer in art and dress, 1955-62; Avery Hill College of Education, London, England, senior lecturer in art, dress, and costume, 1962-70; University of London, London, England, recognised teacher, 1969; West Surrey College of Art and Design, Farnham, England, research lecturer in textiles, 1971-74; free-lance writer, researcher, and lecturer, 1975-78. Consultant to Museum of Costume, Royal Scottish Museum, and National Museum of Antiquities of Scotland. *Member:* Society of Authors, National Society for Art Education, Costume Society. *Awards, honors:* Winston Churchill traveling fellowship from Winston Churchill Memorial Trust, 1973, for Spain, Italy, Germany, and Sweden; Jubilee Research Fellow at Royal Holloway College, London, 1978-81.

WRITINGS: Patterns of Fashion, Volume I: *Englishwomen's Dresses and Their Construction, 1660-1860,* Wace, 1964, revised metric edition, Macmillan, 1977, Drama Book Specialists, 1977, Volume II: *Englishwomen's Dresses and Their Construction, 1860-1940,* Wace, 1965, revised metric edition, Macmillan, 1977, Drama Book Specialists, 1977; (with Pegaret Anthony) *Costume,* (a bibliography), Victoria and Albert Museum and the Costume Society, 1966, revised edition, 1974; *Perukes and Periwigs* (booklet), H.M.S.O., 1970; *A Handbook of Costume,* Macmillan, 1973, S. G. Phillips, 1974; *'Lost From Her Majesties Back,'* Costume Society, 1980; *Queen Elizabeth's Wardrobe Unlock'd* (about Elizabeth I), Macmillan, 1980.

Co-author of "For the Sake of Appearance," a television series, British Broadcasting Corp., 1972-73; "Looking at Costume" and "Fashion and Fabric," two films, British Broadcasting Corp., 1973. Contributor to journals in England and Germany, including *Costume, The Burlington Magazine,* and *Waffen-und-Kostuem-kunde.*

WORK IN PROGRESS: Patterns of Fashions, 1550-1620, for Macmillan; a series of books on the cut and construction of clothes from 1550 to 1950, for Macmillan.

SIDELIGHTS: Janet Arnold told *CA:* "I have visited theatres all over Europe and America, as I am interested in the history of theatrical costume design. During the long vacations from 1962 to 1970 I visited museums and art galleries in America, Sweden, Denmark, France, Italy, and Germany, to carry out research on costume and gathering a collection of more than eighty thousand slides, which I use for research and lectures. From 1970 onwards I have spent an equal amount of time visiting galleries in the United Kingdom.

"I work from the primary sources—specimens of costume, paintings, and archive material, recording as much detailed information as I can for the wide range of people who use my books—conservators working on period costumes in museums, social historians, costume historians, teachers, designers, and people making costumes for the theatre."

Arnold also originated the idea of exhibiting the costumes made for two BBC television series, "The Six Wives of Henry VIII" and "Elizabeth R." The "Henry VIII" exhibit, "originally intended for teachers, students, and children," was displayed at the Bethnal Green Museum in 1970. The "Elizabeth R" exhibition was held at the London Museum in 1971.

*   *   *

ARON, Robert   1898-1975

PERSONAL: Born May 25, 1898, in Le Vesinet, France; died April 19, 1975, in Paris, France; son of Georges and Louise (Lippmann) Aron; married Sabine Pelletier, 1929. *Education:* Attended Sorbonne, University of Paris. *Home:* 2 rue Michel-Ange, Paris 16e, France.

CAREER: Writer. Co-founder of Personalist Movement (Ordre Nouveau) in France, 1930; associated with governments of Henri Giraud and Charles de Gaulle in France, 1943-44; director of theoretical studies in Mouvement Federaliste Francais and La Federation, 1974-75. Literary director of Librairie Fayard. *Military service:* Served with French

Foreign Legion, 1914-18; became chevalier; received Croix de Guerre. *Member:* Academie Francaise. *Awards, honors:* Prix Femina-Vacaresco, 1961; Prix Eve-Delacroix, 1967.

WRITINGS—In English: (With Georgette Elgey) *Histoire de Vichy, 1940-44* (history), Fayard, 1954, translation by Humphrey Hare published as *The Vichy Regime, 1940-44,* Macmillan, 1958, two-volume edition, Fayard, 1966; *Histoire de la liberation de la France, juin 1944–mai 1945* (history), Fayard, 1959, abridged translations by Hare published as *De Gaulle Before Paris: The Liberation of France, June–August, 1944,* Putnam, (London) 1962, Scribner, 1964, and as *De Gaulle Triumphant: The Liberation of France, August 1944–May 1945,* Putnam, 1964, combined two-volume edition published as *The Liberation of France,* Putnam, 1962-64; *Les Annees obscures de Jesus* (biography), 4th edition, B. Grasset, 1960, translation by Frances Frenaye published as *Jesus of Nazareth: The Hidden Years,* Morrow, 1962; *Histoire de Dieu: Le Dieu des origines,* Librairie academique Perrin, 1964, translation by Frenaye published as *The God of the Beginnings,* Morrow, 1966; *An Explanation of de Gaulle,* translated from the French by Marianne Sinclair, Harper, 1966; *The Jewish Jesus,* Orbis, 1971.

Other: *Decadence de la nation francaise,* Rieder, 1931; *Le Cancer americain,* Rieder, 1931; *Dictature de la liberte,* B. Grasset, 1935; *Victoire a Waterloo,* Michel, c. 1937, reprinted, Rombaldi, 1976; *Retour a l'eternel,* Michel, 1946; (with Alexandre Marc) *Principes de federalisme,* Le Portulan, 1948; (editor) *De Marx au marxisme, 1848-1948,* Editions de Flore, 1948; *Les Frontaliers de neant,* Editions de Flore, 1949; *Le Piege ou nous a pris l'histoire,* Michel, 1950; (editor) *Mors et vita,* Plon, 1951; (editor) Pierre Joseph Proudhon, *Portrait de Jesus,* P. Horay, 1951; *Ce que je crois,* B. Grasset, 1955; *L'Ere des federations,* Plon, 1958; *Le Grands Dossiers de l'histoire contemporaine* (history), Librairie academique Perrin, 1962; *Les Origines de la guerre d'Algerie* (history), Fayard, 1962; *Nouveaux Grands Dossiers de l'histoire contemporaine,* Librairie academique Perrin, 1963; *Charles de Gaulle,* Librairie academique Perrin, 1964; (author of introduction) A. D. Arielli, *Israel: Itineraire historique et contemporain,* Editions des deux-Mondes, 1964; *Histoire de l'epuration,* Fayard, 1967; *Les Grandes Heures de la Troisieme Republique* (history), six volumes, Librairie academique Perrin, 1967-68; *Ainsi priait Jesus enfant,* B. Grasset, 1968; *L'Etoile de David et la fleur de lys,* Editions du Jour, 1969; (with others) *L'Histoire contemporaine depuis, 1945* (history), Larousse, 1969; *Discours contre la methode,* Plon, 1974; *Lettre ouverte a l'Eglise de France,* Michel, 1975; *Dossiers de la Seconde Guerre mondiale,* Plon, 1976; *Histoire des annese 40* (history), ten volumes, J. Tallandier, 1976-77; (with Andre Neher and Victor Malka) *Le Judaisme,* Buchet/Chastel, 1977.

SIDELIGHTS: Aron was best known for his books written on the Nazi occupation of France during World War II, *The Vichy Regime* and *The Liberation of France.* Of the latter, Carlyle Morgan commented that "it is written with a fine sincerity, and with that lucidity that makes the best French writing as visual as a scenario." While one reviewer for *Best Sellers* considered *The Liberation of France* "a long, sometimes too-detailed account," D. W. Brogan disagreed, and heralded it a "wise, generous and learned book."

In addition to his historical writings, Aron authored numerous books on religious subjects, and was deeply involved with Judaism. *Jesus of Nazareth: The Hidden Years* is his most popular religious work.

OBITUARIES: New York Times, April 20, 1975; *Washing-*

ton Post, April 20, 1975; *AB Bookman's Weekly*, June 2, 1975.

BIOGRAPHICAL/CRITICAL SOURCES: *Best Sellers*, June 1, 1964, April 1, 1966, May 15, 1966; *Christian Science Monitor*, June 11, 1964; *New York Times Book Review*, July 5, 1964, July 24, 1966; *Book Week*, July 19, 1964, May 1, 1966; *New Yorker*, August 1, 1964, April 16, 1966; *Virginia Quarterly Review*, autumn, 1964; *America*, April 2, 1966; *Harper's*, April 16, 1966; *New York Review of Books*, May 12, 1966; *Saturday Review*, August 6, 1966.*

*   *   *

ASHBEE, Paul 1918-

PERSONAL: Born in 1918, in Maidstone, England; son of Lewis and Hannah M. E. (Brett) Ashbee; married Richmal Crompton Lamburn Disher (a library executive); children: Edward G. C., Catherine R. C. *Education:* Attended Institute of Archaeology (London), University of Bristol, and University of Leicester. *Home:* Old Rectory, Chedgrave, Norwich NR14 6ND, England. *Office:* University of East Anglia, Earlham Hall, Norwich, Norfolk NR4 7TJ, England.

CAREER: Worked for Control Commission in Germany, 1946-49; British Museum, London, England, supervisor of archaeological excavations with Ministry of Public Building and Works, 1949-54; associated with Inner London Education Authority, London, 1954-69; University of East Anglia, Norwich, England, archaeologist, 1969—, member of Centre of East Anglian Studies, 1969-75. Member of Royal Commission on Ancient and Historical Monuments, 1975—; chairperson of Scole Committee for East Anglian Archaeology. *Military service:* British Army, 1939-46. *Member:* Society of Antiquaries (fellow), Prehistoric Society, Royal Archaeological Institute, Cornwall Archaeological Society (president, 1976-80), Wiltshire Archaeological and Natural History Society, Norfolk and Norwich Archaeological Society.

WRITINGS: *The Bronze Age Round Barrow in Britain*, Phoenix House, 1960; *The Earthen Long Barrow in Britain*, Phoenix House, 1970; *Ancient Sicily*, David & Charles, 1975; *The Ancient British: A Social-Archaeological Narrative*, Geo Abstracts, 1978. Contributor to archaeology and antiquarian journals.

WORK IN PROGRESS: Research on the cultural progress of the early British peoples and on the history of antiquarian thought, including ideas about American Indians.

SIDELIGHTS: Ashbee comments: "I have had a life-long fascination with the world of man in which cultural inheritance has increasingly outweighed genetic inheritance as the controlling factor. This is expressed as a preoccupation with the evolution of ideas about the past which emerged in the sixteenth century in a form similar to the present day.

"I am especially attracted by the varieties of landscape and architecture to be found in Britain and Ireland."

AVOCATIONAL INTERESTS: Skiing.

*   *   *

ASHLEY, Bernard 1935-

PERSONAL: Born April 2, 1935, in London, England; son of Alfred Walter (an assistant company secretary) and Vera (a store proprietor; maiden name, Powell) Ashley; married Iris Holbrook (a deputy headteacher), August 2, 1958; children: Christopher, David, Jonathan. *Education:* Trent Park College of Education, certificate, 1957; Cambridge Institute of Education, associate diploma, 1971. *Home:* 128 Heath-

wood Gardens, London SE7 8ER, England. *Office:* Charlton Manor Junior School, Hornfair Rd., London SE7 7BE, England.

CAREER: Teacher at primary school in Gravesend, England, 1957-65, and head-teacher at primary school in Hertford Heath, England, 1965-71; headteacher at junior school in London, England, 1971-76; Charlton Manor Junior School, London, headteacher, 1977—. Member of International Board on Books for Young People. *Military service:* Royal Air Force, 1953-55; became senior aircraftman. *Member:* National Book League, National Association of Head-teachers, Society of Authors. *Awards, honors:* Other Award from Children's Rights Workshop, 1976, for *The Trouble With Donovan Croft;* commended for Carnegie Medal, 1979, for *A Kind of Wild Justice.*

WRITINGS—All for children: *Don't Run Away* (reader), Allman, 1965; *Wall of Death* (reader), Allman, 1966; *Space Shot* (reader), Allman, 1967; *The Big Escape* (reader), Allman, 1967; *The Men and the Boats: Britain's Life-Boat Service* (nonfiction), Allman, 1968; *Weather Men* (nonfiction), Allman, 1970, revised edition, 1974; *The Trouble With Donovan Croft*, (novel), Oxford University Press, 1974; *Terry on the Fence* (novel), Oxford University Press, 1975, S. G. Phillips, 1977; *All My Men* (novel), Oxford University Press, 1977, S. G. Phillips, 1978; *A Kind of Wild Justice* (novel), S. G. Phillips, 1979; *Break in the Sun* (novel), Oxford University Press, 1980; *Dinner Ladies Don't Count*, Julia MacRae Books, in press; *I'm Trying to Tell You* (volume of short stories), Kestrel Books, in press. Contributor to various educational and literary journals.

WORK IN PROGRESS: An untitled novel for Julia MacRae Books.

SIDELIGHTS: The heroes in Bernard Ashley's novels are frequently misunderstood children whose indifferent attitudes towards school reflect concerns they may be having outside the classroom. Worries about home life, he contends, are becoming increasingly evident. "When I was in Gravesend (1957-65) if I had one child in a class with one parent he was special," Ashley explained. "Now there is quite a large proportion of such children."

Typical of Ashley's troubled children is Ronnie, the hero in *A Kind of Wild Justice*. His teacher, who has quit trying to get him to respond to her questions on poetry, sees only one side of his life. A view of the other side, as presented by Ashley, reveals why Ronnie might find concentrating on schoolwork difficult: his dad keeps company with a group of gangsters who have threatened to break Ronnie's back if his father ever leaks information about them; his mother, meanwhile, is plotting to get her husband convicted so that she can skip town with another man.

Ashley hopes that his books will give kids like Ronnie a story they can read. It's not that he objects to animal stories and magical adventure tales, he simply believes children's books should also more closely resemble the lives their readers lead. He knows, too, that they must entertain. "*Wild Justice* is a thriller first and foremost," Ashley reminds. "It is meant to be a pleasure to read. After the pleasure, maybe, there will hopefully be something else a child can take from it, someone else they can identify with or understand a bit better."

As a teacher for more than twenty years, Ashley realizes that the reasons behind a child's behavior are complex. Paul in *All My Men*, for example, finds himself in trouble "not through vice or even laziness but because of a natural desire to be accepted as one of the footballing crowd, and not to become a loner like clever Arthur,'' wrote the *Times Literary Supplement*. Similarly, *A Kind of Wild Justice*, says Ann Thwaite, ''is pretty convincing evidence for those of us (not just soft-hearted social workers) who believe that kids get into trouble not because of original sin but because of what has been done to them and left undone.''

Ashley maintains this same attitude of understanding when dealing with adults. He once tried to subdue a swearing parent in a school corridor and received the parent's fist, and a broken jaw, for his efforts. ''He was Ronnie 30 years on,'' Ashley remarked. ''He had lived a violent life.''

Ashley abstains from giving a moral tone to his stories so that he can emphasize the importance of understanding and sympathy, rather than accusation and blame, in dealing with children's problems. Consequently, as in *Terry on the Fence*, Ashley's moral issues are anything but clear-cut,'' said *Books and Bookmen*. Likewise in *A Kind of Wild Justice*, there are ''no easy answers,'' said the *Times Literary Supplement*. ''Still, . . . many children from quite different backgrounds will feel a stab of sympathy and identification with Ronnie.''

Ashley told *CA:* ''The acid test of a book is how one feels inclined to catalogue it. When it can be as happily placed on the reference shelf under 'adoption,' 'divorce,' or 'death,' as alphabetically under another, then it has already proclaimed its failure as fiction. A need exists in Britain for more books that reflect the multi-racial nature of society, for all of us to read, but if such books emerge other than because their writers have pleasure-giving stories to tell, then they will be as spurious as the worst offerings of the old religious press. A writer with a purpose is no better than the over-devout teacher telling a story in assembly. No hymn book slams closed as loudly as the young mind when the moral is reached.''

BIOGRAPHICAL/CRITICAL SOURCES: Books and Bookmen, December, 1975; *Best Sellers*, May, 1977; *Times Literary Supplement*, October 21, 1977, December 1, 1978; *Times Educational Supplement*, October 27, 1978.

* * *

ASHTON, Winifred   1888-1965
(Clemence Dane)

OBITUARY NOTICE: Born in 1888 in Blackheath, England; died March 28, 1965, in London, England. Portraitist, actress, and author. Ashton began her writing career after several years of teaching, portrait painting, and acting. She chose her pseudonym from the beautiful St. Clements Dane church in London, England, which was later destroyed by a bomb during World War II. Ashton wrote many popular books, including her first novel, *Regiment of Women*, published in 1917. Her first play, ''A Bill of Divorcement,'' was successfully adapted from her 1919 novel, *Legend*, for production in London and New York during the 1920's. She also wrote plays about Shakespeare, the Brontes, and Thomas Chatterton. *Broome Stages, The Moon Is Feminine*, and *He Brings Great News* are among her later novels. Obituaries and other sources: *New York Times*, March 29, 1965; *Newsweek*, April 12, 1965; *The New Century Handbook of English Literature*, revised edition, Appleton, 1967; *Longman Companion to Twentieth Century Literature*, Longman, 1970; *McGraw-Hill Encyclopedia of World Drama*, McGraw, 1972; *Modern World Drama: An Encyclopedia*, Dutton, 1972.

ATKIN, Flora B(lumenthal)   1919-

PERSONAL: Born May 15, 1919, in Baltimore, Md.; daughter of Joseph (a lawyer) and Anna (Levy) Blumenthal; married Maurice David Atkin (an economist), December 25, 1941; children: Joseph, Barrie, Jonathan. *Education:* Attended George Washington University, 1935-38; Syracuse University, A.B. (cum laude), 1940; attended Bennington College, 1941, Catholic University of America, 1959-61. *Politics:* Democrat. *Religion:* Jewish. *Home and office:* 5507 Uppingham St., Chevy Chase, Md. 20015. *Agent:* Pat Whitton, New Plays, Inc., Box 273, Rowayton, Conn. 06853.

CAREER: Jewish Community Center, Washington D.C., director of recreational arts department, 1940-44, founding director of Creative Arts Day Camp, 1941-44; instructor of creative dance, drama, music, and director and choreographer, 1940-68; Adventure Theatre, Glen Echo, Md., founding director and playwright of In-School Players, 1969-79; artist-consultant to public schools and Humanities Project in Arlington, Va., 1977-80. Instructor at Howard University, 1942-43, Jewish Community Center, 1940-44, Coast Guard Auxilary, 1967-73, National Park Service, 1973-74; guest lecturer at Hebrew University, 1970 and 1978, University of Maryland, 1972 and 1980, San Francisco State University, 1978. Consultant to Washington, D.C., recreation department, 1968, and Jewish Community Council Television Program Committee of Greater Washington, D.C., 1968-80. Cultural arts chairperson of Jewish Community Center, 1968-69.

MEMBER: International Association of Theatre for Children and Youth, American Theatre Association, Children's Theatre Association of America, Washington Federation of Music Clubs (District of Columbia; state junior counselor, 1944), Washington Music Teachers Association (District of Columbia; secretary, 1945), Washington Modern Dance Society (District of Columbia), Writer's Center of Glen Echo Park, Phi Sigma Sigma. *Awards, honors:* District of Columbia One-Act Play Tournament, Pauline Eaton Oak Award, 1970, Sybil Baker Award, 1971 and 1973; Eastern States Theatre Association, best director award, 1971, and best production award, 1973; Charlotte B. Chorpenning Cup from Children's Theatre Association of America, 1977, for writing outstanding plays for children; best original script award from Maryland Theatre Festival, 1978, for ''Dig 'N Tel''; special recognition citations from Children's Theatre Association of America, Adventure Theatre, Mid-Atlantic Chapter of American Theatre Association, and Board of Education of Montgomery County, Md.

WRITINGS: Tarradiddle Tales (one-act; first produced in Kennington, Md., 1969; produced in Washington, D.C., at Kennedy Center Opera House, 1969), New Plays, 1970; *Tarradiddle Travels* (one-act; produced in Washington, D.C., 1970), New Plays, 1971; *Golliwhoppers!* (one-act; produced in Washington, D.C., at Smithsonian Institute Theatre, 1972), New Plays, 1973; *Skupper-Duppers* (one-act; produced in Washington, D.C., at Kennedy Center, 1974), New Plays, 1975; *Dig 'N Tel* (one-act; produced in Washington, D.C., at Jewish Community Center Theatre, 1978), New Plays, 1978. Contributor of articles to *Dance Observer, Theatre News, Children's Theatre Review*.

WORK IN PROGRESS: A folklore-motivated play on family relationships for family viewing; a play for junior high students on how to deal with crises.

SIDELIGHTS: Atkin designs her children's plays for in-school productions. They are simple, educational plays which can be performed anywhere with a minimum of stage props and costumes.

Atkin draws most of her dramatic material from folklore. She explained to a *Children's Theatre Review* interviewer: "Folk stories have excitement, humor, and never-ending variety. They have educational value: human problems are presented, even through animals. A child can identify with these stories and yet not be frightened by them. There are problems of sibling rivalry, death, and parental difficulties, but they are removed from the child's own world." Consequently, her plays, "Tarradiddle Tales," "Tarradiddle Travels," "Golliwhoppers!," and "Dig 'N Tel," derive their subjects from American, Jewish, and worldwide folklore. Atkin's most recent play, "Dig 'N Tel," weaves a story around the history of three artifacts found on an archaeological dig at a tel, or hill, in the middle East.

Atkin's plays take a total-theatre approach in which a wide range of dramatic skills are used. She incorporates music, singing, mime, puppetry, narration, dialogue, and dance to give children a taste of the richness of theatre while expanding their knowledge of the adult world. To enhance this goal, Atkin also encourages audience participation: "I want warmth and rapport between the players and the audience. I want the children to feel the production on all levels. Also, the children need a kinesthetic release. Every one of my plays starts with the performers in contact with the children. When children enter the auditorium for *Skupper-Duppers,* they are greeted at the door by the boatswain's 'Welcome aboard! Put your gear on the starboard side and find a deck chair on the port side.' The children's immediate, delighted response is 'We're on a ship,' and they are eager to help swab the decks and pull in the lines. The mood is set."

BIOGRAPHICAL/CRITICAL SOURCES: Children's Theatre Review, spring, 1979.

*　　*　　*

ATYEO, Don 1950-

PERSONAL: Surname is pronounced *At*-yo; born February 10, 1950, in Colac, Australia; son of Leslie George (in business) and Marjorie (Constable) Atyeo. *Education:* University of Melbourne, diploma in journalism, 1970. *Home:* 16 Grove Mansions, Clapham Common, North Side, London S.W.4, England. *Agent:* Deborah Rogers Ltd., 5-11 Mortimer St., London W1N 7RH, England. *Office:* Paddington Press, 21 Bentinck St., London W.1, England.

CAREER: Age, Melbourne, Australia, journalist, 1968-71; free-lance magazine writer in the Far East, India, North Africa, the Netherlands, and England, 1971-74; currently affiliated with Paddington Press, London, England.

WRITINGS: (With Felix Dennis) *Bruce Lee: King of Kung Fu,* Straight Arrow Books, 1974; *Muhammad Ali: The Holy Warrior,* Simon & Schuster, 1975; *Blood and Guts: Violence in Sports,* Paddington Press, 1979; *The Book of Sports Quotes,* Omnibus Press, 1979. Contributor to magazines. Editor of *International Times;* deputy editor of *Oz.*

WORK IN PROGRESS: Another book for Paddington Press.

SIDELIGHTS: Atyeo's books have been published in France and Mexico. He wrote: "I travel at least six months of every year, both for research and relaxation. Although I am based in London, I do much of my writing in the United States and southern France. I am particularly interested in people, hence the travel, the two biographies, the sociological appraisal of sport (*Blood and Guts*), and the new book, which comprises many personal interviews with a broad cross-section of subjects."

AUSLAND, John C(ampbell) 1920-

PERSONAL: Surname is pronounced *Awz*-lund; born July 14, 1920, in La Crosse, Wis.; son of John Engebo and Margaret (Weir) Ausland; married Malory Campbell (a secretary), August 15, 1946 (separated); children: Anne, Hayden, Steven. *Education:* Attended Hardin Junior College, 1940-42, and Laval University, summer, 1946; Princeton University, B.A., 1947, graduate study, 1947-49. *Home:* Sondreveien 4, Oslo 3, Norway.

CAREER: Radio announcer in Vernon and Wichita Falls, Tex., 1939-42; U.S. Department of State, Washington, D.C., foreign service officer in Frankfort and Berlin, West Germany, 1949-51, at East German desk in Washington, D.C., 1951-54, political officer at American embassies in Belgrade, Yugoslavia, 1954-56, and Canberra, Australia, 1956-58, consul in Adelaide, Australia, 1958-61, member of Berlin Task Force in Washington, D.C., 1961-64, member of senior seminar, 1964-65, political adviser to Joint Chiefs of Staff, 1965-67, director of political-military planning, 1967-69, deputy chief of mission at American embassy in Oslo, Norway, 1969-73, executive secretary of U.S. delegation to Strategic Arms Limitation Talks (SALT) in Geneva, Switzerland, 1973-74; writer, 1974—. Attended conferences with foreign ministers of Southeast Asia Treaty Organization (SEATO) and North Atlantic Treaty Organization (NATO). *Military service:* U.S. Army, Infantry, 1942-45; served in European theater; became captain; received Silver Star and Bronze Star.

MEMBER: International Institute for Strategic Studies, American Club (Oslo; president, 1975-77). *Awards, honors:* Superior honor award from U.S. Department of State, 1965; civilian superior service award from U.S. Secretary of Defense, 1967.

WRITINGS: Norway, Oil, and Foreign Policy, Westview Press, 1979; *Bak Ambassadens Murer* (title means "Behind Embassy Walls"), Cappelen, 1979.

WORK IN PROGRESS: "My writing now is concerned with the question, 'What has happened to the United States?'"

SIDELIGHTS: Ausland commented: "I published my first newspaper at age fourteen and, having written my whole life, it was perhaps inevitable that I have drifted into writing since retiring. This has gone so well that it is beginning to interfere with my sailing and skiing."

*　　*　　*

AYRES, Paul
See AARONS, Edward S(idney)

*　　*　　*

AYRES, Robert U(nderwood) 1932-

PERSONAL: Born June 29, 1932, in Plainfield, N.J.; son of John U. (an executive and writer) and Alice (Hutchinson) Ayres; married Leslie Wentz (a computer analyst), June 26, 1954; children: Jennifer Leigh. *Education:* University of Chicago, B.A., 1952, B.S., 1954; University of Maryland, M.S., 1956; King's College, London, Ph.D., 1958. *Religion:* Society of Friends (Quakers). *Home:* 2905 Davenport St. N.W., Washington, D.C. 20008. *Office:* Department of Engineering and Public Policy, Carnegie-Mellon University, Pittsburgh, Pa. 15213.

CAREER: Hudson Institute, Harmon-on-Hudson, N.Y., research associate, 1962-67; International Research & Technology Corp., Arlington, Va., vice-president, 1968-76; Delta Research Corp., Arlington, vice-president, 1977-78;

Carnegie-Mellon University, Pittsburgh, Pa., professor of engineering and public policy, 1979—. Chairperson of board of directors of Variflex Corp.; consultant to United Nations and World Bank. *Member:* American Economic Association, Society of Automotive Engineers, World Future Society, World Future Studies Federation.

WRITINGS: Technological Forecasting and Long-Range Planning, McGraw, 1969; (with A. V. Kneese and R. C. d'Arge) *Economics and the Environment,* Johns Hopkins Press, 1970; (with R. P. McKenna) *Alternatives to the Internal Combustion Engine,* Johns Hopkins Press, 1972; *Resources, Environment, and Economics,* Wiley, 1978; *Uncertain Futures,* Wiley, 1979. Contributor to technical journals. Editorial adviser for *Journal of Technological Forecasting and Social Change* and *Journal of Environmental Economics and Management.*

WORK IN PROGRESS: Research for a book on long-range resource and energy policy, completion expected in 1982.

SIDELIGHTS: Ayres comments: "My wife and I are almost unique among our contemporary acquaintances who have been married to the same person for twenty-five years. Otherwise I am a dilettante. I have worked in physics, ecology, economics, and most recently, engineering. I invent. Some day I hope to design and build a house incorporating a number of new concepts. I also hope to learn to play the piano. I have been in all the continents except Australia. I loathe politics and politicians, lawyers and the medical profession (in the abstract), and 'celebrities.'

'Writing is how I assert myself and (try to) influence the environment I live in. In this, I suppose, I differ from people who seek more direct means of exercising power. Till recently I have only sought to be heard by fellow scientists or academics. *Uncertain Futures* is the first of my books that was intended to reach a wider audience. The original objective was to write for an informed but non-technical 'good citizen,' who is interested in consciously helping to shape the future of this nation—or, for that matter, mankind. I tried, possibly too hard, not to oversimplify or pre-digest difficult ideas to the 'quotable quote' level that seems to be the norm for the popular media. The kind of book I write next depends very much on how this one is received."

AVOCATIONAL INTERESTS: Active sports (tennis, running in road races), painting, making decorative *objets d'art,* reading science fiction and thrillers.

*   *   *

AZORIN
See MARTINEZ RUIZ, Jose

B

BACALL, Lauren   1924-

PERSONAL: Birth-given name, Betty Joan Perske; born September 16, 1924, in New York, N.Y.; daughter of William and Natalie (Bacall) Perske; married Humphrey Bogart (an actor), May 21, 1945 (died January 14, 1957); married Jason Robards, Jr. (an actor), July 4, 1961 (divorced, 1969); children: (first marriage) Stephen, Leslie; (second marriage) Sam. Education: Attended American Academy of Dramatic Arts, 1941. Home: 1 West 72nd St., New York, N.Y. 10023. Agent: Peter Witt Associates, 37 West 57th St., New York, N.Y. 10019.

CAREER: Actress in films and on stage; fashion model. Made stage debut in "Johnny 2 x 4," March 16, 1942; performed on dramatic radio programs, 1942; made film debut in "To Have and Have Not," Warner Bros., 1944; subsequently appeared in films, including "The Big Sleep," 1944, "Dark Passage," 1947, "Key Largo," 1948, "How to Marry a Millionaire," 1953, "Blood Alley," 1955, and "Murder on the Orient Express," 1974; appeared on Broadway in "Goodbye Charlie," 1959, "Cactus Flower," 1965-67, and "Applause," 1969-71; also appeared on television in "Petrified Forest," Producer's Showcase, 1955, and "Blithe Spirit," Hallmark Hall of Fame, 1956. Member: Screen Actors Guild, American Federation of Television and Radio Artists, Actors Equity Association. Awards, honors: Award from American Academy of Dramatic Arts, 1963; Antoinette Perry Award (Tony), 1970, for "Applause."

WRITINGS: Lauren Bacall By Myself, Knopf, 1978.

SIDELIGHTS: "The interesting thing about Bacall," Richard Cohen wrote, "is that she started as a sex kitten, as a woman men were supposed to find attractive, and she wound up as a woman other women find attractive. She is a woman they care about—emulate in some cases." This transition is depicted in her autobiography, Lauren Bacall By Myself, which traces her life from her sudden fame as "Bogey's Baby" through the two decades since Bogart's death.

According to Christopher Lehmann-Haupt, "the big surprise of 'By Myself' is that when the author first went to Hollywood and made 'To Have and Have Not,' at the age of 19, she was a dreamy stagestruck innocent, a 'nice Jewish girl,' as she keeps calling herself, with about as much sexual experience—outside of her imagination, at least—as a fluff of thistledown." But she immediately met Humphrey Bogart, twenty-five years her senior, and their subsequent romance and marriage became Hollywood legend. In her autobiography, Bacall says of Bogart: "I was so much in love with that man that when he left I felt a pain in my heart. I actually did. He was so much my life that I literally couldn't think of anyone else—had to catch my breath when he went away. When I hear the word happy, I think of then. Then I lived the full meaning of the word everyday. Since then it has been elusive." From the start, Bacall's sultry, seductive on-screen image belied the romantic naivete of her private life. Not until Bogart's death in 1957 did she develop that "steely independence" for which she is now known.

Critical response to By Myself has been favorable. Much has been made of the fact that Bacall wrote the book entirely by herself—in long hand on yellow legal paper—as well as of her intimate portrait of Bogart. Nan Robertson was impressed with the book and stated that it is "notable for generosity to others, honesty about herself and restraint—three qualities that are seldom present in show business memoirs." According to Larry McMurty, "The memoirs of performers often fail because the vitality that informs their performances is so volatile and kinetic a strain that it won't submit to print. . . . Lauren Bacall's memoir is an exception. Her writing is not polished, but it carries more than a little of her vitality."

AVOCATIONAL INTERESTS: Fashion, tennis, needlepoint.

BIOGRAPHICAL/CRITICAL SOURCES: Life, February 11, 1966, April 3, 1970; Look, March 22, 1966, April 21, 1970; Saturday Evening Post, March 21, 1966; McCall's, July, 1966, February, 1975; Redbook, July, 1966; Time, July 29, 1966, December 25, 1978; Mademoiselle, August, 1966; Joe Hyams, Bogart and Bacall; A Love Story, McKay, 1975; Howard Greenberger, Bogey's Baby, W. H. Allen, 1976; Harper's Bazaar, February, 1977, November, 1978; Lauren Bacall, Lauren Bacall By Myself, Knopf, 1978; Chicago Tribune, December 25, 1978; Chicago Tribune Magazine, January 7, 1979; New York Times Book Review, January 7, 1979, March 4, 1979; New Yorker, January 8, 1979; New York Times, January 9, 1979, January 11, 1979; Washington Post, January 9, 1979, January 14, 1979, January 25, 1979; People, January 29, 1979.*

*   *   *

BACHMAN, Ingeborg   1926-1973

PERSONAL: Born June 25, 1926, in Klagenfurt, Austria;

died October 16, 1973, in Rome, Italy. *Education:* Attended Universities of Graz, Innsbruck, and Vienna, 1945-50, earned Ph.D.

CAREER: Poet and author of short stories. Member of editorial staff of radio station in Vienna, Austria, 1951-53; Frankfurt University, Frankfurt, West Germany, lecturer in poetry, 1959-60. *Member:* Deutsche Akademie fuer Sprache und Dichtung (corresponding member). *Awards, honors:* Literary award from *Gruppe 47*, 1953; award from Kulturkreis der deutschen Industrie, 1955; award from Freie Hansestadt Bremen, 1957; Buecher Prize, 1964.

WRITINGS—In English: *Das dreissigste Jahr* (short stories), [Germany], 1961, 2nd edition, 1966, translation of original edition by Michael Bullock published as *The Thirtieth Year*, Knopf, 1964. Translations of works represented in anthologies, including *Modern German Poetry*, edited by Michael Hamburge and Christopher Middleton, 1962, *Twentieth Century German Verse*, edited by P. Bridgewater, 1963, and *German Writing Today*, Penguin, 1967.

Other; all published in Germany: *Die gestundete Zeit* (poems; title means "Borrowed Time"), 1953, S. Piper, 1968; *Herrenhaus* (radio play), 1954; *Die Zikaden* (radio play), 1955; *Anrufung des grossen Baeren* (poems; title means "Invocation of the Great Bear"), 1956, S. Piper, 1974; *Der gute Gott von Manhattan* (radio play), 1958; (librettist with H. W. Henze) *Der Prinz von Homburg* (opera), B. Schoot's Soehne, 1960; *Ingeborg Bachmann: Gedichte, Erzaehlungen, Hoerspiel, Essays*, 1964, S. Piper, 1974; *Ein Ort fuer Zufalle*, K. Wagenbuch, 1965; (librettist with Henze) *Der junge Lord* (opera), 1965; *Malina* (novel), 1971; *Simultan* (short stories), 1972, S. Piper, 1974.

SIDELIGHTS: Bachmann was considered an existential lyric poet for she wrote of the meaninglessness of life and of modern man's ultimate failure to understand this.

OBITUARIES: New York Times, October 18, 1973.*

* * *

BACON, Nancy 1940-

PERSONAL: Born August 16, 1940, in Arizona; daughter of Willie A. (a rancher) and Atoka (Harris) Bacon; married Don Wilson (a musician), December 26, 1964 (divorced January, 1969); children: Stacey Layne. *Politics:* Democrat. *Religion:* Baptist. *Agent:* Earl Mills Management Agency, P.O. Box 472, Palm Springs, Calif. 92262. *Office:* P.O. Box 1838, Idyllwild, Calif. 92349.

CAREER: Universal Studios, Hollywood, Calif., actress, 1957-60; *Photoplay*, Hollywood, staff writer in Europe, 1960-63; Africa U.S.A., Newhall, Calif., animal trainer, 1963-65; *Confidential*, Hollywood, editor, 1965-66; model and writer, 1966-71; writer, 1971—.

WRITINGS: I'm Not Ashamed (biography of Barbara Payton), Holloway, 1960; *The Low Price of Fame* (novel), Fawcett, 1967; *Hippie Freakout* (novel), Cimber Press, 1968; *Stars in My Eyes, Stars in My Bed* (autobiography), Pinnacle Books, 1971; *Queen of the Best Sellers*, Avon, 1978; *Love's Lusty Passion*, Pinnacle Books, 1979. Also author of novels *The Professional* and *In the Hollow of His Hand*.

Author of columns "Ask Nancy," and "Inside Hollywood With Nancy Bacon"; guest columnist for "Hollywood Reporter." Contributor to magazines, including *Look, National Tattler, Cosmopolitan, Redbook*, and *Coronet*.

Author of films "Man and Wife," "Black Is Beautiful," and "The Low Price of Fame." Writer for television series "The

Untouchables," "Dobie Gillis," "Zane Grey Theater," "Love American Style," "High Chaparral," and "Mod Squad."

SIDELIGHTS: Nancy Bacon told *CA:* "I didn't finish high school, but took to the road, and traveled in Europe and the Orient. I've traveled so much that I'm now content to stay home.

"Peace and quiet are vital to my writing, and I now live on a mountain top. Clean air and a safe neighborhood provide perfect writing conditions."

* * *

BAGINSKI, Frank 1938-

PERSONAL: Born March 28, 1938, in New York, N.Y.; son of Ernest Ferdinand (a railroad engineer) and Mabel (Aldrich) Baginski. *Education:* Attended School of Visual Arts, 1957. *Home and office:* Box 108, Village Sta., New York, N.Y. 10014.

CAREER: Cartoonist, 1954—. Author and illustrator of cartoon panel, "Little Emily," and comic strips, including "Plain Jane," and "Splitsville." Actor in motion pictures under name Frank Aldrich.

WRITINGS: (With Arnie Silverman and Evelyn Glusko) *Batmensch and Rubin* (cartoon satire), Simon & Schuster, 1966; (illustrator) Henry Walker, *Illustrated Hockey Dictionary for Young People*, Harvey House, 1976; (illustrator) Steve Clark, *Illustrated Basketball Dictionary for Young People*, Harvey House, 1977; (self-illustrated) *Book of Smith*, Nellen Publications, 1978; (with Reynolds Dodson) *Splitsville* (cartoon collection), Hawthorn, 1980. Work represented in numerous anthologies. Contributor of cartoons to more than three hundred newspapers and magazines, including *New York Times, Melbourne Sun* (Australia), *Saturday Evening Post, Collier's, Look, New Yorker*, and *Playboy*.

* * *

BAILEY, Don 1942-

PERSONAL: Born in 1942, in Toronto, Ontario, Canada; married Stella Jane Hance, October 31, 1961 (divorced, 1971); married Anne Walshaw (a social worker), November 11, 1973; children: Estelle, Rebecca, Daniel. *Education:* Attended high school in Bathurst, New Brunswick, Canada. *Home:* 22 Spruce St., Toronto, Ontario, Canada. *Agent:* Larry Hoffman, 51 Spruce St., Toronto, Ontario, Canada.

CAREER: United Church of Canada, project coordinator in Toronto, Ontario, 1970-74, administrator in Winnipeg, Manitoba, 1972-75; Canadian Broadcasting Corp. (CBC), Toronto, script writer, 1975-78; free-lance writer, 1978—. Director of halfway house in Peterborough, Ontario, 1976-78. *Awards, honors:* Recipient of Canada Council grants and Ontario Arts Council grants.

WRITINGS: My Bareness Is Not Just My Body (poems), Fiddlehead, 1971; *If You Hum Me a Few Bars I Might Remember the Tune* (stories), Oberon Press, 1973; *The Shapes Around Me* (poems), Fiddlehead, 1973; *In the Belly of the Whale* (novel), Oberon Press, 1974; *Replay* (stories), Oberon Press, 1976; *The Sorry Papers* (stories), Oberon Press, 1979; *Making Up* (novel), Oberon Press, 1980.

Work represented in anthologies, including *Tigers of the Snow*, NEL, 1973; *New Canadian Stories*, Oberon Press, 1975; *Modern Canadian Stories*, BAN, 1975. Contributor to popular magazines, literary journals, and newspapers, including *West Coast Review, Saturday Night, Canadian Forum,* and *Quarry.*

Author of film, television, and radio scripts.

SIDELIGHTS: Bailey told *CA:* "I have little formal education but have always had an interest in writing. While serving a fifteen-year sentence for bank robbery, I began to write. It became a habit I've yet to break."

* * *

BAIN, Kenneth Bruce Findlater 1921-
(Richard Findlater)

PERSONAL: Born December 23, 1921, in London, England; son of Tom (a journalist) and Elizabeth (Bruce) Bain; married Romany Evens, 1948 (divorced, 1961); married Angela Colbert, 1979; children: Simon, Jennie, Toby, Roualeyn. *Home:* Fuchsia Cottage, High St., Milton-under-Wychwood, Oxfordshire, England. *Agent:* A. P. Watt, 26 Bedford Row, London W.C., England.

CAREER: Tribune, London, England, literary editor and theatre critic, 1946-56; *Books and Art,* editor, 1957-58; *Twentieth Century,* editor, 1961-65; *Author,* London, editor, 1961—. Assistant editor of *Observer,* 1963—. Member of council of English Stage Company. *Military service:* Royal Air Force, 1942-46. *Member:* Society of Authors (member of council).

WRITINGS—Under name Richard Findlater: *The Unholy Trade,* Gollancz, 1952; *Grimaldi,* MacGibbon & Kee, 1955, revised edition published as *Joe Grimaldi: His Life and Theatre,* Cambridge University Press, 1979; *Michael Redgrave, Actor,* Heinemann, 1956; *Banned,* MacGibbon & Kee, 1967; *The Player Kings,* Weidenfeld & Nicolson, 1971; *Lilian Baylis,* Allen Lane, 1975; *The Player Queens,* Weidenfeld & Nicolson, 1976; (with Mary Tich) *Little Tich,* Elm Tree, 1979.

Editor: *Memoirs of Grimaldi,* MacGibbon & Kee, 1968; *Comic Cuts,* Deutsch, 1970; *Public Lending Right,* Deutsch, 1971. Author of pamphlets.

* * *

BAKER, George 1915-1975

PERSONAL: Born May 22, 1915, in Lowell, Mass.; died May 7, 1975, in Los Angeles, Calif.; son of Harry and Mary (Portman) Baker. *Residence:* Santa Monica, Calif.

CAREER: Cartoonist. Walt Disney Studios, Hollywood, Calif., animator, 1937-41. *Military service:* U.S. Army, 1941-45; became staff sergeant.

WRITINGS—Cartoons: *The Sad Sack,* Simon & Schuster, 1944; *The New Sad Sack,* Simon & Schuster, 1946. Author of comic strip, "Sad Sack," appearing in *Yank* and later syndicated in numerous magazines and newspapers, until 1975.

SIDELIGHTS: George Baker was the creator of the popular cartoon character Sad Sack, the hapless Army private in the ill-fitting uniform who never seemed to be able to do anything right. Spotlighted for his shortcomings, overlooked for his few achievements, and forever the brunt of "rank-pulling," Sad Sack became a welcome mascot for millions of American soldiers overwhelmed by the inconsistencies and red tape of military life.

The character of Sad Sack has been capitalized into a sizable industry, including drinking glasses, costume jewelry, appliques for clothing, comic books, animated cartoons, and a radio series featuring the voice of Jim Backus, which was later released as a sound recording by Mark 56 Records in 1975. A movie based on Baker's work was produced by Paramount and starred Jerry Lewis as the bungling private.

OBITUARIES: New York Times, May 9, 1975; *Washington Post,* May 10, 1975; *Newsweek,* May 19, 1975; *Time,* May 19, 1975; *Current Biography,* Wilson, August, 1975.*

* * *

BAKER, Scott (MacMartin) 1947-

PERSONAL: Born September 29, 1947, in Oak Park, Ill.; son of Robert MacMartin (a lawyer) and Sally (an antique clothing collector; maiden name, Underwood) Baker; married. *Education:* New College, Sarasota, Fla., B.A., 1969; attended University of California, Irvine, 1969-70; Goddard College, M.A., 1978; attended Sorbonne, University of Paris, 1978-81. *Home:* 4 rue St. Sulpice, Paris 75006, France. *Agent:* Virginia Kidd, P.O. Box 278, Milford, Pa. 18337.

CAREER: Writer, 1972—; Editions Jean-Claude Lattes, Paris, France, currently a reader. *Member:* Science Fiction Writers of America, World SF.

WRITINGS—Science fiction: *Symbiote's Crown,* Berkley Publishing, 1978; *Nightchild,* Berkley Publishing, 1979; *The Ashlu Trilogy,* Volume I: *Drink the Fire From the Flames,* Berkley Publishing, 1980; (editor) Robert Silverberg, *La Fete de St. Dionysos* (short stories), Editions Jean-Claude Lattes, 1980. Contributor to *New Infinity Review.*

WORK IN PROGRESS: Dhampire, "a tantric vampire novel," publication by Berkley Publishing expected in 1981; *The Ashlu Trilogy,* Volume II: *Firedance* (working title) and Volume III: *Shadows in a Dead Hand* (working title), for Berkley Publishing.

SIDELIGHTS: Baker writes: "I am far more interested in writing about things I haven't done, won't do, or wouldn't do, than about things that have any sort of real-life connection with my personal experience. I have little interest in simplistically realistic or naturalistic fiction, or in fiction whose relationship with the 'world of consensus reality' can be taken for granted. I write out of a need to do so, and for my own personal satisfaction."

* * *

BAKER-CARR, Janet 1934-

PERSONAL: Born October 21, 1934, in Surrey, England; married; children: two daughters. *Education:* Attended Webber-Douglas School of Drama, 1954; Harvard University, certificate in arts administration, 1974, Ed.M., 1979. *Residence:* Cambridge, Mass.

CAREER: WXHR-Radio, Boston, Mass., weekend announcer, 1951-53; teacher of drama and dance at private school for the arts in New York City, 1954-55; WXHR-Radio, assistant program director and announcer, 1955-57; WBAI-Radio, New York City, music director, 1957-59, broadcast manager, 1959-60; WXHR-Radio, announcer for "Evening Concert," 1960-64, and "Morning Concert," 1964-68; Harvard University, Cambridge, Mass., assistant director of Institute in Arts Administration, 1973-79. Actress in Cambridge, summers, 1951-52; interviewer for British Broadcasting Corp., 1958; producer and host of national weekly radio program, "Profiles in Music," 1955-60; guest on radio and television programs; public speaker. Member of board of trustees of Cambridge School of Ballet, 1976—. Member of advisory panel of Massachusetts Council on the Arts and Humanities, 1977—. *Member:* Cambridge Society for Early Music (member of board of trustees, 1977—). *Awards, hon-*

ors: Grant from National Endowment for the Arts and Donner Foundation, 1974.

WRITINGS: (With Douglas Schwalbe) *Conflict in the Arts: The Relocation of Authority,* Arts Administration Research Institute, Volume I: *The Orchestra,* 1975, Volume II: *The Museum,* 1976, Volume III: *The Arts Council,* 1977; *Evening at Symphony: A Portrait of the Boston Symphony Orchestra,* Houghton, 1977. Author of a column in *Manhattan East,* 1958-60. Contributor to magazines. Contributing editor of *Harvard,* 1974—.

WORK IN PROGRESS: Articles for magazines.

*   *   *

BALDERSTON, Katharine Canby   1895-1979

OBITUARY NOTICE: Born January 2, 1895, in Boise, Idaho; died November 21, 1979, in South Natick, Mass. Educator, editor, and author. Balderston, who began teaching at Wellesley College in 1920, was the Martha Hale Shackford Professor of English Literature from 1942 until her retirement in 1960, and professor emeritus until her death. Considered an authority on eighteenth-century literature, she was best known for *Thraliana: The Diary of Mrs. Hester Lynch Thrale.* In 1944 she received the Rose Mary Crawshay Prize from the British Academy for her contributions to the field of English literature. Obituaries and other sources: *Directory of American Scholars,* Volume II: *English, Speech, and Drama,* 6th edition, Bowker, 1974; *New York Times,* November 22, 1979.

*   *   *

BALES, Robert F(reed)   1916-

PERSONAL: Born March 9, 1916, in Ellington, Mo.; son of Columbus Lee (a grocer) and Ada Lois (Sloan) Bales; married Dorothy Louise Johnson (a concert violinist), September 14, 1941. *Education:* University of Oregon, B.S., 1930, M.S., 1940; Harvard University, A.M., 1943, Ph.D., 1945. *Politics:* Democrat. *Religion:* Episcopalian. *Home:* 61 Scotch Pine Rd., Weston, Mass. 02193. *Office:* Harvard University, 1320 William James Hall, Cambridge, Mass. 02138.

CAREER: Harvard University, Cambridge, Mass., instructor, 1945-47, assistant professor, 1947-51, lecturer, 1951-55, associate professor, 1955-57, professor of social psychology, 1957—. *Member:* American Academy of Arts and Sciences, American Psychological Association, American Sociological Association, Society for Experimental Social Psychology, Boston Psychoanalytic Society and Institute (affiliate).

WRITINGS: Interaction Process Analysis, Addison-Wesley, 1950, reprinted, University of California Press, 1976; *Personality and Interpersonal Behavior,* Holt, 1970; (with Stephen P. Cohen and Stephen A. Williamson) *Symlog: A System for the Multiple Level Observation of Groups,* Free Press, 1979. Contributor to academic journals.

WORK IN PROGRESS: Material for groups who want self-studies.

SIDELIGHTS: Bales comments: "Frustrated early in the study of Alcoholics Anonymous, for lack of proper observational methods, I have devoted my whole career to the development of methods for the study of small groups, and am one of the prime advocates of an observational (as opposed to an experimental) approach in social psychology."

BARCYNSKI, Leon Roger   1949-
(Osborne Phillips)

PERSONAL: Born May 23, 1949, in London, England; son of Henry Derek (a catering group manager) and Joan Amelia (McCarthy) Hunt. *Education:* Attended secondary school in London, England; studied Theravada Buddhism with u Maung Maung Ji. *Politics:* Moderate Conservative. *Home:* 1661 Woodbury Dr., Lake Elmo, Minn. 55042.

CAREER: Order Aurum Solis O.S.V., London, England, sodalis, 1971-74, head of psychic research, 1971-75, administrator-general, 1974-77, prior, 1977—. Provost of Ogdoadic Council, 1977—. *Member:* International Biographical Association (fellow), British Astrological and Psychic Society (honorary member), Fellowship of Isis.

WRITINGS—All under pseudonym Osborne Phillips; all with Melita Denning: *The Magical Philosophy,* Llewellyn, Volume I: *Robe and Ring,* 1974, Volume II: *The Apparel of High Magick,* 1975, Volume III: *The Sword and the Serpent,* 1975, Volume IV: *The Triumph of Light,* 1978, Volume V: *Mysteria Magica,* 1979; *The Llewellyn Practical Guide to Astral Projection,* Llewellyn, 1979; *Voudon Fire: The Living Reality of the Voodoo Religion,* Llewellyn, 1979; (editor) *Crowley on Magick,* Llewellyn, 1980; *Creative Visualization,* Llewellyn, 1980; *Group Magick,* Llewellyn, 1980; *Talismanic Magick,* Llewellyn, 1980; *Sex Magick for One,* Llewellyn, 1980; *Voodoo Magick,* Llewellyn, 1980; *Evocation of the Gods,* Llewellyn, 1980; *Sex Magick for Two,* Llewellyn, 1980; *The Mystic Art of Divination,* Llewellyn, 1980.

SIDELIGHTS: Barcynski writes: "In past ages, the great wisdom-teachings have always had their deepest springs and their most fecund cradles in secrecy and monasticism. That has been conspicuously true of Buddhism, whose searching philosophy and immaculate logic fascinated me when first I began searching into the nature of human life. From the Sufis and Dervishes to the recluses of Ireland and Scotland, despite all differences in dogma and tradition, the principles of wisdom based on a life of solitude, of withdrawal, was basically the same.

"This is a matter of history and it worked. Thousands of people lived out their chosen lifetimes of dedication, they handed on and in some cases greatly enriched, their traditions, and despite wars and persecutions and all the betrayals to which life in the world at large has always been subject, they succeeded in preserving at least sufficient to make their ideas and ideals intelligible to succeeding generations.

"However, times change. The grain that has been carefully guarded through the winter must be sown in the spring or it will spoil. The solitaries, the monks, the mystics, have always been those who looked most intently into their own souls, and when all is said, no matter what a man or woman may have learned to believe in religion or philosophy, there is but one kind of human soul. That is why this teaching of the Mystery Schools, the descendant of the ancient wisdoms and monasticisms, is obligated to come forward and proclaim itself, to teach and to guide where guidance is needed at the present day. The modern spread of literacy, and the high value set upon time, are two factors which make it both impractical and needless for numbers of people to take years out of their lives in order to seek out and learn personally from individual teachers.

"The Western Mystery Tradition, growing from its far-off beginnings, has met the challenge of time splendidly. The theory of modern physics is daily growing closer to its likeness, modern psychology is nesting in its branches with every appearance of ease. Religions and social tolerance, desirable though these are as virtues, could breed some dangers of indifference and apathy unless a backbone of commonly-held ideas and knowledge of humanity's nature and needs is held by all.''

* * *

BARFORD, Philip (Trevelyan) 1925-

PERSONAL: Born November 23, 1925, in Leeds, England; son of William (a headmaster) and Alice (a teacher; maiden name, Overend) Barford; married Gwynneth Elizabeth Morgan (a teacher), September 23, 1950; children: Jonathan, Adrian. *Education:* University of Leeds, B.Mus., 1949, M.A., 1950. *Politics:* "Left of Center." *Religion:* Buddhist. *Office:* Institute of Extension Studies, University of Liverpool, P.O. Box 147, Liverpool L6Y 3BX, England.

CAREER: University of Liverpool, Liverpool, England, lecturer, 1950-69, senior lecturer in music, 1969—. Visiting assistant professor at University of California, Davis, 1967-68. *Military service:* Royal Air Force, 1943-46. *Member:* Royal Musical Association.

WRITINGS: The Keyboard Music of C.P.E. Bach, Barrie & Rockliff, 1965; *Mahler: Symphonies and Songs,* British Broadcasting Corp., 1970; (contributor) Denis Arnold and Nigel Fortune, editors, *The Beethoven Companion,* Faber, 1971; *Bruckner Symphonies,* British Broadcasting Corp., 1978. Contributor of more than forty articles to music and Buddhist studies journals.

WORK IN PROGRESS: Two books, *Zen in Piano Playing* and *Buddhist Essays.*

SIDELIGHTS: Barford writes: "I am always aware of the attraction of philosophical and religious preoccupation. This has militated against career ambitions in music. As it is, what I have written about music often strongly reflects the philosophical and religious-mystical preoccupations. This dimension becomes stronger as I grow older, creative aspirations being channeled more and more towards Buddhism.

"However, this is not unrelated to my profession in adult education, as a teacher of adults who see the need for continual mental growth. I feel that adult education could well be the most important kind of education there is, and have strong faith in the idea of continuing education, but this would not stop merely with the training of the analytical intellect. A year in California convinced me of the need for a much more rounded view of education, so that intellectual preoccupations ultimately fan out into a wholeness of vision and a growth of world-awareness.

"Indeed, meeting up with American university students revealed clearly that they certainly feel the limitations of current university provision, and have far wider and deeper ideals about what education should be than many academics. Somewhere along the line a breakthrough has to be made from narrow academicism obsessed with analysis and criticism, towards synthesis and that kind of interdisciplinary study which ultimately reveals the background of all significant human activity.

"I live a quiet life of teaching, study, and meditation. I am totally uninterested in prestigious activities or ambitions, but would like to travel in the Far East.

"Of course I love music, especially French piano music; but feel that I have written enough about the art from an academic, musicological point of view. Buddhism, with which I became acquainted in the RAF, and rambling on the beauti-

ful hills around my home in North Wales have so stimulated the intuitionist aspect of my experience that I have largely lost interest in the abstract analysis of musical structures. All this continues subconsciously anyway; and as musical structure tends to arise spontaneously in a composer's creative depths I am content to respond to his work in the same spirit. The conscious work a composer does on his material is really the attempt to become conscious of what is, in a deeper sense, already there. My strong hunch is that we are approaching the end of a phase of excessive intellectualism not only in music but throughout the entire field of knowledge, and that this has seriously warped our perception of the world and our insight into reality. Musicians, particularly university musicians, should relax more. As I gradually free myself from academicism I find that my personal preferences have moved somewhat away from the Germanic idiom towards the exquisite sensibility of the French; and I now prefer a piece by Debussy or Faure to a fugue by Bach.

"Hegel and Goethe were great influences in my youth, and the Hegel volume in Scribner's Philosophical Library was a pocket bible during the 1950's. I have often quoted from their work in published articles (see, e.g., 'Beethoven the Man' in *The Beethoven Companion*). Reflection on Goethe's theories about plant growth, and Thomas Traherne's *Centuries of Meditations* did much to stir up deeper sensibilities and rectify my perception of the world. I now see this as a kind of salvation. Buddhism confirms this rectification and truly liberates the mind from the tyranny of merely intellectual forms and categories. Whatever I write in the future, and it will not be only about music, will certainly reflect this new perspective."

* * *

BARKER, Charles Albro 1904-

PERSONAL: Born September 15, 1904, in Washington, D.C.; son of Charles Albert (a builder) and Alice (a chemist; maiden name, Albro) Barker; married Louise Cottle (a musician), July 23, 1932; children: John G., Louise B. (Mrs. David S. Cannell). *Education:* Yale University, A.B., 1926, Ph.D., 1932. *Home:* Peacefield, Wonalancet, N.H. 03897.

CAREER: Smith College, Northampton, Mass., instructor in history, 1928-31; Mills College, Oakland, Calif., assistant professor of history, 1932-33; Stanford University, Stanford, Calif., instructor, 1933-36, assistant professor, 1936-42, associate professor of history, 1942-45; Johns Hopkins University, Baltimore, Md., professor of history, 1945-72, professor emeritus, 1972—, head of department, 1961-66. Visiting professor at New York State College for Teachers, 1939-40; Smith-Mundt visiting professor at American University, Beirut, 1953-54; visiting professor at University of Wisconsin, Madison, 1956; Fulbright-Hays lecturer at Punjab University, 1970-71, and University of Melbourne, spring, 1971. Research fellow at Huntington Library, 1944, 1973, and 1974.

MEMBER: American Historical Association, Organization of American Historians, American Studies Association (president, 1953), American Association of University Professors. *Awards, honors:* Beveridge Prize from American Historical Association, 1941, for *Background of the Revolution in Maryland;* Social Science Research Council fellowship, 1962-63; Guggenheim fellowship, 1965; Ralph Waldo Emerson Award from Phi Beta Kappa, 1971, for *American Convictions.*

WRITINGS: Background of the Revolution in Maryland, Yale University Press, 1940, reprinted, Archon Press, 1970;

(editor) *Memoirs of Elisha Oscar Crosky,* Harry E. Huntington, 1945; *Henry George,* Oxford University Press, 1955, reprinted, Greenwood Press, 1976; (editor) *Problems of World Disarmament,* Houghton, 1963; *American Convictions: Cycles of Public Thought, 1600-1850,* Lippincott, 1970; (editor and contributor) *Power and Law: The American Dilemma in World Affairs,* Johns Hopkins Press, 1971.

WORK IN PROGRESS: American Convictions: Crises in Public Thought Since 1840, completion expected in 1982.

SIDELIGHTS: Barker writes: "I was trained at Yale in the Andrews tradition of American colonial history, but shifted early in my career, at Stanford, to the new field (as it then was) of U.S. intellectual history. At Johns Hopkins I concentrated on what I call 'public thought,' or thought concerning the community. I endeavor to synthesize this in *American Convictions.* From colonial beginnings I find public thought to have occurred in long cycles, at least through the nineteenth century. During the twentieth century this interpretation has to yield, as thought in the United States is being ever more affected by the crosscurrents of action and ideas in the world."

*   *   *

BARKER, Ernest 1874-1960

OBITUARY NOTICE: Born September 23, 1874, in Woodley, Cheshire, England; died February 17, 1960. Political scientist, educator, and author of about fifteen books on political theory and history. Barker began teaching in 1899, and was principal of King's College of the University of London from 1920 to 1927. He held the chair in political science at Cambridge University from 1927 until his retirement in 1939. His books include *Greek Political Theory, Political Thought in England From Herbert Spencer to Today, Social and Political Thought in Byzantium,* and an autobiography, *Age and Youth.* Obituaries and other sources: *New York Times,* February 20, 1960; *Illustrated London News,* February 27, 1960; *The New Century Handbook of English Literature,* revised edition, Appleton, 1967; *The Penguin Companion to English Literature,* McGraw, 1971; *Longman Companion to Twentieth Century Literature,* 2nd edition, Longman, 1977.

*   *   *

BARKHOUSE, Joyce 1913-

PERSONAL: Born May 3, 1913, in Woodville, Nova Scotia, Canada; daughter of Harold Edwin (a physician) and Ora (a teacher and secretary; maiden name, Webster) Killam; married Milton Joseph Barkhouse (a bank manager), September 16, 1942 (died, 1968); children: Murray Roy, Janet Louise. *Education:* Provincial Normal College, Truro, Nova Scotia, license, 1932; attended Dalhousie University, summers, 1933, 1935, and Thomas Moore Institute, 1965-66. *Religion:* Protestant. *Home:* 1344 Birmingham St., Halifax, Nova Scotia, Canada B3J 2J2.

CAREER: Teacher at rural elementary schools in Nova Scotia, 1933-38, and Liverpool, Nova Scotia, 1939-42; Protestant School Board of Greater Montreal, Montreal, Quebec, substitute teacher, 1956-66; writer, 1954—. Volunteer promotion and public relations worker for UNICEF. *Member:* Writers Union of Canada, Canadian Children's Authors, Illustrators, and Performers, Canadian Authors Association, Writers Federation of Nova Scotia (member of executive board, 1979—). *Awards, honors:* Grant from Ontario Arts Council, 1976; first prize for children's fiction from Writers Federation of Nova Scotia, 1979, for book-length historical fiction set in Nova Scotia, as yet untitled and unpublished.

WRITINGS: George Dawson: The Little Giant (biography), Clarke, Irwin, 1974; (with niece, Margaret Atwood) *Anna's Pet* (juvenile), James Lorimer, 1980.

Contributor: Robert E. Wilford, editor, *Reading for Little Ones,* Educational Research Council of Greater Cleveland, 1967; *Open Highways,* Gage, 1968; *Teacher's Source Book, Level 4,* Gage, 1970; T. W. Paterson, editor, *Treasure Trails,* Stagecoach Publishing Co., 1976; Stanley Fillmore, editor, *Spirit of Canada,* Canadian Author's Association, 1977; Meguido Zola and Frances Brown, editors, *Hiyou Tillicum,* CommCept Publishing Ltd., 1978; Jack Booth and John R. Linn, editors, *One Banana Step,* Holt, 1978; Elizabeth Thorn and Joan M. Irwin, editors, *Trampolines,* Gage, 1978; *The Seasons of Children,* Simon & Pierre, 1979.

Author of "For Mothers and Others," a column in Nova Scotia weekly newspapers, 1970-74. Reporter for *Camping Guide* and *Trailering Guide,* 1967. Contributor to *Canadian Children's Annuals,* 1976, 1977, 1978, 1980. Contributor of articles, stories, and poems to magazines for adults and children, including *Instructor, Ahoy, Jabberwocky, Bluenose, Canadian Treasure, Family Digest, Family Herald, Onward,* and *Conquest.*

WORK IN PROGRESS—Juveniles: A biography of Abraham Gesner, Nova Scotia inventor, publication by Fitzhenry & Whiteside expected in 1980; *Little Marten* (tentative title), "a tale of Micmac magic," publication by Rhino Books expected in 1980.

SIDELIGHTS: Joyce Barkhouse wrote in *In Review:* "My ancestors came to this province from the United States. My mother's people . . . were New England planters, farmers who came to take up the fertile farmlands around the Minas Basin after the expulsion of the Acadians in 1755. My father's people . . . were United Empire Loyalists who also arrived from New England before the beginning of the nineteenth century . . .

"Most people who have never visited Nova Scotia picture it as a bleak, rocky, foggy peninsula—'Nova Scarcity,' home of the Bluenoses. But the fertile, sheltered Annapolis Valley which stretches for a hundred miles parallel to the Bay of Fundy, from Blomidon to Digby, is one of the best apple-growing belts in the world.

"The 'happy valley' of Longfellow's *Evangeline* was my home; and it was a more beautiful place in the days of my childhood than it is now."

Barkhouse adds: "In 1934, I traveled for six weeks, crossing the continent in a Chevrolet—which had running boards, but no trunk! We—the five of us—ate by the roadside and slept in a tent. This way, we had an intimate association with the country and its people.

"If I have a mission in my writing, it is to help Canadian children to know themselves and their country—to give them a sense of identity. Often they are lost in the shadow of their great next-door neighbor, the United States."

BIOGRAPHICAL/CRITICAL SOURCES: Saturday Night, June, 1976; *In Review,* winter, 1978.

*   *   *

BARLOW, Sanna Morrison
See ROSSI, Sanna Morrison Barlow

*   *   *

BARNER, Bob 1947-

PERSONAL: Born November 11, 1947, in Tuckerman,

Ark.; son of Jewel and Jean (McClure) Barner. *Education:* Columbus College of Art and Design, B.F.A., 1970. *Home and office:* 65 Mount Vernon St., Boston, Mass. 02108.

CAREER: Riverside Hospital, Columbus, Ohio, art therapist, 1970-78; Art Institute of Boston, Boston, Mass., instructor in art, 1978-79; free-lance writer and artist, 1979—. *Member:* Art Directors Club of Boston. *Awards, honors:* Andy Award for Illustration from Children's International Book Fair, 1975, for *The Elephants' Visit.*

WRITINGS—Self-illustrated children's books: *The Elephants' Visit,* Little, Brown, 1975; *Elephant Facts,* Dutton, 1979.

WORK IN PROGRESS: Children's books.

SIDELIGHTS: Barner writes: "Most of my work is inspired by simple doodles. *Elephant Facts* came about after work on the purely fanciful *The Elephants' Visit* aroused my interest in real facts about elephants."

* * *

BARONE, Michael 1944-

PERSONAL: Born September 19, 1944, in Highland Park, Mich.; son of C. Gerald (a physician) and Alice Katherine (a teacher; maiden name, Darcy) Barone; married Joan Carroll Shorenstein (a producer), February 14, 1975; children: Sarah Phyllis. *Education:* Harvard University, A.B. (magna cum laude), 1966; Yale University, LL.B., 1969. *Politics:* Democrat. *Residence:* Washington, D.C. *Agent:* International Creative Management, 40 West 57th St., New York, N.Y. 10019. *Office:* Peter D. Hart Research Associates, Inc., 1529 O St. N.W., Washington, D.C. 20005.

CAREER: Admitted to the Bar of Michigan, 1970; U.S. Court of Appeals for the Sixth Circuit, Detroit, Mich., law clerk, 1969-71; Peter D. Hart Research Associates, Inc., Washington, D.C., associate, 1974-75, vice-president, 1975—. Consultant to CBS News. *Awards, honors:* Nominated for National Book Award, 1972.

WRITINGS: (With Grant Ujifusa and Douglas Matthews) *The Almanac of American Politics 1972,* Gambit, 1971; (with Ujifusa and Matthews) *The Almanac of American Politics 1974,* Gambit, 1973; (with Ujifusa and Matthews) *The Almanac of American Politics 1976,* Dutton, 1975; (with Neal R. Pierce) *The Middle Atlantic States of America,* Norton, 1976; (with Ujifusa and Matthews) *The Almanac of American Politics 1978,* Dutton, 1977; (with Ujifusa) *The Almanac of American Politics 1980,* Dutton, 1979. Contributor of articles to numerous publications, including *Washington Post, New York Times, Wall Street Journal,* and *New Republic.*

* * *

BARROL, Grady
See BOGRAD, Larry

* * *

BART, Peter 1932-

PERSONAL: Born July 24, 1932, in New York, N.Y.; son of M. S. and Clara G. Bart; children: Colby, Dilys. *Education:* Swarthmore College, B.A., 1954; also attended London School of Economics and Political Science, 1955-56. *Home:* 2270 Betty Lane, Beverly Hills, Calif. 90210. *Agent:* Arlene Donovan, International Creative Management, 40 West 57th St., New York, N.Y. 10019.

CAREER: Wall Street Journal, New York City, reporter, 1955-57; *New York Times,* New York City, reporter, 1957-

67; Paramount Pictures, Hollywood, Calif., vice-president in production, 1968-75; president of Lorimar Films Co., 1978—.

WRITINGS: (With Denne Bart Petitclerc) *Destinies* (novel), Simon & Schuster, 1979. Contributor to magazines, including *Harper's, Atlantic, Esquire,* and *Saturday Review.*

WORK IN PROGRESS: Another novel for Simon & Schuster.

SIDELIGHTS: Bart told *CA* that "*Destinies* is a novel describing a family of mixed Cuban and American heritage which is torn apart in the turmoil immediately following the Cuban Revolution and the Bay of Pigs. My next novel is a thriller set against a contemporary American setting.

"At the *New York Times* I was a general assignment reporter but also wrote occasionally about the motion picture industry. I am one of the few people ever to end up working in the field he once wrote about."

* * *

BARTLETT, Jonathan 1931-

PERSONAL: Born February 18, 1931, in Boston, Mass.; son of Arthur Charles (a writer) and Eleonora (Very) Bartlett; married Elsa Jaffe (a psychologist and writer), June, 1967; children: Noah. *Education:* Bowdoin College, B.A., 1953. *Religion:* Society of Friends (Quakers). *Home:* 131 East 19th St., New York, N.Y. 10003. *Office:* Playboy Enterprises, Inc., 747 Third Ave., New York, N.Y. 10017.

CAREER: Alexis Lichine et Cie., Margaux, France, writer, 1955-58; Western Publishing Co., Inc., New York City, held various editorial positions for Golden Press and Odyssey Books, 1959-69; Grosset & Dunlap, Inc., New York City, senior editor, 1969-74; *Newsweek,* New York City, associate editor of Newsweek Books, 1974-75; Winchester Press, New York City, managing editor, 1976-79; Playboy Enterprises, Inc., New York City, special projects editor, 1979—. Director of Multimedia Enterprises. *Military service:* U.S. Army, 1953-55; became first lieutenant.

WRITINGS: The Peasant Gourmet, Macmillan, 1975; (editor) *The Ocean Environment,* H. W. Wilson, 1977; (editor) *The First Amendment in a Free Society,* H. W. Wilson, 1979; *Money,* H. W. Wilson, 1980; *The Playboy Book,* Playboy Press, 1981. Contributor to *Alexis Lichine's Encyclopedia of Wines and Spirits.*

WORK IN PROGRESS: The Story of Islam (juvenile); *Biography of Benjamin Russell.*

SIDELIGHTS: Bartlett comments: "I was subjected early to, and influenced heavily by, the old *New Yorker* magazine, especially the writings of E. B. White. Three years in France on *Alexis Lichine's Encyclopedia of Wines and Spirits* proceeded to make me a francophile. I don't know if Francis Bacon's 'writing (maketh) an exact man' is true, but at least one tries."

* * *

BASCOM, David 1912-
(Milford Poltroon)

PERSONAL: Born in 1912 in Oil City, Pa.; married Harriet Beecher; children: Agnes, Ralph Waldo. *Education:* Attended Academy of Advertising Art, 1931-32. *Home:* 8 Aztec Way, Oakland, Calif. 94611.

CAREER: Worked as gas station attendant, door-to-door salesman, magazine distributor, sign painter, card writer, and lumberman, 1929-36; worked for candymaker in San

Francisco, Calif., 1936-41, became advertising manager; Garfield & Guild (advertising agency), San Francisco, 1943-48, became vice-president and copy chief; Guild, Bascom & Bonfigli (advertising agency), partner, 1949-65.

WRITINGS—Under pseudonym Milford Poltroon: *How to Fish Good,* Winchester Press, 1971; *The Happy Fish Hooker: A Piscatorial Perpetration,* Winchester Press, 1977; *The Phoney Phone Book,* Winchester Press, 1979. Contributor to magazines, including *Angler, Atlantic, Esquire, Sports Afield,* and *Outdoor Life.* Editor and publisher of *Wretched Mess News,* 1962-75.

WORK IN PROGRESS: The 1981 Wretched Mess Calendar, for publication by Wretched Mess Catalog.

SIDELIGHTS: Bascom told *CA:* "I started the *Wretched Mess News* strictly as a fun fish-oriented periodical back in 1962, my sole motivation being to have fun. *Wretched Mess News* carried ads, mostly from national advertisers, but a condition of advertising therein was that I created all the ads and advertisers were not allowed to see them until they were in print, at which point it was too late for them to whinny and snivel, as advertisers are all too prone to do. At its high point the *Mess* had around fifteen thousand paid subscribers. When I retired from the ad agency business in 1968 I expanded the magazine into a humor-oriented mail order business, operating out of West Yellowstone, Montana (wherever that is).

"It is a shame that businesses in the United States must either grow or fail; they can't stay comfortably in place. In the case of the *Mess,* the complexities and responsibilities of growth took much of the fun out of it, for me. So in 1975 I ceased publication of the *Wretched Mess News* and sold my mail order business to a 'gentleman' who moved it to Mountain View, California, a place totally devoid of scenic vistas and with no mountains within 384 miles.

"Since then I've been doing lots of things: writing occasional books, doing pieces (usually so-called funny stuff) for a number of magazines (I'm on the staff of *Angler,* and an abbreviated, piscatorially-pointed version of my *Wretched Mess News* appears in every issue), continuing the *Wretched Mess Calendar,* doing a little consulting for some advertisers, to use the term in its most idiotic sense, occasionally delivering illustrated lectures to groups of culture-hungry illiterates (advertisers and fishermen, mostly), and going fishing on every possible occasion. The audiences I address are not concerned with profundity and in most cases, probably don't know what it means.

"I started the *Wretched Mess Calendar* in 1967 and have perpetrated it annually ever since. Its chief distinction is that it has a famous holiday that no one ever heard of before for each and every day of the year. Some samples from the 1980 edition: Jam 3—A day to try Oil of Olay on your prunes; Fib 14—Call the Wind Harold (Free Maria) Day; Julia 21—Robins return to Baskin."

*   *   *

BASIUK, Victor 1932-

PERSONAL: Born October 19, 1932, in the Ukraine; came to the United States in 1949, naturalized citizen, 1956; son of Walter (an educator) and Nina (a teacher; maiden name, Slowikowska) Basiuk. *Education:* Haverford College, B.A. (with honors), 1952; Columbia University, M.A., 1955, Ph.D., 1956. *Home:* 8360 Greensboro Dr., McLean, Va. 22102.

CAREER: U.S. Naval War College, Newport, R.I., member

of international relations faculty, 1957-60; Washington University, St. Louis, Mo., assistant professor of political science, 1960-61; Columbia University, New York, N.Y., lecturer in government and research associate at Institute of War and Peace Studies, 1961-65; Case Western Reserve University, Cleveland, Ohio, associate professor of political science, 1965-68; Columbia University, research associate at Institute of War and Peace Studies and Institute for the Study of the Science of Human Affairs, 1967-70; U.S. Department of the Navy, Washington, D.C., adviser on international relations to the chief of naval operations, 1970-72; consultant on science and technology policy in Washington, D.C., 1973—. *Military service:* U.S. Navy, 1957-60. U.S. Naval Reserve, 1960—; present rank, captain. *Member:* International Platform Association, International Studies Association, American Political Science Association, American Association for the Advancement of Science, Phi Beta Kappa, Pi Sigma Alpha.

WRITINGS: Technology and World Power, Foreign Policy Association, 1970; (contributor) Lewis M. Alexander, editor, *The Law of the Sea: National Policy Recommendations,* University of Rhode Island Press, 1970; (contributor) William T. R. Fox and W. R. Schilling, editors, *European Security and the Atlantic System,* Columbia University Press, 1973; *Technology, World Politics, and American Policy,* Columbia University Press, 1977. Contributor to political science journals.

WORK IN PROGRESS: Research on technology and the international system and on the impact of technology on the evolution of Soviet society.

SIDELIGHTS: Basiuk remarked to *CA:* "If we took the influence of science and technology away, the advanced societies of today would not be much different from those of the year 200 B.C. Our ability to understand and control the influence of science and technology on society in a comprehensive way could spell the difference between a future which is a product of the best ideals and aspirations of mankind or that of a technological determinism whose outcome is uncertain and probably not very palatable. It is therefore unfortunate that this area has attracted a disproportionately small amount of attention and talent among scholars and policy makers alike."

Basiuk's book, *Technology, World Politics, and American Policy,* received favorable reviews. Peter Fotheringham declared that the "book is essential reading for students of international relations and students of post-industrial society.... Basiuk provides an indispensable framework for anyone who wishes to think about international relations in the next half-century."

BIOGRAPHICAL/CRITICAL SOURCES: Annals of the American Academy, March, 1978; *International Affairs,* October, 1978.

*   *   *

BASSE, Eli 1904-1979

OBITUARY NOTICE: Born in 1904 in Leeds, England; died December 20, 1979, in Brooklyn, N.Y. Comedy writer and scriptwriter. Known as "The Funny Man's Funny Man," Basse wrote material for such stars as Joe E. Lewis, Red Buttons, Milton Berle, Sophie Tucker, and Jackie Gleason. He also wrote scripts for radio and for such shows as "Strip for Action" and "High Heels." Obituaries and other sources: *New York Times,* December 21, 1979.

BATCHELOR, John 1942-

PERSONAL: Born March 15, 1942, in Farnborough, England; son of Aubrey and Hilary (Middleton) Batchelor; married Henrietta Jane Letts; children: William, Clarissa. *Education:* Magdalen College, Cambridge, B.A., 1964, Ph.D., 1968. *Office:* Department of English, New College, Oxford University, Oxford, England.

CAREER: University of Birmingham, Birmingham, England, lecturer in English, 1968-76; Oxford University, Oxford, England, tutor and lecturer in English, fellow of New College, 1976—.

WRITINGS: Breathless Hush (novel), Duckworth, 1974; *Mervyn Peake: A Biographical and Critical Exploration,* Duckworth, 1974.

WORK IN PROGRESS: A book on Edwardian literature, publication by Duckworth expected in 1980 or 1981.

SIDELIGHTS: Batchelor told *CA:* "My study of Edwardian literature centers on Conrad, Ford Madox Ford, Wells, Bennett, Galsworthy, and Forster. My short publications include articles on Virginia Woolf and, in the Edwardian period, on Chesterton, Arthur Machen, and Beerbohm."

*   *   *

BATES, H(erbert) E(rnest) 1905-1974
(Flying Officer X, John Gawsworth)

PERSONAL: Born May 16, 1905, in Rushdon, Northamptonshire, England; died January 29, 1974, in Canterbury, England; son of Albert Ernest and Lucy Elizabeth (Lucas) Bates; married Marjorie Helen Cox, July 18, 1931; children: Ann, Judith, Richard, Jonathan. *Education:* Educated in England. *Address:* The Granary, Little Chart, Ashford, Kent, England.

CAREER: Worked as reporter for *Northamptonshire Chronicle* and as clerk in leather warehouse in England, until 1926; writer, 1926-74. *Military service:* Royal Air Force, 1941-46; became squadron leader. *Member:* Fellow of Royal Society of Literature. *Awards, honors:* Created Commander of the Order of the British Empire, 1973.

WRITINGS—Novels and novellas: The Two Sisters, Viking, 1926, reprinted, Hamilton, 1958; *Catherine Foster,* Viking, 1929, reprinted, Hamilton, 1959; *The Hessian Prisoner,* W. Jackson, 1930; *Charlotte's Row,* J. Cape, 1931, reprinted, Transworld Publishers, 1965; *Mr. Esmond's Life,* privately printed, 1931; *The Fallow Land,* J. Cape, 1932, R. O. Ballou, 1933, reprinted, Transworld Publishers, 1965; *The Poacher,* Macmillan, 1935, reprinted, Sphere, 1969; *A House of Women,* Holt, 1936; *Spella Ho,* Little, Brown, 1938; *Fair Stood the Wind for France,* Little, Brown, 1944; *The Cruise of the Breadwinner,* M. Joseph, 1946, Little, Brown, 1947; *The Purple Plain,* Little, Brown, 1947; *Dear Life,* Little, Brown, 1949; *The Jacaranda Tree,* Little, Brown, 1949, abridged version, edited by G. M. Gore Little, Longmans, Green, 1960.

The Scarlet Sword, M. Joseph, 1950, Little, Brown, 1951; *Love for Lydia,* M. Joseph, 1952, Penguin, 1956; *The Nature of Love: Three Short Novels,* M. Joseph, 1953, Little, Brown, 1954; *The Feast of July,* Little, Brown, 1954; *The Sleepless Moon,* Little, Brown, 1956; *Dear Life [and] The Cruise of the Breadwinner,* Transworld Publishers, 1957; *Death of a Huntsman: Four Short Novels* (also see below), M. Joseph, 1957, Penguin, 1964; *The Darling Buds of May,* Little, Brown, 1958; *A Breath of Fresh Air,* Little, Brown, 1959.

An Aspidistra in Babylon: Four Novellas (also see below), M. Joseph, 1960, Penguin, 1964; *The Grapes of Paradise: Eight Novellas* (includes *Death of a Huntsman: Four Short Novels* and *An Aspidistra in Babylon: Four Short Novels*), Little, Brown, 1960; *When the Green Woods Laugh,* M. Joseph, 1960, Penguin, 1963, published as *Hark, Hark, the Lark!,* Little, Brown, 1961; *The Day of the Tortoise,* M. Joseph, 1961; *A Crown of Wild Myrtle,* M. Joseph, 1962, Farrar, Straus, 1963; *The Golden Oriole: Five Novellas,* Little, Brown, 1962; *Oh! To Be in England,* M. Joseph, 1963, Farrar, Straus, 1964; *The Fabulous Mrs. V.,* M. Joseph, 1964, Penguin, 1970; *A Moment in Time,* Farrar, Straus, 1964; *The Distant Hours in Summer,* M. Joseph, 1967, Penguin, 1969; *The Wild Cherry Tree,* M. Joseph, 1968, Penguin, 1972; *The Triple Echo,* M. Joseph, 1970, Penguin, 1972; *Fair Stood the Wind for France, Yours Is the Earth, A Silas Idyll,* edited by Geoffrey Halson, Longman, 1971.

Short stories: *The Spring Song [and] In Spite of That: Two Stories,* privately printed, 1927; *Day's End, and Other Stories,* Viking, 1928, reprinted, J. Cape, 1961; *Seven Tales and Alexander,* Scholastic Press, 1929, Viking, 1930; *The Black Boxer,* Pharos Editions, 1932, reprinted, Books for Libraries Press, 1971; *Sally Go Round the Moon,* White Owl Press, 1932; *The House With the Apricot, and Two Other Tales,* Golden Cockerel, 1933; *The Woman Who Had Imagination, and Other Stories,* Macmillan, 1934, reprinted, J. Cape, 1964; *Cut and Come Again: Fourteen Stories,* J. Cape, 1935; *Something Short and Sweet,* J. Cape, 1937, reprinted, Lythway Press, 1974; *The Flying Goat,* J. Cape, 1939, reprinted, Lythway Press, 1973; *I Am Not Myself,* Corvinus Press, 1939; *My Uncle Silas,* J. Cape, 1939, Penguin, 1958.

The Beauty of the Dead, and Other Stories, J. Cape, 1940, reprinted, Lythway Press, 1973; *Country Tales: Collected Short Stories,* J. Cape, 1940, reprinted, Lythway Press, 1974; *The Bride Comes to Evensford,* J. Cape, 1943; *The Bride Comes to Evensford, and Other Stories,* J. Cape, 1949; *Colonel Julian, and Other Stories,* M. Joseph, 1951, Little, Brown, 1952; *The Daffodil Sky,* M. Joseph, 1955, Little, Brown, 1956; *Sugar for the Horse,* M. Joseph, 1957; *The Watercress Girl, and Other Stories,* M. Joseph, 1959, Little, Brown, 1960.

Now Sleeps the Crimson Petal, and Other Stories, M. Joseph, 1961, Penguin, 1962, published as *The Enchantress, and Other Stories,* Little, Brown, 1961; *The Wedding Party,* M. Joseph, 1965, Penguin, 1969; *The Four Beauties,* M. Joseph, 1968, Penguin, 1972; *A Little of What You Fancy,* M. Joseph, 1970, Penguin, 1974; *The Song of the Wren,* M. Joseph, 1972, Penguin, 1974; *The Good Corn, and Other Stories,* edited by Geoffrey Halson, Longman, 1974; *The Poison Ladies, and Other Stories,* A. Wheaton, 1976.

Collections: *Thirty Tales,* J. Cape, 1934; *Thirty-One Selected Tales,* J. Cape, 1947; *Selected Short Stories of H. E. Bates,* Pocket Books, 1951; *Twenty Tales,* J. Cape, 1951; *Selected Stories,* Penguin, 1957; *The Best of H. E. Bates,* Little, Brown, 1963; *Seven by Five: A Collection of Stories, 1926-1961,* M. Joseph, 1963, Penguin, 1972; *H. E. Bates,* edited by Alan Cattell, Harrap, 1975.

Plays: *The Last Bread* (one-act), Labour Publishing, 1926; *The Day of Glory* (three-act; first produced in London, England, 1946), M. Joseph, 1945.

Under pseudonym Flying Officer X: *The Greatest People in the World, and Other Stories,* J. Cape, 1942, published as *There's Something in the Air,* Knopf, 1943; *How Sleep the Brave, and Other Stories,* J. Cape, 1943; *The Stories of Flying Officer X,* J. Cape, 1952.

Other: *The Seekers*, J. & E. Bumpus, 1926; *The Tree*, E. Lahr, 1930; *A Threshing Day*, W. & G. Foyle, 1931; *A German Idyll*, Golden Cockerel, 1932; *The Story Without an End* [and] *The Country Doctor*, White Owl Press, 1932; *The Duet*, [London], 1935; *Flowers and Faces*, Golden Cockerel, 1935; *Through the Woods: The English Woodland—April to April*, Macmillan, 1936, reprinted, Gollancz, 1969; *Down the River*, Holt, 1937, reprinted, Gollancz, 1968; *The English Countryside* (travel), [England], 1939; *There's Freedom in the Air*, Ministry of Information (London), 1939.

The Seasons and the Gardener: A Book for Children, Cambridge University Press, 1940; *The Modern Short Story: A Critical Survey*, T. Nelson, 1941, reprinted, Writer Inc., 1972; *In the Heart of the Country* (also see below), Country Life, 1942; *Country Life*, Penguin, 1943; *O! More Than Happy Countryman* (also see below), Country Life, 1943; *The Tinkers of Elstow*, [London], 1946; *Otters and Men*, National Society for the Abolition of Cruel Sports (London), 1947; *The Country Heart* (revised and amended edition of *O! More Than Happy Countryman* and *In the Heart of the Country*), M. Joseph, 1949; *Edward Garnett: A Memoir*, M. Parrish, 1950; *Flower Gardening: A Reader's Guide*, Cambridge University Press, 1950; *The Country of White Clover*, M. Joseph, 1952; *The Face of England*, B. T. Batsford, 1952; *Summer in Salandar*, Little, Brown, 1957.

Achilles the Donkey (juvenile), F. Watts, 1962; *Achilles and Diana* (juvenile), F. Watts, 1963; *Achilles and the Twins* (juvenile), F. Watts, 1964; (editor) *Six Stories* (includes works by Chekhov, Beerbohm, Joyce, Hemingway, and Bates), Oxford University Press, 1965; *The White Admiral* (juvenile), Dobson Books, 1968; *An Autobiography*, University of Missouri Press, Volume I: *The Vanished World*, 1969, Volume II: *The Blossoming World*, 1971, Volume III: *The World in Ripeness*, 1972; *A Love of Flowers* (autobiography), M. Joseph, 1971; *Dulcima*, Penguin, 1971; *A Fountain of Flowers*, M. Joseph, 1974; *The Yellow Meads of Asphodel*, M. Joseph, 1976, Penguin, 1978.

Also author of *Song for December* (poems), 1928; *Christmas, 1930* (poem), 1930; *Holly and Sallow* (poem), 1931; (under name John Gawsworth) *My Beginning*, 1933; *Pastoral on Paper*, 1956.

Author of column, "Country Life," appearing in *Spectator*. Reviewer for magazines, including *Morning Post* and *Spectator*.

SIDELIGHTS: Averaging over one new book each year for a period of more than fifty years, H. E. Bates ranked as one of England's most prolific writers of this century. Often compared to such notables as George Eliot, Thomas Hardy, and D. H. Lawrence, he was regarded for his moving and realistic portrayals of the English countryside. "He was, in no pejorative sense, a prose poet, and his best effects were obtained when his delight in the natural scene, his vivid apprehension of the moods of nature, of the changing seasons and the weather, crystallized into symbols of the states of mind of his characters," expressed one critic for the *London Times*.

The Two Sisters, Bates's first novel, was published when he was twenty. The manuscript greatly impressed Edward Garnett, who immediately recommended it to publisher Jonathan Cape. Bates and Garnett quickly became friends, the latter influencing the former and cultivating the raw talent he saw in the young writer. Bates eventually paid tribute to his long-time mentor in the form of a memoir, written in 1950. So close were the two men, the *London Times* suggested, that "from the very nature of the relation between them, [the

book] was as much a piece of autobiography as of biography."

One of Bates's best-known works is *The Poacher*. It is the story of Luke Bishop who, like his father before him, illegally hunts game. Despite the obvious risks involved in their trade, both pursue it diligently until one event shatters everything: Luke's father is killed by the caretaker of the land. When this man is then shot, all evidence points to Luke. Though innocent of the crime, he flees to another county. Under an assumed name, Luke begins life anew as a farmer, a relatively safe and respectable occupation. He marries and becomes a success in his new livelihood, but feels a strong longing for his native soil. Unfortunately, when he returns as an old man, the temptation to fall into his original profession overcomes him. Eager to teach his young grandson the ancient art of his family, Luke is caught while demonstrating the technique and is sent to jail.

"Beautifully and without affectation Mr. Bates has expressed through the story of Luke Bishop's life, his deep feeling for the life of the English countryside, for the changes which have come over it in the last half century and his own nostalgic regret for the order which has passed," summarized Margaret Wallace in her review of the book. Peter Quennell shared Wallace's enthusiasm: "Nothing that [Bates] writes is indistinguished, and there are many passages in *The Poacher* that must be numbered among the most beautiful he has produced."

While serving with the Royal Air Force during the Battle of Britain in World War II, Bates wrote a number of books under the pseudonym Flying Officer X. Drawing from his own experiences, he attempted to portray the courage, stamina, and determination of his fellow men-in-arms. The first of these works was *There's Something in the Air*, a collection of twenty-one short stories. "Here is sheer beauty in writing. This little volume of short pieces will give the reader a clearer conception of the combat's thinking, fighting, living, than anything that has come before. The little tales are gems cut from purest carbon, handed down so that they spit cold fire," praised Meyer Berger. Other critics were not overly impressed; a reviewer for the *Manchester Guardian* wrote, "An unprecedented form of state patronage seems to have set heavily on the author, whose stories are too slickly turned, whose pilots are a thought too heroic (or seems so to Mr. Bates . . .), and one of whose aircraft, at least, is more than a thought too anthropomorphized."

Another of his wartime writings, though not written under a pseudonym, was *A Moment in Time*. In it, Bates concentrated on those not directly involved in the fighting, yet whose lives were just as drastically altered. The central character is the nineteen-year-old Elizabeth. When her home is requisitioned by the military, she and her grandmother are forced to find shelter elsewhere. She returns often, however, and becomes friendly with the pilots. Finding herself in love with one of the fliers, she marries, but her young husband is soon killed in an attack by German bombers. Though devastated emotionally by her loss, Elizabeth is comforted by a neighbor, Tom Hudson, who has secretly admired and loved her.

The book was criticized by Eric Moon in the *Saturday Review* as nothing more than a "sentimental episode from the past" that "does nothing to interpret that past or give it real meaning for the reader of today," but it was praised by others. J. E. Oppenheimer, for one, was moved to proclaim it "poignant, perceptive," and "splendid, satisfying." Oppenheimer added, "It is . . . in character delineation and in the creation of a recognizably realistic setting for the interplay of intense human emotions under great stress that Mr. Bates reaches the heights and merits literary laurels.''

Bates's writings have proven their popularity not only in England, but in countries all over the world, as is evidenced by the translations into sixteen languages. Four of his novels, *The Darling Buds of May, Dulcima, The Purple Plain,* and *The Triple Echo,* have been produced as motion pictures, and serialized versions of *Love for Lydia* and his books concerning the Larkin family, including *When the Green Woods Laugh* and *Oh! To Be in England,* were broadcast by the British Broadcasting Corp. (BBC-TV) with great success.

BIOGRAPHICAL/CRITICAL SOURCES—Selected sources: *Nation,* June 19, 1935; *New Statesman and Nation,* January 26, 1935, February 5, 1949, November 19, 1955; *New York Times,* March 17, 1935, May 16, 1943, January 30, 1949, November 6, 1949, September 19, 1954, September 30, 1962; *Fortnightly Quarterly,* July, 1936; *Manchester Guardian,* October 23, 1942; *London Times Literary Supplement,* January 22, 1949, October 29, 1954, July 29, 1960, May 25, 1962, September 10, 1964; *New York Herald Tribune Book Review,* January 9, 1949, November 20, 1949, October 23, 1960; *San Francisco Chronicle,* January 23, 1949; *Saturday Review of Literature,* January 8, 1949, November 19, 1949, September 18, 1954, December 29, 1962, August 8, 1964; *Chicago Sunday Tribune,* October 30, 1960, January 22, 1961; *New York Times Book Review,* October 23, 1960, February 5, 1961, September 30, 1962, August 9, 1964; *Time,* October 31, 1960; *Times Literary Supplement,* July 29, 1960, October 8, 1971, October 13, 1972; *New York Herald Tribune Books,* September 23, 1963; *Best Sellers,* August 15, 1964; *New Yorker,* January 8, 1971.

OBITUARIES: London Times, January 30, 1974; *New York Times,* January 30, 1974; *Washington Post,* January 30, 1974; *Newsweek,* February 11, 1974; *Time,* February 11, 1974; *AB Bookman's Weekly,* April 15, 1974.*

—*Sketch by Kathleen Ceton Newman*

*   *   *

BAUM, Vicki 1888-1960

PERSONAL: Born January 24, 1888, in Vienna, Austria; came to the United States, 1931; naturalized U.S. citizen, 1938; died August 29, 1960, in Hollywood, Calif.; daughter of Herman and Mathilde (Donat) Baum; married first husband, c. 1906 (divorced); married Richard Lert (a conductor), July 17, 1916; children: (second marriage) two sons. *Education:* Attended Vienna Conservatory of Music.

CAREER: Novelist, playwright, and writer for motion pictures. Worked as a nurse during World War I; high school teacher of music in Darmstadt, Germany (now West Germany); harpist in German orchestra; Ullstein (publishers), Berlin, Germany, editor of magazines, beginning in 1926; lived permanently in the United States after coming to see the New York staging of her play, ''Grand Hotel,'' in 1931; screenwriter in Hollywood, Calif.

WRITINGS—All novels, except as noted; in English: *Der Eingang zur Buehne,* [Germany], 1920, translation by Felice Harvey and Alan Martin Harvey published as *Once in Vienna,* G. Bles, 1943, Didier, 1947; *Feme,* Ullstein, 1926, translation by Eric Sutton published as *Secret Sentence,* Doubleday, 1932; *Hell in Frauensee,* Ullstein, 1927, translation by Basil Creighton published as *Martin's Summer,* Farrar, 1931; *Stud Chem. Helene Willfueer,* Ullstein, 1928, translation by Felice Bashford published as *Helene,* G. Bles,

1932, translation by Ida Zeitlin, Doubleday, 1933; *Menschem im Hotel,* Ullstein, 1929, translation by Creighton published as *Grand Hotel,* G. Bles, 1930, Doubleday, 1931.

Zwischenfall in Lohwinckel, Ullstein, 1930, translation by Margaret Goldsmith published as *And Life Goes On,* Doubleday, 1931 (published in England as *Results of an Accident,* G. Bles, 1931); *Leben ohne Geheimnis,* Ullstein, 1932, Doubleday, 1932, translation by Zeitlin published as *Falling Star,* Doubleday, 1934; *Men Never Know,* translated by Creighton, Doubleday, 1935; *Die Karriere der Doris Hart,* Querido Verlag (Amsterdam), 1936, translation by Creighton published as *Sing, Sister, Sing,* Doubleday, 1936 (published in England as *Career,* G. Bles, 1936); *Der grosse Ausverkauf,* Querido Verlag, 1937, translation by Paul Seiver published as *Central Stores,* G. Bles, 1940; *Hotel Shanghai,* Querido Verlag, 1937, translation by Creighton published as *Shanghai '37,* Doubleday, 1939 (published in England as *Nanking Road,* G. Bles, 1939); *Das Ende der Geburt,* translation by Creighton published as *Tale of Bali,* Doubleday, 1937 (published in England as *A Tale From Bali,* G. Bles, 1937).

Die grosse Pause, Bermann-Fischer Verlag (Stockholm), 1941, translation published as *Grand Opera,* G. Bles, 1942; *The Ship and the Shore,* Doubleday, 1941; *The Christmas Carp,* Doubleday, 1941; *Marion Alive,* Doubleday, 1942; *The Weeping Wood* (tales), Doubleday, 1943, Greenwood Press, 1971; *Hotel Berlin '43* (Literary Guild selection), Doubleday, 1944 (published in England as *Berlin Hotel,* M. Joseph, 1944, Chivers, 1971); *Mortgage on Life,* Doubleday, 1946; *Headless Angel,* Doubleday, 1948.

Danger From Deer, Doubleday, 1951; *The Mustard Seed,* Dial Press, 1953; *Tiburon,* [Hollywood, Calif.], 1956; *Written on Water,* Doubleday, 1956 (published in England as *Blood on the Sea,* Landsborough Publications, 1960); *Theme for Ballet,* Doubleday, 1958 (published in England as *Ballerina,* M. Joseph, 1958); *It Was All Quite Different* (memoirs), Funk, 1964 (published in England as *I Know What I'm Worth,* M. Joseph, 1964).

Other: *Fruehe Schatten,* [Germany], c. 1919; *Der Tanze der Ina Raffay,* [Germany], 1921; *Die andern Tage* (novelettes), [Germany], 1922; *Die Welt ohne Suende,* [Germany], 1922; *Ulle, der Zwerg,* [Germany], 1924; *Der Weg,* [Stuttgart], 1925; *Tanzpause,* Fleischhauer & Spohn, 1926; *Das grosse Einmaleins,* Querido Verlag, 1935; *Liebe und Tod auf Bali,* Querido Verlag, 1937.

Plays: ''Grand Hotel'' (based on own novel), produced on Broadway at National Theatre, November 13, 1930; (with John Golden) *Divine Drudge* (three-act; based on novel by Baum, *And Life Goes On;* produced on Broadway at Royale Theatre, October 26, 1933), Samuel French, 1934. Also author of ''Pariser Platz,'' 1931.

Screenplays: (Author of screen story) Tess Slesinger and Frank Davis, ''Dance, Girl, Dance,'' RKO, 1940; (contributor to screenplay) Eugene Thackery, ''Unfinished Business,'' Universal, 1941. Contributor of story ideas to ''Honeymoon,'' RKO, 1946, and to ''Powder Town,'' RKO, 1962.

SIDELIGHTS: Though Vicki Baum had been writing since the age of fourteen, she began her career as a novelist quite by accident. While working as a harpist in a German orchestra (her husband, Richard Lert, was the conductor), one of Baum's associates, an actor, discovered Baum's desk filled with stories and novels. The actor sent one of them to a publisher and, to Baum's surprise, it was published. She then abandoned her careers in music and teaching to concentrate fully on writing.

Baum published her first books exclusively in German while working for several years as an editor for her publisher, Ullstein. She might have spent her entire career there, she later admitted, had it not been for a friend who persuaded Baum to dramatize her novel, *Menschem im Hotel* ("Grand Hotel"). Baum did, successfully, and in 1931 she was invited to the United States to see the play's New York staging. What had been intended to be a two-week visit became a permanent stay: Baum spent the rest of her life in the United States.

The novel *Grand Hotel* was a landmark for Baum as well. The first of her many works to be published by Doubleday, the successful "group novel" ensured Doubleday's commitment to its new author. The Baum-Doubleday team lasted twenty years. *Grand Hotel* also marked Baum's emergence as an influential writer: her *Grand Hotel* style became a popular literary convention. In the novel, Baum focused on a large hotel in post World War I Germany, charting her characters as they moved in and out of their rooms and into their common meeting place, the lobby. "The author's pen," said the *Saturday Review*, "is used exactly like a camera, darting among the crowds, picking out individuals here and there, following them for a while through their lives, and all the time nosing out significant detail and cynical contrast."

After the success of *Grand Hotel,* Doubleday published both old and new Baum releases in English translation. Baum's books, meanwhile, continued to be written in German until 1941 and the publication of her first book in English, *The Ship and the Shore.*

Critics found Baum's writing consistently tinged with melodrama and sentimentality. They found, too, that she was very good at what she did. Baum could do more than write a gripping story: she reinforced her work with acute insights into her characters and their worlds. Her 1932 book, *Helene,* for example, "is really good melodrama," said the *Saturday Review of Literature,* "well written, well constructed; more than that, its author has an intuition of right human behavior which gives even the most theatrical of her scenes an air of nature." Years later, Baum's *Mustard Seed* prompted Charles Lee to a similar comment: "Miss Baum writes the most intelligently steam-heated prose of her time; she knows her psychiatry and is glandularly informed. 'The Mustard Seed' is overdone, but it is not to be underrated; there is too much truth among its excess of torments."

Several of Baum's other novels revealed Baum to be equally adept in capturing time and place. In *Tale of Bali* she described the response of the proud Balinese people as they met a Dutch expedition seeking redress for a pillaged ship. "Vicki Baum has caught the very spirit of Bali," said a *Times Literary Supplement* reviewer. Another book, the ambitious *Weeping Wood,* concerns those who have been in some way affected by the marketing of rubber. Stretching from 1740 Brazil to present-day America, "Miss Baum's book has the drama and suspense of a novel, crowded with convincing glimpses of people . . . , times and places," commented Mary Ross.

Judgments of Baum's career have brought consideration of not only what she did as a writer, but also what she could have done. Baum knew how to write books that sold, but never sacrificed her intelligence in doing so, reported Marianne Houser of the *New York Times.* "None of her works can be called outstanding from a literary point of view but all of them are exceptionally entertaining." Baum would likely have had no quarrel with Houser's assessment: in her memoirs she described herself as a "first-class second-rate au-

thor," who had no great ambition to be anything more. Such a view, however, brings more questions than answers. As Bernard Bergonzi pointed out, her attitude may be seen as "genuine humility, but it may also be something of a *gran rifuto,* for one has a feeling that she might have become a somewhat better writer than she allowed herself to be."

CA INTERVIEWS THE AUTHOR
Vicki Baum's fiction was first published in America by Doubleday in 1931. At Doubleday she worked closely with two editors, Donald Elder and Kenneth McCormick. McCormick, editor-in-chief at Doubleday from 1942 until 1971 and vice-president from 1948 until 1971, now serves as senior consulting editor. In an interview at his New York City office on May 18, 1979, McCormick discussed Baum and her relationship with Doubleday.

CA: Did Baum begin writing in English more out of an ideological resentment of the Nazis than out of any real sense that it was necessary in order to succeed in her writing career?

McCORMICK: Yes, because there were perfectly good translators in this country. And although she may have been unhappy about some of the translations, the real purpose was her hatred of the Germans for the way they were treating Jews. She and her husband were both Jewish. They got out of Germany and came to this country in the thirties and settled in Los Angeles. He became the conductor of the Pasadena Symphony.

CA: I've read a great deal of detail about many aspects of her life, but almost nothing about her husband. Did you know him?

McCORMICK: Richard Lert was a sweetheart. He was a wonderful man. He had been the conductor of the Berlin Royal Opera and was a considerable music personality. He was early in that whole Viennese school that moved out of Europe and to Hollywood. I liked him very much. She was Vicki Baum Lert. It was my first acquaintance with a couple that had a sort of easygoing marital relationship in which she went her way and he went his. She did a lot of traveling and went around the world. She would go live in a country and research it. When she went to Bali she did *Tale of Bali.* She was a very quick study. She could go observe an area and feel what was unique about the people and the place. She was an instinctive storyteller. I loved to talk with her because she was always witty and amusing but also filled with the milk of human kindness. But she was *not* a soft touch. She was very tough-minded.

CA: Concerning the switch from German to English, you repeatedly told her after she started working hard on her English that she spoke almost as well as a native. How much editing was necessary to get her texts to the point of publication?

McCORMICK: Not much. What she did is what many writers do when they are going to make a dramatic shift. They will make it on a book that they consider experimental. So she wrote a book called *The Ship and the Shore,* which is a lighthearted book. If it was successful, fine; if it wasn't, it served its purpose of getting her over the line and giving her confidence that she could go ahead in the language. From that she moved into two or three big, long, and really *very* good novels, one of which was *The Weeping Wood.* We did some editing because she was a little longwinded and because she wanted us to. She was very good to work with.

CA: How much editing would you have to do for language?

McCORMICK: Not a tremendous amount. She would once in a while fall into a pitfall that you and I would fall into if we were writing in German for the first time. Really minor awkwardnesses, but the kind of thing that reveals the person is not comfortable in the language. The editor should be a help in erasing that.

CA: But it didn't take up a lot of time in the editing process?

McCORMICK: Oh, no. It was incredible, I thought, because when she came she spoke with a distinct accent, but she was learning all the time.

CA: In a letter from Nelson Doubleday or somebody in the upper levels, in 1930 or 1931, somebody said: 'This woman will not be good for interviews or lectures. She simply doesn't speak sufficiently good English.'

McCORMICK: She became sufficiently good in English to go around the United States on the ladies' book and luncheon circuit. She was a wow. She was selling *Grand Hotel* on that trip. By this time she was a roaring hit. I remember when she got to Minneapolis. She'd begun to get bored with the routine and overenthusiastic ladies and chicken and peas and the speech she gave and everything. But she was a good sport, and so she did it. Afterward the ladies came crowding up and said, 'You're so wonderful.' Finally there was a little lady standing there who said, 'Miss Baum, my son writes stories.' Vicki said, 'Oh, isn't that nice.' Then she thought, 'Maybe I'd better find out who . . . ,' and she said, 'What is your name?' The lady said, 'My name is Hemingway.' Vicki said, 'Are you *Ernest* Hemingway's mother?' 'Yes,' she said. So Vicki blossomed in praise of Ernest Hemingway. When she stopped, Mrs. Hemingway turned to the women and said, 'You see, Miss Baum has heard of my son.' I thought that was the most wistful story. Here's this lady trying to apologize and explain and the local people didn't give a damn for whoever Ernest Hemingway might be.

CA: Did you know her well enough during her period of adjustment to be aware that she had to undergo a transition?

McCORMICK: No. During the actual transition, I was too low down on the totem pole to have done more than meet her, but I later worked with her very closely and absolutely loved her. She was wonderful. There were two of us who worked with her very closely—Don Elder, who is now dead, and myself. He and Vicki were absolute pals. She was terribly nice to me and I enjoyed her enormously, visited her out there on the Coast. There were three or four of us involved. Malcolm Johnson was the executive vice-president and he was very fond of her, but he gradually left the work to Don and me. Ultimately to Don, because by that time I was editor-in-chief and had more than I could do. But I knew her very well and always kept in touch with her. Over the years I kept in touch with her son Wolfgang—Wolfie—until we sort of lost track of each other a few years ago.

CA: Did she ever talk about her experience in moving from Germany to the States?

McCORMICK: No, she did not do a lot of looking back. We used to get her reminiscing about when she was an editor of a magazine in Germany. She was a wonderful raconteur. Don Elder and I would always try to get her talking, because she was incapable of being boring. She was very liberal. And she saw things from a different point of view than we did, because she was a very insightful woman and also because of a

continental point of view. She and Don had an endless correspondence.

CA: Baum mentioned the Red Scare in some of her letters. Was she joking, or was she getting into hot water with the House Un-American Activities Committee?

McCORMICK: I don't think she got into trouble with the House Un-American Activities Committee. She was 150 percent American when she came here. She loved it here. And anything that would be against the Nazis, she would be for. I would think that the House Un-American Activities Committee would have been very grateful for people like Vicki.

CA: A lot of the exiled writers who had very good reputations in Europe simply did not make it commercially or critically in this country. Why did Baum succeed when so many others failed?

McCORMICK: Because she was such a wonderful storyteller. She invented a whole kind of novel which came to be known as the *Grand Hotel* style. Innumerable people write novels using that technique. The fact that everybody took to her and liked her, and that she didn't have to be as wary as she had to be in Germany, gave her confidence. Unlike many of the people who came from Germany and were simply just Germans transplanted here, she became an American. I came to New York from Oregon in 1928, and I very soon became aware of Europeans who used to come to America and insult us in their speeches and write insulting books about the United States, which Americans seemed to love to read. She was not one of them. She wasn't falsely loyal, but she felt she owed something to the country that had given her a place to go on and practice her craft. And although she had become successful before she came here, her success grew while she was here.

CA: Did Doubleday staffers do anything to help her make the transition in her career from German to English?

McCORMICK: I'm sure that we did, as publishers, and in that the publicity we were creating for her made a climate in which she could exist and which was profitable to us. She was an absolute born publicist, and the reason that the publicity department was crazy about her was that they didn't have to explain anything to her. She just knew. Lucy Goldthwaite, who was then in our publicity department, was marvelous with her. She helped a lot.

CA: Was that partly because Baum had worked in a publishing house and was aware of what went on?

McCORMICK: The fact was that she was a writer and a very good editor. She had sat on both sides of the desk.

CA: Did that make her a lot easier to work with?

McCORMICK: Sure, because journalists talked shorthand to her. She understood. You didn't ever have to explain anything all the way with her. She'd get your drift as soon as you began to talk. This is often true of very socially-aware novelists, who just suck up the ambience and begin to appreciate it with an objectivity that surprises the inexperienced. She was very good. I remember asking her a lot about Bali after she had been there. She was so interesting on the subject, because she really got inside those people and understood their society and what made them tick. Also, she was bothered by how they were being corrupted by Americans and other foreigners who came into their Garden of Eden.

CA: What's your recollection of the growing tension that led to Baum's decision that she wanted to write what she called 'the unfriendly book' and work with somebody other than Doubleday?

McCORMICK: She felt that we were a great big manufacturing house and just produced books that would sell. Up to a point that satisfied her because she was a popular writer. She yearned to be a significant writer, and I am not sure that she could have ever achieved that.

CA: Do you think any of the circumstances in her life prevented her from doing the kind of literature she thought she was capable of?

McCORMICK: She overcame some terrible handicaps—the war, being Jewish and being in Germany, and being a mother with two small children, and how to survive. Some of her energy went into surviving. We'll never know the answer, but it is my considered opinion that she would not have been a big, heady, significant writer; that what she should do was what she did—wonderful, human stories that were irresistible. I think that she was a sophisticated superjournalist. I do not think that she was a Thomas Mann, and I don't honestly think that she thought she was, either.

CA: Do you think she thought she was capable of something in between, though?

McCORMICK: I do, but the point remains that we never said, 'No, Vicki, you cannot do that.' I don't think that either Don or I—Don had very high literary standards—would have discouraged her. I don't remember her ever coming in and saying, 'I'm *bursting* to write a novel which is going to get into this philosophical point of view; I'm going to depart from my course. . . .' She was dissatisfied with herself, and because we really adored her, I can't imagine our saying, 'No, stick with what you're doing.' Because we have had authors who have surprised us and themselves and gotten into a high gear and set off in a direction that didn't seem apparent initially.

CA: Could you see that Don Elder was having any effect on what she was writing or how she was writing?

McCORMICK: I think he was tremendously helpful to her because he was very witty, and he encouraged the kind of devil that was in Vicki.

CA: The devil that was in her?

McCORMICK: Oh, she was an absolutely wonderful person with a wonderful sense of humor and would say outrageous things in conversation. She was also very prudent; she knew what would work and what wouldn't work.

CA: Can you remember specific ways in which you or Elder might have helped Baum?

McCORMICK: Both of us wrote to her a lot because she responded to that and because her answers were so entertaining. We felt that she was living in an artificial climate in Hollywood, and I think we had a stereotyped notion of Hollywood. If you keep a close relationship with an author, you can help her keep her own world in perspective. It's very easy in writing a novel to get lost in what you're doing. Baum was not so difficult that way, because she was impatient with herself and impatient with everybody in a pretty good-natured way. Even when she was mad at us, she wasn't really very mad.

CA: When she left Doubleday after twenty years, what were your feelings?

McCORMICK: We missed her terribly. And actually, as far as personal contact was concerned, we continued to be in touch with her. Don and I were individually in touch with her as friends. It's fun to talk about her because, you see, I was really devoted to her.

BIOGRAPHICAL/CRITICAL SOURCES: Times Literary Supplement, October 2, 1930, November 27, 1937, November 11, 1939, September 27, 1941; *Saturday Review,* October 25, 1930, December 12, 1953; *New York Times,* February 1, 1931, August 16, 1931, February 18, 1934, March 17, 1935, August 9, 1936, January 2, 1938, August 6, 1939, January 25, 1942, April 2, 1944, October 13, 1946, May 2, 1948, September 27, 1953, January 13, 1957; *Saturday Review of Literature,* August 15, 1931, August 13, 1932, April 29, 1933, February 24, 1934, August 5, 1939, April 22, 1944, January 27, 1945, February 24, 1951; *Weekly Book Review,* October 24, 1943; *Commonweal,* December 17, 1943; *New Republic,* February 7, 1944; *Chicago Sunday Tribune,* July 6, 1958; *New Statesman,* March 20, 1964; *Newsweek,* April 20, 1964.

OBITUARIES: New York Times, August 30, 1960; *Illustrated London News,* September 12, 1960; *Publishers Weekly,* September 12, 1960; *Time,* September 12, 1960; *Newsweek,* September 12, 1960.

—*Interview by Richard Ziegfeld*

[Sketch approved by Kenneth McCormick]

*   *   *

BAYH, Marvella (Hern) 1933-1979

PERSONAL: Surname is pronounced Buy; born February 14, 1933, in Enid, Okla.; died April 24, 1979, in Bethesda, Md.; daughter of Delbert (a farmer) and Bernett (Monson) Hern; married Birch E. Bayh, Jr. (a U.S. senator), August 24, 1952; children: Evan. *Education:* Attended Oklahoma State University, 1951-52; attended Indiana State University, 1952-54, B.S., 1960. *Residence:* Washington, D.C.

CAREER: Easter Seal Society, co-chairman of Indiana branch, 1965, 1966, and 1967; American Cancer Society, co-chairman of Illinois crusade, 1973, co-chairman of national crusade, 1974, consultant and special representative, 1974-79. Member of speaker's bureau, Democratic National Committee, beginning in 1960; teacher, Girl's State and Girl's Nation, 1962-74. *Member:* National Beautification Speakers Committee, Citizen's Committee for the Conquest of Cancer (sponsor member), Phi Beta Phi, Theta Sigma Pi. *Awards, honors:* Pride of the Plainsmen award, 1967; James Ewing Award from American Society of Oncologists, 1977, for work in disseminating information about cancer; Hubert H. Humphrey Inspirational Award from American Cancer Society, 1979; Matrix award.

WRITINGS: (With Mary Lynne Kotz) *Marvella: A Personal Journey,* Harcourt, 1979. Contributor to publications, including *Day Care Bulletin, McCall's, Today's Health, World Health Magazine,* and *Ladies' Home Journal.*

SIDELIGHTS: Early in 1971, Marvella Bayh, like one out of every fourteen women in the United States of the 1970's, learned she had breast cancer. A modified radical mastectomy was performed in October, 1971, to remove her right breast, a section of chest muscle, and the lymph glands in the armpit. Chemotherapy treatments followed, a grueling eighteen-month regimen. "Wherever you are in the world on April 8, 1973," Marvella informed an interviewer for the *New York Times,* "you are going to hear a world-shaking boom and that will be me celebrating the end of the chemotherapy treatments."

Marvella Bayh lost a breast, but she did not lose her courage, determination, or even her sense of humor. She saw herself as lucky, explaining that if she had to have cancer, this was probably the least disastrous: it wasn't crippling and it did not mean losing an arm, a leg, or her sight. She became very outspoken about cancer, and breast cancer in particular. As co-chair, first with her husband, Senator Birch Bayh, and later with actor Peter Graves, she led both local and national crusades for the American Cancer Society.

Above all, she maintained that a mastectomy did not mean the end of the world. Many women who are faced with this procedure seriously doubt that their husbands will still love them and find them attractive. "In doing so we terribly underestimate the men in this country," she argued in an article for *Ladies' Home Journal.* "In our society," she asserted, "women's breasts have been thought of as a symbol of femininity and sexual adequacy. Actually, they have nothing to do with either. You are the same person that you were before this surgery—with the same desires and the same ability to fulfill them. . . . You have not become maimed or crippled, and the experience should not make you emotionally disabled. You can do anything that you did before."

Through it all, Marvella was aided by her husband, Birch. "He has been my anchor. If I started to be blue, he was there to buoy me up. Birch was right by my side," she reflected to an interviewer for the *New York Times.* Marvella first met her future husband during a speech contest sponsored by the National Farm Bureau. In defeating Birch Bayh, she became the first woman ever to win the nationwide event.

After her mastectomy, Marvella returned to a normal life. Hired as a consultant and special representative by the American Cancer Society, she toured the country giving speeches to community groups and appearing on television talk shows. She cited the horrible facts of breast cancer—it represents about one-fifth of all deaths resulting from cancer and ranks as the number two killer of women—and stressed the importance of self-examination and early detection. "It was the job of a lifetime for me—especially gratifying because so many people wrote that my speaking out about cancer had sent them to the doctor and saved their lives," she declared in her book *Marvella: A Personal Journey.* Despite the disease, she felt her life had not been wasted; she was able, through her own misfortune, to help others in the same situation. She felt that her life was now full.

Then one day it happened. "I had an appointment for my three-times-a-year cancer check-up," she related in her book. "I was not too worried. After all, it had been 6¼ years, with 'all-clear' tests. That afternoon, January 25, 1978, I didn't get an 'all-clear.'" During Marvella's last year of life her diagnostic cancer test rose from a level of 3.5, a relatively safe margin from the warning mark at 5, to 10, and then to a devastating 120. There was absolutely no doubt: her cancer was terminal, inoperable, and spreading like wildfire throughout her entire body.

But she never gave in. When she heard that an article she had written for a magazine had been prefaced by an editor's note that she was dying of cancer, Marvella protested: "I have never, ever said I am dying of cancer. I am living with the knowledge that I have cancer." Mary Lynne Kotz, co-author of Marvella's book, revealed something of Marvella Bayh's spirit in an article for the *Washington Post:* "As she never saw herself as gifted, neither did she see herself as courageous. She was afraid, she had doubts, she was touchingly human. But she continued her life of offering help to other people. Service was nothing new to her; found with the recurrence of cancer, it was what she did."

Close friend and president of the American Cancer Society, Dr. LeSalle Leffall, spoke for many when he eulogized: "She was a powerful figure and a moral force. Even when she lost her own fight she never stopped telling others and counseling them about cancer. Hers was a demonstration of courage beyond description."

BIOGRAPHICAL/CRITICAL SOURCES: New York Times, June 18, 1972, March 26, 1974; *Ladies' Home Journal,* January, 1975; Marvella Bayh and Mary Lynne Kotz, *Marvella: A Personal Journey,* Harcourt, 1979; *People,* May 14, 1979; *Good Housekeeping,* September, 1979, October, 1979; *New York Times Book Review,* October 14, 1979; *Washington Post,* November 25, 1979; *Detroit Free Press,* December 12, 1979.

OBITUARIES: New York Times, April 25, 1979; *Washington Post,* April 25, 1979; *Chicago Tribune,* April 26, 1979.*

—*Sketch by Kathleen Ceton Newman*

* * *

BEACH, Stewart T(aft) 1899-1979

PERSONAL: Born December 17, 1899, in Pontiac, Mich.; died February 21, 1979, in New York. *Education:* University of Michigan, A.B., 1922. *Residence:* Manhattan, N.Y.

CAREER: New York University, New York City, instructor in English, 1922-24; *Independent* (weekly news magazine), Boston, Mass., managing editor, 1924-28; *Theater* (drama magazine), New York City, editor and drama critic, 1928-30; *House Beautiful* (magazine), editor, 1930-39; free-lance writer, 1939-79. *This Week* (weekly magazine), executive editor and fiction editor, 1947-66.

WRITINGS: Short-Story Technique, Houghton, Mifflin, c. 1929; *Racing Start,* Little, Brown, 1941; (editor and contributor) *This Week's Short-Short Stories,* Random House, 1953; (editor and contributor) *This Week's Stories of Mystery and Suspense,* Random House, 1957; *Samuel Adams: The Fateful Years, 1764-1776,* Dodd, 1965; (author of introduction and notes) Samuel Chamberlain, *New England in Color,* Hastings House, 1969; (author of introduction and notes) Chamberlain, *Lexington and Concord in Color,* Hastings House, 1970. Also author of a juvenile book, *Good Morning, Sun's Up,* Scroll Press, and with Philip Wood, of play, "Lend Me Your Ears," 1939.

OBITUARIES: New York Times, February 23, 1979.*

* * *

BEACHCOMBER
See MORTON, John (Cameron Andrieu) Bingham (Michael)

* * *

BEARCHELL, Charles 1925-

PERSONAL: Born October 13, 1925, in Mount Vernon, N.Y.; son of Charles A. and Catharine M. Bearchell; married Ursula M. Herbe, May 3, 1953; children: Charles Raymond. *Education:* San Francisco State University, B.S., 1959, M.S., 1962; Northwestern University, Ph.D., 1971. *Office:* Graduate Studies and Research, California State University, Northridge, Calif. 91330.

CAREER: California State University, Northridge, began as assistant professor, became professor of marketing, 1965—, dean of graduate studies and research, 1977—. *Member:* American Marketing Association, Association of Consumer Research, National Council of University Research Administrators, Council of Graduate Schools, Western Association of Graduate Schools.

WRITINGS: Retailing: A Professional Approach, Harcourt, 1975; (with Wolfgang K. A. Disch) *Marketing Dictionary—English-German, German-English,* Gesellschaft fuer Angewandtes Marketing, 1976, 2nd edition, 1980.

* * *

BEATON, Cecil (Walter Hardy) 1904-1980

OBITUARY NOTICE—See index for CA sketch: Born January 14, 1904, in London, England; died January 18, 1980, in Broadchalke, Wiltshire, England. Photographer, costume and stage designer, painter, and writer. The flamboyant Beaton was one of the most renowned photographers of his time. The favorite photographer of the British royal family, he also snapped pictures of hundreds of other famous people, including T. S. Eliot, Marlon Brando, Rudolf Nureyev, Edith Sitwell, Greta Garbo, and Igor Stravinsky. His photographs are collected in such books as *The Book of Beauty, Royal Portraits,* and *The Best of Beaton.* A stage and costume designer as well, Beaton won Academy Awards for his work on "Gigi" in 1959 and "My Fair Lady" in 1965. Over the years he published a number of best-selling diaries, excerpts of which are contained in *Self Portrait With Friends,* published in 1979. Among his other books are *Ballet, Photobiography,* and a biography of Count Charles Korsetz, *Quail in Aspic.* Obituaries and other sources: *Life,* September 16, 1946; *Current Biography,* Wilson, 1962; *Newsweek,* May 12, 1969, April 16, 1973, January 28, 1980; *Celebrity Register,* 3rd edition, Simon & Schuster, 1973; *Who's Who in the Theatre,* 16th edition, Pitman, 1977; *Who's Who,* 131st edition, St. Martin's, 1979; *New York Times,* January 19, 1980; *Washington Post,* January 19, 1980; *Chicago Tribune,* January 19, 1980.

* * *

BEDFORD, Donald F.
See FEARING, Kenneth (Flexner)

* * *

BEDIKIAN, Antriganik A. 1886(?)-1980

OBITUARY NOTICE: Born c. 1886 in Constantinople (now Istanbul), Turkey; died February 17, 1980, in Orange, N.J. Clergyman, educator, and author of *The Golden Age in Armenia.* Bedikian was a teacher at Robert's College in his native country before coming to the United States in 1913. During the 1940's and 1950's, he taught courses in Armenian studies at Columbia University. He was pastor of the Armenian Evangelical Church of New York for about forty years. Obituaries and other sources: *New York Times,* February 18, 1980.

* * *

BEDOUKIAN, Kerop 1907-

PERSONAL: Born October 15, 1907, in Sivas, Turkey; came to Canada, 1926; naturalized Canadian citizen, 1931; son of Haroutune (a grocer) and Serpouhi (der Mesrobian) Bedoukian; married Marjorie Hayey Clark (a social worker), June 21, 1935; children: Marian Bedoukian Sinn, Harold, Peter. *Politics:* None. *Religion:* None. *Home and office:* 3457 Park Ave., Montreal, Quebec, Canada H2X 2H6.

CAREER: Operated rug cleaning plant in Vancouver, British Columbia; dealer in Oriental rugs in Montreal, Quebec, 1935—. President of Armenian General Benevolent Union,

1956-74. *Member:* Canadian Authors Association (vice-president), Society of Armenians From Istanbul (honorary life president), Armenian Congress (vice-president, 1960-64). *Awards, honors:* Centennial Medal from Government of Canada, 1967; Queen's Jubilee Medal, 1977.

WRITINGS: The Urchin: An Armenian's Escape, J. Murray, 1978, published as *Some of Us Survived: An Armenian's Story,* Farrar, Strauss, 1979.

WORK IN PROGRESS: Biographies of remaining survivors of Turkish massacres, 1915-18.

SIDELIGHTS: Bedoukian writes: "My schooling had started when the war began in 1915 but it ended abruptly because of the general deportation and systematic killings of the Armenian population all over Turkey. From 1915 until my arrival in Canada in 1926, the story is of day-to-day survival; just to be able to exist was quite an achievement. It was only after my arrival in Canada that I could give some thought to my education, well-being, and the future.

"The first two years in Canada were spent on a farm in Ontario, a period of adjustment and building up my health. In 1931, I became a Canadian citizen and also got involved in the needs of the Armenian community. In 1952, upon request of the Canadian Council of Churches and with the help of the World Council of Churches, I sponsored and brought to Canada 750 Armenian refugees from Greece, remnants of the victims of Turkish atrocities.

"This immigrant assistance endeavor never stopped and the number of assisted immigrants grew to over two thousand in the next twenty years. Now, at age seventy-two, I still give most of my time to community services."

* * *

BEESON, Trevor Randall 1926-

PERSONAL: Born March 2, 1926, in Darley Dale, England; son of Arthur William and Matilda (Randall) Beeson; married Josephine Cope, October 2, 1950; children: Jean Elizabeth Beeson Lloyd, Catherine Margaret Beeson Andrews. *Education:* King's College, London, A.K.C., 1950; attended St. Boniface College, 1950-51. *Home:* 2 Little Cloister, Westminster Abbey, London S.W.1, England.

CAREER: Ordained minister of Church of England, 1951; vicar of Church of England in Stockton-on-Tees, England, 1954-65; curate of Church of England in London, England, 1965-71; vicar of Church of England in Ware, England, 1971-76; Westminster Abbey, London, canon-treasurer, 1976—. Chaplain of St. Bride's, 1970—. Chairperson of S.C.M. Press. Consultant to London Weekend Television. *Awards, honors:* M.A. from Archbishop of Canterbury, 1976.

WRITINGS: New Area Mission, Mowbray, 1963; (with Robin Sharp) *Worship in a United Church,* Mowbray, 1964; (editor) *Partnership in Ministry,* Mowbray, 1964; *An Eye for an Ear,* Allenson, 1972; *The Church and England in Crisis,* Davis-Poynter, 1973; *Discretion and Valour: Religious Conditions in Eastern Europe,* Collins, 1974; *Britain Today and Tomorrow,* Collins, 1978. Also author of *New Area Mission,* 1963, and editor of *Partnership in Ministry,* 1964. European correspondent for *Christian Century,* 1970—. Editor of *New Christian,* 1965-70.

* * *

BEETON, (Douglas) Ridley 1929-

PERSONAL: Born August 31, 1929, in Zeerust, South Africa; son of Douglas Arthur Ridley (a bank manager) and

Emma (a teacher; maiden name, Ullmer) Beeton. *Education:* University of Pretoria, M.A., 1952; University of South Africa, D.Litt. et Phil., 1964. *Politics:* Progressive Federal. *Religion:* "A believer without an orthodoxy." *Home:* 269 Polaris Ave., Pretoria 0181, South Africa. *Office:* Department of English, University of South Africa, P.O. Box 392, Pretoria 0001, South Africa.

CAREER: Council for Scientific and Industrial Research, Division of Information, Pretoria, South Africa, 1952-58, began as assistant, later became officer and officer-in-charge; University of South Africa, Pretoria, lecturer, 1958-59, senior lecturer, 1959-63; professor of English, 1963—, head of department, 1963—. Participant in international conferences.

MEMBER: International Joseph Conrad Society, English Academy of South Africa (past vice-president; president, 1969-70, 1973-75; member of council), Human Sciences Research Council (member of council, 1976—), South African Library Association (fellow), Bronte Society (England), Ruskin Association (England). *Awards, honors:* Traveling fellowship from Carnegie Corp., 1966; Ernest Oppenheimer Memorial fellowship from Memorial Trust, 1966 and 1977; grant from Human Sciences Research Council, 1971.

WRITINGS: (Editor with W. D. Maxwell-Mahon) *South African Poetry: A Critical Anthology,* University of South Africa, 1966; (editor) *Four South African One-Act Plays,* Nassau, 1973; *Olive Schreiner: A Short Guide to Her Writings,* Howard Timmins, 1974; (editor with Maxwell-Mahon and J. B. Goedhals) *The Art of Communication,* Oxford University Press, 1974; (with Helen Dorner) *A Dictionary of English Usage in Southern Africa,* Oxford University Press, 1975; (editor) *A Pilot Bibliography of South African English Literature,* University of South Africa, 1976.

Author of a detective novel, under a pseudonym.

Work represented in anthologies, including *The Penguin Book of South African Verse, Meaning in Life,* and *Joseph Conrad: Commemorative Essays.*

Contributor to magazines and newspapers in South Africa, England, and the United States.

WORK IN PROGRESS: Scholars of Mercy, a novel; *The Landscape of Requirement,* poems; a descriptive survey of Olive Schreiner manuscript sources; a dictionary of South African English literature; a critical volume on George Eliot; "Servants," a three-act play.

SIDELIGHTS: Beeton told *CA:* "The aim of my critical work is to find the moral aesthetic that is embedded in the writer's style and approach. The aim of my creative work is to give some personal account, with simplicity (and a firmly acknowledged romantic bias), of the qualities, poignancies, and strengths I find.

"To show the joy and intensity of literature and art has been my constant endeavor as a critic and teacher. The 'life of the thing' is what interests me, and what I try to communicate."

BIOGRAPHICAL/CRITICAL SOURCES: UNISA News, September, 1975, December, 1976.

* * *

BEINE, George Holmes 1893-

PERSONAL: Surname is pronounced *Bine-ee;* born February 13, 1893, in Omaha, Neb.; son of Frank August (a farmer) and Helena (Holmes) Beine; married wife, Anne; children: George K. (deceased), Shirley Beine McDonald. *Education:* Attended school in San Francisco, Calif. *Poli-*

tics: Republican. *Religion:* None. *Home address:* P.O. Box 426, Ross, Calif. 94957.

CAREER: Manager of life insurance company in San Francisco, Calif., 1916-45. Also worked as cowboy and rancher. *Military service:* Served in National Guard and U.S. Navy. *Member:* Life Insurance Managers Association, Chamber of Commerce, Lions, High Twelve Club, Kiwanis, Exchange Club, Olympic Club.

WRITINGS: Land of the Coyote, Iowa State University Press, 1973. Contributor of stories, poems, and articles to magazines.

WORK IN PROGRESS: A humorous book.

SIDELIGHTS: Beine writes: "I was over eighty years old when I took up writing for publication as a hobby."

* * *

BEISER, Arthur 1931-

PERSONAL: Born February 16, 1931, in New York, N.Y.; son of Max (a physician) and Gertrude (Rudin) Beiser; married Germaine Bousquet (a physicist and author), 1953; children: Nadis Louise, Alexa Susan, Isabel Victoria. *Education:* New York University, Ph.D., 1956. *Home:* Ile des Embiez, 83140 Le Brusc, France.

CAREER: New York University, New York City, assistant professor, 1956-59, associate professor of physics, 1959-61, senior research scientist, 1961-62; vice-president of Nuclear Research Associates, Inc., 1961-62; Columbia University, New York City, senior research scientist, 1962-63; writer, 1963—.

WRITINGS: (With wife, Germaine Beiser) *Physics for Everybody,* Dutton, 1956; *Guide to the Microscope,* Dutton, 1957; (with Sidney Borowitz) *Concepts and Principles of Physics,* Addison-Wesley, 1958; *Our Earth: The Properties of Our Planet, How They Were Discovered, and How They Came Into Being,* Dutton, 1959.

The World of Physics: Readings in the Nature, History, and Challenge of Physics, McGraw, 1960; (with Konrad B. Krauskopf) *The Physical Universe,* McGraw, 1960, 4th edition, 1979; *Basic Concepts of Physics,* Addison-Wesley, 1961, 2nd edition, 1972; (with G. Beiser) *Study Guide for Basic Concepts of Physics,* Addison-Wesley, 1962; *The Earth,* Time, 1962, juvenile edition, Time-Life, 1968; *The Mainstream of Physics,* Addison-Wesley, 1962; (with G. Beiser) *Study Guide for the Mainstream of Physics,* Addison-Wesley, 1962; (with G. Beiser) *The Story of Cosmic Rays,* Dutton, 1962; *Concepts of Modern Physics,* McGraw, 1963, 3rd edition, 1981; (with Krauskopf) *Introduction to Physics and Chemistry,* McGraw, 1964, 2nd edition, 1969; *The Foundations of Physics,* Addison-Wesley, 1964; *The Science of Physics,* Addison-Wesley, 1964; *Modern Technical Physics,* Addison-Wesley, 1966, 3rd edition, Benjamin-Cummings, 1979; (with Borowitz) *Essentials of Physics: A Text for Students of Science and Engineering,* Addison-Wesley, 1966, 2nd edition, 1973; (with Krauskopf) *Fundamentals of Physical Science,* McGraw, 1966, new edition, 1971; *The Proper Yacht,* Macmillan, 1966, 2nd edition, International Marine, 1978; *Modern Physics: An Introductory Survey,* Addison-Wesley, 1968; *Essential Math for the Sciences: Algebra, Trigonometry, and Vectors,* McGraw, 1969; *Essential Math for the Sciences: Analytic Geometry and Calculus,* McGraw, 1969; *Perspectives of Modern Physics,* McGraw, 1969.

The Sailor's World, Random House, 1972; *Physics,* Benjamin-Cummings, 1973, 2nd edition, 1978; *Schaum's*

Outline of Theory and Problems of Physical Science, Mc-Graw, 1974; *Schaum's Outline of Theory and Problems of Earth Science,* McGraw, 1975; (with Krauskopf) *Introduction to Earth Science,* McGraw, 1975; *Schaum's Outline of Theory and Problems of Applied Physics,* McGraw, 1976; *Schaum's Outline of Theory and Problems of Mathematics for Electricity and Electronics,* McGraw, 1980; (with Alexander Harvey) *Astronomy,* McGraw, 1981.

WORK IN PROGRESS: Physics, 3rd edition, publication by Benjamin-Cummings expected in 1982.

*   *   *

BELL, David R(obert) 1932-

PERSONAL: Born November 28, 1932, in London, England; son of George Robert (a Salvation Army officer) and O. (a Salvation Army officer; maiden name, Lord) Bell; divorced; children: Hugh David Socrates, Tessa Anne, Adam Aristotle McNiven. *Education:* Attended University of St. Andrews, University of Bristol, and University of Michigan. *Politics:* Whig. *Religion:* "Cricket." *Home:* 29 Falkland St., Glasgow G12 9QZ, Scotland. *Office:* University of Glasgow, Glasgow G12 8QQ, Scotland.

CAREER: Teacher of philosophy at University of Glasgow, Glasgow, Scotland. *Member:* Society of Apothecaries.

WRITINGS: Bertrand Russell, Judson, 1972.

WORK IN PROGRESS: Research on sociology and on philosophy of technique.

SIDELIGHTS: Bell writes: "Subjects I consider vital include truth, credulity, pain, laughter. My motivation is intellectual pride, but petty sums of money are the main reason for my literary effort. Authors, like fighters, are at their best when hungry. I have been well-fed." *Avocational interests:* Women, chess, reading.

*   *   *

BELMONTE, Thomas 1946-

PERSONAL: Born December 8, 1946, in New York, N.Y.; son of Vito and Theodora Belmonte; divorced; children: Christina. *Education:* Hofstra University, B.A., 1969; Columbia University, M.A., 1973, M.Phil., 1974, Ph.D., 1978. *Office:* Department of Anthropology, Hofstra University, Hempstead, N.Y. 11550.

CAREER: Hofstra University, Hempstead, N.Y., assistant professor of anthropology. *Member:* American Anthropological Association.

WRITINGS: The Broken Fountain, Columbia University Press, 1979. Contributor to anthropology journals.

SIDELIGHTS: Belmonte writes: "I am committed to a humanistic literate anthropology which builds not only theories, but also bridges of vital communication and understanding between peoples who are strange and unknown to one another."

BIOGRAPHICAL/CRITICAL SOURCES: New York Times, July 28, 1979.

*   *   *

BELTRAN, Pedro (Gerardo) 1897-1979

PERSONAL: Born February 17, 1897, in Lima, Peru; died of a heart attack, February 16, 1979, in Lima, Peru; son of Pedro and Augusta (Espantoso) Beltran; married Miriam Kropp (an economic analyst), 1950. *Education:* Attended Colegio de la Recoleta and San Marcos University; London School of Economics and Political Science, B.S., 1918. *Residence:* San Francisco, Calif.

CAREER/WRITINGS: Chairman of board of Central Reserve Bank in Peru, 1931-32 and 1948-50; *La Prensa* (newspaper), Lima, Peru, editor and publisher, 1934-75; ambassador to Washington, D.C., 1944-45; member of advisory board of International Bank for Reconstruction and Development, 1948-50; Prime Minister and Minister of Finance in Peru, 1959-61. Delegate to international conferences. Head of Alianza Nacional (private political association) and Los Independientes (political party) in Peru. *Member:* National Agricultural Society (past president). *Awards, honors:* Maria Moors Cabot Prize for inter-American journalism from Columbia University, gold medal, 1955, special citation, 1972; Hero of the Press gold medal from Inter-American Press Association, 1956; LL.D. from Yale University, 1960, and Harvard University, 1968; Theodore Brent Inter-American Award from International House of New Orleans, 1964; decorated Grand Officer of the French Legion of Honor; honorary fellow of London School of Economics and Political Science.

SIDELIGHTS: Pedro Beltran was one of the major proponents of freedom of the press in Peru. His long battle against censorship began in 1934 when he gained control of the formerly dormant newspaper, *La Prensa.* Although the paper had always been moderately popular with the general public, Beltran increased circulation by more than five hundred percent when he modernized the journalistic techniques in 1950 after an extensive study of American newspapers.

Often clashing with the regime of former President Manuel Ordia, *La Prensa* was shut down completely in 1956 for advocating free elections, and Beltran was taken into confinement on the island prison of El Fronton. But he was not discouraged, for as he announced at the time of his arrest, "Like missionaries who go among the savages and must be prepared to be eaten, we independent newspapermen and honest politicians should be prepared for the worst." His imprisonment lasted barely a month, however, for waves of protest and condemnation of Ordia's action came from all corners of the world.

Considered to be due largely to the crusades led by Beltran and *La Prensa,* a free election was held later that same year. The ballot that replaced Ordia with Manuel Prado was later described as "a unique case of a dictator being put out without a single shot fired or a single drop of blood shed." Prado subsequently appointed the newsman to the post of the governor's commissioner in charge of land reform and housing, and three years later, the dual post of Prime Minister and Minister of Finance.

Beltran's experience in these matters stemmed in part from his visits to the United States. By applying the principles of free-enterprise to his own country, he was able to repay Peru's national debt of $14.5 million within his first eight months in office, drastically reduce unnecessary government spending, control tax collections more efficiently, and reduce exports. Beltran was so successful that he sought the presidency in a later election. Despite all efforts, however, he was unable to secure a sufficient majority, and returned to devote himself completely to *La Prensa.*

In 1975, the newspaper was again overrun by the military government of General Juan Velasco Alvarado. Beltran and his wife fled Peru to live in exile in the United States.

BIOGRAPHICAL/CRITICAL SOURCES: Time, February 21, 1972; *Houston Post,* October 25, 1974; *Biography News,* Gale, January/February, 1975.

OBITUARIES: New York Times, February 18, 1979.*

* * *

BENDIXSON, Terence 1934-

PERSONAL: Born August 3, 1934, in Hertfordshire, England; son of Sylvester (a stockbroker) and Evelyn (Palgrave) Bendixson; married Frances Parker (a jeweler), April 5, 1960; children: Adam, Stephen. *Education:* Attended Worcester College, Oxford, 1954-57. *Politics:* "Liberal/Conservative." *Home:* 18 Ifield Rd., London SW10 9AA, England. *Office:* Pedestrians' Association, 1 Wandsworth Rd., London SW8 2LJ, England.

CAREER: Guardian, London, England, planning correspondent, 1963-69; *Observer,* London, member of environment bureau, 1970-71; free-lance writer and broadcaster, 1971—. News editor of *Transportation,* 1972—. Member of council of Royal Borough of Kensington and Chelsea, 1978—. Visiting fellow at University of Southampton. Consultant to British Government and Organization for Economic Cooperation and Development. *Military service:* British Army, Grenadier Guards, 1952-54; became second lieutenant. *Member:* Pedestrians' Association (chairperson, 1976—), Earls Court Youth Club (chairperson, 1976—).

WRITINGS: Instead of Cars, Temple Smith, 1974, published as *Without Wheels: Alternatives to the Private Car,* Indiana University Press, 1975.

WORK IN PROGRESS: Research on charging drivers a fee for using the roads; research on powered hang gliders.

SIDELIGHTS: Bendixson told *CA:* "Perhaps it was the experience of being evacuated to Canada in 1940, and of traveling across the Atlantic in the *Duchess of York,* that explains my interest in transport. I was also for a period excited by sports cars, but today I am more concerned to modernize the obsolete Henry Ford automotive engineering and Macadam highway engineering that makes our cities into stinking, unsafe sinks for children. We have tried the drive-in city and found it does not work. It kills about 20,000 people a year in America and Europe while they are doing nothing more offensive than just trying to walk across the road. Now it is time to try the walk-in city, where short trips are counted as important as long ones, where neighborhood development is ranked above regional development, where cars are small, slow, quiet, and fragile, where bicycling is safe, and where children may play in the streets. Is it really so idealistic to try to make cities fit for people?"

* * *

BENEDICT, Dorothy Potter 1889-1979

OBITUARY NOTICE—See index for *CA* sketch: Born April 15, 1889, in Chicago, Ill.; died December 4, 1979, in Washington, D.C. During World War I Benedict was an American Red Cross worker in France, and during World War II she served as a translator and secretary for the U.S. Air Service. She was the author of three children's books, *Pagan the Black, Fabulous,* and *Bandoleer,* and also contributed short stories and articles to magazines. Obituaries and other sources: *Washington Post,* December 9, 1979.

* * *

BENNETT, Isadora 1900-1980
(Wesley Morgan)

OBITUARY NOTICE: Born July 21, 1900, in Canton, Mo.; died February 8, 1980, in New York, N.Y. Theatrical publicity agent, press representative, reporter, playwright, and author. Bennett, who was the press representative for numerous cultural associations, was affiliated with Martha Graham and her dance company for more than thirty years. She is credited with popularizing modern dance in America. Bennett began her career as a reporter for the *Chicago Daily News,* and often covered gangland stories. In the early thirties she began to work exclusively as a publicity agent. She wrote for such dance groups as the American Dance Festival, the Royal Danish Ballet, the National Ballet of Canada, Argentinita, Jose Greco, and the Joffrey Ballet. Bennett also contributed articles and essays on dance to magazines under the pseudonym Wesley Morgan, and was the author of several plays, including "Soon Bright Day." Obituaries and other sources: *New York Times,* February 10, 1980.

* * *

BENOIT, Pierre 1886-1962

OBITUARY NOTICE: Born July 16, 1886, in Albi, France; died in March, 1962, in Saint-Jean-de-Luz, France. Novelist and short story writer, best known for his first novel, *Koenigsmark.* During his lifetime, Benoit produced about forty adventure novels, including *Pour Don Carlos, Le Lac sale, Chaussee des geants,* and *Lord Dorchester.* Obituaries and other sources: *New York Times,* March 4, 1962; *The Oxford Companion to French Literature,* corrected edition, Oxford University Press, 1966; *Encyclopedia of World Literature in the Twentieth Century,* updated edition, Ungar, 1967; *Everyman's Dictionary of European Writers,* Dent & Sons, 1968; *Cassell's Encyclopaedia of World Literature,* revised edition, Morrow, 1973.

* * *

BENSON, Elizabeth P(olk) 1924-

PERSONAL: Born May 13, 1924, in Washington, D.C.; daughter of Theodore B. (an attorney) and Rebecca (Albin) Benson. *Education:* Wellesley College, B.A., 1945; Catholic University of America, M.A., 1956. *Residence:* Washington, D.C. *Office:* Dumbarton Oaks, 1703 32nd St. N.W., Washington, D.C. 20007.

CAREER: National Gallery of Art, Washington, D.C., museum aide, 1946-51, curator, 1954-60; free-lance editor in New York, N.Y., 1960-62; Dumbarton Oaks (trustees for Harvard University), Washington, D.C., director of Center for Pre-Columbian Studies and curator for Pre-Columbian collection, 1963—. Lecturer at Catholic University of America, 1968, 1969; adjunct professor at Columbia University, 1973; lecturer to Smithsonian Institution Associates, 1978. *Member:* Society for American Archaeology, Society of Women Geographers, Institute of Andean Studies, Columbia University Seminar on Pre-Columbian and Primitive Art.

WRITINGS: The Mohica: A Culture of Peru, Praeger, 1972; *The Maya World,* Crowell, 1972, revised edition, 1977; (editor) *Dumbarton Oaks Collections: Pre-Columbian Art,* University of Chicago Press, 1976. Editor of *Studies in Pre-Columbian Art and Archaeology.* Contributor to professional journals and popular magazines, including *Americas* and *Smithsonian.*

WORK IN PROGRESS: Research on the iconography of early north-coast Peruvian archaeological material.

SIDELIGHTS: Elizabeth Benson commented: "My research aim is to use the art of ancient peoples in an attempt to reconstruct their thought."

AVOCATIONAL INTERESTS: Poetry, fiction, music, painting, travel, Chinese food.

BENTON, Thomas Hart   1889-1975

PERSONAL: Born April 15, 1889, in Neosho, Mo.; died January 19, 1975, of heart disease, in Kansas City, Mo.; son of Maecenus Eason (a U.S. congressman) and Elizabeth (Wise) Benton; married Rita Piacenza, February 19, 1922; children: Thomas P., Jessie P. Lyman. *Education:* Attended Art Institute of Chicago School, 1906-07, and Academie Julian, Paris, 1908-11. *Politics:* Democratic. *Home:* 3616 Belleview Ave., Kansas City, Mo, 64111.

CAREER: Joplin American, Joplin, Mo., cartoonist, 1906; professional painter, 1912-75. Gallery director and art teacher for Chelsea Neighborhood Association, 1917; Kansas City Art Institute and School of Design, teacher, 1926-36, director of department of painting, 1935-40; painter of scenes and characters for the motion picture "The Long Voyage Home," 1940; lecturer; painter of such works as the murals at the Missouri State Capital, Harzfeld Department Store, Lincoln University, New York State Power Authority, Truman Library, New Britain Museum, University of Indiana, New School for Social Research; one-man exhibitions at Lakeside Press Gallery, Chicago, 1927, Ferargil Galleries, New York, 1934, Associated American Artists Gallery, New York, 1931, 1941, 1965, Chicago, 1946, University of Arizona, 1962, Graham Gallery, 1968, 1970, and Madison Art Center, 1971; works included in such collections as Metropolitan Museum of Art, Museum of Modern Art, Brooklyn Museum, Wanamaker Gallery, Pennsylvania Academy of Fine Arts, and Andover/Phillips. *Military service:* U.S. Navy, 1918-19; became draftsman in architectural service. *Member:* American Academy of Arts and Sciences, National Academy of Design, Academia de Bellas Artes (honorary member; Argentine Republic), Academia Sienesa deglia Intronati (honorary member; Siena, Italy), Academia Fiorentina della Arti del Disegno (honorary member; Florence, Italy). *Awards, honors:* Gold medal from Architectes League, 1933; Doctor of Fine Arts from University of Missouri, 1948; Doctor of Letters from Lincoln University, 1957; Doctor of Fine Arts from New School for Social Research, 1968.

WRITINGS: (And illustrator) *An Artist in America* (autobiography), R. M. McBride, 1937, third revision, University of Missouri Press, 1968; (author of introduction) Frederick Shane, *Drawings,* University of Missouri Press, 1964; *Drawings,* University of Missouri Press, 1968; *An American in Art: A Professional and Technical Autobiography,* University Press of Kansas, 1969.

Illustrator: Samuel Langhorne Clemens, *Life on the Mississippi,* Limited Editions, 1944; Jessie Stuart, *Taps for Private Tussie,* World Publishing, 1969.

SIDELIGHTS: Thomas Hart Benton's colorful, folksy, painting became most popular in the 1930's, as it rode on the wave of nostalgia which swept the United States at that time. The country was in the grip of the Great Depression and the face of America was changing. Industrialism and city dwelling were becoming the new mode of living while rural life and farming were taking a less important role. Americans needed reassurance that their great pioneering spirit was not dead and that their country was vital and strong because it was inhabited by people with the same characteristics. Benton, along with his fellow "regionalists," Grant Wood and John Stuart Curry, helped supply such reassurance. They depicted strong, staid characters in their works. Benton painted farmers tending their crops, mountain dwellers strumming fiddles and playing their harmonicas, Jesse James, Negro sharecroppers, soldiers in shantytowns, miners, steamboats on the Mississippi, and railroaders working on steamtrains. His paintings and murals are crowded panoramas of common folk. He tried to show the "real" America, the America he saw so much of while traveling the back roads throughout the country. He visited small towns and the homes of common people. He studied life in the Texas panhandle oil fields, and lived among the mountain people of the Ozarks and Tennessee. He talked, prayed, and sang with the people he met, and put what he experienced into his murals and his autobiography, *An Artist in America.*

Benton, the man Harry S Truman said was the "best damned painter in America," seemed to create controversy wherever he went. He was a strong-willed, outspoken man who spared no one from his opinions and feelings. He did precisely what he wanted to do, despite often harsh criticism. "I furnish the stuff for them—the stuff for them to damn me," he once said of his critics. Although Benton's painting was popular, it was not accepted by the art establishment, and as a result, Benton waged a one-man war against intellectuals, critics, and museums. "If the people didn't demand my representation," he once said, "I wouldn't be in the museums at all." But Benton's work did not always appeal to the common folk, either. In his murals for the Missouri State Capital, he included the figure of a corrupt political boss associating with prominent citizens of the town. Many were outraged at this, but Benton replied: "These incidents are a part of history and should be included. You take the warts with the good stuff."

Benton believed art should depict real things and not artificial abstractions. He felt modern art was unintelligible to the average person, and therefore useless. He believed that only by choosing meaningful subject matter could Americans create an art that was not a blatant copy of the symbolic and abstract paintings so popular in Europe during the 1930's and 1940's. He described the internationalists in favor of modern art "an intellectually diseased lot, victims of sickly rationalizations, psychic inversions and God-awful self-cultivations."

This stance is a strong reaction against his earlier style and schooling. When Benton was studying in Paris, he was very much influenced by the symbolists, led by Gauguin, and by the cubists, with Picasso as their mentor. He said of himself later that "I painted lifeless symbolist and cubist pictures, changing my ways with every whiff from Paris." The drastic change in his style from abstraction to realism occurred while he was in the navy in Norfolk, Virginia. While there, he left behind his "aesthetic drivelings and morbid self-concerns" and started to paint real things: the naval base, the men, and the machinery. This change in style put him at odds with the American art establishment, which was moving in the same direction as Europe—towards abstraction. Benton, once the teacher of Jackson Pollock, became cut off from the mainstream of American art, a man painting for a different time. He attacked the art establishment that rejected him, claiming the intellectuals "don't like art. They like to talk about it, they don't look at it." He vigorously denounced museums, asserting that, "If it was left to me, I wouldn't have any museums ... I'd have people buy the paintings and hang them anywhere anybody had time to look at them." He added that he would rather sell his pictures to saloons, Kiwanis and Rotary clubs, Chambers of Commerce, and "even women's clubs," than to a museum.

BIOGRAPHICAL/CRITICAL SOURCES: Thomas Hart Benton, *An Artist in America,* R. M. McBride, 1937; *Benton Drawings,* University of Missouri Press, 1968; *The Lithographs of Thomas Hart Benton,* edited by Creekmore Fath, University of Texas Press, 1969; Thomas Hart Benton, *An*

American in Art: A Professional and Technical Autobiography, University Press of Kansas, 1969; *Thomas Hart Benton: A Personal Commemorative,* Burd & Fletcher, 1973; *Thomas Hart Benton: An Artist's Selection, 1908-1974,* Nelson Gallery and Atkins Museum, 1974; Matthew Baigell, *Thomas Hart Benton,* Abrams, 1975.

OBITUARIES: New York Times, January 20, 21, 1975; *Washington Post,* January 21, 1975; *Time,* February 3, 1975; *Newsweek,* February 3, 1975.*

* * *

BERG, Rick 1951-

PERSONAL: Born May 16, 1951, in Brooklyn, N.Y.; son of Bernard (a stockbroker) and Irma (a high school physical education teacher; maiden name, Sobin) Berg. *Education:* Wesleyan University, Middletown, Conn., B.A. (magna cum laude), 1972; graduate study at University of California, Berkeley, 1976—. *Home:* 2126 Grant, Berkeley, Calif. 94703.

CAREER: Writer, 1979—. Also worked as deck hand on a tramp steamer in Hong Kong, scuba diver in Greece, Mexico, and Costa Rica, tour guide along the Amazon River, fisherman in Tierra del Fuego, cowboy in the Argentine pampas, and journalist in Costa Rica. *Member:* Phi Beta Kappa.

WRITINGS: The Art and Adventure of Traveling Cheaply, And-Or Press, 1979.

WORK IN PROGRESS: Research on the relationship of inventories to interest rates.

SIDELIGHTS: Berg commented: "Although I've always considered life an adventure, only my years on the road have been truly adventurous. I've climbed in the Andes and Himalayas, descended the Amazon alone in a canoe, and run gold on horseback in South America. I'd like to teach for awhile, then travel again, this time in an ocean-going sailboat. My book is an attempt to make cheap, adventurous foreign travel, including maximum contact with the local people, accessible to those who think there is no alternative to the package tour."

* * *

BERGER, Raoul 1901-

PERSONAL: Born January 4, 1901, in Russia; came to the United States in 1905, naturalized citizen, 1910; son of Jesse and Anna (Kahn) Berger; married Helen Beck, August, 1930 (died, September, 1958); married Patricia Wolcott (a writer), 1967; children: Carl, Andrea Berger Kalodner. *Education:* Attended Institute of Musical Art, 1919-21; University of Cincinnati, A.B., 1932; Northwestern University, J.D., 1935; Harvard University, LL.M., 1938. *Home:* 140 Jennie Dugan Rd., Concord, Mass. 01742.

CAREER: Cleveland Orchestra, Cleveland, Ohio, violin soloist, 1927; Cincinnati Symphony Orchestra, Cincinnati, Ohio, second concertmaster; Cincinnati String Quartet, Cincinnati, first violinist; practiced law in Chicago, Ill., 1935-37; Securities Exchange Commission, Washington, D.C., 1938-40; special assistant to U.S. attorney-general in Washington, D.C., 1940-42; Office of the Alien Property Custodian, Washington, D.C., 1942-46, associate general counsel, then general counsel; private practice of law in Washington, D.C., 1946-62; University of California, Berkeley, visiting professor of law, 1962-65; Harvard University, Cambridge, Mass., Charles Warren Senior Fellow in American Legal History, 1971-76. *Member:* American Bar Association (past chairperson of section on administrative law), Coif. *Awards,*

honors: LL.D. from University of Cincinnati, 1975, and University of Michigan, 1978; Silver Gavel Award from American Bar Association, 1978, for *Government by Judiciary.*

WRITINGS: Congress Versus the Supreme Court, Harvard University Press, 1969; *Impeachment: The Constitutional Problems,* Harvard University Press, 1973; *Executive Privilege: A Constitutional Myth,* Harvard University Press, 1974; *Government by Judiciary: The Transformation of the Fourteenth Amendment,* Harvard University Press, 1977. Contributor to law journals.

WORK IN PROGRESS: Research on constitutional law and history.

* * *

BERMAN, Connie 1949-

PERSONAL: Born January 23, 1949, in Pennsylvania; daughter of Frank Samuel (a grocer) and Violet (Schenck) Stopper; married Richard Berman (a financier), June 28, 1970. *Education:* Duke University, B.A. *Home:* 56 West 82nd St., New York, N.Y. 10024. *Agent:* Writer's House, Inc., 21 West 26th St., New York, N.Y. 10001.

CAREER: Ideal Publishing, New York City, editor, 1971-73; Macfadden Bartell, New York City, editor, 1973-75; Sterling's Magazines, New York City, editor, 1975-78; writer, 1978—. *Member:* Women in Communications.

WRITINGS: The Two Princesses: Caroline Kennedy and Caroline of Monaco, Grosset, 1977; (with Susan Katz) *The Yogurt Book,* Grosset, 1977; *The Official Dolly Parton Scrapbook,* Grosset, 1978. Contributor to magazines, including *Self, Us, Good Housekeeping, Womensports,* and *Working Woman.*

WORK IN PROGRESS: A working woman's guide to business etiquette, based on more than one hundred interviews with other women.

SIDELIGHTS: Berman comments: "I am interested in trends and lifestyles, biographies, working women, and careers."

* * *

BERMAN, Larry 1951-

PERSONAL: Born April 29, 1951, in Bronx, N.Y.; son of Irving (a judge) and Selma (a teacher; maiden name, Genzer) Berman; married Janet Sue Nevins (a teacher), August 19, 1973; children: Scott. *Education:* American University, B.A., 1973; Princeton University, M.A., 1975, Ph.D., 1977. *Home:* 2952 Concord Ave., Davis, Calif. 95616. *Office:* Department of Political Science, University of California, Davis, Calif. 95616.

CAREER: University of California, Davis, assistant professor of political science, 1977—. Member of Davis Recreation and Park Commission. *Member:* American Political Science Association, Academy of Political Science, Academy of Public Administration.

WRITINGS: The Office of Management and Budget and the Presidency, 1921-1979, Princeton University Press, 1979. Contributor to political science journals.

WORK IN PROGRESS: A book on president-adviser relationships and the decision-making process during the presidency of Lyndon Baines Johnson.

SIDELIGHTS: Berman told *CA:* "As a teacher and writer I believe it is my responsibility to get students interested in the political process. The legacy of Vietnam and Watergate was 'stay away from Washington—power corrupts.' No worse lesson could come from these experiences. The country needs creative, honest and sincere leaders.''

*   *   *

BERNARD, Will 1915-

PERSONAL: Born October 17, 1915, in Detroit, Mich. *Education:* University of Michigan, LL.B., 1939. *Agent:* McIntosh & Otis, Inc., 475 Fifth Ave., New York, N.Y. 10017.

CAREER: American Bar Association, Chicago, Ill., author of column "The Family Lawyer," syndicated in approximately three-hundred fifty daily newspapers, 1964—.

WRITINGS: Law for the Family (Kiplinger Book Club selection), Scribner, 1962. Contributor of many articles to magazines, including *Esquire, Woman's Day, Reader's Digest, Coronet, Today's Health,* and *This Week.*

*   *   *

BERRY, Cicely 1926-

PERSONAL: Born May 7, 1926, in Berkhamstead, England; daughter of Cecil V. and Frances (Bachelor); married Harry Moore (a television producer; deceased). *Education:* Attended Central School of Speech and Drama, London, England, 1943-46. *Home:* Old School House, Walton, Warwickshire CV35 9HX, England. *Agent:* Harvey Unna, 14 Beaumont Mews, Marylebone High St., London, England.

CAREER: Central School of Speech and Drama, London, England, teacher of voice and speech, 1948-68; Royal Shakespeare Company, Stratford-upon-Avon, England, voice director, 1969—. Conducted acting studio in London, 1960-66; teacher for British Ministry of Education; voice teacher for priests at St. Patrick's College, Maynooth, Ireland; teacher on BBC-Radio. Lecturer at Brooklyn College of the City University of New York, New York University, University of North Carolina, University of Denver, University of Nebraska at Omaha, and Oberlin College. Works with theatre companies in Germany and Yugoslavia.

WRITINGS: Voice and the Actor, Macmillan, 1974. Also author of *Your Voice and How to Use It Successfully,* 1975, and *The Actor and His Text,* 1980.

SIDELIGHTS: Cicely Berry's students include such actors and performers as Julie Christie, Vanessa and Lynn Redgrave, Sean Connery, Patricia Neal, and Anne Bancroft. But she also works with politicians, physicians, and lecturers, as well as youth clubs and schools, helping anyone who needs to use his or her voice in public.

Berry told *CA* that she is particularly interested in "working on Shakespeare with young people, helping them to relate to the reality of the feelings in the text through an increased awareness of the words, their associations and images. By doing so, they become more articulate about their own feelings."

*   *   *

BERRY, Nicholas O(rlando) 1936-

PERSONAL: Born December 11, 1936, in Passaic, N.J.; son of Henry E. and Grace (a nurse; maiden name, Hellwig) Berry; married Janet Glerum (a teacher), September 18, 1958; children: Lynn, Stephanie. *Education:* Bethany College, Bethany, W.Va., A.B., 1958; University of Pittsburgh, M.A., 1964, Ph.D., 1967. *Home:* 218 South Second St. E., Mount Vernon, Iowa 52314. *Office:* Department of Politics, Cornell College, Mount Vernon, Iowa 52314.

CAREER: Carnegie-Mellon University, Pittsburgh, Pa., instructor in political science, 1965-67; Lynchburg College, Lynchburg, Va., associate professor of political science, 1967-70; Cornell College, Mount Vernon, Iowa, professor of politics, 1970—. Chairperson of Lynchburg City Democratic Committee, 1969-70; mayor of Mount Vernon, Iowa, 1971-75, member of city council, 1977—. *Military service:* U.S. Navy, 1959-62; became lieutenant senior grade. *Member:* American Political Science Association, Midwest Political Science Association (member of executive committee), Iowa Conference of Political Scientists (president, 1974).

WRITINGS: Political Configurations, Goodyear Publishing, 1972; *U.S. Foreign Policy Documents, 1963-1977,* King's Court, 1977; *U.S. Foreign Policy Documents, 1933-1945,* King's Court, 1978; *U.S. Foreign Policy Documents, 1945-1963,* King's Court, 1980. Author of "Viewpoints," a column in *Cedar Rapids Gazette.* Contributor to *Yale Review* and *Orbis.*

WORK IN PROGRESS: U.S. Foreign Policy Documents, 1776-1933, completion expected in 1982.

SIDELIGHTS: Berry commented to *CA:* "Considering the appalling ignorance and the wild gyrations in public moods on U.S. foreign policy, I consider it imperative that analysts go beyond simply writing for themselves by reaching out to the general public. Foreign policy information is too important to be left to journalists who, too often, lack the theoretical and historical bases for understanding what is going on and why. I therefore plan to shift my efforts from the academic press to the popular press."

*   *   *

BERRY, Roland (Brian) 1951-

PERSONAL: Born February 25, 1951, in England; son of John Remy (a parson) and Margaret (a teacher) Berry; married Sheila Margaret Pipes (a nurse), April 9, 1972; children: Oliver. *Education:* Attended Birmingham College of Art and Design. *Religion:* Christian. *Home and office:* 21 Passage Rd., Saul, Gloucestershire GL2 7LB, England.

CAREER: Writer. Worked as college lecturer, manager of advertising studio, artist, illustrator, and designer.

WRITINGS: Berry's Book of How It Works, A. & C. Black, 1976; *Berry's Book of Cunning Contraptions,* A. & C. Black, 1978.

*   *   *

BERRYMAN, James Thomas 1902-1971
(Jim Berryman)

OBITUARY NOTICE: Born June 8, 1902, in Washington, D.C.; died August 11, 1971, in Venice, Fla. Cartoonist, reporter, educator, and author. Berryman, who won the Pulitzer Prize in 1950, began his career as a reporter for the *New Mexico State Tribune* in 1923. He became a staff artist for the *Washington Evening Star* in 1924, and for the next forty years served as its political cartoonist, editorial illustrator, and sports cartoonist. Berryman also illustrated magazines, and was syndicated by King Features Syndicate. From 1937 to 1938 he taught graphic arts at Southeastern University. He was the author of numerous articles about hunting. Obituaries and other sources: *Current Biography,* Wilson, 1950, October, 1971; *New York Times,* August 13, 1971.

*   *   *

BERRYMAN, Jim
See BERRYMAN, James Thomas

BERSON, Lenora E. 1926-

PERSONAL: Born November 30, 1926, in Philadelphia, Pa.; daughter of Matthew Shayne and Sadie (Rosenfield) Ersner; married Norman Scott Berson (a lawyer), August 26, 1955; children: Peter, Erica. *Education:* University of Chicago, Ph.B., 1946; University of Pennsylvania, B.A., 1948, M.A., 1949; also attended University of Oslo. *Religion:* Jewish. *Home:* 2421 Spruce St., Philadelphia, Pa. 19103.

CAREER: Teacher at public schools in Philadelphia, Pa., 1950; Pennsylvania Department of Welfare, case worker, 1950-51; *Time,* New York, N.Y., editorial researcher, 1951-55; City of Philadelphia, Pa., personnel publications specialist, 1962-66; Drexel University, Philadelphia, Pa., lecturer in sociology, 1968-72; Temple University, Philadelphia, Pa., lecturer in political sociology, 1972-79; free-lance writer, 1955—. Correspondent from Democratic National Convention, for National Broadcasting Co., 1972; political speech writer; public lecturer. Coordinator of International Conference of Health Administrators and Educators; project director for Philadelphia Commission for Effective Criminal Justice; member of board of directors of Citizens Committee on Public Education in Philadelphia, Crosstown Community Development Corp., Democratic Women's Forum, Philadelphia City Policy Committee, and Temple University Hospital; member of American Jewish Committee, Center Philadelphia Reform Democrats, and Women's Political Caucus; consultant to Balch Institute of Ethnic Studies. *Member:* Americans for Democratic Action (member of board of directors), Delaware Valley Housing Association, Center City Residents Association, Albert M. Greenfield Home and School Association (member of board of directors).

WRITINGS: Case Study of a Riot: The Philadelphia Riot of 1964, Institute of Human Relations, 1968; *The Dispossessed: A Study of Involuntary Movement Among Philadelphia's Low Income Families,* Philadelphia Housing Association, 1968; *The Negroes and the Jews,* Random House, 1971. Pennsylvania correspondent for *Democratic Forum/Review,* 1974-76; Philadelphia correspondent for *People.* Contributor to magazines and newspapers, including *Region, Ms., City,* and *International Migration Review.*

WORK IN PROGRESS: A documentary film series on social and political life in Philadelphia.

SIDELIGHTS: Berson told *CA:* "I cannot remember a time when I did not write. Although fiction was my original goal, I found that I could sell non-fiction and journalistic articles, too. What comes from writing is intellectual occupation, an opportunity to learn about a variety of subjects, some satisfaction, and some money. People write because they feel compelled. I would never in cold blood advise anyone to be a writer."

*   *   *

BEVERIDGE, Andrew A(lan) 1945-

PERSONAL: Born April 27, 1945, in Madison, Wis.; son of Jacob Melvin (in real estate) and Bonnie (Porter) Beveridge; married Fredrica Rudell (a professor of marketing), April 17, 1970. *Education:* Attended California Institute of Technology, 1963-64; Yale University, B.A., 1967, M.Phil., 1971, Ph.D., 1973. *Politics:* Liberal Democrat. *Home:* 423 West 120th St., New York, N.Y. 10027. *Office:* Department of Sociology, Columbia University, Broadway & West 116th St., New York, N.Y. 10027.

CAREER: Columbia University, New York, N.Y., assistant professor of sociology, 1973—. *Member:* International Soci-

ological Association, American Sociological Association, American Economic Association, African Studies Association, Society for Applied Anthropology, Social Science History Association. *Awards, honors:* National Science Foundation grant, 1976-78; National Endowment for the Humanities grant, 1976; American Philosophical Society grant, 1976; American Council of Learned Societies fellow, 1978-79.

WRITINGS: (With Anthony R. Oberschall) *African Businessmen and Development in Zambia,* Princeton University Press, 1979. Contributor to *African Studies Review* and *New Society.*

WORK IN PROGRESS: Credit to a Community: The Social Effects of Credit Allocation.

SIDELIGHTS: Beveridge writes: "As a sociologist engaged in research on the impact of economic factors on social life, I have tried to avoid the usual jargon afflicting my field. Sometimes I feel that sociology has taken topics of very general interest (who gets ahead and why; how people get rich; how do organizations and bureaucracies work; how do societies develop) and obscured them with heavy doses of jargon. My present research focuses on who gets credit, what they use it for, and how it affects the development of a community over eighty-two years. Bert Lance had many forerunners, that is certain."

*   *   *

BEYE, Charles Rowan 1930-

PERSONAL: Born March 19, 1930, in Iowa City, Iowa; son of Howard Lombard (a surgeon) and Ruth (Ketcham) Beye; married Mary Powers, July 1, 1951 (died August 28, 1955); married Penelope Pendleton (an architect), June 16, 1956 (divorced September 1, 1976); children: Howard, Willis, Helen, Hannah. *Education:* Iowa State University, B.A., 1952; Harvard University, M.A., 1954, Ph.D., 1960. *Residence:* Cambridge, Mass. *Office:* Department of Classics, Boston University, 745 Commonwealth Ave., Boston, Mass., 02215.

CAREER: Wheaton College, Norton, Mass., instructor in classics, 1955-57; Yale University, New Haven, Conn., instructor in classics, 1957-60; Stanford University, Stanford, Calif., assistant professor of classics, 1960-66; Boston University, Boston, Mass., associate professor, 1966-68, professor of classics, 1968—, head of department, 1968-72. Member of managing committee of American School of Classical Studies in Athens, 1966—. *Member:* American Philological Association. *Awards, honors:* Olivia James fellowship from Archaeological Institute of America, 1963-64; National Endowment for the Humanities senior fellowship, 1971-72; senior research fellowship from American School of Classical Studies in Athens, 1978-79.

WRITINGS: The Iliad, the Odyssey, and the Epic Tradition, Doubleday, 1966; *Euripides' Alcestis,* Prentice-Hall, 1969; *Ancient Greek Literature and Society,* Doubleday, 1975. Contributor to classical studies journals.

WORK IN PROGRESS: A study of Apollonios Rhodios's *Argonautika,* publication by University of Southern Illinois Press expected in 1981.

SIDELIGHTS: Beye writes: "When in college I fell in love with ancient Greek and am fortunate that the love affair persisted and that I can earn a livelihood with it. I have spent two years living in Italy, one year in Greece, as well as traveling throughout Europe, Turkey, and Morocco. Now I am ready to stay at home and try writing fiction and learning to live alone, a luxury after fifty years of intense family life of one kind or another. Literature, art, and music remain central to my existence, but love and good conversation are the bedrock foundation beneath.''

* * *

BEYERHAUS, Peter (Paul Johannes)   1929-

PERSONAL: Born February 1, 1929, in Hohenkraenig, Germany; son of Siegfried (a minister) and Fridel (a nurse; maiden name, Korweck) Beyerhaus; married Ingegard Kalen (a teacher), August 6, 1955; children: Karolina, Johannes, Maria, Christoph, Gunilla. *Education:* University of Uppsala, L.Th., 1956, D.Th., 1957. *Home:* Stiffurtstrasse, D 7400 Tuebingen, West Germany. *Office:* Institute of Missiology, Hausserstrasse 43, D 7400 Tuebingen, West Germany.

CAREER: Ordained Lutheran minister, 1955; German Missionary Council, Hamburg, Germany, theological assistant, 1953-54; pastor of Lutheran churches in Berlin, Germany, 1955, and Norrkoeping, Sweden, 1956; missionary in Transvaal, South Africa, 1957-60; Lutheran Theological College, Mapumulo, Natal, lecturer, 1960-65; Tuebingen University, Tuebingen, West Germany, professor of missiology and ecumenics, 1966—, director of Institute of Missiology, 1966—. *Member:* International Christian Network (chairman), Lausanne Continuation Committee on World Evangelism.

WRITINGS: Die Selbstaendigkeit der jungen Kirchen als missionarisches Problem, Rheinischen Missions Gesellschaft, 1956, revised and condensed version (with Henry Lefever) published as *The Responsible Church and the Foreign Mission,* Eerdmans, 1964; (editor) *Begegnung mit messianischen Bewegungen in Afrika,* Evangelischer Missionsverlag, 1967, translation published as *The Encounter With Messianic Movements in Africa,* Scottish Institute of Missionary Studies, 1968; *Humanisierung: Einzige Hoffnung der Welt?,* MKB-Verlag, 1969, translation by Margaret Clarkson published as *Missions: Which Way? Humanization or Redemption,* Zondervan, 1971; *The Church Crossing Frontiers,* [Uppsala], 1969.

Allen Voelkern zum Zeugnis: Biblisch-theologische Besinnung zum Wesen der Mission, R. Brockhaus, 1972; *In Ostasien erlebt,* Evangelischer Missionsverlag, 1972; *In der Inselwelt Suedostasiens erlebt: Zweiter Teil des Reiseberichts* (continuation of *In Ostasien erlebt* [see above]), Evangelischer Missionsverlag, 1973; *Shaken Foundations: Theological Foundations for Mission* (lectures), Zondervan, 1972; *Bangkok '73: Anfang oder Ende der Weltmission* (includes selections of Eighth World Missionary Conference, 1972-73), Liebenzeller Mission, 1973, translation published as *Bangkok '73: The Beginning or End of World Mission?,* Zondervan, 1974; (editor with Walter Kuenneth) *Reich Gottes oder Weltgemeinschaft,* Liebenzeller Mission, 1975; (editor with Ulrich Betz) *Oekumene im Spiegel von Nairobi '75* (title means ''Ecumenism in the Mirror of Nairobi''), Liebenzeller Mission, 1976; *Ideologien: Herausforderung an den Glauben* (title means ''Ideologies as Challenge to the Faith''), Bad Lisbenzell, 1979.

* * *

BHAJAN, Yogi
See YOGIJI, Harbhajan Singh Khalsa

BIBESCO, Marthe Lucie   1887-1973
(Lucile Decaux)

PERSONAL: Born January 28, 1887, in Bucharest, Romania; died November 29, 1973, in Paris, France; daughter of Jean (a diplomat) and Smaranda Mavrocordato Lahovary; married George Bibesco, 1903. *Education:* Educated in France. *Religion:* Catholic. *Residence:* Paris, France.

CAREER: Writer. *Wartime service:* Served as head nurse of hospital in Romania. *Awards, honors:* Elected to Royal Belgian Academy; *Les Huits Paradis* was crowned by the French Academy.

WRITINGS—In English: *Les Huit Paradis: Perse, Asie Mineure, Constantinople,* 3rd edition, Hachette, 1911, translation published as *The Eight Paradises: Travel Pictures in Persia, Asia Minor, and Constantinople,* Dutton, c. 1923; *Alexandre asiatique,* [France], 1912, translation by Enid Bagnold published as *Alexander of Asia,* William Heinemann, 1935; *Isvor: Le Pays des saules,* two volumes, Plon-Nourrit, 1923, translation by Hamish Miles published as *Isvor: The Country of Willows,* William Heinemann, 1924; *Le Perroquet vert* (novel), B. Grasset, 1924, translation by Malcolm Cowley published as *The Green Parrot,* Harcourt, c. 1929; *Catherine—Paris* (novel), B. Grasset, 1927, translation by Cowley published as *Catherine—Paris* (Literary Guild selection), Harcourt, c. 1928; *Une Victoire royale: Ferdinand de Roumanie,* [France], 1927, published as *Royal Portraits,* D. Appleton, 1928; *Au bal avec Marcel Proust,* 3rd edition, Gallimard, 1928, revised edition, 1956, translation by Anthony Rhodes published as *Marcel Proust at the Ball,* Citadel, 1956; *Jour d'Egypte,* Flammarion, 1929, translation by Helen Everitt and Raymond Everitt published as *Egyptian Day,* Harcourt, c. 1930; *Quatre Portraits,* [France], 1929, translation published as *Some Royalties and a Prime Minister: Portraits From Life,* D. Appleton, 1930.

Crusade for the Anemone: Letters From the Holy Land (Catholic Book Club selection), translated by Thomas Kernan, Macmillan, 1932; *Le Destin de Lord Thomson of Cardington,* Flammarion, 1932, published as *Lord Thomson of Cardington: A Memoir and Some Letters,* J. Cape, 1932; *Egalite* (novel), B. Grasset, 1935, translation by Pierce Butler, Jr. published as *Worlds Apart,* D. Appleton, 1935; (under pseudonym Lucile Decaux) *Charlotte et Maximilien: Les Amants chimeriques,* Gallimard, 1937, translation by John Ghika published as *Carlota: The Story of Charlotte and Maximilian of Mexico; A Historical Romance,* William Heinemann, 1956; (under pseudonym Lucile Decaux) *Katia: Le Demon bleu de tsar Alexandre* (novel), Gallimard, 1938, translation by Priscilla Bibesco published as *Katia,* Doubleday, 1939; *Loulou: Prince Imperial,* Gallimard, 1938, translation by Roland Gant published as *Prince Imperial,* Grey Walls, 1949.

Le Voyageur voile, Marcel Proust: Letters au duc de Guiche et documents inedits, La Palatine, 1947, translation by Roland Gant published as *The Veiled Wanderer, Marcel Proust: Letters to the Duc de Guiche and Unpublished Papers,* Falcon Press, 1949; *Tulips, Hyacinths, Narcissi,* Hyperion Press, c. 1948; *La Duchesse de Guermantes: Laure de Sade, comtesse de Chevigne,* Plon, 1930, translation by Edward Marsh published as *Proust's Oriane: A Diptych,* Falcon Press, 1952; *The Sphinx of Bagatelle,* translated by Marsh, Grey Walls Press, 1952; *Churchill; ou, Le Courage,* A. Michel, 1956, translation by Vladimir Kean published as *Sir Winston Churchill: Master of Courage,* J. Day, 1957; *Homage to Marcel Proust, 1871-1971,* Covent Garden Press, 1971. Also author of *Balloons,* 1929.

In French: *Images d'Epinal*, Plon, 1915; *Noblesse de robe*, B. Grasset, 1928; *Portraits d'hommes*, B. Grasset, 1929; *Une Fille inconnue de Napoleon*, Flammarion, 1935; *Le Rire de la naide*, B. Grasset, c. 1935; (under pseudonym Lucile Decaux) *Loulou: Prince Imperial*, Gallimard, 1938; *Feuilles de calendrier*, Plon, c. 1939; (under pseudonym Lucile Decaux) *Pont-l'Abime; ou, La Grande Passion de la duchesse de Baume*, A. Fayard, 1947; (under pseudonym Lucile Decaux) *Caline: La Folle equipee de la duchesse de Berry*, Gallimard, 1948; *La Vie d'une amitie: Ma correspondance avec l'abbe Mungnier, 1911-1944*, Plon, 1951; *Theodore: La Cadeau de Dieu*, Editions francaises d'Amsterdam, 1953; *Elizabeth II*, A. Michel, 1957; *La Nymphe Europe*, Plon, 1960; *Le Confesseur et les poetes*, B. Grasset, 1970; *Echanges avec Paul Claudel*, Mercure de France, 1972.

SIDELIGHTS: Marthe Lucie Bibesco was a woman blessed with beauty, wealth, and according to most reviewers, intelligence and sensitivity. *Catherine—Paris*, declared L. Galantiere, "is the product of a fine analytical intelligence, and an exquisite sensibility, and a superior gift for the writing of delicately cadenced prose." Even her more detracting critics concede that Bibesco's works are "charming," "fanciful," and "glitteringly written." Often metaphors pervade the reviews of her books: *New York Times*, for example, imagined her *Eight Paradises* "filled with the perfume of the East," and expressed that *The Green Parrot* "is a strange and beautiful story, with the faintly arid charm of a miniature painted on the cover of a seventeenth-century snuff box."

BIOGRAPHICAL/CRITICAL SOURCES: Boston Transcript, November 17, 1923, August 16, 1930; *New York Times*, January 13, 1924, November 30, 1924, May 13, 1928, May 19, 1929, August 10, 1930, August 31, 1930, September 1, 1935; *New Republic*, December 24, 1924, August 15, 1928; *New York Tribune*, December 21, 1924; *Saturday Review*, December 6, 1924, May 26, 1928, July 27, 1929; *Outlook*, June 20, 1928, May 29, 1929; *New York Evening Post*, July 5, 1930, May 14, 1932; *Books*, May 15, 1932, September 1, 1935; *New York Herald Tribune Book Review*, May 31, 1959.

OBITUARIES: London Times, November 30, 1973; *AB Bookman's Weekly*, January 14, 1974.*

* * *

BLACK, Betty
  See SCHWARTZ, Betty

* * *

BLACKWELL, Roger D(ale)   1940-

PERSONAL: Born August 7, 1940, in Humansville, Mo.; son of Dale J. (a professor) and Rheva (a treasurer; maiden name, Allen) Blackwell; married Ann Newcomer (a professor), July 31, 1959; children: Christian David, Rebecca Rheva. *Education:* Attended Northwest Missouri State University, 1958-61; University of Missouri, B.S., 1962, M.S., 1963; Northwestern University, Ph.D., 1966. *Religion:* Protestant. *Office:* Department of Marketing, Ohio State University, 1775 College Rd., Columbus, Ohio 43210.

CAREER: Columbia Missourian, Columbia, Mo., in circulation, 1954-56; KNIM-Radio, Maryville, Mo., engineer and announcer, 1956-58; KFEQ-TV, St. Joseph, Mo., announcer, 1958-60; *Columbia Missourian*, in circulation, 1960-62; Ohio State University, Columbus, assistant professor, 1965-68, associate professor, 1969-73, professor of marketing, 1974—. Vice-president and senior research consultant for Management Horizons, Inc., 1969—. Consumer research and marketing consultant. *Member:* American Marketing Association, Association for Consumer Research.

WRITINGS: Consumer Behavior, Holt, 1967, 3rd edition, 1978; *Research in Consumer Behavior*, Holt, 1970; *Strategic Marketing*, Holt, 1972; *American Attitudes Toward Death and Funerals* (monograph), Casket Manufacturers Association, 1974; *Consumer Attitudes Toward Health Care and Medical Malpractice*, Grid Publishing, 1977; *Cases in Consumer Behavior*, Holt, 1977; *Living With Death*, Revell, 1980.

* * *

BLAIR, Frank   1915-

PERSONAL: Born May 30, 1915, in Yemassee, S.C.; son of Frank S. (a telegrapher) and Hannah (Pinckney) Blair; married Lillian Stoddard, October 20, 1935; children: Frank III, John, Tom, Mary Blair Blanchard, Theresa Blair Hahn, Paul, William, Patti. *Education:* Attended College of Charleston, 1933. *Politics:* "Democrat or Republican." *Religion:* Catholic. *Home:* 16 Water Oak Dr., Hilton Head Island, S.C. 29928. *Office address:* P.O. Box 5025, Hilton Head Island, S.C. 29928.

CAREER: WCSC-Radio, Charleston, S.C., newscaster, 1935; WIS-Radio, Columbia, S.C., news editor, 1935-36; WFBC-Radio, Greenville, S.C., news editor and program director, 1936-37; regional correspondent for Transradio Press Service, 1937-42; WOL-Radio, Washington, D.C., news editor and special events director, 1938-42; Mutual Broadcasting System, Washington, D.C., news and special events broadcaster, White House correspondent, and presidential announcer, 1939-42; WOL-Radio, news editor and special events director, 1945-46; WSCR-Radio, Scranton, Pa., general manager, 1947-50; National Broadcasting Co. (NBC), New York, N.Y., newscaster, commercial announcer, and moderator of television programs, including "The American Forum of the Air," "Youth Wants to Know," "Heritage," and "Meet the Press," 1950-52, and newscaster for "The Today Show," 1952-75; records commercials, syndicated radio programs, including "The Financial Page," "Medical Portfolio for Family Doctor," "Medical Horizons of the Air," and "Modern Medical Report," and documentary and industrial films, 1975—. Appeared as host of NBC radio programs, including "Monitor," "Let's Be Frank About It!" (daily commentary), "Emphasis," and "News on the Hour." Originator of syndicated radio program, "Georgetown University Forum," 1946. Instructor in broadcast journalism at Georgetown University, 1939-42, and Scranton University, 1947-50. Member of board of advisers of The Citadel, 1968—. Public speaker. *Military service:* U.S. Navy, 1942-45, served as flight instructor and transport pilot; became lieutenant.

MEMBER: American Federation of Radio and Television Artists, National Epilepsy Foundation (honorary board member), Boy Scouts of America, Screen Actors Guild, Aviation/Space Writers Association, Anchor Mental Health Association (honorary board member), Navy League, Sigma Delta Chi. *Awards, honors:* Medal of honor from Georgetown University, 1965; St. Francis Xavier Medal from Xavier University, 1967; Amelia Earhart Air Medal, 1970, for contributions to aviation; award from University of Missouri, 1971, for journalism expertise; distinguished Eagle Scout award from Boy Scouts of America, 1971. L.H.D. from Nasson College, 1969, and Le Moyne College, 1970, D.F.A. from Niagara University, 1971, and LL.D. from The Citadel, 1979.

WRITINGS: Let's Be Frank About It (autobiography), Doubleday, 1979; *Signs of a Time* (pictorial and narrative), Doubleday, 1980.

SIDELIGHTS: For twenty-three years, millions of Americans began their weekday morning routine listening to Frank Blair, the authoritative, deep-voiced newscaster on NBC-TV's "The Today Show." Whereas the show passed through a succession of hosts and changes of format over the years, Blair's half-hourly news updates remained the one constant. He is a veteran radio broadcaster who has always prided himself "in being an unbiased reporter" and whose retirement in 1975 marked the end of four decades in electronic journalism.

Blair began his career in October, 1935, when he convinced the manager at WCSC-Radio in Charleston, S.C., that the station needed to broadcast news reports between the hillbilly songs and spirituals. He was paid fifteen dollars a week to build a news department and sweep out the studios every morning. After stops in Columbia and Greenville, he moved up to the larger WOL in Washington, D.C., and covered the Roosevelt administration for the Mutual Broadcasting System. Blair tried his hand at managing a radio station after the war, but his real ambitions lay in the new medium of communications, television.

Blair joined the news department at NBC-TV in 1950. His assignments included local and network news telecasts, commercial announcements, and moderating "The American Forum of the Air," a debate program. Largely because of his low-keyed, objective approach to the latter, he was named Washington, D.C., correspondent for an experimental morning news program, "The Today Show," which debuted January 14, 1952. After a shaky start—critics predicted its demise within thirteen weeks—the show found a successful blend of news and personalities with cohosts Dave Garroway and Jack Lescoulie and the reassignment of Blair as newscaster.

During his twenty-three years on "Today," Blair worked with twenty-five hosts, among them Arlene Francis, Faye Emerson, Garroway and Lescoulie, John Chancellor, Hugh Downs, Frank McGee, Jim Hartz, and Barbara Walters, but he preferred not to involve himself in a back-and-forth exchange of banter. Instead, he thought that news should be a thing apart, allowing him to preserve the detachment needed for unbiased reporting. But in his last few years, the pressures of the job led to bouts with alcohol, and, he admits, he "lost control." He resigned from the show on March 14, 1975, and retired to his native South Carolina. His departure drew a wide response from well-wishers: "It never occurred to me I was important to anyone," he reflected. "But I guess I was. And I thank God for that."

BIOGRAPHICAL/CRITICAL SOURCES: Miami Herald, March 30, 1975; *Biography News,* Gale, March/April, 1975; Frank Blair, *Let's Be Frank About It* (autobiography), Doubleday, 1979.

*   *   *

BLAKE, James   1922-1979

PERSONAL: Born in 1922, in Edinburgh, Scotland; came to the United States in 1929; died February 19, 1979, in Arlington, Va. *Education:* Attended University of Illinois and Northwestern University. *Residence:* Arlington, Va.

CAREER: Writer and musician. *Awards, honors:* "The Widow, Bereft" was selected by Martha Foley and Whit Burnett for their "Best American Short Stories of 1971."

WRITINGS: The Joint (collection of letters), Doubleday, 1971. Also author of "The Widow, Bereft," a short story published in *Esquire.* Contributor to periodicals, including

Washingtonian, Paris Review, American Scholar, and *Esquire.*

SIDELIGHTS: By his own admission, James Blake is "the world's indisputably lousiest burglar." As such, most of his adult life was spent behind bars. While in prison he corresponded with a number of notable persons, including Simone de Beauvoir, Studs Terkel, George Plimpton, and Jean Paul Sartre. The collected letters were published in 1971 as *The Joint.*

"He writes lightly, even trippingly, of circumstances which would have broken many men," related Larry McMurty, and added: "Indeed, this book's uniqueness is in its tone. Most prison literature draws its energy from hatred and frustration. Not Mr. Blake's. The joint is his home, as he makes clear. . . . He writes of it with a humor that is finally affectionate in a prose that is entirely free of rancor." Fred Rotondaro agreed, and stated that *The Joint* "is an extremely interesting spiritual journey, a journey taken by a man of fine intellect, not always what we would call a good man but not a bad man either, just a contemporary man trying to find some semblance of meaning in the world and in his own existence."

James Blake was an accomplished pianist, and often accompanied night club acts.

BIOGRAPHICAL/CRITICAL SOURCES: Best Sellers, March 1, 1971; *Washington Post,* March 2, 1971; *New York Times Book Review,* April 25, 1971.

OBITUARIES: New York Times, February 20, 1979; *Washington Post,* February 21, 1979.*

*   *   *

BLAKE, Norman (Francis)   1934-

PERSONAL: Born April 19, 1934, in Ceara, Brazil; son of Harry William (a banker) and Carmen (Fehre) Blake; married Sylvia Valerie Miles, July 6, 1965; children: Dorinda Jane. *Education:* Oxford University, B.A., 1956, B.Litt., 1959, M.A., 1960; attended University of Copenhagen, 1956-57. *Religion:* Church of England. *Home:* 74 Alms Hill Rd., Sheffield S11 9RS, England. *Office:* Department of English Language, University of Sheffield, Sheffield S10 2TN, England.

CAREER: University of Liverpool, Liverpool, England, lecturer, 1959-68, senior lecturer in English language, 1968-73; University of Sheffield, Sheffield, England, professor of English language, 1973—. *Member:* International Association of University Professors of English, Early English Text Society (member of council, 1979—), Society for the Study of Medieval Languages and Literature, Viking Society for Northern Research (member of council, 1974-77).

WRITINGS: (Editor and translator) *The Saga of the Jomsvikings,* Thomas Nelson, 1962; (editor) *The Phoenix,* Manchester University Press, 1964; *Caxton and His World,* Deutsch, 1969; (editor) William Caxton, *Reynard the Fox,* Early English Text Society, 1970; (editor) *Middle English Religious Prose,* Edward Arnold, 1972; (editor) *Selections From William Caxton,* Oxford University Press, 1973; (editor) *Caxton's Own Prose,* Deutsch, 1973; *Caxton: England's First Publisher,* Osprey, 1976; *The English Language in Medieval Literature,* Deutsch, 1977; (editor) Geoffrey Chaucer, *The Canterbury Tales,* Edward Arnold, 1980. Contributor to academic journals.

WORK IN PROGRESS: (With R. E. Lewis and A.S.G. Edwards) *Index of Middle English Prose in Print,* Garland Publishing, 1981.

BLAKE, Richard A(loysius) 1939-

PERSONAL: Born February 21, 1939, in New York, N.Y.; son of Richard A. (an investigator) and Cecelia (a nurse; maiden name, Reilly) Blake. *Education:* Fordham University, A.B., 1962, M.A., 1963; Loyola Seminary, Shrub Oak, N.Y., Ph.L., 1963; Woodstock College, Woodstock, Md., M.Div., 1969; Northwestern University, Ph.D., 1971. *Office:* America Press, 106 West 56th St., New York, N.Y. 10019.

CAREER: Entered Society of Jesus (Jesuits), 1956, ordained Roman Catholic priest, 1969; high school teacher of classics and English at private school in New York City, 1963-66; Loyola College, Baltimore, Md., instructor in film, 1967-69; Northwestern University, Evanston, Ill., instructor in film, 1969-71; America Press, New York City, associate editor of *America* and director of Catholic Book Club, 1971-74; Society of Jesus, New York Province, New York City, director of studies 1974-76; America Press, associate editor of *America*, 1976-77, managing editor, 1977—. *Member:* American Film Institute, Catholic Press Association, University Film Association. *Awards, honors:* First place award from Catholic Press Association, 1977, and 1978, for column, "Films/TV."

WRITINGS: (Contributor) Stuart Kaminsky, editor, *Ingmar Bergman: Essays in Criticism*, Oxford University Press, 1975; *The Luthern Milieu of the Films of Ingmar Bergman*, Arno, 1978. Author of "Films/TV," a column in *America*, 1976—. Contributor to *Catholic Encyclopedia for School and Home*. Contributor to journals, including *Pastoral Life, Media and Methods, Drama Critique, Catholic World, Thought*, and *America*.

SIDELIGHTS: Blake commented: "Writing and editing is, as much as preaching or counseling, a means to help others sort out their reflections on the world and themselves. In a more explicitly religious context, writing is for me a ministry in the service of faith, justice, and culture. I would hope, however, that people of no religious affiliation might find my work thought-provoking."

* * *

BLANK, Joseph P. 1919-

PERSONAL: Born September 9, 1919, in Newark, N.J.; son of Philip and Anna (Olshan) Blank; married Naomi Johnston, June 3, 1945; children: Lisa, Michael. *Education:* Attended University of Missouri, 1938-41. *Politics:* Independent. *Residence:* Yorktown Heights, N.Y. *Office: Reader's Digest*, Pleasantville, N.Y. 10570.

CAREER: Funk & Wagnalls Co., New York, N.Y., associate editor, 1946; free-lance writer, 1947-65; roving editor for *Reader's Digest*, Pleasantville, N.Y. *Military service:* U.S. Army Air Forces, 1941-45; became captain. *Member:* Society of Journalists and Authors, Overseas Press Club of America.

WRITINGS: Nineteen Steps up the Mountain, Lippincott, 1977. Contributor of articles to magazines and newspapers.

* * *

BLANSHARD, Paul 1892-1980

OBITUARY NOTICE: Born August 27, 1892, in Fredericksburg, Ohio; died January 27, 1980, in St. Petersburg, Fla. Editor, columnist, attorney, administrator, and author, best known for his anti-Catholic views. Blanshard held a variety of positions, including field secretary to the League of Industrial Democracy, from 1925 to 1933, and commissioner of investigations and accounts under New York City Mayor LaGuardia, from 1934 to 1938. He practiced law in New York for two years, and later served as economic analyst and consultant to the Caribbean Commission of the U.S. Department of State. Blanshard was the Vatican correspondent for *Nation* for one year, and it was during this time that he began to vocalize his anti-Catholic sentiments in both magazines and books. Among his works are *What's the Matter With New York, Democracy and Empire in the Caribbean, American Freedom and Catholic Power, The Irish and Catholic Power, God and Man in Washington, Paul Blanshard on Vatican II*, and a volume of memoirs, *Personal and Controversial*. Obituaries and other sources: Paul Blanshard, *Personal and Controversial: An Autobiography*, Beacon Press, 1973; *Who's Who in America*, 40th edition, Marquis, 1978; *New York Times*, January 30, 1980; *Time*, February 11, 1980; *Publishers Weekly*, February 22, 1980.

* * *

BLEICH, Harold 1930(?)-1980

OBITUARY NOTICE: Born c. 1930, in New York, N.Y.; died of cancer, January 28, 1980, in Washington, D.C. Educator, rabbi, and author of several books, including *The Philosophy of Herbert Marcuse*. Bleich was director of education at Temple Sinai for two years before becoming director of educational projects for the B'nai B'rith. During the 1960's he became a faculty member at Montgomery College, and was professor of philosophy there until 1979. Obituaries and other sources: *Washington Post*, January 1, 1980.

* * *

BLOCH, Dorothy 1912-

PERSONAL: Born January 13, 1912, in New York, N.Y.; daughter of Joseph and Augusta Bloch. *Education:* Hunter College (now of the City University of New York), B.A., 1931; New York University, M.A., 1955. *Home and office:* 270 West End Ave., New York, N.Y. 10023. *Agent:* Joan Raines, Raines & Raines, 475 Fifth Ave., New York, N.Y. 10017.

CAREER: English teacher at public schools in New York City, 1932-51; private practice of psychoanalysis in New York City, 1952—. Adjunct professor at Long Island University, 1968—. *Member:* National Psychological Association for Psychoanalysis (member of faculty; past dean of Training Institute), Council for Psychoanalytic Psychotherapists, New York Society for Clinical Psychologists.

WRITINGS: (Contributor) Emanuel Hammer, editor, *The Use of Interpretation in Treatment*, Grune, 1968; *"So the Witch Won't Eat Me": Fantasy and the Child's Fear of Infanticide*, Houghton, 1978. Also author of "The Princess and the Swineherd," "Johny Appleseed," "Bunny's Birthday," and "The Brightest Street in Town," all children's plays. Contributor to psychology journals.

WORK IN PROGRESS: The Autobiography of a Worthless Child, a novel; *Child Therapy: A Technique of Treatment*.

SIDELIGHTS: Dorothy Bloch commented: "When I initially decided to write 'So the Witch Won't Eat Me,' I thought of it as a book about the children I had analyzed. As I examined my treatment of one child after another, however, I soon realized that I was actually writing about fantasy. Once I began to probe the function of children's fantasies it became apparent that they were a means of survival and defended the children against their fear that their parents would kill them. It was when I realized that my discussion would have to include the fantasy in homosexuality that I began to understand and became interested in investigating the relationship between the defensive fantasies of children and of adults.

"That what emerged is a single theme with variations has been as much of a surprise to me as it may be to the reader. The discovery that the fear of infanticide may be dominant in early childhood and may remain constant throughout life, although on a diminished and unconscious plane, started as a suspicion and took many years and exposure to many patients before it became what I now consider it to be: a fact. That there is also a continuity between the defensive fantasies of children and of adults follows automatically from their function as a defense against that fear.

"Although the knowledge that can break the chain of psychological trauma transmitted from one generation to the next has existed for some time, it has not been available to most people. My hope in writing '*So the Witch Won't Eat Me*' was therefore to create an understanding of children's preoccupations and the meaning of their communications that may improve the relationship between children and their parents and enable those children, when they become parents, to function more happily. I also hoped that the views expressed in the book might be of some service to professional therapists."

AVOCATIONAL INTERESTS: "Painting, the theater, and travel have been major interests. I have written for children's theater and hope to write a play for adults. I have studied painting in Positano, Italy, in Paris, and New York, and have traveled through Mexico and Europe many times—all before I started writing. Since then I have built a house and spent many summers and long weekends on Martha's Vineyard, Mass. I have found Cuba fascinating and hope to return there, as well as to visit other developing countries."

BIOGRAPHICAL/CRITICAL SOURCES: Boston Globe, December 3, 1978; *London Guardian,* December 15, 1978; *Bergen Record,* March 18, 1979; *New Society,* July 12, 1979.

* * *

BLOCH, Lucienne S(chupf) 1937-

PERSONAL: Born December 11, 1937, in Antwerp, Belgium; came to the United States in 1938, naturalized citizen, 1948; daughter of Jacques (a diamond merchant) and Jana (Beller) Schupf; married Claude Bloch (a physician), August 22, 1961; children: Philippe, Claire, Justine. *Education:* Wellesley College, B.A., 1959. *Residence:* New York, N.Y. *Agent:* Peter H. Matson, Literistic Ltd., 32 West 40th St., New York, N.Y. 10016.

CAREER: New Directions Publishing Corp., New York City, assistant editor, 1959-60; Random House, Inc., New York City, assistant editor, 1961-62; writer, 1977—. Member of collections committee of International Center of Photography; member of Junior Council, Museum of Modern Art. *Member:* Authors Guild, Women's Ink. *Awards, honors:* Award from Academy of American Poets, and Joyce Prize from New England Poetry Society, both 1959.

WRITINGS: On the Great-Circle Route (novel), Simon & Schuster, 1979. Author of "Hers," a column in *New York Times,* 1979.

WORK IN PROGRESS: Another novel, completion expected in 1981; personal essays; short stories.

SIDELIGHTS: Lucienne Bloch told *CA:* "I started to write at the age of forty in order to define a life that was half-way

over, as a way of stopping the clock for a while. My motivation was strictly personal, and temporal. By the time I had written fifty pages, I knew I had something larger than my own experience to deal with, and I also knew that I would spend the rest of my days writing, preparing in my own way for what Rilke calls 'a well-crafted death.'"

* * *

BLONDELL, Joan 1906(?)-1979

OBITUARY NOTICE: Born c. 1906 in New York, N.Y.; died of leukemia, December 25, 1979, in Santa Monica, Calif. Actress and author of the novel *Center Door Fancy.* The daughter of vaudeville parents, Blondell made her stage debut at the age of three and her Broadway debut in the play "Maggie the Magnificent." She made numerous films with such stars as James Cagney, Spencer Tracy, Clark Gable, Leslie Howard, and Robert Taylor. Her screen image was that of the brassy blonde with a heart of gold. In the late 1960's and early 1970's Blondell was featured in the series "Here Come the Brides" and "Banyon." She also made guest appearances on "Name of the Game" and "McCloud." Obituaries and other sources: *Washington Post,* December 26, 1979.

* * *

BLOUET, Brian Walter 1936-

PERSONAL: Born January 1, 1936, in Darlington, England; came to the United States in 1969; son of Raymond Walter and Marjorie (Gargett) Blouet; married Olwen Mary Salt (a professor of history), July 29, 1970; children: Andrew Paul, Helen Clare. *Education:* University of Hull, B.A., 1960, Ph.D., 1964. *Office:* Department of Geography, University of Nebraska, Lincoln, Neb. 68508.

CAREER: University of Sheffield, Sheffield, England, assistant lecturer, 1964-66, lecturer in geography, 1966-69; University of Nebraska, Lincoln, associate professor, 1969-75, professor of geography, 1975—, head of department, 1976—, director of Center for Great Plains Studies, 1979—. *Military service:* Royal Air Force, 1955-57. *Member:* Association of American Geographers, Royal Geographical Society (fellow), British Geographical Association, British Economic History Society, Institute of British Geographers.

WRITINGS: The Story of Malta, Faber, 1967, 3rd edition, 1976; (editor with Merlin P. Lawson) *Images of the Plains,* University of Nebraska Press, 1975; (editor with Fred Luebke) *The Great Plains: Environment and Culture,* University of Nebraska Press, 1979; *Malta: A Short History,* Faber, 1980.

WORK IN PROGRESS: The Origins of Academic Geography in the United States; Halford Mackinder, Pioneer British Geographer, completion expected in 1983.

* * *

BLUMRICH, Josef F(ranz) 1913-

PERSONAL: Surname is pronounced *Bloom*-rick; born March 17, 1913, in Steyr, Austria; came to the United States in 1959, naturalized citizen, 1965; son of Franz and Maria-Theresia (Mayr) Blumrich; married Hilde A. Schmidt Elgers, November 7, 1935; children: Michael Sebastian, Christoph, Stefan. *Education:* Ingenieur Schule, Weimar, Germany (now East Germany), B.S., 1934. *Home and office:* 1139 Noria St., Laguna Beach, Calif. 92651.

CAREER: Gothaer Waggon Fabrik A.G., Gotha, Germany (now East Germany), aircraft department section chief,

1934-44; U.S. Criminal Court, Linz, Austria, court interpreter, until 1951; United Austrian Iron & Steel Works, Linz, deputy department head, 1951-59; National Aeronautics & Space Administration, Marshall Space Flight Center, Huntsville, Ala., branch chief, 1959-74; involved in private research, 1974—. *Military service:* German Army, 1944-45; prisoner of war, April to December, 1945. *Member:* American Institute of Aeronautics and Astronautics, American Association for the Advancement of Science, Ancient Astronaut Society. *Awards, honors:* Exceptional Service Medal from National Aeronautics & Space Administration, 1972.

WRITINGS: Da tat sich der Himmel aur, Econ-Verlag, 1973, translation published as *The Spaceships of Ezekiel,* Bantam, 1974; *Kasskara und die Sieben Welten* (title means "Kasskara and the Seven Worlds"), Econ-Verlag, 1979. Contributor to engineering journals. Editorial consultant to *The Scribner-Bantam English Dictionary,* 1977, 1979.

WORK IN PROGRESS: Continuing research on the technological aspects of ancient writings and traditions; research concerning the possibility of advanced ancient civilizations and/or extraterrestrial visitors.

SIDELIGHTS: Blumrich's first book has been published in eleven languages. He writes: "I knew von Daeniken was wrong even before I began to read his *Chariots of the Gods?.* After forty years' involvement in hardware design and analysis of airplanes, hydraulic structures, and finally large space vehicles, his idea was no more to me than pure fantasy. So I read the book for what I considered its entertainment value. When I came to the passage in which von Daeniken explains what the prophet Ezekiel had seen, I saw in it a wonderful opportunity to refute him: here were statements and claims right in the fields of my professional knowledge. Just for my own satisfaction I began to look critically at individual statements in order to destroy the arguments brought forth in the book. I found one specific description in the Bible which matched exactly something we had designed and tested as actual space hardware at the Marshall Space Flight Center a few years earlier.

"That event reminded me of the old rule of fair play—to give the benefit of doubt both to von Daeniken and the prophet. My attitude changed from negative to neutral and what I found eventually was the distinct possibility of a different viewpoint from which to consider ancient writings and traditions. Later on I discovered to my surprise that aspects of advanced technology were excluded from scientific consideration as a matter of course as far as such records are concerned. However, they frequently contain strong implications in that direction and it seems to me we are obligated to introduce such viewpoints. After all, in our search for the truth, how can we exclude *a priori* any possibility, even if it may look unlikely at first? That is the basis on which I continue my work."

BIOGRAPHICAL/CRITICAL SOURCES: International Herald Tribune, October 22, 1973; *Los Angeles Times,* October 26, 1973; Allan Landsburg and Sally Landsburg, *In Search of Ancient Mysteries,* Bantam, 1974; *New York Post,* February 22, 1974; *Montreal Star,* August 21, 1974; *Newsweek,* June 9, 1975.

*   *   *

BODEN, Margaret A. 1936-

PERSONAL: Born November 26, 1936, in London, England; daughter of Leonard Forbes (a civil servant) and Violet Dorothy (Dawson) Boden; children: Ruskin, Jehane. *Education:* Newnham College, Cambridge, M.A. (with first

class honors), 1959; Harvard University, Ph.D., 1964. *Office:* School of Social Sciences, University of Sussex, Brighton, Sussex, England.

CAREER: University of Birmingham, Birmingham, England, lecturer in philosophy, 1959-65; University of Sussex, Brighton, England, reader in philosophy and psychology, 1965—. Director of Harvester Press. *Member:* British Society for Philosophy of Science, British Psychological Association, American Psychological Association, Society for the Study of Artificial Intelligence and the Stimulation of Behavior, Mind Association (member of executive committee), Cognitive Science Society, Society for Interdisciplinary Study of the Mind. *Awards, honors:* Harkness fellowship from the Commonwealth Fund, 1962-64, for Harvard University.

WRITINGS: Purposive Explanation in Psychology, Harvard University Press, 1972; *Artificial Intelligence and Natural Man,* Basic Books, 1977; *Piaget,* Fontana, 1979, Viking, 1980. General editor of "Harvester Studies in Philosophy" and "Harvester Studies in Cognitive Science." Contributor to philosophy and psychology journals.

WORK IN PROGRESS: Research on philosophy and cognitive science.

SIDELIGHTS: Margaret Boden writes that her interests include "the nature of the human mind and humane values in a basically materialistic universe. How can purpose and consciousness be reconciled with mechanism? The way in which artificial intelligence, and computational models in theoretical psychology, counteract (rather than reinforce) the dehumanizing tendencies of the natural sciences."

*   *   *

BOGRAD, Larry 1953-
(Grady Barrol)

PERSONAL: Born May 5, 1953, in Denver, Colo.; son of Nathan (a physician) and Ruth P. (a community worker) Bograd. *Education:* University of Colorado, B.A., 1975; University of Washington, Seattle, M.A., 1977. *Politics:* "Off-center." *Residence:* New York, N.Y. *Agent:* Carol Mann, 168 Pacific St., Brooklyn, N.Y. 11201.

CAREER: Harvey House Publishers, New York City, managing editor, 1977-79; Children's Television Workshop, New York City, staff writer, 1980—. *Awards, honors:* Irma Simonton Black Award from Bank Street College, 1978, for *Felix in the Attic.*

*WRITINGS—*For children: (Under pseudonym Grady Barrol) *Little Book of Anagrams,* Harvey House, 1978; *Felix in the Attic,* Harvey House, 1978; *Egon,* Macmillan, 1980; *Lost in the Store,* Macmillan, 1980.

WORK IN PROGRESS: First Flush, an adult novel; Four books for children: *Christopher and the Dancer, Caroline in the Woods, Willie in the City,* and *Crumps Search.*

SIDELIGHTS: Bograd told *CA:* "What I'm trying to do with my writing for children—which most children's books do not do—is provide an emotional and psychological field so the reader can 'use' the stories either as an entertaining outlet or to tap their deep-felt feelings about being a child. Loneliness and loss, growth and reconciliation, the search for autonomy and self, the importance of companionship and feelings—these are themes I hope readers can perceive in my writing. My adult writing is more concerned with artistic structure and social issues, but the themes are primarily the same."

BIOGRAPHICAL/CRITICAL SOURCES: New York Times, May 29, 1979.

* * *

BOIKO, Claire Taylor 1925-

PERSONAL: Born May 17, 1925, in Oakland, Calif.; daughter of Clarence Parker (an engineer) and Vivian (Adams) Taylor; married Bernard Boiko (a high school teacher), January 29, 1952; children: Susan Boiko Schwartz, Patricia Boiko Weyranch, Melinda, Robert, Elizabeth. *Education:* University of Redlands, B.A., 1946. *Politics:* Republican. *Religion:* Presbyterian. *Residence:* Bellerose, N.Y.

CAREER: Actress in Clare Tree Major Children's Theater, 1948-50; Department of the Army, Special Services, civilian entertainment and music technician, 1950-52; playwright. *Member:* Dramatists Guild, Sigma Tau Delta.

WRITINGS: Children's Plays for Creative Actors, Plays, 1967; *Plays and Programs for Boys and Girls,* Plays, 1972; *Dramatized Parodies,* Plays, 1979.

Work represented in anthologies; contributor to *Plays.*

SIDELIGHTS: Claire Boiko comments: "The interests reflected in my writing are science, science fiction, mythology and folklore, folk music, social history, astronomy, magic, drama, and those eternally fascinating beings—children."

* * *

BOLCOM, William E(lden) 1938-

PERSONAL: Born May 26, 1938, in Seattle, Wash.; son of Robert (in sales) and Virginia (an elementary school teacher; maiden name, Lauermann) Bolcom; married Fay Levine, December 23, 1963 (divorced, 1967); married Katherine Ling, June 8, 1968 (divorced, 1975); married Joan Morris (a singer), November 28, 1975. *Education:* University of Washington, Seattle, B.A., 1958; Mills College, M.A., 1961; Stanford University, D.M.A., 1964; attended Paris Conservatory of Music, 1959-61, postdoctoral study, 1964-65. *Home:* 3080 Whitmore Lake Rd., Ann Arbor, Mich. 48103. *Office:* School of Music, University of Michigan, Ann Arbor, Mich. 48104.

CAREER: Pianist, 1943—; composer, 1947—; recording artist, 1969—. University of Washington, Seattle, assistant professor of music, 1965-66; Queens College of the City University of New York, Flushing, N.Y., lecturer, 1966-67, assistant professor of music, 1967-68; Yale University, New Haven, Conn., visiting critic in drama school, 1968-69; New York University, New York, composer-in-residence, 1969-70; free-lance writer and record producer, 1970-73; University of Michigan, Ann Arbor, assistant professor, 1973-77, associate professor of music, 1977—. *Member:* American Music Center, American Composers Alliance. *Awards, honors:* William and Noma Copley Award, 1960, for composition; Kurt Weill Award for composition, 1962; Guggenheim fellowship, 1964 and 1968; Marc Blitzstein Award from the American Academy of Arts and Letters, 1965, for excellence in musical theatre; grant from Rockefeller Foundation, 1969-70; National Endowment for the Arts award, 1974 and 1975; Henry Russel Award from University of Michigan, 1977, for teaching excellence; second prize in composition from Paris Conservatory of Music.

WRITINGS: (With Robert Kimball) *Reminiscing With Sissle and Blake,* Viking, 1973. Contributor to *Grove's Dictionary.* Contributor to music journals. Co-editor of *Annals of Scholarship.*

WORK IN PROGRESS: Musical composition.

SIDELIGHTS: Bolcom told *CA:* "I am vitally interested in the American musical language in all its forms. All my literary activity, as well as my activities as a composer and performer, has been involved with its study and pursuit.

"I have been interested in the 1920's black musical because it defined our musical stage as something different from English sources. As a composer of words and music I am naturally interested in how American prosody was affected by this development.

"With one limitation—that my music be comprehensible to others, though not overly simplified—I have forged a style that encompasses everything from jazz and folk elements to extreme dissonance, depending on what the music is meant to express. Many American musicians have slighted the simpler and most basic efforts of our musical language. Without this basis, the most complex piece remains incomprehensible; with it, any complexity is eventually understandable."

BIOGRAPHICAL/CRITICAL SOURCES: Musical America, September, 1978.

* * *

BOLLOTEN, Burnett 1909-

PERSONAL: Born June 24, 1909, in Bangor, Wales; came to United States, 1949; naturalized U.S. citizen, 1955; son of Joseph (a businessman) and Betty (Cohen) Bolloten; married Gladys Evie (an actress), August 27, 1938 (divorced, 1955); married Betty Bieders, May 30, 1955; children: Gregory Max. *Education:* Educated in England and Switzerland. *Home and office:* 491 Raquel Ct., Los Altos, Calif. 94022.

CAREER: Author and journalist. Worked in father's business in London, England, until 1930; worked as English teacher, bookkeeper and hotel receptionist in Bastia, Corsica, as secretary in Tunis, North Africa, for British consulate in Lebanon, and for Royal Air Force station in Ismailia, Egypt, 1929-32; financial writer for stockbroker in London, 1934; journalist with United Press of America and British United Press (now combined as United Press International) in London, 1936-38. Lecturer at Stanford University, 1962-65. Notable assignments include coverage of Spanish civil war.

WRITINGS: The Grand Camouflage: The Communist Conspiracy in the Spanish Civil War, Praeger, 1961, reprinted with introduction by Hugh Trevor-Roper, 1968, revised and greatly expanded edition published as *The Spanish Revolution,* University of North Carolina Press, 1979; (contributor) Raymond Carr, editor, *The Republic and the Civil War in Spain,* Macmillan, 1971.

WORK IN PROGRESS: "I am presently working on the third (and final) volume of the Spanish Revolution, which I hope to complete by 1986 (the 50th anniversary of the outbreak of the Spanish civil war) or at the latest by 1989 (the 50th anniversary of the end of the civil war)."

SIDELIGHTS: Bolloten told *CA:* "On July 18, 1936, I arrived in Spain for my summer vacation only to find myself a few hours later in the midst of the civil war and revolution. Little did I imagine that for the next forty years or more I would be gathering, organizing, digesting, and assimilating the largest collection of materials on the subject ever assembled by a single person. The United Press at first assigned me to the Aragon front, then to Madrid, Valencia, and Barcelona, the main centers of political activity, where I began collecting all available material.

"In 1938, I left Spain, married, and sailed for Mexico, where

I planned to write a brief account of some of the political events of the civil war, but a few months later the war ended and thousands of refugees arrived. I then decided to widen my aim and write a comprehensive history, taking advantage of the new materials and information fortuitously made available to me. Aided by my wife, and financed by my small savings, by a modest legacy, and by the sale of some of my materials to U.S. libraries, I undertook the work of research and investigation on a scale commensurate with the need. From that time on, I consulted and reconsulted more than one hundred thousand issues of newspapers and periodicals published during the civil war and the years of exile, over three thousand books and pamphlets, and a large number of published and unpublished documents. This massive documentation was not available in any one institution or in any one country, but had to be obtained from Spain, Great Britain, France, Germany, Italy, and the U.S., as well as from Mexico and other Latin American republics, where thousands of Spaniards took refuge after the civil war. In the course of forty years of research and inquiry, I corresponded with or interviewed a large number of refugees, and combed and recombed essential institutions and libraries for fresh material. From these sources alone I obtained 125,000 microfilm frames, and years went by in an effort to bring order and meaning into this chaotic welter of material, much of which had to be consulted several times.

"In 1949, I immigrated to the United States. By then, my financial resources were nearing exhaustion, forcing me to lower my sights and settle for a smaller book than the one projected. In 1953, without abandoning my search for new material, I joined Sears, Roebuck & Co. and for five years sold their encyclopedia from door to door. In 1959 I went into the real estate business to make myself financially independent, so that I could eventually resume full-time work on my project."

*   *   *

BOLSHAKOFF, Serge 1901-

PERSONAL: Born July 27, 1901, in St. Petersburg, Russia; son of Nicholas (in business) and Lydia (Balunin) Bolshakoff. *Education:* Studied civil engineering, economics, and sociology in various countries; Christ Church, Oxford, Ph.D., 1943. *Religion:* Russian Orthodox. *Home:* Hauterive Abbey, C.H.-1725 Posieux, Switzerland.

CAREER: Self-employed, 1925—; free-lance writer and lecturer.

WRITINGS—In English: *The Christian Church and the Soviet State,* Macmillan, 1942; *The Foreign Missions of the Russian Orthodox Church,* S.P.C.K., 1943; *The Doctrine of the Unity of the Church in the Works of Khomyakov and Moehler,* S.P.C.K., 1946; *Russian Nonconformity: The Story of "Unofficial" Religion in Russia,* Westminster, 1950, reprinted, AMS Press, 1973; *Father Michael, Recluse of Unsi Valamo,* One Church, 1959; *Russian Mystics,* Cistercian Publications, 1977.

Other: *Na vysotakh dukha* (title means "On the Summit of the Spirit"), Foyer Oriental Chretien (Brussels), 1971; *Auf den Hoehen des Geistes* (title means "On the Summit of the Spirit"), Verlag Kertn Renner, 1976. Also author of books privately printed in Italy. Contributor to magazines and newspapers in several countries and languages.

WORK IN PROGRESS: Light of Thabor; Aux Sommets on souffle l'esprit (title means "On the Summet of the Spirits"); *Souvenirs of Childhood and Adolescence in Imperial Russia;* research on "monastic life and mystics in Russia, Rumania, Athos, and the Holy Land in the nineteenth century."

SIDELIGHTS: Bolshakoff writes: "I have traveled so much in my life and spoken so many languages that it would take a lot of space to enumerate everything. Since 1974 I have lived in Switzerland.

"In the past I wrote mainly on religious and mystical subjects. Now I am engaged in writing my autobiography, concentrating on memoirs of my childhood and adolescence before World War I. This allows me to compare the first years of this century with the modern world. The differences, of course, are enormous, and I was often very near to the great events which shaped this century. The fact that I am not obliged to write for a living gives me a great deal of freedom.

"At present I am interested in the impact of scientific and technological progress on contemporary life and art."

*   *   *

BONETTI, Edward 1928-

PERSONAL: Born September 14, 1928, in Boston, Mass.; son of Michael (a machinist) and Frances (Drinkwater) Bonetti. *Education:* Boston University, B.A., 1960; New York University, M.A., 1962. *Politics:* Democrat. *Religion:* Roman Catholic. *Residence:* Wellfleet, Mass. 02667.

CAREER: Writer, 1967—. Also worked as longshoreman, electronic technician, film actor, and social worker. *Military service:* U.S. Army, radio operator in Signal Corps, 1951-53; served in Europe.

WRITINGS: Apple Wine (poems), R. P. Dickey, 1969; *The Wine Cellar* (stories), Viking, 1977. Contributor to literary journals and little magazines, including *New American Review* and *New Letters.*

WORK IN PROGRESS: The Journal of Cosmo Pike, a novel.

SIDELIGHTS: Bonetti's *The Wine Cellar* is a collection of short works that includes the novella of the same title. Barbara Paul called the works "disturbing stories." She explained that "they achieve the seemingly impossible goal of repelling the reader while holding him captive at the same time. . . . Things build up without our knowing it, the author seems to say; and when they explode, we're surprised."

Paul called the title story one "of Italian immigrants in America—not glamorized gangsters we're so used to . . ."; she continued: "This novella may turn out to be a significant piece of contemporary fiction. The author's prose is as controlled as his characters' emotions are chaotic. Even when you don't like the characters, you're hypnotized by them and need to know what happens to them." Similarly, Gloria Whelan wrote that "it is difficult to believe that this is Bonetti's first book. His descriptions of the making of the wine from the trip to the freight cars to choose the grapes to the final ritualistic tasting of the completed wine are a tour de force." She noted that "Bonetti has bravely taken on the great theme of man struggling against forces he knows will overwhelm him even though he does not have the means to fight—and he has written a masterpiece."

Bonetti told *CA:* "I think there are as many reasons for writing as there are people involved in the act; but for me writing is an act that begins in the imagination, and by this I mean in that kind of world that exists in the imagination. There have been times in my narrow career when one persistent motive dominated my attempt at the craft itself and it was this: to write clearly and simply and as Faulkner once put it, to create something in a story that did not exist before.

"In the short stories I have written, I have tried to show what might be elemental in the sexual violence inherent in human nature; but never do I draw from 'real' people. When I have the arrogance for it, and the good Muse is on my side (always humility before the Muse), I try to lace the stories with elements that one might refer to as universalities. Sometimes I feel the stories succeed in this. Sometimes they end up as ignominious failures.

"In any case I like to write with an economy of words, with little padding, with no 'fleshing out' and with the hope that nothing is wasted. Of course there is the joy of writing, but this is not always forthcoming in a work. After finishing a piece I am no stranger to depression; but since writing can be a defense against internal chaos, the labor is always worth the pain.

"I have been influenced by Poe, Faulkner, Hemingway, Conrad, and inspired by Anderson. I have the feeling that the current literary scene has shrunk to blatant mediocrity."

BIOGRAPHICAL/CRITICAL SOURCES: Norman Mailer, *Of a Fire on the Moon,* Little, Brown, 1971; *Pittsburgh Press,* July 17, 1977; *Detroit Free Press,* August 7, 1977; *State,* August 28, 1977.

*   *   *

BONEWITS, Isaac
See BONEWITS, P(hilip) E(mmons) I(saac)

*   *   *

BONEWITS, P(hilip) E(mmons) I(saac)   1949-
(Isaac Bonewits)

PERSONAL: Surname is pronounced *Bon*-a-wits; born October 1, 1949, in Michigan; son of James Edwin (a home building contractor) and Jeanette (a cook; maiden name, Charlebois) Bonewits; married Deborah Selene Kumin (a dancer, teacher, editor, writer, and graphics designer), August 6, 1978. *Education:* University of California, Berkeley, B.A., 1970. *Politics:* Libertarian. *Office:* Pentalpha, P.O. Box 9398, Berkeley, Calif. 94709.

CAREER: Gnostica, Minneapolis, Minn., editor, 1974-75; *Pentalpha Journal,* Berkeley, Calif., editor, 1978—. Founder and first president of Aquarian Anti-Defamation League, 1974-76. Technical consultant for television and film documentaries. *Member:* Ordo Templi Orientis (minerval, 1975-79), Order of the Feather (illuminatus primus, 1973-79), Pentalpha, Association for the Advancement of Aquarian Age Awareness (member of board of trustees, 1978-79).

WRITINGS: Real Magic, Coward, 1971, revised edition, Creative Arts, 1979; (editor) *The Druid Chronicles (Evolved),* Pentalpha, 1976. Contributor of articles and poems (sometimes under name Isaac Bonewits) to magazines, including *Fate, Psychic, New Realities,* and *Psychic Observer,* and newspapers.

WORK IN PROGRESS: Old Gods Returning, on polytheistic religions; *Understanding Witchcraft; Masculism: A Male Survival Guide for the 1980's; Voodoo: The "Other" Great Religion; Bloodstar,* an occult murder mystery; *Do-It-Yourself Tarot,* with instructions for making a personal tarot deck; screenplays and television plays with occult themes.

SIDELIGHTS: Bonewits writes: "My primary concern as a writer, editor, and speaker is to communicate *accurate* information about metaphysical, occult, and minority religious topics to the general public, in as clear a fashion as I can manage. Although I'm not very interested in academic jargon, I am obsessive about accuracy—which makes me a slow writer. My approach is interdisciplinary and I believe that humor has a definite role to play in demystifying the mystical. Unfortunately, most works published in my field are either turgid or sensationalistic—not to mention sloppily researched!

"My religion is Neopagan and I'm currently an Archdruid in the New Reformed Druids of North America. Neopaganism in general, and the New Reformed Druids in particular, are small religions of recent origin. I mention this to explain why interdisciplinary research, multivalued logic systems, ecological awareness, sensualism, and humor fill my work. In many ways I see my writing and speaking as religious acts, though I try to avoid imposing my worldview on the unwilling.

"There are thousands of minority belief systems growing in the western world today. Some of them are deadly 'cults,' but most are not only harmless, they are actually helpful and growth-oriented. All of them are interesting and deserve accurate presentation of their beliefs and practices to the general public. Understanding an unusual religion is of far more value than hating or fearing it."

BIOGRAPHICAL/CRITICAL SOURCES: San Francisco Examiner, July 25, 1979; Margot Adler, *Drawing Down the Moon,* Viking, 1979.

*   *   *

BONZON, Paul-Jacques   1908-1978

PERSONAL: Born August 31, 1908, in Sainte-Marie du Monte, France; died September 24, 1978; son of Alphonse (a government administrator) and Marie (Flaux) Bonzon; married Aimee Philippon, October 26, 1949; children: Jacques, Isabelle. *Education:* Received degree from teachers college in Saint-Lo, France, 1927. *Address:* 6 rue Louis Barthou, Valence, Drome, France.

CAREER: Teacher at Chabeuil School, France, 1929-49; director of Saint-Laurent School, France, 1949-59; vice-president of French Academy of Letters, Sciences, and Arts, beginning 1960. Author of children's books. *Awards, honors:* Prix Jeunesse, 1952; first prize from Comite National de L'Enfance, 1955; grand prize from Salon de L'Enfance de Paris, 1958, for *L'Eventail de Seville; Book World* award, American Library Association notable book citation, and *New York Times* best book of the year citation, all 1962, all for *The Orphans of Simitra.*

WRITINGS—All juvenile; in English: *Les Orphelins de Simitra,* Hachette, 1955, translation by Thelma Niklaus published as *The Orphans of Simitra,* University of London Press, 1957, Criterion, 1962; *La Ballerine de Majorque,* Hachette, 1956, translation published as *Paquita, the Ballerina From Mallorca,* Sterling, 1958; *L'Eventail de Seville,* Hachette, 1958, translation by Anthony Cappuyns published as *The Spanish Fan,* Heinemann, 1960; *La Croix d'or de Santa-Anna,* Hachette, 1960, translation by Niklaus published as *The Gold Cross of Santa Anna,* University of London Press, 1962, published as *Pursuit in the French Alps,* Lothrop, 1963; *Les Compagnons de la croix-rousse,* Hachette, 1961, translation by Godfrey Burston published as *The Friends of Croix-Rousse,* University of London Press, 1963; *Le Cheval de verre,* Hachette, 1963, translation by Burston published as *The Glass Horse,* University of London Press, 1964; *The Runaway Flying Horse,* translation from the original French edition by Susan Kotta, Parents' Magazine Press, 1976.

Other: *Loutsi-chien et ses jeunes maitres,* Bourrelier, 1945;

Delph, le marin; ou, L'Appel de la mer, Societe Universitaire, 1947; *Le Jongleur a l'etoile*, Hachette, 1948; *Du gui pour Christmas*, Bourrelier, 1953; *Mamadi; ou, le petit roi d'ebene*, Editions Magnard, 1953; *Le Petit Passeur du lac*, Hachette, 1956; *Mon Vercors en feu*, [Paris], 1956, reprinted, Hachette, 1975; *Tout-Fon*, [Paris], 1956; *La Promesse de Primerose*, Hachette, 1957; *La Princesse sans nom*, Hachette, 1958; *Le Voyageur sans visage*, Editions Fleurus, 1958; *Un Secret dans la nuit polaire*, Hachette, 1959.

Contes de l'hiver, Editions Bias, 1960; *J'irai a Nagasaki*, Hachette, 1961; *Contes de mon chalet*, Editions Bias, 1965; *Le Jardin de paradis*, Delagrave, 1967; *La Chalet du bonheur*, Delagrave, 1967; *La Roulotte du bonheur*, Delagrave, 1968.

Le Chateau de Pompon, Delagrave, 1970; *Pompon a la ville*, Delagrave, 1975; *Le Cirque Zigoto*, Delagrave, 1975; *Diablo pompier*, Hachette, 1975; *Diablo jardinier*, Hachette, 1976; *Yani: livre de lectures suivies*, Delagrave, 1976; *Les Espions du X-35*, Hachette, 1976.

"Les Six Compagnons" series; all published by Hachette: *Les Six Compagnons et la disparue de Montelimar*, 1957; *. . . et l'homme au gant*, 1963; *. . . et la pile atomique*, 1963; *. . . et le chateau maudit*, 1965; *. . . et l'emetteur pirate*, 1968; *. . . et les agents secrets*, 1969; *. . . et leurs espions du ciel*, 1971. Also author of *Les Six Compagnons a la Tour Eiffel*, *. . . a Scotland Yard*, *. . . au gouffre marzal*, *. . . au village englouti*, *. . . au concours hippique*, *. . . dans la Citadelle*, *. . . devant la camera*, *. . . en croisiere*, *. . . et la brigade volante*, *. . . et l'ane vart*, *. . . et la perruque rouge*, *. . . et la princesse noire*, *. . . et l'avion clandestin*, *. . . et le mystere du parc*, *. . . et le petit rat de l'opera*, *. . . et le piano a queue*, *. . . et le secret de la calanque*, *. . . et les pirates du rail*, *. . . et les voix de la nuit*, *. . . et l'homme des neiges*, *. . . et l'oeil d'acier*, *. . . se jettent a l'eau*, *. . . et la clef minute*, *. . . et le cigare volant*, and *. . . et la boutielle a la mer*.

"La Famille H. L. M." series; all published by Hachette: *Les Etranges Locataires*, 1966; *L'Homme a la valise jaune*, 1967; *Vol au cirque*, 1967; *Luisa contre-attaque*, 1968; *Rue des chats-sans-queue*, 1968; *Le Perroquet et son tresor*, 1969. Also author of *Le Bateau fantome*, *Un Cheval sur un Volcan*, *L'Homme a la tourterelle*, *L'Homme aux souris blanches*, *Le Marchand de Coquillages*, *Ou est passe l'ane tulipe?*, *Quatre Chats et le diable*, *La Roulotte de l'aventure*, *Le Secret de la malle arriere*, *Le Secret du lac rouge*, *Shalom sur la piste noire*, *Les Espions du x351*, *de Cavalier de la mer*, and *d'homme au noeud papillon*.

Also author of *Devant la rideau*, Amicale, *Diabolo et la fleur qui sourit*, Hachette, *Diabolo le petit chat*, Hachette, *Diabolo et le cheval de bois*, Hachette, *Le Cavalier de la mer*, Hachette, *La Maison aux mille bonheurs*, Delagrave, *Le Relais des ciagales*, Delagrave, *Le Viking au braclete d'argent*, Editions G.P., and *Soleil de monespagne*, Hachette.

SIDELIGHTS: Paul-Jacques Bonzon has received most of his critical attention in the United States for *The Orphans of Simitra*. This is the story of Porphyras and Mina, the orphaned survivors of an earthquake which destroyed their village. The acclaim this book received in France has been echoed in America. A *New York Herald Tribune* reviewer wrote: "This moving story does not soften for children the tragic realities of life but shows an indomitable spirit can make them bearable. Especially fine is the first third of the book when the children are in Greece. The account of the various difficulties Porphyras later encounters seems a little

disconnected and involved, the ending a little pat, though it will satisfy young readers."

BIOGRAPHICAL/CRITICAL SOURCES: New York Herald Tribune, May 13, 1962.*

* * *

BOONE, Gray Davis 1938-

PERSONAL: Born August 27, 1938, in Houston, Tex.; daughter of Edwin Theodore and Martha Lucille (Scholl) Davis; married James B. Boone, Jr. (a publisher), June 30, 1961; children: Kenneth Scholl, James Buford, III, Martha Frances. *Education:* Attended University of Texas, 1956-59, and University of Geneva, 1959; University of Alabama, B.A., 1975. *Home:* 905 21st Ave., Tuscaloosa, Ala. 35401. *Office: Antique Monthly*, P.O. Drawer 2, Tuscaloosa, Ala. 35401.

CAREER/WRITINGS: Antique Monthly, Tuscaloosa, Ala., founder and editor, 1967—; *Horizon* magazine, Tuscaloosa, editor and publisher, 1978—. Editor of *Gray Letter* (weekly news bulletin); publisher of weekly syndicated column, "Gray Boone on Antiques." President of Decorative Arts Trust, 1977—; president and owner of Boone, Inc.; co-owner of De L'Isle/Gray Journeys. Chairman of annual World Antiques Market Conference in New York City; chairman of Tuscaloosa Preservation Authority; co-chairman of bicentennial activities for Tuscaloosa, Tuscaloosa County, and Northport, Ala., bicentennial communities. Member of board of directors: South Central Bell Telephone Co.; Preservation Action; Circle Repertory Theatre, New York City; Triad Playwrights, New York City. Member of advisory committee: Judson College, Marion, Ala.; New College, University of Alabama; Colonial Williamsburg Forum, 1978-81; Carlyle House Restoration, Alexandria, Va.; Governor's Mansion of Alabama. Member of Committee for Decorative Arts, Cooper-Hewitt Museum, New York City; member of Octagon Committee, Washington, D.C.; member of development council for Birmingham Southern College.

MEMBER: Royal Society of Arts (London; fellow). *Awards, honors:* Distinguished service award from Alabama Historical Commission, 1975; Gordon Gray Award from National Trust for Historic Preservation, 1978; Woman of Achievement award from Tuscaloosa Business and Professional Women's Club, 1979.

SIDELIGHTS: Since Gray Boone became the editor and publisher of *Horizon* in 1978 she has managed to keep the magazine in the black, something American Heritage Publishing Co. and other previous owners usually failed to do. By eliminating circulation promotion and moving the office from Rockefeller Center in New York City to Tuscaloosa, Ala., Boone has managed to cut expenses by sixty-five percent. She told a *New York Times* reporter: "We created a vibrant young staff . . . and we have those hungry hordes of Americans who want to assimilate the arts into their life style. Horizon is the perfect vehicle to answer the need."

Gray Boone is actively involved in historic preservation, working not only on community projects, but on personal property as well. She purchased a Greek Revival house in Tuscaloosa that was built about 1835. Archaeological work by the University of Alabama was completed in the summer of 1974 and the house, furnished primarily with Federal-period antiques, is included in the annual Heritage Week pilgrimage in Tuscaloosa. Boone also restored an early nineteenth-century log cabin in rural Alabama that her family uses as a weekend retreat.

Because of her involvement with Heritage Week activities in Tuscaloosa, the mayor of the city proclaimed March 29, 1979 as Gray Boone Day.

BIOGRAPHICAL/CRITICAL SOURCES: New York Daily News, January 5, 1978; *Washington Post,* February 26, 1978; *Houston Chronicle,* October 8, 1978; *New York Times,* April 24, 1979.

* * *

BOOTH, Martin 1944-

PERSONAL: Born September 7, 1944, near Longridge, England; son of William John Kenneth and Alice Joyce (Pankhurst) Booth; married Helen Barber, August 10, 1968; children: Clayer Alexander, Emma Louise. *Education:* University of London, certificate in education, 1968; attended St. Peter's College, Oxford, 1971-72. *Politics:* Democratic Socialist. *Religion:* None. *Home:* Cnot House, Knotting, Bedford M44 1AF, England. *Agent:* Mark Hamilton, A. M. Heath & Co., 40/2 William IV St., London WC2N 4DD, England.

CAREER: Teacher of English literature at schools in Frensham, Surrey, England, 1968-71, and in Wellingborough and Rushden, Northamptonshire, 1971-74; senior assistant in language and English literature, 1974—. Lecturer at Long Island University, Nebraska Wesleyan University, University of Nebraska, and University of New Hampshire; lecturer in Romania. Literary critic, features writer, and presenter for British Broadcasting Corp. Radio; gives poetry readings and creative writing workshops. Founder and director of Sceptre Press and editor for Fuller d'Arch Smith Ltd. Member of London Poets' Workshop. *Member:* Poetry Society (member of general and executive councils, 1967-74), Writers Action Group. *Awards, honors:* E. C. Gregory Award for Poetry from Gregory Foundation, 1970, for *The Crying Embers;* Poets' Yearbook Award from Poets' Yearbook Association, 1978, for *Extending Upon the Kingdom.*

WRITINGS—Books of poems, except as indicated: *Paper Pennies,* privately printed, 1967; *Supplication to the Himalayas,* privately printed, 1968; *In the Yenan Caves,* Sceptre Press, 1969; *The Borrowed Gull,* Sceptre Press, 1970; *White,* Sceptre Press, 1971; *The Crying Embers,* Fuller d'Arch Smith, 1971; *On the Death of Archdeacon Broix,* Second Aeon, 1971; *Winnowing of Silence,* Keepsake Press, 1971; *James Elroy Flecker* (criticism), Keepsake Press, 1971; *Pilgrims and Petitions,* Aquila Publishing, 1971; *Coronis,* Andium Books, 1973; *In Her Hands,* Sceptre Press, 1973; *Teller,* Poet and Printer, 1973; *Yogh,* Ally Press, 1974; *Spawning the Os,* Quarto Press, 1974; *Brevities,* Elizabeth Press, 1974; *Hands Twining Grasses,* Words Etc., 1974; *Snath,* Oasis Books, 1975; *Words Broadsheet 3,* Words Etc., 1975; *Two Boys and a Girl, Playing in the Churchyard,* Mandeville Press, 1975; (editor) *Stalks of Jade,* Menard Press, 1976; *Rider and Horse,* Keepsake Press, 1976; (editor with George MacBeth) *The Book of Cats,* Secker & Warburg, 1976, Morrow, 1978; *Words Broadsheet 27,* Words Etc., 1977; *The Knotting Sequence,* Elizabeth Press, 1977; *Polenul Insidious* (title means "The Insidious Pollens"), Univers Publishing, 1977; *Extending Upon the Kingdom,* Poets Yearbook, 1977; *Martin Booth: Bedfordshire Writer,* Bedford Central Library, 1977; *The Carrier* (novel), W. H. Allen, 1978; *The Dying,* Sceptre Press, 1978; *Calling With Owls,* William B. Ewert, 1979; *The Cnot Dialogues,* Elizabeth Press, 1980; *Devil's Wine,* Colin Smythe Ltd., 1980.

Author of "The Winter Warrior" (television play), broadcast by BBC-TV, December, 1976. Author of scripts for British Broadcasting Corp., including "John of Badsaddle," "Mary Mad," "The Claw of Mammon," and "Beth and the Hand of Glory."

Work represented in about twenty-five anthologies, including *Poetry in the Seventies,* Rondo, 1976; *Writers of East Anglia,* edited by Angus Wilson, Secker & Warburg, 1976; *New Poetry One, Two, & Three,* Arts Council, 1977. Contributor to magazines. Poetry critic for London *Tribune;* political commentator and music critic for *Times Educational Supplement;* literary critic and advisory editor for *Pacific Quarterly.*

WORK IN PROGRESS: Offa's Dyke, publication by David & Charles Ltd. expected in 1981; a book on modern verse and its teaching, publication by Oxford University Press expected in 1981; a book of poems, completion expected in 1981; a novel, publication by Collins expected in 1980; an autobiography covering his years in Hong Kong, 1984.

SIDELIGHTS: Booth wrote: "I was born in Lancashire and later moved to Hong Kong, where (with the exception of a three-year stay in Kenya) I was educated. I came to poetry at the age of sixteen or seventeen through the encouragement of Edmund Blunden, then professor of English at Hong Kong University. It was from him that I learned to see poetically, understand imagery, enjoy reading, and fall in love with books. I returned to England in 1964 and, after a succession of jobs, began teacher education in natural sciences. I've always loved nature and its ways, curiosities, and wonders, but abhorred the formalized teaching of these to 'scientific' ends.

"My work is set in a rural context, even when I'm writing thrillers. The attractions of the history, archaeology, and beauty of the English rural landscape are all that keep me living in England which, in many other ways, I find mundane, parochial, and insular. I am a socialist in the British sense of the term and sickened by seeing how self-indulgent the nation is.

"Travel is a joy to me, once I'm out of the airport and its attendant fears. When I am not writing, my family and the land hold me."

* * *

BOTTOME, Phyllis
See FORBES-DENNIS, Phyllis

* * *

BOULOGNE, Jean 1942-

PERSONAL: Born July 21, 1942, in Alberta, Canada; daughter of Stephen (an engineer) and Olga Zaharichuk; married Jacob Boulogne, September 18, 1963 (divorced December, 1978); children: John, Stephanie. *Education:* University of British Columbia, B.Ed., 1978. *Home and office:* 2780 Keremeos St., Vancouver, British Columbia, Canada V6T 1N5.

CAREER: Teacher in Surrey, British Columbia, 1968-73; writer, 1977—. *Member:* Writers Union of Canada.

WRITINGS: The Making of a Gymnast, Hawthorne, 1978. Contributor to *Canadian Children.*

* * *

BOUMA, Mary La Grand

PERSONAL: Born in Grand Rapids, Mich.; daughter of James (in business) and Katherine (Tornga) La Grand; married Henry Bouma (a minister), March 11, 1957; children: Lisa, Sharon, Mary Lee, Katherine. *Education:* Calvin College, B.A., 1957. *Religion:* Christian. *Home:* 837 North Neel, Kennewick, Wash. 99336.

CAREER: Piano teacher, 1960—. Church organist, 1960-69. Speaker at religious gatherings. President-elect of Mid-Columbia Symphony Guild.

WRITINGS: The Creative Homemaker, Bethany Fellowship, 1973, study guide, 1975; *Divorce in the Parsonage,* Bethany Fellowship, 1979. Contributor to *Banner, Christianity Today,* and *Eternity.*

SIDELIGHTS: Mary Bouma writes: "My husband and I were married in Amsterdam and lived there for two years. During this time I learned to speak Dutch. This took a good deal of determination, since so many Dutch people have a working knowledge of English and are eager to speak it to Americans.

"My experience in counseling as a pastor's wife pointed up the problems in marriage and the family. After a running dialogue with my husband over a number of years, I decided that I could make a positive contribution by writing a book emphasizing the scope and challenge of homemaking as a profession.

"My latest book grew out of my concern about the growing number of divorces among clergy couples of my acquaintance, in addition to the increasing frustration of the many pastors and wives I knew. Over a three-year period I interviewed nearly two hundred pastors, wives, ex-pastors, and ex-wives from California to New York. I found some definite patterns among both the successful and the unsuccessful marriages. I hope the book will be helpful to those already in the ministry, those planning to be pastors, and those who directly influence pastors' marriages, which means all members of congregations."

BIOGRAPHICAL/CRITICAL SOURCES: Family Circle, Western Edition, February, 1979.

*   *   *

BOWYER, (Raymond) Chaz 1926-

PERSONAL: Born September 29, 1926, in Weymouth, England; son of Reginald (a builder) and Dorothy (Northam) Bowyer; married Doreen Scott; children: Katharin, Jeff, Lisa Janine. *Education:* Attended high school in Solihull and Nelson, England. *Home and office:* 33 Laundry Lane, Norwich NR7 0XG, England.

CAREER: Royal Air Force, 1943-69, retiring as sergeant; served as armament technician, airman, and instructor in explosives and armaments; stationed in Egypt, Libya, Palestine, Singapore, and Aden; writer, 1969—. *Member:* Royal Air Force Association (life member).

WRITINGS: The Flying Elephants, Macdonald & Co., 1972; *Mosquito at War,* Ian Allan, 1973; *Hurricane at War,* Ian Allan, 1975; *Airmen of World War I,* Arms & Armour Press, 1975; *Sunderland at War,* Ian Allan, 1976; *Beaufighter at War,* Ian Allan, 1976; *Hampden Special,* Ian Allan, 1977; *Path Finders at War,* Ian Allan, 1977; *Albert Ball, V.C.,* William Kimber, 1977; *History of the R.A.F.,* Hamlyn, 1977; *Sopwith Camel: King of Combat,* Glasney Press, 1978; *For Valour: The Air VCs,* William Kimber, 1978; *Guns in the Sky: The Air Gunners,* Dent, 1979; *Coastal Command at War,* Ian Allan, 1979; *Fighter Command, 1936-68,* Dent, 1980; *Spitfire, a Tribute,* Arms & Armour Press, 1980; *Five Group at War,* Ian Allan, 1980; *Eugene Esmonde, V.C., D.S.O.,* William Kimber, 1981; *Desert Air Force at War,* Ian Allan, 1981.

Editor: *Bomber Pilot, 1916-18,* Ian Allan, 1974; *Fighter Pilot on the Western Front,* William Kimber, 1975; *Wings Over the Somme,* William Kimber, 1976; *Fall of an Eagle: Ernst Udet,* William Kimber, 1980. Author of booklets. Past editor of *Journal of the Cross and Cockade Society.*

WORK IN PROGRESS: A book about veteran aircraft of World War II, publication expected in 1980 or 1981; a book about customs and traditions of the Royal Air Force, publication expected in late 1981.

SIDELIGHTS: Bowyer writes: "My motivation? Simply to place on permanent record *accurate* accounts of men, deeds, and events connected with Royal Air Force history. This is exemplified (perhaps) by *For Valour,* which is now accepted as the standard reference work on the subject. I am tired of reading historical drivel as perpetrated by 'well-known' authors, most of whom are simply novelists or journalists with no background knowledge of genuine aviation history. Too many 'military historians' are simply writers jumping on the history bandwagon only for profit."

*   *   *

**BOYLE, Mark
See KIENZLE, William X(avier)**

*   *   *

BRABEC, Barbara 1937-

PERSONAL: Born March 5, 1937, in Buckley, Ill.; daughter of William J. (a farmer and businessman) and Marcella E. (a nurse; maiden name, Newman) Schaumburg; married Harry J. Brabec (a musician and craft show producer), August, 1961. *Education:* Attended American Conservatory of Music (Chicago, Ill.), 1956-60. *Office:* Countryside Books, 200 James St., Barrington, Ill. 60010.

CAREER: Pennsylvania Railroad, Chicago, Ill., teletype operator, 1955-56; Kaiser Aluminum Co., Chicago, secretary, 1956-60; free-lance musical entertainer for clubs and organizations in Chicago area, 1960-61; Harding Restaurant Co., Chicago, executive secretary, 1961-62; Investment Guide Advertising Inc., Chicago, administrative assistant, 1962-65; designer-craftsman and free-lance secretary, 1965-70; *Artisan Crafts* magazine, Reeds Spring, Mo., editor, co-publisher, and co-owner, 1971-76; writer and secretarial assistant to husband's craft show productions, 1977-79; Countryside Books, Barrington, Ill., began as publisher's assistant, became publisher and general manager, 1979—.

WRITINGS: Creative Cash: How to Sell Your Crafts, Needlework, Designs, and Know-How (alternate selection of Better Homes and Gardens Family Reading Club, Better Homes and Gardens Crafts Club, and Needle Arts Society Book Club), Countryside Books, 1979. Author of "Selling What You Make," a column in *Crafts,* 1979—; author of "The Crafts Spotlight," a column in *Creative Crafts,* 1979—. Contributor to *Craftspirit '76;* contributor to magazines including *Changing Times, Needlecraft for Today,* and *Better Homes and Gardens.* Editor of *Guide to the Craft World,* 1974, revised edition, 1975.

WORK IN PROGRESS: A cookbook.

SIDELIGHTS: Creative Cash is a step-by-step guide for those who want to capitalize on talents in needlework or crafts. It covers pricing, marketing and publicity strategies, starting a home business, selling at fairs, and it offers guidance on finding supply sources and sales outlets, making industry contacts, and coping with things legal and financial. It also covers lecturing, writing, and self-publishing in detail and includes an extensive resource chapter on available craft publications, services, and suppliers.

Among the favorable reviews of Brabec's book is this praise from *Nutshell News:* "With so much being printed on sustaining a hobby or making it into a business that only confuses the reader . . . , it is a pleasure to read this professionally prepared book that is both authoritative and interesting with its positive approaches validated by names and addresses!" An *Interweave 65* reviewer also commended *Creative Cash,* calling it "the liveliest, most down-to-earth, non-intimidating approach to making money from crafts that I've seen."

AVOCATIONAL INTERESTS: Reading, Maori handweaving, ethnic cooking.

BIOGRAPHICAL/CRITICAL SOURCES: Nutshell News, November/December, 1979; *Interweave 65,* winter, 1979-80.

* * *

BRADY, Esther Wood   1905-
    (Esther Wood)

PERSONAL: Born August 24, 1905, in Akron, N.Y.; daughter of Lawrence A. (a minister) and Ida (Eby) Wood; married George W. Brady (an aeronautical engineer), July 29, 1933; children: Caroline F., Barbara (Mrs. William A. Beeker). *Education:* Attended University of Rochester and Denison University; Boston University, B.A., 1928. *Religion:* Presbyterian. *Home:* 3023 44th St. N.W., Washington, D.C. 20016.

CAREER: Woman's Foreign Mission Society, New York, N.Y., editor, 1928-32; writer, 1936—. Past member of board of directors of Montclair Art Museum, Montclair Guidance Center, and Montclair Junior League (all in New Jersey). *Member:* Authors Guild of Authors League of America, Daughters of the American Revolution, Columbia Historical Society, Children's Book Guild of Washington, D.C.

WRITINGS—Children's books; under name Esther Wood: *Great Sweeping Day,* Longmans, Green, 1936; *Pedro's Coconut Skates,* Longmans, Green, 1938; *Silk and Satin Lane,* Longmans, Green, 1939; *Pepper Moon,* Longmans, Green, 1940; *Belinda Blue,* Longmans, Green, 1940; *The House in the Hoo,* Longmans, Green, 1941; *Silver Widgeon,* Longmans, Green, 1942.

Children's books; under name Esther Wood Brady: *Toliver's Secret,* Crown, 1976; *The Toad on Capitol Hill,* Crown, 1978.

WORK IN PROGRESS—Children's books: A historical novel set in Washington, D.C. in 1830; a mystery story set in old New York.

SIDELIGHTS: Esther Brady writes: "I must have been born with wandering feet and a compulsion to see what was beyond the next hill. In school I loved to read about children in foreign countries and always dreamed that someday I'd find a lost wallet or a pot of gold to pay for a trip around the world.

"I never found the pot of gold, but I did earn enough money to travel if I didn't mind traveling on a shoestring. After college I worked for several years in New York, then went with friends for a foot-loose summer of wandering around Europe.

"Two years later, in 1933, I found that a favorable rate of exchange made it possible to go around the world on a series of German freighters. Away from the port cities I found the colorful old China and old Japan and tropical Philippines I

had dreamed of. My most valuable insights and knowledge came from going with missionary nurses as they made their house calls on all classes of people. At length I came back with volumes of notes, a suitcase full of sketches, and a dozen ideas for children's stories.

"A month later I married, and happily put away my passport. We had two little girls and in the next seven years I produced seven books as well. But when the war disrupted our lives and my growing children needed more attention I gave up writing—for a while, I thought. It was thirty years before I got back to it.

"The life of a suburban housewife was a happy one. When our children were in college we moved to Washington, D.C., for the Space Age was upon us and my husband became part of that great venture.

"Because I had recently discovered that my very slow reading ability was due to dyslexia, I became interested in children with that handicap. For ten years I did volunteer tutoring in public schools, and hunted constantly for easy books of high quality for my reluctant readers. This brought me back to my own writing career.

"*Toliver's Secret* was originally much shorter and simpler than it turned out to be when published. The editors at Crown urged me to enlarge it, and I found myself researching more details and absorbed in my second love—history.

"I had grown up with a feeling for history from my grandparents, whose ancestors were early colonists. Because no one in my husband's family ever threw away a letter, our attic has tin boxes crammed with letters from many generations. In addition there are boxes of shawls and mitts and shoe-buckles and tall combs and steel-rimmed glasses. I feel I know all the people who wore them because of their intimate letters. The characters in my books are imaginary, but their times and life-styles seem very real to me.

"I still love to travel, but have not seen the Orient again. We have traveled in Turkey and Greece and several times in Italy, my favorite, as well as other European countries. In the summers we go to a cottage in Leland, Michigan, where I write."

* * *

BRADY, Michael   1928-

PERSONAL: Born December 4, 1928, in Allahabad, India; son of Frank (a soldier) and Kate (Alcock) Brady; married Patricia Catherine Davis, August 18, 1952; children: Kate Alexandra, Marianne Elizabeth. *Education:* University of London, B.Sc., 1948. *Home:* 3 Marlborough Court, Pembroke Rd., London W.8, England. *Agent:* Maximilian Becker, 115 East 82nd St., New York, N.Y. 10028.

CAREER: McNeil & Barry Ltd., Calcutta, India, executive assistant in Tea Division, 1950-52; Trans Empire Oils Ltd., Calgary, Alberta, economic statistician, 1952-57; A. C. Neilsen & Co., London, England, client service executive with TV Index, 1957-58; Beecham Group Ltd., London, marketing director, 1958-64; Allen, Brady & Marsh Ltd. (advertising agency), London, managing director, 1964-76; writer, 1976—. *Military service:* British Army, 1948-50; became lieutenant. *Member:* Marketing Society, Institute of Marketing, Market Research Society.

WRITINGS: American Surrender (novel), Dell, 1979; *The Coda Alliance* (novel), Dell, 1980.

WORK IN PROGRESS: Another thriller, publication expected in 1981.

SIDELIGHTS: Brady wrote: "I gave up a successful business career because it no longer interested me and I no longer found it a challenge. My principal interests are, and always have been, world affairs and military doctrine. The demands of a business life gave me little time to pursue these interests in depth.

"I believe passionately (and am not embarrassed by the word) in freedom. I am acutely aware that nation-states based on liberal democracy are, in historical terms, a very recent advent, and that their ability to survive in a world where the vast majority of states are characterized by very different internal political structures and external objectives is by no means proven.

"There is amongst the people of democracies a complacent assumption that, because democracy is 'best,' it will inevitably prosper. Unfortunately, the lessons of history do not support this comforting proposition. Whether we like it or not, and however unpalatable a truth it may be, history is overwhelming in its evidence that only the strong survive, and further that strength is not only, often not even predominantly, a matter of military and industrial strength, but a matter of national will. This 'national will' expresses itself in the preparedness of a people to pay both in blood and money to defend their societies. Furthermore, in the military environment of today, the survival of a nation depends on its preparedness to spend money on defense *before* a conflict arises and also on the clear perception by a potential adversary that the people of that nation have the will to wage war in their own defense.

"I am only too aware that in popular jargon these views brand me as a hawk. However, pejorative epithets such as 'hawk' and 'dove' are very poor substitutes for informed and rational debate.

"I took up writing after leaving business for two reasons: it was a new challenge and I wished to express my views. Originally I wrote a fictional account of a third world war, but was advised that it was too 'serious' to reach a large audience. *American Surrender* was an attempt to fictionalize three basic propositions—my belief that western Europe no longer has the will to defend itself, my fear that America may be losing hers, and the probability that when Russia achieves decisive strategic nuclear superiority over America the war will be lost without being fought (the best that could be hoped for under such calamitous circumstances).

"My second book, while set in contemporary political context, is far more of a straightforward action-thriller."

*   *   *

BRAITHWAITE, Max 1911-

PERSONAL: Born December 7, 1911, in Nokomis, Saskatchewan, Canada; son of George Albert Warner (a lawyer) and Mary (Copeland) Braithwaite; married Aileen Treleaven, October 12, 1935; children: Beryl Braithwaite Hart, Sharon Braithwaite Siamon, Christopher, Sylvia Braithwaite Skeen, Colin. *Education:* Attended University of Saskatchewan. *Politics:* None. *Religion:* Protestant. *Home address:* P.O. Box 163, Port Carling, Ontario, Canada.

CAREER: Teacher in rural Saskatchewan, 1931-40; freelance writer, 1945—. Member of Orangeville town council, 1964-66. *Military service:* Canadian Navy, 1941-45; became lieutenant commander. *Member:* Writers Union of Canada, Association of Canadian Television and Radio Artists (life member), Academy of Canadian Authors. *Awards, honors:* Stephen Leacock Memorial Medal for Humor, 1972, for *The*

Night We Stole the Mountie's Car; awards from Institute for Education by Radio-Television at Ohio State University for educational radio and television scripts.

WRITINGS: (With E. S. Lambert) *We Live in Ontario* (textbook), Book Society of Canada, 1957; *There's No Place Like Home* (textbook), Book Society of Canada, 1959; *Land, Water, and People* (textbook), Van Nostrand, 1961; *Why Shoot the Teacher* (humor), McClelland & Stewart, 1965; *Canada: Wonderland of Surprises*, Dodd, 1967; *Servant or Master?: A Case Book of Mass Media*, Book Society of Canada, 1968; *Never Sleep Three in a Bed* (humor), Dodd, 1969.

The Western Plains, Natural Science of Canada, 1970; *The Night We Stole the Mountie's Car* (humor), McClelland & Stewart, 1971; *A Privilege and a Pleasure* (novel), J. J. Douglas, 1973; *It's the Family Way* (textbook), Book Society of Canada, 1973; *Max Braithwaite's Ontario* (travel book), J. J. Douglas, 1974; *Sick Kids* (history of Toronto's Hospital for Sick Children), McClelland & Stewart, 1974; *The Hungry Thirties*, Natural Science of Canada, 1977; *Lusty Winter* (novel), McClelland & Stewart, 1978; *The Commodore's Barge Is Alongside* (humor), McClelland & Stewart, 1979; *McGruber's Folly*, McClelland & Stewart, 1980.

Juveniles: *Voices of the Wild*, McClelland & Stewart, 1962; *The Cure Searchers*, Ryerson, 1962; *The Mystery of the Muffled Man*, Little, Brown, 1962; *The Valley of the Vanishing Birds*, Little, Brown, 1963; *The Young Reporter*, Ryerson, 1963.

Author of several hundred radio scripts, dozens of television scripts, and film scripts for National Board of Canada, including "Why Shoot the Teacher," released by Fraser Productions in 1977. Contributor to magazines in Canada and the United States, including *Maclean's Magazine, Chatelaine, Liberty, Saturday Night,* and *Canadian Home Journal.*

SIDELIGHTS: Braithwaite told *CA:* "I have worked hard at one thing or another since I was twelve years old. Writing was the only thing I ever learned to do moderately well. I began writing magazine articles, radio plays, and short stories while teaching in rural Saskatchewan during the 1930's.

"I can think of no better way a person can live and earn a living than by writing ... anything ... but especially novels. The novel is the only form in which a writer can express himself freely, using the language he needs and stating his views of life, whatever they may be, without an editor, producer, or sponsor looking over his shoulder. It is only within the last ten to fifteen years that Canadian book writers have been able to make a living, that Canadian books have become part of school literature courses, and that Canadian publishers have specialized in the publishing of books by Canadians. These are the great days of Canadian writing and I'm proud to be a part of them. Probably my greatest satisfaction (and it's all been satisfying) was when 'Why Shoot the Teacher' was made into a feature film that has been seen by thousands of people in Canada, the United States, England, Europe, Australia, and elsewhere."

AVOCATIONAL INTERESTS: Walking, swimming, canoeing, bucking wood, birdwatching.

*   *   *

BRAKE, Mike 1936-

PERSONAL: Born January 14, 1936, in Plymouth, Devonshire, England; son of Cecil (a clerk) and Hilda (Brookes)

Brake; divorced; children: Johanna. *Education:* University of Leeds, B.A., 1967; London School of Economics and Political Science, London, M.Sc., 1968, Ph.D., 1977. *Politics:* Socialist. *Office:* Keenes College, University of Kent at Canterbury, Canterbury, Kent CT2 7NZ, England.

CAREER: Actor and dancer in various theatrical productions in England, 1954-59; occupational therapist in hospital service in England, 1960-62; British Probation Service, London, England, probation officer and youth worker, 1962-64; Middlesex Polytechnic, London, lecturer in social psychology and criminology, 1968-69; North East London Polytechnic, London, lecturer in social psychology and sociology of deviance, 1969-71; University of Bradford, Bradford, England, lecturer in sociology, 1971-75; University of Kent at Canterbury, Canterbury, England, lecturer in sociology, 1975-79; Carleton University, Ottawa, Canada, visiting professor of sociology, 1979-80. Visiting professor at California State University, summers, 1969, 1970, and 1972. *Member:* British Sociological Association.

WRITINGS: Radical Social Work, Pantheon, 1975; *Radical Social Work and Practice,* Edward Arnold, 1979; *The Sociology of Youth Culture,* Routledge & Kegan Paul, 1979; *Sexual Life,* Penguin, 1981. Contributor of articles to journals in his field.

WORK IN PROGRESS: Research into human sexual relations.

SIDELIGHTS: Brake told *CA:* "Unlike many professors, I came from an unskilled working class family. I entered the ballet, but after an accident, returned to the unskilled working class. I then worked in occupational therapy with mentally ill patients. After working in the youth service and probation service, I became a student at the age of twenty-eight and went on to be an academic. I thus had an extremely distinct view of various types of oppressions both of a class nature and, in various forms, outside class dimensions.

"My interests lie in the forms of class and patriarchial oppression which manifests itself in contemporary life, and in the notion of both radical social work and radical therapy. Obviously the roots of oppression for me lie in poverty. Keeping working people at a low level of material resources prevents any real development of self. This has become a bourgeois luxury in our society. I am interested in assisting people to see beyond the obfuscations of this ideology, realize their relation to the world, and then act to change it personally and collectively.

"My interests in youth culture come from my theatrical background. It seems that much of the youth culture is a form of living theatre which says, more succinctly and immediately, what young people experience and feel than the more formal media of literature. My interest is in human freedom, but not dislocated from a political context of struggle. In this sense we owe much to feminists, gay liberationists, and black activists."

*   *   *

BRANDON-COX, Hugh   1917-

PERSONAL: Born in 1917, in Great Britain; son of Clive (a military colonel) and Eva (a poet) Brandon-Cox; married Ulla-Maija Inkeri, December, 1972 (died, 1977). *Education:* Attended private boys' school in Marlborough, England. *Home:* Moorgate Cottage, Blickling, Norwich, Norfolk, England.

CAREER: Filmmaker for the Educational Foundation for Visual Needs among the Lapps of northern Norway, 1963-

64; surveyor of nature reserves in Poland, 1964-65; naturalist and researcher in Norway, beginning 1965; painter and writer, 1974—. *Member:* Zoological Society (fellow).

WRITINGS: The Trail of the Arctic Nomads, W. M. Kimber, 1968; *Hovran: Swedish Bird Lake,* Tidens, 1968; *Summer of a Million Wings: Arctic Quest for the Sea-Eagle,* Taplinger, 1975. Founding editor of *Westcountryman.*

SIDELIGHTS: Brandon-Cox writes: "I learned Swedish as a boy. After a period of great stress in 1964, I met Ulla-Maija, who changed my life completely. We traveled thousands of miles together each year, searching for knowledge to make nature films. She was from Finland and had a knowledge of the wilderness that was unique.

"Just when we had finished repairing a very old cottage in the Norfolk countryside, Ulla-Maija died, after a few days' illness, at thirty-seven. Since then, I have survived by working on my paintings, but I am determined to find the bridge that will connect me with her again."

BIOGRAPHICAL/CRITICAL SOURCES: Ian Browning, *Call of the Wilderness,* East Countryman Press.

*   *   *

BRANN, Eva T(oni) H(elene)   1929-

PERSONAL: Born January 21, 1929, in Berlin, Germany; came to the United States in 1941, naturalized citizen, 1947; daughter of Edgar (a physician) and Paula (Sklarz) Brann. *Education:* Brooklyn College (now of City University of New York), B.A., 1950; Yale University, M.A., 1951, Ph.D., 1956. *Home:* 71 Wagner St., Annapolis, Md. 21401. *Office:* St. John's College, Annapolis, Md. 21404.

CAREER: Stanford University, Stanford, Calif., instructor in archaeology, 1956-57; St. John's College, Annapolis, Md., tutor, 1957—, Addison E. Mullikin Tutor, 1971—. Arnold Distinguished Visiting Professor at Whitman College, 1978-79. Member of staff of American Agora Excavations at Athens. Member of Institute for Advanced Study, Princeton, N.J., 1958-59. Member of U.S. Advisory Commission for International Educational and Cultural Affairs, 1976-78. *Awards, honors:* Fellow of American School of Classical Studies at Athens, 1952-53; Sibley fellow of Phi Beta Kappa in Greece, 1953-54; fellow of Woodrow Wilson International Center for Scholars, 1976-77.

WRITINGS: Late Geometric and Protoattic Pottery, Princeton University Press, 1962; (translator) Jacob Klein, *Greek Mathematical Thought and the Origin of Algebra,* M.I.T. Press, 1968; (contributor) Leo Paul S. de Alvarez, editor, *The Gettysburg Address and American Constitutionalism,* University of Dallas Press, 1976; (contributor) Samuel S. Kutler, editor, *Essays in Honor of Jacob Klein,* St. John's College Press, 1976; *Paradoxes of Education in a Republic,* University of Chicago Press, 1979; (author of introduction) Raymond Larson, translator and editor, *Plato's Republic,* AHM Publishing, 1979. Contributor to scholarly journals.

WORK IN PROGRESS: Research on the imagination.

SIDELIGHTS: Eva Brann has made a recording, "On the Declaration of Independence," released by Nightingale-Conant Corp. in 1976.

*   *   *

BRAUDEL, Fernand (Paul)   1902-

PERSONAL: Born August 24, 1902, in Lumeville, Meuse, France; son of Charles (a school principal) and Louise (Falet) Braudel; married Paule Pradel, September 14, 1933;

children: Marie-Pierre, Francoise. *Education:* University of Paris, Sorbonne, qualified as teacher, 1923, received doctorate in literature, 1947. *Home:* 59 rue Brillat-Savarin, 75013 Paris, France. *Office:* Maison des Sciences de l'Homme, 54 boulevard Raspail, 75270 Paris, France.

CAREER: High school history teacher in Algiers, Algeria, 1924-32, and Paris, France, 1932-35; University of Sao Paulo, Sao Paulo, Brazil, professor of history of civilization, 1935-37; Ecole Pratique des Hautes Etudes, Paris, director of studies in fourth section, 1937-39, and in sixth section (economic and social sciences), beginning 1947, president of sixth section, beginning 1956; College de France, Paris, professor of modern history, 1949-72, honorary professor, 1972—; Maison des Sciences de l'Homme, Paris, administrator, 1963—. Visiting professor at University of Chicago, 1968. *Military service:* French Army, 1939-45; prisoner of war in Germany, 1940-45; became lieutenant. *Member:* Haut Comite de la Langue Francaise, Commission des Archives Diplomatiques, British Academy, American Philosophical Society, Polish Academy of Science, Academy of History (Spain), Academy of History (Argentina), Bavarian Academy of Sciences, Belgrade Academy of Science, Heidelberg Academy of Science. *Awards, honors:* Officier de la Legion d'Honneur; Commandeur de L'Ordre National du Merite; honorary doctorates from universities of Oxford, Sao Paulo, Brussels, Cologne, Geneva, Madrid, Warsaw, Padua, Chicago, Florence, Cambridge, London, Hull, Leiden, East Anglia, and St. Andrews.

WRITINGS: La Mediterranee et le monde mediterraneen a l'epoque de Philippe II, Colin, 1949, two-volume revised edition, 1966, translation by Sian Reynolds published as *The Mediterranean and the Mediterranean World in the Age of Philip II,* Harper, Volume I, 1972, Volume II, 1974; (with Ruggiero Romano) *Navires et merchandises a l'entree du port de Livourne, 1547-1611* (title means "Vessels and Merchandise Entering the Port of Leghorn, 1547-1611"), Colin, 1951.

(With Suzanne Baille) *Le Monde actuel* (title means "The Contemporary World"), Belin, 1963; (editor) A. Jara and others, *Temas de historia economica hispano-americana* (essays; title means "Themes in the Economic History of Spanish America"), Mouton, 1965; *Civilisation materielle et capitalisme, XVe-XVIIIe siecle,* Colin, 1967, three-volume revised edition, 1979, translation of original edition by Miriam Kochan published as *Capitalism and Material Life, 1400-1800,* Harper, 1973; *Ecrits sur l'histoire* (title means "Writings on History"), Flammarion, 1969; *Afterthoughts on Material Civilization and Capitalism* (translation by Patricia M. Ranum of lectures delivered at 1976 Johns Hopkins Symposium in Comparative History), Johns Hopkins Press, 1977.

Editor of *Annales,* 1956-68, and co-editor, with Ernest Labrousse, of *Histoire economique et sociale de la France,* Presses Universitaires de France, 1970—.

SIDELIGHTS: Fernand Braudel is universally recognized as one of the greatest of contemporary historians. He has been immensely influential, not only as a writer and a teacher, but as leader of the school of historical thought associated with the journal *Annales.* In a "Personal Testimony" published in the *Journal of Modern History,* Braudel described his childhood in a small French village, his early passion for poetry (of which he wrote a great deal as a student), and his entirely orthodox training as a historian at the Sorbonne. He was not a particularly enthusiastic student, he says—his vocation for history came later—but, being blessed with a phenomenal memory, he graduated without difficulty.

Braudel began his career in 1924 at a high school in Algiers, conscientiously passing on what he had been taught—"a superficial history of events ... of politics, of great men." Casting around for a theme for his doctoral thesis, he eventually settled on the Mediterranean policy of Philip II of Spain. Braudel became the proud possessor of an ancient movie camera, with which he learned to photograph documents at the rate of between two and three thousand pages a day: "I was no doubt the first user of true microfilms, which I developed myself and later read, through long days and nights, with a simple magic lantern." Much of this research was conducted during vacations while Braudel was still a teacher in Algiers, and he believes that "this spectacle, the Mediterranean as seen from the opposite shore, upside down, had considerable impact on my vision of history."

Braudel's vision of history was further influenced during the 1930's by the *Annales* historians. *Annales* had been founded in 1929 by Lucien Febvre and Marc Bloch to express their impatience with traditional academic historiography and their demands for a new approach. History, they believed, was not the biography of a few great men; nor was it a steady progress toward some kind of social or spiritual millenium. Rather it was an endless struggle between man's intentions and the limitations imposed by his environment and by his own nature. It followed that "history could not transform itself except by incorporating all the sciences of man as auxiliaries to our profession—by mastering the techniques of the geographer, the economist, the psychologist, the sociologist."

A disciple and soon a close friend of Febvre, Braudel adopted the *Annales* approach in his research for his thesis, the scope of which became steadily wider and deeper as the years went by, so that at times it seemed that the work would never be completed. When at last, in 1939, he was ready to write his thesis, history itself intervened. Braudel served as an army lieutenant on the Maginot Line, was captured, and spent the remainder of the war years as a prisoner in Germany, first at Mainz, then from 1942 to 1945 in a special camp for rebellious prisoners at Luebeck. He was *recteur* of the prison camp—the leader of the French prisoners—but he nevertheless found time, during his imprisonment, to write his long-deferred thesis. Without a single note, a single document, a single book—relying entirely on his prodigious memory—he wrote in a series of school copy books a work which has been described as a "majestic monument of twentieth-century historiography." Braudel returned to France in 1945 and resumed his post at the Ecole Pratique des Hautes Etudes in Paris. He successfully defended his thesis and received his Sorbonne doctorate in 1947, and in 1949 the work was published as *La Mediterranee et le monde mediterraneen a l'epoque de Philippe II.* A second edition in two volumes, much revised and extended, followed in 1966.

The first volume is a "geohistory" of the entire Mediterranean area. In this account, such traditional themes as war, diplomacy, and politics are thoroughly explored. What distinguishes the book, however, is the attention Braudel gives to geography and climate, to transportation, communications, and commerce, and to what one critic called the "barely visible forces of tradition rarely understood or even acknowledged by the participants." Braudel shows how in the sixteenth century these and other factors produced in the two great basins of the Mediterranean, east and west, the embattled empires of Spain and Turkey. "Politics," Braudel has said, "merely follows the outlines of an underlying reality. These two Mediterraneans, commanded by warring rulers, were physically, economically, and culturally different from each other. Each was a separate time zone.'' Hugh Trevor-Roper said of this volume that, ''with its marvellous command of the material, its power to evoke, from literature and history, ancient and modern, Christian or Muslim, the essential timeless character, and the social and economic consequences, of mountains and plains, inland seas and islands, it convinces us that we are in the presence of a great work not merely of scholarship but of imaginative historical literature. From the beginning the multidimensional character of the work is clear. Geography is always related to form of society; mountains and valleys are alive with people; everywhere villages and cities come to life; and the language lives too, vivid, fresh and supple, worthy of the theme.''

There was no less praise for the second volume, which explained how the failure of agriculture to keep pace with a massive increase in the Mediterranean population, and the widening gulf between rich and poor, east and west, led the two empires inevitably into the conflict that ended with Spain's victory at Lepanto in 1571. *The Mediterranean and the Mediterranean World* has been described as ''a work of great seminal influence regarded since its first appearance . . . as the chief masterpiece of the contemporary French historical school,'' and as ''probably the most significant historical work to appear since World War II.'' J. H. Elliott wrote that ''no other book I know of illustrates more graphically the way in which historical writing has been renovated in our time by contact with other disciplines—geography, economics, and the social sciences.'' And J. H. Plumb, describing the work as almost unequalled as ''an intellectual and scholarly tour de force,'' went on: ''Each paragraph is not only erudite, but more often than not pierced with novel insights, at times of such daring that Braudel, who is personally present on every page, rapidly warns the reader not to take them as anything but tentative suggestions.''

Civilisation materielle et capitalisme, translated as *Capitalism and Material Life, 1400-1800*, is a much more general work, studying conditions throughout the world in the four centuries preceding the era of capitalism. It shows how the ''population explosion'' that began in the sixteenth century outstripped the supply of food and other goods, leading in many parts of the world to the same sort of extreme disparity between the living standards of rich and poor that Braudel had already noted in *The Mediterranean*. He analyzes staple diets, housing, and clothes throughout the world, then turns his attention to the three major factors in the growth of the industrial revolution—the spread of technology, the development of sophisticated monetary and credit systems, and the rise of the city. He concludes that the ''capitalist spirit'' of certain medieval towns in northern Europe gave birth to the era of ''pre-capitalism, which is the source of all the economic creativeness in the world,'' as well as ''all the most burdensome exploitation of man by man.''

Hugh Trevor-Roper called this ''a marvelously Braudelian book. It has all the genial erudition, the profusion and variety of illustration, the stimulating (and sometimes paradoxical) suggestions, the delightfully unacademic vitality of his great work [*The Mediterranean*]; but it is more difficult, at first, to deduce the underlying theme. It is also—though this will irritate scholars more than laymen—sadly lacking in documentation, without notes or references.'' J. H. Plumb complained of ''the excess of factual errors'' in the book, ''occasional dubious and portentous generalizations, a cloudy overall structure, and the omission of what for many historians are the critical agents of change.'' Nevertheless, Plumb praised Braudel's ''vivid and exciting style,'' and wrote that ''again and again he strengthens the conviction

that this is the way history will go, and must go.'' Braudel gave a brief preview of the work begun in *Capitalism and Material Life* in the lectures he delivered at Johns Hopkins in 1976. The lectures, translated and published as *Afterthoughts on Material Civilization and Capitalism*, made it clear that this major work-in-progress is expected to run to three, not two, volumes.

The Mediterranean and the Mediterranean World in the Age of Philip II remains the finest achievement to date of the *Annales* school, of which Trevor-Roper has written: ''No group of scholars has had a greater impact, or a more fertilizing effect, on the study of history in this century than the French historians of 'the Annales school.''' When Lucien Febvre died in 1956, Braudel succeeded him as editor of *Annales* and leader of the *Annales* school, which has flourished under his guidance. In 1968 he surrendered the editorship of the journal to younger men, and in 1972 he retired from his professorship at the College de France. He remains president of the economic and social sciences section of the Ecole Pratique des Hautes Etudes, the famous sixth section, and is also administrator of the Maison des Sciences de l'Homme.

BIOGRAPHICAL/CRITICAL SOURCES: Journal of Economic History, November, 1950; *Journal of Modern History*, December, 1950, December, 1972 (Braudel issue); *Times Literary Supplement*, February 15, 1968; *New York Review of Books*, May 3, 1973, December 13, 1973; *History*, June, 1974; *New York Times Book Review*, November 10, 1974; *Time*, May 23, 1977; *Times Higher Education Supplement*, December 9, 1977.

*   *   *

BRAUNTHAL, Alfred   1898(?)-1980

OBITUARY NOTICE: Born c. 1898 in Vienna, Austria; died February 4, 1980, in Boston, Mass. Union executive, journalist, and author of books, including *Salvation and the Perfect Society: The Eternal Quest*. Braunthal was secretary-general of the International Confederation of Free Trade Unions, and worked in Europe from 1950 until his retirement in 1968. He also served as research director for the Hatters and Millinery Workers Union. As a journalist, Braunthal had worked for the *Leipziger Volkszeitung*. Obituaries and other sources: *New York Times*, February 10, 1980.

*   *   *

BRAY, Virginia Elizabeth Nuckolls   1895(?)-1979

OBITUARY NOTICE: Born c. 1895 in Dillon, Mont.; died December 20, 1979, in Washington, D.C. Clinical psychologist, educator, and author of several books on psychology as well as volumes of poetry, short stories, and humorous essays. Bray was a clinical psychologist with the Pennsylvania State Department of Welfare, the Child Guidance Center, and Harrisburg State Hospital. She also taught psychology at Richmond Professional Institute, Richmond, Va., and at Westminster College in New Wilmington, Pa. Obituaries and other sources: *Washington Post*, December 23, 1979.

*   *   *

BREAN, Herbert (J.)   1907-1973

PERSONAL: Born December 10, 1907, in Detroit, Mich.; died of a heart attack, May 7, 1973, in New York, N.Y.; son of Walter Joseph and Eva R. (Dumas) Brean; married Dorothy Skeman, October 6, 1934; children: Judith Ann Travers, Martha Elizabeth Horne. *Education:* University of Michigan, A.B., 1929. *Home:* 500 East 77th St., New York, N.Y. 10021, and 9-39 Vessup Bay, St. Thomas, Virgin Islands 00801.

CAREER: Reporter and rewrite man for United Press (now United Press International) in New York City, and assistant bureau manager in Detroit, Mich.; *Detroit Times*, Detroit, reporter, columnist, feature writer, assistant city editor, and picture editor, 1933-43; *Time, Life*, and *Fortune*, Detroit, news bureau chief, 1943-44, New York City, associate editor of *Life*, 1944, staff writer, 1953-62, assistant editor of national affairs, 1953-73. Lecturer in mystery writing at Columbia and New York Universities. Consultant to General Motors Corp. *Member:* Mystery Writers of America (national director), Crime Writers Association, Baker Street Irregulars, Authors League, Association of Vessup Bay Estates (president), Players Club, Scarsdale Golf Club. *Awards, honors:* American Institute of Arts and Letters fellowship; two Edgar nominations from Mystery Writers of America.

WRITINGS—All mystery novels; all published by Morrow, unless otherwise noted: *Wilders Walk Away*, 1948; *The Darker the Night*, 1949; *Hardly a Man Is Now Alive: A Mystery Novel*, 1950; *The Clock Strikes Thirteen*, 1952; *A Matter of Fact*, 1956; *The Traces of Brillhart: A Novel of Suspense, Detection, and a Curious Immortality*, Harper, 1960; *The Traces of Merrilee*, 1966.

Nonfiction: *How to Stop Smoking*, Vanguard, 1951, revised edition, Penguin, 1975; (editor) *The Mystery Writers Handbook*, Harper, 1956; *How to Stop Drinking: Science Looks at Your Drinking Habits*, Holt, 1958, revised edition published as *A Handbook for Drinkers—And for Those Who Want to Stop*, Collier, 1963; (editor with others) *The Music of Life: Notes, Quotes, and Anecdotes About the Fabulous Music-Makers Who Filled a Tuneful Quarter Century of American Popular Music*, Time, 1962; *The Only Diet That Works*, Morrow, 1965. Also editor of *The Life Treasury of American Folklore*, 1961.

Contributor of fiction stories to magazines and articles to professional journals.

SIDELIGHTS: Brean's first four mysteries revolve around the sleuth Reynold Frame. A free-lance writer and photographer, Frame uncovers the wrongdoer in *Wilders Walk Away, The Darker the Night, Hardly A Man Is Now Alive,* and *The Clock Strikes Thirteen*. These mysteries received favorable reviews, with critic C. K. Kilpatrick venturing to declare *Wilders Walk Away* "a classic in modern crime fiction." Brean abandoned detective Frame in his subsequent novels, and his most successful and highly acclaimed mystery was the later *Traces of Brillhart* about a Broadway playboy who is supposed to be murdered but is apparently still alive. L. G. Oxford praised the novel as "a beautiful sleight-of-hand," while Anthony Boucher asserted that although "it falls just short of the Carr-Christie-Queen standards . . . this is still a who-, how- and whydunit in the classic grand manner."

The nonfiction book, *How to Stop Drinking*, also fared well with the critics. "A highly informative and readable book," contended a *Booklist* reviewer, "the author speaks not as a dour temperance crusader but as a realist, frequently a witty one, who is fully aware of alcohol's uses and abuses." A *Wisconsin Library Bulletin* critic concurred, assessing the book as "practical, informative, and useful for all collections."

BIOGRAPHICAL/CRITICAL SOURCES: Wisconsin Library Bulletin, May, 1958; *Booklist*, May 1, 1958; *Library Journal*, May 1, 1960; *New York Times Book Review*, May 15, 1960; *San Francisco Chronicle*, June 5, 1960.

OBITUARIES: New York Times, May 9, 1973; *AB Bookman's Weekly*, May 25, 1973.*

*   *   *

BREASTED, Charles   1898(?)-1980

OBITUARY NOTICE: Born c. 1898; died January 16, 1980, in Encinitas, Calif. Journalist, executive, editor, and author of *Pioneer to the Past: The Story of James Henry Breasted*. Breasted, who acted as an aide to his father, archaeologist James Henry Breasted, was executive secretary of the Oriental Institute of the University of Chicago, from 1927 to 1936. He was the first science editor of *Life* magazine, and held that position for six years. After World War II he worked as a free-lance writer. Obituaries and other sources: *New York Times*, January 18, 1980.

*   *   *

BREITBART, Vicki   1942-

PERSONAL: Born December 30, 1942, in New York, N.Y.; daughter of M. T. and Belle (Rich) Tanenhaus; married Eric Breitbart (a filmmaker), December, 1966; children: Lela, Joshua. *Education:* Sarah Lawrence College, B.A., 1963; Bank Street College of Education, M.S., 1971; New York University, M.S.W., 1980.

CAREER: New York University, Institute for Developmental Studies, New York City, classroom teacher, 1963-68; director of "head start" program at Children's Aid Society, 1968; Bank Street College of Education, New York City, instructor, 1968-72; Kingsborough Community College of the City University of New York, Brooklyn, N.Y., adjunct lecturer, 1972-78; Brookdale Hospital, Brooklyn, N.Y., educator in "preparing for parenting" program, 1978. Consultant to Odeon Films.

WRITINGS: The Day Care Book: The Why, What, and How of Community Day Care, Knopf, 1974; (with Judith Danoff and Elinor Barr) *Open for Children*, McGraw, 1977.

*   *   *

BREMER, Francis J(ohn)   1947-

PERSONAL: Born January 26, 1947, in New York, N.Y.; son of Francis J. (an accountant) and Marie (Degeilh) Bremer; married Barbara Woodlock, August 24, 1968; children: Heather Jeanne, Kristin Lynn, Megan Elayne. *Education:* Fordham University, B.A., 1968; Columbia University, M.A., 1969, Ph.D., 1972; also attended Union Theological Seminary, New York, N.Y. *Home:* 2225 Coventry Rd., Lancaster, Pa. 17601. *Office:* Department of History, Millersville State College, Millersville, Pa. 17551.

CAREER: Thomas More College, Fort Mitchell, Ky., instructor, 1971-72, assistant professor of history, 1972-74, associate professor of history and director of humanities enrichment program, 1974-77; Millersville State College, Millersville, Pa., associate professor of history, 1977—. Member of Pennsylvania State Coordinating Committee for National History Day. *Member:* Institute of Early American History and Culture (associate), American Association of University Professors, Organization of American Historians, Columbia University Seminar for Early American History. *Awards, honors:* Woodrow Wilson fellow, 1971; National Endowment for the Humanities fellow, 1975; American Philosophical Society fellow, 1978.

WRITINGS: The Puritan Experiment: New England Society From Bradford to Edwards, St. Martin's, 1976; (editor with Alden T. Vaughan) *Puritan New England: Essays on Reli-*

gion, Society, and Culture, St. Martin's, 1977; (with G. Terry Madonna) *Pennsbury Manor: The American Home of William Penn*, Pennsylvania Historical and Museum Commission, 1980; (editor) *Anne Hutchinson, Challenger of the Puritan Zion*, Robert E. Krieger, 1980. Contributor of about thirty articles and reviews to history journals.

WORK IN PROGRESS: A survey of American intellectual history, publication by St. Martin's expected in 1982; a study of trans-Atlantic communication and idea formation in the seventeenth-century Anglo-American Puritan community.

SIDELIGHTS: Bremer told *CA:* "My interest in history originated with a sense of enjoyment experienced from reading historical works and visiting historical restorations in New England while a youth. History has remained fun. My concern with the Puritan past derives from an interest in the relationship between values and behavior and a belief that the communal social philosophy of the early New Englanders offers a contrast to contemporary norms which can provide insight into our society and its problems. I see my writing as an extension of my teaching, offering an opportunity to develop certain themes at greater length and a chance to communicate with (hopefully) a larger audience.

"I am currently very interested in pursuing insights from anthropology and psychology into the non-rational bases of attitudes and beliefs held by the men and women of the seventeenth century. In particular, I am trying to assess the scope of some correspondence networks in the Anglo-American community and the ways in which individuals were influenced towards the adoption of certain views by social forces such as friendship. It is my belief that intellectual historians must make a greater effort to relate the acceptance of ideas to the social milieu in which men lived. I believe that anthropological network theory and psychological studies on attraction and attitude formation may enable historians to move into these new areas."

*　　*　　*

BRESLIN, Catherine   1936-

PERSONAL: Born February 22, 1936, in Springfield, Mass.; daughter of James Edward (a pediatrician) and Adeline (Devereaux) Breslin. *Education:* University of Toronto, B.A. (with honors), 1957. *Politics:* "Gadfly." *Religion:* "Ex-Catholic." *Agent:* Wendy Weil, Julian Bach Literary Agency, 3 East 48th St., New York, N.Y. 10017.

CAREER: Writer.

WRITINGS: The Mistress Condition: New Options in Sex, Love, and Other Female Pleasures (nonfiction), Dutton, 1976; *Unholy Child* (fiction), Dial, 1979. Contributor to periodicals, including *New York, Redbook, Cosmopolitan, Family Circle*, and *Esquire*.

WORK IN PROGRESS: "I am presently brewing a novel about marriage and death, targeted for 1981 publication. For my next effort, I hope to become hooked on a funny, sexy subject."

SIDELIGHTS: Unholy Child, Breslin's first novel, begins as a pregnant nun delivers her own baby in a convent, then smothers it and hides it in a wastebasket. When her actions are discovered a court trial results. The rest of the novel describes the effects of the case on Sister Angela, her fellow nuns, the press, and the community at large.

"From this summary, one might conclude that Catherine Breslin's first novel is sensational in style," observed Joseph McLellan. "But considering her subject matter, the treatment is quite sober and restrained once she gets past the ini-

tial, unavoidable blood and guts." Although McLellan remarked that the book "could have benefited from judicious trimming," he praised Breslin's well drawn characters and her understanding of the subject. *Unholy Child*'s "best moments make the occasional bouts of distaste or tedium worth enduring."

Breslin told *CA:* "My particular fields of expertise in writing are women, personal relationships in the post-sexual revolution; and in the winter months, skiing."

BIOGRAPHICAL/CRITICAL SOURCES: Washington Post, November 26, 1979.

*　　*　　*

BRESSETT, Kenneth E(dward)   1928-

PERSONAL: Born October 5, 1928, in Keene, N.H.; son of George (a printer) and Florence (Forkey) Bressett; married Bertha Britton, October 7, 1950; children: Philip, Richard, Mary. *Education:* Attended Dresser Business College, 1947-48. *Office:* 1220 Mound Ave., Racine, Wis. 53404.

CAREER: Professional coin photographer, 1947-49; Sentinel Printing & Publishing Co., Keene, N.H., member of staff, 1949-59; Western Publishing Co., Racine, Wis., head of editorial staff, 1959-69, manager of coin supply division, 1969—. Managing editor of *Whitman Numismatic Journal*, 1964-68. Speaker on numismatics. *Member:* American Numismatic Society (fellow), American Numismatic Association (life member), Canadian Numismatic Association (life member), Royal Numismatic Society (fellow). *Awards, honors:* Medal of merit from American Numismatic Association, 1966, for work with U.S. Assay Commission; presidential appointment from American Numismatic Association, 1978.

WRITINGS: (With Maurice Gould) *Alaska's Coinage Through the Years*, Whitman Publishing, 1960, 2nd edition (with Gould, Kay Dethridge, and Nancy Dethridge), 1965; (with Gould) *Hawaiian Coins, Tokens, and Paper Money*, Whitman Publishing, 1960, revised edition, 1961; (with Eric P. Newman) *The Fantastic 1804 Dollar*, Whitman Publishing, 1962; *A Guide Book of English Coins*, Western Publishing Co., 1962, 7th edition, 1975; *Let's Collect Coins*, Western Publishing Co., 1966, 7th edition, 1979; *Buying and Selling United States Coins*, Western Publishing Co., 1970, 10th edition, 1979; (contributor) Eric P. Newman and Richard G. Doty, editors, *Studies on Money in Early America*, American Numismatic Society, 1976.

Editor: R. S. Yeoman, *Handbook of United States Coins*, Western Publishing Co., 1963, 37th edition, in press; Yeoman, *Guide Book of United States Coins*, Western Publishing Co., 1963, 19th edition, in press; *Boy Scouts of America Merit Badge Handbook: Coin Collecting*, Boy Scouts of America, 1975; (with Abe Kosoff) *Official A.N.A. Grading Standards for U.S. Coins*, Western Publishing Co., 1977. Contributor to numismatic journals.

WORK IN PROGRESS: Research on American colonial coinage.

SIDELIGHTS: Bressett began collecting coins as a youth, trading most of his earnings as a grocery clerk for valuable coins he found in the store's cash drawer. When he realized he would never be able to afford to buy many of the coins he wanted to own, he built equipment to photograph coins. In the years that followed, he visited the country's leading museum collections and worked with coin experts, polishing his specialties, which include early American coins, odd or unusual money, and East Asian coins, particularly cast copper coins from China, Japan, and Korea. Now he shares his knowledge with beginners as well as veteran coin collectors through his books and journal contributions.

Bressett told *CA:* "As editor of the world's most widely used coin reference book, *Guide Book of United States Coins,* I have achieved my goal of helping others to enjoy the rewarding hobby of collecting coins for fun and entertainment."

BIOGRAPHICAL/CRITICAL SOURCES: Coin World, May 17, 1978.

*   *   *

BRIER, Royce 1894-1975

OBITUARY NOTICE: Born April 18, 1894, in River Falls, Wis.; died January 10, 1975. Journalist and author. Brier, who received the Pulitzer Prize for Journalism in 1934, was affiliated with the *San Francisco Chronicle* for twenty years. His books include *Crusade,* 1931, *Reach for the Moon,* 1934, *Last Boat From Beyrouth,* 1943, and *Western World,* 1946. Obituaries and other sources: *Who's Who in America,* 38th edition, Marquis, 1974; *Who Was Who in America,* 6th edition, Marquis, 1976.

*   *   *

BRIGGS, Jean 1925-

PERSONAL: Born January 7, 1925, in London, England; daughter of Charles (a civil servent) and Ethel (Stevenson) Carpenter; married William Briggs, July 28, 1949 (divorced, 1972). *Education:* King's College, London, B.A. (with honors), 1946, M.A., 1951. *Home:* 5 Denham Dr., Gants Hill, Ilford, Essex LG2 6QU, England.

CAREER: Teacher of English at various schools in London and Essex, England, 1946-62; Brentwood College of Education, Essex, lecturer in English literature, 1962-67; Essex County Council, Essex, director of Educational Closed Circuit Television, 1967-77; London Borough of Redbridge, London, educational adviser, 1977—.

WRITINGS: Jewels and Jewelry, Macmillan, 1967; (with Sidney Bridges, Anthony Kinsey, and Patricia Meldon) *Gifted Children and the Brentwood Experiment,* Pitman, 1969; *The Flame of the Borgias* (novel), Collins, 1974, Harper, 1975.

WORK IN PROGRESS: The Medici Diamond (tentative title), a novel about Giuliano de Medici; research on the Roman occupation of England and Shakespeare's possible Italian connections.

SIDELIGHTS: Jean Briggs writes: "An addiction for Venice stimulated my interest in the background material for my first novel, based on fifteenth- and sixteenth-century letters in Italy. My current novel belongs to the same Renaissance period. Both reflect my interest in forms of government, the nature of personal relationships, and the conflict between these and professional commitments (and/or claims of family ambition)."

*   *   *

BRIGHT, Greg 1951-

PERSONAL: Born April 11, 1951, in Gorseinon, United Kingdom; son of Kenneth (in hotel business) and Mary Elizabeth (in hotel business; maiden name, Hathaway) Bright. *Education:* Attended high school in London, England. *Politics:* None. *Religion:* None. *Address:* c/o Fontana Books, William Collins Sons & Co. Ltd., 14 St. James's Place, London SW1A 1PS, England.

CAREER: Free-lance maze designer, 1973—; writer, 1973—.

WRITINGS: Maze Book, Latimer, 1973, Pantheon, 1975; *Fontana Mazes,* Pantheon, 1975; *Visual Music,* Latimer, 1975; *Ten TV Plays,* Latimer, 1978; *Hole Maze,* Pantheon, 1979.

WORK IN PROGRESS: Musical composition.

*   *   *

BROCK, Michael George 1920-

PERSONAL: Born March 9, 1920, in Bromley, Kent, England; son of Laurence George (a civil servant) and Ellen Margery (Williams) Brock; married Eleanor Hope Morrison, July 28, 1949; children: George L., David M., Paul M. *Education:* Corpus Christi College, Oxford, B.A., 1940, M.A. (with first class honors), 1948. *Home:* 186 Woodstock Rd., Oxford OX2 7NQ, England. *Office:* Office of the Warden, Nuffield College, Oxford University, Oxford OX1 1NF, England.

CAREER: Oxford University, Oxford, England, fellow of Corpus Christi College and tutor in modern history and politics, 1950-66, university lecturer in modern history, 1951-70, vice-president and bursar of Wolfson College, 1967-76; University of Exeter, Exeter, England, professor of education and director of School of Education, 1977-78; Oxford University, warden of Nuffield College, 1978—. *Military service:* British Army, 1940-45; became captain. *Member:* Royal Historical Society (fellow), Athenaeum Club, Oxford Union Society. *Awards, honors:* Honorary fellow of Wolfson College, Oxford, 1977; emeritus fellow of Corpus Christi College, Oxford, 1977.

WRITINGS: The Great Reform Act, Hutchinson, 1973; (with wife, Eleanor Brock) *Letters of H. H. Asquith to Venetia Stanley,* two volumes, Oxford University Press, 1981. Contributor to *Collier's Encyclopedia.* Contributor of articles and reviews to history journals and newspapers.

WORK IN PROGRESS: Editing *The History of the University of Oxford,* Volumes VI-VII, 1800-1914, publication by Oxford University Press expected in 1985.

SIDELIGHTS: Brock comments: "The research and writing for *The Great Reform Act* were done over many years, in the intervals between university teaching and administration. The book is based on a wide range of sources, published and unpublished. I am now working on the extraordinary series of letters in which H. H. Asquith, the British Prime Minister, revealed to his young friend, Venetia Stanley, the inner workings of the Cabinet at the outbreak of World War I."

BIOGRAPHICAL/CRITICAL SOURCES: Times Higher Education Supplement, May 19, 1978; *Oxford,* December, 1978.

*   *   *

BROOKE, (Robert) Tal(iaferro) 1945-

PERSONAL: Born January 21, 1945, in Washington, D.C.; son of Edgar D. (a diplomat) and Frances (Lea) Brooke. *Education:* University of Virginia, B.A., 1969. *Politics:* Conservative. *Religion:* Evangelical Christian. *Home and office:* Shepherd's Hill, Route 1, Box 321, Charlottesville, Va. 22901. *Agent:* Patrick Seale, 2 Motcomb St., Belgrave Sq., London, England; and Scott Meredith Literary Agency, Inc., 845 Third Ave., New York, N.Y. 10022.

CAREER: Free-lance writer, 1971—. Co-founder of Christian Brothers Enterprises. Actor appearing in film, "The Late Great Planet Earth." *Member:* Authors Guild of Authors League of America, Society of Cincinnati.

WRITINGS: *Lord of the Air,* Lion Publishing, 1976; *The Other Side of Death,* Tyndale, 1979; *Sai Baba, Lord of the Air,* Vikas Publishing, 1979. Contributor to *Spiritual Counterfeits Journal.*

WORK IN PROGRESS: A novel "along the lines of George Orwell's *1984*," completion expected in 1981; polemical works on social trends and changes.

SIDELIGHTS: Brooke told *CA:* "Writing came as an inevitable outcropping from a very powerful experience I had in India ten years ago. I did not set out to be a writer, but a consuming passion after the experience drove me into writing—the passion of a perspective, an insight, a revelation so utterly relevant to our age of bafflement that it had to be said, not in the tired old phrases of the past, but with vitality and originality. In the crossfires of an incredible yogic revelation, after two years in India, I jumped from the ancient occult-mystical path I had been on for so long onto the welcome road of Christ.

"I'll never know the full value of this, but one factor in my youth that I believe gave me a wide range of reference points was my exposure to diverse international settings. My family hopped from Haiti, to Georgetown in Washington, to London, Beirut, Brussels, and so on. The one upshot of all this was that I was consumed with the passion to see through the maze of outward events. Human nature, truth, the real direction of world events, and the imposition of the realm of the supernatural on our world greatly occupied my mind. I sensed that ultimate insight was a prize of inestimable value, either to be had by mystics or saints, but not to be found in the academy of human learning. Somewhere in my gut, I also carried an almost apocalyptic feeling about the world's course in my own generation. My burning goal was to somehow find a clue, maybe *the* clue.

"How all this translates artistically is yet to be seen. But certainly one role of the writer is as an expositor of the times. Men from Joyce to Mailer have done this for us, but they have not entered the league of the prophets, they have only been writers. Today we need real penetration. And so the challenge awaits us."

BIOGRAPHICAL/CRITICAL SOURCES: *Richmond Times-Dispatch,* February 28, 1978.

*   *   *

BROOKSHIER, Frank

PERSONAL: Born in Kentucky.

CAREER: Has worked as a sheepherder, copper miner, teacher, and traveling salesman.

WRITINGS: *The Burro,* University of Oklahoma Press, 1974; also author of booklet, *The Philmont Pack-Jacks.* Contributor to *Mr. Longears.*

SIDELIGHTS: Brookshier's adventures have taken him all over the world. He has crossed the Nile, worked on King Ibn Saud's farm in Saudi Arabia, and worked in China, where he was caught one night in cross-fire between Chinese Nationalists and Chinese Communists. He has eaten and danced with the people of Mexico, the Soviet Union, Hungary, and Austria.

But, as he wrote for *Mr. Longears,* "the most difficult task I've ever attempted was when I tried to lead Catrino, my burro, across a ditch of water." Brookshier is considered an authority on the burro.

BROWN, Charles N(ikki)   1937-

PERSONAL: Born June 24, 1937, in New York, N.Y.; son of Lawrence Alexander (in sales) and Yetta (Lamm) Brown; married Marsha Elkin, 1962 (divorced, 1969); married Dena Benatan, 1970 (divorced, 1979). *Education:* City University of New York, B.S., 1968. *Home:* 34 Ridgewood Lane, Oakland, Calif. 94611. *Office:* Locus Publications, P.O. Box 3938, San Francisco, Calif. 94119.

CAREER: American Electric Power, New York, N.Y., electrical engineer, 1962-72; Bechtel Corp., San Francisco, Calif., senior engineer, 1972-75; *Locus* Magazine, San Francisco, Calif., editor and publisher, 1975—; Janus Books, Oakland Calif., partner, 1978—. *Military Service:* U.S. Navy, 1955-59. *Member:* Science Fiction Writers of America. *Awards, honors:* Hugo Awards from World Science Fiction Convention, 1970, 1971, 1976, and 1977, for *Locus* Magazine.

WRITINGS: (Editor) *Far Travelers,* MEWS Books, 1976; (editor) *Alien Worlds,* MEWS Books, 1976; (editor with Dena Brown) *Locus: The Newspaper of the Science Fiction Field,* Volume I: *1968-71,* Volume II: *1972-77,* Gregg, 1978. Editor and publisher of *Locus,* 1968—; magazine reviewer for *Odyssey,* 1976; film reviewer for *Cosmos,* 1976-77; book reviewer for *Isaac Asimov's Science Fiction Magazine,* 1977—.

*   *   *

BROWN, Judith Gwyn   1933-

PERSONAL: Born October 15, 1933, in New York, N.Y.; daughter of Philip and Freda (Robinson) Brown. *Education:* Attended Cooper Union, 1951, and Parsons School of Design, 1957; New York University, B.A., 1956. *Home and office:* 522 East 85th St., New York, N.Y. 10028.

CAREER: Artist, illustrator, and children's author. Worked for Bullard Press (a printer), New York City, 1958-59; freelance book illustrator, 1959—. Work included in the permanent collection of the Metropolitan Museum of Art, New York City, Kerlan Collection, University of Minnesota, and Huntington Library, Calif.

WRITINGS—Juveniles; all self-illustrated: *Max and the Truffle Pig,* Abingdon, 1963; *The Happy Voyage* (Junior Literary Guild selection), Macmillan, 1965; *Muffin,* Abelard, 1972; *Alphabet Dreams,* Prentice-Hall, 1976.

Illustrator: L. J. Bragdon, *It's Fun to Speak French,* Abingdon, 1962; Marjorie Paradis, *Mr. DeLuca's Horse,* Atheneum, 1962; Katherine Dougherty, *A Street of Churches,* Abingdon, 1962; Margaret Hodges, *The Secret in the Woods,* Dial, 1963; Marilyn Sachs, *Amy Moves In,* Doubleday, 1964; Shyrle Hacker, *The Mystery of the Swan Ballet,* F. Watts, 1965; Dale B. Carlson, editor, *The Brainstormers,* Doubleday, 1966; Scott Corbett, *Pippa Passes,* Holt, 1966; Padraic Colum, *The Stone of Victory,* McGraw, 1966; Helen M. Miller, *Janey and Friends,* Doubleday, 1967; Eileen Rosenbaum, *Two for Trouble,* Doubleday, 1967; Beatrice C. Brown, *Jonathan Bing,* Lothrop, 1968; Helene Hanff, *Butch Elects a Mayor,* Parents' Magazine Press, 1969.

Mira Lobe, *The Grandma in the Apple Tree,* McGraw, 1970; Mary Cockett, *Rosanna the Goat,* Bobbs-Merrill, 1970; Daniel Cohen, *Ancient Monuments: How They Were Built,* McGraw, 1971; Julie Edwards, *Mandy,* Harper, 1971; Barbara Robinson, *The Best Christmas Pageant Ever,* Harper, 1972; Wilma Yeo, *The Mystery of the Third Twin,* Simon & Schuster, 1972; Joan Tate, *Ben and Annie,* Doubleday, 1974; Elizabeth Coatsworth, *Daisy,* Macmillan, 1973; Wylly Folk

St. John, *The Secret of the Seven Crows*, Viking, 1973; Patricia Clapp, *King of the Dollhouse*, Lothrop, 1974; Andre Norton, *Lavender-Green Magic*, Crowell, 1974; Marden Dahlstedt, *Shadow of the Lighthouse*, Coward, 1974; Noel Streatfeild, *When the Siren Wailed*, Collins, 1974, published in the United States as *When the Sirens Wailed*, Random House, 1976; Marjorie F. Stover, *Chad and the Elephant Engine*, Atheneum, 1975; Miriam Schlein, *The Girl Who Would Rather Climb Trees*, Harcourt, 1975; Anatolii G. Aleksin, *My Brother Plays the Clarinet*, Walck, 1975; Mary E. Robertson, *Jemimalee*, McGraw, 1977; S. E. Moore, *Secret Island*, Four Winds, 1977; Ida DeLage, *ABC Santa Claus*, Garrard, 1978; M. Schlein, *I Hate It*, Whitman Publishing, 1978; Jack Lovejoy, *The Rebel Witch*, Lothrop, 1978; Daniel Curley, *Hilarion*, Houghton, 1979; Lucile W. Ellison, *Butter on Both Sides*, Scribner's.

Illustrator of text books and book jackets. Contributor of illustrations to anthologies, periodicals, and the *New York Times*.

SIDELIGHTS: Brown told *CA:* "The most pervasive phenomenon common to writers and artists, as I see it, is being alone. Art on any level is not a collective effort, and the aloneness of it, often appearing early in life by circumstance, temperament, or both, is necessary. I think artists and writers, those who work full time at their craft and sustain themselves by it find that they must ultimately make a choice as to the greater importance of a complete life as we generally think of it, or the work itself.

"The working out of art on any level takes so much time; not just the doing of it, but the time spent thinking about it and being concerned with the work of others. I try to read as much as I can and look at pictures of all kinds. I particularly enjoy nineteenth-century fiction, and I make a point of reading poetry every day. I also go to museums so that I might keep in mind what is truly imaginative, rare, and great, and continually affirm to myself what is most important even when I am least sure of my own efforts. When I illustrate a book I consider each particular text as a complete world. The characters and settings for the illustrations come from this concern rather than from a conscious effort to draw in a given mode or style.

"After reading the manuscript I do sketches quite freely, and only for myself, of the people in the story. Sometimes as I work I think of other literary or pictorial connections, that is, the manuscript before me will bring to mind a line of verse or a descriptive passage from another book I have read. Or in my mind's eye I will have a glimpse of a picture I have seen at some past time. The two merge: the text on which I am working and the remembered passage or image I recall. In this way something more dramatic, more amusing, or more deeply felt can be brought to the illustration, and the new picture has an added dimension.

"The next stage is the process of figuring out composition, and the more careful drawing of the characters in the setting. At this point I do research in the picture collection of the New York Public Library for historic or architectural background, costumes, and so on.

"The final putting together of the elements is almost like the first impulse, and has to do with getting down on paper in ink or paint the air and light, the emotion of the situation portrayed. The idea is to make the finished picture correspond as much as possible with the image as originally perceived.

"It is my feeling that an artist's life is lived for the most part in the mind. If this sounds severe I must also say that I do have friends. I like to talk and eat and walk my dog. I care

very much for animals and belong to several groups promoting animal protection.

"In addition to illustrating books I also paint portraits and subjects combining the real world with the world of the imagination."

The *New York Times Book Review* praised Brown's illustrations of *Jonathan Bing*, commenting that "Judith Gwyn Brown's illustrations and jacket are just about perfect, and the whole book demands to be given to a million children quickly."

AVOCATIONAL INTERESTS: Fine arts, reading fiction and poetry.

BIOGRAPHICAL/CRITICAL SOURCES: New York Times Book Review, May 5, 1968.

* * *

BROWN, Julia (Prewitt) 1948-

PERSONAL: Born February 10, 1948, in St. Louis, Mo.; married Deaver Brown (in business), 1978. *Education:* Barnard College, B.A., 1970; Columbia University, M.A., 1971, Ph.D., 1975. *Home:* 23 Commonwealth Ave., Boston, Mass. 02116. *Office:* Department of English, Boston University, Boston, Mass. 02215.

CAREER: Boston University, Boston, Mass., assistant professor of English, 1974—. *Awards, honors:* Mellon fellow at Harvard University, 1979-80.

WRITINGS: Jane Austen's Novels: Social Change and Literary Form, Harvard University Press, 1979.

* * *

BROWN, Lennox (John) 1934-

PERSONAL: Born February 7, 1934, in Trinidad, West Indies; son of Julian and Eldica (Hamlet) Brown. *Education:* University of Western Ontario, B.A., 1961; University of Toronto, M.A., 1969; graduate study at Queen Mary College, London. *Agent:* Emily Goodman, Suite 11, Avenue of the Americas, New York, N.Y. 10019.

CAREER: Playwright and poet. Civil servant for government of Trinidad and Tobago, West Indies, 1952-56; free-lance journalist for West Indies' and Canadian newspapers, including *Trinidad Guardian, Evening News, Globe and Mail, Toronto Star, Telegram,* and *Financial Post,* 1952-63; Canadian Broadcasting Corp. (CBC), editor and producer for National Network Radio News, 1963-67. Visiting playwright-in-residence and lecturer at University of Hartford, 1972-73; lecturer at Queens College, City University of New York, 1975-78; administrator and playwright-in-residence at Keskidee Arts Centre, London, England, 1979-81.

MEMBER: National Black Coalition of Canada, Black Arts of Canada, Canadian Association of Radio and Television Actor's and Writer's Association, Canadian Newspaper and Wireless Guild, Dramatists Guild of America, Caribbean-American Repertory Theatre, Theatre Writers Union of Britain, Ebo Society for Black Art. *Awards, honors:* Canadian national one-act playwriting competition, Yousouf award, and Birk's gold medal, all for "The Captive" in 1965, all for "Night Sun" in 1967, and all for "Jour Ouvert" in 1968; Dorothy White Award, 1966, for "The Meeting"; Canada Council travel grants, 1966, 1975, and 1976; Canada Council promising artist grants, 1967 and 1968; first prize from Canadian National University drama league competition, 1969, for "I Have to Call My Father"; Canada Council short term promising artist grants, 1969, 1971, 1973, and 1976; winner of Canada Council arts bursary contest, 1970; Eugene O'Neill memorial playwriting national competition, 1972, for "Prodigal in Black Stone"; humanitarian art award from Hartford American-West Indian Association, 1974, for "The Winti Train"; nominated for best black playwright by Audience Development Committee, 1976; Canada Council arts grant, 1976; U.S. National Endowments for the Arts fellowship, 1978; New York State Creative Artist Programme fellowship, 1978.

WRITINGS—Published plays: *The Captive* (one-act), Ottawa Little Theatre, 1965; *The Meeting* [one-act; first aired on Canadian Broadcasting Corp. (CBC) television in March, 1969; produced in Holland at Dutch Center for Amateur Theatre, February, 1972], Ottawa Little Theatre, 1966; *Jour Ouvert; or Daybreak* (one-act; sometimes produced as "I Have to Call My Father"), Ottawa Little Theatre, 1968; "Devil Mas'" (three act; first aired on radio by Trinidad Theatre Workshop, 1973; produced in Cleveland, Ohio, at Karamu House Theatre, October, 1976), included in *Kuntu Drama*, edited by Paul Carter Harrison, Grove, 1974; "The Trinity of Four" (one-act; produced in New York City at IRT Theatre, December, 1975), included in *Caribbean Rhythms: The Emerging English Literature of the West Indies*, edited by J. T. Livingston, Pocket Books, 1974; "The Twilight Dinner" (one-act; produced in New York City at St. Mark's Playhouse, 1978), included in *The Twilight Dinner and Other Plays*, Talon Books, 1980.

Produced plays: "Snow Dark Sunday," produced in Toronto at Museum Theatre, September, 1965; "Saturday's Druid," first aired on radio by CBC, March, 1969; "Song of the Spear" (two-act), first aired on radio by CBC, September, 1969; "The Throne in an Autumn Room" (three-act), first aired on radio by CBC, August, 1971, produced in Trinidad at Trinidad Theatre Workshop, January, 1973; "A Ballet Behind the Bridge" (two-act), first aired on CBC television, January, 1971, produced in New York City at St. Mark's Playhouse, 1972; "Wine in Winter" (one-act), first aired on radio by Trinidad Theatre Workshop, March, 1972; "Prodigal in Black Stone" (two-act), produced in Waterford, Conn., at Eugene O'Neill Memorial Theatre, July, 1972; "Ritual of the Ashanti Golden Stool," first aired on radio by CBC, August, 1972; "This Scent of Incense" (two-act), first aired on radio by CBC, 1972.

"The Winti Train" (two-act), produced in Hartford, Conn., at University of Hartford, March, 1974; "Home Is a Long Way" (one-act), first aired on Trinidad and Tobogo television, December, 1974; "The Sisterhood of a Spring Night" (two-act), produced in New York City at Queens College, March, 1975; "A Last Dance in the Sun" (two-act), first aired on Trinidad and Tobogo television, August, 1975; "A Clean Sweep" (one-act), first aired on Trinidad and Tobogo television, August, 1976; "Fog Drifts in the Spring" (one-act), produced in Brooklyn, N.Y., at Billie Holiday Theatre, February, 1976.

Also author of plays: "The Burning Sky" (one-act), 1966; "The Voyage Tonight" (two-act), 1967; "Fire for an Ice Age" (one-act), 1967; "A Ballet in a Bear Pit" (two-act), 1969; "Moon in the Mirror" (one-act), 1969; "Summer Screen" (one-act), 1971; "A Communion in Dark Sun" (two-act), 1972; "A Processional From La Basse" (two-act), 1973; "The Conversion" (two-act), 1973; "Three Colours of a Dream Quartet" (one-act), 1975; "The Blues Smile" (two-act), 1975; "The Gold Coast of Times Square" (one-act), 1976; "Becoming Persons" (two-act), 1977; "Winter Is Coming"; "The Journey."

Contributor of poetry to journals, including *Canadian Poetry Magazine, Alphabet, Canadian Forum,* and *Ebo Voice.* Contributor of articles to journals, including *Black Orpheus, Black Images,* and *Guyana Graphic.*

WORK IN PROGRESS—Eight plays: "The Promise of Yesterday's Flowers," "The Secretary," "The Return," "The Greasy Pole," "Boba-Lee," "Blackout," "Mother," and "The Basement."

SIDELIGHTS: Lennox told *CA:* "The most devastating crisis facing modern American theatre exists unnoticed. This is its basic illiteracy. Although the theatre has become more professional and more substantial in terms of commercial organization, it has declined in an artistic and intellectual sense, and continues to do so at an impressive speed. It has the strongest economic foundation it has ever had in its history: federal funds, state funds, local funds, endowments, investments. It has no mental funds. Producers, writers, actors, directors, and technicians are becoming more and more illiterate. They know the theatre in a technical sense of turning on light switches and positioning bodies on stage, but they do not know theatre as dramatic literature. They are appallingly ill-educated. They have no sense of literature. They do not read or write; therefore the theatre is becoming bigger physically, but smaller mentally every day. If literacy dries up, the funds will dry up too—and the theatre will die."

BIOGRAPHICAL/CRITICAL SOURCES: Women's Wear Daily, March 6, 1972; *New York Times,* March 15, 1972, March 17, 1972, March 23, 1972, April 20, 1978; *New Yorker,* March 25, 1972, May 1, 1978; *Cue,* March 25, 1972; *New York Voice,* February 27, 1976; *Encore,* May 22, 1978.

*   *   *

BRYSON, Conrey 1905-

PERSONAL: Born October 13, 1905, in Cleveland, Utah; son of Samuel C. (a farmer and miner) and Clara E. (Davis) Bryson; married Pearl Hale, May 15, 1935 (died, 1972); married Fay Gardner, August 20, 1974; children: Beth (Mrs. D. E. Hurst), Maurice C. *Education:* Texas Western College (now University of Texas, El Paso), B.A., 1954, M.A., 1959. *Politics:* Democrat. *Religion:* Church of Latter-day Saints (Mormons). *Home:* 600 Gregory Way, El Paso, Tex. 79902.

CAREER: KTSM-Radio and Television, El Paso, Tex., news broadcaster, 1936-64; administrative assistant to Congressman Richard C. White in Washington, D.C., 1965-72; writer, 1972—. Member of El Paso Public Service Board, 1952-64. Instructor at University of Texas, El Paso, 1959-64. *Member:* Western Writers of America, Mormon History Association, El Paso County Historical Society (past president). *Awards, honors:* Sonnichsen Award from Texas Western Press, 1977, for *Down Went McGinty.*

WRITINGS: The Land Where We Live, Aniversario-El Paso Committee, 1973; *Dr. L. A. Nixon and the White Primary,* Texas Western Press, 1974; *Down Went McGinty: El Paso in the Wonderful Nineties,* Texas Western Press, 1977. Contributing editor of *Password* (of El Paso County Historical Society), 1975—.

WORK IN PROGRESS: Winter Quarters, a history of the Mormon community in what is now Omaha, Neb., 1846-47; *The Memphis, El Paso & Pacific Railroad,* on the first railroad in Texas, completion expected in 1981.

SIDELIGHTS: Bryson writes: "During twenty-eight years of radio and television journalism, I accumulated quite a file of subjects on which 'someday I'm going to write a book.' Retirement from government service in 1972 made it possible for me to assemble some of this information in printable form. I have lived for fifty years on the Mexican border, and I'm interested in ancient and modern history of Mexico. I participated in the Smithsonian Institution 'Adventure Tour' of Yucatan Mayan ruins in 1978."

* * *

BUCHMAN, Sidney 1902-1975

PERSONAL: Born March 27, 1902, in Duluth, Minn.; died August 23, 1975, in Cannes, France; children: Susan Silver. *Education:* Attended University of Minnesota, Oxford University, and Columbia University. *Residence:* Cannes, France.

CAREER: Playwright and screenwriter. Assistant stage director at Old Vic Theatre in London, England. Producer and assistant to Harry Cohen at Columbia Studios, 1942-51; writer for Paramount Pictures; writer-producer for Twentieth Century-Fox. *Member:* Screen Writers Guild (president). *Awards, honors:* Academy Award nomination for best screenplay from Academy of Motion Picture Arts and Sciences, 1939, for "Mr. Smith Goes to Washington," and 1942, for "The Talk of the Town"; Academy Award for best screenplay (shared with Seton I. Miller), 1941, for "Here Comes Mr. Jordan"; Academy Award and Writers Guild nominations for best screenplay, both 1949, both for "Jolson Sings Again"; Writers Guild nomination for best screenplay, 1951, for "Saturday's Hero"; Laurel Award from Writers Guild of America, 1965.

WRITINGS—Plays: "This One Man," "Storm Song," "Acute Triangle."

Screenplays: (With Waldemar Young) "Sign of the Cross," Paramount, 1932; "The King Steps Out" (adapted from "Cissy," a play by Gustav Holm, Ernst Decsey, Hubert Marischka, and Ernst Marischka), Columbia, 1936; "Theodora Goes Wild" (adapted from the novel by Mary McCarthy), Columbia, 1936; (with Harry Sauber and Jack Kirkland) "Adventure in Manhattan" (adapted from *Purple and Fine Linen,* a novel by May Edginton), Columbia, 1936; (with Donald Ogden Stewart) "Holiday" (adapted from the play by Philip Barry), Columbia, 1938; "Mr. Smith Goes to Washington," Columbia, 1939.

"The Howards of Virginia" (adapted from *Tree of Liberty,* a novel by Elizabeth Page), Columbia, 1940; (with Seton I. Miller) "Here Comes Mr. Jordon" (adapted from "Heaven Can Wait," a play by Harry Segall), Columbia, 1941; (with Irwin Shaw and Sidney Harmon) "The Talk of the Town," Columbia, 1942; "A Song to Remember," Columbia, 1945; "Over 21" (adapted from the play by Ruth Gordon), Columbia, 1945; "Jolson Sings Again," Columbia, 1949.

(With Millard Lampell) "Saturday's Hero" (adapted from *The Hero,* a novel by Millard Lampell), Columbia, 1951; (with Stanley Mann) "The Mark" (adapted from the novel by Charles Israel), Continental, 1961; (with Joseph L. Mankiewicz and Ranald MacDougall) "Cleopatra" (adapted from the histories of Plutarch, Suetonius, Appian, and other ancient stories, and *The Life and Times of Cleopatra,* a book by C. M. Franzero), Twentieth Century-Fox, 1962; "The Group" (adapted from the novel by Mary McCarthy), United Artists, 1966.

Also author of "Matinee Ladies," 1927, "If I Had a Million," 1932, "Whom the Gods Destroy," 1934, "She Married Her Boss," 1935, "I'll Love You Always," 1935, "Boots Malone," 1951, "Thunder Below," "From Hell to Heaven," "Love Me Forever," "The Deadly Trap."

SIDELIGHTS: Buchman is best known for his comedy screenplays, including "Here Comes Mr. Jordan" and "The Talk of the Town." In 1939, he wrote "Mr. Smith Goes to Washington," which details the efforts of a young, honest, politician in the corrupt and perplexing world of politics. The film was a huge success for Buchman and its director, Frank Capra, and helped establish actor Jimmy Stewart in Hollywood.

Buchman was one of the many people in the motion picture industry to be blacklisted in the 1950's. In 1951, Buchman testified to the House Committee on Un-American Activities that he was a former Communist, but refused to divulge the names of other Communists. Buchman was found guilty of contempt of Congress in 1953 and fined $150 with a one-year suspended sentence. After this affair, he moved to Cannes, France, and made it his permanent home until his death. Buchman produced no credited work between 1951 and 1960, when he was hired by Twentieth Century-Fox as a writer-producer.

He returned to Hollywood in the early 1960's, but the films made from his work were largely rejected by the reviewers. Perhaps his best known effort of this period is "Cleopatra," which he co-wrote with Joseph Mankiewicz and Ranald MacDougall. Though the script seemed a reasonable adaptation of the book *The Life and Times of Cleopatra,* the film ultimately sparked controversy for its gaudy sets and impressive budgets, and is more aptly remembered as the initial setting for the romance between actors Richard Burton and Elizabeth Taylor.

OBITUARIES: New York Times, August 25, 1975.*

* * *

BUCKLEY, Shawn 1943-

PERSONAL: Born May 28, 1943, in Charleston, W.Va.; son of Fred Doyle (an engineer) and Gisela (in real estate; maiden name, Bundig) Buckley. *Education:* University of Pittsburgh, B.S.M.E., 1963; Purdue University, M.S.A.E., 1965; University of California, Berkeley, Ph.D., 1972. *Religion:* None. *Home:* 12504 Venice Blvd., #201, Los Angeles, Calif. 90049. *Office:* Department of Mechanical Engineering, Massachusetts Institute of Technology, Cambridge, Mass. 02139.

CAREER: Group Lotus Ltd., Norwich, England, race-car consultant, 1969-71; National Science Foundation, Washington, D.C., research fellow, 1971-72; Massachusetts Institute of Technology, Cambridge, assistant professor, 1972-76, associate professor of mechanical engineering, 1976—. Solar energy consultant. *Member:* International Solar Energy Society, American Society of Mechanical Engineers. *Awards, honors:* Du Pont grant, 1974; awards from *Industrial Research,* 1979, for thermic diode solar panel and phase monitoring automated inspection system.

WRITINGS: Sun Up to Sun Down: Understanding Solar Energy, McGraw, 1979, textbook edition, 1980. Contributor of about twenty-five articles to scientific journals and magazines, including *Bicycling* and *Solar Age.*

SIDELIGHTS: Buckley writes: "Primarily I am an inventor, with inventions in solar energy, automated manufacturing, and race cars. My doctoral thesis was on race car design for Lotus, and most current Grand Prix cars use my design. I also designed a competition bicycle frame; my students are manufacturing them.

"I wrote *Sun Up to Sun Down* as a way to bring solar energy to the layperson without using mathematics. I do this by analogy: heat flow is made analogous to water flow, which readers can easily visualize with the many accompanying drawings. Since solar energy must ultimately be used by lay-people—in the form of solar heaters for every house—a 'no-math' solar book is very appropriate. I hope to be starting my own business soon, either in solar energy or in auto-mated manufacturing.''

AVOCATIONAL INTERESTS: Motorcycles, Karate (second degree black belt).

* * *

BUENO, Jose de la Torre   1905(?)-1980

OBITUARY NOTICE: Born c. 1905; died January 15, 1980, in Haddam, Conn. Editor, publishing executive, and author of *The American Fisherman's Guide.* Bueno held numerous editorial and promotion positions at such publishing houses as Macmillan, Knopf, and Appleton-Century-Crofts, before joining the staff of Wesleyan University Press. For fourteen years he was senior editor at Wesleyan, and also acted as board member of the Publishing Ad Club, the Coordinating Council of the Literary Magazines, and the Dance Perspectives Foundation. At his retirement both the Dance Perspectives Foundation and Wesleyan University established the Jose de la Torre Bueno Prize, for the most distinguished manuscript on dance. Obituaries and other sources: *Publishers Weekly,* February 8, 1980.

* * *

BULL, Norman John   1916-

PERSONAL: Born October 19, 1916, in Portsmouth, Hampshire, England; son of Edward George and Alice Henrietta Bull; married Margaret Ellen Humm, May, 1942; children: Margaret Jennifer, Peter Edward. *Education:* Trinity College, Oxford, B.A., 1938, M.A., 1949; University of Reading, D.Phil., 1967. *Home:* 21 Wonford Rd., Exeter, Devonshire EX2 4LH, England.

CAREER: Teacher and involved in parish and youth work, 1938-48; St. Luke's College of Education, Exeter, England, lecturer, 1948-58, senior lecturer, 1958-62, principal lecturer in education, 1962-75, head of religious education department, 1948-75; writer, 1952—. Member of Canterbury City Council, 1947-48. *Member:* Society of Authors, Rotary International.

WRITINGS: The Bible Story and Its Background (juvenile), eight volumes, Hulton Educational Publications, 1965-70; *The Rise of the Church,* Heineman, 1967; *Stories Jesus Told* (juvenile), Augsburg, 1969; *The Way of Wisdom* (juvenile), four volumes, Longman, 1970-74; *Moral Education,* Sage Publications, 1970; *Moral Judgment From Childhood to Adolescence,* Sage Publications, 1970; *Symbols* (juvenile), edited by Ronald J. Goldman, four volumes, Morehouse, 1970; *One Hundred Great Lives* (juvenile), Hulton Educational Publications, 1972; *Colours* (juvenile), Burke Books, 1973; *Light and Darkness* (Juvenile), Wheaton Ltd., 1979; *Festivals and Customs,* (juvenile), Wheaton Ltd., 1979. Also author of *Food and Drink* and *You and Me,* published by Wheaton Ltd.

WORK IN PROGRESS: Children's books, for Paul Hamlyn Group, including *100 Bible Stories, The Story of Jesus,* and *My Little Book of Prayers;* research on mythology; collaborating with R. J. Ferris on wide-range readers in religion for primary schools.

SIDELIGHTS: Bull comments: ''I took up writing as an integral part of my professional work in education. I have pub-

lished books for children of all ages, for students and teachers, and, in the publication of my research, for educational psychologists. All my writing has been educational, in the widest sense.'' *Avocational interests:* Music, gardening.

* * *

BULLE, Florence (Elizabeth)   1925-

PERSONAL: Surname is pronounced *Bew*-lee; born January 30, 1925, in Everett, Wash.; daughter of Marshall A. (a minister; in business) and Myrtie U. (a teacher; maiden name, Gray) Schoolcraft; married Al Bulle (a welder; in maintenance), August 3, 1945; children: Marshall, Stephen, Daryl, Janyce Lynn. *Education:* Attended Seattle Pacific College, 1943-44, and Bethany Fellowship Missionary Training Center, 1961-64; Houghton College, B.S., 1977. *Home address:* Route 1, Box 3-A, Houghton, N.Y. 14744.

CAREER: Writer, 1957—. Public speaker.

WRITINGS: (Contributor) W. J. Krutza, editor, *How We Faced Tragedy,* Baker Book, 1968; *Lord of the Valleys,* Logos International, 1972. Contributor to religious and family magazines and newspapers, including *American Weekly, Home Life, Today,* and *Christian Parent.*

WORK IN PROGRESS: A book on deception, publication expected in 1980.

SIDELIGHTS: Florence Bulle's first book describes her Christian faith, strengthened over the years by her successful battles against ill health, hospitalization, and surgery. She told *CA:* ''As I see it, there are two motivating factors from which my writing flows: I'm on speaking terms with God—we even laugh and cry together; and I care about broken people—enough to weep with those who weep, and when God turns their tears to joy to rejoice with them too. Writing, then, is my response to God's love to me by reaching out to touch someone, to take their hand and put it in the hand of God. At least that's what I try to do. And according to the feedback I have received from *Lord of the Valleys,* it is happening. (To date, it has sold around eighty thousand copies—great for a first book with no big name author, I am told.)

''Frankly, I'm disgusted by much of the stuff flooding the religious book market; splashy, sensational, shallow, and sometimes unbelievably stupid, it seems to me. These books remind me of TV commercials dangling promises of health, wealth, and prosperity that they can't possibly deliver. Just read one such book. I have. And when the author says the book was only two weeks in the writing, I wonder why it took that long.

''On the other hand, there are those fine Christian writers I would applaud. They've shorn their writing of pious cliches and religious jargon. They can relate at the gut level. They've made themselves vulnerable by their honesty without sacrificing good taste, neither under-writing or over-writing. They don't have all the answers, and they say so.

''I wish more publishers valued quality rather than quantity. Too many publishers are grinding out books like a circus barker promising the greatest show you've ever seen.

''To a writer aspiring to write Christian books, I would say: Few persons are going to read heavy theological treatises. But this doesn't mean readers want pabulum dripped in their mouths. Put some good red meat in your writing. Live enough so that you have something to say. Don't make wild statements for effect, or those you can't support. You don't have all the answers; neither do I; neither does anyone else. So share your discoveries without claiming they are the last word. Remember, in a very special way, Christian writing must have a life behind it, if it reaches the heart of a fellow pilgrim with consolation and hope.''

Of her work in progress, Bulle remarked: ''Charming, popular super-salespersons who distort the Word of God to promote all sorts of strange teaching are alarmingly successful. How can Christians recognize these deceivers? How can they protect themselves from becoming deceived by the extremes and excesses being taught, from Satan who comes as 'an angel of light'?''

*   *   *

BUNIN, Catherine   1967-

PERSONAL: Born July 31, 1967, in New York, N.Y.; daughter of Norman (a magazine circulation manager) and Sherry (a writer; maiden name, Miller) Bunin. *Education:* Student at junior high school in New York, N.Y. *Home:* 250 West 94th St., New York, N.Y. 10025.

CAREER: Writer, 1976—. Guest on East Coast television and radio programs.

WRITINGS: (With mother, Sherry Bunin) *Is That Your Sister?* (juvenile), Pantheon, 1976.

WORK IN PROGRESS: Growing Up With Color, with mother, Sherry Bunin, an autobiographical account of growing up as a black girl, for Pantheon; poems.

SIDELIGHTS: Catherine Bunin was prompted to write her first book by questions from her friends about her own adoption. The book is aimed at young people like herself.

BIOGRAPHICAL/CRITICAL SOURCES: People, January 8, 1977; *Weekly Reader News Parade,* March 2, 1977.

*   *   *

BUNIN, Sherry   1925-

PERSONAL: Born February 24, 1925, in Tarboro, N.C.; daughter of Louis (a merchant) and Ida (Fader) Miller; married Norman Bunin (a magazine manager), May 1, 1957; children: Alexander, Nicholas, Catherine, Carla. *Education:* University of Cincinnati, B.A., 1946; attended Cincinnati College of Music and Art, New School for Social Research, and Columbia University. *Home:* 250 West 94th St., New York, N.Y. 10025.

CAREER: Junior high school teacher in English in Ashland, Ky., 1947; *Cincinnati Post,* Cincinnati, Ohio, reporter, 1948; WCPO-Radio, Cincinnati, Ohio, writer, 1948-49; Time Inc. Players, New York City, producer, 1954-58; Twentieth Century-Fox, New York City, casting assistant, 1949; Time, Inc., New York City, editorial assistant for *Time, Life,* and *Sports Illustrated,* 1954-58; New York Council on Adoptable Children, New York City, associate director and editor of newsletter, 1972-79; free-lance writer, 1979—. Volunteer tutor in New York City public schools.

WRITINGS: New Voices '64, Macmillan, 1964; (with daughter, Catherine Bunin) *Is That Your Sister?* (juvenile), Pantheon, 1976.

WORK IN PROGRESS: Growing Up With Color, with daughter, Catherine Bunin, a personal account of a black child's experiences; *Exit Beaver,* a novel about a small-town childhood.

SIDELIGHTS: Sherry Bunin's daughter, Catherine, is adopted. Together they have written about adoption, partly to answer common questions Catherine encountered from her friends.

BIOGRAPHICAL/CRITICAL SOURCES: Coronet, August, 1974; *New York Daily News,* February 22, 1977; *Christian Science Monitor,* April 11, 1977; *Philadelphia Inquirer,* May 8, 1977.

*   *   *

BURCKHARDT, C(arl) J(akob)   1891-1974

PERSONAL: Born September 10, 1891, in Basel, Switzerland; died March 3, 1974, in Geneva, Switzerland; married Elisabeth de Reynold; children: Mrs. Andre de Muralt, Mrs. Pierre Chiesa. *Education:* Attended universities of Basel, Munich, Goettingen, Zurich, and Paris.

CAREER: Swiss Diplomatic Service, Vienna, Austria, attache at Swiss legation, 1918-22, minister to France, 1945-49; University of Zurich, Zurich, Switzerland, professor of modern history, 1923-32; Post-graduate School of International Studies, Geneva, Switzerland, professor, 1932-37; League of Nations high commissioner to Free City of Danzig, Poland, 1937-39; writer, 1939-74. President of International Red Cross, 1944-45. *Member:* Austrian Academy of Science and Art (honorary member), Institute of Moral and Political Sciences of the French Academy, Bavarian Academy of Fine Arts, Berlin Academy of Arts, Academy of Salamanca (associate member), Academy of Montpellier. *Awards, honors:* Knight pour le Merite of Germany; Grand Officer of the French Legion of Honor.

WRITINGS: Kleinasiatische reise (travel), [Germany], 1925, reprinted, Callwey, 1942; *Richelieu: Der Aufstieg zur Macht* (history; first volume in trilogy; also see below), Callwey, 1935, translation by Edwin Muir and Willa Muir published as *Richelieu: His Rise to Power,* Oxford University Press, 1940, revised and abridged edition, Vintage, 1964; *Gestalten und Maechte, Reden und Aufsaetze,* Fretz & Wasmuth, 1941; *Erinnerungen an Hofmannsthal und Briefe des Dichters,* Schwabe, 1943; *Maria Theresia* (biography), Coleman, 1944; *Ein Vormittag beim Buchhaendler,* Rinn, 1947; (editor with Martin Huerlimann) *Europa, Bilder seiner Landschaft und Kultur,* Atlantis Verlag, 1947; *Reden und Aufzeichungen,* Manesse Verlag, 1952; *Drei Erzaehlungen,* Manesse Verlag, 1952; *Noris: Zwei Reden* (speech), Deutsches National-Museum, 1953; *Vier historische Betrachtungen* (history), Manesse Verlag, 1953; (with Hugo Hofmannsthal) *Briefwechsel,* S. Fischer, 1956; *Bilder aus der Vergangenheit,* M. Fischer, 1956; *Bildnisse,* S. Fischer, 1958; *Begegnungen,* Manesse Verlag, 1958.

Meine danziger Mission, 1937-1939, Callwey, 1960; *Die Episode Randa,* Tschudy Verlag, 1961; Max Rychner and Hermann Rinn, editors, *Dauer in Wandel: Festschrift zum 70,* Callwey, 1961; *Betrachtungen und Berichte,* Manesse Verlag, 1964; *Hans Erni,* Scheidegger, 1964; *Richelieu: Behauptung der Macht und Kalter Krieg* (second volume in trilogy; also see below), Callwey, 1965, translation by Bernard Hoy published as *Richelieu and His Age,* Allen & Unwin, 1970; (compiler with Fritz Hess) *Auf Heimlichen Faehrten,* Parey, 1965; *Beusuch in Vinzel,* Amriswiler Buecherei, 1966; *Richelieu: Grossmachtpolitik und Tod des Kardinals* (third volume in trilogy), Callwey, 1966, translation published as Volume 3 of *Richelieu and His Age* (see below); *Gedenkworte fuer Albert Schweitzer,* Schneider, 1967; *R. W.: Ein Bericht,* Gute Schriften, 1967; *Richelieu: Nachwort Anmerkungen Literaturhinweise, Personenregister* (supplementary volume to trilogy), Callwey, 1967; *Ueber Werner Bergengruen,* Verlag der Arche, 1968; *Jugendfreundschaften: Erinnerungen,* Verlag der Arche, 1969; *Musik: Erinnerungen,* Verlag der Arche, 1969; *Wolfsjad: Erzaehlungen,* Verlag der Arche,

1970; (editor with Claudia Mertz-Rychner) *Briefe: 1926-1965*, S. Fischer, 1970; *Gasammelte Werke*, six volumes, Scherz, 1971; *Richelieu and His Age* (collected trilogy), three volumes, Harcourt, 1972; *Memorabilien: Erinnerungen und Begegnungen*, edited by Charlotte Koenig, Callwey, 1977.

SIDELIGHTS: As the League of Nations high commissioner to the Free City of Danzig, C. J. Burckhardt played a major role in the League's effort to prevent World War II. The cession of Danzig to Germany was the immediate issue of conflict between Poland and Germany, which finally precipitated the war. Consequently, Burckhardt's position was extremely important. In his efforts to mediate the dispute between the two countries, he met for an interview with Hitler in 1939. At this meeting Hitler informed Burckhardt that he had only contempt for Poland's generals and that he would rather "make war . . . today than tomorrow." Although the war started later that year and Burckhardt failed in his difficult mission, Hitler twice commended him for his "tact and discretion."

Burckhardt was descended from a well-established Basel family of humanistic traditions. As a result of his upbringing, Burckhardt had great faith in human dignity, which marked his literary works. His best-known work, *Richelieu*, was generally well received by critics. Leonard Woolf was very impressed with the book and praised it as "not merely [a] personal biography. Dr. Burckhardt has a profound sense of history, of the great 'movements,' forces, and ideas which appear to mould the shape of human society, and of the relation of persons to them. His Richelieu is not merely a character, which interests us psychologically; his beliefs, ideas, aims, and actions are always related to the current of events, and even in this volume we are enabled to see him as part—a determining part—of history."

BIOGRAPHICAL/CRITICAL SOURCES: London Times Literary Supplement, March 2, 1940; *Spectator*, March 22, 1940; *New Statesman and Nation*, April 13, 1940; *Christian Science Monitor*, May 4, 1940; *Boston Transcript*, September 14, 1940; *Time*, September 23, 1940; *Springfield Republican*, September 26, 1940; *Saturday Review of Literature*, September 28, 1940; *New York Herald Tribune*, September 29, 1940; *Atlantic Monthly*, October, 1940; *New York Times*, December 15, 1940; *Journal of Modern History*, September, 1973.

OBITUARIES: New York Times, March 5, 1974; *Washington Post*, March 5, 1974.*

*   *   *

BURKEY, Richard M(ichael)   1930-

PERSONAL: Born April 25, 1930, in Denver, Colo.; son of Lyle Oran (a bus driver) and Winifred C. (a bookkeeper; maiden name, Richardson) Burkey; married Sally Ann Chambers (a real estate broker), August 15, 1950; children: Richard Michael, Jr. *Education:* University of Denver, B.A., 1953; University of Colorado, M.A., 1963, Ph.D., 1971. *Politics:* Democrat. *Religion:* None. *Home:* 390 Clermont St., Denver, Colo. 80220. *Office:* Department of Sociology, University of Denver, Denver, Colo. 80208.

CAREER: Teacher in public schools in Denver, Colo., 1953-68; University of Denver, Denver, Colo., assistant professor, 1968-72, associate professor of sociology, 1972—. *Military service:* U.S. Marine Corps, 1947-50. *Member:* International Social Science Honor Society, American Sociological Association, Society for the Study of Social Problems, American Association of University Professors, Phi Beta Kappa, Delta Tau Kappa.

WRITINGS: Racial Discrimination and Public Policy in the United States, Lexington Books, 1971; *Ethnic and Racial Groups: The Dynamics of Dominance*, Cummings, 1978. Contributor to *Dictionary of American History*.

WORK IN PROGRESS: Social Inequality in Complex Society.

SIDELIGHTS: Burkey comments: "I am interested in the wide variety and forms of social inequality in complex societies—from Sumeria to the present time, particularly ethnic and racial, gender, and occupational inequality, slavery, and social class. I attempt to merge history and sociology, using the rich descriptive material from history with analysis from a sociological perspective. I believe that inequality is the result of rules of various kinds, and conflict is the basic process that changes the rules and hence the inequality."

*   *   *

BURLINGHAM, Dorothy Tiffany   1891-1979

OBITUARY NOTICE: Born in 1891 in New York, N.Y.; died November 19, 1979, in London, England. Child psychologist and author. In 1924 Burlingham moved to Vienna to continue her study of child psychology. There she met Anna Freud, the daughter of Sigmund Freud, and later lived with the Freud family. Together with the Freuds, Burlingham left Vienna in 1938 to escape the Nazis, and settled in London. During World War II Burlingham and Freud founded three nurseries for British children orphaned or separated from their parents. Their experiences were the basis for the 1943 book *War and Children*. Burlingham also authored two other books, *Twins: A Study of Three Pairs of Identical Twins*, 1953, and *Psychoanalytic Studies of the Sighted and the Blind*, 1972. Obituaries and other sources: *The Author's and Writer's Who's Who*, 6th edition, Burke's Peerage, 1971; *New York Times*, November 22, 1979.

*   *   *

BURRIDGE, Kenelm (Oswald Lancelot)   1922-

PERSONAL: Born October 31, 1922, in St. Julians, Malta; son of William (a professor) and Jane (Torregiani) Burridge; children: Julian Langford. *Education:* Oxford University, B.A., 1948, diploma in anthropology, 1949, M.A., 1950, B.Litt., 1950; Australian National University, Ph.D., 1953. *Home:* Apt. 4, 2265 Acadia Rd., Vancouver, British Columbia, Canada V6T 1R7. *Office:* Department of Anthropology and Sociology, University of British Columbia, Vancouver, British Columbia, Canada.

CAREER: University of Baghdad, Baghdad, Iraq, professor of anthropology, 1953-56; Oxford University, Oxford, England, lecturer in ethnology, 1956-68; University of British Columbia, Vancouver, professor of anthropology, 1968—, head of anthropology and sociology department, 1973—. Visiting lecturer at University of Western Australia, 1968. *Military service:* Royal Navy; became lieutenant. *Member:* American Anthropological Association, Canadian Sociological and Anthropological Association, Royal Society of Canada, Royal Anthropological Institute of Great Britain and Ireland. *Awards, honors:* Research fellow at University of Malaya, 1953-56; Guggenheim fellow, 1972-73; S.S.H.R.C. fellow and Killam fellow, both 1979-80.

WRITINGS: Mambu: A Melanesian Millenium, Methuen, 1967; *Tangu Traditions: A Study of the Way of Life, Mythology, and Developing Experience of a New Guinea People*, Clarendon Press, 1969; *New Heaven, New Earth: A Study of Millenarian Activities*, Schocken, 1969; *Encountering Ab-*

origines, A Case Study: Anthropology and the Australian Aboriginal, Pergamon Press, 1978; *Someone, No One,* Princeton University Press, 1979.

WORK IN PROGRESS: Research on missionaries.

SIDELIGHTS: According to *Anthropology Today,* anthropology is "the comparative study of mankind." The word "comparative" carries special significance for many contemporary cultural anthropologists; Kenelm Burridge is one of these. He believes that a culture must be judged by how well it serves its own people's needs, and not be arbitrarily criticized through another's standards. Nevertheless, it is vital to realize a culture's relevance to every other society. Burridge takes this position in *Encountering Aborigines, A Case Study: Anthropology and the Australian Aboriginal.* Though suggested by the title, his work is not totally devoted to the aborigine; rather, it is "concerned with the way the anthropological enterprise has been shaped by the context of Western civilization, as that enterprise is revealed through its praxis among the Aborigines," explained Philip L. Newman.

Burridge begins his book with a cumulation of much of the published information available on the migratory tribe to date. He then draws generalizations on the society as a whole, leading directly into "motives" or "themes" applicable to any culture. The aborigine is seen as "everyman," reacting in his own unique way to the basic biological and sociological stimuli faced by all humankind. By not taking into account alien cultures such as this one, Burridge insists we cannot ultimately understand our own. And to gain this intrinsic knowledge, the overwhelming conceit in the virtue of our own morals and traditions with its condescending opinion of other cultures must be eradicated.

Burridge sees the unfortunate trend of anthropology today leaning toward "professionalism" rather than "humanism." Cultures are statistically and categorically analyzed with little apparent regard for inherent motivating factors. Rituals and routines alike are duly recorded, but the spirit of the people themselves never emerges. As in most human endeavor, however, a reversal is in sight. Burridge believes the current attitude will soon run its course, with a more humanistic approach resulting.

BIOGRAPHICAL/CRITICAL SOURCES: Times Literary Supplement, March 5, 1970; *Anthropology Today,* Communications Research Machines, 1971; *Science,* June 28, 1974.

* * *

BURTON, H(arry) M(cGuire Philip)   1898(?)-1979

OBITUARY NOTICE: Born c. 1898; died November 15, 1979, in Cambridge, England. Educator, administrator, and author. From 1956 to 1973, Burton served as chief examiner for the Cambridge Local Examination Syndicate. He was the author of several books on education, including *The Education of the Countryman* and *Good English,* and an autobiog-

raphy, *There Was a Young Man.* Obituaries and other sources: *The Author's and Writer's Who's Who,* 6th edition, Burke's Peerage, 1971; *AB Bookman's Weekly,* December 24-31, 1979.

* * *

BUSHYAGER, Linda E(yster)   1947-

PERSONAL: Born September 8, 1947, in Washington, D.C.; daughter of William Henry (a program evaluation and review technique analyst) and Harriette (an administrative assistant; maiden name, Wolk) Eyster; married Ronald R. Bushyager II (a computer systems analyst), August 23, 1969. *Education:* Carnegie-Mellon University, B.S., 1969. *Home:* 1614 Evans Ave., Prospect Park, Pa. 19076. *Agent:* Lea Braff, Jarvis, Braff Ltd., 133 Seventh Ave., Brooklyn, N.Y. 11215.

CAREER: Franklin Institute, Research Laboratories, Philadelphia, Pa., editor of "Air Pollution Abstracts," 1971-75; North American Publishing Co., Philadelphia, editor of *Lab World,* 1975-76; writer, 1976—.

WRITINGS: Master of Hawks (science fiction), Dell, 1979; *Spellstone of Shaltus* (science fiction), Dell, 1980. Editor of science fiction magazines *Granfalloon* and *Karass.*

WORK IN PROGRESS: Several fantasy and science fiction novels.

SIDELIGHTS: Linda Bushyager writes: "I was an avid science fiction fan and reader for many years before becoming a professional science fiction writer. I am currently very active in science fiction fandom." *Avocational interests:* Films (especially science fiction and musicals).

* * *

BUTTRICK, George Arthur   1892-1980

OBITUARY NOTICE—See index for *CA* sketch: Born March 23, 1892, in Seaham Harbour, Northumberland, England; died January 23, 1980, in Louisville, Ky. Preacher, educator, editor, and writer. A Protestant theologian renowned for his liberal beliefs and stirring sermons, Buttrick was the pastor of Madison Avenue Presbyterian Church, New York City's largest Presbyterian congregation, from 1927 to 1954. In 1954 he accepted a position with Harvard University as preacher to the university and professor of Christian morals. Among his books are *The Parables of Jesus; Jesus Came Preaching; God, Pain, and Evil;* and *The Power of Prayer Today.* He was also the editor-in-chief of the twelve-volume *The Interpreters Bible* and the four-volume *The Interpreters Dictionary of the Bible.* Obituaries and other sources: Edgar DeWitt Jones, *Royalty of the Pulpit,* Harper, 1951; *Life,* April 6, 1953; *The Author's and Writer's Who's Who,* 6th edition, Burke's Peerage, 1971; *Who's Who in America,* 40th edition, Marquis, 1978; *New York Times,* January 24, 1980; *Time,* February 4, 1980; *Newsweek,* February 4, 1980; *Publishers Weekly,* February 22, 1980.

C

CABOT, Thomas Dudley 1897-

PERSONAL: Born May 1, 1897, in Cambridge, Mass.; son of Godfrey Lowell and Maria Buckminster (Moors) Cabot; married Virginia Wellington, May 15, 1920; children: Louis Wellington, Thomas Dudley, Robert Moors, Linda (Mrs. L. C. Black), Edmund Billings. *Education:* Harvard University, A.B., 1919. *Politics:* Republican. *Religion:* Unitarian-Universalist. *Home:* 31 Farm Rd., Weston, Mass. 02193. *Office:* 125 High St., Boston, Mass. 02110.

CAREER: Cabot Corp., Boston, Mass., chief executive, 1922-60, chairperson of board of directors, 1960-68, honorary chairperson of board, 1968—. Leader of American Geographic Society's Cabot Colombian Expedition to map the Sierra Nevada de Santa Marta, 1939. Head of Massachusetts Aeronautics Commission, 1942-45, and U.S. International Security Affairs Committee, 1951. President of United Fruit Co., Boston, Mass., 1948-49; co-founder of Controlled Risk Insurance Co.; past member of board of directors of John Hancock Mutual Life Insurance Co., First National Bank of Boston, and American Mutual Liability Insurance Co.; member of board of overseers of Harvard University, 1953-59 and 1962-68, and of governing boards of Massachusetts Institute of Technology, Radcliffe College, and Escuela Agricola Panamericana; consultant to U.S. Department of State. *Military service:* U.S. Army, flying instructor, 1917-18; became second lieutenant; received commendatore Al Merito della Repubblica Italiana; named Chevalier of French Legion of Honor.

MEMBER: International Chamber of Commerce (trustee of national council), American Academy of Arts and Science (fellow), Council on Foreign Relations. *Awards, honors:* L.H.D. from Tufts University, 1951, and Boston University, 1961; LL.D. from Northeastern University, 1952, Morris Harvey College, 1953, and Harvard University, 1970.

WRITINGS: Quick Water and Smooth (guidebook), Stephen Daye Press, 1935; *Beggar on Horseback* (autobiography), David R. Godine, 1979. Contributor to journals, including *Atlantic Monthly, Foreign Service Journal, Appalachia, Harvard,* and *American Geographical Journal.*

*   *   *

CAIN, Michael Peter 1941-

PERSONAL: Born July 3, 1941, in Boston, Mass.; son of Joseph Lambert (an artist and educator) and Matene (an artist and educator; maiden name, Rachoetes) Cain; married Charlotte Modliszewski (an artist and educator) in 1966; children: Vayya Ananda-Jo, Chandra-Lila Matene Maizy. *Education:* Attended Art Students' League, 1961-62; Harvard University, A.B. (cum laude), 1964; Yale University, B.F.A. and M.F.A., both 1967. *Office:* Department of Art, Maharishi International University, Fairfield, Iowa 52556.

CAREER: Yale University, New Haven, Conn., 1967-73, began as research associate, became lecturer in environmental art; Maharishi International University, Fairfield, Iowa, professor of art, 1973—, head of department, 1973-76, director of Institute of the Arts, 1975—. Collaborative artist with Pulsa, 1967-73. Gives public lectures and scholarly seminars and workshops. Paintings and sculptures have been exhibited at shows in New York, New England, Switzerland, and the Midwest, and in galleries in New York City. *Member:* Association for Art, Consciousness and Enlightenment (executive director, 1979—). *Awards, honors:* Grants from Graham Foundation, 1968-72, and from private patrons, industry, Boston Urban Revelopment, Museum of Modern Art, California Institute of the Arts, and Automation House.

WRITINGS: (Contributor) Lucy Lippard, editor, *Six Years,* Praeger, 1972; (with Harold Bloomfield, Robert Kory, and Dennis Jaffe) *TM: Discovering Inner Energy and Overcoming Stress,* Delacorte, 1975; *Images of Consciousness: Boundaries Capturing the Boundless* (video-lecture series), Maharishi International University, 1977. Contributor of articles and poems to art journals and literary magazines.

WORK IN PROGRESS: Additional video lectures; large-scale, multiple-pattern relief paintings in acrylic plastic and routed wood.

SIDELIGHTS: While associated with Pulsa, Cain's work dealt with environmental art. Pulsa's orientation was toward "conceiving, designing, arranging, fabricating, installing, and programming (computer-controlled) or operating various art works; developing alternative life support and communications systems; and public demonstrations."

Cain has exhibited artwork involving microphones, strobe and fluorescent lighting, speakers, infra-red heating devices, mirrors, video projectors, and sonar. More recently he has shown works in watercolor.

AVOCATIONAL INTERESTS: Travel (Afghanistan, Austria, England, France, Germany, Greece, India, Iran, Italy, Mexico, Nepal, Pakistan, Spain, Switzerland, Turkey).

CAIN, Thomas H(enry) 1931-

PERSONAL: Born February 23, 1931, in Toronto, Ontario, Canada; son of Eliot E. (a farmer) and Mary (Ellis) Cain; married Emily J. M. Smith (a graphic designer), June 23, 1963; children: Patrick E. M. *Education:* University of Toronto, B.A., 1953, M.A., 1956; University of Wisconsin, Madison, Ph.D., 1959. *Religion:* Anglican. *Office:* Department of English, McMaster University, Hamilton, Ontario, Canada.

CAREER: Yale University, New Haven, Conn., lecturer, 1959-62, assistant professor of English, 1962-66; McMaster University, Hamilton, Ontario, associate professor, 1966-79, professor of English, 1979—. Past member of Te Deum Singers. *Member:* Association of Canadian University Professors of English, Renaissance Society of America.

WRITINGS: Common Sense About Writing, Prentice-Hall, 1966; *Praise in "The Faerie Queene,"* University of Nebraska Press, 1978. Contributor to literature journals.

WORK IN PROGRESS: Research on concealed structures in Spenser.

SIDELIGHTS: Cain's interests are Renaissance literature, Irish studies, the teaching of writing, and university liaison with secondary schools.

AVOCATIONAL INTERESTS: Gardening (especially old and wild plants), early music (especially choral), liturgy, organ, church and concert choirs.

*   *   *

CALVERT, Mary 1941-
(Mary Danby)

PERSONAL: Born May 26, 1941, in Dorking, England; daughter of Denys (a veterinary surgeon) and Doris (a writer and teacher; maiden name, Dickens) Danby; married Brian Calvert (an airline pilot), April 15, 1972; children: Diana May. *Education:* Attended technical high school in Kingston-upon-Thames, England. *Home:* Noakes Hill Cottage, Ashampstead, Berkshire RG8 8RY, England.

CAREER: Westward Television, Plymouth, England, production assistant, 1962-65; American Broadcasting Companies (ABC-TV), London, England, production assistant, 1965-68; Fontana Paperbacks, London, fiction editor, 1969-72; free-lance writer, 1972—; Armada Books, London, consulting editor, 1973—.

WRITINGS: Turnip Tom and Big Fat Rosie (juvenile), BBC Publications, 1972; (under name Mary Danby) *A Single Girl* (novel), McGraw, 1972; (under name Mary Danby) *The Best of Friends* (novel), McGraw, 1975; *The Big Fat Rosie Storybook* (juvenile), BBC Publications, 1977; (under name Mary Danby; with Jane Allen) *Hello to Ponies* (juvenile nonfiction), Heinemann, 1979; (with Allen) *Hello to Riding* (juvenile nonfiction), Heinemann, 1980. Work represented in anthologies, including *Spectre 1*, edited by Richard Davis, Abelard-Schuman, 1973; *Creepies*, edited by Helen Hoke, Franklin Watts, 1977, and *Horrors, Horrors, Horrors*, edited by Hoke, Franklin Watts, 1978. Also editor of horror anthologies and children's puzzle books, for Fontana and Armada, 1970-79.

*   *   *

CAMP, John (Michael Francis) 1915-

PERSONAL: Born July 31, 1915, in England; son of Harold Walter (a government official) and Marguerite (a teacher; maiden name, Dervin) Camp; married Rose Elizabeth Anstis (a pharmacist), April 18, 1938; children: John Edward. *Education:* Attended West Ham Technical College, London, England, 1932-36. *Home and office:* Thurston House, Wingrave, Aylesbury, Buckinghamshire HP22 4QE, England.

CAREER: Apprentice at a private pharmacy in Dagenham, England, 1932-36; cosmetics salesman for D. R. Collins Ltd., 1936-40 and 1946-52; ran own business in agricultural chemicals, Amersham, England, 1952-66; Wellcome Foundation Ltd., medical writer in London, 1966-70; writer, 1970—. Justice of the Peace, 1964—. *Military service:* British Army, 1940-46; became counter-intelligence warrant officer; received American Bronze Star. *Member:* Society of Authors, Society for the History of Pharmacy, Medico-Legal Society, Magistrates Association.

WRITINGS: Oxfordshire and Buckinghamshire Pubs, B. T. Batsford, 1965; *Discovering Bells and Bellringing*, Shire, 1968; *Discovering London Railway Stations*, Shire, 1971; *Portrait of Buckinghamshire*, Hale, 1972; *Magic, Myth, and Medicine*, Priory Press, 1973; *Bellringing: Chimes, Carillons, Handbells; The World of the Bellringer*, David & Charles, 1974; *Holloway Prison: The Place and the People*, David & Charles, 1974; *The Healers Art: The Doctor Through History*, Muller, 1978. Contributor of articles to more than twenty journals and magazines, including *World Medicine, Good Housekeeping, Reader's Digest, Guardian,* and *Chemist and Druggist*.

WORK IN PROGRESS: A history of Mentmore Towers, a large Victorian mansion in Buckinghamshire, England, once owned by the Rothschilds and now by the Transcendental Meditation Movement.

SIDELIGHTS: John Camp told *CA:* "I have been engaged in selling and writing since being paid for an article by a local newspaper at the age of ten. I believe that life is a constant process of salesmanship, largely of ourselves, though I am by no means an extrovert or 'pushy' person. In my writings, I do not indulge in fiction (except when writing advertising copy) but specialize in legal and medical history and also in crime."

*   *   *

CAMPBELL, E. Simms 1906-1971

OBITUARY NOTICE: Born January 2, 1906, in St. Louis, Mo.; died January 25, 1971, in White Plains, N.Y. Illustrator, cartoonist, and author. Campbell was a regular cartoonist for *Esquire* since the magazine's inception in 1933; he is credited with the creation of Eski, the connoisseur of female beauty who appeared on numberous *Esquire* covers. His cartoons also appeared in such publications as *New Yorker, Playboy, Life,* and *Saturday Evening Post*. He also illustrated children's books and wrote articles on American jazz. Obituaries and other sources: *Current Biography*, Wilson, 1941, March, 1971; *New York Times*, January 29, 1971.

*   *   *

CANADA, Lena 1942-

PERSONAL: Born July 18, 1942, in Ljusdal, Sweden; came to United States in 1963; daughter of Ake (in Swedish navy) and Britt (Moberg) Svensson; divorced; children: Herbie, Patrick. *Education:* Statens Normalskola, Stockholm, Sweden, graduate, 1961; also attended University of California, Los Angeles. *Home:* 2657 South Bedford St., Los Angeles, Calif. 90034. *Agent:* Julian Bach Literary Agency, Inc., 3 East 48th St., New York, N.Y. 10017.

CAREER: Legal secretary in and near Los Angeles, Calif., 1967—.

WRITINGS: To Elvis, With Love, Everest House, 1978.

WORK IN PROGRESS: An autobiographical novel, dealing mainly with child abuse.

SIDELIGHTS: Lena Canada writes: "I have spent my entire life writing and dreaming of being a 'writer.' *To Elvis* was extremely intimate and personal writing, based entirely on my own pain, and was never intended as a manuscript. On a fluke, however, I sent it to my agent, who turned it into a *real* book. I am now facing the ordeal of finding out, for myself, whether I am—really and truly—a writer."

To Elvis, With Love is currently being made into a screenplay.

BIOGRAPHICAL/CRITICAL SOURCES: McCalls, August, 1978; *Working Woman,* November, 1978; *Detroit Free Press,* November 26, 1978; *Hollywood Reporter,* December 8, 1978.

*   *   *

CANAWAY, W(illiam) H(amilton)   1925-

PERSONAL: Born June 12, 1925, in Altrincham, Cheshire, England; married Pamela Mary Burgess; children: five. *Education:* University of Wales, B.A. (with honors), 1948, Dp.Ed., 1949, M.A., 1951. *Agent:* Curtis Brown Ltd., 1 Craven Hill, London W2 3EW, England.

CAREER: Writer. *Military service:* British Army, Queen's Royal Regiment and Intelligence Corps, 1943-46; served in Italy and the Middle East. *Member:* International P.E.N., Bronte Society. *Awards, honors:* Grant from Welsh Arts Council, 1973.

WRITINGS: A Creed of Willow (nonfiction), M. Joseph, 1957; *A Snowdon Stream (the Gwyrfai) and How to Fish It* (nonfiction), Putnam, 1958; *The Ring-Givers,* M. Joseph, 1958; *The Seal,* M. Joseph, 1959; *Find the Boy,* Viking, 1961 (published in England as *Sammy Going South,* Hutchinson, 1961); *The Hunter and the Horns,* Harper, 1962; *My Feet Upon a Rock,* Hutchinson, 1963; *Crows in a Green Tree,* Doubleday, 1965; *The Grey Seas of Jutland,* Hutchinson, 1966; *The Mules of Borgo San Marco,* Hutchinson, 1967; *A Moral Obligation,* Hutchinson, 1969; *A Declaration of Independence,* Hutchinson, 1974; *The Willow-Pattern War,* Hutchinson, 1976. Also author of *The Solid Gold Buddha,* 1979, and *Deserters.*

Plays: "Horse on Fire," first produced in England, at Hawkesyard Priory, 1961; "Roll Me Over," first produced in Birmingham, England, 1971.

Screenplays: (With James Doran) "The Ipcress File," 1965; "Rendezvous in Black," 1972. Also author of "Dan, Badger and All the Coal" and "Love of Life."

Contributor of short stories and articles to magazines and journals.

SIDELIGHTS: Canaway told *CA:* "Though Richard Griffith said it about Robert Flaherty, I view my own writing in much the same way: 'His was the search for what he called the spirit of man . . . a search which has been almost abandoned in our time . . . and many, to whom his films are an experience almost like racial memory, ponder what sent him forth on this alchemical quest in a day when science, or some of her voices, say there is no spirit to be found, but only a handful of dust.'"

*   *   *

CANNON, Le Grand, Jr.   1899-1979

OBITUARY NOTICE: Born December 1, 1899, in New Haven, Conn.; died December 12, 1979, in Hamden, Conn. Novelist, best known for *Look to the Mountain,* a story of America's early pioneers. Cannon, who received an M.B.A. from Harvard University, pursued a business career until 1932, when he decided to try his hand at full-time writing. Among his other works are *The Kents, A Mighty Fortress,* and *Come Home at Even.* He was an associate fellow of Saybrook College, Yale University. Obituaries and other sources: *Current Biography,* Wilson, 1943; *The Author's and Writer's Who's Who,* 6th edition, Burke's Peerage, 1971; *New York Times,* December 15, 1979; *AB Bookmen's Weekly,* January 14, 1980.

*   *   *

CAPTAIN X
See POWER-WATERS, Brian

*   *   *

CARMODY, Denise Lardner   1935-

PERSONAL: Born December 10, 1935, in Baltimore, Md.; daughter of Denis and Martha (Coman) Lardner; married John Tully Carmody (a writer), December 12, 1971. *Education:* College of Notre Dame of Maryland, B.A. (summa cum laude), 1958; Boston College, M.A., 1966, Ph.D., 1970. *Home:* 3425 East English, #108, Wichita, Kan. 67218. *Office:* Department of Religion, Wichita State University, Wichita, Kan. 67208.

CAREER: Boston College, Chestnut Hill, Mass., instructor in philosophy, 1967-68; College of Notre Dame of Maryland, Baltimore, assistant professor of philosophy, 1969-70; St. Patrick's college, Mountain View, Calif., assistant professor of philosophy, 1970-73; Pennsylvania State University, University Park, assistant professor of religion, 1973-77; Wichita State University, Wichita, Kan., chair of religion department, 1977—. *Member:* American Academy of Religion (chair of academic study of religion section, 1979-81).

WRITINGS: Women and World Religion, Abingdon, 1979; *Ways to the Center,* Wadsworth, 1980; *The Oldest God,* Abingdon, in press; *Catholic Theology,* Harper, in press.

WORK IN PROGRESS: Collaborating with husband, John Carmody, on *Religious Wisdom,* publication by Wadsworth expected in 1982.

SIDELIGHTS: Carmody told *CA:* "I am especially interested in furnishing undergraduates with lively texts on world religions. I am also interested in feminist issues and contemporary Christian spirituality."

AVOCATIONAL INTEREST: Jogging, international travel.

*   *   *

CARPENTER, Andrew   1943-

PERSONAL: Born June 26, 1943, in Frimley, England; son of Philip (a clergyman and carpenter) and Anne Faithfull (Monier-Williams) Isdell-Carpenter; married Mary Jean Stewart, 1967; children: Jonathan, Simon. *Education:* Oxford University, B.A. (with honors), 1964, M.A., 1967; National University of Ireland, Ph.D., 1970. *Office:* Department of English, University College, National University of Ireland, Belfield, Dublin 4, Ireland.

CAREER: British Institute, Oporto, Portugal, lecturer in English, 1964-65; University of Victoria, Victoria, British Columbia, lecturer in English, 1965-67; National University of Ireland, University College, Dublin, lecturer, 1970-74, senior lecturer in English, 1974—. *Member:* International

Association for the Study of Anglo-Irish Literature, Dublin Association of An Taisce (chairperson, 1975-78).

WRITINGS: Miscellanies in Prose, Cadenus Press, 1972; *Miscellanies in Verse,* Cadenus Press, 1973; *Miscellanies in Correspondence,* Cadenus Press, 1974; (editor) *My Uncle John: Recollections of J. M. Synge,* Oxford University Press, 1974; (editor) William King, *Sermon on Predestination,* Cadenus Press, 1975; (editor) Charles Ford, *Adventure in Siena,* Cadenus Press, 1977; *Place, Personality, and the Irish Writer,* Barnes & Noble, 1977; (editor with Peter Fallon) *The Writers: A Sense of Ireland 1980,* O'Brien Press, 1980; (editor) *A New Guide to Anglo-Irish Literature,* Volume I, Irish Academy Press, 1980. Editor of quarterly journal of Dublin Association of An Taisce, 1976-79.

SIDELIGHTS: Carpenter commented: "I have been instrumental in bringing to fruition the ten-volume Cadenus Press series, 'Irish Writings From the Age of Swift.' I have also been publishing (and sometimes printing) limited editions of works by modern Irish writers."

* * *

CARPENTER, Rhys 1889-1980

OBITUARY NOTICE—See index for *CA* sketch: Born August 5, 1889, in Cotuit, Mass.; died January 2, 1980, in Devon, Pa. Archaeologist, educator, and writer. Carpenter served as the head of the archaeology department at Bryn Mawr and as director of the American School of Classical Studies in Athens. Among the many books he wrote on archaeology and classical studies are *The Greeks in Spain, The Humanistic Value of Archaeology,* and *The Architects of the Parthenon.* A poet as well, his volumes of verse include *The Tragedy of Etarre* and *The Plainsman and Other Poems.* Obituaries and other sources: *Who's Who in America,* 39th edition, Marquis, 1976; *Who's Who,* 131st edition, St. Martin's 1979; *New York Times,* January 4, 1980.

* * *

CARR, Janet Baker
See BAKER-CARR, Janet

* * *

CARR, Robert K(enneth) 1908-1979

PERSONAL: Born February 15, 1908, in Cleveland, Ohio; died of a brain tumor, February 21, 1979, in Elyria, Ohio; son of Clifford A. and Sue (Stewart) Carr; married Olive Grabill (a child Guidance worker), August 25, 1933; children; Norman Stewart, Elliot Grabill, Robert Clifford. *Education:* Dartmouth College, B.A., 1929; Harvard University, M.A., 1930, Ph.D., 1935. *Residence:* Oberlin, Ohio.

CAREER: University of Oklahoma, Norman, 1931-37, began as instructor, became associate professor and director of Bureau of Municipal Research; Dartmouth College, Hanover, N.H., instructor, 1937-48, Joel Parker Professor of Law and Political Science, 1948-59; Oberlin College, Oberlin, Ohio, president, 1960-70, instructor, 1975; American Council on Education, Washington D.C., executive associate, 1970-72; consultant to Association of Governing Boards of Universities and Colleges, 1972-79. Executive secretary of President's Committee on Civil Rights, 1947; Carnegie Foundation for the Advancement of Teaching, trustee, 1962-66, member of executive committee, 1966-70; trustee of American Council of Education, 1963-67. Consultant to U.S. Civil Rights Commission, 1959; member of advisory committee for higher education of Department of Health, Education

and Welfare, 1967-68; member of academic advisory board of U.S. Naval Academy, 1969-71.

MEMBER: American Association of University Professors (vice-president, 1955-57; general secretary, 1957-58), Association of American Colleges, American Political Science Association, American Academy of Arts and Sciences (fellow), New England Political Science Association (president, 1955-56), Phi Beta Kappa. *Awards, honors:* Rockefeller Foundation fellowship, 1945 and 1947; Franklin D. Roosevelt Book Prize from American Political Science Association, 1948; Guggenheim fellow, 1954-55; LL.D. from Dartmouth College, Ohio Wesleyan University, and Concord College, all 1960, from University of Pittsburgh, 1962, and from Ripon College, 1967; L.H.D. from Denison University, 1970.

WRITINGS: Democracy and the Supreme Court, University of Oklahoma Press, 1936; *State Control of Local Finance in Oklahoma,* University of Oklahoma Press, 1937; *The Supreme Court and Judicial Review,* Farrar & Rinehart, 1942, reprinted, Greenwood Press, 1970; *Federal Protection of Civil Rights: A Quest for a Sword,* Cornell University Press, 1947; (with others) *American Democracy in Theory and Practice: The National Government,* Holt, 1951, revised edition published as *American Democracy in Theory and Practice: National, State, and Local Government,* 1955, published as *American Democracy in Theory and Practice: Essentials of National, State, and Local Government,* 1961, 4th edition published under original title, 1963, 5th and revised edition published as *American Democracy* 1968, 6th edition published both as *American Democracy* and as *Essentials of American Democracy,* 1971, 8th edition published as *Carr and Bernstein's American Democracy,* 1977; (editor) *Civil Rights in America,* American Academy of Political and Social Science, 1951; *The House Committee on Un-American Activities, 1945-50,* Cornell University Press, 1952; (with Daniel K. VanEyck) *Collective Bargaining Comes to the Campus,* American Council on Education, 1973. Contributor of articles to newspapers and legal journals.

SIDELIGHTS: Robert K. Carr was a highly respected authority on constitutional law and civil rights. His books on these topics were praised for their thorough scholarship and lucid style of writing. E. S. Corwin declared that in *The Supreme Court and Judicial Review,* Carr "writes most engagingly. His selection and arrangement of materials reflect a high degree of literary craftsmanship. He has a quick eye for the significant issue, and notable skill in making its significance evident to lay comprehension."

Carr's next book, *Federal Protection of Civil Rights,* was very well received by critics. A. T. Mason remarked that "Carr has given us a timely and effective book, admirably conceived, balanced in organization and presentation—a work that meets the requirements of scholarship as well as literary artistry. In all these respects it may well serve as a model of research and writing in political science." In *The House Committee on Un-American Activities, 1945-1950,* according to R. L. Duffuss, the author "has made a real attempt to evaluate the committee's work." Similarly, Clair Wilcox claimed that Carr "has gone over the record with a fine-tooth comb. He supports his every statement with a citation of chapter and verse. He leans over backward to be fair. His tone is objective, scholarly, dispassionate. He allows the Committee to speak for itself—and to condemn itself."

On Carr's last book, *Collective Bargaining Comes to the Campus,* J. W. Garbarino observed: "The strengths of the book are its comprehensive discussion of virtually all of the evidence and experience available. It is particularly strong in its review of the hearings and court cases that have been such an important part of the record of faculty unionism so far. . . . This is clearly the book to read to find the most complete statement of the issues involved.''

BIOGRAPHICAL/CRITICAL SOURCES: Social Studies, May, 1942; *American Political Science Review,* June, 1942, June, 1948, September, 1953; *New York Herald Tribune Book Review,* July 12, 1942; *Saturday Review of Literature,* August 22, 1942, February 28, 1948; *Annals of the American Academy of Political and Social Science,* September, 1942, March, 1953; *American Economic Review,* December, 1942; *Survey Graphic,* April, 1948; *Harvard Law Review,* May, 1948; *New York Times,* May 2, 1948, December 14, 1952; *New Republic,* September 28, 1953; *Journal of Higher Education,* March, 1974.*

* * *

CARRACO, Carol Crowe
   See CROWE-CARRACO, Carol

* * *

CARRIGHAR, Sally

PERSONAL: Born in Cleveland, Ohio. *Education:* Attended Wellesley College.

CAREER: Writer and naturalist. Wrote for various motion picture companies, 1923-28, and for radio, 1928-38. *Awards, honors:* Guggenheim fellowship for field work in the Arctic.

WRITINGS: One Day on Beetle Rock, Knopf, 1944, reprinted, University of Nebraska Press, 1978; *One Day at Teton Marsh,* Knopf, 1947, reprinted, University of Nebraska Press, 1979; *Icebound Summer,* Knopf, 1953; *As Far as They Could Go* (play), [Fairbanks, Alaska], 1956; *Moonlight at Midday,* Knopf, 1958; *Wild Voice of the North,* Doubleday, 1959 (published in England as *A Husky in the House,* M. Joseph, 1959); *The Glass Dove* (novel), Doubleday, 1962; *Wild Heritage,* Houghton, 1965; *Home to the Wilderness* (autobiography), Houghton, 1973; *The Twilight Seas,* Weybright, 1975 (published in England as *Blue Whale,* Gollancz, 1978).

Also author of screenplay, ''One Day at Teton Marsh'' (adapted from the book by Carrighar), Walt Disney, 1966. Contributor of articles to magazines, including *Saturday Evening Post, Atlantic Monthly,* and *Reader's Digest.*

SIDELIGHTS: Sally Carrighar was introduced to nature at an early age—she spent her childhood at her grandparent's home in Ohio where her playground was the outdoors. From those grandparents she gained her deep-seated interest in animals and plants, and as a result, much of her life has been spent in the appreciation and study of nature—several summers in the Canadian woods, with a guide who taught her how to track wild animals; trips into northern Michigan, the Rockies and the Ozarks, where she spent six months as a guide at a fishing lodge.

In 1937 she turned to writing about her experiences. Material for her first book was collected after spending months at Beetle Rock in Sequoia National Park, in the Sierra Nevada Mountains, where she spent her time learning about every part of the living world around her. *One Day at Beetle Rock* was the outcome, and it was widely acclaimed. Said the *New York Times,* ''[It] is a book of rare distinction, at once a record of objective facts, of deep feeling without sentimentality and intense and subtle perception expressed in beauty. The

reader must, indeed, be hardened whom it does not lead into the paths of nature study, whether these paths are familiar or explored for the first time.'' And *Book Week* also praised it: ''The book is beautifully written, but there is more here than mere beautiful writing. With a skillful, expansive style the author succeeds in imparting the 'feel' of nine diverse lives, each as different from the others as though they existed in different worlds. Each chapter is a new experience for the reader, each animal a new study in actions and emotions.''

Her next book, *One Day at Teton Marsh,* focused on the habits and behavior of marsh animals when caught in an equinoctial storm. Illustrated by George and Patritia Mattson, the book was another critical success, ''both beguiling to look at and to read and own,'' wrote David McCord. Another reviewer, William Beebe, held that ''For a minimum of anthropomorphism, and in faithful representation of activities possible in a day in the life of each of these creatures, Miss Carrighar's book deserves a place near the top of fictional natural history.'' Noted J. H. Jackson: ''Wise, observant, patient, able to set down what she sees and learns in simple, admirable prose, Miss Carrighar is like no one else who has ever written about animals, birds and insects. Better still, she has the kind of sensitivity that doesn't need a conflict on man-scale in order to produce tension. . . . She can build a drama even—well, even around a mosquito.''

Thanks to a Guggenheim fellowship, received as a result of her studies of natural animal behavior, she was able to take up the study of the Eskimos and wild animals of the Arctic. She stayed nine years, part of the time in Unalakleet, a primitive, isolated village, supporting herself through writing when her fellowship ran out. From her years in the Arctic came *Icebound Summer, Moonlight at Midday,* and *Wild Voice of the North.*

With *Icebound Summer,* critics were again struck by the virtues of Carrighar's prose and her special sensitivity to animal life. ''Her writing is delicate and precise,'' noted P. L. Adams, ''and she has a fine touch with the physical maneuvers of her subjects and the look of the country itself, the visual effects of cold, sunlight, wind, and water.'' W. M. Teller found that ''Throughout her book Miss Carrighar inspires confidence in her accuracy as a wildlife observer. But she does more—she communicates her excitement and fervor. Her stories are informed with drama, pathos and surprise.'' T. M. Longstreth concluded: ''Few first books have founded a reputation unanimously as did Sally Carrighar's 'One Day on Beetle Rock.' Few second books uphold a reputation better than 'One Day at Teton Marsh.' When a third book is finest yet, congratulations and purchases are in order, for we have fame in the making.''

The Alaskan people themselves are treated in *Moonlight at Midday,* offering both a description and an analysis of the problems brought to the Arctic by Western civilization. Though R. L. Neuberger thought that ''more thorough analyses of Alaska's economic plight'' had already been written, he conceded that ''as an interpreter and analyst of those fetching native residents, the Eskimos, Sally Carrighar is without any superior.'' Added F. H. Guidry: ''With humor, warmth, good taste, and scientific thoroughness . . . Miss Carrighar covers a broad range of questions that any newcomer to the region might ask.''

The third book of her Alaskan period, *Wild Voice of the North,* presents what Rose Feld called ''a highly personal and deeply moving story'' about the author's seven-year association with Bobo, an Eskimo lead dog. Living in a house of the gold-rush days, Carrighar weathered an Alaskan winter in Nome and learned to communicate with her companion "by inflection of voice as well as through Bobo's intuition and insight," Feld remarked. She also "has a good deal to say about lemmings, huskies, Eskimos and life in the North," commented a writer for *Kirkus Reviews*. "And she says it in a prose in which the cooly scientific is balanced by the haunting warmth and loneliness left in the wake of a profound and unique friendship."

In her novel, *The Glass Dove*, Carrighar tells of Sylvia MacIntosh's efforts to run a station on the underground railroad during the American Civil War. Sylvia's task is complicated, however, by a romance with a suspected Confederate spy. According to Henry Cavendish, "The narrative, tho more leisurely than brisk, is packed with suspense thruout," whereas William Hogan "found the book tough going; the characters surprisingly lifeless." But P. P. Stiles observed that the book "examines the subtle intricacies of human nature—specifically the origins of a selfish love. . . . Characterizations are delicate and skillful." Another reviewer, Henrietta Buckmaster, remarked that "The resolution is not glib; it sustains the quiet probing tone of the whole book. This is one of the best things that can be said about this good book, that however melodramatic are the events, the human beings invariably move at a level of complete credibility and also with moral strength."

In 1965 Carrighar returned to her naturalist concerns with *Wild Heritage*. The book purports to show "how close is our behavior to that of other animals and how much we can discover from them about ourselves," she wrote. Edward Weeks thought that the "chapter on sex . . . is the most fascinating and provocative portion of Wild Heritage, and here, as throughout her text, Miss Carrighar supplements her own findings with the absorbing testimony she has garnered from other behaviorists. . . . The passages she selects are not only colorful; they tend to corroborate a central line of reasoning." As Marston Bates explained in the *New York Times Book Review*, Carrighar "is in rebellion against the school of thought, most fashionable early in the century, which regards animals as machines, without feelings or insights. . . . I think that [she] tends to overstress the cooperative aspects of the system of nature; but many other writers have overstressed conflict." Noted Weeks: "[The] book is delightfully written, packed with episodes one pauses to enjoy for a second time, and well illustrated by Rachel S. Horne."

Eight years later, Carrighar's autobiography, *Home to the Wilderness*, drew this response from H. T. Anderson: "I have just finished reading [one] of the most fascinating autobiographies to come my way in quite some time. . . . A great portion of Sally Carrighar's life was spent living in baroque hostility with her mother. For reasons profound, disturbing, and tragic, the child was hated by a mother who was unquestionably paranoic. Even a dog was taken away from her while she was very young, her mother admonished, 'You have to be learned not to be loved.' . . . The book chronicles monstrous, disturbing cruelty that ends in triumph. . . . From poverty to attempted suicide to psychoanalysis to the point of becoming an extraordinarily perceptive if not mystical writer of the world of nature—this author writes from the deepest level and withholds nothing."

Another work of fiction published in 1975, *The Twilight Seas*, depicts the life of a blue whale from birth to death. "Inspired by the grace and playfulness of these creatures, the writing at times becomes almost as liquid and as graceful as the blue whale itself," remarked John Ruppe. "In attempting to disclose the animal's point of view, its probable 'thought patterns,' as one might say, there is of course the danger of making the creature think like a human. I am always impressed, however, by the subtlety and delicacy with which Miss Carrighar copes with the problem." Reviewer V. M. Gilboy commented that this "is a very beautifully written book—a real delight to read. Miss Carrighar certainly has a wonderful knowledge of the ways of the oceans and the living beings within them. She spent many months of research and of correspondence with whale scientists at oceanographic institutes from Oslo to San Diego and the result is apparent in this work."

BIOGRAPHICAL/CRITICAL SOURCES: Book Week, November 19, 1944; *New York Times*, December 10, 1944, July 19, 1953, October 26, 1958; *San Francisco Chronicle*, September 25, 1947, July 28, 1953, November 9, 1958, March 7, 1962; *New York Herald Tribune Book Review*, September 28, 1947, July 19, 1953, August 2, 1953, October 26, 1958, December 6, 1959; *Atlantic Monthly*, November, 1947, August, 1953, April, 1965; *New York Times Book Review*, July 19, 1953, March 28, 1965; *Christian Science Monitor*, July 23, 1953, October 23, 1958, December 7, 1959, March 22, 1962, May 7, 1975; *Kirkus Reviews*, September 15, 1959; *Library Journal*, March 15, 1962; *Chicago Sunday Tribune*, April 1, 1962; *Saturday Review*, March 20, 1965; Sally Carrighar, *Home to the Wilderness* (autobiography), Houghton, 1973; *Best Sellers*, May 15, 1973, May, 1975.*

* * *

CARTLIDGE, Michelle 1950-

PERSONAL: Born October 13, 1950, in London, England. *Education:* Attended Hornsea College of Art, 1967-68, and Royal College of Art, 1968-70.

CAREER: Writer and illustrator. *Awards, honors:* Mother Goose Award, 1979, for *Pippin and Pod*.

WRITINGS—Self-illustrated children's books: *Pippin and Pod*, Pantheon, 1978; *The Bear's Bazaar* (craft book), Lothrop, 1979. Also author of *A Mouse's Diary*, 1980.

WORK IN PROGRESS: Another self-illustrated children's book.

SIDELIGHTS: Michelle Cartlidge began drawing in 1970 and had her initial exhibition in the same year. Her first book is set in Hampstead, but a Hampstead populated entirely by mice. Her second book is a creative crafts book for children, emphasizing projects that are inexpensive to make and require only a minimum of adult assistance.

* * *

CASALS, Pablo
See CASALS, Pau Carlos Salvador Defillo de

* * *

CASALS, Pau Carlos Salvador Defillo de 1876-1973
(Pablo Casals)

PERSONAL: Born December 29, 1876, in Vendrell, Catalonia, Spain; died of a heart attack, October 22, 1973, in Rio Piedras, Puerto Rico; son of Carles (an organist) and Pilar (Defillo) Casals; married Guilhermina Suggia (a cellist), 1906 (divorced); married Susan Metcalfe (a soprano), 1914 (divorced, 1920); married Marta Montanez, August, 1957. *Education:* Attended Barcelona Municipal School of Music and Royal Conservatory of Music, 1894-97. *Religion:* "A sort of intimate dialogue between my conscience and the Divinity." *Residence:* Santurce, Puerto Rico.

CAREER: Cellist, conductor, composer, and instructor.

Made Paris debut with Lamoureux Orchestra, and London debut at Crystal Palace, both 1899; U.S. concert tour, 1901-02, 1903-04, 1914-17; played at White House in Washington, D.C., and made New York City debut, both 1904; member of Cortot-Thibaud-Casals trio, 1905; soloist for British Broadcasting Orchestra, 1945; played at United Nations in New York City, 1958, and at White House, 1961; performed in numerous other cities throughout the world, including Rome, Prague, Berlin, Zurich, Havana, Buenos Aires, and Mexico City. Teacher of cello at Paris Conservatory, 1897; professor of cello at Barcelona Conservatory, 1897-99; founder and teacher of Paris Normal School of Music, 1914; founder and principal conductor of Pau Casals Orchestra in Barcelona, Spain, 1920-36; founder of Workers Concert Society in Barcelona, 1923; founder and musical director of Prades Bach Bicentennial Festival Society, 1950-53, and Festival Casals in San Juan, Puerto Rico, 1957; teacher and conductor on summer staff of Marlboro School of Music, 1961-79; guest conductor of New York Symphony, London Symphony, and Vienna Philharmonic. President of Puerto Rico Conservatory of Music.

MEMBER: Spanish Academy (honorary member), Hispanic Society, Royal Philharmonic Society, Philharmonic Society of London, Friends of Music Society of Vienna (honorary member), Academy of Sciences and Letters of Montpellier, Friends of Music. *Awards, honors:* Beethoven gold medal, 1912; doctor honoris causa from University of Edinburgh, 1934; gold medal from Worshipful Co. of Musicians, 1937; doctor honoris causa from University of Barcelona, 1939; medal of city of Toulouse, 1946; grand officer of Legion of Honor, 1946; doctor honoris causa from University of Montpellier, 1946; U.S. Presidential Medal of Freedom, 1963; freedom awards, 1968; United Nations Peace Medal, 1971; American Man of Music, 1973; Grand Cross of Isabella the Catholic; Grand Cross for services to the Republic of Austria; Grand Cross of the Republic of Spain; fellow of Royal College of Music; made citizen of honor of Barcelona, 1934, Madrid, 1935, Prades, 1941, Perpignan, 1945, Beziers, 1946, Foix, 1947, Narbonne, 1948, New York, 1973, and also several South American cities.

WRITINGS—Under name Pablo Casals: (Contributor) Juan Alavedra, *Poema del pessebre* (title means "Poems of the Manger"), [Barcelona], 1948; (with J. Ma. Corredor) *Conversations avec Pablo Casals: Souvenirs et opinions d'un musicien,* A. Michel, 1955, translation by Andre Mangeot published as *Conversations With Casals,* Dutton, 1956; (editor) *Libro blanco de Cataluna,* Revista Catalunya, 1956; *The Memoirs of Pablo Casals as Told to Thomas Dozier,* Life en Espanol, 1959; *Joys and Sorrows: Reflections by Pablo Casals as Told to Albert E. Kahn,* Simon & Schuster, 1970; Lluis Carulla and Maria Font Carulla, editors, *Homenatge a Pau Casals en el seu 95 aniverdari: 29 desembre 1876 Nadal del 1971,* Carulla i Canals, 1971.

Also author of music, including "El Pessebre" (oratorio), "La Creche" (oratorio), "La Vision de Fray Martin," (choral), "El Passelera," and "La Sardana"; contributor of music to sound recording by W. H. Auden, "Hymn to the United Nations," Tetra Music Corp., 1972.

SIDELIGHTS: Casals first heard the cello at the age of ten. "I felt as if I could not breathe," he recounted later. "There was something so tender, beautiful and human about the sound. A radiance filled me." Thus began Casal's lifelong fascination and preoccupation with the cello. The gifted musician revolutionized and modernized the playing techniques of the cello, single-handedly elevating it to the status of a serious solo and orchestral instrument.

Casals mastered the piano at the age of four, the violin at eight, the organ at nine, and the cello at eleven. He composed music at seven years and could sing in tune before he learned to speak clearly. "From my earliest days, music was for me a natural element, an activity as natural as breathing," he reflected. When Casals was introduced to the cello, he convinced his reluctant father to teach him on a homemade cello with a gourd as sounding board. The young Casals soon mastered the primitive instrument and exhausted his father's knowledge. Casals wanted to continue his study of the cello in Barcelona. His mother supported him, but his father disapproved, thinking the boy should have become a carpenter instead of a musician. A lasting family argument ensued and resulted in Casals and his mother going to Barcelona.

At the Municipal School of Music, Casals excelled in his cello studies. He rebelled against the traditional method of playing the cello and devised a totally new style. Formerly, cellists were taught to bow with their arms held rigidly at their sides—for practice they placed a book under their armpits. Also, the fingering of the left hand was restricted to an up and down motion. Casals bowed more freely and experimented with more liberal movements for the left hand. His techniques "transformed the cello from the ugly duckling to the swan of solo instruments," one *Newsweek* writer contended. "Casals's system of fingering purified phrasing, enriched intonation, increased speed and accuracy. His new cello tone was warm and singing; the intonation was purity itself, spare, yet somehow passionate."

It was at this time that Casals, at the age of thirteen, stumbled upon six Bach suites for unaccompanied cello while rummaging through a music shop with his father. The suites were ignored pieces of music that were regarded as academic, abstract, finger exercises. "I forgot entirely the reason of my visit to the shop and could only stare at this music which nobody had told me about," Casals remembered. "I took the suites home and read and reread them. For 12 years after that I studied and worked every day at them. I was nearly 25 before I had the courage to play one of them in public." Casals played all six suites publicly, becoming the first cellist ever to accomplish the feat. Single-handedly, Casals resurrected the Bach pieces and transformed them into "a transcendent musical experience," Alden Whitman of the *New York Times* asserted.

During his school years, Casals supported himself and his mother by playing with a trio at a Barcelona cafe. Casals convinced the cafe owner to host a night of classical music each week. The venture became popular and drew a number of serious musicians. One of these musicians gave Casals a letter of recommendation to Count Guillermo de Morphy, a patron of music and adviser to Maria Cristina, queen mother and regent of Spain. The count in turn introduced Casals to the queen and she awarded the budding musician a monthly allowance of fifty dollars.

After attending the Royal Conservatory in Madrid, Casals played the cello in Brussels and Paris and returned to Barcelona to teach at the music school for two years. In 1899, he journeyed again to Paris with a letter of introduction from the Count de Morphy to Charles Lamoureux, conductor of the Lamoureux Orchestra. When the twenty-two-year-old began his audition, the brusque and crippled conductor stood in amazement and embraced Casals at the finish of his piece, exclaiming, "My boy, you are one of the elect!"

Casals made his professional debut with the orchestra in Paris on November 12, 1899, playing the Lalo Concerto. The young artist's success was instantaneous. Casals premiered the same year in London and played for Queen Victoria; he also performed for the king and queen of Portugal and Belgium's Queen Elizabeth.

Casals made Paris his permanent home and traveled from there to play in cities throughout the world until the end of World War I. During this period, Casals helped popularize chamber music once again. In 1905, he became part of a trio with pianist Alfred Cortot and violinist Jacques Thibaud. The musician also played his Gofriller cello with pianist Harold Bauer and violinist Fritz Kreisler. The "king of the bow" (as Kreisler called him) developed friendships with such well-known people as Maurice Ravel, Camille Saint-Saens, George Clemenceau, Henri Bergson, and Sergei Rachmaninoff.

Casals returned to Spain in 1919, and founded the Pau Casals Orchestra in Barcelona a year later. The cellist personally funded the symphony until it became financially independent seven years later at a total cost to himself of $320,000. As conductor of the orchestra, Casals felt he had discovered his true vocation. He claimed the orchestra was "the greatest of all instruments" because of the cooperation required by all its members. In his later years, Casals preferred conducting to playing the cello.

The artist also created the Workers Concert Society in 1923. Believing that the working class should have the opportunity of listening to good music, he created a society in which laborers paid only one dollar in dues per year to hear a series of concerts given by the Pau Casals Orchestra. The society also encouraged and helped workers to create their own musical ensembles.

In 1931, Spain's Second Republic was established by popular election. Casals vigorously supported the new government mainly because it had the mandate of the Spanish people, but also because it allowed the region of his birth, Catalonia, to act autonomously. During the Spanish civil war, when Francisco Franco led the rebellion against the republic, Casals supported the Loyalist cause by giving benefit concerts and donating his personal savings for the defense of the moribund government. Casals abandoned his fight in 1939 when a Franco victory was inevitable and escaped, dejected and bitter, to Prades, France. The musician swore never to play in his beloved Spain while it remained under the hated Franco regime.

Casals opposed any kind of political oppression. He contended that "we are before anything men and we have to take part in the circumstances of life. Who indeed should be more concerned than the artist with the defense of liberty and free inquiry, which are essential to his very creativity." Stating that "I am a man first and an artist second" and that "an affront to human dignity is an affront to me," Casals refused to play in countries ruled by dictators and totalitarian governments, just as he had also declined in protest from playing in Communist Russia, Fascist Italy, and Nazi Germany.

In the border city Prades, Casals aided the Franco refugees pouring into France, but with the fall of France to Hitler in 1940, the cellist retired in seclusion until the end of the war. In 1945, Casals made his first public appearance in England. He believed that after the war and the defeat of the Axis powers, Britain and the United States would also oust Franco. The musician, however, was soon disillusioned when he realized the Allies meant to do nothing about the Spanish dictator. In sorrow, Casals vowed never to play again in England and the United States, or in any country

that supported Franco. He soon extended this ban to all commercial appearances. Casals explained that "I love the Americans and I love the British. I once had faith in their governments, but I have been deceived. It would not be dignified to go to these countries to earn money." The cellist later added: "I knew that in a world where cynicism widely held sway, my action would hardly affect the course of the nations—it was, after all, only the action of a single individual. But how else could I act? One had to live with oneself." Casals fulfilled all his prior commitments and withdrew in silent protest to Prades in 1947.

In 1950, however, violinist Alexander Schneider, with Casals's permission, led an entourage of musicians from all over the world to Prades to commemorate the two hundredth anniversary of Bach's death. Casals, who once commented "I see God in Bach," played and conducted in the festival. The event became an annual affair, with Casals participating for the next three years. Gradually the artist relented in his resolve never to play in public. In a 1951 conversation between Casals and humanitarian Albert Schweitzer, the latter remarked that "it is better to create than to protest." Casals replied: "Why not do both—why not create and protest both?" Even so, Casals remained in isolation until 1956, when he made his first commercial appearance in nine years. In the same year he also moved to Puerto Rico, the birthplace of his mother and of his wife, Marta. From then until his death, Casals made regular concert appearances in the United States and abroad.

Throughout his career, Casals was considered a "living anachronism" in music. Born in 1876, the cellist was a romantic who, "along with other great musicians of his generation," claimed Harold C. Schonberg of the *New York Times*, "tried to look beyond the printed note." Casals always told his students that "the important thing in music . . . is what is *not* in the notes. The important thing is the re-creation of an emotion, a mood, an experience." During the 1930's, 1940's, and 1950's, when strict interpretation of music was taught and practiced, many musicians tended to look down on Casals's work. In recent decades, however, Casals's romanticized interpretations of such composers as Bach and Beethoven are considered closer to their intended spirit than a strict rendering. "Casals the interpreter was an apostle of warmth, free tempos and the right—no, the necessity—of the player to add his own ideas to the ideas of the composer," noted Schonberg. Critic Howard Taubman added that the cellist's "tone is pure gold, mellow, resonant, infinitely flexible."

Casals wrote his musical compositions in the same style that he played cello. Alfred Frankenstein declared in *Newsweek* that "Casals is the only composer who can write a long work as if the twentieth century had never existed and make one take it seriously." Schonberg conceded that Casals's "approach was so big that it simply negated criticism."

BIOGRAPHICAL/CRITICAL SOURCES: New York Times, May 28, 1950, March 3, 1957; *Spectator*, April 27, 1956; *Christian Science Monitor*, February 28, 1957; *New York Herald Tribune Book Review*, March 3, 1957; *Newsweek*, April 30, 1962; *McCall's*, May, 1966; *Time*, August 12, 1966; *Life*, November 11, 1966, April 17, 1970; *Saturday Review*, December 31, 1966, June 22, 1968, May 2, 1970; *New York Times Book Review*, April 12, 1970; *New Yorker*, April 25, 1970, May 2, 1970; *Best Sellers*, May 1, 1970; *American Record Guide*, January, 1971; *Americas*, May, 1971, August, 1973; *New York Times Biographical Edition*, October, 1973; *Christian Century*, November 21, 1973; *Commonweal*, December 14, 1973; *Reader's Digest*, June, 1975.

OBITUARIES: New York Times, October 23, 1973; *Washington Post,* October 23, 1973; *Detroit News,* October 23, 1973; *Newsweek,* November 5, 1973; *Time,* November 5, 1973; *National Review,* November 9, 1973.*

—*Sketch by Anne M. Guerrini*

*   *   *

CASCIO, Chuck 1946-

PERSONAL: Surname is pronounced *Cash*-ee-yo; born October 27, 1946, in Brooklyn, N.Y.; son of Morris Frank (a federal employee) and Blanche (a bank clerk; maiden name, Borzomati) Cascio; married Bonnie Wells (a teacher), August 17, 1968; children: Marc, Ross. *Education:* Wagner College, B.S., 1968; American University, M.A., 1972. *Home and office:* 12613 Pinecrest Rd., Herndon, Va. 22070.

CAREER: Fairfax County Public Schools, Fairfax, Va., teacher, 1969—. Lecturer at American University, 1976—. *Awards, honors:* Certificate of merit from Virginia Press Association, 1977, for sports column.

WRITINGS: (With Brig Owens) *Over the Hill to the Super-bowl,* Luce, 1973; *Soccer U.S.A.,* Luce, 1975. Author of a weekly sports column. Special writer for *Washington Post,* 1976—. Contributor of several hundred articles to newspapers.

WORK IN PROGRESS: The Ambassador of Ill Will, with Paul Cannell; *A Matter of Timing,* a novel.

SIDELIGHTS: Cascio commented to *CA:* "I've worked in some area of writing ever since 1962 because I enjoy it. I enjoy the discipline and even the frustration and pain of it. I like to think of people reading my work and having it provide some emotion for them. I've been motivated by a belief that I can write as well as, or better than, most writers, given the chance. I enjoy quick humor, which I try to inject into my work where appropriate."

AVOCATIONAL INTERESTS: Exercise.

*   *   *

CASONA, Alejandro
See ALVAREZ, Alejandro Rodriguez

*   *   *

CASOTTI, Fred 1923-

PERSONAL: Born November 3, 1923, in Fraser, Iowa; son of Fred A. (a merchant) and Pia (Marzi) Casotti; married L. Darlene Mitchell, June 22, 1947; children: Candace Lee Casotti Nesheim, Christine Mitchell Casotti Reischmann. *Education:* Attended Boone Junior College, 1940-42; University of Colorado, B.A., 1949. *Home:* 320 31st St., Boulder, Colo. 80303. *Office:* Department of Intercollegiate Athletics, University of Colorado, Boulder, Colo. 80309.

CAREER: Nonpareil (newspaper), Council Bluffs, Iowa, sports writer, 1949-52; University of Colorado, Boulder, sports information director, 1952-68, assistant athletic director, 1968-72, associate athletic director, 1972—. *Military service:* U.S. Army, Medical Corps, 1943-46; became sergeant.

WRITINGS: Football, C.U. Style, Pruett, 1972.

WORK IN PROGRESS: A comprehensive book on football at University of Colorado, publication by Strode expected in 1980.

SIDELIGHTS: Casotti told *CA:* "At the conclusion of twenty-five year's work with the athletic department at Uni-

versity of Colorado, I decided to write what had built up inside me during that time. Inasmuch as my job was basically involved with writing, this was not particularly difficult, and the result was a highly personalized account of events and people with whom I had very close contact during that time. I felt the book was more readable than most of its type because of the personal nature in contrast to the rather detached descriptions which characterize most history-type books. My next book will not have this advantage; it begins in 1876."

*   *   *

CAZAMIAN, Louis Francois 1877-1965

OBITUARY NOTICE: Born April 2, 1877, in Saint-Denis, Reunion, of the Mascarene Islands; died in 1965. Educator, literary critic, and author. Cazamian taught at the Sorbonne, University of Paris from 1925 to 1945, but was best known as a critic of English literature. His most important work was *A History of English Literature,* written with Emile Legouis, which incorporated two of his earlier books on the history of English humor and humor in Shakespeare. He also wrote several French publications, and co-edited the *Revue Anglo-Americaine* for twelve years. Obituaries and other sources: *The Oxford Companion to French Literature,* corrected edition, Oxford University Press, 1966; *Longman Companion to Twentieth Century Literature,* Longman, 1970.

*   *   *

CENDRARS, Blaise
See SAUSER-HALL, Frederic

*   *   *

CHALMERS, John W. 1910-

PERSONAL: Born April 18, 1910, in Winnipeg, Manitoba, Canada; son of James H. (a lawyer) and Eva L. (a teacher; maiden name, West) Chalmers; married Dorothy Niddrie, August 23, 1938; children: John J., William F., Ronald S., David A., Margaret A., D. Elizabeth. *Education:* University of Manitoba, B.A., 1931; University of Alberta, M.A., 1935, M.Ed., 1941; Stanford University, Ed.D., 1946. *Politics:* "Eclectic, pragmatic." *Religion:* Protestant.

CAREER: Teacher and principal in high schools in Alberta, 1932-39; Civil Service Association of Alberta, school administrator, 1939-69; University of Alberta, Edmonton, professor of educational foundations, 1969-75, professor emeritus, 1975—; Concordia College, Edmonton, sessional instructor in education, 1975—. Visiting instructor at Eastern Montana State College, McGill University, University of New Brunswick, and University of Regina. Chairperson of Edmonton Historical Board. *Military service:* Royal Canadian Air Force, air navigator, 1942-45; became flying officer.

MEMBER: Canadian Authors Association (past vice-president), Alberta Teachers Association (past local president), Historical Society of Alberta (past president; local president), Educational Society of Edmonton, Phi Delta Kappa (historian). *Awards, honors:* Award from Historical Society of Alberta.

WRITINGS: Red River Adventure, Macmillan (Canada), 1956; *Fur Trade Governor,* Institute of Applied Art, 1960; *Horseman in Scarlet,* Gage, 1961; (editor) *Philips' Historical Atlas of Canada,* George Philip & Sons, 1966; *Schools of the Foothills Province,* University of Toronto Press, 1967; *Teachers of the Foothills Province,* University of Toronto Press, 1968; (editor) *On the Edge of the Shield,* Boreal Institute, 1971; (editor) *The Land of Peter Pond,* Boreal Institute, 1974; (editor) *Profiles of Canadian Educators,* Heath, 1974; *Gladly Would He Teach,* Alberta Teachers Association, 1978; (editor) *Alberta Diamond Jubilee Anthology,* Hurtig, 1979.

Work represented in anthologies. Contributor of poems, stories, articles, and reviews to scholarly journals and popular magazines, including *Alberta History, Canadian Geographical Journal, Alaska Journal, Monday Morning,* and *Islander,* and newspapers. Past editor of *Canadian Author and Bookman.*

WORK IN PROGRESS: A history of the department of secondary education at University of Alberta; a biography of David Laird, the first lieutenant-governor of Northwest Territories, 1876-81.

SIDELIGHTS: Chalmers comments: "Since high school days I have written for fun, love, and money, and been successful in all three aspects. I regard myself as an artisan or craftsman rather than an artist. I do not seem to have either the temperament or the imagination to be a creative artist."

*   *   *

CHALON, Jon
See CHALONER, John Seymour

*   *   *

CHALONER, John Seymour   1924-
(Jon Chalon)

PERSONAL: Born in 1924 in London, England; married Katharine Joan Horton (divorced, 1974); children: two sons. *Education:* Attended Royal Military College, Sandhurst. *Home:* 29 Eccleston Sq., London S.W.1, England.

CAREER: Information Service Division, Germany, press chief, 1945-48; farmer in Sussex, England, 1960—. Founder and president of Seymour Press Group. Member of London Borough Council, 1968-74. *Member:* Society of Authors, National Farmers Union.

WRITINGS—Novels; under name Jon Chalon: *Three for the Road,* Hutchinson, 1956; *The Eager Beaver,* Anthony Blond, 1963; *Family Hold Back,* Dobson, 1969; *To the Manner Born,* Cassell, 1978, St. Martin's, 1979.

Juveniles; under name Jon Chalon: *The Green Bus,* Hutchinson, 1958, Grosset, 1979; *The Flying Steamroller,* Anthony Blond, 1962; *The House Next Door,* Dobson, 1967; *Sir Lance a Little and the Knights of the Kitchen Table,* Bobbs-Merrill, 1971; *The Voyage of the Floating Bedstead,* Bobbs-Merrill, 1973; *To Europe With Love,* Bantam, 1974; *The Dustmen's Holiday,* Bobbs-Merrill, 1975. Contributor to radio, television, and farm journals and to newspapers.

AVOCATIONAL INTERESTS: Riding, skiing, sailing.

BIOGRAPHICAL/CRITICAL SOURCES: Anthony Sampson, *The New Emperors,* Hodder & Stoughton, 1968; *Bracknell News,* January 25, 1979.

*   *   *

CHAMBERLAIN, Muriel Evelyn   1932-

PERSONAL: Born November 1, 1932, in Syston, England; daughter of Arthur John (a railway worker) and Gladys Ellen (a teacher; maiden name, Shortland) Chamberlain. *Education:* St. Hilda's College, Oxford, B.A., 1954, M.A., 1958, D.Phil., 1961. *Agent:* Curtis Brown Ltd., 1 Craven Hill, London W2 3EP, England. *Office:* Department of History, University College of Swansea, University of Wales, Singleton Park, Swansea SA2 8PP, Wales.

CAREER: University of London, Royal Holloway College, London, England, assistant lecturer in history, 1955 and 1957-58; University of Wales, University College of Swansea, Swansea, began as lecturer, 1958, became senior lecturer in history, dean of faculty of arts, 1975-77.

WRITINGS: The New Imperialism, Historical Association, 1970; *Britain and India: The Interaction of Two Peoples,* Archon Books, 1974; *The Scramble for Africa,* Longman, 1974; *British Foreign Policy in the Age of Palmerston,* Longman, 1980. Contributor to *Times Atlas of World History.* Contributor to history journals.

WORK IN PROGRESS: Life of the Fourth Earl of Aberdeen; Imperialism and Social Reform, publication expected by Macmillan.

*   *   *

CHANDLER, Caroline A(ugusta)   1906-1979

OBITUARY NOTICE—See index for *CA* sketch: Born December 7, 1906, in Ford City, Pa.; died of emphysema, December 18, 1979, in Washington, D.C. Pediatrician, educator, and writer. An authority on child mental health and hygiene, Chandler held a number of jobs with the National Institute of Mental Health and with various government agencies. From 1959 to 1961 she was chief of the Office of Mental Health and Child Health in Maryland. At one time she served as an instructor of preventive medicine at Johns Hopkins University. In addition to writing specialized books and articles on medicine, Chandler was the author of several books for the general reader, including *Susie Stuart, M.D.; Dr. Kay Winthrop, Intern;* and *Nursing as a Career.* Obituaries and other sources: *American Men and Women of Science: The Social and Behavioral Sciences,* 12th edition, Bowker, 1973; *Who's Who in America,* 40th edition, Marquis, 1978; *Washington Post,* December 21, 1979.

*   *   *

CHANTLER, David T(homas)   1925-

PERSONAL: Born May 24, 1925, in Pittsburgh, Pa.; children: Angela, Peter. *Education:* Earned B.S. from Northwestern University. *Home:* Santa Monica Bay Club, Apt. 209, 2210 Third St., Santa Monica, Calif. 90405. *Agent:* Eisenbach-Greene-Duchow, Inc., 760 North La Cienega Blvd., Los Angeles, Calif. 90069.

CAREER: Writer. *Military service:* U.S. Army Air Corps, 1943. *Member:* Writers Guild of America, Writers Guild of Great Britain, National Academy of Television Arts and Sciences.

WRITINGS: Fellow Creature (novel), Gollancz, 1970; *The Man Who Followed in Front* (novel), Cassell, 1974; *The Capablanca Opening* (novel), St. Martin's, 1976.

Screenplays: "Magic Fire," released by Republic, 1957; "Last of the Badmen," released by Allied Artists, 1957; "Face of a Fugitive," released by Columbia, 1959; "Cash on Demand," released by Columbia, 1961; "Follow the Boys," released by Metro-Goldwyn-Mayer, 1963; "She," released by Metro-Goldwyn-Mayer, 1965. Also author of television plays in United States and England.

WORK IN PROGRESS: The Girl With the Pink Umbrella, a novel.

*   *   *

CHAPIN, Henry   1893-

PERSONAL: Born in 1893 in Toledo, Ohio; married Paula

Van Dyke; children: one son, two daughters. *Education:* Attended Princeton University, 1913-17. *Residence:* Stonington, Conn. *Office:* c/o William L. Bauhan, Inc., Dublin, N.H. 03444.

CAREER: Writer. *Military service:* U.S. Army, 1917-19; became captain. *Member:* Century Association.

WRITING—Poetry: *Leifsaga,* Farrar & Rinehart, 1934; *West Walking Yankee,* Howell, Soskin, 1940; *To the End of West,* Bauhan, William, 1970; *A Celebration,* Bauhan, William, 1974; *The Constant God,* Bauhan, William, 1978.

Other: *The Adventures of Johnny Appleseed,* Coward, 1930; (with Frederick George Walton Smith) *The Ocean River,* Scribner, 1952; (with Smith) *The Sun, the Sea, and Tomorrow: Potential Sources of Food, Energy, and Minerals From the Sea,* Scribner, 1954; *The Remarkable Dolphin and What Makes Him So* (juvenile), W. R. Scott, 1962; *Spiro of the Sponge Fleet* (juvenile), W. R. Scott, 1965; *The Search for Atlantis,* Crowell, 1968; *Countdown at Eighty,* Bauhan, William, 1977.

SIDELIGHTS: Chapin is an author of books for children, magazine articles, scientific studies, and epic-scale narrative poetry. For the most part, his efforts have been well-received by the critics.

One of his books, *The Remarkable Dolphin and What Makes Him So,* has been widely recommended. As stated in the *Christian Science Monitor,* "this excellent book is intended to acquaint readers 12 to 16 with the remarkable abilities of dolphins.... For younger readers in the age group it does this very well. But the book suffers from a fault often found in works aimed at this awkward age span. While it should interest and challenge the young readers, it probably is too sketchy and immature in style for today's scientifically inclined high school juniors and seniors. Nevertheless, this reservation aside, the author has turned out an informative little book."

Chapin's efforts at narrative poetry have also received critical acclaim. One comment in the *New York Herald Tribune* concerning *Leifsaga,* Chapin's account of the Norse discoveries of America, summarizes the sentiments of the reviewers: "The beauty of this long narrative epic lies chiefly in the poet's excellent handling of his material, his very reputable verse, and his love and knowledge of the folk customs of the Icelandic heroes. Out of fragments of legend, true folk song and epic, Mr. Chapin makes a consistent modern narrative, exalted in tone, true to the spirit of epic poetry in its selection of detail and in its ethical standards."

Written in collaboration with F. G. Walton Smith, one of Chapin's scientific studies, *Ocean River,* received praise from the *San Francisco Chronicle:* "Mr. Chapin is a historian-anthropologist with a talent for illustrating the eternal connection between nature and Man; Mr. Smith is one of the world's foremost oceanographers and marine biologists. The team works smoothly together, and between them the two members have written an exceedingly interesting book."

AVOCATIONAL INTERESTS: Fishing, gardening, wine making, drinking.

BIOGRAPHICAL/CRITICAL SOURCES: New York Herald Tribune, December 16, 1934; *San Francisco Chronicle,* September 11, 1952; *Christian Science Monitor,* November 15, 1962.

*   *   *

CHAPMAN, M(ary) Winslow 1903-

PERSONAL: Born August 30, 1903, in Raleigh, Tenn.; daughter of E. Eveleth and Anne (Goodwin) Winslow; married Charles S. Chapman (deceased); children: Margaret, Winslow, Mary. *Education:* Attended University of California, Berkeley, 1919-20; Vassar College, A.B., 1923; attended University of Geneva, 1923-24. *Politics:* Independent. *Religion:* Episcopal. *Home and office:* 4066 James, Memphis, Tenn. 38128.

CAREER: In farming and real estate, 1959-62; *Raleigh Bartlett Star,* sports reporter and author of weekly column, "The Ivory Bomb Shelter," 1960-63.

WRITINGS—Books of poems: *The Keyhole,* Windemere Press, 1966; *The Gelded Centaur,* Golden Quill, 1968; *Seen From Space,* Golden Quill, 1972; *I Remember Raleigh,* Riverside Press, 1977; *Temples: Selected Poems,* Golden Quill, 1979.

SIDELIGHTS: Chapman writes: "My poems are the outgrowth of my newspaper column. Having found how little time people will give to serious thought, I decided to condense my conservative 'propaganda' into short—very short—poems to be swallowed whole. It seems to have worked."

*   *   *

CHARLES, David
See MONDEY, David (Charles)

*   *   *

CHARNAS, Suzy McKee 1939-

PERSONAL: Born October 22, 1939, in Manhattan, N.Y.; daughter of Robinson (an artist) and Maxine (an artist; maiden name, Szanton) McKee; married Stephen Charnas (a lawyer), October 4, 1968; children: (stepchildren) Charles N., Joanna. *Education:* Barnard College, B.A., 1961; New York University, M.A.T., 1965. *Politics:* "Disgusted; liberal when active." *Religion:* Jewish. *Agent:* Virginia Kidd, Box 278, Milford, Pa. 18337. *Office:* 8918 Fourth St. N.W., Albuquerque, N.M. 87114.

CAREER: U.S. Peace Corps, Washington, D.C., teacher of history and English at girls' high school in Ogbomosho, Nigeria and lecturer in economic history at University of Ife, Ibadan, Nigeria, both 1961-63; junior high school teacher of ancient history and African studies in New York City, 1965-67; Flower Fifth Avenue Hospital, New York City, in curriculum development, with Division of Community Mental Health, 1967-69; writer, 1969—. *Member:* Authors Guild of Authors League of America, Science Fiction Writers of America, Poets and Writers.

WRITINGS: Walk to the End of the World (first novel in trilogy; also see below), Ballantine, 1974; *Motherlines* (second novel in trilogy), Putnam, 1978; (contributor) Marleen Barr, editor, *Future Females: A Critical Anthology,* Bowling Green Popular Press, 1980; *Scorched Supper on New Niger* (novelette), edited by R. R. Martin, Berkley Publishing, 1980; *The Unicorn Tapestry,* edited by Marta Randall, Pocket Books, 1980; *The Vampire Tapestry* (novel), Pocket Books, 1980. Contributor to magazines, including *Khatru* and *Omni.*

WORK IN PROGRESS: The third volume of a trilogy begun with *Walk to the End of the World* and *Motherlines,* publication expected by Berkley Publishing; *The Ancient Mind at Work,* a novella.

SIDELIGHTS: Suzy Charnas writes: "I think of myself as a late bloomer, since my first book was published when I was thirty-four. This was good: I didn't leap in all at once as a youth to write the typical autobiographical first novel that so often leads to a one-book career.

"I am a devoted researcher. For *Walk to the End of the World,* I tried to learn everything there is to know about, for instance, crude plastics and the agricultural production of seaweed. For *Motherlines* I read about all sorts of nomadic stock herders, from Mongols to Lapps.

The Vampire Tapestry comprises a sequential group of inter-related incidents during a period of the protagonist's life when matters have gone seriously out of control, so that he's forced to confront vital challenges to his freedom and his existence. I began with the idea of a vampire not as a figure of romance, a tarted-up Byronic hero with fangs, but as a natural creature. Frankly, he is a predator, and we are his prey. He has, of necessity, a scholarly turn of mind (there's a lot to study up on when you wake up after a fifty-year snooze that began before the turn of the century). So while he has his primitive side, ancient and ruthless, he's also a bit too intelligent for his own mental serenity—otherwise he could not cope with the computer age and the gas shortage, among other things. I don't mean to indicate a tongue-in-cheek approach; the work is serious, but shows, I hope, some wit. Again, much of the fun of doing this book has been the opportunity for research—studying gestalt therapy, the Santa Fe Opera and Puccini's 'Tosca,' and consulting people whose paths would not normally cross mine, such as the local zoo veterinarian.

"My interests extend to other arts because I am convinced that the arts feed each other. To someone like myself who has a very active inner eye, the images provided by the visual arts, stage performances of any kind, and of course those called up by words are all stimulating and rich. The arts also nourish the life of my dreams, which I feel is a distinct and powerful part of my working life.

"Reading is sometimes a problem. Sometimes the writer is obvious, and I get bored. Often I find I can't bring myself to stomach a writer's stated or implied sexism. No matter how excellent the work, this kind of rotten place at the core invalidates all and is too insulting and distressing to put up with for the sake of whatever fragmentary insight the person may have. This does not mean that I consider myself the perfect feminist. It does mean that I try not to be either a purveyor or a victim of cultural distortions demeaning to my sex, and I have no patience with those who are proponents of those distortions.

"My advice to aspiring writers is simply what works for me: hand over the work, at a point where it has already gelled and taken a firm shape of its own, to certain friends whose judgment can be trusted. After they have read it, they report back on the actual effects achieved, as opposed to what I had intended and think I have done. While I do not bow to every wind of criticism that blows, I do value very highly the insights that come from other's perspectives. Without that, I tend to get stuck in obsessive ruts inside my own head and to communicate very little, and that faultily. A novel is not, for me, a group effort, but it invariably benefits from some outside feedback from those for whom, after all, it is intended: readers."

AVOCATIONAL INTERESTS: Hiking, running.

* * *

CHAVEZ, Angelico 1910-
PERSONAL: Born April 10, 1910, in Wagon Mound, N.M.; son of Fabian (a carpenter) and Nicole (a teacher; maiden name, Roybal) Chavez. *Education:* Attended Franciscan seminaries in Cincinnati, Ohio, and Detroit, Mich. *Home:* 236 Johnson St., Santa Fe, N.M. 87501.

CAREER: Entered Franciscan religious order, 1929, ordained Roman Catholic priest, 1937-72; missionary among Pueblo Indians in New Mexico, 1937-72; laicized, 1972; writer, 1972—. Lecturer at University of Albuquerque, 1972-74. Member of board of regents of Museum of New Mexico, 1946-57. *Military service:* U.S. Army, Infantry, chaplain, 1943-46, 1951-52; served in Pacific theater and Germany; became major.

AWARDS, HONORS: University of New Mexico, M.A., 1947, D.H.L., 1974; Catholic Poetry Award from Catholic Poetry Society of New York, 1948, for body of lyric poetry; D.Litt. from University of Albuquerque, 1963; award from National Council of Christians and Jews, 1963; LL.D. from Southern University of New Mexico, 1975; literary award from governor of New Mexico, 1976, for body of literature.

WRITINGS: Clothed With the Sun (poems), Rydal, 1939; (self-illustrated) *New Mexico Triptych* (short stories), St. Anthony Guild Press, 1940, 3rd edition, 1976; *Eleven Lady-Lyrics* (poems), St. Anthony Guild Press, 1945; *The Single Rose* (poems), Los Santos Bookshop, 1948; *Our Lady of the Conquest* (nonfiction), Historical Society of New Mexico, 1948; *La Conquistadora: The Autobiography of an Ancient Statue* (nonfiction), St. Anthony Guild Press, 1954; *Origins of New Mexico Families in the Spanish Colonial Period* (nonfiction), Historical Society of New Mexico, 1954, 3rd edition, 1975; (with E. B. Adams) *The Missions of New Mexico, 1776,* University of New Mexico Press, 1956; *Archives of the Archdiocese of Santa Fe,* Academy of American Franciscan History, 1957; *From an Altar Screen* (short stories), Farrar, Straus, 1957, 2nd edition, 1976; *The Virgin of Port Lligat* (poems), Academy Guild Press, 1959.

(Self-illustrated) *The Lady From Toledo* (historical novel), Academy Guild Press, 1960; *Coronado's Friars* (nonfiction), Academy of American Franciscan History, 1968; *Selected Poems,* Territorian Press, 1969; (editor and translator) *The Oroz Codex,* Academy of American Franciscan History, 1972; *The Song of Francis* (poetic *resume* of the life of St. Francis of Assisi), Northland Press, 1973; *My Penitente Land: Reflections on Spanish New Mexico,* University of New Mexico Press, 1975, second edition, 1979; (translator) *The Dominguez-Escalante Expedition, 1776,* Brigham Young University Press, 1976.

Work represented in *Best Poems,* edited by Moult, J. Cape, 1938, 1940, 1941. Contributor of articles, poems, and reviews to history and literary journals.

WORK IN PROGRESS: Books on southwestern history.

SIDELIGHTS: Chavez writes: "I have loved English literature since childhood. I started publishing poetry and prose in my teens. I left the Franciscan Order and active priesthood at age sixty-two, obviously not for wine, women, and song at that age, but because of having outgrown former ideals. I started a new life, as happy as the first, with no regrets for the past."

* * *

CHELMINSKI, Rudolph 1934-
PERSONAL: Born February 21, 1934, in Wilton, Conn.; son of Roman (an engineer) and Pauline Chelminski; married Brien Mutrux, December 29, 1966; children: Roman Michael, Stephane Aimee. *Education:* Harvard University, B.A., 1956; attended Institut d'Etudes Politiques, 1961-62.

Home and office: 68 rue Murger, 77780 Bourron-Marlotte, France. *Agent:* Paul R. Reynolds, Inc., 12 East 41st St., New York, N.Y. 10017.

CAREER: Rocky Mountain News, Denver, Colo., worked as copy editor and general assignment reporter; *Life,* New York, N.Y., worked as reporter, correspondent from Paris, bureau chief in Moscow, Soviet Union, and deputy bureau chief in Paris, France; free-lance writer, 1972—. *Military service:* U.S. Army, Field Artillery, 1957-58; served in Korea. *Member:* American Society of Journalists and Authors.

WRITINGS: Prisoner of Mao, Coward, 1973; *Paris,* Time-Life, 1976. Contributor to magazines.

* * *

CHERNISS, Harold 1904-

PERSONAL: Born March 11, 1904, in St. Joseph, Mo.; son of David Benjamin (a health inspector) and Theresa (Hart) Cherniss; married Ruth Meyer, January 1, 1929. *Education:* University of California, Berkeley, A.B., 1925, Ph.D., 1929; attended University of Chicago, 1926, University of Goettingen, 1927, and University of Berlin, 1928. *Politics:* None. *Religion:* None. *Office:* c/o School of Historical Studies, Institute for Advanced Study, Princeton, N.J. 08540.

CAREER: Cornell University, Ithaca, N.Y., instructor in classics, 1930-33; Johns Hopkins University, Baltimore, Md., associate in Greek, 1933-36, associate professor of Greek, 1936-46; University of California, Berkeley, professor of Greek, 1946-48; Institute for Advanced Study, Princeton, N.J., professor of Greek, 1948-74, professor emeritus, 1974—. *Military service:* U.S. Army, 1942-46; served in European theater, became captain.

MEMBER: American Philosophical Society, American Academy of Arts and Sciences, American Philological Association, British Academy, Royal Academy of Arts and Sciences of Goeteborg, Academie Royale Flamande des Sciences, Lettres, et Beaux Arts. *Awards, honors:* D.H.L. from University of Chicago, 1950, Johns Hopkins University, 1965, and Brown University, 1976; laurea honoris cause from University of Rome, 1976; Charles J. Goodwin Award of Merit from American Philological Association, 1977, for *The Platonic and Stoic Essays of Plutarch.*

WRITINGS: Aristotle's Criticism of Presocratic Philosophy, Johns Hopkins Press, 1935; *Aristotle's Criticism of Plato and the Academy,* Volume I, Johns Hopkins Press, 1944; *The Riddle of the Early Academy,* University of California Press, 1945; (editor and translator) Plutarch, *De Facie in Orbe Lunae* (title means "Concerning the Face Which Appears in the Orb of the Moon"), Harvard University Press, 1957; (editor and translator) *The Platonic and Stoic Essays of Plutarch,* Harvard University Press, 1976; *Selected Papers,* edited by Leonrado Taran, Brill, 1977. Assistant editor of *American Journal of Philology,* 1936-40, editor, 1940-42.

WORK IN PROGRESS: Aristotle's Criticism of Plato and the Academy, Volume II.

* * *

CHERRY, Colin 1914-1979

OBITUARY NOTICE—See index for *CA* sketch: Born June 23, 1914, in St. Albans, England; died November 23, 1979, in England. Educator and writer. The Henry Mark Pease Professor of Telecommunication at the University of London, Cherry was an expert on the social, psychological, and philosophical aspects of human communications. He wrote *Pulses and Transients in Communication Circuits, On Human Communication,* and *World Communication: Threat or Promise?.* Obituaries and other sources: *AB Bookman's Weekly,* December 24-31, 1979.

* * *

CHILD, John 1922-

PERSONAL: Born March 18, 1922, in Dunedin, New Zealand; son of Paul Gabriel (a fencer) and Sarah (Cousens) Child; married Shirley Ruth Hardcastle, May 7, 1948; children: Sally Ruth, Jennifer Mary, Richard Harold, Madeleine Jill, Rosemary Ann. *Education:* University of Otago, M.A. (with first class honors), 1947, B.Comm., 1951; Oxford University, D.Phil., 1953. *Politics:* Socialist. *Religion:* None. *Home:* 136 Queen St., Dunedin, New Zealand. *Office:* Department of Economic History, University of Otago, Dunedin, New Zealand.

CAREER: High school teacher in Lawrence, New Zealand, 1948-50, and Tauranga, New Zealand, 1954-56; University of New South Wales, Sydney, Australia, lecturer, 1958-64, senior lecturer in industrial relations, 1965-67; University of Otago, Dunedin, New Zealand, fellow, 1968-74, lecturer in economic history, 1974—. *Military service:* Royal New Zealand Air Force, 1943-46. *Member:* New Zealand Ecological Society, New Zealand Entomological Society, Royal Society of New Zealand, Friends of Otago Museum, Ecology Action, Native Forests Action Council.

WRITINGS: (With Ellic Howe) *The Society of London Bookbinders, 1780-1951,* Sylvan Press, 1952; (with others) *Vietnam and Australia,* University Study Group, 1966; *Industrial Relations in the British Printing Industry: The Quest for Security,* Allen & Unwin, 1967; *Unionism and the Labor Movement,* Macmillan, 1971.

Biology books: *Shellfish of the Bay of Plenty,* Periwinkle Press, 1956, revised edition, 1957; *Australian Seashells: An Introduction for Young Biologists and Collectors,* Periwinkle Press, 1959, revised edition, Cheshire-Lansdowne, 1968; *Australian Insects: An Introduction for Young Biologists and Collectors,* Periwinkle Press, 1960, revised edition, Cheshire-Lansdowne, 1968; *Australian Rocks and Minerals: An Introduction to Geology,* Periwinkle Press, 1963, revised edition, Cheshire-Lansdowne, 1968; *Australian Spiders,* Periwinkle Press, 1965, 3rd edition, 1971; *Australian Seashore Life,* revised edition, Cheshire-Lansdowne, 1968; *Australian Pond and Stream Life,* Cheshire-Lansdowne, 1968; *Wildflowers of the Sydney Region,* Cheshire-Lansdowne, 1968; *Trees of the Sydney Region,* Cheshire-Lansdowne, 1968; *Collecting Specimens,* Periwinkle Press, 1969; *Australian Alpine Life,* Cheshire-Lansdowne, 1969.

(With K. W. Allison) *The Mosses of New Zealand,* University of Otago Press, 1971; (with brother, Peter Child) *Australian Dictionary of Biology,* Periwinkle Books, 1971; (with John Currey) *Australia's Insects,* Lansdowne, 1971; (with William Martin) *Lichens of New Zealand,* A. H. & A. W. Reed, 1972; (with Currey) *Shells and the Seashore,* Lansdowne, 1972; (with P. Child) *New Zealand Dictionary of Biology,* Periwinkle Books, 1974; *New Zealand Insects,* Periwinkle Books, 1974; *New Zealand Shells,* Periwinkle Books, 1974; *Practical Natural History,* Periwinkle Books, 1974; (with Allison) *The Liverworts of New Zealand,* University of Otago Press, 1975.

WORK IN PROGRESS: Research into the economic history of New Zealand, its alpine plants, and the natural history of the Rock and Pillar mountain range.

SIDELIGHTS: Child told *CA:* "After graduating in economics, I took up secondary school teaching, became fascinated by biology, and began writing introductory books on shells and other subjects. When I took a university post in Sydney, I attended classes in biology and continued writing. My great ambition is to write a natural history of one limited area, and I hope to do this on the Rock and Pillar mountain range in the south island of New Zealand.''

* * *

CHOTZINOFF, Samuel 1889-1964

OBITUARY NOTICE: Born July 4, 1889, in Vitebsk, Russia (now U.S.S.R.); died February 9, 1964. Pianist and music critic. After immigrating to New York City as a young boy, Chotzinoff learned to play the piano and eventually became an accompanist for Alma Gluck, Jascha Heifetz, and violinist Efrem Zimbalist. In 1925, he became a music critic with the *New York World* and remained there for five years. During the 1930's he joined the *New York Post* in the same capacity. Chotzinoff was also known for his work with the National Broadcasting Co. as commentator of a weekly symphony program and as director of the company's music division. Obituaries and other sources: *Current Biography,* Wilson, April, 1940, April, 1964; *New York Times,* February 11, 1964.

* * *

CHRIST, Carol T(ecla) 1944-

PERSONAL: Born May 21, 1944, in New York, N.Y.; daughter of John George and Tecla (Bobrick) Christ; married Larry Sklute (a professor), August 15, 1975; children: Jonathan Michael. *Education:* Rutgers University, B.A., 1966; Yale University, M.Ph., 1969, Ph.D., 1970. *Residence:* Berkeley, Calif. *Office:* Department of English, University of California, Berkeley, Calif. 94720.

CAREER: University of California, Berkeley, assistant professor of English, 1970—. *Member:* Phi Beta Kappa. *Awards, honors:* Woodrow Wilson fellowship, 1966; National Endowment for the Humanities fellowship, 1978-79.

WRITINGS: The Finer Optic: The Aesthetic of Particularity in Victorian Poetry, Yale University Press, 1975. Contributor to *Novel* and *Women's Studies.*

WORK IN PROGRESS: A book on Victorian and modern poetics.

* * *

CHRISTIAN, Roy Cloberry 1914-

PERSONAL: Born October 8, 1914, in Riddings, Derbyshire, England; son of Frederick Ewan (an Anglican priest) and Ethel M. T. (Rogers) Christian; married Mary Elizabeth Mansfield, April 20, 1940 (died August 11, 1979); children: Susan Mary. *Education:* Daneshill College of Education, certificate, 1947. *Politics:* Liberal. *Religion:* Church of England. *Home:* 53 Littleover Lane, Derby DE3 6JH, England. *Agent:* David Higham Associates Ltd., 5-8 Lower John St., London W1R 4HA, England.

CAREER: Teacher of English and history at various schools in Derby, England, 1947-55; lecturer in English in Derby and at District College of Technology, 1955-62; Derby College of Further Education, Derby, lecturer in English, 1962-66, lecturer in charge of mature students, 1966-76. Free-lance writer and broadcaster, 1950—. Part-time lecturer in local history for University of Nottingham and Workers' Educational Association. Member of board of governors of Homeland School and Mickleover School. Member of Council for

the Protection of Rural England, Derbyshire Naturalists Trust, and Derbyshire Historic Buildings Trust. *Military service:* Royal Naval Volunteer Reserve, active duty, 1940-46; mentioned in dispatches. *Member:* Derbyshire Archaeological Society, Derby Civic Society. *Awards, honors:* Member of the Order of the British Empire (MBE).

WRITINGS: Ships and the Sea, Studio Vista, 1962; *Old English Customs,* David & Charles, 1966; *Ghosts and Legends,* David & Charles, 1972; (editor) *The Nature-Lover's Companion,* Eyre Methuen, 1972; *Nottinghamshire,* Batsford, 1974; *Factories, Forges, and Foundries* (juvenile), Routledge & Kegan Paul, 1974; *Peak District,* David & Charles, 1976; *Vanishing Britain,* David & Charles, 1977; *Derbyshire,* Batsford, 1978. Radio writer for British Broadcasting Corp. (BBC). Contributor to magazines, including *Country Life.* Author of monthly feature for *Derbyshire Life and Countryside.*

WORK IN PROGRESS: Writing three local history series on BBC-Radio.

SIDELIGHTS: Christian comments: "I am interested in all aspects of the British countryside, past, present, and future. I am impressed by the continuity of British history and believe that we must understand the past in order to move into a successful future. I see a need for top-level discussions about the future use of land in Britain. Ours is a small, heavily populated island with too many bodies fighting to use what land is left for agriculture, roads, defense, housing, minerals, and other purposes (often legitimate). There is a danger that we may soon have no beautiful areas left to enjoy in peace. That was the major theme of my *Vanishing Britain,* but it also runs as a minor theme through most of my other books and much of my broadcast work.

"I am a compulsive writer and have been since schooldays. In the past I have been prepared to write on almost anything, but I try now to be slightly more selective, concentrating on subjects that interest me—though there are rather too many of those. I try to write something each day, working more or less office hours, in order to combat my natural idleness. I am sure this is the only way to be a successful writer. Success owes much more to perspiration than inspiration."

* * *

CLARIE, Thomas C(ashin) 1943-

PERSONAL: Born December 21, 1943, in Providence, R.I.; son of T. Emmet (a federal judge) and Gertrude (Reynolds) Clarie. *Education:* College of the Holy Cross, B.S., 1965; Southern Connecticut State College, M.S.L.S., 1972; University of Connecticut, M.A., 1973. *Politics:* Democrat. *Religion:* Roman Catholic. *Home:* Jefferson Woods, No. 197, Branford, Conn. 06405. *Office:* Buley Library, Southern Connecticut State College, New Haven, Conn. 06515.

CAREER: Hamden Public Library, Hamden, Conn., librarian, 1967-69; school librarian in Avon, Conn., 1969-71; University of Connecticut, Storrs, reference librarian, 1973; Southern Connecticut State College, New Haven, head reference librarian at Buley Library, 1973—. *Member:* American Library Association, American Association of University Professors, American Society for Psychical Research, Society for Psychical Research (England), Connecticut Library Association. *Awards, honors:* Prize from Carrollton Press, 1978, for best reference book idea.

WRITINGS: Occult Bibliography, Scarecrow, 1978. Also author of *Connecticut News Handbook, 1977-1978,* 1979, and *Pharos, Lighthouse of Alexandria,* 1980.

SIDELIGHTS: Clarie told *CA:* "The two most important fields for the future are the occult/psychic sciences and the knowledge industry (libraries, publishing, computerized data bases). I am deeply committed to both.

"I consider all library work as a fierce battle to preserve for humanity as much knowledge as possible. Each generation must be allowed to rediscover the past. If one generation of librarians, publishers, and readers forgets or mislays a book, a chain to the past is broken, perhaps losing that writer's knowledge forever. I look forward to a lifetime of chain-building (writing nonfiction and reference books).

"My occult bibliography is one small attempt at this knowledge preservation. I have been interested in the field for twenty years, due to my mystical, religious nature. The occult, particularly its spiritualism side, has given me peace and confidence. Once you realize that life goes on forever, on many levels, and that we are all part of vast flows and cycles, it is difficult to get too worried about anything. I have a healthy respect for the occult and the contact with chaos that it can bring. I do not actively practice the field, since I believe that I am in this current life not to study my past reincarnations, but to experience thousands of new things. One should consciously strive to live the life of one's period in history (right now it is rock music, sports, condominiums, inflation, personal religion, and love).

"Hermann Hesse has had a great influence on me, because I feel we are so alike (the typical Hesse hero travels through life making others happy, then dies in a snowbank). Another author I like is Mary Renault, who understands the complexities of the human soul better than anyone I know. I feel emotionally very close to Nietzsche, love to languish in Joseph Conrad's moody atmospheres, and enjoy Ortega y Gasset's twists of thought. The music and words of Jackson Browne and Dan Fogelberg have held me together through life's buffetings."

AVOCATIONAL INTERESTS: Collecting books on the occult, studying the stock market, playing tennis and basketball, following New Haven's professional ice hockey team and the New York Rangers, playing the organ.

* * *

CLARK, Jean C(ashman) 1920-

PERSONAL: Born February 19, 1920, in Waterbury, Conn.; daughter of George Kellas (a teacher) and Marion (Peck) Cashman; married Jack H. Whittington, September 23, 1944 (divorced February 15, 1946); married Jason G. Clark (a designer and engineer), October 14, 1948. *Education:* Attended Post Junior College, 1938-39, and Schauffler College, 1939-41; Western Connecticut State College, B.S., 1968; Wesleyan University, Middletown, Conn., M.A., 1972. *Home address:* P.O. Box 336, West Cornwall, Conn. 06796. *Agent:* Dorothy Olding, Harold Ober Associates, Inc., 40 East 49th St., New York, N.Y. 10017.

CAREER: Secretary, 1944-47; *Angler's Almanac,* New York, N.Y., associate editor, 1947-51; Northwestern Regional School, Winsted, Conn., high school English teacher, 1968-79; writer, 1979—. *Member:* Authors Guild of Authors League of America, National Council of Teachers of English, New England Council of Teachers of English, Connecticut Council of Teachers of English, Litchfield Hills Audubon Society (member of board of directors, 1962-63). *Awards, honors:* Award from League of Connecticut Historical Societies, 1977, for *Untie the Winds.*

WRITINGS: Untie the Winds (novel), Macmillan, 1976.

Contributor of stories to popular magazines, including *Redbook, McCall's, Ladies' Home Journal, Cosmopolitan,* and *Woman's Day.*

WORK IN PROGRESS: A modern novel; research for a historical novel set in early New York and the Hudson River area.

SIDELIGHTS: Jean Clark comments: "Like many others, I developed an early and enduring love for the printed word as I escaped the frustrations of childhood through reading. This naturally led to the desire to write. I have been writing for as long as I can remember, am restless and unhappy if circumstances prevent me from doing so, and recently gave up an enjoyable teaching position for this reason.

"My return to college was important to my career in that it deepened my interest in history and sharpened my research skills. As a result, while reading through old colonial records of Connecticut, I discovered Ann Eaton, the controversial wife of the first governor of New Haven Colony and the subject of my novel, *Untie the Winds.* It seemed to me that a woman of the early seventeenth century who dared to challenge the beliefs of not only her husband but also the equally powerful John Davenport, head of New Haven's church, even though this challenge led to an embarrassing church trial and eventual excommunication, deserved to be commemorated."

AVOCATIONAL INTERESTS: "My most pleasurable relaxation is walking or snowshoeing on a quiet country road or in a silent woods with my binoculars in hand. My privately-acquired knowledge of birds has recently been increased through an extension course in ornithology.

"Beyond going to our favorite haunts in Vermont, I do little traveling. I am interested in Greek history, language, and drama, and twice have nearly gone to Greece, but a fear of flying keeps me at home."

* * *

CLARK, Joan 1934-

PERSONAL: Born October 12, 1934, in Liverpool, Nova Scotia, Canada; married John Clark (an engineer); children: three. *Education:* Acadia University, B.A., 1957; attended University of Alberta, 1960. *Address:* 364 Wildwood Dr. S.W., Calgary, Alberta, Canada T3C 3E6.

CAREER: Teacher in Sussex, New Brunswick, 1957-58, Edmonton, Alberta, 1960-61, Calgary, Alberta, 1962-63, and Dartmouth, Nova Scotia, 1969-70. *Member:* Writers Union of Canada, Children's Book Centre.

WRITINGS—Juveniles: Girl of the Rockies, Ryerson, 1968; *Thomasina and the Trout Tree,* Tundra Books, 1971; *The Hand of Robin Squires,* Clarke, Irwin, 1977. Contributor of stories to magazines, including *Canadian Fiction, Waves, Dalhousie Review, Journal of Canadian Fiction,* and *Wascana Review.* Editor of *Dandelion.*

WORK IN PROGRESS: A children's book; short stories.

* * *

CLARK, Kenneth (Mackenzie) 1903-

PERSONAL: Born July 13, 1903, in London, England; son of Kenneth Mackenzie (an industrial tycoon) and Margaret Alice (McArthur) Clark; married Elizabeth Martin, 1927 (died, 1976); married Nolwen de Janze-Rice, 1977; children: Alan, Rolin, Colette. *Education:* Trinity College, Oxford, received A.B., M.A., Ph.D. *Home:* B5 Albany, Picadilly, London W.1, England.

CAREER: Worked with Bernard Berenson in England, Italy, and France, 1926-28; Ashmolean Museum, Oxford, England, keeper of department of fine art, 1931-33; National Gallery, London, England, director, 1934-45; surveyor of king's pictures, Hampton Court, Buckingham Palace, and Windsor Palace, England, 1934-44; U.K. Ministry of Information, controller of home publicity and director of films division, 1939-41; Oxford University, Oxford, Slade Professor of Fine Arts, 1946-50 and 1961-62; University of York, Heslington, York, England, chancellor, 1969—. Chairman of Arts Council of Great Britain, 1953-60, and Independent Television Authority, 1954-57. *Member:* British Academy (fellow), Royal College of Art (fellow), National Art Collection Fund, Contemporary Art Society, Covent Garden Opera Trust, Victoria and Albert Museum (member of advisory council). Committee member of numerous organizations, including National Theatre Board, Conseil Artistique des Musees Nationaux, and Art Collection Fund. Honorary member of organizations, including Royal Scottish Academy, Swedish Academy, American Academy of Arts and Letters, Commendatore della Corona d'Italia, Commendatore al Ordine de Merito, Florentine Academy, American Institute of Architects, fellow of the Royal Institute of British Architects.

AWARDS, HONORS: Created Knight Commander of the Bath, 1938; knighted by Queen Elizabeth II, 1953; Serena Medal from British Academy for Italian Studies, 1955; Companion of Honor, 1959; fellow at University of Oxford, 1968; created Baron of Saltwood (life peerage), 1969; U.S. National Gallery of Art Award for distinguished services, 1970, for "Civilisation"; named Companion of Literature by Royal Society of Literature, 1974; Order of Merit, 1976; gold meal from New York University; commander of French Legion of Honor; Knight of the Lion of Finland. Honorary degrees from more than ten universities and colleges.

WRITINGS: The Gothic Revival: An Essay in the History of Taste, Constable, 1929; (with David Lindsay) *A Commemorative Catalogue of the Exhibition of Italian Art,* [London], 1931; *A Catalogue of the Drawings of Leonardo da Vinci in the Collection of His Majesty the King, at Windsor Castle,* three volumes, Macmillan, 1935, 2nd edition, Phaidon Press, 1968-69; *Leonardo da Vinci: An Account of His Development as an Artist,* Macmillan, 1939, 2nd edition, Cambridge University Press, 1952; (editor) *The Penguin Modern Painters,* Penguin, 1943; *Landscape Into Art,* John Murray, 1949, Penguin, 1956, 2nd edition, John Murray, 1979; (author of introduction) *Paintings of Graham Bell,* Lund Humphries, 1947.

Landscape Painting, Scribner, 1950; *Piero della Francesca,* Phaidon Press, 1951; *Moments of Vision,* Oxford University Press, 1954, variant edition, John Murray, 1975; *Selected Drawings From Windsor Castle: Leonardo da Vinci,* three volumes, Phaidon Press, 1955; *The Nude: A Study in Ideal Form,* Pantheon Books, 1956, Penguin, 1960; *Looking at Pictures,* Holt, 1960; (author of introduction and notes) Walter H. Pater, *The Renaissance: Studies in Art and Poetry,* Collins, 1961; *Sidney Nolan,* Thames & Hudson, 1961; *Provincialism,* Oxford University Press, 1963; (author of introduction) Douglas Cooper, editor, *Great Private Collections,* Macmillan, 1963; (editor) *Ruskin Today* (anthology), John Murray, 1964; *Rembrandt and the Italian Renaissance,* John Murray, 1966; (editor) R. M. Slyth, *Guides to the Published Work of Art Historians,* Bournemouth, 1968; *Civilisation: A Personal View,* John Murray, 1969, Harper, 1970, 2nd edition, John Murray, 1971.

The Artist Grows Old, Cambridge University Press, 1972;

Studies in the History of the Renaissance, Fontana, 1973; *Blake and Visionary Art,* University of Glasgow, 1973; *The Romantic Rebellion: Romantic Versus Classic Art,* John Murray, 1973; *Another Part of the Wood: A Self-Portrait,* John Murray, 1974, Harper, 1975; (editor) *Henry Moore Drawings,* Thames & Hudson, 1974; *Concept of Universal Man,* Ditchley Foundation, 1976; *The Drawings by Sandro Botticelli for Dante's "Divine Comedy": After the Originals in the Berlin Museums and the Vatican,* Thames & Hudson, 1976; *Animals and Men: Their Relationship as Reflected in Western Art From Prehistory to the Present Day,* Thames & Hudson, 1977; *The Other Half: A Self-Portrait,* John Murray, 1977; *Introduction to Rembrandt,* John Murray, 1978; *The Best of Aubrey Beardsley,* John Murray, 1979; *Happiness,* University of Birmingham, 1979. Also author of *A Failure of Nerve,* 1967.

Also author of television series broadcast by the British Broadcasting Corp. (BBC), "Civilisation," 1969, and "Romantic Versus Classic Art," 1973.

SIDELIGHTS: Sir Kenneth Clark, English art authority and historian, has been called a "Renaissance grandee," the "picture of patrician grace," and the "quintessential English gentleman." Heir to a vast fortune amassed by his tycoon father, he describes his parents as belonging "to a section of society known as the 'idle rich,' and although, in that golden age, many people were richer, there can be few who were idler.... They were two of the most irresponsible people I have ever known." His father, though he encouraged young Kenneth in his passion for art, spent his days with drink, and his mother, whose harsh indifference left him frequently in the care of servants who mistreated him, revealed to him early the cruel injustices of life. "Kenneth Clark was left in no doubt," stated John Russell, "... that life has its vicissitudes. He developed two lines of defense: a lifelong passion for works of art and a highly developed sense for the ridiculous."

After completing his studies at Oxford University, Clark journeyed to Florence with renowned art authority Bernard Berenson to work on a revision of the latter's *Florentine Drawings.* Upon returning to England, Clark published his first book, *The Gothic Revival,* at the age of twenty-six. A year later he was named keeper of the fine art department of the Ashmolean Museum at Oxford, and by the time he reached thirty, was appointed to the prestigious post of Director of London's National Gallery, the youngest ever so honored.

The following years saw Clark's career skyrocketing in several different directions at once. So successful were his endeavors that he himself dubbed the years 1932-39 the "Clark Boom." But even in the midst of such meteoric rise, he never lost sight of his goal to bring art to the masses. With the advent of World War II, when all the art works of the National Gallery had to be moved to Wales for protection from the German bombers, he brought back a different work each month and presented lunch-time concerts in the abandoned Gallery to lift the morale of his fellow countrymen and women.

One of Clark's major projects has been the undertaking of a television series on art and culture for the British Broadcasting Corp. In discussing the enterprise with one of the directors, the word "civilisation" was mentioned. "I had no clear idea what he meant, but I thought it was preferable to barbarism and fancied that this was the moment to say so," recalled Clark in the foreword to *Civilisation.* He went on to express that he "would like to think that these programmes have done two things: they have made people feel that they are part of a great human achievement, and be proud of it; and they have made them feel humble in thinking of the great men and women of the past. Also, I like to think that they are entertaining.'' While the televised version of ''Civilisation'' was praised highly, the book version, for some, was disappointing. Oswell Blakeston felt that the ''idea of presenting a selection of crucial civilising episodes from the Fall of the Roman Empire to the present day was a serious one—for TV; but when a book raises such profound issues as the nature of civilisation, it needs backbone, an all-over philosophy which is fully reasoned and unclouded. . . . I'm not impressed with the book as book, which is another way of saying that I'm not impressed with the trivialisation of the TV medium.''

While there are critics who have condemned Clark as a fraud who attempts to be an expert on everything from Gothic architecture to Renaissance music to Classical painting, Clark himself has protested: ''I've never tried to be an expert on all of those things. If you like to say I'm a popularizer, I have no objection. My main aim has been to make things understandable to people.'' Regarding the success of Clark's intention, Nigel Nicolson declared, ''He is our greatest communicator, a scholar with the boldness to believe that whatever is intelligible to him can be made intelligible to people with little learning, a popularizer who never surrendered his integrity, who talked up, never down, who has a historical perspective in both directions, who has provided three generations with a set of scales on which to weigh the past and present achievement, never pontifical, always lucid, always enthusiastic, believing that people, anybody, can be brought to care for what he most cares for himself.''

The Romantic Rebellion was another book derived from a televised series, though not so well received as was ''Civilisation.'' ''On the whole,'' claimed Ruth Berenson, ''it offers the neophyte a well written, if incomplete, introduction to some of the great artists of the late eighteenth and nineteenth centuries. For readers with more than a passing acquaintance with the subject, however, Lord Clark hasn't much new to say—though he does say it very well indeed.'' Comprised of essays on thirteen artists of the Classic and Romantic periods, Clark presented *The Romantic Rebellion* as a broad survey of the age. '''The Romantic Rebellion,''' assessed Peter Conrad, ''is remarkable in dealing not only in great confident arcs of generalisation about cultural history but in those small, unique apprehensions of detail which are Kenneth Clark's signature.''

In *Animals and Men*, Clark takes us on a ''delightful romp'' through the animal kingdom as depicted by the Lascaux cave drawings of pre-literate man and into the abstract world of Picasso. The book was written at the urgings of Fleur Cowles, the international trustee of the World Wildlife Fund (which, incidentally, receives a percentage of the royalties). Howard Fox related that Clark ''pursues his thesis that a dual relationship of love and worship, enmity and fear, has persisted between men and animals since prehistory.'' Jan Morris, however, suggested that it is an ''irony that a book professing to examine the immemorial relationship between man and beast should disregard the very territories where they have come closest to understanding one another.'' Fox disagreed, stating that ''it is very much to Clark's credit that in his brevity he piques the reader's curiosity rather than lays it to rest. For lovers of animals and art, the book is a delight; for those who like one but not the other, the book could provide just enough substance for a second look.''

Clark's two autobiographies, *Another Part of the Wood* and *The Other Half*, have received contrasting reviews. The latter, for example, has been deemed by Christopher Booker ''one of the most unconsciously self-revealing books ever written,'' but was also referred to by Rene Kuhn Bryant as one that details a life ''without revealing more than the merest minimum of the man who has written it.'' Clark's style of writing is another aspect that invites opposing opinions. Robert Melville flatly stated that part of the fascination is ''his attempt to find a style in which to present himself to the general reader as an ordinary chap who happens to be a wealthy aesthete, and one of the most sensitive and stylish writers we have ever had. He makes a glorious hash of it. His false modesty is excruciating.'' On the other hand, Bryant asserted that ''Clark marries substance with style, links wit to criticism, and demonstrates yet again his extraordinary ability to convey complex conceptions to a diverse and random audience with clarity and concision.''

Another Part of the Wood, which recalls Clark's life until his late thirties, confirms that he was ''brought face to face at a very early age with the fragility and instability of our human lot,'' observed John Russell. Though he is the product of a wealthy family and has had tremendous success in his career, Clark himself conceded that he learned from Ibsen ''how full of cruel surprises life can be, how mixed are all motives, how under each layer of deception lies a still deeper layer of self-deception.'' He sees his life as one long string of good luck and feels somewhat awed by it all: ''How my small talents came to arouse this kind of mass hysteria I shall never understand.'' In fact, he admits to being almost bullied by his own phenomenal rise and reputation as the foremost authority on art and culture, and revealed that he was afflicted by ''that subtle corruption that attacks almost everyone when he can no longer be contradicted or prevented from doing things, and when everyone except a few old friends kow-tows him.''

BIOGRAPHICAL/CRITICAL SOURCES: Kenneth Clark, *Civilisation*, John Murray, 1969, Harper, 1970, 2nd edition, John Murray, 1971; *Saturday Review*, August 28, 1971; *Books and Bookmen*, September, 1971; *New Statesman*, November 30, 1973, October 11, 1974; Clark, *Another Part of the Wood: A Self-Portrait*, John Murray, 1974, Harper, 1975; *National Review*, April 26, 1974; *New York Times Book Review*, March 30, 1975, July 2, 1978; Clark, *The Other Half: A Self-Portrait*, John Murray, 1977; *Spectator*, November 12, 1977; *Washington Post Book World*, November 13, 1977.

—*Sketch by Kathleen Ceton Newman*

*   *   *

CLARKSON, Jan Nagel   1943-

PERSONAL: Born June 26, 1943, in Pittsburgh, Pa.; daughter of Carl E. (an executive recruiter) and Grace (a real estate broker; maiden name, Wilkie) Nagel; married James A. Clarkson III (an attorney), November 25, 1967; children: Blair. *Education:* Connecticut College, B.A., 1965; graduate study at Columbia University, 1965-66. *Home:* 9917 East Bexhill Dr., Kensington, Md. 20795.

CAREER: Fortune, New York, N.Y., researcher, 1966-69; National Geographic Society, Washington, D.C., editor, researcher, and writer, 1969-75; currently free-lance writer. *Awards, honors: Tricks Animals Play* was listed among outstanding books for children by National Science Teachers Association and Children's Book Council, 1975.

WRITINGS: Tricks Animals Play (juvenile), National Geographic Society, 1975.

SIDELIGHTS: Jan Clarkson writes: "Despite a background in economics, specifically corporation analysis and finance, I am strongly interested in the natural sciences."

* * *

CLAY, Grady E. 1916-

PERSONAL: Born November 5, 1916, in Ann Arbor, Mich.; son of Grady E. (a physician) and Eleanor (Hall) Solomon; married Judith McCandless (an architect), August 28, 1976; children: Grady E. III, Theodore H., Peter M. *Education:* Emory University, A.B., 1938; Columbia University, M.S., 1939; attended Harvard University, 1948-49. *Residence:* Louisville, Ky. *Office: Landscape Architecture,* 1190 East Broadway, Louisville, Ky. 40204.

CAREER: St. Simons Island Star, St. Simons Island, Ga., editor and publisher, 1938; *Louisville Courier-Journal,* Louisville, Ky., urban affairs editor, 1964-66; Grady Clay & Co. (editors and publishers), Louisville, president, 1976—. Research associate at Joint Center for Urban Studies, of Massachusetts Institute of Technology and Harvard University, 1960-61; visiting lecturer at University of Kentucky, 1960, 1965, and Northwestern University, 1966-68; Lorado Taft Lecturer at University of Illinois, 1963, 1975; member of faculty at Salzburg Seminar in American Studies, 1968; Dennis O'Harrow Memorial Lecturer of American Society of Planning Officials, 1969; visiting member of faculty at Massachusetts Institute of Technology, 1973; Metroversity Lecturer at University of Louisville, 1975, Bingham Professor of Humanities, 1978. Head of waterfront panel of White House Conference on Natural Beauty, 1965; member of President's Task Force on Suburban Problems, 1967-68; chairperson of Environmental Planning Advisory Council of Amelia Island, Fla., 1971-75; co-founder of Louisville's Citizens' Metropolitan Planning Council; member of Kentucky governor's Design Advisory Council, 1976-80.

MEMBER: American Society of Planning Officials (president, 1973-74), American Institute of Architects (honorary member), American Society of Landscape Architects (honorary member), National Association of Real Estate Editors (past president), Urban Writers Society (founding member). *Awards, honors:* Nieman fellow at Harvard University, 1948-49; Ford Foundation grant, 1960-61; Guggenheim fellowship, 1973-74; grants from National Endowment for the Arts and National Endowment for the Humanities, 1974-78, 1976-77.

WRITINGS: This Is the Place, City of Louisville, Ky., 1966; *Close-Up: How to Read the American City,* Praeger, 1973; *Alleys: A Hidden Resource,* Grady Clay & Co., 1978; (editor) *Water in the Landscape,* McGraw, 1978; (editor) *Landscapes for Living,* McGraw, 1980. Also co-author of *New Towns for Appalachian America,* 1962.

Contributor: *The Exploding Metropolis,* Doubleday, 1958; *The Potomac,* U.S. Government Printing Office, 1967; *The Changing Metropolis,* Houghton, 1969; *Interpreting Environmental Issues,* Dembar Educational Research Services, 1973. Contributor to professional journals, popular magazines, and newspapers, including *Horizon, Fortune, House Beautiful, Ekistics,* and *Southern Living.* Editor of *Landscape Architecture.*

* * *

CLEMENTS, Frank A. 1942-

PERSONAL: Born January 10, 1942, in Edinburgh, Scotland; son of Alan Lawrence and Janet (Moore) Clements;

married Maureen Victoria (a hairdresser), August 13, 1966; children: Mark Francis. *Education:* Educated in Scotland. *Home:* 11 Frenshaw Ave., Plymouth, Devonshire, England.

CAREER: Writer. Worked as civil servant in England, 1960-61, and Australia, 1961-64; librarian in England, 1964—. *Member:* British Society for Middle Eastern Studies, Royal Asiatic Society, Council for Anglo-Arab Understanding, Library Association (fellow).

WRITINGS: T. E. Lawrence: A Reader's Guide, Shoe String Press, 1973; *The Emergence of Arab Nationalism,* Scholarly Resources, 1977, 2nd edition, Mansell Publishing, 1981; *Saudi Arabia,* ABC—Clio, 1979; *Oman: The Reborn Land,* Longman, 1980.

WORK IN PROGRESS: The Arabian Gulf States, publication by ABC—Clio expected in 1982.

SIDELIGHTS: Clements commented to *CA:* "I became interested in Arabia purely by accident and found that it became an all-consuming interest which I could not stop even if I so desired. I write in addition to holding a full-time post as librarian, but would ideally wish to write full time. Unfortunately, the type of book that I write is not commercial in the sense of bringing in a full-time income and I have no interest in writing fiction or popular travelogues."

* * *

CLOUD, Preston (Ercelle) 1912-

PERSONAL: Born September 26, 1912, in West Upton, Mass.; son of Preston E. and Pauline L. (Wiedemann) Cloud; married Janice Gibson, 1972; children: (previous marriage) Karen, Lisa, Kevin. *Education:* George Washington University, B.S., 1938; Yale University, Ph.D., 1940. *Home:* 400 Mountain Dr., Santa Barbara, Calif. 93103. *Office:* Department of Geology, University of California, Santa Barbara, Calif. 93106.

CAREER: University of Missouri, Rolla, instructor in geology, 1940-41; U.S. Geological Surveys, geologist, 1942-46 and 1948-61, chief of paleontology and stratigraphy branch, 1949-59, representative in oceanography, 1959-61; Harvard University, Cambridge, Mass., assistant professor and curator of invertebrate paleontology, 1946-48; University of Minnesota—Minneapolis, professor of geology and geophysics, 1961-65, chairman of department of geology and geophysics, 1961-63, head of School of Earth Science, 1962-63; University of California, Los Angeles, professor of geology, 1965-68; University of California, Santa Barbara, professor emeritus, 1968—. Lecturer in geology, University of Texas, 1962, Salzburg Seminar on American Studies, 1973; served on numerous congressional panels and on advisory panels of organizations, including National Aeronautics and Space Administration (NASA), U.S. Department of the Interior, and Smithsonian Institution. *Military service:* U.S. Navy, 1930-33. *Member:* American Philosophical Society, American Geophysical Union, American Association for Advancement of Science, American Academy of Arts and Sciences (fellow), National Academy of Sciences (council member, 1972-75; executive committee member, 1973-75), National Research Council (governmental board member, 1972-75), Geological Society of America (council member, 1972-75; life fellow), Paleontological Society of America, American Society of Naturalists (fellow), Paleontological Society of India (honorary member), Phi Beta Kappa, Sigma Xi. *Awards, honors:* A. Cressy Morrison Prize for Natural History, 1941; Yale University research fellow, 1941-42 and 1973; U.S. Department of the Interior Medal, 1959; Lucius Wilbur Cross Medal, 1973.

WRITINGS: *The Ellenburger Group of Central Texas,* University of Texas, 1948; (contributor) *Geology of Saipan and the Mariana Islands,* three volumes, U.S. Government Printing Office, 1956-57; *Environment of Calcium Carbonate Deposition West of Andros Island, Bahamas,* U.S. Government Printing Office, 1962; *Resources and Man,* W. H. Freeman, 1969; *Cosmos, Earth, and Man: A Short History of the Universe,* Yale University Press, 1978. Contributor of articles to journals in his field. Associate editor of *American Journal of Sciences, Quarterly Review of Biology,* and *Precambrian Research.*

* * *

COBB, Jonathan 1946-

PERSONAL: Born March 7, 1946, in Summit, N.J.; son of Raymond W. (an insurance executive) and Helen (Baker) Cobb; married Susanna Hawley Dodds, December 30, 1967; children: Alyssa, Alexander. *Education:* Columbia University, B.A., 1968. *Home and office:* 1329 Henry St., Apt. 2-D, Berkeley, Calif. 94709.

CAREER: Urban Family Study, Cambridge, Mass., co-director, 1969-72; factory worker in Boston, Mass., 1973; free-lance writer and editor, 1974—. Fellow of Cambridge Institute for Policy Studies, 1969-71.

WRITINGS: (With Richard Sennett) *The Hidden Injuries of Class,* Knopf, 1972. Reviewer for *Progressive.*

* * *

COBURN, Kathleen 1905-

PERSONAL: Born September 7, 1905, in Stayner, Ontario, Canada; daughter of John and Susannah (Emerson) Coburn. *Education:* University of Toronto, B.A., 1928, M.A., 1930; St. Hugh's College, Oxford, B.Litt., 1932. *Office:* c/o Department of English, Victoria College, 91 Charles St. W., Toronto, Ontario, Canada M5S 1K7.

CAREER: Victoria College, Toronto, Ontario, instructor, 1932-53, professor of English, 1953-71, professor emerita, 1971—. *Member:* Royal Society of Canada (fellow), Royal Society of Literature (fellow), British Academy (corresponding fellow). *Awards, honors:* Senior fellow of International Federation of University Women, 1947; Leverhulme fellow in England, 1948; Guggenheim fellow, 1953-54, 1957-58; Rosemary Crawshay Prize from British Academy, 1958; senior Commonwealth visiting research fellow at University of London, 1962-63; LL.D. from Queen's University, Kingston, Ontario, 1964; D.H.L. from Haverford College, 1972; D.Litt. from Trent University, 1973, Cambridge University, 1975, University of British Columbia, 1976, and University of Toronto, 1978; officer of Order of Canada, 1974.

WRITINGS: *The Grandmothers,* Oxford University Press, 1949; *Discourse,* Royal Institution, 1972; *In Pursuit of Coleridge,* Clarke, Irwin, 1977; *Experience Into Thought: Some Perspectives on Coleridge From His Notebooks,* University of Toronto Press, 1979; *Inquiring Spirit: A New Presentation of Coleridge From His Published and Unpublished Prose Writings,* revised edition, University of Toronto Press, 1979. Also contributor to *Riddell Memorial Lectures,* 1972.

Editor: *The Notebooks of Samuel Taylor Coleridge,* Bollingen Foundation, Volume I, 1957, Volume II, 1961, Volume III, 1973; *Coleridge: A Collection of Critical Essays,* Prentice-Hall, 1967. General editor of "The Collected Works of Samuel Taylor Coleridge," twenty-four volumes, Bollingen Foundation, 1968—. Also editor of *The Philosophical Lectures of S. T. Coleridge, Hitherto Unpublished,* 1949, and *The Sara Hutchinson Letters,* 1954.

COHN, Dorrit 1924-

PERSONAL: Born August 9, 1924, in Vienna, Austria; daughter of Herbert and Emma (Hirsch) Zucker-Hale; married Robert G. Cohn, July 3, 1947 (divorced, 1963); children: Stephen, Richard. *Education:* Radcliffe College, B.A., 1945, M.A., 1946; attended Yale University, 1946-49; Stanford University, Ph.D., 1964. *Home:* 221 Mount Auburn, Cambridge, Mass. 02138. *Office:* Department of Germanic Languages, Harvard University, Boylston Hall, Cambridge, Mass. 02138.

CAREER: Indiana University, Bloomington, assistant professor, 1964-68, associate professor of German, 1968-71; Harvard University, Cambridge, Mass., professor of German, 1971—. *Member:* Modern Language Association of America, American Association of Teachers of German, American Comparative Literature Association. *Awards, honors:* Guggenheim fellowship, 1970-71.

WRITINGS: *The Sleepwalkers: Elucidations of Herman Bloch's Trilogy,* Mouton, 1966; *Transparent Minds: Narrative Modes for Presenting Consciousness in Fiction,* Princeton University Press, 1978.

* * *

COHN, Ruby 1922-

PERSONAL: Born August 13, 1922, in Columbia, Ohio. *Education:* Hunter College (now of the City University of New York), B.A., 1942; University of Paris, D.Univ., 1952; Washington University, St. Louis, Mo., Ph.D., 1960. *Office:* Department of Comparative Literature, University of California, Davis, Calif. 95616.

CAREER: University of California, lecturer in English, 1960-61; San Francisco State College, San Francisco, Calif., 1961-70, began as assistant professor, became associate professor and professor of English and world literature; California Institute of the Arts, Valencia, fellow, 1970-72; University of California, Davis, professor of comparative drama, 1972—. *Member:* Modern Language Association of America, American Comparative Literature Association. *Awards, honors:* Guggenheim fellow, 1965-66.

WRITINGS: *Samuel Beckett: The Comic Gamut,* Rutgers University Press, 1962; (editor) *Moonlight Monologues,* Macmillan, 1963; (editor) *Classics for Contemporaries,* Indiana University Press, 1969; *Currents in Contemporary Drama,* Indiana University Press, 1969; *Dialogue in American Drama,* Indiana University Press, 1971; *Back to Beckett,* Princeton University Press, 1973; *Modern Shakespeare Offshoots,* Princeton University Press, 1976; *Just Play: The Theater of Samuel Beckett,* Princeton University Press, 1979.

* * *

COKER, Gylbert 1944-

PERSONAL: Born May 14, 1944, in New York, N.Y.; daughter of Myles Alan (in business) and Anita (a cataloger at a television station; maiden name, Garvin) Coker. *Education:* Attended Universidad de Mexico, 1962; Pratt Institute, B.F.A., 1968; also attended Herbert H. Lehman College of the City University of New York, 1972, and Hunter College of the City University of New York, 1975.

CAREER: Museum of Modern Art, New York City, cataloger, 1969-71; Negro Action Group Daycare Center, New York City, teacher, 1971-74; Children's Art Carnival, New York City, art teacher, 1974; Studio Museum in Harlem, New York City, artist-in-residence, 1973-74, art teacher,

1974-76, curator, 1978-79; art editor for *Black American*, 1979. Auditor for New York State Council of the Arts. Member of Art Commission of the City of New York. *Member:* American Association of Museums, National Conference of Artists, Smithsonian Institution. *Awards, honors:* Rockefeller Foundation fellowship, 1976.

WRITINGS: (Self-illustrated) *Naptime* (picture book), Delacorte, 1978. Reviewer for *Amsterdam News, Black American,* and *Art in America.*

SIDELIGHTS: Coker writes: "Because I have worked with very small children (ages two to four) I have become aware of their need for books that afford them an opportunity to get into reading readiness. My picture book provides this kind of experience.

"Every third Sunday I read to small children at a local book store. This kind of experience keeps me in touch with the response children have to the language, the rhythm, and the visuals of stories. I know that most writers write for themselves. I write for children and in order to give them what they enjoy I need to listen, watch, and learn from them."

*   *   *

COLCHIE, Elizabeth Schneider 1943-

PERSONAL: Born April 8, 1943, in New York, N.Y.; daughter of Herman (a writer of science books for children) and Nina (a science writer and novelist; maiden name, Zimet) Schneider; married Thomas James Colchie, August 28, 1966 (divorced, 1974); children: Daisy Juliana. *Education:* New York University, B.A., 1966. *Home and office:* 215 East 80th St., New York, N.Y. 10021. *Agent:* Harriet Wasserman, Russell & Volkening, Inc., 551 Fifth Ave., New York, N.Y. 10017.

CAREER: Free-lance editor of children's books and language texts, 1966-71; free-lance food writer, developing recipes in her test kitchen, 1971—. *Member:* Les Dames d'Escoffier (charter member), Phi Beta Kappa.

WRITINGS: (Contributor) *The Cooks' Catalogue,* Harper, 1975; (with Helen Witty) *Better Than Store-Bought,* Harper, 1979. Author of "Fete Accomplie," a monthly column in *International Review of Food & Wine.* Historical consultant and picture researcher, *The International Cooks' Catalogue,* Random House, 1977. Contributor of articles and recipes to popular magazines and newspapers, including *Family Circle, Gourmet, Ladies' Home Journal, Bon Appetit, House & Garden, Cuisine,* and *The Pleasures of Cooking.* Contributing editor of *International Review of Food & Wine.*

WORK IN PROGRESS: A book of menus, recipes, and historical discussions based on made-ahead food for entertaining; a book to teach children about food and cooking.

SIDELIGHTS: Elizabeth Schneider Colchie wrote: "In *Better Than Store-Bought* we devised recipes to provide alternatives to some of the commercially prepared foods that have become, through industrialization, either tasteless or unhealthy. We hoped that informally presented advice and reliable recipes could interest (and 'convert') some cooks who might not have known that they could make at home their own cream cheese, dill pickles, or English muffins. I expect that in books to come, my interests will lead me to the same general question; that is, what to do about maintaining a pleasurable and nutritionally sound way of eating in a time and place (the twentieth century, America) where the demands upon our time and money are seemingly endless."

COLE, John N(elson) 1923-

PERSONAL: Born February 26, 1923, in New York, N.Y.; son of John N. (a stockbroker) and Helen (an artist; maiden name, Dodd) Cole; married Cynthia Waterbury (divorced, 1963); married Jean Gurley (a typist), June 19, 1964; children: Marshall, Darrah; (stepchildren) Chris, Robert, Tracy, Sam. *Education:* Yale University, B.A., 1948. *Home address:* Box 3137, Simpson's Point Rd., Brunswick, Maine 04011. *Office: Maine Times,* 47 Main St., Topsham, Maine 04086.

CAREER: Worked as public relations representative, writer, and commercial fisherman in New York; *York Country Coast Star,* Kennebunk, Maine, editor, 1956-60; *Bath-Brunswick Times Record,* Brunswick, Maine, editor, 1961-68; *Maine Times,* Topsham, co-founder and editor, 1968-76, contributing editor, 1976—, president of Maine Times, Inc. Member of adjunct faculty at Bowdoin College. Co-founder of WorldPaper; private investigator for Dunfey Brothers. Member of National Parks Advisory Council; member of board of directors of national Media Access Project, Washington, D.C.; member of U.S. Office of Technology Assistance task force for appropriate technology. Member of New England Regional Energy Council and Maine Natural Resources Council; chairperson of local Town Common committee and shellfish conservation committee. Director of Center for Constructive Change, Durham, N.H.; member of board of directors and past president of Allagash Group; consultant to Maine Coast Heritage Trust. *Military service:* U.S. Army Air Forces, combat gunner, 1941-45; served in England; received Purple Heart, Air Medal, and Distinguished Flying Cross.

MEMBER: National Audubon Society (member of board of directors), St. Botolph's Club. *Awards, honors:* Journalism awards include Yankee Quill Award from New England Academy of Journalists, 1973; Environmental Achievement Award from U.S. Environmental Protection Agency, 1974; Missouri Medal for Journalism, 1976, for *Maine Times.*

WRITINGS: In Maine, Dutton, 1974; *From the Ground Up,* Little, Brown, 1976; *Striper: The Story of Fish and Man,* Little, Brown, 1978; *The Amaranth,* Rodale Press, 1979. Author of a column in *Boston Globe,* 1974—, and in *Newsday,* 1977—. Contributor to magazines and newspapers, including *Harper's, Yankee, Esquire, Reader's Digest, Sports Illustrated,* and *Atlantic Monthly.*

WORK IN PROGRESS: Pinion, a novel; *The Sun Book,* nonfiction.

BIOGRAPHICAL/CRITICAL SOURCES: Audubon, July, 1973; *Washington Post Book World,* November 11, 1979.

*   *   *

COLE, Sonia (Mary) 1918-

PERSONAL: Born in 1918, in London, England; children: one son, one daughter. *Education:* Attended University of London. *Home:* 23 Whitehead's Grove, London S.W.3, England.

CAREER: Borax Consolidated Ltd., editor of *Twenty Mule Team.* Associate of British Museum (Natural History).

WRITINGS: An Outline of the Geology of Kenya, Pitman, 1950; *The Prehistory of East Africa,* Penguin, 1954, 2nd edition, New American Library, 1965; *Counterfeit,* J. Murray, 1955; *Early Man in East Africa,* Macmillan, 1958, 3rd edition, 1970; *The Neolithic Revolution,* Department of Geology and Paleontology, British Museum (Natural History), 1959, 5th edition, 1971; *Races of Man,* British Museum (Natural History), 1963, 2nd edition, 1965; *Animal Ancestors,* Dutton, 1964; *Calibration of Hominoid Evolution: Recent Advances in Isotopic and Other Dating Methods Applicable to the Origin of Man,* Scottish Academic Press, 1972; *Leakey's Luck: The Life of Louis Seymour Bazett Leakey, 1903-1972,* Collins, 1975.

SIDELIGHTS: Cole's biography of Louis Leakey was praised by critics as an entertaining, fair, and balanced study of the anthropologist. An *Economist* reviewer commented, "Cole, who knew Leakey for nearly 30 years, has written an admirable biography with the support of his family: highly readable, full of affection, but hiding no warts." Derek Roe agreed, stating that Cole "has performed her daunting task quite brilliantly. For those who never knew him at all, *Leakey's Luck* is an admirable and entertaining biography."

BIOGRAPHICAL/CRITICAL SOURCES: Economist, June 14, 1975; *New York Times Book Review,* November 16, 1975; *Times Literary Supplement,* November 21, 1975.

* * *

COLEMAN, Dorothy Gabe 1935-

PERSONAL: Born March 26, 1935, in Swansea, Wales; daughter of Rufus (an accountant) and Bessie (a teacher; maiden name, Lewis) Gabe; married Robert Coleman (a university lecturer), June 28, 1958; children: Ian Gilbert. *Education:* Graduated from Girton College, Cambridge, 1957; University of Glasgow, Ph.D., 1960. *Politics:* Labour. *Religion:* None. *Home:* 60 Gilbert Rd., Cambridge, England.

CAREER: University of Glasgow, Glasgow, Scotland, assistant lecturer in French, 1957-60; Cambridge University, Cambridge, England, college lecturer in French and director of studies in modern languages at New Hall, 1960, university assistant lecturer, 1961-67, university lecturer in French, 1967—. *Member:* Association of University Lecturers, Society for French Studies.

WRITINGS: Rabelais: A Critical Study of Prose Fiction, Cambridge University Press, 1971; *Sceve: Poet of Love—Tradition and Originality,* Cambridge University Press, 1975; *The Gallo-Roman Muse: Aspects of Roman Literary Tradition in Sixteenth-Century France,* Cambridge University Press, 1979; *The Chaste Muse: A Study of Joachim du Bellay's Poetry,* E. J. Brill, 1979; *Maurice Sceve's Illustrated "Canzoniere,"* University of Turin, in press. Contributor to French studies and Renaissance studies journals.

WORK IN PROGRESS: Articles on Montaigne and the classics; a book on Montaigne.

SIDELIGHTS: Dorothy Coleman comments: "Being brought up bilingually (Welsh and English) made me interested in modern languages from an early age. Earning a degree in Latin and French (with a sideline in Italian) makes me fascinated by the period of the Renaissance, where bilingualism was very much to the fore (Latin plus the vernacular)."

AVOCATIONAL INTERESTS: International travel (especially France, Italy, and Greece).

* * *

COLLIER, Gaydell M(aier) 1935-

PERSONAL: Born June 28, 1935, in Long Island, N.Y.; daughter of Harry (a building manager) and Jean (Gaydell) Maier; married Roy Hugh Collier (a rancher), December 27, 1955; children: Sam Patrick, Frank Robert, Jenny Gay, Fred Melder. *Education:* Attended Middlebury College, 1953-55,

and University of Wyoming, 1955-56. *Home and office address:* Backpocket Ranch, Sundance, Wyo. 82729. *Agent:* Ellin K. Roberts, Box 391A, R.D. 1, Woodstock, N.Y. 12498.

CAREER: Free-lance writer and editor, 1962—. Member of library staff at University of Wyoming, 1970-73, head of circulation department, 1973-74; owner and manager of Backpocket Ranch Bookshop, 1977—. Member of board of trustees of Albany County Public Library, 1967-72; member of Wyoming State Advisory Council on Libraries, 1971-72. *Member:* American Booksellers Association, Western Writers of America, Wyoming Writers, Wyoming Library Association.

WRITINGS: (Editor) John Gorman, *The Western Horse: Its Types and Training,* 5th edition (Collier was not associated with earlier editions), Interstate, 1967; (with Eleanor Prince) *Basic Horsemanship, English and Western: A Complete Guide for Riders and Instructors,* Doubleday, 1974; (with Prince) *Basic Training for Horses: English and Western,* Doubleday, 1979. Contributor of articles and reviews to magazines and newspapers, including *Smithsonian, National Wildlife, Science News, Discovery,* and *Horse of Course.* Member of advisory board of *WLA Roundup* (of Wyoming Library Association), 1973.

WORK IN PROGRESS: A book on basic horse care, with Eleanor Prince; a historical biography, with Allen G. Richardson.

SIDELIGHTS: Gaydell Collier writes: "I have always had to do with books—reading, sorting, reviewing, editing, selling, writing. Now my main occupation is chief ranch hand and bottle washer, especially during the winter when the boys are away at college. We raise Hereford cattle, Morgan horses, Jersey milk cows, and Rambouillet sheep. We also have a small bookstore here on the ranch. From bookselling, fence building, horse training, cattle feeding, haying, milking, cooking, entertaining guests, and so on, I mine nuggets of time for writing with all the dedication of a prospector digging for gold. There is rarely a windfall of an uninterrupted two to three hours; an hour-and-a-half, three days in a row, is like tapping the mother lode. Don't ever say, 'I don't have time to write.' Somehow, some way, a writer will write."

* * *

COLLIER, Joy
See MILLAR, (Minna Henrietta) Joy

* * *

COLVER, A(nthony) Wayne 1923-

PERSONAL: Born December 23, 1923, in Oakland, Calif.; son of Wayne Cundiff and Viva (Davison) Colver; married Virginia Sanders, April 9, 1949; children: Clinton Anthony, Christopher Russell. *Education:* University of California, Los Angeles, B.A., 1948; Harvard University, M.A., 1951, Ph.D., 1957. *Home:* 4564 East Rialto, Fresno, Calif. 93726. *Office:* Department of Philosophy, California State University, Fresno, Calif. 93740.

CAREER: Reed College, Portland, Ore., instructor in philosophy and humanities, 1953-55; California State University, Fresno, assistant professor, 1957-62, associate professor, 1962-66, professor of philosophy, 1966—. *Military service:* U.S. Army, 1943-45; served in New Guinea, the Philippines, and Korea. *Member:* American Philosophical Association, Phi Beta Kappa, Pi Gamma Mu.

WRITINGS: (With Robert D. Stevick) *Composition and*

Research: Problems in Evolutionary Theory, Bobbs-Merrill, 1963; (editor with Alex Vavoulis) *Science and Society: Selected Essays*, Holden-Day, 1966; (editor) David Hume, *Natural History of Religion* (critical edition), Oxford University Press, 1976.

WORK IN PROGRESS: Editing Hobbe's *Leviathan*, from the British Library manuscript (Edgerton, 1910); critical editions of Hume's *Enquiries* and *Political Discourses*.

SIDELIGHTS: Colver wrote: "I am currently working on an edition of the manuscript of Hobbe's *Leviathan*, presented by Hobbes to the future Charles II in 1651. It deviates from the text of the first edition in numerous respects, most of them trivial, but some few of them interesting."

*   *   *

COMINI, Alessandra 1934-

PERSONAL: Born November 24, 1934, in Winona, Minn.; daughter of Raiberto (a composer and photographer) and Megan (a professor of Italian; maiden name, Laird) Comini. *Education:* Barnard College, B.A., 1956; University of California, Berkeley, M.A., 1964; Columbia University, Ph.D., 1968. *Home:* 2900 McFarlin, Dallas, Tex. 75205. *Office:* Department of Art History, Southern Methodist University, Dallas, Tex. 75222.

CAREER: Columbia University, New York, N.Y., instructor, 1967-68, assistant professor of art history, 1968-74; Southern Methodist University, Dallas, Tex., professor of art history, 1974—. Guest professor at University of California, Berkeley, 1966, and Yale University, 1973; Alfred Hodder Resident Humanist at Princeton University, 1972-73. *Member:* American Society of Composers, Authors and Publishers, College Art Association of America, Texas Institute of Letters. *Awards, honors:* National Book Award nomination, 1975, for *Egon Schiele's Portraits;* Charles Rufus Morey Book Award from College Art Association of America, 1976.

WRITINGS: Schiele in Prison, New York Graphic Society, 1973; *Egon Schiele's Portraits*, University of California Press, 1974; *Gustav Klimt*, Braziller, 1975; *Egon Schiele*, Braziller, 1976; *The Fantastic Art of Vienna*, Knopf, 1978. Guest editor of *Art Journal*, December, 1979; associate editor of *Arts*, 1977—.

WORK IN PROGRESS: Alfred Kubin; The Changing Image of Beethoven; Foreign Artists in Rome, 1775-1910.

*   *   *

CONN, Martha Orr 1935-

PERSONAL: Born March 12, 1935, in McKeesport, Pa.; daughter of Laird Earle (a stationary engineer) and Edna (Brown) Orr; married Kenneth A. Conn (an airline captain), December 21, 1953; children: Richard Laird, Robert William, David Jesse. *Education:* Attended Muskingum College, 1953-54, University of Virginia, 1962, 1966-68, 1970, and George Washington University, 1963; George Mason University, B.S., 1973. *Religion:* Methodist. *Home:* 4114 Burke Rd., Fairfax, Va. 22032.

CAREER: Nursery school teacher in Fairfax County, Va., 1969-71; Rose Hill Elementary School, Fairfax County, teacher, 1972-74; writer, 1974—. Adult education teacher, 1978. *Member:* Authors Guild of Authors League of America, National League of American Pen Women, Society of Children's Book Writers, Washington Area Writers, Children's Book Guild of Washington, D.C., United Pilot's Wives Club.

WRITINGS: Petey and I (juvenile), Western Publishing, 1973; *Crazy to Fly* (juvenile), Atheneum, 1978. Author of "Budget Redecorating," a column in *Trail-R-News*, 1963-64. Contributor of stories and articles to magazines.

WORK IN PROGRESS: A sequel to *Crazy to Fly;* a humorous autobiography, *Not That Kind of Girl;* an adult novel set in the behind-the-scenes world of airline flying.

SIDELIGHTS: Martha Conn writes: "One of the most surprising things that has happened to me lately was being invited to attend a conference for aviation writers. Although many of my stories in the past, as well as my planned adult novel, center around flying, I never thought of myself as a 'specialized' writer. I'm just following the old rule: Write what you know. After all, I have a husband, two brothers, and two sons who have been, are, or are planning to be professional pilots. It's as natural for me to write about people who love airplanes as it is for Jacques Cousteau to talk about sea creatures.

"Combining my two loves—writing and flying—has been a real joy for me. I have flown to various writers' meetings in all parts of the country and have studied under some of the outstanding writers for children. When I meet authors like Madeleine L'Engle, Carol Farley, and Katherine Paterson, who are writing some of the best fiction available today (note I did not limit that to *juvenile* fiction), I wonder how I dare to work in the same field. (Perhaps this explains why I'm currently outlining a novel for grownups!) Yet I do believe there is room in the wide world of children's books for a simple historical adventure like *Crazy to Fly*, as well as for the more complicated, stunningly realistic or engrossingly fantastic stories.

"The only writing for which there is no room in the children's book field is that with a theme of utter despair. There are those who do not agree, but I feel very strongly about this. If we fail to give our children a sense of hope, a feeling that they *do* have a chance of making the world better, where will we ever find the leaders who are willing to try?

"Speaking of a sense of hope, I have just had mine renewed by moving into a Fairfax office building. Shortly after publication of *Crazy to Fly*, I made the mistake (never make important decisions right after major surgery!) of moving my writing place from a dear little office in Falls Church, Virginia, back to my home. My writing output was reduced to almost nothing—and most of that strictly wastebasket material. But at last I have escaped once more from the telephone, washing machine, and Bad Housekeeper's Guilt to revel in the quiet (and be spurred on by the rent!) of a real office.

"Somehow this explanation of my lack of progress makes me think of the mouse who explained to the elephant why he couldn't match the pachyderm's feats of strength: 'I've been *sick!*' No more excuses—it's time to find out whether I'm an elephant or a mouse."

*   *   *

CONNIFF, Frank 1914-1971

OBITUARY NOTICE: Born April 24, 1914, in Danbury, Conn.; died May 25, 1971, of a heart attack, in New York, N.Y. Journalist. During his many years with the Hearst newspapers, Conniff served as war correspondent during World War II and the Korean war, director of Hearst Headline Services, and author of a syndicated column, "East Side, West Side." Conniff also was editor of the *World Journal Tribune* from 1966 to 1967, when the paper ceased publication. He was co-recipient of a Pulitzer Prize for international reporting in 1955 for an interview with Russian Premier Nikita Khrushchev. Obituaries and other sources: *New York Times,* May 27, 1971; *Newsweek,* June 7, 1971; *Time,* June 7, 1971.

* * *

CONROY, Patricia 1941-

PERSONAL: Born May 22, 1941, in Ohio; daughter of Howard Joseph (in sales) and Marion (Kiel) Conroy. *Education:* Rutgers University, B.A., 1963; University of California, Berkeley, M.A., 1968, Ph.D., 1974. *Residence:* Seattle, Wash. *Office:* Scandinavian Department, University of Washington, Seattle, Wash. 98195.

CAREER: University of Washington, Seattle, assistant professor of medieval Scandinavian literature, 1972—. *Member:* Modern Language Association of America, Scandinavian Studies Association, American Folklore Society, Mediaeval Academy of America, Viking Society for Northern Research, Medieval Association of the Pacific.

WRITINGS: Ballads and Ballad Research, University of Washington Press, 1978.

WORK IN PROGRESS: Translating and writing introduction to *H. C. Andersen's Tales and Stories,* with Sven H. Rossel; *A Complete Concordance to Heidreks saga ins visa; A Complete Concordance to Volsunga saga; Faroese Ballad Tradition.*

* * *

CONSIDINE, Bob
See CONSIDINE, Robert (Bernard)

* * *

CONSIDINE, Robert (Bernard) 1906-1975
(Bob Considine)

PERSONAL: Born November 4, 1906, in Washington, D.C.; died of a stroke, September 25, 1975, in New York, N.Y.; son of James William (a tinsmith) and Sophie (Small) Considine; married Mildred Anderson, July 21, 1931; children: Michael Riley, Robert Barry, Dennis Joel, Deborah Joan. *Education:* Attended George Washington University. *Religion:* Roman Catholic. *Home:* 171 West 57th St., New York, N.Y. 10019.

CAREER: Messenger, typist, and clerk for U.S. Government in Census Bureau, Bureau of Public Health, Treasury Department, and Department of State, Washington, D.C., 1923-30; *Washington Post,* Washington, D.C., reporter on sports and drama, writer of Sunday features, 1930-33; *Washington Herald,* Washington, D.C., sports editor, editorial and feature writer, 1933-37; *New York American,* New York City, syndicated sports columnist, trial reporter, feature writer, 1937; *New York Daily Mirror,* New York City, sports columnist, 1937-42; International News Service, sports and news reporter in Washington, D.C., war correspondent in England, China-Burma-India theater, Korea, 1942-50; Hearst newspapers, King Features, and Hearst Headline Service, columnist and news reporter in New York City, war correspondent in Vietnam, 1950-75. Notable assignments include coverage of execution of Julius and Ethel Rosenberg, trial of Jack Ruby, death and funeral of Pope Pius XII, and interview of Nikita Khrushchev. Host of own weekly radio show; script writer, commentator, and interviewer for radio programs; appeared regularly on television news show "America After Dark."

MEMBER: Overseas Press Club (president, 1947), National Press Club, Artists and Writers Club (president), Sigma Alpha Epsilon, Sigma Delta Chi. *Awards, honors:* George R. Holmes Memorial Award, 1947, for stories on the hydrogen bomb test on Bikini Island; Catholic Writers Guild award, 1949; Catholic Institute of the Press award, 1949; Sigma Delta Chi award for distinguished service in journalism, 1949, for series on Frank Costello, and voted one of the ten outstanding living journalists, 1975; Albert and Mary Lasker Foundation award, 1952; Overseas Press Club award, 1957, for exclusive interview with Nikita Khrushchev, and 1959, for best reporting from abroad on the death and funeral of Pope Pius XII; American Jewish Congress award; Christian Athletic Foundation award; Los Angeles City Council award.

WRITINGS—All under name Bob Considine, unless otherwise noted: *MacArthur the Magnificent,* McKay, 1942; *The Babe Ruth Story,* Dutton, 1948; (under name Robert Considine) *Innocents at Home,* Dutton, 1950; (under name Robert Considine) *The Maryknoll Story* (nonfiction), Doubleday, 1950; (under name Robert Considine) *The Panama Canal,* Random House, 1951; (under name Robert Considine) *Man Against Fire: Fire Insurance—Protection From Disaster,* Doubleday, 1955; (with Bill Slocum) *Dempsey: By the Man Himself,* Simon & Schuster, 1960.

(With William Randolph Hearst, Jr. and Frank Conniff) *Ask Me Anything: Our Adventures With Khrushchev,* McGraw, 1960, revised edition published as *Khrushchev and the Russian Challenge,* Avon, 1961; *The Men Who Robbed Brink's: The Inside Story of One of the Most Famous Holdups in the History of Crime,* Random House, 1961; (compiler) *True War Stories: A Crest Anthology,* Fawcett, 1961; (under name Robert Considine) *It's the Irish,* Doubleday, 1961; (under name Robert Considine) *Ripley: The Modern Marco Polo,* Doubleday, 1961; (under name Robert Considine) *The Unreconstructed Amateur: A Pictorial Biography of Amos Alonzo Stagg,* Amos Alonzo Stagg Foundation, 1962; *The Long and Illustrious Career of General Douglas MacArthur,* Fawcett, 1964; *It's All News to Me: A Reporter's Deposition* (autobiography), Meredith, 1967; (with Fred G. Jarvis) *The First Hundred Years: A Portrait of the NYAC,* Macmillan, 1969; *Toots* (biography), Meredith, 1969.

The Remarkable Life of Dr. Armand Hammer, Harper, 1975; *They Rose Above It: True Stories About Men, Women, and Children Who Fought Back in the Face of Pain, Doubt, and Dismay,* Doubleday, 1977. Also author of *Christmas Stocking, Madison Square Garden,* and *They Gave You Wings,* 1971.

Editor—All under name Robert Considine, unless otherwise noted: Ted W. Lawson, *Thirty Seconds Over Tokyo* (Book-of-the-Month Club selection), Random House, 1943; Sammy Schulman, *Where's Sammy?,* Random House, 1943; Jonathan Wainwright, *General Wainwright's Story,* Doubleday, 1946; (under name Bob Considine) Robert E. Stripling, *The Red Plot Against America,* Bell, 1949.

Motion picture screenplays: "Ladies Day," RKO, 1942; "Thirty Seconds Over Tokyo," Metro-Goldwyn-Mayer (MGM), 1944; "The Beginning of the End," MGM, 1947; "The Babe Ruth Story," Allied Artists, 1948; "Hoodlum Empire," Republic, 1952.

Columnist, "On the Line" in *Washington Herald* and in more than one hundred other newspapers, 1933-75. Contributor of fiction and articles to magazines.

SIDELIGHTS: Bob Considine has become a legend in the newspaper business, ranking with the great journalist Da-mon Runyon. Stories of Considine's amazing talent as a writer and his unbelievable speed and accuracy are numerous. He was known to work at two typewriters at once, writing a news story on one and his column or a book on the other. His colleagues at the *Washington Post* timed him once: he wrote a column about the 1942 World Series in exactly nine minutes—in a train, with his typewriter on a baggage wagon, while the conductor shouted "All Aboard." Others recalled Considine's remarkable ability in smoking and pounding away at the typewriter without a pause. Considine would have a cigarette in the right corner of his mouth while typing and when it was half consumed, he would, without looking, exhale from the left side of his mouth and send the ash flying three feet into the air, to land exactly center in a nearby ashtray. Another co-worker at the old International News Service mused: "Bob writes more good words than any newsman I ever knew—and faster. He's a quiet operator and never seems to rush or tear up leads. There's no fussing. The machine always holds the story he wants. All he's got to do is push buttons."

For a man of such brilliant talent, Considine surprisingly entered the field of journalism by accident. While working for the government, Considine was an early tennis enthusiast, and played in many amateur tournaments in his home town, Washington, D.C. The *Washington Post* covered one of these tournaments and spelled Considine's name incorrectly in the article. Considine went to the paper and complained, asserting that he could do a better job himself. The paper decided to give him a chance and hired him to write a weekly sports column. A year later, he was hired as a regular full-time employee.

Considine then moved to the *Washington Herald* where he began writing his famous column "On the Line." Considine wrote the column for over forty years, from 1933 to 1975, and it was printed in over one hundred newspapers. His last column, written in the week he died, stated prophetically: "I'll croak in the newspaper business. Is there any better way to go?"

During his career, Considine covered the great historical events of his time. Working for Hearst publications for almost four decades, Considine reported on World War II, the Korean War, and Vietnam. He accompanied Presidents Eisenhower, Kennedy, Johnson, and Nixon on their world travels, including Nixon's momentous trips to China and the U.S.S.R. Perhaps Considine's most heralded achievement was obtaining an exclusive interview with Nikita Khrushchev in 1957. As a member of the famed "Hearst Task Force," with William Randolph Hearst, Jr. and Frank Conniff, Considine interviewed the Russian leader for four hours. Afterwards, he sat down at his typewriter for thirteen hours without a break and finished with forty pages of copy. Considine also earned much praise in 1952, when he obtained the information that Eisenhower and General MacArthur planned to meet to discuss MacArthur's plan for settling the Korean conflict. Considine had this scoop twelve hours before any other reporter in the world.

Considine wrote that he loved newspaper reporting. In his final column he observed: "In what other trade can a man hope to build a bridge between himself and others every day of every week and every year. On what other field of endeavor is a competitor called upon to come up each day with words and thoughts he did not use the day before. Every time a reporter picks a phone to call in a story, swings aboard a plane on an assignment, or spins a fresh sheet of copy paper into his typewriter, he shoots his roll—like a craps player going for broke."

BIOGRAPHICAL/CRITICAL SOURCES: Saturday Review of Literature, January 21, 1950; *New York Herald Tribune Book Review,* January 22, 1950; *New York Times Book Review,* May 15, 1960; *Saturday Review,* October 28, 1961; *Book Week,* April 30, 1967; *Variety,* October 29, 1969; *Authors in the News,* Volume 2, Gale, 1976.

OBITUARIES: New York Times, September 26, 1975; *Washington Post,* September 26, 1975; *News-American,* September 26, 1975; *Long Island Press,* September 26, 1975; *Time,* October 6, 1975; *Newsweek,* October 6, 1975; *Current Biography,* November, 1975.*

* * *

COOK, F(rederick) P. 1937-

PERSONAL: Born October 20, 1937, in Lakewood, N.J.; son of Fred J. (a writer) and Julia (Simpson) Cook; married Georgianna Carol Wolfe (a medical secretary), August 15, 1965; children: Robert, Colleen. *Education:* Rutgers University, B.A., 1958; Michigan State University, M.A.T., 1964. *Religion:* Methodist. *Home address:* Four Corners Rd., Blairstown, N.J. 07825.

CAREER: West Morris Central High School, Chester, N.J., history teacher, 1969—. *Member:* West Morris Regional Education Association (president), Blairstown Democratic Club (president).

WRITINGS: The American Struggle, Doubleday, 1974.

* * *

COOK, Mary Jane 1929-

PERSONAL: Born March 31, 1929, in Stevens Point, Wis.; daughter of John Morgan (a contractor) and Nita (Smith) Donahue; married Howard C. Belt, July 23, 1949 (divorced November 8, 1971); married Thomas C. Cook, November 12, 1972; children: (first marriage) Joy Dusel, Shari Manney, John Howard, Candi. *Education:* Attended Central State Teachers College, 1946-49. *Politics:* Republican. *Religion:* Dutch Reform. *Home and office:* 5037 North 127th St., Butler, Wis. 53007.

CAREER: Waupaca Police Department, Waupaca, Wis., radio operator and matron, 1961-63; Bob Knerr Pontiac-Olds, Waupaca, Wis., bookkeeper and car salesperson, 1963-67; Automotive Services, Inc., Brookfield, Wis., bookkeeper, 1972—. *Member:* National Speakers Association, Wisconsin Poets, Wisconsin Professional Speakers.

WRITINGS: From My Heart to Yours, T.J.C. Publishing, 1977; *God Loves You and I Do Too* (poems), edited by husband, Thomas C. Cook, Ideals Publishing, 1978; (contributor) Jim Kuse, editor, *Success Secrets,* Royal C.B.S. Publishing, 1978.

WORK IN PROGRESS: Five books of poetry, *Come Share With Me, Thoughts Along Life's Way, To Care Is to Share, I Give You My Heart, By Caring We Learn Love;* short stories.

SIDELIGHTS: Mary Jane Cook told *CA:* "My motivation is life and living, reaching out and touching people through my speeches, poetry, radio, television, and musical poetic tapes. I have no specific book that I refer to other than the book of life and people. That book is all I need for a wealth of material enough to fill a dozen books.

"I traveled very little until I met and married my present husband. Now when my health allows, we travel a great deal.

"My special interest is people. Children and older people are a great source for learning. It's important to me to make people realize, through my speeches and poetry, that life is good and beautiful. Even when there is pain, it is a growing experience. I want to let them know that if they are scarred by life, it is only because they have let themselves be scarred.

"My poetry is simple, everyday poetry. It seems there are a great many unhappy people in this world, searching for answers, looking to find someone who cares, and that is what I try to do through my outreach: to let people know they are not alone, they are not different. I want to make them realize that there is honor in any field of endeavor, if they love and respect themselves, and when they grow, as they will, a new door will open for them."

BIOGRAPHICAL/CRITICAL SOURCES: Success Secrets, Royal C.B.S. Publishing, 1978; Positive Living, September, 1979.

*   *   *

COOK, Michael   1933-

PERSONAL: Born February 14, 1933, in London, England; came to Canada, 1966; naturalized Canadian citizen, 1971; son of George William Cook (a civil servant); married Joyce Horner, 1951 (divorced, 1966); married Janis Jones, 1967 (divorced, 1973); married Madonna Decker (a researcher), December 28, 1973; children: Michael, Diane, Graham, Elaine, Adrian, Etain, Rowena, Christopher, Sarah, Sebastian, Fergus, Perdita. Education: University of Nottingham, T.T.C. (with honors), 1966. Home and office address: Box 327, R.R. 1, Petley, Random Island, Trinity Bay, Newfoundland, Canada AOE IJO. Agent: Guild of Canadian Playwrights, 24 Ryerson Ave., Toronto, Ontario, Canada M5T 2P3.

CAREER: Steelworker and farmer in Nottinghamshire, England, 1961-63; Memorial University, St. John's, Newfoundland, drama adviser, 1967-69, lecturer, 1969-74, assistant professor, 1974-79; writer, 1979—. Host and scriptwriter of "Our Man Friday" (weekly television review), Canadian Broadcasting Corp. (CBC-TV), 1971-72; St. John's Evening Telegram, St. John's, Newfoundland, drama critic and television columnist, 1967-77. Artistic director of St. John's Summer Festival of the Arts, 1968-75; director of Newfoundland Arts and Culture Centre productions, 1971-74; occasional actor. Member of executive board of Canadian Theatre Review; governor of Canadian Conference of the Arts, 1975-79; member of grants and awards committee of Department of Cultural Affairs, 1979—. Military service: British Army, Royal Electrical and Mechanical Engineers and Intelligence Corps, 1949-61; served in Korea, Japan, Malaya, and Europe; became staff sergeant. Member: Guild of Canadian Playwrights (vice-chairman, 1977—), Playwright's Canada, Association of Canadian Radio and Television Artists, Newfoundland Arts Council. Awards, honors: Canada Council senior arts grant, 1973 and 1979, for significant contribution to the arts; Labatt's Award for the best Canadian play, 1974, for "Head, Guts, and Soundbone Dance," 1975, for "Jacob's Wake," 1978, for "On the Rim of the Curve," and 1979, for "The Gayden Chronicles"; Queen's Medal, 1979, for service to the arts.

WRITINGS—Plays: "Colour the Flesh the Colour of Dust" (two-act; first produced in Ottawa, Ontario, at National Arts Centre, 1972; also adapted for radio [see below]), published in A Collection of Canadian Plays, Simon & Pierre, 1972; "Tiln" (one-act; adpated from own radio play of same title [see below]), published in Encounter: Canadian Drama in

Four Media, Methuen, 1973; The Head, Guts, and Soundbone Dance (two-act; first produced in Montreal, Quebec, at Saidye Bronfman Centre, 1974; also adapted for radio [see below]), Breakwater, 1974; Jacob's Wake (three-act; first produced in Lennoxville, Ontario, at Lennoxville Festival Theatre, 1975), Tallonbooks, 1975; Quiller [and] Therese's Creed (both one-act; first produced in Montreal, Quebec, at Centaur Theatre, 1977; "Quiller" also adapted for radio [see below]), Tallonbooks, 1977; "On the Rim of the Curve" (two-act; first produced in Ontario, 1977; also adapted for radio [see below]), published in Three Plays, Breakwater, 1977; "The Gayden Chronicles" (three-act; first produced in Waterford, Conn., at O'Neill Centre, 1978), published in Canadian Theatre Review, January, 1977; Not as a Dream (two-act; first produced in Halifax, Nova Scotia, at Dalhousie University, 1976), Doubleday, 1979; "The Fisherman's Revenge" (one-act; first produced in Newfoundland, 1978), Doubleday, 1979; "The Apocalypse Sonata: Sex and St. John" (two-act; first produced in Regina, Saskatchewan, 1980).

Radio plays; first broadcast on Canadian Broadcasting Corp. (CBC)-Radio, except as noted: "He Should Have Been a Pirate," 1967; "No Man Can Serve Two Masters," 1967; "Or the Wheel Broken," 1968; "A Walk in the Rain," 1968; "The Concubine," 1969; (television) "In Search of Confederation," first broadcast on CBC-TV, 1969; "A Time for Doors," 1970; "The Truck," 1970; "To Inhabit the Earth Is Not Enough," 1971; "Love Is a Walnut," 1971; "A Walk Into the Unknown," 1972; "The Ballad of Patrick Docker," 1972; "Tiln," 1972; "There's a Seal at the Bottom of the Garden," 1973; "Colour the Flesh the Colour of Dust," 1973; "Apostles for the Burning," 1974; "Travels With Aunt Jane," 1974; "Knight of Sorrow, Lady of Darkness," 1975; "The Head, Guts, and Soundbone Dance," 1975; "Ireland's Eye," 1976; "The Producer, the Director," 1976; "On the Rim of the Curve," 1977; "Quiller," 1978.

Radio adaptations; all broadcast by CBC-Radio: Homer, "The Illiad," 1967; Shakespeare, "Midsummer Night's Dream," 1969; Ibsen, "Enemy of the People," 1971.

Other: The Island of Fire (novel), Doubleday, 1980. Also author of an autobiographical novel, The Elusive Conversationalist, held in Canadian Archives at University of Calgary, 1966, and a juvenile, The Fogo Island Caper, 1972, both unpublished.

Work represented in anthologies, including The Blasty Bough, Breakwater, 1967; Tiln and Other Plays, Tallonbooks, 1976; Cues and Entrances, Gage, 1977; Transitions, Short Plays, Comcept, 1978; 31 Newfoundland Poets, Breakwater, 1979; And What Are You Going to Do for Us?, Simon & Pierre, 1980. Contributor of reviews, articles, and short stories to periodicals, including Macleans, Performing Arts in Canada, Canadian Theatre Review, Vie Des Arts, and Canadian Broadcasting Corp. (CBC)-Radio.

WORK IN PROGRESS: "The End of the Road," a two-act play.

SIDELIGHTS: Cook told CA: "If you are committed to the living theatre, why the hell live so far away from anywhere that theatre is happening? I get letters from friends in New York asking 'When are you coming?'—as if it is the only place to be. I know professionally it is a hell of a place to be. But I also know my own nature and given that amount of stimulus, I'd probably blow up or scatter myself in all directions or become a faded story teller in bars.

"Looking back over this hodge podge of literary and dramatic activity, though, I'm astonished to discover that virtually none of it took place before I emigrated to Canada, more specifically, Newfoundland, in 1966. Twelve years in the army, any army I suppose, although providing a not always pleasant treatment book on the magnificent corruption of life, isn't exactly conducive to reflection, prompting instead alternate moods of anger and despair, which bouts of absurdity and alcohol do not always dissipate.

"This is the place I love. It informs my sensibility and I suppose I cling, desperately, to the old belief that if I write anything good enough, it will get done somewhere out there. Certainly Canada has been good to me, and the stuff has been done out there—if not as often as I've liked simply because I am not readily available. It is a conscious choice, and one that I agonize over every year. But I'm still here.

"Perhaps most important to me is the fact that Newfoundland is itself a stage, afloat in the Atlantic, a rocky plug in the fundament of the St. Lawrence River, beautiful and savage at once, whose people, isolated for centuries, kept their own seventeenth- and eighteenth-century idioms of speech and a brand of humor that was, in the face of a merciless environment, exploitive colonialism, black and cruel and ribald. Artaud would have loved it. Although I doubt if he could have lived there.

"Myself, half Irish, half English, the island, itself half and half, acted as a catalyst. It was like coming home, both physically and emotionally, and the people and the environment seemed to open an artistic floodgate. I had always known I was a playwright. And now I was surrounded by the artifacts to make that boast either come to fruition or die.

"Initially, my emotional and theatrical response was to the brutal effects of the inevitable patterns of change that took place when, to quote one of our premiers, 'Newfoundland was dragged kicking and screaming into the twentieth century.' Since then my base has broadened, as it must, but still at some point, no matter what I'm writing, this often bleak and stormbound island, littered with the droppings of millions of sea birds, stirs the true and ancient Celtic responses which at the core of the subconscious inform all of my work. Which is also to say, myself."

Many of Michael Cook's radio plays have been translated for broadcast on Radio Berlin and Radio Switzerland.

BIOGRAPHICAL/CRITICAL SOURCES: Canadian Theatre Review, Issue 16, fall, 1977; *Stage Voices,* Doubleday, 1978.

*   *   *

COOK, Stanley 1922-

PERSONAL: Born April 12, 1922, in Austerfield, England; son of Joseph (an engineer's patternmaker) and Dora (a dressmaker; maiden name, Jacques) Cook; married Kathleen Mary Daly, August 26, 1947; children: Sarah, Paul, Ann. *Education:* Christ Church, Oxford, B.A., 1943, M.A., 1948. *Home:* 600 Barnsley Rd., Sheffield, South Yorkshire S5 6UA, England. *Office:* Department of English Studies, Huddersfield Polytechnic, Huddersfield, West Yorkshire, HD1 3DH, England.

CAREER: Poet and writer. Assistant master at grammar school in Barrow-in-Furness, England, 1944-48; master at grammar school in Bury, England, 1948-55; senior English master at school in Sheffield, England, 1955-68; Huddersfield Polytechnic, Huddersfield, England, senior lecturer, 1969—. *Member:* Sheffield Writers Club (chairman, 1962—). *Awards, honors:* British Broadcasting Corp. (BBC) poetry competition prize from Hull Arts Centre, 1969; Cheltenham festival poetry competition prize, 1972.

WRITINGS—All poetry, except as noted: *Form Photograph,* edited by Harry Chambers, Peterloo Poets, 1971; *Signs of Life,* edited by Chambers, Morten, 1972; *Seeing Your Meaning: Concrete Poetry in Language and Education* (criticism), Huddersfield Polytechnic, 1975, 2nd edition, 1980; *Staff Photograph,* edited by Chambers, Peterloo Poets, 1976; *Alphabet,* edited by Chambers, Peterloo Poets, 1976; *Come Along: Poems for Infants,* privately printed, 1978; *Word Houses: Poems for Juniors,* privately printed, 1979; *Woods Beyond a Cornfield,* Keepsake Press, 1979.

Contributor of poems to British Broadcasting Corp. (BBC) Radio programs "Poetry Corner" and "Stories and Rhymes." Contributor of poems to magazines, including *Listener, New Statesman, Poetry Review, London Times Literary Supplement, English in Education, School Librarian,* and *Use of English.*

WORK IN PROGRESS: Concrete poetry for and by younger children; a long poem written in Spenserian stanzas, completion expected in 1980.

SIDELIGHTS: Cook told *CA* and observed in the introduction to *Form Photograph:* "In a democratic country with universal primary and secondary education, poets should aim at a much wider readership than many of them do. (Whatever its greatness, T. S. Eliot's 'Waste Land' was as remote from the common man as poetry was from the illiterate majority two centuries before.) I hope the steelworker and his wife next door would never need a dictionary to read my poems. I like to feel, too, that I have been as practical and unsentimental with a poem as if I had farmed, smithed, or carpentered it—that the rest of the family would think I had done some 'real work' and had not let them down.

"Arising out of my belief that a poet has an obligation to work to be enjoyed as widely as possible and by the accident of my working for some of my time with teachers and intending teachers at Huddersfield Polytechnic, I write poems for infants (a neglected audience) and juniors. Most of my concrete poetry (though I try to achieve an adult standard) has these children in mind. It is a great pleasure to go into a school and get children of six to eight to do their own concrete poems, some of which are better in some ways than anything that adults can do.

"In our poetry the past is not very far away and while I admire William Carlos Williams I admire at least equally Pope, Dryden, Spenser, Chaucer, and the poet of 'Beowulf'. I especially admire (one reviewer referred to my 'Form Photograph' as 'a South Yorkshire "Spoon River"') their interest in people."

BIOGRAPHICAL/CRITICAL SOURCES: London Times, February 10, 1972, December 14, 1972; *Teacher,* March 3, 1972, October 27, 1972; *Critical Quarterly,* spring, 1972; *London Times Literary Supplement,* August 17, 1973; *Manchester Guardian,* November 23, 1976.

*   *   *

COOMBS, H. Samm 1928-

PERSONAL: Born March 19, 1928, in California; son of Sam W. and Edith V. Coombs; married Peggy Walsh, July 4, 1952 (divorced, June, 1967); married Shirley Martha Muir (an actress), October 7, 1967; children: Maureen, Bridget, Jefferson. *Education:* St. Mary's College, Moraga, Calif., A.A., 1948; University of the Pacific, B.A., 1949. *Politics:* Libertarian. *Religion:* "Mind Science." *Home:* 446 Mesa Rd., Santa Monica, Calif. 90402. *Office:* Samm Coombs' Co., 9024 Olympic Blvd., Beverly Hills, Calif. 90211.

CAREER: Batten, Barton, Durstine & Osborne (advertising firm), San Francisco, Calif., advertising copywriter and copy group head, 1955-60; McCann Erickson (advertising firm), 1960-62, creative supervisor for special projects in San Francisco, Calif., Honolulu, Hawaii, and New York, N.Y.; Kenyon & Eckhardt (advertising firm), San Francisco, Calif., creative director, 1962-65; Wilton, Coombs & Colnett (advertising agency), San Francisco, Calif., president, 1965-70; Advocacy Advertising Associates (public service communications firm), San Francisco, Calif., managing director, 1970-73; C. Brewer & Co., Honolulu, Hawaii, director of sales administration and creative services, 1973-75; Great American Broadcasting, Los Angeles, Calif., vice-president and director of marketing, 1975-76; Samm Coombs' Co. (consultants in creative services), Beverly Hills, Calif., president, 1976—. Lecturer in communication arts. Member of San Francisco Council of Churches. *Military service:* U.S. Navy, 1946-48.

MEMBER: American Motorcycle Association, California Arts Society, San Francisco Press Club, San Francisco Advertising Club, Honolulu Press Club, Involvement Corps, Intersection, Windward Theatre Guild, Montgomery Street Motorcycle Club, Kailua Racquet Club. *Awards, honors:* Advertising awards include "best of the year" award from *Ad Age;* New York Art Directors award; Los Angeles Art Directors award; San Francisco Art Directors award.

WRITINGS: The Last President, Sherbourne, 1969; *The Last Time I Saw Darris,* Discovery Books, 1976; *Teen Age Survival Manual,* Seed Center, 1977.

WORK IN PROGRESS: The Book for People Who Are New at Being Old (tentative title).

SIDELIGHTS: Coombs's advertising clients have included such firms as Lincoln-Mercury, Labatts, U.S. Steel, and Gallo Wines. In 1975 he teamed up with Playboy Enterprises to create Great American Broadcasting, aimed at disseminating "The Sound of Playboy" on affiliated major-market radio stations. Later, Samm Coombs' Co. marketed time-shared vacation rights for Playboy Clubs International.

At the same time he created KiiS Broadcasting Workshop and KiiS Radio Workshop Theatre, lecturing for broadcast training programs, and working in outreach management, curriculum development, and program syndication.

*   *   *

COOMBS, Herbert Cole   1906-

PERSONAL: Born February 24, 1906, in Kalamunda, Australia; son of Francis Robert (a railway officer) and Rebecca (Elliott) Coombs; married Mary Alice Ross (a teacher); children: Janet, John, James, Jerome. *Education:* University of Western Australia, B.A. (with honors), 1930, M.A., 1931; London School of Economics and Political Science, London, Ph.D., 1933. *Home:* 119 Milson Rd., Cremorne, New South Wales 2090, Australia. *Office:* Australian National University, Canberra, Australian Capital Territory 2600, Australia.

CAREER: Commonwealth Bank of Australia, Sydney, assistant economist, 1935-39; Commonwealth Treasury, Canberra, Australia, economist, 1939-41; Commonwealth Government, director of rationing in Melbourne, Australia, 1941-43, director-general of PWR in Canberra, Australia, 1943-48; Commonwealth Bank of Australia, governor, 1949-60; Reserve Bank of Australia, Sydney, chairperson, 1968-76; Australian National University, Canberra, visiting fellow, 1977—. Chairperson of Australian Council for Aboriginal

Affairs and Sydney's Council for the Arts, 1968-76. *Member:* Australian Academy of Science (fellow), Academy of Social Sciences in Australia (fellow). *Awards, honors:* Fellow of Australian Academy of the Humanities and London School of Economics and Political Science, London; LL.D. from University of Western Australia, University of Sydney, and Australian National University.

WRITINGS: The Fragile Pattern, Australian Broadcasting Commission, 1970; *Other People's Money,* Australian National University Press, 1971; *Kulinma: Listening to Aboriginal Australians,* Australian National University Press, 1978.

WORK IN PROGRESS: With Nine Prime Ministers; a review of episodes and issues from 1939 to 1979.

*   *   *

COOPER, Jeremy (Francis Peter)   1946-

PERSONAL: Born July 25, 1946, in Christchurch, Hampshire, England; son of Basil (a schoolmaster) and Doreen (a nurse; maiden name, Thompson) Cooper; married Helen Koch (an actress). *Education:* Cambridge University, M.A. 1969. *Home:* 48 Portland Rd., London W.11, England. *Agent:* Curtis Brown Ltd., 1 Craven Hill, London W.2, England. *Office:* Jeremy Cooper Ltd., 9 Galen Place, Bury Place, London WC1A 2JR, England.

CAREER: Sotheby & Co., London, England, art expert and auctioneer, 1969-1977, head of department of furniture and works of art at Belgravia office, 1971-75, established office in Tehran and head of its Middle East business department, 1975, assistant director and personal assistant to company's chairman, 1976-77; Jeremy Cooper Ltd., London, England, managing director and art dealer, 1978—. Managing director of Overseas Art Consultants Trust. Lecturer in the United States and England, including Inchbald School of Design and National Association of Decorative and Fine Art Societies; guest on British radio and television programs.

WRITINGS: (Contributor) *Antiques: A Popular Guide to Antiques for Everyone,* David & Charles, 1973; *The Complete Guide to London's Antique Street Markets,* Thames & Hudson, 1974; *Nineteenth-Century Romantic Bronzes,* David & Charles, 1975; *Under the Hammer: The Auctions and Auctioneers of London,* Constable, 1978. Contributor to magazines, including *Connoisseur, Apollo,* and *Collector's Guide.*

WORK IN PROGRESS: Guide to the Auctioneers of Great Britain, completion expected in 1980; *Artistic Life in London, 1965-75,* completion expected in 1982.

SIDELIGHTS: Cooper told *CA:* "Jeremy Cooper Ltd. is the only gallery specializing in all aspects of the decorative arts of the period 1830 to 1930. It offers museum quality works of art in under-appreciated fields. I am also interested in television and radio, with two series currently running. My publishing and lecturing interests are now confined to the nineteenth-century decorative arts, the contemporary international auction and antiques markets, and the feasibility of investment in the art market."

*   *   *

COOPER, Wayne   1938-

PERSONAL: Born November 22, 1938, in Elba, Ala.; son of Oscar E. (a carpenter) and Mary (Foley) Cooper; married Eleanor Williams, January 21, 1961 (separated, 1972). *Education:* Tulane University, B.A., 1961, M.A., 1965; Rutgers University, Ph.D., 1980. *Politics:* "The politics of democratic justice." *Religion:* Baptist. *Home:* 370 Chestnut Hill

Ave., Brookline, Mass. 02146. *Agent:* Carl Cowl, 91 Remsen St., Brooklyn, N.Y. 11201.

CAREER: Writer. Worked in New York City, 1964-68; Fairleigh Dickinson University, Rutherford, N.J., adjunct instructor of world history, 1968-70; Georgian Court College, Lakewood, N.J., adjunct instructor of Afro-American history, 1977. *Member:* American Historical Association.

WRITINGS: (Contributor) C.W.E. Bigsby, editor, *The Black American Writer,* Penguin, 1969; (contributor) Seth Scheiner and Tilden Edelstein, editors, *The Black Americans: Interpretive Readings,* Holt, 1971; (author of introduction) *Dialect Poetry of Claude McKay,* Books for Libraries, 1972; (editor) *The Passion of Claude McKay: Selected Poetry and Prose, 1912-1948,* Schocken, 1973. Contributor to *Encyclopaedia Britannica.* Contributor to *Race* and *New Beacon Review.*

WORK IN PROGRESS: A biography of Claude McKay, publication by University of Illinois Press expected in 1981; *Class Consciousness and Racial Conflict: Mobile, Alabama, 1941-1945; A Social History of Jamaica, 1865-1938.*

SIDELIGHTS: Cooper told *CA:* "I am interested in narrative history as an art form and as a major method of ordering and interpreting our knowledge of the growth of human societies and individuals over time.

"Having grown up in the South, I developed an early interest in the history of race relations. In my research on Claude McKay and other black writers, I have attempted to demonstrate how black creative writers can illuminate for the general reader the realities of black existence as it is reflected in their works and careers—in Africa, Latin America, the Caribbean, and the United States. To me, literature and art provide ways of penetrating the shrouds of color and other prejudices which ordinarily separate various human groups."

* * *

CORDINGLY, David 1938-

PERSONAL: Born December 5, 1938, in London, England; son of Eric W. B. (a bishop) and Mary (Mathews) Cordingly; married wife, Shirley Robin; children: Matthew, Rebecca. *Education:* Studied at Christ's Hospital, Horsham, 1948-57; Oriel College, Oxford, M.A., 1960; graduate work at Sussex University. *Home:* 1 Lovers Walk, Brighton, England. *Agent:* A. D. Peters, 10 Buckingham St., London W.C.2, England. *Office:* Museum of London, London Wall, London, England.

CAREER: David Ogle Associates, Letchworth, England, graphic designer, 1960-63; Peter Hatch Partnership, Picadilly, London, England, graphic designer, 1963-65; Paul Hamlyn Publishers, Covent Gardens, London, book designer, 1965-67; British Museum, London, exhibition designer, 1967-71; Royal Pavilion Art Gallery and Museum, Brighton, England, keeper, 1971-78; Museum of London, London, England, assistant director, 1978—. *Member:* Royal Society of Arts (fellow), Society of Industrial Artists and Designers. *Awards, honors:* Leverhulme Trust Fund award, 1974.

WRITINGS: Marine Painting in England, 1700-1900, C. N. Potter, 1974; *Painters of the Sea,* Lund, Humphries, 1979. Contributor to magazines, including *Apollo, Connoisseur,* and *Art and Antiques Weekly.*

WORK IN PROGRESS: English Marine Watercolours, publication by Batsford expected in 1981; research on the life and work of John Brett.

CORNEHLS, James V(ernon) 1936-

PERSONAL: Born November 16, 1936, in Dallas, Tex.; son of Charles (an electrician) and Nola (Roper) Cornehls; married Paloma Gaos (a teacher), September 26, 1959; children: Paula, Lee, Diego. *Education:* University of the Americas, B.A. (summa cum laude), 1961; University of Texas, Ph.D., 1965; postdoctoral study at American University, 1979—. *Home:* 4209 Sparkford Court, Arlington, Tex. 76013. *Office:* Institute of Urban Studies, University of Texas, Arlington, Tex. 76019.

CAREER: Columbia University, Teachers College, New York, N.Y., assistant professor of economics and consultant to Peruvian National Planning Institute mission to Lima, 1964-66; State University of New York at Stony Brook, assistant professor of economics, 1966-70, faculty director of Theodore Dreiser College, 1968-70; University of Texas, Arlington, associate professor, 1970-74, professor of urban affairs and economics, 1974—, counselor at Institute of Urban Studies, 1974-76, director of urban and regional affairs program, 1975-77, director of Center for Comparative Urban Research, 1978—. Visiting adjunct professor at Columbia University, 1967-68. Congressional fellow, U.S. Office of Technology Assessment, 1979. Consultant to local governments and law firms. *Military service:* U.S. Army, 1955-58. *Member:* American Economic Association, Association for Evolutionary Economics, Social Science Society, Delta Sigma Pi, Omicron Delta Epsilon.

WRITINGS: (With Carlos Malpica and Fred Scholten) *Recursos humanos, educacion y desarrollo economico en el Peru* (title means "Human Resources, Education and Economic Development in Peru"), Peruvian National Planning Institute, 1966; (contributor) Thomas J. Labelle, editor, *Education and Development: Latin America and the Caribbean,* Latin American Center, University of California, Los Angeles, 1971; (editor) *Economic Development and Economic Growth,* Quadrangle, 1972; *Report on the Taxation of Intangible Personal Property,* Institute of Urban Studies, University of Texas, Arlington, 1973; (editor and contributor) *Mexico City: Essays in Comparative Urbanization,* Institute of Urban Studies, University of Texas, Arlington, 1974; (with Del Taebel) *The Political Economy of Urban Transportation,* Kennikat, 1977; (contributor) Mark Rosentraub, editor, *Financing Local Government: New Approaches to Old Problems,* Western Social Science Association, 1977. Contributor to scholarly journals.

WORK IN PROGRESS: Research on land use planning based on environmental criteria, global food futures, and low-income housing in urban Mexico.

SIDELIGHTS: Cornehls comments: "I have been motivated by the absurd contradictions in society: between extremes of wealth and poverty, between private wealth and public squalor, and the irrational waste of the natural environment. My writing, research, and teaching have all reflected this concern and an interest in promoting rational humane change."

* * *

CORWEN, Leonard 1921-

PERSONAL: Born October 17, 1921, in Philadelphia, Pa.; son of Herman and Ann (Richstone) Corwen; married Bernice Roth, September 3, 1958; children: Carol. *Education:* Temple University, degree, 1949; New York University, degree, 1952. *Home:* 2632 West Second St., Brooklyn, N.Y. 11223. *Office:* Corwen/Marchant Associates, Inc., 527 Madison Ave., New York, N.Y. 10022.

CAREER: American Traveler, New York City, editor, 1950-55; Griffith Personnel Agency, New York City, owner, 1955-66; Corwen/Marchant Associates, Inc. (personnel career consultants and executive recruiters), New York City, president, 1959—. *Military service:* U.S. Army Air Forces, 1942-46, 1948; became captain. *Member:* National Association of Corporate and Professional Recruiters, National Association of Personnel Consultants, Association of Business Press Editors, Sales Executive Club, Advertising Club of New York.

WRITINGS: Find Your Job and Land It, Arco, 1964; *The Job Hunters' Handbook,* Arco, 1975; *Your Future in Publishing,* Richards Rosen, 1976; *Your Resume: Key to a Better Job,* Arco, 1978; *The Job You Want—How to Find It—How to Get It,* Gnome Press, 1980. Editor of *Travel Agent.*

SIDELIGHTS: Corwen told *CA:* "I write books on the subject of jobs and careers because I believe there is an urgent need for this kind of information. Almost everyone has been in the position, at some time or another, of having to change jobs or careers. Since success in this endeavor depends upon avoiding the pitfalls in the path of the hit-or-miss job seeker, I try in my writings to offer sound advice based upon long experience in guiding people toward more productive activities in their search for better jobs and more rewarding careers."

*   *   *

COSTELLO, Peter 1946-

PERSONAL: Born April 3, 1946, in Dublin, Ireland; son of James (a professor) and Margaret (Walsh) Costello; married Mary Litton, December 28, 1974; children: Timothy James Peter. *Education:* University of Michigan, B.A., 1969. *Home:* 15 Wellington Place, Dublin, Ireland. *Agent:* Murray Pollinger, 4 Garrick St., London, England.

CAREER: Writer, 1970—. Consultant for television series, "Arthur C. Clark's Mysterious World," 1979.

WRITINGS—Nonfiction: In Search of Lake Monsters, Coward, 1974; *The Heart Grown Brutal,* Gill & Macmillan, 1977; *Jules Verne,* Scribner, 1978; *The Magic Zoo,* St. Martin's, 1979; *James Joyce: A Brief Life,* Gill & Macmillan, 1980; *Under Ben Bulben,* Gill & Macmillan, 1981.

WORK IN PROGRESS: Research into unknown animals; a book on sea serpents; research into the film and culture of Ireland.

SIDELIGHTS: Costello told *CA:* "My prime motivation in writing is a desire to discover the truth behind legend and myth, both scientific and cultural.

"In *The Heart Grown Brutal* I have tried to present the reality behind the myths and legends surrounding the Irish revolution by showing how the events of the period 1891-1939 are dealt with in Irish writing of that time. Thus, new and surprising aspects of a well-known story are revealed, some for the first time. Benedict Kiely remarked in the *Dublin Sunday Press,* that *The Heart Grown Brutal* "is an important, thought-provoking and complicated book."

"In writing *In Search of Lake Monsters,* a very different book, which was the product of over a decade of research in Europe and America, I tried to show what sort of real animals existed in Loch Ness and elsewhere around the world. *The Magic Zoo* deals with the natural history of many 'imaginary animals' such as the dragon and the unicorn, tracing them back to real animals or real biological facts.

"Future work will continue the exploration of these fields, dealing with the interface between imagination and reality, myth and sober fact.

"From my late father I have inherited a rational approach to life, but this has been tempered with an imaginative outlook which comes from my mother. By straddling two cultures in this way, it is often difficult to persuade people of the seriousness of some of my interests, but in the end I hope to broaden other people's minds rather than narrow down my own views."

BIOGRAPHICAL/CRITICAL SOURCES: Dublin Sunday Press, January 8, 1978.

*   *   *

COTHRAN, Jean 1910-

PERSONAL: Born in 1910 in Los Angeles, Calif.; daughter of Gilbert John (a rancher) and Inez (Hollett) Syminton; married Francis Eugene Cothran, 1934; children: William S. *Education:* Scripps College, B.A., 1931; University of California, Berkeley, M.A., 1933; University of Southern California, B.L.S., 1944. *Religion:* Episcopal. *Home:* 604 Brook Lane, Greenwood, S.C. 29646.

CAREER: Los Angeles Public Library, Los Angeles, Calif., children's librarian, 1945-50; writer, 1950—. *Member:* Authors League of America, Phi Kappa Phi.

WRITINGS—For children: (Editor) *Magic Bells,* Aladdin, 1949; *With a Wig, With a Wag,* McKay, 1954; *The Magic Calabash,* McKay, 1956; *The Whang Doodle and Other Stories,* Sandlapper Store, 1972.

SIDELIGHTS: Cothran told *CA:* "I worked in the Los Angeles Central Children's Library Room for five years. Youngsters of many backgrounds, including Asian, Hispanic, and Black American, came to our story hours. The Library contained a marvelous collection of juvenile folk and fairy tales. My first book grew from a desire to present a common motif, that of bells, in tales from around the world.

"In the 1940's, there were few juvenile American folk tale collections. It was, then, an innovation when we decided to feature American tales, songs, and dances in our summer programs. Searching for tales led me to adult reference sources for material which, while respecting the integrity of its sources, could be edited and rewritten for children.

"The next two books grew from the experiences of these story hours. In 1950 my husband and I returned to South Carolina and spent our summers in the Blue Ridge Mountains. There existed no children's collection of Carolina tales which included the region's diverse strands: Indian, British, and Black; as such, my most recent book, *The Whang Doodle* attempted to provide such a collection."

*   *   *

COVENTRY, John 1915-

PERSONAL: Born January 21, 1915, in Deal, England; son of Bernard Seton (a surveyor) and Annie (Cunningham) Coventry. *Education:* Heythrop College, L.Phil., 1938, L.Th., 1949; Oxford University, M.A., 1945. *Home:* St. Edmund's House, Cambridge University, Cambridge CB3 0BN, England.

CAREER: Entered Society of Jesus (Jesuits), 1932, ordained Roman Catholic priest, 1947; prefect of studies at secondary school in Old Windsor, England, 1950-56, headmaster, 1956-58; Jesuit provincial in England, 1958-64; Heythrop College, Oxfordshire, England, lecturer in Christian doctrine, 1965-70; University of London, London, England, lecturer in

Christian doctrine, 1970-76; Cambridge University, Cambridge, England, master of St. Edmund's House, 1976—.

WRITINGS: Morals and Independence, Burns & Oates, 1949; *The Breaking of Bread,* Sheed, 1950; *Faith Seeks Understanding,* Sheed, 1951; *The Life Story of the Mass,* Harvill, 1960; *The Theology of Faith,* Mercier Press, 1968; *Christian Truth,* Darton, Longman & Todd, 1975.

WORK IN PROGRESS: Faith in Jesus Christ, a booklet; a course of lectures.

SIDELIGHTS: Coventry writes: "I am now a college administrator, but still spend much time on ecumenical matters, with a special interest and involvement in the problems and opportunities of the two-church marriage."

* * *

COWLE, Jerome Milton 1917-
(Jerry Cowle)

PERSONAL: Born October 26, 1917, in Utica, N.Y.; son of Lewis (a merchant) and Minerva (a merchant; maiden name, Michaels) Cowle; married Betty Bell Seeman, November 8, 1958 (died September 10, 1979); children: Edward Arthur, Jay, Sally Ann. *Education:* Syracuse University, B.S., 1939; also attended U.S. Coast Guard Academy, 1942-43, Columbia University, 1946-47, and University of Chicago, 1956-57. *Home:* 1000 Glenhaven Dr., Pacific Palisades, Calif. 90272. *Agent:* Sanford J. Greenburger & Associates, Inc., 825 Third Ave., New York, N.Y. 10022. *Office:* Foote, Cone & Belding, K-727 West Sixth St., Los Angeles, Calif. 90057.

CAREER: Erwin Wasey & Co., New York City, copywriter, 1946-50; Platt-Forbes, New York City, copywriter, 1950-52; Anderson & Cairns, New York City, senior copywriter, 1952-54; Campbell-Ewald, Detroit, Mich., senior copywriter, 1954-55, copy supervisor, 1955; Grant Advertising, Detroit, copy chief, 1955-56; Leo Burnett Co., Chicago, Ill., copy supervisor, 1956-60; Kenyon & Eckhardt, Chicago, vice-president and creative director, 1960-62; Compton Advertising, Los Angeles, Calif., vice-president and creative director, 1962-63; creative consultant, 1963-68; Needham, Harper & Steers, Inc., Los Angeles, creative supervisor, 1968-72; Parker Advertising, Palos Verdes, Calif., creative supervisor, 1972-77; Foote, Cone & Belding, Los Angeles, senior copywriter, 1977—. Member of board of directors of Pacific Palisades Civic League. *Military service:* U.S. Coast Guard Reserve, active duty, 1942-46; served in Europe; became lieutenant senior grade. *Member:* Mensa. *Awards, honors:* Golden Thirty Award from Chicago Copywriters Club, 1958, for Pillsbury and Bissell print campaigns; first prize from *Advertising Age,* 1966, for contest presentation.

WRITINGS—Under name Jerry Cowle: *How to Make Big Money as an Advertising Copywriter,* Parker & Son, 1966; *Discover the Trees* (children's nonfiction), Sterling, 1977; *How to Survive Getting Fired,* Follett, 1979. Author of "A View From the Palisades," a column in *Media/Agencies/Clients,* 1966-68. Contributor to popular magazines, including *Sports Illustrated, Reader's Digest, Sports Afield, Ford Times, Glamour,* and *Doc Savage,* and newspapers.

SIDELIGHTS: Cowle told *CA:* "After many years of fruitless fiction writing, it became apparent to me, with my wife's encouragement, that nonfiction was my forte. From that moment on, I started selling a good percentage of my writing. I would advise any young writer to be realistic and to learn what it is that he or she does best, then concentrate on it, and never give up." *Avocational interests:* Swimming, hiking, forestry, travel.

COWLE, Jerry
See COWLE, Jerome Milton

* * *

COX, Allan 1937-

PERSONAL: Born June 13, 1937, in Berwyn, Ill.; son of Brack C. and Ruby (Cline) Cox; married Jeanne Brazier, June 10, 1961 (divorced, 1966); married Bonnie Welden, May 13, 1966; children: (first marriage) Heather; (second marriage) Laura. *Education:* Attended Wheaton College, Wheaton, Ill., 1956-57; Northern Illinois University, received B.A., M.A., 1961. *Home:* 1515 Astor, Chicago, Ill. 60610. *Agent:* Dominick Abel Literary Agency, 498 West End Ave., Apt. 12-C, New York, N.Y. 10024. *Office:* Allan Cox & Associates, 410 North Michigan Ave., Chicago, Ill. 60611.

CAREER: Wheaton College, Wheaton, Ill., instructor in sociology, 1963-65; Case & Co., Inc., Chicago, Ill., associate, 1965-66; Spencer Stuart & Associates, Chicago, Ill., associate, 1966-68; Westcott Associates, Chicago, Ill., vice-president, 1968-69; Allan Cox & Associates, Chicago, Ill., president, 1969—. Member of Chicago Crime Commission and Chicago Committee on Foreign Affairs; member of board of directors of Illinois Council on Family Relations, 1964-66, and Chicago Center for Urban Projects, 1966-68. *Member:* International Wine and Food Society, North American Society of Adlerian Psychology, American Sociological Association, Association for Humanistic Psychology, Chicago Club, Tavern Club, University Club (New York City), Alpha Kappa Delta.

WRITINGS: Confessions of a Corporate Headhunter, Trident, 1973; *Work, Love, and Friendship,* Simon & Schuster, 1974. Contributor of more than one hundred articles to professional and popular magazines and newspapers, including *Family Weekly, California, Commerce,* and *Advertising Age.*

WORK IN PROGRESS: The Cox Report on American Corporations.

SIDELIGHTS: Cox's firm, which he views as a practice rather than a business, specializes in executive development and search, recruiting senior executives for some of America's leading corporations, and presenting workshops "to help executives learn how to make their strengths more productive," explained Cox to *CA.*

"My beliefs about managing are good-humored Machiavellian. I think I proved that in my book, *Confessions of a Corporate Headhunter.* In human development, they take the form that man is a little good and a little evil.

"By my definition, human development is radically different from management development. I have elected to do something about what I consider an oversight in fostering human development among executives in today's corporation. What is needed is a new approach. Not one that manipulates, but accepts man as he is and aids him in human growth. The Action Perspectives Workshop is committed to the ultimate dignity of the individual and to the belief that if one is not effective in all areas of his life when it comes to problem-solving, neither will he be effective in problem-solving in his work."

BIOGRAPHICAL/CRITICAL SOURCES: Chicago Tribune, July 21, 1974; *Crain's Chicago Business,* July 17, 1978; *Industry Week,* December 11, 1978.

COX, Hugh Brandon
See BRANDON-COX, Hugh

*   *   *

COYNE, John
CAREER: Writer.

WRITINGS: (With Tom Hebert) *This Way Out: A Guide to Alternative College Education in the United States, Europe, and the Third World,* Dutton, 1972; (editor) *Better Golf,* Follett, 1972; (editor) *The New Golf for Women,* Doubleday, 1973; (with Hebert) *By Hand: A Guide to Schools and Careers in Crafts,* Dutton, 1974; (editor) *The Penland School of Crafts Book of Jewelry Making,* Bobbs-Merrill, 1975; (editor) *The Penland School of Crafts Book of Pottery,* Bobbs-Merrill, 1975; (with Hebert) *Getting Skilled: A Guide to Private Trade and Technical Schools,* Dutton, 1976; (with Jerry Miller) *How to Make Upside-Down Dolls,* Bobbs-Merrill, 1977; *The Piercing* (a novel), Putnam, 1979; *The Legacy* (novel), Berkley, 1979.

SIDELIGHTS: Coyne's two *Penland School of Crafts* books contain conversations with craftsmen from the famous Penland school in North Carolina, as well as instructions in each craft. Penland faculty members are among the best craftsmen in the country and have earned Penland School a fine reputation in its field. The *New York Times Book Review* declared that "if you have some experience in one of these crafts, and if the work and the talk in these handsome books fails to move you, feel your pulse to see if you're alive."

The Piercing, Coyne's first novel, is the story of a stigmatic girl. At the age of twelve, Betty Sue Wadkins is molested in the Appalachian woods by the devil, who is disguised as a hillbilly. From that time on the girl begins bleeding from wounds in her hands and feet each week. Five years later this fact becomes public, and, as the *Critic* described, "Betty Sue is turned into a full-flowing stigmatic who does her thing on National TV."

Although *Critic* called *The Piercing* a "putrid puddle of gagging, sensational, tasteless, ultimately pointless fiction," Michele Slung contended that Coyne "has concocted a swift-moving plot, one that's intelligently done, if not terribly subtle," and asserted that the book provides readers with "an interlude of ghastly pleasure."

Coyne's most recent novel, *The Legacy,* is a suspenseful story of witchcraft and the supernatural set in England. A film version was released by Universal in 1979.

BIOGRAPHICAL/CRITICAL SOURCES: Saturday Review World, February 9, 1974; *Smithsonian,* November, 1975; *New York Times Book Review,* December 7, 1975; *Critic,* February 1, 1979; *Washington Post Book World,* March 25, 1979.*

*   *   *

CRAIG, Eleanor   1929-
PERSONAL: Born October 17, 1929, in Boston, Mass.; daughter of John Michael (a lawyer) and Marie Louise (a teacher; maiden name, O'Brien) Russell; married William Craig (a writer), 1951 (divorced, 1978); married Paul Richard Green (a publisher), August 30, 1978; children: (first marriage) Anne Marie, Richard Russell, William Michael, Ellen Louise; (stepchildren from second marriage) Andrew, Alex, Kathy, Douglas, Peter. *Education:* Framingham Teachers College, B.S.Ed., 1951; University of Bridgeport, M.Ed., 1968. *Religion:* Roman Catholic. *Residence:* Westport, Conn. *Agent:* Don Congdon, Harold Matson Co., Inc., 22

East 40th St., New York, N.Y. 10016. *Office:* Mid Fairfield Child Guidance Center, 74 Newtown Ave., Norwalk, Conn.

CAREER: Elementary school teacher in Massachusetts, Ohio, and Connecticut; special education teacher in Connecticut, 1961-65; Mid Fairfield Child Guidance Center, Norwalk, Conn., therapist, 1968—, director of day treatment program. *Member:* Authors Guild, National Organization for Women, Connecticut Association for Children With Learning Disabilities.

WRITINGS: One Two Three: The Story of Matt, a Feral Child, McGraw, 1968; *P.S. Your Not Listening,* Dutton, 1973.

WORK IN PROGRESS: Therapy with troubled families.

SIDELIGHTS: Eleanor Craig reflected to *CA:* "I grew up in a Boston Irish Catholic family. The men were lawyers, the women teachers.

"After teaching a pilot program for emotionally disturbed children, I felt committed to share the experience and began my first book. I have lived in Germany and Italy and visited children's facilities in Egypt, Japan, and Korea."

*   *   *

CREIGHTON, Donald Grant   1902-1979
OBITUARY NOTICE: Born July 15, 1902, in Toronto, Ontario, Canada; died December 19, 1979, near Toronto. Educator, historian, and author. Creighton taught history at the University of Toronto from 1927 to 1971. He earned several awards for his books on the history of Canada, such as the Tyrrel Medal for History from the Royal Society of Canada in 1951. His most important book is *The Commercial Empire of the St. Lawrence: 1760-1850,* which studies the impact of the St. Lawrence River trading system on Canada's political and economic development. Other notable works are *Dominion of the North: A History of Canada, John A. Macdonald: The Young Politician,* and *Harold Adams Innis: Portrait of a Scholar.* Obituaries and other sources: *The Oxford Companion to Canadian History and Literature,* Oxford University Press, 1967; *The Author's and Writer's Who's Who,* 6th edition, Burke's Peerage, 1971; *Who's Who in Canada,* International Press, 1973; *Directory of American Scholars,* Volume I: *History,* 7th edition, Bowker, 1978; *Who's Who,* 131st edition, St. Martin's, 1979; *AB Bookman's Weekly,* February 11, 1980.

*   *   *

CRISP, Norman James   1923-
PERSONAL: Born in 1923 in Southampton, England; son of James Henry (a taxicab owner) and Edith Mary (Sims) Crisp; married Marguerite Lowe; children: Brian, Robert, Simon, Annette. *Education:* Attended grammar school in Southampton, England. *Home:* 4 Abbotts Way, Southampton, England. *Agent:* Murray Pollinger, 4 Garrick St., London W.C.2, England. *Office:* 1 St. Peters Villas, London W6 9BQ, England.

CAREER: In administration and sales, 1947-59; writer, 1959—. *Military service:* Royal Air Force, pilot, 1943-47. *Member:* Writers Guild of Great Britain (chairman, 1968-70). *Awards, honors:* Best series award from Writers Guild of Great Britain, 1967, for "Dixon of Dock Green" and "The Revenue Men," 1973, for "Colditz," "Spy Trap," and others, and best children's series award, 1972, for "The Long Chase."

*WRITINGS—*Novels: *The Gotland Deal,* Viking, 1976; *The*

London Deal, St. Martin's, 1979; *The Odd Job Man,* St. Martin's, 1979; *A Family Affair,* Macdonald & Jane's, 1979.

Plays: "Jet Set" (two-act), first produced in Windsor, England, at Theatre Royal, October 9, 1979.

Writer for television series, including "Dixon of Dock Green," "The Revenue Man," "Dr. Finlay's Casebook," "The Expert," "Colditz," "The Brothers," and "A Family Affair." Contributor of nearly a hundred stories to popular magazines, including *Today, Saturday Evening Post, Mc-Call's,* and *John Bull.*

WORK IN PROGRESS: A novel about a festival theatre, entitled *Festival!.*

SIDELIGHTS: Crisp told *CA:* "I write fiction, and I dislike the present day urge to imply that there is always some real life event or experience behind a story. Whatever happened to the art of imaginative writing, of invention, of fictional truth?"

*   *   *

CRISPIN, Ruth Helen Katz 1940-

PERSONAL: Born December 30, 1940, in Brooklyn, N.Y.; daughter of Joseph (a manufacturer; in sales) and Esther (Malkoff) Katz; married John Crispin (a professor), June 9, 1966; children: Melissa Leah. *Education:* Brandeis University, B.A., 1962; University of Wisconsin, Madison, M.A., 1965; George Peabody College for Teachers, M.L.S., 1975; attended Estudio Internacional Sampere, summer, 1978. *Politics:* Democrat. *Religion:* Jewish. *Home:* 3305 Orleans Dr., Nashville, Tenn. 37212. *Office:* Department of Language, Literature, and Communicative Arts, Belmont College, Belmont Blvd., Nashville, Tenn. 37203.

CAREER: Boston Public Library, Jamaica Plain, Mass., children's librarian, 1962; junior high school teacher of Spanish and French in Levittown, N.Y., 1962-63; St. Olaf College, Northfield, Minn., instructor in Spanish, 1965-66; Fisk University, Nashville, Tenn., instructor in Spanish, 1966-68; free-lance writer, reviewer, and translator, 1968-71; University of Tennessee, Nashville, instructor in Spanish, 1971-73; Belmont College, Nashville, assistant professor of Spanish, 1976—. Adult education teacher of English as a second language, 1976—. *Member:* American Association of Teachers of Spanish and Portuguese, National Association for Public Continuing Adult Education, American Civil Liberties Union, Tennessee Association for Public Continuing Adult Education, Beta Phi Mu.

WRITINGS: (With husband, John Crispin) *Progress in Spanish: Grammar and Composition,* Scott, Foresman, 1972, 2nd edition published as *Progress in Spanish: Grammar and Practice,* with workbook, 1978; (translator of poems) Crispin, *Pedro Salinas,* Twayne, 1974. Contributor to *Kentucky Language Quarterly.*

WORK IN PROGRESS: An intermediate cultural reader; a college-level Spanish textbook; translations, including children's books from Spanish.

*   *   *

CROCKER, Mary Wallace 1941-

PERSONAL: Born January 15, 1941, in Clarksdale, Miss.; daughter of Wallace Glen (a cotton farmer) and Emma (a nurse; maiden name, Willis) Bailey; married William Jack Crocker (an editor), September 2, 1961. *Education:* Delta State University, B.S.E., 1961; University of Mississippi, M.A., 1963; Florida State University, Ph.D., 1968; studied

at Winterthur Museum, 1976. *Home:* 1483 Goodbar, Memphis, Tenn. 38104. *Office:* Memphis State University, Memphis, Tenn. 38152.

CAREER: Florida Extension Service, home economist, 1963-64; Mississippi University for Women, Columbus, instructor, 1965-67, assistant professor, 1969-70, associate professor of home economics, 1970-74; Memphis State University, Memphis, Tenn., associate professor of housing and home furnishings, 1974-75; Texas Tech University, Lubbock, associate professor of housing and home furnishings, 1975-77; Memphis State University, professor of housing and home furnishings, 1977—. Visiting professor at University of Mississippi, summers, 1969-71. Photographs have been exhibited throughout the United States; guest on television programs; public speaker.

MEMBER: American Home Economic Association, American Association of Housing Educators (head of research committee, 1975; co-chairperson, 1978), National Trust for Historic Preservation, Society of Architectural Historians, Victorian Society of America, West Tennessee Historic Society. *Awards, honors:* Grants from Mississippi Department of Education, 1971, and American Philosophical Society, 1977; award of merit from American Association for State and Local History for *Historic Architecture in Mississippi.*

WRITINGS: Historic Architecture in Mississippi (with own photographs), University Press of Mississippi, 1974. Also author of *Memphis Architecture* (with own photographs). Contributor of photographs to Calder Lath, *The Only Proper Style* and William Pierson, *American Architects and Their Buildings.* Contributor of articles and photographs to home economic, architecture, education, and regional journals. Guest editor of *Housing and Society,* March, 1979; contributing editor of *New South,* 1971-72, and *Mississippi Architect,* 1972-73; member of advisory board of *Tips and Topics,* 1976-77.

WORK IN PROGRESS: Research on architects and decorative arts craftsmen in antebellum Memphis, Tennessee.

SIDELIGHTS: Mary Crocker writes: "When I began the task of researching the history of selected buildings in Mississippi and photographing their outstanding features, I was interested in the social and economic aspects of the buildings as well as the design."

*   *   *

CROSBY, Alexander L. 1906-1980

OBITUARY NOTICE—See index for *CA* sketch: Born June 10, 1906, in Catonsville, Md.; died January 31, 1980, in Quakertown, Pa. Journalist, editor, and writer. Crosby was an editorial writer for the *Staten Island Advance* from 1929 to 1934, when he was fired for trying to organize a chapter of the American Newspaper Guild. After his dismissal he held jobs as editor of the *Paterson Press,* assistant New Jersey Supervisor of the Federal Writers Project, news editor of the Federated Press, and executive director of the National Housing Conference. In 1944 he became a free-lance writer of pamphlets and children's books. His books include *The Rio Grande* and *Steamboat Up the Colorado.* Obituaries and other sources: *Authors of Books for Young People,* 2nd edition, Scarecrow, 1971; *More Books by More People,* Citation Press, 1974; *New York Times,* February 1, 1980.

*   *   *

CROSS, Ralph D(onald) 1931-

PERSONAL: Born December 31, 1931, in Quincy, Ill.; son

of Raymond B. and Dorothy (a teacher; maiden name, Cook) Cross; married Madolyn Rachel Estrich (a registered nurse), June 30, 1955; children: Angela Cross Pickett, Pamela, Jeffrey, Janet. *Education:* Flint Community College, A.A., 1958; Eastern Michigan University, A.B., 1960; University of Oklahoma, M.A., 1961; Michigan State University, Ph.D., 1968. *Religion:* Methodist. *Home:* 109 Parkwood Dr., Hattiesburg, Miss. 39401. *Office:* Box 8352, University of Southern Mississippi, Southern Station, Hattiesburg, Miss. 39401.

CAREER: Southeast Missouri State College (now University), Cape Girardeau, instructor in earth science, 1961-63; Michigan State University, East Lansing, assistant instructor in geography, 1963-65; Northeast Oklahoma State College, Tahlequah, assistant professor of social science, 1965-66; Oklahoma State University, Stillwater, assistant professor of geography, 1966-68; Boston University, Boston, Mass., assistant professor of geography, 1968-71; University of Southern Mississippi, Hattiesburg, associate professor of geography, 1971—. Instructor at Flint Community College, 1964-65. Speaker at scholarly meetings. Market analyst with Paul E. Smith & Associates; air quality analyst for Leaf River Forest Products. Member of Lamar County Planning Commission. *Military service:* U.S. Navy, radar operator, 1952-55.

MEMBER: American Meteorology Society, American Water Resources Association, Association of American Geographers, National Weather Association, Soil Conservation Society of America, Southeastern Association of American Geographers, Southwestern Social Science Association, Mississippi Academy of Sciences (section head), Phi Kappa Phi. *Awards, honors:* Grants from *Southern Quarterly*, 1973, Mississippi Marine Resources Council, 1975, Mississippi Water Resources Research Institute, 1976, Southeast Mississippi Air Ambulance District, 1976, and U.S. Forest Service, 1977.

WRITINGS: (Contributor) Clifford Humphreys, editor, *Parameters of Water Quality,* Michigan State University Press, 1966; (editor and contributor) *Atlas of Mississippi,* University Press of Mississippi, 1974; *Denton's Army* (mystery), Tower, 1979; *The Key to Murder* (mystery), Tower, 1980; *When the Old Man Died* (mystery), Tower, 1980. Contributor of articles and reviews to geography and scientific journals. Regional editor of *National Weather Digest;* editor of *Hub Elks Times.*

SIDELIGHTS: Cross comments: "My motivation to write seems to be a compulsive need to string words together. Essentially, I write to please myself and would probably continue to do so even if I couldn't publish my work.

"My first book fits into my specialty field. Actually the book contains more narrative than maps or pictures. Despite all the local publicity from its publication, which included autograph parties, appearances on television talk shows, and seeing the book in bookstores, I received no thrill of any kind. It all seemed mundane.

"On the other hand, when I received the contract for my first novel—a paperback yet—I was on a high which lasted for weeks. Maybe if I work hard, I can re-experience that thrill. I'll keep trying, no matter what."

*   *   *

CROWE-CARRACO, Carol 1943-

PERSONAL: Born October 27, 1943, in Athens, Ga.; daughter of Hugh Dorsey (a merchant) and Rosa Lee (West) Crowe; married Robert Arthur Carraco (an attorney), July 24, 1976. *Education:* University of Georgia, A.B. (cum laude), 1965, M.A., 1966, Ph.D., 1971. *Religion:* Episcopalian. *Home:* 2508 Stonebridge Lane, Bowling Green, Ky. 42101. *Office:* Department of History, Western Kentucky University, Bowling Green, Ky. 42101.

CAREER: Western Kentucky University, Bowling Green, assistant professor, 1970-74, associate professor, 1974-77, professor of history, 1978—. Member of Southern Kentucky Bar Auxiliary, Warren County-Bowling Green Art Commission, and Warren County Women's Political Caucus. *Member:* American Historical Association, American Association of University Women, Southern Historical Association, Kentucky Archivists, Kentucky Historical Society, Big Sandy Valley Historical Society, Filson Club, Phi Beta Kappa, Phi Kappa Phi, Sigma Delta Pi, Phi Alpha Theta.

WRITINGS: The Big Sandy (nonfiction), University Press of Kentucky, 1979; *Cry for the Children: A Biography of Mary Breckinridge, 1881-1965,* University Press of Kentucky, 1980.

WORK IN PROGRESS: Slide shows on Appalachian history to be used in high school classrooms.

SIDELIGHTS: Carol Crowe-Carraco writes: "Although English history has been my vocational interest, I have found it necessary to branch out into areas where more publication is possible. However, the work on Mary Breckinridge fulfills many interests: women's history, Appalachian history, and English history."

*   *   *

CURL, David H. 1932-

PERSONAL: Born June 2, 1932, in Columbus, Ohio; son of John W. (a certified public accountant) and Florence (a teacher; maiden name, Davidson) Curl; married Dorothy A. Goodwin, May 13, 1961 (divorced); married Ardyce E. Hoffer Czuchna (a free-lance writer), April 6, 1979; children: Laura E., Steven D. *Education:* Ohio University, B.F.A., 1954; Indiana University, M.S., 1958, Ed.D., 1961. *Politics:* Independent. *Religion:* Unitarian-Universalist. *Home and office:* 2243 South 11th St., Kalamazoo, Mich. 49009.

CAREER: Indiana University, Bloomington, assistant professor of education, 1957-63; University of Connecticut, Storrs, assistant professor of education, 1963-65; University of Chicago, Chicago, Ill., audiovisual director, 1965-66; Western Michigan University, Kalamazoo, associate professor of education, 1966-69, professor of education, 1969—. Consultant with Oak Woods Media, 1976—. *Military service:* U.S. Air Force Reserve, 1954—; present rank, colonel. *Member:* Association for Educational Communications and Technology, Professional Photographers of America, Association for Multi-Image, Society for Photographic Education, Air Force Association, Phi Delta Kappa.

WRITINGS: Photography for Publication, U.S. Agency for International Development, 1963, 2nd edition, 1965; (with C.W.H. Erickson) *Fundamentals of Teaching With Audiovisual Technology,* Macmillan, 1972; *Photocommunication,* Macmillan, 1979; *Instructional Technology,* 3rd edition, Macmillan, in press. Author of film scripts. Author of "AV Training," a column in *Training,* 1964-74, "AV at Meetings," a column in *Meetings and Conventions,* 1970-74, "Audiovisual," a column in *Photomethods,* 1970-75, and "Sight and Sound," a column in *Photomethods,* 1978—. Contributor of more than two hundred articles and reviews to magazines. Contributing editor of *Photomethods.*

WORK IN PROGRESS: Instructional filmstrips.

SIDELIGHTS: Regarding his book *Photocommunication,* Curl told *CA:* "Although this book includes essential technical information, I have learned as a teacher to encourage each student to photograph first and to ask questions later. The technical processes are merely means to an end—means to creating an image that communicates something to someone else or expresses the photographer's feelings or impressions of a situation or subject. I believe it is a mistake to treat technique as if it were an end in itself."

* * *

CURREY, R(alph) N(ixon) 1907-

PERSONAL: Born December 14, 1907, in Mafeking, South Africa; son of John (a missionary) and Edith (Vinnicombe) Currey; married Helen Estella Martin (a writer), August 4, 1932; children: James Martin, Andrew John Colborne. *Education:* Wadham College, Oxford, M.A. (with honors), 1930. *Home:* 3 Beverley Rd., Colchester, Essex CO3 3NG, England.

CAREER: Royal Grammar School, Colchester, Essex, England, senior English master, 1946-72, senior master for arts subjects, 1964-72; writer and broadcaster, 1972—. *Military service:* British Army, 1941-46; became subaltern in Royal Regiment of Artillery in England and India, and major in Army Bureau of Current Affairs publications in Royal Education Corps. *Member:* P.E.N. International (fellow), Royal Society of Literature (fellow), Eastern Arts Association Literature Panel, Suffolk Poetry Society (president, 1965-79), Colchester Literary Society. *Awards, honors:* Viceroy's Prize from the All-India Poetry Competition for Forces, 1945, for "Burial Flags, Sind"; South African Poetry Prize (shared with Anthony Delius), 1960, for "Africa and the East."

WRITINGS: Tiresias and Other Poems, Oxford University Press, 1940; *This Other Planet* (poems), Routledge & Kegan Paul, 1945; (editor with R. V. Gibson) *Poems From India by Members of the Forces,* Oxford University Press, 1945; *Indian Landscape: A Book of Descriptive Poems,* Routledge & Kegan Paul, 1947; (translator) *Formal Spring: French Renaissance Poems of Charles d'Orleans, Villon, Ronsard, du Bellay, and Others,* Oxford University Press, 1950; *Poets of the 1939-1945 War,* Longmans, Green for the British Council, 1960, revised edition, 1967; (editor) *Letters and Other Writings of a Natal Sheriff: Thomas Phipson, 1815-1876,* Oxford University Press, 1968; *The Africa We Knew* (poems), David Phillip, 1973.

Radio plays: "Between Two Worlds," first broadcast by BBC Radio, December 15, 1948; "Early Morning in Vaaldorp," first broadcast by BBC Radio, August 29, 1961.

Contributor of articles to magazines and newspapers, including *Time and Tide, Manchester Guardian, New English Weekly, Dublin Magazine, Poetry Chicago, Contrast, Spectator, Listener, Observer,* and *Times Literary Supplement.*

WORK IN PROGRESS: A biography of a South African pioneer, Thomas Vinnicombe, 1854-1932, who kept a record in verse of gold-mining, transport-riding, and the Zulu and Boer wars.

SIDELIGHTS: Currey told *CA:* "In the 1930's, I published short stories and poems in England and the United States and was very much preoccupied with the coming of World War II. I became particularly aware during my army service of the modern phenomenon of killing by machines at a distance. This is apparent in my poems on "Unseen Fire," which are in several war and general anthologies. I have an-

thologized war poets and have written war poems, poems about war service overseas, and a standard study of the poets of World War II. T. S. Eliot said of my book, *This Other Planet,* that it contained 'the best war poetry in the correct sense of the term, that I have seen in the last six years.'

"I am also very aware of topography—the relationship between topography, architecture, and history in India, Morocco, Italy, France, and other countries I have visited. In recent years, the focus of my work has been South Africa—research into the early history of Natal and Transvaal, as well as poems about my experience of it. My interest in South Africa (where my mother's family went in 1849) has led me to devote most of my time to researching early family papers that have come into my hands. Perhaps because I passed my formative years in South Africa, I have never fitted into any of the writing groups in England. My 'colonial' fascination with European civilization found expression in my translations from medieval French. My wartime experience of India fascinated me as it was, in one respect, a direct experience of the Middle Ages which I had previously only read about. In Morocco I found echoes of India and of South Africa; in the far west of the United States, the South African echoes were audible despite the powerful new voice."

BIOGRAPHICAL/CRITICAL SOURCES: G. M. Miller and Howard Sergeant, *A Critical Survey of South African Poetry in English,* Balkema, 1957; D. R. Beeton and W. D. Maxwell Mahon, *South African Poetry: A Critical Anthology,* University of South Africa Press, 1966.

* * *

CUSHION, John P(atrick) 1915-

PERSONAL: Born March 2, 1915, in London, England; son of John (a jeweler) and Daisy (Abbot) Cushion; married Irene Howard, December 19, 1937; children: Patricia Esme Cushion Arnell, Peter John. *Education:* Attended technical school in London, England. *Religion:* Church of England. *Home:* Rockingham, Hurston Close, Worthing, Sussex BN14 0AX, England.

CAREER: Victoria and Albert Museum, London, England, 1931-75, began as boy assistant, became senior research officer; writer, 1975—. Lecturer at University of London; lecturer in the United States, Canada, Europe, and England. Member of council of Attingham Park Summer School. *Military service:* Royal Air Force, 1940-46; became sergeant. *Member:* English Ceramic Circle (honorary member), Morley College Ceramic Circle (president).

WRITINGS: Connoisseur's Guide to Pottery and Porcelain, Connoisseur, 1972; *The Pocket-Book of British Ceramic Marks,* Faber, 1976, revised edition published as *Handbook of Pottery and Porcelain Marks,* 1980; *Animals in Pottery and Porcelain,* Crown, 1976; *Pottery and Porcelain Tablewares,* Morrow, 1977. Contributor to *Antique Dealer and Collector's Guide.*

SIDELIGHTS: Cushion lectures on ceramics and on appreciation and recognition of antique decorative pottery and porcelain. He has served as art lecturer on tours of major art museums and ceramics collections in England and the United States. Cushion also holds sessions devoted to the discussion of ceramic wares brought to meetings, and is in great demand by museums and universities where the ceramic collections are unfamiliar to the curators, who often specialize in other art fields.

CUSHMAN, Clarissa Fairchild   1889-1980

OBITUARY NOTICE: Born January 13, 1889, in Oberlin, Ohio; died February 18, 1980, of heart failure, in Annandale, Va. Editor and novelist. In addition to their hardcover publication, Cushman's nine novels were serialized in national magazines. Her book, *Young Widow,* was adapted as a motion picture of the same name starring Jane Russell in 1946. Cushman won the Mary Roberts Rhinehart Mystery Novel Prize in 1940 for *I Wanted to Murder.* Obituaries and other sources: *Washington Post,* February 23, 1980.

D

DANBY, Mary
See CALVERT, Mary

*   *   *

DANE, Clemence
See ASHTON, Winifred

*   *   *

DANIELS, Mary   1937-

PERSONAL: Born February 18, 1937, in Chicago, Ill.; daughter of Dan (a businessman) and Virginia (Jankiewicz) Aisanich; married Richard Daniels (an agronomist; deceased); children: Roxana. *Education:* University of Texas, El Paso, B.A., 1960; graduate study at University of the Americas. *Religion:* Roman Catholic. *Agent:* Robert Lantz, Lantz Office, Inc., 114 East 55th St., New York, N.Y. 10022. *Office: Chicago Tribune,* 435 North Michigan Ave., Chicago, Ill. 60611.

CAREER: Free-lance writer in Mexico City, Mexico, 1960-68; *Chicago Tribune,* Chicago, Ill., feature writer, 1969—; *Midwest Equine Market* (horse magazine), features editor, 1977—.

WRITINGS: Morris, an Intimate Biography: The Nine Lives of Morris the Cat, Morrow, 1974; *Cat Astrology,* Morrow, 1975. Contributor to magazines, including *Chronicle of the Horse, Equine Events, Equus, Midwest Equine Market, Northwest Horseman, Cosmopolitan,* and *Cats.*

SIDELIGHTS: Daniels told *CA:* "Write about what you're interested in or feel passionate about. Getting some culture shock in another country is also important to the writer. Since childhood I have been interested in dressage, or classical, horsemanship; I am a circus freak, too. I love folk art and folk jewelry, especially from Mexico. I could never live without sharing my life with a cat."

*   *   *

DARLEY, John M(cConnon)   1938-

PERSONAL: Born April 3, 1938, in Minneapolis, Minn.; son of John Gordon (a professor and psychologist) and Kathleen (a psychologist; maiden name, McConnon) Darley; married Susan Ellen Ancell (a clinical psychologist), July 2, 1966; children: Lea Shannon, Piper Eve. *Education:* Swarthmore College, B.A., 1960; Harvard University, M.A., 1962,

Ph.D., 1965. *Religion:* Episcopalian. *Home:* 33 Cameron Ct., Princeton, N.J. 08540. *Office:* Department of Psychology, Princeton University, Princeton, N.J. 08544.

CAREER: New York University, New York, N.Y., assistant professor of psychology, 1964-68; Princeton University, Princeton, N.J., associate professor, 1968-72, professor of psychology, 1972—. *Member:* American Association for the Advancement of Science, American Psychological Association (fellow), American Sociological Association, Society of Experimental Social Psychologists, Society for the Psychological Study of Social Issues. *Awards, honors:* Shared socio-psychological essay prize from American Association for the Advancement of Science, 1968, for "The Unresponsive Bystander: Why Doesn't He Help?"

WRITINGS: (Contributor) Jacqueline Macauley and Leonard B. Berkowitz, editors, *Altruism and Helping,* Academic Press, 1969; (with Bibb Latane) *The Unresponsive Bystander: Why Doesn't He Help?,* Appleton, 1970; (with Susan Darley) *Conformity and Deviation,* General Learning Press, 1973; (with Latane) *Help in a Crisis: Bystander Response to an Emergency,* General Learning Press, 1976; (contributor) Lawrence Pervin and Michael Lewis, editors, *Perspectives in Interactional Psychology,* Plenum, 1978. Also co-author, with George R. Goethals, of *Approaches to Attribution Theory,* 1979. Contributor to *International Encyclopedia of Neurology, Psychology, Psychoanalysis, and Psychiatry.* Contributor of about thirty articles and reviews to psychology journals.

WORK IN PROGRESS: Research on moral judgment principles of children and adults; research on energy conservation in "an increasingly energy scarce world."

SIDELIGHTS: Darley writes: "Like most academics, I write for a variety of audiences. Increasingly, I've felt the need or obligation to put the research social psychologists do in a context in which it can be understood and used by a wide range of people."

*   *   *

DARLING, Jay Norwood   1876-1962
  (J. N. Ding)

OBITUARY NOTICE: Born October 21, 1876, in Norwood, Mich.; died February 12, 1962. Cartoonist. Darling's often controversial cartoons were featured in the *Des Moines Register, New York Globe,* and the *New York Tribune* for nearly fifty years. He won the Pulitzer Prize for best cartoon in 1924 and in 1943. The first award was for a four-strip cartoon illustrating three men who rose from their beginnings as an orphan, a plasterer's son, and a printer's apprentice to become a great mining engineer, a neurologist, and president of the United States. The last caption read "But they didn't get there by hanging around the corner drugstore!" Darling published several cartoon books, including *Ding Goes to Russia, Aces and Kings, Condensed Ink,* and *The Education of Alonzo Applegate,* the latter featuring one of his best known cartoon characters. Obituaries and other sources: *Current Biography,* Wilson, 1942, March, 1962; *New York Times,* February 13, 1962; *Time,* February 23, 1962; *Newsweek,* February 26, 1962.

* * *

DARLING, John R(othburn)   1937-

PERSONAL: Born March 30, 1937, in Holton, Kan.; son of John Rothburn, Sr. (a minister) and Beatrice (Deaver) Darling; married Melva Jean Fears, August 20, 1958; children: Stephen, Cynthia, Gregory. *Education:* Graceland College, A.A., 1957; University of Alabama, B.S., 1959, M.S., 1960; University of Illinois, Ph.D., 1967. *Religion:* Reorganized Church of Jesus Christ of Latter-day Saints. *Home:* 3212 West Kent Dr., Carbondale, Ill. 62901. *Office:* Office of the Dean, College of Business and Administration, Southern Illinois University, Carbondale, Ill. 62901.

CAREER: J. C. Penney Co., Kansas City, Mo., divisional manager, 1960-63; University of Illinois, Urbana, accountant and administrative assistant, 1963-65; University of Alabama, University, assistant professor of marketing, 1966-68; University of Missouri, Columbia, associate professor of marketing, 1968-71; Wichita State University, Wichita, Kan., professor of administration and coordinator of marketing, 1971-76; Southern Illinois University, Carbondale, professor of marketing and dean of College of Business and Administration, 1976—. Instructor at University of Kansas City (now University of Missouri), 1961-62; visiting professor at University of Montana, summer, 1971, and Helsinki School of Economics and Business Administration, 1974-75; visiting distinguished professor at Vaasa School of Economics and Business Administration, autumn, 1978; guest lecturer at colleges and universities all over the United States and in Finland, Thailand, Egypt, Korea, Taiwan, Australia, and the Netherlands. President of Business Research Associates, Inc., 1972-76, senior research consultant, 1976—; member of board of directors of National Family Institute, 1969-72, 1977—, and Outreach Foundation, 1973-79 (vice-president, 1975-77); member of board of trustees of Graceland College, 1976—, management committee of Park College, 1976-79, and advisory council of Illinois Two Thousand Foundation, 1977-79. Special U.S. representative and marketing consultant, Shopbank, Helsinki, Finland, 1979—. Participant and administrator at seminars and workshops in the United States and abroad; consultant to U.S. Department of Justice and Federal Trade Commission. *Military service:* U.S. Army Reserve, 1954-62.

MEMBER: Sales and Marketing Executives International, Academy of International Business, American Marketing Association, American Economic Association, Southern Marketing Association, Southern Economic Association, Midwest Business Administration Association, Beta Gamma Sigma, Alpha Kappa Psi, Chi Alpha Phi, Alpha Phi Omega.

WRITINGS: (With Harry A. Lipson) *Introduction to Marketing Administration,* University of Alabama Press, 1967,

revised edition, three volumes, 1968, study guide, 1969; (with Lipson) *Introduction to Marketing: An Administrative Approach,* Wiley, 1971; (with Lipson) *Decision Exercises in Marketing,* Wiley, 1971; (with Lipson) *Cases in Marketing,* Wiley, 1971; (with Lipson) *Marketing Fundamentals: Text and Cases,* Wiley, 1974; (contributor) Subhash C. Jain and Lew Tucker, editors, *Readings in International Marketing,* C.B.I. Publishing, 1979; (with Donald L. Perry) *Sales Management: Strategies and Concepts,* Goodyear Publishing, in press; (contributor) Iqbal Mathur, editor, *Cases in Finance,* Dame Publications, in press. Contributor of about forty articles to business journals in the United States and abroad. Member of editorial board of *Journal of Research,* 1979—.

SIDELIGHTS: Darling writes that his current projects include studies "of the attitudes of administrators in not-for-profit organizations toward marketing and the performance of marketing activities; the attitudes of consumers in the Far East, Middle East, Western Europe, and Scandinavia toward products and marketing practices in such countries as England, Finland, France, West Germany, Italy, Japan, Spain, Sweden, the United States, and the Soviet Union; the attitudes of such professionals as accountants, attorneys, dentists, and physicians toward advertising of their services and fees; attitudes toward marketing and the marketing concept by business executives in developing countries; and productivity differentials encountered by business firms with regard to marketing efforts in foreign countries, especially developing countries."

* * *

DAVIDSON, Bill
See DAVIDSON, William

* * *

DAVIDSON, Mildred   1935-

PERSONAL: Born March 2, 1935, in Silksworth, England; daughter of John Thomas (in merchant navy) and Elizabeth (McManners) Davidson. *Education:* University of London, B.A. (with first class honors), 1957, M.Phil., 1959; Cambridge University, certificate in education, 1960. *Home:* 39 Belsize Sq., London N.W.3, England.

CAREER: Teacher of English at grammar school in Belfast, Northern Ireland, 1960-64; University of Baghdad, Baghdad, Iraq, lecturer in English, 1964-65; Middlesex Polytechnic (formerly Hendon College of Technology), London, England, lecturer, 1966-71, senior lecturer in English, 1971—.

WRITINGS: The Poetry Is in the Pity (criticism), Chatto & Windus, 1972; *The Last Griffin* (juvenile), Macdonald & Jane's, 1974; *Dragons and More* (juvenile), Chatto & Windus, 1976; *Link of Three* (juvenile), Chatto & Windus, 1980.

SIDELIGHTS: Mildred Davidson told *CA:* "I wrote creatively from a very young age. University and academic life, however, channeled me into assessing other people's work rather than developing my own. During the last few years I have been able to go back to the beginning. I am drawn to fantasy not because it seems to me an escapist route but rather, when properly handled, just the opposite. Our innermost hopes and fears have always been confronted through myth, ever since Stone Age man totemized the natural world on the walls of his cave. The child accepts this naturally. I have written fiction for children that attempts to make fantasy bear out the realities of life."

AVOCATIONAL INTERESTS: Chess, spiritualism.

DAVIDSON, William 1918-
(Bill Davidson)

PERSONAL: Born in 1918, in Jersey City, N.J. *Education:* Attended New York University. *Address:* c/o Simon & Schuster, Inc., The Simon & Schuster Building, 1230 Ave. of the Americas, New York, N.Y. 10020. *Residence:* New York, N.Y.

CAREER: Author and journalist. Former associate editor of *Collier's* magazine, and contributing editor to *Look* magazine and *Saturday Evening Post. Military service:* U.S. Army; served as publications correspondent in Europe. *Awards, honors:* Sigma Delta Chi Award, for magazine reporting; Albert Lasker Award, for medical journalism.

WRITINGS—Under name Bill Davidson: *The Real and the Unreal,* Harper, 1961; *President Kennedy Selects Six Brave Presidents* (juvenile), Harper, 1962; *The Crickets All Look Alike,* Harper, 1962; *Indict and Convict: The Inside Story of a Prosecutor and His Staff in Action,* Harper, 1971; *Cut Off: Behind Enemy Lines in the Battle of the Bulge With Two Small Children, Ernest Hemingway, and Other Assorted Misanthropes,* Stein & Day, 1972; (with Sherman Chavoor) *The Fifty-Meter Jungle: How Olympic Gold Medal Swimmers Are Made,* Coward, 1973; *Return to Rainbow Country: The Television Heroes in a New Adventure,* Paper-Jacks, 1975; *Collura: Actor With a Gun,* Simon & Schuster, 1977. Contributor to periodicals, including *McCall's, Ladies' Home Journal,* and *Good Housekeeping.*

SIDELIGHTS: This popular contributor to magazines has also written a number of books on subjects ranging from criminal justice to movie stars. A versatile writer, Bill Davidson has even written a humorous chronicle of his family's experiences while buying a house, *The Crickets All Look Alike.* Another autobiographical work, *Cut Off,* is more serious in nature, describing Davidson's experiences as a World War II war correspondent. *Best Sellers* has commented that *Cut Off* includes "so many unexpected and even fantastic happenings that one finds it hard to believe that Mr. Davidson did not make some of them up out of whole cloth. . . . There is a small account of battlefield language but it is not overly offensive. The reader gets a little bit of the fluidity of modern warfare as an added bonus. All that needs to be said further is that those who miss this ride will be most unfortunate."

Davidson's *Collura: Actor With a Gun* is the story of an actor who works as a narcotics agent for the New York Police Department. The author's "account of Mr. Collura's police life, based on his recollections, has the ring of authenticity to it," reported Alden Whitman. "A skillful magazine writer, Mr. Davidson develops a suspenseful running story that highlights the dangers and the dramas of Mr. Collura's experiences." Aside from wishing to see more of Collura's "moments of introspection," Whitman thought Davidson's work "a crackling good book."

BIOGRAPHICAL/CRITICAL SOURCES: Best Sellers, July 1, 1972; *Detroit News,* August 6, 1972; *New York Times,* August 11, 1977.*

* * *

DAVIES, Christie
See DAVIES, John Christopher Hughes

* * *

DAVIES, John Christopher Hughes 1941-
(Christie Davies)

PERSONAL: Born December 25, 1941, in Sutton, Surrey, England; son of Christopher G. H. (an inspector of schools) and Marian (a teacher; maiden name, Johns) Davies. *Education:* Emmanuel College, Cambridge, B.A. (with first class honors), 1964, M.A., 1968. *Politics:* "Libertarian Conservative." *Religion:* "Protestant Agnostic." *Residence:* Reading, England. *Agent:* Laurence Pollinger Ltd., 18 Maddox St., London W.1, England. *Office:* Department of Sociology, University of Reading, Whiteknights, Reading, Berkshire, England.

CAREER: British Broadcasting Corp., London, England, radio producer for Third Programme, 1967-69; University of Leeds, Leeds, England, lecturer in sociology, 1969-72; University of Reading, Reading, England, lecturer, 1972-75, senior lecturer in sociology, 1975—, acting head of department, 1976-77. Visiting lecturer at University of Bombay, University of Delhi, Maharaja Sayajirao University of Baroda, and University of Punjab, all 1973-74. *Member:* Cambridge Union Society (president, 1964).

WRITINGS—All under name Christie Davies: (With Ruth Brandon) *Wrongful Imprisonment, Mistaken Convictions, and Their Consequences,* Allen & Unwin, 1973; (with Russell Lewis) *The Reactionary Joke Book,* Wolfe, 1973; *Permissive Britain: Social Change in the Sixties and Seventies,* Pitman, 1975; (with Rajeev Dhavan) *Censorship and Obscenity,* Martin Robertson, 1978; *Welsh Jokes,* John Jones, 1978. Contributor to magazines and newspapers in India and England, including *Quest, New Quest, Banker,* and *Daily Telegraph.*

WORK IN PROGRESS: Ethnic Jokes and Society, publication expected in 1981; *Sexual Taboos and Prejudices,* completion expected in 1982; *Bastards,* 1982.

SIDELIGHTS: Davies writes: "Throughout my work I have been interested in questions of ambiguity. Initially this led me to study the ways in which ethnic minorities maintain their identities in the face of the mixture of acceptance and discrimination that accompanies success. I have studied the Welsh, the Jews, and Indians abroad; hence, my interest in jokes, especially ethnic jokes. Later I became interested in similar problems involving sexual minorities and the illegitimate."

* * *

DAVIS, Bette J. 1923-

PERSONAL: Born April 18, 1923, in Joplin, Mo.; daughter of Clyde Wilbur (an engineer) and Opal (Morgan) Davis. *Education:* Pratt Institute, B.F.A., 1944. *Politics:* Liberal. *Religion:* Catholic.

CAREER: Illustrator and writer. U.S. Signal Corps Publication Agency, Fort Monmouth, N.J., illustrator, 1948-54; Norcross Greeting Card Co., New York, N.Y., designer, 1956-58; White Pines College, Chester, N.H., instructor of design and director of publicity, 1974-77. *Military service:* U.S. Marine Corps, Woman's Reserve, 1944-46; became sergeant in special services. *Member:* National Wildlife Federation, Society of Children's Book Writers, Audubon Society. *Awards, honors:* Outstanding Science Book Award from National Science Teachers Association, 1973, for *Winter Buds.*

WRITINGS—All self-illustrated: *Animals With Pockets,* Random House, 1968; *Working Animals,* Random House, 1969; *Mole From the Meadow,* Lothrop, 1970; *Musical Insects,* Lothrop, 1971; *Freedom Eagle,* Lothrop, 1972; *Winter Buds,* Lothrop, 1973; *World of Mosses,* Lothrop, 1975. Also illustrator of many other books.

DAVIS, Jan Haddle   1950-

PERSONAL: Born August 17, 1950, in San Francisco, Calif.; daughter of Gillian P. (a professor) and Dorothy (Jones) Haddle; married James V. Davis (a corporate farm manager), January 7, 1978; children: Joyce Ann. *Education:* Marietta Cobb School of Business, graduated, 1969. *Home and office address:* Quailwood Farm, Inc., Route 1, Box 111-A, Shady Dale, Ga. 31085.

CAREER: Secretary in commercial real estate, 1970-73; free-lance writer, 1974—. Owner of J-Bar-D Livestock, a livestock marketing and livestock advertising agency. *Awards, honors:* Appreciation award from Georgia Appaloosa Association, 1979, for *Complete Book of the Appaloosa.*

WRITINGS: Complete Book of the Appaloosa, A. S. Barnes, 1975. Contributor to *Appaloosa News, Spotted Horse,* and *Working Dog.*

WORK IN PROGRESS: A book on Australian kelpie dogs.

SIDELIGHTS: Jan Davis writes: "Both my business and personal interests lie with horses, dogs, and nature. As owner of a show and breeding kennel for rare-breed dogs, and after years of association with showing Appaloosa horses, I have been motivated to promote these unknowns.

"My first inquiry to a publisher was met with a contract, sent by return mail, quite a feat for an interested person with no formal training in journalism.

"My style has been termed 'lively.' In all my writing I try to look for the humor in the event, an 'unstuffy' approach to presenting facts and figures. Personally I enjoy an informal country lifestyle and I enjoy life to the hilt."

BIOGRAPHICAL/CRITICAL SOURCES: Appaloosa News, July, 1975.

*   *   *

DAVIS, Patrick (David Channer)   1925-

PERSONAL: Born January 7, 1925, in Aldershot, England; son of David (a forest officer) and Joan Bridgeman (Channer) Davis; married Mary Snowdon Catherall (a teacher), February 23, 1952; children: Allyson Julie, Mark David. *Education:* Jesus College, Oxford, B.A., 1951. *Home:* 6 Mount Harry Rd., Sevenoaks, Kent, England. *Agent:* Bolt & Watson Ltd., 8 Storey's Gate, London S.W.1, England.

CAREER: CMS Bookshops, Nigeria, bookseller, 1952-55; Oxford University Press, London, England, in publicity and sales, 1955-59; J. M. Dent & Sons Ltd., London, publicity manager and editor, 1959-64; University of London, London School of Economics and Political Science, London, publications officer, 1964—. *Military service:* Indian Army, 1943-47; became major; mentioned in dispatches. *Member:* Royal Geographical Society (fellow). *Awards, honors:* Award from *Yorkshire Post,* 1971, for *A Child at Arms.*

WRITINGS: A Child at Arms (autobiography), Hutchinson, 1970; *An Experience of Norway* (travel), David & Charles, 1974. Also author of two unpublished novels, *Mildred* and *Lise.* Contributor of stories to magazines. Contributing editor of *LSE,* 1967—.

WORK IN PROGRESS: Three novels.

*   *   *

DAY, Albert M.   1897-1979

PERSONAL: Born April 2, 1897, in Humboldt, Neb.; died January 21, 1979, in Harrisburg, Pa.; son of John Breece (a farmer and rancher) and Laura (Thayer) Day; married Gertrude Wichmann, August, 1923 (marriage ended); married Eva Kendall, September 2, 1944; children: (first marriage) Doris Jeanne, Richard Thayer; (second marriage) John Kendall. *Education:* Received degree from Jireh Junior College, 1916; University of Wyoming, B.S., 1923. *Residence:* Camp Hill, Pa.

CAREER: U.S. Department of Agriculture, Bureau of Biological Survey (now Department of Fish and Wildlife Service), Washington, D.C., field assistant in Wyoming branch, 1918-19, leader of rodent control in Laramie, Wyo., 1920-28, leader of predatory animal control in Cheyenne, Wyo., 1928-30, assistant chief of Division of Predator and Rodent Control in Washington, D.C., 1930-34, chief, 1934-38, chief of Division of Federal Aid in Wildlife Restoration, 1938-42; U.S. Department of Interior, Department of Fish and Wildlife Service, Washington, D.C., liason officer, 1942-43, assistant director in Chicago, Ill., and Washington, D.C., 1943-46, 1953-55, director, 1946-53; director of wildlife resources for the Arctic Institute of North America, 1955-58; executive director of the Oregon Fish Commission, 1958-60, and of the Pennsylvania Fishing Commission, 1960-64. Conservation consultant, 1964-65; national resource specialist for U.S. Department of Interior, 1965-66; conservation consultant to U.S. Department of Agriculture, 1966-71; environmental consultant, beginning 1971.
Member of International Pacific Salmon Fisheries Commission, 1947; member of special advisory committee to secretary of interior, 1956; adviser to International North Pacific Salmon Fisheries Commission, 1958-60; member of U.S. section at United Nations conference on law and sea; member of Pacific Marine Fisheries Commission. Consultant to National Park Service, Bureau of Sports Fisheries and Wildlife, Bureau of Outdoor Recreation, and Bureau of Land Management. *Military service:* U.S. Signal Corps, served in World War I; became corporal. *Member:* American Forestry Association, National Audubon Society, American Wildlife Institute, American Society of Mammalogists, American Fisheries Society, Wildlife Society, Merchants and Manufacturers Club (Chicago), Cosmos Club.

WRITINGS: North American Waterfowl, Stackpole & Heck, 1949; (with Milo Moore) *A Review of the Japanese Salmon Fishery,* Oregon Fish Commission, 1957; (with John T. Day and Bessie Day Amiss) *John Breese Day, 1860-1942: A Brief Sketch of His Life,* [Camp Hill, Pa. (?)], 1966; *Wildlife Habitat Management as a Means of Increasing Recreation on Public Lands,* U.S. Department of Interior, Bureau of Land Management, 1966; *Making a Living in Conservation: A Guide to Outdoor Careers,* Stackpole, 1971. Also author of *Hunters Handbook,* 1932.
Contributor of articles to periodicals, including *American Forests, Field and Stream, Sports Afield, Audubon Magazine* and *Outdoors.*

SIDELIGHTS: Environmentalist Albert Day's career is highlighted by the seven years he spent as director of the U.S. Department of Interior's Fish and Wildlife Service. He believed that the nation's wealth hinged on its natural resources and that sound land and water management would ensure the preservation of the country's wildlife.
Day's *North American Waterfowl* is an account of waterfowl conservation efforts as well as a study of sanctuaries and refuge systems. His *Making a Living in Conservation* discusses careers in oceanography, forestry, wildlife, fisheries, park administration, and other related areas. It contains guidelines on where to get an education, where to find job information, and how to find employment in conservation.

OBITUARIES: Washington Post, January 24, 1979.*

DAY, David   1944-

PERSONAL: Born February 6, 1944, in Kent, England; son of Julian Lister (a textile cutter) and Ellen Harriet (Street) Day; married Jacqueline Madeleine Walsh, July, 1967; children: Jason, Alexander, Nicholas. *Education:* Ravensbourne College of Art, N.D.D., 1964; Royal College of Art, M.Des.R.C.A., 1967. *Religion:* Church of England. *Home and office:* 39 Gourock Rd., Eltham, London SE9 1JA, England.

CAREER: Jackson Day Designs (industrial designers), London, England, partner, 1970—. Consultant to *Reader's Digest,* 1967-69; free-lance consultant, 1969—.

WRITINGS: (With Albert Jackson) *Good Housekeeping Decorating and Do-It-Yourself,* Good Housekeeping Books, 1977 (published in England as *Good Housekeeping Do-It-Yourself Book,* Ebury Press, 1977); (with Jackson) *Tools and How to Use Them,* Knopf, 1978; (with Jackson) *Complete Book of Tools,* M. Joseph, 1978; (with Jackson) *Simply Fix-It,* Ebury Press, 1979; (with Jackson) *Handbook of Model-making,* 1980.

SIDELIGHTS: Day told *CA:* "My work in publishing has always dealt with practical subjects. I have been involved as project designer, writer, and illustrator for books and magazines. In recent months my partner and I have acted as consultants and co-presenters of a television series for the British Broadcasting Corp. The ten-week series, 'Make Your Own Furniture,' deals with making furniture for the home, beginning with simple projects, leading to the more complex."

AVOCATIONAL INTERESTS: Golf, interior design, designing and making furniture, rebuilding old automobiles.

*   *   *

d'AZEVEDO, Warren L.   1920-

PERSONAL: Born August 19, 1920, in Oakland, Calif.; son of Joseph L. (a physician) and Helen (Finley) d'Azevedo; married Kathleen Addison (in child development), January 25, 1944; children: Anya d'Azevedo-Rosen, Erik. *Education:* Attended Modesto Junior College, 1937-39, and Fresno State College, 1940-41; University of California, Berkeley, B.A., 1942, graduate study, 1949-53; Northwestern University, Ph.D., 1962. *Office:* Department of Anthropology, University of Nevada, Reno, Nev. 89557.

CAREER: Northwestern University, Chicago Division, Chicago, Ill., instructor in anthropology, spring, 1958; University of California, assistant professor of anthropology, 1958-60; University of Utah, Salt Lake City, assistant professor of anthropology, 1960-62; University of Pittsburgh, Pittsburgh, Pa., assistant professor of anthropology, 1962-63; University of Nevada, Reno, associate professor, 1963-69, professor of anthropology, 1969—, head of department of sociology and anthropology, 1965-66, and department of anthropology, 1967-72, chairperson of executive board of Center for Western North American Studies, 1964-66. Visiting professor at Indiana University, spring, 1970. Conducted field studies in Liberia and the United States; participant and coordinator of conferences in the United States and abroad. Member of staff of Nevada Intertribal Council communication and self-study project, 1968—.

MEMBER: American Anthropological Association, African Studies Association, American Association of University

Professors, Annual American Conference on Liberian Research (founding member), National Society of Professors, National Research Association of Liberia (founding member), Southwestern Anthropological Association (vice-president, 1977-78; president, 1978-79). *Awards, honors:* Ford Foundation fellowship for Africa, 1955-57; National Science Foundation grant, 1964-70; Social Science Research Council grants, 1965, 1966-67.

WRITINGS: (With Marvin D. Solomon) *A General Bibliography of the Republic of Liberia,* Northwestern University Press, 1962; (editor) *The Washo of California and Nevada,* University of Utah, 1963; (editor and contributor) *Current Status of Anthropological Research in the Great Basin,* Desert Research Institute, University of Nevada, 1964; *The Artist Archetype in Gola Culture* (monograph), Desert Research Institute, University of Nevada, 1966; *Some Terms From Liberian Speech,* U.S. Peace Corps in Liberia, 1967.

The Gola of Liberia, two volumes, Human Relations Area File Press, 1972; (contributor) Ruth M. Houghton, editor, *Native American Politics: Power Relationships in the Western Great Basin Today,* Bureau of Governmental Research, University of Nevada, 1973; (editor and contributor) *The Traditional Artist in African Societies,* Indiana University Press, 1973; (contributor) Anthony Forge, editor, *Primitive Art and Society,* Oxford University Press, 1973; *American Indian and Black Students at the University of Nevada, Reno, 1874-1974,* Department of Anthropology, University of Nevada, 1975; *Straight With the Medicine: Washoe Peyotist Narratives,* Black Rock Press, 1978. Editor of *Handbook of North American Indians: Great Basin,* Smithsonian Institution Press.

Co-author of "Nevada Indian Historical Map." Contributor of about twenty articles to anthropology and African studies journals. Contributing editor of *Indian Historian,* 1966—, and *California Anthropology,* 1973—; associate editor of *Ethnology: A Journal of Social and Cultural Anthropology,* 1962-63; member of advisory board of *Liberian Studies Journal,* 1968—.

SIDELIGHTS: D'Azevedo made a recording, "Washo-Peyote Songs: Songs of the Native American Church," released by Ethnic Folkways Library in 1972.

*   *   *

DeARMENT, Robert K(endall)   1925-

PERSONAL: Born August 29, 1925, in Johnstown, Pa.; son of John R. (an insurance adjuster) and Madeleine (a secretary; maiden name, Young) DeArment; married Rose Marie Nowakowski (a vice-president and general manager of a fishing tackle manufacturing company); children: Rosemary, Paul, Joan, Diana. *Education:* University of Toledo, B.A., 1952. *Politics:* Conservative. *Religion:* "No church affiliation." *Home:* 5912 Brookson, Sylvania, Ohio 43560. *Office:* Champion Spark Plug Co., 900 Upton Ave., Toledo, Ohio 43607.

CAREER: Champion Spark Plug Co., Toledo, Ohio, factory work, 1950-55, production scheduler, 1956-70, manager of sales order department, 1971-79, assistant manager of marketing services, 1980—. President of Stillfish Corp. (fishing tackle manufacturers), 1959—. *Military service:* U.S. Army, Combat Infantry, 1943-46; became staff sergeant. *Member:* National Association and Center for Outlaw and Lawman History (life member; member of board of directors), Kansas State Historical Society (life member).

WRITINGS: Bat Masterson: The Man and the Legend, University of Oklahoma Press, 1979.

WORK IN PROGRESS: Knights of the Green Cloth, on gamblers of the frontier West; research for a biography of cowboy, frontier detective, and writer, Charlie Siringo, publication expected in 1982.

SIDELIGHTS: DeArment commented: "Although most of my adult life has been devoted to business, I have maintained a keen interest in the history of the American West. I have delved deeply into this area and my writing is based on thirty years of research."

*   *   *

DEASY, C(ornelius) M(ichael)   1918-

PERSONAL: Born July 19, 1918, in Mineral Wells, Tex.; son of Cornelius and Monetta (Palmo) Deasy; married Lucille Laney, September 14, 1941; children: Diana, Carol, Ann. *Education:* University of Southern California, B.Arch., 1941. *Home and office:* Davenport Creek Farm, Route 3, Box 161-S, San Luis Obispo, Calif. 93401.

CAREER: Private practice of architecture in Los Angeles, Calif., 1946-60; practice of architecture with Robert D. Bolling, Los Angeles, Calif., 1960-75; private practice of architecture in Los Angeles, Calif., 1975—. Vice-president of Los Angeles Beautiful; commissioner of Los Angeles Board of Zoning Appeals, 1973-74; chairperson of board of directors of Booth Memorial Hospital. *Military service:* U.S. Naval Reserve, active duty, 1943-46; became lieutenant junior grade. *Member:* American Institute of Architects (fellow; president of southern California chapter; head of research committee), Regional Plan Association (member of board of directors), Los Angeles Library Association (member of board of directors). *Awards, honors:* Governor's design award 1964, for student lounge at California State University, Los Angeles; merit design award, 1966, for Lincoln Savings building in Los Angeles; merit award from American Institute of Architects and U.S. Navy, 1974, for enlisted men's housing in El Toro, Calif.

WRITINGS: Design for Human Affairs, Schenkman, 1974. Contributor to architecture and psychology journals.

WORK IN PROGRESS: Directory of Human Behavior in Public Places for Designers, completion expected in 1981.

SIDELIGHTS: Deasy writes: "Most of my non-professional writing has dealt with the effect of the physical environment on human behavior. As an architect, it is my position that the only rational basis for constructing any building is to make people more effective in whatever they do. Since individual effectiveness is influenced far more by psychological and social factors than by the color of the walls or the quality of the plumbing, it follows that the primary commitment of the design profession should be to create physical environments that permit people to interact with the maximum amount of benefit and the minimum amount of stress. Having practiced what I am preaching for a number of years, I am keenly aware of how inappropriate many buildings are in human terms and how much better they could be; hence, my writing. The number of people whose lives are touched by an individual building design is limited. The number whose lives are touched, directly or indirectly, by writing, is without limit."

*   *   *

DEATON, Charles W.   1942-

PERSONAL: Born October 21, 1942, in Nacogdoches, Tex.; son of William P. (in business) and Iva (Whitton) Deaton; married Suzan McCallister (a secretary), August 7, 1971.

Education: Stephen F. Austin State University, B.B.A., 1964, M.A., 1967. *Office address:* Texas Government Newsletter, P.O. Box 12814, Austin, Tex. 78711.

CAREER: Del Mar College, Corpus Christi, Tex., professor of government, 1969-71; *Texas Government Newsletter,* Austin, editor and publisher, 1971—. Professional philatelist, specializing in rare stamps and postal history. Reporter and analyst for KEYS-Radio.

WRITINGS: The Year They Threw the Rascals Out, Shoal Creek Publishers, 1973; *A Voter's Guide to the 63rd Legislature,* Texas Government Newsletter, 1973; *A Voter's Guide to the 64th Legislature,* Texas Government Newsletter, 1975; *A Voter's Guide to the 65th Legislature,* Texas Government Newsletter, 1977; *A Voter's Guide to the 66th Legislature,* Texas Government Newsletter, 1979; *Textbook on Texas Politics,* West Publishing, 1980.

SIDELIGHTS: Deaton began publishing his newsletter in 1973 to provide the public with information then unavailable in concise, readable form. He felt that mass media didn't allow enough time for complete reporting on the state legislature, and that bulky official records of meetings and vote counts discouraged ordinary citizens from seeking informed answers to their questions. His weekly newsletter is now used by high school and college students throughout Texas.

BIOGRAPHICAL/CRITICAL SOURCES: Nacogdoches Sunday Sentinel, March 10, 1974; *Dallas Morning News,* January 9, 1978, October 5, 1978.

*   *   *

DEATS, Randy   1954-

PERSONAL: Born July 1, 1954, in Newton, Mass.; son of Paul Kindred, Jr. (a professor) and Ruth (Zumbrunen) Deats. *Education:* Boston University, B.A., 1977. *Home and office:* 106 Berkeley St., West Newton, Mass. 02165.

CAREER: Dancer and teacher of ballroom and disco dancing in West Newton and Boston, Mass., and around the world, 1974—. *Member:* Dance Masters Association, Dance Teachers Club of Boston.

WRITINGS: (With Laurie Devine) *Dancing Disco,* Morrow, 1979. Contributor to *Dancer's Digest.*

WORK IN PROGRESS: A series of disco variations for *Dancer's Digest.*

SIDELIGHTS: Deats writes: "American culture is uniquely and sadly lacking in that social dance is not yet integral to it. The long-heralded return to ballroom dancing is illusory. Ballroom dancing is a complex form: varied, artistic, and athletic. Now, with the advent of disco, and particularly the simpler freestyle dances, the first *universal* folk dance approaches. It is my ambition to promote the growth and longevity of dance in the United States and elsewhere. There is a vital sensuality in partner dancing, a need long denied by our society and met by few (if any) other activities. Anything I can do to share the excitement and joy in social dancing with others, I will do."

BIOGRAPHICAL/CRITICAL SOURCES: Patriot Ledger, July 3, 1979; *Boston Globe,* July 7, 1979; *Boston Herald American,* August 21, 1979.

*   *   *

DECAUX, Lucile
See BIBESCO, Marthe Lucie

de EXTRAMUROS, Quixote
  See ESPINO, Federico (Licsi, Jr.)

*   *   *

de GAMEZ, Cielo Cayetana Alba
  See ALBA de GAMEZ, Cielo Cayetana

*   *   *

de GAMEZ, Tana
  See ALBA de GAMEZ, Cielo Cayetana

*   *   *

DEGENSHEIN, George A.   1918(?)-1979

OBITUARY NOTICE: Born c. 1918 in New York; died of a heart attack, December 13, 1979, in Brooklyn, N.Y. Educator, surgeon, and author. Degenshein was director of surgery at Maimonides Medical Center in Brooklyn, N.Y., and a clinical professor of surgery at the State University of New York. He also co-edited *Milestones in Modern Surgery.* Obituaries and other sources: *New York Times,* December 16, 1979.

*   *   *

deGUZMAN, Daniel   1911-

PERSONAL: Surname is accented on last syllable; born December 4, 1911, in Mexico City, Mexico; came to the United States in 1916, naturalized citizen, 1952; son of Octavio J. (a writer) and Grace (Ketcham) deGuzman. *Education:* Columbia University, B.A., 1933; New York University, M.A., 1951; Yale University, Ph.D., 1957. *Politics:* Independent. *Religion:* Roman Catholic. *Home and office:* 116 East 73rd St., Apt. 8, New York, N.Y. 10021. *Agent:* Russ Perry, 1550 North Hayworth Ave., Los Angeles, Calif. 90046.

CAREER: Worked as a journalist, in exports and imports, and as an instructor of romance languages at Latin American Institute, New York City, 1933-52; Xavier University, Cincinnati, Ohio, instructor in romance languages, 1952-54; Yale University, New Haven, Conn., instructor in romance languages, 1954-58; free-lance journalist, 1958-61; Queens College of the City University of New York, Flushing, N.Y., associate professor of Spanish language and literature, 1961-76, director of program in Barcelona, 1965-66; writer, 1976—. Chairperson of Educational Testing Service committee to revise graduate record examination, 1957. *Member:* American Association of Teachers of Spanish and Portuguese, Congreso Nacional de Historia (associate member).

WRITINGS: (With Henriette Betourne) *Tests and Drills in French Grammar,* Latin American Institute Press, 1954; *Mexico epico* (title means "Epic Mexico"), Costa-Amic Editorial, 1962; (with Hyman Alpern) *Cuatro novelas modernas de la America Hispana* (title means "Four Modern Novels of Spanish America"), Chilton, 1965; (with Betourne and Charles Starr) *Direct French Conversation,* Latin American Institute Press, 1966; *Carlos Fuentes,* Twayne, 1972; *The Literature of Intervention,* Stockton Press, 1980; *Journey Into Now* (novel), Stockton Press, in press. Contributor to *Hispania.*

WORK IN PROGRESS: *All About Cuqui,* memoirs, publication by Stockton Press expected in 1982.

SIDELIGHTS: DeGuzman describes *Mexico epico* as "a new critical and aesthetic evaluation of the impact of the Mexican Revolution of 1910 on the formative literary and artistic currents in that country between 1910 and 1940. It presents a new theory on the psychological coming-of-age of Mexico, and was well-received by the Mexican press on its publication."

He adds: "My goal has been to help young people understand and deal with their world, to learn and think. Born in Mexico, raised and educated both in Mexico and the United States, I was fortunate to be brought up bilingually in both cultures, and my secondary interest has been in furthering Mexican-U.S. relations."

*   *   *

De JAEGHER, Raymond-Joseph   1905-1980
  (Lei Chen Yuan)

OBITUARY NOTICE—See index for *CA* sketch: Born September 13, 1905, in Courtrai, Belgium; died of cancer, February 6, 1980, in Manhattan, N.Y. Roman Catholic priest, missionary, educator, editor, and writer. During the 1930's De Jaegher was a missionary in China. When World War II broke out, he was captured by the Japanese and spent time in a concentration camp; later he was held prisoner by Chinese Communists. After his release he did relief work in Peking and worked for a time at Seton Hall University's Far Eastern Studies Institute. From 1954 to 1964 De Jaegher lived in Vietnam. In addition to serving as a special adviser to Vietnamese President Ngo Dinh Diem, he founded the Free Pacific News Agency, the *Free Pacific Magazine,* and the *New Vietnam* newspaper. While in that country he also edited the periodicals published in English as *Free Front* and in French as *Front de la Liberte.* De Jaegher's books include *The Enemy Within,* which has been translated into eight languages, and *Peking's Red Guards.* Obituaries and other sources: *New York Times,* February 8, 1980; *Washington Post,* February 9, 1980.

*   *   *

DeKOSKY, Robert K.   1945-

PERSONAL: Born January 14, 1945, in Camden, N.J.; son of Aaron (in adult education) and Evelyn (a teacher; maiden name, Gorlen) DeKosky; married Deborah Padway (an artist), August 19, 1973. *Education:* Pennsylvania State University, B.S., 1966; University of Kansas, M.S., 1968; University of Wisconsin—Madison, Ph.D., 1972. *Office:* Department of History, University of Kansas, Lawrence, Kan. 66045.

CAREER: University of Wisconsin—Milwaukee, assistant professor of history, 1972-77; University of Kansas, Lawrence, assistant professor, 1977-79, associate professor of history, 1980—. *Member:* American History of Science Society, Alpha Chi Sigma. *Awards, honors:* Grant from National Science Foundation, for England, 1977.

WRITINGS: (Contributor) Gerhart Hoffmeister, editor, *The Renaissance and Reformation in Germany,* Ungar, 1977; *Knowledge and Cosmos: Development and Decline of the Medieval Perspective,* University Press of America, 1979. Contributor to history journals.

WORK IN PROGRESS: Research on the physical and chemical work of Sir William Crookes and on the evolution of experimental science in the sixteenth and seventeenth centuries.

*   *   *

DeLANCEY, Mark W(akeman)   1939-

PERSONAL: Born December 26, 1939, in Rochester, N.Y.;

son of Blaine M. (a professor) and Floy (a professor and writer; maiden name, Winks) DeLancey; married Virginia Valchar (a professor), August 12, 1961; children: Blaine Fubara, Mark Dike, Elise. *Education:* Syracuse University, B.A., 1961; Indiana University, M.A., 1967, Ph.D., 1973. *Politics:* Democrat. *Religion:* None. *Home:* 20 Hillstar Court, Columbia, S.C. 29206. *Office:* Department of Government and International Studies, University of South Carolina, Columbia, S.C. 29208.

CAREER: U.S. Peace Corps, Washington, D.C., volunteer teacher in Nigeria, 1962-64; University of South Carolina, Columbia, assistant professor, 1971-77, associate professor of government and international studies, 1977—, vice-chairman of department, 1978-79. Reader at University of Nigeria, 1976-77. *Member:* International Studies Association (associate director), International African Institute, American Political Science Association, Nigerian Political Science Association, African Studies Association, Southern Association of Africanists (member of executive committee).

WRITINGS: (With wife, Virginia DeLancey) *A Bibliography of Cameroon Folklore,* African Studies Association, 1972; (editor) *The United States and World Problems,* University of South Carolina Press, 1972; (editor with Robert Charlick and John Holmes) *An African Data Bank* (monograph), University of South Carolina Press, 1973; (editor) *World Affairs and U.S. Foreign Policy: A Collection of Readings,* University of South Carolina Press, 1973; *Teaching the International Relations of Africa* (monograph), University of South Carolina Press, 1975; (with V. DeLancey) *A National Bibliography of Cameroon,* Africana Publishing, 1975; (with V. DeLancey) *Tinkering Around With School,* Intercultural Association, 1978; (with Christopher Herrick) *African Politics at American Universities and Colleges: A Survey of Purposes, Methods, and Materials* (monograph), University of South Carolina Press, 1978; (editor) *Aspects of International Relations in Africa,* Indiana University Press, 1979; (editor) *Bibliography of African International Relations,* Westview Press, 1979; *Political Economy of Cameroon,* Westview Press, 1980; (with Michael Olisa) *Introduction to Political Science,* Longman, 1980; (editor) *Readings in African Politics,* Longman, 1980; (editor) *Readings in African International Relations,* Westview Press, 1980. Contributor to political science and African studies journals. Editor of *Bulletin* of Southern Association of Africanists, 1973-75; associate editor of *African Book Publishing Record,* 1977—.

WORK IN PROGRESS: Research in Africa on national food policies and conflict between urban and rural populations as a major factor in contemporary African politics.

SIDELIGHTS: DeLancey comments: "The major motivating factor in my career has been my two years as a Peace Corps volunteer in Nigeria. This changed my views and my career interest."

*   *   *

DENHAM, Bertie   1927-

PERSONAL: Born October 3, 1927, in Weston Underwood, Buckinghamshire, England; son of George (a politician; member of House of Lords) and Daphne (Mitford) Denham; married Jean McCorquodale, February 14, 1956; children: Jocelyn, Richard, Harry, George. *Education:* King's College, Cambridge, B.A., 1951. *Politics:* Conservative. *Religion:* Church of England. *Home:* Laundry Cottage, Weston Underwood, Olney, Buckinghamshire MK46 5JZ, England. *Agent:* Michael Shaw, Curtis Brown Ltd., 1 Craven Hill, London W.2, England. *Office:* House of Lords, Westminster, London, England.

CAREER: House of Lords, London, England, government junior whip and lord-in-waiting to Queen Elizabeth, 1961-64, opposition junior whip, 1964-70, government junior whip and lord-in-waiting to Queen Elizabeth, 1970-71, government deputy chief whip and captain of yeomen of the guard, 1971-74, opposition deputy chief whip, 1974-78, opposition chief whip, 1978-79, government chief whip and captain of gentlemen-at-arms, 1979—. *Military service:* British Army, Oxford and Buckinghamshire Light Infantry, 1946-48, Honourable Artillery Company, 1955-61; became lieutenant. *Member:* Society of Authors, Crime Writers Association, White's Club, Pratt's Club.

WRITINGS: The Man Who Lost His Shadow (suspense novel), Scribner, 1979. Also author of *Two Thyrdes,* 1980.

SIDELIGHTS: Lord Denham commented: "Several years ago I started to write humorous short stories based on the British Parliament, and these were unsuccessful. I was told that the style would have been quite acceptable in the 1930's, but not today. I realized the reason for this was that that is the period of humorous stories which I enjoy reading most. Accordingly, when I decided to try writing again, I chose suspense thrillers because my preference in those is for the very latest and most up-to-date, and I thought that this too might show in my writing and therefore be more acceptable to a publisher." He noted that his thrillers are set in "a background of politics, country life, and country sports, which is my own background."

*   *   *

DENNIS, Lane T(imothy)   1943-

PERSONAL: Born September 7, 1943, in Evanston, Ill.; son of Clyde H. (a publisher) and Muriel (a publisher; maiden name, Benson) Dennis; married Ebeth Garrison, September 28, 1963; children: Geoffrey, Jon, Jenay, Sasha, Rachel, Joshua. *Education:* Northern Illinois University, B.S., 1965; McCormick Theological Seminary, M.Div., 1973; Northwestern University, Ph.D., 1980. *Religion:* Christian. *Home:* 419 Ellis Ave., Wheaton, Ill. 60187. *Office:* Good News Publishers, Westchester, Ill. 60153.

CAREER: Lithocolor Press (printer), Westchester, Ill., production manager, 1965-69; Good News Publishers (religious publisher), Westchester, Ill., general manager, 1969-71; Verlag Grosse Freude (Swiss branch of Good News Publishers), Zurich, Switzerland, interim director, 1971-72; ordained minister of United Presbyterian Church, 1973; Anchor House, Sault Ste. Marie, Mich., campus minister, 1972-74; Good News Publishers, general manager, 1974-76, vice-president, 1976—, member of board of directors, 1969—. *Member:* Evangelical Christian Publishers Association.

WRITINGS: A Reason for Hope, Revell, 1976; (contributor) Robert Webber and Donald Bloesch, editors, *The Orthodox Evangelicals,* Thomas Nelson, 1978; (author of prologue) Muriel B. Dennis, *Chosen Children,* Good News Publishers, 1978.

WORK IN PROGRESS: Research on evangelical Christianity, especially L'Abri Fellowship of Switzerland, and on the social sources of Christian traditions.

SIDELIGHTS: Dennis writes: "Everything that I have written has grown out of a deep concern for understanding the meaning of life and how we are to live in our age. This quest has led me to Europe a number of times. I traveled around the world, lived deep in the North woods for two years, and eventually returned to a suburb of Chicago. Throughout this quest my wife, Ebeth, has been a constant source of strength, insight, and happiness.

"I am interested in issues of justice and of a more humane and ecologically sound way of living. Two of our children are racially mixed adopted children, and I thank God for the irreplaceable dimension they (and our other children) bring to our life. Over the years I have become deeply committed to the Christian faith as the only hope for today and forever."

* * *

DETZER, David William 1937-

PERSONAL: Born September 29, 1937, in Washington, D.C.; son of August Jarvis (a Navy captain) and Dorothy (Allee) Detzer; married Marta Moret (a research director); children: Christopher, Curtis, Katrina. *Education:* Pennsylvania State University, A.B., 1960, M.A., 1961; University of Connecticut, Ph.D., 1970. *Home:* 349 Rimmon Rd., Woodbridge, Conn. 06525. *Agent:* Paul R. Reynolds, Inc., 12 East 41st St., New York, N.Y. 10017. *Office:* Department of History, Western Connecticut State College, Danbury, Conn. 06810.

CAREER: Northern Illinois University, DeKalb, instructor in history, 1962-63; University of Pittsburgh, Bradford, Pa., instructor in history, 1963-66; Western Connecticut State College, Danbury, assistant professor, 1966-70, associate professor, 1970-74, professor of history, 1974—, head of department, 1977—. Member of board of directors of WINE-Radio and WRKI-Radio; consultant to U.S. Department of Defense. *Member:* Organization of American Historians. *Awards, honors:* Grant from Harry S Truman Library, 1973-74.

WRITINGS: Thunder of the Captains, Crowell, 1977; *The Brink: The Cuban Missile Crisis, 1962,* Crowell, 1979. Also author of more than twenty scripts produced for noncommercial television. Contributor of articles and reviews to scholarly journals.

WORK IN PROGRESS: Research on exploration, and on World War II, especially as it involved the war in the Pacific.

SIDELIGHTS: Detzer commented to *CA:* "I am driven to write, as I am driven to eat, by forces I do not understand, by some internal pressure. It is not that writing makes me exceptionally happy or that I feel I have so much to contribute. I'm not even sure I really like it that much. But when I'm not involved in some project—gathering materials, doing research, organizing my thoughts, writing and rewriting—I become edgy. I feel incomplete, like a jigsaw puzzle with a piece missing."

* * *

DEUTSCH, Eberhard Paul 1897-1980

OBITUARY NOTICE: Born October 31, 1897, in Cincinnati, Ohio; died January 16, 1980, in New Orleans, La. Lawyer and author. Deutsch gained recognition in the 1930's for his efforts in fighting the tax on newspaper advertising that had been advocated by Huey P. Long. An expert in international law, Deutsch was also known for his work in re-establishing Austria as an independent nation after World War II, and in 1967 received Austria's Gold Badge of Merit. Deutsch practiced law in New Orleans since 1925. He edited *The International Lawyer,* an American Bar Association periodical, and wrote two books, *An International Rule of Law* and *A Model Ocean Bill of Lading.* Obituaries and other sources: *Who's Who in Finance and Industry,* 21st edition, Marquis, 1979; *New York Times,* January 18, 1980.

DEUTSCH, Hermann Bacher 1889-1970

OBITUARY NOTICE: Born March 16, 1889, in Brux, Austria (now Czechoslovakia); died June 25, 1970. Restaurateur and journalist. Deutsch worked on the *New Orleans Item* from 1943 to 1970, beginning as associate editor and becoming editorial page editor and columnist. He was also the owner of Brennan's Restaurant in New Orleans. In addition to contributing short stories and articles to periodicals, Deutsch wrote *Incredible Yanqui, The Wedge,* and *The Huey Long Murder Case.* Obituaries and other sources: *New York Times,* June 27, 1970; *Who's Who in the South and Southwest,* 13th edition, Marquis, 1973.

* * *

DEUTSCHER, Max 1916(?)-1979

OBITUARY NOTICE: Born c. 1916; died November 20, 1979, in New York, N.Y. Psychologist, psychoanalyst, and author. A practicing analyst at Manhattan's William Alanson White Institute of Psychiatry, Psychoanalysis, and Psychology, Deutscher was a founder and editor of *Contemporary Psychoanalysis.* His *Psychological Effects of Enforced Segregation,* written with Isadore Chein, was cited in the landmark Supreme Court desegregation ruling, *Brown v. Board of Education,* in 1954. Deutscher also contributed articles and papers to professional journals. Obituaries and other sources: *New York Times,* November 22, 1979.

* * *

DHIEGH, Khigh (Alx)

PERSONAL: Name is pronounced Kai Dee; son of Nath Ani (an engineer) and Kasatola (Deeimutu) El Zuzuzan; married wife, Mary, 1933. *Education:* Golden State College, B.A. and M.A., Ph.D., 1938. *Home address:* P.O. Box 27806, Tempe, Ariz. 85282. *Agent:* Bertha Klausner International Literary Agency, Inc., 71 Park Ave., New York, N.Y. 10016.

CAREER: University of California, Los Angeles, instructor in philosophy of theatre, 1969 and 1972-76; Taoist Sanctuary, North Hollywood, Calif., rector, 1971—. Actor in motion pictures, including "The Manchurian Candidate," "Seconds," "The Hawaiians," and "The Mephisto Waltz"; actor on stage, radio, and television, including appearances on "Hawaii Five-O," "Judge Dee," and "Khan"; theatrical director. Executive administrator of Five Powers (Wu Te Unlimited). Guest lecturer at colleges throughout the United States. Member of Arizona governor's Film and Television Commission.

WRITINGS: The Eleventh Wing: An Exposition on the Dynamics of I Ching for Now, Nash Publishing, 1973. Editor of *I Ching: Taoist Book of Days* (annual calendar), 1975-80. Editor of *Tao and Change,* 1972-77.

WORK IN PROGRESS: Prosperity via Chance, Cycles, and Synchronicity, publication by Prentice-Hall expected in 1981; research on Chinese philosophy and cosmology.

SIDELIGHTS: Dhiegh wrote: "The public often recognizes me because of my role as Wo Fat, the occasional antagonist to Mr. Jack Lord, as the masterful McGarrett in 'Hawaii Five-O.' But, in addition to my long career in theatre, radio, and television, I am active on the academic platform as an educator and lecturer. I also recorded an arrangement of 'The Poems of St. John of the Cross,' released by Folkway Records in 1965, and did a specially edited rendition of 'The Rubiyat of Omar Khayyam,' released by CMS Records.

"As executive administrator of Five Powers, I am sincerely

concerned with initiating a harmonious working-together relationship with others who are aware and creative.''

* * *

DIDINGER, Ray 1946-

PERSONAL: Born September 18, 1946, in Philadelphia, Pa.; son of Raymond G. (a steel company executive) and Marie (Curran) Didinger; married Denise Daly, June 17, 1972; children: David John, Kathleen. *Education:* Temple University, B.S., 1968. *Religion:* Roman Catholic. *Home:* 101 Gainsboro Rd., Cherry Hill, N.J. 08003. *Office: Philadelphia Bulletin,* 30th & Market Sts., Philadelphia, Pa. 19101.

CAREER: Delaware County Daily Times, Chester, Pa., reporter, 1968-69; *Philadelphia Bulletin,* Philadelphia, Pa., high school sports reporter, 1969-77, columnist, 1977—. *Member:* Baseball Writers Association of America, Professional Hockey Writers Association, Philadelphia Sportswriters Association. *Awards, honors:* Keystone Award from Pennsylvania Newspaper Publishers Association, 1972, for ''Lance Rentzel Says He's Sorry,'' 1973, for ''Brian Spencer Skates for Glory,'' and 1977, for ''Philadelphia Fans: Boobirds or Lovebirds?''; award from Philadelphia Press Association, 1974, for ''Larry Brown: King of the Hill.''

WRITINGS: (With Norm Evans and Sonny Schwartz) *On God's Squad,* Creation House, 1971; *The Pittsburgh Steelers,* Macmillan, 1974; *The Complete Handbook of Pro Football,* Signet, 1975.

Work represented in anthologies, including *More Than a Game,* Prentice-Hall, 1974, and *Best Sports Stories of the Year,* Dutton, 1974. Contributor to *The NFL's Official Encyclopedic History of Professional Football.* Contributor to national magazines, including *Sports Illustrated, Sporting News, Pro!, Football Digest,* and *Baseball Digest.*

WORK IN PROGRESS: Research for a book on the Philadelphia Phillies.

SIDELIGHTS: Didinger wrote: ''Sports has been the driving force in my life for as long as I can recall. The first books I remember reading for enjoyment were the Chip Hilton sports books. Chip Hilton was a blonde-haired, blue-eyed high school phenomenon. He captained the football, baseball, and basketball teams, worked nights to keep the family afloat, made straight A's, and still found time to fight ignorance and injustice on the side.

''For the longest time I wanted to be Chip Hilton. I assumed his athletic interests, if not his skills, and adopted his lofty principals, if not his commitment. Finally I realized Chip was giving me a terrible inferiority complex, so I gave the books away.

''By then, of course, it was too late. I was hooked on sports and I've stayed that way ever since. When I took physics in high school, the first thing I learned to do with a slide rule was figure out batting averages.

''I developed an affinity for the written word about this time. Every night when the *Philadelphia Bulletin* was delivered to our home, I would turn to the sports section and read the column written by Sandy Grady, then spend hours at my typewriter, imitating Grady's delightful style. I told my friends that one day I would be the sports columnist at the *Philadelphia Bulletin.*

''In 1969, I was hired by the *Bulletin*'s sports editor to be his high school writer. He gave me the desk right next to Sandy Grady's. It was a thrill not unlike a rookie having the locker next to Babe Ruth.

''I still haven't shaken the Chip Hilton complex. In 1977 I went to a pro football camp and tried out as a quarterback. The past two years, I've played professional softball with the Philadelphia Athletics.''

* * *

DIMOND, Mary Clark

PERSONAL: Born in New York, N.Y.; daughter of Grenville (an attorney) and Fanny (an ornithologist and horticulturist; maiden name, Dwight) Clark; married E. Grey Dimond (a physician); children: Clarie Crosier, Louisa Peterson, Greenville Clark Thoron, Molly D. Thoron, Thomas Thoron. *Education:* Radcliffe College, received degree in 1939. *Home and office:* 2501 Holmes St., Kansas City, Mo. 64108.

CAREER: Writer, 1965—. Resident at Rockefeller Foundation Conference and Study Center, Bellagio, Italy, 1978. President of board of directors of Grenville Clark Fund at Dartmouth College, and supervisor of ''Papers of Grenville Clark''; charter member of board of directors of KCPT-TV; founder of Edgar Snow Memorial Fund, and member of board of directors of Friends of the Library, both at University of Missouri, Kansas City; founder of Center for World Community; member of board of directors of Institute for World Order; member of board of overseers committee on East Asian studies at Harvard University; supervisor of lemon ranch in California.

WRITINGS: (Compiler) *Memoirs of a Man: Grenville Clark,* edited by Norman Cousins and J. Garry Clifford, Norton, 1975. Author of filmstrip on China. Contributor to magazines and newspapers, including *Eastern Horizon.*

SIDELIGHTS: Mary Dimond has made seven trips to China since 1971. These trips have been with groups or with her husband, often having to do with the exchange of Chinese and American physicians, medical care and medical education. She and her husband frequently lead groups of medical students to examine health care systems and medical education in foreign countries such as Israel, China, and the Navajo nation.

BIOGRAPHICAL/CRITICAL SOURCES: Kansas City Star, September 16, 1970, October 26, 1970, October 25, 1973, January 16, 1975, April 20, 1975; *San Diego Union,* January 2, 1976; *Radcliffe Quarterly,* June, 1979.

* * *

DING, J. N.
See DARLING, Jay Norwood

* * *

DINGMAN, Roger 1938-

PERSONAL: Born October 19, 1938, in Los Angeles, Calif.; son of Alvin Boyd (an architect) and Rose Irene (a teacher; maiden name, Brennan) Dingman; married Linda Story (a teacher), August 21, 1965; children: Charles, Margaret, Zachary, Andrew. *Education:* Stanford University, B.A. (cum laude), 1960; Harvard University, M.A., 1963, Ph.D., 1969; attended Inter-University Center for Japanese Studies, Tokyo, Japan, 1965-66. *Politics:* Democrat. *Religion:* Roman Catholic. *Home:* 1532 West 238th St., Harbor City, Calif. 90710. *Office:* Department of History, University of Southern California, Los Angeles, Calif. 90007.

CAREER: Harvard University, Cambridge, Mass., instructor, 1968-69, lecturer in history, 1969-71; University of Southern California, Los Angeles, assistant professor, 1971-

76, associate professor, 1976-77; U.S. Naval War College, Newport, R.I., professor of strategy, 1977-78; University of Southern California, Los Angeles, associate professor of history, 1978—. Consultant to Q-Ed Films. *Military service:* U.S. Navy, 1960-62; became lieutenant junior grade.

MEMBER: American Historical Association, Society of Historians of American Foreign Relations, International House of Japan, California Japan Seminar, Southern California Japan Seminar (member of executive committee), University of Southern California-University of California, Los Angeles East Asian International Relations Seminar, Phi Beta Kappa. *Awards, honors:* Woodrow Wilson fellowship, 1960; National Defense Education Act language fellowship (Japan), 1965-66; Harvard American East Asian research fellowships, 1967-68, 1969-70; grants from American Philosophical Society, 1969, University of Southern California, 1972, 1973, Asia Society (Japan), 1973, and Social Science Research Council, 1973; Harvard Canaday Award, 1970; Stanford University Hoover Institution national fellow, 1973-74; Haynes Foundation award, 1975; American Philosophical Society research award, 1976; Bernath Prize from Society of Historians of American Foreign Relations, 1977, for *Power in the Pacific;* U.S. Naval War College Center for Advanced Research award, 1978.

WRITINGS: (Editor with Sato Seizaburo, and contributor) *Kindai Nihon no taigai taido* (title means "Japan and World Order"), University of Tokyo Press, 1974; *Power in the Pacific,* University of Chicago Press, 1976. Contributor of articles and reviews to journals. Member of board of editors of *Pacific Historical Review.*

WORK IN PROGRESS: The Price of Peace (tentative title), on the making of the peace settlement with Japan in 1951; *From Enmity to Alliance: American-Japanese Relations, 1945-1952;* a series of essays on the Korean conflict.

SIDELIGHTS: Dingman comments: "My intellectual and professional interests have grown out of three related circumstances: my birth and education on the Pacific coast; exposure to the life of the professional military, first as an officer and then as a teacher to them; and prolonged, repeated residence in Japan. I am passionately interested in the history and current affairs of Japan. I have been fortunate to travel there and learn the language, and have had the opportunity to see other Asian and Pacific countries with which to compare Japan. Consequently, I am interested in the interaction—at all levels, not just in political or diplomatic terms—between Americans and the peoples of Eastern Asia and the Pacific.

"My first book dealt with the efforts of Americans, Japanese, and Britons to preserve peace in the Pacific by limiting naval armaments. I have collaborated with Japanese scholars in studying the underlying premises that have guided modern Japanese foreign policy. My current work is an attempt to understand the multiple interactions among Americans, Japanese, and other Pacific people which led to the signing of the 1951 peace treaty with Japan and the establishment of a kind of international system for the Pacific.

"My principal objectives, as a scholar and teacher, are to learn and to make others more aware of the importance and inner dynamics of the American relationship with the nations and peoples of eastern Asia."

AVOCATIONAL INTERESTS: International travel, sailing.

*   *   *

DODD, Anne W(escott) 1940-

PERSONAL: Born April 24, 1940, in Bangor, Maine; daugh-

ter of Archie Hanson and Felicia (Ferrara) Wescott; married James H. Dodd, February 26, 1965; children: (stepchildren) Vickie Dodd Gehm, Sue. *Education:* Attended Pennsylvania State University, 1957-58; University of Maine, Orono, B.A., 1961, graduate study, 1977—; California State University, Los Angeles, M.A., 1967. *Home address:* Mere Point Rd., R.F.D. 3, Box 3095, Brunswick, Maine 04011. *Office:* Brunswick High School, Spring St., Brunswick, Maine 04011.

CAREER: High school teacher of English in Hallowell, Maine, 1961-62; junior high school teacher of English, French, and social studies in Pasadena, Calif., 1962-67, and Montebello, Calif., 1967-68; elementary school supervisor in Machias, Maine, 1968-69; curriculum coordinator and teacher of English at high school in Machias, Maine, 1969-71; high school teacher of English and department head in Wiscasset, Maine, 1971-72; Brunswick High School, Brunswick, Maine, English teacher, 1972-77, assistant principal, 1977—. Presents composition workshops. Former member of board of directors of Machias Young Men's Christian Association. Consultant to Coronet Films.

MEMBER: National Association of Secondary School Principals, National Council of Teachers of English, Association for Supervision and Curriculum Development, New England Association of Teachers of English (member of executive board, 1974-78), Maine State Principals Association (chairperson of Joint Legislative Committee with Maine State Elementary Principals Association, 1978—), Maine Council of Teachers of English (vice-president, 1977-78), Brunswick League of Women Voters, Machias Valley Women's Club.

WRITINGS: Write Now!, Globe Book Co., 1973. Contributor of articles, poems, and reviews to education journals and other magazines, including *English Journal.*

WORK IN PROGRESS: A book on organizing time and resources for more leisure-time availability, publication expected in 1981; a novel about tour groups, publication expected in 1982; a children's book, publication expected in 1982.

SIDELIGHTS: Anne Dodd writes: "I am currently very involved in 'invading' the traditionally male-controlled world of secondary school administration and am finding precious little time to write. Attending my first conference of secondary school principals was an experience I'll never forget. I was the only female in a group of 150 males. I found out what it feels like to be a member of a minority group: I was generally ignored socially during the two days, reference to my presence in the audience was made by every speaker, and I was overcharged for my room because the desk clerk assumed I wasn't part of the principals' group. In all fairness, I must admit that I am now fairly well accepted by most members of this association.

"Travel is also very important to me, being an escape as well as an education. Reading books about places is not the same as being there. No photograph or description can capture the immensity of the temple at Karnak or the sand that is the air one breathes in the Valley of the Kings. The Russian character must be affected by the climate: in April I was colder there than I ever thought possible and wondered how anyone could tolerate a winter in Moscow. Visiting most countries, especially the Soviet Union, has made me appreciate the United States even more. Places visited include England, France, Mexico, Greece, Italy, Switzerland, Luxembourg, Austria, West Germany, the Netherlands, Iceland, Canada, the U.S. Virgin Islands, and Puerto Rico.

"The future of American public education is of great concern to me now. Drastic changes must come if we are to cope with tight budgets, declining enrollments, the back-to-basics movement, teacher and administrator 'burnout,' and the problems of society as a whole. Creative thinking and research are needed to make our schools effective in teaching students to live in the chaotic present and in the future, the shape of which we cannot imagine.''

BIOGRAPHICAL/CRITICAL SOURCES: Media and Methods, January, 1975.

* * *

DONALD, Larry W(atson) 1945-

PERSONAL: Born March 10, 1945, in Dayton, Ohio; son of Carl V. (a train dispatcher) and Ruth (a librarian; maiden name, Sanders) Donald; married Nanci Higgins (an educator), January 27, 1969; children: David. *Education:* Bowling Green State University, B.S., 1967. *Home:* 6578 Emerald Lake Dr., Troy, Mich. 48098. *Office:* Donald Publications, Inc., 811 Oakwood Ct., Rochester, Mich. 48063.

CAREER/WRITINGS: Review Times, Fostoria, Ohio, sports editor, 1967-71; *Football News,* Detroit, Mich., managing editor, 1971-79; *Basketball Weekly,* Grosse Pointe, Mich., editor, 1971-79; Donald Publications, Inc., Troy, Mich., editor and publisher of *Baseball Bulletin,* 1979—. Contributor to *Street & Smith Basketball Yearbook,* and *NCAA Basketball Guide.* Columnist and editor of *Medalist Sports News.* Notable assignments include coverage of eight NCAA basketball championships, eight National Basketball Association championships, two World Series, and one National Football League Championship. *Member:* U.S. Basketball Writers Association (member of board of directors), U.S. Professional Football Writers Association, National Association of Sportswriters and Broadcasters, Baseball Writers of America. *Awards, honors:* National Newspaper Association Sports Contest, 2nd place, 1969; U.S. Basketball Writers Association Contest, 1st and 3rd place, 1977, 2nd and 3rd place, 1978.

SIDELIGHTS: "My career," writes Larry Donald, "has been motivated by a desire to become one of a vanishing breed in journalism today—that is. the person capable of doing all things (editing, writing, graphics, and photography), and doing them well.

"In an era which appears to emphasize the specialist, I suspect mine is a lost cause. Nonetheless, I perceive it to be one worth pursuing.

"I've sought throughout to elevate the role of the sports journalist from its pedestrian level to one of more importance in the newspaper world. As the games we watch and play have changed over the years, so too have the demands on our sports journalist changed. No longer is the hack writer who drones on about the who, what, where, when, and why an acceptable part of our business. The sports journalist of today needs a thorough understanding of psychology and law as well as the athletic events he covers. Being able to write about events and people, being able to edit and refine what others say about events and people, and being able to present it graphically are the goals I pursue."

* * *

DONICHT, Mark Allen 1946-
(Marcus Allen, Mark Allen)

PERSONAL: Born July 1, 1946, in Roseau, Minn.; son of William A. (in business) and Anne M. (a beautician; maiden name, Nyland) Donicht. *Education:* University of Minnesota, B.A. (magna cum laude), 1968; graduate study at Nyingma Institute, 1972. *Politics:* "I tend toward the left, but don't like to be classified." *Religion:* "New Age, my own blend of East and West." *Residence:* Mill Valley, Calif. *Office:* Whatever Publishing, 158 East Blithedale #4, Mill Valley, Calif. 94941.

CAREER: Professional actor in Minnesota and California, 1968-72; writer, astrologer, teacher, and songwriter in northern California, 1972-76; Whatever Publishing, Mill Valley, Calif., founder, editor, and chairperson of board of directors, 1976—. Co-founder of Rising Sun Records, 1978—. *Member:* Phi Beta Kappa.

WRITINGS—Under pseudonym Mark Allen: *Chrysalis* (nonfiction), Ross Books, 1978; *Seeds to the Wind: Poems, Songs, Meditations,* Whatever Publishing, 1979.

Under pseudonym Marcus Allen: *Reunion: Tools for Transformation,* Whatever Publishing, 1976, revised edition, 1978; *Astrology for the New Age,* Whatever Publishing, 1979; *B'Nai Or* (science fiction novel; also see below), Whatever Publishing, 1980; *Tantra for the West: A Guide to Personal Freedom,* Whatever Publishing, 1980. Author of ''B'nai Or'' (film script).

WORK IN PROGRESS: Another book.

SIDELIGHTS: Donicht told *CA:* "*Chrysalis* explores my motivation and circumstances at length. I had a very unique education, which began when I left the university in 1968. It was a rough time for me and for the country in general; I was in an intensely negative space, exhausted, into drugs, not well physically, and very cynical. It was my existential period. Then I traveled around the country, first with a theatre company, then later on my own. I got interested in the 'spiritual' activities which were so abundant on the West Coast.

"I studied everything I could get my hands on which related to Eastern philosophy and practice. I spent an entire summer reading my way around a bookstore in Berkeley. I spent a year studying yoga and Vedantic philosophy, two years studying Zen (including six months at a Zen retreat center on Maui), and over three years studying Tibetan Buddhism at the Nyingma Center.

"Then I left my Eastern studies, looking for parallels in the West, or at least for more successful adaptations of the Eastern teachings to the West. I stayed as a staff member at the Living Love Center in Berkeley for a year, and found what I was looking for. For the past five years I have been on my own, writing and recording music. My main focus almost always seems to involve translating clearly for the West the deep teachings I have encountered in my period of intensive study.

"I'm very optimistic, in some ways. I feel there is hope for our planet—but I feel that everyone needs to take responsibility for the condition it's in and for trying to clean it up in every way possible. It starts in our homes and in our heads, and it is spreading, organically, to big business and to government. Time will tell.

"Although basically I am a writer and musician, I divide my time between creative work and my business. I am involved in the management of Whatever Publishing and Rising Sun Records. Our business is unique in that it was set up by creative artists for themselves. One of our partners started with some good, solid business experience, but the rest of us have just developed it as we've developed the business. Initial response has been very encouraging. We feel that a lot of creative artists have given too much power to the business people. It's time to take care of business ourselves, and do exactly the kinds of books and music that we want to do in our hearts, and not what some big corporation's marketing people think will sell.

"I also play and record music. I'm just finishing my third album for Rising Sun Records. The music is mellow, meditative. The albums are 'Eveningsong: Songs of Love and Moon-Filled Nights,' 'Seeds: Hymns for a New Age,' and 'Breathe.'

"My book, *Tantra for the West,* is an attempt to translate for the West the things I have learned in my studies of Eastern thought and practice. I have found, within the Tibetan tradition, that tantra is defined not as just 'the yoga of sex,' as most people think, but 'the art and science of finding personal freedom within every moment of daily life, rejecting nothing.' There are chapters which relate to many of the most important areas of our lives: work, relationship, sex, money, creativity, food and drink, and aging."

BIOGRAPHICAL/CRITICAL SOURCES: Uni-Com Guide, December, 1978.

* * *

DONIS, Miles 1937-1979

OBITUARY NOTICE—See index for *CA* sketch: Born December 6, 1937, in Scranton, Pa.; died in an automobile accident, December 20, 1979, in Burbank, Calif. Novelist and screenwriter. Miles was the author of three novels, *Falling Up, The Fall of New York,* and *Cloud Eight.* He adapted *Falling Up* for the screen. Obituaries and other sources: *AB Bookman's Weekly,* January 14, 1980.

* * *

DONNELLY, John 1941-

PERSONAL: Born March 30, 1941, in Worcester, Mass.; son of Donald Smith (a state official) and Viola (Norton) Donnelly; married Joyce Mattress (a computer analyst), June 10, 1967. *Education:* Holy Cross College, Worcester, Mass., B.S., 1963; Boston College, M.A., 1965; Brown University, M.A., 1967, Ph.D., 1969. *Politics:* Democrat. *Religion:* Roman Catholic. *Home:* 1773 Glidden Court, San Diego, Calif. 92111. *Office:* Department of Philosophy, University of San Diego, San Diego, Calif. 92110.

CAREER: University of Notre Dame, Notre Dame, Ind., assistant professor of philosophy, 1969-70; Fordham University, Bronx, N.Y., assistant professor of philosophy, 1970-75; State University of New York College at Fredonia, visiting professor of philosophy, 1975-76; University of San Diego, San Diego, Calif., associate professor of philosophy and head of department, both 1976—. *Member:* American Philosophical Association, Kierkegaard Society (co-founder).

WRITINGS: (Editor) *Logical Analysis and Contemporary Theism,* Fordham University Press, 1972; (editor with Leonard Lyons) *Conscience,* Alba, 1973; (editor) *Language, Metaphysics, and Death,* Fordham University Press, 1978.

Contributor: Keith Lehrer, editor, *Analysis and Metaphysics,* D. Reidel, 1975; Marvin Kohl, editor, *Infanticide and the Value of Life,* Prometheus Books, 1978; Florence Hetzler and Austin Kutscher, editors, *Philosophical Aspects of Thanatology,* Arno Press, 1978; Robert L. Perkins, editor, *Kierkegaard's Fear and Trembling: Critical Appraisals,* University of Alabama Press, 1980. Contributor to philosophy and theology journals. Book review editor of *International Philosophical Quarterly,* 1972-75.

WORK IN PROGRESS: A book on Kierkegaard; continuing research on thanatology.

AVOCATIONAL INTERESTS: Playing basketball.

* * *

DOOLEY, Thomas A(nthony) 1927-1961

OBITUARY NOTICE: Born January 17, 1927, in St. Louis, Mo.; died January 18, 1961. Physician, medical missionary, and author. Dooley is known primarily for his tireless relief work during the war in Indochina. In 1954 he aided refugees from northern Vietnam in their flight from advancing Communist Viet Minh armies. On a ship of two thousand refugees, Dooley was the only medical officer available to treat numerous cases of disease and malnutrition. Later in Haiphong he helped build and maintain camps that sheltered nearly six hundred thousand refugees awaiting safe passage to Saigon. Most importantly, Dooley made friends with the Vietnamese and helped dispel the prejudices that they had learned from years of exposure to anti-American propaganda. In 1956, Dooley organized a small civilian unit to do similar work in Laos, funded in part by profits the doctor received from his book, *Deliver Us From Evil,* an account of his experiences in Vietnam. His other books are *The Edge of Tomorrow, The Night They Burned the Mountain,* and *Before I Sleep.* Obituaries and other sources: *Current Biography,* Wilson, 1957, March, 1961; *Newsweek,* November 23, 1959, January 30, 1961; *New York Times,* January 19, 1961; *Time,* January 27, 1961; Agnes Dooley, *Promises to Keep: The Life of Doctor Thomas A. Dooley,* Farrar, Straus, 1963; Glenn D. Kittler, *Wings of Eagles,* Doubleday, 1966.

* * *

DORIN, Patrick C(arberry) 1939-

PERSONAL: Born February 12, 1939, in Chicago, Ill.; son of Aloysius (a foreman) and Grace (a nurse; maiden name, Maebius) Dorin; married Karen M. Foley, May 13, 1961; children: Thomas, Michael, Susan, Amy, John. *Education:* Northland College, B.S., 1961; Northern Michigan University, M.A., 1966; Michigan State University, Ed.Spec., 1971; University of Minnesota, Ph.D., 1977. *Residence:* North Branch, Minn. 55056. *Office:* North Branch Public Schools, North Branch, Minn. 55056.

CAREER: Elgin, Joliet & Eastern Railway, Milwaukee Road, Chicago, Ill., cost analyst in marketing and train operation research, 1961-64; public school teacher in Marquette, Mich., 1965-66, Duluth, Minn., 1966-69, and East Lansing, Mich., 1969-73; North Branch Public Schools, North Branch, Minn., data processing coordinator, 1973-78, principal of North Branch Elementary School, 1978—. Vice-chairperson of transportation committee of East Central Minnesota Development Council; vice-president of public relations for Lake Superior Transportation Museum in Duluth, Minn., 1975. Member of advisory board of Young Men's Christian Association (YMCA); consultant. *Member:* National Elementary Principal's Association, Lake Superior Transportation Club (vice-president), Chicago and North Western Historical Society.

WRITINGS—All published by Superior; except as noted: *Lake Superior Iron Ore Railroads,* 1969; *Commuter Railroads,* 1970; *C&NW Motive Power,* 1971; *The Domeliners,* 1973; *Canadian Pacific,* 1974; *Coach Trains and Travel,* 1975; *Canadian National Railways,* 1975; *Everywhere West,* 1976; *Grand Trunk Western,* 1977; *Milwaukee Road East,* 1978; *Young Railroader's Book of Steam* (juvenile), 1978; *Soo Line Railroad,* 1979; *Amtrak Trains and Travel,* 1979; *Chesapeake and Ohio Railway,* 1980; *Yesterday's Trains,* Lerner, 1980. Contributor to journals.

WORK IN PROGRESS: Textbooks on railway transportation; novel on his grandfather's life; a textbook on methods, operations, and administration of public schools.

SIDELIGHTS: Dorin comments: "Both railroads and writing are very important hobbies of mine. By combining the two, I attain a high level of relaxation and enjoyment. Hopefully, I can help preserve some of the history of the railroads as well as helping other individuals with their own hobbies."

*   *   *

DORN, Edward (Merton) 1929-

PERSONAL: Born April 2, 1929, in Villa Grove, Ill.; son of William and Louise Abercrombie (Ponton) Dorn. *Education:* Attended University of Illinois, Urbana, 1949-50; Black Mountain College, 1950 and 1954, received B.A. *Home:* 1035 Mapleton, Boulder, Colo. 80302.

CAREER: Poet. Idaho State University, Pocatello, lecturer, 1961-65; *Wild Dog*, Pocatello, co-editor, 1964-65; University of Essex, Colchester, England, Fulbright lecturer, 1965-67, visiting professor of English, 1967-68, 1974-75; University of Kansas, Lawrence, visiting professor, 1968-69; University of California, Riverside, regent's lecturer, 1973-74; University of California at San Diego, La Jolla, writer-in-residence, 1976; University of Colorado, Boulder, visiting professor, 1977-80. *Awards, honors:* D. H. Lawrence fellowship, summer, 1969.

WRITINGS—Poetry: *The Newly Fallen*, Totem Press, 1961; *Hands Up!*, Totem Press, 1964; *From Gloucester Out*, Matrix Press, 1964; *Idaho Out*, Fulcrum Press, 1965; *Geography*, Fulcrum Press, 1965; *The North Atlantic Turbine*, Fulcrum Press, 1967; *Gunslinger*, Black Sparrow Press, 1968; *Gunslinger: Book II*, Black Sparrow Press, 1969; *The Midwest Is That Space Between the Buffalo Statler and the Lawrence Eldridge*, T. Williams, 1969; *The Cosmology of Finding Your Spot*, Cottonwood, 1969; *Twenty-four Love Songs*, Frontier Press, 1969.

Gunslinger I & II, Fulcrum Press, 1970; *Songs: Set Two, a Short Count*, Frontier Press, 1970; *Spectrum Breakdown: A Microbook*, Athanor Books, 1971; *By the Sound*, Frontier Press, 1971; *The Cycle*, Frontier Press, 1971; *A Poem Called Alexander Hamilton*, Tansy-Peg Leg Press, 1971; *The Hamadryas Baboon at the Lincoln Park Zoo*, Wine Press, 1972; *Gunslinger, Book III: The Winterbook, Prologue to the Great Book IV Kornerstone*, Frontier Press, 1972; *Recollections of Gran Apacheria*, Turtle Island, 1974; *Slinger* (contains *Gunslinger*, Books I-IV and *The Cycle*), Wingbow Press, 1975; *The Collected Poems, 1956-1974*, Four Seasons Foundation, 1975; (with Jennifer Dunbar) *Manchester Square*, Permanent Press, 1975; *Hello, La Jolla*, Wingbow Press, 1978; *Selected Poems*, edited by Donald Allen, Grey Fox Press, 1978.

Other: *What I See in the Maximum Poems*, Migrant Press, 1960; (with Michael Rumaker and Warren Tallman) *Prose 1*, Four Seasons Foundation, 1964; *The Rites of Passage: A Brief History*, Frontier Press, 1965; *The Shoshoneans: The People of the Basin-Plateau*, Morrow, 1966; (translator with Gordon Brotherston) *Our Word: Guerrilla Poems From Latin America*, Grossman, 1968; (translator with Brotherston) Jose Emilio Pacheco, *Tree Between Two Walls*, Black Sparrow Press, 1969; (author of introduction) Daniel Drew, *The Book of Daniel Drew*, Frontier Press, 1969; *Some Business Recently Transacted in the White World* (short stories), Frontier Press, 1971; (translator) Cesar Abraham Vallejo, *Selected Poems of Cesar Vallejo*, Penguin, 1976.

SIDELIGHTS: Dorn spent several years at Black Mountain College, a North Carolina school founded in 1933 as a liberal alternative for teachers and students seeking a creative educational environment. Breaking away from tradition, those affiliated with the school created art and literature that had a profound affect on American culture even after the school closed in 1956. Over the years numerous noteworthy artists and writers, including Charles Olson, Robert Creely, Allen Ginsberg, Denise Levertov, William Carlos Williams, and Gary Snyder, were associated with the college as teachers, students, or contributors to Black Mountain publications.

Although poets who attended the college have often been grouped together as the "Black Mountain poets," Dorn told David Ossman that he has "been unable to find any similarity" among the writers who are associated with Black Mountain. Speculating on his own inclusion in the group, Dorn added: "I think I'm rightly associated with the Black Mountain 'school,' not because of the way I write, but because I was there. I always thought of the place not as a school at all, but as a climate in which people work closely together and talk."

While at Black Mountain, Dorn was admittedly influenced by Charles Olson. Several critics have commented that Dorn's use of free verse and breath-determined rhythms is similar to Olson's. For example, the *Virginia Quarterly Review* heralded Dorn as "an experienced and accomplished poet who has absorbed Olson, Williams, and Pound and moved beyond them." Marjorie Perloff, however, suggested that other than some "thematic links, Dorn is really quite unlike Olson; he is, for that matter, quite unlike any poet writing today." Dorn denied using "Olson's 'breath'" as a method of line division "because I'm not sure I understand that unit exactly, although I know what he's talking about." Dorn explained: "The way I write is really in clots of phrase. . . . When the individual line ceases to have energy for me . . . I usually break the line there."

Dorn's most influential and highly acclaimed work was the four-volume epic poem, *Slinger*, which evolved from his earlier poem, "An Idle Visitation." Calling the first volume, *Gunslinger*, "one of the fine poems of the decade," Charles Stein predicted that it was "the first part of what promises to be a major American narrative poem." Perloff later stated that the completed poem is "one of the masterpieces of contemporary poetry."

The epic is a fantasy about a demigod-cowboy, the poet-narrator, a madam of a saloon, and a talking horse named Claude Levi-Strauss, who travel southwest America in search of Howard Hughes, a symbol of everything that can and has gone wrong with the modern world. Although *Slinger* "tends to resist description," Donald Wesling observed that the poem "is 'about' how and why we spend money and words in this 'cosmological' place; about . . . surreal imagery, personifications, the texture of jokes, the paradoxical aspects of thinking . . . ; and about how a self or voice can be differentiated into a cluster of other selves."

In *Slinger*, Dorn cleverly mixes the jargon of junkies, Westerners, structuralists, and scientists to reflect the jumble of American speech. He intentionally frustrates the reader: syntax is ambiguous, punctuation is sparse, and puns, homonyms, and nonsense words become an integral part of conversation. Wesling declared that such frustration is "one of the pleasures of the poem when you finally discover the mechanism." Perloff pointed out that *Slinger*'s collage of language "perfectly embodies Dorn's theme that nothing is what it seems to be."

This poem and many of Dorn's other writings were set in the western states. In fact, he has referred to himself as "a poet of the West—not by nativity but by orientation." William J. Lockwood speculated that "the southwestern landscape would seem to supply to his creative imagination those elements of brightness, clarity, and austerity that correspond to the forms of his own mind and appear as the distinctive qualities of the best of his early poems."

In some of Dorn's earlier poetry, critics have commented that his "prosy manner and chopped-up lines" detract from the ideas he tries to present. Martin Dodsworth noted that although Dorn tackles important themes in *The North Atlantic Turbine,* "I kept on getting the feeling that he could argue it all much better if he weren't trying to write poetry at the same time." A *Times Literary Supplement* critic echoed those feelings in a review of *Geography,* suggesting that "Edward Dorn might do better to publish his fulminations against America . . . as prose."

Dorn's writing is nearly all socially and politically oriented. From his earlier studies of Shoshoni Indians and the transients near Puget Sound, to his reflections on the state of America in *Slinger,* Dorn's concern for his countrymen is evident. Peter Ackroyd declared that "Dorn has become the only plausible, political poet in America" because of "the quality of his response to public situations, not whether that response is 'right' or 'wrong.'" During the middle 1960's Dorn moved to England and "his work for a time grew overtly political, that is, preachy," noted Bill Zavatsky. "His (perhaps temporary) need to slam his reader over the head with politics is unfortunate, for all of Dorn's work is inherently political, needing no soapbox."

In Ackroyd's opinion, "Dorn's proper achievement has been to create single-handedly a language of public reference, and to have brought within the sphere of expressive language and poetic experience objects and feelings which had been, literally, *unimaginable* in those terms. It is in this context that he is one of the masters of our contemporary language."

CA INTERVIEWS THE AUTHOR
Edward Dorn was interviewed by telephone May 4, 1979, at the University of Colorado at Boulder, where he was a visiting professor of writing in the English department.

CA: Was it a coincidence that there were several writers with similar ideals at Black Mountain?

DORN: Yes. There were lots of people there throughout its history, and they were all noteworthy and peculiar for having been there at all. I've always thought that the whole usage of "Black Mountain Poets" only has an existence in the minds of the people who use it. I don't even know of such a thing myself.

CA: Is it just a convenient grouping?

DORN: I think it's pure convention—convention based on nothing. I don't notice writing that is cohesive enough as a group to demand that it be referred to as a school.

CA: Isn't it notable that you were all there at one time?

DORN: Well, I'll tell you one thing. I think Black Mountain as a school, irrespective of poets, denotes a certain value toward learning and the analysis of ideas. The perspective that I refer to as a school would refer to the whole school and its history and its conception and its principles and its various periods of authority and so forth—and not to poets,

necessarily. I certainly believe that it was a school, in the old sense.

CA: Charles Olson apparently was a great influence on you there. In what specific ways did he help you?

DORN: I think actually I was saying that at the same time. I think he made it possible for me to know how to value the school in that conceptual sense I was talking about just now. That was an education. In fact, that was my only education. So the institution's importance to me would be incalculable.

CA: Were there specific ways Olson could bring out the best in a writer?

DORN: Yes, I think so. It seems to me his habit and inclination was to run everything as wide as possible all over the lot all the time. In other words, the way he conveyed one's possibilities as a writer to the writer was to penetrate as deeply as possible every aspect of the linguistic reality. It wasn't ordered so much as intensified.

CA: You teach writing. Are you able to do that? Is your approach the same?

DORN: Well, no, I'm different, although naturally I share some attitudes with Olson; but for one thing, my ranges aren't actually so great, which tends to concentrate me a little more.

CA: In teaching itself or in writing?

DORN: In writing.

CA: Do you think that one can be taught to write?

DORN: I think one can be provoked to write.

CA: What do you mean by "provoked"?

DORN: I wouldn't say someone can't be taught to write, although I'd be inclined to say it. So that's why I would prefer to say "provoked," because it doesn't involve that question. And I believe it completely. But of course that presupposes an intelligence that's provokable.

CA: Do you have students who struggle very hard to write and just never seem to get there?

DORN: I think students have changed. Struggle has traditionally been linked with writing. I don't know whether it's proper that it should be or not, but I don't notice much struggle now. I think the things that seem easy are also the things that have the most market value.

CA: You've said that you felt it was important to be published by individuals rather than publishing houses. Why do you feel that?

DORN: Well, I said that in an introduction to my *Collected Poems.* But I don't particularly hold that view any longer, and in fact, I don't think it's important who you get published by if that's what you want to do.

CA: You have mostly been published by an individual—even the Collected Poems—*have you not?*

DORN: Yes, but actually Donald Allen is the most high-class editor in the country, really, and of much background experience. So he's not just any individual. The fact is that individuals are often a lot more able than "non-individuals." But all I mean by that is that when I came to write the introductory statement I was thinking about the background of my own work, and that's one of the things that I felt I could say which was true and a principle which I still honor. On the other hand, maybe it was so noticed or noticeable that I'd just like to add that it's only an idea about how that work came out and mainly has to do with my life in print. It's not necessarily anything I'd recommend or anything final, or anything definitive or about anybody.

CA: Can we discuss your poetry?

DORN: I'd rather say, since this is an interview, that the library at the University of California at San Diego (La Jolla) brought out an interview conducted by Steve Fredman last year [1978] that really brings all my positions and opinions up to date. It's a library publication, and it's quite a long interview. Also Donald Allen is just about to publish two volumes, *Views* and *Interviews,* which will catch all the statements I care to maintain for now.

CA: May I ask just one question about your poems? You've criticized America for several things: its imperialism, its carelessness with natural resources and the landscape, its treatment of minority groups. Are these still concerns of yours?

DORN: I take democracy very seriously, but on the other hand, it's a form of government that you have to change your mind about a lot because its form is protean, and its instinct, essentially, comes from a mob psychology. Unlike an adherent to a dogmatic position like Marxism, about which there is very little to change your mind, a democrat is liable to change his mind a lot. So none of those concerns and principles ever leave my mind much, but I vary my attitude according to the angles of perspective I'm able to get on them. Democracy literally has to be cracked on the head *all the time* to keep it in good condition. But all other forms are more or less sudden death.

CA: Have you been a large part of the tradition of street poetry and coffee house poetry in San Francisco?

DORN: I was around it. I lived in North Beach, and I hung out quite a lot with Jack Hirschman, who's really the doyen of North Beach literary cafe life, and delightfully so. I don't feel altogether comfortable in that atmosphere for reading, although I like to go myself to hear readings.

CA: Is that tradition still alive?

DORN: Last summer, which is the last time I knew anything about it, it was still going quite strong. You know, San Francisco is a city of poets. It's quite social in that sense.

CA: That must be a very nice atmosphere for a poet to work in.

DORN: It is. A lot of the time it is indeed. It's a spiritually satisfying city.

CA: There are many classical allusions in your work. Were you trained in the classics?

DORN: No, I was not. Absolutely not. It's quite superficial, of course, and it comes entirely from my own interests in reading over the years. Just trying to absorb as much of the subject as I could.

CA: What poets do you read?

DORN: I'm reading Keats right now. I read Jonson's poetry, and I've also been reading Leigh Hunt because I'm reading Keats. And I've been reading quite a lot of Wordsworth off and on recently. I'm just reading for what strikes me as the

most pleasure and beauty.

BIOGRAPHICAL/CRITICAL SOURCES: David Ossman, *The Sullen Art,* Corinth Books, 1963; *Times Literary Supplement,* January 27, 1966; *Illustrated London News,* May 6, 1967; *Hudson Review,* winter, 1967-68; *Listener,* February 1, 1968; *Poetry,* March, 1969; *Nation,* May 12, 1969; *Virginia Quarterly Review,* summer, 1969, autumn, 1970; *New Statesman,* August 21, 1970; Martin B. Duberman, *Black Mountain: An Exploration in Community,* Doubleday, 1973; *Spectator,* January 10, 1975; *New Republic,* April 24, 1976; *New York Times Book Review,* October 17, 1976; *Parnassus: Poetry in Review,* spring-summer, 1977; *Contemporary Literature,* winter, 1978; Steve Fredman, *Documents for New Poetry 1,* University of California, San Diego, 1978; Donald Allen, editor, *Interviews,* Four Seasons Foundation, 1979; *Contemporary Literary Criticism,* Volume 10, Gale, 1979; Allen, editor, *Views,* Four Seasons Foundation, 1980.

—*Sketch by Martha G. Winkel*
—*Interview by Jean W. Ross*

*   *   *

DOUGLAS, William O(rville)   1898-1980

OBITUARY NOTICE—See index for *CA* sketch: Born October 16, 1898, in Maine, Minn.; died January 19, 1980, in Washington, D.C. U.S. Supreme Court justice, educator, and writer. As a child, Douglas suffered from polio, and his classmates often taunted him about this affliction and about his family's poverty. This early experience helped develop in him a deep sympathy for the downtrodden, a quality which he often displayed during his thirty-six year stay on the U.S. Supreme Court. Those years, from 1939 to 1975, were fraught with controversy (twice his foes tried to impeach him), but many observers now regard Douglas as one of the finest justices in the Court's history. Although Douglas had several opportunities to run for political office, he turned them down, feeling that his position on the Court as a defender of civil rights, civil liberties, and the right of dissent was more important. His judicial opinions, which are esteemed for their clarity and eloquence, total 1,306. He also wrote a number of books on law, including *The Rule of Law in World Affairs, The Anatomy of Liberty,* and *The Bible and the Schools.* A world traveler, Douglas gave accounts of his journeys to other lands in such books as *Beyond the High Himalayas* and *Russian Journey.* In addition, he was the author of several works on conservation. Obituaries and other sources: *Current Biography,* Wilson, 1950; Sidney H. Asch, *Supreme Court and Its Great Justices,* Arco, 1971; Vern Countryman, *Judicial Record of Justice William O. Douglas,* Harvard University Press, 1974; *New Republic,* November 29, 1975; Catherine A. Barnes, *Men of the Supreme Court: Profiles of the Justices,* Facts on File, 1978; *Who's Who in America,* 40th edition, Marquis, 1978; *Washington Post,* January 20, 1980; *New York Times,* January 20, 1980.

*   *   *

DRABEK, Jan   1935-

PERSONAL: Born May 5, 1935, in Prague, Czechoslovakia; son of Jaroslav (a lawyer and journalist) and Jarmila (Kucerova) Drabek; married Joan M. Sanders (a university instructor), October 24, 1979; children: Katherine, Alexandra. *Education:* Attended Washington and Lee University, 1953-56; American University, B.A., 1960; University of Mysore, diploma, 1964; University of British Columbia, teaching certificate, 1966. *Politics:* "A fanatical democrat." *Religion:*

Protestant. *Home:* 3330 West King Edward, Vancouver, British Columbia, Canada V6S 1M3. *Agent:* Michael Hamilburg, Mitchell J. Hamilburg Agency, 292 South La Cienega Blvd., Suite 212, Beverly Hills, Calif. 90211.

CAREER: Washington Star, Washington, D.C., member of editorial staff, 1958-60; Radio Free Europe, Munich, West Germany, announcer, 1961-63; American Express Co., New York, N.Y., travel agent, 1964-65; Vancouver School Board, Vancouver, British Columbia, teacher, 1966-76; writer, 1976—. Worked in refugee resettlement in Vienna, Austria, 1961. *Military service:* U.S. Navy, 1956-58. *Member:* Canadian Authors Association, Writers Union of Canada, Council for Free Czechoslovakia, Czechoslovak National Association of Canada (vice-president). *Awards, honors:* Canada Council grant, 1978.

WRITINGS: Blackboard Odyssey (on education in Europe), J. J. Douglas, 1973; *Whatever Happened to Wenceslas?* (novel), Peter Martin, 1975; *Melvin the Weathermoose* (juvenile), Holt, 1976; *Report on the Death of Rosenkavalier* (novel; alternate Literary Guild selection), McClelland & Stewart, 1977; *The Lister Legacy* (novel), General Publishing, 1980; *The New Salisbury Statement* (novel), McClelland & Stewart, 1980. Television and radio writer (and narrator) for Canadian Broadcasting Corp. (CBC) and Radio Canada International. Contributor of stories and articles to magazines, including *Reader's Digest, Weekend, Canadian,* and *Malahat Review.*

SIDELIGHTS: Drabek writes: "I spent the war and postwar years in Prague, until 1948. After escaping with my family to West Germany, I lived in the United States, 1948-60, Austria and Germany, 1961-63, India, 1963-64, and New York, 1964-65. Since 1965 I have been living in Vancouver. I took two research trips for my books, each lasting several months: in 1972 through England and Europe, and in 1978 to New Zealand and the South Pacific.

"The ethnic consciousness and the awareness of the tragedy of foreign totalitarian rule in my native Czechoslovakia run through most of my work. Both of my major works of fiction have been translated into Czech and published."

*   *   *

DRAKE, David (Allen) 1945-

PERSONAL: Born September 24, 1945, in Dubuque, Iowa; son of Earle Charles (a maintenance foreman) and Maxine (Schneider) Drake; married Joanne Kammiller (a teacher), June 5, 1967; children: Jonathan. *Education:* University of Iowa, B.A., 1967; Duke University, J.D., 1972. *Home address:* P.O. Box 904, Chapel Hill, N.C. 27514. *Agent:* Kirby McCauley Ltd., 60 East 42nd St., New York, N.Y. 10017.

CAREER: Town of Chapel Hill, N.C., assistant town attorney, 1972—. Partner of Carcosa (publisher). *Military service:* U.S. Army, 1969-71; served in Viet Nam and Cambodia. *Member:* International Fortean Organization, Science Fiction Writers of America, Phi Beta Kappa.

WRITINGS: Hammer's Slammers (science fiction), Ace Books, 1979; *The Dragon Lord* (fantasy novel), Putnam, 1979. Contributor of more than forty stories to magazines. Assistant editor of *Whispers.*

WORK IN PROGRESS: Research for a historical novel; short stories.

SIDELIGHTS: Drake writes: "I am a military history buff, though with no particular affection for the military as an institution. (I was drafted out of law school to serve as an interrogator in Viet Nam and Cambodia.) I tend to write on

themes of violence and to explore interplays between society on the one hand and personal values on the other; that is, friendship, love, honor, et cetera. I try to be a careful writer, seeing myself as a craftsman, rather than an artist. While writing is a hobby with me, I am dead damned serious about it, as much as any golfer or tournament bridge-player ever was about his hobby."

*   *   *

DRANE, John (William) 1946-

PERSONAL: Born October 17, 1946, in Hartlepool, England; son of John Wallace (an interior decorator) and Marjorie (Ireland) Drane; married Olive Mary Fleming, September 16, 1967; children: Andrew James Jonathan, Mark Samuel Paul. *Education:* University of Aberdeen, M.A. (with first class honors), 1969; Victoria University of Manchester, Ph.D., 1972. *Home:* Louise Villa, Fountain Rd., Bridge of Allan, Stirlingshire FK9 4AJ, Scotland. *Office:* Department of Religious Studies, University of Stirling, Stirling FK9 4LA, Scotland.

CAREER: Ordained Baptist minister, 1969; pastor of Baptist church in Manchester, England, 1969-73; University of Stirling, Stirling, Scotland, lecturer in religious studies, 1973—. *Member:* Society of Authors, Society for New Testament Studies, Tyndale Fellowship for Biblical Research.

WRITINGS: Paul: Libertine or Legalist?, Allenson, 1975; *Paul: An Illustrated Documentary,* Lion, 1976, Harper, 1977; (contributor) I. H. Marshall, editor, *New Testament Interpretation,* Eerdmans, 1977; (editor with Pat Alexander, David Field, and Alan Millard) *The Lion Encyclopedia of the Bible,* Eerdmans, 1978; *Jesus and the Four Gospels,* Harper, 1979. Contributor to *New Bible Dictionary Revised.* Contributor to religious journals, including *Christianity Today.*

WORK IN PROGRESS: A commentary on Galatians, publication by Harper expected in 1982; a book on techniques for understanding the Bible, publication by Lion expected in 1982.

SIDELIGHTS: Drane commented: "Much of my writing has simply grown out of my everyday work, teaching the New Testament to university students. But I have also consciously aimed my writings at the person who is not committed to any religious faith, but who is curious to understand the Bible, and to know what modern theologians think about it. I hope that my writings will aid the Christian church in its outreach programs, and with *Paul* in a dozen foreign language editions (including an Italian one with a Roman Catholic imprimatur), I can lay some claim to success. But my books are not simply platitudes for the pious. In that I am a committed Christian, I suppose my work is conservative, but in most ways I like to think that I adopt a radical open stance toward the Bible, allowing it to speak to me, rather than putting my own preconceived notions onto its pages."

AVOCATIONAL INTERESTS: Beekeeping.

*   *   *

DRASKOVICH, Slobodan M. 1910-

PERSONAL: Born April 18, 1910, in Belgrade, Serbia (now part of Yugoslavia); came to the United States in 1947, naturalized citizen, 1956; son of Milorad (a member of the Serbian cabinet) and Jovanka (Milanovich) Draskovich; married, June, 1938 (divorced, 1945). *Education:* University of Belgrade, degree in law, 1930; University of Munich, doctorate in economics (magna cum laude), 1933. *Religion:* Serbian Orthodox. *Residence:* Chicago, Ill. *Office:* 448 Barry Ave., Chicago, Ill. 60657.

CAREER: University of Belgrade, Belgrade, Yugoslavia, assistant professor, 1935-40, associate professor of economics and sociology, 1940-41; *Srpska Borba* ("The Serbian Struggle"; weekly newspaper), Chicago, Ill., chief editor, 1946—. Political editor of weekly newspaper, *Srpski Glas* ("The Serbian Voice"), 1939-40. Secretary general of Serbian Cultural Club of Yugoslavia, 1939-41; member of Institute of National Defense of Ministry of War (Belgrade), 1940-41; member of Serbian Central National Committee (Chicago), 1947-53; president of Serbian Cultural Club "St. Sava," 1951—. Testified before various committees of U.S. Congress on problems pertaining to Communist strategy and tactics. Lecturer at universities, army groups, church groups, and service clubs; has made numerous guest appearances on radio and television programs. *Military service:* Yugoslav Army, Infantry, prisoner of war in Italy and Germany, 1941-45; became lieutenant. *Awards, honors:* Invited by University of Wyoming to donate papers to university's Archive of Contemporary History, 1970; elected life member of International Social Science Honor Society, 1973, for "outstanding scholastic achievement"; received Annual Bella V. Dodd Memorial Award from New York County Committee of Conservative party of State of New York, 1978, for "service to the people and government of the United States of America by pioneering in the delineation of the Communist maneuver known as 'Titoism.'"

WRITINGS: Srpski narod i srpska politica (title means "The Serbian People and Serbian Politics"), [Germany], 1947, 2nd revised edition, Serbian Cultural Club "St. Sava," 1974; *Tito, Moscow's Trojan Horse,* Regnery, 1956; *Kojim putem?* (title means "At the Crossroads"), Serbian Cultural Club "St. Sava," 1967; *Will America Surrender?,* Devin-Adair, 1973. Also author of *History of Yugoslavia, 1918-1941* and *Liberalism and Democracy in Postwar Europe,* both manuscripts destroyed by prisoner-of-war camp authorities during World War II. Contributor of articles on economic and political subjects to periodicals and newspapers, including *Saturday Evening Post, National Review,* and *Modern Age.*

WORK IN PROGRESS: Their War and Our Peace (tentative title), "pertaining to the policy of the free world, headed by the United States, toward the Communist world, headed by the Soviet Union," completion expected in 1980; *The Problem of SALT,* "viewed as a preeminently political problem," completion expected in 1980; several projects in Serbian.

SIDELIGHTS: Tito, Moscow's Trojan Horse and *Will America Surrender?* comprise the first two volumes of a trilogy to be completed by the work in progress, *Their War and Our Peace.* The opening work, *Tito,* was the first study of Titoism as a phenomenon of the Communist world strategy and contended that the Yugoslav leader was still, regardless of all differences with the U.S.S.R., a most active member of the Communist world movement, working, in somewhat different ways, for the same goal as Moscow. "Mr. Draskovich's book is the work of a passionate Serbian patriot who is a keen student of communism and a deep unhappy observer of Western, especially American, foreign policy," wrote E. S. Pisko of the *Christian Science Monitor.* The second volume, *Will America Surrender?,* is a "critique of America's response to Communist global political warfare," commented a *National Review* critic, and "exposes the consequences of the view that avoiding nuclear war is the chief concern proper to policy." Draskovich, who maintains that the United States is engaged in a policy of surrender to communism, recommends a new strategy, one that promotes U.S. self-assertion and a global political war against communism.

Draskovich told *CA:* "To me there is no more important problem in the world than communism, challenging the free world in all spheres of human activity and contemptuously denying all the values of civilization. The true and decisive battle is above all spiritual (not military, economic, or scientific). It will be decided in the realm of the spirit and of the mind. That is the broad framework of my writing. I write because I believe that the word is mightier than the sword or the nuclear bomb or any other material force. I write because I feel that I can contribute to shape and develop the thinking and spiritual awareness needed to fight and win the good battle.

"What we need is to assert America, wage a political war against communism, stand by our friends and allies, and rally all freedom-loving people in the world (free and enslaved) in the struggle against slavery and oppression. Only so can we fatally weaken the Communists, put them on the road to inevitable defeat, and open unsuspected avenues toward a world of freedom and justice for all nations."

BIOGRAPHICAL/CRITICAL SOURCES: Christian Science Monitor, May 21, 1957; *Springfield Republican,* May 26, 1957; *New York Herald Tribune Book Review,* July 14, 1957; *Catholic World,* August, 1957; *American Academy of Politics and Social Science: Annals,* September, 1957; *Best Sellers,* April 1, 1973; *National Review,* March 15, 1974.

*   *   *

DRINKLE, Ruth Wolfley 1903-

PERSONAL: Born February 23, 1903, in Prospect, Ohio; daughter of Harvey Wilson (in business) and Mary (Wieland) Wolfley; married Charles H. Drinkle (an attorney), February 4, 1928; children: Charles Henry, Jr., Mary Alice Drinkle Kuhn. *Education:* Ohio Wesleyan University, B.A., 1924. *Home:* 110 West Mulberry St., Lancaster, Ohio 43130. *Office:* Fairfield Heritage Association, 105 East Wheeling St., Lancaster, Ohio 43130.

CAREER: High school teacher in Massillon, Ohio, 1925-28; founder of Fairfield Heritage Association, Lancaster, Ohio, 1963, president, 1963-64, honorary president, 1964—. Volunteer worker in community and educational activities. *Member:* National Trust for Historic Preservation, Ohio Historical Society, Delta Gamma.

WRITINGS: Heritage of Architecture and Arts of Fairfield County, Ohio, Fairfield Heritage Association, 1979. Co-editor of *Fairfield Heritage Quarterly.*

SIDELIGHTS: In 1963 Ruth Drinkle became a founder and first president of the Fairfield Heritage Association in Fairfield County, Ohio. During the last fifteen years the group has sparked local interest in historical preservation by purchasing and restoring an 1830 Georgian house for use as a county museum and center for community activities and by spearheading "Downtown Preservation" and numerous county projects. In 1970, under the guidance of the Ohio Historical Society, the group conducted a survey of all structures in Fairfield County more than one hundred years old.

Drinkle told *CA:* "To arouse awareness I developed a slide program of local architecture and furnishings which was presented to more than one hundred organizations and schools. In 1976 I was invited by Ohio University, Lancaster, to help formulate their Bicentennial project, and wrote the outline for a sound-slide history of Fairfield County, which was funded by the Gand Foundation of Cleveland. This book was written to put in permanent form the results of former research. It presents a microcosm of nineteenth-century architecture, all found within the borders of one midwest county, illustrating that 'architecture and furniture are history in its most tangible form.'"

Heritage of Architecture and Arts of Fairfield County, Ohio contains four hundred photographs of nineteenth-century architectural forms found within the county. Included are exteriors with details of masonry, wood, and stone carving, and interiors with fine furniture and other work of local craftsmen. Mary Louise Baker noted that Drinkle's commentary is "direct, informative and gracefully presented. . . . This masterful volume is not just a catalog, but a celebration of a proud and unique culture."

BIOGRAPHICAL/CRITICAL SOURCES: Columbus Dispatch, February 18, 1979; *Ohio Antiques Review,* April, 1979; *Ohioana Quarterly,* autumn, 1979.

* * *

DUFFY, Edmund 1899-1962

OBITUARY NOTICE: Born March 1, 1899, in Jersey City, N.J.; died September 13, 1962. Cartoonist. During his twenty-four years with the *Baltimore Sun,* Duffy won Pulitzer Prizes for his political cartoons in 1931, 1934, and 1940. The prize-winning cartoon for the last award depicted Hitler with his right hand outstretched and dripping in blood, labeled "the peace offer," and his left hand holding torn papers marked "broken promises, treaty and no more territorial demands." His cartoons also appeared in other newspapers and periodicals, including *Saturday Evening Post, New York Evening Post, Brooklyn Daily Eagle, New York Tribune,* and *Collier's.* Obituaries and other sources: *Current Biography,* Wilson, 1940, November, 1962; *New York Times,* September 13, 1962; *Time,* September 21, 1962; *Newsweek,* September 24, 1962.

* * *

DUNCAN, Chester 1913-

PERSONAL: Born May 4, 1913, in Strasbourg, Saskatchewan, Canada; son of Alexander Gladstone (a banker) and Isabella Madge (Winchester) Duncan; married Adah Margaret Elwick, May 29, 1943; children: Alexe, Mark, Laurie. *Education:* University of Manitoba, B.A., 1934, M.A., 1939; further graduate study at University of Toronto, 1945-46. *Politics:* Socialist. *Religion:* Anglican. *Home:* 295 Ashland Ave., Winnipeg, Manitoba, Canada R3L 1L5.

CAREER: University of Manitoba, Winnipeg, lecturer, 1942-46, assistant professor, 1946-60, associate professor, 1960-74, professor of English, 1974-78, professor emeritus, 1978—. Musician and composer; music teacher. Critic on Canadian Broadcasting Corp. programs, "Critically Speaking," "The Passing Show," "In Town and Out," and "Arts National."

WRITINGS: Wanna Fight, Kid? (autobiographical essays), Queenston House Press, 1975.

Work represented in anthologies, including *Winnipeg Stories,* Queenston House Press, 1974.

WORK IN PROGRESS: A book of songs; *Shorts and Longs; or, The Long and Short of It,* "a group of essays, mainly on the inter-relationships between music and literature."

SIDELIGHTS: Duncan comments: "In my retirement, which was mandatory, I am interested mainly in musical composition. I have had a number of commissions and a fair number of performances. I write in the genre of art-song."

DUNNING, John 1942-

PERSONAL: Born January 9, 1942, in Brooklyn, N.Y.; son of Elmo Michael and Helen (Hulst) Dunning; married Helen Rose Korupp (a caseworker), May 30, 1969; children: James, Katharine. *Education:* Attended school in Charleston, S.C. *Home and office:* 4457 South Eagle Circle, Aurora, Colo. 80015. *Agent:* Harold Ober Associates, 40 East 49th St., New York, N.Y. 10017.

CAREER: Pittsburgh Plate Glass and William M. Bird & Co., both Charleston, S.C., glass cutter, 1959-64; groom for horse trainer Lawrence Kidd, Idaho Falls, Idaho, 1964-65; groom for various horse trainers in California, 1965; *Denver Post,* Denver, Colo., clerk, 1966, reporter, 1966-69; freelance writer, 1970-74; *Denver Post,* investigative reporter, 1974; writer, 1974—. Press secretary for various political campaigns, including Pat Schroeder, U.S. congresswoman from Denver, and Dale Tooley, Denver district attorney; part-time instructor at University of Denver and Metropolitan State College; radio show producer and host, KFML, 1972-78, KADX, 1978—; worked on the sound track for the motion picture "Thieves Like Us," 1973. *Member:* Colorado Authors' League. *Awards, honors:* Colorado Association for Retarded Children award, 1974, for *Denver Post* series exposing conditions in state homes for the retarded.

WRITINGS: The Holland Suggestions (Mystery Guild selection), Bobbs-Merrill, 1975; *Tune In Yesterday* (nonfiction), Prentice-Hall, 1976; *Looking for Ginger North,* Fawcett, 1980; *Denver,* New York Times Co., 1980.

WORK IN PROGRESS: A Civil War novel; another suspense novel, publication by Fawcett expected in 1981.

SIDELIGHTS: Dunning told *CA:* "Having no formal education (I quit school in the tenth grade to join the army), I found it tough getting the kind of jobs I wanted. I've always wanted to write, but no newspaper would touch me. I read constantly, even took a professional speedreading course, but that's no substitute for degrees on a resume. One frustrated city editor in Sacramento, who badly needed help, took one look at my 'experience' and said, 'God, why do they send me guys like this?' Eventually, after pestering the personnel director for several years, I landed at the *Denver Post* as a file clerk in the library. From there I was able to move up and into writing. First I wrote book reviews and later some news stories. Finally a great city editor named John Snyder gave me a job. After my first year, Snyder put me onto the *Post*'s three-man investigative team.

"I've learned that to stay alive as a writer, you have to do a lot of things in addition to writing. Once, interviewing University of Denver chancellor Maurice Mitchell for the *Christian Science Monitor,* I found out that Mitchell had never graduated from college. How, I asked him, can you be chancellor at a university that requires doctorates of its professors if you don't have a degree of your own? He said that when his lack of education became a factor in his life, he went to his local college and asked to teach a course. 'Once you've taught something, they never question your competence in that area again.' So I started teaching a course, which I still do on occasion, at the University of Denver. In addition, I've taught journalism courses at Metropolitan State College."

Dunning is also an avid collector of old-time radio tapes. He has one of the most extensive radio libraries in the country, with more than fifteen thousand old radio shows on tape. This collection of six thousand hours of radio history includes such classics as "Fibber Magee and Molly," "Fred Allen," "Inner Sanctum," and complete seasons of "The

Jack Benny Show." Dunning also owns hundreds of newscasts, including six hours of news coverage of the D day invasion and dress rehearsals from the old "Gunsmoke" series.

"My interest in radio history led to a job on a feature motion picture, 'Thieves Like Us,' released by United Artists in 1974 and directed by Robert Altman of 'M*A*S*H,' 'Nashville,' and 'McCabe and Mrs. Miller' fame. Altman had heard of my interest in radio, and since his film was about bank robbers holed up in Mississippi in 1937, he wanted to score it with old shows. I went to Altman's Lion's Gate Films office and worked there for five weeks, writing a few simulated newscasts that were used in part in the film."

The Holland Suggestions has been translated into German.

BIOGRAPHICAL/CRITICAL SOURCES: Denver Post, March 25, 1973; *Houston Chronicle,* February 23, 1976; *Rocky Mountain News "Now,"* February 29, 1976; *Denver,* June, 1978; *Rocky Mountain News,* March 9, 1979.

*   *   *

DURANTE, James Francis   1893-1980
(Jimmy Durante)

OBITUARY NOTICE: Born February 10, 1893, in New York, N.Y.; died January 29, 1980, in Santa Monica, Calif., of pneumonitis. Entertainer and author of *Night Clubs.* Commonly referred to as the "Ol' Schnozzola," Durante was best known for his large nose and raspy delivery. Durante began playing the piano in dance halls and saloons at seventeen. It was not until he teamed with Lou Clayton though, in 1923, that he was bound for greater success. They performed together throughout the decade in nightclubs and on Broadway. With Clayton, Durante managed to develop his comedic skills as well as his musical ones. By 1930 he was in demand in Hollywood, so the act broke up and Clayton became Durante's manager. Durante made a number of popular films, including "Jumbo" and "Red, Hot and Blue," and quickly became one of America's favorite entertainers. Though he suffered a brief lapse in success toward the end of the 1930's, Durante still managed to parlay his early popularity into a career that also embraced radio and television. He remained active until suffering a stroke in 1972. Durante consistently ended his performances, whether for radio, television, or the stage, with the closing, "Good night Mrs. Calabash, wherever you are." Obituaries and other sources: *Current Biography,* Wilson, 1946, March, 1980; Gene Fowler, *Schnozzola: The Story of Jimmy Durante,* Viking, 1951; *The ASCAP Biographical Dictionary of Composers, Authors, and Publishers,* American Society of Composers, Authors, and Publishers, 1966; *The Biographical Encyclopaedia and Who's Who of the American Theatre,* James Heineman, 1966; *Celebrity Register,* 3rd edition, Simon & Schuster, 1973; *Who's Who in America,* 40th edition, Marquis, 1978; *New York Times,* January 30, 1980; *Newsweek,* February 11, 1980; *Time,* February 11, 1980.

*   *   *

DURANTE, Jimmy
See DURANTE, James Francis

*   *   *

DYE, H(ershel) Allan   1931-

PERSONAL: Born July 21, 1931, in Union City, Ind.; son of Herschell Llewelyn (a mechanic) and Ruth (Risley) Dye; married Marcia Gettinger, June 30, 1957 (died October,

1966); married Celeste Lombardi, October 4, 1969 (divorced October, 1973); children: (first marriage) Leigh Ann, Christy Jo. *Education:* Ball State University, B.S., 1953, M.A., 1959; Purdue University, Ph.D., 1964. *Residence:* West Lafayette, Ind. *Office:* Department of Education, Purdue University, West Lafayette, Ind. 47907.

CAREER: Hardy Manufacturing Corp., purchasing agent, 1955-57; teacher at public schools in Dayton, Ohio, 1957-58; Ball State University, Muncie, Ind., curricular adviser and assistant dean of men, 1958-61; Purdue University, West Lafayette, Ind., instructor, 1963-64, assistant professor, 1964-73, associate professor of education, 1973—, director of Counseling and Guidance Center, 1976—. Visiting lecturer at University of Michigan, summer, 1968. Private practice of psychology. Director of workshops; member of Horizons. *Military service:* U.S. Army, 1953-55. *Member:* American Personnel and Guidance Association, Association for Specialists in Group Work (chairperson of publication committee, 1978-79; president-elect, 1978-79), Association for Counselor Educators and Supervisors, American College Personnel Association, American Psychological Association, Planned Parenthood Association (member of advisory board, 1968-70). *Awards, honors:* Service award from Association for Specialists in Group Work, 1977.

WRITINGS: Fundamental Group Procedures for Counselors (monograph), Houghton, 1968; (editor with Richard C. Diedrich) *Fundamentals of Guidance,* 2nd edition (Dye was not associated with earlier edition), Houghton, 1976; (with H. L. Hackney) *Gestalt Approaches to Counseling* (monograph), Houghton, 1975. Contributor to education and guidance journals.

SIDELIGHTS: Dye commented: "I am fascinated by human behavior and am particularly attracted to changing nonproductive behavior. Specifically, my interests are in learning and teaching, both individual and group counseling. I regard these as the most exciting and satisfying activities I could possibly be engaged in."

*   *   *

DYKEMAN, Richard M(ills)   1943-

PERSONAL: Born January 3, 1943, in Seattle, Wash.; son of Glenn H. and Carol (Taylor) Dykeman; married Winnifred Saroch (a musician), October 26, 1975; children: Marcus Andrew, Jeffrey Briggs. *Education:* University of Washington, Seattle, B.A., 1971. *Politics:* Republican. *Religion:* Protestant. *Home:* 237 Anchorage Court, Annapolis, Md. 21401. *Office:* Creative Communications Consultants, 800 18th St. N.W., Suite 600, Washington, D.C. 20006.

CAREER: Free-lance writer, 1973-75; U.S. Congress, Washington, D.C., member of staff, 1975-76; free-lance writer and editor, 1976-77; Opticians Association of America, Washington, D.C., associate editor of *Dispensing Optician,* 1977—. President of Creative Communications Consultants. *Member:* Ripon Society (member of national board of governors), Providence Community Association, Toastmasters (president).

WRITINGS: (Contributor) Clifford W. Brown, Jr., editor, *Jaws of Victory,* Little, Brown, 1974; (editor and contributor) *Financing the 1972 Election,* Heath, 1975. Editor of *Layman Speaks.*

WORK IN PROGRESS: Teaching manuals for U.S. Foreign Service Institute of U.S. Department of State; a political novel.

SIDELIGHTS: Dykeman comments: "Writing has always

been a release—an opportunity to sort out the confusion of daily existence—a kind of sacred counselor. I chose early to make a living as a writer and have sought many mediocre assignments in pursuit of family survival. I feel largely unfulfilled as a writer—but I predict that will change and perhaps sooner than I think. Each new assignment, mundane or not, adds a new dimension to cumulative skills. The day will come when all this experience forms the foundation for a 'successful writer.'"

E

EASTMAN, Robert E. 1913-

PERSONAL: Born April 29, 1913, in Battle Creek, Mich.; son of Roy Oliver (a researcher) and Fannie (Garton) Eastman; married Anne S. Strom, January 14, 1940; children: Spencer, Robert, Stephanie, Victoria Eastman Ohlandt. *Education:* Graduated from Ohio Wesleyan University, 1935. *Home:* 351 Palmetto Point, John's Island, Vero Beach, Fla. 32960. *Agent:* Clyde Taylor, 34 Perry St., New York, N.Y. 10014.

CAREER: NBC-Radio, New York City, in sales and program executive, 1937-40; Blue Network, New York City, in sales, 1940-41; John Blair & Co., New York City, executive vice-president, 1942-57; ABC-Radio, New York City, network president, 1957-58; Robert E. Eastman & Co., New York City, founder and chief executive officer, 1958-73; writer, 1973—. Owner of Vermont Arabian Horse Farm, 1966-72. Past member of board of directors of Radio Advertising Bureau. *Member:* John's Island Country Club (member of board of directors), Grandfather Golf and Country Club, Vero Beach Country Club, Green Mountain Horse Association (member of board of trustees).

WRITINGS: Pendulum, Harcourt, 1979.

WORK IN PROGRESS: Three novels: *Punch Catterson's Cache, The Archer,* and *The Rider.*

SIDELIGHTS: Eastman comments: "Writing is a second career. During my thirty years in the broadcasting business, writing was one of my principal tools. Now I enjoy writing, drawing from the experience of a rich life. My younger son is the world's leading archer, and this will provide the background for a quasi-biographical novel, *The Archer.* I am myself an experienced equestrian. This will feed a future novel, *The Rider.*"

*   *   *

EBERHART, Dikkon 1946-

PERSONAL: Born October 30, 1946, in Boston, Mass.; son of Richard G. (a poet) and Elizabeth (Butcher) Eberhart; married Channa Alperin (an editor), March 6, 1976; children: Lena Elizabeth. *Education:* Dartmouth College, B.A., 1968; Pacific School of Religion, M.A. and M.Div., both 1972; Graduate Theological Union, Berkeley, Calif., Ph.D., 1980. *Address:* RFD Camden, Me. 04843.

CAREER: Teacher at private academy in Thetford, Vt.,

1968-69; assistant headmaster at private academy in East Burke, Vt., 1972-75; Harry's Restaurant, Camden, Me., first cook, 1978—.Worked at various times as actor in summer stock, cab driver, sailor, carpenter, gardener, and bookstore clerk.

WRITINGS: On the Verge (novel), Stemmer House, 1979.

WORK IN PROGRESS: A historical novel set in the sixth century, publication by Stemmer House expected in 1980; a contemporary novel set in Maine, publication by Stemmer House expected in 1981 or 1982.

SIDELIGHTS: Eberhart writes: "Being raised in a literary family made the desire to write ambiguous. For ten years or so, I wondered whether this was learned habit or innate. I no longer concern myself with this inner debate, freed from it by the pleasure of having published a book of my own. Fortunately, the book was not published before I was old enough to be my father's friend.

"I am interested in the land: the way it works, looks, feels, and what has happened on it, and travel, with the object of exploring the land. I have crossed the United States fourteen times, up and down, following the trails of explorers, consciously or unconsciously, stirred by climbing in the Wind River Range, the Sangre de Cristo range, and the California Coastal Range. I like the light in the mountains."

Eberhart's first novel, *On the Verge,* is the first-person narrative of Noah, a young man seeking self-reliance and solitude in the woods of Vermont. Poet-novelist James Dickey commented: "This remarkably sensitive novel is not only a beautifully written evocation of nature, but a frightening look at the illegitimate refuge that nature, in our day, has become for those who wish to use it as a retreat from responsibility, an excuse for not taking on the human commitments that a full life requires.... *On the Verge* is a novel that needed to be written, and it is good that a writer as perceptive and incisive as Dikkon Eberhart was around to write it." Another reviewer, Philip Corwin, called the book "a lyrical and very private novel, refreshingly unpolitical. At times the tone and language seem calculatedly naive and too consciously poetic, but those are minor flaws in an otherwise invigorating performance."

AVOCATIONAL INTERESTS: Ships, sailing, history in general (especially of the ancient Near East), history of exploration.

BIOGRAPHICAL/CRITICAL SOURCES: Christian Science Monitor, July 5, 1979.

EDELEN, Georges 1924-

PERSONAL: Born July 18, 1924, in Great Lakes, Ill.; son of John R. (in U.S. Navy) and Suzanne (a secretary; maiden name, Keller) Edelen; married Virginia Rhinelander, June 29, 1957; children: Susan, Philip, Frederick. *Education:* Georgetown University, B.S., 1949; Harvard University, M.A., 1953, Ph.D., 1955. *Religion:* Roman Catholic. *Home:* 3710 Leonard Springs Rd., Bloomington, Ind. 47401. *Office:* Department of English, Indiana University, Bloomington, Ind. 47401.

CAREER: Harvard University, Cambridge, Mass., instructor in English, 1955-58; Indiana University, Bloomington, assistant professor, 1958-64, associate professor, 1964-68, professor of English, 1968—. *Military service:* U.S. Army Air Forces, 1943-46; became sergeant. *Member:* Modern Language Association of America.

WRITINGS: (Editor) Harrison's *"Description of England,"* Cornell University Press, 1968; (editor) Hooker's *"Laws of Ecclesiastical Polity,"* Books I-IV, Harvard University Press, 1977.

WORK IN PROGRESS: A biography of Richard Hooker, publication expected in 1985.

*   *   *

EGREMONT, Max 1948-

PERSONAL: Born April 21, 1948, in London, England; son of John (a member of House of Lords) and Pamela (Wyndham-Quin) Egremont; married Caroline Nelson, April 15, 1978; children: Jessica. *Education:* Christ Church, Oxford, B.A., 1971, M.A., 1975. *Home:* Petworth House, Petworth, Sussex, England. *Agent:* Diana Avebury, Strathmore Literary Agency, 34 Cathcart Rd., London S.W.10, England.

CAREER: Associated with Crowell, Collier, and Macmillan publishing companies, London, England, 1970-72; farmer and writer, 1972—. *Awards, honors:* First book award from *Yorkshire Post,* 1977, for *The Cousins.*

WRITINGS: The Cousins (about Wilfred Blunt and George Wyndham), Collins, 1977; *Balfour* (biography of Arthur James Balfour), Collins, 1980. Contributor to magazines and newspapers, including *Books and Bookmen, Encounter,* and *Spectator.*

WORK IN PROGRESS: A general book on the customs and thought of Edwardian England.

*   *   *

EICH, Guenter 1907-1971
(Erich Guenter)

OBITUARY NOTICE: Born February 1, 1907, in Lebus on the Oder, Germany; died in 1972 in Salzburg, Austria. Poet and playwright. A pioneer of modern German radio plays, Eich's works were noted for their terse, abstract, and dream-like qualities. His poetry, inspired by everyday objects and events, was also influential in post-World War II German literature. Eich's most successful radio plays were "Das festliche Fahr," "Die Maedchen von Viterbo," and "Allah hat hundert." A collection of his radio plays written between 1950 and 1964 was published as *Fuenfzehn Hoerspiele.* Obituaries and other sources: *Encyclopedia of World Literature in the Twentieth Century,* updated edition, Ungar, 1967; *The Penguin Companion to European Literature,* McGraw, 1969; Egbert Krispyn, *Guenter Eich,* Twayne, 1971; *Cassell's Encyclopaedia of World Literature,* revised edition,

Morrow, 1973; *The International Who's Who,* Europa, 1974; *The Oxford Companion to German Literature,* Clarendon Press, 1976.

*   *   *

EICHELBERGER, Clark M(ell) 1896-1980

OBITUARY NOTICE: Born July 29, 1896, in Freeport, Ill.; died January 26, 1980, in Manhattan, N.Y. Association executive and author. Throughout his life, Eichelberger crusaded for the aims of the old League of Nations and for his own personal credo: "That all the men, in all the lands, may live out their lives in freedom from fear and want." He began as a midwest officer of the League of Nations Association in 1929, and became the national director of the organization when its name was changed to the American Association for the United Nations in 1934. For thirty years Eichelberger remained at this post, seeking to garner support and understanding for the United Nations among the American public. His efforts on behalf of the organization included lectures, radio broadcasts, and a series of books, the last entitled *Organizing the Peace: A Personal History of the Founding of the United Nations.* Obituaries and other sources: *Current Biography,* Wilson, 1947, March, 1980; *Who's Who in America,* 40th edition, Marquis, 1978; *New York Times,* January 27, 1980.

*   *   *

ELIS, Islwyn Ffowc 1924-

PERSONAL: Birth-given name, Islwyn Foulkes Ellis; name is pronounced *Iss*-lou-in Foulke *El*-lis; born November 17, 1924, in Wrexham, Wales; son of Edward Ivor (a farmer) and Catherine (Kenrick) Ellis; married Eirlys R. Owen, October 28, 1950; children: Sian (Mrs. Amode Mohamed Iqbal Lado). *Education:* University of Wales, University College of North Wales, B.A., 1946; Aberystwyth Theological College, B.D., 1949; also attended Bala Theological College, 1949-50. *Politics:* Plaid Cymru (Welsh National Party). *Home:* Pengwern, Falcondale Dr., Lampeter, Dyfed, Wales. *Office:* Department of Welsh, St. David's University College, University of Wales, Lampeter, Dyfed, Wales.

CAREER: Ordained Presbyterian minister, 1950; pastor of Llanfair and Meifod churches in Montgomeryshire, Wales, 1950-54, and Newborough church in Anglesey, Wales, 1954-56; free-lance writer and broadcaster, 1956-63; Trinity College, Carmarthen, Wales, lecturer in Welsh, 1963-68; Welsh Books Council, Aberystwyth, Dyfed, Wales, literary director, 1968-71; free-lance writer and broadcaster, 1971-75; University of Wales, St. David's University College, Lampeter, lecturer in modern Welsh literature, 1975—. Member of Board of Celtic Studies and National Eisteddfod Court. *Member:* Welsh Academy, Welsh Writers Union, Honorary Society of Cymmrodorion. *Awards, honors:* Gold medal for prose from National Eisteddfod of Wales, 1951, for ten essays subsequently included in *Cyn oeri'r gwaed;* prize from Arts Council of Great Britain, 1962, for *Tabyrddau'r Babongo.*

WRITINGS: Cyn oeri'r gwaed (essays; title means "Before the Blood Cools"), Gomer, 1952; *Cysgod y cryman* (novel; title means "Shadow of the Sickle"), Gomer, 1953; *Ffenestri tua'r gwyll* (novel; title means "Windows Towards the Dusk"), Gomer, 1955; *Yn ol i Leifior* (novel; title means "Return to Lleifior"), Gomer, 1956; *Wythnos yng nghymru fydd* (political novel; title means "A Week in the Wales to Be"), Plaid Cymru, 1957; *Blas y cynfyd* (novel; title means "A Taste of the Pre-World"), Gomer, 1958.

Tabyrddau'r Babongo (novel; title means "Drums of the Babongo"), Gomer, 1961; *Y blaned dirion* (science fiction novel; title means "The Gentle Planet"), Gomer, 1968; *Y gromlech yn yr haidd* (novel; title means "The Cromlech in the Barley"), Gomer, 1970; *Eira mawr* (novel; title means "The Big Snow"), Gomer, 1971; *Harris* (play; first produced in Harlech, Wales, at Theatr Ardudwy, November 5, 1973), Gomer, 1973; *Marwydos* (stories; title means "Embers"), Gomer, 1974; *Daniel Owen*, University of Wales Press, in press.

Editor: *Edward Tegla Davies*, Brython Press, 1956; *Storiau'r deffro* (stories; title means "Stories of the Awakening"), Plaid Cymru, 1959; (with Gwyn Jones; also contributor) *Twenty-Five Welsh Short Stories*, Oxford University Press, 1971.

Author of ten radio musicals for children (including music and lyrics), two unpublished plays, and six television plays, including "Rhai yn Fugeiliaid" (title means "Some as Shepherds"), a weekly serial first broadcast by British Broadcasting Corp., March 25, 1962.

Stories, in translation, represented in anthologies, including *The Language of Love*, edited by Michael Martin, Bantam, 1959; *The Penguin Book of Welsh Short Stories*, edited by Alun Richards, Penguin, 1976.

Translator of radio plays from Italian into Welsh. Contributor to Welsh and British journals.

WORK IN PROGRESS: Research on the Welsh novel and the structures of Welsh prose.

SIDELIGHTS: Elis wrote: "Belonging as I do to an endangered species of wildlife—five hundred thousand Welsh speakers—I have a natural sympathy with all threatened or depressed minorities, ethnic, linguistic, cultural, or religious. My work is largely concerned with the necessity for roots and a sense of belonging and the fear of a world-wide standardization of human life. I write in my native tongue, which is more than fourteen hundred years old, because I cannot write creatively in any other, but also as an act of faith in its survival and in defiance of the growing mass culture which threatens all variety and can only cause worldwide boredom and the stagnation of the arts."

AVOCATIONAL INTERESTS: Travel (France, Germany, Switzerland, the Netherlands, Greece, Belgium, Italy, and Yugoslavia), folk music, ancient history, visual arts (including sketching), politics.

BIOGRAPHICAL/CRITICAL SOURCES: Anglo-Welsh Review, Volume IX, number 24, winter, 1958; J. Maxwell Jones, Jr., *Islwyn Ffowc Elis*, [Philadelphia], 1970; Meic Stephens, editor, *Artists in Wales*, Gomer, 1971.

*   *   *

ELKIN, Stephen L(loyd) 1941-

PERSONAL: Born March 1, 1941, in New York, N.Y.; son of Max and Mildred (Miller) Elkin; married Diana Wilson (an account representative), March 26, 1967. *Education:* Alfred University, B.A., 1961; Harvard University, M.A., 1963, Ph.D., 1969. *Home:* 3000 Tilden St. N.W., Washington, D.C. 20008. *Office:* Department of Government and Politics, University of Maryland, College Park, Md. 20742.

CAREER: Smith College, Northampton, Mass., lecturer in political science, 1966-68; University of Pennsylvania, Philadelphia, assistant professor of political science, 1968-75; University of Maryland, College Park, associate professor of government and politics, 1975—. *Member:* American Politi-

cal Science Association. *Awards, honors:* Fellow of Social Science Research Council, Ford Foundation, and American Philosophical Society, all 1969-70; Leverhulme fellow at University of Leicester, 1969-70.

WRITINGS: Politics and Land Use Planning: The London Experience, Cambridge University Press, 1974. Contributor to political science journals.

WORK IN PROGRESS: City Politics and Liberal Democracy.

*   *   *

ELLIOTT, Aubrey (George) 1917-

PERSONAL: Born August 11, 1917, in East London, South Africa; son of Percival C. (a farmer) and Florence (Hearn) Elliott; married Lesley Sutton, 1943 (divorced, 1968); married Irma Leonie Webster, June 20, 1969; children: Margaret (Mrs. Martin Rudd), Wayne. *Education:* Attended high school in East London, South Africa. *Religion:* Anglican. *Home and office:* 350 Lawley St., Waterkloof, Pretoria 0181, South Africa.

CAREER: South African Reserve Bank, Pretoria, 1936-74, clerk in East London, 1936-39, teller in East London, 1942-48, in foreign exchange control department, Pretoria, 1948-52, pro sub-accountant in Cape Town, 1952-56, in department of economic research and statistics, Pretoria, 1956-58, in foreign exchange control department, 1958-64, assistant head, 1964-74; retired from banking to begin work in social anthropology, concentrating on the study and photographing of South African tribes, 1974—. Photographer, with exhibits at the University of South Africa; judge of photography contests. *Military service:* South African Army, Kaffrarian Rifles Infantry Regiment, 1939-42; served in Egypt and Libya. *Member:* Photographic Society of Southern Africa (past member of board of directors), Pretoria Photographic Society (past president), Rotary International. *Awards, honors:* Awards from Pretoria Photographic Society and Photographic Society of Southern Africa.

WRITINGS—With own photographs: *The Magic World of the Xhosa*, Collins, 1971, Scribner, 1975; *Pretoria* (booklet), Purnell (South Africa), 1975; (contributor of photographs) *The Republic of Transkei*, Chris van Rensburg Publications (South Africa), 1976; *Sons of Zulu*, Collins, 1978. Contributor of articles and photographs to South African journals, including *Lantern, Creative Photography*, and *South Africa Digest*.

WORK IN PROGRESS: Research on tribal people of southern Africa, including the Ndebele (Mapoch); classifying and indexing photographs; directing design of statuettes of tribal men and women in full regalia.

SIDELIGHTS: Since spending his childhood on a farm in the heart of Xhosa tribal territory, Elliott has had three major interests: social anthropology, photography, and writing. His books on the Xhosa and Zulu peoples have allowed him to combine his interests. Since and before his retirement from banking, he has spent much of his time traveling in remote tribal areas of Natal, Zululand, and the Transkei, with his notebook and cameras and his knowledge of Xhosa and Zulu languages.

What motivates his writing? He says: "When I ask myself *why* I write—as I often do—I invariably end up romanticising on the mysteries in the creation about me. What makes any man do anything which a dictionary may define as *work* when he does not have to? I am not sure . . . but perhaps it is a part of nature's plan that all her children must or should give something back to the world. I write because I have an irresistible urge to write. I enjoy it. I enjoy, too, playing with language. Writing, in my case, is one of three allied interests as closely linked as the three sides of a triangle. The other two are the study of tribespeople's customs and photography.

"My inclination to write is inborn. My father was a farmer and I grew up in an area of the Cape Province of South Africa which has a high percentage of rural black people of the Xhosa tribe. I learned to speak Xhosa at the same time as I learned my own English. Xhosa beliefs and superstitions fascinated me and I got to believing that I knew Tikoloshe, their mischievious little water sprite, and Mpundulu, their mighty lightning bird. I looked for other creatures and found them—many of them. But I found not only 'creatures': Xhosa ideas and explanations of scientific phenomena around them, like the migration of birds, life after death, the powers of witches and witch-doctors (diviners), fascinated me. My third interest, photography, was not an 'automatic.' With the progress of my anthropological research and studies, I saw the need to capture the tribal kraal scene in pictures before it too, was lost forever. That was 1960. In no time I was carried away with it and after I won a few competitions and one or two 'pictures of the year' awards, I found it difficult to keep my enthusiasm in check and my priorities on an even keel. Photography has now become an integral part of my writing.

"In conclusion, a brief analysis: In my book *The Magic World of the Xhosa* I concentrated for the greater part on the beliefs, superstitions, witchcraft, and ancestor worship of the uneducated rural Xhosa tribesfolk. My book *Sons of Zulu*, which deals more extensively with the physical aspects of tribal life, complements it in a way, even though dealing with a completely different tribe. The common Nguni heritage of the Xhosa and the Zulu provides a broad basis for this link. It must, however, always be borne in mind that both these books are about the rural, uneducated branches of their tribes and not about their brothers who have become urbanised."

Elliott's books have been valued both by students of his subjects and lay readers as well. His range of appeal was measured by a *Mankind Quarterly* reviewer of *The Magic World of the Xhosa*: "This full account of the Xhosa is written in nontechnical language and is one which should be in the library of anyone interested in the nationalities of Southern Africa. The pictures alone are a valuable record of the racial type—much better than can be found elsewhere."

AVOCATIONAL INTERESTS: Ornithology, woodworking.

BIOGRAPHICAL/CRITICAL SOURCES: Photography and Travel, July, 1971; *Mankind Quarterly,* Number 2, 1971; *Lantern,* September, 1973; *Creative Photography,* December, 1978; *South African Digest,* March 9, 1979.

*   *   *

ELLISON, Lucile Watkins   1907(?)-1979

OBITUARY NOTICE: Born c. 1907, in Pennington, Ala.; died of cancer, December 20, 1979, in Washington, D.C. Associate executive and author. Ellison spent thirty-three years with the National Education Association, serving her last nine years there as executive secretary of the citizenship committee. After learning in 1974 that she had terminal cancer, Ellison began to write children's books based on her own childhood experiences. The first book, *Butter on Both Sides,* was published in 1979. Obituaries and other sources: *Washington Post,* December 17, 1979, December 22, 1979.

ELSY, (Winifred) Mary

PERSONAL: Born in London, England; daughter of Albert Edward (a court photographer) and Ethel Jeffrey (Forster) Elsy. *Education:* Attended Oakley Training College for Teachers. *Politics:* "Left-wing Conservative." *Religion:* Church of England. *Home and office:* 519-C Finchley Rd., Hampstead, London N.W.3, England. *Agent:* Gerald Pollinger, Laurence Pollinger Ltd., 18 Maddox St., Mayfair, London W1R OEU, England.

CAREER: Teacher at state school in Littlebury, Essex, England, 1947-48; teacher at state school in London, England, 1948-49; teacher at private school in Hampstead, England, 1949-51; worked at various odd jobs and as a free-lance writer while traveling extensively throughout Europe, 1951-57; associated with Realist Film Unit, London, 1957-58; Associated-Rediffusion Television, London, assistant to script writer, 1958-59; Fleetway Publications, London, sub-editor and caption writer for *The Children's Encyclopedia,* 1960-62; B.P.C. Publishing Ltd., London, writer and editorial assistant, 1963-64; Evans Bros., London, sub-editor, 1965-66; Abelard Schuman Ltd., London, children's book editor, 1967-68; free-lance writer, 1968—. Secretary to director of British Institute of Human Rights, 1979. *Member:* International P.E.N., Society of Authors, Institute of Journalists, Contemporary Art Society, Camden History Society, Hampstead Scientific Society.

WRITINGS: Travels in Belgium and Luxembourg, Deutsch, 1966; *Brittany and Normandy,* Batsford, 1974.

Author of television programs, each previously published in magazines and newspapers: "The Bus That Wouldn't Budge," first aired on Children's Television, March 17, 1954; "The Bed That Ran Away," first aired on Welsh Regional British Broadcasting Corp. (BBC), May 26, 1955; "The Adventures of Hetty the Hat," first aired on Welsh Home Service BBC, December 1, 1955. Contributor to *Odham's Children's Encyclopedia.* Contributor of articles and children's stories to magazines, including *Observer, Elizabethan, Voyager, She, Art and Antique,* and *Illustrated London News,* and newspapers.

WORK IN PROGRESS: Cycle Camping Tour of Europe, based on her own tour in the 1950's; *Travel Guide to France.*

SIDELIGHTS: Elsy comments: "It is difficult to say what factors and circumstances have been important in my career. Most opportunities in my life have happened by chance. I started writing when a teenager, gave it up for a period, and started again when I was a teacher. I wrote a large number of children's stories and tried my hand at novels, but unfortunately for me, it was a bad period, because it was not long after the war and there was a shortage of paper; there were also few magazines to sell them to. I suppose writing eventually became a habit, and/or it was necessary for me to have some form of self expression. I am not sure what sort of message, if any, I am trying to put over. Certain things, like hyprocrisy and injustice, make me angry, and I am somewhat cynical, but I would never presume to try to reform the human race.

"When I am writing, I work an office day, that is, I start at nine, take a lunch hour, and continue until about five. The two travel books I have had published were commissioned, although I chose the subjects. I enjoy traveling and see myself as a sort of pioneer, maybe an advance party, or even spy, telling people what to do, see, and look out for, etc. Traveling is an enjoyable way of educating myself. I find it difficult to know what to say to an aspiring writer, because writing is such an individualistic profession, and no two people will have the same experiences. If someone decides to follow a writing career, however, they will have to be prepared to give it all their attention, which is a big sacrifice to ask of anyone.

"I do not know exactly which writers have influenced me. My parents' business/home stood opposite the main Hampstead Public Library, which was very convenient for me when a child, as I was a great reader. Two writers who I particularly admire are George Orwell and Alexander Solzhenitsyn. I am afraid I do not follow the current literary trends, and therefore do not have any specific opinions on them."

"I would next like to write about a country or place in depth, rather than write a travel guide. I would then like to try my hand at adult fiction.

"My motivation is self-expression. I like to write, and would have liked to be an artist. I believe in internationalism and like people, but don't always practice what I preach. I often change my mind. I don't believe in dogma, but in pragmatism. I find life interesting, but am not very clear why I'm here."

*   *   *

ENGHOLM, Eva   1909-

PERSONAL: Born November 1, 1909, in Beckenham, England; married Geoffrey Engholm (a lecturer in political science; divorced). *Education:* Newnham College, Cambridge, M.A. *Politics:* "Apolitical." *Religion:* "Disciple of Drs. Albert Schweitzer and Jung." *Home:* Lame Ducks, Catsfield, East Sussex, England.

CAREER: Government of Southern Rhodesia, senior woman H.M.I. for European and Colored Schools, 1940-44; St. Gabriel's Teacher Training College, London, England, senior lecturer in education, 1945-52; University of East Africa (now Makerere University), Kampala, Uganda, lecturer in education and head of Demonstration School, 1953-56; Language Tuition Centre, Eastbourne, England, principal of Residential International College for Girls, beginning 1958; writer. Volunteer worker with school-age delinquents. *Member:* National Association for Teachers of English, Society of Authors.

WRITINGS: Education Through English: The Use of English in African Schools, Cambridge University Press, 1965; *Practical English for the Foreign Student,* Pitman, 1967; *Company of Birds,* Neville Spearman, 1970. Also author of *Omukazi Omukadde n'Embuz: Ye,* Eagle Press. Contributor to education journals and popular magazines, including *New Era* and *Athene.*

WORK IN PROGRESS: An autobiography, covering the first twenty years of her life; translating Charitas Bischoff's biography of her mother, nineteenth-century botanist and naturalist, Amalie Dietrich; translating Bischoff's autobiography; poetry (ballads and folk).

SIDELIGHTS: Eva Engholm writes: "My parents were both on the stage. Their stage names were Frank Warden Reed and Jennie Stevens. My cousin was a producer for Denver University Civic Theatre, and the theatre is in my bones. I was an acting member of the Unnamed Society's Experimental Theatre in Manchester in the early thirties, and have since done production work in schools. I have written about this in my autobiographical account and study of the profound (I believe primary) importance to the individual of his first twenty years of life.

"I was brought up in the country, and mountains, streams, and lakes are my great loves. I love the silence—except for nature's own voice.

"I now have a small wild birds' rescue hospital; hence, my book, *Company of Birds.* This year I have been more deluged with patients than ever before. I have no assistance, so my other work suffers. My motivation is to be on the side of the victim, to be a voice for those who are voiceless."

AVOCATIONAL INTERESTS: Climbing, skiing, swimming, canoeing (especially in unfrequented mountain lakes and pools).

*   *   *

ENTWISTLE, Noel (James)   1936-

PERSONAL: Surname is pronounced *En*-twistle; born December 26, 1936, in Bolton, England; son of Joseph (a leather merchant) and Gladys (a secretary; maiden name, Jackson) Entwistle; married Dorothy May Bocking, August 8, 1964; children: Abigail. *Education:* University of Sheffield, B.Sc., 1960; University of Aberdeen, Ph.D., 1967. *Office:* Department of Education, University of Edinburgh, 10 Buccleuch Place, Edinburgh EH8 9JT, Scotland.

CAREER: Physics teacher at private boys' school in Fleetwood, England, 1961-64; University of Aberdeen, Aberdeen, Scotland, research fellow, 1964-67; University of Lancaster, Bailrigg, England, lecturer, 1968-70, senior lecturer, 1970-71, professor of education, 1971-78; University of Edinburgh, Edinburgh, Scotland, Bell Professor of Education and director of Godfrey Thomson Unit for Educational Research, 1978—. *Military service:* Royal Air Force, 1955-57. *Member:* British Psychological Society (fellow).

WRITINGS: (With J. S. Nisbet) *The Age of Transfer to Secondary Education,* University of London Press, 1966; (with Nisbet) *The Transition to Secondary Education,* University of London Press, 1969; (with Nisbet) *Educational Research Methods,* University of London Press, Volume II, 1970, Volume III, 1973; (editor with Nisbet) *Educational Research in Action,* University of London Press, 1972; (editor with D. J. Hounsell) *How Students Learn,* University of Lancaster, 1975; (editor) *Strategies for Research and Development in Higher Education,* Swets & Zeitlinger, 1976; (with J. D. Wilson) *Degrees of Excellence: The Academic Achievement Game,* Hodder & Stoughton, 1977.

Contributor: *Research Into Higher Education,* Society for Religion and Higher Education, 1970, 1973; *Contemporary Problems in Higher Education,* McGraw-Hill, 1972; *Research Perspectives in Education,* Routledge & Kegan Paul, 1973; *Personality and Academic Progress,* Association of Educational Psychologists, 1974; *Methodological Problems in Research and Development in Higher Education,* Swets & Zeitlinger, 1974; *Strategies for Research and Development in Higher Education,* Swets & Zeitlinger, 1977; *Proceedings of the Second Congress,* Association for Research and Development in Higher Education, 1977. Contributor to academic journals. Editor of *British Journal of Educational Psychology,* 1970-75.

WORK IN PROGRESS: A book on educational psychology, publication by Wiley expected in 1981; research on students' learning strategies in higher education.

SIDELIGHTS: Entwistle writes: "My initial interest in educational research was in the application of scientific methodology (based on my training as a physicist) to the elucidation of educational issues. My current interests are still in empirical research, but with a broader definition, related more to thought than behavior, and one which is embedded in social situations."

ERENS, Patricia 1938-

PERSONAL: Born May 31, 1938, in Washington, D.C.; daughter of Benjamin (a pharmacist) and Nettie Brett; married Jay Erens (an attorney), August 21, 1960; children: Pamela, Bradley. *Education:* George Washington University, B.A., 1959; University of Chicago, M.A., 1963; doctoral study at Northwestern University, 1972-79. *Politics:* Liberal. *Religion:* Jewish. *Home:* 2920 Commonwealth Ave., Chicago, Ill. 60657. *Office:* Department of Communications, Rosary College, 7900 West Division, River Forest, Ill. 60305.

CAREER: University of Illinois at Chicago Circle, Chicago, instructor in English, 1963-64; Art Institute of Chicago, Chicago, staff assistant, 1963-70; University of Chicago, Chicago, lecturer in humanities, 1965-66; Northwestern University, Evanston, Ill., lecturer in film, 1975; Rosary College, River Forest, Ill., instructor in film, 1977—. Lecturer at Hebrew University, Jerusalem, Israel, 1979. Member of Film Center advisory board at Art Institute of Chicago, advisory board of Midwest Women's Center, and Chicago executive board of American Jewish Committee. *Member:* Modern Language Association of America, Society of Cinema Studies, Popular Film Association, University Film Association, National Organization for Women, Zero Population Growth, Planned Parenthood. *Awards, honors:* Grants from International Communications Agency, 1978, for Japan, and 1979, for Israel.

WRITINGS: Masterpieces: Famous Chicagoans and Their Paintings, Chicago Review Press, 1969; (editor with Steve Fagin, Joseph Hill, and William Horrigan) *Film Reader I,* Northwestern University, 1975; (editor with Horrigan) *Film Reader II,* Northwestern University, 1977; *The Films of Shirley MacLaine,* A. S. Barnes, 1978; *Akira Kurosawa: A Guide to References and Resources,* G. K. Hall, 1979; *Sexual Stratagems: The World of Women in Film,* Horizon Press, 1979. Contributing editor of *Quarterly Review of Film Studies.*

WORK IN PROGRESS: The Portrayal of the Jew in the American Cinema, publication expected in 1982.

SIDELIGHTS: Patricia Erens writes: "I have spent time during the last several years in Japan and Israel, where I have discussed filmmaking and feminism, and researched material for future writing.

"Although my primary focus remains the cinema, a medium which combines art with the social aspects of contemporary culture, I am also interested in all the humanities—art, literature, music, photography, and dance—and have involved myself in these areas as observer, participant, and critic."

* * *

ERICKSON, Millard J. 1932-

PERSONAL: Born June 24, 1932, in Stanchfield, Minn.; son of Andrew Olaf (a farmer) and Ida (Sundstrom) Erickson; married Virginia Nepstad (a school teacher), August 20, 1955; children: Kathryn Sue, Sandra Lynne, Sharon Ruth. *Education:* Attended Bethel College, St. Paul, Minn., 1949-51; University of Minnesota, B.A., 1953; graduate study at Bethel Theological Seminary, 1953-54; Northern Baptist Theological Seminary, B.D., 1956; University of Chicago, M.A., 1958; further graduate study at Garrett Theological Seminary, 1959-61; Northwestern University, Ph.D., 1963. *Home:* 2000 Greenview Dr., New Brighton, Minn. 55112. *Office:* Bethel Theological Seminary, 3949 Bethel Dr., St. Paul, Minn. 55112.

CAREER: Ordained Baptist minister; pastor of Baptist churches in Chicago, Ill., 1956-61, and Minneapolis, Minn., 1961-64; Wheaton College, Wheaton, Ill., assistant professor, 1964-68, associate professor of Bible and apologetics, 1968-69, head of department, 1967-69; Bethel Theological Seminary, St. Paul, Minn., associate professor, 1969-71, professor of theology, 1971—. Interim pastor at nearly thirty Baptist churches. Member of publications board of Baptist General Conference, 1957-62, 1965-70, chair of board, 1959-61, 1966-68, member of conference's board of trustees, 1960-62, 1965-69. *Member:* American Society of Christian Ethics, American Theological Society, American Academy of Religion, American Philosophical Association, American Association of University Professors, Evangelical Theological Society, Evangelical Philosophical Society, Phi Beta Kappa.

WRITINGS: The New Evangelical Theology, Revell, 1968; (editor) *The Living God,* Baker Book, 1973; *Relativism in Contemporary Christian Ethics,* Baker Book, 1974; (editor) *Man's Need and God's Gift,* Baker Book, 1976; *Contemporary Options in Eschatology,* Baker Book, 1977; *Salvation: God's Amazing Plan,* Victor, 1978; (editor) *The New Life,* Baker Book, 1979.

AVOCATIONAL INTERESTS: Golf, photography, flying, horseback riding.

* * *

ERICKSON, Russell E(verett) 1932-

PERSONAL: Born July 8, 1932, in Hartford, Conn.; son of John Waldemar (a factory inspector) and Emily (in sales; maiden name, Billings) Erickson; married Agnes Gruber (a lithographer), May 30, 1964. *Education:* Attended public schools in Canton, Conn. *Residence:* Bristol, Conn.

CAREER: Photographic laboratory technician in Hartford, Conn., 1951-52; typesetter in Hartford, 1952-53; lithographer in Elmwood, Conn., and Farmington, Conn., 1955-76; freelance writer of children's books, 1976—. *Military service:* U.S. Army, radio operator in Signal Corps, 1953-55; served in Korea. *Awards, honors: A Toad for Tuesday* was named notable children's book by the American Library Association, among best books of the year by *School Library Journal,* outstanding book for young readers by the *New York Times,* and among the year's ten best books by *Learning,* all 1974; *Warton and Morton* was listed among books of the year by Child Study Association of America, 1976.

WRITINGS—Juvenile: The Snow of Ohreeganu, Lothrop, 1974; *A Toad for Tuesday,* Lothrop, 1974; *Warton and Morton,* Lothrop, 1976; *Warton's Christmas Eve Adventure,* Lothrop, 1977; *Warton and the King of the Skies,* Lothrop, 1978; *Warton and the Traders,* Lothrop, 1979; *Warton and the Castaways,* Lothrop, 1980. Contributor of stories to children's magazines, including *Friend, Cricket,* and *Highlights for Children.*

SIDELIGHTS: Erickson told *CA:* "When describing my vocation I usually say that I write children's books. Actually, I think of it a bit differently. I write stories that children might enjoy, the difference to me being that while a child may not give a hoot about carrying on a conversation with an adult, he or she will often listen with great interest when one adult is talking with another, especially if the conversation is of a story-telling sort. In that sense there are two kinds of children's stories: one is written *for* children, the other is a story that they might enjoy, and it could be any story at all.

"When I write my books, which are naturalistic animal fantasy, I try to keep this in mind. The nature description comes from my own experiences fishing rivers and streams and camping in woods and forests, and the adventures are kept within the realm of real-life possibility. Therefore it's relatively easy for me to write in an adult conversational sort of way—a conversation to be overheard, so to speak.

"There are several possibilities for future stories floating around in my head at the moment, but I hesitate to say more about them. The very act of putting a few thoughts on paper or telling them to someone often removes an important part of the incentive I need to write the story—the surprise factor. Not having the slightest idea about what's going to happen next keeps me interested, and that keeps me writing. Sadly, this also creates impossible situations and unsolvable predicaments and I have vowed many times never again to write a single word without knowing exactly where I was headed. So far I have decided to wait until after my *next* story is written before I actually try that."

AVOCATIONAL INTERESTS: Fresh and salt water fishing, vegetable gardening, carpentry, hiking in the woods.

* * *

ESCOTT, Paul David 1947-

PERSONAL: Born July 31, 1947, in St. Louis, Mo.; son of William Edwin (a machinist) and Fannie (Espy) Escott; married Durant Williams (an attorney), October 12, 1968; children: Lauren Elizabeth. *Education:* Harvard University, B.A., 1969; Duke University, M.A., 1972, Ph.D., 1974. *Politics:* Democrat. *Religion:* None. *Home:* 1418 Lexington Ave., Charlotte, N.C. 28203. *Office:* Department of History, University of North Carolina, Charlotte, N.C. 28223.

CAREER: University of North Carolina, Charlotte, assistant professor, 1974-79, associate professor of history, 1979—. Member of advisory board of North Carolina Institute of Applied History. Member of Charlotte-Mecklenburg Historic Properties Commission. *Member:* Social Science History Association, Southern Historical Association. *Awards, honors:* Whitney M. Young, Jr. academic fellowship, 1975-76; Rockefeller Foundation fellow, 1979-80.

WRITINGS: After Secession: Jefferson Davis and the Failure of Confederate Nationalism, Louisiana State University Press, 1978; *Slavery Remembered: A Record of Twentieth-Century Slave Narratives,* University of North Carolina Press, 1979. Contributor to history journals.

WORK IN PROGRESS: A study of race, class, and social organization in North Carolina, 1850-1890.

SIDELIGHTS: Escott comments: "I am a historian specializing in the history of the southern United States. My interest lies primarily in social history, the contours of people's lives as these are shaped by events and by forces such as race and social class."

* * *

ESPINO, Federico (Licsi, Jr.) 1939-
(Quixote de Extramuros)

PERSONAL: Born April 10, 1939, in Pasig, Rizal, Philippines; son of Federico Lopez (a dentist) and Paula (a teacher; maiden name, Dimacali-Licsi) Espino. *Education:* University of Santo Tomas, Litt.B., 1959. *Home:* 178 Marcelo H. del Pilar, Pasig, Rizal, Philippines.

CAREER: Free-lance writer, 1959-60; *Mirror Magazine,* Manila, Philippines, feature writer, 1960-63, assistant editor, 1964-71; free-lance writer, 1972—. *Awards, honors:* Fellowship from Asia Foundation and Silliman University, 1966;

Palanca Memorial Award, 1967, for *Toreng Bato, Kastilyong Pawid,* 1969, for *Dark Sutra* and *Counterclockwise,* and 1972, for *Tinikling: A Sheaf of Poems;* short story prize from *Free Press,* 1972, for "Segkopoulos"; short story prize from *Graphic,* 1972, for "Bituin sa Palasingsingan"; Premio de Poesia Ramon de Basterra from Association Artistica Vizcaina, 1977, for *Tambor de sangre.*

WRITINGS—Poetry: In Three Tongues: A Folio of Poems in Tagalog, English, and Spanish, Bustamante Press (Quezon City), 1963; *Apocalypse in Ward 19 and Other Poems,* Journal Press (Quezon City), 1965; *The Shuddering Clavier,* Journal Press, 1965; *Sa Paanan ng parnaso* (title means "At the Foot of Mount Parnassus"), Journal Press, 1965; *Toreng bato, kastilyong pawid* (title means "Tower of Stone, Castle of Nipa"), Journal Press, 1966; *Balalayka ni Pasternak at iba pang tula* (in Pilipino and English; title means "Pasternak's Balalaika and Other Poems"), Pioneer Press (Manila), 1967; *A Rapture of Distress,* Pioneer Press, 1968; *Alak na buhay, hinog na abo, phoenix na papel* (in Pilipino and English; title means "Living Wine, Dead Sea Fruit, Phoenix of Paper"), Pioneer Press, 1968; *Dark Sutra,* Pioneer Press, 1969; *Burnt Alphabets: Poems in English, Tagalog, and Spanish,* Pioneer Press, 1969; *Dawn and Downsitting: Poems,* Pioneer Press, 1969; *Counterclockwise: Poems, 1965-1969,* Bustamante Press, 1969.

A Manner of Seeing: A Folio of Poems, privately printed, 1970; *Caras y Caretas de Amor* (title means "Faces and Masks of Love"), Bustamante Press, 1970; *The Winnowing Rhythm,* Bustamante Press, 1970; *Makinilya at lira, tuluyan at tula* (title means "Typewriter and Lyre: A Collection of Poems and Prose"), Pioneer Press, 1970; *Letters and Nocturnes: Poems, 1972-1973,* Pioneer Press, 1973; (translator) *Makabagong panulaan* (English, American, and European poems; title means "Contemporary Poetry"), Manlapaz Publishing (Quezon City), 1974; *Tambor de sangre,* Association Artistica Vizcaina (Spain), 1977.

Short stories: *The Country of Sleep,* Bustamante Press, 1969; *Percussive Blood,* Pioneer Press, 1972.

Other: *English-Pilipino Thesaurus* (lexicography), Soller Press, 1980.

Contributor of poems to *Literature East and West* and *Hemisphere.* Contributor of articles, under pseudonym Quixote de Extramuros, to magazines, including *Fina* and *Pic.*

WORK IN PROGRESS: A novel in Pilipino, *Sarung banggi: Kasaysayan ng isang magdamag,* completion expected in 1982.

SIDELIGHTS: Philippine culture and literature have been influenced both by the East and the West. From the East came the influence of the Indonesians, the Chinese, and the Muslims. After Magellan discovered these South Pacific islands in 1521, the West began to have an impact on Philippine society. From the sixteenth to the nineteenth centuries, the national literature was written both in the native tongues of the Philippines as well as in Spanish, the language of the colonial overlords. When the United States took control of the Philippines after the Spanish-American War in 1898, the Americans officially introduced the English language. In an article on Philippine poetry in English, Cirilo F. Bautista wrote about the consequences of the American takeover: "Because we had to learn a new language, our literature in Spanish seemed to have lost relevance ... because we had to assimilate a new culture we achieved a dichotomous personality: we wrote in English what we thought in our native tongues."

Bautista went on to say that it is difficult to express the Filipino consciousness in a foreign language, but some writers have managed to do so. Among the authors he cited was Federico Espino, who writes with equal facility in English, in Spanish, and in the vernacular. Espino is considered by some critics to be the foremost writer in Pilipino (formerly known as Tagalog), which is the language spoken in Manila and the surrounding area. He told *CA* that he also writes in Ilocano (another Philippine tongue spoken by the people of northern Luzon); however, he still considers himself to be "a literary apprentice" when it comes to writing Ilocano poetry.

In an overview of Espino's work, Bautista observed that Espino "is the country's most prolific poet. He comes out regularly with one or two slim volumes with exceptional poetic quality. . . . He is at his best in English, though his Tagalog and Spanish are no less remarkable. Of him it is said that he was born with a fountain pen in his hand and that as a child he spoke in sprung rhythm." According to Bautista, Espino's poetry tends to be preoccupied with French symbolism, Japanese folk songs, and the Eros myth. He also noted that Espino is a romanticist: "At the core of his poetic consciousness are the love for the past, emphasis on the imagination, and freedom for experimentation."

Among the writers who have influenced Espino are Jose Garcia Villa, Wallace Stevens, Robert Lowell, and Jorge Guillen. On this subject, Espino told *CA:* "Some critics say that my poetry in Spanish shows the influence of Federico Garcia Lorca, and my poetry in English shows the influence of T. S. Eliot and John Crowe Ransom, though my early poetry is not just an echo of the poems of other writers.

"My most recent poems in English, Spanish, Pilipino, and Ilocano are couched in a style which is no longer reminiscent of the manner of my former literary exemplars. I have long ago buried Lorca, Ransom, and Eliot. My poem, 'Lament for Prufrock,' is my way of exorcizing my muse from the astral body of T. S. Eliot—the Eliot of the *Four Quartets* and 'The Wasteland' who has also influenced other Filipino poets whether they are writing in English or Pilipino."

BIOGRAPHICAL/CRITICAL SOURCES: Books Abroad, winter, 1967, autumn, 1970, winter, 1971, spring, 1971; *Sunburst Magazine,* August, 1977; *Solidarity,* December, 1970.

* * *

EVANS, Barbara Lloyd
See LLOYD EVANS, Barbara

* * *

EVANS, Sara 1943-

PERSONAL: Born December 1, 1943, in McCormick, S.C.; daughter of J. Claude (a minister) and Maxilla (an environmentalist; maiden name, Everett) Evans; married Harry C. Boyte (a writer), June 5, 1966; children: Craig Evans. *Education:* Duke University, B.A., 1966, M.A., 1968; University of North Carolina, Ph.D., 1976. *Office:* Department of History, University of Minnesota, Minneapolis, Minn. 55455.

CAREER: University of North Carolina, Greensboro, instructor in history, 1974; Duke University, Durham, N.C., instructor in history, 1974-75; University of North Carolina, Chapel Hill, assistant professor of history, 1975-76; University of Minnesota, Minneapolis, assistant professor, 1976-79, associate professor of history, 1979—. *Member:* American Historical Association, Organization of American Historians, Women Historians of the Midwest.

WRITINGS: Personal Politics: The Roots of Women's Liberation in the Civil Rights Movement and the New Left, Knopf, 1979. Contributor to magazines, including *Radical America, Southern Exposure, Counseling and Values,* and *Working Papers for a New Society.*

WORK IN PROGRESS: "Research and writing on women in the southern textile industry and on cultural contact between white and native American women on the Minnesota frontier."

SIDELIGHTS: Evans writes: "*Personal Politics* was both a work of academic scholarship and an expression of my feminism."

* * *

EVERETT, Walter 1936-

PERSONAL: Born November 28, 1936, in Mississippi; son of Nathan C. (a teacher) and Ollie (a teacher; maiden name, Ekes) Everett; married Shirley Watkins (a teacher), August 23, 1959; children: Emily. *Education:* Mississippi College, B.A., 1959, M.A., 1962; University of North Carolina, Ph.D., 1974. *Home:* 2216 East Gum St., Evansville, Ind. 47714. *Office:* Department of English, Indiana State University, Evansville, Ind. 47712.

CAREER: Mississippi University for Women, Columbus, instructor in English, 1962-65; University of Southern Mississippi, Hattiesburg, assistant professor of English, 1968-77; Indiana State University, Evansville, assistant professor of English, 1977—. Community representative to Mississippi Committee for the Humanities; member of Leadership Evansville (civic training group) and Evansville Philharmonic Chorus; member of board of directors of Evansville Arts and Education Council. *Member:* Modern Language Association of America, Mediaeval Academy of America, Association of Teachers of Technical Writing, Early English Text Society, South Central Modern Language Association.

WRITINGS: Faulkner's Art and Characters, Barron's, 1969. Associate editor of *Mississippi Review,* 1970-77; co-editor of *Mississippi Folklore Register,* 1974-77.

WORK IN PROGRESS: A book of grammatical terminology and concepts.

AVOCATIONAL INTERESTS: Canoeing, fishing, singing.

* * *

EXCELLENT, Matilda
See FARSON, Daniel Negley

F

FABRICAND, Burton Paul 1923-

PERSONAL: Born November 22, 1923, in New York, N.Y.; son of Irving Kermit and Frances (Sobler) Fabricand; married Heather C. North (a nurse and teacher), December 15, 1972; children: Nicole Diane, Lorraine Stewart. *Education:* Columbia University, A.B., 1947, A.M., 1949, Ph.D., 1953. *Home:* 47 Plaza St., Brooklyn, N.Y. 11217. *Agent:* Elizabeth McKee, McIntosh, McKee & Dodds, Inc., 22 East 40th St., New York, N.Y. 10016. *Office:* Pratt Institute, 215 Ryerson St., Brooklyn, N.Y. 11205.

CAREER: Philco Corp., Philadelphia, Pa., project engineer, 1952-54; University of Pennsylvania, Philadelphia, lecturer in physics and research associate, 1954-56; Columbia Hudson Laboratories, Dobbs Ferry, N.Y., senior research scientist, 1957-69; Pratt Institute, Brooklyn, N.Y., professor of physics, 1969—. Managing partner of Fabricand Associates (investment firm), 1970—; consultant to Industrial Electronic Hardware Corp. and Ocean and Atmospheric Science, Inc. *Military service:* U.S. Army, 1943-46; became staff sergeant. *Member:* American Physical Society, Sigma Xi.

WRITINGS: Horse Sense: A New and Rigorous Application of Mathematical Methods to Successful Betting at the Track, McKay, 1965, revised edition, 1976; *Beating the Street,* McKay, 1969; *The Science of Winning: A Random Walk on the Road to Riches,* Van Nostrand, 1979. Contributor to physics journals.

WORK IN PROGRESS: The Hole, a novel about "Project Mohole"; a how-to book on finance.

SIDELIGHTS: Fabricand writes: "My writings are fundamentally concerned with the random walk, a mathematical game that underlies all real-world phenomena from particle physics to the affairs of men. I believe the twentieth century will be remembered as the 'century of the random walk,' a time when man gained a revolutionary new idea of his place in the universe. To explain and capitalize on this concept in my three vocations (physics, finance, and writing) is my present aim in life.

"Death, taxes, the various markets in which we as human beings participate, the evaluation of information—these are some of the vital areas where the random walk operates. For example, with the use of mortality tables, actuaries can predict accurately the number of people of any given age who will be alive years into the future. But they cannot predict just which individuals will survive and which will not. Put another way, each of us has a known probability of survival. At birth, a male baby has an expectation of seventy-one years of life, a female seventy-six years. Who dies earlier, who lives longer, who can say? We are subject to random forces that an uncaring God, so to speak, inflicts on us at the flip of a coin or the roll of dice.

"The random walk in economics is the sophisticated efficient-markets theory, first put forth by Adam Smith in 1776 in his mystical principle of the 'invisible hand.' It forms the theoretical basis of capitalism and is essential to an understanding of the operation of and, as Karl Marx wrote, 'the colossal productive forces' of free markets. Unfortunately, neither Marx nor his disciples show any comprehension of the random walk in their writings; hence, their theories must be considered naive and fallacious by modern standards."

* * *

FABRIZIUS, Peter
See KNIGHT, Max

* * *

FAINSTEIN, Susan S. 1938-

PERSONAL: Born September 27, 1938, in Cleveland, Ohio; daughter of Jacob (a physician) and Rose (a teacher; maiden name, Horwitz) Saltzman; married Roger Bove, June 3, 1959 (divorced, May 10, 1969); marrried Norman I. Fainstein (a professor), May 18, 1969; children: (first marriage) Eric, Paul. *Education:* Radcliffe College, A.B. (magna cum laude), 1960; Boston University, A.M., 1962; Massachusetts Institute of Technology, Ph.D., 1970. *Home:* 808 South First Ave., Highland Park, N.J. 08904. *Office:* Department of Urban Planning and Policy Development, Livingston College, Rutgers University, New Brunswick, N.J. 08903.

CAREER: Queens College of the City University of New York, Flushing, N.Y., lecturer in political science, 1970; Rutgers University, Livingston College, New Brunswick, N.J., assistant professor, 1970-73, associate professor, 1973-77, professor of urban planning and policy development, 1977—. Senior research associate at University of Pennsylvania, 1978—. Adjunct associate professor at Columbia University, 1975-76. Member of advisory board of Eagleton Institute of Politics, 1975-77; consultant to Russell Sage Foundation. *Member:* Society for the Study of Social Problems (head of Community Research and Development Division, 1977-79), American Sociological Association.

WRITINGS: (Editor with husband, Norman I. Fainstein, and contributor) *The View From Below: Urban Politics and Social Policy,* Little, Brown, 1972; (contributor) Dorothy B. James, editor, *Outside Looking In: Critiques of American Policies and Institutions, Left and Right,* Harper, 1972; (contributor) H. George Frederickson, editor, *Neighborhood Control in the 1970's,* Chandler Publishing, 1973; (with N. I. Fainstein) *Urban Political Movements,* Prentice-Hall, 1974; (contributor) Allen Barton and other editors, *Decentralizing City Government,* Heath, 1977; (contributor) George Sternlieb and James Hughes, editors, *Revitalizing the Northeast,* Center for Urban Policy Research, Rutgers University, 1978. Contributor of about a dozen articles to urban affairs and social science journals. Associate editor of *International Organization,* 1962-63; American editor of *Ethnic and Racial Studies,* 1977—.

*   *   *

FARNWORTH, Warren 1935-

PERSONAL: Born in 1935 in Manchester, England; son of Lawrence (an electrical engineer) and Emily (Cooke) Farnworth; married Jennifer Anne Bizzell, April 3, 1972; children: Emily, Ruth, Lucy. *Education:* Salford College of Art, N.D.D. and A.R.T.C.S., both 1955; University of London, A.T.D., 1967; attended University of Wales, 1972-73. *Politics:* "Royalist." *Home:* 11 Maxwell Close, Gresford, Clwyd LL12 8UD, Wales. *Office:* Cartrefle College of Education, Wrexham, Clwyd, Wales.

CAREER: Teacher in schools and colleges in England, 1957-67; Cartrefle College of Education, Wrexham, Wales, senior lecturer in art and craft, 1967—.

WRITINGS: First Art, Evans Brothers, 1972; *Clay in the Primary School,* Batsford, 1973; *Railways* (juvenile), Mills & Boon, 1973; *Pressing Flowers and Leaves* (juvenile), Chatto & Windus, 1974; *Canals* (juvenile), Mills & Boon, 1974; *Folk Toys Around the World* (juvenile), Chatto & Windus, 1974; *Creative Work With Plaster,* Batsford, 1975; *Pin and Thread Craft,* Batsford, 1975; *Shops and Markets* (juvenile), Mills & Boon, 1976; *Industry* (juvenile), Mills & Boon, 1977; *Techniques and Designs in Pin and Thread Craft,* Batsford, 1977; *Approaches to Collage,* Batsford, 1978; *Roman Britain* (juvenile), Mills & Boon, 1980; *Britain in the Eighteenth Century* (juvenile), Mills & Boon, 1981; *The Industrial Revolution* (juvenile), Mills & Boon, 1981.

SIDELIGHTS: Farnworth commented to *CA:* "I agree with Dr. Johnson when he said in 1776, 'No man but a blockhead ever wrote, except for money!' "

*   *   *

FARRELL, Robert T(homas) 1938-

PERSONAL: Born November 16, 1938, in New York, N.Y.; son of Raymond Edward (an elevator operator) and Gertrude (Klesius) Farrell; married Caroline Pearce-Higgins, October 8, 1958 (divorced, 1972); married Nancy A. Kaplan (a university lecturer), December, 1975; children: (second marriage) Eva Klesius. *Education:* Fordham University, B.A., 1960, M.A., 1961, Ph.D., 1967; Merton College, Oxford, B.Phil., 1967; also studied at New York University and University of London. *Politics:* Democrat. *Religion:* Roman Catholic. *Home:* 1017 Cayuga Heights Rd., Ithaca, N.Y. 14850. *Office:* Department of English, Cornell University, Ithaca, N.Y. 14853.

CAREER: Fordham University, Bronx, N.Y., assistant professor of English, 1961-65; Oxford University, Oxford, England, lecturer in English, 1965-67; Cornell University, Ithaca, N.Y., assistant professor, 1967-72, associate professor, 1972-79, professor of English, medieval studies, and archaeology, 1979—. Lecturer at Oxford University, 1971-72, 1976. *Member:* Modern Language Association of America, Mediaeval Academy of America, Society for Medieval Archaeology (England), Society of Antiquaries (Scotland; fellow). *Awards, honors:* Scandinavian studies fellow at University of London, 1971-72, 1976.

WRITINGS: Beowulf: Swedes and Geats, Viking Society, London, 1972; *Daniel and Azarias,* Methuen, 1974; *Bede and Anglo-Saxon England,* Oxford University Press, 1978; (with Mary Salu) *J.R.R. Tolkien, Scholar and Storyteller: Essays in Memoriam,* Cornell University Press, 1979. Also author of *"Beowulf" and the Northern Heroic Age,* 1980. Contributor to art history, archaeology, and medieval literature journals.

WORK IN PROGRESS: Archaeological studies; research on Chaucer.

SIDELIGHTS: Farrell writes: "I have spent a good deal of time on marine archaeological research, assisting and co-directing excavations on 'H.M.S. Coronation' (1691), Plymouth, the Shetland Viking expedition, and inland lake sites in New York state. Since 1967 my work has been concentrated on the meeting points between literature, art history, and archaeology."

*   *   *

FARSON, Daniel Negley 1927-
(Matilda Excellent)

PERSONAL: Born January 8, 1927, in London, England; son of Negley (a writer and foreign correspondent) and Eve (Stoker) Farson. *Education:* Cambridge University, B.A., 1950. *Home address:* Appledore, North Devonshire, England. *Agent:* Irene Josephy, 35 Craven St., London W.C.2, England.

CAREER: Lobby correspondent in House of Commons, London, England, 1945-46; *Picture Post,* London, staff photographer, 1951-53; free-lance writer and photographer, 1954; British Merchant Navy, seaman, 1955; Instructional Television (ITV), London, television interviewer, 1956-64, host of "Farson's Guide to the British," 1959, "Farson in Australia," 1961, and "Time Gentlemen Please!," 1962; operator of public house in Waterman's Arms, England, 1962-66; free-lance writer, 1964—. Interviewer on "The Dracula Business," on BBC-TV, 1974—. *Military service:* U.S. Army Air Forces, 1947-48. *Awards, honors:* Voted best television interviewer by British critics, 1960.

WRITINGS: Jack the Ripper (nonfiction), M. Joseph, 1972; *Marie Lloyd and Music Hall,* Staley, 1972; (editor) *Wanderlust,* White Lion Publishers, 1972; *Out of Step* (autobiography), M. Joseph, 1972; *The Man Who Wrote Dracula* (biography of author's great-uncle, Bram Stoker), St. Martin's, 1975; *Vampires, Zombies, and Monster Men,* Doubleday, 1975; (editor) *In Praise of Dogs* (stories), Harrap, 1976; *The Dan Farson Black and White Picture Show,* Lemon Tree Press, 1976; *A Window on the Sea,* M. Joseph, 1977; *The Hamlyn Book of Ghosts* (juvenile), Hamlyn, 1978; *The Clifton House Mystery* (juvenile), Arrow, 1978; *The Hamlyn Book of Horror,* Hamlyn, 1979; (under pseudonym Matilda Excellent) *The Dog Who Knew Too Much,* Jay Landesman, 1979; *Curse,* Hamlyn, 1980; *Transplant,* Hamlyn, 1980.

Plays: "The Marie Lloyd Story" (two-act musical), first produced in London at Theatre Royal, 1967; "The Funniest Man in the World" (two-act musical), first produced in London at Theatre Royal, 1977; "Clifton House Mystery" (serial for children), first aired on ITV Britain, 1978. Contributor to newspapers including the *Telegraph Magazine* and *Men Only*.

WORK IN PROGRESS: Jonah and the Joneses, a children's book, for ITV Books.

SIDELIGHTS: Farson writes: "Though born in London, my father was an American foreign correspondent, and much of my childhood was spent in traveling abroad. At the age of seventeen I became the youngest-ever lobby correspondent in the House of Commons. I chose British nationality at the age of twenty-one, and went to Cambridge University, where I started my own magazine, *Panorama.* In 1962, an entertainment program, 'Time Gentlemen Please!' led to my taking over a pub on the Isle of Dogs and started a boom in pub entertainment. At this time I lived on the River Thames at Limehouse, but in 1964 I resigned from television, gave up the pub, and went to live in North Devon to concentrate on writing. Today, I live in the fishing village of Appledore, in an old boat-house overlooking the water.

"I believe it is fair to say that I am the leading authority in the world on Jack the Ripper, having named the police suspect in my book of the same name, and Dracula, which was written by my great-uncle Bram Stoker. Consequently, I am immersed in the subject of horror, often for children who seem more able to accept it than adults, with the occasional, racier sortie into such magazines as *Men Only.* Having been a successful 'television personality,' I gave up this security in order to write. This was a hazardous move financially, but I gain more satisfaction from writing and seeing the printed page than I did from the ephemeral fame and transient glory of television. Now I am writing a series of modern horror novels and hope this will bring a degree of security as well! I shall persevere, even though the climate in England today is hostile to the independent writer."

*   *   *

FARSON, (James Scott) Negley   1890-1960

OBITUARY NOTICE: Born May 14, 1890, in Plainfield, N.J.; died December 13, 1960. Journalist and novelist. Bored with office jobs, Farson became a foreign correspondent for the *Chicago Daily News* from 1924 to 1935. While in Europe he bought a yawl and wrote about his cruises in *Sailing Across Europe.* Other books chronicling his adventures in India, Egypt, and Russia include *Black Bread and Red Coffins, The Way of a Transgressor,* and *Transgressor in the Tropics.* Obituaries and other sources: *New York Times,* December 14, 1960; *Newsweek,* December 26, 1960; *Time,* December 26, 1960.

*   *   *

FASSBINDER, Rainer Werner   1946-

PERSONAL: Born May 31, 1946, in Bad Woerishofen, Germany (now West Germany); married Ingrid Caven (an actress), 1970 (divorced). *Education:* Attended Fridi-Leophard Studio, c. 1966. *Residence:* Munich, West Germany. *Office:* c/o New Yorker Films, 16 West 61st St., New York, N.Y. 10023.

CAREER: Writer and director of plays and films; actor. Actor in Munich Action Theatre, 1967-68, and in motion pictures, including "Tonys Freunde," 1967, "Baal," 1969,

"Katzelmacher," 1969, "Warnung vor einer heiligen Nutte," 1971, and "Faustrecht der Freiheit," 1975. Director of Theatre am Turm in Frankfurt, West Germany, 1974-75. Founder of Antitheatre, 1968; co-founder of Film-verlag der Autoren, 1970. *Awards, honors:* West German Film Critics Prize and Federal Film Prize, both 1969, both for "Katzelmacher"; Federal Film Prize, 1970, for "Warum laeuft Herr R. amok?"; Critics Award from Cannes Film Festival, 1974, for "Angst isst die Seele auf"; and other film awards.

WRITINGS—In German; published plays; produced in Munich, West Germany, at the Antitheater; all as director: *Katzelmacher* (also see below), Verlag der Autoren, 1969; (with John Gay) *Die Bettleroper* (also see below), Verlag der Autoren, 1970; (with Gay) *Antiteater* (contains "Katzelmacher," "Preparadise sorry now," and "Die Bettleroper," latter with Gay; also see above), Suhrkamp, 1970; *Das brennende Dorf* (adapted from writings of Lope de Vega; also see below), Verlag der Autoren, 1970; *Blut am Hals der Katze* (also see below), Verlag der Autoren, 1970; *Bremer Freiheit. Ein buergerliches Trauerspiel* (two plays; also see below), Verlag der Autoren, 1971; *Antiteater 2* (contains "Bremer Freiheit," "Blum am Hals der Katze," and "Das Kaffeehaus"; latter adapted from the play by Carlo Goldoni; also see above), Suhrkamp, 1972; *Die bitteren Traenen der Petra von Kant* (also see below), Verlag der Autoren, 1973; (with Hans Guenther Pflaum) *Das bisschen Realitaet, das ich brauche,* Hanser, 1976; *Stuecke 3* (contains "Die bitteren Traenen der Petra von Kant," "Das brennende Dorf," and "Der Muell, die Stadt und der Tod"; also see above), Suhrkamp, 1976.

Other plays; performed in Munich at the Antitheater; all as director: "Iphigenie auf Tauris" (adapted from the play by Johann Wolfgang von Goethe), 1968; "Pioniere in Ingolstadt" (adapted from the play by Marie-Louise Fleisser), 1968; "Ajax" (adapted from writings of Sophocles), 1968; "Orgie Ubu" (adapted from the play by Alfred Jarry, *Ubu Roi*), 1968; "Anarchie in Bayern," 1969; "Werwolf," 1969.

Screenplays; screenwriter and director, unless otherwise indicated: "Der Stadtstreicher" (short; released in the U.S. as "The City Bums"), Roser-Film, 1965; "Das kleine Chaos" (short; released in the U.S. as "The Small Chaos"), Roser-Film, 1966; "Liebe ist kaelter als der Tod" (released in the U.S. as "Love Is Colder Than Death"), Antiteater-X-Film, 1969; "Katzelmacher," Antiteater-X-Film, 1969; "Gotter der Pest" (released in the U.S. as "Gods of the Plague"), Antiteater, 1969; (with Michael Fengler) "Warum laeuft Herr R. amok?" (released in the U.S. as "Why Does Herr R. Run Amok?"), Antiteater and Maran-Film, 1969.

"Der amerikanische Soldat" (released in the U.S. as "The American Soldier"), Antiteater, 1970; (with Fengler) "Die niklashauser Fahrt" (released in the U.S. as "The Niklashauser Drive"), Janus Film und Fernsehen, 1970; "Rio das Mortes," Janus Film und Fernsehen/Antiteater-X-Film, 1970; "Whity," Atlantis Film/Antiteater-X-Film, 1970; "Warnung vor einer heiligen Nutte" (released in the U.S. as "Beware of a Holy Whore"), Antiteater-X-Film/Nova International, 1970.

"Haendler der vier Jahreszeiten" (released in the U.S. as "The Merchant of Four Seasons"), Tango Film, 1971; "Die bitteren Traenen der Patra von Kant" (released in the U.S. as "The Bitter Tears of Petra von Kant"), Tango Film, 1972; "Effi Briest" (adapted from the novel by Theodor Fontane), Tango Film, 1974; (with Christian Hohoff) "Faustrecht der Freiheit" (released in the U.S. as "Fox and His Friends" and as "Survival of the Fittest"; also released as "Fist-Right of Freedom''), Tango Film, 1975; (with Kurt Raab) "Mutter Kuesters fahrt zum Himmel" (released in the U.S. as "Mother Kusters Goes to Heaven"), Tango Film, 1975.

"Satansbraten" (released in the U.S. as "Satan's Brew"), Albatros Productions, 1976; (screenplay only) "Schatten der Engel" (released in the U.S. as "Shadows of Angels"; adapted from the play by Fassbinder, "Der Muell, die Stadt und der Tod"), [West Germany], 1976; "Chinesisches Roulette" (released in the U.S. as "Chinese Roulette"), Albatros-Film/Les Films du Losange, 1977; "Die dritte Generation" (released in the U.S. as "The Third Generation"), [West Germany], 1978; "Die Ehe der Maria Braun" (released in the U.S. as "The Marriage of Maria Braun"), [West Germany], 1978; "In einem Jahr mit 13 Monden" (released in the U.S. as "In a Year With 13 Moons"), [West Germany], 1978.

Screenplays for television productions; all as writer and director: "Pioniere in Ingolstadt" (released in the U.S. as "Recruits in Ingolstadt"; adapted from writings of Marieluise Fleisser), Janus Film und Fernsehen/Antiteater, 1971; "Acht Stunden sind kein Tag" (released in the U.S. as "Eight Hours Don't Make a Day"; contains "Jochen und Marion," "Oma und Gregor," "Franz und Ernst," "Harald und Monika," and "Irmgard und Rolf"), WDR-TV, 1972-73; "Wildwechsel" (released in the U.S. as "Game Pass"; adapted from the play by Franz Xaver Kroetz), Intertel, 1973; (with Fritz Mueller-Scherz) "Welt am Draht" (released in the U.S. as "World on a Wire"; adapted from the novel by Daniel F. Galouye), WDR-TV, 1973; "Angst isst die Seele auf" (released in the U.S. as "Ali: Fear Eats the Soul"), Tango Film, 1974; "Martha," WDR-TV, 1974; "Ich will doch nur, dass ihr mich liebt" (released in the U.S. as "I Only Want You to Love Me"), [West Germany], 1976.

SIDELIGHTS: Though Fassbinder is the most prolific filmmaker of the German "new wave," his popularity is considerably less than peers Werner Herzog and Wim Wenders. This is due, in part, to Fassbinder's synthesis of style and content in a manner that American audiences find flashy, yet detached. His pessimistic intertwining of politics and love is especially evident in "Ali: Fear Eats the Soul," in which the love affair between a Moroccan immigrant and an elderly German woman is undermined by racism in their community, and "Fox and His Friends," where the homosexual communtiy is a metaphor for class struggle. Many critics have intimated that "Fox and His Friends" is a painfully autobiographical film, for Fassbinder himself plays Fox, a poor homosexual who finds himself surrounded by potential lovers after winning a lottery. When Fox finally exhausts his funds, he once again finds himself unattended. "Love," Fassbinder asserts, "is the best, most insidious, most effective instrument of social repression."

Fassbinder attributes his pessimism to an unhappy childhood. "My father was chaotic," he recalls, "and I still bear the scars of that so deeply that I can never settle down in a stable home. The terrible quarrels of my parents in my early years have warped me forever." Appropriately enough, Fassbinder calls his first film "Love Is Colder Than Death."

The theme of human relationships as power struggles is a recurring one in Fassbinder's films. Gerald Clark notes that Fassbinder is concerned with "power, its uses and abuses. His movies assert that in any relationship, personal or political, there will always be the oppressor and the oppressed." Clark's assessment is born out in "The Bitter Tears of Petra von Kant," in which the tyranical Petra finds herself the oppressed in a relationship with another woman. Fassbinder

sympathizes with neither woman. Instead, he dedicates the film to Maria, a character in the film who is forced to witness Petra's degradation. Penelope Gilliatt called Maria the heroine, for she "has been tortured by the sight of sadistic love's punishments."

Fassbinder's political beliefs are similarly pessimistic, as evidenced in "Mother Kusters Goes to Heaven," the story of a widow attempting to redeem her husband's reputation after his murder-suicide. Because her husband was a factory worker, Mother Kusters is approached by a bourgeois Communist couple trying to convince her that her husband was a martyr. Of course, they next try to involve her in a political campaign. Mother Kusters's dealings with anarchists and other Communists also prove exploitive. "As a social critic," writes Canby, "Mr. Fassbinder is equally skeptical of all prefabricated solutions. His sympathies are with the left, but he doubts everything except the will to survive. All other impulses . . . can be co-opted and exploited by the Establishment."

Fassbinder's nihilism also covers rebellion. In films such as "Love Is Colder Than Death" and "The American Soldier," he depicts the hopelessness and boredom that comes from living apart from society. He is especially fond of portraying the rebel as a Humphrey Bogart-like gangster. In "The American Soldier," a Vietnam veteran-turned-killer is psychologically undermined by the isolation of his occupation; and in "The Gods of Plague," the gangster dies unceremoniously in a supermarket. For Fassbinder, the rebel, especially one taking his cues from the cinema, is doomed to failure.

In later films, Fassbinder's condemnation of resistance is usurped by one of participation. His despair for cooperation is obvious in "Why Does Herr R. Run Amok?," in which the boredom of Herr R.'s lower-middle-class existence sparks a moment of insanity resulting in Herr R.'s killing of his family and himself. Herr R.'s behavior equals that of the husband in "Mother Kusters Goes to Heaven." In the end of that film, Fassbinder depicts Mother Kusters's decision to join society as hopeless. As Canby notes, Fassbinder "sees a gradual, peaceful accommodation to outrageous circumstances as the worst surrender of all."

Some critics suggest that Fassbinder's cinematic style works detrimentally with his screenplays. Following the work of Douglas Sirk, director of such films as "The Tarnished Angels" and "Imitation of Life," Fassbinder relies heavily on mirrors, enclosures, and exaggerated angles to emphasize the melodrama. But Sirk's films tend to be glamourized soap operas, and his direction brings both humor and irony to the films. Fassbinder, however, only confuses reviewers by favoring Sirk's techniques over realist ones. Stanley Kauffmann believes that "there's a sense of a real ability with greased fingers—the form of the work keeps slipping through them." He claims that Fassbinder "envies Sirk his American phase . . . , and, out of a different base, has tried to emulate it. But the result is neither sound high art nor sound pop art—just one more display of talent in an unfilled work." Other reviewers insist that Fassbinder's Sirkian style obliviates the content. Gilliatt writes, "The extreme formalism of his best later work tends to hide their warmth."

Fassbinder's prolificity appears to be his means for amending the flaws in previous films. "Like many prodigal artists," declares Gilliatt, "he seems to correct any mistake he finds in a film by immersing himself in the next picture." Andrew Sarris asserts: "I think that artists should be measured by quantity as well as by quality. . . . Too many contemporary artists futz around by meditating on the one Great Work that shall redeem them. More often ... great works emerge not in splendid isolation, but in fruitful communion with many lesser works.''

Fassbinder attributes his productivity to his fear of isolation. He told a reporter, ''I want to build a house with my films.'' And when a friend asked, ''Why do you work so hard,'' Fassbinder replied, ''To escape the loneliness.''

BIOGRAPHICAL/CRITICAL SOURCES: Film Quarterly, summer, 1975, winter, 1976; *New Yorker,* June 14, 1976, May 30, 1977; *Washington Post,* December 19, 1976; *New York Post,* March 7, 1977; *New York Times,* February 16, 1977, March 7, 1977, March 17, 1977; *Village Voice,* July 11, 1977; *Horizon,* September, 1977; *Time,* March 20, 1978; *New Republic,* September 29, 1979.*

—*Sketch by Les Stone*

* * *

FAULKNER, (Herbert Winthrop) Waldron 1898-1979

PERSONAL: Born January 21, 1898, in Paris, France; died May 11, 1979, of cancer, in Washington, D.C.; son of Herbert Waldron (a painter) and Mary (John) Faulkner; married Elizabeth Ferry Coonley, November 18, 1926; children: Winthrop W., Avery C., Celia F. Clevenger. *Education:* Yale University, Ph.B., 1919, B.F.A., 1924, M.Arch., 1973. *Home:* 3415 36th St. N.W., Washington, D.C. 20016.

CAREER: Architect. Waldron Faulkner, New York, N.Y., and Washington, D.C., principal, 1927-39; Faulkner & Kingsbury, Washington, D.C., partner, 1939-46; Faulkner, Kingsbury & Stenhouse, Washington, D.C., partner, 1946-65; Faulkner, Stenhouse, Fryer & Faulkner, Washington, D.C., senior partner, 1965-68. Works include Washington, D.C., buildings: American Association for the Advancement of Science Headquarters, 1956, Evening Star Newspaper Plant and Offices, 1958, and American Chemical Society Headquarters, 1959. President of Washington Urban League, 1938-41; president of Washington Housing Association, 1947-50. Member of Washington, D.C., Board for Examining and Registering Architects, 1945-51; secretary of board of Lisner-Louise Home, 1954-79; member of Shipstead Panel of Commission of Fine Arts, 1957-60. Trustee, gunnery school, 1967-71.

MEMBER: American Institute of Architects (fellow; president of Washington-Metropolitan Chapter, 1942-43; delegate and chairman to International Society Color Council, 1950-79; chairman of library committee, 1954-63). *Awards, honors:* Diploma of merit from Washington Board of Trade, 1938, for Hall of Government, 1961, for Washington, D.C., Evening Star Newspaper Building and American Chemical Society Headquarters, and also for George Washington University, Suburban Hospital, Providence Hospital, and Holy Cross Hospital; first award from Washington-Metropolitan Chapter of American Institute of Architects, 1954, for Bethesda Library; honor award from Middle Atlantic Region of American Institute of Architects, 1969, for National Collection of Fine Arts and National Portrait Gallery; national honor award from American Institute of Architects, 1970, for National Collection of Fine Arts and National Portrait Gallery.

WRITINGS: Architecture and Color, Wiley-Interscience, 1972. Also illustrator of *Woodwork Displayed in the American Wing at the Metropolitan Museum of Art,* 1929.

OBITUARIES: Washington Post, May 14, 1979.*

FAUSSET, Hugh I'Anson 1895-1965

OBITUARY NOTICE: Born June 16, 1895, in Killington, Westmorland, England; died in 1965. Poet, critic, and novelist. At one time Fausset reviewed three to four hundred books per year for newspapers in England, but he is best known for his critical volumes on Keats, Tennyson, Donne, Coleridge, Tolstoy, Wordsworth, and Whitman. He also wrote several novels and poetry books, and was a student of Eastern philosophies. Obituaries and other sources: *The New Century Handbook of English Literature,* revised edition, Appleton, 1967; *Longman Companion to Twentieth Century Literature,* Longman, 1970.

* * *

FEARING, Kenneth (Flexner) 1902-1961
(Donald F. Bedford, a joint pseudonym)

PERSONAL: Born July 28, 1902, in Oak Park, Ill,; died June 26, 1961; son of Harry L. (an attorney) and Olive (Flexner) Fearing; married Nan Lurie, 1945; children: one son. *Education:* University of Wisconsin, B.A., 1924. *Residence:* New York, N.Y.

CAREER: Poet and novelist. Worked at various jobs, including newspaper reporter, salesman, mill hand, and clerk. Free-lance writer and editor, 1927-61. *Awards, honors:* Guggenheim fellowship, 1936 and 1939.

WRITINGS: Angel Arms (poems), Coward, 1929; *Poems,* Dynamo, 1935; *Dead Reckoning: A Book of Poetry,* Random House, 1938; *Collected Poems of Kenneth Fearing,* Random House, 1940, reprinted, AMS Press, 1977; *Afternoon of a Pawnbroker and Other Poems,* Harcourt, 1943; *Stranger at Coney Island and Other Poems,* Harcourt, 1948; *New and Selected Poems,* Indiana University Press, 1956.

Novels: *The Hospital,* Random House, 1939; *Dagger of the Mind,* Random House, 1941; *Clark Gifford's Body,* Random House, 1942; *The Big Clock,* Harcourt, 1946, reprinted, Garland, 1976; (with Donald Friede and H. Bedford Jones under joint pseudonym Donald F. Bedford) *John Barry,* Creative Age Press, 1947; *Lonliest Girl in the World,* Harcourt, 1951; *The Generous Heart,* Harcourt, 1954; *The Crozart Story,* Doubleday, 1960.

SIDELIGHTS: Kenneth Fearing's writings deal with the urban, mechanized society, a world where faith and love no longer have meaning. He portrays the everyday in a macabre light, simultaneously evoking ''horror and delight.'' Dudley Fitts declared that ''it is a frightening poetry, thank God, a poetry of angry conviction, few manners and no winsome graces. It is stubborn in its Old Guard attitude, stubborn in its technique: so unfashionable, indeed, in its resistance to the prevalent obsession with metrical vacuity, that a well-bred young new-classicist might regard it as almost theatrically conservative.''

The Big Clock, which was produced as a motion picture in 1948, is Fearing's best-known work. In stark journalistic style, the book relates the events following a murder. Tired of his mistress, a publisher of a large metropolitan magazine kills her, pinning the crime on a stranger seen leaving her apartment that evening. He subsequently assigns the story to his ace crime reporter who, in fact, was the very stranger seen the night of the murder: the hunter and hunted are one.

Kenneth Fearing's work, according to Eugene Davidson, ''is readable, often brilliant writing of innuendo, of things seen out of the corner of his eye, of fears and doubts and strange characters in the background.''

BIOGRAPHICAL/CRITICAL SOURCES: Poetry, January,

1941, December, 1943, August, 1957; *New York Times,* October 24, 1948, February 17, 1957; *Nation,* November 13, 1948, January 19, 1957; *Saturday Review,* June 29, 1957.*

* * *

FEDER, Jane 1940-

PERSONAL: Born September 23, 1940, in Brooklyn, N.Y.; daughter of Jules (a lawyer) and Patricia (a bookkeeper; maiden name, Brechner) Gaynor; married Michael Feder (a retailer), February 5, 1961; children: Jonathan Paul. *Education:* Attended Skidmore College, 1957-59; New York University, B.A., 1960. *Office:* Pantheon Books, 201 East 50th St., New York, N.Y. 10010.

CAREER: Random House, Inc., School and Library Services, New York City, promotion assistant, 1963-65; Pantheon Books, Juvenile Division, New York City, editorial assistant, 1965-67, assistant editor, 1968-70, editor, 1970-75, senior editor, 1975—. *Member:* Society of Children's Book Writers, Children's Book Council.

WRITINGS—For children: *Beany,* Pantheon, 1978; *The Nightlight,* Dial, 1980.

WORK IN PROGRESS: A sequel to *Beany,* publication by Pantheon expected in 1981.

SIDELIGHTS: Jane Feder writes: "Watching a child grow, attempting to help him deal with the complexities of the world, made it clear that children as well as adults need to know that their fears and joys are shared by others. Seeing themselves in characters in books, dealing with similar situations or feelings, hopefully provides a connection with humankind and with the self."

* * *

FEELINGS, Muriel (Grey) 1938-

PERSONAL: Born July 31, 1938, in Philadelphia, Pa.; married Thomas Feelings (an author and illustrator), February 18, 1969 (divorced, 1974); children: Zamani, Kamili. *Education:* Attended Philadelphia Museum School of Art, 1957-60; Los Angeles State College (now California State University, Los Angeles), B.A., 1963. *Address:* c/o Dial Press, 1 Dag Hammarskjold Plaza, New York, N.Y. 10017.

CAREER: Writer. Teacher of Spanish and art in elementary and secondary schools in Philadelphia, Pa., and New York, N.Y.; teacher of art at a boys' secondary school in Kampala, Uganda. *Member:* Columbian Design Society. *Awards, honors: Moja Means One* and *Jambo Means Hello* were American Library Association Notable Books; *Moja Means One* was a runner-up for the Caldecott Medal, 1972, and was cited by the Brooklyn Art Books for Children, 1973.

WRITINGS—Juvenile: *Zamani Goes to Market* (illustrated by husband, Thomas Feelings), Seabury, 1970; *Moja Means One: Swahili Counting Book* (illustrated by T. Feelings), Dial, 1971; *Jambo Means Hello: Swahili Alphabet Book* (illustrated by T. Feelings), 1974.

SIDELIGHTS: Muriel Feelings spent two years in Africa. During her stay there, she taught at a boys' secondary school in Kampala and traveled extensively in Uganda, Kenya, Tanzania, and Central Africa. Her experiences in Africa served as the inspiration for her three books, all of which are about African culture and language.

BIOGRAPHICAL/CRITICAL SOURCES: Saturday Review, January 15, 1972.*

FENTON, William N(elson) 1908-

PERSONAL: Born December 15, 1908, in New Rochelle, N.Y.; son of John William (a painter) and Anna (a teacher; maiden name, Nourse) Fenton; married Olive Ortwine (a teacher of English), April 4, 1936; children: Elizabeth Fenton Snyder, John William II, Douglas Bruce. *Education:* Dartmouth College, A.B., 1931; Yale University, Ph.D., 1937. *Politics:* Democrat. *Religion:* Episcopalian. *Home:* 7 North Helderberg Parkway, Slingerlands, N.Y. 12159. *Office:* 210 University Library, State University of New York at Albany, 1400 Washington Ave., Albany, N.Y. 12222.

CAREER: U.S. Indian Field Service, Tonawanda, N.Y., community worker, 1935-37; St. Lawrence University, Canton, N.Y., instructor, 1937-38, assistant professor, 1938-39; Smithsonian Institution, Washington, D.C., associate anthropologist, 1939-43, senior ethnologist for Bureau of American Ethnology, 1943-51, research associate with ethnogeographic board, 1942-45; National Academy of Sciences and National Research Council, Washington, D.C., executive secretary for anthropology and psychology, 1952-54; New York State Museum and Science Service, Albany, assistant commissioner, 1954-68; State University of New York at Albany, research professor, 1968-76, distinguished professor of anthropology, 1976-79, emeritus distinguished professor, 1979—. Visiting professor at Northwestern University, 1947, and University of Michigan, 1951; lecturer at Johns Hopkins University, 1949-50, and Catholic University of America, 1950-52. Member of board of trustees of Museum of the American Indian, 1976—.

MEMBER: American Anthropological Association (past member of executive board), American Folklore Society (fellow; president, 1962), American Ethnological Society (president, 1961); Trout Unlimited (president of Clearwater Chapter, 1979—). *Awards, honors:* Cornplanter Medal for Iroquois Research from Cayuga County Historical Society, 1965, for contributions to Iroquois research; LL.D. from Hartwick College, 1968; Citizen Laureate Award from University Foundation at Albany, 1978; National Endowment for the Humanities fellowship, 1978-79; Dartmouth College Class of 1930 Award, 1979; named "Dean in Perpetuum of Iroquois Studies" by Conference on Iroquois Research, 1979.

WRITINGS: Reports on Area Studies in American Universities, Ethnogeographic Board, Smithsonian Institution, 1945; *Area Studies in American Universities,* American Council on Education, 1947; *The Roll Call of the Iroquois Chiefs: A Study of a Mnemonic Cane From the Six Nations Reserve,* Smithsonian Institution Press, 1950; (editor and contributor) *Symposium on Local Diversity in Iroquois Culture,* U.S. Government Printing Office, 1951, reprinted, Scholarly Press, 1976; *The Iroquois Eagle Dance: An Offshoot of the Calumet Dance* (bound with *An Analysis of the Iroquois Eagle Dance and Songs,* by Gertrude Prokosch Kurath), U.S. Government Printing Office, 1953; *American Indian and White Relations to 1830: Needs and Opportunities for Study,* University of North Carolina Press, 1957; (editor) *Symposium on Cherokee and Iroquois Culture,* U.S. Government Printing Office, 1961; (editor) Arthur Caswell Parker, *Parker on the Iroquois,* Syracuse University Press, 1968; (editor and translator, with Elizabeth L. Moore) J. F. Lafitau, *Customs of the American Indians, Compared With the Customs of Primitive Times,* Champlain Society, Volume I, 1974, Volume II, 1977.

WORK IN PROGRESS: A Documentary History of the Iroquois: The Colonial Treaties of the Five (Later Six) Nations,

1640-1842; "The Iroquois False Face Society" for the Museum of the American Indian.

SIDELIGHTS: Fenton writes: "My artist father was a collector of Seneca Indian ethnographic art. As a boy I accompanied him to the Allegany Reservation of the Seneca Nation in western New York. I returned there as a graduate student at Yale to do my first field work for a dissertation—a trip that shaped my career afterward. In the 1940's, at the Smithsonian, I wrote several monographs on Iroquois medicine societies." *Avocational interests:* Angling, fly fishing.

* * *

FETTERMAN, John (Davis) 1920-1975

PERSONAL: Born February 25, 1920, in Danville, Ky.; died of a heart attack, June 21, 1975, in Louisville, Ky.; son of John Lawrence and Zora (Goad) Fetterman; married Evelyn Alline Maner, November 2, 1944; children: Phyllis Lee (Mrs. John Terry), Mindy Nelle. *Education:* Murray State University, B.S., 1948. *Religion:* Methodist. *Home:* 4425 Greenbriar Rd., Louisville, Ky. 40207.

CAREER: Teacher in public schools in Illinois, 1948-50; associated with the *Nashville Tennessean,* 1950-57; *Louisville Courier-Journal* and *Courier-Journal & Times Magazine,* Louisville, Ky., writer and photographer, 1957-75. *Military service:* U.S. Naval Reserve, 1942-45. *Awards, honors:* Co-recipient of Pulitzer Prize in journalism, 1967, for *Courier-Journal & Times Magazine* edition on strip mining; Pulitzer Prize in journalism, 1969, for news story, "Pfc. Gibson Comes Home"; National Headliner Award, 1969; named Outstanding Alumnus of Murray State University, 1971.

WRITINGS: Stinking Creek: The Portrait of a Small Mountain Community in Appalachia, Dutton, 1967.

SIDELIGHTS: One of John Fetterman's goals as a writer was to attempt "to discover and record some of the truth of people and events of my time." That time, as his book and his Pulitzer Prize-winning efforts in journalism reveal, was one that saw the destruction of much of the nation's land and many of its people. His book, *Stinking Creek,* explored the poverty in an Appalachian hillbilly community; his study of the damage caused by strip mining was part of a Pulitzer Prize-winning edition of the *Courier-Journal & Times Magazine;* his Pulitzer-Prize-winning article, "Pfc. Gibson Comes Home," followed the corpse of a Vietnam soldier as it returned to its native Kentucky town.

Fetterman researched *Stinking Creek* from February and throughout the summer of 1965, recording life among the shacks in the eastern Kentucky hamlet through interviews and photographs, letting the words and pictures speak for themselves. The result is a composite impression unlike any stereotypical image of hillbilly life. Fetterman interviewed one man, a father of seven, who drove five hours to Cincinnati each Monday to spend the week working at a job that paid as much as a welfare check would have supplied. "I guess I ain't made for the welfare," the man reasoned. "Sometimes I wonder how the men do it and live with themselves—stay on the welfare. I don't want none of that welfare 'til I can't work and then I want my share."

After touring the Appalachian community by way of *Stinking Creek,* former Secretary of the Interior Stewart L. Udall concluded that "we must rethink 'progress,' strive to save the character of the hill folk—and Indians—and not just push them into the city after 'jobs.' And to do that we have to know them. It is much simpler to translate from one language into another than from one psychology into another.

To those who would accelerate the pace of our attempt to do the latter in Appalachia, I would urge an evening with, a visit to, *Stinking Creek.*"

Response to Fetterman's work indicates that he did more than "discover and record": he provoked his readers, if not to action, then at least to thought. His "simple but deeply moving" story on Private Gibson "attracted a tremendous response," said the *New York Times.* The *Times* also reported that Fetterman and his paper's feature on strip mining "resulted in a tough strip-mining control law." Finally, Fetterman's book forced us to "rethink the approaches we have established to eliminate poverty," said Udall. *Stinking Creek* "should hit at our collective conscience."

BIOGRAPHICAL/CRITICAL SOURCES: Life, August 18, 1967; *New York Times,* June 23, 1975.*

* * *

FIELDEN, Charlotte

PERSONAL: Born in Toronto, Ontario, Canada; daughter of Bernard (a coat designer and manufacturer) and Mae (Wultz) Schrager; married Hubert Fielden, May 12, 1956 (separated, 1976); children: Jerry, Thomas. *Education:* Royal Conservatory of Toronto, A.R.C.T., 1951; University of Toronto, B.A. (with honors), 1955; also attended Marcel Marceau School of Mime, 1956. *Politics:* "A-political." *Religion:* "Non-religious, but into cosmic light and meditation." *Home:* 44 Walmer Rd., #801, Toronto, Ontario, Canada M5R 2X5. *Agent:* Helene Hoffman, 51 Spruce St., Toronto, Ontario, Canada.

CAREER: University of Sherbrooke, Sherbrooke, Quebec, teacher in drama department, 1965, 1966; Jeunesses Musicales Arts Camp, Orford, Quebec, teacher, 1965-68; Melanie Theatre, Montreal, Quebec, founder and artistic director, 1973-76; currently teacher and writer. Lecturer at universities, including Dalhousie University, Queen's University, Vanier College, Concordia University, and University of Quebec; adult education teacher of improvisation and developmental drama in Montreal, Quebec. Actress on stage, film, television, and radio; puppeteer, including regular appearance on television program, "Chez Helene," 1961-64. Gives poetry and prose readings, 1974—. *Member:* Writers Union of Canada (founding member; member of national council, 1977-78), Association of Canadian Television and Radio Artists, Playwrights Cooperative of Canada, Guild of Canadian Playwrights (founding member). *Awards, honors:* Epstein Award for Poetry from University of Toronto, 1955, for "Metamorphosis" and "African Nights"; gold honor medal from University of Toronto, 1955, for work in theatre; Canada Council grants, 1971, 1972, 1974; prize from National Playwriting Competition for Women, of Playwrights Cooperative of Canada, 1976, for "One Crowded Hour"; Ontario Arts Council grants, 1977, 1978, 1979; fleur-de-lys from *Montreal Star,* 1977, for French version of "One Crowded Hour."

WRITINGS: Crying as She Ran (novel), Macmillan, 1970; *One Crowded Hour* (three-act play; first produced in Montreal, Quebec, at Centaur Theatre, 1976), Playwrights Cooperative of Canada, 1977. Also author of *Travelling Together,* 1980.

Unpublished plays: "The Honeymoon" (one-act), first produced in Montreal, Quebec, at Centaur Theatre, 1976; "Summer Holidays" (one-act), first produced in Montreal, Quebec, at Centaur Theatre, 1976. Writer for television programs, including "Chez Helene" and "Family Court." Contributor of articles and stories to magazines, including *Tamarack, Impulse,* and *Canadian Theatre Review.*

WORK IN PROGRESS: The Tree Speaks, "an adventure in consciousness"; four three-act plays, "The Nowhere Girl," "The Dido," "The Morning Needs Me," and "The Hacks"; a musical comedy, with Robert Swerdlow.

SIDELIGHTS: Charlotte Fielden writes: "My life has been and still is very 'gestalty,' and that has to do with growth. Every time I achieve or accomplish something, I consider it an opportunity for growth, and then I move on to something else. There's a parallel movement or process on another level, or on several levels. There's the evolving of talents and gifts, along with that, emotional growth, but the most important kind of growth I'm aware of is the evolution of consciousness. The more I consider this last kind of growth, the more important it becomes in my life, until now I realize that it is the whole point of life, my life, without any doubt. With this attitude, I have lost my desperate clutch on this life, and in so doing have let flow the reality of ages. How can I fear death when life is all there is? How can I fear loneliness when I am linked to the loving realities of trees and earth and water and air? How can I imagine abandonment when in all those things there is a Presence that shows me, always, the way to serve, the way to love?"

BIOGRAPHICAL/CRITICAL SOURCES: Canadian Theatre Review, autumn, 1975.

* * *

FIELDS, Dorothy   1905-1974

PERSONAL: Born July 15, 1905, in Allenhurst, N.J.; died March 28, 1974, in New York, N.Y.; daughter of Lewis Maurice (a comedian under name Lew M. Fields) and Rose (Harris) Schoenfeld; married Eli Lahm, 1939 (died, 1958); children: David, Eliza. *Residence:* New York, N.Y.

CAREER: Lyricist, librettist, and writer. *Awards, honors:* Academy Award, 1936, for "The Way You Look Tonight"; elected to Songwriter's Hall of Fame, 1971; Antoinette Perry Award (Tony) and Grammy Award for "Redhead."

WRITINGS: (With brother, Herbert Fields) *Annie Get Your Gun* (original version produced on Broadway by Richard Rogers and Oscar Hammerstein), Dramatists Publishing, 1952; (with brother, Jack Fields) *South Pacific* (travel), Kodansha, 1972; (with J. Fields and Isamitsu Kitakoji) *Cherry Blossoms* (travel), Harper, 1973.

Lyricist of Broadway stage scores: "Blackbirds of 1928," 1928; "Hello, Daddy," 1928; "The International Revue," 1930; "The Vanderbilt Revue," 1930; "Rhapsody in Black," 1931; "Shoot the Works," 1931; "Singin' the Blues," 1931; "Stars in Your Eyes," 1939; "A Tree Grows in Brooklyn," 1951; (also librettist) "Redhead," 1959.

Librettist; all with H. Fields except as noted: "Let's Face It," 1941; "Something for the Boys," 1943; "Mexican Hayride," 1944; (also lyricist) "Up in Central Park," 1945; "Annie Get Your Gun," 1946; (also lyricist) "By the Beautiful Sea," 1954; (with Neil Simon) *Sweet Charity,* Random House, 1966; (with Cy Coleman) *Seesaw,* Samuel French, c. 1975.

Film scores: "Excuse My Dust," "The Farmer Takes a Wife," "I Dream Too Much," "Mr. Imperium," "Swingtime."

Involved in musical production: (With H. Fields) "Arms and the Girl"; "Joy of Living"; "The King Steps Out"; (with Jerome Kern) "Roberta."

Also lyricist of television musical, "Junior Miss," 1957.

SIDELIGHTS: Dorothy Fields wrote the lyrics for more

than four hundred songs, including the songs for over twenty-five motion pictures. Her most famous works are "On the Sunny Side of the Street," "I'm in the Mood for Love," "The Way You Look Tonight," and "I Can't Give You Anything But Love."

OBITUARIES: New York Times, March 29, 1974; *Washington Post,* March 30, 1974; *Newsweek,* April 8, 1974; *Time,* April 8, 1974.*

* * *

FINDLATER, Richard
    See BAIN, Kenneth Bruce Findlater

* * *

FIRSOFF, V(aldemar) Axel   1910-

PERSONAL: Born in 1910, in England. *Home:* 7 Wells Rd., Glastonbury, Somerset BA6 9DN, England.

CAREER: Writer, translator, and scientist. *Member:* Royal Astronomical Society (fellow).

WRITINGS: (Translator) E. E. Hauge, *Odds Against Norway,* Lindsay Drummond, 1941; *The Tatra Mountains,* Lindsay Drummond, 1942; *Ski Track on the Battlefield,* A. S. Barnes, 1943; *The Unity of Europe,* Lindsay Drummond, 1947; *The Cairngorms on Foot and Ski,* R. Hale, 1949.

Aran With Camera and Sketchbook, R. Hale, 1951; *Our Neighbour Worlds,* Philosophical Library, 1952; *In the Hills of Breadalbane,* R. Hale, 1954; *Strange World of the Moon,* Basic Books, 1959.

The Surface of the Moon, Hutchinson, 1961; *Moon Atlas,* Viking, 1961; *The Crust of the Earth,* Weidenfeld & Nicolson, 1962; *Life Beyond the Earth,* Basic Books, 1963; *The Moon,* Signet, 1964; *Exploring the Planets,* A. S. Barnes, 1964; *On Ski in the Cairngorms,* W. R. Chambers, 1965; *On Foot in the Cairngorms,* W. R. Chambers, 1965; *Facing the Universe,* A. S. Barnes, 1966; *Life, Mind, and Galaxies,* Oliver & Boyd, 1967; *The Interior Planets,* Oliver & Boyd, 1968; *The Old Moon and the New,* Oliver & Boyd, 1969.

Gemstones of the British Isles, Oliver & Boyd, 1971; *Working With Gemstones,* Arco, 1974; *Life Among the Stars,* Wingate, 1974; (with G. I. Firsoff) *The Rockhound's Handbook,* Arco, 1975; *The Solar Planets,* Crane, Russak, 1977; *At the Crossroads of Knowledge,* Ross-Erikson, 1977; *The New Face of Mars,* Ian Henry, 1979.

WORK IN PROGRESS: In Search of Reality.

SIDELIGHTS: Firsoff writes: "I have written numerous technical papers on astronomical subjects, and have lately branched off into parascience or parapsychology, and presented papers at international congresses. I have also written some fiction and poetry."

* * *

FISHER, A(rthur) Stanley T(heodore)   1906-
    (Michael Scarrott)

PERSONAL: Born January 10, 1906, in Hoima, Uganda; son of Arthur Bryan (a minister and missionary) and Ruth (a missionary; maiden name, Hurditch) Fisher; married Elizabeth Rose, January 1, 1936; children: Margaret (Mrs. Barry Surie), Jeremy. *Education:* Christ Church, Oxford, B.A., 1927, M.A., 1931; attended Cuddesdon Theological College, 1928-29. *Home:* 72 Rosamund Rd., Oxford, England.

CAREER: Teacher at school in Darjeeling, India, 1929-31; ordained minister of Church of England, 1931; chaplain of school in Blandford, Dorset, England, 1931-34; teacher at private schools in Buckinghamshire and Sussex, England, 1935-37; chaplain of grammar school in Leeds, England, 1937-43; chaplain and house tutor of De Aston school, Market Rasen, Lincolnshire, England, 1943-46; Magdalen College School, Oxford, England, chaplain and senior English master, 1946-60, fellows chaplain of Magdalen College, 1950-56; rector of Westwell and vicar of Holwell, Oxfordshire, England, 1961-74. Honorary secretary of the Oxford Diocesan Advisory Committee for the Care of Churches, 1978—. *Awards, honors:* Prize from Oxford University, 1950, for English Poem on a Sacred Subject, "The Prodigal Son."

WRITINGS: An Anthology of Prayers, Longmans, Green, 1934, 5th edition, 1950; *The Reach of Words* (poems), Macmillan, 1935; *Voice and Verse: An Anthology in Three Parts for Community Speaking,* Cambridge University Press, 1946; *The Comet and Earlier Poems,* Muller, 1948; *Happy Families: The Story of Sex for Boys and Girls,* Alliance, 1950; (under pseudonym Michael Scarrott) *Ambassador of Loss* (novel), Fortune Press, 1955; *Notes on Three Gospels and the Acts,* Basil Blackwell, 1956; *The Story of Life,* Basil Blackwell, 1957.

Fifty Days to Easter, Mowbray, 1964; *The History of Broadwell, Oxfordshire, with Filkins, Kelmscott and Holwell,* privately printed, 1968; *The History of Kencot,* privately printed, 1970; (with David G. O. Ayerst) *Records of Christianity,* Basil Blackwell, Volume I: *In the Roman Empire,* 1970, Volume II: *Christendom,* 1977; *The History of Westwell,* privately printed, 1972; *Selected Poems,* privately printed, 1978. Contributor to journals, including *Notes and Queries.*

WORK IN PROGRESS: At Auden's Oxford: An Autobiography.

SIDELIGHTS: Fisher attended Oxford University with W. H. Auden, John Betjeman, Cecil Day Lewis, Louis Macneice, and Stephen Spender, and introduced Auden to Christopher Isherwood. "It was the most brilliant generation of poets that Oxford has produced," says Fisher. He writes that the main themes of his own poems concern "love, nature—especially insects, religion, and the human predicament," and his work includes light verse.

Fisher added: "As a teacher of English I was concerned to interest my pupils in the sound of poetry as part of its sense, hence my anthology of *Voice and Verse,* and practical demonstrations of the Department of Education at Oxford. As a local historian I was concerned at the disappearance of the traditional patterns of life in English villages, the loss of schools and resident minister, so as last rector and vicar of two such villages, I compiled their histories and those of four neighbouring ones. In the two large source books of Christian history compiled with David Ayerst, we were concerned to show, by the use of contemporary records of all kinds, what it felt like to be a Christian in those times, to bring the history of Christianity alive."

AVOCATIONAL INTERESTS: Sculpting in stone, wood, and ivory.

*   *   *

FISHER, Bob
   See FISHER, Robert Percival

*   *   *

FISHER, Johanna   1922-

PERSONAL: Born July 6, 1922, in New Brunswick, N.J.; daughter of Frank (an engineer) and Lenore (a musician; maiden name, Berman) Szerlip; married Solomon Fisher (a lawyer); children: four. *Education:* Attended Brooklyn College (now of the City University of New York); Central Connecticut State College, B.S., 1960; University of Hartford, M.Ed., 1972; further graduate study at New School for Social Research; Columbia University, Ph.D., 1979; also studied at Ackerman Family Institute, Metropolitan Institute for Psychoanalytic Studies, and Psychiatric and Counseling Associates. *Residence:* Stamford, Conn. *Office:* Fairfield Public Schools, Fairfield, Conn. 06430.

CAREER: Elementary school teacher in Plainville, Conn., 1959-61; junior high school guidance counselor in Canton, Conn., 1961-63; psychological examiner for public schools in Bristol, Conn., 1963-65; Marian Hall Residential Treatment Center (for emotionally disturbed adolescent girls), Hartford, Conn., psychologist, 1965-66; school psychologist for public schools in Stamford, Conn., 1966-68; Fairfield Public Schools, Fairfield, Conn., school psychologist, 1968—. Instructor at University of Connecticut, 1970-73; instructor in parent effectiveness training, 1973-75. Private practice in family counseling, 1974—. *Member:* American Association of Marriage and Family Therapists (clinical member).

WRITINGS: A Parent's Guide to Learning Disabilities, Scribner, 1979.

WORK IN PROGRESS: Research on learning disabled children.

SIDELIGHTS: Johanna Fisher writes: "My special interest in learning disabilities began when one of my children showed signs of being dyslexic. I have pursued all the current information about learning problems avidly and have worked for the past fifteen years as a school psychologist with a major interest in the learning disabled. As I became an expert in the field, I began to realize that there was a great deal that parents could do to prevent and ameliorate the deficits that lead to learning disabilities, but no one had communicated this information to them. It was to correct this situation that I wrote my book."

*   *   *

FISHER, Robert Percival   1935-
   (Bob Fisher)

PERSONAL: Born April 20, 1935, in Brightlingsea, England; son of William Henry (a government official) and Nora (Percival) Fisher; married Sallie Ireland (a store director), October 29, 1956; children: Carolyne Sallie, Alice. *Education:* Attended University of London. *Home:* 54-56 Neal St., #4, London WC2H 9PA, England.

CAREER: Free-lance journalist, 1952-63; British Broadcasting Corp., London, England, television producer and director, 1963-71; free-lance journalist, 1971—. Marine consultant to businesses and advertising agencies. *Member:* International Yacht Racing Union, Royal Yachting Association (committee chairperson).

WRITINGS—All under name Bob Fisher: (With Reg White) *Catamaran Racing,* Cassell, 1968; (with Peter Cook) *The Longest Race,* Stamford Maritime, 1974; *Crewing Racing Dinghies and Keel Boats,* Stamford Maritime, 1975; *Small Boat Racing With the Champions,* Barrie & Jenkins, 1977. Contributor to yachting magazines and newspapers, including *Yachts and Yachting.*

WORK IN PROGRESS: A book on yacht racing, for Octopus Books.

SIDELIGHTS: Fisher writes: "I write about a sport in which I have participated on a high level for the past twenty-five years. It allows me to promote the sport and to compare and understand those who enjoy it. In an age where sport is beginning to replace war as a means of establishing national superiority, the role of the sportswriter becomes more and more important."

* * *

FITTS, Dudley 1903-1968

PERSONAL: Born April 28, 1903, in Boston, Mass.; died July 10, 1968; married Cornelia Butler Hewitt, 1939; children: one son, one daughter. *Education:* Harvard University, A.B., 1925.

CAREER: Poet, critic, and translator. Choate School, Wallingford, Conn., instructor in English, beginning 1927; Phillips Academy, Andover, Mass., instructor in English, beginning 1941. Worked at both the MacDowell and Yaddo colonies for writers. *Awards, honors:* Grant from American Academy of Arts and Letters, 1948; appointed to Emilie Beldon Cochran Foundation, 1948.

WRITINGS: Poems, 1929-1936, New Directions, 1937. Also author with Genevieve Taggard, *Ten Introductions: A Collection of Modern Verse,* 1934, reprinted, Century Bookbindery, 1977.

Translator: *One Hundred Poems From the Palatine Anthology,* New Directions, 1938; *More Poems From the Palatine Anthology in English Paraphrase,* New Directions, 1941; (with Robert Fitzgerald) Sophocles, *Oedipus Rex: An English Version,* Harcourt, 1949; Aristophanes, *Lysistrata: An English Version,* Harcourt, 1954; Aristophanes, *The Frogs: An English Version,* Harcourt, 1955; *Poems From the Greek Anthology in English Paraphrase,* New Directions, 1956 (published in England as *From the Greek Anthology: Poems in English Paraphrase,* Faber, 1957); Aristophanes, *The Birds: An English Version,* Harcourt, 1957; (with Fitzgerald) Sophocles, *The Oedipus Cycle: An English Version,* Harcourt, 1958; Aristophanes, *Ladies' Day: An English Version* (translation of *Thesmophoriazusae*), Harcourt, 1959; Aristophanes, *Four Comedies: An English Version,* Harcourt, 1962; *Sixty Poems of Martial,* Harcourt, 1967. Also translator of *The Alcestis of Euripedes* (with Fitzgerald), 1936.

Editor: *Anthology of Contemporary Latin-American Poetry,* New Directions, 1942, reprinted, Greenwood Press, 1976; (and author of introduction) *Greek Plays in Modern Translation,* Dial Press, 1947; *Six Greek Plays in Modern Translation,* Dryden Press, 1955; (and contributor of translations; with Louis MacNeice) *Four Greek Plays,* Harcourt, 1960. Also editor with C. F. Pfatteicher of *Office Hymns of the Church,* 1951.

Also author of sound recording, "Dudley Fitts Reads From His Own Works," 1975; author of several short collections of poetry, including *Two Poems,* 1932. Editor of "Yale Series of Younger Poets," beginning 1960. Contributor of poems and critical articles to numerous periodicals, including *Hound and Horn, Poetry, Transition, Atlantic Monthly,* and *Criterion.*

SIDELIGHTS: Dudley Fitts was one of the foremost translators from the ancient Greek in this century. Differing from the procedure many scholars follow, Fitts attempted to evoke the inherent character from the work by taking certain liberties with the text. The result, most reviewers agreed, was a version as pertinent and meaningful to the modern reader as it was to the audiences of Sophocles and Aristophanes.

"This modern, colloquial translation [of *The Birds* by Aristo-

phanes] is, of course, aimed at introducing the comic literary and dramatic genius of Aristophanes to the general reader," explained Paul H. Cubeta, "but the apparatus of scholarly and critical notes and the index of proper names have a fresh exuberance that Aristophanes would surely have enjoyed. Fitts, moreover, has the imaginative insight to meet the Greek dramatist on his own literary grounds."

BIOGRAPHICAL/CRITICAL SOURCES: Saturday Review, July 3, 1937, June 22, 1957; *Poetry,* November, 1937; *Nation,* June 14, 1954; *New York Times,* September 11, 1955, October 29, 1967.

OBITUARIES: New York Times, July 11, 1968; *Washington Post,* July 12, 1968; *Antiquarian Bookman,* July 22, 1968; *Publishers Weekly,* August 5, 1968; *Books Abroad,* spring, 1969.*

* * *

FITZGERALD, John Dennis 1907-

PERSONAL: Born in 1907, in Utah. *Office:* c/o Dial Press, 1 Dag Hammarskjold Plaza, New York, N.Y. 10017.

CAREER: Writer. Worked as journalist and jazz drummer. *Awards, honors:* Young Readers' Choice Award from Pacific Northwest Library Association, 1976, for *Great Brain Reforms;* Surrey School Book of the Year Award, 1976, for *Me and My Little Brain.*

WRITINGS: Papa Married a Mormon (memoir), Prentice-Hall, 1955; *Mamma's Boarding House* (memoir), Prentice-Hall, 1958; *Uncle Will and the Fitzgerald Curse* (memoir), Bobbs-Merrill, 1961; (with Robert C. Meredith) *The Professional Story Writer and His Art,* Crowell, 1963; (with Meredith) *Structuring Your Novel: From Basic Idea to Finished Manuscript,* Barnes & Noble, 1972; *Brave Buffalo Fighter (Waditaka Tatanka Kisisohitika)* (juvenile), Independence Press, 1973; *Private Eye* (juvenile), Thomas Nelson, 1974.

"Great Brain" series; juvenile; published by Dial: *The Great Brain,* 1967; *More Adventures of the Great Brain,* 1969; *Me and My Little Brain,* 1971; *The Great Brain at the Academy,* 1972; *The Great Brain Reforms,* 1973; *The Return of the Great Brain,* 1974; *The Great Brain Does It Again,* 1975.

SIDELIGHTS: John Fitzgerald began his writing career by reaching back into his childhood and youth for material. The result was *Papa Married a Mormon.* A *San Francisco Chronicle* reviewer wrote of the book: "Papa built an extraordinary life and family in the alien West; Mama sounds like one of the nicest people in the Utah of her time; others pop up with humor, lustiness, rage and spirit—one of the best family albums I have run across in a long time." In contrast, a *New York Times* critic noted: "In these pages, papa and mama talk to each other like a couple of lovers out of *Godey's Lady's Book.* The other family and community portrayals read like the over-sentimentalized and romanticized eulogies at a family reunion. There remains a pretty valid, if sketchy, picture of how the Mormons and the miners built Utah."

Fitzgerald turned his hand to children's books in the early 1970's. The characters in the "Great Brain" series are drawn from his childhood. The relationship and schemes of two brothers growing up in the wilds of Utah is seen through the eyes of the younger brother, John Dennis (J.D.). Of *The Great Brain,* the first book in this series, a commentator for the *New York Times Book Review* wrote: "Tom [the oldest brother] would be enough to send most younger brothers stuttering off to the psychiatrist. But not J.D. The plucky youth is a willing Watson to his brother's Holmes, a Tonto to his Lone Ranger, and, as this charming memoir testifies, a Boswell to his Johnson." *Me and My Little Brain*, another book in this series, earned these words of praise from a *Children's Book Review* critic: "[*Me and My Little Brain*] is Tom Sawyer country—we are some miles further west and a decade or two later but the feeling's just the same.... Mr. Fitzgerald has humor, ingenuity, and a light touch with character and situation; he also has sympathy, insight and depth."

BIOGRAPHICAL/CRITICAL SOURCES: *San Francisco Chronicle*, November 10, 1955; *New York Times*, November 13, 1955; *New York Times Book Review*, November 19, 1967; *Children's Book Review*, autumn, 1974.*

*   *   *

FITZLYON, Kyril 1910-

PERSONAL: Born in 1910, in St. Petersburg, Russia; son of Leo (a member of Russian parliament) and Olga (Baranoff) Zinovieff; married April Mead (a writer), January 7, 1941; children: Sebastian, Julian. *Education:* University of London, B.Sc., 1932. *Religion:* Russian Orthodox. *Home:* 2 Arlington Cottages, Sutton Lane, London W.4, England.

CAREER: Former economist with Ministry of Defence, London, England; writer. *Military service:* British Army, 1941-46. *Member:* Society of Authors.

WRITINGS: (Translator, with wife, April Fitzlyon) *The Woman in the Case: Chekhov*, Neville Spearman, 1953; (translator and author of introduction) Theodor Mikhailovich Dostoevsky, *Summer Impressions*, J. Calder, 1955; (editor and translator) Ekaterina R. Dashkova, *The Memoirs of Princess Dashkov*, J. Calder, 1958; (translator) Leo Tolstoy, *Anna Karenina*, Harper, 1966; (translator) Konstantin Georgievich Paustovsky, *Southern Adventure*, Harvill, 1969; (translator) Tolstoy, *A Landowner's Morning*, Harper, 1969; (translator) Paustovsky, *Story of a Life*, Volume VI: *The Restless Years*, Harvill, 1974; (translator with Hayward) Abram Tertz, *A Voice From the Chorus*, Octagon, 1974; (with Tatiana Browning) *Before the Revolution: A View of Russia Under the Last Tsar*, Allen Lane, 1977. Contributor to magazines and newspapers, including *London, Soviet Studies*, and *Books and Bookmen*.

WORK IN PROGRESS: Translating the diary of Waslaw Nijinsky.

SIDELIGHTS: Fitzlyon's languages include French, Russian, Italian, German, Danish, and Norwegian. *Avocational interests:* Reading, travel.

*   *   *

FITZMAURICE, George 1877-1963

OBITUARY NOTICE: Born in 1877 in Listowel, Ireland; died in 1963 in Dublin, Ireland. Playwright. Although Fitzmaurice was one of the pioneer playwrights of the Abbey Theatre in Dublin, he was soon forgotten after the successful production of his play, "The Country Dressmaker," in 1907. He subsequently wrote over twenty plays, but none were produced and only a few were published. Fitzmaurice's reputation grew after his death, and since then some critics have heralded him as one of Ireland's most important playwrights. "The Pie Dish," "The Dandy Dolls," "The Magic Glasses," "'Twixt the Giltinans and the Carmodys," and "The Enchanted Land" were among his most noteworthy plays. Obituaries and other sources: *The Reader's Encyclopedia of World Drama*, Crowell, 1969; *McGraw-Hill Encyclopedia of World Drama*, McGraw, 1972; *Modern World Drama: An Encyclopedia*, Dutton, 1972; *Cassell's Encyclopaedia of World Literature*, revised edition, Morrow, 1973; *A Concise Encyclopedia of the Theatre*, Osprey, 1974.

*   *   *

FLANAGAN, William G(eorge) 1940-

PERSONAL: Born November 21, 1940, in Queens, N.Y.; son of William G. (a police detective) and Margaret (White) Flanagan; married Rosemary Harrigan, October 4, 1965 (divorced, January, 1978). *Education:* Brooklyn College of the City University of New York, B.A., 1962. *Home:* 277 West 10th St., New York, N.Y. 10014. *Agent:* Barbara Lowenstein, 250 West 57th St., New York, N.Y. 10019. *Office:* Esquire, 2 Park Ave., New York, N.Y. 10016.

CAREER: *Electrical World*, New York City, news editor, 1964-68; *Business Week*, New York City, staff writer, 1968-71, author of column, "Personal Business," 1971-76; *New York*, New York City, editor and author of column, "Your Own Business," 1976-78; *Esquire*, New York City, contributing editor and author of column, "Personal Finance," 1978—. *Military service:* U.S. Army, newspaper editor, 1962-64; served in Korea. *Member:* New York Financial Writers Association (president, 1974-75).

WRITINGS: *The Smart Executive's Guide to Major American Cities*, Morrow, 1975; *The Executive's Guide to Major American Cities*, Simon & Schuster, 1979; *Outsmarting Inflation*, Doubleday, 1980; *The Chairman* (novel), Dell, in press. Author of "Money," a monthly column in *Vogue*. Contributor to magazines, including *Diversion, Prime Time, TWA Ambassador*, and *Travel Illustrated*.

WORK IN PROGRESS: *Thoroughbred*, a novel.

SIDELIGHTS: Flanagan writes: "I guess there are two prime movers for every writer, from the newspaperman to the novelist. First, and most important, is a burning need to tell somebody something. Maybe it's only a weather report, maybe it is the death of a president or the good/bad/indifferent nature of man. Be it a lengthy yarn or a wire report, the writer has to express something which he knows or thinks he knows. It is, basically, a noble instinct.

"The other motive is, of course, fame. Writers *do* think they are better than most other people, and maybe they are. They are certainly willing to suffer for their craft. Writing is a lonely and difficult business; the writer cannot be blamed for wanting ample rewards, those being a byline (first) and money (if possible).

"Writers are naive and idealistic, and are often taken advantage of, especially when young. Witness the platoons of kids working on magazines, newspapers, and in publishing houses who are paid a pittance for the 'glory' of being in publishing. Eventually, the better ones learn that there is simply no other way of making it in this business but the typewriter. Editors come and go, but the writer cannot be denied.

"I see a danger, though, a complicating factor in this writers' law of nature that generally works toward the good of a society. That is the distortion caused by electronic journalism, and the instant fame and megabucks it generates. Idiots are entrusted with incredible faith by an unassuming public. The inflatability of the ego takes a quantum jump. The 'writer' sits on a back bench punching up copy for a talking head, and the pure transmission of information, the basic prime mover of the writer to communicate, is frustrated. The tube is an aberration; it upsets the basic equation of what it is to be a writer."

BIOGRAPHICAL/CRITICAL SOURCES: *New York*, March 29, 1976.

FLEESON, Doris 1901-1970

OBITUARY NOTICE: Born May 20, 1901, in Sterling, Kan.; died August 1, 1970. Journalist. Fleeson was a Washington correspondent for the *New York Daily News* for fifteen years and a Washington columnist for United Feature Syndicate for another twenty-one years. Known for her wit, impartiality, and outspoken commentary on the political scene, Fleeson was twice awarded the New York Newspaperwoman's Club prize for distinguished reporting, and several other awards. Obituaries and other sources: *Current Biography*, Wilson, 1959, October, 1970; *New York Times*, August 2, 1970; *Who's Who of American Women*, 8th edition, Marquis, 1973.

* * *

FLEMING, David A(rnold) 1939-

PERSONAL: Born April 14, 1939, in Topeka, Kan.; son of Ambrose D. (in business) and Mildred (in business; maiden name, Williams) Fleming. *Education:* St. Mary's University, San Antonio, Tex., B.A., 1959; University of Chicago, M.A., 1963, Ph.D., 1965; University of Fribourg, S.T.B., 1967, S.T.L., 1969; postdoctoral study at University of Munich, 1967-68. *Home address:* P.O. Box 23130, St. Louis, Mo. 63156. *Office:* 4528 Maryland, St. Louis, Mo. 63108.

CAREER: Entered Society of Mary (S.M.), 1956, ordained Roman Catholic priest, 1969; St. Mary's University, San Antonio, Tex., assistant professor of English and theology, 1969-76; Society of Mary, St. Louis, Mo., provincial assistant, 1976-79, provincial superior, 1979—. Chairperson of board of trustees of St. Mary's University, 1979—. Consultant to Leadership Conference of Women Religious. *Member:* American Academy of Religion, Renaissance Society of America, Association of Governing Boards of Colleges and Universities, Conference of Major Superiors of Men of the United States of America. *Awards, honors:* Woodrow Wilson fellowship, 1962; Fulbright grant, 1967; Bavarian State scholarship, 1967; American Council of Learned Societies grant, 1971; Hoepfner Literary Prize from *Southern Humanities Review*, 1972, for article, "Literary Interpretation Today."

WRITINGS: (Editor) William Chaminade, *Notes d'instruction*, Etudes Marianistes, 1967; (editor) John Barclay, *Euphormio's Satyricon*, de Graaf, 1973; *The Fire and the Cloud: An Anthology of Catholic Spirituality*, Paulist/Newman, 1977. Contributor to scholarly journals.

WORK IN PROGRESS: Research on contemporary movements of monastic religious life for men and women, especially in the United States.

SIDELIGHTS: Fleming writes: "My interests have shifted over the years from comparative Renaissance literature, through the Western tradition of mysticism, and into contemporary trends in Roman Catholic religious communities. In all this I feel a common thread, hard to define, but certainly summarized in the discipline of hermeneutics—the interpretation of the wealth of the past in a way that enters into dialogue with the concerns and challenges of the present. My experiences of recent years have given me the chance to share this dialogue and search with people from several parts of the world and to expand horizons to global concerns through conferences in Europe, Asia, and South America. I feel that we are at a challenging turning point in Western civilization, painful but full of promise for the future."

FLOWERS, Charles E(ly, Jr.) 1920-

PERSONAL: Born July 20, 1920, in Zebulon, N.C.; son of Charles Ely and Carmen (Poole) Flowers; married Juanita Bays, November 23, 1944 (deceased); married Jaunzetta Shew, September 25, 1972; children: (first marriage) Charles Ely III, Carmen Eva. *Education:* Citadel, B.S., 1941; Johns Hopkins University, M.D., 1944. *Home:* 3757 Rockhill Rd., Birmingham, Ala. 35223. *Office:* Medical Center, University of Alabama, Birmingham, Ala. 35294.

CAREER: Johns Hopkins Hospital, Baltimore, Md., intern, 1944, resident, 1945-50; State University of New York at Brooklyn, instructor, 1950-51, assistant professor of obstetrics and gynecology, 1951-53; University of North Carolina, Chapel Hill, associate professor, 1953-61, professor of obstetrics and gynecology, 1961-66; Baylor University, Houston, Tex., professor of obstetrics and gynecology and head of department, 1966-69; University of Alabama, Birmingham, professor of obstetrics and gynecology and head of department at Medical Center, 1969—, obstetrician-and-gynecologist-in-chief at university hospital, 1969—. Diplomate of American Board of Obstetrics and Gynecology (associate examiner); member of oral contraceptives advisory committee of International Planned Parenthood, and member of its national medical services advisory committee; consultant to National Institute of Mental Health. *Military service:* U.S. Army, Medical Corps, 1946-48; became captain.

MEMBER: International College of Anesthetists, American Medical Association, American College of Surgeons, American Gynecological Society, American Association of Obstetricians and Gynecologists, American College of Obstetricians and Gynecologists (chairperson of committee on anesthesia and analgesia), Continental Gynecological Society, Central Association of Obstetricians and Gynecologists.

WRITINGS: Obstetric Analgesia and Anesthesia, Harper, 1967; (with Maxine Abrams) *A Woman Talks With Her Doctor: A Comprehensive Guide to Women's Health Care*, Morrow, 1979. Editor of *Journal of Continuing Education in Obstetrics and Gynecology;* member of editorial board of *Obstetrics and Gynecology;* member of editorial advisory board of *Physician*.

WORK IN PROGRESS: Research into female sexuality.

* * *

FLYING OFFICER X
See BATES, H(erbert) E(rnest)

* * *

FOIN, Theodore C(hin) 1940-

PERSONAL: Born September 27, 1940, in Chicago, Ill.; son of Theodore C. and Lai Sheung (Luke) Foin; married Alice Angela Terry (a laboratory technician), July 30, 1966; children: Erika Meilin, Jeremy Chin. *Education:* Stanford University, A.B., 1962; University of North Carolina, Ph.D., 1967. *Home:* 1019 Deodara Court, Davis, Calif. 95616. *Office:* Department of Environmental Studies, University of California, Davis, Calif. 95616.

CAREER: University of California, Davis, assistant professor, 1970-76, associate professor of environmental studies, 1976—. *Member:* Society of Naturalists, Ecological Society of America, American Association for the Advancement of Science, California Botanical Society, Sigma Xi. *Awards, honors:* Shared in certificate of merit from the American Institute of Planners, 1971, for "The California Tomorrow Plan," a proposal for statewide planning for California development to the year 2000.

WRITINGS: *Ecological Systems and the Environment,* Houghton, 1976. Contributor of more than forty articles to scientific and environmental studies journals.

WORK IN PROGRESS: Research on ecology, with emphasis on grassland ecology.

SIDELIGHTS: Foin writes: "I have attempted to build a career of broad interests within my discipline. My book represents a synthesis of many of these interests, and was written in the belief that environmental problem-solving would stimulate a cross-disciplinary program of research in both government laboratories and academic institutions.

"Since the publication of my book I have devoted my time to teaching and research in more theoretical ecology, particularly in grassland and range communities. However, I remain committed to the idea that ecology as a science is potentially useful for sophisticated insight into environmental problem solving. A real science of applied ecology, such as is hinted at in *Ecological Systems and the Environment,* has hardly been developed even while the measures for resource development and better environmental assessment continue to grow. If I write a book in the future, it will be based on experience in this area of environmental analysis."

*   *   *

FOLDS, Thomas M.

PERSONAL: Married; children: Charles W. *Education:* Yale University, B.A., 1930, B.F.A., 1934. *Home and office:* 909-B Heritage Village, Southbury, Conn. 06488.

CAREER: English teacher at private school in Exeter, N.H., 1934-35, art director, 1935-46; Northwestern University, Evanston, Ill., professor of art, 1946-60, head of department; Metropolitan Museum of Art, New York, N.Y., dean of education, 1960-73, educator emeritus and guest lecturer, 1973—. President of School of the Art League of New York City, 1968-73. Chairperson of committee for education and cultural action of International Council of Museums, 1968. Designer of nationally circulated art exhibitions. Performer on national television programs, 1953-56. Art consultant to business corporations. *Member:* College Art Association of America.

WRITINGS: (Self-illustrated) *Where Is the Fire?* (juvenile), Houghton, 1946; (self-illustrated) *Your Taste and Good Design,* Science Research Associates, 1953; (author of commentary with Edith A. Standen) *Masterpieces of Painting in the Metropolitan Museum of Art,* New York Graphic Society, 1970.

Script writer for about twenty-five television art programs, 1953-56. Co-editor of art section of English literature textbooks, for Harcourt, 1968. Contributor to art and education journals.

WORK IN PROGRESS: Research on nineteenth-century English painting, contemporary American painting, and Romance sculpture and architecture.

SIDELIGHTS: Folds writes: "Though retired from the staff of the Metropolitan Museum in 1973, I have continued to give a program of art history lectures there and elsewhere, especially in Connecticut. My wife and I travel abroad every year to prepare material for future lecture programs."

*   *   *

FOLEY, Duncan K(arl)   1942-

PERSONAL: Born June 15, 1942, in Columbus, Ohio; son of Gerard M. (a research physicist) and Ruth C. (Johnson) Foley; married Helene Marie Peet (a professor of classics), June 11, 1966. *Education:* Swarthmore College, B.A., 1964; Yale University, Ph.D., 1966. *Home:* 404 Riverside Dr., #5-C, New York, N.Y. 10025. *Office:* Department of Economics, Barnard College, Columbia University, New York, N.Y. 10027.

CAREER: Massachusetts Institute of Technology, Cambridge, assistant professor of economics, 1966-69, associate professor of economics, 1969-73; Stanford University, Stanford, Calif., associate professor of economics, 1973-79; Columbia University, Barnard College, New York, N.Y., professor of economics, 1977—. *Member:* American Economic Association, Union for Radical Political Economy.

WRITINGS: (With Miguel Sidrauski) *Monetary and Fiscal Policy in a Growing Economy,* Macmillan, 1971. Contributor to professional journals.

WORK IN PROGRESS: Research on labor theory of value and macroeconomic instability.

*   *   *

FONG-TORRES, Ben   1945-

PERSONAL: Born January 7, 1945, in Alameda, Calif.; son of Richard (a chef) and Connie (a seamstress; maiden name, Joe) Fong-Torres; married Dianne Sweet (a probation officer), May 1, 1976. *Education:* San Francisco State University, B.A., 1966. *Residence:* San Francisco, Calif. *Agent:* International Creative Management, 8899 Beverly Blvd., Los Angeles, Calif. 90048. *Office: Rolling Stone,* 625 Third St., San Francisco, Calif. 94107.

CAREER: Writer. KFOG-Radio, San Francisco, Calif., announcer and writer, 1967; Pacific Telephone Co., San Francisco, editor and writer, 1968; *Rolling Stone,* San Francisco, senior editor and writer, 1968—. Announcer on weekends for KSAN-Radio, 1970—. Consultant to Population Institution, 1977-78. Member of board of directors of Youth Advocates, San Francisco, 1977. *Member:* Writers Guild. *Awards, honors:* Deems Taylor Award from American Society of Composers, Authors, and Publishers, 1974, for interview with Ray Charles; award for broadcasting excellence from *Billboard,* 1976, for narration of "San Francisco: What a Long Strange Trip It's Been"; Northern California Emmy Award, 1977, for interview with Steve Martin.

WRITINGS—Editor: *The Rolling Stone Rock 'n' Roll Reader,* Bantam, 1974; *What's That Sound?,* Anchor Press/Doubleday, 1976. Editor and writer of *East-West,* 1969-70. Contributor to periodicals.

WORK IN PROGRESS: Screenplay, tentatively entitled "Somebody to Love," for Paramount.

SIDELIGHTS: Fong-Torres told *CA:* "I started writing because I was a ham and wanted attention, and from reading my favorite magazines, *Mad* and *Dig,* it seemed easy. Now I write because, although it ain't easy, it's the best work in the world."

BIOGRAPHICAL/CRITICAL SOURCES: *Dallas Times-Herald,* April 16, 1976; *Bam,* December 3, 1976; *Mountain Express,* July 7, 1977; *City Adventure,* February 6, 1978.

*   *   *

FOOTE, Timothy (Gilson)   1926-

PERSONAL: Born May 3, 1926, in London, England; son of John Taintor (a writer) and Jessica Florence (Todhunter) Foote; married Audrey Chamberlain (a writer and teacher), June 18, 1948; children: Colin, Victoria, Valerie, Andrew.

Education: Harvard University, A.B., 1949, M.A., 1952. *Religion:* Episcopalian. *Home:* 63 Orchard St., Nyack, N.Y. 10960. *Agent:* John Cushman Associates, Inc., 174 Sullivan St., New York, N.Y. 10012. *Office: Time,* 1271 Avenue of the Americas, New York, N.Y. 10020.

CAREER: Life, New York City, reporter and writer, 1949-51, assistant editor, 1953-54; teacher, 1952-53; Time-Life News Service, Paris, France, foreign correspondent, 1954-58; *Life,* 1958-62, associate editor, then senior editor; *Time,* New York City, book reviewer, 1962-64; International Book Society, Paris, European editor, 1964-66; *Time,* associate editor, 1968, senior editor and book critic, 1969-77. Fiction judge for National Book Awards, 1974. *Military service:* U.S. Navy, 1944-46; served in Pacific theater and Asia; received two battle stars. *Member:* National Book Critics Circle (member of executive board, 1976-77), Phi Beta Kappa, Signet Society, Harvard Club, Nyack Boat Club, Nyack Field Club.

WRITINGS: The World of Peter Bruegel, Time-Life, 1968; *The Great Ringtailed Island Caper,* Houghton, 1979; *A Sailor's History of the American Revolution,* Knopf, in press. Contributor to popular magazines, including *Esquire, New York, Harper's,* and *Horizon.* Member of advisory board of *Sea History,* 1977-78.

WORK IN PROGRESS: An anthology of fishing stories, publication by David R. Godine.

SIDELIGHTS: Foote commented: "I see less and less that I think is cheerful in America, and at the same time I think it is mainly in America and among the Western countries that forces are struggling, often unwittingly, which will decide whether Europe and America will have much of a future in the next century."

* * *

FORBES-DENNIS, Phyllis   1884-1963
   (Phyllis Bottome)

OBITUARY NOTICE: Born May 31, 1884, in Rochester, Kent, England; died August 22, 1963. Author of more than twenty novels under the pseudonym Phyllis Bottome. She was best known for her anti-Nazi novel, *The Mortal Storm.* Obituaries and other sources: *New York Times,* August 24, 1963; *Time,* August 30, 1963; *Publishers Weekly,* September 9, 1963; *The Reader's Encyclopedia,* 2nd edition, Crowell, 1965; *The New Century Handbook of English Literature,* revised edition, Appleton, 1967; *Twentieth Century Writing: A Reader's Guide to Contemporary Literature,* Transatlantic, 1969; *Longman Companion to Twentieth Century Literature,* Longman, 1970; *The Penguin Companion to English Literature,* McGraw, 1971.

* * *

FORD, Murray J(ohn) S(tanley)   1923-

PERSONAL: Born February 20, 1923, in Calgary, Alberta, Canada; son of Stanley (a contractor) and Margaret (Budds) Ford; married Gwynneth Ney, May 21, 1959; children: Donald, Margaret, Jane. *Education:* McMaster University, B.A., 1948, B.D., 1951; Columbia University, M.A., 1953; Chicago Theological Seminary, D.Rel., 1968. *Politics:* Liberal. *Home:* 177 Old Ancaster Rd., Dundas, Ontario, Canada L9H 3R3. *Office:* Divinity College, McMaster University, Hamilton, Ontario, Canada L8S 4K1.

CAREER: Ordained Baptist minister, 1951; pastor of Baptist churches in New York, N.Y., 1951-56, and Toronto, Ontario, 1956-62; McMaster University, Hamilton, Ontario, pro-

fessor of theology, 1962—. Professor of Christian ministry and director of field education at Toronto School of Theology, 1968; member of coordinating committee on theological education in Canada. Life member of board of directors of Brooklyn Young Men's Christian Association. *Military service:* Royal Canadian Air Force, 1941-45. *Member:* Association for Professional Education in Ministry (vice-president), Association for Theological Schools (Canadian member of executive committee), American Academy of Homiletics.

WRITINGS: Church Vocations: A New Look, Judson, 1951; *A Call to Discipleship,* Department of Communications, Baptist Convention of Ontario and Quebec, 1976; *Planning, Preparing, Praising,* Judson, 1978. Contributor to religious magazines.

WORK IN PROGRESS: What Shall We Share With the Children?

SIDELIGHTS: Ford comments: "Most of my writing has been motivated by a desire to reach a wider audience with helpful background information to guide their personal growth."

* * *

FORD, W(illiam) Clay(ton, Jr.)   1946-

PERSONAL: Born July 18, 1946, in El Paso, Tex.; son of William Clay (in business) and Virginia (Morrow) Ford; married Cheryl Jean Verkler, March 15, 1979; children: Billy, Hannah. *Education:* Davidson College, B.A., 1968; American Baptist Seminary of the West, M.Div., 1972; Eastern Baptist Theological Seminary, D.Min., 1980. *Home and office:* 219 Ford St., West Conshohocken, Pa. 19428.

CAREER: Ordained American Baptist minister, 1971; assistant youth minister at Baptist church in Pomona, Calif., 1969-70; American Baptist Home Missions Society, Valley Forge, Pa., missionary in Berkeley, Calif., summer, 1970; assistant pastor of Baptist churches in San Bernardino, Calif., 1971-72, and Chula Vista, Calif., 1972-78; Balligomingo Baptist Church, West Conshohocken, Pa., pastor, 1978—. Member of American Baptist Ministers Council. Member of Chula Vista Commission on Housing for Low and Moderate Income Citizens, 1977-78, and Commission on Racial and Ethnic Balance in Schools, 1978.

WRITINGS: Berkeley Journal: Jesus and the Street People—A First-Hand Report, Harper, 1972. Also author of *The Shepherding,* 1980. Contributor to *New Covenant.*

WORK IN PROGRESS: Christian Communal Living, a critique based on five years' experience, publication expected in 1981; a systematic approach to the study of cults in contrast to the Christian church, publication expected in 1981; research on "Gospel saturation" in a small depressed community, building the body, and community involvement program development.

SIDELIGHTS: Ford writes: "I have a vital concern for the Christian church, that it become renewed, that it live out its message. I am also concerned about a 'wholistic' approach to the ministry: the whole gospel for the whole world, balancing personal piety with corporate awareness, identity, and responsibility; spiritual vitality with social action and involvement; evangelism with the practical application of Christ's love; and gifts of the spirit with fruits of the spirit. I have a deep desire for revival, for the spiritual awakening to Christ to sweep through our land. I believe it is our only hope."

BIOGRAPHICAL/CRITICAL SOURCES: American Baptist, winter, 1971; *Dimensions,* spring, 1971.

FORSYTHE, Elizabeth 1927-

PERSONAL: Born May 25, 1927, in London, England; daughter of George (a banker) and Margaret (Harvey) Webber; married John Forsythe (a merchant banker), October 1, 1955; children: Nicola, Peter, Joanna. *Education:* King's College Hospital Medical School, London, M.R.C.S., L.R.C.P., 1950; Royal Institute of Public Health and Hygiene, D.P.H., 1966. *Home:* Lybster Harbour, Lybster, Caithness, Scotland. *Agent:* Peter Grose, Curtis Brown Ltd., 1 Craven Hill, London W.2, England. *Office:* Rhind House, Wick, Caithness, Scotland.

CAREER: Deputy medical officer of health in Saffron Walden, England, 1966-73; family planning medical officer in Saffron Walden, 1965-73; Highland Health Board, Wick, Scotland, clinical medical officer, 1974—. Lecturer to Women's Royal Naval Service. Member of local Disablement Income Group. *Member:* British Medical Association, Medical Journalists Association.

WRITINGS: Asthma, Hay Fever, and Other Allergies, Luscombe, 1975; *A Less Anxious You,* Luscombe, 1978; *Living With Multiple Sclerosis,* Faber, 1979; *Grow Your Own Health,* Pelham, 1979; *Low Fat Gourmet,* Pelham, 1979; *Your Child's Health at Primary School,* Faber, 1979. Also editor of *Faber's Pocket Medical Dictionary.* Contributor to *Scotsman.*

SIDELIGHTS: Elizabeth Forsythe told *CA:* "I started freelance journalism about twenty years ago because I wanted to stay at home while my children were small, but not lose touch with medicine. I had multiple sclerosis diagnosed in 1976, although I have had the disease for many years. I am still able to do medical work part-time, but it was obviously sensible at that point to increase my writing commitment.

"I do not attempt to write medical books for professional workers; I write my books *to* other people, not *for* other people, about medical problems. Perhaps I am now able to explain medicine and health and illness in a readable way without medical jargon. My own illness has certainly deepened my understanding of human problems."

* * *

FOSS, Christopher F(rank) 1946-

PERSONAL: Born April 8, 1946, in Portsmouth, England; son of Frank Victor and Doris (Dorsett) Foss; married Elaine Jean Jenkins, March 11, 1972; children: Robert James. *Education:* Attended high school in Portsmouth, England. *Office:* Jane's Yearbooks, Macdonald & Jane's Publishers Ltd., Paulton House, 8 Shepherdess Walk, London N1 7LW, England.

CAREER: Macdonald & Jane's Publishers Ltd., London, England, editor of "Jane's Armour and Artillery," and *Jane's Combat Support Equipment. Member:* Fortress Study Group.

WRITINGS: Armoured Fighting Vehicles of the World, Ian Allan, 1971, 3rd edition, 1977; *Profile Number 51: Abbot S.P.G.,* Profile, 1972; *Profile Number 53: FV 432 Series,* Profile, 1973; *Profile Number 62: Commando, Twister, and H.M.V.,* Profile, 1973; *Profile Number 65: PT-76 Light Amphibious Tank,* Profile, 1974; *Artillery of the World,* Ian Allan, 1974, 2nd edition, 1976; *Jane's Pocket Book of Modern A.F.V.'s,* Macdonald & Jane's, 1974, 2nd edition, 1977.

Jane's World Armoured Fighting Vehicles, Macdonald & Jane's, 1976; *Military Vehicles of the World,* Ian Allan, 1976, 2nd edition, 1979; *Infantry Weapons of the World,* Ian Allan, 1977, 2nd edition, 1979; *Jane's Pocket Book of Towed Artil-*lery, Macdonald & Jane's, 1977; (editor-in-chief) *Encyclopedia of Tanks and Armoured Fighting Vehicles,* Salamander Books, 1977; *Jane's Combat Support Equipment, 1978-79,* Macdonald & Jane's, 1978; (contributor) *The American War Machines,* Salamander Books, 1978.

Weapons correspondent for *Defence,* 1974—. Contributor to *Encyclopedia of Land Warfare.* Contributor of nearly two hundred articles to magazines, including *Battle, Armour, Military Technology, Airfix,* and *Defence Africa.*

WORK IN PROGRESS: Jane's Pocketbook of Military Vehicles; a second edition of *Jane's Combat Support Equipment;* a third edition of *Artillery of the World.*

* * *

FOSTER, Dorothy 1936-

PERSONAL: Born September 15, 1936, in Clintonville, Wis.; daughter of Frank A. (a director of industrial relations) and Norma (Dohrman) Sinkewicz; married Donald Foster, December 7, 1968 (divorced, 1976); children: Edward. *Education:* University of Wisconsin—Milwaukee, B.A., 1968, M.A., 1969; further study at University of British Columbia, 1970-71. *Politics:* None. *Religion:* None. *Home:* 1625 East Prince Rd., Tucson, Ariz. 85719.

CAREER: English teacher at a private college in West Germany, 1974-77; Arizona Center for Occupational Safety and Health, Tucson, library researcher and editor, 1979—.

WRITINGS: (Editor) *In Praise of Cats: A Book of Poems About Cats,* Crown, 1974.

WORK IN PROGRESS: Editing *The Silver Chain of Sound,* poems and illustrations of birds; editing *The Animal Fair,* animal poems for children; a vegetarian cookbook; a baby-food cookbook.

* * *

FOWLER, Elaine W(ootten) 1914-

PERSONAL: Born March 22, 1914, in New York, N.Y.; daughter of Irving (an actor; stage name, Alan Brooks) and Marion (an actress and writer; maiden name, Wootten) Hayward; married Gordon Fowler (a Navy captain), June 5, 1938; children: Gordon, Jr., Terry Fowler Fiumi, Eric Raymond. *Education:* Wellesley College, B.A., 1935; graduate study at George Washington University. *Home:* 7900 Curtis St., Chevy Chase, Md. 20015. *Office:* National Geographic Society, Room 338, Sixteenth Street Building, Washington, D.C. 20036.

CAREER: International Business Machines, systems representative, 1935-37; reporter, 1937-38; writer and broadcaster of radio program, Long Beach, Calif., 1942; Folger Shakespeare Library, Washington, D.C., head of reading room services, 1955-71, research associate, 1968-71, associate editor of publications, 1968-71; free-lance writer and editor, 1971—. Research associate at National Geographic Society, 1971—; film consultant. *Member:* International Shakespeare Association.

WRITINGS: English Seapower in the Early Tudor Period, 1485-1558, Cornell University Press, 1965; (with Louis B. Wright) *English Colonization of North America,* Edward Arnold, 1968; (contributor) *The Renaissance: Maker of Modern Man,* National Geographic Society, 1970; (with Wright) *West and by North: North America Seen Through the Eyes of Its Seafaring Discoverers,* Delacorte, 1971; (with Wright) *Everyday Life in the New Nation, 1787-1860,* Putnam, 1972; (with Wright) *The Moving Frontier: North Amer-*

ica as Seen Through the Eyes of Its Pioneer Discoverers, Delacorte, 1972; (with Wright) *A Visual Guide to Shakespeare's Life and Times,* Washington Square Press, 1975. Consultant for educational filmstrips and co-author and editor of educational film series, "The World of William Shakespeare," for National Geographic Society. Contributor to magazines, including *Shipmate.*

WORK IN PROGRESS: A study of Spanish conquistadors from Extremadura, Spain, with Louis B. Wright; a book on Patrol Wing Ten, a U.S. Navy air wing in early days of World War II, completion expected in 1982.

SIDELIGHTS: Elaine Fowler commented: "My major areas of professional interest are Renaissance English and European history, with special emphasis on early seafaring and exploration, and on William Shakespeare and his milieu. Thanks to parents in the diplomatic service and my husband's career in the Navy, I have lived in China, Canada, England, and Italy. In recent years professional travel has taken me to Great Britain, Italy, Portugal, Spain, and the Middle East. The unifying thread in all this is a fascination with the ways in which cultural ideas are transmitted and changed over time and space."

*   *   *

FOX, Richard Wightman 1945-

PERSONAL: Born November 27, 1945, in Boston, Mass.; son of Matthew Bernard (a television producer and writer) and Lucy (Pope) Fox; married Frances Diane Niblack, September 16, 1967; children: Rachel, Christopher. *Education:* Stanford University, B.A., 1966, M.A., 1974, Ph.D., 1975; attended Yale University, 1966-67. *Home:* 154 Franklin Rd., Hamden, Conn. 06517. *Office:* Department of History, Yale University, New Haven, Conn. 06520.

CAREER: Chinese University of Hong Kong, Chung Chi College, Hong Kong, instructor in western civilization, 1967-68; Lycee Ibn Rouchd, Blida, Algeria, teacher of English, 1968-70; Yale University, New Haven, Conn., assistant professor of history and American studies, 1975—. *Member:* Organization of American Historians, American Studies Association. *Awards, honors:* Fellowship from Stanford University, 1977; Morse fellowship from Yale University, 1979-80.

WRITINGS: So Far Disordered in Mind: Insanity in California, 1870-1930, University of California Press, 1978; (editor with T. J. Jackson Lears) *The Culture of Consumption in America,* Pantheon, 1981. Contributor of about forty articles and reviews to scholarly and popular journals.

WORK IN PROGRESS: A biography of Reinhold Niebuhr.

SIDELIGHTS: Fox writes: "The most pressing concern for the scholarly writer in an age of over-specialized disciplines is to cultivate a style accessible to non-specialists. Like Reinhold Niebuhr, the subject of my biography in progress, I am trying to bridge the gap between journalism and scholarship, between a wide audience of ordinary readers and a narrow one of academic professionals. There are few models in America of the serious 'writer' in the British sense. We tend to equate 'writer' with 'writer of fiction' rather than with 'essayist.' What we need are more essayists who are equally comfortable with scholarly methods and literate, nonesoteric expression."

*   *   *

F.P.A.
See ADAMS, Franklin P(ierce)

FRANCE, Richard 1938-

PERSONAL: Born May 5, 1938, in Boston, Mass.; son of N. R. Zagami (in military) and Rita (Foster) France; married Annette Ruth Darling, September, 1960 (divorced, 1965); married Rachel Anne Mehr (a writer and professor), March 21, 1969; children: Rebecca Foster, Miriam Sellin. *Education:* Attended Yale University, 1964-65; Carnegie-Mellon University, M.F.A., 1970, Ph.D., 1973. *Agent:* Susan Schulman, 165 West End Ave., New York, N.Y. 10023.

CAREER: Writer. Worked as foreign language programmer, radio announcer, actor, short-order cook, and trophy maker, 1957-68; WQED-TV, Pittsburgh, Pa., film and drama critic, 1969-72; Rhode Island College, Providence, assistant professor, 1972-73; Lawrence University, Appleton, Wis., assistant professor, 1974-80; Hofstra University, Hempstead, N.Y., associate professor, 1980—. American Theatre Association (vice-chairman, 1972-75, and chairman of playwrights program), Dramatists Guild, Screen Actors Guild. *Awards, honors:* Grants from Ford Foundation, Rockefeller Foundation, and National Endowment for the Arts; National Endowment for the Humanities Fellowship for independent study and research; *The Theatre of Orson Welles* was selected by *Choice* as one of the "most outstanding academic books" in 1978.

WRITINGS: The Magic Shop (juvenile play), Performance Publishing, 1972; *The Adventure of the Dying Detective* (juvenile play), I. E. Clark, 1974; *One Day in the Life of Ivan Denisovich* (play; adapted from the novel by Alexander Solzhenitsyn), Performance Publishing, 1974; *The Theatre of Orson Welles* (nonfiction), Bucknell University Press, 1977; *Feathertop* (juvenile play), Dramatic Publishing Co., 1979.

Other plays: "Don't You Know It's Raining" first produced in Dallas, Tex., at Dallas Theater Center, 1970; "A Day in the Life," first produced in Syracuse, N.Y., at Salt City Playhouse, 1973; "Station J," first produced in Chicago, Ill., at Body Politic Playhouse, 1979.

Work represented in anthology *The Best Short Plays of 1979,* Chilton, 1979.

Contributor to periodicals, including *Theatre Quarterly, Theatre Survey,* and *Yale/Theatre.*

WORK IN PROGRESS: A screenplay, "War Is. . . ."; a trilogy for the stage, "The Massachusetts Saga"; editing the correspondence between Virgil Thomson and Gertrude Stein.

SIDELIGHTS: France told *CA:* "It was my very good fortune to spend some seven years abroad (Europe, Japan, and Australia) by the time I was eighteen. Those experiences, and the decade I spent wandering about this country and Canada and Mexico, made school seem unnecessary to me. I still have a bad case of wanderlust and hope it will stay with me always. When I returned to school, it was with a sense of purpose that pitifully few students have who are caught up in the usual progression of high school to college. There is no substitute for experience, a message I don't hesitate to tell my own students.

"For all its politicking and all its self-deceptions, I still see teaching as an attractive livelihood for a writer—just so long as you know when to walk away and have the fortitude to do so."

*   *   *

FRANCOIS, Andre 1915-
PERSONAL: Original name, Andre Farkas; name legally

changed; born November 9, 1915, in Timisoara, Rumania; naturalized French citizen; son of Albert (a civil servant) and Olga (Plon) Farkas; married Margaret Edmunds; children: Pierre, Catherine. *Education:* Attended Cassandre's School of Fine Arts and Poster Design, 1935-36. *Home:* 95 Grisyles-Platres, Seine-et-Oise, France.

CAREER: Began career as commercial artist, with advertisements for Standard Oil, Olivetti, Perrier, and Dutch Master Cigars; illustrator and cartoonist, with work appearing in magazines, including *Vogue, Holiday, Femina, Punch,* and *New Yorker;* painter, with exhibitions at several one-man shows, including Librairie La Hune, 1955, and Club du Meilleur Livre, 1958; set and costume designer for theatre and ballet, including work for the Roland Petit Ballet of Paris, 1956, Peter Hall, 1958, and Gene Kelly, 1960. Author and illustrator of children's books. *Member:* Royal Designers for Industry (honorary member). *Awards, honors:* New York Times "Best Illustrated Children's Book" citation, 1952, for *The Magic Currant Bun,* 1956, for *Crocodile Tears,* 1958, for *Roland,* and 1970, for *You Are Ri-di-cu-lous;* gold medal from Art Directors Club of New York; honorary doctorate from Royal College of Art, London, 1978.

WRITINGS—All juvenile: *Double Bedside Book,* Deutsch, 1952, published as *The Tattooed Sailor, and Other Cartoons From France,* introduction by Walt Kelly, Knopf, 1953; (self-illustrated) *Crocodile Tears,* Faber, 1955, Universe, 1956, revised edition, 1964; *The Half-Naked Knight* (cartoons and drawings), Knopf, 1958; *Heikle Themen,* Diogenes, 1959; *The Biting Eye of Andre Francois* (caricature and comic art), Perpetua, 1960; (with John Symonds; self-illustrated) *Dapple Gray: The Story of a Rocking Horse,* Harrap, 1962; *The Penguin Andre Francois* (collection), Penguin, 1964; (self-illustrated) *You Are Ri-di-cu-lous,* Pantheon, 1970; *Les Rhumes,* Melisa, 1971; *Qui est le plus Marrant?,* L'Ecole des Loisirs, 1971; *Santoun,* S.E.R.G., 1972; *Toi et moi,* L'Ecole des Loisirs, 1973; (with Roger McGough) *Mr. Noselighter,* Deutsch, 1977.

Illustrator; juvenile: John Symonds, *William Waste,* Sampson Low, 1946; Jacques LeMarchand, *L'Odyssee d'Ulysse,* Leprat, 1947, translation by E. M. Hatt published as *The Adventures of Ulysses,* Criterion, 1960; Isobel Harris, *Little Boy Brown,* Lippincott, 1949; Symonds, *Magic Currant Bun,* Lippincott, 1952; Symonds, *Travelers Three,* Lippincott, 1953; Nelly Stephane, *Roland,* Harcourt, 1958; Symonds, *The Story George Told Me,* Harrap, 1963, Pantheon, 1964; Symonds, *Grodge-Cat and the Window Cleaner,* Pantheon, 1965; Symonds, *Tom and Tabby,* Universe, 1964.

Other: Diderot, *Jacques le Fataliste,* Reunis, 1946; Jacques Prevert, *Lettres des Iles Baladar,* NRF, 1952; R. Vailland, *Beau Masque,* NRF, 1954; J. Anselme, *On vous l'a Dit,* Delpire, 1955; Balzac, *Contes Drolatiques,* Diogenes, 1957; Alfred Jarry, *Ubu Roi* (five-act play), Le Club du Meilleur Livre, 1958.

SIDELIGHTS: Andre Francois is renowned for his work in a variety of different art fields, from the graphic arts and advertising to set and costume design to cartoons. He has even received commissions from Simpson's of Piccadilly in London to design a pack of playing cards and from UNICEF to draw a series of Christmas cards. He feels he has been influenced by the works of George Grosz and Paul Klee, and perhaps the strongest imprint on his career resulted from the time spent in the studio of Cassandre, noted French poster painter.

His artistic ability serves him well when he turns his hand to children's books. His first book illustrations published in the United States were those for *Little Boy Brown* in 1949. Children's author and illustrator Marcia Brown said of his work, "Entering the spirit of the text completely, M. Francois has enriched it as he creates in pen and ink and warm brown wash the world that is so exciting to a child. So directly is he concerned with telling the story that artistic considerations seem to fall naturally into place. Each line is drawn with feeling and control of feeling. Little Boy Brown sometimes appears in different actions on the same page, the way a child draws. . . . Author and artist are so successful in effacing themselves that it is Little Boy Brown who tells his story. To almost any small child this is a most personal book, because it is a book about himself."

With *Crocodile Tears* Andre Francois became creator of the story as well as of the illustrations. A *New Yorker* reviewer wrote, "Knowing juveniles will think everything about this piece of absurdity by the French cartoonist is funny—from its size, three by ten inches, down to the carton it comes in." And the *New York Times* commented, "This jaunty excursion into fantasy is told by M. Francois in a very few words and in witty pictures. His invention is fresh and ingenious, his line is sophisticated."

BIOGRAPHICAL/CRITICAL SOURCES: Horn Book, January, 1950; *New York Times,* November 4, 1956; *New Yorker,* November 24, 1956; *Graphis,* March, 1958, November, 1959; Barbara Bader, *American Picturebooks,* Macmillan, 1976.

*   *   *

FRANK, R., Jr.
  See ROSS, Frank (Xavier), Jr.

*   *   *

FRANK, Waldo (David)   1889-1967
  (Search-light)

PERSONAL: Born August 25, 1889, in Long Branch, N.J.; died January 9, 1967; son of Julius J. (a lawyer) and Helen (Rosenberg) Frank; married Margaret Naumberg, 1916 (divorced); married Alma Magoon, 1927 (marriage ended); married Jean Klemper, 1943; children: (first marriage) Thomas; (second marriage) Michael, Deborah. *Education:* Yale University, B.A. and M.A., 1911.

CAREER: Novelist, editor, playwright, and literary and social critic. Free-lance writer for the *New York Times* and *New York Evening Post,* 1911-13; correspondent for *La Nouvelle Revue Francaise* and *Europe,* 1917-19. Lecturer on modern art and literature at the New School for Social Research, 1917-19; lecturer throughout Europe and Latin America. Chief American delegate at International Congress of Writers for the Defense of Culture, Paris, France, 1936. *Member:* League of American Authors (chairman at first Congress of American Writers, 1936), Phi Beta Kappa. *Awards, honors:* L.H.D. from National University of San Marcow (Lima, Peru); guest of honor at National Congress of Writers and Artists, Mexico City, 1937.

WRITINGS—Novels: *The Unwelcome Man,* Little, Brown, 1917; *The Dark Mother,* Boni & Liveright, 1920, reprinted, AMS Press, 1979; *City Block,* privately printed, 1922, Scribner, 1932, reprinted, AMS Press, 1970; *Rehab,* Boni & Liveright, 1922; *Holiday,* Boni & Liveright, 1923; *Chalk Face,* Boni & Liveright, 1924; *The Death and Birth of David Markand: An American Story,* Scribner, 1934, reprinted, Johnson Reprint, 1971; *The Bridegroom Cometh,* Gollancz, 1938, Doubleday, 1939; *Summer Never Ends: A Modern Love Sto-*

ry, Duell, Sloan & Pearce, 1941; *Island in the Atlantic*, Duell, Sloan & Pearce, 1946, reprinted, Greenwood Press, 1970; *The Invaders*, Duell, Sloan & Pearce, 1948; *Not Heaven: A Novel in the Form of Prelude, Variations, and Theme*, Hermitage House, 1953.

Other: *The Art of Vieux Colombier: A Contribution of France to the Contemporary Stage*, Nouvelle Revue Francaise (Paris), 1918; *Our America*, Boni & Liveright, 1919, reprinted, AMS Press, 1970 (published in England as *The New America*, J. Cape, 1922); *Salvos: An Informal Book About Books and Plays*, Boni & Liveright, 1924; (under pseudonym Search-light) *Time Exposures*, Boni & Liveright, 1924; (translator) Jules Romains, *Lucienne*, Boni & Liveright, 1925; *Virgin Spain: Scenes From the Spiritual Drama of a Great People*, Boni & Liveright, 1926, revised edition, 1942; *The Re-Discovery of America: An Introduction to a Philosophy of American Life*, Scribner, 1929 (also see below); (with others) *Five Arts*, D. Van Nostrand, 1929.

America Hispana: A Portrait and a Prospect, Scribner, 1931; *Dawn in Russia: The Record of a Journey*, Scribner, 1932; *In the American Jungle, 1925-1936*, Farrar & Rinehart, 1937, reprinted, Books for Libraries Press, 1968; *Chart for Rough Water: Our Role in a New World*, Doubleday, 1940 (also see below); *South American Journey*, Duell, Sloan & Pearce, 1943; *The Re-Discovery of America* [and] *Chart for Rough Water*, Duell, Sloan & Pearce, 1947; *The Jew in Our Day*, Duell, Sloan & Pearce, 1944; *Birth of a World: Bolivar in Terms of His Peoples*, Houghton, 1951; *Bridgehead: The Drama of Israel*, Braziller, 1957; *The Rediscovery of Man: A Memoir and a Methodology of Modern Life*, Braziller, 1958; *Cuba: Prophetic Island*, Marzani & Munsell, 1961; *The Memoirs of Waldo Frank*, University of Massachusetts Press, 1973.

Plays: *New Year's Eve* (seven-scene), Scribner, 1929; *Dot* (four-act), Rosenfeld, 1933.

Editor: Moliere, *Plays by Moliere*, Boni & Liveright, 1924; (and author of foreword) *Tales From the Argentine*, Farrar & Rinehart, 1930, reprinted, Books for Libraries Press, 1970; Hart Crane, *The Collected Poems of Hart Crane*, Boni & Liveright, 1933; *America and Alfred Stieglitz: A Collective Portrait*, Doubleday, 1934, reprinted, Octagon Books, 1975.

Contributor to *Scribner's*, *Harper's*, and *Adelphi*; contributor to major Mexican and South American magazines; contributing editor of *Masses* and *New Republic*, 1917-19. Cofounder, with James Oppenheim, of *Seven Arts*, 1916-17.

SIDELIGHTS: Waldo Frank was on the scene when literary criticism emerged in the United States as a genre in its own right. He was ranked among the "literary radicals" who, in the second decade of the twentieth century, shared an antagonism toward the moral and social standards upheld by the "genteel tradition" of the nineteenth century. He was associated with such critics as Randolph Bourne, Van Wyck Brooks, H. L. Mencken, and Lewis Mumford, who were calling for a closer connection between art and the vital experiences of life than had been tolerated by traditional morality. In both his fiction and cultural commentary, Frank conveyed this dissatisfaction with old modes of thought and accepted forms of literature.

Like the other "anti-traditionalists," Frank was strongly influenced by the natural and social sciences, particularly the theories of Freud and Marx. According to Frederick J. Hoffman, "Frank's debt to Freud is extensive . . . his preoccupation with the unconscious life of his later characters is not merely a deeper study of motivation, for the unconscious of

his central character is always the point to which events are referred." In the 1920's, along with such writers as Max Eastman and John Reed, Frank was also drawn to the dialectical materialism of Marx, making it not only a social but a spiritual cause in his writing. In *The Re-Discovery of America*, for example, he sought to discern the economic imperatives underlying cultural phenomena. Lewis Mumford considered this book "one of the most vigorous positive criticisms of our civilization that has been made. No one else in America that I know combines anything like Mr. Frank's interior resources and insight with such wide scholarship and such ample observation of contemporary affairs in Europe and America."

In the 1930's, Marxist criticism solidified. Critics moved away from viewing large bodies of literature in terms of larger patterns of social forces; instead they considered how an individual work contributed to the cause of "social truth," i.e., Marxism. But as criticism tended to conform more and more to socialist and communist orthodoxy, a rift developed among writers and artists. There were those who followed official party line and those who criticized growing authoritarianism. As an editor of the *New Republic* and the *Masses*, two left-wing publications, and as an active participant in the three American Writers' Congresses held during the decade, Waldo Frank was at the center of the controversy.

Although a Marxist, Frank did not follow orthodox patterns of thought. Nor did he ever fully abandon the Whitmanesque mysticism of the early literary radicals. In fact, he often referred to himself as a "philosophical social revolutionary." Thus his work was frequently attacked from both sides: traditionalists dismissed him because of his politics; Marxists dismissed him because of his style. But there were also those for whom the diversity of his ideas held together. Max Lerner, for instance, reviewing *Chart for Rough Water*, perceived Frank's multiple voices: he is "at once religious prophet, moral exhorter, fashioner of new myths, social analyst, historial of ideas, political polemicist." Similarly, Charles I. Glicksberg described Frank as "the most metaphysical of native critics—a strange mixture of mysticism rooted in the culture of the west, science employed against the pretensions of science, Marxism combined with a romantic conception of cosmic mystery."

The critical split can be seen in the reviews of Frank's novels. Reviewing *The Unwelcome Man* in *The Dial*, Van Wyck Brooks approvingly wrote: "The vitality of Mr. Frank's conception is shown by the fact that it provides a concrete touchstone for most of the problems of our contemporary civilization." On the other hand, H. W. Boynton in *Bookman* regretted that "the book with all its realism of scene and episode is less a story than a parable; and it is a parable based upon despair."

Of *Rehab*, Carl Van Vechten said in *Nation*: "Both story and doctrine call for careful statement, but both instead are clapper-clawed and mauled and dragged through keyholes and kept in the cellar until only God and Waldo Frank can quite guess what the row is all about." In contrast, Lewis Mumford wrote in the *New Republic*: "If anyone takes exception to the fact that Mr. Frank speaks of physical things in spiritual terms, and spiritual things in almost physical terms; if anyone dislikes to see the naked bodies of thoughts before they get dressed for society and leave the chamber of the mind, the fault is not with Mr. Frank's method but with the code of mental etiquette it infringes."

Sometimes, as with *The Death and Birth of David Markand*,

Frank received mixed reviews from an individual critic. The *Boston Transcript* considered this novel "rich and heavy with life, but ... for all that very unpleasant." The *New York Times* called its prose excellent but its mysticism "as cloudy as ever." Even Malcolm Cowley, who claimed to be paying to the book the "tribute it requires," equivocated: "I admired its scope and its close texture, but I was repelled by the style in which the more emotional passages are written."

Interestingly, Frank's reception in Spanish-speaking countries was wholeheartedly enthusiastic. Recognized as an authority on the culture of South America, he has been called "the only serious North American author who exercised a direct influence in America Hispana during the twenties." Fluent in literary Spanish, he lived for a time in Mexico City and lectured all over the hemisphere as well. His book of impressionistic sketches, *Virgin Spain,* was described by Laura Benet as "a singularly poetic interpretation of a great people ... a spiritual poem"; Gorham Munson called it "definite, intricate, dense, jewelled, aspirant, gracious and mastered to a harmony that appears peculiarly fitting for Spain." Gardner Harding considered *America Hispana* "indispensible to any one who would understand America Hispana." And Ernest Gruening described it as "a beautiful and dynamic interpretation of the Hispanic hemisphere," adding, "Waldo Frank is a poet. His prose is poetry. His imagination is poetic. His vision and his visions are those of the poet."

BIOGRAPHICAL/CRITICAL SOURCES: The Dial, March 22, 1917, October 22, 1922, January 27, 1926; *Bookman,* April, 1917; *New York Herald Tribune Books,* March 31, 1921; *Nation,* April 26, 1922; *New Republic,* August 16, 1922, May 26, 1926, October 17, 1934.

Gorham Munson, *Waldo Frank: A Study,* Boni & Liveright, 1923; *International Book Review,* May, 1926; M. J. Benardete, editor, *Waldo Frank in America Hispana,* Instituto de las Espanas in los Estados Unidos (New York), 1930; *Saturday Review of Literature,* October 3, 1931, May 25, 1940, June 15, 1940; *New York Times,* October 18, 1931, October 21, 1934, January 10, 1967.

Sewanee Review, October, 1932; *Boston Transcript,* November 24, 1934; *South Atlantic Quarterly,* January, 1936; *Kenyon Review,* winter, 1940; Oscar Cargill, *Intellectual America,* Macmillan, 1941; *New York Times Book Review,* April 15, 1942; F. J. Hoffman, *Freudianism and the Literary Mind,* Louisiana State University Press, 1957; W. R. Bittner, *The Novels of Waldo Frank,* University of Pennsylvania Press, 1958; R. L. Perry, *The Shared Vision of Waldo Frank and Hart Crane,* University of Nebraska Press, 1966.*

—*Sketch by Andrea Geffner*

* * *

FRASCA, John (Anthony) 1916-1979

OBITUARY NOTICE—See index for *CA* sketch: Born May 25, 1916, in Lynn, Mass.; died December 3, 1979, in Tampa, Fla. While working as an investigative writer for the *Tampa Tribune,* Frasca received a Pulitzer Prize for his series on Robert Lamar Watson, a man unjustly accused of armed robbery and sentenced to ten years in prison. In 1968 Frasca became a free-lance writer. One of his books, *The Mulberry Tree,* won an Edgar Award. He was also the author of *The Unstoppable Glenn Turner* and *A Sharecropper's Best Short Stories.* Obituaries and other sources: *Who's Who in America,* 40th edition, Marquis, 1978; *New York Times,* December 5, 1979.

FRAZIER, Sarah
See WIRT, Winola Wells

* * *

FREEHOF, Solomon B(ennett) 1892-

PERSONAL: Born August 8, 1892, in London, England; came to the United States; married Lillian Simon (a writer), October 29, 1934. *Education:* Attended University of Cincinnati; Hebrew Union College, Rabbi, 1915, D.D., 1922. *Politics:* Democrat. *Home:* 128 North Craig St., Pittsburgh, Pa. 15213. *Office:* Rodef Shalom Temple, 4905 Fifth Ave., Pittsburgh, Pa. 15213.

CAREER: Hebrew Union College, Cincinnati, Ohio, faculty member, 1915-24; rabbi of Jewish congregation in Chicago, Ill., 1924-34; Rodef Shalom Temple, Pittsburgh, Pa., rabbi, 1934-66, rabbi emeritus, 1966—. *Military service:* American Expeditionary Forces, chaplain. *Member:* World Union for Progressive Judaism (honorary life president; past president). *Awards, honors:* D.H.L. from Hebrew Union College, 1944, Jewish Institute of Religion, 1945, and St. Vincent College, 1964; D.Litt. from Dropsie College, 1957; D.Letters from University of Pittsburgh, 1958.

WRITINGS: Stormers of Heaven, Harper, 1931; *What Is Reform Judaism?* (pamphlet), Tract Commission, Union of American Hebrew Congregations and Central Conference of American Rabbis, 1937; *The Book of Psalms: A Commentary,* Union of American Hebrew Congregations, 1938.

(Editor and contributor) *The Union Prayerbook for Jewish Worship,* two volumes, new edition (Freehof was not associated with earlier editions), Central Conference of American Rabbis, 1940-45; *Modern Jewish Preaching,* Bloch Publishing, 1941; *The Small Sanctuary: Judaism in the Prayerbook,* Union of American Hebrew Congregations, 1942; *Reform Jewish Practice and Its Rabbinic Background,* Hebrew Union College Press, Volume I, 1944, Volume II, 1952; *Responsa in War Time,* Responsa Committee, Division of Religious Activities, Jewish Welfare Board, 1947; (contributor) *Reform Judaism: Essays by Alumni of Hebrew Union College,* Hebrew Union College Press, 1949.

Preface to Scripture: A Guide to the Understanding of the Bible in Accordance With the Jewish Tradition, Union of American Hebrew Congregations, 1950; *In the House of the Lord: Our Worship and Our Prayer Book,* Union of American Hebrew Congregations, 1951; (contributor) Jacob Zallel Lauterbach, editor, *Rabbinic Essays,* Hebrew Union College Press, 1951; *Union Home Prayer Book,* Central Conference of American Rabbis, 1951; (contributor) *Magazine of Building,* Time-Life, 1953; (contributor) *Aspects of Progressive Jewish Thought,* Gollancz, 1954; *The Responsa Literature,* Jewish Publication Society, 1955, reprinted (bound with *A Treasury of Responsa*), Ktav, 1973; *The Book of Job: A Commentary,* Union of American Hebrew Congregations, 1958.

Reform Responsa, Hebrew Union College Press, 1960, reprinted (bound with *Recent Reform Responsa*), Ktav, 1973; (editor and contributor) *Israel Bettan Memorial Volume,* Central Conference of American Rabbis, 1961; *Studies in Bibliography and Booklore,* Volume V, Library, Hebrew Union College, 1961; (contributor) *Studies and Essays in Honor of Abraham A. Neuman,* E. J. Brill, 1962; *Treasury of Responsa,* Jewish Publication Society, 1962, reprinted (bound with *The Responsa Literature*), Ktav, 1973; *Recent Reform Responsa,* Hebrew Union College Press, 1963, reprinted (bound with *Reform Responsa*), Ktav, 1973; *Books of Thirty Years: Reviewed Before the Modern Literature Class, 1934-1963,* Rodef Shalom Sisterhood, 1964; (author of introduction) David Philipson, *The Reform Movement in Judaism,* revised edition (Freehof was not associated with 1st edition), Ktav, 1967; *Current Reform Responsa,* Hebrew Union College Press, 1969.

(With Vigdor W. Kavaler) *J. Leonard Levy: Prophetic Voice,* Rodef Shalom Congregation, 1970; *Modern Reform Responsa,* Hebrew Union College Press, 1971; *The Book of Isaiah: A Commentary,* Union of American Hebrew Congregations, 1972; *Spoken and Heard: Sermons and Addresses,* Rodef Shalom Congregation, 1972; *Bible Sermons for Today,* Ktav, 1973; *Preaching the Bible: Sermons for Sabbaths and High Holy Days,* Ktav, 1974; *Contemporary Reform Responsa,* Hebrew Union College Press, 1974; *The Book of Jeremiah: A Commentary,* Union of American Hebrew Congregations, 1977; *Reform Responsa for Our Time,* Hebrew Union College Press, 1977; *The Book of Ezekiel: A Commentary,* Union of American Hebrew Congregations, 1978. Also contributor to *Jewish Life in America,* 1955, and *Religious Authority in Progressive Judaism,* 1960. Also author of *On the Collecting of Jewish Books,* 1962.

Contributor to *Central Conference of American Rabbis Yearbook, Universal Jewish Encyclopedia,* and *Encyclopaedia Britannica.* Contributor of several hundred articles and reviews to theology journals, religious and popular magazines, and newspapers, including *Carnegie* and *Commentary.*

SIDELIGHTS: Freehof's editor, Daniel Syme, wrote: "It is rare, indeed, when the teacher of one's youth remains a teacher of one's adult years. There are few individuals whose powers of expression and explanation can move and expand the minds of pupils of all ages, crystalizing concepts and making complex ideas accessible in terms that each student can easily comprehend. . . .

"As a young boy, I would often sit at Rabbi Freehof's feet, listening carefully as he patiently elucidated a small piece of our Jewish tradition. Today, some thirty years later, it has been my distinct privilege to help bring the blessings of his brilliance and wisdom . . . to a Jewish community eager for intensified Jewish study and learning."

BIOGRAPHICAL/CRITICAL SOURCES: Walter Jacob, Frederick C. Schwartz, and Vigdor W. Kavaler, editors, *Essays in Honor of Solomon B. Freehof,* privately printed, 1964.

*   *   *

FREEMAN, Gary 1945-

PERSONAL: Born February 5, 1945, in Atlanta, Ga.; son of Peter James (a sheet metal worker) and Sarah (Kagelmacher) Freeman. *Education:* Emory University, B.A. (summa cum laude), 1967; University of Wisconsin—Madison, M.A., 1968, Ph.D., 1975. *Office:* Department of Government, University of Texas, Austin, Tex. 78712.

CAREER: University of Pennsylvania, Philadelphia, assistant professor of political science, 1975-76; University of Texas, Austin, assistant professor of government, 1976—. Visiting professor at University of Pennsylvania, 1979-80. *Member:* American Political Science Association, Policy Studies Organization, Council for European Studies, Midwest Political Science Association, Southwest Political Science Association, Phi Beta Kappa. *Awards, honors:* Woodrow Wilson fellow, 1967-68; Danforth graduate fellow, 1967-75; National Endowment for the Humanities fellow, 1978.

WRITINGS: *Immigrant Labor and Racial Conflict in Industrial Societies: The French and British Experience, 1945-1975,* Princeton University Press, 1979.

WORK IN PROGRESS: A comparative study of social security policy in western capitalism, with Paul Adams.

*   *   *

FREEMAN, Thomas 1919-

PERSONAL: Born November 16, 1919, in Glasgow, Scotland; son of Phillip and Rebecca (Bernard) Freeman; married Joan Goldslatt, 1943. *Education:* Queen's University of Belfast, M.D., 1942. *Home:* Little Marlow, Longforgan, Dundee, Scotland. *Office:* Royal Dundee Liff Hospital, Dundee, Scotland.

CAREER: Belmont Hospital, Surrey, England, senior registrar, 1948-50; Tavistock Clinic, London, England, senior registrar, 1950-52; University of Glasgow, Glasgow. Scotland, lecturer, 1952-54; private practice of psychiatry and psychoanalysis, 1954—. Consulting psychiatrist with Glasgow Royal Mental Hospital, 1954-65, Royal Dundee Liff Hospital, 1965-68, 1977—, and Holywell Hospital, Antrim, Northern Ireland, 1968-77; consultant to Hampstead Child Therapy Clinic. *Military service:* British Army, Royal Medical Corps, 1943-47; became major. *Member:* Royal College of Psychiatrists (fellow), British Psychoanalytical Society, Royal College of Physicians of Edinburgh (fellow).

WRITINGS: (With John L. Cameron and Andrew McGhie) *Chronic Schizophrenia,* International Universities Press, 1958, 3rd edition, 1972; *Studies on Psychosis,* International Universities Press, 1965; *Psychopathology of the Psychoses,* International Universities Press, 1969; *A Psychoanalytic Study of the Psychoses,* International Universities Press, 1973; *Childhood Psychopathology and Adult Psychoses,* International Universities Press, 1976. Contributor of about sixty articles to medical journals. Editor of *British Journal of Medical Psychology,* 1962-68.

WORK IN PROGRESS: A textbook on psychoanalytic psychiatry, with Clifford Yorke and Stanley Weinberg, in collaboration with Anna Freud; comparative studies of child and adult mental disorders.

SIDELIGHTS: Freeman told *CA:* "The basic aim of the published work has been to demonstrate the value and relevance of psychoanalysis for clinical psychiatry, in particular the role which psychoanalytic concepts can play in extending the range of clinical observation. The purpose of childhood studies is to show, wherever possible, the normal prototypes of later mental pathology. This developmental approach to clinical problems acts as a corrective to the mechanistic, 'medical' model of mental illness."

*   *   *

FRENCH, Doris
See SHACKLETON, Doris (Cavell)

*   *   *

FRIED, Mary McKenzie Hill 1914-

PERSONAL: Born December 6, 1914, in Baltimore, Md.; daughter of Robert (a bank clerk) and Susanah B. (a teacher; maiden name, Banks) Hill; married Frederick Fried; children: Robert, Rachel. *Education:* Attended Maryland Institute, and art schools in France and Germany. *Religion:* Presbyterian. *Home:* 875 West End Ave., New York, N.Y. 10025.

CAREER: Free-lance illustrator and writer. Active in local preservation work. *Member:* International Carousel Association, National Association of Watch and Clock Collectors, Musical Box Society.

WRITINGS: (With husband, Frederick Fried) *America's Forgotten Folk Arts,* Pantheon, 1978.

* * *

FRIEDMAN, Jerrold David
  See GERROLD, David

* * *

FRIPP, Patricia 1945-

PERSONAL: Born April 18, 1945, in England; came to the United States; daughter of Arthur H. (in real estate) and Edith (a shop manager; maiden name, Greene) Fripp. *Education:* Attended high school in England. *Politics:* Republican. *Religion:* Baptist. *Home:* 527 Hugo St., San Francisco, Calif. 94122. *Office:* Take Charge of Your Life, 465 California St., San Francisco, Calif. 94104.

CAREER: Men's and women's hair stylist in England; currently affiliated with Take Charge of Your Life, San Francisco, Calif. *Member:* Sales and Marketing Executives International, National Speakers Association, Women Entrepreneurs.

WRITINGS: (With Keith De Greene) *Stand Up, Speak Out, and Win,* Summit Publishing, 1977; (with De Greene) *The Joy of Selling,* Summit Publishing, 1978; (with Dottie Walters) *Success Secrets,* Royal Publications, 1978.

* * *

FRISON, George C(arr) 1924-

PERSONAL: Born November 11, 1924, in Worland, Wyo.; son of George S. (a rancher) and Meta (Carr) Frison; married wife, Carolyn, September 8, 1946; children: Carol L. Frison Grace. *Education:* University of Wyoming, B.A. (with honors), 1964; University of Michigan, M.A., 1965, Ph.D., 1967. *Home:* 4619 Oriole Lane, Laramie, Wyo. 82070. *Office:* Department of Anthropology, University of Wyoming, Laramie, Wyo. 82071.

CAREER: Rancher in Ten Sleep, Wyo., 1946-62; University of Wyoming, Laramie, professor of anthropology, 1973—, head of department, 1967—. Conducted and directed archaeological and anthropological field work all over Wyoming. Wyoming state archaeologist, 1967—; member of state advisory board on land quality, 1973—; consultant to *National Geographic* and to writer James Michener. *Military service:* U. S. Navy, in fire control, 1942-45; served in Pacific theater.

MEMBER: American Anthropological Association, Society for American Archaeology (member of executive board, 1973), American Association for the Advancement of Science (fellow), American Quaternary Association, Plains Anthropological Association (member of board of directors, 1970—; president of board, 1972), Phi Beta Kappa. *Awards, honors:* Woodrow Wilson fellowship, 1964; grants from National Science Foundation, 1969, 1970, 1971-72, 1973-75, 1974-77, 1976-78, Carter Corp. and Kerr-McGee Corp., 1977-78, and National Parks Service, 1978; Asa Hill Award from Nebraska Historical Society, 1975.

WRITINGS: (Contributor) James E. Fitting, editor, *The Development of North American Archaeology,* Anchor Books, 1973; *The Casper Site: A Hell Gap Bison Kill on the High Plains,* Academic Press, 1974; (contributor) Charles E. Cleland, editor, *Cultural Change and Continuity: Essays in Honor of James Bennet Griffin,* Academic Press, 1975; *Prehistoric Hunters of the High Plains,* Academic Press, 1978. Contributor to *Wyoming Geological Association Guidebook* and *Handbook of North American Indians.* Contributor of about forty articles and reviews to anthropology and archaeology journals.

WORK IN PROGRESS: Folsom Tools and Technology, with Bruce Bradley, publication expected by University of New Mexico Press; research on Medicine Lodge Creek Site, prehistoric bison procurement on the Plains, prehistoric high altitude cultural adaptations, the Hanson and Colby sites, prehistoric occupations during the Altithermal Period on the Northwestern Plains, and prehistoric mountain sheep procurement in the Absaroka and Wind River Mountains; re-evaluating the Agate Basin Site in eastern Wyoming, the Finley Site in western Wyoming, and the Horner Site in northern Wyoming.

SIDELIGHTS: Frison writes: "Prehistoric animal strategies are interpreted from my own experience handling livestock (including bison) and from nearly three decades' experience as a professional big game guide."

* * *

FRITZ, Leah 1931-

PERSONAL: Born May 31, 1931, in New York, N.Y.; daughter of Harry (an architect) and Esther (Bloom) Hurwit; married Howard W. Fritz (a printing executive), December 25, 1955; children: Monica, Amy. *Education:* Attended Syracuse University, 1949, and Columbia University, 1961-63. *Politics:* "Feminist." *Residence:* New York, N.Y. *Agent:* Emily Jane Goodman, Esq., 1414 Sixth Ave., New York, N.Y. 10019.

CAREER: Film promoter and clerk at Museum of Modern Art in New York City; *Aeronautical Engineering Review,* New York City, technical abstractor, 1955-56; Harlem Parents Union, New York City, coordinator of tutoring program, 1974-75; free-lance writer and journalist. Lecturer on women's studies.

WRITINGS: Thinking Like a Woman, WIN Books, 1975; *Dreamers and Dealers: An Intimate Appraisal of the Women's Movement,* Beacon Press, 1979. Contributor to *Village Voice, Ms., Sojourner,* and other publications.

WORK IN PROGRESS: Bureau de Change, poems, publication expected in 1982; a novel, completion expected in 1982.

SIDELIGHTS: Fritz writes: "I have made yearly trips to Europe since 1970, visiting England, France, Italy, Spain, Ireland, Denmark, Sweden, Finland, Czechoslovakia, and the Soviet Union. I write for the love and magic of words, the need to argue and persuade, and the hope (still) of changing the world. As a Gemini, I particularly enjoy direct communication—reading my work publicly and engaging in discussion about the ideas I have presented. There's a frustrated actor in me which comes out when I lecture or read poetry."

* * *

FRY, John 1930-

PERSONAL: Born January 22, 1930, in Montreal, Quebec, Canada; came to the United States in 1957; son of J. Stevenson and Beatrice (Pratt) Fry; married Marlies Strillinger, February 19, 1965; children: Leslie, William, Nicole. *Educa-*

tion: McGill University, B.A., 1951. *Home:* 318 Second Ave., New York, N.Y. 10003. *Office:* 380 Madison Ave., New York, N.Y. 10017.

CAREER: Forster McGuire & Co. Ltd., Montreal, Quebec, writer, 1951-57; *American Metal Market*, New York City, associate editor, 1957-59, managing editor, 1960-63; *Ski*, New York City, editor-in-chief, 1964-74, editorial director, 1975—. Editorial director of *Ski Business*, 1964—, *Golf*, 1968-71, 1977—, *Guide to Cross-Country Skiing*, 1975—, and *Outdoor Life*, 1975—. President of Mens Sana Publishing, Inc. Member of World Cup committee of International Ski Federation; founder of National Standard Ski Race. *Member:* American Society of Magazine Editors.

WRITINGS: America's Ski Book, Scribner, 1973; *Winners on the Ski Slopes* (juvenile), F. Watts, 1978.

SIDELIGHTS: Fry told *CA:* "I am presently developing a new magazine about cross-country skiing and am looking for natural history stories related to winter and also adventure and ordeal on skis.

"Both the ski books I have done were assignments from publishers; I have been unable to assign to publishers the ski books *I* would like to do.

"Most queries and story suggestions I see from writers indicate they have done little or no reading of the magazine they hope to sell to. And I don't mean just reading. I mean they need to study the magazine and see how it is edited.

"The decline in the simple, raw ability to tell a story today is not only evident to me as an editor; it also is appalling, steep, and becoming precipitous."

*   *   *

FRYER, William T.   1900(?)-1980

OBITUARY NOTICE: Born c. 1900 in Colora, Md.; died of pneumonia, February 8, 1980, in Bethesda, Md. Educator, lawyer, and author. Fryer taught law for many years at George Washington University. He wrote *Cases and Materials on Legal Method and Legal Systems,* as well as several textbooks, including *Selected Readings on Evidence and Trial.* Obituaries and other sources: *Washington Post,* February 12, 1980.

*   *   *

FUOSS, Robert Martin   1912-1980

OBITUARY NOTICE: Born December 16, 1912, in Saline, Mich.; died January 27, 1980, in Natick, Mass. Retailing executive and journalist. As an employee of Curtis Publishing Co. for over twenty years, Fuoss was associated with its publication, the *Saturday Evening Post,* as managing editor, executive editor, and editor-in-chief before leaving the company. With a talent for both advertising and editing, Fuoss contributed many new ideas to the *Post,* such as the "Adventures of the Mind" series. He became vice-president in public relations and later executive vice-president for Federated Department Stores after leaving the *Post* in 1962. Fuoss contributed jokes, verse, and epigrams to the *Wall Street Journal*'s "Salt and Pepper" column and was a senior editor for *Reader's Digest* in 1964. Obituaries and other sources: *Current Biography,* Wilson, 1959, March, 1980; *Newsweek,* May 22, 1961; *Who's Who in Finance and Industry,* 18th edition, Marquis, 1973; *New York Times,* January 29, 1980; *Washington Post,* January 30, 1980.

G

GABLE, Tom 1944-

PERSONAL: Born July 4, 1944, in San Diego, Calif.; son of Tom P. (a physician) and Mary Ellen (Kilfoy) Gable; married Laura Lee Rickerson, December 17, 1966; children: Michelle, Brian. *Education:* San Diego State College (now University), B.A., 1967. *Home address:* P.O. Box 1986, Rancho Santa Fe, Calif. 92067. *Office:* The Gable Agency, Inc., 409 Camino del Rio South, San Diego, Calif. 92108.

CAREER/WRITINGS: Evening Tribune, San Diego, Calif., investigative reporter, 1969-70, business editor, 1970-75; The Gable Agency, Inc., San Diego, president, 1975—. Contributor to *Where to Eat in America,* edited by Beard, Glaser, and Wolf, Random House, 1977, 2nd edition, 1979. Author of column on food and wine for *San Diego Magazine;* monthly feature columnist for *California* magazine; weekly wine columnist for Copley News Service. *Military service:* U.S. Army, 1967-69; combat correspondent in Vietnam; received two Bronze Stars and two Army Commendation medals. *Member:* Southern California Wine Writers, Southern California Restaurant Writers, San Diego Press Club (vice president and director), North San Diego County Press Club (past president), San Diego State University Alumni Association (member of board of directors; member of business advisory committee). *Awards, honors:* Numerous local, regional, and national awards for newspaper and magazine writing, including first place awards for news, feature, and investigative reporting from the San Diego Press Club, Sigma Delta Chi, and California Newspaper Publishers; nominated for Pulitzer Prize in 1974.

WORK IN PROGRESS: The Easter Agenda, a novel about the changes in American life from 1967 to 1999; a ranking of every winery in California, *The 1980 Classification of California Wines.*

SIDELIGHTS: Gable told *CA* that although his public relations agency specializing in corporate, political and problem accounts is very successful, he writes because "of the pleasure of working with words in many different ways." He reads three to four books a month, mostly histories, political treatises, essays, satire, and novels. His favorite books include *Catch-22, Miss Lonely Hearts,* and *The Challenge of Man's Future.* Most of Gable's free-lance writing consists of restaurant and wine reviews; he is a wine connoisseur and teaches wine appreciation classes. He also judges at wine competitions in California.

AVOCATIONAL INTERESTS: Tennis, jogging, skiing.

GABRIEL, Jueri (Evald) 1940-

PERSONAL: Born July 27, 1940, in Tallinn, Estonia; son of Edgar Alois and Leida (Luther-Leetjaerv) Gabriel; married Margaret Lynette Hemmant (an illustrator), August 25, 1962. *Education:* Jesus College, Oxford, B.A., 1962. *Politics:* "Liberal with a *small* '1'." *Religion:* None. *Home:* 16 Roseneath Rd., Battersea, London SW11 6AH, England.

CAREER: Associated-Rediffusion Television, London, England, camera operator, 1963-65; Thames & Hudson, London, England, editor, 1965-67; free-lance writer, photographer, translator, editor, and consultant, 1967—. Associate of Adrian Knowles Associates. Creative writing teacher at Morley College. Member of British Copyright Council, 1978—. *Member:* Writer's Guild of Great Britain, Writers' Action Group, Authors' Lending and Copyright Society.

WRITINGS: Victoriana, Hamlyn, 1969, published in the United States as *Victorian Furniture and Furnishings,* Grosset, 1971; (with wife, Lynette Hemmant) *Europa: Gastronomic Guide to Europe,* three volumes, Rand McNally, 1971; (self-illustrated) *Thinking About Television,* Oxford University Press, 1973; (with Hemmant) *European Campground Guide,* Rand McNally, 1974, 5th edition, 1978; (editor and contributor) *Guide to European Campgrounds,* Rand McNally, 1974, 5th edition, 1978; *Unqualified Success,* Kestrel, 1981.

Translator: Wolfgang Fritz Volbach, *Early Decorative Textiles,* Hamlyn, 1969; Gottfried Tritten, *Colour and Form: Methods and Ideas for Children's Art,* Batsford, 1971; Robert Girard, *Color and Composition: A Guide for Artists,* Van Nostrand, 1974; Beatrix von Rague, *A History of Japanese Lacquerwork* (edited by Annie R. de Wassermann), University of Toronto Press, 1976.

Contributor: (Photographer) Stephen Knight, *The Inside Eye: A Study in Pictures of Oxford University Life* (edited by Philip D. Roberts), Abbey Press, 1961; *Art Treasures of Germany,* Hamlyn, 1970.

Author of pamphlets for Manpower Services Commission. Contributor of articles, photographs, and reviews to *Times Educational Supplement.*

SIDELIGHTS: Gabriel was active in the long, and ultimately successful, campaign for centrally-funded loans based on the Public Lending Right in the United Kingdom.

He told *CA:* "I have specialized in the logical presentation of information, whether in words, or pictures, or both. But as I approach my forties, I am becoming ever more conscious of the fact that art is life, and I am not living enough. I would like to tackle fiction; I hope I have the necessary courage and energy—energy because, unfortunately, I am far from being a natural writer.''

* * *

GABRIEL, Philip L(ouis)   1918-

PERSONAL: Born in 1918, in Fort Fairfield, Maine; son of Samuel and Amelia Gabriel; children: Ronald S., Dennis Jon (deceased), Phyllis Mary, Robert Philip. *Education:* Attended Washington State University, 1937, and Southwestern Law School, 1940. *Politics:* Republican. *Religion:* Roman Catholic. *Home:* 2130 Miramar Dr., Newport Beach, Calif. 92661. *Office:* P.O. Box 718, Whittier, Calif. 90608.

CAREER: President of Crystal Ice Manufacturing Co., 1935-64; president of Gabriel Brothers (department stores), 1947-56, and Smithy Muffler Manufacturing Co. (also partner), 1948-56. Vice-president and member of board of directors of Del Mar Turf Club, 1947-54; member of board of trustees of General Service Studios, 1949-55; member of board of directors of Office of Price Administration during World War II. *Member:* Tri-State Ice and Cold Storage Association (president, 1947-49), Tau Kappa Epsilon (Alpha Gamma chapter), Knights of Columbus (grand knight, 1946-47; district deputy, 1947-48), Elks, Rotary (president, 1946). *Awards, honors:* Medal of honor from Government of Lebanon.

WRITINGS: I Found America, Vantage, 1952; *Citizen From Lebanon* (novel), Citadel, 1957; *The Executive* (nonfiction), Citadel, 1959; *Tomorrow-Tomorrow* (novel), Whitmore, 1971; *In the Ashes: The Story of Lebanon* (nonfiction), Whitmore, 1978.

WORK IN PROGRESS: Fiction.

AVOCATIONAL INTERESTS: Fishing, hunting.

* * *

GABRIELSON, Frank   1911(?)-1980

OBITUARY NOTICE: Born c. 1911; died January 24, 1980, in Woodland Hills, Calif. Television and radio script writer. Gabrielson wrote many of the scripts for the television series, ''Mama,'' in the 1950's, and introduced such actors as Paul Newman, Jack Lemmon, James Dean, and Dick Van Patten on the show. After studying at the Yale Drama School, he moved to Hollywood, where he became a bit actor before joining the studios of Twentieth Century-Fox and Walt Disney. Among numerous other radio shows, Gabrielson wrote the ''Shirley Temple Playhouse.'' Obituaries and other sources: *Chicago Tribune,* February 3, 1980; *New York Times,* February 20, 1980.

* * *

GAGER, Nancy Land   1932(?)-1980

OBITUARY NOTICE: Born c. 1932; died of leukemia, February 1, 1980, in Baltimore, Md. Author and editor. Founding president of the Washington, D.C., chapter of the National Organization for Women (NOW), Gager wrote numerous feminist works, including *Sexual Assault: Confronting Rape in America.* Her best-known book, *Women's Rights Almanac,* was commended by the *Washington Post* as ''a remarkable document, balanced, interesting and well informed.'' She also wrote the Emmy award-winning documentary, ''How We Got the Vote,'' in 1976. She was at one time a member of the staff of *National Geographic* and

served during the 1970's as president and editor of the Elizabeth Cady Stanton Publishing Co. in Bethesda, Md. Gager served as a civilian intelligence analyst with the U.S. Army in Korea, and edited the LEAA newsletter. She was a frequent contributor to periodicals, including the *Chicago Tribune,* the *Washingtonian,* and the *Armed Forces Journal.* Obituaries and other sources: *Washington Post,* February 4, 1980.

* * *

GALLE, William   1938-

PERSONAL: Born October 21, 1938, in New York, N.Y.; son of Benjamin (a merchant) and Ruth (Stein) Galle. *Education:* Rutgers University, B.A., 1960; Columbia University, M.A., 1962. *Home:* 2001 North Adams St., Arlington, Va. 22201.

CAREER/WRITINGS: Journal of Commerce, New York City, reporter, 1968-69; *Investment Dealers' Digest,* New York City, financial writer, 1969-72; National Association of Securities Dealers, Washington, D.C., financial writer, 1972-73. Editor and publisher of *Financial Analysts Report.* Contributor of articles to magazines, including *Barron's, Investment Dealers' Digest,* and *Financial Analysts Report. Member:* National Press Club, New York Financial Writers Association.

* * *

GAMOW, George   1904-1968

OBITUARY NOTICE: Born March 4, 1904, in Odessa, Russia (now U.S.S.R.); died August 19, 1968. Author and scientist. A renowned researcher in such fields as radioactivity, nuclear and thermonuclear physics, and cosmology, Gamow was also praised as a popularizer of science. His ''Mr. Tompkins'' series of books, for example, introduced the layman to the theories of relativity, physiology, and genetics, among others. In 1956 he received the Kalinga Prize for his work in making science understandable to the general public. Before his professorships at George Washington University and the University of Colorado, Gamow held positions with the universities of London and Paris, in addition to participating in several scientific congresses in Rome, Brussels, and Warsaw. He was also the author of numerous books for both the layman and the specialist, including *The Structure of Atomic Nuclei and Nuclear Transformations; Matter, Earth, and Sky;* and *One, Two, Three . . . Infinity.* Obituaries and other sources: *Current Biography,* Wilson, 1951, October, 1968; *New York Times,* August 22, 1968; *Time,* August 30, 1968; *Newsweek,* September 2, 1968; *Publishers Weekly,* September 9, 1968.

* * *

GARDINER, Dorothy   1894-1979

OBITUARY NOTICE: Born in 1894 in Naples, Italy; died December 4, 1979, in Buffalo, N.Y. Author. Gardiner was the author of several historical and mystery novels. Colorado and the West were often her subjects in such books as *West of the River, Golden Lady,* and *Great Betrayal.* In addition to writing mystery novels, including *The Seventh Mourner,* Gardiner served as executive secretary for the Mystery Writers of America. Obituaries and other sources: *The Author's and Writer's Who's Who,* 6th edition, Burke's Peerage, 1971; *A. B. Bookman's Weekly,* December 24, 1979.

GARROW, David J(effries) 1953-

PERSONAL: Born May 11, 1953, in New Bedford, Mass.; son of Walter J. (in business) and Barbara (Fassett) Garrow. *Education:* Wesleyan University, Middletown, Conn., B.A., 1975; Duke University, M.A., 1978. *Office:* Institute for Advanced Study, Princeton, N.J. 08540.

CAREER: Duke University, Durham, N.C., instructor in political science, 1978—. Visiting member in the School of Social Science at Institute for Advanced Study, Princeton, N.J., 1979-80.

WRITINGS: Protest at Selma: Martin Luther King, Jr. and the Voting Rights Act of 1965, Yale University Press, 1978.

WORK IN PROGRESS: A study of the surveillance and harassment of Martin Luther King, Jr. by the Federal Bureau of Investigation; a study of King's entire public career, publication by Yale University Press expected in 1982.

SIDELIGHTS: Garrow writes: "*Protest at Selma* began as my undergraduate honors thesis. It argues that Dr. King should be viewed as an insightful and pragmatic political strategist whose foremost goal was winning the enactment of federal civil rights laws, and not simply as the charismatic orator the media have portrayed him as. My book on the FBI's pursuit of King will focus on the motives behind the bureau's activities, and will be based largely on FBI files released to me under the Freedom of Information Act. My major, forthcoming study of King's entire career will expand upon the argument concerning King's political growth and evolution that I made in *Protest at Selma.* I believe I'll continue writing on the civil rights movement for many years to come. At present, the amount of serious scholarship on the movement is far too limited."

According to James Button, *Protest at Selma* "is a thorough and astute analysis of the crucial role of black protest in the emergence of the revolutionary Voting Rights Act of 1965." Specifically, Garrow examines both the dynamics of protest and what he calls "nonviolent coercion," the tactic "used to induce white southern officials to brutalize black demonstrators and thereby gain publicity and nationwide support for the cause," Button observed. Another reviewer, Francis M. Wilhoit, stated that the book "merits high marks for its excellent integration of a wide variety of data into a unified explanation of what contributes to the success or failure of protest appeals in an open society.... The strengths of the work are, in fact, so considerable that the book could well serve as a model of scholarly insight and research design implementation."

BIOGRAPHICAL/CRITICAL SOURCES: Perspective, December, 1978; *Social Science Quarterly,* June, 1979; *American Historical Review,* June, 1979.

* * *

GATES, Frieda 1933-

PERSONAL: Born May 30, 1933, in New York, N.Y.; daughter of Herman Herbert (a chef) and Bella (Alexander) Wolff; married David Lloyd Gates (a professor of art), June 18, 1955; children: Alexander Edward, Katherine Isabel, Beatrice Ellen. *Education:* Attended New York University; also studied at Brooklyn Museum, Art Students League, and New School for Social Research. *Home:* 32 Hillside Ave., Monsey, N.Y. 10952. *Office:* Department of Art, Rockland Community College, 145 College Rd., Suffern, N.Y. 10901.

CAREER: Worked as illustrator and graphic designer at J. Walter Thompson Co., Peter Pan Co., Julian Mansfield Associates, and Comart Associates; free-lance graphic designer in commercial and book illustration; art teacher in East Ramapo adult education program, 1965-74; art instructor at Parsons School of Design; Rockland Community College, Suffern, N.Y., art instructor, 1973—. Professional puppeteer with Hudson Valley Vagabond Players, 1972-75; taught puppet workshop at Finkelstein Memorial Library, 1975; lecturer on history and art of the puppet at Hopper House Museum.

WRITINGS—All self-illustrated; all juveniles: *Easy to Make Puppets,* Harvey House, 1976; *Easy to Make Costumes,* Harvey House, 1978; *Glove, Mitten, and Sock Puppets,* Walker & Co., 1978; *Easy to Make Monster Masks and Disguises,* Harvey House, 1979; *Easy to Make American Indian Crafts,* Harvey House, 1980; *Monsters and Ghouls: Costumes and Lore,* Walker & Co., 1980.

Illustrator: Carolyn Ramirez, *Foot and Feet,* Harvey House, 1973.

WORK IN PROGRESS: A book on early American crafts.

SIDELIGHTS: Gates told *CA:* "I sort of 'fell into' writing books for children. By profession, I am a visual artist. I first became involved in writing when I illustrated *Foot and Feet* by Carolyn Ramirez and helped solve some of the writing problems. Since I had been a puppeteer, the editor I had been working with asked if I would be interested in writing an easy-to-make puppet book. I found that I enjoyed the research and writing as much as the illustrations. I am now working on my eighth book."

* * *

GAWAIN, Shakti 1948-

PERSONAL: Born September 30, 1948, in Trenton, N.J.; daughter of Theodore H. (an aeronautical engineer) and Elizabeth (a yoga teacher; maiden name, Miller) Gawain. *Education:* Attended Reed College, 1966-69; University of California, Irvine, B.A., 1971. *Residence:* Mill Valley, Calif. *Agent:* Rosalie Heacock, 1121 Lake St., Venice, Calif. 90291.

CAREER: Dance teacher, 1968-71; therapist, 1975-80; writer. Leader of personal growth workshops.

WRITINGS: (With Mark Allen and Jon Bernoff) *Reunion: Tools for Transformation,* Whatever Publishing, 1978; *Creative Visualization,* Whatever Publishing, 1979. Also author of a book on relationships in the context of spiritual and personal growth, Whatever Publishing, 1981.

WORK IN PROGRESS: Research on individual human potential and transformation of human consciousness.

SIDELIGHTS: Gawain writes: "From 1971 to 1973 I traveled around the world. I spent several months in Asia, particularly India. I developed a deep interest in Eastern spiritual philosophy and meditation. I am now deeply involved in the 'human potential movement,' particularly the marriage of Eastern spiritual understanding and Western psychology. I am devoted to transforming the quality of life on our planet to make it a nourishing, beautiful, and fulfilling place for all beings."

* * *

GAWSWORTH, John
See BATES, H(erbert) E(rnest)

* * *

GEDYE, George Eric Rowe 1890-1970

OBITUARY NOTICE: Born May 27, 1890, in Clevedon, Somerset, England; died March 21, 1970. Author and journalist. Gedye worked as a reporter and special correspondent for numerous London newspapers, including the *Daily Express, Daily Telegraph,* and *Daily Herald,* in addition to working for the *New York Times* and *Manchester Guardian.* For his services during the war, he was decorated Member of the Order of the British Empire. Numbered among Gedye's books are *A Wayfarer in Austria, The Revolver Republic,* and *Betrayal in Central Europe.* Obituaries and other sources: *Who Was Who in America,* 5th edition, Marquis, 1973.

*   *   *

GENDRON, George M. 1949-

PERSONAL: Born April 19, 1949, in New York, N.Y.; son of George J. (a mechanical engineer) and Elizabeth (Downey) Gendron; married Hollis Lyons, June 26, 1971. *Education:* Attended United States Air Force Academy, 1967-68; Manhattan College, B.A., 1976. *Home:* 83 Elm St., Hingham, Mass. *Office: Boston* Magazine, 38 Newbury St., Boston, Mass. 02116.

CAREER/WRITINGS: New York Magazine, New York, N.Y., editor, 1972-75; *Boston* Magazine, Boston, Mass., editor-in-chief, 1976—. Contributor of articles to *New York* and *Village Voice.*

*   *   *

GENTZLER, J(ennings) Mason 1930-

PERSONAL: Born January 5, 1930, in Hackensack, N.J.; son of Jennings Mason (an engineer) and Miriam (a teacher; maiden name, Herr) Gentzler; married Li Yu-ning (a professor), July 31, 1970. *Education:* Columbia University, B.A., 1951, Ph.D., 1966. *Home:* 1 Center Knolls, Bronxville, N.Y. 10708. *Office:* Department of Asian Studies, Sarah Lawrence College, Bronxville, N.Y. 10708.

CAREER: Columbia University, New York, N.Y., instructor, 1964-66, assistant professor of East Asian languages and cultures, 1966-70; Duke University, Durham, N.C., visiting associate professor of history, 1970-71; Sarah Lawrence College, Bronxville, N.Y., teacher of Asian studies, 1971—. *Military service:* U.S. Army, 1951-54. *Member:* Association for Asian Studies. *Awards, honors:* Columbia University Cutting Traveling fellowship, 1961-63; Ford Foundation Foreign Area fellowship, 1963-64; Fulbright fellowship, 1969-70.

WRITINGS: A Syllabus of Chinese Civilization, Columbia University Press, 1968, 2nd edition, 1972; (editor) *Changing China: Readings in the History of China From the Opium War to the Present,* Praeger, 1977. Contributor to *Encyclopedia International.*

WORK IN PROGRESS: A Literary Biography of Liu Tsung-yuan, 773-819; The Buddhist Sociology of "Dream of the Red Chamber".

*   *   *

GEORGIANA, Sister
See TERSTEGGE, Mabel Alice

*   *   *

GERNSBACK, Hugo 1884-1967

OBITUARY NOTICE: Born August 16, 1884, in Luxembourg City, Luxembourg; died August 19, 1967. Author and publisher. In addition to ranking as a major science fiction writer, Gernsback founded numerous magazines, including

Amazing Stories, Modern Electrics, Sexology, and *Short Wave Craft.* He manufactured the first wireless home radio and was founder of the Wireless Association of America. Among his science fiction writings are *Evolution of Modern Science Fiction, Ultimate World,* and *Ralph 124C 41+: A Romance of the Year 2660.* Gernsback was also an avid inventor of such things as the hypnobioscope, an instrument used to instruct sleeping individuals, and the osophone, a device enabling those with hearing impairments to "hear" by conducting sound waves through their teeth. Obituaries and other sources: *New York Times,* August 20, 1967; *Publishers Weekly,* September 4, 1967.

*   *   *

GERROLD, David 1944-

PERSONAL: Birth-given name, Jarrold David Friedman; born January 24, 1944, in Chicago, Ill.; son of Lewis (a photographer) and Johanna (Fleischer) Friedman. *Education:* Attended University of Southern California; California State University at Northridge, earned B.A. degree. *Home and office address:* Box 1190, Hollywood, Calif. 90028. *Agent:* Henry Morrison, Inc., 58 West Tenth St., New York, N.Y. 10011.

CAREER: Science-fiction writer, 1967—. *Awards, honors:* Hugo Award nomination, 1968, for "The Trouble With Tribbles"; Nebula Award nomination, 1972, for *In the Deadlands,* and, 1977, for *Moonstar Odyssey;* Hugo and Nebula Award nominations, 1972, for *When Harlie Was One,* 1973, for *The Man Who Folded Himself,* and 1977, for *Moonstar Odyssey;* Skylark Award, 1979.

WRITINGS: (With Larry Niven) *The Flying Sorcerers* (novel), Ballatine, 1971; (editor with Stephen Goldin) *Protostars,* Ballantine, 1971; (editor with Goldin) *Generation,* Dell, 1972; *Space Skimmer* (novel), Ballantine, 1972; *When Harlie Was One* (Science Fiction Book Club selection), Doubleday, 1972; *With a Finger in My I* (short stories), Ballantine, 1972; *Yesterday's Children* (novel), Dell, 1972; *Battle for the Planet of the Apes* (novel; adapted from the screenplay by John William Corrington and Joyce Hooper Corrington), Universal Publishing & Distributing, 1973; *The Man Who Folded Himself* (Science Fiction Book Club selection), Random House, 1973; *The World of Star Trek,* Ballantine, 1973; (editor) *Alternities* (anthology), Dell, 1974; (editor) *Emphasis* (anthology), Ballantine, 1974; (contributor) Alan Dean Foster, editor, *Star Trek Log,* Corgi, 1976; (editor) *Ascents of Wonder* (anthology), Popular Library, 1977; *Moonstar Odyssey* (novel), New American Library, 1977; *Deathbeast* (novel), Popular Library, 1978.

Teleplays: *The Trouble With Tribbles* (first produced as episode of "Star Trek" television series by NBC-TV, telecast December 29, 1967), Ballantine, 1973. Also author of a revision of "I, Mudd," first produced in 1967, and "The Cloud Minders," first produced in 1968, both as episodes for "Star Trek," and of "More Troubles, More Tribbles" and "BEM," both for the animated "Star Trek" series.

Columnist in *Starlog* and *Galileo.* Story editor of "Land of the Lost," 1974.

WORK IN PROGRESS: "It's bad luck to talk about them prior to completion."

SIDELIGHTS: Gerrold's science fiction novel, *Yesterday's Children,* is, according to the *Times Literary Supplement,* "that rare thing in the genre: a study of character." Aboard the starship *Burlingame,* a weak and tired captain contends with his mutinous crew, gives reluctant chase to an enemy space craft, and struggles with an ambitious, power-usurping officer for control of the ship. Like the *Caine Mutiny*, it examines the emotional and moral conflicts generated by the shifting balance of military authority. The *Times Literary Supplement* concluded: "*Yesterday's Children* remains a solidly worked-out SF novel with unusually good characterization."

Another book, *The Man Who Folded Himself*, looks at the paradoxical implications of time travel. With the aid of a special belt, a nineteen-year-old student confronts a half-dozen versions of himself at different ages. The awkward repercussions that follow gradually leave the narrator in complete loneliness and displacement. In the judgment of *Publishers Weekly*, "Gerrold is such a good writer that he keeps us reading through the most confusing shifts of time, space and character—right into pre-history." It is a story, noted the *Times Literary Supplement*, of "uncanny allegorical force" that explores the limits of self-knowledge being set by one's compulsive behavior. "Altogether most impressive."

CA INTERVIEWS THE AUTHOR
CA interviewed David Gerrold by telephone September 13, 1979, at his office in Los Angeles.

CA: You've emphasized the need for writers to learn traditional writing skills. How do you think that can best be accomplished?

GERROLD: When a beginning writer asks me "What is the most important course I can take?" I usually say "Remedial English." The English language is a very precise tool. If you understand the ways each word is meant to be used, it forces you to think clearly. Clear thinking demands clear language. Fuzzy use of language indicates difficulty in handling concepts. So my emphasis has always been on learning how to use the language, learning the tools. Once you know what a tool can do, then you are better able to make it work for you.

CA: You started writing very early. What led you into science fiction?

GERROLD; The same thing that leads a lot of people to science fiction: it's an escape literature. Children who have trouble adjusting to their environment for one reason or another seek escape; some go into drugs, some go into some kind of fantasy world, some go into science fiction. I had always been an inveterate reader, and I stumbled into science fiction by a fellow named Heinlein. There was this book labeled *Rocketship Galileo*, and I said, "Gee, I like rocketships. That's terrific." After I'd gone through about six of Heinlein's juveniles, I used the card catalogue to discover that there were about twenty more Heinleins I hadn't read, and that led me into adult science fiction. I was there for ten years, and then "Star Trek" came on the air. By that time I was convinced I had read every science-fiction book ever written. I was already studying theatre arts and had had a couple of writing courses, so I sent them some story ideas to demonstrate what I thought a good science-fiction story for television should be. Of course it was terribly prideful to think that with no experience at all I could be writing for tv, but it turned out there were very few television writers who really understood science fiction. Someone who had a grasp of science fiction was more in demand for "Trek" than someone who understood tv writing, because tv writing doesn't require much intelligence, as the current state of television demonstrates.

CA: Do you share Harlan Ellison's concern about television and what it's doing to us?

GERROLD: He's more than concerned; he's livid. I share that feeling. I think, if anything, Harlan understates the danger. So much of it is so banal and uninteresting; there isn't a program on the air that requires you to exercise your mind muscles, except "Lou Grant" and PBS programming. I just went through the new *TV Guide* today looking for something that I might want to set the videotape machine for next week, and in a schedule for twenty-four hours a day, eleven local channels, I found three shows that I want to watch, and one of them is a rerun of a movie. I find that offensive, because the programming is being aimed at the lowest common denominator. That means there's nothing left for us smart people. The networks discovered that prime time hours of the television set are controlled by the children. Most families would rather not argue with the kids about what to watch, and if they have a videotape recorder, the parents tape what they want to watch for later, but the kids control the tv set. Because of that the programming is aimed at the kids and the commercials are aimed at mom. That's why the average program today is written for a twelve-year-old. They don't want it to be better than that, because they're aware of the twelve-year-old hand on the dial. I think this is a serious cultural defect, that we are allowing twelve-year-olds to determine the shape of the culture instead of allowing the mature members of our society to say, "Hey. We are the ones who must run this society. We don't turn over the direction of our culture to adolescents and immature minds who have not yet learned how to handle responsibility."

The only hope for it is the videodisc and pay tv, and also the home computer, which will lure people away from the television set on a scale unprecedented. I think ten years from now the menace of television will be lessened considerably, because any home that has a home computer will have something far more interesting than a television set. A computer is much more entertaining. The computer is going to be the new direction of home entertainment because it's an interactive device, whereas television is a passive one. You become involved with the computer on a more complete level. This is why I'm convinced that the threat of television is only a temporary one.

CA: What do you think accounts for the critical acceptability of science fiction after the long period when it was considered inferior?

GERROLD: There was a time when science fiction was a bastard child; but science-fiction people didn't worry about it, we just concentrated on doing good science fiction. Now science fiction has become an important literary genre. There are large advances being paid for books; writers are considered important because we can predict the future, and all of the other headtrips that they lay on science fiction as being respectable. I find this to mean that society is trying to assimilate something that it can't understand and by assimilating it, is destroying it. Science fiction was at its most vital and alive time before there was this pressure to be respectable.

I don't think respectability is a viable end if truth is the victim. And today we have a wide spectrum of writing being passed off as science fiction: on one end it's one step removed from masturbation fantasies, and on the other end are self-indulgent, self-cathartic works that aren't intended for readers. In the middle there are a few guys, and women, too—in fact, the women are doing a large part of the responsible work—who are exploring ideas; and that's always been the essence of science fiction.

CA: There seems to be an attempt in your writing to make some moral implication.

GERROLD: What I'm interested in is growth. Everybody has that one thing inside that he doesn't want to look at too closely because it hurts too much—like being picked last to play ball—that gives him a feeling of insecurity. Whatever it is, there's that one thing. My stories are about the person who suddenly finds himself in a situation where, in order to survive, he must get right down in there, find that part of him that hurts, and deal with it. That's called growth. That fascinates me, the idea of how much it is possible for an individual to grow beyond his or her apparent limitations. That is my central theme, and whether I intend it to or not, it shows up in anything I write, even the easy stuff that's meant just for fun. *Deathbeast* was just for fun, yet there are scenes in there where the characters have to deal with their own feelings.

CA: You've called science fiction "the twentieth century morality play." Do you think science fiction—or any other kind of writing—must have a message to be valid?

GERROLD: The writing that pleases me the most is that which, in one way or another, enriches me, provides me with the knowledge of something I didn't know before. It gives me an experience that I can incorporate into my own life and thereby increases my spectrum of awareness of the world around me. What I'm looking for in something to read or a movie to go to is something in which the authors believed in what they were doing. I subscribe to the Cracker Jack theory of storytelling. A story is like a box of Cracker Jacks—there's a prize in it. If they forgot to put the prize in, you feel cheated. That prize is that piece of truth that the author believed in.

CA: Is there a closeness among science-fiction writers?

GERROLD: There used to be more closeness than there is today, and I think that's because ten years ago there was a feeling that we were all suffering together. Now some of us are suffering with $50,000 and $100,000 book contracts, and it's difficult for us to all suffer together when some of us are not suffering at all, apparently. So I would say that the field is beginning to experience the same sort of growing pains as any successful literary genre. The question in my mind is whether science fiction can survive its own success. I suspect that science fiction, as we know it today, is doomed, and that there is a whole new area which is just going to be called fantastic fiction, of which science fiction will be just a subgenre, and that all the old truths that we know about science fiction are in the process of evolving into something else.

CA: Do you feel sad about that?

GERROLD: I feel sad to lose some of the old stuff; I feel excited by some of the new things that are happening.

CA: What trends do you see?

GERROLD: I do see the growth of the home computer as an entertainment medium of incredible importance. Right now the home computer is where television was in 1947—for hobbyists; there are just a few devices available to the general public, but it really requires a technical mind. But by 1954 television was having the most important cultural impact in the century, and by the end of the decade it was in

almost every home in the country. The home computer is going to have the same kind of impact, or even greater impact, on the culture.

CA: What trends do you see in science fiction?

GERROLD: Science fiction in the 1970's has been very much like rock music in the 1970's. Nothing specific has happened except that we've assimilated what happened in the 1960's. In the 1960's there was a lot of experimentation, most of it bad. In the 1970's we've been assimilating those experiments and rediscovering what it was that made science fiction strong in the first place. In the 1980's? On the one hand, the science fiction that is being written by women tends to be more character-oriented than idea-oriented. Someone like Larry Niven or John Varley will take an idea and take it apart to see what makes it work, to see what the implications are. It's a terrific way of structuring a story, and it's a very masculine kind of science fiction. The feminine science fiction tends to be oriented toward character and experience within an environment. I hate to call it masculine and feminine, but this is the perception I've been getting. I think both trends are important. We must never lose sight of the fun of ideas, but I think it's important to understand what the experiences feel like. I think what we're growing toward is a literary field that incorporates the best of both kinds.

CA: Are you still involved with "Star Trek"?

GERROLD: Not really. What is happening with the fan movement is that it's turning into a nostalgia thing more than anything else. It's strange to be nostalgic for the future, but that's really what "Star Trek" is now.

CA: Are you interesting in doing other kinds of writing?

GERROLD: As a matter of fact, I'm moving out of writing into directing. Writing has been satisfying and fun, but it's not where I'm going to be in the future.

CA: Would you elaborate on what you said earlier about the distinction between mediocre writing and good writing, on what makes a writer a good writer?

GERROLD: I believe there's nothing inherently special about a writer; he's just a human being who has learned to use the language precisely enough to be coherent in the communication of his ideas. There are lots of people who have the skill to be writers who just never have the determination to sit down at a typewriter, or the feeling that what they have to say is important enough. But what distinguishes the real writer from the guy who's just putting words on paper is that he is reporting back his experiences; that is, he uses his life as a laboratory and reports back on what he has discovered in that laboratory. It is a continual process of discovery of self, and when a writer is able to report something he has discovered about himself, he is reporting something he has discovered about the human condition. When he does that, and other people recognize the truth of it, there is one more piece of truth in the world than there was before, and more understanding.

I'm very involved with computer science and psychiatry and what it is that makes a thing function as if it's intelligent. Consider what Freud did. Freud was the first human being to say, "Way down at the bottom level of my mind are these urges." And he put down on paper, "Way down at the bottom level of the human mind are these urges." But he had to recognize them inside himself first. When he wrote about them, a lot of people who had spent their whole lives denying these urges said, "No, this is wrong." But as more and more people began to recognize that here was a piece of truth, the whole idea of psychiatry gained in validity.

Psychiatry is a very young science. If we had had a thousand years of psychiatric study, psychiatry could be as precise as medicine is today. And medicine isn't all that precise yet either, but doctors can accomplish a lot more today than they ever could before; and I find myself thinking that when psychiatrists have had a chance to build up several centuries of practice, our knowledge of what makes the human mind work and how to make it work more efficiently is going to be very advanced. So my feeling is that anybody who can record a piece of truth is serving a function for the betterment of the human race, and that those writers who are merely using up paper and ink are stealing from us, because they are not only *not* giving us a piece of truth, they are using up our resources in distracting us from the *real* search for truth. The whole idea of truth is that you keep questioning it, to make sure it *is* truth.

BIOGRAPHICAL/CRITICAL SOURCES: Publishers Weekly, February 4, 1974, May 13, 1974, January 3, 1977, June 5, 1978; *Times Literary Supplement*, February 15, 1974, June 14, 1974; *Village Voice*, June 13, 1974; *Book World*, March 30, 1975.

—*Interview by Jean W. Ross*

*   *   *

GERSON, Corinne 1927-

PERSONAL: Born January 19, 1927, in Allentown, Pa.; daughter of Henry and Selma (Deutsch) Schreibstein; married Everett W. Gerson (an attorney), February 1, 1953; children: Risa, Roger. *Education:* Moravian College, B.A., 1949. *Home:* 71 Glenwood Ave., New Rochelle, N.Y. 10801.

CAREER: Harcourt Brace, Inc. (now Harcourt Brace Jovanovich, Inc.), New York City, editorial assistant in high school English textbook department, 1949; assistant editor of pulp fiction and confession magazines, 1949-57; Funk & Wagnalls Co., New York City, editor of general nonfiction and adult and teenage fiction, 1952-54; free-lance writer, 1949—; free-lance editor, 1954—. *Member:* International P.E.N., Forum of Writers for Young People, Authors Guild, Authors League of America.

WRITINGS: Like a Sister (teenage novel), Funk, 1954; *The Closed Circle* (juvenile novel), Funk, 1968; *Passing Through* (teenage novel), Dial, 1978; *Tread Softly* (juvenile novel), Dial, 1979; *Son for a Day* (juvenile novel), Atheneum, 1980; *Choices* (contemporary adult novel), Tower, 1980. Contributor to teenage and romance magazines.

WORK IN PROGRESS: How I Put My Mother Through College, a teenage novel, publication by Atheneum expected in 1981; a collection of literary sketches; a play; short stories.

SIDELIGHTS: Corinne Gerson writes: "Most of my published work so far has been books for 'younger readers'—anywhere from eight to sixteen. The first was a teenage novel written not terribly long after my own teen years. It was a labor of loving utilization of ideas held dear, done with the seriousness of purpose that directed my life. I continued to deal with what I considered the important realities in my books for kids before the term 'problems' was invented. Now that children's literature seems to have used up that genre I have veered off toward the lighter side of kids' experiences. But they're the same kids, living with the same difficulties that reality hands out indiscriminately. Recently I wondered why my principal success has been with writing for younger people and realized it is because I unconsciously

project how they react to particular incidents and situations. I have no idea why I do this; I just know I do it as naturally as I yawn or laugh or cry. For me, the writing itself is something almost organic—something I never learned but just did."

*   *   *

GIBSON, D. Parke 1930-1979

PERSONAL: Born October 8, 1930, in Seattle, Wash.; died of a heart attack, May 12, 1979, in New York, N.Y.; children: (stepchildren) Dale Hall, Frank Turner. *Education:* Graduated from City College of the City University of New York. *Residence:* New York, N.Y.

CAREER: Partner of Laws Gibson Associates, 1952-54; advertising representative for Interstate Newspapers, 1954-56; manager of public relations for Johnson Publishing Co., 1956-59; promotion director for Sengstacke Publications, 1960; president of D. Parke Gibson Associates, Inc. (management consulting firm), 1960-79. Publisher of *Gibson Report* and *Race Relations and Industry*. *Member:* American Marketing Association, Public Relations Society of America, National Association of Market Developers. *Awards, honors:* Doctor of Humane Letters from King Memorial College, South Carolina.

WRITINGS: The $30 Billion Negro, Macmillan, 1969, revised edition published as *$70 Billion in the Black: America's Black Consumers*, 1978.

SIDELIGHTS: Gibson's book, *The $30 Billion Negro*, is an examination of the purchasing power of the blacks. Divided into three sections—a basic history of the market, ways to predict the market, and ways to develop the market—the book explains that in order to tap the resources of the Negro population, large corporations must alter advertising strategies to appeal to this group. A reviewer for the *Christian Science Monitor* felt that Gibson's handling of this concept was ironic in that he treated the black population as remaining "isolated, unsophisticated, and heavily reliant upon cultural idiosyncrasy and corporate magnanimity," but concluded that "we should be heading for a mixed economy. . . . It might also, if only incidentally, make for a better America."

BIOGRAPHICAL/CRITICAL SOURCES: New York Times, May 20, 1969; *Christian Science Monitor*, January 8, 1970.

OBITUARIES: New York Times, May 14, 1979.*

*   *   *

GIBSON, E(dward) Lawrence 1935-

PERSONAL: Born December 25, 1935, in Alta Vista, Va.; son of Frank James (a restaurateur) and Jessie (Blackwell) Gibson. *Education:* Attended University of Richmond, 1954-56, World Centre of Shakespeare Studies, 1971; Towson State University, B.S., 1961; Princeton Theological Seminary, M.A., 1966. *Residence:* Brooklyn, N.Y. *Agent:* Wender & Associates, 30 East 60th St., New York, N.Y. 10022.

CAREER: Teacher of English, history, and drama in schools in Annapolis, Md., 1962-64 and 1967-75; writer, 1973—. Director of nearly eighty productions, and actor in dramas and musicals; production manager and board member of Colonial Players of Annapolis, 1969-71; director, designer, and choreographer for U.S. Naval Academy drama and musical groups, 1971-74; civilian instructor for U.S. Navy Pre-Reenlistment Education Program (PREP), 1975. Copy Laurent Studio, Annapolis, Md., and New York, N.Y., co-founder of studio and creator of books, graphic arts, photography, 1974—. *Member:* Alpha Psi Omega, Gamma Theta Upsilon, Kappa Delta Pi.

WRITINGS: Get Off My Ship: Ensign Berg vs. U.S. Navy, Avon, 1978. Also author of *Flashpoints* (novel), 1980.

Plays: "A Return to Jerusalem" (one-act dramaturgy), first produced in Baltimore, Md., at Central Presbyterian Church, 1963; "The Tempest" (two-act; adaption for young people), first produced in Annapolis, Md., at Annapolis Fine Arts Festival Theatre, 1964; "Dawn of Deliverance" (one-act dramaturgy), first produced in Annapolis at First Presbyterian Church, 1964; "A Lover's Quarrel With the World" (one-act), first produced in Princeton, N.J., at Princeton Seminary, 1966; "The Lament of Job" (one-act), first produced in New York, N.Y., at Fifth Avenue Presbyterian Church, 1966; "Snow White and the Seven Dwarfs" (two-act), first produced in Annapolis at Children's Theatre of Annapolis, 1968; "Dixie Rose" (one-act), first produced in Annapolis at Summer Garden Theatre, 1969; "Rip Van Winkle" (two-act), first produced in Annapolis at Children's Theatre of Annapolis, 1969; "Secrets of Spoon River" (two-act), first produced in Annapolis at Colonial Players Workshop, 1970; "Peter Pan" (two-act; adaption for young people), first produced in Annapolis at Children's Theatre of Annapolis, 1972; "Six Characters in Search of Christmas" (one-act), first produced in Annapolis at St. Johns College, 1972; "The Christmas Story" (a telescript), first produced in Baltimore by WBAL-TV, 1972; "Huckleberry" (two-act), first produced in Annapolis at Key School, 1973; "Night Season: Oedipus" (one-act), first produced in Annapolis at Key School, 1973. Also author of "Get Off My Ship" (three-act), 1980.

Contributor of articles to *Blueboy, Club, Advocate, Gaysweek, Social Action/Engage,* and *Dimension.*

WORK IN PROGRESS: And Who Told You You Are Naked?, a theological/social criticism; dramatic adaptions of five Shakespearean plays for young people.

SIDELIGHTS: Regarding his book, *Get Off My Ship: Ensign Berg vs. U.S. Navy,* Gibson told *CA* that while teaching enlisted personnel aboard the U.S.S. *Little Rock* as a civilian instructor in the Pre-Reenlistment Education Program (PREP) in Gaeta, Italy, "I was removed from my classroom without warning and confronted by agents of the Naval Investigative Service. Within two hours of the questioning, the Navy extended its jurisdiction and, without granting a hearing, unilaterally barred me from the ship and terminated my civil service position. No accusation of indiscretion or misconduct was ever made. Yet Ensign Vernon E. Berg III and I found ourselves facing a Kafkaesque ordeal that subjected us to continual surveillance, the monitoring of our mail, illegal searches of our home, the theft of documents and private property, suppression of vindicating documents, the use of unidentified informants, and the dissemination of fabricated and defamatory information, and the collusion of men sharing a common prejudice against homosexuals.

"Berg decided to fight for retention in the Navy. His case was filed in the federal courts because of violations of due process during the hearing and other basic constitutional considerations.

"The Berg case has evolved into a landmark judicial case that made public the Navy's covert maneuvers and abuse of power. As a result of the litigation, Navy policies toward homosexuals have been changed significantly, requiring a fully honorable discharge to be awarded to any person separated for reasons of homosexuality. A unanimous decision by the U.S. Court of Appeals in Berg's favor on December 6, 1978, ruled that the Navy had wrongly discharged Berg, and required that the Navy produce a reason other than Berg's homosexuality to justify his discharge from military service.

"Since our initial confrontation with naval authorities in July, 1975, Berg and I have appeared nationally on television and radio, and have spoken throughout the nation at colleges, medical schools, church conferences, community groups and before the American Bar Association.

"Forced into a posture of self-defense and self-assertion, Berg and I remain committed to the task of focusing on the personal and social consequences of discrimination against individuals solely because of sexual orientation or affectional preferences."

BIOGRAPHICAL/CRITICAL SOURCES: New York Times, March 24, 1976, April 28, 1977; *Boston Gay Community News,* May 8, 1976, December 23, 1978, January 27, 1979; *Annapolis Evening Capital,* February 24, 1977, October 20, 1978; *Philadelphia Inquirer,* May 11, 1977; *Us,* June 14, 1977; *Advocate,* June 15, 1977, January 11, 1979, March 22, 1979; *Club,* November, 1977; *Washington Blade,* December 4, 1978; *Washington Post,* December 7, 1978; *Baltimore Sun,* December 8, 1978; *Soho News,* December 14, 1978; *Philadelphia Gay News,* January, 1979; *Mandate,* March, 1979; *Gaysweek,* March 12, 1979.

* * *

GILBERT, Milton 1909(?)-1979

OBITUARY NOTICE: Born c. 1909 in Philadelphia, Pa.; died of a heart attack, September 28, 1979, in Washington, D.C. Economist and author. Before joining the Bank for International Settlements in Basel, Switzerland, as an adviser in 1960, Gilbert served as chief of the national income division of the U.S. Commerce Department, where he helped to develop the concept of a gross national product. An international authority on gold, he wrote *The Gold Dollar System: Conditions of Equilibrium and the Price of Gold* in 1968. His other books deal with international, national, and economic matters. Obituaries and other sources: *Washington Post,* September 30, 1979.

* * *

GILES, Frederick John 1928-

PERSONAL: Born December 30, 1928, in Toronto, Ontario, Canada; son of Charles Louis (a civil servant) and Kathleen Ellen (Cottle) Giles. *Education:* University of Toronto, B.A., 1950, M.A., 1951; doctoral study at University of Michigan, 1951-52, and University of Chicago, 1952-53; University of London, Ph.D., 1960. *Politics:* "Slightly right of center." *Office:* F. J. Giles & Associates, Suite 5, Third Floor, King York House, 32-4 York St., Sydney, New South Wales 2000, Australia.

CAREER: F. J. Giles & Associates (opal merchants), Sydney, Australia, founder and chairperson, 1962—. Special part-time lecturer at University of Sydney. Senior director of Holiday Resort of Gloucester Park.

WRITINGS: Ikhnaton: Legend and History, Hutchinson, 1970. Contributor to *Journal Aegyptus.*

WORK IN PROGRESS: Continuing research on the Amarna period, to update *Ikhnaton.*

* * *

GILLION, Kenneth Lowell (Oliver) 1929-

PERSONAL: Born August 2, 1929, in New Zealand; son of Oliver William (a journalist) and Jessie Helen (MacGregor) Gillion; married Barbara Hamblyn, 1959 (divorced, 1968);

children: Rachel Barbara. *Education:* Victoria University of Wellington, M.A., 1951; Fletcher School of Law and Diplomacy, A.M., 1952; Australian National University, Ph.D., 1958. *Home:* 5 Jalanga Cres., Aranda, Australian Capital Territory 2614, Australia.

CAREER: New Zealand Department of External Affairs, diplomatic trainee and third secretary, 1950-54; University of Western Australia, Nedlands, 1958-62, began as lecturer, became senior lecturer in history; University of Adelaide, Adelaide, Australia, 1963-72, began as senior lecturer, became reader in history; Australian National University, Canberra, senior research fellow in Pacific and Southeast Asian history, 1973-78; writer, 1978—. *Awards, honors:* Fulbright and Smith-Mundt scholarships, 1951; Carnegie Foundation grant, 1965; Leverhulme grant, 1969.

WRITINGS: Fiji's Indian Migrants: A History to the End of Indenture in 1920, Oxford University Press, 1962; *Ahmedabad: A Study in Indian Urban History,* University of California Press, 1968; *The Fiji Indians: Challenge to European Dominance, 1920-1946,* Australian National University Press, 1977.

WORK IN PROGRESS: Research on modern history of Fiji and India.

*   *   *

GILMORE, Alec 1928-

PERSONAL: Born January 23, 1928, in Bacup, England; son of Leonard and Martha (Spraggon) Gilmore; married Enid Ruth Batten (a social worker), July 1, 1952; children: Ian Stuart, David John. *Education:* Attended Manchester Baptist College, 1946-52; Victoria University of Manchester, B.A., 1949, B.D., 1951, M.A., 1952. *Home:* 112 St. Lawrence Ave., Worthing, West Sussex BN14 7JL, England. *Office:* United Society for Christian Literature, Luke House, Farnham Rd., Guildford, Surrey GU1 4XD, England.

CAREER: Ordained Baptist minister, 1952; pastor of Baptist churches in Kingsthorpe, England, 1952-62, and West Worthing, England, 1962-74; United Society for Christian Literature, Guildford, England, editor of Lutterworth Press, 1975—, general secretary of society, 1976—. Pastor of Baptist church in Philadelphia, Pa., 1974; lecturer at Louisville Baptist Theological Seminary, 1979. Member of Baptist Union Council, 1959—. Radio and television broadcaster. *Member:* Society for Old Testament Study, Athenaeum.

WRITINGS: Reading the Bible, Carey Kingsgate Press, 1956; (editor) *Christian Baptism,* Judson, 1959, 3rd edition, 1959; (editor) *The Pattern of the Church,* Lutterworth, 1963; *The Family of God,* Carey Kingsgate Press, 1964; *Baptism and Christian Unity,* Judson, 1966; (editor) *Ministry in Question,* Darton, Longman & Todd, 1971; *Tomorrow's Pulpit,* Judson, 1975; *Have a Good Day!,* Hodder & Stoughton, 1975; *Praise God,* Baptist Union (London), 1980. Part-time editor for Carey Kingsgate Press, 1962-67. Contributor to religious and secular journals in England and the United States, including *Upper Room, Christian World,* and *American Baptist.* Review editor of *Baptist Quarterly,* 1960-64.

WORK IN PROGRESS: Research for a book on the Christian gospel as it is reflected by contemporary playwrights.

SIDELIGHTS: Gilmore writes: "As general secretary of United Society for Christian Literature I traveled in Africa, India and Bangladesh, South and Central America, and the Caribbean.

"My motivation? The preacher's urge to talk, lecture, write,

and teach; to engage people both in thought and discussion with a view toward enlightening them and deepening their grasp of what is going on around them: not so much to push a line as to help people to discover for themselves.

"Currently, my main motivation is the raising of funds to provide support for writers, publishers, and booksellers in Third World countries, as well as to fund religious and theological libraries in colleges, seminaries, and lay-training centers. At the same time, I am anxious not to lose touch with preaching, so I am building up more and more broadcasting both with radio and with television."

*   *   *

GIRAGOSIAN, Newman H. 1922-

PERSONAL: Born July 18, 1922, in Binghamton, N.Y.; son of Samuel B. and Victoria (Garabedian) Giragosian. *Education:* Pennsylvania State University, B.S. (chemistry), 1943, B.S. (chemical engineering), 1947; University of Pennsylvania, M.B.A., 1951; New York University, Ph.D., 1965. *Religion:* Protestant. *Home and office:* 400 East 89th St., New York, N.Y. 10028.

CAREER: Allied Chemical Corp., Philadelphia, Pa., production control supervisor, 1947-49; Shell Chemical Corp., New York City, senior technologist, 1951-61; G.A.F. Corp., New York City, director of marketing research, 1961-74; Delphi Marketing Services, Inc., New York City, president, 1974—. *Military service:* U.S. Navy, 1944-46. U.S. Naval Reserve; became captain.

MEMBER: Chemical Marketing Research Association (president, 1972-73), Commercial Development Association (member of board of directors, 1971-72), American Chemical Society (chairperson of Chemical Marketing Division, 1968-69; member of council, 1973-75), American Institute of Chemists (fellow), Drug, Chemical, and Allied Trades, Synthetic Organic Chemical Manufacturers Association, Army and Navy Club, Chemists Club, New York University Club. *Awards, honors:* Distinguished service award from Chemical Marketing Research Association.

WRITINGS: A Marketing Guide to the Chemical Industry, Technomic, 1965; *Chemical Marketing Research,* Reinhold, 1968; *Fundamentals of Commercial Development,* American Chemical Society, 1970; *Successful Product and Business Development,* Dekker, 1979.

AVOCATIONAL INTERESTS: Travel (Europe and Latin America).

*   *   *

GIROUX, Joan 1922-

PERSONAL: Born February 15, 1922, in Ottawa, Ontario, Canada; daughter of R. Francis and Elizabeth (Trottier) Giroux. *Education:* University of Ottawa, B.A., 1943, M.A., 1968. *Politics:* Liberal. *Home and office:* 3-6 Hanazono Cho, Fukushima Shi, Japan 960.

CAREER: Entered Congregation of Notre Dame of Montreal, 1943, became Roman Catholic nun, 1945; teacher of English and history at high schools in Toronto, Ontario, 1945-52, and Kingston, Ontario, 1952-54; principal of Roman Catholic elementary school in Ottawa, Ontario, 1954-56; teacher of English at schools in Kitakyushu, Japan, 1956-61, and Fukushima, Japan, 1961-66; Sakura no Seibo Junior College, Fukushima, Japan, professor of English and head of department, 1968—. *Member:* Association of Foreign Teachers in Japan, Tokyo English Literature Society.

WRITINGS: The Haiku Form, Tuttle, 1974. Contributor to junior college bulletin.

WORK IN PROGRESS: Translating Buson's haiku.

SIDELIGHTS: Joan Giroux writes: "Brought up largely in the care of housekeepers, I was a voracious reader. This stimulated my interest in writing. In 1943 I entered a Catholic teaching community of sisters. After arriving in Japan in 1956, I 'went native' for a short time and became very interested in haiku. On my first home leave ten years later I had time to do research on haiku. In my free time since, I have tried to keep up with developments in the subject. Although I speak Japanese, I have to depend on my colleagues for help in reading the difficult ideographs."

In *The Haiku Form,* Giroux provides a history of haiku in Japan, explains the various poetic techniques, and studies representative works by master poets. The author, noted Atsuo Nakagawa, "has read and closely studied Japanese haiku and most books and articles available on English haiku, and presents in her book a thorough review and intelligent, reasonable perspective. She has mastered and digested them all to make her own theory." Another reviewer, James R. Morita, added: "The true value of the book . . . lies in the fact that it penetrates deep into the interior of haiku, and guides the reader to the haiku moment, which is the highest state of man's understanding of the universe. . . . This is an amazing work, succeeding where many failed. Few scholars or critics have ever explored, in clear beautiful English, this depth of haiku, a deceptively simple but really complex art."

BIOGRAPHICAL/CRITICAL SOURCES: Poetry Nippon, March, 1975; *Books Abroad: An International Literary Quarterly,* Volume 49, number 4.

* * *

GLYNN, Thomas P(eter)   1935-

PERSONAL: Born March 8, 1935, in Montreal, Quebec, Canada; came to the United States in 1937, naturalized citizen, 1953; son of John H. (a physician) and Eleanor (a nutritionist; maiden name, Schmidt) Glynn; married Patricia Jane Weaver (a teacher), July 14, 1962; children: Brendan, Siobhan, Julie. *Education:* Attended Northwestern University, 1953-55; University of Chicago, B.A., 1958. *Politics:* "Ecological People's party." *Religion:* "Pantheist." *Home and office:* 278 Sterling Place, Brooklyn, N.Y. 11238. *Agent:* Ellen Levine, Curtis Brown Ltd., 575 Madison Ave., New York, N.Y. 10022.

CAREER: Associated with McCann Erickson, 1966-68, Foote, Cone, Belding, 1968-69, and Scali, McCabe, Sloves, 1974-76; New York Urban Coalition, producer and director of films, 1977, managing editor of *Neighborhood,* 1978—; free-lance writer, 1978—. *Military service:* U.S. Army, 1959-64. *Member:* Union of Concerned Scientists, Sierra Club, Audubon Society, Fiction Collective, Prospect Heights Neighborhood Association.

WRITINGS: Temporary Sanity (novel), Fiction Collective, 1977.

Author of filmstrips. Contributor of stories to literary journals and popular magazines, including *Playboy* and *Paris Review.*

WORK IN PROGRESS: Two novels, *The Instruction Manual* and *Survival Conditions.*

SIDELIGHTS: Glynn comments: "I write to share outrageous fantasies, secrets, exposes, constructions, inventions.

I write to raise spirits, create joy, to sing. I write to celebrate the beauty of words in print, to taste paragraphs, to scatter sentences. I write to make a film for the mind. I write for fun, though many times it is not fun, and I write for money, though often there is little money. I write, for it is there to be written."

* * *

GOBLE, Dorothy

PERSONAL: Born in Singapore; married Paul Goble (a children's author and illustrator), 1960 (divorced, 1978); children: one son, one daughter. *Residence:* London, England.

CAREER: Industrial designer; children's author, 1969—. *Awards, honors:* Notable book citation from American Library Association, 1970, for *Red Hawk's Account of Custer's Last Battle;* three prizes for industrial designs, 1961, 1963, and 1967.

WRITINGS—Juvenile; all with husband, Paul Goble; all illustrated by Paul Goble: *Red Hawk's Account of Custer's Last Battle,* Pantheon, 1969; *Brave Eagle's Account of the Fetterman Fight, 21 December 1866,* Pantheon, 1972 (published in England as *The Hundred in the Hands: Brave Eagle's Account of the Fetterman Fight, 21st December 1866,* Macmillan, 1972); *Lone Bull's Horse Raid,* Macmillan, 1973; *The Friendly Wolf,* Bradbury, 1974.

SIDELIGHTS: Commenting on *Red Hawk's Account of Custer's Last Battle,* the *New York Times Book Review* asserted: "It all rings true, with an air of excitement, compassion for victor and vanquished and an awareness of the main echoes that come down to us today. . . . The realities conveyed to the young reader are the closest to the final layer of truth that one can hope for." A *New Statesman* reviewer noted that "the illustrations, filled with drama, movement and occasional moments of stillness, are based on the work of Plains Indians of the period. The account of the fighting is stern, straightforward, quite shocking, and a model of how reality may be presented to children in poetic terms: something, I feel, that every writer of non-fiction for children should at least set his sights on."

A reading of *Red Hawk's Account of Custer's Last Battle* was recorded by Caedmon Records in 1972.

BIOGRAPHICAL/CRITICAL SOURCES: New Statesman, November 6, 1970; *New York Times Book Review,* November 9, 1970.*

* * *

GOBLE, Paul   1933-

PERSONAL: Born September 27, 1933, in Surrey, England; son of Robert John (a harpsichord maker) and Marion Elizabeth (Brown) Goble; married wife, Dorothy (an author and industrial designer), 1960 (divorced, 1978); married Janet Tiller; children: one son, one daughter. *Education:* Central School of Arts and Crafts, London, England, N.D.D., 1959. *Address:* Nemo Route 104Y, Deadwood, S.D. 57732.

CAREER: Free-lance industrial designer, 1960-68; visiting lecturer at Central School of Arts and Crafts, England, 1960; senior lecturer in three-dimensional design at Ravensbourne College of Art and Design, London, 1968-77; painter; illustrator and author of children's books. *Military service:* British Army, 1951-53. *Awards, honors: Red Hawk's Account of Custer's Last Battle* was named an American Library Association Notable Book of 1970; Caldecott Medal, 1979, for *The Girl Who Loved Wild Horses.*

WRITINGS—Juvenile; all with Dorothy Goble, except as noted; all self-illustrated: *Red Hawk's Account of Custer's Last Battle*, Pantheon, 1969; *Brave Eagle's Account of the Fetterman Fight, 21 December 1866*, Pantheon, 1972 (published in England as *The Hundred in the Hands: Brave Eagle's Account of the Fetterman Fight, 21st December 1866*, Macmillan, 1972); *Lone Bull's Horse Raid*, Macmillan, 1973; *The Friendly Wolf*, Bradbury, 1974; (illustrator) Richard Erdoes, editor, *The Sound of Flutes and Other Indian Legends*, Pantheon, 1976; (sole author) *The Girl Who Loved Wild Horses*, Bradbury, 1978.

WORK IN PROGRESS: The Gift of the Sacred Dogs, for publication by Bradbury Press.

SIDELIGHTS: Paul Goble in his books tries to dispel the stereotypical image of the American Indian. His concern in portraying Indians as they really were is the result of his numerous visits to the United States and to Indian reservations. In 1959, Goble became a member of the Yakima and Sioux tribes and assumed the Indian name of *Wakinyan Chikala* or "Little Thunder."

Goble's work, both as an illustrator and an author, has been praised by many critics. A *New York Times Book Review* critic commented that in *Red Hawk's Account of Custer's Last Battle* "the pictures are among the best I have seen in any children's history, and the realities conveyed to the young reader are the closest to the final layer of truth that one can hope for."

Goble told *CA:* "My first four books were written when I was living in England and I had young Indian readers very much in mind. On my long summer visits I only made contact with native Americans, and back in England when working on the books I was, in a sense, doing it with them in mind. And I am glad to say that they have responded warmly to the books. Some will speak no English, and yet the lively discussions amongst themselves which the illustrations provoke tell me they are happy that a white man has admiration for their culture."

BIOGRAPHICAL/CRITICAL SOURCES: New York Times Book Review, November 9, 1970, September 24, 1972, November 11, 1973.

*   *   *

GODARD, Jean-Luc 1930-
(Hans Lucas)

PERSONAL: Born December 30, 1930, in Paris, France; son of Paul (a physician) and Odile (Monod) Godard; married Anna Karina (an actress), March 1, 1961 (divorced, 1964); married Anne Wiazemsky (an actress), July 21, 1967; children: one daughter. *Education:* Sorbonne, University of Paris, Certificate d'Ethnologie, 1949. *Residence:* Grenoble, Austria.

CAREER: Writer and director of motion pictures; film critic. Actor in motion pictures, including "Contempt." Co-founder of *Gazette du Cinema;* founder of Anouchka Films. *Awards, honors:* Prix Jean Vigo and best director award from Berlin Film Festival, both 1960, both for "A bout de souffle"; jury's special prize from Berlin Film Festival, 1961, for "Une Femme est une femme"; jury's special prize and Italian critics' prize, both from Venice Film Festival, and German critics' prize for best foreign film, all 1962, all for "Vivre sa vie"; jury's special prize from Venice Film Festival, 1967, for "La Chinoise, ou plutot a la chinoise"; and other film awards.

WRITINGS—Screenplays, unless otherwise indicated; also

director: (With Macha Meril) *Journal d'une femme mariee* (journal), Denoeel, 1965; *Alphaville* (Chaumiane Productions and Filmstudio, 1965), translation from the French by Peter Whitehead, Lorrimer Publishing, 1966, Simon & Schuster, 1968; (with Jean Gruault and Roberto Rossellini) *Les Carabiniers* (released in the U.S. as "The Riflemen" and as "The Soldiers"; Rome-Paris Films and Laetitia, 1963; adapted from Jacques Audiberti's adaptation of the play by Benjamin Joppolo, *I Carabinieri*), Verlag Filmkritik, 1967; *Made in America* (Rome-Paris Films, 1966; adapted from the novel by Richard Stark, *Rien dans le coffre*), Lorrimer Publishing, 1967; *La Petit Soldat* (also released in the U.S. as "The Little Soldier"; Georges de Beauregard, S.N.C., 1969), translated by Nicholas Garnham, Lorrimer Publishing, 1967, Simon & Schuster, 1970; *Jean-Luc Godard ... articles, essais, entretiens* (title means "Jean-Luc Godard ... Articles, Essays, and Interviews"), P. Belfond, 1968; *Pierrot le fou* (Rome-Paris Films, 1965; adapted from the novel by Lionel White, *Obsession*), Simon & Schuster, 1969; *Masculine-feminin* (Anouchka Films, Argos Films, Svensk Filmindustri, and Sandrews, 1966; adapted from two short stories by Guy de Maupassant, "La Femme de Paul" and "Le Signe"), Grove, 1969.

La Chinoise, ou plutot a la chinoise (Anouchka Films, Les Productions de la Gueville, Athos Films, Parc Films, and Simar Films, 1967), L'Avant-Scene, 1971; (with Daniel Cohn-Bendit) *Weekend* [and] *Wind From the East* (former by Godard; Films Copernic, Ascot Cineraied, Comacico, and Lira Films, 1967; latter by Cohn-Bendit; CCC, Poli Films, and Anouchka Films, 1969), edited by Nicholas Fry, translated by Marianne Sinclair and Danielle Adkinson, Simon & Schuster, 1972; *Godard on Godard* (criticism and interviews), edited and translated by Tom Milne, Viking, 1972; *A bout de souffle* (released in the U.S. as "Breathless"; Georges de Beuregard and Societe Nouvelle de Cinema, 1959; adapted from the screen story by Francois Truffaut), Balland, 1974; *Godard: Three Films* (contains "Une Femme est une femme" [released in the U.S. as "A Woman Is a Woman"], Rome-Paris Films, 1961; "La Femme mariee" [released in the U.S. as "A Married Woman"], Anouchka Films and Orsay Films, 1964; and "Deux ou trois choses que je sais d'elle" [released in the U.S. as "Two or Three Things I Know About Her"], Anouchka Films, Argos Films, Les Films du Carosse, and Parc Films, 1966), translated by Jan Dawson, Susan Bennet, and Marianne Alexander, Harper, 1975 (published in England as *A Woman Is a Woman; A Married Woman; Two or Three Things I Know About Her: Three Films by Jean-Luc Godard*, Lorrimer Publishing, 1975).

Unpublished screenplays; also director: "Vivre sa vie" (released in the U.S. as "My Life to Live"), Les Films de la Pleieade, 1962; "Le Mepris" (released in the U.S. as "Contempt"; adapted from the novel by Alberto Moravia, *Il Disprezzo*), Rome-Paris Films, Films Concordia, and Compagnia Cinematografica Champion, 1963; "Band a part" (released in the U.S. as "Band of Outsiders" and as "The Outsiders"; adapted from the novel by D. Hitchens and B. Hitchens, *Fool's Gold*), Anouchka Films and Orsay Films, 1964; "Le Gai Savoir" (released in the U.S. as "Merry Wisdom" and as "The Joy of Learning"), O.R.T.F., Anouchka Films, and Bavaria Atelier, 1967; "Un Film comme les autres" (released in the U.S. as "A Film Like All the Others"), Leacock-Pennebaker Films, 1968; "One Plus One" (also released in the U.S. as "Sympathy for the Devil"), Cupid Productions, 1968; (with D. A. Pennebaker) "One P.M." (adapted from the unfinished film by Godard, "One A.M."), Leacock-Pennebaker, 1971.

"Dziga-Vertov" series; all with Jean Pierre Gorin: "British Sounds" (also released in the U.S. as "See You at Mao"), Kestrel Productions, 1969; (with Jean-Henri Roger and Paul Burron) "Pravda," Centre Europeen Cinema Radio Television, 1969; "Lotte in Italia" (title means "Struggle in Italy"), Cosmoseion, 1969; "Vladimir et Rosa," Grove Press Evergreen Films, 1971; "Tout va bien," Anouchka Films, Vicco Films, and Empire Films, 1972; "Letter to Jane," 1972.

Short films; also director: "Operation Beton," Actua Films, 1954; (under pseudonym Hans Lucas) "Une Femme coquette" (adapted from the short story by de Maupassant, "Le Signe"), Jean-Luc Godard, 1955; "Charlotte et son Jules," Les Films de la Pleieade, 1958; "Une Histoire d'eau" (title means "A History of Water"; adapted from footage by Truffaut), Les Films de la Pleieade, 1958; "La Paresse," Films Gibe and Franco-London Films, 1962; "Le Nouveau Monde," Lyre Cinematographique, 1962; "Montparnasse-Levallois," Les Films du Losange, 1963; "Le Grande Escroc," Ulysse Productions, Primec Films, Vides, Toho, and Caesar Films, 1964; "Anticipation, ou L'Amour en l'an 2000," Francoriz Films, Films Gibe, Rialto Films, and Rizzoli Films, 1966; "L'Enfant prodigue," Castoro Films and Anouchka Films, 1967.

Other; all as director: "L'Amour," 1970; "Moi je," 1973; "Ici et Ailleurs" (adapted from the unfinished film by Godard and Gorin, "Till Victory"), 1974; "Numero deux," 1975; "Comment ca va," 1976.

Contributor to periodicals, sometimes under the Lucas pseudonym, including *Cahiers du Cinema* and *Arts*.

WORK IN PROGRESS: A film, "Sauve qui peut," to be released in the U.S. as "Every Man for Himself."

SIDELIGHTS: Godard insists that his films are really essays, ones that examine and raise questions, as opposed to traditional narratives. James Monaco writes that "Godard's films require participation." He adds: "Trained as we have been to expect instant gratification from our cinematic commodities, we have too little preparation for appreciating the kind of open dialectic which form Godard's films. They are not machines designed to measure out quanta of entertainment in effective rhythms, but, as he has said many times, essays—*tries*. They form questions; they don't draw conclusions."

Godard's approach to filmmaking as a medium for posing problems probably derives from his early years as a film critic. Since 1949, when he was only nineteen, Godard has been concerned with the nature of film and its potential. While agreeing with Andre Bazin's notion of realism as the absence of montage, Godard expands Bazin's original concept to accommodate montage within the realist framework, or *mise-en-scene*. Monaco writes that "Godard sees montage doing in time what mise-en-scene does in space," and he quotes Godard as saying, " 'If direction is a look, montage is a heartbeat.' "

With its furious pace and abrupt scene-switching, "Breathless," Godard's first full-length film, can almost be termed a self-contained montage. The film is essentially a homage to the *film noir*—dark films of immorality such as the detective story "The Big Sleep" and the melodramatic "The Postman Always Rings Twice." But in "Breathless," Godard emphasizes the presentation, the actual filmmaking process, instead of the presented—the characters. "What is important

for Godard," writes Monaco, "is not what we are, but what we think we are; not the object, but the medium through which it is expressed and which modifies it." It is as an exploration of the cinema's potential that "Breathless" best conforms to Godard's notion of "film as essay." In fact, Godard contends that the film made a star of his cameraman as much as it did either of its principal performers, Jean Seberg and Jean-Paul Belmondo.

Neither of Godard's following films, "The Little Soldier" and "A Woman Is a Woman," is usually ranked among his finer works. In the former, he abandoned his jump-cut style in favor of political content. Godard examines the ambiguity of war through the title character in "The Little Soldier," a youth who refuses to align himself with the cause for which he is fighting. The film was banned in France until 1963, when that country's own military activities in Algeria ended.

"A Woman Is a Woman" is a comedy about a woman who responds to her husband's inattentiveness by seeking his best friend's sexual interest for the purpose of bearing a child. Despite receiving the jury's special prize from the Berlin Film Festival, the film was lampooned by French critics who abhorred its frenzied style and technique. Godard confesses: "There's a basic weakness in the film. It's a color film . . . theoretically made to be shot a la [Luchino] Visconti. By that I mean with a great deal of care and with a taste for details. A set-designer's film. I deliberately shot it in a manner that was the opposite from what it should have been. By going fast, by rushing over things, by improvising."

Godard returned to critical and popular favor with "My Life to Live," the story of a housewife's decline into prostitution that results in her murder. The film is almost the antithesis of "Breathless." Godard acknowledges that it "owes very little to the editing, as it is really a collection of shots placed side by side, each one of which should be self-sufficient." He also notes: "The curious thing is that I think the film looks carefully constructed, whereas I made it extremely rapidly, almost as if I were writing an article without going back to make any corrections. I wanted to make the film like this, without shooting a scene and then trying it another way."

After the release of "My Life to Live," Godard revealed that he was trying to make a film which audiences could easily comprehend. "I think one must aim to attract the widest possible audience," he said. "One must be sincere, believe that one is working for the public, and aim at them. In my early days I never asked myself whether the audience would understand what I was doing, but now I do."

Oddly enough, "The Riflemen," Godard's next film, has proved to be one of his least understood. It is essentially the story of two men persuaded to fight during wartime after being told that, as conquerors, they will reap the spoils of victory and be allowed to vent their long-suppressed desires to rape, murder, and steal. When the men return from the war, they bring with them photographs and post cards depicting the country and people they have defeated. In a bizarre finish, as Jean Collet notes, "yesterday's enemies have become today's friends, and the . . . soldiers are shot."

The objective, or documentary, style of "The Riflemen" often confuses its audience. "The misunderstanding," Godard explains, "springs plainly from the fact that I filmed the war objectively on all levels including that of conscience. . . . Now conscience is always subjective to a more or less greater degree. . . . All films, and in particular war films, have alway staked themselves upon this notion." He concludes that "the making of a documentary is not achieved by robbing the life which lays dormant in film archive store-rooms, but is accomplished only by stripping reality of its appearance by restoring its unpolished aspect, where it suffices unto itself, and by seeking at the same time the moment when it takes on meaning."

"The Riflemen" is succeeded by an equally controversial film, "Contempt." Ostensibly the story of a screenwriter's failing marriage during his work on the filming of *The Odyssey*, "Contempt" is an extremely complex modernization of the lost-love theme. Toby Mussman writes that "Contempt" "confronts us with a myriad of ambiguities, contradictions, and what amounts ultimately to a metaphysical labyrinth of existence." Godard describes the film as the story of a "misunderstanding," and reveals that "at the beginning nothing ought to be bad. At the end it is a catastrophe. At bottom, I believe that there are more catastrophes which come about because of stupidities than because of things which are truly important. This is the kind of misunderstanding which is truly the worst." He sees the characters in the film as "men who have been cut off from themselves, from the world, from reality. They try awkwardly to find the light again, but they have been locked into a black play."

Much of the controversy regarding "Contempt" arose during filming. Producers Carlo Ponti and Joseph E. Levine presumed that Godard would provide them with a marketable film when they supplied him with a $1 million budget, especially since the film featured popular French actress Brigitte Bardot. Since Bardot had attracted considerable attention for appearing nude in films, Ponti and Levine were piqued to discover that Bardot not only remained fully clothed throughout "Contempt," but paraded through portions of the film wearing a black wig that completely hid her blonde hair. The producers demanded that Godard shoot some additional footage featuring a nude Bardot. He refused and ordered his name removed from the credits. Later though, he recanted and delivered the additional scenes. "The problem did not come from Bardot herself," Godard insists. "Rather, it arose from what she represents today in the cinema and in industry."

Because of his disagreements with Ponti and Levine, Godard formed his own production company, Anouchka Films. He wanted "Band of Outsiders," his first film for the company, to be a huge box-office success. As Pauline Kael observes, "Godard intended to give the public what it wanted. His next film was going to be about a girl and a gun—'A sure-fire story which will sell a lot of tickets.'" But, Kael writes, Godard then "proceeded to make a work of art that sold fewer tickets than ever."

"Band of Outsiders" is about two men who play at being gangsters. When a woman convinces them that money is hidden in her villa, they set to the task of stealing the cash. Kael writes that the film "is like a reverie of a gangster movie as students in an expresso bar might remember it or plan it.... It's as if a French poet took an ordinary banal American crime novel and told it to us in terms of the romance and beauty he read between the lines; that is to say, Godard gives it his imagination, recreating the gangsters and the moll with his world of associations—seeing them as people in a Paris cafe, mixing them with Rimbaud, Kafka, Alice in Wonderland." Godard recalls that he "wanted to make a simple film that would be perfectly understandable.... But that didn't stop me from putting everything I really like into the film."

Although "Band of Outsiders" was not the huge commercial

success Godard envisioned, an agreement between his Anouchka Films and Columbia Pictures assured his continuance as a filmmaker. His next film, "A Married Woman," is often seen by critics as a link between "My Life to Live" and the later "Two or Three Things I Know About Her." In the film, Charlotte pursues her day's activities and debates whether to remain with her husband or leave him for her lover. Monaco describes her as "*the* married woman—a concept rather than a human being, for she has been formed and molded by the languages of the media that surround her." Godard fused the two—woman and imposing medium—by breaking from the conventional means of filmmaking. He defines the film as one "where subjects are seen as objects, where pursuits by taxi alternate with ethnological interviews, where the spectacle of life finally mingles with its analysis." Monaco asserts, "Those abrupt shifts of the level of discourse ... should no longer trouble us as they once might have, since now, for the first time, we approach the film as an essay rather than a fiction." "A Married Woman" marks a turning point in Godard's artistry. "The relationship between character and observer is no longer in focus," writes Monaco. "It has been replaced by the relationship between filmmaker and observer."

Godard's next film, "Alphaville," is essentially a summary of his previous efforts. Like "Breathless," "Alphaville" is inverted *film noir*: private detective Lemmy Caution tries to break from a future society in which emotion is deemed detrimental to progress. By integrating his ever-developing political philosophy with his filmmaking abilities, Godard fashioned "Alphaville" as both a summary of his filmmaking past and a forecast of future intentions. Michael Benedikt declares that "it is no longer possible to view a creator like Godard as operating solely ... out of a background of the visual arts—even the cinematic—developments of the past few years. It seems to me that *Alphaville* is an excellent place from which to launch a useful series of fresh confrontations."

But "Pierrot le fou" is also a summary of other Godard films. It combines the narrative device of the diary from "Alphaville" with the disdain for commercialism so evident in "A Married Woman." The plot resembles yet another film, "Contempt," in its chronicling of a declining relationship. But despite its dim view of relationships, the film inspires the same celebration of Godard's talents as the previous "Alphaville." "In *Pierrot*," writes Peter Harcourt, "Godard seems to have discovered a form that has enabled him to express his most private and apparently autobiographical obsessions in such a way that by the end of the film they have the liberating quality of a work of art."

In 1966, Godard said: "Two or three years ago I felt that everything had been done, that there was nothing left to do today. I couldn't see anything to do that hadn't been done already.... After *Pierrot*, I no longer feel this.... Everything remains to be done." As proof, Godard offers three films of vastly different style and content, all made in 1966.

Godard describes "Masculine-feminin," his first film of that year, as one about "the children of Marx and Coca-Cola." The plot revolves around the efforts of a Communist, Paul, to win the love of Madeleine, who works in publishing but wishes to be a singer. Within this simple story, Godard invests numerous observations on Vietnam, politics, and youth. The men in the film are intensely dedicated to their causes. The women, however, are defined by Monaco as commodities "formed by the newly powerful youth culture." Richard Roud contends that their motto is "Give us this day our TV and automobile, but deliver us from freedom." Through the conflicting interests of Paul and Madeleine, Godard examines the conflicting interests of "the children of Marx and Coca-Cola." "When we read between the press-agented lines," observes Monaco, "we have the real Madeleine, a true child of the Pepsi generation, whose emptiness is a void in which Paul loses himself. She not only strives to create a universe all her own, she denies his."

Throughout the remainder of 1966, Godard labored simultaneously on both "Made in U.S.A." and "Two or Three Things I Know About Her." The former is in the pseudo-*film noir* vein of "Breathless" and "Alphaville," and was inspired by Raymond Chandler's novel, *The Big Sleep.* Conceived as the relatively straightforward story of a woman searching for her husband's murderers, the film took on added dimensions when Godard interjected references to the assassinations of both John Kennedy and Ben Barka. "I tried to make a simple film," explains Godard, "and . . . to tell a story. But it's not in my nature. I don't know how to tell stories. I want to mix everything, to restore everything, to tell all at the same time."

In "Made in U.S.A.," Godard abandoned his usual style of contrasting form and content. "Chandler's world was dark, impenetrable, and paranoid," writes Monaco, "and the angst which pervaded it had first attracted the critics of the New Wave in the fifties; Godard is simply transferring the breakdown of logic and ethics which frightened Philip Marlowe from the Private Eye metaphor to a more specific mode." By paralleling form and content, though, Godard has created a film which confuses audiences, especially those accustomed to his particular style. "It is wholly proper to have the form express the content," states Roud. "But this has not been Godard's way before, and it doesn't work too well here."

"Two or Three Things I Know About Her" is yet another reworking of themes already familiar from "My Life to Live" and "A Married Woman," for it combines the element of prostitution of the former with the one-day-in-the-life-of-a-housewife structure of the latter. Critics seem divided on the merits of this film; some complain that Godard was merely returning to themes he had successfully explored already, others insist that it is the quintessential Godard film, surpassing even "Alphaville" and "Pierrot le fou" in its recitation of his pet themes and obsessions.

By 1967, Godard was becoming more political in his subjects. "La Chinoise," one of his most successful fusions of politics and entertainment, portrays several Maoist students in Paris. Many scenes are simply conversations among the students. By photographing each speaker objectively, Godard leaves it to the viewer to determine the value of each philosophy. "From the strict point of view of the film itself," writes Royal S. Brown, "the whole thing remains at the level of unresolved dialectic."

In "Weekend," Godard offers a scathing indictment of the French bourgeoisie—a class in almost total submission to American commercialism and ideals. The plot centers around the efforts of Roland and Corinne to arrive at the latter's home and abscond with her dying father's funds before her mother arrives. En route, they become involved in a huge traffic tie-up, try to steal a car, and are harassed by revolutionaries and cannibals. Themselves members of the bourgeoisie, they exhibit the symptoms of American influence. By journey's end, they encounter the results of that influence. Roger Greenspun wrote that "Weekend" "moves from casual killing to purposeful killing, from merely poison-ing your loved ones to eating them, from erotic abuse of bodies to murderous use of bodies, from civilization and its discontents to totem and taboo."

After "Weekend," Godard began devoting more attention to his interest in politics and film form. In "Le Gai Savoir," Godard suggests that filmmakers "return to zero" and redefine cinematic concepts. Calling for a rewriting of cinematic language, Godard employs outlines and math-related formulas in the detailing of his new design for film. He suggests that accepted notions of the cinema be analyzed and decomposed so that more accurate ones may be reconstructed. The emphasis should not be on the object, Godard asserts, but on the *sign*—the meaning of the object as interpreted through the filmmaker's approach. He claims that "realism does not consist in reproducing reality, but in showing how things really are."

In revising his views of the cinema, Godard forced himself to abandon aspects of his work that had been admired by audiences and critics. In "One Plus One," he juxtaposes scenes of the Rolling Stones recording their song "Sympathy for the Devil," with footage depicting war and strife. The characters in the film, however, are not well-rounded individuals, but personifications of political ideologies. Though these characters seem a logical extension of those in "Weekend" and "La Chinoise," they're much less human than those in "A Married Woman" or "Two or Three Things I Know About Her." "It seems to me that Godard is uniquely unfitted to make the kind of films he thinks he ought to be making," Roud muses, "it would seem he cannot do without the lyricism which recently he has been trying so hard to suppress."

Godard became even more removed from that "lyricism" in 1969 when he began collaborating with Jean-Pierre Gorin, a young Marxist, as a two-man filmmaking cooperative called Dziga-Vertov, a reference to the famed Russian filmmaker of the 1920's. Godard renounced his previous films as "bourgeois movies for bourgeois producers" and dedicated his filmmaking future to "the revolution." "In order to use the right violence at the right time in the right place," he observes, "you must first use nonviolence. Through an ideological struggle, we can proceed to an armed struggle. And the mass media are very important in this struggle."

Godard was so taken with his new direction that he even envisioned a time when he might cease making films and opt for something more beneficial to his cause. "Movies are merely chapters in ideology," he announces. "As Lenin said, 'Art and literature are just tiny elements—a screw of the revolution.' Maybe in time we'll find that our task will not be to make movies, but to perform a different task in a different sector."

Critics generally agree that the first film from Dziga-Vertov, "British Sounds," is their most successful synthesis of politics and Godard's concept of image/sound. In the opening sequence, the camera follows the assemblage of an automobile as it moves through the factory; the soundtrack features both the chaotic din of the factory and quotations from Marx. It is a powerful scene that both depicts the plight of the proletariat and suggests the solution in the form of an alternate ideology.

In another sequence, Godard and Gorin question sexism in much the same way as Godard questioned the validity of existing rules of cinema language in "Le Gai Savoir." The image is that of a nude woman photographed from waist to knee and the soundtrack features the same woman reading a feminist tract while a male voice pronounces inane political-sexist remarks. Though the immediate male reaction may be a leering, voyeuristic one, and the female reaction one of embarrassment and exploitation, the image and soundtrack work to revise the *sign*—what the image represents—so that preconceived notions prove useless (in fact, harmful) to an understanding of the sequence.

Dziga-Vertov made three more films in 1969. Unlike the earlier "British Sounds" however, the remaining works quickly become mired in their own dogma. "Pravda," a study of Czechoslovakia's reaction to Western politics, begins as documentation but quickly evolves into analysis. It exemplifies the strengths and weaknesses of Dziga-Vertov: its ability to conceptualize and its inability to analyze. Monaco notes the collective's "tendency for baroque, dogmatic, effulgent ideology to cloud the images and sounds of 'concrete analysis of concrete situations.'" He concludes: "The two failures are linked, for both make it possible for the Dziga-Vertov films to ignore people in order to celebrate the esthetics of dogma. In the battle between theory and practice, the former too often wins out."

Dziga-Vertov's over-reliance on theory ultimately sabotaged "Wind From the East." The first half of the film is devoted to a relentless contrasting of image and sound: two people lie chained together in a field while numerous voices talk of a strike. The film then develops into an exploration of a different strike through an exploration of various film styles. The second half imposes a paradigm of theory and practice regarding political behavior. Unfortunately, "Wind From the East" is considered so complex in its elaborate theorization that it burdens the viewer by presupposing a working knowledge of both radical politics and the cinema, thus making it largely incomprehensible to many viewers.

By 1971, Dziga-Vertov had completed two more films, the rarely shown "Struggles in Italy" and "Vladimir et Rosa." The latter is reminiscent of "One Plus One" in its dual narrative—in this case a bourgeois tennis match is interwoven with re-enactments of the trial of the Chicago Seven. Neither film proved to be effective in either elucidating Dziga-Vertov's previous films or developing new theories.

A breakthrough for the group came in 1972 when they signed controversial actors Yves Montand and Jane Fonda to appear in "Tout va bien," Dziga-Vertov's first entertaining venture. The film is an attempt to determine the role of the intellectual in the "revolution"; Montand plays Jacques, a filmmaker reduced through his own disinterest to making commercials; Fonda plays Susan, a television journalist acutely aware of her political stagnation. Political holdovers from the sixties, both Jacques and Susan are mired in the repetition of their marriage and their careers, but they become aware of their problems during their coverage of a strike at a sausage factory. While observing the strike, they are re-awakened to their own potential—emotionally, politically, and professionally. The film ends with the two in a cafe analyzing their past and anticipating their future.

"Tout va bien" did moderately well at the French box office and if it was not the success it could have been, the fault lies primarily with Gorin. In late 1971, Godard suffered a near-fatal motorcycle accident. Since "Tout va bien" was already in preparation, much of the filmmaking was handled by Gorin, who had little experience aside from the other Dziga-Vertov films. After "Tout va bien" though, Godard and Gorin collaborated for the final time on "Letter to Jane," a film in which they tried once again to determine the role of the intellectual in the "revolution." "Letter to Jane" is little more than an analysis of an expression—an image of concern exemplified in a photograph of Fonda among North Vietnamese citizens. Godard calls her expression "an expression of an expression" for, according to Monaco, the expression "is quantitative and emotional rather than qualitative and analytic." "Letter to Jane" suggests that a revision of perceiving reality is in order in much the same way that "Le Gai Savoir" pushes for a restructuring of cinematic language.

Godard has maintained a low profile since the disbanding of Dziga-Vertov in 1972. Relocating first in Switzerland and then Austria, he divided his attention among three films, "Numero deux," "Comment ca va," and "Ici et ailleurs," a reworking of footage of the Palestinian Liberation Organization originally intended for Dziga-Vertov's "Till Victory." When the films were shown in New York City in late 1977, there was virtually no attention accorded them. Apparently, Godard's overt political and cinematic theorizing proved too complex for even attentive filmgoers, and his refusal to compromise spelled his commercial demise. "The artist and the scientist are similar," he offers. "I mix images and sounds like a scientist, I hope. The mystery of the scientific is the same as the mystery of the artistic. So is the misery."

BIOGRAPHICAL/CRITICAL SOURCES—Books: Susan Sontag, *Against Interpretation*, Farrar, Straus, 1966; Toby Mussman, editor, *Jean-Luc Godard*, Dutton, 1968; Sontag, *Styles of Radical Will*, Farrar, Straus, 1969; Ian Cameron, editor, *The Films of Jean-Luc Godard*, Praeger, 1969; Richard Roud, *Godard*, Indiana University Press, 1970; Jean Collet, *Jean-Luc Godard*, Crown, 1970; Royal S. Brown, editor, *Focus on Godard*, Prentice-Hall, 1972; Jean-Luc Godard, *Godard on Godard*, edited and translated by Toby Mussman, Viking, 1972; Peter Harcourt, *Six European Directors: Essays on the Meaning of Film Style*, Penguin, 1974; James Monaco, *The New Wave*, Oxford University Press, 1976; Monaco, *How to Read a Film*, Oxford University Press, 1977.

Periodicals: *Cahiers du Cinema*, April, 1960, November, 1962, December, 1962, August, 1963, October, 1964, November, 1966, June, 1967; *L'Express*, June 16, 1960, January 12, 1961, July 27, 1961; *Film Culture*, summer, 1961, winter, 1962, spring, 1972; *Sight and Sound*, winter, 1962-63, winter, 1963-64, spring, 1964, summer, 1965, winter, 1965-66, summer, 1966, summer, 1967, winter, 1967-68, summer, 1968, autumn, 1969, spring, 1971, summer, 1971, summer, 1972, summer, 1973; *Les Signes du temps*, July, 1963; *Le Monde*, December 20, 1963; *Film Quarterly*, spring, 1964, summer, 1966, summer, 1968, winter, 1968-69, winter, 1970-71, fall, 1972, summer, 1974; *Moviegoer*, summer-autumn, 1964; *Telerama*, August 16, 1964; *Village Voice*, November 12, 1964, April 20, 1970, October 31, 1977; *New Republic*, September 10, 1966; *New Left Review*, September-October, 1966; *Take One*, June, 1968, March, 1971, June, 1971, October, 1972, July, 1974, January, 1976; *New York Free Press*, October 17, 1968; *New York Times*, October 27, 1968, April 27, 1970, May 17, 1970; *Rolling Stone*, June 14, 1969; *Films and Filming*, June, 1970; *Evergreen Review*, October, 1970; *Partisan Review*, July, 1971; *Film Comment*, May-June, 1974.*

—*Sketch by Les Stone*

*   *   *

GOLDBERG, Moses H(aym)   1940-

PERSONAL: Born May 25, 1940, in New Orleans, La.; son of Leon (a social worker) and Celia (Draisen) Goldberg; married Patricia Davis (an educator), December 27, 1964; children: Ruth, Joel. *Education:* Attended University of London, 1959-60; Tulane University, B.S., 1961; Stanford

University, M.A. (child psychology), 1963; University of Washington, Seattle, M.A. (drama), 1965; University of Minnesota, Ph.D., 1969. *Home:* 5301 Chenoweth Park Lane, Louisville, Ky. 40291. *Office:* Stage One, 2117 Payne St., Louisville, Ky. 40206.

CAREER: Conducted training program for camp counselors in Hendersonville, N.C., 1963-65; University of Minnesota, Minneapolis, director of youth theatre series, 1967; Southwest Texas State College (now University), San Marcos, instructor in speech, 1967-69; Florida State University, Tallahassee, assistant professor, 1969-73, associate professor of theatre, 1973-76, also administrator of children's theatre program and founding director of Children's Theatre Tour; PAF Playhouse, Huntington, N.Y., director of youth theatre, 1976-77; Stage One (children's theatre), Louisville, Ky., director, 1978—. Teacher of creative dramatics for children in public schools; director of children's theatre tour to elementary schools in Florida, 1970; director at Asolo State Theatre, 1970-75, and Aspen Theatre Institute, 1973; judge of playwriting contests.

MEMBER: International Association of Theatre for Children and Youth (vice-chairperson of U.S. Centre, 1972—), American Theatre Association (member of International Commission), American Camping Association, Children's Theatre Association of America (member of national board of directors, 1972-74; vice-president for research, 1975-77), Southeastern Theatre Conference (chairperson of Children's Theatre Division and member of board of directors, 1972-74), Florida League of the Arts, Florida Alliance for Arts Education (member of board of directors, 1975-77), Tallahassee Arts Council, Sigma Xi, Alpha Epsilon Pi. *Awards, honors:* Grants from Florida State Arts Council, 1970, and National Endowment for the Arts, 1970, 1975-76; special recognition award from Children's Theatre Association of America, 1975.

WRITINGS: (Contributor) Pat Whitton, editor, *Participation Plays: A Handbook for Directors,* New Plays for Children, 1972; *Children's Theatre: A Philosophy and a Method,* Prentice-Hall, 1974; (contributor) Don Rapp, editor, *What Is a Fine Art?,* Office of Publications, Florida State University, 1975; (contributor) Nellie McCaslin, editor, *Children and Drama: Perspectives,* McKay, 1975.

Published plays: *Hansel and Gretel* (one-act; first produced in Tallahassee, Fla., at Florida State University, October, 1970), New Plays for Children, 1972; *Wind in the Willows* (one-act; first produced in Seattle, Wash., at Showboat Theatre, April 15, 1965), Anchorage Press, 1974; *Aladdin: A Participation Play* (one-act; first produced in Sarasota, Fla., Asolo State Theatre, December, 1972), Anchorage Press, 1977; *The Outlaw Robin Hood* (one-act; first produced in Minneapolis, Minn., at Scott Hall, April, 1968), Anchorage Press, 1979; *The Men's Cottage* (one-act; first produced in Louisville, Ky., at Stage One, February, 1979), Anchorage Press, 1980.

Unpublished plays: "Puss in Boots" (one-act), first produced in Minneapolis at Peppermint Tent, July, 1968; "Rumpelstiltskin" (one-act), first produced in Tallahassee at Florida State University, February, 1969; "Jack and the Beanstalk" (one-act), first produced in Seattle at A Contemporary Theatre, July, 1971; "Johnny Tremain" (two-act musical), first produced in Tallahassee at Florida State University, April, 1973; "Herakles" (one-act musical), first produced in Tallahassee at Asolo Touring Theatre, November, 1974; "The Shepherd's Play" (one-act adaptation from Wakefield Cycle), first produced in Newark, Del., at Dela-

ware Summer Festival, June, 1974; "Antigone" (one-act adaptation from Sophocles), first produced in Tallahassee at Asolo Touring Theatre, November, 1975; "The Queen Bird and the Golden Fish" (one-act), first produced in New York City at PAF Playhouse, October, 1976; "Vasilia" (one-act), first produced in Sarasota at Asolo Touring Theatre, October, 1977.

Contributor to theatre journals. Editor of regional newsletter of Children's Theatre Conference, 1966-67; U.S. theater editor of *Childhood and Youth,* 1970-72.

WORK IN PROGRESS: Plays about real young people of junior high age.

SIDELIGHTS: Goldberg wrote: "My position is, simply stated, that every human being should be offered aesthetic development as part of the education furnished to him by society in an attempt to help him reach his fullest human potential. The individual should be exposed to a series of arts experiences, sequenced to maximize the development of his aesthetic powers. The individual should be exposed to participatory experiences which exercise and develop his 'right-brain' processes. I place slightly more emphasis on the former than on the latter.

"I feel that the product exposure should come from adult professional artists, performing either in the school or in a nearby theatre or auditorium, and the training of the aesthetic processes of the mind should rest with the classroom teachers. I see a need for another kind of practitioner who can design the structured lessons and train the actors to perform them and who can work to develop the classroom teachers' ability. These tasks do not require artistic ability; they require ability in instructional design, techniques of teacher training, and great sympathy with the aesthetic process."

AVOCATIONAL INTERESTS: Cooking, science fiction.

*   *   *

GOLDMAN, Alan H(arris)   1945-

PERSONAL: Born August 7, 1945, in New York, N.Y.; son of Larry I. (in business) and Florence (Goodman) Goldman; married Joan Berkowitz (a teacher), May 29, 1968; children: Michael. *Education:* Yale University, B.A., 1967; Columbia University, M.A., 1968, Ph.D., 1972. *Home:* 7771 Southwest 103rd Place, Miami, Fla. 33173. *Office:* Department of Philosophy, University of Miami, Coral Gables, Fla. 33124.

CAREER: Columbia University, New York, N.Y., instructor in philosophy, 1970-72; Ohio University, Athens, assistant professor of philosophy, 1972-74; University of Idaho, Moscow, assistant professor of philosophy, 1974-77; University of Miami, Coral Gables, Fla., associate professor of philosophy, 1977—. *Member:* American Philosophical Association. *Awards, honors:* National Endowment for the Humanities fellow; grant from Phi Beta Kappa.

WRITINGS: Justice and Reverse Discrimination, Princeton University Press, 1979; *Moral Foundations of Professional Ethics,* Littlefield, 1980. Contributor to philosophy journals.

*   *   *

GOLDMAN, Richard Franko   1910-1980

OBITUARY NOTICE—See index for *CA* sketch: Born December 7, 1910, in New York, N.Y.; died January 19, 1980, in Baltimore, Md. Translator, conductor, composer, educator, musicologist, and author of works in his field. Goldman conducted the Goldman Band in free concerts in New York

City from 1956 to 1979. He also conducted the Baltimore Symphony and taught at both the Peabody Conservatory of Music and the Julliard School. His writings include *The Wind Band: Its Literature and Technique* and *Harmony in Western Music*. Obituaries and other sources: *The ASCAP Biographical Dictionary of Composers, Authors, and Publishers*, American Society of Composers, Authors, and Publishers, 1966; *Who's Who in the World*, 2nd edition, Marquis, 1973; *The Writers Directory, 1976-78*, St. Martin's, 1976; *Director of American Scholars*, Volume I: *History*, 7th edition, Bowker, 1978; *Washington Post*, January 24, 1980.

*   *   *

GOLDRING, Douglas   1887-1960

OBITUARY NOTICE: Born January 7, 1887, in Greenwich, England; died in 1960. Novelist, critic, and travel writer. In his early career, Goldring served on the editorial staffs of several periodicals, including *Country Life, English Review,* and his own literary magazine, *Tramp.* An avid devotee of rural England and Georgian architecture, he founded the Georgian Group, a branch of the Society for the Protection of Ancient Buildings. Numbered among Goldring's more than twenty-five books are *Northern Lights and Southern Shores, Sardinia: The Island of the Nuraghi,* and *Margot's Progress,* in addition to two autobiographies, *Odd Man Out* and *Facing the Odds.* Obituaries and other sources: *New Century Handbook of English Literature,* revised edition, Appleton, 1967; *Longman Companion to Twentieth Century Literature,* Longman, 1970.

*   *   *

GOLDSTEIN, Howard   1922-

PERSONAL: Born February 12, 1922, in Hamilton, Ontario, Canada; came to United States in 1924; naturalized citizen; son of David (a self-employed shoe salesman) and Jennie (Frohman) Goldstein; married Linda Lehmann (a writer), 1971; children: Janis Bouc, Marcy, Lora, James, Lani. *Education:* Santa Monica City College, A.A., 1951; University of Southern California, B.A. (magna cum laude), 1952, M.S.W., 1954, D.S.W., 1970. *Politics:* Democrat. *Religion:* Jewish. *Home:* 1649 Compton Rd., Cleveland Heights, Ohio 44118. *Office:* School of Applied Social Sciences, Case Western Reserve University, Cleveland, Ohio 44106.

CAREER: Traveler's Aid Society of Los Angeles, Los Angeles, Calif., caseworker with transients, 1953-54; Family Service Association of Cleveland, Cleveland, Ohio, caseworker, 1954-56; Family Service of San Diego, San Diego, Calif., social worker, 1956-63; San Diego State College (now University), San Diego, assistant professor of social work, 1964-70; University of South Carolina, Columbia, professor of social work, 1971-73; Dalhousie University, Halifax, Nova Scotia, professor of social work, 1973-77; Case Western Reserve University, Cleveland, Ohio, professor of social work, 1977—. Private practice of social work, 1957-70. Director of research for Homemaker Service of San Diego, 1964-66. Seminar leader; workshop participant. *Military service:* U.S. Army, combat photographer, 1943-46. *Member:* International Association of Social Work, Council on Social Work Education, Academy of Certified Social Workers, National Association of Social Workers, Canadian Association of Schools of Social Work, Phi Beta Kappa.

WRITINGS: Social Work Practice: A Unitary Approach, University of South Carolina Press, 1973; *Change Through Social Learning: A Cognitive Approach to Human Service Practice,* University of South Carolina Press, 1980. Contrib-utor to *Handbook of Social Work Programs and Methods.* Contributor to American and Canadian social work journals. Corresponding editor of *Canadian Journal of Social Work Education,* 1974—; co-editor of *Social Work in Atlantic Canada,* 1974—; member of editorial board of *Journal of Applied Social Sciences,* 1977—.

SIDELIGHTS: Goldstein told *CA:* "The impetus for writing stemmed from two major sources: (1) a mid-life decision regarding my future and career and (2) a need to see if I could reconceptualize the theoretical foundations of social work using my experience in teaching and practice and the emergence of new knowledge in the social and behavior sciences. Thus, in 1970 I rejected my teaching contract at San Diego State College, closed a lucrative private practice in psychotherapy and counseling, and moved to New York. There I spent the next year writing *Social Work Practice: A Unitary Approach* which was published in 1973. This book was well received and has had considerable impact on sectors of the profession that were ready to jettison traditional Freudian, psychiatric models." Reviewing the book in *Social Work,* Carol H. Meyer remarked: "On every page I had to stretch my mind. When I agreed with Goldstein I found myself nodding; and when I disagreed, I felt like telephoning him to discuss it. The reader of this book will be engaged with the ideas of a scholar, a humanist, and a sensitive social worker."

"The second book was begun in 1974," Goldstein commented. "Although it does build from the first, it is an entity in its own right and is to depart rather totally from well-entrenched psychodynamic and behaviorist models to construct a theory of practice with a rational, common-sense, and cognitive orientation. Moreover, this book is concerned with practice with populations who would usually resist aforementioned traditional models, such as the disenfranchised, poor, deviant, stigmatized, and disadvantaged.

"I have some questions regarding how the book will be received. With some dismay, I see my colleagues in the helping professions clinging uncritically to well-worn, traditional and rhetorical models of practice—this despite any solid evidence that their efforts are producing significant results. The helping professions have become guilds that are concerned mainly with self-perpetuation. The human and social service organizations similarly are concerned with self-maintenance. A good many educational institutions make cosmetic changes in their curricula but continue to teach in conservative and traditional ways. Occasional fads (such as de-institutionalization) capture the fancy of the professions, but again without a critical and analytical eye.

"These conditions persist despite lack of evidence of the effectiveness of these approaches, despite the fact that so many people are not receiving the help and service they require, and despite the emergence of ideas and theories of behavior, interaction, and change that cast new light on the human and social condition. My hope is that this book will at least stir some thinking about these serious issues.

"I have a goodly number of other interests which, to some extent, compensate for the frustration I feel about not having three or four simultaneous careers. I am most interested in animal life and in addition to surrounding myself with the usual dogs and cats, also raise parrot-type birds. I do my best writing when Blue, my blue front amazon parrot, is looking over my shoulder. Photography is another interest. I was formerly a medical and combat photographer but circumstances transformed this career into a hobby. Gardening is yet another avocation, abetted by that fact that my wife, Linda, spent her developing years on a farm."

BIOGRAPHICAL/CRITICAL SOURCES: Social Work, March, 1974.

* * *

GOLDSTEIN, Laurence 1943-

PERSONAL: Born January 5, 1943, in Los Angeles, Calif.; son of Cecil (in sales) and Helen (a secretary; maiden name, Soltot) Goldstein; married Nancy Jo Copeland (a registered nurse), April 28, 1968; children: Andrew William, Jonathan Lee. *Education:* University of California, Los Angeles, B.A., 1965; Brown University, Ph.D., 1970. *Politics:* Democrat. *Religion:* Jewish. *Office:* University of Michigan, 3032 Rackham Building, Ann Arbor, Mich. 48109.

CAREER: University of Michigan, Ann Arbor, assistant professor, 1970-78, associate professor of English, 1978—. *Awards, honors:* Andrew Mellon fellowship from University of Pittsburgh, 1975-76.

WRITINGS: Ruins and Empire: The Evolution of a Theme in Augustan and Romantic Literature, University of Pittsburgh Press, 1977; *Altamira* (poems), Abattoir, 1978. Editor of *Michigan Quarterly Review,* 1977—.

WORK IN PROGRESS: A book on the response of poets to the achievements of aerial technology; a volume of poems about southern California.

SIDELIGHTS: Goldstein wrote: "An editor's taste may be defined as his *sense of the significant* in contemporary writing. This sense, or intuition, must be formed by an immersion in all kinds of literature: past and present, foreign and national, fiction, nonfiction, poetry—anything written with such passionate intelligence it engages a modern reader. Taste becomes the editor's worst handicap when it ossifies into a set of predictable and inflexible standards. Editors must keep in training by reading the apparently *dis*-tasteful, eccentric, obscure, and far-fetched, as well as the clearly authentic works honored by critics. Editors, like writers (and most editors are writers), must believe that their productions will have an impact on the society at large; this belief provides energy though it can also lead to a preference for the modish or false sublime over more confined but evidentially precise expression. For this reason all editors need independent-minded staff members to consult and negotiate with.

"Speaking personally, I think southern California is a good place for an editor to grow up. One is nourished there first by a progressive and offbeat lifestyle, and then by nostalgia for a greater degree of order and meaning in life. The opposite combination can lead to frantic iconoclasm, *vide* H. L. Mencken (Mencken had wit but no taste; *American Mercury* published no single enduring essay, story, or poem).

"Finally, one must emphasize that editors should begin as and remain writers, not only for the sake of alertness and for survival purposes—the tenure of editors is notoriously short—but to constantly renew their sympathy with the authors whose manuscripts and egos they process daily."

* * *

GOOCH, Bryan Niel Shirley 1937-

PERSONAL: Born December 31, 1937, in Vancouver, British Columbia, son of Niel C. S. (a naval commander) and Mary A. Bryan (a teacher; maiden name, Williams) Gooch; married Jane Lytton Tryon (a university teacher), June 24, 1974. *Education:* University of British Columbia, B.A., 1959, M.A., 1962; Royal Conservatory of Music, Toronto, Ontario, A.R.C.T., 1957; Trinity College of Music, London,

L.T.C.L., 1959, F.T.C.L., 1961; University of London, Ph.D., 1968. *Religion:* Church of England. *Home:* 2791 West 43rd Ave., Vancouver, British Columbia, Canada V6N 3H8. *Office:* Department of English, University of Victoria, Victoria, British Columbia, Canada V8W 2Y2.

CAREER: Pianist and piano teacher in Vancouver, British Columbia, 1955—; University of Victoria, Victoria, British Columbia, instructor, 1964-68, assistant professor, 1968-76, associate professor of English, 1976—. Member of faculty at Victoria Conservatory of Music, 1967-70. Musical director and conductor of Nanaimo Symphony Orchestra, 1968-71, and New Westminster Symphony Orchestra, 1975-77. Performer for Canadian Broadcasting Corp. Member of advisory academic panel of Social Sciences and Humanities Research Council of Canada, 1978—. *Military service:* Royal Canadian Sea Cadets, 1957-62; became lieutenant.

MEMBER: Humanities Association of Canada (member of executive committee, 1968-70), Association of Canadian University Teachers of English, American Musicological Society, Modern Language Association of America, Renaissance Society of America, Royal Commonwealth Society (life fellow). *Awards, honors:* Canada Council grants, 1972-80, fellowship, 1976-77.

WRITINGS: (Editor with Tory I. Westermark) *Poetry Is for People,* Macmillan, 1973; (with David S. Thatcher) *Musical Settings of Late Victorian and Modern British Literature: A Catalogue,* Garland Publishing, 1976; (with Thatcher) *Musical Settings of Early and Mid-Victorian Literature: A Catalogue,* Garland Publishing, 1979. Author of radio scripts for Canadian Broadcasting Corp. Contributor to *Encyclopedia of Music in Canada.* Contributor to music, literature, and other academic journals, including *Commonwealth Journal, English Journal,* and *Music Review.*

WORK IN PROGRESS: Musical Settings of British Romantic Literature: A Catalogue, with David S. Thatcher, publication by Garland Publishing expected in 1982.

SIDELIGHTS: Gooch writes that his main research interests "involve the relationship of poetry and music in England between 1660 and 1760 and the musical settings of British literature from the Romantics to the present day. I would always hope that the results of my work would be of value to other people and that what is a personal concern or love for me may be shared by a wider community, both inside and outside the world of the universities.

"My main interests as a pianist are accompanying and chamber music. I thoroughly enjoy working with other performers and find the exchange of ideas and views with respect to interpretation enormously stimulating. Playing for singers has its literary side, too. After all, one is dealing with both text and music."

* * *

GOODE, James M. 1939-

PERSONAL: Born September 17, 1939, in Statesville, N.C.; son of George Browne (a corporation treasurer) and Dorothy (Wagg) Goode. *Education:* University of South Carolina, B.A., 1964; University of Virginia, M.A., 1966. *Politics:* Democrat. *Religion:* Episcopalian. *Home:* 2039 New Hampshire Ave. N.W., Washington, D.C. 20009. *Office:* Smithsonian Institute, Washington, D.C. 20560.

CAREER: George Mason University, Fairfax, Va., lecturer in history, 1966-68; Library of Congress, Washington, D.C., reference librarian, 1969; Smithsonian Institute, Washington, D.C., curator of Smithsonian Building, 1970—. Member of board of directors of Art for Humanities Foundation. Active in local preservation movement. *Military service:* U.S. Army, 1958-61. *Member:* Victorian Society in America, Manuscript Society of America (local president, 1967-68), Society of Architectural Historians, Columbia Historical Society (member of board of managers), White House Historical Association.

WRITINGS: The Outdoor Sculpture of Washington, D.C.: A Comprehensive Historical Guide, Smithsonian Institute Press, 1974; *Capital Losses: A Cultural History of Washington's Destroyed Buildings,* Smithsonian Institute Press, 1979.

WORK IN PROGRESS: Research on American studies, cultural history, nineteenth-century American furniture and architecture, and urban history.

BIOGRAPHICAL/CRITICAL SOURCES: Washington Star, March 18, 1979; *Washington Post Book World,* October 14, 1979.

* * *

GOODNOUGH, David L. 1930-

PERSONAL: Born August 6, 1930, in Binghamton, N.Y.; son of Bruce (an electrical engineer) and Norine (Hanrahan) Goodnough; married Doris Bloodgood (a free-lance editor), July 1, 1965; children: Jonathan, Norine. *Education:* Harpur College, B.A., 1953. *Home:* 18 Pines Bridge Rd., Ossining, N.Y. 10562. *Office:* Arco Publishing Co., Inc., 219 Park Ave. S., New York, N.Y. 10003.

CAREER: Holt, Rinehart & Winston, Inc., New York City, editor, 1962-64; A. S. Barnes & Co., Inc., New York City, senior editor, 1964-66; Grosset & Dunlap, Inc., New York City, senior editor, 1966-72; Arco Publishing Co., Inc., New York City, editor-in-chief, 1972—. *Military service:* U.S. Army, 1953-55.

WRITINGS—Juvenile: The Cherry Valley Massacre, F. Watts, 1968; *Pontiac's War,* F. Watts, 1970; *The New York Colony,* F. Watts, 1972; *Christopher Columbus,* Troll Associates, 1978; *Sir Francis Drake,* Troll Associates, 1978; *John and Sebastian Cabot,* Troll Associates, 1978.

WORK IN PROGRESS: That Jap Can Sing!, a mystery novel.

* * *

GOODSPEED, Edgar Johnson 1871-1962

OBITUARY NOTICE: Born October 23, 1871, in Quincy, Ill.; died January 13, 1962. Educator, author, and translator. Goodspeed began his life-long affiliation with the University of Chicago in 1894 as a teacher. He subsequently became professor of the Bible and Patristic Greek, secretary to the president, chairman of the department, distinguished services professor, and professor emeritus, a post he held since 1937. Of his more than fifty books, Goodspeed's translations of both the Old and New Testaments brought him popularity for their modernized texts. He also wrote books on different aspects of the Bible, including *The Story of the Bible* and *How to Read the Bible.* His autobiography, *As I Remember,* was published in 1953. Obituaries and other sources: *New York Times,* January 14, 1962; *Time,* January 26, 1962; *Publishers Weekly,* January 29, 1962; *Current Biography,* Wilson, 1946, March, 1962.

* * *

GOODWIN, Derek 1920-

PERSONAL: Born February 26, 1920, in Woking, England; son of H. and Amy (Lane) Goodwin. *Education:* Attended school in Egham, England. *Politics:* "Dislike Communism, Fascism, *and* Bureaucracy." *Religion:* Agnostic. *Office:* Department of Zoology, British Museum (Natural History), Tring, Hertfordshire HP23 6AS, England.

CAREER: British Museum (Natural History), London, England, 1946—, currently principal scientific officer in subdepartment of ornithology in Tring. *Military service:* British Army, 1940-46; served in Libya and Malta. *Member:* British Ornithologists' Union, Avicultural Society, American Ornithologists' Union (corresponding fellow), Deutschen Ornithologen-Gesellschaft (corresponding fellow).

WRITINGS: Bird Behaviour, Museum Press, 1961; *Domestic Birds,* Museum Press, 1965; *Pigeons and Doves of the World,* Cornell University Press, 1967, 3rd edition, 1980; *Crows of the World,* Cornell University Press, 1976; *Birds of Man's World,* Cornell University Press, 1978. Contributor to ornithology journals.

WORK IN PROGRESS: A book on Estrildid finches, publication by Cornell University Press expected in 1980 or 1981.

SIDELIGHTS: Goodwin writes: "I think conservation of the world's resources and wildlife is important, human freedom and happiness (or the possibility of it) equally important, and both impossible unless birth control becomes more widely practiced, and not *only* by the more intelligent."

* * *

GORDON, Beverly 1948-

PERSONAL: Born January 30, 1948, in New York, N.Y.; daughter of Daniel M. and Irene (Bodin) Gordon; married Steven R. Vedro (a television-radio specialist), 1975; children: Rhea. *Education:* University of Wisconsin—Madison, B.A., 1969, doctoral study, 1979—; Goddard College, M.A., 1975. *Home:* 908-B Eagle Heights, Madison, Wis. 53705. *Office:* Department of Environment, Textiles, and Design, University of Wisconsin—Madison, Madison, Wis. 53706.

CAREER: Educators Publishing Service, Cambridge, Mass., editorial assistant, 1969-70; Educational Development Center, Newton, Mass., research assistant, 1970-72; Hancock Shaker Village, Pittsfield, Mass., textile interpreter, 1973-77; Historic Deerfield, Deerfield, Mass., volunteer costume accessioner, 1977-78; University of Wisconsin—Madison, assistant textile curator for Helen Allen Textile Collection, 1979—. Weaving teacher; teacher in alternative education and adult education programs and at high schools; gives lectures and workshops. *Member:* International Guild of Craft Journalists and Photographers, Costume Society of America, Handweavers Guild of America, Center for the History of American Needlework (member of advisory board, 1976—).

WRITINGS: Domestic American Textiles: A Bibliographic Sourcebook, Center for the History of American Needlework, 1977; *Shaker Textile Arts,* University Press of New England, 1979; *Feltmaking: Traditions and Explorations,* Watson-Guptill, 1980. Contributor to craft, textile, and popular culture journals, including *Centerpeace, East West Journal, Fiberarts, Shuttle,* and *Spindle and Dyepot.*

WORK IN PROGRESS: Research on dress codes in American religious-utopian societies, fancywork in America, textile activities, and work songs.

SIDELIGHTS: Beverly Gordon writes: "Since we first began fashioning clothes for ourselves out of animal skins, people have been concerned with textiles. Throughout our lives we are literally surrounded by cloth and fiber construction—from diapers and swaddling clothes at birth to burial clothes at death, with all forms of clothing, bedding, and decorative textiles in between. These textiles, born out of practical necessity, have often been constructed and embellished with amazingly intricate and rich designs, incorporating every imaginable material from wild grasses to solid gold. The fiber medium itself offers unique and rich artistic possibilities which have been explored in depth throughout the world and throughout time.

"Unfortunately, the pervasive importance—both physical and psychic—of textiles, and the rich artistic fiber traditions are all too often ignored. They are considered minor arts, 'busy' work, and are simply not seen, remembered, or understood by many otherwise sophisticated and art-conscious people.

"I write about textiles and how they fit into people's lives. My approach is unique. I incorporate an anthropological/sociological/art historical/historical perspective. I believe that textiles have not been given their due, and am committed to bringing to public attention what textiles and costumes have meant and mean in people's lives.

"My background is North American textiles, and I am now an authority on Shaker textiles, but my interest has no geographical or cultural boundaries. I am also interested in writing profiles and critiques of textile artists and their work.

"I believe that life has a purpose and we all have a need to find realms higher than those of our usual consciousness. I am particularly concerned with material (often textile) manifestations of our spiritual searching."

* * *

GORDONE, Charles 1925-

PERSONAL: Born October 12, 1925, in Cleveland, Ohio; son of William and Camille (Morgan) Gordon; married Jeanne Warner (a stage and film producer), 1959; children: Stephen, Judy, Leah Carla, David. *Education:* Los Angeles State College of Applied Arts and Sciences (now California State University, Los Angeles), B.A., 1952; also attended University of California, Los Angeles. *Home:* 200 West 79th St., New York, N.Y. 10024. *Office address:* c/o Springer-Warner Productions, 365 West End Ave., New York, N.Y. 10024.

CAREER: Playwright, actor, and director. As actor, has appeared in plays, including "Of Mice and Men," 1953, "The Blacks," 1961-65, and "The Trials of Brother Jero," 1967. Director of about twenty-five plays, including "Rebels and Bugs," 1958, "Peer Gynt," 1959, "Tobacco Road," 1960, "Detective Story," 1960, "No Place to Be Somebody," 1967, "Cures," 1978, and "Under the Boardwalk," 1979. Co-founder of Committee for the Employment of Negro Performers, 1962, and chairman; member of Commission on Civil Disorders, 1967; instructor at Cell Block Theatre, Yardville and Bordontown Detention Centers, New Jersey, 1977-78; judge, Missouri Arts Council Playwriting Competition, 1978; instructor at New School for Social Research, 1978-79; member of Ensemble Studio Theatre and Actors Studio. *Military service:* U.S. Air Force. *Awards, honors:* Obie Award for best actor, 1953, for performance in "Of Mice and Men"; Pulitzer Prize for Drama, Los Angeles Critics Circle Award, and Drama Desk Award, all 1970, all for "No Place to Be Somebody"; grant from the National Institute of Arts and Letters, 1971.

WRITINGS—Plays: (With Sidney Easton) "Little More Light Around the Place," first produced in New York City at

Sheridan Square Playhouse, 1964; *No Place to Be Somebody: A Black-Black Comedy* (first produced in New York City at Sheridan Square Playhouse, November, 1967; produced Off-Broadway at New York Shakespeare Festival Public Theatre, May, 1969; produced on Broadway at American National Theatre and Academy (ANTA) Theatre, December 30, 1969), introduction by Joseph Papp, Bobbs-Merrill, 1969; "Willy Bignigga" [and] "Chumpanzee," first produced together in New York City at Henry Street Settlement New Federal Theatre, July, 1970; "Gordone Is a Muthah" (collection of monologues; first produced in New York City at Carnegie Recital Hall, May, 1970), published in *The Best Short Plays of 1973*, edited by Stanley Richards, Chilton, 1973; "Baba-Chops," first produced in New York City at Wilshire Ebel Theatre, 1975; "The Last Chord," first produced in New York City at Billie Holliday Theatre, 1977. Also author of an unproduced musical, "The Block."

Screenplays: "No Place to Be Somebody" (adapted from the play); "The W.A.S.P." (adapted from the novel by Julius Horwitz); "From These Ashes"; "Under the Boardwalk"; "Liliom."

WORK IN PROGRESS: A play, "Anabiosis"; lyrics for a musical adaptation of "No Place to Be Somebody"; stage adaptation of "Under the Boardwalk."

SIDELIGHTS: Charles Gordone's "No Place to Be Somebody," a production of Joseph Papp's Public Theatre, opened on Broadway to rave reviews. Walter Kerr hailed Gordone as "the most astonishing new American playwright since Edward Albee," while other critics compared him to Eugene O'Neill. According to Norman Nadel, Gordone finds, as did O'Neill, "the gritty truths in bars, where pretense is too much trouble and deceit too futile." Set in a tawdry bar in Greenwich Village, "No Place" belongs in the category of American saloon dramas, and follows in the tradition of such plays as "The Iceman Cometh" and "The Time of Your Life." But, as a *Time* critic pointed out, "'Johnny's Bar' is no oasis for gentle day-dreamers. It is a foxhole of the color war—full of venomous nightmares, thwarted aspirations and trigger-quick tempers."

The owner of the bar, Johnny Williams, is also a pimp who takes on the syndicate in an effort to obtain control of the local rackets. His ambition is to organize his own black mafia, and he uses the affections of a white female student to further his aims. Although he has "learned early to hate white society and not to trust anybody," Johnny supports an out-of-work actor and retains an incompetent white employee. Other characters include a bartender who has "drug-induced daydreams of having once been a jazz musician," Johnny's two whores, a disillusioned ex-dancer and short-order cook, and Gabe Gabriel, an unemployed, light-skinned black actor who is too white for black roles. Gabe is Gordone's spokesman, introducing the acts of the play, and reciting monologues that "use humor and candor to express the absurdity and tragedy of racism." He is also, as Molly Haskell observed, "by nature witness rather than activist." At the end of the play, however, he shoots Johnny, at the request of Machine Dog, a black militant who exists only in Gabe's mind.

Although many critics noted that the play had some flaws, all praised Gordone's ability for characterization and dialogue. Some indicated that the play's only problem came from Gordone's ambition of trying to say too much in one work. As Edith Oliver noted: "There are several plots . . . and subplots running through the script, but what is more important is the sense of life and intimacy of people in a place, and of the diversity of their moods—the sudden, sometime inexplicable, spurts of anger and wildness and fooling—and their understanding of one another.'' Kerr highlighted Gordone's ''excellent habit'' of pressing ''his confrontations until they become reversals, until the roles are changed.''

''Written with a mixture of white heat and intellectual clarity,'' wrote Jack Kroll, ''it is necessarily and brilliantly grounded in realism but takes off from there with high courage and imagination; it is funny and sad and stoical, revolutionary and conciliatory.'' Brendon Gill concurred: ''Mr. Gordone is as fearless as he is ambitious, and such is the speed and energy with which he causes his characters to assault each other—every encounter is, in fact, a collision—that we have neither the time nor the will to catch our breath and disbelieve. The language is exceptionally rough and exceptionally eloquent; it is a proof of Mr. Gordone's immense talent that the excrementitious gutterances of his large cast of whores, gangsters, jailbirds, and beat-up drifters stamp themselves on the memory as beautiful.''

Criticism from black reviewers was not, however, totally favorable. Along with Clayton Riley and Peter Bailey, some black critics found evidence of self-hate—''a hint of contempt for black people''—in Gordone's play. But Jeanne-Marie Miller disagreed: ''[The play] depicts the black experience, but it is also concerned with people, black and white, who are filled with despair but who continue to hold on to their dreams, dreams shaped by their surroundings.'' Other reviewers were also quick to stress Gordone's concern with the total human experience. ''In Gordone's work,'' declared Ross Wetzsteon, ''rage and wit and dignity are ultimately aspects not so much of black consciousness as of humanity.''

CA INTERVIEWS THE AUTHOR

Charles Gordone was interviewed by phone at his office in New York City on April 18, 1979.

CA: You've said there's no such thing as black theatre. Has this provoked a lot of criticism?

GORDONE: Oh, Yes.

CA: Will you discuss that?

GORDONE: First of all, I don't know what people are referring to when they say black theatre. I just left St. Louis, where they were having a ''Black Theatre Week.'' First of all, how do we give color names to groups of people? We know what we mean when we say white people in this country; that means anyone that is not a Caucasian would not be white. So those people who are not Caucasians, why don't we refer to them as yellow or brown or green or blue? White people—that is not their identity. Are we talking about Russians? Are we talking about the Irish? Are we talking about the British? Are we talking about Germans? On the other side, do we have a whole world of blacks? The opposite of white here is not black. There are many opposites of what is white. I think what they do is very self-consciously accept the definition that they presume whites to give. If we look in the dictionary, it takes a while before we find out that a group of people called Negroes have very dark skin and we call that black. It's very hard in this world to find a skin that is absolutely black. So we obscure it.

Now, when you apply this to areas of life, are there black painters? Is there black basketball? I went to see the Nicks and the Lakers. The teams are predominantly black, to use the term black here. Does that mean I went to see black bas-

ketball subsidized by white money? So I don't know what they're talking about. Black music, we say, when everybody knows that jazz is still formulated on the musicology of the so-called white people in the Western culture. So the music is now Occidental music. All art borrows. We borrow; we are influenced; we respect. That's what makes it art. It's the same with painting, music, sculpture, or whatever. So to single out, to isolate, is just another way of segregating yourself, setting yourself apart.

This is a multiracial country; and certainly anytime there is a culture that is born out of this country, it is American culture. I was hearing Jesse Jackson this morning on Phil Donahue's show. He was talking about the diversity of culture in this country. We've always had a diversity of culture; but if we're going to point specifically to black people in this country, their culture is about as American as you're going to get. The American music is a jazz form, not an African form. It may take its roots from Bach; it may take its roots from the African ethnic. But it borrows everywhere. So you can't just single something out and say, ''This is black theatre'' or ''This is black music.'' Now I think there are those that want to have some kind of pride in the fact that, well, if we're not accepted over here, we'll just make our own and we'll be separate. If they don't accept us in the theatre, we'll make our own and call it black theatre. Why don't they call it Negro theatre or whatever? It becomes very confused. Theatre is theatre.

For myself, I write out of an American experience. I don't write out of a black experience or a white experience; it's American. If my color happens to be different from someone else's, that doesn't make any difference. I write for whites just as well as I write for blacks. I write out of the American experience as I observe it and as I live it, and I would not like to chop it up there.

CA: In a New York Times *article in 1970, you also made the point that good, lasting drama is that because it draws on a common experience, not an isolated kind of experience.*

GORDONE: It has to be human experience, you know. In the front of the Samuel French edition of *No Place To Be Somebody* I think is my philosophy as well as the social scientist's who wrote it. The truth is not merely the truth about Negroes. It reflects the deeper torments and anguish of the total human predicament. Certainly we have our stories to tell. We can't deny the history of this country. We can't deny the fact that there was slavery, and later it was turned into racial politics. I think had not the Negro been here, someone else would have taken the brunt of the blow, with the systems that were set up. Persons of color in this country have no corner on soul or suffering. (Need I mention the native Americans?)

There are those who would like you to believe that. Lois P. McGuire, executive director of Karamu House, Cleveland, recently stated that ''black people are no longer popular, the problem being that since the initial emergence of the black theatre movement, other ethnic theatre has crowded the arena vying for the public's interest and support.'' I say we must not continue to try to make good, fair, just people feel guilty for four hundred years of racial prejudice in this country.

And, of course, where you find one kind of prejudice, you'll find many others. What about the women in this country? There are those who would not like to include women as part of this whole human rights struggle. In the world we live in today, there can be no seniority or preferential treatment. Everything is part of the whole.

CA: How did you become interested in theatre?

GORDONE: There are many reasons. Theatre is my life. I began by wanting to be a musician; I wanted to be a singer. But I got sidetracked. I think my new play explains that, the one I just directed in St. Louis.

CA: What's the new play?

GORDONE: "Anabiosis." It's due for Broadway next March [1980]. I was trying it out in St. Louis. We may try it out in Washington at the Arena again. It needs another rewrite. Literally, the dictionary translates as resuscitation, new life, rebirth. We did it with the City Players in St. Louis as a work-in-progress tryout. It got rave reviews there. Standing ovation opening night.

CA: You've won a number of awards, including the Pulitzer Prize in 1970 for "No Place to Be Somebody." Was the Pulitzer a great thrill?

GORDONE: Well, at first you're delighted and you're very proud. But the weight of it all comes on you as the years go. Everybody starts introducing you as a Pulitzer Prize playwright, and it scares the hell out of you.

CA: You have to live up to that forever?

GORDONE: You have to try to live it *down*.

CA: Do you think the Off-Off-Broadway of the 1960's, the so-called avant-garde theatre, made a lasting impact on drama?

GORDONE: In my day there wasn't any Off-Off-Broadway; everything was just considered Off-Broadway. But do I think it had any impact on theatre? Oh yes, it always does. It still does. Sam Shepard just got a Pulitzer Prize, and for an Off-Broadway play [April, 1979, for "Buried Child"]. Now that's the second time. Mine was the first Off-Broadway play to receive a Pulitzer. The writing more and more is coming from playwrights whose plays for some reason are Off-Broadway. They're not money-making propositions like the Tennessee Williamses or the Arthur Millers or the Inges. Seems the people who are doing the writing are only doing it for Off-Broadway. Sam's play closed the night before he got the Pulitzer, 152 performances. That's not very many. Slim pickings.

CA: But the experimental type of theatre that was going in the 1960's—did it have any impact?

GORDONE: I don't think it had much impact.

CA: Is it still going on?

GORDONE: No. I think it was a little too far out, and it was only faddist theatre. It only spoke to those who were trying to move with the avant-garde. There were a lot of antiplays, or nonplays, going. Anybody who wanted to write wrote. They competed with each other to see how obscure they could be. Call it absurdist.

CA: In an Esquire *interview you described public enemy number one—the WASP, club-member type who takes his family on a vacation every year and works hard to get ahead. Is this class changing or growing smaller?*

GORDONE: Oh, no. I don't want to put that down completely. We're a highly competitive country, and we all are middle-class headed. To accumulate. We all want the good things. It moves into conspicuous consumption. We overspend, and then we cry about the fact that we owe, and

prices are so high. But we still accumulate, and we still look like we're very affluent. We look affluent, but we still owe our bodies to the company store. But the Jones idea in this country will always be there, at least in my time. That means we're our worst enemies. Me just as much. All those things I described—I'm very much like that.

CA: How much change do you see in theatre since "No Place To Be Somebody"?

GORDONE: I don't see any change. "No Place"—they still call it a black play. As long as something's by a black playwright, they call it a black play. I called it "A Black-Black Comedy," and it wasn't long after that until I was sorry I did. What I was trying to do, really, was write a human play. I'm a humanist; I'm not on a soapbox, a propagandist. The only story I have to tell is the human comedy.

I think the work you'll see that's coming out is more so, because I treat it much more seriously. It's almost as if a different playwright had written it. If there's anyone writing on the subject that I write about, which has to do—there's no denying—with the interpersonal relationships, the confrontations, between whites and blacks in this country, it all comes out still a humanist story which has nothing to do with color. I just use that as my fabrication, because this social problem is going to be with us for quite some time. And we have to give it as much understanding and as much light on the subject as possible. And those of us that can do it should. We owe it to everyone here, if we're writers or anybody in the arts, I think, to open this most vital subject, that is always with us, in many different ways. It expresses itself in many ways—how one combats it, is controlled by it, or succumbs to it.

CA: Do you think of yourself more as a writer, an actor, or a director?

GORDONE: I work at the theatre. They say, "That Gordone, he just works in the theatre." I go out into the hinterlands. I just love the experience, and it keeps my ear to the drum, because I know where the theatre is in this country. I helped establish the Missouri Playwrights Association last year. So they are putting their playwrights to work.

CA: Do you think regional theatre is very important at this time?

GORDONE: I do, but I think regional theatre has a lot of work to do in terms of educating their audiences, because they want to see what is popular. It's hard to slip in a serious play, but more and more they're doing that. In many instances, it's the only theatre going in this country.

CA: Is any of your family involved in theatre?

GORDONE: No. Except my daughter—my youngest daughter. She goes to the High School for the Performing Arts, and she wants to be an actress.

CA: Are you all for that?

GORDONE: Oh yes. She's a good one, too. She's fifteen.

CA: Did you study classical and the various schools of theatre? Do your plays have conscious roots in other schools of drama?

GORDONE: Yes. It has been pointed out to me on several occasions that my classical background very often shows up in my work. For instance, the visitations of the character Machine Dog in "No Place"; he functions as a messenger or chorus. Also, he speaks in the Greek declamatory style. A good example of Shakespearean influence is Gabe's last speech, "Dying into that new life." It's even spoken in an Elizabethan-British dialect.

CA: You once said that a writer has to be "obsessive, compulsive—impulsive—about writing." Are you these things?

GORDONE: Right! I'm that way about everything! There's no love's labor lost.

CA: Do you write every day?

GORDONE: Yeah. Well, I have some stretches, like if I'm directing a play, I'm not on the typewriter. But I'm getting ready to really go at it in the coming week. I've just come up for air, because I've been working hard for the past year. I've just had a chance to go to the dentist, and to have a checkup with my doctor—and I haven't had one of those in almost a year. Here's a bit of news, and a lot of people are groaning about it. I'm about to start work on the book and lyrics for the Broadway production of "No Place To Be Somebody" as a musical drama. I'll be able to try some of my ideas about how I think the American musical should be in the future. I'm very excited.... So with "No Place" and "Anabiosis" to deal with in the coming year, I will have my hands quite full.

The artist, if he is to be relevant, must seize the logic of the moment—must deal with the true stuff of his time and place himself and his work within this broader human context. Otherwise his perspectives might become distorted and his truths not totally true.

BIOGRAPHICAL/CRITICAL SOURCES: Village Voice, May 8, 1969, May 22, 1969; *Time,* May 16, 1969; *New Yorker,* May 17, 1969, January 10, 1970; *New York Times,* May 18, 1969, December 31, 1969, May 17, 1970; *Variety,* May 28, 1969, June 10, 1970, August 26, 1970, January 14, 1970, September 15, 1971; *Saturday Review,* May 31, 1969; *Newsweek,* June 2, 1969; *New York,* June 9, 1969; *Critic's Choice,* September, 1969; *Negro Digest,* April, 1970; *Christian Science Monitor,* September 21, 1970; *Journal of Negro Education,* spring, 1971; *Black World,* December, 1972.

—*Interview by Jean W. Ross*

*   *   *

GOSDEN, Peter Henry John Heather 1927-

PERSONAL: Born August 3, 1927, in Fittleworth, England; son of Alfred John and Elizabeth Ann (Richardson) Gosden; married Margaret Sheila Hewitt (an educator), February 9, 1964. *Education:* Emmanuel College, Cambridge, M.A., 1949; University of London, Ph.D., 1959. *Office:* School of Education, University of Leeds, Leeds LS2 9JT, England.

CAREER: University of Leeds, Leeds, England, lecturer, 1960-67, senior lecturer, 1967-71, reader, 1971-79, professor of history of education, 1979—, chairperson of School of Education, 1976-80. *Military service:* Royal Air Force, education officer, 1949-51. *Member:* Royal Historical Society (fellow), Association of University Teachers, Economic History Society, Agricultural History Society, History of Education Society, Universities Council for the Education of Teachers (member of executive committee).

WRITINGS: The Friendly Societies in England, 1815-75, Manchester University Press, 1963; *The Development of Educational Administration in England and Wales,* Basil Blackwell, 1967; *How They Were Taught: Learning and Teaching, 1800-1950,* Basil Blackwell, 1969; *The Evolution*

of a Profession, Basil Blackwell, 1972; *Self-Help: Voluntary Associations in Nineteenth-Century Britain,* Batsford, 1973; *Education in the Second World War: A Study in Policy and Administration,* Methuen, 1976; (with P. R. Sharp) *The Development of an Education Service: The West Riding, 1889-1974,* Martin Robertson, 1978. Also author of *Education Since World War II,* 1981. Contributor to education and history journals.

WORK IN PROGRESS: Research on the development of educational policy in England and Wales since 1945.

SIDELIGHTS: Gosden comments: "I have approached the study of education from and through history."

*   *   *

GOTTLIEB, Paul 1936-

PERSONAL: Born June 29, 1936, in Budapest, Hungary; son of Arnold and Rose Gottlieb; married Erika Simon (a lecturer and artist); children: Peter John, Julia Veronica. *Education:* Sir George Williams University, B.A., 1964, M.A., 1970. *Residence:* Toronto, Ontario, Canada. *Office:* D'Arcy MacManus & Masius, 250 Bloor St. E., Toronto, Ontario, Canada.

CAREER: Ronalds-Reynolds, Montreal, Quebec, vice-president and creative director, 1968-78; Baker-Lovich Co., Toronto, Ontario, vice-president, 1978-79; D'Arcy, MacManus & Masius, Toronto, vice-president and director of creative services, 1979—. President of Amadeus Creative Enterprises Ltd. Lecturer at Ryerson Polytechnical Institute. *Member:* Association of Canadian Television and Radio Artists, Academy of Canadian Cinema, Writers Union of Canada.

WRITINGS: Agency (suspense novel), Musson, 1974.

Screenplays: "In Praise of Older Women," R. S. L. Productions, 1978; "Agency," R. S. L. Productions, 1979; "Command Performance," Canadian Broadcasting Corp., in production. Contributor of articles, stories, and reviews to magazines, including *Prism* and *Exchange.*

WORK IN PROGRESS: A screenplay, "Stonewalls."

*   *   *

GOULD, Ed(win Orrin) 1936-

PERSONAL: Born February 26, 1936, in Turner Valley, Alberta, Canada; son of Elmo Floyd (a plumber) and Janet (Logie) Gould; married Janet Green (a writer), May 13, 1959 (divorced); children: Jay. *Education:* Attended University of British Columbia, 1959-60. *Politics:* Liberal. *Religion:* Protestant. *Home:* 1406-415 Michigan St., Victoria, British Columbia, Canada V8V 1R8. *Agent:* Lucinda Vardey, 36 Maitland St., Toronto, Ontario, Canada M4Y 1C5.

CAREER: CKNL-Radio, Fort St. John, British Columbia, news editor, 1962-66; Canadian Press, Edmonton, Alberta, editor, 1966-68; *Victoria Times,* Victoria, British Columbia, reporter, 1968-71; *Victorian* (newspaper), Victoria, British Columbia, assistant editor and author of column, "Ed Gould," 1971-75; free-lance writer, 1975—. Operated a trucking firm in Vancouver, British Columbia. Host of "Gould on Books," on Victoria Cable 10 Television; instructor at Camosun College. Information officer for provincial government officials; director of Greater Victoria Public Library Board. Past president of "The Smile Show," a music hall show; past director of local Community Arts Council and Open Space Cultural Center.

MEMBER: Writers Union of Canada, Canadian Authors

Association (local president), Canada/China Friendship Society, Vancouver Island Psychical Research Society (honorary life member). *Awards, honors:* Award from Media Club of Canada for best article in a British Columbia publication, 1972; Canada Council grant, 1977.

WRITINGS: Just Like Sweet Cream (stories), Modern Press, 1965; *Bridging the Gulf* (satire), Review Publishing, 1971; *The Lighthouse Philosopher: The Adventures of Bill Scott*, Hancock House, 1975; *Logging: The Logging History of British Columbia*, Hancock House, 1975; *Oil: The History of Canada's Oil and Gas Industry*, Hancock House, 1976; *Ranching in Western Canada*, Hancock House, 1978; *Ralph Edwards: Crusoe of Lonesome Lake*, Hancock House, 1979; (with Marguerite Mahay) *Fire at Sea* (nonfiction), Hancock House, 1981.

Editor: Humphrey Golby and Shirley Hewett, *Swiftsure: The First 50 Years*, Pacific Yachting; Charles Keenan, *Environmental Anarchy*, Douglas & MacIntyre.

Screenplays: (Co-author) "The Big Country," released by Wilf Gray Films, 1971; "Raw Empire," National Film Board, 1980. Author of semi-fictional stories for Canadian Broadcasting Corp.

WORK IN PROGRESS: Is There Intelligent Life on Earth?, a humorous novel; *All Hell for a Basement,* a history of Medicine Hat, Alberta.

SIDELIGHTS: Gould writes: "I find the snobbishness of so-called academics toward 'commercial' writers particularly galling. The jealousy expressed is more intense than toward their peers (which is expectable), particularly when a writer has consistently published more work and makes a living from writing. I dabble in teaching and other media (television and radio), but my main source of income is from writing books, and many academics find such success intolerable. I feel there is a place for both popular and academic histories."

* * *

GOULD, Leroy C. 1937-

PERSONAL: Born December 30, 1937, in Sheridan, Wyo.; son of Delmer Leroy (a pipefitter) and Gladys (Clemens) Gould; married Carolyn Presley (a lawyer), June 5, 1959; children: Juli, Ellen, Anne. *Education:* Harvard University, B.A., 1959; University of Washington, Seattle, M.A., 1962, Ph.D., 1964. *Home:* 299 Mansfield Rd., North Haven, Conn. 06473. *Office:* Institution for Social and Policy Studies, Yale University, P.O. Box 16-A, Yale Station, New Haven, Conn. 06520.

CAREER: Yale University, New Haven, Conn., assistant professor of sociology, 1964-69, research associate, 1969-73, assistant professor of psychiatry, 1973-75, lecturer in sociology and senior research associate at Institution for Social and Policy Studies, 1976—. Research director at Seattle Atlantic Street Center, 1963-64; project director for President's Commission on Law Enforcement and Administration of Justice, 1966-67; director of epidemiology and evaluation for Connecticut Mental Health Center's drug dependence unit, 1969-73. Member of governor's special committee to study educational and custodial programs for youthful wards of the state, 1966-69; member of research advisory committee of State of Connecticut Department of Corrections, 1971-73; participant in professional meetings; consultant to Vera Institute of Justice. *Member:* American Sociological Association, Society for the Study of Social Problems, Alpha Kappa Delta. *Awards, honors:* Grants from U.S. Department of

Health, Education and Welfare, 1970-74, 1974-75, and National Science Foundation, 1976—.

WRITINGS: (With Egon Bittner, Sol Chaneles, and others) *Crime as a Profession* (monograph), Office of Law Enforcement Assistance, U.S. Department of Justice, 1967; (contributor) Jack Douglas, editor, *Crime and Justice in American Society*, Bobbs-Merrill, 1971; (with Andrew L. Walker, Lansing E. Crane, and Charles W. Lidz) *Connections: Notes From the Heroin World*, Yale University Press, 1974; (contributor) James Inciardi and Carl Chambers, editors, *Drugs and the Criminal Justice System*, Sage Publications, 1974; (contributor) Lloyd Johnston, David Nurco, and Lee Robins, editors, *Conducting Follow-Up Research on Drug Treatment Programs*, National Institute on Drug Abuse, 1977. Contributor of about twenty articles and reviews to academic journals.

WORK IN PROGRESS: Editing *Too Hot to Handle: Social and Policy Issues in Radioactive Waste Management* (tentative title), with Charles A. Walker, publication by Yale University Press.

* * *

GOULD, Milton Samuel 1909-

PERSONAL: Born October 8, 1909, in New York, N.Y.; son of David H. and Ida (Berman) Gould; married Eleanor Greenburg, 1936; children: Patricia, Judson, Jonathan. *Education:* Cornell University, B.A., 1930, L.B., 1933. *Home:* 35 East 75th St., New York, N.Y. 10021. *Office:* 330 Madison Ave., New York, N.Y. 10017.

CAREER: Admitted to the Bar of New York State, 1933; associate with Judge Samuel H. Kaufman in New York City, 1933-38; Kaufman & Cronan, New York City, law partner, 1938-48; Gallop, Climenko & Gould, New York City, law partner, 1948-64; Shea, Gould, Climenko & Casey, New York City, senior partner, 1964—. Special attorney for U.S. Department of Justice, 1935-37. Lecturer at Practicing Law Institute and Cornell University, 1969-70, Stevens Memorial Lecturer, 1971, adjunct professor, 1974-77; adjunct professor at New York Law School, 1977. Member of New York City mayor's committee on the judiciary; head of Lawyers Division of Anti-Defamation League, 1972. Chairperson of board of directors of Elgin National Industries, Inc.; member of board of directors of Texas Oil & Gas Corp. and Toys 'R' Us.

MEMBER: New York County Lawyers Association, Association of the Bar of New York City, Cornell Law Association (president), Newcomen Society of North America, Statler Club, Tower Club, Lake Waramaug Golf Club, Cornell Club, Sky Club. *Awards, honors:* Award from Lawyers Division of United Jewish Appeal, 1972; Joseph M. Proskauer Award from New York Federation of Jewish Philanthropes, 1977.

WRITINGS: The Witness Who Spoke With God and Other Tales From the Courthouse, Viking, 1979. Member of board of editors of *New York Law Journal*.

* * *

GRABBE, Paul 1902-

PERSONAL: Surname is pronounced *Grah*-beh; born February 14, 1902, in St. Petersburg, Russia; came to the United States in 1923, naturalized citizen, 1932; son of Count Alexander (a general and aide-de-camp to the czar) and Marie (Bezak) Grabbe; married Laura Harris, May, 1930 (divorced, 1943); married Beatrice Chinnock (an editor), June

16, 1944; children: Alexandra (Mrs. Jacques Boutin), Nicholas. *Education:* Attended Juilliard Graduate School of Music, 1929-30. *Home address:* Box 882, Old Kings Highway, Wellfleet, Mass. 02667.

CAREER: Teacher and free-lance writer, 1930-42; Office of Facts and Figures, Washington, D.C., chief of graphic unit, 1942-43; Office of War Information, Washington, D.C., research officer, 1943-44; Office of Strategic Services, Washington, D.C., operations officer, 1944; fellow in visual sciences at Dartmouth College, 1944-45; communication consultant to vice-president in personnel at American Telephone & Telegraph Co., 1945-48; City College (now of the City University of New York), New York, N.Y., instructor in psychology, 1949-50; U.S. Department of State, Washington, D.C., policy presentation officer, 1951-52, chief of project control section, 1952-53, assistant chief of Division of Visual and Technical Services, 1952-53; U.S. Information Agency, Washington, D.C., adviser on visual projects and special assistant to assistant director for administration, 1955-65, and senior representative on foreign affairs information management effort in Department of State, 1965-69; writer, 1969—. *Awards, honors:* Denver Allied Arts grant, 1928-29; Juilliard Graduate School of Music fellowship, 1929-30; Rockefeller Foundation grant, 1950-51.

WRITINGS: Minute Stories of the Opera, Grosset, 1932; (with Gardner Murphy) *We Call It Human Nature,* Harper, 1939; *The Story of One Hundred Symphonic Favorites,* Grosset, 1940; *Outdoors With the Camera,* Harper, 1941; (with Joseph Sherman) *The Story of Orchestral Music and Its Times,* Grosset, 1942; *Windows on the River Neva* (memoirs), Pomerica Press, 1977. Contributor to magazines, including *Journal of Social Issues, Harper's,* and *Good Housekeeping.*

WORK IN PROGRESS: The second volume of his memoirs.

SIDELIGHTS: Grabbe was raised as a Russian aristocrat during the last years of the czar. He was tutored privately and isolated from the events of everyday life, as was the custom of the Russian upper class. Immediately after the revolution in 1917, his family took him to the Caucasus, seeking the safety of the countryside for the duration of the rebellion. But civil war came to the Caucasus, and the family attempted to escape the country altogether. They were taken prisoner by the German Army in the Crimea, and made their way to Riga, Latvia, where they remained until the British fleet arrived in 1918 and took them to Denmark.

Grabbe remained in Copenhagen for four years before coming to the United States. His early years as a new immigrant, at the bottom of the social scale, included a wide variety of colorful occupations: gold miner, pallbearer and organist at a San Francisco cemetery, film extra, streetcar conductor, companion to an elderly playwright, and rent collector in the "Hell's Kitchen" district of New York City.

He writes: "At first my writing was in the field of information, motivated by a desire to understand a non-native environment (the United States). Self-taught, I chose to write about certain subjects as a means of learning more about them: my published books are in music, psychology, and photography. I also have unpublished studies on the Russian language and immigrant adjustment.

"Since my retirement in 1970, my writing has been autobiographical. The first volume, *Windows on the River Neva,* recreates my childhood in pre-revolutionary Russia. Here my motivation has been to recreate a style of life which is gone. In Volume II I am attempting to give an immigrant's reaction to the United States and to describe the process of acculturation as I have experienced it here.

"At present I am bi-lingual; in the past I have also been fluent in Danish and French. I have come to realize that even at the age of seventy-seven growth is important to survival. A person need not commit an evil act to deteriorate; passive acceptance of an unhealthy condition of life also has a deteriorating effect on an individual. While trying to develop my mind, I have depended a great deal on intuition and have found it is sometimes superior to logic."

BIOGRAPHICAL/CRITICAL SOURCES: Paul Grabbe, *Windows on the River Neva* (memoirs), Pomerica Press, 1977.

* * *

GRADE, Chaim 1910-

PERSONAL: Born in 1910 in Vilna, Lithuania; came to United States in 1948, naturalized citizen, 1960; son of Schlomo-Motte (a teacher) and Vella (Blumenthal) Grade. *Education:* Educated in Lithuania.

CAREER: Writer. Member of Young Vilna writers' group in 1930's. *Awards, honors:* William and Janice Epstein Fiction Award from Jewish Book Council of the National Jewish Welfare Board, 1968, for *The Well;* Remembrance Award from World Federation of Bergen-Belsen Associations, 1969, for excellence in literature on the Nazi atrocities against European Jewry for *The Seven Little Lanes;* award from American Academy for Jewish Research; award for excellence from B'nai B'rith; Doctorate of Hebrew Letters from Jewish Theological Seminary, 1961, and Union College, 1972; Jewish Heritage Award for excellence in literature, 1976.

WRITINGS—In English: Ha-Anuga (novel), Am oved (Tel-Aviv), 1962, translation by Curt Leviant published as *The Agunah,* Bobbs-Merrill, 1974; *The Well* (novel; translation by Ruth Wisse of "Der brunem," originally published in *Der Shulhoyf* [see below]), Jewish Publication Society of America, 1967; *Tsemah Atlas* (novel), two volumes, 1968, translation by Leviant published as *The Yeshiva,* Bobbs-Merrill, Volume I, 1976, Volume II, 1977; *The Seven Little Lanes* (stories), translated by Leviant from the original Yiddish, Bergen-Belson Memorial Press, 1972.

Other writings: *Yo* (verse; title means "Yes"), 1936; *Mussernikes* (narrative poem), [Vilna], 1939, reprinted, 1969; *Dereth* (title means "Generations"), [New York], 1945; *Farwaksene vegn* (verse; title means "Dangerous Paths"), [Paris], 1947; *Oyf di khurves* (verse; title means "On the Ruins"), [Lodz], 1947; *Peletim* (title means "The Refugees"), [Buenos Aires], 1947; *Der mamme's tsavue* (verse; title means "The Mother's Will"), [New York], 1949.

Shain fun farlorene shtern (verse; title means "The Light of Extinguished Stars"), [Buenos Aires], 1950; *Shabtoteha shel ima* (stories; title means "My Mother's Sabbath Days"), [Tel-Aviv], 1958; *Der shulhoyf* (prose; title means "The Synagogue Courtyard"), Natsyonaler Arbeterfarband, 1958; *Der mamme's shabbosim* (prose; title means "My Mother's Sabbaths"), 1959.

Der mentsh fun fayer (title means "The Man of Fire"), 1962; *Oyf mayn veg tsu dir* (title means "On My Way to You"), 1969; *Milhemet ha yetser* (novel; title means "The Moralists"), 1970; *Di kloyz un di gas* (stories; title means "Synagogue and Street"), [New York], 1974; *Der shtumer minzen* (title means "The Silent Minzen"), 1976.

Work represented in *A Treasury of Yiddish Stories,* edited by Irving Howe and Eliezer Greenberg, Holt, Rinehart, 1969.

WORK IN PROGRESS: The Old House.

SIDELIGHTS: Chaim Grade is one of the few surviving writers in Yiddish. His stories and books concern the religious and secular intellectual controversies of Eastern European Jewish communities. Grade was raised in that environment in Vilna, Lithuania, and in his youth was trained in the Musar movement, an ascetic, ethical-religious sect of Judaism. This experience was the basis for many of his works of fiction.

When he was twenty-two, Grade abandoned his religious studies and began to write poetry. He was associated with that group of artists called the "Young Vilna," who were advocates of modernism. Grade was able to flee Vilna in 1941, although his wife, mother, and many of his friends were murdered in the Holocaust. In 1948, Grade settled in New York City, where he still lives, and turned to writing fiction.

Grade's works are relatively unknown to American audiences, even though he is a major Yiddish writer, because they are quite complex and full of religious allusions that are difficult to translate. Only a few of his novels and one short story have been published in English. The short story, "My Quarrel with Hersh Rasseyner," is a furious debate between a secular Jewish writer and a Mussarist teacher. "There is in this story a remarkable exhilaration," critic Ruth R. Wisse wrote, "deriving not only from the tension of the debate—which remains a draw—but from the combined victory of the debaters over time and circumstance." Irving Howe stated: "Indeed, the clash between these two world-outlooks forms a dominant theme in his work, which is notable for a fierce, sometimes overwrought sense of historical pressure."

Grade returns to the subject of this debate time and again. In his recent novel, *The Yeshiva,* he covers the same ground and further illuminates his subject. As Wisse commented: "There is greater psychological depth in this work than in any of Grade's earlier prose, but even here he stays within his single context, probing underlying motives and subconscious desires—just as *mussar* does—not in the interests of an integrated personality but as part of the search for true moral perfection." And Howe remarked: "Grade is one of those writers who seems most concrete when dealing with the abstract. There are fine passages on the torments and trickeries of ethical self-conquest, the way, for instance, the self can gain a triumph of wickedness through the very denials it exacts from itself."

Noting that Grade's books are very densely written and difficult for those unfamiliar with Talmudic scholarship, Thomas Lask wrote of *The Yeshiva:* "Although the religious concerns in the book may seem puzzling, the intensity with which they are argued is effectively, sometimes movingly conveyed. Everyone in the novel lives at his nerves' end. Women weep, turn ashen, waste away; men groan, shriek, bare their teeth in anger. The 19th century novel is well-preserved in 'The Yeshiva.' It is a hothouse world and the blooms and weeds have a hectic, feverish flush."

Grade has often been compared to the more popular Yiddish writer, Isaac Bashevis Singer. Howe, in a detailed discussion of the two writers, wrote, "Though Grade and Singer seem to deal with similar situations and settings, they are radically different in literary method and their outlooks upon human existence." Morton A. Reichek wrote: "Comparison of his work with Singer's is inevitable. Singer is a highly gifted storyteller who disclaims any concern with social or philosophical messages. His mystical and often erotic tales appeal to modern tastes and his exotic color is relatively easy for an outsider to absorb. Grade's work is markedly different. The Jewish particularism is much stronger in his writing. In focusing so clinically on Jewish ethics, Grade is immersed in more formidable themes and makes considerably greater demands on the reader. He is less immediately accessible to the non-Jew, and to Jews who are unfamiliar with Orthodox religious ritual and Talmudic dialectic." Howe concluded, "Singer wants to charm us into surrendering to his magic; Grade to force us to share his rages of thought."

BIOGRAPHICAL/CRITICAL SOURCES: Washington Post Book World, June 2, 1968; *New York Times Book Review,* October 22, 1967, January 8, 1978; *New Republic,* February 26, 1977; *New York Times,* March 18, 1977; *Commentary,* April, 1977; *Judaica Book News,* spring/summer, 1979; *Contemporary Literary Criticism,* Volume 10, Gale, 1979.

*   *   *

GRAHAM, J. W. 1925-

PERSONAL: Born March 6, 1925, in Montreal, Quebec, Canada; son of William Creighton (a professor) and Ella (Cook) Graham; married Angela Baird (a social worker), September 14, 1957; children: Gillian, Kathleen, Anne. *Education:* University of Manitoba, B.A., 1945; University of Toronto, M.A., 1947, Ph.D., 1952. *Home:* 432 Huron St., London, Ontario, Canada N5Y 4J3. *Office:* Department of English, Faculty of Arts, University of Western Ontario, London, Ontario, Canada N6A 3K7.

CAREER: University of Western Ontario, London, professor of English, 1949—. *Member:* Association of Canadian University Teachers of English, Canadian Association of University Teachers, Modern Language Association of America.

WRITINGS: (Editor) *The Waves: The Two Holograph Drafts,* University of Toronto Press, 1976. Member of editorial board of *Twentieth Century Literature.*

WORK IN PROGRESS: Research on theory of narrative, theory of the novel, and William Faulkner.

*   *   *

GRAHAM, Kennon
See HARRISON, David L(ee)

*   *   *

GRAHAM, Stephen 1884-1975

OBITUARY NOTICE: Born in 1884 in England; died in 1975. Author. Graham spent his life traveling around the world. For years he journeyed through Russia, mostly on foot, writing of the people and their land in such books as *A Vagabond in Caucasus, The Life of Peter the Great,* and *Undiscovered Russia.* As a private with the British Scots Guard, Graham wrote of his World War I experiences in *A Private in the Guards.* The conditions depicted in the book subsequently led to an investigation by the British Parliament. His autobiography, *Part of the Wonderful Scene,* was published in 1964. Obituaries and other sources: *The Reader's Encyclopedia,* 2nd edition, Crowell, 1965; *The New Century Handbook of English Literature,* revised edition, Appleton, 1967; *Longman Companion to Twentieth Century Literature,* Longman, 1970; *The Author's and Writer's Who's Who,* 6th edition, Burke's Peerage, 1971.

*   *   *

GRAHAM, Victor E(rnest) 1920-

PERSONAL: Born May 31, 1920, in Calgary, Alberta, Canada; son of William J. (a sales manager) and Mary E. (Wark) Graham; married Mary H. Faunt, August 1, 1946; children: Ian R., Gordon K., Miriam E. Graham Pilkey, Ross W. *Education:* University of Alberta, B.A., 1946; Oxford University, B.A., 1948, M.A., 1952; Columbia University, Ph.D., 1953. *Home:* 100 Glenview Ave., Toronto, Ontario, Canada M4R 1P8. *Office:* University College, University of Toronto, Toronto, Ontario, Canada M5S 1A1.

CAREER: University of Alberta, Calgary, assistant professor of English and French, 1948-53, associate professor of French, 1953-58, professor of French, 1958; University of Toronto, Toronto, Ontario, associate professor, 1958-60, professor of French, 1960—, head of department, 1965-67, associate dean of graduate studies, 1967-69, vice-principal of University College, 1969-70. Church organist and choir director. *Member:* Royal Society of Canada. *Awards, honors:* Rhodes scholar at Oxford University, 1946; Canada Council senior fellow, 1963; D.Litt. from Oxford University, 1968; Guggenheim fellow, 1970; Connaught senior fellow, 1978.

WRITINGS: How to Learn French in Canada: A Handbook for English Canadians, University of Toronto Press, 1965; *The Imagery of Proust,* Barnes & Noble, 1966; (contributor) Richard Schoek, editor, *Editing Sixteenth-Century Texts,* University of Toronto Press, 1966; (with W. McAllister Johnson) *Estienne Jodelle: Le Recueil de inscriptions, 1558; A Literary and Iconographical Exegesis,* University of Toronto Press, 1972; (with Johnson) *The Paris Entries of Charles IX and Elisabeth of Austria, 1571; With an Analysis of Simon Bouquet's Bref et sommaire recueil,* University of Toronto Press, 1974; *Bibliographie des etudes sur Marcel Proust et son oeuvre* (title means "Bibliography of Studies on Marcel Proust and His Works"), Droz, 1976; *The Royal Tour of France by Charles IX and Catherine de Medici, 1564-66,* University of Toronto Press, 1979; *Triumphal Entries: Court Festivals in Sixteenth-Century France,* University of Toronto Press, 1979.

Editor: Philippe Desportes, *Cartels et masquarades* (critical edition; title means "Cartels and Masquerades"), Droz, 1958; Desportes, *Epitaphes,* Droz, 1958; Desportes, *Les Amours de Diane* (title means "The Loves of Diana"), two volumes, Droz, 1959; Desportes, *Les amours d'Hippolyte* (critical edition; title means "The Loves of Hippolyta"), Droz, 1960; Desportes, *Elegies* (critical edition), Droz, 1961; Desportes, *Cleonice: Dernieres Amours* (title means "Cleonice: Last Loves"), Droz, 1962; *Representative French Poetry,* University of Toronto Press, 1962, 2nd edition, 1965; Desportes, *Diverses Amours et autres oeuvres meslees* (title means "Diverse Loves and Other Miscellaneous Works"), Droz, 1963; *Sixteenth-Century French Poetry,* University of Toronto Press, 1964; Andre Chamson, *Le Chiffre de nos jours* (title means "The Number of Our Days"), Burns & MacEachran, 1965; Pernette Du Guillet, *Rymes,* Droz, 1968. Contributor to language and literature journals.

AVOCATIONAL INTERESTS: Chinese snuff bottles.

*   *   *

GRATUS, Jack 1935-

PERSONAL: Born in 1935, in Johannesburg, South Africa; son of Victor and Flora (Maneshewitz) Gratus; married wife, Estelle, 1959 (divorced); married wife, Christine (an advertising executive), October, 1971; children: David, Jonathan. *Education:* King Edward VII School, B.A., 1955, LL.B., 1958. *Home:* 17 Cunnington St., London W4 5ER, England.

Agent: Carol Smith, 2 John St., London WC1N 2HJ, England.

CAREER: Pritchard Englefield & Co. (solicitors), London, England, legal executive, 1960-62; Oxford College, Johannesburg, South Africa, deputy principal and teacher of English and commercial law, 1963-66; free-lance writer, 1967—; City Literary Institute, London, tutor in charge of nonfiction writing, 1974—. Tutor at Glamorgan Summer School, 1968-77; senior tutor at Regent Institute, 1973-76; member of faculty at London extension of University of California, Los Angeles. *Member:* Writers Guild of Great Britain (member of books committee and executive council).

WRITINGS: (With Estelle Gratus) *Cooking in Season* (edited by P. H. Hargreaves), L. Hill, 1967; *A Man in His Position* (novel), Hutchinson, 1968; *The Victims* (nonfiction), Hutchinson, 1969; *Mister Landlord Appel* (novel), Hutchinson, 1971; (with Trevor Preston) *Night Hair Child* (novel), Sphere Books, 1971; *The Great White Lie: Slavery, Emancipation, and Changing Racial Attitudes,* Hutchinson, 1973; *The False Messiahs: Prophets of the Millenium,* Gollancz, 1975, Taplinger, 1976; *The Jo'burgers* (novel), Corgi, 1979; *The Redneck Rebel* (novel), Corgi, 1980.

WORK IN PROGRESS: A third volume in the fiction series begun with *The Jo'burgers.*

SIDELIGHTS: Gratus told *CA:* "I started as a fiction writer (of very small books written for proud parents) when I was about eight or nine, but a university education in an English department put an end temporarily to any ambitions as a writer. So I became a lawyer instead. After a few years of this and then another few years of teaching, I realized that I could not avoid my destiny. The call to write was too strong to be ignored any longer and I started writing short stories, which won prizes in the *Transatlantic Review,* and then my first novel, which was praised for its 'psychological insights,' among other things.

"Financial needs drove me to journalism, which in turn led to a desire to find out about things, such as the effect of slavery on race relations (*The Great White Lie*), what makes people victim-prone (*The Victims*), and the kind of people who claim to be gods (*The False Messiahs*). But I wanted to return to my original love, the novel, so I combined my research techniques with my fiction writing to produce a historical novel set in the early mining camp days of my home town, Johannesburg.

"I find it more congenial to write about the past than the present and about the experiences of others than about my own life, but this is not always the case. Though I've not made a great deal of money out of my chosen profession, I am proud of the fact that I've managed so far to survive as a full-time writer, not an easy thing to do.

"I care about the quality of my writing and consider myself more of a craftsman in words than an artist. The praise of critics is pleasing to me, but that of ordinary readers who actually go out to buy my books even more so. I am also concerned about the writing profession in general and that is why I now devote time and energy to my work on the Writers' Guild of Great Britain, which represents writers of all kinds and which strives to improve their lot."

*   *   *

GRAY, Eden 1907-

PERSONAL: Born June 9, 1907, in Chicago, Ill.; daughter of Albert Jerome (in real estate) and Florence (Myers) Pardridge; married Lester Cohen (deceased); children: Peter

Gray. *Education:* Attended Purdue University. *Religion:* "Charismatic." *Residence:* Vero Beach, Fla.

CAREER: Writer and actress on Broadway. Inspiration House (bookstore), New York, N.Y., owner, 1954-64. Hostess of talk show on WNCN-FM Radio, 1961-64. *Military service:* U.S. Army, Women's Army Corps. *Member:* Mental Health Association.

WRITINGS: Recognition: Themes on Inner Perfection, Inspiration House, 1969; *A Complete Guide to the Tarot,* Crown, 1970; *Guide to the Tarot,* Wehman, 1970; *Mastering the Tarot: Basic Lessons in an Ancient Mystic Art,* Crown, 1971; *Tarot Revealed: A Modern Guide to Reading the Tarot Cards,* New American Library, 1971.

WORK IN PROGRESS: Diary of a Metaphysician.

*   *   *

GRAYSON, Benson Lee   1932-

PERSONAL: Born December 1, 1932, in New York, N.Y.; son of Jay Benson (a writer) and Sadie (a social worker; maiden name, Greene) Grayson; married Helen Donovan (an economist), May 30, 1960; children: Richard Andrew, Winifred Hope. *Education:* New York University, B.A., 1953, M.A., 1954; Harvard University, M.P.A., 1962; Columbia University, Ph.M., 1979. *Home:* 7006 Capitol View Dr., McLean, Va. 22101.

CAREER: U.S. Department of State, Washington, D.C., foreign service officer, 1957-65, political officer in Hong Kong, 1959-61, economic officer in Bangkok, Thailand, 1962-64; writer, 1965—. Member of board of directors of Continental Software Corp., 1968-70. *Military service:* U.S. Army Reserve, 1953-65; became captain. *Member:* International Institute for Strategic Studies, National Economists Club, Royal Asian Society, Cosmos Club.

WRITINGS: The American Image of Russia, Ungar, 1978; *Russian-American Relations in World War I,* Ungar, 1979; *The American Image of China,* Ungar, 1979. Also author of *United States Relations With Iran,* 1980, and *Millard Fillmore, America's Unknown President,* 1980. Contributor to military journals.

WORK IN PROGRESS: United States Relations With Saudi Arabia, publication expected in 1981.

SIDELIGHTS: Grayson told *CA:* "I believe that the greatest danger facing the United States is our failure in recent years to project to the Soviets, Chinese, and other nations our determination to protect and defend America's independence and the survival of democratic ideas around the world. I hope that my books will help show where we have succeeded and where we have failed and contribute to a more sustained policy of maintaining American vital interests in the years ahead."

*   *   *

GRAZIANO, Anthony M(ichael)   1932-

PERSONAL: Born February 18, 1932, in Nyack, N.Y.; son of Michael and Theresa (Dattio) Graziano; married Sheila Ginsberg (an attorney), 1958; children: Amy, Lisa, Michael. *Education:* Columbia University, B.A., 1954; Michigan State University, M.A., 1956; Purdue University, Ph.D., 1960. *Residence:* Buffalo, N.Y. *Office:* Department of Psychology, State University of New York at Buffalo, 4230 Ridge Lea Rd., Buffalo, N.Y. 14226.

CAREER: U.S. Veterans Administration, Washington, D.C., intern at hospitals and clinics in Michigan and Indiana,

1955-59; child clinical psychologist at schools in Devon, Pa., 1960-61; University of Bridgeport, Bridgeport, Conn., assistant professor, 1961-65, associate professor of psychology, 1965-69; State University of New York at Buffalo, associate professor, 1969-72, professor of psychology, 1972—. Director of Nomic Child Development Center, 1963-67; acting director of Kennedy Center Diagnostic and Treatment Center, 1965-67; director of behavior research at Foundation School. Guest on television and radio programs; consultant to correctional and mental health facilities.

MEMBER: American Psychological Association, Eastern Psychological Association, Psychological Association of Western New York, Sigma Xi, Psi Chi. *Awards, honors:* Grants from Connecticut State Department of Mental Health, 1965-66, 1966-68, Connecticut State Department of Education, 1966, 1967, 1968-69, and New York State Department of Mental Hygiene, 1970-71, 1974-76; Baldy summer fellowship from Baldy Foundation, 1974.

WRITINGS: (Editor) *Behavior Therapy With Children,* Aldine, Volume I, 1971, Volume II, 1975, Volume III, 1980; (contributor) Stuart Golann and Charles Eisdorfer, editors, *Handbook of Community Psychology and Mental Health,* Appleton, 1972, revised edition, 1978; (contributor) Jack Zusman and David L. Davidson, editors, *Practical Aspects of Mental Health Consultation,* C. C Thomas, 1972; *Child Without Tomorrow,* Pergamon, 1974; (contributor) Michele Hersen, R. M. Eisler, and P. M. Miller, editors, *Progress in Behavior Modification,* Academic Press, 1977; (contributor) Benjamin Wolman, Alan O. Ross, and James Egan, editors, *Handbook of Treatment of Mental Disorders in Childhood and Adolescence,* Prentice-Hall, 1978; (with B. R. Bugelski) *An Encyclopedia of Practical Psychology,* Prentice-Hall, 1980. Also author of *Goodbye Chautauqua,* 1980, and co-author with wife, S. G. Graziano, of *Child Abuse: American Style,* 1980. Contributor of about twenty articles to journals in psychology and the behavioral sciences.

SIDELIGHTS: Graziano writes: "My major concerns are with the status and optimum development of children in our physically and psychologically polluted environment. *Child Without Tomorrow* and *Goodbye Chautauqua* are autobiographical, and discuss my personal concerns as they were evidenced in both professional work and private life."

*   *   *

GREEN, Georgia M.   1944-

PERSONAL: Born April 16, 1944, in Atlanta, Ga.; daughter of Lester Victor and Marjorie (a writer and editor; maiden name, Fishbein) Marks; married Tucker Green, September 8, 1964 (divorced); married Jerry Morgan (a linguist), March 26, 1969; children: (second marriage) Robin Leslie, Dylan Kay. *Education:* University of Chicago, A.B., 1966, A.M., 1969, Ph.D., 1971. *Office:* Department of Linguistics, University of Illinois, Urbana, Ill. 61801.

CAREER: University of Illinois, Urbana, fellow of Center for Advanced Study, 1970-71, assistant professor, 1971-73, associate professor of linguistics, 1973—, research associate professor at Center for the Study of Reading, 1978—. Fellow of Center for Advanced Study in the Behavioral Sciences, 1978-79. *Member:* Linguistic Society of America (chairperson of committee on the status of women), Modern Language Association of America, Chicago Linguistic Society.

WRITINGS: Semantics and Syntactic Regularity, Indiana University Press, 1974.

Contributor: Braj B. Kachru and other editors, *Issues in*

Linguistics: Papers in Honor of Henry and Renee Kahane, University of Illinois Press, 1970; R. Shuy, editor, *Some New Directions in Linguistics,* Georgetown University Press, 1973; M. Saltarelli and D. Wanner, editors, *Diachronic Studies in Romance Linguistics,* Mouton, 1975; P. Cole and J. Morgan, editors, *Syntax and Semantics,* Volume III: *Speech Acts,* Academic Press, 1975. Also contributor to C. H. Frederiksen, M. F. Whiteman, and J. D. Dominic, editors, *Writing: The Nature, Development, and Teaching of Written Communication;* R. C. Spiro, B. C. Bruce, and W. F. Brewer, editors, *Theoretical Issues in the Study of Reading.*

Editor of "Studies in the Linguistic Sciences," Department of Linguistics, University of Illinois, 1972; advisory editor of "Syntax and Semantics," a series for Academic Press. Contributor of about a dozen articles and reviews to linguistic journals.

WORK IN PROGRESS: Research on organization of newswriting and sports announcing and on the relation between text and illustration in children's literature.

*   *   *

GREENAWAY, Gladys 1901-
(Julia Manners)

PERSONAL: Born in 1901, in London, England; daughter of John William (a confidential foreman) and Sarah Eliza (Allen) Marshall; married William Ernest Greenaway (deceased); children: two sons, two daughters (one deceased). *Education:* Educated privately. *Religion:* Agnostic. *Home and office:* 43 Queens Ave., Winchmore Hill, London N.21, England. *Agent:* Laurence Pollinger Ltd., 18 Maddox St., London W.1, England.

CAREER: Writer. *Member:* Crime Writers Association, Romantic Novelists Association, Women's Press Club.

WRITINGS—Novels: Girl on the Heights, Hurst & Blackett, 1968; *Cousin Alison,* Hurst & Blackett, 1969; *The Wheel of the Potter,* Hurst & Blackett, 1969; *The Late Summer of Christine Hargreave,* Hurst & Blackett, 1970; *Girl on a Ladder,* Hurst & Blackett, 1972.

Novels; under pseudonym Julia Manners: *Shadows on Bright Waters,* R. Hale, 1975; *The Small Circle,* R. Hale, 1979. Also author of *The Dark Places.*

WORK IN PROGRESS: Alice and Lissy, a novel; another novel.

SIDELIGHTS: In the 1920's, Gladys Greenaway lived on a small island off the coast of China. Later she spent six years in Malta. She has also traveled in the United States and Aden. *Avocational interests:* Embroidery.

*   *   *

GREENBERG, Pearl 1927-

PERSONAL: Born January 29, 1927, in New York, N.Y.; daughter of Abe (a plastics manufacturer) and Lucille (a nurse; maiden name, Berlin) Katz; married Murray Greenberg (a professor and engineer), September 12, 1947; children: Kenneth. *Education:* Cooper Union College, certificate, 1948, B.F.A., 1976; New York University, B.A., 1957, M.A., 1960; Columbia University, Ed.D., 1970. *Home:* 212 East Broadway, New York, N.Y. 10002. *Office:* Department of Fine Arts, Kean College of New Jersey, Union, N.J. 07083.

CAREER: Art teacher at private school in New York, N.Y., 1950-65; Kean College of New Jersey, Union, associate pro-

fessor, 1965-71, professor of fine arts, 1971—, coordinator of art education, 1969—. *Member:* International Society for Education Through Art, American Crafts Council, National Art Education Association (vice-president, 1978-80), University Council for Art Education (president, 1974-78), New York State Craftsmen, Art Educators of New Jersey. *Awards, honors:* Award from National Art Education Association, 1980, for work in enhancing the status of art education for people of all ages in New Jersey.

WRITINGS: Art in Early Childhood, Early Childhood Council, 1965; *Children's Experiences in Art: Drawing and Painting,* Reinhold, 1966; *Art and Ideas for Young People,* Van Nostrand, 1970; (editor) *Art Education: Elementary,* National Art Education Association, 1972; (editor with Donald Hoffman and Dale Fitzner) *Lifelong Learning in the Arts: A Book of Readings,* National Art Education Association, 1980. Author of filmstrips. Contributor of more than forty articles to education and art journals.

WORK IN PROGRESS: "Outline of a book on the arts and the elderly, introducing retired people to the pleasure of creating, using a variety of art materials, to enhance the passage of their newly found leisure time."

SIDELIGHTS: Pearl Greenberg made a record and two filmstrips, "Art: How Does a Child Grow?," released by International Film Bureau, 1968. '

She writes: "I have always been interested in combining my visual art, my teaching, and my writing. Each seems to flow from the other. I had my first article published in 1957, and was thrilled at the idea, so I kept writing—partly for pleasure, and partly to share my ideas and thoughts with art teachers all over the country. My own art work is what I call 'wool painting.' I adhere naturally dyed yarns to canvas, and weave, mostly in the form of tapestry."

*   *   *

GREENWOOD, Kathryn Moore 1922-

PERSONAL: Born May 25, 1922, in Hartford, Ark.; daughter of William Erwin (a barber) and Pauline (a school teacher; maiden name, Edwards) Moore; children: W. Hayes, Paula Mae Greenwood Fonfara. *Education:* Oklahoma State University, B.S., 1943, Ed.D., 1972; New York University, M.S., 1944. *Religion:* "Born-again" Baptist. *Home:* 1523 West Fourth, Stillwater, Okla. 74074. *Office:* Department of Clothing, Textiles & Merchandising, Oklahoma State University, Stillwater, Okla. 74074.

CAREER: Brown Dunkins Department Store, Tulsa, Okla., assistant buyer, 1942; John Wanamaker Department Store, New York City, assistant buyer and fashion coordinator, 1943; Bonwit Teller Department Store, New York City, assistant buyer, 1943; high school teacher of distributive education in Tulsa, Okla., 1944-45; Oklahoma State University, Stillwater, assistant professor, 1945-60, associate professor and chair of undergraduate program, 1963-68, professor in clothing, textiles, and merchandising department, 1968—, fashion merchandising coordinator, 1960-63. Adjunct professor at University of Massachusetts, summer, 1976; director of workshops and study tours to Dallas, New York City, and abroad; personnel assistant for Lord & Taylor in New York City, 1969; member of consumer advisory board of Springs Mills.

MEMBER: International Home Economics Association, American Home Economics Association, American Association of University Women, Association of College Professors of Textiles and Clothing, Association for Consumer

Research, Fashion Group, Inc., Oklahoma Home Economics Association (vice-president, 1973), Oklahoma Education Association, Danforth Faculty Association, Phi Kappa Phi, Omicron Delta Kappa, Omicron Nu, Oklahoma State University Alumni Association, New York University Alumni Association. *Awards, honors:* Research grants from U.S. Office of Education, 1975-78; creative program award from National Association of University Extensions, 1979.

WRITINGS: (With Mary Murphy) *Fashion Innovation and Marketing,* Macmillan, 1978. Contributor to home economics and education journals.

WORK IN PROGRESS: Research on merchandising management and inventory control learning guides for small apparel shop owners and managers; guidelines for fashion merchandising curriculum; apparel shop entrepreneurship learning packages for individualized instruction; initiating Faculty Professional Development Internship Program in fashion merchandising.

SIDELIGHTS: Kathryn Greenwood told *CA:* "I established the fashion merchandising program at Oklahoma University in 1947. My twenty-five years of experience in teaching fashion merchandising and supervising student work experience have been most rewarding. Among my former students are two vice-presidents, one at Neiman-Marcus in Dallas, and one at Foley's in Houston, and prominent buyers at major stores in other cities.

"I believe that women are especially adept at buying fashion goods and have a sixth sense when it comes to perceiving seasonal changes in fashion. My concepts of fashion innovation and marketing led me to propose that fashion merchandising techniques can and should be used in controlling inventories and anticipating the demand for consumer goods other than just for apparel.

"I believe that faculty teaching fashion merchandising should have opportunities for internship in major retail stores which hire college graduates. Faculty Professional Development Internships should serve as an update and renewal experience and would lead to more relevancy in the classroom. Competency based curriculum for fashion merchandising programs and other career oriented options can be achieved in higher education in areas where job profiles can be established. Continuous evaluation and development of educational programs should be based on updated job profiles.

"I am presently attempting to obtain a research grant to fund the implementation of a model Faculty Professional Development Internship (FPDI) program for faculty in four career oriented areas of home economics: fashion merchandising, interior design, child care, and food services. We are presently pretesting the model for the FPDI with two faculty members from other universities who are enrolled for graduate study at Oklahoma State University. Eight weeks have been spent 'on campus' in competency based curriculum study and ten weeks will be spent 'off campus' in a major retail store to provide an opportunity to update knowledge of retailing and verify the job profiles for buyers and assistant buyers. I believe this interface between the academic and the business worlds is vital for higher education programs which aim to prepare young people for careers in retailing or in other occupational areas."

*　　*　　*

GREENWOOD, Walter 1903-1974

PERSONAL: Born December 17, 1903, in Salford, Lancastershire, England; died September 13, 1974, in Isle of Man, England; son of Thomas (a hairdresser) and Elizabeth M. (a waitress; maiden name, Walter) Greenwood; married Pearl Alice Osgood (an actress), 1937. *Education:* Educated in England. *Home:* Whitegates Cannon Ave., Kirk Michael, Isle of Man, England.

CAREER: Novelist and dramatist. Worked variously as pawnbroker's clerk, office boy, stable boy, packing case maker, sign writer, chauffeur, cab driver, warehouseman, salesman, and automobile factory worker. *Awards, honors:* D.Litt. from Salford University, 1971.

WRITINGS—Novels: Love on the Dole: A Tale of the Two Cities, J. Cape, 1933, reprinted, 1966, Doubleday, 1934; *His Worship the Mayor; or, It's Only Human Nature After All,* J. Cape, 1934, published as *The Time Is Ripe,* Doubleday, 1935; *Standing Room Only; or, A Laugh in Every Line,* Doubleday, 1936; *Only Mugs Work: A Soho Melodrama,* Hutchinson, 1938, reprinted, H. Baker, 1969; *The Secret Kingdom,* J. Cape, 1938; *How the Other Man Lives,* Labour Book Service, c. 1939; *So Brief the Spring,* Hutchinson, 1952; *What Everybody Wants,* Hutchinson, 1954; *Down by the Sea,* Hutchinson, 1956; *Something In My Heart,* Morley-Baker, 1969.

Other: *The Cleft Stick; or, It's the Same the World Over* (short stories), Selwyn & Blount, 1937, Stokes Publishing, 1938; *Lancashire* (travel), Hale, 1951; *There Was a Time* (autobiography), J. Cape, 1967.

Plays: (With Ronald Gow) "Love on the Dole," first produced in Manchester, England, 1934; (with D. H. Lawrence) "My Son's My Son," first produced in London, England, 1936; "The Practiced Hand" (one-act), 1936; "Only Mugs Work," 1938; "Give Us This Day" (adaptation of own novel, *His Worship the Mayor*), first produced in London, 1940; "So Brief the Spring," first produced in London, 1946; *The Cure for Love: A Lancashire Comedy* (three-act; first produced in Oldham, England as "Rod of Iron," 1947), Samuel French, 1947; *Never a Dull Moment* (first produced in Oldham, 1950), Samuel French, 1952; *Saturday Night at the Crown* (three-act; first produced in Morecambe, England, 1954), Samuel French, 1958; "Happy Days," first produced in Oldham, 1958; "Happy Birthday," 1959; "Fun and Games," first produced in Salford, England, 1963; "There Was a Time," first produced in Dundee, England, 1967.

Screenplays: "No Limit," 1935; "Merchant Navy," 1942; "Six Men of Dorset," 1944; "Chance of a Lifetime," 1947; "Eureka Stockade," 1947; "Love on the Dole," 1940; "The Cure for Love," 1949; "The Secret Kingdom," 1960; "Hanky Park," 1971.

Also author of novel, "It Takes All Sorts," and television play for British Broadcasting Corp. (BBC), "The Secret Kingdom."

SIDELIGHTS: After the overwhelming success of his first novel, *Love on the Dole,* Walter Greenwood was proclaimed one of the leading "proletarian novelists" in England. Born into a poor family himself, he wrote from his own experiences of the miseries of the lower classes: the inhuman factory working conditions, the unemployment, and the rationing system known as the "dole." *Love on the Dole* raised questions that were later discussed in Parliament, leading to investigations and programs of reform. The book was critically acclaimed, and as one reviewer remarked, "What might have been a tale of unmitigated squalor is relieved by the zest of [Greenwood's] narrative."

Greenwood's autobiography, *There Was a Time,* again clearly depicted life on the poor side of town. Although criticized for its "sentimentality" and "over-lush" style, a reviewer for the *Times Literary Supplement* felt that "for all its gusto—indeed, largely because of it—the book projects a sense of angry desolation, as though a killing tide had rolled over natural living and destroyed its creatures, like slag or oil."

BIOGRAPHICAL/CRITICAL SOURCES: Walter Greenwood, *There Was a Time,* J. Cape, 1967; *Times Literary Supplement,* May 25, 1967; *Books and Bookmen,* August, 1967; *Plays, Players,* June, 1970, May, 1971; *Stage,* July 2, 1970, July 30, 1970.

OBITUARIES: New York Times, September 14, 1974; *Washington Post,* September 15, 1974; *AB Bookman's Weekly,* November 18, 1974.*

*   *   *

GREY, David Lennox   1935-

PERSONAL: Born August 14, 1935, in Chicago, Ill.; son of Lennox B. (a professor) and Charlotte (Montgomery) Grey; married Helen Lucanna Marquardt (a psychiatric nurse), September 6, 1959; children: Eric, Mark, Leah. *Education:* University of Michigan, B.A., 1957; Stanford University, M.A., 1960; University of Minnesota, Ph.D., 1966. *Religion:* Unitarian-Universalist. *Home:* 444 Tennyson Ave., Palo Alto, Calif. 94301. *Office:* Department of Journalism and Advertising, San Jose State University, JC-147, San Jose, Calif. 95192.

CAREER: Ann Arbor News, Ann Arbor, Mich., reporter, correspondent, and copy news editor, 1957-59; *Wall Street Journal,* New York, N.Y., staff reporter at San Francisco bureau, 1960-61; *Toledo Blade,* Toledo, Ohio, staff reporter, 1961-62; University of Minnesota, Minneapolis, instructor in journalism and mass communications, 1962-65; Northwestern University, Evanston, Ill., instructor, 1965-66, assistant professor of journalism, 1966-67; Stanford University, Stanford, Calif., assistant professor of journalism and mass communications, 1967-73; San Jose State University, San Jose, Calif., lecturer , 1973-74, associate professor, 1974-76, professor of journalism and mass communications, 1976—. *Member:* Association for Education in Journalism (head of Law Division, 1975-77), Sigma Delta Chi, Kappa Tau Alpha, Phi Kappa Phi, Michigamua (life member).

WRITINGS: The Supreme Court and the News Media, Northwestern University Press, 1968; *The Writing Process,* Wadsworth, 1972; (with Maxwell McCombs and Donald Shaw) *Handbook of Reporting Methods,* Houghton, 1976; (with Everette Dennis and Donald Gillmor) *Justice Hugo Black and the First Amendment,* Iowa State University Press, 1978. Contributor to journalism and communication journals.

WORK IN PROGRESS: The Writing Process, 2nd edition, publication expected in 1980.

SIDELIGHTS: Grey writes: "I have concentrated on connecting better communication theory and methodology with basic and advanced news writing courses. My continuing interests are First Amendment issues in general, and the U.S. Supreme Court as a 'communication institution,' as an interactor with the press."

*   *   *

GRIERSON, Herbert John Clifford   1886-1960

OBITUARY NOTICE: Born January 16, 1886, in Lerwick, Shetland, Scotland; died in 1960. Author, critic, and translator. Grierson was associated with the University of Aberdeen before joining the staff of the University of Edinburgh as professor of English in 1915, a position he held for twenty years. He subsequently became rector of that university. Knighted in 1936, he was considered a leading authority on Milton, Donne, and Scott. His books include *Lyrical Poetry From Blake to Hardy, Letters of Sir Walter Soctt,* and *The Poems of John Milton,* in addition to several translations from the original Dutch. Obituaries and other sources: *New York Times,* February 21, 1960; *Time,* February 29, 1960; *The Reader's Encyclopedia,* 2nd edition, Crowell, 1965; *Longman Companion to Twentieth Century Literature,* Longman, 1970; *The Penguin Companion to English Literature,* McGraw, 1971; *Cassell's Encyclopaedia of World Literature,* revised edition, Morrow, 1973.

*   *   *

GRIFFIN, (Henry) William   1935-

PERSONAL: Born February 7, 1935, in Waltham, Mass.; son of Henry Francis and Margaret Mary (Burke) Griffin; married Emilie Dietrich (an advertising vice-president), August 31, 1963; children: Lucy Adelaide, Henry Francis II, Sarah Jeannette. *Education:* Boston College, A.B., 1960; Catholic University of America, M.A., 1962. *Office:* Macmillan Publishing Co., Inc., 866 Third Ave., New York, N.Y. 10022.

CAREER: Member of Society of Jesus (Jesuits), 1952-60; Macmillan Publishing Co., Inc., New York City, assistant editor in school department, 1962-64; Harcourt Brace Jovanovich, Inc., New York City, associate editor in school department, 1964-68; Macmillan Publishing Co., Inc., senior editor in General Books Division, 1969—. Translator for International Committee on English in the Liturgy, 1973; president of Religion Publishing Group, 1979-80.

WRITINGS—Editor; all published by Macmillan: C. S. Lewis, *The Joyful Christian: One Hundred Twenty-Seven Readings,* 1977; Dorothy L. Sayers, *The Whimsical Christian: Eighteen Essays,* 1978; J. B. Phillips, *The Newborn Christian: One Hundred Fourteen Readings,* 1978; Fulton J. Sheen, *The Electronic Christian: One Hundred Five Readings,* 1979; *Endtime: The Doomsday Catalog,* 1979.

Plays: "A Fourth for the Eighth" (two-act), first produced in Hollywood, Calif., at Evergreen Playhouse, March, 1964; "Campion," first produced in Waterford, Conn., at Eugene O'Neill Playwrights' Conference, August, 1971. Film reviewer for National Catholic Office for Motion Pictures, 1960-70; play reviewer for *Sign,* 1971-75.

*   *   *

GRINDLE, Carleton
See PAGE, Gerald W(ilburn)

*   *   *

GROENOSET, Dagfinn   1920-

PERSONAL: Born April 4, 1920, in Trysil, Norway; son of Daniel and Minda (Skogli) Groenoset; married Rise Vestergaard, August 6, 1957. *Education:* Attended school in Trysil, Norway. *Religion:* Protestant. *Home:* Storgt. 16, 2400 Elverum, Norway. *Office: Oestlendingen,* Elverum, Norway.

CAREER: Oestlendingen, Elverum, Norway, reporter, 1939-56, editor, 1956—. *Member:* Norsk Presseforbund, Norsk Forfattenforening. *Awards, honors:* Christopher Book Award, 1976, for *Anna;* Oesterdal Fjellpris; grant from Norsk Forfattenforening.

WRITINGS: Anna, translated by Ingrid B. Josephson, Nordon Publications, 1977.

Other—All published by Aschehoug: Vandring i Villmark, 1952; Finnskog og Trollskap, 1953; Gull i sporet, 1956; Nitahaa-Fussi, 1957; Villmarksfolk, 1959; Med Kong Olav mot nord, 1959; I Vinges fotspor, 1960; Langs bygdevegen, 1960; Bella Capri, 1961; Folk fraskogene, 1970; Anna i oedemanka, 1972; Taler-Milla, 1974. Reporter for radio and television.

* * *

GROSS, Michael (Robert) 1952-
(Robert Alexander)

PERSONAL: Born July 16, 1952, in New York, N.Y.; son of Milton (a sports columnist) and Estelle (a registered nurse; maiden name, Murov) Gross. Education: Vassar College, B.A., 1974. Residence: New York, N.Y. Agent: Ellen Levine, Curtis Brown Ltd., 575 Madison Ave., New York, N.Y. 10022. Office: Bantam Books, Inc., 666 Fifth Ave., New York, N.Y. 10019.

CAREER: Zakin & Comerford Advertising, Inc., New York City, copywriter, 1975-76; Rock, New York City, editor-in-chief, 1976-77; Fire Island News, Ocean Beach, N.Y., editor-in-chief, 1978; Bantam Books, Inc., New York City, copywriter, 1978—. Member: Authors Guild, Authors League of America. Awards, honors: Andy Award from New York Advertising Club, 1975, for radio commercials.

WRITINGS: I, a Groupie (novel), Pinnacle Books, 1975; Robert Plant (biography), Popular Library, 1975; Bob Dylan: An Illustrated History, Grosset, 1978; (contributor under pseudonym Robert Alexander) Robert Atwan, Barry Orton, William Vesterman, editors, American Mass Media: Industry and Issues, Random House, 1978; The Hits Just Keep Coming In, Ace Books, 1980.

Co-author of "Lucky's Strike" (filmscript). Author of radio commercials. Author of "Music in Review," a column in Interview, 1973-74. Contributing editor of Circus, 1974-76, Rush, 1976-77, and Swank, 1976-79; music editor of Club, 1975-76.

SIDELIGHTS: Gross told CA: "Writing about rock music was initially exciting and ultimately frustrating. Publishers have hardly an inkling of how to publish books for and that reach out to people under the age of thirty-five. They have few if any of the marketing skills of the record companies. Their morality is often as questionable as that of their music business counterparts, while their bottom line is far lower.

"I began writing (about rock) to get free records. I quit writing about music because it had never been commercially viable. I now write for my own satisfaction, expecting no compensation, enjoying it when it comes.

"I believe in the power of words to alter men's minds. I believe that unless publishers learn to effectively compete against electronic media, words will lose their power. When that happens, I wonder what will happen to men's minds."

* * *

GROSS, Phyllis P(ennebaker) 1915-

PERSONAL: Born July 18, 1915, in Exeter, Calif.; daughter of William Glen and Palma (Buckman) Pennebaker; married Joseph A. Gross, October 10, 1940 (divorced, 1954); children: William, Patricia Gross Grimm Lillywhite. Education: San Mateo Junior College, A.A., 1935; San Jose State College (now University), B.S., 1937; Stanford University, M.A., 1939. Residence: Hayward, Calif.

CAREER: High school biology teacher in Madera, Calif., 1939-41, Redwood City, Calif., 1949-51, and Modesto, Calif., 1954-64; California State University, Hayward, associate professor, 1964-70, professor of biology, 1970-78, professor emeritus, 1978—. Lecturer at Fresno State College, 1963-64. Member: American Association for the Advancement of Science, National Science Teachers Association, National Association of Biology Teachers, National Association for Research in Science Teaching, California Teachers Association, California Science Teachers Association. Awards, honors: Shell merit fellow at Stanford University, summer, 1968.

WRITINGS: (With Esther P. Railton) Teaching Science in an Outdoor Environment: Handbook for Students, Parents, Teachers, and Camp Leaders, University of California Press, 1972, revised edition, 1978. Contributor to government and business publications.

SIDELIGHTS: Phyllis Gross commented that her recent writing has consisted of "materials for use with biology teacher trainees and biology classes for non-majors. Making the subject fascinating was the prime mover for my approach to teaching."

* * *

GROSSEN, Neal E. 1943-

PERSONAL: Born June 5, 1943, in Ely, Nev. Education: California State University, Sacramento, earned B.A., M.A., 1967; earned Ph.D. from University of Washington, Seattle. Office: Department of Psychology, 6000 J St., California State University, Sacramento, Calif. 95819.

CAREER: California State University, Sacramento, associate professor, 1970—. Principal of Research Consulting Corp., Sacramento, 1972—. Member: Psychonomic Society.

WRITINGS: (With Lawrence S. Meyers) Behavioral Research: Theory, Design, and Procedure, W. H. Freeman, 1974, 2nd edition, 1978. Also author of Psychological Testing: An Introduction. Contributor to psychology journals.

* * *

GROSVENOR, Gilbert (Hovey) 1875-1966

OBITUARY NOTICE: Born October 28, 1875, in Constantinople (now Istanbul), Turkey; died February 4, 1966. Geographer, editor, publisher, and author. Grosvenor was associated with the National Geographic magazine for over fifty years. Beginning as assistant editor and rising to editor-in-chief, he simultaneously held the presidential post of the National Geographic Society before being elected to its board of trustees in 1954. Under his supervision the magazine became the first to utilize advanced photoengraving, and it also pioneered aerial, underwater, and wildlife photography. The number of subscribers rose dramatically with the introduction of these innovations: from less than one thousand in 1899 to ten thousand in 1905, and surpassing one million by 1940. In addition to his role as editor-in-chief, Grosvenor wrote numerous articles and contributed frequent photographs to the National Geographic. Numbered among his books are Discovery and Exploration, The Hawaiian Islands, and The National Geographic Society and Its Magazine. Obituaries and other sources: Current Biography, Wilson, 1946, March, 1966; New York Times, February 5, 1966.

* * *

GROVES, Paul 1930-

PERSONAL: Born in 1930, in Oxford, England; son of

Charles Hubert Warburg and Doris (Watson) Groves; married June Griggs; children: Wendy, Sally. *Education:* Royal Academy of Dramatic Art, diploma, 1950, L.R.A.M., 1955; attended College of St. Mark and St. Joann, 1955-57. *Politics:* Labour. *Home:* Willows, Casthorpe Rd., Barrowby, Grantham, Lincolnshire, England.

CAREER: Professional actor, 1950-53; clerk for Colgate Palmolive, 1953-55; teacher at Lancastrian school in Chichester, 1957-61; teacher of English and head of department at St. Hugh's C.E. Comprehensive School, 1961—. *Military service:* British Army, Royal Electrical and Mechanical Engineers, 1949-50. *Member:* National Association for the Teaching of English.

WRITINGS—All juveniles; all published by Longman, except as noted: *Egbert Nosh,* Childrens Press, 1970; *The Hat Trick,* 1975; *Eggs,* 1975; *Wiggly Worms,* 1975; *The Clock,* 1975; *The Best Duster,* 1975; *In a Jam,* 1975; *Ding Dong Baby,* 1975; *Red Indians and Red Spots,* 1975; *The Bee and the Sea,* 1975; *Wet Paint,* 1975; *Toothday and Birthday,* 1975; *Bikes and Broomsticks,* 1975; *The Hole Story,* 1975; *The Cow and the Bull Story,* 1975; *The Third Climber,* Hutchinson, 1977; *Not That I'm Workshy,* Hutchinson, 1978; *Hatching Is Catching,* 1979; *Tea Break,* 1979; *Jumpers,* 1979; *Bubble Bath,* 1979; *Garden Trouble,* 1979; *Snatch and Grab,* 1979; *Sticky Trousers,* 1979; *The C.P.O.,* 1979; (with Jennifer Bromley) *Bangers and Mash Workbooks,* three volumes, 1979; *Into Action,* Edward Arnold, 1980; *Smudge and Chewpen Word Book,* Edward Arnold, 1980; *Tempo Plays,* two volumes, in press, 1981.

With Leslie Stratta; all published by Longman: *The Swinging Kings,* 1965; *The Big Drop,* 1965; *Lost in the Fog,* 1965; *The Club Dance,* 1966; *Sandra Helps the Gang,* 1966; *At the Market,* 1966; *Bonfire Night,* 1967; *The Trap,* 1967; *The Fair,* 1967; *At the Circus,* 1967; *On the Mountain,* 1979; *The Swindle,* 1979; *Please Help,* 1979; *Happy Christmas,* 1979.

With Nigel Grimshaw; all published by Edward Arnold: *Up Our Way,* 1972; *Living Our Way,* 1973; *Join the Action,* 1973; *Action Replay,* 1975; *Thirteen Ghosts,* 1976; *The Goodbodys,* 1976; *Smudge and Chewpen,* 1976; *Action Stations,* 1977; *Thirteen Weird Tales,* 1977; *Monsters of Myth and Legend,* 1977; *Call to Action,* 1978; *Thirteen Horror Stories,* 1978; *Smudge and Chewpen Tests,* 1978; *Stops and Starts,* 1978; *Thirteen Science Fiction Stories,* 1979. Author of "Egbert Nosh" cartoon strips for BBC-TV.

WORK IN PROGRESS: Four more *Bangers and Mash* books; a *Bangers and Mash* alphabet book.

SIDELIGHTS: Groves comments: "As a writer I am a leader in the use of phonics in learning to read. I am also a pioneer in the use of humor, particularly for slow-learning pupils. I have received many letters from teachers who say that pupils who had initially failed to read found the humorous approach of *Bangers and Mash* the impetus they needed. I write a lot of realistic and fantasy stories for older pupils."

Egbert Nosh has been translated into German and Czech.

* * *

GRUTZ, Mariellen Procopio 1946-
(Mariellen Procopio)

PERSONAL: Born July 9, 1946, in Portchester, N.Y.; daughter of Anthony Peter and Anne (Wagner) Procopio; married Juergen Grutz, November 27, 1976; children: Anthony. *Education:* Emmanuel College, Boston, Mass., B.A., 1968. *Home:* 4-8 Scheidstrasse 16, 1600 Frankfurt am Main 1, West Germany.

CAREER: U.S. Peace Corps, Washington, D.C., volunteer worker in Niger, 1969; African-American Institute, Washington, D.C., program assistant, 1969-73; Sheraton Corp., Boston, Mass., personnel assistant, 1973-75; U.S. Catholic Conference, Washington, D.C., researcher and writer, 1975-76; International Monetary Fund, Washington, D.C., Secretary, 1977-78. Escort and interpreter for U.S. Department of State.

WRITINGS: (Under name Mariellen Procopio; with Frederick J. Perella, Jr.) *Poverty Profile, U.S.A.,* Paulist/Newman, 1976.

SIDELIGHTS: Grutz told *CA:* "Working on *Poverty Profile, U.S.A.* with Fred Perella was a most satisfying and interesting task. Because my work as a public health volunteer in the Peace Corps was cut short, I always hoped to work on another project, however limited in scope or notoriety, through which I could express my desire to help improve the human condition of those who have yet to enjoy the basic requirements of life. All present activities center around my new experiences in motherhood and life in Germany."

* * *

GUENTER, Erich
See EICH, Guenter

* * *

GUERNEY, Bernard G(uilbert), Jr. 1930-

PERSONAL: Born February 28, 1930, in New York, N.Y.; son of Bernard G. (a translator, author, and editor) and Elizabeth (an office worker; maiden name, Langer) Guerney; married Louise Fisher (a professor of human development), June 20, 1953; children: Janis, Bruce, Robert. *Education:* Brooklyn College (now of the City University of New York), B.A. (cum laude), 1951; Pennsylvania State University, M.S., 1953, Ph.D., 1956. *Home:* 442 Park Lane, State College, Pa. 16801. *Office:* Individual and Family Consultation Center, Catharine Beecher House, Pennsylvania State University, University Park, Pa. 16802.

CAREER: Wichita Guidance Clinic, Wichita, Kan., intern, 1953-54; Wayne State University, Detroit, Mich., instructor in psychology, 1956-57; Rutgers University, New Brunswick, New Jersey, assistant professor, 1957-62, associate professor, 1962-68, professor of psychology, 1968-69, director of Psychological Clinic, 1962-69; Pennsylvania State University, University Park, professor of human development and head of Individual and Family Consultation Center, 1969—. Diplomate of American Board of Professional Psychology. Psychologist at Lafayette Clinic, 1956-57; founder and president of Institute for the Development of Emotional and Life Skills, 1972—. Vice-president of Raritan Valley Community Services Council, 1966-67; member of professional advisory committee of Middlesex County Mental Health Board, 1966-67. Participates in and directs professional meetings and workshops; consultant.

MEMBER: American Psychological Association (fellow), American Association of University Professors, Psychologists Interested in the Advancement of Psychotherapy, Association for the Development of Clinical Psychology as an Experimental-Behavioral Science, Association for the Advancement of the Behavior Therapies, Groves Conference on Marriage and the Family, Eastern Psychological Association, Pennsylvania Psychological Association. *Awards, honors:* Grants from National Institute of Mental Health, 1963-64, 1965-66, 1966-69, 1974-77.

WRITINGS: (Editor with G. E. Stollak and Myer Rothberg, and contributor) *Psychotherapy Research: Selected Readings,* Rand McNally, 1966; (with Salvador Minuchin, Braulio Montalvo, Bernice Rosman, and Florence Schumer) *Families of the Slums: An Exploration of Their Structure and Treatment,* Basic Books, 1967; (editor and contributor) *Psychotherapeutic Agents: New Roles for Nonprofessionals, Parents, and Teachers,* Holt, 1969; *Relationship Enhancement: Skill-Training Programs for Therapy, Problem Prevention, and Enrichment,* Jossey-Bass, 1977.

Contributor: Charles Schaefer, editor, *The Therapeutic Use of Child's Play: Basic Readings,* Jason Aronson, 1976; (author of introduction) T. F. Reif and G. E. Stollak, *Sensitivity to Young Children: Training and Its Effects,* Michigan State University Press, 1972; D.H.L. Olson, editor, *Treating Relationships,* Graphic Publishing (Lake Mills, Iowa), 1976; (author of foreword) *Microcounseling: Innovations in Interview Training,* Holt, 1978; Theodor Vallance, editor, *Society's Stepchildren: Mental Health Services in Transition,* Hemisphere, 1979.

Co-author of films: "Conjugal Relationship Enhancement," Pennsylvania State University, 1976; "The Relationship Enhancement Program for Family Therapy and Enrichment," Pennsylvania State University, 1977; "Filial Therapy," Pennsylvania State University, 1979.

Contributor to *Psychotherapy Handbook.* Contributor of more than forty articles to psychology and education journals. Member of editorial board of *International Journal of Family Therapy,* 1978—, and of the *American Journal of Family Therapy,* 1979—.

SIDELIGHTS: Guerney's special interests are "new forms of psychotherapy, particularly those employing an educational model, combining preventive with therapeutic goals, implemented with the help of significant persons in the environment, and emphasizing specific demonstrable goals, training of paraprofessionals, mental health education, and developing new mental health programs."

*   *   *

GUICHARNAUD, June 1922-

PERSONAL: Born June 15, 1922, in Elizabeth, N.J.; daughter of William M. (an investment banker) and Miriam (a pianist; maiden name, Steiner) Beckelman; married Jacques E. H. Guicharnaud (a professor of French), May 28, 1957. *Education:* Attended Beaver College, Tobe-Coburn School for Fashion Careers, and Columbia University; New York University, B.A., 1953, graduate study, 1954; Sorbonne, University of Paris, certificate, 1954. *Politics:* Independent. *Religion:* High Episcopal. *Residence:* New Haven, Conn.

CAREER: Macy's, Newark, N.J., buyer, 1942-46; *American Girl,* New York City, associate editor, 1947-48; French Cultural Services, New York City, director of educational service, 1955-56; free-lance writer, editor, and translator, 1957—. Interim managing editor of *Yale Review,* 1971-72. *Awards, honors:* National Book Award nomination, 1979, and Christophers Award, both for translating, abridging, and editing *The Horse of Pride.*

WRITINGS: (With husband, Jacques Guicharnaud) *Modern French Theatre: From Giraudoux to Genet,* Yale University Press, 1961, revised edition, 1967.

Translator: (And abridger) *Self-Portraits: The Gide-Valery Letters, 1890-1942,* University of Chicago Press, 1955; Jean Delay, *The Youth of Andre Gide,* University of Chicago Press, 1963; Jacques Guicharnaud, *Raymond Queneau,* Co-

lumbia University Press, 1965; Auguste Toussaint, *History of the Indian Ocean,* University of Chicago Press, 1966; Villiers de L'Isle d'Adam, *Axel,* Prentice-Hall, 1970; Jose Cabanis, *The Joyless Years* (novel), Prentice-Hall, 1970; Simone Berteaut, *Piaf,* Harper, 1972; Daniel Halevy, *The End of the Notables,* edited by Alain Silvera, Wesleyan University Press, 1974; Gisele Freund, *The World in My Camera,* Dial, 1974; (with Madeleine Kamman) Robert J. Cortine, *Feasts of a Militant Gastronome,* Morrow, 1974; Andre Malraux, *Picasso's Mask,* Holt, 1976; (and editor and abridger) Pierre-Jakez Helias, *The Horse of Pride: Life in a Breton Village,* Yale University Press, 1978. Editor of art catalogs. Contributor of more than thirty-five translations of articles and reviews to magazines, anthologies, and dictionaries.

WORK IN PROGRESS: A short novel; translations.

SIDELIGHTS: Guicharnaud commented: "I dislike 'confessional' literature in any form, especially Robert Lowell's. Most autobiographers rewrite their own lives as historians tend to rewrite history. So I have wiped out my past and shredded all reviews, accolades, letters, and so on, although I was especially pleased with historian J. H. Plumb's letter complimenting me on 'sub-editing' his prose and with Cyril Connally's review of the Gide/Valery correspondence.

"I started translating, copy-editing, and editing when I married and moved to New Haven in 1957, because there were no top jobs for women here in those days. But I am heartily sick of *re*-writing the illiterate prose of young academics and thus getting them promotions.

"I translate merely because I enjoy it. What the future will hold, I do not know. What I do know is that eighty percent of the fiction being published today is mediocre or pure trash. Like Flannery O'Connor, I believe that such writers 'should be stifled with all deliberate speed.' Long live Beckett, Anthony Powell, Walker Percy, and Robert Penn Warren."

*   *   *

GUILD, Nicholas M. 1944-

PERSONAL: Born November 5, 1944, in San Mateo, Calif.; son of Walter Francis and Gertrude (Mowry) Guild; married Joan Suzanne Weil, March 19, 1966. *Education:* Occidental College, A.B., 1966; University of California, Berkeley, M.A., 1968, Ph.D., 1972. *Home:* 1500 McCoy Rd., Columbus, Ohio 43220. *Agent:* Scott Meredith Literary Agency, Inc., 845 Third Ave., New York, N.Y. 10022.

CAREER: Clemson University, Clemson, S.C., assistant professor of English, 1973-75; Ohio State University, Columbus, assistant professor of English, 1975—. *Member:* Modern Language Association of America, American Association of University Professors. *Awards, honors:* Ohioana Book Award, 1978, for *The Summer Soldier.*

WRITINGS—Novels: The Lost and Found Man, Harper Magazine Press, 1975; *The Summer Soldier,* Seaview Books, 1978; *Old Acquaintances,* Seaview Books, 1978. Contributor of more than a dozen articles and reviews to language and literature journals, popular magazines, including *Harper's,* and newspapers.

WORK IN PROGRESS: The Legend of Good Women, a novel; another novel.

*   *   *

GUILLEVIC, (Eugene) 1907-
(Serpieres)

PERSONAL: Born August 5, 1907, in Carnac, Brittany,

France; son of Eugene (a sailor and a gendarme) and Jeanne (a seamstress; maiden name, David), Guillevic; married Alice Munch, September 15, 1930; children: Simone, Irene. *Education:* Received degree from College of Altkirch, 1925. *Politics:* Communist. *Home:* 11 rue Emile-Dubois, 75014 Paris, France.

CAREER: Civil servant in Huningen, Bas-Rhin, France, 1926; receiver of registration fees in Rocroi and Charleville, France, 1932-35; Government of France, Paris, worker in ministry of finance, 1935-42; chief of bureau of ministry of national economy, 1942-47, inspector of the national economy for ministry of finance, 1947-63, member of cabinet of ministry of reconstruction, 1945-47. Poet, 1929—. Member of directing committees of Comite National des Ecrivains and of Comite de l'Union des Ecrivains; member of French commission for United Nations Educational, Scientific, and Cultural Organization (UNESCO), 1976-79; member of administration council of Centre National des Lettres, 1978; vice-president of Conseil Permanent des Ecrivains, 1979. *Military service:* French Army, 1927; served in Besancon, France, and Mainz, Germany (now West Germany). *Member:* Academy Mallarme (president), Peu Club. *Awards, honors:* Created chevalier de la Legion d'Honneur, 1950, chevalier du Merite Agricole, c. 1960, and chevalier de l'Economie Nationale, c. 1960; Golden Eagle at Nice book fair, 1973; Brittany Prize, 1975; grand prize for poetry of the French Academy, 1976; Couronne d'Or des Soirees Poetiques de Struga (Macedonia, Yugoslavia), 1976.

WRITINGS—In English: Elegies, Dubuffet, Point de Jour, 1946, translation by Maurice O'Meara published under same title (text in English and French), Southern Illinois University Press, 1976; *Euclidiennes,* Gallimard, 1967, translation by Teo Savory published as *Euclidians,* Unicorn Press, 1977; *Guillevic: A Selection,* edited and translated by Teo Savory, Unicorn Press, 1968; *Selected Poems,* translated and introduced by Denise Levertov, New Directions, 1969; *Selected Poems,* edited and introduced by Savory, Penguin, 1974.

Other: *Requiem* (title means "Requiem"), Tschann, 1938; *Terraque* (title means "Landwater"), Gallimard, 1942; *Amulettes* (title means "Amulets"), Seghers, 1946; *Fractures* (title means "Breakages"), Editions de Minuit, 1947; *Executoire* (title means "Writ of Execution"), Gallimard, 1947; *Coordonnees* (title means "Coordinates"), Trois Collines (Geneva), 1948; *L'Homme qui se ferme* (title means "Man Closing Up"), Reclame, 1949; *Gagner* (title means "To Earn"), Gallimard, 1949; *Les Chansons d'Antonin Blond* (title means "The Songs of Antonin Blond"), Seghers, 1949; *Les Murs* (title means "The Walls"), Les Editions du Livre, 1950; *Envie de vivre* (title means "Envy of Life"), Seghers, 1951; *Le Gout de la paix* (title means "The Taste of Peace"), Au Colporteur, 1951; *Terre a bonheur* (title means "Land of Happiness"), Seghers, 1952; *Trente-et-un sonnets* (title means "Thirty-One Sonnets"), Gallimard, 1954; *L'Age mur* (title means "The Ripe Age"), Editions Cercle d'Art, 1955.

Carnac (title means "Carnac"), Gallimard, 1961; *Guillevic* (selected works), Seghers, 1962; *Sphere* (title means "Sphere"), Gallimard, 1963; *Avec* (title means "With"), Gallimard, 1966; (compiler) *Mes Poetes hongrois* (title means "My Hungarian Poets"), Editions Corvina (Budapest), 1967; *Ville* (title means "City"), Gallimard, 1969; *Temple du merle* (title means "Blackbird's Chapel"), Galanis, 1969.

De la Prairie, Petithony, 1970; *Paroi* (title means "Wall"), Gallimard, 1970; *Choses* (title means "Things"), Le Bou-
quet, 1970; *Encoches* (title means "Notches"), Les Editeurs Francais Reunis, 1970; *De l'hiver* (title means "Of Winter"), Galanis, 1971; *Inclus* (title means "Enclosed"), Gallimard, 1973; *Racines,* Robert Blanchet, 1973; *Hippo et Hippa,* Hachette, 1973; *Cymbaleem,* Le Veut d'Arles, 1973; *Supposer,* Edition Commune Mesure, 1974; *L'Hubier de la Bretagne,* Tchou-Laffont, 1974; *Medor. Tudor,* Farandole, 1975; *La Danse des Korrigans* (title means "Goblins' Dance"), Farandole, 1976; *Du Domaine,* Gallimard, 1977; *Babioles,* Regard-Parole, 1977; *Magnificat,* Carmen Martinez, c. 1977; *Conjugaison,* Commune Mesure, 1978; *Etier,* Gallimard, 1979; *Suppose,* Marc Pessin, 1979; *Fifre,* Maeght, 1980; *Autres,* Gallimard, 1980; *Vivre eu poesie,* Stock, 1980; *Harpe,* Galanis, 1980. Also author of *Delta,* 1976.

Also author of poems under pseudonym Serpieres. Translator of poems from Hungarian, German, and Russian.

SIDELIGHTS: Guillevic (who signs his poems with his surname only) was born of peasant stock in Brittany at Carnac, a small city famous as the site of a vast and enigmatic assemblage of megalithic stone monuments. Carnac, like most of the great ritual places of the Celts is, as Denise Levertov has written, a landscape "of a profound austerity. In such landscapes the senses are undistracted from the elements: rock, sky, sea are there not backgrounds but presences. Beginning in such a place, Guillevic learned to recognize all else in life likewise as *presence,* not as incidental properties."

The poet's father, a sailor, became a gendarme in 1909 and was assigned to Jeumont, an industrial town on the Belgian border where the family lived in police barracks. Three years later they returned to Brittany, living, again in barracks, in a village about forty kilometers from Carnac. Guillevic's father was mobilized in 1914 and the family remained in Brittany throughout World War I, a period of considerable poverty for them. After the war, in 1919, they moved to Ferrette in Alsace, close to the Swiss border. It was here that Guillevic spent his adolescence, learning Alsatian and German, and developing an intense enthusiasm for poetry—Lamartine, Rousseau, Rilke, the French symbolists, and later Trakl, an important influence. Living first among Bretons, then in Alsace, Guillevic heard French spoken only at school until he was nearly twenty, when he served in the military. This early detachment from the language in which he writes, Jean Tortel has suggested, may have helped to form "the consideration with which he approaches words, the space he leaves between them and himself. For him each vocable (plate, chair, nightingale) is not something taken for granted, something everyday."

Guillevic's first pamphlet of poems, *Requiem,* published when he was thirty-one, made no great impact, but *Terraque,* which appeared four years later, was greeted as a revelation. From the beginning, Guillevic's poems were brief, plain, and concentrated, reminding some critics of haiku. Many of them contemplate a stone or a flower, the sea or the sky, a bird or an animal, seeking to discover the true essence of such things, as distinct from man's sentimental or intellectual conception of them. These poems have been seen as an attempt to close the gap that has opened between man and nature, providing a revelatory introduction to the natural world in all its strangeness. According to a critic in the *Times Literary Supplement,* "Guillevic is notable above all for having discovered a way of writing genuinely cosmic poetry without the least hint of strained portentousness. Using the simplest of means, in a verse that is sparing of images and normally refuses intensity, in short, sharp phrases that are not 'suggestive' through any of the traditional devices, he manages to convey an apprehension of the universal and the infinite.''

After his demobilization at Terrasson, Dordogne, in 1940, Guillevic returned to Paris where he again worked for the ministry of finance. Also at that time he befriended the poet Paul Eluard. He joined the clandestine Communist party in 1942, and played a part in the Resistance, not least in the powerful poems he wrote under the pseudonym ''Serpieres,'' several of which were later collected in *Executoire.* For a time after the war, specifically *Trente et un sonnets* (1954), Guillevic adopted traditional verse forms in a number of overtly ''Marxist'' poems. Many critics feel that, as C. A. Hackett wrote, these poems ''have with few exceptions lost the virtues of their brevity; they are no longer the concise expression of personal feeling, but have become the formulae of a political creed.''

Guillevic himself must have felt that this was the wrong path for him, and in the major sequence he published in 1961 as *Carnac,* he reverted to the condensed and unrhymed forms, and regained and refined the distinctive voice of his earlier poetry, a process which has continued in subsequent volumes. Denise Levertov, one of Guillevic's translators, says that he ''avoids the easily opulent image, the blurred emotive impression. He trusts the hard, the plain, the stripped, to speak for itself. He refuses to say more than he feels.''

BIOGRAPHICAL/CRITICAL SOURCES: Pierre Daix, *Guillevic,* Seghers, 1954; C. A. Hackett, editor, *An Anthology of Modern French Poetry,* Blackwell, 1967; Guillevic, *Selected Poems,* New Directions, 1969; Graham Dunstan Martin, editor, *Anthology of Contemporary French Poetry,* Edinburgh University Press, 1972; *Times Literary Supplement,* May 27, 1974; Guillevic, *Selected Poems,* Penguin, 1974; Guillevic, *Elegies,* Southern Illinois University Press, 1976.

*   *   *

GURNEE, Jeanne 1926-

PERSONAL: Born December 11, 1926; daughter of Jacques Henri (a lecturer and writer) and Ruth (a library director; maiden name, Heckert) Bustanoby; married Russell Hampton Gurnee (a writer); children: Susan Tenbrook, Wendy Leigh Gurnee Gustafson. *Education:* Attended New York University, Columbia University, Bergen Community College, and Rutgers University; New York School of Interior Decoration, graduated, 1950. *Home:* 231 Irving Ave., Closter, N.J., 07624. *Office:* R. H. Gurnee, Inc., 15 William St., Closter, N.J. 07624.

CAREER: Prang Studio, New York, N.Y., assistant to art director, 1945-51; R. H. Gurnee, Inc., Closter, N.J., vice-president, 1951—. Chairperson of Closter Environmental Commission, 1976—; public relations chairperson of International Congress of Speleology, 1981; consultant to governments of Puerto Rico and Barbados. *Member:* National Speleological Society (fellow; chairperson of New York group, 1972-75), Society of Women Geographers (vice-president, 1972-75; member of national executive council, 1972—).

WRITINGS: (With husband, R. H. Gurnee) *Discovery at the Rio Camuy,* Crown, 1974; (editor with Joan Bastable; also contributor) *Historic Homes in Closter,* privately printed, 1979; (with R. H. Gurnee) *The Gurnee Guide to American Caves,* Zephyrus Press, 1979. Contributor to magazines, including *Explorers Journal* and *Natural History.* Editor for National Speleological Society, 1952-60.

SIDELIGHTS: Jeanne Gurnee told *CA:* ''I have explored wild caves throughout the United States since 1951. I am also interested in caves exhibited to the public. I hope to encourage commercial caves and improve guide training and obtain better technical, scientific, and conservation information during the development process.''

Gurnee has explored caves throughout Venezuela, Mexico, Yucatan, and Puerto Rico. As a result of reports on Rio Camuy Cave, the Commonwealth of Puerto Rico has set aside that area as a park and preserve for the people.

In 1972 and 1975 she was a member of a team that explored the Tanama River in rubber boats, and ran this whitewater river two of the three times it has been done. The team's follow-up report prevented the dumping of copper mining residue into this river.

In Guatemala she explored caves in the Cuchumatanes Mountains, to investigate whether or not they are still being used for Mayan ceremonials. In the 1960's she explored caves and volcanos in El Salvador (and was there at the time of the 1964 earthquake), Antigua, Barbuda, Ecuador, and Europe.

In Greece, Gurnee examined caves on the islands and mainland which were believed to have been those on which Greek legends were based. In 1973 she drove from Belgium to Czechoslovakia with her daughters, exploring ice caves and salt mines, hiking to other natural phenomena along the way. The 1970's have also taken her to Barbados, Bermuda, Hawaii, Peru, Cuba, Jamaica, Egypt, England and Scotland, St. Maarten, and Anguilla.

*   *   *

GUTHRIE, Woodrow Wilson 1912-1967
(Woody Guthrie)

OBITUARY NOTICE: Born July 14, 1912, in Okemah, Okla.; died October 3, 1967, of a nervous affliction. Folksinger, songwriter, and author. One of the pioneering modern folksingers, Guthrie wrote approximately one thousand songs, including ''This Land Is Your Land'' and ''Tom Joad,'' throughout a career that was often as philanthropic as it was musical. During the Depression Guthrie performed in migrant camps and at union rallies, and in the 1940's he toured union halls with Pete Seeger, Lee Hays, and others. Similar tours of Mexico and the farm belt also preoccupied Guthrie during World War II, as did his overseas broadcasts for serving troops. In 1955 Guthrie's career was halted by a nervous affliction that required constant hospitalization; he died from the disease twelve years later. His writings include an autobiography, *Bound for Glory,* a collection of songs and sketches entitled *American Folksong,* and articles on music and folklore for periodicals, including *People's World* and *Daily Worker.* Though Guthrie was relatively inactive during the 1960's, interest in him was revived by Bob Dylan, who credited the former with being a profound influence on his own music. Obituaries and other sources: *Current Biography,* Wilson, 1963, December, 1967; *New York Times,* October 4, 1967; *Time,* October 13, 1967; *Newsweek,* October 16, 1967.

*   *   *

GUTHRIE, Woody
See GUTHRIE, Woodrow Wilson

H

HADAS, Pamela White 1946-

PERSONAL: Born October 31, 1946, in Holland, Mich.; daughter of James Floyd (in business) and Phyllis (Pelgrim) White; married David Elkus Hadas (a professor), December 31, 1970. *Education:* Washington University, St. Louis, Mo., B.A., 1968, M.A., 1970, Ph.D., 1973. *Home:* 6628 Pershing Ave., St. Louis, Mo. 63130.

CAREER: Washington University, St. Louis, Mo., part-time lecturer, 1976—. Part-time lecturer at Webster College, 1976—. *Member:* Missouri Playwrights Association, Phi Beta Kappa. *Awards, honors:* Woodrow Wilson fellowship; Norma Lowry Memorial Prize for Poetry; prize from American Academy of Poets; fellow of MacDowell Colony and Bread Loaf Writers Conference.

WRITINGS: The Passion of Lilith, Cauldron Press, 1976; *Marianne Moore: Poet of Affection,* Syracuse University Press, 1977; *Designing Women,* Knopf, 1979; *In Light of Genesis,* Jewish Publication Society, in press. Contributor of articles and reviews to literary journals and popular magazines, including *Poetry, Mademoiselle,* and *Poetry Northwest.* Poetry editor of *Webster Review.*

WORK IN PROGRESS: A novel; two books of poems; "Mother's Day," a play; research on the work of Gertrude Stein.

SIDELIGHTS: Pamela Hadas writes: "I have studied music seriously, particularly baroque (flute and harpsichord). I have also studied drawing, and am particularly interested in figure drawing. I read science, especially physics. London is the only city in which I feel comfortable, and I take every opportunity to go there to see plays, the gardens, and the National Gallery."

*   *   *

HAGEN, Richard L(ionel) 1935-

PERSONAL: Born May 20, 1935, in Orlando, Fla.; son of Richard Todd (in U.S. Navy) and Edith (Lilley) Hagen; married Alberta Carolyn Nielsen, May 30, 1958 (divorced June 8, 1978); children: Barbara June, Raymond Charles. *Education:* Moody Bible Institute, diploma, 1956; American Conservatory of Music, Mus.B., 1961; University of Illinois, A.B., 1964, M.A., 1968, Ph.D., 1970. *Religion:* Protestant. *Home:* 2311 San Pedro, Tallahassee, Fla. 32304. *Agent:* Glenn Cowley, 60 West 10th St., New York, N.Y. 10011.

Office: Department of Psychology, Florida State University, Tallahassee, Fla. 32306.

CAREER: Moody Bible Institute, Chicago, Ill., concert manager in department of sacred music, 1956-58, assistant to director of department, 1958-61; Veterans Administration Hospital, Danville, Ill., psychological trainee, 1967-68; State of Illinois, Division of Mental Health, Adolf Meyer Zone Center, Decatur, psychologist, 1968-69; Leon County Guidance Center, Tallahassee, Fla., clinical psychologist, 1969-70; Florida State University, Tallahassee, associate professor of psychology, 1970—. *Member:* American Psychological Association, National Association for Retarded Children, Association for the Advancement of Behavior Therapy, Midwestern Psychological Association, Southeastern Psychological Association, Florida Psychological Association (member of executive council, 1970-74).

WRITINGS: (With James C. Coleman) *Abnormal Behavior,* W. C. Brown, 1973; (contributor) J. P. Foreyt, B. J. Williams, and Sander Martin, editors, *Obesity: Behavioral Approaches to Dietary Management,* Brunner, 1976; (contributor) J. Calhoun, editor, *Abnormal Psychology: Current Perspectives,* Random House, 1976; (contributor) Foreyt, editor, *Behavioral Treatments of Obesity,* Pergamon, 1977; *The Bio-Sexual Factor;* Doubleday, 1979. Contributor to *Advances in Behavioral Medicine,* J. M. Ferguson and C. B. Taylor, editors, Spectrum. Contributor to psychology journals.

WORK IN PROGRESS: A book on free will and determinism; research on philosophy and psychology.

SIDELIGHTS: Hagen wrote: "The idea for *The Bio-Sexual Factor* floated into mind one evening while I was awakening from a brief nap. Chapter headings seemed to flow along in my head. I jumped up, began writing, and wrote way into the morning. I knew little about the subject, and had to do many hours of library research; nevertheless, three months from the time of the initial idea, I mailed the completed manuscript to my agent. Because I felt the book contained an important message, I often worked until one or two o'clock in the morning, after a full day of work at the university, and even then I had trouble turning loose of the project and going to sleep. The experience was thoroughly enjoyable."

*   *   *

HAGGAI, Thomas Stephens 1931-

PERSONAL: Surname is pronounced *Hag*-gy-eye; born

201

January 29, 1931, in Kalamazoo, Mich.; son of Waddy A. (a Baptist minister) and Mildred (Steere) Haggai; married Joan Randall, October, 1951 (divorced, 1970); married Buren Cashatt (a radio producer), August 25, 1971; children: Martha Christine, Janice Lynn, Natalie Jayne, James Allan. *Education:* Attended North Greenville College, 1947-49, and Furman University, 1949-51. *Politics:* Republican. *Home:* 2116 Guilford College Rd., Jamestown, N.C. 27282. *Agent:* Larry Stone, Box 843, Nashville, Tenn. *Office:* Tom Haggai & Associates Foundation, 209 North Main St., High Point, N.C. 27260.

CAREER: "Licensed Baptist minister, 1943"; ordained Baptist minister, 1951; pastor of Baptist churches in Rock Hill, N.C., 1952-56, and High Point, N.C., 1956-59; "Values for Better Living" (national radio program), High Point, commentator, 1958—. President of Tom Haggai & Associates Foundation, 1963—; lecturer for General Motors Speakers Bureau, 1970—. Chairperson of board of directors of Independent Grocers Alliance, 1976—; member of board of directors of Super Foods, Inc. and Myrtle Desk Co.; national director of personnel for Boy Scouts of America, 1975-77. *Member:* High Point Executives Club (president, 1978-79). *Awards, honors:* D.D. from High Point College, 1965; D.Hum. from Salem College, 1966; Silver Buffalo from Boy Scouts of America, 1971; Chauncey Rose Award from Rose-Hulman Institute of Technology, 1972; Gold Medallion from National Association of Secretaries of State, 1976; International Speakers Hall of Fame, 1979.

WRITINGS: Will America Be Spared, Christie Press, 1963; *Chrissie, I Never Had It So Bad* (on youth and their problems), Thomas Nelson, 1974.

Author of "How to Get What You Want," a film, released by John Hammond Associates. Author of columns in trade journals, including *Now,* 1963-70, *Grocergram,* 1967, *SuperNews,* 1970, *Aerogram,* 1974—, and *Torch.* Contributor to magazines.

WORK IN PROGRESS: A book of radio scripts; research for books on economics and business.

SIDELIGHTS: Haggai commented: "I believe in the total development of man—his spiritual, mental, and physical development. I think we've done a good job with the physical and mental, but not with the spiritual. And I find that businessmen are hungry . . . when I get through speaking they almost smother me, wanting to . . . talk about how to make a certain decision."

Haggai's radio program, which consists of brief daily messages, is not so much religious as it is inspirational. He aims his anecdotes, interviews, and observations at people of all ages and circumstances. His career as a public speaker involves nearly a speech a day in all corners of the world, including each of the U.S. Air Force overseas bases.

Haggai told *CA:* "After suffering a serious illness I became a minister as a lad of twelve. My feeling is that God is interested in the total man, so I'm motivated to apply ageless ethics and morals to contemporary problems."

AVOCATIONAL INTERESTS: Boy Scout activities, jazz.

BIOGRAPHICAL/CRITICAL SOURCES: Furman University Magazine, fall, 1968.

* * *

HAILEY, Elizabeth Forsythe 1938-

PERSONAL: Born August 31, 1938, in Dallas, Tex.; daughter of Earl Andrew (an attorney) and Janet (Kendall) Forsythe; married Oliver D. Hailey (a writer), June 25, 1960; children: Elizabeth Kendall, Melinda Brooke. *Education:* Hollins College, B.A., 1960. *Home:* 11747 Canton Place, Studio City, Calif. 91604. *Agent:* Geoffrey Sanford, The Artists Agency, 190 North Canon Dr., Beverly Hills, Calif. 90210.

CAREER: Writer. Worked as creative consultant on television series, "Mary Hartman, Mary Hartman," Tandem Productions, 1976; co-producer of television series, "Another Day," James Komack Productions, 1977. *Awards, honors:* Silver Medal for best first novel from Commonwealth Club of California, 1979.

WRITINGS: A Woman of Independent Means (novel), Viking, 1978.

WORK IN PROGRESS: A novel, *Life Sentence,* to be completed by January, 1981.

SIDELIGHTS: Hailey's first novel, *A Woman of Independent Means,* attends to Bess Steed Garner, a woman born at the end of the nineteenth century who dies during the 1960's. The entire book consists of letters written by Garner to both friends and relatives. A reviewer for *Ms.* noted that "the letters are a tour de force that unfolds a multiple view of Bess." The writer also declared, "Without the benefit of a single word from the other 'characters,' we know exactly how they see her. What emerges is a complex, moving, and entertaining portrait."

Hailey told *CA:* "Though I have always wanted to write, the women's movement caused me to begin questioning the value of an individual life—especially one devoted to home and family. In the life of my grandmother I found not only a subject for my first novel but an affirmative answer to the question of whether it is possible to make permanent emotional commitments to other people and still retain one's integrity as an individual."

BIOGRAPHICAL/CRITICAL SOURCES: Christian Science Monitor, June 14, 1978; *Ms.,* July, 1978; *Virginia Quarterly Review,* autumn, 1978.

* * *

HALBACH, Edward C(hristian), Jr. 1931-

PERSONAL: Born November 8, 1931, in Clinton, Iowa; son of Edward C. (a lawyer) and Lewella (Sullivan) Halbach; married Janet E. Bridges, July 25, 1953; children: Kristin, Edward, Kathleen, Thomas, Elaine. *Education:* University of Iowa, B.A., 1953, J.D., 1958; Harvard University, LL.M., 1959. *Home:* 679 San Luis Rd., Berkeley, Calif. 94707. *Office:* School of Law, University of California, Berkeley, Calif. 94720.

CAREER: University of California, Berkeley, acting associate professor, 1959-62, professor of law, 1962—, dean of School of Law, 1966-75. Visiting professor at University of Chicago, Harvard University, and Stanford University. Member of board of directors of California Indian Legal Services, advisory board of American Indian Lawyer Training Program, and advisory committee for Restatement of Property. *Military service:* U.S. Air Force, 1953-55; became first lieutenant.

MEMBER: International Academy of Estate and Trust Law (vice-president), American Bar Association (director of Probate and Trust Division; chairperson-elect of section of Real Property, Probate, and Trust Law), American Law Institute, American College of Probate Council (fellow), American Academy of Political and Social Sciences, California State Bar Association, Iowa State Bar Association. *Awards, honors:* LL.D. from University of Redlands, 1971.

WRITINGS: (With Eugene F. Scoles) *Materials on Decedents' Estates and Trusts,* Little, Brown, 1965, 2nd edition, 1973; (contributor, and editor with Robin Foster) *California Will Drafting,* University of California Extension, Berkeley, 1965; (contributor) *Uniform Probate Code,* National Conference of Commissioners on Uniform State Laws, 1969; *The Uses of Trusts in Estate Planning,* American College of Probate Council, 1975; (with Scoles) *Materials on Future Interests,* Little, Brown, 1977; (editor and contributor) *Death, Taxes, and Family Property,* West Publishing, 1977; *Income Taxation of Estates, Trusts, and Beneficiaries,* University of California Extension, Berkeley, 1978, 2nd edition (with Paul G. Hoffmann), 1980; *Materials on Estate Taxation and Planning,* West Publishing, 1979. Contributor to law journals.

* * *

HALE, William Harlan 1910-1974

PERSONAL: Born July 21, 1910, in New York, N.Y.; died June 30, 1974, in New York, N.Y.; son of William Bayard (a journalist) and Olga (Unger) Hale; married Jean Laughlin Barker, August 19, 1941; children: Katherine, Jonathan, Elizabeth. *Education:* Yale University, A.B., 1931. *Politics:* Democrat. *Religion:* Episcopalian. *Home:* Goodhill Rd., Weston, Conn. 06880.

CAREER: Vanity Fair, New York City, associate editor, 1932-33; *Washington Post,* Washington, D.C., columnist, 1933; *Fortune,* New York City, editorial associate, 1934-35; free-lance writer, 1935-41; *New Republic,* New York City, 1946-47; *Reporter,* New York City, senior writer, 1948-49, contributing editor, 1954-58; *Horizon* (magazine), New York City, managing editor, 1958-61, editor, 1961-63; Horizon Books, New York City, editor, 1963-67, senior writer, 1967-68; writer, 1968-74. *Wartime service:* Office of War Information (OWI) and Supreme Headquarters of Allied Expeditionary Forces (SHAEF), 1941-45; served in New York, in London as chief of German propaganda operations, in Luxembourg as chief of psychological warfare division, and in Germany as policy adviser for information control division. U.S. Foreign Service, 1950-53; served with Office of High Commander at American Embassy in Vienna, Austria, as press attache and director of public affairs division.

WRITINGS: Challenge to Defeat: Modern Man in Goethe's World and Spengler's Century (philosophy), Harcourt, 1932; *Hannibal Hooker: His Death and Adventures* (novel), Random House, 1939; *A Yank in the R.A.F.* (novel), Random House, 1941; *The March of Freedom: A Layman's History of the American People,* Harper, 1947; *Horace Greeley: Voice of the People* (biography), Harper, 1950; (author and editor in charge) *The Horizon Book of Ancient Greece,* American Heritage Publishing, 1965, abridged edition published as *Ancient Greece,* American Heritage Press, 1970; (editor in charge) *The Horizon Book of Ancient Rome,* American Heritage Publishing, 1966; (with others) *The Horizon Cookbook and Illustrated History of Eating and Drinking Through the Ages,* American Heritage Publishing, 1968; (with others) *The World of Rodin, 1840-1917* (biography and history), Time-Life, 1969. Also author of *Innocence Abroad,* 1957.

SIDELIGHTS: William Hale wrote his first book, *Challenge to Defeat,* at the age of twenty-one. The book is a philosophical argument spanning a century of thought in art and literature. The protagonists are Goethe, the prophet of affirmation, and Spengler, the prophet of negation. The work was generally well received albeit with a large amount of astonishment. Critics were amazed that a twenty-one-year-old freshly graduated from college wrote such a work. L. W.

Dodd heralded *Challenge to Defeat* as "the most significant utterance that has yet come from our youngest literary generation." He added: "Hale—as each of his successive reviewers points out with an astonishment more than a little patronizing—is but twenty-one; and he has actually dared to publish a thoughtful, eloquent, fighting book—a rallying cry to Youth." Leon Whipple declared further that "the generation that can discover already so much poise, clarity and defiance in its striplings need not be wept over."

Hale's next book, *Hannibal Hooker,* a picaresque novel, was not so warmly received. Although it was agreed that this young author definitely had talent, he still had to make many improvements in his style. F. T. Marsh cuttingly expounded that the book "is a novel of words, words, words. The words are the best things about it, for many of them are very good words—a few of them witty, a few others stimulating, a few other critical or revealing. . . . But there are no people and there is no story." W. L. White was more optimistic when he asserted that "it is a novel of ideas, scrambled though they sometimes may be. Some of the dialogue is brilliant. And on every page are bits of keen observation and good writing. There is also a deeper bite to Mr. Hale's irony than a cursory reader would suspect. But that is hardly the reader's fault, because Mr. Hale firmly steers his allegories so as to avoid both the Scylla of clarity and the Charybdis of common sense. Yet his literary virtues are such that the book shows much promise if Mr. Hale can be coaxed out from among his stoles, naves and flying buttresses, and wheedled into writing simply, directly and steadily about a world he knows."

Hale's first attempt at writing history in *The March of History* was not considered an auspicious one. Many critics felt his rendition of American history too brief and unoriginal except for his often unwanted opinions. J. A. Krout claimed that "Hale is usually in a hurry" and "the pace he sets for himself prevents him from making necessary explanations." Another critic, H. F. Pringle, railed that the book was too opinionated. "He has a lot of opinions and a good many people will find the book cocky and brash. Clever, upstanding, opinionated Yaleman Hale writes a good deal like his fellow-Yalemen on *Time* magazine."

If Hale's stab at history was less than propitious, his try at biography was not. *Horace Greeley* was highly praised. Ralph Korngold remarked that Hale "tells the story interestingly, in a style without adornment and with admirable objectivity." More enthusiastically, Allan Nevins claimed the book "may safely be pronounced the best of the existing lives of Greeley: a work which throws new light not only upon the man but his time, and a delightfully readable biography to boot."

BIOGRAPHICAL/CRITICAL SOURCES: Springfield Republican, May 16, 1932, October 7, 1950; *New York Herald Tribune,* May 22, 1932, February 19, 1939; *New York Times,* May 22, 1932, February 19, 1939, June 29, 1947, October 8, 1950; *Boston Evening Transcript,* May 28, 1932; *Saturday Review of Literature,* June 4, 1932, February 18, 1939, June 14, 1947, October 7, 1950, September 28, 1968; *Nation,* June 8, 1932, March 11, 1939, November 11, 1950; *Christian Science Monitor,* June 11, 1932, May 24, 1947; *Survey,* July 1, 1932, November, 1950; *New Republic,* August 3, 1932, November 13, 1950; *Commonweal,* September 14, 1932; *San Francisco Chronicle,* May 13, 1947, September 22, 1950; *New York Herald Tribune Weekly Book Review,* May 18, 1947; *New York Herald Tribune Book Review,* October 1, 1950; *Chicago Sunday Tribune,* October 8, 1950.

OBITUARIES: New York Times, July 1, 1974.*

HALL, Frederic Sauser
  See SAUSER-HALL, Frederic

*   *   *

HALL, Gene E(rwin)   1941-

PERSONAL: Born June 19, 1941, in Rutland, Vt.; son of Walter and Ruth Hall; married Betsey Hudson; children: Gregory Walter, Jeffrey Michael. *Education:* Castleton College, B.S., 1964; Syracuse University, M.S., 1965, Ph.D., 1968. *Office:* Research and Development Center for Teacher Education, University of Texas, Austin, Tex. 78712.

CAREER: Eastern Regional Institute for Education, Syracuse, N.Y., administrative assistant and staff associate in science program, 1967-68; University of Texas at Austin, assistant professor of education, 1968-71, staff member of Research and Development Center for Teacher Education, 1968-71, program director, 1971—. Participant in professional meetings.

WRITINGS: (With D. P. Butts) *Children and Science: The Process of Teaching and Learning,* Prentice-Hall, 1974; (with H. L. Jones) *Competency-Based Education: A Process for the Improvement of Education,* Prentice-Hall, 1976; (editor) *Vantage Point 1976,* Association for the Education of Teachers in Science, 1976. Contributor to education journals.

SIDELIGHTS: Hall writes: "My research continues to be trying to understand the change process in schools, colleges, and industry, using the individual and the innovation as the frame of reference. The conceptual basis for this research is the 'Concerns-Based Adoption Model' which proposes that change is a process and not an event and that individuals move through identifiable developmental levels when they are involved in change. The research thrust presented is upon trying to understand better how managers can focus their 'interventions' according to the diagnosed developmental level of their staff members. I am also involved in establishing national priorities for research in teacher education and beginning several new initiatives in this area.

"My motivations probably come out of the basic set of assumptions that believe in the worth of the individual and that individual growth is possible even in the midst of our complex society. Motivation also comes from the success that our concepts and research have had in being recognized as useful by practitioners, researchers, evaluators, and policymakers. This success has also had its drawbacks, since it has meant more travel within and outside the United States than anyone should be subjected to."

*   *   *

HALL, J. De P.
  See McKELWAY, St. Clair

*   *   *

HALL, John   1937-

PERSONAL: Born June 2, 1937, in Philippi, W. Va.; son of J. Harold (a teacher) and Grace (a teacher; maiden name, Wolfe) Hall; married Susie Deem; children: Mark, Doug. *Education:* West Virginia University, B.S. *Home:* 7125 Carol Lane, Falls Church, Va. 22042. *Office:* Media General, 214 National Press Bldg., Washington, D.C. 20004.

CAREER/WRITINGS: United Press International, reporter in Columbus, Ohio, 1959-60, in Trenton, N.J., 1960-64, and in Washington, D.C., 1964-73; Hearst Newspapers, Washington, D.C., reporter, 1973-78; Media General, Washington, D.C., bureau chief, 1979—. Notable assignments include coverage of all national conventions since 1964, Hubert Humphrey, George McGovern, and James E. Carter presidential campaigns, the Watergate scandal, the antiballistic missile (ABM) debates of the 1960's, and the Strategic Arms Limitation Talks (SALT). *Military service:* U.S. Army National Guard. *Member:* National Press Club.

SIDELIGHTS: Hall is "primarily a political writer," he told *CA.* He also specializes in national security reportage.

*   *   *

HALL, Manly Palmer   1901-

PERSONAL: Born March 18, 1901, in Peterborough, Ontario, Canada; came to the United States in 1904; son of William S. and Louise (Palmer) Hall; married Marie Bauer, December 6, 1950. *Education:* High school graduate. *Residence:* Los Angeles, Calif. *Office:* Philosophical Research Society, Inc., 3910 Los Feliz Blvd., Los Angeles, Calif. 90027.

CAREER: Philosophical Research Society, Inc., Los Angeles, Calif., founder, president, and member of board of trustees, 1934—. *Member:* International Society for General Semantics, Pythagorean Society, Chinese Culture Society (life member), Societas Rosecrucina in Civitatibus Folderatis (honorary member), Indian Association of American, American Federation of Astrologers, American Society for Psychical Research, Baconian Society, New Mexico Historical Society (life member). *Awards, honors:* Distinguished service award from city of Los Angeles, Calif., 1970.

WRITINGS: The Initiates of the Flame, [Los Angeles], 1922; *The Ways of the Lonely Ones: When the Sons of Compassion Speak,* privately printed, 1923, 4th edition published as *The Ways of the Lonely Ones: A Collection of Mystical Allegories,* Phoenix Press, 1934, reprinted, Philosophical Research Society; *Notes on the Culture of the Mind,* 1927, 2nd edition, Hall Publishing, 1929, reprinted, Philosophical Research Society; *An Encyclopedic Outline of Masonic, Hermetic, Qabbalistic, and Rosicrucian Symbolical Philosophy,* H. S. Crocker Co., 1928, 11th edition published as *The Secret Teachings of All Ages: An Encyclopedic Outline of Masonic, Hermetic, Qabbalistic, and Rosicrucian Symbolical Philosophy—Being an Interpretation of the Secret Teachings Concealed Within the Rituals, Allegories, and Mysteries of All Ages,* Philosophical Research Society, 1957, 19th edition, 1973.

The Occult Anatomy of Man; to Which Is Added a Treatise on Occult Masonry, 3rd edition, Hall Publishing, 1929; *Melchizedek and the Mystery of Fire: A Treatise in Three Parts,* 3rd edition, Hall Publishing, 1929; *Magic: A Treatise on Natural Occultism,* 3rd revised edition, Hall Publishing, 1929, 6th edition, Philosophical Research Society, 1960; *The Lost Keys of Masonry: The Legend of Hiram Abiff,* 3rd revised edition, Hall Publishing, 1929, 4th edition published as *The Lost Keys of Freemasonry; or, The Secret of Hiram Abiff,* Macoy Publishing, 1931, 11th edition, 1976; *An Essay on the Fundamental Principles of Operative Occultism,* 2nd revised edition, Hall Publishing, 1929, reprinted as *Spiritual Centers in Man,* Philosophical Research Society, 1978; *What the Ancient Wisdom Expects of Its Disciples: A Study Concerning the Mystery Schools,* 2nd edition, Hall Publishing, 1929; *Unseen Forces: Nature Spirits, Thought Forms,*

Ghosts and Specters, the Dweller on the Threshold, 3rd revised edition, Hall Publishing, 1929, 7th edition, Philosophical Research Society, 1960; *Talks to Students on Occult Philosophy*, 2nd edition, Hall Publishing, 1929; *Evolution and the Orthodox Church: A Plea for Theological Reform*, 2nd revised edition, Hall Publishing, 1929; *The Hermetic Marriage: A Study in the Philosophy of the Thrice Greatest Hermes*, 3rd revised edition, Hall Publishing, 1929; *The Sacred Magic of the Qabbalah: The Science of the Divine Names and Numbers*, 3rd revised edition, Hall Publishing, 1929.

Lectures on Ancient Philosophy: An Introduction to the Study and Application of Rational Procedure, Hall Publishing, 1929, reprinted, Philosophical Research Society; *The Mysteries of Asia: The Wonders of the Golden Dragon, the Land of the Living Saints, the Secrets of the Gobi Desert, the Sorcery of Tibet, the Astronomer's City, the Towers of Silence, Magic and Sorcery of the Far East*, Hall Publishing, 1929; *KFI-Radio Talks on Philosophy and Psychology*, Hall Publishing, 1929; *From a Philosopher's Scrap-Book: The Sand Magic of the Navahos, the Mystery of the Thunderbird, Ju-Jitsu, a Secret of the Samurai, the Whirling Dervishes, Java's Dancing Shadows, the Temple of Heaven, the Seven Days of Creation*, Hall Publishing, 1929; *The Noble Eightfold Path: The Doctrine of Dharma*, Hall Publishing, 1929, 7th edition, Philosophical Research Society, 1964.

The Space-Born, Skelton Publishing, 1930; (editor) *Astrological Keywords: Compiled From Leading Authorities*, 2nd enlarged edition, McKay, 1931, 7th edition, Philosophical Research Society, 1973; *The Phoenix: An Illustrated Review of Occultism and Philosophy*, Hall Publishing, 1931, 5th edition, Philosophical Research Society, 1968; *Man: The Grand Symbol of the Mysteries*, Hall Publishing, 1932, 6th edition, Philosophical Research Society, 1972; *Facing the Facts: Social and Political Essays*, Hall Publishing, 1932; *The Story of Astrology: The Belief in the Stars as a Factor in Human Progress*, Phoenix Press, 1933, reprinted, Philosophical Library, 1959; *First Principles of Philosophy: The Science of Perfection*, Phoenix Press, 1935, 2nd edition published as *First Principles of Philosophy: Direction of Mental Activity in the Science of Perfection*, Philosophical Research Society, 1949; *Words to the Wise: A Practical Guide to the Occult Sciences*, Philosophical Research Society, 1936, 2nd edition, 1963; *Twelve World Teachers: A Summary of Lives and Teachings*, Philosophers Press, 1937, reprinted, Gordon Press; *Freemasonry of the Ancient Egyptians; to Which Is Added an Interpretation of the Crata Repoa Initiation Rite*, Philosophers Press, 1937, 4th edition, Philosophical Research Society, 1973; *Questions and Answers: Fundamentals of the Occult Sciences*, Philosophers Press, 1937, 3rd edition, Philosophical Research Society, 1965; *Reincarnation: The Cycle of Necessity*, Philosophers Press, 1939, 6th edition, Philosophical Research Society, 1971.

How to Understand Your Bible: A Philosopher's Interpretation of Obscure and Puzzling Phrases—A Study of the Bibles of the World Revealing One Spiritual Tradition, Philosophical Research Society, 1942, revised edition published in three volumes, including Volume I: *Old Testament Wisdom: Keys to Bible Interpretation*, 1957; *Self-Unfoldment by Disciplines of Realization: Releasing and Developing the Inward Perceptions—Practical Instruction in the Philosophy of Disciplined Thinking and Feeling*, Philosophical Research Society, 1942, 4th edition, 1961; *The Philosophy of Astrology*, Philosophical Research Society, 1943, 3rd edition, 1970; *Healing, the Divine Art*, 2nd edition, Philosophical Research Society, 1944, reprinted as *The Story of Healing:*

The Divine Art, Citadel, 1958; *The Guru, by His Disciple: The Way of the East as Told to Manly Palmer Hall*, Philosophical Research Society, 1944; *The Secret Destiny of America*, Philosophical Research Society, 1944, 3rd edition, 1958; *Journey in Truth*, Philosophical Research Society, 1945; *The Way of Heaven, and Other Fantasies Told in the Manner of the Chinese*, Philosophical Research Society, 1946; *Pathways of Philosophy*, Philosophical Research Society, 1947; *Very Sincerely Yours: A Collection of Personal Letters to Students*, Philosophical Research Society, 1948; *The Adepts in the Western Esoteric Tradition*, Philosophical Research Society, 1949.

The Mystical Christ: Religion as a Personal Spiritual Experience, Philosophical Research Society, 1951, 2nd edition, 1956, reprinted, Gordon Press; *The Adepts in the Eastern Esoteric Tradition*, Philosophical Research Society, 1952; (with Henry L. Drake) *The Basic Ideas of Man: A Program of Study Founded Upon Man's Heritage of Wisdom*, Philosophical Research Society, 1953; *Lectures*, Philosophical Research Society, 1956; *Studies in Character Analysis: Phrenology, Palmistry, Physiognomy, Graphology*, Philosophical Research Society, 1958; *Collected Writings*, two volumes, Philosophical Research Society, 1958; *Search for Reality: Ten Lectures on Personal Growth*, Philosophical Research Society, 1959.

Survey Course in Philosophy: Based Upon the Introduction to An Encyclopedic Outline of Symbolical Philosophy, Philosophical Research Society, 1960; *The Western Paradise of Amitabha*, Philosophical Research Society, 1962; (editor and author of introduction) *The Most Holy Trinosophia of the Comte de Saint-Germain*, 4th edition, Philosophical Research Society, 1963; *The White Bird of Tao*, Philosophical Research Society, 1964; *Daily Words of Wisdom: A Calendar of Inspiring Thoughts*, Philosophical Research Society, 1964; *The Mystical and Medical Philosophy of Paracelsus; to Which Is Added "The Nature Spirits" According to Paracelsus*, Philosophical Research Society, 1964; *Psychoanalyzing the Twelve Zodiacal Types*, 7th edition, Philosophical Research Society, 1965; *Studies in Dream Symbolism*, Philosophical Research Society, 1965; *The Four Seasons of the Spirit; and, Achieving the Miracle of Contentment*, Philosophical Research Society, 1965; *The Text of Three Recordings*, Philosophical Research Society, 1966; *Great Books on Religion and Esoteric Philosophy*, Philosophical Research Society, 1966; *Buddhism and Psychotherapy*, Philosophical Research Society, 1967; *Ralph Waldo Emerson's Essays on Friendship, Love, and Beauty: An Interpretation*, Philosophical Research Society, 1967; *Right Thinking: The Royal Road to Health—A Study in Psychotherapy*, 7th edition, Philosophical Research Society, 1968; *Death and After and the Theory of Reincarnation*, 8th edition, Philosophical Research Society, 1968; *Invisible Records of Thought and Action: The Theory and Practice of Psychometry; and, The Use and Abuse of the Natural Psychic Powers Within Us and Around Us*, Philosophical Research Society, 1969; *Adventures in Understanding*, Philosophical Research Society, 1969.

Codex rosae crucis: A Rare and Curious Manuscript of Rosicrucian Interest, revised edition, Philosophical Research Society, 1971; (author of introduction) Max Heindel, *Blavatsky and the Secret Doctrine*, 2nd edition, DeVorss, 1972; *Atlantis: An Interpretation*, revised edition, Philosophical Research Society, 1976; *"Very Unusual": The Wonderful World of Mr. K. Nakamura*, Philosophical Research Society, 1976; *Past Lives and Present Problems: How to Prepare for a Fortunate Rebirth*, 3rd edition, Philosophical Research Society, 1977.

All published by Philosophical Research Society: *Incompatability: A Crisis in Modern Living; An Introduction to Dream Interpretation; America's Assignment With Destiny; Arhats of Buddhism; Basic Fears; Basic Principles of Domestic Philosophy; Blind Spot in the Mind; Dark Night of the Soul; Drugs of Vision; From Death to Rebirth; Impressions of Modern Japan; Initiation of Plato; The Inner Lives of Minerals, Plants, and Animals; Invisible Records of Thoughts and Actions; Is Each Individual Born With a Purpose?; Koyasan: Sanctuary of Buddhism; Lady of Dreams; Life Planning; Light of the Vedas; Lone Traveler; The Lord Giveth and Taketh; Medicine of the Sun and Moon; Mystery of Human Birth; Mysticism and Mental Healing; Old Testament Wisdom; Planetary Influence and the Human Soul; Psychic Self-Reproach; Psychic Symbolism of Headaches; Psychology of Religious Ritual; Quiet Way; Sages of China; Sermon on the Mount; Ten Basic Rules for Living; The Therapeutic Value of Music; Wisdom Beyond the Mind; Woman: The Mother of All Living; Zen of the Bright Virtue.*

Author of pamphlets. Contributor to magazines. Editor and publisher of *Philosophical Research Society Journal*, 1941—.

* * *

HALL, Steven (Leonard) 1960-

PERSONAL: Born November 3, 1960, in San Francisco, Calif.; son of George (a teacher) and Mary-Anne (a teacher; maiden name, Sheflott) Hall. *Education:* University of Missouri, student, 1978—. *Politics:* Youth International Party. *Home:* 16 Berkeley Ave., New London, Conn. 06320. *Agent:* Jim Dickson, 408 Bel Air, Jefferson City, Mo. 65101.

MEMBER: Delta Chi.

WRITINGS: Down Came the Sun (poems), Barlenmir, 1972. Contributor of poems to magazines.

SIDELIGHTS: Hall writes: "Significance in a personal form came to me due to a matter of authorship. When I was twelve, a new publishing firm, Barlenmir House Inc. of New York, brought forth a small volume of my poetry entitled *Down Came the Sun*. The book contained free verse either penned or dictated by myself between the ages of four and eleven. A friend of my mother's, a distinguished avant-garde artist and writer from California named Ed Stone, collected and sought publishing outlets for my work and it is to him that I owe my accomplishment. The poetry was bad and the book was a commercial failure. I stopped writing free verse poetry when I was thirteen, and the whole thing became a nearly forgotten episode as I tangled with adolescence and a new step-father. In the back of my mind, however, a thought remained. In the future, when my mortal being would become one with the universe, my name would survive, because in Washington, D.C., in the Library of Congress there would be a card stating that I existed and created *Down Came the Sun*, copyright 1972 by Steven L. Hall."

* * *

HALLE, Jean-Claude 1939-

PERSONAL: Born February 26, 1939, in France; son of Jean and Heber (Emanuele) Halle; married Marie-Francoise Place, July 9, 1966; children: Olivier, Frederique. *Education:* Attended Institut d'etudes politiques, 1958-62, and Centre de formation des journalistes, 1962-64. *Home:* 6 Pare de Bearn, Saint-Cloud, France 92210. *Office: Journal du Dimanche*, 6 Rue Ancelle, Neuilly, France 92211.

CAREER: L'Express, Paris, France, staff reporter, 1966-73; *Paris-Match*, Paris, staff reporter, 1974-78; *Journal du Dimanche*, Paris, editor in chief, 1979—. *Military service:* French Army Reserve; became captain.

WRITINGS: (Contributor) Pierre Desgraupes and Pierre Dumayet, editors, *Prague: L'Ete des tanks*, Tchou, 1968; *Guide secret des courses et du tierce*, Tchou, 1969; *Francois Cevert: La Mort dans mon contrat*, Flammarion, 1974, translation by Denis Frostick and Michael Frostick published as *Francois Cevert: A Contract With Death*, Kimber, 1975; *Glasgow 76: Le Defi des "Verts,"* Flammarion, 1976; *Football Story*, Flammarion, 1978; (with Paul Chantrel) *Le Marginal* (novel), Julliard, 1979.

* * *

HALLOWELL, Christopher L. 1945-

PERSONAL: Born October 14, 1945, in Boston, Mass.; son of William Ladd and Margaret (Barney) Hallowell; married Willa Zakin (a photographer), September 30, 1978. *Education:* Harvard University, B.A., 1968; Columbia University, M.S.J., 1971. *Home:* 245 West 74th St., New York, N.Y. 10023. *Agent:* Peter L. Ginsberg, James Brown Associates, Inc., 25 West 43rd St., New York, N.Y. 10036.

CAREER: Interamerican Research and Development Corp., Cambridge, Mass., vice-president, 1969-70; *Springfield Union*, Springfield, Mass., reporter, 1971-72; *Natural History*, New York City, senior editor, 1973-78; *Human Nature*, New York City, senior editor, 1978-79; free-lance writer, 1979—.

WRITINGS: People of the Bayou, Dutton, 1979. Contributor to magazines, including *Audubon* and *Geo*, and newspapers.

WORK IN PROGRESS: Research on the family.

SIDELIGHTS: Hallowell comments: "I am interested in writing about man's relationship to his environment, and on anthropological and ecological subjects. Although quantities of information have appeared on these subjects, very little of it bears on people as individual human beings. I am drawn to describing people and if I can relate them to their environment and vice versa, a surprising, subtle relationship, I am satisfied. That subtlety is so often unrealized. People do have a relationship to their environment. They are denying themselves an entire psychological framework by being blinded to its importance. I don't like all the mobility in this country—the population shift to the sunbelt, or that so few people in California are Californians. It indicates a lack of awareness of where you are as well as a certain subservience to lesser values."

* * *

HALPERN, Howard Marvin 1929-

PERSONAL: Born March 5, 1929, in New York, N.Y.; married, 1961; children: Shari, Dina. *Education:* Syracuse University, B.A., 1950; Columbia University, M.A., 1952, Ph.D., 1954. *Home:* 2211 Broadway, New York, N.Y. 10024. *Agent:* Curtis Brown Ltd., 575 Madison Ave., New York, N.Y. 10022.

CAREER: Trainee at Veterans Administration, 1951-54; Columbia University, Teachers College, New York City, instructor in psychology, 1954-60; New York Student Consultation Center, New York City, co-director, 1961—. Private practice in psychology, 1954—. Clinical psychologist at Bronx Veterans Administration Hospital, 1955-57; child therapist with Bleuler Psychotherapy Group, 1955—. Lecturer at Bar-Ilan University, summer, 1960; member of faculty at Metropolitan Institute for Psychoanalytic Studies, 1963—. *Member:* American Psychological Association, American Group Psychotherapy Association, American Academy of Psychotherapy (past president), Society for the Scientific Study of Sex.

WRITINGS: A Parent's Guide to Child Psychotherapy, A. S. Barnes, 1963; *Cutting Loose: An Adult Guide to Coming to Terms With Your Parents,* Simon & Schuster, 1977; *No Strings Attached,* Simon & Schuster, 1979. Contributor to psychology journals.

SIDELIGHTS: Halpern writes: "I am increasingly interested in the relationship between parents and children at all ages, from the toddler to the seventy-year-old child and ninety-year-old parents."

*　　*　　*

HAMILTON, George Rostrevor   1888-1967

OBITUARY NOTICE: Born in 1888 in London, England; died in 1967. Author. A member of the civil service in England for more than fifty years, Hamilton was knighted in 1951. He wrote several books of verse, including *Collected Poems and Epigrams* and *Apollyon,* as well as volumes of literary essays such as *The Tell-Tale Article.* His autobiography, *Rapids of Time: Sketches From the Past,* was published in 1965. Obituaries and other sources: *New Century Handbook of English Literature,* revised edition, Appleton, 1967; *Longman Companion to English Literature,* Longman, 1970.

*　　*　　*

HAMLIN, Wilfrid G(ardiner)   1918-

PERSONAL: Born May 18, 1918, in New York, N.Y.; son of Talbot Fancher (an architectural historian) and Hilda Blanche (a teacher; maiden name, Edwards) Hamlin; married Elizabeth Brett (a poet), June 11, 1944 (died April 19, 1968); children: Christopher Stone. *Education:* Attended Antioch College, 1937-40, and Black Mountain College, 1940-43; Wayne State University, B.A., 1947; Putney Graduate School, M.A., 1954; further graduate study at Harvard University, 1960-62; Union Graduate School, Cincinnati, Ohio, Ph.D., 1972. *Home address:* P.O. Box 87, Plainfield, Vt. 05667. *Office:* Goddard College, Plainfield, Vt. 05667.

CAREER: Worked as public relations writer, photographer, and printer; Johnson O'Connor Research Foundation, New York City, in aptitude testing and research, 1943-44; U.S. Air Force, Air Technical Service Command, New York City, civilian public relations writer, 1944-45; Johnson O'Connor Research Foundation, in aptitude testing and research, 1947-48; Goddard College, Plainfield, Vt., member of faculty in literature, education, and psychology, 1948—, director of information, 1950-59, college editor, 1959-66, dean of adult degree program, 1965-70, assistant to president, 1971-73, director of evaluation, 1973-77. Consumer member of district advisory council of Vermont Health Policy Corp., 1977-79.

WRITINGS: (Editor and contributor) *Teacher: School: Child,* Goddard College, 1964; (with Margaret Skutch) *To Start a School,* Little, Brown, 1971; (contributor) Dwight W. Allen and Jeffrey C. Hecht, editors, *Controversies in Education,* Saunders, 1974. Contributor to education journals.

WORK IN PROGRESS: Research on the relationship between children and parents, as seen mainly in nursery or preschool education; research on philosophy of education.

SIDELIGHTS: Hamlin writes: "I hate jargon and sometimes find myself not only drowning in it, but beginning to use it. I am fascinated with the relationship between language structures and the nonverbal world they presume to be about. When I teach literature, the philosophy of education, or psychology—as I sometimes do—this relationship always becomes one focus of the work, and it has also been a focus in work I've done in drama. So my writing is an attempt to build something out of words which will evoke, but also in some sense create, a nonverbal reality."

*　　*　　*

HANENKRAT, Frank (Thomas)   1939-

PERSONAL: Born May 24, 1939, in Appomattox, Va.; son of William Frank and Vara (Conner) Hanenkrat; divorced. *Education:* University of Richmond, B.A., 1961, M.A., 1968; Emory University, Ph.D., 1971. *Agent:* Scott Meredith Literary Agency, Inc., 845 Third Ave., New York, N.Y. 10022. *Office:* Department of English, Lynchburg College, Lynchburg, Va. 24501.

CAREER: Part-time instructor at University of Washington, Seattle; University of Richmond, Richmond, Va., part-time instructor in English, 1962-67; Virginia Commonwealth University, Richmond, part-time instructor in English, 1965-67; University of Georgia, Athens, instructor in English, 1970-71; Lynchburg College, Lynchburg, Va., assistant professor, 1971-74, associate professor of English, 1974—. Freelance photographer. *Military service:* U.S. Army, Infantry, 1963-65; became first lieutenant. *Member:* Authors Guild of Authors League of America, Phi Beta Kappa.

WRITINGS: Position Rifle Shooting, Winchester Press, 1973; *The Education of a Turkey Hunter,* Winchester Press, 1974; *Wildlife Watcher's Handbook,* Winchester Press, 1977. Contributor to magazines, including *American Rifleman, Virginia Wildlife,* and *Shooter's Bible,* and newspapers.

WORK IN PROGRESS: A mystery novel.

SIDELIGHTS: Hanenkrat writes: "I'm interested in the politics and wildlife of southern Africa, and spent two months there in 1979. I would like to return and write a book on the area, if circumstances permit. My current writing tends toward magazine-directed nonfiction and book-length fiction."

*　　*　　*

HANNING, Robert William   1938-

PERSONAL: Born April 21, 1938, in New York, N.Y.; son of Howard B. (a dentist) and Mary (Bavetta) Hanning; married Barbara Russano (a professor of music history), June 15, 1963; children: Biagina, Robert C. *Education:* Columbia University, B.A., 1958, Ph.D., 1964; Oxford University, B.A., 1960, M.A., 1964. *Religion:* Roman Catholic. *Home:* 410 Riverside Dr., New York, N.Y. 10025. *Office:* Department of English and Comparative Literature, Columbia University, 410 Hamilton Hall, New York, N.Y. 10027.

CAREER: Columbia University, New York, N.Y., instructor, 1963-65, assistant professor, 1965-69, associate professor, 1969-71, professor of English, 1971—. Visiting professor at Yale University, 1977, and Johns Hopkins University, 1979. Member of faculty at Bread Loaf School of English, 1974-76, 1978, director of its summer program at Lincoln College, Oxford, 1980. *Member:* Modern Language Association of America, Mediaeval Academy of America, Renaissance Society of America, Society for Study of Mediaeval Languages and Literature. *Awards, honors:* American Council of Learned Societies fellowship, 1966-67; Guggenheim fellowship, 1972-73; National Endowment for the Humanities fellowship, 1979-80.

WRITINGS: The Vision of History in Early Britain: From Gildas to Geoffrey of Monmouth, Columbia University Press, 1966; (contributor) George Economou, editor, *Geoffrey Chaucer: Contemporary Studies in Literature,* McGraw, 1975; (editor with Paul Delany and P. J. Ford) *Sixteenth-Century English Poetry and Prose: A Selective Anthology,* Holt, 1976; (contributor) Aldo Scaglione, editor, *Ariosto 1974 in America,* Longo, 1976; *The Individual in Twelfth-Century Romance,* Yale University Press, 1977; (translator with J. M. Ferrante) *The Lais of Marie de France,* Dutton, 1978; *The Wakefield Master and Contemporaries: Medieval English Cycle Drama,* E. J. Brill, in press. Contributor to academic journals.

WORK IN PROGRESS: Chaucer's Word Games: Language and Society in the Canterbury Tales; (with David Rosand) *The Equivocating Muse: Essays in the Art and Literature of the Renaissance.*

SIDELIGHTS: Hanning wrote: "My study of the Middle Ages and Renaissance aims at exploring the issues in our cultural heritage that help explain our attitudes toward language and society today. Above all I want to communicate to my readers my sense that human problems and decisions are substantially the same in all ages."

*   *   *

HANSEN, Flemming 1938-

PERSONAL: Born July 16, 1938, in Copenhagen, Denmark; son of Arne and Grethe Hansen; married Birgit Hallum Andersen, January 5, 1962; children: Morten, Jan, Karin. *Education:* Copenhagen School of Business Administration and Economics, H.A., 1960, H.D., 1962, Lic.merc., 1967; University of Lund, Ekon.dr., 1972. *Home:* Brodersens Alle 13, Hellerup 2900, Denmark. *Office:* Copenhagen School of Business Administration and Economics, Howitzvej 60, Copenhagen 2000, Denmark.

CAREER: University of New Hampshire, Durham, assistant professor of marketing, 1967-70; T.Bak-Jensen, Denmark, director, 1970-73; president of AIM A/S Institute for Opinion Research, 1973-74; Aalborg University Center, Aalborg, Denmark, professor of economic psychology, 1974-77; Copenhagen School of Business Administration and Economics, Copenhagen, Denmark, professor of economic psychology, 1977—. Chairperson and part owner of board of directors of AIM, A/S Institute for Opinion Research. *Awards, honors:* Danish Business Societies Award for Research in Marketing, 1972; A. C. Nielsen Foundation award, 1967, for Scandinavian marketing.

WRITINGS: Consumer Choice Behavior: A Cognitive Theory, Free Press, 1972; (with J. C. Nielson and M. Nielson) *Marketing Handbog* (title means "Marketing Handbook"), Birsom Forlag, 1977; (with S. R. Christensen and Christian Raon) *Handbog i Marked Analyse* (title means "Handbook in Marketing Research"), Borsens Forlag, 1978; *Maleproblemeri Samtundsvidn Skabene* (title means "Measurement Problems in the Social Sciences"), NYT Nordish Forlag, 1979; *Borns Mediavane* (title means "Children's Use of Information"), Berlingske Tidendes Forlag, 1979. Contributor to marketing journals.

WORK IN PROGRESS: Research on the use of information in low-involvement situations.

SIDELIGHTS: Hansen told *CA:* "Being involved with consumer psychology with a background in economics, I am

concerned with the application of behavioral research in decision processes at various levels of society."

*   *   *

HAPGOOD, Fred 1942-

PERSONAL: Born January 16, 1942, in Washington, D.C.; son of Charles Hutchins and Tamsin (Hughes) Hapgood. *Education:* Harvard University, B.A., 1963. *Home address:* P.O. Box 490, Cambridge, Mass. 02139.

CAREER: Harvard University, News Office, Cambridge, Mass., science reporter, 1978; Sloan Commission on Government and Higher Education, Cambridge, Mass., editor, 1978-79; writer, 1979—.

WRITINGS: Space Shots, New York Times Co., 1979; *Why Males Exist,* Morrow, 1979. Contributor to popular magazines, including *Atlantic.*

WORK IN PROGRESS: Research on the structure and dynamics of ethical intuition, or "common sense."

SIDELIGHTS: Hapgood told *CA:* "The point of writing, at least for me, is to use it as leverage to jimmy one deeper into that small number of dreaded issues which constitute one's life."

*   *   *

HARDEN, (John) William 1903-

PERSONAL: Born August 22, 1903, in Graham, N.C.; son of Peter Ray (a farmer) and Nettie (Abbott) Harden; married Josephine Holt, June 13, 1928 (deceased); married Sarah Plexico (a merchandising consultant), October 15, 1953; children: John William, Jr., Glenn Harden Springer-Miller, Holmes and Mark (twins), Jonathan. *Education:* University of North Carolina, A.B., 1927. *Politics:* Democrat. *Religion:* Episcopalian. *Home:* 2700 Twin Lakes Dr., Greensboro, N.C. 27407. *Office:* John Harden Associates, 1215 West Bessemer Ave., Greensboro, N.C. 27408.

CAREER: Burlington Times-News, Burlington, N.C., staff member, 1922-23; *Raleigh News and Observer,* Raleigh, N.C., staff member, 1923-24; University of North Carolina, News Bureau, Chapel Hill, N.C., staff member, 1924-28; *Charlotte News,* Charlotte, N.C., author of daily column, "Snap Shots," 1928-37; *Salisbury Post,* Salisbury, N.C., author of daily column, "Post Scripts," 1937-44; *Greensboro Daily News,* Greensboro, N.C., author of daily column, "Newsettes," 1944-45; private secretary to North Carolina Governor Gregg Cherry, 1945-48; vice-president and director of public relations, Burlington Industries, 1948-58; John Harden Associates, Greensboro, N.C., owner, 1958—. Aired weekly program, "Tales of Tar Heelia," over WPTF-Radio; served as special assistant to the president, Cannon Mills Co., Kannapolis, N.C. Vice-president of Rowan Printing Co.; member of board of directors of Rowan Corp., Penick Home, Carolina Motor Club (of Automobile Club of America), and Carolina Regional Theatre; member of board of trustees of Crossnore School; member of visitors committee of Guilford College. President of Greensboro Chamber of Commerce.

MEMBER: University of North Carolina General Alumni Association (president), Rotary Club (local president; district governor), Greensboro Country Club, Greensboro City Club, Grandfather Golf and Country Club (member of board of directors), Grandfather Lake Club (president), Linville Golf Club. *Awards, honors:* Public Relations Infinity Award from Public Relations Society (Charlotte, N.C.), 1977.

WRITINGS: Alamance County Economic and Social, University of North Carolina Press, 1927; *The Devil's Tramping Ground and Other North Carolina Ghost Stories,* University of North Carolina Press, 1949; *Tar Heel Ghosts,* University of North Carolina Press, 1954; *North Carolina Roads and Their Builders,* Edwards & Broughton, 1966; *Cannon* (history of Cannon Mills), Cannon Mills, 1979. Contributor to trade journals and popular magazines.

WORK IN PROGRESS: A book on the seventy-five-year history of Boling Co., a furniture manufacturer in Siler City, N.C., publication by Boling Co.

SIDELIGHTS: Harden told *CA* that in *The Devil's Tramping Ground* he adapted some of the stories used on his radio program, "Tales of Tar Heelia." "Most of the stories are old classics," he said. "Some are new. At least one had never before been written. A principal service in this collection lies in the fact that North Carolina's best-known true story mystery classics have, for the first time, been collected together between one set of covers.

"In 1954 the University of North Carolina Press brought out *Tar Heel Ghosts,* a collection of North Carolina ghost stories in which I attempted to bring together the active and hard-working spooks found ghosting across North Carolina. Some of them are delicate, ladylike, and of gentle manner. Others, roister and roughneck. These ghosts have righted wrongs, brought criminals to justice, punished wayward husbands, avenged cruel deeds, and even gotten themselves into court records. Some of the stories have amazing authenticity."

*   *   *

HARDING, William Harry   1945-

PERSONAL: Born September 26, 1945, in Paterson, N.J.; son of Raymond T. (a postal supervisor) and Gaynell (a teacher; maiden name, Zigarelli) Harding. *Education:* Attended Bucknell University, 1962-65; Upsala College, B.A., 1968. *Residence:* Southern California. *Agent:* Curtis Brown Ltd., 575 Madison Ave., New York, N.Y. 10022; and John Johnson Agency, Clerkenwell House, 45/47 Clerkwell Green, London ECIR OHT, England.

CAREER: Writer, 1971—; independent film producer and director, Los Angeles, Calif., 1973-74. Founder of American Ink (nonprofit foundation for the arts); member of board of directors of Harding Enterprises, Inc.; president of WHH Productions, 1973, and of Astroscope, Inc., 1974. *Military service:* U.S. Navy, 1968-74; became lieutenant and naval flight officer; received seventeen air medals and two Navy commendation medals. *Member:* International Platform Association, Lambda Chi Alpha.

WRITINGS: Rainbow (Book-of-the-Month Club featured alternate), Holt, 1979. Contributor of articles to *Los Angeles Times Sunday Book Review* and *Bachy.*

WORK IN PROGRESS: A second novel.

SIDELIGHTS: William Harry Harding told *CA:* "I had the great good fortune to serve an apprenticeship with a gifted working writer, Joseph Hansen. Without his patient help, my learning would have been much slower, my growth as a writer stunted. I don't write about what I know because I know so little. I write to explore and discover. And I try to write honest fiction."

Carolyn See of the *Los Angeles Times* called *Rainbow* "both attractive and enraging. Prodigious research obviously was involved. . . . Only the characters aren't quite real."

A motion picture adaptation of *Rainbow* is scheduled for production by Warner Bros. in 1980 or 1981.

BIOGRAPHICAL/CRITICAL SOURCES: Los Angeles Times Book Review, October 7, 1979.

*   *   *

HARNIK, Bernard   1910-

PERSONAL: Born May 10, 1910, in Nova-Sulita, Austria; son of Mendel (in business) and Rosa (Winkler) Harnik; married Betty Wuescher, September 3, 1939; children: Avo, Gratia-Noelle Harnik-Amadasun. *Education:* Attended medical schools in Vienna, Austria, 1928-29, Leipzig, Germany, 1929, Rostock, Germany, 1929-31, and Berlin, Germany, 1931-32; medical school in Basel, Switzerland, M.D., 1934. *Politics:* Liberal. *Religion:* Reformed Church of Switzerland. *Home and office:* Eidmattstrasse 55, Zurich 8032, Switzerland.

CAREER: Private practice of pediatrics in Bucharest, Rumania, 1936-48; general practice of medicine in Switzerland, 1948-53; marriage and youth counselor for the Reformed Church in St. Gallen, Switzerland, 1953-60, and in private practice in Zurich, Switzerland, 1960—. Leader of church groups for the training of physicians, ministers, teachers, and social workers; lecturer at schools all over the world, including the United States. Past chairperson of Swiss Board of Christian Doctors; vice-president of executive committee of International Congress of Christian Physicians; member of group of physicians for "medicine of the whole person." *Military service:* Rumanian Army, Sanitation Corps, 1930 and 1940-43; became lieutenant. *Member:* Swiss Society of Gynecology and Obstetrics (honorary member), Christian Association of Marriage and Family Counseling (Switzerland; honorary member).

WRITINGS: Risk and Chance in Marriage, Word Books, 1972; (editor and contributor) Paul Tournier, *Medicine of the Whole Person,* Word Books, 1973; *Toward a Healthy Marriage,* Word Books, 1976.

In German: *Zwischen 16 und 25* (title means "Between Sixteen and Twenty-five"), Gotthelf Verlag, 1960; *Erziehung und Selbsterziehung zur Ehe* (title means "Education and Self-Education for Marriage"), Gotthelf Verlag, 1960; *Der Sinn der Sexualitaet* (title means "The Meaning of Sexuality"), Reinhardt, 1961; *Ehekrankheiten: Ihre Behandlung und Vorbeugung aus der Praxis der Eheberatung und Vorberatung* (title means "Marriage Sickness: Treatment and Prevention Seen From the Practice of Marriage and Premarital Counseling"), Gotthelf Verlag, 1961; (contributor) Ernst Sieber, editor, *H. . . S . . . , der Homosexuelle* (title means "H. . . S . . . : The Homosexual"), Gotthelf Verlag, 1964; *Probleme der Jugend: Hilfe zur Selbsterziehung des Jugendlichen* (title means "Youth Problems: Aid for the Self-Education of Young People"), Habegger, 1966; *Freundschaft und Liebe: Kleine Ehe-und Ledigenschule* (title means "Friendship and Love: A Small School of Marriage and Single Life"), Habegger, 1967; *Jugend, Ehe und Familie: Eine Lebenskunde fuer jung und alt* (title means "Youth, Marriage, and Family: A Life Manual for Young and Old"), Habegger, 1967; *Unser Leben: Ein Schatten* (autobiography; title means "Our Life: A Shadow"), Gotthelf Verlag, 1978.

SIDELIGHTS: Harnik has made sound tape recordings in English, including "Conflicts: How to Cope With Them," "How to Mature," and "The Meaning of Person in Light of the Bible," all released by Creative Resources.

Harnik writes: "I have been greatly influenced by the Bible and by the writings of my friend, Dr. Paul Tournier; also by my experience during the Second World War and my emigration to Switzerland. Travels and lecture tours have taken me to the United States, Australia, England, France, Germany, Scandinavia, Japan, Hong Kong, and Thailand. The motivation for my life and my marriage and family counseling is faith in Jesus Christ and love for all people.''

* * *

HARRIS, Aurand   1915-

PERSONAL: Born July 4, 1915, in Jamesport, Mo.; son of George Dowe (a physician) and Myrtle (a teacher; maiden name, Sebastian) Harris. *Education:* University of Kansas City, A.B., 1936; Northwestern University, M.A., 1939; graduate study at Columbia University, 1945-47. *Agent:* Anchorage Press, Box 8067, New Orleans, La. 70182. *Office:* Department of Drama, University of Texas, Austin, Tex. 78712.

CAREER: Teacher of drama at public schools in Gary, Ind., 1939-41; William Woods College, Fulton, Mo., head of drama department, 1942-45; Grace Church School, New York, N.Y., instructor in drama, 1946-77; University of Texas at Austin, lecturer in drama, 1978—. Lecturer at Columbia University Teachers College, summers, 1958-63; lecturer at Western Connecticut State College, summer, 1976. Playwright-in-residence at University of Florida, 1972; playwright-in-residence at Youtheatre in Fort Wayne, Ind., 1979. Director and designer at summer theatres in Cape May, N.J., 1946, Bennington, Vt., 1947, Peaks Island, Me., 1948, and Harwich, Mass., 1963-75. Member of advisory board of Institute for Advanced Studies in Theatre Arts. *Member:* Children's Theatre Association of America. *Awards, honors:* John Golden Award from Columbia University, 1945, for "Circus in the Wind"; Anderson Award from Stanford University, 1948; Marburg Prize from Johns Hopkins University, 1956; Horatio Alger Newsboy Award, 1967, for "Rags to Riches"; Chorpenning Cup from American Theatre Association, 1967, for "continued contributions to the field of children's drama in the writing of superior plays for young audiences"; creative writing fellowship from National Endowment for the Arts, 1976.

WRITINGS—Plays; all juvenile, except as noted: *Once Upon a Clothesline* (four-act; first produced in Fulton, Mo., 1944), Baker, 1945; *Ladies of the Mop* (one-act; adult), Row Peterson, 1945; *The Doughnut Hole* (three-act; adult), Samuel French, 1947; *The Moon Makes Three* (three-act; adult), Samuel French, 1947; *Madam Ada* (three-act; adult), Samuel French, 1948; *Seven League Boots* (three-act; first produced in Cleveland, Ohio, 1947), Baker, 1948; *Circus Day* (three-act; first produced in Seattle, Wash., 1948), Samuel French, 1949, revised edition published as *Circus in the Wind*, 1960; *Pinocchio and the Indians* (three-act; first produced in Seattle, 1949), Samuel French, 1949.

And Never Been Kissed (three-act; adult; adapted from the novel by Sylvia Dee), Samuel French, 1950; *Simple Simon; or, Simon Big-Ears* (three-act; first produced in Washington, D.C., 1952), Children's Theatre Press, 1953; *Buffalo Bill* (three-act; first produced in Seattle, 1953), Children's Theatre Press, 1954; *We Were Young That Year* (three-act; adult), Samuel French, 1954; *The Plain Princess* (three-act; adapted from the book by Phyllis McGinley; first produced in Kalamazoo, Mich., 1954), Children's Theatre Press, 1955; *The Flying Prince* (two-act; first produced in Washington, D.C., 1965), Samuel French, 1958; *Junket: No Dogs Allowed* (three-act; adapted from story by Anne H. White; first produced in Louisville, Ky., 1959), Children's Theatre Press, 1959.

The Brave Little Tailor (three-act; first produced in Charles-

ton, W.Va., 1960), Children's Theatre Press, 1961; *Pocahontas* (two-act; first produced in Birmingham, Ala., 1961), Children's Theatre Press, 1961; *Androcles and the Lion* (two-act; first produced in New York City, 1964), Children's Theatre Press, 1964; *Rags to Riches* (two-act; adapted from stories by Horatio Alger; first produced in Harwich, Mass., 1965), Anchorage Press, 1966; *Pinocchio and the Fire-Eater* (one-act; first produced in Gary, Ind., 1940), McGraw, 1967; *A Doctor in Spite of Himself* (two-act; adapted from a play by Moliere; first produced in New York City, 1966), Anchorage Press, 1968.

The Comical Tragedy or Tragical Comedy of Punch and Judy (two-act; first produced in Atlanta, Ga., 1969), Anchorage Press, 1970; *Just So Stories* (three-act; adapted from stories by Rudyard Kipling; first produced in Tallahassee, Fla., 1971), Anchorage Press, 1971; *Ming Lee and the Magic Tree* (one-act), Samuel French, 1971; *Steal Away Home* (two-act; adapted from the story by Jane Kristof; first produced in Louisville, Ky., 1972), Anchorage Press, 1972; *Peck's Bad Boy* (three-act; adapted from the novel by George Wilbur Peck; first produced in Harwich, Mass., 1973), Anchorage Press, 1974; *Yankee Doodle* (two-act; first produced in Austin, Tex., 1975), Anchorage Press, 1975; *Star Spangled Salute* (two-act; first produced in Harwich, 1975), Anchorage Press, 1975; *Six Plays for Children*, edited by Coleman A. Jennings (contains "Androcles and the Lion," "Rags to Riches," "Punch and Judy," "Steal Away Home," "Peck's Bad Boy," and "Yankee Doodle"), University of Texas Press, 1977; *Robin Goodfellow* (two-act; first produced in Harwich, 1974), Anchorage Press, 1977; *A Toby Show* (three-act; first produced in Austin at University of Texas Theatre, 1978), Anchorage Press, 1978; *Ralph Roister Doister* (one-act; adapted from a play by Nicholas Udel), Baker, 1978; *Cyrano de Bergerac* (one-act; adapted from the play by Edmond Rostand), Baker, 1979; *The Romancers* (one-act; adapted from the play by Edmund Rostand), Baker, 1979; *Candida* (one-act; adapted from the play by George Bernard Shaw), Baker, 1979.

Contributor: Dorothy Schwartz, editor, *Give Them Roots and Wings*, American Theatre Association, 1972; Nellie McCaslin, editors, *Children and Drama*, Longman, 1977, revised edition, 1981.

Work represented in anthologies, including *Twenty Plays for Young People* and *Contemporary Children's Theatre.*

WORK IN PROGRESS: "The Arkansaw Bear," a fantasy play dealing with the theme of death for youth theatre; co-editing an anthology of plays for children, for Doubleday.

SIDELIGHTS: Harris told *CA:* "I write plays for youth theatre because I like theatre, I like children, and I like what children like in the theatre—a good story, interesting characters, visual excitement and beauty, suspense, music, and comedy. In youth theatre there is the freedom to write in any style or use any appropriate dramatic form. There is the challenge of breaking new ground. And there is the reward of the spontaneous applause of a young, critical, and appreciative audience. There is also the practical side. Children's theatre is one area in American drama that is growing both in quality and quantity, which means a present and increasing market for good scripts.

"With the exception of a few professional companies, I think the best children's drama is produced in regional theatres across the nation. There is no 'Little Broadway' for a children's playwright, which is healthy. Instead of being bound by the provincial tastes of a New York Broadway, children's theatre is a part of the varied tastes, demands, and mores of the entire country.

"I am proud to be part of a growing movement in American drama and have no regrets about giving up a promising career of writing for adults. I once suggested to the late Pulitzer Prize-winning playwright William Inge that he write a play for youth theatre. Inge replied, ''I have nothing to say to children.' In the same manner, perhaps I have nothing to say to adults. But happily I do have many stories to 'show and tell' to children.''

Androcles and the Lion has been translated into four languages and has been performed more than six thousand times around the world.

* * *

HARRIS, Janet   1932-1979

OBITUARY NOTICE—See index for *CA* sketch: Born April 17, 1932, in Newark, N.J.; died December 6, 1979, in Freeport, N.Y. Political activist, historian, educator, and writer. A firm opponent of racism, sexism, and war, Harris wrote a number of books on social revolution. Among her publications, which include both adult and juvenile titles, are *The Long Freedom Road: The Civil Rights Story, Students in Revolt, Crisis in Corrections,* and *The Prime of Ms. America.* Obituaries and other sources: *Publishers Weekly,* January 18, 1980.

* * *

HARRIS, John   1916-
(Mark Hebden, Max Hennessy)

PERSONAL: Born October 18, 1916, in Kimberworth, England; son of Ernest Joseph and Helen (Hough) Harris; married Betty Wragg, January 31, 1947; children: Max Richard, Juliet (Mrs. John Dottridge). *Education:* Attended grammar school in England. *Home:* Merston Cottage, Jerusalem Bottom, West Wittering, Sussex, England. *Agent:* Michael Shaw, Curtis Brown, 1 Craven Hill, London W2 3EW, England.

CAREER: Worked as clerk, reporter, cartoonist, sailor, airman, history teacher, and travel courier; full-time writer, 1955—. *Military service:* Merchant Navy, 1938-39. Royal Air Force, 1939-45.

WRITINGS: The Lonely Voyage, Hutchinson, 1951, reprinted, 1975; *Hallelujah Corner,* Hutchinson, 1952, reprinted, 1975; *The Undaunted,* W. Sloane, 1953 (published in England as *The Sea Shall Not Have Them,* Hurst & Blackett, 1953); *The Claws of Mercy,* Hurst & Blackett, 1955; *Close to the Wind,* W. Sloane, 1956 (published in England as *Getaway,* Hurst & Blackett, 1956); *The Sleeping Mountain,* W. Sloane, 1958, simplified edition, Longmans, Green, 1969; *Adventure's End,* W. Sloane, 1959 (published in England as *The Road to the Coast,* Hutchinson, 1959).

Sunset at Sheba, W. Sloane, 1960; *Covenant With Death,* W. Sloane, 1961; *The Spring of Malice,* W. Sloane, 1962; *The Unforgiving Wind,* Hutchinson, 1963, W. Sloane, 1964; *Vardy,* Hutchinson, 1964, W. Sloane, 1965; *The Cross of Lazzaro,* Morrow, 1965; *The Charge of the Light Brigade* (juvenile), M. Parrish, 1965; *The Old Trade of Killing,* Morrow, 1966; *The Wonderful Ice Cream* (juvenile), self-illustrated, Hutchinson, 1966; *The Somme: Death of a Generation,* Hodder & Stoughton, 1966; *The Big Slump,* Hodder & Stoughton, 1967; *Light Cavalry Action,* Morrow, 1967; *The Sword of General Frapp* (juvenile), self-illustrated, Hutchinson, 1967, adapted as juvenile play, Samuel French, 1972; *Sir Sam and the Dragon* (juvenile), Hutchinson, 1968; *Sam and the Kite* (juvenile), Hutchinson, 1968; *Right of Re-*

ply, Coward, 1968; *The Jade Wind,* Doubleday, 1969 (published in England as *The Mercenaries,* Hutchinson, 1969).

The Courtney Entry, Doubleday, 1970; *A Matter of Luck,* Hutchinson, 1971; *The Fledglings* (juvenile), Hutchinson, 1971; *The Mustering of the Hawks,* Hutchinson, 1972; *A Kind of Courage,* Hutchinson, 1972; *The Gallant Six Hundred: A Tragedy of Obsessions,* Mason & Lipscomb, 1973; *The Professionals,* Hutchinson, 1973; *The Indian Mutiny,* Hart-Davis, 1973; *Smiling Willie and the Tiger,* Hutchinson, 1974; *Ride Out the Storm: A Novel of Dunkirk,* Mason, 1975; *Much Sounding of Bugles: The Siege of Chitral, 1895,* Hutchinson, 1975; *A Tale of a Tail,* Hutchinson, 1975; *The Victors* (juvenile), Hutchinson, 1975; *Take or Destory: A Novel of Alamein,* Hutchinson, 1976; *The Interceptors* (juvenile), Hutchinson, 1977; *Army of Shadows,* Hutchinson, 1977; *The Fox From His Lair: A Novel of D-Day,* Hutchinson, 1978; *The Revolutionaries* (juvenile), Hutchinson, 1978; *Corporal Cotton's Little War: A Novel of the Aegean Campaign,* Hutchinson, 1979; *Toll to the Devil,* Hutchinson, in press; *Sea Mysteries,* Methuen, in press. Also author of *Swordpoint,* 1980.

Under pseudonym Mark Hebden: *What Changed Charley Farthing,* Harrap, 1965; *Eyewitness,* Harrap, 1966, Harcourt, 1967; *The Errant Knights,* Harcourt, 1968; *Portrait in a Dusty Frame,* Harrap, 1969, published as *Grave Journey,* Harcourt, 1970; *Mask of Violence,* Harcourt, 1970; (editor) H.N.H. Williamson, *Farewell to the Don,* John Day, 1971; *A Killer for the Chairman,* Harcourt, 1972; *The Dark Side of the Island,* Harcourt, 1973; *A Pride of Dolphins,* M. Joseph, 1974, Harcourt, 1975; *The League of Eighty-Nine,* Hamish Hamilton, 1977; *Death Set to Music,* David & Charles, 1979; *Pel and the Faceless Corpse,* Hamish Hamilton, 1979; *Dunkirk, the Storm of War,* David & Charles, 1980; *Pel Under Pressure,* Hamish Hamilton, 1980.

Under pseudonym Max Hennessy: *The Lion at Sea* (part I of trilogy), Hamish Hamilton, 1977, Atheneum, 1978; *The Dangerous Years* (part II of *The Lion at Sea* trilogy), Atheneum, 1979; *Back to Battle* (part III of *The Lion at Sea* trilogy), Atheneum, 1980; *Soldier of the Queen* (part I of a cavalry trilogy), Atheneum, in press.

WORK IN PROGRESS: A fourth "Pel" book under pseudonym Mark Hebden.

SIDELIGHTS: A prolific writer of adventure stories, John Harris is "adept at making original entertainments out of obsolete military personnel," noted Martin Levin. "His recipe is compounded of crisply plotted adventure, exotic background, and a generous dash of charm—all ingredients *frapped* with the skill of a first-rate story teller."

One of Harris's most popular books was *Light Cavalry Action.* The story concerns British officer Henry Prideaux, who had been honored for leading the last charge of the British horsed cavalry against the Bolsheviks at Dankoi in 1919. Twenty years later, just as Prideaux has a chance at becoming commander of the British Expeditionary Force for World War II, a letter is published accusing Prideaux of not being present when needed at Dankoi. A libel trial ensues and "almost every possible military notion is discussed, explored, turned inside out, as the jury tries to decide whether General (then Colonel) Prideaux was a coward, whether his Light-Brigade-like charge at the Reds was successful, whether he merited the honours which the next 20 years were to bring," stated *Books and Bookmen.*

Harris unfolds the story by means of narrative flashback. During the court testimony, "the author allows the story action to unfold much as if we were replaying the part of the combat of which the witness speaks," explained Eugene J. Linehan. "The device is much like the camera which moves from the spoken testimony to reliving on film the actuality."

Although a *Times Literary Supplement* critic commented that "Harris is unable to convey a sense of time and place and he has little ear for idiom of period and class," he also applauded the author for his "carefully carpentered narrative" and "resourceful plotting." Other critics noted Harris's excellent characterization and skill at keeping the suspense mounting in both the court and the battlefield scenes.

In *Eyewitness,* which was published under the pseudonym Mark Hebden, a young boy known for telling tall tales witnesses an attempt to assassinate Charles de Gaulle. When the killers go after the boy, nobody believes his story. Anthony Boucher remarked that the story "can be summed up in the words 'Wolf! Wolf!' . . . [Harris uses a] simple and predictable story-line, but [with] a good deal of charm and spirit in the telling." The novel was adapted as a motion picture of the same name by Metro-Goldwyn-Mayer in 1970.

Harris told *CA:* "My interests are military history, flying, and bird watching, all of which have been and continue to be covered in my books. I have traveled widely and regularly visit France, which has provided the background for many of my books, including a new series featuring a French detective.

"I started at the age of thirteen writing stark adult books which terrified me as I grew older. They were mostly written during physics lessons at school, which was why I failed in physics. I saw myself then as a well-known and successful author, living in a very pleasant house in the country, with a beautiful wife and beautiful children. That's exactly how it has been.

"As a cartoonist, I was often told by my editor that I had so many ideas they were an "embarrassment of riches,' and that is how it is as an author. I have so many ideas, I shall have to go on writing forever to get even half of them down on paper. It makes up for not being the best writer in the world of prose."

BIOGRAPHICAL/CRITICAL SOURCES: New York Times Book Review, March 26, 1967, May 21, 1967, June 16, 1968, October 5, 1969; *Time,* April 21, 1967; *Books and Bookmen,* May, 1967; *Best Sellers,* May 1, 1967, November 1, 1970; *Times Literary Supplement,* May 25, 1967; *Punch,* November 29, 1967, December 11, 1968; *Christian Science Monitor,* August 22, 1968; *Variety,* January 21, 1970, September 16, 1970, December 30, 1970; *Observer,* September 6, 1970; *Detroit News,* June 4, 1972.

* * *

HARRIS, Robert Dalton 1921-

PERSONAL: Born December 24, 1921, in Jamieson, Ore.; son of Charles S. and Dorothy (Cleveland) Harris; married Ethel Imus Hagen, June 26, 1971. *Education:* Whitman College, B.A., 1951; University of California, Berkeley, M.A., 1953, Ph.D., 1959. *Politics:* Democrat. *Religion:* Methodist. *Home:* 928 East Eighth St., Moscow, Idaho 83843. *Office:* Department of History, University of Idaho, Moscow, Idaho 83843.

CAREER: University of Idaho, Moscow, instructor, 1959-62, assistant professor, 1962-68, associate professor, 1968-74, professor of history, 1974—. *Military service:* U.S. Army Air Forces, 1942-46; served in North Africa, Italy, and the Western Pacific; became captain; received Distinguished Flying Cross and Air Medal with nine oak leaf clusters.

Member: American Historical Association, Society for French Historical Studies.

WRITINGS: Necker: Reform Statesman of the Ancien Regime, University of California Press, 1979. Contributor to history journals.

WORK IN PROGRESS: A sequel to the 1979 book, *Necker and the French Revolution,* publication expected in 1982.

SIDELIGHTS: Harris told *CA:* "It is now almost a truism to say that each generation rewrites the history of the past to suit its own needs and preoccupations. The eighteenth century was certainly one of the most vital periods in the history of European civilization, and it loses nothing of its fascination for succeeding generations. 'The springtime of the modern world,' Carl Becker has described it. It was also the seedtime of our own nation.

"One subject that has always attracted me is the role of France in the formation of the United States. During the bicentennial celebration of our independence in 1976 we frequently heard that France's participation in the war of American independence eventually brought about her own bankruptcy, that it was a principal cause for the French Revolution. Having studied French finances and the ministry of Jacques Necker from 1776 through 1781, I knew that this was not true. For about twelve years, in the time that could be spared from teaching, I had poured over French documents and found that a great many common notions about both Necker and the finances of Louis XVI were flagrantly in error. My first book, published in 1979, attempts a complete rehabilitation of Necker's first ministry.

"I am now working on a second volume which will continue the story of Necker's career through the early years of the French Revolution. I am finding as much rehabilitation to do here as on his first ministry.

"There is some bias today against political history because so much has already been done in the field. Young historians are often advised to pursue some social or cultural topic, especially if it lends itself to present-day quantitative techniques. But when history students ask me if there is any room for more work in political history, I reply: 'If what has been written about Necker is any indication of how political history has been written, then *everything* is to be re-done!'"

* * *

HARRIS, Roy J. 1903(?)-1980

OBITUARY NOTICE: Born c. 1903; died February 21, 1980, in Los Angeles, Calif. Journalist. For Harris's work with others on a series of articles on the Republican administration of Illinois Governor Dwight H. Green, the *St. Louis Post Dispatch* shared a Pulitzer Prize for public service with the *Chicago Daily News.* Through the expose, fifty-one journalists in Illinois were discovered to be on the state payroll. Harris was subsequently involved in the coverage of three additional incidents that brought the newspaper Pulitzer Prizes: the story of the St. Louis election frauds in 1936, the case of poor mining conditions in Centralia, Ill., that resulted in an explosion and took the lives of eleven men in 1947, and the campaign aimed at the problem of smoke pollution in the St. Louis area in 1939-40. Obituaries and other sources: *New York Times,* February 22, 1980.

* * *

HARRIS, Thomas A(nthony) 1913(?)-

PERSONAL: Born c. 1913 in Mineola, Tex. *Education:* Temple University, M.D., 1940. *Office address:* P.O. Box 255039, Sacramento, Calif. 95825.

CAREER: U.S. Navy, 1941-54, became commander; intern at U.S. Navy Hospital, Philadelphia, Pa., 1940-41; resident in psychiatry at St. Elizabeth's Hospital, Washington, D.C., 1942-43, and at Philadelphia Child Guidance Clinic, Philadelphia, 1946-47; fellow at Washington-Baltimore Psychiatric Institute, 1947; chief of neuropsychiatry on U.S.S. *Haven*, at U.S. Navy Hospital, Philadelphia, and at Philadelphia Bureau of Medicine and Surgery, Philadelphia. Director of Department of Institutions of State of Washington, after 1955; former associate professor of child psychiatry at University of Arkansas, Fayetteville; currently president of Institute for Transactional Analysis, Sacramento, Calif. *Member:* International Transactional Analysis Association, American Psychiatric Association (fellow).

WRITINGS: I'm OK—You're OK: A Practical Guide to Transactional Analysis, Harper, 1969 (published in England as *The Book of Choice,* J. Cape, 1969); (author of introduction) Richard Blackstock, *Study Guide for I'm OK—You're OK,* Harper, 1971.

SIDELIGHTS: Harris's *I'm OK—You're OK* is a primer on Transactional Analysis, "one of the most promising breakthroughs in psychiatry in many years." Harris realized the validity of complaints about psychiatry's specialized language, its foggy purpose, its arguable benefits, and saw the potential in Dr. Eric Berne's concept of Transactional Analysis as a practical answer to some of psychiatry's problems. Berne "has created a unified system of individual and social psychiatry that is comprehensive at the theoretical level and effective at the applied level," wrote the author in his preface. His book, then, is "the product of a search to find answers for people who are looking for hard facts in answer to their question about how the mind operates, why we do what we do, and how we can stop doing what we do if we wish."

The key to Transactional Analysis, said Harris, is its vocabulary. "It is the precision toll of treatment because, in a language anyone can understand, it identifies things that really are, the reality of experiences that really happened in the lives of people who really existed." Words such as "Parent," "Adult," and "Child" have special significance for Harris: in his early chapters he defines these three personalities as elements of every individual. Richard Todd explained these personality categories: "the Child, who is a collection of those impressions and emotions we experienced in childhood, predominantly feelings of inferiority; the Parent, who represents the unexamined views, prejudices, and habits of our parents or their surrogates; the Adult, the autonomous creature of reason who is able to mediate among the various claims of the Child and the Parent, to test their fixed ideas against the situation, to be flexible, to change." The book's title refers to the response of the mature adult, at peace with himself and others.

Public enthusiasm over Harris's ideas was evident in the book's popularity. *I'm OK—You're OK* enjoyed months on bestseller lists, selling more than a million hardcover copies.

BIOGRAPHICAL/CRITICAL SOURCES: Life, August 11, 1972, December 29, 1972; *Christian Century,* November 22, 1972; Thomas A. Harris, *I'm OK—You're OK,* Avon, 1973; *Washington Post Book World,* July 15, 1973; *Time,* August 20, 1973; *Atlantic,* November, 1973; *Scholastic Teacher,* Junior/Senior High Teacher's Edition, October, 1974.*

*   *   *

HARRISON, Bernard   1933-

PERSONAL: Born May 29, 1933, in Bristol, England; son of William Bernard (a railway clerk) and Camilla Victoria (Davis) Harrison; married Dorothy White (a teacher of English), July 21, 1956; children: Eva, Katherine, David. *Education:* University of Birmingham, B.Sc., 1954, B.A., 1956, M.A., 1957; University of Michigan, Ph.D., 1961. *Home:* The Old Anchor, South St., Lewes, Sussex, England. *Agent:* Curtis Brown Ltd., 1 Craven Hill, London W2 3EW, England. *Office:* School of English and American Studies, University of Sussex, Arts Building, Falmer, Brighton, Sussex BN1 9QN, England.

CAREER: University of Toronto, Toronto, Ontario, lecturer in philosophy, 1960-62; University of Birmingham, Birmingham, England, assistant lecturer in philosophy, 1962-63; University of Sussex, Brighton, England, lecturer, 1963-71, reader in philosophy, 1971—. Associate professor at University of Cincinnati, 1967-68; visiting professor at University of Western Australia, 1978. Fellow of Humanities Research Center at Australian National University, 1976. *Awards, honors:* Fulbright senior scholar, 1967-68; essay prize from American Council for Philosophical Studies, 1969, for "Violence and the Rules of Law"; Leverhulme fellow, 1976-77.

WRITINGS: (With Robert Andi, Robert L. Holmes, and Ronald B. Miller) *Violence* (philosophical essays), McKay, 1971; *Meaning and Structure: An Essay in the Philosophy of Language,* Harper, 1972; *Form and Content,* Basil Blackwell, 1973; *Fielding's "Tom Jones": The Novelist as Moral Philosopher,* Chatto & Windus, 1975; (contributor) Gabriel Josipovici, editor, *The Modern English Novel,* Open Books, 1976; *An Introduction to the Philosophy of Language,* Macmillan, 1979. Contributor to philosophy journals.

WORK IN PROGRESS: A book on the analytical tradition in philosophy, publication by Methuen expected in 1981; a book on the concept of sense, 1983; a collection of literary-critical essays on the relationship of literature to reality, 1984.

SIDELIGHTS: Harrison writes: "Over the last decade I have come to write both as a philosopher and as a literary critic. The two activities are radically distinct, the particular kinds of analytic rigour required in philosophy being unnecessary to, and on the whole destructive to, good criticism, and the particular kinds of perceptiveness required in good criticism being unnecessary to, and on the whole destructive to, good philosophy. Nevertheless the subject matter of the two disciplines is intimately interwoven and connected beneath the surface; and I think there are advantages to be gained from allowing both modes of response to hold sway simultaneously in a single mind."

*   *   *

HARRISON, David L(ee)   1937-
(Kennon Graham)

PERSONAL: Born March 13, 1937, in Springfield, Mo.; son of John A. (in business) and L. Neva (Justice) Harrison; married Sandra Kennon (a high school counselor), May 23, 1959; children: Robin L., Jeffrey S. *Education:* Drury College, A.B., 1959; Emory University, M.S., 1960; also attended Evansville College (now University of Evansville), 1960-63. *Home:* 4214 Cherry, Springfield, Mo. 65804. *Office:* Glenstone Block Co., 928 South Glenstone, Springfield, Mo. 65802.

CAREER: Mead Johnson Co. (pharmaceutical company), Evansville, Ind., pharmacologist, 1960-63; Hallmark Cards, Inc., Kansas City, Mo., began as editor of juvenile greeting cards, became editorial manager and administrative head of editorial division's greeting card departments, 1963-73; Glenstone Block Co., Springfield, Mo., owner and president, 1973—. Gives readings and lectures; greeting card consultant. *Awards, honors:* Juvenile writing fellowship from Bobbs-Merrill Co., 1964; award from *Writer's Digest* short-short story competition, 1968, for "The Gate"; Christopher Award, 1973, for *The Book of Giant Stories;* award from Central Missouri State University, 1978.

WRITINGS—All juveniles: *The Boy With a Drum*, Golden Press, 1969; *Little Turtle's Big Adventure*, Random House, 1969; *The Little Boy in the Forest*, Whitman Publishing, 1969; *About Me*, Childcraft Education Corp., 1969; *The World of American Caves*, Reilly & Lee, 1970; *The Case of Og the Missing Frog*, Rand McNally, 1972; (with Mary Loberg) *The Backyard Zoo*, Hallmark, 1972; (with Loberg) *The Kingdom of the Sea*, Hallmark, 1972; (with Loberg) *The World of Horses*, Hallmark, 1972; (with Loberg) *The Terrible Lizards*, Hallmark, 1972; *The Book of Giant Stories*, McGraw, 1972; *The Little Boy and the Giant*, Golden Press, 1973; *Let's Go Trucks!*, Golden Press, 1973; *Children Everywhere*, Rand McNally, 1973; *Piggy Wiglet and the Great Adventure*, Golden Press, 1973; *The Huffin Puff Express*, Whitman Publishing, 1974; *The Busy Body Book*, Whitman Publishing, 1975; *Monster! Monster!*, Golden Press, 1975; *The Pink Panther in Z-Land*, Whitman Publishing, 1976; *The Circus Is in Town*, Golden Press, 1978.

Under pseudonym Kennon Graham: *Smokey Bear Saves the Forest*, Whitman Publishing, 1971; *Lassie and the Big Clean-Up Day*, Golden Press, 1971; *Eloise and the Old Blue Truck*, Whitman Publishing, 1971; *Lassie and the Secret Friend*, Golden Press, 1972; *My Little Book of Cars and Trucks*, Whitman Publishing, 1973; *Woodsy Owl and the Trail Bikers*, Golden Press, 1974; *Land of the Lost: Surprise Guests*, Golden Press, 1975; *The Pink Panther in the Haunted House*, Golden Press, 1975; *The Pink Panther Rides Again*, Whitman Publishing, 1976; (with others) *The Witch Book*, edited by Dorothy F. Haas, Rand McNally, 1976; *My Little Book About Flying*, Whitman Publishing, 1978.

Editor; all published by Hallmark: *Peter Pan*, 1964; *Cinderella*, 1964; *Pinnochio*, 1964; *The Adventures of Doctor Dolittle*, 1965; *A Christmas Carol*, 1965; *The Three Pigs*, 1966; *Goldilocks and the Three Bears*, 1966. Also editor of numerous other books for Hallmark.

Contributor to magazines, including *Family Circle* and *Highlights for Children*.

WORK IN PROGRESS—All juveniles; all under name David L. Harrison: A question and answer book, publication by Rand McNally expected in 1980; a new collection of giant stories, publication by McGraw expected in 1981; a teenage adventure novel set in eleventh-century England, completion expected in 1982; a book of poems, completion expected in 1982; a book of farmer stories; a teenage adventure novel set in South America.

SIDELIGHTS: Harrison's stories have been included in school textbooks; his books have been distributed by Weekly Reader Book Club, Book-of-the-Month Club, and Best Book Club Ever, and have been translated into German, Japanese, Italian, Afrikaans, Norwegian, and French. His works have been read on national television and have been videotaped for public television.

Harrison told *CA:* "I wrote my first poetry before my sixth birthday and illustrated my own comic books at eight, but I didn't recognize any special need to write until I was in college.

"As a boy I collected butterflies, snakes, fossils, skulls, arrowheads, minerals, bird wings, stamps, and coins. I played (and later taught) trombone, was an amateur taxidermist and spelunker, and earned summer money as a musician, assistant to an entomologist, pet shop flunky, and clean-up man in a bakery. I also operated a jackhammer, poured concrete, and unloaded boxcars.

"I've traveled to Mexico, Canada, the Virgin Islands, England, and Wales. The trip to England/Wales was to research the eleventh-century novel in progress.

"In a picture book, every word must count; every sentence must be stout enough to bear the weight of endless readings without caving in. Few forms of expression are read aloud more often (during a brief span) than a favorite picture book. The writer must therefore reach out at once both to the child listening and to the adult reading his work.

"Too few men spend enough time in this field to learn it and contribute to it. The stories of our youth may play a significant role in shaping our tastes, preferences, even ideals, as adults. More men should add their voices to those who speak to each generation's developing imagination."

*   *   *

HARSENT, David 1942-

PERSONAL: Born December 9, 1942, in Devonshire, England; married; children: Ysanne, Simon, Barnaby. *Education:* Educated in England. *Residence:* London, England. *Office:* Andre Deutsch, 105 Great Russell St., London WC1B 3LJ England.

CAREER: Poet. Bookseller in Aylesbury, Buckinghamshire, England; worked for Eyre Methuen (publisher); Arrow Books, London, England, editorial director, 1977-79; Andre Deutsch (publisher), London, editor-in-chief and director, 1979—. *Awards, honors:* Gregory Award, 1967, for *A Violent Country;* first prize from Cheltenham Festival of Literature, 1968, for poem "Legendry"; poetry bursary from Arts Council of Great Britain, 1970; Geoffrey Faber Memorial Award, 1978, for *Dreams of the Dead.*

WRITINGS—Poetry: *Tonight's Lover*, The Review, 1968; *A Violent Country*, Oxford University Press, 1969; *Ashridge*, Sycamore Press, 1970; *After Dark*, Oxford University Press, 1973; *Truce*, Sycamore Press, 1973; *Dreams of the Dead*, Oxford University Press, 1977. Fiction critic for *Times Literary Supplement*, 1965-73; poetry critic for *Spectator*, 1970-73; contributor of reviews and critical essays to periodicals, including *New Statesman*, *Agenda*, and *New Review*.

WORK IN PROGRESS: "A poem sequence which continues the theme explored in the 'Punch' poems in *Dreams of the Dead*"; short stories.

SIDELIGHTS: Though Harsent's poetry often describes a world of madness, violence, and death, it also allows for softer reflections and the hope of love. Whether evoking violence or love, critics have remarked on the strength of the poet's precise imagery: in "The Woman and the Cat" he records the eyes of a cat cracking "like a trodden grape" under the wheels of a car; but the poem "Acid Landscapes" considers how lovers might lie awake "breathing each other's breath / and feeling the island slipping with the tides." As Alan Brownjohn claimed in the *New Statesman*, Harsent's is "an honest voice, sparing with its effects, and meticulous in its ordering of resonant detail."

Other general critical comments include an early observation made by the *Virginia Quarterly Review:* "Certainly his work, operating always in the sparest economy, stands with the best of his contemporaries." In 1978, Craig Raine of the

New Statesman held that Harsent's *Dreams of the Dead* "is crammed with ... powerful images ... focused to a hard edge and convincingly lucid in their enigmatic contexts.... [His] world is reminiscent of early Auden: there is the same precision, the same vague menace." And a reviewer for the *Times Literary Supplement* wrote: "The characteristic atmosphere of his poems derives from the contrast between their musical exactness of measure and the uncharted menacing territory it is their business to explore. He is a writer of extreme assurance and precision; poem after poem sounds irresistably right, its rhythmic and sensuous components perfectly interlocking.... One of our most gifted younger poets."

AVOCATIONAL INTERESTS: "I like to ride horses and to shoot (though not simultaneously)."

BIOGRAPHICAL/CRITICAL SOURCES: Times Literary Supplement, May 22, 1969, January 11, 1974, December 30, 1977; *New Statesman,* May 30, 1969, March 6, 1970, January 4, 1974, February 10, 1978; *Observer,* June 22, 1969, December 30, 1973, December 18, 1977, January 15, 1978; *Listener,* August 28, 1969; *Virginia Quarterly Review,* spring, 1970; *Poetry,* May, 1971; *Encounter,* February, 1974.

*   *   *

HARSH, George   1908(?)-1980

OBITUARY NOTICE: Born c. 1908; died January 25, 1980, in Toronto, Ontario, Canada. Convicted murderer, war hero, and author. Imprisoned for the "thrill killing" of a drugstore clerk, Harsh served eleven years of his sentence before being paroled in 1940 for saving the life of a fellow convict with an emergency appendectomy. He then joined the Royal Canadian Air Force in World War II and was captured by the German Army. While at a prisoner-of-war camp, Harsh helped plan the escape of 126 Allied soldiers, 80 of whom eventually made it to safety. These experiences served as the basis of the film, "The Great Escape." His autobiography, *Lonesome Road,* was published in 1971. Obituaries and other sources: *Newsweek,* February 11, 1980; *Time,* February 11, 1980.

*   *   *

HART, Archibald D(aniel)   1932-

PERSONAL: Born April 27, 1932, in Kimberly, South Africa; came to the United States in 1973; son of Daniel H. (a builder) and Gertrude (Smith) Hart; married Kathleen Armstrong (a public relations director), December 4, 1954; children: Kathryn, Sharon, Sylvia. *Education:* Institution of Civil Engineers, London, England, degree in civil engineering, 1955; University of Natal, M.Sc., 1967, Ph.D., 1969. *Religion:* Presbyterian. *Home:* 1042 Cyrus, Arcadia, Calif. 91006. *Office:* 177 North Madison Ave., Pasadena, Calif. 91101.

CAREER: Civil engineer in Pietermeritzberg, South Africa, 1955-65; clinical psychologist in Pietermeritzberg, 1965-72; Graduate School of Psychology, Fuller Theological Seminary, Pasadena, Calif., assistant professor, 1973-75, associate professor of psychology, 1975—. *Member:* American Psychological Association, American Electroencephalographic Society, California Psychological Association, Biofeedback Society of California (president, 1980—). *Awards, honors:* C. W. Weyerhauser Award from Fuller Theological Seminary, 1977, for faculty excellence.

WRITINGS: Feeling Free, Revell, 1979; *Stress and the Christian,* Revell, 1981. Contributor to scientific journals.

WORK IN PROGRESS: Techniques of Biofeedback, completion expected in 1981; *The Mental Health of the Minister,* for Eerdmans; research on brain stem-evoked potentials and biofeedback.

SIDELIGHTS: Hart told *CA:* "I am particularly interested in the integration of psychology and Christian theology. Much research and writing is directed at establishing a relationship between mental health and faith.

"The current state of theology as it is preached in Protestant churches leaves much to be desired. Rather than alleviating guilt, it often provokes increased guilt tendencies. Rather than furthering brotherly love and forgiveness, it often breeds judgmental behavior and criticism. As a Christian psychologist, I find this a challenging situation to write about. One way of addressing the problem is to write directly for ministers—which is my next major work. It is a topic I teach in the seminary associated with the Fuller Graduate School of Psychology."

*   *   *

HART, George L. III   1942-

PERSONAL: Born September 28, 1942, in Washington, D.C.; son of George L., Jr. (a judge) and Louise (Neller) Hart; married Kausalya Shenbagam (a lecturer), November 12, 1966; children: Alexander. *Education:* Harvard University, B.A., 1964, M.A., 1968, Ph.D., 1969. *Home:* 1915 Napa Ave., Berkeley, Calif. 94707. *Office:* Department of South Asian Studies, University of California, Berkeley, Calif. 94720.

CAREER: University of Wisconsin, Madison, assistant professor, 1969-74, associate professor of South Asian studies, 1974-75; currently associate professor of South Asian studies at University of California, Berkeley. *Member:* Association of Asian Studies, American Oriental Society.

WRITINGS: A Rapid Sanskrit Method, Department of South Asian Studies, University of Wisconsin, Madison, 1972; *A Tamil Printer,* Department of South Asian Studies, University of Wisconsin, Madison, 1974; *The Poems of Ancient Tamil,* University of California Press, 1975; *Poets of the Tamil Anthologies,* Princeton University Press, 1979.

*   *   *

HARVEY, John Robert   1942-

PERSONAL: Born June 25, 1942, in Bishops Stortford, England; son of Eric William Spurrier (in nursery business) and Muriel (Bigg) Harvey; married Julietta Chloe Papadopoulou (a university teacher), September 1, 1968; children: Ekaterini. *Education:* Magdalene College, Cambridge, B.A. (with first class honors), 1964, M.A., 1967, Ph.D., 1969. *Home:* 30 Alpha Rd., Cambridge, England. *Office:* Department of English, Emmanuel College, Cambridge University, Cambridge, England.

CAREER: Cambridge University, Cambridge, England, fellow of Emmanuel College, 1967—, lecturer in English, 1974—. Artist and printmaker, with exhibitions in the Cambridge area. *Awards, honors:* David Higham Prize, 1979, for *The Plate Shop.*

WRITINGS: Victorian Novelists and Their Illustrators, Sidgwick & Jackson, 1970; *The Plate Shop* (novel), Collins, 1979. Contributor to magazines, including *Cambridge Review, Delta, Encounter,* and *Listener.* Editor of *Cambridge Quarterly.*

WORK IN PROGRESS: A novel about Greece during the

period of the Colonel's Junta, publication by Collins expected in 1981.

SIDELIGHTS: In discussing his first novel, *The Plate Shop,* John Harvey told *CA:* "There have been factories in England for two hundred years, but they haven't appeared much in fiction. Even when a novel is supposed to be about industrial life, the factory itself is usually only a backdrop to, for instance, a worker's affair with the boss's wife. It seemed to me that fiction should not be so shy of the place where most people spend most of their lives. In *The Plate Shop* I have tried to give a direct picture of life *inside* the factory."

"This is an uncomfortable book," assessed one reviewer, "and not always easy to read, but Mr. Harvey has a powerful style, a strong visual sense, and an impressive understanding of men who have a right to survive." *The Plate Shop* revolves around Edward Clyde, aging foreman in the factory, a man firmly rooted in days gone by. He is skeptical of the new ideas and modern machinery that surround him. Spanning two days, the novel is packed with action: a strike by the workers, a death from heat-stroke, accidents with equipment, the "sacking" of employees, and the ultimate rebellion and take-over of the plant. While Thomas Hinde found it difficult to accept that these events could have happened within only thirty-six hours when they were "more likely to occur over months or years," John Mellors had only praises for the author's style: "John Harvey has something of Zola's ability to describe physical work so that you can almost hear 'the beating iron heart' of the workshop and see across the floor the acid-blue flames of the profile burner."

Chosen by the *Observer* as one of the best books of 1979, reviewer Hermione Lee summarized that *The Plate Shop* is "precise, subtle, authoritative and unexpectedly exciting."

AVOCATIONAL INTERESTS: Travel in Greece.

BIOGRAPHICAL/CRITICAL SOURCES: Listener, March 15, 1979; *London Sunday Telegraph,* March 18, 1979; *London Daily Telegraph,* March 23, 1979; *Observer,* March 25, 1979, December 9, 1979; *Guardian,* April 12, 1979; *Cambridge Evening News,* April 19, 1979; *London Morning Star,* April 19, 1979; *London Tribune,* April 20, 1979; *London Times,* November 24, 1979; *London Sunday Times,* December 9, 1979.

* * *

HARWARD, Donald W. 1939-

PERSONAL: Born December 1, 1939, in Baltimore, Md.; son of Stewart McFadden (a banker) and Lucille (West) Harward: married Ann M. McIlhenny (a university project coordinator), August 26, 1961; children: Sharon West, Brian McIlhenny. *Education:* Maryville College, Maryville, Tenn., B.A., 1961; American University, M.A., 1963; University of Maryland, Ph.D., 1968. *Home:* 209 Winslow Rd., Newark, Del. 19711. *Office:* Honors Program, University of Delaware, Newark, Del. 19711.

CAREER: In departments of philosophy at State University of New York College at Geneseo and Millikin University, Decatur, Ill., 1963-69; University of Delaware, Newark, currently associate professor of philosophy, named H. Fletcher Brown Professor of Humanities, 1972-73, head of department of philosophy, 1970-74, director of honors program. *Member:* National Forum for Philosophical Reasoning in the Schools (member of board of directors, 1975—), American Philosophical Association, American Association of University Professors, Omicron Delta Kappa.

WRITINGS: (Editor and author of introduction) *The Crisis in Confidence,* Little, Brown, 1974; *Wittgenstein's Saying and Showing Theories,* Bouvier, 1976; (contributor) *Wittgenstein and His Impact on Contemporary Thought,* Hoelder, 1978; (editor and author of introduction) *The Nature of Power,* Schenkman & Hall, 1979. Member of advisory board of "Philosophical Monographs." Contributor of articles and reviews to philosophy journals. Member of editorial board of *Journal of Pre-College Philosophy,* 1975—.

* * *

HASSEL, Sven 1917-

PERSONAL: Took mother's maiden surname as own surname; born April 19, 1917, in Fredriksborg, Denmark; son of Peder Oluf and Hansigne (Hassel) Pedersen; married Dorthe Jensen, January 6, 1951; children: Michael. *Education:* Attended military academy in Berlin, Germany. *Politics:* Democrat. *Religion:* Protestant. *Home:* Avda. Pau Casals 17, Barcelona 21 Spain.

CAREER: Danish Merchant Navy, shipboy, 1931-36; Mercedes Benz, Copenhagen, Denmark, production chief, 1949-51; Free Port of Copenhagen, shipping manager, 1951-55; writer, 1955—. *Military service:* German Army, Panzer Regiment, 1936-45, prisoner of war, 1945-49; became first lieutenant; received Iron Cross first and second class, Gold Medal, Finnish Mannerheim Cross, and Italian Military Cross. German Tank Corps, reserve officer, 1970.

WRITINGS—Novels: De fordomtes legion, Grafisk Forlag, 1953, translation by Maurice Michael published as *The Legion of the Damned,* Farrar, Straus, 1957; *Doden pa larvefodder,* Grafisk Forlag, 1958, translation by I. O'Hanlon published as *Wheels of Terror,* Souvenir Press, 1960, Fawcett, 1965.

Frontkammerater, Grafisk Forlag, 1960, translation by Sverre Lyngstad published as *Comrades of War,* Fawcett, 1963; *Marchbattailion,* Grafisk Forlag, 1962, translation by Jean Ure published as *Marchbattalion,* Transworld, 1970; *Gestapo,* Grafisk Forlag, 1963, translation by Ure published as *Assignment Gestapo,* Bantam, 1972; *Monte Cassino,* Bellum, 1965, translation by Michael published as *Beast-Regiment,* Bantam, 1973 (published in England as *Monte Cassino,* Transworld, 1973); *Likvider Paris!,* Bellum, 1967, translation by Ure published as *Liquidate Paris,* Transworld, 1974; *SS-generalen,* Bellum, 1969, translation by Ure published as *SS-General,* Bantam, 1972.

Kommando Reichsfuehrer Himmler, Bellum, 1971, translation by Ure published as *Reign of Hell,* Transworld, 1975; *Jegsa dem do,* Bellum, 1973, translation by Tim Bowie published as *Blitzfreeze,* Transworld, 1975; *Glemt af Gud,* Bellum, 1975, translation by Bowie published as *The Bloody Road to Hell,* Transworld, 1977; *Krigsret,* Bellum, 1978, translation by Bowie published as *Court Martial,* Transworld, 1979; *Kampvognen,* Bellum, in press.

WORK IN PROGRESS: The Tank, translation of *Kampvognen,* publication by Transworld, expected in 1982.

SIDELIGHTS: Hassel writes: "I was born in a small village in Denmark and grew up in a typical Danish working class family. At fourteen I embarked in the merchant navy. In 1936 I joined the German Army as a volunteer, because of the great unemployment in Denmark. I fought on all fronts, including the North of Africa, was wounded eight times, and was a prisoner of war in Russian, American, French, and Danish prison camps. In 1957 I was attacked by Caucasian fever, a sickness caught in the war, provoking total paralysis. I was not cured until 1959. Since 1964 I have lived in Barcelona.

"My books have been translated into eighteen languages, published in more than fifty countries, and have sold about forty million copies all over the world. The same characters appear in all my books: Porta, Tiny, the Little Legionnaire, the Old 'Un, Heide, Gregor Martin, Colonel Hinka, and myself. Of these real people only Tiny, the Legionnaire, and I are alive.

"My books are strictly antimilitary. They correspond to my personal view of what I experienced. I write to warn the youth of today against war. I am writing the story of the small soldiers, the men, who neither plan nor cause wars, but have to fight them. War is the last arm of bad politicians."

*   *   *

HATCH, Robert McConnell 1910-

PERSONAL: Born July 6, 1910, in Brooklyn, N.Y.; son of William Henry Paine and Marion Louise (Townsend) Hatch; married Helen Crocker Addison, June 15, 1940; children: Martha Addison, Louise Townsend. *Education:* Harvard University, A.B., 1933; Columbia University, A.M., 1935; Episcopal Theological School, Cambridge, Mass., B.D., 1939. *Home address:* P.O. Box 302, Gorham, N.H. 03581.

CAREER: Ordained minister of Protestant Episcopal Church, 1939; curate of Episcopal church in Boston, Mass., 1939-41, rector in Arlington, Mass., 1941-45; dean of Episcopal cathedral in Wilmington, Del., 1945-48; rector of Episcopal church in Waterbury, Conn., 1948-51; suffragan suffragan of Connecticut in Hartford, 1951-57; Episcopal bishop of western Massachusetts in Springfield, 1957-70; writer, 1970—. *Member:* Company of Military Historians, Massachusetts Historical Society, New Hampshire Historical Society, Arnold Expedition Historical Society. *Awards, honors:* D.D. from Trinity College, Hartford, Conn., 1951; S.T.D. from Berkeley Divinity School, 1951; Litt.D. from Norwich University, 1963.

WRITINGS: Thrust for Canada, Houghton, 1979. Author of pamphlets. Contributor to religious magazines.

SIDELIGHTS: Hatch commented: "My book describes the American invasion of Canada at the start of the revolution. Two armies, one led by General Richard Montgomery, the other by Benedict Arnold, converged on Quebec and attacked the city during a snowstorm on the night of December 31, 1775. It was a desperate, if valiant, attempt, and it ended in overwhelming defeat. The Americans continued to lay siege to the city throughout the harsh Canadian winter but were driven back to Lake Champlain when heavy British reinforcements arrived in the spring of 1776. The book gives a detailed description of Arnold's famous march through the Maine woods, of Montgomery's advance by way of Lake Champlain and the capture of Montreal, and of the battle of Valcour Island in the fall of 1776, whereby a British invasion of the United States was forestalled until the following year. It is a story of brave hopes and faulty planning, rarely given its proper emphasis in most histories of the Revolution.

"I chose this subject because of my familiarity with the terrain involved and my interest in the enigmatic Benedict Arnold, who had a genius for leadership as well as his darker side."

*   *   *

HATCHER, Robert Anthony 1937-

PERSONAL: Born June 2, 1937, in New York, N.Y.; son of Robert Lee (an economist) and Meta (Lieber) Hatcher; married Carolyn Jean Boyd; children: Robert Lee, Peter Woolverton, Carrie-Anne. *Education:* Attended Williams College, 1955-59; Cornell University, M.D., 1963; University of California, Berkeley, M.P.H., 1973. *Religion:* Episcopalian. *Home:* 3246 Cochise Dr. N.W., Atlanta, Ga. 30339. *Office:* Family Planning Program, Emory University, 69 Butler St. S.E., Atlanta, Ga. 30303.

CAREER: Grady Memorial Hospital, Atlanta, Ga., intern, 1963-64, resident in pediatrics, 1964-66; Emory University, Atlanta, Ga., associate professor of obstetrics and gynecology, 1968—, director of Emory University-Grady Memorial Hospital family planning program, 1968—. Chairperson of Atlanta Area Family Planning Council, 1969-71, 1975-77; member of Georgia Governor's Citizens Environmental Council, 1971-72. *Military service:* U.S. Public Health Service, Epidemic Intelligence Service, 1966-68.

MEMBER: American Public Health Association, American Association of Planned Parenthood Physicians, National Association for the Repeal of Abortion Laws (member of board of directors, 1969—), Planned Parenthood Federation of America (member of board of directors, 1971), Georgia Conservancy, Planned Parenthood Association of Atlanta (member of board of directors, 1966-72), Atlanta Chamber of Commerce, Phi Beta Kappa. *Awards, honors:* New England heavyweight wrestling champion, 1958-59.

WRITINGS: The People Problem (pamphlet), Atlanta Constitution, 1968; (contributor) Mary Calderone, editor, *Manual of Contraception,* 2nd edition (Hatcher was not included in 1st edition), Williams & Wilkins, 1970; (with Gary K. Stewart) *Contraceptive Technology,* Family Planning Program, Emory University, 1971, 10th revised edition, Irvington Books, 1979; (with T. J. Trussell) *Women in Need,* Macmillan, 1972; (with J. S. Terry and P. Galle) *Case Histories in Family Planning, 1972,* Family Planning Program, Emory University, 1972; (with W. B. Beck and others) *Case Histories in Family Planning, 1976,* Family Planning Program, Emory University, 1976; *My Body, My Health,* Wiley, 1979. Contributor of about eighty-five articles to medical journals and local newspapers.

AVOCATIONAL INTERESTS: Gardening, tennis.

*   *   *

HATLO, Jimmy 1898-1963

OBITUARY NOTICE: Born September 1, 1898, in Providence, R.I.; died November 30, 1963. Cartoonist. Creator of the "They'll Do It Every Time" and "Little Iodine" series, Hatlo began his career as a sports and editorial cartoonist for the *Los Angeles Times.* He subsequently spent fifteen years with the Hearst newspaper chain as an editorial cartoonist. Hatlo's works were syndicated in the United States and abroad. Obituaries and other sources: *New York Times,* December 2, 1963; *Time,* December 13, 1963; *Newsweek,* December 16, 1963.

*   *   *

HAUGLAND, Vern(on Arnold) 1908-

PERSONAL: Surname is pronounced *Hoag*-land; born May 27, 1908, in Litchfield, Minn.; son of Olaus Olson (a rancher) and Hannah (Blom) Haugland; married Tesson Courtney McMahon, June 3, 1944; children: Taya Theresa, Marcia Maria (Mrs. Hathaway Watson III). *Education:* Attended University of Washington, Seattle, 1927-29; University of Montana, B.A.J., 1931. *Religion:* Roman Catholic. *Home:* 702 Camino de los Mares, San Clemente, Calif. 92672.

CAREER: Reporter for *Daily Missoulian*, 1931-33; *Montana Standard*, Butte, reporter, 1933-36; Associated Press, reporter in Salt Lake City, Utah, 1936-38, and Los Angeles, Calif., 1938-41, war correspondent in the South Pacific and Southeast Asia, 1941-45, reporter on the Indonesian War in Java, 1945-46, reporter in Washington, D.C., 1947-73, aviation editor, 1952-73; free-lance writer, 1973—. *Member:* Aviation Writers Association (national president, 1955-56), Aviation-Space Writers Association, National Press Club, Sigma Delta Chi. *Awards, honors:* Silver Star from U.S. Army, 1942, for civilian war correspondence; medal of valor from Headliners Club, 1942, for reporting in New Guinea, and 1945 for reporting in Okinawa; Lauren D. Lyman Award from Aviation-Space Writers Association, 1976, for outstanding achievement in aviation writing.

WRITINGS: Letter From New Guinea, Farrar & Rinehart, 1943; *The A.A.F. Against Japan*, Harper, 1948; *The Eagle Squadrons: Yanks in the R.A.F., 1940-1942*, Ziff-Davis, 1979. Contributor to aviation and military journals.

WORK IN PROGRESS: Research for another book on the Eagle Squadrons, for Ziff-Davis.

BIOGRAPHICAL/CRITICAL SOURCES: Air California, June, 1977.

*   *   *

HAYEK, Friedrich August von   1899-

PERSONAL: Born May 8, 1899, in Vienna, Austria; naturalized British citizen, 1938; son of August (a physician and educator) and Felizitas (von Juraschek) von Hayek; married Helene von Fritsch, 1926 (marriage ended); married Helene Bitterlich, 1950; children: (first marriage) Christine, Laurence. *Education:* University of Vienna, Dr. Jur., 1921, Dr.Sc.Pol., 1923; graduate study at New York University, 1923-24. *Home:* Urachstrasse 27, D-7800, Freiburg in Breisgau, Federal Republic of Germany. *Office:* University of Freiburg, D-7800, Kozzegiengebaude II, Federal Republic of Germany.

CAREER: Employed with Austrian Civil Service, 1921-26; Austrian Institute for Economic Research, Vienna, director, 1927-31; University of Vienna, Vienna, lecturer in economics and statistics, 1929-31; University of London, London, England, Tooke Professor of Economic Sciences and Statistics, 1931-50; University of Chicago, Chicago, Ill., professor of social and moral sciences, 1950-62; University of Freiburg, Freiburg, West Germany, professor of economics, 1962-69, professor emeritus, 1969—. Visiting professor at University of Salzburg, Salzburg, Austria, 1970-77. *Member:* British Academy (fellow), Austrian Academy of Science (honorary fellow), Academia Sinaica (honorary fellow). *Awards, honors:* D.Sc. from University of London, 1941; Dr.Jur.Hon.C. from University of Rikkyo, Tokyo, 1964; Nobel Prize for economic science, 1974.

WRITINGS: Geldtheorie und Konjunkturtheorie, Hoelder-Pichler-Tempsky, 1929, translation by N. Kaldor and H. M. Cromme published as *Monetary Theory and the Trade Cycle*, Harcourt, 1933, reprinted, Augustus M. Kelley, 1966; *Prices and Production*, G. Routledge & Sons, 1931, 2nd edition, 1935, reprinted, Augustus M. Kelley, 1967; *Freedom and the Economic System*, University of Chicago Press, 1939; *Profits, Interest, and Investment, and Other Essays on the Theory of Industrial Fluctuations*, G. Routledge & Sons, 1939; *The Pure Theory of Capital*, Macmillan, 1941, University of Chicago Press, 1962; *The Road to Serfdom*, University of Chicago Press, 1944; *Individualism and Economic Order*, University of Chicago Press, 1948, reprinted, Routledge & Kegan Paul, 1977.

The Sensory Order: An Inquiry Into the Foundations of Theoretical Psychology, University of Chicago Press, 1952; *The Counter-Revolution of Science: Studies on the Abuse of Reason*, Free Press (England), 1952; *The Political Ideal of the Rule of Law*, [Cairo], 1955; *The Constitution of Liberty*, University of Chicago Press, 1960; *Monetary Nationalism and International Stability*, Augustus M. Kelley, 1964; *Dr. Bernard Mandeville*, Oxford University Press, c. 1966; *Studies of Philosophy, Politics, and Economics*, University of Chicago Press, 1967; *Confusion of Language in Political Thought*, Transatlantic, 1968; *Freiburger Studien* (title means "Freiburg Studies"; includes ten essays translated from the original English), Mohr, 1969; *Roads to Freedom*, Routledge & Kegan Paul, 1969.

Toward Liberty, California Institute for Humane Studies, 1971; *A Tiger by the Tail: A Forty-Year's Running Commentary on Keynsianism*, Transatlantic, 1972; *Verdict on Rent Control*, London Institute of Economic Affairs, 1972; *Economic Freedom and Representative Government*, Transatlantic, 1973; *Law, Legislation, and Liberty: A New Statement of the Liberal Principles of Justice and Political Economy*, University of Chicago Press, Volume I: *Rules and Order*, 1973, Volume II: *The Mirage of Social Justice*, 1977, Volume III: *The Political Order of a Free People*, 1979; *Full Employment at Any Price*, Transatlantic, 1975; *Rent Control*, Fraser Institute, 1975; *Denationalisation of Money: An Analysis of the Theory and Practice of Concurrent Currencies*, London Institute of Economic Affairs, 1976; *Choice in Currency: A Way to Stop Inflation*, Transatlantic, 1977; *New Studies in Philosophy, Politics, Economics, and the History of Idea*, University of Chicago Press, 1978.

Editor: Marco Fanno, Marius W. Holtrop, Johan G. Koopmans, *Beitraege zur Geldtheorie*, J. Springer, 1933; N. G. Pierson, Ludwig von Mises, Georg Halm, and Enrico Barone, *Collectivist Economic Planning: Critical Studies on the Possibilities of Socialism*, G. Routledge & Sons, 1935, reprinted, Augustus M. Kelley, 1967; John Stuart Mill, *John Stuart Mill and Harriet Taylor: Their Correspondence*, University of Chicago Press, 1951; Henry Thornton, *An Enquiry Into the Nature and Effects of the Paper Credit of Great Britain*, Augustus M. Kelley, 1962; T. S. Ashton, *Capitalism and the Historians*, University of Chicago Press, 1963.

SIDELIGHTS: Hayek's earliest writings were contributions to theoretical economic thought. In his first book, *Monetary Theory and the Trade Cycle*, he theorized that economic cycles are caused, not by changes in the value of money, but by changes in the volume of money. A reviewer for the *Times Literary Supplement* was impressed by the strength of his abstract ideas and attributed the "unquestionable importance" of the work "as much to the challenging nature of his conclusions as to the great erudition, the logical austerity and the unusual power of sustained abstract reasoning which he has at his command." Similarly, in a review of *Prices and Production*, A. W. Marget praised both Hayek's "scholarly appreciation of the achievement of monetary theory in the past" and his ability to recombine various elements "in the construction of the monetary theory of the future."

Hayek continued his abstract analyses in subsequent books. In *Monetary Nationalism and International Stability*, he argued for an international monetary standard, and in *The Pure Theory of Capital*, he described "the role of capital in a dynamic, capitalist economy." When *The Road to Serfdom* appeared in 1944, it too was considered an abstract, scholarly work. Despite this appraisal, it became a popular success and was a nonfiction bestseller in the United States. The book was later dramatized on the radio program

"Words at War," condensed by *Reader's Digest*, reprinted as a pamphlet by the Book-of-the-Month Club, and serialized by Hearst's King Features Syndicate.

The Road to Serfdom is an argument against socialism. It is based on two premises: that economic security is not as important as freedom, and that socialized planning leads to totalitarianism. Written during World War II, the book sets up events in Germany as a model to avoid and calls for the maintenance of competition and laissez-faire as prerequisite to the maintenance of political liberty.

L. M. Hacker of the *Weekly Book Review* described *The Road to Serfdom* as "written with austerity and learning; it is reasoned closely; it is as devoid of passion and special pleading as is a text in geometry." T. V. Smith, in an article for *Ethics*, however, called the book "'hysterical' because, though calm in exterior, it is agitated at heart and in turn agitates others . . . rather than activates." Some critics, like James Harrington of the *New Statesman*, criticized Hayek for repeating nineteenth-century economic concepts without taking into account such changes in the contemporary world as revolutions and world wars. But Henry Hazlitt of the *New York Times* found value in the book, for "it restates for our time the issue between liberty and authority with the power and rigor of reasoning that John Stuart Mill stated the issue for his own generation in his great essay 'On Liberty.'"

Hayek's more recent works digressed only occasionally from economic theory. *Counter-Revolution of Science* criticized the use by social scientists of the methods of natural scientists, while *Sensory Order: An Inquiry Into the Foundations of Theoretical Psychology* was a study of sense perception and memory. But with his three-volume work, *Law, Legislation, and Liberty*, Hayek returned to earlier themes. In *The Denationalisation of Money*, he examined how the power to issue currency could be taken away from government and placed in the private sector, a scheme John Porteous of the *New Statesman* considered "anarchic" despite Hayek's "conservative ideals."

BIOGRAPHICAL/CRITICAL SOURCES: Journal of Political Economy, April, 1932; *Times Literary Supplement*, May 4, 1933, February 5, 1938, April 1, 1944, December 12, 1952, July 22, 1960, July 25, 1968; *Boston Transcript*, June 28, 1933; *Spectator*, December 17, 1937, March 31, 1944, July 1, 1960; *Annals of the Academy of Political and Social Science*, January, 1942, May, 1945, November, 1952, May, 1954; *New Statesman*, May 13, 1944, November 24, 1967, December 7, 1973, January 14, 1977; *New York Times*, September 24, 1944, September 5, 1948; *Commonweal*, September 29, 1944, February 12, 1954; *Saturday Review of Literature*, October 21, 1944, May 12, 1945, October 23, 1948, October 11, 1952, April 2, 1960; *Nation*, October 21, 1944, April 28, 1945, September 25, 1948; *Weekly Book Review*, October 29, 1944; *Atlantic*, December, 1944.

Christian Century, January 3, 1945, October 12, 1960; *American Economic Review*, March, 1945, September, 1954; *Ethics*, April, 1945; *American Political Science Review*, June, 1945, February, 1949, December, 1960, September, 1968; *Political Science Quarterly*, September, 1945; *New Yorker*, September 25, 1948; *New York Herald Tribune Weekly Book Review*, September 26, 1948; *New Republic*, October 4, 1948; *New York Times Book Review*, February 21, 1960.

*   *   *

HAYES, John P(hillip)   1949-

PERSONAL: Born August 17, 1949, in Dover, Ohio; son of Paul Raymond and Dolores Constance (Contini) Hayes;

married Jo Ann Pickenstein, September 19, 1970; children: Holly Lynne, Elizabeth Constance. *Education:* Kent State University, B.A., 1971, M.A., 1973; student at Temple University, 1977—. *Religion:* Roman Catholic. *Agent:* Ray Lincoln Literary Agency, 4 Surrey Rd., Melrose Park, Pa. 19126. *Office:* Department of Journalism, Temple University, Philadelphia, Pa. 19122.

CAREER: Kent Record Courier, Kent, Ohio, entertainment editor, 1969-72; Kent State University, Kent, assistant professor of journalism, 1972-76; Temple University, Philadelphia, Pa., assistant professor of journalism, 1976—. *Member:* Association for Education in Journalism.

WRITINGS: Mooney: The Life of the World's Master Carver, Dove Bible Publishers, 1977; *Lonely Fighter: One Man's Battle With the God of the United States*, Lyle Stuart, 1979. Contributor to magazines.

WORK IN PROGRESS: A biography of writer James Michener; a self-help psychology book, for publication by Prentice-Hall.

SIDELIGHTS: Hayes told *CA:* "I want my books to help people by entertaining them, teaching them, or in some way satisfying human interests."

*   *   *

HAYS, Paul R.   1903-1980

OBITUARY NOTICE—See index for *CA* sketch: Born April 2, 1903, in Des Moines, Iowa; died February 13, 1980, in Tucson, Ariz. Educator, lawyer, judge, and author. A member of the United States Court of Appeals since 1961, Hays was involved in decisions that allowed the film "I Am Curious—Yellow" to be shown and prevented the *New York Times* from printing what later became *The Pentagon Papers*. Though Hays was a proponent of judicial restraint, his decisions sometimes disappointed his more liberal peers. He is well known for his reversed ruling whereupon he allowed Con Edison to construct a power plant after determining that the company had made the necessary environmental precautions. As a reporter for the *New York Times* noted, "The decision disappointed environmentalists, who had considered him a champion for the antinuclear cause." His writings include *Labor Arbitration: A Dissenting View* and *Cases and Materials on Civil Procedure*. Obituaries and other sources: *Directory of American Scholars*, Volume IV: *Philosophy, Religion, and Law*, 6th edition, Bowker, 1974; *Who's Who in America*, 40th edition, Marquis, 1978; *New York Times*, February 15, 1980.

*   *   *

HAYWARD, Max   1925(?)-1979

PERSONAL: Born c. 1925, in London, England; died March 18, 1979, of cancer, in Oxford, England. *Education:* Attended Oxford University, c. 1939-45. *Home:* Spetsai, Greece.

CAREER: Translator and author. Editor of *London Daily Telegraph*. Professor. Associated with British embassy in Moscow and Russian Institute at Columbia University. Adviser to Harvill Press, Chekhov Press, and Harcourt Brace Jovanovich. *Awards, honors:* Oxford University fellow; Harvard University fellow, 1959.

WRITINGS: The Ideological Consequences of October, 1956, St. Anthony's Press, 1957.

Translator from the Russian: (With Manya Harari) Boris Pasternak, *Doctor Zhivago*, Pantheon, 1958; (with George

Reavey) Vladimir Mayakovski, *The Bedbug and Selected Poetry*, Weidenfeld & Nicolson, 1961, World Publishing, 1962; (with Ronald Hingley) Alexander Solzhenitsyn, *One Day in the Life of Ivan Denisovich*, Praeger, 1963; (with Ronald Hingley) Abram Tertz, pseudonym of Andrei Sinyavsky, *Fantastic Stories*, Pantheon, 1963 (under author's own name, published in England as *The Icicle and Other Stories*, Collins, 1963); (with David Floyd) Alexander Solzhenitsyn, *For the Good of the Cause*, Pall Mall, 1964; Issac Babel, *You Must Know Everything*, Farrar, Straus, 1969; Nadezhda Mandelstam, *Hope Against Hope*, Atheneum, 1970; (with Manya Harari, and author of introduction) Andrei Amalrik, *Involuntary Journey to Siberia*, Harcourt, 1970; (also compiler and author of introduction with Stanley Kunitz) Anna Akhmatova, *Poems of Akhmatova*, Little, Brown, 1973; Nadezhda Mandelstam, *Hope Abandoned*, Atheneum, 1974; (with Paul Stevenson) Eugenia Ginzburg, *Journey Into the Whirlwind*, Harcourt, 1975; Olga Ivinskaya, *A Captive of Time*, Doubleday, 1978; (with Dyril Fitzlyon) Abram Tertz, *A Voice From the Chorus*, Bantam, 1978.

Editor: (With Patricia Blake) *Dissonant Voices in Soviet Literature*, Harper, 1964; (with Blake) *Half-way to the Moon: New Writing From Russia*, Holt, 1964; (also translator and author of introduction) *On Trial: The Soviet State Versus "Abram Tertz" and "Nikolai Arzhak,"* Harper, 1966 (with Leopold Labedz, and translator with Manya Harari; published in England as *On Trial: The Case of Sinyavsky (Tertz) and Daniel (Arzhak)*, Collins, 1967); (with Blake) Andrei Voznesensky, *Antiworlds and the Fifth Ace*, Anchor Books, 1967 (published in England as *Antiworlds*, Oxford University Press, 1967); (with William C. Fletcher) *Religion and the Soviet State*, Pall Mall, 1969; (also translator and author of introduction) Aleksander Gladkov, *Meetings With Pasternak: A Memoir*, Harcourt, 1977; (with Vera Dunham) Andrei Voznesensky, *Nostalgia for the Present*, Doubleday, 1978.

Adaptations: (With William Jay Smith) *The Telephone* (fiction; adapted from the Russian text, *Telefon*, by Kornei Chukovsky), Delacorte, 1977.

SIDELIGHTS: Max Hayward was an expert in contemporary Russian literature and devoted himself to preserving the Russian culture in the West. As a translator, Hayward saved many banned works of dissident Soviet authors from obscurity. "Max acted as the custodian of Russian literature in the West, until such time as it could be restored to Russia," said Patricia Blake, his former student and co-editor on a number of books.

Hayward became committed to this cause when employed at the British Embassy in Moscow. There he witnessed Stalin's purges of artists, writers, and the intellectual community. He was determined to keep alive the culture Stalin tried to destroy.

Hayward learned to read Russian while still a teenager. In his youth, he traveled England extensively with his father who was an itinerant worker. This lifestyle sparked an early interest in Gypsies and the boy bought a second-hand book on the subject written in Russian. He taught himself the language from that book.

OBITUARIES: New York Times, March 20, 1979; *AB Bookman's Weekly*, April 16, 1979.*

* * *

HEALY, John D(elaware) 1921-

PERSONAL: Born September 12, 1921, in Philadelphia, Pa.; son of Raymond John (in sales) and Kathryn (Hood) Healy; married Nancie L. Trotman; children: Debra, Douglas, Diane, Davina, Duncan, Dorinda, Dierdra. *Education:* Attended University of Alabama, 1942, and Georgetown University, 1943; Gettysburg College, B.A., 1948; University of Pennsylvania, M.A., 1949, doctoral study, 1950; also attended University of Marburg and Foreign Service Institute. *Religion:* Protestant. *Home:* 30 Country Club Lane, Marlton, N.J. 08053; (summers) 121 Brigantine Dr., Ocean City, N.J. 08226.

CAREER: U.S. Department of State, Washington, D.C., foreign service officer in Dillenburg, Kassell, and Hanover, West Germany, 1950-53, cultural affairs officer in Stuttgart, West Germany, 1953-55, public affairs officer in Isfahan, Iran, 1955-56; American Cancer Society, executive director in Mason City, Iowa, 1957-60, national director of trades and industry relations, 1960-61; International Rescue Committee, executive director, 1961-62; Leukemia Society, Inc., national executive vice-president, 1962-64; G. A. Brakeley & Co., Inc., New York, N.Y., national development counselor, 1964-66, vice-president and member of board of directors, 1966-68; Philadelphia Orchestra Challenge Program, Philadelphia, Pa., resident manager, 1966-68; Philadelphia Orchestra Association, Philadelphia, director of financial development, 1968—. Assistant to president of Academy of Music of Philadelphia, 1970—; president and chief executive officer of Greater Philadelphia Cultural Alliance, 1973-76. Treasurer of Philadelphia 76 (official bicentennial agency), 1973-76. Instructor at University of Pennsylvania, 1974-76; guest on television and radio programs (also producer). Artist, with exhibitions of paintings in Connecticut. Member of music panel of Pennsylvania Council on the Arts, 1973-75; director and vice-president of Philadelphia Style 200, Inc., 1974-76. Volunteer worker with youth groups. *Military service:* U.S. Army, Combat Infantry, 1942-46; received Bronze Star. U.S. Army Reserve, 1946-55.

MEMBER: International City Managers Society, American Society for Public Administration, National Fund Raisers Society, Western Governmental Research Association, Macogen Club, Scabbard and Blade Military Society. *Awards, honors:* National citation from American Cancer Society, 1959.

WRITINGS: Klauen (novel), Ashley Books, 1980. Author of radio and television commercial advertisements. Guest editorial writer for *Mason City Globe* and *Des Moines Register and Tribune*. Past editor of *New Horizons*.

WORK IN PROGRESS: Three novels, *The Language Tutor's Legacy, The Recorder*, and *Beyond the Seed*; research on the Franco-Prussian War.

SIDELIGHTS: As a foreign service officer, Healy was partly responsible for European tours of notable Americans, including Ernest Hemingway and Herbert Hoover, and performing groups, including the New York City Ballet. Since then he has lectured throughout the United States on such subjects as foreign policy and Chinese communism.

Healy told *CA:* "During World War II, as an infantryman, I decided that if I made it through I would devote further training to the study of 'why we fight' through research in liberal arts, history, philosophy, and political science. All this was in the successful pursuit of a career with the State Department.

"I thoroughly enjoyed all assignments in Germany, but in 1953 I switched from the State Department to the U.S. Information Agency in a desire for more people contact. By then both my wife and I had conquered the language barrier.

"While in Iran I found that I was functioning on only four cylinders whereas I had been accustomed to the demands of having to call upon sixteen cylinders in Germany. I requested more responsibility. When nothing happened, I resigned rather than jeopardize a very good record.

"When I returned to the United States I decided I wanted to remain in a service oriented field where people, rather than a nut or a bolt, were the end product. Since organization and administration were my strong points, a series of assignments in the non-profit sector have been rewarding.

"I returned to my home town of Philadelphia, Pa., in 1966, essentially to conduct a management study of the Philadelphia Orchestra Association. They requested I remain and since I had always been a fan of the orchestra and my parents still lived in the area, I did.

"Culture in Philadelphia is 'big business.' Looked at as an industry, it draws more people than the combined attendance at all professional sports events. Payrolls, services purchased, and other aspects of the association are equal to those in a major industry.

"One manages in the non-profit sector by indirection—suggesting leadership to the volunteer rather than implying what shall be done, giving credit away rather than taking credit. Publicity is arranged; public relations are practiced. Logic and organization, projecting a good community image, and leveling with the public as to honest needs result in successful fund raising.

"In the summer I commute from Ocean City, N.J., using a quaint little train through the meadows. Most summers since 1968 I read during the one and one-half hour ride (three hours a day). In 1977 I decided to attempt writing a novel in longhand during the ride. I finished *Klauen* in 1977, a second book in 1978, and a third in 1979. I hope to finish the fourth in 1980."

AVOCATIONAL INTERESTS: Collecting and playing percussion instruments (especially jazz), sports (as coach and participant), cooking.

*   *   *

HEATH, Catherine   1924-

PERSONAL: Born November 17, 1924, in London, England; daughter of Samuel Michael (an accountant) and Anna (de Boer) Hirsch; married Dennis Heath, July 19, 1949 (divorced, 1977); children: Anne Lindsay, Anthony David. *Education:* St. Hilda's College, Oxford, B.A. (with honors), 1946. *Home:* 14 Grosvenor Ave., Carshalton, Surrey SM5 3EW, England. *Agent:* Curtis Brown Ltd., 1 Craven Hill, London W.2, England.

CAREER: University of Wales, Cardiff, assistant lecturer in English literature, 1948-50; Carshalton College of Further Education, Carshalton, England, lecturer, 1964-70, senior lecturer in English, 1970—. Member of social services committee of London Borough of Sutton, 1967-77. *Member:* International P.E.N., Society of Authors.

WRITINGS—All novels: *Stone Walls*, J. Cape, 1973; *The Vulture*, J. Cape, 1974; *Joseph and the Goths*, J. Cape, 1975; *Lady on the Burning Deck*, J. Cape, 1978, Taplinger, 1979.

WORK IN PROGRESS: Radio plays.

SIDELIGHTS: "Joseph and the Goths" was broadcast by British Broadcasting Corp. in 1977.

Catherine Heath commented: "I grew up within the Dutch community in England, so my love of England and the English language has in it an element of yearning. I am a purist where language is concerned, believing that any artist must always love and have control of his medium. While I doubt the possibility or value of teaching creative writing, I think it is of intense importance, and a great delight, to teach the ability to handle words accurately, sensitively, powerfully, and grammatically. One can teach the craft, but artists then make themselves."

BIOGRAPHICAL/CRITICAL SOURCES: Washington Post, August 21, 1979.

*   *   *

HEBDEN, Mark
See HARRIS, John

*   *   *

HEGNER, William   1928-

PERSONAL: Born May 11, 1928, in Sandusky, Ohio; son of Edward and Ada Louise (Knabke) Hegner; married Martha Boitel (divorced, November 6, 1968); children: Robert Leonard. *Education:* Attended Bowling Green State University, 1948, and Ohio Wesleyan University, 1949; Western Reserve University (now Case Western Reserve University), B.A., 1951. *Residence:* Caldwell, N.J. *Agent:* Knox Burger Associates Ltd., 39½ Washington Sq. S., New York, N.Y. 10012.

CAREER: George Shearing Quintet, New York City, road manager, 1953-55; in public relations in New York City, 1955-68; writer, 1968—. Member of board of trustees of Riverside School. *Military service:* U.S. Army Air Forces, 1945-46. *Member:* Authors Guild of Authors League of America.

WRITINGS—Novels: *The Scandal Goddess*, Delacorte, 1970; *The Host*, Pocket Books, 1971; *The Drumbeaters*, Pocket Books, 1972; *Three Loose Women*, Pocket Books, 1972; *The Idolaters*, Trident, 1972; *King Corso*, Pocket Books, 1973; *The Adopters*, Pocket Books, 1974; *Stars Cast No Shadows*, Pocket Books, 1974; *The Worshipped and the Damned*, Pocket Books, 1975; *The Chaperone*, Pocket Books, 1975; *The Lovelorners*, Pocket Books, 1976; *The Bigamist*, Pocket Books, 1977; *Rainbowland*, Playboy Press, 1977; *The Creator*, Pocket Books, 1978. Author of a dozen novels under pseudonyms, including *The Concessionaire*, 1980. Author of unproduced screenplay, "The Scandal Goddess."

SIDELIGHTS: Hegner comments: "I have always written to please myself as well as to survive. The marketplace for authors is complex and frustrating, but compulsion overwhelms that. A free press, a free literature, is the last hope of mankind in an increasingly contained society. I love writers—I think they represent the most reasoned hope for emotional survival in our world."

*   *   *

HEIDE, Florence Parry   1919-
(Alex B. Allen, Jamie McDonald)

PERSONAL: Surname is pronounced *High*-dee; born February 27, 1919, in Pittsburgh, Pa.; daughter of David W. (a banker) and Florence (a columnist and drama critic; maiden name, Fisher) Parry; married Donald C. Heide (a lawyer), November 27, 1943; children: Christen, Roxanne (Mrs. Richard Krogh), Judith, David, Parry. *Education:* Attended Wilson College; University of California, Los Angeles, B.A., 1939. *Politics:* Republican. *Religion:* Protestant. *Home:* 6910 Third Ave., Kenosha, Wis. 53140. *Agent:* Curtis Brown, 575 Madison Ave., New York, N.Y. 10022.

CAREER: Associated with Radio-Keith-Orpheum in New York City; worked at advertising and public relations agencies in New York City; Pittsburgh Playhouse, Pittsburgh, Pa., public relations director.

MEMBER: International Board on Books for Young People, American Society of Composers, Authors, and Publishers (ASCAP), Authors Guild, National League of American Pen Women, Society of Children's Book Writers, Council for Wisconsin Writers, Children's Reading Round Table. *Awards, honors:* American Institute of Graphic Arts selection as one of the fifty best books of the year, 1971, American Institute of Graphic Arts Children's Book Show selection, 1971-72, *New York Times* "Best Illustrated Children's Book" citation, 1971, Children's Book Showcase selection, 1972, Jugendbuchpreis for best children's book in Germany, 1977, Graphic Arts Prize from Bologna Book Fair, 1977, and American Library Association notable book citation, all for *The Shrinking of Treehorn;* second prize for juvenile fiction from Council for Wisconsin Writers and selected by Social Studies—Children's Book Council as notable trade book in field of social studies, both 1975, both for *When the Sad One Comes to Stay;* Golden Kite award, first prize for juvenile fiction from Council for Wisconsin Writers, and named honor book by Society for Children's Book Writers, all 1976, all for *Growing Anyway Up;* Golden Archer award, 1976; American Library Association notable book citation for *Banana Twist;* Litt.D. from Carthage College, 1979.

WRITINGS: Benjamin Budge and Barnaby Ball, Four Winds Press, 1967; (under pseudonym Jamie McDonald; with Anne Theiss and others) *Hannibal,* Funk, 1968; *Maximilian Becomes Famous,* Funk, 1969; *Alphabet Zoop,* McCall Publishing, 1970; *Giants Are Very Brave People,* Parents' Magazine Press, 1970; *The Little One,* Lion Press, 1970; *Sound of Sunshine, Sound of Rain,* Parents' Magazine Press, 1970; *The Key,* Atheneum, 1971; *Look! Look! A Story Book,* McCall Publishing, 1971; *The Shrinking of Treehorn,* Holiday House, 1971; *Some Things Are Scary,* School Book Service, 1971; *Who Needs Me?,* Augsburh, 1971; *My Castle,* McGraw, 1972; (with brother, David Fisher Parry) *No Roads for the Wind* (textbook), Macmillan, 1974; *God and Me,* Concordia, 1975; *When the Sad One Comes to Stay,* Lippincott, 1975; *You and Me,* Concordia, 1975; *Growing Anyway Up,* Lippincott, 1976; *Banana Twist,* Holiday House, 1978; *Changes,* Concordia, 1978; *Secret Dreamer, Secret Dreams,* Lippincott, 1978; *Who Taught Me?,* Concordia, 1978; *By the Time You Count to Ten,* Concordia, 1979.

With Sylvia W. Van Clief: *Maximilian,* Funk, 1967; *The Day It Snowed in Summer,* Funk, 1968; *How Big Am I,* Follett, 1968; *It Never Is Dark,* Follett, 1968; *Sebastian,* Funk, 1968; *That's What Friends Are For,* Four Winds Press, 1968; *The New Neighbor,* Follett, 1970; (lyricist) *Songs to Sing About Things You Think About,* Day, 1971; (lyricist) *Christmas Bells and Snowflakes* (songbook), Southern Music Publishing, 1971; (lyricist) *Holidays! Holidays!* (songbook), Southern Music Publishing, 1971; *The Mystery of the Missing Suitcase,* Whitman, 1972; *The Mystery of the Silver Tag,* Whitman, 1972; *The Hidden Box Mystery,* Whitman, 1973; *Mystery at MacAdoo Zoo,* Whitman, 1973; *Mystery of the Whispering Voice,* Whitman, 1974; *Who Can?* (primer), Macmillan, 1974; *Lost and Found* (primer), Macmillan, 1974; *Hats and Bears* (primer), Macmillan, 1974; *Fables You Shouldn't Pay Any Attention To,* Lippincott, 1978.

With daughter, Roxanne Heide; all published by Whitman, except as noted: *Lost!* (textbook), Holt, 1973; *I See America Smiling* (textbook), Holt, 1973; *Tell About Someone You Love* (textbook), Macmillan, 1974; *Mystery of the Melting*

Snowman, 1974; *Mystery of the Vanishing Visitor,* 1975; *Mystery of the Bewitched Bookmobile,* 1975; *Mystery of the Lonely Lantern,* 1976; *Mystery at Keyhole Carnival,* 1977; *Brillstone Break-In,* 1977; *Mystery of the Midnight Message,* 1977; *The Face at the Brillstone Window,* 1978; *Fear at Brillstone,* 1978; *Mystery at Southport Cinema,* 1978; *I Love Every-People,* Concordia, 1978; *Body in the Brillstone Garage,* 1979; *Mystery of the Mummy Mask,* 1979; *Mystery of the Forgotten Island,* 1979.

Under pseudonym Alex B. Allen; all with S. W. Van Clief, except as noted; all published by Whitman: *Basketball Toss Up,* 1972; *No Place for Baseball,* 1973; *Danger on Broken Arrow Trail,* 1974; *Fifth Down,* 1974; (with son, David Heide) *The Tennis Menace,* 1975.

WORK IN PROGRESS: Juvenile novels; an adult thriller; several mystery novels in collaboration with daughter, Roxanne Heide.

SIDELIGHTS: Many of Heide's early books, written in collaboration with Sylvia Van Clief, were highly recommended by the critics. Typical of the early work is *Maximilian,* a story about a mouse who wants to be a bird. *Book World* praised this story as "a perfect 'Fun and Frolic' book" in which "no child is going to resent the obvious moral: It's always better to be oneself. Not when a story is as funny as this one or has such hilarious illustrations."

Heide told *CA:* "Writing for young people is the most exciting and rewarding thing I've done, and I hope to continue happily ever after."

BIOGRAPHICAL/CRITICAL SOURCES: Book World, December 31, 1967; *Vilas County News-Review,* June 3, 1976; *Kenosha News,* December 10, 1976, May 15, 1979; *Pittsburgh Post Gazette;* April 26, 1979.

*   *   *

HEINRICH, Willi 1920-

PERSONAL: Born August 9, 1920, in Heidelberg, Germany; son of Wilhelm and Berta (Koch) Heinrich; married Erika Stocker, June 23, 1955. *Education:* Attended commercial school in Germany. *Religion:* Roman Catholic. *Home:* Im Schoenbrunn 7, 7580 Buehl-Neusatz, West Germany. *Agent:* Albrecht Leonhardt, Studiestraede 35, Copenhagen K, Denmark.

CAREER: Writer. *Military service:* German Army, 1938-45; received Iron Cross, first and second class, and Casualty Badge.

WRITINGS—In English: *Das geduldige Fleisch* (novel), Deutsche Verlags-Anstalt, 1955, translation by Richard and Clara Winston published as *The Cross of Iron,* Bobbs-Merrill, 1956 (published in England as *The Willing Flesh,* Weidenfeld & Nicolson, 1956); *Der goldene Tisch* (novel), Stahlberg, 1956, reprinted as *In stolzer Trauer,* Bertelsmann, 1970, translation by Oliver Coburn published as *Crack of Doom,* Farrar, Straus, 1958 (translation by Coburn and Ursula Lehrburger published in England as *The Savage Mountain,* Weidenfeld & Nicolson, 1958); *Die Gezeichneten,* Stahlberg, 1958, translation by Sigrid Rock published as *Mark of Shame,* Farrar, Straus, 1959; *Rape of Honor,* translated by Rock, Dial, 1961, original German edition published as *In einem Schloss zu wohner,* Bertelsmann, 1976; *Gottes zweite Garnitur,* Ruetten & Loening, 1962, translation by Rock published as *The Lonely Conqueror,* Dial, 1962; *Alte Haeuser sterben nicht* (novel), S. Fischer, 1960, translation by Michael Glenny published as *The Crumbling Fortress,* Macdonald & Co., 1963, Dial, 1964; *Ferien im Jenseits* (novel), Ruetten & Loening, 1964, translation by Hans Konings-berger published as *The Devil's Bed*, Dial, 1965.

Other: *Vom inneren Leben*, Ullirch-Verlag, 1961; *Maigloeckchen oder aehnlich: Die Aufzeichnungen der Simone S. Roman* (title means "Lilies of the Valley or Something: The Sketches of Simon S. Roman"), Ruetten & Loening, 1965; *Mittlere Reife* (novel; title means "Middle-Aged Maturity"), Ruetten & Loening, 1966; *Geometrie einer Ehe* (novel; title means "Geometry of a Marriage"), Ruetten & Loening, 1967; *Schmetterlinge weinen nicht* (novel; title means "Butterflies Do Not Cry"), Bertelsmann, 1969; *Jahre wie Tau* (novel; title means "Years Like Dew"), Bertelsmann, 1971; *So Long, Archie* (novel), Bertelsmann, 1972; *Liebe und was sonst noch zaehlt* (novel; title means "Love and What Else Counts"), Bertelsmann, 1974; *Eine Handvoll Himmel* (novel; title means "A Handful of Heaven"), Bertelsmann, 1976; *Eine Mann ist immer unterwegs* (novel), Bertelsmann, 1978; *Herzbube und Madchen*, Bertelsmann, 1980.

* * *

HEINTZELMAN, Donald S(haffer) 1938-

PERSONAL: Born May 25, 1938, in Allentown, Pa.; son of Rewellien G. (a pattern maker) and Florence May (Shaffer) Heintzelman. *Education:* Muhlenberg College, A.B., 1965; graduate study at Lehigh University, 1965. *Home and office:* 629 Green St., Allentown, Pa. 18102.

CAREER: Rodale Press, Emmaus, Pa., staff photographer, 1958-66; William Penn Memorial Museum, Harrisburg, Pa., associate curator of natural science, 1966-69; New Jersey State Museum, Trenton, curator of ornithology, 1969-73; ornithological and wildlife writer, lecturer, and consultant, 1973—. Conducted field research in North America, East Africa, Bermuda, the West Indies, the Galapagos and Falkland Islands, South America, and Antarctica. Film producer and photographer. *Member:* American Ornithologists' Union, American Birding Association, Northeastern Bird Banding Association, Wilson Ornithological Society, Delaware Valley Ornithological Club (fellow). *Awards, honors:* Louis Agassiz Fuertes grant from Wilson Ornithological Society, 1962; Delaware Valley Ornithological Club, Witmer Stone Award, 1964, for studies on autumn hawk migrations, and Julian K. Potter Award, 1972, for high quality of ornithological work.

WRITINGS: The Hawks of New Jersey, New Jersey State Museum, 1970; *A Guide to Northeastern Hawk Watching*, privately printed, 1972; *Finding Birds in Trinidad and Tobago*, privately printed, 1973; *Autumn Hawk Flights: The Migrations in Eastern North America*, Rutgers University Press, 1975; *A Guide to Eastern Hawk Watching*, Pennsylvania State University Press, 1976; *North American Ducks, Geese, and Swans*, Winchester Press, 1978; *A Manual for Bird Watching in the Americas*, Universe Books, 1979; *Hawks and Owls of North America* (Birding Book Club selection), Universe Books, 1979; *A Guide to Hawk Watching in North America*, Pennsylvania State University Press, 1979; *The Bird Watcher's Dictionary*, Winchester Press, 1980; *A Guide to Whales, Dolphins, and Porpoises of the World*, Winchester Press, 1980. Contributor of about eighty articles and numerous photographs to ornithology and wildlife journals, including *National Wildlife, Explorers Journal, New Jersey Outdoors*, and *Cassinia*. Past book review editor for *New Jersey Nature News* and *EBBA News*.

WORK IN PROGRESS: A semi-autobiographical book about his wildlife adventures around the world, publication expected in 1981; development of conservation methods for birds of prey; exploring new bird-watching sites.

SIDELIGHTS: Heintzelman's experience is extensive on all four continents, but his specialties are Pennsylvania and New Jersey, and the eastern United States and Canada in general. His emphasis is on birds of prey (biology, ecology, and migrations), waterfowl, seabirds, and non-game and endangered wildlife.

He writes that his interests are "wildlife and natural history photography, collecting bird books, and travel to remote corners of the world, seeking wildlife information and photographs."

BIOGRAPHICAL/CRITICAL SOURCES: New York Times, December 23, 1959; *Trenton Times-Advertiser*, May 30, 1971; *Allentown Call-Chronicle*, September 14, 1975; *Northampton Suburban Scene*, September 14, 1978; *Allentown Evening Chronicle*, February 21, 1979.

* * *

HENDEE, John C(lare) 1938-

PERSONAL: Born November 12, 1938, in Duluth, Minn.; son of Clare W. (a forester) and Myrtle (a teacher; maiden name, Parker) Hendee; married Juanita Louise Wilson (a registered nurse) September 4, 1957 (separated March, 1979); children: John, Jr., James, Joy, Joni. *Education:* Michigan State University, B.S., 1960; Oregon State University, M.S., 1962; University of Washington, Seattle, Ph.D., 1967. *Home:* 24 Audubon Dr., Asheville, N.C. 28804. *Office:* Southeast Forest Experiment Station, Forest Service, U.S. Department of Agriculture, Asheville, N.C. 28802.

CAREER: U.S. Department of Agriculture, Forest Service, Washington, D.C., in timber management at Suislaw National Forest in Oregon, 1961-63, fire researcher at Pacific Southwest Experiment Station, Berkeley, Calif., 1964, recreation researcher at Pacific Northwest Forest and Range Experiment Station, Seattle, Wash., 1964-76, congressional fellow, Washington, D.C., 1976-79, legislative affairs staff, Washington, D.C., 1977-78, assistant director of Southeastern Forest Experiment Station, Asheville, N.C., 1978—. Affiliate associate professor at University of Washington, Seattle, 1968-76. Member of Durward Allen Committee to write a new North American wildlife policy, 1972-73. *Awards, honors:* Research award from Keep America Beautiful, 1972; conservation award from American Motors, 1974; federal Congressional fellow, 1976-77.

WRITINGS: (With William Robert Catton, Jr.) *Wilderness Users in the Pacific Northwest: Their Characteristics, Values, and Management Preferences*, Pacific Northwest Forest and Range Experiment Station, 1968; (with Dale R. Potter) *Human Behavior Aspects of Fish and Wildlife Conservation*, Pacific Northwest Forest and Range Experiment Station, 1973; (editor with Clarence Schoenfeld) *Human Dimensions in Wildlife Programs*, Wildlife Management Institute, 1974; (with Schoenfeld) *Wildlife Management in Wilderness*, Boxwood Press, 1978; (with George Stankey and Robert Lucas) *Wilderness Management*, U.S. Government Printing Office, 1978. Contributor of more than seventy-five articles to professional journals.

WORK IN PROGRESS: Revision of *Wilderness Management* and *Wildlife Management in Wilderness*.

SIDELIGHTS: Hendee Commented: "Having moved to a research administration position I no longer do research but still guest lecture and write on topics such as wilderness management, wildlife values and use, public involvement in resource decisions, and diffusion of innovations."

HENDERSON, Archibald   1877-1963
(Erskine Steele)

OBITUARY NOTICE: Born June 17, 1877, in Salisbury, N.C.; died December 6, 1963. Educator, historian, mathematician, and author. A onetime student of Albert Einstein, Henderson taught mathematics at the University of North Carolina for nearly fifty years, becoming professor emeritus in 1948. In addition to his more technical works such as *The Derivation of the Brianchon Configuration of Two Special Point-Triads,* he wrote several books on the life and works of George Bernard Shaw. His other books include a two-volume history of North Carolina and a history of the University of North Carolina. In 1949, a number of friends and colleagues paid tribute to him by publishing *Archibald Henderson: The New Crichton.* Obituaries and other sources: *New York Times,* December 7, 1963; *Time,* December 13, 1963.

*   *   *

HENDRICKSON, Donald E(ugene)   1941-

PERSONAL: Born January 27, 1941, in Muncie, Ind.; son of Howard B. and Ethel L. (Whitmire) Hendrickson; married Karen S. Wimmer (a teacher), August 9, 1964; children: Jennifer, Michael, Todd, Sean, Paula. *Education:* Huntington College, B.A., 1964; St. Francis College, Fort Wayne, Ind., M.A., 1965; Indiana University, Ed.D., 1968; postdoctoral study at Michael Reese Psychiatric Hospital and Menninger Foundation. *Office:* Counseling and Psychological Services Center, Ball State University, Lucina Hall, Muncie, Ind. 47306.

CAREER: Richmond State Hospital, Richmond, Ind., recreational therapist, 1962; Allen County Department of Public Welfare, Fort Wayne, Ind., caseworker and psychometrist, 1963-65; City of Fort Wayne, Ind., social worker and coordinator of Headstart Project, 1965; Ball State University, Muncie, Ind., assistant professor, 1968-72, associate professor, 1972-77, professor of psychology, 1977—, counseling psychologist, 1968—. Psychologist and partner at Muncie Psychiatric Clinic, 1972—; project director for Regional Diagnostic and Evaluation Center, Inc., 1974-79. Co-founder and member of board of directors of Crisis Intervention Center of Delaware County, 1969-73; psychologist at Bethel Home for Boys, 1969-75; co-founder and president of board of directors of Cambridge House (for girls), 1970-77. Consulting psychologist for Delaware Juvenile Court, 1968-72; member of board of directors of local Parole Commission, 1969; co-founder of Youth Services Bureau of Delaware County, 1972. Member of Indiana State Board of Examiners in Psychology.

MEMBER: American Psychological Association, American Personnel and Guidance Association, American Academy of Psychotherapists, National Register of Health Care Providers in Psychology, Association for the Advancement of Psychology, Mental Health Counselors Association, Society for Clinical and Experimental Hypnosis, Indiana Psychological Association. *Awards, honors:* Grants from Huntington College, 1969-70; chosen alumnus of the year of Huntington College, 1977.

WRITINGS: (With Frank Krause) *Counseling Techniques With Youth,* C. E. Merrill, 1972; (with Krause) *Counseling and Psychotherapy: Training and Supervision,* C. E. Merrill, 1972; *Relaxation Manual,* Contemporary Press, 1975; (with Stephen P. Janney and James E. Fraze) *How to Establish Your Own Private Practice,* Professional Consultants Associates, 1978.

Author of five-part film series, "Techniques and Processes of Counseling and Psychotherapy," for Ball State University, 1971, and scripts for audio tapes. Contributor to psychology journals.

WORK IN PROGRESS: Behavior Modification With Children for Parents; Weight Loss Through the Use of Hypnosis and Behavior Modification; Dealing With Stress Through Hypnosis.

*   *   *

HENNESSY, Max
See HARRIS, John

*   *   *

HEPPENHEIMER, T(homas) A(dolph)   1947-

PERSONAL: Born January 1, 1947, in New York, N.Y.; son of Henry Gunther (a toolmaker) and Betty Lorraine (a secretary; maiden name, Amitin) Heppenheimer; married Phyllis Marcia Safdy, December 9, 1967 (divorced May 9, 1977); children: Laurie, Alex, Connie. *Education:* Michigan State University, B.S., 1967, M.S., 1968; University of Michigan, Ph.D., 1972. *Politics:* Republican. *Religion:* None. *Home:* 11040 Blue Allium Ave., Fountain Valley, Calif. 92708. *Agent:* Neil McAleer, R.D. 1, Box RV-230, Etters, Pa. 17319. *Office:* K.R.G., Inc., 27526 Sunnyridge, Palos Verdes Peninsula, Calif. 90274.

CAREER: Science Applications, Inc., Chicago, Ill., scientist, 1972-73; Rockwell International Corp., Downey, Calif., member of technical staff in systems engineering, 1973-74; California Institute of Technology, Pasadena, research fellow in planetary science, 1974-75; Max Planck Institute for Nuclear Physics, Heidelberg, West Germany, Alexander von Humboldt Research Fellow, 1976-78; K.R.G., Inc., Palos Verdes Peninsula, Calif., vice-president, 1978—. Technical vice-president of Forum for the Advancement of Students in Science and Technology, 1971-73. *Member:* American Institute of Aeronautics and Astronautics (associate fellow), American Association for the Advancement of Science, American Astronomical Society (Division of Dynamical Astronomy), British Interplanetary Society (fellow), Sigma Xi, Tau Beta Pi, Pi Tau Sigma, Phi Kappa Phi, Phi Eta Sigma.

WRITINGS: (Contributor) Jerry Grey, editor, *Space Manufacturing Facilities: Space Colonies,* American Institute of Aeronautics and Astronautics, Volumes I and II, 1977, Volume III, 1979; *Colonies in Space* (Book-of-the-Month Club selection), introduction by Ray Bradbury, Stackpole, 1977; (contributor) R. A. Van Patten, Paul Siegler, and E.V.B. Stearns, editors, *The Industrialization of Space: Advances in the Astronautical Sciences,* American Astronautical Society, 1977; (contributor) S. F. Dermott, *The Origin of the Solar System,* Wiley-Interscience, 1978; (contributor) G. K. O'Neill, editor, *Space Manufacturing From Nonterrestrial Materials: Progress in Aeronautics and Astronautics,* American Institute of Aeronautics and Astronautics, 1977; *Toward Distant Suns* (Book-of-the-Month Club selection), Stackpole, 1979; (editor) *Power Satellites and the Industrial Use of Lunar Resources,* American Institute of Aeronautics and Astronautics, 1981. Also author of *The Lamps of Atlantis* with Archie Roy, 1981. Contributor of more than fifty articles to scientific journals. Book review editor of *Journal of the Astronautical Sciences,* 1979—.

WORK IN PROGRESS: A trilogy, *Man and the Solar System, Into the Galaxy, Perspectives on the Future;* continuing research on problems of lunar resources transport and on the early history of asteroids.

SIDELIGHTS: Heppenheimer comments: "To be a good science writer, it is important first to be a good scientist. This means carrying forward a program of original research. Such research does several good things. It gives me a most unique source of material to write about, but more importantly, it keeps me current on the most significant insights and critical thinking in my areas of interest. It also gains me access to conferences—and to colleagues' offices, who welcome me as one who knows their world intimately. It is by going forward in this fashion, by spending time at seminars and keeping up with the journals, that I maintain the flow of new, significant ideas which contribute to the standard of quality which I seek to maintain in my work. And there is more. I find true science to be more imaginative, more stimulating, more exciting than all but the very best in science fiction. There is a pleasure in actually doing science, in wrestling with nature and in seeking to make discoveries, which to me is quite thrilling."

BIOGRAPHICAL/CRITICAL SOURCES: Jerry Grey, *Enterprise*, Bantam, 1980.

*   *   *

HERBERT, Eugenia W(arren) 1929-

PERSONAL: Born September 8, 1929, in Summit, N.J.; daughter of Robert B. (an economist) and Mildred (Fisk) Warren; married Robert L. Herbert (an art historian), June 6, 1953; children: Timothy, Rosemary, Catherine. *Education:* Wellesley College, B.A., 1951; attended University of Vienna, 1951-52; Yale University, M.A., 1953, Ph.D., 1957, postdoctoral study, 1967-68; also studied at Sorbonne, University of Paris, 1955-56, 1968-69. *Home:* 34 Beacon Rd., Bethany, Conn. 06525. *Agent:* Paul R. Reynolds, Inc., 12 East 41st St., New York, N.Y. 10017. *Office:* Department of History, Mount Holyoke College, South Hadley, Mass. 01075.

CAREER: Quinnipiac College, Hamden, Conn., assistant professor of African history, 1970; Yale University, New Haven, Conn., lecturer in African history, 1972-73; Mount Holyoke College, South Hadley, Mass., assistant professor of history, 1978—. Lecturer at Yale University, summer, 1976, research affiliate, 1976—; senior associate of St. Antony's College, Oxford, 1978. Founder and first president of New Haven's Center for Independent Study.

MEMBER: American Historical Association, African Studies Association, Historical Metallurgy Society, Royal Geographical Society (fellow), Phi Beta Kappa. *Awards, honors:* Fulbright scholar at University of Vienna, 1951-52; American Association of University Women fellow in France, 1955-56; Mary Elvira Stevens fellowship from Wellesley College for France and Africa, 1968-69; Frank Luther Mott Award from Kappa Tau Alpha, Laurence L. Winship Award from *Boston Globe,* and book award from Colonial Dames of America, all 1975, for *The Private Franklin.*

WRITINGS: The Artist and Social Reform: France and Belgium, 1885-1898, Yale University Press, 1961; (with C. A. Lopez) *The Private Franklin: The Man and His Family,* Norton, 1975; (contributor) B. K. Swartz and R. E. Dumett, editors, *West African Culture Dynamics: Archaeological and Historical Perspectives,* Mouton, 1979. Contributor of articles and reviews to history, art, and African studies journals.

WORK IN PROGRESS: Copper in Africa: The Cultural History of a Metal.

SIDELIGHTS: Eugenia Herbert writes that *Copper in Africa* is "an interdisciplinary astudy of the role of copper in tropical Africa from the Early Iron Age to the eve of the colonial period.

"My work deals with the metallurgy of copper and its alloys in Africa, the economic importance of these metals, and their function in the artistic, social, religious, and ritual life of a range of African societies. I seek to illuminate not only the symbolic character of materials in pre-industrial cultures, but also the notion of value itself.

"My current research is an interdisciplinary study combining history of technology, trade, political, and ritual life in an attempt to reformulate the notion of value and emphasize the symbolic qualities of materials in pre-industrial cultures. I am particularly interested in African history as a means of breaking out of our own ethnocentric view of the world with its 'norms' of behavior and historical development."

*   *   *

HERTLING, James E. 1935-

PERSONAL: Born November, 1935, in New Albany, Ind.; son of Glen E. (a jeweler) and Margaret Hertling; married Sandra Lee Dyer (a music teacher), June 24, 1962; children: Heather S. *Education:* Indiana University, B.S., 1959, M.S., 1961, Ph.D., 1968. *Home:* 1935 Locust Court, Bloomington, Ind. 47401. *Office:* School of Continuing Studies, Indiana University, 202 Owen Hall, Bloomington, Ind. 47405.

CAREER: High school business education teacher in Delphi, Ind., 1959-61, guidance counselor, 1961-62, guidance director, 1962-63, principal, 1963-67; Indiana University, Bloomington, visiting lecturer in education, 1967-69; Northern Illinois University, DeKalb, assistant professor of education, 1969-71; Indiana University, associate professor, 1971-75, professor of continuing studies, 1975—, director of continuing education program, 1971-75, and Division of Continuing Studies, 1975—. *Member:* National University Extension Association (member of board of directors, 1976-78; chairperson of Council on Human Resources), National Association of Secondary School Principals, Phi Delta Kappa.

WRITINGS: (Editor with Roy L. Bragg) *Foundations of Secondary Education,* Simon & Schuster, 1970; (with Bragg, E. Leland Brode, and Vernon L. Wills) *A Teacher's Guide to Practical Evaluation,* Kendall/Hunt, 1971; (editor with Howard G. Getz) *Education for the Middle School Years: Readings,* Scott, Foresman, 1971; (co-editor of revision) Robert W. Richey, *Planning for Teaching,* 5th edition (Hertling was not associated with earlier editions), McGraw, 1973. Contributor to education journals.

*   *   *

HERZ, Irene 1948-

PERSONAL: Born April 26, 1948, in Brooklyn, N.Y.; daughter of Emanuel Albert (a lawyer) and Florence (a secretary; maiden name, Hirschberg) Herz; married Kenneth Stow, June, 1968 (divorced, 1972). *Education:* Barnard College, A.B., 1968; Hunter College of the City University of New York, M.S.W., 1970; Pratt Institute, M.L.S., 1973. *Religion:* Jewish. *Home:* 7002 Boulevard East, Guttenberg, N.J. 07093. *Agent:* Ruth Cantor, 156 Fifth Ave., Room 1005, New York, N.Y. 10010. *Office:* Document Management Group, 30 Vesey St., New York, N.Y. 10007.

CAREER: Brooklyn Public Library, Brooklyn, N.Y., librarian, 1973-77; King's Bay Young Men's/Young Women's Hebrew Association Senior Citizen's Center, Brooklyn, N.Y., social worker, 1977-79; Document Management Group, New York, N.Y., marketing program manager,

1979—. Performed with Regina Opera Society and Oratorio Society. *Member:* National Organization for Women, Barnard College Club.

WRITINGS: Hey! Don't Do That (juvenile), Prentice-Hall, 1978.

Work represented in anthologies, including "Sprint Skills Books," Scholastic Book Services.

WORK IN PROGRESS: The King's Highway Cooking Contest and Kidnapping, a novel for children.

SIDELIGHTS: Irene Herz writes: "I wrote *Hey! Don't Do That* with my two nephews, Adam and Scott, in mind. The older character changed sexes in the course of my writing and I found, to my surprise, when the book was finished she had a little bit of me in her. My experience has been that, when I pick up a pencil, my fears and hopes come tumbling onto the page, whether I intend it or not."

*   *   *

HESKES, Irene   1928-

PERSONAL: Born June 15, 1928, in New York, N.Y.; daughter of Abraham and Elsie (Weiss) Newman; married Jacob Heskes (a certified public accountant), May, 1946; children: Deborah Aviva (Mrs. Alan M. Kraut), Walter Morris. *Education:* Attended Juilliard School, 1946-50; New York University, B.A. (summa cum laude), 1948; Hebrew Union College, music educator's certificate, 1952; attended Jewish Theological Society of America, 1959-63, and Eastman School of Music, 1966-69; Harvard University, certificate in arts administration, 1971. *Religion:* Jewish. *Residence:* Forest Hills, N.Y. *Office:* Jewish Music Council, National Jewish Welfare Board, 15 East 26th St., New York, N.Y. 10010.

CAREER: Music consultant and lecturer, 1958-76; Jewish Music Council, National Jewish Welfare Board, New York, N.Y., director, 1968—. Lecturer at schools and synagogues; performer of Jewish music; consultant to organizations and educational groups. *Member:* International Musicological Society, American Musicological Society, Music Librarians Association, Music Educators National Conference, American Council of the Arts, Association of Jewish Center Workers, Phi Beta Kappa.

WRITINGS—All published by Jewish Music Council, National Jewish Welfare Board, except as noted: *A. W. Binder: His Life and Work,* 1965; *The Cantorial Art,* 1966; (editor with Arthur M. Wolfson) *The Historic Contribution of Russian Jewry to Jewish Music,* 1967; *Supplement: Historic Contribution,* 1968; *Studies in Jewish Music: The Collected Writings of A. W. Binder,* Bloch Publishing, 1971; *Jewish Music Programs, 1973,* 1973; (editor) Artur Halde, *Jews in Music: Holde,* revised edition, Bloch Publishing, 1974; (with Suzanne Bloch) *Ernest Bloch, Creative Spirit: A Program Source Book,* 1976; *Jewish Music Programs and Commissioning Guidelines, 1978,* 1978; (with Judith Kaplan Eisenstein) *Israeli Music: A Program Aid,* 1978; (editor) *Jerusalem in Music: Guidelines and Resources,* 1980. Author of resource manuals. Contributor to *Jewish Book Annual* and *Encyclopaedia Judaica.* Contributor to Anglo-Jewish periodicals in the United States, Canada, and Israel.

WORK IN PROGRESS: A collection of previously published journal articles, publication expected in 1982; resource materials on music contests, Holocaust music, and music of the Jewish holidays.

SIDELIGHTS: Irene Heskes writes: "The focus of my career—my direction and motivation—stems from a keen awareness and appreciation for my Judaic heritage and the cultural achievements of my Jewish people. I realize the devastation to Jewish historic continuity of the Holocaust, and cannot let such destruction mean that all the creativity of generations could slip away into oblivion with the concentration camp dust and ashes. I am heartened to find more and more non-Jewish artists and communal as well as religious leaders who wish to learn much about the Jewish musical heritage and to help me perpetuate it. I welcome, therefore, contact and happy associations with my Christian brothers and sisters in behalf of a noble musical art."

*   *   *

HESLIN, Jo-Ann   1946-

PERSONAL: Born February 16, 1946, in Bayshore, N.Y.; daughter of Joseph Martin (an upholsterer) and Anna (a secretary; maiden name, Hodl) Saufl; married Joseph Heslin (a credit manager), January 3, 1969; children: Kristen, Karen. *Education:* State University of New York College at Oneonta, B.S., 1967; New York University, M.A., 1970. *Office:* N.R.H. Nutrition Consultants, 100 Rosedale Rd., Valley Stream, N.Y. 11581.

CAREER: Family Circle, New York City, associate in foods department, 1967-68; Dairy Council of Metropolitan New York, New York City, nutritionist, 1968-69; City University of New York, New York City, lecturer in nutrition, 1969-70; State University of New York Downstate Medical Center, Brooklyn, assistant professor of nutrition, 1970-76; Adelphi University, Garden City, N.Y., adjunct assistant professor of nutrition, 1976—. Principal with N.R.H. Nutrition Consultants, 1975—. Assistant professor at New York University, 1976. *Member:* American Dietetic Association, American Home Economics Association, Dietitians in Pediatric Practice, Home Economists in Business, Kappa Delta Pi, Omicron Nu.

WRITINGS: (With Annette Natow and Barbara Raven) *No Nonsense Nutrition for Your Baby's First Year,* C.B.I. Publishing, 1978; (with Natow) *Geriatric Nutrition,* C.B.I. Publishing, 1980. Contributor to nutrition journals and popular magazines, including *American Baby* and *Baby Talk.*

WORK IN PROGRESS: Research on the nutritional status of urban children, infant feeding practices, and the nutrition practices of pregnant women.

SIDELIGHTS: Heslin wrote: "'Nutrition is the most important environmental factor in good health.' Because I strongly believe and live this philosophy, I have attempted through my writing to answer some of the needs of the general public. I see my role as a liaison between the professional and the public, as a translator of complex nutrition information into useful and practical day-to-day concepts that can be incorporated into one's way of life. In private practice, as a nutrition consultant, my partner and I have concentrated on pediatric and geriatric nutritional needs. Our philosophy of infant nutrition is that there is *no one* correct way to nourish your baby. Each parent must decide for himself what is appropriate based on facts, their feelings, and their lifestyle. We provide the facts and let the parents provide their decision. An optimum quality of life is a right each human should enjoy. Inadequate nutrition leading to poor health is a risk faced by many older people; by upgrading the quality of their diet we can often upgrade the quality of their life. We feel that working toward the improvement of care for the aged is self-serving since age is a great universalizing factor and something we all have in common."

HESPRO, Herbert
  See ROBINSON, Herbert Spencer

*   *   *

HETHERINGTON, John (Aikman)   1907-1974

PERSONAL: Born October 3, 1907, in Sandringham, Victoria, Australia; died September 17, 1974, in Melbourne, Australia; son of Hector and Agnes (Bowman) Hetherington; married Olive Meagher, March 15, 1943 (marriage ended); married Mollie Roger Maginnis, July 26, 1967. *Education:* Educated in Australia. *Residence:* Malvern, Victoria, Australia.

CAREER: Reporter and feature writer for *Melbourne Herald* group in Australia, 1925-35; journalist in London, England and New York, N.Y., 1935-38; *Melbourne Herald*, Melbourne, Australia, feature editor, 1938-39; war correspondent in Middle East and Europe, 1940-45; editor-in-chief of *Adelaide News*, 1945-49; *Melbourne Argus*, Melbourne, department editor, 1952-54; *Melbourne Age*, Melbourne, feature writer, 1954-67; author and free-lance journalist, 1967-74. *Member:* Australian Society of Authors, Fellowship of Australian Writers. *Awards, honors:* Recipient of *Sydney Morning Herald* war novel prize, 1947; Walkley Award for best magazine story, 1960; Commonwealth of Australia Literary fellow, 1967 and 1972; Sir Thomas White Memorial Prize, 1968; decorated Officer of Greek Royal Order of the Phoenix.

WRITINGS: Airborne Invasion: The Story of the Battle of Crete, Duell, Sloan & Pearce, 1943; *The Australian Soldier: A Portrait,* F. H. Johnston, 1943; *The Winds Are Still,* Georgian House, 1947; *Blamey, Controversial Soldier: A Biography of Field Marshall Sir Thomas Blamey,* F. W. Cheshire, 1954; *Australians: Nine Profiles,* F. W. Cheshire, 1960; *Norman Lindsay: The Embattled Olympian,* Lansdowne Press, 1961, 2nd edition, 1962; *Forty-Two Faces,* F. W. Cheshire, 1962; *John Monash,* Oxford University Press, 1962; *Australian Painters: Forty Profiles,* F. W. Cheshire, 1963; *Witness to Things Past: Stone, Brick, Wood, and Men in Early Victoria,* F. W. Cheshire, 1964; *Uncommon Men,* F. W. Cheshire, 1965; *Pillars of Faith: Churchmen and Their Churches in Early Victoria,* F. W. Cheshire, 1966; *Melba: A Biography,* Faber, 1967.

SIDELIGHTS: One of Hetherington's best-known books, *Airborne Invasion: The Story of the Battle of Crete,* chronicles the author's eye-witness account of the military actions on the island of Crete in 1941. In a review of the book for the *New York Times,* Lawrence Thompson claimed that it was "thrown together without sufficient consideration for the reader's desire to analyze sequences of time and timing." A reviewer for the *Christian Science Monitor,* however, felt that *Airborne Invasion* "is more than just another war book, it is an attempt to record history, to sort out and set down accurately and in proper sequence the tangled tragedy and heroism of these heroic days."

BIOGRAPHICAL/CRITICAL SOURCES: Springfield Republican, July 25, 1943; *New York Times,* August 1, 1943; *Chicago Sun Book Week,* August 8, 1943; *New York Herald Tribune Weekly Book Review,* August 8, 1943; *Christian Science Monitor,* August 11, 1943, April 11, 1968; *Saturday Review of Literature,* August 21, 1943; *Observer Review,* September 17, 1967; *Listener,* October 5, 1967; *Times Literary Supplement,* December 14, 1967; *New Yorker,* June 15, 1968; *Economist,* April 13, 1974.

OBITUARIES: AB Bookman's Weekly, November 18, 1974.*

HEWARD, Edmund (Rawlings)   1912-

PERSONAL: Born August 19, 1912, in London, England; son of Thomas Brown (a minister) and Kathleen Amy Rachel (Rawlings) Heward; married Constance Mary Sandiford Crossley, July 14, 1945. *Education:* Trinity College, Cambridge, M.A., 1933, LL.M., 1961. *Home:* 36A Dartmouth Row, Greenwich, London SE10 8AW, England. *Agent:* Laurence Pollinger Ltd., 18 Maddox St., London W1R 0EU, England.

CAREER: Rose, Johnson & Hicks, London, England, law partner, 1946-59; Supreme Court, London, master of Chancery Division, 1959—. *Military service:* British Army, gunner in Royal Artillery, 1940-46; became major. *Member:* United Oxford and Cambridge University Club, Travellers' Club.

WRITINGS: Guide to Chancery Practice, Butterworth & Co., 1962, 5th edition, 1979; *Matthew Hale,* R. Hale, 1972; *Lord Mansfield,* Barrie Rose, 1979. Also editor of the twenty-fourth and twenty-fifth editions of *Probate Practice* by T. H. Tristram and H. C. Coote, and the fourth edition of *Judgments and Orders,* by Halsbury.

*   *   *

HEXT, Harrington
  See PHILLPOTTS, Eden

*   *   *

HEYER, Georgette   1902-1974
  (Stella Martin)

PERSONAL: Born August 16, 1902, in London, England; died July 4, 1974, in London, England; daughter of George and Sylvia (Watkins) Heyer; married George Ronald Rougier (a barrister), August 18, 1925; children: Richard George. *Education:* Privately educated. *Address:* c/o Deborah Owen, 78 Narrow St. Limehouse, London N.W. 8, England.

CAREER: Writer, 1921-74; lived in Africa, 1925-28, and Yugoslavia, 1928-29.

WRITINGS: The Black Moth, Houghton, 1921, reprinted, Bantam, 1976; *The Great Roxhythe,* Hutchinson, 1922, reprinted, Buccaneer Books, 1976; *Instead of the Thorn,* Hutchinson, 1923, Buccaneer Books, 1976; (under pseudonym Stella Martin) *The Transformation of Philip Jettan,* [London], 1923, published as *Powder and Patch: The Transformation of Philip Jettan,* Heinemann, 1930, reprinted, Bantam, 1976; *Simon the Coldheart,* Small, Maynard, 1925, reprinted, Dutton, 1979; *These Old Shades,* Heinemann, 1926, Dutton, 1966; *Helen,* Longmans, Green, 1928, reprinted, Buccaneer Books, 1976; *The Masqueraders,* Heinemann, 1928, reprinted, Fawcett, 1977; *Beauvallet,* Heinemann, 1929, reprinted, Dutton, 1968; *Pastel,* Longmans, Green, 1929, reprinted, Buccaneer Books, 1976.

The Barren Corn, Longmans, Green, 1930, reprinted, Buccaneer Books, 1976; *The Conqueror,* Heinemann, 1931, Dutton, 1964; *Footsteps in the Dark* (mystery), Longmans, Green, 1932, Buccaneer Books, 1976; *Why Shoot a Butler?* (mystery), Longmans, Green, 1933, reprinted, Dutton, 1973; *The Unfinished Clue* (mystery), Longmans, Green, 1934, Harmondsworth, 1943, reprinted, Dutton, 1970; *The Convenient Marriage,* Heinemann, 1934, Dutton, 1966; *Devil's Cub,* Heinemann, 1934, Dutton, 1966; *Merely Murder* (mystery), Doubleday, 1935 (published as *Death in the Stocks,* Longmans, Green, 1935, Harmondsworth, 1942, reprinted, Dutton, 1970); *Regency Buck,* Heinemann, 1935, Dutton, 1966; *Behold, Here's Poison!* (mystery), Doubleday, 1936, reprinted, Fawcett, 1979; *The Talisman Ring* (mystery), Heinemann, 1936, Dutton, 1967; *They Found Him Dead* (mystery), Hodder & Stoughton, 1937, Dutton, 1973; *An Infamous Army* (historical novel), Heinemann, 1937, Dutton, 1965; *A Blunt Instrument* (mystery), Doubleday, 1938, reprinted, Garland Publishing, 1976; *Royal Escape*, Heinemann, 1938, Dutton, 1967; *No Wind of Blame*, Hodder & Stoughton, 1939, Dutton, 1970.

The Spanish Bride (historical novel), Heinemann, 1940, Dutton, 1965; *The Corinthian*, Heinemann, 1940, Dutton, 1966; *Envious Casca* (mystery), Hodder & Stoughton, 1941, Sun Dial Press, 1942, reprinted, Bantam, 1978; *Faro's Daughter*, Heinemann, 1941, Dutton, 1967; *Beau Wyndham*, Doubleday, 1941; *Penhallow* (mystery), Heinemann, 1942, Doubleday, 1943, reprinted, Dutton, 1971; *Friday's Child*, Heinemann, 1944, Putnam, 1946, reprinted, Berkley, 1977; *The Reluctant Widow*, Putnam, 1946, reprinted, Berkley, 1977; *The Foundling*, Putnam, 1948; *Arabella*, Putnam, 1949, reprinted, Buccaneer Books, 1978.

The Grand Sophy, Putnam, 1950; *Duplicate Death* (mystery), Heinemann, 1951, Bantam, 1977; *The Quiet Gentleman*, Heinemann, 1951, Putnam, 1952; *Detection Unlimited* (mystery), Heinemann, 1953, Dutton, 1969; *Cotillion*, Putnam, 1953, reprinted, Buccaneer Books, 1978; *The Toll-Gate*, Putnam, 1954; *Bath Tangle*, Putnam, 1955, reprinted, Berkley, 1979; *Sprig Muslin*, Putnam, 1956; *April Lady*, Putnam, 1957; *Sylvester; or, The Wicked Uncle*, Putnam, 1957; *Venetia*, Heinemann, 1958, Putnam, 1959; *The Unknown Ajax*, Heinemann, 1959, Putnam, 1960.

Pistols for Two and Other Stories, Heinemann, 1962, Dutton, 1964; *A Civil Contract*, Heinemann, 1961, Putnam, 1962; *The Nonesuch*, Heinemann, 1962, Putnam, 1963; *False Colours*, Bodley Head, 1963, Dutton, 1964; *Frederica*, Dutton, 1965; *Black Sheep*, Bodley Head, 1966, Dutton, 1967; *Cousin Kate*, Bodley Head, 1968, Dutton, 1969; *Charity Girl*, Dutton, 1970; *Lady of Quality*, Dutton, 1972; *My Lord John*, Dutton, 1975.

Omnibus volumes: *The Georgette Heyer Omnibus* (contains *Faro's Daughter*, *The Corinthian*, and *The Nonesuch*), Dutton, 1973; *These Old Shades* [and] *Sprig Muslin* [and] *Sylvester* [and] *The Corinthian* [and] *The Convenient Marriage*, Heinemann, 1977.

SIDELIGHTS: Author of nearly sixty romance and mystery novels, Georgette Heyer attracted a large and devoted readership in both England and the United States. From her first book, written when she was seventeen, to her last, Heyer entertained her readers for over fifty years with her "waggishly frolicsome, pertly paced" novels.

Most of Heyer's novels are set in the Regency period of England and are filled with descriptions of customs, clothes, and manners of that era. Some critics have complained that her books are "overstuffed" because of her tendency to "give her readers too much rather than too little history," and have claimed that a few of her romances, such as *April Lady*, contain inaccurate details. Nevertheless, other reviewers have agreed with I. W. Lawrence that Heyer "knows her history thoroughly and seldom takes liberties with it." In 1964 *Time* declared: "By knowing more about Regency fops, rakes, routs and blades than anyone else alive, Georgette Heyer has turned what otherwise could be dismissed as a long series of sugary historical romances into a body of work that will probably be consulted by future scholars as the most detailed and accurate portrait of Regency life anywhere."

One of Heyer's techniques for setting the historical tone of her period pieces was to liberally sprinkle the dialogue with Regency slang. Some critics found this irritating and suggested that readers skip over it. Others thought this aspect of dialogue delightful, and Lucille Crane noted that "the slang which should puzzle the American reader, does not. In itself it brings alive an era."

Throughout the years, Heyer has often been compared to Jane Austen because of her wit, her leisurely detailed manner, and her tongue-in-cheek description of early nineteenth-century manners. "Like Jane Austen (to whom she can hold a dim candle) Miss Heyer has a gift for painting one or two magnetic characters who stand out in bright relief among a host of lesser ones, always well and amusingly drawn," noted Nancie Matthews. A few critics, however, pointed out that Heyer's books did not contain enough ironic commentary to qualify as social satire in the tradition of Austen.

Regardless of their historically accurate accounts of the Regency period, Heyer's novels are for many readers best known as lively and entertaining "escape" literature. *Chicago Sunday Tribune* critic Henry Cavendish observed that Heyer's stories stack up "as something of a literary bubble bath wherein readers so inclined may take a delightful and frothy dip."

Although some reviewers have complained of her stock characters and predictable conclusions, Heyer earned a better reputation for quality than did many other romance writers of her time. A *Times Literary Supplement* reviewer declared that Heyer's works are "redeemed from the ruck of such productions by the author's light-hearted wit and her peculiar skill in the delineation of silly women." Richard Match agreed that Heyer's stories are rescued from the category of "trashy novels" by several saving graces, including her "sardonic, elegantly turned eighteenth-century prose." Discussing an early Heyer romance, *Instead of the Thorn*, a *Literary Review* critic declared: "It is so easy to read, it is so recognizably human, the characters are so completely in their role, and the conclusions grow so quietly out of the premises that one has gone straight through the story almost without realizing what skill and insight have gone into its creation."

Heyer's humor and characterization helped make her mysteries as popular as her romances. Critics such as Isaac Anderson maintained that even though "there are not so many shudders in Georgette Heyer's murder mysteries as there are in those of some other writers, . . . there is a lot more fun." And although a few reviewers complained that her plots were hardly mysterious, others noted that they were logical, ingenious, and free from messy details. The *Times Literary Supplement* declared that *Death in the Stocks* "is an excellent example of what can be achieved when the commonplace material of detective fiction is worked up by an experienced novelist."

Stephanie Nettell has attributed Georgette Heyer's tremendous popularity to her wit, charm, warmth, and gusto, her good story lines and talented use of language, and most of all her sharp delineation of character. "All the characters are attractive, even the villains. They are all alive," exclaimed Nettell. Heyer is one of those people "who like[s] to write, never mind the actual chore of it, and this gets across to the reader." Her steady stream of best sellers testifies to Crane's observation that "Heyer's efforts are always enjoyable . . . in spite of the defects in technique we are all so fond of criticising. My recommendation is: Read and Enjoy!"

BIOGRAPHICAL/CRITICAL SOURCES: New York Times, April 12, 1924, February 21, 1937, June 13, 1937, August 8,

1937, October 9, 1938, February 17, 1946, March 21, 1948, April 6, 1952, April 12, 1953, August 29, 1954, September 4, 1955; *Literary Review*, June 21, 1924; *Boston Transcript*, May 23, 1925, July 10, 1937, September 25, 1937; *Saturday Review of Literature*, June 6, 1925; *Times Literary Supplement*, April 18, 1935, June 12, 1937, October 1, 1938, November 8, 1941, January 18, 1957; *Manchester Guardian*, June 23, 1936, June 25, 1937; *Chicago Daily Tribune*, March 6, 1937; *Spectator*, June 17, 1938; *New Statesman and Nation*, June 25, 1938; *New Yorker*, October 15, 1938, May 28, 1949, October 7, 1950, September 4, 1954; *Weekly Book Review*, February 24, 1946; *Chicago Sun Book Week*, March 2, 1947; *Commonweal*, June 17, 1949; *Chicago Sunday Tribune*, October 22, 1950, April 12, 1953, September 1, 1957, May 22, 1960; *Saturday Review*, March 22, 1952; *New York Herald Tribune Book Review*, August 26, 1956, June 5, 1960; *Library Journal*, July, 1957, March 15, 1958; *Christian Science Monitor*, April 24, 1958, May 12, 1960, January 4, 1962, November 5, 1964; *Time*, February 21, 1964; *Best Sellers*, March 1, 1964, September 15, 1967, December 1, 1967, March 1, 1968, June 15, 1968, October 15, 1970, April 15, 1973, May 15, 1973; *Book Week*, March 15, 1964; *Books and Bookmen*, September, 1965, November, 1968.

OBITUARIES: New York Times, July 6, 1974; *Washington Post*, July 6, 1974; *Publishers Weekly*, July 29, 1974.*

—*Sketch by Martha G. Winkel*

*   *   *

HIGGINBOTHAM, (Prieur) Jay   1937-

PERSONAL: Born July 16, 1937, in Pascagoula, Miss.; son of Prieur Jay (a contractor) and Vivian (Perez) Higginbotham; married Alice Louisa Martin, June 27, 1970; children: Jeanne-Felicie, Denis Prieur, Robert Findlay. *Education:* University of Mississippi, B.A., 1960; graduate study at Hunter College of the City University of New York and American University. *Home:* 60 North Monterey St., Mobile, Ala. 36604.

CAREER: State House of Representatives, Jackson, Miss., assistant clerk, 1955-61; Mobile (Ala.) Public Schools, teacher, 1962-73; Mobile Public Library, head of local history department, 1973—. *Member:* Alabama Library Association. *Awards, honors:* General L. Kemper Williams Prize from the Louisiana Historical Association, 1977; award of merit from Mississippi Historical Society, 1978; Alabama Library Association nonfiction award, 1978; Gilbert Chinard Prize from Institut francais de Washington and Society for French Historical Studies, 1978.

WRITINGS: The Mobile Indians, Colonial Books, 1966; *Family Biographies*, Colonial Books, 1967; *The Pascagoula Indians*, Colonial Books, 1967; *Pascagoula-Singing River City*, Gill Press, 1968; *Mobile—City by the Bay*, Mobile Jaycees, 1968; *The Journal of Sauvole*, Colonial Books, 1969; *Fort Maurepas—The Birth of Louisiana*, Colonial Books, 1969; *Brother Holyfield*, Thomas-Hull, 1972; *A Voyage to Dauphin Island*, Museum of the City of Mobile, 1974; *Old Mobile: Fort Louis de la Louisiane, 1702-1711*, Museum of the City of Mobile, 1977. Contributor of articles to newspapers, magazines, and journals, including *Louisiana Studies*, *Alabama Review*, *Journal of Mississippi History*, and *New Orleans Times—Picayune*.

WORK IN PROGRESS: A book about journeys through Siberia, tentatively entitled *Fast Train Russia*.

HIKMET, Nazim   1902-1963

OBITUARY NOTICE: Born in 1902 in Salonika, Turkey (now Greece); died in 1963. Poet and playwright. An advocate of international communism, Hikmet was imprisoned several times in Turkey before fleeing to the Soviet Union in 1951. Considered one of the few outstanding poets that Turkey has ever produced, he is often compared to Federico Garcia Lorca. In addition to his multi-volume poem, *Human Landscapes From My Country*, he has written numerous books of verse, including *A City Which Lost Its Voice* and *1 + 1 = One*. An autobiographical novel was published in Turkey a year before his death. Obituaries and other sources: *New York Times*, June 4, 1963; *Twentieth Century Writing: A Reader's Guide to Contemporary Literature*, Transatlantic, 1969; *Who's Who in Twentieth Century Literature*, Holt, 1976.

*   *   *

HILL, Fiona
   See PALL, Ellen Jane

*   *   *

HILLCOURT, William   1900-

PERSONAL: Birth-given name, Wilhelm Hans Bjerregaard-Jensen; name legally changed; born August 6, 1900, in Auarhus, Denmark; came to United States, 1926; naturalized U.S. citizen, 1939; son of Johannes Hans and Andrea Kristina (Pedersen) Bjerregaard-Jensen; married Grace Constance Brown, June 3, 1933. *Education:* Pharmaceutical College (Copenhagen), M.S., 1924. *Home:* 43 Pardun Rd., North Brunswick, N.J. 08902.

CAREER: Writer. Associated with Boy Scouts of America. *Military service:* U.S. Army, 1941-45. *Member:* Authors League of America. *Awards, honors:* Certificate of Merit from Freedom Foundation and Medal of Merit from Danish Boy Scout Association, both 1951; numerous awards from Boy Scout troops throughout the world, 1953-57.

WRITINGS: Handbook for Patrol Leaders, Boy Scouts of America, 1929; *The Boy Campers*, Brewer, Warren, 1931; (with James E. West) *The Scout Jamboree Book*, Putnam, 1933; (contributor) *Handbook for Scoutmasters*, 16th edition, Boy Scouts of America, 1936; (with West) *Scout Field Book*, Boy Scouts of America, 1944; *Field Book of Nature Activities*, Putnam, 1950, reprinted as *Field Book of Nature Activities and Conservation*, 1961, revised edition published as *The New Field Book of Nature Activities and Hobbies*, 1970, reprinted, 1978; (with Lady Baden-Powell) *Baden-Powell: The Two Lives of a Hero*, Putnam, 1964; *Physical Fitness for Boys*, Golden Press, 1967; *Physical Fitness for Girls*, Golden Press, 1967; *Fun With Nature Hobbies*, Putnam, 1970; *The Golden Book of Camping*, Golden Press, 1971; *Outdoor Things to Do: Year-Round Nature Fun for Girls and Boys*, Golden Press, 1975; *Norman Rockwell's World of Scouting*, Abrams, 1977; *Official Boy Scout Handbook*, Boy Scouts of America, 9th edition, 1979.

SIDELIGHTS: Most of Hillcourt's books deal with nature and how to enjoy it. A reviewer in *Saturday Review of Literature* described *The Boy Campers* as "a book for boys, on the pages of which are written lessons on the life in the woods, aided by enlivening drawings, aimed not at the earning of medals and insignia to be worn on the sleeve of the coat, but to engender confidence and inspire a yearning for the open in the heart of the juvenile camper."

BIOGRAPHICAL/CRITICAL SOURCES: Springfield Re-

publican, November 1, 1931; *Saturday Review of Literature*, November 14, 1931.*

*   *   *

HIRSCHHORN, Howard H(arvey) 1931-

PERSONAL: Born April 26, 1931, in Baltimore, Md.; son of Robert E. (an artist) and Rita (Sugar) Hirschhorn; married Nelly Marie de Brauwer, September 30, 1960; children: Christina, Ingrid. *Education:* University of Miami, Coral Gables, Fla., B.A., 1954; University of Florida, M.A., 1958; University of Heidelberg, certificates in basic medical sciences, 1959. *Religion:* Roman Catholic. *Home:* 1215 Pizarro St., Coral Gables, Fla. 33134.

CAREER: U.S. Department of the Army, Office of the Surgeon-General, Washington, D.C., civilian researcher in medical intelligence, 1960-61; Miami-Dade Community College, Miami, Fla., instructor in English, German, and Spanish, 1961-66; Hoffmann-La Roche, medical writer and editor, 1966-73; independent technical writing consultant, 1973—; University of Miami, Coral Gables, Fla., lecturer in scientific and technical English, 1975—. *Military service:* U.S. Army, interpreter in military intelligence, 1954-57, in military police, 1964; became first lieutenant. *Member:* American Association of Physical Anthropologists, American Medical Writers Association, Chambre Belge des Traducteurs, Interpretes et Philologues, Verband Deutschsprachiger Uebersetzer Literarischer und Wissenschaftlichen Werke.

WRITINGS: Scientific and Technical German Reader, Odyssey, 1964; *Spanish-English Medical Interviewing Guide*, Regents Publishing, 1968; *Technical and Scientific English* (for Spanish-speakers), Regents Publishing, 1970; *A Jew Is* ... ("socio-psychological study of a Catholic Jew"), Christopher, 1972; *All About Rabbits*, T.F.H. Publications, 1974; *All About Mice*, T.F.H. Publications, 1974; *All About Rats*, T.F.H. Publications, 1974; *All About Guard Dogs*, T.F.H. Publications, 1976; (with James E. Fulton) *Farewell to Pimples*, Acne Research Center, 1977; *Pain-Free Living*, Parker, 1977; *The Moon Is a Heart*, privately printed, 1977; *Health From the Sea*, Parker, 1979; *Writing for Science, Industry, and Technology*, Van Nostrand, 1980. Contributor to scientific journals and *Dining Out*.

WORK IN PROGRESS: Treatment Methods of European Doctors, and novels.

BIOGRAPHICAL/CRITICAL SOURCES: Current Anthropology, June, 1979.

*   *   *

HOBAN, Tana

PERSONAL: Born in Philadelphia, Pa.; married Edward Gallob; children: Meila. *Education:* Graduate of Moore College of Art. *Office:* c/o Macmillan Publishing Co., Inc., 866 Third Ave., New York, N.Y. 10022.

CAREER: Writer and artist. Worked as photographer; instructor in graphics and photography at University of Pennsylvania, 1966-69. *Awards, honors:* John Frederick Lewis fellowship; Children's Book Showcase Title, 1972, for *Look Again!*, and 1973, for *Count and See;* second place in Fourth Annual Children's Science Competition, 1975, for *Circles, Triangles, and Squares.*

WRITINGS—Juvenile; all self-illustrated: *Shapes and Things*, Macmillan, 1970; *Look Again!*, Macmillan, 1971; *Count and See*, Macmillan, 1972; *Push, Pull, Empty, Full: A Book of Opposites*, Macmillan, 1972; *Over, Under, and*

Through, and Other Spatial Concepts, Macmillan, 1973; *Where Is It?*, Macmillan, 1974; *Circles, Triangles, and Squares*, Macmillan, 1974; *Dig, Drill, Dump, Fill*, Greenwillow, 1975; *Big Ones, Little Ones*, Greenwillow, 1976; *Is It Red? Is It Blue?*, Greenwillow, 1978.

Other: *How to Photograph Your Child*, Crown, 1953. Also illustrator of books.

BIOGRAPHICAL/CRITICAL SOURCES: Saturday Review, November 14, 1970; *New York Times Book Review*, May 2, 1971.*

*   *   *

HODGINS, Jack 1938-

PERSONAL: Born October 3, 1938, in Comox, British Columbia, Canada; son of Stanley (a logger) and Reta (Blakely) Hodgins; married Dianne Child (a teacher), December 17, 1960; children: Shannon, Gavin, Tyler. *Education:* University of British Columbia, B.Ed., 1961. *Home and office:* Rutherford Rd., RR1, Lantzville, British Columbia, Canada V0R 2H0.

CAREER: Teacher of English at secondary schools in Nanaimo, British Columbia, 1961-79; full-time writer, 1979—. Writer-in-residence at Simon Fraser University, 1977, and University of Ottawa, 1979. *Member:* Writers Union of Canada. *Awards, honors:* President's medal from University of Western Ontario, 1973, for short story "After the Season"; award for best book by a British Columbian from Eaton, 1976, for *Spit Delaney's Island;* Gibson's First Novel Award, 1977, for *The Invention of the World;* periodical distributors award, 1979, for short story "The Concert Stages of Europe."

WRITINGS: (Editor with W. H. New) *Voice and Vision*, McClelland & Stewart, 1972; (editor) *The Frontier Experience* (anthology), Macmillan, 1975; (editor) *The West Coast Experience* (anthology), Macmillan, 1976; *Spit Delaney's Island* (short stories), Macmillan, 1976; *The Invention of the World* (novel), Macmillan, 1977; *The Resurrection of Joseph Bourne* (novel), Macmillan, 1979.

Stories represented in anthologies, including: Andreas Schroeder and Rudy Wiebe, editors, *Stories From Pacific and Arctic Canada*, Macmillan, 1974; David Arnason, editor, *Isolation in Canadian Literature*, Macmillan, 1975; Gary Geddes, editor, *Skookum Wawa*, Oxford University Press, 1975; John Metcalf and Joan Harcourt, editors, *Best Canadian Stories*, Oberon Press, 1977; Robert Weaver, editor, *Canadian Short Stories*, Oxford University Press, 1978; Metcalf, editor, *Stories Plus*, McGraw, 1979.

WORK IN PROGRESS: A collection of short stories tentatively entitled *The Invasions*, publication by Macmillan expected in 1981.

SIDELIGHTS: Hodgins's books and stories are usually set on Vancouver Island, British Columbia, where he has been a lifelong resident. Because of its location on the far western shore of Canada, the island has long been the final frontier for pioneers heading west. Hodgins explained: "Many people came here because they wanted a place to set up the perfect society. Then once they got on the island, they immediately started making even smaller islands for themselves."

In *The Invention of the World*, Hodgins described the mythic attempts of Donal Keneally, a character loosely based on a real life islander of the 1920's, to create his own version of utopia. The egocentric Keneally convinces an entire Irish village to follow him to Vancouver Island, telling them it is the only place where they will be safe from the end of the world. But after their arrival on the island he forces them all to become his slaves. A *Vancouver Free Press* reviewer noted that in addition to being "a good yarn," the novel also emphasizes that man's spirit of self-determination can be "crushed by the 'invention' of a new world, a counterfeit culture of 'pornography shops and slot machines and periodic festivals of idiocy.' . . . Or to put it bluntly, the Almighty Buck usurps the Almighty Lord. Greed gobbles human spirituality."

The Resurrection of Joseph Bourne returns to the world Hodgins invented in his first novel. With its improbable events and strange names such as Fat Annie Fartenburg, the book "can mislead casual readers into thinking it's superficial, which would be a serious mistake," observed William French. In a place where finding a fishing boat lodged in a fir tree and a Peruvian freighter washed into town by a tidal wave are typical occurrences, "the most apt word to describe his work is fantastical; he hovers somewhere between reality and the surreal, but even the surreal is dealt with as though it were an everyday commonplace." French also asserted that all Hodgins's work "is dedicated to his belief that we need more myth and legend in this country. Without them, he seems to be saying, without the imaginative perspective they can provide, we are merely a nation of materialists and consumers."

Hodgins has been praised for his ability to capture the voice, the lifestyle, and the spirit of Vancouver Islanders, especially in *Spit Delaney's Island*. The *Montreal Gazette* declared that "he has burned [the people of Vancouver Island] into the national consciousness in a series of vivid and unforgettable portraits of ordinary folks, loggers and farmers and small town women, seen through the eyes of one of their own kind." Hodgins told a reporter that he seeks to create characters recognizable the world over. "There's a danger, I think, in making too much of the uniqueness of a people in a region. That could lead a writer into writing stuff which is nothing but regional. Of course it's important to get Vancouver Island right, but if I were only interested in writing about Vancouver Island, I'd write a geography book. Mostly I'm interested in writing about human beings."

BIOGRAPHICAL/CRITICAL SOURCES: Canadian Magazine, June, 1977; *Vancouver Free Press,* July 27-August 2, 1979; *Books in Canada,* August-September, 1979; *Toronto Globe and Mail,* September 15, 1979; *Quill and Quire,* December, 1979; *Canadian Forum,* December, 1979; *Canadian Fiction Magazine,* January, 1980; *Canadian Literature,* winter, 1980.

*   *   *

HOEHLING, Mary   1914-

PERSONAL: Born December 8, 1914, in Worcester, Mass.; daughter of Philip H. (in real estate) and Clara (Mulvey) Duprey; married Adolph A. Hoehling (an editor and writer), September 30, 1936; children: Barbara Hoehling Vinal, Dorothea C., Adolph A. IV, Clara Hoehling Pierson. *Education:* Attended Wheaton College, Norton, Mass., 1934-36, and American University. *Politics:* Independent. *Religion:* Christian. *Home:* 7601 Hemlock St., Bethesda, Md. 20034.

CAREER: Stamford Museum Puppet Theater, Stamford, Conn., writer and performer, 1950-55; free-lance writer, 1956—; in real estate sales, 1970-80. Member of board of directors of Episcopal Center for Children, Washington, D.C.

WRITINGS: (With husband, A. A. Hoehling) *The Last Voy-*

age of the Lusitania, Holt, 1956; *Thaddeus Lowe: America's One-Man Air Corps* (Encyclopaedia Britannica Book Club selection), Messner, 1958; *Girl Soldier and Spy: Sarah Emma Edmundson,* Messner, 1959; *Yankee in the White House: John Quincy Adams,* Messner, 1963; *The Real Sherlock Holmes: Arthur Conan Doyle,* Messner, 1965; (with Betty Randall) *For Life and Liberty: The Story of the Declaration of Independence,* Messner, 1969; (with A. A. Hoehling) *The Day Richmond Died; or, The Last Days of Richmond as the Capital of the Confederacy,* A. S. Barnes, 1980.

SIDELIGHTS: Mary Hoehling writes: "My children were coming home from school complaining of the dullness of history. No wonder, when battle dates and politics took precedence over the people involved! People and their experiences and reactions to the impact of history are important and exciting to me, so I was motivated to write biography. *For Life and Liberty, Lusitania,* and *Richmond* are also primarily concerned with people.

"*The Day Richmond Died* is a detailed account of the events of April 3, 1865, when the proud capital of the Confederacy was abandoned to Federal troops, as told by those who lived through the historic moments."

*   *   *

HOGARTH, Burne   1911-

PERSONAL: Born December 25, 1911, in Chicago, Ill.; son of Max (a carpenter) and Pauline (Lerman) Hogarth; married Rhoda Simons, February 29, 1936 (divorced); married Constance Green, June 27, 1955; children: Michael Robin, Richard Paul, Ross David. *Education:* Attended Crane College, 1928-30, University of Chicago, 1930-31, Northwestern University, 1931-33, and Columbia University, 1956-58. *Home and office:* 234 Mountain Rd., Pleasantville, N.Y. 10570.

CAREER: Bonnet-Brown, Inc., Chicago, Ill., artist and illustrator, 1933; Leeds Features, Chicago, Ill., editor, 1935; McNaught Syndicate, Inc., New York City, staff artist, 1935; King Features Syndicate, New York City, staff artist, 1936; United Feature Syndicate, Inc., New York City, illustrator and cartoonist for "Tarzan," 1937-50, and "Miracle Jones," 1948; Post-Hall Syndicate, New York City, illustrator and cartoonist for "Drago," 1947; School of Visual Arts, New York City, co-founder and vice-president, 1947-70, curriculum coordinator and instructor of anatomy, drawing, art history, and design analysis, 1947-50; Parsons School of Design, New York City, instructor of anatomy and interpretive and conceptual drawing, 1976-79. Work has been exhibited in numerous museums, including Louvre's Museum of Decorative Arts, Palace of Fine Arts in Brussels, Academy of Art in Berlin, Berne Art Museum, Kennedy Cultural Center, and museums in Italy, the Netherlands, Mexico, and Canada. Participant in comics conferences and conventions, 1967-77. President of Pendragon Press, 1975-79.

MEMBER: U.S. Committee for the World Health Organization (Graphic Arts Section), Het Stripschap (Amsterdam), National Cartoonists Society (president, 1977-79), National Art Education Association, American Society for Aesthetics, Society of Illustrators, Museum of Cartoon Art. *Awards, honors:* Scarp Award from New York Comicon, 1968; plaque from Dallas Comicon, 1973; three silver awards from National Cartoonists Society, 1974, 1975, 1976, for best illustration; artist of the year awards from Montreal's Man and His World, 1975; Ignatz Gold Brick Award from Orlando, 1975; Premio Emilio Freixas from International Salon (Gijon, Spain), 1978; Ink Pot plaque from San Diego Comicon, 1978.

WRITINGS—All published by Watson-Guptill, unless otherwise noted: *Dynamic Anatomy,* 1958; *Drawing the Human Head,* 1965; *Dynamic Figure Drawing,* 1970; (author of preface) Francis Lecassin, *Tarzan ou le chevalier crispe* (title means "Tarzan or the Intense Knight"), Union generale d'editions, 1971; (illustrator) Robert M. Hodes, *Tarzan of the Apes* (based on the original text by Edgar Rice Burroughs), 1972; (illustrator) Hodes, *Jungle Tales of Tarzan* (based on the original text by Burroughs), 1976; *Drawing Dynamic Hands,* 1977; (illustrator) Burroughs, *Burne Hogarth's The Golden Age of Tarzan, 1939-1942,* Chelsea House, 1977; *Dynamic Light and Shade,* in press.

WORK IN PROGRESS: The Savage Champion of God, an illustrated graphic narrative; *Life of King Arthur,* a portfolio, for Collector's Press.

SIDELIGHTS: After illustrating his famed "Tarzan" comic strip for fourteen years, Burne Hogarth gave up the strip in 1950 to co-found and teach at the School of Visual Arts in New York City. Seventeen years later, Hogarth was amazed to be hailed as a hero by European art critics. The French, first to treat films as a serious art form, were the first to recognize the art of the comic strip, especially that of Hogarth's "Tarzan." In 1967 the Society for the Study of the Comic Strip (SOCERLID), a group of French critics and scholars, staged the first worldwide exhibition of comic strip art at the Louvre's Museum of Decorative Arts: Hogarth's illustrations were the highlight of the show, and the French critics dubbed Hogarth "the Michelangelo of the comic strip."

"Hogarth is now widely recognized as the greatest living artist of the comics," wrote Maurice Horn, author of *A History of the Comic Strip.* Another critic, Francis Lacassin, observed that "most of the work of adventure strip artists . . . bears Hogarth's stamp. Hogarth fascinates because he is the only artist to have thoughts on the comic strip, its techniques, its artifices, its mission, its destiny." Specifically, Hogarth brings to his art "a sophisticated sense of mannerism (Tarzan as a post-Michelangelesque male) and of Japanese art (in the flat patterning of jungle flora)," according to Lawrence Alloway.

In his essay, "Hogarth Between Wonder and Madness," Lacassin described the dynamic point of view of Hogarth's art: "[His] universe is unremittingly shaken by a frightful tempest which dislocates its angles and deforms its perspectives, at the same time that a brutal and frigid wind moves across it." Overall, it is a vision rooted in diverse interests: "Hogarth is fascinated by Oriental art, by the vehemence of Goya's work, by the suffering portrayed by Gruenewald, by the vitality portrayed by Rubens' compositions, by the narrative technique of cinema, by the classicism of Greek sculpture, and by the ideas of German expressionism."

The influence of film is especially apparent in Hogarth's work. Visually, "Tarzan" is "a montage of images composed in accordance with cinematic techniques . . . closeup, cross-cutting, downward shot, upward shot, panning," commented Lacassin. Another "Tarzan" admirer, French film director Alain Resnais, disclosed that Hogarth's original strip provided the inspiration for many cinematic sequences in his film, "Hiroshima mon amour."

After an absence of twenty-two years from illustrating the "Tarzan" comic strip, Hogarth returned in 1972 as the artist of *Tarzan of the Apes.* The new work was a book-length version of the Edgar Rice Burroughs novel in an adult format, described by Hogarth as "pictorial fiction" or "graphic narrative art." In contrast to the small, checkerboard drawings of traditional comic strips, Hogarth's *Tarzan* consists of large format drawings—limited to three or four per page—that develop a cinematic visualization of the action. Four years later, Hogarth illustrated a sequel edition, *Jungle Tales of Tarzan,* hailed by one Parisian critic as "an exceptional success whose pages provoke an emotional impact equal to that which one experiences before an authentic work of art."

In his introduction to *Jungle Tales of Tarzan,* Walter James Miller of New York University reflected on the significance of Hogarth's work: "The social and cultural revolutions of the sixties brought new dignity to Burne Hogarth. Suddenly he was recognized as one of the great iconographers. He had done the almost impossible; he had grafted a soul into the comic strip by deepening mood in that medium." Maurice Horn arrived at a similar conclusion: "A work of singular genius, Hogarth's *Tarzan* marks one of the supreme moments of the comic strip."

Hogarth told *CA:* "For the greater part of my life, it would appear I have pursued an activity which would not sustain the notion of a 'fine arts' career. While my training and orientation originated in the fine arts as a prior and continuing commitment, I had, as an art student entering the workaday world, never thought to pursue a career without expecting to make a decent living from my professional work. It never entered my mind to take a monastic stance of ascetic self-denial and sacrifice like some inspired artist afflicted with a 'divine madness' for whom the daily pain of slow death approaches the mystic ecstasy of martyrdom. As much as I may stand in awe or admiration of such dramatic integrity, this kind of sacrifice for art does not excite my imagination.

"Nevertheless, the path I chose was perhaps equally austere as that of our artistic visionary and laid down for much the same reasons: my father died when I was fifteen because of unrelieved physical difficulties aggravated under the duress of sustained hard work to keep our family from want. This is dull stuff and nobody cares about silent heroism anymore—except when the obscure paint radiant sunflowers and commit suicide or die building Chartres cathedral. My brother and I stepped into the breach. What does a 'fine arts' student do in a time of personal disaster? Like my father who set the example, you become a good workman, you sell honest art work like a professional, if that's your job.

"But what could I sell, still in high school, studying art? Almost by instinct I turned to an art I could perform without effort: cartoons. I could free-lance, work uniquely to myself (since this was no bar) and, raw as it might be, reflect my own style and signature.

"I became a cartoonist. From this time on, I was to continue in a field which I had entered accidentally, but strangely, was natively congenial to me and could permit all my abilities to flourish. All the while, I could go on painting, carving, etching, work in every medium I desired, keep my stance as an artist, yet adapt my knowledge with equal persuasiveness and drive to satirical commentary or broad farcical humor. Either way, to journalistic or museum art, I felt at home.

"Nevertheless, let me reiterate: Art for me is no sacred duty, nor is it a sacrificial act. My pictures are neither 'fine' nor 'creative' art. They do not arise from some hermetic predicament or orgiastic crisis, neither do they lead to some inconclusive effusion or inarticulate embarrassment. I will therefore not admit to being 'fine' because (a) I will not help the legions of amateurs and incompetents to traumatize or tranquilize shows and galleries with vacuous corner store abstractions and supermarket painted goods, and I abjure 'creative' because (b) this is an accolade given by history (like the term 'great') and cannot be attached by voluntary enlistment.

"As the illustrator of the Sunday newspaper feature 'Tarzan,' it was clear to me from the start that I had in my hands not merely a popular comic figure, but an epic personality, a latter-day analog of those age-old mythic culture heroes of antiquity; a modern man belonging to that class of universally-recognized beings who leap to magical life in daydreams, the emancipated other side of ourselves. I was intrigued with the idea that this archetypal man, who came into his realm naked like Adam, learns that his inherited dawn-world is no Paradise or primeval Arcadia, but a jungle of ordeal, trial, and adversity. Like the Osiris-Adonis/Hercules-Samson mythic heroes with their labors and tribulations, here was a theme for a civilization in the dust, a paradigm for a nation and a people caught in a web of turmoil and depression—wherein a man-not-god fights in a fang and claw environment and survives, a totem symbol of the victory of intelligence over malice and brute force.

"When I gave up the 'Tarzan' assignment, I had been at the job for sixteen years; I was tired of the job, and I was missing an ingredient. My training in the 'fine' arts had left me without the other side of my capabilities, that is to say, the desire to do art in a different scale, to paint, to use color and media with a richer surface and texture than was possible in reproduced media, and to apprehend a sense of the syncretic, synergistic matter which accrues to form and symbol when it arises from an independent and personal source. Yet I wanted to be responsible to some form of environmental consciousness, to work to the full of my training and awareness, to jettison nothing of my history and my experience, but to create an art object which could stand in the midst of the real world and perhaps relate, envision, even tangentially, the 're-alia,' a new reality of that 'other thing,' the felt consciousness of a *new* nature and a new man (different in a marked degree from *old* nature and man), in whom freedom (not food) must become an urgent, compelling necessity as a force for his survival against the precarious drift of his mindless, maniacal world.

"Now, I want you to know I am speaking strictly for myself, from my own convictions, toward a definition of what I want to do. This is my point of orientation, my ground, my argument. I have reached a point of conviction. Cezanne is right; the artist does not learn from nature, he learns in the museum. With the emergence of Pop art, the New Realism, the Neo-Dada, I have been forcibly struck with the fact that our art can never again promote the Precious Object as the lodestone of forms, as the magnetic center of attraction around which all modern concepts turn. The nature of form is not the form of Nature; nor is it the form of Beauty; neither the Ideal, nor the Perfect; nor is the beautiful implied in the form of the Ugly. Today the form of art is in the nature of Ruin—*Technological Ruin*.

"The technological supersystem had produced The Affluent Society. We are a society whose cultural format is a gathering together of wealth in such abundance that any measure by past standards is meaningless. Our capacity to produce superabundance has made us become a colossal model of gaud, glitter, and glut. No past period of history has produced a society like ours, whose wealth and opulence is *not* measured by accumulation, but by *discard*. The Affluent Society has produced a culture of *planned waste*.

"In the society of planned waste, the making of commodities must be conceived from the proposition of continual change; not revision, but total replacement is the goal because super-

abundance needs ever-increasing change to keep pace with the computerized instant schedules of superproductive machines. As planned waste and instant objects become social necessity, a new reorientation must occur in relation to custom, religion, and history. Because all religion is based on austerity and need and promises a return to eternal good beyond mortal time and space; and because history is a reaction in the search of a great myth-man, an ancestor, a hero, or god who possesses the Tree of Life and shows how to reach its everlasting abundance—today such needs are gone. Man, not God, creates superabundance. If the needs are gone, the myth of the hero and the god must die.

"Man as the arbiter of push-button superabundance has redefined slow-time transformation-evolution into instant-time creation-annihilation. As these overturn the old myths of history and speed toward unimpeded chaos, chaos in its finite term is infinite good. Waste and chaos as Infinite Good become analogous to God. In the era of waste, we see the wreck of the Hero and the death of God. Cybernetic routine man has atomized them, sent them to oblivion. This is why we delight in the wreck. This is why great concretions of junk abound in our world.

"No human use can effectively reduce the gargantuan output, the superglut. There is only one means which can keep pace with machine superglut, and that equivalent is to use the *machine* to use up the output of the machine. In other words, the equivalent of technological hyperproduction can only be *technological ruin*.

"The name of this solution is war—but war that is not for plunder, not for annexation of territory, not rape of cities, not taking of slaves—none of these things. The object is the sudden ruin of instant objects, the immediate annihilation of hyperproduced material. There the equation of use—destruction—begins to meet the equation of production. Against all progress, Technological Ruin is the paradox of our time, the precious ideal form of the perverse Cybernetic Society."

BIOGRAPHICAL/CRITICAL SOURCES: Bizarre (Paris), numbers 29-30, 1963; Pierre Couperie and Maurice Horn, *A History of the Comic Strip,* Crown, 1968; *Nation,* August 30, 1971; Francis Lacassin, *Tarzan ou le chevalier crispe,* Union generale d'editions, 1971; Burne Hogarth and Robert M. Hodes, *Jungle Tales of Tarzan,* Watson-Guptill, 1976; Horn, *World Encyclopedia of Comics,* Chelsea House, 1976; *Arts/Lettres* (Paris), June, 1977.

*   *   *

HOGG, Oliver Frederick Gillilan   1887-1979

PERSONAL: Born December 22, 1887, in Bedford, England; died in 1979; son of Arthur Melvill Hogg (an army officer); married Ella Harold Hallam, 1919; children: one son. *Education:* Attended Royal Military Academy, Woolwich, England. *Home:* 1 Hardy Rd., Blackheath SE3 7NS, England.

CAREER: British Army, Royal Artillery, 1907-46, retired as brigadier, 1946. During World War I served in France; received British War and Victory Medals; became major, 1926; Armaments Inspection Department, assistant inspector, 1921-25, inspector, 1927-30; became colonel, 1935; secretary of Ordnance Board, 1936-39; became brigadier, 1939; Ministry of Supply, deputy director, 1939-41, director, 1941-46; received War and Defense Medals. *Member:* Society of Antiquaries (fellow; member of council, 1953-55), Royal Society of Arts (fellow), Royal Geographical Society (fellow), Royal Historical Society (fellow), Ancient Monuments

Society (fellow), Society of Genealogists (fellow; member of executive committee, 1959-62), Society for Army Historical Research, Greenwich Conservative Association (vice-president, 1957-79). *Awards, honors:* Commander, Order of the British Empire, 1943; Leverhulme research fellowship, 1950-51; third class, Order of Polonia Restituta.

WRITINGS: The Royal Arsenal: Its Background, Origin, and Subsequent History, Oxford University Press, 1963; *English Artillery, 1326-1716: Being the History of Artillery in This Country Prior to the Formation of the Royal Regiment of Artillery,* Royal Artillery Institution, 1963; *Further Light on the Ancestry of William Penn,* Society of Genealogists, 1964; *Clubs to Cannon: Warfare and Weapons Before the Introduction of Gunpowder,* Duckworth, 1968; *Artillery: Its Origin, Heyday, and Decline,* Archon Books, 1970. Also author of *The History of the Third Durham Volunteer Artillery, 1860-1960,* 1960, and *The Woolwich Mess,* 2nd edition, 1971. Contributor to *Chamber's Encyclopaedia,* and to journals and magazines.

AVOCATIONAL INTERESTS: Walking and boating.*

*   *   *

HOLMAN, Mary A(lida) 1933-

PERSONAL: Born June 26, 1933, in West Point, N.Y.; daughter of Jonathan Lane (an army officer) and Anna Alida (Johnson) Holman; married Theodore Suranyi-Unger (a professor), December 15, 1962. *Education:* George Washington University, B.A., 1955, M.A., 1957, Ph.D., 1963. *Politics:* Independent. *Religion:* Episcopalian. *Home:* 8900 Jeffery Rd., Great Falls, Va. 22066. *Office:* Department of Economics, George Washington University, Washington, D.C. 20052.

CAREER: Continental Oil Co., Houston, Tex., statistical analyst, 1957; National Planning Association, Washington, D.C., economic research assistant, 1957-58; U.S. Department of Agriculture, Washington, D.C., economist, 1958-59; Resources for the Future, Washington, D.C., economist, 1960-61; George Washington University, Washington, D.C., instructor, summers, 1959-61, 1962-65, associate research professor and associate professorial lecturer, 1963-66, professor of economics, 1966—, head of department, 1976—, director of Natural Resources Policy Center, 1970-76. Professorial lecturer at Industrial College of the Armed Forces, 1965-75; guest lecturer at National War College, 1966-73. Consultant to U.S. Office of Management and Budget, Stanford Research Institute, and National Aeronautics and Space Administration. *Awards, honors:* Robert C. Watson Award from American Patent Law Association, 1964; certificate from Industrial College of the Armed Forces, 1966.

WRITINGS: (Co-author) *Evaluation of the Patent Policy of the National Aeronautics and Space Administration,* U.S. Government Printing Office, 1966; (contributor) *Conservation in the United States,* 2nd edition (Holman was not included in 1st edition), Rand McNally, 1968; (contributor) J. L. Harris, editor, *Nurturing New Ideas: Legal Rights and Economic Roles,* Bureau of National Affairs, 1969; *The Political Economy of the Space Program,* Pacific Books, 1974; (with D. S. Watson) *Price Theory and Its Uses,* 4th edition (Holman was not associated with earlier editions), Houghton, 1977. Contributor of about twenty articles to economic, technical, and scientific journals.

WORK IN PROGRESS: The Economics of Science and Technology; Public Policy Economics.

SIDELIGHTS: Mary Holman writes that she is motivated by "a deep belief that extensive federal funding for science and technology will do much to increase productivity and solve short-run problems of such a nature as the energy crisis, and a strong belief in the effectiveness of the private market mechanism."

*   *   *

HOLMES, Frederic L(awrence) 1932-

PERSONAL: Born February 6, 1932, in Cincinnati, Ohio; son of Frederic Everett (a clinical biochemist) and Florence (Jauch) Holmes; married Harriet Vann (a university teacher of English), December 29, 1959; children: Catherine, Susan, Rebecca. *Education:* Massachusetts Institute of Technology, B.S., 1954; Harvard University, M.A., 1957, Ph.D., 1962. *Politics:* Democrat. *Religion:* Protestant. *Home:* 74 Edgemere Rd., Hamden, Conn. 06517. *Office:* School of Medicine, Yale University, 333 Cedar St., New Haven, Conn. 06510.

CAREER: Massachusetts Institute of Technology, Cambridge, assistant professor of humanities and history of science, 1962-64; Yale University, New Haven, Conn., assistant professor, 1964-70, associate professor of history of science, 1970-72; University of Western Ontario, London, professor of history of medicine and science and head of department, 1972-79; Yale University, professor of history of medicine, 1979—. Member of Hamden Human Relations Area Council, 1970-72. *Military service:* U.S. Air Force, 1955-57; became first lieutenant.

MEMBER: History of Science Society (vice-president, 1978-80; president-elect, 1980-82), American Association for the History of Medicine, Canadian Society for the History and Philosophy of Science (second vice-president, 1977-79). *Awards, honors:* Schumann Prize from History of Science Society, 1961; Pfizer Prize from History of Science Society, 1975, and William Welch Medal from American Association for the History of Medicine, 1978, both for *Claude Bernard and Animal Chemistry.*

WRITINGS: Claude Bernard and Animal Chemistry, Harvard University Press, 1974. Contributor of about a dozen articles and reviews to journals on the history of science and medicine.

WORK IN PROGRESS: Hans Krebs: The Formation of a Scientific Life (tentative title).

SIDELIGHTS: Holmes writes: "For many years the normal patterns of education have continued to divide students sharply into scientists and humanists. Recently the growing sense that most public issues have at least some scientific component has renewed my hope that the history of science may still sometime play a mediating role.

"My first two teaching years gave me limited scope to develop my interest in the history of science, but by a fortunate chance I was asked to spend a year at Yale. I stayed for eight years. There I had the opportunity to specialize in the history of the biological sciences and to benefit from a splendid library for the history of medicine.

"I left Yale in 1972 for the University of Western Ontario. I found it a rewarding experience to live in that very comfortable, attractive region of Canada, and came to recognize and appreciate the real differences between the outlook of Canadians and Americans, to feel a sense of rapport with the Canadian way of life, and at the same time to view our country from the perspective of those who live just beyond its borders.

"I had not considered myself to be a historian of medicine,

since I am not medically trained, and my historical research has been principally in such areas as the history of biochemistry and physiology. The dean of medicine at Yale assured me, however, that at Yale they consider this to be a part of medicine."

AVOCATIONAL INTERESTS: Tennis, playing the clarinet.

* * *

HOLROYD, Stuart 1933-

PERSONAL: Born August 10, 1933, in Bradford, England; son of Thomas (a sales representative) and Edith (King) Holroyd; married Susan Joy Bennett (a writer and teacher), September 23, 1961; children: Helen and Ruth (twins), Piers Jonathan. *Education:* Attended University College, London, 1957-58. *Home:* 55 Filsham Rd., St. Leonards-on-Sea, Sussex TN38 OPA, England. *Agent:* David Bolt, 8/12 Old Queen St., London S.W.1., England.

CAREER: Inlingua School of Languages, Hastings, England, founder and owner, 1962-75; writer, 1975—.

WRITINGS: Emergence From Chaos, Houghton, 1957; *Flight and Pursuit,* Gollancz, 1959; *The English Imagination,* Longmans, Green, 1969; *Contraries: A Personal Progression,* Bodley Head, 1975; *Magic, Words, and Numbers,* Doubleday, 1976; *Minds Without Boundaries,* Doubleday, 1976; *PSI and the Consciousness Explosion,* Taplinger, 1977; *Dream Worlds,* Doubleday, 1977; *Psychic Voyages,* Doubleday, 1977; *Prelude to the Landing on Planet Earth,* W.H. Allen, 1977, reprinted as *Briefing for the Landing on Planet Earth,* Corgi Books, 1979; *Mysteries of the Gods,* Aldus Books, 1979; *Mysteries of Life,* Aldus Books, 1979; *Alien Intelligence,* Everest House, 1979; *Mysteries of the Past,* Aldus Books 1980; (with wife, Susan Holroyd) *The Complete Book of Sexual Love,* Aldus Books, 1980; *The Philosophy of Krishnamurti,* Aquarian Press, 1980.

Author of "The Tenth Chance" (three-act play), first produced in London, England, at Royal Court Theatre, 1958. Contributor to magazines, including *London, Declaration,* and *Encounter,* and newspapers.

WORK IN PROGRESS: The New Age Book of Mind, Body, and Environment; Sex and the New Age; Man Alone (tentative title), literary criticism and essays on changing images of man in literature, from the beginnings of Romanticism to the present day; *The Call From Tomorrow* (tentative title), "a comic psychic/science fiction novel."

SIDELIGHTS: Holroyd wrote: "My literary career has been in two stages. At the rather early age of twenty-three, I published my first book, a discussion of the psychology and significance of religious experience as expressed in some modern poets, and at twenty-five I had the temerity to publish an account of my own inner life and experience.

"This was in the late 1950's, when the British press made much of the 'angry young men,' and that was probably one reason why I ventured to write autobiographically: all the publicity we had received made us feel that what we were and what we had to say was important.

"Then, in 1959, something happened that seemed more important and more valuable: I fell in love. Love, marriage, and the bearing and rearing of children absorbed virtually all my time and energies for nearly fifteen years.

"My literary work was resumed in 1975, with the publication of *Contraries,* an autobiographical volume about the late fifties. By the mid-seventies the interests and ideas that some friends and I had entertained and advocated in the fifties were considered by many more people to be important and/or interesting, and I was able to embark on a spate of work, developing the interest in questions of the psychology and relevance of religious or spiritual experience that had been central in my first books.

"*PSI and the Consciousness Explosion,* an examination of the evidence for paranormal functions of mind and a discussion of the relevance of the existence of these functions for philosophy, psychology, and our concept of man and of his future, is probably my most condensed and coherent statement to date, although *Alien Intelligence* carries the discussion into new areas.

"Fundamentally, I feel that we are living through a time of very great and salutary changes in human consciousness, and it is my hope that my work may report, reflect, and possibly even contribute to these changes."

* * *

HOLZNER, Burkart 1931-

PERSONAL: Born April 28, 1931, in Tilsit, Germany; came to the United States in 1957, naturalized citizen, 1965; son of Hans Otto (a publisher) and Brigitte Holzner; married Anne Segel; children: Steven, Daniel, Claire. *Education:* Attended University of Wisconsin—Madison, 1952-53, 1957-59; University of Munich, diploma, 1954; University of Bonn, diploma, 1957, Ph.D. (summa cum laude), 1958. *Office:* Department of Sociology, University of Pittsburgh, Pittsburgh, Pa. 15260.

CAREER: University of Pittsburgh, Pittsburgh, Pa., assistant professor, 1960-63, associate professor, 1963-66, professor of sociology and head of department, 1966—, director of board of visitors field staff of Learning Research and Development Center, 1966-69, 1973-78. Associate director of program development at University of Hawaii's Social Science Research Institute, 1965-66; visiting professor at Chinese University of Hong Kong, 1969-70, and University of Augsburg, 1977; member of national advisory board of Center for the Study of Educational Evaluation, at University of California, Los Angeles, 1968-70.

MEMBER: International Society for the Comparative Study of Civilizations (U.S. vice-president, 1977), American Sociological Association, Conference Group on German Politics, Sozialwissenschaftlicher Studienkreis fuer international Probleme (member of council), Eastern Sociological Association, North Central Sociological Association. *Awards, honors:* U.S. State Department scholar, 1952-53.

WRITINGS: Reality Construction in Society, Schenkman, 1968, revised edition, 1972; (with John Marx) *Knowledge Application: The Knowledge System in Society,* Allyn & Bacon, 1978; (editor with Roland Robertson) *Identity and Authority,* Basil Blackwell, 1979.

In German: (Editor) *Der Staatsbuerger fragt* (handbook of political institutions in West Germany), 2nd edition (Holzner was not associated with 1st edition), Menzen Verlag, 1955; (translator from English) Leslie C. Steven, *Russian Assignment,* Holzner Verlag, 1956; *Amerikanische und deutsche Psychologie* (title means "Psychology in America and Germany"), Holzner Verlag, 1958; (editor) Howard Becker, *Soziologie als Wissenschaft vom sozialen Handeln* (title means "Sociology as the Study of Social Action"), Holzner Verlag, 1959; *Volkerpsychologie: Leitfaden mit Bibliographie* (title means "National Psychologies: An Outline and Bibliography"), Holzner Verlag, 1960.

Contributor to *English Language Dictionary of Central So-*

cial Science Concepts. Contributor of about thirty articles and reviews to sociology journals.

* * *

HONG, Jane Fay 1954-
(Adora Sheridan, a joint pseudonym)

PERSONAL: Born October 30, 1954, in San Francisco, Calif.; daughter of Lim Chong (in laundry work) and Choon Ong (in laundry work; maiden name, Chow) Hong. *Education:* San Francisco City College, A.A., 1973; San Francisco State University, B.S.W., 1977. *Office:* Day Center, Garden Sullivan Hospital, 2700 Geary Blvd., San Francisco, Calif. 94118.

CAREER: Garden Sullivan Hospital, Day Center, San Francisco, Calif., outreach social worker, 1977—. Member of San Francisco Coalition for In-Home Services.

WRITINGS—With Evelyn Marie Pavlik under joint pseudonym Adora Sheridan: *The Signet Ring* (novel), Ballantine, 1979; *The Season* (novel), Ballantine, 1979.

WORK IN PROGRESS—With Evelyn Marie Pavlik under joint pseudonym Adora Sheridan: *Hightower,* a Regency romance; *The Walking Stick,* a late Georgian romance.

SIDELIGHTS: Jane Hong comments: "These romances were meant originally only to entertain ourselves. They were never intended for publication, but became so large that it was decided that we might as well try to publish them. I personally write for the pleasure of it and only write what I would like to read myself."

* * *

HOOVER, Mary B(idgood) 1917-

PERSONAL: Born July 3, 1917, in Tuscaloosa, Ala.; daughter of Lee (a professor) and Emily (Smith) Bidgood; married Rolle R. Rand (divorced); married Gilbert Corwin Hoover, Jr. (an advertising director), January 19, 1952; children: Mallory S., Lee (Mrs. Ivan Suzman), Gilbert Corwin IV. *Education:* University of Alabama, A.B., 1938; Columbia University, M.A., 1939. *Residence:* New York, N.Y. *Agent:* McIntosh & Otis, Inc., 475 Fifth Ave., New York, N.Y. 10017.

CAREER: Writer, 1952—. Chairperson of book review committee of Jewish Board of Family and Children's Services, 1969—. *Awards, honors:* Brotherhood Award from National Conference of Christians and Jews, 1962, for article, "Values to Live By."

WRITINGS: (With Greta Mayer) *When Children Need Special Help With Emotional Problems* (pamphlet), Child Study Press, 1961, revised edition, 1974; (with Mayer) *Learning to Love and Let Go* (pamphlet), Child Study Association of America, 1965; (editor) *Guiding Your Child From Five to Twelve,* revised edition (Hoover was not associated with 1st edition), Parents' Magazine Press, 1969; (with Ada Daniels) *When Children Ask About Sex* (pamphlet), Child Study Association of America, 1969; (with Marsha Berent) *Mnemonic Phonetics: A Total Language Program,* Wadsworth, 1969; *You, Your Child, and Drugs* (Book-of-the-Month Club selection), Child Study Press, 1971; *The Responsive Parent,* Parents' Magazine Press, 1972; *Home Study Course in Day Care Services,* Child Welfare League of America, 1973.

Author of filmstrip series. Author of "Parents Want to Know," a monthly column in *True Story,* 1970-73, 1976—. Editor-in-chief of "Parents' Magazine's Self-Guidance Program to Successful Parenthood," a book series, Parents'

Magazine Press, 1972. Contributor to *Childcraft Encyclopedia.* Contributor of about thirty articles to *Parents' Magazine, Redbook, McCall's, Seventeen,* and *New York Times Magazine.*

WORK IN PROGRESS: A book about ways in which children become inhibited by sex stereotyping, regardless of their rearing, and what parents can do about it at each age level; continuing research on child development.

AVOCATIONAL INTERESTS: Apartment gardening, reading, fishing, travel, cooking, sewing.

* * *

HOPE, Karol

PERSONAL: Born in Pennsylvania. *Education:* University of California, Los Angeles, B.A., 1970. *Home address:* c/o General Delivery, Caspar, Calif. 95420. *Agent:* Virginia Barber Literary Agency, Inc., 44 Greenwich Ave., New York, N.Y. 10011.

CAREER: Founding member of Momma (national organization for single mothers), president, 1970-72. *Awards, honors:* Named woman of the year by *Mademoiselle,* 1974.

WRITINGS: (With Nancy Young) *Momma: The Sourcebook for Single Mothers,* New American Library, 1976; *Out of the Frying Pan: A Decade of Change in Women's Lives,* Doubleday, 1979. Founder and editor of *Momma* (newspaper), 1970-72.

* * *

HOPE-WALLACE, Philip (Adrian) 1911-1979

OBITUARY NOTICE: Born November 6, 1911; died September 2, 1979, in Guildford, England. Drama critic. Hope-Wallace began his journalistic career as a correspondent for the *London Times.* He subsequently became a drama critic for various publications, including *Time and Tide, Listener,* and *Manchester Guardian.* In 1939 he wrote *A Key to Opera.* Hope-Wallace served with the Air Ministry as a press officer during World War II and was created Commander of the Order of the British Empire in 1975. Obituaries and other sources: *Who's Who in Music and Musicians' International Directory,* 6th edition, Hafner, 1972; *Who's Who in the Theatre,* 15th edition, Pitman, 1972; *Who's Who,* 131st edition, St. Martin's, 1979; *Chicago Tribune,* September 9, 1979.

* * *

HOWARD, Dorothy Gray 1902-
(Dorothy Mills)

PERSONAL: Born July 8, 1902, in Greenville, Tex.; daughter of Leonidas Menno (an educator) and Lou Florence (an educator; maiden name, Gray) Mills; married James Howard, June 26, 1925 (died, 1945); children: James, Ann Howard Wilson. *Education:* North Texas State University, B.S., 1923; New York University, M.A., 1932, Ed.D., 1938. *Politics:* Independent. *Religion:* Unitarian-Universalist. *Home:* 2009 North Louisiana, Roswell, N.M. 88201.

CAREER: Public school teacher and principal in Texas, New York, and New Jersey, 1919-44; Frostburg State College, Frostburg, Md., professor of English, 1944-67, head of department, 1944-61; University of Nebraska, Lincoln, visiting professor of English, 1967-69; writer, 1969—. Director of Westchester County Recreation Camp (for girls), 1930-36. Conducted sociological research in Jalisco, Mexico, 1962-63. *Member:* American Folklore Society. *Awards, honors:* Fulbright grant for study at University of Melbourne, 1954-55.

WRITINGS: (With Eloise Ramsey) *Folklore for Children and Young People* (bibliography), American Folklore Society, 1952; (author of introduction) A. B. Gomme, *The Traditional Games of England, Scotland, and Ireland*, two volumes, Dover, 1964; *Dorothy's World: Childhood in Sabine Bottom, 1902-1910*, Prentice-Hall, 1977. Contributor of about thirty-five articles and poems to scholarly journals, literary and popular magazines, including *New Yorker* (under name Dorothy Mills), *Jack and Jill*, *Texas Poets*, and *Lantern*.

WORK IN PROGRESS: Pedro of Tonala, a sociological study of a Mexican boy; *Travel Guide for the Young*, completion expected in 1982; *The Education of Wesley Wyler*, a novel, publication expected in 1985.

SIDELIGHTS: Dorothy Howard began studying children's verses and play in the 1930's. She has observed children of different cultures and different generations and has noted the similarities of many of their activities. Her book, *Dorothy's World*, chronicles her own pioneer childhood in Texas from her own notes and family letters and documents.

She writes: "Since retirement from teaching, I have been writing and communing with nature. According to my writing plan, I hope to complete four or five books (based on forty-five years of research on children's play life) before creeping senility overtakes me. Be that as it may, writing does not interfere with communion with nature. I live in a little fake-adobe house facing Sierra Blanca and El Capitan mountains seventy to one hundred miles to the west. Western meadowlarks court in my backyard, nest in the pasture west of my house, and bring their brood to breakfast in my front yard. Hummingbirds feed on the honeysuckle which I planted for them and nest in nearby mulberry trees. Spring and fall, sandhill cranes from the Dakotas vacation for a month at Bitter Lakes, nearby. They mark the hour of the day for us, honking as they fly westward at dawn to feed on pastures and fields and eastward at sunset to Bitter Lakes. And they tell us the season by their arrivals and departures."

BIOGRAPHICAL/CRITICAL SOURCES: Albuquerque Journal, March 8, 1977; *Cumberland News*, March 15, 1977; *Roswell Daily Record*, June 5, 1977; *NRTA Journal*, March-April, 1978.

*   *   *

HOWARD, Roger   1938-

PERSONAL: Born June 19, 1938, in Warwickshire, England; married Anne Mary Zemaitis (a teacher), August 13, 1960; children: Bjorn Axel. *Education:* Attended Royal Academy of Dramatic Art, 1956-57, and University of Bristol, 1958; University of Essex, M.A., 1976. *Home:* Church Road, Little Waldingfield, Sudbury, Suffolk CO10 0SN, England. *Office:* Department of Literature, University of Essex, Wivenhoe Park, Colchester CO4 3SQ, England.

CAREER: Poet, playwright, novelist, and biographer. Nankai University, Tientsin, People's Republic of China, teacher of English, 1965-67; Collets Bookshop, Peterborough, England, manager, 1967-68; Bookshop 85, London, England, manager, 1968-72; Peking University, Peking, People's Republic of China, lecturer in English literature, 1972-74; Mercury Theatre, Colchester, England, playwright-in-residence, 1976; University of York, York, England, fellow in creative writing, 1976-78; University of East Anglia, Norwich, England, Henfield Writing Fellow, 1979; University of Essex, Colchester, lecturer in literature, 1979—. Member of editorial committee of *China Now* magazine and of *Platform* theatre magazine. *Military service:* Royal Armoured Service Corps, 1958; sentenced to imprisonment after refusing to wear uniform; dishonorably discharged. *Member:* British Theatre Institute, Society of Anglo-Chinese Understanding (member of council of management, 1971-72), Union of Theatre Writers. *Awards, honors:* Playwright's bursary from Arts Council of Great Britain, 1975-76.

WRITINGS: A Phantastic Satire (novel), Chapple, 1960; *From the Life of a Patient* (novel), Chapple, 1961; *Four Stories* [and] *Twelve Sketches* (the former by Howard; the latter by Tony Astbury), Mouthpiece, 1964; *To the People* (poems), Mouthpiece, 1966; *Praise Songs* (poems), Mouthpiece, 1966; *The Technique of the Struggle Meeting* (nonfiction), Clandestine, 1968; *The Use of Wall Newspapers* (nonfiction), Clandestine, 1968.

The Hooligan's Handbook (essay), Action Books, 1971; (editor) *Culture and Agitation: Theatre Documents*, Action Books, 1972; *Method for Revolutionary Writing*, Action Books, 1972; *Mao Tse-Tung and the Chinese People* (biography), Allen & Unwin, 1976, Monthly Review Press, 1977; *Contemporary Chinese Theatre*, Heinemann, 1976.

Plays: "Bewitched Foxes Rehearsing Their Roles," first produced in London, England, 1968; *Fin's Doubts* (first produced in London, 1968), privately printed, 1968; "The Love Suicides at Havering," first produced in London, 1969 (also see below); "Season," first produced in London, 1969; "Simon Murdering His Deformed Wife With a Hammer," first produced in London, 1969.

"Seven Stages on the Road to Exile," first produced in Carlisle, England, 1970 (also see below); "The Carrying of X From A to Z," first produced in Papua, New Guinea, 1971 (also see below); "Dis," first produced in York, England, 1971 (also see below); "The Meaning of the Statue," first produced in London, 1971 (also see below); "Writing on Stone," first produced in London, 1971 (also see below); "The Auction of Virtues," first produced in London, 1972 (also see below); "Sunrise" first produced at Peking University, 1973.

"The Travels of Yi Yuk-sa to the Caves at Yenan," first produced in Colchester, England, 1976 (also see below); "The Drum of the Strict Master," first produced in Colchester at Essex University Theatre, February, 1976 (also see below); "Klong 1, Klong 2, and the Partisan," first produced in Colchester, 1976; "Notes for a New History," first produced in Colchester at Essex University Theatre, February, 1976; "The Tragedy of Mao in the Lin Piao Period," first produced, under title "History of the Tenth Struggle," in London at ICA Theatre, September, 1976; "The Great Tide," first produced in Colchester at Mercury Theatre, 1976; "A Feast During Famine," first produced by Wakefield Tricycle Co., 1977; "Travelling Players of the Dawn," first produced in York, 1977.

"Women's Army," first produced by Omoro Theatre Co., 1978; "Margery Kempe," first produced in London at ICA Theatre, May, 1978; "Korotov's Ego-Theatre," first produced in Edinburgh, Scotland, by Cambridge Mummers' Theatre, 1978 (also see below); "Report From the City of Reds in the Year 1970," first produced in Cambridge, England, by Cambridge Mummers' Theatre, 1978 (also see below); "Episodes From Fighting in the East," first produced in Edinburgh by Cambridge Mummers' Theatre, 1978 (also see below); "Queen," first produced in Alsager, England, at Alsager College, March, 1979; "The Society of Poets," first produced in Edinburgh, 1979 (also see below); "Memorial of the Future," first produced in Norwich, England, 1979 (also see below); "A Break in Berlin," first produced at Essex University in Theatre Underground, 1979.

Other plays: (Contributor) *New Short Plays* (includes "Dis," "The Carrying of X from A to Z," "The Love Suicides at Havering," and "Seven Stages on the Road to Exile,"), Methuen, 1968; *Slaughter Night and Other Plays* (contains "Slaughter Night," "The Meaning of the Statue," "The Travels of Yi Yuk-sa to the Caves at Yenan," "Returning to the Capital," "Writing on Stone," "Korotov's Ego-Theatre," "Report From the City of Reds in the Year 1970," "The Drum of the Strict Master," "Episodes From the Fighting in the East," "A New Bestiary," and "The Play of Iron"), Calder & Boyars, 1971; *The Society of Poets* [and] *Memorial of the Future*, Action Books, 1979. Contributor to *Scripts* (includes "The Travels of Yi Yuk-sa to the Caves at Yenan," "Episodes From the Fighting in the East," and "Returning to the Capital"), February, 1972, and to *Yorrick* (includes "The Auction of Virtues"), No. 9, 1977.

Unpublished and unproduced plays: "A, B and C"; "Bread, Meat and Higher Learning: Interludes Between Life and Death From the History of the Reformation"; "Brothers"; "Cage"; "The Career of Solus Altissimus"; "Cells"; "Ceremony"; "The Charter of the Word"; "Courier"; "Datien"; "The Death of Hunger"; "The Earth-Founding"; "Elements"; "The Flight of the Birds"; "For"; "The Force in the Land"; "Idol"; "'Ism' Isn't Right, Right?"; "Joseph Arch"; "Looking at the Finger Pointing to the Moon"; "Poetry and Documents From My Occupation"; "A Propaganda Play"; "Rising"; "The Robbers: A Jubilee Pageant"; "Seven Days of Correction: A Radio Play"; "Song of the Eight Points"; "Still Birth"; "Stone"; "The Struggle of the On Guard Group"; "Testimony of the Accused X23Z"; "Tower"; "Uncadre Li"; "The Use of Burning"; "The Verdict: A Comedy"; "Wants"; "Wartext"; "The Weight of Many Masters"; "White Sea."

Contributor of stories to magazines and journals, including *Works, Wordworks,* and *Transatlantic Review;* contributor of poems to magazines and journals, including *New Poetry, Minnesota Review,* and *Times Literary Supplement;* contributor of book reviews to magazines, including *Books and Bookmen* and *New Society;* contributor of play reviews to *Gambit* and *Plays and Players.*

WORK IN PROGRESS: A book on the idea content of new English theatre writing; a full-length play about the Siege of Colchester in 1648, for the Mercury Theatre, Colchester.

SIDELIGHTS: Though Roger Howard has written a "sympathetic biography" of Mao Tse-tung, he had earned his "Maoist" label long before his study of the revolutionary Chinese leader. His plays, as he says, fall under a number of headings, but the recurring theme of revolution reinforces his belief that the purpose of art is to "divide and agitate." Having raised their class consciousness to the point of overcoming fear of action, the heroes of Howard's plays are revolutionaries. Howard relies on his heroes to shake the "great sleep" encouraged by society's oppressors—those that preserve its class divisions.

But the 'Maoist' label may be misleading. An outline of some of Howard's plays, while it reveals his preoccupation with the revolutionary theme, also shows his roots in English popular tradition. Manifest in the revolutionary theme is the author's belief in the ability of individuals to influence the conditions under which they live. "My early short plays are most of them highly stylised abstractions," Howard remarked. "They have a rather international subject matter—decolonisation in Africa, the Cultural Revolution in China, ancient Britain, modern Ireland. The recent long plays include a series of plays dealing with moments in En-

glish history, in the lives of people struggling. 'The Earth-Founding' is about slaves and farmers in St. Edmund's time. 'Margery Kempe' is about an unorthodox medieval mystic and brewer. 'Bread, Meat and Higher Learning' deals with the Catholic suppression of the Protestants during Mary's reign. 'The Weight of Many Masters' traces the rise of the agricultural workers' union in the late nineteenth century and the career of one of its first leaders, Joseph Arch. . . . A number of my plays on contemporary England, like 'Still Birth' and 'Women's Army,' deal with people who, as it were, resist 'fitting in.'"

Closely related to an understanding of Howard's definition of socialism is the difference between what is and what could be. In "A Break in Berlin," for example, a German woman realizes there are two sides to the invading Red Army. First, said Howard, when she "sees the easy informality between officers and men and listens to their optimistic ideas, she is struck by the contrast between the Nazi propaganda version of the Red Army, raping, looting and killing, and the actuality." Eventually this woman finds that the Red Army does indeed rape, loot and kill, but, ironically, in a socialist way. "This lonely, prejudiced, and suffering middle-class woman had her first experience of the realities of 'actually-existing socialism' lying on her back," noted Howard.

The subject matter of "A Break in Berlin" "draws attention to the primary matter I'm dealing with in all my plays," the author continued. "It is that I am concerned to show the person, from whatever class, in a material way, from many angles, containing a multitude of facets—expressed in anguish, suffering, sorrow, hopes, happiness, joy—from a personal point of view and a social point of view simultaneously, so that the person's private self is shown in relation to that person's public persona."

Howard's plays are considered easily stagable, but he has had little success in having them widely performed in larger theatres. One reason, he speculated, is the current state of socialist theatre: "As we are not yet free to operate in properly based socialist theatre companies and not yet free, as writers to write completely as socialists, we must still usually put our meaning in obliquely, sometimes hide behind conundrums, often compromise, resort to prevarication and occasionally be agitationally bold in order to get our plays performed at all."

BIOGRAPHICAL/CRITICAL SOURCES: Times Literary Supplement, November 10, 1978.

*   *   *

HOWAT, Gerald Malcolm David   1928-

PERSONAL: Born June 12, 1928, in Glasgow, Scotland; son of Dean Rudolph (a minister) and Agatha (Cooke) Henderson-Howat; married Anne McGillivray Murdoch (a psychiatrist), July 8, 1951; children: David Barclay, Gillian Mary, Michael Gerald. *Education:* University of Edinburgh, M.A. (with honors), 1950; University of London, diploma in education, 1959; Exeter College, Oxford, M.Litt., 1962. *Home:* Old School House, North Moreton, Didcot, Oxford OX11 9BA, England. *Office:* Lord Williams's School, Thame, Oxford, England.

CAREER: High school history teacher and department head in Tavistock, England, 1955-60; Culham College of Education, Oxford, England, principal lecturer in history and head of department, 1960-73; high school history teacher and department head in Oxford, England, 1973-77; Lord Williams's School, Oxford, England, tutor, 1977—. Vice-chairman of board of governors of Wallingford School, 1968-73. *Military service:* Royal Air Force, 1950-52; became flying officer. *Member:* Royal Historical Society (fellow), Marylebone Cricket Club (playing member). *Awards, honors:* Jubilee Award from Cricket Society, 1975, for outstanding cricket book of the year.

WRITINGS: From Chatham to Churchill: British History, 1760-1965, Thomas Nelson, 1966; (editor) *Essays to a Young Teacher,* Pergamon, 1966; (with wife, Anne Howat) *The Story of Health,* Pergamon, 1967; *The Teaching of Empire and Commonwealth History,* Historical Association, 1967; (editor) *Dictionary of World History,* Thomas Nelson, 1973; *Documents in European History, 1789-1970,* Edward Arnold, 1974; *Stuart and Cromwellian Foreign Policy,* A. & C. Black, 1974; *The Oxford and Cambridge Examination Board, 1873-1973,* Oxford University Press, 1974; (editor) *Who Did What: The Lives and Achievements of the 5000 Men and Women—Leaders of Nations, Saints and Sinners, Artists and Scientists—Who Shaped Our World,* Mitchell Beazley, 1974, revised edition published as *Who Did What: The Mitchell Beazley Illustrated Biographical Dictionary; 5000 Men and Women Who Have Shaped the World's Destiny,* 1975; *Learie Constantine,* Allen & Unwin, 1975; *Village Cricket,* David & Charles, 1980; *Victoria and Her Times,* Ward, Lock, 1981.

WORK IN PROGRESS: Cricketer Militant, publication expected in 1982; *Cricket and the Victorians,* 1983.

*　　*　　*

HOWELL, William C(arl)　1932-

PERSONAL: Born June 26, 1932, in Morristown, N.J.; son of William (a musician) and Elisabeth (Baraniecki) Howell; married wife, Patricia A., December 21, 1954; children: Karen, Stephen, Carol, Stuart. *Education:* University of Virginia, B.A., 1954, M.A., 1956, Ph.D., 1958. *Home:* 10218 Briar Forest, Houston, Tex. 77042. *Office:* Department of Psychology, Rice University, Houston, Tex. 77001.

CAREER: Ohio State University, Columbus, research associate, 1957-62, assistant professor, 1960-62, associate professor, 1962-65, professor of psychology, 1965-68, director of Human Performance Center, 1962-68; Rice University, Houston, Tex., professor of psychology, 1968—, professor of administrative science, 1977—, head of department of psychology, 1970—. Consultant to government and industry. *Member:* American Psychological Association (fellow), Psychonomic Society, American Association for the Advancement of Science, Phi Beta Kappa, Sigma Xi.

WRITINGS: (With I. Goldstein) *Engineering Psychology: Current Perspectives in Research,* Appleton, 1971; *Essentials of Industrial and Organizational Psychology,* Dorsey, 1976. Contributor of about seventy articles to academic journals. Member of editorial board of *Organizational Behavior and Human Performance* and *Journal of Experimental Psychology,* 1966-73.

WORK IN PROGRESS: A second edition of *Essentials of Industrial and Organizational Psychology;* editing *Human Performance and Productivity,* for Erlbaum Associates.

BIOGRAPHICAL/CRITICAL SOURCES: Contemporary Psychology, April, 1977.

*　　*　　*

HUDSON, Gossie Harold　1930-

PERSONAL: Born February 22, 1930, in New Bern, N.C.; son of Gossie Mark (a soldier) and Bertha Elizabeth (a nurse; maiden name, Nelson) Hudson; married Florence Delores

McCall (a teacher), June 30, 1956; children: Gossie Harold, Jr., Florence Elizabeth. *Education:* North Carolina Central University, B.A., 1956, M.A., 1967; Ohio State University, Ph.D., 1970. *Religion:* Christian. *Home:* 2406 Overland Ave., Baltimore, Md. 21214. *Office:* Department of History, Morgan State University, Baltimore, Md. 21239.

CAREER: High school teacher of history, German, and music in Sarasota, Fla., Eatonton, Ga., Warrenton, N.C., and Durham, N.C., 1956-67; Ohio State University, Columbus, instructor in history, 1968-70; Southern Illinois University, Carbondale, assistant professor of history, 1970-72; Lincoln University, Jefferson City, Mo., professor of history, head of department of history and government, and chairperson of Division of Social Sciences, all 1973-77; Morgan State University, Baltimore, Md., professor of history, 1977—. Visiting associate professor at University of Maryland, 1978-79. Director of symposia; conductor of workshops. Volunteer parole officer. *Military service:* U.S. Army, 1952-54; served in Germany.

MEMBER: Association for the Study of Afro-American Life and History (member of executive committee), Missouri Sheriff's Association (honorary member), Phi Alpha Theta, Pi Gamma Mu. *Awards, honors:* Citations from *Teaching History,* Connectional Lay Council of African Methodist Episcopal Church, and Kaleidoscope of Black Fine Arts, all 1977.

WRITINGS: Forward for Freedom: Mr. Lincoln and the Negroes (booklet), American Education Association, 1971; (editor) *Research Journal,* Department of History and Government, Lincoln University, Volume I, 1973, Volume II, 1975; (contributor) Jean Dorsett Robinson, editor, *The Black Elderly,* College of Human Resources, Southern Illinois University, 1974; (editor) *Directory of Black Historians, Ph.D.'s, and Others, 1975-1976: Essays, Commentaries, and Publications,* Council of Planning Librarians, 1975; (with Edward S. Jenkins) *American Black Scientists and Inventors* (for young people), National Science Teachers Association, 1975; (editor with Jay Martin) *The Paul Laurence Dunbar Reader,* Dodd, 1975; (contributor) Martin, editor, *A Singer in the Dawn,* Dodd, 1975; (contributor) Frank Emory, editor, *Paths Toward Freedom,* Center for Urban Affairs, North Carolina State University, 1976; (editor) *Directory of School Songs and Histories of Black Heritage Institutions in the United States,* National Black Bibliographic and Research Center, 1980; *Slavery: An Extended Bibliography,* National Black Bibliographic and Research Center, in press.

Author of "Connectional Lay Council Column of the American Methodist Episcopal Zion Church," a column in *Star of Zion.* Contributor to *Encyclopedia of Black America* and *Encyclopedia of Southern History.* Contributor of more than forty articles and reviews to history and black studies journals in the United States and abroad. Assistant editor of education and history for *Afro-American Journal;* member of editorial board of *Journal of Ethnic and Special Studies, Teaching History: A Journal of Methods,* and *Burning Heart Newsletter.*

WORK IN PROGRESS: Paul Laurence Dunbar in History, completion expected in 1980; *Prophet Jones: Saint,* completion expected in 1980.

SIDELIGHTS: Hudson told *CA:* "The myth that black studies and the need for instructors in this field are passing into oblivion needs correcting. While it does appear that the job market is closed, the fact is that in the colleges and universities where these courses and programs operate, the instructors are generally young and not inclined to resign. Recent investigations, observations, discussions, and research, however, show that black studies are gaining in academic respectability; programs at new institutions are increasing, and in most colleges, at least some black studies courses are being taught. This trend toward permanency is due in part to the recent appointments in the last seven years of scholarly, research-oriented teachers, and competent administrators to head these programs.''

*   *   *

HUDSON, Jean B(arlow) 1915-

PERSONAL: Born August 21, 1915, in Sugar Grove, Pa.; daughter of Wesley C. (a farmer) and Vesta (Abbott) Barlow; married Benjamin R. Hudson (a hydrogeologist), October 12, 1940; children: Jon Barlow, Rexford Alan, Christopher Giles, Holly Maria. *Education:* Ohio Wesleyan University, B.A., 1939. *Religion:* Unitarian-Universalist. *Residence:* Yellow Springs, Ohio. *Agent:* Norman Darden, 325 East 41st St., New York, N.Y. 10017.

CAREER: Worked as secretary and schoolteacher, 1939-74; writer, 1974—. *Member:* Authors Guild of Authors League of America, Feminist Writers Guild, Women, Inc.

WRITINGS: Rivers of Time (novel), Avon, 1979. Also author of *A Call to Remembrance* (novel).

WORK IN PROGRESS: A third novel, *Earth Tenure.*

SIDELIGHTS: Hudson told *CA:* "After many years of raising a family and following my husband about the world, it became important to me to realize my own development as a person and a writer. I have been enthusiastically pursuing this goal since the fall of 1974, although I am still a part-time homemaker with one teenager at home. My need to write is partly the need to communicate my enthusiasms and goals, feminism, world peace, and international understanding, yet my convictions will always take second place to the characters my imagination creates. They will have their own things to say if they are to be alive. They expand my world; my brain, my energy, my fingers writing, are instruments of the creative process, and I shall follow wherever it takes me.''

*   *   *

HUFF, T(om) E. 1938(?)-
(Edwina Marlow, Beatrice Parker, Katherine St. Clair, Jennifer Wilde)

PERSONAL: Born c. 1938; son of Beatrice (Parker) Huff. *Education:* Attended Texas Wesleyan College; graduate study at Columbia University. *Residence:* Fort Worth, Tex.

CAREER: Former high school teacher. Currently full-time writer.

WRITINGS—All novels: Nine Bucks Row, Hawthorn, 1973; *Meet a Dark Stranger*, Hawthorn, 1974; *Susannah, Beware*, Dell, 1976; *Whisper in the Darkness*, Dell, 1977; *Marabelle*, St. Martin, 1979. Also author of *In Every Window.*

Under pseudonym Edwina Marlow: *Danger at Dahlkari*, Berkley, 1975; *Midnight at Mallyncourt*, Berkley, 1975; *When Emmalyn Remembers*, Ace Books, 1976. Also author of *Falconridge.*

Under pseudonym Beatrice Parker: *Jamintha*, Dell, 1975; *Wherever Lynn Goes*, Dell, 1975.

Under pseudonym Katherine St. Clair: *Room Beneath the Stairs*, Bobbs-Merrill, 1975.

Under pseudonym Jennifer Wilde: *Love's Tender Fury*, Warner Books, 1976; *Dare to Love*, Warner Books, 1978.

SIDELIGHTS: Erotic historical romances can usually be spotted, if not judged, by their covers. The cover of such a book typically depicts a couple locked in a passionate embrace. Sprawled in huge letters across the front, the title usually contains words like "love," "fury," and "tumult." Also on the cover is the author's name, which often sounds as aristocratic and sexy as the name of the fictional heroine. While the author's name does not attract nearly so much attention as the title or the picture on the cover, it too is a matter of interest. For, although erotic historical romances are geared almost exclusively toward the female reader, many of them are written by men who hide behind feminine pseudonyms.

One man who has made a living by writing for women is Tom Huff. Huff began turning out novels when he was in high school, but it was many years before he discovered his proper market. While working as a teacher, he noticed that his female students were always engrossed in gothic novels. Determined to capitalize on this trend, Huff wrote a gothic novel in his spare time. To his delight, the book was snapped up by a publisher.

There was one hitch. His publishers didn't think that a gothic novel written by a man would sell, so Huff was forced to come up with a pen name. He settled upon Edwina Marlow. In the years since then, he has written under other female pseudonyms—Beatrice Parker, Katherine St. Clair, and Jennifer Wilde. Huff doesn't feel that it is unusual for men to write gothic novels. "I think at least 40 per cent of the gothic writers are male," he told a reporter for the *Dallas News.* Nor does he worry about his ability to portray women: "A writer, if he's any kind of writer, is able to project and get under the skin of the character.''

Huff's books, many of which were paperback originals, provided him with such a comfortable income that he was able to quit his teaching job and devote all his time to writing. He writes five days a week, ten to fourteen hours a day. The best rule for writing, he insists, is "put the seat of the pants in the seat of the chair in front of the typewriter and do it.''

Although gothic novels are not Huff's favorite type of book (he prefers detective and mystery novels), he has no difficulty justifying what he is doing. His books supply readers with a necessary escape from reality. "I feel like you need more entertainment," he explained. "Happy people don't start wars, rob banks, shoot people.''

When Huff originally began writing gothic novels, his heroines were true to form—passionate but chaste young women. In one of his books Huff included a scene in which the heroine lost her virginity, but when his editor read the manuscript, that passage was immediately axed. In the 1970's however, it became permissible to put sex scenes in popular romances. In 1972 the publication of Kathleen Woodiwiss's *The Flame and the Flower*, which was filled with torrid love scenes, marked a new trend away from the gothic novel toward the erotic historical romance. Accordingly, Huff began to put more sexually explicit passages into his own books.

Thus far Huff's most lucrative nom de plume has been Jennifer Wilde. There are 2.5 million copies of *Love's Tender Fury*, which was written under the Wilde pseudonym, in print. *Dare to Love*, another book by Wilde, made the best-sellers list.

BIOGRAPHICAL/CRITICAL SOURCES: Authors in the News, Volume 2, Gale, 1976; *Dallas News*, February 18, 1976; *New York*, February 13, 1978; *Chicago Tribune*, July 14, 1978.*

HUISKEN, Ronald H(erman) 1946-

PERSONAL: Born June 17, 1946, in The Hague, Netherlands; came to the United States in 1979; son of Herman Jan (a mechanic) and Catherina (von Splunteren) Huisken; married Meiling Lew, June 22, 1968; children: Jan Greger, Marc Greger. *Education:* University of Western Australia, B.Econ. (with first class honors), 1967; University of Stockholm, M.S.Sc., 1971; doctoral study at Australian National University. *Residence:* New York, N.Y. *Office:* United Nations Organization, First Ave., New York, N.Y. 10017.

CAREER: University of Malaya, Kuala Lumpur, assistant lecturer in economics, 1970-72; Stockholm International Peace Research Institute, Stockholm, Sweden, research fellow, 1972-76; Strategic Defence Studies Centre, Canberra, Australia, visiting fellow, 1976-77, 1979; United Nations, New York, N.Y., consultant to Center for Disarmament, 1977-79, political affairs officer, 1980—.

WRITINGS: The Meaning and Measurement of Military Expenditure (monograph), Almqvist & Wiksell, 1973; (with Frank Barnaby) *Arms Uncontrolled,* Harvard University Press, 1975; *Arms Limitation in Southeast Asia: A Proposal* (monograph), Australian National University Press, 1979; *The Cruise Missile and Arms Control* (monograph), Australia National University Press, 1980. Contributor to *Bulletin of Peace Proposals, Australian Outlook,* and *Australian Journal of Defence Studies.*

WORK IN PROGRESS: A decision-making study of long-range cruise missiles; research on disarmament and development.

SIDELIGHTS: Huisken wrote: "I came to the arms control/disarmament field quite by accident. The field's intrinsic interest and the manifest urgency of doing something about the arms race made the switch from economics easy and irreversible. The arms control process is badly in need of rejuvenation after the marathon of SALT II and its relatively disappointing outcome."

*   *   *

HUMPHREY, J(ames) Edward 1918-

PERSONAL: Born March 2, 1918, in St. Pauls, N.C.; son of Stinson Earl (a farmer) and Caroline (Graham) Humphrey; married Sadie Rachel Thompson, May 23, 1947; children: Stinson Edward, Neal Susan Humphrey Perkins, Edna Rachel Humphrey Miller. *Education:* Wake Forest College (now University), A.B., 1946; Southern Baptist Theological Seminary, B.D., 1948, Th.D., 1960; also attended Graduate Theological Union, Berkeley, Calif., 1962-63. *Politics:* "Registered Democrat, but vote quite independently." *Religion:* Baptist. *Home:* 24 Platt Court, Mill Valley, Calif. 94941. *Office:* Department of Theology, Golden Gate Baptist Theological Seminary, Mill Valley, Calif. 94941.

CAREER: Ordained minister of Baptist Church. Moncure Baptist Church, Moncure, N.C., interim pastor, 1945; Tates Creek Baptist Church, Richmond, Ky., pastor, 1946-48; Iwo Baptist College, Iwo, Nigeria, teacher of Christian doctrine, 1948; Baptist Teacher Training College, Ede, Nigeria, principal, 1949-50; Nigerian Baptist Theological Seminary, professor of theology and church history, 1951-65; Golden Gate Baptist Theological Seminary, Mill Valley, Calif., professor of systematic theology and historical theology, 1966—. *Member:* American Academy of Religion.

WRITINGS: Emil Brunner, Word Books, 1976. Contributor to religious journals.

WORK IN PROGRESS: Pilgrimage to Maturity: Christian

Life in Doctrinal Perspective, publication expected by Broadman.

SIDELIGHTS: Humphrey commented to *CA:* "My interest in writing on Brunner reflected the great influence which he had on my own thought, both as a Christian and as a teacher of theology. My current interest grows out of my desire to combine theology as a way of thinking with theology as a way of life.

"I have a deep interest in systematic, historical, and biblical theology and in philosophy as academic disciplines. All historical subjects hold a strong attraction for me. As a committed Christian, I am inclined to hold sustained interest in a subject only in the measure that it seems to me to offer the means of enhancement of life as it is actually lived.

"I love the great classics in both music and literature. Biographies of great persons have holding power for me. I have an abiding interest in Christian world mission. I am also basically ecumenical in outlook and commitment as a practicing churchman."

*   *   *

HUNT, Earl B. 1933-

PERSONAL: Born January 8, 1933, in San Francisco, Calif.; son of Robert W. (a physician) and Beryl (Busby) Hunt; married Mary Lou Smith (a counselor), December 20, 1954; children: Robert, Susan, Alan, Steven. *Education:* Stanford University, B.A., 1954; Yale University, Ph.D., 1960. *Residence:* Bellevue, Wash. *Office:* Department of Psychology, N1-25, University of Washington, Seattle, Wash. 98195.

CAREER: Yale University, New Haven, Conn., assistant professor of psychology, 1960-61; University of California, Los Angeles, senior research associate in psychology, 1961-62; University of Sydney, Sydney, Australia, senior lecturer in computer science, 1963-65; University of California, Los Angeles, associate professor of business administration, 1965-66; University of Washington, Seattle, professor of psychology, 1966—. President of Bellevue Youth Soccer Club, 1978. Consultant to National Institute of Mental Health, National Science Foundation, and U.S. Navy. *Military service:* U.S. Marine Corps, 1954-57. *Member:* American Association for the Advancement of Science (fellow), American Psychological Association (fellow), Psychonomic Society.

WRITINGS: Concept Learning: An Information Processing Problem, Wiley, 1962; (with J. Marin and P. Stone) *Experiments in Induction,* Academic Press, 1966; *Artificial Intelligence,* Academic Press, 1975. Contributor of articles and reviews to psychology journals. Editor of *Cognitive Psychology.*

WORK IN PROGRESS: Research on human intelligence and mathematical models of cognitive processes.

SIDELIGHTS: Hunt comments: "I have been interested in human intelligence from a 'bioengineering' point of view. What are the abstract information processing capacities of the brain? Paradoxically, I have focused more and more on motor skills analogies. In what way do our ideas about the 'conceptual' reasoning of the mathematician relate to our ideas about the 'perceptual' reasoning displayed by, say, basketball players? Also, how much does our thought depend on biological factors—drug state, age, fever, et cetera? At a vast level, I sometimes wonder how much *great decisions,* even at the foreign policy level, are influenced by transient or permanent biological or personal effects—and their interaction with the particular social situation in which they occurred?"

HUNT, Frazier 1885-1967

OBITUARY NOTICE: Born December 1, 1885, in Rock Island, Ill.; died December 24, 1967. Journalist. Hunt was a correspondent for publications, including the American Red Cross magazine, the *Chicago Tribune,* and the *New York Sun,* where he created the character of the drafted soldier, "Yaphank Bernie." During World War I, he covered the front in France and interviewed both Lenin and Bolshevik leaders. Numbered among his books are *Blown in by the Draft, This Bewildered World,* and *MacArthur and the War.* Obituaries and other sources: *New York Times,* December 26, 1967; *Time,* January 5, 1968; *Publishers Weekly,* January 8, 1968.

* * *

HUNT, William R(aymond) 1929-

PERSONAL: Born August 1, 1929, in Seattle, Wash.; son of William R. and Annastacia (Gleason) Hunt; married Irmgard Elsner, 1963; children: Tom, Maria, Alexander. *Education:* Seattle University, B.S.S., 1951; University of Washington, Seattle, J.D., 1958, M.A., 1966, Ph.D., 1967. *Home:* 4315 Northeast 87th St., Seattle, Wash. 98115.

CAREER: High school history teacher in Seattle, Wash., 1959-67; University of Alaska, Fairbanks, assistant professor, 1967-70, associate professor, 1970-74, professor of history, 1974-79, head of department, 1970-74; free-lance writer in Seattle, Wash., 1979—. Exchange teacher in Kobe, Japan, 1963-64; assistant professor at Memorial University of Newfoundland, summer, 1969.

WRITINGS: Dictionary of Rogues, Philosophical Library, 1970; *North of Fifty-Three Degrees: A Social History of the Alaska-Yukon Mining Frontier,* Macmillan, 1974; *Arctic Passage: A History of the Bering Sea,* Scribner, 1975; *Alaska: A Bicentennial History,* Norton, 1976. Contributor of more than thirty articles and reviews to scholarly journals and popular magazines, including *Explorers Journal, Alaska Journal, Journal of Popular Culture,* and *Pacific Northwest Quarterly.*

WORK IN PROGRESS: A biography of Vilhjalmur Stefansson (in press); a history of Seattle; a book on celebrated Northwest crimes.

* * *

HUNTER, Mel 1927-

PERSONAL: Born July 27, 1927, in Oak Park, Ill.; son of Milford J. (a business executive) and Lucille (Clarkson) Hunter; married Nan Forster (divorced, April, 1969); married Nancy O'Connor (an art gallery director), August 23, 1969; children: Lisa, Scott, Amy. *Education:* Attended Northwestern University. *Home address:* Townshend Rd., Grafton, Vt. 05146. *Office:* Mel Hunter Graphics, P.O. Box 2, Grafton, Vt. 05146.

CAREER: Free-lance writer and illustrator, 1950-72; Mel Hunter Graphics, Grafton, Vt., president. *Member:* National Arts Club, Southern Vermont Artists, Drawing Society, Salmagundi Club. *Awards, honors: Strategic Air Command* was named best aviation book of the year by Aviation and Space Writers Association, 1962.

WRITINGS—Self-illustrated children's books: *The Missilemen,* Doubleday, 1960; *Strategic Air Command,* Doubleday, 1961; *How the Earth Began,* World Publishing, 1972; *How Man Began,* World Publishing, 1972; *How Fishes Began,* World Publishing, 1972; *How Plants Began,* World Publishing, 1972.

Nonfiction: (Editor and contributor) *The Mylar Manifesto: The New Hand-Drawn Lithography,* Atelier North Star, 1979; *Mylar Method Lithography,* Van Nostrand, 1980. Contributor to *American Artist.*

SIDELIGHTS: Hunter writes: "Since 1972 I have been working entirely in the field of fine art original prints, especially hand-drawn color lithography, producing to date eighty-three editions, most in many colors. All during this period, I have been continuously pressing the medium for improvement in techniques and tools, to make this difficult medium much more accessible to artists. Many breakthroughs have been made, and a whole new field of color printmaking has appeared, now used by hundreds of artists who could not have made their prints by the old methods. My books are my effort to spread the how-to information as broadly as I can."

* * *

HUNTER, Norman (George Lorimer) 1899-

PERSONAL: Born November 23, 1899, in Sydenham, Kent, England; son of Joseph (an insurance clerk) and Minnie Elizabeth (Smith) Hunter; married Sylvia Mary Rangel (a secretary), September 1, 1923; children: one son, two daughters. *Education:* Educated in England. *Home:* 23 St. Olave's Close, Penton Rd., Middlesex TW18 2LH, England.

CAREER: S. H. Benson Ltd., London, England, senior copywriter, 1938-49; P. N. Barret & Co., Johannesburg, South Africa, chief copywriter, 1949-59, staff member in central advertising, 1959-70; author. Magician in over two-hundred performances at Maskelyne's Theatre of Magic, St. George's Hall, London, and at Little Theatre, London. *Military service:* London Irish Rifles; member of Ninth Division, 1918-19. *Member:* Inner Magic Circle (associate).

WRITINGS—All juvenile, except as noted; nonfiction: *Simplified Conjuring for All* (adult), C.A. Pearson, 1923; *Advertising Through the Press* (adult), Pitman, 1925; *New and Easy Magic* (adult), C.A. Pearson, 1925; *Hey Presto: A Book of Effects for Conjurers* (adult), E. Bagshawe, 1931; *New Conjuring Without Skill* (adult), John Lane, 1935; *Successful Conjuring for Amateurs* (adult), C. A. Pearson, 1951, published as *Successful Magic for Amateurs,* Arco, 1952, revised edition published as *Successful Conjuring,* Arco, 1964; *The Puffin Book of Magic,* Penguin, 1968, reprinted as *Norman Hunter's Book of Magic,* Bodley Head, 1974; *Professor Branestawm's Dictionary,* Bodley Head, 1973, Penguin, 1974; *Professor Branestawm's Compendium of Conundrums, Riddles, Puzzles, Brain Twiddlers, and Dotty Descriptions,* Bodley Head, 1975, Penguin, 1978; *Professor Branestawm's Do-It-Yourself Handbook,* Bodley Head, 1976; *The Wizard Book of Magic,* Sterling, 1978.

Fiction: The Bad Barons of Crashbania, Blackwell, 1932; *The Incredible Adventures of Professor Branestawm,* John Lane, 1933, Penguin, 1970; *Professor Branestawm's Treasure Hunt, and Other Incredible Adventures,* John Lane, 1937, Penguin, 1966; *Larky Legends,* John Lane, 1938, abridged edition published as *The Dirbblesome Teapots, and Other Incredible Stories,* Bodley Head, 1969, Penguin, 1971; *Stories of Professor Branestawm,* E. J. Arnold, 1939; *Jingle Tales,* Warne, 1941; *The Peculiar Triumph of Professor Branestawm,* Bodley Head, 1970, Penguin, 1972; *The Home-Made Dragon, and Other Incredible Stories,* Bodley Head, 1971, Penguin, 1974; *Professor Branestawm Up the Pole,* Bodley Head, 1972, Penguin, 1975; *The Frantic Phantom, and Other Incredible Stories,* Bodley Head, 1973, Penguin, 1976; *Wizards Are a Nuisance,* British Broadcasting Corp.,

1973; *Professor Branestawm's Great Revolution, and Other Incredible Adventures*, Bodley Head, 1974, Penguin, 1977; *Dust-Up at the Royal Disco, and Other Incredible Stories*, Bodley Head, 1975, Penguin, 1978; *Professor Branestawm 'Round the Bend*, Bodley Head, 1977; *Count Bakwerdz on the Carpet, and Other Incredible Stories*, Bodley Head, 1979; *Professor Branestawm's Perilous Pudding*, Bodley Head, 1979; *Sneeze and Be Slain*, Bodley Head, 1980.

Other: *Vanishing Ladies, and Other Magic*, Bodley Head, 1978.

WORK IN PROGRESS: The Best of Branestawn, for Bodley Head.

SIDELIGHTS: Hunter told *CA:* "I began my writing career after working in a secretarial capacity for Louise Heilgers, a well-known short story writer of the 1920's.

"I write in the morning, doing all of the twelve stories for a book. Then I go back to the beginning and revise when I have forgotten what I wrote and can assess it impartially. I write to give pleasure to my readers and to please myself, not with an eye on the market. Another purpose, of course, is to earn a living.

"I never read children's stories by other writers because there is always the risk of unconsciously using an idea from them. I have been influenced by the writings of G. K. Chesterton and W. S. Gilbert, especially their use of the unexpected word and their habit of turning things upside down and seeing the absurd side of ordinary things.

"One of my current hobbies is the re-assembling of a scale working model of Drury Lane Theatre which I built in South Africa and brought home in pieces. The model has four-color lighting, electrically operated scenery, and stage lifts, and is a lovely toy to build and play with.

"For some years I have been doing a little magic show for children at libraries, schools, book shows, and bookshops. Some of the tricks were connected with the adventures or inventions of Professor Branestawn. I don't do this much now, but I still give talks to children and do one or two tricks. I have done my magic show for children in South Africa, Australia, New Zealand, Ireland, Scotland, and pretty well all over England.

"I agree with H. G. Wells's advice to aspiring writers: 'The art of writing consists of the application of the seat of the trousers to the seat of the chair.'"

* * *

HUNTER, Robert Grams 1927-

PERSONAL: Born November 12, 1927, in Milbank, S.D.; son of Donald R. and Esther (Grams) Hunter; married Anne Ziesmer, August 25, 1956; children: Timothy, Catherine. *Education:* Harvard University, B.A., 1949; Columbia University, M.A., 1958, Ph.D., 1963. *Home:* 3612 Hampton Ave., Nashville, Tenn. 37215. *Office:* Department of English, Vanderbilt University, Nashville, Tenn. 37203.

CAREER: Robert College, Istanbul, Turkey, instructor in English, 1949-52; Dartmouth College, Hanover, N.H., instructor, 1959-64, assistant professor, 1964, associate professor of English, 1965-70, faculty fellow, 1964-65; Vanderbilt University, Nashville, Tenn., Kenan Professor of English, 1970—. *Military service:* U.S. Army, 1952-54.

WRITINGS: Shakespeare and the Comedy of Forgiveness, Columbia University Press, 1965; *Shakespeare and the Mystery of God's Judgments*, University of Georgia Press, 1976.

HUTSON, Anthony Brian Austen 1934-

PERSONAL: Born December 28, 1934, in England; son of Philip and Olga (Barker) Hutson; married Pamela Smith (a teacher), April 7, 1958; children: Nadienne, Philip, Elrand (daughter). *Religion:* Roman Catholic. *Home:* 100-A Whitehaven Rd., Glendowie, Auckland, New Zealand.

CAREER: Teacher at girls' high school in Wanganui, New Zealand, 1971-77; St. Mary's College, Auckland, New Zealand, teacher and head of department, 1979—. *Military service:* British Army, Royal Engineers, 1953-55.

WRITINGS: Sample Studies Around the World, Allmans, 1970; *The Navigator's Art*, Allmans, 1974; *Top Dressing Pilot*, A. H. & A. W. Reed, 1974; *Cheesemaker*, A. H. & A. W. Reed, 1975; *Auckland*, A. H. & A. W. Reed, 1975; *Your Book of Tall Ships*, Faber, 1978. Contributor to magazines. Book reviewer for Radio New Zealand.

WORK IN PROGRESS: Notable Churches of New Zealand, with own photographs; a children's novel based on Captain Cook's first voyage.

SIDELIGHTS: Hutson comments: "I started writing in 1964, with an article for *Yachting Monthly* about a somewhat harrowing and foolhardy voyage from the Thames to Devon. Since then, writing comes on like a rash every so often."

* * *

HYATT, Carole S. 1935-

PERSONAL: Born April 29, 1935, in New York, N.Y.; daughter of Arthur (in business) and Shirley (Unger) Schwartz; married Gordon Hyatt (a documentary filmmaker), October 25, 1971; children: Ariel. *Education:* Syracuse University, B.S.; University of Denver, M.A. *Home:* 7 West 81st St., Apt. 6-A, New York, N.Y. 10024. *Agent:* Julie Coopersmith Literary Agency, 10 West 15th St., New York, N.Y. 10011. *Office:* Child Research Service, Inc., 18 East 48th St., Suite 1202, New York, N.Y. 10017.

CAREER: Peppermint Players, New York City, producer-director, 1960-66; Child Research Service, New York City, president, 1966—. President of Childways, Inc., 1961-70, and Center for Family Research, Rutherford, N.J., 1970—; member of board of directors of *Womensweek* (newspaper). Creator of children's special programs for WCBS-TV. Public speaker. *Member:* National Association of Female Executives, Women's Forum.

WRITINGS: The Woman's Selling Game: How to Sell Yourself . . . And Anything Else, M. Evans, 1979.

* * *

HYMAN, Irwin A(braham Meltzer) 1935-

PERSONAL: Born March 22, 1935, in Neptune, N.J.; son of Henry Samuel Meltzer and Harriet (Greenetz) Hyman; married Nada Elizabeth Pospisil, February 6, 1960; children: Nadine Meltzer, Deborah Nan. *Education:* University of Maine, B.A., 1958; Rutgers University, M.Ed., 1961, Ed.D., 1964. *Home:* 207 Carter Rd., Princeton, N.J. 08540. *Office:* Department of School Psychology, College of Education, Temple University, Ritter Hall, Philadelphia, Pa. 19122.

CAREER: Elementary school teacher in Millstone Township, N.J., 1957-61; school psychologist and coordinator of special services in Trenton, N.J., 1962-66; American Institute for Mental Studies, Training School Unit, Vineland, N.J., chief of clinical services, 1966-67; Newark State College, Union, N.J., professor of special education, 1967-68; Temple University, Philadelphia, associate professor, 1968-

77, professor of school psychology, 1977—, director of National Center for the Study of Corporal Punishment and Alternatives in the Schools, 1977—. Diplomate of American Board of Professional Psychology. Founder of New Jersey Coordinating Committee on Child Advocacy, 1975-76; chairperson of workshops. Testified before New Jersey state legislature; consultant to Stanford Research Institute, American Civil Liberties Union, and U.S. Department of Health, Education & Welfare.

MEMBER: American Psychological Association (fellow; coordinator of Eastern Regional Institute, Division of School Psychology, 1973-74; member of council of representatives, 1974-77; president of Division of School Psychology, 1977-78; member of Board of Social and Ethical Responsibility in Psychology, 1977-79), American Educational Research Association, American Association on Mental Deficiency, American Association for the Advancement of Science, American Association of University Professors, National Association of School Psychologists, New Jersey Psychological Association, New Jersey Association for School Psychologists (president, 1969-70; chairperson of child advocacy committee, 1974-76), New Jersey Education Association, Phi Delta Kappa.

WRITINGS: (Contributor) G. R. Gredler, editor, *Ethical and Legal Factors in the Practice of School Psychology*, Pennsylvania Department of Education, 1974; (editor with Joel Meyers and Roy P. Martin) *School Consultation: Readings About Preventive Approaches for Pupil Personnel Workers*, C. C Thomas, 1977; (contributor) *Inequality in Education*, Center for Law and Education (Cambridge, Mass.), 1978; (editor with James Wise) *Corporal Punishment in American Education: Readings in History and Practice*, Temple University Press, 1979; (contributor) John Money and Gertrude Williams, editors, *Traumatic Abuse and Neglect in the Home*, Johns Hopkins Press, 1979.

Contributor to *International Encyclopedia of Psychiatry, Psychology, Psychoanalysis, and Neurology*. Contributor of about forty articles and reviews to psychology and education journals. Founding editor of *Rutgers School Psychology Newsletter*, 1962-64; school news editor for *New Jersey Psychologist*, 1965-70; editor of *School Psychology in New Jersey*, 1965-68; associate editor of *School Psychologist*, 1969-71, editor, 1971-74; member of editorial board of *American Psychologist*, 1976.

SIDELIGHTS: In a paper on psychology, education, and schooling presented at the 1979 annual meeting of the American Psychological Association, Hyman pointed out: "Generally, the old saying that the rich get richer and the poor get poorer is still applicable. The core of the problem is related to the myth that we live in a free enterprise system in which all have an opportunity to get ahead. While there are exceptions to the rule, it just isn't so. . . . And the discrepancy between the promise of the myth and the reality of the world is reflected in the actions and hearts of every American who keeps reaching deeper into his or her savings to stay ahead of inflation."

I

IANNUZZI, John Nicholas 1935-

PERSONAL: Born May 31, 1935, in New York, N.Y.; son of Nicholas Peter (a lawyer) and Grace M. (Russo) Iannuzzi. *Education:* Fordham College (now University), B.S., 1956; New York Law School, J.D., 1962. *Religion:* Roman Catholic. *Agent:* Owen Laster, William Morris Agency, 1350 Avenue of the Americas, New York, N.Y. 10019. *Office:* Iannuzzi, Russo & Iannuzzi, 233 Broadway, New York, N.Y. 10007.

CAREER: Iannuzzi, Russo & Iannuzzi, New York, N.Y., attorney specializing in criminal work, 1962—.

WRITINGS: What's Happening? (fiction), A. S. Barnes, 1963; *Part Thirty-Five* (fiction), Baron, 1970; *Sicilian Defense* (fiction), Baron, 1973; *Courthouse* (fiction), Doubleday, 1976.

WORK IN PROGRESS: A novel, publication by Jove expected in 1981; a textbook on cross-examination, publication by Prentice-Hall expected in 1981.

*   *   *

INAYAT-KHAN, Pir Vilayat 1916-

PERSONAL: Born June 19, 1916, in London, England; son of Inayat (spiritual head of Sufi Order) and Ora Ray (Baker) Inayat-Khan. *Education:* Received license es lettres and diplome d'estudes superieures de philosophie from Sorbonne, University of Paris; also attended Oxford University. *Office:* Sufi Order, P.O. Box 396, New Lebanon, N.Y. 12125.

CAREER: Sufi Order, Paris, France, president of international order, 1957—, and American order, 1962—. President of Ecole International de la Meditation, 1960—. Producer of Cosmic Mass, an inter-religious pageant. International lecturer and teacher of meditation and comparative religion. *Military service:* Served with Royal Navy; became lieutenant.

WRITINGS: Toward the One, Harper, 1974; *The Message in Our Time,* Harper, 1978; *Transformation,* Sufi Order, 1980. Also author of *Sufi Masters* and *Eine Meditation nach Sufitum.*

WORK IN PROGRESS: A book on science and mysticism to be published by Sufi Order.

SIDELIGHTS: In *Toward the One,* Inayat-Khan outlines his teachings on spirituality and the practices he prescribes to aid in realizing the divinity within oneself. *The Message in Our Time* is a biography of Inayat-Khan's father, the Sufi master, Pir-O-Murshid Inayat-Khan. The author based the book on the accounts of relatives and disciples, personal letters, and his father's unpublished autobiography. The book includes descriptions of his father's meetings with such notable men as Mahatma Gandhi, Khalil Gibran, Claude Debussy, Count Serge Tolstoy, Luther Burbank, and Henry Ford. Inayat-Khan's latest book, *Transformation,* traces the whole process of personal transformation, the basis of spiritual training.

Inayat-Khan made a sound recording, "Sufi Meditation," released by Big Sur Recordings in 1971.

*   *   *

IRVIN, Rea 1881-1972

OBITUARY NOTICE: Born August 26, 1881, in San Francisco, Calif.; died of a stroke, May 28, 1972, in Frederiksted, Virgin Islands. Artist and cartoonist. The first employee of the *New Yorker,* Irwin created its initial cover, introducing what would become his best-known character, "Eustace Tilley." In addition to his other duties as art editor, Irwin produced numerous covers and drew many cartoons for the magazine. Obituaries and other sources: *New York Times,* May 29, 1972; *New Yorker,* June 10, 1972; *Newsweek,* June 12, 1972.

*   *   *

IRWIN, Margaret 1889-1967

OBITUARY NOTICE: Born in 1889 in London, England; died in 1967. Author. Irwin made a reputation as a writer of mysteries and historical novels both in the United States and England. Her first historical novel, *None So Pretty,* won the competition organized by the publishing company, Chatto & Windus, in 1930. Her other books include *Still She Wished for Company* and the author's own favorite, *The Royal Flush.* Obituaries and other sources: *Current Biography,* Wilson, 1946; *Twentieth Century Writing: A Reader's Guide to Contemporary Literature,* Transatlantic, 1969; *Longman Companion to Twentieth Century Literature,* Longman, 1970.

*   *   *

IVANOV, Vsevolod Vyacheslavovich 1895-1963

OBITUARY NOTICE: Born February 4, 1895, in Lbyazhen,

Siberia, Russia (now U.S.S.R.); died Autust 15, 1963, in Moscow, U.S.S.R. Considered the epic poet of the Russian Civil War, Ivanov wrote of the conflict from his own experiences, first as a soldier with the White Army and later with the Red Forces. His best-known work, *Armored Train 14-69*, was based on an actual incident in the civil war. First published as a short novel, it was later successfully adapted as a play—the only purely Russian play to be produced by the Moscow Art Theatre. Ivanov held various positions during his lifetime, including employment as a circus clown and fakir, a sorter in the emerald mines, a sailor, and a news correspondent covering the Nuremburg war-crimes trial for a Russian periodical. Numbered among his books are *The Taking of Berlin, Skyblue Sands,* and *Journey to a Country That Does Not Yet Exist*. An autobiographical novel, *Adventures of a Fakir*, initially published in 1935, was also released under the titles *I Live a Queer Life* and *Patched Breeches*. Obituaries and other sources: *Encyclopedia of World Literature in the Twentieth Century,* updated edition, Ungar, 1967; *Everyman's Dictionary of European Writers,* Dent & Sons, 1968; *Twentieth Century Writing: A Reader's Guide to Contemporary Literature,* Transatlantic, 1969; *McGraw-Hill Encyclopedia of World Drama,* McGraw, 1972; *Modern World Drama: An Encyclopedia,* Dutton, 1972; *World Authors, 1950-1970,* Wilson, 1975.

* * *

IZENOUR, George Charles 1912-

PERSONAL: Born July 24, 1912, in New Brighton, Pa.; son of Charles S. and Wilhelmina (Freseman) Izenour; married Hildegard Hilt, September 7, 1937; children: Steven. *Education:* Wittenberg College, A.B., 1934, M.A., 1936. *Home:* 10 Alston Ave., New Haven, Conn. 06515.

CAREER: Director of lighting at theatres in California, 1938-39; Yale University, New Haven, Conn., director of Electromechanical Laboratory at School of Drama, 1939-77, professor of theatre design and technology, 1960-77; theatre design consultant, 1977—. Inventor of lighting systems for the theatre and television, as well as rigging and computer control systems. Associated with Office of Scientific Research and Development, 1943-46.

MEMBER: American Association for the Advancement of Science, American National Theatre and Academy, U.S. Institute of Theater Technology, Institute of Electrical and Electronics Engineers, Connecticut Academy of Arts and Sciences. *Awards, honors:* Rockefeller Foundation fellow, 1939-43, 1946-47; Ford Foundation fellow, 1960-61; D.F.A. from Wittenberg College, 1960; Rodgers and Hammerstein Award from Hammerstein Foundation, 1960; M.A. from Yale University, 1961; Guggenheim fellow, 1971-72; award from U.S. Institute for Theater Technology, 1975; Benjamin Franklin fellow of Royal Society, 1975; honor award from American Theatre Association, 1977.

WRITINGS: Theater Design, McGraw, 1977. Contributor to *Encyclopaedia Britannica* and *Dictionary of Architecture and Construction.*

WORK IN PROGRESS: Theater Technology, publication by McGraw expected in 1984; *Roofed Theaters of Antiquity,* publication by Garland Publishing expected in 1984.

J

JACKSON, Albert 1943-

PERSONAL: Born October 4, 1943, in Brighton, England; son of Arthur and Rosina (Rose) Jackson; married Pauline Flanagan; children: Beth, Eva. *Education:* Royal College of Art, M.Des.R.C.A., 1967. *Home:* 26 Chalcroft Rd., Lewisham, London SE13 5RF, England. *Office:* Jackson Day Designs, 39 Gourock Rd., Eltham, London SE9 1YR, England.

CAREER: Contracted to Reader's Digest Association, England, beginning 1967; free-lance designer and illustrator, 1969; Jackson Day Designs (industrial designers), London, England, partner, 1970—. Lecturer at Medway College of Design.

WRITINGS: (With David Day) *Good Housekeeping Decorating and Do-It-Yourself,* Good Housekeeping Books, 1977 (published in England as *Good Housekeeping Do-It-Yourself Book,* Ebury Press, 1977); (with Day) *Tools and How to Use Them,* Knopf, 1978; (with Day) *Complete Book of Tools,* M. Joseph, 1978; (with Day) *Simply Fix-It,* Ebury Press, 1979.

WORK IN PROGRESS: Handbook of Modelmaking, with David Day, completion expected in 1980.

AVOCATIONAL INTERESTS: Philately, golf, modelmaking.

*   *   *

JACKSON, Guida 1930-

PERSONAL: Given name is pronounced *Guy-*da; born August 29, 1930, in Amarillo, Tex.; daughter of James Hurley (a merchant) and Ina (Benson) Miller; married Prentice Lamar Jackson (an anesthesiologist), June 15, 1951; children: Jeffrey Allen, William Andrew, James Tucker, Annabeth. *Education:* Attended Musical Arts Conservatory, Amarillo, Tex., 1945-47; Texas Tech University, B.A., 1951; also attended University of Houston, 1953. *Home:* 339 Fawnlake, Houston, Tex. 77079. *Agent:* Aaron M. Priest Literary Agency, 150 East 35th St., New York, N.Y. 10016.

CAREER: English teacher at public high schools in Houston, Tex., 1951-54; music teacher and free-lance writer in Houston, Tex., 1956-71; Monday Shop (antiques store), Houston, Tex., owner, 1971-75; *Houston Town and Country* (magazine), Houston, Tex., contributing editor, 1975; *Texas Country* (magazine), Houston, Tex., editor, 1976-78; free-lance writer, 1978—. *Member:* Authors Unlimited of Houston, Houston Area Writers Workshop.

WRITINGS: Passing Through (novel), Simon & Schuster, 1979; *A Common Valor,* Simon & Schuster, 1980. Contributor to magazines. Editor of *Touchstone Literary Quarterly* and *Texas Anesthesiologists Newsletter.*

SIDELIGHTS: Guida Jackson writes: "As a child of Pollyanna persuasion, growing up in the Panhandle Dust Bowl Depression days, I sometimes had to strain to ferret out delights—especially visual ones in nature. This was a marvelous hone for sharpening the powers of observation. Very early I decided the finest calling was that of a reporter, and I started a newspaper at about eleven to report the 'facts' as I saw them. The same year I wrote two books, which I handprinted and passed around at a penny a read. I believe that's what a fiction writer does: just reports the facts from the imagination.

"My adult fiction writing experience is limited to short stories, written for my own pleasure and stored away to eliminate possible rejection slips. I wrote *Passing Through* in odd moments during the day for a year, took a chapter to a writers' conference for critique. The judge put me in touch with his agent, who sold it in a couple of weeks, the first time out. So I still have my fear of rejection slips to conquer. I write for fun."

*   *   *

JACKSON, Louise A(llen) 1937-

PERSONAL: Born March 20, 1937, in Killeen, Tex.; daughter of Robert King (a rancher; in business) and Mattie (a teacher; maiden name, Darter) Allen; married Donny R. Jackson (a chemical engineer), December 27, 1969. *Education:* Southwest Texas State University, B.S., 1957, M.A., 1959; University of Wyoming, Ed.D., 1965. *Politics:* Independent. *Religion:* Baptist. *Home:* 1719 South Oak, Casper, Wyo. 82601. *Office:* College of Education, University of Wyoming, 200 North Wolcott, Room 118, Casper, Wyo. 82601.

CAREER: Elementary teacher in Freeport, Tex., 1957-60; University of Wyoming, Caspar, instructor in education, 1960-63; North Texas State University, Denton, assistant professor, 1965-68, associate professor of education, 1968-70; learning coordinator for public schools in Austin, Tex., 1971-74, language arts consultant, 1974-77, remedial reading teacher, 1977-78; University of Wyoming, Casper, associate professor of education, 1978—. Visiting lecturer at University of Houston, Clear Lake City Branch, summer, 1978. *Member:* International Reading Association, Texas State Teachers Association (life member), Alpha Chi, Kappa Delta Pi, Phi Delta Kappa.

WRITINGS: The Key in Student Teaching: A Handbook for the Supervising Teacher, University of Wyoming, 1961; *Handbook for Supervising Teachers,* North Texas State University Press, 1966; *Grandpa Had a Windmill, Grandma Had a Churn* (juvenile), Parents' Magazine Press, 1977; *Over on the River* (juvenile), Lothrop, 1980. Contributor to education journals.

WORK IN PROGRESS—Children's books: *John Franklin's Exciting Adventure,* a pioneer story; *The Butterfly Girl.*

SIDELIGHTS: Louise Jackson told *CA:* "The summer after I was ten years old, my mother decided that the school wasn't doing a very good job of teaching creative writing. She liked to write herself and had her first poem published when she was twelve. So she saw her duty clearly. She would teach me, as she had always done.

"We packed a picnic lunch, drove to the back pasture, and parked where we had a view of hills and lake. There my brother and I had our first lesson in descriptive writing.

"My interest was kindled. I continued writing off and on until I entered high school. From then until three years ago, my writing was primarily in response to class assignments and professional requirements.

"Then, three years ago, I stayed at home for awhile. It seemed a good time to get back to writing and I did. I went to the public library and checked out two books on how to write juvenile fiction. I read them carefully, did exactly what they said to do, and submitted a manuscript to Parents' Magazine Press. It was accepted and I was off and running."

*   *   *

JACKSON, Teague 1938-

PERSONAL: Born April 10, 1938, in Buffalo, N.Y.; son of Richard Wagner (a journalist) and Catherine (a teacher; maiden name, Teague) Jackson; married Sandra Dallas (an artist and teacher), July 21, 1963; children: Kristin Camille, Cheryl Karen. *Education:* University of Michigan, B.A., 1960. *Home address:* P.O. Box 386, New York, N.Y. 10011. *Agent:* Mitch Douglas, International Creative Management, 40 West 57th St., New York, N.Y. 10019. *Office:* Travel Trade Publications, 605 Fifth Ave., New York, N.Y. 10017.

CAREER: Atlanta Journal, Atlanta, Ga., sports reporter and golf editor, 1967-71; David Pearson Associates, Coral Gables, Fla., account executive, 1971-73; Bahia Mar Hotel, Fort Lauderdale, Fla., director of public relations, 1973-76; free-lance writer in New York City, 1976-78; Travel Trade Publications, New York City, managing editor of Guides Division, 1978—. *Military service:* U.S. Army, 1961-63; became first lieutenant. *Member:* Commerce Club of Fort Lauderdale (member of board of directors).

WRITINGS: Encore (biography; American Dance Guild Book Club selection), Prentice-Hall, 1978. Contributor to magazines, including *Golf Digest* and *Black Enterprise,* and newspapers.

WORK IN PROGRESS: Connee (tentative title), a biography of jazz singer Connee Boswell; a novel; a screenplay treatment of Mario Biaggi, U.S. Congressman from Bronx, N.Y., "former cop-on-the-beat and unsuccessful candidate for mayor of New York in 1973"; short stories.

SIDELIGHTS: Jackson comments: "My given name is a

curse/ethnic slur in the Gaelic. This is a source of pride and a fine starting point for my writing. I am an instinctive liberal, espousing many causes, yet I grew up in a doctrinaire conservative atmosphere. Thus I have walked in both worlds. My psychology/journalism education, joined with the foregoing (which I consider attributes), have led my thinking—and writing—into a sociological/psychological contemplation of human relationships, from one-to-one, through family, community and city/state, to universal.

"Both words, 'psychological' and 'sociological' include the word 'logical'—the thing that fascinates me most about the study of relationships is that they are not logical at all, and thus a function as well of mysticism, dreams, and fate.

"*Encore* is the story of dancer Emily Frankel, who recovered from an auto wreck, danced on Broadway a year after the accident, then went on a world tour. But this is not the story of a dancer; it is a story of a human being with unusual resources of courage, intelligence, self-awareness, and commitment. And in the psychological sense, these qualities lead not only to triumph but to peril."

*   *   *

JANES, Edward C. 1908-

PERSONAL: Born in 1908, in Westfield, Mass. *Education:* Attended Williams College.

CAREER: Writer. Editor of *Outdoor Magazine;* travel editor of *Hunting and Fishing Magazine.*

WRITINGS—Juvenile: (With Oliver H. P. Rodman) *The Boy's Complete Book of Fresh and Salt Water Fishing,* Little, Brown, 1949; *A Boy and His Gun,* A. S. Barnes, 1951; *Wilderness Warden,* Longmans, Green, 1955; *A Boy and His Boat: An Introduction to Boating,* Macrae, 1963; *The First Book of Camping,* F. Watts, 1963, revised edition, 1977; *The Story of Knives,* Putnam, 1968; *When Men Panned Gold in the Klondike,* Garrard, 1968; *When Cape Cod Men Saved Lives,* Garrard, 1968.

Other: (With Ray Bergman) *Trout,* Knopf, 1952; *Hunting Ducks and Geese,* Stackpole Co., 1954; *Trouble at Clear Lake,* Macrae, 1956; *Fresh-Water Fishing Complete,* Holt, 1961; *Nelson's Encyclopedia of Camping,* Nelson, 1963; *Westfield, Massachusetts, 1669-1969: The First Three Hundred Years,* Westfield Tri-Centennial Association, 1968; (with Bergman) *Fishing with Ray Bergman,* Knopf, 1970; (with Lee Wulff) *Fishing with Lee Wulff,* Knopf, 1972; *Salmon Fishing in the Northeast,* Stone Wall Press, 1973; *I Remember Cape Cod,* S. Greene Press, 1974; *Ringneck!: Pheasants and Pheasant Hunting,* Crown, 1975.

SIDELIGHTS: Edward C. Janes is a hunting and fishing enthusiast who has written a number of informative books on these subjects. Most of his works have been highly recommended for their clarity and practical advice. *A Boy and His Boat,* for example, has been cited by the *New York Times* as "a well-written book of sound good sense.... There is even a chapter on water skiing and one on fishing from boats. Altogether one of the best of its kind around."

Janes has also written some fiction dealing with outdoor adventure themes. These efforts have been well received. *Wilderness Warden,* the story of a young game warden's fight against a poaching ring, elicited this favorable comment from the *Saturday Review of Literature:* "The story is closely knit. It is also full of courage and suspense, of good characterizations, and of fast action; and in addition there are the feel and smell of the outdoors and appreciation for the magnificent forests of northern Maine.... This is an outstanding adventure story."

BIOGRAPHICAL/CRITICAL SOURCES: *Saturday Review of Literature*, November 12, 1955; *New York Times*, September 22, 1963.*

* * *

JANOWITZ, Phyllis

PERSONAL: Born in New York, N.Y.; daughter of Morris (a circus manager) and Lillian (a psychiatrist; maiden name, Reiner) Winer; married Julian F. Janowitz, May 6, 1960 (died, 1968); children: Thomas A., David H. *Education:* Queens College of the City University of New York, B.A. (magna cum laude), 1961; University of Massachusetts, M.F.A., 1970. *Politics:* "Eclectic." *Religion:* "Yes." *Home:* 5-R Hibben, Faculty Rd., Princeton, N.J. 08540. *Office:* Council of the Humanities, Princeton University, 122 East Pynne, Princeton, N.J. 08540.

CAREER: Massachusetts Bay Community College, Waltham, instructor in creative writing, 1970-71; Middlesex Community College, Bedford, Mass., instructor in creative writing, 1974-75; Radcliffe College, Radcliffe Institute, Cambridge, Mass., instructor at poetry seminar, 1975-76; Washington College, Chestertown, Md., visiting assistant professor of English, 1976-77; writer, 1977—. Visiting assistant professor at St. Cloud State University, spring, 1978; writer-in-residence at Indiana Central University, spring, 1979. Gives readings from her works.

MEMBER: Poetry Society of America, New England Poetry Club, Society of Fellows of Mary Bunting Institute. *Awards, honors:* Fellow at Radcliffe Institute, 1971-73, Macdowell Colony, summers, 1972-74, National Endowment for the Arts, 1974-75, and Eastern Washington State College, 1975; Power Dalton Award from Poetry Society of New England, 1978, for "Reunion With Jake at Still Pond Creek"; Gretchen Warren Award, 1978, for "Harmony: Four Rites," and 1979, for "Luncheon at the Marshalls"; Bernice Ames Award from Poetry Society of America, 1978, for "Cells"; Alfred Kreymborg Award, 1978, for "A Family Portrait," and Emily Dickinson Award, 1978, for "A Formal Feeling"; award from Stroud International Poetry Festival, 1978, for "A Formal Feeling"; Alfred Hodder Fellow in the Humanities at Princeton University, 1979-80.

WRITINGS: Dancing With Mr. D. (poetry chapbook), Quark Press, 1978; *Rites of Strangers* (poems), University Press of Virginia, 1978; *Lives on a Leaf* (poems), Archival Press, 1979.

Work represented in anthologies, including *Blacksmith Anthology,* edited by Gail Mazur, Blacksmith Press, 1976; *The Best of the Radcliffe Quarterly,* edited by Thea Singer and Aida Press, March, 1979; and *Anthology of Magazine Verse and Yearbook of American Poetry,* edited by Alan F. Pater, Monitor. Contributor of poems, articles, and reviews to magazines, including *Feminist Art Journal, Atlantic Monthly, Esquire, Nation, Paris Review, Prairie Schooner,* and *New Yorker.*

WORK IN PROGRESS: Diminuendo (poems).

SIDELIGHTS: Janowitz wrote: "Fish. Poets are fish. A school of sardines. Needle-points. Swimming round and round the bait. Eyes bulging with wonder and hope. Thieves, stealing cream and roses. Stealing paintings and cakes. Their mothers in tears. Taxman knocking. Phone ripped out. Words filling ditches and gullies. River banks overflowing. The essential always escaping. An angel blinking on and off from the top of an unclimbable pine. The picture scraped down with a palette knife. Everything wrecked by a twig of a

line, a graft rejected. Starting over. A hot-orange field. A sky green as a traffic light. Hounds. Sniffing the tail of the fox. The fox flying off at the last second, short barks of laughter falling from the sky, fading. And the sky always ready for changes."

Rites of Strangers contains "taut, sometimes sardonic, poems about broken connections and abortive communication," noted the *Radcliffe Quarterly.* "The loneliness of moving to a new town, the disjunction of body and spirit, and the absurdity of human expectation about love, childbirth, and old age motivate clever, controlled images and humor that is often cutting and occasionally more gently playful."

BIOGRAPHICAL/CRITICAL SOURCES: *Radcliffe Quarterly,* June, 1979; *Lexington Minute-Man,* July 12, 1979.

* * *

JASSY, Marie-France Perrin
See PERRIN JASSY, Marie-France

* * *

JAY, Ruth I(ngrid) 1920-
(Ruth Johnson Jay, Ruth I. Johnson)

PERSONAL: Born September 20, 1920, in Rockford, Ill.; daughter of Simon (a carpenter) and Olga (Soderstrom) Johnson; married Morris Delbert Jay (a fabric shop owner), March 15, 1969. *Education:* Moody Bible Institute, graduated, 1946; also attended University of Chicago and University of Nebraska. *Religion:* "Protestant Christian Believer." *Home:* 1229 Dakota St., Fremont, Neb. 68025. *Office:* "Back to the Bible Broadcast," P.O. Box 82808, Lincoln, Neb. 68501.

CAREER: Amerok, Inc., Rockford, Ill., time clerk, 1937-43; worked as church youth and music director, 1946-48; "Back to the Bible Broadcast," Lincoln, Neb., youth counselor and magazine editor, 1948-75, youth music director, 1948—. Conducted Christian writers' conference in Italy, 1974.

WRITINGS:—Under name Ruth I. Johnson: *Programs for Special Occasions,* Zondervan, 1950; *Joy Sparton of Parsonage Hill* (juvenile fiction), Moody, 1958; *Devotions for the Family,* Moody, Volume I, 1958, Volume II, 1959, Volume III, 1960; *Sam at Bible School* (juvenile fiction), Moody, 1959; *Joy Sparton and the Vacation Mix-Up* (juvenile fiction), Moody, 1959; *Joy Sparton and the Money Mix-Up* (juvenile fiction), Moody, 1960; *Christians You Should Know* (biography), Moody, 1960; *Devotions for Early Teens,* Moody, Volume I, 1960, Volume II, 1961, Volume III, 1962, Volume IV, 1963; *Christians With Courage* (biography), Back to the Bible Publishers, 1961; *Joy Sparton and Her Problem Twin* (juvenile fiction), Moody, 1963; *Years Between* (missionary tips for teenagers), Back to the Bible Publishers, 1964; *Daily Devotions for Juniors,* Moody, Volume I, 1964, Volume II, 1965, Volume III, 1967; *Reflections: Devotions on the Life of Christ* (for women), Back to the Bible Publishers, 1968, revised edition, 1979.

Under name Ruth Johnson Jay; all published by Back to the Bible Publishers, except as noted: *Devotions With the Hymnbook* (adult devotionals), Volume I, 1970, Volume II, 1971; *Bible Stories for Little People,* Volume I, 1973, Volume II, 1974, Volume III, 1975, Volume IV, 1976; *Joy Sparton and the Mystery of Room Seven* (juvenile fiction), Moody, 1974; *Time Out With God* (teen devotionals), Volume I, 1975, Volume II, 1976, Volume III, 1977; *Mystery of the Missing Campers* (juvenile fiction), 1978; *Alaskan Smoke Eaters* (juvenile fiction), 1979.

Also author of two audio cassette series, including "Bible Stories for Little People" and "Sing Along Story Time." Musical composer. Contributor to magazines. Past editor of *Young Ambassador*.

WORK IN PROGRESS: Books for the "Tyler Series" (juvenile fiction), for Back to the Bible Publishers.

SIDELIGHTS: Jay told *CA:* "I began writing when, as a college graduate, I got rheumatic fever and spent several months in bed. We lived across the street from a library, and my mother would go there and get all the books on creative writing and journalism. I studied during those months and had my first story accepted before I was over the disease.

"Now I assist my husband in our fabric shop two days a week, write a fifteen-page drama for 'Back to the Bible Broadcast' once a week, and act as producer-director for this radio taping."

AVOCATIONAL INTERESTS: Ceramics, listening to music, sewing.

*   *   *

JAY, Ruth Johnson
See JAY, Ruth I(ngrid)

*   *   *

JEFFERS, H(arry) Paul   1934-

PERSONAL: Born in 1934, in Phoenixville, Pa. *Education:* Attended Temple University; University of Iowa, M.A.

CAREER: Instructor in journalism at Boston University, Boston, Mass.; producer and news writer for American Broadcasting Co. (ABC); Fulbright professor in Thailand; writer, 1967—. *Military service:* U.S. Army, linguist.

WRITINGS: The CIA: A Close Look at the Central Intelligence Agency, Lion Press, 1970; (with Dick Levitan) *See Parris and Die: Brutality in the U.S. Marines,* Hawthorn, 1971; (with Levitan) *Sex in the Executive Suite,* Playboy Press, 1972; *Wanted by the FBI,* Hawthorn, 1972; (editor) *The Adventure of the Stalwart Companions: Heretofore Unpublished Letters and Papers Concerning a Singular Collaboration Between Theodore Roosevelt and Sherlock Holmes,* Harper, 1978.

Juvenile: (With Everett M. Dirksen) *Gallant Men* (based on the recording of the same name by Jeffers), McGraw, 1967; (with Margaret Chase Smith) *Gallant Women,* McGraw, 1968; *How the U.S. Senate Works,* McGraw, 1970.

Recordings: "Gallant Men," narrated by Everett M. Dirksen, Capitol Records, 1966; "Confrontation at Harvard," narrated by Charles Osgood, Buddah Records.

BIOGRAPHICAL/CRITICAL SOURCES: Washington Post Book World, November 5, 1967; *Best Sellers,* April 15, 1971, November 15, 1972; *New York Times Book Review,* May 30, 1971.*

*   *   *

JEFFERYS, Allan

PERSONAL: Born in New Jersey; married June Hoopes (in real estate), September 30, 1950; children: Douglas, Laura. *Home:* 46 Little Brook Rd., Wilton, Conn. 06897. *Agent:* Robert P. Mills Ltd., 156 East 52nd St., New York, N.Y. 10022. *Office:* ABC-TV, 1330 Avenue of the Americas, New York, N.Y. 10019.

CAREER: WTOP-TV, Washington, D.C., actor, singer, and program host, 1950-54; ABC-TV, New York, N.Y., announcer, newscaster, and writer, 1955—, drama critic and entertainment editor, 1961-69. *Military service:* U.S. Army Air Forces, pilot, 1941-45; became captain; received Air Medal. *Member:* American Federation of Television and Radio Artists, Camp Fire Club of America, Authors Guild of Authors League of America, Screen Actors Guild, Actors Equity Association.

WRITINGS: (With Bill Owen) *D.J.,* Popular Library, 1972.

WORK IN PROGRESS: A novel.

SIDELIGHTS: Jefferys commented: "I am interested in theatre, golf, fly fishing, music, and dance, and tend to weave those interests into my writing. My new novel will cover the period since World War II, with an accent on theatre and dance. Although I am past fifty, I recently began to take classes in ballet, jazz, and tap dancing. I also returned to the stage after a more than twenty-year hiatus. I am a firm believer in change of pace—in writing, performing, and living."

*   *   *

JEFFREY, Julie Roy   1941-

PERSONAL: Born March 20, 1941, in Boston, Mass.; daughter of James Charles (a judge) and Grace Roy; married Christopher Jeffrey (a transportation architect), August 27, 1963; children: Michael, Sophia. *Education:* Radcliffe College, B.A., 1962; Rice University, Ph.D., 1972. *Home:* 913 St. Paul St., Baltimore, Md. 21202. *Office:* Department of History, Goucher College, Baltimore, Md. 21204.

CAREER: Goucher College, Baltimore, Md., assistant professor, 1972-78, associate professor of American history, 1978—, director of historic preservation, 1976—, and director of faculty development. Member of Baltimore Commission for Historic and Architectural Preservation; member of board of directors of Hampton Mansion, Grace and St. Peters School, and National Publications and Records Commission. *Member:* Organization of American Historians, National Trust for Historic Preservation, Coordinating Committee of Women in the Historical Profession, Berkshire Conference of Women Historians. *Awards, honors:* Fellow of Newberry Library, 1979.

WRITINGS: Education for Children of the Poor: A Study of the Intellectual Origins and Implementation of the Elementary and Secondary Education Act of 1965, Ohio State University Press, 1978; *Frontier Women: The Trans-Mississippi West, 1840-1880,* Hill & Wang, 1979. Contributor to history and women's studies journals.

WORK IN PROGRESS: Research on women in the nineteenth century, and on architectural and social history.

SIDELIGHTS: Jeffrey wrote: "My recent research and writing has focused on the lives and experiences of American women. I have found that my work has affected my personal outlook and has broadened my perspective. My work on western women, for example, was initiated by a feminist urge to see the nineteenth-century pioneers eagerly take on the 'freedoms' the West offered (mainly the opportunity to do mens' work). I discovered that the women did the work but failed to assume a 'liberated' viewpoint; more importantly, I discovered why these women were so eager to climb back up on the Victorian pedestal. In short, I learned not only about these women's choices, but also to understand and even sympathize with them. That kind of experience which I seek out through research and writing is what I really consider to be liberating.

"One other thing I might say is how amazed I am that writing never gets any easier. I used to think that would happen, but it hasn't. But I continue to write, hard though it is."

BIOGRAPHICAL/CRITICAL SOURCES: Washington Post Book World, August 10, 1979; *New York Times Book Review*, September 9, 1979; *Los Angeles Times Book Review*, October 7, 1979.

*   *   *

JESSNER, Lucie Ney   1896-1979

OBITUARY NOTICE: Born September 15, 1896, in Frankfurt am Main, Germany (now West Germany); died of emphysema, December 18, 1979, in Washington, D.C. Psychiatrist, educator, and author. Before coming to the United States in the late 1930's, Jessner practiced and taught psychiatry in both Germany and Switzerland. She subsequently helped to develop and direct the psychiatric services for children at the Massachusetts General Hospital in Boston from 1943 to 1955, and later was affiliated with the Washington Psychoanalytic Institute as a supervising and training analyst. A clinical associate of Harvard University, she was also professor of psychiatry at the School of Medicine at the University of North Carolina and the Georgetown University Medical Center, becoming professor emerita of the latter in 1973. In addition to her numerous articles in scholarly journals, Irwin collaborated on two books, *Shock Treatment in Psychiatry* and *Dynamic Psychopathology in Childhood*. Obituaries and other sources: *American Men and Women of Science: The Physical and Biological Sciences*, 12th edition, Bowker, 1971-73; *Who's Who of American Women*, 11th edition, Marquis, 1979; *Washington Post*, December 23, 1979.

*   *   *

JEWETT, Ann E(lizabeth)   1921-

PERSONAL: Born July 30, 1921, in Newburgh, N.Y.; daughter of Eva M. Jewett. *Education:* Oberlin College, B.A., 1941; University of Michigan, M.A., 1947; Stanford University, Ed.D., 1951. *Home:* 160 Gatewood Place, Athens, Ga. 30606. *Office:* Division of Health, Physical Education, and Recreation, University of Georgia, Athens, Ga. 30602.

CAREER: High school physical education teacher in Kingston, Pa., 1941-44; State University of New York College at Cortland, instructor in physical education, 1947-50; Stanford Consultation Service, Stanford, Calif., research assistant, 1950-51; University of Illinois, Urbana, associate professor of education and physical education, 1951-63; Springfield College, Springfield, Mass., professor of physical education and director of women's physical education, 1963-66; University of Wisconsin—Madison, professor of physical education and head of department of health, physical education, and recreation, 1974—. Visiting professor at Stanford University, University of Wisconsin—Madison, University of Michigan, State University of New York at Buffalo, and University of Tennessee; Fulbright lecturer at Hague Academy for Physical Education, 1954-55; Laura J. Huelster lecturer, 1972; distinguished professor at University of Bridgeport, 1972; visiting scholar at Piedmont University, 1973. Member of civilian advisory committee of U.S. Marine Corps Physical Fitness Academy, 1969—; delegate to conferences in the United States and abroad; workshop coordinator; consultant to U.S. Army and U.S. Navy. *Military service:* U.S. Navy Women's Reserve, 1944—, active duty in Women Accepted for Volunteer Emergency Service, 1944-46; present rank, captain.

MEMBER: International Association of Physical Education

and Sports for Girls and Women, American Academy of Physical Education (fellow; member of executive committee, 1970-71; president, 1973-74), American Alliance for Health, Physical Education, and Recreation (vice-president and chairperson of Physical Education Division, 1965-66), American Educational Research Association, American Association for Higher Education, National Education Association, National Association for Physical Education in Higher Education (vice-president, 1969-71; president, 1973-75), Association for Supervision and Curriculum Development, Southern Association for Physical Education of College Women, Midwest Association for Physical Education of College Women, Eastern Association for Physical Education of College Women, Illinois Association for Health, Physical Education, and Recreation (district president, 1953; vice-president for physical education, 1962), Illinois Association for Professional Preparation in Health, Physical Education, and Recreation, Massachusetts Association for Health, Physical Education, and Recreation, Wisconsin Association for Health, Physical Education, and Recreation, Georgia Association for Health, Physical Education, and Recreation. *Awards, honors:* Honor award from American Alliance for Health, Physical Education, and Recreation, 1974; Golden Award from city of Athens, Ga., 1976.

WRITINGS: (With Clyde Knapp) *Physical Education: Student and Beginning Teaching*, McGraw, 1957; (with Knapp) *Physical Education Student Teaching Guide*, Stipes, 1962; (editor with Knapp; and contributor) *The Growing Years: Adolescence*, American Alliance for Health, Physical Education, and Recreation, 1962; (with John Nixon) *Physical Education Curriculum*, Ronald, 1964; (with Eloise Jaeger, Margie Hanson, and Lorena Porter) *Professional Preparation of the Elementary School Physical Education Teacher* (monograph), American Alliance for Health, Physical Education, and Recreation, 1969; (with Nixon) *Introduction to Physical Education*, 8th edition (Jewett was not associated with earlier editions), Saunders, 1974, 9th edition, 1979; (editor) *NAPECW Biennial Record, 1973-1975*, Printing Department, University of Georgia, 1977; (with Marie R. Mullan) *Curriculum Design: Purposes and Processes in Physical Education Teaching-Learning*, American Alliance for Health, Physical Education, and Recreation, 1977.

Contributor: Merle M. Ohlson, editor, *Modern Methods in Elementary Education*, Dryden, 1959; *Innovations in Curriculum Design for Physical Education*, University of Pittsburgh Press, 1970; *Curriculum Improvement in Secondary School Physical Education*, American Alliance for Health, Physical Education, and Recreation, 1972; William J. Ellena, editor, *Curriculum Handbook for School Executives*, American Association for School Administrators, 1973; Allan J. Ryan and Fred L. Allman, Jr., editors, *Sports Medicine*, Academic Press, 1974. Contributor of about twenty-five articles to education and physical education journals and popular magazines, including *Quest*. Member of editorial board of *Physician* and *Sports Medicine Journal*, 1979—.

*   *   *

JOBSON, Gary Alan   1950-

PERSONAL: Born July 17, 1950, in Hackensack, N.J.; son of Thomas W. and Helyn (Burrows) Jobson; married Janice Murphy, August 9, 1974. *Education:* State University of New York Maritime College, Bronx, B.S., 1973. *Office:* Jobson Sailing Associates, 3 Church Circle, Annapolis, Md. 21401.

CAREER: Jobson Sailing Associates (consultants), Annapolis, Md., founder and owner, 1979—. Former member of faculty at U.S. Merchant Marine Academy and U.S. Naval Academy. Licensed by U.S. Merchant Marine. Chairperson of Collegiate Hall of Fame selection committee; member of U.S. Olympic yachting committee; public speaker. *Military service:* U.S. Naval Reserve, 1973-78; became lieutenant. *Member:* U.S. Yacht Racing Union, Annapolis Yacht Club, Beachwood Yacht Club, Corinthians, Corinthian Yacht Club, Fort Worth Boat Club, Kings Point Sailing Squadron, Maritime College Sailing Squadron, Naval Academy Sailing Squadron, New York Yacht Club, Storm Trysail Club, Toms River Yacht Club. *Awards, honors:* Named All-American Sailor, 1971, 1972, and 1973, and College Sailor of the Year, 1972 and 1973, by Intercollegiate Yacht Racing Association.

WRITINGS: A Sailing Instructor's Manual, U.S. Yacht Racing Union, 1977; (with Ted Turner) *The Racing Edge,* Simon & Schuster, 1979; *Gary Jobson's How to Sail,* Ziff-Davis, 1980; *Offshore Sailing,* Ziff-Davis, in press. Author of "Sailing Slants," a weekly column in *Evening Capital;* author of a monthly column in *Yachting.* Contributor to magazines, including *Yachting, Sail,* and *Yacht Racing/Cruising,* and newspapers. American editor of *Yachtsman's Pocket Alamanac,* 1980.

SIDELIGHTS: Jobson wrote: "I was Ted Turner's tactician on *Courageous* in 1977, and most recently was watch captain on *Tenacious* in the Fastnet Race.

"From all my experiences I have put together a lecture series, which I presented to over a hundred groups in 1978 and 1979. I also bring this experience and expertise together at Jobson Sailing Associates. I advise companies in product development, and on how best to market their products in the marine marketplace—how to reach the yachtsman."

*   *   *

JOHNSON, Audrey P(ike) 1915-

PERSONAL: Born November 17, 1915, in Pittsburgh, Pa.; daughter of Earl (an engineer) and Mae (a secretary; maiden name, Reynolds) Pike; married Gordon Hollis Johnson (a produce broker; deceased); children: Richard, Roger, Robert. *Education:* Graduated from high school. *Religion:* Catholic. *Home:* 16 Fuller Ave., Webster, N.Y. 14580. *Agent:* Dorothy Markinko, McIntosh & Otis, Inc., 475 Fifth Ave., New York, N.Y. 10017.

CAREER: Area reporter for *Rochester Times Union* and *Rochester Democrat and Chronicle,* c. 1950-59; *Webster Herald,* Webster, N.Y., editor, 1960-67; writer. *Member:* Mystery Writers of America, Genesee Valley Writers.

WRITINGS: The Pet Show, Ginn, 1972; *Thunder Waters,* Montana Reading Publications, 1974; *Hush, Winifred Is Dead,* Bouregy, 1976; *Nurse of the Thousand Islands,* Bouregy, 1978. Contributor of articles and short stories to magazines.

WORK IN PROGRESS: The Apple Hangs So High and Bright, a novel for teenagers.

*   *   *

JOHNSON, Dave W(illiam) 1931-

PERSONAL: Born April 7, 1931, in Chicago, Ill.; son of Fred Howard (in sales) and Ruth O. (Borg) Johnson; married Carolyn Joan Powelson (a decorator; in sales), July 29, 1952; children: David G., Stanford S., Heidi K. *Education:* Attended University of the Pacific, 1949-50; San Francisco State College, B.A., 1955. *Politics:* Republican. *Religion:* Born-Again Christian. *Home:* 40647 Canyon Heights Dr., Fremont, Calif. 94538.

CAREER: Gulbransen CBS (CBS Musical Instrument Co.), Deerfield, Ill., marketing manager, 1972-76, regional sales manager, 1976-79; Universal Piano Co., director of marketing and sales, 1980—. Presents sales seminars; consultant to sales organizations. *Military service:* U.S. Army, Special Services, 1953-55. *Member:* National Speaker's Association.

WRITINGS: The Success Principle, Harvest House, 1976; *The Power of Positive Intimidation in Sales,* Prentice-Hall, 1980; *Spiritual Meditation,* Spring House, 1980. Contributor of about fifty articles to magazines, including *Success Unlimited, Salesmen's Opportunity,* and *American Salesman.*

WORK IN PROGRESS: The Game of Inner Selling, completion expected in 1981.

SIDELIGHTS: Johnson writes: "My background includes that of being a concert pianist and organist for ten years, and arranging for and directing an orchestra and choir for three radio stations. I taught school for five years, and private piano and organ lessons for twenty years. I developed a computerized audio-visual organ teaching program. Now I am into motivation and sales through seminars and writing. I also teach an adult Sunday school class and feel that success in the spiritual area of life brings complete success in all other areas."

*   *   *

JOHNSON, Hugh 1939-

PERSONAL: Born March 10, 1939, in London, England; son of Guy (a barrister) and Enid (Kittel) Johnson; married Judith Eve Grinling, (a graphic designer), 1965; children: Lucy, Redmond, Kitty-Alice. *Education:* King's College, Cambridge, M.A., 1960. *Home:* Saling Hall, Great Saling, Braintree, Essex, England.

CAREER: Staff writer, Conde Nast Publications, 1960-63; editor of *Wine and Food,* Wine and Food Society, 1963-65; author of column on wine, 1965-67, and travel editor, 1967, *London Times;* editor of *Queen,* 1968-70; free-lance writer. *Member:* Sunday Times Wine Club (president, 1973—).

WRITINGS: Wine, Simon & Schuster, 1965; *The World Atlas of Wine,* Simon & Schuster, 1971; *The International Book of Trees,* Simon & Schuster, 1973; (with Robert Thompson) *The California Wine Book,* Morrow, 1975; *Hugh Johnson's Pocket Encyclopedia of Wine,* Simon & Schuster, 1978; *The Principles of Gardening,* Simon & Schuster, 1979; *Understanding Wine,* Gainsburg, 1980. Editorial director of *Journal of the Royal Horticultural Society.*

WORK IN PROGRESS: A Pocket Encyclopedia of Garden Plants.

*   *   *

JOHNSON, John M(yrton) 1941-

PERSONAL: Born June 1, 1941, in Peru, Ind.; son of John Wilmer and Thelma (Boyd) Johnson; married Suzanne Marie McNelley, August 29, 1964 (divorced November 15, 1978); married Kathleen Joan Ferraro, August 1, 1979. *Education:* Indiana University, B.A., 1963; San Diego State University, M.A., 1969; University of California, San Diego, C.Phil., 1971, Ph.D., 1973. *Home:* 2401 South College Ave., #103, Tempe, Ariz. 85282. *Office:* Department of Sociology, Arizona State University, Tempe, Ariz. 85281.

CAREER: San Diego State University, San Diego, Calif., acting assistant professor of sociology, 1971-72; Arizona State University, Tempe, assistant professor, 1972-76, associate professor of sociology and associate of Center for Family Studies, 1976—. Founder and executive vice-president of Friends of the Family Ltd. (for battered women and children), 1977—. Chairperson of scholarly meetings; public speaker; consultant to state and local agencies. *Military service:* U.S. Navy, 1964-67; served in Vietnam; became lieutenant senior grade.

MEMBER: American Academy of Political and Social Science, American Association of University Professors, American Humane Association, American Society of Criminology, American Sociological Association, Environmental Sociology Network, Society for the Study of Social Problems, Society for the Study of Symbolic Interaction, Subterranean Sociology Association, Pacific Sociological Association (chairperson of publications committee, 1977-78), North Central Sociological Association, Alpha Kappa Delta. *Awards, honors:* Grant from Shell Foundation, 1976.

WRITINGS: Doing Field Research, Free Press, 1975; (editor with Jack D. Douglas, and contributor) *Official Deviance: Readings in Official Misfeasance, Malfeasance, and Other Forms of Corruption,* Lippincott, 1977; (editor with Douglas, and contributor) *Existential Sociology,* Cambridge University Press, 1977; (editor with Douglas) *Crime at the Top: Deviance in Business and the Professions,* Lippincott, 1978; *The Sociology of Sport,* Sage Publications, 1978; (with David L. Altheide) *Bureaucratic Propaganda* (monograph), Allyn & Bacon, 1979; *The Bureaucratic File* (monograph), Greenwood Press, 1979. Co-author with F. L. Bolton, Jr., *Structures of American Violence,* 1980.

Contributor: Robert A. Scott and Jack D. Douglas, editors, *Theoretical Perspectives on Deviance,* Basic Books, 1972; Douglas, editor, *Situations and Structures: An Introduction to Sociology,* Free Press, 1973; Douglas, editor, *Observations of Deviance,* 2nd edition (Johnson was not included in 1st edition), Random House, 1979.

Editor of Sage Publications, 1976—, editor of "Sociological Observations," a monograph series, 1977—. Contributor of more than a dozen articles and reviews to journals in the social sciences. New ethnographies editor of *Urban Life,* 1974-83, editor, January, 1977, October, 1977, July, 1978, 1979—; associate editor of *Pacific Sociological Review,* 1974—; member of editorial advisory board of Society for the Study of Symbolic Interaction, 1976-77, advisory editor of *Symbolic Interaction,* 1977-80; associate editor of *Western Sociological Review,* Volume VIII, number 1, 1977.

SIDELIGHTS: Johnson writes: "Most of my publications have been in the fields of deviance, social problems, qualitative sociological research, and social theory. I became inspired to pursue these interests during my four years at University of California, largely because of the personal influence of many fellow graduate students from that era.

"My first publications described the processes whereby official military records and reports were put together and distributed by the mass media, and were inspired by my experiences as a Navy officer and by the weekly Vietnam 'body count' reports disseminated by television. These interests carried over to my doctoral dissertation, a lengthy field study of social welfare offices in southern California. One portion of this research described the problems and practices of field work in sociology, and led to the publication of *Doing Field Research.* Another portion described how official records and reports were done by those individuals in the welfare offices who were mandated with the responsibility for doing them. These early studies led to other research, involving different problems and settings, and even ten years after my first article about official records and reports, *Bureaucratic Propaganda* indicates that I have continued these interests, for reasons even I do not fully understand.

"My first writings were strongly guided by my desire to seek membership in the social science community, as well as a desire to address matters concerning public policy. As the presumptive scientific community dissipates and fragments and as the debates over public policies become characterized by sociological technicism and mumbo-jumbo, I find that my earlier desires have waned. Thus have my inspirations for writing changed as well. I now find myself writing for a more limited audience, and my pretensions about changing the world have become more realistic too."

*   *   *

JOHNSON, Ruth I.
   See JAY, Ruth I(ngrid)

*   *   *

JOHNSON, Vernon E(dwin)   1920-

PERSONAL: Born August 23, 1920, in Ironwood, Mich.; son of Edwin and Josephine (Wilson) Johnson; married Mary Ann Phelps, June 12, 1944; children: Stephen, Bromley, Merodie Johnson Valdovinos, Gary. *Education:* Carleton College, B.A., 1941; Seabury Western Theological Seminary, B.D., 1944, M.Div., 1944. *Home:* 9128 Neill Lake Rd., Eden Prairie, Minn. 55344. *Office:* 6440 Flying Cloud Dr., Eden Prairie, Minn. 55344.

CAREER: Ordained Episcopalian priest, 1944; pastor of Episcopal churches in Windom, Minn., 1944-47, Winona, Minn., 1947-50, and Minneapolis, Minn., 1962—; Johnson Institute, Minneapolis, Minn., president, 1966—. Member of summer faculty at Rutgers University. Member of Southeast Conference on Alcohol and Drug Abuse; consultant to Air Line Pilots Association. *Awards, honors:* D.D. from Seabury Western Theological Seminary, 1969.

WRITINGS: I'll Quit Tomorrow, Harper, 1973, revised edition, 1980. Contributor to theology and social work journals.

SIDELIGHTS: Johnson told *CA* that *I'll Quit Tomorrow* was written "to inform the general public that alcoholism is a disease of such a nature that its victims cannot be expected to have spontaneous insight into the severity of their own symptoms. Therefore, intervention by caring people around the victim should be viewed as a norm rather than the exception."

*   *   *

JOHNSTON, Norman   1921-

PERSONAL: Born August 5, 1921, in Marion, Mich.; son of Dean (a school administrator) and Lila (a social service administrator; maiden name, Madison) Johnston. *Education:* Central Michigan University, B.A. (summa cum laude), 1943; University of Chicago, A.M. (with honors), 1951; University of Pennsylvania, Ph.D., 1958. *Home address:* P.O. Box 66, Hatboro, Pa. 19040. *Office:* Department of Sociology and Anthropology, Beaver College, Glenside, Pa. 19038.

CAREER: Illinois State Penitentiary System, Pontiac and Joliet, Ill., sociologist, 1948-51; University of Pennsylvania, Philadelphia, instructor in sociology, 1952-59, research associate, 1959-62; Beaver College, Glenside, Pa., professor of sociology and head of department, 1962—. Visiting professor at University of Missouri, St. Louis, 1968-69. Member of Pennsylvania Committee for Correctional Staff Training, Philadelphia Commission on the Detention, Sentencing, and

Release of Prisoners, and Citizens Crime Commission of Philadelphia; consultant to United Nations Social Defense Research Institute, U.S. Department of Justice, and American Foundation Institute of Corrections. *Military service:* U.S. Army Air Forces, 1943-45.

MEMBER: Societe International de Criminologie, Societe Internationale de Defense Sociale (joint national delegate), American Correctional Association, American Sociological Association (fellow), National Council on Crime and Delinquency, American Society of Criminology. *Awards, honors:* Fulbright fellow at University of London, 1958-59; Ford Foundation fellow, 1959-62.

WRITINGS: (With Otto Pollak) *Studies in Juvenile Delinquency: A Selected Bibliography, 1939-1954,* U.S. Children's Bureau, 1956; (contributor) Hermann Mannheim, editor, *Pioneers in Criminology,* Patterson Smith, 1960, revised edition, 1972; (editor with Marvin E. Wolfgang and Leonard Savitz) *The Sociology of Crime and Delinquency,* Wiley, 1962, 2nd edition, 1970; (editor with Wolfgang and Savitz) *The Sociology of Punishment and Correction,* Wiley, 1962, 2nd edition, 1970; (author of introduction to reprint) William Crawford, *Report on the Penitentiaries of the United States,* Patterson Smith, 1969; *The Human Cage: A Brief History of Prison Architecture,* Walker & Co., 1973; (with Savitz) *Crime in Society,* Wiley, 1978; (with Savitz) *Justice and Corrections,* Wiley, 1978; (author of introduction to reprint) Alexis de Tocqueville and Gustave de Beaumont, *On the Penitentiary System in the United States,* Patterson Smith, in press. Contributor to *Collier's Encyclopedia.* Contributor of more than a dozen articles and reviews to professional journals.

WORK IN PROGRESS: A worldwide history of prison architecture from earliest times to the present.

SIDELIGHTS: Johnston writes: "My primary scholarly research interest for many years has continued to be the history of prison architecture. I have been in hundreds of prisons in the United States and abroad, as well as ancient prisons in old castles and fortresses. One of my books has been translated into Russian and several journal articles have appeared in translation in foreign journals. I have most recently visited prisons in the People's Republic of China."

* * *

JONES, Andrew 1921-

PERSONAL: Born June 20, 1921, in West Orange, N.J.; son of H. Seaver (a contractor) and Jean (Gillespie) Jones; married Janet Wallace, October 15, 1949; children: Brooke, H. Seaver II, Audrey. *Education:* Princeton University, A.B., 1947; Yale University, M.F.A., 1952. *Religion:* Episcopalian. *Home address:* Long Meadow Rd., Bedford, N.Y. 10506. *Agent:* Dorothy Olding, Harold Ober Associates, Inc., 40 East 49th St., New York, N.Y. 10017. *Office: Reader's Digest,* Pleasantville, N.Y. 10570.

CAREER: Newark News, Newark, N.J., reporter, 1947-48; *Field and Stream,* New York, N.Y., contributing editor, 1952-55; *Reader's Digest,* Pleasantville, N.Y., senior editor, 1955—. Creative writing teacher at Bedford Hills Correctional Facility for Women. *Military service:* U.S. Marine Corps, fighter pilot, 1942-45; served in Pacific theater; became captain.

WRITINGS: Flight Seaward (novel), Morrow, 1978. Contributor to *Reader's Digest.*

WORK IN PROGRESS: Another novel, *More Than Conquerors* (tentative title); a book on the "recent debacle dur-

ing the 1979 Fastnet Rock yacht race in the Irish Sea," to be published as a *Reader's Digest* magazine book supplement in March, 1980.

SIDELIGHTS: Jones writes: "I am a lifelong birdwatcher and fisherman. I was a waterfowler and deerhunter, but gave up scattergunning ten years ago and hung up the rifle. I read most of Faulkner every five years, also dip regularly into Joyce Cary, J. P. Donleavy, and Saul Bellow."

* * *

JONES, E(li) Stanley 1884-1973

PERSONAL: Born January 3, 1884, in Clarksville, Md.; died January 25, 1973, in Bareilly, India; son of Albin Davis and Sarah Alice (Peddicord) Jones; married Mabel Lossing (a missionary), February 11, 1911; children: Eunice Jones Mathews. *Education:* Attended City College of Baltimore; Asbury College, M.A., 1912; received D.D. from Duke University and S.T.D. from Syracuse University. *Residence:* Sitapur, Uttar Pradesh, India.

CAREER: Minister of Methodist Episcopal Church; missionary in India, Ceylon, Burma, Japan, China, Malaya, Singapore, Latin America, and the Philippines. Pastor of English Church in Lucknow, India, superintendant of Lucknow district, and principal of Sitapur Boarding School, 1907-15; co-founder of Nur Manzil Psychiatric Center, Lucknow, 1951. Conducted retreats in the United States and India; speaker for Federal Council of Churches.

WRITINGS—All published by Abingdon, except as noted: *The Christ of the Indian Road,* 1925; *Christ at the Round Table,* 1928, reprinted, Arden Library, 1978; *The Christ of Every Road: A Study in Pentecost,* 1930; *The Christ of the Mount: A Working Philosophy of Life,* 1931; *Christ and Human Suffering,* 1933; (with others) *The Christian Message for the World Today: A Joint Statement of the World-Wide Mission of the Christian Church,* 1934, reprinted, Books for Libraries Press, 1971; *Christ's Alternatives to Communism,* 1935 (published in England as *Christ and Communism,* Hodder & Stoughton, 1935); *Victorious Living,* 1936; *The Choice Before Us,* 1937; *Along the Indian Road,* 1939; *Is the Kingdom of God Realism?,* 1940; *The Christ of the American Road,* 1944; *The Way,* 1946, reprinted, Doubleday, 1946; *Abundant Living,* Hodder & Stoughton, 1946, reprinted, 1976; *Mahatma Gandhi: An Interpretation,* 1948; *The Way to Power and Poise,* 1949.

How to Be a Transformed Person, 1951, reprinted, 1978; *Growing Spiritually,* 1951, reprinted, 1978; *Mastery: The Art of Mastering Life,* 1955; *Christian Maturity,* 1957; *Conversion,* 1959; *In Christ,* 1961; *The Word Became Flesh,* 1963; *Victory Through Surrender,* 1966; *A Song of Ascents: A Spiritual Autobiography,* 1968; *The Reconstruction of the Church—on What Pattern?,* 1970; *The Unshakable Kingdom and the Unchanging Persons,* 1972; *Selections From E. Stanley Jones: Christ and Human Need,* compiled by Eunice Jones Mathews and James K. Mathews, 1972; *The Contribution of E. Stanley Jones* (anthology), introduction by Richard W. Taylor, Christian Literature Society, 1973; (with daughter, Eunice Jones Mathews) *The Divine Yes,* 1975. Contributor of articles to newspapers and periodicals, including *Christian Herald* and *Christian Advocate.*

SIDELIGHTS: In 1907 E. Stanley Jones decided to become a missionary, and spent the next fifty years of his life preaching in India and in other Asian countries. He was beloved by both low and high castes, and counted among his dearest friends and confidants was the Indian leader Mahatma Gandhi. At one point during his ministry, Jones questioned Gandhi about the best approach to bring Christian doctrine to his fellow countrymen. Gandhi pointed out the lack of appreciation for Indian culture so often present in Christian missionaries. Jones then spent the next few months studying Indian culture and religion with the Christian Indian poet Tabindranath Tagore.

In addition to his missionary work in India, Jones also conducted retreats, both in the United States and abroad. He maintained an *ashram*—"a place of spiritual retreat"—in the Himalayas, along with five retreat centers in the United States, and one in Canada. During his lifetime Jones was elected a Methodist bishop three times; he refused the appointments in favor of his missionary work. Among his more than twenty inspirational books, *The Divine Yes*, published after his death, summarizes and affirms his steadfast faith in Christian doctrine and his vocation. "E. Stanley Jones left us," wrote Malcolm Boyd, "an inspiring, exciting final testament concerning a vital Christian's relationship with Jesus Christ. His book is courageous, honest, intensely human and often deeply moving."

BIOGRAPHICAL/CRITICAL SOURCES: E. Stanley Jones, *A Song of Ascents: A Spiritual Autobiography*, Abingdon, 1968; E. S. Jones and Eunice Jones Mathews, *The Divine Yes*, Abingdon, 1975; *Christian Century*, May 15, 1975.

OBITUARIES: New York Times, January 26, 1973; *Washington Post*, January 26, 1973; *Newsweek*, February 5, 1973.*

*   *   *

JONES, Harold
See PAGE, Gerald W(ilburn)

*   *   *

JONES, Maynard Benedict   1904-1972
(Nard Jones)

OBITUARY NOTICE: Born April 12, 1904, in Seattle, Wash.; died September 3, 1972. Journalist, editor, and novelist. Early in his career, Jones was a reporter for the *Walla Walla Daily Bulletin* and editor of *Pacific Motor Boat* magazine. He was also the author of several novels, under name Nard Jones, including the critically acclaimed *Oregon Detour* and *Swift Flows the River*. Obituaries and other sources: *Who's Who Among Pacific Northwest Authors*, 2nd edition, Pacific Northwest Library Association, 1969; *Who Was Who in America*, 5th edition, Marquis, 1973.

*   *   *

JONES, Nard
See JONES, Maynard Benedict

*   *   *

JONES, Richard M(atthew)   1925-

PERSONAL: Born June 10, 1925, in New Brunswick, N.J.; son of Richard M. (a musician) and Marie (Pfeiffer) Jones; married Susan Smullin (a translator), September 8, 1967; children: Andras, Gabriel. *Education:* Stanford University, A.B., 1950; Harvard University, Ph.D., 1956. *Home:* 603 Governor Stevens Ave., Olympia, Wash. 98501. *Agent:* Gerard McCauley Agency, Inc., 209 East 56th St., New York, N.Y. 10022. *Office:* The Evergreen State College, Olympia, Wash. 98505.

CAREER: Veterans Administration, Boston, Mass., trainee in clinical psychology, 1951-54; Judge Baker Guidance Cen-

ter, Boston, intern, 1954-55, staff psychologist, 1955-57; Brandeis University, Waltham, Mass., assistant professor, 1957-61, associate professor, 1961-65, professor of psychology, 1965-67, staff psychologist at Psychological Counseling Center, 1957-67, director of counseling center, 1965-67; University of California, Santa Cruz, lecturer in psychology, 1967-69, and education, 1968-69; Harvard University, Cambridge, Mass., professor of education, 1969-70; The Evergreen State College, Olympia, Wash., member of faculty, 1970—. Instructor at Smith College, 1956-57; research associate at Harvard University, 1957. Private practice of psychotherapy, 1955-68; chief of psychological services for Massachusetts Department of Mental Health, 1969-70. *Military service:* U.S. Coast Guard, 1943-46.

MEMBER: American Psychological Association, American Orthopsychiatric Association, American Group Psychotherapy Association, American Academy of Psychotherapists, Association for the Psychophysiological Study of Sleep, Council for the Advancement of Small Colleges, Massachusetts Psychological Association, Phi Beta Kappa. *Awards, honors:* National Institute of Mental Health fellow, 1963-64.

WRITINGS: An Application of Psychoanalysis to Education, C. C Thomas, 1960; *Ego Synthesis in Dreams*, Schenkman, 1962; (with Eugenia Hanfmann and Elliot Baker) *Psychological Counseling in a Small College*, Schenkman, 1963; (with Hanfmann and Andras Angyal) *Neurosis and Treatment: A Holistic Theory*, Wiley, 1965; *Contemporary Educational Psychology*, Harper, 1967; *Fantasy and Feeling in Education*, New York University Press, 1968; *The New Psychology of Dreaming*, Grune, 1970; *The Dream Poet*, Schenkman, 1979; *Experiment at Evergreen*, Oxford University Press, 1980.

Contributor: Milton Kornrich, editor, *Psychological Test Modification*, C. C Thomas, 1965; *Topical Problems in Group Psychotherapy*, Volume V, Karger, 1964; Milton Kramer, editor, *Dream Psychology and the New Biology of Dreaming*, C. C Thomas, 1969; M. D. Faber, editor, *The Design Within*, Science House, 1970; Ernest Hartmann, editor, *Sleep and Dreaming*, Little, Brown, 1970; James Fadiman, editor, *The Proper Study of Man*, Macmillan, 1971; Louis J. Rubin, editor, *Facts and Feelings in the Classroom*, Walker & Co., 1973; Barry McWaters, editor, *Humanistic Perspectives: Current Trends in Psychology*, Brooks/Cole, 1977; Arthur Foshay and Irving Morrissett, editors, *Beyond the Scientific*, Social Science Education Consortium (Boulder, Colo.), 1978. Contributor to *Collier's Encyclopedia*. Contributor of about twenty-five articles and reviews to psychology and education journals and to popular magazines, including *Nation*.

SIDELIGHTS: In the preface to *The Dream Poet*, Jones wrote: "This has been a troublesome book to organize. Writing it involved coming to grips with a serendipitous confluence of professional interests that I had thought to be disparate enough to be safely beyond the need to live together. On the one side were interests in enlisting modern psychotherapeutic perspectives in the service of making modern compulsory educational practices more lively than they routinely are.... On the other side, enduring interests in dreams as such led me to develop some expertise as a scientific onierologist.... The prevailing notion ... is that the manifest content and the transformation of day residue are at least as important in understanding dreams as are Freud's concepts of the 'latent content' and 'the censorship'....

"In 1969 I found myself in the painful grip of the 'Peter Principle' in a professorship at Harvard.... The position turned out to be one in which I could do nothing that was relevant to the further pursuit of either interest: dreaming about teaching or teaching about dreams. An opportunity came along to help plan, and then to teach in, an 'alternative' college . . . , The Evergreen State College, founded in 1970; and I took it.

"The college which we planned, now in its eighth controversially successful year, has no departments, requirements, majors, courses, or grades. Instead, groups of students and small teams of faculty contract to work together full time . . . to study a theme, solve a problem or complete a project of interdisciplinary scope. When we are done with such a project, we write to each other as candidly as is possible about the influences we had on each other in the process. Considerations of *what* is learned are secondary to considerations of *how* to learn. For neither students nor faculty can there be competing commitments. Whatever it takes to get the job done well and satisfactorily—skills to be learned, information to be acquired, research to be done—cannot be arbitrarily obstructed. There is no place to hide, and almost anything can be tried. And the system of evaluation by mutual reflection tends to keep most of us honest.

"During my first year at Evergreen . . . I had become truly less interested in what my dreams could say to me and more interested in what I, as their author, *could say to them*.

"Increasingly, I wanted to 'talk back' to the dreams' play with words and images, to their sound symbolisms and flourishes of synesthesia, to their visually alliterative sequences, to their amusing and sometimes profound deployments of the figurative and the literal, to their double entendres, to their stagings, artifices, puns and jokes. . . . [W]hereas Freud was bent on understanding the rational truths which lay dissembled in dreams, I seemed to be primarily interested in simply appreciating their prerationative artistry. In short, I realized that what had imperceptibly become the first reward for the disciplines of remembering and recording my dreams was not their mental health value, but the pleasure that came from exercising these disciplines. . . . So, what I wrote about was not only the ways that had been invented to interpret dreams, but how one might hope to *enjoy* dreams after having learned those ways."

*   *   *

JONES, Ruth Dorval

PERSONAL: Born in Lynbrook, N.Y.; daughter of Claude O. (a chemist) and Katharine (an artist; maiden name, Crane) Dorval; married William Wright Jones (a state commissioner of banks; deceased); children: Charles Lawrence, William Wright, Jr., Ronald Arthur, Dorval Thompson. *Education:* Attended high school in Upper Darby, Pa. *Religion:* Episcopal. *Home:* 507 Cleveland St., Raleigh, N.C. 27605.

CAREER: Writer, 1947—. Directed civic programs on food and money management. *Member:* North Carolina Literary and Historical Society, Women's Club of Raleigh (vice-president), Creative Writers Club, Raleigh Writers Club. *Awards, honors:* First place awards for plays and songs from North Carolina Federation of Women's Clubs, including awards, 1977, for song, "I Saw the Lovely Jesus," and 1979, for song, "Your Shadow on My Mind."

WRITINGS: (With Mary Lee McMillan) *Make Your Own Merry Christmas*, Moore, 1971; *My Helenka* (biography of Helenka Paderewski), Moore, 1972; (with Lee Parker) *China and the Golden Weed*, Herald, 1976; (with McMillan) *Beautiful North Carolina and the World of Flowers*, Moore, 1979.

Plays: *Belles of the Nineties* (three-act farce), Walter H. Baker, 1944; *The Glory of a Thousand Years* (cantata), Harold Flammer Co., 1953.

Also author of radio programs. Contributor of stories to adult and juvenile magazines, including *Seventeen, American Girl, Young Catholic Messenger, Chatelaine,* and *Cavalier,* and newspapers. Past editor of *Tela-Woman.*

WORK IN PROGRESS: Barney, a biography, with Barbara Bernard McGee; *Some Great Ladies of North Carolina;* "Sweet Adeline," a three-act play.

SIDELIGHTS: Ruth Jones writes: "I have been writing short stories practically all my life from observations of bits of life around me. My favorite, 'Goodbye Indian Prince,' that appeared in *American Girl,* is the story of a girl's struggle to escape from her dream world into reality.

"*My Helenka* was done with Mary Lee McMillan, who was Madame Paderewska's secretary during the time she organized the Polish White Cross. It is the bittersweet love story of the great Polish genius and his Helenka, daughter of a Baltic nobleman, and called the most beautiful woman in Europe. It is also the story of their love for Poland and their travels about the country in their private railway car to raise money for the displaced masses of Polish people by means of concerts, the sale of dolls, and Paderewski's own impassioned pleas.

"*China and the Golden Weed* is the story of a young man's travels in China, 1916-1921, selling tobacco for the British American Tobacco Company when travel was both dangerous and hard, the story of a young man's hopes and aspirations.

"*Barney* is the story of Harry V. Bernard, who went to China in 1911 to set up a sales organization for the Singer sewing machine company. It is a story of danger and adventure as well as the tender story of his love for his family. He was acting consul-general of Shanghai before he left China in 1946, and was recognized by the American and Chinese governments for his great service to the Chinese people."

*   *   *

JONES-RYAN, Maureen 1943-

PERSONAL: Born September 12, 1943, in Auburn, Mass.; daughter of Harold Douglas and Margaret (Buckley) Jones; married Robert Martin Ryan (an investment counselor), March 2, 1963; children: Robert Martin, Jr., Margaret. *Education:* Atlantic Christian College, B.A., 1965; Clark University, A.G.S., 1968; Assumption College, Worcester, Mass., M.A., 1972. *Religion:* "Humanist." *Home address:* P.O. Box 889, Carefree, Ariz. 85377.

CAREER: Counselor and director at Middlesex Family Counseling Service, Sudbury, Mass.; professor of psychology and public relations director at Quinsigamond Community College, Worcester, Mass.; president of Harold Douglas Publishing Co., Carefree, Ariz. *Member:* World Congress of Poets, Mensa, National League of American Penwomen, Arizona Authors Association (vice-president), Arizona Poetry Association (president), Arizona State Poetry Society, Phoenix Writers Club.

WRITINGS: Meditation Without Frills, Schenkman, 1977; *Thirty-Three and Mortgage-Free,* Schenkman, 1978; *Colorful Seasons of Arizona,* Carlos Elmer, 1979; *An Arizona Christmas,* Harold Douglas, 1979. Author of newspaper columns, "Poets Corner" and "Arizona Authors and Their Books." Contributor to magazines, including *Worcester Poetess, Images and Rainbows,* and *M-Muse.* Editor of newsletter of National League of American Penwomen and Mensa's international poetry journal.

WORK IN PROGRESS: Some of My Best Friends Are In-Laws.

SIDELIGHTS: Maureen Jones-Ryan wrote: "It is high time poetry is brought down from the ivory tower and made accessible to the people. It is the most human of activities—the basic form of meaningful communication.

"Regarding my nonfiction, it is hoped that my experience in counseling troubled families can be passed on to as many individuals as possible."

*   *   *

JORDAN, David William 1940-

PERSONAL: Born July 7, 1940, in Wilson, N.C.; son of William Alexander (a printer) and Mildred (Ferrell) Jordan; married Kay Smith (a teacher), November 25, 1967; children: Anna Carole, Leah Bryant. *Education:* Davidson College, A.B., 1962; Princeton University, M.A., 1964, Ph.D., 1966. *Politics:* Democrat. *Religion:* Presbyterian. *Home:* 1415 Park St., Grinnell, Iowa 50112. *Office:* Department of History, Grinnell College, Grinnell, Iowa 50112.

CAREER: Grinnell College, Grinnell, Iowa, assistant professor, 1969-72, associate professor, 1972-78, professor of history, 1978—. *Military service:* U.S. Army, 1967-69; became captain. *Member:* American Association of University Professors, Organization of American Historians, Institute of Early American History and Culture (associate), Southern Historical Association, Phi Beta Kappa. *Awards, honors:* National Endowment for the Humanities grant, 1974-76.

WRITINGS: (With Lois Green Carr) *Maryland's Revolution of Government, 1689-1692,* Cornell University Press, 1974; (editor with Edward Papenfuse, Alan Day, and Gregory Stiverson) *Biographical Dictionary of the Maryland Legislature, 1635-1789,* two volumes, Johns Hopkins Press, 1979-80.

WORK IN PROGRESS: A study of the evolution of representative government in Maryland, 1634-1715.

*   *   *

JOSEPH, Dov 1899-1980

OBITUARY NOTICE: Born in 1899 in Montreal, Quebec, Canada; died January 6, 1980, in Tel Aviv, Israel. Soldier, government minister, and author. Joseph was one of Israel's founding fathers who fought alongside David Ben-Gurion against the British in Palestine. He held several ministerial posts in the government of Israel and served as Jerusalem's military governor during the siege of April, 1948. He was the author of several books, including *British Rule in Palestine* and *The Faithful City.* Obituaries and other sources: *Who's Who in World Jewry,* Pitman, 1972; *Who's Who in the World,* 4th edition, Marquis, 1978; *The International Who's Who,* 42nd edition, Europa, 1978; *Washington Post,* January 7, 1980; *New York Times,* January 7, 1980.

*   *   *

JUDD, Dennis R. 1943-

PERSONAL: Born March 12, 1943, in Provo, Utah. *Education:* Oregon College of Education, B.S., 1965; University of Illinois, A.M., 1968, Ph.D., 1972. *Home:* 1801 East Jewell, Denver, Colo. 80208. *Office:* Department of Political Science, University of Denver, Denver, Colo. 80208.

CAREER: Washington University, St. Louis, Mo., assistant

professor of political science and urban studies, 1970-78, head of urban studies program and assistant director of Institute of Urban and Regional Studies, both 1972-74; University of Denver, Denver, Colo., associate professor of political science and head of department, 1978—. *Member:* Western Social Science Association, Midwest Political Science Association.

WRITINGS: (With Robert Mendelson) *The Politics of Urban Planning: The East St. Louis Experience,* University of Illinois Press, 1973; (contributor) Alan Stone and Theodore Lowi, editors, *Public Policies in America,* Sage Publications, 1978; *The Politics of American Cities: Private Power and Public Policy,* Little, Brown, 1979; (contributor) Gary Tobin, editor, *The Changing Structure of the City,* Sage Publications, 1979. Contributor to professional journals and popular magazines, including *Focus/Midwest.* Book review editor of *Urban Affairs Quarterly,* 1973-79.

WORK IN PROGRESS: The National Policy Process: Implementing Social Policy in a Complex Federal System, with Francis N. Kopel; research on the social class composition of progressive and municipal reform, 1900-1920, and on the four stages of suburbanization.

*   *   *

JUDSON, David (Malcolm) 1941-

PERSONAL: Born July 20, 1941, in Keighley, England; son of William Jason (an engineer) and Hilda (Rhodes) Judson; married Penelope Wendy Tutt (an accountant), April 14, 1979. *Education:* Leeds College of Art, Dipl.Arch., 1965; also attended University of Aston in Birmingham, 1967-69. *Residence:* Littleborough, England. *Agent:* John Farquharson Ltd., 35 Red Lion Sq., London, England.

CAREER: Redditch New Town Corp., Redditch, Worcestershire, England, architect, 1965-70; Manchester City Council, Manchester, England, senior architect, 1970-72; Bury Metropolitan Borough Council, Bury, Lancashire, England, principal architect, 1972-74, chief architect, 1974—. Conservation officer for British Cave Research Association. Co-founder and member of board of trustees of Ghar Parau Foundation. *Member:* National Caving Association (secretary, 1979—).

WRITINGS: Ghar Parau, Macmillan, 1973; (with Arthur Champion) *Caving and Potholing,* Granada, in press.

SIDELIGHTS: Judson commented: "*Ghar Parau* was written after two successful cave exploration expeditions to the Zagros Mountains in Iran, and tells the story of these journeys. A result of the financial success of these ventures was that the Ghar Parau Foundation was set up. It is a charitable trust which makes annual grants to British caving expeditions going abroad. I am actively involved in all aspects of the conservation of caves.

"My interest in caves first came from walks in the Pennine Hills of Yorkshire, England. Natural curiosity was aroused which led to a passion to explore all known caves and then, logically, to find new and unexplored caves. After reaching the bottom of the Gouffre Bergen (France) with an all-British team in 1962 (the first national team to achieve this depth, 3,840 feet), there followed a period of searching Europe for an even deeper one. There were expeditions to Spain in 1963, Austria and Czechoslovakia in 1964 and 1965, Italy in 1967, 1969, and 1970, and then to Iran in 1971 and 1972. The record was always elusive, but the search was often exciting!

"In recent years, inspired by the appalling mess made by cavers, quarry firms, and landowners on revisits to British caves, an interest in cave conservation has developed. A desire to improve the image of cavers has led through conservation to representation on national park committees and other quasi-government bodies. Recently, I have been instrumental in the production of a film on cave conservation in Britain.''

K

KAHAN, Stuart 1936-

PERSONAL: Born September 10, 1936, in Philadelphia, Pa.; son of Jack D. (an executive) and Violet (a ballerina; maiden name, Sadoff) Kahan; married Judith Amstell, 1963 (divorced, 1972); married Nancy White, 1972 (divorced, 1978); children: Brian, Pamela, William. *Education:* Pennsylvania State University, B.A., 1958; graduate study at New York Law School, 1960-64. *Office:* American Society of Magazine Photographers, 205 Lexington Ave., New York, N.Y. 10016.

CAREER: William Morris Agency (theatrical agency), New York City, in business affairs, 1959-66; Paramount Pictures Corp., New York City, in business affairs, 1966-71; independent negotiator and consultant, 1972-77; American Society of Magazine Photographers, New York City, executive director and editor-in-chief of *ASMP Bulletin,* 1978—. *Military service:* U.S. Marine Corps, 1958-64; became captain. *Member:* Authors League of America, National Theatrical Fraternity, Authors Guild, Beta Sigma Rho, Androcles Club, Skull and Bones Club, Thespians Club (president), Carriage House Players (member of board of directors).

WRITINGS: Photography: What's the Law?, Crown, 1976, revised edition, 1979; *The Expectant Father's Survival Kit,* Simon & Schuster, 1977; *For Divorced Fathers Only,* Simon & Schuster, 1978; *Do I Really Need a Lawyer?,* Chilton, 1979; *The Business of Photography,* Crown, 1980. Contributor to magazines and newspapers.

WORK IN PROGRESS: Confessions of an Emancipated Man; The New Yorkers.

SIDELIGHTS: Kahan wrote: "Ninety-nine and forty-four one hundredths percent of the time, I write about what I know. That's usually me. This has been the case in the books I have written thus far and in the articles and columns I have done for magazines and newspapers.

"In the fiction area (I am completing my first novel), the book is based solidly on what has transpired in my own life and in the lives of people I know or have known.

"I am terrible at making up things. I couldn't tell a fairy tale to save my hair. But who needs fairy tales? Fact is more overwhelming than make-believe. Why try to make up something when by looking a little closer at what's around, you can find anything you need in almost any way you need?"

"I have published six books and each has been taken from my own life. Two more are now in the hopper: one on emerging men will show how the male is experiencing a greater awareness of his own capacity for creativity and emotion, and as a result, is using such capabilities in all aspects of daily living, from his relationships with friends, neighbors, and business associates, to his sharing in child care, homemaking, and financial responsibilities. In short, it's the confessions of an emancipated man. Again, it is drawn from my own background."

BIOGRAPHICAL/CRITICAL SOURCES: Photographic, August, 1976; *New York Times,* June 18, 1978, July 16, 1978, December 30, 1979, January 6, 1980; *Us,* March 20, 1979; *Richmond News Ledger,* March 28, 1979.

*   *   *

KAISER, Edward J(ohn) 1935-

PERSONAL: Born February 26, 1935, in Evanston, Ill.; son of Alphonse and Anna (Ficker) Kaiser; married Patricia Ann Brodie (a secretary), June 7, 1958; children: E. Michael, Kathleen, Karen, Joanne, Christopher. *Education:* Illinois Institute of Technology, B.Arch., 1958; University of North Carolina, Ph.D., 1966. *Home:* 1605 Ferrell Rd., Chapel Hill, N.C. 27514. *Office:* Department of City and Regional Planning, University of North Carolina, Chapel Hill, N.C. 27514.

CAREER: University of North Carolina, Chapel Hill, instructor, 1965-66, assistant professor, 1966-69, associate professor, 1969-74, professor of city and regional planning, 1974—. Vice-chairperson of Chapel Hill Planning Board. *Military service:* U.S. Navy, 1958-61; became lieutenant junior grade. *Member:* American Planning Association, Association of Collegiate Schools of Planning (vice-president).

WRITINGS: Residential Mobility in New Communities: An Analysis of Recent In-Movers and Prospective Out-Movers, Ballinger, 1976; (with F. Stuart Chapin, Jr.) *Urban Land Use Planning,* 3rd edition (Kaiser was not associated with earlier editions), University of Illinois Press, 1979; *Energy Conservation in the Production of Residential Environments,* Oelgeschlager, Gunn & Hain, 1980; *Flood Plain Land Use and Management,* Center for Urban and Regional Studies, University of North Carolina, 1980. Book review editor of *Journal of the American Planning Association.*

WORK IN PROGRESS: Urban Development Guidance Systems.

KALDOR, Mary 1946-

PERSONAL: Born March 16, 1946, in England; daughter of Nicholas (an economist) and Clarissa (a politician; maiden name, Goldschmidt) Kaldor; married Julian Perry Robinson (a researcher); children: Joshua. *Education:* Attended Somerville College, Oxford, 1963-67. *Politics:* Socialist. *Home:* 35 Sussex Sq., Brighton, England. *Agent:* Anthony Sheil, 2/3 Morwell St., London WC1B 3AR, England. *Office:* Science Policy Research Unit, University of Sussex, Falmer, Brighton, Sussex BN1 9QX, England.

CAREER: International Peace Research Institute, Stockholm, Sweden, consultant, 1967-69; associated with University of Sussex, Institute for the Study of International Organisation, Brighton, England, 1969-76, research fellow of Science Policy Research Unit, 1976—, and Institute of Development Studies, 1978—, faculty member, 1977—. Research fellow at Massachusetts Institute of Technology, 1972; visiting fellow at Free University of Berlin, 1974, and Institute for Policy Studies, 1978. Member of national executive committee of Labour party, 1975—. *Member:* International Peace Research Association, Pugwash.

WRITINGS: European Defence Industries (monograph), Institute for the Study of International Organisation, University of Sussex, 1972; *The Disintegrating West*, Allen Lane, 1978; *The World Military Order: The Impact of Military Technology on the Third World*, Macmillan, 1979. Also author of *The Arms Trade With the Third World*, 1971.

WORK IN PROGRESS: The Baroque Arsenal.

*   *   *

KALLEN, Horace M(eyer) 1882-1974

PERSONAL: Born August 11, 1882, in Berenstadt, Silesia, Germany; came to United States in 1887; naturalized citizen; died February 16, 1974; son of Jacob David (a rabbi and Hebrew scholar) and Esther Rebecca (Glazier) Kallen; married Rachel Oatman Van Arsdale, 1926; children: Harriet S., David J. *Education:* Harvard University, A.B., 1903, Ph.D., 1909; also studied at Princeton University, Oxford University, and Sorbonne, University of Paris. *Residence:* New York, N.Y.

CAREER: Clark College, Worcester, Mass., instructor in logic, 1910; University of Wisconsin—Madison, instructor in psychology and philosophy, 1911-18; New School for Social Research, New York, N.Y., co-founder in 1919, member of faculty, 1919-1952, professor emeritus, 1952-74. Member of Mayor's Committee on City Planning, New York City, 1923-37; chairman of American Labor Conference on International Relations, 1942-43. Vice-president of American Jewish Congress; chairman of academic council, Yiddish Scientific Institute of New York City; trustee of Rochdale Institute of New York. *Member:* American Philosophical Society, Society for Psychological Research, Society of Physical Research, Western Philosophical Society.

WRITINGS: (Editor) William James, *Some Problems of Philosophy: A Beginning of an Introduction to Philosophy*, 1911, reprinted, Greenwood Press, 1968; *William James and Henri Bergson: A Study in Contrasting Theories of Life*, University of Chicago Press, 1914; *The Structure of Lasting Peace: An Inquiry Into the Motives of War and Peace*, Marshall Jones Co., 1918, reprinted, Haskell House, 1974; (editor) *The Book of Job as a Greek Tragedy*, Moffat, 1918; *The League of Nations, Today and Tomorrow: A Discussion of International Organization, Present and to Come*, Marshall Jones Co., 1919.

Zionism and World Politics: A Study in History and Social Psychology, Doubleday, Page & Co., 1921, reprinted, Greenwood Press, 1975; *Culture and Democracy in the United States: Studies in the Group Psychology of the American Peoples*, Boni & Liveright, 1924, reprinted, Arno Press, 1970; *Education, the Machine and the Worker: An Essay in the Psychology of Education in Industrial Society*, New Republic, 1925; *Why Religion*, Boni & Liveright, 1927; (editor) *Freedom in the Modern World*, Coward-McCann, 1928, reprinted, Books for Libraries Press, 1969; *Frontiers of Hope*, H. Liveright, 1929, reprinted, Arno Press, 1977.

Indecency and the Seven Arts, and Other Adventures of a Pragmatist in Aesthetics, H. Liveright, 1930; *Judaism at Bay: Essays Toward the Adjustment of Judaism to Modernity*, Bloch Publishing Co., 1932, reprinted, Arno Press, 1972; *Individualism: An American Way of Life*, Liveright, 1933; *A Free Society*, R. O. Ballou, 1934; (editor with Sidney Hook) *American Philosophy Today and Tomorrow*, reprinted, Books for Libraries Press, 1968; *The Decline and Rise of the Consumer: A Philosophy of Consumer Cooperation*, D. Appleton-Century, 1936, reprinted, Arno Press, 1976.

(Editor with John Dewey) *The Bertrand Russell Case*, 1941, reprinted, Da Capo Press, 1972; *Art and Freedom: A Historical and Biographical Interpretation of the Relations Between the Ideas of Beauty, Use and Freedom in Western Civilization From the Greeks to the Present Day*, Duell, Sloan & Pearce, 1942, reprinted, Greenwood Press, 1969; *Modernity and Liberty: The University of Buffalo Centenary Lectures on the Problems of Freedom in the Modern World*, University of Buffalo, 1947; *The Liberal Spirit: Essays on Problems of Freedom in the Modern World*, Cornell University Press, 1948; *Ideals and Experience*, New School for Social Research, 1948; *The Education of Free Men: An Essay Toward a Philosophy of Education for Americans*, Farrar, Straus, 1949.

Patterns of Progress, Columbia University Press, 1950; *Secularism Is the Will of God: An Essay in the Social Philosophy of Democracy and Religion*, Twayne, 1954; "*Of Them Which Say They Are Jews,*" *and Other Essays on the Jewish Struggle for Survival*, edited by Judah Pilch, Bloch Publishing Co., 1954; *Cultural Pluralism and the American Idea: An Essay in Social Philosophy*, University of Pennsylvania Press, 1956; *Utopians at Bay*, Theodor Herzl Foundation, 1958; *A Study of Liberty*, Antioch Press, 1959.

Philosophical Issues in Adult Education, Thomas, 1962; *Liberty, Laughter, and Tears: Reflections on the Relations of Comedy and Tragedy to Human Freedom*, Northern Illinois University Press, 1968; *What I Believe and Why—Maybe: Essays for the Modern World*, edited by Alfred J. Marrow, Horizon Press, 1971; *Creativity, Imagination, Logic: Meditations for the Eleventh Hour*, Gordon & Breach, 1973; *Toward a Philosophy of the Seas*, University Press of Virginia, 1973. Also author of numerous pamphlets on Zionism, education, and political philosophy. Contributing editor, *Dial*, 1917-22; managing editor, *Advance*, 1923-25.

SIDELIGHTS: In 1919 Horace Kallen, together with James Harvey Robinson, Charles Beard, Thorstien Veblen, and Robert Bruerre, founded the New School for Social Research in New York City. Their intent, according to a New York newspaper, was "to seek an unbiased understanding of the existing order, its genesis, growth and present working." The founders incorporated into the curriculum their own philosophies of education, and narrowed down their instruction to almost entirely economics. Kallen, who had been an associate of both William James and George Santanya, espoused James's pragmatist philosophy, and believed education to be part of the whole of life. From the school's inception, he taught two classes exclusively: "Beauty and Use" and "Dominant Ideals of Western Civilization."

He was also the author of more than thirty books on education, Zionism, and philosophy. One of Kallen's later works, *What I Believe and Why,* is considered to be a good introduction to his philosophy. M. R. Konvitz observed: "In this collection Kallen attempts to refocus his powers, his instincts, his memories, and his inspiration into a new harmony of insight. If the ideas are no longer novel, it is because he has been such a superbly effective teacher. But, familiar as they may be, their tone remains pristine and clear.... This book proves that the stream of Kallen's thought, with its freshness and agitation, still has power to excite and incite."

AVOCATIONAL INTERESTS: Painting surrealistic pictures; reading detective novels.

BIOGRAPHICAL/CRITICAL SOURCES: New York Times, September 30, 1919; *Saturday Review,* October 12, 1968, July 31, 1971; *Journal of Aesthetics,* Winter, 1969.

OBITUARIES: New York Times, February 17, 1974.*

*   *   *

KALTENBORN, Hans Von   1878-1965

OBITUARY NOTICE: Born July 9, 1878, in Milwaukee, Wis.; died June 14, 1965. In 1922, Kaltenborn became radio's first news analyst and was later so closely identified with his war reports that he was popularly dubbed "the suave Voice of Doom." During the Spanish civil war, he made the first live radio broadcasts of combat when, with a coil of cable tucked under his arm, he tapped into a telephone line, took shelter in a haystack, and sent back reports punctuated by the sound of machine gun fire and exploding shells. From 1930 to 1940, he covered every major crisis for the Columbia Broadcasting System and performed the amazing feat of making eighty-five broadcasts in eighteen days during the Czechoslovakian crisis. The Harvard-educated broadcaster, who never allowed commercials to interrupt his reports, became famous for his rapid, distinctive delivery and his facility for extemporaneous reporting. After 1940, he covered World War II for the National Broadcasting Co., then worked as that network's news analyst until his retirement in 1955. Kaltenborn wrote several books, including *We Look at the World, Kaltenborn Edits the News, Europe Now,* and his autobiography, *Fifty Fabulous Years.* Obituaries and other sources: *Current Biography,* Wilson, 1940, September, 1965; *New York Times,* June 15, 1965.

*   *   *

KALU, Ogbu Uke   1944-

PERSONAL: Born June 2, 1944, in Ohafia, Nigeria; son of Uke Kalu Onwuchekwa (a trader and retailer) and Uzumma Uchendu; married wife, Wilhemina Josephine (a child psychologist and lecturer), June 6, 1970; children: one son, two daughters. *Education:* University of Toronto, B.A. (with honors), 1967, Ph.D., 1973; McMaster University, M.A. (cumma cum laude), 1968; attended Institute of Historical Research, London, 1970-72; Princeton Theological Seminary, M.Div., 1974. *Office:* Department of Religion, University of Nigeria, Nsukka, Nigeria.

CAREER: University of Nigeria, Nsukka, lecturer, 1974-78,

professor of church history and director of division of general studies, 1978—.

MEMBER: Conference of African Theological Institutions (executive member), African Studies Association, Nigerian Historical Association, National Association for the Study of Religions, Historical Society of Nigeria, Nigerian Association for the Study of Religions (executive member), Canadian Society for Church History, Conference of British Historians, West African Association of Theological Institutions (secretary-general), Institute of Church and Society (Ibadan; member of board of management). *Awards, honors:* Waring fellowship from University of Toronto, 1968; Province of Ontario graduate award, 1969-70; Canada Council for the Arts fellowship, 1970-72; grant from Ecumenical Commission, 1973; Grier-Davies Award in Homiletics from Princeton Theological Seminary, 1974; Pollack Trust Fund grant, 1979.

WRITINGS: (Editor and contributor) *Christianity in West Africa: The Nigerian Story,* Daystar Press, 1978; *Divided People of God: The Church Union Movement in Nigeria, 1875-1966,* NOK Publishers, 1978; (editor and contributor) *Readings in African Humanities: African Cultural Development,* Fourth Dimensions Publishers, 1978; (editor and contributor) *The History of Christianity in West Africa,* Longman, 1979.

Contributor: *The Future of the Historical Missionary Enterprise,* IDOC International, 1974; Richard Gray, editor, *Christianity in Post-Independence Africa,* Rex Collings, 1978; Kofi Appiah Kubi and Sergio Torres, editors, *African Theology En Route,* Orbis, 1979; Elocknkwu Amucheadi, editor, *Issues in Nigerian National Development,* Fourth Dimensions Publishers, 1979; H. N. Nwosu, editor, *Public Administration in Nigeria,* Fourth Dimensions Publishers, 1980.

Contributor of about thirty articles and poems to theology journals, *Omabe,* and *Victoriana Acta.* Chief editor of *University of Nigeria Journal of the Social Sciences;* editor of *Religions and West African Religion;* member of editorial board of *Journal of African Theology, Caribbean and African Journal of Theology,* and *Bulletin Theologie Africaine.*

WORK IN PROGRESS: Religious Policy and Practice in Jacobean England; Religion and Society in Cross River Igboland.

SIDELIGHTS: Kalu wrote: "The history of Christianity in Africa is not primarily concerned with what missionaries did or did not do. Rather it is a story of how communities with viable religious, political, and cultural structures reacted to new change agents—Christian missionaries, traders, and colonial administrators. The *encounter* produced a spectrum of reactions ranging from full acceptance to total rejection, but with many medial positions. The encounter also changed both the culture bearers and their hosts. Therefore, the study of Christianity must start with a reconstruction of the structures of the various African communities. It is argued that the patterns of Christian expansion and the African responses were determined by the patterns of social, political, economic, and other ecological and cultural factors. History is ideology. Therefore, for the African, church history should start with his traditional religious base and worldview and endeavor to explain why some Africans abandoned the gods of their fathers. Obviously, an understanding of the *home base* of the missionaries is essential. But the religious history of Africa does not begin in Europe.

"It should also be added that African church history does not end with the Golden Age of Missionaries, i.e. the pre-

Independence period. Rather it should take seriously the form of Christian presence in the post-Independence period, the contributions of the church in the task of nation building, and the challenges of realizing her mission, maturing into an independent, self-supporting body, combatting non-Christian ideologies, and restructuring her relationship with other members of the universal church.''

*   *   *

KANNAPPAN, Subbiah 1927-

PERSONAL: Born June 8, 1927, in Bombay, India; came to the United States; naturalized citizen, 1962; son of Subbiah (a banker) and Parvathi (Ramalingam) Arumugam; married Nancy Kenney (a stockbroker), June 13, 1956 (divorced, March 19, 1971); children: Maryann, Ken, Sheila. *Education:* University of Madras, B.A., 1948, M.A. (economics), 1949; University of Geneva, diploma in French, 1949; Fletcher School of Law and Diplomacy, M.A., 1950, Ph.D., 1956; postdoctoral study at University of Chicago, 1958-59. *Home:* 1540 Ridgewood Dr., East Lansing, Mich. 48823. *Office:* Department of Economics, Michigan State University, East Lansing, Mich. 48824.

CAREER: Massachusetts Institute of Technology, Cambridge, research associate in economics and social sciences, 1952-56, director of research, 1956-58; Michigan State University, East Lansing, assistant professor, 1961-64, associate professor, 1964-68, professor of economics, 1968—. Visiting professor at International Institute for Labour Studies, 1965-66, 1973-75, and Indian Institute of Management, 1968-69. Economist for Delhi Regional Planning Team; member of Government of India Team on Workers' Education; member of United Nations mission to Sudan, 1975, also Security Council intern. Editorial assistant for Carnegie Endowment for International Peace. Workshop and seminar director; consultant to National Planning Association. *Member:* Common Cause (district chairperson, 1971-73), Midwest Universities Consortium for International Affairs (chairperson, 1972-73), Delta Tau Kappa.

WRITINGS: Aluminum Limited in India, National Planning Association, 1962; (with C. A. Myers) *Industrial Relations in India,* Asia Publishing House, 1971; (contributor) J. S. Uppal, editor, *India's Economic Problems: An Analytical Approach,* McGraw, 1975; (editor) *Research Conference on Urban Labour Markets in Developing Areas: Discussions and Notes,* International Institute for Labour Studies, 1975; (editor and contributor) *Studies on Urban Labour Market Behavior,* International Labor Organization, 1977. Contributor to learned journals, including *Annals of the American Academy of Political and Social Sciences.* Member of editorial board of *Journal of Asian Studies,* 1962-65.

WORK IN PROGRESS: A report on urban labor markets in developing areas, for Macmillan; a monograph on urban employment problems in developing nations.

*   *   *

KAPLAN, Martin F(rancis) 1940-

PERSONAL: Born April 20, 1940, in Brooklyn, N.Y.; son of Ben (a truck driver) and Bebe (Wulinsky) Kaplan; married Lydia M. Eagle (in social services), July 9, 1960; children: Jonathan, Jeremy, Jaymie. *Education:* City College of the City University of New York, B.B.A., 1960, M.S., 1962; University of Iowa, Ph.D., 1965. *Politics:* "Every now and then." *Religion:* Jewish. *Office:* Department of Psychology, Northern Illinois University, DeKalb, Ill. 60115.

CAREER: Veterans Administration Hospital, Iowa City, Iowa, intern, 1964-65; Northern Illinois University, DeKalb, assistant professor, 1965-68, associate professor, 1968-75, professor of psychology, 1975—. Research visitor at University of California, Center for Human Information Processing, San Diego, 1970-71. Member of publication board of Northern Illinois University Press, 1976-79. Grant proposal reviewer for National Science Foundation and Canada Council of the Arts. *Member:* American Psychological Association (fellow), Psychonomic Society, Society of Experimental Social Psychologists, American Psychology-Law Society, American Association of University Professors, Midwestern Psychological Association (program chairperson, 1976), Sigma Xi. *Awards, honors:* National Science Foundation grants, 1971, 1975-77; National Institute of Mental Health grants, 1971-72, 1973-76.

WRITINGS: (Editor) *Readings for Social Psychology,* MSS Information, 1972; (editor with Steven Schwartz, and contributor) *Human Judgment and Decision Processes,* Academic Press, 1975; (editor with Schwartz, and contributor) *Human Judgment and Decision Processes in Applied Settings,* Academic Press, 1977; (contributor) B. D. Sales, editor, *Perspectives in Law and Psychology,* Volume II, Plenum, 1979; (contributor) Sales and Paul Lipsitt, editors, *New Directions in Psycholegal Research,* Van Nostrand, 1979; (contributor) Robert Bray and Norbert Kerr, editors, *The Psychology of the Courtroom,* Academic Press, 1981. Contributor of more than forty articles to journals in the behavioral sciences. Member of editorial board of *Journal of Personality and Social Psychology,* 1975—.

WORK IN PROGRESS: Several articles.

SIDELIGHTS: Kaplan told *CA:* "I consider myself primarily as a researcher, but secondarily as one who can help others to apply my knowledge to their concerns in human affairs. My belief as a social psychologist is that my contribution is best given by alerting decision-makers to the implications of research, and for that research to be helpful, it has to be rigorous and conclusive. For example, speculation and poorly run research has led many to fear and expect strong effects for bias in juror decisions, while more careful research suggests that a number of means are available within the present system for controlling and reducing biases—other than currently popular, though wasteful and ethically questionable modes of 'scientific' (a misnomer) jury selection. The manifestation and reduction of biasing which I've been finding is understandable in light of research and theory in social psychology. I'm presently designing courses and workshops to bring the relevant social-psychological knowledge to the legal profession.

"Generally speaking, my interest in social-psychological behavior is in how we judge and evaluate other people in *any* context. Juror decision-making is but one aspect of this endeavor. Other sorts of judgment which I'm working with include studies of the moral judgments children and adults form of others' actions, the evaluation of suspects in murder mysteries by readers, and judgments by experts and nonexperts of contestants in old-time fiddle contests. The last reflects a wedding of my research with my personal interests in old-timey music, which I play badly (guitar and autoharp) but listen to well. Underlying these strange research projects is the belief that all human judgment, regardless of the thing being judged, involves basically the same fundamental process.

"Background . . .? Lower-middle class-New York-liberal-educated at City College-Jewish. The sort that Woody Allen has repeatedly publicized, and of the denomination that populates academia. How such a person got to be fanatic and knowledgeable about fiddles, banjos, old-time and country music is a long story, which I'll tell the reader about, if s/he's interested, over a Lone Star beer while listening to Bob Wills and Willie Nelson.''

*   *   *

KASCHNITZ, Marie Luise
See von KASCHNITZ-WEINBERG, Marie Luise

*   *   *

KATTERJOHN, Arthur D.   1930(?)-1980

OBITUARY NOTICE: Born c. 1930; died January 8, 1980, in Wheaton, Ill. Educator and band director. Katterjohn was an associate professor at Wheaton College, where he directed the school's concert band and symphony orchestra. He wrote two religious books, Tribulation People and Lord, When? Obituaries and other sources: Chicago Tribune, January 10, 1980.

*   *   *

KATZ, Albert M(ichael)   1938-

PERSONAL: Born May 20, 1938, in New York, N.Y.; son of Harry Joseph (a certified public accountant) and Esther (Gottesman) Katz; married Virginia Teare (a professor of speech), September 2, 1962; children: Rachel Susannah, Rebecca Miriam. Education: Union College, Schenectady, N.Y., B.A., 1958; University of Michigan, M.A., 1960, Ph.D., 1966. Religion: Jewish. Home: 2105 Harvard Ave., Duluth, Minn. 55803. Office: Department of Communicating Arts, University of Wisconsin, Superior, Wis. 54880.

CAREER: University of Michigan, Ann Arbor, instructor in speech and theatre, 1960-62; Alma College, Alma, Mich., assistant professor of speech and theatre, 1962-65; University of Wisconsin—Superior, associate professor, 1966-74, professor of speech and theatre, 1974—, director of theatre, 1966-80. Member of theatre evaluation panel of Wisconsin Arts Board, 1979-81. Actor, including performances at Great Lakes Shakespeare Festival, and with summer stock and civic theatre groups.

MEMBER: International Listening Association (founding member), Speech Communication Association, American Theatre Association (member of regional board of governors, 1973-76), American Association of University Professors, Wisconsin Theatre Association (founding president of board of directors, 1972-76), Wisconsin University and College Theatre Association (president, 1977-78), Association of University of Wisconsin Faculties, Alpha Psi Omega, Phi Kappa Phi. Awards, honors: Grants from Wisconsin State Universities Research Board, 1970-71, 1971-72, Wisconsin Fine Arts Council, 1972-73, and U.S. Department of Health, Education, and Welfare, 1977-78.

WRITINGS: Stage Violence: Offense, Defense, and Safety, Richards, Rosen, 1976.

Scripts based on The Odyssey: A Modern Sequel, by Nikos Kazantzakis: "The Reabduction of Helen" (two-act), first produced at University of Michigan, Ann Arbor, May, 1971; "The Destruction of Knossos," first produced at University of Wisconsin—Superior, May, 1972; "The Flight Out of Egypt" (two-act), first produced at University of Wisconsin, May, 1973; "They Build the Perfect City" (two-act), first produced at University of Wisconsin, October, 1973.

Author of "The Moebus Ring" (opera libretto). Contributor to theatre journals and Modern Gymnast.

WORK IN PROGRESS: Research on the relationship between interpersonal communication training and theatre.

SIDELIGHTS: Albert Katz commented: "Since 1966, I have taught in a department which includes programs in speech-communication, theatre, mass communication, and journalism. I have taught courses in both acting and speech-communication and, like many of my colleagues, I have both taught and thought of them as separate entities. In recent years, my interests have increasingly focused on the problems of one-to-one communication. As a result of this interest in interpersonal communication, I have come to the conclusion that acting and interpersonal communication are separate, but convergent. The study of each enhances our knowledge of the other.''

*   *   *

KATZENSTEIN, Mary Fainsod   1945-

PERSONAL: Born February 2, 1945, in Boston, Mass.; daughter of Merle and Elizabeth (Stix) Fainsod; married Peter Joachim Katzenstein (a professor), June, 1970; children: Tai, Suzanne. Education: Radcliffe College, B.A., 1966; London School of Oriental and African Studies, London, M.Sc., 1968; Massachusetts Institute of Technology, Ph.D., 1975. Residence: Ithaca, N.Y. Office: Department of Government, Cornell University, Ithaca, N.Y. 14850.

CAREER: Cornell University, Ithaca, N.Y., professor of government, 1973—.

WRITINGS: Ethnicity and Equality: The Shiv Sena Party and Preferential Policies in Bombay, Cornell University Press, 1979.

*   *   *

KATZENSTEIN, Peter J(oachim)   1945-

PERSONAL: Born February 17, 1945, in Bremerhaven, Germany; came to the United States in 1964, naturalized citizen, 1979; son of Gerhard (in business) and Gerda (Hertz) Katzenstein; married Mary Fainsod (a professor), June 18, 1970; children: Tai, Suzanne. Education: Swarthmore College, B.A. (with highest honors), 1967; London School of Economics and Political Science, London, M.Sc. (with distinction), 1968; Harvard University, Ph.D., 1973. Office: Department of Government, Cornell University, Ithaca, N.Y. 14853.

CAREER: University of Massachusetts, Boston, instructor in politics, 1972-73; Cornell University, Ithaca, N.Y., assistant professor, 1973-77, associate professor of government, 1977—. Fellow of Center for Advanced Study in the Behavioral Sciences, 1981-82. Member: International Studies Association, European Consortium for Political Research, American Political Science Association, Conference Group on German Politics, Council on European Studies, Phi Beta Kappa. Awards, honors: Helen Dwight Reid Award from American Political Science Association, 1974, for doctoral dissertation; Ford Foundation grant, 1974-77; U.S. Office of Education grant, 1975-77; fellowship from Andrew W. Mellon Foundation and Aspen Institute for Humanistic Studies, 1976-77; Rockefeller Foundation fellowship, 1977-79; German Marshall Fund fellowship, 1979-81.

WRITINGS: From Many One and From One Many: Political Unification, Political Fragmentation, and Cultural Cohesion in Europe Since 1815 (monograph), Cornell University, 1974; (with Douglas Ashford and T. J. Pempel) Bibliography of Comparative Public Policy in Britain, West Germany, Japan, and France, American Society for Public

Administration, 1976; *Disjoined Partners: Austria and Germany Since 1815,* University of California Press, 1976; (contributor) Richard Rosecrance, editor, *America as an Ordinary Country: United States Foreign Policy and the Future,* Cornell University Press, 1976; (contributor) Milton J. Esman, editor, *Ethnic Conflict in the Western World,* Cornell University Press, 1977; (with Ashford and Pempel) *Comparative Public Policy: A Cross-National Bibliography,* Sage Publications, 1978; (editor with Sidney Tarrow and Luigi Graziano; also contributor) *Territorial Politics in Industrial Nations,* Praeger, 1978; (editor and contributor) *Between Power and Plenty: Foreign Economic Policies of Advanced Industrial States,* University of Wisconsin Press, 1978. Contributor of articles and reviews to political science journals. Member of editorial board and executive committee of *International Organization,* 1976—.

WORK IN PROGRESS: Comparative Foreign Economic Policies of Advanced Industrial States; In Search of Germany: The National and Social Question in Central Europe; Comparative Analysis of Public Policy, with Douglas Ashford and T. J. Pempel.

* * *

KAUFMAN, George S(imon) 1889-1961

OBITUARY NOTICE: Born November 16, 1889, in Pittsburgh, Pa.; died June 2, 1961. Journalist, playwright, and director. Called the greatest success in the American theatre, Kaufman was a *New York Times* drama critic who in 1921 collaborated with Marc Connelly on his first Broadway hit, "Dulcy," and thereafter wrote at least one play a year. Fifteen of his plays ran for 200 performances or more, and more than twenty were sold to motion picture studios. Kaufman, believing his solo efforts as a playwright were never as good as his collaborations, almost always teamed with the freshest, most promising young writers in the theatre, and, because it usually meant success, a collaboration with Kaufman became one of the most prized assignments on Broadway. During the 1920's, Kaufman and Connelly were regarded as the premiere writing team of the decade, but Kaufman then went on to work with such luminaries as Alexander Woollcott, Ring Lardner, Edna Ferber, John Steinbeck, and Howard Dietz. One of those Kaufman introduced to Broadway was Moss Hart, perhaps his most successful partner after Connelly, and together they wrote seven plays, including the 1936 Pulitzer Prize-winning "You Can't Take It With You." Kaufman had earlier shared the award with Morrie Ryskind for their 1931 play, "Of Thee I Sing." A member of the now-legendary fellowship of writers, actors, and journalists who met daily for lunch at the Algonquin Hotel, Kaufman was famous for his terse sarcasms and witticisms, including the oft-quoted "One man's Mede is another man's Persian." And though recognized as one of America's leading satirists, Kaufman claimed that "satire is something that closes on Saturday night." He directed several successful plays, among them "My Sister Eileen," "Guys and Dolls," and "Front Page," and wrote dozens more, including "Merton of the Movies," "The Beggar on Horseback," "The Coconuts," "The Royal Family," "Animal Crackers," "Once in a Lifetime," "The Man Who Came to Dinner," "The Late George Apley," and "Silk Stockings." Obituaries and other sources: *Current Biography,* Wilson, 1941, September, 1961; *New York Times,* June 3, 1961; *The Oxford Companion to American Literature,* 4th edition, Oxford University Press, 1965; *Twentieth Century Writing: A Reader's Guide to Contemporary Literature,* Transatlantic, 1969; *The Penguin Companion to American Literature,*

McGraw, 1971; *McGraw-Hill Encyclopedia of World Drama,* McGraw, 1972; *A Concise Encyclopedia of the Theatre,* Osprey, 1974.

* * *

KAUFMAN, Lloyd 1927-

PERSONAL: Born September 6, 1927, in New York, N.Y.; son of Samuel and Mildred (Feldman) Kaufman; married Elaine Morganstern (a teacher), February 22, 1954; children: Laura Kaufman Foreman, Robin, James. *Education:* San Diego State University, B.A., 1950; New School for Social Research, M.A., 1957, Ph.D., 1961. *Residence:* Roslyn Heights, N.Y. *Office:* Department of Psychology, New York University, 6 Washington Pl., New York, N.Y. 10003.

CAREER: Sperry Rand Corp., engineer in Long Island City, N.Y., 1952-57, head of human factors section in Great Neck, N.Y., 1957-62, member of research staff in Sudbury, Mass., 1962-67; Yeshiva University, New York City, associate professor of psychology, 1967-69; New York University, New York City, professor of psychology, 1969—. Visiting lecturer in psychology at State University of New York, 1958; visiting associate professor of psychology at New York University, 1967-79. Member of National Academy of Sciences-National Research Council vision committee. *Military service:* U.S. Army, 1945-46. *Member:* American Psychological Association (fellow), American Association for the Advancement of Science, Eastern Psychological Association, Association for Research in Vision and Ophthalmology. *Awards, honors:* Grants from Department of Health, Education, and Welfare, 1975-78 and 1978-81, from National Science Foundation, 1973-77 and 1975-77, from Office of Naval Research, 1976-77 and 1977-78, from New York State Health Research Council, 1976-77 and 1977-78, and from Public Health Service, 1975-80.

WRITINGS: Sight and Mind, Oxford University Press, 1974; *Perception: The Word Transformed,* Oxford University Press, 1979. Contributor of more than fifty articles to professional journals. Member of board of editors of *Contemporary Psychology* and *Perception.*

WORK IN PROGRESS: Revising *Sight and Mind.*

SIDELIGHTS: Kaufman writes: "My primary areas of professional interest are visual perception and study of the electrical activity of the human brain."

Reviewing Kaufman's most recent work on these topics, *Perception: The World Transformed,* Maya Pines noted that the author "allows himself few flights of fancy and sometimes seems to drown in detail." Nonetheless, she concluded, it is a "highly informative book."

AVOCATIONAL INTERESTS: Gardening, working with tools, running, reading recent history.

BIOGRAPHICAL/CRITICAL SOURCES: New York Times Book Review, April 29, 1979.

* * *

KAUFMANN, William J(ohn) III 1942-

PERSONAL: Born December 27, 1942, in New York, N.Y.; son of William J., Jr. (a teacher) and Katherine (a teacher; maiden name, Dunne) Kaufmann; married Barbara Smith, 1964 (divorced, 1972); married Lee Johnson (a psychologist), September 13, 1972; children: Kristine Nicole, William J. IV. *Education:* Adelphi University, B.A., 1963; Rutgers University, M.S., 1965; Indiana University, Ph.D., 1968. *Politics:* None. *Religion:* None. *Home and office:* 385 Paraiso Dr., Danville, Calif. 94526.

CAREER: Griffith Observatory, Los Angeles, Calif., director, 1970-75; San Diego State University, San Diego, Calif., adjunct professor of physics, 1976—. Member of visiting faculty at California Institute of Technology, 1974-75; visiting scholar at Jet Propulsion Laboratory, Pasadena, Calif., 1976. *Member:* American Astronomical Society, Astronomical Society of the Pacific (member of board of directors, 1975-79). *Awards, honors:* Dorothea Klumpke-Roberts Award from Astronomical Society of the Pacific, 1979, for "outstanding contributions to better public understanding and appreciation of astronomy."

WRITINGS: Relativity and Cosmology, Harper, 1973; *Astronomy: The Structure of the Universe,* Macmillan, 1977; *Exploration of the Solar System,* Macmillan, 1978; *Stars and Nebulas,* W. H. Freeman, 1978; *Planets and Moons,* W. H. Freeman, 1979; *Galaxies and Quasars,* W. H. Freeman, 1979; *Black Holes and Warped Spacetime,* W. H. Freeman, 1979; *Particles and Fields,* W. H. Freeman, 1980.

WORK IN PROGRESS: The Communication, a novel.

* * *

KAVNER, Richard S. 1936-

PERSONAL: Born February 12, 1936, in Brooklyn, N.Y.; son of Saul (a maritime captain) and Sylvia (a clothing designer) Kavner; married wife, Carole (an interior designer), 1940; children: Theodore, William. *Education:* Attended Long Island University, 1953-55; Massachusetts College of Optometry, B.S., 1959, O.D., 1960; also studied at Queens College of the City University of New York and Gesell Institute of Child Development. *Residence:* Millwood, N.Y. *Office:* 245 East 54th St., New York, N.Y. 10022.

CAREER: Private practice of optometry, specializing in binocular vision and perception, 1960—. Chief of Behavioral Vision Laboratory of State University of New York College of Optometry, 1971-74, assistant clinical professor, 1972-73; lecturer at Brown University, 1977. Affiliated with Daughters of Israel Home and Hospital, 1961—, and Optometric Center of New York, 1962— (chairperson of vision training department, 1966-70). Chief of orthoptic department of Harlem Eye and Ear Hospital, 1964-69; chief of Optometry Clinic at Fort Hamilton Army Dispensary, 1961—. Member of Optometric Extension Program, 1959—. Gives lectures and workshops.

MEMBER: American Academy of Optometry (fellow), American Optometric Association, American Public Health Association, Council for Exceptional Children, New York Academy of Optometry (fellow), New York Optometric Association, New York Academy of Sciences, Bronx County Optometric Society (chairperson of children's vision committee, 1964-66), Omega Epsilon Phi. *Awards, honors:* Grant from National Institutes of Health, 1966.

WRITINGS: Pleoptics Handbook, Optometric Center of New York, 1966, revised edition, 1969; (with Lorraine Dusky) *Total Vision,* A & W Publishing, 1978. Contributor of about fifteen articles to optometry journals.

WORK IN PROGRESS: Vision and Creativity.

* * *

KAWABATA, Yasunari 1899-1972

PERSONAL: Born June 11, 1899, in Osaka, Japan; died by his own hand in Zushi, Japan, April 16, 1972; son of a physician; married wife, Hideko; children: one daughter. *Education:* Tokyo Imperial University, degree in Japanese literature, 1924.

CAREER: Japanese novelist, playwright, short story writer, and critic. Conducted seminars at various American universities, 1960. Author-in-residence at University of Hawaii, 1969. *Member:* P.E.N. Club of Japan (vice-president, 1959-69). *Awards, honors:* Bungei Konwa Kai prize, 1937; Geijutsuin-sho literary prize, 1952; prize from Japanese Academy of Arts, 1952; Noma literary prize, 1954; elected member of Japanese Academy of Arts, 1954; Goethe Medal from Frankfurt, West Germany, 1959; Ordre des Arts et Lettres from France, 1960; French Prix du Meilleur Livre Etranger, 1961; cultural medal from the Japanese government, 1961; Nobel Prize in literature, 1968; recipient of Akutagawa Prize.

WRITINGS—In English: *Izu no odoriko* (fiction), [Japan], 1925, translation by Edward Seidensticker published as *The Izu Dancer* (text in English and Japanese), Harashobo, 1964; *Kinju* (title means "Of Birds and Beasts"), [Japan], 1933, translation published in *The House of the Sleeping Beauties and Other Stories,* 1969 (see below); *Yukiguni* (fiction), [Japan], 1937, revised edition, 1969, translation by Seidensticker of original edition published as *Snow Country,* Knopf, 1957; *Yama no oto,* [Japan], 1952, translation by Seidensticker published as *The Sound of the Mountain,* Knopf, 1970; *Hokuro no nikki* (title means "The Mole"), [Japan], 1940, translation published in *The Izu Dancer and Others,* 1964 (see below); *Meijin,* Shincho magazine, 1951, published as *Go Sei-gen kidan,* [Japan], 1954, translation by Seidensticker of original edition published as *The Master of Go,* Knopf, 1972; *Sembazuru,* [Japan], 1952, translation published as *Thousand Cranes,* Knopf, 1959; *Suigetsu* (title means "The Moon on the Water"), [Japan], 1953, translation published in *The Izu Dancer and Others,* 1964 (see below).

Nemureru bijo (title means "The House of the Sleeping Beauties"), [Japan], 1961, translation published in *The House of the Sleeping Beauties and Other Stories,* 1969 (see below); *Mizuumi,* [Japan], 1961, translation by Reiko Tsukimura published as *The Lake,* Kodansha International, 1974; *Kataude* (title means "One Arm"), [Japan], 1965, translation published in *The House of the Sleeping Beauties and Other Stories,* 1969 (see below); *Utsukushisa to kanashimi to* (fiction), [Japan], 1965, translation by Howard Hibbett published as *Beauty and Sadness,* Random House, 1975; *Bi no sonzai to hakken/The Existence and Discovery of Beauty* (text in English and Japanese), English text translated by V. H. Viglielmo, Mainichi Newspapers, 1969; *Utsukushii Nihon no watakushi/Japan, the Beautiful, and Myself* (Nobel Prize acceptance speech; text in English and Japanese), English text translated by Seidensticker, Kodansha International, 1969.

Omnibus volumes: *The Izu Dancer and Others* (text in English and Japanese; contains "The Izu Dancer," "Reencounter," "The Mole," and "The Moon on the Water"), translated by Seidensticker and others, [Tokyo], 1964; *The House of the Sleeping Beauties and Other Stories* (contains "House of the Sleeping Beauties," "One Arm," and "Of Birds and Beasts"), translated by Seidensticker, introduction by Yukio Mishima, Ballantine, 1969; *Snow Country and Thousand Cranes,* translated by Seidensticker, Knopf, 1969.

In Japanese; all published in Japan; fiction: *Matsugo no me,* 1930; *Asakusa Kurenaidan* (title means "Red Group of Asakusa"), 1930; *Hana no Warutsu,* 1936; *Utsukushii tabi,* 1947; *Otome no minato,* 1948; *Hi mo tsuki mo,* 1953; *Kawa no aru shitamachi no hanashi,* 1954; *Tokyo no hito,* 1955; *Onna de aru koto,* 1956-58; *Kawabata Yasunari sakuhin sen,*

1968; *Shosetsu nyumon,* 1970; *Tampopo,* 1972; *Aru hito no sei no naka ni,* 1972.

Short stories: *Jojoka,* 1938, reprinted, 1950; *Shiroi mangetsu,* 1948; *Maihime,* 1951; *Bungei tokuhon Kawabata Yasunari,* edited by Yukio Mishima, 1962; *Kogen,* 1969; *Tenohira no shosetsu,* 1969; *Shui yuch,* 1971; *Tenju no ko,* 1975; *Honehiroi,* 1975.

Other: *Jurokusai no Nikki* (title means "Diary of a Sixteen-Year-Old"), 1925; *Yugashima onsen,* 1925; *Kanjo shushoku,* 1926; *Bungakuteki Jijoden* (title means "My Literary Biography"), 1934; *Kyucho no tantei,* 1937; *Asakusa Monogatari,* 1950; *Saikonsha,* 1953; *Shosetsu no kenkyu,* 1955; *Fuji no hatsuyuki,* 1958; *Kawabata Yasunari no hito to sakuhin,* 1964, published as *Kawabata Yasunari tokuhon,* 1969; *Koto,* 1968; *Kawabata Yasunari* (catalog of exhibition), 1969; *Kawabata Yasunari ten* (catalog of exhibition), 1972; *Isso ikka* (essays), 1973; *Nihon no bi no kokoro* (essays), 1973; *Take no koe momo no hana* (essays and short stories), 1973.

Omnibus volumes: *Kawabata Yasunari zenshu,* twelve volumes, including volume of short stories and essays, 1948-54, volume of fiction, 1956, two volumes of collected works, 1959-60 and 1969; *Kawabata Yasunari shu* (selected works), volume of short stories, 1951, volume from "Gendai bungo meisaku zenshu" series, 1954, volume of fiction, 1968, three volumes of fiction, each 1975; *Izu no odoriko* [and] *Kinju,* 1951; *Jojoka* [and] *Kinju,* 1952; *Rakka Ryusui* (collection of essays), 1966; *Kawabata Yasunari jisen shu* (fiction), 1966; *Kawabata Yasunari no ningen to geijutsu,* 1971; *Kawabata Yasunari seishun shosetsu shu* (short stories and essays), 1972; *Kawabata Yasunari no bungaku,* 1972-73; *Kawabata Yasunari* (volume from "Nihon bungaku kenkyu shiryo sosho" series), 1973; *Kawabata Yasunari* (volume from "Bungei tokuhon" series), 1977.

Editor: (With Mimei Ogawa and Tsunatake Furuya) *Gendai jido bungaku jiten,* 1955; (with Naoya Shiga and Haruo Sato) *Gendai kiko bungaku zenshu,* 1958; (with Kazuo Mabuchi and Umetomo Saeki) *Kokugo jiten,* Kodansha, 1964; (with Jiro Osaragi, Sen'ichi Hisamatsu, and Tatsuro Inagaki) *Nihon kindai bungaku zuroku,* 1964; *Shonen shojo sekai no meisaku bungaku,* 1965-68; *Kyoto jiten,* 1967; (with Saeki) *Gakushu shin kokugo jiten,* 1968; (with Yoshimoto Endo) *Bunsho no giho,* 1970; *Ocho monogatari shu,* 1971-72; (with Seizo Hayashiya and Tetsuzo Tanikawa) *Nihon no toji,* 1971-73.

Translator: *Ocho monogatari shu,* 1956-58; *Isoppu* (Aesop's fables), 1968.

Contributor: *Taketori monogatari,* 1937, reprinted, 1976; *Bunsho gairon,* 1954; *Bunsho hyogen,* 1954; *Bunsho kosei,* 1954; *Bunsho koza,* 1954; *Bunsho kansho,* 1955; *Jitsuyobun no riron to hoho,* 1955; *Sosaku hoho,* 1955; *Showa meisaku shu,* 1956; *Yaidan Nihon no bungaku,* 1971; *Watarai jimbutsushi,* 1975; *Echizen, Suzu,* 1976; *Hajiki sueki,* 1976; *Sansai ryokuyo kaiyu,* 1976; *Seto Mino,* 1976; *Shigaraki bizen tamba,* 1976; *Tokoname Atsumi Sanage,* 1976.

Work represented in anthologies, including *Modern Japanese Literature,* edited by Donald Keene, Grove, 1956, and *Modern Japanese Stories,* edited by Ivan Ira Morris, translated by Seidensticker, Tuttle, 1961.

SIDELIGHTS: In 1968 internationally acclaimed novelist and short story writer Yasunari Kawabata became the first Japanese ever to receive the Nobel Prize in literature. By this time he had already been honored with every major literary award in Japan, as well as several French awards.

Kawabata's literary prominence began early when as a stu-

dent in 1924 he joined with Riichi Yokomitsu and other young writers to found the literary journal *Bungei Jidai,* the mouthpiece of the Shinkankaku-ha, or Neo-Sensualist movement. Members of this short-lived but important avantgarde literary movement experimented with cubism, dadaism, futurism, and surrealism in an effort to capture the pure feelings and sensations of life. For a time Kawabata was also influenced by stream-of-consciousness techniques, but later returned to a more traditional style which critics have had difficulty categorizing because of its uniqueness.

Kawabata's distinctively Japanese writings are characterized by nostalgia, eroticism, and melancholy. He presents these elements with a poetic style sometimes described as a series of linked haiku, thus making his work "most resistant to translation," noted Ivan Morris. Lance Morrow agreed that Kawabata's "fiction seems to be most valued in Japanese for those qualities that are most difficult to render in translation: precision and delicacy of image, the shimmer of haiku, an allusive sadness and minute sense of the impermanence of things."

Western readers often find Kawabata's novels to be troublesome because of the unusual writing style and also because "some of the nuances may well be lost on people who do not know the Japanese scene and do not fully understand the nature of Japanese social and family relationships," observed a *Times Literary Supplement* reviewer. D. J. Enright claimed that even "the most attentive reader, and the most prurient, will be hard put to know what exactly is going on at times" in some of Kawabata's books. Nevertheless, Gwenn R. Boardman promised that "careful reading of his work . . . offers an aesthetic experience not to be found in the west."

Snow Country and *Thousand Cranes* were the first of Kawabata's novels to be translated into English. Although eroticism and cosmopolitan settings made the books accessible to Westerners, they attracted only a small readership. Comparing the two novels, Enright declared that *Snow Country* "is distinctly superior to *Thousand Cranes.*" In the latter, Enright explained, "the characters are so faintly drawn as to seem hardly two-dimensional" and the end of the story is so cryptic that the reader is unable to discern "what is being done and who is doing it to whom." Enright praised *Snow Country,* which Kawabata spent over fourteen years perfecting, for its sensitive and adroit portrayal of the relationship of man and nature. Boardman also extolled the book, saying that "Kawabata's characterization is such a subtle web of allusion and suggestion, that [any] summary cannot do justice to *Snow Country.*"

Sadness pervades Kawabata's writing and this is undoubtedly a reflection of his early years. He was orphaned by the age of three, and his sister and maternal grandmother with whom he had been sent to live died soon afterward. Later, when his grandfather died, sixteen-year-old Kawabata was left entirely alone in the world.

In a larger context, Kawabata's pensive writing reflects his cultural background. Boardman noted that "sadness is a characteristic of much Japanese literature, the *mono-no-aware* or *aware* that is a delicate perception of transcience, of sadness, of the implication of gesture, or of the intersection of silence and time." Mary DeJong Obuchowski suggested that "melancholy is pleasurable, perhaps one of the most appealing of moods to the Japanese." Because of this, writers like Kawabata often dwell on transitory natural events such as cherry blossoms and moonlight, which "inevitably produce sadness and reminders of our mortality."

As a youngster Kawabata had intended to become a painter,

and this interest in art strongly influenced his writing. "There are many exquisitely visual passages," a *New Yorker* critic observed. "Sometimes it seems that a splendid pageant is taking place when all that is happening is that someone is lifting a teacup." Color was an especially important factor in Kawabata's descriptive writing. With it he could set the mood or suggest an association between certain hues and events from the past. His deft use of color is prominent in *The House of the Sleeping Beauties,* where the red velvet curtains are associated with blood, the blackness of night with death, and a girl's white skin with mother's milk, camellias, and virginity.

The House of the Sleeping Beauties also incorporates the themes that Kawabata dealt with most often: loneliness, alienation, love, guilt, impermanence of life, old age, and death. In this story Eguchi, nearly seventy years old, visits a secret house where old men come to spend the evening with beautiful young girls who are deep in a drug-induced sleep. Lying in one of the dark crimson rooms beside a sleeping girl, Eguchi is confronted with memories of his past—his mother's death, his daughter's wedding, and the first woman in his life. The girl's youth and beauty remind him of his own old age and ugliness, and her death-like sleep emphasizes his nearness to death. Kawabata fills the story "with countless examples of paradoxical or contradictory thoughts and appearance/reality opposites," related Arthur G. Kimball, thus creating a tension, a feeling that Eguchi is "trapped, immobilized by the certainty that death is inevitably approaching but that he can only remain fixed and gasp for air."

The Sound of the Mountain was another study of the self-analysis provoked by approaching old age. Although the book "is not distinguished by a clear plot line, suspense, climax or denouement," Obuchowski noted, "the cumulative effects of imagery, repetition and parallels work together to provide theme and build a total picture of a man aging in the midst of his memories and concerns." In this story death is suggested by the sounds of the mountain, imaginary sounds that are heard by an elderly businessman as he contemplates the personal failures of his life. Howard Hibbett called the book "an engrossing novel" that "leaves no doubt as to the strength that underlies Kawabata's notoriously elliptical methods of characterization and narrative construction."

Kawabata's first book also examined death, but from a very personal viewpoint. *Juro kusai no nikki* ("Diary of a Sixteen-Year-Old") described the last days before his grandfather died, when Kawabata was torn between irritation at the old man's demands and compassion for his suffering. The book, considered remarkably well written for so young an author, was published in 1925, ten years after its completion.

During the same year Kawabata achieved his first popular success with *Izu no odoriko* (*The Izu Dancer*), a short novel about a student's interest in a young dancing girl. He intends to buy the girl's favors, but when he realizes that she is just a child his feelings develop into an innocent affection. Masao Miyoshi commented that "the atmosphere of freshness and innocence enveloping 'The Izu Dancer' comes, I think, from Kawabata's utterly simple language which sets the experience down among the trees and clean air and wet grass of a country resort.... Kawabata, instead of explaining the characters' thoughts and feelings, merely suggests them by mentioning objects which, in a country setting, are certain to reverberate with tangible, if not identifiable, emotions."

Kawabata's short novel, *The Lake*, features a typically un-conventional plot and a main character named Gimpei Momoi, described by Lance Morrow as "another of literature's repellent voyeurs—a wincing, hypersensitive defective on the sad trail of ineffable beauty." Intimating the tie between sex and death, victim and criminal, Kawabata returns again and again to a specific moment in time, creating "circles upon circles of memory, coincidence after coincidence, innocent themes followed by their sinister, scarcely audible overtones and echoes," observed Edmund White.

In *The Lake* Kawabata "plunges 'love' into an acid bath in which it disintegrates into its constituents of vanity, lust, an itch for adventure and an old, inconsolable ache to be whole, to be fulfilled by someone else," White declared. Some critics thought that his representation of love gave the novel an air of misery and perverseness, but Susan Heath declared that "this dredging of the sexual depths is at once so intriguing and sordid, poetic and allusive, that one senses here the presence of an intensely Japanese, yet universal, master of the erotic."

In April of 1972, without leaving any note or explanation, Kawabata committed suicide by gassing himself in his workroom at Zushi, Japan. It was speculated that his death had been influenced by the 1970 ritual suicide of his protege, Yukio Mishima.

Edward Weeks noted that it was in character that Kawabata's "brooding death" was one of "the distinguishing elements in his posthumous novel," *Beauty and Sadness*. Begun in 1961, the novel "is not Kawabata's sensuous best, certainly not his richest work," asserted A. G. Mojtabai, "but it is endlessly provocative to the mind and, as is everything else he wrote, original, indisputably his own."

The story centers around a famous novelist, Oko Toshio, who journeys to Kyoto in hopes of hearing the New Year's bells with Otoko, who had been his mistress twenty-four years earlier. Other characters include Oki's wife and son, and Keiko, a beautiful young girl who is fiercely devoted to Otoko. Aware of Otoko and Oki's previous tragic affair, Keiko seeks revenge upon the novelist by trying to seduce either him or his son.

Most Western critics seemed to find the book somewhat inaccessible. While John Skow called *Beauty and Sadness* "a consummately skillful arrangement of space and stillness, a brush drawing of love and vengeance," he also contended that the "characters and their pain disappear from the mind with the turn of the last page." Edward Weeks complained that the characters "talk around and about; they repeat themselves to the point where the reader yearns for them to decide. It is a mark of Kawabata's genius that what one remembers is Keiko's painting of the plum blossom, the soothing summer evening on the balcony of Ofusa's tea house," and other visually beautiful passages. On the contrary, a *New Yorker* critic commented that "the endless spate of rich kimonos, serene mountains, elegant sunsets, and sombre stone gardens and temples tends to overwhelm the few tortured, lost souls that inhabit this strange, frozen book."

Such weaknesses in Kawabata's writings are apparent to most readers. As Kimball pointed out: "Even for Japanese readers the Nobel prize winner's works sometimes appear strange and even uninviting. . . . In any case, however 'traditionally Japanese,' however much 'of the past,' and however puzzling, Kawabata's artistry has much which declares its timeliness and relevance for the present." Ivan Morris agreed, heralding Kawabata's novels as "among the most affecting and original works of our time."

BIOGRAPHICAL/CRITICAL SOURCES: New York Times, October 18, 1968, October 29, 1968; *Critique: Studies in Modern Fiction,* Volume XI, number 2, 1969, Volume XIII, number 1, 1970; *New Statesman,* August 1, 1969; *Pacific Affairs,* winter, 1969-1970; *Newsweek,* June 1, 1970; *Saturday Review,* June 6, 1970; *New York Times Book Review,* June 14, 1970, October 27, 1972, June 23, 1974, September 8, 1974, March 2, 1975; *Christian Science Monitor,* September 15, 1970, October 11, 1972, August 21, 1974; *Times Literary Supplement,* August 20, 1971, October 3, 1975, March 11, 1977; *London Magazine,* December, 1971/January, 1972; D. J. Enright, *Man Is an Onion: Reviews and Essays,* Open Court, 1972; *Time,* October 9, 1972, July 29, 1974, February 24, 1975; *Contemporary Literary Criticism,* Gale, Volume 2, 1974, Volume 5, 1976, Volume 9, 1978; Masao Miyoshi, *Accomplices of Silence: The Modern Japanese Novel,* University of California Press, 1974; *Saturday Review/World,* July 27, 1974; *Atlantic Monthly,* March, 1975; *New Yorker,* March 17, 1975; *World Literature Today,* spring, 1977.

OBITUARIES: New York Times, April 17, 1972; *Washington Post,* April 17, 1972; *L'Express,* April 24-30, 1972; *Newsweek,* May 1, 1972; *Time,* May 1, 1972.*

—*Sketch by Martha G. Winkel*

* * *

KAYE, Bruce (Norman) 1939-

PERSONAL: Born June 30, 1939, in Sydney, Australia; son of John Harold and Elsie (Whitehead) Kaye; married Rosemary Jeanette Hutchinson, 1965; children: Alison, Nigel. *Education:* University of London, B.D., 1964; University of Sydney, B.A., 1966; University of Basel, Dr.Theol., 1976. *Home:* 17 South Bailey, Durham DH1 3EE, England.

CAREER: Metropolitan Water Board, Sydney, Australia, civil engineer, 1955-60; ordained as minister of Church of England, 1964; pastor of St. Jude's Church, Dural, New South Wales, Australia, 1964-66; University of Durham, St. John's College, Durham, England, tutor, 1968-75, senior tutor, 1975—. Part-time lecturer in theology, University of Durham, 1969—. Chairman of Friends of St. Margaret's Junior School, 1978-79.

WRITINGS: Using the Bible in Ethics, Grove, 1956; (editor) *Obeying Christ in a Changing World,* Volume III, Collins, 1977; *The Supernatural in the New Testament,* Lutterworth, 1977; (with John Rogerson) *Miracles and Mysteries in the Bible,* Westminster, 1978; (editor and contributor) *Law, Morality, and the Bible,* Inter-Varsity Press, 1978; *The Argument of Romans,* Scholarly Press, in press. Contributor of articles and reviews to professional journals. Member of editorial board and council of reference, *Christian Weekly* newspaper (London).

WORK IN PROGRESS: Research on the institutional development of early Christianity.

SIDELIGHTS: Kaye writes: "I have traveled and studied in Germany, Switzerland, and Austria. My research interests include interpretation of the Bible, Christianity and the social order, and law and society. My work at the University of Durham has stimulated a keen interest in the philosophy of education (particularly of testiary education) and the practice of research." It has also resulted in a "firm commitment to inter-disciplinary studies."

* * *

KEANE, Betty Winkler 1914-

PERSONAL: Born April 19, 1914, in Berwick, Pa.; daughter of David Louis (a merchant) and Paula (Harris) Winkler; married George Keane (an actor and pension planner), 1948; children: Jonathan Alfred. *Education:* Attended Western Reserve University (now Case Western Reserve University), 1930-32, and Brooklyn College (now of the City University of New York), 1958-59. *Home:* 470 West End Ave., New York, N.Y. 10024. *Agent:* Lucy Kroll Agency, 390 West End Ave., New York, N.Y. 10024.

CAREER: Actress, 1930-50; New School for Social Research, New York, N.Y., faculty member in Human Relations Center, 1965—. Member of faculty at William Alanson White Institute of Psychiatry and Zen Studies Society of New York; speaker at growth centers and universities all over the United States and in Mexico. Affiliated with New York City Bureau of Child Guidance; and Bellevue Hospital. Private practice in sensory awareness training. Member of C. G. Jung Foundation. *Member:* American Federation of Television and Radio Artists (charter member). *Awards, honors:* Named best radio actress by *New York Radio-Mirror,* 1945, for performance in "Rosemary."

WRITINGS: Sensing: Letting Yourself Live, Harper, 1979.

SIDELIGHTS: Betty Keane, who began her acting career at the age of six, told *CA:* "For most of my life I have been involved in the field of the experiential. Participating in such an exacting field as acting has made me well aware of the effects of tension in the human organism and has provided me with the sensitivity to individual character differences crucial to the work of sensory awareness. As we become more aware we come to a deepening of concentration and a more direct communication with the creative, self-activating sources within us that provide natural vitality and joy.

"My main emphasis in my work and in my life is a deep interest in human function and human growth and development, including how human beings respond to their conditioning and to cultural change."

* * *

KEEFE, Michael 1946-

PERSONAL: Born November 6, 1946, in Santa Rosa, Calif.; son of Raymond Thomas and Rae Laverne (Ferrin) Keefe; married Jerry Lynn Harper, April 18, 1970 (divorced, 1975). *Education:* University of Missouri, Kansas City, B.S., 1973, M.S., 1974. *Home:* 2383 Albion, Denver, Colo. 80207. *Office: Denver Post,* 650 15th St., Denver, Colo. 80202.

CAREER: Denver Post, Denver, Colo., editorial page cartoonist, 1975—. *Military service:* U.S. Marine Corps, 1969-71. *Member:* American Association of Editorial Cartoonists.

WRITINGS: Running Awry (cartoons and text), McGraw, 1979.

WORK IN PROGRESS: Another book; an animated film.

SIDELIGHTS: Keefe told *CA: "Running Awry* is a humorous look at the running phenomenon. A very simple exercise that requires a person to simply place one foot in front of the other in rapid succession has exploded into a cult activity complete with sophisticated clothing and equipment, elder statesmen, gurus, and groupies.

"I am an enthusiastic runner. I ran my first marathon in 1965 wearing a pair of high school gym shorts and frayed U.S. Keds. Today I would be laughed off the bike paths in that outfit. For those who would scoff at my attire, *Running Awry* is revenge.

"Rock climbing, handball, and racquetball may provide subjects for future satirical books. Eventually, I would like to compile my editorial cartoons in book form, and I would like to experiment with a short story-cartoon format on social issues."

* * *

KEELEY, Steve 1949-

PERSONAL: Born February 8, 1949, in New York, N.Y.; son of Gilbert S. (a nuclear engineer) and Mary Jane (Abbott) Keeley. *Education:* Michigan State University, degree, 1969, D.V.M., 1972. *Home and office:* 6369 Reynolds Rd., Haslett, Mich. 48840.

CAREER: Practiced veterinary medicine, 1973; professional racquetball player, 1973—. Publisher of Service Press, Inc., 1977—.

WRITINGS: The Complete Book of Racquetball, DBJ Books, 1976; *Racquetball Lessons Made Easy,* McDonald Associates, 1977; *The Kill and Rekill Gang* (racquetball cartoons), Service Press, 1979; *It's a Racquet* (short stories), Service Press, 1979; (with Shanon Wright) *The Women's Book of Racquetball,* Service Press, 1980; *It's Still a Racquet,* Service Press, 1980; *The Cerebral Game* (advanced racquetball instruction), Service Press, 1980.Contributor to racquetball magazines, including *Racquet, National Racquetball, Racquetball, Racqueteer,* and *Racquetball and Handball News.*

WORK IN PROGRESS: The History of Racquetball, for Service Press.

SIDELIGHTS: Keeley was national paddleball champion five times, 1971-77, and runner-up national racquetball champion in 1973 and 1974. He writes: "*The Complete Book of Racquetball* is the top-selling book on the game. I publish my own racquetball books and those of others at Service Press."

AVOCATIONAL INTERESTS: Marathon running, bicycling (across the United States from California to Michigan and from Canada to Mexico).

* * *

KEEN, Geraldine
See NORMAN, Geraldine (Lucia)

* * *

KELLY, Eric Philbrook 1884-1960

OBITUARY NOTICE: Born March 16, 1884, in Amesbury, Mass.; died January 3, 1960. Journalist, educator, and author. Kelly worked as a reporter in Illinois and for the *Boston Herald* before his career as a teacher at Dartmouth College. He was a professor of journalism from 1929 to 1954. His books were largely of two kinds: authoritative works on Poland and those directed at young readers. His writings included the Newberry Medal-winning *The Trumpet of Krakow, The Blacksmith of Vilno, A Girl Who Would Be Queen, The Amazing Journey of David Ingram,* and *In Clean Hay.* Obituaries and other sources: *Who Was Who in America,* 3rd edition, Marquis, 1960; *New York Times,* January 4, 1960; *Publishers Weekly,* January 18, 1960.

* * *

KELLY, George V(incent) 1919-

PERSONAL: Born April 29, 1919, in Leadville, Colo.; son of James J. (an ore miner) and May I. (a bookkeeper and cashier; maiden name, Arnold) Kelly; married Catherine A. Floyd, July 15, 1941; children: Ann Terese. *Education:* Cit-

rus Junior College, A.A., 1936; Register College of Journalism, B.A., 1939, M.J., 1941. *Politics:* Democrat. *Religion:* Roman Catholic. *Home and office:* 641 Columbine St., Denver, Colo. 80206.

CAREER: Azusa Herald, Azusa, Calif., assistant editor, 1935-37; Register System of Newspapers, associate editor, 1938-43, newscaster, 1946; KFEL-Radio, Denver, Colo., copy editor and reporter, 1946-49; *Denver Post,* Denver, reporter, 1949-52; *Rocky Mountain News,* Denver, publications officer, 1952-55; City of Denver, member of city council, 1959-63, president of council, 1960-61, assistant to mayor, 1955-61 and 1965-70; William Kostka & Associates, public relations consultant, 1963-65; Bezoff-Kelly, Inc., public relations consultant, 1970-71; Denver Regional Council of Governments, Denver, public affairs director, 1971-76; writer, 1976—. Public relations consultant to Health Screening Centers, Inc. *Military service:* U.S. Army Air Forces, 1943-45; served in North Africa and Italy; became staff sergeant. *Member:* American Newspaper Guild (local president), Colorado Municipal League (district president, 1969), Denver Press Club.

WRITINGS: The Old Gray Mayors of Denver, Pruett, 1974.

WORK IN PROGRESS: Laradon Hall, Garden of Hope, with Harry Farrar, a history of the school for the retarded, publication expected in 1980.

SIDELIGHTS: Kelly commented: "In all my writings, which have dealt chiefly with facts, I have had a single aim: to report accurately, directly, and objectively."

* * *

KELMAN, Mark 1951-

PERSONAL: Born August 20, 1951, in New York, N.Y.; son of Kurt (a patent agent) and Sylvia (a lawyer; maiden name, Etman) Kelman; married Ann Richman, August 26, 1979. *Education:* Harvard University, B.A., 1972, J.D., 1976. *Home:* 1376 University Ave., Palo Alto, Calif. 94301. *Office:* School of Law, Stanford University, Stanford, Calif. 94305.

CAREER: Fund for the City of New York, New York, N.Y., director of criminal justice projects, 1976-77; Stanford University, Stanford, Calif., assistant professor of law, 1977—.

WRITINGS: What Followed Was Pure Lesley (novel), Dutton, 1973. Contributor to law journals, *Dissent,* and *Working Papers for a New Society.*

WORK IN PROGRESS: Life's Little Mysteries, a novel in part about child prostitution in New York City, completion expected in 1980.

SIDELIGHTS: Kelman told *CA:* "I am interested a great deal in the connection between political and personal life: whether the impoverishment of public life and the pressure to live an empty public role puts undue pressure on fantasy and romance. I am also quite interested in the ways in which people deal with the opacity of the external world, and whether it is possible to act in a satisfactorily moral fashion in the presence of uncertainty about the consequences of our own conduct."

* * *

KEMP, John C(rocker) 1942-

PERSONAL: Born August 8, 1942, in Fitchburg, Mass.; son of William S., Jr. and Rosemary (Crocker) Kemp; married Joyce Coster (a teacher of mathematics), February 22, 1969; children: Shane Cushing, Carolyn Sumner. *Education:* Harvard University, B.A., 1964, M.A.T., 1966; University of Pennsylvania, Ph.D., 1975. *Home:* 20 Sanderson Dr., Plymouth, Mass. 02360.

CAREER: High school English teacher in Scarsdale, N.Y., 1964-65; teacher of language arts at secondary school in Winston-Salem, N.C., 1966-67, and Philadelphia, Pa., 1967-68; University of Pennsylvania, Philadelphia, teaching fellow of English, 1970-75; Kanazawa University, Kanazawa City, Japan, visiting lecturer in English and American literature, 1975-78; Massasoit Community College, Brockton, Mass., instructor in English, 1978-79. Member of faculty at North Carolina School of the Arts, 1967, and Fort Knox Community College, 1968-70. *Military service:* U.S. Army, 1968-70.

WRITINGS: Robert Frost and New England: The Poet as Regionalist, Princeton University Press, 1979.

WORK IN PROGRESS: A novel about the international community in Japan.

SIDELIGHTS: Kemp commented: "My study of Robert Frost leaves me dissatisfied with the current climate of opinion on regionalism in general and New England poetry in particular. I hope over several years to examine regional elements in the work of perhaps a dozen poets, ranging from the older generation of Emerson, Whittier, Longfellow, and J. R. Lowell, through transitional figures like Dickinson, Robinson, Millay, Amy Lowell, and Cummings, to such 'modern poets' as Robert Lowell, Eberhart, and Charles Olson."

* * *

KENDALL, R(obert) T(illman) 1935-

PERSONAL: Born July 13, 1935, in Ashland, Ky.; son of Wayne E. and Lucille (McCurley) Kendall; married Louise E. Wallis, June 28, 1958; children: Robert Tillman II, Melissa Louise. *Education:* Trevecca Nazarene College, A.B., 1970; Southern Baptist Theological Seminary, M.Div., 1972; University of Louisville, M.A., 1973; Oxford University, D.Phil., 1977. *Residence:* London, England. *Office:* Westminster Chapel, Buckingham Gate, London S.W.1, England.

CAREER: In private business, 1956-64; ordained Southern Baptist minister, 1964; minister of Baptist churches in Fort Lauderdale, Fla., Salem, Ind., and Lower Heyford, Oxfordshire, England, 1955-77. Westminster Chapel, London, England, senior minister, 1977—. *Member:* United Oxford and Cambridge University Club.

WRITINGS: Jonah, Hodder & Stoughton, 1978; *Jonah: An Exposition,* Zondervan, 1979; *Calvin and English Calvinism to 1649,* Oxford University Press, 1979. Editor of *Redeemer's Witness,* 1964-67, and *Westminster Record.*

WORK IN PROGRESS: An exposition of Hebrews, chapter eleven; book on Calvin for Oxford University Press.

SIDELIGHTS: Kendall commented: "My books on Jonah are sermons that were first preached at Westminster Chapel, London, in 1977. *Calvin and English Calvinism to 1649* is written at the academic level. It has wide interest, however, for it challenges the traditional view that English Calvinists followed Calvin. I argue that they followed Theodore Beza, Calvin's successor, and that they thought that Beza represented Calvin's views. I also show that Calvin did *not* believe in 'limited atonement,' whereas Beza did. I trace the nature of 'saving' faith from William Perkins (d. 1602), prominent English Puritan, to the Westminster Assembly (1643-49) which produced the Westminster Confession of Faith

and two catechisms. Perkins followed Beza, the Puritans generally followed Perkins; the Westminster Confession of Faith is the credal culmination of the Beza-Perkins tradition. The book, in the words of Carl F. H. Henry (who reviewed it for *Christianity Today*), raises Calvin to 'controversial new prominence.'"

* * *

KENEALY, James P. 1927-
(Jim Kenealy)

PERSONAL: Born June 4, 1927, in Dorchester, Mass.; son of William V. and Margaret (McConville) Kenealy; children: Nancy, Mike, Deane. *Home address:* R.D. 1, Rensselaer, N.Y. 12144.

CAREER: WQBK-AM Radio, Albany, N.Y., outdoor editor, 1972—. Owner of J. P. Kenealy Associates (marine and environmental consultants). Director of Rensselaer Boys' Club. *Military service:* U.S. Navy, 1944-46. *Member:* Outdoor Writers of America.

WRITINGS—All under name Jim Kenealy: *Boating From Bow to Stern,* Dodd, 1967; *Better Fishing for Boys,* Dodd, 1969; *Better Camping for Boys,* Dodd, 1973. Author of outdoor column in *Knickerbocker News,* 1973—. Contributor to state and national magazines.

WORK IN PROGRESS: Hunting and Fishing in New York State, for Donlevy Press.

* * *

KENEALY, Jim
See KENEALY, James P.

* * *

KENNEDY, Hubert (Collings) 1931-

PERSONAL: Born March 6, 1931, in Pierce, Fla.; son of Glenn Hubert (an electrical engineer) and Verna (Collings) Kennedy. *Education:* University of Florida, B.A., 1952; University of Michigan, M.A., 1957; further graduate study at University of Milan, 1957-58; St. Louis University, Ph.D., 1961. *Religion:* None. *Home:* 33 Huxley Ave., Providence, R.I. 02908. *Office:* Department of Mathematics, Providence College, Providence, R.I. 02918.

CAREER: Providence College, Providence, R.I., assistant professor, 1961-63, associate professor, 1963-70, professor of mathematics, 1970—. *Military service:* U.S. Army, 1952-54; became sergeant. *Member:* Mathematical Association of America, American Association of University Professors, Canadian Society for the History and Philosophy of Mathematics, Phi Beta Kappa. *Awards, honors:* Fulbright fellowships for Italy, 1957-58, 1966-67, and Germany, 1974-75.

WRITINGS: (Editor, translator, and author of notes) *Selected Works of Giuseppe Peano,* University of Toronto Press, 1973; *Giuseppe Peano* (monograph; translated into German by Ruth Amsler), Birkhaeuser Verlag, 1974; *Peano: The Life and Work of Giuseppe Peano,* D. Reidel, 1980. Contributor of about seventy-five articles, poems, and reviews to mathematics and education journals, gay liberation publications, and newspapers.

WORK IN PROGRESS: A biography of James Mills Peirce, completion expected in 1985.

SIDELIGHTS: Kennedy writes: "My interest in the history of nineteenth-century mathematics and in the origins of the gay liberation movement, in which I am active, have led to my current research on the lives of nineteenth-century gay mathematicians. I consider myself a historian of mathematics, rather than a mathematician." *Avocational interests:* European travel.

* * *

KENNEDY, Lena
See SMITH, Lena (Kennedy)

* * *

KENNETT, (Houn) Jiyu 1924-

PERSONAL: Birth-given name, Peggy Teresa Nancy Kennett; name changed to Houn Jiyu Kennett at ordination, 1962; born January 1, 1924, in England; came to the United States in 1970, naturalized citizen, 1975; daughter of Walter James Carthew (a clothing designer) and Sarah Annie (a governess; maiden name, Miles) Kennett. *Education:* University of Durham, B.Mus., 1960; Trinity College of Music, London, L.T.C.M., 1960; Dai Hon Zan Soji-ji, teaching diploma and science degree, 1967. *Politics:* Conservative. *Home and office:* Order of Buddhist Contemplatives, Shasta Abbey, P.O. Box 478, Mount Shasta, Calif. 96067.

CAREER: Professional musician, performing and teaching in London, England, 1943-61; Buddhist priest and foreign guest master at Buddhist temple in Yokohama, Japan, 1963-69; Shasta Abbey, Mount Shasta, Calif., abbess, 1970—, president, 1970-76, chairperson of board of directors, 1976—. Lecturer at University of California, Extension, 1971—. *Awards, honors:* First prize from Wesak Anthem contest in Malaysia, 1961, for composing "Welcome Joyous Wesak Day."

WRITINGS—Under name Jiyu Kennett: *Selling Water by the River*, Pantheon, 1972, revised edition published as *Zen Is Eternal Life*, Dharma, 1976; *How to Grow a Lotus Blossom*, Shasta Abbey Press, 1977; *The Wild White Goose*, Shasta Abbey Press, Volume I, 1977, Volume II, 1978; (with Daizui MacPhillamy) *The Book of Life*, Shasta Abbey Press, 1979; *The Shasta Abbey Book of Ceremonies*, Shasta Abbey Press, 1979; *The Shasta Abbey Psalter*, Shasta Abbey Press, 1979; *The Book of Universal Law*, Shasta Abbey Press, in press; *Where to Find It*, Shasta Abbey Press, in press.

Composer of a motet, "O Sacrum Convivium," and operas, "The Great Enlightenment" and "Agni the Fire God"; also composer of Buddhist service music.

Religious correspondent for *Japan Times*, 1967-69. Contributor to religious magazines.

SIDELIGHTS: Kennett told *CA:* "The books I write are not meant in any way to proselytize or convert people to Buddhism. If they are of use in helping someone find what they are looking for, I am glad. I am in religion for one reason only, to help people find their full spiritual potential in whatever tradition is right for them as individuals."

* * *

KENNETT, Peggy Teresa Nancy
See KENNETT, (Houn) Jiyu

* * *

KERKVLIET, Benedict J(ohn) 1943-

PERSONAL: Born October 28, 1943, in Great Falls, Mont.; son of John Benedict (a business machines technician) and Dorothy (a secretary; maiden name, Grasseschi) Kerkvliet; married Jerene Peterson, December, 1962 (divorced); married Melinda Castro Tria, June 16, 1972; children: Brian B.,

Jodie K. *Education:* Whitman College, B.A., 1965; University of Wisconsin—Madison, M.A., 1966, Ph.D., 1972. *Office:* Department of Political Science, University of Hawaii, Honolulu, Hawaii 96822.

CAREER: University of Hawaii, Honolulu, assistant professor, 1971-76, associate professor of political science, 1976—. *Member:* Association for Asian Studies (member of board of directors, 1979-81; member of Southeast Asia Regional Council), Phi Beta Kappa. *Awards, honors:* Fellow of Woodrow Wilson International Center for Scholars, 1973-74; National Endowment for the Humanities fellow, 1978.

WRITINGS: (Editor and contributor) *Political Change in the Philippines*, University Press of Hawaii, 1974; *The Huk Rebellion*, University of California Press, 1977. Contributor to Asian studies journals.

WORK IN PROGRESS: A book on political-economic conditions in the rural Philippines, completion expected in 1982.

SIDELIGHTS: Kerkvliet comments: "I write primarily to help people (including myself) to learn about their fellow human beings.

"Eighteen months of research in the Philippines during 1978 to 1979 included living one year in a village in central Luzon. Through observation, talking at length with peasants and others there, and joining work and social activities, I became more aware of how most people just manage to scrape by, while a very few within the village and in Philippine society in general live very well. One of my research interests became understanding to what extent people saw the injustice of these gross inequities, as I did, and what their justifications or explanations are. I have not yet formulated the answer to the second, but to the first I think the answer is that people do see the inequities, but most—both the poor and the rich—do not regard this as unjust."

* * *

KERN, Seymour 1913-

PERSONAL: Born November 3, 1913, in Brooklyn, N.Y.; son of Abraham and Anna (Friedman) Kern; married Jessie Kraus, May 29, 1936; children: Hartley, Stephen. *Residence:* California. *Agent:* Desmond Elliott, 3 Clifford St., London W1, England.

CAREER: Worked as an actor, cigarmaker, door-to-door salesman, roofing salesman, grocer, and department store clerk, 1931-37; real estate agent in Los Angeles, Calif., 1937-75. Co-chairman of Dissenting Democrats, 1967-68. *Member:* International P.E.N., American Civil Liberties Union, Author's Guild.

WRITINGS: *The Golden Scalpel*, John Day, 1960; *Samson Duke*, Sherbourne, 1972; *Fifty*, New English Library, 1975, Sherbourne, 1978. Also author of *The Passion of Jennie Cortland*. Author of television scripts. Contributor of articles to periodicals, including *Look*, *Scope*, and *Frontier*.

WORK IN PROGRESS: A satire on the U.S. political scene.

SIDELIGHTS: Praising Kern as "a talented and gifted storyteller," Robert Kirsch declared: "Seymour Kern's massive novel SAMSON DUKE has that quality rare in fiction nowadays, the increasing illusion that we have entered and are part of the world portrayed in its pages." Kirsch also applauded the absence of artificial plotting, introspection, and sermonizing in this "highly readable and very exciting fiction."

Kern told *CA:* "The material for my stories emanates from my experiences. Most of my principal characters are composites of persons I have known or observed. Though I sometimes wish I had started writing earlier in life (I began to write when I was thirty-nine), I am inclined to believe that the late start has been an advantage. I was able to accumulate experiences that can only be garnered by putting in the years. My life, up until the time I began writing, was one of varied occupations, moving about, struggle, disappointments, and some successes. This rich and varied material provided the ingredients out of which I was able to weave my tales and develop characters that I hope were visceral, three-dimensional.

"My novel, *The Golden Scalpel*, was written after I had spent five years working with a group of doctors in the construction of a medical building during the frenzied years after World War II. It tells of the battle for patients after the war, especially the mink-coated women and the silk-suited men with real and imaginary diseases to cure, for which no fee was too high. This novel was one of the first to expose the fee-splitting and unnecessary surgeries that appear to have become a not uncommon practice of the medical profession, and caused much consternation in medical circles.

"*Samson Duke*, a novel of real estate, high finance, money juggling, and perfidy, was the product of nearly twenty years of my work in that field. *Fifty* was a novel about the male menopause and the problems of a man who reached this critical age and was not prepared to cope with its problems.

"Though the contents and characters in the better fiction surely are created out of the experiences in the writer's life, conscious or subconscious, there are some who can spin a yarn out of total imagination and make it work. Unless they are fantasy or satire, such good books are rare and I envy their creators. I find it difficult to accomplish. I must live and observe, travel and taste, and from this I gather my stories and people.

"I have traveled much during the past twenty years, lived in other countries and with other cultures. This is my avocation and my source. It has enriched my life and I hope my work, and I intend to be on the move as long as I am able."

BIOGRAPHICAL/CRITICAL SOURCES: Los Angeles Times, September 26, 1972.

* * *

KERR, (Anne-) Judith   1923-

PERSONAL: Born June 14, 1923, in Berlin, Germany; married Nigel Kneale (a writer), 1954; children: one son, one daughter. *Education:* Attended Central School of Arts and Crafts, 1945. *Office:* c/o William Collins Sons & Co. Ltd., 14 St. James Place, London SW1A 195, England.

CAREER: Writer and illustrator. Worked as textile designer and teacher, 1946-53; reader, scriptwriter, and editor for BBC-TV, 1953-58. *Wartime service:* Worked as secretary for Red Cross in London, England, 1941-45.

WRITINGS—Juvenile; all self-illustrated: *The Tiger Who Came to Tea*, Coward, 1968; *Mog, the Forgetful Cat*, Collins, 1970, Parents' Magazine Press, 1972; *When Hitler Stole Pink Rabbit*, Collins, 1971, Coward, 1972; *When Willy Went to the Wedding*, Collins, 1972, Parents' Magazine Press, 1973; *The Other Way Round*, Coward, 1975; *Mog's Christmas*, Collins, 1976, Collins, 1977; *A Small Person Far Away*, Collins, 1978.

SIDELIGHTS: Kerr's juvenile books deal with World War II and her own childhood as a refugee from Nazi Germany. She relates the changes and disasters of this historic period in an easily understood style. In *When Hitler Stole Pink*

Rabbit, Kerr introduces nine-year-old Anna and her family who have left Hitler's Germany for Switzerland, France, and finally England where they settle permanently. Critic Lore Segal claimed that Kerr "is good at showing how in a child's world—and an adult's too—the little businesses of life overshadow the monstrous ones: The Reichstag burns, but will Anna's friend Elsbeth buy a wooden Yo-Yo which works best or the tin one which is a lovely color?" An *Economist* critic further observed that "Hitler is still a fact of life that most parents find they have to explain to their young. Antisemitism is another. This excellent . . . novel . . . will go a long way to help the questioning child understand some of what happened during those years."

The Other Way Around continues the story begun in *When Hitler Stole Pink Rabbit*. In the book, Anna is eighteen and fully assimilated into English society. Christopher Wordsworth asserted that "the triumph of the novel is its avoidance of sententiousness. . . . Almost alarmingly evocative, tinged with quiet wisdom, it touches tellingly on the pecking order of the refugee community and the sadness when one generation adapts and another is left marooned."

BIOGRAPHICAL/CRITICAL SOURCES: Economist, December 18, 1971; *Book World*, May 7, 1972; *London Times Literary Supplement*, April 4, 1975; *New Statesman*, May 23, 1975.*

* * *

KERSLAKE, Susan   1943-

PERSONAL: Born April 20, 1943, in Chicago, Ill.; daughter of Youart (a lawyer) and Martha E. (a teacher; maiden name, Muckley) Kerslake. *Education:* Attended Montana State University, 1960-61, and Beloit College, 1961. *Home:* 5713 Victoria Rd., Halifax, Nova Scotia, Canada B3H 2Y3.

CAREER: Kroch's and Brentano's Bookstore, Chicago, Ill., sales clerk, 1962-66; Dalhousie University, Halifax, Nova Scotia, library assistant, 1966-73, archives apprentice at Medical Library, 1972-73; St. Joseph's Children's Centre, Halifax, Nova Scotia, child care worker, 1974—. Part-time Montessori teacher. *Member:* Writers Union of Canada, Preschool Education Association of Nova Scotia, Writers Federation of Nova Scotia (executive).

WRITINGS: Middlewatch (magic-realism adult novel), Oberon Press, 1976.

WORK IN PROGRESS: Penumbra, a novel; *Creance*, a novel; *Book of Fears*.

SIDELIGHTS: Susan Kerslake told *CA:* `Having begun writing when I was five years old, I feel that it is just what I do: living one life on a level that is unlike another one, that shows; thinking about things on paper, though story and impression, mood and word are what emerge. Achievement is personal, as I do not seem to begin a book with anything particular to say, but rather find out myself, as the book progresses (admitting to unconsciousness!). I tend to work in the evening, it being a time when distractions cease, and, of course, indulge in the little rituals that accompany the descent into blessed solitude and isolation. Always, the writing itself is the best part.

"I am influenced by anyone who loves words (some favorite authors: Joyce Carol Oates, Loren Eiseley, Christopher Fry, Dylan Thomas, Norman Cousins, Sylvia Ashton-Warner, Toni Morrison). My advice to anyone who wants to write is simply to do so, and read. The current 'scene' is discouraging to me, but not everyone is being lost. Lofty image of goals, courtesy of Robinson Jeffers: `. . . for to equal a need /

Is natural, animal, mineral: but to fling / Rainbows over the rain. . . .' ''

AVOCATIONAL INTERESTS: Travel (Japan, Thailand, India, Israel, Jordan, Lebanon, Egypt, Greece), making stuff.

* * *

KESSELL, John L(ottridge)   1936-

PERSONAL: Born April 2, 1936, in East Orange, N.J.; son of John S. (a physician) and Dorothy L. (a physician; maiden name, Lottridge) Kessell; married Marianne R., July 1, 1961; children: Kristen Anne. *Education:* Fresno State College (now California State University, Fresno), B.A., 1958; University of California, Berkeley, M.A., 1961; University of New Mexico, Ph.D., 1969. *Home:* 823 Girard N.E., Albuquerque, N.M. 87106.

CAREER: National Park Service, Washington, D.C., historian at Saratoga National Historical Park, 1961-62, and Tumacacori National Monument, 1963-66; University of New Mexico, Albuquerque, visiting assistant professor of history, 1969-70; historian and writer, 1970—. *Member:* Western Writers of America, Western History Association, Historical Society of New Mexico, Arizona Historical Society. *Awards, honors:* Annual award from *New Mexico Historical Review,* 1966, for "The Puzzling Presidio: San Phelipe de Guevavi, alias Terrante"; Herbert E. Bolton Award from *Western Historical Quarterly,* 1973, for "Friars Versus Bureaucrats: The Spanish Mission as a Threatened Institution on the Arizona-Sonora Frontier"; Spur Award from Western Writers of America, 1976, for *Friars, Soldiers, and Reformers;* award of honor from New Mexico Cultural Properties Review Committee, 1979, for *Kiva, Cross, and Crown.*

WRITINGS: (With Fay Jackson Smith and Francis J. Fox) *Father Kino in Arizona,* Arizona Historical Foundation, 1966; *Missions of Sorrows: Jesuit Guevavi and the Pimas, 1691-1767,* University of Arizona Press, 1970; *Friars, Soldiers, and Reformers: Hispanic Arizona and the Sonora Mission Frontier, 1767-1856,* University of Arizona Press, 1976; *Kiva, Cross, and Crown: The Pecos Indians and New Mexico, 154^ 1840,* National Park Service, 1979; *The Missions of New Mexico Since 1776,* University of New Mexico Press, 1979; *Pecos: The Gateway Pueblo, From 1300 to the Present,* National Park Service, in press. Contributor to *Reader's Encyclopedia of the American West.* Contributor of articles and reviews to history journals. Assistant editor of *New Mexico Historical Review,* 1970-72.

WORK IN PROGRESS: "I have a proposal pending before the National Historical Publications and Records Commission for a selective five- or six-volume edition of the papers of Diego de Vargas, governor and recolonizer of New Mexico, 1690-1704."

SIDELIGHTS: Kessell told *CA:* "After ten years as a free-lance historical researcher, or contract historian, I do not recommend it as a career. It has been precarious. I have achieved neither fame nor financial security. I have done local history, which I feel deserves one's best shot. Never presuming that it might free the locals from repeating their errors, I do reckon that it may at times enlighten and reassure them, even make them laugh. It has been good fun. And there is something to be said for getting out on one's cross-country skis right when the snow falls, especially in the Southwest."

KHAN, Pir Vilayat Inayat
See INAYAT-KHAN, Pir Vilayat

* * *

KHER, Inder Nath   1933-

PERSONAL: Born October 12, 1933, in Gujrat, Panjab, India; Canadian citizen; son of Gopal Dass and Kaushalya Devi (Ohri) Kher; married Salochna Chopra, July 13, 1963; children: Rshmi. *Education:* Panjab University, B.A., 1954, M.A., 1959; McMaster University, M.A., 1966; University of Alberta, Ph.D., 1969. *Religion:* Hindu. *Home:* 306-2010 Ulster Rd. N.W., Calgary, Alberta, Canada T2N 4C2. *Office:* Department of English, University of Calgary, Calgary, Alberta, Canada T2N 1N4.

CAREER: Panjab University, Jullundur, India, lecturer in English, 1960-65; University of Calgary, Calgary, Alberta, assistant professor, 1969-74, professor of English, 1974—. Member of Canada committee of World University Services India seminar planning group, 1972-73; participant in scholarly meetings.

MEMBER: Canadian Association of University Teachers, Canadian Association for South Asian Studies (member of board of directors, 1976-78), Association of Canadian University Teachers of English, Canadian Association for American Studies, Canadian Association for Commonwealth Literature and Language Studies, Modern Language Association of America (member of board of directors of South Asian Literary Association, 1977—), Poe Studies Association of America, Philological Association of the Pacific Coast. *Awards, honors:* Canada Council grants, 1970, 1975-79, fellowship, 1975-76; grant from Folger Shakespeare Library, 1972; fellow of Calgary Institute for the Humanities, 1978-79.

WRITINGS: The Landscape of Absence: Emily Dickinson's Poetry, Yale University Press, 1974. Contributor to literature journals and literary magazines. Associate editor of *Emily Dickinson Bulletin,* 1973-74, and *Journal of South Asian Literature,* 1978—; member of editorial board of *Emily Dickinson Bulletin* and *Higginson Journal of Poetry,* 1974—, and *Ariel,* 1978—; guest editor of *Journal of South Asian Literature,* 1975-76.

WORK IN PROGRESS: Nissim Ezekiel, a study of the works of the Indo-Anglian poet, playwright, and art critic, publication by Twayne; *The Epic of the Eyes: The Poetry of Theodore Roethke.*

SIDELIGHTS: Inder Kher writes: "My teaching and research interests include American literature of the nineteenth and twentieth centuries, British Romantic literature, the modern European novel, post-independence Indo-Anglian poetry and fiction, the literature of existential thought and imagination, and Oriental thought (Eastern philosophy and religions).

"I enjoy teaching literature and treat literary criticism as a creative act. I believe that a work of criticism should be able to recreate the writer's consciousness and enact the imaginative perceptions contained in the language of the art work. *The Landscape of Absence* is written from such a critical and creative perspective.

"I have traveled extensively in Canada and the United States, and am completely at home in North America. I like to visit different places and meet different people, continually absorbing them into my being. Highly tolerant in religious and cultural matters, I detest physical violence and vulgarity in any form."

AVOCATIONAL INTERESTS: Indian music, Urdu poetry, films.

BIOGRAPHICAL/CRITICAL SOURCES: American Literature, November, 1975.

* * *

KIECKHEFER, Richard 1946-

PERSONAL: Born June 1, 1946, in Minneapolis, Minn.; son of E. W. (a journalist) and Virginia (a nurse; maiden name, Kelley) Kieckhefer; married Margaret Lauer (a librarian), August 24, 1968; children: Daniel Robert, Christine Anastasia. *Education:* St. Louis University, B.A., 1968; University of Texas, M.A., 1970, Ph.D., 1972. *Religion:* Roman Catholic. *Residence:* Evanston, Ill. *Office:* Department of History and Literature of Religions, Northwestern University, Evanston, Ill. 60201.

CAREER: University of Texas, Austin, instructor in history, 1973-74; Phillips University, Enid, Okla., assistant professor of history, 1975; Northwestern University, Evanston, Ill., assistant professor, 1975-79, associate professor of history and literature of religions, 1979—. *Member:* Mediaeval Academy of America.

WRITINGS: European Witch Trials: Their Foundations in Popular and Learned Culture, 1300-1500, University of California Press, 1976; *Repression of Heresy in Medieval Germany,* University of Pennsylvania Press, 1979. Contributor to history and theology journals.

WORK IN PROGRESS: Research on Meister Eckhart and on fourteenth-century spiritual biographies; studies of saints.

SIDELIGHTS: Kieckhefer related to *CA:* "For some time I have been interested in the role of tradition, and the problems that arise when a significant number of people within a culture begin to reject or neglect their own heritage. Given my personal background and my education as a historian, I have more than a casual or nostalgic interest in the past. I am persuaded that there are important psychological and social reasons for being aware of one's heritage. Yet I am enough of a realist to recognize that this awareness both cannot and need not be sustained today in traditional ways. Much of what once was 'living tradition' cannot be resuscitated in its original form. And while scholarly understanding of the past seems essential for many reasons, it cannot substitute for that living sense of a shared and perpetuated past. It strikes me that one of the most important tasks for Western culture is to develop new ways of keeping in touch with our own cultural heritage—while at the same time becoming more open to other traditions."

* * *

KIENZLE, William X(avier) 1928-
   (Mark Boyle)

PERSONAL: Born September 11, 1928, in Detroit, Mich.; son of Alphonzo and Mary Louise (Boyle) Kienzle; married Javan Herman (an editor and researcher), 1974. *Education:* Sacred Heart Seminary College, B.A., 1950; also attended St. John's Seminary, 1950-54, and University of Detroit, 1968. *Politics:* Independent. *Religion:* Catholic. *Home:* 1612 Lafayette Towers East, Detroit, Mich. 48207.

CAREER: Ordained Roman Catholic priest, 1954-74; Roman Catholic Archdiocese of Detroit, Detroit, Mich., archdiocesan priest in five parishes, 1954-74; *MPLS.* magazine, Minneapolis, Minn., editor-in-chief, 1974-77; Western Michigan University, Kalamazoo, associate director of Center for

Contemplative Studies, 1977-78; University of Dallas, Irving, Tex., director of Center for Contemplative Studies, 1978-79; writer, 1979—. *Member:* Mystery Writers of America. *Awards, honors:* Michigan Knights of Columbus journalism award, 1963, for general excellence; honorable mention from Catholic Press Association, 1974, for editorial writing.

WRITINGS: The Rosary Murders (mystery novel; Mystery Guild selection; Literary Guild and Doubleday Book Club alternate selection), Andrews & McMeel, 1979; *Death Wears a Red Hat* (mystery novel), Andrews & McMeel, 1980. Contributor under pseudonym Mark Boyle to *MPLS.* magazine. Editor-in-chief of *Michigan Catholic,* 1962-74.

WORK IN PROGRESS: The Fugue Murders, completion expected in 1980.

SIDELIGHTS: Kienzle commented: "When I was ordained a Catholic priest at age twenty-five, I was painfully conscious of my lack of experience. I had no stories to tell. And I knew that effective communication was directly proportional to good stories well told.

"Twenty-five years later, I have abundant stories to tell. A senior editor at St. Martin's Press advised me that there was a readership of at least six people who were eager to learn of my autobiographical memoirs. However, an agent assured me nearly everyone enjoyed mystery novels.

"Thus, one reason I write mystery novels is to use the plots as skeletons over which to hang all these marvelous stories I've gathered over the years as a priest and as a journalist.

"Another reason I write is to entertain. I believe it is almost an apostolic mission these days to bring productive distraction to people.

"Finally, I write because after twenty years of conscientious service, the Archdiocese of Detroit decided to take my vested interest in a pension and run. I must rebuild a nest egg for our tender years."

BIOGRAPHICAL/CRITICAL SOURCES: Washington Post, April 1, 1979; *Los Angeles Times,* June 10, 1979; *Chicago Tribune,* August 5, 1979.

* * *

KILBURN, Henry
   See RIGG, H(enry Hemmingway) K(ilburn)

* * *

KIMBALL, John W(ard) 1931-

PERSONAL: Born January 13, 1931, in Portland, Maine; son of C. Carleton (a banker) and Elizabeth O. (Ward) Kimball; married Margaret D. Wilkerson, March 31, 1953; children: Christopher W., Nicholas Holt. *Education:* Harvard University, A.B., 1953, A.M., 1970, Ph.D., 1972. *Politics:* Republican. *Home and office:* 89 Prospect Rd., Andover, Mass. 01810.

CAREER: Biology teacher at private secondary school in Andover, Mass., 1956-69; Tufts University, Medford, Mass., assistant professor, 1972-77, associate professor of biology, 1977—. Warden and local committee chairman of Charles W. Ward Reservation, 1956—; member of standing committee of Trustees of Reservations, 1971—, and board of trustees of Memorial Hall Library, 1976—. *Military service:* U.S. Air Force, 1953-56; became captain. *Member:* American Association of Immunologists, Andover Historical Society (president, 1960-62).

WRITINGS: Biology, Addison-Wesley, 1965, 4th edition,

1978; *Cell Biology*, Addison-Wesley, 1970, 2nd edition, 1978; *Man and Nature: Principles of Human and Environmental Biology*, Addison-Wesley, 1975. Contributor to scientific journals.

WORK IN PROGRESS: A university-level immunology textbook, publication expected in 1982.

SIDELIGHTS: Kimball writes: "Each of my books has grown out of a course that I developed and taught. And I hope that each has been strengthened by the interplay of my professional interests—the laboratory world of test tubes, incubators, centrifuges, and the like—with my avocational interests—the ecology and conservation of natural areas."

Biology has been translated into Spanish, and *Cell Biology* into German and Japanese.

* * *

KIMBROUGH, Sara Dodge   1901-

PERSONAL: Born July 14, 1901, in New York, N.Y.; daughter of William de Leftwich (a painter) and Frances (Pryor) Dodge; married Hunter S. Kimbrough (an insurance agent), February 20, 1933; children: Leftwich Dodge. *Education:* Attended Cooper Union Art School and Grand Central Art School; also studied art privately. *Religion:* Protestant. *Home:* 806 North Beach, Bay Saint Louis, Miss. 39520.

CAREER: Portrait painter and art teacher from the 1940's to the 1960's. *Member:* Gulf Coast Art Council, Mississippi Art Association, Mississippi Institute of Arts and Letters (member of board of directors). *Awards, honors:* First prize from National League of American Pen Women, 1936, for an oil portrait; grand national finalist of American Artists Professional League, 1953.

WRITINGS: Drawn From Life, University Press of Mississippi, 1976.

SIDELIGHTS: Sara Kimbrough told *CA:* "*Drawn From Life* is the story of four American artists (my father, Frederick MacMonnies, George Grey Barnard, and George Bridgman), whose friendship and work began in Paris during the 1880's. I knew them, admired their work, had access to their personal papers and letters, and thought that era of American art had not been sufficiently covered."

BIOGRAPHICAL/CRITICAL SOURCES: Apollo, June, 1979.

* * *

KINGHORN, A(lexander) M(anson)   1926-
(James Sharp)

PERSONAL: Born October 12, 1926, in London, England; son of Alexander (a chemist) and Susan (a musician; maiden name, Burgess-Davidson) Kinghorn; married Marion Gurling (a scientific bibliographer), September 1, 1956. *Education:* University of Aberdeen, M.A., 1951; Pembroke College, Cambridge, Ph.D., 1953. *Politics:* None. *Religion:* None. *Home:* Tiuccia, Derringstone, Barham, Canterbury, Kent, England. *Office:* P.O. Box 2992, Doha, Qatar.

CAREER: University of Texas, Austin, Fulbright visiting lecturer in English, 1953-55; McGill University, Montreal, Quebec, lecturer in English and warden of Wilson Hall, 1955-57; Dalhousie University, Halifax, Nova Scotia, assistant professor of English, 1957-60; University of the West Indies, Kingston, Jamaica, 1960-75, began as senior lecturer, became reader in medieval literature; University of Aarhus, Aarhus, Denmark, professor of English, 1975-77; University of Qatar, Doha, professor of English, 1977—. *Member:* Royal Commonwealth Society.

WRITINGS: (Editor) *Barbour's Bruce*, Oliver & Boyd, 1960; (editor with Alexander Law) *Works of Allan Ramsay*, four volumes, Johnson Reprint, 1961-74; *Mediaeval Drama*, Evans Brothers, 1968; *The Middle Scots Poets*, Northwestern University Press, 1970; *The Chorus of History, 1485-1558*, Barnes & Noble, 1971; *Peblis: To the Play*, Quarto Publishing, 1974; (editor with Law) *Poems by Ramsay and Fergusson*, Rowman & Littlefield, 1974; (under pseudonym James Sharp) *The Life and Death of Michael X*, Volturna Press, 1980. Member of editorial board of "Studies in Scottish Literature," University of South Carolina Press. Contributor of about thirty articles to language and literature journals.

WORK IN PROGRESS: A literary history to 1650, for students to whom English is a second language; a book on medieval literary backgrounds, with emphasis on "death vision."

SIDELIGHTS: Kinghorn writes: "My recent work has been topical: research on criminal cases and trials and ephemeral journalistic contributions. I write this under other names.

"I've resided abroad for thirty years altogether, but return to England for a few months each year—this is important to me.

"I have been disenchanted with the academic life for some years now, and hope to retire soon and devote my time entirely to writing. I doubt if I shall write much more in the 'heavyweight' or scholarly line."

AVOCATIONAL INTERESTS: Oil painting, playing the piano.

* * *

KIRCHWEY, Freda   1893-1976

PERSONAL: Born September 26, 1893, in Lake Placid, N.Y.; died January 3, 1976, in St. Petersburg, Fla.; daughter of George W. (an educator, criminologist, and law school dean) and Dora (Wendell) Kirchwey; married Evans Clark (a director of the Twentieth Century Fund), November 9, 1915 (died, 1970); children: Brewster (deceased), Michael, Jeffrey (deceased). *Education:* Barnard College, B.A., 1915.

CAREER: New York Morning Telegraph, New York City, reporter, 1915-16; *Every Week*, New York City, member of editorial staff, 1917-18; member of editorial staff of *Sunday Tribune*, 1918; *Nation*, New York City, began as cub reporter, became assistant editor and editor of international relations section, 1918-22, managing editor, 1922-28, literary editor, 1928-29, editor, 1932-55, publisher, 1937-55. Member of Committee for World Development and World Disarmament and Committee for a Democratic Spain. *Member:* Women's International League for Peace and Freedom, Women's International League for Rights of Man, League of Women Voters, National Association for the Advancement of Colored People (NAACP), Union for Democratic Action, Museum of Modern Art, Cosmopolitan Club (New York City). *Awards, honors:* D.H.L. from Rollins College, 1944; created chevalier of French Legion of Honor, 1946.

WRITINGS: (Editor and author of introduction) *Our Changing Morality: A Symposium*, A. & C. Boni, 1924, reprinted, Arno Press, 1972; (editor) *The Atomic Era—Can It Bring Peace and Abundance?*, McBride, 1950.

SIDELIGHTS: With her background as a campaigner on behalf of striking garment workers, and with her collegiate acclaim as "most popular, most militant, most likely to be famous in the future," Freda Kirchwey blended perfectly into the left-leaning mold of the *Nation*. According to one associate, Joseph Wood Krutch, Kirchwey was a "natural born Bohemian who would undoubtedly be talking to people over cocktails about the state of the world every day of her life if she did not have The Nation as an outlet." With Kirchwey as managing editor, the magazine headed even further left in the early 1920's, increasing its support of social and economic reform. When she bought the magazine in 1937, it became *her* outlet for commenting on the turbulent world events of the next eighteen years.

Though she was accused by one *Saturday Evening Post* writer of being a timid liberal in hesitating to condemn Stalin, Kirchwey was, by other reports, a much bolder spirit. She supported the Spanish Loyalists and belonged to the Committee for a Democratic Spain; she advocated sanctions against Japan and Italy in the early 1940's, and she worked for the League of Women Voters and the Women's International League for Rights of Man. Her Barnard reputation for militancy remained with her throughout her career. As another *Saturday Evening Post* writer once remarked, "She goes merrily on her crusading way, smiting evildoers and letting the howls of pain rise where they may."

In his article, "The Freda Kirchwey I Knew," former *Nation* editor Carey McWilliams recalled "her courage, her unflappability, her indominatable spirit," as being Kirchwey's finest qualities. "Throughout the searing experiences we shared, she remained self-confident, high-spirited, and never lost her poise or sense of humor," McWilliams continued. "That she was addicted to biting her fingernails was about the only outward manifestation of tension I ever observed. . . . I have never known a less self-righteous person than Freda or one who made less of her position and achievements. She was quite without pretense."

AVOCATIONAL INTERESTS: Sailing, traveling.

BIOGRAPHICAL/CRITICAL SOURCES: Saturday Evening Post, February 9, 1946; *Nation,* January 17, 1976.

OBITUARIES: New York Times, January 4, 1976; *Newsweek,* January 19, 1976.*

* * *

KIRKMAN, James S(pedding) 1906-

PERSONAL: Born December 22, 1906, in London, England; son of Benjamin Spedding (a rubber planter) and Ada Eleanor (Wright) Kirkman; married Dorothy Constance Layton, April 9, 1942; children: Richard Neo. *Education:* Gonville and Caius College, Cambridge, B.A., 1928, Ph.D., 1969. *Politics:* "Anti-socialist." *Religion:* Church of England. *Home:* 11 Blanford Walk, Cambridge CB4 3NQ, England.

CAREER: Administrative officer in British North Borneo, 1929-32; conducted private archaeological and historical research, 1932-34; tea planter in Nuwara Eliya, Ceylon, 1934-36; Wellcome-Marston Expedition to the Near East, Lachish, Palestine, field assistant at Tell Duweir, 1937-38; Royal Iraq Legation, London, England, education officer, 1945-47; British Broadcasting Corp., London, England, program assistant for Arabic broadcast, 1947-48; Kenya National Parks, Kenya, warden of coastal historical sites, 1948-60; Fort Jesus, Mombasa, Kenya, curator, 1960-72; writer, 1972—. *Military service:* Royal Air Force, air gunner and political officer, 1940-45; served in Iraq. *Member:* Society of Antiquaries (fellow). *Awards, honors:* Officer of Order of Dom Henrique, 1960; officer of Order of the British Empire, 1967.

WRITINGS: Gedi the Great Mosque: Architecture and Finds, Oxford University Press, 1954; *Gedi, the Palace,*

Mouton, 1963; *Men and Monuments on the East African Coast,* Lutterworth Press, 1964; *Ungwana on the Tana,* Mouton, 1966; *Fort Jesus: A Portuguese Fortress on the East African Coast,* Oxford University Press, 1974. Assistant editor of *International Journal of Nautical Archaeology.*

WORK IN PROGRESS: Editing and translating *Two Contemporary Histories of the Siege of Fort Jesus by the Arabs, 1696-1698,* for Juntade Investigacoes Cientificas de Ultra-man Lisbon.

SIDELIGHTS: Kirkman writes: "From my earliest years, I wished to devote myself to the study of the past, with no particular field preferred, but concentrating on urban and civilized, rather than primitive, communities. My main interest has been in the archaeological aspect (architecture, numismatics, weapons, ceramics), rather than literature or economics, except insofar as they relate to the material culture. This interest does not normally extend beyond the end of the seventeenth century, except with regard to military affairs. At present I am particularly concerned with the conception of the western Indian Ocean as a cultural unity, similar to the Mediterranean, in spite of the diversity of its parts."

* * *

KIRKPATRICK, Doris (Upton) 1902-

PERSONAL: Born August 29, 1902, in Fitchburg, Mass.; daughter of Bradford Farnum (a railroad engineer) and Flora (Smith) Upton; married Clifford Kirkpatrick (a professor of sociology), July 16, 1927 (deceased); children: Judith Kirkpatrick Paterson. *Education:* Middlebury College, A.B., 1924; graduate study at University of Chicago. *Religion:* Unitarian-Universalist. *Residence:* Whitingham, Vt.

CAREER: Social worker in Philadelphia, Pa., 1926; freelance newspaper journalist, 1926-45; *Fitchburg Sentinel,* Fitchburg, Mass., reporter, 1945-57; reporter for the Associated Press, in Vermont, 1957-64; free-lance journalist, 1964—. *Awards, honors:* Five awards from Associated Press, 1945-57; D.Letters from Fitchburg State College, 1977.

WRITINGS: In Houses Like These, Fitchburg Council of Social Agencies, 1945; *The City and the River,* Fitchburg Historical Society, 1971; *Around the World in Fitchburg,* Fitchburg Historical Society, 1975; *Honey in the Rock,* American Elsevier, 1979. Also author of pageant, "This Land Was Made for You and Me," 1964.

WORK IN PROGRESS: Changing Vermont.

SIDELIGHTS: Doris Kirkpatrick writes: "I spent a year in Germany, 1936-37, and wrote numerous articles about the Nazis."

BIOGRAPHICAL/CRITICAL SOURCES: Montachusett Review, February 18, 1976.

* * *

KIRKWOOD, G(ordon) M(acdonald) 1916-

PERSONAL: Born May 7, 1916, in Toronto, Ontario, Canada; came to the United States in 1946, naturalized citizen, 1960; son of George Leslie (an insurance agent) and Gertrude (Marlatt) Kirkwood; married Patricia Frueh (a university lecturer), September 16, 1940; children: Michael John, David Hoyt. *Education:* University of Toronto, B.A., 1938; Cornell University, M.A., 1939; Johns Hopkins University, Ph.D., 1942. *Home:* 516 Cayuga Heights Rd., Ithaca, N.Y. 14850. *Office:* Department of Classics, Goldwin Smith Hall, Cornell University, Ithaca, N.Y. 14853.

CAREER: Senior Latin master at secondary school in Montreal, Quebec, 1945-46; University of Saskatchewan, Saskatoon, lecturer in Latin, summer, 1946; Cornell University, Ithaca, N.Y., instructor, 1946-48, assistant professor, 1948-54, associate professor, 1954-59, professor of classics, 1959-74, head of department, 1963-72, Frederic J. Whiton Professor of Classics, 1974—. *Military service:* Royal Canadian Navy, 1943-45; became lieutenant. *Member:* American Philological Association, American Association of University Professors, Classical Association of the Atlantic States, Phi Beta Kappa. *Awards, honors:* Ford Foundation fellowship, 1953-54; Guggenheim fellowship, 1956-57; award of merit from American Philological Association, 1959, for *A Study of Sophoclean Drama;* American Council of Learned Societies fellowship, 1962-63; National Endowment for the Humanities fellowship, 1977.

WRITINGS: *A Study of Sophoclean Drama,* Cornell University Press, 1958; *A Short Guide to Classical Mythology,* Holt, 1959; *Early Greek Monody,* Cornell University Press, 1974; (editor) *Poetry and Poetics: Studies in Honor of James Hutton,* Cornell University Press, 1975; (editor, and author of introduction and notes) *Pindar: Selected Poems and Fragments,* American Philological Association, 1980. Contributor of articles and reviews to classical studies journals.

* * *

KIRN, Ann Minette 1910-

PERSONAL: Born April 4, 1910, in Montgomery City, Mo. *Education:* Columbia University, B.A. and M.A.; also attended William Woods College, Chicago Academy of Fine Arts, St. Louis School of Fine Arts, and University of California, Los Angeles. *Home:* 1020 San Luis Rd., Tallahassee, Fla. 32304.

CAREER: Fashion illustrator and elementary schoolteacher; faculty member in art department at Florida State University, Tallahassee; free-lance writer and illustrator, 1958—. *Awards, honors: Full of Wonder* was named one of the ten best illustrated children's books of the year by the *New York Times,* 1959.

WRITINGS—Juvenile; all self-illustrated: *Leopard on a String,* World Publishing, 1959; *Full of Wonder,* World Publishing, 1959; *Tinkie,* World Publishing, 1960; *Two Pesos for Catalina,* Rand McNally, 1962; *I Spy,* Norton, 1965; *Bamboo,* Putnam, 1966; *Nine in a Line, From an Old, Old Folktale,* Norton, 1966; *In a Garden,* World Publishing, 1967; *Beeswax Catches a Thief,* Norton, 1968; *Tale of a Crocodile,* Norton, 1968; *Let's Look at Tracks,* Putnam, 1969; *Let's Look at More Tracks,* Putnam, 1970; *Tip for Tap,* Norton, 1970; *Never Run Scared,* Four Winds Press, 1974.

Illustrator: Lynda Graham, *Pinky Marie,* Saalfield, 1939; Flora M. Hood, *One Luminaria for Antonio: A Story of New Mexico,* Putnam, 1966.*

* * *

KLEIN, Herbert Sanford 1936-

PERSONAL: Born January 6, 1936, in New York, N.Y.; son of Emil A. and Florence (Friedman) Klein; married Harriet E. Manelis (an anthropologist), September 3, 1956; children: Rachel, Daniel, Jacob. *Education:* University of Chicago, A.B., 1957, M.A., 1959, Ph.D., 1963. *Home:* 157 Ames Ave., Leonia, N.J. 07605. *Office:* Department of History, Columbia University, New York, N.Y. 10027.

CAREER: University of Chicago, Chicago, Ill., instructor, 1962-63, assistant professor, 1963-67, associate professor of history, 1967-69; Columbia University, New York, N.Y., associate professor, 1969-71, professor of history, 1971—. *Member:* Conference on Latin American History. *Awards, honors:* Henry L. and Grace Doherty fellow in Bolivia, 1960-61; Fulbright grant for Bolivia, summer, 1963; Social Science Research Council fellow in Spain, 1964-65, 1971-72; Ford Foundation fellow in Argentina and Brazil, 1965-67; American Council of Learned Societies fellow, 1973; grants from National Science Foundation, 1974-76, and from Tinker and National Endowment for the Humanities, both 1975-77.

WRITINGS: *Slavery in the Americas: A Comparative Study of Cuba and Virginia,* University of Chicago Press, 1967; *Parties and Political Change in Bolivia, 1880-1952,* Cambridge University Press, 1970; *The Middle Passage: Comparative Studies in the Atlantic Slave Trade,* Princeton University Press, 1978. Contributor of numerous articles and reviews to professional journals.

* * *

KLEIN, Milton M(artin) 1917-

PERSONAL: Born August 15, 1917, in New York, N.Y.; son of Edward and Margaret (Greenfield) Klein; married Margaret Gordon, August 25, 1963; children: Edward Gordon, Peter Gordon. *Education:* City College (now of the City University of New York), B.S.S., 1937, M.S.Ed., 1939; Columbia University, Ph.D., 1954. *Home:* 8124 Kingsdale Dr., Knoxville, Tenn. 37919. *Office:* Department of History, University of Tennessee, Knoxville, Tenn. 37916.

CAREER: High school social studies teacher in New York City, 1938-41, 1947-57; Columbia University, New York City, lecturer in history, 1954-58; Long Island University, Brooklyn, N.Y., professor of history and head of department, 1958-62, dean of College of Liberal Arts and Sciences, 1962-66; State University of New York College at Fredonia, dean for graduate studies and research, 1966-69; University of Tennessee, Knoxville, professor, 1969-77, alumni distinguished service professor of history, 1977—. Fulbright professor at University of Canterbury, 1962; Walter E. Meyer visiting professor at New York University, 1976-77. *Military service:* U.S. Army Air Forces, 1942-46; received Army commendation ribbon and oak leaf cluster. U.S. Air Force Reserve, 1946-77; became lieutenant colonel.

MEMBER: American Association of University Professors (member of national council, 1977-80), American Historical Association, Organization of American Historians, American Society for Eighteenth-Century Studies, American Society for Legal History (secretary, 1975-77, vice-president, 1978-79, president, 1980—), Conference on British Studies, Southeastern Society for Eighteenth-Century Studies (member of board of directors, 1978—), Columbia University Seminar on Early American History (associate, 1967, chairperson, 1971-72), Phi Beta Kappa, Phi Kappa Phi, Phi Alpha Theta, Omicron Delta Kappa. *Awards, honors:* Ford Foundation fellowship, 1955-56; Lilly Foundation fellowship, summer, 1961; American Philosophical Society grant, summer, 1973; outstanding teacher award from University of Tennessee Alumni Association, 1974; Kerr History Prize from New York State Historical Association, 1975, and prize from American Society for Eighteenth-Century Studies, 1976, both for "New York Lawyers and the Coming of the American Revolution."

WRITINGS: *Social Studies for the Academically Talented Student,* National Education Association, 1960; (editor) *The Independent Reflector,* Harvard University Press, 1963; *New York in the American Revolution,* New York State

American Revolution Bicentennial Commission, 1974; *The Politics of Diversity: Essays in the History of Colonial New York*, Kennikat, 1974; (editor) *New York: The Centennial Years, 1676-1976*, Kennikat, 1976; (editor with Leo Hershkowitz) *Courts and Law in Early New York*, Kennikat, 1978. General editor of "A History of the American Colonies," a thirteen-volume series, Scribner and KTO Press, 1973—. Contributor to history and literary journals.

WORK IN PROGRESS: Editing *New York City Under British Rule: The Letterbook of General James Robertson*, publication by New York State Historical Association expected in 1981.

SIDELIGHTS: Klein writes: "What I have sought in my historical writing is to correct the imbalance in the literature of our colonial past which makes New England and the South the sole progenitors of our American tradition. I have tried to arouse interest in the Middle Colonies and states and to demonstrate how much later America owes to developments during the colonial period in New York, New Jersey, and Pennsylvania.

"I am also convinced that unless professional historians address their writings to the general public as well as to other historians, they will have missed their obligation to educate and inform the public of our heritage. All too often historians write for other historians. How then can a sense of history be conveyed to the general public and Americans be made aware of their identity?"

BIOGRAPHICAL/CRITICAL SOURCES: William and Mary Quarterly, July, 1979.

*   *   *

KLEMM, W(illiam) R(obert) 1934-

PERSONAL: Born July 24, 1934, in South Bend, Ind.; son of Lincoln W. and Helen (DeLong) Klemm; married Doris Mewha (a history teacher), August 27, 1957; children: Mark Dolan, Laura Margaret. *Education:* Attended University of Tennessee, 1952-54; Auburn University, D.V.M., 1958; University of Notre Dame, Ph.D., 1963. *Religion:* Presbyterian. *Home address:* Route 3, Box 179, Bryan, Tex. 77801. *Office:* Department of Biology, Texas A & M University, College Station, Tex. 77843.

CAREER: Iowa State University, Ames, assistant professor, 1963-64, associate professor of pharmacology, 1964-66; Texas A & M University, College Station, assistant professor, 1966-70, professor of biology, 1970—. Consultant to Surgeon General of U.S. Air Force. *Military service:* U.S. Air Force Reserve, 1958—; present rank, lieutenant colonel. *Member:* American Association for the Advancement of Science, American Physiological Association, Society for Neuroscience, Sigma Xi. *Awards, honors:* Book of the month award from *Medical Electronics and Data*, 1969, for *Animal Electroencephalography.*

WRITINGS: Animal Electroencephalography, Academic Press, 1969; *Science, the Brain, and Our Future*, Bobbs-Merrill, 1972; *Applied Electronics for Veterinary Medicine and Animal Physiology*, C. C Thomas, 1976; (editor) *Discovery Processes in Modern Biology*, Robert E. Krieger, 1977. Associate editor of *Communications in Behavioral Biology* and *Journal of Electrophysiological Techniques.*

SIDELIGHTS: Klemm wrote: "I don't ordinarily think of myself as an author, because my writings are mostly scientific and technical. However, I did put together two books which were aimed more or less at a general audience.

"*Science, the Brain, and Our Future* was written expressly

for the general public. Its aim is to provide a quick and readable account of what is known about the brain and, moreover, to give the public some insight into how brain research is going to affect us all in the very near future. The book also points up the need to consider human values in the context of the recent and impending discoveries of brain research.

"My book on discovery processes is designed, in part, to help inspire young biological researchers. It is a collection of autobiographies of famous biologists, who tell some of the more personal aspects of their careers and how these related to the discoveries they have made. Another focus of the book is to help the general public, which provides the funds for most biological research, understand better the nature of the discovery process. Hopefully, the book gives the layman a whole new perspective on science and its practitioners; maybe it even shows why appropriation of public money cannot purchase 'discovery' in any linear, orderly, or even predictable way."

*   *   *

KLOOS, Peter 1936-

PERSONAL: Born June 21, 1936, in Haarlem, Netherlands; son of Jan Piet (an architect) and Maria (Moolenaar) Kloos; children: Esther, Bart. *Education:* University of Amsterdam, M.A., 1962, Ph.D., 1971. *Religion:* None. *Home:* Damloperwerf 1, 2317 DS, Leiden, Netherlands. *Office:* Institute of Social and Cultural Studies, State University of Leiden, Stationsplein 10, Leiden, Netherlands.

CAREER: University of Amsterdam, Amsterdam, Netherlands, junior lecturer in cultural anthropology, 1969-74; State University of Leiden, Leiden, Netherlands, senior lecturer in cultural anthropology, 1974—. *Member:* Netherlands Sociological and Anthropological Society (president of anthropological branch, 1971-75), Academic Council (head of anthropological section, 1975—).

WRITINGS—In English: *The Maroni River Caribs of Surinam*, Humanities, 1971; (editor with K. W. van der Veen) *Rule or Reality: Essays in Honour of A.J.F. Koebben*, University of Amsterdam, 1975; (editor with Henri J. M. Claessen) *Current Anthropology in the Netherlands*, Anthropological Branch, Netherlands Sociological and Anthropological Society, 1975.

Other: *Culturele antropologie: Een inleiding* (title means "Cultural Anthropology: An Introduction"), Van Gorcum, 1972; *Het Indianenprobleem in Zuid-Amerika* (title means "The Amerindian Problem in South America"), Van Gorcum, 1974; *Galibi: Een Karaibendorp in Suriname* (title means "Galibi: A Carib Village in Surinam"), Bureau Volkslectuur Paramaribo, 1975; (editor) *Culturele antropologie: Portret van een wetenschap* (title means "Cultural Anthropology: Portrait of a Discipline"), Intermediair, 1976; (with Henri J. M. Claessen) *Evolutie en evolutionisme* (title means "Evolution and Evolutionism"), Van Gorcum, 1978.

Editor of series "Studies of Developing Countries" and "Terreinverkenningen in de culturele antropologie," both published by Van Gorcum.

WORK IN PROGRESS: Kurunduwila: The Structure of Social Relations in a Sinhalese Village; Land and the People of Kurunduwila, Sri Lanka; The Integration of Anthropological Theories.

SIDELIGHTS: Kloos has carried out field studies in the Netherlands, in the modern reclamation Eastern Flevoland, in Surinam, South America, and in Sri Lanka.

KLOTMAN, Phyllis Rauch

PERSONAL: Born in Galveston, Tex.; daughter of Isadore and Esther (Schreiber) Rauch; married Robert H. Klotman (a professor of music), April 4, 1943; children: Janet Klotman Cutler, Paul Evan. *Education:* Cleveland College, B.A. (summa cum laude), 1961; Western Reserve University (now Case Western Reserve University), M.A., 1963, Ph.D., 1969; graduate study at Wayne State University. *Home:* 2740 Spicewood Lane, Bloomington, Ind. 47401. *Office:* Department of Afro-American Studies, Indiana University, Bloomington, Ind. 47401.

CAREER: Lawrence Institute of Technology, Southfield, Mich., instructor in English, 1967-68; Indiana State University, Terre Haute, assistant professor of English, 1969-70; Indiana University, Bloomington, assistant professor, 1970-73, associate professor, 1973-78, professor of Afro-American studies, 1978—. Guest lecturer at University of Toronto, 1976, Western Maryland College, 1977, University of Rhode Island, 1978, and Gutenberg University, 1978; visiting professor at University of Hamburg, 1978. Member of advisory board of Black American Literature Forum, 1976—; consultant to National Endowment for the Humanities. *Member:* Modern Language Association of America, College Language Association, College English Association, Popular Culture Association, American Association of University Professors, National Council of Black Studies, American Association of Interdisciplinary Studies for Native American, Black, Chicano, Puerto Rican, and Asian Americans, Midwest Modern Language Association.

WRITINGS: Another Man Gone: The Black Runner in Contemporary Afro-American Literature, Kennikat, 1977; (editor with David Baker and others, and contributor) *Humanities Through the Black Experience,* Kendall/Hunt, 1977; (with Wilmer Baatz) *The Black Family and the Black Woman,* Arno, 1978; *Frame by Frame: A Black Filmography,* Indiana University Press, 1979. Contributor of about twenty articles and reviews to literature journals. Guest editor of *Balf,* winter, 1978.

WORK IN PROGRESS: A literary biography of Harlem Renaissance writer and critic, Wallace Thurman; a work of fiction; research on Afro-Americans in film and on Black women in literature.

SIDELIGHTS: Klotman writes: "Writing for me is the most difficult and yet the most rewarding of all my activities. My first work of fiction was completed when I was stumbling into adolescence. My academic writing is a result of some compelling need I feel, usually connected with actual classroom experiences or to some research frustration. My book *Frame by Frame* was the result of such frustration. The research necessary to begin a new course for the Afro-American Studies Department on 'Images of Blacks in Film' (from 1903 to the mid 1950's) took me all over the country trying to assemble materials, and the information I finally put together marked my first foray into academic computing. One of my audio-visual associates impressed upon me the need to share such information with other scholars, teachers, students. It is a book which I believe will help community groups—both black and white—in learning more about the contributions of black people to still another art medium."

*   *   *

KLOTTER, John C(harles)   1918-

PERSONAL: Born November 6, 1918, in Louisville, Ky.; son of John J. and Lillie (Fischer) Klotter; married Jane Rid-

dle, November 3, 1954; children: James C., Douglas A., Ronald L. *Education:* Western Kentucky University, A.B., 1941; University of Kentucky, J.D., 1948; studied law at U.S. Department of Justice, 1948; attended Judge Advocate General School, 1961. *Home:* 11905 Cedardale Rd., Anchorage, Ky. 40223. *Office:* School of Justice Administration, University of Louisville, Louisville, Ky. 40208.

CAREER: Admitted to Bar of Kentucky Supreme Court, 1948, and U.S. Supreme Court, 1967. Teacher in schools in Hardin County, Ky., 1934-41; Louisville Board of Education, Louisville, Ky., secondary school teacher, 1941-42; Federal Bureau of Investigation (FBI), Washington, D.C., special agent, 1948-50; Kentucky State Police, Frankfort, legal officer, 1951-52, director of division of probation and parole, 1952-56; University of Louisville, Louisville, assistant professor, 1957-63, associate professor, 1963-66, professor, 1966—, associate director of Southern Police Institute, 1957-71, director, 1971-77, chairman of undergraduate division at School of Justice Administration, 1969-71, dean, 1971—. Member of many committees, including Kentucky Law Enforcement Council and Kentucky Attorney General Prosecutor Advisory Council. *Military service:* U.S. Army, 1942-46; became captain. U.S. Army Reserve, 1946—; became colonel. *Member:* International Association of Chiefs of Police, Academy of Criminal Justice Sciences, Reserve Officers Association, Society of Former Special Agents of the FBI, Kentucky Bar Association, Honorable Order of Kentucky Colonels, Louisville Bar Association. *Awards, honors:* Ford Foundation grant, 1968, for research project, "Burglary: Prevention, Investigation, and Prosecution"; Dictograph Public Safety Award, 1978; Shein award from Kentucky Law Enforcement Council for most outstanding contribution to law enforcement in Kentucky.

WRITINGS: Techniques for Police Instructors, C. C Thomas, 1963, 3rd edition, 1978; (with Jacqueline R. Kanovitz) *Constitutional Law for Police,* W. H. Anderson, 1968, 3rd edition, 1977; (with Carl L. Meier) *Criminal Evidence for Police,* W. H. Anderson, 1971, 2nd edition, 1975; *Legal Guide for Police: Detention, Arrest, Search and Seizure, Questioning, Identification,* W. H. Anderson, 1977; (with Joseph Rosenfeld) *Criminal Justice Instructional Techniques,* C. C Thomas, 1979; (with Arthur Bilek) *Legal Aspects of Private Security,* W. H. Anderson, 1979; *Criminal Evidence in Justice Administration,* Anderson, 1980. Also author with Richard J. Brzeczek of *Legal Considerations in Justice Management,* 1980.

SIDELIGHTS: Klotter told *CA:* "I am convinced that writers of textbooks have as much influence on the attitudes of students as do the instructors. One might argue that in a textbook the material should be presented without reflecting the writer's position on points presented. Anyone who has written a book or reads textbooks extensively, however, recognizes that this is impossible. Either knowingly or unknowingly, the author of the book, even if only by the style of his writing, influences the interpretation placed upon the material by the reader. When discussing writing with young writers and with co-authors, I emphasize the necessity of considering the reader and the long-range influence of the concepts being presented."

*   *   *

KNIGHT, Janet M(argaret)   1940-

PERSONAL: Born May 15, 1940, in New York, N.Y.; daughter of Arnol J. (an opera singer and carpenter) and Lottie (Haase) Knight. *Education:* City College of the City University of New York, B.A., 1961; attended New School for Social Research, 1961-63. *Politics:* Liberal. *Religion:* "Mormon upbringing." *Home and office:* 5601 Riverdale Ave., Bronx, N.Y. 10471.

CAREER: German Federal Railroad, New York City, public relations manager, 1963; Facts on File (publisher), New York City, associate editor, 1963-70; free-lance writer and editor, 1970-74; Yeshiva University, New York City, assistant director of public relations, 1974—. Opera reviewer and commentator for WNYC-Radio. Involved in community and political activities; editorial consultant. *Member:* Word Guild.

WRITINGS: (Editor) *Three Assassinations: The Deaths of John and Robert Kennedy and Martin Luther King,* Facts on File, 1971. Contributor to *Collier's Encyclopedia* and *Funk & Wagnalls Encyclopedia.* Contributor to magazines and newspapers, including *Ms., Coronet,* and *Opera News.*

WORK IN PROGRESS: The Onlookers, a novel, completion expected in 1982; short stories.

SIDELIGHTS: Janet Knight writes: "In all my writing I try to adhere to three guidelines: maintaining objectivity, believing in my subject, and most importantly, keeping my sense of humor. If I can then interest and stimulate my readers, I consider the work successful."

*   *   *

KNIGHT, John Shively 1894-

PERSONAL: Born October 26, 1894, in Bluefield, W.Va.; son of Charles Landon (a publisher) and Clara Irene (Scheifly) Knight; married Katherine McLain, November 21, 1921 (died, 1929); married Beryl Zoller Comstock, January 24, 1932 (died August, 1974); married Elizabeth Good Augustus, January 6, 1976; children: (first marriage) John Shively (died May, 1945), Charles Landon, Frank McLain (died, 1958); (second marriage) Mrs. Kenneth Hewitt. *Education:* Attended Cornell University, 1914-17. *Religion:* Episcopalian. *Home:* 255 North Portage Path, Akron, Ohio 44303. *Office:* 44 East Exchange St., Akron, Ohio 44328.

CAREER/WRITINGS: Newspaper reporter and executive, 1920-25; *Akron Beacon-Journal,* Akron, Ohio, managing editor, 1925-33, editor, 1933-71, editorial chairman, 1971-76, editor emeritus, 1976—; *Springfield Sun,* Springfield, Ohio, editorial director, 1925-27; *Massilion Independent,* Massilion, Ohio, editorial director, 1927-33, president, 1933-37; *Miami Herald,* Miami, Fla., publisher and chairman of the board, 1937-67, editorial chairman, 1967-76, editor emeritus, 1976—; Beacon-Journal Publishing Co., Knight Newspapers, Inc. (now Knight-Ridder Newspapers, Inc.), Akron, president, until 1966, editorial chairman, 1967-76, editor emeritus, 1976—; *Detroit Free Press,* Detroit, Mich., president and editor, 1940-67, editorial chairman, until 1976, editor emeritus, 1976—; *Chicago Daily News,* Chicago, Ill., owner, editor, and publisher, 1944-59; *Charlotte Observer,* Charlotte, N.C., vice-president, 1954; *Charlotte News,* Charlotte, vice-president, 1959-76. Former vice-president of *Tallahassee Democrat,* Tallahassee, Fla. Author of column, "The Editor's Notebook," appearing in *Akron Beacon-Journal, Detroit Free Press,* and *Miami Herald,* 1933-76, and *Chicago Daily News,* 1944-59. Chief liaison officer of United States Office of Censorship in London, England, 1943-44. Vice-president, director, chairman of finance committee, and member of executive committee of Associated Press. Trustee emeritus at Cornell University and University of Miami. *Military service:* Served with Army Air Corps and American Expeditionary Forces, 1917-19. *Member:* Ameri-

can Newspaper Publishers Association (past committee member), American Society of Newspaper Editors (past president), Inter-American Press Association (past president), Forty and Eight (American Legion), Phi Sigma Kappa, Sigma Delta Chi.

AWARDS, HONORS: Medal from Syracuse University, 1946, for achievement in journalism; Brotherhood of Children award, 1946; citation of merit from Poor Richard Club, 1946; Frank M. Hawks Memorial Trophy, 1947; honor award from University of Missouri, 1949, for distinguished service journalism; named outstanding Chicagoan in Inter-American relations from United States/Uruguay alliance, 1952; La Prensa award, 1954; Americas Foundation award, 1959; John Peter Zenger Award, 1967; Pulitzer Prize, 1968, for distinguished editorial writing; Carr Van Anda Award from Ohio University, 1970; William Allen White Award of journalistic merit, 1972; gold medal of achievement from Poor Richard Club, 1972; Fourth Estate award from National Press Club, 1976; LL.D. from University of Akron, 1945, Northwestern University, 1947, Kent State University, 1958, Ohio State University, 1961, University of Michigan, 1969, Oberlin College, 1969, and Colby College, 1969.

SIDELIGHTS: Before choosing a journalistic career, John Shively Knight considered both cattle ranching and the field of law for his life's work. At the urging of his father, owner and publisher of the *Akron Beacon-Journal,* however, he entered the family business. Beginning as a reader of news dispatches in 1920, the young Knight quickly advanced his career, becoming managing editor within five years. With the death of his father in 1933, he took over as owner and editor of the *Beacon-Journal.* Contrary to the then-popular opinion that he fell effortlessly into a plush career, Knight worked diligently and saved the newspaper from ruin. When the United States was in the midst of a devastating depression, the *Beacon-Journal* consistently lost money, often paying its employees partially in scrip. It was only after the younger Knight took the newspaper under his wing did it begin to turn around and show profit.

Knight subsequently bought and published five more newspapers—the *Chicago Daily News, Detroit Free Press, Miami Herald, Miami Tribune,* and *Akron Times Press.* He then discontinued the latter two, acquisitions he had made basically to eliminate competition. He felt that in Miami, for example, three major newspapers were simply unnecessary.

Whenever he gained a new publication, Knight altered the journalistic policies toward a completely unbiased view of news events and urged the coverage of purely local stories. He supported individuality, allowing each regional editor a free hand with the advocacies and management of his own paper. According to John M. Johnston, this practice of "local autonomy" sometimes led to difficulties: "Once a professional liberal took after [Knight] as an 'unprincipled opportunist' because 'in liberal, labor Detroit' his paper had supported control of the rates of independent gas producers, while 'for his conservative, Republican readers in Chicago' his paper took the opposite side."

Far from uninvolved, Knight participated actively in his publications. His popular column, "The Editor's Notebook," which ran from 1933 until his retirement, served as a vehicle for his own thoughts and convictions. Because the column appeared in all of his papers, the possibility of opposing views, even within a single publication, again existed. Johnston related that at one time an interviewee for an editorial writing position had queried the publisher as to the consequences if an opinion expressed in his column differed from one already set forth by another of Knight's newspapers. Nonplussed, Knight replied, "If I'm willing to take that chance, why should it bother you?"

Knight established both the Knight Memorial Fund in honor of his father, and the La Prensa Scholarship for the furtherance of Inter-American understanding.

CA INTERVIEWS THE AUTHOR

On October 24, 1979, John S. Knight, editor emeritus of Knight-Ridder Newspapers, Inc., replied to the questions posed by Peter Benjaminson. Benjaminson, whose sketch is in *CA* 73-76, is the co-author, with David Anderson, of *Investigative Reporting,* published by Indiana University Press, 1976, and the author of *The Story of Motown,* published by Grove Press, 1979.

CA: Do you think the future of newspapers lies in the sunbelt, the big northern cities, the small towns, or the suburbs? Knight-Ridder now has papers in all these areas (and the new Detroit Free Press *plant in downtown Detroit indicates you're still committed to the inner cities), yet one of your executives has said you're looking for papers with circulations up to 200,000.*

KNIGHT: Yes, I think newspapers do better in the sunbelt than in the "big northern cities." However, many small town and suburban papers do quite well.

We built a new plant in Detroit because we are committed to that city and believe it has a future despite its present problems. The statements you read about guidelines for future acquisitions are simply guidelines, and never will be observed to the letter.

CA: The Miami Herald *is working on a project that would put in each subscriber's home a screen on which he would read his newspaper. Do you think newspapers will be replaced by these screens, stay as they are, or be eliminated by competition from radio and television?*

KNIGHT: No, I don't think newspapers will be replaced by some of the new methods of distributing news and advertising. The venture to which you refer is purely experimental, as we believe in investigating all future methods of news distribution.

CA: You've improved the readability of many of the papers you acquired by making them brighter and more attractive and cutting story length. If you were starting now to build the Knight group from scratch again, would you take the same or a different approach?

KNIGHT: I will agree generally that we try to make newspapers brighter and more attractive, but we have no rule about cutting story length. That is a myth. We give stories whatever they deserve, including many which run over a large number of pages.

CA: What was the central reason for the merger with Ridder? Would you call the merger successful so far?

KNIGHT: The Ridder merger provided a broader distribution of newspapers between medium-sized and large cities. It has been most successful so far.

CA: Did you buy the Miami Herald *partly to continue your competition with Governor Cox?*

KNIGHT: No. We simply saw an unusually fine opportunity in the acquisition of the *Miami Herald.*

CA: How did you manage to get the Detroit Free Press *out of debt so quickly after you took it over? How have you managed to keep so many newspapers going, especially big city newspapers, while so many other publishers have failed?*

KNIGHT: The *Free Press* debt was paid off so rapidly because the late John H. Barry, our general manager, wanted to show me what could be done while I was serving as director of censorship in Europe during World War II.

CA: What is the one act in your career you're proudest of? What newspaper acquisition do you value most?

KNIGHT: I guess I am most proud of my early and continuing opposition to the Vietnam war. The *Miami Herald* has been our most profitable acquisition.

CA: Why did you first oppose U.S. entry into World War II, and then support it?

KNIGHT: I opposed our entry into World War II so long as I thought opposition could be effective. When it became obvious that the die was cast, I supported our effort in the interests of national unity.

CA: Do you consider Knight-Ridder powerful in national affairs?

KNIGHT: No.

CA: You editorialized against the Vietnam War for years in your column, but the war continued, even expanded, in spite of your opposition to it. Did this make you cynical about the virtues or usefulness of trying to change national policy through a newspaper or a newspaper column? Why did you start writing your column, and why did you stop?

KNIGHT: No, I am not cynical about the fact that I was unable to change national policy on Vietnam. My only regret is that more fellow editors and columnists did not join me in this endeavor.

I started writing my column in 1933. I stopped when I retired, as I believe there is a time to stop.

CA: You shortened the foreign dispatches printed in the Chicago Daily News *when you owned it. Yet, at present, the Knight-Ridder group is opening new foreign bureaus while other newspapers are closing theirs. Is this contradictory? How would you recommend balancing readability with completeness in foreign news coverage?*

KNIGHT: There is no comparison between the *Chicago Daily News* foreign service and what I inherited and what we are doing in opening foreign bureaus for Knight-Ridder. When I bought the *Chicago Daily News,* many of the correspondents were closer to the governments of the foreign countries than they were to the newspapers they represented. We tried to change this and we did. We will not attempt to become a newspaper of record on foreign coverage. I do not think that is essential nor do I think people would read it.

CA: Nixon Smiley has written that you didn't like H. Bond Bliss's column in the Miami Herald *but tolerated it because many readers liked it. Where do you draw the line, in terms of what you'll allow in a newspaper, between what you or your editors like and what the readers like?*

KNIGHT: I did not subscribe to the opinions of H. Bond Bliss. He was much too didactic for me. However, I saw no reason to cancel it because I did not agree with what he had to say. I am sure many of our readers did enjoy it.

CA: Are the editors really free, in the long run, if they are replaced or promoted on the basis of what you or your executives read?

KNIGHT: Actually, I no longer exercise any editorial influence. I would say that our editors are mostly free, although their policies are subject to debate. Obviously, if an editor pursues a consistently erratic course, he is replaced.

CA: The Miami Herald *crusaded for pasteurized milk and the Everglades Park and against gambling clubs. Do you approve, in general, of such advocacy journalism? How do such crusades square with your notion of objective journalism?*

KNIGHT: Yes, I do approve of advocacy journalism. I think both advocacy and crusading journalism can be kept consistent with the facts.

CA: You and your newspapers seem to know how to make the best of being beaten—or at least losing your lead—on some stories, such as the Eagleton affair and the errant Miami IRS squad story. On other occasions, when the Miami News beat the Miami Herald on the story of the war against Nazi subs off Florida during World War II, for example, you've been beaten and haven't even bothered to attempt a recovery. On still other stories, such as your prediction that Eisenhower and Nixon would be the Republican nominees in 1952, you've been way out in front. How important do you think it really is for a paper to be first with a story?

KNIGHT: I think it is important for a newspaper to be first with a story provided its information has been fully checked out and is completely accurate. I do not feel that newspapers suffer irreparable damage when they are "scooped."

CA: You once said you didn't want to buy the Miami News *because competition was healthy for the* Miami Herald, *yet you bought and closed competing newspapers in both Akron and Miami and the* Miami Herald *now prints the* Miami News. *Have you changed your feelings about the benefits of competition between newspapers published in the same town? Do you still consider the* Miami News *and the* Miami Herald *to be in competition?*

KNIGHT: Yes, I like competitive cities. I am sorry we became entangled with the *Miami News.* The *Miami News* and the *Miami Herald* are in competition editorially, but business administration is handled by the *Herald.* I am not happy with this arrangement.

CA: Is there one underlying goal behind your many newspaper acquisitions?

KNIGHT: To expand a growing organization. We don't like to stand still.

CA: Does running a group of newspapers take the fun out of owning an individual newspaper?

KNIGHT: No, I wouldn't say so.

CA: You have said you believe in the virtues of competition, yet you supported the Newspaper Preservation Act, at least passively. This also seems to contradict your belief that newspapers shouldn't be exempt from controls applied to other businesses. Was your support of the failing newspaper act a victory of economics over idealism?

KNIGHT: I am not enthusiastic about the Newspaper Pres-

ervation Act. I don't think it has worked very well. I think newspapers have a right to fail.

CA: What do you think of federal policies restricting cross-ownership of newspapers and broadcasting outlets?

KNIGHT: While I do not give blanket approval to federal policies of restricting cross-ownership of newspapers and broadcasting outlets, I can see some validity in limiting the number.

CA: Why did you decide to have the Knight group go public?

KNIGHT: Largely because of government taxation policies. A public group has a listed price which appears on the New York Stock Exchange every day. The value of newspapers can be more accurately ascertained. The shareholders know what their stock is worth. Newspapers sell to larger newspaper groups almost entirely because of unfair and inequitable inheritance tax laws.

CA: In many cases, you've used your ownership of newspapers to improve them. But some day some other person, or group of people, will be in command of all your papers and may let them slide. Or, the Knight-Ridder group may be taken over by someone who believes in tight editorial control from the very top. Do you think these are real possibilities? If so, wouldn't your linking of so many newspapers under one management then turn out to have been a disservice? Does your insistence on calling Knight-Ridder a group indicate you have fundamental reservations about newspaper chains?

KNIGHT: There is no way that I can provide for the future, but I think Knight-Ridder Newspapers will continue to operate on many of the same principles which we have followed through the years.

CA: Your foundation contributes to journalism education, yet you have said you prefer liberal arts graduates as reporters on your own newspapers. Would you advise people who wish to enter the newspaper business to go to journalism school? Would you advise them to enter the newspaper business at all?

KNIGHT: I believe in a strong liberal arts education for people who intend to go into journalism. The schools of journalism do provide some instruction in direct approaches to journalism, but much of this can be learned under the guidance of good editors. I have no advice as to whether anyone should enter the newspaper business and/or profession. If a young man or woman has any doubt about their interest, I would suggest they forget it.

CA: To what extent did your father, by example or advice, influence your career, especially in its early stages?

KNIGHT: My father influenced my career by the expression of his ideals and his literary qualities. I did not always agree with my father on policies. We were alike in some respects but quite different in others. I am proud to say that our relationship was always useful, productive and highly educational, to me at least.

BIOGRAPHICAL/CRITICAL SOURCES: Time, May 13, 1940, July 3, 1944, October 30, 1944; *Newsweek,* May 15, 1944; *Miami Herald,* December 12, 1965; *Akron Beacon-Journal,* December 8, 1975; *Authors in the News,* Volume 2, Gale, 1976.

—Interview by Peter Benjaminson

KNIGHT, Max 1909-
(Peter Fabrizius, a joint pseudonym)

PERSONAL: Born June 8, 1909, in Austria; came to United States in May, 1941; naturalized U.S. citizen, 1942; son of Bernhard (a stock broker) and Margarethe (Hoffer) Kuehnel; married Charlotte Lowes, July 11, 1942; children: Anthony C., Martin L. *Education:* University of Vienna, J.Sc.D., 1933; post graduate study at University of California, Berkeley. *Home and office:* 760 Grizzly Peak Blvd., Berkeley, Calif. 94708.

CAREER: Newspaper editor and feature writer in Vienna, London, and Shanghai, 1935-41; Office of War Information, San Francisco, Calif., script writer and analyst, 1943-45; *San Francisco Daily Commercial News*, San Francisco, Calif., financial editor, 1945-47; Stanford University, Hoover Institute, Stanford, Calif., deputy executive secretary of Carnegie Project, 1949; University of California, Berkeley, research assistant in political science, 1950; University of California Press, Berkeley, principal editor, 1950-76; writer, 1976—.

WRITINGS: The German Executive, 1890-1933 (nonfiction), Stanford University Press, 1952; *Return to the Alps*, Friends of the Earth, 1970; *The Original Blue Danube Cookbook*, Lancaster-Miller, 1979.

Translator from the German, except as noted: (From the English) Lawrence Price, *Die Aufnahme englischer Literatur in Deutschland*, Francke, 1962; *Christian Morgenstern's Galgenlieder*, University of California Press, 1963; (with Joseph Fabry) *Johann Nestroy: Three Comedies*, Ungar, 1967; Hans Kelsen, *The Pure Theory of Law*, University of California Press, 1967; Heinrich Kuenzel, *Upper California*, Book Club of California, 1967; Christian Morgenstern, *Three Sparrows*, Scribner, 1968; (with Fabry) Willy Haas, *Bert Brecht*, Ungar, 1968; Morgenstern, *The Great Lalula*, Putnam, 1969; (with Edward Gans) *Goethe's Italian Renaissance Medals*, Malter-Westerfield, 1969; *Galgenlieder/Gallows Songs*, Piper, 1972; Morgenstern, *The Daynight Lamp*, Houghton, 1973; (with Fabry) Helen Mustard, editor, *Heinrich Heine: Selected Works*, Random House, 1973; (contributor of translation) Ralph Manheim, editor, *Bertold Brecht: Collected Works*, Volume VII, Random House, 1975; *A Confidential Matter: The Letters of Richard Strauss and Stefan Zweig*, University of California Press, 1977; (contributor of translation) Karl Kraus, *In These Great Times*, edited by Harry Zohn, Engendra Press, 1977; (from the English; with Karl Ross) Ogden Nash, *Der Kuckuck fuehrt ein Lotterleben*, Paul Zsolnay, 1977.

With Fabry under joint pseudonym Peter Fabrizius; all collections of German short stories: (Editor) *Der schwarze Teufel*, J. Murray, 1942; (editor) *Der Komet*, J. Murray, 1942; (editor) *Die Siebzehn Kamele*, J. Murray, 1949; *Wer zuletzt lacht . . .*, edited by Clair Hayden Bell, Appleton, 1952; *. . . lacht am besten*, edited by Bell, Appleton, 1957.

Editor: Otto Maenchen-Helfen, *The World of the Huns*, University of California Press, 1973; Albert Ehrenzweig, *Law: A Personal View*, Sijthoff, 1977; (and translator from the German) Albert Friedemann, *The Stamps of the German Colonies*, Part I: *Offices in China*, German Colonies Collectors Group, 1978.

Other: (With Ernst Friese) "Lisa, benimn dich" (musical comedy; four-act), first produced in Vienna, Austria, at Kammerspiele Theatre, March, 1939; (translator of songs) *Monuments of Renaissance Music* (poems of chansonnier 1490 A.D.), Volume VII, University of Chicago Press, 1980.

Contributor of translations to proceedings of International Josquin Festival Conference, 1980.

WORK IN PROGRESS: Translation from the German of the novel, *Gripsholm*, by Kurt Tucholsky.

SIDELIGHTS: Knight told *CA:* "Raised in the German-language orbit, yet living most of my adult life in the United States, I am thoroughly bilingual. I consider myself as part of a bridge between the two cultures, an attitude that finds expression in my translations. I travel to Europe frequently; whether I arrive in Austria or California, I am always 'coming home.' I am happiest in the mountains, as indicated in my *Return to the Alps*."

*   *   *

KNOWLES, Yereth K(ahn) 1920-

PERSONAL: Born November 17, 1920, in Hartsdale, N.Y.; daughter of Leon S. (in business) and Yereth (a landscape architect; maiden name, Frank) Kahn; divorced; children: Christine Knowles Hmiel, Timothy M. *Education:* University of Wisconsin (now University of Wisconsin—Madison), B.A., received M.A., 1945; University of Geneva, Ph.D., 1972. *Home:* Ramal, 362 Guama, San German, P.R. 00753. *Office:* Inter American University of Puerto Rico, Box 1807, San German, P.R. 00753.

CAREER: Inter American University of Puerto Rico, San German, professor of political science, 1962—, head of department, 1972-74. Visiting associate of University of the Pacific, 1969-70. Director of Caribbean Institute and Study Center for Latin America, 1977-79. *Member:* American Political Science Association (member of Women's Caucus), Caribbean Studies Association, Phi Delta Kappa.

WRITINGS: Beyond the Caribbean States: A History of Regional Cooperation in the Commonwealth Caribbean, Caribbean Institute and Study Center for Latin America, 1972. Contributor of articles and reviews to academic journals.

WORK IN PROGRESS: Nationalism in the Caribbean.

SIDELIGHTS: Yereth Knowles has traveled in China, Uruguay, Europe, and eastern Europe. She lived in the Netherlands from 1962 to 1963.

*   *   *

KOBRYN, A(llen) P(aul) 1949-

PERSONAL: Born September 29, 1949, in Utica, N.Y. *Education:* Attended Johns Hopkins University, New York University, and City University of New York. *Residence:* New York, N.Y. *Agent:* Jane Rotrosen Agency, 318 East 51st St., New York, N.Y. 10022.

CAREER: Poet and novelist. WBAI-FM, New York, N.Y., worked as producer in drama and literature department, hosted "Big Al's Literary Salon . . . and Pool Hall."

WRITINGS: Poseidon's Shadow (novel), Rawson, Wade, 1979.

SIDELIGHTS: Kobryn remarked in an article for *Library Journal:* "The current status of fiction in our society is fictive—or furtive—or futile. . . . The sole distinguishing characteristic of art is that it is utterly without redeeming social value."

BIOGRAPHICAL/CRITICAL SOURCES: Library Journal, June 15, 1979.

KOCH, H(annsjoachim) W(olfgang) 1933-

PERSONAL: Born November 23, 1933, in Munich, Germany; son of Hanns Peter (an archaeologist) and Charlotte (von Ludwigsdorf) Koch; married Verona Williams, 1955; children: Roger Wolfgang, Freya Agathe, Marcus Hanns Joachim. *Education:* University of Keele, B.A. (with honors), 1965. *Home:* 13 Manor Park Close, Shipton Rd., York, England. *Office:* Department of History, University of York, York, England.

CAREER: University of York, York, England, senior lecturer in history, 1965—. Visiting professor at Free University of Berlin and Freidrich-Meinecke-Institut. *Member:* Royal Historical Association (fellow). *Awards, honors:* Wedgwood Memorial Prize in History from Wedgwood Foundation, 1964, for essay, "The Geographic, Strategic, and Ideological Bases of the Anglo-German Naval Rivalry, 1896-1906."

WRITINGS: Can I Forget?: The True Life of a Hitler Youth, Brown, Watson, 1960; *The Origins of the First World War: Great Power Rivalry and German War Aims,* Macmillan, 1972; *The Hitler Youth: Origins and Development,* Macdonald & Jane's, 1975, Stein & Day, 1976; *A History of Prussia,* Longman, 1978; *Medieval Warfare,* Prentice-Hall, 1979; *The Rise of Modern Warfare,* Prentice-Hall, 1980.

Not in English: *Der Sozialdarwinismus: Seine Genese und Einfluss auf das imperialistische Denken* (title means "Social Darwinism: Its Influence Upon Imperialist Thinking"), [Munich], 1973; *Der deutsche Buergerkrieg* (title means "The German Civil War"), [Berlin], 1978. Contributor to British and German professional journals.

WORK IN PROGRESS: A History of the Third Reich, publication expected in 1981.

SIDELIGHTS: "I must admit that I did not come as an innocent to history," reflected Koch to *CA.* "From my childhood onwards I lived on the periphery of the historical process, be that as a member of the Hitler Youth, and at the age of eighteen as a news editor for Radio Free Europe in Munich and London. As an American prisoner of war at the age of eleven, I realized that one day I should like to investigate how events in Germany in particular, and the world in general, could take such a tragic and disastrous turn. I also realized that this could hardly be done with the traditional methodological tools of historiography. Before one can produce differentiated analyses in contemporary history, it is necessary to return to Ranke's dictum and aim—fully realizing that one could never completely achieve it—at doing the spade work along the lines of 'history as it actually happened.' This demands, first and foremost, an approach which avoids clever theses and the endless repetition of cliches. It demands empathy and the kind of self-discipline in which the historian lets the documents speak while he puts his own person, as much as this is possible, into the background."

*   *   *

KOEPKE, Wulf 1928-

PERSONAL: Born September 24, 1928, in Luebeck, Germany; came to United States in 1965; son of Otto (a teacher) and Emma (a teacher; maiden name, Jahnke) Koepke; married Monique Lehman-Lukas, June 8, 1953; children: Niels, Detlev, Rebekka, Jens. *Education:* Attended University of Hamburg, 1949; attended University of Paris, 1951-52; University of Freiburg, Ph.D., 1955. *Home:* 728 Inwood, Bryan, Tex. 77801. *Office:* Department of Modern Language, Texas A & M University, College Station, Tex. 77843.

CAREER: Lecturer in German, University of Singapore and University of Malaya, 1955-59; Goethe-Institute, Munich, Germany, head of teacher training and new course material department, 1959-65; University of Illinois, Chicago Circle Campus, Chicago, associate professor of German, 1965-68; Rice University, Houston, Tex., associate professor of German, 1968-71; Texas A & M University, College Station, professor of German, 1971—. *Member:* American Association of Teachers of German, American Society for Eighteenth-Century Studies, Modern Language Association of America, Western Association for German Studies, Lessing Society, Jean-Paul Society. *Awards, honors:* Jean-Paul silver medal, 1960, for work on Jean Paul Richter; faculty distinguished achievement award for teaching from Texas A & M University, 1978.

WRITINGS: (Editor) *Berichte aus Deutschland* (title means "Reports From Germany"), Bertelsmann, 1965; (with K. Blohm) *Begegnung mit Deutschland* (title means "Meet Germany"), Max Hueber, 1966, 4th edition, 1973; *Die Deutschen* (title means "The Germans"), Holt, 1971, revised edition, 1980; *Erfolglosigkeit* (title means "Lack of Success"), Wilhelm Fink, 1977.

WORK IN PROGRESS: Textbooks on German language and culture; research on German exile authors in the United States; book on Lion Feuchtwanger.

SIDELIGHTS: Koepke told *CA:* "I am researching the material conditions of the German exile writers in the United States after 1933 insofar as these conditions affected their writing. The authors were accustomed to a very different type of book market and publishing industry where the author was not expected to conform to rigid concepts about length and style of a novel, and the playwrights were used to a highly experimental and political theatre. Thus, even apart from the question of language, they found it very hard to adjust. The older and more famous writers were hardest hit, except for a few authors of best-sellers (Feuchtwanger and Werfel, for example) or somebody with the reputation of a Thomas Mann. Younger authors were able to switch language and style more easily; poets and playwrights were worse off than novelists. The most favorable genre was that of the historical novel or biography. All in all, there is a full scale of response to the exile condition in the United States from total refusal and isolation to complete assimilation. This situation presents a unique chance to study the way in which external conditions affect the work of a writer: form, style, content."

*   *   *

KOFOED, Jack
See KOFOED, John C.

*   *   *

KOFOED, John C. 1894-1979
(Jack Kofoed)

OBITUARY NOTICE—See index for *CA* sketch: Born December 17, 1894, in Philadelphia, Pa.; died December 27, 1979, in Miami, Fla. Journalist and writer. Kofoed served on the staffs of several different newspapers, including the *Philadelphia Public Ledger,* the *New York Evening Post,* and the *Miami Post.* Hundreds of his short stories and articles appeared in major periodicals. From 1945 to 1979 he was a columnist for the *Miami Herald.* Among his books are *Behind the Green Lights, Brandy for Heroes,* and *The Florida Story.* Obituaries and other sources: *New York Times,* December 29, 1979.

KOKOSCHKA, Oskar 1886-1980

OBITUARY NOTICE: Born March 1, 1886, in Poechlarn, Austria; died February 22, 1980, in Montreux, Switzerland. Artist, teacher, and writer. Kokoschka was a leading figure in the school of painting and drama known as expressionism. According to Grace Glueck of the *New York Times,* he was "known especially for the penetrating portraits of his early years, in which he achieved psychological and emotional depth by means of a nervous, tense line and an expressive use of distortion." Labeled a "decadent" artist by pre-World War I critics, he was similarly attacked by the Nazis in 1937, when eight of his paintings were featured in the "Degenerate Artists" show staged in Munich. He later came to symbolize those artists whose beliefs compelled them into exile following the Nazi occupation of Europe. Prior to 1933, he had resigned his teaching post at the Prussian Academy of Art to protest the expulsion of Jewish artists and, in 1938, fled to England, where he could turn his art to the ideological expression of humanist ideals. As a writer, Kokoschka produced three plays, "Sphinx and Straw Man," "Murder, the Hope of Women," which sparked a riot in Vienna in 1909, and "The Burning Thornbush." He was writing his memoirs at the time of his death. Obituaries and other sources: *Current Biography,* Wilson, 1956; *Encyclopedia of World Literature in the Twentieth Century,* updated edition, Ungar, 1967; *Everyman's Dictionary of European Writers,* Dent & Sons, 1968; *The Reader's Encyclopedia of World Drama,* Crowell, 1969; *McGraw-Hill Encyclopedia of World Drama,* McGraw, 1972; *The Oxford Companion to German Literature,* Clarendon Press, 1976; *New York Times,* February 23, 1980.

*   *   *

KOLBAS, Grace Holden 1914-

PERSONAL: Born December 20, 1914, in Wilson, N.Y.; daughter of Benjamin Harrison (a custodian) and Mabel (Sherriff) Holden; married Ervin Bernhard Kolbas (a metallurgist), June 10, 1939; children: Judith Grace (Mrs. Peter Prochaska-Kolbas) Richard Bernhard. *Education:* State University of New York at Buffalo, B.S. (cum laude), 1961, M.S., 1964. *Religion:* Protestant. *Home address:* Outdoor Resorts, P.O. Box 2093, South Padre Island, Tex. 78597.

CAREER: Comptometer operator in Buffalo, N.Y., 1932-56; Kenmore West High School, Kenmore, N.Y., biology teacher, 1961-71; writer, 1971—.

WRITINGS: Ecology: Cycle and Recycle (self-illustrated), Sterling, 1972. Contributor of about twenty-five articles to magazines.

WORK IN PROGRESS: Quest for Health (tentative title), on "a new way of life through chiropractic naturopathic physicians."

SIDELIGHTS: Grace Kolbas commented: "I have to write and don't know why. I need to communicate, even though I am shy and find it difficult to voice my opinions and feelings.

"I have succeeded in reducing my daily duties to a minimum, to allow time for writing. I am an enthusiastic traveler and my needs are satisfied by living in a trailer. There is little work, time for writing, and endless topics of interest.

"I am a naturalist, a biologist with a vitally active personality, but for some time I was grounded and depressed by creeping poor health. By 1971 I had lost confidence, patience, and enthusiasm for teaching, writing, and other activities, and even harbored fears of senility. Gradually I abandoned whatever I could in daily responsibilities in my determination to fight a confining, painful, depressing way of life.

"Now the typewriter is out again. Enthusiasm is building, intelligence is returning. Life is worth living again in a slim, tall, straight, painless body.

"Each quest for fulfillment is a personal one whether for health, family life, retirement, career, or other. I have learned to use all my senses and available knowledge to aid my cause. I must shop around for the right books, doctors, and friends who enrich my life by adding to my knowledge and understanding of myself and my immediate needs.

"Being a biologist with the precise thinking of a mathematician presents a weird combination of interests. Natural health, photography, conservation, physical fitness, and the application of logic in all my contacts keep me alert. Travel has added dimension to my life, and I hope to do more of it as health permits. Europe, Canada, Mexico, Hawaii, and many of the contiguous United States make up my list of travel experiences."

*   *   *

KOLODIN, Irving 1908-

PERSONAL: Born February 21, 1908, in New York, N.Y.; son of Benjamin (a book and stationary shopkeeper) and Leah (Geller) Kolodin; married Irma Rose Levy, June 19, 1936. *Education:* Attended Columbia University, 1925-27; Institute of Musical Art, certificate, 1943. *Home:* 1 Lincoln Plaza, New York, N.Y. 10023. *Office: Saturday Review,* 1290 Avenue of the Americas, New York, N.Y. 10019.

CAREER: Institute of Musical Art, New York City, instructor in harmony and theory, 1930-31; *Brooklyn Eagle,* Brooklyn, N.Y., member of musical staff, 1931-32; *New York Sun,* New York City, music critic, associate music critic, and first critic, 1932-50; *Saturday Review,* New York City, editor of recordings supplement, 1950-52, associate editor, 1952—; Julliard School of Music, New York City, lecturer on music criticism, summers, 1938 and 1939, member of faculty, 1968—. Program annotator for New Friends of Music concerts, 1936—, Duke Ellington's concerts in New York City, Boston, and Cleveland, 1943, and New York Philharmonic Orchestra, 1953-58. Script writer for CBS-Radio's "Jazz Laboratory," 1943. *Wartime service:* Staff member of *Official Guide to AAF* and *Air Force* magazine, 1943-45. *Member:* National Arts Group, Ltd. (vice-president and editor).

WRITINGS: The Metropolitan Opera, 1883-1935, Oxford University Press, 1936, revised edition published as *The Metropolitan Opera, 1883-1939,* 1940; (with Benny Goodman) *The Kingdom of Swing,* Stackpole, 1939; (editor) *The Critical Composer: The Musical Writings of Berlioz, Wagner, Schumann, Tchaikovsky, and Others,* Howell, Soskin, 1940; *A Guide to Recorded Music,* Doubleday, 1941; *Mozart on Records,* Four Corners, 1942; *The New Guide to Recorded Music,* Doubleday, 1946; (with others) *The Saturday Review Home Book of Recorded Music and Sound Reproduction,* Prentice-Hall, 1952; *The Story of the Metropolitan Opera, 1883-1950: A Candid History,* Knopf, 1953, revised 4th edition published as *The Metropolitan Opera, 1883-1966: A Candid History,* 1966; *Orchestral Music,* Knopf, 1955; *The Musical Life,* Knopf, 1958; (editor) *The Composer as Listener: A Guide to Music,* Horizon, 1958; *The Continuity of Music: A History of Influence,* Knopf, 1969; *The Interior Beethoven: A Biography of the Music,* Knopf, 1975; *The Opera Omnibus: Four Centuries of Critical Give and Take,* Dutton, 1976.

Contributor to *International Cyclopedia of Music and Musicians, Grove's Dictionary of Music and Musicians,* and various magazines, including *Theatre Arts, Harper's, New Republic, Vogue, Vanity Fair,* and *American Mercury.*

SIDELIGHTS: Kolodin's books, which range in subject from opera to jazz, provide his readers with a plethora of musical information. His first book, *The Metropolitan Opera, 1883-1935,* along with its subsequent revision, is a historical survey of the Metropolitan Opera and its activities. With a particular emphasis on the casts, the author traces the evolution of the Met and changes in musical taste. According to Richard Aldrich, the book "is something more than a record, complete as it is in that way. It is a narrative circumstantial but rapidly moving, vigorous and picturesque in style, written with a keen sense of all the importance it carries and all the implications it yields." Similarly, Edward Reed wrote: "Mr. Kolodin has heightened the inherent flatness of a thoroughgoing record by a keen perception of the place of the Metropolitan as an individual unit, as a part of the city's history, and as a reflection of the city's society."

Kolodin's later work, *The Story of the Metropolitan Opera, 1883-1950: A Candid History,* added substantially to the facts. For it is, as Winthrop Sargeant described it, "a massive encyclopedic volume in which the persevering reader can find virtually every item of expense, every cast, every production in the seventy-year history of the opera house."

The flip side of Kolodin's work is represented by *The Kingdom of Swing,* which he co-authored with Benny Goodman. Like *The Metropolitan Opera,* this book is "a narrative of names, places, events," but this time the focus is the life and music of a swing artist and band leader. Kolodin provides two solo written chapters, one on Chicago, where the music originated, and one on the nature of swing. H. H. Taubman described this latter chapter, "Swing Is Here," as "a penetrating summary of the ingredients and character of swing, one of the best short essays on the subject that has appeared in print."

Several of Kolodin's next books were guides to musical recordings, evaluated by critics as comprehensive surveys "conducted with normal good taste." These were followed by two volumes of criticism. *The Musical Life,* a collection of essays and articles, was highly praised. Edward Barry said that reading the book was "much like listening to the conversation of a highly articulate person with a well stocked mind." Herbert Kupferberg felt the diverse essays "share a common clarity of thought and geniality of expression." And Neville Cardus wrote, "I have found in Irving Kolodin's 'The Musical Life' much more refreshment to mind and spirit than in any book on music I have seen for decades."

The Continuity of Music, however, met with less enthusiasm. The book is a highly detailed and illustrated demonstration of the influences that composers from Bach to Stravinsky have exerted on one another, as well as an explanation of what Kolodin sees as the barrenness of contemporary music. Richard Freeman found Kolodin's argument "ingenious, but slightly fallacious." Alfred Frankenstein took issue with half the volume: "While Mr. Kolodin's antimodernist arguments must be taken with the highest degree of skepticism, his history of musical influence within his given framework is extremely interesting." On the other hand, Gerald Abraham felt that "while *The Continuity of Music* sustains a thesis—and amply proves it—it will be enjoyed by many intelligent music-lovers who don't care a damn for a musicological thesis."

On *The Interior Beethoven,* D. R. de Lerma wrote that "Kolodin provides a popular book for the musically literate . . . and for musicology amateurs." As in *The Continuity of Music,* he explores the relationship of melodic and harmonic ideas between compositions but does not examine the music in detail. *Choice* found fault in Kolodin's failure to consider influences on Beethoven, and Alan Tyson questioned the veracity of Kolodin's scholarship. Yet H.C.R. Landon saw value in "the refocused perspective he gives to Beethoven's early music . . . and the number and accuracy of musical examples, which make it a book for the professional as well as (hopefully) for the amateur."

Kolodin's most recent work, *The Opera Omnibus,* is "a miscellany of opera lore" cast in a framework of an imaginary two-act opera. In it he remembers performances, relates anecdotes, and profiles famous figures, all from the point of view of his own experience. P. L. Miller explained the book's wide appeal: "Writing chiefly for the opera goer of some experience, Kolodin is careful to translate and explain for the novice."

BIOGRAPHICAL/CRITICAL SOURCES: New York Times, May 17, 1936, June 18, 1939, June 9, 1940, July 28, 1940, April 30, 1950, November 22, 1953, May 8, 1955, April 6, 1958; *Saturday Review of Literature,* May 30, 1936, April 22, 1939, July 6, 1940, April 29, 1950, April 26, 1952, April 25, 1953, April 5, 1958, August 23, 1958, December 17, 1966, May 24, 1969, May 31, 1975; *Theatre Arts Monthly,* June, 1936, October, 1939; *New Republic,* August 12, 1936, August 2, 1939, August 5, 1940, March 2, 1942; *Nation,* June 29, 1940, January 31, 1942, July 19, 1952; *Music Library Association Notes,* June, 1950, September, 1953, September, 1955, September, 1958; *Christian Science Monitor,* April 23, 1953; *New York Herald Tribune Book Review,* May 3, 1953, July 10, 1955, August 17, 1958; *Chicago Sunday Tribune,* August 31, 1958; *Book Week,* January 22, 1967; *Kenyon Review,* Volume XXXI, number 4, 1969; *New York Times Book Review,* July 13, 1969; *New York Review of Books,* May 29, 1975; *Library Journal,* June 1, 1975, September 15, 1976; *Choice,* July/August, 1975, February, 1977.*

*   *   *

KOPAL, Zdenek 1914-

PERSONAL: Born April 4, 1914, in Litomysl, Czechoslovakia; son of Joseph (a professor) and Ludmila (Lelek) Kopal; married Alena Muldner, September 7, 1938; children: Georgiana L., Zdenka A., Eva M. *Education:* Charles University, R.N.Dr., 1936, D.Sc., 1937; postdoctoral study at Cambridge University, 1938, and at Harvard University, 1939-40. *Home:* Greenfield, Parkway, Wilmslow, Cheshire, England. *Agent:* Christopher Busby Ltd., 44 Great Russell St., London WC1B 3PA, England. *Office:* Department of Astronomy, Victoria University of Manchester, Oxford Rd., Manchester M13 9PL, England.

CAREER: Harvard University, Cambridge, Mass., Agassiz research fellow, 1938-40, research associate in astronomy, 1940-46; Massachusetts Institute of Technology, Cambridge, associate professor of astronomy, 1942-46 and 1947-51; Victoria University of Manchester, Manchester, England, professor of astronomy, 1951—. Lecturer at Harvard University, 1948; Pahlavi Lecturer in Iran, 1977; visiting professor at numerous universities. President of Fondation Internationale du Pic-du-Midi. Chairperson of British National Committee for Space Research's committee for lunar and planetary exploration; member of U.S. National Space Board's lunar-planetary committee, 1961-66; consultant to the aircraft industry, National Aeronautic and Space Administration (NASA), and the U.S. military. *Member:* International Academy of Astronautical Sciences, Greek National Academy of Athens (foreign member). *Awards, honors:* Gold medal from Czechoslovak Academy of Sciences, 1969; D.Sc. and Copernicus Medal from Cracow University, 1974; named honorary citizen of Delphi, Greece, 1978.

WRITINGS: An Introduction to the Study of Eclipsing Variables, Harvard University Press, 1946; (editor) *Tables of Supersonic Flow Around Cones of Large Yaw,* three volumes, Center of Analysis, Department of Electrical Engineering, Massachusetts Institute of Technology, 1947-49.

Numerical Analysis, With Emphasis on the Application of Numerical Techniques to Problems of Infinitesimal Calculus in Single Variable, Wiley, 1955, 2nd edition, 1961; (editor) *Proceedings of a Symposium on Astronomical Optics and Related Subjects,* North-Holland Publishing, 1956; *Close Binary Systems,* Wiley, 1959.

Figures of Equilibrium of Celestial Bodies, With Emphasis on Problems of Motion of Artificial Satellites, University of Wisconsin Press, 1960; *The Moon: Our Nearest Celestial Neighbour,* Chapman & Hall, 1960, Academic Press, 1961, 2nd edition, Chapman & Hall, 1963, Academic Press, 1964; (editor with Ellen B. Finlay) *Problems of Lunar Topography,* Manchester University Press, 1960; (with others) *Studies in Lunar Topography,* Geophysics Research Directorate, Air Force Cambridge Research Laboratories, 1961; *Thermal History of the Moon and of the Terrestrial Planets: Numerical Results,* Jet Propulsion Laboratory, California Institute of Technology, 1962; (editor) *The Moon,* Academic Press, 1962; (editor) *Advances in Astronomy and Astrophysics,* nine volumes, Academic Press, 1962-72; (editor) *The Physics and Astronomy of the Moon,* Academic Press, 1962, 2nd edition, 1971; *Radiative Transport of Heat in Lunar and Planetary Interiors,* Geo-Astrophysics Laboratory, Boeing Scientific Research Laboratories, 1964.

(With Josef Klepesta and Thomas W. Rackham) *Photographic Atlas of the Moon,* Academic Press, 1965; *Lunar Coordinates and Their Determination,* Manchester University Press, 1965; *Internal Structure of the Moon,* Mathematics Research Laboratory, Boeing Scientific Research Laboratories, 1965; *An Introduction to the Study of the Moon,* Gordon & Breach, 1966, published as *The Moon,* D. Reidel, 1970; (editor with C. L. Goudas) *Measure of the Moon,* D. Reidel, 1967; *Telescopes in Space,* Faber, 1968, Hart Publishing, 1970; *Exploration of the Moon by Spacecraft,* Oliver & Boyd, 1968; *The Moon: An Outline of Astronomy and Physics of Our Satellite on the Eve of the Apollo Era,* D. Reidel, 1969.

Widening Horizons: Man's Quest to Understand the Structure of the Universe, Kahn & Averill, 1970, Taplinger, 1971; *A New Photographic Atlas of the Moon,* Taplinger, 1971; *The Solar System,* Oxford University Press, 1972; *Man and His Universe,* Morrow, 1972; (editor) *Lunar Geophysics,* D. Reidel, 1972; (editor) *Conference on Lunar Dynamics and Observational Coordinate Systems,* D. Reidel, 1973; *The Moon in the Post-Apollo Era,* D. Reidel, 1974; (with Robert W. Carder) *Mapping of the Moon: Past and Present,* D. Reidel, 1974; *Dynamics of Close Binary Systems,* D. Reidel, 1978; *The Realm of Terrestrial Planets,* Institute of Physics (England), 1978, Halsted, 1979; *Language of the Stars: A Discourse on the Theory of the Light Changes of Eclipsing Variables,* D. Reidel, 1979.

Contributor of more than three hundred articles to scientific journals. Editor-in-chief of *Astrophysics and Space Science,* 1968; founding editor of *Icarus,* 1963, and *Moon,* 1969—.

WORK IN PROGRESS: Life and the Universe; Stability of the Stars.

SIDELIGHTS: Kopal reflected to *CA:* "Being sixty-five years young, I believe my best works are still in the future. But of the past, my greatest day had to have been July 20, 1969, when *Apollo II* landed on the moon. You may have seen me that day on television—not on the moon, to be sure, but on the CBS national network." *Avocational interests:* Mountaineering, music.

*   *   *

KOPLINKA, Charlotte
See LUKAS, Charlotte Koplinka

*   *   *

KORN, Alfons L(udwig) 1906-

PERSONAL: Born March 15, 1906, in Davenport, Iowa; son of Harry Henry (a baker and businessman) and Ernestine (Teegen) Korn; married Laura V. (a professor of English; maiden name, Schwartz), July 31, 1945. *Education:* University of Oregon, B.A., 1927; Christ Church, Oxford, B.A., 1930, M.A., 1968; University of California, Berkeley, M.A., 1936. *Politics:* Democrat. *Agent:* University Press of Hawaii, 2840 Kolowalu St., Honolulu, Hawaii 96822.

CAREER: University of Illinois, Urbana, instructor in English, 1931-32; Historical Records Survey, Portland, Ore., assistant state director, 1937-39; Bonneville Power Administration, Portland, information specialist and writer, 1940-41; University of Hawaii, Honolulu, instructor, 1944-47, assistant professor, 1947-53, associate professor, 1953-58, professor of English, 1958-66, emeritus professor, 1966—. Pacific literature consultant, Hawaii Curriculum Center, English Project, 1967-69; senior specialist in Pacific studies at East-West Center, Honolulu, 1970. *Military service:* U.S. Army, 40th Infantry Division, 1942-44; stationed on islands of Hawaii and Oahu and at Armed Forces Institute. *Member:* Association of American Rhodes Scholars, Hawaiian Historical Society. *Awards, honors:* Rhodes scholarship, 1927-30; fellowship from University of California, 1936; award of merit from American Association for State and Local History, 1959, for *The Victorian Visitors;* Hawaii award for literature from State Council on the Hawaiian Heritage, Hawaii Literary Arts Council, and State Foundation on Culture and the Arts, 1975, for writings on Hawaii.

WRITINGS: The Victorian Visitors: An Account of the Hawaiian Kingdom, Including the Journal Letters of Sophia Cracroft, Extracts From the Journals of Lady Franklin, and Diaries and Letters of Queen Emma of Hawaii, University of Hawaii Press, 1958; (with Mary Kawena Pukui) *The Echo of Our Song: Chants and Poems of the Hawaiians,* University Press of Hawaii, 1973; (editor, and author of introduction and notes) *News From Molokai: Letters Between Peter Kaeo and Queen Emma, 1873-1876,* University Press of Hawaii, 1976; (translator and author of introduction) Charles de Varigny, *Quatorze Ans aux Iles Sandwich* (title means "Fourteen Years in the Sandwich Islands"), University Press of Hawaii, 1980.

Contributor: (Author of introduction) Isabella L. Bird, *Six Months in the Sandwich Islands,* University of Hawaii Press, 1958; H. T. Swedenberg, editor, *Essential Articles for the Study of John Dryden,* Archon Books, 1966; Phyllis Thompson, editor, *Festival: Poems From Hawaii,* Hawaii State Foundation on Culture and the Arts, 1966; Edward T. James, editor, *Notable American Women, 1607-1950: A Biographical Dictionary,* Belknap Press of Harvard University

Press, 1971; (contributor of translations) Ruth Finnegan, editor, *A World Treasury of Oral Poetry,* Indiana University Press, 1978; Frank Stewart and John Unterecker, editors, *Poetry Hawaii: A Contemporary Anthology,* University Press of Hawaii, 1979. Contributor of articles to journals, including *Huntington Library Quarterly, Comparative Literature, Pacific Historical Review, Oceanic Linguistics,* and *Journal of Hawaiian History.*

SIDELIGHTS: Korn told *CA:* "My concentration on Hawaiian studies began only after 1944 and the end of World War II, when I first started teaching courses in literature and composition at the University of Hawaii. My initial, rather random interest in the history of the Hawaiian monarchy soon found a chronological focus in the twenty-year period (c. 1854-74) under Kamehameha IV and Kamehameha V, when British influences in the Hawaiian Kingdom tended to offset, in important political and religious ways, the earlier (1830—), preponderating American and missionary interests in the islands. My two books concerned with this interim period of precarious British ascendance in Hawaii have significant features in common.

"*The Victorian Visitors* and *News From Molokai* are based chiefly on out-of-the-way primary source materials, including journal letters, diaries, and miscellaneous family papers (some of native Hawaiian provenance as well as British) hitherto unknown in Hawaii and not duplicated nor easily accessible elsewhere. In addition to their illuminating historical value, the materials, although non-literary, possess at times a descriptive appeal and spontaneous narrative quality that can hold the interest of the general as well as the specialist reader. Thus, the major section of *The Victorian Visitors,* 'The Island Kingdom,' contains an account of life in Hawaii as viewed, judged, and minutely reported through the eyes of two energetic world travelers. These far from unbiassed witnesses of mid-Victorian Hawaii were Sophia Cracroft, the Lincolnshire-born niece of Admiral Sir John Franklin, and the lost arctic explorer's devoted widow, Jane Franklin, who visited several main islands of the Hawaiian chain in the summer of 1861.

"In thematic pattern and overall point of view, *The Victorian Visitors* can be described as a composite of travel narrative, informal social history, and lively regional anecdote. *News From Molokai: Letters Between Peter Kaeo and Queen Emma* is essentially a biographical study, judiciously sympathetic, of two bilingual Hawaiian *ali'i* (nobles), during a period of political crisis and mounting ethnic and cross-cultural tensions in Hawaii's internal and foreign affairs. An annotated compilation of the correspondence carried on during the early 1870's by the dowager Queen Emma, widow of Kamehameha IV, and her favorite cousin, Peter Young Kaeo, a leper of Kalaupapa, Molokai, the book is built around the 122 letters—and the *mea hou,* 'latest news' (often in the form of startling Honolulu gossip)—exchanged between Peter and the queen during Kaeo's three-year exile at the leprosy settlement. Though not documents of oral history in the modern sense, the Kaeo-Emma letters possess distinctive ethnological, ethnolinguistic, and indeed medical interest, and provide true 'speaking likenesses' of the two authors at a dramatic turning-point in Hawaiian history and their interwoven lives.

"My third book, *The Echo of Our Song,* a collaborative anthology of oral poetry, is for the most part likewise based on hitherto unavailable documents and texts. Translated, edited, and annotated with the help of Mary Kawena Pukui, a leading authority on the Hawaiian people and their ancient language, the anthology contains some thirty chants, dance-

songs, and post-missionary poems, accompanied by their original versions in Hawaiian (the latter printed with their diacritical and phonetic markings). The time span of the selections, many of which are especially illustrative of the impact of Western influences upon the older unwritten Hawaiian poetic tradition, is generous. It ranges from the late eighteenth century and the discovery of the archipelago by Captain Cook to the downfall of the Hawaiian throne under Queen Liliuokalani and on into the political aftermath, when the century-old kingdom of the Kamehameha and Kalakaua dynasties became an overseas territory of the United States."

BIOGRAPHICAL/CRITICAL SOURCES: New Mexico Quarterly, Volume 29, 1959; *Journal de la Societe des Oceanistes,* Volume 15, 1959, Volume 19, 1963, Volume 30, 1977; *Pacific Historical Review,* August, 1959; *Times Literary Supplement,* September 18, 1959; *Revue d'Histoire Moderne et Contemporaine,* January, 1960, May, 1960; *Journal of Pacific History,* Volume 5, 1970, Volume 14, 1979; *Books Abroad,* summer, 1974; *Journal of the Polynesian Society,* September, 1975; A. Grove Day, *Books About Hawaii: Fifty Basic Authors,* University Press of Hawaii, 1977; *Book Exchange* (London), April, 1977; *Brigham Young University Studies,* Spring, 1977; *Hawaii Observer,* June 2, 1977.

*   *   *

KOTOWSKA, Monika 1942-

PERSONAL: Born September 5, 1942, in Cracow, Poland; daughter of Kazimierz (an engineer) and Maria (Hotynska) Kotowska; married Sylvester Porowski (a professor of physics), January 30, 1965. *Education:* Warsaw University, student, 1967—. *Politics:* Independent. *Home:* Rutkowskiego 35m. 182, 00021 Warsaw, Poland.

CAREER: Writer. *Member:* Society of Writers, Authors and Composers Society.

WRITINGS: Most na druga strone, Czytelnik, 1963, translation by Maia Wojciechowska published as *Bridge to the Other Side,* Doubleday, 1970; *Piekna droga* (title means "Beautiful Road"), Czytelnik, 1972; *Kolorowe Lato* (title means "Colored Summer"), Iskry, 1980. Also author of "Straw Moon" (play) and "Beautiful Road" (screenplay).

WORK IN PROGRESS: "Silver and Rain," a novel.

SIDELIGHTS: Monika Kotowska told *CA:* "The principal problem which interests me most in all my works consists of searching for and finding the poetry in life and in the world."

AVOCATIONAL INTERESTS: Travel, theatre, music, movies.

*   *   *

KRANZLER, David 1930-

PERSONAL: Born May 19, 1930, in Wurzburg, Germany (now West Germany); son of Meier Leib and Hannah (Adler) Kranzler; married Judy Bein (a teacher), April 24, 1957; children: Moshe, Shani, Yaakov Meir. *Education:* Brooklyn College (now of the City University of New York), B.A., 1953, M.A., 1958; Columbia University, M.L.S., 1957; Yeshiva University, Ph.D., 1971. *Politics:* Independent. *Religion:* Jewish. *Home:* 729 Avenue N, Brooklyn, N.Y. 11230. *Office:* Library, Queensborough Community College of the City University of New York, Bayside, N.Y. 11364.

CAREER: Junior high school library teacher in Brooklyn, N.Y., 1956-66; high school librarian in Brooklyn, 1966-69;

Queensborough Community College of the City University of New York, Bayside, N.Y., professor of library science, 1969—, chief of library's Social Science Division. *Member:* Association of Orthodox Jewish Teachers (founding member; vice-president, 1961-64), Association of Orthodox Jewish University Faculty (founder; president, 1971-75), Association of Jewish Studies, Association of Jewish Libraries, Association for the Sociological Study of Jewry, Jewish Genealogical Society, Jewish Social Studies Association, New York Jewish Historical Society, Library Association of New York, Library Association of the City University of New York.

WRITINGS: Japanese, Nazis, and Jews: The Jewish Refugee Community of Shanghai, 1938-1945, Yeshiva University Press, 1976; (with Samuel Gross) *My Jewish Roots: A How-to Guide to Jewish Genealogy and Family History,* Hermon, 1978; (contributor) *Contemporary Iraqi Jewry,* Hebrew University, 1980. Also co-editor of *Contemporary Issues in Light of Jewish Tradition,* ten volumes, 1979. Contributor to Jewish studies and Asian studies journals, and *Forum.* Founder of *Orthodox Jewish Archives,* 1978. Member of editorial board of *Jewish Life,* 1977—.

WORK IN PROGRESS: Relief and Rescue Attempts During the Holocaust; Spiritual Resistance: Personal Vignettes; Chiang, Mao, and Moishe: The Decline of the Jewish Community of Shanghai, 1945-1960; A Millenia of Jewish Life in China; The Sephardim of the Far East.

SIDELIGHTS: Kranzler wrote: "My research and writings reflect my background, training, and interests. These include a deep commitment to Torah-true Judaism, general history, especially of the Far East, and its relation to Jewish history, an abiding concern for the understanding of anti-semitism, the Holocaust and its aftermath, and a personal enthusiasm for Jewish genealogy, family history, and Jewish migrations."

AVOCATIONAL INTERESTS: Photography, Hebrew and English calligraphy.

BIOGRAPHICAL/CRITICAL SOURCES: American Libraries, February, 1977; *Newsletter* of National Foundation for Jewish Culture, autumn, 1978.

*   *   *

KRASNE, Betty
See LEVINE, Betty K(rasne)

*   *   *

KROMER, Helen

PERSONAL: Born in Columbus, Ohio; daughter of Edward (an architect and engineer) and Mary (Creamer) Kromer; divorced. *Education:* Ohio State University, B.A.; also attended American Academy of Dramatic Art and Columbia University. *Home:* 173 West 78th St., New York, N.Y. 10024. *Agent:* McIntosh & Otis, Inc., 475 Fifth Ave., New York, N.Y. 10017.

CAREER: Free-lance writer. Worked as instructor at Rutgers University; public relations representative and public speaker; conducts writing workshops. *Awards, honors:* Golden Reel Award from American Film Festival, 1956, and George Washington Honor Medal from Freedoms Foundation, 1957, both for film, "Broken Mask"; blue ribbon from American Film Festival, 1956, for script of filmstrip "Matter of Fact," 1959, for filmstrip series "Ways Youth Learn," and 1964, for filmstrip "Face to Face"; Danforth grant, 1960; honorary doctor of humanities from Christian Theolog-

ical Seminary, Indianapolis, Ind., 1967; Popular Panel awards from American Society of Composers, Authors, and Publishers, 1963-71, for "For Heaven's Sake!"

WRITINGS: Communes and Communitarians in America, Grossman, 1972; *The Amistad Revolt, 1839: The Slave Uprising Aboard the Spanish Schooner* (juvenile), F. Watts, 1973.

Plays: *Caught Between* (one-act), Friendship Press, 1955; *Stolen Goods* (one-act), Friendship Press, 1956; *Under One Roof* (one-act), Friendship Press, 1958; *Acres to Cross* (one-act), Friendship Press, 1959; *Verdict of One* (one-act; first produced in Oberlin, Ohio, at Oberlin College), Baker's Plays, 1963; *For Heaven's Sake!* (first produced in Ann Arbor, Mich.), Baker's Plays, 1963; *Hannah: A Parable in Music* (first produced in Columbus, Ohio, at Veteran's Memorial, 1965), Baker's Plays, 1965; "Sure As You're Born," first produced in Indianapolis, Ind., 1967. Also author of "They Made a Path" (one-act); "Take Any Street" (one-act); "No Hiding Place," first produced in Lafayette, Ind., at Purdue University; and "Like It Is," first produced in St. Louis, Mo.

Scripts: "Presbyterian Panorama," first produced in New York City at Madison Square Garden, 1954; "Festival of Faith," first produced in Chicago, Ill., at Soldier Field, 1954; "This City Under God," first produced in Brooklyn, N.Y., at Brooklyn Academy of Music, 1955; "God's Man Alone," first produced in Hollywood, Calif., at Hollywood Bowl, 1956 (adapted for NBC-TV as "That Unpleasant Protestant"); "Measure of a Moment," first produced in Omaha, Neb., at Omaha Arena, 1957; "The Visited Planet," first produced in Pittsburgh, Pa., at Pitt Stadium, 1958.

Feature writer for United Methodist Church.

WORK IN PROGRESS: Lyrics for a musical play about Diego Velazquez and his servant, Juan de Pareja.

SIDELIGHTS: Helen Kromer commented that her assignments have taken her to cities and towns in over forty states to research films and articles, to serve as public relations representative or reporter at conventions, to manage dramatic productions, and to give talks or teach in summer conferences or writing workshops. She has been on location for documentary film production at the Navajo and Pima Indiana reservations, the Protestant missions of pre-revolutionary Cuba, and the Spanish-American towns of New Mexico. Feature writing assignments have taken her to Panama, Nicaragua, Belize, and most recently from Lebanon to Laos, from Pakistan to Taiwan and to seven other countries in Asia.

BIOGRAPHICAL/CRITICAL SOURCES: Christian Century, August 25, 1954, October 4, 1961, June 28, 1967; *Christian Science Monitor,* August 16, 1954; *Chicago Sun-Times,* August 16, 1954; *New York Herald Tribune,* August 16, 1954; *Newsweek,* September 4, 1961; *Saturday Evening Post,* September 22, 1962; *Intelligencer Journal,* April 20, 1966.

*   *   *

KUHN, Edward, Jr.   1924(?)-1979

OBITUARY NOTICE: Born c. 1924 in Cincinnati, Ohio; died December 20, 1979, in Mount Kisco, N.Y. Editor, publishing executive, and novelist. Kuhn was an editor for the McGraw-Hill Book Co. from 1947 to 1965, where he edited the memoirs of Herbert Hoover, Harry S Truman, General Douglas MacArthur, and other works of nonfiction. He later worked as executive vice-president of New American Library and as editorial director of Playboy Press and the Playboy Book Club. Kuhn wrote two novels, *The American Princess* and *Ski Week*. Obituaries and other sources: *New York Times,* December 22, 1979; *Publishers Weekly,* January 11, 1980; *AB Bookman's Weekly,* January 14, 1980.

*   *   *

KUHNE, Cecil   1952-

PERSONAL: Born May 26, 1952, in Louisville, Miss.; son of Cecil C., Jr. (an attorney) and Emma Lou (a teacher; maiden name, Miller) Kuhne. *Education:* Texas Christian University, B.A., 1973; Texas Tech University, J.D., 1976, M.A., 1978. *Home:* 3304 56th St., Lubbock, Tex. 79413.

CAREER: Attorney in Lubbock, Tex., 1977—. Consultant with Pacific Northwest Natural Resource Consultants, 1978—. *Awards, honors:* Award from American Trial Lawyers Association environmental law essay contest, 1976, for "Cost-Benefit Analysis in the Development of Water Resources"; agricultural law essay award from Kasmir, Willingham & Krage, 1976, for "Clearcutting as Management Policy of National Forest Lands."

WRITINGS: River Rafting, World Publications, 1979; *Advanced River Rafting,* World Publications, 1980; *Rafting the Wild Rivers,* World Publications, in press. Contributing editor of *River World.*

SIDELIGHTS: Kuhne wrote: "So far most of my work has dealt with the technical aspects of the sport of river rafting, but I would like to publish photo-essay journals of actual rafting trips in the future."

BIOGRAPHICAL/CRITICAL SOURCES: River World, October, 1978.

*   *   *

KULLMAN, Harry   1919-

PERSONAL: Born February 22, 1919, in Malmo, Sweden; son of Emil (a factory foreman) and Olga (Gustafsson) Kullman; married Lilian Svenningson, September 10, 1949. *Education:* University of Stockholm, M.A., 1944. *Home:* 152 Hornsgatan, Stockholm, Sweden.

CAREER: Advertising copywriter, 1946-51; Sven Rygaards Advertising Agency, advertising consultant, 1951-65; freelance writer, 1965—. *Member:* International Board on Books for Young People (vice-president of Swedish section, 1969-79), International P.E.N., Swedish Society of Authors, Society of Authors (England). *Awards, honors:* Nils Holgerson Plaque from Swedish Library Association, 1955, for *Hemlig Resa;* award for best children's book of the year, 1968; Astrid Lindgren Prize from Raben & Sjoegren Bokfoerlag, 1970, for collected works.

WRITINGS—Juvenile: *Med hemlig order,* [Sweden], 1948, translation by L. W. Kingsland published as *Under Secret Order,* Harcourt, 1968; *Hemlig Resa,* [Sweden], 1953, translation by Evelyn Ramsvew published as *The Secret Journey,* University of London Press, 1959; *Ponyexpressen,* Raben & Sjoegren, 1955, revised edition, 1973, translation by Ramsvew published as *Pony Express,* University of London Press, 1965; *Rymlingen,* Raben & Sjoegren, 1957, translation by Ramsvew published as *Runaway,* Methuen, 1961.

In Swedish; all juvenile; all published by Raben & Sjoegren, except as indicated: *Den svarta flaecken* (title means "The Black Spot"), 1949; *Den tomma staden* (title means "The Empty City"), 1951, reprinted, 1979; *Den spanska vaerjan* (title means "The Spanish Sword"), 1952; *Buffalo Bill,* 1953;

Leve konungen (title means "Long Live the King"), 1956; *Paa jakt efter vilda vaestern* (title means "Looking for the Old West"), 1958; *Spejarna* (title means "The Scouts"), 1958; *Gaardarnas krig* (title means "War of the Backyards"), 1959.

Beundraren: Roman (title means "The Beaux"), 1961; *Natthaemtaren: Roman* (title means "The Nightman"), 1962; *Mannen fraan moerkrummet* (title means "The Man From the Darkroom"), 1963; *Boskapstjuvarna* (title means "The Rustlers"), 1965; *Moete med aeventyret: En samlingsvolym, innehaallande—Hemlig resa—Rymlingen* (title means "A for Adventure"), 1965; *De roedas uppror* (title means "Red Uprising"), 1968; *Mannen fraan Montana* (title means "The Mountain"), 1970; *Faangarna paa Fattigmannagatan* (title means "The Prisoners of Poor Man's Street"), 1972; *Den Amerikanske faarngen* (title means "The American Prisoner"), 1975; *Stridshaesten* (title means "The War Horse"), 1977; *Slagskampen* (thriller for adults; title means "The Fighter"), 1980.

Contributor to Swedish magazines.

WORK IN PROGRESS: The Body-Guard; a second thriller.

SIDELIGHTS: Kullman writes: "My books for young people have been translated into thirteen languages. I have also written two novels and nonfiction on the West. I have traveled extensively in the United States, and have written five books on the American West of yesterday and today." *Avocational interests:* Classical music, science fiction, tennis, movies.

*   *   *

KUNHARDT, Dorothy Meserve   1901(?)-1979

OBITUARY NOTICE: Born c. 1901; died December 23, 1979, in Beverly, Mass. Author and illustrator. Kunhardt was the author and illustrator of numerous children's books, including *Pat the Bunny,* first published in 1940 and still listed as a bestseller on the list of children's classics. She also collaborated with her son, Philip B. Kunhardt, Jr., on *Twenty Days,* a book about the period of national mourning that followed President Abraham Lincoln's assassination, and *Matthew Brady and His World.* Her other books included the popular "tiny" series— *Tiny Animal Stories* and *Tiny Nonsense Stories*—and such juveniles as *The Telephone Book, Junket Is Nice, Lucky Mrs. Ticklefeather,* and *Feed the Animals.* Obituaries and other sources: *New York Times,* December 25, 1979; *Publishers Weekly,* January 18, 1980.

*   *   *

KUNIHOLM, Bruce Robellet   1942-

PERSONAL: Born October 4, 1942, in Washington, D.C.; son of Bertel E. (a diplomat) and Berthe E. (a government employee; maiden name, Robellet) Kuniholm; married Elizabeth Fairbank (a lawyer), June 29, 1968; children: Jonathan Fairbank, Erin Fairbank. *Education:* Dartmouth College, B.A., 1964; Duke University, M.A., 1972, M.A.P.P.S. and Ph.D., both 1976. *Residence:* Durham, N.C. *Office:* Institute of Policy Sciences and Public Affairs, Duke University, 4875 Duke Station, Durham, N.C. 27706.

CAREER: Robert College, Istanbul, Turkey, instructor in English at Robert Academy, 1964-67; Duke University, Durham, N.C., lecturer, 1975-77, assistant professor of policy sciences and history and director of undergraduate studies, both 1977—. U.S. Department of State's Bureau of Intelligence and Research, political analyst for Arabian

Peninsula and Persian Gulf, 1979, member of policy planning staff, 1979—. *Military service:* U.S. Marine Corps, 1967-71; became captain; received Bronze Star with "V" and Navy Achievement medal. *Member:* American Historical Association, Organization of American Historians, Society for Historians of American Foreign Relations, Middle East Institute, Council on Foreign Relations, Phi Beta Kappa. *Awards, honors:* International Affairs fellow of Council on Foreign Relations, National Endowment for the Humanities, 1978-79.

WRITINGS: The Origins of the Cold War in the Near East: Great Power Conflict and Diplomacy in Iran, Turkey, and Greece, Princeton University Press, 1980.

WORK IN PROGRESS: A book on the meaning of American involvement in Vietnam; research on the current Palestine problem and its historical background.

* * *

KUNIN, Madeleine May 1933-

PERSONAL: Born September 28, 1933, in Zurich, Switzerland; daughter of Ferdinand and Renee (Bloch) May; married Arthur S. Kunin (a physician), 1959; children: Peter, Julia, Adam, Daniel. *Education:* University of Massachusetts, B.A., 1956; Columbia University, M.S., 1957; University of Vermont, M.A., 1967. *Religion:* Jewish. *Home:* 122 Dunder Rd., Burlington, Vt. 05401.

CAREER: Burlington Free Press, Burlington, Vt., reporter, 1957-58; Trinity College, Burlington, instructor in English, 1971-72; Vermont House of Representatives, Montpelier, Democratic representative, 1973-78; State of Vermont, Montpelier, lieutenant-governor, 1978—. Member of governor's Commission on the Status of Women, 1966-68.

WRITINGS: (With Marilyn Stout) *The Big Green Book: A Four-Season Guide to Vermont,* Crown, 1976. Contributor to magazines, including *Vermont Life.*

* * *

KUNZE, Reiner 1933-

PERSONAL: Born August 16, 1933, in Oelsnitz im Erzgebirge, East Germany; son of Ernst (a miner) and Martha (Friedrich) Kunze; married Elizabeth Mifka; children: Marcela, Ludwig. *Education:* University of Leipzig, diploma, 1955. *Home:* am Sonnenhang 8, D-8391 Obernzell 1-Erlau, Hungary.

CAREER: Poet, novelist, script writer, and translator. Worked as locksmith. *Member:* Deutschen Akademie fuer Sprache und Dichtung (Darmstadt section), Akademie der Kuenste (Bavarian and West German sections). *Awards, honors:* Translator prize from Czechoslovakian literary society, 1968; German book prize for children's literature, 1971; literature prize from Akademie der Kuenste, Bavaria, 1973; Molle literature prize, Sweden, 1973; Goerg Trakl Prize, Austria, 1977; Andreas Gryphius Prize, 1977; Georg Buechner Prize, 1977, for *The Wonderful Years;* Bavarian film prize, 1979.

WRITINGS—In English: *Zimmerlautstaerke* (poems), S. Fischer, 1972, translation by Ewald Osers published as *With the Volume Turned Down, and Other Poems,* London Magazine Editions, 1973; *Die wunderbaren Jahre* (novel), S. Fischer, 1976, translation by Joachim Neugroschel published as *The Wonderful Years,* G. Braziller, 1977 (translation by Osers published in England as *The Lovely Years,* Sidgewick & Jackson, 1979), adaptation of original novel as screenplay published as *Die wunderbaren Yahre* (released by United Artists, 1980), S. Fischer, 1979.

Other: *Voegel ueber dem Tau* (poems; title means "Birds on the Dew"), Mitteldeutscher Verlag, 1959; *Aber der Nachtigall jubelt* (poems; title means "But the Nightingale is Rejoicing"), Mitteldeutscher Verlag, 1962; *Widmungen* (poems; title means "Dedications"), Hohwacht-Verlag, 1963; *Reiner Kunze* (poems), Verlag Neues Leben, 1968; *Sensible Wege* (poems; title means "Sensitive Ways"), Rowohlt, 1969; *Der Loewe Leopold* (stories; title means "Lion Leopold"), S. Fischer, 1970; *Der Dichter und die Loewenzahnweise* (title means "The Poet and the Dandelion Meadow"), Berliner Handpresse, 1971; *Brief mit blauem Siegel* (poems; title means "Letter with a Blue Seal"), Reclam Verlag, 1973; *Das Kaetschen* (poems; title means "The Kitten"), S. Fischer, 1979.

WORK IN PROGRESS: A book of poems.

SIDELIGHTS: Compared to Reiner Kunze, "Hemingway was a chatterbox," wrote John Leonard in the *New York Times,* for Kunze's prose is minimalist, "nothing flashy, no rhetorical fatty tissue, just bone words." Similarly, in a review for *Books Abroad,* Diether H. Haenicke described the style of Kunze's poetry as "laconic, terse and concise," while Alexandra Johnson said in the *Christian Science Monitor* that his short stories were "etched with such fine, understated realism that one believes it all."

The appearance of *The Wonderful Years* was a political as well as a literary event. *New York Times Book Review* critic Martin Greenberg called the book "an act of heroism" and compared its author's courage to that of Boris Pasternak and Alexander Solzhenitsyn. When the volume was first published in West Germany, Kunze, who now lives in exile, expected to be arrested; instead, the East German regime expelled him from the writer's union and impounded his passport. Yet his earlier work had been equally controversial, for as Haenicke said: "Kunze's poems, with very few exceptions, all reflect in one way or another the political conditions in his country: intimidation through government officials, the monotony of the party celebrations, travel restrictions imposed on the citizenry by the government, the iron curtain and so on."

Heinrich Boll called *The Wonderful Years* "The first that weeps." Its vignettes describe life in East Germany, the repression by the government as well as the solidarity of the people. Indeed, Roger Garfitt called Kunze "one of the wittiest critics of repressive aspects of the East German regime."

BIOGRAPHICAL/CRITICAL SOURCES: Books Abroad, winter, 1971, winter, 1974; *Times Literary Supplement,* January 12, 1973, August 17, 1973, June 17, 1977; *London Magazine,* June-July, 1974; *New York Times,* November 26, 1976, December 17, 1976, April 21, 1977; *Library Journal,* April 15, 1977; *New York Times Book Review,* April 24, 1977; *Christian Science Monitor,* May 4, 1977; *Saturday Review,* May 28, 1977; *New Yorker,* September 26, 1977; *Contemporary Literary Criticism,* Volume 10, Gale, 1979.

* * *

KURTZ, Donna Carol 1943-

PERSONAL: Born December 6, 1943, in Cincinnati, Ohio; daughter of Louis Daniel and Carolyn Kurtz. *Education:* University of Cincinnati, B.A., 1964; Yale University, M.A., 1965; Oxford University, D.Phil., 1968. *Religion:* Presbyterian. *Home:* 2805 Harrison Ave., Cincinnati, Ohio; Wolfson, Oxford, England. *Office:* Ashmolean Museum, Oxford, England.

CAREER: Oxford University, Oxford, England, Beazley archivist and lecturer in classical archaeology; fellow of Wolfson College.

WRITINGS: (With John Boardman) *Greek Burial Customs,* Thames & Hudson, 1971; *Athenian White Leicythoi,* Clarendon Press, 1975.

WORK IN PROGRESS: The Berlin Painter, to be published by Clarendon Press.

* * *

KWANTEN, Luc 1944-

PERSONAL: Born January 8, 1944, in Brussels, Belgium; married Susan Hesse (a librarian); children: Alexandre, Pascal. *Education:* University of Ghent, B.A., 1965; University of Louvain, M.A., 1968; University of South Carolina, Ph.D., 1972. *Home:* 330 West Diversey Parkway, Chicago, Ill. 60657. *Office:* Far Eastern Library, University of Chicago, Chicago, Ill. 60637.

CAREER: Ramapo College of New Jersey, Mahwah, assistant professor of Chinese history, 1972-74; Indiana University, Bloomington, associate professor of Chinese history, 1974-78; University of Chicago, Chicago, Ill., associate professor of Chinese history and curator of Far Eastern Library, 1978—. *Military service:* Belgian Army Reserve; became captain. *Member:* Association for Asian Studies, American Oriental Society, American Historical Association, Committee on East Asian Libraries.

WRITINGS: Imperial Nomads: A History of Central Asia, 500-1500, University of Pennsylvania Press, 1979.

L

LANDERS, Gunnard W(illiam) 1944-

PERSONAL: Born November 12, 1944, in Tomahawk, Wis.; son of Gunnard E. (a guide) and Louise (Yunker) Landers; married Kathleen M. Harings (a riding instructor and horse trainer), 1972. *Education:* University of Wisconsin—Madison, B.B.A., 1967. *Politics:* Independent. *Religion:* None. *Residence:* Fall Creek, Wis. *Agent:* Jane Rotrosen Agency, 318 East 51st St., New York, N.Y. 10022.

CAREER: Writer, 1970—. Also worked as butcher, bank examiner, and construction worker. *Military service:* U.S. Army, rifle platoon leader and airborne pathfinder platoon leader, 1967-69; served in Vietnam; became first lieutenant.

WRITINGS: The Hunting Shack (novel), Arbor House, 1979; *Rite of Passage* (novel), Arbor House, 1980.

SIDELIGHTS: Landers writes: "People have bodies and minds—I believe in using both. With good characterization and good plotting you can't miss. Through writing I hope to have an influence on our evolving culture."

* * *

LANE, James B(uchanan) 1942-

PERSONAL: Born February 24, 1942, in Easton, Pa.; son of Victor Cowan and Mary Virginia Lane; married Antoinette Trojecka (an artist), January 16, 1965; children: Philip Anthony, David Victor. *Education:* Bucknell University, B.A., 1964; University of Hawaii, M.A., 1966; University of Maryland, Ph.D., 1970. *Office:* Department of History, Indiana University—Northwest, 3400 Broadway, Gary, Ind. 46408.

CAREER: Indiana University—Northwest, Gary, assistant professor, 1970-76, associate professor of history, 1976—. Co-director of Calumet Regional Archives. *Awards, honors:* Charles M. Gates Memorial Award from *Pacific Northwest Quarterly*, 1971, for "Joseph B. Poindexter and Hawaii During the New Deal."

WRITINGS: (Editor with David Goldfield) *The Enduring Ghetto*, Lippincott, 1972; *Jacob A. Riis and the American City*, Kennikat, 1974; *City of the Century: A History of Gary, Indiana*, Indiana University Press, 1978. Contributor to history journals and *Gary Post-Tribune*. Editor of *Steel Shavings*.

WORK IN PROGRESS: Editing a book of readings on urban history, publication expected in 1985.

SIDELIGHTS: Lane comments: "I am interested in local history and the writing of family history. In my book, *City of the Century*, I have tried to write history in a style that can be appreciated by the residents of Gary as well as by the academic community. In fact, I have written approximately two hundred fifty articles concerning local history for the *Gary Post-Tribune* and have profited from the critical reaction to them."

* * *

LANGTON, Daniel J(oseph) 1927-

PERSONAL: Born September 6, 1927, in Paterson, N.J.; son of Daniel P. (a poet) and Martha Langton; married Eva Heymann (a counselor), February 1, 1949; children: Mark. *Education:* San Francisco State College (now University), B.A., 1952, M.A., 1954; attended University of Aix-Marseilles, 1961-63; University of California, Berkeley, Ph.D., 1970. *Home:* 1673 Oak St., San Francisco, Calif. 94117. *Agent:* James Oliver Brown, James Brown Associates, Inc., 22 East 60th St., New York, N.Y. 10022. *Office:* Department of English, San Francisco State University, San Francisco, Calif. 94132.

CAREER: Metropolitan Life Insurance Co., San Francisco, Calif., assistant auditor, 1955-61; foreign correspondent in Europe, 1961-63; high school teacher of English in San Rafael, Calif., 1963-67; San Francisco State University, San Francisco, Calif., lecturer, 1967-69, assistant professor, 1969-72, associate professor, 1972-77, professor of English and creative writing, 1979—. *Military service:* U.S. Army Air Forces, 1945-47. *Member:* Academy of American Poets (associate), American Civil Liberties Union, American Association of University Professors. *Awards, honors:* Browning Society Prize from Browning Society, 1970, for "The Three Visits"; Hart Crane Memorial Award from Hart Crane Memorial Fund, 1971, for poem in *Saturday Review*; Devins Award from University of Missouri, 1976, for *Querencia*; London Prize from London Press Ltd., 1976, for "Waking in Winter."

WRITINGS: Querencia (poems), University of Missouri Press, 1976; *The Inheritance: A Poem for the Stage*, Julian Press, 1977. Contributor of more than a hundred articles and reviews and about two hundred fifty poems to magazines.

WORK IN PROGRESS: Another book of poems; research on preliterate poetry.

SIDELIGHTS: Langton writes: "My first enthusiasm was

Yeats, my first master Williams, my second master Wilbur. None of this was clear to me when it was happening. I liked Yeats because my father was Irish, Williams because I was born in Paterson, and Wilbur because I met him. But they now seem to sum up the forces I was trying to cope with.

"My first poems were earnest and philosophical, and my idea of technique was to judiciously employ the semi-colon. I was pretty good, but I saw no way to get better. Yeats's lines, 'Irish poets, learn your trade / Sing whatever is well made,' haunted me, but I wanted to write in the American language, the flow and energy and rhythms are there for me. Williams turned me into a poet by demanding I be one, providentially the poem he dedicated to me was 'Sonnet in Search of an Author.' Wilbur was cool, ice-blue, reserved, fastidious: but he wrote of clotheslines and dead dogs, and that reality called to me. I knew what I wanted from poetry, the tension of molecules in a rock, and he had that. And then there was Williams. Fire and ice.

"There is a French poem that demands that the young poets of France stop writing sonnets. It is a sonnet. Another kind of tension I wanted. I want the test, the stricture, the stolidity of form. I want demands on me, more and more demands all the time. But I want to write in the attractive everyday language I hear all about me. I want to prove if I can, and if I may, that these are not incompatible, that they complement each other, that they contribute.

"That is not *the* way to write poetry. It is just my way."

* * *

La PATRA, Jack W(illiam) 1927-

PERSONAL: Born September 19, 1927, in Watertown, N.Y.; son of Kenneth Roswell (a farmer) and Mildred (Miller) La Patra; married Jesalee Beilby (a teacher), May 22, 1977; children: Scott, William, Ann. *Education:* Clarkson College, B.E.E., 1955; University of Iowa, M.S., 1956, Ph.D., 1963. *Home:* 625 Amberidge Trail, Atlanta, Ga. 30328. *Agent:* Jane Jordan Browne, 410 South Michigan, Chicago, Ill. 60605. *Office:* School of Health Systems, Georgia Institute of Technology, Atlanta, Ga. 30332.

CAREER: Westinghouse, Pittsburgh, Pa., design engineer, 1956-57; University of California, Berkeley, research associate in electrical engineering, 1957-58; Naval Postgraduate School, Monterey, Calif., instructor in electrical engineering, 1958-61; University of the Pacific, Stockton, Calif., assistant professor of electrical engineering, 1961-62; University of California, Davis, associate professor of electrical engineering, 1963-77, and community health, 1970-77; Georgia Institute of Technology, Atlanta, professor of health systems and research associate at Health Systems Research Center, 1977—. Visiting associate professor at University of California, Riverside, 1975-76. *Military service:* U.S. Navy, 1945-46. U.S. Air Force, 1949-53; became first lieutenant. *Member:* Eta Kappa Nu. *Awards, honors:* National Science Foundation grant, 1965-66; fellow of National Aeronautics and Space Administration and American Society for Engineering Education, summers, 1968, 1970; National Institutes of Health fellow, 1969-70.

WRITINGS: Applying the Systems Approach to Urban Development, Dowden, 1973; *Health Care Delivery Systems: Evaluation Criteria,* C. C Thomas, 1975; *Public Welfare Systems,* C. C Thomas, 1975; (with Gabor Temes) *Introduction to Circuit Synthesis and Design,* McGraw, 1977; *Healing: The Coming Revolution in Holistic Medicine,* McGraw, 1978; *Analyzing the Criminal Justice System,* Lexington Books, 1978; (with Walton Dowdle) *Informed Consent: In-*

fluenza Facts and Myths, Nelson-Hall, 1980; *The Age Factor,* M. Evans, 1980. Contributor of more than twenty-five articles to engineering and education journals.

SIDELIGHTS: La Patra writes: "My early professional education was as an electrical engineer. At the outset I focused on systems theory; then there was a steady movement through applied systems analysis to social systems. For the last decade I have been doing research on social problem-solving using the systems approach. My professional expertise is in the areas of systems analysis, modeling, information systems, social problem-solving, public policy and administration, and evaluation. I have worked on urban problems, welfare, crime and have emphasized, in recent years, health."

* * *

LAPEDES, Daniel N. 1913(?)-1979

OBITUARY NOTICE: Born c. 1913; died of a heart attack, December 14, 1979, in Princeton, N.J. Editor, publishing executive, and author. Lapedes was editor-in-chief of McGraw-Hill's encyclopedia division, where he supervised the publication of such reference works as the *McGraw-Hill Encyclopedia of Science and Technology.* In 1979, he became vice-president of Garland STPM Press after a career of twenty-one years at McGraw-Hill. Lapedes wrote *Helpful Microorganisms* in 1968. Obituaries and other sources: *Publishers Weekly,* February 1, 1980.

* * *

LaPOINTE, Frank 1936-

PERSONAL: Born November 1, 1936, in Rosebud, S.D.; son of Elmer C., Sr. (a rancher) and Neva (a clerk; maiden name, Herman) LaPointe; married Elizabeth Randall (an educational coordinator), February 3, 1964; children: Lema, Francis, Shizue, Randall, Thomasine. *Education:* Rockhurst College, B.A., 1958; also attended Black Hills State College. *Politics:* Democrat. *Religion:* Roman Catholic. *Home address:* Spotted Tail Lane, Rosebud, S.D. 57570. *Agent:* Barthold Fles Literary Agency, 507 Fifth Ave., New York, N.Y. 10017. *Office:* Sicangu Oyate Ho, Inc., St. Francis Indian School, St. Francis, S.D. 57572.

CAREER: Custodian and ranch worker, 1954-58; *Rosebud Sioux Herald: Eyapaha,* Rosebud, S.D., reporter and editor, 1963-71; *Littleton Independent and Arapahoe Herald,* Littleton, Colo., intern-reporter, beginning in 1967; Sicangu Oyate Ho, Inc. (Indian-controlled contract school), St. Francis, S.D., executive director, 1971-77, fiscal officer, 1977—. Member of Rosebud Sioux Council; charter member of American Indian Leadership Council. Instructor at Sinte Gleska College. Elected member of Tripp-Todd County Commission (later invalidated by U.S. Commission of Civil Rights). *Military service:* U.S. Navy, journalist, 1959-63. *Member:* American Indian Press Association (charter member). *Awards, honors:* John Hay Whitney fellowship, 1967; named South Dakota Indian Educator of the Year from South Dakota Indian Education Association, 1979.

WRITINGS: The Sioux Today, Macmillan, 1972.

Work represented in anthologies, including an American Indian collection, Blue Cloud Quarterly, 1971. Past editor of *Indian.*

SIDELIGHTS: LaPointe told *CA* his advice for aspiring young writers: "Always look to your own life, times, and locality for your first book. It will be a lot easier."

LARDNER, John (Abbott) 1912-1960

OBITUARY NOTICE: Born May 4, 1912, in Chicago, Ill.; died March 24, 1960. Journalist and author. The son of humorist and short-story writer Ring Lardner, John Lardner began his career as a reporter for the *New York Herald Tribune* in 1931. He was subsequently a sports columnist for the North American Newspaper Alliance, a columnist and correspondent for *Newsweek*, and a critic and reviewer for *New Yorker* magazine. Lardner wrote several books, including *The Crowning of Technocracy, It Beats Working, White Hopes and Other Tigers,* and *Strong Cigars and Lovely Women.* Obituaries and other sources: *Who Was Who in America,* 3rd edition, Marquis, 1960; Roger Kahn, editor, *The World of John Lardner,* Simon & Schuster, 1961.

* * *

LARSEN, Paul E(manuel) 1933-

PERSONAL: Born October 5, 1933, in Minneapolis, Minn.; son of David Paul (a lumber manufacturer) and Myrtle (Grunnet) Larsen; married Elizabeth Helen Taylor (a lecturer), March 19, 1966; children: Kristin Julianne, Kathleen Kerry. *Education:* Stanford University, B.A., 1955; Fuller Theological Seminary, M.Div., 1958; San Francisco Theological Seminary, S.T.D., 1978. *Home:* 803 Shepard Way, Redwood City, Calif. 94062. *Office:* Peninsula Covenant Church, 3560 Farmhill Blvd., Redwood City, Calif. 94061.

CAREER: Ordained minister of the Evangelical Covenant Church of America, 1963; assistant pastor of Covenant church in Eaglerock, Calif., 1958-59, founding pastor in Orangevale, Calif., 1959-63, pastor in Pasadena, Calif., 1963-70; Peninsula Covenant Church, Redwood City, Calif., pastor, 1971—. Member of board of directors of Samarkand of Santa Barbara and Mount Miguel Covenant Village; member of board of trustees of MacLoughlin Trust; member of Covenant Executive Board and Fuller Theological Seminary, Bay Area Extension; chairperson of Hearthstone Manor, 1963. Chairperson of Pasadena Town Hall, 1969; past member of Pasadena human relations committee and founding committee of PRIDE of Pasadena, Inc. *Member:* National Association of Evangelicals (past regional director), National Association for the Advancement of Colored People (past member of local board of directors).

WRITINGS: Wise Up and Live: The Book of Proverbs, Regal Books, 1974. Contributor to *Journal of the American Scientific Affiliation.*

WORK IN PROGRESS: Writing about psychology and religion, worship, preaching, biblical studies, suburban sociology, and training for the lay ministry.

SIDELIGHTS: Larsen wrote: "I prefer to write from the standpoint of the active pastoral perspective. I am interested in a scholarly approach to the contemporary issues of church and society."

* * *

LARSON, Gerald James 1938-

PERSONAL: Born April 24, 1938, in Chicago, Ill.; children: three. *Education:* Blackburn College, A.B., 1960; Union Theological Seminary, New York, N.Y., M.Div., 1963; Columbia University, Ph.D., 1967. *Home:* 550 Sussex Court, Goleta, Calif. 93107. *Office:* Department of Religious Studies, University of California, Santa Barbara, Calif. 93106.

CAREER: University of Tennessee, Knoxville, assistant professor, 1967-69, associate professor of religious studies, 1969-70; University of California, Santa Barbara, associate professor, 1970-72, professor of religious studies, 1972—, head of department, 1971-76. Banaras Hindu University, research scholar, 1968-69, honorary visiting professor, 1976-77; visiting associate professor at Union Theological Seminary, New York, N.Y., summer, 1971.

MEMBER: American Oriental Society (division vice-president, 1973-74), American Academy of Religion, Association for Asian Studies, Society for Asian and Comparative Philosophy (vice-president, 1976-78), Society for the Scientific Study of Religion. *Awards, honors:* Fellow of Society for Religion in Higher Education, 1968-69, for study in Asia; senior fellow at University of Hawaii's East-West Center, summer, 1971; American Institute of Indian Studies grant, summer, 1974, senior fellow, 1976-77; senior fellow of Indo-U.S. Subcommission on Education and Culture, 1976-77, for study in India.

WRITINGS: Classical Samkhya: An Interpretation of Its History and Meaning, Motilal Banarsidass, 1969, 2nd edition, 1979; (editor and contributor) *Myth in Indo-European Antiquity,* University of California Press, 1974; (contributor) B. Smith, editor, *Religion and the Legitimation of Power,* E. J. Brill, 1977.

Editor of "Aids to the Study of Religion" series, American Academy of Religion. Contributor to *World Book Encyclopedia.* Contributor of about thirty articles and reviews to religious, philosophy, and Indian studies journals. Member of editorial board of *Journal of Religious Ethics,* 1973-78, *Dharma,* and *Encyclopedia of Indian Philosophies.*

WORK IN PROGRESS: Editing *Encyclopedia of Indian Philosophies,* Volume III, on Samkhya and Yoga systems; *Consciousness as Freedom: A Cross-Cultural Essay on Samkhya Philosophy,* a monograph.

* * *

LARSSON, Flora (Benwell) 1904-

PERSONAL: Born May 31, 1904, in Buenos Aires, Argentina; daughter of Alfred James (a Salvation Army officer) and Matilda Gustava (a Salvation Army officer; maiden name, Byden) Benwell; married Sture William Larsson, September 11, 1934 (deceased); children: David (deceased), John, Miriam Larsson Frederiksen. *Education:* Attended high school in Newcastle, Liverpool, and Leicester, England. *Politics:* Conservative. *Home:* 72 Hope Park, Bromley, Kent BR1 3RQ, England.

CAREER: Salvation Army, officer, serving in England, France, Sweden, Denmark, Chile, Argentina, Finland, and Norway, 1926-74.

WRITINGS: Just a Moment, Lord, Hodder & Stoughton, 1973, Shaw, 1974; *My Best Men Are Women,* Hodder & Stoughton, 1974; *Between You and Me, Lord,* Hodder & Stoughton, 1975, Shaw, 1976; *Towards You, Lord,* Hodder & Stoughton, 1978, published as *I'm Growing, Lord,* Shaw, 1979.

SIDELIGHTS: Flora Larsson commented: "I have British, Swedish, and Argentine nationality, but reckon myself a Britisher. My late husband, my mother, and my children have Swedish nationality.

"My parents had been missionaries in Argentina, but I left Buenos Aires when only a year old, so my growing-up years were spent in England. After a few years of secretarial work I became a Salvation Army officer, and as such have served in England, France, Chile, Argentina, Denmark, Finland, Sweden, and Norway, finally retiring in London.

"For many years I wrote articles and brief biographies. It is only now 'in old age' that I have published books."

All of Larsson's books have been translated into Swedish, Finnish, German, Dutch, and Norwegian.

* * *

LAUCK, Carol 1934-

PERSONAL: Born May 5, 1934, in Philadelphia, Pa.; daughter of Howard C. (a banker) and Florence (a bookkeeper; maiden name, Monroe) Strong; married Donald G. Lauck, Jr. (a marketing executive), June 18, 1955; children: Nancy Carolyn, Kay Elizabeth. *Education:* Pennsylvania State University, B.S., 1955. *Home:* 1406 Pueblo Dr., Mount Lebanon, Pa. 15228.

CAREER: Elementary school teacher in Ardmore, Pa., 1955, Warwick, Va., 1955-57, Castle Shannon, Pa., 1957-58, and Summit, N.J., 1962-63; Junior League of Pittsburgh, Pittsburgh, Pa., vice-president, c. 1963-72; Little Lake Theatre, Canonsburg, Pa., director of Children's Theatre, 1972—, member of board of directors, 1979—. Actress in television commercials, films, and summer stock productions in Pittsburgh, 1967—; coordinator of First Stage: Performing Arts for Children, 1975-77; industrial films casting consultant, 1979—; member of Pittsburgh Public Theatre Advisory Council. Affiliated with Girl Scouts of America, c. 1963-72. *Awards, honors:* Cultural Service to Youth Award from Pittsburgh Young Men's Christian Association, 1976.

WRITINGS—For children: *Marmalade Gumdrops* (two-act play; first produced in Canonsburg, Pa., at Little Lake Theatre, June 27, 1973), Samuel French, 1974; *Heads and Tales* (one-act play; first produced in Canonsburg at Little Lake Theatre, July 19, 1978), Samuel French, 1978.

Unpublished plays: "Loudmouse" (musical; two act; adapted from book of the same name by Richard Wilbur), first produced in Canonsburg, Pa., at Little Lake Theatre, June 26, 1974; "Reflections and Refractions" (one-act), first produced in Mt. Lebanon, Pa., at Sunset Hills United Presbyterian Church, May 4, 1975.

WORK IN PROGRESS: "Cleo's Cafe," a play for children.

SIDELIGHTS: Carol Lauck commented to *CA:* "I could say that I always wanted to be a writer, but it wouldn't be true. Even though I edited high school and college newspapers, what I truly wanted was a career in theatre. The writing came after I achieved my first desire. As a director of theatre for children, I sought scripts with more to offer than a tale of a poor orphan child who had been stolen by bad fairies. The selection at that time was poor, so I wrote my own. It's become a habit.

"Directing my own plays has its advantages; I can see what works and not worry about offending the playwright by suggesting cuts or changes. Above all, I am assured that the script, at least for the first production, is interpreted exactly as intended. My message to young audiences is that they keep alive the gift of imagination. As stated in my first play, 'Marmalade Gumdrops,' 'Imagination is like a marmalade gumdrop; once you've tasted it, you'll never settle for just plain.'"

BIOGRAPHICAL/CRITICAL SOURCES: Pittsburgh Press, March 2, 1978, April 27, 1978.

* * *

LAUDER, Phyllis 1898-

PERSONAL: Born June 16, 1898, in London, England; daughter of Alfred Lynn (a solicitor) and Edith (Carty) Thompson; married Harold Victor Lauder (a physician), October 3, 1925; children: Iris, James. *Education:* Attended schools in Tunbridge Wells, England. *Politics:* "Tory." *Religion:* Church of England. *Home:* Mulberry Cottage, Exlade St., Woodcote, Reading, England.

CAREER: Writer, 1950—. *Member:* Siamese Cat Association, Colourpoint, Rex, Any Other Variety Club, Burmese Cat Club.

WRITINGS: Siamese Cats, Benn, 1950, 3rd edition, 1953; *New Siamese Cats,* Benn, 1953; *The Siamese Cat,* Batsford, 1971, 2nd edition, 1978; *The Batsford Book of the Siamese Cat,* Batsford, 1974; *The Rex Cat,* David & Charles, 1978; *Burmese Cats,* T.F.H. Publications, 1980. Editor of *Reading Conservative Journal,* 1943-60.

SIDELIGHTS: Phyllis Lauder commented: "I judge cats in Europe and am bilingual in English and French. In 1977, I judged on tour in Australia and New Zealand. For me, writing is recreation—fairy tales, poetry, anything at all—I just like writing for its own sake. My husband, for recreation, wrote adventure stories, some of which were published. His agent, a very nice woman, once asked me if I could write a book about Siamese cats for a little firm called Williams & Norgate, later acquired by Ernest Benn. I have been writing about cats ever since. My favorite authors are Sir Julian Huxley, Jacob Bronowski, and D.A.G. Searles, but I dearly love a whodunnit!"

* * *

LAUDICINA, Paul A(ndrew) 1949-

PERSONAL: Born August 9, 1949, in Brooklyn, N.Y.; son of Thomas P. (a machinist) and Catherine (Caroniti) Laudicina; married Susan Sammartano (a health budget analyst), June 17, 1973. *Education:* Attended Maryknoll College, 1966-68; University of Chicago, B.A., 1970. *Politics:* Democrat. *Religion:* Roman Catholic. *Home:* 4231 47th St. N.W., Washington, D.C. 20016. *Office:* U.S. Senate, 431 Russell Bldg., Washington, D.C. 20510.

CAREER: United Nations Center for Economic and Social Information, New York City, political and economic researcher in Latin America, 1970; Overseas Development Council, Washington, D.C., associate fellow in public affairs, 1971-74; Mobil Oil Corp., New York City, foreign affairs analyst in planning department and senior staff adviser, 1974-77; U.S. Senate, Washington, D.C., legislative director and chief adviser on national and international energy policy issues for Senator Joseph R. Biden, Jr., 1977—. Vice-president and member of executive committee of Coordination in Development, Inc.; corporate member of U.S. Committee for UNICEF.

WRITINGS: World Poverty and Development: A Survey of American Public Opinion, Praeger, 1974. Contributor to magazines.

SIDELIGHTS: Laudicina's career began with studies of the impact of U.S. foreign investment in selected Latin American countries. After that he conducted economic research in East Africa. He has worked closely with the U.S. Department of State and many non-governmental and international organizations concerned with U.S. foreign policy and international energy developments. His current work on national and international policy issues includes analysis of worldwide energy developments, U.S. activities in the area of international exploration and production, U.S. consumption and conservation patterns, policies of the Organization of

Petroleum Exporting Countries (OPEC), and alternate energy supplies. As director of a U.S. senator's legislative staff, Laudicina concerns himself with major current policy issues.

* * *

LAVORI, Nora 1950-

PERSONAL: Born August 11, 1950, in Staten Island, N.Y.; daughter of William P. (a dentist) and Mary (a teacher; maiden name, Agoliati) Lavori; married David B. Sterling (a real estate developer), August 27, 1974. *Education:* Bryn Mawr College, A.B., 1971; Brooklyn Law School, J.D., 1976. *Office:* 1 East 42nd St., Suite 1002, New York, N.Y. 10017.

CAREER: New York City Environmental Protection Administration, New York City, member of general counsel's staff, 1971-73; private practice of law in New York City, 1976-78; principal in real estate development, New York City, 1978—. *Member:* New York County Lawyers Association, Association of the Bar of the City of New York.

WRITINGS: Living Together, Married or Single: Your Legal Rights, Harper, 1976.

* * *

LAWRENCE, Mary Margaret 1920-

PERSONAL: Born September 27, 1920, in Boulder, Colo.; daughter of James Henry (a farmer) and Grace (Bower) Roosa; married Walter David Lawrence (a consulting engineer), July 4, 1941; children: Randy (deceased), Sheri Lawrence Lodge, Kirk, Glen. *Education:* Attended University of Colorado, 1940-41. *Religion:* Christian. *Home and office:* 6423 Princeton Dr., Alexandria, Va. 22307. *Agent:* Steve Roday, Roday Literary Agency, Inc., 663 Fifth Ave., New York, N.Y. 10022.

CAREER: U.S. Information Service, New Delhi, India, contract writer, 1965; *Time,* New York, N.Y., stringer in New Delhi, 1965-66; General Federation of Women's Clubs, Washington, D.C., program coordinator, 1967-68; Office of U.S. Economic Coordinator for Central Treaty Organization, Ankara, Turkey, technical editor, 1969-73; free-lance writer, 1973—. Volunteer listener for Northern Virginia Hotline. *Member:* National Federation of Press Women (Capital Affiliate), Washington Independent Writers. *Awards, honors:* First place award from National Federation of Press Women's communications contest, 1975, for *Seven Thunders.*

WRITINGS: Seven Thunders (novel), Dell, 1974. Editor of twenty-five collections of conference, seminar, and symposium proceedings, all published by Central Treaty Organization (Ankara, Turkey). Contributor of articles, stories, and poems to magazines and newspapers in the United States and abroad, including *Ingenue, Short Story International,* and *Canadian Home Journal.*

WORK IN PROGRESS: By Moon and by Market, a novel; stories and poems.

SIDELIGHTS: Mary Margaret Lawrence wrote: "After spending some years in India, Lebanon, Ceylon, Turkey and Indonesia, I write with the hope that my stories and novels will entertain my readers, and at the same time nudge them toward a deeper understanding of the people who live, love, work and breathe in other houses, other professions, other countries. I believe that there is throughout life a universality in the most basic emotions. Joy and laughter may be shared in a split-second glance, a gesture. The death of a child speaks a common language. Fear recognizes no dialect. Love and friendship grow long deep roots inside skin of any color.

"Now that I have returned to the United States to live, I find that the fullness of my life challenges me. I want to stand in the shoes of many people, watching the world through their eyes. If I succeed, you will meet them in print."

BIOGRAPHICAL/CRITICAL SOURCES: Publishers Weekly, September 23, 1974.

* * *

LEAKEY, Richard E(rskine Frere) 1944-

PERSONAL: Born December 19, 1944, in Nairobi, Kenya; son of Louis Seymour Bazett (a paleontologist) and Mary Douglas (an archaeologist; maiden name, Nicol) Leakey; married Margaret Cropper (divorced, 1970); married Meave Gillian Epps (a zoologist), 1971; children: (first marriage) Anna; (second marriage) Louise, Samira. *Education:* Attended Duke of York School, Nairobi, 1956-59. *Address:* P.O. Box 24926, Nairobi, Kenya. *Office:* National Museums of Kenya, P.O. Box 40658, Nairobi, Kenya.

CAREER: Paleoanthropologist. Conducted safaris in Kenya, 1960-63; leader of expeditions to West Lake Natron, Tanzania, 1963-64, West Lake Baringo, Kenya, 1966, Omo River, Southern Rhodesia, 1967, and East Lake Rudolf (now Lake Turkana), Kenya, 1968; National Museums of Kenya, Nairobi, administrative director, 1968-74, director, 1974—; leader and coordinator of Koobi Fora research project, Lake Turkana, 1969—. Research associate of International Louis Leakey Memorial Institute for African Prehistory. Curle lecturer for Royal Anthropological Institute; lecturer at universities in the United States, England, Sweden, and China. Trustee of East African Wildlife Society, 1972-77, and vice-chairman, 1977; trustee of Foundation for Social Rehabilitation. *Member:* Pan African Association for Prehistoric Studies (secretary), Wildlife Clubs of Kenya (chairman, 1969—), Kenya Exploration Society (chairman, 1969-72), Foundation for Research Into Origin of Man (chairman), Explorers Club, Royal Anthropological Institute (fellow), Sigma Xi. *Awards, honors:* Franklin L. Burr Prize for Science from National Geographic Society, 1965 and 1973.

WRITINGS: (Contributor) S. L. Washburn and P. C. Jay, editors, *Perspectives on Human Evolution,* Holt, 1968; (contributor and editor) *Fossil Vertebrates of Africa,* Academic Press, 1969; *The Fossil Hominids and an Introduction to Their Context, 1968-1974,* Volume 1, Clarendon Press, 1977; (with Roger Lewin) *Origins: What New Discoveries Reveal About the Emergence of Our Species and Its Possible Future,* Dutton, 1977; (with Roger Lewin) *People of the Lake: Mankind and Its Beginnings,* Doubleday, 1978; (editor with Isaac Glynn) *Human Ancestors: Readings from "Scientific American,"* W. H. Freeman, 1979; (editor and author of introduction) Charles Darwin, *The Illustrated Origin of Species,* Hill & Wang, 1979. Also contributor to *General History of Africa,* Volume 1. Contributor to scientific journals.

SIDELIGHTS: Richard Leakey has spent many years puzzling over the mystery of man's origins, but it is Leakey's more immediate ancestry that interests biographers. "If anyone doubts the power of heredity, let him examine the lineage—or the books—of the Leakey family," declared Peter Stoler. Leakey's lineage is an impressive one. His parents, Louis and Mary Leakey, are two of the most famous figures in anthropology. Their excavations at the Olduvai Gorge in Tanzania have been documented in books and on television. Because he accompanied his parents on their expeditions, Leakey learned to identify fossils almost as soon as he could talk. As a boy he helped his father conduct research work. In one notable experiment, the father and son, using animal bones as their only weapons, attacked a pack of hyenas that had surrounded a dead zebra. They managed to snatch some meat from the carcass before the hyenas closed in, a feat that lent credence to Louis Leakey's theory that early man had survived by scavenging.

Although he grew up surrounded by talk about artifacts and bones, Richard Leakey had not intended to pursue the family profession. He dropped out of high school and established a lucrative business as a safari operator. Soon, however, he grew weary of truckling to tourists, and before long he was back in the digs. After finding the lower jaw of an *Australopithecus* (an ape-man who lived 3.5 to 1.5 million years ago) during an expedition at Lake Natron, Leakey became so enthused about anthropology that he resolved to broaden his scientific background. He traveled to England, where after several months of study he was able to pass his college entrance examinations. But Leakey became impatient—and impoverished—before he could enroll at a university. Determined to gain his education in the field and not in the classroom, he returned to Kenya without a college degree.

Leakey's lack of a college degree was not an insurmountable barrier to his getting established as an anthropologist. In 1967 he participated in an international fossil hunting expedition at the Omo River Valley. This experience deepened his conviction that he was capable of directing his own expedition. On the way home, he flew over Lake Turkana (then known as Lake Rudolf). Later Leakey recalled his feelings when he first caught sight of the lake's eastern shore: "Looking down at the harsh-sun-baked patchwork of that virtually unknown volcanic terrain, with its eroded sediment layers, I felt certain that I was looking at a great anthropological adventure and a major challenge." Shortly afterwards he returned to Lake Turkana, where a quick search yielded some primitive tools. Accompanied by his father, Leakey went to Washington, D.C., and asked the National Geographic Society for funding to pursue further research at Lake Turkana. Impressed by the chutzpah of the twenty-three-year-old Leakey, the trustees granted his request.

Their decision to finance the expedition was a wise one: Lake Turkana turned out to be a treasure trove for anthropologists. Although the region is arid and desolate now, the fossil evidence indicates that three million years ago it was a lush tropical paradise with abundant wildlife, including now-extinct hippos, pelicans, monkeys, lions, crocodiles, impalas, rodents, and man-like creatures. Leakey and his team of Kenyan researchers, dubbed the "Hominid Gang," made their first major discovery at Lake Turkana in 1969. In a remarkable stroke of luck, they stumbled across the skull of an *Australopithecus*, missing only its teeth and lower jaw. Only a short distance away they found some chopping tools. Leakey thought there was little likelihood that the owner of the newly discovered skull had fashioned these implements, for the australopithecines were vegetarians who would not have needed such tools. Instead, he hypothesized that the tools had been devised by another type of early man who had lived during the same period but who had hunted for his food.

Leakey was soon to find more evidence to support this theory. In 1972 Bernard Negeno, Leakey's assistant, uncovered some fragments of a demolished skull. Eventually more than three hundred bits of bone were collected, and the skull was then painstakingly reconstructed by Meave Leakey and Bernard Wood. Called simply "1470" after its catalog number at the National Museums of Kenya, the skull created quite a stir in scientific circles. In comparison to other hominids, it had a smaller face, less aquiline profile, and lacked a beetle brow. Its cranial capacity was 800 cubic centimeters, nearly twice the size of that of *Australopithecus* and more than half the size of that of modern man. Most significant of all, the skull, probably that of a *Homo habilis*, was estimated to be about 2.2 million years old.

Prior to the discovery of 1470, most anthropologists had argued that man's family tree was one straight branch—successively *Australopithecus*, *Homo habilis*, *Homo erectus*, and then *Homo sapiens*. Louis Leakey had been one of the few dissenters; he had insisted that the australopithecines and other hominids had co-existed. Now his son had provided convincing evidence that the older man's theory was correct. "While the skull is different from our own species, Homo sapiens, it is also different from all other known forms of early man and thus does not fit into any of the presently held theories of human evolution," Richard Leakey asserted in a discussion about 1470. He concluded that *Homo habilis* was not a descendant of *Australopithecus*; rather, the *Australopithecus* line (including both *Australopithecus africanus* and *Australopithecus robustus*) and the *Homo habilis* line had existed contemporaneously. The australopithecines eventually became extinct, while the *Homo habilis* line evolved into modern man.

As Leakey's discoveries at Lake Turkana caused his fame to grow, his relationship with his father became strained. A flamboyant figure who loved the limelight, Louis Leakey resented his son's easy success in the field. Louis and Mary had labored at the digs in Olduvai Gorge from 1931 to 1959 before making a major discovery, whereas Richard had unearthed important fossils in only a few years' time. For a while the father and son barely spoke to one another, but later the two men were reconciled. Richard allowed his father to examine the 1470 skull before it was completely restored, and Louis reiterated his belief that *Homo* and *Australopithecus* had co-existed. He also acknowledged that his son had made more important discoveries than he had. Shortly afterwards Louis died. Richard later paid these words of tribute to his father: "I think his sheer dogged persistence—and his follow-through on ideas to the point where they were proved either right or wrong—was his greatest gift. In many ways, his greatest achievement was his ability to stimulate others."

Although Leakey and his father were in agreement that *Homo habilis* and *Australopithecus* had lived side by side, at first other experts challenged this claim. Some anthropologists held that the 1470 skull had not been put together correctly, while others maintained that 1470 was merely an aberrant form of *Australopithecus*. Subsequently Leakey found more evidence to bolster his theory of parallel evolutionary development. In 1975 a complete *Homo erectus* skull, dated at 1.5 to 1.8 million years, was discovered at the Lake Turkana site. "This is a very, very exciting development for us, particularly because it is uncontroversially Homo and it is from deposits that have also yielded uncontroversial evidence of Australopithecus," Leakey remarked. Yet another significant clue was turned up in 1975: the upper part of a skull and the hipbone of a hominid that had clearly walked on two legs. Leakey noted jubilantly that this new skull was "a dead ringer" for the 1470 skull, and thus refuted the argument of those who had claimed that the 1470 was merely a variation of *Australopithecus*.

Although it is now generally acknowledged that from two

million years ago onward at least two types of hominids existed, *Homo* and *Australopithecus,* anthropologists are far from agreement on other matters. As Elizabeth Peer pointed out, "all known remnants of our ancestors from 1 million to 5 million years ago could be spread out on two large trestle tables." Because there is so little evidence about early man, the discovery of a new fossil can launch a heated debate. One such debate came to a head in February of 1979, when Leakey and Donald Carl Johanson appeared at a symposium in Pittsburgh. Johanson, a highly regarded anthropologist who discovered a collection of bones at a site in eastern Africa, argued that these fossils were from thirteen individuals who had perished simultaneously in a natural disaster. These individuals, he claimed, are all examples of a previously unrecognized ancestor of man called *Australopithecus afarensis.* He asserted that *Australopithecus afarensis* was the forerunner both of *Homo* and other forms of australopithecines. Leakey challenged this theory, contending that the bones are specimens of two types of hominids, *Homo* and *Australopithecus.*

Boyce Rensberger explained the implications of the dispute: "If Dr. Johanson is correct, it would mean that the human species emerged from more primitive ancestors more recently, perhaps only two million years ago. On the other hand, if Mr. Leakey is correct, mankind appeared on the scene so long ago—more than four million years—that there is no clear evidence of a fossil form that could have been ancestral to human beings." It will probably be many years before the dispute is settled.

Anthropology is a popular as well as a controversial topic. In addition to his scientific writing, Leakey has written two books on anthropology for the general reader, *Origins* and *People of the Lake.* The two books, both written in collaboration with Roger Lewin, trace man's evolutionary path and speculate as to how early man behaved. After reading the best-selling *Origins,* Carl Sagan commented, "In a field replete with pseudo-scientific special pleadings and secondhand accounts it is a pleasure to see in print an authentic representation of what are, with only minor exceptions, the views held by most of the professionals in the field." Ashley Montagu, however, felt that the "minor exceptions" should have been set forth more clearly: "This volume would have been more lively and well balanced had Leakey and Lewin provided a sense of the ongoing debate over the significance of these finds. Surely they should have let the readers know that many other authorities disagree with some of their views."

In *Origins,* Leakey and Lewin repudiated the idea, popularized by Robert Ardrey, that humans are basically belligerent. "The notions of territorial and aggressive instincts and our evolutionary career as killer apes are dangerous myths," Leakey told an interviewer. "In the book we reject the conventional wisdom that violence and war are in our genes. Our long pre-history as food gatherers argues more persuasively that we are a cooperative rather than an aggressive animal." *People of the Lake* elaborated on this idea. Citing as evidence the fossils of early man, the living habits of primates, and the social ties in modern-day primitive societies, Leakey argued that early man was a cooperative, gentle creature rather than a murderous brute. "Sharing, not hunting or gathering as such, is what made us human," Leakey wrote. "We are human because our ancestors learned to share their food and their skills in an honored network of obligation." He went on to say that it was not until farming was invented some 10,000 years ago that man became warlike. Once man had fields and wealth to protect, wars ensued.

Leakey's studies of ancient man have provided him with many other insights into current problems. When he was a schoolboy, Leakey was shunned by the other students for daring to defend blacks and the concept of Kenyan nationalism. As he grew older and learned more about man's origins, he became even more convinced that the color of one's skin is unimportant. "I regard black and white as divisive terms, but I'm sure the ancestors of man were, shall we say, dark-skinned," he once commented. "Like it or not, most pale-skinned Caucasians can trace their origins to a darker form of humanity in Africa."

An ardent conservationist, Leakey is deeply worried about the problems of overpopulation and pollution. His field work has taught him that any living organism, including man, may become extinct. While he is not a doomsayer, Leakey has said time and time again that the human race must learn to reflect upon its past and upon its future if it wishes to survive. For this reason Leakey is certain that his own fascination with early man will never diminish. "As I grow older my interests continue to broaden," he explained. "I'm interested in Kenyan affairs and international affairs and I would hope that I am able to make contributions in these areas. But, I'm sure I'll always be interested in human evolution. After all, our past, as a species, may help guide us in the future."

BIOGRAPHICAL/CRITICAL SOURCES: Life, September 12, 1969; *National Geographic,* May, 1970, June, 1973; *Science News,* February 26, 1972, November 18, 1972, March 13, 1976; *New York Times,* November 10, 1972, February 18, 1979; *Newsweek,* November 20, 1972, July 15, 1974, March 22, 1976, September 4, 1978; *Esquire,* October, 1973; *New York Times Magazine,* March 3, 1974; *International Wildlife,* May, 1975; *Psychology Today,* October, 1977, July, 1978; *New York Times Book Review,* October 30, 1977, February 19, 1978, November 19, 1978; *Time,* November 7, 1977, August 14, 1978; *Saturday Review,* November 12, 1977; *Washington Post Book World,* December 25, 1977, August 27, 1978; *Human Behavior,* February, 1978, December, 1978; *Times Educational Supplement,* March 17, 1978; *Times Literary Supplement,* January 20, 1978; *Christian Science Monitor,* September 18, 1978; *Washington Post,* October 3, 1978; *People,* January 8, 1979.

—*Sketch by Ann F. Ponikvar*

*   *   *

LEARY, William M., Jr. 1934-

PERSONAL: Born May 6, 1934, in New Jersey; son of William M. and Beatrice A. (Bloemeke) Leary; married Margaret M. MacGregor, July 16, 1977; children: Patricia, Douglas, Maureen, Peter. *Education:* Wayne State University, B.A., 1963; Princeton University, M.A., 1965, Ph.D., 1966. *Home:* 295 Wildwood Dr., Watkinsville, Ga. 30677. *Office:* Department of History, University of Georgia, Athens, Ga. 30602.

CAREER: Princeton University, Princeton, N.J., research associate, 1966-68; San Diego State University, San Diego, Calif., assistant professor of history, 1968-69; University of Victoria, Victoria, British Columbia, associate professor of history, 1969-73; University of Georgia, Athens, currently faculty member in history department. *Military service:* U.S. Air Force, 1951-55. *Member:* Phi Beta Kappa. *Awards, honors:* Woodrow Wilson fellow, 1963; history manuscript award from American Institute of Aeronautics and Astronautics, 1973, for *The Dragon's Wings;* Air Force Historical Foundation fellow, 1977.

WRITINGS: (Editor with A. S. Link) *The Progressive Era and the Great War, 1896-1920,* Appleton, 1969, revised edition, AHM Publishing Corp., 1978; (editor with Link) *The Diplomacy of World Power: The United States, 1889-1920,* Edward Arnold, 1970; *The Dragon's Wings: The China National Aviation Corporation and the Development of Commercial Aviation in China,* University of Georgia Press, 1976.

WORK IN PROGRESS: The Post Office Air Mail Service and the Development of Commercial Aviation in the United States, 1918-1927.

*   *   *

LeBOEUF, Michael   1942-

PERSONAL: Born February 27, 1942, in New Orleans, La.; son of Maurice Paul (in sales) and Winifred (Fatherree) LeBoeuf. *Education:* Louisiana State University, B.S., 1966, M.B.A., 1967, Ph.D., 1969. *Home:* 1328 Homestead Ave., Metairie, La. 70005. *Agent:* Arthur Pine Associates, Inc., 1780 Broadway, New York, N.Y. 10019. *Office:* Department of Management and Marketing, University of New Orleans—Lakefront, New Orleans, La. 70122.

CAREER: University of New Orleans—Lakefront, New Orleans, La., assistant professor, 1969-73, associate professor of management, 1973—.

WRITINGS: Working Smart, McGraw, 1979.

WORK IN PROGRESS: Imageering, "a book on how to think up new ideas and transform them into successful realities," for McGraw.

SIDELIGHTS: LeBoeuf told *CA:* "My career as a lecturer and consultant in the area of time management led me to write. It is my first book, and, as a main selection of the Macmillan Book Club and a Fortune Book Club alternate, has been well received. In addition, portions have appeared in *Reader's Digest* and *Glamour.*

"In my writings, I try to give people practical ideas and present them in the most entertaining and simple way possible. Hopefully, people come away from *Working Smart* feeling better about life, themselves, and their ability to lead a more productive and fulfilling life."

*   *   *

LEE, Eric
See PAGE, Gerald W(ilburn)

*   *   *

LEE, Gerard (Majella)   1951-

PERSONAL: Born November 23, 1951, in Melbourne, Australia; son of Brian Reynolds (a banker) and Dorothea (Galvin) Lee. *Education:* University of Queensland, received degree, 1973, diploma, 1975. *Politics:* "Politics in Australia don't seem to offer a means of reform for our society." *Home:* 11 Jones, West End, Brisbane, Queensland 4101, Australia.

CAREER: Writer, 1975—. Affiliated with *Brisbane Telegraph,* 1969-71, and *Bundaberg News-Mail,* 1971-72; also worked as mail carrier and rock musician.

WRITINGS: Manual for a Garden Mechanic (prose poems), Ragman Productions, 1976; *Pieces for a Glass Piano* (fiction), University of Queensland Press, 1978.

Author of "Here I Am," a script for a children's educational program, first broadcast by Queensland Education Dept.,

October, 1979. Contributor to Australian magazines, including *River Run, Magic Sam, Cane,* and *Time Off.*

WORK IN PROGRESS: A novel, "spoofing the affluent society's strivings for romance, ultimate orgasms, and other signs of cultural with-it-ness."

SIDELIGHTS: Lee wrote: "Philosophically, at present, I'm interested in the role desire plays in our lives, what it makes us do, whether that is developmental or destructive. I am also interested in the differences between New York City luxury apartments and Third World slums." *Avocational interests:* Music, women, work situations.

*   *   *

LEE, J(erry) W(allace)   1932-

PERSONAL: Born September 21, 1932, in Orange, Tex.; son of Wallace Paul (a minister) and Mildred (a teacher; maiden name, Corley) Lee; married Joyce Bilbo, 1952; children: Jerolyn, Jody, Jay. *Education:* Louisiana College, B.A., 1955; New Orleans Baptist Theological Seminary, M.Div., 1958, Th.D., 1964. *Home:* 1303 Sanders Ave., Graceville, Fla. 32440. *Office:* Baptist Bible Institute, 1306 College Dr., Graceville, Fla. 32440.

CAREER: Ordained Baptist minister, 1952; pastor of Baptist churches in Natchez, Miss., 1962-65, and Jennings, La., 1965-69; Baptist Bible Institute, Graceville, Fla., professor of Old Testament, 1969—. Member of Trans-Pacific Crusade in New Zealand, 1965; member of executive board of Louisiana Baptist Convention, 1967-69; camp pastor and Bible teacher; conducts Bible conferences and revival crusades; interim pastor in Florida, Alabama, and Georgia; leads tours to Bible lands and Europe. Member of board of directors of Baptist Student Union of McNeese College, 1966-68, and trustee of Louisiana College, 1968-69. *Member:* Kiwanis International.

WRITINGS: Preaching From Genesis: The Perfecting of the Believer's Faith, Baker Book, 1975. Author of church school curriculum material for adults.

WORK IN PROGRESS: Preaching From Psalms.

*   *   *

LEE, Meredith   1945-

PERSONAL: Born July 11, 1945, in St. Louis, Mo.; daughter of Russell E. (an auditor) and Agnes (a high school teacher; maiden name, Erickson) Lee; married N. Anthony Battaglia (a professor), November 18, 1977. *Education:* St. Olaf College, B.A. (summa cum laude), 1968; Yale University, M.Phil., 1971, Ph.D., 1976. *Religion:* Lutheran. *Office:* Department of German, University of California, Irvine, Calif. 92717.

CAREER: Yale University, New Haven, Conn., part-time instructor in German, 1973-74; University of California, Irvine, assistant professor of German, 1974—. *Member:* Modern Language Association of America, American Association of Teachers of German, Society for Values in Higher Education, Lessing Society, Eighteenth Century Society, American Goethe Society, Goethe-Gesellschaft. *Awards, honors:* Fulbright scholarship, 1972-73.

WRITINGS: Studies in Goethe's Lyric Cycles, University of North Carolina Press, 1978. Contributor to *Lessing Yearbook.*

WORK IN PROGRESS: Research on Norwegian-German literary relations and Goethe and the eighteenth century.

LEECH, Bryan Jeffery 1931-

PERSONAL: Born May 14, 1931, in Buckhurst Hill, England; came to the United States in 1955; son of Harold Cayzer (in business; an inventor) and Lillian (Gothard) Leech. *Education:* London Bible College, A.L.B.C.; Barrington College, B.A.; also attended University of London, and North Park Seminary, Chicago, Ill. *Politics:* "In England, Conservative." *Home and office address:* P.O. Box 5595, Santa Barbara, Calif. 93108.

CAREER: Ordained minister of Evangelical Covenant Church of America, 1959; pastor of Evangelical Covenant churches in Boston, Mass., 1957-58, Montclair, N.J., 1958-63, and San Francisco, Calif., 1963-68; Montecito Covenant Church, Santa Barbara, Calif., senior minister, 1968-75; free-lance writer and composer, 1975—. Broadcaster on "Morning Song," on KBLS-Radio. Gives seminars on worship; performs at concerts. Secretary for Samarkand Retirement Residence, 1968-77; member of president's council of Westmont College, 1972-77. *Military service:* Royal Navy, Medical Branch, 1949-51. *Member:* American Society of Composers, Authors and Publishers. *Awards, honors:* Lutheran Key 73 Hymn Award for "Let God Be God."

WRITINGS: (With Glenn Edward Sadler) *It Must Have Been McNutt* (juvenile), Regal Books (Glendale), 1974; (assistant editor and contributor) *Hymns for the Family of God,* Paragon, 1977; (editor with Fred Bock, and contributor) *Companion to Hymns for the Family of God,* Paragon, 1979. Also editor and contributor to *The Covenant Hymnal.*

Author of musical plays, "Simon," 1978, "A Tale of Two Brothers," 1978, and "Ebenezer," 1978. Co-author of "Dove Descending" and "The Best of News," cantatas, published in one volume, with sound recording, Lillenas, 1978. Composer of eighty-five songs and anthems, published by Presser, Fred Bock Music Co., Shawnee, Singspiration, and Lillenas, including "The Hiding Place." Script writer for Mel White Productions and "Haven of Rest Broadcast." Contributor to magazines, including *Covenant Companion* and *Hymn Society.*

SIDELIGHTS: Leech wrote: "My songs have been recorded and performed by Norma Zimmer, Paul Sandberg, and Bruce Leafblad. My best known song, 'The Hiding Place,' has been recorded eight times and in 1976 was performed at the Royal Albert Hall in London. *Hymns for the Family of God* was chosen as the hymn book for use at the 1978 Presidential Prayer Breakfast. So universal is its appeal that it has been chosen by all the major denominations as a worship hymnal.

"My aim is to try to express my Christian faith in fresh ways that will appeal to people who have no understanding of the conventional jargon so often used by the church. I am very interested in drama as a means of presenting this challenge, and feel that we have now gone full circle, as it was the Mystery Plays in Europe, all of a religious nature, which gave birth to the theatre as we know it."

*   *   *

LEECH, Margaret (Kernochan) 1893-1974

PERSONAL: Born November 7, 1893, in Newburgh, N.Y.; died of a stroke, February 24, 1974, in New York, N.Y.; daughter of William and Rebecca (Taggart) Leech; married Ralph Pulitzer (a publisher), August 1, 1938 (died June 14, 1939); children: Susan Freedberg, Margaretta (deceased). *Education:* Vassar College, B.A., 1915. *Residence:* New York, N.Y.

CAREER: Novelist, biographer, and historian. Worked variously for publishing company and advertising agency in New York, N.Y. *Wartime service:* Worked as publicity agent for numerous fund-raising organizations during World War I, including Anne Morgan's American Committee for Devastated France. *Awards, honors:* Pulitzer Prize for History, 1942, for *Reveille in Washington, 1860-1865;* Pulitzer Prize for History and Bancroft Prize from Columbia University, both 1960, both for *In the Days of McKinley.*

WRITINGS: The Back of the Book (novel), Boni & Liveright, 1924; *Tin Wedding* (novel), Boni & Liveright, 1926; (with Heywood Broun) *Anthony Comstock: Roundsman of the Lord* (biography; Literary Guild selection), Boni & Liveright, 1927; *The Feathered Nest* (novel), H. Liveright, 1928; *Reveille in Washington, 1860-1865* (history of Civil War; Book-of-the-Month Club selection), Harper, 1941, reprinted, Greenwood Press, 1971; *In the Days of McKinley* (biography and history; Book-of-the-Month Club selection), Harper, 1959; (with Harry J. Brown) *The Garfield Orbit* (biography and history), Harper, 1978. Also author with Beatrice Kaufman of play, "Divided by Three," first produced in 1934. Contributor to periodicals, including *Harper's.*

SIDELIGHTS: Margaret Leech's best-known work, *Reveille in Washington, 1860-1865,* encompasses many aspects of the American Civil War from the bloody battlefields to the gay ballrooms of Washington, D.C., and highlights such individuals as Abraham and Mary Todd Lincoln, and Rose Greenhow, the Confederate spy whose advanced warning to the Southern forces resulted in the Union defeat at the first battle of Bull Run. In preparation for the book, Leech conducted extensive research at the Library of Congress and the National Archives studying numerous old photographs, correspondences, personal accounts, newspapers, government documents, and reports. The result of her efforts was a best-selling book that received a Pulitzer Prize in 1942 and, according to Clifton Fadiman of the *New Yorker,* placed "Miss Leech at once among the foremost contemporary historians of America."

Although considered "fair and accurate" by R. E. Canielson of the *Atlantic Monthly,* James Orrick complained that *Reveille in Washington* "remains a panorama, a picture, something looked at rather than lived through." MacKinlay Kantor, however, insisted that it "[embodies], along with faultless exactitude and respect for documentation, the power and excitement of a story in which living men perform." Katherine Woods of the *New York Times* concurred, "[The book] comes to us with enlightenment and wit, brilliance in scene and universality in insight."

Another of Leech's successful historical works is *In the Days of McKinley,* a biography of William McKinley, the twenty-fifth president of the United States. The book, which was written over a period of twelve years, was lauded for bringing considerable new and little-known information to light. "Her book is excellent biography, sympathetic, indeed compassionate, but not uncritical," assessed J. Blum in the *New York Times.* Charles Rolo also praised Leech in that she "does not in any way minimize [McKinley's] limitations, but, from her meticulous documentation of his life, he emerges as a firmer, more principled, and more attractive figure than the established image suggests."

BIOGRAPHICAL/CRITICAL SOURCES: New Yorker, August 30, 1941; *Saturday Review,* August 30, 1941, December 12, 1959; *Books,* August 31, 1941; *New York Times,* August 31, 1941, November 1, 1959; *Springfield Republican,* August 31, 1941; *Yale Review,* autumn, 1941; *Atlantic*

Monthly, September, 1941, December, 1959; *New Republic,* September 1, 1941; *Time,* September 1, 1941, November 16, 1959; *Nation,* September 6, 1941, November 28, 1959; *Commonweal,* September 26, 1941; *Chicago Sunday Tribune,* November 1, 1959; *New York Herald Tribune Book Review,* November 1, 1959; *Christian Science Monitor,* November 5, 1959; *San Francisco Chronicle,* November 18, 1959.

OBITUARIES: New York Times, February 25, 1974; *Newsweek,* March 11, 1974; *Time,* March 11, 1974.*

* * *

LEEFELDT, Christine 1941-

PERSONAL: Born February 28, 1941, in Alameda, Calif.; daughter of Earl Frank (in business) and Helen (a dietitian; maiden name, Arthur) Leefeldt; married Ernest William Callenbach (a writer and editor), May 19, 1978; children: Joanna Margaret, Hans Christopher (stepchildren). *Education:* University of California, Berkeley, B.A., 1963, M.A., 1965, Ph.D., 1971; attended University of Paris, 1960-61. *Home:* 1963 El Dorado Ave., Berkeley, Calif. 94707. *Agent:* Richard Kahlenberg, 225 Santa Monica Blvd., Santa Monica, Calif. 90401. *Office:* Department of Humanities, San Francisco Conservatory of Music, 1201 Ortega St., San Francisco, Calif. 94122.

CAREER: University of California, Berkeley, instructor, 1970—; San Francisco Conservatory of Music, San Francisco, Calif., director of department of humanities, 1972—. Active in state and local politics. *Member:* Modern Language Association of America, Association for Humanistic Psychology, American Association of University Women, University of California Alumni Association.

WRITINGS: (With husband, Ernest Callenbach) *The Art of Friendship,* Pantheon, 1979.

WORK IN PROGRESS: Research and interviews for a book on power and how it is viewed and worked with in the helping professions, publication expected in 1981; editing an anthology on friendship for college and university use, publication expected in 1981.

SIDELIGHTS: Christine Leefeldt commented to *CA:* "The book on friendship came out of my husband's and my preparation of a marriage contract at the time we married. Both of us realized how highly we valued friendship in our lives, and were anxious not to have the usual marriage pattern of 'compulsory coupledom' friendships. Talking it over, we suspected that this was territory nobody had thoroughly explored before.

"We did some informal interviews with friends, and discovered there were many other intriguing and often problematic issues that had been almost totally ignored in literature, both professional and popular. After some two hundred interviews and more than a year of intensive collaboration, plus four weeks of promotion travel, I am happy to say that we are still friends."

A reviewer for the *Washington Post* declared *The Art of Friendship* to be "a sensitive, much-needed attack on the myths surrounding friendship.... [It] explores every conceivable aspect of human relations, and reaches some profound and undeniable conclusions about the state of the art."

AVOCATIONAL INTERESTS: Travel in Europe, Mexico, Central and South America, Japan, China, and the South Seas.

BIOGRAPHICAL/CRITICAL SOURCES: Los Angeles Times, September 30, 1979; *Washington Post,* November 3, 1979.

* * *

LEESON, C(harles) Roland 1926-

PERSONAL: Born January 26, 1926, in Halifax, England; came to United States in 1963; son of Charles E. (a teacher) and Gladys (Stott) Leeson; married Marjorie Martindale, April 24, 1954; children: Mark, Jane, Christine, Neil, Paula. *Education:* St. Catharine's College, Cambridge, B.A., 1947, M.B., B.Chir., 1950, M.A., 1951, M.D., 1959, Ph.D., 1971. *Politics:* Conservative. *Home:* 2503 Melrose Dr., Champaign, Ill. 61820. *Office:* Department of Anatomy, University of Illinois, Urbana, Ill. 61801.

CAREER: King's College Hospital, London, England, intern, 1950-51; University of Wales, University College of South Wales, Cardiff, lecturer in anatomy, 1955-58; Dalhousie University, Halifax, Nova Scotia, associate professor of anatomy, 1958-61; Queen's University, Kingston, Ontario, associate professor of anatomy, 1962-63; University of Iowa, Iowa City, professor of anatomy, 1963-66; University of Missouri, Columbia, professor of anatomy and head of department, 1966-78; University of Illinois, Urbana, professor of anatomy, 1978—. Visiting professor at London Hospital, 1973-74. *Military service:* Royal Air Force, Medical Branch, 1951-55; became squadron leader. *Member:* American Association of Anatomists, Electron Microscopy Society of America, Anatomy Society of Great Britain and Ireland, Canadian Association of Anatomists.

WRITINGS—With brother, Thomas S. Leeson: *Histology,* Saunders, 1966, 4th edition, in press; *Human Structure: A Companion to Anatomical Studies,* Saunders, 1972; *A Brief Atlas of Histology,* Saunders, 1979. Also author of *Practical Histology,* 1973.

SIDELIGHTS: Leeson commented: "As a teacher and researcher I enjoy attempting to write medical texts for students that stress the basic concepts, rather than details. In the study of anatomy as a basic medical science, it is important that students gain an understanding of the complexity of organization of the human body before they proceed into clinical studies."

* * *

LEHRMAN, Nat 1929-

PERSONAL: Born August 5, 1929, in Brooklyn, N.Y.; son of Louis (in needle trades) and Lena (Goldfarb) Lehrman; married Kazuko Miyajima (an interpreter), November 13, 1956; children: Jerome Masato, Cynthia Hanako. *Education:* Brooklyn College (now of the City University of New York), B.A., 1953; New York University, M.A., 1960. *Residence:* Chicago, Ill. *Agent:* Sterling Lord Agency, Inc., 660 Madison Ave., New York, N.Y. 10021. *Office:* Playboy Enterprises, Inc., 919 North Michigan Ave., Chicago, Ill. 60611.

CAREER: American Automobile Association, New York City, travel writer and editor in international travel department, 1955-57; West Park Publishing, New York City, editor of *Relax,* 1957-58, managing editor, 1958-61, editor of *Dude,* 1961-63, and *Gent,* 1961-63; Playboy Enterprises, Inc., Chicago, Ill., associate editor of *Playboy,* 1963-70, assistant managing editor, 1970-72, editor of new publications, 1972—, editor of *Oui,* 1973-75, associate publisher, 1975-76, associate publisher of *Playboy,* 1976—, group executive and director of Magazine Publishing Division, 1977—. Member of faculty at Columbia College, Chicago, Ill., 1967; member of board of directors of Publishers Information Bureau, Inc. and Playboy Foundation. *Military service:* U.S. Army, 1953-55; served in Japan. *Member:* American Civil Liberties Union, Midwest Classical Guitar Society, Lincoln Park Tennis Club.

WRITINGS: Masters and Johnson Explained, Playboy Press, 1970, revised edition, 1976; (editor with Frank Robinson) *Sex, American Style,* Playboy Press, 1976. Contributor to *Playboy.* Literary adviser of *Guitarra.*

WORK IN PROGRESS: Research on male/female roles.

SIDELIGHTS: Lehrman told *CA:* "I think writing is the hardest work in the world, and would rather edit the writing of others (because I'm more analytical than creative), play the classical guitar, hit a tennis ball, or fool with languages. As editor and associate publisher of *Oui,* I loved the opportunity to brave two years of frequent visits to Paris and play with French.

"Now, as de facto publisher of *Playboy* and associated publications, I'm removed, at least at one level, from the substance of the magazines, the fun part. Do I regret it? I don't know. I'll consider the question again next year. I used to be one of the world's greatest authorities on sex, journalistic division. Publishing also pulls me away from this vocation. Advancing age helps me not regret it too much."

*   *   *

LEITER, Samuel Louis 1940-

PERSONAL: Surname is pronounced "lighter"; born July 20, 1940, in Brooklyn, N.Y.; son of Joseph and Frieda (Pekofsky) Leiter; married Marcia Frieda Lerner, February 3, 1963; children: Bambi Lani, Justin Leigh. *Education:* Brooklyn College of the City University of New York, B.A., 1962; University of Hawaii, M.F.A., 1964; New York University, Ph.D., 1968. *Home:* 137-29 79th St., Howard Beach, N.Y. 11414. *Office:* Department of Theatre, Brooklyn College of the City University of New York, Bedford Ave., Brooklyn, N.Y. 11210.

CAREER: Brooklyn College of the City University of New York, Brooklyn, N.Y., lecturer, 1965-68, assistant professor, 1968-73, associate professor, 1973-76, professor of theatre, 1977—. *Member:* American Society for Theatre Research, American Theatre Association. *Awards, honors:* Grant from University of Hawaii's East-West Center, 1963, and Fulbright grant, 1974, both for study in Japan.

WRITINGS: The Art of Kabuki: Famous Plays in Performance, University of California Press, 1979; *Kabuki Encyclopedia: An English Language Adaptation of "Kabuki Jiten,"* Greenwood Press, 1979; *Stage Directors of the Century,* Drama Book Specialists, 1981. Author of filmstrip series, "The Classical Theatre of Japan." Contributor to theatre journals. Editor of *Asian Theatre Bulletin,* 1970-78.

WORK IN PROGRESS: Research for *Danjuro: Kabuki's Greatest Acting Dynasty,* completion expected in 1982.

SIDELIGHTS: Leiter writes: "For fifteen years, my primary writing interests have been with Japanese theatre subjects, especially *Kabuki.* I hope to continue writing in this field, expanding to studies of other genres such as *kagura,* folk theatre (*minzoku geino*), *Noh,* puppet theater, *shinpa,* and so on. If all goes well, I would one day like to write a comprehensive account of all forms of classical Japanese theatre. I am interested not only in the production techniques and history of these forms, but in the world behind the scenes. A book I want to write is about the world of

Kabuki, the people who make it live—costumiers, actors, producers, stage hands, prop makers, and so forth. I also want to provide translations of important Japanese theatre reference works and plays. If only traveling to and living in Japan were not so terribly expensive I would be there every year doing research. My two extended stays were the most fruitful research periods of my life.

"I am also deeply involved in the world of Western theatre. Stage production fascinates me, whether it be Eastern or Western. The forces, the people, the ideas that go into making theatre work will continue to inspire me to write in this field."

*   *   *

LEMERT, Edwin M(cCarty) 1912-

PERSONAL: Born May 8, 1912, in Norwood, Ohio; son of Blaine E. (an insurance manager) and Gertrude (McCarty) Lemert; children: James E., Blaine C., Sean E., Deborah Lemert Ackerman, Deirdre Lemert Welch, Teheurra M. *Education:* Miami University, Oxford, Ohio, A.B., 1934; Ohio State University, Ph.D., 1939. *Residence:* Winters, Calif. *Office:* Department of Sociology, University of California, Davis, Calif. 95616.

CAREER: Kent State University, Kent, Ohio, instructor in social science, 1939-41; Western Michigan University, Kalamazoo, assistant professor of sociology, 1941-44; University of California, Los Angeles, assistant professor, then associate professor of sociology, 1944-53; University of California, Davis, 1953—, began as associate professor, currently professor of sociology. Member of National Advisory Commission on Alcohol, 1968; consultant to President's Commission on Law Enforcement and Administration of Justice. *Member:* Society for the Study of Social Problems (president, 1973), Pacific Sociological Society (president, 1974). *Awards, honors:* Sutherland Award in Criminology from American Society of Criminology, 1974.

WRITINGS: Social Pathology, McGraw, 1951; *Alcohol and the Northwest Coast Indians,* University of California Press, 1954; *Human Deviance: Social Problems and Social Control,* Prentice-Hall, 1970, revised edition, 1972; *Social Action and Legal Change,* Aldine, 1970; *Offenders in the Community,* Heath, 1978. Member of editorial board of *Quarterly Journal on the Study of Alcohol.*

WORK IN PROGRESS: Social Control of Youth in Comparative Perspective; Law and Society.

SIDELIGHTS: Lemert writes that he is one of the originators of "societal reaction and the labeling theory of deviance." His research has taken him to the South Pacific, New Zealand, England, France, Italy, and Hong Kong. He also notes that his "perspective is interdisciplinary, combining sociology, anthropology and clinical psychology." He advises young social scientists to "learn everything there is to know about the subject of your research and follow your own leads."

*   *   *

LEONE, Mark P(aul) 1940-

PERSONAL: Born June 26, 1940, in Waltham, Mass.; son of Frank (in sales) and Eleanor (Flynn) Leone. *Education:* Tufts University, B.A., 1963; University of Arizona, M.A., 1965, Ph.D., 1968. *Office:* Department of Anthropology, University of Maryland, College Park, Md. 20742.

CAREER: Princeton University, Princeton, N.J., assistant professor of anthropology, 1968-76; University of Maryland,

College Park, associate professor of anthropology, 1976—. Visiting associate professor at Johns Hopkins University. *Member:* American Anthropological Association, Society for American Archaeology. *Awards, honors:* National Endowment for the Humanities fellow, 1975-76.

WRITINGS: (Editor) *Contemporary Archaeology,* Southern Illinois University Press, 1972; (editor with Irving I. Zaretsky) *Religious Movements in Contemporary America,* Princeton University Press, 1974; *Roots of Modern Mormonism,* Harvard University Press, 1979. Contributor to anthropology journals.

WORK IN PROGRESS: Past Time in America, on the social functions of archaeological research at colonial Williamsburg, Va.

SIDELIGHTS: When asked to comment on Mormonism and contemporary American religions, Mark Leone stated: "Mormonism is a way of thinking used by increasingly powerless people in modern society. It is a religion for subordinates. Despite the wealth, certainty, and authoritarian stance of Mormons, the religion, like almost all other invented in America, serves to trap its members in our society, not, as all Christians suppose, to free believers from the demands of society. My purpose in studying contemporary American religions and our outdoor history museums like Williamsburg is to examine how those institutions, which are supposed to create understanding of everyday life, actually, though inadvertently, prevent it."

BIOGRAPHICAL/CRITICAL SOURCES: New York Times, September 6, 1979.

* * *

LERNER, Richard M(artin) 1946-

PERSONAL: Born February 23, 1946, in Brooklyn, N.Y.; son of Max and Sara (Goldfarb) Lerner; married Jacqueline R. Verdirame (a psychologist), July 24, 1977. *Education:* Hunter College of the City University of New York, B.A. (with honors), 1966, M.A., 1967; City University of New York, Ph.D., 1971. *Home:* 124 Sandy Ridge Rd., State College, Pa. 16801. *Office:* College of Human Development, Pennsylvania State University, University Park, Pa. 16802.

CAREER: Hunter College of the City University of New York, New York, N.Y., lecturer in psychology, 1967-69; Eastern Michigan University, Ypsilanti, 1969-76, began as assistant professor, became associate professor of psychology; Pennsylvania State University, University Park, associate professor of child development, 1976—. Fellow of Center for Advanced Study in the Behavioral Sciences, 1980-81; consultant to National Institutes of Health. *Member:* American Psychological Association (fellow), Society for Research in Child Development, Society for the Psychological Study of Social Issues, American Association for the Advancement of Science, American Association of University Professors, Eastern Psychological Association, New York Academy of Sciences, Sigma Xi, Psi Chi.

WRITINGS: (Contributor) H. D. Thornburg, editor, *Contemporary Adolescence,* 2nd edition (Lerner was not included in 1st edition), Brooks/Cole, 1975; *Concepts and Theories of Human Development,* Addison-Wesley, 1976; (editor with G. B. Spanier, and contributor) *Child Influences on Marital and Family Interaction: A Life Span Perspective,* Academic Press, 1978; (contributor) P. B. Baltes, editor, *Life-Span Development and Behavior,* Volume I, Academic Press, 1978; (contributor) R. L. Burgess and T. L. Huston, editors, *Social Exchange in Developing Relationships,* Aca-

demic Press, 1979; (with Spanier) *Adolescent Development: A Life-Span Perspective,* McGraw, in press; (editor with N. A. Busch-Rossnagel, and contributor) *Individuals as Producers of Their Development: A Life-Span Perspective,* Academic Press, in press.

Contributor to *International Encyclopedia of Neurology, Psychiatry, Psychoanalysis, and Psychology.* Contributor of about sixty articles to journals in the behavioral sciences. Editor of *Michigan Psychologist,* 1971-74, and *Newsletter of the Association of Aviation Psychologists,* 1973-74; member of editorial board of *Child Development,* 1978—.

WORK IN PROGRESS: Human Development: A Life-Span Perspective, with D. F. Hultsch and S. Friedman, publication by McGraw expected in 1982.

* * *

LESIKIN, Joan 1947-

PERSONAL: Born February 25, 1947, in Suffern, N.Y.; daughter of Jack B. (in business) and May (Goldman) Lesikin. *Education:* Syracuse University, B.F.A., 1968; Rutgers University, M.F.A., 1970. *Home:* 172-B Kearsing Parkway, Monsey, N.Y. 10952.

CAREER: American School of Tangier, Tangier, Morocco, junior high school teacher of English and art, high school teacher of art, 1972-74; Sunflower Designs, New York City, textile designer, 1974-76; free-lance color consultant to textile industry in New York City, 1976—.

WRITINGS: Down the Road, self-illustrated, Prentice-Hall, 1978.

WORK IN PROGRESS—All self-illustrated; all juveniles: *Boy of the Rif;* a book about death; picture books for beginning readers.

SIDELIGHTS: "I'm a visual artist who fell in love with children while teaching art and English in Morocco," Lesikin told *CA.* "Now those two areas are meshed in my own life through writing and illustrating children's literature.

"The struggle to learn to write and refine, then to capture in drawing what I expressed in words, is my own. Hopefully the end products will not show the labor, but rather a clarity, a beauty that will enrich."

* * *

LESLEY, Cole 1910(?)-1980

OBITUARY NOTICE: Born c. 1910 in Farningham, Kent, England; died January 4, 1980, in Les Avants sur Montreux, Switzerland. Aide and biographer. Lesley was playwright Noel Coward's valet and cook for thirty-seven years and the author of *Remembered Laughter: The Life of Noel Coward.* The book is a massive, sympathetic biography of the famed English actor and writer, assembled from the letters, diaries, and notebooks Coward made available to the author. With Graham Payne and Sheridan Morley, Lesley wrote a second book in 1979, *Noel Coward & Friends.* Obituaries and other sources: *New York Times,* January 9, 1980; *Newsweek,* January 21, 1980.

* * *

LESLIE, Kenneth 1892-1974

PERSONAL: Born November 1, 1892, in Pictou, Nova Scotia, Canada; died October 7, 1974, in Halifax, Nova Scotia, Canada; son of Robert Jamieson and Rebecca (Starratt) Leslie; married Beth Moir (deceased); married Nora S. Totten, 1960; children: (first marriage) Gloria, Kathleen, Rosaleen,

Kenneth Alexander. *Education:* Dalhousie University, B.A., 1912, Nebraska University, M.A., 1914; attended Harvard University. *Religion:* Baptist. *Residence:* Halifax, Nova Scotia, Canada.

CAREER: Poet. Former editor of *Protestant* and *New Man. Awards, honors:* Tweedsmuir Prize, 1938; Governor General's Award, 1939, for *By Stubborn Stars, and Other Poems.*

WRITINGS—Poetry: Windward Rock, Macmillan, 1934; *Such a Din,* John McCurdy, 1935; *Lowlands Low,* John McCurdy, 1936; *By Stubborn Stars, and Other Poems,* Ryerson Press, 1938; *Songs of Nova Scotia,* privately printed, 1964; *The Poems of Kenneth Leslie,* Ladysmith Press, 1971; *O'Malley to the Reds, and Other Poems,* privately printed, 1972. Work represented in *The Book of Canadian Poetry.*

OBITUARIES: New York Times, October 9, 1974; *A. B. Bookman's Weekly,* December 2, 1974.*

*   *   *

LESSER, Margaret 1899(?)-1979

OBITUARY NOTICE: Born c. 1899; died November 21, 1979, in New York, N.Y. Editor. Lesser was a children's book editor at Doubleday for thirty years. She worked on several award-winning books, including Thomas Handforth's *Mei Li* and Leonard Weisgard's *The Little Island,* both of which won the Caldecott Medal. Obituaries and other sources: *Publishers Weekly,* December 24, 1979.

*   *   *

LEVIN, Harold L(eonard) 1929-

PERSONAL: Born March 11, 1929, in St. Louis, Mo.; son of Harry (a tailor) and Anna (Millman) Levin; married Kay Helen Tamarkin (a dental assistant); children: Linda Suzann, Stephen David, Janet Caroline. *Education:* University of Missouri, A.B., 1951, M.A., 1952; Washington University, St. Louis, Mo., Ph.D., 1956. *Home:* 12506 Trammell, Creve Coeur, Mo. 63141. *Office:* Campus Box 1169, Washington University, St. Louis, Mo. 63130.

CAREER: Standard Oil Co. of California, Bakersfield, Calif., research geologist, 1956-62; Washington University, St. Louis, Mo., assistant professor, 1962-65, associate professor, 1965-76, professor of geology, 1976—, head of department of earth and planetary sciences, 1973-76, associate dean of College of Arts and Sciences. Lecturer; participant in (and director of) scholarly meetings. Consultant to U.S. Army Corps of Engineers. *Military service:* U.S. Army, Artillery, 1952-53, Corps of Engineers, 1953-55; became second lieutenant. *Member:* Paleontological Society, Society of Economic Paleontologists and Mineralogists, American Association for the Advancement of Science, Association of Missouri Geologists.

WRITINGS: (With J. C. Brice) *Studies in Earth History,* W. C. Brown, 1969, 2nd edition, 1977; (self-illustrated) *Life Through Time,* W. C. Brown, 1975; *The Earth Through Time* (with study manual), Saunders, 1978; *Contemporary Physical Geology,* Saunders, 1980. Contributor of about twenty articles and reviews to geology and paleontology journals.

SIDELIGHTS: Levin wrote: "Since childhood the history of this planet and the living things on it have held a fascination for me. I enjoy sharing this fascination with others as a teacher, and, for me, writing is an extension of the task of teaching. I believe that even abstract and complex scientific concepts can be put into prose that even the non-science students can understand and appreciate.

"My specialization has been in the general area of micropaleontology, and specifically the study of fossil and living calcareous oceanic phytoplankton known as coccolithophorids. My objectives have been to increase the usefulness of coccolithophorids in dating and correlating strata and thereby contribute to a better understanding of events and conditions in the geologic past. The research has, in addition, value in the exploration for petroleum."

AVOCATIONAL INTERESTS: Sketching, sculpture, nature.

*   *   *

LEVINE, Betty K(rasne) 1933-
(Betty Krasne)

PERSONAL: Born May 25, 1933, in New York, N.Y.; daughter of Israel (in wholesale grocery business) and Hannah (Goldstein) Krasne; married Robert Phillip Levine (an attorney), May 4, 1958; children: Thomas Krasne, Jonathan Newman, Kate Israel. *Education:* Mount Holyoke College, B.A. (cum laude), 1955; Columbia University, M.A. (with highest honors), 1957; Union Graduate School, Yellow Springs, Ohio, Ph.D., 1979. *Home:* 42 Eastern Dr., Ardsley, N.Y. 10502. *Office:* Department of English and Humanities, Mercy College, 555 Broadway, Dobbs Ferry, N.Y. 10522.

CAREER: Equitable Life Assurance Co., New York City, editorial assistant, 1955-56; Gimbel's (department store), New York City, assistant director of public relations, 1957-58, advertising copywriter, 1958-59; Mercy College, Dobbs Ferry, N.Y., lecturer, 1967-68, instructor, 1968-70, assistant professor, 1970-78, associate professor of English and humanities, 1979—. *Member:* Modern Language Association of America, American Association of University Professors, Mercy College Faculty Association (president, 1979), Phi Beta Kappa, Kappa Delta Phi. *Awards, honors:* Greenburgh Poetry Prize, 1977, for "The Good Daughter"; prize from Aspen Writer's Conference, 1978.

WRITINGS: Hex House (novel), Harper, 1973; *Hawk High* (novel), Atheneum, 1980; *The Great Burgerland Disaster* (novel), Atheneum, 1980. Contributor of stories and poems to magazines.

WORK IN PROGRESS: Playing the Part, poems; *Another Time in the Same Place,* a novel; (under name Betty Krasne) *Beware of Death by Water: A Thematic Study of Women in Myth and Fiction,* literary criticism.

SIDELIGHTS: Betty Levine writes: "All my writings reflect an interest in exploring the role of women in society and in examining the way literature, interacting with life, reflects traditional roles and expresses new models. My work has moved increasingly from the former (descriptive) position to the latter (prescriptive) one.

"In addition, my fiction is inextricably involved with places where I have lived. A sense of place plays a significant part in each work of fiction.

"My fiction has also tended to change in direct relation to the ages of our children. As the three of them grow older, so do the characters in the novels, whose concerns thus become more sophisticated and complex."

*   *   *

LEVISON, Andrew 1948-

PERSONAL: Born September 20, 1948, in New York, N.Y.; son of Stanley David and Beatrice Levison; married Judith Luna (a medical laboratory technician), March 19, 1974.

Education: University of Wisconsin—Madison, B.A., 1970. *Home:* 1437 Wessyngton Rd., Atlanta, Ga. 30306.

CAREER: Martin Luther King Center for Social Change, Atlanta, Ga., research associate, 1970—. Researcher, National Committee for Full Employment, 1975—. *Awards, honors: The Working Class Majority* was nominated for a National Book Award in 1974.

WRITINGS: The Working Class Majority, Coward, 1974; *The Full Employment Alternative,* Coward, 1980.

SIDELIGHTS: Levison's first book counters the widely-held notion that the United States constitutes a middle class society. He emphasizes that the working class is still in the majority, and while workers' problems and resentments have mounted, sometimes resulting in conservative or reactionary behavior, they are in reality a far more progressive force in society than government officials and academicians have admitted. His book attempts to bridge the gap between the working and middle classes.

BIOGRAPHICAL/CRITICAL SOURCES: New York Times Book Review, October 20, 1974.

*   *   *

LEVOY, Myron

PERSONAL: Born in New York, N.Y. *Education:* Received M.Sc. from Purdue University.

CAREER: Chemical engineer and writer. *Awards, honors: The Witch of Fourth Street, and Other Stories* was a Children's Book Showcase Selection, 1973.

WRITINGS: A Necktie in Greenwich Village (novel), Vanguard, 1968; *Penny Tunes and Princesses* (juvenile), Harper, 1972; *The Witch of Fourth Street, and Other Stories* (juvenile), Harper, 1972; *Alan and Naomi* (juvenile), Harper, 1977.

Plays: "Eli and Emily," first produced in New York City in 1969; "The Sun is a Red Dwarf" (one-act), first produced in New York City at New York Theatre Ensemble, 1969; "Sweet Tom" (two-act), first produced in New York City at the Playbox, 1969; *Footsteps* (first produced in New York City in 1970), Breakthrough, 1971; "Smudge," first produced in New York City in 1971.

SIDELIGHTS: Myron Levoy's *The Witch of Fourth Street* consists of eight short stories about the immigrants who settled in New York City's lower East Side in the twenties. Natalie Babbit paid tribute to the book: "[These stories] have extraordinary freshness and charm. . . . But Myron Levoy does not compromise with truth: there is pain too, and frustration—and in the final story, death. What makes this such a good book is the author's compassion, imagination, and humor; his clear eye for detail and craftsman's sense of what language means and can be made to do. It is a first book for children by a first-rate writer."

BIOGRAPHICAL/CRITICAL SOURCES: Washington Post Book World, May 7, 1972; *New York Times Book Review,* June 18, 1972.*

*   *   *

LEWALD, (Theo) Roon 1942-

PERSONAL: Name is pronounced Rawn *Lair*-vult; born June 19, 1942, in Durban, South Africa; son of Otto Albrecht (a singing teacher) and Helen (van Pletzen) Lewald; married Lyn Joanna Kock (a computer programmer), November 30, 1968; children: Lewald and Katherine Helen (twins). *Education:* Attended University of Pretoria, 1961, and University

of Cape Town, 1962. *Home:* Julius-Pluecker-Strasse 13, 5300 Bonn 1, West Germany. *Office:* McGraw-Hill World News, Pressehaus I/12, 5300 Bonn 1, West Germany.

CAREER/WRITINGS: South African Broadcasting Corp., Cape Town, South Africa, news cadet, 1963; *Cape Argus,* Cape Town, South Africa, accident and court reporter, 1964; South African Broadcasting Corp., regional news reporter in Cape Town, 1965, national news and audio report editor in Johannesburg, 1965-68; Associated Press, news staffer in Johannesburg, 1968-71, and in Bonn, West Germany, 1971-78; McGraw-Hill World News, Bonn, West Germany, news staffer, 1978—. Notable assignments include resignation of Willy Brandt, 1974, OPEC ministerial conferences, 1975 and 1976, and the Rhodesia constitutional conference, 1977. *Military service:* South African Air Force, 1960. *Member:* Verein der Auslaendischen Presse in der Bundesrepublik Deutschland, American Embassy Club. *Awards, honors:* Nomination for Associated Press Managing Editors' Award, 1973, for writing the feature "Aerial Pollution Is Decaying Cologne Cathedral."

WORK IN PROGRESS: Currently reporting on energy, business, and political issues for McGraw-Hill magazines; political articles for Argus Printing and Publishing Co.

SIDELIGHTS: Roon Lewald told *CA:* "Relentless objectivity and an ability to put yourself in the shoes of a person or group of persons whose stated viewpoint may be inimical to your own principles are the keys to fair reporting in a confusing and complex world." Lewald is interested in politics, economics, energy, and history.

*   *   *

LEWANDOWSKI, Stephen 1947-

PERSONAL: Born February 27, 1947, in Canandaigua, N.Y.; son of Stanley J. (a painter) and Faith (Sterling) Lewandowski. *Education:* Hamilton College, B.A., 1969; also studied at Pendle Hill, 1969-70, and Washington University, St. Louis, Mo., 1971-72. *Home:* 639 Boughton Hill Rd., Honeoye Falls, N.Y. 14472. *Office:* Ontario County Soil and Water Conservation District, 482 North Main, Canandaigua, N.Y. 14424.

CAREER: Ontario County Soil and Water Conservation District, Canandaigua, N.Y., laborer, 1974—. Member of New York State Poets-in-the-Schools program, 1974-77; teacher at University of Rochester, 1976. *Member:* Rochester Poetry Central.

WRITINGS: Whispering Grass (poems), Farm Museum Press, 1974; *Visitor* (poems), White Pine Press, 1976; (editor) *1888 Farmer's and Housekeeper's Cyclopedia,* Crossing Press, 1977; *Water* (poems), Uroboros Press, 1978; *Inside and Out* (poems), Crossing Press, 1979; (editor) *Openers* (poems for young people), Crossing Press, 1981. Editor of *Common Sense.*

SIDELIGHTS: Lewandowski told *CA:* "I am an unabashed regionalist. I am interested, first of all, in developing an audience in upstate New York. I try to write about what I know, or what extensions of my knowing I can make with words. I believe poetry is a by-product of a well-lived life. Not necessarily a life lived by this or that religious precept, but a full life, sometimes ecstatically engaged, sometimes curiously inspected."

*   *   *

LEWIS, Hilda (Winifred) 1896-1974

PERSONAL: Born in 1896 in London, England; died February, 1974, in England; married Michael Lewis (a professor); children: one son. *Residence:* England.

CAREER: Writer. Former teacher in London, England.

WRITINGS—Novels: Madam Gold, Hurst & Blackett, 1933; *Pegasus Yoked,* Hurst & Blackett, 1933; *Full Circle,* Hurst & Blackett, 1935; *Pelican Inn,* Jarrolds, 1937; *Because I Must,* Jarrolds, 1938; *Said Dr. Spendlove,* Jarrolds, 1940, published as *Case of the Little Doctor,* Random House, 1949; *Penny Lace,* Jarrolds, 1942; *Imogen Under Glass,* Jarrolds, 1943; *Strange Story,* Jarrolds, 1945, Random House, 1947; *Gone to the Pictures,* Jarrolds, 1946; *The Day Is Ours,* Jarrolds, 1947.

More Glass Than Wall, Macdonald & Co., 1950; *No Mate, No Comrade,* Macdonald & Co., 1951; *Enter a Player,* Macdonald & Co., 1952; *Wife to Henry V,* Jarrolds, 1954, Putnam, 1957; *The Witch and the Priest,* Jarrolds, 1956, Mc-Kay, 1970; *I, Jacqueline,* Jarrolds, 1957; *Wife to Great Buckingham,* Jarrolds, 1959, Putnam, 1960; *Call Lady Purbeck,* Hutchinson, 1961, St. Martin's, 1962; *A Mortal Malice,* Hutchinson, 1963; *Wife of Charles II,* Hutchinson, 1965, published as *Catherine,* Putnam, 1966; *Wife to the Bastard,* Hutchinson, 1966, McKay, 1967.

Harlot Queen, McKay, 1970; *I Am Mary Tudor,* Hutchinson, 1971, McKay, 1972; *Mary the Queen,* Hutchinson, 1973; *Bloody Mary,* Hutchinson, 1974; *Rose of England,* Hutchinson, 1977; *Heart of a Rose,* Hutchinson, 1978.

Children's books: *The Ship That Flew,* Oxford University Press, 1939, Criterion Books, 1958; *The Gentle Falcon,* Oxford University Press, 1952, Criterion Books, 1957; *Here Comes Harry,* Criterion Books, 1960; *Harold Was My King,* Oxford University Press, 1968, McKay, 1970.

SIDELIGHTS: With more than twenty-five novels to her name, Hilda Lewis earned the reputation as one of England's finest historical novelists. Her two-volume work on Mary, the wife of King Louis XII of France, was published posthumously, and editions of her earlier books are still being reprinted. Building stories on actual historical events and characters, Lewis excelled at the meticulous research needed for her craft. Indeed, more than a few critics pointed out that her novels were both "interesting and authentic," and that she had adeptly combined "good fiction" with "good history."

"The extensiveness of the author's research," wrote P. A. Duhamel in a review of *Wife to Henry V,* "is apparent in the description of feminine dress and the rejection of the legendary pictures of Henry V." Edward Wagenknecht of the *Chicago Tribune* agreed: "It [the book] is sound and sensible in its values. It is excellently written and technically adroit, developed mainly in terms of an endless series of ever shifting scenes of a cinematic vividness." Although Phyllis Kerr thought *I Am Mary Tudor* to be "unfulfilled, lacking some needed spark," she nevertheless called it a "thought provoking" book which "captures superbly the Catholic viewpoint of the period."

Of Lewis's four children's books, three are historical novels: *The Gentle Falcon,* a story about the child bride of Richard II; *Here Comes Harry,* the life of Henry VI, King of England; and *Harold Was My King,* a novel about Edmund Edmundson, the eleventh-century English steward who refused to accept the authority of William the Conqueror. "The background detail [in *Here Comes Harry*]," wrote Aileen Pippett, "brings life and color into several otherwise bewildering and boring pages of English history." M. S. Libby concurred, "Fifteenth-century London springs to life in this tale with the action kept continuously interesting."

BIOGRAPHICAL/CRITICAL SOURCES: New Yorker, July 5, 1947; *New York Times,* July 6, 1947, March 3, 1957, July 20, 1958; *New York Herald Tribune Book Review,* March 24, 1957, May 11, 1958, July 24, 1960, November 13, 1960; *Chicago Tribune,* March 31, 1957; *Times Literary Supplement,* December 11, 1959; *Best Sellers,* October 1, 1967, May 15, 1970, April 1, 1971; *Library Journal,* May 1, 1972.*

* * *

LEWIS, Linda 1927-

PERSONAL: Born May 29, 1927, in New York, N.Y.; daughter of John (a planner) and Sher (a social worker; maiden name, Sooch) Rannells; married Anthony Lewis (a columnist), July 8, 1951; children: Eliza, David, Mia. *Education:* Cornell University, A.B., 1948; Columbia University, M.A., 1949. *Politics:* "Vaguely Democratic." *Residence:* Cambridge, Mass. *Agent:* Liz Darhansoff, 52 East 91st St., New York, N.Y. 10028.

CAREER: High school teacher of American history in Phoenix, Ariz., 1949-51; New Lincoln School, New York, N.Y., teacher, 1952-53; teacher of modern dance in Washington, D.C., 1953-64; writer, 1973—. Chairperson of Young Audiences of Massachusetts, 1977—; member of board of directors of Boston Athenaeum, Commonwealth School, Boston Fulbright Committee, and Anglo-American Contemporary Dance Trust.

WRITINGS: Birthdays, Little, Brown, 1976. Contributor to *Boston Globe.*

WORK IN PROGRESS: Essays.

SIDELIGHTS: Linda Lewis wrote: "I am writing essays on parents and children, art, solitude, pleasure, England, academic towns, and music.

"There have always been women who have known what was important—connection, learning, loving, families, fortitude, beauty, joy, decency, self-respect. Within the last ten years more and more women have begun to explain what they have come to understand about living. Although I would choose living itself, over writing about it, I would like to count myself among them—standing well back in the crowd."

* * *

LEWIS, Willie Newbury 1891-

PERSONAL: Born October 28, 1891, in Dallas, Tex.; daughter of Henry Lee (a banker and merchant) and Anna Letitia (Perkins) Newbury; married William Jenks Lewis, September 15, 1912 (deceased); children: William Jenks, Betty Lewis Young, Anne Lewis David, Joan Lewis Tatum. *Education:* Attended a private school in Texas. *Politics:* Republican. *Religion:* "Unorthodox." *Home:* 3131 Maple Ave., Dallas, Tex. 75201. *Agent:* Frank Wardlaw, 777 Marlin Dr., Fripl Island, S.C. 29920.

CAREER: Writer. Co-founder and research chairperson of Women's Council of Dallas County. *Member:* Garden Club of America (president of Dallas founders), Dallas Shakespeare Club (president), Dallas Women's Club (vice-president), Dallas Historical Society (member of board of trustees).

WRITINGS: Between Sun and Sod (informal history of Texas, based on interviews), Clarendon Press, 1938, reprinted, Texas A & M University Press, 1976; *Tapadero,* University of Texas Press, 1972.

WORK IN PROGRESS: Another book, partly autobiographical, *Dallas and a Girl Called Willie* (tentative title).

SIDELIGHTS: Willie Lewis comments: "My husband had wide experience on the Texas frontier. My married life provided me with much experience, including world travel."

* * *

LIEBERMAN, Philip 1934-

PERSONAL: Born October 25, 1934, in Brooklyn, N.Y.; son of Harry Israel (a plumber) and Miriam (Mendelson) Lieberman; married Marcia Rubinstein (a writer), June 2, 1957; children: Benjamin, Daniel. *Education:* Massachusetts Institute of Technology, B.S.E.E. and M.S.E.E., both 1958, Ph.D. (linguistics), 1966. *Home:* 141 Elton St., Providence, R.I. 02906. *Office:* Brown University, Box E, Providence, R.I. 02912.

CAREER: Air Force Communication Research Laboratories, Bedford, Mass., research scientist, 1958-67; University of Connecticut, Storrs, associate professor of linguistics and electrical engineering, 1967-70, professor of linguistics, 1970-74; Brown University, Providence, R.I., professor of linguistics, 1978—. Member of research staff, Haskins Laboratories, 1967-74; guest of Research Laboratory for Electronics, Massachusetts Institute of Technology, 1967-70. *Military service:* U.S. Air Force, 1958-62; became first lieutenant. *Member:* Modern Language Association of America, Linguistic Society of America, Acoustical Society of America, American Association of Physical Anthropology, American Anthropological Association, Swiss Alpine Club.

WRITINGS: Intonation, Perception, and Language, M.I.T. Press, 1967; *Speech Acoustics and Perception,* Bobbs-Merrill, 1970; *The Speech of Primates,* Mouton, 1972; *On the Origin of Languages: An Introduction to the Evolution of Human Language,* Macmillan, 1975; *Speech Physiology and Acoustic Phonetics,* Macmillan, 1977. Contributor of articles to journals, including *Language, Journal of the Acoustical Society of America, American Anthropologist, Brain and Language,* and *Linguistic Inquiry.*

WORK IN PROGRESS: Research into the development of speech in infants and children, "speech" communication in chimpanzees, and the evolution of language; analysis of speech pathologies and the acoustic detection of cancer and stress.

SIDELIGHTS: Lieberman told *CA:* "It's probably comforting for many people to think that human beings, as a class, are unique. The evidence for human uniqueness has, however, been transitory. In the eighteenth century, certain bones were supposed to be present only in human beings; in the nineteenth century, the structure of the human brain was supposed to be unique. Similar bones and similar neural structures were, however, found in apes. The differences which did exist were of degree rather than kind. In recent years the case for human uniqueness seems to be based on language. The problem is that chimpanzees do, in fact, behave in a linguistic mode when they are taught a modified version of American sign language. The counter-argument from advocates of uniqueness is that the chimpanzees are either not really using sign language, or that even if they are, the situation is artificial and they don't exhibit any linguistic behavior when we observe them in the wild.

"I believe that chimpanzees in the state of nature use a linguistic mode of communication and that we will ultimately be able to decode this system. The problem is that chimpanzees are not human beings and the special mechanisms that we know exist in human beings to facilitate the acquisition of human language are probably not appropriate for their language. Research on the biological bases of human language

shows that human infants, for example, are equipped to perceive some of the phonetic contrasts that are productive in human speech. The situation is similar for ducklings and duck calls. It is very difficult for humans to hear the distinctions that are meaningful to ducks; we need complex instruments or careful auditory training to differentiate the duck calls that are distinct to ducklings.

"Ultimately I believe that we will find that chimpanzees communicate in a linguistic mode—i.e., by means of an open system that can transmit new information in contrast to the closed communication systems of animals like ducks. I doubt that chimpanzees will have a language that is equivalent in its logical power to human language—they are not, after all, human beings. The difference, however, will be one of degree rather than kind.

"Some of the controversy that has emerged regarding my own work on the evolution of human language is based on the rejection of the theory that linguistic ability is a continuum. My work, for example, indicates that the speech of Neanderthal hominids was less effective than the speech of present day humans. Australopithecines, in turn, were probably closer to present day apes. If linguistic ability is the key to humanness, then the human-nonhuman distinction is not sharp. Thus, people sometimes become emotional in discussing the linguistic abilities of fossil hominids or present-day chimpanzees. The debate really isn't about language but the human-nonhuman distinction.

"The next decade will be interesting. It will be curious, to say the least, to establish ethical standards if the human-nonhuman distinction is a continuum."

* * *

LIEBLICH, Amia 1939-

PERSONAL: Born November 24, 1939, in Tel Aviv, Israel; daughter of Moshe Aryeh (a welfare worker) and Hanna (a pharmacist; maiden name, Schidlowski) Kurtz; married Israel D. Lieblich (a psychologist), July, 1963; children: Yuval, Matat. *Education:* Hebrew University, B.A., 1961, M.A., 1964, Ph.D., 1967; attended Gestalt Therapy Institute (Los Angeles), 1969-70. *Religion:* Jewish. *Home:* 6 Aluf Simkhoni St., Jerusalem, Israel. *Office:* Department of Psychology, Hebrew University, Jerusalem, Israel.

CAREER: Hebrew University, Jerusalem, Israel, student services counselor, 1970-74, and professor of psychology, 1970—. Part-time private practice as gestalt therapist, 1971—.

WRITINGS: Tin Soldiers on Jerusalem Beach, Pantheon, 1978.

WORK IN PROGRESS: An Oral History of a Kibbutz (tentative title), publication by Pantheon expected in 1980.

SIDELIGHTS: Lieblich told *CA:* "I see my life and career as based on two main components: my Israeli identity and strong identification with the struggle of the state of Israel and Jews everywhere, and my education and training as an existential psychologist, with the major impact of gestalt therapy approach. The synthesis of these two components is what produced my first book."

In *Tin Soldiers on Jerusalem Beach,* Lieblich studies some of the psychological conditions peculiar to Israeli life. She observes that, having lived under the constant threat of war, Israeli women will too often indulge the demands of their sons and husbands. One mother said of her thirteen-year-old son, "You have to compensate him now, give him the best possible childhood, since a young man in Israel, who knows?'' This tendency of women to spoil their sons, Lieblich contended, is extended to the grown men as well. Women are reluctant to press for the changes made elsewhere by the women's movement ''because they suffer from guilt vis-a-vis the fighting men who protect them in war.''

One particular problem for Israeli men, argues Lieblich, is the need to conform to the hero mystique. According to one young man, ''We are all born to be heroes, to fulfill the expectations of generations of Jews out there.'' As a result, the obsession with stoic strength and courage leaves the Israeli male emotionally crippled during times of peace. In one case, Lieblich documents the struggle of a tank commander to regain his capacity to feel; a man who begs his hidden, teen-age self to ''give me back the ability to cry.''

According to *Newsweek,* Lieblich identifies several other subsidiary effects of the hero-ethos, but while she touches upon the unusual lack of creativity and tolerance among Israelis and the overbearing need to conform, she does not give these themes a full examination. Concluded Elizabeth Peer: ''But in a nation where emotional repression is as common as olive trees, and where a single-minded obsession with survival means that negativity rarely surfaces at all, her report is extremely valuable.''

BIOGRAPHICAL/CRITICAL SOURCES: Newsweek, November 27, 1978; *New York Times Book Review,* December 10, 1978.

* * *

LIEDERBACH, Clarence Andrew 1910-

PERSONAL: Born November 29, 1910, in Cleveland, Ohio; son of James F., Sr. and Louise (Tucaur) Liederbach. *Education:* Attended Marquette University, Our Lady of the Lake Seminary, Kent State University, and St. John College. *Home and office:* 906 College Ave., Cleveland, Ohio 44113. *Agent:* Robert J. Liederbach, 2720 East Blvd., Cleveland, Ohio 44104.

CAREER: Ordained Roman Catholic priest; assistant principal and athletic director at Roman Catholic high school in Youngstown, Ohio, 1941-42; associate pastor of Roman Catholic churches in Great Falls, Mont., and Springfield, Mass.; pastor of Roman Catholic churches in Cleveland, Ohio, and Rittman, Ohio. Cruise chaplain for major cruise ship lines. Member of Cleveland Regional Transit Authority Committee. *Member:* Knights of Columbus, Rittman Rotary Club.

WRITINGS: The Way of the Cross for Crossbearers, Abbey Press, 1945; *When a Catholic Marries,* Bruce Publishing, 1946; *Instructio pro Confessariis,* Bruce Publishing, 1948; *America's Thousand Bishops,* Bona Ventura Press, 1970; *Canada's Bishops,* Bona Ventura Press, 1971; *Mexico's Bishops,* Bona Ventura Press, 1977. Contributor to church magazines, including *Our Sunday Visitor.*

WORK IN PROGRESS: Research on two Confederate priest-poets, Ryan and Tabb.

SIDELIGHTS: Liederbach writes that he maintains a ''conservative Roman Catholic stance, with the conviction that the Roman Catholic Church prospers or disintegrates as its hierarchy leads.''

* * *

LIGHT, Albert 1927-

PERSONAL: Born June 19, 1927, in New York, N.Y.; son of David and Sarah (Edinoff) Light; married Tobia Lipsher (a teacher), May 18, 1952; children: Pamela S., Audrey L. *Education:* City College (now of the City University of New York), B.S., 1948; Yale University, Ph.D., 1955. *Home:* 2307 Carmel Dr., West Lafayette, Ind. 47906. *Office:* Department of Chemistry, Purdue University, West Lafayette, Ind. 47907.

CAREER: Cornell University, Ithaca, N.Y., fellow at Medical College, 1955-57; University of Utah, Salt Lake City, assistant professor of chemistry, 1957-63; University of California, Los Angeles, associate professor of chemistry, 1963-65; Purdue University, West Lafayette, Ind., associate professor, 1965-77, professor of chemistry, 1977—. Participant in international meetings. *Military service:* U.S. Navy, 1944-45. *Member:* American Chemical Society, American Society of Biological Chemists, American Association for the Advancement of Science, American Association of University Professors, Sigma Xi. *Awards, honors:* U.S. Public Health Service postdoctoral fellowship.

WRITINGS: (Contributor) Sidney P. Colowick and Nathan O. Kaplan, editors, *Methods in Enzymology,* Academic Press, 1972. *Proteins: Structure and Function,* Prentice-Hall, 1974; Contributor to *Encyclopedia Americana.* Contributor to chemistry journals.

WORK IN PROGRESS: Enzyme and protein research.

AVOCATIONAL INTERESTS: International travel.

* * *

LIKERT, Rensis 1903-

PERSONAL: Born August 5, 1903, in Wyoming; son of George Herbert (an engineer) and Cornelia (Zonne) Likert; married Jane Gibson (an editor and consultant), August 31, 1928; children: Elizabeth Likert David, Patricia Likert Pohlman. *Education:* University of Michigan, A.B., 1926; Columbia University, Ph.D., 1932. *Religion:* Unitarian-Universalist. *Home:* 860 Mokulua Dr., Kailua, Hawaii 96734. *Office:* Rensis Likert Associates, 630 City Center Bldg., Ann Arbor, Mich. 48104.

CAREER: New York University, New York, N.Y., 1930-35, began as instructor, became assistant professor; Sarah Lawrence College, Bronxville, N.Y., faculty member, 1935-36; U.S. Department of Agriculture, Bureau of Agricultural Economics, Washington, D.C., head of Division of Program Surveys, 1935-46; University of Michigan, Ann Arbor, professor of psychology and sociology, 1946-70, professor emeritus, 1971—, director of Survey Research Center, 1946-48, and Institute for Social Research, 1948-70, director emeritus, 1971—; Rensis Likert Associates, Inc., Ann Arbor, chairperson of board of directors, 1971—. Research director for Life Insurance Agency Management Association, 1935-39; director of Morale Division of U.S. Strategic Bombing Survey, 1944-46.

MEMBER: American Psychological Association (fellow; past member of board of directors), American Statistical Association (past president), National Academy of Public Administration. *Awards, honors:* Paul D. Converse Award from University of Illinois, 1955; publication award from Organization Development Council, James A. Hamilton Award, and book award from McKinsey Foundation, all 1962, for *New Patterns of Management;* Stockberger Award from Society for Personnel Administration, 1963; D.H.C. from University of Tilburg, 1967; human relations award from Society for the Advancement of Management, 1968; professional achievement award from American Board of Examiners of Professional Psychologists, 1968; outstanding achievement awards from American Society for Training and Development, 1969, and American Association for Public Opinion Research, 1973.

WRITINGS: (With G. Murphy) *Public Opinion and the Individual,* Harper, 1938, reprinted, Russell, 1970; (with J. M. Willits) *Morale and Agency Management,* four volumes, Life Insurance Agency Management Association, 1940-41; (editor with S. P. Hayes) *Some Applications of Behavioral Research,* Publications Division, United Nations Educational, Scientific, and Cultural Organization, 1957; *New Patterns of Management,* McGraw, 1961; *The Human Organization: Its Management and Value,* McGraw, 1967; (with wife, Jane Gibson Likert) *New Ways of Managing Conflict,* McGraw, 1976.

Contributor: W. D. Dennis, editor, *Current Trends in Psychology,* University of Pittsburgh Press, 1947; Lerner and Lasswell, editors, *The Policy Sciences,* Stanford University Press, 1951; R. A. Walker, editor, *America's Manpower Crisis,* Public Administration Service, 1952; L. Festinger and D. Katz, editors, *Research Methods in the Behavioral Sciences,* Dryden, 1953; *Manpower Problems in the United States,* McGraw, 1954; R. H. Cole, editor, *Consumer Behavior and Motivation,* University of Illinois Press, 1955; *Some Applications of Behavioural Research,* Publications Division, United Nations Educational, Scientific and Cultural Organization, 1957; *Operations Research,* Industry Program, University of Michigan, 1957; F. E. May, editor, *Increasing Sales Efficiency: Conference on Sales and Marketing Management, 1959,* Bureau of Business Research, University of Michigan, 1959; D. L. Bowen and R. H. Pealy, editors, *Administrative Leadership in Government: Selected Papers,* Institute of Public Administration, University of Michigan, 1959; M. Haire, editor, *Modern Organization Theory,* Wiley, 1959.

Contributor: J. G. Peatman and E. L. Hartley, editors, *Festschrift for Gardner Murphy,* Harper, 1960; L. Petrullo, editor, *Leadership and Interpersonal Behavior,* Holt, 1961; F. A. Bond, editor, *Business Schools and Economic Growth: CIC Conference on Productivity and Economic Growth,* Bureau of Business Research, University of Michigan, 1964; L. L. Cummings and W. E. Scott, editors, *Readings in Organizational Behavior and Human Performance,* Irwin, 1969; D. Allison, editor, *The R & D Game,* M.I.T. Press, 1969; (author of introduction) *Human Resource Accounting: Development and Implementation in Industry,* Foundation for Research on Human Behavior, 1969; Harper Boyd and Robert Davis, editors, *Readings in Sales Management,* Irwin, 1970; *A New Rationale for Corporate Social Policy,* Committee for Economic Development, 1970; D. E. Johnson, editor, *Concepts of Air Force Leadership,* Air University, 1971; A. L. Hite, editor, *Organizational Development: The State of the Art,* Foundation for Research on Human Behavior, 1971; B. T. King and E. McGinnies, editors, *Attitudes, Conflict, and Social Change,* Academic Press, 1972; B. Strumpel, J. N. Morgan, and E. Zahn, editors, *Human Behavior in Economic Affairs: Essays in Honor of George Katona,* Elsevier Publishing, 1972; A. H. Rosenthal, editor, *Public Science Policy and Administration,* University of New Mexico Press, 1973; H. Koontz and C. O'Donnell, editors, *Management: A Book of Readings,* 3rd edition (Likert was not affiliated with earlier editions), McGraw, 1972; E. A. Fleishman and A. R. Bass, editors, *Studies in Personnel and Industrial Psychology,* 3rd edition (Likert was not affiliated with earlier editions), Dorsey, 1974; Dale S. Beach, editor, *Managing People at Work: Readings in Personnel,* 2nd edition (Likert was not affiliated

with 1st edition), Macmillan, 1975; *Evaluating Governmental Performance: Changes and Challenges for G.A.O.,* U.S. Government Printing Office, 1975.

Contributor to *International Encyclopedia of Neurology, Psychiatry, Psychoanalysis, and Psychology.* Contributor of more than sixty articles to a wide variety of professional and popular periodicals, including *Scientific American,* and to U.S. Congress hearings.

*   *   *

LINDBERGH, Charles A(ugustus, Jr.) 1902-1974

PERSONAL: Born February 4, 1902, in Detroit, Mich.; died August 26, 1974, of cancer, in Maui, Hawaii; buried in Maui, Hawaii; son of Charles Augustus (a lawyer) and Evangeline Lodge (Land) Lindbergh; married Anne Spencer Morrow (a writer), May 27, 1929; children: Charles Augustus III (died, 1932), Jon Morrow, Land Morrow, Scott, Reeve, Anne Spencer. *Education:* Attended University of Wisconsin, 1920-22, and Nebraska Aircraft Corp. flying school, 1922. *Politics:* Conservative.

CAREER: Stunt flier, barnstormer, and mechanic in Midwest, 1922-24; Robertson Aircraft Corp., airmail pilot between Chicago and St. Louis, 1926; solo-pilot of transcontinental flight between New York and Paris, 1927; goodwill ambassador to Central America, West Indies, and Cuba, 1927-28; Rockefeller Institute, inventor and designer, 1930-35; researcher and inventor with Alexis Carrel in France, 1935-39; Ford Motor Co., Detroit, Mich., and U.S. War Department, consultant, 1939-44; civilian consultant to United Aircraft Corp. in Connecticut and in Pacific theater, 1943-44; consultant and writer, 1944—; conservationist, 1964—. Consultant and technical adviser to Pan American Airways; chairman of technical committee of Transcontinental Air Transport Co.; member of Army Ordinance's CHORE project at University of Chicago; consultant to secretary of Air Force; member of scientific ballistic-missile committee of Air Force and Defense Department; reorganizer of Strategic Air Command (SAC). *Military service:* U.S. Army Air Service Reserve, 1924-41, 1954—; became brigadier general.

AWARDS, HONORS—All for transcontinental flight, 1927: Distinguished Flying Cross and Congressional Medal of Honor from the United States by special act of Congress; Chevalier of the Legion of Honor from France; Order of Leopold from Belgium; Royal Air Cross from Great Britain; Woodrow Wilson medal and $25,000 good will flight to Mexico, Central America, and West Indies; Orteig prize of $25,000 from Raymond B. Orteig. Other: Master of Aeronautics from New York University, 1928; Doctor of Laws from Northwestern University and University of Wisconsin, 1928; Master of Science from Princeton University, 1931; Service Cross of the German Eagle from Hermann Goering, 1938; Wright Brothers Memorial Trophy, 1949; Daniel Guggenheim International Aviation Award, 1953; Pulitzer Prize in biography for *Spirit of St. Louis,* 1954; Langly Medal from Smithsonian Institute; Hubbard Medal from National Geographical Society; Cross of Honor from U.S. Flying Association; Medal of Valor from State of New York.

WRITINGS: We, Putnam, 1927; (with Alexis Carrel) *Culture of Organs,* Harper, 1938; *Of Flight and Life,* Scribner, 1948; "Thirty-Three Hours to Paris," published in *Saturday Evening Post,* 1953, published as *The Spirit of St. Louis* (Book-of-the-Month Club selection), Scribner, 1953, condensed version, Reader's Digest Press, 1953; *The Wartime Journals of Charles A. Lindbergh,* Harcourt, 1970; *Boyhood on the*

Upper Mississippi, Minnesota Historical Society, 1972; *Banana River*, Harcourt, 1976; *Autobiography of Values*, Harcourt, 1978.

SIDELIGHTS: The world held its breath as Charles A. Lindbergh flew alone for thirty-three hours over the Atlantic Ocean to complete the first non-stop plane flight from New York to Paris. Will Rogers wrote in his column on that day, May 20, 1927, that there would be "no attempts at jokes today. A slim, tall, bashful, smiling American boy is somewhere over the middle of the Atlantic Ocean, where no lone human being has ever ventured before." When the "Lone Eagle" finally landed shortly after 10 P.M. on May 21, at Le Bourget Airport in Paris, the world exhaled a triumphant sigh of relief and smothered him with adulation. "Lucky Lindy" became the symbol for a new age: The Age of Aviation. His deed had changed the course of history.

Lindbergh, the son of a populist lawyer and U.S. representative, became interested in aviation as a boy of ten, after seeing a plane flying above Washington, D.C. His fascination never dulled, so Lindbergh quit the University of Wisconsin and concentrated on learning to fly at the Nebraska Aircraft Corporation flying school. He took his first flight on April 9, 1922, and within a month became a barnstormer and stunt pilot. At the price of five dollars for five minutes, he traveled through southern Nebraska giving farmers and small-towners rides on his plane. The "Flying Fool," who experimented with such stunts as the double parachute jump, decided to make flying his career. "I began to feel that I lived on a higher plane than the skeptics of the ground. In flying, I tasted a wine of the gods of which they could know nothing. Who valued life more highly, the aviators who spent it on the art they loved, or these misers who doled it out like pennies through their antlike days? I decided that if I could fly for ten years before I was killed in a crash, it would be a worthwhile trade for an ordinary lifetime," he wrote many years later.

Lindbergh started to fly airmail between Chicago and St. Louis, which was a risky proposition. It was on one of these night flights in the autumn of 1926 that he seriously considered attempting to win the $25,000 prize offered by Raymond B. Orteig to anyone who could successfully complete the first non-stop flight from New York to Paris. Lindbergh acquired the financial backing of some St. Louis businessmen and bought a mono-plane with a single radial air cooled engine. One writer described the plane as "one giant gasoline tank with wings, a propeller and a bucket seat." The plane was christened the *Spirit of St. Louis*.

When Lindbergh took off, with only a bag of sandwiches to sustain him, his craft was so laden with gas that he cleared the telephone lines near Long Island's Roosevelt Field by barely twenty feet. When the "Lone Eagle" arrived in Paris, after traveling more than 3600 miles, he was a hero and an instant celebrity. He was deluged with awards, honors, and testimonials. He was so popular and well-known that "if he sent shirts to the laundry, they were not sent back. If he wrote a check, it was never cashed. If he checked a hat, it was somehow lost. All became souvenirs, precious talismans of the otherwise cynical Jazz Age." Lindbergh said later that he was "so filled up with listening to this hero guff that I was ready to shout murder."

After the initial excitement, Lindbergh became a tireless promoter of the aviation industry. He flew the *Spirit of St. Louis* to all forty-eight states and embarked on a good will tour to Mexico, Central America, Cuba, and the West Indies. It was in Mexico that he met Anne Spencer Morrow,

the daughter of Dwight Morrow, an associate of banker J. P. Morgan and the U.S. ambassador to Mexico. The two married in 1929. Meanwhile, Lindbergh continued his work in aviation by helping to lay out transatlantic, transcontinental, and Caribbean air routes for Pan American and Trans World Airlines. He also branched out into other fields by designing and building a tissue-perfusion apparatus to be used in a mechanical heart and by inventing a quick method of separating serum from blood by means of a centrifuge.

On March 1, 1932, tragedy struck Lindbergh and his wife when their twenty-month-old, Charles, Jr., was kidnapped from his crib in their house in New Jersey. After paying $50,000 in ransom, and waiting over two months, their child was found dead in a shallow grave near his home. A carpenter, Bruno Richard Hauptmann, was convicted in 1935 and executed for the crime. As a result of this sensational trial, the "Lindbergh laws" were enacted in 1932 and 1934, imposing severe penalties for interstate abduction, with the death sentence for cases in which the victim was harmed.

Lindbergh and his wife, previously always in the public eye, were mercilessly hounded by the press after the kidnapping of their son. One photographer went so far as to break into the child's casket in the morgue to take a picture of his body. To escape the attentions of the press, Lindbergh moved to England and later France with his wife and new son. They stayed there until the beginning of World War II. When the family returned to the United States, Lindbergh, a member of the isolationist group America First, again entered the public spotlight to express his opinion that America remain isolated and not become involved in the war. He was very impressed with Germany's war machine after inspecting its air force in 1938. He felt that Great Britain and France were so appallingly unprepared for war that the conflict would ultimately result in Germany and Russia being the main contenders and that they would destroy each other. This view was very unpopular. President Roosevelt openly criticized Lindbergh and the aviator was accused of being unpatriotic, a fascist, and anti-Semitic.

When Pearl Harbor was bombed, Lindbergh volunteered immediately, but was refused by President Roosevelt. In retaliation, Lindbergh angrily resigned his position in the Army Air Corps. Nevertheless, he did see action in the Pacific theater. As a civilian technician for the United Aircraft Corp., Lindbergh was sent to the Pacific to study the Navy Corsair F4U planes. During his six-month stay, he flew over fifty missions and shot down two Japanese planes. After the war, Lindbergh became a consultant to a number of organizations, including the U.S. Government and Pan American Airlines again, where he worked on the design specifications for the Boeing 747. Although most of his work with the government was secret, it is known that he worked on developing missiles and rockets. Lindbergh had been a close friend and financial supporter of Dr. Robert Goddard, the pioneer of the development of rockets.

In his later years, until his death, Lindbergh became very interested in conservation. "I have felt the godlike power man derives from his machines. . . . But I have seen the science I worshiped and the aircraft I loved destroying the civilization I expected them to serve." Lindbergh came to this realization in Africa in 1964, while "lying under an acacia tree with the sounds of the dawn around me." "I realized more clearly the fact that man should never overlook: that the construction of an airplane, for instance, is simple when compared to the evolutionary achievement of a bird; that airplanes depend on an advanced civilization, and that where civilization is most advanced few birds exist. I realized that if I had to choose, I would rather have birds than airplanes.'' Lindbergh worked to save the humpbacked and blue whales from extinction and also studied monkey-eating eagles and primitive tribes in the Philippines.

BIOGRAPHICAL/CRITICAL SOURCES: New York World, January 16, 1927; *New York Evening Post,* August 6, 1927; *New York Times,* August 7, 1927, August 22, 1948, September 13, 1953, September 23, 1970, August 27, 1974; *Nation,* August 10, 1927; *New York Herald Tribune Book Review,* August 14, 1927, September 13, 1953; *Survey,* October 1, 1927; Anne Morrow Lindbergh, *North to the Orient,* Harcourt, 1935; A. Lindbergh, *Listen! the Wind,* Harcourt, 1938; *Saturday Review of Literature,* August 21, 1948; *Christian Science Monitor,* August 28, 1948, September 17, 1953, October 1, 1970; *New Republic,* August 30, 1948, October 3, 1970; *Newsweek,* December 5, 1949, September 14, 1953, September 28, 1970, September 9, 1974.

Saturday Evening Post, March 8, 1952; *Aero Digest,* May, 1952; *Saturday Review,* September 12, 1953, October 3, 1970; *Chicago Sunday Tribune,* September 13, 1953; *Time,* September 14, 1953, September 9, 1974; *Atlantic,* October, 1953, November, 1970; Kenneth Sydney Davis, *Hero: Charles A. Lindbergh and the American Dream,* Doubleday, 1959; *Life,* October 4, 1963; *Reader's Digest,* February, 1964, December, 1974; *New York Times Book Review,* September 20, 1970; *Book World,* September 27, 1970; *New York Review of Books,* October 8, 1970; *National Review,* November 17, 1970; *Commentary,* February, 1971; A. Lindbergh, *Locked Rooms and Open Doors,* Harcourt, 1974; A. Lindbergh, *Flower and the Nettle,* Harcourt, 1976.

OBITUARIES: New York Times, August 27, 1974; *Washington Post,* August 27, 1974; *Newsweek,* September 9, 1974; *Time,* September 9, 1974; *National Review,* September 13, 1974.*

—*Sketch by Anne M. Guerrini*

* * *

LIPTON, Lawrence 1898-1975

PERSONAL: Born in 1898 in Poland; died July 9, 1975, in Venice, Calif.; married wife, Nettie; children: James. *Residence:* Venice, Calif.

CAREER: Writer. Worked as instructor at universities in California.

WRITINGS: Brother, the Laugh Is Bitter (novel), Harper, 1942; *Rainbow at Midnight* (verse), Golden Quill Press, 1955; *The Holy Barbarians* (criticism), Messner, 1959; *The Erotic Revolution: An Affirmative View of the New Morality* (nonfiction), Sherbourne Press, 1965; *Bruno in Venice West* (verse), Venice West Publishers, 1976. Also author of the novel *In Secret Battle.*

SIDELIGHTS: Lipton is best known for *The Holy Barbarians,* his critical work on the Beat writers, including Allen Ginsburg and Jack Kerouac. Years later, after Kerouac died, and the Beats were passe, Lipton compared himself to Mother Goddam. "Most have gone, but I've survived," he claimed. "I'm a tough hombre."

BIOGRAPHICAL/CRITICAL SOURCES: New York Times, July 11, 1975.*

* * *

LITTELL, Robert 1896-1963

OBITUARY NOTICE: Born May 15, 1896, in Milwaukee, Wis.; died December 5, 1963. Editor, journalist, and author.

Littell began his career as an associate editor of *New Republic* in 1922, a post he left five years later to become a drama critic for the *New York Evening Post.* When he joined the *New York World* in 1929, he worked as both drama critic and columnist. In 1927, he began his long association with *Reader's Digest,* becoming its senior editor in 1942. Littell was the author of *Read America First, Candles in the Storm, It Takes All Kinds,* and co-author of the play "Gather Ye Rosebuds." Obituaries and other sources: *Who Was Who in America,* 4th edition, Marquis, 1968; *American Authors and Books, 1640 to the Present Day,* 3rd revised edition, Crown, 1972.

* * *

LLOYD EVANS, Barbara 1924-

PERSONAL: Born April 5, 1924, in Malvern, Worcestershire, England; daughter of Ernest Joseph (a civil servant) and Edith Mary (Kings) Bowen; married Gareth Lloyd Evans (a lecturer and writer), August 29, 1949; children: Lynette Lloyd Evans Lowthian, Jeremy, Martin. *Education:* University of Birmingham, B.A., 1944, M.A., 1946; Oxford University, teaching diploma, 1945. *Home:* 1 Hunts Rd., Stratford-upon-Avon, Warwickshire, England.

CAREER: University of Birmingham, Birmingham, England, lecturer in English, 1959-76; teacher of English in high school in England, 1960—.

WRITINGS: (Editor) *Something to Offer: A Selection of Contemporary Prose and Verse,* Blackie & Son, 1968; (with husband, Gareth Lloyd Evans) *Everyman's Companion to Shakespeare,* Dent, 1978; (with G. Lloyd Evans) *Everyman's Companion to the Brontes,* Dent, 1980.

Plays: "The Three Bears," first broadcast by British Broadcasting Corp. (BBC); "Chirp the Bold Bad Chick," first broadcast by BBC.

Contributor of stories, poems, and articles to adult and juvenile magazines.

WORK IN PROGRESS: Plays for BBC; poems; children's stories.

SIDELIGHTS: Barbara Lloyd Evans told *CA:* "There are two things that give me great joy—writing poetry and traveling, and I suppose writing poetry could be seen as a way of traveling. The first poems I remember were 'composed' in my head and written down by my mother. I had an uncle, now dead, who had little formal education, but great sensitivity who, in a light-hearted way, kept the flame alive. As a teenager, the magic of my home—a house perched up on the side of the Malvern Hills where I roamed day and night to my heart's content, encouraged that flame into a small fire. Now, as well as lecturing, writing, and acting as some kind of anchor for my family, I teach, and find that I spend most of my time trying to arouse in my pupils that sense of delight and curiosity that is at the root, not only of most poetry, but of being alive—as distinct from merely living.

"I think, at the moment, I have got over the stage of wanting to pour out my soul in verse—it's a dull old soul, anyway. Poetry is a need, as I see it. It has a public as well as a private face. Believing this has led me to write a series of poems for a local group of mentally retarded children, who respond eagerly to poetry, but who, alas, can find very little poetry that is right for them.

"Travel? Well, it's like living a poem. You plan ahead, but you are never quite sure what may happen until you are back at home base again. I think that somewhere I must have had gypsy sea-faring forebears—the itch to get away, particularly to the sea, is so overwhelming.

"Writing *Everyman's Companion to Shakespeare* has proved to be one of the happiest experiences of my life. We couldn't live in a better place (Stratford-upon-Avon) to catch a glimpse of his ghost disappearing round old corners."

* * *

LOASBY, Brian John 1930-

PERSONAL: Born August 2, 1930, in Kettering, England; son of Frederick T. and Mabel (Burrett) Loasby; married Judith Ann Robinson, September 7, 1957; children: Caroline, Sarah. *Education:* Emmanuel College, Cambridge, B.A., 1952, M.Litt., 1957. *Home:* 8 Melfort Dr., Stirling FK7 0BD, Scotland. *Office:* Department of Economics, University of Stirling, Stirling FK9 4LA, Scotland.

CAREER: University of Aberdeen, Aberdeen, Scotland, research assistant in political economy, 1955-58; University of Birmingham, Birmingham, England, Bournville research fellow, 1958-61; University of Bristol, Bristol, England, tutor in management studies, 1961-67; University of Stirling, Stirling, Scotland, lecturer, 1967-68, senior lecturer, 1968-71, professor of management economics, 1971—. Management fellow with Arthur D. Little, Inc., 1965-66; visiting fellow at Oxford Center for Management Studies, 1974. *Military service:* British Army, 1948-49; became sergeant. *Member:* Royal Economic Society, British Institute of Management (associate member), Scottish Economic Society, American Economic Association.

WRITINGS: The Swindon Project, Pitman, 1973; *Choice, Complexity, and Ignorance,* Cambridge University Press, 1976. Contributor to economic and management journals.

WORK IN PROGRESS: Studying scientific research programs in economics; research on coordination and innovation in economic systems.

SIDELIGHTS: Loasby told *CA:* "I am currently concerned to see how adequately one can explain decision-making in organizations by treating decision-makers as scientists, that is as people who base their decisions on theories—be they roughly or precisely formulated—which are amended in the light of experience, but amended within some persistent overall framework. The conception of scientific method thus used derives from the work of Sir Karl Popper, supplemented by Imre Lakatos: science progresses by conjecture and refutation, contained within a research program. Furthermore, I am attempting to link this approach with the ideas of Herbert A. Simon, Nobel prize-winner in economics, on the implication of bounded rationality and of the extent to which, and the conditions in which, the interdependence of complex systems may be safely ignored."

* * *

LOCKRIDGE, Frances Louise ?-1963

OBITUARY NOTICE: Born in Kansas City, Mo.; died February 17, 1963. Journalist and author. After working four years as a reporter and feature writer for the *Kansas City Post,* Lockridge moved to New York City in 1922, where she met and married *New York Sun* reporter Richard Lockridge. In 1940, she and her husband began collaborating on a series of mystery novels that centered around a charming, domestic pair of sleuths, Mr. and Mrs. North. Among the numerous volumes of the series are *The Norths Meet Murder, A Pinch of Poison, Death on the Aisle, Killing the Goose,* and *Quest of the Bogeyman.* For many years a publicity worker at State Charities Aid Association, Lockridge also wrote a book called *Adopting a Child.* Obituaries and other sources: *Who Was Who in America,* 4th edition, Marquis, 1968; *Encyclopedia of Mystery and Detection,* McGraw, 1976.

* * *

LOEB, William 1905-

PERSONAL: Born December 26, 1905, in Washington, D.C.; son of William (a private secretary to President Theodore Roosevelt) and Katherine W. (Dorr) Loeb; married Elizabeth V. Nagy, May 29, 1926 (marriage annulled October 11, 1932); married Eleanor McAlister, September 26, 1942 (divorced, 1952); married Nackey Scripps, July 15, 1952; children: (second marriage) Penelope; (third marriage) Elizabeth (adopted, daughter of Nackey and George Gallowher), Edith. *Education:* Williams College, A.B., 1927; attended Harvard University, 1929-31. *Politics:* "Nineteenth-century liberal." *Religion:* Baptist. *Home:* Nevada Star Ranch, 6995 Franktown Rd., Carson City, Nev. 89701. *Office: Manchester Union Leader,* 35 Amherst St., Manchester, N.H. 03105.

CAREER/WRITINGS: Springfield Republican and *Springfield Union,* Springfield, Mass., part-time reporter; *New York World,* New York City, part-time reporter; worked as reporter for Paul Block newspapers; worked in sales and public relations; *St. Albans Daily Messenger,* St. Albans, Vt., publisher, 1941—; *Vermont Sunday News,* St. Albans, publisher, 1942—; *Burlington Daily News,* Burlington, Vt., publisher, 1942-61; *Manchester Union Leader,* Manchester, N.H., publisher, 1946—; *New Hampshire Sunday News,* Manchester, publisher, 1948—; *Haverhill Journal,* Haverhill, Mass., publisher, 1957-65; *Connecticut Sunday Herald,* Bridgeport, Conn., publisher, 1964-74. Regular contributor of editorials to his newspaper, *Manchester Union Leader.* President of American China Policy Association, 1941-43; chairman of Council of Profit-Sharing Industries, 1949-52; director of National Rifle Association. Secretary of American Foundation for Tropical Medicine, 1940-44; trustee of Lahey Clinic Fund (Boston).

MEMBER: Zeta Psi, Seawanhaka Corinthian Yacht Club (Oyster Bay), Harvard Club (Boston), Prospectors' Club (Reno). *Awards, honors:* Named "an outstanding American conservative" by National Economic Council, 1972; decorated commander; Knight of Malta; received Order of St. John of Jerusalem; Polonia Restitute from Government in Exile of Poland, 1975.

SIDELIGHTS: As the publisher of the *Manchester Union Leader,* William Loeb enjoys an especially influential position in New Hampshire's political life. Explained Bill Kovach for the *New York Times Magazine:* "The newspaper's importance results from a position of power unequaled in any other state. The Union Leader—circulation 63,000 'and growing'—is the only statewide newspaper serving New Hampshire's 740,000 people [and] it is the only morning paper in the state. . . . Because The Union Leader is their biggest client in the state, the wire services feel its influence. If it concentrates on an issue, the wire services are hard put not to cover that issue for their clients." As a result, he continued, Loeb can—almost without fail—"turn political novices into threatening candidates, and he can regularly name the Democratic gubernatorial nominee" as well as "determine the issues in an election."

But once every four years, Loeb and the *Union Leader* become a national force in the opening round of presidential primaries. His hard-hitting and often controversial front-page editorials have been instrumental in affecting the outcome of the New Hampshire primary: he is generally credited with derailing Senator Edmund S. Muskie's drive for the 1972 Democratic nomination. In other election years, he had called Dwight Eisenhower a "stinking hypocrite," John Kennedy the "No. 1 liar in the U.S.A.," and Eugene McCarthy the "skunk's skunk's skunk." He is a man who believes in absolutes ("Things are either right or they are wrong"), including "honor, good manners, the country, patriotism"; and if good manners seem incommensurate with some of his more personal, bitter editorial attacks, he commented, it is because they were designed for "shock value" or to "get people thinking." His conservative views and attitudes remain unchanged since they were first refined in the 1930's: "I guess seen from the viewpoint of that age I was an idealist, but seen from the viewpoint of today, I'm called reactionary.... You are supposed to adjust, and if you don't you are called a reactionary. I just haven't changed much from those days."

AVOCATIONAL INTERESTS: Skiing, horseback riding, tennis, trap shooting, goose shooting, salmon fishing.

CA INTERVIEWS THE AUTHOR

William Loeb, president and publisher of the *Manchester Union Leader* and *St. Albans Daily Messenger*, was interviewed by Peter Benjaminson in Loeb's somewhat spartan second-floor office at the *Union Leader* in Manchester on September 11, 1979. Loeb's wife, Nackey Scripps Loeb, and a secretary were also present. Benjaminson, whose sketch is in *CA* 73-76, is the co-author, with David Anderson, of *Investigative Reporting*, published by Indiana University Press in 1976, and the author of *The Story of Motown*, published by Grove Press in 1979.

CA: I just wanted to ask you a few general questions about your philosophy and some of the operations here. I'll try not to take up too much of your time.

LOEB: That's perfectly all right. I'm just one of those fellows that doesn't care about publicity. I don't seek it. I get enough of it my way anyhow. I take what I believe seriously; I don't take myself seriously. So I really don't give a damn about most of these things that most people want; they want to be in *Who's Who*, in all kinds of reference books and everything else, but I couldn't care less. But go ahead anyhow.... Interesting project on your part. I hope you can make a buck out of it....

CA: One of the things I wanted to ask you about was the New Hampshire primary. Your newspapers have a lot of influence on it; it's certainly an unusual institution in that New Hampshire's primary is first and it does have an effect. I'm sure you've heard all the arguments about New Hampshire not being totally representative of the country and that perhaps the primary has more influence on the national scene than it should. There have been suggestions for a regional primary, and other states have tried to move their primaries back earlier than New Hampshire's.

LOEB: Well, there's one very good argument in favor of it: that it's a small state and somebody like Carter can come in—and I don't know if this is a very good example—a guy like Carter can come in with very little funds, nothing very elaborate, and can make an impression in New Hampshire, and if he wins in New Hampshire he can then get national support and go on to bigger campaigns. If you make it a regional campaign, say a regional primary for New England, then you get into big money; now you're limiting it to candidates who can either have big personal resources, such as the Kennedys, or can put together a group of conglomerates

or labor leaders, labor parties, labor organizations that'll finance him. I think it's a very healthy thing to have a state where almost anybody of modest means can go in and test the waters and see whether people really want what he represents.

And then going back on the other part about we're not typical, the thing that's noticeable over the years has been that it's significant that no one who's ever lost the New Hampshire primary has gone on to be President. So it seems to be a good political barometer.

CA: You were answering the argument about New Hampshire not being typical.

LOEB: I said, as the example, no one's ever lost it who's gone on to be President.

CA: If I'm not mistaken, you were a student at Harvard Law School for at least a couple of years. Were you considering going into law at the time?

LOEB: No, no. I grew up in an age which is hard for you to imagine: If your parents said, "Go to law school," you went to law school without any murmur. I probably would have been much happier going to medical school. I had no interest in the law. So in the middle of my third year—which was a wonderful year, just coast around, very easy—some things came up and I left, and that's the answer to that.

CA: Did you have the idea at the time that you wanted to be a newspaper publisher? Was that an early ambition?

LOEB: Yes, I think so. I was on the college paper when I was in college. I got out of Williams College in 1927, and the summer of 1929, while I was at Harvard Law School, I started working for Hearst's International News Service, for $15 a week, because nobody else wanted to work it for that small sum. I covered the Institute of Politics in Williamstown, which was sort of a prerunner of the United Nations, financed by Barney Baruch, and brought world figures from all over the globe to Williamstown on pleasant summer days.

CA: That sounds like kind of a liberal organization.

LOEB: No, it was designed to try to settle international questions and brought political figures from all over the globe to discuss everything from the freedom of India to disarmament to almost every problem you could think of. Baruch had the naive idea that if you just bring people together and they could talk it over, why, you'd have a better world.

This was a fairly important operation from a news standpoint, because the second year I covered it for the *New York World* and the managing editor of the *World* told me that they didn't have much money left for telegraph charges any more, so I had to confine my report to three-quarters of a column a day. But I needn't think that was going to be an easy job, coasting along, because I was supposed to include in that three-quarters of a column everything that Arthur Ruhl of the *New York Herald Tribune* got into two and one-half columns and everything that Louis Stark of the *New York Times* got into three and one-half columns. So that gives you some idea of the importance with which the *New York Times* and *Tribune* regarded the affair.

CA: When you thought about becoming a newspaper publisher, did you have any particular goals in mind in terms of what newspapers you were interested in?

LOEB: I'd gone to prep school, and college, and law school in New England, so I naturally turned towards New England, and I acquired the *St. Albans Daily Messenger* up in St. Albans.

CA: Did you gravitate to New England for other reasons, such as liking the area?

LOEB: Well, I was just here, that's all. I really like the West better in many ways than I do New England. The West is much less inhibited and much less ingrown and in many ways a friendlier place.

CA: Would you be able to define what a publisher's role is in a community, from your point of view?

LOEB: Well, from my standpoint, we're interested in making enough money to pay our bills and all that, but this is not our primary goal. The difficulty with the press in the United States today is it's largely in the hands of people, they're not evil people, who're just interested in the bottom line, and they don't give a God damn about anything else, and anything that interferes with the maximizing of profit is discarded. As a result, I don't think the papers are doing the job that they ought to be doing for their communities or for their readers.

We attempt to support everything that we think is good for the community, that will bring along the highest rate of employment and produce the best life that you can imagine. New Hampshire has no sales or income tax—we fought against those for years on the theory that they don't relieve property taxes, all they do is give politicians more money to spend.

The results of this campaign have been rather good for the state of New Hampshire. We have consistently almost the lowest unemployment in the nation, and that's because many companies have moved up to New Hampshire. They want to get into a state which has some economic common sense.

Very often we take unpopular positions. Opposing a sales and income tax probably is a popular position with the average citizen, but certainly is not popular with a great many special interests in this state. We don't pander to any special interests. We're completely independent of advertisers or any interests.

CA: What special interests are you referring to?

LOEB: Before I took over, one of the reporters was fired for printing a story that the utility rates in New Hampshire were the highest in the nation at the time. Now, we supported, we still do support the Public Service Company in connection with Seabrook [proposed New Hampshire nuclear facility], but we don't hesitate to tell them when we think they're acting like a bunch of damn fools.

We're not the voice of any political party or any political machine. The liberal elements in the Republican Party centering around Peterborough and that area there always had in the past a pretty good hold on this newspaper. They don't today, which infuriates them. In other words, we just don't play ball with the establishment. We're interested in protecting what we consider the best interests of our readers. To hell with anything else. In other words we intend to "afflict the comfortable, and comfort the afflicted."

CA: New Hampshire has a reputation for being ingrown.

LOEB: We couldn't give a damn. Let me tell you about a few things which you probably don't know. For instance, it costs us one-half what it costs the state of Massachusetts to educate a pupil, a high school pupil. Therefore the liberals on the

Boston Globe went on to say, "My God, what are they doing to those poor children?" Then the SAT tests come out, the national ones, and our students rank highest of any of the students in New England. We rank higher than the national average.

In other words, what we've done in New Hampshire is simply learn how to have good government without going broke in the process. The Campbells at Dartmouth, Professor and Mrs. Campbell, made a study of state and local taxes in New Hampshire and Vermont, and they found it costs New Hampshire people forty-eight percent, almost fifty percent less than Vermont. Well, you might say Vermont just opted for luxurious government services. The Campbells checked that and found out that the government services in New Hampshire were as good as those in Vermont, sometimes better. We pay our schoolteachers more. We have so many firsts in the nation that it's hard even to enumerate them all. We have the lowest rate of tuberculosis per 100,000 in the nation, so we must be doing something right with our health and on and on. We're first in almost everything you can think of.

CA: You didn't grow up here, and perhaps you might have been seen as an outsider initially.

LOEB: I've been here thirty-three years, so there's not much problem with that anymore. People are quite used to the fact that I live in Massachusetts and this is my main interest up here.

CA: Was there a problem at the beginning, some kind of resistance?

LOEB: There may have been. I don't know anything about it. I don't worry about those kind of things. I'm not in business to try and make myself popular. I couldn't care less.

CA: I read somewhere that your almost daily, I guess they are daily, front page editorials began in 1962.

LOEB: No, they began long before that. I don't remember when they began.

CA: Why did you choose that particular format?

LOEB: Well, when I think of something, when I believe in something, I'll put it on the front page where people will read it.

CA: Is there any reaction, or bad reaction to that? Do people think you're coming on too strong?

LOEB: People sometimes don't like the subjects that I write about and react, but otherwise I haven't heard any.

CA: Is the fact that the editorials are forcefully worded—they're on the front page, the headlines are very direct, at least they're forceful headlines—is that always a reflection of how you feel about the subject matter?

LOEB: Yes.

CA: Do you write the editorials that are on the editorial page as well, or is that done by the editors here?

LOEB: They're written by various people.

CA: Some people have said that journalism in general in this country is too negative, that newspapers tend to go after public figures, call them all sorts of names and so on. You are sometimes very, perhaps, abrasive, with politicians.

LOEB: It's the only way to keep the bastards straight. This

country is in a terrible mess. Imagine having a choice between a stupid nut like Jerry Ford on the one hand and a sniveling, double-dealing, phony, poor white trash on the other hand in the form of Carter. That was an awful choice. There are so many brilliant people in the United States, in engineering, in medicine, architecture, business, finance, almost every other field. In God's name why do we have to turn over the government to the most incompetent members of society, rich or poor? The media often does not help. This adulation over Ted Kennedy, whether he's going to run or not going to run, if I hear that damn story on national television again I'm going to puke. I probably will have to puke, too, because I'm sure to hear it. You'd think the whole world was hung on this little bastard that never did anything in the world except not be able to get a girl home safely from a party.

CA: What do you think of his chances here, if he were to run?

LOEB: I think, I hate to tell you, but I think if he were to run in New Hampshire tomorrow he'd snow Carter under and Brown as well. I mean you have so many nuts in the world that I don't know what you do about them. They don't know when they're committing political suicide. They usually enjoy doing it in the process. I think, if Kennedy doesn't repudiate the write-in, and I don't think he's going to, I think the write-in will swamp Carter. The Democratic Party's got some very good men in it. To be a Democrat and to be reduced to picking between a California flake and Carter and Kennedy seems to me a horrible fate.

CA: Some of your newspapers have been very successful and some perhaps haven't been as successful.

LOEB: We try, we try. When we think something needs to be done, we do it, whether it's financially possible or not.

CA: Are you able to say in some kind of capsulated way why a couple of them closed? For example the Haverhill Journal.

LOEB: Well, the *Haverhill Journal* closed [in 1965] because we had a Federal judge who gave us a completely wrong [antitrust case] decision. That's the reason why Haverhill did. In Connecticut [*Connecticut Sunday Herald*, closed in 1974] we tried simply to see whether there was any interest in it. As a matter of fact, that paper was established long before I had it, and we did our best to keep it going.

CA: Then there was the other one. Burlington Daily News, *I believe?*

LOEB: Burlington was an afternoon paper against a very strong morning paper. That was only closed as part of the Haverhill situation.

CA: You were way ahead of other publishers, I think, with your profit-sharing plan for employees. What was it that caused you to establish that plan in the first place?

LOEB: Well, I was one of the founding directors of the Council of Profit-Sharing Industries. I was its third national president, Jim Lincoln was the first one, and I've always believed that profit-sharing, if you could adopt it universally, would stop most of the friction, the ridiculous friction, between labor and management, which does really prove nothing. And I think it's a hell of a good way to run a society; it's a good way, as Lincoln proved.

I was testifying as an expert in a case for him once. The government was trying to say, "Look, before you pay profits, you've got to pay us first, and then you can take it out of

your profits after corporate taxes." And Lincoln said, "No, profit sharing is the reason for high productivity, which in turn is the reason why I have such good profits." We won that case because we showed that on similar products, the price at Lincoln was going down, the price at Sylvania and General Electric was going up. What was the one difference? It wasn't engineering skill or anything else; it was profit-sharing, which got the workers really producing.

If the purpose of the free-enterprise system is to get people the most goods at the lowest possible price, and to pay good wages to your employees at top prices and stockholders a good return, what could be better proof of that fact than that profit-sharing works? The judge apparently felt the same way on this thing. Unfortunately, a great many people in the world don't understand that you can get more by giving more.

I don't believe in inherited wealth to any great scale. Mrs. Loeb and I both decided the best people to have the paper after our deaths would be the employees. My stock is now all in trust. She's the trustee, and when she dies there will be seven or eight executives of the paper who will be trustees, three of them in their early thirties. Over the years I've watched them work, I think I know their philosophy, I think they'll continue the paper along the lines that I run it for at least forty years. After that it'll be distributed to the employees and they can do whatever they want to with it. Anybody who tries to control the future that far ahead has to be a little unrealistic.

CA: Maybe I'm getting into events that are a little too recent here, but wasn't that somehow involved in that recent situation? [A suit against Loeb in Federal Court charging pension law violations. Loeb agreed to settle the suit on terms that will cause him to lose control of twenty-five percent of the newspaper's stock and result in the pension fund being removed from Loeb's control and put in the hands of a court-approved financial manager.]

LOEB: It wasn't in any way involved. That recent situation was the most outrageous miscarriage of justice I've ever heard of. No employees ever gave a nickel to the employees pension fund; it was all out of my own pocket.

[According to the *New York Times*, the pension fund's stock has been valued at $375,000 on its books since Loeb sold it to the fund for $300 a share in 1956. Recent appraisals by the newspaper have valued the shares at close to $3 million, a change that, according to the *Times*, has not been reflected in pension benefits.]

I sold the quarter of the stock at a nominal figure and I kept it at a nominal figure because that stock was going to be given to the employees. How do you value stock under those circumstances?

In comes this Labor Department—interestingly enough, right after [U.S. Senator Thomas J.] McIntyre was defeated. We feel that this was only politics. They objected because we had borrowed half a million dollars from the pension fund of the paper to buy a press for the paper. Well, what better investment could you make for a pension fund than to pay ten percent at a time when the prime rate was about seven percent? And to do something which would enhance the newspaper on which the pension fund in turn depends?

Well, we said, "All right, if that's the way you feel about it," so Mrs. Loeb and I advanced the money to the company, we paid off that. And they objected to the fact that, well, maybe the Teamster loan took priority over the pension fund or something. They couldn't prove it but we said, "All right, we'll settle that.'' So we retired that loan, which was a wonderful loan at six and one-half percent, and borrowed it at thirteen percent, which is certainly not a smart thing from their standpoint. We satisfied all those points and then my lawyer said, ''Well, what else do you want?'' They said, ''We want to get Loeb out of there!'' [Remove the pension fund from his control.] Purely political. And now they're forcing the sale of a quarter of the stock. This might give present employees a little more money, but it deprives them in the long run of an asset which can't help but increase in value. This is especially so when it's attached to the other three-quarters. So it's just the case of the utter vindictiveness of the Federal Government.

CA: They were trying to force you out of ownership entirely?
LOEB: That's it exactly. They were. They failed.

CA: You mentioned the Teamsters Pension Fund loan. I'm sure you're aware that some critics—you have a lot of critics, obviously—
LOEB: Oh yeah.

CA: Some of them have said that that might not have been such a good idea, getting a loan from the Teamsters, because of all the charges that have been thrown at them.
LOEB: I couldn't care less. In 1954, I heard from Bill Miller when he was [Republican] National Chairman, before he was Goldwater's running mate, that I'd have to support Rockefeller because the Teamsters were supporting Rockefeller. I said, ''Well, I don't know anything about that.''

I went right on supporting Goldwater, and the Teamsters went right on supporting Rockefeller. Afterwards, I found out that Rockefeller had gone to [James R.] Hoffa and said, ''I want that paper to support me,'' and Jim had said: ''No, I didn't loan money to Bill for that purpose, of controlling anything. He can support anybody he wants to in the United States and I'll support anybody I want and I think that's the way they should run this country, Governor. Don't you?'' So that's the kind of guy Hoffa was, one of the most misunderstood people in the nation, pilloried by the Kennedys. So nobody has ever exercised any control of any kind on us, no attempt to exercise any control, and it was a damned good loan at six and one-half percent.

CA: You campaigned pretty forcefully, I think, to have Hoffa released.
LOEB: You're darn right I did. Hoffa became a very close personal friend of mine in later years, and he was framed, and I know how he was framed, but proving it is another proposition.

CA: Do you, incidentally, it may be off the subject, have any theories about his death?
LOEB: Yes, nothing that's unique or anything. I know Jim, and I once said to him, ''Why don't you have a bodyguard?'' and he said: ''The only people that need bodyguards are people who cheat their wives or cheat their partner, Bill. I don't do either. I don't need a bodyguard.'' I also know, growing from very early association, that he trusted people that he shouldn't trust. There was nothing innately evil or mean in the man. He didn't realize some people are evil. In spite of his background and associations, he sometimes didn't realize who his friends were.

CA: Just to switch back a minute, is there any advice you'd give to someone now who wanted to be a newspaper publisher and was looking for some way to get in it or some principles on which they could run the paper, run any paper they published?
LOEB: Well, I just hope they would get back to the ways of my wife's grandfather, E. W. Scripps, the father of Scripps-Howard newspapers and United Press, etc., and his contemporaries, Hearst and Pulitzer. They were outspoken people. They made a lot of money and were very successful, but they also were interested in what was in their papers. Today, Gannett and all the rest of these chains, with them it's just a business operation, how much money can we make out of it, Newhouse, Gannett. They don't really do the job that should be done to protect the interests of the people. All they discuss at Gannett is how they can cut down labor costs.

Newspapers are not doing themselves any good by indicating they're something special in society, that they have privileges under the First Amendment that shouldn't accrue to anybody else in society. I think that doesn't go down with the general public, and I think they're having less and less confidence in their newspapers.

CA: Let me get you on one more question if I could, then I'll skip out of here. Two very quick ones. You seem to be getting a lot of competition from the Boston Globe, *at least on Sunday.*
LOEB: Hasn't made any dent on us at all.

CA: Someone's written that their circulation is equal or perhaps even more than yours on Sundays [in New Hampshire].
LOEB: No. That's that crazy guy who'll never get inside these doors again. We try to treat everybody nicely, but that fellow out in Chicago wrote that. Declining!? Our Sunday circulation's at an all-time high and exceeds the total of both Boston papers.

CA: On Sunday?
LOEB: Yeah.

CA: Well, that was wrong information.
LOEB: Well sure, they lie, lie. Listen, we're raising a bunch of journalistic whores in the United States who don't care what they say about anybody. They don't like somebody, truth is the last thing that bothers or inhibits them. I think they're just a bunch of lice, as far as I'm concerned.

CA: In a way, you may have answered this already, but is there a perfect kind of government that you'd like to see in the United States?
LOEB: I'd just like to see some competent people. I don't care whether they're Democrats, Republicans, or Hottentots, who have some integrity, and some honesty, and some intelligence. We've just turned the government over to the most incompetent members of our society and you can't survive that way. Our opponents may be thoroughly evil but they're not crazy in Russia, they're not crazy, like our people are. Damn Carter letting out those four Puerto Ricans who should have been sent to the chair and killed immediately after that attack. Now they come out and say, ''We're not grateful to Carter. Viva the Revolution!'' Crazy, you've got to be nuts to be nice to people like that.

CA: Thank you very much.
LOEB: Well, nice to see you. Sorry I had to cut it off.

BIOGRAPHICAL/CRITICAL SOURCES: Newsweek, May

20, 1957, February 17, 1964, February 28, 1972, January 12, 1976; *Time,* May 20, 1957, February 23, 1968, January 31, 1972, March 13, 1972, January 12, 1976; *New York Times Magazine,* December 12, 1971; *New Republic,* March 11, 1972, January 31, 1976; *National Review,* March 17, 1972; Kevin Cash, *Who the Hell Is William Loeb?,* Amoskeag Press, 1975; *Nation,* December 20, 1975; *People,* March 26, 1979.

—*Interview by Peter Benjaminson*

* * *

LOGAN, Spencer 1912(?)-1980

OBITUARY NOTICE: Born c. 1912 in Elizabeth, N.J.; died January 17, 1980, in Annapolis, Md. Government worker and author. Logan worked for the U.S. Army as coordinator of the Army Staff Management Intern Program and for the National Institutes of Health as an equal employment opportunity officer. He wrote an award-winning book, *A Negro's Faith in America.* Obituaries and other sources: *Washington Post,* January 19, 1980.

* * *

LOMAS, Geoffrey (Robert) 1950-

PERSONAL: Born January 5, 1950, in Brisbane, Australia; son of Robert George (a retailer) and Vera (Fisher) Lomas. *Education:* University of Queensland, B.V.S. (with honors), 1971. *Religion:* Anglican. *Home:* 48 Aberfeldy St., Kenmore, Brisbane 4069, Australia. *Agent:* Gerald Pollinger, Laurence Pollinger Ltd., 18 Maddox St., London W1R 0EU, England.

CAREER: Veterinarian in private practice in England and Australia, 1972-77; University of Sydney, Sydney, Australia, clinical veterinary microbiologist, 1978—. Founding partner, Top Deck Travel Ltd., 1973-74. *Military service:* Royal Australian Air Force Reserve, pilot, five years. *Member:* Australian Society of Authors, Australian Jockey Club, Royal College of Veterinary Surgeons (England).

WRITINGS: Hostages (suspense novel), Scribner, 1979. Composer of songs, with lyrics.

WORK IN PROGRESS: When the Black Rains Fall, an adventure novel set in Scotland, about North Sea oil rigs and pipelines; *Forty Days to Death,* "a medical thriller," about cancer and contemporary developments in genetic engineering.

SIDELIGHTS: Lomas writes: "Unlike James Herriot, my writing has nothing to do with my career as a veterinary surgeon. I like both jobs, but am aiming to be able to write full-time. I would like to write musical plays for the stage, and will begin work on the first one soon. I am also interested in writing for films.

"In 1973, in England, I did some veterinary work with small and large animals. Then, with a partner, I established a double-decker bus touring company. On our first trips we drove passengers on six-week trips around Spain and Morocco. The company now runs trips all over Europe and overland, through Asia, to Australia. I intend to write a book of my experiences on these trips.

"My next project will be a novel set in Australia. It will tell the story of a family of sheep and cattle graziers. This will not be an adventure thriller like my first three books. Rather, it will describe the fortunes of this family, their life in the bush, and the contrast between those on the land and those who went to the city. It will be based on my own experiences in the bush (I spent some time 'jackarooing' on various

sheep stations) and those of my own family, who have sheep properties in Queensland."

* * *

LONGSTREET, Wilma S. 1935-

PERSONAL: Born July 3, 1935, in New York, N.Y.; married Shirley H. Engle, September 11, 1978. *Education:* Hunter College (now of the City University of New York), B.A., 1956; Indiana University, M.A., Ph.D., 1970. *Office:* School of Education, DePaul University, Chicago, Ill. 60604.

CAREER: Globus and American Express, London, England, tour director, summers, 1961-67; University of Illinois, Champaign-Urbana, assistant professor of education, 1970-72; University of Michigan, Flint, associate professor, 1972-76, professor of education, 1976-79; DePaul University, Chicago, Ill., professor of education and dean of School of Education, 1979—. *Member:* Association for Supervision and Curriculum Development (past member of board of directors), National Council for the Social Studies, Professors of Curriculum.

WRITINGS: (With husband, Shirley H. Engle) *A Design for Social Education in the Open Classroom,* Harper, 1972; *Beyond Jencks: The Myth of Equal Educational Opportunity,* Association for Supervision and Curriculum Development, 1973; *Aspects of Ethnicity: Understanding the Differences in Pluralistic Classrooms,* Teachers College Press, 1978. Contributor to education journals.

WORK IN PROGRESS: Applying research on ethnic studies for the public school to the field of nursing; developing a theoretical research framework for "action research."

SIDELIGHTS: Wilma Longstreet writes: "It seems to me ethnic studies entered the university politically—they have yet to make their *intellectual* mark. I hope to be able to contribute to the development of ethnic studies as a vital intellectual university enterprise as important to students as English or history.

"I am also very concerned at the exclusive translation of educational benefit into quantitative terms and am trying to develop qualitative criteria of such a format that they may be used in the public arena."

* * *

LONGWORTH, Alice Lee (Roosevelt) 1884-1980

OBITUARY NOTICE: Born February 12, 1884, in New York; died of cardiac arrest and bronchial pneumonia, February 20, 1980, in Washington, D.C. Social leader. Longworth, known to her friends as Mrs. L., was the daughter of President Theodore Roosevelt, the wife of Congressman and Speaker of the House Nicholas Longworth, and the grand dame of Washington's social life for most of the twentieth century. She was famous for her charm, beauty, intelligence, and wit, her political acumen and friendships, and her frank and honest opinions about presidents, congressmen, their wives and children, and her own family. In her opinion, Warren G. Harding was "just a slob," Calvin Coolidge "looked as if he had been weaned on a pickle," and her cousin, Eleanor Roosevelt, was "one-third sap and two-thirds Eleanor." According to Myra MacPherson of the *Washington Post,* she was "capable of cruelty and malice in her scorn, distaste and mockery of sentimentality, emotionalism, do-gooders and other things she simply did not understand." Nevertheless, her favor and company were courted by the elite of Washington who recognized and valued her thorough understanding of behind-the-scenes life and politics in the nation's capital. She knew President Benjamin Harrison and all those who followed, was a skilled poker-playing partner of President Harding, and a close confidante of Presidents Truman and Kennedy. In her later years, she presided over afternoon teas at her Dupont Circle mansion, hosting a steady stream of world leaders and journalists. And like Citizen Kane's "Rosebud," the clue to Longworth's abiding passion in life was prominently displayed on her drawing room divan: a needlepoint pillow that advertised, "If you haven't got anything nice to say about anyone, come and sit here by me." Longworth was the author of an autobiography, *Crowded Hours*. Obituaries and other sources: Alice Longworth, *Crowded Hours*, Scribner, 1933; *Current Biography*, Wilson, 1943, April, 1980; *Saturday Evening Post*, December 4, 1965; *Vogue*, February 1, 1966; *Newsweek*, May 23, 1966; *Celebrity Register*, 3rd edition, Simon & Schuster, 1973; *Washington Post*, February 21, 1980; *New York Times*, February 21, 1980.

*   *   *

LOOMIS, Albertine 1895-

PERSONAL: Born January 8, 1895, in Grand Rapids, Mich.; daughter of Vincent Hazen (a musician and piano tuner) and Jennie (Hulburt) Loomis. *Education:* University of Michigan, A.B., 1917; University of Chicago, M.A., 1934. *Politics:* Democrat. *Religion:* United Church of Christ. *Home:* 21 Craigside Place, Apt. 5-C, Honolulu, Hawaii 96817.

CAREER: High school English teacher in St. Louis, Mich., 1917-19, Highland Park, Mich., 1919-29, Grand Rapids, Mich., 1929-36, and Highland Park, Mich., 1936-51; Highland Park Junior College, Highland Park, Mich., teacher of English and head of department, 1951-57; writer, 1957—. Member of board of trustees of Mission Houses Museum, Honolulu, 1960-70. *Member:* Pan Pacific and South East Asia Women's Association, National League of American Pen Women, Hawaiian Mission Children's Society, Hawaiian Historical Society, Friends of the Library of Hawaii, Friends of Iolani Palace, Phi Beta Kappa. *Awards, honors:* Prize from Honolulu Commission on Culture and the Arts, 1978, for article, "Summer of 1898"; third annual award from Associates of the Library of the University of Hawaii, Manoa, 1979, for writings about Hawaii.

WRITINGS: Grapes of Canaan: Hawaii, 1820, Dodd, 1951; *To All People,* Hawaii Conference, United Church of Christ, 1970; (with A. Grove Day) *Ka Pa'i Palapala: Early Printing in Hawaii,* Printing Industries of Hawaii, 1973; *For Whom Are the Stars?,* University Press of Hawaii, 1976; *The Best of Friends,* Friends of the Library of Hawaii, 1979; (contributor) Emerson C. Smith and others, editors, *The Queen's Song Book,* Hui Hanai, 1980.

SIDELIGHTS: Albertine Loomis writes: "I was not particularly interested in writing until, in 1935, I discovered the journals of my great-grandparents who had spent seven years, 1820-27, in Hawaii as missionaries. Since that time I have been deeply interested in Hawaii and its remarkable history. Until I retired from teaching my writing had to be confined to vacations. I spent four summers in Hawaii and after retirement came to live here.

"Ever since I studied journalism in college I have been convinced that what *really* happened, either yesterday or in times long past, is more dramatic and exciting that anything anyone could make up. To be sure, fiction is an art, and good fiction can illuminate history; but I myself feel challenged to find out as exactly as possible what happened in an era and make that story come alive for readers.

"I have been twice to Europe, once to Japan and Hong Kong, have explored Hawaii quite extensively, and visited Micronesia, Fiji, and Tahiti."

*   *   *

LORD, Jeremy
See REDMAN, Ben Ray

*   *   *

LOSSKY, Andrew 1917-

PERSONAL: Born May 27, 1917, in St. Petersburg, Russia (now Leningrad, U.S.S.R.); son of Nicolas (a professor of philosophy) and Ludmila (Stoyunine) Lossky; married Irene Nekhorocheff (a physician), June 25, 1956 (deceased); children: Marie, Alexis. *Education:* University of London, B.A. (with honors), 1938; Yale University, M.A., 1942, Ph.D., 1948. *Religion:* Russian Orthodox. *Home:* 16930 Bollinger Dr., Pacific Palisades, Calif. 90272. *Office:* Department of History, University of California, Los Angeles, Calif. 90024.

CAREER: Yale University, New Haven, Conn., instructor in history, 1947-50; University of California, Los Angeles, assistant professor, 1950-56, associate professor, 1956-62, professor of history, 1962—. *Military service:* U.S. Army, 1941-45; became lieutenant; received Legion of Merit and Bronze Star. U.S. Army Reserve, 1945-67; became major. *Member:* International Committee for the Study of Parliamentary and Representative Institutions, Society for French Historical Studies, Societe d'Etude du Dix-Septieme Siecle, Societe d'Histoire Moderne, Western Society for French History. *Awards, honors:* Guggenheim fellow, 1961-62.

WRITINGS: Louis XIV, William III, and the Baltic Crisis of 1683, University of California Press, 1954; *The Seventeenth Century,* Free Press, 1967; (editor with George Vernadsky, Ralph Fisher, and others) *Source Book for Russian History From Early Times to 1917,* three volumes, Yale University Press, 1972; (contributor) Ragnhild Hatton, editor, *Louis XIV and Absolutism,* Macmillan (England), 1976. Contributor to *New Cambridge Modern History.* Contributor to history journals.

WORK IN PROGRESS: Louis XIV and the Ascendancy of France.

SIDELIGHTS: Lossky's languages include Russian, French, Latin, German, Dutch, Czech, and Italian. He describes his scholarly interests as "early modern European history, especially seventeenth-century France and France's political, diplomatic, and religious history, with occasional forays into medieval Russian history," up to and including the eighteenth century.

*   *   *

LOVETT, Clara Maria 1939-

PERSONAL: Born August 4, 1939, in Trieste, Italy; came to the United States in 1962, naturalized citizen, 1968. *Education:* University of Trieste, diploma, 1962; attended Cambridge University, 1960; University of Texas, M.A., 1967, Ph.D., 1970. *Office:* Department of History, Bernard M. Baruch College of the City University of New York, New York, N.Y. 10010.

CAREER: Retail Credit Co., Corpus Christi, Tex., service reviewer, 1963-64; State University of New York College at Oneonta, assistant professor of history, 1970-71; Bernard M. Baruch College of the City University of New York, New York, N.Y., assistant professor, 1971-76, associate professor of history, 1976—, and head of department, 1979—.

Member of board of trustees of Park Slope Civic Council, 1975-76. *Member:* American Historical Association, Society for Italian Historical Studies, Conference Group for Italian Politics. *Awards, honors:* National Endowment for the Humanities grant, 1972; Radcliffe Institute fellowships, 1975-77; Phi Alpha Theta manuscript award, 1976, for *Giuseppe Ferrari and the Italian Revolution;* American Council of Learned Societies fellowship, 1976; Guggenheim fellowship, 1978-79; Woodrow Wilson International Center fellowship, 1979.

WRITINGS: Carlo Cattaneo and the Politics of the Risorgimento, Nijhoff, 1972; *Giuseppe Ferrari and the Italian Revolution,* University of North Carolina Press, 1979; (editor with Carol Ruth Berkin, and contributor) *Women, War, and Revolution: Original Essays,* Holmes & Meier, 1979. Contributor of articles and reviews to history and Italian studies journals. Editor of newsletter of League of Women Voters, 1969-70.

WORK IN PROGRESS: The Democratic Movement in Italy, 1830-1876: Ideology, Social Foundations, and Political Behavior.

SIDELIGHTS: Lovett told *CA:* "My work on Italian and European history focuses on the intellectual origins, formation, and political legacy of various nineteenth-century radical movements and leaders. Its primary purpose is to illuminate the indigenous roots, issues, and perspectives of the contemporary Italian Left. My book-in-progress is an attempt to provide an analytical view of the development of the Italian Left during the period of national unification. It seeks to integrate recent scholarship on the nineteenth-century Italian democrats (most of it by Italian scholars virtually unknown in this country) with my own original contributions to the field.

"The book on *Women, War, and Revolution,* which I have co-edited with C. R. Berkin, brings together twelve groundbreaking contributions by historians and social scientists. The essays, with appropriate introductions by the editors, explore the impact of wartime political and economic mobilization upon the status and self-consciousness of women. They also explore the persistence of patriarchal values and relationships in the midst of revolutionary change. Finally, they discuss the ideal of 'civic motherhood' as a possible compromise between persistent patriarchy and revolutionary change."

AVOCATIONAL INTERESTS: Urban development and rehabilitation, restoring old houses, travel, canoeing, fishing, hiking.

* * *

LOWDER, Paul D(aniel) 1929-

PERSONAL: Born June 20, 1929, in Albemarle, N.C.; son of Charles Ernest (a mechanic) and Victoria (Harwood) Lowder; married Martha Blackburn, August 17, 1955 (separated August 10, 1979); children: Paula Marisa Lowder Cole, Karen Kay. *Education:* Attended Pfeiffer Junior College, 1947-49; Albion College, B.A., 1951; Emory University, B.D., 1954. *Home:* 23 West I St., Newton, N.C. 28658. *Office:* First United Methodist Church, P.O. Box 926, Newton, N.C. 28658.

CAREER: Ordained United Methodist minister, 1953; pastor of Methodist churches in Harmony, N.C., 1954-58, Conover, N.C., 1958-63, Davidson, N.C., 1963-67, Greensboro, N.C., 1967-72, and Winston-Salem, N.C., 1972-77; First United Methodist Church, Newton, N.C., pastor, 1977—. Chairperson of Conference Board of Discipleship.

WRITINGS: Let Us Pray, Upper Room, 1963; *Feed Whose Sheep?,* Word, Inc., 1973. Contributor to Christian magazines. Book editor of *North Carolina Christian Advocate.*

WORK IN PROGRESS: The Late Liz and *Prayers for the Wounded.*

* * *

LOWENSTEIN, Tom 1941-

PERSONAL: Born August 15, 1941, in Chalfont St. Peter, England; son of Edgar H. and Jane (Herrmann) Lowenstein. *Education:* Queens' College, Cambridge, B.A., 1965, M.A., 1967; University of Leicester, certificate, 1966. *Home:* 66 Lady Margaret Rd., London N.W.5, England. *Agent:* Deborah Rogers, 5-11 Mortimer St., London W.1, England.

CAREER: Teacher in London, England, 1967-71; Northwestern University, Evanston, Ill., instructor in English, 1971-74; writer, 1974—. *Awards, honors:* Guggenheim fellow, 1979.

WRITINGS: Our After-Fate (poems), Softly Loudly, 1971; (editor) *Eskimo Poems From Canada and Greenland,* University of Pittsburgh Press, 1974; *Booster* (game of divination), Many Press, 1977; *The Death of Mrs. Owl* (poems), Anvil Press, 1977; *La Tempesta* (poems; title means "The Tempest"), Oasis Books, 1980.

Author of "An Eskimo Storyteller," for BBC-Radio.

WORK IN PROGRESS: Editing Alaskan Eskimo texts in translation, publication by University of California Press expected in 1984; *Letter From Uivvaq: A Comedy of Divagations in the Arctic; Booster N!ow; La Tempesta* (open poem).

* * *

LOWERY, Lynn 1949-

PERSONAL: Born July 3, 1949, in Cleveland, Ohio; daughter of James William (a boilermaker) and Mona (an instructor in cosmetology; maiden name, Benjamin) Lowery; married James Hahn (a writer), April 17, 1971. *Education:* Northwestern University, B.S., 1971. *Politics:* Independent. *Religion:* United Church of Christ. *Home and office:* 2202 Sherman Ave., #D-2, Evanston, Ill. 60201.

CAREER: Free-lance writer, 1971—.

WRITINGS—Romantic historical novels: *Sweet Rush of Passion,* Bantam, 1978; *Loveswept,* Bantam, 1978; *Larissa,* Bantam, 1979. Contributor to newspapers.

WORK IN PROGRESS: Charmaine (tentative title), another romantic historical novel.

SIDELIGHTS: Lynn Lowery writes: "The inspiration for *Sweet Rush of Passion,* set in the Russian Empire of the 1820's and 1830's, came from several sources. My great-grandmother was Russian, and I grew up around icons and samovars, and was fascinated by the gilded onion domes of the Russian Orthodox church in her neighborhood. In college I studied Russian language, history, literature, and culture, and visited Russia on a summer study trip. This fermented in my head for several years, until I came up with the story line for the book. As I wrote, I found that notes and photographs I had taken on my trip were invaluable in recreating the specific settings in my story.

"Intrigued by an article describing Sitka, Alaska, once the capital of the Russian colony in North America, I began doing more research on Alaska in the mid-1800's, and about the period and circumstances of the transfer of the colony from the Russian Empire to the United States. This led to

Loveswept, which follows the adventures of the heroine, Tasha, through Moscow, Siberia, Alaska, and the United States.

"*Larissa* is set in the United States, China, and India during the days of the clipper trade. I have always thought of the clippers as beautiful, romantic vessels, and the clipper trade provided a romantic, exciting setting.

"*Charmaine* is set in the Austrian Empire, France, Mexico, and the United States during the 1860's. This was the period when Maximilian of Hapsburg and his wife Carlota attempted to set up a monarchy in Mexico, and much of the book is set in their court. I've just returned from a trip to Mexico, where I researched many of the settings for the novel. Hours spent wandering in Maximilian and Carlota's Chapultepec Castle in Mexico City were especially inspiring.

"In all my books I have researched carefully, since I think it is important to be historically accurate. Sometimes I find my own enjoyment of historical research becomes a problem. I get so absorbed in research that I read much more than necessary for my books, sometimes reading when I should be writing!"

BIOGRAPHICAL/CRITICAL SOURCES: Cleveland Press, January 3, 1978; *Chicago Tribune,* February 8, 1978; *Evanston Review,* March 2, 1978; *Chicago Sun-Times,* March 16, 1978; *Berea Sun News,* January 4, 1979.

* * *

LOWNEY, Paul Benjamin 1922-

PERSONAL: Born March 25, 1922, in Butte, Mont.; son of Mark (a plumbing contractor) and Bessie (Wicks) Lowney; children: Ivy (Mrs. Jack Laurance). *Education:* Montana State University, B.A., 1943; also attended Cornish School of Music, 1950, and University of Washington, Seattle, 1950-52, 1954-56. *Politics:* Republican. *Home:* 1808 40th Ave. E., Seattle, Wash. 98112. *Office:* 1219 Westlake N., Seattle, Wash. 98109.

CAREER: Photo Publishing Co., Seattle, Wash., owner, 1959—. Owner of Lowney Advertising, 1968—. *Member:* Alpha Tau Omega (president, 1941).

WRITINGS: Offbeat Humor, Peter Pauper, 1962; *The Best in Offbeat Humor,* Peter Pauper, 1968; *Gleeb,* Dodd, 1973; *The Big Book of Gleeb,* Dodd, 1975. Author of "The Pookas," a comic strip distributed by Los Angeles Times Syndicate, 1977-78, and "Gleeb," a weekly cartoon distributed by Copley News Service, 1980.

WORK IN PROGRESS: The Best of Gleeb.

SIDELIGHTS: Lowney writes: "*Gleeb* is the culmination of my search for a substantive and challenging type of humor—one in which I am able to deal with the nonsensical and frivolous aspects of human existence, as well as the fascinating data found in the physical sciences, philosophy, psychology, and sociology.

"Humor writing has always intrigued me. My first attempt was a column for my high school newspaper. I went through the usual juvenile addiction to word play, and then proceeded to a love affair with 'offbeat humor' with its wildly incongruous situations. After writing two books in this vein, I evolved the ideal format for my particular brand of humor—*Gleeb.*

"This format is a short dialogue form, usually running from six to eighteen lines. A 'gleebism' most always ends with a humorous line and, with only one exception, each has been confined to a single book page; and no paragraph—no matter now long—ever contains more than one sentence.

"I have arrived at a point in my life where I see little purpose in writing—or for that matter, engaging in any of the art forms—unless there is something in it for human knowledge and human betterment. It is not enough simply to entertain. I want the additional ingredient of saying something which informs, gives insight, and provokes thought. I like to believe that I succeed in this goal with each book I write."

* * *

LOWRY, Nan
See MacLEOD, Ruth

* * *

LUCAS, Hans
See GODARD, Jean-Luc

* * *

LUCAS, Scott 1937-

PERSONAL: Born November 7, 1937, in Fremont, Ohio; son of Robert Burger (an attorney) and Virginia (Shaffer) Lucas; married Sue Oliver (a legal secretary); children: Dana, Joseph. *Education:* Attended University of Michigan; graduate study at University of Copenhagen. *Politics:* Republican. *Religion:* Lutheran. *Home and office:* 3823 T St. N.W., Washington, D.C. 20007.

CAREER: Wittrup Motel, Inc., Copenhagen-Taastrup, Denmark, general manager, 1959-60; Sterling Associates, Inc., Vaduz, Liechtenstein, area manager for southern Europe, 1960-63; Greenbelt Consumers, Inc., Falls Church, Va., assistant manager in SCAN Division, 1963-64; SCAN-AM Products Ltd., Jacksonville, Fla., president, 1963-65; Northwestern Mutual Life Insurance Co., Washington, D.C., special agent, 1966-67; Modern Design, Inc., Chevy Chase, Md., designer, 1967-68; Greenbelt Consumers, Inc., Washington, D.C., in sales and design in SCAN Division, 1968; free-lance writer and investigative reporter, 1968—. Commercial and residential designer. *Military service:* U.S. Navy, in naval aviation, 1955-66.

WRITINGS: The F.D.A., Celestial Arts, 1978; *The Forging of Jacob Taylor* (first novel in trilogy; also see below), Celestial Arts, 1980; *Jacob Taylor* (second novel in trilogy), Celestial Arts, 1981.

WORK IN PROGRESS: A short story collection.

SIDELIGHTS: Lucas writes: "Almost from birth, it was assumed that I would study at the University of Michigan, go on to law school either there or at Harvard, and practice criminal law. Naval aviation came first, causing me to select a different road.

"I gained vast experience not only in export/import problems, but also from manufacturing and purchase to final accounting. In the course of my working life, I have spent twenty-odd years in supervision and training personnel. There has also been active participation in new product marketing, new area marketing, and all facets of corporate accounting and advertising.

"I devoted a lot of time last year to energy research, seeking information for use in articles and documentaries. It is a timely, relevant, and fascinating area for writers.

"I have always written for personal pleasure; I find the discipline and certainly the results exhilarating. Everything is maximized in writing, both successes and failures."

AVOCATIONAL INTERESTS: Travel, sailing, painting in oils.

LUCKHARDT, C(harles) Grant 1943-

PERSONAL: Born October 25, 1943, in Palm Beach, Fla.; son of Roy E. and Leona (Rue) Luckhardt; married Arabelle Davies (a Montessori director), August 25, 1967; children: Cassandra. *Education:* St. John's College, Annapolis, Md., A.B., 1965; Emory University, M.A., 1968, Ph.D., 1972. *Home:* 2058 Palifox Fr. N.E., Atlanta, Ga. 30307. *Office:* Department of Philosophy, Georgia State University, University Plaza, Atlanta, Ga. 30303.

CAREER: Georgia State University, Atlanta, assistant professor, 1971-76, associate professor of philosophy, 1977—. Visiting tutor at St. John's College, Santa Fe, N.M., summers, 1976-77; speaker at academic gatherings. *Member:* American Philosophical Association, Society for Ancient Greek Philosophy, American Society for Value Inquiry, Society for the Philosophical Study of Marxism, Southern Society for Philosophy and Psychology, Georgia Philosophical Society. *Awards, honors:* National Endowment for the Humanities fellowships, 1974, 1978; American Philosophical Society grant, 1976.

WRITINGS: (Contributor) Elisabeth Leinfellner, editor, *Wittgenstein and His Impact on Contemporary Thought*, Hoelder, Pichler, Tempsky, 1978; (editor) *Wittgenstein: Sources and Perspectives*, Cornell University Press, 1979; (translator with M.A.E. Aue) Ludwig Wittgenstein, *Remarks on the Foundations of Psychology*, Volumes II and III, Basil Blackwell, 1979; (contributor) Mark Woodhouse, editor, *A Preface to Philosophy*, 2nd edition (Luckhardt was not included in 1st edition), Wadsworth, 1979. Contributor of articles and reviews to philosophy journals.

WORK IN PROGRESS: Books on the political thought of Socrates and on Wittgenstein's philosophical psychology.

AVOCATIONAL INTERESTS: Canoeing, music, woodworking, photography.

* * *

LUKAS, Charlotte Koplinka 1954-
(Charlotte Koplinka)

PERSONAL: Born March 3, 1954, at Mitchell Air Force Base, N.Y.; daughter of George B. (a sales representative) and Margaret (a home economics teacher; maiden name, Landon) Koplinka; married Andrew A. Lukas (an English teacher), June 23, 1979. *Education:* Middlebury College, B.A., 1976, graduate study, 1977—. *Home address:* P.O. Box 43, Star Route, Windsor, Vt. 05089.

CAREER: English teacher at public schools in New City, N.Y., 1977-79; Whitney Point Central Schools, Whitney Point, N.Y., English teacher, 1979—. *Member:* Phi Beta Kappa. *Awards, honors:* Fellow of Bread Loaf Writers' Conference, 1977.

WRITINGS—Under name Charlotte Koplinka: *The Silkies: A Novel of the Shetlands* (young-adult fiction), Paul Eriksson, 1978. Contributor to *Co-Ed*.

WORK IN PROGRESS: An adult novel; poems.

SIDELIGHTS: Charlotte Lukas writes: "Details are essential. I think we overlook too much in this fast-paced civilization. I urge attention to the smallest of things. A piece of old Christmas tree tinsel in the dirt on the side of a mountain highway, its forlorn hopelessness and tragic beauty, became part of a short story I wrote. It is the small things which count, whether the laugh of a handicapped child or the feel of rough bark in your hand."

LUKES, Steven (Michael) 1941-

PERSONAL: Born March 8, 1941, in Newcastle-on-Tyne, England; son of Stanley and Martha Lukes; married Nina Stanger (a barrister-at-law), 1977; children: Daniel Nicholas Timothy, Michael Jonathon Anthony. *Education:* Balliol College, Oxford, B.A. (with first class honors), 1962; Nuffield College, Oxford, D.Phil., 1968. *Home:* 18 Beaumont Buildings, Oxford, England. *Agent:* Michael Sissons, A. D. Peters & Co. Ltd., 10 Buckingham St., London WC2N 6BU, England. *Office:* Balliol College, Oxford University, Oxford OX1 3BJ, England.

CAREER: University of Keele, Keele, England, assistant lecturer in philosophy, 1963; Oxford University, Oxford, England, lecturer in politics at Worcester College, 1964-66, fellow and tutor in politics and sociology at Balliol College, 1966—, fellow of Nuffield College, 1964-66. Visiting lecturer in Canada, the United States, and Europe, including Sorbonne, University of Paris, Free University of Berlin, Harvard University, and Princeton University; director of studies at Ecole Pratique des Hautes Etudes, 1972; associate professor of public law at University of Paris, 1974; participant in scholarly meetings in England and the United States. *Member:* International Sociological Association (president of research committee on history of sociology, 1974—), Group d'Etudes Durkheimiennes.

WRITINGS: (Editor with Anthony Arblaster) *The Good Society: A Book of Readings*, Harper, 1971; *Emile Durkheim, His Life and Work: A Historical and Critical Study*, Harper, 1973; *Individualism*, Harper, 1973; *Power: A Radical View*, Macmillan (England), 1974, Humanities, 1975; *Essays in Social Theory*, Macmillan (England), 1976.

Contributor: H. S. Kariel, editor, *Frontiers of Democratic Theory*, Random House, 1970; B. R. Wilson, editor, *Rationality*, Basil Blackwell, 1970; Dorothy Emmet and Alasdair Macintyre, editors, *Sociological Theory and Philosophical Analysis*, Macmillan (England), 1970; Geoffrey Mortimore, editor, *Weakness of the Will*, Macmillan (England), 1971; A. W. Finifter, editor, *Alienation and the Social System*, Wiley, 1972; Robin Horton and Ruth Finnegan, editors, *Modes of Thought: Essays Presented to E. E. Evans-Pritchard*, Faber, 1973; Leszek Kolakowski and Stuart Hampshire, editors, *The Socialist Idea: A Reappraisal*, Weidenfeld & Nicolson, 1974; T. B. Bottomore and Robert A. Nisbet, editors, *A History of Sociological Analysis*, Basic Books, 1978; Stuart Brown, editor, *Philosophical Disputes in the Social Sciences*, Harvester, in press; Alkis Kontos, editor, *Festschrift for C. B. Macpherson*, University of Toronto Press, in press.

Co-editor of "Marxism and . . . ," a series published by Clarendon Press. Contributor to *International Encyclopedia of the Social Sciences*, *Dictionary of the History of Ideas*, and *Dictionary of World History*. Contributor of more than twenty-five articles and reviews to sociology, history, and philosophy journals. Associate editor of *Political Studies*, 1976—; member of editorial board of *Archives europeennes de sociologie*.

WORK IN PROGRESS: Editing *Durkheim's Sociology of Law* with Andrew Scull, for Basil Blackwell; *Marxism and Morality*.

* * *

LYGRE, David G(erald) 1942-

PERSONAL: Surname is pronounced La-*gree;* born August 10, 1942, in Minot, N.D.; son of C. Gerald (a minister) and Esther R. (an organist; maiden name, Fossum) Lygre; married Laurae Yvonne Johnson (a nurse), August 20, 1966; children: Jedd, Lindsay. *Education:* Concordia College, Moorhead, Minn., B.A. (summa cum laude), 1964; University of North Dakota, Ph.D., 1968; postdoctoral study at Case Western Reserve University, 1968-70. *Home:* 805 North B St., Ellensburg, Wash. 98926. *Office:* Department of Chemistry, Central Washington State University, Ellensburg, Wash. 98926.

CAREER: Central Washington State University, Ellensburg, assistant professor of chemistry, 1970-73, associate professor of chemistry, 1973—, director of water analysis laboratory, 1972-73. Visiting professor at University of York, 1976-77. *Member:* American Chemical Society, Sigma Xi. *Awards, honors:* American Cancer Society fellowship, 1968-70; Research Corp. grant, 1970-71.

WRITINGS: Life Manipulation, Walker & Co., 1979. Contributor to scientific journals and newspapers.

WORK IN PROGRESS: Research on carbohydrate metabolism and aging.

SIDELIGHTS: Lygre told *CA:* "My current research interests are in two areas. For many years I've been studying an enzyme that helps regulate our blood sugar levels. I've found that cyclamate and saccharin inhibit the ability of this enzyme to function, and now I'm studying the effects of certain pesticides. The other area of research I'm interested in is aging—specifically, trying to identify the cause(s) of aging. I'm not doing laboratory work on this (yet), but I have a theory I'm keeping under my hat for now. I need to do much more reading and thinking before talking about it, but I'm excited about it.

"My book, *Life Manipulation,* deals with techniques for manipulating life ('artificial' methods of reproduction, prenatal analysis, genetic engineering, replacing worn-out or diseased body parts, and more) and the social, ethical, and legal implications of these tools. We used to leave most of these matters to nature because we couldn't do much about it anyway. But now we are wresting that power, and responsibility, from nature. We have options we've never had before, and we have to decide when to use our growing powers.

"I think the greatest fear most people have of these tools, in the long run, is that they will depersonalize us and turn people into objects—objects to be produced when we want them, for a particular purpose, and made according to a particular blueprint. But technology itself will not dehumanize us; only people can dehumanize people. Whether these tools will help us achieve a more (or less) humane society depends on how we use them, what values we bring to bear as we face these excruciatingly difficult decisions—using surrogate mothers, preselecting the sex of our children, gene transplants, keeping people physically alive for progressively longer periods, and many more.

"As far as my personal values are concerned, I view myself as fairly middle-of-the-road. For example, I favor allowing the 'test tube baby' technique to be used in the U.S. under tightly defined conditions (at least for a trial period), but I oppose using prenatal diagnosis solely for determining the sex of the fetus so that an abortion decision may be made on that basis. (I've been intrigued, though, by book reviewers variously categorizing me as liberal or conservative.) I also have a moderate amount of faith in man's basic goodness and common sense. What I fear most, however, is that people will not be sufficiently aware of our new powers to insist on public discussion and debate over what boundaries to draw for the application of these tools. We must not leave these decisions to the scientists alone, nor accept by default the technological imperative: what can be done will be done. Instead, we must struggle together to decide as best we can what kind of society and people we are to become."

AVOCATIONAL INTERESTS: Marathon running.

BIOGRAPHICAL/CRITICAL SOURCES: Yakima Herald-Republic, March 3, 1978; *St. Paul Pioneer Press,* August 10, 1979; *Tacoma News Tribune,* September 9, 1979; *Yakima Valley Community News,* December 12, 1979.

* * *

LYMAN, Marilyn F(lorence) 1925-

PERSONAL: Born August 17, 1925, in Detroit, Mich.; daughter of Ellis E. (an engineer) and Florence (a secretary; maiden name, Gowman) Smauder; married George F. Lyman (an industrial engineer), January 29, 1948; children: Claudia Ann (Mrs. Harvey Sarkisian), George David. *Education:* Attended Albion College and Wayne State University. *Religion:* Congregational. *Home:* 3886 Wedgewood Dr., Birmingham, Mich. 48010.

CAREER: Birmingham Eccentric (now *Observer Eccentric*), Birmingham, Mich., staff and feature writer, 1965-70. Speaker at Oakland University and at elementary and secondary schools; organizer of writers' conferences. *Member:* Detroit Women Writers (president, 1967-69).

WRITINGS—For children: *The Girl Who Knew Rule One,* Scholastic Book Services, 1972; *That Face in the Mirror,* Scholastic Book Services, 1974. Contributor to magazines and newspapers, including *Ingenue.*

WORK IN PROGRESS: A nonfiction book about a well-known resident of Michigan; a teenage novel viewing child abuse; research for a novel about a teenage boy.

* * *

LYNCH-WATSON, Janet 1936-

PERSONAL: Born June 11, 1936, in London, England; daughter of C. W. (a company director) and M. L. (Bentley) Meadows; married Graham Lynch-Watson (a minister), January 6, 1962; children: Frances, Sam. *Education:* University of St. Andrews, M.A. (with honors), 1958. *Home:* 51 Galsworthy Dr., Caversham, Reading, Berkshire, England.

CAREER: Writer, 1966—. Also worked as teacher, secretary, shop assistant, and public examiner.

WRITINGS: My Prayer Scrapbook (juvenile), Falcon, 1972; *Ben's Giraffe* (juvenile), Abelard, 1973; *Pressing Plants* (juvenile), Muller, 1975; *The Saffron Robe* (adult), Hodder & Stoughton, 1975; *A Patchwork Prayerbook* (juvenile), Hodder & Stoughton, 1976; *The Shadow Puppet Book* (juvenile), Sterling, 1979; *Good Luck, Kelverton United* (juvenile), Evans, 1980.

SIDELIGHTS: Janet Lynch-Watson commented: "I write, when I have time, because I enjoy it, because I need the money, because books fascinate me. I buy them, covet them, collect them, read them, and write them."

* * *

LYONS, Barbara (Baldwin) 1912-

PERSONAL: Born September 16, 1912, in Honolulu, Hawaii; daughter of Samuel Alexander (a cattle rancher) and Kathrine (Smith) Baldwin; married Raymond Lyons (a naval admiral), August 30, 1934; children: Michael Henry II, Samuel Alexander Baldwin, Shaun Baldwin Lyons McKay. *Education:* Attended Dominican College of San Rafael,

1930-31, and University of Hawaii, 1931-32. *Politics:* Republican. *Religion:* Congregational. *Address:* c/o Charles E. Tuttle Co., 28 South Main St., Rutland, Vt. 05701. *Residence:* Makawao, Maui, Hawaii 96768.

CAREER: Writer. *Member:* Hawaiian Mission Children's Society, Hawaiian Historical Society, Daughters of Hawaii, Maui Historical Society.

WRITINGS: Maui, Mischievous Hero, Petroglyph, 1969; *Fire and Water* (Hawaiian legends), Tuttle, 1973; *The Brook,* Topgallant Publishing, 1976. Author of "Legends of Hawaii," a column in *Honolulu Advertiser,* 1957-58, and in *Maui News,* 1964-65.

WORK IN PROGRESS: "Mountain," an article on Haleakala, Maui; sketches of Hawaiian life during the 1920's; sketches of Island girls in England during the early 1930's.

SIDELIGHTS: Barbara Lyons related to *CA:* "My interest in writing about Honolulu and Maui, especially of childhood in a world that is no more, stems from my background. My family has lived in Hawaii for four generations, beginning with missionaries a hundred and fifty years ago.

"I wrote *The Brook* for our grandchildren, but also as a love letter to the people, places, and animals I knew fifty and sixty years ago.

"In doing research for the Maui Historical Society, I could find no books composed entirely of legends of the Maui region. Because of this, I wrote both *Maui, Mischievous Hero* and *Fire and Water* largely from the abundant oral history of the legends of Maui."

*   *   *

LYONS, Len 1942-

PERSONAL: Born July 24, 1942, in Albany, N.Y.; son of Irving D. and Gertrude (Siagel) Lyons; married Maxine Iris Schoenbrun (a gerontologist), June 26, 1977; children: Gila Rachel. *Education:* University of Rochester, B.A., 1964; Brown University, M.A., 1966, Ph.D., 1969. *Religion:* Jewish. *Address:* P.O. Box 2156, Berkeley, Calif. 94702. *Agent:* Michael Larsen/Elizabeth Pomada, 1029 Jones St., San Francisco, Calif. 94109.

CAREER: University of Santa Clara, Santa Clara, Calif., assistant professor of philosophy, 1969-73; writer, 1973—. *Awards, honors:* Ralph J. Gleason Memorial Fund Award from Monterey Jazz Festival, 1976, for jazz criticism.

WRITINGS: (With John Donnelly) *Conscience: A Philosophical Analysis,* Alba, 1972; *The One Hundred Best Jazz Albums: A History of Jazz on Records,* Morrow, 1980.

Author of "Tyranny: A Case in Point," first broadcast by KPIX-TV, San Francisco, Calif., November 5, 1978. Contributor of more than one hundred articles to magazines and newspapers.

AVOCATIONAL INTERESTS: Playing the piano, reading, jogging, playing tennis.

*   *   *

LYTLE, Clifford M(erle) 1932-

PERSONAL: Born May 11, 1932, in Youngstown, Ohio; son of Clifford M. (in sales) and Ethel Mae (Warner) Lytle; married Elizabeth Holmes, December 21, 1958; children: Christian, Carrie, Jamie. *Education:* Denison University, B.A., 1954; Case Western Reserve University, LL.B., 1957; University of Pittsburgh, Ph.D., 1963. *Politics:* Democrat. *Religion:* None. *Home:* 7215 Princeton Dr., Tucson, Ariz. 85710. *Office:* Department of Political Science, University of Arizona, Tucson, Ariz. 85721.

CAREER: Carson, Vogelgesang & Sheehan, Canton, Ohio, attorney, 1958-59; University of Pittsburgh, Johnstown Campus, Johnstown, Pa., instructor in political science, 1961; University of Arizona, Tucson, assistant professor, 1962-65, associate professor, 1966-69, professor of political science, 1970—, head of department of government, 1969-73, 1978-79, director of Institute of Government Research, 1978-79. *Member:* American Political Science Association, American Civil Liberties Union, Western Political Science Association.

WRITINGS: (With David Bingham) *Public Land Use, Transfer, and Ownership in Arizona,* Arizona Academy, 1965; *The Warren Court and Its Critics,* University of Arizona Press, 1968; *The Public Defender System in Arizona: A Study of Policymaking at the State Level,* Institute of Government Research, University of Arizona, 1969; (with Richard Cortner) *Constitutional Politics in Arizona,* Institute of Government Research, University of Arizona, 1969; (with Cortner) *Modern Constitutional Law: Cases and Commentaries,* Free Press, 1971; (with John Garcia) *Mexican Juveniles and Crime in U.S. Border Communities,* Institute of Government Research, University of Arizona, 1974. Contributor of about a dozen articles and reviews to political science and law journals.

WORK IN PROGRESS: Research on criminal sentencing, the role of the probation officer in judicial decision-making, and judicial reliance on pre-sentence investigations in criminal sentencing.

M

MAAS, Peter 1929-

PERSONAL: Born June 27, 1929, in New York, N.Y.; married Audrey Gellen (a producer and writer), April 4, 1962 (died July 2, 1975); married Laura Parkins (a real estate broker), September 14, 1976 (separated, 1979); children: John Michael. *Education:* Duke University, B.A., 1949. *Religion:* Roman Catholic. *Agent:* Sam Cohn, International Creative Management, 40 West 57th St., New York, N.Y. 10019.

CAREER: Writer. *New York Herald Tribune*, Paris, France, reporter; *Collier's*, New York City, reporter, 1955-56; *Look*, New York City, senior editor, 1959-62; *Saturday Evening Post*, New York City, senior writer, 1963-66. Special consultant for "David Brinkley's Journal," National Broadcasting Co., 1961-62. *Military service:* U.S. Navy, 1952-54. *Member:* P.E.N.

WRITINGS: The Rescuer (nonfiction), Harper, 1968; *The Valachi Papers* (nonfiction), Putnam, 1969; *Serpico* (biography; Literary Guild selection), Viking, 1973; *King of the Gypsies* (nonfiction), Viking, 1975; *Made in America* (novel), Viking, 1979. Contributing editor and author of column in *New York*, 1968-71; author of column in *New York Times*, 1978.

WORK IN PROGRESS: Another novel, which "will deal with a subject that has preoccupied [me] lately: women."

SIDELIGHTS: Peter Maas built a reputation as one of New York's preeminent investigative reporters during the fifties and sixties. A staff writer for *Collier's, Look,* and the *Saturday Evening Post,* Maas broke headline stories about crime and corruption, an insider's view of life in the Mafia, and the emergence of the lone hero under life-and-death circumstances. When he turned to book writing, he applied a journalist's expertise for research and narrative to tell the stories of mafioso Joseph Valachi and police detective Frank Serpico. Since 1969, Maas has parlayed an unbroken string of best sellers—*The Valachi Papers, Serpico,* and *King of the Gypsies*—into film and paperback bonanzas and scored new riches with *Made in America,* his first novel. The writer's progress has been accorded the rewards of success, but he has also incurred many of its special hazards, including a prolonged, court-tested case of government suppression.

Maas's friend, Robert Alan Aurthur, once wrote, "I've learned that Peter Maas refers to himself as an Investigative Reporter much as Tom Wolfe uses the term Personal Journalist: always in caps, with pride, and a sense of ownership." Maas first worked for the *New York Herald Tribune* in Paris, then moved to *Collier's* in 1955. When the magazine folded one year later, he joined the crew of a lobster boat before resuming his journalism career at *Look* and the *Saturday Evening Post*. Two articles in particular drew national attention: a 1960 story for *Look* led to the release of a Louisiana black man who had been on death row longer than any other prisoner in the United States; later, at the *Post*, he exposed syndicated columnist Cholly Knickerbocker as an agent of the Dominican Republic. But his big break came in 1963, when he stumbled onto the story of racketeer and Mafia hitman Joseph Valachi.

While doing research for a story on Roy Cohn, Maas visited the New York office of U.S. Attorney Robert Morgenthau, where he first learned that an important underworld figure had turned government informer. Two months later, at a luncheon interview with his friend Attorney General Robert Kennedy, he suddenly asked about "the mob guy who's talking." Maas recalled: "I knew absolutely nothing, but Bobby thought I did. . . . Kennedy'd had no intention of surfacing Valachi, but now he told me he'd discuss it with his people and let me know later. When I returned I was told that since the story was going to break anyway—it really wasn't—they'd decided to tell me all."

Valachi had confirmed for the FBI the existence of the Cosa Nostra, disclosed its organizational structure, and named the heads of various units. Maas broke the story in a series of three articles for the *Saturday Evening Post*, accounts which also made the front page of the *New York Times*. Meanwhile, members of the Justice Department were urging Valachi to write his memoirs, reasoning that, with a book, "law enforcement can be benefited substantially." After completing his testimony before televised Congressional hearings on organized crime in 1965, the mobster set down his recollections in a 1,180-page manuscript called *The Real Thing*. According to Maas, "It was just one long sentence. No one could read it. But I discovered it made sense if you read it aloud." The Department retained Maas as the book's editor and allowed him to interview Valachi in his Washington, D.C., jail cell. Word of the project leaked early in 1966, however, and Maas soon found himself mired in a federal law suit.

"The Italian-American community, angered by any implication that Italians hold an exclusive franchise on crime, anticipated nothing but substantial harm" if the book went to press, reported *Newsweek* magazine. A delegation of twelve prominent Italian-Americans, including Congressmen Peter Rodino, Dominick Daniels, Joseph Minish, and Frank Annunzio, went to Attorney General Nicholas Katzenbach and protested against the planned book. Within a week, the project was virtually dead, but Maas refused to back out of his contract, claiming that the Department had succumbed to political pressure, and declared his intention to complete the book.

On May 10, 1966, the Justice Department filed suit in Washington's Federal District Court seeking an injunction against the publication or dissemination of Valachi's memoirs. The government brief charged that publication would "be detrimental to law enforcement" and cause the United States "immediate and irreparable harm." It also alleged that Maas violated the terms of his original agreement with the Justice Department when he applied for a copyright on the book and showed excerpts of the manuscript to a literary agent before receiving the Department's final approval. Maas's attorneys fired back, "The action of the Justice Department flies in the face of . . . free speech. This appears to be the first time so far as we know that the [department] has ever undertaken censorship of a work." Maas added that his application for copyright was not a breach of contract insofar as a completed book did not exist and could not therefore be submitted for final approval.

The court finally resolved the dispute in 1968, upholding a government regulation that prohibits a prisoner from writing and publishing a book about his life of crime. Maas, however, could not be prevented from writing a book based on what he knew from personal interviews, tape recordings, and other sources.

Twenty publishers rejected *The Valachi Papers,* a book that became a run-away best seller for Putnam in 1969. (On the walls of Maas's study now hang the framed jackets of thirteen foreign editions of the book.) Emanuel Perlmutter, writing in the *New York Times Book Review,* asserted that "Peter Maas . . . has produced a narrative that is exciting as well as informative, as fascinating as fiction, a bloody history of the Mafia as lived by one of its members for three decades." Maas was practically an overnight success: the motion picture made by Dino De Laurentiis, after every studio turned it down, grossed $20 million; paperback sales reached 2.5 million; and the author, suddenly boosted into the seventy percent tax category, had to borrow money to pay his income taxes. Even greater success awaited his next book.

In a February, 1971, narcotics raid, New York City police detective Frank Serpico was shot in the face by a drug dealer. Some reports later held that he had been set up by fellow police officers, though the charge was never proved. Nevertheless, Serpico had delivered documented evidence of widespread police corruption to the *New York Times,* and many believed the shooting was not an accident. Maas told the story in *Serpico,* a biography of the policeman the author has described as "maybe the only pure man I've ever known."

In the fall of '71, Serpico agreed to work with Maas on a book about his life. Maas, though, was careful to acquire full editorial control over the project; a few policemen had suggested that Serpico would be exposed, and "the burden of proof was on me," the author said, "to show that Frank was not on the pad." A thorough investigator, he conducted six months of tape-recorded interviews with Serpico at his Greenwich Village apartment and spent six months corroborating the detective's story. He combed confidential police

files and inter-office memos kept on Serpico, questioned hundreds of witnesses, and visited the scenes of crimes. "And you know what? Frank Serpico never took a quarter," Maas reported. "I couldn't believe what I discovered: as a cop Serpico is the *first* police officer in the history of the New York department who on his own tried to reveal corruption."

It took Maas nine months to write the book. Putnam turned it down: cop stories didn't sell. But *Serpico* was published by Viking in 1973 and has since topped sales of three million copies. *New York Times* critic R. R. Lingeman commented: "Maas tells this story with effortless smoothness. . . . I don't think anyone can come away from *Serpico* without admiration for one man's lonely integrity." The book became a hot movie property, and again De Laurentiis bought the screen rights. Maas decided that half of the $400,000 he was paid should go to Serpico. "After all," he remarked, "it's his life."

Success admitted Maas to the "good life," or at least allowed him to live better than he had. In the lean days, when he was working on the Valachi book, his wife, movie and television producer Audrey Gellen, supported them both. Now they could afford to buy a house in the country and move into the Manhattan apartment once owned by Marilyn Monroe. But Maas then suffered two personal setbacks. In 1973, Mafia Godfather Frank Costello died soon after he and Maas began collaborating on a book. "He promised to tell me everything," Maas revealed. "*Everything!*" Two years later, Maas's wife was killed in an auto accident. There was no will, and the ensuing legal and financial settlements cost him "a fortune" to untangle.

The author recouped some of his losses in 1975 with *King of the Gypsies,* another work of nonfiction about an unlikely hero, gypsy Steve Tene. In the book Maas chronicles a power struggle involving three generations of the "royal" gypsy family headed by King Tene Bimbo. When Bimbo nears death, he bequeaths the kingship to his grandson, Steve, rather than Carranza, his homicidal son, sparking a violent father-and-son feud. "Steve, as Maas presents him to us, is a man in transition," explained *Newsweek,* "anxious to become Americanized and to help other gypsies learn to read, to enter the professions, and to break the repetitive cycle that has enslaved them for thousands of years." The film rights sold for $350,000.

In his review of *King of the Gypsies,* P. S. Prescott described an underlying concern of Maas's work, observing that the author "writes books about people who live on the margin of our heterogeneous society and attack its center. These are vicious people—mafiosi, corrupt cops, gypsies—who act often violently, but always so unobtrusively that most of us do not notice them. . . . It is to Maas's credit that except for a wistful admiration for the gypsies' skill at eluding the ubiquitous computer, he does not romanticize their way of life." Nancy Naglin's review called the book a "masterful play-by-play expose of gypsy violence, revenge, con games, and shams as well as an amazing collection of gypsy folklore . . . irresistible." Jim Hampton of the *National Observer* stated: "It's readable, it's dramatic, and, like a novel, it tells the story of an entire people principally through the travail of one of them. . . . Maas has captured the gypsy's soul."

After *King of the Gypsies,* Maas was urged by friends, especially novelist E. L. Doctorow, to make an earnest attempt at fiction writing. Despite a tempting $1 million offer to write a book about the Shah of Iran, Maas decided to take up the greater challenge: "As one of the leading practitioners of what has been called the 'new journalism,' even with its use of fictional techniques, I became increasingly frustrated by the necessary limitations of observable or ascertainable facts," he explained. "Fiction, it seemed to me, was in fact the only way to come to grips with the human condition." The book, *Made in America,* proved that "the leap [from nonfiction to fiction] was well worth chancing," concluded Evan Hunter. "He has every right to be proud of this novel."

Made in America tells of an ordinary man's once-in-a-lifetime opportunity to strike it rich. Richie Flynn, an ex-pro football player turned beer salesman, dreams of buying an abandoned synagogue in the Bronx, converting it into a daycare center, and leasing it back to the city for a windfall profit of $2 million. For his plan to succeed, however, he needs a $10,000 stake for a down payment on the building, and his only source for the money is Albert "King Kong" Karpstein, "surely one of the most frightening creations in recent fiction," allowed Evan Hunter. The dream quickly sours as Flynn sinks deeper into the loan shark's debt and wakes up as the government's star witness against Mafia boss Frank Donato and his enforcer, Karpstein.

"'Made in America' is written as if it were told across the table at Maas' New York hangout, P. J. Clarke's, or read on the front page of the New York Daily News," wrote James F. Vesely. "It is a delightful, funny book, as though Maas, Jimmy Breslin and Pete Hamill all sat around a bottle of Kessler's and spilled the beans. But the credit goes entirely to Maas, one of the best writers around." Feature writer Ron Base called it "a sardonic and cynical book, written by a man who suspects the whole world is out to make the easy score and is not particularly concerned about how it's accomplished. One hundred years hence sociologists, if they are smart, may pass up Mailer and Barth and John Cheever in favor of books like 'Made in America' in order to probe the moral climate of the times."

The present state of morality, Maas maintains, has promoted a "great disillusionment in America." Citing Watergate as an example, he noted that "if the stakes are high enough, there is no difference between the good guys and the bad guys. It's who wins that counts. . . . There is cynicism and corruption of a profound sort. People are acting corrupt and they don't even know it." *Made in America,* he observed, stands as an illustration of "the corruption of the human spirit, conscious and unconscious, individual and societal."

Meanwhile, De Laurentiis has purchased the film rights to *Made in America* for $450,000, and a similar figure was paid for the paperback rights. Success continues, though problems remain. Gypsies angered by *King of the Gypsies* have kept Maas embroiled in numerous law suits, and he has separated from his second wife. But the writer is confirmed in his ambitions: he has started work on a second novel.

CA INTERVIEWS THE AUTHOR
Peter Maas was interviewed by *CA* in June, 1979.

Maas is a trim, athletic figure who looks considerably younger than his fifty years, with a shock of gray hair, big bushy eyebrows over Irish blue eyes—the perfect face, as a recent story in the *Soho Weekly News* put it, for a beer commercial. And in fact the first thing Maas did when he met *CA*'s interviewer in his midtown New York office (he has a couple of nondescript rooms in an office building between two famous delicatessens on Seventh Avenue; a writing neighbor is Paddy Chayevsky) was offer him a beer to go with the one he was already nursing.

Maas has already achieved considerable success with three of his four previous nonfiction books, including sales totaling 2.5 million copies for *The Valachi Papers* and three million for *Serpico.* He is now branching out into fiction with high hopes.

"I'm very possessive about my novel," he said recently in reference to *Made in America.* "I think it's much more important than anything else I've done. And it's far more exciting, I find, to write a novel than the other kind of books I've done. The others all had intrinsically dramatic stories to tell, so that once the research was complete, the problem was simply a tactical one of putting it all together.

"I guess another reason I wanted to write a novel was that I'd been accused so often of writing fiction when I wasn't that I thought I'd try it in fact. And I could have gone on doing the kind of books I was doing but I think it's important for a writer to challenge himself."

As usual, Maas planned out his novel before writing it. But like many beginning novelists he found the plot getting away from him. *Made in America* is the story of Richie Flynn, a former football star who dreams of riches via a welfare swindle but becomes involved with a loan shark and the Mafia. While writing the novel Maas found that he "got more interested in some characters than others." Among the characters that clearly fascinated him was Karpstein, the hulking and brutal loan shark, whom Maas had planned on portraying as a complete villain but converted into a strange mixture of a character. "By the time I finished the first time around I had a sort of unwieldy balloon," Maas noted. "I had to go back and redo the whole thing; I expanded rather than subtracted, and it ended up a much bigger book than I expected. The biggest change in it came out of the act of discovery while writing."

Maas was surprised that *Made in America* had already been sold to film producers. "I don't think of it as exactly an upbeat sort of story—anyway, I never think about the movies while I'm writing."

Maas's three previous books have caused a certain amount of controversy upon publication. *The Valachi Papers,* for instance, outraged the Italian community as one of the first in what eventually became a wave of literature focusing on Mafia figures. Maas was an investigative reporter, writing "inside" stories about civic corruption and organized crime, when he happened upon the Joe Valachi story. Maas recalled that he was in a prosecutor's office in New York seeking information when he overheard a phone conversation which suggested to him that a major underworld figure was talking. "I didn't ask about it because I was afraid they'd tell me about it and tell me not to write anything," he revealed. Later, however, he asked Attorney General Robert Kennedy who in the "mob" was talking and Kennedy, thinking there had already been a leak, gave him Joe Valachi's story and access to tapes of the mobster's FBI interviews. Maas also learned later that Valachi was writing his autobiography and was provided with that material.

"The Mafia whipped up the Italian-American community against me and they even went so far as to send a group to the White House to complain about the book," claimed Maas. "I think it was the first time the White House actually tried to suppress a book." The fight to publish went on for two years until a judge agreed that Maas could write *about* Valachi as long as the book was not published as the Mafia figure's own memoirs. "That meant I had to set to work to check most of what he'd told me because if it was me writing it, I had to get it right. If it was his version of the truth, it didn't matter." In the end, Maas observed proudly, "No one has found any factual error in the book." But the book still went to a number of publishers before being accepted by Putnam. Many publishers informed Maas that books about the Mafia were poor sellers. "It was probably true before Valachi," Maas commented, "but afterward it seemed as if I had created a new industry."

Maas also encountered considerable difficulty while writing *Serpico.* "A lot of the story about police corruption had been in papers," Maas related, "and everyone was after Serpico, but he was wary of being used. When he finally agreed to talk to me, I asked him why he had done so, and he said he'd been up against it so often himself, looking for help, that he felt he couldn't turn down his own help when it was asked for." Maas reported that other policemen constantly told him that Serpico was only talking because he was eventually going to be revealed as a crook, too. "In the end," stated Maas, "I got a copy of an investigation of Serpico by the cops themselves, and believe me, they did a thorough job, but they couldn't find the slightest blemish on his record—not even that he had ever given a desk officer a few bucks to type up his report for him, which almost every cop does."

Maas also said that one of the reasons that he was particularly drawn to the story of Serpico was that it would help to show he had no bias. "You couldn't imagine two people more different than Valachi and Serpico," he remarked, "yet they both originally came from Neopolitan stock—it shows there are really no stereotypes."

One of the complaints made about *Serpico* was that it didn't go into great detail about police corruption. "But," Maas contended, "that wasn't what I was after—the thing that fascinated me was Serpico as an individual, a man who actually stood up for what he believed in; he was the story, not the corruption he was fighting. It was at the time of Watergate and he began to seem like a metaphor for everything that was happening.

"Everyone was assuming everyone was a crook, and here was someone who really did what he was supposed to do—no more than that, after all, but it came to seem so unusual that he was a hero. Everyone became deeply involved with Serpico because at that time the country needed heroes so badly."

Serpico was more successful than Maas expected and he now confesses that he is not entirely pleased with it. "I think it didn't cover Serpico's personal side as thoroughly as it might have," he allowed. "It didn't explain sufficiently *why* he was the sort of person he was. I should have gone more into the influence on him of his family, especially his father. Here was a man who really believed everything he'd been told about America, and although Serpico was a pretty argumentative guy, he'd really listen to his father."

The pattern of controversy was repeated with *King of the Gypsies* which, according to Maas, provoked $18 million worth of lawsuits from the gypsy community. "But I'm winning them one by one," he declared.

With his first novel completed, Maas is now readying a second one. "My only real worry about *Made in America,*" he confessed, "is that the female characters are not very thoroughly explored. Next time around I'd like to make a woman the central character." And Maas is doubtful about repeating the writing formula which brought him success. "It would have to be a really enormous story to persuade me to do another nonfiction book," he said. In fact, he feels that it would be difficult to return to such writing after the "exhila-

ration" of creating a novel. "But I might do some essays," he admitted, "much more personal than any writing I've done before—*my* attitudes, *my* reactions. I wrote a sports column for the *New York Times* last year and I enjoyed that, but when they asked me to continue it I refused. Still, that's a way I could go, and eventually pieces like that could make a collection. Otherwise I think I'll stick to fiction."

BIOGRAPHICAL/CRITICAL SOURCES: Publishers Weekly, May 23, 1966; *Newsweek,* May 23, 1966, January 6, 1969, May 7, 1973, October 20, 1975; *New York Times Book Review,* October 8, 1967, January 12, 1969, May 27, 1973, November 9, 1975, September 2, 1979; *Time,* January 17, 1969; *New York Review of Books,* April 19, 1973; *New York Times,* May 26, 1973, October 28, 1975; *New Republic,* May 26, 1973; *Christian Science Monitor,* May 30, 1973; *Esquire,* June, 1973; *New Yorker,* July 2, 1973, October 22, 1979; *Commentary,* October, 1973; *Atlanta Journal & Constitution,* February 3, 1974; *Chicago Daily News,* February 16-17, 1974; *Biography News,* Gale, March, 1974; *Chicago Tribune Book World,* October 12, 1975; *National Observer,* November 1, 1975; *Library Journal,* June 15, 1979; *Detroit News,* September 5, 1979; *Detroit News Magazine,* September 9, 1979; *Washington Post Book World,* September 9, 1979; *Chicago Tribune Arts and Fun/Books,* September 23, 1979.

—*Sketch by B. Hal May*
—*Interview by John F. Baker*

*   *   *

MacCORMICK, Austin H(arbutt)   1893-1979

OBITUARY NOTICE: Born April 20, 1893; died October 24, 1979, in New York, N.Y. Penologist, educator, and author. MacCormick was an assistant director of the U.S. Bureau of Prisons, the Commissioner of Corrections in New York City under Mayor Fiorella La Guardia, and a professor of criminology at the University of California. He was awarded the Presidential Medal of Merit for his work in the rehabilitation of Army prisoners during World War II and was the author of a 1931 book, *The Education of Adult Prisoners.* Obituaries and other sources: *Current Biography,* Wilson, 1951, January, 1980; *New York Times,* October 25, 1979.

*   *   *

MacDONAGH, Donagh   1912-1968

OBITUARY NOTICE: Born in 1912 in Dublin, Ireland; died January 1, 1968. Barrister, editor, poet, and dramatist. MacDonagh, a barrister and later a district justice in Wexford and Dublin, wrote two verse plays, "Happy as Larry" and "Step-in-the-Hollow." He edited *Poems From Ireland* and co-edited *The Oxford Book of Irish Verse.* His works of poetry include *Veterans, The Hungry Grass,* and *A Warning for Conquerors.* Obituaries and other sources: *The Reader's Encyclopedia,* 2nd edition, Crowell, 1965; *Twentieth Century Writing: A Reader's Guide to Contemporary Literature,* Transatlantic, 1969; *Longman Companion to Twentieth Century Literature,* Longman, 1970; *McGraw-Hill Encyclopedia of World Drama,* McGraw, 1972; *Cassell's Encyclopaedia of World Literature,* revised edition, Morrow, 1973.

*   *   *

MACGOWAN, Kenneth   1888-1963

OBITUARY NOTICE: Born November 30, 1888, in Winthrop, Mass.; died April 27, 1963. Drama critic, editor, publicity director, stage director, producer, educator, and author. Macgowan was a drama critic for several newspapers and magazines, including the *New York Globe* and *Vogue*, editor of *Theatre Arts* magazine, and a publicity director for Goldwyn Pictures Corp. During the 1920's, he directed plays for the Provincetown Players, the Greenwich Village Theatre, and the Actors Theatre, after which he worked as a producer of motion pictures at RKO-Radio Pictures, Twentieth Century-Fox, and Paramount. In 1947, Macgowan became a professor of theatre arts at the University of California at Los Angeles, where the theatre arts building was named in his honor in 1963. He wrote numerous books about theatrical and anthropological subjects, including *The Theatre of Tomorrow, Masks and Demons, Footlights Across America, Early Man in the New World,* and *Behind the Screen: The History and Techniques of the Motion Picture*. Obituaries and other sources: *Who Was Who in America,* 4th edition, Marquis, 1968; *American Authors and Books, 1640 to the Present Day,* 3rd revised edition, Crown, 1972.

* * *

MacGREGOR, David Roy 1925-

PERSONAL: Born August 26, 1925, in London, England; son of Walter William (an army officer) and Rachel (Bryan-Smith) MacGregor; married Patricia Margaret Aline Purcell-Gilpin (a teacher), October 26, 1962. *Education:* Trinity College, Cambridge, B.A., 1948, M.A., 1950; also attended Hammersmith School of Building, 1954-55. *Home:* 99 Lonsdale Rd., London SW13 9DA, England.

CAREER: Fulham Borough Council, London, England, assistant architect, 1949-61; free-lance writer and researcher, 1961—. Member of Maritime Trust ships' committee; member of board of directors of Catamaran Cruisers Ltd. *Member:* Royal Historical Society (fellow), Society for Nautical Research (member of council, 1959-63, 1965-69, 1974-77), Society of Antiquaries (fellow), Royal Institute of British Architects (associate), Hurlingham Club. *Awards, honors:* Gold medal from *Daily Express,* 1973, for *Fast Sailing Ships.*

WRITINGS: (Contributor) Basil Greenhill, *The Merchant Schooners,* Percival Marshall, Volume I, 1951, revised edition, 1968, Volume II, 1957, revised edition, 1968; *The Tea Clippers,* Percival Marshall, 1952, reprinted, Conway, 1972; *The China Bird,* Chatto & Windus, 1961; *Fast Sailing Ships: Their Design and Construction, 1775-1875,* Nautical Publishing, 1973; *Square-Rigged Sailing Ships,* Argus, 1977; *Clipper Ships,* Argus, 1979; *Merchant Sailing Ships,* Argus, Volume I, 1979, Volume II, 1980, Volume III, 1980. Contributor to magazines and newspapers, including *Trident* and *Mariner's Mirror.*

WORK IN PROGRESS: Research for a book on the history of ship fittings.

SIDELIGHTS: MacGregor writes: "It must have been in 1950 that Basil Greenhill, now director of the National Maritime Museum at Greenwich, introduced me to Percival Marshall for whom he was writing a book on schooners, and it was suggested that I write for them on clippers. I had no ambition before this to become an author. My first two books were written when I worked full-time in an architect's office. Although I qualified as an architect, I gave this work up in 1961 to devote my time to sailing ship research. The principal result was *Fast Sailing Ships.* I drew most of the ship plans first and then wrote about them. The American, Howard I. Chapelle, was my great inspiration: he drew plans of ships, analyzed them, but produced a readable narrative. I have tried to copy his methods for British ships, although I

am not a naval architect. I measure actual vessels or models or work from old plans.

"I have no regular working habits when writing, although I find the hours of 7:00 A.M. to noon a good period. As a result of my books, I seem to have become an authority on merchant sailing ships, but this always brings problems. The field of sailing ship history is so vast and it has barely been covered, but unfortunately many publications merely cover the same ground to appeal to popular tastes. In the method I have adopted in my more serious books of employing ship plans and analyzing them, I am reluctantly obliged to notice that there are very few others using these methods."

In his review of *Fast Sailing Ships,* Richard Hough wrote: "It is difficult to envisage any work that can ever take its place as the most exhaustively researched and important study of all sailing ships built with speed as a high priority." The book incorporates "exquisite little colour drawings . . . and hauntingly evocative photographs."

BIOGRAPHICAL/CRITICAL SOURCES: Daily Telegraph, October 18, 1973.

* * *

MacKAYE, Milton 1901-1979

PERSONAL: Born December 23, 1901, in Redfield, Iowa; died March 21, 1979, in Miami, Fla.; son of Donald John (a clergyman) and Catherine (Stacey) McKay; married Dorothy Cameron Disney (a writer), November 15, 1927; children: William Ross. *Education:* Attended Simpson College. *Residence:* Madison, Conn.

CAREER: Reporter for newspapers, including *Des Moines News, Des Moines Tribune, Kansas City Post,* and *Washington Daily News,* 1920-24; *New York Evening News,* reporter, 1924-32; Paramount Pictures, Hollywood, Calif., member of writing staff, 1933; member of Washington bureau of United Press; free-lance journalist and writer, 1931-79. *Wartime service:* Served with Office of War Information in Washington, D.C., and later as chief of its London office. *Member:* National Press Club, Overseas Press Club of America, Authors Club, Cosmos Press Club, Alpha Tau Omega, Players, Madison Beach Club.

WRITINGS: Dramatic Crimes of 1927: A Study in Mystery and Detection, Crime Club, 1928; *The Tin Box Parade: A Handbook for Larceny,* McBride, 1934; (with Robert Laurence Eichelberger) *Our Jungle Road to Tokyo,* Viking, 1950; (with Ernest N. Harmon and son, William Ross MacKaye) *Combat Commander: Autobiography of a Soldier,* Prentice-Hall, 1970. Contributor of articles to periodicals, including *New Yorker, Saturday Evening Post, Scribner's,* and *Reader's Digest.*

SIDELIGHTS: MacKaye was known for his articles on politicians. His most notable pieces included profiles of Franklin D. Roosevelt and Adlai Stevenson.

OBITUARIES: Washington Post, March 23, 1979; *New York Times,* March 24, 1979.*

* * *

MacKENZIE, Jean 1928-

PERSONAL: Born March 22, 1928, in Traynor, Saskatchewan, Canada; daughter of F. J. (a free-lance writer) and Jean (a teacher; maiden name, Irving) Whiting; married Edward D. MacKenzie (a data processing consultant), July 5, 1952; children: two. *Education:* Educated in Vancouver, British Columbia. *Home:* 3815 Merriman Dr., Victoria, British Columbia V8P 2S8, Canada.

CAREER: Free-lance writer. R. W. Large Memorial Hospital, Bella Bella, British Columbia, assistant cook and children's nurse, 1947-48; Birk's Jewelers, Vancouver, British Columbia, display assistant, 1948-52, display manager, 1952-54; Firbank's, Vancouver, display manager, 1954-55. *Member:* Canadian Authors Association. *Awards, honors:* Prize from Canadian Centennial Commission, 1967, for *Storm Island.*

WRITINGS: Storm Island (juvenile), Macmillan, 1968; *River of Stars* (juvenile), McClelland & Stewart, 1971. Contributor of more than one hundred articles to periodicals, including *Western Living, Islander, United Church,* and *Beautiful British Columbia.*

WORK IN PROGRESS: Researching history of British Columbia; a juvenile historical book.

SIDELIGHTS: MacKenzie told *CA:* "My father was a free-lance writer, so I grew up knowing that writing, for me, was a real possibility, not just a dream, as it is for so many would-be writers. If Dad could do it, I could do it. I'm still very much a learner at my craft. Each book breaks a new frontier for me. It doesn't really concern me that much if the book is successful. If I feel I've done a better job than last time, and have written the best book I could at that stage of development, then I'm content ... or reasonably so. It doesn't bother me in the slightest if the writing community feels 'juvenile' writers are a 'lesser breed.' That's not my problem. My problem is growing to be a better writer. And that's what I aim for."

*   *   *

MacLEOD, Ruth 1903-
(Nan Lowry)

PERSONAL: Born December 29, 1903, in Hanford, Calif.; daughter of William O. and Myrtle (Sutton) Pickerill; married Guy Derby, 1930 (died, 1953); married Horace MacLeod, 1954 (died, 1964); children: (first marriage) Lorna Derby Johnston, William. *Education:* Attended Eugene Bible University, 1922-23, and University of California, Los Angeles, 1925-26. *Politics:* Democrat. *Religion:* Christian. *Home:* 2526 East Andrews, 204, Fresno, Calif. 93726. *Agent:* Julie Fallowfield, McIntosh & Otis, Inc., 475 Fifth Ave., New York, N.Y. 10017.

CAREER: Burnett Sanitarium, Fresno, Calif., student nurse, 1923-24; San Francisco City and County Hospital, San Francisco, Calif., student nurse, 1924-25; writer, 1930—; Civil Aeronautics Administration, Seattle, Wash., bookkeeper and auditor, 1942-46. *Member:* Authors Guild, California Writers Club, California Writers of the San Joaquin Valley.

WRITINGS—Novels: *Murder on Vacation,* Bouregy, 1962; *Nurse for Dr. Sterling,* Ace Books, 1962; *Dr. Grayson's Crisis,* Berkley, 1962; *Waikiki Nurse,* Avon, 1963; *Cheryl Downing, School Nurse,* Messner, 1964; *Nurse Ann in Surgery,* Ace Books, 1965; *A Love to Cherish,* Paperback Library, 1966; *Arlene Perry,* Messner, 1966; *Bitter Legacy,* Tower, 1966; *Arlene Perry, Orthopedics Nurse,* Messner, 1966; *Mistress of Shadows,* Tower, 1968; *Born to Be a Nurse,* Paperback Library, 1969.

Buenos Dias, Teacher, Messner, 1970; *Mendocino Menace,* Avon, 1973; *Make Way for Love,* Bantam, 1973; *Hawks of Glenaerie,* Manor, 1977.

Under pseudonym Nan Lowry: *Clayton Richards, M.D.,* Paperback Library, 1962; *Crystal Manning, Maternity Nurse,* Paperback Library, 1964. Contributor of nearly four hundred stories to periodicals, including confession magazines.

WORK IN PROGRESS: A paramedic nurse romance novel; a long historical romance.

SIDELIGHTS: Ruth MacLeod commented: "I sold my first story to a love pulp in 1931. Since then, several of my books have been printed in French, Spanish, Portuguese, German, and Norwegian.

"I wrote my first story at age nine for an audience of one—my younger sister who is still my most enthusiastic critic. For the past decade through 1979, my files have been donated to the University of Oregon Library for research by students who, it is hoped, will profit by my struggles and mistakes."

AVOCATIONAL INTERESTS: Piano, organ, choir.

*   *   *

MacMANUS, Seumas 1869-1960

OBITUARY NOTICE: Born in 1869 in Donegal, Ireland; died October 23, 1960. Lecturer, poet, playwright, short story writer, and compiler. MacManus grew up in the mountainous region of northwestern Ireland, where he farmed his father's hillside, wrote patriotic poems, and listened to the rich lore of stories told by the mountain people. He worked briefly as a schoolmaster, then sailed to America with a collection of folk tales and short stories that were quickly sold to New York magazines. He spent the remainder of his life writing and collecting stories, poems, and plays about the Irish people and commuting between his home in Donegal and the lucrative college lecture circuit in the United States. His works include *Shuilers* (poems), *The Bewitched Fiddle, Donegal Fairy Stories, Top o' the Mornin', The Donegal Wonder Book,* and *The Rocky Road to Dublin,* his autobiography. Obituaries and other sources: *Who Was Who in America,* 4th edition, Marquis, 1968; *American Authors and Books, 1640 to the Present Day,* 3rd revised edition, Crown, 1972.

*   *   *

MacRAE, Donald E. 1907-

PERSONAL: Born March 10, 1907, in Humeston, Iowa; son of Burnett and Mabel (Evans) MacRae; married Ruth Wilhite, July 19, 1935; children: Jean Margaret, Patricia Katherine. *Education:* Drake University, B.A., 1928; University of Iowa, M.A., 1932, Ph.D., 1934. *Politics:* "Variable—more interesting that way." *Religion:* "A true one—my own." *Home:* 8118 Southeast 39th Ave., Portland, Ore. 97202.

CAREER: Central Washington State College, Ellensburg, chairman of English department, 1934-43; Reed College, Portland, Ore., lecturer, 1944-45, associate professor, 1945-48, professor of literature, 1948-73; writer, 1973—. Exchange professor at University College of North Staffordshire (now University of Keele), 1959-60. Member of Oregon State Curriculum Study, 1965-68. *Member:* American Association of University Professors, Modern Language Association of America, Phi Beta Kappa, Sigma Delta Chi. *Awards, honors:* American Council of Learned Societies fellowship, 1952-53.

WRITINGS: Dwight Craig (novel), Houghton, 1947; (contributor) Albert R. Kitzhaber, editor, *The Oregon Curriculum: A Sequential Program in Literature,* six volumes, Holt, 1968-70, revised edition published as *Concepts in Literature,* four volumes, 1974. Contributor of articles and stories to journals, including *Midland, Frontier and Midland,* and *American Prefaces.*

WORK IN PROGRESS: Editing an anthology of stories by such writers as Sherwood Anderson, Ernest Hemingway, Flannery O'Connor, and Jean Stafford.

SIDELIGHTS: MacRae wrote: "I hope to write my critical commentaries in such a way that they might be attractive enough to interest both the general reader, the 'trade,' and bright but off-beat students at the college-university level. I intend, among other things, to make my commentaries personal, to suggest, that is, that I really do exist; and since my reader is *you,* perhaps I can guarantee your reality simply by reminding you now and then of mine.

"I began writing my first book, *Dwight Craig,* sometime in 1940 and of course made use of some of my own experiences—my protagonist growing up in a very small Iowa town and hating it (as I did not), a kind of sullen competitive spirit forced upon him quite early but without much satisfaction. Then college, a year of high school teaching, then graduate school and advanced degrees in education, along with the discovery of a passionate ambition, realized finally in the presidency of a western state university. Before long there is even some talk about the possibility of a political career.

"I tried to tell enough in the book about the personal problems he had to face early on to inspire *some* sympathy for him, but by the end of the book he has become a very simple creature: he is a pure bastard. He married for money, and his wife, who was simple, decent, and handsome in her way, and with no trace of boldness in her, ends as pure victim.

"The narrative did not grow out of just my professional life, but of living and growing up in the Midwest of fifty years ago, the hopes and fears of that time, perhaps not much different in substance from what we have now, but radically different in form, in the texture of life, in the habits that both keep us together and pull us apart. And underneath it all was the nonverbal data that cannot be clarified, the things unseen, unheard, untouchable, and odorless that really control our lives.

"I find myself, at the age of seventy-two, beginning to consider trying fiction again after all these years. Or, if not that, something in the way of a perhaps slightly slaphappy autobiography."

*   *   *

MAGNARELLA, Paul J(oseph)

PERSONAL—Education: University of Connecticut, B.S., 1959; Fairfield University, M.A. (secondary education), 1962; Harvard University, A.M. (social anthropology), 1969, Ph.D., 1971. *Office:* Department of Anthropology, University of Florida, Gainesville, Fla. 32611.

CAREER: University of Vermont, Burlington, assistant professor, 1971-75, associate professor of anthropology, 1975-78; University of Florida, Gainesville, professor of anthropology, 1979—.

WRITINGS: Tradition and Change in a Turkish Town, Wiley, 1974; *The Peasant Venture,* G. K. Hall, 1979. Contributor to sociology, anthropology, and Middle East journals.

WORK IN PROGRESS: Models of Human Nature, examining the basic assumptions about human nature by leading thinkers of past and present.

*   *   *

MAGNUSON, Keith (Arlen) 1947-

PERSONAL: Born April 27, 1947, in Wadena, Saskatchewan, Canada; son of Joseph and Birdie Magnuson; married Cynthia White, June 7, 1975; children: Kevin. *Education:* University of Denver, B.B.A., 1969. *Home:* 1694 Clendenin Lane, Riverwoods, Ill. 60015. *Office:* Chicago Black Hawk Hockey Team, Inc., 1800 West Madison St., Chicago, Ill. 60612.

CAREER: Chicago Black Hawk Hockey Team, Inc., Chicago, Ill., professional hockey player, 1969—, team captain, 1977-78. Account executive for Joyce Beverages, 1970—. *Awards, honors:* Western Collegiate Hockey Association (WCHA) Sophomore of the Year, 1967; member of WCHA First All-Star Team, 1967, 1968, 1969; member of National Collegiate Athletic Association (NCAA) Second All-American Team, 1967, member of First Team, 1968, 1969; named most valuable player in NCAA tournament, 1969; member of National Hockey League (NHL) First All-Star Team, West Division, 1971, 1972.

WRITINGS: (With Robert Bradford) *None Against!,* Dodd, 1973.

SIDELIGHTS: Magnuson began playing hockey at the age of six, and was collecting awards in hockey, baseball, football, and track while still in elementary school in Saskatchewan. After starring for the Denver Pioneers in college, Magnuson realized his goal of playing in the NHL when he made the Chicago Black Hawks as a rookie defenseman in 1969. Magnuson has since enjoyed several seasons as an NHL all-star, and has led the Black Hawks to a number of division championships.

AVOCATIONAL INTERESTS: Stamp collecting.

*   *   *

MAGUBANE, Bernard (Makhosezwe) 1930-

PERSONAL: Born August 26, 1930, in South Africa; son of Xengwana E. (a laborer) and Ella (Khumalo) Magubane; married Thembie E. Khaula (a nurse); children: Suzu, Bonjit, Vukani, Ziwe. *Education:* University of Natal, B.A., B.A. (with honors) and M.A., c. 1960; University of California, Los Angeles, M.A. and Ph.D., c. 1966. *Home:* 379 Middle Turnpike, Storrs, Conn. 06268. *Office:* Department of Anthropology, University of Connecticut, Storrs, Conn. 06268.

CAREER: University of Connecticut, Storrs, member of anthropology department, 1970—. *Member:* American Anthropological Association, American Sociological Association.

WRITINGS: The Continuing Class Struggle in South Africa, University of Denver, 1975; *Magubane's South Africa,* Knopf, 1978; *The Political Economy of Race and Class in South Africa,* Monthly Review Press, 1979.

WORK IN PROGRESS: National and Class Struggle in South Africa, 1800-1980.

*   *   *

MAHL, George F(ranklin) 1917-

PERSONAL: Surname is pronounced like "mail"; born November 27, 1917, in Akron, Ohio; son of Floyd A. (in business) and Margaret (Strecker) Mahl; married Martha Fenn, January 3, 1944; children: Barbara Mahl Hardwig. *Education:* Oberlin College, A.B., 1939, M.A., 1941; Yale University, Ph.D., 1948; Western New England Institute for Psychoanalysis, certificate, 1962. *Office:* Department of Psychiatry, Yale University, New Haven, Conn. 06520.

CAREER: Yale University, New Haven, Conn., research assistant at Institute of Human Relations, 1947-50, instructor, 1947-50, assistant professor, 1950-53, associate professor, 1953-64, professor of psychology, 1964—. Instructor at Western New England Institute for Psychoanalysis, 1961—, president of institute, 1972-74. Fellow of Center for Advanced Studies in the Behavioural Sciences, 1963-64. Speaker at scientific meetings. *Military service:* U.S. Army, clinical psychologist, 1942-46. *Member:* American Psychological Association (fellow), American Association for the Advancement of Science (fellow), Eastern Psychological Association, Western New England Psychoanalytic Society. *Awards, honors:* Foundations' Fund for Research in Psychiatry fellow, 1956-58.

WRITINGS: (With Irving Janis, Jerome Kagan, and Robert Holt) *Personality: Dynamics, Development, and Assessment,* Harcourt, 1969; *Psychological Conflict and Defense,* Harcourt, 1971.

Contributor: Ithiel de Sola Pool, editor, *Trends in Content Analysis,* University of Illinois Press, 1959; L. A. Gottschalk, editor, *Comparative Psycholinguistic Analysis of Two Psychotherapeutic Interviews,* International Universities Press, 1961; Peter Knapp, editor, *Expression of Emotions in Man,* International Universities Press, 1963; Thomas Sebeok, Albert Hayes, and Catherine Bateson, editors, *Approaches to Semiotics,* Mouton, 1964; Daniel Rioch, editor, *Disorders of Communication,* Association for Research in Nervous and Mental Diseases, 1964; John Shlein, editor, *Research in Psychotherapy,* Volume II, American Psychological Association, 1968; Arnold Siegman and Benjamin Pope, editors, *Studies in Dyadic Interaction,* Pergamon, 1972; Norbert Freedman and Stanley Grand, editors, *Communicative Structures and Psychic Structures,* Plenum, 1977. Contributor of about thirty-five articles and reviews to scientific journals.

* * *

MAILLARD, Keith 1942-

PERSONAL: Surname is pronounced Muh-*lard;* born February 28, 1942, in Wheeling, W.Va.; son of Eugene Charles and Aileen (a payroll office manager; maiden name, Sharp) Maillard. *Education:* Attended West Virginia University, 1961-63. *Residence:* Vancouver, British Columbia, Canada. *Agent:* Felicia Eth, Writers House, Inc., 21 West 26th St., New York, N.Y. 10010.

CAREER: Writer in Boston, Mass., 1967-70, and Vancouver, British Columbia, 1970—. *Member:* Writers' Union of Canada (member of national council, 1979-80). *Awards, honors:* Grants from Canada Council, 1974, 1977-78, 1978, and Ontario Arts Council, 1976, 1977.

WRITINGS: (Contributor) Howard Reiter, editor, *Instead of Revolution,* Hawthorn, 1971; *Two Strand River* (novel), Press Porcepic, 1976; *Alex Driving South* (novel), Dial, 1980. Writer for Canadian Broadcasting Corp. radio programs, "This Country in the Morning," "Our Native Land," and "Five Nights." Contributor to magazines, including *Fusion, Body Politic, Malahat Review, Books in Canada,* and *Canadian Literature,* and newspapers.

WORK IN PROGRESS: Two novels—*Motet* and *Difficulty at the Beginning: Magic Realism in British Columbia Fiction.*

SIDELIGHTS: Maillard worked his way through the United States (including Alaska) and Canada during the 1960's as a folksinger, photographer, music teacher, and writer. In 1970 he settled in Canada, becoming a Canadian citizen in 1976, and continued his work as writer, musician, and music teacher.

He writes: "Although much of my fiction to date is set in the United States where I grew up, I believe that my current writing is firmly in the Canadian (and specifically British Columbian) tradition. Contact with other Canadian writers is very important to me, and I see myself as a member of a loose 'school' of people working in a post-realist mode that has recently been labeled 'magic realism.'"

BIOGRAPHICAL/CRITICAL SOURCES: Canadian Fiction, spring-summer, 1977.

* * *

MAINS, David R(andall) 1936-

PERSONAL: Born August 6, 1936, in Aurora, Ill.; son of Douglas L. (an advertising executive) and Faith (an editor; maiden name, Jess) Mains; married Karen Burton (a writer), June 24, 1961; children: Randall, Melissa, Joel, Jeremy. *Education:* Wheaton College, Wheaton, Ill., B.A., 1958; also attended Southwestern Seminary, Fort Worth, Tex. *Home:* 29-W-377 Hawthorne Lane, West Chicago, Ill. 60185. *Office:* "Chapel of the Air," North Main Place, Wheaton, Ill. 60187.

CAREER: Ordained Evangelical Free Church minister, 1969; associate pastor of Moody Memorial Church in Chicago, Ill., 1965-66; pastor of Circle Church in Chicago, 1967-76; "Chapel of the Air" (radio broadcast), Wheaton, Ill., co-host, 1977-79, director, 1979—.

WRITINGS: Full Circle, Word Books, 1971.

WORK IN PROGRESS: A twelve-volume series of books, publication by David Cook expected in 1980; radio sermons.

SIDELIGHTS: Full Circle is about the birth and growth of the Chicago church that Mains led for ten years. Even before he left the pastorate for radio broadcasting, his influence was felt outside his own congregation through his speaking and writing efforts on such subjects as urban ministry, church renewal, and national revival.

Mains shares his broadcast with his uncle, John D. Jess, who founded "Chapel of the Air" in 1939. It is now heard six days a week on about two hundred fifty radio stations throughout North America and overseas.

* * *

MAKIN, Peter (Julian) 1946-

PERSONAL: Born March 23, 1946, in London, England; son of S. Noel (a lecturer in education) and Vicki (a handcraft teacher) Makin; married Stella Irene Correa (a painter), December 3, 1973. *Education:* King's College, London, B.A., 1968, Ph.D., 1972; also attended Sorbonne, University of Paris, 1968-69. *Home:* Ozu 1-chome 19-10, Fuchu-machi, Aki-gun, Hiroshima-ken 735, Japan. *Office:* Department of English, Faculty of Letters, University of Hiroshima, Hiroshima 730, Japan.

CAREER: Cours Normal de Sevare, Mopti, Mali, volunteer teacher, 1964-65; University of Birmingham, Birmingham, England, lecturer in British and American literature, 1971-72; University of Warwick, Coventry, England, lecturer in British and American literature, 1972-73; University of Hiroshima, Hiroshima, Japan, foreign lecturer in English, 1973-75; University of Warwick, lecturer in British and American literature, 1975-78; University of Hiroshima, foreign lecturer in English literature, 1978—.

WRITINGS: (Contributor) Philip Grover, editor, *Ezra Pound: The London Years, 1908-1920,* AMS Press, 1978; *Provence and Pound,* University of California Press, 1978. Contributor to language and literature journals.

WORK IN PROGRESS: "I am pondering on the prosody of Basil Bunting, Louis Zukofsky, and Ezra Pound, and its relation to the thought in their verse; also upon the way in which the prosodic theories of these three men developed while they were in close contact during Pound's time at Rapallo."

SIDELIGHTS: Makin wrote: "I try to clarify the materials and the methods that poets use. My preferred tools: a grasp of the material, common sense, and a visible structure of argument."

*   *   *

MALINA, Frank J(oseph) 1912-

PERSONAL: Born October 2, 1912, in Brenham, Tex.; son of Frank (a musician) and Caroline (a musician; maiden name, Marek) Malina; married Lilian Darcourt, July 14, 1933 (divorced, 1946); married Marjorie Duckworth, March 12, 1949; children: (second marriage) Roger Frank, Alan Jan. *Education:* Texas A & M University, B.S.M.E., 1934; California Institute of Technology, M.S. (mechanical engineering), 1935, M.S. (aeronautical engineering), 1936, Ph.D., 1940. *Politics:* Democrat. *Religion:* None. *Home and office:* 17 rue Emile Dunois, 92100 Boulogne-sur-Seine, France.

CAREER: California Institute of Technology, Pasadena, chief engineer on Air Corps Jet Propulsion Research Project, 1938-44, co-founder and director of Jet Propulsion Laboratory, 1944-46, assistant professor of aeronautics, 1942-46; National Advisory Committee for Aeronautics, Washington, D.C., member of subcommittee on propulsion systems, 1945-47; United Nations Educational, Scientific & Cultural Organization, Paris, France, science councelor, 1947-48, deputy director, 1948-51, head of Division of Scientific Research, 1951-53; artist, 1953—. Cooperative agent for Soil Conservation Service of U.S. Department of Agriculture, 1939-43; co-founder and director of Aerojet General Corp., 1942-44. Founder and director of Electre Lumidyne International Corp., 1959-76. Art work exhibited all over the world, including Smithsonian Institution and French Musee d'Art National. Representative of International Astronautical Federation to United Nations Educational, Scientific & Cultural Organization, 1959-64, and United Nations Economic and Social Council, 1964-76. Member of board of trustees of Theodore von Karman Memorial Foundation, 1961-62, 1975—; member of Fulbright Commission; member of Franco-American Commission for Educational and Cultural Exchange, 1969—; member of correspondence committee of Center for Integrative Education, 1972-74, and board of governors of Institute of American Studies in France, 1974—.

MEMBER: International Academy of Astronautics (member of founding committee; vice-president, 1960-63; president, 1963; member of board of trustees, 1963—; chairperson of Lunar International Laboratory Committee, 1960-68, and Manned Research on Celestial Bodies Committee, 1968—), American Association for the Advancement of Science, American Astronautical Society, American Federation of Arts, French Astronautics Society, French Society for the Encouragement of Research and Invention (commander), British Interplanetary Society, New York Academy of Science, Association of Former Students of Texas A & M University (member of international council, 1969-76), Sigma Xi. *Awards, honors:* French Prix d'Astronautique from French Astronomical Society, 1939, for "contributions to the study of rocket propulsion and flight"; certificate of commendation from U.S. Army Ordnance Department, 1946, for "contributions to the development of rocket en-

gines and missiles"; C. M. Hickman Award from American Rocket Society, 1948, for "development of the WAC Corporal sounding rocket"; Prix Yvonne Valensi from *Salon Compaisons*, 1958, for art exhibit, "Changing Times"; order of merit from French Society for the Encouragement of Research and Invention, 1962, for "contributions to aeronautics"; recognition from U.S. House of Representatives, 1967, for service to Committee on Science and Astronautics; medal of honor from city of Mendon, France, 1970; Prix Signature from *Salon Signature,* 1970, for "development of kinetic electric light artworks."

WRITINGS: (Editor) *Proceedings of the First Lunar International Laboratory (LIL) Symposium: Research in Geosciences and Astronomy,* Springer-Verlag, 1966; (editor) *Proceedings of the Second Lunar International Laboratory (LIL) Symposium: Life Sciences Research and Lunar Medicine,* Pergamon, 1967; (editor) *Proceedings of the Third Lunar International Laboratory (LIL) Symposium: Research in Physics and Chemistry,* Pergamon, 1969; (editor) *Proceedings of the Fourth Lunar International Laboratory (LIL) Symposium: Applied Sciences Research and Utilization of Lunar Resources,* Pergamon, 1970; (editor) *Kinetic Art: Theory and Practice—Selections From the Journal "Leonardo,"* Dover, 1974; (editor) *Visual Art, Mathematics, and Computers: Selections From the Journal "Leonardo,"* Pergamon, 1979.

Contributor: *Collected Works of Theodore von Karman,* Volume IV, Butterworth & Co., 1956; O. E. Lancaster, editor, *Jet Propulsion Engines: High Speed Aerodynamics and Jet Propulsion,* Volume XII, Princeton University Press, 1959; Eugene M. Emme, editor, *The History of Rocket Technology,* Wayne State University Press, 1964; Anthony Hill, editor, *DATA: Directions in Art, Theory, and Aesthetics,* Faber, 1968; F. C. Durant III and G. S. James, editors, *First Steps Toward Space: Smithsonian Annals of Flight,* Smithsonian Institution Press, 1974; *Collected Works of Theodore von Karman, 1952-1963,* Von Karman Institute for Fluid Dynamics, 1975. Also contributor to *Essays on the History of Rocketry and Astronautics,* Volume II, edited by R. Cargill Hall, National Aeronautics and Space Administration.

Contributor to *Encyclopaedia Britannica.* Contributor of more than eighty articles and reviews to scientific and visual arts journals and popular magazines, including *Bulletin of the Atomic Scientists, Listener, New Scientist,* and *Popular Educator.* Founding editor of *Leonardo,* 1967—; co-editor of *Astronautica Acta,* 1960-65, member of editorial advisory board, 1965-74, honorary editor, 1974—; member of editorial advisory board, *Computer Graphics and Art,* 1976-78.

WORK IN PROGRESS: Research on the relationships between visual art, science, and technology; paintings and kinetic artworks.

SIDELIGHTS: In 1944, Malina conceived and directed the construction and testing of the world's first successful high altitude sounding rocket, the WAC Corporal. But even then he was active as a visual artist and illustrator of technical books. He began concentrating on the visual arts in 1953, in Paris. Soon after, he incorporated electric light into his art work, with static "Electro-paintings," and later, kinetic paintings. He also painted hundreds of miniature pictures.

In 1956 he invented the "Lumidyne" system for making pictorial kinetic artworks, much later he also developed audio-kinetic artworks.

Malina has combined his artwork artistic creation with his background of engineering research, and his efforts have spread beyond his work as an artist. *Leonardo,* which he launched and has been editing since 1968, is an international journal of contemporary visual artists that provides a bridge between developments in art and science and an opportunity for artists to discuss their own art work of any tendency.

AVOCATIONAL INTERESTS: Chess, traveling.

* * *

MALININ, Theodore I 1933-

PERSONAL: Born September 13, 1933, in Krasnodar, Soviet Union; came to the United States in 1949, naturalized citizen, 1956; son of Ivan M. (a physician) and Olga (a musician; maiden name, Senitzky) Malinin; married Dorothy Rearick (a chemist), September 4, 1960; children: Ellen, Alexander, Catherine, Michael. *Education:* Concord College, B.S., 1955; University of Virginia, M.S., 1958, M.D., 1960. *Religion:* Eastern Orthodox. *Home:* 360 Atlantic Rd., Key Biscayne, Fla. 33149. *Office:* School of Medicine, University of Miami, Coral Gables, Fla. 33101.

CAREER: Johns Hopkins University, Baltimore, Md., research fellow in pathology, 1960-61; National Cancer Institute, Washington, D.C., pathologist, 1961-64; Georgetown University, Washington, D.C., assistant professor of pathology, 1964-69; University of Miami, Coral Gables, Fla., clinical associate professor, 1969-70, professor of surgery and pathology, 1970—. Guest scientist at Tissue Bank of Naval Medical Research Institute, 1964-70; member of staff at Veterans Administration Hospital, Miami, Fla., 1970—; consultant to U.S. Public Health Service. *Military service:* U.S. Public Health Service, surgeon, 1961-64.

MEMBER: American Association for the Advancement of Science, American Medical Association, American Association of Pathologists and Bacteriologists, American Society for Experimental Pathology, American Society of Tissue Banks, Pathologic Society of Great Britain and Ireland, Society for Cryobiology.

WRITINGS: Processing and Storage of Viable Human Tissues, National Cancer Institute, 1966; (editor) *Microcirculation, Perfusion, and Transplantation of Organs,* Academic Press, 1970; (editor) *The Reversibility of Cellular Injury,* C. C Thomas, 1972; (editor) *Acute Fluid Replacement in the Therapy of Shock,* Stratton Intercontinental Medical Book Corp., 1974; *Surgery and Life: The Extraordinary Career of Alexis Carrel,* Harcourt, 1979. Editor of *Cryobiology,* 1964-70.

WORK IN PROGRESS: A book dealing with cancer researchers.

SIDELIGHTS: Malinin told *CA:* "I have a very strong interest in tissue banking and transplantation, and I serve as director of the University of Miami Tissue Bank. My research endeavors include surgical research and tissue culture."

* * *

MALONE, Ruth 1918-

PERSONAL: Born October 4, 1918, in Philadelphia, Pa.; daughter of Robert Montgomery (in sales) and Marguerite Ruth (McGuigen) Edgar; married James Leland Malone (a college administrator and engineer), May 28, 1949; children: Molly, Kathy, James Leland, Jr. *Education:* Charles Morris Price School of Advertising and Journalism, A.A., 1940; Temple University, B.S., 1949. *Politics:* Democrat. *Religion:* Episcopalian. *Home:* 312 Harvard Ave., Swarthmore, Pa. 19081. *Office:* Cloisters, Swarthmore College, Swarthmore, Pa. 19081.

CAREER: Director of news office, Swarthmore College, Swarthmore, Pa.; writer. Volunteer worker for American Friends Service Committee, 1950-53. Member of steering committee of Philadelphia Children's Reading Round Table; member of board of directors of Swarthmore Co-Operative. *Member:* Newspaper Guild of America (vice-president, 1947-48), Word Guild (senior member), League of Women Voters of Swarthmore (member of board of directors). *Awards, honors:* William Leidt Award, 1966, for a magazine article on the "God-Is-Dead theologians."

WRITINGS: Here No Evil, Westminster, 1972; *Mystery of the Golden Ram* (juvenile), Westminster, 1976. Also author of *Death of a Hostile Psychiatrist,* 1959, and *Death of a Lighthearted Lady,* 1960.

Contributor of articles, stories, and poems to magazines, including *Saturday Review, Prairie Schooner, Writer's Digest, Mike Shayne Mystery,* and *Philadelphia.* Associate editor of *Episcopalian,* 1963-64.

WORK IN PROGRESS: Green of Spring, a novel; *The Trouble at Tree Farm; The Search for Mrs. Jefferson,* a biography of Martha Wayles Jefferson; a children's mystery novel based on Edgar Allan Poe in Philadelphia; short stories.

SIDELIGHTS: Ruth Malone wrote: "In directing a short story workshop for Philadelphia Writers Conference this year, I came to understand at last that the only way I understand the world around me is by writing about it; and the only important thing about the form I use is that it should fit the subject. The Greeks felt that writing was action; the Elizabethans, character. Today, writing seems focused on the writer—wrongly, I feel. To make a part of the world real to the reader would be the greatest accomplishment possible—especially in this world of nuclear accident and vanishing leadership."

* * *

MAN, John 1941-

PERSONAL: Born May 15, 1941, in Tenterden, England; son of John Henry Garnet (a farmer) and Peggy (a tennis coach; maiden name, Durnford) Man; married Angela Strange (an actress), January 27, 1967; children: Jonathan, Thomas, Emily. *Education:* Keble College, Oxford, B.A., diploma in history and philosophy of science. *Home:* 27 Polstead Rd., Oxford, England.

CAREER: Reuters, London, England, correspondent in London and in Bonn, West Germany, 1965-68; British Publishing Corp., London, editor, 1968-69; Time-Life Books, New York, N.Y., editor in London, 1969-72, European editor in London, 1972-74, senior editor in New York, 1974-75; director of John Man Books Ltd., London. *Member:* Anglo-Mongolian Society.

WRITINGS: Berlin Blockade, Ballantine, 1973; (with Henry Kyemba) *State of Blood,* Ace Books, 1977; *The Day of the Dinosaur,* Dutton, 1978; *Assault at Mogadishu,* Corgi, 1978; *Walk! It Could Change Your Life,* Paddington, 1979.

WORK IN PROGRESS: The Valium Connection, with publication by Paddington.

SIDELIGHTS: Man commented: "My particular interests are contemporary history, popular science and history, and Mongolia (I studied the language for a year)."

* * *

MANCUSO, Joe
See MANCUSO, Joseph R.

MANCUSO, Joseph R.   1941-
(Joe Mancuso)

PERSONAL: Born May 6, 1941, in Hartford, Conn.; son of Anthony J. (an engineer) and Helen (a teacher; maiden name, Silvester) Mancuso; married Judith Abair, April 20, 1963 (divorced, November, 1979); children: Karyn, Amy. *Education:* Worcester Polytechnic Institute, B.S.E.E., 1963; Harvard University, M.B.A., 1965; Boston University, Ed.D., 1975. *Politics:* Republican. *Religion:* Roman Catholic. *Office:* Center for Entrepreneurial Management, Inc., 311 Main St., Worcester, Mass. 01608.

CAREER: Applied Marketing, Inc., Wellesley, Mass., founder and president, 1965-71; Worcester Polytechnic Institute, Worcester, Mass., head of department of management, 1971-78, associate professor of management, 1974-78; Center for Entrepreneurial Management, Worcester, founder and director, 1978—. Adjunct professor at Clark University and Worcester Polytechnic Institute. Director of Worcester Corporation Council and more than one dozen small entrepreneurial ventures; member of board of directors of Laser, Briox Technology, Polyform, Vee-Arc, Rural Properties (Worcester), Worcester Surface Grinders, New Technology Precision Machining, and Moore Survey & Mapping. Member of White House Commission to Reduce Federal Paperwork and Massachusetts Task Force on Equity Capital Formation. Public speaker; guest on radio and television programs; business consultant. *Member:* International Council for Small Business Management Development, American Management Association, American Society for Engineering Education, Institute of Electrical and Electronics Engineers. *Awards, honors:* Small business award from Small Business Institute, 1976.

WRITINGS—Under name Joe Mancuso: *Fun and Guts: The Entrepreneur's Philosophy,* Addison-Wesley, 1973; *The Entrepreneur's Handbook,* two volumes, Horizon House, 1974; (with Cliff Baumback) *Entrepreneurship and Venture Management,* Prentice-Hall, 1974; *Marketing and Managing Technology Products,* two volumes, Horizon House, 1974; *No Guts, No Glory: How to Fight Dirty Against Management,* Ashley Books, 1976; *How to Start, Finance, and Manage Your Own Small Business,* Prentice-Hall, 1978; *Four Hundred Two Things You Must Know Before You Start a Business,* Prentice-Hall, 1980; *The Small Business Survival Guide,* Prentice-Hall, 1980; (with Alexandria Thatcher) *The Entrepreneurial Women,* Prentice-Hall, in press. Author of "Management Strategies," a column in *Electro-Mechanical Design.* Contributor to business and marketing journals and newspapers.

SIDELIGHTS: Mancuso told *CA:* "I have been called the entrepreneur's entrepreneur, and my life has been dedicated to serving the independent way of life in a small business. It's okay to be independent, but there is no reason to be alone. While the professional manager seeks to protect resources, the entrepreneurial manager creates them."

*   *   *

MANDEL, Sidney Albert   1923-

PERSONAL: Born March 14, 1923, in Chicago, Ill.; son of Arthur and E. Mollie Mandel; married Judith E. Lazowick, May 16, 1949; children: Debra Mandel Bertram, Daniel. *Education:* University of Illinois, B.S., 1945. *Politics:* Independent. *Religion:* Jewish. *Home:* 5252 Bell Wood Way, Carmichael, Calif. 95608.

CAREER: Public relations worker in Chicago, Ill., 1945-47;

worked in radio broadcasting in Chicago, 1947-49; KGST-Radio, Fresno, Calif., owner and manager, 1949-53; freelance writer in Los Angeles, Calif., 1961-68, and Sacramento, Calif., 1968—. Past president (and member of boards of trustees and directors) of Belmont Memorial Park. *Military service:* U.S. Army Air Forces, 1942-45; served in European theater; became first lieutenant.

WRITINGS: Gigante (novel), Avon, 1972. Author of about fifty teleplays for series, including "Dr. Kildare," 1963, "Please Don't Eat the Daisies," 1964, "Gilligan's Island," 1965, the "Andy Griffith Show," 1965, and the "Phyllis Diller Show," 1965. Contributor to magazines and newspapers.

WORK IN PROGRESS: A novel, publication expected in 1980.

SIDELIGHTS: Mandel writes: "I wrote both my novels as a weekend author."

*   *   *

MANDER, Gertrud   1927-

PERSONAL: Born November 5, 1927, in Stuttgart, Germany; daughter of Theodor (a civil servant) and Gertrud Bracher; married John Mander, December, 1956 (divorced, 1966); children: Mark. *Education:* Attended University of Tuebingen, 1949-51; Free University of Berlin, D.Phil., 1954. *Home:* 24 Chalcot Cres., London N.W.1, England.

CAREER: Rundfunk in Amerikanischen Sektor Berlins (radio network), West Berlin, Germany, script editor, 1954-58; free-lance writer, critic, translator, and reviewer, 1958—. *Member:* Foreign Press Association (London, England).

WRITINGS: Jean-Baptiste Moliere, Friedrich, 1967, translation by Diana Stone Peters published as *Moliere,* Ungar, 1973; (contributor) Ronald Hagman, editor, *The German Theatre,* Barnes & Noble, 1975.

Not in English: *George Bernard Shaw,* Friedrich, 1965; *Shakespeares Zeitgenossen: Von Marlowe bis Massinger* (title means "Shakespeare's Contemporaries: Marlow to Massinger"), Friedrich, 1966; *Jean Giraudoux,* Friedrich, 1969.

Translator from German, unless otherwise noted: George Lukaks, *The Meaning of Contemporary Realism,* Merlin Press, 1962; Erwin Leiser, *Nazi Cinema: Cinema Two,* Secker & Warburg, 1974; Lotte H. Eisner and Fritz Lang, editors, *David Robinson,* Secker & Warburg, 1976; Georg Groddeck, *The Meaning of Illness,* Hogarth Press, 1976; (into German) George Nikes, *Britain,* Reich Verlag, 1980.

Contributor to German periodicals, newspapers, and radio.

WORK IN PROGRESS: Translation into German of *Memoirs,* edited by Paula Heimann.

SIDELIGHTS: Gertrud Mander told *CA:* "My main interests are in the performing and fine arts, literature and criticism. I have recently become interested in psychoanalytical theory and practice, which has given my criticism a new angle. For twenty years I have been interested in explaining English culture and the London scene to German readers, though I also write in English, explaining German culture and literature to the English reader."

*   *   *

MANN, Peter (Clifford)   1948-

PERSONAL: Born November 17, 1948, in St. Louis, Mo.; son of Harvey H. (a country club manager) and Bridget (a teacher; maiden name, Adler) Mann; married Deborah

Rock, June 11, 1968 (died, 1971); married Carol Lehr, August 22, 1973; children: Abigail Elizabeth. *Education:* Washington University, St. Louis, Mo., A.B., 1970; University of Missouri, D.V.M., 1979. *Religion:* None. *Residence:* Silver Spring, Md. *Office:* National Zoological Park, Washington, D.C. 20008.

CAREER: Ralston-Purina Co., St. Louis, Mo., dog food scientist, 1974-75; National Zoological Park, Washington, D.C., resident in pathology, 1979—. Also worked as electrician, plumber, and musician. *Member:* American Veterinary Medical Association, American Association of Laboratory Animal Science.

WRITINGS: How to Buy a Used Car Without Getting Gypped, Harper, 1975. Contributor to veterinary medical journals.

WORK IN PROGRESS: Research on rodent mycoplasmosis.

SIDELIGHTS: Mann commented: "I have wandered off into veterinary medicine where I plan to spend the next several years. It is my goal to make scientific literature (starting with my own) more closely related to the English language."

*   *   *

MANNERS, Julia
See GREENAWAY, Gladys

*   *   *

MANVILLE, W(illiam) H(enry)   1930-
(Henry Williams)

PERSONAL: Born August 5, 1930, in New York, N.Y.; son of Philip M. (a contractor) and Betty Manville; married Nancy Friday (a writer), October 20, 1966. *Education:* University of the Mediterranean, Nice, France, B.A., 1953. *Residence:* New York, N.Y., and Key West, Fla. *Agent:* Lynn Nesbit, International Creative Management, 40 West 57th St., New York, N.Y. 10019.

CAREER: Writer, 1958—. Worked as copywriter for Grey Advertising, 1958-64; vice-president of J. M. Hickerson, Inc., 1964-65.

WRITINGS: Saloon Society: The Diary of a Year Beyond Aspirin (nonfiction), Duell, Sloane & Pearce, 1960; *Breaking Up* (autobiographical novel), Simon & Schuster, 1962; *The Palace of Money* (novel), Delacorte, 1966; (with James Wright) *Am I Too Heavy, Dear?* (cartoon), New American Library, 1970; *Goodbye* (novel; Book-of-the-Month Club alternate selection), Simon & Schuster, 1977. Author of movie novelizations under pseudonym Henry Williams, including *How to Murder Your Wife* (adapted from the screenplay by George Axelrod) and *A New Kind of Love* (adapted from the screenplay by Melville Shavelson). Author of column, "Saloon Society," in *Village Voice.* Contributor of articles to magazines, including *Saturday Evening Post* and *Cosmopolitan.*

WORK IN PROGRESS: Another novel, *Dark,* publication expected in 1980 or 1981.

CA INTERVIEWS THE AUTHOR

W. H. Manville was interviewed by *CA* July 12, 1979.

Manville (who writes as W. H. Manville) is an attractive, sophisticated man in his middle years who dresses with casual elegance and commutes between a penthouse apartment in New York and a house in Key West, Florida, where he

and his wife, Nancy Friday (*My Secret Garden, My Mother/Myself*), are part of the winter literary scene. Appropriately enough, *CA* met Manville at a small New York French restaurant for lunch to discuss his life and work.

W. H. Manville's writing career to date has been that of a man skilled from the start in the techniques of commercial writing, who has gradually grown in ambition—a prolonged attempt, in a sense, to show that serious work can be done in a highly accessible style.

"I like to think I work like my friend Alan Pakula, the movie director," he says. "He's not interested in only commercial success, or only artistic success. He believes, as I do, that something of value can be done which also has commercial appeal. Too many people think in such black-and-white terms—you either sell out, or you do noble work and starve. The suggestion that you might be able to avoid either extreme is not even mentioned."

Manville spent the early 1950's in Europe—he went to college there and spent a year and a half writing a novel—then came back to the United States and settled down to work. "I realized that first novel was awful, and didn't even try to get it published," he says. "I looked at it again recently, and it's still awful." He became an advertising copywriter at Grey Advertising, but found that insufficiently interesting to occupy his full attention. "One day I was sitting in my office and I realized there was a typewriter and paper, and I might as well do something with it."

So he wrote what he calls "a funny little anecdotal piece" about bar life in Greenwich Village called "Let's Start a Saloon Society." "Some friends had started the *Village Voice* a couple of years earlier, so I sent it over there. They said they'd publish it, but only if I did it as a regular column for six months." Manville obliged, doing a regular column called "Saloon Society," which recounted the doings and conversations of his drinking companions. "It floundered at first but eventually became quite popular, and some publishers asked to put a collection into book form." Duell, Sloan & Pearce brought the book out, he notes, just as they were going into bankruptcy; "it was rather as if the book was published by the C.I.A. in secrecy." Still, he says, it seems to have developed something of an underground following, and Jove is bringing it out in paperback shortly.

Having got into the habit of regular writing for the *Voice,* Manville now set to work on a second novel called *Breaking Up,* partly autobiographical, "perhaps not fully shaped as a novel," about the end of a marriage. A few years after it was published, he met Nancy Friday. "She urged me to give up my job, and we would run off to Europe together. I thought why not? I think each of us thought the other was rich." They lived in the south of France, where Manville wrote another novel called *The Palace of Money.* "It was an ambitious idea, but I'm not sure I was quite up to it at the time." The two were married in Rome early in 1966.

Manville was supporting himself now with regular professional writing assignments. He wrote some movie "novelizations"—he recalls *How to Murder Your Wife* and *A New Kind of Love*—which he wrote rapidly, under the pseudonym Henry Williams, for flat fees of around $3,000 apiece. He also did a paperback original for Dell with a title he still cherishes: *The Man Who Left His Wife and Had a Nifty Time,* although he doesn't object if it is left off the list of his published works.

In 1968 he became a contributing editor of *Cosmopolitan* magazine, and for the next five years wrote "about eight to twelve pieces a year" for them: "I think I wrote more than their next two most prolific writers combined." Sometimes he would write one of these pieces in a day. He would usually deliberately sober up to do so, because during these years he was drinking more and more. Eventually, after a couple of hospital stays, he entered Chit Chat Alcoholic Rehabilitation Center in Pennsylvania. That was in 1972, and he hasn't drunk a drop since.

The following year he began to write *Goodbye,* and Nancy began work on *My Mother/Myself.* From the start Manville had hoped and expected that *Goodbye* would be the book that would really make his mark as a writer. It drew on memories of his Greenwich Village drinking days, had some strong sex scenes, and an intriguing murder mystery. "I thought I finally knew how to balance real quality and a big commercial appeal." There was a lot of advance publicity about *Goodbye,* as it was a Book-of-the-Month Club alternate selection and made a big paperback sale ($400,000, to Ballantine); still, somehow "it wasn't the breakthrough I'd hoped for," says Manville. Meanwhile, Nancy Friday's *My Mother/Myself* had a remarkable best-selling success in hardcover and paperback, and Manville loyally supported her through the hectic public appearance schedule of a highly popular author.

Currently, he is working on a novel called *Dark.* Once again it is a thriller in outline about a mysterious millionaire living on an island off Key West and a bomb squad detective who becomes involved in investigating his past, and perhaps his own as well. It is, says Manville, "a re-telling of Oedipus, but in murder mystery form."

He feels that his writing has been steadily improving: "I was especially pleased with *Goodbye,* and I'm working very hard on *Dark.*" He rewrites a great deal on his books, but no longer does magazine work. His favorite authors, rather surprisingly, are Britain's Anthony Powell ("my favorite living novelist") and Evelyn Waugh.

These days he reads mostly contemporary thrillers ("I like to see how it's done") and popular science writers like Isaac Asimov and Carl Sagan. Manville believes that most American novelists write their best book first, and rarely thereafter live up to the early promise. "At least you can't say that of me."

BIOGRAPHICAL/CRITICAL SOURCES: New York Times Book Review, October 30, 1960, May 15, 1977; *New Yorker,* December 10, 1960; *Best Sellers,* April 15, 1966; *Book Week,* April 17, 1966; *Rolling Stone,* September 8, 1977; *Village Voice,* July 11, 1977; *Ms.,* March, 1978.

—*Interview by John F. Baker*

*   *   *

MARANGELL, Virginia J(ohnson) 1924-

PERSONAL: Born July 8, 1924, in New Haven, Conn.; daughter of Henry Enoch (a farmer) and Hope Ann (an entertainer; maiden name, Hokanson) Johnson; married Joseph Marangell (a government auditor), May 10, 1947; children: Joseph, Ronald (deceased), Randall. *Education:* Stone College, diploma, 1943; Newspaper Institute of America, certificates in journalism and fiction, 1944. *Religion:* Nondenominational Christian. *Home:* 165 Fairfield St., New Haven, Conn. 06505.

CAREER: Delaware, Lackawanna & Western Railroad, New Haven, Conn., stenographer, 1943-47; writer, 1968—.

WRITINGS: Gianna Mia (novel), Dodd, 1979. Contributor to adult and juvenile periodicals, including *Youth Alive, Christian, Young Teen Power, Encounter,* and *Sunday Digest.*

WORK IN PROGRESS: A novel about a young widow left, in the 1930's, with three children to support.

SIDELIGHTS: Virginia Marangell comments: "I have been writing since I was ten years old. During the years of raising three sons I completed four novels but had no success with them, although I did publish seventy short stories.

"*Gianna Mia* is about an Italian-American family living in New Haven in the 1930's and 1940's, a story inspired by my admiration for my Italian in-laws who struggled against great difficulties to educate their children. In this book I showed a way of life that seems to be passing from the American scene, that of the strong, supportive family circle where the material things are secondary to love.

"I have always written with the hope of helping people, which is why I wrote for religious and teenage publications for many years. I have a philosophy that I would like to pass on to others, the belief that no matter what bad things happen to you in life you can still find peace and joy and purpose. This came to me through my religious beliefs and through two particular circumstances: having to leave high school because of tuberculosis, and the shooting death of a twenty-one-year-old son who was about to graduate from college. I feel that my personal experiences have helped me to gain a deeper insight into other people's problems and to feel more compassion for their sorrow."

*   *   *

MARGADANT, Ted W(inston) 1941-

PERSONAL: Born February 22, 1941, in Los Angeles, Calif.; son of Edward (in business) and Clarys (a teacher; maiden name, Allison) Margadant; married Lenore Timm, 1967 (divorced, 1972); married Jo Burr Fredrickson, 1977; children: (stepchildren) Ashley Dunning, Thad Dunning. *Education:* Harvard University, B.A., 1962, Ph.D., 1972; Christ's College, Cambridge, A.B., 1964. *Politics:* Democrat. *Home:* 717 Bianco Court, Davis, Calif. 95616. *Office:* Department of History, University of California, Davis, Calif. 95616.

CAREER: University of California, Davis, assistant professor, 1969-75, associate professor of history, 1976—. *Member:* American Historical Association, French Historical Association, American Civil Liberties Union, National Audubon Society, Sierra Club, Common Cause.

WRITINGS: French Peasants in Revolt: The Insurrection of 1851, Princeton University Press, 1980.

WORK IN PROGRESS: Research on towns in conflict, and the administrative revolution of 1790 in France.

*   *   *

MARGER, Mary Ann 1934-

PERSONAL: Surname is pronounced *Mar*-jer; born October 27, 1934, in New York, N.Y.; daughter of Herman (an electrical engineer and columnist) and Theresa (a secretary; maiden name, Teiser) Baum; married Bruce Marger (an attorney), February 5, 1956; children: William Gary, David Scott, Susan Teiser. *Education:* University of North Carolina, Greensboro, A.B., 1956. *Home:* 1901 80th St. N., St. Petersburg, Fla. 33710.

CAREER: Elementary school teacher at Patrick Air Force Base, Fla., 1956-57, in Malden, Mass., 1957-59, and in St. Petersburg, Fla., 1967-70; *St. Petersburg Times,* St. Petersburg, correspondent and reporter, 1976—. Member of board of directors of local arts council, 1972-75, 1976-79. *Member:* St. Petersburg Chamber of Commerce.

WRITINGS—Novels for young adults: *Winner at the Dub-Dub Club,* American Elsevier, 1979; *Justice at Peachtree,* American Elsevier, 1980. Author of "Two Schools of Thought," a column in *St. Petersburg Evening Independent, Fort Myers News Press,* and *Palm Beach Post,* 1975-79. Contributor to magazines and newspapers, including *Good Housekeeping, Instructor,* and *Teacher.*

WORK IN PROGRESS: Another novel.

SIDELIGHTS: Mary Ann Marger writes: "My first book was written as a challenge, to see if I could produce a book-length manuscript. My second book concerns South Carolina in 1950 and 1951. It reflects my own impressions there as a transplanted Yankee teenager."

* * *

MARGOLIS, Michael (Stephen) 1940-

PERSONAL: Born March 27, 1940, in Chicago, Ill.; son of Ralph V. (a physical education teacher) and Annette (an elementary education teacher; maiden name, Krassner) Margolis; married Ellen Freedman (a pregnancy counselor), December, 1964; children: Karen, Jennifer, Abby, Matthew, Nicola. *Education:* Oberlin College, B.A., 1961; University of Michigan, M.A., 1962, Ph.D., 1968. *Home:* 5546 Forbes Ave., Pittsburgh, Pa. 15217. *Office:* Department of Political Science, University of Pittsburgh, 4N22 Forbes Quadrangle, Pittsburgh, Pa. 15260.

CAREER: University of Strathclyde, Glasgow, Scotland, visiting lecturer in politics, 1965-67; University of Pittsburgh, Pittsburgh, Pa., instructor, 1967-68, assistant professor, 1968-73, associate professor of political science, 1973—. Visiting lecturer at University of Glasgow, 1973-74; guest lecturer at Indiana University of Pennsylvania, summers, 1975, 1977; guest on local television and radio programs. Official representative of Inter-University Consortium for Political Research, 1967-73, 1974-76; consultant to Policy Innovations, Inc., and to WTAG-TV news. *Member:* American Political Science Association.

WRITINGS: (With Ian Budge, J. A. Brand, and A.L.M. Smith) *Political Stratification and Democracy,* Macmillan, 1972; (author of instructor's manual) Dennis J. Palumbo, *American Government,* Appleton, 1972; (contributor) Jeff Fishel, editor, *Parties and Elections in an Anti-Party Age,* Indiana University Press, 1978; *Viable Democracy,* St. Martin's, 1979. Contributor of about twenty articles and reviews to scholarly journals, popular magazines, and newspapers. Member of editorial advisory board of *Historical Methods Newsletter,* 1972-78.

WORK IN PROGRESS: "Local Party Organization: From Disaggregation to Disintegration," with Lee S. Weinberg and David F. Ranck; "Pressure Politics Revisited: The Anti-Abortion Campaign," with Kevin Neary; "Applied Tolerance or Fear of Government?: An Alternative Interpretation of Jackman's Findings," with Khondaker E. Haque; "Toward an Ultimate Model of Rational Party Choice," a satiric critique of formal models; *Issues and Election Campaigns,* a study of changes in issue positions held by American voters over several presidential election campaigns.

SIDELIGHTS: Margolis commented: "I believe that social scientists have a responsibility to convey their ideas to the general public as well as to their professional colleagues. For me the challenge is to communicate complex ideas about social problems in an interesting and intelligible manner to the general reader without sacrificing the scholarly integrity of the research upon which those ideas are based."

MARGOLIUS, Sidney 1911-1980

OBITUARY NOTICE—See index for *CA* sketch: Born May 3, 1911, in Perth Amboy, N.J.; died of a heart attack, January 30, 1980, in Roslyn, N.Y. Journalist, free-lance writer, and author of *The Consumer's Guide to Better Buying.* As the consumer editor of the New York City newspaper *PM,* Margolius pioneered consumer affairs reporting at a time when stories critical of American business practices were considered bold and even radical. Before joining *PM* in 1940, he worked for the United Press, *Market Observer,* and *Retailing.* His column was syndicated by the North American Newspaper Alliance and the Women's News Service and appeared in numerous newspapers, including the *Boston Globe* and the *Washington Star.* He was the author of twenty books about consumer and financial issues, including *Your Guide to Financial Security, The Innocent Consumer vs. the Exploiters,* and *The Great American Food Hoax.* Obituaries and other sources: *Who's Who in the East,* 14th edition, Marquis, 1973; *New York Times,* February 1, 1980; *Time,* February 11, 1980.

* * *

MARIMOW, William K. 1947-

PERSONAL: Born August 4, 1947, in Philadelphia, Pa.; son of Jack (a retail store owner) and Helen (Gitnig) Marimow; married Diane Macomb (a potter and art teacher), October 18, 1969; children: Ann Esther. *Education:* Trinity College, Hartford, Conn., B.A., 1969. *Home:* 321 South 44th St., Philadelphia, Pa. 19104. *Office: Philadelphia Inquirer,* 400 North Broad St., Philadelphia, Pa. 19101.

CAREER/WRITINGS: Chilton Book Co., Bala Cynwyd, Pa., assistant editor, 1969-70; *Philadelphia Bulletin,* Philadelphia, Pa., assistant to economics columnist, 1970-72; *Philadelphia Inquirer,* Philadelphia, staff writer, 1972—. Lecturer at University of Pennsylvania, 1979—. *Member:* Pen and Pencil Club. *Awards, honors:* Award for deadline reporting from Pennsylvania Associated Press Managing Editors, 1977, public service award, 1978; first place award for team reporting from Philadelphia Press Association, 1977; Pulitzer Prize for distinguished public service, 1978; national public service award from Sigma Delta Chi, 1978; public service award from Scripps-Howard Foundation, 1978; Robert F. Kennedy Journalism Award, 1978; silver gavel from American Bar Association, 1978.

WORK IN PROGRESS: A book examining the frailty of the American criminal justice system.

* * *

MARK, Jan 1943-

PERSONAL: Born June 22, 1943, in Welwyn, England; daughter of Colin Denis and Marjorie Brisland; married Neil Mark (a computer operator), March 1, 1969; children: Isobel, Alexander. *Education:* Canterbury College of Art, N.D.D., 1965. *Politics:* Labour. *Religion:* None. *Home:* 10 Sydney St., Ingham, Norfolk NR12 9TQ, England. *Agent:* Murray Pollinger, 4 Garrick St., London WC2E 9BH, England.

CAREER: Southfields School, Gravesend, England, teacher of art and English, 1965-71; full-time writer, 1975—. *Awards, honors:* Penguin/*Guardian* Award, 1975, and Carnegie Medal from The Library Association, 1976, both for *Thunder and Lightnings.*

WRITINGS: Thunder and Lightnings (for children), Kestrel, 1976, Crowell, 1979; *Under the Autumn Garden* (for children), Kestral, 1977, Crowell, 1979; *The Ennead*, Crowell, 1978; *Divide and Rule*, Kestrel, 1979, Crowell, 1980; *The Short Voyage of the Albert Ross* (for children), Granada, 1980; *Nothing to Be Afraid Of* (stories for children), Kestrel, 1980. Contributor of stories and articles to magazines.

SIDELIGHTS: Jan Mark comments: "I believe reading and writing is the nearest most of us will ever come to telepathy. If I write stories about children they are normally read by children—I do not otherwise aim at any particular audience. I write about people, the ways in which they use each other and allow themselves to be used. I am not interested in victims, only in the men and women who are authors of their own downfalls. There can be no external intervention. The forces of evil currently fashionable are not supernatural, but human ignorance and complacency.

"My prime motive in becoming a professional writer was the need to earn a living. Although writing gives me more pleasure than does anything else, I do not write for pleasure: I write for money. I am singularly fortunate in getting both, but I fear that if I did not have to choose between writing and starving I should have begun self-indulgent and made no subsequent progress. I started well by winning a competition for new fiction but this has imposed on me the challenge to produce always something at least as good as the first book. I dare not fall below that standard.

"I did not begin writing seriously until I was in my thirties and am in retrospect glad of it, since I had by then developed a voice of my own, an intelligible one, moreover. One writer I know of, who was published very young, describes herself as having 'learned to write in public.' I was spared that, but only through lack of self-confidence.

"When writing about children I like to present readers with a situation they may recognize and supplement with their own experience. In novels for older readers I prefer to place a character in an unfamiliar environment and watch him struggle (or in one case disintegrate) in the best traditions of tragedy, through his own shortcomings. They tend to be studies in failure. *The Ennead* dealt with the results of total self-absorption; *Divide and Rule* with the liberal conscience under attack from extremists and unable to defend itself. Exploitation is always rife."

BIOGRAPHICAL/CRITICAL SOURCES: Guardian, July 17, 1975; *Times Educational Supplement*, November 24, 1978; *Washington Post*, December 12, 1978.

*   *   *

MARK, Michael L(aurence)   1936-

PERSONAL: Born December 1, 1936, in Schenectady, N.Y.; son of David (a tool maker) and Ruth (a bookkeeper; maiden name, Garbowit) Mark; married Lois Nitekman (a real estate agent), October 21, 1962; children: Michelle, Diana. *Education:* Catholic University of America, B.Mus., 1958, D.M.A., 1969; George Washington University, M.A., 1960; University of Michigan, M.Mus., 1962. *Home:* 23 Franklin Ave., Silver Spring, Md. 20901. *Office:* School of Music, Catholic University of America, Washington, D.C. 20064.

CAREER: Music teacher at public schools in Prince George's County, Md., 1958-66; Morgan State University, Baltimore, Md., assistant professor, 1966-69, associate professor of music, 1970; music supervisor at public schools in Auburn, N.Y., 1970-72; director of music at public schools in Elmira, N.Y., 1972-73; Catholic University of America, Washington, D.C., associate professor of music, 1973—.

President of Cayuga County Arts Council, 1972. *Member:* Music Educators National Conference, Council for Research in Music Education, Council for Basic Education, American Association of University Professors, Council of Higher Education for Maryland and the District of Columbia (president, 1975-77), Maryland Music Educators Association, District of Columbia Music Educators Association.

WRITINGS: Contemporary Music Education, Schirmer Books, 1978. Contributor to music and music education journals.

WORK IN PROGRESS: Research on history and philosophy of music education, with a book expected to result.

SIDELIGHTS: Mark told *CA:* To be most effective, professional people must know enough of the history of their profession to understand how and why current practices developed, and the causative factors of current professional problems. The purpose of *Contemporary Music Education* is to provide a recent history of the profession of music education so that music education students and in-service music teachers will better understand the current status of their profession."

*   *   *

MARKHAM, James M(orris)   1943-

PERSONAL: Born March 7, 1943, in Washington, D.C.; son of James M. and Mary Paul (Rix) Markham; married Stephanie Reed, June 25, 1966; children: Katharine, Samuel. *Education:* Princeton University, B.A., 1965; graduate study at Balliol College, Oxford, 1965-67. *Agent:* Susan Ann Protter, 156 East 52nd St., New York, N.Y. 10022. *Office address:* c/o Foreign Desk, *New York Times*, 229 West 43rd St., New York, N.Y. 10036.

CAREER/WRITINGS: Time magazine, New York City, stringer in New Delhi, India, summer, 1966; Associated Press, New York City, reporter in New Delhi, 1968-69, West Africa correspondent based in Lagos, Nigeria, 1970-71; *New York Times*, New York City, reporter, 1971-73, Saigon bureau chief, 1973-75, Beirut bureau chief, 1973-75, Madrid bureau chief, 1976—. Most notable assignments include coverage of wars in Indochina and the Lebanese civil war. *Member:* Phi Beta Kappa. *Awards, honors:* Woodrow Wilson fellow, 1965; Rhodes Scholar, 1965-67.

*   *   *

MARLOW, Edwina
See HUFF, T(om) E.

*   *   *

MARSHALL, Donald R.   1934-

PERSONAL: Born November 25, 1934, in Panguitch, Utah; son of Wilford Earl (a pharmacist) and Eva (Daly) Marshall; married Jean Stockseth, August 14, 1964; children: Robin (daughter), Jordan (daughter), Reagan (son). *Education:* Brigham Young University, B.A., 1960, M.A., 1964; University of Connecticut, Ph.D., 1970. *Religion:* Church of Jesus Christ of Latter-day Saints (Mormons). *Home:* 2765 Oneida Lane, Provo, Utah 84601. *Office:* Department of Humanities, Brigham Young University, A-262 JKBA, Provo, Utah 84602.

CAREER: University of Hawaii, Honolulu, instructor in English, 1964-66; Brigham Young University, Provo, Utah, assistant professor, 1971-76, associate professor of humanities and film, 1976—, director of international cinema program, 1975—. Painter, free-lance photographer, and musical composer. *Military service:* U.S. Army, 1960-62. *Member:* Western Writers of America. *Awards, honors:* Best short story award from *Dialogue*, 1973, for "The Weekend"; Spur Award from Western Writers of America, 1977, for "Fugues and Improvisations on a Theme"; two regional Emmy Awards from Public Broadcasting Service (PBS), 1979, for "Christmas Snows, Christmas Winds."

WRITINGS: The Rummage Sale (stories), Peregrine Smith, 1972; *Frost in the Orchard* (stories), Brigham Young University Press, 1977.

Author and composer of "The Rummage Sale" (two-act musical play), first produced in Salt Lake City, Utah, at Shire West Theatre, July, 1979. Also author of unproduced play, "In the Dark Backward Abysm of Time," 1979.

Author of "Christmas Snows, Christmas Winds," a film, first broadcast by PBS-TV, December, 1978. Contributor to magazines.

WORK IN PROGRESS: A novel and a children's book, publication of both expected in 1981.

SIDELIGHTS: Marshall comments: "I am interested in writing, as was Hawthorne, about the truth of the human heart. I write not to entertain (though many have found my stories 'delightful' and 'immensely entertaining') but to move, to stir, to change lives. I want readers to come away from my works knowing that they have had an *experience*—that their perception of the world will never be quite the same because of the insight they are beginning to get into human nature."

AVOCATIONAL INTERESTS: Travel (Tahiti, Spain, France).

*   *   *

MARSHNER, Connaught Coyne 1951-
(C. P. Sarsfield)

PERSONAL: Born June 26, 1951, in St. Louis, Mo.; daughter of William Dougherty and Vinette Coyne; married William H. Marshner (a professor of theology); children: Pearse Raphael Dennis, Michael William Dougherty. *Education:* Attended College of Notre Dame of Maryland, 1967-69; University of South Carolina, B.A., 1971. *Religion:* Melchite Catholic. *Office:* Free Congress Foundation, 4 Library Court S.E., Washington, D.C. 20003.

CAREER: Office of Economic Opportunity, Washington, D.C., confidential assistant, 1973; Heritage Foundation, Washington, D.C., education director, 1973-75; Free Congress Foundation, Washington, D.C., director of Family Policy Division and editor of *Family Protection Report*, 1978—. Field coordinator for Committee for Survival of a Free Congress, 1976-78. Member of board of directors of Young Americans for Freedom, 1973-75, and Committee for Responsible Youth Politics, 1975—.

WRITINGS: Federal Child Development: What's Developing? (monograph), Heritage Foundation, 1974; *Blackboard Tyranny*, Arlington House, 1978. Contributor to magazines, sometimes under pseudonym C. P. Sarsfield.

WORK IN PROGRESS: Research on family policy issues, coalition politics, the emergence of Christian activists into the political process, and "New Right" politics.

SIDELIGHTS: Connaught Marshner writes: "The issue of parents' rights in education first came to my attention when I was working on Capitol Hill in 1971. I observed the difference that concerned parents could make in the outcome of political questions. After the 1973 Supreme Court abortion

decision, as the women's liberation movement became prominent, it became obvious that the moral majority of middle-class and lower-middle-class parents felt threatened by what they perceived as anti-Christian, anti-traditionalist trends in government actions and cultural shifts. These people are alienated; they need a spokesman to express their family-related values and to help them connect with the political process. I intend to perform that function to the extent that I can."

*   *   *

MARTIN, Augustine 1935-

PERSONAL: Born November 14, 1935, in Leitrim, Ireland; son of Patrick and Mary Kate Martin; married Claire Kennedy (a radiographer); children: Brefni (son), Grainne (daughter), Niamh (daughter), Aengus (son). *Education:* Attended Cistercian College, Roscrea, Ireland, and National University of Ireland, University College, Dublin. *Religion:* Roman Catholic. *Home:* 5 Cambridge Ter., Dublin 6, Ireland. *Office:* Department of English, Room J-203, University College, National University of Ireland, Belfield, Dublin 4, Ireland.

CAREER: National University of Ireland, University College, Dublin, lecturer, 1965-79, professor of Anglo-Irish literature and drama, 1979—. Senator of Ireland, 1973-80. Director of Yeats International, Sligo, Ireland. Irish member of European advisory committee of Salzburg Seminar of American Studies.

WRITINGS: (Editor with James J. Carey) Veronica O'Brien, *Exploring English*, Gill & Macmillan, 1968; *Soundings*, Gill & Macmillan, 1969; *Introducing Literature*, Gill & Macmillan, 1970; (editor) *Introducing English*, Gill & Macmillan, 1970; (editor) *Winter's Tales From Ireland*, Gill & Macmillan, 1971; (editor and author of introduction) James Stephens, *The Charwoman's Daughter*, Gill & Macmillan, 1972; *James Stephens: A Critical Study*, Gill & Macmillan, 1977; *Anglo-Irish Literature Surveyed*, Irish Department of Foreign Affairs, 1980. Contributor of articles and reviews to magazines, including *Chicago Review*, *Ariel*, and *Anglo-Irish Studies*, and newspapers.

WORK IN PROGRESS: Alchemy and Priestcraft and a History of the Irish Short Story, on Yeats and Joyce.

*   *   *

MARTIN, Charles B(asil) 1930-

PERSONAL: Born August 9, 1930, in Pittsburg, Kan.; son of William R. and Vera (Fletcher) Martin; married Darlyn Dossey (a kindergarten teacher), August 25, 1961; children: Bradley Stephen, Gregory Scott, Randall Clark. *Education:* University of New Mexico, B.A., 1952; University of Florida, M.A., 1954; University of Missouri, Ph.D., 1959. *Home:* 1510 Kendolph, Denton, Tex. 76201. *Office:* Department of English, North Texas State University, Denton, Tex. 76203.

CAREER: University of Missouri, Columbia, instructor in English, 1954-59; East Central State College, Ada, Okla., associate professor of English, 1959-64; North Texas State University, Denton, professor of English, 1964—. Fulbright professor at University of Seville, 1967-68. *Member:* Modern Language Association of America, National Council of Teachers of English, Teachers of English to Speakers of Other Languages, American Name Society, Texas Folklore Society.

WRITINGS: (With Curt M. Rulon) *The English Language: Yesterday and Today*, Allyn & Bacon, 1973. Contributor of articles and reviews to scholarly journals.

MARTIN, Esmond Bradley 1941-

PERSONAL: Born April 17, 1941, in New York, N.Y.; son of Esmond Bradley, Sr. (an orchid grower) and Edwina (Atwell) Martin; married Chryssee MacCasler Perry (a writer), October 22, 1966. *Education:* University of Arizona, B.S., 1964, M.A., 1966; University of Liverpool, Ph.D., 1970. *Home address:* P.O. Box 15510, Mbagathi, Nairobi, Kenya. *Office:* Department of Geography, University of Nairobi, P.O. Box 30197, Nairobi, Kenya.

CAREER: University of Nairobi, Nairobi, Kenya, research associate in geography, 1967—. Research associate at University of Dar es Salaam, 1974-75; researcher for Zanzibar Department of Education, 1975-76; consultant to International Union for the Conservation of Nature, Survival Service Commission, and Elephant Group. *Member:* Explorers Club, Association of American Geographers, American Geographic Society, African Studies Association, Royal Geographical Society, Royal African Society, Institute of British Geographers, East African Natural History Society, Geographical Society of Kenya (vice-chairperson), Kenya Museum Society (head of publications committee), Geological Club, Historical Association of Kenya, Karen and Langata Association.

WRITINGS: Malindi Past and Present, National Museums of Kenya, 1970; *The History of Malindi: A Geographical Analysis of an East African Coastal Town From the Portuguese Period to the Present,* East African Literature Bureau, 1973; (with wife, Chryssee MacCasler Perry Martin) *Quest for the Past: An Historical Guide to the Lamu Archipelago,* Marketing & Publishing, 1973; (with C. M. P. Martin) *Cargoes of the East: The Ports, Trade, and Culture of the Arabian Seas and Western Indian Ocean,* Hamish Hamilton, 1978; *Zanzibar: Tradition and Revolution,* Hamish Hamilton, 1978. Contributor to *Kenya Historical Review.*

WORK IN PROGRESS: Writing on conservation issues in Africa.

SIDELIGHTS: Martin told *CA:* "I have lived in Kenya for the past fourteen years, and my interests in Africa range from the geography of the east coast to the history of the slave trade from Somalia, Kenya, and Tanzania in the eighteenth and nineteenth centuries (on which I have had published an article in the *Kenya Historical Review*). For my book *Cargoes of the East,* I spent several months in 1978 in Oman and India studying the dhow trade. Because of the tremendous pressures on wildlife in Africa today, my most recent work has been concerned with the trade and use of wild animal products, in particular rhino horn and ivory."

*   *   *

MARTIN, Stella
See HEYER, Georgette

*   *   *

MARTINEZ RUIZ, Jose 1873-1969
(Azorin)

PERSONAL: Born June 8, 1873, in Monovar, Alicante, Spain; died March 2, 1969, in Madrid, Spain; son of Isidro Martinez (a lawyer) and Luisa Ruiz; married Julia Guinda Urzanqui, 1908. *Education:* Attended University of Valencia and University of Granada. *Residence:* Madrid, Spain.

CAREER: El Pais, Madrid, Spain, staff member, beginning in 1896; American Broadcasting Co. (ABC), Paris, France, correspondent, 1917; *La Nacion,* Buenos Aires, Argentina, columnist, 1930-69; writer. Deputy of public instruction, 1907 and 1914; undersecretary of public instruction, 1917 and 1919. *Awards, honors:* Elected to the Spanish Academy, May 28, 1924.

WRITINGS—All under pseudonym Azorin; in English: *Un hora de Espana (entre 1560 y 1590),* Raggio, 1924, translation by Alice Raleigh published as *An Hour of Spain Between 1560 and 1590,* Routledge & Kegan Paul, 1930; *Don Juan,* translated by Catherine Alison Phillips, Chapman & Dodd, 1927; *Old Spain,* Century, 1928; *The Syrens and Other Stories,* translated by Warre B. Wells, Scholartis, 1931, reprinted as *The Sirens and Other Stories,* Richard West, 1978.

Other works: *Buscapies,* F. Fe, 1893; *Moratin esboza por Candido* (title means "Moratin's Outline by Candide"), F. Fe, 1893; *Literatura* (title means "Literature"), F. Fe, 1896; *La intrusa: Drama en un acto y en prosa* (title means "The Intruder: A Play in One Act and in Prose"), F. Vives Moro, 1896; *Bohemia,* [Madrid], 1897; *La sociologia criminal* (title means "The Criminal Sociology"), F. Fe, 1899; *La evolucion de la critica* (title means "The Evolution of Criticism"), F. Fe, 1899.

Los hidalgos (title means "The Noblemen"), F. Fe, 1900; *El alma castellano* (title means "The Castilian Soul"), [Madrid], 1900; *Diario de un enfermo* (title means "Diary of a Patient"), F. Fe, 1901; *La fuerza del amor: Tragicomedia* (title means "The Force of Love: A Tragicomedy"), [Madrid], 1901; *Antonio Azorin: Pequeno libro en que se habla de la vida de este peregrino senor* (title means "Antonio Azorin: A Little Book in Which the Life of This Wandering Man Is Told"), Renacimiento, 1913; *Los valores literarios* (title means "The Literary Values"), Renacimiento, 1913; *La voluntad* (title means "The Will"), Renacimiento, 1913; *Los pueblos: Ensayos sobre la vida provinciana* (title means "The Villages: Essays About the Provincial Life"), Renacimiento, 1914; *La ruta de Don Quijote* (title means "The Route of Don Quixote"), Renacimiento, 1915; *Al margen de los clasicos* (title means "To the Margin of the Classics"), Clasica espanola, 1915; *Lecturas de Azorin* (title means "Lectures of Azorin"), Grenas, 1915; *Parlamentarismo espanol* (title means "Spanish Parliamentarism"), Calleja, 1916; *Entre Espana y Francia: Paginas de un francofilo,* (title means "Between Spain and France: Pages of a Francophile"), Bloud y Gay, 1917; *Paginas escogidas* (title means "Selected Pages"), Calleja, 1917.

Castilla (title means "Castle"), Raggio, 1920; *Un pueblecito, Riofrio de Avila* (title means "A Little Village, Riofrio of Avila"), Raggio, 1921; *Paris, bombardeado, y Madrid sentimental, mayo y junio 1918* (title means "Paris, Bombarded, and Sentimental Madrid, May and June, 1918"), Raggio, 1921; *El licenciado vidriera* (title means "The Licensed Glassblower"), Raggio, Oxford, 1939; *Los dos Luises, y otros ensayos* (title means "The Two Louises, and Other Essays"), Raggio, 1921; *Un discurso de la cierva* (title means "A Discourse About the Doe"), Raggio, 1921; *Rivas y Larra: Razon social del romanticismo en Espana* (title means "Rivas and Larra: The Firm Name of Romanticism in Spain"), Raggio, 1921; *De Granada a Castelar* (title means "From Granada to Castile"), Raggio, 1922; *Las confesiones de un pequeno filosofo* (title means "The Confessions of a Little Philosopher"), Heath, 1923; *El chirrion de los politicos: Fantasia moral* (title means "The Squeak of the Politicians: A Moral Fantasy"), Raggio, 1923; *Racine y Moliere,* [Madrid], 1924; *Discursos leidos ante la real academia espanola en la recepcion de don Joaquin Quintero el dia 19 de abril de 1925* (title means "Discourses Read Before the Royal Spanish Academy at the Reception for Mr. Joaquin Quintero, April 19, 1925"), Clasica Espanola, 1925; *Los quinteros, y otros paginas* (title means "The Draftees, and Other Pages"), Raggio, 1925; *Dona Ines*, Raggio, 1926, text edition edited by Livingstone, Irvington, 1969; *Brandy, mucho brandy: Sainete sentimental en tres actos* (title means "Brandy, Much Brandy: A Sentimental Farce in Three Acts"), Raggio, 1927; *Felix Vargas*, Biblioteca Nueva, 1928; (with Munoz Seca) *El Clamor: Farsa en tres actos* (title means "The Clamor: A Farce in Three Acts"), Artes graficos, 1928; *Lo invisible* (title means "The Invisible One"), Prensa Moderna, 1928; *Comedia del arte: En tres actos*, Prensa Moderna, 1928; *Doctor Fregoli; o, La comedia de la felicidad; Comedia en tres actos* (title means "Doctor Fregoli; or, the Comedy of Happiness; A Comedy in Three Acts"), Prensa Moderna, 1928; *Leyendo a los poetas* (title means "Reading to the Poets"), Libreria General, 1929; *Palabras al viento* (title means "Words to the Wind"), Libreria General, 1929; *Blanca en azul* (title means "White on Blue"), Biblioteca Nueva, 1929; *Andando y pensando: Notas de un transeunte* (title means "Walking and Thinking: Notes of a Transient"), Editorial Paez, 1929; *Superrealismo, prenovela* (title means "Surrealism, prenovel"), Biblioteca Nueva, 1929.

Pueblo: Novela de los que trabajan y sufren (title means "Village: A Novel of Those Who Work and Suffer"), Biblioteca Nueva, 1930; *Angelita: Auto sacramental* (title means "Angelita: A One-Act Religious Play"), Biblioteca Nueva, 1930; *Nuevas obras* (title means "New Works"), Biblioteca Nueva, 1930; *Lope en silueta*, Arbol, 1935; *La guerilla: Comedia en tres actos* (title means "The Skirmish: A Comedy in Three Acts"), Rivadeneyra, 1936; *Lecturas espanolas* (title means "Spanish Lectures"), Espasa-Calpe (Buenos Aires), 1938; *Trasuntos de Espana*, Espasa-Calpe, 1938; *Clasicos y modernos* (title means "Classics and Moderns"), Losada (Buenos Aires), 1939; *En torno a Jose Hernandez* (title means "Around to Jose Hernandez"), Editorial sudamericana (Buenos Aires), 1939; *Espanoles in Paris* (title means "Spaniards in Paris"), Espasa-Calpe, 1939.

Pensando en Espana (title means "Thinking in Spain"), Biblioteca Nueva, 1940; *Madrid*, Biblioteca Nueva, 1941; *El paisaje de Espana visto por los espanoles* (title means "The Landscape of Spain Seen by the Spanish"), Espasa-Calpe, 1941; *Vision de Espana* (title means "Vision of Spain"), Espasa-Calpe, 1941; *Tomas Rueda*, Espasa-Calpe, 1941; *Valencia*, Biblioteca Nueva, 1941; *Sintiendo a Espana*, Tartessos, 1942; *El escritor* (title means "The Writer"), Espasa-Calpe, 1942; *Cavilar y contar*, Destino, 1942; *Capricho* (title means "Caprice"), Espasa-Calpe, 1943; *El enfermo* (title means "The Patient"), Adan, 1943; *Veraneo sentimental* (title means "Sentimental Summer Vacation"), Libreria General (Zaragoza, Mexico), 1944; *Salvadora de Olbena*, Cronos (Zaragoza), 1944; *Maria Fontan*, Espasa-Calpe, 1944; *Paris*, Biblioteca Nueva, 1945; *La farandula*, Libreria General, 1945; *Los clasicos redivivos, los clasicos futuros*, Espasa-Calpe, 1945; *El artista y el estilo* (title means "The Artist and Style"), Aguilar, 1946; *Memorias inmemoriales* (title means "Immemorial Memories"), B.N., 1946; *El politico: Con un epilogo futurista* (title means "The Politician: With a Futuristic Epilogue"), Espasa-Calpe, 1946; *Prosas selectas* (title means "Selected Prose"), Secretoria de Educacion Publica (Mexico), 1946; *Ante Baroja* (title means "Before Baroja"), Libreria General, 1946; *Ante las candilejas* (title means "Before the Oil Lamp"), Libreria General, 1947; *Con Cervantes* (title means "With Cervantes"), Espasa-Calpe, 1947; *Escena y sala* (title means "Scene and Parlor"), Libreria General, 1947; *Obras completas* (title means "Complete Works"), Aguilar, 1947; *Con permiso de*

los cervantistas (title means "With the Permission of the Cervanteites"), Biblioteca Nueva, 1948.

La cabeza de castilla (title means "The Head of the Castle"), Espasa-Calpe, 1950; *Con bandera de Francia* (title means "With the Flag of France"), Biblioteca Nueva, 1950; *El oasis de los clasicos* (title means "The Oasis of the Classics"), Biblioteca Nueva, 1952; *El libro de Levante* (title means "The Book of Levante"), Losada, 1952; *Dos comedias: Comedia del arte* [and] *Old Spain* (title means "Two Comedies . . ."), Houghton, 1952; *Verano en Mallorca* (title means "Summer in Majorca"), Palma, 1952; *El cine y el momento* (title means "The Movies and the Moment"), Biblioteca Nueva, 1953; *Pintar como querer* (title means "Painting as Loving"), Biblioteca Nueva, 1954; *El buen Sancho* (title means "The Good Sancho"), [Madrid], 1954; *El pasado* (title means "The Past"), Biblioteca Nueva, 1955; *El efimero cine* (title means "The Ephemeral Film"), Aguado, 1955; *Cuentos de Azorin* (title means "Stories of Azorin"), Aguada, 1956; *Escritores* (title means "Writers"), Biblioteca Nueva, 1956; *Dicho y hecho* (title means "No Sooner Said Than Done"), Destino, 1957; *De un transeunte* (title means "Concerning a Transient"), Aguado, 1958; *Sin perder losestribos* (title means "Without Losing One's Balance"), Taurus, 1958; *La isla sin aurora* (title means "The Island Without Dawn"), Destino, 1958; *Agenda*, Biblioteca Nueva, 1959; *De Valera a Miro* (title means "From Valera to Miro"), Aguado, 1959; *Espana* (title means "Spain"), Espasa-Calpe, 1959; *Pasos quedos* (title means "Quiet Passages"), Escelicer, 1959; *Posdata* (title means "Postscript"), Biblioteca Nueva, 1959.

Ejercicios de castellano (title means "Exercises of a Castilian"), Biblioteca Nueva, 1960; *Mis mejores paginas* (title means "My Best Pages"), Mateu, 1961; *La Generacion del 98* (title means "The Generation of '98"), Anayas (Salamania, Mexico), 1961; *Lo que paso una vez* (title means "That Which Happens Once"), Lumen, 1962; *Varios hombres y alguna mujer* (title means "Various Men and Any Woman"), Aidos, 1962; *Historia y vida* (title means "History and Life"), Espasa-Calpe, 1962; *En lontananza* (title means "In the Background"), Bullon, 1963; *Los recuadros*, Biblioteca Nueva, 1963; *El caballero inactual* (title means "The Nonpresent Cowboy"), Espasa-Calpe, 1965; *Ni si, ni no* (title means "Neither Yes, Nor No"), Destino, 1965; *Los medicos* (title means "The Doctors"), Prometco, 1966; *Ultramarinos* (title means "Those From Overseas"), Editora y Distribudora Hispano Americana, 1966; *Espana clara* (title means "Clear Spain"), Doncel, 1966; *La amada Espana* (title means "The Loved Spain"), Destino, 1967; *Azorin y los libros* (title means "Azorin and the Books"), Instituto Nacional del Libro Espanol, 1967; *Critica de anos cercanos* (title means "Criticism of Neighboring Years"), Taurus, 1967; *Politica y literatura: Fantasias y devaneos* (title means "Politics and Literature: Fantasies and Frenzies"), Alianza, 1968; *Tiempo y paisaje: Vision de Espana* (title means "Time and Landscape: Vision of Spain"), Ediciones Cultura Hispanica, 1968.

Albacite, siempre (title means "Albacite, Always"), Ayuntamiento de Albacite, 1970; *Tiempos y cosas* (title means "Times and Things"), Salvat, 1970; *Reflejos de Espana* (title means "Reflections on Spain"), Moreno (Buenos Aires), 1971; *Rosalia de Castro y otros motivos gallegos* (title means "Rosalia de Castro and Other Gallician Motifs"), Celta, 1973; *Cada cosa en su sitio* (title means "Everything in Its Place"), Destino, 1973; *La Andalucia tragedia* (title means "The Tragic Lady of Andalusia"), Castalia, 1974; *Obras completas* (title means "Complete Works"), Aguilar, 1975.

SIDELIGHTS: Early in his career Jose Martinez Ruiz played with pseudonyms such as "Ahriman" and "Candido." But when he adopted the name "Azorin" for the protagonist of his autobiographical trilogy, the character gradually became an alter ego of the author, providing not only his literary identity, but his personal identification as well. As Azorin, he wrote in such diverse genres as essays, plays, novels, and short stories, and came to be considered one of Spain's greatest twentieth-century writers.

Azorin was a stylistic revolutionary, using the Spanish language in new and striking ways. According to Charles K. Colhoun, he "replaced the sonorous and rolling periods of his predecessors with short, clear-cut luminous sentences." Ida Farnell noted how his use of Arabic terms and revival of fine old words "has enlarged the vocabulary and given a new harmony to modern Spanish." In a review of *Hour of Spain,* the *Christian Science Monitor* maintained that, in their "magic clarity," his essays give the impression "that each word has been distilled."

Azorin's principal themes are "time and space, repetition in time, *paisaje, ensueno,* and love as a force which solves the most difficult problems." He presented these themes by means of an impressionistic treatment of details, interpreting objective reality through his sensibility. For this he is sometimes described as a miniaturist with "a gift of compressing the history of a lifetime within a couple of pages."

In 1947 Madrid sponsored a public meeting in Martinez Ruiz's honor, accompanied by a ten-day exposition of his works by the city's book dealers.

BIOGRAPHICAL/CRITICAL SOURCES: Ida Farnell, *Spanish Poetry and Prose,* [Oxford, England], 1920; *New York Times,* January 27, 1924; *Nation,* March 19, 1924; Aubrey Fitz Gerald Bell, *Contemporary Spanish Literature,* Knopf, 1928: *Christian Science Monitor,* January 17, 1931; *Bookman,* September, 1931; Anna Krause, *Azorin: The Little Philosopher,* University of California, 1948; *Books Abroad,* spring, 1953; Lawrence Anthony LaJohn, *Azorin and the Spanish Stage,* Hispanic Institute, 1958; *PMLA,* April, 1958, Volume 79, 1964; Edward Inman Fox, *Azorin as a Literary Critic,* Hispanic Institute, 1960; *Times Literary Supplement,* June 23, 1966; Ernest Boyd, *Studies from Ten Literatures,* Kennikat, 1968; *Contemporary Literary Criticism,* Volume 2, Gale, 1979.

OBITUARIES: New York Times, March 3, 1967; *Antiquarian Bookman,* March 27, 1967; *Books Abroad,* spring, 1968.*

*   *   *

MARTINSON, Floyd M(ansfield) 1916-

PERSONAL: Born November 12, 1916, in Montevideo, Minn.; son of John Elmer (a farmer) and Mathilda (Bang) Martinson; married Beatrice Awes (a clerk), June, 1946; children: John, Anne, Stephen, Peter, Sarah. *Education:* Concordia College, Moorhead, Minn., B.A., 1942; University of Minnesota, M.A., 1947, Ph.D., 1953; postdoctoral study at Tulane University, 1957-58, and University of Uppsala, 1968-69. *Religion:* Lutheran. *Office:* Department of Sociology and Anthropology, Gustavus Adolphus College, St. Peter, Minn. 56082.

CAREER: High school teacher of social science, biology, business law, and history in Belle Plaine, Minn., 1943; Gustavus Adolphus College, St. Peter, Minn., assistant professor, 1945-51, associate professor, 1951-56, professor of sociology, 1956—, head of department, 1945-70, 1976-77.

Visiting professor at University of Uppsala, 1968-69, guest lecturer, 1973, 1978; guest lecturer at University of Oslo, spring, 1969, 1975-76, and University of Lund, spring, 1969; visiting scientist at National Institute of Mental Health's Center for Studies in Child and Family Mental Health, spring, 1973. Organized and presented national and international workshops and seminars; directed study tour of England, Norway, Sweden, and Denmark.

MEMBER: International Sociological Association, American Sociological Association (fellow), National Council on Family Relations (member of board of directors, 1965-68), Association for Humanistic Sociology, Society for the Scientific Study of Sex, Sex Information and Education Council of the United States (associate), Midwest Sociological Society, Minnesota Council on Family Relations.

WRITINGS: Marriage and the American Ideal, Dodd, 1960; *Sexual Knowledge, Values, and Behavior Patterns: With Especial Reference to Minnesota Youth,* Gustavus Adolphus College, 1966.

The Family in Society, Dodd, 1970; *Infant and Child Sexuality: A Sociological Perspective,* Book Mark, 1973; *The Quality of Adolescent Sexual Experiences,* Book Mark, 1974; (contributor) Evelyn Oremland and Jerome Oremland, editors, *Sexual and Gender Development of Young Children,* Ballinger, 1977. Contributor to *Handbook of Human Sexuality.* Contributor to sociology journals. Member of editorial board of *Family Coordinator,* 1972-77, and *Journal of Sex Research,* 1978—.

WORK IN PROGRESS: Research on the social psychology of childhood, infant and child sexuality, family sexuality, in Norway and Sweden as well as the United States.

SIDELIGHTS: Martinson told *CA:* "I started out as a rural sociologist and my Ph.D. thesis and subsequent early writings were in that area. It was my experience teaching sociology in a liberal arts college along with the attention given by professionals and the press to one of my first articles in a professional journal—an article on high school dating and early marriage—that had most to do with turning my attention from rural sociology to the sociology of dating, mate selection, marriage, and the family. This interest resulted in several books. The first was *Marriage and the American Ideal* (1960) in which I analyzed marriage as an institution of permanence within a society that emphasizes personal freedom. In another book, *Family in Society* (1970), I was motivated by an interest in bringing a balance to sociological writing on the American family. It was my impression that too much attention was being paid to what occurred in the bedroom and in the bathroom, in other words inside the family, to the neglect of the place of the family in the structures and functioning of the society.

"One semester while teaching a course on the sociology of marriage and family, I invited students to write term papers on their experiences as an alternative to writing the traditional paper based on library research. I was unprepared for the large number who chose this option, the intimate experiences they described and analyzed, and the large number who wrote on childhood sexual experiences. It was the latter that sent me to the library on an extensive and intensive search for sources of information on sexuality in the young. This literature search and subsequent research in the United States and in Sweden led me to write several articles, two book-length monographs—*Infant and Child Sexuality* (1973) and *The Quality of Adolescent Sexual Experiences* (1974)—as well as a forthcoming book, co-edited with Larry Constantine, tentatively entitled *Children and Sex: New Findings, New Perspectives.*

"I spent the 1975-76 academic year on a peace research leave of absence in Oslo, Norway, at the University and at the International Peace Research Institute. A paper based on some of the work I did that year will appear under the title "The Family, The Child, and Social Change" in a forthcoming book edited by Jan Trost, *The Family in Change.*

"I have determined that my work on infant and child sexuality has been carried on in too great isolation from the family which is the context of most childhood experiences. For this reason, the topic of my research while on leave of absence at Sweden's Uppsala University in 1980-81 will be on family interaction with special attention given to intimacy and affection within the family."

*   *   *

MASLOWSKI, Raymond M(arion) 1931-

PERSONAL: Born August 19, 1931, in Mount Ephraim, N.J.; son of Casper (an accountant) and Cecilia (Wilinski) Maslowski; married Ann Marie McManus (a nurse), June 10, 1967; children: Ann Marie, Raymond Marion. *Education:* Alliance College, B.A. (cum laude), 1954; Edinboro State College, teaching certificate, 1954; Villanova University, M.A. (with honors), 1963; Catholic University of America, Ph.D. (with honors), 1968; postdoctoral study at Temple University, 1968-69. *Religion:* Roman Catholic. *Home:* 404 Echo Place, Woodcrest, Cherry Hill, N.J. 08003. *Office:* Northwest Center for Community Mental Health/Mental Retardation Programs, 27 East Mount Airy Ave., Philadelphia, Pa. 19119; and Rittenhouse Medical Center, 1900 Spruce St., Philadelphia, Pa. 19103.

CAREER: Teacher of accounting and social studies, counselor, and athletic coach at Roman Catholic high school in Camden, N.J., 1956-61; Radio Corp. of America (RCA), Electronic Data Processing Division, Cherry Hill, N.J., systems analyst, 1961-65; Catholic University of America, Washington, D.C., instructor in counseling psychology and guidance services, 1965-68; Veterans Administration Hospital, Mental Hygiene Clinic, Wilmington, Del., intern and staff psychologist, 1968-70; Villanova University, Villanova, Pa., assistant professor, 1970-74, associate professor of counseling and guidance, 1974-75; Northwest Center for Community Mental Health/Mental Retardation Programs, Philadelphia, Pa., principal psychologist, 1975—. Psychologist at Wilmington College, 1968-72, and Rosemont College, 1970-72; psychologist in vocational rehabilitation for public schools of Wilmington, 1969-70. Adjunct associate professor at Wilmington College, 1968-72; public speaker. *Military service:* U.S. Army, Military Police, 1954-56; served in Germany.

MEMBER: American Psychological Association, American Personnel and Guidance Association, Eastern Psychological Association, Pennsylvania Psychological Association, Pennsylvania Personnel and Guidance Association, Delaware Psychological Association, New Jersey Psychological Association, Philadelphia Society of Clinical Psychologists.

WRITINGS: Analysis and Appraisal in Counseling, Simon & Schuster, 1971; *Psychology and Life: Selected Readings,* Simon & Schuster, 1971; (editor) *Educational and Psychological Appraisal in Counseling,* Simon & Schuster, 1972; (editor with Lewis B. Morgan) *Interpersonal Growth and Self Actualization in Groups,* MSS Information, 1973. Contributor to academic journals and newspapers.

WORK IN PROGRESS: A rationale for cognitive therapy.

SIDELIGHTS: Maslowski told *CA:* "I am a firm believer in a healthy set of values, including truth, honesty, integrity, and patriotism." *Avocational interests:* Gardening, fishing, boating.

*   *   *

MASNATA, Albert 1900-

PERSONAL: Born March 16, 1900, in Odessa, Russia; son of Paul (a banker) and Isabella Masnata; married Irene Krafft (an educator), July 18, 1925; children: Marianne Masnata Dolivo, Francois, Elisabeth. *Education:* Attended Petrograd State University (now Leningrad A.A. Zhdanov State University), 1917-18, and University of Lausanne, 1918-23. *Religion:* Presbyterian. *Home and office:* 29 Av. de Senaleche, Pully-Lausanne, Switzerland.

CAREER: Swiss Industrial Bureau, Lausanne, Switzerland, general secretary, 1924-27; Swiss Office for Development of Trade, Lausanne, director in Lausanne and Zurich, 1928-66; University of Lausanne, 1936-70, began as lector, became associate professor; honorary professor at University of Lausanne and Lausanne People's University; visiting professor at Montpelier University, University of Brussels, Ohio Wesleyan University, Northwestern University, Stanford University, and Harvard University. Deputy to Great Council of Canton Vaud (state Parliament); president of Swiss Federal Economic Commission, 1935-70. Member of International Chamber of Commerce; member of council of international commercial center of General Agreement on Tariffs and Trades (GATT) and United Nations Conference on Trade and Development; member of United Nations Organization and Swiss development missions to Panama and Madagascar. *Military service:* Swiss Army, translator for general staff; became lieutenant.

MEMBER: International Development Society, Association Internationale d'economistes de langue francaise, Societe Suisse d'economie politique et de statistique. *Awards, honors:* Officer of French Legion d'Honneur; grants from Swiss National Scientific Research Fund.

WRITINGS: Le Destin des echanges ouest-est: Problemes et solutions, Editions de la Baconniere, 1972, translation by John Cuthbert-Brown published as *East-West Economic Cooperation: Problems and Solutions,* Lexington Books, 1974; *Collective Planning Versus Free-Market Economy,* Lexington Books, 1975.

In French: *Emigration des industries suisses,* [Lausanne], 1924; *Nationalites et federalisme,* Payot, 1933; *Les Echanges internationaux au vingtieme siecle: Introduction a la connaissance des structures, institutions et problemes generaux,* Editions Generales, 1961; *Le Systeme socialiste-sovietique: Essai d'une generale de son economie,* Editions de la Baconniere, 1965; *Planification collectiviste et economie de marche confrontees: Une Economie concurrentielle socialment ordonee?,* Editions de la Baconniere, 1976; *Le Monde marxiste: Son Empire par lui meme,* University of Lausanne, 1979. Contributor to European political science journals.

WORK IN PROGRESS: Research on the Soviet socialist system.

*   *   *

MATHEWS, Anthony Stuart 1930-

PERSONAL: Born August 22, 1930, in Pretoria, South Africa; son of Lorenzo (a lawyer) and Enid Mabel Mathews; married Pamela Joan Steward (a secretary), May 15, 1954; children: Catherine, Richard Anthony, Elizabeth, Stephen

John. *Education:* University of Natal, B.A., 1956, LL.B. (cum laude), 1959, Ph.D., 1969. *Office:* Department of Private Law, University of Natal, Durban, South Africa.

CAREER: Attorney in Transvaal, South Africa, 1953-55; University of Natal, Durban, South Africa, member of faculty, 1959, senior lecturer in law, 1960-64, professor of private law, 1965—, head of department, 1965—, dean of faculty of law, 1966-67, 1971-74, 1979-80. Head of Natal region of South African Institute of Race Relations; chairman of Political Commission of Spro-cas. *Member:* Society of University Teachers of Law (member of council). *Awards, honors:* Visiting scholar at Harvard University, 1968-69; Butterworth overseas legal fellow, 1971; visiting fellow of Clare Hall, Cambridge, 1975-76.

WRITINGS: Law, Order, and Liberty in South Africa, University of California Press, 1972; (contributor) J. Midgley, J. H. Steyn, and R. Grazer, editors, *Crime and Punishment in South Africa,* McGraw, 1975; *The Darker Reaches of Government,* University of California Press, 1978. Contributor of about twenty articles to law journals.

WORK IN PROGRESS: A chapter on public safety for *The Law of South Africa* publication by Butterworth expected in 1982.

SIDELIGHTS: Mathews told *CA:* "My first book, *Law, Order, and Liberty in South Africa* begins with a full analysis of the concept of the rule of law. It is an in-depth study of South Africa's internal security legislation with comparative references to the laws of the United States. *The Darker Reaches of Government,* my second book, is an examination of the problem of secrecy in democracies and the relation between secrecy and power. The bulk of the work consists of a detailed analysis of secrecy and information laws in America, Britain, and South Africa. The book concludes with a chapter on possible reforms in each of the three societies."

*   *   *

MATTHEWS, Victor Monroe 1921-

PERSONAL: Born February 6, 1921, in Montesano, Wash.; son of Victor M., Sr. (a farmer) and Ethyl (Taylor) Matthews; married Bonnie L. Reeme (a secretary), September 9, 1941; children: Victor M. III, Susan L. Matthews Marshall. *Education:* Attended Simpson Bible Institute, 1939-42; Calvin College, A.B., 1953; Grand Rapids Baptist Seminary, B.D., 1949; Calvin Seminary, Grand Rapids, Mich., Th.M., 1956; Lutheran Theological Seminary, Chicago, Ill., S.T.D., 1965. *Home:* 2859 Bird Ave. N.E., Grand Rapids, Mich. 49505. *Office:* Grand Rapids Baptist College and Seminary, 1001 East Beltline, Grand Rapids, Mich. 49505.

CAREER: Ordained Baptist minister, 1949; pastor of Baptist churches in Grand Rapids, Mich., 1946-50, and Greenville, Mich., 1950-51; Grand Rapids Baptist College and Seminary, Grand Rapids, Mich., associate professor of Bible and philosophy, 1951-65, professor of systematic theology and apologetics, 1965—. *Member:* Evangelical Theological Society.

WRITINGS: Confessions to a Counselor, Zondervan, 1969; *Growth in Grace,* Zondervan, 1970; *Neo-Evangelicalism,* Regular Baptist Press, 1971; *Biblical Inspiration, Textual Inerrancy, Theological Integrity,* Grand Rapids Baptist College and Seminary, 1979. Contributor to *Tyndale Family Bible Encyclopedia.*

WORK IN PROGRESS: Books on the Christian life and counseling; *Understanding Ourselves,* three volumes.

MATTSON, Lloyd 1923-

PERSONAL: Born August 29, 1923, in Duluth, Minn.; son of David J. (a police officer) and Beatrice L. Mattson; married Elsie E. Heaton (a nurse), November 19, 1942; children: Sally Mattson Rogers, Keith, Joel, David, Kevin. *Education:* Bethel Theological Seminary, St. Paul, Minn., Th.B., 1947; John Wesley College, B.A., 1979. *Politics:* "Generally Republican though wavering." *Home and office:* 5118 Glendale St., Duluth, Minn. 55804.

CAREER: Ordained Baptist minister; pastor of Baptist congregations in Wisconsin, Michigan, and Alaska, 1947-62; Baptist General Conference, Evanston, Ill., executive, 1962-72; free-lance writer, photographer, and camp counselor in Minnesota, 1972-77; North Shore Baptist Church, Duluth, Minn., pastor, 1977—. Producer of filmstrips. *Member:* Outdoor Writers Association of America, Association of Great Lakes Outdoor Writers.

WRITINGS: Camping Guideposts, Moody, 1964, revised edition, 1972; *Wilderness Way,* Baptist Men's Board, 1971, revised edition, Accent Books, 1979; *Family Camping,* Moody, 1973; *Devotions for Men: Good Morning, Lord,* Baker Book, 1979; (co-editor) *Introduction to Christian Camping,* Moody, 1979; *Things to Do With Families,* Victor, 1980. Author of religious booklets. Author of a column in *Trails-a-Way.* Contributor to religious and camping journals. Editor of *Journal of Christian Camping,* 1970-73.

SIDELIGHTS: Mattson wrote: "I have found a blending of outdoor interests with professional religious leadership a satisfying, effective career, and have traveled in my work to every state, as well as Canada, Mexico, and Europe. I have special interests in the North Country, with frequent trips to Alaska to work with remote camps for native Americans. Camping plays an important role in my parish work as minister of a small congregation on Lake Superior."

*   *   *

MATUS, Greta 1938-

PERSONAL: Born November 13, 1938, in New York, N.Y.; daughter of Irving L. (an architect) and Helen (Silverman) Levett; married Stanley Matus (an account executive); children: Adam, Jason. *Education:* Attended Cooper Union, New York, N.Y., 1956-59; California School of Fine Arts, 1959-62. *Home:* 3608 Noble Ave., Richmond, Va. 23222. *Office:* Richmond Newspapers, 333 E. Grace St., Richmond, Va. 23219.

CAREER: New York Public Schools, New York, N.Y., teacher of art, 1963-65, teacher of painting and sculpture, 1967-73; free-lance illustrator, 1973—; Richmond Newspapers, Richmond, Va., research copywriter, 1975—.

WRITINGS: (Self-illustrated) *Where Are You, Jason?,* Lothrop, 1974; (illustrator) Genevieve Gray, *Ghost Story,* Lothrop, 1975.

*   *   *

MAXWELL, Gilbert 1910-1979

OBITUARY NOTICE—See index for *CA* sketch: Born February 13, 1910, in Washington, Ga.; died November 29, 1979, in South Miami, Fla. Poet and novelist best known for three volumes of poetry, *Look to the Lightning, Stranger's Garment,* and *The Dark Rain Falling.* He also wrote a novel, *The Sleeping Trees,* and a biography of playwright Tennessee Williams called *Tennessee Williams and Friends.* Obituaries and other sources: *New York Times,* December 4, 1979.

MAXWELL, William (Keepers, Jr.) 1908-

PERSONAL: Born August 16, 1908, in Lincoln, Ill.; son of William Keepers (an insurance executive) and Eva Blossom (Blinn) Maxwell; married Emily Gilman Noyes, May 17, 1945; children: Katharine Farrington, Emily Brooke. *Education:* University of Illinois, B.A., 1930; Harvard University, M.A., 1931. *Home:* 544 East 86th St., New York, N.Y. 10028.

CAREER: University of Illinois, Urbana, member of English faculty, 1931-33; *New Yorker,* New York, N.Y., member of editorial staff, 1936-76. Novelist and short story writer. *Member:* National Institute of Arts and Letters (president, 1969-72). *Awards, honors:* Friends of American Writers Award, 1938; grant from National Institute of Arts and Letters, 1958.

*WRITINGS—*All novels, except as noted: *Bright Center of Heaven,* Harper & Bros., 1934; *They Came Like Swallows,* Harper & Bros., 1937, revised edition, Vintage Books, 1960; *The Folded Leaf,* Harper, 1945; *The Heavenly Tenants* (fantasy for children), Harper, 1946; *Time Will Darken It,* Harper, 1948; *Stories,* Farrar, Straus, 1956; *The Chateau,* Knopf, 1961; *The Old Man at the Railroad Crossing and Other Tales* (stories), Knopf, 1966; *Ancestors* (nonfiction), Knopf, 1971; *Over by the River, and Other Stories* (stories), Knopf, 1977; *So Long, See You Tomorrow,* Knopf, 1980. Contributor of stories and book reviews to the *New Yorker.*

SIDELIGHTS: Although he is perhaps best known for his work on the *New Yorker,* William Maxwell is the author of eleven books, including a family history which traces his ancestry back to such American pioneers as Henry Maxwell and Charles Blinn. Both his novels and stories alike have drawn praise from critics, and he has, on occasion, been compared to Sinclair Lewis, Henry Fuller, and Sherwood Anderson. With a "gentle wit" and a true appreciation of rural America, Maxwell paints a picture of small-town life in the Midwest, untouched by the worldliness and loneliness of the big city. Maxwell once said that he doesn't consider his books to be nostalgic "in the strict sense." "I write about the past," he stated, "not because I think it is better than the present but because of things that happened that I do not want to be forgotten."

Out of his six novels, *The Folded Leaf* has been singled out by a number of critics as a good example of his "genuine artistry." A sensitive portrayal of the friendship between two adolescent boys of different temperament, the novel is, according to Diana Trilling, an "important social document." Edmund Wilson wrote that Maxwell "approaches such matters as fraternity initiations and gratuitous schoolboy fights, the traditional customs of childhood, from an anthropological point of view . . . : with careful, unobtrusive art, [he] has made us feel all the coldness and hardness and darkness of Chicago, the prosaic surface of existence which seems to stretch about one like asphalt or ice. But there are moments when the author breaks away into a kind of poetic reverie that shows he is able to find a way out." Colby Walworth emphasized the difficulty of the theme, and praised Maxwell's "affectionate insight into the frailities of immaturity" in the characterizations of Lymie Peters and Spud Latham. Richard Sullivan concluded: "[The novel] does precisely, beautifully and completely what it sets out to do. . . . It is a satisfaction to read prose always so admirably controlled, so governed with distinction."

They Came Like Swallows, an account of the effects of a Spanish influenza epidemic on a close-knit family, has also drawn praise from critics. David Tilden called it an "unpre-tentious book, simple and straightforward and natural, unspoiled by sentimentality." Fanny Butcher concurred, "The children are as real as any children in literature. There is neither oversentimentalizing nor that sometimes too obvious . . . lack of sentiment in these simple and memorable pages." V. S. Pritchett mentioned the "lack of unity" in the novel, but noted that "otherwise the book is a sensitive, wistful reminiscence of family life."

Maxwell turned to a different theme in *The Chateau:* the American experience in Europe. According to Richard Gilman, he exercised "a trained, cool-tempered sensibility" in portraying the predicament of an American couple in postwar France. David Boraff called the work "a beguilingly old-fashioned novel, almost Jamesian in its restraint and in its delineation of subtle shifts in consciousness." For Naomi Bliven, "*The Chateau* . . . is a large-scale work whose smallest details are beautifully made. The author has labored for the reader's case. His style is a joy—exact, moderate, from time to time amused or amusing, always compassionate, sometimes as startling as lightning. . . . This novel is fiction with the authenticity of a verified document, a history of what some citizens of the splintered Western World might say or mean to each other in our period." Elizabeth Bowen declared, "I can think of few novels, of my day certainly, that have such romantic authority as *The Chateau,* fewer still so adult in vitality, so alight with humor."

In her review of *Over by the River, and Other Stories,* Joyce Carol Oates praised "Maxwell's gifts as a writer" which "allow him to impose upon his material a gentle, rather Chekhovian sense of order: whatever happens is not Fate but the inevitable working-out of character, never melodramatic, never pointedly 'symbolic.'" This collection of stories includes work written from as early as 1941 to 1977. Oates pointed out a few stories that she especially liked, and spoke of Maxwell's "vision." "He is not unaware of what might be called evil," she commented, "and he is willing to explore the possibility that, yes, civilization is in decline."

So Long, See You Tomorrow is his latest work and, according to Robert Wilson, "a summing up by Maxwell at the age of 71 of many of the most powerful experiences and concerns from his past work." In this novel, Maxwell recalls the death of his mother in the 1918 flu epidemic, and the family's subsequent move to Chicago. He also describes the tragedy which struck another Lincoln household: tenant farmer Clarence Smith finds out about his wife's love affair, kills her lover, and then commits suicide. Years later in Chicago, Maxwell comes face to face with Cletus Smith, Clarence's son, and the meeting stirs up painful memories for both boys.

A *New York Post* critic noted that the book "is filled with the sense of desolation and bewilderment which adults inflict upon their young, wounds like those of war, never fully healing, aching with each twinge of recollection. There is compressed into this small work the scope of Greek tragedy, a sense of time and place and the accumulated perception of a thoughtful and moving writer. William Maxwell makes one believe that the best traditions of American fiction continue to survive." White agreed, "His accomplishment is to present a fascinating tragedy enacted by sincere, gentle, reluctant participants—and to give his account the same integrity that marks their deeds." Likewise, Wilson praised Maxwell for "a marvelously evocative prose style, which suggests in its grace and simplicity a gentle wind brushing autumn leaves across the yards of those stately old house that seemingly exist outside time compared to the lives of the families who pass through them."

William Maxwell was interviewed by phone at his home in New York City on April 13, 1979.

CA: How did you become a part of the New Yorker *staff in 1936?*

MAXWELL: I had had one book published, and my publisher gave me three letters—one to the *New Republic,* one to *Time,* and one to the *New Yorker.* I was unsuited for the *New Republic* because I was politically uninformed. I don't know if I was unsuited to *Time* as well; I got to the *New Yorker* before I got to *Time,* and they hired me, and that was that. There was a vacancy in the art department, and I found myself sitting in at the weekly art meeting, and on the following day I would tell the artists whether or not their work had been bought, and any changes in their drawings that the meeting wanted. Technically, I guess I was an assistant to Rea Irvin, the art director, who lived in the country and only came to town for the art meeting, but the *New Yorker* has no masthead, and I never asked what I was.

CA: You have primarily been fiction editor for the New Yorker?

MAXWELL: I was *a* fiction editor—one of, usually, six or seven; I was never the head of the fiction department. I retired from the *New Yorker* three years ago, after roughly forty years. Most of the time, I worked only two or three days a week so that I would have the rest of the week for writing.

CA: As a fiction editor, you must have had to deal with a great many manuscripts from unknown or unpublished writers. How did you manage it?

MAXWELL: The usual way: I would read them quickly for signs of talent. When there were such signs I would put the manuscript aside and read it again later, carefully. One of the best of all the *New Yorker*'s fiction writers turned up for the first time in that pile, but she was discovered by Mildred Wood, not by me.

CA: Brendan Gill has said there has never been a conscious New Yorker *style. Do you agree?*

MAXWELL: I do, definitely. *New Yorker* editors tend to cut out unnecessary words and to punctuate according to the house rules, and most often the prose advances sentence by sentence in its effects, rather than by paragraphs in which any given sentence may not carry that much weight. The result is a certain density that may appear to be a "style." But when you consider the fiction writers who have appeared frequently in the magazine, for example, John Updike, John Cheever, John O'Hara, Vladimir Nabokov, Mary McCarthy, Mavis Gallant, Sylvia Townsend Warner, Shirley Hazzard, Eudora Welty, J. D. Salinger, Frank O'Connor, Maeve Brennan, and Larry Woiwode—it is immediately apparent that there is no style common to all of them.

CA: Gill has also commented on the amount of work you did behind the scenes to turn out good finished stories from manuscripts. Was there a lot to be done?

MAXWELL: Some manuscripts arrive in a virtually perfect state; others require a certain amount of cutting and clarifying—in short, editing.

CA: What writers have you been instrumental in developing?

MAXWELL: I'd rather not answer that question. I'm not sure I know, anyway. If a writer continues to grow in stature, it is because he has put everything he has into his work, and not because an outsider has been steering him in the right direction. Most writers could do with a little appreciation, though. An editor can offer that.

CA: How was your association with O'Hara?

MAXWELL: Agreeable. He was a fine writer, and my dealings with him were always very pleasant.

CA: What about Cheever?

MAXWELL: What about him? He's a marvel, isn't he?

CA: Behind the scenes, has the magazine undergone many changes?

MAXWELL: American fiction has undergone so many changes, and these have been reflected in the magazine as changes in length, in subject matter, in technique, in language. Essentially, with fiction at least, a magazine has no choice but to go the way its most talented contributors are going. Anything else would probably be highly destructive.

CA: Were you writing in your undergraduate days at the University of Illinois?

MAXWELL: I was writing poetry.

CA: What influenced you to become a writer?

MAXWELL: Well, I suppose I always had my nose in a book, from an early age. I also met certain people—the Wisconsin novelist and playwright Zona Gale, and the poet Robert Fitzgerald, who was a Harvard undergraduate when I went there for an M.A.—who set fires blazing in my mind. I was lucky in my teachers. Lucky generally.

CA: Do you still write poetry?

MAXWELL: No, I gave up poetry. I realized I wasn't a poet. All the true poets I have ever known agreed that it is given to them in that it comes from a source outside themselves. Prose is, on the contrary, something you work at until it achieves the effects you want it to achieve.

CA: You've written many stories—"fables"—in fairy-tale form.

MAXWELL: I've also published a volume of stories that are not in this form, but the ones you are referring to are half fable, half fairy tale.

CA: Does your fondness for this genre go back to childhood reading?

MAXWELL: It probably does.

CA: In the New York Review of Books, *the person reviewing* The Old Man at the Railroad Crossing (1966), *discusses the combination of this form with your concern for contemporary issues and calls the result "something midway between the Brothers Grimm and Kafka, with perhaps a touch of Zen." Do you like this description?*

MAXWELL: Well, at least it places me in good company.

CA: Much of your writing—the novels especially—shows a great pride in your Midwestern heritage, unlike the satire in some of the earlier Midwestern writers. Would you comment on that?

MAXWELL: I grew up in the Midwest; I think and speak as a Midwesterner. I've lived in New York City most of my adult life, and I like it here, but I still think of myself as a Midwesterner.

CA: Are the experiences of living in New York City heightened by contact with your Midwestern background?

MAXWELL: No. I'm afraid I've tried to create a small-town life in the middle of a great city.

CA: Do you see any trends in fiction today?

MAXWELL: I don't think about it. I just enjoy reading.

CA: Unlike the New Yorker, *many good magazines haven't been able to stay in business. What do you attribute this to?*

MAXWELL: Postal rates have gone up tremendously over the years. The very thing the government should subsidize is instead being penalized out of existence. It's lamentable.

CA: What do you think is in the future for magazines?

MAXWELL: Oh, I'm no good at predicting the future. Some people can do it, unusually thoughtful people, perhaps, but I'm not one of them.

BIOGRAPHICAL/CRITICAL SOURCES: Chicago Daily Tribune, May 1, 1937; *Books,* May 2, 1937; *Christian Science Monitor,* May 26, 1937, December 17, 1946, September 9, 1948; *Times Literary Supplement,* August 21, 1937; *New Statesman and Nation,* August 28, 1937; *New Yorker,* March 31, 1945, September 4, 1948, March 25, 1961; *New York Times,* April 8, 1945, September 5, 1948; *Weekly Book Review,* April 8, 1945; *Nation,* April 21, 1945; *Saturday Review of Literature,* November 9, 1946, September 4, 1948; *Time,* September 20, 1948; *New York Times Book Review,* March 26, 1961, March 13, 1966, August 8, 1971; *Reporter,* May 25, 1961; *Commonweal,* December 10, 1971; *New Republic,* September 10, 1977; *Publishers Weekly,* December 10, 1979; *Chicago Tribune Book World,* December 12, 1979; *New York Post,* January 12, 1980; *Washington Post Book World,* January 13, 1980.

—Sketch by Nancy M. Rusin
—Interview by Jean W. Ross

* * *

MAYER, Marianna 1945-

PERSONAL: Born November 8, 1945; married Mercer Mayer (an author and illustrator). *Education:* Attended Art Students League. *Address:* Four Winds Press, Scholastic Book Services, 50 West 44th St., New York, N.Y. 10036. *Residence:* Connecticut.

CAREER: Worked as commercial artist and copywriter; free-lance writer and illustrator. *Awards, honors:* Brooklyn Art Books for Children citation, 1973, for *A Boy, a Dog, a Frog and a Friend.*

WRITINGS—With husband, Mercer Mayer, except as noted: *Mine* (picture book), Simon & Schuster, 1970; *A Boy, a Dog, a Frog and a Friend* (picture book), Dial, 1971; *Me and My Flying Machine* (fantasy), Parents' Magazine Press, 1971; *One Frog Too Many* (picture book), Dial, 1975; (sole author) *Beauty and the Beast* (based on the French classic by Marie Leprince de Beaumont), Four Winds Press, 1978.

* * *

MAZZOTTA, Giuseppe 1942-

PERSONAL: Born January 1, 1942, in Curinga, Italy; son of Pasquale and Rose Mazzotta; married Carol Carlson, March 2, 1972; children: Rosanna, Antony, Paula. *Education:* University of Toronto, B.A., 1965, M.A., 1966; Cornell University, Ph.D., 1969. *Religion:* Roman Catholic. *Home:* 206 Delaware Ave., Ithaca, N.Y. 14850. *Office:* Department of Romance Studies, Cornell University, Ithaca, N.Y. 14853.

CAREER: Cornell University, Ithaca, N.Y., assistant professor, 1969-70; Yale University, New Haven, Conn., assistant professor, 1970-72; University of Toronto, Toronto, Ontario, associate professor, 1972-73; Cornell University, associate professor, 1973-78, professor of Romance studies, 1978—.

WRITINGS: Dante, Poet of the Desert: History and Allegory in the Divine Comedy, Princeton University Press, 1979.

WORK IN PROGRESS: A reading of the *Decameron.*

SIDELIGHTS: Mazzotta comments that his interests include theology, literature, and political life.

* * *

McCAGG, William O., Jr. 1930-

PERSONAL: Born June 16, 1930, in New York, N.Y.; married wife, Louise (a sculptress); children: Alexandra, Dorothy. *Education:* Harvard University, B.A., 1952; Columbia University, M.A., 1960, Ph.D., 1965. *Home:* 6204 Coleman Rd., East Lansing, Mich. 48822. *Office:* Department of History, Michigan State University, East Lansing, Mich. 48824.

CAREER: Fairleigh Dickinson University, Rutherford, N.J., assistant professor of history, 1962-64; Michigan State University, East Lansing, assistant professor, 1964-71, associate professor, 1971-77, professor of history, 1977—.

WRITINGS: (Editor with Arthur Adams and Ian Matley) *Atlas of Russian and East European History,* Praeger, 1967; *Jewish Nobles and Geniuses in Modern Hungary* (monograph), Columbia University Press, 1972; *Stalin Embattled, 1943-1948,* Wayne State University Press, 1978; (editor with Brian Silver) *Soviet-Asian Ethnic Frontiers,* Pergamon, 1979.

Contributor of articles and reviews to history journals.

* * *

McCARTHY, Edward V., Jr. 1924-

PERSONAL: Born November 16, 1924, in Boston, Mass.; son of Edward V. (a letter carrier) and Margherite (a secretary; maiden name, Griffin) McCarthy; married Margaret Ann O'Leary (a secretary), October 26, 1957; children: Margaret Katherine, Eileen Elizabeth, Patricia Ann. *Education:* Georgetown University, B.S.F.S., 1950. *Religion:* Catholic. *Home:* 4 Maple Road, Winchester, Mass. 01890. *Office:* Foxboro Co., 38 Neponset Ave., Foxboro, Mass. 02035.

CAREER: Self-employed communication and training consultant, Wakefield, Mass., 1960-63; General Electric Co., Lynn, Mass., communication manager, 1950-60 and 1963-69; Foxboro Co., Foxboro, Mass., public relations manager, 1969—. Speechwriter for Massachusetts Governor John A. Volpe and various company presidents and corporate officers. Teacher of public speaking at Daytona Beach Junior College. *Military service:* U.S. Army, 1943-46, Signal Intelligence Service, served in China, Burma, and India; became technical sergeant. *Member:* National Investor Relations Institute, Mystery Writers of America, Georgetown University Alumni Association, Gold Key Society, Pi Gamma Mu.

WRITINGS: The Pied Piper of Helfenstein, Doubleday, 1975.

WORK IN PROGRESS: A mystery novel based on the solution of a twenty-four-year-old crime.

SIDELIGHTS: McCarthy commented: "I consider myself an entertainer. I try to write for fast reading, giving my readers a well-engineered plot, some amusing characters, and a few hours of release from their chores and troubles. I also consider my stories my primary legacy—and I'm including unpublished as well as published work."

* * *

McCONKEY, Dale Durant 1928-

PERSONAL: Born March 10, 1928, in Washington Court House, Ohio; son of Edwin D. and Ora (Emrich) McConkey; married Eleanor A. Intoccia, September 4, 1948; children: Dale D., Lori L., Dean E., Todd E. *Education:* New York University, B.S., 1951, M.B.A., 1953. *Home address:* P.O. Box 1746, Madison, Wis. 53701.

CAREER: Worked as examiner for National Labor Relations Board, 1949-50; personnel manager of American Sugar Refining Co., 1952-55; Beech-Nut Life Savers, Inc., Canajoharie, N.Y., manager of industrial relations, 1955-56, director of industrial relations, 1956-59, vice-president, 1959-60; vice-president of United Fruit Co., 1960-62, executive assistant to president and vice-president in administration, 1962-66, group vice-president, 1966-68; Dale D. McConkey Associates, Madison, Wis., president, 1968—. Instructor at Eastern University, 1952; lecturer at Brooklyn College (now of City University of New York), 1952; professor at University of Wisconsin, Madison, 1973—. Member of board of directors of American and Canadian corporations, including A & W Root Beer Co. and Baskin-Robbins 31 Ice Cream Co.; member of board of trustees of Amsterdam City Hospital. Member of New York governor's business assistance committee. *Military service:* U.S. Army Air Forces. U.S. Air Force; served in Korea; became first lieutenant.

MEMBER: Pan American Society (member of board of governors), National Association of Manufacturers, Grocery Manufacturers Association, American Management Association, Society for the Advancement of Management, Ecuadorian-American Association (member of board of directors), Pan American Society of New England (member of board of trustees), Alpha Kappa Psi, New York University Club, University Club (Boston), Canajoharie Golf and Country Club. *Awards, honors:* Distinguished service award from Alpha Kappa Psi, 1951.

WRITINGS: How to Manage by Results, American Management Association, 1965, 3rd edition, 1976; *Planning Next Year's Profits,* American Management Association, 1968; *Updating the Management Process,* American Management Association, 1971; *Management by Objectives for Staff Managers,* Vantage, 1972; *No-Nonsense Delegation,* American Management Association, 1974; *Management by Objectives for Nonprofit Organizations,* American Management Association, 1975; (with Ray Vander Weele) *Financial Management by Objectives,* Prentice-Hall, 1976. Also author of *Management by Objectives for Financial Managers,* 1976. Contributor to professional journals.

* * *

McCORMICK, Ernest J(ames) 1911-

PERSONAL: Born August 22, 1911, in Indianapolis, Ind.; son of Malcolm E. and Bessie G. (Gibbons) McCormick; married Emily Arnold Stetson, June 13, 1936; children: Wynne G. (Mrs. Frank D. Lewis), Jan S. (Mrs. Thomas D. Edging), Colleen Clark (deceased). *Education:* Ohio Wesleyan University, B.A., 1933; attended American University, 1939-41; Purdue University, M.S., 1947, Ph.D., 1948. *Home:* 1315 Sunset Lane, West Lafayette, Ind. 47906.

CAREER: Cotton Garment Code Authority, New York, N.Y., statistician, 1933-35; U.S. Employment Service, Washington, D.C., chief of planning unit, job analysis and information section, Division of Standards and Research, 1935-39; U.S. Bureau of the Census, Washington, D.C., chief occupational expert in Population Division, 1939-41; U.S. Selective Service System, Washington, D.C., chief of occupational statistics section, Division of Research and Statistics, 1941-43; Purdue University, West Lafayette, Ind., assistant professor, 1948-51, associate professor, 1951-55, professor of psychological sciences, 1955-77, professor emeritus, 1977—. Co-founder and president of PAQ services, Inc. Diplomate of American Board of Examiners in Professional Psychology.

Fulbright lecturer at Catholic University, Milan, Italy, 1964-65; lecturer at workshops and professional meetings throughout the world, including India, Hong Kong, Manila, Okinawa, and South Africa; seminar leader. Adviser to director of Selective Service System, 1947; panel chairperson of U.S. Department of Defense Research & Development Board, 1948-53; member of Research and Engineering Advisory Council to U.S. Postmaster-General, 1967-69; vice-chairperson of Navy Advisory Board for Human Resources, 1971-77; member of committees and panels of Human Resources Research Institute, Army Scientific Advisory Panel, General Electric Co., U.S. Employment Service, and National Research Council of the National Academy of Science; consultant to Shri Ram Centre of Industrial Relations, New Delhi, 1969-70. *Military service:* U.S. Navy, chief of classification analysis unit, Bureau of Naval Personnel, 1943-48; became lieutenant commander.

MEMBER: International Association of Applied Psychology, American Psychological Association (fellow; member of executive committee of Division of Industrial and Organizational Psychology, 1961-64), Society of Engineering Psychologists (fellow; member of executive committee, 1971-73), Human Factors Society (fellow), Association of Applied Psychology (India), Midwestern Psychological Association (member of council, 1961-63). *Awards, honors:* James McKeen Cattell Award from American Psychological Association, 1964, for outstanding research design; Franklin V. Taylor Award from Society of Engineering Psychologists, 1966, for outstanding contributions to human factors education; named honorary president of Center of Ergonomic Studies, Milan, Italy, 1966; Paul M. Fitts Award from Human Factors Society, 1972, distinguished contribution award, 1977; Gordon A. Barrows Memorial Award from Indiana Psychological Association, 1979, for distinguished contribution to psychology.

WRITINGS: (Contributor) John F. Mee, editor, *Personnel Handbook,* Ronald, 1951; (with Joseph Tiffin) *Workbook for Industrial Psychology,* 3rd edition (McCormick was not associated with earlier editions), Tri-State Offset, 1953, 6th edition (with Tiffin and J. R. Terborg), 1974; (contributor) C. H. Lawshe, editor, *The Psychology of Industrial Relations,* McGraw, 1953; (contributor) H. B. Maynard, editor, *Industrial Engineering Handbook,* McGraw, 1956, 2nd edition, 1963; *Human Engineering,* McGraw, 1957, 2nd edition published as *Human Factors Engineering,* 1964, 4th edition published as *Human Factors in Engineering and Design,* 1976, workbook for 3rd edition (with Mark S. Sanders), Tri-State Offset, 1970, workbook for 4th edition, Kendall/Hunt, 1976; (with Tiffin) *Industrial Psychology,* 4th edition (McCormick was not associated with earlier editions), Prentice-Hall, 1958, 7th edition (with Daniel R. Ilgen), 1980.

(Contributor) M. D. Dunnette, editor, *Handbook of In-*

dustrial and Organizational Psychology, Rand McNally, 1976; (contributor) Dale Yoder and H. G. Heneman, Jr., editors, *ASPA Handbook of Personnel and Industrial Relations,* Bureau of National Affairs, 1979; *Job Analysis: Methods and Applications,* American Management Association, 1979. Contributor of about forty articles to scholarly journals.

WORK IN PROGRESS: A fifth edition of *Human Factors in Engineering and Design,* with Sanders, publication by McGraw expected in 1981.

SIDELIGHTS: McCormick's books have been published in Mexico, France, Japan, Brazil, India, Poland, and Italy. He and his associates created PAQ Services, Inc. "to provide data processing services, to develop additional technical materials, and to conduct further research in support of the Position Analysis Questionnaire and its utility to the behavioral sciences and its application in personnel administration. The Position Analysis Questionnaire was characterized in the *Annual Review of Psychology,* 1979, as one of the most important personnel selection milestones in the past sixty years."

McCormick added: "The books I have initiated myself were triggered by the fact that there appeared to be 'voids' in the publishing field in the areas in question. This was the case, for example, in writing *Human Engineering* in 1957, since there was no available text dealing with the developing field of human factors. This was also the instigation for writing *Job Analysis: Methods and Applications,* since the material dealing with job analysis was generally scattered to the four winds and had not been organized into any single, comprehensive volume. In connection with the field of job analysis, a major focus that I have had in my research and writing has been in terms of encouraging the development of systematic, quantifiable approaches to the analysis of human work."

An award in McCormick's honor, the Ernest J. McCormick Award in Industrial/Organizational Psychology, was established at Purdue University in 1977.

* * *

McCOY, Samuel (Duff) 1882-1964

OBITUARY NOTICE: Born April 17, 1882, in Burlington, Ia.; died April 7, 1964. Journalist and author. McCoy began writing for magazines in 1898, then worked for years as a publicity man for newspapers and magazines. In 1923, he wrote a series of fifty articles for the *New York World* about the flogging death of Martin Tabert, a convict leased to a lumber camp in Florida, and other abuses in that state's prison system. McCoy's articles resulted in the revision of Florida laws relating to the practice of convict leasing and corporal punishment. He also served on the American Committee for Relief in Ireland in 1921, a group that successfully negotiated with the British to supply $5 million of aid to Irish non-combatants. McCoy's other writings include *Tippecanoe, Merchants of the Morning,* and *This Man Adams.* Obituaries and other sources: *Who Was Who in America,* 4th edition, Marquis, 1968; *American Authors and Books, 1640 to the Present Day,* 3rd revised edition, Crown, 1972.

* * *

McCRADY, Lady 1951-

PERSONAL: Born October 13, 1951, in Indianapolis, Ind.; daughter of Harry E. (a jazz musician and engineer) and Louise (Benson) McCrady. *Education:* Attended Sir John Cass School of Art, London; Syracuse University, B.F.A.

(cum laude), 1973. *Address:* c/o Holiday House, 18 East 53rd St., New York, N.Y. 10022; and 35 North St., Hingham Harbor, Mass. 10043; and 17 Park Ave., New York, N.Y. 10016.

CAREER: Free-lance writer, artist, and illustrator, with paintings and illustrations exhibited at shows in New England. Guest lecturer and illustrator at schools, libraries, and colleges. *Member:* Illustrators Guild, Kappa Kappa Gamma.

WRITINGS: (Self-illustrated) *Miss Kiss and the Nasty Beast,* Holiday House, 1979; *Mildred and the Mummy,* Holiday House, 1980; *Junior's Tune,* Holiday House, 1980.

Illustrator: Parents' Nursery School, *Kids Are Natural Cooks,* Houghton, 1971; Charles Keller, *Glory, Glory, How Peculiar,* Prentice-Hall, 1976; Tobi Tobias, *An Umbrella Named Umbrella,* Knopf, 1976; Inez Maury, *My Mother the Mail Carrier,* translated by Norah Alemany, Feminist Press, 1976; Mary Calhoun, *The Witch's Pig,* Morrow, 1977; Rose Lagerkrantz, *Tulla's Summer,* Harcourt, 1977; Steven Kroll, *If I Could Be My Grandmother,* Pantheon, 1977; Calhoun, *Jack the Wise and the Cornish Cuckoos,* Morrow, 1978; Bonnie Carey, *Grasshopper to the Rescue,* Morrow, 1979; Jan van Pelt, *The Day the Zoo Caught the Flu,* Harvey House, 1979; Jane Feder, *The Night Light,* Dial, 1979.

WORK IN PROGRESS: Writing and illustrating a pirate book, publication by Dial expected in 1980; three other books, *The Gypsy,* for Houghton, *Monkey in Space,* and *The Orchestra.*

SIDELIGHTS: "I'm as concerned with pictorial language as with written language," says Lady McCrady. "Art should be more than a mirror of a written theme. Drawings are gestures that mean different things to each of us. As separate entities, they should be read for their content. They give us information we take for granted by setting a stage. If they are filled with whimsy and intrigue they encourage the mind to wander, express movement and change and allow the imagination to flow. The imagination is the key to problem solving, and this is what picture books are all about."

McCrady's paintings and book illustrations are in the Hartford Collection in Hartford, Conn., and in various private collections in New England and New York. Her mother is the inventor of the Shirret needlepoint technique; McCrady's own Shirret rugs have been featured in *Family Circle* and *American Home.*

BIOGRAPHICAL/CRITICAL SOURCES: Hartford Courant Sunday Magazine, June, 1978.

* * *

McDANIELS, Carl 1930-

PERSONAL: Born September 29, 1930, in Sioux City, Iowa; son of Oscar E. (a teacher) and Janetta (a teacher; maiden name, Miller) McDaniels; married Ann Eller, August 18, 1951; children: Janetta Lynn McDaniels Beaty, Lisa C., Diane E. *Education:* Bridgewater College, Bridgewater, Va., B.A., 1951; University of Virginia, M.Ed., 1957, Ed.D., 1964. *Religion:* Methodist. *Home:* 713 Broce Dr., Blacksburg, Va. 24060. *Office:* Virginia Polytechnic Institute and State University, Blacksburg, Va. 24061.

CAREER: High school counselor in Arlington, Va., 1957-59; American Personnel and Guidance Association, Washington, D.C., associate director, 1959-65; George Washington University, Washington, D.C., professor, 1965-69; Virginia Polytechnic Institute and State University, Blacksburg, professor of counselor education, 1969—. *Military service:* U.S. Navy, elementary school supervisor at U.S. Naval Prison in

Portsmouth, N.H., 1952-56. *Member:* National Vocational Guidance Association (president, 1973-74), American Personnel and Guidance Association (member of board of directors), Rotary International. *Awards, honors:* Career service award from Virginia Personnel and Guidance Association, 1976; merit award from National Vocational Guidance Association, 1978.

WRITINGS: Vocational Aspects of Counselor Education, George Washington University Press, 1965; *Finding Your First Job,* Houghton, 1975; *Preparing a Professional Vita or Resume,* Garrett Park Press, 1978; (with Dean Hummel) *How to Help Your Child Plan a Career,* Acropolis Books, 1979. Contributor to guidance journals.

WORK IN PROGRESS: Revising *Finding Your First Job; Leisure and Career Development.*

SIDELIGHTS: McDaniels comments: "My research and writing have been in the area of career development throughout the life span, with special emphasis on job placement of high school graduates and the implications of leisure in career development."

*   *   *

McDONALD, Jamie
See HEIDE, Florence Parry

*   *   *

McDOWELL, Michael 1950-
(Nathan Aldyne, a joint pseudonym)

PERSONAL: Born June 1, 1950, in Enterprise, Ala; son of Thomas Eugene (an accountant) and Marian (a social worker; maiden name, Mulkey) McDowell. *Education:* Harvard University, B.A. (magna cum laude), 1972; Brandeis University, Ph.D., 1978. *Residence:* Medford, Mass. *Agent:* Jane Otte, Otte Co., 9 Goden St., Belmont, Mass. 02178.

CAREER: Writer, 1978—. Member of National Gay Task Force and Massachusetts Fair Share.

WRITINGS—Novels: The Amulet, Avon, 1979; (with Dennis Schuetz, under joint pseudonym, Nathan Aldyne) *Vermilion: A Mystery,* Avon, 1980; *Cold Moon Over Babylon,* Avon, 1980; *The Black Triangle,* Avon, in press. Contributor of articles and reviews to magazines.

WORK IN PROGRESS: A novel, *Hammers of Heaven,* with Dennis Schuetz, publication expected in 1980.

SIDELIGHTS: McDowell told *CA:* "I began writing fiction when I was an undergraduate at Harvard, and had completed six novels before I sold the seventh, *The Amulet,* to Avon, in 1977. The first six had been written more or less to my own taste; *The Amulet,* however, was written specifically with the hope of interesting a publisher. I was gratified that it did, and soon came to see that this commercial property was probably the best written of all my work, if only because the constrictions of writing within a specific form, in this case, the occult novel, had sharpened my literary wits. Now, I am happiest working within a specific genre: detective, occult, historical-adventure, because the constraints discourage my tendencies towards self-indulgence.

"In general, I write in haste and revise at leisure. Of particular use in writing, I have found Eric Partridge's *Usage and Abusage,* not only as a specific work of reference, but for inculcating his dicta of clarity, brevity, and simplicity. Three things I would recommend to any writer, because they have been indispensable to me: keeping a journal, extensive reading (of practically anything at all), and steadiness of working habits, whatever they may be."

McGANN, George T(homas) 1913-

PERSONAL: Born July 9, 1913, in New York, N.Y.; son of John and Celia (Conroy) McGann; married Louise Kenney, October 1, 1937; children: Jeffrey, Patricia. *Education:* Attended University of Notre Dame, 1931-32. *Politics:* "Always voted Democratic, not always wisely." *Home:* 71-26 Juno St., Forest Hills, N.Y. *Agent:* Arthur Pine Associates, Inc., 1780 Broadway, New York, N.Y. 10019. *Office:* Australian Consolidated Press, 444 Madison Ave., New York, N.Y.

CAREER: New York Times, New York City, reporter, 1938-41; Australian Associated Press, New York City, correspondent, 1941-47; Australian Consolidated Press, New York City, correspondent, 1947-73, U.S. manager and editor, 1973—. *Member:* Foreign Press Association, National Press Club, U.S. Tennis Writers Association. *Awards, honors:* Allison Danzig Trophy for Tennis Reporting, 1969.

WRITINGS: (With Clive Cottingham) *The Game of Billiards,* Lippincott, 1964; *Court Hustler, Bobby Riggs,* Lippincott, 1973; *Court on Court, Margaret Court,* Dodd, 1975. Contributor to *World Tennis.*

SIDELIGHTS: McGann wrote: "I have enjoyed a lifelong fascination with the game of tennis, and have covered major tournaments throughout the world for twenty-five years, including Wimbledon, Forest Hills, and the Davis Cup matches. I am still a competent club player." *Avocational interests:* Playing piano ("bar-room version with accent on Cole Porter, Rogers & Hart, anything written before the Age of the Beatles").

*   *   *

McGINNIS, Lila S(prague) 1924-

PERSONAL: Born May 29, 1924, in Ashtabula Harbor, Ohio; daughter of Lynn A. (a teacher) and Florence (White) Sprague; married Richard W. McGinnis (a regional planner), June 1, 1944; children: Richard, Ralph, Leslie, Benjamin. *Education:* Attended Kent State University, 1941-43; Ohio State University, B.Sc., 1948. *Religion:* Episcopal. *Home:* 120 Park Ave., Elyria, Ohio 44035. *Office:* Elyria Public Library, 320 Washington Ave., Elyria, Ohio 44035.

CAREER: Elementary school teacher in Orwell, Ohio, 1943-45, in Columbus, Ohio, 1949, and Interlaken, N.Y., 1949-50; Elyria Public Library, Elyria, Ohio, children's librarian, 1973—.

WRITINGS: What Will Simon Say?, Logos International, 1974; *Secret of the Porcelain Cats* (juvenile), Albert Whitman, 1978. Contributor of about thirty stories to magazines, including *Good Housekeeping.*

WORK IN PROGRESS: Another children's book, completion expected in 1980.

SIDELIGHTS: Lila McGinnis comments: "I write because I enjoy it and feel more alive doing it. When I am working on a story or a book I am sure I am easier to live with—perhaps that is why I have such a supportive family!

"I like the short story form and have done most of my writing in that form, but the market for it is small. The last few years I have tried writing for children and enjoy it immensely. Working with children each day as a children's librarian brings me much pleasure too, and probably accounts for my turning to the juvenile field."

*   *   *

McGRAW, James R. 1935-
PERSONAL: Born December 3, 1935, in Fort Wayne, Ind.;

son of Kenneth M. and Rose (Duthie) McGraw. *Education:* Northwestern University, B.S., 1958; Yale University, B.D., 1961. *Home:* 85 Columbia St., New York, N.Y. 10002. *Agent:* Jeannette Hopkins, 301 East 47th St., New York, N.Y. *Office:* Adherent, 460 Park Ave. S., New York, N.Y. 10016.

CAREER: Ordained Methodist minister; pastor of Methodist church in Brooklyn, N.Y., 1961-63, co-pastor in Brooklyn, N.Y., 1963-65; editor of *Renewal,* 1965-70; *Adherent: A Journal of Comprehensive Employment Training and Human Resource Development,* New York, N.Y., managing editor. Research assistant with Ministerial Interfaith Association of Harlem; consultant to Opportunities Industrialization Center of New York.

WRITINGS—All with Dick Gregory: *The Shadow That Scares Me,* Doubleday, 1968; *Write Me In!,* Bantam, 1968; *No More Lies: The Myth and Reality of American History,* Harper, 1971; *Dick Gregory's Political Primer,* Harper, 1972; *Dick Gregory's Natural Diet for Folks Who Eat: Cookin' With Mother Nature,* Harper, 1974; *Dick Gregory's Bible Tales With Commentary,* Stein & Day, 1974; *Up From Nigger,* Stein & Day, 1976. Contributing editor of *Christianity and Crisis.*

SIDELIGHTS: McGraw comments: "Writing for publication came to me by accident and association. I began collaborating with Dick Gregory because of the friendship which evolved from our common participation in the civil rights movement. One book led to another, which in turn led to writing articles on my own.

"I also made a comedy album with Sandy Baron, 'God Save the Queens,' for A & M Records in 1972, another example of the association of friendship leading to just doing it."

* * *

McGUIRE, Jerry 1934-

PERSONAL: Born March 30, 1934, in Denver, Colo.; son of Donald W. (in highway construction) and Faye E. (a nurse; maiden name, Fleming) McGuire; married Judith K. Burghardt, July 5, 1953 (divorced, December, 1969); married Judee Lea Thimgan (a free-lance writer and photographer), May 7, 1971; children: Kathleen McGuire Maddox, Pam, Mindy McGuire Porter, Marci McGuire Penman, Michael. *Education:* Colorado State University, B.S., 1959; also attended University of Colorado and University of California, Los Angeles. *Politics:* Republican. *Religion:* Episcopalian. *Home and office address:* P.O. Box 95, Indian Hills, Colo. 80454; and, P.O. Box 94, Haxtun, Colo. 80731. *Agent:* Richard Huttner Agency, Inc., 330 East St., New York, N.Y. 10016; and Florence Feiler, 1524 Sunset Plaza Dr., Los Angeles, Calif. 90069.

CAREER: Pan American Petroleum Corp., Denver, Colo., geologist, 1959-60; Riddle & Associates Advertising, Denver, Colo., copywriter, 1960-61; Broyles, Alebaugh & Davis Advertising, Denver, Colo., copywriter, 1961; free-lance writer in Denver, Colo., and San Francisco, Calif., 1961-62; Coors Porcelain Co., Golden, Colo., assistant advertising manager, 1962-64; Barbre Productions, Denver, Colo., film writer, director, and producer, 1964-66; free-lance writer, director, and producer, 1966—. Co-founder of BRAVO! Productions, 1969. Instructor at University of Colorado, 1972. *Military service:* U.S. Marine Corps, radar navigator, 1953-55; became sergeant.

MEMBER: National Writers Club, American Legion. *Awards, honors:* Nominated for National Book Award,

1974, for *Elijah;* special trustee's award from National Cowboy Hall of Fame, award for creative excellence from U.S. Film Festival in Chicago, Ill., best documentary award from Colorado Broadcasting Association, all 1972, all for "Harry Jackson: A Man and His Art"; and award from State of Ohio.

WRITINGS: Elijah (novel), Northland Press, 1973; *How to Write, Direct, and Produce Effective Business Films and Documentaries,* TAB Books, 1978; *Learning How to Fly an Airplane,* TAB Books, 1979.

Author of more than two hundred and fifty film scripts, including "Harry Jackson: A Man and His Art," first broadcast by KB-TV, 1972, and "Wild Champions."

Writer for television series, including "Run for Your Life" and "Death Valley Days."

Ghost writer. Author of "Colorado Crossroads," a column syndicated in thirty newspapers, 1974-77. Contributor of several hundred articles and stories to regional and national magazines, including *Writer's Digest, Argosy, Saturday Evening Post,* and *Empire.*

WORK IN PROGRESS: A novel; two nonfiction books; five motion picture scripts; three films for the U.S. Department of Energy.

SIDELIGHTS: McGuire writes: "Projects in the mill at this time would throw most writers into a tailspin. But I've always had to do that to stay alive as a writer. Versatility—being able to write a film, a book, a magazine article, a speech, advertising copy for print, radio, or television—has provided me with a way to make a good living. Certain writers have been critical of me because of that. If I can be regarded as successful it is because I have tried my best to be a writer, not a specialist who devotes all of his time to novels or films or cookie boxes. Working on hundreds of subjects has given me a wonderful, very broad education, and each project has helped me do a better job on the next one.

"One day soon I hope to begin a long list of best selling material, and I prefer fiction. But I will never lose touch with the film business or writing magazine material. Every script or article is a new, exciting challenge which enables me to see more of life and share it with millions of people I don't know. To me, the most important participant in what I do is the reader or the viewer, not the publisher or the producer."

BIOGRAPHICAL/CRITICAL SOURCES: Canyon Courier, August 2, 1973, December 18, 1975; *Denver Post,* October 22, 1978; *Movie Maker,* May, 1979.

* * *

McJIMSEY, George T(ilden) 1936-

PERSONAL: Born March 9, 1936, in Dallas, Tex.; son of Joseph Bailey (in sales) and Harriet (a university professor; maiden name, Tilden) McJimsey; married Sandra Kay Bryant, January 3, 1970; children: Anne Katherine. *Education:* Grinnell College, B.A., 1958; Columbia University, M.A., 1959; University of Wisconsin—Madison, Ph.D., 1968. *Politics:* Democrat. *Religion:* Presbyterian. *Home:* 2236 Storm St., Ames, Iowa 50010. *Office:* Department of History, Iowa State University, Ames, Iowa 50011.

CAREER: Portland State University, Portland, Ore., instructor in history, 1964-65; Iowa State University, Ames, instructor, 1965-68, assistant professor, 1968-71, associate professor of history, 1971—. *Member:* Iowa Civil Liberties Union, Phi Beta Kappa. *Awards, honors:* Woodrow Wilson fellowship, 1958-59.

WRITINGS: Genteel Partisan: Manton Marble, 1834-1917, Iowa State University Press, 1977.

WORK IN PROGRESS: The Dividing and Reuniting of America, 1848-1877, for Forum Press; a biography of Harry Hopkins, 1890-1946.

*   *   *

McKELWAY, St. Clair   1905-1980
(J. De P. Hall)

OBITUARY NOTICE—See index for *CA* sketch: Born February 13, 1905, in Charlotte, N.C.; died January 10, 1980, in New York, N.Y. Screenwriter and staff writer of *New Yorker.* McKelway contributed numerous profiles and short stories to *New Yorker* during his career of more than thirty years. Among his more notable subjects are Walter Winchell and dancer Bill Robinson. Many of his pieces were also published in volumes such as *True Tales From the Annals of Crime and Rascality* and *The Edinburgh Caper.* Obituaries and other sources: *New York Times,* January 11, 1980; *Newsweek,* January 21, 1980.

*   *   *

McKENDRICK, Melveena (Christine)   1941-

PERSONAL: Born March 23, 1941, in Glamorgan, Wales; daughter of James Powell (a teacher) and Catherine Letitia Jones; married Neil McKendrick (a historian), March 18, 1968; children: Olivia, Cornelia. *Education:* King's College, London, B.A. (first class honors), 1963; Girton College, Cambridge, Ph.D., 1967. *Home:* Howe House, Huntingdon Rd., Cambridge CB3 0LY, England. *Office:* Girton College, Cambridge University, Cambridge CB3 0JG, England.

CAREER: Cambridge University, Girton College, Cambridge, England, research fellow, 1967—, tutor, 1970-74, senior tutor, 1974—, lecturer in Spanish, 1970—.

WRITINGS: Ferdinand and Isabella, American Heritage, 1968; *A Concise History of Spain,* McGraw, 1972; *Woman and Society in the Spanish Drama of the Golden Age,* Cambridge University Press, 1974. Contributor to *Calderon: Critical Studies,* edited by J. E. Vasey, 1973, and to language and Spanish studies journals.

WORK IN PROGRESS: A composite edition of Calderon's *El magico prodigioso* with A. A. Parker; a "literary life" of Cervantes for Little, Brown.

*   *   *

McKENNA, J(ane) J(essica)   1945-

PERSONAL: Born June 25, 1945, in Bristol, England; daughter of George Alec (an engineer) and Hilda Kathleen (Lanfear) Reid; married. *Education:* Received Ordinary National Certificate from a technical college. *Residence:* Bristol, England. *Agent:* McIntosh & Otis, Inc., 475 Fifth Ave., New York, N.Y. 10017.

CAREER: Technician in various fields, including dentistry, nutrition, and cancer research in Bristol and London, England, 1961-73; self-employed caterer in Bristol, 1974-76; College of Further Education, Bristol, technician, 1977-78; writer, 1978—.

WRITINGS: Sarah and Joshua, Avon, 1979; *Ask of the Wind,* Avon, 1980.

WORK IN PROGRESS: Last Time on the Rocking Horse.

SIDELIGHTS: McKenna told *CA:* "I have the same problem about writing as I do about painting or playing golf: the vision of perfection, forever flaunting itself as a real possibility, yet constantly soiled by my own ineptitude. If creativity is a search for truth, I can only say that I am never wholly content with what I find, and will continue in this passion to discover until I am satisfied—at which point I will know I have failed. This is no original thought—would that I possessed the genius to invent one—but nevertheless forms my motivation for that strange symbiosis of self and characters called fiction writing.''

*   *   *

McKENNEY, Ruth   1911-1972

PERSONAL: Born November 18, 1911, in Mishawaka, Ind.; died July 25, 1972, in New York, N.Y.; daughter of John Sidney and Marguerite (Flynn) McKenney; married Richard Bransten (a writer sometimes under pseudonym Bruce Minton), 1937; children: Eileen, Patrick, Thomas. *Education:* Attended Ohio State University.

CAREER: Worked as printer, book salesperson, waitress, and newspaper reporter. *Akron Beacon-Journal,* Akron, Ohio, reporter, 1932-33; *New York Post,* New York, N.Y., feature writer, 1934-36; writer, 1936-72. *Awards, honors:* Received several awards from Ohio Newspaper Women's Association; Best Fiction Book award at Writer's Congress, 1938 and 1939, for *Industrial Valley.*

WRITINGS: My Sister Eileen, Harcourt, 1938; *Industrial Valley* (fiction), Harcourt, 1939; *The McKenneys Carry On,* Harcourt, 1940; *Jake Home,* Harcourt, 1943; *The Loud Red Patrick,* Harcourt, 1947; (with husband, Richard Bransten) *Here's England: An Informal Guide,* Harper, 1950, 3rd edition, 1971; *Love Story,* Harcourt, 1950; *All About Eileen,* Harcourt, 1952; *Far, Far From Home,* Harper, 1954; *Mirage,* Farrar, Strauss & Cudahy, 1956. Author of column, "Strictly Personal." Contributor to *Harper's* and *New Yorker.* Editor, *New Masses.*

SIDELIGHTS: Ruth McKenney is best remembered for her first book, *My Sister Eileen.* Subsequently made into a Broadway play, a musical, and a full-length motion picture, it chronicles the author's relationship with her beautiful and popular sister. McKenney writes "lovingly" of the sometimes funny, sometimes poignant experiences the two shared. The book enjoyed immediate popularity, "for the incidents which assume such entertaining guise in her reminiscences of her sister and herself lie within the experience of every one of us and are the more delightful because they might have been our own," explained Amy Loveman.

McKenney was also a dedicated and sincere sociological writer. In *Industrial Valley,* her second and in her own opinion, her best book, she tells of the culmination of events that led to the rubber worker's strike in early 1936. G. E. Shipler, Jr. claimed that "the book's sharp portrayal of the apathy of thousands of unemployed makes the reader visualize the rise and fall of the morale of the union and other rubber-workers as though registered on a chart." McKenney made use of actual newspaper clippings and used only two ficticious names in this most "readable piece of American labor history ever written."

BIOGRAPHICAL/CRITICAL SOURCES: Books, July 24, 1938, February 19, 1939, September 29, 1940; *New Republic,* August 24, 1938, February 22, 1939; *Commonwealth,* March 3, 1939, February 26, 1943; *New York Times,* March 5, 1939, February 28, 1943, August 5, 1950; *Christian Science Monitor,* April 5, 1939, July 22, 1950; *Springfield Republican,* October 10, 1940, February 28, 1943; *New York Herald Tribune Weekly Book Review,* February 28, 1943, November 9,

1947, February 12, 1950, July 9, 1950, December 2, 1956; *Nation*, March 13, 1943; *Saturday Review of Literature*, March 13, 1943, February 11, 1950, February 13, 1954; *Book Week*, March 28, 1943; *San Francisco Chronicle*, February 12, 1950; *Time*, December 3, 1956.

OBITUARIES: New York Times, July 27, 1972; *Washington Post*, July 28, 1972; *Newsweek*, August 7, 1972; *Variety*, August 8, 1972; *Publishers Weekly*, August 14, 1972; *Antiquarian Bookman*, September 25, 1972; *Current Biography*, October, 1972.*

*   *   *

McKIM, Donald K(eith)   1950-

PERSONAL: Born February 25, 1950, in New Castle, Pa.; son of Keith B. (an accountant) and Mary (a teacher; maiden name, Leslie) McKim; married LindaJo Horton (a United Presbyterian minister), February 28, 1976. *Education:* Westminster College, New Wilmington, Pa., B.A. (cum laude), 1971; Pittsburgh Theological Seminary, M.Div. (magna cum laude), 1974; doctoral study at University of Pittsburgh. *Home:* 776 Scott Rd., Pittsburgh, Pa. 15228.

CAREER: Ordained United Presbyterian minister, 1975; Friendship United Presbyterian Parish, Slippery Rock, Pa., student pastor, 1970-74, supply pastor, 1975—. Visiting member of faculty at Westminster College, New Wilmington, Pa., 1979. *Member:* Karl Barth Society of North America (charter member), American Society of Church History, Presbyterian Historical Society, Pennsylvania Small Arms Company.

WRITINGS: The Church: Its Early Life, Cooperative Uniform Series, 1978; (with Jack B. Rogers) *The Authority and Interpretation of the Bible: An Historical Approach*, Harper, 1979; (with Rogers) *Biblical Inerrancy*, Harper, 1980. Contributor to *International Standard Bible Encyclopedia*. Contributor of articles and reviews to history and theology journals.

WORK IN PROGRESS: Research on Ramism in William Perkins.

SIDELIGHTS: McKim told *CA: "The Authority and Interpretation of the Bible: An Historical Approach* was written to fill a pressing scholarly need. Until now there has been no detailed study of the history of the doctrine of Scripture in the Christian church from the early church to the present. Specialists have provided much help with specific historical periods or with the doctrine of certain theologians. But co-author Jack B. Rogers and I saw that a much broader picture was needed. So we tried to draw it.

"Our book is the result of over ten years of individual and joint study. I built on Jack's 1967 doctoral dissertation, *Scripture in the Westminster Confession*, with several articles. Our individual research and published pieces through the years formed the initial basis for our book. But for three years we worked specifically to 'fill in the cracks.' We needed to flesh out our story, to reassess what we had already learned in light of new research, and to tie together the themes we found running through the church's understandings of Scripture from the earliest times till the present. Our collaboration was carried on long-distance: Jack in Pasadena, Calif.; I in Pittsburgh, Pa. Several chances to meet personally in those 'research' years helped us gain perspective and plot our further course.

"We wrote with scholars in mind. But we were most aware of the difficulties of Christian people faced with multiple options of belief about the Bible and the nature of its authority

and means of interpretation. Some have claimed the church has always seen the Scriptures as an errorless (inerrant) source of information on topics ranging from astronomy to geography and philosophy. We found that this was not the case. Instead there is a central tradition extending from the early church through the Protestant reformers of the sixteenth century and extending to our own times which has regarded the Bible rather as the primary way by which people are informed about salvation—how to have a right relationship with God. The Bible *is* an infallible source about this. So Jack and I wanted to set the historical record straight. We wanted lay people in the church as well as scholars to realize that their trust in the Scriptures as the real word of God does not have to rest on whether or not the Bible presents totally accurate scientific information on any topic under the sun! So we wrote our book to bring the insights of the best of the Church's past thinking to present problems. Our next book will be telling this same story in a non-technical fashion. It will be aimed at a much wider reading public.

"It was hard work. But it was thrilling to see our project progress and to trace the story of the development of the doctrine of Scripture in the church. It's much like detective work. At many points, various historical and philosophical influences caused some to turn away to an extreme position regarding Scripture, rather than following the church's central tradition. Our job was to pinpoint what these influences were and who led people in that direction. Both Jack and I grew up in the Presbyterian or Reformed tradition of theology. So part of our emphasis was to see how this tradition's understanding of the Bible has developed—especially in America. And we found some startling information! But our study, we hope, will also aid people in other theological traditions. It was a real attempt to discover 'roots' and to anchor our attitudes for the present in the richness and depth of our understandings in the past."

AVOCATIONAL INTERESTS: Reading, chess, sports.

*   *   *

McLAUGHLIN, Elizabeth Taylor   1923-

PERSONAL: Born August 30, 1923, in Washington, D.C.; daughter of Andrew Ruffner (a manufacturer) and Elizabeth (a teacher; maiden name, Glascock) Taylor; married Chester B. McLaughlin (a business executive), May, 1947 (divorced August, 1957); children: Margaret Elizabeth (Mrs. Jeffrey McKim), Chester B. *Education:* Wellesley College, B.A. (with honors in English and French), 1944; Radcliffe College, M.A. (English), 1946, Ph.D., 1949; New School for Social Research, M.A. (clinical psychology), 1978. *Politics:* Democrat. *Religion:* Society of Friends (Quakers). *Home:* 400 Riverside Dr., New York, N.Y. 10025.

CAREER: George Washington University, Washington, D.C., instructor in English, 1944-45; New York University, New York City, instructor in English, 1948-51; Mills College of Education, New York City, part-time assistant to dean of admissions, 1954-56; George Washington University, lecturer in English, 1957-58; Bucknell University, Lewisburg, Penn., instructor, 1958-60, assistant professor, 1960-66, associate professor of English, 1966-75; St. Paul's Halfway House, Baltimore, Md., co-director, 1976. *Member:* Modern Language Association of America, Milton Society of America. *Awards, honors:* Fellow of Radcliffe Institute, 1967-68.

WRITINGS: Ruskin and Gandhi, Bucknell University Press, 1974. Contributor of articles to journals, including *Bucknell Review* and *Studies in Philology*.

McLEAN, Malcolm Dallas 1913-

PERSONAL: Born March 10, 1913, in Rogers, Tex.; son of Dallas Duncan and Gladys (Robertson) McLean; married Margaret Stoner, February 11, 1939; children: John Robertson. Education: University of Texas, B.A. (with highest honors), 1936, Ph.D., 1951; Universidad Nacional Autonoma de Mexico, M.A., 1938. Home: 409 Baylor Dr., Arlington, Tex. 76010. Office: Robertson Colony Collection, University Library, University of Texas, Arlington, Tex. 76019.

CAREER: Texas Historical Records Survey, San Antonio, field editor in charge of Spanish translators, 1938-39; San Jacinto Museum of History, Houston, Tex., assistant director and archivist, 1939-41; U.S. War Department, Washington, D.C., research analyst on Mexico and Central America for Military Intelligence, 1941-46; University of Texas, Austin, Spanish translator at library, 1946-47, instructor in Romance languages, 1947-51; University of Arkansas, Fayetteville, assistant professor, 1951-55, associate professor of Romance languages, 1955-56; U.S. Information Agency, Washington, D.C., director of Binational Center in Tegucigalpa, Honduras, 1956-59, and Guayaquil, Educador, 1959-61; Texas Christian University, Fort Worth, associate professor, 1961-68, professor of Spanish, 1968-76, professor emeritus, 1977—, associate dean of AddRan College of Arts and Sciences, 1964-74, director of summer programs in Mexico, 1961-64; University of Texas, Arlington, professor of history and Spanish, 1976—. Vice-president of Humanities, Inc., 1964—; member of Texas Historical Foundation.

MEMBER: American Historical Association, Organization of American Historians, American Association for State and Local History, Western Writers of America, Collector's Institute, Western History Association, Westerners, Southwestern American Literature Association, Tennessee Historical Society, Texas Folklore Society, Texas Foreign Language Association (honorary member; president, 1964-65), Texas State Genealogical Society (fellow), Texas State Historical Association (fellow; life member), Sons of the Republic of Texas, East Texas Historical Association, Tarrant County Historical Society, Bell County Historical Society, Friends of Texas Christian University Libraries, Phi Beta Kappa (local founding president, 1971), Phi Alpha Theta, Phi Delta Kappa, Phi Eta Sigma, Phi Sigma Iota, Sigma Delta Pi (local honorary founding member), Knights of the Order of San Jacinto. Awards, honors: Citation from Military Intelligence Division of U.S. War Department, 1945; distinguished service award from Sons of the Republic of Texas, 1971, for founding the Spanish Texas Microfilm Center; Dr. Malcolm D. McLean Scholarship was endowed at Texas Christian University, 1972; Coral Horton Tullis Memorial Prize from Texas State Historical Association, 1974, Summerfield G. Roberts Award, 1974, and award of merit from American Association for State and Local History, 1976, all for Papers Concerning Robertson's Colony in Texas.

WRITINGS: (With J. Villasana Haggard) Handbook for Translators of Spanish Historical Documents, Semco Color Press, 1941; Vida y obra de Guillermo Prieto (title means "Life and Works of Guillermo Prieto"), Fondo de Cultura Economica, 1960; (editor with Eugenio del Hoyo) Josseph Antonio Fernandez de Juaregui Urrutia, Descripcion del Nuevo Reino de Leon, 1735-1740, Talleres de Impresiones, 1963, translation by McLean published as Description of Nuevo Leon, Mexico, 1735-1740, 1964; Contenido literario de "El Siglo Diez y Nueve" (title means "Literary Content of the Newspaper Entitled The Nineteenth Century"), Secretaria de Hacienda y Credito Publico, 1965; Fine Texas Horses: Their Pedigrees and Performance, 1830-1845, Texas Christian University Press, 1966; (editor with del Hoyo) Fray Juan Agustin de Morfi, Diario y derrotero, 1777-1781 (title means "Diary and Itinerary, 1777-1781"), Instituto Tecnologico y de Estudios Superiores de Monterrey, 1967; Notas para una bibliografia sobre Guillermo Prieto, Secretaria de Hacienda y Credito Publico, 1968, translation published as Bibliography on Guillermo Prieto, Mexican Poet-Statesman, Texas Christian University Press, 1968.

(Editor) Papers Concerning Robertson's Colony in Texas, Volume I: 1788-1822: The Texas Association, Texas Christian University Press, 1974, Volume II: 1823 Through September, 1826: Leftwich's Grant, Texas Christian University Press, 1975, Volume III: October, 1826, Through April, 1830: The Nashville Colony, Texas Christian University Press, 1976, Volume IV: May Through October, 1830: Tenoxtitlan, Dream Capital of Texas, University of Texas at Arlington Press, 1977, Volume V: October 11, 1830, Through March 5, 1831: The Upper Colony, University of Texas at Arlington Press, 1978.

Contributor: (Author of preface) Mercedes Ruiz Garcia, La obra novelistica de Jaime Torres Bodet (title means "The Novels of Jaime Torres Bodet"), Secretaria de Hacienda y Credito Publico, 1971, Texas Christian University Press, 1977; (author of preface) Delia Leonor M. Sutton, Antonio Caso y su impacto cultural en el intelecto mexicano (title means "Antonio Caso and His Cultural Impact on the Mexican Mind"), Texas Christian University Press, 1974; (author of preface) Cecilia Silva de Rodriguez, Vida y obra de Ermilo Abreu Gomez (title means "Life and Works of Ermilo Abreu Gomez"), Texas Christian University Press, 1975; (author of introduction) Brownson Malsch, Indianola: The Mother of Western Texas, Shoal Creek Publishers, 1977, 3rd edition, 1978.

Member of editorial advisory board of "The Papers of the Texas Revolution, 1835-1836," 1973. Contributor to Handbook of Texas and Encyclopaedia Britannica. Contributor of about one hundred articles to scholarly journals. Associate editor of Belton Journal, 1932-33; history editor of Texas Parade, 1948-49; founding editor of Arkansas Foreign Language Bulletin, 1954-56; member of editorial board of Boletin Bibliografico de la Secretaria de Hacienda y Credito Publico, 1969-74.

SIDELIGHTS: McLean writes: "Papers Concerning Robertson's Colony in Texas is the story of a piece of land and how it influenced the lives of men. Others have written of the men and what they did for the land, but this is an account of the land and what it did to the men. The characters may change, the scene may shift, but the constantly recurring theme is the lure of the land.

"This fascinating region occupied an area 100 miles wide and 200 miles long in the fertile valley of the rich old restless Brazos River in the heart of Texas. It came into being officially as Leftwich's Grant more than a century ago when Mexico was trying to colonize Texas under the empresario system. Later it was called the Nashville Colony, then the Upper Colony and, finally, Robertson's Colony. Today it is broken up into thirty counties.

"Men spent entire fortunes in a futile attempt to gain control of this region. For it, special commissioners spent years in chilly ante-rooms in Mexico City, brokers schemed in Wall Street, and politicians plotted in Washington. That it might change hands, perjury and libel were committed, the chink of coin lent its telling argument, and the would-be assassin's knife gleamed in the dark.

"From this maze of plots and counter-plots there emerged a sandy-haired Tennessean by the name of Sterling C. Robertson, who wore long silver spurs and a brace of Castilian pistols on his belt. Despite all opposition he managed to introduce hundreds of colonists into the region, many of them from his native state. Among the Tennesseans who were attracted to Texas by the lure of this land were George C. Childress, author of the Texas Declaration of Independence, and Sam Houston, commander-in-chief of the victorious Texas Army at San Jacinto. The story of the extraordinary influence which this region exercised over the lives of men is recounted in the documents reproduced here in these volumes, written by the participants themselves.

"Every reader will find here something that he did not know, and some of our most eager historians will find more than they wanted to know, for some of their history-book heroes are going to emerge from the printed page as three-dimensional human beings of flesh and blood. May these readers have sufficient breadth of vision to encompass the grandeur of their favorites in this new dimension, and enough understanding to forgive them for their weaknesses."

BIOGRAPHICAL/CRITICAL SOURCES: Hispanic American Historical Review, February, 1954, February, 1955.

* * *

McLENDON, Winzola Poole

PERSONAL: Born in Cardwell, Mo.; daughter of Mactie Ulysses and Ethel (Romines) Poole; married John Benjamin McLendon, August 6, 1953; children: Martha Elizabeth Beardsley. *Education:* Attended public schools in Long Beach, Calif. *Home and office:* 414-B Westchester, 4000 Cathedral Ave. N.W., Washington, D.C. 20016.

CAREER: Honolulu Advertiser, Honolulu, Hawaii, columnist, 1950-51; *Philadelphia Inquirer,* Philadelphia, Pa., columnist, 1951-53; *Washington Post,* Washington, D.C., staff reporter, 1954-67; writer, 1967—. *Member:* American Newspaper Women's Club, White House Correspondents Association, Washington Press Club, Theta Sigma Phi.

WRITINGS: (With Scottie Fitzgerald Smith) *Don't Quote Me!,* Dutton, 1970; *Martha: The Life of Martha Mitchell,* Random House, 1979. Contributor of articles to *McCall's, Good Housekeeping, Ladies' Home Journal, Town and Country, Family Circle,* and others.

WORK IN PROGRESS: A book for Random House.

SIDELIGHTS: Commenting on breaking into the field of journalism, McLendon told *CA:* "It seems to be a good idea to start early. When Scottie and I were writing *Don't Quote Me!,* we were amazed at the number of newswomen (the book was about Washington newswomen) who had worked on their high school papers—I started as managing editor of my *junior* high paper."

BIOGRAPHICAL/CRITICAL SOURCES: Los Angeles Times Book Review, July 15, 1979.

* * *

McPOLK, Andre (Hans) 1935-

PERSONAL: Born February 6, 1935, in Ludlow, Mass.; son of Palmero (a lexicographer) and Irma (Fluellen) McPolk; married Hilda Doalot (a poet), September 29, 1961; children: E. Brooks, Edwin N., Mario P. *Education:* Legein College,

B.A., 1956, M.A., 1958. *Home and office:* 221 Lewiston Rd., Grosse Pointe Farms, Mich. 48236.

CAREER: Libro's Books, Mahanoy City, Pa., salesman, 1955-57; teacher of English, linguistics, and Romance languages in public schools in Delphos, Ohio, Thorold, Ontario, and Quincy, Mich., 1958-76; free-lance writer, critic, and editor, 1976—. Lecturer at colleges and universities, 1972-75; consultant to publishing firms, including Oratio Press and Phonein Publishing Co. *Member:* Association of Midwestern Linguists, Writers Against Rhetoric (WAR). *Awards, honors:* Bronze Quill from Writers Against Rhetoric, 1973, for *Far Out: Language and the Counterculture of the Sixties.*

WRITINGS: Rhetoric for High Schoolers, Oratio Press, 1965; *Latin Revisited,* Oratio Press, 1967; *Parlez-Vous Too?* (for children), Hors d'Oeuvres Presse, 1972; *Far Out: Language and the Counterculture of the Sixties,* Hyperbole Publications, 1973; *Homeric Homonyms,* Oratio Press, 1978. Contributor to lexicography journals.

WORK IN PROGRESS: "A 'Who's Who' of popular poets who, at one time or another, have wallowed in obscurity"; a biography of John Simon.

SIDELIGHTS: McPolk told *CA:* "A primary concern of importance to me has been to purge written English of all effusive and redundant tendencies which tend to serve as hindrances to direct and noncircumlocutory communication. During my years spent teaching in high schools located in the eastern and midwestern United States, I was appalled at the shocking disintegration of students' ability to compose even the most simple and unburdensome paragraph without committing an abundance of sins of style and grammar. I was rather annoyed with these pupils' performances with the pen, perturbed especially at the fact that they were often incapable of spelling words properly as well. These problems I am attributing to the prolificity of television and relaxed—or, should I say, virtually nonexistent—standards of discipline in education, which are pernicious byproducts of student revolts which occurred in the late 1960's and early 1970's as well.

"It really goes without saying that what is necessary in these beleagured times is an all-out effort to thrust English education back to the basics: reading and writing. To do this is imperative. The time has now come for a multilateral organizational effort between teachers, television executives, journalists, and other media personnel to get their heads together and come up with a consistently uniform example of model English for our blighted students to follow and—hopefully—to emulate."

* * *

MEDVED, Harry 1961(?)-

PERSONAL: Born c. 1961 in San Diego, Calif.; son of David (a physicist) and Renate (a chemist; maiden name, Hirsch) Medved. *Education:* Student at University of California, Los Angeles. *Politics:* "Slightly to the left of James Madison." *Religion:* Jewish. *Agent:* Arthur Pine Associates, Inc., 1780 Broadway, New York, N.Y. 10019. *Office:* 1224 Ashland Ave., Santa Monica, Calif. 90405.

CAREER: Writer, 1978—. *Member:* American Federation of Television and Radio Artists.

WRITINGS: The Fifty Worst Films of All Time, Popular Library, 1978; (with brother, Michael Medved) *The Golden Turkey Awards: The Worst Achievements in Cinema History Receive Their Proper Recognition,* Putnam, 1980. Contributor to *Book of Lists.*

SIDELIGHTS: Medved commented: "I am fortunate to have an older brother who is a professional writer and has done his duty in bringing me into the family business. I've been interested in film since the age of four, with 'cinematic worsts' a consistent specialty."

*   *   *

MEEHL, Paul E(verett) 1920-

PERSONAL: Born January 3, 1920, in Minneapolis, Minn.; son of Otto John (a clerk) and Blanche (Duncan) Swedal; married Alyce Roworth, September 6, 1941 (died, 1972); married Leslie Jane Yonce (a psychologist), November 17, 1973; children: Karen Meehl Hill, Erik. *Education:* University of Minnesota, B.A., 1941, Ph.D., 1945. *Politics:* Libertarian. *Home:* 1544 East River Ter., Minneapolis, Minn. 55414. *Office:* Mayo Box 392, University of Minnesota, Minneapolis, Minn. 55455.

CAREER: University of Minnesota, Minneapolis, assistant professor, 1945-48, associate professor, 1948-52, professor of psychology, 1952-68, chairman of department of psychology, 1951-57, adjunct professor of law, 1967—, Regents' Professor, 1968—, professor of philosophy, 1971—. Private practice of psychotherapy at Nicollet Clinic, 1970—. *Member:* American Psychological Association (president, 1962), Psychometric Society, American Psychology-Law Society, Classification Society, Philosophy of Science Association, American Academy of Arts and Sciences. *Awards, honors:* Two distinguished contributor awards from American Psychological Association, 1958, 1967, for published research and theory of diagnosis and prediction, and distinguished scientist award, 1976.

WRITINGS: Atlas for the Clinical Use of MMPI, University of Minnesota Press, 1951; *Clinical Versus Statistical Prediction,* University of Minnesota Press, 1954; *Modern Learning Theory,* Appleton, 1954; *What Then Is Man?,* Concordia, 1958; *Psychodiagnosis,* University of Minnesota Press, 1973; *Taxometrics and Schizoidia,* Academic Press, 1980. Contributor to philosophy, psychology, law, and genetics journals.

WORK IN PROGRESS: Revising *Clinical Versus Statistical Prediction,* for University of Minnesota Press.

SIDELIGHTS: Meehl comments: "I was attracted to psychology in my teens by reading Freud. I was trained at Minnesota in a tough-minded behavioristic and statistical tradition. Much of my work has been a struggle to integrate—to be scientific about the complex human mind. I write for me, plus a tiny minority of first-class psychologists."

*   *   *

MEEKS, M(errill) Douglas 1941-

PERSONAL: Born April 24, 1941, in Memphis, Tenn.; son of Merrill Douglas (a railroad official) and Evelyn (an art shop proprietor; maiden name, Yost) Meeks; married Helen Blair Gilmer (a teacher), June 5, 1963; children: Merrill Douglas III, John William. *Education:* Attended Vanderbilt University, 1959-60; Southwestern College at Memphis, B.A., 1963; Duke University, B.D., 1966, Ph.D., 1968; postdoctoral study at University of Tuebingen, 1968-70. *Religion:* United Methodist. *Home:* 121 Park Rd., St. Louis, Mo. 63119. *Office:* Department of Systematic Theology and Philosophy, Eden Theological Seminary, 475 East Lockwood, St. Louis, Mo. 63119.

CAREER: Ordained United Methodist minister, 1964; assistant pastor in Durham, N.C., and Clifton Forge, Pa.; Duke University, Durham, instructor in theology, 1966-68; Huntingdon College, Montgomery, Ala., assistant professor of philosophy and religion, 1970-71; Eden Theological Seminary, St. Louis, Mo., assistant professor, 1971-74, associate professor, 1974-78, professor of systematic theology and philosophy, 1978—. Member of directorate of United Church Office for Church and Society. *Member:* Karl Barth Society of North America, American Academy of Religion (chairperson of Liberation Theology Group), American Society of Christian Ethics, American Theological Society, Society for Values in Higher Education. *Awards, honors:* Fulbright fellowship for West Germany, 1968-70.

WRITINGS: (Translator) Juergey Moltmann, *Religion, Revolution, and the Future,* Scribner, 1969; *Origins of the Theology of Hope,* Fortress, 1974; (editor and translator) Moltmann, *The Experiment Hope,* Fortress, 1975; (translator) Gerhard M. Martin, *Fest: The Transformation of Everyday,* Fortress, 1977; (editor and translator) Moltmann, *The Passion for Life: A Messianic Lifestyle,* Fortress, 1978; *Hope for the Church,* Abingdon, 1979. Contributor of articles and reviews to theology journals.

WORK IN PROGRESS: Research for books on the church and the city and on theology and economics, for Fortress Press.

SIDELIGHTS: Meeks told *CA:* "My present research and writing deal with the Church's mission within the city. It is often thought that the Bible gives the city a 'bad press' as the center of all human sin, and we usually think of church and city in disjunction. But biblical traditions stress that while the first 'earth creatures' began in a garden, their ultimate destiny is the city created by God. God accepts the human decision to build and live in cities as a kind of counter-creation. This decision culminates in the image of the ultimate 'new creation' in the form of the 'new city.' All of creation aims at and finds its completion in the 'new city,' and I am attempting to show the ways in which the church is called to bring that city into being.

"My writing in the area of theology and economics is an attempt to work out the biblical 'logic of superabundance' over and against every economic theory which begins with the assumption of scarcity."

*   *   *

MELLICHAMP, Josephine 1923-

PERSONAL: Born September 30, 1923, in Helton, N.C.; daughter of James Thomas Hampton (a farmer) and Bonnie Clyde (a teacher; maiden name, Bauguess) Weaver; married F. M. Stafford Smith, December 15, 1944 (divorced, 1959); married Stiles A. Mellichamp, Sr. (a sales representative), December 16, 1961; children: Stiles A., Jr. and Joseph Capers III (stepsons). *Education:* Emory and Henry College, A.B. (cum laude), 1943; graduate study at Emory University, 1950-51. *Religion:* Methodist. *Home:* 1124 Reeder Circle N.E., Atlanta, Ga. 30306.

CAREER: High school English teacher in Lansing, N.C., 1943-48, and Jefferson, N.C., 1948-50; Emory University, Atlanta, Ga., editorial assistant in Office of Public Information, 1951-53; free-lance writer, 1953-57; *Atlanta Journal and Constitution,* Atlanta, Ga., librarian in reference department, 1957-66, assistant head librarian, 1966-79; writer, 1979—. *Member:* National League of American Pen Women, Southeastern Writers Association, Dixie Council of Authors and Journalists, Atlanta Writers Club. *Awards, honors:* Named Georgia nonfiction author of the year by Dixie Council of Authors and Journalists, 1976, for *Senators From Georgia.*

WRITINGS: Senators From Georgia, Strode, 1976; *Georgia Heritage*, Strode, 1980. Contributor of articles and children's stories to newspapers and magazines, including *Georgia, Constitution, Birmingham News, Modern Woodmen, Grit*, and *Atlanta Journal*.

WORK IN PROGRESS: A biography of Georgian Anne Nichols, author of "Abie's Irish Rose"; *Flukey*, a children's book on oceanography; *Winklewood and Other Stories*, a children's book.

SIDELIGHTS: Josephine Mellichamp told *CA:* "Before researching and writing *Senators From Georgia*, I neither expected to present history nor to find it so fascinating I would want to present more. Until then, I had lived in a world laced with fantasy, and to me every road was a ribbon of enchantment leading to some fairy castle. I never looked back.

"I wrote my first little book when I was about eight years old. There were no reprints, no royalties, and no readers except my parents. But ever since, I have enjoyed putting my thoughts on paper, for I just knew I was born to write. A writer is what he writes and writes what he is, I said, and kept writing what I thought I was. However, few publishers cared how I made a rainbow.

"I'm glad I kept circling that rainbow, for at its end was a publisher looking for a certain kind of writer—one who would write about what he wanted to publish. He was looking for a certain non-scholarly style, for a history book with lots of anecdotes. So, going from fantasy to fact, I did my research, put one word after another, and came up with *Senators From Georgia*. If the reader becomes better informed about these fifty-two men and one woman (the nation's first female United States Senator), my purpose has been achieved."

BIOGRAPHICAL/CRITICAL SOURCES: Constitution, December 24, 1976; *Georgia Life*, winter, 1976; *Skylark Post*, January 27, 1977; *Enquirer and Ledger*, July 4, 1978; *Headliner*, June, 1979.

*　　*　　*

MELLINI, Peter 1935-

PERSONAL: Born August 16, 1935, in Hermosa Beach, Calif.; son of Oscarre (a sea captain) and Helen (an art teacher; maiden name, Scheck) Mellini; married Verna Adams (an attorney), December, 1970 (divorced December, 1975); married Gisela Doppelgatz (a flight attendant), October 7, 1977. *Education:* Stanford University, B.A., 1962, M.A., 1965, Ph.D., 1971. *Politics:* "Generally Democrat." *Home:* 141 Ward St., Larkspur, Calif. 94939. *Agent:* Michael Larson/Elizabeth Pomada, 1029 Jones St., San Francisco, Calif. 94109. *Office:* Department of History, Sonoma State University, Rohnert Park, Calif. 94939.

CAREER: Stanford University, Stanford, Calif., instructor in history, 1968-70; Sonoma State University, Rohnert Park, Calif., assistant professor, 1970-73, associate professor, 1973-79, professor of history, 1979—. Consultant to Monterey County, Calif. *Military service:* U.S. Army, 1956-58; served in Germany. *Member:* National Trust for Historic Preservation, Conference on British Studies, United Oxford and Cambridge University Club.

WRITINGS: Sir Eldon Gorst: The Overshadowed Proconsul, Hoover Institution, 1977; (with Kent L. Seavey) *Historic Preservation Field School: Jolon California*, Monterey County Department of Parks, 1979; (with Roy T. Matthews) *In Vanity Fair*, Scolar Press, 1980. Reviewer for history journals; columnist for local papers.

WORK IN PROGRESS: Research on British/English caricature and on nineteenth-century photography; *Marin County in Words and Pictures.*

SIDELIGHTS: Mellini comments: "*In Vanity Fair* emerged from the search for illustrations for my first book and led to my assembling a major collection of these lithographs. For the moment, my writing is concentrated on my locale, where I hope to reach a larger audience, using not only prose but color photography.

"To return to the *Vanity Fair* caricatures, few tasks have been so rewarding, even before publication. My co-author and I learned more history, met a number of delightful people, and now feel that our book will be of interest to a wide variety of types. As wide, we hope, as the caricatures themselves."

In reviewing Mellini's *Sir Eldon Gorst*, critic Robert Heussler said the author "threads his way through the minefield of intrigue, emotionalism, naivete, and misconception with perspicacity and skill. . . . The conclusions of this valuable book are just, for all their ferocity."

AVOCATIONAL INTERESTS: European travel, photography, newspapers ("I am a newspaper junkie").

BIOGRAPHICAL/CRITICAL SOURCES: American Historical Review, October, 1978.

*　　*　　*

MELTZOFF, Nancy 1952-

PERSONAL: Born March 26, 1952, in New York, N.Y.; daughter of Julian (a psychologist) and Judith (a psychologist; maiden name, Novikoff) Meltzoff. *Education:* Simmons College, B.A., 1974; University of Redlands, M.A., 1977; also attended Chapman College, World Campus Afloat. *Home:* 1650 16th St., Apt. F-301, Newport Beach, Calif. 92663.

CAREER: Substitute teacher at elementary schools in Huntington Beach and Newport Beach, Calif., both 1975-76; Village View School, Huntington Beach, teacher, 1976-79; writer. Nursery school teacher, summer, 1975; public speaker. *Member:* Society of Children's Book Writers, Southern California Council on Literature for Children and Young People.

WRITINGS: A Sense of Balance (juvenile novel), Westminster, 1978.

WORK IN PROGRESS: An adult book on weight control; an adult romance; three novels for young people, *Legs, A Summer Story, Smokejumpers.*

SIDELIGHTS: Nancy Meltzoff told *CA:* "What drives me to write is my desire to reach young people. Young teenagers and I seem to be attracted to each other. I like to watch young people reading one of my books, and see them cry or laugh. They are so alive, so present in their lives; they are giving and are able to receive.

"I taught eighth grade for three years, but found that teachers spend more time and energy being secretaries, disciplinarians, and 'adults' than being listening, responding 'people.' Close relationships with students, exploring their dreams and fears, and urging them to love books, kept me deeply involved, but now I want to reach a greater audience through writing.

"I like to include my interest in sports in novels for girls. Young women are involved in athletics as never before, and I am eager to promote this as much as I can.

"My major message to young people is that they are okay.

No matter what anyone says, no matter what they tend to believe about themselves, they are okay and someone cares. Underneath all the bravado of the teens there is a strong current of self-doubt. I'd like to help teenagers swim past that current rather than be trapped in it.''

AVOCATIONAL INTERESTS: Travel, athletics (gymnastics, skiing, water sports), the sea, reading.

* * *

MENSHIKOV, Marina 1928(?)-1979

OBITUARY NOTICE: Born c. 1928; died November 6, 1979, in Moscow, U.S.S.R. Scholar, editor, translator, and author. Menshikov, who worked for the United Nations as an editor and translator, was one of the first Soviet scholars to study American agriculture. She was the author of *Capital Accumulation and Technical Revolution in United States Agriculture* and *Structural Change in United States Agriculture.* Obituaries and other sources: *New York Times,* December 7, 1979.

* * *

MENZEL, Roderich 1907-
(Clemens Parma)

PERSONAL: Born April 13, 1907, in Reichenberg, Czechoslovakia; son of Ernst (in business) and Leopoldine (Kahl) Menzel; divorced; children: Michael, Christian, Renate, Carola, Peter. *Education:* Attended business schools in Czechoslovakia. *Religion:* "Self-Realization." *Home:* Gartenstrasse 12, D-8120 Weilheim, West Germany. *Office:* Pacellistrasse 8/III, Munich 2, West Germany.

CAREER: Writer in Prague, Czechoslovakia, 1927-38; *Reichsrundfunk,* Berlin, Germany, sub-editor, 1939-45; Military Government, interpreter and instructor in Friedberg, Germany, 1945-48, and Munich, Germany, 1946-48; *Echo der Woche,* Munich, chief editor of culture, 1948-51; editor of culture for *Das Schoenste,* 1953-55; chief editor of culture for *Wissen,* 1961-62; writer, 1962—. *Military service:* Czechoslovak Army, 1929-31.

MEMBER: International Academy of Poets, Freie Deutsche Autoren (vice-president), Knut Hamsun Society, Die Kogge, Red and White Tennis Club. *Awards, honors:* Greif Medal from Sudeten Germans in Czechoslovakia, 1934; first prize from Ministry of the Interior, 1962, for best children's book; Stifter Medal from Adalbert Stifter Society, 1962, for best literature; Liebieg Medal from Reichenberger Society, 1968, for *Liebe zu Boehmen;* Leutelt Medal from Polzen-Neisse-Niederland, 1970; Sudeten German prize from Sudeten German Organization, 1970; certificate of merit from Biographical Centre of Cambridge, 1974; Lodgman Medal from speaker of Sudeten Germans, 1977, for *Als Boehmen noch bei Oesterreich war: Die Tannhoffs—Roman einer Familie;* Pforten Prize for literature, 1978; more than three hundred tennis awards, including Davis Cup victories, and championships in Germany, Czechoslovakia, Egypt, India, Greece, Hungary, Yugoslavia, and France.

WRITINGS: (Under pseudonym Clemens Parma) *Der wandernde Schuh,* Parabel, 1964, translation published as *Wandering Shoe,* Lerner, 1966.

Not in English: Zwischen Mensch und Gott (poems; title means "Between Man and God"), H. Meister, 1937; *Mit Schlaeger und Schreibmaschine, Tennisaufsaetze und Tennisgeschichten* (title means "With Racket and Typewriter"), 2nd edition, H. Meister, 1942; *Ein Mann—wie neugeboren!: Ein vorwiegend heiterer Sport-Roman* (title means "A Man

Like New-born"), R. Moelich, 1947; *Gesaenge und Balladen* (poems; title means "Songs and Ballads"), R. Moelich, 1948.

Abenteuer, Geheimnis und grosse Fahrt (title means "Adventure, Secrets, and Great Peril"), C. Wegner, 1952; *Maenner, die Krebs bekaempfen* (title means "Men Against Cancer"), Kindler & Schiermeyer, 1953; *Geliebte Tennispartnerin: Zeichnungen Karlheinz Grindler* (title means "Beloved Tennis-Partner"), W. Limpert, 1957; *Die Maenner sind so wankelmuetig, und andere lustige Geschichten* (title means "Men Are So Fickle, and Other Funny Stories"), Schmitz, 1958; *Lied am Brunnenrand* (poems; title means "Song on the Edge of the Well"), H. Meister, 1958.

Weltmeister auf dem Eis: Kilius/Baeumler (title means "World Champions on Ice: Kilius/Baeumler"), F. Schneider, 1963; *Wunder geschehen jeden Tag* (title means "Miracles Happen Every Day"), [Germany], 1958, revised edition published as *Die Herren von Morgen: Neue Wege der Forschung* (title means "New Ways of Research Work"), Lichtenberg, 1963; *Geheimer Treffpunkt: Waldhuette* (title means "Hidden Meeting Place: Hut in the Forest"), F. Schneider, 1964; *Mein Fussball und ich* (title means "My Football and I"), F. Schneider, 1964; *Ruhm war ihr Begleiter: Die kuehnsten Expeditionen unserer Zeit* (title means "Glory Was Their Companion: The Boidest Expeditions in Our Time"), Hoch, 1964; *Schneewittchen: Nach dem Maerchen der Brueder Grimm in Verse gebracht* (title means "Snow White: Fairy Tale in Verse From the Brothers Grimm"), Peters, 1964; (with Johanna Sengler) *Neue Ruebezahl-Geschichten* (fairy tales; title means "New Ruebezahl Tales"), Aufstieg-Verlag, 1965; *Sportregeln: Die jeder kennen sollte* (title means "Sports Rules That Everybody Should Know"), F. Schneider, 1966; *Leo der Loewe* (title means "Leo the Lion"), Sellier, 1966; *Zotti der Baer* (title means "Zotti the Bear"), Sellier, 1966; *Meine Freunde, die Weltmeister* (title means "My Friends, The World Champions"), Hoch, 1966; *Sie haben die Welt verzaubert* (title means "They Have Enchanted the World"), F. Pustet, 1967; (with Sengler) *Maerchenreise ins Sudetenland: Ein neuer, bunter Maerchenschatz* (fairy tales; title means "Fairy-tale Voyage Into Sudetenland"), Aufstieg-Verlag, 1967; *Mario und Grissi,* Sellier, 1967; (with Sengler) *Der fliegende Teppich* (title means "The Flying Carpet"), F. Pustet, 1968; *Adam schuf die Erde neu: Ein Buch von der schoepferischen Veraenderung der Erdoberflaeche in unserer Zeit* (title means "Adam Creates the Earth Anew"), Econ-Verlag, 1968; *Sabu spielt die Hirtenfloete* (fairy tale; title means "Sabu Plays the Shepherd's Flute"), A. Betz, 1968; *Sieben mal Sieben: Weltwunder* (title means "Seven Times Seven World Wonders"), Hoch, 1968; *Heimat und Volk im Zeitalter der Raumfahrt* (title means "Homeland and People in the Times of Spaceflight"), Witikobund, 1969.

Die besten elf Skilaeufer (title means "The Eleven Best Skiers"), Hoch, 1970; *Bis ans Ende der Welt: Die Eroberung der Erde durch die Eisenbahn* (title means "To the End of the World: The Conquest of the World by the Railway"), Hoch, 1971; *Der Vogelkoenig* (fairy tales; title means "The Bird King"), [Germany], 1972; *Als Boehmen noch bei Oesterreich war: Die Tannhoffs—Roman einer Familie* (novel; first volume of the trilogy; title means "When Bohemia Belonged to Austria: The Tannhoffs, A Family Saga"), Amalthea, 1972; *Liebe zu Boehmen* (title means "Love for Bohemia"), Sudpress, 1972; *Staerker als tausend Pferde: Der Siegeszug des Automobils* (title means "Stronger Than One Thousand Horses: The Victorious March of the Automobile"), Hoch, 1972; *Maenner gegen Eis und Wueste: Expedi-*

tionen und Abenteuer (title means "Men Against Ice and Deserts: Expeditions and Adventures"), Kraft, 1974; *Oesterreichische Maerchen* (title means "Austrian Fairy Tales"), [Germany], 1978; *Der Pulverturm* (novel; second volume of the trilogy; title means "The Powder Tower"), [Germany], 1978; *Schlesische Maerchen* (title means Silesian Fairy Tales"), [Germany], 1979; *Die Sieger* (novel; third volume of the trilogy; title means "The Victors"), Amalthea, 1980. Also author of *Mit Glanz und Gloria* (title means "With Glow and Glory").

Under pseudonym Clemens Parma: *Ein Herz fuer das Volk: Die Geschichte der Koenigin von Griechenland* (title means "A Heart for the People: The Story of the Queen of Greece, Friederike"), Kindler, 1956; *Max Reinhardt: Ein Lebensbild* (title means "Max Reinhardt: A Living Picture"), Pforten-Verlag, 1959; *Pitt und das verzauberte Fahrrad* (fairy tale; title means "Pitt and the Enchanted Bicycle"), Obpacher, 1963; *Peter und die Turmuhr* (title means "Peter and the Tower Clock"), Parabel Verlag, 1966; *Kitti das Kaetzchen* (fairy tale; title means "Kaetzchen the Kitten"), Sellier, 1966; *Juri das Zauberpony: Eine Geschichte* (fairy tale; title means "The Magic Pony"), Sellier, 1966; *Thomas der grosse Fussballheld* (a modern fairy tale; title means "Thomas, The Great Football Hero"), Globi-Verlag, 1968. Contributor to magazines. Editor of *Die Tennisbuehne*, 1932-33.

WORK IN PROGRESS: Writing on history, Christianity, music, natural medicine, tennis, football, skiing.

SIDELIGHTS: Menzel told *CA:* "I have been influenced by Nikolai Lesskow and Knut Hamsun in literature, Mozart and Bruckner in music, da Vinci and Hobbema in painting, King Ashoka as a model ruler, and Yogananda as a spiritual leader.

"I have learned of human nature from my world travels as a tennis player and from the study of history. I have tried to defend humanity (often in vain, as with the Czechs and Jews in the time of the Nazis) and to correct the false conception of history. I love children, fight against Communism, and for truth."

Some of Menzel's books have been translated into fourteen languages.

* * *

MERLE, Robert (Jean Georges) 1908-

PERSONAL: Born August 29, 1908, in Tebessa, Algeria; son of Felix (an interpreter) and Eugenie (Ollagne) Merle; married third wife, Magali Boudou; children: (second marriage) Francoise, Philippe, Pierre, Olivier; (third marriage) Frederic. *Education:* Sorbonne, University of Paris, received licentiate and doctorate degrees; also attended University of Cleveland. *Home:* La Malmaison, 78125 Grosrouvre, France. *Office:* Faculty of Letters, University of Paris X, 200 Avenue de la Republique, 92000 Nanterre, France.

CAREER: Novelist, dramatist, critic, and biographer. Teacher of English literature at high schools in Bordeaux, France, 1934-36, and Neuilly, France, 1936-39; University of Rennes, Rennes, France, professor of English and American literature, 1949-57; University of Toulouse, Toulouse, France, professor of English and American literature, 1957-60; University of Caen, Caen, France, professor of English and American literature, c. 1960-63; University of Rouen, Rouen, France, professor of English and American literature, c. 1960-63; University of Algiers, Algiers, Algeria, pro-

fessor of English and American literature, 1963-65; University of Paris X, Nanterre, France, professor of English and American literature, 1965—. *Military service:* French Army, 1939-43; prisoner of war, 1940-43; received Croix du combattant. *Awards, honors:* Prix Goncourt, 1949, for *Weekend a Zuydcoote;* Prix de la Fraternite, 1962, for *L'Ile;* Prix Franz Hellens, 1974, for *Les Hommes proteges.*

WRITINGS—In English: *Weekend a Zuydcoote,* Gallimard, 1949, translation by K. Rebillon-Lambley published as *Weekend at Zuydcoote,* Lehmann, 1950, published as *Weekend at Dunkirk,* Knopf, 1951; *La Mort est mon metier,* Gallimard, 1952, translation by Alan Ross published as *Death Is My Trade,* Verschoyle, 1954; *L'Ile,* Gallimard, 1962, translation by Humphrey Hare published as *The Island,* St. Martin's, 1964; *Ahmed Ben Bella,* Gallimard, 1965, translation by Camilla Sykes published under same title, Walker & Co., 1967; *Un Animal doue de raison,* Gallimard, 1967, translation by Helen Weaver published as *The Day of the Dolphin,* Simon & Schuster, 1969; *Derriere la vitre,* Gallimard, 1970, translation by Derek Coltman published as *Behind the Glass,* Simon & Schuster, 1972; *Malevil,* translation by Coltman published under same title, Simon & Schuster, 1974; *Les Hommes proteges,* Gallimard, 1974, translation by Martin Sokolinsky published as *The Virility Factor,* McGraw-Hill, 1977.

Other works: *Oscar Wilde: Appreciation d'une oeuvre et d'une destinee* (title means "Oscar Wilde: Appreciation of a Life's Work and of a Destiny"), Hachette, 1948; *Theatre 1* (collected plays; contains "Falmineo," "Sisyphe et la mort," and "Les Sonderling"), Gallimard, 1950; *Theatre 2* (collected plays; contains "Nouveau Sisyphe," "Justice a Miramar," and "L'Assemblee des femmes"), Gallimard, 1950; *Oscar Wilde; ou, La 'Destinee' de l'homosexuel* (title means "Oscar Wilde; or, The 'Destiny' of the Homosexual"), Gallimard, 1955; *Vittoria princesse Orsini* (title means "Vittoria, Princess Orsini"), Del Duca, 1958; *Moncado, premier combat de Fidel Castro* (title means "Moncado, Fidel Castro's First Battle"), Laffont, 1965; *Madrapour* (novel), Editions du Seuil, 1976. Translator of works by John Webster, Jonathan Swift, Erskine Caldwell, and others.

SIDELIGHTS: Robert Merle has spent his working life as a teacher of English and American literature—in high schools before World War II and since then at a series of universities. His first book, which was also his doctoral thesis, was a study of Oscar Wilde. It was followed by something very different, a stark novel drawing on his own experiences during the war, when he was captured by the Germans at Zuydcoote, near Dunkirk. *Weekend a Zuydcoote* describes the Dunkirk debacle from the point of view of a French sergeant who tries to join the British withdrawal from the beaches. He fails, and then dies. It received the coveted Prix Goncourt and was praised for its vividness and deftness, "its qualities of unflinching honesty and understated compassion." Henri Peyre described Merle as "one of a number of French writers ... born and trained in North Africa who have lately brought new vigor into French fiction." It seemed to Peyre that *Weekend a Zuydcoote* revealed a close acquaintance with the modern American novel. He continued: "It was criticized [in France] as brutal, tough, and artificial, but wrongly so in our estimation. It is one of the few true, convincing, and even moving novels written as yet on the catastrophe of 1940." The book was filmed in 1965 by Twentieth Century-Fox.

La Mort est mon metier ("Death Is My Trade") is the imaginary autobiography of a dedicated Nazi, Rudolf Lang, who becomes the commandant of the Auschwitz death camp. It begins with his account of his appallingly bleak childhood, which teaches him, as one critic wrote, "that there is no peace but in obedience. . . . Once freed from his father's terrible will, [he] can only transfer his absolute submission to a more congenial master." This professional butcher, according to a reviewer in the *Times Literary Supplement*, "is honest, hard-working, fearless, loyal and ready for any sacrifice. What turns him into a monster is his utter lack of sense of proportion and his belief that his conscience was given him only so that he could surrender it to his superiors. . . . By blocking out the windows of common sense and leaving the reader alone in the darkness where the flames of fanaticism achieve an unnatural brightness," Lang is made credible and even understandable.

This "brilliant feat" was followed by *L'Ile* ("The Island"), an adventure story which is also a moral fable. It is about a party of mutineers who colonize a South Pacific island (much as the Bounty mutineers did Pitcairn). Several themes are examined in this long and ambitious novel, including the contrast between the innocence of the islanders and the corruption of the Europeans, the dangers of appeasement and collaboration (highly relevant in postwar France), and conflicts over power, sex, and territory. The book was found vivid, powerful, and highly readable, but seemed to some reviewers excessively long and marred at times by melodrama.

The corruption of innocence is studied in a different context in *Un Animal doue de raison* ("The Day of the Dolphin"), another Merle novel that has been adapted for the cinema (United Artists, 1973). A dedicated and brilliant scientist working in Florida manages to achieve the rudiments of communication with a pair of dolphins. This achievement, promising a new era in the relations between man and his fellow creatures on earth, is wickedly perverted when the Pentagon and the security services decide that Professor Sevilla's experiments have military and political possibilities. N. W. Ross called the book "an absorbing, unusual and blood-chilling novel."

Derriere la vitre ("Behind the Glass") adopts the "simultaneism" of John Dos Passos to give a fictional account of the political ferment that erupted in 1968 at the Nanterre campus of the University of Paris, where Merle teaches. Merle contrasts the political attitudinizing of the students with the real hardships of Algerian construction workers on the site, and shows how political fanaticism can turn people into slogan-ridden abstractions. Some reviewers, however, found the author's own point of view frustratingly ambivalent.

This was followed by *Malevil,* an ingenious and immensely readable fantasy about life after "the bomb." "Seldom has that old reader-pleaser—the dilemma of a group of survivors making do with what has survived with them—been in the hands of a more skillful suspense-builder," wrote Pamela Marsh. "And while M. Merle has us pinned to the page he shows his characters slowly growing, changing, developing into a community. His story, we soon discover, is more than just a well-plotted tale."

There was a more mixed reception for *Les Hommes proteges* ("The Virility Factor"), another instructive fantasy, which envisages an America ruled by a power-crazed woman president and a crew of fanatical feminists. The book, though it had its admirers, seemed to some readers no more than a caricature of the American political scene and of the feminist movement. One reviewer called it "not so much a nightmare as a private and ultimately rather delectable sexual fantasy on the part of the author."

AVOCATIONAL INTERESTS: Tennis, swimming, rowing.

BIOGRAPHICAL/CRITICAL SOURCES: Times Literary Supplement, April 21, 1950, March 20, 1953, December 10, 1954, December 14, 1962, January 15, 1971, June 2, 1972; Henri Peyre, *French Novelists of Today,* Oxford University Press, 1967; *New York Times Book Review,* July 3, 1977.*

* * *

MERLIN, David
See MOREAU, David Merlin

* * *

MESHACK, B(illie) A(ugusta) 1922-

PERSONAL: Born March 25, 1922, in Texas; son of Benjamin (a farmer and teacher) and Mary (Peterson) Meshack; married Lula M. Sanford; children: Phyllis Yvonne, Betty Laverne. *Education:* Attended Los Angeles City College, 1958-65; California State University, Dominguez Hills, B.A., 1973, M.A., 1975. *Politics:* Democrat. *Home:* 8214½ Hooper Ave., Los Angeles, Calif. 90001.

CAREER: Manager of family business, 1939-52; U.S. Postal Service, Los Angeles, Calif., mail carrier, 1952-76. Ordained Baptist minister, 1959; pastor of Baptist church in Los Angeles, 1959-71; Christian Missionary Baptist Church, Los Angeles, pastor, 1976—. Substitute teacher at local community colleges and adult schools. Chairperson of board of directors of Paradise Mortuary, 1972-78; member of Florence-Firestone Community Coordinating Council; member of advisory board of local Neighborhood Adult Participation Project. *Military service:* U.S. Army, 1943. *Member:* National Association for the Advancement of Colored People (NAACP), Urban League, Baptist Ministers Conference, Black Caucus of American Baptist Convention Churches, Southern Christian Leadership Conference. *Awards, honors:* Scribe of the year awards from *Angel City Carrier,* 1972, 1973.

WRITINGS: Is the Baptist Church Relevant to the Black Community?, R & E Research Associates, 1976. Author of a column in *Angel City Carrier,* 1966-76.

WORK IN PROGRESS: The Theological Imperative, a study of the validity of black people's quest for freedom as it relates to theological concepts proscribed in biblical literature.

SIDELIGHTS: Meshack writes: "In spite of the gains of black people toward freedom and equality, it has been observed that we are yet a long way from attaining the rights provided by the U.S. Constitution. Consequently, it becomes imperative that black people remain, or become, fully aware of their present status, as opposed to the status expressed as the 'will of God' for all peoples, thereby motivating them to continuous involvement. This view is based on both the proclamation of Jesus, as pronounced in Luke 4: 18-19, and his demonstration of those things he proclaimed throughout the Gospels."

* * *

MESHENBERG, Michael J(ay) 1942-

PERSONAL: Born April 15, 1942, in Brooklyn, N.Y.; son of Herman M. (in business) and Diane (Cohen) Meshenberg; married Kathryn A. Duffell (a health researcher), May 30, 1968; children: Ronald, Andrew, Alisa. *Education:* Brooklyn College of the City University of New York, B.A., 1963; University of Pennsylvania, M.C.P., 1965. *Politics:* Liberal Independent. *Religion:* Jewish. *Home:* 5524 South Kenwood

Ave., Chicago, Ill. 60637. *Office:* Argonne National Laboratory, 9700 South Cass Ave., Argonne, Ill. 60439.

CAREER: American Society of Planning Officials, Chicago, Ill., principal research associate, 1966-78; Argonne National Laboratory, Argonne, Ill., environmental scientist, 1978—. President of Hyde Park-Kenwood Community Conference, 1976. *Member:* American Planning Association.

WRITINGS: Health Planning and the Environment, American Society of Planning Officials, 1974; *Environmental Planning Information Guide,* Gale, 1976; *The Administration of Flexible Zoning Techniques,* American Society of Planning Officials, 1976; *The Language of Zoning: A Glossary of Words and Phrases,* American Society of Planning Officials, 1976.

*   *   *

MESSAGER, Charles   1882-1971
(Charles Vildrac)

OBITUARY NOTICE: Born November 23, 1882, in Paris, France; died June 25, 1971, in Saint-Tropez, France. Poet, essayist, and playwright. Vildrac is best known for his empathetic portrayal of the struggling classes in plays such as "The Steamer Tenacity." Obituaries and other sources: *The Reader's Encyclopedia,* 2nd edition, Crowell, 1965; *The Oxford Companion to French Literature,* corrected edition, Oxford University Press, 1966; *Everyman's Dictionary of European Writers,* Dent & Sons, 1968; *McGraw-Hill Encyclopedia of World Drama,* McGraw, 1972; *Modern World Drama: An Encyclopedia,* Dutton, 1972; *Cassell's Encyclopaedia of World Literature,* revised edition, Morrow, 1973.

*   *   *

METOS, Thomas H(arry)   1932-

PERSONAL: Born June 14, 1932, in Salt Lake City, Utah; son of Harry G. (a lawyer) and Grace (Milner) Metos; married Marilyn Oberg, September 3, 1955; children: Jeffery, Melissa. *Education:* University of Utah, B.S., 1954, M.S., 1958, Ph.D., 1963. *Home:* 1427 North Sunset Dr., Tempe, Ariz. 85281. *Office:* College of Education, Arizona State University, Tempe, Ariz. 85281.

CAREER: History teacher at public schools in Salt Lake City, Utah, 1954-62, curriculum supervisor, 1962-63; University of Utah, Salt Lake City, assistant professor of education, 1963-64; San Diego County Department of Schools, San Diego, Calif., curriculum coordinator in social studies, 1964-65; Arizona State University, Tempe, assistant professor, 1965-67, associate professor, 1967-71, professor of educational administration, 1965—, director of Research Services of Bureau of Educational Research and Services, 1965-78. Consultant to government agencies. *Member:* American Educational Research Association, National Conference of Professors of Educational Administration, Western Psychological Association. *Awards, honors:* Joint committee of National Science Teachers Association and Children's Book Council named *Exploring With Metrics* an outstanding science book for children in 1975, and named *Exploring With Solar Energy* in 1978.

WRITINGS—All for children: (With C. D. Montgomery) *Workbook: The Free and the Brave,* Rand McNally, 1967, 3rd edition, 1977; (with Montgomery) *Workbook: The Adventure of the American People,* Rand McNally, 1968; (with Gary Bitter) *Exploring With Metrics,* Messner, 1975; (with Bitter) *Exploring With the Pocket Calculator,* Messner, 1977; *Exploring With Solar Energy,* Messner, 1978.

Contributor: E. T. Demars, editor, *Utah School Organization and Administration,* University of Utah Press, 1964; Locke Bowman, editor, *Education for Volunteer Teachers,* Scottsdale, Ariz., 1971.

Co-author of film scripts: "Using the Pocket Calculator," Centron Corp., 1978; "Introducing the Pocket Calculator," Centron Corp., 1978; "Using the Pocket Calculator," Centron Corp., 1978. Contributor to school surveys and education journals. Editor of *Arizona Professor,* 1969-72; member of editorial review board of *Louisiana Education Research Journal,* 1977—.

WORK IN PROGRESS: A book on the impact of automation and automatic devices on society, publication by Messner.

SIDELIGHTS: Metos told *CA:* "I have found writing for children to be the most satisfying and challenging of tasks. It has given me the opportunity to research topics in depth that are of interest to me and that I would not probably investigate without the pressure of contracts and deadlines.

"Also, it has given me the opportunity to work with my own children in developing the manuscripts. I have relied heavily on their advice as to what will or will not work."

*   *   *

METTLER, George B(arry)   1934-

PERSONAL: Born May 18, 1934, in Tampa, Fla.; son of John H. (a manager) and Velma Grace (Hickman) Mettler; married Patsy Farrington, January, 1961 (divorced December, 1971); married Darlene Debault (a college English teacher), June 1, 1972; children: Jaime, Sean. *Education:* Loyola University, New Orleans, La., B.A., 1956; attended Mercer Law School, 1956-57; Stetson College of Law, J.D., 1961. *Agent:* Carole Abel, 160 West 87th St., New York, N.Y. 10024. *Office:* 412 East Madison, Suite 1211, Tampa, Fla. 33602.

CAREER: Federal Bureau of Investigation, Washington, D.C., special agent, 1961-62; private practice of law in Tampa, Fla., 1962-65; free-lance writer in the British West Indies, 1965-68; private practice of law in Tampa, 1968-70; free-lance writer in Europe, Mexico, and North Africa, 1970-73; Georgia University System, Macon, associate professor of criminal justice, 1973-79; free-lance writer with private practice of law in Tampa, 1979—. *Military service:* U.S. Army, 1958-60; became first lieutenant. *Member:* American Association of University Professors, Former Special Agents Association, Florida Bar Association, American Club (London, England).

WRITINGS: The Sensualist (novel), Dell, 1970; *The Handyman* (novel), Dell, 1971; *Carey and Julie* (novel), Dell, 1973; *Criminal Investigation,* Holbrook, 1977; *Down Home* (novel), Fawcett, 1980; *Criminology,* Harcourt, 1980; *Criminal Law and Procedure,* Holbrook, 1981. Author of column "Free Press-Fair Trial," 1978—.

WORK IN PROGRESS: A novel; two other books, *Criminology* and *Criminal Law and Procedures.*

SIDELIGHTS: Mettler writes: "I practice law full time, I write fiction and nonfiction obsessively, and I lecture on the subjects of criminal justice and creative writing at the drop of a hat. I travel incessantly." *Avocational interests:* Painting in oils, farming.

*   *   *

MEVES, Christa   1925-

PERSONAL: Born March 4, 1925, in Neumuenster, Germany (now West Germany); daughter of Carl and Else (Rohweder) Mittelstaedt; married Harald Meves (a doctor), December 18, 1946; children: Antje Meves Oppermann, Ulrike. *Education:* Received degrees from University of Breslau, 1943, University of Kiel, 1953, University of Hamburg, 1954, and Psychotherapeutic Institute of Hannover and Goettingen, 1955. *Religion:* Evangelical Lutheran. *Home:* Albertstrasse 14, 3110 Uelzen 1, West Germany.

CAREER: Child psychotherapist in private practice, Uelzen, Germany, 1960—. Co-editor of weekly magazine, *Rheinischer Merkur* (title means "Rhenanian Gazette"). *Awards, honors:* Wilhelm Boelsche medal; gold medal of Herderbuecherei; Niedersaechsischer Verdienstorden first class; Konrad-Adenauer prize.

WRITINGS—In English: Die Bibel antwortet uns in Bildern, Herder-Verlag, 1973, translation by Hal Taussig published as *The Bible Answers Us With Pictures,* Westminster Press, 1977.

Other: *Die Schulnoete unserer Kindern: Wie Eltern ihnen vorbeungen abhelfen koennen,* Furche-Verlag, 1969, 4th edition, Guetersloher Verlagshaus Mohn, 1976; *Mit zum Erziehen: Erfahrungen aus der psychagogischen Praxis* (title means "Courage for Education: Experiences in Psychological Work"), Furche-Verlag, 1970; (with Joachim Illies) *Lieben, was ist das?: Ein Grenzgespraeche zwischen Biologie und Psychologie* (title means "Love—What Does It Mean? Biological and Physical Aspects"), Herder-Verlag, 1970; *Manipulierte Masslosigkeit: Psychologie Gefahren im technistierten Leben* (title means "Manipulated Uncontrollability: Psychic Dangers in Technological Life"), Herder-Verlag, 1971, revised edition, 1975; *Erziehen lernen in tiefenpsychologischer Sicht* (title means "Learning to Educate"), Bayerischer Schulbuch-Verlag, 1971, revised edition, 1973; *Erziehen und Erzaelen* (title means "Educating and Telling"), Kreuz-Verlag, 1971; *Verhaltensstoerungen bei Kindern* (title means "Behavioral Disturbances in Children"), Piper-Verlag, 1971; *Wunschtraum und Wirklichkeit* (title means "Illusion and Reality"), Herder-Verlag, 1972; *Ich reise fuer die Zukunft: Vortragserfahrungen und Erlebnisse einer Psychagogin* (title means "I Travel for the Future: Life of a Psychagogin"), Herder-Verlag, 1973.

Ehe-Alphabet (title means "Alphabet of Marriage"), Herder-Verlag, 1973; *Ermutingung zum Leben* (title means "Encouragement for Life"), Kreuz-Verlag, 1974; *Ich will leben: Briefe an Martina* (title means "I Want to Live!"), Verlag Weisses Kreuz, 1974; *Wer passt zu mir?* (title means "Who Is Suited to Me?"), Verlag Weisses Kreuz, 1974; *Ninive darf nicht untergehen* (title means "Ninive Must not Die!"), Verlag Weisses Kreuz, 1974; *Erziehung zur Reife und Verantwortung* (title means "Education for Maturity and Responsibility"), Verlag Weisses Kreuz, 1974; *Kinderschicksal in unserer Hand: Erfahrungen aus der psychagogie* (title means "Children's Fate in Our Hand: Experiences in a Psychagogian Practice"), Herder-Verlag, 1974; *Freiheit will gelernt sein* (title means "Freedom Must Be Learned"), Herder-Verlag, 1975; (with Joachim Illies) *Mit der Agression leben* (title means "To Live With Aggressions"), Herder-Verlag, 1975.

Unser Leben muss anders werden (title means "Our Life Must Change"), Herder-Verlag, 1976; *Lange Schatten—helles Licht* (title means "Long Shadows—Bright Light"), Herder-Verlag, 1976; *Wer wirft den ersten Stein?* (title means "Who Throws the First Stone?"), Verlag Weisses Kreuz, 1977; *Chancen und Krisen der modernen Ehe* (title means "Chances and Crisis of Modern Mar

riage"), Verlag Weisses Kreuz, 1977; *Antrieb, Charakter, Erziehung: Werden wir ein Volk Neurotikern?* (title means "Shall We Become a Nation of Neurotics?"), Fromm-Verlag, 1977; *Antworten Sie gleich* (title means "Please, Answer Soon"), Herder-Verlag, 1977; *Typisch Mutter* (title means "Typical Mother"), Herderbuecherei, 1978; (with H. D. Ortlieb) *Macht Gleichheit gluecklich?* (title means "Makes Equality Happy?"), Herderbuecherei, 1978; *Seelische Gesundheit und biblisches Heil* (title means "Psychic Healthiness and Biblic Salvation"), Herder-Verlag, 1979; *So ihr nicht werdet wile die Kinder,* Kreuz-Verlag, 1979. Also author of, with Lothar Kaiser, *Zeitloses Mass in massloser Zeit* (title means "Timeless Measure in Measureless Time"), 1976.

Contributor of numerous articles to journals.

SIDELIGHTS: Christa Meves told *CA* that she has attempted to demonstrate and promote the concept that nonobservance of the biological dependencies of people —particularly in the first year of life—may result in severe psychological depressions. Her writings stress the necessity of prophylaxis and therapy as preventive measures.

*   *   *

MEYER, Linda D(oreen)   1948-

PERSONAL: Born April 2, 1948, in Santa Barbara, Calif.; daughter of John Floyd (an assistant fire chief) and Dorothy (Baker) Potter; married Lee Meyer (an electrical engineer), September 6, 1969; children: Joshua Scott, Matthew Sean. *Education:* Attended University of California, Santa Barbara, 1966-68; San Jose State University, B.A., 1971. *Politics:* Social Democrat. *Religion:* Born-again Christian. *Home:* 18409 90th Ave. W., Edmonds, Wash. 98020.

CAREER: Women's Community Clinic, San Jose, Calif., pregnancy counselor, 1973-75; Childbirth Education Association of Snohomish County, Wash., cesarean childbirth educator, 1978—, and founding member of board of directors of Cesarean Family; Birthplace, Seattle, Wash., baby care instructor, 1979—. *Member:* International Childbirth Education Association, Cesarean Birth Council International, Cesareans/Support Education and Concern (C/SEC), Cesarean Family Concern, Childbirth Education Association of Snohomish County.

WRITINGS: The Cesarean (R)evolution: A Handbook for Parents and Childbirth Educators, Chas. Franklin, 1979. Also author of script for video cassette dealing with cesarean postpartum recovery, 1980.

WORK IN PROGRESS: Greater Love Hath No Man, a novel, publication by Chas. Franklin, expected in 1984; a television script on child abuse, for Churches Impact Project.

SIDELIGHTS: Meyer told *CA:* "After having my own two children in births by surgery, I became sensitive to the cesarean situation and studied to receive my certification to teach cesarean childbirth classes. In my exposure to the field as mother, student, and instructor, I learned many behind-the-scene things that were not covered elsewhere. Most importantly, I wanted to assure parents that in this age of involved childbirth they needn't relinquish control and responsibility over the birth simply because it may be by surgery. So over the year preceding the start of the book, I kept a sheet of paper on which I would occasionally jot down a subject 'which somebody ought to write about someday.' Then a few weeks before Christmas, 1978, the words started pouring into my head. Inspiration is the only word for it. I was compelled to sit down and write or I couldn't sleep at night.

"Some people wonder how the mother of two pre-schoolers finds the time and energy to write a book. My secret was that I napped every day with the children. Then I wrote most evenings from eight o'clock when the children went to bed until midnight or 1:00 A.M. The first draft took about five weeks while the second and third each took about two weeks. Some people wonder how I write so fast. I don't know the answer other than that my talent is a gift from God.

"I was tremendously influenced by a fellow childbirth educator and writer, Vicki Walton, whose book *Have It Your Way* was first 'self-published' and then taken over by a big publishing firm. Without her encouragement and guidance, I would never have attempted this project, much less completed it. Having her example to emulate was of inestimable value and impressed on me the importance of a mentor."

* * *

MICHELSON, Stephan 1938-

PERSONAL: Born February 28, 1938, in Cambridge, Mass.; son of Morris and Harriet S. Michelson. *Education:* Attended New York University, 1958-59; Oberlin College, B.A. (with honors), 1960; Stanford University, M.A., 1962, Ph.D., 1968. *Office:* Econometric Research, Inc., 1701 K St. N.W., 11th Floor, Washington, D.C. 20006.

CAREER: Reed College, Portland, Ore., instructor in economics, 1964-66; Brookings Institution, Washington, D.C., research associate, 1966-68; Harvard Universtiy, Cambridge, Mass., lecturer in education and research associate at Center for Educational Policy Research, 1968-72, research fellow in economics, 1968-70, research associate at Center for Law and Education, 1972-74; Center for Community Economic Development, Cambridge, Mass., senior economist and director of research, 1974-78; Urban Institute, Washington, D.C., senior fellow, 1978-79; Econometric Research, Inc., Washington, D.C., senior partner, 1979—. Owner of Physical World (recording studio and record company). Visiting instructor at Stanford University, summer, 1966; lecturer at University of California, Irvine, 1974; guest lecturer at colleges and universities and on radio programs. Organizer and chairperson of conferences and workshops; expert witness in court proceedings; consultant to Rand Corp., Children's Defense Fund, U.S. Department of Labor, and other organizations. *Member:* American Statistical Association, Association for Political and Legal Anthropology, Union for Radical Political Economics, Planners Network.

WRITINGS: (Contributor) *Do Teachers Make a Difference?*, U.S. Office of Education, 1970; (contributor) Joseph, Bach, and Seeber, editors, *Economic Analysis and Social Policy*, Prentice-Hall, 1971; (with Christopher Jencks and others) *Inequality: A Reassessment of the Effect of Family and Schooling in America*, Basic Books, 1972; (contributor) Martin Carnoy, editor, *Schooling in a Corporate Society*, McKay, 1972; (with W. Norton Grubb) *States and Schools: The Political Economy of Public School Finance*, Lexington Books, 1974; (contributor) Benjamin Chinitz, editor, *Central City Economic Development*, Abt Books, 1978; (contributor) Carol Weiss and Allen Barton, editors, *Bureaucratic Maladies and Remedies*, Sage Publications, 1980. Contributor of more than twenty articles and reviews to academic journals and newspapers.

WORK IN PROGRESS: A book on social science and the judicial system, for the Urban Institute.

SIDELIGHTS: Michelson is a member of the Red Shadow, the economics rock and roll band.

* * *

MIDGLEY, E(rnest) B(rian) F(rancis) 1927-

PERSONAL: Born September 16, 1927, in Huddersfield, England; son of Ernest (a company secretary) and Dorothy Mary (Tyas) Midgley; married Mary Richardson (a teacher), August 18, 1951; children: Janet (deceased), Catherine, Robert, Peter, Michael, Dominic, Margaret, Paul, David. *Education:* Victoria University of Manchester, B.A. (with first class honors), 1951; London School of Economics and Political Science, London, M.Phil., 1967. *Religion:* Roman Catholic. *Home:* 111 Brighton Place, Aberdeen AB1 6RT, Scotland. *Office:* Department of Politics, Kings College, University of Aberdeen, Aberdeen AB9 2UB, Scotland.

CAREER: Ministry of Supply (subsequently Ministry of Aviation), London, England, assistant principal, 1951-56, principal, 1956-61; Ministry of Health, London, principal, 1961-65; University of Aberdeen, Kings College, Aberdeen, Scotland, assistant lecturer, 1967-68, lecturer, 1968-72, senior lecturer in politics, 1972—. *Military service:* Royal Air Force, 1945-48; became flight sergeant. *Member:* British International Studies Association, Association for Legal and Social Philosophy.

WRITINGS: *The Natural Law Tradition and the Theory of International Relations*, Barnes & Noble, 1975. Contributor to *Year Book of World Affairs*. Contributor to international studies, philosophical, and social studies journals.

WORK IN PROGRESS: *The Ideology of Max Weber; The Scavenger's Daughter* (tentative title), a novel; a philosophical critique of Hobbes's *Leviathan;* research on philosophical critiques of modern atheistic ideologies—"this academic work is undertaken on the intellectual foundation of the Thomist philosophy."

* * *

MILES, Sylva
See MULARCHYK, Sylva

* * *

MILKS, Harold Keith 1908-1979

OBITUARY NOTICE: Born June 28, 1908, in South Milford, Ind.; died December 12, 1979, in Paradise Valley, Ariz. Journalist. Milks was an editor of the *Arizona Republic* and a former correspondent and bureau chief for the Associated Press. During his thirty-three-year career with the Associated Press, he covered such stories as Mao Tse-tung's rise to power in China, the Bay of Pigs invasion of Cuba, and the recovery of hydrogen bombs lost off the coast of Spain. He became Latin affairs editor of the *Arizona Republic* in 1967, managing editor in 1971, and a foreign affairs reporter in 1978. Obituaries and other sources: *Who's Who in America*, 38th edition, Marquis, 1974; *New York Times*, December 14, 1979.

* * *

MILLAR, (Minna Henrietta) Joy 1914-
(Joy Collier)

PERSONAL: Born February 15, 1914, in London, England; daughter of James (a neurologist) and Minna (Summerhayes) Collier; married Anthony Kendal Millar, June 21, 1941; children: James, Alastair. *Education:* Attended Polytechnic Art School of Central London, 1931-33. *Politics:* "Cosmopolitan

Conservative!'' *Religion:* Church of England. *Home:* 4 Kensington Cres., Oranjezicht, Cape Town, South Africa. *Agent:* Curtis Brown Ltd., 1 Craven Hill, London W.2, England.

CAREER: Writer, 1939—; farmer in South Africa, 1947-56; artist, with four exhibitions, 1957-71, 1974—. *Military service:* Royal Air Force, Women's Auxiliary Air Force, fighter command, 1940-44; became section officer. *Member:* International P.E.N., Royal Air Force Club.

WRITINGS—All under name Joy Collier: (Self-illustrated) *Algerian Adventure* (travelogue), Allen & Unwin, 1944; (self-illustrated) *Stellenbosch Revisited*, Univ. Pub., 1957; (self-illustrated) *Portrait of Cape Town*, Longmans, Green, 1961; (self-illustrated) *Purple and Gold: Johannesburg and Pretoria*, Longmans, Green, 1965; *King Sun* (biography of Egyptian pharaoh Akhenaten), Ward, Lock, 1970, published as *The Heretic Pharaoh*, John Day, 1972; (self-illustrated) *Joy Collier's Cape*, Purnells, 1976.

WORK IN PROGRESS: Two Georgian romances, *The Spy From the Parsonage* and *The Heroine*.

SIDELIGHTS: Collier believes Cape Town, South Africa, ''is one of the most beautiful capital cities in the world to live in. Looking at a map of Africa and taking into account such regimes as Uganda and Mozambique, I still think think South Africa is one of the best countries of this continent to live in *for all* races—it now has a promising future.''

Among her ''loves'' Collier lists her family and grandchildren, ''people generally, pasties, animals, the natural world, and gardens, flowers, and antiques, from houses through pictures to *objets d'art*.'' Collier ''hates concrete jungles, 'isms,' closed minds, and cruelty in all its forms.''

*   *   *

MILLER, David Merlin   1934-

PERSONAL: Born September 5, 1934, in Citronelle, Ala.; son of Richard Joseph (a mail carrier) and Merle (a teacher; maiden name, King) Miller; married Nancy Templeton, December 27, 1957 (divorced); married Joanne Ervin (a teacher), July 11, 1972; children: Garth, Dain, Erik. *Education:* University of Minnesota, B.A., 1958, M.A., 1961; University of California, Davis, Ph.D., 1966. *Home:* 6827 State Rd. 43 N., West Lafayette, Ind. 47906. *Office:* Department of English, Purdue University, West Lafayette, Ind. 47907.

CAREER: English teacher at junior high school in Minneapolis, Minn., 1958-59, and high school, 1961-62; Mankato State University, Mankato, Minn., instructor in English, 1964-66; Purdue University, West Lafayette, Ind., assistant professor, 1966-72, associate professor of English, 1972—. *Military service:* U.S. Army, 1954-56. *Member:* Modern Language Association of America, Midwest Modern Language Association.

WRITINGS: The Net of Hephaestus, Mouton, 1971; *John Milton: Poetry*, Twayne, 1978; *Frank Herbert*, Starmont Press, 1979. Contributor to literature journals.

WORK IN PROGRESS: Milton and Myth; *Generation*, a science fiction novel.

SIDELIGHTS: Miller writes that his interests include myth, seventeenth-century English poetry, creative writing, literary theory, science fiction, and fantasy. He told *CA:* ''All my work is guided by the belief that an educated man must know both what he is doing and why. John Milton can tell us important things, so can Frank Herbert. . . . A man who can't fix a light switch is not likely to do anything very well.''

AVOCATIONAL INTERESTS: Youth's football and baseball coaching, automobile repair, house building, tuba playing, Beethoven quartets, ''arguing the defects of linear imaginations.''

*   *   *

MILLER, Gerald R(aymond)   1931-

PERSONAL: Born October 18, 1931, in Muscatine, Iowa; son of Raymond R. and Mabel Anna (Bridges) Miller; married Pearl Ann Parsons (a librarian), August 2, 1952; children: Patricia Anne (Mrs. David C. Bender), Greg A., Caleb D. *Education:* University of Iowa, B.A., 1957, M.A., 1958, Ph.D., 1961. *Politics:* Democrat. *Religion:* Unitarian-Universalist. *Home:* 1323 Beech St., East Lansing, Mich. 48823. *Office:* Department of Communication, Michigan State University, 527 South Kedzie Hall, East Lansing, Mich. 48824.

CAREER: High school teacher of speech and supervisor of student teachers in Iowa City, Iowa, 1956-58; University of Iowa, Iowa City, instructor in communication skills, 1958-61; University of Washington, Seattle, assistant professor of speech, 1961-62; Michigan State University, East Lansing, assistant professor, 1962-66, associate professor, 1966-69, professor of communication, 1969—, director of graduate studies, 1967-73. Lecturer on radio in West Berlin, Germany, 1966. *Military service:* U.S. Army, 1952-54.

MEMBER: International Communication Association (president, 1979-80), American Psychological Association, American Association for the Advancement of Science, Speech Communication Association of America, Central States Speech Association. *Awards, honors:* Golden anniversary award from Speech Communication Association of America, 1967, for ''Some Recent Research in Fear-Arousing Message Appeals,'' 1974, for ''Counterattitudinal Advocacy: A Current Appraisal,'' and 1976, for ''The Effects of Videotaped Testimony in Jury Trials''; grants from National Institutes of Health, 1968-69, and National Science Foundation, 1973-75, 1976-78.

WRITINGS: Speech Communication: A Behavioral Approach, Bobbs-Merrill, 1966, revised edition published as *An Introduction to Speech Communication*, 1972; (editor with T. R. Nilsen) *Perspectives on Argumentation*, Scott, Foresman, 1966; (with H. M. Burgoon) *New Techniques of Persuasion*, Harper, 1973; (editor with H. W. Simons) *Perspectives on Communication in Social Conflict*, Prentice-Hall, 1974; (with Mark Steinberg) *Between People: A New Analysis of Interpersonal Communication*, Science Research Associates, 1975; (with H. E. Nicholson) *Communication Inquiry: A Perspective on a Process*, Addison-Wesley, 1975; (editor) *Explorations in Interpersonal Communication*, Sage Publications, 1976; (with F. J. Boster) *Communicating in the Small Group: The Eternal Dilemma*, Wiley, 1979; (with N. E. Fontes) *Video Technology and the Legal Process*, Sage Publications, 1979.

Contributor: O. W. Haseloff, editor, *Kommunikation*, Colloquium Verlag, 1969; A. H. Monroe and Douglas Ehninger, editors, *Principles of Speech Communication*, Scott, Foresman, 1969; R. J. Kibler and L. L. Barker, editors, *Conceptual Frontiers in Speech Communication*, Speech Association of America, 1969; Philip Emmert and W. D. Brooks, editors, *Methods of Research in Communication*, Houghton, 1970; R. H. Budd and B. D. Ruben, editors, *Approaches to Communication*, Spartan Press, 1972; C. D. Mortensen and K. K. Sereno, editors, *Advances in Communication Research*, Harper, 1973; W. R. Fisher, editor, *Rhetoric: A*

Tradition in Transition, Michigan State University Press, 1974; G. J. Hannenman and W. J. McEwen, editors, *Communication and Behavior*, Addison-Wesley, 1975; Gordon Bermant, editor, *Psychology and the Law: Research Frontiers,*Heath, 1976; B. D. Sales, editor, *Psychology in the Legal Process*, Spectrum, 1977; B. D. Ruben, editor, *Communication Yearbook I*, Transaction Books, 1977; Sales, editor, *Perspectives in Law and Psychology*, Volume II: *The Jury, Judicial, and Trial Process*, Plenum, 1979; B. D. Ruben, editor, *Communication Yearbook II*, Transaction Books, 1979; F.E.X. Dance, editor, *Comparative Theories of Human Communication*, Harper, in press; C. C. Arnold and J. W. Bowers, editors, *Handbook of Rhetorical and Communication Theory*, Allyn & Bacon, in press.

Contributor of about a hundred articles and reviews to speech, communication, psychology, and law journals. Member of editorial board of *Human Communication Research* (past editor), and of *Law of Human Behavior;* past member of editorial board of *Speech Monographs, Speech Teacher,* and *Journal of Communication.*

SIDELIGHTS: Miller writes: "Writing is like making love: it is impossible to do right unless the urge is there, but if the urge is present it is a totally consuming passionate activity. So few young academic writers take time to curry and brush their work that it is no wonder we find the academy swimming in ambiguity and verbiage."

*   *   *

MILLER, John (Laurence) 1947-
(Johnny Miller)

PERSONAL: Born April 29, 1947, in San Francisco, Calif.; son of Laurence O. (a cable traffic supervisor) and Ida (Meldrum) Miller; married Linda Strouse, September 17, 1969; children: five. *Education:* Attended Brigham Young University, 1965-68, and Professional Golf Association School. *Home address:* Napa, Calif. 94558. *Office:* Suite 1800, 10880 Wilshire Blvd., Los Angeles, Calif. 90024.

CAREER: Rancher; professional golfer, 1969—. *Awards, honors:* Winner of U.S. Open at Oakmont Country Club, Lacome Trophy tournament in Paris, and World Cup championship in Marbella, Spain, all in 1973; Hickok Professional Athlete of the Year award, 1973; winner of Bing Crosby National Phoenix Open, Dean Martin Tucson Open, Heritage Classic, Tournament of Champions, Westchester Classic, World Open, and Kaiser International, all in 1974; Professional Golfers Association (PGA) Player of the Year award, 1974; winner of Phoenix Open, Tucson Open, Bob Hope Classic, and Kaiser Open, all in 1975; member of U.S. Ryder Cup team; winner of British Open, Bob Hope Classic, and Kaiser Open, all in 1975; winner of British Open, Bob Hope Classic, and Tucson Open, all in 1976; Jackie Gleason Inverary Classic, 1980.

WRITINGS: (With Dale Shankland; under name Johnny Miller) *Pure Golf*, foreword by John Geersten, illustrations by Jim McQueen, Doubleday, 1976.

SIDELIGHTS: A protege of Billy Casper, Johnny Miller joined the ranks of the professional golfers in 1970. A year later he became known on the national circuit when he tied for second place with Jack Nicklaus in the Masters tournament, losing to Charles Coody.

Miller went on to become the victor of the U.S. Open in 1973, scoring a low 63 in a final eighteen-hole round that has been described as the greatest in golf history. The outcome of the tournament was especially surprising because, at the beginning of the round, Miller was outranked by twelve of his competitors, half of whom had formerly held the U.S. Open title. During that same year, Miller teamed with Jack Nicklaus to represent the United States in the World Cup Championship in Marbella, Spain. Miller won that tourney as well, having again established a new record with a score of 65 in the second round. The following year, Miller took the title at the first three major tournaments of the season, "the first time that had ever been done and the hottest stretch since Arnold Palmer took three straight back in 1962," Bill Lyon pointed out.

The difference between a professional golfer and a champion is a positive attitude, Miller's father once told him. It is to this advice that Johnny attributes his success. A skilled amateur golfer himself, Laurence Miller taught his son, then age five, how to swing at his first golf ball. While Johnny displayed a definite talent for the sport, his father "encouraged [him] to have fun, never pushed [him], and that kept sports in the level of enjoyment rather than a job," he recounted in a *Parade* interview.

Labeled a "thinking golfer," Miller carefully plans his moves on the green, taking notes as he plays. Bill Lyon classified him as "one of a new breed who has brought computer strategy to the land of double knits and 5-woods." As calculated as his play is, Miller also relies on his vintage 1947 iron clubs and an old Bullseye putter to see him through a tournament.

"Tempo, alignment, and address position" are Miller's strong points, he once commented. He asserted that he plays best when he does not practice while on tour, unless a certain aspect of his performance requires polishing. Those who do practice habitually become "tired, their reflexes are slow, their legs are dead, and they're not taking time with the shots," Miller explained.

In addition to competing on the golf circuit and playing in exhibition games, Miller endorses products varying from tomato juice to cars to golf balls for over twenty national and international companies. Articulate, well-mannered, and attractive, Miller projects an image of the "natural, all-American boy," observed Ed Barner, and, because of this winning image, Miller's endorsement is in great demand. A faithful Mormon and family man, Miller was also described by Philip Taubman as "one of the most unpretentious people in sport[s]."

AVOCATIONAL INTERESTS: Sports car driving, fishing, hiking, tennis, hunting ducks.

BIOGRAPHICAL/CRITICAL SOURCES: Sports Illustrated, February 21, 1972, January 28, 1974, April 1, 1974, June 10, 1974, January 20, 1975, February 3, 1975, March 24, 1975, August 18, 1975, April 5, 1976, January 24, 1977, March 27, 1978; *Newsweek*, July 2, 1973, February 4, 1974, October 14, 1974, February 3, 1975, April 14, 1975; *New York Times*, March 24, 1974; *Saturday Evening Post*, June, 1974; *Sport*, June, 1974; *Parade*, June 2, 1974; *Philadelphia Inquirer*, June 7, 1974; *Biography News*, Gale, July, 1974; Johnny Miller and Dale Shankland, *Pure Golf*, Doubleday, 1976; *Esquire*, November 7, 1978.*

*   *   *

MILLER, Johnny
See MILLER, John (Laurence)

*   *   *

MILLER, Joseph C(alder) 1939-

PERSONAL: Born April 30, 1939, in Cedar Rapids, Iowa;

son of John W. (in business) and Harriet C. Miller; married Janet K. Knapp, September 9, 1961; children: Julia Carolyn, John Russell, Laura Andree. *Education:* Wesleyan University, Middletown, Conn., B.A., 1961; Northwestern University, M.B.A., 1963; University of Wisconsin—Madison, M.A., 1967, Ph.D., 1972. *Home:* 1621 Rugby Ave., Charlottesville, Va. 22901. *Office:* Department of History, University of Virginia, Randall Hall, Charlottesville, Va. 22903.

CAREER: Buyer and manager in retail department store in Cedar Rapids, Iowa, 1963-65; University of Wisconsin—Madison, instructor, 1971, visiting assistant professor of history, 1971-72; University of Virginia, Charlottesville, assistant professor, 1972-75, associate professor of history, 1975—, director of history graduate program, 1979—. Lecturer at University of Washington, Seattle, 1972, and Haverford College, 1977; discussant at Wiles Lectures at Queen's University, Belfast, 1978. Associate member of Columbia University's Seminar on Modern African Studies, 1973-76; coordinator and participant at seminars in the United States and abroad. *Member:* International African Institute, International Conference Group on Modern Portugal, African Studies Association, American Historical Association, Social Science History Association, African Studies Association (England), Southern Association of Africanists, Southeastern Regional Seminar on African Studies. *Awards, honors:* Fellow of American Council of Learned Societies in London, England, 1974-75, and National Endowment for the Humanities, 1978-79; grants from American Philosophical Society, 1976, National Endowment for the Humanities, 1977, joint committee on Africa of the Social Science Research Council and American Council of Learned Societies, 1977, Fundacao Calouste Gulbenkian, 1978, and from National Library of Medicine, 1978-80.

WRITINGS: Kings and Kinsmen: Early Mbundu States in Angola, Clarendon Press, 1976; *Equatorial Africa* (pamphlet), American Historical Association, 1976; *Slavery: A Comparative Teaching Bibliography,* African Studies Association, 1977; (editor and contributor) *The African Past Speaks: Essays on Oral Tradition and History,* Dawson Publishing, 1979.

Contributor: Franz-Wilhelm Heimer, editor, *Social Change in Angola,* Weltforum Verlag, 1973; Martin L. Kilson and Robert I. Rotberg, editors, *The African Diaspora: Interpretive Essays,* Harvard University Press, 1976; Suzanne Miers and Igor Kopytoff, editors, *Slavery in Africa: Historical and Anthropological Essays,* University of Wisconsin Press, 1977; Henry A. Gemery and Jan S. Hogendorn, editors, *The Uncommon Market: Essays in the Economic History of the Atlantic Slave Trade,* Academic Press, 1979. Contributor of more than twenty-five articles and reviews to scholarly journals. Member of editorial advisory board of *History in Africa,* 1974—, and *Journal of African History,* 1976—.

WORK IN PROGRESS: Way of Death: The Angolan Slave Trade, 1750-1830; research on Angolan economic history.

SIDELIGHTS: Miller has conducted research in England, Belgium, Portugal, France, Brazil, and Angola. He writes: "I set out somewhat naively ten years ago to outline the history of an African kingdom, Kasanje, located in what later became the Portuguese colony (and now nation) of Angola. My first pass at the subject got me only to the antecedents of the formation of the state during the 1620's, and that research became *Kings and Kinsmen.* The work was based in significant part on the use of oral traditions as historical sources and raised methodological issues that I explored with several colleagues in *The African Past Speaks.* Since

the African kingdom of Kasanje had been an important source of slaves during the period of the Atlantic slave trade from Angola to Brazil, I am still edging up on the history I set out to do ten years ago by looking at the economic history of Angola as a slaving colony in the Portuguese empire. Eventually I will get to Kasanje in the eighteenth and nineteenth centuries, probably looking at it together with several neighboring regions in north-central Africa . . . if nothing else interesting comes up first."

*   *   *

MILLER, Lewis (Ames) 1928-

PERSONAL: Born August 4, 1928, in Brooklyn, N.Y.; son of Joseph Burke (an attorney) and Charlotte (Keller) Miller; married Jean Chandler, December 28, 1949; children: David C., Kathryn A. *Education:* Princeton University, B.A., 1949; Columbia University, M.S., 1976. *Religion:* Congregational. *Home:* 90 Goodwives River Rd., Darien, Conn. 06820. *Office:* Miller Communications, Inc., 322 Westport Ave., Norwalk, Conn. 06856.

CAREER: Glastonbury Citizen, Glastonbury, Conn., editor and publisher, 1950-52; *Newark Star-Ledger,* Newark, N.J., reporter and copy editor, 1952-53; *New York World-Telegram & Sun,* New York, N.Y., copy editor, 1953-56, night editor, 1956-58, assistant managing editor, 1958-59; *Medical Economics,* Oradell, N.J., executive editor, 1960-66; *Patient Care,* Darien, Conn., editor-in-chief and president, 1967-78; Miller Communications, Inc., Norwalk, Conn., president, 1978—. Lecturer at Newark Medical School, 1977—. President of United Church of Christ Residences, 1961-65; director of Term-Care Resources, Inc., 1976-78, and Darien Community Homes, 1978—. Speaker to medical groups; consultant to National Institutes of Health.

MEMBER: Alliance for Continuing Medical Education (member of council and secretary-treasurer, 1976—), Society of Prospective Medicine (member of board of directors, 1978—), Society of Teachers of Family Medicine, Direct Mail Marketing Association, Beta Gamma Sigma, Princeton Club of New York, Landmark Club of Stamford, Conn. *Awards, honors:* Editorial awards from American Business Press, 1976-78, for articles in *Patient Care.*

WRITINGS: The Life You Save: A Guide to the Best Possible Care From Doctors, Hospitals, and Nursing Homes, Morrow, 1979. Author of "You and the Doctor," a column distributed by New York Times Syndication Service, 1970-72.

SIDELIGHTS: Miller told *CA:* "My career has been characterized by a ubiquitous interest in people and their problems, and by a persistent desire to be an entrepreneur. I've satisfied both, after a good deal of trial and error.

"My newspaper career began when I helped revive the *Daily Princetonian* at the end of World War II; I gave up my original objective of entering the Foreign Service to pursue a news job. By 1950, I was ready to chart my own course, and started a weekly (the *Glastonbury Citizen*) in Glastonbury, Conn., a farming/suburban town. After two years, my money was running out. I didn't like selling advertising, nor was I any good at it. My wife was unhappy, so I sold out (the paper is thriving today) and returned to a daily newspaper.

"Seven years later, I tried again, this time to start a daily in the Maryland suburbs of Washington, D.C. But I couldn't raise enough money; my family wanted to eat, and I wanted to pay the mortgage, so I answered an ad in the *New York Times* (just as the promotion says!). That was the start of my new career in medical magazines.

"After six years of learning the business, I tried for a third time and was successful—editorially and financially—with *Patient Care*, a practical journal for family physicians. That led me into close relationships with practicing physicians and medical educators, which became the basis of my book, *The Life You Save*.

"I believe that individuals should learn to use the medical care system effectively, without being intimidated by it. *The Life You Save* is full of practical ideas on how to do just that."

* * *

MILLER, Luree 1926-

PERSONAL: Born February 10, 1926, in Seattle, Wash.; daughter of W. Virgil (a professor and administrator) and Margaret (an artist; maiden name, Watson) Smith; married William J. Miller (a foreign service officer); children: Scott, Blair, Stacy. *Education:* Attended Reed College, 1943-46; Stanford University, B.A., 1949; George Washington University, M.A., 1977.

CAREER: Writer. *Member:* Authors Guild, Society of Women Geographers, Washington Independent Writers.

WRITINGS: Bala, Child of India, Methuen, 1962, Hastings House, 1964; *Gurkas and Ghosts: The Story of a Boy in Nepal,* Methuen, 1964, Criterion, 1965; *On Top of the World: Five Women Explorers in Tibet,* Paddington, 1977; *Late Bloom: New Lives for Women,* Paddington, 1979.

SIDELIGHTS: As the wife of a foreign service officer, Luree Miller has lived in Dacca, Bombay, and London. Her main interest is women's history.

* * *

MILLER, Perry (Gilbert Eddy) 1905-1963

OBITUARY NOTICE: Born February 25, 1905, in Chicago, Ill.; died December 9, 1963. Educator, editor, and author. Miller was a professor of American literature at Harvard University from 1946 until his death. He was the author of the highly-regarded, two-volume study, *The New England Mind*, a work noted for its erudition, profundity, and wit. He also edited a collection of Jonathan Edwards's writings called *Images; or, Shadows of Divine Things*. Miller's other writings include *Orthodoxy in Massachusetts, The Puritans, The Raven and the Whale, Errand Into the Wilderness,* and *Life of the Mind in America*. Obituaries and other sources: *The Reader's Encyclopedia,* 2nd edition, Crowell, 1965; *Who Was Who in America,* 4th edition, Marquis, 1968; *The Penguin Companion to American Literature,* McGraw, 1971.

* * *

MILLER, Shirley 1920-

PERSONAL: Born September 15, 1920. *Education:* Western Michigan University, B.S., 1942; University of Michigan, B.A.L.S., 1950. *Home:* 2431 Outlook St., Kalamazoo, Mich. 49001. *Office:* Reference Division, Kalamazoo Public Library, 315 South Rose St., Kalamazoo, Mich. 49007.

CAREER: Worked as elementary school teacher and junior high school librarian; currently reference librarian at Kalamazoo Public Library, Kalamazoo, Mich. Lecturer at Western Michigan University; conducts workshops. *Member:* American Library Association, National Librarians Association, National Education Association, Michigan Library Association, Michigan Education Association.

WRITINGS: The Vertical File and Its Satellites, Libraries Unlimited, 1971, revised edition, 1979. Contributor to library and education journals. Reviewer for *American Reference Books Annual,* 1971—.

BIOGRAPHICAL/CRITICAL SOURCES: Wilson Library Bulletin, May, 1971.

* * *

MILLIKEN, Stephen F(rederick) 1928-

PERSONAL: Born July 3, 1928, in New London, Conn.; son of Frederick (a mechanic) and Ruth (a secretary; maiden name, Smith) Milliken; married Michelle Henriette Vallette (a teacher), December 19, 1972. *Education:* City College (now of the City of New York), B.S. (magna cum laude), 1951; Middlebury College, Graduate School in Paris, France, M.A., 1953; Columbia University, Ph.D. (with distinction), 1965. *Politics:* Democrat. *Religion:* Roman Catholic. *Home address:* c/o Maynard, 1705 Purdy St., Bronx, N.Y. 10462.

CAREER: Cottey College, Nevada, Mo., instructor in languages, 1953-55; English teacher at military academy in Lebanon, Tenn., 1956-61; Rocky Mountain College, Billings, Mont., assistant professor, 1962-66, associate professor, 1966-70, professor of English, 1970-73; Ecole Normale Superieure, Bamako, Mali, professor of English, 1975-77; University of Abidjan, Abidjan, Ivory Coast, Fulbright lecturer in American literature, 1977-79; University of Niamey, Niamey, Niger, professor of English, 1979—. Fulbright lecturer at Ecole Nationale d'Administration, Abidjan, 1977—. Research associate at University of California, Berkeley, 1970-71. *Member:* Modern Language Association of America, American Association of University Professors (local president), Phi Beta Kappa.

WRITINGS: (With Otis Fellows) *Buffon,* Twayne, 1972; (contributor) John Pappas, editor, *Essays on Diderot and the Enlightenment,* Droz, 1974; *Chester Himes: A Critical Appraisal,* University of Missouri Press, 1976. Contributor to *Diderot Studies.*

WORK IN PROGRESS: A critical work on Francophone African novelists.

SIDELIGHTS: Milliken comments: "I consider a literary critic's function to be much the same as that of a teacher of literature: to make difficult books more accessible to the general reader. My studies center on authors who present difficulties of a cross-cultural or intellectual nature. Buffon's thought was anchored in outmoded scientific assumptions. Himes expressed an extreme minority militancy, a hatred directed at the reader himself. The African writers I am working on at present are in the process of constructing a wholly new composite literary culture."

BIOGRAPHICAL/CRITICAL SOURCES: French Review, May, 1974; *Times Literary Supplement,* December 24, 1976; *New York Times Book Review,* February 13, 1977; *Etudes Anglaises,* Volume XXXI, number 3, 1978.

* * *

MILLIN, Sarah Gertrude 1889-1968

OBITUARY NOTICE: Born March 19, 1889, in Barkly, South Africa; died July, 1968. Author of several novels, including *God's Stepchildren, The South Africans,* and *Herr Witch Doctor.* Obituaries and other sources: *The Reader's Encyclopedia,* 2nd edition, Crowell, 1965; *The New Century Handbook of English Literature,* revised edition, Appleton, 1967; *Encyclopedia of World Literature in the Twentieth*

Century, updated edition, Ungar, 1967; *The Penguin Companion to English Literature,* McGraw, 1971; *Cassell's Encyclopaedia of World Literature,* revised edition, Morrow, 1973; *Longman Companion to Twentieth Century Literature,* Longman, 1970.

* * *

MILLMAN, Lawrence 1946-

PERSONAL: Born January 13, 1946, in Kansas City, Mo.; son of Daniel S. (a lawyer) and Zelma (Lawrence) Millman. *Education:* Washington University, St. Louis, Mo., B.A., 1968; Rutgers University, M.A., 1971, Ph.D., 1974. *Politics:* None. *Religion:* None. *Home address:* P.O. Box 235, York, Maine 03909. *Agent:* John Sterling, 40 West 57th St., New York, N.Y. 10019.

CAREER: University of New Hampshire, Durham, assistant professor of English, 1973-74; writer in western Ireland, 1974-77; University of Minnesota, Minneapolis, assistant professor of English, 1977-78; full-time writer, 1978—. *Awards, honors:* Grant from International P.E.N., 1977; Bush Foundation fellowship, 1979-80.

WRITINGS: Our Like Will Not Be There Again (nonfiction), Little, Brown, 1977; *Jesse* (novel), Little, Brown, 1980. Contributor of stories, poems, and reviews to journals.

WORK IN PROGRESS: Sweet Stone Lives, a prose-poem cycle about sea creatures, publication expected in 1981.

SIDELIGHTS: Millman writes: "I tend to react eternally against a shady past: a Ph.D. in English. My point of view was formed when I lived in Ireland for two years, among old story-tellers, and learned the verbal eloquence with which uneducated and illiterate people can speak. Since then I have tried to capture in my writings the stark and beautiful rhythms of this kind of speech, speech that lived before the onslaught of television."

BIOGRAPHICAL/CRITICAL SOURCES: Kansas City Star, June 5, 1977; *Orcadian,* August 9, 1977, September 6, 1979.

* * *

MILLS, Dorothy
See HOWARD, Dorothy Gray

* * *

MILLS, Jeannie 1939-

PERSONAL: Born July 2, 1939, in Angels Camp, Calif.; daughter of Edwin P. and Mary P. Gustafson; married Thomas Updyke, August 7, 1960 (divorced October, 1968); married Al J. Mills (a carpenter), November 2, 1968; children: (second marriage) Nathan, Linda Mertle, Diana, Eddie, Daphene. *Education:* Attended Southern Missionary College, 1958. *Home:* 2731 Woolsey St., Berkeley, Calif. 94705. *Agent:* Michael Larsen, Michael Larsen/Elizabeth Pomada, 1029 Jones St., San Francisco, Calif. 94109.

CAREER: Bookkeeper and accountant, 1958-73; Valley Publishing Co., Redwood Valley, Calif., manager, 1973-75; Mertle Rest Home, Berkeley, Calif., administrator, 1975-78; Human Freedom Center, Cult Rehabilitation Center, Berkeley, research director, 1978-79; writer, 1979—.

WRITINGS: Six Years With God: Life Inside Reverend Jim Jones' Peoples Temple, A & W Publishers, 1979.

WORK IN PROGRESS: Research on cults and authoritarian groups in America.

SIDELIGHTS: Jeannie Mills writes: "The six years I spent as one of the leading members of the Peoples Temple convinced me that the human mind is a very fragile thing. We need to understand more about the mind control techniques that are used by some cult leaders. To this end I am studying cults, hoping to find the answers to some of the questions that have been raised by the tragedy that happened in November, 1978, in Jonestown, Guyana, when 912 people died so needlessly."

* * *

MINETREE, Harry 1935-

PERSONAL: Surname is pronounced Min-*uh*-tree; born April 7, 1935, in Poplar Bluff, Mo.; son of Richard H. (a broker) and Ruth (a teacher; maiden name, Esther) Minetree; married Judith Garner, November 13, 1955; children: Harry II, Lee, Elizabeth, Hugh, Garner, Judith McVay. *Education:* Attended Harvard University, 1958; Vanderbilt University, B.A., 1959; University of Iowa, M.F.A., 1962. *Religion:* Society of Friends (Quaker). *Home address:* P.O. Box 10, East Hampton, N.Y. 11937. *Agent:* Irving Paul Lazar Agency, 211 South Beverly Dr., Beverly Hills, Calif. 90212.

CAREER: Christian College, Columbia, Mo., instructor in English, 1962-64; Memphis State University, Memphis, Tenn., assistant professor of English, 1964-66; Lindenwood College, St. Charles, Md., assistant professor of English, 1966-69; writer, 1969—. *Member:* Overseas Press Club of America.

WRITINGS: (Contributor) J. W. Corrington and M. Williams, editors, *Southern Writing in the Sixties,* two volumes, Louisiana State University Press, 1968; *Cooley: The Career of a Great Heart Surgeon,* Harper, 1973. Contributor to magazines, including *Delta Review, Arlington Quarterly, Kenyon Review, Town and Country, People, Money, Time, Penthouse, Family Circle, Cosmopolitan, Quest, US, Sports Afield, New York, Science Digest, Rolling Stone,* and numerous publications abroad. Founding editor of *Confluence.*

WORK IN PROGRESS: Afrika, Afrika, a novel, publication by Doubleday expected in 1981; "The Woods," a screenplay, for Paramount; *Houston Blue Leader,* a novel.

SIDELIGHTS: Minetree writes: "For the past five years, I've spent a great deal of time in Africa writing for American and European magazines while compiling background material for a novel, a political adventure novel which, I hope, will inform the public where the media and the popular press have failed. Although I came to free-lance magazine writing out of duress—broke, unable to find a book subject that interested me—I would recommend it as a training ground for any young writer who is long on insight, short of experience, and overly concerned with literary style. Working for a newspaper is no good, since the tendency is to bend to editorial policies. The same holds true for being on the staff of a magazine. Magazines, though, are finally, in every sense, disposable—no space to develop an idea that is truly worthwhile. Moreover, they pay poorly and slowly. But, if you're lucky, they'll pay the rent and feed the kids while you see the world and get sufficiently outside yourself to recognize important truth and then go write a book about it. By then you will know how to deal with editors . . . or anyone else, including all the frauds in what someone called 'the quality lit. game.'"

* * *

MINGUS, Charles 1922-1979

PERSONAL: Born April 22, 1922, in Nogales, Arizona; died

of a heart attack, January 5, 1979, in Cuernavaca, Mexico; married fourth wife, Susan Graham (a music agent); children: three sons, two daughters. *Education:* Studied music privately with Red Callendor and H. Rheinshagen. *Residence:* New York, N.Y.

CAREER: Bass player with jazz bands, including those of Lee Young, 1940, Louis Armstrong, 1941-43, Lionel Hampton, 1946-48, Red Norvo Trio, 1950-51, Billy Taylor Trio, 1952-53, Charlie Parker, Stan Getz, Duke Ellington, Art Tatum, and his own Jazz Workshop. Founder of Debut (recording company), 1952. Actor in motion pictures, including "Higher and Higher," "Road to Zanzibar," and "All Night Long." Featured in television documentary, "Mingus," 1968. *Awards, honors:* Co-recipient of New Star award from *Down Beat* critics poll on bass, 1953; grant from Guggenheim Foundation, 1971-72; holder of Slee Chair in Music from State University of New York, 1972; honorary degree from Brandeis University, 1974.

WRITINGS: Beneath the Underdog: His World as Composed by Mingus (autobiography), edited by Nel King, Knopf, 1971.

SIDELIGHTS: "Don't call me a jazz musician," Charles Mingus once protested to a writer for *Time.* "The word jazz means nigger, discrimination, second-class citizenship, the back-of-the-bus bit." Mingus was haunted by the bitter racism he first encountered in Watts, a rough ghetto district in Los Angeles, California, where he grew up. Throughout his career, he battled hatred and was painfully aware of the subjugation of his black ancestors. Even his own name represented racism to him. "Don't call me Charlie, that's a slave name, that's what you would name a dog," he once raged to a reporter.

Often referred to as "jazz's angry man," Mingus had a reputation as a "voluble and occasionally violent" man. When at one time many patrons at jazz festivals attended simply because it was fashionable to be seen there, most of the performing artists suffered the noise and lack of attention and interest without comment. Mingus, however, was known to stop a performance midway through to lecture the audience on their behavior, sometimes refusing to continue if they did not listen attentively. Even his own musicians could not escape a reprimand on stage if Mingus felt they were not giving their best.

In 1974 Mingus wrote his autobiography, *Beneath the Underdog.* Meant to be read as "an ongoing act of therapeutic self-investigation," explained Geoffrey Wolff of *Newsweek,* a reviewer for the *Times Literary Supplement* noted that it "is very different from the usual anecdote-dropping jazz memoir." According to Jonathan Yardley in the *New Republic,* the book is "an account of one man pursued by his particular demons and trying to make something of his talents."

In *Beneath the Underdog,* Mingus describes what it is like to be black in a "white man's world." He tells how black musicians were replaced before recording sessions in the 1950's, as interracial groups were at that time frowned upon. In another episode he recalls the long treks after each performance in a strange and hostile town to find a hotel that would accommodate blacks. He depicts the world of pimps and whores; in fact, his own life as a pimp. Mingus is, assessed Wolff, "an unusually gifted pornographer, in part because he is an inventive soul, in part because he chases his dreams of tail with astonishing single-mindedness, in part because his sensual vocabulary . . . is most exotic." Some critics, however, felt that Mingus spent too much time glorifying his

sexual exploits. A reviewer for *Best Sellers,* for instance, applauded the depiction of injustices to black musicians and commended his expositions on music, but complained that "when he talks about sex, and at least half the time he is doing so, he is coarse, dirty, brutal, explicit, and disgusting." Mingus's editor, Nel King, probably summed up the essence of *Beneath the Underdog* most accurately: "It's neither all true nor all fiction, not an autobiography or a novel. I guess it's Mingus."

Like his book, Mingus's music has also defied catagories. Try as they might, critics have never been able to pin him down to one style. When a reviewer once complained about this, Mingus retorted: "He just doesn't understand that I don't want to be caught in any one groove. Everything I do is Mingus. That's why I don't like to use the word 'jazz' for my work. I write what I think is classical music too." Hollie I. West of the *Washington Post* agreed. "His music was always serious, sometimes reaching a brooding intensity of Wagnerian scope."

In the late 1950's, Mingus formed his famous Jazz Workshop. Ted Curson, former member of the workshop, explained that it "was definitely a university thing. Usually, when you think of a guy going with a band, that's it. With Mingus, it was more like a school in the real sense of being a school." Another member, Danny Richmond, added that "a workshop is a means for musicians to come together and work on tunes, so we just carried it on over to the professional side of music, right on the bandstand at gigs. Mingus would explain to the audience. 'Everything is cool; this is the way we do it in the Jazz Workshop. We're just stoppin' the band, we're going to start over again, it's just that I want to tell the piano player the right harmonies for this chord sequence. Then we're going to play the piece in its entirety.'"

Mingus's last endeavor was his unusual collaboration with popular recording artist, Joni Mitchell. Although considered by many as a folk-pop-rock star, Mitchell had in recent years broadened her scope to include aspects of jazz in her music. It was, in fact, one of her more experimental pieces, "Paprika Plains," that first attracted Mingus to her music. For the joint album, Mingus decided that Mitchell would write lyrics to music he first created. He sent her several pieces, though she only composed lyrics for four of them. "See, I can only work from inspiration," she conceded to Leonard Feather in *Down Beat* magazine. "I have a certain amount of craft, granted, but I cannot work only from craft. A piece that is merely craft doesn't mean anything to me. It has to be inspired. . . . The four that I did complete were all inspired: either I stumbled across pieces of the poetry in the street, or they came to me in mysterious ways—they were meant to be." The remaining two pieces on the album were written by Mitchell alone as a tribute to Mingus. "God Must Be a Boogie Man," for example, is based on the first four pages of his book, *Beneath the Underdog.*

In the early 1970's, Mingus was diagnosed as having amyotrophic lateral sclerosis, a degenerative muscle disorder sometimes called "Lou Gehrig's disease." Despite failing health, Mingus extended his tour schedule and became a regular at musical events such as the Newport Jazz Festival. "He composed steadily, even when he was no longer able to play or even sing," related John Rockwell in the *New York Times.* He was already confined to a wheelchair when he and Mitchell began their collaboration. "I never knew him when he was well," lamented Mitchell, "and I never heard him play; he was paralyzed then."

To the people who knew him, Mingus was a special person.

Fellow musician Jaki Byard commented: "Once you get to know him, he's really a gentle man. A cool person. He's a very soft man. It's unbelievable once you get to know him as a friend, he has a smile for you all and all that."

BIOGRAPHICAL/CRITICAL SOURCES: Time, October 2, 1964; *National Observer,* September 6, 1965; *Newsweek,* May 17, 1971; *New Yorker,* May 29, 1971; *Best Sellers,* June 1, 1971; *New Republic,* June 3, 1971; *Christian Science Monitor,* June 10, 1971; *Times Literary Supplement,* September 10, 1971; *Down Beat,* January 12, 1978, December 7, 1978, September 6, 1979.

OBITUARIES: Chicago Tribune, January 9, 1979; *New York Times,* January 9, 1979; *Washington Post,* January 9, 1979.*

—*Sketch by Kathleen Ceton Newman*

* * *

MISCHE, Patricia M(ary) 1939-

PERSONAL: Born August 14, 1939, in Shakopee, Minn.; daughter of Clarence T. and Rose H. (Hahn) Schmitt; married Gerald F. Mische (an educational administrator and writer), April 18, 1964; children: Ann Elizabeth, Monica Luz, Nicole Stephanie. *Education:* College of St. Benedict, B.A., 1961; graduate study at University of London and University of East Africa, both 1961; Columbia University, M.A., 1969. *Office:* Global Education Associates, 552 Park Ave., East Orange, N.J. 07017.

CAREER: Mukumu Girls High School, Kakamega, Kenya, teacher, 1961-63; Riverside Nursery and Kindergarten, New York, N.Y., teacher, 1969-70; Glen Ridge Public Schools, Glen Ridge, N.J., teacher, 1970-71; teacher of English and communications at Essex County Community College, 1971-72; Clark School, East Orange, N.J., teacher, 1972-73; Seton Hall University, South Orange, N.J., teacher of humanistic studies, 1974-78; Global Education Associates, East Orange, N.J., co-founder and director of educational development, 1973—. Founder and director of Seton Hall University's Institute for Education in Justice, Peace, and Human Values, 1974-78; conducted more than three hundred workshops and seminars in the United States, Africa, Asia, Latin America, and Europe. *Member:* World Future Studies Federation, International Studies Association, Consortium on Peace, Research, Education, and Development (member of executive committee, 1978—), American Association of University Women.

WRITINGS: (With husband, Gerald Mische) *Toward a Human World Order: Beyond the National Security Straitjacket,* Paulist Press, 1977; *Women, Power, and Alternative Futures* (monograph), two volumes, Global Education Associates, 1978; (contributor) Mary Evelyn Jegen, editor, *The Earth is the Lord's,* Paulist Press, 1978; *Education and World Order,* Global Education Associates, 1979; *Alienation and World Order,* Global Education Associates, 1980. Wrote and presented four segments for television series "Alternative Futures," on CBS-TV, 1978. Editor of and contributor to "The Whole Earth Papers" (monograph series), Global Education Associates. Contributor to magazines.

WORK IN PROGRESS: Mission and World Order, publication by Pro Mundi Vita expected in 1979 or 1980; research on human development and world futures.

SIDELIGHTS: Mische comments: "We are caught up, whether we choose to be or not, in a struggle for human survival and a viable future on the planet. There are dangers ahead, especially in the forms of environmental destruction, the escalating arms race, growing economic disparities be-

tween rich and poor within and among nations, competition for diminishing resources, and human rights violations. But there are also tremendous opportunities for human growth and advancement.

"As I see it, global education is not a luxury or peripheral subject. It is at the core of human survival and humanization. It is concerned with full human development for each person and the species as a whole. It is concerned not only with human survival in a world of growing populations and diminishing resources, but also deeper communion among diverse but interdependent human groups and between humans and the whole natural and physical world on which we are utterly dependent.

"The present system of competing nation-states is inadequate for the new era of global interdependence. More effective structures need to be created at a world level, based on values of war-prevention, social justice, economic well-being, and participation in decision-making.

"A more humanizing future is dependent on the imagination, wisdom and courage of people living in the present, people bold enough to take initiatives toward preferred alternatives. I want to be part of the ferment, to contribute what I can in this exciting, formative period of history."

BIOGRAPHICAL/CRITICAL SOURCES: Sign, March, 1978.

* * *

MITCHELL, Giles 1928-

PERSONAL: Born October 7, 1928, in Dyer, Ark.; son of N. C. (a school superintendent) and Edith (Standfield) Mitchell; married Angela May (divorced, 1973); children: Brent. *Education:* East Central Oklahoma State University, B.A.; University of Oklahoma, M.A. and Ph.D. *Home:* 105-D Heritage, Denton, Tex. 76203. *Office:* Department of English, North Texas State University, Denton, Tex. 76203.

CAREER: North Texas State University, Denton, professor of English, 1962—. *Military service:* U.S. Army, Infantry, 1952-54. *Member:* Modern Language Association of America, Association for Psychoanalytic Criticism, South Central Modern Language Association.

WRITINGS: The Art Theme in Joyce Cary's First Trilogy, Mouton, 1971. Contributor to literature journals. Associate editor of *D. H. Lawrence Review* and *Studies in the Novel.*

WORK IN PROGRESS: Virgin and Prostitute: A Theory of Tragedy; co-author, *Darwin and Death: The Descent of Darwin;* co-author of a monograph, *The Freeing of the Waters in Romantic Poetry.*

SIDELIGHTS: Mitchell commented: "The two most important books that I have read in many years are E. Becker's *The Denial of Death* and D. Dinnerstein's *The Mermaid and the Minotaur.*"

* * *

MITCHELL, Ken(neth Ronald) 1940-

EDUCATION: University of Saskatchewan, M.A., 1967. *Agent:* Bella Pomer Agency, 9 Ardmore Rd., Toronto, Ontario, Canada M5P 1V4. *Office:* University of Regina, Regina, Saskatchewan, Canada.

CAREER: University of Regina, Regina, Saskatchewan, professor, 1967—. *Awards, honors:* Canada-Scotland exchange fellowship, 1979-80.

WRITINGS: Wandering Rafferty (novel), Macmillan, 1972; *The Meadowlark Connection: A Saskatchewan Thriller* (adapted from his own radio dramatic serial, "The Meadowlark Caper"), Pile of Bones Publisher, 1975; *In Forest, by Stream,* Highway Book Shop, 1975; (editor) *Horizon: Writings of the Canadian Prarie,* Oxford University Press, 1977; *Everybody Gets Something Here* (stories), Macmillan, 1977; *Davin: The Politician,* NeWest Press, 1979.

Plays: *Heroes* (one-act), Playwrights Co-op, 1973; *This Train,* Playwrights Co-op, 1973; (with Humphrey and the Dumptrucks) *Cruel Tears* (country opera), Talonbooks, 1977. Also author of screenplay, "Striker," released by National Film Board.

WORK IN PROGRESS: A critical study of Sinclair Ross; "The Shipbuilder," a play for voices and percussion.

* * *

MITCHELL, William E. 1936-

PERSONAL: Born December 16, 1936, in Cincinnati, Ohio; son of William E. (a contractor) and Annarose (Rebholz) Mitchell; married Lee Labbe (an accountant); children: Carey Anne, Sharon Lee, Leslie Jean, Jason Louis. *Education:* University of Cincinnati, B.B.A., 1960; Duke University, Ph.D., 1967. *Home:* 12459 Hollister Dr., Bridgeton, Mo. 63044. *Office:* Department of Economics, University of Missouri, St. Louis, Mo. 63121.

CAREER: Bache & Co. (brokerage firm), Cincinnati, Ohio, representative, 1960-62; University of Missouri, St. Louis, assistant professor, 1965-70, associate professor of economics, 1970—, head of department, 1978—. Chairperson of finance for city of Bridgeton, Mo. *Military service:* U.S. Navy, 1954-57. *Member:* Bridgeton Historical Society (president, 1970-71). *Awards, honors:* Grant from American Life Insurance Association, 1975.

WRITINGS: The Effectiveness of Debt Limits on State and Local Government Borrowing, Institute of Finance, New York University, 1967; (contributor) M. E. Polakoff and others, editors, *Financial Institutions and Markets,* Houghton, 1970; (editor with Ingo Walter) *State and Local Finance,* Ronald, 1970; (with Walter and John H. Hand) *Exercises in Macroeconomics: Development of Concepts,* McGraw, 1973; (editor with Walter and Hand, and author of introduction) *Readings in Macroeconomics: Current Policy Issues,* McGraw, 1974; (contributor) A. W. Sametz and P. Wachtel, editors, *Understanding Capital Markets: Financial Modeling and Forecasting in a Flow of Funds Framework,* Heath, 1977; (contributor) Polakoff and others, editors, *Financial Institutions and Markets,* Houghton, 1979. Contributor to economic and finance journals.

WORK IN PROGRESS: Research on default risk and interest rate differentials and on interstate variations in refunding by state and local governments.

* * *

MODELL, John 1941-

PERSONAL: Born June 3, 1941, in New York, N.Y.; son of Walter (a physician) and Merriam (a writer; maiden name, Levant) Modell; married Judith Schachter (an anthropologist), June 2, 1963; children: Jennifer, Matthew Thelonious. *Education:* Columbia University, B.A., 1962, M.A., 1963, Ph.D., 1969; postdoctoral study at University of Pennsylvania, 1970. *Politics:* "Unaffiliated." *Religion:* Jewish. *Home:* 2610 Irving Ave. S., Minneapolis, Minn. 55408. *Office:* Department of History, University of Minnesota, Minneapolis, Minn. 55455.

CAREER: Kingsborough Community College of the City

University of New York, Brooklyn, N.Y., lecturer in history, 1965-66; University of California, Los Angeles, director of research of Japanese-American research project, 1966-69; University of Minnesota, Minneapolis, assistant professor, 1969-72, associate professor, 1972-77, professor of history, 1977—, acting director of Center for Immigration Studies, 1973-74. Research associate at University of Pennsylvania, 1974—, visiting associate professor, 1974-76. Member of Minnesota State Historical Records Advisory Board. *Member:* International Union for the Scientific Study of Population, American Historical Association, Organization of American Historians, Social Science History Association, Phi Beta Kappa. *Awards, honors:* Social Science Research Council fellowship, 1970; Guggenheim fellowship, 1978-79.

WRITINGS: (Contributor) Charles Wollenberg, editor, *Ethnic Conflict in California History,* Tinnon-Brown, 1970; (editor and author of introduction) *The Kikuchi Diary: Chronicle of an American Concentration Camp,* University of Illinois Press, 1973; (contributor) Richard Ehrlich, editor, *Immigrants and Industry,* University Press of Virginia, 1976; *The Economics and Politics of Racial Accommodation: The Japanese of Los Angeles, 1900-1942,* University of Illinois Press, 1977; (contributor) John Demos and Sarane S. Boocock, editors, *Turning Points,* University of Chicago Press, 1978; (contributor) T. K. Hareven and Maris Vinovskis, editors, *The Nineteenth-Century Family and Demographic Behavior,* Princeton University Press, 1978; (contributor) Hareven, editor, *Life-Course Perspectives on the Nineteenth-Century Family,* Academic Press, 1978; (contributor) Allan Lichtman and Joan Challinor, editors, *Kin and Communities,* Smithsonian Institution Press, 1979; (with Edna Bonacich) *The Economic Basis of Ethnic Solidarity: The Case of the Japanese Americans,* University of California Press, 1980.

Contributor to *Harvard Encyclopedia of American Ethnic Groups.* Contributor of more than thirty articles and reviews to history and social science journals. Member of editorial board of *American Studies.*

* * *

MOEHLMANN, F. Herbert 1893-

PERSONAL: Born June 4, 1893, in Watertown, Wis.; son of Henry and Ruby (Keuling) Moehlmann; married Cora A. Kepke, September 5, 1918 (died August 22, 1976). *Education:* Wartburg College, graduate, 1915, D.D., 1978; Wartburg Theological Seminary, B.D., 1918, M.D., 1977; also attended University of Wisconsin—Madison, 1918-19, and Lutheran Theological Seminary, 1946. *Home and office:* 1845 Ivanhoe Rd., Orlando, Fla. 32804.

CAREER: Ordained Lutheran minister, 1918; pastor of Lutheran church in Spragueville, Iowa, 1918-20; in charge of war work for National Lutheran Council, 1918-20; organized Trinity American Lutheran Church in Waterloo, Iowa, 1920-30; U.S. Army, chaplain, 1930-46, retiring as colonel; pastor of Lutheran church in Canal Zone, Panama, 1932-34; St. John Lutheran Church, Winter Park, Fla., visitation pastor, 1953—. Assisted in rehabilitation program for returning soldiers, National Lutheran Council, 1945. Chaplain at Sunland Training Center, 1962. Chairman of Lutheran Council of Jackson County, Iowa, 1917-18, and Eastern District of Iowa Synod, 1930. *Member:* National Historical Society, Wartburg College Centenary Club, Lions International (honorary life member). *Awards, honors—Military:* Bronze Star, seven battle stars. Other: For God and Country award from Service Committee of National Lutheran Council; distinguished achievement award from International Biographical Institute; tribute from Boy Scouts of America, 1966; Lutheran Brotherhood award, 1967, for distinguished service; awards from Civitan International, including outstanding service award, 1968, for stimulating citizenship; distinguished service award, 1973, for helping humankind; and distinguished service citation, 1977.

WRITINGS: Bible Name Quiz Contests Relating to Famous Bible Characters, Zondervan, 1942; *Bible Challenges: Quiz Book Number One,* Concordia, 1957; *Have Fun With Bible Quizzes,* Zondervan, 1973. Also author of twenty-three other Bible quiz books published by Concordia and Zondervan. Contributor of articles to *Army Chaplain* and *Lutheran.*

WORK IN PROGRESS: Another Bible quiz manuscript.

SIDELIGHTS: Moehlmann comments: "My purpose has been to interest our youth in the Holy Bible."

* * *

MOLTMANN, Juergen 1926-

PERSONAL: Born April 8, 1926, in Hamburg, Germany; son of Herbert (a teacher) and Gerda (Stuhr) Moltmann; married Elisabeth Wendel (a writer), March 16, 1952; children: Susanne, Anne-Ruth, Esther, Friederike. *Education:* University of Goettingen, D.Th., 1952, D.Th.H., 1957. *Home:* Biesingerstrasse 25, D-74 Tuebingen, Germany. *Office:* University of Tuebingen, Liebermeisterstrasse 12, D-74 Tuebingen, Germany.

CAREER: Ordained minister of Reformed Church; pastor of evangelical church in Bremen, Germany, 1953-58; high school teacher in Wuppertal, Germany, 1958-63; University of Bonn, Bonn, Germany, professor, 1963-67; University of Tuebingen, Tuebingen, Germany, professor, 1967—. *Awards, honors:* Premio letterario d'isola d'elba, 1971; D.D. from Duke University, 1972, and Moravian College, 1976.

WRITINGS: Theology of Hope, Harper, 1967; *Religion, Revolution, and the Future,* Scribner, 1968; *Theology of Play,* Harper, 1972; *Gospel of Liberation,* translated from the German by H. Wayne Pipkin, Word Books, 1973; *The Crucified God,* Harper, 1974; *Man: Christian Anthropology in the Conflicts of the Present,* translated from the German by John Sturdy, Fortress, 1974; *Religion and Political Society,* Harper, 1974; *The Experiment Hope,* translated from the German by M. Douglas Meeks, Fortress, 1975; *The Church in the Power of the Spirit,* Harper, 1977; *The Passion for Life,* Fortress, 1978; (editor with Hans Kung) *An Ecumenical Creed?,* Seabury, 1978. Editor of *Evangelische Theologie.*

BIOGRAPHICAL/CRITICAL SOURCES: D. Meeks, *Origins of the Theology of Hope,* Fortress, 1972; W. Capps, *Hope Against Hope: Moltmann to Merton,* Fortress, 1976; C. Morse, *The Logic of Promise in Moltmann's Theology,* Fortress, 1978.

* * *

MONAHAN, Brent J(effrey) 1948-

PERSONAL: Born June 28, 1948, in Fukuoka, Japan; son of Martin Joseph (in sales) and Rosemarie (a teacher and accountant; maiden name, Squillante) Monahan. *Education:* Rutgers University, B.A., 1971, M.Mus., 1974; Indiana University, D.M.A., 1979. *Home:* 50 Jonathan Dr., Trenton, N.J. 08619. *Agent:* Peter R. Knipe, 44 Nassau St., Princeton, N.J. 08540.

CAREER: Private voice teacher in Trenton, N.J., 1977—. Performer in concert and musical theatre, 1977—. *Member:* Phi Beta Kappa.

WRITINGS: The Art of Singing, Scarecrow, 1978; (with Michael Maryk) *Deathbite,* Andrews & McMeel, 1979. Also author of *The Highwayman* (novel), 1980.

WORK IN PROGRESS: A novel about the restoration of the United States after World War III.

SIDELIGHTS: Monahan writes: "I'm just writing until I can play hoary character roles (meaning: it is too hard to earn a living on Broadway—even tougher than writing). Although I find straight dialogue difficult, I would very much like to write plays (dramas and thrillers) because they deal with people's favorite subject: people. They truly distill the essences of life and enable us to have vicarious revelations that are both entertaining and educational.

"I also hope to remain in music because it is the purest of all art forms, needing no transfer media for its impression upon the mind (as sculptors need marble or metal, writers need words, painters need pigments). I wrote a set of songs to poems by R. W. Service for my final doctoral voice recital. This combination of music and the word is particularly pleasing to me. In summation, I enjoy giving others enjoyment and hope I can continue to earn a living doing so."

* * *

MONDEY, David (Charles) 1917-
(David Charles)

PERSONAL: Surname is pronounced like "Monday"; born October 24, 1917, in Skegness, England; son of David (an engineer) and Helen (Husband) Mondey; married Joyce Doreen Meredith (an artist), December 12, 1938; children: Richard David. *Education:* Attended high school in Wellingborough, England. *Politics:* Conservative. *Religion:* Church of England. *Home and office:* 175 Raeburn Ave., Surbiton, Surrey KT5 9DE, England.

CAREER: Thames Valley Services, Kingston-upon-Thames, England, manager, 1946-66, general manager and member of board of directors, 1967-72; writer, 1972—. *Military service:* Royal Air Force, 1939-45; became flight sergeant. *Member:* Royal Aeronautical Society, Royal Historical Society (fellow).

WRITINGS: Pictorial History of the U.S.A.F., Ian Allan, 1971; *Rockets and Missiles,* Hamlyn, 1971; (with J.W.R. Taylor) *Spies in the Sky,* Ian Allan, 1972; (with J.W.R. Taylor and M. J. Taylor) *Air Facts and Feats,* Guinness Superlatives, 1973, 3rd edition, 1977; *Aircraft: A Colour History of Modern Flight,* Octopus Books, 1973; (under pseudonym David Charles) *The Story of Aircraft,* Octopus Books, 1974; *World Airliner Registrations,* Ian Allan, 1974; *The Schneider Trophy,* R. Hale, 1975; *A Pictorial History of Aircraft,* Sundial Books, 1976; *The All Colour World of Aircraft,* Octopus Books, 1978; *Fighter Aircraft of the West,* Ian Allan, 1979; *Aircraft of World War II,* Volume I, Hamlyn, 1980.

Editor: *The Luftwaffe at War, 1939-45,* Ian Allan, 1972; *Pictorial History of Japanese Military Aviation,* Ian Allan, 1974; *Air War Over Spain,* Ian Allan, 1974; *International Encyclopaedia of Aviation,* Octopus Books, 1977; *Illustrated Encyclopaedia of World Aircraft,* Quarto Publishing, 1978.

British correspondent for *Avia.* Contributor to *Guinness Book of World Records* and *All the World's Aircraft.* Contributor to magazines, sometimes under pseudonym David Charles.

WORK IN PROGRESS: A book on postwar civil transport aircraft, for Hamlyn; *Aircraft of World War II,* Volume II.

SIDELIGHTS: Mondey writes: "My motivation is easy—I always wanted to be a writer, but acquired too many responsibilities too young, and had to wait until I could devote the enormous number of hours necessary to succeed. I think I now spend the greatest part of my life with a pen in hand, and love every minute of it. After waiting for so many years for the opportunity to write, I find that every minute is sheer joy, as if I am on permanent holiday. How better could one earn one's living?

"In addition to compiling the American aircraft section of *All the World's Aircraft,* I also write up the German, most of the British, and lighter-than-air sections, complete the index, and, of course, we have bi-monthly supplements which appear in the United States in *Air Force* and in the leading German aviation magazine. For years I have written articles, either on natural history subjects (mainly birds) or on aviation, but since compiling *Pictorial History of the U.S.A.F.* I have had no time for anything but aviation books."

* * *

MONK, Janice J(ones) 1937-

PERSONAL: Born March 13, 1937, in Sydney, Australia; came to the United States in 1961; daughter of Harold F. and Edith E. Jones; married David Monk (an environmental educator and artist), July 31, 1964. *Education:* University of Sydney, B.A. (with honors), 1958; University of Illinois, A.M., 1963, Ph.D., 1972. *Home:* 717 Breen Dr., Champaign, Ill. 61820. *Office:* Department of Geography, University of Illinois, Urbana, Ill. 61801.

CAREER: University of Illinois, Urbana, instructor, 1968-71, assistant professor of geography, 1972—, research associate in instructional resources, 1968-71. Member of board of directors of Educational Resources in Environmental Science, 1977. *Member:* Association of American Geographers (member of national council, 1978-81), National Council for Geographic Education, American Association for the Advancement of Science, American Association of University Professors, Geographical Society of New South Wales, Illinois Geographical Society, Society of Women Geographers.

WRITINGS: (Contributor) L. J. Evendon and F. F. Cunningham, editors, *Cultural Discord in the Modern World,* Tantalus Press, 1974; (with C. S. Alexander) *Physical Geography: Analytical and Applied,* Duxbury, 1977; (with Alexander and John Oliver) *Investigations in Applied Physical Geography,* Duxbury, 1979; (contributor) W. P. Avery, R. E. Lonsdale, and Ivan Volgyes, editors, *Rural Change and Public Policy in Eastern Europe, Latin America, and Australia,* Pergamon, 1979. Contributor to geography, education, and international studies journals.

WORK IN PROGRESS: Teaching materials on women for college geography classes; research on Asian professionals as immigrants and on rural development and social change in the Caribbean.

SIDELIGHTS: Janice Monk writes: "My main professional interests are geographic research, including rural social change (particularly in the Caribbean), and minority group studies. In addition, I am interested in problems of curriculum development and evaluation in higher education. I am particularly concerned with enhancing the status and professional participation of women in academia and the geographic profession, and with improving the quality of undergraduate education. My professional travel has been extensive for research in Australia and the Caribbean, and to professional meetings in Canada, Nigeria, New Zealand, Mexico, and the Soviet Union."

* * *

MONTAGU, Jeremy (Peter Samuel) 1927-

PERSONAL: Born December 27, 1927, in London, England; son of Ewen Edward Samuel (a judge) and Iris Rachel (Solomon) Montagu; married Gwen Ellen Ingledew (a researcher), July 29, 1955; children: Rachel Mary, Sarah Ruth, Simon Joseph Samuel. *Education:* Attended Trinity College, Cambridge, and Guildhall School of Music. *Politics:* "Uncommitted." *Religion:* Jewish. *Home:* 7 Pickwick Rd., Dulwich Village, London SE21 7JN, England. *Agent:* A. P. Watt & Son, 26/28 Bedford Row, London WC1R 4HL, England.

CAREER: Musician and musicologist; performed with all major British orchestras. Ethno-organologist and lecturer specializing in early music at universities in England, the United States, Sweden, and Israel. *Military service:* British Army, Royal Artillery Corps and Royal Education Corps, 1946-48. *Member:* International Folk Music Council, Fellowship of Makers and Restorers of Historical Instruments (founding member), Society for Ethnomusicology, Royal Anthropological Institute, Union of Liberal and Progressive Synagogues (member of council), Galpin Society.

WRITINGS: The World of Medieval and Renaissance Musical Instruments, Overlook Press, 1976; (with James Blades) *Early Percussion Instruments,* Oxford University Press, 1976; *Making Early Percussion Instruments,* Oxford University Press, 1976; *The World of Baroque and Classical Musical Instruments,* Overlook Press, 1979; (editor and contributor) *Choose Your Instrument,* Gollancz, 1979; *The World of Romantic and Modern Musical Instruments,* Overlook Press, 1980. Contributor of articles and reviews to music journals.

WORK IN PROGRESS: Research for books on non-European musical instruments, for Overlook Press, and a series of books for young people on the history of musical instruments.

SIDELIGHTS: Montagu writes: "My obsessive interest in musical instruments—their history, function, use, and distribution—has led to the formation of the largest private collection of instruments in Britain. Most of my time is spent writing and lecturing about them and exhibiting them. The rest is spent working for the Jewish community, both in synagogues and at Leo Baeck College, the only training seminary for progressive rabbis in Britain and the most important one in Europe."

* * *

MONTAGUE, Gene Bryan 1928-

PERSONAL: Born October 27, 1928, in Santa Ana, Calif.; son of William B. (a grocer) and Gladys (Finkbeinen) Montague; married Barbara Holliday (a nurse), January 1, 1950; children: Christopher, Elisabeth, Tony, Andrew. *Education:* Central Washington State College, B.A., 1950; University of Texas, M.A., 1952, Ph.D., 1957; graduate study at Florida State University, 1952-53; Episcopal Theological School, certificate in divinity, 1967. *Politics:* Democrat. *Religion:* Episcopalian. *Home:* 5151 Crooked Lake Rd., Howell, Mich. 48843. *Office:* College of Liberal Arts, University of Detroit, Detroit, Mich. 48221.

CAREER: University of Texas (now University of Texas at

Austin), Austin, instructor in English, 1955-57; Arizona State University, Tempe, instructor, 1957-68, began as assistant professor, became associate professor of English; University of Detroit, Detroit, Mich., professor of English, 1967—, head of department, 1970-74, dean of College of Liberal Arts, 1978—. Assistant minister, Cathedral Church of St. Paul, 1967-68. *Member:* Modern Language Association of America.

WRITINGS: (Editor with Marjorie Henshaw) *Colloquium,* Little, Brown, 1962; (editor with Henshaw) *The Experience of Literature: Anthology and Analysis,* Prentice-Hall, 1966, 2nd edition (with Henshaw and Nicholas A. Salerno), 1970; *Poetry and a Principle,* Lippincott, 1972; (with Louis McCorry Myers) *Guide to American English,* 5th edition (Montague was not associated with earlier editions), Prentice-Hall, 1972; (editor with Robert Stahr Hosmon) *Man: Paradox and Promise,* Prentice-Hall, 1973; (with J. Lauer) *The Four Worlds of Writing,* Harper, 1979. Contributor to literature journals and literary magazines, including *Sewanee Review.*

* * *

MONTGOMERY, Nancy S(chwinn)

PERSONAL: Born in Claxton, Ga.; daughter of Karl Christian (a military officer) and Nancy Elmore (a film producer and editor) Schwinn; married Howard H. Montgomery, Jr. (separated, 1974); children: Nancy O'Neil M. Dickson, Morgan O'Neille. *Education:* Mt. Holyoke College, B.A. (with honors), 1942; Sorbonne, University of Paris, certificate, 1959; further graduate study at American University, 1964-65. *Home:* 2413 Huidekoper Place N.W., Washington, D.C. 20007. *Office:* Washington National Cathedral, Mount Saint Alban, Washington, D.C.

CAREER: Free-lance editor and public relations consultant until 1966; Washington National Cathedral, Washington, D.C., director of communications and publications, 1967—, also producer of weekly programs, "Forum" and "Focus on Religion," on WRC-TV. Vice-president of Associated Church Press, 1977-79. *Member:* Public Relations Society of America, National Press Club, Religious Public Relations Council (member of board of directors), Mt. Holyoke Alumnae Association. *Awards, honors:* Awards of merit from Associated Church Press, 1971, 1973, 1975, 1976, 1977, 1978, and 1979, for *Cathedral Age* magazine; Paul M. Hinkhouse/Victor DeRose Award from Religious Public Relations Society, 1976, 1977, for public relations projects.

WRITINGS: (With Michael P. Hamilton) *Ordination of Women: Pro and Con,* Morehouse, 1975; (editor) *A Scenario for Disaster,* Eerdmans, 1977; (editor) *To Stand in the Cross,* Seabury, 1978. Also editor of *The Herb Cottage Cook Book.* Contributing editor of series, "A Guide to Washington Cathedral." Contributor to newspapers. Editor of *Cathedral Age.*

WORK IN PROGRESS: A new and revised edition of *The Herb Cottage Cook Book.*

SIDELIGHTS: Montgomery told *CA:* "Most of my writing has been done for Washington Cathedral or as a result of my position here. Interests in medieval architecture, music, and modern art are constantly stimulated here." *Avocational interests:* Gourmet cooking, entertaining, food research.

* * *

MOODY, Raymond Avery, Jr. 1944-

PERSONAL: Born June 30, 1944, in Porterdale, Ga.; son of Raymond Avery (a physician) and Josie Merrill (Waddleton) Moody; married Louise Lamback, June 26, 1966; children: Raymond Avery III, Samuel Palmer. *Education:* University of Virginia, B.A., 1966, M.A., 1967, Ph.D., 1969; Medical College of Georgia, M.D., 1976. *Politics:* Democrat. *Religion:* Presbyterian. *Agent:* J. P. Jones, P.O. Box 41544, Jacksonville, Fla. 32203. *Office:* 731 May St., Jacksonville, Fla. 32203.

CAREER: East Carolina University, Greenville, N.C., assistant professor of philosophy, 1969-72; University of Virginia, Charlottesville, resident in psychiatry, 1976-77, visiting associate professor of philosophy, 1976.

WRITINGS: Life After Life, Mockingbird Books, 1975; *Reflections on Life After Life,* Mockingbird Books, 1977; *Laugh After Laugh: The Healing Power of Humor,* Headwaters Press, 1978.

* * *

MOORE, William L(eonard, Jr.) 1943-

PERSONAL: Born October 31, 1943, in Sewickley, Pa.; son of William L. (a steelworker) and Dorothy M. (an archivist and historian; maiden name, McClirk) Moore; married Lynne Rose Applbaum, August 10, 1970; children: Melissa Anne, Susan Joy, Jeffrey William, Scott Patrick. *Education:* Thiel College, A.B., 1965; attended Duquesne University, 1968-72. *Politics:* Independent. *Religion:* Lutheran. *Home:* 573 Prescott Heights Dr., Prescott, Ariz. 86301. *Office address:* P.O. Box 189, Dewey, Ariz. 86327.

CAREER: Teacher of French and Russian at public schools in McKees Rocks, Pa., 1966-69; high school teacher of English and French at community schools in Herman, Minn., 1969-79; full-time writer and lecturer, 1979—. Collective bargaining consultant to public employees, 1972—; research consultant to Sunn Classic motion picture, "The Bermuda Triangle." *Member:* National Education Association, National Investigations Committee on Aerial Phenomena, Mutual Unidentified Flying Objects Network (MUFON; state section director and investigator), Aerial Phenomena Research Organization (field investigator), Borderland Sciences Research Foundation (associate member), Society for the Investigation of the Unexplained, Alpha Psi Omega.

WRITINGS: Just a Little Soul (one-act play; first produced in Herman, Minn., at Herman Community Theatre, November, 1973), Eldridge Publishing, 1974; *The Philadelphia Experiment: Project Invisibility,* Grosset, 1979; (with Charles Berlitz) *The Roswell Incident,* Grosset, 1980. Contributor of articles to magazines, including *Saga UFO Report.*

WORK IN PROGRESS: UFOs: Earth's Cosmic Watergate, completion expected in 1981; a one-act drama tentatively entitled "Judgment in Perspective."

SIDELIGHTS: William Moore began his interest in the "Philadelphia experiment" when he heard author Charles Berlitz lecture about a bizarre U.S. Navy experiment that reportedly made a ship disappear. In 1943, the story goes, the Navy caused a ship to vanish from its Philadelphia port, only to have it appear minutes later in the same place. In the meantime, the ship had been sitting in the harbor at Norfolk, Va.

A disbelieving Moore scoffed at Berlitz's story and set out to prove it a myth. But, after his research had taken him more than twenty-five thousand miles through two foreign countries and twenty-five states, he found that his opinion had changed. There is a good possibility that the Navy actually did make the ship disappear, Moore concluded, and he offered his evidence for the phenomenon in his book, *The Philadelphia Experiment.*

In a *Washington Post* review of *The Philadelphia Experiment,* critic Henry Allen questioned Moore's findings. Much of the book's information, reported Allen, came from the letters of Carlos Miguel Allende (or Carl Allen), a seaman who allegedly witnessed the disappearance. The problem with this and other "proof," remarked the *Post,* is that "Allen/Allende is missing. All other witnesses, be they second-hand, circumstantial or material, are either missing, dead, or refusing to let their names be used." Furthermore, the book's last lines—"If the Philadelphia Experiment never happened as described, what actually *did* happen in a high-security area of the Philadelphia Navy Yard in October, 1943?"—prompted Allen to ask a question of his own, a question about the motives of the book's publisher. "After all, if this book isn't true, what actually did happen in a high-security area of Grosset & Dunlap in 1978?"

Moore responded: "One of the greatest challenges facing anyone who chooses to write about strange and unexplained phenomena is how to anticipate the reactions that the skeptics and critics are sure to have, and then demolish them beforehand with as much evidence or logic as it is possible to muster in the text. Such is the case with *The Philadelphia Experiment,* which sets out not so much to prove that an experiment in invisibility actually happened as to show that in spite of diligent research, it is impossible to dismiss the possibility of this bizarre rumor/event on the basis of the evidence at hand.

"Even so, no matter how much evidence is amassed and presented, it is impossible to defend against the critic who chooses to ignore the text of the book in favor of doing an in-depth critical analysis of the flap copy. So it is with Allen of the *Washington Post,* who, had he troubled to read the book more closely, would have instantly recognized that an entire chapter is devoted to the fact that the 'missing' seaman Carlos Allende was located and interviewed by the authors (myself and Berlitz). The other evidence in the book, I feel, speaks for itself, and readers are purposely left to draw their own conclusions.

"Probing the unexplained is sometimes tedious and always time consuming. The satisfaction comes when enough research has been collected to begin the actual writing process. The challenge is then similar to that posed by a giant jigsaw puzzle with some of its key pieces missing: Is it possible to construct enough of the puzzle with the pieces at hand to venture a guess at what the complete picture must be, while at the same time convincing the skeptics that all of the pieces in your possession really belong to the same puzzle? My preference for working on jigsaw puzzles tends to be as late at night as possible. Only then do the pieces actually talk."

BIOGRAPHICAL/CRITICAL SOURCES: Philadelphia Bulletin, January 25, 1979; *Washington Post,* March 6, 1979; *Der Stern,* March 14, 1979; *Der Spiegel,* March 26, 1979; *Fergus Falls Daily Journal,* April 5, 1979; *Parade of Books,* May 13, 1979; *Pursuit,* summer, 1979; *Minneapolis Tribune,* June 24, 1979; *Manchester Evening News,* July 19, 1979; *Glascow Daily Record,* July 20, 1979; *Yorkshire Evening Post,* August 4, 1979; *UFOs and Outer Space Quarterly,* fall, 1979; *Skeptical Inquirer,* fall, 1979; *Fate,* October, 1979; *Pittsburgh Press,* November 28, 1979.

MOREAU, David Merlin 1927-
(David Merlin)

PERSONAL: Born October 9, 1927, in Cairo, Egypt; son of Reginald Ernest (a biologist) and Winifred Muriel (a botanist; maiden name, Bradberry) Moreau; married Elizabeth Mary Rees (an editor), December 22, 1956; children: Sally Prinia, Alexander Piers. *Education:* Jesus College, Cambridge, B.A. (modern languages), 1950, B.A. (law), 1951, M.A., 1956. *Home:* Rowley Cottage, Langley Park, Buckinghamshire SL3 6DT, England. *Office:* Elga Products Ltd., Lane End, Buckinghamshire HP14 3JH, England.

CAREER: John Wyeth & Brothers (pharmaceutical company), London, England, export manager, 1952-56; Beecham Pharmaceuticals, London, market controller, 1956-65; Syntex Pharmaceuticals, Maidenhead, England, founder and first managing director, 1965-70; Weddel Pharmaceuticals, London, chairperson, 1970-79; Elga Products Ltd., Lane End, England, managing director, 1972—. *Military service:* Royal Air Force, 1946-48; served as radar specialist. *Member:* Royal Society of Medicine (fellow), British Institute of Management (fellow), Institute of Directors (fellow), Association of British Pharmaceutical Industries (past member of council), Society of Authors, Chemical Society (fellow), Zoological Society (London; fellow), Guild of Air Pilots and Navigators (freeman).

WRITINGS: (Under pseudonym David Merlin) *The Simple Life* (novel), Pan Books, 1962; (under pseudonym David Merlin) *That Built-In Urge* (novel), Elek, 1963; *Summer's End* (novel), Dell, 1966; *Look Behind You* (nonfiction), Morrow, 1973. Flying correspondent for *Director.* Contributor to magazines and newspapers, including *Vogue* and *Ideal Home.*

WORK IN PROGRESS: Eclipse (tentative title), a novel; a book on self-management, for McGraw.

SIDELIGHTS: Moreau wrote: "As a chief executive I am impatient, optimistic, innovative, and a great believer in proverbs such as 'least said soonest mended.' I find that you can get people to do almost anything as long as you sell the idea to them.

"As a writer I am disorganized, satirical, solitary, shy, and easily overwhelmed by such things as unreasonable tax demands. Andre Gide said, 'je sens deux personnes en moi' [I sense two people in myself], and I would have to agree with him. But this irreconcilable conflict is a bizarre source of energy to me. I will write about almost anything—water, graphology, hypnotism, flying, hepatitis, jet lag, and motor cars are recent examples—and I can get interested in almost anything, so that material crowds in on me.

"I have traveled all over the world, and as a consequence speak some six languages. Medicine has always been my hobby, hence the fact that I have managed pharmaceutical companies for over twenty-five years. Flying light aircraft and driving are hobbies as well as minor vocations."

BIOGRAPHICAL/CRITICAL SOURCES: Financial Times, January 2, 1979.

*   *   *

MOREWEDGE, Parviz 1934-

PERSONAL: Born January 30, 1934, in Babulsar, Iran; came to the United States in 1948, naturalized citizen, 1952; son of Hossein and Gamar (Qaim Magami) Morewedge; married Rosemarie Thee (a professor of German), September 1, 1962; children: Karim G. *Education:* University of California, Los Angeles, B.A., 1957, M.A., 1967, Ph.D.,

1969. *Home:* 220 Madison Ave., New York, N.Y. 10016. *Office:* Department of Philosophy, Bernard M. Baruch College of the City University of New York, 17 Lexington Ave., New York, N.Y. 10010.

CAREER: Bendix Corp., Los Angeles, Calif., mathematician in Computer Division, 1960-62; General Motors Corp., Los Angeles, senior research engineer in Computer Division, 1962-64; University of California, Los Angeles, instructor in philosophy, 1964-68; State University of New York at Binghamton, assistant professor of philosophy, 1968-71; New York University, New York City, adjunct associate professor of Near Eastern languages and literature, 1971-76; Fordham University, Bronx, N.Y., adjunct associate professor of philosophy, 1976-79. Assistant professor at California State College, Los Angeles, 1964-68; instructor at California State University, Long Beach, 1965-67; lecturer and research associate at Columbia University, 1969-70; adjunct associate professor at Fairleigh Dickinson University, 1971—; associate professor at Bernard M. Baruch College of the City University of New York, 1971—. *Member:* Middle East Studies Association of North America, American Oriental Society, American Philosophical Association, Society for the Study of Islamic Philosophy and Science.

WRITINGS: The Metaphysics of Avicenna, Columbia University Press, 1973; (editor) *Islamic Philosophical Theology,* State University of New York Press, 1979; (editor) *Philosophies of Existence,* Fordham University Press, 1980; (editor) *Essays in Islamic Philosophy and Mysticism,* Caravan Books, 1980. Editor of "EIDOS: Monographs in Islamic Religion and Theology." Contributor to professional journals. Coordinate editor of *Studies in Islamic Philosophy and Science,* 1971—.

WORK IN PROGRESS: Philosophies of Mysticism; Ancient and Medieval Epistemology; Mathematics and Ontology; The Physica of Avicenna.

SIDELIGHTS: Morewedge commented: "Plato and Spinoza more than other thinkers have influenced my own philosophical views. In my writing I have attempted to clarify for the English reader the philosophical themes embedded in Near Eastern texts."

*　　*　　*

MORGAN, Michael Croke   1911-

PERSONAL: Born October 13, 1911, in Guildford, England; son of Richard Croke (an estate agent) and Mabel (Bovill) Morgan; married Estelle McIlvenna (a university lecturer), July 29, 1945. *Education:* Oxford University, B.A., 1933, M.A., 1943. *Home:* Worlds End House, Bristol BS8 4TH, England.

CAREER: History teacher at private schools in Long Eaton, England, 1935-38, and Blandford, England, 1938-40, 1945-50; Cheltenham College, Cheltenham, England, teacher of history and head of department, 1950-65; writer, 1965—. *Military service:* Intelligence Corps., 1940-45; became major. *Member:* English-Speaking Union.

WRITINGS: Freedom and Compulsion, Edward Arnold, 1954; *Cheltenham College,* Richard Sadler, 1968; *Lenin,* Ohio University Press, 1971; *Foreign Affairs, 1886-1914,* Collins, 1973; *Bryanston, 1928-1978,* Bryanston School, 1978. Contributor to *Encyclopaedia of World History.*

WORK IN PROGRESS: Research on Byron and Pushkin.

AVOCATIONAL INTERESTS: Music, gardening, travel (Europe, North Africa, United States, Mexico, Peru), conversation.

MORGAN, Roberta   1953-

PERSONAL: Born May 1, 1953, in New York, N.Y.; daughter of Bernard (in sales) and Belle (a bookkeeper; maiden name, Pollock) Goldin; married Brian L. G. Morgan (a professor of nutrition), April 8, 1973. *Education:* New York University, B.A., 1973. *Home:* 16 West 16th St., #10-RS, New York, N.Y. 10011. *Agent:* Writers House, Inc., 21 West 26th St., New York, N.Y. 10010.

CAREER: Chelsea House Publishers, New York City, managing editor, 1974-75; Dale Books, New York City, editor-in-chief, 1976-78; writer, 1978—. Professional musician, 1974-78. *Member:* Women in Communications, Kappa Tau Alpha.

WRITINGS: Main Event: The World of Professional Wrestling (nonfiction), Dial, 1979; *Disco,* Crown, 1980; *How to Break Into Publishing,* Harper, 1980; *Brain Food, Mind Food,* Dial, 1980. Contributor to *Seventeen.*

WORK IN PROGRESS: Fiction.

SIDELIGHTS: Roberta Morgan writes: "I am a performer and a writer, with varied interests—music, theatre, dance, literature, and sports. I have been writing since I was seven (starting out with fiction, to which I am returning) and believe my wide range of interests (from professional wrestling to the publishing industry) has been the key to my success in nonfiction, since I can handle and enjoy many different topics. I enjoy writing nonfiction because it gives the writer a chance to become part of a whole world, while doing interviews, and to learn about new fields. It is not as lonely a practice to me as writing fiction is, but I suppose I view fiction writing as more satisfying, because the emotional input is usually greater."

*　　*　　*

MORGAN, Wesley
See BENNETT, Isadora

*　　*　　*

MORRIS, Clyde M(cMahon)   1921-

PERSONAL: Born August 14, 1921, in Fort Atkinson, Wis.; son of Virgil (an engineer) and Bonnie (a teacher; maiden name, Hamilton) Morris; married second wife, Sally Georgia Lund (a dancer, teacher, and artist), March 24, 1949; children: Bonnie Morris Hollenbeck, Elizabeth Morris Hendrickson, Stanley C. *Education:* Attended University of Wisconsin—Whitewater, 1939-42; University of Wisconsin—Madison, B.S., 1947, M.S., 1948, Ph.D., 1957. *Home:* 417 Fourth Ave. S., Grand Forks, N.D. 58201. *Office:* Mor-Lun Studios, 417 Fourth Ave. S., Grand Forks, N.D. 58201.

CAREER: Teacher and administrator at public schools in Wisconsin and Illinois; University of North Dakota, Grand Forks, professor of education, 1965-68, head of department of education, 1965—; writer. Member of Greater Grand Forks Community Theater. *Military service:* U.S. Army Air Forces, 1942-45; became major. *Member:* National Organization for Legal Problems in Education, American Federation of Musicians, Midwest Council for Educational Administrators, North Dakota Association of School Administrators, Grand Forks Musicians Association, Grand Forks Symphony Association.

WRITINGS: (With Ed Kramer) *Reading and Evaluating Educational Research,* Macmillan, 1974. Contributor to education journals and *Congressional Record.* Past editor of *West Virginia School Boards Journal;* editor of *Appellate Decisions and the Schools.*

WORK IN PROGRESS: A cook book, "for the uninitiated and inexperienced who are intimidated by standard cook books"; *School Law and the Classroom Teacher; Play Piano by Ear.*

SIDELIGHTS: Morris writes: "I began restoring a late nineteenth-century house in 1978. Both the work and the historical tidbits have been fascinating and might lead to a publication. I am also interested in drawing, painting, and ceramics. My wife and I prepare note cards which are currently being marketed on a limited basis, and many drawings are in preparation.

"About *Playing Piano by Ear*—it has been my experience that many people have studied piano for years but can't play without the music. The success I've enjoyed with serious students has led me to conclude that there is room in the market for a book on the subject."

* * *

MORRIS, R(oger) J(ohn) B(owring) 1946-

PERSONAL: Born June 13, 1946, in Abergavenny, Wales; son of Timothy George Bowring (a municipal accountant) and Mabel (a civil servant; maiden name, Baxter) Morris. *Education:* Cambridge University, B.A., 1967, LL.B., 1970, M.A., 1971, LL.M., 1975. *Religion:* Church of England. *Home:* 16 Pelham Rd., Grimsby, South Humberside DN34 4SU, England. *Office:* Great Grimsby Borough Council, Municipal Offices, Town Hall Sq., Grimsby, South Humberside DN31 1H4, England.

CAREER: St. Helens County Borough Council, St. Helens, England, articled clerk and first assistant solicitor, 1968-72; Grimsby County Borough Council, Grimsby, England, assistant and associate town clerk, 1973-74; Great Grimsby Borough Council, Grimsby, director of administration and associate town clerk, 1974—. *Member:* Royal Institute of Public Administration, Royal Society of Arts (fellow), Law Society, Association of District Secretaries (vice-president, 1978-79; president, 1979-80), Union of County and District Secretaries (vice-president, 1978-79; president, 1979-80), Grimsby Rotary Club.

WRITINGS: A Short History of St. Helen's Parks (booklet), privately printed, 1976; *Parliament and the Public Libraries,* Mansell, 1977; *The Public Lending Right Handbook,* Barry Rose, 1980. Contributor of articles and reviews to various periodicals.

WORK IN PROGRESS: A textbook of local government law.

SIDELIGHTS: Morris writes: "I am interested in the history of libraries, especially British public libraries, and in local government. The interest in library history originally stemmed from a Cambridge University research degree project, and has since been extended so that I now review books and occasionally contribute articles on library and information science projects and on public lending rights."

* * *

MORRISON, Carl V(incent) 1908-

PERSONAL: Born February 7, 1908, in Stanberry, Mo.; son of Oliver M. (a teacher and farmer) and Marguerite (a music teacher; maiden name, Hunsicker) Morrison; married Dorothy Nafus (a writer), April 25, 1936; children: James, Anne Morrison Feighner, David, John. *Education:* Attended Simpson College, Indianola, Iowa, 1925-26, and Northwest Missouri State University, 1926-27; University of Iowa, M.D., 1933. *Home:* 8600 Southwest 170th Ave., Beaverton, Ore. 97007.

CAREER: Junior high school teacher in Iowa, 1927-29; Highland Park General Hospital, Highland Park, Mich., intern, 1933-34; Wilder Child Guidance Clinic, St. Paul, Minn., child psychiatrist, 1941-42; Iowa State Hospital, Independence, staff physician, 1934-36; Lansing Children's Center, Lansing, Mich., director, 1942-47; Morrison Center for Youth and Family Services, Portland, Ore., medical director, 1947-76; writer, 1976—. Professor at University of Oregon, Health Sciences Center, 1947-77, professor emeritus, 1977—. Director of veterans' psychiatric clinic in Lansing, Mich., 1946-47; consultant. *Military service:* U.S. Public Health Service, psychiatrist with Bureau of Prisons, 1937-41. *Member:* American Psychiatric Association (life member), American Medical Association, Oregon Medical Society (life member). *Awards, honors:* Fellow of Commonwealth Fund, 1941-42; professional awards from Oregon Mental Health Association, 1967, 1973.

WRITINGS: (With wife, Dorothy Nafus Morrison) *Can I Help How I Feel?* (juvenile), Atheneum, 1976. Contributor to *Today's Health.*

SIDELIGHTS: Morrison comments: "My chief motivation was the observed need for preventive work in mental health. *Can I Help How I Feel?* was directed at ten- to fifteen-year-old children to give them some understanding of the more common disturbing feelings of these crucial years. I have done extensive work with delinquent adolescents and see the need for much more research.

"While parents who fail need compassionate understanding, professionals as well as the general public must give abused and neglected children adequate protection to prevent the perpetuation of a vicious cycle. I have found active cooperation with the juvenile courts very productive to this end."

* * *

MORTON, Jane 1931-

PERSONAL: Born November 13, 1931, in Colorado Springs, Colo.; daughter of William Ernest (a rancher) and Eva (Wolowsky) Ambrose; married Richard John Morton (an elementary school principal), June 7, 1953; children: John, Lizabeth Morton Duckworth, Mary Morton Crawford. *Education:* Attended Colorado State University, 1949-50; University of Northern Colorado, B.A., 1952. *Politics:* Democrat. *Religion:* Methodist. *Home:* 6162 South Kearney, Englewood, Colo. 80111. *Agent:* Carol Mann, 168 Pacific St., Brooklyn, N.Y. 11201.

CAREER: Junior high school English teacher in Englewood, Colo., 1952-53; high school journalism teacher in Seaside, Ore., 1955-56, and Twin Falls, Idaho, 1956-57; teacher and substitute teacher at public schools in Denver, Colo., 1961-78; Denver District Attorney's Crime Advisory Commission, Denver, Colo., office manager of Whistlestop Crime Prevention Program, 1978-79; free-lance writer, 1979—. *Member:* Colorado Authors League.

WRITINGS: (With husband, Richard J. Morton) *Innovation Without Renovation in the Elementary School,* Citation Press, 1974; *Running Scared* (juvenile), Elsevier/Nelson, 1979. Contributor to juvenile magazines, including *Wee Wisdom, Working for Boys, Friend, Child Life,* and *American Girl.*

WORK IN PROGRESS: A teen-age novel about a troubled boy.

SIDELIGHTS: Jane Morton writes: "When I was in high school I won two cans of peanuts for my last line in a jingle contest. It was years before I could see myself writing for anything more than that.

"I entered every contest that came along. I completed sentences in twenty-five words or less, wrote jingle last lines, and named everything from Kool-Aid pitchers to race horses. Prizes ranged from refrigerators to vibrating bar bells, and my winnings almost furnished our house.

"But I tired of praising soaps and toothpastes and cooking oils about the same time my family tired of eating from cans without labels, boxes without tops, and using the same brand of soap for months on end. So I took a juvenile writing course at University of Colorado, Denver Center, and shortly after published my first story for young people.

"While I was working on *Running Scared,* I read a chapter about juvenile hall to a high school class I was teaching. After I'd finished, one of the boys said, 'He didn't get beat up.'

"I realized then that when I visited the halls, those in charge didn't tell me everything. I talked to the students, and they filled me in, so I think my book is realistic about the way it is."

AVOCATIONAL INTERESTS: Running a mile a day, hiking, skiing.

*   *   *

MORTON, John (Cameron Andrieu) Bingham (Michael) 1893-1979 (Beachcomber)

PERSONAL: Born June 7, 1893, in London, England; died May 10, 1979, in Worthington, England; son of Edward (a journalist and dramatist) and Rosamond (Bingham) Morton; married Mary O'Leary, 1927. *Education:* Attended Oxford University. *Residence:* Sussex, England.

CAREER: London Daily Express, London, England, resident poet, 1920-22, reporter, 1922-24, author of column, "By The Way," under pseudonym Beachcomber, 1924-75. *Military service:* Served with British Army in France, 1914-18. *Awards, honors:* Created Commander of the Order of the British Empire, 1952.

WRITINGS: Maladetta, Chapman & Hall, 1932; *1933 and Still Going Wrong!,* Eyre & Spottiswoode, 1932; *Sobieski: King of Poland,* Eyre & Spottiswoode, 1932; *Who's Who at the Zoo* (poetry), Houghton, 1933; *The Death of the Dragon: New Fairy Tales,* Eyre & Spottiswoode, 1934; *Skylighters,* Heinemann, 1934; *The Bastille Falls, and Other Studies of the French Revolution,* Longmans, Green, 1936; *The Dauphin,* Longmans, Green, 1937; *Sideways Through Borneo: An Unconventional Journey,* J. Cape, 1937; *The New Ireland,* Paladin Press, 1938; *Pyrencan: Being the Adventures of Miles Walker on His Journey From the Mediterranean to the Atlantic,* Longmans, Green, 1938; *A Bonfire of Weeds,* J. Cape, 1939; *Saint-Just,* Longmans, Green, 1939.

(With Nathaniel Gubbins, F. W. Thomas, and Frederick Karinthy) *Bridge Over the Rainbow: A Survey of Humorous Sketches,* Pallas, 1940; *The Gascon: A Story of the French Revolution,* Macmillan, 1946; *Here and Now,* Hollis & Carter, 1947; *Brumaire, the Rise of Bonaparte: A Study of French History From the Death of Robespierre to the Establishment of the Consulate,* Laurie, 1948; *Camille Desmoulins, and Other Studies of the French Revolution,* Laurie, 1950; *The Tibetan Venus,* Sheed, 1951; *St. Therese of Lisieux: The Making of a Saint,* Burns & Oates, 1954; *Hilaire Belloc: A Memoir,* Sheed, 1955; *Springtime: Tales of the Cafe Rieu,* Constable, 1956; *Marshal Ney,* Barker, 1958; *Merry-Go-Round,* Oldbourne, c. 1959.

Under pseudonym Beachcomber: *Mr. Thake: His Life and Letters,* Bles, 1929; *By The Way,* Sheed, 1931, Doubleday, 1932; *Mr. Thake Again,* Chapman & Hall, 1931; *Hag's Harvest,* Doubleday, 1933; *Morton's Folly,* Sheed, 1933, Doubleday, 1934; *Mr. Thake and the Ladies,* J. Cape, 1935; *I Do Not Think So,* Burns, Oates & Washbourne, 1940; *Captain Foulenough & Company,* Macmillan, 1944; *The Misadventures of Dr. Strabismus,* Sheed, 1949; *The Best of Beachcomber,* Heinemann, 1963; *Beachcomber: The Works of J. B. Morton,* edited by Richard Ingrams, Muller, 1974.

Also author of *The Barber of Putney,* 1919, *Enchanter's Nightshade,* 1920, *Penny Royal,* 1921, *Tally-Ho!,* 1922, *Old Man's Beard,* 1923, *The Cow Jumped Over the Moon,* 1924, *St. Martin of Tours,* 1932, and *The Dancing Cabman: Collected Verse,* 1938.

SIDELIGHTS: Morton's column, "By The Way," which he wrote under the pseudonym Beachcomber, ran in the *London Daily Express* for over fifty years. Originally authored by D. B. Syndham Lewis who used the same alias, Morton met with much criticism when he assumed the position. According to his readers, he had two weaknesses: he was an unknown, and he did not copy Lewis's style. Because of these complaints, he initially lacked appeal; in time, however, public opinion softened, and the new Beachcomber enjoyed lasting popularity.

Though the column was intended to be purely fictional, fact had a way of creeping in. Morton would often use his characters to drive home a point or to illustrate a current opinion. His characters, with such names as Dr. Smart-Allick and Captain Foulenough, became so fashionable that a television comedy series, "The World of Beachcomber," was created around them in 1969. It was broadcast by the British Broadcasting Corp. (BBC) through 1970.

BIOGRAPHICAL/CRITICAL SOURCES: Observer, November 3, 1974, December 8, 1974; *Punch,* November 6, 1974; *New Statesman,* December 20, 1974.

OBITUARIES: Chicago Tribune, May 13, 1979.*

*   *   *

MOSELEY, Spencer A(ltemont) 1925-

PERSONAL: Born July 18, 1925, in Bellingham, Wash.; son of Roswell L. (a businessman) and R. Ferne (a businesswoman; maiden name, Sutton) Moseley; married Aileen A. Lofquist (a teacher), February 17, 1952; children: Grendl Anna Christina, Max Lars Spencer. *Education:* University of Washington, B.A., 1948, M.F.A., 1951; studied with Fernand Leger in Paris, 1949. *Residence:* Seattle, Wash. *Office:* School of Art, University of Washington, Seattle, Wash. 98195.

CAREER: University of Washington, Seattle, 1951-77, began as instructor, became professor of art history and painting, chairman of general education program, 1951-63, director of School of Art and acting director of Henry Art Gallery, 1967-77. Artist, 1977—, with exhibitions at one-man shows in Reno, Nev., Seattle, Wash., New York, N.Y., and Fresno, Los Angeles, and Santa Barbara, Calif.; has also shown work in more than fifteen group exhibitions in the United States and in Auckland, New Zealand. *Member:* National Council of Art Administrators, National Association of Schools of Art, College Art Association, Phi Beta Kappa. *Awards, honors:* Ford Foundation Purchase Award, 1966; recipient of numerous purchase awards in regional exhibitions.

WRITINGS: (With Pauline Johnson and Hazel Koenig) *Crafts Design,* Wadsworth, 1952; *Ed Rossbach: Non Loom*

Fabrics; Katherine Westphall: Quilted Textiles (catalog), Museum of Contemporary Crafts (New York City), 1967; (with Millard B. Rogers) *Wendel Brazeau: A Search for Form*, University of Washington Press, 1977.

Reproductions of Moseley's art have appeared in books, including *Optical Illusions and the Visual Arts*, by Ronald G. Carraher and Jacqueline B. Thurston, Reinhold Press, 1966; *The Principles of Pattern for Craftsmen and Designers*, by Richard M. Proctor, Reinhold Press, 1969; and *Illusion in Nature and Art*, edited by Ernst Hans Josef Gombrich and Richard Langton Gregory, Duckworth, 1974. Contributor of articles to publications, including *Crafts Horizons, Art Education Journal*, and *Lincoln Library of Essential Information*.

WORK IN PROGRESS: A biography with Gervais Reed, *Walter F. Isaacs: An Artist in America, 1886-1964*, for University of Washington Press.

* * *

MOSES, Anna Mary Robertson   1860-1961
(Grandma Moses)

OBITUARY NOTICE: Born September 7, 1860, in Greenwich, N.Y.; died December 13, 1961. Author and artist who began painting at the age of seventy-eight. Moses is considered "an authentic American primitive" painter. Her nostalgic paintings depicting scenes of her New England childhood were exhibited in museums, including the Museum of Modern Art, the Metropolitan Museum of Art, and the Phillips Gallery. She wrote an autobiography called *My Life's History*. Obituaries and other sources: *Current Biography*, Wilson, 1949, February, 1962; *New York Times*, December 14, 1961; *The Reader's Encyclopedia*, 2nd edition, Crowell, 1965; *Authors of Books for Young People*, 2nd edition, Scarecrow, 1971.

* * *

MOSES, Grandma
See MOSES, Anna Mary Robertson

* * *

MOSHER, (Christopher) Terry   1942-
(Aislin)

PERSONAL: Born November 11, 1942, in Ottawa, Ontario, Canada; married; children: two daughters, eldest named Aislin. *Education:* Attended Ontario College of Art, 1963-64; Ecole des Beaux-Arts, Quebec City, Quebec, graduated, 1966. *Office:* Montreal Gazette, 1000 St. Antoine St., Montreal, Quebec, Canada.

CAREER: Free-lance political cartoonist, 1968-69; *Montreal Star*, Montreal, Quebec, staff cartoonist, 1969-71; *Montreal Gazette*, Montreal, staff cartoonist, 1972—. Art director for *Take One*, 1969-71; designer of book and magazine covers. Faculty member at Montreal Museum of Fine Arts, 1973, 1974. Creator and producer of "The Hecklers," a documentary film released by National Film Board of Canada, 1976. *Awards, honors:* Canada Council grant, 1971; journalism awards include first prize from International Salon of Caricature, 1970, for editorial cartoon; Graphica Award, 1971, 1973; Canadian National Newspaper Award, 1977, 1978, for political cartoons; Quill Award from Windsor Press Club.

WRITINGS—All under pseudonym Aislin: *Aislin: 100 Caricatures*, Reporter Publications, 1971; (with Jack Ludwig) *Hockey Night in Moscow*, McClelland & Stewart, 1972, published as *The Great Hockey Thaw*, Doubleday, 1973; *Aislin,*

73: 150 Caricatures, Content Publishing, 1973; *'Ello, Morgentaler?: Aislin—150 Caricatures*, Hurtig, 1975; (with Patrick Brown, Robert Chodos, and Rae Murphy) *Winners, Losers*, Lorimer, 1976; (with Bill Mann) *The Retarded Giant* (self-illustrated joke book), Tundra Books, 1977; *O.K., Everybody Take a Valium!: Aislin—150 Caricatures*, Hurtig, 1977; *L'Humour d'Aislin* (cartoons), Editions Quinze, 1978. Also author with Peter Desbarats of a book on Canadian political cartooning, McClelland & Stewart, 1979.

Cartoons are distributed by Toronto Star Syndicate to newspapers and magazines in Canada. Contributor of cartoons to journals in Canada, England, and the United States, including *Harper's, Atlantic Monthly, National Lampoon, Punch*, and *Time*, and to newspapers. Co-founder and associate editor of *Last Post*, 1970—.

* * *

MOSKVITIN, Jurij   1938-

PERSONAL: Took mother's maiden surname as own legal surname, 1955; born January 6, 1938, in Copenhagen, Denmark; son of Arthur Thorkild (a publisher) and Maria (Moskvitina) Hansen; married Grete Bentsen (a philologist), June 20, 1978; children: Nathalie, Andrei, Alexander. *Education:* Royal Danish Academy of Music, graduated (with honors), 1959; University of Copenhagen, M.A., 1979. *Home:* Oesterbrogade 57, Q 22, 2100 Copenhagen, Denmark.

CAREER: Musical composer and author. *Member:* Neo-Platonic Society (president).

WRITINGS: An Essay on the Origin of Thought, Ohio University Press, 1974; *Det er spaendende at taenke* (young adult book; title means "Thought Is Our Adventure"), Sommer & Soerensen, 1976. Also composer of "various occasional music." Contributor to journals in Denmark and France. Co-editor of *Savoy*; music critic and book reviewer for *Politiken*.

WORK IN PROGRESS: The Diamond Stylus, about Leibniz; *The Enthropy of Ideas; Thought Forms and Thought Levels*, on the nature of mathematical reasoning.

SIDELIGHTS: Moskvitin told *CA* that his book *Det er spaendende at taenke* "was a kind of experiment. There had been a discussion in the papers whether serious scientific ideas should be popularized, and whether it would altogether be possible to do so without distorting and vulgarizing the whole thing. I claimed that it was possible and accepted a bet with the Copenhagen daily newspaper, *Politiken*, that I would be able successfully to convey serious and advanced philosophical ideas to persons at the age from twelve to sixteen.

"The book in question appeared as a series of weekly installments during 1975-76 and was a great success. The book itself is a slightly revised version of the original articles, now brilliantly illustrated by Jakob Hoffmeyer."

Moskvitin added: "I am personally convinced that we are living in a transitional era leading possibly to an epoch in human civilization which will resemble a renaissance: we will become aware of the practically unlimited potentialities of the individual, and also the conditions for actualizing these potentialities. Today morality and intelligence are things completely apart. But there will be a growing realization that intelligence is morality—in the sense that true creativity depends on the desire to enter into contact with the deeper and more hidden levels of one's consciousness."

MUEHSAM, Gerd 1913(?)-1979

OBITUARY NOTICE: Born c. 1913 in Berlin, Germany; died December 14, 1979. Educator, librarian, and author. Muehsam taught at Queens College and was the art librarian at the Cleveland Museum of Art. Her works include *Painters and Painting From the 14th Century to Post-Impressionism* and *Guide to Basic Information Sources in the Visual Arts.* Obituaries and other sources: *A Biographical Directory of Librarians in the United States and Canada,* 5th edition, American Library Association, 1970; *AB Bookman's Weekly,* January 28, 1980.

* * *

MUELLER, Lisel 1924-

PERSONAL: Born February 8, 1924, in Hamburg, Germany; came to United States in 1939, naturalized in 1945; daughter of Fritz C. (a teacher) and Ilse (a teacher; maiden name, Burmester) Neumann; married Paul E. Mueller, June 15, 1943; children: Lucy, Jenny. *Education:* University of Evansville, B.A., 1944; graduate study at Indiana University, 1950-53. *Residence:* Lake Forest, Ill. *Office:* Master of Fine Arts Writing Program, Goddard College, Plainfield, Vt. 05667.

CAREER: Worked as social case worker, receptionist, library assistant, and free-lance writer and reviewer. Instructor in poetry writing, Elmhurst College, 1969-72; participating poet, Poets In The Schools, 1972-77; instructor in master of fine arts writing program, Goddard College, 1977—. *Awards, honors:* Robert M. Ferguson Memorial Award from Friends of Literature, 1966, for *Dependencies;* Helen Bullis Award, 1974 and 1977; Lamont Poetry Selection 1975, for *The Private Life;* Emily Clark Balch Award, 1976.

WRITINGS: Dependencies, University of North Carolina Press, 1965; *Life of a Queen* (chapbook), Juniper Press, 1970; *The Private Life,* Louisiana State University Press, 1976; *Voices From the Forest* (chapbook), Juniper Press, 1977; *The Need to Hold Still,* Louisiana State University Press, 1980. Also co-translator of performing version of Hugo von Hofmannsthal's play, "Das Salzburger Grosse Welttheater," produced in Chicago at Goodman Theatre. Poems represented in anthologies, including *The Contemporary American Poets, The Poetry Anthology,* and *Rising Tides: 20th Century Women Poets.* Poems published in numerous magazines and literary journals, including *New Yorker, Poetry, Saturday Review, Virginia Quarterly Review, Shenandoah, Poetry Northwest, Ohio Review,* and *Chicago Review.* Contributor of critical essays to numerous journals.

WORK IN PROGRESS: The Selected Later Poems of Marie Luise Kaschnitz, a volume of translations, to be published in a bilingual edition by Princeton University Press in 1980 or 1981.

SIDELIGHTS: In her second book of poems, *The Private Life,* Lisel Mueller probes the enigma of our public and private selves. So blazingly accurate are her insights into the human psyche that Warren Slesinger remarked "we are transfixed and filled with fascination," and Dick Allen reported "shocks of recognition. . . . She goes after our secrets, this poet; often, she finds them."

The Private Life is a collection of forty-three short poems on subjects ranging from highways to a child's bed-time story to an old brooch that had at one time belonged to her grandmother. As Russell Brignano noted, her verses are filled with "captivating figures and metaphors, projecting an imagina-tive, deeply reflective, subtle intelligence. Her voice quivers here and there; a misplaced beat jars us now and then; but *The Private Life* is well worth entering."

BIOGRAPHICAL/CRITICAL SOURCES: Book Forum, summer, 1976; *Yale Review,* autumn, 1976; *London Times Literary Supplement,* October 29, 1976; *America,* April 2, 1977; *Poetry,* summer, 1977; *Three Rivers Poetry Journal,* March, 1978; *Contemporary Literary Criticism,* Volume 13, Gale, 1980.

* * *

MUIR, Malcolm 1885-1979

PERSONAL: Born July 19, 1885, in Glen Ridge, N.J.; died January 30, 1979, in New York, N.Y.; son of James and Susan (Brown) Muir; married Linda Kelly, May 14, 1914 (divorced, 1942); married Frances Tener Brown, August 19, 1943; children: (first marriage) Malcolm, Eleanor Warfield (Mrs. Collister Johnson). *Education:* Attended public and private secondary schools. *Politics:* Republican. *Religion:* Episcopalian. *Residence:* New York, N.Y.

CAREER/WRITINGS: James H. McGraw (publisher), New York City, 1905-17, began as file clerk, became vice-president; McGraw-Hill Publishing Co., New York City, vice-president, 1917-28, president, 1928-37, founder of *Business Week* magazine, 1929; *Newsweek,* New York City, editor-in-chief, 1937-61, president and director, 1937-59, chairman of the board, 1959-61, honorary chairman, 1961-70. Deputy administrator, National Recovery Administration, 1933-34; chairman of War Committee, 1942-43; member of National Industrial Conference Board, Labor-Management Council, 1943; member of Council on Foreign Relations, and chairman of capital funds program, 1964-67; chairman of American advisory council, Ditchley Foundation, 1967-73, and of U.S. Commission for United World Colleges, 1967-73. Chairman of New York State Committee on Medical Education, 1962-63; member of advisory committee, Associated Medical Schools of Greater New York, 1964-65. Member of board of trustees, Committee for Economic Development, U.S. Council of the International Chamber of Commerce, and International Press Institute. Author of *Trade Associations and Code Authorities as an Integral Part of Business Management,* American Management Association, 1934, reprinted, 1967. Contributor of articles to periodicals and journals. *Member:* American Arbitration Association (member of board), Foreign Policy Association (member of board), Burns Society, St. Andrews Society, St. George's Society. *Awards, honors:* Knight commander, Order of the British Empire; Chevalier, Legion of Honor (France); Lebanese Order of Cedar.

SIDELIGHTS: Malcolm Muir, who was editor of *Newsweek* magazine for more than twenty years, is credited with revitalizing the publication and increasing its circulation. Subtitling it "The Magazine of News Significance," he placed a greater emphasis on international editions and interpretative columns. In December, 1942, Muir reported as a foreign correspondent for *Newsweek* on the British industrial war effort. He became honorary chairman of the board for the publication when it was purchased by the *Washington Post* in 1961.

OBITUARIES: New York Times, January 31, 1979; *Washington Post,* January 31, 1979; *Chicago Tribune,* February 1, 1979.*

MULARCHYK, Sylva
(Sylva Miles, a joint pseudonym)

PERSONAL: Born in Washington, D.C.; daughter of Jens O. (a merchant and farmer) and Mary (a teacher; maiden name, Hazlett) Nelson; divorced; children: Beverley Mularchyk Sadoski, Bill Wynn Stotts, Ted Mike. *Home:* Conde de las Posadas, 2-4D. Madrid 22, Spain. *Office:* 401 CSG, Box 4849, APO New York 09283.

CAREER: Worked at Puget Sound Naval Shipyard in Bremerton, Wash.; Moron Air Base, Seville, Spain, secretary to comptroller, 1960-70; Torrejon Air Base, Madrid, Spain, secretary to comptroller, 1970-77; writer, 1977—. *Military service:* U.S. Naval Reserve, Seabees, 1958-62.

WRITINGS: (With Dorien K. Miles, under joint pseudonym Sylva Miles) *Shadow Over Beauclaire,* Bouregy, 1975.

Contributor of stories, poems, and articles to magazines in the United States and abroad, including *Mankind, Popular History, Cricket, Americans Abroad,* and *Lookout.*

WORK IN PROGRESS: Three novels, *Cousin Charlene, The Beautiful Young Men,* and *Killwoman Country;* "My Cousin Charlene," a three-act play.

SIDELIGHTS: Sylva Mularchyk told *CA:* "I have traveled extensively throughout Europe, concentrating on Spain. For many years I have been collecting material on Spanish history, arts, and particularly castles, with the hope of writing a worthwhile book. I am also an amateur photographer and have many photographs which could be used as illustrations. I have written short stories, some with a bullfighting theme. Living in Spain has been exciting and rewarding."

* * *

MULLANEY, Thomas E. 1922(?)-1978

PERSONAL: Born c. 1922 in Brooklyn, N.Y.; died of cancer, October 21, 1978, in Flushing, N.Y.; married wife, Dolores; children: Thomas E., Jr., Robert, Gerard, James, Vincent. *Education:* St. John's University, bachelor's degree. *Residence:* Flushing, N.Y. *Office: New York Times,* 229 West 43rd St., New York City, N.Y. 10036.

CAREER/WRITINGS: New York Times, New York City, copy boy, 1942, business reporter, 1946-62, editor of *Times* West Coast edition, 1962-63, business and financial editor, 1963-76, author of weekly column "The Economic Scene," 1963-76, column expanded to thrice weekly, 1976-78. Instructor in journalism at St. Johns University. *Military service:* U.S. Navy, World War II, served aboard battleship *New Jersey.*

OBITUARIES: Washington Post, October 25, 1978; *New York Times,* November 6, 1978.*

* * *

MULLOY, Elizabeth D(ibert) 1945-

PERSONAL: Born December 27, 1945, in Tyler, Tex.; daughter of Philip Landis (a district clerk) and Marjorie Iris (a mental health director; maiden name, Dodd) Dibert; married Michael F. Mulloy (in historic preservation), July 11, 1970; children: Margaret Elizabeth. *Education:* Stephens College, B.A., 1967; University of Missouri, M.A., 1969. *Home:* 1792 Ivy Oak Square, Reston, Va. 22090.

CAREER: University of Missouri, Columbia, instructor in English, 1968-72; General Services Administration, Washington, D.C., public relations and speech writer, 1972; American Institute of Architects, Washington, D.C., promotional and technical writer, 1973-75; National Trust for Historic Preservation, Washington, D.C., writer and editor, 1974-76.

WRITINGS: (With Tony P. Wrenn) *America's Forgotten Architecture,* Pantheon, 1976; *The History of the National Trust for Historic Preservation,* Preservation Press, 1976.

SIDELIGHTS: Mulloy wrote: "In 1973 I became a Christian. The motivation for my writing began to change at that point from promoting my own career to sharing the reality of Jesus Christ and God's love for His fallen world. Since 1976 I have been engaged in a full-time study of the Bible, teaching classes in Scripture for children as well as adults. I am currently teaching English composition in a Bible college extension program in the Washington, D.C., area, helping people involved in Christian ministry improve their writing skills.

"I am convinced that if, in a world changing with rhetoric and 'hype,' the Gospel can be presented with honesty and clarity, the truth will surely set us free. Nobody in our time has done this as superlatively as the British scholar, C. S. Lewis, who mastered a whole spectrum of genres to glorify his Lord (*Mere Christianity, The Screwtape Letters, The Narnia Chronicles, Surprised by Joy,* and so on). The erudition, the grace, and the wit of his work represents the best of Christian writing, as far as I'm concerned. I'd be happy just to introduce others to his books for the duration of my career."

* * *

MULTHAUF, Robert P(hilip) 1919-

PERSONAL: Born June 8, 1919, in Sioux Falls, S.D.; son of Philip J. (in sales) and Rose (Broderick) Multhauf; married Mary Smith, May, 1948 (divorced, 1959); married Lettie Stibbe (a translator), February 19, 1960; children: Ben, Bram, Stephen (stepchildren). *Education:* Iowa State University, B.S., 1941; University of California, Berkeley, M.A., 1950, Ph.D., 1953. *Home:* 4504 Salem Lane N.W., Washington, D.C. 20560. *Office:* National Museum of History and Technology, Smithsonian Institution, Washington, D.C. 20007.

CAREER: Smithsonian Institution, National Museum of History and Technology, Washington, D.C., historian of science, 1954—. *Military service:* U.S. Navy, 1943-46. *Member:* Society for the History of Technology (president, 1968-69), History of Science Society (president, 1979-80). *Awards, honors:* Usher Award from the Society for the History of Technology, 1965, for "Sal Ammoniac: A Case History of Industrialization."

WRITINGS: A Historical Collection of Instruments and Machines: A Catalogue of Instruments and Models, American Philosophical Society, 1961; *The Origins of Chemistry,* Oldbourne Press, 1967; *Neptune's Gift: A History of Common Salt,* Johns Hopkins Press, 1978. Contributor of about fifty articles to learned journals. Editor of *Isis,* 1964-78.

WORK IN PROGRESS: A history of the exploitation of nitrogen.

SIDELIGHTS: Multhauf comments: "I am writing a history of our exploitation of nitrogen, to which we owe such commodities as gunpowder and fertilizer. It is not a trivial subject, but alas, my last book, on salt, led a correspondent to ask if I would next write on ketchup or mustard.

"I try, with what could overoptimistically be called moderate success, to bridge the gap between the 'scholarly' exposition of the history of science and technology and the popular exposition of these topics. The gap is not only wide, but separates rocky, forbidding cliffs and a swamp."

MUNITZ, Milton K(arl) 1913-

PERSONAL: Born July 10, 1913, in New York, N.Y.; son of Samuel H. and Anna (Blumberg) Munitz; married Lenore D. Bloom, December 22, 1946; children: Charles S., Andrew S. *Education:* City College (now of the City University of New York), B.A., 1933; Columbia University, M.A., 1935, Ph.D., 1939. *Home address:* Marlborough Rd., Scarborough, N.Y. 10510. *Office:* Graduate Center, Graduate School and University Center of the City University of New York, 33 West 42nd St., New York, N.Y. 10036.

CAREER: City College (now of the City University of New York), New York City, 1935-43, began as tutor, became instructor in philosophy; Queens College (now of the City University of New York), Flushing, N.Y., instructor in philosophy, 1945-46; New York University, New York City, assistant professor, 1946-51, associate professor, 1951-58, professor of philosophy, 1958-73, head of department, 1968-73, director of Institute of Philosophy, 1968-73; Bernard M. Baruch College of the City University of New York, New York City, distinguished professor of philosophy, beginning 1973; staff member at Graduate School and University Center of the City University of New York, New York City. Instructor at Columbia University, 1945-46; visiting lecturer at Princeton University, 1952; distinguished visiting professor at State University of New York College at Brockport, 1967-68; visiting professor at Bar-Ilan University, 1972. Resident scholar at Villa Serbelloni, 1972; head of Fulbright screening committee of Association of Research Council's conference board, 1965-69. *Military service:* U.S. Army Air Forces, 1943-45; became second lieutenant.

MEMBER: American Philosophical Association, Aristotelian Society, Conference on Methods in Philosophy and Science, Royal Astronomical Society (fellow). *Awards, honors:* Ford Foundation fellow, 1954-55; senior Fulbright fellow at Cambridge University, 1960-61; Guggenheim fellow, 1960-61; Nicholas Murray Butler Medal from Columbia University, 1963; Rockefeller Foundation fellow, 1972.

WRITINGS: The Moral Philosophy of Santayana, Columbia University Press, 1939, reprinted, Greenwood Press, 1972; *Space, Time, and Creation: Philosophical Aspects of Scientific Cosmology*, Free Press, 1957; (editor) *Theories of the Universe: From Babylonian Myth to Modern Science*, Free Press, 1957; (editor and author of introduction) *A Modern Introduction to Ethics: Readings from Classical and Contemporary Sources*, Free Press, 1958.

The Mystery of Existence: An Essay in Philosophical Cosmology, Appleton, 1965; (editor) Immanuel Kant, *A Universal Natural History and Theory of the Heavens*, University of Michigan, 1969; (editor with Howard Keifer) *Contemporary Philosophic Thought*, State University of New York Press, 1970; (editor) *Ethics and Social Justice*, State University of New York Press, 1970; (editor) *Language, Belief, and Metaphysics*, State University of New York Press, 1970; (editor) *Mind, Science, and History*, State University of New York Press, 1970; (editor) *Perspective in Education, Religion, and the Arts*, State University of New York Press, 1970; (editor) *Identity and Individuation*, State University of New York Press, 1971; (editor) *Logic and Ontology*, New York University Press, 1972; *Existence and Logic*, New York University Press, 1974; (editor with Peter K. Unger) *Semantics and Philosophy*, New York University Press, 1974.

MURPHY, Gardner 1895-1979

PERSONAL: Born July 8, 1895, in Chillicothe, Ohio; died March 18, 1979, in Washington, D.C.; son of Edgar (a clergyman) and Maud (King) Murphy; married Lois Barclay (a psychologist), November 27, 1926; children: Alpen Gardner, Agatha Margaret Small. *Education:* Yale University, B.A., 1916; Harvard University, M.A., 1917; Columbia University, Ph.D., 1923. *Home:* 2810 Cortland Pl. N.W., Washington, D.C. 20008.

CAREER: Columbia University, New York City, lecturer, 1921-25, instructor, 1925-29, assistant professor of psychology, 1929-40; City College (now of the City University of New York), New York City, professor of psychology and chairman of department, 1940-52; Menninger Foundation, Topeka, Kan., director of research, 1952-68; George Washington University, Washington, D.C., professor of psychology, 1968-73. UNESCO consultant to Ministry of Information, 1950. *Military service:* U.S. Army, 1917-19, served with American Expeditionary Forces as medical corpsman. *Member:* American Academy of Arts and Sciences, American Psychological Association (president, 1943-44), American Society for Psychical Research (president, 1961-71), Eastern Psychological Association (president, 1941-42). *Awards, honors:* Hodgson fellow in psychology, 1922-25; Butler Medal from Columbia University, 1932; Gold Medal from the American Psychological Association, 1972.

WRITINGS: An Historical Introduction to Modern Psychology, Harcourt, 1929, 3rd edition, 1972; (with wife, Lois Barclay Murphy, and Theodore M. Newcomb) *Experimental Social Psychology: An Interpretation of Research Upon the Socialization of the Individual*, Harper, 1931, revised edition, 1937, reprinted, Greenwood Press, 1970; (with Friedrich Jensen) *Approaches to Personality: Some Contemporary Conceptions Used in Psychology With Psychiatry*, Coward, 1932; *General Psychology*, Harper, 1933, revised edition published as *A Briefer General Psychology*, 1935; (with Rensis Likert) *Public Opinion and the Individual: A Psychological Study of Student Attitudes on Public Questions, With a Retest Five Years Later*, Harper, 1938.

Personality: A Biosocial Approach to Origins and Structure, Harper, 1947; (editor) Muzafer Sherif, *An Outline of Social Psychology*, Harper, 1948; (editor) Milton L. Blum, *Industrial Psychology and Its Social Foundations*, Harper, 1949; (with Herbert Spohn) *An Introduction to Psychology*, Harper, 1951; *In the Minds of Men: The Study of Human Behavior and Social Tensions in India*, Basic Books, 1953; (editor with Arthur J. Bachrach) *An Outline of Abnormal Psychology*, revised edition, Modern Library, 1954; *Human Potentialities*, Basic Books, 1958.

(With Charles Marion Solley) *Development of the Perceptual World*, Basic Books, 1960; (editor) William James, *William James on Psychical Research*, Viking, 1960; (with Laura A. Dale) *Challenge of Psychical Research: A Primer of Parapsychology*, Harper, 1961; *Freeing Intelligence Through Teaching: A Dialectic of the Rational and the Personal*, Harper, 1961; (editor with L. Murphy) *Asian Psychology*, Basic Books, 1968; (with Spohn) *Encounter With Reality: New Forms for an Old Quest*, Houghton, 1968; *Psychological Thought From Pythagorus to Freud: An Informal Introduction*, Harcourt, 1968; (with Morton Leeds) *Outgrowing Self-Deception*, Basic Books, 1975.

Also author of sound recordings; all published by Big Sur Recordings; "Parapsychology," c. 1960; "Science, Man, and Parapsychology," 1965; "Toward a General Theory of the Paranormal," 1969.

SIDELIGHTS: According to Murphy, the scientific and analytical study of parapsychology is imperative to the ultimate understanding of ourselves and the world around us. He felt it necessary to study the unknown recesses of the mind and the psychic ''phenomena'' that accompany them. His basic argument for research into psychic phenomena was that science, by its own definition, precludes the notion of disclaiming things simply because they appear to be impossible. Where, Murphy asked, would science be today had not all the Galileos and Madame Curies questioned the inconceivable and delved into the unknown?

BIOGRAPHICAL/CRITICAL SOURCES: New Yorker, January 18, 1969; *New York Times,* July 4, 1975; *New York Times Book Review,* July 13, 1975; *Contemporary Psychology,* April, 1976.

OBITUARIES: New York Times, March 21, 1979; *Washington Post,* March 21, 1979.*

*   *   *

MUSHKIN, Selma J.   1913-1979

OBITUARY NOTICE: Born December 31, 1913, in Centerville, N.Y.; died of cancer, December 2, 1979, in Washington, D.C. Author, educator, and an expert in health and public management. Mushkin was the chief of financial studies with the Social Security Administration and also worked with the Public Health Service. She taught at Georgetown University and was a research professor at Johns Hopkins University. Mushkin's work includes *Functional Federalism* and *Economics of Higher Education.* Obituaries and other sources: *American Men and Women of Science: The Social and Behavioral Sciences,* 12th edition, Bowker, 1973; *Who's Who of American Women,* 8th edition, Marquis, 1973; *Washington Post,* December 4, 1979.

*   *   *

MUSIAL, Stan(ley Frank)   1920-

PERSONAL: Born November 21, 1920, in Donora, Pa.; son of Lukasz (a steelworker) Musial; married Lillian Labash, November 21, 1939; children: Dickie, Geraldine. *Education:* Graduated from high school, 1938. *Office:* c/o St. Louis Cardinals, 250 Stadium Plaza, St. Louis, Mo. 63102.

CAREER: St. Louis Cardinals baseball team, St. Louis, Mo., player with minor league teams, 1938-41, player with parent team, 1941-63, general manager, 1967, senior vice-president, 1967—. Owner and operator of St. Louis restaurant. Director of President Lyndon Johnson's Physical Fitness Program, 1964. *Military service:* U.S. Navy, 1945. *Awards, honors:* Named most valuable player of National League, 1943, 1946, and 1948; named as outfielder on *Sporting News* All-Star major league teams, 1943, 1944, 1948, 1949, 1950, 1951, 1952, 1953, and 1954, named as first baseman, 1946, 1957, and 1958; named top National League player by *Sporting News,* 1943, 1948, 1951, and 1957; named major league player of the year by *Sporting News,* 1946 and 1951; Sid Mercer Award from New York Baseball Writers, 1947; Kenesaw Mountain Landis Memorial Plaque, 1948; named player of the decade by *Sporting News,* 1956; elected to baseball's Hall of Fame, 1974.

WRITINGS: (With Bob Broeg) *Stan Musial: ''The Man's'' Own Story, as Told to Bob Broeg,* Doubleday, 1964; *U.S. Official Physical Fitness Program: A Fitness Program for All That Takes Only a Few Minutes a Day,* J. Dienhart, 1964; (with Jack Buck and Broeg) *We Saw Stars,* Bethany Press, 1976. Contributor of articles on physical fitness to magazines, including *Parents'* Magazine, *Parks & Recreation,* and *American Education.*

SIDELIGHTS: Musial hoped for a career in baseball from the time he was eight years old. At sixteen, he was offered both an athletic scholarship to the University of Pittsburgh and a professional baseball contract with the St. Louis Cardinals. Though Lukasz Musial wanted his son to attend college, he was eventually persuaded to let Stan begin a baseball career upon his graduation from high school in 1938. By August of 1948, Musial had already joined the ranks of the best in the game. Jimmy Cannon, sports writer for the *New York Post,* contended that only five players of the day might be considered great: Bob Feller, Joe DiMaggio, Ted Williams, Lou Boudreau, and Stan ''The Man'' Musial.

Recruited as a pitcher, the southpaw improved his 1938 performance of six wins, six losses by posting a nine-and-two record in 1939, the year he married Lillian Labash. The following season, Musial alternated between the pitcher's mound and the outfield. But when he made a difficult shoestring catch of a fly ball, he fell and injured his left shoulder. The mishap ended his pitching career.

Married, not yet twenty, and his wife expecting a baby, Musial might have had to leave baseball altogether but for the kindness of his team manager, Dick Kerr, a former star pitcher for the Chicago White Sox. Kerr and his wife rented a larger house and invited the Musials to live with them, an arrangement that allowed Musial to continue playing as an outfielder. In honor of Kerr's hospitality, the Musials named their son after the manager, and many years later, when the Kerrs faced financial difficulties of their own, Musial secretly bought a house for them in Houston. A newsman, not Musial, disclosed the secret.

At the start of the 1941 season, his fourth year in the minor leagues, no team wanted ''dead-arm Musial'' who wound up playing for the Class C Springfield club in Missouri. By mid-season, Musial was slugging an amazing .379 and was promoted in July to the Class AA Rochester team. There he hit for a .336 average, good enough to be called up by the Cardinals who were locked in a pennant race with the Brooklyn Dodgers. In twelve games with the parent club, Musial batted .426, collecting twenty hits and driving in seven runs. On September 23, 1941, the Cardinal management held a ''Stan Musial Day,'' an honor that capped ''perhaps the most spectacular season in the life of any young ballplayer in all baseball history.''

Over the next three years, Musial established himself as one of the most feared hitters in baseball. After a slow start in 1942, he finished the season at .315, fourth-best in the league. Then, in 1943, he played in his first All-Star game, won his first batting title, and was named the most valuable player in the National League. His .357 average dropped slightly the next year, when he was runner-up to Dixie Walker for the batting championship. Though military service interrupted his career in 1945, Musial used his spare time to improve his home run hitting technique.

Moved from the outfield to first base in 1946, ''Stash,'' as his teammates called him, again won the batting crown and was voted most valuable player. Before Musial, only Hank Greenburg had been voted MVP at two different positions. But, as in 1942, Musial struggled at the plate the following spring and blamed his .171 pace on too much golf. When doctors discovered that he was actually suffering from acute appendicitis, Musial had the organ frozen and postponed surgery until after the season. Meanwhile, he again competed in the All-Star game, raised his average to .312, and hit more home runs (nineteen) than in previous seasons.

Musial reached his peak as a hitter in 1948. He led the league in hitting (.376), hits, runs, doubles, triples, runs batted in, and came within one of tying for the home run lead with thirty-nine. Both John Mize and Ralph Kiner picked up forty homers that year. Musial also set a National League record when he connected for five hits in a single game for the fourth time that season, equaling Ty Cobb's mark in the American League. For his play that year, he was honored with a record-breaking third MVP award, the Kenesaw Mountain Landis Memorial Plaque, and an Associated Press poll that ranked him third among world athletes. That October, Musial's contract negotiations with Cardinal president Robert Hannegan took only fifteen minutes; he signed up for another two years at a reported annual salary of fifty thousand dollars.

Over the next fifteen years, until his retirement in 1963, Musial accumulated a .331 lifetime batting average, 3,630 base hits, a record 1,951 runs batted in, 10,972 times-at-bat, and 475 home runs. His most notable accomplishments as a home run hitter include the times he belted five of the long-balls in a 1954 doubleheader and racked up four others in four consecutive times at bat in 1962. In the twelfth inning of the 1955 All-Star game, American League catcher Yogi Berra complained to Musial of aching feet. The Cardinal star stepped up to the plate, told Berra he wouldn't have long to wait, and promptly tagged the first pitch for a home run, giving the National League a 6-5 victory. The record also shows that Musial played in more All-Star games, twenty-four, than any other player in history.

In addition to all his hitting, Musial led the National League in fielding as an outfielder three times. In 1961, his best season of fielding, he committed only one error. However, he also recalls the time he misjudged a fly ball in a 1944 game with the Phillies; the ball somehow hit him squarely on top of the head, caromed high and away, and allowed two runs to score.

After his 1963 retirement, Musial returned to the Cardinals as general manager in 1967. The Redbirds won both the league pennant and the world championship that year. It marked the first time in major league history that a league flag and the World Series were won in a general manager's first year of office. Because of other business interests, though, Musial resigned his office after ten months and became the club's vice-president.

In *Stan Musial: "The Man's" Own Story*, Musial relates the highlights of his baseball life, presents his philosophy on the sport, offers some tips on hitting, and appraises the managers and players he has known. "For anyone who has an interest in baseball . . . ," wrote J. P. McNicholas, "this book will make engrossing reading. It is full of good sound advice for our younger generation." It also includes "some rather piquant remarks about the Yankees . . . , Durocher and the Dodgers, . . . Jackie Robinson's reception in the big leagues,

and . . . the peculiar situation in left field at Yankee Stadium."

BIOGRAPHICAL/CRITICAL SOURCES: Stan Musial and Bob Broeg, *Stan Musial: "The Man's" Own Story, as Told to Bob Broeg*, Doubleday, 1964; *Sports Illustrated*, March 20, 1967, August 23, 1976; *New York Times Magazine*, September 17, 1967; Robert Liston, *The Pros*, Platt, 1968; Joseph Reichler, *30 Years of Baseball's Great Moments*, Crown, 1974; Mac Davis, *100 Greatest Baseball Heroes*, Grosset, 1974; Frank Litsky, *Superstars*, Derbibooks, 1975.*

*   *   *

MUTKE, Peter H(ans) C(hristoph)   1927-

PERSONAL: Born April 30, 1927, in Ohlau/Schlesien, Germany; came to the United States in 1952; son of Ernst (a physician) and Magalene (an artist and craftsperson; maiden name, Adler) Mutke; children: Lorraine. *Education:* University of Heidelberg, M.A., 1949, M.D., 1952; attended Chines College of Acupuncture, 1972. *Office:* Department of Psychology, John F. Kennedy University, Orinda, Calif. 94563; and Box 4977, Carmel, Calif. 93921.

CAREER: Orange General Hospital, Orange, Calif., intern, 1953-54; St. Joseph Hospital, Orange, resident and surgeon, 1954-57; physician and surgeon in Carmel, Calif., 1960-72; John F. Kennedy University, Orinda, Calif., instructor in selective awareness therapy, 1972—. Private practice in selective awareness therapy, 1974-76. Medical director of Foundation for Humanistic Medicine and Psychology. Lecturer at University of California, Berkeley, 1968—. Senior member of National Ski Patrol; detective with Berkeley Police Department; professional artist and photographer. *Military service:* U.S. Army, Medical Corps, 1957-59; became captain; received Commanders Trophy. *Member:* American Medical Association, Academy of Psychosomatic Medicine, American Society of Clinical Hypnosis, California Medical Association. *Awards, honors:* Fellowships from American Society of Clinical Hypnosis, 1965, American Society of Clinical Hypnosis, 1968, and Academy of Psychosomatic Medicine, 1975.

WRITINGS: Selective Awareness, Celestial Arts, 1977; *Selective Awareness Therapy*, Westwood Publishing, 1980.

WORK IN PROGRESS: Psychophysiological Responses of the Thermographic Image, completion expected in 1981.

SIDELIGHTS: Mutke told *CA:* "Of all my creative talents, I find writing the most difficult. It would be great if there were thinking machines that would put all my thoughts on paper, because my head is always full of thoughts.

"In my writing, I want to show that health is a very personal matter and that healing and getting well are much simpler than is accepted today."

N

NAGEL, Ernest 1901-

PERSONAL: Born November 16, 1901, in Novemesto, Czechoslovakia; came to the United States in 1911, naturalized citizen, 1919; son of Isidor (a shopkeeper) and Frida (Weisz) Nagel; married Edith Haggstrom (a physicist), January 23, 1935; children: Alexander, Sidney. *Education:* City College (now of the City University of New York), B.S., 1923; Columbia University, A.M., 1925, Ph.D., 1931. *Politics:* None. *Religion:* None. *Home:* 25 Claremont Ave., New York, N.Y. 10027. *Office:* Philosophy Hall, Columbia University, New York, N.Y. 10027.

CAREER: Teacher at public schools in New York City, 1923-29; City College (now of the City University of New York), New York City, instructor in philosophy, 1930-31; Columbia University, New York City, instructor, 1931-37, assistant professor, 1937-39, associate professor, 1939-46, professor, 1946-55, John Dewey Professor of Philosophy, 1955-66, university professor, 1967-70, professor emeritus, 1970—. Fellow of Center for Advanced Studies in the Behavioral Sciences, 1959-60.

MEMBER: International Union for the Philosophy and History of Science (chairperson of national committee, 1958-59), British Academy (corresponding fellow), American Association for the Advancement of Science (fellow; section vice-president, 1951, 1973), American Academy of Arts and Sciences (fellow), American Philosophical Society (fellow), American Philosophical Association (president of Eastern Division, 1954), National Academy of Sciences, Association for Symbolic Logic (president, 1947-49), Philosophy of Science Association (president, 1960-62), Institute for the Unity of Science (vice-president), Conference on Methods in the Philosophy of Science (chairperson, 1946-47), New York Philosophical Society, Phi Beta Kappa. *Awards, honors:* Guggenheim fellowships, 1934-35, 1950-51; L.H.D. from Bard College, 1964, and City University of New York, 1972; D.Sc. from Brandeis University, 1965; D.Litt. from Rutgers University, 1967, Case Western Reserve University, 1970, Columbia University, 1971, and University of Guelph, 1979.

WRITINGS: On the Logic of Measurement, privately printed, 1932; (with Morris R. Cohen) *Introduction to Logic and Scientific Method,* Harcourt, 1934; *Principles of the Theory of Probability,* University of Chicago Press, 1939; *Sovereign Reason,* Free Press, 1954; *Logic Without Metaphysics,* Free Press, 1957; (with J. R. Newman) *Goedel's Proof,* New York University Press, 1958; *The Structure of Science,* Harcourt, 1961; *Teleology Revisited,* Columbia University Press, 1979. Contributor to learned journals. Editor of *Journal of Symbolic Logic,* 1939-45, *Journal of Philosophy,* 1940-56, and *Philosophy of Science,* 1956-59.

WORK IN PROGRESS: The Dimensions of Critical Philosophy (tentative title), publication by Open Court Publishing Co. expected in 1981.

SIDELIGHTS: Nagel writes: "I have been interested in philosophy since my high school days. I have been strongly influenced by my former teachers, Morris R. Cohen, Bertrand Russell, George Santayana, Rudolf Carnap, Phillip Frank, and John Dewey. I would characterize myself as an empirical rationalist and naturalist, with special interest in the natural and social sciences, and also in the philosophy of law. I suppose I should classify myself as a liberal in my social outlook, even though that label does not really reveal much."

Goedel's Proof has been translated into Dutch, German, Italian, Japanese, Portuguese, and Spanish. Another book, *The Structure of Science,* has been translated into Dutch, Italian, Polish, and Spanish.

* * *

NAGEL, Shirley 1922-

PERSONAL: Born May 20, 1922, in Youngstown, Ohio; daughter of Fred E. (a business manager) and Jane Addams (a teacher; maiden name, Moore) Stansbury; married William V. Ward, October 11, 1944 (divorced, 1959); married Richard Nagel, June 25, 1975; children: (first marrige) Rob, Flint. *Education:* Attended University of Arizona, 1942-44, Occidental College, 1955, University of California, Los Angeles, and California State University, Los Angeles. *Home:* 16001 Pacific Coast Highway, #1 Vista, Pacific Palisades, Calif. 90272.

CAREER: Elementary school teacher, 1955-65; La Canada School District, La Canada, Calif., library assistant, 1967; independent researcher, 1970-72; Regional Research Institute, Los Angeles, Calif., consultant, 1972-74; writer, 1974—. *Member:* Society of Children's Book Writers. *Awards, honors: Tree Boy* was named a notable book in the field of social studies by National Council for the Social Studies, 1978.

WRITINGS: Tree Boy, Scribner, 1978; *Escape From the Tower,* Bowmar, 1978; *Six Short Stories,* Bowmar, 1978.

Contributor of articles and stories to magazines and newspapers, including *Highlights for Children.*

WORK IN PROGRESS: When the Dogwood Blooms, an adventure story for young adults, set during the Civil War; a children's book about the handicapped; research in England for a gothic novel.

SIDELIGHTS: Shirley Nagel writes: "I have a passionate concern about good literature for children, encouraging and motivating their interest in books. In my own writing, I like to show that children count, that they are important for the present and the future, and that, as individuals, they can make a difference."

* * *

NAGORSKI, Andrew 1947-

PERSONAL: Born May 3, 1947, in Edinburgh, Scotland; children: two. *Education:* Attended secondary schools in Cairo, Egypt, Paris, France, and Seoul, Korea; Amherst College, B.A., 1969; attended Jageillonian University of Cracow, 1968-69. *Home:* 31A Repulse Bay Towers, 119A Repulse Bay Rd., Hong Kong, Hong Kong. *Office:* Newsweek, 2A Gardena Ct., 2 Kennedy Terr., Hong Kong, Hong Kong.

CAREER/WRITINGS: Wayland High School, Wayland, Mass., teacher of social studies, 1969-73; *Newsweek,* New York City, associate editor, writer, and reporter, 1973-76, general editor, 1976-77, assistant managing editor, 1977-78, Asian regional editor, based in Hong Kong, 1978—. Most notable assignments include more than twenty cover stories for *Newsweek,* including oil diplomacy, inflation, Sun Myung Moon, and the rise of African nationalism. Contributor to *Africa and the United States: Vital Interests,* edited by Jennifer S. Whitaker, New York University Press, 1978. *Awards, honors:* Overseas Press Club citation for best magazine reporting from abroad, 1974, for cover story "Black Africa Moves South," and award for best business reporting from abroad, 1978, for cover story "Japan vs. the World."

* * *

NAMIKAWA, Ryo 1905-

PERSONAL: Born December 26, 1905, in Matsue, Japan; son of Yoshitaka and Hide Namikawa; married Shimomura Hisako; children: Banri. *Education:* Tokyo University, D.Litt., 1977. *Home:* 5-2-14 Kugayama, Suginami-ku, Tokyo, Japan.

CAREER: Educator and writer. Nihon University, Tokyo, Japan, professor of drama and English literature, 1970-79; Tamagawa University, Tokyo, Japan, lecturer in drama, 1971—. Member of council of UNESCO Asian Cultural Centre. *Member:* Japanese Association for the Reconstruction of Borobudur (member of council). *Awards, honors:* Ten art prizes from Cultural Department of Japanese government and Commercial Broadcasting Association of Japan, for television and radio scripts, including Grand Prix from the Art Festival of Japan.

WRITINGS: John Dos Passos, U.S.A., three volumes, Kaizo-sha, Shincho-sha, 1954; (editor) Banri Namikawa, Daigoro Chihara, and Ryusho Hikata, *Borobudoru* (text in English and Japanese), [Japan], 1971, published as *Borobudur: The World of Gandhavyuha,* Kodansha, 1978; (with son, Banri Namikawa) *Istanbul: Tale of Three Cities,* Kodansha, 1972; *William Blake,* Hara-shobo, 1978; *Blake's Life and Works,* Hara-shobo, 1979.

In Japanese: *Sugata naki buki* (title means "Weapon With-

out Arms"), Taisei Shuppan, 1943; *Hyakunen no burei* (title means "One Hundred Years' Humiliation"), Taisei Shuppan, 1944; *Jazu monogatari* (title means "Story of New Orleans"), Hasegawa Shoten, 1949; *Jazu ongaku,* [Japan], 1953; *Kami o tazunete sammankiro* (title means "Seeking the God: My Long Travel"), [Japan], 1966.

Hoso no daihon to enshutsu (title means "Directing Radio and Television"), [Japan], 1970; *Shiruku Rodo o yuku hotoke* (title means "Buddha Images on the Silk Road"), [Japan], 1974; *Chichukai: Ishi to suna no sekai* (title means "Mediterranean: Stone and Sand"), [Japan], 1977; (with B. Namikawa) *Butsuzo no nagai tabiji* (title means "Long Journey of the Buddha Image"), [Japan], 1978; (with B. Namikawa) *Chichukai: Kami to hito no sekai* (title means "Mediterranean: God and Man"), [Japan], 1978; *Persepolis,* Kodansha, 1978, revised edition, 1980.

Also author of *Rafukadio Hahn Shisetsu* (title means "Lafcadio Hearn Reconsidered"), 1980, and *Central Silkroad,* 1980. Author of more than three hundred television and radio scripts, including "Men of Bunraku," "Hiroshima," and "Bell of Nagasaki." Translator of *Upton Sinclair's Works,* 1952-56.

SIDELIGHTS: Namikawa wrote: "The *Mainichi* criticized *Persepolis* as 'the best separate volume in quality depicting the grand drama of Iran from ancient to Islam Revolution of 1979.' The *Nihon Dokusho Shimbun* valued *William Blake* as 'the most voluminous, epochal book dealing with the vision of Blake.' As for *Borobudur,* many scholars in Europe and the United States valued the work of identification of the hitherto unidentified reliefs as the 'most plausible and elaborate work,' and 'the great contribution in the field of . . . ancient Asian art.'

"I was one of Upton Sinclair's disciples. When I translated his twelve works into Japanese, they impressed the Japanese people deeply just after the surrender of World War II."

* * *

NASH, David T(heodore) 1929-

PERSONAL: Born October 15, 1929, in New York, N.Y.; son of Sam (a tailor) and Pearl (Middlepunkt) Nash; married Ellen Cohn (a singer), September 26, 1956; children: Stephen D., Robert M. *Education:* New York University, B.A. (magna cum laude), 1949, M.D., 1953. *Home:* 4 Meadow Dr., Fayetteville, N.Y. 13066. *Office:* 600 East Genesee St., Syracuse, N.Y. 13202.

CAREER: Mount Sinai Hospital, New York City, rotating intern, 1953-54; University Hospital, Syracuse, N.Y., assistant resident in medicine, 1954-57; Mount Sinai Hospital, New York City, resident in medicine, 1957-58; fellow in cardiology, Harvard University, Cambridge, Mass., and Beth Israel Hospital, Boston, Mass., both 1958-59. Attending physician at St. Joseph's Hospital, Syracuse, 1959—; associate attending physician at University Hospital, Syracuse. Clinical associate professor at State University of New York Upstate Medical Center. *Military service:* U.S. Air Force, 1955-57; served in Guam; became major. *Member:* American College of Physicians (fellow), American College of Cardiology (fellow).

WRITINGS: Dr. Nash's Natural Diet Book, Grosset, 1978; *Coronary: Prediction and Prevention,* Scribner, 1979. Contributor to *Yearbook of Drug Therapy.* Contributor of about thirty-five articles to medical journals in the United States and abroad.

WORK IN PROGRESS: A novel "based on in-hospital epidemics and the roles professionals play."

SIDELIGHTS: Nash writes: "I am interested in providing the average reader with a more accurate picture of the medical world stripped of its mystique."

*   *   *

NAUMANN, Marina 1938-

PERSONAL: Born July 15, 1938, in Princeton, N.J.; daughter of John (a professor) and Ludmilla (a professor; maiden name, Buketoff) Turkevich; married Robert Alexander Naumann (a professor), September 16, 1961; children: Kristin Ragnhild, Andrew John Bruno. *Education:* Wellesley College, B.A., 1960; graduate study at Brown University, 1960-61; University of Pennsylvania, M.A., 1962, Ph.D., 1973. *Religion:* Russian Orthodox. *Home:* 29 Oxford Circle, Skillman, N.J. 08558. *Office:* Department of Russian, Douglass College, Rutgers University, New Brunswick, N.J. 08903.

CAREER: Rutgers University, Douglass College, New Brunswick, N.J., assistant professor of Russian language and literature, 1974—. *Member:* North American Dostoevski Society, Modern Language Association of America, American Association for the Advancement of Slavic Studies, American Association of University Professors, Vladimir Nabokov Society, American Association of Teachers of Slavic and East European Languages, Slavic Conference on Slavic Studies, Wellesley Club of Central New Jersey, Princeton University League, Dobro Slovo. *Awards, honors:* Grant from Andrew W. Mellon Foundation, 1978.

WRITINGS: Blue Evenings in Berlin: Nabokov's Short Stories of the 1920's, New York University Press, 1978; (contributor) Victor Terras, editor, *American Contributions to the Eighth International Congress of Slavists,* Slavica Publishers, 1978. Contributor to language and Slavic studies journals.

WORK IN PROGRESS: Emblems of Exile in Modern Russian Literature, publication expected in 1982.

SIDELIGHTS: Marina Naumann writes: "Literary criticism in American and Russian literature is my central professional interest. Due to my heritage I have been particularly attracted to the study of Russian emigre accomplishments. As a native-born American I am alarmed by the increasing neglect of foreign language training in the United States, and particularly in the essential Slavic area."

AVOCATIONAL INTERESTS: Philately, photography, playing the piano, travel (Denmark, Germany).

*   *   *

NAYLOR, John 1920-
(Orion)

PERSONAL: Born December 15, 1920, in Knaresborough, Yorkshire, England; son of R. H. (an astrologer) and E. (Thropp) Naylor; married V. McGurk, September 15, 1943; children: Patricia Naylor Kilbane, Christine Naylor Gavin, Lloyd, Michele. *Education:* Attended University of London, 1937-39. *Politics:* "Nonpolitical." *Religion:* Church of England. *Home and office:* Skerry Vore, Undercliffe, Sandgate, Folkestone, Kent, England. *Agent:* K. Singer, BP Singer Features, Inc., 3164 West Tyler Ave., Anaheim, Calif. 92801; and Rupert Crew, King's Mews, Gray's Inn Rd., London WC1 N2JA, England.

CAREER: British Thomson Houston, London, England, apprentice electrical engineer, 1936-39; conducted astrological research with father, R. H. Naylor, 1940-49; independent writer, publisher, researcher, and consultant, 1949—. *Mem-*

ber: Federation of British Astrologers (president, 1965-79), Federation of American Astrologers.

WRITINGS: Your Stars, Naylor Press, 1963, 15th edition, 1977; *Your Stars,* twelve volumes, Bantam, 1965, 20th edition, 1975; *Your Luck,* Naylor Press, 1967, 11th edition, 1977; *Your Life,* Naylor Press, 1968; *Your Romance,* Naylor Press, 1970; *Your Stars,* twelve volumes, Globe Communications Corp., 1979. Author of syndicated feature, "What the Stars Foretell," published weekly in England, West Indies, India, South Africa, New Zealand, and Australia. Author, under pseudonym Orion, of daily feature, "Stars," in *London Daily Mail.* Contributor of weekly features to *Love Affair* and of monthly features to *19, Annabel, Puzzler,* and *Panache.*

WORK IN PROGRESS: Continuing research on political and financial astrology.

SIDELIGHTS: Naylor writes: "I have only two major interests: family life and astrology. My father pioneered popular astrology in England and internationally during the 1930's. I followed in his footsteps. Delighted about the increasing public interest in astrology and the extent to which modern scientific research is confirming ancient astrological theories, I look forward to the day when it is generally accepted that man is not 'master of his fate, captain of his soul' but an instrument responsive to forces operating both in the solar system and in the universe as a whole. Unless there is this recognition and acceptance and an appreciation that safeguards are necessary, I foresee the day when populations will be politically manipulated by the use of power plants which duplicate radiations reaching the earth from outer space. Conversely, just as bacteriology revolutionized medicine to the benefit of mankind, so I consider a greater understanding of extra-terrestrial forces will result in control and elimination of what are generally regarded as natural hazards, to universal benefit."

*   *   *

NEIL, Randolph L. 1941-
(Randy Neil)

PERSONAL: Born December 16, 1941, in Kansas City, Mo.; son of Randolph Steele and Elizabeth (Laning) Neil; married Debra Panknin, October 4, 1974 (divorced November 6, 1978); children: Merritt Angeline. *Education:* Attended University of Kansas, 1962-65. *Religion:* Episcopalian. *Home:* 5100 West 111th Ter., Leawood, Kan. 66211. *Agent:* Wendy Lipkind Agency, 225 East 57th St., New York, N.Y. 10022. *Office:* International Cheerleading Foundation, Foxhill Village, Shawnee Mission, Kan. 66211.

CAREER: Kansas City Chiefs, Kansas City, Mo., head cheerleader, 1963-64; International Cheerleading Foundation, Shawnee Mission, Kan., founder and president, 1964—. Originator of annual "National Collegiate Cheerleading Championships" on Columbia Broadcasting System, Inc. (CBS-TV). Vice-chairperson of county Democratic party, 1976-77. Associate of Kansas City Philharmonic Orchestra, 1978—. *Member:* National Film Society (founder; president, 1975—), American Society of Association Executives, National Collegiate Athletic Association, Bibliographical Society of America, National Trust for Historic Preservation, Cousteau Society, Southern Poverty Law Center, Greater Kansas City Chamber of Commerce. *Awards, honors:* Named motion picture preservationist of the year by Women of the Motion Picture Industry, 1977.

WRITINGS—Under name Randy Neil: *Faculty Cheerleader Advisor's Handbook,* Traditions Press, 1967; *The Encyclo-*

pedia of Cheerleading, Traditions Press, 1974; *You Can Become a Cheerleader*, Traditions Press, 1975; *The Official Cheerleader's Handbook*, Simon & Schuster, 1979; *The Booster's Handbook: A Guide to American School Spirit*, Simon & Schuster, 1980. Publisher of *American Classic Screen*, 1976—.

WORK IN PROGRESS: Governor Jefferson, a history of Thomas Jefferson's years as governor of Virginia, 1779-1781.

SIDELIGHTS: Neil describes his beginnings as a professional cheerleader in the preface to *The Official Cheerleader's Handbook:* "I was never big enough to quarterback a football team or push and shove under a basketball goal. But from the time I saw my first cheerleader I knew what I wanted to do. Back in 1955 I joined my first pep club. In 1962 I was on my first cheerleading squad . . . and in 1963, I initiated a group of cheerleaders for the Kansas City Chief pro-football team."

He adds: "I have been one of a handful of people in America who have made a career being a professional cheerleader . . . teaching, writing, and running an educational association in this field. After the *Washington Post* called me 'Mr. Spirit' in 1973, my work has been covered in over five hundred newspapers and has caused appearances on all major television networks."

In 1978, Neil was instrumental in bringing the organization he founded, International Cheerleading Foundation, to network television with the CBS-TV special, "The National Collegiate Cheerleading Championships." That same year he began a series of instructive texts on school spirit for Simon & Schuster.

An ardent film preservationist, Neil is the founder and current president of the National Film Society. In 1975 he initiated the annual "Artistry in Cinema Awards," the only honors program that pays tribute to the people who pioneered the American motion picture industry.

AVOCATIONAL INTERESTS: Motion picture history, colonial American history (especially the life of Thomas Jefferson), collecting rare books.

BIOGRAPHICAL/CRITICAL SOURCES: Newsweek, April 10, 1978; *Sports Illustrated*, April 24, 1978.

*   *   *

NEIL, Randy
     See NEIL, Randolph L.

*   *   *

NEIL, William   1909-1979

OBITUARY NOTICE—See index for *CA* sketch: Born June 13, 1909, in Glasgow, Scotland; died November 10, 1979. Clergyman, educator, Bible historian, and author of works in his field. Neil's numerous writings include *The Bible as History, The Plain Man Looks at the Bible*, and *The Bible Story*. Obituaries and other sources: *The Author's and Writer's Who's Who*, 6th edition, Burke's Peerage, 1971; *The Writers Directory, 1976-78*, St. Martin's, 1976; *Who's Who*, 131st edition, St. Martin's, 1979; *AB Bookman's Weekly*, January 28, 1980.

*   *   *

NELSON, Beth
     See NELSON, Mary Elizabeth

NELSON, Harold L(ewis)   1917-

PERSONAL: Born November 28, 1917, in Fergus Falls, Minn.; son of Charles (a dentist) and Drusilla (Hodgson) Nelson; married Ann Sullivan, January 14, 1942; children: Susan Lene (Mrs. Richard M. Goldsmith), Eric Charles. *Education:* University of Minnesota, B.A., 1941, M.A., 1950, Ph.D., 1956. *Politics:* Democrat. *Religion:* Unitarian-Universalist. *Home:* 5805 Anchorage Ave., Madison, Wis. 53705. *Office:* School of Journalism, University of Wisconsin, Vilas Hall, Madison, Wis. 53706.

CAREER: Time Life, Inc., Minneapolis, Minn., in public relations, 1941; Northwestern National Bank, Minneapolis, Minn., in public relations, 1946-47; United Press Associations, Minneapolis, Minn., reporter and editor, 1947-50; Texas Tech University, Lubbock, assistant professor of journalism, 1950-51; State University of Iowa, Iowa City, instructor, 1951-52; University of California, Berkeley, assistant professor of journalism, 1954-55; University of Wisconsin—Madison, assistant professor, 1955-59, associate professor, 1959-63, professor of journalism, 1963—, director of School of Journalism, 1966-75. Gonzales Professor of Journalism at University of South Carolina, 1976. *Military service:* U.S. Naval Reserve, active duty, 1941-46; became lieutenant.

MEMBER: International Association for Mass Communications Research, American Historical Association, Organization of American Historians, Wisconsin Historical Society, Madison Press Club, Milwaukee Press Club, Madison Literary Club, Association for Education in Journalism (president, 1967), Society of Professional Journalists, Sigma Delta Chi, Kappa Tau Alpha. *Awards, honors:* Shared in special citation from Sigma Delta Chi, 1969, for *Law of Mass Communications*.

WRITINGS: Libel in News of Congressional Investigating Committees, University of Minnesota Press, 1961; (editor) *Freedom of the Press From Hamilton to the Warren Court*, Bobbs-Merrill, 1967; (with D. L. Teeter, Jr.) *Law of Mass Communications*, Foundation Press, 1969, 3rd edition, 1978. Contributor to journalism and law journals. Member of editorial board of *Journalism History*.

WORK IN PROGRESS: Law of Mass Communications, 4th edition, with D. L. Teeter, Jr., publication expected by Foundation Press; continuing research on freedom of the press in eighteenth-century America.

SIDELIGHTS: Nelson writes: "My central research interest is the history of the First Amendment and freedom of the press. It emerged in my graduate-school days, stimulated by my major professor and by the historical work of Frederick S. Siebert. I consider myself a litertarian in freedom of expression, but not an 'absolutist.' I like to teach journalistic writing and editing, and the law and history of mass communications."

AVOCATIONAL INTERESTS: "Anything to do with trees, and life close to nature."

*   *   *

NELSON, Mary Elizabeth   1926-
     (Beth Nelson)

PERSONAL: Born October 5, 1926, in Douglas, Ariz.; daughter of John R. and Ruth (a telephone operator; maiden name, Butler) Nelson. *Education:* Attended University of Chicago, Johns Hopkins University, and Harvard University; University of California, B.A., 1953, Ph.D., 1966. *Office:* Department of English, University of Colorado, Boulder, Colo. 80309.

CAREER: Worked variously as reporter and editor; Sacramento State College (now California State University, Sacramento), Sacramento, Calif., instructor in English, 1964-66; University of Colorado, Boulder, associate professor of English, 1966—. *Member:* Modern Language Association of America, American Association of University Women, American Federation of Teachers.

WRITINGS—Under name Beth Nelson: *George Crabbe and the Progress of Eighteenth-Century Narrative,* Bucknell University Press, 1977.

WORK IN PROGRESS: A study of women prophets and the emergence of the woman writer in the seventeenth and eighteenth centuries; a biographical study of Lady Eleanor Davies.

*   *   *

NELSON, Oswald George   1907-1975
(Ozzie Nelson)

PERSONAL: Born March 20, 1907, in Jersey City, N.J.; died June 3, 1975, of cancer, in San Fernando, Calif., buried in Hollywood Hills, Calif.; son of George Waldumar (a banker) and Ethel Irene (Orr) Nelson; married Peggy Lou Snyder (actress under name Harriet Hilliard), October 8, 1935; children: David Ozzie, Eric Hilliard (actor and singer under name Rick Nelson). *Education:* Rutgers University, B.Litt., 1927, LL.B., 1930. *Politics:* Republican. *Residence:* San Fernando Valley, Calif.

CAREER: Actor, producer, director, bandleader and musician, lawyer, and author under the name of Ozzie Nelson. Dance orchestra leader for hotels, theatres, ballrooms, and radio programs such as "Believe It or Not," "Seeing Stars," for Joe Penner, Bob Ripley, Red Skelton, recording such songs as "And Then Your Lips Met Mine," "Baby Boy," "Size 37 Suit," "Swinging on the Golden Gate," 1943-44; actor on radio program, "The Ozzie and Harriet Show," 1944-52; actor, director, and producer of television series, "The Adventures of Ozzie and Harriet," 1952-66; actor in plays, including "Impossible Years," "State Fair," "Marriage-Go-Round," 1966-73; actor and director of television series "Ozzie's Girls," and occasional director of "Adam 12," 1973-75. Actor in motion pictures, including "Sweethearts of the Campus," 1942, "Strictly in the Groove," 1942, "Honeymoon Lodge," 1943, "Take It Big," 1944, "People Are Funny," 1946, "Big City," 1948, "Here Come the Nelsons," 1952, "Impossible Years," 1969; director of "Love and Kisses," 1965. *Awards, honors:* Winner of *Daily Mirror* Popularity Contest for orchestra leaders, 1931; National Family Week Radio Citation from Inter-Council Committee on Christian Family Life; distinguished achievement award for comedy script writing from Radio Life, 1947; with wife, voted best husband and wife team in television by readers of *TV-Radio Mirror* for seven consecutive years; Doctor of Humane Letters from Rutgers University, 1957; Distinguished Eagle Scout Award, 1973.

WRITINGS: (Under name Ozzie Nelson) *Ozzie,* Prentice-Hall, 1973.

SIDELIGHTS: Many magazine writers and newspaper reporters have referred to Ozzie Nelson as the stereotypical All-American male, on radio and television and off. As a boy of thirteen, he became the youngest Eagle Scout on record in the United States and was chosen to attend the Boy Scouts of America First International Jamboree in London, England. In high school, the ever active Nelson played the saxophone in his own band. At Rutgers University, Nelson was the ideal college student. He was an All-American varsity

quarterback, a varsity letter-man in swimming and lacrosse, and welter-weight boxing champion. In addition to these activities, he was also captain of the debate team, head of the student council, and art editor of the *Chanticleer,* Rutgers University's humor magazine. Nelson was very talented and originally wanted to become a cartoonist. He was also an honor student, being elected in his senior year to the Cap and Skull honor society.

When he graduated from law school in 1930, the Depression was in full swing, and not favorable to the legal profession, so Nelson turned to music. He became a big-time band leader and by 1931 was highly successful and rumored to have one of the largest salaries ever paid to an orchestra leader. Nelson could play all the instruments used by his band except the trumpet. His favorite was the saxophone. In 1932, Nelson hired Harriet Hilliard to be a singer for his band. The association was profitable, and evidently a happy one, for they were married two years later.

Ozzie and Harriet, household words to a whole generation of Americans, began their famous "Ozzie and Harriet" show on radio in 1944. It ran for a total of twenty-two years: eight years on radio and fourteen years on television. By the time it finally went off the air, Ozzie and Harriet were working with their two sons, David and Eric (Ricky), and both their sons' wives. "The fact is, we went on a little longer than we should—I guess we could still be at it, but I decided we had operated as a clan long enough unless we wanted to start writing the scripts to bring up our grandchildren," Nelson said many years later.

AVOCATIONAL INTERESTS: Golf, tennis, swimming, weight-lifting.

BIOGRAPHICAL/CRITICAL SOURCES: New York Daily Mirror, April 18, 1931, March 8, 1933; *New York Daily News,* September 11, 1936, July 29, 1937, March 3, 1939; *New York Herald Tribune,* March 29, 1937, January 9, 1947, January 12, 1949; *New York World-Telegram,* December 7, 1940, November 24, 1941, April 3, 1945; *Look,* September 4, 1945; *Time,* February 16, 1948.

OBITUARIES: New York Times, June 4, 1975; *Washington Post,* June 4, 1975; *Newsweek,* June 16, 1975; *Current Biography,* August, 1975.*

*   *   *

NELSON, Ozzie
See NELSON, Oswald George

*   *   *

NEMETH, Laszlo   1901-1975

PERSONAL: Born April 18, 1901, in Nagybanya, Hungary (now Baia-Mare, Romania); died March 8, 1975, in Budapest, Hungary; son of Jozsef (a teacher) and Vilma (Gaal) Nemeth; married Gabriella Demusz, December 26, 1925; children: Magda, Judit, Agnes, Csilla. *Education:* Semmelweis University of Medicine, M.D., 1925. *Residence:* Sajkod, Hungary.

CAREER: Essayist, physician, translator, critic, novelist, and playwright. Practiced medicine in Hungary, 1925-43; director of Hungarian Radio department of literature, 1934-35; grammar school teacher in Hodmezovasarhely, Hungary, 1945-50; literary translator, 1945-75. Founder and manager of essay-periodical, *Tanu* (title means "Witness"), 1932. *Awards, honors:* Kossuth Prize, 1957, for *Eszter Egeto;* Hungarian National Merit prize, 1957; Herder Prize, 1965.

WRITINGS—In English; books: *Bun*, Franklin-Tarsulat, 1936, two-volume edition, Szepirodalmi Konyvkiado, 1961, 4th edition, 1966, translation by Gyula Gulyas published as *Guilt*, revised by Anna Tauber, Owen, 1966; *Iszony*, Szepirodalmi Konyvkiado, 1957, 6th edition, 1967, translation by Kathleen Szasz published as *Revulsion*, Eyre & Spottiswoode, 1965, Grove Press, 1966.

Plays: *The Plough and the Pen* (Act IV of "Galilei" [see below]), [London], 1963.

In Hungarian; books: *A minoseg forradalma* (essays; title means "The Revolution of Quality"), six volumes published in three, Magyar Elet, 1940-43; *Emberi szinjatek*, Franklin-Tarsulat, 1944, two-volume edition, Magveto Konyvkiado, 1973; *Egeto Eszter*, Magveto Konyvkiado, 1956, 5th edition, 1965; *Gyasz* (title means "Mourning"), 2nd edition, Szepirodalmi Konyvkiado, 1957; *Torteneti dramak*, Szepirodalmi Konyvkiado, 1957; *Tarsadalmi dramak*, two volumes, Szepirodalmi Konyvkiado, 1958, 2nd edition, 1964.

Alsovarosi bucso, two volumes, Franklin-Tarsulat, c. 1960; *Sajkodi estek* (title means "Evenings at Sajkod"), Magveto Konyvkiado, 1961; *Hrich*, Umeni, 1962; *Lanyaim*, Magveto Konyvkiado, 1962; *Valtozatok egy temara*, 2nd edition, Szepirodalmi Konyvkiado, 1962; *A kiserletezo ember* (title means "The Experimenting Man"), Magveto Konyvkiado, 1963; *Mai temak* (title means "Today's Themes"), Szepirodalmi Konyvkiado, 1963; *Irgalom* (title means "Charity"), two volumes, Szepirodalmi Konyvkiado, 1965; *Ujabb dramak: Csapda, Gandhi halala, Negy profeta*, Szepirodalmi Konyvkiado, 1966; *Puskin*, Gondolat, 1967; *Kiadatlan tanulmanyok*, two volumes, Magveto Konyvkiado, 1968; *Az en katedram: Tanulmanyok*, Magveto es Szepirodalmi Konyvkiado, 1969; *Nemeth Laszlo munkai*, Szepirodalmi Konyvkiado, 1969; *Negyven ev palyatortenet* (collection of works, including "Mrs. Harvath Dies" and "Mourning"), Magveto es Szepirodalmi Konyvkiado, 1969; *Utolso kiserlet* (title means "The Last Trial"), two volumes, Magveto es Szepirodalmi Konyvkiado, 1969.

Erbarmen, Corvina, 1970; *Ket nemzedek: Tanulmanyok*, Magveto es Szepirodalmi Konyvkiado, 1970; *Bun* [and] *Iszony* (novels; title means "Guilt" and "Revulsion"), Magveto es Szepirodalmi Konyvkiado, 1971; *Szerettem az igazasagot: Dramak, 1931-55*, Magveto es Szepirodalmi Konyvkiado, 1971; *Kiserleti dramaturgia: Dramak, 1960-69*, two volumes, Magveto Konyvkiado, 1972; *Europai utas: Tanulmanyok*, Magveto Konyvkiado, 1973; *Megmentett gondolatok*, Magveto Konyvkiado, 1975; *Dramak*, Magveto Konyvkiado, 1977; *Homalybol homalyba: Eletrajzi frasok*, Szepirodalmi Konyvkiado, 1977.

Plays; all published in Hungary: *Villamfenynel* (four-act; title means "Stroke of Lightning"; first produced in 1937), 1937; *VII. Gergely* (five-act; title means "Gregory VII"; first produced in 1939), 1939; *Apaczai* (five-act), 1956; *Eklezsiamegkovetese* (four-act; title means "Public Penance"), 1956; *Galilei* (four-act; title means "Galileo"; first produced in 1956), 1956; *Husz Janos* (four-act; title means "Jan Hus"), 1956; *II. Jozsef* (five-act; title means "Joseph II"), 1956; *Petofi Mezoberenyben* (one-act; title means "Petofi in Mezobereny"), 1956.

Szechenyi (four-act), 1956; *Bodnarne* (four-act; title means "Mrs. Bodnar"), 1958; *Cseresznyes* (four-act; title means "Cherry Patch"; first produced in 1942), 1958; *Erzsebet-nap* (title means "Elizabeth Day"), 1958; *Gyozelem* (four-act; title means "Victory"), 1958; *Mathiaszpansio* (four-act; title means "Mathias's Boardinghouse"), 1958; *Papucshos* (four-act; title means "Henpecked Husband"; first produced in

1938), 1958; *Pusztulo Magyarok* (three-act; title means "Vanishing Hungarians"), 1958; *Samson* (three-act), 1958; *Szornyeteg* (four-act; title means "The Monster"), 1958; *A ket Bolyai* (four-act; title means "The Two Bolyais"), 1962; *Apai dicsoseg* (three-act; title means "Father's Glory"), 1962; *Utazas* (four-act; title means "The Journey"), 1962; *Az arulo* (four-act; title means "The Traitor"), 1963; *Nagy csalad* (two-part play; title means "The Great Family"; Part 1: "Elso este" [four-act; title means "First Night"], Part 2: "Masadik este" [three-act; title means "Second Night"], 1963.

Also author of "Gandi halala" (title means "The Death of Gandhi"; first produced in 1963).

SIDELIGHTS: In 1925, within a fortnight, Laszlo Nemeth began his medical career, got married, and published his first work, a prize-winning short story for the literary review *Nyugat*. His story, along with most of his later writings, stressed the inherent conflict between the individual and society. Nemeth was deeply troubled by contemporary society and urged both political and social reform. He became a spokesman for the cause, subsequently founding the essay-periodical *Tanu* as a medium for expounding his views. As chief critic and leader of the folk-writer's movement, his philosophies spread quickly across Hungary.

Like many young Hungarians at the time, Nemeth soon became involved with the "Third Road" concept of socialism excluding Marxism. So devoted was he that the authorities during the Stalin regime considered him a dangerous subversive and prohibited him from writing. Basically, he believed in a return to the land, finding a national identity through realization of Hungarian folk-lore and traditions. He was thoroughly engrossed with Hungarianism and advocated the purification of a "master race."

Nemeth resumed publishing in 1954, letting loose a flurry of suppressed literary activity. Continuing in the same vein as his earlier works, many of his historical dramas of this period reflected the lives of great men caught between their ideals and reality, struggling desperately to convince their contemporaries that drastic upheavals in social and political thinking were in order, but frustrated in their attempts.

Laszlo Nemeth was one of the most widely published authors in Hungary as well as a skillful translator of both Shakespeare and the Russian classics.

BIOGRAPHICAL/CRITICAL SOURCES: Books Abroad, August, 1974.

OBITUARIES: Washington Post, March 8, 1975; *AB Bookman's Weekly*, April 21, 1975.*

*   *   *

NETHERCLIFT, Beryl (Constance) 1911-

PERSONAL: Born September 26, 1911, in Woodford Green, England; daughter of Edward Ernest and Edith (Leighton) Netherclift. *Education:* Attended high school in Burgess Hill, England. *Home:* 83 Graham Ave., Brighton, Sussex BN1 8HB, England.

CAREER: Free-lance writer, 1928-40; secretary for Railway Assessment Authority in Burgess Hill, England, 1940-47, and London, England, 1947-49; Inland Revenue Valuation Office, London, secretary, 1949-50; Howard King & Partners (chartered surveyors), London, secretary, 1950-59; free-lance writer, 1959—. *Member:* Sussex Archaeological Society, Society of Authors.

WRITINGS: No Road Runs By (essays), Heffer, 1935;

Greensleeves (essays), Heath Cranton, 1939; *The Snow-storm* (juvenile; Foyles Children's Book Club selection), Knopf, 1967; *Castle Steep* (juvenile), Knopf, 1970; *The Certain Spring* (novel), Hurst & Blackett, 1971. Contributor to adult and juvenile magazines, including *This England* and *Sussex Life,* and newspapers.

WORK IN PROGRESS: An autobiography; various articles.

SIDELIGHTS: Nethercliff commented to *CA:* "I began writing at the ripe old age of seven. Living in the country, far from libraries and bookshops, I decided to write my own books. My first story was published in my sixteenth year, a school story in the Girl Guide magazine, *The Guide.* The following year my first adult story, a romance, was published in a woman's magazine. The instinct to put pen to paper was always with me.

"Later, a growing awareness of the beauty of the English countryside led me to write almost exclusively on country matters, with a view of sharing my delight with others similarly minded, particularly those who lived in towns and were unable to get out. This is chiefly what I hoped to achieve with the books of essays and poems, *No Road Runs By* and *Greensleeves.*

"My advice to aspiring authors is never be discouraged and never give up trying. As Erasmus said, 'The desire for writing grows with writing.'"

AVOCATIONAL INTERESTS: Gardening, music, walking.

*   *   *

NEWELL, Helen M(arie)   **1909-**

PERSONAL: Born August 10, 1909, in Salmon Dam, Idaho; daughter of Robert J. (a civil engineer) and Mary J. (a teacher; maiden name, LeGore) Newell. *Education:* Attended Link's Business College and College of Idaho; University of Washington, Seattle, B.A., 1933. *Religion:* Protestant. *Home:* 334 Hulbe Rd., Boise, Idaho 83705.

CAREER: U.S. Bureau of Reclamation, Grand Coulee Dam, Wash., secretary in engineering office, 1935-41; Lowry Air Force Base, Denver, Colo., civilian aircraft engine mechanic, 1942-45; high school English teacher in Balmorhea, Tex., 1945-46; secretary in engineering, construction, and aeronautical offices, 1946-54; free-lance writer, 1955-63; AFL-CIO state office, Boise, Idaho, secretary, 1964-69; free-lance writer, 1970—. *Awards, honors:* Won essay contest sponsored by Broadcast Music, American Association for State and Local History, and *This Week,* 1960, for "Reflections While Standing Before the Lincoln Memorial."

WRITINGS: The Hardhats (novel), Houghton, 1956 (published in England as *The Dam,* Eyre & Spottiswoode, 1956); *Idaho's Place in the Sun* (high school textbook), Syms-York Co., 1975, revised edition, 1977.

Work represented in anthologies, including *Lincoln for the Ages,* edited by Ralph G. Newman, Doubleday, 1960.

WORK IN PROGRESS: Shoestring Valley, a novel set in the 1930's, about an Idaho community of relocated farm families who lost their farms in all the states of the Dust Bowl.

SIDELIGHTS: Helen Newell writes: "I was born in a construction camp, and grew up in similar camps and on a cattle ranch. I have worked at jobs (some interesting, some dull, all rich in human nature) in engineering, construction, aeronautical, and union offices.

"Some conclusions of a writer with a fair share of birthdays: No life is grim throughout. Everybody has something good, sometime. Lives are made up of a few jubilant summits, a few tragic depths, and very many plodding everydays. These are the things a writer works with. Because people are put together with some goodness and some meanness, and varying mixtures of the ordinary and the idiosyncratic, they are the one commodity eternally interesting. The warmest and most attractive qualities are kindness, generosity, humor, and courage. The coldest and most repelling are selfishness, intolerance, cruelty, and a narrow mind."

*   *   *

NICELY, Thomas S(hryock), Jr.   **1939-**
  (Tom Nicely)

PERSONAL: Born January 23, 1939, in Philadelphia, Pa.; son of Thomas S. (a sales manager) and Marian (Hamming) Nicely; married Cynthia Leapley (a stoneware potter), January 16, 1965; children: Megan Vineta, Alexis Hamming. *Education:* Williams College, B.A., 1960; University of Michigan, M.A., 1968, Ph.D., 1975. *Residence:* Ann Arbor, Mich. *Office:* Leaves of Grass, 2433 Whitmore Lake Rd., Ann Arbor, Mich. 48103.

CAREER: Doubleday & Co., Inc., New York, N.Y., college traveler, 1961-63, chief copywriter, 1964-65; high school English teacher in Kampala, Uganda, 1965-67; University of Michigan Press, Ann Arbor, copywriter, 1968-76; Leaves of Grass (dealer in rare books), Ann Arbor, Mich., owner, 1973—. *Military service:* U.S. Marine Corps Reserve, 1960-66, active duty, 1960-61.

WRITINGS—Under name Tom Nicely: (Contributor) *The Mother Earth News Handbook of Home Business Ideas and Plans,* Bantam, 1976; *Adam and His Work: A Bibliography of Sources by and About Paul Goodman (1911-1972),* Scarecrow, 1979. Contributor to periodicals, including *AB Bookman's Weekly* and *New Letters,* and newspapers.

WORK IN PROGRESS: Revising *Adam and His Work,* for inclusion in an anthology on Paul Goodman; "future projects may include antiquarian checklists or articles, based upon my own interests as a used and rare book dealer and book collector."

SIDELIGHTS: Nicely told *CA:* "Aside from numerous dust jackets for Doubleday and the University of Michigan Press, my most fugitive pieces must be many 'Letters to the Editor' (c. 1965-73+), often protesting the war in Vietnam and other hair-brained projects reported in local papers."

*   *   *

NICELY, Tom
  See NICELY, Thomas S(hryock), Jr.

*   *   *

NICHOLAS, Anna Katherine   **1917-**

PERSONAL: Born June 16, 1917, in Cohoes, N.Y.; daughter of M. J. (a lawyer and realtor) and Gretchen (McElwain) Nicholas. *Education:* Privately educated. *Home:* 15 Ledgemere Dr., Danbury, Conn. 06810.

CAREER: Writer, 1930—. Judge of multi-breed show dogs in the United States and Canada, 1934—. *Member:* American Pomeranian Club (honorary member), Southern New York Beagle Club (honorary member), Queensboro Kennel Club (honorary member). *Awards, honors:* Best Technical Book Award from Dog Writers Association of America, 1970, for *The Nicholas Guide to Dog Judging,* honorable mention, 1975, for *The Wonderful World of Beagles and Beagling;* named dog writer of the year by *Kennel Review,* 1974, 1977; named journalist of the year by Gaines's Dog Research Center, 1977.

WRITINGS: The Pekingese, Judy Publishing, 1939; *The Skye Terrier Book*, Skye Terrier Club of America, 1960; *The Nicholas Guide to Dog Judging*, Howell Book, 1969, 2nd edition, 1979; (with Joan Brearley) *This Is the Bichon Frise*, T.F.H. Publications, 1973; (with Brearley) *The Wonderful World of Beagles and Beagling*, T.F.H. Publications, 1975; (with Brearley) *This Is the Skye Terrier*, T.F.H. Publications, 1975; (with Brearley) *The Book of the Pekingese*, T.F.H. Publications, 1975; (with Brearley) *The Book of the Boxer*, T.F.H. Publications, 1977; *Successful Dog Show Exhibiting*, T.F.H. Publications, 1980.

Columns: "Peeking at the Pekingese," in *Dogdom*, during 1930's and 1940's, and *Popular Dogs*, during 1940's; columnist for *Boxer Briefs*, during 1940's; "It Seems to One," in *Kennel Review*, 1970—; "Here, There, and Everywhere," in *Dog World*, 1977; also currently author of column "Seen, Heard, and Overheard," in *Canine Chronicle*. Contributor to dog magazines, including *American Kennel Gazette*.

SIDELIGHTS: Anna Nicholas writes: "From earliest childhood, I have been involved with dogs. My earliest pets were a Boston terrier, an airedale, and a German shepherd. Then, in 1925, came the first Pekingese, a gift from a friend, which led to more than thirty years' ownership of this breed. Now my home is shared with beagles.

"I am approved to judge all hound breeds, all terriers, all toys and all non-sporting dogs, plus pointers, English and Gordon setters, Vizslas, weimaraners, and wire-haired pointing griffons, and the miscellaneous class. In 1970 I became the third woman in history to judge 'best in show' at the prestigious Westminster Kennel Club event.

"In writing about exhibiting, I am doing so through the eyes of a judge, as I have been far more concerned with the study and judging of dogs than I have with showing them. But I do occasionally exhibit my beagles, and I feel that everyone who judges should do so upon occasion in order to keep their perspective and consideration for what it is like to *show* dogs as well as *judge* them."

*   *   *

NICHOLS, (John) Beverley 1899-

PERSONAL: Born September 9, 1899, in Bristol, England; son of John (a solicitor) and Pauline (Shalders) Nichols. *Education:* Balliol College, Oxford, B.A., 1921. *Home:* Sudbrook Cottage, Ham Common, Surrey, England.

CAREER: Journalist, novelist, playwright, and composer. Press correspondent in India, 1939-45. *Member:* Oxford Union Debating Society (president, c.1922).

WRITINGS—Juvenile: The Tree That Sat Down, J. Cape, 1945; *The Stream That Stood Still*, J. Cape, 1948; *The Mountain of Magic*, J. Cape, 1950; *The Wickedest Witch in the World*, W. H. Allen, 1971.

Novels: *Prelude*, Chatto & Windus, 1920; *Patchwork*, Chatto & Windus, 1921, Holt, 1922; *Self*, Chatto & Windus, 1922; *Crazy Pavements*, G. H. Doran, 1927; *Evensong*, Doubleday, 1932; *Revue*, Doubleday, 1939; *Men Do Not Weep*, J. Cape, 1941, Harcourt, 1942; *No Man's Street*, Dutton, 1954; *The Moonflower Murder*, Dutton, 1955 (published in England as *The Moonflower*, Hutchinson, 1955); *Death to Slow Music*, Dutton, 1956; *The Rich Die Hard*, Hutchinson, 1957, Dutton, 1958; *Murder by Request*, Dutton, 1960.

Plays: *The Stag* (first produced in London in 1929), P. Smith, 1933; *Avalanche* (first produced in Edinburgh in 1931; produced in London in 1932), P. Smith, 1933; (with Edward Knoblock) *Evensong* (three-act; based on own novel; first produced in London in 1932; produced in New York City in 1933), Samuel French, 1933; *When the Crash Comes* (first produced in Birmingham in 1933), P. Smith, 1933; *Failures: Three Plays* (contains "The Stag," "Avalanche," and "When the Crash Comes"), P. Smith, 1933; *Mesmer* (first produced in London in 1938), J. Cape, 1937; *Shadow of the Vine* (three-act; first produced in London in 1954), J. Cape, 1949.

Nonfiction: *Twenty-five: Being a Young Man's Candid Recollections of His Elders and Betters*, G. H. Doran, 1926; *Are They the Same at Home?*, G. H. Doran, 1927; *The Star Spangled Manner*, Doubleday, 1928; *Women and Children Last*, Doubleday, 1931; *Down the Garden Path*, Doubleday, 1932, reprinted, Norwood Editions, 1978; *For Adults Only*, J. Cape, 1932, Doubleday, 1933; *Cry Havoc!*, Doubleday, 1933; *A Thatched Roof*, Doubleday, 1933; *A Village in a Valley*, Doubleday, 1934, reprinted, Arden Library, 1980; (with others) *How Does Your Garden Grow?* (broadcast talks), Doubleday, 1935; *The Fool Hath Said*, Doubleday, 1936, reprinted, Norwood Editions, 1978; *No Place Like Home*, Doubleday, 1936; *News of England; or, A Country Without a Hero*, Doubleday, 1938; *Green Grows the City*, Harcourt, 1939.

Verdict on India, Harcourt, 1944; *All I Could Never Be: Some Recollections*, J. Cape, 1949, Dutton, 1952; (with Monica Dickens) *Yours Sincerely*, G. Newnes, 1949; *Uncle Samson*, Evans Brothers, 1950; *Merry Hall*, J. Cape, 1951, Dutton, 1953; *A Pilgrim's Progress*, J. Cape, 1952; *Laughter on the Stairs*, J. Cape, 1953, Dutton, 1954, reprinted, Dynamic Learning Corp., 1979; *The Queen's Coronation Day: The Pictorial Record of the Great Occasion*, Pitkin Pictorials, 1953; *Beverley Nichols' Cat Book*, T. Nelson, 1955; *Sunlight on the Lawn*, Dutton, 1956; *The Sweet and Twenties*, Weidenfeld & Nicolson, 1958.

Cats A. B. C., Dutton, 1960; *Cats X. Y. Z.*, Dutton, 1961; *Garden Open Today*, Dutton, 1963; *Forty Favourite Flowers*, Studio Vista, 1964, St. Martin's, 1965; *Powers That Be*, St. Martin's, 1966; *A Case of Human Bondage*, Award Books, 1966; *The Art of Flower Arrangement*, Viking, 1967; *Garden Open Tomorrow*, Heinemann, 1968, Dodd, 1969; *The Sun in My Eyes; or, How Not to Go Around the World*, Heinemann, 1969; *Father Figure*, Simon & Schuster, 1972; *Down the Kitchen Sink*, W. H. Allen, 1974; *The Unforgiving Minute: Some Confessions From Childhood to the Outbreak of the Second World War*, W. H. Allen, 1978; *The Romantic Garden*, Gordon-Cremonesi, 1980.

Collections: *The Tree That Sat Down [and] The Stream That Stood Still*, St. Martin's, 1966; *The Gift of a Garden; or, Some Flowers Remembered*, edited by John E. Cross, W. H. Allen, 1971, Dodd, 1972; *The Gift of a Home*, W. H. Allen, 1972, Dodd, 1973; *Beverley Nichols' Cats A-Z*, W. H. Allen, 1977.

Other: (Author of introduction) Charles Sedley, *The Faro Table; or, The Gambling Mothers*, Nash & Grayson, 1931; (contributor) *Official Handbook of the Corporation of Brighton*, Corporation of Brighton, 1933; (compiler) *A Book of Old Ballads*, Hutchinson, 1934; (author of foreword) *The Making of a Man*, Nicholson & Watson, 1934; (author of preface) *Receipt Book*, Woolf, 1968; (author of preface) Jan Styczynski, *Cats in America*, A. Deutsch, 1962.

Founder and editor of *The Oxford Outlook*; editor of *American Sketch*, 1928-29, and *Isis*; contributor to newspapers and periodicals.

BIOGRAPHICAL/CRITICAL SOURCES: Guardian, July 29, 1960; *New York Times Book Review*, October 8, 1972; *Times Literary Supplement*, March 10, 1972.*

NICHOLS, Bill
   See NICHOLS, William James

*   *   *

NICHOLS, Robert (Molise Bowyer) 1919-

PERSONAL: Born July 15, 1919, in Worcester, Mass.; son of Charles and Clare (Lalone) Nichols; married Grace Paley; children: Kerstin, Duncan, Eliza. *Education:* Harvard University, B.A., 1941. *Home:* 126 West 11th St., New York, N.Y. 10011.

CAREER: Writer and landscape architect.

WRITINGS: Slow Newsreel of Man Riding Train (poems), City Lights, 1962; *Daily Lives in Nghsi-Altai,* New Directions, Book I: *Arrival,* 1977, Book II: *Garh City,* 1978, Book III: *The Harditts in Sawna,* 1979, Book IV: *Exile,* 1979. Also author of *Address to the Smaller Animals, Red Shift,* and *Anthology of War Poetry, 1914-1918.*

*   *   *

NICHOLS, William James 1942-
   (Bill Nichols)

PERSONAL: Born August 19, 1942, in New York, N.Y.; son of James William and Nellie Mae (Register) Nichols. *Education:* Duke University, B.A., 1964; graduate study at Stanford University, 1964-65; University of California, Los Angeles, M.A., 1972, Ph.D., 1978. *Home:* 251 William St., Kingston, Ontario, Canada K7L 2E5. *Office:* Film Studios, Queen's University, Kingston, Ontario, Canada K7L 3N6.

CAREER: KMET-AM Radio, Los Angeles, Calif., assistant news director, 1972-73; Queen's University, Kingston, Ontario, lecturer, 1974-75, assistant professor, 1976-78, associate professor of film studies, 1978—. Visiting professor at Griffith University, spring, 1978.

WRITINGS—Under name Bill Nichols: (Editor) *Movies and Methods,* University of California Press, 1976; *Ideology and Image: The Politics and Aesthetics of Visual Representation,* Indiana University Press, 1980. Associate editor of *Cine-Tracts;* film and book reviewer for *Film Quarterly.*

WORK IN PROGRESS: A novel, completion expected in 1980.

SIDELIGHTS: Nichols writes: "My interests are in the nature and function of ideology and art, especially in relation to the cinema, but also in other media. The relations between everyday life, ideology, and social change interest me more and more. I am presently working on a novel examining romantic love as a particularly acute obfuscation of the interrelationship between the personal and the political."

*   *   *

NICHOLSON, W(illiam) G(eorge) 1935-

PERSONAL: Born September 18, 1935, in Greenfield, Mass.; son of George W. Nicholson; married Cornelia Downes (a counselor), August 30, 1958; children: Alexandra, Christopher, Hugh. *Education:* Brown University, A.B., 1958; Ohio State University, M.A., 1963. *Politics:* Democrat. *Religion:* None. *Home and office:* 110 Woodbury Rd., Watertown, Conn. 06795. *Agent:* James Seligmann Agency, 280 Madison Ave., New York, N.Y. 10016.

CAREER: Taft School, Watertown, Conn., English teacher and director of college placement, 1969—. *Member:* National Association of College Admissions Counselors, Northeastern Association of College Admissions Counselors.

WRITINGS: Pete Gray: One-Armed Major Leaguer, Prentice-Hall, 1976. Contributor to journals.

WORK IN PROGRESS: Jim Folsom, Alabama Populist, publication expected in 1982.

SIDELIGHTS: Nicholson told *CA:* "My interest in Pete Gray goes back to my boyhood. His accomplishments were a tribute to his indomitable will and an inspiration to all handicapped people. My view of Jim Folsom's importance resulted from a year spent in Alabama and through contact with that state's Byzantine political and social structure. *Avocational interests:* Baseball, politics, travel.

*   *   *

NICOLSON, Victoria Mary
   See SACKVILLE-WEST, V(ictoria Mary)

*   *   *

NIELSEN, Dulcimer 1943-

PERSONAL: Born May 20, 1943, in Altadena, Calif.; daughter of John C. and Heath (Hamilton) Ainsworth; married Thor Nielsen (a writer), December 18, 1975; children: (from previous marriage) Julie, Robert, Margie. *Education:* Attended high school in Oroville, Calif. *Home address:* P.O. Box 1961, Ormond Beach, Fla. 32074.

CAREER: Rancher and horse breeder in Oregon, 1969-74; writer, 1975—. Worked as swimming instructor, 1960.

WRITINGS: Hanging and Rattling, Caxton, 1979. Contributor to *Saturday Evening Post, Pets of the World, Woman's Own,* and *She.*

WORK IN PROGRESS: Do It, with husband, Thor Nielsen, a book on alternative lifestyles; an animal story book; travel writing.

SIDELIGHTS: Dulcimer Nielsen writes: "Writing as a career was, for me, an evolutionary process rather than a conscious decision. Ed James, the subject of my first book, and a friend for years, had such an interesting life that I thought someone should write a book about him. My husband said, 'Don't talk about it; do it.' Taking the challenge, I plunged off the deep end into the world of writing and came up with a manuscript that was accepted by the first publisher to whom I submitted it. This was an unusual and encouraging bit of luck which befalls very few authors.

"I had reached the age of thirty as Little Susie Rancher and Housewife, pretty much caged within four walls with my head in a diaper pail. After a typical experience with Divorce—American Style and a readjustment period amongst the Swinging Singles, I remarried.

"My husband has broadened my horizons immensely through our extensive travels (Europe, the Middle East, Africa, the Caribbean). While we were living in England, I submitted an article to a woman's magazine that was also snapped up first time out. With the ego-boosting status of an internationallly accepted writer, I became addicted."

*   *   *

NIHAL SINGH, Surendra 1929-

PERSONAL: Born April 30, 1929, in Rawalpindi, India; son of Gurmukh (an academician) and Lachchmi Nihal Singh; married Geertje Zuiderweg, November 4, 1957. *Education:* University of Delhi, B.A. (honors), 1948. *Home:* 12-C Minto Park, 13 Debendralal Khan Rd., Calcutta 700 027, India. *Office: Statesman,* 4 Chowringhee Sq., Calcutta 700 001, India.

CAREER: Statesman, Calcutta, India, staff reporter, 1954-57, political reporter, 1958-62, author of weekly parliamentary column, "Week in Parliament," correspondent from Singapore, 1962-67, Pakistan, 1967, and Moscow, Soviet Union, 1968-69; political correspondent in New Delhi, India and author of column on Indian and international affairs, 1969-71, political correspondent from London, England, 1971-74, resident editor in Calcutta, 1974-75, editor, 1975—. Guest member of staff of *Quincy Patriot Ledger*, 1957. *Member:* International Press Institute, Press Club of India, Authors Guild of India, Institute of Defense Analysis, Commonwealth Press Club, Twentieth Century Fund. *Awards, honors:* Named international editor of the year by Atlas World Press Service, 1978.

WRITINGS: Malaysia: A Commentary, Barnes & Noble, 1971; *From the Jhelum to the Volga*, Nachiketa Publications, 1972; *Indira's India*, Nachiketa Publications, 1978; *The Gang and 900 Million*, Nachiketa Publications, 1979.

WORK IN PROGRESS: "A broad, interpretive look at India, seeking to bring out the basic features and characteristics of its people and its leaders," publication expected in 1980.

SIDELIGHTS: In 1962, Nihal Singh was sent to Singapore to report and comment on events in Southeast Asia and the Far East. His five years there coincided with the birth of Malaysia, Singapore's exit from the Federation, the 'confrontation' phase between Indonesia and Malaysia, the big American buildup in Vietnam, the abortive Communist coup in Indonesia, and Sukarno's downfall.

From Singapore he went to Pakistan. He was the first, and so far the only, Indian correspondent permitted in Pakistan since the 1965 Indo-Pakistani war. His next assignment was in Moscow, where he covered the Soviet intervention in Czechoslovakia. Nihal Singh returned to India in 1969. The two years he served as political correspondent coincided with the events that led to the split in India's Congress party. Next he went to London to report on political developments in western Europe. During his stay there industrial strife arose in England, and England entered the European Economic Community.

Nihal Singh became editor of the *Statesman* in 1975, and bore the brunt of the Indira Gandhi government's confrontation policy toward the dissenting press, especially the *Statesman*. With the lifting of the internal emergency in 1977, he was able to resume his weekly signed column.

Nihal Singh writes: "My motivation in writing a book is to put across a viewpoint. In the political domain, I feel strongly that in this multi-polar world, the media are still inevitably biased in favor of a Western view. This is not for any diabolical reasons, but is due to the fact that the developed world has had the resources and power to get its point of view across to the rest of the world.

"In writing fiction, my objective is to try to bare an aspect of human life or experience and to try to assess what makes human beings behave as they do in a particular situation. In short, a writer's metier is to try to divine the mystery of human life and human motivation."

*   *   *

NOJIRI, Kiyohiko 1897-1973
(Jiro Osaragi)

PERSONAL: Born October 9, 1897, in Yokohama, Japan; died April 30, 1973, in Tokyo, Japan; son of a shipping company official. *Education:* Attended First High School (now part of Tokyo University), 1915-18; Imperial University, graduated, 1921.

CAREER: Author, historian, playwright, and translator. Worked variously as teacher at girls' school in Kamakura, Japan, and as member of treaties bureau of Ministry of Foreign Affairs in Japan. *Member:* Japan Academy of Arts. *Awards, honors:* National Culture Prize, 1964; Japan Academy Prize for *The Homecoming*.

WRITINGS—All under pseudonym Jiro Osaragi; in English: *Kikyo* (fiction), [Japan], 1949, translation by Brewster Horwitz published as *The Homecoming*, Knopf, 1954; *Tabiji* (fiction), [Japan], 1953, translation by Ivan Morris published as *The Journey*, Knopf, 1960; *Kyoto*, translated from the original Japanese by Donald Keene, Otis Cary, and Thomas I. Elliott, Tanko-Shinsha, 1962.

In Japanese; all published in Japan; fiction: *Ako roshi* (title means "The Ronin of Ako"), 1927, four volume edition, 1949-50; *Kurama tengu jigoku no mon*, 1948; *Tengu kaijo*, 1948; *Teru hi kumoru hi*, 1948; *Nichiren*, two volumes, 1949; *Shinju*, 1949; *Yama o mamoru kyodai*, 1949; *Munakata shimai*, 1950; *Shijuhachininme no otoko*, 1952; *Gento*, 1956; *Mito komon*, 1964; (editor) *Kokumin no bungaku*, twenty-six volumes, 1967-69; *Osaraji Jiro*, 1968; *Nezumikozi jirokichi*, 1970; (editor with Matsutaro Kawaguchi and Ki Kimura) *Taishu bungaku taikei*, 1971; *Fuyo no shinshi*, 1972; *Okubo hikozaemon*, 1973; *Oboro kago*, 1974; *Yui shosetsu*, 1975; *Gorotsukibune*, 1976; *Satsuma bikyaku*, 1976; *Yugao koji*, 1977.

Selected works: *Osaragi Jiro nonfikushon zenshu*, five volumes, 1971-72; *Osaragi Jiro shu*, two volumes, 1972; *Osaragi Jiro jisen shu, gendai shosetsu*, 1972-73; *Osaragi Jiro jidai shosetsu zenshu*, two volumes, 1975; *Shijin*, 1976.

Essays: *Kamakura tsushin*, 1924; *Kamakura rekishi sampo*, 1957; *Yoshitsune no shui*, 1967; *Zuihitsushu kyo no yuki*, 1970; *Fuyo no hana*, 1973; *Osaragi Jiro zuihitsu zenshu*, three volumes, 1973-74.

Other: *Dorefyusu jiken* (biography; title means "The Dreyfus Case"), 1930, reprinted, 1974; *Furansu ningyo*, 1932; *Muteki* (short stories), 1934; *Buranje shogun no higeki* (title means "The Tragedy of General Boulanger"), 1935; *Mikumari monogatari* (short stories), 1944; *Hatsukoi*, 1950; *Zuihitsu mizu ni kaku* (reminiscences), 1959; *Pari moyu* (history; title means "Paris in Flames"), 1961, four-volume edition, 1975; (editor with Yasunari Kawabata and Sen'ichi Hisamatsu) *Nihon kindai bungaku zuroku*, 1964; *Ishi no kotoba* (reminiscences), 1966; *Nara kasugano*, 1968; *Sanshimai* (plays), 1968; *Nihon no bi to shizen* (travel), 1969; *Tenno no seiki* (history), 1969, seventeen-volume edition, 1977-78; *Sengoku no hitobito* (plays), 1970; *Gikyoku sanshimai hoka* (plays), 1971; *Sugao no kamakura*, 1971; *Kokohu fukiji* (art), 1972; *Miyako sodachi* (reminiscences), 1972; (with Jojiro Ishizaka) *Gendai nihon bungaku zenshu* (series), 1975; (with Chogoro Kaionji) *Chikuma gendai bungaku* (series), 1977; (with Teiji Ito) *Shugakuin rikyu*, 1977; *Neko no iru hibi* (cat legends), 1978.

Contributor of stories and abridged translations to literary magazines and newspapers.

BIOGRAPHICAL/CRITICAL SOURCES: New York Herald Tribune Book Review, January 16, 1955; *New York Times Book Review*, January 16, 1955, July 17, 1960; *Saturday Review*, January 22, 1955; *Times Literary Supplement*, September 9, 1955; *New Yorker*, October 1, 1960.

OBITUARIES: New York Times, May 1, 1973.*

NORMAN, Geraldine (Lucia) 1940-
(Geraldine Keen)

PERSONAL: Born May 13, 1940, in Wales; daughter of Harold Hugh (an accountant) and Catherine (Cummins) Keen; married John Frank Norman (a writer), July 16, 1971. *Education:* St. Anne's College, Oxford, B.A. (with honors), 1961; attended University of California, Los Angeles, 1961-62. *Home:* 5 Seaford Court, 220 Great Portland St., London W.1, England.

CAREER: Times, London, England, sale room correspondent, 1969—. Member of board of directors of Co-Operative Development Agency, 1978—, and Job Ownership Ltd. *Awards, honors:* Named news reporter of the year, 1977.

WRITINGS: (Under name Geraldine Keen) *Money and Art,* Putnam, 1971 (published in England as *The Sale of Works of Art,* Thomas Nelson, 1971); (editor) *Marius' Dutch Painters of the Nineteenth Century,* Antique Collectors Club, 1973; (with husband, Frank Norman, and T. Keating) *The Fake's Progress,* Hutchinson, 1977; (editor) *The Tom Keating Catalogue,* Hutchinson, 1977; *Nineteenth-Century Painters and Painting: A Dictionary,* University of California Press, 1977; (with A. Campbell, C. Keen, and R. Daveshott) *Worker-Owners: The Mondragon Achievement,* Anglo-German Foundation for the Study of Industrial Society, 1978.

*   *   *

NORRIS, Gunilla Brodde 1939-

PERSONAL: Born in 1939 in Argentina; married David A. Norris. *Education:* Attended Sarah Lawrence College. *Office:* c/o E. P. Dutton, 2 Park Ave., New York, N.Y. 10016. *CAREER:* Writer. Worked as counselor.

WRITINGS—Juvenile: The Summer Pastures, Knopf, 1965; *A Feast of Light,* Knopf, 1967; *Lillan,* Atheneum, 1968; *The Good Morrow,* Atheneum, 1969; *A Time for Watching,* Knopf, 1969; *Take My Waking Slowly,* Atheneum, 1970; *The Top Step,* Atheneum, 1970; *Green and Something Else,* Simon & Schuster, 1971; *If You Listen,* Atheneum, 1971; *Josie on Her Own,* Scholastic Book Service, 1972; *The Friendship Hedge,* Dutton, 1973; *Standing in the Magic,* Dutton, 1974.

SIDELIGHTS: Some of Norris's books are set in Sweden, including *A Time for Watching* and *The Top Step.* The former is the story of Joachim, a young boy who sets about doing a number of things to break the boredom of his lonely summer. He becomes interested in a clockmaker, Gubban, who repays him with scorn. By story's end, though, the two have befriended.

The Top Step is a rather serious tale about Mikael, a Swedish lad burdened with asthma and a father who doesn't comprehend his affliction. Mikael's father encourages him to frolic vigorously and Mikael sets himself the goal of outgrowing the asthma before his birthday. The birthday passes and still Mikael suffers from asthma. However, his father begins treating him as an adult and the book ends with Mikael being extended an invitation to join his father on his walks in the country.

Another of Norris's books, *The Good Morrow,* is equally solemn in its tone. In it, Josie, a black girl, leaves the city for a stay at a summer camp. There, she encounters animosity from a fellow camper. Because the girl is white, Josie assumes that she is the victim of prejudice. In the end, Josie discovers the real reason for the other girl's behavior, which has nothing to do with skin color. Robin Gottlieb described it as "a tense story which . . . touches the mind but not the heart."

BIOGRAPHICAL/CRITICAL SOURCES: Book World, May 4, 1969.*

*   *   *

NORTON, Bettina A(ntonia) 1936-

PERSONAL: Born August 22, 1936, in Boston, Mass.; daughter of Carmen (an architect) and Rosa (a secretary; maiden name, Tirabassi) di Stefano; married John Merrill Norton (a banker), June 16, 1956; children: James A., Benjamin R., Giulia di S., Laura E. *Education:* Attended Wellesley College, 1954-57, earned degree (with honors), 1976. *Politics:* Democrat. *Religion:* Episcopalian. *Home:* 6 Rollins Place, Boston, Mass. 02114.

CAREER: Boston Athenaeum, Boston, Mass., print cataloger, 1972-75; Essex Institute, Salem, Mass. print cataloger, 1976-78, registrar, 1978-79; archivist and historian for Trinity Church in Boston. Founder and first president of Hill House, Inc. *Member:* Victorian Society of America (member of New England board of directors), American Print Symposium. *Awards, honors:* Award from Northeast Conference of American Association of Museums, 1978, for *Prints at the Essex Institute.*

WRITINGS: History of the Boston Naval Shipyard, Bostonian Society, 1975; *Edwin Whitefield: Nineteenth-Century North American Scenery,* Barre, 1977; *Trinity Church: The Story of an Episcopal Parish in the City of Boston,* privately printed, 1978; *Prints at the Essex Institute* (booklet), Essex Institute, 1978. Contributor to journals, including *Antiques.*

WORK IN PROGRESS: A murder mystery; research on nineteenth-century lithography in Boston.

SIDELIGHTS: Bettina Norton comments: "My father's interest in art history, especially in relation to American social and cultural history, led me to a love for American prints, and early professional associations with three men—Sinclair Hitchings, Charles D. Childs, and Walter M. Whitehill—established a sound footing for me.

"I did not work when my children—except the last—were growing up. Since employed, I have cut down on volunteer commitments; that of archivist and historian of one of the most important churches in America is both interesting and demanding.

"I am currently writing a mystery set in a library; development of characters and complexities is a welcome diversion from concern for factual accuracy and working up a thesis."

*   *   *

NORWAY, Nevil Shute 1899-1960
(Nevil Shute)

OBITUARY NOTICE: Born January 17, 1899, in Ealing, Middlesex, England; died January 12, 1960, in Melbourne, Australia. Airplane engineer, aviator, and author. Norway worked as an airplane designer and builder for many years in England. He combined his technical knowledge with fast-paced plots in his books, which include *The Far Country, On the Beach,* and *Pied Piper.* Obituaries and other sources: *Current Biography,* Wilson, 1942, March, 1960; *The Reader's Encyclopedia,* 2nd edition, Crowell, 1965; *The New Century Handbook of English Literature,* revised edition, Appleton, 1967; *Twentieth Century Writing: A Reader's Guide to Contemporary Literature,* Transatlantic, 1969; *Longman Companion to Twentieth Century Literature,* Longman, 1970; *The Penguin Companion to English Literature,* McGraw, 1971.

NOSCO, Peter 1950-

PERSONAL: Born March 13, 1950, in New York, N.Y.; son of John and Beatrice (Votavova) Nosco; married Margaret Button, June 19, 1976; children: John Alexander. *Education:* Columbia University, B.A., 1971, M.Phil., 1975, Ph.D., 1978; Cambridge University, B.A., 1973, M.A., 1977. *Home:* 255-23 74th Ave., Glen Oaks, N.Y. 11004. *Office:* Center of Asian Studies, St. John's University, Jamaica, N.Y. 11439.

CAREER: Cambridge University, Cambridge, England, supervisor in classical Japanese, 1977-78; University of Maryland, College Park, visiting lecturer in East Asian thought, spring, 1979; St. John's University, Jamaica, N.Y., assistant professor of Asian studies, 1979—. *Member:* Association of Asian Studies. *Awards, honors:* Fulbright scholarship for Japan, 1975-76; award from Translation Center at Columbia University, 1978, for translating *Some Final Words of Advice.*

WRITINGS: (Translator and author of introduction) Ihara Saikaku, *Some Final Words of Advice,* Tuttle, 1979.

WORK IN PROGRESS: A study of nostalgic and patriotic themes in Japanese nativist thought from the seventeenth to the early nineteenth century; a study of the development of Japanese historical theory.

SIDELIGHTS: Nosco told *CA:* "If there is any guiding principal to the topics I select for research, then it is simply to ask interesting questions in the hope that they may yield interesting answers."

*   *   *

NOSSACK, Hans Erich 1901-1978

PERSONAL: Born January 30, 1901, in Hamburg, Germany; son of Eugen (a coffee merchant) and Elita (Krohnke) Nossack; married Gabriele Knierer, November 10, 1925. *Education:* Attended Jena University, 1919-22. *Home:* Hansastrasse 20, 2 Hamburg 13, Federal Republic of Germany.

CAREER: Writer. Factory worker, 1919-22; employed by commercial firms, 1925-33; proprietor of coffee and cocoa import business in West Germany, 1933-78. Guest professor of poetry at Frankfort University, 1968. *Member:* German Academy of Science and Literature, Germany Academy of Language and Poetry. *Awards, honors:* George Buchner Prize, 1961; Wilhelm Raabe Prize, 1963.

WRITINGS—In English: *Unmoegliche Beweisaufnahme* (also see below), Suhrkamp, 1959, translation by Michael Lebeck published as *The Impossible Proof,* Farrar, Straus, 1968; *Der Fall d'Arthez* (novel), Suhrkamp, 1968, translation by Lebeck published as *The d'Arthez Case,* Farrar, Straus, 1971; *Dem unbekannten Sieger,* Suhrkamp, 1969, translation by Ralph Manheim published as *To the Unknown Hero,* Farrar, Straus, 1974.

Other: *Gedichte* (title means "Poems"), [Hamburg], 1947; *Nekyia: Bericht eines Ueberlebenden* (novel: title means "Nekya: Report of a Survivor"), [Hamburg], 1947; *Interview mit dem Tode* (Short stories; title means "Interview With Death"), [Hamburg], 1948, 2nd edition published as *Dorothea,* [Hamburg], 1950; *Die rotte Kain* (play), [Hamburg], 1949; *Die Begnadigung,* [Zurich], 1955; *Spaetestens im November* (novel; title means "In November at the Latest"), Suhrkamp, 1955; *Der Neugierige* (short stories), [Munich], 1955; *Spirale* (stories; title means "Spirals"; contains *Unmoegliche Beweisaufnahme;* also see above), Suhrkamp, 1956; *Begegnung im Barraum* (short stories; title means "Meeting in the Anteroom"), [Olten], 1958; *Der juen-*

gere Bruder (novel; title means "The Younger Brother"), Suhrkamp, 1958.

Der Untergang (short stories; title means "The Defeat"), Suhrkamp, 1961; *Nach dem letzten Aufstand* (novel; title means "After the Last Rebellion"), Suhrkamp, 1961; *Ein Sonderfall* (play), Luchterhand, 1963; *Sechs Etueden* (short stories), Insel-Verlag, 1964; *Das kennt Man* (title means "The Known Man"), Suhrkamp, 1964; *Das Testament des Lucius Eurinus* (story; title means "The Testament of Lucius Eurinus"), [Zurich], 1964; *Das Mal und andere Erzaehlungen,* Suhrkamp, 1965; *Die schwache Position der Literatur* (essays; title means "The Weak Position of Literature"), Suhrkamp, 1966.

Pseudoautobiographische Glossen, Suhrkamp, 1971; *Die gestohlene Melodie* (novel; title means "The Stolen Melody"), Suhrkamp, 1972; *Bereitschaftsdienst* (novel), Suhrkamp, 1973; *Ein gluecklicher Mensch* (novel), Suhrkamp, 1975; *Um es kurz zu machen: Miniaturen,* Suhrkamp, 1975; *Dieser Andere: Ein Lesebuch,* Suhrkamp, 1976.

Also translator of works into German.

SIDELIGHTS: Nossack was virtually unknown in America for most of his writing career. A prolific writer of plays and novels during the 1930's and early 1940's, Nossack was prohibited by ruling Nazis from having his works published because of his past support of left-wing politics. An extremely important moment in his life was the fire bombing of Hamburg in 1943 that destroyed all his writings. Nossack likened his fate to that of the city, and his novel *Nekyia* details the mental anguish involved in enduring such a disaster. H. M. Waidson observed that *Nekyia* "ruthlessly abandons the narrative conventions of place and time, and plunges us into a dreamworld which is to symbolize the transition from death to reincarnation, and in addition the interim period of chaos immediately after the collapse of Germany in 1945." Nossack later returned to this theme in his collection of short stories, *Interview mit dem Tode.*

Jean Paul Sartre helped popularize Nossack outside Germany by considering him an existentialist. But while Nossack profited from the popularity, he did not consider himself as an existentialist. He turned to writing plays in the early 1950's before receiving more fame for his novel *Spaetestens im November.* Narrated by a woman who trades one egocentic mate for another, the novel warns against the psychological dangers of living through another person's experiences.

Der juengere Bruder is similar to *Spaetestens im November* in its devotion to revealing the foolishness of assuming roles. "In the course of his quest," wrote H. M. Waidson, "Nossack's protagonist turns from the world of moneymaking and middle-class standards to a bohemian half-world which he finds more congenial. However, he meets a sudden and unexpected end." In both *Spaetestens im November* and *Der juengere Bruder,* untimely death strikes the people who assume roles other than their own.

Spirale, a collection of stories, features a style more stark than its predecessors. "The individual stories are composed in an economical, distinctly poetic prose without any ornamentation," wrote Eberhard Horst. He added, "The sentences are short, and the statements are pregnant with meaning. In place of feeling and sentiment, which are misused in literature as anywhere else, there is an alert sensibility that relentlessly uncovers the subsoil and fragility of human existence."

The Impossible Proof, a story from *Spirale* which became

Nossack's first published work in America, deals with a man's judgment of himself in regard to his wife's disappearance. The story reveals the more positive side of assuming roles. Michael Wood noted that "there is a sense of irreducible difference, a sense of being radically unlike other people, and . . . there is a great emphasis on the idea of acting as at least a partial protection against danger and distress." Calling the story "a tour de force of great brilliance," Wood also declared that *The Impossible Proof* "is both funny and disturbing . . . , and it is strictly metaphysical, preoccupied, that is, by problems of guilt and anxiety which are offered to us as universal, or at least as international, stripped of all local psychological and historical resonances."

To the Unknown Hero in many ways resembles *The Impossible Proof.* As Wood stated, "*The Impossible Proof* is presented as the product of a single brain during a sleepless night; the narrator of *To the Unknown Hero* is telling a friend about a book he has written, and about a long conversation he has had with his father about that book—the father's recreated speech forms the body of the novel." Valentine Cunningham wrote that *To the Unknown Hero* "is tellingly and absorbingly put together, and its theme becomes more than captivating by the links made between its immediate subject and more recent German events." Sheldon Frank noted that "Nossack may appear to represent a kind of atavism, as a postwar existentialist still running changes on familiar themes of despair and ambiguity." Frank called *To the Unknown Hero* "a parable about the limitations of historical understanding, but it is also a very clever, often very funny story of adventure and detection."

The lack of critical attention in America regarding Nossack has itself resulted in critical attention. Writing in 1975, Frank observed, "In 1948 Jean-Paul Sartre called [Nossack] 'the most interesting contemporary German writer,' yet *To the Unknown Hero* is only his third novel to appear in English translation. Why this neglect of a writer with such a distinguished European reputation? Well, I'm not sure, but I suspect we had an overdose of Camus. Nossack is very much an 'existentialist' novelist, mining a by-now familiar vein of metaphysical bewilderment in a world without sense. And perhaps this attitude seems outmoded, just another dated product of postwar Europe. Whatever the reason, this neglect of Nossack is regrettable, for he is an artist of disconcerting power, offering us a series of unsettling reports from the abyss." Rosmarie Waldrop also called for recognition of Nossack. "It is time that Nossack be recognized as a major novelist outside Germany," she wrote. "The lack of English translations is scandalous."

BIOGRAPHICAL/CRITICAL SOURCES: German Life and Letters, 1953-54, 1958-59; *Neu deutsche Hefte,* January-February, 1957, January-February, 1962; *Books Abroad,* summer, 1973, summer, 1974; *Listener,* March 28, 1974; *Nation,* May 23, 1975; *New York Review of Books,* September 18, 1975; *Contemporary Literary Criticism,* Volume 6, Gale, 1976.*

—*Sketch by Martha J. Abele*

*   *   *

NOTTINGHAM, Elizabeth K.   1900-

PERSONAL: Born May 9, 1900, in York, England; daughter of Edward Emil (a priest of Church of England) and Ada A. (Smalley) Nottingham. *Education:* Cambridge University, B.A., 1922; attended University of London, 1922-23; Columbia University, Ph.D., 1938. *Politics:* Democrat. *Religion:* "Ecumenical." *Home:* 2615-C Ridge Rd., Berkeley, Calif. 94709.

CAREER: Wheaton College, Norton, Mass., 1935-42, began as instructor, became assistant professor of sociology; Tulane University, Newcomb College, New Orleans, La., associate professor of sociology, 1942-46; Queens College of the City University of New York, Flushing, N.Y., 1946-68, began as assistant professor, became associate professor and professor of sociology. Fulbright associate professor at University of Rangoon, 1957-58; resident at Center for the Study of World Religions, Harvard University, 1961-62. *Member:* American Sociological Association, Society for the Scientific Study of Religion (vice-president, 1950), Eastern Sociological Association.

WRITINGS: The Making of an Evangelist: A Study of John Wesley's Early Years, privately printed, 1938; *Methodism and the Frontier,* Columbia University Press, 1942; *Religion and Society,* Random House, 1954; *Religion: A Sociological View,* Random House, 1971.

WORK IN PROGRESS: The Politics of American Churches; an autobiography.

SIDELIGHTS: Elizabeth Nottingham writes: "The Fulbright award which took me to Burma sparked a lasting interest in world religions and Asian society: a prelude to much world travel, including Thailand, India, Ceylon, and Japan."

*   *   *

NOVAK, David   1941-

PERSONAL: Born August 19, 1941, in Chicago, Ill.; son of Syd (a stockbroker) and Sylvia (a ballerina; maiden name, Wien) Novak; married Melva Ziman (an educator), July 3, 1963; children: Marianne, Jacob George. *Education:* University of Chicago, A.B., 1961; Jewish Theological Seminary of America, M.H.L., 1964, rabbi, 1966; Georgetown University, Ph.D., 1971. *Politics:* Republican. *Home:* 1008 Colonial Ave., Norfolk, Va. 23507. *Office:* Congregation Beth El, 422 Shirley Ave., Norfolk, Va. 23517.

CAREER: Rabbi of Jewish congregations in Washington, D.C., 1966-68, Oklahoma City, Okla., 1969-72, and Baltimore, Md., 1972-77; Congregation Beth El, Norfolk, Va., rabbi, 1977—. Lecturer at Oklahoma City University, 1971-72; visiting associate professor at Baltimore Hebrew College, 1975-76; adjunct assistant professor at Old Dominion University, 1978—. Director of Jewish chaplaincy at St. Elizabeth's Hospital, Washington, D.C., 1967-69; member of Rabbinical Assembly's committee on Jewish law, 1972—; member of board of directors of Americans Concerned for Life, 1974—. Panelist on Baltimore television program, "Question and Answer," 1974-77. *Member:* American Academy of Religion, American Philosophical Association, Tidewater Board of Rabbis. *Awards, honors:* Hyman Enelow Prize from Jewish Theological Seminary of America, 1975, for essay, "Parents and Children in Jewish Ethics."

WRITINGS: Law and Theology in Judaism, Ktav, Volume I, 1974, Volume II, 1976; *Suicide and Morality,* Scholars' Press, 1975; (contributor) Seymour Siegel, editor, *Contemporary Jewish Ethics,* Behrman, 1980; (contributor) David W. Silverman, editor, *Conservative Jewish Thought Today,* Ktav, 1980. Contributor of about thirty articles and reviews to theology, law, and philosophy journals. Contributing editor of *SH'MA: A Journal of Jewish Responsibility.*

WORK IN PROGRESS: The Human Prelude: A Foundation for Jewish Philosophy, publication expected in 1981.

SIDELIGHTS: Novak writes: "My literary work is the result of my research and thought as a Jewish theologian. This work is concerned with the foundations of Jewish theology, philosophically considered, and with the application of Jewish theology to contemporary problems, especially ethical ones. Because of this abiding interest, my education has been in the classical sources of Jewish theology, the classical sources of Western civilization, and philosophical method, especially phenomenology as developed by Edmund Husserl and Max Scheler. Although I make my living as a congregational rabbi and part-time teacher of philosophy, I consider theological research and writing to be my primary vocation.

"Since languages are a necessary tool in my work, I speak Hebrew, Yiddish, and German, and have a reading knowledge of Aramaic, Greek, Latin, and French."

BIOGRAPHICAL/CRITICAL SOURCES: Commentary, March, 1977.

* * *

NOVAK, William (Arnold)   1948-

PERSONAL: Born August 1, 1948, in Toronto, Ontario, Canada; son of George (a stockbroker) and Esther (Brill) Novak; married Linda Mali Manaly (a psychiatric social worker), June 19, 1977; children: Benjamin Joseph. *Education:* York University, B.A., 1969; Brandeis University, M.A., 1972. *Religion:* Jewish. *Residence:* Newton Center, Mass. *Agent:* Steven Axelrod, Curtis Brown Ltd., 575 Madison Ave., New York, N.Y. 10022. *Office:* 17 Commonwealth Ave., Boston, Mass. 02116.

CAREER: Response, New York, N.Y., editor in New York and Boston, 1969-74; *Moment,* Boston, Mass., executive editor, 1975—. Member of faculty at Tufts University, 1975—.

WRITINGS: High Culture: Marijuana in the Lives of Americans, Knopf, 1980. Contributor of articles and reviews to magazines and newspapers.

WORK IN PROGRESS: A book on friendship; a book on "the inner experience of Jewishness."

* * *

NUGENT, Jeffrey B(ishop)   1936-

PERSONAL: Born March 8, 1936, in New York, N.Y.; son of J. Rolf (an economist) and Natalie (an actress; maiden name, Burggraf) Nugent; married Patricia Cameron (an advertising writer), June 21, 1961; children: Daphne Dorian, Nikaela Cameron. *Education:* Amherst College, B.A., 1957; New School for Social Research, M.A., 1961, Ph.D., 1965. *Office:* Department of Economics, University of Southern California, Los Angeles, Calif. 90007.

CAREER: University of Southern California, Los Angeles, assistant professor, 1964-68, associate professor, 1968-76, professor of economics, 1976—. Economist for U.S. Agency for International Development, 1967; economic affairs officer for United Nations Economic Commission for Western Asia, Beirut, Lebanon, 1971-73; consultant to International Monetary Fund and Pan American Health Organization. *Military service:* U.S. Marine Corps Reserve, 1958-62. *Member:* American Economic Association, Econometric Society, Royal Economic Society, Western Economic Association, Omicron Delta Epsilon (district director, 1978-79).

WRITINGS: Programming the Optimal Development of the Greek Economy, Center of Planning and Economic Research, 1966; *Economic Integration in Central America,* Johns Hopkins Press, 1974; (with Pan A. Yotopoulos) *Economics of Development: Empirical Investigations,* Harper,

1976. Contributor to economic and Latin American studies journals.

WORK IN PROGRESS: Dynamics of Rural Development: A Multi-Disciplinary Analysis of Health, Social, and Economic Interactions.

* * *

NUSSBAUMER, Paul (Edmund)   1934-

PERSONAL: Born May 2, 1934, in Lucerne, Switzerland; son of Paul (a technician) and Roesli (Dreher) Nussbaumer; married Mares Jans (a marionette puppeteer), February 2, 1962; children: Nicolas Emanuel, Melchior Peter. *Education:* Attended an art school in Lucerne, Switzerland; attended Grafisches Atelier, Olten, Switzerland. *Religion:* Catholic. *Home:* Sonnhalden, CH—6024 Hildisrieden, Lucerne, Switzerland.

CAREER: Painter, illustrator, and writer. *Awards, honors:* Grants from the Federal Department of the Interior, 1956, 1966, and 1967; Kiefer-Hablitzel Grant, 1967; Biennale der Illustrationene Bratislava Silbermedaille, 1967, for *William Tell and His Son;* Jugendbuchpreis der Schweiz, 1974.

WRITINGS—Self-illustrated; juvenile: (With Palmer Brown) *Anna Lavinias wunderbare Reise* (title means "The Wonderful Journey of Anna Lavinia"), Benziger (Zurich), 1958; (with Ulrich Gisiger) *Arrah der Zigeuner* (title means "Arrah the Gypsy"), Benteli (Bern), 1964; (with wife, Mares Nussbaumer) *Ihr Kinderlein kommet,* Atlantis (Zurich), 1964, published as *Away in a Manger,* Harcourt, 1965; (with Bettina Huerlimann) *Der Knabe des Tell,* Atlantis, 1965, published as *William Tell and His Son,* Harcourt, 1966; (with Alfred Eidenbenz) *Onkel Toms wundersame Reise* (title means "Uncle Tom's Wonderful Journey"), Schweizerspiegel (Zurich), 1965; (with Ursule Williams) *Der schwarze Max* (title means "Black Max"), Benziger, 1966.

(With Bettina Huerlimann) *Barry,* Atlantis, 1967, published as *Barry: The Story of a Brave St. Bernard,* Harcourt, 1968; (with Johan Fabricius) *Hentjes ganz besonderer Winter* (title means "Hentje's Very Special Winter"), Sauerlaender (Aarau), 1969; (with Rudolf Reichling) *Der Bauernhof* (title means "The Farm"), Atlantis, 1969; (with Ludwig Bechstein) *Hans im Glueck* (title means "Lucky John"), Harlekin-Verlag (Lucerne), 1970; (with Gottfried Burgin) *Pony-Ranch,* Atlantis, 1972; (with Retus de Selva) *Die rote Katzenfamilie* (title means "The Red Cat Family"), Werner Classen Verlag (Zurich), 1974.

Illustrator: *Im Wunderland* (textbook; title means "In Wonderland"), two volumes, Kant. Lehrmittelverlag (Lucerne), 1966; *Daheim* (textbook; title means "At Home"), Kant. Lehrmittelverlag, 1966; Alexander Pushkin, *Eugen Onegin Dramen* (title means "Eugen Onegin Dramas"), Edito-Service (Geneva), 1967; Guy de Maupassant, *Mademoiselle Fifi: Une Vie* (title means "Mademoiselle Fifi: A Life"), Maurice Goron Editeur d'art (Paris), 1968; Sagenmappen, *Wallis* (title means "Traditions"), Wallis, Mengis & Sticher (Lucerne), 1968; Sagenmappen, *Innerschweiz* (title means "Traditions of Inner Switzerland"), Mengis & Sticher, 1969.

Sagenmappen, *Luzern,* Mengis and Sticher, 1970; Grimm Brothers, *Hansel and Gretel,* Harlekin-Verlag, 1971; Johanna Spyri, *Heidi,* Volume 1, Benziger, 1971; Alain Fournier, *Le Grand Maulnes* (title means "The Big Maulnes"), Edito-Service, 1971; Hans Bender, *Wunschkost,* Edito-Service, 1971; C. F. Meyer, *Juerg Jenatsch,* Edito-Service, 1971; *Als die Eisenbahn noch Konig war* (title means "The Time the Train Was Still King"), Harlekin-Verlag, 1972;

Sagenmappen, *Berner Oberland* (title means "Traditions of Berner Oberland"), Mengis & Sticher, 1972; Sagenmappen, *Bundner* (title means "Traditions of Graubuenden"), Mengis & Sticher, 1973.

Sagenmappen, *Ostschweizer* (title means "East Switzerland"), Mengis & Sticher, 1974; Silvia Sempert, *Na meh Guet Nacht-Geschichtli* (title means "Some More Good-Night Stories"), Ex-Libris (Zurich), 1974; *Solothurner Sagen* (title means "Traditions of Kanton"), Solothurn, Mengis & Sticher (Lucerne), 1975; Hans Manz, *Der schwarze Wasserbutz* (also titled as *Die schoensten Sagen der Schweiz;* title means "The Most Beautiful Traditions of Switzerland"), Huber Fraunfeld, 1976; Gilbert Cesbron, *La Tradition Fontquernie* (title means "Tradition of Fontquernie"), Edito-Service, 1976; Johanna Spyri, *Heidi,* two volumes, Benziger, 1976; Adolf Heizmann, *Der Kaiser bracht Soldaten* (title means "The Emperor Needs Soldiers"), Schweizer Jugendschriftenwork (Zurich), 1977; Grimm Brothers, *Die zertanzten Schuhe* (title means "The Shoes Used by Dancing"), Aktion Blindenhoerbuecherei (Zurich), 1978; *Das Eselein,* Aktion Blindenhoerbuecherei (Zurich), 1979.

SIDELIGHTS: Nussbaumer told *CA:* "For twenty years, I have been painting and expressing my rather sorrowful, but occasionally happy world. I don't illustrate objects, but instead endeavor to capture the hidden essence or interior of a figure or group. Action, play, work, or social expression are of no conscious importance to me. My intention is to put a figure or group into a peaceful, restful stance, similar to the static compositions found in classical paintings.

"If I'm illustrating for children, though, I become their servant. I strive to be comprehensible while providing pleasure and happiness. I play the small buffoon, the clown who gives out happiness, color, and excitement.

"These two worlds are very important to me, for my natural tendency is a rather sorrowful one. The part of my personality which finds expression in my juvenile illustrations is very optimistic and happy."

*   *   *

NYBAKKEN, Oscar Edward   1904-

PERSONAL: Born February 2, 1904, in Hawley, Minn.; son of Ole A. (a farmer) and Elizabeth (Welo) Nybakken; married Gertrude Njus (a teacher), December 27, 1933; children: Lorraine (Mrs. Fredy Perlman), Ruth Elaine. *Education:* Moorhead State Teachers College (now Moorhead State College), two-year degree, 1923; Luther College, B.A., 1928; University of Iowa, M.A., 1930, Ph.D., 1937; graduate study at Harvard University, 1931, and American Academy of Rome, 1932. *Office:* Department of Classics, University of Iowa, Iowa City, Iowa 52240.

CAREER: University of Iowa, Iowa City, assistant professor, 1938-45, associate professor, 1945-59, professor, 1959-71, professor emeritus, 1971—, chairman of department of classical studies, 1958-66. Member of managing committee of American School of Classical Studies, 1965-72; member of advisory council of American Academy in Rome, 1959-71, and chairman, 1962-63. Director of Classical Backgrounds Tour of Europe, summers, 1949, 1950, and 1952. Trustee of Vergilian Society, 1956-61. *Member:* American Philological Association, Archeological Institute of America, Classical Association of Middle West and South (president, 1958-59), Kiwanis, Eta Sigma Phi (chairman of board of trustees, 1964-68). *Awards, honors:* L.H.D. from Luther College, 1966.

WRITINGS: An Analytical Study of Horace's Ideas, Mennonite Press, 1937; *Guide for Readings on Roman Civilization,* American Classical League Service Bureau, 1940; *Greek and Latin in Scientific Terminology,* Iowa State College Press, 1959, reprinted, 1970.

O

O'BRIEN, Kate   1897-1974

PERSONAL: Born December 3, 1897, in Limerick, Ireland; died August 13, 1974, in Faversham, England; daughter of Thomas and Catherine (Thornhill) O'Brien. *Education:* Attended University College, Dublin. *Home:* 177 The Street Boughton, Faversham, Kent, England.

CAREER: Novelist and playwright. Journalist for *Manchester Guardian* and worked in Bilbao, Spain. *Awards, honors:* James Tait Black Memorial Prize and Hawthornden Prize, both 1931, both for *Without My Cloak.*

WRITINGS—Novels; except as noted: *Without My Cloak,* Doubleday, 1931, reprinted, Portway Press, 1969; *The Anteroom,* Doubleday, 1934, reprinted, Chivers, 1969; *Mary Lavelle,* Doubleday, 1936, reprinted, Large Print Ltd., 1977; *Farewell Spain* (travel), Doubleday, 1937; *Pray for the Wanderer,* Doubleday, 1938, reprinted, Large Print Ltd., 1976; *The Land of Spices,* Doubleday, 1941, reprinted, Millington, 1973; *English Diaries and Journals* (history and criticism), Collins, 1943; *The Last of Summer,* Doubleday, 1943; *For One Sweet Grape,* Doubleday, 1946 (published in England as *That Lady,* Heinemann, 1946, reprinted, Large Print Ltd., 1976); *Teresa of Avila* (biography), Sheed, 1951; *The Flower of May,* Harper, 1953; *As Music and Splendour,* Harper, 1958; *My Ireland* (travel), Hastings House, 1962; *Presentation Parlour* (nonfiction), Heinemann, 1963. Also contributor to *English Association: Essays and Studies,* 1956.

Plays: *Distinguished Villa* (three-act; first produced in London at Aldwych Theatre, May 2, 1926), Benn, 1926; "The Bridge," first produced at Arts Theatre Club, May 31, 1927; (with Geoffrey Gomer and W. A. Carot) "The Ante-Room" (adapted from O'Brien's own novel), first produced in London at Queen's Theatre, August 14, 1936; "The Schoolroom Window," first produced at Manuscript Club, 1937; *That Lady* (adapted from own novel; first produced on Broadway at Martin Beck Theatre, November 22, 1949), Harper, 1949.

SIDELIGHTS: Although first known as a playwright, Kate O'Brien is best known as a novelist. In her books, she was most concerned with the Irish middle class and the emotional tensions created by Catholic puritanism. O'Brien was one of the few contemporary Irish writers who dealt with the cultured middle class instead of the working or peasant class. In her first and most highly praised novel, *Without My Cloak,* critic V. P. Ross claimed: "O'Brien seizes and impales a whole era, a whole attitude and a whole racial stamp.

You feel, at the end of her book, that she has nourished you with a particularly large, particularly juicy slab from life's well laden feast."

O'Brien also lived in Spain for a time, which sparked her interest in Spanish history and culture. She wrote a number of works reflecting this interest. *Mary Lavelle,* her first novel set in Spain, also incorporates O'Brien's Irish affiliations. The heroine is an Irish governess, and O'Brien explores the conflicts caused by extreme religious beliefs. Grant O'Harrah wrote that the book "has a rare objectivity for the most part; yet the all-pervasive Catholic doctrines cannot be mistaken." Her most famous and successful novel, *For One Sweet Grape,* chronicles the romantic and political intrigues of the Spanish court of Phillip II. A *New Yorker* critic noted: "O'Brien has taken the strange superficial facts of the case and, without reconstructing a moment of history, has created a tragic study of three absorbing and very disparate personalities. An original and impressive work, reflecting the same lofty, thoughtful Catholicism that distinguished the author's *The Land of Spices.*" *For One Sweet Grape* was adapted for the stage and was also made into a motion picture in 1955, starring Olivia De Havilland.

In her last two novels, *The Flower of May* and *As Music and Splendour,* O'Brien returned to the Irish middle class as seen against a European backdrop. Elizabeth Janeway sums up O'Brien's work in these novels, observing that "it is the upper bourgeoisie with whom this Irish-Catholic novelist is concerned, but an upper bourgeoisie allied with landed gentry, unprovincial and European-minded. Superimposed upon its 'middle class morality' is a delicate sense of honor and code of behavior." Janeway continued: "Within the precise limits she has set—and they are limits of depth as well as of breadth—Miss O'Brien tells a delightful story."

BIOGRAPHICAL/CRITICAL SOURCES: Outlook and Independent, December 9, 1931; *New York Herald Tribune Book Review,* October 25, 1936; *New Yorker,* May 25, 1946; *New York Times,* September 6, 1953.

OBITUARIES: New York Times, August 15, 1974; *Washington Post,* August 18, 1974; *Publishers Weekly,* September 16, 1974; *AB Bookman's Weekly,* October 7, 1974.*

*   *   *

OCHSE, Orpha Caroline   1925-

PERSONAL: Born May 6, 1925, in St. Joseph, Mo.; daughter of Franklin Lewis and Della (Poindexter) Ochse. *Education:* Central Methodist College, Fayette, Mo., B.Mus., 1947; University of Rochester, M.Mus., 1948, Ph.D., 1953. *Office:* Department of Music, Whittier College, 13046 East Philadelphia, Whittier, Calif. 90608.

CAREER: Central Methodist College, Fayette, Mo., member of faculty, 1948-50; Western Illinois State College (now Western Illinois University), Macomb, member of faculty, 1950-51; Phoenix College, Phoenix, Ariz., member of faculty, 1952-57; music director at Congregational church in Pasadena, Calif., 1958-70; Whittier College, Whittier, Calif., professor of music, 1969—. Lecturer at California Institute of Technology, 1969-76. Organist. Member of board of directors of Ruth and Clarence Mader Memorial Scholarship Fund.

MEMBER: Organ Historical Society, Sonneck Society, American Guild of Organists (dean of central Arizona chapter, 1956-57, and Pasadena chapter, 1967-68; member of national council, 1975—), Boston Organ Club. *Awards, honors:* American Philosophical Society grant.

WRITINGS: The History of the Organ in the United States, Indiana University Press, 1975.

Composer of organ music, including "Allegro," 1962, "Chaconne," 1962, "Monogram," 1963, "Trio Pastorale," 1966, "Trio and Allegro," 1966, "Dust and Fanfare," 1967, and "Prelude and Fugue," 1975.

*   *   *

O'CONNOR, Edwin (Greene)   1918-1968

PERSONAL: Born July 29, 1918, in Providence, R.I.; died March 23, 1968, in Boston, Mass.; son of John Vincent (a doctor) and Mary (Greene) O'Connor; married Veniette Caswell Weil, September 2, 1962; children: one son. *Education:* University of Notre Dame, A.B., 1939. *Residence:* Boston, Mass.

CAREER: Writer. Worked as radio announcer, writer, and producer. *Military service:* U.S. Coast Guard, served as information officer. *Awards, honors:* Golden Book Award from Catholic Writer's Guild, 1957, and Atlantic Prize, both for *The Last Hurrah;* Pulitzer Prize for fiction, 1962, for *The Edge of Sadness;* Catholic Press Institute Award, 1962.

WRITINGS: The Oracle, Harper, 1951; *The Last Hurrah* (Book-of-the-Month Club selection), Little, Brown, 1956; *Benjy: A Ferocious Fairy Tale,* Little, Brown, 1957; *The Edge of Sadness,* Little, Brown, 1961; *The Last Hurrah* [and] *The Edge of Sadness,* Little, Brown, 1962; *I Was Dancing* (novel), Little, Brown, 1964, adaptation as play published under same title, Dramatists Play Service, 1966; *All in the Family,* Little, Brown, 1966; *The Best and the Last of Edwin O'Connor,* Little, Brown, 1970. Contributor to publications, including *Atlantic Monthly* and *McCall's.*

WORK IN PROGRESS: Two novels left unfinished at time of death.

SIDELIGHTS: Edwin O'Connor's two most popular books, *The Last Hurrah* and *The Edge of Sadness,* have won him praise and recognition as a spokesman of the Irish-American people. In addition to this, O'Connor "is unquestionably one of the most skillful writers of the day," noted J. K. Galbraith. "He has a gift for quick description and a singular purity of style."

The Edge of Sadness, O'Connor's Pulitzer Prize winner, relates the saga of three generations in an Irish-American family as seen through the eyes of a Father Hugh Kennedy. So well does *The Edge of Sadness* portray its characters that John V. Kelleher observed, "It is well to admit that the reader will find here, or recognize, closer and more informed observation of middle-class, Irish-American Catholics than he could get from a platoon of sociologists."

The Last Hurrah chronicles the career of a "corrupt and powerful, yet understanding and generous" politician. Most reviewers insisted the book was nothing more than a poorly masked account of former Massachusetts governor and long-time Boston mayor James Michael Curly, a suspicion Curly himself held, but O'Connor denied this interpretation. The politician, however, fought the release of O'Connor's book as a motion picture and took the author to court. Despite Curly's efforts, the case was settled privately, and the movie reached the theatres in 1958. Both book and movie proved a huge success. In the words of H. M. Jones, *The Last Hurrah* "is atrociously funny, it is acute, it is tolerant, it is a triumph of style."

BIOGRAPHICAL/CRITICAL SOURCES: Atlantic Monthly, May, 1951, October, 1966; *New Yorker,* May 12, 1951, February 11, 1956, June 24, 1961, October 15, 1966; *New York Times,* June 10, 1951; *San Francisco Chronicle,* June 29, 1951; *New York Herald Tribune Book Review,* July 15, 1951; *Saturday Review,* June 10, 1961, October 1, 1966; *New York Times Book Review,* March 22, 1964, September 25, 1966, June 4, 1971; *Critic,* April, 1964; *New York Review of Books,* April 30, 1964, June 1, 1970; *America,* October 1, 1966, May 21, 1970; *Commonweal,* October 23, 1970.

OBITUARIES: New York Times, March 24, 1968; *Washington Post,* March 24, 1968; *Time,* March 29, 1968; *Newsweek,* April 1, 1968; *Publishers Weekly,* April 1, 1968; *Antiquarian Bookman,* April 15, 1968; *Atlantic Monthly,* May, 1968; *Current Biography,* May, 1968; *Books Abroad,* spring, 1969.*

*   *   *

O'CONNOR, Frank
See O'DONOVAN, Michael John
*   *   *

O'DONOVAN, Michael John   1903-1966
(Frank O'Connor)

PERSONAL: Born in 1903 in Cork, Ireland; came to United States, 1952; died March 10, 1966, of a heart attack in Dublin, Ireland; son of Michael (a laborer) and Mary (O'Connor) O'Donovan; married Evelyn Bowen; married Harriet Rich, 1953; children: (first marriage) two sons, one daughter, (second marriage) one child. *Education:* Educated in Cork, Ireland. *Politics:* Republican.

CAREER: Writer. Librarian in Sligo, Cork, and Dublin, 1923; director of Abbey Theatre, 1935-39; teacher at Harvard University, Northwestern University, and Stanford University. Associated with the Irish Republican Army (IRA), 1921-23. *Awards, honors:* Doctor of Letters from Dublin University.

WRITINGS—Under name Frank O'Connor; short stories, unless otherwise noted: *Guests of the Nation,* Macmillan, 1931; *The Saint and Mary Kate,* Macmillan (London), 1932, reprinted, Proscenium, 1970; *Three Old Brothers and Other Poems,* Thomas Nelson, 1936; *Bones of Contention and Other Stories,* Macmillan, 1936, reprinted, Core Collection, 1978; *Death in Dublin: Michael Collins and the Irish Revolution* (history), Doubleday, 1937 (published in England as *The Big Fellow: A Life of Michael Collins,* Thomas Nelson, 1937), revised edition published as *The Big Fellow: Michael*

Collins and the Irish Revolution, Burns & Oates, 1965, revised edition, Corgi, 1969.

Dutch Interior (novel), Knopf, 1940; *Three Tales*, Cuala Press, 1941, reprinted, Irish University Press, 1971; (author of introduction) Eric Cross, *The Tailor and Ansty*, Chapman & Hall, 1942, 2nd edition, Mercier, 1970; *A Picture Book* (travel), Cuala Press, 1943; *Crab Apple Jelly*, Knopf, 1944; (author of preface) *Selected Poems*, translated by Nigel Heseltine, Cuala Press, 1944, reprinted, Piers Press, 1968, reprinted as *Twenty-Five Poems*, Piers Press, 1968, reprinted as *Selected Poems*, Irish University Press, 1971; *Selected Stories*, Fridberg, 1946; *Irish Miles* (travel), Macmillan (London), 1947; *The Common Cord*, Macmillan (London), 1947, Knopf, 1948.

Leinster, Munster, and Connaught (travel), Robert Hale, 1950; *Traveller's Samples*, Knopf, 1951; *The Stories of Frank O'Connor*, Knopf, 1952; *More Stories by Frank O'Connor*, Knopf, 1954; *Domestic Relations*, Knopf, 1957; (with Michael Aldenhoff) *Die Amerikanerin: Ihre Macht und Ihre Moral* (nonfiction), Hellas-Verlag, 1958.

An Only Child (autobiography), Knopf, 1961; *My Oedipus Complex and Other Stories*, Penguin Books, 1963; *Collection Two*, Macmillan (London), 1964; *Collection Three*, Macmillan, 1969; *A Life of Your Own and Other Stories*, Pan Books, 1969; *Masculine Protest and Other Stories*, Pan Books, 1969; *A Set of Variations*, Knopf, 1969; *My Father's Son* (autobiography), Knopf, 1969.

Literary criticism: *Towards an Appreciation of Literature*, Metropolitan, 1945, reprinted, Haskell House, 1974; *The Art of the Theatre*, Fridberg, 1947, reprinted, Norwood, 1977; *The Road to Stratford*, Methuen, 1948, revised edition published as *Shakespeare's Progress*, World Publishing, 1960; *The Mirror in the Roadway* (and history), Knopf, 1956; *The Lonely Voice: A Study of the Short Story*, World Publishing, 1963; *A Short History of Irish Literature: A Backward Look*, Putnam, 1967 (published in England as *The Backward Look: A Survey of Irish Literature*, Macmillan, 1967).

Translator from the Irish: *The Wild Bird's Nest*, Cuala Press, 1932, reprinted, Irish University Press, 1971; *Lords and Commons*, Cuala Press, 1938, reprinted, Irish University Press, 1971; *The Fountain of Magic*, Macmillan (London), 1938; Eileen O'Connell, *A Lament for Art O'Leary*, Cuala Press, 1940, reprinted, Irish University Press, 1971; *The Little Monasteries*, Oxford University Press, 1963; Brian Merriman, *The Midnight Court*, Haskell House, 1974.

Plays; and director: (With Hugh Hunt) "The Invincibles" (one-act), first produced in Dublin at Abbey Theatre, 1937; (with Hugh Hunt) "Moses' Rock" (one-act), first produced in Dublin at Abbey Theatre, 1938; "Time's Pocket" (one-act), first produced in Dublin at Abbey Theatre, 1938; "The Statue's Daughter" (one-act), first produced in Dublin at Abbey Theatre, 1940.

Editor: (And author of introduction) *Modern Irish Short Stories*, Oxford University Press, 1957; *A Book of Ireland*, Collins, 1960; (and translator) *Kings, Lords, and Commons*, Knopf, 1959; (with David Green; and translator) *A Golden Treasury of Irish Poetry: A.D. 600 to 1200*, Macmillan (London), 1967.

Contributor of more than forty short stories to *New Yorker*, *Irish Statesman*, *Atlantic*, *Harper's*, *Holiday*, and *Esquire*.

SIDELIGHTS: "Storytelling is the nearest thing one can get to the quality of a pure lyric poem," Frank O'Connor wrote. "It doesn't deal with problems; it doesn't have any solutions to offer; it just states the human condition." Written in a deceptively simple style, O'Connor's stories admirably recorded the realities and intricacies of life in Ireland under the often heavy rule of the Catholic church and small-town life. His stories exhibit a poetic sensitivity with a delightful sense of humor. W. B. Yeats once declared that "O'Connor is doing for Ireland what Chekov did for Russia."

O'Connor was the only son of a very poor family. His father was a hard working laborer who saved his money to periodically go on drinking sprees, which would devastate the family financially and emotionally. His father would become violent and cruel when he drank. O'Connor wrote that he hated and loved his father, but was mainly jealous of him. He loved his mother intensely and was jealous of the love and understanding she had for his father. O'Connor identified his conflict as an Oedipus Complex, which became the subject of many of his written works. He dealt with it in both of his autobiographies, *An Only Child* and *My Father's Son*, and in a short story entitled "My Oedipus Complex," among others. When Michael O'Donovan changed his name to Frank O'Connor for political reasons, it was not surprising that he chose his beloved mother's maiden name.

The O'Donovan family was so poor it could not afford to provide a formal education for O'Connor. Although he briefly attended the Christian Brothers School in Cork, O'Connor was mainly self-educated. "I had to content myself with a make-believe education, and the curious thing is that it was the make-believe that succeeded," O'Connor claimed much later. O'Connor began writing while very young, and at the age of twelve he turned out his first collection of writings: poems, biographies, and essays on history. O'Connor observed, "I was intended by God to be a painter, but I was very poor and pencil and paper were the cheapest. Music was out for that reason as well. Literature is the poor man's art."

While still in his teens, O'Connor joined the Irish Republican Army (IRA) and fought in the civil war from 1919 to 1921. In 1921, a treaty ended seven centuries of English occupation, but the Republicans, and with them, O'Connor, continued the fight to include Ulster in the Irish Free State. O'Connor was arrested and imprisoned after about a year of living as a homeless fugitive. In jail, O'Connor continued to educate himself and became a librarian when he was released in 1923. He was hired by the playwright Lennox Robinson who was then the secretary of the Irish Carnegie United Kingdom Trust, which was organizing rural libraries.

O'Connor became involved in the tail end of the Irish Literary Revival that was sweeping Ireland and endeavoring to create a literature that was purely Irish in scope and tone. The writers of this nationalistic movement also strove to reawaken in the Irish people an awareness of Ireland's rich history and colorful mythological past.

O'Connor began contributing stories to *Irish Statesman*, edited by George Russell (also known as "A.E."). Russell, one of the principal leaders of the Irish Literary Revival, with Yeats and Synge, made the magazine a forum for writers of all schools and the focal point of literature in Ireland. O'Connor and Russell grew to be good friends, each admiring the other's talents. "I haven't discovered any writer so good as O'Connor since I found James Stephens," Russell asserted.

In 1935, O'Connor became director with Yeats of the Abbey Theatre Company in Dublin. The theatre was the voice box of Irish nationalism and the hub of the Irish Literary Revival. Here, O'Connor became acquainted with the other greats of the revival, including Lady Gregory, Sean O'Casey, Sean

O'Faolain, Liam O'Flaherty, and F. R. Higgins. O'Connor served with Yeats in a tumultuous partnership. O'Connor commented that he never argued so much with anyone since his father. Despite the frequent squabbles, the two men were friends, encouraging and supporting each other. Yeats was so impressed with O'Connor's translations of old Irish literature and poetry from the Gaelic that he arranged to have them published by his sisters at the Cuala Press. A number of O'Connor's good lines also found their way into Yeats's poetry.

O'Connor left the Abbey Theatre in 1939, on the issue of censorship, an unfortunate fact of life in Ireland. In the 1940's, a number of his books, including *Traveller's Samples, The Common Cord,* and *Dutch Interior,* were officially banned by the Irish government. O'Connor fought against such censorship his entire life. He was still writing about the issue in Irish newspapers and magazines as late as 1962.

James H. Matthews observed that the stories of O'Connor have a wonderful oral quality, a natural, seemingly effortless style, which often gives "the reader the feeling that he is overhearing them." Critic William Troy claimed O'Connor's "language is a realization of the improbable flights of Irish speech of a sort to make the more famous passages of Synge seem like the insincerities of a tired litterateur." O'Connor sought to capture the drama of oral transmission. He believed that writers "from Chekov to Katherine Mansfield and James Joyce had so fashioned the short story that it no longer rang with the tone of a man's voice, speaking." This is why O'Connor always set his stories in Ireland. "I prefer to write about Ireland and Irish people merely because I know to a syllable how everything in Ireland can be said." Nevertheless, O'Connor's stories are not merely provincial in flavor. Critic Muriel Spark claimed that O'Connor had "a miraculous technique which universalizes the stories without impairing their local virtue." He portrayed people and human nature, which never change from one culture to another. "People are all that matters," O'Connor once remarked.

O'Connor wrote about his theories on the short story in his critical work, *The Lonely Voice.* He felt that the short story is "the literature of submerged population groups," and the product of an "intense awareness of human loneliness." Short stories deal with people living on the fringes of society, outcasts, and "out-lawed figures." "While we often read a familiar novel again for companionship, we approach the short story in a very different mood," O'Connor contended. The short story "began, and continues to function, as a private art intended to satisfy the standards of the individual, solitary, critical reader." The critics generally praised the book for its perceptive approach and William Barrett went so far as to say that O'Connor "has written an analysis of the shorter fictional form that, for the charm of its writing and for depth of insight, deserves to be set beside E. M. Forster's classic *Aspects of the Novel.*"

O'Connor strove throughout his career to achieve an "organic form," a form which captured a human event in all its complexities and which embraced the past, present, and future. This goal determined the form a story was to take. On this point, many of O'Connor's stories have been criticized for their sketchiness, a "certain inconclusiveness" or "lack of shape." If the critics, though, sometimes thought his stories needed reworking, O'Connor always thought they needed rewriting. "As a writer I like the feeling I get when some story which I've been trying to bring up in the right way gets up and tells me to go to hell," O'Connor explained. His wife Harriet described him as a "tinkerer." William

Maxwell, a fiction editor at *New Yorker,* where O'Connor published many stories, affirmed that "he rewrote and rewrote. After he was published, he rewrote and was republished. Everything he wrote was an unfinished work, not so much because of any dissatisfaction, but because of the pleasure he got out of a story. He liked his stories."

Many of O'Connor's short stories have been adapted into plays for the stage. Neil McKenzie adapted one of O'Connor's first stories, "Guests of the Nation," into a one-act play that premiered on Broadway in 1958. Paul Avila Mayer's book, *Three Hand Reel,* was published in 1964, and contains three one-act plays, "The Frying Pan," "Eternal Triangle," and "The Bridal Night," all based on short stories by O'Connor. Another story, "In the Train," was adapted by Hugh Hunt into a one-act play that premiered at the Abbey Theatre in 1937. The same story was also adapted by Hunt into a radio play in four scenes.

O'Connor was also an expert on Russian authors and interested in eighteenth-century music.

BIOGRAPHICAL/CRITICAL SOURCES: New Statesman and Nation, October 17, 1931; *Nation,* April 29, 1936; *Atlantic,* April, 1963; Maurice Sheehy, editor, *Michael/Frank: Studies on Frank O'Connor,* Knopf, 1969; *Sewanee Review,* winter, 1976.

OBITUARIES: New York Times, March 11, 1966; *Publishers Weekly,* March 21, 1966; *Antiquarian Bookman,* April 1, 1966; *Books Abroad,* spring, 1967; *Britannica Book of the Year,* 1967.*

—*Sketch by Anne M. Guerrini*

*   *   *

OFOMATA, G(odfrey) E(zediaso) K(ingsley)   1936-

PERSONAL: Born August 28, 1936, in Nnewi, Nigeria; son of Ofomata Ezeatuma Ezebube and Ndayagwa (Nzuko) Ofomata; married Obiageli Hope Ejimbe (a high school teacher), August 2, 1969; children: Obianuju, Kenechukwu, Chijioke, Ogochukwu, Chukwudum. *Education:* University of Ibadan, B.A. (with honors), 1961; University of Strasbourg, Doctorat de Troisieme Cycle, 1963. *Religion:* Christian. *Home:* 17 Sir Louis Mbanefo St., University of Nigeria, Nsukka, Nigeria. *Office:* Department of Geography, University of Nigeria, Nsukka, Nigeria.

CAREER: University of Nigeria, Nsukka, lecturer, 1963-70, senior lecturer, 1970-74, reader, 1974-76, professor of geography, 1976—, dean of faculty of environmental studies. President of Nigerian National Committee on Geography, of International Geographical Union, 1978-82; chairperson of Nigerian National Committee on Soil Conservation, 1978—. *Military service:* Biafran Army, 1967-70; became lieutenant colonel. *Member:* Nigerian Geographical Association (president, 1974 and 1975).

WRITINGS: (Editor and contributor) *Nigeria in Maps: Eastern States,* Ethiope, 1975; (editor and contributor) *The Nsukka Environment,* Fourth Dimension, 1978; *Geography for Africa: Landforms,* Ethiope, 1979.

WORK IN PROGRESS: Soil and Environment; Man and Environment; Erosion and Soil Conservation.

SIDELIGHTS: Ofomata writes that his motivation is "the urge to reveal part of the mysteries of Nigeria, especially the southeastern part, to the general public, and to make available to my students what I consider suitable texts for their education. For instance, *Geography for Africa: Landforms* is the result of several years of reflection on how best to present the essential contents of geomorphology to African students. That is why the title is 'for' and not 'of' Africa. Again, *The Nsukka Environment* provides an impulse towards literary creativity and attempts to present a coherent study of continuity and change typical of rural Igboland—change which has led to visible transformations in the way of life of a people who, while retaining the essential elements of their tradition, are receptive of such innovations as make for progress in their social and economic well-being. The search continues for a better understanding of the interaction between man and his environment."

*   *   *

OGBU, John U(zor)   1939-

PERSONAL: Born May 9, 1939, in Onicha, Nigeria; came to the United States in 1961; son of Ogbu nw'Onu nw'Igbo (a farmer) and Ugo nw'Uzor (a farmer); married second wife, Marcellina Ada nw'Igwe, 1976; children: (first marriage) Grace Ugo; (second marriage) Elizabeth Ijeoma, Cecilia Chinyere Mgboro, Nnanna Ibiam. *Education:* Methodist Teachers College, Uzuakoli, Nigeria, teaching certificate, 1958; studied at Africa Writing Center, Kitwe, Zambia, 1961; Princeton University and Princeton Theological Seminary, 1961-62; University of California, Berkeley, A.B. (with honors), 1965, M.A., 1969, Ph.D., 1971. *Office:* Department of Anthropology, University of California, Berkeley, Calif. 94720.

CAREER: High school teacher of Latin, math, and geography in Calabar, Nigeria, 1959-61; ethnographer for public schools in Stockton, Calif., 1968-69; University of California, Berkeley, acting assistant professor, 1970-71, assistant professor, 1971-76, associate professor of anthropology, 1976—. Research associate at Yale University, 1973-75; adjunct professor at San Francisco Theological Seminary, 1973—; distinguished visiting professor at University of Delaware, 1979; lecturer at colleges and universities. Chairperson of committee of experts on transfer of knowledge for United Nations Educational, Scientific and Cultural Organization, 1978; member of advisory panels of National Science Foundation and National Institute of Education; delegate to U.S.-Israel Joint Colloquium on the Education of the Disadvantaged.

MEMBER: International African Institute, African Studies Association, American Anthropological Association (fellow), American Association for the Advancement of Science, American Ethnological Society, Council on Anthropology and Education (co-chairperson of committee on cognitive and linguistic studies), Society for Applied Anthropology (fellow), Kroeber Anthropological Society, Royal Anthropological Society (fellow). *Awards, honors:* National Institute of Mental Health grant, 1974; Margaret Mead Award from Society for Applied Anthropology, 1979, for *The Next Generation* and *Minority Education and Caste.*

WRITINGS: The Next Generation: An Ethnography of Education in an Urban Neighborhood, Academic Press, 1974; (contributor) George M. Foster and Robert V. Kemper, editors, *Anthropologists in Cities,* Little, Brown, 1974; *Minority Education and Caste: The American System in Cross-Cultural Perspective,* Academic Press, 1978; (contributor) Michael Cohen, editor, *School Organization and Effectiveness,* National Institute of Education, 1979; (contributor) Robert H. Koff and Hendrick D. Gideonse, editors, *Values Imposed by the Behavioral and Social Sciences,* National Society for the Study of Education, 1979; (contributor) Kathryn Borman, editor, *Socialization in a Changing Society,* Pergamon, 1980. Contributor of about twenty-five articles and reviews to academic journals.

WORK IN PROGRESS: Transmission of Oral Literature Among the Ibos of Nigeria; Urbanization in a Stratified Community: The Case of Stockton, California; research comparing caste and social change in the United States and Nigeria; research on ethnic stratification, politics, and social change in Stockton, and on domestic roles and diet in a Poka village.

SIDELIGHTS: Ogbu writes: "As an African (Nigerian) anthropologist it is both very educational and very interesting to be doing research on American society and writing about Americans. I think that many Third World scholars should consider studying Western societies and Western peoples because the knowledge gained from such studies could be very valuable in examining the nature and problems of Third World societies."

*   *   *

O'GRADY, John F(rancis)   1939-

PERSONAL: Born September 6, 1939, in Philadelphia, Pa.; son of Joseph P. (in sales) and Nora (an office worker; maiden name, Gallagher) O'Grady. *Education:* Mary Immaculate College, B.A., 1962; University of St. Thomas, Rome, Italy, S.T.D., 1969; Pontifical Bible Institute, S.S.D., 1976. *Home address:* P.O. Box 235, Monterey, Mass. 01245. *Office:* 2260 Lake Ave., Rochester, N.Y. 04612.

CAREER: Ordained Roman Catholic priest, 1966; Niagara University, Niagara University, N.Y., assistant professor of theology, 1969-71; Siena College, Loudonville, N.Y., assistant professor of religious studies, 1975-77; St. Bernard's Seminary, Rochester, N.Y., associate professor of New Testament and dean of seminary, 1977—. Diocese of Albany, Albany, N.Y., founder and director of liturgy office, 1971-73, and office for clergy education, 1975-78. *Member:* American Academy of Religion, Catholic Biblical Association of America, Catholic Theological Society of America, Society of Biblical Literature.

WRITINGS: Jesus, Lord and Christ, Paulist/Newman, 1972; *Christian Anthropology,* Paulist/Newman, 1975; *The Johannine Community and the Individual Believer,* Duquesne University Press, 1981. Also author of *Models of Jesus,* 1980. Author of weekly column appearing in *Evangelist.* Contributor to theology journals. Editor of *Biblical Theology Bulletin.*

SIDELIGHTS: O'Grady told *CA:* "I am particularly interested in integrating the contemporary findings of biblical scholarship with the needs of ordinary people. There is a definite relationship between understanding ourselves and understanding Jesus. People believe, but need help in understanding their faith. It is also important to understand the psychological aspects of people and their faith, and so I am concerned always to respond to felt needs of people of faith."

AVOCATIONAL INTERESTS: European travel.

*   *   *

O HEHIR, Diana

PERSONAL: Surname is pronounced O-*Hare;* born in Lexington, Va.; daughter of Willard (an educator) and Corinee (an educator; maiden name, Cassard) Farnham; married Brendan O Hehir (an educator), June 8, 1958; children: Michael, Andrew. *Education:* Johns Hopkins University, M.A., 1958, Ph.D., 1970. *Home:* 5610 Denton Place, Oakland, Calif. 94619. *Office:* Department of English, Mills College, Oakland, Calif. 94613.

CAREER: Mills College, Oakland, Calif., began as instructor, became professor of English and creative writing. *Awards, honors:* Second prize from Borestone Poetry Award, 1973, for "Summoned"; Devins Award, 1976, for *Summoned;* Helen Bullis Prize from *Poetry Northwest,* 1977.

WRITINGS: Summoned (poems), University of Missouri Press, 1976; *The Power to Change Geography,* Princeton University Press, 1979.

WORK IN PROGRESS: A new collection of poems.

SIDELIGHTS: Diana O Hehir writes: "I want to take chances in my poetry, not just for the shock value or for excitement, but also because there seem to be some things that can be said only with risk. I think of my poetry as rhythmic, visual, and surreal. I hope that the poems communicate strong feelings; I have strong feelings when I write them."

* * *

OKIN, Susan Moller 1946-

PERSONAL: Born July 19, 1946, in Auckland, New Zealand; came to the United States in 1971; daughter of Erling Leth (an accountant) and Kathleen (Morton) Moller; married Robert Laurence Okin (a psychiatrist), July 29, 1972; children: Laura Moller. *Education:* University of Auckland, B.A., 1967; Somerville College, Oxford, B.Phil., 1970; Harvard University, Ph.D., 1975. *Religion:* None. *Residence:* Lincoln, Mass. *Office:* Department of Politics, Brandeis University, Waltham, Mass. 02154.

CAREER: McKinsey & Co., New York, N.Y., temporary associate, 1970; University of Auckland, Auckland, New Zealand, lecturer in political theory, 1971; McKinsey & Co., temporary associate, 1972; Vassar College, Poughkeepsie, N.Y., visiting assistant professor of political theory, 1975-76; Brandeis University, Waltham, Mass., assistant professor of political theory, 1976—. *Member:* American Association of University Women, Amintaphil.

WRITINGS: Women in Western Political Thought, Princeton University Press, 1979. Contributor to philosophy and political science journals.

WORK IN PROGRESS: Research for a book on the philosophical problems of human rights.

SIDELIGHTS: Susan Okin comments: "My interest in the history of political thought and my feminism combined to inspire my first book."

According to *Washington Post* reviewer Vivian Gornick, Okin's book asks, "Why is it that the political enfranchisement of women has not led to substantive equality between the sexes?" The author answers that question by studying the ideas of four political philosophers—Plato, Aristotle, Rousseau, and Mill—who shared a concern for liberty but could not declare women capable of political equality. Okin's explanation, summarized Gornick, is that "none of the four can or will get past the conviction that the family, rather than the individual adult, is the central institution of higher human life."

Gornick concluded her review by saying: "The patient recital of the obvious illogic with which the philosophers had to argue in order to exclude women from political equality is the heart of this excellent book. . . . Her thesis is not original, but what a powerful reminder of revolutionary times her work is."

BIOGRAPHICAL/CRITICAL SOURCES: Washington Post Book World, February 10, 1980.

OLFSON, Lewy 1937-

PERSONAL: Born April 2, 1937, in Boston, Mass.; son of Samuel (in sales) and Bella (Glickman) Olfson. *Education:* Carnegie Institute of Technology (now Carnegie-Mellon University), B.F.A., 1958. *Home address:* P.O. Box 8, South Lyme, Conn. 06376.

CAREER: Copeland & Lamm, Inc. (editorial consultants), New York City, editor, 1959-63; Croft Educational Services (publisher), New London, Conn., editor, 1963-65; Bantam Books, Inc., New York City, marketing manager in School and College Division, 1966; free-lance writer, 1967—. Member of faculty at Boston Center for Adult Education, University of Connecticut, and Mohegan Community College. *Member:* Dramatists Guild (associate member), Council for Interracial Education and Cooperation (past chairperson), New London County Civil Liberties Union (past chairperson).

WRITINGS: Radioplays of Famous Stories, Plays, 1956, reprinted as *Dramatized Readings of Famous Stories,* 1969; *Radioplays From Shakespeare,* Plays, 1958; *Dramatized Classics for Radio-Style Reading,* two volumes, Plays, 1966; *Plot Outlines of One Hundred Famous Novels: The Second Hundred,* Doubleday, 1969; *Glimmer, Glimmer, Glumpkin* (poems for children), Grosset, 1969.

Fifty Great Scenes for Student Actors, Bantam, 1970; *Classics Adapted for Acting and Reading,* Plays, 1971; *You Can Act!,* Pendulum Press, 1971, Sterling, 1972; *The Great American Folk Heroes,* American Education Publications, 1971; *Let's Give a Party!,* American Education Publications, 1972; *Read-Aloud Plays From Around-the-World Tales,* Young Readers Press, 1972; *It's Fun to Act!,* American Education Publications, 1973; *Skits and Short Farces for Young Actors,* Plays, 1974; *You Can Put on a Show!,* Sterling, 1976; *Paco and the Pizza* (juvenile), Xerox Education Publications, 1977.

Co-author with Sue Lawless of "The $400,000 J." (three-act play), first produced as "The President's Mistress" in Cincinnati, Ohio, at Beef 'n Boards Dinner Theatre, June 7, 1972.

Work represented in twenty-one anthologies, including *Under Canadian Skies,* edited by F. Henry Johnson, Dent, 1962; *Starting Points in Reading,* edited by Cross and Julland, Ginn, 1974; and *On the Air: A Collection of Radio and TV Plays,* edited by Sylvia Z. Brodkin and Elizabeth J. Pearson, Scribner, 1977.

WORK IN PROGRESS: Special combined editions of *You Can Act!* and *You Can Put on a Show!,* for publishers in England and Germany.

SIDELIGHTS: Olfson writes: "In addition to my books for young people, I specialize in the field of educational journalism, writing on assignment for a number of publisher clients and educational associations. Whether it's aimed at the school board member, superintendent, teacher, school attorney, school custodian, or the pupils themselves, at one time or another I'm likely to write it."

* * *

OLIN, Spencer C(arl), Jr. 1937-

PERSONAL: Born February 13, 1937, in Los Angeles, Calif.; son of Spencer Carl (an attorney and corporation executive) and Mary Cecelia (Junior) Olin. *Education:* Pomona College, B.A., 1958; Claremont Graduate School and University Center, M.A., 1961, Ph.D., 1965. *Office:* Department of History, University of California, Irvine, Calif. 92717.

CAREER: Pomona College, Claremont, Calif., instructor in history, 1964-65; University of California, Irvine, assistant professor, 1965-69, associate professor, 1969-78, professor of history, 1978—, head of department, 1977—. Visiting lecturer at University of Stirling, 1971-72.

WRITINGS: California's Prodigal Sons: Hiram Johnson and the Progressives, 1911-1917, University of California Press, 1968; (editor with Roger Daniels) *Racism in California: A Reader in the History of Oppression,* Macmillan, 1972; (with Keith L. Nelson) *Why War?: Ideology, Theory, and History,* University of California Press, 1979; *California Politics Through the Progressive Era,* Boyd & Fraser, 1980. Contributor to history journals.

SIDELIGHTS: Olin told *CA:* "My research and writing on California history have focused on social conflict, reform movements, race relations, and communitarianism. Future work includes an analysis of California legal institutions and social change."

*   *   *

OLIVIER, Robert L(ouis) 1903-

PERSONAL: Born October 25, 1903, in Grand Coteau, La.; son of George L. and Antoinette (Stelly) Olivier; married Mildred Speyrer, August 22, 1931; children: Robert, Charles, James, Anne Olivier Wolverton, Paul, John. *Education:* Loyola University, New Orleans, La., B.A., 1925. *Religion:* Roman Catholic. *Residence:* Arlington, Washington, La. 70589.

CAREER: Teacher of French and English at public schools in New Orleans and St. Landry County, La.; principal of Roman Catholic boys' school in Opelousas, La., and public school in Washington, La.; principal of Krotz Springs Academy (private elementary school) in Krotz Springs, La.; currently writer.

WRITINGS: Pierre of the Teche (novel), Pelican, 1936; *Pap Puppies and Papas* (nonfiction), Pelican, 1937; *Reducation* (nonfiction), Meador, 1956; *Tidoon* (novel), Pelican, 1972; *Tinonc* (novel), Pelican, 1974; *Spare Not the Rod,* Carlton, 1976.

WORK IN PROGRESS: Books on religion.

SIDELIGHTS: Olivier told *CA:* "My interest has always been in education and in the Cajun people of Louisiana. My books on education condemned permissiveness in the schools and in all our institutions, a permissiveness breeding crime and immorality and bringing our country to the very brink of ruin."

In 1965, Olivier and his wife purchased the Arlington house, restored and refurnished it completely with antiques, and opened it to the public.

*   *   *

OLLARD, Richard (Laurence) 1923-

PERSONAL: Born November 9, 1923, in Bainton, Yorkshire, England; married Mary Buchanan Riddell; children: two sons, one daughter. *Education:* New College, Oxford, M.A., 1952. *Agent:* Curtis Brown Ltd., 1 Craven Hill, London W.2, England. *Office:* William Collins & Sons, 14 St. James's Place, London S.W.1, England.

CAREER: Royal Naval College, Greenwich, England, lecturer, 1948-52, senior lecturer in history and English, 1952-59; William Collins & Sons (publisher), London, England, senior editor, 1960—. *Military service:* Royal Navy, 1942-45. *Member:* Royal Society of Literature (fellow).

WRITINGS: (Editor with H. E. Bell) *Historical Essays, 1600-1750,* Barnes & Noble, 1963; *The Escape of Charles II After the Battle of Worcester,* Scribner, 1966; *Man of War: Sir Robert Holmes and the Restoration Navy,* Hodder & Stoughton, 1969; (compiler) *Pepys and the Development of the British Navy,* Jackdaw Publications, 1971; *Pepys: A Biography,* Holt, 1974; *This War Without an Enemy,* Atheneum, 1978.

*   *   *

OLLIF, Lorna (Anne) 1918-

PERSONAL: Born March 19, 1918, in Stawell, Victoria, Australia; daughter of Herbert John and Elizabeth (Pyke) Box; married Frank Edward Ollif (an accountant), October 19, 1946; children: Elizabeth Anne (Mrs. John Piercy), Cathryn Ellen. *Education:* Attended technical colleges in Melbourne and Hornsby, Australia. *Politics:* "No rigid political convictions." *Religion:* Baptist. *Home:* 41 Galston Rd., Hornsby, New South Wales 2077, Australia.

CAREER: Stenographer and secretary in Melbourne, Australia, 1931-43; writer, 1932—; government stenographer in Brisbane, Australia, 1946; secretary in London, England, 1950-51, and Sydney, Australia, 1967-75. *Military service:* Australian Women's Army Service, driver and stenographer in Military Intelligence, 1943-46; became sergeant. *Member:* International P.E.N., Fellowship of Australian Writers, New South Wales Military History Society, Royal Blind Society, Society of Women Writers of New South Wales, Baptist Historical Society of New South Wales, Canberra and District Historical Society, Ashfield and District Historical Society, Hornsby Historical Society (president, 1971-73), North Shore Historical Society. *Awards, honors:* Literary awards include president's trophy from Smith Family View Clubs, 1966 and 1967, for best contribution of the year to *View World;* grant from Literature Board of Australia Council, 1974, for re-publication of *There Must Be a River;* second prize from Maryborough Golden Wattle Festival, 1977, for short story, "The Wedding Cake"; grant from Literature Board of the Australia Council, 1978, for research and completion of *Women in Khaki;* grant from Australian War Memorial, 1978, for research in connection with a work of military history.

WRITINGS: Andrew Barton Paterson, Twayne, 1971; *There Must Be a River* (history of Hornsbyshire), Ollif Publishing, 1973, 2nd edition, 1975; *Early Australian Crafts and Tools,* Rigby, 1977; *Louisa Lawson,* Rigby, 1978; (contributor) Susan Yorke and Val Thompson, editors, *Australian Women of Two Centuries,* Society of Women Writers of New South Wales, 1980; *A Centenary History,* Royal Blind Society of New South Wales, 1980; *Around the World in a Hundred-Sixty Days* (travel), Rigby, 1981; *Women in Khaki,* University of Queensland Press, 1981. Contributor to magazines, including *View World, Home and Motor, So You Want to Be a Writer,* and *Viscare News.*

SIDELIGHTS: Lorna Ollif told *CA:* "As soon as I could write, I was putting stories together. When I left school, I wrote articles for magazines and newspapers, for which I was sometimes paid. I progressed to short stories, for which I sometimes received placings in competitions. Then, in the mid-1960's, a friend, with many books to his credit, encouraged me to offer to write a biography of Andrew Barton Paterson, one of Australia's best-known earlier writers.

"I had always had a deep curiosity about history and an ever-increasing desire to understand people and their motivations. To this end, I had collected all the information I could about the area in which I lived. I became known as a local authority on the district. Its history had never been published, so, mainly as a buffer against continual enquiry from students, I wrote *There Must Be a River.*

"I later discovered that Louisa Lawson was one of Australia's most important women. Among other things, she had started Australia's first magazine for women and ran it for seventeen years, using women alone on her staff. Her biography had never been written—I just had to do it.

"I consider a firm faith in God to be essential to understanding and appreciating people. I do not believe that men and women are 'equal,' but were meant to be—and are—supplementary to each other. We should be able to work *together* for the common good, and I am always on the lookout for any opportunity to ensure that women obtain equal *legal* rights.

"I have taken every opportunity to travel, to try to see people in their own settings, and I am of the opinion that, despite their differing circumstances, people themselves differ very little throughout the world. I deplore the current materialism in the more 'civilized' countries. I have never been dependent on my writing for my livelihood, so remuneration has never been a major consideration, which has enabled me to do what I felt needed to be done. However, a good royalty check is welcome, as it enables me to indulge my desire to travel.

"My advice to aspiring writers is to find their own style, but to be forever on the lookout for ways of improving it; to clearly establish the goal for which they are striving, and to spare no effort in trying to achieve it.

"I think there is more general encouragement and opportunity for writers than there has ever been previously. I think, however, that there is not enough movement of contemporary literature between countries.

"Australians are said to be the keenest buyers of new books in the world—our shops are full of all the latest English and American literature—yet it is exceedingly difficult for Australian literature to reach other countries. It is hard to get manuscripts published outside Australia, and if published here, are seldom available in other countries. This is a pity, for many Americans, in particular, visit here and profess interest in literature produced by Australians about Australia."

BIOGRAPHICAL/CRITICAL SOURCES: Auckland Herald, March 29, 1979; *Northampton Mercury-Courier,* August 7, 1979.

* * *

OLMSTED, John Charles 1942-

PERSONAL: Born January 24, 1942, in Windsor, Ontario, Canada; came to the United States in 1964; son of Charles W. (in business) and Kathleen (Smith) Olmsted. *Education:* University of Western Ontario, B.A., 1964; Harvard University, A.M., 1965, Ph.D., 1972. *Home:* 170 Woodland, Oberlin, Ohio 44074. *Office:* Department of English, Oberlin College, Oberlin, Ohio 44074.

CAREER: Oberlin College, Oberlin, Ohio, assistant professor, 1970-78, associate professor of English, 1978—. *Awards, honors:* Woodrow Wilson fellowship, 1964; Canada Council fellow, 1965-68; National Endowment for the Humanities fellowship, 1978.

WRITINGS: Thackeray and His Twentieth-Century Critics, Garland Publishing, 1977; (with Jeffrey E. Welch) *The Repu-*

tation of Trollope, Garland Publishing, 1978; *A Victorian Art of Fiction,* three volumes, Garland Publishing, 1979; *George Meredith: An Annotated Bibliography,* Garland Publishing, 1979; (with Welch) *Victorian Novel Illustration,* Garland Publishing, 1979; *Victorian Painting: Essays and Reviews,* three volumes, Garland Publishing, 1980.

* * *

O'NEILL, Gerard Kitchen 1927-

PERSONAL: Born February 6, 1927, in Brooklyn, N.Y.; son of Edward G. (a lawyer) and Dorothy (Kitchen) O'Neill; married Sylvia Turlington, 1950 (divorced, 1966); married Renate Steffen (a treasurer), April, 1973; children: Janet, Roger, Eleanor. *Education:* Swarthmore College, B.A., 1950; Cornell University, Ph.D., 1954. *Politics:* Independent. *Home:* 127 McCosh Circle, Princeton, N.J. 08540. *Agent:* John Brockman, 200 West 57th St., Suite 1207, New York, N.Y. 10019. *Office:* Department of Physics, Princeton University, Princeton, N.J. 08544.

CAREER: Princeton University, Princeton, N.J., instructor, 1954-56, assistant professor, 1956-59, associate professor, 1959-65, professor of physics, 1965—. President of Space Studies Institute; member of advisory board, National Air and Space Museum. *Military service:* U.S. Navy, radar technician, 1944-46; became radio tech II. *Member:* American Institute of Aeronautics and Astronautics, American Physical Society, American Association for the Advancement of Science, Phi Beta Kappa, Sigma Xi. *Awards, honors:* Glover Medal, 1977, for *The High Frontier;* D.Sc. from Swarthmore College, 1978; Phi Beta Kappa Science Book Award, 1978, for *The High Frontier.*

WRITINGS: The High Frontier: Human Colonies in Space, Morrow, 1977; (editor) *Space-Based Manufacturing from Non-Terrestrial Materials,* American Institute of Aeronautics and Astronautics, 1977; (with David Cheng) *Elementary Particle Physics: An Introduction* (graduate textbook), Addison-Wesley, 1979. Contributor of over one hundred articles to scientific journals, including *Physical Review, Science,* and *Nature.* Associate editor of *Space Solar Power Review,* 1979—.

WORK IN PROGRESS: A book.

SIDELIGHTS: In his book, *The High Frontier,* Gerard O'Neill advocates the establishment of space colonies as a means of ensuring solar power for the earth, and alleviating some of the present human problems. But as Joanne Omang commented, O'Neill "makes the case for a great leap forward into space at a time when more and more people are worrying about even standing still successfully here on Earth."

Even though he argued his case both in his book and on CBS-TV's news program, "Sixty Minutes," O'Neill has not convinced everyone that an escalation of space exploration is necessary. For example, Doug Boucher of the American Association for the Advancement of Science raised the question of priorities with regard to space exploration. Space colonies are possible, Boucher believes, "but lots of things are possible and we have to decide which ones to do on the basis of benefiting the majority."

Carl Sagan, noted professor, astronomer, and author, stated: "Planetary exploration is uplifting to the human spirit. It is a mistake to require that the federal budget go entirely to immediately practical enterprises." O'Neill agrees: "I have always felt strongly a personal desire to be free of boundaries and regimentation. . . . The steady-state society, ridden with rules and laws, proposed by the early workers on the limits to growth was, to me, abhorrent."

BIOGRAPHICAL/CRITICAL SOURCES: Washington Post, March 14, 1978.

* * *

OOSTERWAL, Gottfried 1930-

PERSONAL: Born February 8, 1930, in Rotterdam, Netherlands; came to the United States in 1968; son of Hillebrand and Margaretha (Obrikat) Oosterwal; married Emilie Tilstra (a teacher), October 31, 1957; children: Waronne, Dantar, Erik. *Education:* Attended John Calvin College, 1945-50, and Cambridge University, 1954; University of Utrecht, Ph.D., 1956, D.Litt., 1961. *Office:* Department of Missiology and Religion, Andrews University, Berrien Springs, Mich. 49104.

CAREER: Minister in Netherlands, 1950-56; professor at theological seminary in Huister Heide, Netherlands, 1950-56; missionary in New Guinea, 1957-63, and Philippines, 1963-68; ordained Seventh-day Adventist minister, 1963; professor of historical theology at Philippines Union College, 1963-68; University of the Philippines, Quezon City, professor of anthropology, 1964-68; Andrews University, Berrien Springs, Mich., professor of missiology and religion, 1968—. Consultant to Netherlands New Guinea government. *Member:* International Association for the History of Religion, International Association of Mission Studies, North American Society for Social Anthropology in Oceania, American Anthropological Association, American Academy of Religion, American Society of Missiology, Royal Anthropological Society.

WRITINGS: People of the Tor, Royal Van Gorum Association, 1961; *Mission: Possible,* Southern Publishing, 1972; *Modern Messianic Movements,* Herald Press, 1976; *Patterns of Church Growth in North America,* Andrews University Press, 1977; *A Theology of Healing,* Southern Publishing, 1980.

Not in English: (With Jan E. Tekulve and Jan Achterstraat) *Zandvoort* (title means "Zandvoort: A Socio-Economic Study"), University of Utrecht, 1957; *Papoeas Mensen zoals wij* (title means "Papuas, People Such as We Are"), Wereldvenster, 1961; *Die Papua* (title means "The Papuas"), Kohlhammer, 1963. Contributor to scientific journals and popular magazines. Co-editor of *Missiology,* until 1976.

WORK IN PROGRESS: Missions: Which Way?, publication expected in 1981.

SIDELIGHTS: Oosterwall told *CA:* "I write about people for people, so that we all may become a people."

* * *

ORGA, Ates 1944-

PERSONAL: Name is pronounced *A*-tesh *Au*-ger; born November 6, 1944, in England; son of Irfan (an air force officer, diplomat, and writer) and Margaret Veronica (a publisher and writer; maiden name, D'Arcy-Wright) Orga; married Josephine Prior, November 23, 1974. *Education:* University of Durham, B.Mus., 1968; Trinity College of Music, F.T.C.L., 1972. *Home address:* Spike Island, Wadhurst, East Sussex, England. *Office:* Department of Music, University of Surrey, Guildford, Surrey, England.

CAREER: British Broadcasting Corp. (BBC), London, England, music presentation and information assistant, 1971-75; University of Surrey, Guildford, England, lecturer in music, 1975—. Artistic director of Institute of Armenian Music, 1976—. Director of Authors Agency Ltd. *Member:* Royal Musical Association.

WRITINGS: The Proms, David & Charles, 1974; *Chopin: His Life and Times,* Midas Books, 1976, revised edition, 1978; *Beethoven: His Life and Times,* Midas Books, 1978; (editor) *Proceedings of Music Armenia, 1978,* Kahn & Averill, 1980; (with Mozelle Moshansky) *Piano Rolls: The Golden Age,* Midas Books, 1980.

Also editor of two editions of *Records and Recording Classical Guide,* Midas Books, 1977 and 1978. Contributor to music journals. Editor of *International Music Guides,* 1977—.

WORK IN PROGRESS: Research on Vorisek, a Bohemian contemporary of Beethoven.

* * *

ORION
See NAYLOR, John

* * *

ORNSTEIN, J. L.
See ORNSTEIN-GALICIA, J(acob) L(eonard)

* * *

ORNSTEIN, Norman J(ay) 1948-

PERSONAL: Born October 14, 1948, in Grand Rapids, Minn.; son of Joseph and Dorothy (Latz) Ornstein. *Education:* University of Minnesota, B.A. (magna cum laude), 1967; University of Michigan, M.A., 1968, Ph.D., 1972. *Home:* 6618 31st St. N.W., Washington, D.C. 20015. *Office:* Department of Politics, Catholic University of America, Washington, D.C. 20064.

CAREER: Eastern Michigan University, Ypsilanti, instructor in political science, winter, 1971; Johns Hopkins School of Advanced International Studies, Washington, D.C., assistant professor of political science in Bologna, Italy, 1971-72; Catholic University of America, Washington, D.C., assistant professor, 1972-76, associate professor of politics, 1976—, director of Congressional studies program, 1977—. Professional staff member of U.S. Senate temporary select committee, 1976-77, staff director, 1977; adjunct scholar at American Enterprise Institute, 1978—. Lecturer at U.S. Civil Service Commission General Management Training Center, 1973—, and Brookings Institution, 1977—; lecturer to government officials, academic gatherings, and journalists in Egypt, Turkey, Spain, Britain, Iran, Cuba, and the Soviet Union; guest on television and radio programs. Member of joint discussion group on Congress and foreign policy; member of Council on Foreign Relations and Carnegie Endowment for International Peace, 1978-79; consultant to National Opinion Research Center, Public Broadcasting Service, and U.S. International Communications Agency. *Member:* American Political Science Association, Academy of Political Science, Council on Foreign Relations, American Film Institute, Midwest Political Science Association, Southern Political Science Association, National Capitol Area Political Science Association (member of council, 1975—). *Awards, honors:* American Political Science Association Congressional fellowship, 1969-70; Russell Sage Foundation grant, 1973-74.

WRITINGS: (Editor and contributor) *Congress in Change: Evolution and Reform,* Praeger, 1975; (with Shirley Elder) *Interest Groups: Lobbying and Policymaking,* Congressional Quarterly Press, 1978.

Contributor: James J. Heaphey and Alan P. Balutis, editors, *Legislative Staffing: A Comparative View*, Sage Halsted Press, 1976; Charles Peters and James Fallows, editors, *Inside the System*, 3rd edition (Ornstein was not included in earlier editions), Praeger, 1976; Robert L. Peabody and Nelson W. Polsby, editors, *New Perspectives on the House of Representatives*, 3rd edition (Ornstein was not included in earlier editions), Rand McNally, 1977; Susan Welch and John G. Peters, editors, *Legislative Reform and Public Policy*, Praeger, 1977; Larry Dodd and Bruce Oppenheimer, editors, *Congress Reconsidered*, Praeger, 1977, 2nd edition, Holt, 1979; Allan P. Sindler, editor, *America in the 1970's*, Little, Brown, 1977; *Senators: Offices, Ethics, and Pressures*, U.S. Government Printing Office, 1977; Jeff Fishel, editor, *Politics and Parties in an Anti-Party Age*, Indiana University Press, 1978; *Global Economic Issues*, U.S. Government Printing Office, 1979.

Editor of "The New Congress: People and Process on Capitol Hill," a *National Journal*, reprint series, 1978-79. Contributor of about forty articles and reviews to professional journals, popular magazines, and newspapers, including *Current, Fortune, Washington Post, Wall Street Journal,* and *Washington Monthly*. Special editor of *Annals of the American Academy of Political and Social Science*, January, 1974.

WORK IN PROGRESS: A book on the U.S. Senate in the 1970's and 1980's; a study of the new congress; a book on the role of the legislature in Western democracies; a study of congress and foreign policy.

SIDELIGHTS: Ornstein told *CA:* "Unlike many academics, I attempt in many of my writings to reach a wider audience—policy makers, journalists, and the interested public. I try to combine my academic training, practical experience in Washington politics and public affairs, and my Washington base to analyze political events, processes, and policies."

*   *   *

ORNSTEIN-GALICIA, J(acob) L(eonard) 1915-
(J. L. Ornstein)

PERSONAL: Original name Jacob Leonard Ornstein, name legally changed; born August 8, 1915, in Cleveland, Ohio; divorced; children: one daughter. *Education:* Ohio State University, B.S., 1936, M.A., 1937; University of Wisconsin—Madison, Ph.D., 1940; attended University of Mexico, summer, 1940; postdoctoral study at Harvard University, 1957-58. *Politics:* "Best candidate." *Religion:* Reformed Jewish. *Home:* 315 West Schuster, Apt. 12, El Paso, Tex. 79902. *Office:* Department of Linguistics, University of Texas at El Paso, El Paso, Tex. 79968.

CAREER: University of Wisconsin—Madison, instructor in Spanish, until 1940; Washington University, St. Louis, Mo., instructor in Spanish, 1940-41; Office of Strategic Services, Washington, D.C., linguistic specialist and interrogator, 1942-43; Waldorf College, Forest City, Iowa, assistant professor of Spanish, French, and German, 1947-51; U.S. Department of Defense, Washington, D.C., associate of Russian Research Center, 1951-68; University of Texas, El Paso, professor of modern languages and linguistics, 1968-75, professor emeritus, 1975—, co-director of Cross-Cultural Southwest Ethnic Study Center, until 1975. Visiting associate professor at Catawba College, summer, 1948; assistant professor at New Mexico State University, 1949-51; language teacher for U.S. Department of Agriculture, 1951-63; lecturer at Georgetown University, 1964-68. Assistant managing editor of *Modern Language Journal*, 1961-64. Created

and produced radio series, "Voyage to Latin America." Public speaker; guest on radio programs; consultant to Southwest Cooperative Educational Laboratory. *Military service:* U.S. Army, Office of Strategic Services, 1943-45; served in Mediterranean theater.

MEMBER: Linguistic Society of Canada and the United States, Modern Language Association of America (member of executive committee, 1975-77), Linguistic Society of America, American Dialect Society, Teachers of English to Speakers of Other Languages, American Association of Teachers of Spanish and Portuguese, Asociacion de Linguistica y Filologia de America Latina, Association of Borderland Scholars, Border Linguistics Circle, Linguistic Association of the Southwest. *Awards, honors:* Grants from Hogg Foundation for Mental Health and Spencer Foundation.

WRITINGS—All under name J. L. Ornstein: *A Critical Study of Luis de Lucena and His "Repeticion de amores,"* University of North Carolina Press, 1954; (with Robert C. Howes) *Elements of Russian*, Allyn & Bacon, 1964; (with W. W. Gage) *The ABC's of Language and Linguistics*, Chilton, 1964, revised edition (with Gage and C. W. Hayes) published as *The New ABC's of Language and Linguistics*, Institute of Modern Languages, 1977; (with Ewton and Theodore Mueller) *Programmed Instruction and Educational Technology in the Language Teaching Field: New Approaches to Old Problems*, Center for Curriculum Development, Inc., 1971; *A Sociolinguistic Study of Mexican-American and Anglo Students in a Border University* (monograph), Institute of Public and Urban Affairs, California State University, San Diego, 1975; *Three Essays on Linguistic Diversity in the Spanish-Speaking World: The U.S. Southwest and the River Plate Area*, Mouton, 1975; (with W. F. Mackey) *The Bilingual Education Movement: Essays on Its Progress*, Texas Western Press, 1977.

Editor: (With R. W. Ewton, Jr., and contributor) *Studies in Language and Linguistics*, Texas Western Press, Volume I; *1969-70*, 1970, Volume II: *1971-72*, 1972; (and contributor) *Linguistic Diversity in the Spanish-Speaking World: Three Cases*, Mouton, 1975; (with J. Donald Bowen) *Studies in Southwest Spanish*, Newbury House, 1976; (with Glenn L. Gilbert) *Problems in Applied Educational Sociolinguistics: Readings on Language and Cultural Problems of U.S. Ethnic Groups*, Mouton, 1978.

Contributor: E. Goldhagen, editor, *Ethnic Minorities in the Soviet Union*, Praeger, 1968; G. E. Perren and J.L.M. Trim, editors, *Applications of Linguistics: Selected Papers of the Second International Congress of Applied Linguistics*, Cambridge University Press, 1971; Paul R. Turner, editor, *Bilingualism in the Southwest*, University of Arizona Press, 1972; Peter A. Reich, editor, *Second Lacus Forum*, Hornbeam Press, 1976; A. Makkai, V. B. Makkai, and L. Heilman, editors, *Linguistics at the Crossroads*, Jupiter Press, 1977. Also contributor to *Language and Society: Anthropological Issues*, edited by William F. McCormack, and *Applied Educational Sociolinguistics*, edited by Bernard Spolsky.

Stringer for *New York Times*, 1960-64. Founder and co-editor of "Studies in Language and Linguistics" series, Texas Western Press, 1969—. Contributor to *Reader's Encyclopedia of the American West*. Contributor of about thirty-five articles and reviews to education, linguistic, and Hispanic studies jourals, popular magazines, including *Parents' Magazine, Woman's Day, Think,* and *American*, and newspapers. Member of editorial board of *Language Problems and Language Planning*.

WORK IN PROGRESS: Editing *Sociolinguistic Issues in Language Contact,* with W. F. Mackey, publication expected by Laval University Presses; editing *Bilingualism and Bilingual Education: New Readings and Insights,* with Robert St. Clair; editing *Perspectives on Politics and Society in the U.S. Southwest,* with Z. A. Kruszewski; collaborating on a book about Mexican-American English and *Learning a Language by Yourself Can Be Fun; Farm Saga: Growing Up Jewish on an Ohio Farm,* an autobiography.

AVOCATIONAL INTERESTS: Travel, conversation, gourmet cooking.

* * *

OSARAGI, Jiro
See NOJIRI, Kiyohiko

* * *

OSBORN, Carolyn 1934-

PERSONAL: Born July 11, 1934, in Nashville, Tenn.; daughter of William and Katherine (Truett) Culbert; married Joe A. Osborn (an attorney), June 11, 1955; children: William, Claire, Celia. *Education:* University of Texas, B.J., 1955, M.A., 1959. *Home:* 3002 Gilbert, Austin, Tex. 78703. *Agent:* Emilie Jacobson, Curtis Brown Ltd., 575 Madison Ave., New York, N.Y. 10022. *Office:* 601 West 14th, Austin, Tex. 78701.

CAREER: Augusta Chronicle and Herald, Augusta, Ga., reporter, 1955; KEPO-Radio, El Paso, Tex., continuity writer, 1955-56; University of Texas, Austin, instructor in English, 1968-78; Culbert-Osborn Cattle, Austin, Tex., partner, 1973—. Teacher at Writers' Workshop International at Universidad de las Americas, Puebla, Mexico. *Awards, honors:* Shared award from *Texas Books in Review,* 1977, for *A Horse of Another Color,* and short story award from Texas Institute of Letters, 1979, for "The Accidental Trip to Jamaica."

WRITINGS: A Horse of Another Color (stories), University of Illinois Press, 1977. Contributor of short stories to periodicals, including *Ascent, Paris Review,* and *Antioch Review.*

WORK IN PROGRESS: Having Cake and Eating It Sometimes, a novel; *The Fields of Memory,* short stories; *Allowable Perversions,* short stories.

SIDELIGHTS: Carolyn Osborn writes: "Though I was born in Tennessee, I was brought to Texas at the age of twelve. I'm continually fascinated and appalled by the state. Most of my work deals with city people. Since I lived in a small Texas town for five years and am involved in managing my stepmother's ranch, ninety miles from Austin, I also write about country folks, but they are generally in conflict with the twentieth century. (The nineteenth century has been a long time dying in rural Texas.)

"My first book is simply a collection of stories. One, "The Accidental Trip to Jamaica," has been translated into Spanish. However, the next two books are centered around themes. In *The Fields of Memory* I'm interested in the way memory affects people's lives. In *Allowable Perversions* I'm dealing with rule-breakers, how they operate, and how they manage to get away with it.

"I have lived abroad and traveled in Europe, particularly England and France."

* * *

OSMAN, Betty B(arshad) 1929-

PERSONAL: Born September 1, 1929, in New York, N.Y.; daughter of Maurice S. (a dentist) and Rose (Bush) Barshad; married Albert I. Osman (a business executive), June 24, 1951; children: Richard M., Nancy Osman Korda, Meg J. *Education:* Vassar College, B.A., 1951; Columbia University, M.A., 1965, Ed.M., 1970; doctoral study at Fordham University, 1977—. *Office:* 36 Fenimore Rd., Scarsdale, N.Y. 10583.

CAREER: Department of Family and Child Welfare, White Plains, N.Y., social case worker, 1951-58; learning disabilities specialist at public schools in White Plains, N.Y. 1966-70; Bank Street College, New York, N.Y., instructor in learning disabilities, 1970-74; Manhattanville College, Purchase, N.Y., adjunct professor of learning disabilities, 1974—. Private practice of educational therapy, 1966—. President of board of visitors of Rockland Children's Psychiatric Center; member of board of advisers of Hallen School. *Member:* National Foundation for Children With Learning Disabilities (member of board of directors), American Association of University Professors, Association for Children With Learning Disabilities, Council for Exceptional Children, Orton Society, Westchester County Psychological Association, Columbia University Alumni Council, Kappa Delta Pi.

WRITINGS: Learning Disabilities: A Family Affair (Literary Guild selection), Random House, 1979. Contributor to *Redbook* and *Ladies' Home Journal.*

WORK IN PROGRESS: A book on social problems of children, publication by Random House expected in 1980.

SIDELIGHTS: Betty Osman writes: "In my present work with children, I have combined social work and teaching. My approach is a clinical one, to help youngsters with learning disabilities and their families. While learning problems are centered in school, they are rarely confined to the classroom. Children bring home with them the failure and frustration incurred in school, and their problems quickly become a 'family affair' with widespread repercussions. I wrote *Learning Disabilities* on the premise that with knowledge and understanding come the ability to help one's child, and thereby all members of the family. In the book, I discuss ways that parents and professionals can help the youngster with learning disabilities at home, at school, and in the world outside."

AVOCATIONAL INTERESTS: Travel, tennis.

BIOGRAPHICAL/CRITICAL SOURCES: New York Daily News, April 5, 1979; *Parents' Magazine,* May, 1979.

* * *

OSMER, Margaret

PERSONAL: Born in New York, N.Y.; daughter of Herbert and Margaret (Brunjes) Osmer. *Education:* Earned B.A. from Cornell University. *Home:* 1124 Conn Ave., Washington, D.C. 20036. *Agent:* N. S. Bienstock, 10 Columbus Cir., New York, N.Y. 10019.

CAREER/WRITINGS: Columbia Broadcasting System (CBS-TV), New York City, writer, reporter, and producer, 1962-73, producer and reporter for "Sixty Minutes," 1969-73; American Broadcasting Co. (ABC-TV), New York City, producer and correspondent of "The Reasoner Report," 1973-75, co-anchor of morning news on "Good Morning America," 1975-77, news correspondent for evening news, 1975—, producer of "Saturday Closeup" feature on "ABC News With Ted Koppel." Lecturer. Member of Defense Advisory Committee on Women in the Service; member of Council on Foreign Relations. Notable assignments include coverage of events involving the United Nations; coverage of Pope Paul VI's visit to the United States; producer of coverage of Cuban missile crisis, 1962, and the war in the Middle East, 1967; coverage of Apollo space missions, and the 1964 and 1968 Democratic and Republican national conventions and subsequent elections; producer of "Kissinger," "Trudeau's Canada," and "Cry for Help" (a documentary on child abuse), all for "Sixty Minutes"; producer of "No Tears for Rachel" (a documentary on rape), for "Bill Moyer's Journal," Public Broadcasting Service (PBS-TV); first interview with exiled financier Robert Vesco; producer of "Come Fly a Kite," "The Arabs Are Bullish on America," and "Master of Mobiles."

MEMBER: Radio and Television Correspondents Association, Association of Radio and Television News Analysts, Washington Press Club, Sigma Delta Chi. *Awards, honors:* National Photographers award for "Come Fly a Kite."

* * *

OSMUN, Mark 1952-

PERSONAL: Born July 25, 1952, in Montclair, N.J.; son of James W. (a geophysicist) and Hazel I. (Young) Osmun. *Education:* George Mason University, B.A., 1975. *Home and office:* 95 Lovell Ave., Mill Valley, Calif. 94941.

CAREER: Arlington News, Arlington, Va., news and feature reporter, 1971-72; *Fort Collins Coloradoan,* Fort Collins, Colo., sports and feature reporter, 1972-73; free-lance reporter for newspapers, 1973-75; *Honolulu Advertiser,* Honolulu, Hawaii, sports and feature reporter, 1975-78; free-lance writer, 1978—.

WRITINGS: The Honolulu Marathon, Lippincott, 1979.

Work represented in anthologies, including *The Runners,* Jove Press, 1979. Contributor to magazines, including *Runner* and *City Sports,* and newspapers.

WORK IN PROGRESS: Research for a novel on gambling, completion expected in 1982.

SIDELIGHTS: Osmun writes: "I have just this hour dropped out of law school after a very short sampling of it. Law school represented one thing to me—a hedge against the life of insecurity faced by writers. A writer's lot is one partially characterized by heavy anxiety, waiting, risk, anonymity, poverty, and rejection. After going through the grind a few times—whether it be with book publishers, miserly magazine people, or self-righteous newspaper editors—a good writer might sensibly opt for another profession.

"But that nasty element is only *part* of a writer's lot. There are also those benefits of excitement, freedom, creative satisfaction, and sense of . . . well, integrity, maybe.

"At some point one must choose. The choice may be between 'straight' work and writing, material success and writing, lovers and writing . . . whatever. And the choice may come up again and again. It gets to be a very difficult situation.

"My first book was an experiment for me, an exercise in research and in using the elements of the new journalism, participatory journalism, or whatever that stuff is called these days. The fact that I applied that style to running was not dictated by the subject. Rather the reverse. I was always attracted to that style, but unable to make much use of it until I wrote *The Honolulu Marathon.* It was not conceived in response to a fad, as so many subsequent 'running books' have been, for there was no fad at the time."

BIOGRAPHICAL/CRITICAL SOURCES: Sports Illus-

trated, February 27, 1978; *Honolulu Star-Bulletin,* July 19, 1979; *Honolulu Advertiser,* August 1, 1979; *Windward Sun-Press,* August 1, 1979; *San Rafael Independent Journal,* August 28, 1979; *City Sports,* October, 1979; *Runner,* January, 1980.

* * *

O'SULLIVAN, P. Michael 1940-

PERSONAL: Born April 15, 1940, in Jackson, Mich.; son of Emmett Michael (a social worker) and Freda Ann (a factory worker and waitress) O'Sullivan; married Victoria Oltean, February 19, 1966; children: Siobhan, Sean. *Residence:* Chicago, Ill. *Office:* O'Sullivan Group, 118 West Kinzie St., Chicago, Ill. 60610.

CAREER: Has worked as photojournalist for *Business Week,* and for *Life* in New York, N.Y.; film producer and director, 1972-78; affiliated with O'Sullivan Group, Chicago, Ill. Member of faculty at Columbia College, Chicago, 1973-74. *Military service:* U.S. Army, 1960-62; airborne pathfinder.

WRITINGS: Patriot Graves, Follett, 1972.

* * *

OTTLEY, Reginald Leslie

PERSONAL: Born in London, England. *Education:* Educated in England. *Address:* 37 Henry St., Chapel Hill, Brisbane, Queensland 4069, Australia.

CAREER: Writer. Worked as a seaman, cattle worker and horsebreaker in Australian Outback, and manager of a cattle station in Fiji, until 1939; trained race horses in Sydney, Australia, beginning 1945; cattle ranch manager in New Caledonia. *Military service:* Served in Australian Remount Corps, 1939-45. *Member:* Authors Guild Association. *Awards, honors:* Notable book award from American Library Association, 1966, runner-up for Best Book of the Year Award from Australian Children's Book Council, 1966, Children's Spring Book Festival Award from *New York Herald Tribune,* 1966, and National Mass Media Award from Thomas Alva Edison Foundation, 1967, all for *Boy Alone;* runner-up for Best Book of the Year Award from Australian Children's Book Council, 1970, for *The Bates Family.*

WRITINGS—Juvenile: By the Sandhills of Yamboorah, Deutsch, 1965, published as *Boy Alone,* Harcourt, 1966; *The Roan Colt of Yamboorah,* Deutsch, 1966, published as *The Roan Colt,* Harcourt, 1967; *Rain Comes to Yamboorah,* Deutsch, 1967, Harcourt, 1968; *Giselle,* Harcourt, 1968; *The Bates Family,* Harcourt, 1969; *Brumbie Dust: A Selection of Stories,* Harcourt, 1969; *Jim Grey of Moonbah,* Harcourt, 1970; *No More Tomorrow,* Harcourt, 1971; *The War on William Street,* Collins, 1971, Thomas Nelson, 1973; *A Word About Horses,* Collins, 1973; *Mum's Place,* Collins, 1974.

Novels: *Stampede,* Laurie, 1961.

Radio plays: "The Feather Shoes."

SIDELIGHTS: Ottley spent many years working in the Australian Outback, and this experience is reflected in his books. Critics repeatedly describe his fiction about the Outback as authentic and unsentimental. H. L. Maples had these words of praise for *Boy Alone:* "One comes to live fully in this boy's world, and the setting . . . is powerfully real. The adults who share the story and from whom the boy unconsciously draws strength and wisdom will linger in the memory. . . . A book of unflagging vitality, authentic and sometimes grim, yet compassionate and unexpectedly comforting."

Ottley's subsequent books also aroused the admiration of critics. "Reginald Ottley's special virtues are honesty, toughness, and a real, unsentimental eye for nature," Taliaferro Boatwright commented in a review of *The Roan Colt*. The vividly drawn atmosphere in *Rain Comes to Yamboorah* prompted a *Times Literary Supplement* critic to remark: "[The story] has an extraordinarily strong atmosphere. The author describes conditions in the early 1930s, and indeed today, in the dry, burning heart of Australia, and his characters are based on real people, just as his setting is in every detail authentic."

BIOGRAPHICAL/CRITICAL SOURCES: Times Literary Supplement, June 17, 1965, May 25, 1967, June 26, 1969, December 4, 1969; *Washington Post Book World,* May 8, 1966, April 30, 1967, May 5, 1968, May 4, 1969; *New York Times Book Review,* May 7, 1967, May 2, 1971.*

*   *   *

OUTERBRIDGE, David E(ugene)   1933-

PERSONAL: Born August 12, 1933, in New York, N.Y.; son of Kenneth Boyd and Florence (Lockwood) Outerbridge; married Lilias Hollins (a teacher), February 15, 1958; children: Benoni, Oliver, Thomas, Joshua. *Education:* Harvard University, A.B., 1955; New York University, M.A., 1968. *Home:* 700 Acre Island, Islesboro, Maine 04848.

CAREER: Outerbridge & Lazard, Inc., New York, N.Y., publisher and editor-in-chief, 1969-74; writer, 1974—. Film director and producer. *Military service:* U.S. Navy, 1955-58. *Member:* Harvard Club. *Awards, honors:* First prize from American Film Festival, 1974, for directing "The Art of the Potter."

WRITINGS: (Editor) *The Potter's Challenge,* Dutton, 1975; (with Julie Thayer) *The Last Shepherds,* Viking, 1979; *Without Makeup: Liv Ullmann,* Morrow, 1979.

WORK IN PROGRESS: Fog, with photographs by Jacques Minassian, publication expected in 1981; *Coach,* on coaching in America, with Arthur Tobier; editing *On Acting.*

SIDELIGHTS: Outerbridge comments: "I am interested in recording, in a nonsentimental way, the passing of different ways of traditional work. I am also interested in exploring the underside of everyday phenomena (such as coaches as builders of the American dream)."

BIOGRAPHICAL/CRITICAL SOURCES: New York Times Book Review, October 7, 1979.

P

PACHAI, Bridglal 1927-

PERSONAL: Born November 30, 1927, in Ladysmith, Natal, South Africa; son of Sukrani (Mardan) Pachai; married Leelawathie Ramnath (a dental assistant), December 28, 1952; children: Jairaj, Indira, Santosh, Ansuya, Pradeep. *Education:* University of South Africa, B.A., 1954, B.A. (honors), 1956, M.A., 1958; University of Natal, Ph.D., 1962. *Religion:* Hindu. *Office:* Department of History, University of Sokoto, Sokoto, Nigeria.

CAREER: High School teacher of English and history in Ladysmith, Natal, 1958-62; University College of Cape Coast, Cape Coast, Ghana, lecturer in history, 1962-65; University of Malawi, Zomba, professor of history, 1965-75; Dalhousie University, Halifax, Nova Scotia, Senior Killam Professor, 1975-76; Dalhousie University and Mount Saint Vincent University, Halifax, professor of history, 1976-77; Saint Mary's University, Halifax, director of International Education Centre, 1977-79; University of Sokoto, Sokoto, Nigeria, professor of history, 1979—. *Awards, honors:* Senior Killam fellow at Dalhousie University, 1975-76.

WRITINGS: History of Indian Opinion, Government Printer (Cape Town, South Africa), 1963; (editor with R. K. Tangri and G. W. Smith) *Malawi, Past and Present,* Christian Literature Association of Malawi, 1970; (editor) *The Memoirs of Lewis Mataka Bandawe,* Christian Literature Association of Malawi, 1971; (editor) *Early History of Malawi,* Longman, 1971; *The International Aspects of the South African Indian Question,* Struik, 1971; *Malawi: The History of the Nation,* Longman, 1973; (editor) *Livingstone, Man of Africa: Memorial Essays,* Longman, 1973; *Land and Politics in Malawi, 1875-1975,* Limestone Press, 1978; *South Africa's Indians: The Evolution of a Minority,* University Press of America, 1979. Also author of a biography on Dr. William Pearly Oliver, Nova Scotia Museum, in press. Contributor to scholarly journals.

WORK IN PROGRESS: History of the Malawi Ngoni, completion expected in 1982.

SIDELIGHTS: Pachai comments: "My upbringing in South Africa has created a deep awareness of the experiences of black persons and minorities, and the relevance of objective studies in race relations. I have written articles on multiculturalism in Canada and the experience of blacks in Nova Scotia and these have flowed spontaneously from my background in Africa and my entry into North American society as a new Canadian.

"My publications on South Africa examine the experiences of persons of Indian origin in the context of the total situation in that country. They draw attention to the extremely difficult position in which South African Indians find themselves, surrounded as they are by pressures emanating from many quarters. In spite of their extreme vulnerability, my studies show that this minority community has adapted—and responded—with resilience.

"My decade in Malawi was most enjoyable, rewarding, and memorable. My writings bear evidence of the growth situation in which the academic fraternity found itself in a newly-independent country and in a brand new university. In many ways, it is fair to consider my historical studies on Malawi to be part of the pioneering products of a difficult and trying period."

*   *   *

PAGE, Gerald W(ilburn) 1939-
(Carleton Grindle, Harold Jones, Eric Lee, Kenneth Pembrooke, Leo Tifton)

PERSONAL: Born August 12, 1939, in Chattanooga, Tenn.; son of Horace Wilburn (an air operations controller) and Polly (Grindle) Page. *Home and office:* 193 Battery Place N.E., Atlanta, Ga. 30307.

CAREER: TV Guide, Atlanta, Ga., local editions editor, 1969—. Guest lecturer at Atlanta College of Art, 1976; speaker at science fiction-fantasy conventions. *Military service:* U.S. Army, 1963-65.

WRITINGS—Editor of speculative fiction anthologies: (And contributor) *Nameless Places,* Arkham, 1975; *The Year's Best Horror Stories,* Daw Books, Series IV, 1976, Series V, 1977, Series VI, 1978, Series VII, 1979; (with Hank Reinhardt, and contributor) *Heroic Fantasy,* Daw Books, 1979.

Work represented in anthologies, including *Future Pastimes,* edited by Scott Edelstein, Aurora, 1977.

"The View from Antan," a column in *Chicago Fantasy Newsletter.* Contributor, under pseudonyms Carleton Grindle, Harold Jones, Eric Lee, Kenneth Pembrooke, and Leo Tifton, of more than fifty articles, stories, and poems to magazines, including *Analog, Magazine of Horror, Startling Mystery, Whispers,* and *Famous Science Fiction.* Editor and publisher of *Lore,* 1965-68.

WORK IN PROGRESS: Novels and stories in science fiction, horror, and heroic fantasy.

SIDELIGHTS: Page wrote: "I have always thought of myself as a science fiction writer, but somehow readers (and some editors, I fear) seem to know me only as a fantasist. I'm currently working on a cycle of short stories set in a dream world. These stories are a bit different from the run of the mill of their type in being less action-oriented, more dependent on mood and character. Also in progress is a science fiction series, utilizing the far-future background that first appeared in 'Worldsong' in *Nameless Places,* and a background fantasy series set around a fictitious inland sea called the Orchar.

"At present, the best statement of one of the things I hope to do is probably to be found in *Heroic Fantasy.* The book shows, I think, a commitment to more character development and emotion, as well as a stronger authenticity than has been the rule. But I'm also at work on other types of fantasy writing, as well as science fiction, and wouldn't want to emphasize any one type of writing as more important than any other. Basically, I follow the tradition: my most important work is whatever I'm hard at work on now."

*   *   *

PALEY, Vivian Gussin   1929-

PERSONAL: Born January 25, 1929, in Chicago, Ill.; daughter of Harry A. (a physician) and Yetta (Meisel) Gussin; married Irving Paley (in public relations), June 20, 1948; children: David, Robert. *Education:* University of Chicago, B.A., 1947; Tulane University, B.A., 1950; Hofstra University, M.A., 1962. *Religion:* Jewish. *Home:* 5422 South Blackstone, Chicago, Ill. 60615. *Office:* Laboratory School, University of Chicago, 1362 East 59th St., Chicago, Ill. 60637.

CAREER: Teacher in New Orleans, La., 1952-56, and Great Neck, N.Y., 1963-70; University of Chicago, Chicago, Ill., teacher at Laboratory School, 1971—.

WRITINGS: White Teacher, Harvard University Press, 1979; *Wally's Stories,* Harvard University Press, 1980.

SIDELIGHTS: Vivian Paley commented: "My point of view is that of the classroom teacher, not often heard because few classroom teachers write books or articles. It is subjective and personal.The teacher observes the child in ways that are quite different from the psychologist and academic researcher, who watch and measure human behavior in the classroom. The teacher watches, becomes involved in, and practices human behavior in the classroom.

"As a writer I am primarily interested in the attitudes and beliefs of teacher and child. This hidden current influences and often supersedes the formal curriculum but is seldom examined or discussed openly.

"My subject is differences. In *White Teacher* those differences are racial; in *Wally's Stories* they are the gulf between the adult and child's point of view. The message for me is that differences, when recognized and studied, make the classroom the exciting place it ought to be."

*   *   *

PALL, Ellen Jane   1952-
(Fiona Hill)

PERSONAL: Born March 28, 1952, in New York, N.Y.; daughter of David B. (a scientist) and Josephine (an artist; maiden name, Blatt) Pall. *Education:* Attended University of Michigan, 1969-70; University of California, Santa Barbara, B.A., 1973. *Religion:* Jewish. *Residence:* Pacific Palisades, Calif. *Agent:* Harvey Klinger Literary Agency, 250 West 57th St., New York, N.Y. 10019.

CAREER: Teacher of French in Glendale, Calif., 1974; writer, 1975—. *Member:* Phi Beta Kappa.

WRITINGS—Novels, all under pseudonym Fiona Hill: *The Trellised Lane,* Berkeley, 1975; *The Wedding Portrait,* Berkley, 1975; *The Practical Heart,* Berkley, 1975; *Love in a Major Key,* Berkley, 1976; *Sweet's Folly,* Berkley, 1977; *The Love Child,* Putnam, 1977; *The Autumn Rose,* Putnam, 1978.

WORK IN PROGRESS: Research on Harriette Wilson and her circle.

SIDELIGHTS: Ellen Pall wrote: "Several years ago I began to write songs, learned to sing (in my fashion), and for a year or so pursued a career as a singer and songwriter. As my knowledge of the world of professional popular music increased, however, I became disenchanted and finally abandoned the idea of a public career for now.

"Why does anyone become a writer? I became a writer because I was moved by the things people do not say. I became a writer to impress my father. I became a writer because I *could* become a writer. I became a writer because I wrote well. I became a writer because writing became me.

"I write historical fiction because when I had my wisdom teeth removed I read a Gothic novel to keep my mind off my mouth, and came away crying 'I can do that!' I had no knowledge or feeling for the Regency period when I began. I wanted to show John Keats in a scene, and he lived a short life. Certainly I had no intention of continuing in the genre once I had sold that first effort. But when you do something well the world encourages you to continue."

*   *   *

PALMS, Roger C(urtis)   1936-

PERSONAL: Born September 13, 1936, in Detroit, Mich.; son of Nelson C. and Winifred J. Palms; married Andrea Sisson, 1959; children: Grant Curtis, Andrea Jane. *Education:* Wayne State University, B.A., 1958; Eastern Baptist Theological Seminary, B.D., 1961, M.Div., 1971, D.D., 1977; Michigan State University, M.A., 1971; further graduate study at Princeton Theological Seminary. *Residence:* Bloomington, Minn. *Office: Decision,* 1300 Harmon Place, Minneapolis, Minn. 55403.

CAREER: Ordained American Baptist minister, 1961; pastor of Baptist churches in Ronceverte, W.Va., 1961-64, and Highland Park, N.J., 1964-67; Michigan State University, East Lansing, chaplain of American Baptist Student Foundation, 1967-73; *Decision,* Minneapolis, Minn., assistant editor, 1973-74, associate editor, 1975-76, editor, 1976—. Gives workshops.

WRITINGS: The Jesus Kids, Judson, 1971; *The Christian and the Occult,* Judson, 1972; *God Holds Your Tomorrows,* Augsburg, 1976; *God's Promises for You,* Revell, 1977; *Upon a Penny Loaf,* Bethany Fellowship, 1978.

SIDELIGHTS: Palms comments: "Teaching other writers is important to me. I do workshops, lectures, and classes. Travel is part of my work, and I've written and taught on six continents."

*   *   *

PANGER, Daniel   1926-

PERSONAL: Born May 16, 1926, in New York, N.Y.; son of Morris Herman (a lawyer) and Henrietta (an office manager; maiden name, Breger) Panger; married Mary Ann Miner (a physician), March 26, 1978. *Education:* University of California, Los Angeles, A.B., 1948; New York University, M.A., 1950; Starr King School for the Ministry, M.Div., 1971. *Home:* 9615 Lona Lane N.E., Albuquerque, N.M. 87111. *Office:* First Unitarian Church, 3701 Carlisle Blvd. N.E., Albuquerque, N.M. 87110.

CAREER: Ordained Unitarian-Universalist minister, 1971; Los Angeles County Probation Department, Los Angeles, Calif., probation officer, 1957-61; State of California, Fair Employment Practices Division, supervising consultant, 1961-69; pastor in Godalming, England, 1971-72; pastor of Fellowship Church in San Francisco, Calif., 1972-75, and First Unitarian Church in San Jose, Calif., 1975-78; First Unitarian Church, Albuquerque, N.M., pastor, 1978—. *Military service:* U.S. Navy, 1943-45.

WRITINGS: Ol' Prophet Nat, Fawcett, 1968; (with Lloyd Zimpel) *Business and the Hard Core Unemployed,* Fell, 1970; *The Dance of the Wild Mouse* (a novel), Entwhistle Books, 1979. Also author of *Thoughts and Meditations,* 1978. Contributor of articles and stories to magazines.

WORK IN PROGRESS: Joanna the Woman Pope, a novel about John VIII; *Armed Only With the Cross,* a novel about sixteenth-century explorer Cabeza de Vaca.

SIDELIGHTS: Panger commented: "My main interest is in the ministry. My two works in progress have a historical/religious theme, which I found exciting to explore."

* * *

PAPACHRISTOU, Judy 1930-

PERSONAL: Born July 17, 1930, in New York, N.Y.; daughter of Max and Rose (Bradie) Reisner; married Tician Papachristou (an architect), June 11, 1951; children: Alexander, Nicholas. *Education:* Barnard College, B.A., 1952; University of Colorado, M.A., 1963, Ph.D., 1968. *Home:* 190 East 72nd St., New York, N.Y. 10021. *Office:* Department of History, Sarah Lawrence College, Bronxville, N.Y. 10708.

CAREER: Educational Testing Service, Princeton, N.J., psychometrist, 1951-53; Western Interstate Commission on Higher Education, Boulder, Colo., writer and researcher, 1957-58; Hunter College of the City University of New York, New York, N.Y., lecturer in history, 1967-68; York College of the City University of New York, Jamaica, N.Y., assistant professor, 1968-76, associate professor, 1976-79; Sarah Lawrence College, Bronxville, N.Y., member of history faculty, 1979—. *Member:* American Historical Association, Organization of American Historians, Institute on Women in the Historical Profession, City University of New York Women's Coalition, Phi Beta Kappa.

WRITINGS: (With Carol Wald) *Myth American,* Pantheon, 1975; *Women Together: A History in Documents of the Women's Movement in the United States,* Knopf, 1976. Contributor to scholarly journals.

WORK IN PROGRESS: A History of Abortion in Nineteenth-Century America.

* * *

PARADIS, James G(ardiner) 1942-

PERSONAL: Born October 3, 1942, in Walker, Minn.; son of Louis Adelard and Rosalie (Gardiner) Paradis; married Judith Ellen Kler. *Education:* St. John's University, Collegeville, Minn., B.S., 1964; New York University, M.A., 1970; University of Washington, Seattle, Ph.D., 1975. *Office:* Department of Humanities, Massachusetts Institute of Technology, Cambridge, Mass. 02139.

CAREER: Massachusetts Institute of Technology, Cambridge, assistant professor of humanities, 1975—. *Member:* Modern Language Association of America, History of Science Society, Society for Technical Communication.

WRITINGS: T. H. Huxley: Man's Place in Nature, University of Nebraska Press, 1978; (editor and contributor) *Victorian Science and Victorian Values,* New York Academy of Sciences, 1980.

WORK IN PROGRESS: Editing *The Letters of T. H. Huxley.*

SIDELIGHTS: Paradis commented: "I am interested in the personal, biographical element in science, and in the origins and evolution of the modern concept of the scientist. Thomas Henry Huxley seems to me to represent one of the great social voices of Victorian science at the important historical juncture when science itself was rapidly becoming institutionalized. Huxley became the first great popularizer of science, answering a particularly vital need at a time when the descriptive and conceptual systems of the specialist were drifting increasingly beyond the grasp of the generalist. Victorian technology had become a physical force capable of radically altering society, and Victorian science had become a conceptual force capable of altering assumptions as fundamental as man's conception of himself. Hence the institutionalization and professionalization of science and technology, which removed them from the social mainstream, created a profound sense of ambiguity among Victorians (and their twentieth-century descendents) who could no longer understand the sources of the realities they faced in daily life.

"I see Huxley, then, as a man who understood the perils facing a society which, largely, was unable to comprehend the nature of its most powerful and influential creations. Huxley's campaign to educate the public remains one of the great *tours de force* in the social history of science."

* * *

PARCHMAN, William E(ugene) 1936-

PERSONAL: Born July 30, 1936, in Louisville, Ky.; son of George Rufus and Mabel Parchman; married Roma Satterfield, December 5, 1959 (died November, 1977); children: Melia. *Education:* Received degree from Murray State College (now University), 1956; attended American Theatre Wing, 1957-58, and New School for Social Research, 1961-62. *Home:* 65 Fourth Ave., Mineola, N.Y. 11501. *Agent:* Ellen Neuwald, Inc., 905 West End Ave., New York, N.Y. 10025.

CAREER: New Dramatists, New York City, play reader and member of executive board, 1960-79; Asolo Theatre, Sarasota, Fla., writer-in-residence, 1969-70; Wantagh CAP-712 Association, Wantagh, N.Y., playwright-in-residence, 1974-76; New Nassau Repertory Company, Mineola, N.Y., director, 1977—. Guest director at Garden City Little Theater. Acting credits include appearances on "TV Playhouse 90," at Pasadena Playhouse, and in summer stock. Teacher of acting and theater games. *Military service:* U.S. Army, 1952-54; served in Korea.

MEMBER: New Dramatists, Eugene O'Neill Theatre Centre. *Awards, honors:* John Golden grant from the John Golden Fund, 1962-63; grant from Dramatists Guild, 1964-65; Stanley Award from New York City Writers Conference, 1967, for "The Prize in the Crackerjack Box"; fellow of Florida State University at Asolo Theatre, 1969-70; fellow of Audrey Wood-O'Neill Foundation at Wesleyan University, Middletown, Conn., 1970-71.

WRITINGS—Plays: "The Prize in the Crackerjack Box" (three-act), first produced on Staten Island, N.Y., at Wagner College, 1967; "The Party" (one-act), first produced in Waterford, Conn. at Eugene O'Neill Theatre Conference, 1969; "Mocking Bird" (one-act), first produced in Waterford at Eugene O'Neill Theatre Conference, 1969; "Needmore" (one-act), first produced in New York City at New Dramatists workshop, 1968; "Needmore's Mother" (one-act), first produced in Sarasota, Fla., at Asolo Theatre, 1970; "The King of the Hill Is Down" (three-act), first produced in New York City at New Dramatists, 1975; "A Trip to Oz" (two-act), first produced in Mineola, N.Y., at Mineola High School, 1973; "Fable Theatre" (one-act), first produced in Wantagh, N.Y., at Wantagh High School, 1975. Writer for "Captain Kangaroo," on CBS-TV.

WORK IN PROGRESS: "Sexual Incompatibility," a three-act play.

SIDELIGHTS: Parchman commented: "Growing up on the East Side of Detroit, in a tough lower middle-class working neighborhood in the late forties and early fifties, gave me only three ways out—sports, crime, or the entertainment field. The only people I knew that had ever been to college were my public school teachers.

"Luckily, though I didn't think so at the time, I was drafted during the Korean Conflict. Uncle Sam jerked me off my street corner and away from my auto assembly-line job. In the military I met up with young men who had been to college and had ambitions, and that got me to thinking. Utilizing the G.I. Bill, I attended college and found I was interested in drama and theatre production, partly because I thought I might like to be a movie star.

"But there was more interest in the scenes that I wrote for fellow actors than in my ability to act. Although I did get as far as reading for a part in a Broadway play, my acting career fell by the wayside and eventually I concentrated on writing for the theatre and television.

"What I most enjoy from an audience viewing something I have written is hearty laughter where I've intended for them to laugh. Well, why not? My introduction to live theatre was, after all, the old Gaiety Burlesque in downtown Detroit. Otherwise I saw every movie ever made in the forties and fifties. Burlesque comedy intrigued me and still does. I incorporate burlesque techniques and movie techniques in all my plays. And I hope to be funny. I may write about the futility of war, the despair of loneliness, the self-destruction of divorce, but I hope the audience never realizes that my plays are telling them something, because they should be too busy laughing. I sugar-coat the pill.

"Because a playwright cannot be too proficient in his field, I have grabbed every opportunity to teach or to direct plays on a professional level. It is all fodder for my writing mill. I learn as much each time I direct or run a class as anyone working with me."

* * *

PARDEY, Larry
   See PARDEY, Lawrence Fred

* * *

PARDEY, Lawrence Fred 1939-
   (Larry Pardey)

PERSONAL: Born October 31, 1939, in Victoria, British Columbia, Canada; son of Francis Henry and Beryl (Peterson) Pardey; married Mary Lin Zatkin (a writer), October 30, 1968. *Education:* Attended high school in Vancouver, British Columbia, Canada. *Home:* "On board our yacht, *Seraffyn.*" *Address:* c/o W. W. Norton, 500 Fifth Ave., New York, N.Y. 10036.

CAREER: Worked in sawmills in British Columbia, 1960-62; in sales service for paper company in Vancouver, British Columbia, 1962-64; charter yacht captain in Newport Beach, Calif., 1965-66; operated yacht repair business and chandlery in Costa Mesa, Calif., 1966-69; writer, 1969—. *Member:* West Vancouver Yacht Club.

WRITINGS—Under name Larry Pardey: (With wife, Lin Pardey) *Cruising in Seraffyn,* Seven-Seas Press, 1976; (with Lin Pardey) *Seraffyn's European Adventures,* Norton, 1979.

Work represented in anthologies, including *The Best of Sail-Cruising,* Sail, 1978. Contributor to American and foreign boating magazines, including *Sail, Cruising World,* and *Yachting Monthly.*

WORK IN PROGRESS: A technical book on boat-building, publication expected in 1982.

SIDELIGHTS: In 1969 the Pardeys began a ten-year cruise on their sailing yacht *Seraffyn.* Pardey writes: "Our motivation for writing was to explode the myth that to enjoy yacht cruising, you had to have a large fifty-foot expensive complicated vessel."

BIOGRAPHICAL/CRITICAL SOURCES: New York Times Book Review, June 17, 1979.

* * *

PARDEY, (Mary) Lin 1944-

PERSONAL: Born August 1, 1944, in Detroit, Mich.; daughter of Sam (a tool maker) and Marion (an office manager; maiden name, Adelman) Zatkin; married Lawrence Fred Pardey (a writer), October 30, 1968. *Education:* Attended California State University, Northridge, 1964-65. *Home:* "On board our yacht, *Seraffyn.*" *Address:* c/o W. W. Norton, 500 Fifth Ave., New York, N.Y. 10036.

CAREER: Small business accountant, 1965-68; writer, 1969—. Member of faculty at Wooden Boat Festival, 1978-79. *Member:* Ocean Cruising Club, Perak Yacht Club (Malaysia).

WRITINGS: (With husband, Larry Pardey) *Cruising in Seraffyn,* Seven-Seas Press, 1976; (with Larry Pardey) *Seraffyn's European Adventures,* Norton, 1979; *Care and Feeding of the Offshore Crew,* Norton, 1980. Work represented in anthologies, including *The Best of Sail-Cruising,* Sail, 1978. Contributor to American and foreign boating magazines, including *Sail, Cruising World,* and *Yachting World.*

WORK IN PROGRESS: The third in a series of *Seraffyn's* adventures, publication by Norton expected in 1981.

SIDELIGHTS: In 1969, Lin Pardey and her husband embarked on a ten-year cruise aboard their sailing yacht, *Seraffyn.* She writes: "Writing has been the perfect complement to our voyaging way of life—in a way, it's like the chicken and the egg. If we didn't sail, we wouldn't have so much to write about. If we didn't write, we wouldn't have the funds to travel so freely. But the voyaging came long before the writing, and we never plan a day of our life by thinking, 'This would make a good story.'

"I've found our method of writing as joint author/editors most successful. The two of us discuss any ideas we have, suggesting additions or other insights. Then, whoever feels most interested in a particular idea or subject will sit down and write an outline. We again discuss and suggest changes.

The final article or story is written by whoever did the outline, with final editing a joint effort. Since Larry is a far more practical person than I, a joke has developed: he tells the truth while I tell the sea stories."

BIOGRAPHICAL/CRITICAL SOURCES: *New York Times Book Review,* June 17, 1979.

* * *

PARISI, Joseph 1944-

PERSONAL: Born November 18, 1944, in Duluth, Minn.; son of Joseph C. and Phyllis (a musician; maiden name, Quaranta) Parisi. *Education:* Attended Duns Scotus College, 1962-64; College of St. Thomas, St. Paul, Minn., B.A. (with honors), 1966; University of Chicago, M.A., 1967, Ph.D. (with honors), 1973. *Home:* 3440 North Lake Shore Dr., Chicago, Ill. 60657. *Office: Poetry,* 601 South Morgan St., Chicago, Ill. 60680.

CAREER: Roosevelt University, Chicago, Ill., assistant professor of English, 1969-78; *Poetry,* Chicago, associate editor, 1976—. Visiting professor at University of Illinois at Chicago Circle, 1978-79. *Member:* Delta Epsilon Sigma, Cliff Dwellers.

WRITINGS: (Editor) *The Poetry Anthology, 1912-1977: Sixty-Five Years of America's Most Distinguished Verse Magazine,* Houghton, 1978. Contributor of articles, photographs, and reviews to magazines, including *TriQuarterly, New Leader, Sewanee Review,* and *Shenadoah,* and newspapers.

AVOCATIONAL INTERESTS: Music, photography.

BIOGRAPHICAL/CRITICAL SOURCES: *Chicago,* March, 1979.

* * *

PARKER, Beatrice
See HUFF, T(om) E.

* * *

PARKER, Dorothy 1922-

PERSONAL: Born December 8, 1922, in Reading, Mass.; daughter of Robert E. (a civil engineer) and Edith (Ives) Parker; married A. J. Slep (divorced); married Saul Maloff (a critic and novelist): children: (first marriage) Peter A. *Education:* University of New Hampshire, B.A., 1944. *Home address:* Second Hill Rd., Bridgewater, Conn. 06752.

CAREER: McGraw-Hill Book Co., New York City, editor in trade book department, 1944-52; Popular Library, Inc., New York City, editor, 1952-57; free-lance writer, editor, and consultant, 1957-59; Atheneum Publishers, New York City, editor, 1959-76; free-lance writer, editor, and consultant, 1976—. Member of faculty at Columbia University, New York University, Pratt Institute, and New School for Social Research; conducts workshops and seminars. Member of Bridgewater Conservation Commission.

WRITINGS: *The Wonderful World of Yogurt,* Hawthorn, 1972; *Feeling Fine, Looking Great,* Crowell, 1974; (with Vera Gewanter) *Home Preserving Made Easy,* Viking, 1975; *Ms. Pinchpenny's Book of Kitchen Management,* Penguin, 1976; *Ms. Pinchpenny's Book of Interior Design,* Van Nostrand, 1979.

Contributor: Wendy Rieder and Kate Slate, editors, *The Great Cook's Guide to Cookies,* Beard, Glaser & Wolf, 1978; Rieder and Slate, editors, *The Great Cook's Guide to Ice Cream and Other Frozen Desserts,* Random House, 1978;

(author of introduction) Rieder and Slate, editors, *The Great Cook's Guide to Rice Cookery,* Random House, 1978. Contributor to magazines, including *Writer* and *Country Journal.* Book reviewer for *Christian Science Monitor.*

WORK IN PROGRESS: Two nonfiction books, one about housing, one about food.

SIDELIGHTS: Dorothy Parker wrote: "I never intended to be a writer and couldn't afford the free-lance life now, except that my knowledge is encyclopedic on beating the system, making it or doing it yourself, and matching your appetites to your budget. These are the subjects of much of my writing. As a lecturer, my favorite topic is how to enjoy life to the utmost while saving time, energy, nerves, and money: that's the kind of conservationist I am.

"My own unfinished books may never be completed, especially if I'm lured away from them into collaboration, editing, or rewriting of enough 'work in progress' of other authors. On several publishers' lists are a number of silk purses that began life as sow' ears in my hands. Since I'm just as happy writing other people's books as my own, I'm equally gratified when a book published under another name is as successful as my own have been."

BIOGRAPHICAL/CRITICAL SOURCES: *Bridgeport Post,* April 29, 1979; *Hartford Courant,* May 18, 1979; *Danbury News-Times,* May 24, 1979.

* * *

PARMA, Clemens
See MENZEL, Roderich

* * *

PARRISH, Thomas (Douglas) 1927-

PERSONAL: Born October 12, 1927, in Richmond, Ky.; son of H. Douglas (a lawyer) and Julia M. (Gourley) Parrish; divorced. *Education:* University of Chicago, A.B., 1949, A.M., 1979; also attended New York University, 1955. *Home:* 110 Crescent Dr., Berea, Ky. 40403.

CAREER: Henry Regnery Co., Chicago, Ill., editor, 1949-50; University of Chicago, Chicago, radio producer, 1952-54; Maco Magazine Corp., New York City, editor, 1954-59; Berkley Publishing Corp., New York City, editor, 1959-60; free-lance work, 1960-64; Council of the Southern Mountains, Inc., Berea, Ky., editor and executive, 1964-70; writer, 1970—. *Military service:* U.S. Army, 1946-47. *Member:* American Committee on the History of the Second World War.

WRITINGS: *Victory at Sea: The Submarine* (juvenile), Scholastic Book Services, 1959; *Great Battles of History: The Bulge* (juvenile), World Publishing, 1966; (contributor) David S. Walls and John B. Stephenson, editors, *Appalachia in the Sixties,* University Press of Kentucky, 1972; (contributor) Fritz F. Heimann, editor, *The Future of Foundations,* Prentice-Hall, 1973; *The American Flag,* Simon & Schuster, 1973; (editor) *Encyclopedia of World War II,* Simon & Schuster, 1978.

Editor of "Men and Battle" series; published by Dutton, 1978: *Anzio: Edge of Disaster; Carrier Victory: The Air War in the Pacific; Decision at Sea: The Convoy Escorts; The Men Who Bombed the Reich; Okinawa: The Great Island Battle; Tigers Over Asia.*

Contributor to *Reporter.*

WORK IN PROGRESS: *Strategic Questions in World War II.*

SIDELIGHTS: Parrish commented: "In my introduction to *Encyclopedia of World War II*, I quoted Josh Billings's saying: 'The trouble with people is not that they don't know but that they know so much that ain't so.' I find this a valuable principle to keep in mind."

* * *

PARRY, Ellwood C(omly) III 1941-

PERSONAL: Born August 9, 1941, in Abington, Pa.; son of Ellwood Comly, Jr. (a business and school executive) and Elizabeth (Graham) Parry; married Carol Jacqueline Newman, February 1, 1964 (divorced November 15, 1971); married Pamela Jeffcott (an art librarian and editor), November 20, 1971. *Education:* Harvard University, A.B., 1964; University of California, Los Angeles, M.A., 1966; Yale University, Ph.D., 1970. *Home:* 143 Bowling Green Place, Iowa City, Iowa 52240. *Office:* School of Art and Art History, University of Iowa, Iowa City, Iowa 52242.

CAREER: Columbia University, New York, N.Y., assistant professor of art history, 1969-75; University of Iowa, Iowa City, associate professor of art history, 1976—. *Military service:* U.S. Naval Air Reserve, 1961-69. *Member:* College Art Association, Mid-America College Art Association, Midwest Art History Society. *Awards, honors:* National Endowment for the Humanities fellowship, 1975-76.

WRITINGS: The Image of the Indian and the Black Man in American Art, 1590-1900, Braziller, 1974; *Reflections of 1776: The Colonies Revisited,* Viking, 1974. Contributor to art journals.

SIDELIGHTS: Parry writes: "In dealing with nineteenth-century American art and photography, I am primarily interested in the interface between the fine arts and the more popular forms that image-making could take—from panoramas and dioramas to stereo photographs. While continuing to do research and writing on two major nineteenth-century American painters, Thomas Cole and Thomas Eakins, I am also beginning to explore more fully the relationship between art and science—particularly art and geology. Eventually, I hope to publish a book entitled *On Common Ground: Artists and Geologists in the American Landscape, 1790-1890.*"

* * *

PARSONS, Louella (Oettinger) 1881-1972

PERSONAL: Born August 6, 1881, in Freeport, Ill.; died December 9, 1972; daughter of Joshua and Helen Ida (Wilcox) Oettinger; married John Parsons (in real estate), 1910 (died, 1914); married Harry Martin (a physician), 1931; children: Harriet.

CAREER: Journalist, screenwriter, and actress. *Dixon Morning Star,* Dixon, Ill., drama editor and assistant city editor, c. 1909; worked as story editor for Essanay Co., 1912; *Chicago Tribune,* Chicago, Ill., reporter, 1914; *Chicago Record-Herald,* Chicago, columnist, 1914-18; *New York Morning Telegraph,* New York, N.Y., film critic, 1918; columnist for Hearst newspapers, including *Los Angeles Herald-Examiner,* 1922-65. Appeared on radio programs, including "Hollywood Hotel," 1934-38. Actress in motion pictures, including "Hollywood Hotel," 1938.

WRITINGS: How to Write for the "Movies," A. C. McClurg & Co., 1915; *Jean Harlow's Life Story,* [U.S.], 1937, reprinted, Dell, 1964; *The Gay Illiterate* (autobiography), Doubleday, 1944; *Tell It to Louella* (memoirs), Putnam, 1961. Also author of the screenplay, "Chains," 1912.

SIDELIGHTS: From her literary beginning as a drama critic for the *Dixon Morning Star,* Parsons has been associated, in one way or another, with the entertainment world. She married in 1910 and abandoned journalism for a career as a story editor for Essanay, a prominent filmmaking studio during the silent era. Unfortunately, after selling a screenplay, "Chains," Parsons and Essanay became mutually disenchanted. Her dissatisfaction with the studio, coupled with the tragic, premature death of her husband, drove Parsons back into journalism, as a reporter in Chicago.

Parsons cultivated a steady readership in Chicago before her abrupt dismissal by publisher William Randolph Hearst. Then, just as suddenly, she was rehired after it was relayed to Hearst that Parsons had made flattering references to his mistress, actress Marion Davies. Parsons returned as a film critic for the *New York Morning Telegraph.* Troubles continued to plague her, though, when a doctor informed her that she had a fatal respiratory ailment.

When Hearst learned about the prognosis, he invited Parsons to write her column in California, where the southern climate would be less taxing on her health. Parsons accepted Hearst's offer and resettled in Hollywood. She became vigorously involved in many aspects of the film industry: chronicling everything from actors' and actresses' alliances to business contracts and gala parties. It soon became obvious from all Parsons' activities that her doctor's evaluation was false. She was not only enjoying the Hollywood scene but becoming an important member of it.

Together with her feuding fellow-columnist Hedda Hopper, Parsons began using her influence in the media to sway the opinions of both the public and other members of the film industry. This resulted in an embarrassing calamity in 1940 when Parsons took offense at Orson Welles's film "Citizen Kane" because she believed that Kane was a detrimental characterization of Hearst, her employer. Parsons launched a campaign against Welles, depicting him alternately as a gloating egomaniac and an opportunistic fraud. Largely through her efforts, Welles and his film were ignored by the Academy of Motion Picture Arts and Sciences during their awards ceremony.

By the late 1950's, Parsons was content to write about the various affairs being carried on by those in the film business. Audiences, though, had become disinterested in gossip, as had actors and actresses, who became increasingly reluctant to reveal intimate details. The lack of information then sufficiently reduced Parsons's power within the industry. She retired in 1965.

BIOGRAPHICAL/CRITICAL SOURCES: Louella Parsons, *The Gay Illiterate,* Doubleday, 1944; George Eells, *Hedda and Louella,* Putnam, 1972; *Newsweek,* March 20, 1972; Kenneth Anger, *Hollywood Babylon,* Simon & Schuster, 1975.*

* * *

PASCARELLA, Perry (James) 1934-

PERSONAL: Born April 11, 1934, in Bradford, Pa.; son of James and Lucille (Monti) Pascarella; married Carol Ruth Taylor, May 4, 1957; children: Cynthia, Elizabeth. *Education:* Kenyon College, A.B., 1956. *Religion:* Presbyterian. *Home:* 29701 Wolf Rd., Bay Village, Ohio 44140. *Office: Industry Week,* 1111 Chester Ave., Cleveland, Ohio 44114.

CAREER: Dun & Bradstreet, Cleveland, Ohio, credit reporter, 1960-61; *Industry Week,* Cleveland, Ohio, executive editor, 1961—. Guest lecturer at Cleveland State University. *Military service:* U.S. Navy, Intelligence, 1957-60; became lieutenant commander. *Member:* World Future Society (local vice-president), Society of Professional Journalists, American Teilhard Association for the Future of Man, National Association of Business Economists, Cleveland Press Club.

WRITINGS: Technology: Fire in a Dark World, Van Nostrand, 1979; *Humanagement in the Future Corporation,* Van Nostrand, 1980. Contributor of several hundred articles to business, economic, and future studies journals.

SIDELIGHTS: Pascarella told *CA:* "In the preface to *Technology: Fire in a Dark World,* I wrote: 'We live in a technological society which is struggling to be more humane.'

"The primary subject of my research and writing is the role of business in meeting society's changing needs. I strive to strengthen the business sector, sensitize it to the world around it, and make known its needs so it can serve more effectively.

"The business sector is our problem-solving mechanism. It is the steward of our know-how and a primary agent of change. In recent years, we have allowed apathy and anti-technology feelings to restrain technological innovation in ways that threaten both our economic security and our freedom to create new solutions for our limitless problems.

"Business managers are becoming more and more responsive to society's needs. In the future, the most effective manager will be the person who can direct our know-how in a humanistic manner to serve humanistic ends. Combining a sensitivity to people and an understanding of technology, he or she will help us build a future where progress is measured in the many dimensions of human values.

"The future will always hold risks for us. There is no such thing as a risk-free life. A key role of the business manager will be to present for us the facts regarding the risk, cost, and benefits of any proposed action. It is we, then, who determine the shape of the future. For that reason, the excitement I see in the future lies in the development of man and his cultures, not in rockets and robots."

*   *   *

PASOLINI, Pier Paolo   1922-1975

PERSONAL: Born March 5, 1922, in Bologna, Italy; died November 2, 1975, in Ostia, Italy; son of Carlalberto (an army officer) and Susanna (Colussi) Pasolini. *Education:* Earned Ph.D. from University of Bologna. *Address:* Via Eufrate 9, Rome 00144, Italy.

CAREER: Director of motion pictures; writer. Founder of Academiuta di lenga Furlana (Academy of Friulan Language); actor in "Il gobbo" and "Requiescant," in addition to many of his own screenplays. *Military service:* Served with Italian Army, 1943. *Awards, honors:* Silver Bear Award, 1971, for "Il Decamerone"; Golden Bear Award, 1972; special jury prize from Cannes Film Festival, 1974; Karlovy Vary Festival award for "Accatone"; Viareggio Prize for *Le ceneri de Gramsci;* director award for "Edipo re."

WRITINGS—Novels: *Ragazzi di vita,* Garzanti, 1955, 12th edition, 1963, translation by Emile Capouya published as *The Ragazzi,* Grove Press, 1968; *Una vita violenta,* Garzanti, 1959, translation by William Weaver published as *A Violent Life,* J. Cape, 1968, reprinted edition by Bruce S. Kupelnick, Garland Publishing, 1978; *Il sogno di una cosa,* Garzanti, 1962; *Teorema,* Garzanti, 1968.

Poetry: *Le ceneri di Gramsci,* Garzanti, 1957, 5th edition,

1965; *L'usignolo della Chiesa Cattolica,* Loganesi, 1958; *Passione e ideologia, 1948-1958,* Garzanti, 1960; *La religione del mio tempo,* Garzanti, 1961, 4th edition, 1963; *Poesia in forma di rosa,* Garzanti, 1964, 2nd edition, 1964; *Poesie dimenticate,* Societa Filologica Friulana, 1965; (with Laura Betti) *Potentissima signora,* Loganesi, 1965; *Poesie,* Garzanti, 1970; *Trasumanar e organizzar,* Garzanti, 1971; *Tal cour di un frut: Nel cuore di un fanciullo,* 2nd edition, Doretti, 1974; *La Nuova giovento: Poesie friulane, 1941-1974,* Einaudi, c. 1975; *Le poesie,* Garzanti, 1975.

Other: (Translator) Aeschylus, *Orestiade,* Einaudi, 1960; (contributor) Sam Waagenaar, *Donne di Roma,* Saggiatore, 1960; (contributor) Enzo Siciliano, editor, *Scrittori della realta dell'VIII al XIX secolo,* Garzanti, 1961; *L'odore dell'India,* Loganesi, 1962; (translator) Titus Maccius Plautus, *Il vantone [di] Plauto,* Garzanti, 1963; *Ali dagli occhi azzurri,* Garzanti, 1965, 2nd edition, 1976; (contributor) Gioacchino Colizzi, *Attalo,* Lara, 1968; (compiler) *Canzoniere italiano* (anthology), two volumes, Garzanti, 1972; *Empirismo eretico,* 2nd edition, Garzanti, 1972; *Il padre selvaggio,* Einaudi, 1975; *La divina mimesis,* Einaudi, c. 1975; *Scritti corsari,* Garzanti, 1975; *Lettere agli amici,* edited by Luciano Serra, Guanda, 1976; *Lettere luteranc,* Einaudi, 1976; *Pasolini in Friuli, 1943-1949,* Arti grafiche friulane, 1976; *Con Pier Paolo Pasolini* (interview), edited by Enrico Magretti, Bulzoni, 1977; *Le belle bandiere: Dialoghi 1960-1965,* edited by Gian Carlo Ferretti, Editori riuniti, 1977; Mario Ricci, editor, *Pier Paolo Pasolini e Il Setaccio 1942-1943,* Cappelli, 1977; *I disegni 1941-1975,* edited by Giuseppe Zigaina, Edizioni di Vanni Scheiwiller, 1978.

Plays: "Orgia," 1969; *Affabulazione: Pilade* (first produced in Taormina, Italy, at Greek Theatre, August 30, 1969), Garzanti, 1977; *Calderon,* Garzanti, 1973.

Screenplays; all as director: *Accattone* (released by Cino del Duca/Arco, 1961; adapted from own novel, *Una vita violenta*), Edizioni FM, 1961; *La commare secca,* Zibetti, 1962(?); *Mama Roma* (released by Arco/Cineriz, 1962), Rizzoli, 1962; *Il vangelo secondo Matteo* (released by Arco/Lux, 1964; released in the U.S. as "The Gospel According to St. Matthew"), Garzanti, 1964; *Uccellacci e uccellini* (released by Arco, 1966), Garzanti, 1966; *Edipo re* (released by Arco, 1967; released in the U.S. as "Oedipus Rex"; adapted from the tragedy by Sophocles), Garzanti, 1967; *Medea* (released by San Marco/Rosima Anstaldt/New Line Cinema, 1970; released in the U.S. as "Medea"; adapted from the tragedy by Euripides), Garzanti, 1970; *Ostia,* Garzanti, 1970; *Il Decamerone* (film in trilogy; also see below; released by Produzione Europee Associate/United Artists, 1971; released in the U.S. as "The Decameron"; adapted from the work by Giovanni Boccaccio), Cappelli, 1975; *I racconti di Canterbury* (film in trilogy; also see below; released by United Artists; released in the U.S. as "The Canterbury Tales"; adapted from the work by Geoffrey Chaucer), Cappelli, 1975; *Il fiore delle Mille e una notte* (film in trilogy; also see below), Cappelli, 1975; *Trilogia della vita* (trilogy; includes *Il Decamerone, I racconti di Canterbury, Il fiore della Mille una notte*), Cappelli, 1975.

Other screenplays: "La ricotta," released by Arco/Cineriz/Lyre, 1962; "La rabbia," released by Opus, 1963; "Comizi d'amore," released by Arco, 1964; "Sopraluoghi in Palestina," 1964; "La terra vista dalla luna," released by Dino de Laurentis/United Artists, 1965; "Che cosa sono le nuvole?," released by Dino de Laurentis, 1967; "Le sequenza del fiore de corta," 1967; "Teorema" (adapted from own novel), released by Aetus, 1968; "Porcile," 1969; "Appunti per un' Orestiade africana," 1970. Also author of screenplays "Salo, or 120 Days of Sodom," "On Any Street," "From a Roman Balcony," "Bell' Amore," "Woman of the River," "La donna del fume" (with Mario Soldati), "Il prigioniero della montagna" (with Luis Trenker), "Le notti de Cabiria" (with Federico Fellini), "La notte brava" and "Il bell'Antonio" (with Mauro Bolognini), "Il carro armato dell' settembre" (with Gianni Puccini), "La ragazza in vetrina" (with Luciano Emmer).

SIDELIGHTS: Pier Paolo Pasolini bore a great affinity with the poor. Upon being conscripted into the Italian Army only a week before its surrender to the German forces, Pasolini fled the ominous prison camps to Casarsa, a small impoverished town in the Friulan section of northern Italy. It was here that Pasolini wrote his early poetry, in the language of the district. He was sympathetic to the plight of the peasants, and joined them in their revolts against the notorious war lords. Pasolini learned a lesson in Casarsa that was to remain with him always: the frightening reality of class struggle.

Pasolini's first novel, *The Ragazzi,* gives evidence of this concern. Though drawing no conclusions, it is an almost clinical study of "the street urchins of Rome, specifically the ones who came of age in the disjointed and disillusioning years after the war, the way they were. Pasolini's *ragazzi* lie and steal. They are cruel and cynical; they despise authority, mock the church, experience sexual intercourse while still in short pants," reported Robert Crichton. The novel unleashed a fury of rage against the author. His readers were appalled at the audacity of Pasolini to imply that all the young people of Italy behaved in such a manner, for the Italian word *ragazzi* literally means youth in general.

In this novel, which was later produced as a film, Pasolini acted as a nonjudgmental, detached observer, unfeeling and unemotional, duly recording what he saw. In addition to this, the work has no discernible form, no unifying motif linking it all together. "This is not a novel," asserted Crichton, "but a loosely connected series of sketches, verbal pictures, unresolved short stories and fragments of life. . . . The result is an imbalanced mass of behavioristic description, whose intent is not to re-create a life, but to expose a condition of life." This, it seems, was Pasolini's crime. He broke Italian film tradition by revealing "a condition of life" long ignored, the wretched poor.

His next novel, *A Violent Life,* also involves the peasant class. The main character, the young Tomasso, lives a life of petty thievery. He is eventually caught by the police and imprisoned. When released, he decides to try an honest living only to be fired by his first employer when found to be tubercular. Still determined to make good, he joins the rescue operations of the slum in which he was raised that had recently been ravaged by flood. He dies in the attempt. "Fatalistic yet exuberant," remarked one reviewer, "the youngsters at the centre of his books are social outcasts for any number of reasons—through ignorance, through lack of the means or the will to change, through lack of sympathy, on anyone else's part, for their plight; above all through a social system that has totally excluded them, failed to harness their exuberance, failed to make anything of their possibilities."

Pasolini assumes the same stance in his films as in his novels: sober objectivity. He is the instrument through which we see that the reality of life is not always pleasant. A particularly sordid slice of life is chronicled in "Salo, or 120 Days of Sodom," one of his later films. Based on the Marquis de Sade's work of the same name, Pasolini's version takes place in fascist Italy rather than the original seventeenth century Swiss villa. The four "gentlemen" are presented by Pasolini as well-read and cultured intellectuals, a judge, a banker, a duke, and a bishop, who "exercise every conceivable form of torture and excess on innumerable victims," asserted Gideon Bachmann.

"I have in no way tried to arouse sympathy, and in fact the film would lose its sting if I had," Pasolini disclosed to Bachmann. "In this I am also very true to de Sade: I have not shown victims whose side the viewer could be on. Pity would have been horrible as an element in this film, nobody would have stood for it. People who cry and tear their hair out would have made everybody leave the cinema after five minutes. In any case, I don't believe in pity." Above all, Pasolini strives for the stark and unidealized truth. "My ambition in making films," he has said, "is to make them political in the sense of being profoundly 'real' in intent: in choosing the characters, in that which they say and in that which they do . . . I do nothing to console, nothing to embellish reality, nothing to sell the goods."

"The Decameron" has become one of Italy's biggest money-making motion pictures of all time, and although enjoying somewhat less success in its U.S. release, it did meet with high critical acclaim. Based on ten stories from Boccaccio's fourteenth century work, the film "lyrically" interweaves the tales by means of a giant fresco. Characters slip in and out of the design almost at will, appearing in several tales. Due to its explicit sexuality, however, dissension arose among some reviewers. "Pier Paolo Pasolini's *The Decameron* strikes the senses like an early spirit of spring, and it's one of the most innocent dirty movies ever made," expressed Tom Shales. Kathleen Carroll disagreed, describing it as a "strangely lifeless film," and summarized: "In the end Pasolini proves only that he is a dull pornographer."

Pasolini's version of Euripides' *Medea* saw the film debut of operatic superstar Maria Callas, and while most reviewers agreed that she gave a surprisingly effective and artistic performance as the tragic heroine, they rendered decidedly opposing estimations on the screenplay itself. Paul Zimmerman, for example, announced "Medea" to be "educational, respectable, boring," but Vincent Canby protested, claiming the film "superb" and "full of eccentric imagination and real passion." Much of the controversy stemmed from Pasolini's rather loose adaptation of the original, but, as Canby noted, "Euripides was not, after all, a movie maker."

BIOGRAPHICAL/CRITICAL SOURCES: Observer Review, January 28, 1968; *Times Literary Supplement,* February 8, 1968, September 12, 1968, October 12, 1973, October 31, 1975, February 13, 1976; *New York Times Book Review,* November 10, 1968; *Best Sellers,* December 1, 1968; *Variety,* December 11, 1968, March 19, 1969; *Saturday Review,* May 3, 1969; *Newsweek,* September 13, 1971; *New York Times,* October 5, 1971, October 29, 1971; *New Statesman,* November 19, 1971; *New York Daily News,* December 13, 1971; *Los Angeles Times,* January 7, 1972; *Washington Post,* February 11, 1972; *Film Quarterly,* winter, 1973-74, winter, 1975-76; *Nation,* December 6, 1975.

OBITUARIES: New York Times, November 3, 1975; *Time,* November 17, 1975; *Current Biography,* January, 1976.*

—*Sketch by Kathleen Ceton Newman*

*   *   *

PATERSON, Allen P(eter) 1933-

PERSONAL: Born September 14, 1933, in Haverhill, England; son of Harry Poole (a naval officer) and Olive (Wiseman) Paterson; married Penelope Anne Worthington (a physiotherapist), April 5, 1969; children: Mark Christopher John, Eve Louise Flora. *Education:* Attended University Botanic Garden, Cambridge, 1949-52, 1954-55; Royal Botanic Garden, diploma in horticulture, 1958; University of Bristol, certificate in education, 1959; University of Reading, M.Ed., 1972. *Home and office:* Chelsea Physic Garden, 66 Royal Hospital Rd., London SW3 4HS, England.

CAREER: Teacher of rural studies at Portchester secondary school in Hampshire, England, 1959-62; Culham College, Oxford, England, lecturer in rural studies, 1962-66, senior lecturer in rural and environmental studies, 1962-73; Chelsea Physic Garden, London, England, curator, 1973—. Extramural lecturer at University of London, 1974—; director of Garden Design School at Inchbald School of Design, 1978—. Lecturer in Britain and abroad. Member of executive committee of National Garden Plant Conservation Committee. *Military service:* Royal Air Force, 1952-54. *Member:* Royal Horticultural Society, Linnean Society (fellow), Garden History Society (member of executive committee).

WRITINGS: Trees, Transworld, 1974; *The World of a Tree,* Transworld, 1977; *Growing Plants,* Transworld, 1977; *The Gardens of Britain,* Volume II (Paterson was not associated with Volume I), Batsford, 1978; *The Hamlyn Book of Garden Ideas,* Hamlyn, 1979; *The History of the Rose,* Mirage Editions, 1980; *The Origins of Garden Plants,* South Leigh Press, 1981. Also author of *Shade Plants and the Woodland Garden,* Dent. Contributor to specialist publications, horticulture journals, and popular magazines, including *Country Life* and *Amateur Gardening.*

WORK IN PROGRESS: Herbs in the Garden, publication by Dent expected in 1982; text for botanical drawings by Graham Rust, publication by Compton Press in 1981 or 1982.

SIDELIGHTS: Paterson comments: "I consider the study and cultivation of plants for economic reasons and as an amenity among the prime pleasures of life, as well, obviously, as vital to man's survival on this earth.

"My own interests range from cultivated plants and the planned landscape to wild species in their natural habitats. I have led plant study expeditions to Greece three times, Crete five times, as well as Corfu, Kashmir, Ecuador, and the Galapagos, and more expeditions are planned. The flora of the Mediterranean is of particular interest, because it has been so much a part of the development of Western civilization. This was emphasized in my research on the history and mythology of garden roses."

AVOCATIONAL INTERESTS: Visual and aural arts in general, opera, eighteenth-century architecture and artifacts, wild country, walking and fishing near his vacation home in a remote part of Scotland.

*   *   *

PATTERSON, Craig E(ugene)   1945-

PERSONAL: Born April 6, 1945, in Wellsboro, Pa.; son of Preston Lewis (an engineer) and Grace (Becker) Patterson; married Carol Wagner, July, 1967 (divorced October, 1971). *Education:* Pennsylvania State University, B.S., 1967. *Politics:* None. *Religion:* None. *Home address:* P.O. Box 551, Yosemite, Calif. 95389. *Office:* National Park Service, Yosemite, Calif. 95389.

CAREER: Amoco Oil Co., petroleum engineer in Houston, Tex., 1967-68, and Glendive, Mont., 1968-71; construction worker and member of expedition, 1971-73; Yosemite Mountaineering School, Yosemite, Calif., instructor, 1973-77; National Park Service, Yosemite, park ranger, 1977—. Nordic examiner for Far West Ski Instructors Association.

WRITINGS: Mountain Wilderness Survival, And-Or Press, 1979.

WORK IN PROGRESS: Desert Survival, publication by And-Or Press expected in 1982.

SIDELIGHTS: Patterson's main interests are wilderness travel and mountaineering. He has participated in expeditions on Mt. McKinley, *Cordillera Blanca* in Peru, and the St. Elias Mountains. He is active in search and rescue work and emergency medicine.

Patterson told *CA:* "In the course of my search and rescue work it became apparent that existing texts on survival did not adequately treat contemporary wilderness problems. I knew of no one who had starved to death in the back country, or who needed to make a bow and arrow, or to fashion a rope from grass fibers. But I knew of many people who had died of exposure, or had been struck by lightning, buried in an avalanche, or swept away in swift mountain streams. My own wilderness experience corroborated the thesis that those abstruse survival techniques would not keep people out of trouble in the mountains. So I wrote a book full of practical information that would keep them alive."

AVOCATIONAL INTERESTS: River running, scuba diving, sky diving.

*   *   *

PAUL, Sheri
See RESNICK, Sylvia (Safran)

*   *   *

PAUSTOVSKY, Konstantin (Georgievich)   1892-1968

PERSONAL: Born May 31, 1892, in Moscow, Russia (now U.S.S.R.); died July 14, 1968, in Moscow; married twice; children: (second marriage) one stepdaughter. *Education:* Attended Kiev University.

CAREER: Memoirist, novelist, dramatist, and short story writer. During World War I worked throughout Russia as a tram driver, as a medical orderly on a hospital train, and with a field unit; later became a factory worker in the Donbas, a fisherman in the Sea of Azov, and a journalist in Moscow; revived periodical, *Moryak* ("The Seaman"), in Odessa, 1920-21; worker for railway newspaper, *Gudok;* settled in central Russia during the 1930's; war correspondent for the southern front during World War II; conducted seminars for young writers for ten years during the 1950's and 1960's.

WRITINGS—In English: Kara-Bugaz, [Moscow], 1936, reprinted, 1969 (also see below), translation by Eugenia Schimanskaya published as *The Black Gulf,* Hutchinson, 1946; *Selected Stories* (contains "The Gulf of Kara-Bugaz," "Colchis," "The Australian From Pilyevo Station," "Snow," "A Night in October," "The Cowherd," and "Boys"), Foreign Languages Publishing House, 1949; *Zolotaya roza,* [Moscow], 1956 (also see below), translation by Susanna Rosenberg published as *The Golden Rose: Literature in the Making,* Foreign Languages Publishing House, c. 1957; *The Flight of Time: New Stories,* translated by Lev Navrozov, Foreign Languages Publishing House, 1956; *Rabbit's Paws* [and] *Zinochka* (the former by Paustovsky; the latter by N. Novoselova), D. Van Nostrand, 1961; *Zolotoi Lin,* [Moscow], 1962, bilingual edition published as *Zolotoi Lin; or, The Golden Tench,* Ungar, 1966; *Stal'noe kolechko,* [Moscow], 1963, translation by Thomas P. Whitney published as *The Magic Ringlet,* Young Scott Books, 1971; *The Story of a Life* (autobiography; translation of first three volumes of *Povesti' o zhizni;* also see below), translated by Joseph Barnes, Pantheon, 1964; *Selected Stories*, introduction and notes by Peter Henry, Pergamon Press, 1967; *Selected Stories*, translated from the original Russian, Progress Publishers, 1970.

Povesti' o zhizni (autobiography; title means "The Story of a Life"), six volumes, Volume I: *Dalekie gody* (title means "The Distant Years"), [Moscow], 1946, translation by Manya Harari and Michael Duncan published as *The Story of a Life: Childhood and Schooldays*, Harvill Press, 1964; Volume II: *Bespokoynaya yunost*, [U.S.S.R.], translation published as *Slow Approach of Thunder*, Harvill Press, 1965; Volume III: *Nachalo nevedomogo veka* (title means "The Beginning of an Unknown Era"), [Moscow], 1958, translation by Harari and Duncan published as *In That Dawn*, Harvill Press, 1967; Volume IV: *Vremya bol'shikh ozhidaniy*, [Moscow], 1960, translation by Harari and Andrew Thompson published as *Years of Hope*, Pantheon, 1968; Volume V: *Brosok na yug*, Sovetskiy pisatel, 1961, transaltion by Kyril FitzLyon published as *Southern Adventure*, Harvill Press, 1969; Volume VI: *Kniga skitanii* (title means "The Book of Wanderings"), [U.S.S.R.], 1946(?), translation by FitzLyon published as *The Restless Years*, Harvill Press, 1974.

Other: *Morskiye nabroski* (title means "Sea Sketches"), [U.S.S.R.], 1925; *Minetoza*, [U.S.S.R.], 1927; *Vstrechniye korabi*, [U.S.S.R.], 1928; *Blistayushchiye oblaka*, [U.S.S.R.], 1929; *Sud'ba Sharlya Lonsevilya* (biography; title means "The Fate of Charles Lonceville"), [U.S.S.R.], 1933; *Velikan na Kame*, [Moscow], 1934; *Kolkhida* (title means "Colchis"), [U.S.S.R.], 1934; *Romantiki* (title means "The Romantics"), [U.S.S.R.], 1935; *Chernoe more* (title means "The Black Sea"), [Moscow], 1937; *Isaak Levitan* (biography), [U.S.S.R.], 1937; *Orest Kiprenski* (biography), [U.S.S.R.], 1937; *Marshal Blykher*, [Moscow], 1938; *Zhizn' Grina* (biography), [U.S.S.R.], 1939-56; *Severnaya povest* (title means "Tale of the North"), [U.S.S.R.], 1939; *Taras Shevchenko* (biography), [Moscow], 1939; *Meshcorskaya storona*, [Moscow], 1939; *Aleksei Tolstoi* (biography), [Moscow], 1939.

Poruchnik Lermontov, [U.S.S.R.], 1941; *Leningradskaya noch'*, [Moscow], 1943; *Stepnaya gross*, [Moscow], 1945; *Novye rasskazy*, [Moscow], 1946; *Izbrannoe* (selected works), [Moscow], 1947; *Povest' o lesakh* (title means "Tales of the Woods"), [Moscow], 1948; *Nash sovremennik: Pushkin*, [U.S.S.R.], 1949.

Talye vody, [Moscow], 1950; *Severyanka* (drama), [Moscow], 1950; *Izbrannoe* (selected works), [Moscow], 1953; *Rozhdenie morya*, [Moscow], 1953; *Rodnye prostory*, [Moscow], 1954; *Beg vremeni*, [Moscow], 1954; *Izbrannye proizvedenniya* (contains "Povesti" and "Malen'kie povesti"), two volumes, [Moscow], 1956; *Sobranie sochineniy* (title means "Collected Works"; includes "Romantiki," "Kara-Bugaz," "Kolkhida," "Chernoe more," "Povest' o lesakh," "Zolotaya roza," and "Povest' o zhizni"), six volumes, [Moscow], 1957-58; *Zhil'tsy starogo doma; rasskazy*, Gos. izd-vo detskoi lit-ry, 1958.

Izbrannoe (selected works), Moskovskiy rabochii, 1961; *Letnie dni; rasskazy*, Gos. izd-vo detskoi lit-ry, 1962; *Poteryannye romany*, [U.S.S.R.], 1962; *Rasskazy*, [Moscow], 1962; *Prostye serdtsa; p'esa*, Iskusstvo, 1963; *Dym otechestva*, [Moscow], 1964; *Kniga skitanii*, Sov. Rossiia, 1964; *Izbrannaya proza*, [Moscow], 1965; *Kniga o khudozhnikakh*, [Moscow], 1966; *Povesti, rasskazy, skazki*, [Moscow], 1966; *Povesti*, Izd-vo "Khudozh lit-ra," 1967; *Naedine s osen'yu*, [Moscow], 1967; *Pokhozhdeniya zhuka-nosoroga*, [Moscow], 1968; *Teplyi khleb*, [Moscow], 1968; *Rastrepanni vorobel*, [Moscow], 1969; *Severnye povesti*, [U.S.S.R.], 1969.

Zlatovlaska, [Moscow], 1970; *Rasskazy* (selected works), Librarie des Cinq Continents, 1970; *Rodina*, [Moscow], 1972; *Razlivy rek*, [Moscow], 1973; *Chernoe more. Povest', rasskazy, ocherki, stat'i*, Simferopol', 1973.

SIDELIGHTS: During a time when many of his contemporaries were being silenced by their own government, Konstantin Paustovsky continued to publish his stories of the Russian landscape and its people. But while writing on these subjects, he never forgot the events, many of which he witnessed, that shaped his time: revolution, civil war, tyrannical oppression. His works, capturing both the old and new Russia, reveal both his tremendous love for his own country and his responses to many of its dramatic changes. Known to foreign readers primarily for his autobiography, to generations of Soviet readers he was one of their greatest storytellers.

Paustovsky's varied experiences in Russia provided him with a wealth of material for his writings, revealed most memorably in his six-volume autobiography, *Povesti' o zhizni* ("The Story of Life"). There he focused on his schooldays, his experiences during World War I and the Russian Revolution, his years in Odessa after the revolution, and his wanderings during the following decade through the mid 1930's. He witnessed many of the climactic events of the time—and the wrenching effects they had on the Russian people. As a medical orderly he saw starving, epidemic-stricken troops; he saw a nurse he loved die of smallpox in a ravaged village; he saw the passing train from which anarchist chief Nester Mahkno shot, "for the hell of it," and killed a standing guard at a railway station. But, as critic Konstantin Bazarov pointed out, Paustovsky saw another Russia as well. By Volume Six of the autobiography, "Paustovsky is well away from the center of things, exploring the remote corners from the White Sea to the Black Sea, from the Caucasus to the Northern Urals, which were still unchanged and unaffected either by the revolution or the new industrialization."

Paustovsky was virtually unknown to American readers until the publication of the various volumes of *The Story of a Life*. The first, *Childhood and Schooldays*, recounts his early family life, his education in Kiev, and his earliest writings. The author's personal life merges into the broad spectrum of Russian history in the second volume, *Slow Approach of Thunder*. Against the backdrop of World War I, Paustovsky began his "restless youth," wandering from job to job across the vast Russian landscape. He worked on sea and on land, on trucks and on trams, before becoming a journalist in Moscow. It was during that time that he, along with his fellow countrymen, saw light in the February Revolution of 1917.

In That Dawn captures those years, 1917 through 1920, when the shadow of civil war obscured the light of the revolution. The fallen czarist regime had been replaced by a new provisional government, which would later fall to the Bolsheviks. "In the course of a few months," wrote Paustovsky, "Russia spoke out everything she had kept to herself for centuries. Day and night, from February to the autumn of 1917, the country seethed from end to end like one continuous rowdy meeting." Paustovsky first greeted the revolution "with a schoolboy's delight," reported the *Times Literary Supplement*; but he soon "realized that 'the majority of the intellectuals—heirs to the great humanistic tradition of Pushkin and Herzen, Chekhov and Tolstoy—were utterly confused. Capable of creating high spiritual values, they had proved themselves, with few exceptions, powerless to lay the foundations of a state.'"

The focus of Paustovsky's work is his own experiences in this time. A prisoner of the Anarchists, a conscriptee of Hetman Skoropadsky, and always a close observer, Paustovsky recorded these apocalyptic personal and political events convincingly. Edward Crankshaw commented: "This unassuming but exquisitely managed narrative of a poet caught up in a convulsion of unimaginable violence and extent—a young man, as he then was, shocked and appalled by the destruction of all his idealistic dreams under the impact of Russian reality—somehow makes that reality comprehensible."

Paustovsky and a host of other writers withdrew from the mainstream of civil war-torn Russia in the early 1920's. Odessa became their colony, and 1920 and 1921 were their "years of hope." The spiritual writers could do little else—Odessa had been devastated by the Whites and lay waiting for the Reds to restore order. Camped in a Soviet food rationing office, the journalists were victimized by food shortages and an inflation which rendered the ruble practically worthless. They survived on rations of bread for food, and stolen wood and newspapers for fuel. They prospered by their art and their newspaper, *The Seaman,* which they printed on old tobacco wrappers. On these dull pages appeared the stories of the Odessa writers, including some of the first works by Isaac Babel. Paustovsky devotes three chapters to Babel in *Years of Hope,* which was praised for its preservation of a segment of Russian life. As Katherine Gauss Jackson wrote, "though the background of the book is dire poverty and physical hardship, what comes through is the tough strength of the intellect, the ability to laugh, the closeness to nature. Russia becomes believable."

After accounting for his years in the Caucasas in *Southern Adventure,* Paustovsky concluded his unfinished autobiography with his sixth volume, *The Restless Years.* While the author spent these years wandering throughout the Soviet Union, the direction his writing had taken was clear: he was trying to break away from journalism and become an artist. "Journalism," said V. S. Pritchett, "was killing Russian prose"; Paustovsky sought to revive it. Moved by the country's liberating spirit, Paustovsky declared: "Language must suit the nation. It must define its face, its beauty, its character as graphically as does the actual landscape of the country, a hill rising gently and losing itself in the evening mist over a river so dear to one that it makes the heart throb." *The Restless Years* is an account of both Paustovsky's search for himself as a writer and his search for material to write about. Apparently, he found both: this last segment of the autobiography ends in the mid 1930's, at the time when two of his most popular works, *Kara-Bugaz* and *Colchis,* were published.

Though Paustovsky's autobiography recalls a lively period of Russian history, his work is not generally valued for its historical accuracy. In reviewing *The Restless Years,* a *Times Literary Supplement* critic acknowledged Paustovsky's "consummate skill" in evoking the events of his time, but added that "his work is basically a record of the vicissitudes of one man's life with remarkably little reflection on political and public events." Another *Times Literary Supplement* reviewer noted that in *In That Dawn,* "Paustovsky's chronology is a little uncertain, and his real strength lies not in the description of historical events but in his accounts of 'atmosphere' and of people." Sidney Heitman recognized the same trait in *Years of Hope.* "What comes through these short pieces," he said, "is not history as personal narrative so much as the exquisite artistry of a master storyteller and the nobility of a gentle human being."

Paustovsky began his storytelling career in the 1920's. His early stories and novels, imaginative tales of adventurous and noble men in faraway lands, were shunned by the author himself in 1929 when he realized that much of what he had written was "artificial." His characteristic work in the following years, according to the *New York Times,* "combined his romantic spirit with the ideological requirements of purposeful literature in short novels that set exotic adventures against backgrounds of industrialization and land reclamation." These simple stories, noted for their brilliant nature descriptions, earned Paustovsky the distinction as one of the Soviet Union's foremost storytellers.

In addition to his love of nature, Paustovsky's gentle spirit pervaded his work, often manifesting itself in his own characters. In *In That Dawn,* said the *Times Literary Supplement,* "he writes beautifully and his narrative has something of that human warmth and that blend of sympathy, understanding, gentle humor and an occasional touch of angry satire which one associates with some of the best prerevolutionary writing." In the same vein, Vera Alexandrova wrote that "clarity and softness—these two qualities are characteristic of Paustovsky's talent.... But most of all, Paustovsky's works are peopled with ordinary folk, lovers of their native regions.... Although Paustovsky tries to be impartial toward the people he describes, it is easy to see that his warmest feelings are for the 'adventurers,' like his Uncle Yuzya and his father, who had taught throughout his lifetime that man does not live 'by bread alone.'"

Known as an "old-time liberal intellectual," Paustovsky survived the Stalin era with remarkably few scars. His own stories of his beloved Russian landscape had kept him free from rebuke until the post-Stalin era, when he publicly defended Soviet writers under fire. Paustovsky was one of the strongest supporters of Vladimir Dudintsev and his controversial book, *Not By Bread Alone.* In 1963 Nikita Kruschev publicly censured Paustovsky after the author had traveled to western Europe with Viktor Nekrasov and poet Andrei Voznesensky. Later, Paustovsky spoke in defense of Yuli Daniel and Andrei Sinyavsky as well as Aleksandr Solzhenitsyn and Yuri Galanskov. But Paustovsky's reputation alone could shield him from censure. According to *Time,* the author was "so well entrenched" as a leader in Russian letters that "the Kremlin could only let him have his say."

BIOGRAPHICAL/CRITICAL SOURCES: Soviet Literature, October, 1955, number 10, 1962, number 9, 1967, number 4, 1978; Vera Alexandrova, *A History of Soviet Literature,* Doubleday, 1963; *New York Times Book Review,* May 3, 1964; *Book Week,* May 10, 1964; *Nation,* May 11, 1964; *Christian Science Monitor,* May 14, 1964; *Saturday Review,* May 16, 1964, May 17, 1969; *New York Review of Books,* August 20, 1964; *Times Literary Supplement,* October 22, 1964, November 11, 1965; February 16, 1967, September 12, 1968, May 1, 1969, April 12, 1974; *New Statesman,* October 30, 1964, January 7, 1966, February 10, 1967, November 15, 1968, April 25, 1969, March 15, 1974.

Observer, February 5, 1967; *New York Times,* July 15, 1968; *Time,* July 26, 1968; *Illustrated London News,* February 18, 1969; *Book World,* March 30, 1969; *Harper's,* May, 1969; *Punch,* October, 1969; *Commonweal,* November 19, 1971; *Books and Bookmen,* July, 1974.*

—*Sketch by David Versical*

*   *   *

PEMBERTON, Margaret 1943-

PERSONAL: Born April 10, 1943, in Yorkshire, England;

daughter of George Arthur (an architect) and Kathleen (an artist; maiden name, Ramsden) Hudson; married Mike Pemberton (an advertising executive), October 13, 1968; children: Amanda, Rebecca, Polly, Michael, Natasha Christina. *Education:* Attended girls' school in Bradford, Yorkshire, England. *Politics:* "Variable." *Home:* 13 Manor Lane, London S.E.13, England. *Agent:* Carol Smith Agency, 2 John St., London WC1N 2MJ, England.

CAREER: Free-lance writer, 1974—. Has worked as secretary, actress, model, nurse, overseas telegraphist, and catering manager. *Member:* Romantic Novelists Association, Crime Writers Association.

WRITINGS: Rendezvous With Danger, Macdonald & Jane's, 1974; *The Mystery of Saligo Bay,* Macdonald & Jane's, 1975; *Shadows Over Silver Sands,* Berkeley, 1976; *The Guilty Secret,* R. Hale, 1979.

WORK IN PROGRESS: A book on lace-making in late medieval France.

SIDELIGHTS: Margaret Pemberton writes: "My main passions in life are Mike Pemberton, smaller Pembertons, Shakespeare, theatre, acting, and travel, in that order. I am a keen amateur actress and will travel anywhere at the slightest excuse. I write because I love it, because it is the only thing I can do!"

*　　*　　*

PEMBROOKE, Kenneth
　　See PAGE, Gerald W(ilburn)

*　　*　　*

PENDERGAST, Richard J.   1927-

PERSONAL: Born March 24, 1927, in Brooklyn, N.Y.; son of Thomas Vincent (an insurance broker) and Harriet Elizabeth (Fitzpatrick) Pendergast. *Education:* Manhattan College, B.E.E. (with highest honors), 1949; St. Louis University, Ph.L., 1955, Ph.D., 1960; Woodstock College, Woodstock, Md., S.T.L., 1964; postdoctoral study at University of Chicago, 1974-75. *Home and office:* Loyola Retreat House, 161 James St., Morristown, N.J. 07960.

CAREER: Entered Society of Jesus (Jesuits), 1949, ordained Roman Catholic priest, 1963; Loyola University, New Orleans, La., research assistant, 1955-56; St. Peter's College, Jersey City, N.J., associate professor of physics, 1966-72, adjunct professor of theology, 1971-72; St. Louis University, St. Louis, Mo., minister at Medical Center, resource person, and director of medical ethics, 1972-74; Gonzaga Renewal Center, Monroe, N.Y., director of Ignatian retreats, 1975-76; Roman Catholic priest in Newark, N.J., 1976—. *Military service:* U.S. Navy, 1945-46.

WRITINGS: Cosmos, Fordham University Press, 1973. Contributor to magazines, including *America* and *Downside Review.*

WORK IN PROGRESS: The Problem of Evil; a book on Christology.

SIDELIGHTS: Pendergast writes: "Since I was trained as a physicist, my theological interests were initially concerned with 'theological cosmology,' as the title of my first book indicates. That led me to the problem of evil, the subject of my current book. Partly as a result of my interest in the 'cosmic Christ' concept of Teilhard de Chardin, I have been led to a study of Trinitarian-Christological problems, the subject on which I am now writing."

PENN, Asher   1908(?)-1979

OBITUARY NOTICE: Born c. 1908, in Ukraine, Russia (now U.S.S.R.); died December 24, 1979, in New York, N.Y. Editor, author, journalist, and founder of *Havaner Lebn,* Cuba's first Jewish weekly. Penn also wrote for the *Day-Jewish Journal* and the *Jewish Daily Forward,* two Yiddish newspapers in the United States. His work includes *Judaism in America.* Obituaries and other sources: *AB Bookman's Weekly,* February 11, 1980.

*　　*　　*

PENNINGTON, M. (Robert John) Basil   1931-

PERSONAL: Born July 28, 1931, in Brooklyn, N.Y.; son of Dale K. (an engineer) and Helene J. Pennington. *Education:* Cathedral College of the Immaculate Conception, 1951; Pontifical University of St. Thomas Aquinas, S.T.L. (cum laude), 1959; Pontifical University of the Gregoriana, J.C.B. (summa cum laude), 1962, J.C.L. (summa cum laude), 1963; graduate study at Pontifical University of St. Thomas Aquinas and Benedictine International College of St. Anselm. *Office:* School of Theology, St. Joseph's Abbey, Spencer, Mass. 01562.

CAREER: Entered Order of Cistercians of the Strict Observance (OCSO), 1951, ordained Roman Catholic priest, 1957; St. Joseph's Abbey, Spencer, Mass., professor of moral theology, 1959-61, professor of theology and church law, 1963—, pastoral counselor at Retreat House, 1959-61, 1963—, librarian at Institute of Monastic Studies, 1960-61, lecturer at institute, 1971-72, assistant director of novices, summer, 1962. Lecturer at Mount St. Mary's Abbey, 1969-70. Head of Monastic Council on Church Law, 1964—; member of Commission of Law, Order of Cistercians of the Strict Observance, 1969—; member of Ecumenical Institute of Spirituality; head of Interreligious Monastic Colloquium, 1977. Managing editor of Cistercian Publications, 1968-73, chairperson, 1973-76. Organizer and director of ecumenical conferences and symposia; consultant to Second Vatican Council. *Member:* Canon Law Society of America, Academie Nationale de Reims.

WRITINGS: Daily We Touch Him: Practical Religious Experiences, Doubleday, 1977; *O Holy Mountain: Diary of a Visit to Mount Athos,* Doubleday, 1978; (with Sergius Bolshakoff) *In Search of True Wisdom: Visits to Spiritual Fathers,* Doubleday, 1979; *Centering Prayer,* Doubleday, 1980; *The Spirituality of the Priest Today,* Doubleday, 1980; *A Master of Friendship: Aelred of Rievaulx,* Paulist Press, 1980.

Editor and author of introductions and notes; published by Cistercian Publications, except as noted: *The Cistercian Spirit: A Symposium in Memory of Thomas Merton,* 1969; Thomas Merton, *The Climate of Monastic Prayer,* 1969; William of St. Thierry, *Exposition on the Song of Songs,* 1970; Guerric of Igny, *Liturgical Sermons I,* 1971; Igny, *Liturgical Sermons II,* 1971; St. Thierry, *On Contemplating God, Prayer, Meditations,* 1971; *Rule and Life: An Interdisciplinary Symposium,* 1971; Bernard of Clairvaux, *On the Song of Songs I,* 1971; Aelred of Rievaulx, *Treatise, Pastoral Prayer,* 1971; St. Thierry, *The Golden Epistle: A Letter to the Brethren at Mont Dieu,* 1971; (also contributor) *Contemplative Community: An Interdisciplinary Symposium,* 1972; *Bernard of Clairvaux: Studies Presented to Dom Jean Leclercq,* 1973; *One Yet Two: Monastic Tradition East and West,* 1976; *Two Yet One: The Cistercian-Orthodox Symposium,* 1976; *Prayer and Liberation,* Alba, 1976; *Clairvaux, Five Books on Consideration: Advice to a Pope,* 1976; Clairvaux, *On the Song of Songs II*, 1976; *Saint Bernard of Clairvaux: Studies Commemorating the Eighth Centenary of His Canonization*, 1977; (also contributor) *Finding Grace at the Center*, St. Bede Publications, 1978; *The Cistercian Fathers: Collected Essays*, Doubleday, 1980.

In Latin: *Propositum monasticum de Codice iuris canonici recognoscendo* (title means "Monastic Proposal for the Renewal of the Code of Canon Law"), St. Joseph's Abbey, 1966.

Syndicated writer for National Catholic News Service. Contributor of nearly two hundred articles and reviews to theology and law journals. Member of board of editors of *Citeaux*, 1968—, *Monastic Studies*, 1971—, and *Studies in Medieval Culture*, 1972—.

SIDELIGHTS: Pennington writes: "My main interest is to help as many as I can to come to experience how much God loves them, so that their lives can be fuller and happier in a union of love with him. I am also deeply concerned about the union of the churches and all religions as a basis for a world spirituality that will undergird true fraternal collaboration in the social, political, and economic spheres."

* * *

PERDUE, Theda 1949-

PERSONAL: Born April 2, 1949, in McRae, Ga.; daughter of Howard (in business) and Ouida (Davis) Perdue. *Education:* Mercer University, A.B., 1972; University of Georgia, M.A., 1974, Ph.D., 1976. *Office:* Department of History, Western Carolina University, Cullowhee, N.C. 28723.

CAREER: Western Carolina University, Cullowhee, N.C., assistant professor of history, 1975—. *Member:* Organization of American Historians, Association for the Study of Afro-American Life and History, Society for Eighteenth-Century Studies, Council on Appalachian Women, Southern Historical Association, Southern Anthropological Society, Southern Association of Women Historians, Phi Beta Kappa, Phi Alpha Theta, Sigma Epsilon. *Awards, honors:* Grants from National Endowment for the Humanities, summer, 1977, American Association of University Women, 1977-78, and American Philosophical Society, 1978-79; fellow of Newberry Library, 1978.

WRITINGS: (Contributor) Lucien Mandeville, editor, *Tradition et changement dans les systemes militaires occidentaux*, Centre d'Etudes et Recherches sur l'Armee de Toulouse, 1978; *Slavery and the Evolution of Cherokee Society, 1540-1866*, University of Tennessee Press, 1979; (with James M. Gifford and James H. Horton) *Our Mountain Heritage*, Mountain Heritage Center, Western Carolina University, 1979; (contributor) Duane King, editor, *Cherokees in Historical Perspective*, University of Tennessee Press, 1979; *Forgotten Nations: An Oral History of the Oklahoma Indian Territory*, Greenwood Press, 1979. Contributor of articles and reviews to history journals.

WORK IN PROGRESS: The Changing Status of Cherokee Women; Elias Boudinot; research on utopian schemes for the Cherokee Nation and on a post-Civil War freedmen's commune in North Carolina.

* * *

PERERA, Gretchen G(ifford) 1940-

PERSONAL: Born October 6, 1940, in Kingston, N.Y.; daughter of Esmond W. and Ruth W. (Nelson) Gifford; married Thomas B. Perera (a professor of psychology); children: Daniel G., Thomas B., Jr. *Education:* Attended Bennett College, Millbrook, N.Y., 1958-59; Lenox Hill Hospital School of Nursing, R.N., 1962; attended Columbia University, 1962-65 and 1968-70; Montclair State College, B.A., 1977; attended Caldwell College, 1977-78. *Home:* 11 Squire Hill Rd., North Caldwell, N.J. 07006.

CAREER: Lenox Hill Hospital, New York City, staff nurse, 1962-63; health education teacher at private school in New York City, 1970-76, school nurse, 1970-75; Columbia University, New York City, nurse and administrator at Psychphysics Laboratory, 1976-77; North Caldwell Schools, North Caldwell, N.J., substitute school nurse, 1977—. Nursery school teacher, 1966-68; part-time nurse at Camp Killooleet, 1968—. Member of board of trustees of Thompkins Hall Nursery School, 1968-75.

WRITINGS—For children: (With husband, Thomas B. Perera) *Louder and Louder*, F. Watts, 1973; (with T. B. Perera) *Your Brain Power*, Coward, 1975; (with T. B. Perera) *The Eye Book*, Coward, 1980.

* * *

PERES, Richard 1947-

PERSONAL: Born January 23, 1947, in Passaic, N.J.; son of Leo (a broker) and Henrietta (Wolffe) Peres. *Education:* Franklin and Marshall College, B.A., 1968; Miami University, Oxford, Ohio, M.A., 1969. *Politics:* Democrat. *Religion:* Jewish. *Home:* 1-E Meadowland Apartments, Princeton, N.J. 08540. *Office:* New Jersey Division on Civil Rights, 436 East State St., Trenton, N.J.

CAREER: New Jersey Division on Civil Rights, Trenton, conciliator, 1971—.

WRITINGS: Dealing With Employment Discrimination, McGraw, 1978; *Preventing Discrimination Complaints*, McGraw, 1979.

SIDELIGHTS: Peres told *CA:* "I wrote the first concise and understandable book for managers on the employment discrimination law."

* * *

PEREZ de AYALA, Ramon 1881-1962

OBITUARY NOTICE: Born August 9, 1881, in Oviedo, Spain; died August 5, 1962, in Madrid, Spain. Author and poet who won the Spanish National Prize of Literature in 1926. Perez de Ayala helped overthrow the monarchy in Spain and was appointed ambassador to London by the newly-created republic. He also served as the director of the National Library and the Prado Museum. His works include *Prometheus, The Fall of the House of Limon,* and *Tiger Juan.* Obituaries and other sources: *The Reader's Encyclopedia,* 2nd edition, Crowell, 1965; *Encyclopedia of World Literature in the Twentieth Century,* updated edition, Ungar, 1967; *Everyman's Dictionary of European Writers,* Dent & Sons, 1968; *The Penguin Companion to European Literature,* McGraw, 1969; *Twentieth Century Writing: A Reader's Guide to Contemporary Literature,* Transatlantic, 1969; *Cassell's Encyclopaedia of World Literature,* revised edition, Morrow, 1973.

* * *

PERKINS, Hugh V(ictor) 1918-

PERSONAL: Born June 9, 1918, in Toledo, Ohio; son of Hugh V. (an educator) and Frances (Adams) Perkins; married Cynthia Demaree (a teacher), March 30, 1946; children: Frances, David, Elizabeth Perkins Follin, Kenneth, Douglas. *Education:* Oberlin College, A.B. and Mus.B., both 1941; University of Chicago, M.A., 1946, Ph.D., 1949; New York University, Ed.D., 1956. *Politics:* Independent. *Religion:* Protestant. *Home:* 2200 Lackawanna St., Adelphi, Md. 20783. *Office:* Institute for Child Study, University of Maryland, College Park, Md. 20783.

CAREER: Teacher of English and band at public schools in Bay Village, Ohio, 1941-42; history teacher at public schools in Norwalk, Ohio, 1946-47; University of Maryland, College Park, assistant professor, 1948-51, associate professor, 1951-56, professor of human development, 1956—. Fulbright professor in Pakistan, 1958-59. *Military service:* U.S. Army, 1942-45; received Croix de Guerre. *Member:* American Psychological Association (fellow), Society for Research in Child Development, Gerontological Society, Association for Supervision and Curriculum Development.

WRITINGS: (With others) *Research Evaluating a Child Study Program,* Society for Research in Child Development, 1956; *Human Development and Learning,* Wadsworth, 1969, 2nd edition, 1974; *Human Development,* Wadsworth, 1975. Contributor to education and child study journals.

WORK IN PROGRESS: Research on adult learning and on retirement.

*   *   *

PERKINS, John Bryan Ward
    See WARD-PERKINS, John Bryan

*   *   *

PERL, Teri (Hoch)   1926-

PERSONAL: Born November 19, 1926, in New York, N.Y.; daughter of Nathan (a furrier) and Rose (Gross) Hoch; married Martin Lewis Perl (a physicist), June 18, 1948; children: Jed, Anne, Matthew, Joseph. *Education:* Brooklyn College (now of the City University of New York), B.A., 1947; San Jose State University, teaching credential, 1969; Stanford University, Ph.D., 1979. *Home:* 140 Iota Court, Madison, Wis. 53703. *Office:* University of Wisconsin, Teacher Education Building, 225 North Mills St., Madison, Wis. 53706.

CAREER: Mathematics consultant at elementary school in Palo Alto, Calif., 1971-77; San Jose State University, San Jose, Calif., instructor in mathematics, 1977; San Francisco State University, San Francisco, Calif., lecturer in mathematics, 1977-79; University of Wisconsin, Madison, project specialist, 1979—. Instructor at San Jose State University and University of California, Santa Cruz, 1973; instructor at workshops. Member of California Mathematics Council; co-director of evaluation of Math Science Conferences for Girls, 1978. *Member:* National Council of Teachers of Mathematics, American Educational Research Association, Association for Women in Mathematics, Mathematical Association of America, Santa Clara Valley Mathematics Association.

WRITINGS: (With M. K. Freedman) *A Sourcebook for Substitutes,* Addison-Wesley, 1974; *Patches,* Cuisenaire Co., 1975; *Math Equals: Biographies of Women Mathematicians Plus Related Activities,* Addison-Wesley, 1978; *Alphagrams,* Cuisenaire Co., 1979. Author of "Activity Cards for the Relationships," Cuisenaire Co., 1975. Contributor to mathematics and education journals.

WORK IN PROGRESS: Editing book of readings based on newsletters from Association for Women in Mathematics, with Carol Langbort; research and papers for professional journals.

SIDELIGHTS: Teri Perl's current interests include discriminating factors and sex differences that affect choosing mathematics as a field of study. Her research showed that reluctance on the part of contemporary women to study mathematics was not shared by other women throughout history.

She reported, for instance, that eighteenth-century women were not considered to be intellectual inferiors of men and in fact had a periodical, *The Ladies' Diary or Woman's Almanack,* published from 1704-1841, which was largely devoted to mathematics and mathematical games and puzzles.

However, Perl found that the social role of women in the 1800's kept them at home where the study of mathematics had little value except as a pastime. At the same time, mathematics itself became more of a tool in the world of work, which was inhabited mainly by men, and changing attitudes about women relegated them to the position of weaker people, intellectually as well as physically.

Her book, *Math Equals,* is about nine women, from fourth-century Alexandria to twentieth-century Germany, who persisted and excelled in their field, despite the social attitudes of the times in which they lived.

*   *   *

PERRIN JASSY, Marie-France   1942-

PERSONAL: Born March 17, 1942, in Tarbes, France; daughter of Claude (a lawyer) and Marie Andre (an artist; maiden name, Francon) Perrin Jassy; married Josef Rott (an agricultural engineer), July 5, 1971; children: Michaela, Gabrielle, Raphaela, Ourielle. *Education:* Institut d'Etudes Politiques, diploma, 1965; Sorbonne, University of Paris, doctorate, 1970. *Religion:* Roman Catholic. *Home:* 2 Hutackerstrasse, St. Wolfgang 8251, West Germany.

CAREER: Maryknoll Missionary Society, Musoma and Shinyanga, Tanzania, pastoral assistant, 1966, 1969, 1970-75; researcher, writer, and lecturer, 1975—.

WRITINGS: Forming Christian Communities, Gaba Pastoral Institute, 1967; *La Communaute de base dans les Eglises Africaines,* Hermann Hochegger, 1970, translation by Sr. Jeanne Lyons published as *Basic Community in African Churches,* Orbis, 1973; *Leadership,* Gaba Pastoral Institute, 1974.

WORK IN PROGRESS: A dictionary of rites in Zaire; research on liturgy and the sacred in the current Roman Catholic crisis; translation of *Forming Christian Communities* into French, with a new chapter on urban communities in Europe.

SIDELIGHTS: Marie-France Perrin Jassy wrote: "In East Africa, working with missionaries, I discovered the importance of the religious dimension in life. Without it, society loses its soul, it disintegrates. My work is geared to finding religious models adapted to our time and culture. I have traveled all around Africa, in most European countries, and the United States."

AVOCATIONAL INTERESTS: Occult sciences, medicine (homeopathy and herbs), painting, singing.

*   *   *

PERRY, John Oliver   1929-

PERSONAL: Born April 9, 1929, in Paris, France; American citizen born abroad; son of John Edmond (an engineer) and Norma (a teacher, secretary, and artist; maiden name, Stewart) Perry; married Lucy Holt, February, 1953 (divorced,

1972); married Sue Baxter (a psychiatric social worker), April 15, 1974; children: (first marriage) John Gavin, Celia Ann. *Education:* Kenyon College, A.B. (magna cum laude), 1949; University of Florida, M.A., 1951; University of California, Berkeley, Ph.D., 1958. *Politics:* "Democratic socialist; civil rights, anti-war, and anti-nuclear activist." *Religion:* "Humanist." *Residence:* Newton, Mass. *Office:* Department of English, Tufts University, Medford, Mass. 02155.

CAREER: University of Colorado, Boulder, instructor in English, 1955-58; State University of New York at Binghamton, Harpur College, assistant professor of English, 1958-64; Tufts University, Medford, Mass., assistant professor, 1964-66, Goldthwaite Associate Professor of Rhetoric, 1966—. Fulbright professor at Delhi University, 1971-72; lecturer at Sahitya Akademi, Hindu College in Delhi, Institute for English in Bhopal, Hyderabad University, and Mysore University; speaker for U.S. International Communications Agency in India, Thailand, Korea, and Japan; guest on All-India Radio. Public speaker; gives poetry readings. *Member:* American Association of University Professors, Citizens for Participation in Political Action (member of executive board), India Society (member of executive board). *Awards, honors:* State University of New York faculty research grant, 1963; Whiting Foundation travel/research grant in India, 1978.

WRITINGS: (Editor and contributor) *Approaches to the Poem: Modern Essays in the Analysis and Interpretation of Poetry,* Chandler Publishing, 1965; (editor and contributor) *Backgrounds to Modern Literature,* Chandler Publishing, 1968; *The Experience of Poems,* Macmillan, 1972. Contributor of articles, poems, and reviews to journals in the United States and abroad, including *Kenyon Review, Carleton Miscellany,* and *Criticism.* Associate editor of *Indian Review.*

WORK IN PROGRESS: Collecting, co-translating, and editing *Protest Poems of Indian Emergency.*

SIDELIGHTS: Perry writes: "I toured the subcontinent of India in 1978, renewing and deepening my experience of its culture, both past and present. Besides revisiting many of the archaeological and architectural monuments seen during my year at Delhi University in 1971-72, I was able to visit several less accessible and hitherto missed sites. Some of the richest experiences of the journey involved returning to such places as the Shalimar Gardens in the Kashmir, the Himalayas, the Taj Mahal by moonlight, the Ajanta caves, and especially the crowded markets of old Delhi.

"A deep and more lasting impact came from seeing the enormously multiplied, apparently archaic, but deeply coherent and intensely resourceful working ways and social forms of the Indian people coping with modern technological and Western commercial values from a still very traditional and Eastern perspective, often feudal and to us apparently irrational.

"During November of 1978 I focused on a research project that involved collecting literature in various Indian regional languages, dealing in a non-journalistic way with the intensely controversial period of recent Indian history called 'the Emergency.' Combining literature and politics, the project gave me the opportunity to talk with writers, politicians, editors, social activists, academic intellectuals, journalists, and often just people met on trains or in the street. The question I asked was 'How did the Indian people, particularly the literate (and even smaller literary) minority react to the censorship and other strict social disciplines imposed by then Prime Minister Indira Gandhi from June, 1975 to March, 1977?'"

PERSICO, Joseph E(dward) 1930-

PERSONAL: Born July 19, 1930, in Gloversville, N.Y.; son of Thomas L. (a glove maker) and Blanche (a glove maker; maiden name, Perrone) Persico; married Sylvia Lavista (an administrator), May 23, 1959; children: Vanya, Andrea. *Education:* State University of New York at Albany, B.A., 1952; also attended Columbia University, 1955. *Home:* 5602 Jordan Rd., Washington, D.C. 20016. *Agent:* Morton Janklow, 375 Park Ave., New York, N.Y. 10022.

CAREER: Consumer advocate for governor of New York, in Albany, 1956-59; U.S. Information Agency, Washington, D.C., foreign service officer in Rio de Janeiro, Brazil, and Buenos Aires, Argentina, 1959-62; speechwriter for Nelson A. Rockefeller, 1966-77; writer, 1977—. *Military service:* U.S. Navy, 1952-55; became lieutenant junior grade. *Member:* Authors Guild of Authors League of America, American Film Institute. *Awards, honors:* Book award from National Intelligence Study Center, 1979, for *Piercing the Reich.*

WRITINGS: My Enemy My Brother: Men and Days of Gettysburg, Viking, 1977; *Piercing the Reich,* Viking, 1979; *The Spiderweb* (novel), Crown, 1979. Contributor to *American Heritage.*

WORK IN PROGRESS: A memoir of his years with Nelson Rockefeller, publication by Simon & Schuster expected in 1981; *The Fornix,* a "sexual, sociological thriller."

SIDELIGHTS: Persico told *CA:* "The creative process remains to me the holiest mystery. The capacity to leave something where nothing existed before is the ultimate glory of the human mind. I write out of no such conscious awareness, but out of unreasoned compulsion. When I do not write, I experience actual mental and emotional anguish. The obsession is chronic and seemingly incurable, a disease, benign, one hopes.

"My private pleasure is in moving with some success between nonfiction and fiction. I draw equal but differing satisfactions from each. Nonfiction is the reward of the detective, the explorer, the scholar, adding to the sum of knowledge. Fiction is the joy of releasing a lifetime of observation, emotion, prejudice, and occasionally, wisdom, and the satisfaction of making one's loves and hates come alive in a world where the writer plays God.

"I am unusually sensitive to the freedom a (solvent) writer possesses, having passed my life until age forty-six in someone else's harness. I enjoy now that rarest of freedoms: the ability to get up in the morning and ask, 'What will I do with my life today?'"

AVOCATIONAL INTERESTS: Cooking, hiking, tennis, baroque music.

BIOGRAPHICAL/CRITICAL SOURCES: Washington Post, October 27, 1979; *Detroit News,* December 16, 1979.

*   *   *

PERTWEE, Roland 1885-1963

OBITUARY NOTICE: Born in 1885 in Brighton, England; died in 1963. Actor, playwright, and novelist. Pertwee was a successful actor when he began writing plays, short stories, and novels. He contributed short stories to the *Saturday Evening Post* and *Strand* magazine. Pertwee's work includes the plays "Seein' Reason," "Interference," and "Hell's Loose," and the novels *The Eagle and the Wren* and *Rivers to Cross,* in addition to an autobiography entitled *Master to None.* Obituaries and other sources: *New York Times,* April

28, 1963; *Illustrated London News,* May 4, 1963; *The Reader's Encyclopedia,* 2nd edition, Crowell, 1965; *Longman Companion to Twentieth Century Literature,* Longman, 1970.

* * *

PETERS, Arthur Anderson   1913-1979
(Fritz Peters)

OBITUARY NOTICE: Born in 1913 in Madison, Wis.; died of heart disease, December 19, 1979, in Las Cruces, N.M. Author of psychological novels, including *The World Next Door, Finistere,* and *The Descent,* and a memoir, *Boyhood With Gurdjieff.* Obituaries and other sources: *Saturday Review of Literature,* September 17, 1949; *New York Times,* December 28, 1979.

* * *

PETERS, Fritz
See PETERS, Arthur Anderson

* * *

PETERS, Virginia Bergman   1918-

PERSONAL: Born May 13, 1918, in Lac qui parle County, Minn.; daughter of Samuel Oscar (a farmer) and Ruth (Erlandson) Bergman; married J. Shelton Peters (an education specialist), April 27, 1946 (died August 18, 1978); children: Emory Bergman. *Education:* University of Minnesota, B.S.Ed., 1941; attended University of Richmond, 1947-48; George Washington University, M.A., 1965. *Politics:* Democrat. *Religion:* Episcopal. *Home and office:* 3320 Executive Ave., Falls Church, Va. 22042.

CAREER: High school teacher of English and journalism in Appleton, Minn., 1941-43; Lewis Publishing Co., Richmond, Va., office worker, 1947; elementary school teacher in Richmond, 1948-49; U.S. Department of Defense, Washington, D.C., research analyst, 1951-55; elementary school teacher in Fairfax County, Va., 1957-61; University of Virginia, Arlington, instructor in anthropology, 1965-67; high school teacher of history, geography, and English in Fairfax County, 1965-71; writer, 1971—. Archaeology member of Fairfax County History Commission, 1974—; archival technician at National Archives, summer, 1976. *Military service:* U.S. Navy, 1943-46; became lieutenant junior grade.

WRITINGS: Legato School: A Centennial Souvenir, privately printed, 1976; *The Florida Wars,* Archon Books, 1979. Contributor to history journals, church magazines, and newspapers.

WORK IN PROGRESS: History of North America to the European Conquest, with completed chapters to be used as the basis for a series of books for junior high school students, including a book about the Seminoles; a novel.

SIDELIGHTS: Virginia Peters has toured archaeological sites all over Mexico, and has visited Indian mound sites along the Mississippi River, pueblos throughout the southwestern United States, and effigy mounds in the Midwest.

She writes: "While teaching American civilization and history, I had to dig to find facts about (and literary works by) minorities. I hope to give some of them their due by recognizing their contributions to our culture in my writing. My other concerns are conservation of our natural resources on this fragile planet and concern over pollution, particularly from atomic waste.

"When I graduated from college in the 1940's, I should have

had the courage to attempt a career in journalism or writing since the men were all at war and opportunities for women might have been better than in the thirties, but at that time I chose the safer career of teaching. My only defense is that, as a child of the depression, security was a prime consideration in making choices. When my husband retired in 1971, I decided to quit teaching in order to share more time with him and to do what I had always wanted to do—write. As a result, my first book published by a nationally known house came out after I was sixty years old. I hope that, like Edith Hamilton, Grandma Moses, and Arthur Fiedler, I can continue to do what I love best for another quarter century.

"After *The Florida Wars* was finally in the hands of the printers, I found myself unable to go back to historic research and turned instead to a novel. After I had written it, I realized that through it I had worked out much of the grief, pain, and guilt that comes with the death of someone as close as a husband of thirty-three years. How fortunate those of us are who can write, paint, compose, or perform our agonies away. I believe the novel I have written will help others who read it to face age and widowhood, just as writing it has helped me. After editing and re-typing it, I will be ready to go back to writing history again."

AVOCATIONAL INTERESTS: Travel (Scandinavia, the Far East, Europe, North Africa), local archaeology.

* * *

PETITCLERC, Denne Bart   1929-

PERSONAL: Surname is pronounced *Pet*-a-clair; born May 15, 1929, in Montesano, Wash.; son of Edmund (a rancher) and Grace (a teacher; maiden name, Meyers) Petitclerc; married W. Leigh Daley, November, 1971; children: Gayle, Jacqueline, Charles, Scot, Patricia. *Education:* Attended Santa Rosa Junior College, 1949-50. *Residence:* Ketchum, Idaho. *Agent:* Jeff Berg, International Creative Management, 8899 Beverly Blvd., Los Angeles, Calif. 90048.

CAREER: Santa Rosa Press Democrat, Santa Rosa, Calif., reporter, 1949-56; *Miami Herald,* Miami, Fla., reporter, 1956-59; *San Francisco Chronicle,* San Francisco, Calif., reporter, 1960-65; free-lance writer, 1965—. *Member:* Writers Guild of America (West). *Awards, honors:* National Headliners Award, 1952, for "The Story of a Killer's Siege"; award from California Newspaper Publishers, 1952, for spot news reporting, and 1954, for investigative reporting; award from Florida Publishers, 1957, for feature writing; award from San Francisco Press Club, 1960, for series on farm-worker's union in California.

WRITINGS: Rage of Honor (novel), Doubleday, 1965; *Lemans 24* (novel), Harcourt, 1971; *Destinies* (novels), Simon & Schuster, 1979.

Screenplays: "Red Sun," released by Warner Brothers, 1969; "Islands in the Stream," released by Paramount, 1976. Writer for television programs "Shane" (also producer), American Broadcasting Co. (ABC), 1966-67, "High Chapparal," National Broadcasting Co. (NBC), 1967, and "Then Came Bronson" (also creator), NBC, 1968.

Executive story editor of "Bonanza," NBC-TV, 1965-66.

WORK IN PROGRESS: A screenplay; a novel.

SIDELIGHTS: Petitclerc told *CA:* "I am most concerned about the survival of the individual in a hostile world. My novels to date reflect this theme."

PHILLIPS, Debora R(othman) 1939-

PERSONAL: Born December 8, 1939, in Brooklyn, N.Y.; daughter of Samuel (a social worker) and Iris (an educator; maiden name, Weinstein) Rothman; married William Phillips (a physicist), January 25, 1959; children: Ronald Eric, Wendy Jill. *Education:* Attended Barnard College, 1956-59; Chatham College, B.A., 1960; Rutgers University, M.Ed., 1966; Institute for the Advanced Study of Human Sexuality, D.Arts, 1977. *Politics:* Independent. *Religion:* Jewish. *Home:* 14 Philip Dr., Princeton, N.J. 08540. *Agent:* Jay Acton, Acton Rights Associates, 17 Grove St., New York, N.Y. 10014. *Office:* Princeton Center for Behavior Therapy, 245 Nassau St., Princeton, N.J. 08540.

CAREER: Princeton Center for Behavioral Consultation, Princeton, N.J., member of faculty, 1968—. Supervisor of Temple University's Behavior Therapy Institute, 1969-74, director of clinical training in children's program, 1971—, and sex therapy program, 1974—, assistant clinical professor of psychiatry, 1976—; sex counselor at Princeton University, 1973—; consultant to Children's Television Workshop. *Member:* American College of Sexology (member of board of directors), American Personnel and Guidance Association, American Association of Sex Educators, Counselors, and Therapists, Society for the Scientific Study of Sex, Behavior Therapy and Research Society (charter clinical fellow), Association for the Advancement of Behavior Therapy, Eastern Academy of Sex Therapy (charter member).

WRITINGS: (Contributor) L. K. Daniels, editor, *The Management of Childhood Behavior Problems in School and at Home,* C. C Thomas, 1974; (with William Kirby and Manford Wright-Saunders) *Sexual Dysfunction: The Hidden Agenda,* American Bar Association, 1978; (with Robert Judd) *How to Fall Out of Love,* Houghton, 1978. Contributor of about a dozen articles and reviews to medical journals.

WORK IN PROGRESS: A book on sexual confidence for publication by Houghton.

SIDELIGHTS: Phillips told *CA:* "The idea for *How to Fall Out of Love* grew out of my clinical work at Temple University Medical School and Princeton University. A reporter for the *Philadelphia Inquirer* heard about the work and wrote an article on the subject. The response to the article sparked the idea for the book."

*   *   *

PHILLIPS, Osborne
See BARCYNSKI, Leon Roger

*   *   *

PHILLPOTTS, Eden 1862-1960
(Harrington Hext)

OBITUARY NOTICE: Born November 4, 1862, in Mount Aboo, India; died December 29, 1960, in Exeter, England. Author and poet best known for his series of novels depicting life in Dartmoor, England. Phillpotts wrote more than two hundred fifty books during his lifetime in a style that has been compared to that of Thomas Hardy. His works include *Through a Glass Darkly, Down Dartmoor Way,* and *The Changeling.* Obituaries and other sources: *The Reader's Encyclopedia,* 2nd edition, Crowell, 1965; *The New Century Handbook of English Literature,* revised edition, Appleton, 1967; *The Who's Who of Children's Literature,* Schocken, 1968; *Who Was Who in America,* 4th edition, Marquis, 1968; *Twentieth Century Writing: A Reader's Guide to Contemporary Literature,* Transatlantic, 1969; *Longman Companion to Twentieth Century Literature,* Longman, 1970.

PILE, John F(rederick) 1924-

PERSONAL: Born December 3, 1924, in Philadelphia, Pa.; son of Wilson H. and Clara D. (Auch) Pile; married Naomi Freilicoff; children: Helen L., W. Henry. *Education:* University of Pennsylvania, B.Arch., 1946. *Home and office:* 25 Bethune St., New York, N.Y. 10014.

CAREER: Donald Deskey Associates, New York City, designer, 1946-50; Paul McCobb Design Associates, New York City, designer, 1950-52; George Nelson & Co., New York City, designer, 1952-62; independent consultant designer, 1962—. Adjunct professor at Pratt Institute, 1948—; lecturer at Hampshire College, New School for Social Research, New York University, Queens College of the City University of New York, and Philadelphia College of Art. Photographer and filmmaker. *Member:* Society of Architectural Historians. *Awards, honors:* Grant from Graham Foundation for Advanced Studies in the Fine Arts, 1973.

WRITINGS: Drawings of Architectural Interiors, Whitney Library of Design, 1967; *Interiors Second Book of Offices,* Whitney Library of Design, 1969; (with Arnold Friedmann and Forrest Wilson) *Interior Design,* American Elsevier, 1970, 2nd edition, 1976; *Interiors Third Book of Offices,* Whitney Library of Design, 1976; *Open Office Planning,* Whitney Library of Design, 1978; *Modern Furniture,* Wiley, 1979; *Design: Purpose, Form, and Meaning,* University of Massachusetts Press, 1979; *Architectural Drawing as Process,* Whitney Library of Design, 1980. Contributor to magazines, including *Time, Progressive Architecture,* and *Industrial Design.*

SIDELIGHTS: Pile commented: "My primary focus is analysis and criticism of design of objects, buildings, and the environment."

*   *   *

PITSEOLAK, Peter 1902-1973

PERSONAL: Born in November, 1902, on Nottingham Island, Northwest Territories, Canada; died, 1973; son of Innukjvarjuk (a camp leader) and Kooyoo; married wife, Annie (deceased); married second wife, Aggeok; children: Udluriak Manning, Kooyoo Ottochie; (adopted children) Mark Tapungai, Annie, Maralak. *Religion:* Anglican.

CAREER: Hunter.

WRITINGS: (With Dorothy Eber) *People From Our Side: An Eskimo Life Story,* Hurtig, 1975, Indiana University Press, 1977; *Peter Pitseolak's Escape From Death,* edited by Dorothy Eber, McClelland & Stewart, 1977, Seymour Lawrence, 1978.

SIDELIGHTS: Pitseolak's co-author and editor, Dorothy Eber, wrote: "Peter Pitseolak is called the historian of South Baffin Island. He spoke only Eskimo and wrote only in Eskimo syllabecs, but recorded his people's history by drawing and photography and through his writings. A solo show of his photographs and drawings opened at McCord Museum in Montreal, Quebec, in January, 1980."

BIOGRAPHICAL/CRITICAL SOURCES: Natural History, February, 1977.

[Sketch verified by Dorothy Eber]

*   *   *

PODMARSH, Rollo
See SALTER, Donald P. M.

POE, James 1921-1980

OBITUARY NOTICE: Born October 4, 1921, in Dobbs Ferry, N.Y.; died of a heart attack, January 24, 1980, in Malibu, Calif. Author, journalist, and screenwriter. Poe started his career working for the *March of Time* and then wrote radio plays, screenplays, and documentaries in Hollywood. He won an Academy Award for his screenplay "Around the World in Eighty Days." Poe's other screenplays include "Cat on a Hot Tin Roof," "Lilies of the Field," and "They Shoot Horses, Don't They?" Obituaries and other sources: *Who's Who in America*, 38th edition, Marquis, 1974; *Chicago Tribune*, February 3, 1980; *New York Times*, February 6, 1980.

* * *

POLING, Daniel Alfred 1884-1968

OBITUARY NOTICE: Born November 30, 1884, in Portland, Ore.; died February 7, 1968. Clergyman, lecturer, radio commentator, editor, and author. A Protestant clergyman, Poling was president and editor of the *Christian Herald* and the *Christian Endeavor Quarterly.* He lectured extensively and was the prohibition candidate in the Ohio gubernatorial race of 1912. In the 1920's, Poling gave talks on a radio show for the National Broadcasting Co. (NBC), which were subsequently published in three volumes, *Radio Talks to Young People, Radio Talks,* and *Youth and Life.* Poling was also author of several books, including *Mothers of Men, The Heretic, Youth Marches,* and *He Came From Galilee.* Obituaries and other sources: *Current Biography,* Wilson, 1943, March, 1968; *American Authors and Books, 1640 to the Present Day,* Crown, 1972.

* * *

POLK, Stella Gipson 1901-

PERSONAL: Born November 27, 1901, in Mason, Tex.; daughter of Beck (a farmer) and Emma Gipson; married Pascal Polk (a rancher), December 24, 1921 (died June 14, 1977); children: Jack Gordon (deceased). *Education:* Attended San Marcos Normal School (now San Marcos University). *Politics:* Democrat. *Religion:* Methodist. *Home address:* P.O. Box 642, Mason, Tex. 76856.

CAREER: Elementary school teacher in Mason County, Tex., 1918-66. Writer, 1930—.

WRITINGS: Mason and Mason County: A History, Pemberton Press, 1966; *Glory Girl,* Pemberton Press, 1970. Author of "Ranch Life," a column in *Mason County News.* Contributor of about six hundred pioneer stories to magazines.

WORK IN PROGRESS: "Somebody Like You," for *Ms.;* a book on one-room schoolhouses, publication by Eakin expected in 1980.

SIDELIGHTS: Polk writes: "I am a Texas rancher. I love the life, though I am now too old to ride my pony to round up cattle, sheep, or goats in these hills.

"*Glory Girl* is a novel set in my beloved Texas hill country. I wanted to place a twelve-year-old girl against a background of frontier life so she could experience first-hand all its rugged beauty."

Polk's main motivation for writing is her "longing to set down my love of pioneer life and my love of the Texas Hill Country." Her present goal, she says, is to publish her book, *Someone Like You.* "It is nonfiction written in fiction form. It is a true story of over fifty years of life together. I assure you it is not dull—but where do I go with it?

"My publisher, Ed Eakin, is having me write *Child's History of the Hill Country,* aimed at third or fourth graders. When he comes again I'm going to ask him to read my *Someone Like You;* however, he publishes only history. My manuscript is history, but a little off the beaten trail. Perhaps, though, he can advise me where to market it."

* * *

POLTROON, Milford
See BASCOM, David

* * *

PORTER, Cole 1893-1964

OBITUARY NOTICE: Born June 9, 1893, in Peru, Ind.; died October 15, 1964. Composer and lyricist best known for his songs, "Kiss Me Kate," "You're the Top," "Night and Day," and "Begin the Beguine." Porter wrote the scores for more than thirty Broadway and Hollywood musical comedies. His songs are characterized by their witty, sophisticated, and impertinent lyrics. Porter's work includes the musical scores of "Anything Goes," "Dubarry Was a Lady," "Gay Divorcee," and "Can-Can." Obituaries and other sources: *Current Biography,* Wilson, 1940, December, 1964; *New York Times,* October 16, 1964; *The Reader's Encyclopedia,* 2nd edition, Crowell, 1965; *Longman Companion to Twentieth Century Literature,* Longman, 1970; *McGraw-Hill Encyclopedia of World Drama,* McGraw, 1972; *Biography News,* Volume I, Gale, 1974.

* * *

PORTES, Alejandro 1944-

PERSONAL: Born October 13, 1944, in Havana, Cuba; came to the United States in 1959, naturalized citizen, 1968; son of Helio (an educator) and Eulalia (a teacher; maiden name, Cortada) Portes; married Nancy Brazie, January 26, 1966 (divorced, 1975); married Kristin Neva (a marketing representative), June 30, 1976; children: Elizabeth Marie, Charles Alexander, Andrea Renee. *Education:* Attended University of Havana, 1959-60, and Catholic University of Argentina, 1963; Creighton University, B.A. (summa cum laude), 1965; University of Wisconsin, Madison, M.A., 1967, Ph.D., 1970. *Office:* Department of Sociology, Duke University, Durham, N.C. 27706.

CAREER: University of Wisconsin—Madison, lecturer in sociology, 1969-70; University of Illinois, Urbana, assistant professor of sociology, 1970-71; University of Texas, Austin, associate professor of sociology, 1971-75; Duke University, Durham, N.C., professor of sociology, 1975—. Guest lecturer at University of Chile, 1968, and at American universities; guest researcher at Torcuato di Tella Institute, 1972-73; visiting professor at University of Brasilia, 1976. Member or director of committees and panels of Social Science Research Council, National Research Council, National Academy of Sciences, and Smithsonian Institution; program director for National Institute of Mental Health; member of fellowship selection board of Inter-American Foundation, 1978—; witness before U.S. House of Representatives subcommittees. Co-chairperson of symposium at University of Sussex, 1978; speaker in Chile and Colombia; consultant to Ford Foundation, Development Foundation of Honduras, and Santiago's Latin American Population Center.

MEMBER: American Sociological Association, Latin American Studies Association, Southern Sociological Association. *Awards, honors:* Manford Kuhn Award from Midwest

Sociological Society, 1967, for "An Hypothesis of Reference Group Selection"; fellow of Midwestern Universities Consortium for International Activities (in Chile), 1968, Latin American Teaching Fellowship Program (in Chile), 1968-69, and Council on Foreign Relations, 1972-73; grants from Council on Foreign Relations, 1972-73, National Institute of Mental Health and National Science Foundation, 1973-81.

WRITINGS: *Cuatro Poblaciones: Situacion y aspiraciones de Grupos Marginados en el Gran Santiago* (monograph; title means "For Squatter Settlements: Conditions and Aspirations of Marginalized Groups in the Greater Santiago [Chile] Region"), Sociology of Development Program, University of Wisconsin—Madison, 1969; (with John Walton) *Urban Latin America: The Political Condition From Above and Below,* University of Texas Press, 1976; (editor with Harley L. Browning) *Current Perspectives in Latin American Urban Research,* University of Texas Press, 1976.

Contributor: Hubert M. Blalock, editor, *Causal Models in the Social Sciences,* Aldine, 1971; Herman J. Peters and James C. Hansen, editors, *Vocational Guidance and Career Development,* 2nd edition (Portes was not included in 1st edition), Macmillan, 1971; J. M. Armer and A. D. Grimshaw, editors, *Comparative Social Research: Methodological Problems and Strategies,* Wiley, 1973; R. S. Byars and J. L. Love, editors, *Quantitative Social Science Research on Latin America,* University of Illinois Press, 1973; Phillip Brickman, editor, *Social Conflict,* Heath, 1974; Arturo Valenzuela and Samuel Valenzuela, editors, *Chile: Politics and Society,* Transaction Books, 1976; Janet Abu-Lughod, editor, *Third World Urbanization: Inequalities in Development,* Maaroufa Press, 1977; Irving L. Horowitz, editor, *Equity, Income, and Policy: Comparative Studies in Three Worlds of Development,* Praeger, 1977; Abdul Asiz Said, editor, *Human Rights and World Order,* Praeger, 1978; George A. Kourvetaris and Betty Dobratz, editors, *Political Sociology,* Transaction Books, 1979; (with Robert L. Bach) *Dual Labor Markets and Immigration: A Test of Competing Theories of Income Inequality,* Center for International Studies, Duke University, 1979; (with Robert N. Parker and Jose A. Cobas) *Assimilation or Consciousness: Immigrants to the United States,* Center for International Studies, Duke University, 1979.

Contributor of more than fifty articles and reviews to sociology journals in the United States and abroad, and to popular magazines, including *Nation.* Guest editor of *Journal of Political and Military Sociology* and *International Migration Review,* both 1978; associate editor of *Sociological Methods and Research,* 1971-72, *Sociology of Education,* 1975-77, *Cuban Studies* and *Journal of Political and Military Sociology,* both 1975—, and *American Sociological Review,* 1979-81; member of editorial board of *Studies in International Sociology,* 1977-81.

WORK IN PROGRESS: "Immigrant Enclaves: An Analysis of the Labor Market Experiences of Cubans in Miami," with Kenneth L. Wilson, for *American Journal of Sociology;* a book on international development and inequality, with John Walton; a book on recent Mexican immigration into the United States.

SIDELIGHTS: Portes's current research includes comparative urbanization, international migration, and class and ethnicity. He told *CA:* "My major career goal is to contribute to clarification of the sources of poverty and inequality in the Third World. The 'new wave' of immigrants from Mexico and other countries in the U.S. periphery has given rise to a number of misperceptions and simplifications about the causes of immigration and the immigrants themselves. My major present task is to help dispel such mythologies and contribute to a more enlightened policy toward this new sector of the U.S. population. To do this, I find it necessary to take a more 'activist' role (congressional testimony, publications in popular journals, speeches, etc.) than that which has characterized my career in the past."

*   *   *

PORUSH, David H(illel) 1952-

PERSONAL: Born October 23, 1952, in New York, N.Y.; son of Abraham (in business) and Judith (in business; maiden name, Gudin) Porush. *Education:* Massachusetts Institute of Technology, B.S., 1973; State University of New York at Buffalo, M.A. and Ph.D., both 1977. *Home:* 221 Richmond Rd., Williamsburg, Va. 23185. *Office:* Department of English, College of William and Mary, Williamsburg, Va. 23185.

CAREER: Golden Alligator, Inc., New York, N.Y., antiques dealer, 1971; Maclean's Hospital, Belmont, Mass., mental hospital aide, 1972; State University of New York at Buffalo, instructor in English, 1973-77, director of Buffalo writer's project, 1974-77; College of William and Mary, Williamsburg, Va., assistant professor of English, 1977—.

WRITINGS: *Rope Dances* (short fictions), Fiction Collective, 1979. Contributor to *Spree* and *American Book Review.*

WORK IN PROGRESS: *Astonishment of Heart; or, The Blind Woman Tapes,* a novel; research for *Cybernetic Fiction: Technology and Postmodernism,* a critical work.

SIDELIGHTS: Porush comments: "I write because it is what I do best; indeed, it is the only thing I do well. At present, the idea most important to me is that the world is a dissipative structure, in the sense that it is a momentary aberration of order building on the general dissipation of the universe. I have traveled all through Europe and the Middle East and discovered this is generally true, though more true is some places than in others. I would describe my fictions as dissipative structures as well."

*   *   *

POSEY, Sam 1944-

PERSONAL: Born May 26, 1944, in New York, N.Y.; son of Samuel Felton and Mary (Jameson) Posey; married Ellen Griesedieck (an artist), September 10, 1979. *Education:* Rhode Island School of Design, B.F.A., 1966. *Home address:* Low Rd., Sharon, Conn. 06069. *Agent:* International Literary Management, Inc., 767 Fifth Ave., Suite 601, New York, N.Y. 10022.

CAREER: Professional artist, 1958—. Professional race car driver, 1965—. Sports commentator for American Broadcasting Co. (ABC-TV), 1974—.

WRITINGS: *Mudge Pond Express* (autobiography), Putnam, 1976. Contributor to magazines, including *Quest, Reader's Digest, TV Guide, Sports Illustrated,* and *Road and Track.*

WORK IN PROGRESS: Articles for magazines, primarily about racing.

SIDELIGHTS: Posey told CA: "I write in longhand on yellow legal pads, very slowly, and I dread it. Mostly I write about my experiences in racing. Without my writing I would have gone down in racing history as a mediocre driver, easily forgotten. Now I'll be remembered as a mediocre driver."

POWERS, Bob
    See POWERS, Robert L(eroy)

*   *   *

POWERS, Robert L(eroy)   1924-
    (Bob Powers)

PERSONAL: Born June 7, 1924, in Kernville, Calif.; son of Marvin P. (a cattle rancher) and Isabel (Anderson) Powers; married Marjorie Martin (a secretary), April 7, 1951; children: Thomas C., David M., Kenneth W., Robert S., Susan M. *Education:* Attended Bob Jones Academy, 1945-47. *Religion:* Protestant. *Residence:* Wofford Heights, Calif. *Office address:* P.O. Box 204, Kernville, Calif. 93238.

CAREER: Worked on family cattle ranch in Onyx, Calif., 1949-52; U.S. Forest Service, Washington, D.C., Sequoia National Forest, Greenhorn Ranger District, Bakersfield, Calif., forestry aid, 1956-59, Kern County Sequoia National Forest, Cannel Meadow Ranger District, Kernville, Calif., fire control aid, 1959-1960, fire prevention technician, 1960-63, recreation foreman, 1963-70, range and recreation officer, 1970-73; writer, 1974—. President of local cemetery board, 1971-79. *Military service:* U.S. Navy, 1942. *Member:* Western Writers of America, Kern Valley Historical Society (member of board of directors, 1975-79), Kern River Historical Society (member of board of directors, 1976-78).

WRITINGS—Under name Bob Powers: *South Fork Country,* Westernlore, 1971; *North Fork Country,* Westernlore, 1974; *Hot Springs Country,* Westernlore, 1979; *Kern River Country,* Westernlore, 1979.

WORK IN PROGRESS: Indian Country.

SIDELIGHTS: Powers writes: "The Lord willing, I will write many more books during my lifetime, but my first book will always hold a special place in my heart. It gave me my start, and enabled me to tell of my love for the beautiful mountain country of central California, and the great people who helped make history here.

"In the fifth generation of my family to live in the Kern River Valley, I have been steeped in its history. The old-timers who were, and in some cases still are, my neighbors each have their own special story to tell. Many of these stories would never have been recorded on the printed page if I hadn't taken on this project.

"The experiences I have had during my life all seem to be of value in writing about rural America. The first thirty years of my life were spent on the family cattle ranch where I worked the range used by four generations of my family. I worked teams in the hay fields. I attended school and worked on ranches with Indians of the local tribe. I have worked with a chuck wagon, and know the excitement of discovering a rich mineral deposit. I worked for a neighbor who was a top bootlegger during Prohibition, and I was also active in the local churches that were so much a part of our early beginnings. I worked for the U.S. Forest Service, riding the same trails my grandfather rode when he was a ranger for the same agency. In most cases I know my subject extremely well.

"It was no small undertaking for me to write a book, as I had no formal training in writing. The most rewarding part of my writing is that my books are used in elementary and high schools and colleges. The verbal and written thanks from the school children, and knowledge that I have had a small part in making them aware of their rich heritage, is what makes any amount of work worthwhile."

POWER-WATERS, Brian   1922-
    (Captain X)

PERSONAL: Born December 19, 1922, in London, England; came to the United States in 1927, naturalized citizen, 1949; son of Percey (a producer of Broadway plays) and Alma (a writer; maiden name, Shelley) Power-Waters; married Roberta Kay Lawrence (a book shop owner), December 19, 1956; children: Lisette, Laurette, Linette, Lanette. *Education:* Attended Columbia University, 1946, and University of Miami, 1947-48. *Religion:* Roman Catholic. *Home:* Flying P-W Ranch, Church Hill, Md. 21623. *Office:* U.S. Air, Washington National Airport, Washington, D.C. 20001.

CAREER: Bricklayer, 1946-49; Mohawk Airlines, Utica, N.Y., pilot, 1954-56, captain, 1956-70; U.S. Air (formerly Allegheny Airlines), Washington, D.C., senior captain, 1970—. Instrument instructor; flight instructor for sea planes; ground instructor in meteorology, radio navigation, civil air regulations, aircraft, and engines. *Military service:* Royal Canadian Air Force, 1943-45; became flight sergeant. U.S. Air Force Reserve, pilot, 1949-54; became major. U.S. Air National Guard, pilot, 1954-70. *Member:* International Acrobatic Club, International Masons Union, Parachute Club of America, Aviation Space Writers Association, Professional Air Traffic Controllers Association, Experimental Aircraft Association. *Awards, honors:* Presidential award from Professional Air Traffic Controllers Association, 1976, for air safety.

WRITINGS: (Under pseudonym Captain X) *Safety Last: The Dangers of Commercial Aviation—An Indictment by an Airline Pilot,* Dial, 1972.

WORK IN PROGRESS: No Margin for Error (tentative title), on air traffic controllers, publication expected in 1980.

SIDELIGHTS: Years before the aircraft disasters of 1979, which resulted in massive inspections of jet aircraft for design and maintenance problems, Power-Waters sought the passage of enforceable legislation that would make his job as an airline pilot a safer one.

In *Safety Last* he wrote: "All airlines are guilty of some unsafe practices, but some airlines are guilty of them all. . . . There isn't a pilot in the sky today who doesn't break at least one regulation every time he flies. It is practically impossible to comply with one regulation without infringing on another."

Power-Waters told *CA:* "Very little has changed since I wrote *Safety Last.* In fact, if I were asked to update the book I could do so easily by simply relating the numerous disasters that have happened since 1972.

"The Federal Aviation Administration has two jobs. One is to promote aviation, and the other is to regulate it. It is obvious that these two hats cannot fit the same head. There are still hundreds of outlying airports that lack the luxury of approach lights, control towers, instrument landing systems, taxi lights, radar, and overruns.

"The potential for midair collisions is still the greatest threat to the traveling public. The air traffic system must be updated and the number of controllers has to be increased. At present we are short some three thousand controllers, and that isn't counting normal attrition. Were it not for the exceptional work of the professional air traffic controllers, there would be far more accidents than there are."

AVOCATIONAL INTERESTS: His home-built Starduster II biplane, sky diving, jogging, skiing, sailing, bobsledding, tennis, body building, photography, gliding.

POYNTER, Margaret 1927-

PERSONAL: Born May 30, 1927, in Long Beach, Calif.; daughter of John Benjamin (in business management) and Dorothy Juanita (a seamstress; maiden name, Garvin) Lewis; married Carl Stanton Olsen, September 4, 1946 (divorced, 1956); married Robert Louis Poynter (in space science), September 18, 1960; children: Geraldine Olsen Tannahill, Carlene Olsen Ray, Eric, Mark. *Education:* Attended San Diego State College (now University) and Pasadena City College, 1945-65. *Politics:* Liberal Republican. *Religion:* Church of Jesus Christ of Latter-day Saints (Mormons). *Home:* 2541 North Marengo, Altadena, Calif. 91001. *Office: Chronicle,* 2396 North Lake, Altadena, Calif. 91001.

CAREER: Free-lance writer, 1972-79; *Chronicle,* Altadena, Calif., news writer, in advertising design and sales, 1979—. Also worked as waitress and restaurant manager. *Member:* International P.E.N., Society of Children's Book Writers, Southern California Council on Literature for Children and Young People. *Awards, honors:* First prize for nonfiction from International P.E.N., 1976, for part of *The Zoo Lady.*

WRITINGS—Juvenile: Frisbee Fun, Messner, 1977; *Miracle at Metlakatla,* Concordia, 1978; *The Jimmy Carter Story,* Messner, 1978; *Crazy Minnie,* Bowmar, 1978; *The Weeping Ghost,* Scholastic Book Services, 1978; *Gold Rush!,* Atheneum, 1979; *The Zoo Lady,* Dillon, 1979; *Racquetball for You,* Messner, 1980; *The Rocking Chair Doctor,* Dillon, 1980; *Search and Rescue!,* Atheneum, 1980; *Volcanoes,* Messner, in press. Contributor of more than sixty stories and articles to magazines.

WORK IN PROGRESS: Voyager: The Story of a Space Mission, with Arthur Lane, and *Humane Societies and the Stray Animal Problem,* publication by Atheneum expected in 1981.

SIDELIGHTS: Margaret Poynter told *CA:* "I write young people's nonfiction because I want to learn about those subjects myself. Each book I write involves so much research that by the time I'm done, I feel as if I'd taken a year of college classes. During that time I'm caught up in an entire new world of people, facts, and ideas. (And when I'm done with the subject, I really don't want to hear anything more about it for a long while.) The world of writing is a magical one. My only regret is that I didn't start sooner."

* * *

PRATT, Edwin John 1883-1964

OBITUARY NOTICE: Born February 4, 1883, in Western Bay, Newfoundland, Canada; died April 26, 1964, in Toronto, Ontario, Canada. Educator, editor, and poet. Pratt was a professor of English at the University of Toronto and editor of the *Canadian Poetry* magazine. His works include *Fables of the Goats and Other Poems, The Witches' Brew, Dunkirk,* and *Verses of the Sea.* Obituaries and other sources: *New York Times,* April 27, 1964; *The Reader's Encyclopedia,* 2nd edition, Crowell, 1965; *Canadian Writers: A Biographical Dictionary,* revised edition, Ryerson Press, 1966; *The New Century Handbook of English Literature,* revised edition, Appleton, 1967; *The Oxford Companion to Canadian History and Literature,* Oxford University Press, 1967; *Longman Companion to Twentieth Century Literature,* Longman, 1970; *Cassell's Encyclopaedia of World Literature,* revised edition, Morrow, 1973.

* * *

PRATTE, Richard (Norman) 1929-

PERSONAL: Born September 8, 1929, in Norwich, Conn.; son of Severin and Rosilda (Duquette) Pratte; married Janet C. Howard in 1951; children: Thomas, Lorraine, Dianne, Gil. *Education:* American International College, B.A., 1955, M.A., 1957; University of Connecticut, Ph.D., 1967. *Office:* College of Education, 145 Ramseyer Hall, Ohio State University, Columbus, Ohio 43210.

CAREER: High school history teacher in Agagam, Mass., 1956-62; University of Bridgeport, Bridgeport, Conn., assistant professor of education, 1962-67; University of Akron, Akron, Ohio, associate professor of education, 1967-70; Ohio State University, Columbus, professor of philosophy of education, 1970—. Lecturer at Syracuse University, summer, 1964, and University of Connecticut, summer, 1965. *Member:* Philosophy of Education Society (president-elect), American Educational Studies Association (member of executive council), John Dewey Society, Ohio Valley Philosophy of Education Society (past president; member of executive board, 1969-70).

WRITINGS: Contemporary Theories of Education, Intext Educational, 1971; *The Public School Movement: A Critical Study,* McKay, 1973; (editor) *Proceedings of the Philosophy of Education Society,* Philosophy of Education Society, 1975; *Ideology and Education,* McKay, 1977; *Pluralism in Education: Conflict, Clarity, and Commitment,* C. C Thomas, 1979. Contributor of about forty articles to education journals. Member of editorial board of *Educational Theory* and advisory editorial board of *Review Journal of Social Science and Philosophy.*

WORK IN PROGRESS: Research on "schools and schooling, and the tensions between theories and strategies of educational social change."

* * *

PRELUTSKY, Jack

PERSONAL: Born in New York, N.Y. *Residence:* Cambridge, Mass.

CAREER: Poet and translator.

WRITINGS—All for children: (Translator) Rudolf Neuman, *The Bad Bear,* Macmillan, 1967; *A Gopher in the Garden and Other Animal Poems,* Macmillan, 1967; (translator) *No End of Nonsense: Humorous Verses,* Macmillan, 1968; *Lazy Blackbird and Other Verses,* Macmillan, 1969; *Three Saxon Nobles and Other Verses,* Macmillan, 1969.

The Terrible Tiger, Macmillan, 1970; *Toucans Two and Other Poems,* Macmillan, 1970 (published in England as *Zoo Doings and Other Poems,* Hamilton, 1971); *Circus,* Macmillan, 1974; *The Pack Rat's Day and Other Poems,* Macmillan, 1974; *Nightmares: Poems to Trouble Your Sleep,* Greenwillow Books, 1976; *It's Halloween,* Greenwillow Books, 1977; *The Snopp on the Sidewalk and Other Poems,* Greenwillow Books, 1977; *The Mean Old Mean Hyena,* Greenwillow Books, 1978; *The Queen of Eene,* Greenwillow Books, 1978.

SIDELIGHTS: Critics have noted that Prelutsky has a delightful manner of presenting nonsense in rhymed, rhythmic verse designed to appeal to children. In reviewing *The Queen of Eene,* Natalie Babbitt remarked, "This is a wicked, irreverent, splendid book of 14 verses, with admirable scansion." A critic for *Young Readers' Review* also praised Prelutsky's earlier verse: "Mr. Prelutsky writes clever, funny poems with definite child appeal and a lovely use of words. These verses bring to mind poems by Shel Silverstein, Ian Serraillier, John Ciardi, Eve Merriam—the best of contemporary poets of nonsense for children."

BIOGRAPHICAL/CRITICAL SOURCES: Young Readers'

Review, November, 1967; *New York Times Book Review,* April 23, 1978.*

*   *   *

PREM, Dhani   1904(?)-1979

OBITUARY NOTICE: Born c. 1904; died November 11, 1979, in India. Film director, screenwriter, physician, and author. Prem was a screenwriter and film director in Bombay, India, in the 1930's, but later practiced medicine in Britain. He was a speaker for Anglo-Indian relations and a supporter of Asian relief organizations. Prem's work includes *Injection Theory* and *Colour and British Politics.* Obituaries and other sources: *AB Bookman's Weekly,* December 24, 1979.

*   *   *

PREST, Alan Richmond   1919-

PERSONAL: Born March 1, 1919, in York, England; son of Fred and Eliza (Hornshaw) Prest; married Pauline C. Noble, May 31, 1945; children: Michael R., Harriet F. Prest Carr-West, Nicholas M. *Education:* Clare College, Cambridge, B.A., 1940; Christ's College, Cambridge, Ph.D., 1948. *Home:* 21 Leeward Gardens, Wimbledon Hill, London S.W.19, England. *Office:* Department of Economics, London School of Economics and Political Science, University of London, Houghton St., Aldwych, London W.C.2, England.

CAREER: Cambridge University, Cambridge, England, lecturer in economics, 1949-64; Victoria University of Manchester, Manchester, England, professor of economics, 1964-70; University of London, London School of Economics and Political Science, London, England, professor of economics, 1971—. *Military service:* British Army, 1941-45; became captain. *Member:* Royal Economic Society.

WRITINGS: Public Finance in Theory and Practice, Weidenfeld & Nicolson, 1960, 6th edition, 1979; *Public Finance in Developing Countries,* Weidenfeld & Nicolson, 1962, 2nd edition, 1972; (editor) *The United Kingdom Economy,* Weidenfeld & Nicolson, 1966, 7th edition, 1978.

WORK IN PROGRESS: Continuing research on public finance.

*   *   *

PREZIOSI, Donald   1941-

PERSONAL: Born January 12, 1941, in New York, N.Y.; son of Romulus Michael and Mary (Fazioli) Preziosi. *Education:* Harvard University, M.A. and Ph.D. *Home address:* P.O. Box 554, Ithaca, N.Y. 14850. *Office:* Department of Art and Art History, State University of New York at Binghamton, Binghamton, N.Y. 13901.

CAREER: Yale University, New Haven, Conn., assistant professor, 1967-72; Massachusetts Institute of Technology, Cambridge, assistant professor, 1972-77; Cornell University, Ithaca, N.Y., associate professor, 1978; State University of New York at Binghamton, associate professor of art and art history, 1978—. Fellow of Center for Advanced Study in the Behavioral Sciences, 1981-82. *Member:* International Association of Semiotic Studies, Linguistic Association of Canada and the United States, College Art Association of America, Society of Architectural Historians, American Anthropological Association, Canadian Society for the History and Philosophy of Science. *Awards, honors:* National Endowment for the Humanities fellow, 1973; Wenner-Gren Foundation fellow, 1979—.

WRITINGS: The Semiotics of the Built Environment, Indiana University Press, 1979; *Architecture, Language, and Meaning,* Mouton, 1979. Contributor to journals in art, architecture, and aesthetics.

WORK IN PROGRESS: Editing *Nonverbal Communication Today: Current Research,* with Mary Ritchie Key; a book on metaphor and metonymy in visual and verbal systems in culture, with L. R. Waugh; a book on Paleolithic art; a book on the semiotics of art and culture; *Minoan Architectural Design: Formation and Signification;* a novel; poetry.

SIDELIGHTS: Preziosi writes: "My research and writing interests include the area of aesthetics, semiotics, art and architectural history and theory, nonverbal communication, and visual and spatial perception. I am concerned with understanding the nature of communication in general, and visual communication, representation, and expression in particular. The general framework of my research and writing has been the area of semiotics, an interdisciplinary approach to the study of human significative behavior in its various aspects. This framework synthesizes my formal educational background in art history, linguistics, and anthropology.

"Another area of interest is the origins of art and architecture. *Architecture, Language, and Meaning* explores the subject of the origins and earliest evolution of human-built environments, and the relationship of that evolution to concurrent evolutions in human culture, language, and cognition during the Paleolithic period."

*   *   *

PRICE, Christine (Hilda)   1928-1980

OBITUARY NOTICE—See index for *CA* sketch: Born April 15, 1928, in London, England; died January 13, 1980, in Albuquerque, N.M. Illustrator and writer of children's books on art history, dance, and folklore. Among Price's books are *Three Golden Nobles, Sixty at a Blow, The Mystery of Masks,* and *Dance on the Dusty Earth.* Obituaries and other sources: *Authors of Books for Young People,* 2nd edition, Scarecrow, 1971; *Who's Who of American Women,* 10th edition, Marquis, 1977; *The Writers Directory, 1980-82,* St. Martin's, 1979; *Publishers Weekly,* February 22, 1980.

*   *   *

PROCOPIO, Mariellen
See GRUTZ, Mariellen Procopio

*   *   *

PUCCETTI, Roland (Peter)   1924-

PERSONAL: Born August 11, 1924, in Oak Park, Ill.; son of George (in sales) and Marie (McKone) Puccetti; married Rose-Marie Jeanne Maroun (a language teacher), November 9, 1959; children: Maia Clara, Peter Harry. *Education:* University of Illinois, B.A., 1948; University of Toronto, M.A., 1950; Sorbonne, University of Paris, Dr. de l'Univ., 1952. *Politics:* Democrat. *Religion:* Atheist. *Home:* 14 Oceanview Dr., Halifax, Nova Scotia, Canada B3P 2H3. *Agent:* Sheila Watson, Bolt & Watson Ltd., 8/12 Old Queen St., London S.W.1, England. *Office:* 1400 Henry St., Halifax, Nova Scotia, Canada B3H 3J5.

CAREER: American University of Beirut, Beirut, Lebanon, instructor, 1954-56, assistant professor, 1956-62, associate professor of philosophy, 1962-65; University of Singapore, Singapore, professor of philosophy, 1965-71; Dalhousie University, Halifax, Nova Scotia, professor of philosophy,

1971—. *Military service:* U.S. Army, Parachute Infantry, 1942-44. *Member:* Canadian Philosophical Association, Canadian Association of University Teachers, American Philosophical Association, Dalhousie Faculty Association (president, 1976-77). *Awards, honors:* Canada Council fellowship, 1977-78.

WRITINGS: Persons: A Study of Possible Moral Agents in the Universe, Macmillan, 1968, B. Herder, 1969; *The Death of the Fuehrer* (novel), Hutchinson, 1972, Fawcett, 1973; *The Trial of John and Henry Norton* (novel), Hutchinson, 1973; *Brain and Mind: A Study of Consciousness,* Macmillan, 1980. Contributor of more than fifty articles to philosophy and scientific journals.

WORK IN PROGRESS: A Journey Through the Brain, for the general reader, publication expected in 1981; *The Story of Steven,* a novel.

SIDELIGHTS: Puccetti writes: "Though a philosopher and university teacher, I write fiction as a hobby on subjects related to my research interests. For the past ten years, these interests have focused on the human brain. I argue two radical hypotheses in *Brain and Mind,* namely: that despite currently fashionable materialistic theories of the mind, closer inspection of the brain reveals it cannot be the mind; and that the mind is entirely brain-dependent, nevertheless, and the duplicated structure of the brain supports the view that there are two minds inside our heads, only one being able to talk and write."

BIOGRAPHICAL/CRITICAL SOURCES: New Yorker, November 8, 1976.

*   *   *

PURDON, Eric (Sinclaire)   1913-

PERSONAL: Born October 25, 1913, in Manila, Philippines; son of Eric St. Clair and Mary (Morgan) Purdon; married Mary Benjamin, March 15, 1941; children: Henry Prime, Eric St. Clair, Pamela Purdon Link. *Education:* Attended St. Columba's College, Rathfarnham, Ireland, 1927-31; Trinity College, Hartford, Conn., B.S., 1935; Boston University, M.S., 1958. *Religion:* Episcopal. *Home:* Arden, Harwood, Md. 20776. *Agent:* Martin Caan, William Morris Agency, 151 El Cimino, Beverly Hills, Calif. 90202.

CAREER: Desiccated Coconut Factory, Calamba Sugar

Estate, Canlubang, Luzon, Philippines, assistant manager, 1935-36; Farrar & Rinehart, Inc., New York, N.Y., associate editor, 1937-41; writer, 1946-48; U.S. Navy, speechwriter for chief of naval operations, 1948-50, chief of magazine and book branch of Department of Defense, 1950-52, chief of information for U.S. European Command, 1952-54, public information officer for 1st Naval District in Boston, Mass., 1954-58, assigned to Office of Information and Education at Department of Defense, 1958-60, public information officer for U.S.-Taiwan Defense Command in Formosa, 1960-61, officer-in-charge at Navy Training Publications Center, 1961-63, retiring as commander, 1963; U.S. Department of Commerce, Washington, D.C., information officer, 1963-64; Job Corps, Office of Economic Opportunity, Washington, D.C., 1964-66; U.S. Department of Labor, Manpower Administration, Washington, D.C., began in 1966, became special assistant to director of Job Corps, 1971-73; writer, 1973—. Photographer, Inner Mongolia Historical Expedition, 1936. *Military service:* U.S. Navy, 1941-46; became captain; received China's Order of Cloud and Banner. *Member:* National Press Club, U.S. Naval Institute, International Club (Washington, D.C.).

WRITINGS: The Valley of the Larks: A Story of Inner Mongolia, Farrar & Rinehart, 1939; (with Walter Karig) *Battle Report: The Middle Phase,* Rinehart & Co., 1946; *Black Company: The Story of Subchaser 1264,* Luce, 1972. Contributor of articles and stories to magazines, including *Atlantic, Naval Institute Proceedings, Nation, American,* and *Shipmate.*

SIDELIGHTS: Purdon told *CA:* "My first book, *The Valley of the Larks,* was an adventure story for children and came from my experiences as a photographer for an expedition into Inner Mongolia that was collecting stories and legends of Ghenghis Khan, the thirteenth-century world conqueror. *Battle Report: The Middle Phase* was the third volume of a series about the Navy's operations during World War II, emphasizing the experiences of the sailors themselves rather than the grand strategy. *Black Company* is the account of a small Navy submarine chaser that had the job of determining whether American Blacks could be sailors and not only steward's mates. The ship was a primary factor in the desegregation of the U.S. Navy. I had the colossal good fortune to be her captain during the war years."

Q

QUINN, Jane Bryant 1939-

PERSONAL: Born February 5, 1939, in Niagara Falls, N.Y.; daughter of Frank Leonard and Ada (Laurie) Bryant; married David Conrad Quinn, June 10, 1967; children: Matthew Alexander, Justin Bryant. *Education:* Middlebury College, B.A., 1960. *Home:* 7 Berrybrook Circle, Chappaqua, N.Y. 10514. *Office: Washington Post,* 444 Madison Ave., New York, N.Y. 10020.

CAREER: Insider's Newsletter, New York City, reporter, 1962-66, editor, 1967; Cowles Book Co., New York City, senior editor, 1968; *Business Week Letter,* New York City, editor-in-chief, 1969-72, general manager, 1973-74; *Washington Post,* New York City, author of syndicated financial column, 1974—. Business news analyst for WPIX-TV, 1973; business reporter for WCBS-TV, 1979—. *Member:* Phi Beta Kappa. *Awards, honors:* John Hancock Award from John Hancock Mutual Life, 1975, for business and financial journalism.

WRITINGS: Everyone's Money Book, Delacorte, 1979. Author of a regular column in *Newsweek,* 1978—. Editor of *Skilled Collector,* 1966-68.

*   *   *

QUIRIN, William L(ouis) 1942-

PERSONAL: Born November 29, 1942, in New York, N.Y.; son of Karl Louis (an engineer) and Cecelia (White) Quirin; married Diane Davino (a high school teacher), April 7, 1974. *Education:* St. Peter's College, B.S., 1964; Rutgers University, M.S., 1966, Ph.D., 1969. *Politics:* None. *Religion:* Roman Catholic. *Home:* 232-21 Hillside Ave., Bellerose Manor, N.Y. 11427. *Office:* Department of Mathematics, Adelphi University, Garden City, N.Y. 11530.

CAREER: Adelphi University, Garden City, N.Y., assistant professor, 1969-74, associate professor of mathematics, 1974—. *Member:* Mathematical Association of America, Association for Computing Machinery.

WRITINGS: Fortran IV Programming for the CDC 3300, Adelphi University Press, 1972; *Turf Racing in North America,* Millwood, 1975; *Par Times,* Millwood, 1978; *Probability and Statistics,* Harper, 1978; *Winning at the Races,* Morrow, 1979.

WORK IN PROGRESS: A textbook combining Fortran and Cobol programming; a book on thoroughbred handicapping techniques and procedures.

SIDELIGHTS: Quirin discussed his theories for winning at the races: "I consider myself an 'intuitionist.' In order to be successful playing the races, a person must have a solid foundation in the basics of handicapping, an 'arsenal of weapons' (successful techniques) at his command, and the ability to know which one to use in any given situation. Handicapping is an art, rather than a science, although it can be studied scientifically. The 'art' comes in when applying the lessons learned from the scientific study—that is what I mean by my 'intuitionist' approach to handicapping. I do not subscribe fully to the tenets of any of the major schools of handicapping—class, speed, formula, trip, etcetera—yet I am familiar with the basic principles of each and use them when the situation warrants their use.'' Quirin breeds thoroughbred race horses, works as a consultant in the thoroughbred bloodstock field, and conducts seminars on thoroughbred handicapping.

R

RAIMY, Eric 1942-

PERSONAL: Born February 9, 1942, in Columbus, Ohio; son of Victor and Ruth Raimy; married Jean McGillivray (a computer specialist), December 26, 1978. *Education:* Antioch College, B.A., 1965; University of Colorado, M.P.A., 1970. *Home:* 3160 Lewiston Ave., Berkeley, Calif. 94705. *Agent:* Michael Larsen, Michael Larsen/Elizabeth Pomada, 1029 Jones St., San Francisco, Calif. 94109.

CAREER: Writer. Worked as reporter for Associated Press. *Member:* American Society for Training and Development.

WRITINGS: Shared Houses, Shared Lives: The New Extended Families and How They Work, St. Martin's, 1979.

* * *

RAJNEESH, Acharya 1931-
(Bhagwan Shree Rajneesh)

PERSONAL: Born December 11, 1931, in Kutchwara, India; son of Swami Dev Teertha (in business) and Saraswati (Devi) Bharati. *Education:* Jabalpur University, B.A., 1955; University of Saugar, M.A., 1957. *Home:* Shree Rajneesh Ashram, 17 Koregaon Park, Poona 411 001, Maharashtra, India. *Agent:* Ma Yoga Laxmi, Rajneesh Foundation, 17 Koregaon Park, Poona 411 001, Maharashtra, India.

CAREER: Currently a Zen, Taoist, and Tantric master, known as Bhagwan Shree Rajneesh, at Shree Rajneesh Ashram, Poona, India.

WRITINGS—Under name Bhagwan Shree Rajneesh, except as indicated; published by Rajneesh Foundation, except as indicated: *I Am the Gate,* 1972, 2nd edition, 1976; *The Book of Secrets: Vigyana Bhairava Tantra,* Volume I, 1974, 2nd edition, 1975, Harper, 1976, Volume II, 1975, Harper, 1979, Volume III, 1976, Harper, in press, Volumes IV-V, 1976.

The Way of the White Clouds, 1975, revised edition published as *My Way: The Way of the White Clouds,* 1978, Grove, in press; *No Water, No Moon,* 1975, 2nd edition, 1978; *The Mustard Seed: The Gospel According to Thomas,* 1975, 2nd edition, 1978, Harper, 1978; *Roots and Wings,* 1975; *. . . And the Flowers Showered,* 1975, De Vorss, 1978; *Tantra, the Supreme Understanding: Tilopa's ''Song of Mahamudra,''* 1975, published in the United States as *Only One Sky,* Dutton, 1976; *Neither This Nor That: Sosan,* 1975.

Yoga, the Alpha and Omega: Patanjali, Volumes I-III, V, 1976, Volumes IV, VI-VIII, 1977, Volumes IX-X, 1978; *Just Like That,* 1976; *Hammer on the Rock,* 1976, Grove, in press; *The Hidden Harmony: The Fragments of Heraclitus,* 1976; *When the Shoe Fits: The Sayings of Chuang Tzu,* 1976, De Vorss, 1978; *Returning to the Source,* 1976; *Tao, the Three Treasures: The Tao Te Ching of Lao Tzu,* Volumes I-III, 1976, Volume IV, 1977; *The Ultimate Alchemy: Atma Pooja Upanishad,* Volume II, 1976, Volume I, 1977; *Until You Die,* 1976, published in the United States as *Straight to Freedom,* Harper, in press; *The Grass Grows by Itself,* 1976, De Vorss, 1978; *Come Follow Me: The Four Gospels,* Volume I, 1976, Volumes II-IV, 1977; *Vedanta, Seven Steps to Samadhi: Akshya Upanishad,* 1976; *The True Sage,* 1976; *Nirvana: The Last Nightmare,* 1976; *The Empty Boat: The Stories of Chuang Tzu,* 1976; *Meditation: The Art of Ecstasy,* Harper, 1976 (published in India as *Meditation: The Art of Inner Ecstasy,* 1977).

Above All, Don't Wobble, 1977; *The Supreme Doctrine: Kenopanishad,* 1977; *Nothing to Lose But Your Head,* 1977; *The Search: The Ten Zen Bulls,* 1977; *Dang Dang Doko Dang,* 1977; *Ancient Music in the Pines,* 1977; *The Beloved: The Baul Mystics,* Volume I, 1977, Volume II, 1978; *Be Realistic: Plan for a Miracle,* 1977; *A Sudden Clash of Thunder,* 1977; *The Psychology of the Esoteric,* Harper, 1977.

(Under name Acharya Rajneesh) *The Mysteries of Life and Death,* translated from the Hindi by Malini Bisen, Motilal Banarsidass (India), 1978; *The Cypress in the Courtyard,* 1978; *Get Out of Your Own Way,* 1978; *The New Alchemy: To Turn You On—Mabel Collins' ''Light on the Path,''* 1978; *The Discipline of Transcendence: The Sutra of Forty-Two Chapters,* four volumes, 1978; *Ecstasy, the Forgotten Language: Kabir,* 1978; *The Art of Dying,* 1978; *Beloved of My Heart,* 1978; *A Rose Is a Rose Is a Rose,* 1978; *Dance Your Way to God,* 1978; *The Great Nothing,* 1978; *God Is Not for Sale,* 1978; *The Divine Melody: Kabir,* 1978; *The Path of Love: Kabir,* 1978; *The Heart Sutra: The Prajnaparamita Hridayam Sutra,* 1978; *The Passion for the Impossible,* 1978; *Tao, the Pathless Path: The Sayings of Lieh Tzu,* Volume II, 1978, Volume I, 1979; *Zen: The Path of Paradox,* Volume I, 1978, Volumes II-III, 1979; *The Shadow of the Whip,* 1978; *This Very Body the Buddha: Hakuin's ''Song of Meditation,''* 1978; *The Supreme Understanding,* Sheldon Press, 1978; *Dimensions Beyond the Known,* Sheldon Press, 1978.

The Tantra Vision: The Royal Song of Saraha, Volumes I-II, 1979; *The Diamond Sutra: The Vajrachchedika Prajnapar-*

amita Sutra, 1979; *The Rajneesh Nothing Book* (blank pages), 1979; *Blessed Are the Ignorant*, 1979; *Walk Without Feet, Fly Without Wings, and Think Without Mind*, 1979; *The Buddha Disease*, 1979; *This Is It*, 1979; *The Revolution: Kabir*, 1979; *Take It Easy: Ikkyu*, Volume I, 1979, Volume II, in press; *From Sex to Superconsciousness*, 1979; *Sufis: The People of the Path*, Volume I, 1979, Volume II, in press; *The Zero Experience*, 1979; *For Madmen Only—Price of Admission: Your Mind*, 1979; *A Cup of Tea: Letters*, in press; *I Say Unto You: The Four Gospels*, in press; *The Secret*, in press.

Author of more than a hundred books in Hindi, all published by Rajneesh Foundation, 1975—. Author of *Sannyas* and *Rajneesh Newsletter*.

WORK IN PROGRESS—All to be published by Rajneesh Foundation: *The First Principle; The Wisdom of the Sands; The Sun Rises in the Evening; The Perfect Master; The Secret of Secrets*, Volumes I-II; *Unio Mystica; Philosophia Perennis; The Book of Wisdom; The Fish in the Sea Is Not Thirsty; The Guest; The Book of Books*, Volumes I-II; *What Is, Is, What Ain't, Ain't; The Open Secret; The Sun Behind the Sun Behind the Sun; Let Go!; Turn On, Tune In, and Drop the Lot; Zorba the Buddha; You Ain't Seen Nothing Yet; The Madmen's Guide to Enlightenment; Hallelujah!; The Tongue-Tip Taste of Tao; The Sacred Yes; The Further Shore; The No Book; Only Losers Can Win in This Game; Believing the Impossible Before Breakfast; The Ninety-Nine Names of Nothingness; Snap Your Fingers, Slap Your Face, and Wake Up!*

SIDELIGHTS: Rajneesh's books have been translated into Japanese, Dutch, Italian, French, German, Spanish, and Portuguese.

His associate, Ma Yoga Pratima, told *CA:* "Bhagwan Shree Rajneesh is an enlightened Master, a rare example of the ultimate flowering of human consciousness, whose life work is dedicated to helping and encouraging others to realize the same potential in themselves. His books are direct transcripts of discourses which he gives every morning to disciples at his Poona *ashram*, speaking for an hour and a half, and alternating each month with talks in Hindi and English. These lectures, rather than a transmission of knowledge, are an opportunity to be in his presence and share his being."

Rajneesh has said: "I am here to create millions of mystics in the world—that's my sole purpose, and that's my joy and my celebration. I use words to take you to a place that is beyond words. I am not here to explain certain things to you, but to create a certain quality within your being. I am here to transform you. . . ."

BIOGRAPHICAL/CRITICAL SOURCES: R. C. Prasad, *The Mystic of Feeling*, Motilal Banarsidass, 1970, 2nd edition, 1978; Ma Prem Divya, *Lord of the Full Moon: Life With Bhagwan Shree Rajneesh*, Rajneesh Foundation, 1979; Bernard Gunther, *Dying for Enlightenment*, Harper, 1979; Ma Satya Bharti, *The Ultimate Risk*, Wildwood House, 1979.

*   *   *

RAJNEESH, Bhagwan Shree
   See RAJNEESH, Acharya

*   *   *

RAKOVE, Jack N(orman)   1947-

PERSONAL: Born June 4, 1947, in Chicago, Ill.; son of Milton L. (a professor) and Shirley (Bloom) Rakove; married Helen Scharf (an attorney), June 22, 1969; children: Robert

Benjamin. *Education:* Attended University of Edinburgh, 1966-67; Haverford College, A.B., 1968; Harvard University, Ph.D., 1975. *Home:* 24 Hamilton St., Hamilton, N.Y. 13346. *Office:* Department of History, Colgate University, Hamilton, N.Y. 13346.

CAREER: Colgate University, Hamilton, N.Y., assistant professor of history, 1975—. *Military service:* U.S. Army Reserve, 1968-74. *Member:* Organization of American Historians, American Association of University Professors. *Awards, honors:* Fellow at Brookings Institution, 1980-81.

WRITINGS: The Beginnings of National Politics, Knopf, 1979. Contributor to *Perspectives in American History*.

WORK IN PROGRESS: Foreign Affairs and the Power of the Presidency: The Original Understanding; The Recruitment of a National Elite, 1774-89.

BIOGRAPHICAL/CRITICAL SOURCES: Washington Post Book World, December 30, 1979.

*   *   *

RANSOME, Eleanor   1915-

PERSONAL: Born March 24, 1915, in Bramhall, England; daughter of Ernest and Mary (Clayton) Dean; married Patrick Ransome, June 29, 1948 (deceased). *Education:* St. Hilda's College, Oxford, M.A., 1937. *Home:* 39 Lansdowne Rd., London W.11, England.

CAREER: British Broadcasting Corp., London, England, in radio news and current affairs, 1941-65.

WRITINGS: (Editor and author of introduction) *The Terrific Kemble: A Victorian Self-Portrait From the Writings of Fanny Kemble*, Hamish Hamilton, 1978.

*   *   *

RASH, J(esse) Keogh   1906-

PERSONAL: Born October 5, 1906, in New Providence, Iowa; son of Junius D. (a farmer) and Matilda Jane (Chance) Rash; married Faye Wood, August 22, 1928 (died October 14, 1957); married Mary Kathryn Strain Fulwider (a registered nurse), August 25, 1962; children: Marjorie Faye Rash Miller, William E. *Education:* Penn College (now William Penn College), A.B., 1928; Young Men's Christian Association Graduate School, Nashville, Tenn., M.A., 1933; Indiana University, H.S.Dir., 1948, H.S.D., 1949; University of California, Berkeley, M.P.H., 1957. *Politics:* Republican. *Religion:* Society of Friends (Quakers). *Home:* 1415 Hunter Ave., Bloomington, Ind. 47401.

CAREER: Berea College, Secondary Normal School, Berea, Ky., instructor in mathematics and general science and athletic coach, 1928-31; Iowa State Training School for Boys, Burlington, instructor and athletic coach, 1933-34; Young Men's Christian Association, Burlington, Iowa, physical director and boys' secretary, 1934-35; William Penn College, Oskaloosa, Iowa, instructor in health and physical education and athletic coach, 1935-37; Pikeville College, Pikeville, Ky., instructor in health and physical education and athletic director and coach, 1937-42; Wilmington College, Wilmington, Ohio, professor of health and physical education and business manager, 1942-47; Indiana State Department of Public Welfare, Indianapolis, health educator, 1948-49; Indiana University, Bloomington, professor of health and safety education, 1949-76, professor emeritus, 1976—, head of department, 1952-72. Visiting lecturer at North Dakota State University, summer, 1961, Union College, Barbourville, Ky., 1965-68, and Western Kentucky University, 1969-73.

President of Indiana State Health Council, 1959-60, and Indiana Council on Family Relations, 1960-62; chairperson of Indiana Interagency Council on Smoking and Health, 1973-74.

MEMBER: American School Health Association (fellow; president, 1959-60), Indiana Association of Health Educators, Indiana Association of Health, Physical Education and Recreation, Indiana Public Health Association, Public Health Nursing Association of Monroe County (member of board of directors; president of board, 1970-72, 1974), Phi Delta Kappa, Phi Epsilon Kappa, Delta Omega (Zeta chapter), Eta Sigma Gamma (Nu chapter), Bloomington Lions Club (president, 1960-61). *Awards, honors:* Distinguished service award from American School Health Association, 1965, certificate of recognition, 1967, William A. Howe Award, 1969; certificate of recognition from Indiana Public Health Association, 1967; leadership award from Indiana Association for Health, Physical Education and Recreation, 1967; honor award from Eta Sigma Gamma, 1974; awards from Mid America College Health Association, 1975, Indiana Health Careers, 1976, and Indiana Association of Health Educators, 1976.

WRITINGS: Score Sheet for School Health Surveys, Indiana University Bookstore, 1951, 3rd edition, 1960; *Tentative Standards for School Health Survey,* Indiana University Bookstore, 1954, 3rd edition, 1959; (with W. W. Patty) *Health Education Test Construction and Refinement,* Indiana University Bookstore, 1953; *Health Education Curriculum Development,* privately printed, 1958; *Combined Standards and Score Card for School Health Programs,* Indiana University Bookstore, 1964, 4th edition, 1973; *The Health Education Curriculum,* privately printed, 1966, 4th edition, 1974; (editor) *Pathways to Health,* Globe Book Co., 1975; (with R. Morgan Pigg, Jr.) *The Health Education Curriculum,* Wiley, 1979; *A History of the American School Health Association,* American School Health Association, 1980.

Contributor: *Planning Areas and Facilities for Health, Physical Education, and Recreation,* Athletic Institute, 1956, 2nd edition, 1965; *Health and Physical Education in Junior High Schools,* Indiana Association of Junior and Senior High School Principals, 1960; *Teamwork in School Health,* American Association for Health, Physical Education and Recreation, 1962; *Health Education,* National Education Association, 1962; *Planning Facilities for College and University Health and Safety Education, Physical Education, and Recreation,* Athletic Institute, 1967. Contributor to *World Book Encyclopedia.* Contributor to health and education journals.

SIDELIGHTS: Rash writes: "I believe the health education of students (of all ages) to be the most important responsibility of parents and educational institutions. Education to conserve health can prevent much debilitating illness."

*   *   *

RASMUSSEN, R. Kent   1943-

PERSONAL: Born October 11, 1943, in Albany, Calif.; son of Clyde L. and Marian (Bambrough) Rasmussen; married Nancy Carpenter (a teacher), July 2, 1966; children: Christopher, Erik. *Education:* University of California, Berkeley, B.A., 1966; University of California, Los Angeles, M.A., 1969, Ph.D., 1975. *Religion:* "Bokononism." *Home and office:* 14317 Miranda St., Van Nuys, Calif. 91401.

CAREER: University of California, Los Angeles, lecturer in history, 1976; free-lance writer and researcher, 1976—. Coach for American Youth Soccer Organization, 1977—. *Military service:* U.S. Coast Guard Reserve, 1962-70. *Mem-*

ber: Authors Guild, Authors League of America. *Awards, honors:* Fulbright-Hays fellowship, 1971-72.

WRITINGS: Mzilikazi of the Ndebele, Heinemann, 1977; (with Mark R. Lipschutz) *Dictionary of African Historical Biography,* Aldine, 1978; *Migrant Kingdom: Mzilikazi's Ndebele in South Africa,* Rex Collings, 1978; *Historical Dictionary of Rhodesia/Zimbabwe,* Scarecrow, 1979. Contributor to encyclopedias and reference books, including *Book of Lists 2.* Contributor to history and African studies journals and newspapers.

WORK IN PROGRESS: A book on the Mfecane, in collaboration with William E. Rau, for G. K. Hall; *King Solomon's Mines: The True Story* (tentative title), an adventure novel set in late nineteenth-century Zimbabwe; *A Child's Dictionary of Forbidden Words;* science fiction stories.

SIDELIGHTS: Rasmussen writes: "I love to write, I want to go on learning forever, and I—like my fellow writers—dream of becoming rich and famous. I'm slowly moving away from the kind of arcane historical books I have been writing, and I have high hopes for the historical novel in progress."

*   *   *

REA, Gardner   1892-1966

OBITUARY NOTICE: Born August 12, 1892, in Ironton, Ohio; died December 28, 1966. Cartoonist, writer, and journalist. Rea is best known for his wiggly-lined, sparsely detailed cartoons that appeared in several magazines, including *Collier's, New Yorker, Saturday Evening Post, Life,* and *Judge.* He was also a drama critic for the *Ohio State Journal.* Collections of Rea's cartoons include *The Gentleman Says It's Pixies* and *Gardner Rea's Sideshow.* Obituaries and other sources: *Current Biography,* Wilson, 1946, February, 1967; *New York Times,* December 29, 1966; *Time,* January 6, 1967; *Newsweek,* January 9, 1967; *Publishers Weekly,* January 9, 1967.

*   *   *

REAMS, Bernard Dinsmore, Jr.   1943-

PERSONAL: Born August 17, 1943, in Lynchburg, Va.; son of Bernard Dinsmore (an Army major) and Eloise (a librarian; maiden name, Hickman) Reams; married Rosemarie Bridget Boyle, October 26, 1968; children: Andrew Dennet. *Education:* Lynchburg College, B.A., 1965; Drexel University, M.S. in L.S., 1966; University of Kansas, J.D., 1972. *Home:* 2353 Hollyhead Dr., Des Peres, Mo. 63131. *Office:* School of Law, Washington University, St. Louis, Mo. 63130.

CAREER: Rutgers University, College of South Jersey, Camden, N.J., assistant librarian, 1966-69; University of Kansas, Lawrence, assistant professor of law and law librarian, 1969-74; Washington University, St. Louis, Mo., assistant professor and law librarian, 1974-76, associate professor, 1976, professor of law and law librarian, 1976—. *Member:* American Bar Association, American Library Association, American Association of Law Libraries, American Society for Information Science, Special Libraries Association, Southwestern Association of Law Libraries (president, 1977-79), Beta Phi Mu, Phi Delta Phi, Coif.

WRITINGS: Law for the Businessman, Oceana, 1974; (with Paul E. Wilson) *Segregation and the Fourteenth Amendment in the States: A Survey of State Segregation Laws, 1865-1953,* William S. Hein & Co., 1975; (with Ellen L. Kettler) *Historic Preservation Law: An Annotated Bibliography,* National Trust for Historic Preservation, 1976; *Reader in*

Law Librarianship, Information Handling Services, 1976; *Immigration and Nationality Law Review,* William S. Hein & Co., Volume 1, 1976, Volume 2, 1979; (with Charles R. Haworth) *Congress and the Courts: A Legislative History, 1787-1977,* William S. Hein & Co., 1978; (with J. Ray Ferguson) *Federal Consumer Protection: Laws, Rules, Regulations,* Oceana, 1979. Book review editor of *International Journal of Law Libraries;* member of editorial advisory board of Trans-Media Co.

WORK IN PROGRESS: Studying documentary material on federal price and wage control programs, 1917—; research on legal bibliography and immigration and nationality law.

SIDELIGHTS: Reams told an interviewer for the *St. Louis Countian* that "being a lawyer and a librarian is a nice blend of two professions. Identification of areas ripe for publishing is a natural outcome. I am constantly exposed to new trends in the law and at the same time involved in the day-to-day challenge of library development."

BIOGRAPHICAL/CRITICAL SOURCES: St. Louis Countian, March 14, 1978.

* * *

REDMAN, Ben Ray   1896-1961
(Jeremy Lord)

OBITUARY NOTICE: Born February 21, 1896, in Brooklyn, N.Y.; died August 1, 1961. Editor, journalist, author, translator, and poet. Redman was editor of *Travel* and *Spur* magazines, and also editor of the column "Old Wine in New Bottles" in the *New York Herald-Tribune.* He worked as vice-president in charge of production at Universal Pictures and wrote scenarios for Twentieth Century-Fox. Redman's works include *Masquerade, Edwin Arlington Robinson,* and *The Meeker Case,* in addition to several translations of French and Italian works into English. Obituaries and other sources: *New York Times,* August 3, 1961; *Publishers Weekly,* August 14, 1961; *Saturday Review,* August 19, 1961; *Who Was Who in America,* 4th edition, Marquis, 1968; *The Author's and Writer's Who's Who,* 6th edition, Burke's Peerage, 1971.

* * *

REED, Mark L(afayette) III   1935-

PERSONAL: Born September 26, 1935, in Asheville, N.C.; son of Mark L., Jr. (a businessman) and Edith (a teacher; maiden name, Murphy) Reed; married Martha B. Sibley (in special education), August 30, 1958; children: Victoria, Christina. *Education:* Yale University, B.A., 1957; Harvard University, M.A., 1958, Ph.D., 1962. *Home address:* Iris Lane, Chapel Hill, N.C. 27514. *Office:* Department of English, University of North Carolina, Chapel Hill, N.C. 27514.

CAREER: Harvard University, Cambridge, Mass., instructor in English, 1962-63; University of North Carolina, Chapel Hill, assistant professor, 1963-66, associate professor, 1966-71, professor of English, 1971—. Member of executive board of North Carolina Poetry Council, 1978—. Associate trustee of Dove Cottage Trust, 1968—; member of board of advisers of Warren Wilson College, 1973—. *Member:* Modern Language Association of America, South Atlantic Modern Language Association. *Awards, honors:* Fulbright scholar at Cambridge University, 1960-61; visiting fellow at Clare Hall, Cambridge, 1965-66; Guggenheim fellowship, 1965-66, 1970-71; fellowship from American Council of Learned Societies, 1980; grants from National Endow-

ment for the Humanities and American Philosophical Society.

WRITINGS: Wordsworth: The Chronology of the Early Years, 1770-1799, Harvard University Press, 1967; (contributor) A. R. Jones and William Tydeman, editors, *Coleridge: The Ancient Mariner and Other Poems,* Macmillan, 1973; *Wordsworth: The Chronology of the Middle Years, 1800-1815,* Harvard University Press, 1975. Associate editor of "Cornell Wordsworth Series," Cornell University Press, 1975—. Contributor of more than fifteen articles and reviews to literature journals.

WORK IN PROGRESS: An edition of Wordsworth's *The Prelude, 1800-1820,* for the Cornell Wordsworth series; *Wordsworth: The Chronology of the Later Years, 1815-1850,* with Paul F. Betz.

* * *

REEL, A(dolf) Frank   1907-

PERSONAL: Born June 30, 1907, in Milwaukee, Wis.; son of Herman (a merchant) and Blanche (Ullman) Reel; married Virginia Wentworth (a nurse), March 29, 1947; children: Thomas, Christopher, Jeffrey, Judy. *Education:* Harvard University, B.S., 1928, LL.B., 1931. *Politics:* Democrat. *Home address:* Leroy Ave., Tarrytown, N.Y. 10591. *Agent:* William Morris Agency, 1350 Avenue of the Americas, New York, N.Y. 10019. *Office:* Hess, Segall, Guterman, Pelz & Steiner, 230 Park Ave., New York, N.Y. 10017.

CAREER: Private practice of law in Boston, Mass., 1931-34; Roewer & Reel, Boston, law partner, 1934-47; American Federation of Radio Artists, New York City, executive secretary, 1947-54; Ziv Television Programs, Inc., New York City, executive vice-president, 1954-68; Metromedia Producers Corp., New York City, president, 1968-77; Hess, Segall, Guterman, Pelz & Steiner, New York City, attorney, 1977—. Member of board of trustees of Tarrytown, N.Y., 1958-62, corporation counsel, 1977—. *Military service:* U.S. Army; defense counsel for Japanese General Tomyuki Yamashita, 1942-46; became captain.

WRITINGS: The Case of General Yamashita, University of Chicago Press, 1949, reprinted, Farrar, Straus, 1971; *The Networks: How They Stole the Show,* Scribner, 1979.

* * *

REEVE, William Charles   1943-

PERSONAL: Born March 25, 1943, in Toronto, Ontario, Canada; son of Charles Frederick (a hydrotherapist) and Ena (Erskine) Reeve; married Katsue Hiraga, July 5, 1970. *Education:* University of Toronto, B.A. (with honors), 1966; Cornell University, M.A., 1967, Ph.D., 1970. *Home address:* R.R.1, Glenburnie, Ontario, Canada K0H 1S0. *Office:* Department of German, Queen's University, Kingston, Ontario, Canada.

CAREER: CORNELL University, Ithaca, N.Y., assistant professor of Germanic languages and literature, 1970-71; Queen's University, Kingston, Ontario, assistant professor of German, 1971—. *Member:* Canadian Association of University Professors of German.

WRITINGS: Georg Buechner, Ungar, 1979. Contributor to *Germanic Review.*

WORK IN PROGRESS: Heinrich von Kleist.

SIDELIGHTS: Reeve told *CA:* "Theatre has always been a major source of attraction and interest for me and hopefully I can add something to a greater appreciation of the German theatre by a North American audience."

REID, William H(oward) 1945-

PERSONAL: Born April 10, 1945, in Dallas, Tex.; son of Howard C. (a psychiatrist) and Lucile (an artist) Reid. *Education:* University of Minnesota, B.A., 1966, M.D., 1970; University of California, Berkeley, M.P.H., 1975. *Office:* Nebraska Psychiatric Institute, 602 South 45th St., Omaha, Neb. 68106.

CAREER: University of California, Davis, resident in psychiatry, 1970-71, 1973-75; University of Nebraska, Omaha, clinical and research psychiatrist at Medical Center and Nebraska Psychiatric Institute, 1977—. Lecturer at Northwestern University, 1978—; visiting associate professor at Rush Medical College, 1979—. Consultant in forensic psychiatry. *Military service:* U.S. Army, Medical Corps, chief of mental hygiene, 1971-73; became captain. *Member:* American Medical Association, American Psychiatric Association, American Public Health Association, American Academy of Psychiatry and Law, Association for the Advancement of Psychotherapy, American Association for the Advancement of Science.

WRITINGS: (Editor) *The Psychopath: A Comprehensive Study of Antisocial Disorders and Behavior,* Brunner, 1978; *Psychiatry for the House Officer,* Brunner, 1979; *Basic Intensive Psychotherapy,* Brunner, 1980; (editor) *Treatment of Antisocial Syndromes,* Van Nostrand, 1980.

Contributor: J. R. Lion, editor, *Diagnosis and Management,* Williams & Wilkins, 2nd edition, 1980; H. L. Morrison, editor, *Children of Depressed Parents,* Van Nostrand, 1980. Contributor of more than thirty articles to medical journals. Reviewer for *American Journal of Psychotherapy.*

WORK IN PROGRESS: Editing *The American Psychiatric Association International Symposium on Terrorism,* with David Soskis and Burr Eichelman, publication expected in 1981.

SIDELIGHTS: Reid told *CA:* "I am a clinical and research psychiatrist with professional interests in areas related to antisocial behavior, forensic psychiatry, terrorism, and intensive psychotherapy. My work involves living in two cities (Omaha and Chicago), and I enjoy travel for both professional meetings and recreation. My trusty dog Jock and I like to fish. He eschews my other habits, such as playing guitar and sitting in hot tubs. I should enjoy trying my hand at writing fiction; however, to date academic work has been both vocation and avocation."

*   *   *

REIDA, Bernice 1915-

PERSONAL: Born March 15, 1915, in Brooklyn, Iowa; daughter of George (a farmer) and Maude (Keysor) Lyman; married Truman W. Reida (a judge), September 26, 1934; children: Larry T., Linda Kay Reida Downey. *Education:* Buena Vista College, B.A. (magna cum laude), 1958; University of South Dakota, M.A., 1968; also attended Simpson College and Drake University. *Politics:* Republican. *Religion:* Methodist. *Home and office:* 312 Third St., Lakeview, Iowa 51450.

CAREER: Sac City High School, Sac City, Iowa, history teacher, 1953-77; writer, 1977—. Instructor at Buena Vista College, 1970-74. *Member:* P.E.O. Sisterhood, National Education Association (member of national board of directors, 1963-67), United Methodist Women, Iowa Council for Social Studies (member of board of directors), Iowa State Education Association (member of board of directors, 1963-67), Eastern Star.

WRITINGS—All with Ann Irwin: *Hawkeye Adventure,* Graphic Publishing (Lake Mills, Iowa), 1966, revised edition, 1975, teacher's manual, 1967, student workbook, 1967; *Hawkeye Lore,* Pella Publishing, 1967; *Moon of the Red Strawberry* (juvenile novel), Aurora, 1975; *Until We Reach the Valley* (juvenile novel), Avon, 1979. Author of "Merry Christmas in the Past," a series syndicated by Des Moines Register and Tribune Syndicate, 1972. Contributor to education journals, regional magazines, and newspapers, including *Iowan.*

WORK IN PROGRESS: A romance novel.

SIDELIGHTS: Bernice Reida told *CA:* "My interest in writing came from the dearth of material on Iowa history. *Hawkeye Adventure* was written for students, but adults also enjoy it (an unexpected bonus). It proved to be a springboard for the next three books. *Hawkeye Lore* contains tidbits of Iowa history.

"The juvenile novels are based on historical events. *Moon of the Red Strawberry* is the story of Little Cloud, a young Sioux Indian who participates in the Battle of the Little Big Horn. Little Cloud's bravery during the battle wins him a place of honor, but his youthful triumph is soon replaced by the grim reality of the price to be paid for bravery. The white man's vengeance makes it necessary for the Sioux to move to a reservation or escape to Canada. The title, *Moon of the Red Strawberry,* is Sioux language for the 'Month of June.'

"*Until We Reach the Valley* is the story of a group from Wales who had been converted to the Mormon faith and emigrated to America to live in the 'Land of Zion'—Utah. The year is 1856 and the railroad had been built no farther west than Iowa City, Iowa. They built handcarts on the banks of the Iowa River and walked the rest of the way to Salt Lake City, a distance of twelve hundred miles. Fourteen-year-old Sara Lewis and her family are part of the expedition and Sara is full of excitement as they begin the long trek across the country."

*   *   *

REIFEN, David 1911-

PERSONAL: Born July 30, 1911, in Plauen, Germany; son of Abraham and Ester Reifen; married Helena Gross, 1942 (deceased); children: Judith (Mrs. E. Ronen). *Education:* Attended London School of Economics and Political Science, London, 1945-48; University of Heidelberg, D.Phil. (magna cum laude), 1975. *Politics:* Labour. *Religion:* Jewish. *Home:* 7 Witkinstreet, Tel-Aviv 63 474, Israel.

CAREER: Tel-Aviv Municipality, Tel-Aviv, Palestine (now Israel), child welfare officer, 1935-44; Juvenile Court, Jerusalem, Israel, judge, 1950-65, chief judge, 1965-74; conducted research on juvenile delinquency in Israel, 1974-78; chief editor of *Society and Welfare* in Israel, 1978—. *Military service:* Israel Defence Army, 1948-49; became captain. *Member:* International Association of Youth Magistrates (vice-president, 1962—), Israel Society of Criminology. *Awards, honors:* First Chanan Rubin Book Prize from Chanan Rubin Fund, 1968, for *Ye'ud Umatarah;* First Chazani Prize in Social Work from Ministry of Welfare, 1976, for community service.

WRITINGS: The Juvenile Court in Israel, Ministry of Justice, 1964; *Patterns of Juvenile Delinquency Among Israeli Arabs,* Ministry of Welfare, 1964; *The Juvenile Court in a Changing Society,* University of Pennsylvania Press, 1973.

Not in English: *Noar Bamishpat* (title means "Youth in Court"), Mifaley Tarbut We-Chinuch, 1961; *Ye'ud Umatara* (title means "Mission and Vocation"), *Mifaleh Tarbut Wechinuch*, 1968; *Das Jugendgericht in Israel* (title means "The Juvenile Court in Israel"), de Gruyter, 1974; *Hakatin Ubet-Hamishpat Lanoar* (title means "The Minor and the Juvenile Court"), Hakibuth Hameuchad, 1978. Contributor to Hebrew, English, and French professional journals.

WORK IN PROGRESS: Cultural Components in Juvenile Delinquency Within a Changing Society (working title).

* * *

REIFF, Stephanie Ann 1948-

PERSONAL: Born September 14, 1948, in New York, N.Y.; daughter of Sol (a shoe manufacturer) and Sylvia (a shoe manufacturer; maiden name, Finkelstein) Reiff; married Michael Luftglass (an advertising and marketing director), January 2, 1977; children: Scott Brian. *Education:* Adelphi University, B.A., 1970; graduate study at Queens College of the City University of New York, 1970. *Politics:* Democrat. *Religion:* Jewish. *Home:* 279 Park Ave., Elberon, N.J. 07740. *Office:* Conceptual Designs, 2500 Johnson Ave., Riverdale, N.Y. 10463.

CAREER: Language arts teacher at junior high school in Lido Beach, N.Y., 1971; remedial reading specialist and literature teacher at elementary school in Watchung, N.J., 1972; *Reader's Digest*, Pleasantville, N.Y., senior educational editor, 1972-75; Conceptual Designs, Riverdale, N.Y., president and chief writer, 1976—.

WRITINGS: The Story Behind the Exorcist, Crown, 1974; *Bio-Modes: A Biology Lab Program*, Contemporary Perspectives, 1976; *Top-Pics Readers*, Reader's Digest Press, 1976; *The European Experiences*, Reader's Digest Press, 1976; *The American Experience*, Reader's Digest Press, 1976; *Industrial Training Systems for Business*, Contemporary Perspectives, 1977; *The Myths, Magic, and Superstition Series* (juvenile), twenty volumes, Raintree, 1977; *The Great Unsolved Mysteries Series* (juvenile), twenty volumes, Raintree, 1977; *Magic Numbers and Cards: Visions of the Future* (juvenile), Raintree, 1977; *Secrets of Tut's Tomb and the Pyramids* (juvenile), Raintree, 1977; *Elizabeth Blackwell: The First Woman Doctor* (juvenile), Contemporary Perspectives, 1978; *Counterpoint: The Sights and Sounds of Reading* (to accompany film), Contemporary Perspectives, 1978. Editor of *Together* and *Guidelines*, 1972-75.

WORK IN PROGRESS: Tell Me You Love Me, Stanley Lipshitz, a novel.

SIDELIGHTS: Reiff told *CA:* "My father asked for a refund because he thought private schooling did little for his rebellious daughter. With the birth of my son I have entered early retirement, though I am working on my first novel about the rise and fall of a Jewish American princess's empire. All resemblances to family members are purely intentional. I thought it was about time for a change of ratings from PG to R."

* * *

REIFLER, Samuel 1939-

PERSONAL: Surname is pronounced *Rye*-fler; born March 27, 1939, in Poughkeepsie, N.Y.; son of Nathan L. (in business) and Martha (an educator; maiden name, Gold) Reifler; children: Nelly. *Education:* Attended Columbia University, 1956-61. *Home and office address:* Hollow Rd., Clinton Corners, N.Y. 12514.

CAREER: Clerk at bookstore in New York, N.Y., 1961-65;

Bennett Junior College, Millbrook, N.Y., visiting lecturer in philosophy, 1969-71; writer, 1971—.

WRITINGS: I Ching: A New Interpretation for Modern Times, Bantam, 1973. Editor of *Regulation News*, 1975—, and *Barrytown Explorer*, 1978–.

WORK IN PROGRESS: "Literature in various forms."

* * *

REILLY, Edward R(andolph) 1929-

PERSONAL: Born September 10, 1929, in Newport News, Va.; son of John Randolph (a naval architect) and Florence (a musician; maiden name, Cowan) Reilly; married Evangeline Broderick (a custodian of a historic home), August 31, 1957; children: Sean, Catherine, Christopher. *Education:* University of Michigan, B.Mus., 1949, M.Mus., 1952, Ph.D., 1958. *Home:* 358 Hooker Ave., Poughkeepsie, N.Y. 12603. *Office:* Department of Music, Vassar College, Poughkeepsie, N.Y. 12601.

CAREER: Converse College, Spartanburg, S.C., associate professor, 1957-58, professor of music, 1958-62; University of Georgia, Athens, associate professor, 1962-64, professor of music, 1964-69; Vassar College, Poughkeepsie, N.Y., visiting professor of music, 1969-70; University of Georgia, professor of music, 1970-71; Vassar College, professor of music, 1971—, chairman of department, 1976-79. Visiting professor at San Francisco State College, summer, 1962, and at Boston University, summer, 1979. *Military service:* U.S. Army, 1953-55. *Member:* Internationale Gustav Mahler Gesellschaft (member of board of directors, 1978—), American Musicological Society (member of national council), Music Library Association, Gustav Mahler Society of America (vice-president, 1979—).

WRITINGS: (Translator and author of notes) J. J. Quantz, *On Playing the Flute*, Faber, 1966; *Quantz and His Versuch: Three Studies*, American Musicological Society, 1971; *Gustav Mahler und Guido Adler* (translated by Herta Singer-Blaukopf), Universal Editions (Vienna, Austria), 1978. Contributor to music journals and *Georgia Review*.

WORK IN PROGRESS: A Catalogue of the Musical Manuscripts of Gustav Mahler; Mussorgsky's Boris Godunov: A Musical and Dramatic Study.

SIDELIGHTS: Reilly writes: "My serious interest in music history developed during my high school days. Although no longer active as a performer, during my first ten years in college teaching I also functioned as an instructor of percussion students, and took part in a considerable number of concerts and opera productions. I have been most interested in improving the library holdings at all of the institutions at which I have served. At Converse College I instituted a series of Baroque music festivals. I also wrote and announced a number of radio and television programs.

"For some years my interests have taken me into research on composers Mahler and Mussorgsky, and on the whole range of musical developments in the latter part of the nineteenth century and the first decades of the twentieth."

* * *

REIMAN, Jeffrey H. 1942-

PERSONAL: Born July 23, 1942, in New York; son of Max Albert (a jeweler) and Shirley (Hoch) Reiman. *Education:* Queens College of the City University of New York, B.A., 1963; Pennsylvania State University, Ph.D., 1968. *Residence:* Washington, D.C. *Office:* School of Justice, American University, Washington, D.C. 20016.

CAREER: American University, Washington, D.C., assistant professor, 1970-73, associate professor, 1973-77, professor of criminal justice, 1977—. *Member:* American Society of Criminology, American Philosophical Association, Phi Beta Kappa.

WRITINGS: In Defense of Political Philosophy, Harper, 1972; (editor with Emilio Viano) *The Police in Society,* Lexington Books, 1974; *The Rich Get Richer and the Poor Get Prison,* Wiley, 1979.

SIDELIGHTS: Reiman comments: "Much of my work reflects my unique position as a trained philosopher teaching in a criminal justice program."

* * *

REIN, Martin   1928-

PERSONAL: Born April 17, 1928, in New York, N.Y.; son of Max and Esther (Stranger) Rein; married Mildred Steinberg, February 5, 1927; children: two. *Education:* Brooklyn College (now of the City University of New York), B.A., 1950; Columbia University, M.S.S.W., 1954; Brandeis University, Ph.D., 1961. *Home:* 40 Crafts Rd., Chestnut Hill, Mass. 02167. *Office:* Department of Urban Studies and Planning, Massachusetts Institute of Technology, Cambridge, Mass. 02139.

CAREER: Brownsville Boys Club, Brooklyn, N.Y., program director, 1950-52; James Weldon Johnson Community Center, New York, N.Y., supervisor of gang project, 1954-56; East Tremont Young Men's-Young Women's Hebrew Association, Bronx, N.Y., executive director, 1956-59; Clark University, Worcester, Mass., lecturer in sociology, 1960-62; Bryn Mawr College, Bryn Mawr, Pa., began as associate professor, became professor of social work and social research, 1962-70; Massachusetts Institute of Technology, Cambridge, professor of urban studies and planning, 1970—. Lecturer at University of Pennsylvania, 1965, 1967, 1968, University of Pittsburgh, 1968, and Albert Einstein College of Medicine, 1968; visiting professor at London School of Economics and Political Science, 1972, and Harvard University, 1976-80; adjunct professor at University of Michigan, fall, 1979. Fellow at Center for Advanced Study in the Behavioral Sciences, 1976. Member of executive committee of Harvard University-Massachusetts Institute of Technology Joint Center for Urban Studies, 1971—; member of National Research Council-National Academy of Sciences committees; consultant to Organization for Economic Cooperation and Development, Office of Child Development, and President's Task Force for the War on Poverty.

AWARDS, HONORS: National Institute of Mental Health grants, 1961 (for Barbados), 1963; senior Fulbright fellowship for London School of Economics and Political Science, 1966-67; Ford Foundation grant, 1969-71; fellow of Centre for Environmental Studies, London, 1969-70, 1971; grants from Department of Housing and Urban Development, 1972-73, Ford Foundation and Office of European and International Affairs, 1973-75, and Department of Health, Education and Welfare, 1975-77.

WRITINGS: An Organizational Analysis of National Agency's Local Affiliates in Community Contexts, Planned Parenthood Federation in America, 1961; *The Network of Agencies Providing Child Protective Services in Massachusetts,* Research Center, Graduate School of Advanced Study in Social Welfare, Brandeis University, 1964; (with Robert Morris and Robert Binstock) *Social Planning: A Feasible Approach,* Columbia University Press, 1966; (with Peter Marris) *Dilemmas of Social Reform: Poverty and Community Action in the United States,* Aldine-Atherton, 1967, 2nd edition, Aldine, 1973; *Social Policy: Issues of Choice and Change,* Random House, 1970; (with Sar Levitan and David Marwick) *Work and Welfare Go Together,* Johns Hopkins Press, 1972, 2nd edition, 1974; (with Judy Areen) *Youth Service Agencies,* Ballinger, 1976; *Social Science and Public Policy,* Penguin, 1976; *Knowledge and Action,* M. D. Sharpe, 1979.

Contributor: *Social Work Practice, 1963,* Columbia University Press, 1963; *Social Welfare Forum,* Columbia University Press, 1964; L. A. Ferman, J. L. Kornbluth, and A. Haber, editors, *Poverty in Affluence,* University of Michigan Press, 1965; Ben Seligman, editor, *Poverty as a Public Issue,* Free Press, 1965; Benjamin Schlesinger, editor, *Poverty in Canada and the U.S.A.,* University of Toronto Press, 1966; Howard S. Becker, editor, *Social Problems: A Modern Approach,* Wiley, 1966; W. A. Glaser and David Sills, editors, *The Government of Associations,* Bedminster Press, 1966; Leonard Goodman, editor, *Economic Progress and Human Welfare,* Columbia University Press, 1966; Mayer Zald, editor, *Organizing for Community Welfare,* Quadrangle, 1967; William C. Kvaraceus, John S. Gibson, and Thomas J. Curtin, editors, *Poverty, Education, and Race Relations: Studies and Proposals,* Allyn & Bacon, 1967; Chaim J. Waxman and J. Green, editors, *Poverty, Power, and Politics,* Grosset, 1968; Ferman and Kornbluth, editors, *Poverty in America,* University of Michigan Press, 1968; E. G. Jaco, editor, *Patients, Physicians, and Illness,* Free Press, 1969; Roland Warren, editor, *Politics in the Ghetto,* Atherton, 1969; William Ryan, editor, *Distress in the City,* Press of Case Western Reserve University, 1969; Harry Schatz, editor, *Social Work Administration: A Source Book,* Council on Social Work Education, 1969; Ralph Kramer and Harry Specht, editors, *Readings in Community Organization Practice,* Prentice-Hall, 1969.

Social Workers at Work: An Introduction to Social Work Practices, Simon & Schuster, 1970; Marc Pilisuk and Phyllis Pilisuk, editors, *Poor Americans: How the White Poor Live,* Transaction Books, 1971; F. G. Caro, editor, *Research,* Russell Sage Foundation, 1971; *The National Administration System,* Wiley, 1971; Harold Demone Jr. and Dwight Harshbarger, editors, *Handbook of Human Service Organizations in Context,* Behavioral Publications, 1973; J. E. Tropman and other editors, *Strategic Perspectives in Social Policy,* Markham, 1973; Allan P. Sindler, editor, *Policy and Politics in America: Six Case Studies,* Little, Brown, 1973; S. M. Miller and Bruno Stein, editors, *Incentives and Planning in Social Policy,* Aldine-Atherton, 1973; Lee Rainwater, editor, *Social Problems and Public Policy: Inequality and Justice,* Aldine, 1974; Alvin L. Schorr, editor, *Children and Decent People,* Basic Books, 1974; David Jones and Marjorie Mayo, editors, *Community Work II,* Routledge & Kegan Paul, 1975; Carol Weiss, editor, *Using Social Research for Public Policy Making,* Lexington Books, 1977. Also contributor to *The City,* edited by Murray Stewart, 1970.

Editor of social policy series for Random House, 1970; co-editor of *Encyclopedia of Social Work,* 1969-70. Contributor to *International Encyclopedia of the Social Sciences.* Contributor of about fifty articles to scholarly journals, including *Annals of the American Academy of Political and Social Science.*

WORK IN PROGRESS: A comparative study of family income in Britain, Sweden, and the United States, with Lee Rainwater.

SIDELIGHTS: Rein told *CA:* "I approach policy analysis from what I call a 'value critical' perspective. In this approach I try to uncover the critical value assumptions on which practice and policy rests, that is, the implicit normative framework that organizes thought and action."

*   *   *

REINHARDT, Gottfried 1913-

PERSONAL: Born March 20, 1913, in Berlin, Germany; son of Max (a director) and Else (an actress; maiden name, Heims) Reinhardt; married Silvia Hanlon (a writer), March 15, 1944; children: Stephen. *Education:* Attended University of Berlin, 1931-32. *Home:* Hoyos Schloessl, Salzburg-Klessheim 5071, Austria. *Agent:* Irving Paul Lazar Agency, 211 South Beverly Dr., Beverly Hills, Calif. 90212.

CAREER: Writer, producer, and director of films and stage plays in the United States, England, Germany, and Austria. Worked for Metro-Goldwyn-Mayer, 1933-54, and Columbia Pictures, 1957-58. Director of motion pictures, including "Invitation," 1952, "Story of Three Loves," 1953, "Town Without Pity," 1961, and "Situation Hopeless—But Not Serious," 1965. Producer of motion pictures, including "Comrade X," 1940, "The Red Badge of Courage," 1951, and "Young Man With Ideas," 1952. *Military service:* U.S. Army, 1942-45; became sergeant.

WRITINGS: Der Liebhaber, Droemer, 1973, translation and adaptation by Reinhardt published as *The Genius: A Memoir of Max Reinhardt,* Knopf, 1979. Co-author of librettos for "Rosalinda," 1942, "Helen Goes to Troy," 1944, and "Polonaise," 1945. Also author of screenplays, including "I Live My Life," 1937, and "The Great Waltz," 1938.

WORK IN PROGRESS: I Almost Didn't Get Out of Bed, "a panorama of personal impressions."

SIDELIGHTS: Gottfried Reinhardt's *The Genius* is a memoir of his father, Austrian director and producer, Max Reinhardt. It is "both less and more than a formal biography," summarized Dorothy Samachson of the *Chicago Tribune.* "It is a living tribute from a son to an admired, famous father. It is a knowledgable survey of theater by a man who was himself a screenwriter and producer, and who also collaborated with his father in the American theater; it is a spirited defense of Max Reinhardt's methods, although Gottfried does, in all fairness, quote those who were less than wholehearted admirers of his father. And 'The Genius' is crowded with names and entertaining gossip about the notables with whom Reinhardt worked, those who took advantage of him, and those who loved him."

BIOGRAPHICAL/CRITICAL SOURCES: New York Times, November 2, 1979; *New York Times Book Review,* December 2, 1979; *Chicago Tribune Book World,* February 10, 1980.

*   *   *

REIT, Seymour 1918-
(Sy Reit)

PERSONAL: Born November 11, 1918, in New York, N.Y.; married wife, Edmee. *Education:* New York University, A.B., 1938. *Address:* c/o Golden Press, Western Publishing Co., Inc., 850 Third Ave., New York, N.Y. 10022.

CAREER: Animated cartoonist, editor, author. Bank Street College of Education, New York City, writer and editor, 1950—. Creator of "Casper the Friendly Ghost" cartoon character for television, 1940; has made television appearances on behalf of New York Board of Education. *Military*

service: U.S. Army Air Forces, World War II; camofleur and photo intelligence officer.

WRITINGS—Juvenile: *The King Who Learned to Smile,* Golden Press, 1960; (with Fred Dietrich) *Wheels, Sails, and Wings,* Golden Press, 1961; *Where's Willie?,* Golden Press, 1961; (with Frances Giannoni) *The Golden Book of Gardening,* Golden Press, 1962; *Look! Look! A Clown Book,* Golden Press, 1962; *Coins and Coin Collecting,* Golden Press, 1965; (editor) *America Laughs: A Treasury of Great Humor,* Crowell-Collier, 1966; *Count, Write and Read About What Goes Up and Down,* Golden Press, 1966; *Read and Write About What Is Big and Little,* Golden Press, 1966; (with Anne Bailey) *The West in the Middle Ages,* Golden Press, 1966; *Growing Up in the White House,* Crowell-Collier, 1968; *Dear Uncle Carlos,* McGraw, 1969; *Jamie Visits the Nurse,* McGraw, 1969; *Round Things Everywhere,* McGraw, 1969; (with Louis Goldman) *A Week in Hagar's World: Israel,* Crowell-Collier, 1969.

Animals Around My Block, McGraw, 1970; (with Claudia Andujar) *A Week in Bico's World: Brazil,* Crowell-Collier, 1970; *Child of the Navajos,* Dodd, 1971; *The Easy How-To Book,* Golden Press, 1973; *Rice Cakes and Paper Dragons,* Dodd, 1973; *Benvenuto,* Addison-Wesley, 1974; *Benvenuto and the Carnival,* Xerox Education Publications, 1976; *Race Against Death: A True Story of the Far North,* Dodd, 1976; *Bugs Bunny's Space Carrot,* Golden Press, 1977; *Ironclad! A True Story of the Civil War,* Dodd, 1977; *Tweety and Sylvester: Birds of a Feather,* Golden Press, 1977; *All Kinds of Planes,* Golden Press, 1978; *All Kinds of Ships,* Golden Press, 1978; *All Kinds of Trains,* Golden Press, 1978; *Bugs Bunny Goes to the Dentist,* Golden Press, 1978; *Sails, Rails, and Wings,* Golden Press, 1978.

Under name Sy Reit: (With Frank Jacobs) *Canvas Confidential: A Backward Glance at the World of Art* (humor), Dial, 1963; *The Ginghams* (juvenile), Golden Press, 1977; *Tiny and Tony* (juvenile), Golden Press, 1977; (with Jacobs) *Masquerade: The Amazing Camouflage Deceptions of World War II,* Hawthorn, 1978, published in England by R. Hale. Contributor to *Pre-School Library,* Encyclopaedia Britannica, 1972. Contributor to television shows, including "Captain Kangaroo."

SIDELIGHTS: Reit told *CA:* "*Masquerade* is my current book and a fairly important one. It deals with the whole story of camouflage in World War II, with many secrets revealed for the first time. (I served as both a camoufleur and a photo intelligence officer during the war on the staff of General Hoyt Vandenberg of the fabled Ninth Air Force.) The book is now in an English edition, and early in 1980 will be brought out by New American Library in paperback. My other books are almost all books for various younger readers, but with *Masquerade* I am broadening my efforts and horizons."

BIOGRAPHICAL/CRITICAL SOURCES: Times Literary Supplement, July 2, 1971.

*   *   *

REIT, Sy
See REIT, Seymour

*   *   *

RESNICK, Sylvia (Safran) 1927-
(Sheri Paul)

PERSONAL: Born February 22, 1927, in Chicago, Ill.; daughter of Abe (a tailor) and Sarah (an actress; maiden name, Green) Safran; married Max Resnick (an aeronautical designer), July 9, 1948; children: Barry Paul. *Education:* Attended Wright Junior College, 1945, and Los Angeles Junior College, 1946. *Religion:* Jewish. *Residence:* Canoga Park, Calif. *Agent:* Margo VanderMullen, 4317 Skillman Ave., Sunnyside, N.Y. 11104; and Amy Berkower, Writers House, Inc., 21 West 26th St., New York, N.Y. 10010.

CAREER: Free-lance writer, 1964-67; *Movie Life,* New York, N.Y., Hollywood editor, 1967-69; *Rona Barrett's Hollywood,* Hollywood, Calif., associate editor, 1970-72; *Bestways,* La Canada, Calif., feature writer and beauty editor, 1973-77; free-lance writer, 1977—. *Member:* Academy of Television Arts and Sciences, Hollywood Women's Press Club.

WRITINGS: Heat Wave (novel), Chariot Publishing, 1961; *Willing Flesh* (novel), Chariot Publishing, 1962.

Young adult novels: *Debbie Preston, Teenage Reporter: The Case of the Gypsy's Warning,* New American Library, 1972; *Debbie Preston and the Hollywood Mystery,* New American Library, 1972; *Debbie Preston and the Donny Osmond Mystery,* New American Library, 1973; *The Partridge Family Cookbook,* Curtis Books, 1973; *The Walton Family Cookbook,* Bantam, 1976; *Kristy McNichol* (biography), Xerox Education Publications, 1979.

Columns: "Las Vegas Go-Round," in *TV Star Parade,* 1967-70; "Daytime Television News," in *Rona Barrett's Hollywood,* 1970-72; "Film Reviews," in *Rona Barrett's Hollywood,* 1970-72, and *Hollywood Now,* 1972; "Your Beauty," in *Bestways,* 1973-77. Also author of column "A Word to the Wives," 1958-59. Contributor to magazines (sometimes under pseudonym Sheri Paul) and newspapers, including *Coronet, Pageant, Ladies Home Companion, Photoplay,* and *Big Valley.*

WORK IN PROGRESS: Nothing Ever Stays the Same, a young adult novel; *Hearts Are for Loving,* a family saga, 1938-75; *Intimate Strangers All,* an adult novel.

SIDELIGHTS: Sylvia Resnick told *CA:* "I feel that writers have an obligation to reflect an aura of hope, especially in the climate of uncertainty and noncommitment in which we presently live. Although I write about the everyday lives of my characters, often presenting them with real and tragic problems, in the end I must always leave them and my readers with *hope.* I think that there is too much of the negative being published: dwelling on and elaborating on sensational crimes in the name of literature. Readers should be involved with the characters in a book, but in a way that is enriching rather than merely titillating or shocking.

"When I was a child, the books of Pearl Buck and Louisa May Alcott were my mainstay. They were not works of pure sweetness and light, but they were uplifting and inspiring in their positive influence, in which the family was of uppermost importance even in the midst of strife and war or the sorrows of sickness and death. I am no Pollyanna, but I do feel I have a responsibility to use whatever talents I have to do whatever little or (hopefully) much I can to uplift while entertaining with words.

"Travel is my second love, and whenever there is enough time and money I am off on a trip. Although I have a passion for antiquity, it is primarily centered on the people of the past, rather than the things. The remnants of other times in the form of furniture, art, and especially old houses set up a chain reaction that eventually spins a story about the people to whom those objects belonged. And whenever I travel I manage to get to know as much as I can about one or more of the natives. I love people, and am excited by meeting with them and with the past that has shaped all of us.

"Another of my activities is the study of metaphysics and its entire scope of the mental and spiritual. I have taken classes in learning how to expand my psychic awareness, which I found fascinating. I believe very deeply in the need of all of us to return to the basics of caring for one another, and perhaps this can be made possible through an expansion of spiritual consciousness, tuning in to one another in a positive way."

AVOCATIONAL INTERESTS: Cooking, reading, dancing, watching old movies.

* * *

REYNOLDS, Valrae 1944-

PERSONAL: Born December 18, 1944, in San Francisco, Calif.; daughter of Ralph S. (an engineer) and Valberta (a secretary; maiden name, Eversole) Reynolds; married Richard Lee Huffman (an attorney), September 14, 1974; children: Elizabeth Anne, Margaret Lee. *Education:* Attended University of the Seven Seas (now Chapman College), 1964-65; University of California, Davis, B.A. (with honors), 1966; New York University, M.A., 1969. *Office:* Newark Museum, 43 Washington St., Newark, N.J. 07101.

CAREER: Metropolitan Museum, New York, N.Y., Ford Foundation museum intern, 1968; Brundage Collection, San Francisco, Calif., Ford Foundation museum intern, 1969; Newark Museum, Newark, N.J., assistant curator, 1969-70, curator of Oriental Collections, 1970—. Lecturer at museums and scholarly meetings; chairperson of symposia. *Member:* Asia Society, China Institute in America, Japan Society, Tibet Society, Phi Beta Kappa. *Awards, honors:* National Endowment for the Humanities grant, 1974.

WRITINGS: (Editor) *Tibetan Resources in America,* Asia Society, 1977; *Japanese Textiles,* Newark Museum, 1978; *Tibet: A Lost World,* Indiana University Press, 1979; *Chinese Art From the Newark Museum,* China Institute in America, 1980.

Co-author of films: "Journey to a Lost World," released by Newark Museum, 1974; "Beyond the Hidden Frontier," released by Newark Museum, 1975. Contributor of articles and reviews to museum and Asian studies journals. Editor of *Newark Museum Quarterly,* winter-spring, 1976, and *Tibetan Journal,* autumn, 1976.

SIDELIGHTS: Valrae Reynolds's research on Asian art and culture has taken her to Europe and Asia in 1968, 1969, 1974, and 1977.

She told *CA:* "I don't think of myself as an 'author' as all of my publications have developed out of museum projects. These have led me all across Asia (Iran to Korea) and forced me to be a generalist rather than a specialist. The focus, if these is any, on Tibet arises out of Newark's wonderful Tibetan collection and the enduring fascination of that land and its people (and the sad circumstances of the last twenty years)."

* * *

RHINE, J(oseph) B(anks) 1895-1980

OBITUARY NOTICE—See index for *CA* sketch: Born September 29, 1895, in Juniata County, Pa.; died February 20, 1980, in Hillsborough, N.C. Parapsychologist and writer. A pioneer in experimental parapsychology, Rhine added a new word to the lexicon: extrasensory perception (ESP). In his 1934 book by that name, Rhine gave an account of some 90,000 experiments in clairvoyance and mental telepathy. These experiments were conducted at Duke University's

Parapsychology Laboratory, which he helped to establish. A subsequent book, *New Frontiers of the Mind*, was a bestseller and made ESP a household term. Other publications by Rhine include *The Reach of the Mind* and *Parapsychology Today*. After his retirement from Duke University in 1965, Rhine founded his own research center, the Foundation for Research on the Nature of Man. Obituaries and other sources: *Current Biography*, Wilson, 1949; *American Men and Women of Science: The Social and Behavioral Sciences*, 12th edition, Bowker, 1973; *Who's Who in America*, 40th edition, Marquis, 1978; *Who's Who*, 131st edition, St. Martin's, 1979; *New York Times*, February 21, 1980; *Time*, March 3, 1980.

* * *

RHODE, Robert D(avid)   1911-

PERSONAL: Born May 30, 1911, in Jourdanton, Tex.; son of Hiram David (a teacher and school administrator) and Tennie P. (a teacher; maiden name, Tumlinson) Rhode; married Dorothy A. Kidd (a teacher), January 24, 1941; children: Janet Kay Rhode Sublett, David Leland. *Education:* University of Texas, B.A., 1933, M.A., 1935, Ph.D., 1940. *Politics:* Independent. *Religion:* Baptist. *Home:* 1001 West Yoakum, Kingsville, Tex. 78303. *Office:* Department of English, Texas A & I University, Kingsville, Tex. 78363.

CAREER: High school teacher of English in Clegg, Tex., and Harlandale, Tex., 1929-35; part-time teacher of English at Texas Wesleyan Academy in Austin, Tex., 1935-36; University of Texas, Austin, part-time tutor in English, 1936-38; Oklahoma College for Women, instructor in English and philosophy, 1938-39; Texas A & I University, Kingsville, assistant professor, 1940-43, professor of English, 1946-76, head of department, 1946-51, dean of Graduate School, 1951-62, vice-president and dean of university, 1962-71. *Military service:* U.S. Naval Reserve, active duty as instructor in naval aviation, 1942-46; became lieutenant commander. *Member:* Texas Association of College Teachers (past vice-president), Association of Texas Graduate Schools (president, 1958-59), Texas Joint English Conference (honorary life member), Kingsville Rotary Club (president, 1972-73), Kingsville Chamber of Commerce (past member of board of directors).

WRITINGS: (Editor) *Silver Spur*, Seton Village Press, 1942; (editor) *Cenizo Spray*, Banks Upshaw, 1947; (editor) *Yucca Trail*, Kingsville Publishing Co., 1951; (editor) *Cactus Tongues*, Edwards Bros., 1957; (contributor) Richard Cary, editor, *Appreciations of Sarah Orne Jewett: Twenty-Nine Interpretive Essays*, [Waterville, Me.], 1973; *Setting in the American Short Story of Local Color*, Mouton, 1975. Contributor of articles, poems, and reviews to professional journals, literary magazines, including *College English, Modern Language Quarterly*, and *Personalist*, and to newspapers.

WORK IN PROGRESS: A collection of poems; historical fiction about South Texas and Mexico in the last century.

SIDELIGHTS: Rhode writes: "Growing up in a family of itinerant school teachers in rural south Texas, I was at first a typical native son, with dog, pony, twenty-two rifle, and wanderlust. When no field work or produce-sorting job was available—and that was most of the time—I explored the mesquite and cactus trails through the neighboring ranch country. Later I hitchhiked to San Antonio and more distant cities, and then took up riding box cars across the country. Doubtlessly worried about my prospects, my father called me in out of the heat one summer afternoon and proudly presented me a massive set of books: 'Harvard Classics.' Reading, as an alternative to baseball, rodeo, and aimless wander-

ing, took hold of me with such ferocity that my parents became even more worried about my prospects.

"I have always had to deal with two strong conflicting yearnings: the desire for reading, contemplation, and writing, and the desire for full engrossment in practical and material affairs. As I reached maturity I was able to maintain a tentative, eclectic truce fashioned out of small segments of the thought of Emerson, Whitman, Plato, Jefferson, Franklin, Shelley, Arnold, and a host of others. Gradually I was able to confirm my ambition to be a university teacher, scholar, and writer of sorts. At first I assumed that, for a person working at such a lofty level, wealth and leisure for extensive travel and public involvement would be taken for granted. Indeed, as a beginning eighteen-year-old country high school teacher I enjoyed one of the highest cash incomes in the community. But ironically, twenty-odd years later, in a totally different economic situation, mature teachers with families were on the fringe of poverty.

"My response to this was not to abandon my profession, but to divert as much time and energy as necessary to other work with a higher income. I began to climb the academic-administrative ladder. I took each step with increasing reluctance because it carried me farther away from my proper element, though the new work and responsibility were always absorbing. Greedy for still more income, I diverted a great deal of spare time to private investment in business and land development and other speculative ventures in real estate. Though I regret the loss of time I have given over to business, I am happy that it has enabled me to travel through the world at will.

"To me writing has always been a collateral activity, not a proper means for earning a living. This is not to say that writing is not important; in fact, it stands near the peak of quality in all of human experience. A writer should never become a merchant, fashioning his wares for the market. His writing should be an intense function of his total personality, conscious and subconscious, releasing a body of thought as naturally as a woman gives birth to a child. The concept is an old one, but none could be more apt. Though some art is always involved in writing, as in any repeated human activity, the result is generally better when there is more matter and less art."

* * *

RHODES, Laura
See ROBINSON, Lisa

* * *

RICE, Max M(cGee)   1928-

PERSONAL: Born August 19, 1928, in Belton, S.C.; son of Max (an executive) and Janie (Haynie) Rice; married Vivian Barker, February 17, 1956; children: Vivian Ann, Carolyn B., Eunice T. *Education:* Furman University, B.A., 1949. *Religion:* Baptist. *Home and office:* Look Up Lodge, Route 1, Box 322-B, Travelers Rest, S.C. 29690.

CAREER: Rice Corp., Travelers Rest, S.C., president, 1961—. Director of Look Up Lodge, 1965—. *Military service:* U.S. Air Force, 1950-53; became first lieutenant.

WRITINGS: Common Sense Christianity, Moody, 1974; *When Can I Say I Love You?*, Moody, 1977.

WORK IN PROGRESS: You Can Take It With You.

SIDELIGHTS: Rice told *CA:* "My books result from leading retreats at Look Up Lodge. Numerous analogies are used to present practical Christianity in easily understood terms."

RICHARD, Lionel (Camille Paul) 1938-

PERSONAL: Born February 10, 1938, in Ormes-sur-Voulzie, France; son of Rene (an electrician) and Marcelle (Magnen) Richard; married Michelle Cayrol (a government electricity engineer); children: Stephane, Fanny. *Education:* Sorbonne, University of Paris, Ph.D., 1973. *Office:* Faculte des Lettres, University de Besancon, 30 rue Megevand, 25000 Besancon, France.

CAREER: High school teacher in Constantine, Algeria, 1964-65, Wassy, France, 1965-67, and Ermont, France, 1967-69; University of Besancon, Besancon, France, professor of comparative literature, 1970—. Poet, author, and translator. *Member:* Societe Francaise de Litterature Generale et Comparee (member of board of administrators, 1979-81), Societe des Gens de Lettres de France.

WRITINGS—In English: *Encyclopedie de l'Expressionnisme*, Somogy, 1978, translation by Stephen Tint published as the *Phaidon Encyclopedia of Expressionism*, Dutton, 1978. Translations of some of Richard's poems have appeared in *Poet* (Madras, India), July, 1971, and *Small Pond* (Stratford, Conn.), winter, 1972.

Other: *La Voix des flammes* (poems; title means "The Voice of the Flames"), [Paris], 1957; *Le Bois et la cendre* (poems; title means "The Wood and the Ashes"), [France], 1959; (translator) Nelly Sachs, *Brasier d'enigmes et autres poemes* (title means "Flame of Enigmas and Other Poems"), Denoel, 1967; (translator) Sachs, *Presence a la nuit* (poems; title means "Presence to the Night"), Gallimard, 1969; (translator with Paul Wiens) Eugene Guillevic, *Geheimnis der Dinge* (poems; title means "In the Secret of the Things"), Verlag Volk & Welt, 1969.

Nazisme et litterature (title means "Nazism and Literature"), F. Maspero, 1971; *Expressionnistes allemands: Panorama bilingue d'une generation* (text in French and in German), F. Maspero, 1974; *D'une apocalypse a l'autre* (title means "From One Apocalypse to Another"), Union Generale d'editions, 1976; *Le Nazisme et la culture* (title means "Nazism and Culture"), F. Maspero, 1978.

Contributor: (Author of introduction and notes) Ernst Glaeser, *La Paix* (novel; title means "The Peace"), F. Maspero, 1977; *Marinetti*, L'Age d' omme editeur, 1978; Jean Cassou, editor, *Encyclopedie du symbolisme* (title means "Encyclopedia of Symbolism"), Somogy, 1979; *L'Activisme hongrois, art pouvoir* (title means "The Hungarian Activism . . ."), Goutal-Darly, 1979-81; (author of introduction and notes) Rosa Meyer-Levine, *Vie et mort d'un revolutionnaire*, F. Maspero, 1980.

Screenplays; produced by French educational television: "Pierre Reverdy," 1970; "Regards critiques sur le surrealisme" (title means "Critical Regards on Surrealism"), 1972.

Director of publication: Roger Borderie, *Obliques*, Les Pilles, Volume I: *L'Expressionnisme allemand*, 1976, Volume II: *Lulu*, 1979, Volume III: *Brecht*, 1979. Contributor to literary journals, including *Mosaic* (Canada) and *Scena* (Italy).

WORK IN PROGRESS: A history of the Weimar Republic, publication by Hachette expected in 1981; a novel; books of selected poems and short stories.

SIDELIGHTS: Lionel Richard began writing poetry during his youth and considers it his only real need. Though he has not published poetry for several years, he continues to write it. He believes that his activity as a journalist and university specialist of literature is a consequence of his admiration for art and literature, and also a way to defend them. Richard is particularly interested in some of the lesser-known authors of the late nineteenth and the twentieth century.

* * *

RICHARDS, David Adams 1950-

PERSONAL: Born October 17, 1950, in Newcastle, New Brunswick, Canada; son of William Angus and Margaret (Adams) Richards; married Margaret McIntyre (a secretary), November 19, 1971. *Education:* Attended St. Thomas University. *Home:* 376 King George Highway, Newcastle, New Brunswick, Canada.

CAREER: Writer, 1970—. *Member:* Writers Union of Canada.

WRITINGS: Small Heroics (poems), New Brunswick Chap Books, 1973; *The Coming of Winter* (novel), Oberon Press, 1974; *Blood Ties* (novel), Oberon Press, 1976; *Dancers at Night* (short stories), Oberon Press, 1978.

Work represented in anthologies, including *Stories From Atlantic Canada*, 1972; *East of Canada*, 1976.

WORK IN PROGRESS: Another book, completion expected in 1980, for Oberon Press.

SIDELIGHTS: Richards told *CA:* "I write about the people of the Miramichi region in northeastern New Brunswick, a place famous for the birth of the Cunnard Shipping line, Lord Beaverbrook, and the Atlantic Salmon River of North America. It's one of the poorest parts of the poorest province in Canada, and in a strange way the most gifted, exuberant place I've been."

* * *

RICHARDSON, Arleta 1923-

PERSONAL: Legally changed surname to Richardson, 1944; born March 9, 1923, in Flint, Mich.; daughter of Clarence A. and Alma (Williams) Wright. *Education:* Spring Arbor College, A.A., 1944; Western Michigan University, B.S., 1949. *Religion:* Free Methodist. *Residence:* Los Angeles, Calif.

CAREER: Teacher at public school in Flint, Mich., 1945-47; Spring Arbor College, Spring Arbor, Mich., teacher of English and sociology, 1949-53; Los Angeles Pacific College, Los Angeles, Calif., instructor in speech and sociology and librarian, 1953-63; Light and Life Day School, Los Angeles, Calif., teacher, 1963-69; writer, 1969—. *Awards, honors:* Teacher of the year award from California Association of Christian Schools, 1968.

WRITINGS: It Takes a Spy (three-act play; first prodcued in Los Angeles, Calif. at Pacific Christian High School, May 10, 1975), Eldridge Publishing, 1977; *In Grandma's Attic,* (stories), David Cook, 1974; *More Stories From Grandma's Attic,* David Cook, 1979; *Still More Stories From Grandma's Attic,* David Cook, 1980. Contributor of articles and stories to religious periodicals, including *Christian Herald, Upper Room,* and *Church of God.*

WORK IN PROGRESS: A New Heart for Cami, a juvenile book about open-heart surgery; *There's One in Every Church,* short sketches.

SIDELIGHTS: Arleta Richardson told *CA:* "I began writing for Christian publications because I felt the quality of material for children and adults was not all it could be. I believe that Christian material should be decidedly superior to secular work, or there is no need for it at all. I do not mean that secular writers are inferior, but that being a Christian is not enough for a religious writer—he must also be a superior craftsman.

"My first book of stories, *In Grandma's Attic,* was first a series published in Sunday school newspapers. I had no idea that it would become a best-seller. The stories are memories of my grandmother's childhood, and apparently I have been in the right place at the right time with a return to a simple way of life. Of all the writing I've done, I've enjoyed the 'Grandma stories' the most.

"I also enjoy travel. I have been to Europe twice, Mexico, and more recently the Holy Land. I no longer teach school, but I am happy and thankful for the opportunity to write. God has been good to me, and I would like to have my life and my writings reflect my gratitude."

AVOCATIONAL INTERESTS: Reading, knitting.

*   *   *

RIDENOUR, George M(eyer)   1928-

PERSONAL: Surname is pronounced *Ride*-nour; born August 30, 1928, in Findlay, Ohio. *Education:* Wooster College, B.A., 1950; attended University of Vienna, 1951-52; Yale University, M.A., 1953, Ph.D., 1955. *Home:* 166 East 35th St., Apt. 16-E, New York, N.Y. 10016. *Office:* Graduate Center of the City University of New York, 33 West 42nd St., New York, N.Y. 10036.

CAREER: Yale University, New Haven, Conn., instructor, 1955-60, assistant professor of English, 1960-63; Haverford College, Haverford, Pa., associate professor of English, 1963-64; University of New Mexico, Albuquerque, professor of English, 1964-69; Graduate Center of the City University of New York, New York, N.Y., professor, 1969—. *Member:* Modern Language Association of America, Keats-Shelley Association, Wordsworth-Coleridge Association. *Awards, honors:* Fulbright scholar in Austria, 1951-52.

WRITINGS: The Style of Don Juan, Yale University Press, 1960; (editor and author of introduction) *Shelley: A Collection of Critical Essays,* Prentice-Hall, 1965; (editor and author of introduction) *The Selected Poetry of Browning,* New American Library, 1966; (editor and author of introduction) *Romantic Poetry,* Prentice-Hall, 1973. Contributor of articles and reviews to literature journals.

WORK IN PROGRESS: Studying Blake, Shelley, and Swinburne.

*   *   *

RIDGEWAY, Rick   1949-

PERSONAL: Born August 12, 1949, in Long Beach, Calif.; son of William (a sailor) and Elizabeth (in computer field; maiden name, White) Ridgeway. *Education:* Attended University of the Americas, 1969-70; University of Hawaii, B.A., 1971; graduate study at Catholic University, Lima, Peru. *Agent:* Perry Knowlton, Curtis Brown Ltd., 575 Madison Ave., New York, N.Y. 10022. *Office address:* P.O. Box 83, Malibu, Calif. 90265.

CAREER: Professional sailor and navigator, 1970-73; mountain climbing guide, 1973-76; actor and filmmaker, 1976—. *Member:* Screen Actors Guild, American Alpine Club (member of board of directors, 1979-82).

WRITINGS: The Boldest Dream: Twelve Who Climbed Everest, Harcourt, 1979; *The Last Step: The American Ascent of K2,* The Mountaineers, 1980. Contributor to *Outside.*

WORK IN PROGRESS: An article for *National Geographic;* a novel.

SIDELIGHTS: Ridgeway writes: "I am a filmmaker and writer, and consider my two nonfiction books stepping stones to my goal, which is writing adventure fiction.

"I am an active mountain climber. In 1978, I was one of the group of four who were the first Americans to climb the world's second highest mountain, and the first group to climb it without oxygen. In 1980, I participated in expeditions to an unexplored island in Tierra del Fuego and to West Irian, New Guinea."

BIOGRAPHICAL/CRITICAL SOURCES: National Geographic, May, 1979.

*   *   *

RIEGER, James H(enry)   1936-

PERSONAL: Born September 5, 1936, in New York, N.Y.; son of Henry George and Grace (Vargo) Rieger. *Education:* Harvard University, B.A., 1958, Ph.D., 1963; University of California, Berkeley, M.A., 1959. *Office:* Department of English, University of Rochester, River Station, Rochester, N.Y. 14627.

CAREER: Harvard University, Cambridge, Mass., instructor in English, 1963-65; University of California, Berkeley, assistant professor of English, 1965-69; University of Rochester, Rochester, N.Y., associate professor, 1969-76, professor of English, 1976—. *Member:* Modern Language Association of America, Keats-Shelley Association of America, Wordsworth-Coleridge Association, Byron Society, Rydal Mount Summer School Association. *Awards, honors:* American Philosophical Society grant, 1968; American Council of Learned Societies grant, 1969.

WRITINGS: The Mutiny Within: The Heresies of Percy Bysshe Shelley, Braziller, 1967; (contributor) Stuart Curran and Joseph A. Wittreich, Jr., editors, *Blake's Sublime Allegory,* University of Wisconsin Press, 1973; (editor) Mary Shelley, *Frankenstein,* Bobbs-Merrill, 1974; (contributor) Wittreich, editor, *Milton and the Line of Vision,* University of Wisconsin Press, 1975.

*   *   *

RIGG, H(enry Hemmingway) K(ilburn)   1911-1980
(Henry Kilburn)

OBITUARY NOTICE—See index for *CA* sketch: Born January 11, 1911, in Newcastle, Del.; died of cancer, February 11, 1980, in Annapolis, Md. Yachtsman and writer. An experienced yachtsman who sailed in many of the major ocean races, Rigg worked as the yachting editor of *New Yorker* from 1935 to 1939. Later he became editor and publisher of *Skipper* magazine. He was the author of *Rigg's Handbook of Nautical Etiquette.* Obituaries and other sources: *New York Times,* February 12, 1980; *Washington Post,* February 13, 1980.

*   *   *

RIGHTER, Carroll   1900-

PERSONAL: Born February 2, 1900, in Salem, N.J.; son of John Charles and Mary Caroline (Burch) Righter. *Education:* Attended University of Pennsylvania, 1917-19; Dickinson School of Law, LL.B., 1922. *Home:* 1801 North Curson Ave., Los Angeles, Calif. 90046. *Office:* P.O. Box 1921, Hollywood, Calif. 90028.

CAREER: Practicing astrologer, 1939—. Founder and president of Carroll Righter Astrological Foundation. Public speaker; involved in civic activities. *Awards, honors:* LL.D. from Dickinson School of Law, 1975.

WRITINGS: Astrology and You, Fleet Publishing, 1957; *Astrological Guide to Marriage and Family Relations,* Putnam, 1964; *Astrological Guide to Health and Diet,* Putnam, 1967; *Dollar Signs,* Putnam, 1971. Author of "Carroll Righter Astrological Forecast," a monthly column syndicated by McNaught Syndicate to about three-hundred-fifty newspapers around the world, 1950-77. Contributor to magazines and newpapers.

WORK IN PROGRESS: Planetary Aspects, publication expected in 1981; an autobiography, publication expected in 1982; research on career potentials.

SIDELIGHTS: Righter considers astrology to be one of God's gifts to humanity. He writes: "God, Creator of the heavens and the earth, of man and of woman, clearly and specifically interrelated the influence of the heavenly bodies on the Planet Earth and on human affairs. However, man alone, of all things on earth, is impelled by the awesome powers of the heavenly bodies, but, because God gave man free will, man is not compelled to behave according to the pressures from outer space to which he is subjected.

"Astrology provides man with alternatives, and choices, and of times in which to make his own judgments. Astrology does not make decisions. The proper function of the competent astrologian is to determine the effect of the stars and planets on individual humans and their enterprises every twenty-four hours, to the end that celestial and human power will best be coordinated and harmonized to the best possible achievements of the individual's desired wishes.

"While I recognize the symptoms of the general malaise of our times—stress, violence, social breakups, poverty, and unemployment—I view the near and the distant future as hopefully promising for mankind.

"It is in my charts that I am to be of service, and I endeavor to live up to the very best I can, that I can fulfill that heavenly demand."

AVOCATIONAL INTERESTS: European travel.

BIOGRAPHICAL/CRITICAL SOURCES: Time, March 21, 1969.

*   *   *

RIKHYE, Indar Jit   1920-

PERSONAL: Surname is pronounced "Ricky"; born July 30, 1920, in Lahore, India; came to United States in 1960; son of Madan Lal (a physician) and Raj (Rani) Rikhye; married Usha Erry, March 5, 1946 (divorced, December, 1973); married Cynthia de Haan (a United Nations employee), February 13, 1974; children: (first marriage) Ravi Indar Lall, Bhalinder. *Education:* Attended Government College, Lahore, India, 1935-38, and Defence Services Staff College, Wellington, India, 1951-52. *Religion:* Hindu. *Home:* 320 East 42nd St., New York, N.Y. 10017. *Office:* International Peace Academy, 777 United Nations Plaza, New York, N.Y. 10017.

CAREER: Indian Army, 1939-67, served in Middle East and Italy, 1941-45, commander of Indian contingent and chief of staff of United Nations Emergency Force in Gaza, 1957-60, commander of independent infantry brigade group in Ladakh, India, 1960, military adviser to secretary-general of United Nations in New York City, 1960-67, retiring as major general; United Nations, New York City, military adviser to secretary-general, 1967-69; International Peace Academy, New York City, president, 1970—. Chairperson of Symphony for the United Nations, 1975-79; consultant to Earthsat, Velsicol Corp., and Sungold International. *Member:* International Institute of Strategic Studies, India International Centre, India Institute of World Affairs, Royal Insti-

tute of International Affairs, Defense Services Club (New Delhi), Amateur Dramatic Club, Cavalry and Guards Club (London).

WRITINGS: Preparation and Training of United Nations Peacekeeping Forces, International Institute of Strategic Studies, 1964; *United Nations Peacekeeping Operations Higher Conduct,* International Information on Peace-Keeping Operations, 1964; (editor) *Peacekeeping in the Oceans,* Pacem in Maribus Publications, 1972; (with Michael Harbottle and Bjorn Egge) *Thin Blue Line,* Yale University Press, 1973; (with John Volkmar) *The Middle East and the New Realism,* International Peace Academy, 1975; *The Sinai Blunder,* Frank Cass, 1978; *Negotiating the End of Conflicts: Namibia and Zimbabwe,* International Peace Academy, 1979; (contributor) Henry Wiseman, editor, *Peacekeeping: An Appraisal and Proposal,* University of Guleph, 1979. Contributor to international affairs and military journals.

WORK IN PROGRESS: United Nations Peacekeeping Operations in the Congo, publication by Frank Cass expected in 1981; research on the use of technology for peacekeeping, third party roles in international peacekeeping in the Middle East and Cyprus, negotiating the end of South African conflicts, and developing skills for third party international mediation and negotiation.

SIDELIGHTS: Rikhye writes: "During my United Nations service I led several special missions for the secretary-general, including the Spinelli-Rikhye mission to Israel and Jordan in 1965 to deal with border raids. I was an observer in the Dominican Republic in 1965, and special adviser to U Thant during the Cuban missile crisis. I have traveled extensively to crisis areas in Cyprus, the Middle East, Southeast Asia, Africa, and Latin America.

"I am motivated by Gandhi's philosophy for nonviolent social change, Nehru's doctrine of *Panch Sheel* (nonalignment), and Hammarskjold's advocacy of the role of international organisations in promoting peaceful settlement of disputes and strengthening international systems for the maintenance of peace and security."

*   *   *

RITTER, Henry, Jr.   1920-

PERSONAL: Born April 14, 1920, in New York, N.Y.; son of Henry Hausmann (a physician) and Beatrice (Kamsler) Ritter; married Mary Caroline Loewe (a teacher and interior designer), June 10, 1949; children: Caroline Victoria, Mark Henry. *Education:* Lafayette College, B.A., 1941; New York University, M.D., 1945. *Home:* 349 Selby Lane, Atherton, Calif. 94025. *Office:* 2946 Broadway, Redwood City, Calif. 94062; and 888 Oak Grove Ave., Menlo Park, Calif. 94025.

CAREER: Bellevue Hospital, New York City, intern, 1945-46; Lincoln Hospital, New York City, intern, 1948, assistant resident in surgery, 1949-50; New York Polyclinic Hospital, New York City, resident in urology, 1950-52; private practice of urology in New York City, 1952-53, 1954-55, Redwood City, Calif., 1955—, Palo Alto, Calif., 1955-72, San Carlos, Calif., 1968-71, and Menlo Park, Calif., 1972—. Diplomate of American Board of Urology. Instructor at University of California, San Francisco, 1955-60; clinical instructor at Stanford University, 1960. Member of attending staff at Chope Community Hospital, Sequoia Hospital, and Stanford Hospital. Assistant visiting urologist at Morrisania City Hospital, assistant attending urologist at New York Polyclinic Medical School and Hospital, and clinical assistant urologist at Goldwater Memorial Hospital, all 1952-55. Instructor in cardiopulmonary resuscitation (CPR). Member of Holbrook-Palmer Foundation; former member of board of directors of San Mateo County Junior Museum. Public speaker; guest on radio and television programs. *Military service:* U.S. Army, surgeon in Medical Corps, 1946-48; became captain. U.S. Air Force, Medical Corps, 1953; became captain.

MEMBER: International College of Surgeons (regent for California, 1972-75; member of executive committee, 1975), International Wine and Food Society (member of governing board, 1973-75), International Family Planning Research Association, World Adoption International Fund International Social Service Organization (member of men's advisory board), World Health Organization, World Medical Association, Pan American Medical Association (member of board of directors, 1970-71), American Medical Association, American Urological Association, American Society for the Study of Sterility, National Kidney Foundation (member of board of directors, 1970-74), American College of Surgeons, Association of Military Surgeons of the United States, Industrial Medical Association, Society of the Medical Friends of Wine (Member of board of governors, 1967-70), American Association of Clinical Urologists, English Speaking Union, Royal Society of Health (fellow), American Medical Association of Vienna, Pacific Coast Sterility Society, Northwestern Medical Association, California Medical Association, California Academy of Medicene, New York Academy of Medicene, Northern California Urological Association, San Mateo County Medical Society (member of board of directors, 1972-75), Santa Clara County Medical Society, San Mateo County Surgical Society, Menlo Town Club, Redwood City Rotary Club, Atherton Civic Betterment League. *Awards, honors:* Certificates from California Medical Association, 1969-72, 1972-75, 1975-78, 1978-81; physicians' recognition awards from American Medical Association, 1973, 1974, 1975, 1976, 1977, 1978, 1979, 1980.

WRITINGS: From Man to Man, Harper, 1979. Contributor of about fifteen articles to medical journals.

SIDELIGHTS: Ritter comments: "I have a strong interest in dispelling the ignorance of the lay public regarding medical matters, particularly those concerning the male urinary tract and sexual apparatus. Great unhappiness with sex education as it exists in the schools and laying to rest many myths regarding the male life-style are discussed at length in my book, *From Man to Man.*"

*　　　*　　　*

ROADARMEL, Paul 1942-

PERSONAL: Born May 28, 1942, in Ithaca, N.Y.; son of Kenneth (a minister) and Catherine (a nurse; maiden name, Bobel) Roadarmel. *Education:* Syracuse University, B.F.A., 1964, M.F.A., 1971. *Politics:* Liberal. *Religion:* Protestant. *Home and office:* 118 East 91st St., New York, N.Y. 10028. *Agent:* Anita Diamant, Writer's Workshop, Inc., 51 East 42nd St. New York, N.Y. 10017.

CAREER: Painter and sculptor, 1966—; Hariana State Health Department, Chandigarh, India, director of art (publicity), 1968; commercial artist in Bangkok, Thailand, 1969; Syracuse University, Syracuse, N.Y., theatre instructor, 1971; painter, sculptor, and free-lance photographer in New York City, 1974; Dalton School, New York City, teacher, 1976; writer, 1979—.

WRITINGS: The Kaligarh Fault, Harper, 1979.

WORK IN PROGRESS: Research for *Good-by, Nina Rose,* a novel about refugees and Americans in Bangkok.

SIDELIGHTS: Roadarmel wrote: "I had been an artist for a number of years before starting off on a writing career. On reflection I have come to feel that the experience that I gained from my painting was essential because of the common need in both arts for composition in form and in reason.

"*The Kaligarh Fault* is a novel of adventure set, for the most part, in the high Himalayas. I chose this format because I felt I understood it and because I liked the idea of placing such a purposeful structure against the melange of Asian detail.

"India can be an almost miraculous experience for the Westerner, a confrontation with the best and the worst of the human drama. There is a modern nation there, waiting in the midst of its own history, and to participate in its daily life is to be granted witness to a remarkable epic.

"*Good-by, Nina Rose,* a new novel, is well along at the time of this writing. It is set in Bangkok in the mid-seventies and it deals with Indochina and her real refugees: the Laotians, the boat people, and the left-over foreigners, victims and derelicts like the rest, who are lost in the wake of the passing war."

*　　　*　　　*

ROALFE, William R(obert) 1896-

PERSONAL: Born August 22, 1896, in Mexico City, Mexico; son of William Robert (in business) and Isabel (Dunlop) Roalfe; married Mary Elizabeth Holland, July 7, 1934 (died, 1958); married Helen S. Snook, November 26, 1960 (died February 24, 1974); married Emma M. Brubaker, July 10, 1975; children: William Robert, Jr. *Education:* University of Southern California, LL.B., 1922. *Home:* 2404 Loring St., San Diego, Calif. 92109.

CAREER: Admitted to the Bar of California, 1921, and to the Bar of North Carolina, 1932; associated with O'Melveny, Millikan & Tuller, Los Angeles, 1922-23; in private practice, 1924-25; University of Southern California, Los Angeles, law librarian, 1927-30; Duke University, Durham, N.C., law librarian and professor of law, 1930-43; Office of Price Administration, Washington, D.C., attorney for Research and Opinion Bureau, 1943, chief counsel for Cereals, Feeds and Agricultural Chemicals Bureau, Food Price Division, 1944-45; Duke University, law librarian and professor of law, 1946; Northwestern University, Evanston, Ill., law librarian and professor of law, 1946-64, professor emeritus, 1964—; writer and researcher, 1964—. Member of executive committee of Commission to Study the Organization of Peace, 1966-73. *Member:* International Association of Law Librarians (president, 1959-62; member of board of directors, 1962-65), American Association of Law Librarians (member of executive committee, 1931-32, 1934-37; president, 1935-36), American Library Association, Coif (member of executive committee, 1949-52). *Awards, honors:* LL.D. from Temple University, 1959.

WRITINGS: The Libraries of the Legal Profession, West Publishing, 1953; (editor and contributor) *How to Find the Law,* 5th edition (Roalfe was not associated with earlier editions), West Publishing, 1957, 6th edition, 1975; *John Henry Wigmore, Scholar and Reformer,* School of Law, Northwestern University, 1962; *Poetic Utterance,* privately printed, 1976. Contributor to law, library, and education journals.

*　　　*　　　*

ROBBEN, John 1930-

PERSONAL: Born February 27, 1930, in New York, N.Y.;

son of Herman (a toy manufacturer's representative) and Edith (Ferris) Robben; married Margaret Burger (a psychiatric social worker), January 2, 1954; children: Susan, Janet, Ellen, John, Robert. *Education:* Fordham University, B.S., 1952. *Residence:* Old Greenwich, Conn. *Agent:* Al Hart, Fox Chase Agency, Inc., 419 East 57th St., New York, N.Y. 10022. *Office:* Robtoy, Inc., 177 Sound Beach Ave., Old Greenwich, Conn. 06870.

CAREER: Robtoy, Inc. (sales agency for toy manufacturers), Old Greenwich, Conn., president, 1954—. Member of board of directors of Dolly Toy Co. and Old Greenwich-Riverside Community Center (also vice-president). *Military service:* U.S. Navy, 1952-54.

WRITINGS: Coming to My Senses (autobiographical), Crowell, 1973. Contributor to magazines and newspapers, including *Reader's Digest* and *Cosmopolitan.*

WORK IN PROGRESS: Know Me From Adam, a personal account of a psychotherapeutic experience.

* * *

ROBERTSON, Heather Margaret 1942-

PERSONAL: Born March 19, 1942, in Winnipeg, Manitoba, Canada; daughter of Harry (a teacher) and Margaret (Duncan) Robertson; married David Hildebrandt, May 16, 1968 (divorced, 1974); married Andrew Marshall (a broadcaster and publisher), July 11, 1975; children: (second marriage) Aaron. *Education:* University of Manitoba, B.A., 1963; Columbia University, M.A., 1964. *Politics:* National Party of Canada. *Religion:* None. *Home:* 379 Hillsdale Ave. E., Toronto, Ontario, Canada M4S 1T9. *Agent:* Nancy Colbert, 44 Charles St. W., Toronto, Ontario, Canada M4Y 1R5.

CAREER: Winnipeg Tribune, Winnipeg, Manitoba, reporter and critic, 1964-66; radio producer in public affairs for Canadian Broadcasting Corp., 1969-71; *Maclean's* magazine, author of television column, "Television," television critic, and feature writer, 1971-75; free-lance writer, 1975—. *Member:* Periodical Writers Association of Canada (president, 1977-78), Writers Union of Canada, Association of Canadian Radio and Television Artists. *Awards, honors:* Woodrow Wilson fellow, 1963-64.

WRITINGS: Reservations Are for Indians (nonfiction), James Lorimer, 1970; *Grass Roots* (nonfiction), James Lorimer, 1973; *Salt of the Earth* (nonfiction), James Lorimer, 1974; *A Terrible Beauty: The Art of Canada at War,* James Lorimer, 1977. Contributor to Canadian magazines. Book review editor of *FM Guide.*

WORK IN PROGRESS: A historical novel covering the period 1914-45, publication by James Lorimer expected in 1981; research on twentieth-century Canadian history.

SIDELIGHTS: Heather Robertson comments: "I am fascinated by the literary potential of real people and real events, the attempt to render the raw material of specific human experience into words which not only capture its truth but reveal its meaning. I like to explore the boundaries between journalism and fiction, the point at which a real human being becomes a 'character' in a book."

* * *

ROBINSON, Corinne H(ogden) 1909-

PERSONAL: Born February 21, 1909, in Ettrick, Wis.; daughter of Albert Julius (a builder) and Nora Amanda (Onsrud) Hogden; married Howard West Robinson, September 9, 1944 (died, December, 1970); children: Glenn Adrian.

Education: University of Wisconsin, Madison, B.S., 1930; University of Cincinnati, M.S., 1934. *Politics:* Republican. *Religion:* Lutheran. *Home:* 3552 Woodcrest Ave., Newton Square, Pa. 19073.

CAREER: University of Michigan Hospital, Ann Arbor, intern, 1930-31; Children's Hospital, Research Foundation, Cincinnati, Ohio, research dietitian, 1931-41; Columbia-Presbyterian Medical Center, New York, N.Y., supervising dietitian and instructor in nursing, 1941-44; part-time instructor in nutrition and diet therapy at University of Pennsylvania Hospital and Temple University Hospital, 1947-52; Temple University, School of Medicine, Philadelphia, Pa., lecturer in nutrition, 1948-52; Temple University Hospital, Philadelphia, director of department of dietetics, 1952-53; Drexel University, Philadelphia, professor of nutrition and head of department of nutrition and food, 1953-67, professor emeritus, 1967—. Member of advisory committee of Delaware County Services for the Aging (president of committee, 1977, 1978); member of board of directors of Community Nursing Service, Chester, Pa.; member of Delaware County Human resources committee.

MEMBER: American Dietetic Association (past chairperson of diet therapy section), American Home Economics Association, Society for Nutrition Education, Nutrition Today Society, American Association of University Women, League of Women Voters. *Awards, honors:* Lindbach Award from Drexel University, 1962; named dietitian of the year by Pennsylvania Dietetic Association, 1968; D.Sc. from Drexel University, 1976; Marjorie Hulsizer Copher Award from American Dietetic Association, 1978.

WRITINGS: (With Fairfax T. Proudfit) *Nutrition and Diet Therapy,* 9th edition (Robinson was not associated with earlier editions), Macmillan, 1946, 12th edition published as *Normal and Therapeutic Nutrition,* 1961, 13th edition (sole author) published as *Proudfit-Robinson's Normal and Therapeutic Nutrition,* 1967, 14th edition published as *Normal and Therapeutic Nutrition,* 1972, 15th edition (with Marilyn R. Lawler), 1977; (with C. S. Davidson, L. E. Clifcorn, and others) *Sodium Restricted Diets,* National Academy of Sciences—National Research Council, 1954; (with Beth Heap) *Your Five-Hundred Milligram Sodium Diet,* American Heart Association, 1957; (with Heap) *Your One Thousand Milligram Sodium Diet,* American Heart Association, 1957; (with Heap) *Your Mildly Restricted Sodium Diet,* American Heart Association, 1957.

Basic Nutrition and Diet Therapy, Macmillan, 1965, 4th edition, 1980; *Nutrition Education for Nursing Students: A Teacher's Manual,* Macmillan, 1968; *Fundamentals of Normal Nutrition,* Macmillan, 1968, 3rd edition, 1978; (contributor) Irene L. Beland, editor, *Clinical Nursing: Pathophysiological and Psychosocial Approaches,* Macmillan, 1970; (with Lawler and Anne E. Garwick) *Case Studies in Clinical Nutrition,* Macmillan, 1977.

Contributor to *Cyclopedia of Medicine, Surgery, and Specialties.* Contributor of about thirty-five articles to nutrition and other scientific journals. Section editor of *American Journal of Clinical Nutrition,* 1952-62.

WORK IN PROGRESS: Revising *Normal and Therapeutic Nutrition,* with Marilyn R. Lawler, 16th edition, publication by Macmillan expected in 1982.

SIDELIGHTS: Corinne Robinson writes: "I am especially interested in furthering nutrition education as a coordinated, sequential program for all pupils in elementary and secondary schools, and as continuing education for adults through responsible use of the mass media. I believe that good nutritional practices can enhance the health, vigor, and longevity of people and, together with other health measures, can reduce the incidence of some chronic diseases.''

BIOGRAPHICAL/CRITICAL SOURCES: Journal of the American Dietetic Association, November, 1978.

* * *

ROBINSON, Helen Caister   1899-

PERSONAL: Born August 16, 1899, in Tavistock, Ontario, Canada; daughter of Edwin (a farmer) and Margaret (a teacher; maiden name, Ross) Caister; married Norman James Robinson, August 1, 1925 (died April, 1979); children: Donald C. *Education:* Attended high school in Tavistock and Stratford, Ontario. *Religion:* Anglican. *Home:* 35 Wynford Heights Cres., #1704, Don Mills, Ontario, Canada M3C 1L1.

CAREER: Writer, 1920—. Member of Big Sister Association of Metropolitan Toronto (past president and former member of board of directors) and local social planning council. *Member:* Writers Union of Canada, Canadian Authors Association, Canadian Society of Children's Authors, Illustrators, and Performers, Canadian Conference of the Arts, Women's Press Club of Toronto.

WRITINGS: Joseph Brant: A Man for His People, Longman, 1971; *Decades of Caring: The Big Sister Story,* Dundurn Press, 1979; *Miss Molly, the Brown Lady,* Dundurn Press, 1980. Work represented in juvenile anthology; contributor of adult and juvenile articles, stories, and poems to newspapers and to Canadian and American magazines, including *Canada, Presbyterian Life, Jack and Jill,* and *Outdoor Canada.* Contributing editor of *Your Home.*

WORK IN PROGRESS: A biographical novel for teenagers; a mystery novel for teenagers; a juvenile fantasy; an adult novel set in Stratford, Ontario.

SIDELIGHTS: Helen Robinson comments: ''I spent my childhood years on the farm on which my great-great-grandfather settled when he came to upper Canada from England in the early 1800's. From the age of eighteen I have lived in Toronto.

''In addition to my writing, I have for a number of years been interested in the promotion of better opportunities for youth.

''An ardent lover of nature, I spend many hours on back roads, and in woods in Ontario and elsewhere, where I get ideas for the natural history articles I write.''

AVOCATIONAL INTERESTS: Golf.

BIOGRAPHICAL/CRITICAL SOURCES: In Review, winter, 1972; *Quill & Quire,* October, 1979.

* * *

ROBINSON, Herbert Spencer
(Herbert Hespro)

RESIDENCE: New York, N.Y. *Address:* c/o Littlefield, Adams & Co., 81 Adams Dr., Totowa, N.J. 07512.

CAREER: Former professor of English at Pace College (now Pace University), New York City, and at City College of City University of New York, New York City.

WRITINGS: English and Shakesperian Criticism in the Eighteenth Century, Wilson, 1932, reprinted, Gordian Press, 1968; (under pseudonym Herbert Hespro) *What Your Dreams Mean,* Permabooks, 1949; (editor) Nathaniel Hawthorne, *The Scarlet Letter,* Globe Book Co., 1954; (with Knox Wilson) *The Encyclopaedia of Myths and Legends of*

All Nations, Garden City Books, 1960, revised edition, Ward, 1962, published as *Myths and Legends of All Nations,* Littlefield, Adams, 1976; (with others) *Dictionary of Biography,* Doubleday, 1966, revised edition, Littlefield, Adams, 1975.*

* * *

ROBINSON, Horace W(illiam)   1909-

PERSONAL: Born October 26, 1909, in Apache, Okla.; son of William Wesley (farm machinery wholesaler) and Ora (Moran) Robinson; married Gwendolyn Pauline West; children: Douglas John, Thomas Keith, Pamela Gayle Robinson Knowlton. *Education:* Oklahoma City University, B.A., 1931; University of Iowa, M.A., 1932; further graduate study at Stanford University. *Home:* 1671 Sylvan St., Eugene, Ore. 97403.

CAREER: University of Oregon, Eugene, instructor, 1933-42, assistant professor, 1942-49, associate professor, 1949-56, professor of theatre, 1956-75, professor emeritus, 1975—, director, designer, actor, and producer, artistic director of university and head of theatre area, 1946-71, founder of Festival of Arts and Carnival Theatre. Member of summer faculty at University of Montana; visiting professor at University of California, Los Angeles; Fulbright lecturer in Australia. Conducted overseas entertainment tour for United Service Organization and U.S. Department of Defense. Executive director of Northwest Drama Conference; theatre architecture consultant.

MEMBER: American Educational Theatre Association (past president), National Association of Schools of Theatre (past president), American Theatre Association (fellow), National Collegiate Players Association, Speech Association of America, U.S. Institute of Theatre Technology, National Theatre Conference, American National Theatre and Academy, American Association of University Professors, Western Speech Association, Lane County Auditorium Association (member of board of directors), Friars Club. *Awards, honors:* Fulbright fellow in Finland, 1963-64; gold award from American College Theatre Festival, 1973, for ''distinguished service to American theatre.''

WRITINGS: Architecture for the Educational Theatre, University of Oregon Books, 1970. Contributor to *Senior Adult Theatre,* Pennsylvania State University Press, 1980. Contributor to professional journals, including *Educational Theatre Journal, World Theatre, Shakespeare Quarterly, Theatre Arts, Exchange,* and *ARC News Letter, London.*

SIDELIGHTS: Robinson wrote: ''Although I have a high regard for my colleagues who write for publication, I regret that most of my literary output has been in the form of 'a prospectus for action.' Such writings include a number of one-act plays which have been produced extensively, but not published; a series of historical pageants on the Pacific Northwest with as many as three thousand actors on stage at one time; and extensive planning of theatres and auditoriums in the United States and elsewhere for high schools, colleges, universities, community theatres, and civic auditoriums. My national work (now after retirement) is concentrated largely in theatre architecture, college and university standards and accreditation, and the Senior Adult Theatre movement. Last year I was co-author of a national survey of that SAT activity (I covered the area west of the Mississippi) which was sponsored by the John F. Kennedy Center.

''As indicated by the above, I do not consider myself an author. I have been in academic theatre most of my life and this has required some skills as a writer, but they are all things to be implemented. In my case the finished product is not publication but 'the thing done.'''

* * *

ROBINSON, Lisa 1936-
(Laura Rhodes)

PERSONAL: Born September 3, 1936, in Baltimore, Md.; daughter of Walter H. (a clothing manufacturer) and Evalyn (a pianist; maiden name, Moritz) Swartz; married Neil Robinson, June 5, 1960 (divorced November, 1977); married Norman Kirmayer (an engineer), May 24, 1979; children: (first marriage) Karen, Susan, Bruce. *Education:* Attended Carleton College, 1954-55, and Johns Hopkins University, 1955-56; Union Memorial Hospital School of Nursing, R.N., 1959; American University, B.S.N.Ed., 1961; University of Maryland, Baltimore, M.S., 1965; University of Maryland, College Park, Ph.D., 1970. *Residence:* Baltimore, Md. *Office:* School of Nursing, University of Maryland, 655 West Lombard St., Baltimore, Md. 21201.

CAREER: Spring Grove State Hospital, Baltimore, Md., instructor in psychiatric nursing, 1965; Sinai Hospital, Baltimore, clinical specialist in psychiatry, 1965-67; University of Maryland, Baltimore, instructor, 1969-70, associate professor of nursing, 1972, assistant professor, 1972-74, associate professor, 1974-76, professor of psychiatry, 1976—. Distinguished visiting professor at Lackland Air Force Base, 1978, 1979; participant in and director of numerous seminars, workshops, and professional conferences; consultant. *Member:* International Association of Transactional Analysis, American Nurses Association, National League for Nursing, American Association of University Professors, Foundation of Thanatology, Sigma Theta Tau.

WRITINGS: (Under pseudonym Laura Rhodes) *Chastise Me With Scorpions,* Putnam, 1963; *Psychological Aspects of the Case of Hospitalized Patients,* F. A. Davis, 1968, 3rd edition, 1976; *Psychiatric Nursing as a Human Experience,* Saunders, 1972, 2nd edition, 1977; *Liaison Nursing: A Psychological Approach to Patient Care,* F. A. Davis, 1974.

Author of "Who Shall Riddle Me the How and the Why?," a film distributed by University of Maryland School of Nursing, 1972. Author of study guides. Staff writer for *Nursing '74,* 1974. Contributor of more than a dozen articles and reviews to nursing and health care journals, and to *McCall's.* Member of editorial board of *RN,* 1968-70, and *Journal of Psychiatric Nursing,* 1972-79; editor of *Free Associations,* 1974, 1976-77.

WORK IN PROGRESS: Psychiatric Liaison Nursing: A Theoretical Basis.

SIDELIGHTS: Robinson told *CA:* "I started to write my first book because I challenged myself to complete such a project. Now that I know I can do that, I write to share my thoughts and feelings with others. Sometimes my writing is an effort to communicate some nuance that I think nurses might not generally be aware of and I try to create some sort of situation in which they can see the event unfold before them, so that they do not have to grasp the nuance in the abstract.

"I became interested in liaison nursing because as a child I spent much time in the hospital. It was a lonely and frightening time, and I believe that my current efforts to comfort people have been, in part, an effort to comfort the child in myself."

ROBISON, David V.   1911(?)-1978

PERSONAL: Born c. 1911; died of cancer, November 30, 1978, in Woodstock, N.Y.; married wife, Naomi; children: Paula Robison Nickrenz, Deborah Robison Cohen, Joshua. *Education:* Attended University of Vienna; Columbia University, M.A., 1937. *Residence:* Woodstock, N.Y.

CAREER: Playwright. Writer for radio, movies, television, and documentary films in California for twenty-five years; instructor in music at Columbia University and Fisk University; assistant conductor of San Francisco Symphony Orchestra; chairman of Maverick Concerts, Woodstock, N.Y. *Member:* National Audubon Society. *Awards, honors:* Straw Hat award, Council of Stock Theatres, for the best play of the summer theatre season, 1971, for "Promenade, All!"

WRITINGS—Plays: "My Little Boy/My Big Girl," first produced in London at Mercury Theatre, c. 1968; "The Jew as a Character in Drama," first produced in Los Angeles, c. 1968; *Promenade, All!* (two-act; first produced on Broadway at Alvin Theatre, April 16, 1972), Samuel French, 1971.

SIDELIGHTS: "Promenade, All!" was Robison's best known play. This comedy opened at the Alvin Theatre in 1972 with such notable actors as Hume Cronym, Anne Jackson, Eli Wallach, and Richard Backus. The *New York Times* described the play as "amiable, at times rather too bland, and often too obvious, but it has a few really sharp lines and well-crafted performances."

For a time Robison served as chairman of the Maverick Concerts, a chamber-music series in Woodstock, N.Y.

OBITUARIES: New York Times, December 5, 1978.*

* * *

ROBISON, Nancy L(ouise)   1934-

PERSONAL: Born January 20, 1934, in Compton, Calif.; daughter of Iver and May (Ingersoll) Johnson; married Robert B. Robison (an administrative assistant), August 14, 1954; children: Jeff, Todd, Eric, Glenn. *Education:* Attended University of California, Los Angeles, and Pasadena City College, 1951, 1972-75. *Home:* 1700 Euclid Ave., San Marino, Calif. 91108.

CAREER: Film and television actress and model in Los Angeles, Calif., 1954-74; full-time writer, 1974—. *Member:* International P.E.N., Society of Children's Book Writers, California Writers Club, Southern California Council on Writing for Children and Young People.

WRITINGS—All juveniles: *Where Is Zip?,* Ginn, 1974; *Hang Glider Mystery,* Lantern Press, 1976; *Department Store Model Mystery,* Scholastic Book Services, 1977; *Where Did My Little Fox Go?,* Garrard, 1977; *The Missing String Ball,* Garrard, 1977; *Hang Gliding* (nonfiction), Harvey House, 1978; *Tracy Austin* (nonfiction), Harvey House, 1978; *UFO Kidnap!,* Lothrop, 1978; *The Other Place* (science fiction), Walker & Co., 1978; *On the Balance Beam,* Albert Whitman, 1978; *Space Hijack!,* Lothrop, 1979; *The Lizard Hunt,* Lothrop, 1979; *Baton Twirling* (nonfiction), Harvey House, 1979; *Nancy Lopez* (nonfiction), Childrens Press, 1979; *Janet Guthrie* (nonfiction), Childrens Press, 1979; *Mystery at Hilltop Camp,* Garrard, 1979; *Games to Play in the Pool,* Lothrop, 1980; *The Space Collection!,* Lothrop, 1980. Contributor of more than fifty stories and articles to magazines, including *Jack and Jill, Christian Science Monitor, Young World,* and *Boston Research,* and to newspapers.

WORK IN PROGRESS: Fiction, nonfiction, and science fiction for children and young people.

SIDELIGHTS: Nancy Robison writes: "I come from a Scandinavian background. My grandmother on my mother's side was a vaudeville actress and later a motion picture and television actress. She also wrote plays, so I came by my acting and writing careers naturally. When I was three years old I was adopted from that family into another one.

"My first article was published when I was fifteen, and it had to do with my experiences as a television actress. At this time I couldn't choose between careers. I loved to act and I loved to write, but writing meant I had to sit still and I wasn't ready to do that. I pursued a career in the theatre. It wasn't until 1974 that I got serious about writing children's books, and now I enjoy it so much I write every day.

"At this time I still haven't written the book I want to write or feel I am capable of writing. I suppose when I do write it my career will be over, so I'll just keep putting it off until I'm ready to retire.

"I enjoy travel and have been to Mexico, England, Scotland, and Wales, Norway, Sweden, Denmark, France, Belgium, and Germany. I find travel educational and plan to do more."

AVOCATIONAL INTERESTS: Tennis, skiing, sailing, swimming, baking breads and pastries.

*   *   *

ROBYNS, Gwen   1917-

PERSONAL: Born January 29, 1917, in Australia; daughter of William Arthur (a business director) and Margaret Jane (O'Connor) Robyns; married Paul von Stemann (a writer), October 22, 1946. *Education:* Attended girls' high school in Wellington, New Zealand. *Politics:* Liberal. *Religion:* Church of England. *Home:* Hollycourt Farm, North Leigh, Witney, Oxfordshire, England. *Agent:* Marchesa Ray Corsini, 12 Beekman Place, New York, N.Y. 10022.

CAREER: Journalist in New Zealand and England, 1938-64; free-lance writer, 1964—. *Awards, honors:* Edgar Award from Mystery Writers of America, 1978, for *The Mystery of Agatha Christie.*

WRITINGS: Vivien Leigh, A. S. Barnes, 1970; *Margaret Rutherford,* Leslie Frewin, 1972; *Wimbledon,* David & Charles, 1973; *Princess Grace,* McKay, 1976; *The Potato Book,* Stemmer House, 1977; *The Mystery of Agatha Christie,* Doubleday, 1978; *Princess Grace's Book of Flowers,* Doubleday, 1980. Contributor to British magazines and newspapers.

SIDELIGHTS: Gwen Robyns writes: "People, all kinds of people, are my main interest. As a trained reporter I like to draw the character of the person I am writing about and leave the reader to make his own decisions."

*   *   *

ROE, Daphne A(nderson)   1923-

PERSONAL: Born January 4, 1923, in London, England; came to the United States in 1953, naturalized citizen, 1958; daughter of Adrian (in business) and Lillian Marion (Adler) Anderson; married Albert S. Roe (a professor), May 18, 1954; children: David, Laura, Adrian. *Education:* University of London, M.B., B.S., 1945, M.R.C.P., 1948, M.D., 1950. *Politics:* Democrat. *Religion:* Episcopalian. *Home:* 116 North Sunset Dr., Ithaca, N.Y. 14850. *Office:* Division of Nutritional Sciences, Cornell University, Ithaca, N.Y. 14850.

CAREER: Royal Free Hospital, London, England, intern, 1946, A. M. Bird scholar in pathology, 1946-47; Bristol General Hospital, Bristol, England, senior house officer, 1948; St. John's Hospital for Diseases of the Skin, registrar, 1948-52, first assistant, 1952-53; Massachusetts General Hospital, Boston, research fellow, 1953-54; University of Pennsylvania, Philadelphia, research associate, 1954-57; Wilmington General Hospital, Wilmington, Del., attending physician, 1958-61; Cornell University, Ithaca, N.Y., 1961—, clinical nutritionist, 1961-63, began as assistant professor, 1963, became professor of nutrition, director of health rehabilitation project, 1974-78. Consulting dermatologist; adjunct professor at State University of New York Upstate Medical Hospital; attending physician at Tompkins County Hospital, Ithaca, N.Y. Registrar at Royal Free Hospital and Hospital for Sick Children, London, England, 1948-52. Research fellow at Harvard University, 1953-54.

MEMBER: American Medical Association, American Institute of Nutrition, American Association for the Advancement of Science, Academy of Dermatology, Society for Investigative Dermatology, American Public Health Association, Royal Society of Medicine (fellow), British Medical Association. *Awards, honors:* Chesterfield Medal, 1950; distinguished service award from *New York State Journal of Medicine,* 1966; book award from American Medical Writers Association, 1977.

WRITINGS: A Plague of Corn: The Social History of Pellagra, Cornell University Press, 1973; *Drug Induced Nutritional Deficiencies,* Avi, 1976; *Alcohol and the Diet,* Avi, 1979; *Clinical Nutrition for the Health Scientist,* CRC Press, 1979. Contributor to nutrition journals.

WORK IN PROGRESS: Research on drug-nutrient interactions and drug-induced fetal malnutrition.

SIDELIGHTS: Daphne Roe writes: "*A Plague of Corn* reflects my major interest in man-made diseases and the relationships between social issues and health problems."

AVOCATIONAL INTERESTS: History of science and art, children's books and their illustrators, travel (Europe, Virgin Islands, Guyana), painting, French cooking.

*   *   *

ROE, Kathleen Robson   1910-

PERSONAL: Born March 17, 1910, in London, Ontario, Canada; daughter of James L. (a farmer) and Inez (Taylor) Robson; married A. E. Roe. *Education:* University of Western Ontario, B.A., 1931. *Home:* 14 Nottawa Ave., Toronto, Ontario, Canada.

CAREER: Secretary for Ontario Provincial Government in Toronto; writer, 1975—. *Military service:* Canadian Women's Army Corps, 1939-45; mentioned in dispatches; received Oak Leaf Medal. *Member:* Theosophical Society.

WRITINGS: War Letters From the C.W.A.C., Kakabeka Publications, 1975.

WORK IN PROGRESS: "An oral history of a group of people living on an island in Toronto Harbour. These residents have been fighting expropriation for decades and consequently have become an unique community, many of whom are descendants of the original settlers."

SIDELIGHTS: Kathleen Roe comments: "*War Letters* is a book of letters written home to my parents during World War II, edited and published as written. Some of the flavor of the times, events, and places of that period of history has been preserved in these letters from a young girl."

ROGERS, Jack 1934-

PERSONAL: Born January 23, 1934, in Lincoln, Neb.; married Sharon Mangold; children: Matthew, John, Toby. *Education:* University of Nebraska, A.B., 1955; Pittsburgh Theological Seminary, B.D., 1959, Th.M., 1964; Free University of Amsterdam, Th.D., 1967. *Religion:* United Presbyterian. *Office:* Fuller Theological Seminary, 135 North Oakland, Pasadena, Calif. 91101.

CAREER: Westminster College, New Wilmington, Pa., associate professor of religion and philosophy, 1963-71; Fuller Theological Seminary, Pasadena, Calif., professor of philosophical theology, 1971—. Fellow of Case Study Institute, Cambridge, Mass. *Member:* American Academy of Religion, American Philosophical Society.

WRITINGS: Scripture in the Westminster Confession: A Problem of Historical Interpretation for American Presbyterians, Eerdmans, 1967; *Confessions of a Conservative Evangelical,* Westminster, 1974; (editor and translator) G. C. Berkouwer, *Holy Scripture,* Eerdmans, 1975; (with wife, Sharon Rogers) *The Family Together,* Acton House, 1976; (with Louis Weeks and Ross Mackenzie) *Case Studies in Christ and Salvation,* Westminster, 1977; (editor) *Biblical Authority,* Word Books, 1977; (with Donald K. McKim) *The Authority and Interpretation of the Bible: An Historical Approach,* Harper, 1979.

* * *

ROHRER, Norman B(echtel) 1929-

PERSONAL: Born January 25, 1929, in Strasburg, Pa.; son of Walter M. (a farmer) and Naomi (Bechtel) Rohrer; married Virginia Rose Page (a nutritionist and writer), August 4, 1956; children: Randall Page, Russell Norman. *Education:* Wheaton College, Wheaton, Ill., B.A., 1953; Grace Theological Seminary, Winona Lake, Ind., M.Div., 1956. *Politics:* Conservative Republican. *Religion:* Presbyterian. *Home:* 5306 Stardust Rd., La Canada-Flintridge, Calif. 91011. *Office:* P.O. Box 707, La Canada-Flintridge, Calif. 91011.

CAREER: International Students, Inc., Washington, D.C., publications director, 1956-57; The King's Business, Los Angeles, Calif., editorial coordinator, 1957-58; *World Vision* (magazine), Pasadena, Calif., editor, 1958-64; Evangelical Press News Service, La Canada-Flintridge, Calif., director, 1965-78; Christian Writers Guild, La Canada-Flintridge, Calif., founder and director, 1968—. *Member:* Evangelical Press Association (executive secretary, 1965-78).

WRITINGS: Convict's Cry, Moody, 1968; *The Explo Story,* Regal Books, 1972; (with Peter Deyneka, Jr.) *Peter Dynamite, "Twice-Born Russian,"* Baker Book, 1975; *How to Eat Right and Feel Great,* Tyndale, 1977; *Why Am I Shy?,* Augsburg, 1978. Ghostwriter. Contributor of more than a thousand articles to magazines.

WORK IN PROGRESS: Why Am I Angry?, with Philip Sutherland, for Augsburg; a biography of Leighton Ford, brother-in-law of evangelist Billy Graham.

SIDELIGHTS: Rohrer comments: "I write chiefly for the inspirational press. I have a rather ordinary mind, but have been gifted with a strong constitution and a propensity toward hard work. I've traveled to sixteen foreign countries as director of the Evangelical Press News Service, a weekly collection of top religious news. I now teach writing by mail through the Christian Writers Guild."

He tells prospective students: "Throughout human history men have been materialistic and insensitive to higher values. Nothing too new about that. But until our day the majority of men and women have had *some* concern for their souls and for the life to come. How tragic it is that, in an age when we challenge the frontiers of the universe, the 'typical American' is chiefly absorbed in playing games. The writer is in a position to help change the picture."

* * *

RONNS, Edward
See AARONS, Edward S(idney)

* * *

RORTY, Winifred Raushenbush 1894(?)-1979

OBITUARY NOTICE: Born c. 1894, in New York; died of a heart attack, December 30, 1979, in Princeton, N.J. Sociologist and author of a number of books dealing with social science. Rorty was the secretary of the American Civil Liberties Union's committee on race relations during the 1940's. She also contributed articles to magazines, including *Commentary* and *Harper's*. Her works include *How to Dress in Wartime* and *Robert Park: Biography of a Sociologist.* Obituaries and other sources: *New York Times,* January 1, 1980.

* * *

ROSE, Alan Henry 1938-

PERSONAL: Born May 23, 1938, in New York, N.Y.; son of Mannie and Frances (Zimmern) Rose; married Maureen Kearney (a banker), September 26, 1976. *Education:* University of Pennsylvania, B.A., 1960; Indiana University, Ph.D., 1970. *Home:* 20 West 64th St., #27c, New York, N.Y. 10023. *Office:* Davis Publications, 380 Lexington Ave., New York, N.Y. 10017.

CAREER: University of New Hampshire, Durham, professor of English, 1969-76; Davis Publications, New York, N.Y., managing editor, 1976—.

WRITINGS: Demonic Vision: Racial Fantasy and Southern Fiction, Archon Books, 1978. Contributor to literature journals and literary magazines, including *Centennial Review* and *New England Quarterly.*

* * *

ROSE, Jeanne 1940-

PERSONAL: Born January 9, 1940, in Stockton, Calif.; daughter of Arnold M. and Aline LaRamee (LaLancette) Colon; married Ernest Kamamo Dias (a moving van employee; marriage ended); married Orville Jock Griffis (in sales; marriage ended); married Michael Shannon Moore (an artist; marriage ended, 1978); children: Amber Antonia, Bryan LaRamee. *Education:* Studied at University of Hawaii, 1958, and Hopkins Marine Station, 1959; San Jose State College, B.S., 1960; graduate study at University of Miami, Coral Gables, Fla. *Politics:* "Man working with nature." *Religion:* "Earth, sun, moon." *Home:* 219 Carl St., San Francisco, Calif. 94117.

CAREER: Agricultural Research Station, Leesburg, Fla., field assistant, 1961-63; Rock 'n' Roll Coutouriers, San Francisco, Calif., designer, 1965-71; New Age Body Care Products, San Francisco, Calif., owner, 1969—. Co-founder and organizer of Planned Layman Accessibility to Natural Studies; conducts seminars. Instructor at University of California extensions in Santa Cruz and San Francisco, 1972—, and California Community Colleges, 1975—; marine docent at Steinhart Aquarium, of California Academy of Science, 1974—; herbalist at Wholistic Health and Nutrition Institute, 1975-78; consulting herbalist. *Member:* Society of Herbalists, Herbalist Society of England.

WRITINGS: Herbs and Things: Jeanne Rose's Herbal, Grosset, 1972; *The Herbal Body Book,* Grosset, 1976; *Kitchen Cosmetics,* Panjandrum, 1978; *The Herbal Guide to Inner Health,* Grosset, 1979; *The Herbal: A Guide to Living,* Bantam Books, 1981. Contributor to magazines, including *Well-Being, McCall's, Harper's Bazaar, Town and Country, Herbalist,* and *Prevention.*

WORK IN PROGRESS: The Herbalist Mother and Child Book; Aromatherapy: Inhalations for the Mind, completion expected in 1982.

SIDELIGHTS: Jean Rose includes as a part of her education "several useless correspondence courses in herbal medicine," but adds that she has "a lifetime spent in the study of herbs and their uses." Her more formal education has included zoology, marine biology, ethnobotanical studies in Hawaii, honey bees, pesticides, and fungicides. She maintains her own aromatic garden and a laboratory where she manufactures herbal cosmetics.

Her lectures include herbal studies programs on subjects ranging from herbs for women through herbs for pets. Her present concentration is on aromatherapy and her audiences include New York City perfumers.

She writes: "The focal point of my research is the art and practice of using essential oils of flowers, fruits, and herbs to effect rejuvenation of the mind, skin, and body cells. Approaching the subject less from a chemical viewpoint than from a botanical and historical one, I am in accord with the medieval herbalists who felt that to smell green herbs continuously would keep anyone in the best of health. I make sleep or dream pillows that are mixtures of herbs, flowers, and scents designed to make insomniacs drowsy or stimulate the narcoleptics. By applying certain herbal oils during pressure point massage, deeper relaxation can be achieved and rejuvenation of cells can occur. Other custom-brewed potions are designed to relieve chronic headaches and will induce dreams. Scents such as vanilla, woodruff, tonka, and melilot seem to recall childhood, while thyme is used for its antiseptic, quieting smell.

"I want to demystify herbal use for people's health and well-being. I would like to see everyone taking a real and active part in their own health, using fewer chemical medicines and chemical cosmetics, and using more natural and wholesome products on and in their bodies."

*   *   *

ROSEN, Elliot A(lfred)   1928-

PERSONAL: Born July 20, 1928, in New York, N.Y.; son of Victor (a shoe worker) and Goldie (a seamstress; maiden name, Kuperman) Rosen; married Carol Mendes (an artist and teacher), June 30, 1957. *Education:* New York University, B.A., 1949, M.A., 1951, Ph.D., 1954. *Home address:* Beavers Rd., R.R. 3, Box 57, Califon, N.J. 07830. *Office:* Department of History, Rutgers University, 175 University Ave., Newark, N.J. 07102.

CAREER: Long Island University, Brooklyn, N.Y., lecturer in history and government, 1956-57; Rutgers University, Newark, N.J., instructor, 1957-61, assistant professor, 1961-66, associate professor, 1966-77, professor of history, 1977—, head of department, 1968-71. Visiting assistant professor at New York University, summer, 1962, visiting associate professor, summer, 1967. Chair of grants committee of Eleanor Roosevelt Institute, at Franklin D. Roosevelt Library, 1975-76. *Military service:* U.S. Army, 1955-56. *Member:* American Historical Association, Organization of

American Historians, American Academy of Political Science, Columbia University Seminar in American Civilization (associate). *Awards, honors:* Grants from Penrose Fund, American Philosophical Society, 1965-67 and 1977, Eleutherian Mills Hagley Foundation, 1977, Herbert Hoover Presidential Library Association, 1979, and Eleanor Roosevelt Institute, 1980.

WRITINGS: (With Raymond Moley) *The First New Deal,* Harcourt, 1966; *Hoover, Roosevelt, and the Brains Trust,* Columbia University Press, 1977. Contributor to history and political science journals.

WORK IN PROGRESS: The Age of the Conservative Coalition, 1934-44.

*   *   *

ROSENBERG, David A(aron)   1940-

PERSONAL: Born October 25, 1940, in New Jersey; son of Samuel and Sophie (Pinsky) Rosenberg; married Jean Gibson (an economist), July 6, 1969; children: Eli S., Elizabeth S. M. *Education:* University of Pennsylvania, B.S., 1963; Cornell University, M.P.A., 1967, Ph.D., 1972. *Home address:* R.D.1, Middlebury, Vt. 05753. *Office:* Department of Political Science, Middlebury College, Middlebury, Vt. 05753.

CAREER: U.S. Peace Corps, Washington, D.C., volunteer in Panchayat development program in Nepal, 1963-65; U.S. Department of State, Washington, D.C., research associate on policy planning staff, 1967; University of the Philippines, Quezon City, visiting research fellow in public administration, 1969-70; Cornell University, Ithaca, N.Y., visiting professor of comparative government, 1971-72; Middlebury College, Middlebury, Vt., assistant professor of political science, 1972—. Visiting professor at Cornell University, 1975, 1977-78, University of Philippines, and Australian National University. *Member:* American Political Science Association, Association for Asian Studies.

WRITINGS: (Contributor) Benedict Kerkvliet, editor, *Political Change in the Philippines,* University Press of Hawaii, 1974; *Economic Growth and Social Equity in Developing Countries,* Dartmouth College, 1976; *Guided Press in Southeast Asia: National Development Versus Freedom of Expression,* State University of New York at Buffalo, 1976; (contributor) Kimberley A. Bobo, compiler, *World Food and Hunger Studies,* Institute for World Order, 1977, 2nd edition, 1978; *Landlessness and Near-Landlessness in Developing Countries,* Center for International Studies, Cornell University, 1978; *Landless Peasants and Rural Poverty in Asia,* Center for International Studies, Cornell University, 1978; *Marcos and Martial Law in the Philippines,* Cornell University Press, 1979; *Landless Peasants and Rural Poverty in Indonesia and the Philippines,* Center for International Studies, Cornell University, 1979.

Co-author of "The World Room," a script for "20/20," aired by ABC-TV August 15, 1978. Contributor to Asian studies journals and U.S. Senate hearings.

WORK IN PROGRESS: The Politics and Morality of Foreign Aid for Population Control.

SIDELIGHTS: Rosenberg's studies have taken him to the Philippines, Thailand, Laos, Burma, Nepal, and India.

*   *   *

ROSENBLUM, Davida   1927-

PERSONAL: Given name is pronounced Da-*vee*-da; born

January 1, 1927, in New York, N.Y.; daughter of William Daniel (in insurance sales) and Augusta (a pianist; maiden name, Schwartz) Gottlieb; married Ralph B. Rosenblum (a film director), November 7, 1948; children: Emily, Paul. *Education:* Brooklyn College (now of the City University of New York), B.A., 1947; Columbia University, M.A., 1961; Graduate Center of the City University of New York, Ph.D., 1976. *Home:* 344 West 84th St., New York, N.Y. 10024. *Agent:* Wendy Lipkind Agency, 225 East 57th St., New York, N.Y. 10022. *Office:* Department of Speech and Theater, Herbert H. Lehman College of the City University of New York, Bronx, N.Y. 10468.

CAREER: Folksinger, live and on radio, 1945-49; teacher of speech and hearing handicapped children at public schools in New Rochelle, N.Y., 1961-71; Herbert H. Lehman College of the City University of New York, Bronx, N.Y., assistant professor of speech science, 1972—. Private practice in speech pathology, 1968-74. *Member:* American Speech, Language, and Hearing Association, Acoustical Society of America, Orton Society, New York State Speech and Hearing Association, New York Academy of Sciences, New York City Speech and Hearing Association.

WRITINGS: Relatives: A Family Memoir, Dial, 1979. Contributor of articles to *Brain and Language.*

WORK IN PROGRESS: Friends and Other Hardships (tentative title), nonfiction; research on speech perception and a method of grammatical assessment.

SIDELIGHTS: Davida Rosenblum told *CA:* "I am a living example of a late bloomer. I took my first job at age thirty-four, earned my Ph.D. just before I turned fifty, and published my first book just before the age of fifty-three.

"I also find myself an anachronism. I've been married to the same man for over thirty years, out of choice, and with (I think) increasing success. Looking back I can see that I've practiced a personal (but not political) feminism, often with great struggle. I'm grateful that my life is being lived *now,* at a time of transition for women, since I was able to partake from both the worlds I straddled. *Relatives* is, in part, a celebration of this."

*   *   *

ROSS, Frank (Xavier), Jr.   1914-
(R. Frank, Jr.)

PERSONAL: Born February 8, 1914, in Manhattan, N.Y.; married; wife's name, Rose Laura. *Education:* Attended Columbia University, 1936. *Home and office:* 20 Lillian Lane, Southampton, N.Y. 11968.

CAREER: Worked as an engineering draftsman in New York, N.Y., 1941-46; writer.

WRITINGS—Juvenile; all published by Lothrop, except as noted: *Trail Blazers of the Sky,* Wallace Hebberd, 1945; *Young People's Book of Jet Propulsion,* R. M. McBride, 1948, revised edition, Lothrop, 1959; *Guided Missiles: Rockets and Torpedoes,* 1951, revised edition, 1959; *Ben Franklin, Scientist,* 1952; *Flying Windmills: The Story of the Helicopter,* 1953; *Space Ships and Space Travel,* 1954, revised edition, 1961; *Radar and Other Electronic Inventions,* 1954; *Superpower: The Story of Atomic Energy,* 1955, revised edition, 1960; *Modern Miracles of the Laboratory,* 1957; *The World of Engineering,* 1958; *Automation: Servant to Man,* 1958.

New Worlds in Science: The Story of Scientific Research, 1960; *Partners in Science: The Story of the International Geophysical Year,* 1961; *The Con Men,* World Distributors,

1962; *The World of Medicine,* 1963; *Weather: The Science of Meteorology From Ancient Times to the Space Age,* 1965; *The World of Power and Energy,* 1967; *Transportation of Tomorrow,* 1968; *Stories of the States: A Reference Guide to the Fifty States and the U.S. Territories,* Crowell, 1969; *Model Satellites and Spacecraft: Their Stories and How to Make Them,* 1969.

Undersea Vehicles and Habitats: The Peaceful Uses of the Ocean, Crowell, 1970; *Space Science and You,* 1970; *Storms and Man,* 1971; *Racing Cars and Great Races,* 1972; *Historic Plane Models: Their Stories and How to Make Them,* 1973; *The Metric System: Measures for all Mankind,* S. G. Phillips, 1974; *Jobs in Marine Science: Commercial Fishing, Marine Construction, and Salvage,* 1974; *Flying Paper Airplane Models,* 1975; *Car Racing Against the Clock: The Story of the World Land Speed Record,* 1976; *Antique Car Models,* 1978; *Arabs and the Islamic World,* S. G. Phillips, 1978; *Space Shuttle,* 1979.

Juvenile; under pseudonym R. Frank, Jr.; all published by Crowell: *Work Boats,* 1954; *Experimental Planes: Subsonic and Supersonic,* 1955; *Ice Island: The Story of Antarctica,* 1957; *Flashing Harpoons: The Story of Whales and Whaling,* 1958; *Frozen Frontier: The Story of the Arctic,* 1961; *Burning Lands and Snow-Capped Mountains: The Story of the Tropics,* 1963.

WORK IN PROGRESS: The Model T Ford, a craft book.

*   *   *

ROSS, Ishbel   1897-1975

PERSONAL: Born in 1897 in Sutherlandshire, Scotland; came to United States in 1919, naturalized in 1922; died September 21, 1975, in New York, N.Y.; daughter of David and Grace (McCrone) Ross; married Bruce Rae (an editor), 1922; children: Catriona. *Education:* Educated in Scotland. *Residence:* New York, N.Y.

CAREER: New York Herald Tribune, New York, N.Y., general-assignment reporter and member of editorial staff, 1919-33; writer, 1933-75.

WRITINGS: Through the Lich-Gate: A Biography of the Little Church Around the Corner, W. F. Payson, 1931; *Marriage in Gotham,* A. L. Burt, 1933; *Ladies of the Press: The Story of Women in Journalism by an Insider,* Harper, 1936, reprinted, Arno, 1974; *Fifty Years a Woman,* Harper, 1938; *Isle of Escape,* Harper, 1942; *Child of Destiny: The Life Story of the First Woman Doctor,* Harper, 1949; *Margaret Fell: Mother of Quakerism,* Longman, 1949; *Journey Into Light: The Story of the Education of the Blind,* Appleton, Century, Crofts, 1951; *Proud Kate: Portrait of an Ambitious Woman,* Harper, 1953; *Rebel Rose: Life of Rose O'Neal Greenhow, Confederate Spy,* Harper, 1954; *Angel of the Battlefield: The Life of Clara Barton,* Harper, 1956; *First Lady of the South: The Life of Mrs. Jefferson Davis,* Harper, 1958; *The General's Wife: The Life of Mrs. Ulysses S. Grant,* Dodd, 1959.

Silhouette in Diamonds: The Life of Mrs. Potter Palmer, Harper, 1960; *Grace Coolidge and Her Era: The Story of a President's Wife,* Dodd, 1962; *Crusades and Crinoline: The Life and Times of Ellen Curtis Demorest and William Jennings Demorest,* Harper, 1963; *An American Family: The Tafts, 1678 to 1964,* World Publishing, 1964; *Charmers and Cranks: Twelve Famous American Women Who Defied the Conventions,* Harper, 1965; *Taste in America: An Illustrated History of the Evolution of Architecture, Furnishings, Fashions, and Customs of the American People,* Crowell, 1967;

Sons of Adam, Daughters of Eve, Harper, 1969; *The Expatriates*, Crowell, 1970; *The Uncrowned Queen: The Life of Lola Montez*, Harper, 1972; *The President's Wife: Mary Todd Lincoln*, Putnam, 1973; *Power With Grace: The Life of Mrs. Woodrow Wilson*, Putnam, 1975. Also author of novel, *Promenade Deck*, and numerous magazine articles for Office of War Information, 1933-36.

SIDELIGHTS: Prior to becoming a highly praised author of novels, nonfiction, and biographies, Ishbel Ross enjoyed a successful career as a journalist with various newspapers in Canada and the United States. During her fourteen-year stint with the *New York Herald Tribune*, she covered such notable stories as the Hall-Mills murder case, the kidnapping of Charles A. Lindbergh's child, and the death of Thomas Alva Edison. In 1933, however, Ross left the newspaper world to devote herself more completely to her writings and her family.

Ross is primarily known for her books dealing with the lives of the women behind famous men. In *The President's Wife: Mary Todd Lincoln,* Ross attempts to portray Mrs. Lincoln as an important historical figure in her own right. The rather erratic first lady "emerges as a complex woman who suffered not only during her own lifetime, but afterwards at the hands of the Lincoln myth makers," related E. G. Detlefsen.

Ishbel Ross departs from biography in *The Expatriates* to concentrate on a two-hundred year survey of Americans who have extensively lived, worked, or traveled abroad. "In this fast-paced account," reported Donald Gropman, "Miss Ross presents a quick history of expatriates from Ben Franklin through the travelers on the Grand Tour, from Hemingway and Fitzgerald through the Peace Corps and the Hippies.... The book has enough scholarship to be sound and enough style to be fun."

BIOGRAPHICAL/CRITICAL SOURCES: Harper's, April, 1970; *Time*, May 15, 1972; *Best Sellers*, May 15, 1972, July 1, 1973, August, 1975; *Booklist*, July 15, 1972, October 1, 1973, October 15, 1973; *Atlantic*, August, 1975.

OBITUARIES: New York Times, September 23, 1975; *AB Bookman's Weekly*, December 1, 1975.*

* * *

ROSSI, Sanna Morrison Barlow   1917-
(Sanna Morrison Barlow)

PERSONAL: Born October 10, 1917, in Johnson City, Tenn.; daughter of James Stanley (a lawyer) and Emily (Miller) Barlow; married Anthony Rossi (in business), September 11, 1959. *Education:* Attended Columbia Bible College, 1936-39, and East Tennessee State Teachers College (now Tennessee State Universtiy), 1940-41. *Religion:* Baptist. *Home:* 1800 Point Pleasant Ave., Bradenton, Fla. 33505.

CAREER: Bible teacher at schools in Reidsville, N.C., 1941-43, and Union, S.C., 1943-45; director of child evangelism in Greensboro, N.C., 1945-47; junior high school teacher in Jonesboro, Tenn., 1947-48; Gospel Recordings, Los Angeles, Calif., missionary, 1949-59; writer, 1959—.

WRITINGS—All under name Sanna Morrison Barlow: *Mountains Singing*, Moody, 1952; *Light Is Sown*, Moody, 1956; *Arrows of His Bow*, Moody, 1960; *A Man's Hand*, Gospel Recordings, 1965; *God's City in the Jungle*, Tyndale, 1975.

WORK IN PROGRESS: An account of India and New Guinea, for Gospel Recordings; poems.

SIDELIGHTS: Sanna Rossi writes: "The urgency of reaching out to the earth's primitive people with the Christian message that uplifts them has been the motivation for my books. The earlier ones were to make known the dynamic ministry of records in tribal tongues, and the last was to reveal the challenging life-investment of missionaries working with a Peruvian tribe that resulted in the tribe's transformation."

* * *

ROTH, Leland M(artin)   1943-

PERSONAL: Born March 22, 1943, in Harbor Beach, Mich.; son of Leland Monroe (a minister) and Margaret (an organist; maiden name, Martin) Roth; married Carol Mangold (an editor and typist), June 25, 1965; children: Amanda Catherine. *Education:* University of Illinois, B.Arch., 1966; Yale University, M.Phil., 1970, Ph.D., 1973. *Residence:* Eugene, Ore. *Office:* Department of Art History, University of Oregon, Eugene, Ore. 97403.

CAREER: University of Illinois, Urbana, instructor in architecture, 1966-67; Ohio State University, Columbus, instructor in art history, 1971-73; Northwestern University, Evanston, Ill., assistant professor of art history, 1973-78; University of Oregon, Eugene, assistant professor of art and architectural history, 1978—. *Member:* College Art Association of America, Society of Architectural Historians (member of board of directors, 1977-80), National Trust for Historic Preservation.

WRITINGS: (Editor) *A Monograph of the Work of McKim, Mead, and White, 1879-1915*, B. Blom, 1974; *A Concise History of American Architecture*, Harper, 1979. Contributor to architectural history journals.

WORK IN PROGRESS: Planned Company Towns, 1860-1925; research on Stanford White as an artist and on railroad stations for the Northern Pacific Railroad.

SIDELIGHTS: Roth told *CA:* "My research and writing interests are simultaneously broad and highly focused in scope. My *Concise History of American Architecture*, originally written for an encyclopedic history of American art, has been published separately. This surveys the full sweep of building aesthetics, building technology, landscape architecture, and planning from before European settlement to the present. As I finished this I found myself tending towards guarded optimism concerning the future of American architecture in the 1980's, for though it may prove a difficult decade, architects and their clients seem to be more receptive to a pluralism of solutions. The rub will be in providing good housing for all groups of people. The more focused writing concerns the work of the prominent turn-of-the-century architects, McKim, Mead, and White. Continuing research on selected aspects of their work has led me into broader areas concerning industrial housing, and, most recently, building commissioned by the railroads from 1860 to 1940. I am also interested in the development of architectural rendering from 1860 to 1900, but my immediate interest is in visiting and documenting the major planned industrial housing villages from 1865 to 1920, from Maine to Washington and Ontario to Mississippi. The architects of these villages believed architecture has the power to interfere for good in human affairs, and the towns need to be studied to see what their long term effect has been."

* * *

ROTHMAN, Stanley   1927-

PERSONAL: Born August 4, 1927, in Brooklyn, N.Y.; son

of Jack (a cab driver) and Rose (Kleinberg) Rothman; married Eleanor Ruth Berman (a college administrator), August 12, 1956; children: David, Michael. *Education:* City College (now of the City University of New York), B.S.S., 1949; Brown University, A.M., 1951; Harvard University, Ph.D., 1958. *Politics:* Independent. *Religion:* Jewish. *Home:* 67 Country Way, Northampton, Mass. 01060. *Office:* Department of Government, Smith College, Northampton, Mass. 01060.

CAREER: City College (now of the City University of New York), New York, N.Y., lecturer in social science, summer, 1950; Smith College, Northampton, Mass., instructor, 1956-59, assistant professor, 1959-62, associate professor, 1962-67, professor, 1968-77, Mary Huggins Gamble Professor of Government, 1978—. Instructor at Harvard University, summers, 1957-58; senior lecturer at University of Massachusetts, summers, 1959-65; visiting assistant professor at Yale University, spring, 1962; visiting professor at Catholic University of Santiago, 1963, and Universidad Ibero America, 1966-67. Senior research fellow at Columbia University's Institute on International Change, 1979-81. Adviser to National Humanities Center; seminar director. *Military service:* U.S. Navy, 1945-46.

MEMBER: International Society of Political Psychology, American Political Science Association, Group for Applied Psychoanalysis, Phi Beta Kappa. *Awards, honors:* Fellowships from Ford Foundation, 1962-63, 1973-75, and Social Science Research Council, 1966-67; grants from National Institute of Mental Health, 1970-71, 1971-72, and National Science Foundation, 1972-74; honorary research associate in social relations at Harvard University, 1972-73.

WRITINGS: European Society and Politics, Bobbs-Merrill, 1970, 2nd edition (with David Scarrow and Martin Schein), West Publishing, 1977; (with Peter Rose and William Wilson) *Through Different Eyes,* Oxford University Press, 1973; (with George Breslauer) *Soviet Society and Politics,* West Publishing, 1977; (with S. Robert Lichter) *The Radical Impulse,* Oxford University Press, 1980.

Contributor: J. S. Roucek, editor, *Contemporary Ideologies,* Philosophical Library, 1961; Frank Munger and Douglas Price, editors, *Readings in Political Parties and Pressure Groups,* Crowell, 1964; Richard Rose, editor, *Studies in British Politics,* St. Martin's, 1966; Peter Rose, editor, *A Nation of Nations,* Random House, 1972; Vernon Van Dyke, editor, *Political Sciences: The Teacher and the Polity,* Humanities, 1977; Seweryn Bialer, editor, *Sources of Contemporary Radicalism,* Westview Press, 1977; S. M. Lipset, editor, *Emerging Coalitions in American Politics,* Institute for Contemporary Studies (San Francisco, Calif.), 1978; Sherman C. Feinstein, editor, *Adolescent Psychiatry,* Volume VII, University of Chicago Press, 1978; Lipset, editor, *America in the Third Century,* The Hoover Institution, Stanford University, 1979. Contributor of more than forty articles and reviews to academic journals and popular magazines, including *New Leader, America, Race,* and *Reporter.* Reviewer for *Quill.*

WORK IN PROGRESS: The New Class: A Psycho-Social Study, with S. Robert Lichter.

SIDELIGHTS: Rothman writes: "Most of my research experience prior to 1970-71 was in what might be called traditional political science, enabling me to broaden my understanding of motivational theory and research techniques. Since 1972 I have been involved in a large-scale study of the relationship between personality and political variables, using projective tests and associative interviews."

ROUSMANIERE, John 1944-

PERSONAL: Surname is pronounced Ru-ma-*near;* born March 10, 1944, in Louisville, Ky.; son of James A. (a fundraiser) and Jessie (a nurses' aide; maiden name, Pierce) Rousmaniere; children: William Pierce, Dana Starr. *Education:* Attended University of Pennsylvania, 1962-63; Columbia University, B.S. (with honors), 1967, M.A., 1968. *Home and office:* 100-23 Hope St., Stamford, Conn. 06906. *Agent:* Russell & Volkening, Inc., 551 Fifth Ave., New York, N.Y. 10017.

CAREER: U.S. Military Academy, West Point, N.Y., assistant professor of history, 1970-72; *Yachting,* New York City, associate editor, 1972-77; *Natural History,* New York City, senior editor, 1978; free-lance writer, 1978—. *Military service:* U.S. Army, 1969-72; became first lieutenant. *Member:* New York Yacht Club.

WRITINGS: A Glossary of Modern Sailing Terms, Dodd, 1975; (with Dennis Conner) *No Excuse to Lose,* Norton, 1978; (editor) *The Enduring Great Lakes,* Norton, 1979; *Fastnet, Force Ten,* Norton, 1980; *The Annapolis Book of Seamanship,* Simon & Schuster, 1981. Editor of newsletter of U.S. Yacht Racing Union; book review editor of *Yachting.*

WORK IN PROGRESS: A biography of Richard Henry Dana.

SIDELIGHTS: Rousmaniere told *CA:* "As editor and writer, I have tended to specialize in the subjects of boats and the sea, although my last two books have taken me into slightly different areas. *The Enduring Great Lakes* is a scientific study of the ecology of those bodies of water, which are so vulnerable in this day of proliferation of toxins. *Fastnet, Force Ten* is about the killer gale that swept across the three hundred boats sailing in the 1979 Fastnet yacht race, off England, a book about how people deal with overwhelming, irrational forces—a nautical war story, if you will."

*   *   *

ROWE, Erna (Dirks) 1926-

PERSONAL: Born March 24, 1926, in Winnipeg, Manitoba, Canada; daughter of Peter Henry (an educator and owner of a printing business) and Katarina (Goerzen) Dirks; married Beverley William Rowe, February 15, 1963. *Education:* Attended Hamilton Teachers College, 1943-44; Bethel College, North Newton, Kan., A.B., 1957; McMaster University, B.A., 1959; received Primary Education Supervisor's Certificate, 1960, and Special Education Specialist Certificate, 1976. *Religion:* General Conference Mennonite. *Home:* 33 King St., Apt. 1404, Weston, Ontario, Canada M9N 3R7. *Office:* Yorkwoods Public School, 25 Yorkwoods Gate, Downsview, Ontario, Canada M3N 1K1.

CAREER: Teacher at public elementary schools in Ontario, 1944-57; teacher at Hopi Indian reservation in Arizona, 1957-59; Mallow Road Public School, Don Mills, Ontario, teacher, 1959-66; Board of Education of Bourough of North York, Toronto, Ontario, teacher consultant, 1966-73; Yorkwoods Public School, Downsview, Ontario, teacher of perceptually handicapped children, 1973—.

WRITINGS: Giant Dinosaurs (juvenile), Scholastic Book Services, 1973.

WORK IN PROGRESS: Swimming and Flying Reptiles in the Days of the Dinosaurs (juvenile) for Scholastic Book Services.

SIDELIGHTS: Erna Rowe told *CA:* "As a teacher I have

been greatly frustrated in choosing library books for the first-grade level that were easy enough for a young reader to read himself. At one time, I was trying to teach a group of third and fourth-grade boys who were reading at first-grade level and were very difficult to motivate. However, their interest in dinosaurs, especially big ones, was insatiable. When I suggested branching out to another subject, they were unwilling, unless the subject was another huge creature like the woolly mammoth.

"In due time, I had quite a collection on dinosaurs, which I refined to be as easy-to-read as possible, and added humorous take-offs to balance the factual information. Many children have since enjoyed *Giant Dinosaurs* immensely.

"I am personally pleased that Tyrannosaurus Rex is the only meat-eater in my book. I would rather not write about violence, since I feel that there are better ways to settle disagreements than by force.

"I believe that helping underprivileged people during peacetime goes a long way to prevent bursts of discontent and violence. It was this belief that motivated me to work on an Indian reservation as a volunteer teacher. I sincerely believe that if many young people would donate a summer or a year or two to work with underprivileged people, much goodwill would be spread and perhaps wars prevented."

AVOCATIONAL INTERESTS: Music, reading, plants, cats.

* * *

ROWE, George E(rnest), Jr. 1947-

PERSONAL: Born September 9, 1947, in Hartford, Conn.; son of George Ernest (an engineer) and Selma (Schindler) Rowe; married Kathleen Karlyn, July 12, 1969; children: Elizabeth, Miranda, Helen. *Education:* Brandeis University, B.A. (magna cum laude), 1969; Johns Hopkins University, M.A., 1971, Ph.D., 1973. *Home:* 3920 East First St., Wichita, Kan. 67208. *Office:* Department of English, Wichita State University, Wichita, Kan. 67208.

CAREER: Wichita State University, Wichita, Kan., assistant professor, 1973-79, associate professor of English, 1979—. *Member:* Modern Language Association of America, American Association of University Professors, Phi Beta Kappa.

WRITINGS: Thomas Middleton and the New Comedy Tradition, University of Nebraska Press, 1979. Contributor to literature journals.

WORK IN PROGRESS: A book on the relationship between certain seventeenth-century dramatists and the literary tradition, completion expected in 1985; research on the relationship between historiography and literature during the English Renaissance.

SIDELIGHTS: Rowe comments: "My motivation is a desire to become the best possible scholar and teacher. I do not plan to publish an extraordinarily large number of books and articles; rather, I hope to publish works that make a genuine contribution to knowledge. My major area of interest is Renaissance literature."

* * *

ROY, John (Flint) 1913-

PERSONAL: Born February 19, 1913, in Yarmouth, Nova Scotia, Canada; son of Louis Joseph (in sales) and Hattie (Lewis) Roy; married Eveleen Leigh, September 9, 1944. *Education:* Attended high school in Arcadia, Nova Scotia. *Religion:* Anglican. *Home:* 27 Cunningham St., Ridgetown, Ontario, Canada N0P 2C0.

CAREER: Royal Canadian Mounted Police, policeman in training in Regina, Saskatchewan, and Ottawa, Ontario, 1937-39, policeman in Toronto, Ontario, 1939-50, in St. John's, Newfoundland, 1950-54, in Ottawa, Ontario, 1954-71, retiring as sergeant; writer, 1971—. Member of local museum board. *Member:* Burroughs Bibliophiles (honorary life member), Edgar Rice Burroughs Society (honorary life member), Ridgetown Historical Society (president, 1980—), Ridgetown Horticultural Society (past president). *Awards, honors:* Hugo Award from World Science Fiction Convention, 1965, for *ERB-dom;* Royal Canadian Mounted Police long service medal, 1957, with bar and two stars, 1962 and 1967.

WRITINGS: A Guide to Barsoom, Ballantine, 1976. Contributor to *ERBania* and *ERBivore.* Assistant editor of *ERB-dom,* 1963-68, associate editor, 1968-76.

SIDELIGHTS: Roy told *CA:* "I was an avid reader from early childhood, raised by an uncle who allowed me to read whatever I wanted and taught me to treasure my books. Everything from Tom Swift to Tarzan to the whole world of fantasy and science fiction was as natural to me as breathing. My twenty or so years in the records branch of the Royal Canadian Mounted Police, checking and correlating field reports, proved invaluable experience for reviewing and researching the Burroughs books. In quiet retirement, I now sit back and enjoy my library of science fiction books, juveniles, and 'pulp' magazines."

BIOGRAPHICAL/CRITICAL SOURCES: Ottawa Journal, February 29, 1964; *RCMP Quarterly,* January, 1973; *London Free Press,* June 24, 1974; *Windsor Star,* October 5, 1974; *Chatham Daily News,* January 6, 1978.

* * *

RUBINSTEIN, David M(ichael) 1942-

PERSONAL: Born November 9, 1942, in Chicago, Ill.; son of Jack (in business) and Florence (a teacher; maiden name, Atkin) Rubinstein; children: Jacob. *Education:* University of Colorado, B.A., 1965, Ph.D., 1974. *Religion:* Jewish. *Home:* 744 Bittersweet, Chicago, Ill. 60613. *Office:* Department of Sociology, University of Illinois at Chicago Circle, Chicago, Ill. 60680.

CAREER: Colorado College, Colorado Springs, instructor in sociology, 1972; University of Illinois at Chicago Circle, Chicago, associate professor of sociology, 1972—.

WRITINGS: (Contributor) Phil Weinberger, editor, *Sociology for Our Times,* Scott, Foresman, 1976; *Marx and Wittgenstein: Social Praxis and Social Explanation,* Routledge & Kegan Paul, 1980. Contributor to sociology journals. Book review editor of *Sociology of Work and Occupations,* 1974-77.

* * *

RUDD, Robert D(ean) 1924-

PERSONAL: Born January 10, 1924, in Terre Haute, Ind.; son of Paul Adams (a telegrapher) and Caroline (Rapp) Rudd; married Patricia Wampler (a librarian), June 6, 1944; children: Stephen M. *Education:* Indiana State University, B.S., 1947; University of Wisconsin—Madison, M.S., 1949; Northwestern University, Ph.D., 1953. *Politics:* Independent. *Religion:* Protestant. *Home:* 2927 East Dry Creek Place, Littleton, Colo. 80122. *Office:* Department of Geography, University of Denver, Denver, Colo. 80208.

CAREER: Ohio University, Athens, instructor, 1951-53, assistant professor of geography, 1953-56; University of Utah,

Salt Lake City, visiting assistant professor of geography, 1956-57; Oregon State University, Corvallis, assistant professor, 1957-60, associate professor, 1960-65, professor of geography, 1965-70; University of Denver, Denver, Colo., professor of geography, 1970—, head of department, 1973—. Research associate at University of Denver, 1963; research geographer for U.S. Geological Survey, 1977—; member of remote sensing subcommittee of Colorado Mapping Advisory Commission, 1978—. Participates in and directs professional meetings; consultant. *Military service:* U.S. Army Air Forces, weather officer, 1942-46; served in China-Burma-India theater; became first lieutenant.

MEMBER: Association of American Geographers (head of Remote Sensing Commission, 1971), American Society of Photogrammetry, Sigma Xi. *Awards, honors:* Grants from U.S. Geological Survey and Association of American Geographers, 1968-69; National Science Foundation fellow, 1969, 1971; grant from U.S. Geological Survey, 1974.

WRITINGS: (Contributor) Richard M. Highsmith, editor, *Case Studies in World Geography,* Prentice-Hall, 1961; (with Highsmith and J. Granville Jensen) *Conservation in the United States,* Rand McNally, 1962, 2nd edition, 1969; (contributor) John E. Estes and Leslie W. Senger, editors, *Readings in Remote Sensing: Techniques for Environmental Analysis,* Hamilton Publishing, 1973; *Remote Sensing: A Better View,* Duxbury, 1974, revised edition, 1981. Author of technical reports. Contributor to *Atlas of the Pacific Northwest* and *Encyclopedia Americana.* Contributor of more than a dozen articles to geography and other scientific journals. Guest editor of *RSEMS,* January, 1977.

WORK IN PROGRESS: Research on remote sensing applications to U.S. Geological Survey's geography program on land use mapping.

SIDELIGHTS: Rudd writes: "I had taught photointerpretation for ten years when remote sensing began to evolve. Fortunate to have been in on the developmental stages, I was afforded a perspective from which I could see the rapid advances of the technique for the remarkable phenomenon they represented. I also began to perceive a widening gap between those working in the field and those who were uninformed. The significance of the potential of the technique for all the world's people is such that I felt an effort to bridge that gap was necessary. I guess my own enthusiasm played a part also. At any rate, the result was a book which I hoped any educated lay person could read. It would have been easier to have used formulas in some sections, but formulas turn off many of the very people I wanted to reach. The book is not intended to be a textbook; its purpose is to introduce the subject and, hopefully, intrigue some to read beyond it."

*   *   *

RUDDELL, Robert B(yron)   1937-

PERSONAL: Born May 27, 1937, in West Virginia; son of Byron B. and Nell (Hossett) Ruddell; married Annette Arnold, June, 1961; children: Amy Rebecca, Robert Thomas. *Education:* West Virginia University, B.A., 1958, M.A., 1960; George Peabody College for Teachers, M.A., 1960; Indiana University, Ed.D., 1963. *Office:* School of Education, University of California, Berkeley, Calif. 94720.

CAREER: Developmental and Remedial Reading Clinic, Uniontown, Pa., director, 1959-61; elementary school teacher in Charleston, W.Va., 1955-57; reading supervisor for public schools in Uniontown, Pa., 1959-61; West Virginia University, Morgantown, instructor in graduate extension program, 1959-61; Indiana University, Bloomington, re-

search associate, 1961-63; University of California, Berkeley, assistant professor, 1963-67, associate professor, 1967-72, professor of education, 1972-79, co-director of language and reading development program, 1971-79, acting dean of graduate school, 1978-79. Past member of state education committees and task forces.

MEMBER: International Reading Association (past chairperson of committee on studies and research; member of board of directors, 1975-78), National Council of Teachers of English (past director of Commission on Reading), National Conference for Research in English, National Reading Conference, American Educational Research Association, Phi Delta Kappa, Kappa Delta Pi. *Awards, honors:* Outstanding dissertation award from International Reading Association, 1963; grants from International Reading Association, 1964, and U.S. Office of Education; international reading research award from Capitol University, Columbus, Ohio, 1979, for outstanding research in reading.

WRITINGS: Reading Skill Builder, Parts A-B, with teacher's manual, Reader's Digest Press, 1965; *Linguistics and Language Learning* (textbook to accompany television series), Bay Region Instructional Television for Education, 1966; *How It Is Nowadays,* with teacher's edition and workbook, Ginn, 1969; *All Sorts of Things,* with teacher's edition and workbook, Ginn, 1969; *Decoding Skills in Reading 360: Scope and Sequence,* Ginn, 1969.

(Editor) *The Dynamics of Reading,* Blaisdell, 1970; (editor with Harry Singer, and contributor) *Theoretical Models and Processes of Reading,* International Reading Association, 1970, 2nd edition, 1978; *Program BUILD: Basic Understandings in Language Development,* Ginn, 1972; (editor) *Accountability and Reading Instruction: Critical Issues,* National Council of Teachers of English, 1973; *Reading-Language Instruction: Innovative Practices,* Prentice-Hall, 1974; *Resources in Reading-Language Instruction,* Prentice-Hall, 1974; (with Evelyn J. Anern, Eleanor V. Hartson, and JoEllyn Taylor) *Pathfinder: The Allyn & Bacon Reading Program,* twenty-two volumes, Allyn & Bacon, 1978.

Contributor: *The Psycholinguistic Nature of the Reading Process,* Wayne State University Press, 1968; *Reading and Realism,* International Reading Association, 1969; Richard E. Hodges and E. Hugh Rudorf, editors, *Language and Reading,* Houghton, 1970; Malcolm Douglas, editor, *Reading, Thought, and Language,* Claremont Graduate School, 1974; *Modular Preparation for Teaching Reading,* International Reading Association, 1974; S. J. Samuels, editor, *What Research Has to Say About Reading Instruction,* International Reading Association, 1978.

Author of "Linguistics and Language Learning," a series for KQED-TV, 1966; "Language Stages and Styles," Nebraska Educational Television Council, 1971; "Exploring Edges of Language," Nebraska Educational Television Council, 1971. Contributor of about thirty-five articles to education journals. Member of editorial board of *Journal of Educational Research* and *Reading Research Quarterly.*

WORK IN PROGRESS: Research on early identification of children with high-risk reading and writing failure characteristics.

*   *   *

RUFF, Howard J.

PERSONAL: Married; children: eight. *Education:* Attended Brigham Young University. *Religion:* Church of Jesus Christ of Latter-day Saints (Mormons). *Address: Ruff Times* Newsletter, P.O. Box 2000, San Ramon, Calif. 94583.

CAREER: Professional actor and singer, appearing on radio and television programs; soloist and announcer with the U.S. Air Force Band and Singing Sergeants; host of television talk show, "Ruffhouse"; investment counselor and stockbroker; chairman of board of Target Publishers. Founder of Evelyn Wood Reading Dynamics in western United States.

WRITINGS: Famine and Survival in America, Ruff, 1974; *How to Prosper During the Coming Bad Years,* Times Books, 1979. Editor of *The Ruff Times* newsletter. Contributor of articles to magazines, including *Prevention.*

SIDELIGHTS: One of the founders of the Evelyn Wood Reading Dynamics organization in the western United States, Howard Ruff reads over three thousand words a minute and devotes three to five hours each day to research in economics, money markets, investments, nutrition, politics, and other areas that affect our future.

Ruff claims that his book, *Famine and Survival in America,* accurately forecasted the recession and weather problems of the last few years. In *How to Prosper During the Coming Bad Years,* Ruff explains how to survive inflation by investing in gold, silver, and diamonds, and he describes how to avoid the starving and rioting he predicts will occur when a depression strikes. A. J. Giunta remarked: "The unfortunate part of a book such as this is the effect that it will have on the prices of the items that the author recommends to buy and store away. If readers are foolish enough to follow his advice, their spending would cause prices to rise and thus add fuel to the fire of inflation."

BIOGRAPHICAL/CRITICAL SOURCES: Best Sellers, May, 1979.*

* * *

RUGH, Roberts 1903-1978

PERSONAL: Born April 16, 1903, in Springfield, Ohio; died November 10, 1978, in Bethesda, Md.; son of Arthur (a missionary) and Gertrude (a missionary; maiden name, Roberts) Rugh; married Harriette Sheldon, July 24, 1926; children: Mary Elizabeth (Mrs. A. J. Downs), William Arthur. *Education:* Oberlin College, A.B., 1926, M.A., 1927; Columbia University, Ph.D., 1935. *Residence:* Rockville, Md.

CAREER: Lawrence College, Appleton, Wis., member of faculty, 1927-28; Hunter College (now of the City University of New York), New York City, member of faculty, 1929-39; New York University, New York City, member of faculty, 1939-48; Columbia University, College of Physicians and Surgeons, New York City, professor of radiology and director of radiological research laboratory, 1948-71; National Institutes of Health, biologist and radiologist, 1971-78; Department of Health, Education and Welfare, research biologist, 1971-78. *Member:* American Association of Anatomists, American Society of Zoologists, American Association of Roentgenology, American Society of Neuropathologists, American Roentgen Ray Society, American Academy of Arts and Sciences, Radiological Society of North America, British Institute of Radiology, Society for Cancer Research, Society for Experimental Biology and Medicine, Harvey Society, Tissue Culture Association, Teratology Society (American and Japanese sections), Radiation Research Society. *Awards, honors:* American Academy of Arts and Sciences grant, 1934-37; American Philosophical Society grant, 1938, 1940, and 1941.

WRITINGS: Experimental Embryology: A Manual of Techniques and Procedures, New York University Bookstore, c.

1941, 3rd edition, Burgess, 1962; *A Laboratory Manual of Vertebrate Embryology,* Burgess, 1944; *The Frog: Its Reproduction and Development,* Blakiston, 1951, revised edition, McGraw, 1953; *A Laboratory Manual of Experimental Embryology,* Burgess, 1956; *Vertebrate Embryology: The Dynamics of Development,* Harcourt, 1964; *The Mouse: Its Reproduction and Development,* Burgess, 1968; (with Landrum B. Shettles and Richard Einhorn) *From Conception to Birth: The Drama of Life's Beginnings,* Harper, 1971; *A Guide to Vertebrate Development,* 7th edition, Burgess, 1977.

BIOGRAPHICAL/CRITICAL SOURCES: Scientific American, October, 1971; *Catholic Library World,* November, 1971.

OBITUARIES: Washington Post, November 13, 1978.*

* * *

RUIZ, Jose Martinez
See MARTINEZ RUIZ, Jose

* * *

RUKEYSER, Muriel 1913-1980

OBITUARY NOTICE—See index for *CA* sketch: Born December 15, 1913, in New York, N.Y.; died February 12, 1980, in New York, N.Y. Social activist, teacher, poet, biographer, screenwriter, novelist, dramatist, translator, and author of children's books. Rukeyser united her personal and political interests in her poetry. While covering the Scottsboro trial in 1932 for the *Student Review,* she was detained briefly because she had been observed talking with some black journalists. This experience is recorded in one of her early poems, "The Trial." Rukeyser's voice of protest was to be heard again in the succeeding years. During the Spanish civil war she lobbied for the cause of the Spanish loyalists. An early advocate of women's rights, in her later years she protested the Vietnamese War and expressed concern about the persecution of the Kurds in Iran. Counted among her volumes of verse are *Theory of Flight, Soul and Body of John Brown, The Green Wave,* and *The Gates. The Collected Poems of Muriel Rukeyser* was published in 1979. Rukeyser was the recipient of the Shelley Memorial Award and the Copernicus Award. Although she won wide acclaim as a poet of social protest, she also ventured successfully into other genres. She translated the work of such authors as Octavio Paz and Bertold Brecht, wrote a biography of Wendell Willkie, and produced several children's books, including *I Go Out* and *Bubbles.* Obituaries and other sources: *Current Biography,* Wilson, 1943; *Contemporary Poets,* 2nd edition, St. Martin's, 1975; *Biography News,* Volume II, Gale, 1975; *Who's Who in America,* 40th edition, Marquis, 1978; *The Writers Directory, 1980-82,* St. Martin's, 1979; *Ms.,* January, 1979; *New York Times,* February 13, 1980; *Chicago Tribune,* February 15, 1980; *Time,* February 25, 1980; *Newsweek,* February 25, 1980.

* * *

RUSHDOONY, R(ousas) J(ohn) 1916-

PERSONAL: Born April 25, 1916, in New York, N.Y.; son of Y. K. (a minister) and Rose G. Rushdoony; married Dorothy Barbara Ross; children: Ronald Haig, Rebecca J. Rushdoony Rouse, Joanna M. Rushdoony Manesajian, Sharon R. Rushdoony North, Martha L. Rushdoony Coie, Mark Rousas. *Education:* University of California, Berkeley, B.A., M.A.; Pacific School of Religion, B.D., 1943. *Home address:* Hilltop Ranch, Vallecito, Calif. 95251. *Office:* Chalcedon Foundation, P.O. Box 158, Vallecito, Calif. 95251.

CAREER: Ordained Presbyterian minister, 1944; missionary to American Chinese in San Francisco, Calif., 1940-44, Paiute and Shoshone Indians in Owyhee, Nev., 1944-52; pastor of Presbyterian churches in Santa Cruz, Calif., 1952-62; William Volker Fund, Burlingame, Calif., consultant, 1962-63; Center for American Studies, Burlingame, Calif., staff member, 1963; Chalcedon Foundation (educational foundation), Vallecito, Calif., president, 1965—. Lecturer at colleges, universities, and theological seminaries. *Member:* American Society of Church History. *Awards, honors:* Grants from William Volker Fund, 1959-61, 1963-65; D.Letters from Brainerd Seminary, 1975, and Grove City College, 1978.

WRITINGS—All published by Thoburn Press, except as noted: *Van Til*, Presbyterian & Reformed, 1960; *Intellectual Schizophrenia*, 1961; *The Messianic Character of American Education*, Presbyterian & Reformed, 1963; *This Independent Republic*, 1963; *The Nature of the American System*, 1965; *Freud*, Presbyterian & Reformed, 1965; *The Mythology of Science*, 1967; *The Foundations of Social Order*, 1968; *By What Standard?*, 1968; *Bread Upon the Waters*, 1969; *The Biblical Philosophy of History*, 1969; *The Myth of Over-Population*, 1969.

Politics of Guilt and Pity, Craig Press, 1970; *Thy Kingdom Come: Studies in Daniel and Revelation*, Presbyterian & Reformed, 1970; *Law and Liberty*, 1971; *The One and the Many*, Craig Press, 1971; *The Flight From Humanity*, 1973; *The Institutes of Biblical Law*, Craig Press, 1973; *The Politics of Pornography*, Arlington House, 1974; *The Word of Flux*, 1975; *God's Plan for Victory*, 1977; *Revolt Against Maturity*, 1977; *Infallibility: An Inescapable Concept*, Ross House, 1979; *Tithing and Dominion*, Ross House, 1979; *Salvation and Godly Rule*, 1979; *The Necessity for Systematic Theology*, Ross House Books, 1979; *Law and Society*, Ross House Books, 1980. Contributor to scholarly journals.

WORK IN PROGRESS: The Philosophy of the Christian Curriculum; The Meaning of Inflation; The Family and Society.

SIDELIGHTS: R. J. Rushdoony wrote that the purpose of the Chalcedon foundation is "to further Christian reconstruction in every area of life and thought." He is "hostile to the pietistic retreat from life which has long marked much of orthodox and evangelical Christianity," and seeks "to relate Biblical faith to every area of life and thought."

*   *   *

RYAN, Charles W(illiam)   1932-

PERSONAL: Born August 8, 1932, in Pittsburgh, Pa.; son of Cornelius F. (in electronics) and Catherine Ryan; married Elizabeth Gail Hartigan (an educator), August 22, 1959; children: Mary, Charles, Katherine. *Education:* Slippery Rock State College, B.S.Ed., 1959; Colgate University, M.A., 1961; University of Toledo, Ph.D., 1966. *Home:* 381 Wedgewood Dr., Veazie, Maine 04401. *Office:* Department of Counselor Education, University of Maine, Orono, Maine 04469.

CAREER: Teacher at public school in Williamson, N.Y., 1961-63; University of Maine, Orono, assistant professor, 1966-69, associate professor, 1969-74, professor of education, 1974-79, assistant dean, 1979—. *Military service:* U.S. Army, 1954-56. *Member:* American Personnel and Guidance Association, National Vocational Guidance Association (member of board of trustees, 1976-79), American Vocational Association.

WRITINGS: (With Glenn Saltzman and Gene Wysong) *Career Education: Kindergarten Through Grade Twelve*, Houghton, 1973, 2nd edition published as *Career Education in the Elementary School*, 1979; *Career Education: A Handbook for Funding Resources*, Houghton, 1973, 5th edition, Time-Share, 1979; (with E. G. Johnson) *Career Education and Maine*, State Department of Education (Augusta, Maine), 1973; (with Peter White, Edward Revello, and Robert J. Drummond) *Presenting a Planned Program of Career Information to Elementary School Children*, Bureau of Vocational Education, State Department of Educational and Cultural Services (Augusta), 1973; (with Mary A. Beattie) *Counseling Women: Ideas for School Counselors*, College of Education, University of Maine, 1975; (with R. R. Hammond and Drummond) *An Evaluation of the Effects of a Planned Career Education Program for Grades Seven, Eight, Nine, and Ten in a Rural Area*, Bureau of Vocational Education, State Department of Educational and Cultural Services, 1973; (with Donna Brown and others) *Maine Trainer's Manual for Career Education*, College of Education, University of Maine, 1975; (with G. G. Work) *Research Priorities for Vocational-Technical Education in Maine, 1975-1977*, Bureau of Vocational Education, State Department of Educational and Cultural Services, 1975; (with J. W. Miller and Anne Pooler) *Coping Skills for Citizenship Participation*, College of Education, University of Maine, 1976; (with Drummond and John M. Sutton, Jr.) *A Handbook for the Development of Local Career Education Plans*, College of Education, University of Maine, 1978; *Career Development Theory for Women*, University of Maine Press, 1980.

Contributor: C. W. Ryan, editor, *Career Development in the Elementary School*, State Department of Educational and Cultural Services, 1971; R. E. Norton, editor, *Career Education: An Integrating Process*, Center for Vocational and Technical Education, Ohio State University, 1973; D. P. Garner, editor, *The Career Educator*, Eastern Illinois University Press, Volume II, 1976, Volume III, 1978. Contributor of about thirty-five articles and reviews to education and counseling journals. Member of editorial board of *Counseling and Values*.

SIDELIGHTS: Ryan writes: "In retrospect, my early experiences in American public schools profoundly influenced the direction of future writing and research efforts. The lack of career guidance and development activity in public schools results in considerable floundering for a substantial portion of our youth. As one of those 'flounderers' I experimented with a variety of jobs (about thirteen) prior to 'accidentally' finding a career field that provided both intrinsic and extrinsic satisfactions. As a result, my research focus is on investigating problems associated with career guidance and development as they relate to providing effective services to youth and adults. A recent area of concern is the inadequacy of career counseling for older adults, in particular women, who wish to enter new fields or resume careers that were interrupted by child raising. It is particularly noticeable that our society continues to ignore the potential of older citizens to contribute as volunteers or mentors to youth.

"The future direction of my writing will probably have sharper focus in relation to adults. I'm concerned that schools, colleges, universities, and other learning agencies have failed to acquire a perspective that embraces life-long learning for all citizens. A narrow view of learning as occurring only in grades kindergarten through twelve or from ages eighteen to twenty-two must be addressed by learned scholars now. Without doubt, my writing efforts produce materials that blend a strong sense of midwestern pragmatism with intellectual values molded by teaching in an eastern university. A continuing search for excellence in the field, both as practitioner and teacher, is important to me.''

*   *   *

RYAN, Maureen Jones
     See JONES-RYAN, Maureen

S

SACKVILLE-WEST, V(ictoria Mary) 1892-1962
(Victoria Mary Nicolson)

OBITUARY NOTICE: Born March 9, 1892, in Kent, England; died June 2, 1962, in Kent, England. Author, poet, and winner of the Hawthornden prize in 1927 for her long poem, *The Land.* Sackville-West was a member of the "Bloomsbury group," a loose association of writers, including such well-known authors as E. M. Forster, Virginia Woolf, John Maynard Keynes, and Lytton Strachey. Her works include *The Edwardians, All Passion Spent,* and *Andrew Marvell.* Obituaries and other sources: *New York Times,* June 3, 1962; *Time,* June 8, 1962; *Publishers Weekly,* June 25, 1962; *The Reader's Encyclopedia,* 2nd edition, Crowell, 1965; *The New Century Handbook of English Literature,* revised edition, Appleton, 1967; *Twentieth Century Writing: A Reader's Guide to Contemporary Literature,* Transatlantic, 1969; *Longman Companion to Twentieth Century Literature,* Longman, 1970; *The Penguin Companion to English Literature,* McGraw, 1971; *The Reader's Adviser: A Layman's Guide to Literature,* Volume I: *The Best in American and British Fiction, Poetry, Essays, Literary Biography, Bibliography, and Reference,* 12th edition, Bowker, 1974.

*   *   *

SAFER, Morley 1931-

PERSONAL: Born November 8, 1931, in Toronto, Ontario, Canada; came to United States in 1964; son of Max (an upholsterer) and Anna (Cohn) Safer; married Jane Fearer (an anthropologist), 1968; children: Sarah. *Education:* Attended University of Western Ontario, 1952. *Residence:* Manhattan, N.Y. *Office:* CBS News, 524 West 57th St., New York, N.Y. 10019.

CAREER/WRITINGS: Rueters (writer's news agency), London, England, 1955; Canadian Broadcasting Corp. (CBC-TV), correspondent and producer, 1955-60, writer and London correspondent, 1961-64; British Broadcasting Corp. (BBC-TV), London, correspondent and producer, 1961; Columbia Broadcasting System, Inc. (CBS-TV), New York, N.Y., London correspondent, 1964, head of Saigon bureau, 1965-70, chief of London bureau, 1967-70, co-editor and co-host of television news program "Sixty Minutes," 1970—. *Awards, honors:* Polk Award, 1965; Overseas Press Club of America award, 1965 and 1966; Sigma Delta Chi award, 1965; George Foster Peabody Radio and Television Award, 1966; National Academy of Television Arts and Sciences Award (Emmy) nominations.

SIDELIGHTS: "Sixty Minutes," the CBS weekly television news show, is the only nonfiction program to be ranked consistently in Nielsen's "top ten" rated shows. And Morley Safer helped put it there. He joined the staff in 1970 when the show was going through a critical period. Shuffled around from one time-slot to another, it never quite mustered a steady following, and with the loss of Harry Reasoner, the show's original correspondent, to the American Broadcasting Co. (ABC-TV) News, the future of "Sixty Minutes" looked dim. The choice of replacement was crucial. "We're looking for Reasoner's wit and style, his craggy good looks," explained executive producer Don Hewitt at the time. Morley Safer satisfied all those requirements. "It was one of the better fits of all time in television," proclaimed Donovan Moore. "A man of average television conceit, though in a humble way, Safer glided into the '60 Minutes' operation, his essays and softer features balancing [Mike] Wallace's hard stuff. In a medium growing fat on pedestrian entertainment, Safer brought writing—not just reporting, but writing, *good* writing—to the air." Since that time, "Sixty Minutes" has steadily worked its way into the weekly routine of millions of Americans.

"I think we're popular because you never know how the show is going to end," suggested Safer to Ron Base. "I defy you to name any other regular broadcast where you don't know in the first 10 minutes how it's going to end." Another ingredient of its success is the dedication of the staff. Safer and Wallace, co-hosts and co-editors of the show, work six and seven days a week, logging more than 200,000 miles apiece each year as well as writing most of their own material. Dan Rather, until Reasoner's return in 1979 the newest member of the team, denies the existence of regular working hours at "Sixty Minutes." The work simply never stops. "Once in a while," he admitted to Base, "when I'm flying around in the middle of the night, I ask myself why I'm doing this. The answer is that this is what most of us got into journalism for. Hell, I'd pay cash money to do this." Safer agrees: "It's the best job in the world. No question."

Before joining the "Sixty Minutes" team and CBS-News, Safer worked for both the Canadian and British Broadcasting Corporations. During that time he reported on a variety of news events, though was best known for his commentary on battle. In his twenty-odd years as a foreign correspondent, Safer "covered nine wars, took a bit of shrapnel, suffered nightmares about Nigeria and made his reputation in Vietnam," summarized Mary Vespa.

Morley Safer was sent to southeast Asia in 1965 for a stint as war correspondent in a campaign that was expected to last no longer than six months. In late August of that year, Safer set out for the Marine staging area in Da Nang, where he found them readying for a mission to be carried out the next day. When a young lieutenant suggested he accompany them, the newsman thought it an ideal way to delve into the character of the current military action. En route to their destination, Safer queried the officer for details of the operation. He was told that the village of Cam Ne had turned hostile, often firing on U.S. troops; the province chief wanted it stopped. It was supposedly for retribution that the Marines had been called in. Years later, however, it was learned that "the reason Cam Ne was leveled had nothing to do with the Vietcong; rather, the Vietnamese province chief was furious that the locals had refused to pay their taxes, and he wanted the village punished; and the Americans, who were to do the punishing, were not aware of that," revealed David Halberstam.

What lay in store at Cam Ne was more than Safer or the American public expected. Instead of a militant populace showering the U.S. forces with artillery, the small community did not fire a single shot in their own defense. The Marines, indiscriminately bombarding and setting fire to villager's homes like so many torches, met with no resistance. The film footage documenting these maneuvers was to shock America into recognizing the harsh realities of the war. President Lyndon Johnson was outraged and accused Safer of being a Communist. He immediately launched an investigation into Safer's past, and charged the newsman with bribing and/or tricking the senior officer into staging the entire "farce." Much to Johnson's dismay, however, none of his accusations could be substantiated.

Because of Morley Safer, Halberstam concluded, the way was cleared for other newsmen and women to seek out the truth and report it fully without self-imposed censorship: "Overnight, one correspondent with one cameraman could have as much effect as ten or fifteen or twenty senators turned dissident."

AVOCATIONAL INTERESTS: Painting, reading, playing tennis, watching television, baking.

BIOGRAPHICAL/CRITICAL SOURCES: Milwaukee Journal, June 1, 1975; *Authors in the News,* Volume 2, Gale, 1976; *Atlantic Monthly,* February, 1976; *Rolling Stone,* January 12, 1978; *People,* January 15, 1979, May 28, 1979; *Detroit News Magazine,* September 16, 1979.

—*Sketch by Kathleen Ceton Newman*

*   *   *

St. CLAIR, Katherine
See HUFF, T(om) E.

*   *   *

SAINTY, John Christopher   1934-

PERSONAL: Born December 31, 1934, in London, England; son of Christopher Lawrence (an engineer) and Nancy Lee (Miller) Sainty; married Elizabeth Frances Sherlock, January 7, 1965; children: Christopher James, Henry John, Edward Francis. *Education:* New College, Oxford, M.A., 1956. *Home:* 22 Kelso Place, London W.8, England. *Office:* House of Lords, London S.W.1, England.

CAREER: Clerk in the House of Lords, London, England, 1959-70; Institute of Historical Research, London, research assistant and editor, 1970-74; reading clerk in House of Lords, 1974—. *Member:* Royal Historical Society (fellow), Society of Antiquaries (fellow).

WRITINGS: (Editor) *Office-Holders in Modern Britain,* Athlone Press, Volume I: *Treasury Officials, 1660-1870,* 1972, Volume II: *Officials of the Secretaries of State, 1660-1782,* 1973, Volume III: *Officials of the Boards of Trade, 1660-1870,* 1974, Volume IV: *Admiralty Officials, 1660-1870,* 1975, Volume V: *Home Office Officials, 1782-1870,* 1975, Volume VI: *Colonial Office Officials: Officials of the Secretary of State for War, 1794-1801, of the Secretary of State for War and Colonies, 1801-54, and of the Secretary of State for Colonies, 1854-70,* 1976; (with D. Dewar) *Divisions in the House of Lords: An Analytical List 1685-1857,* H.M.S.O., 1976. Contributor to history journals.

WORK IN PROGRESS: Personnel of the Exchequer, 1307-1834.

*   *   *

SALIH, H(alil) Ibrahim   1939-

PERSONAL: Born February 26, 1939, in Kyrenia, Cyprus; came to the United States in 1959, naturalized citizen, 1969; son of Ismail and Sabire Salih; married Sharon Kettlewell, January 30, 1965; children: David Kerim, Julie Shermin. *Education:* University of the Pacific, B.A., 1963; American University, M.A., 1965, Ph.D., 1967. *Politics:* Democrat. *Religion:* Muslim. *Home:* 6404 Franwood Ter., Fort Worth, Tex. 76112. *Office:* Department of Political Science, Texas Wesleyan College, Fort Worth, Tex. 76105.

CAREER: Cyprus Auxiliary Police Force, Nicosia, transportation statistics correlator, 1957; Foreign Broadcast Information Service, Kyrenia, Cyprus, clerk, 1958-59; Texas Wesleyan College, Fort Worth, assistant professor, 1968-71, associate professor of political science, 1971—, head of department, 1973—, director of summer program in Mexico, 1978. Lecturer at American University, 1966, and other colleges and universities; participant in scholarly meetings; guest on television programs.

MEMBER: Middle East Institute, American Association of University Professors, Western Social Science Association, Southwestern Social Science Association, Phi Kappa Alpha, Phi Alpha Theta (charter member), Masons. *Awards, honors:* Distinguished service award from Pi Kappa Alpha, 1978; Danforth associate, 1979.

WRITINGS: Cyprus: A Nation in Name Only (monograph), Pakistan Press Syndicate, 1966; *Cyprus: An Analysis of Cypriot Political Discord,* Gaus, 1968; *Cyprus: The Impact of Diverse Nationalism,* University of Alabama Press, 1978. Contributing editor of *Encyclopedia of the Middle East.* Contributor of articles and reviews to political science and history journals and newspapers.

WORK IN PROGRESS: International Drug Traffic: An Introduction to the Middle East.

SIDELIGHTS: Salih writes: "I am deeply committed to teaching and to my subject, but I do not teach for the financial reward or the gratitude of students (both of which are adequate, but not abundant). My reward is the development of my students as individuals. There is further satisfaction in my own self-development and in being able to challenge students to use their minds for their own well-being and that of their fellow human beings.

"I was motivated to write about Cyprus because I wanted to

gather all the information on Cyprus and synthesize it into books which could be a resource for better understanding of the many facets of Cypriot politics and the importance of Cyprus internationally. I also wanted, if possible, to suggest new political alternatives to the deadlock which has persisted since 1964. It is my belief that the ultimate settlement must rest with the Cypriots themselves, and these books are my contribution to that solution of the Cyprus problem.

"As a step toward accommodation, the Cypriot constitutional institutions based on the Zurich-London agreements of 1959 must be replaced by a federal constitutional system. A two-zone federation, which Turkey has proposed, may be the answer since the two ethnic communities are already separated physically and politically. If an amicable settlement cannot be reached, the partition of Cyprus will become permanent and the two communities will seek to legitimatize the independence of their sovereign political units."

* * *

SALPETER, Eliahu (Arnost) 1927-

PERSONAL: Born November 1, 1927, in Slatina, Czechoslovakia; son of Nahman and Cornelia (Horowitz) Salpeter; married Ruth Freiman (an attorney), 1960; children: Ron, Noam, Vered. *Education:* Attended Charles University, 1947-49, and Hebrew University of Jerusalem, 1949-51. *Home:* 9 Ben Ezra St., Tel Aviv, Israel. *Office:* Ha'aretz House, Schocken St., Tel Aviv, Israel.

CAREER: Associated with Associated Press, Prague, Czechoslovakia, 1948-49, and *Jerusalem Post,* Jerusalem, Israel, 1950-53; *Ha'aretz,* Tel Aviv, Israel, Washington correspondent, 1953-56, diplomatic correspondent, 1957-61, Washington correspondent, 1961-65, managing editor, 1965-68, columnist, 1965—, editorial writer and member of editorial board, 1968—. Chief of Jerusalem bureau of Jewish Telegraphic Agency, 1956-61. *Member:* International Press Institute, Israel Journalists Association, Israel Foreign Policy Association, National Press Club (Washington, D.C.).

WRITINGS: (With Y. Elizur) *Who Rules Israel?,* Harper, 1973; (editor) *Israeli Humor and Satire* (anthology), Sadan, 1974.

SIDELIGHTS: Salpeter writes: "I specialize in international relations and technology-induced social developments. I also write occasional brief satirical pieces." His languages include Hebrew, English, Czech, Hungarian, German, and French.

* * *

SALTER, Donald P. M. 1942-
(Rollo Podmarsh)

PERSONAL: Born November 7, 1942, in Budapest, Hungary; son of Istvan (in sales) and Grace (a horticulturist; maiden name, Gargrave) Molnar; married Sheila Browne (a teacher), October 4, 1969; children: Katherine Mary, Robert Stephen. *Education:* University of Leicester, B.A., 1963, M.A. (with distinction), 1970; University of Exeter, M.Ed., 1973. *Politics:* "Vacillating toward Little Englandism." *Religion:* "Vestigial Church of England." *Home:* 28 Grosvenor Place, Newcastle-upon-Tyne, England. *Agent:* D. Timms, 37 Eastbourne Ave., Bath, Avon, England. *Office:* 6 Grosvenor Place, Newcastle-upon-Tyne, England.

CAREER: Worcester College of Higher Education, Worcester, England, senior lecturer in English, 1972-79; University of Newcastle-upon-Tyne, Newcastle-upon-Tyne, England, lecturer in education, 1979—. Visiting professor at Trenton

State College, 1975-76. Member of Working Party Against Sexism in Education and Severn Stoke Old Folks' Parcel Fund, 1978-79; past member of Leicester Group for Comprehensive Education. *Member:* National Association for the Teaching of English.

WRITINGS: The Hard Core of Children's Fiction, Ward, Locke, 1972; *That Is My Ticket,* London, 1975; (editor) *The Ward, Locke English Library,* Ward, Locke, 1979. Contributor of articles and reviews (sometimes under pseudonym Rollo Podmarsh) to magazines and newspapers, including *Critical Quarterly.*

WORK IN PROGRESS: Research on E. M. Forster's homosexual writings.

SIDELIGHTS: Salter writes: "The seminal influence on my writing career has been provided by Evelyn Waugh. In his novel, *Decline and Fall,* his Dr. Fagan states: 'It is vision I need, Mr. Pennyfeather, not diplomas.'"*

* * *

SALU, Mary 1919-

PERSONAL: Born August 30, 1919, in England; daughter of Hubert Francis (a confectioner) and Mary Elizabeth (Burns) Salu. *Education:* University of Newcastle upon Tyne, B.A. (with first class honors); Lady Margaret Hall, Oxford, B.Litt. *Religion:* Roman Catholic. *Home:* 197 Wingrove Rd., Newcastle upon Tyne, Northumbria, England.

CAREER: Associated with University of Newcastle upon Tyne, Newcastle upon Tyne, England, Department of English; writer.

WRITINGS: (Editor with Robert T. Farrell) *J. R. R. Tolkien, Scholar and Storyteller: Essays in Memoriam,* Cornell University Press, 1979. Also translator of Ancrene Wisse, *Attitudes to English Usage.*

WORK IN PROGRESS: Essays on *Troilus and Criseyde.*

* * *

SAMARIN, William J. 1926-

PERSONAL: Born February 7, 1926, in Los Angeles, Calif.; son of John A. and Hazel (Kornoff) Samarin; married Ruth Marie Custer, 1947; children: George Egerton, Per Furst. *Education:* Bible Theological Seminary, Los Angeles, Calif., B.Th., 1948; University of California, Berkeley, B.A., 1950, Ph.D., 1962. *Religion:* Protestant. *Office:* Department of Linguistics, University of Toronto, 43 Queen's Park Crescent E., Toronto, Ontario, Canada M5S 1A1.

CAREER: Worked as missionary and linguist in Foreign Missionary Society of the Brethren Church, 1951-60; Hartford Seminary Foundation, Hartford, Conn., assistant professor, 1961-65, associate professor, 1965-68, professor of linguistics, 1968; University of Toronto, Toronto, Ontario, began as associate professor, 1968, became professor of linguistics. Visiting lecturer at University of Oklahoma, summer, 1964; visiting professor at University of Leiden, 1966-67; consultant to Agency for International Development and Republic of Mali.

MEMBER: Linguistic Society of America, American Anthropological Association, Canadian Linguistic Association, West African Linguistic Society (charter member). *Awards, honors:* Grants from National Science Foundation, for Senegal, 1962, American Council of Learned Societies, for Congo Republic, 1962, African Studies Association, 1963, Canada Council, 1970-71, American Philosophical Society, 1972-73, and Social Science and Humanities Research Council of Canada, 1979-80.

WRITINGS: The Gbeya Language: Grammar, Text, Vocabularies, University of California Press, 1966; *A Grammar of Sango,* Mouton, 1967; *Field Linguistics: A Guide to Linguistic Field Work,* Holt, 1967; *Basic Course in Sango,* two volumes, U.S. Department of Health, Education, and Welfare, 1968; *Sango: Langue de l'Afrique centrale,* E. J. Brill, 1970; (contributor) *Pidginization and Creolization of Languages,* Cambridge University Press, 1971; *Tongues of Men and Angels: The Religious Language of Pentecostalism,* Macmillan, 1972; *Language in Religious Practice,* Newbury House Publishers, 1976. Contributor to linguistic journals.

WORK IN PROGRESS: Research on the emergence of linguae francae (Sango, Lingala, and Kituba) in central Africa in the colonial period.

*   *   *

SAMUELS, Harold   1917-

PERSONAL: Born July 9, 1917, in New York, N.Y.; married wife, Peggy (a writer and antiques dealer); children: Peter, Amy, Matt, Joany. *Education:* Ohio University, A.B., 1937, M.A., 1938; Harvard University, LL.B., 1941; also attended Art Students League. *Home address:* P.O. Box 465, Locust Valley, N.Y. 11560.

CAREER: Dealer in antique American paintings (specializing in the American West); public speaker.

WRITINGS: (With wife, Peggy Samuels) *The Illustrated Biographical Encyclopedia of Artists of the American West,* Doubleday, 1976; (editor with P. Samuels) *The Collected Writings of Frederic Remington,* Doubleday, 1979. Also author of *The Life of Frederic Remington* and *Catalog Raisonne of the Paintings of Frederic Remington.*

*   *   *

SANDBACH, Francis Henry   1903-

PERSONAL: Born February 23, 1903, in Birmingham, England; son of F. E. (a professor) and Ethel Sandbach; married Mary Warburton Mathews (a translator from Swedish), 1932; children: Catherine, Martin. *Education:* Trinity College, Cambridge, B.A., 1924. *Home:* 2 Hedgerley Close, Cambridge CB3 0EW, England.

CAREER: Victoria University of Manchester, Manchester, England, assistant lecturer in classics, 1926-28; Cambridge University, Cambridge, England, lecturer, 1929-67, professor of classics, 1967-70, Brereton Reader in Classics, 1951-67, tutor at Trinity College, 1945-52, senior tutor, 1952-56, fellow of Trinity College, 1927—. *Member:* British Academy (fellow).

WRITINGS: (Editor) *Plutarch's Moralia,* Harvard University Press, Volume IX, 1961, Volume XI, 1965, Volume XV, 1969 (Sandbach was not associated with other volumes); (editor) *Plutarchus Moralia,* Volume VII (Sandbach was not associated with other volumes), Teubner, 1967; (editor) *Menandri Reliquiae Selectae* (title means "Selected Remains of Menander"), Clarendon Press, 1972; (with A. W. Gomme) *Menander: A Commentary,* Clarendon Press, 1973; *The Stoics,* edited by M. I. Finley, Norton, 1975; *The Comic Theatre of Greece and Rome,* edited by Finley, Norton, 1977. Contributor to classical studies journals.

WORK IN PROGRESS: Research on Aristotle and the Stoics; research on Terence.

*   *   *

SANDROF, Ivan   1912(?)-1979

PERSONAL: Born c. 1912 in Gardner, Mass.; died February

1, 1979, in Worcester, Mass.; children: Mark, Martha Sacks.

CAREER: Worcester Telegram, Worcester, Mass., member of staff, 1941-60, literary editor, 1960-76; founder, president, and editor of newsletter of National Book Critics Circle, 1974-76. *Military service:* U.S. Army. Served in Infantry and as staff writer for *Stars and Stripes. Awards, honors:* Recipient of several awards from Associated Press for feature writing.

WRITINGS: More Massachusetts Towns (local history), Barre Publishers, 1965; *Yesterday's Massachusetts* (history), E. A. Seemann, 1977. Author of book column in *Worcester Evening Gazette.* Contributor to periodicals, including *Esquire, New York Times,* and *New Yorker.*

OBITUARIES: New York Times, February 3, 1979; *Publishers Weekly,* February 12, 1979.*

*   *   *

SANTESSON, Hans Stefan   1914(?)-1975

PERSONAL: Born c. 1914 in Sweden; died February 21, 1975, in Edgewater, N.J. *Residence:* Edgewater, N.J.

CAREER: Editor for Unicorn Mystery Book Club, 1945-52; editor of *Saint Mystery Magazine* and *Fantastic Universe Science Fiction,* 1956-67; editor for Walker & Co. (publisher); science fiction editor for Paperback Library. *Awards, honors:* Edgar Award from Mystery Writers of America, 1964, for reviews of mysteries.

WRITINGS: Gods for Tomorrow (science fiction), Award Books, 1967; *The Mighty Barbarians: Great Sword and Sorcery Heroes* (science fiction), Lancer Books, 1969; *Reincarnation,* Award Books, 1969; *Understanding Mu,* Paperback Library, 1970; *The Case for Exorcism,* Warner Books, 1974.

Editor; science fiction: *The Fantastic Universe Omnibus,* Prentice-Hall, 1960; *Rulers of Men,* Pyramid Books, 1965; (compiler with Leslie Charteris) *The Saint Magazine Reader,* Doubleday, 1966; *The Locked Room Reader,* Random House, 1968; (compiler) *Crime Prevention in the Thirtieth Century,* Walker, 1969; (compiler) *The Days After Tomorrow,* Little, Brown, 1971; (compiler) *Mirror, Mirror, Fatal Mirror: An Anthology of Mystery Stories by the Mystery Writers of America,* Doubleday, 1973.

Other edited works: *Flying Saucers in Fact and Fiction,* Lancer Books, 1968.

OBITUARIES: New York Times, February 22, 1975; *Publishers Weekly,* March 10, 1975; *AB Bookman's Weekly,* March 17, 1975.*

*   *   *

SARETT, Morton R(euben)   1916-

PERSONAL: Born September 30, 1916, in New York, N.Y.; son of Max (a manufacturer) and Mary (Goodman) Sarett; married Helen Lyons (a public relations and television consultant), June 14, 1952. *Education:* Brooklyn College (now of the City University of New York), A.B., 1937; Brooklyn Law School, LL.B., 1940. *Home:* 400 East 55th St., New York, N.Y. 10022. *Agent:* Helmut Meyer, 330 East 79th St., New York, N.Y. 10021. *Office:* 608 Fifth Ave., New York, N.Y. 10020.

CAREER: Admitted to the Bar of New York State; general practice of law in New York, N.Y., 1941—. President of Jewelry Industry Council, 1962—; member of jewelry industry advisory council of Fashion Institute of Technology. *Member:* American Gem Society, American Society of Association Executives, Twenty-Four Karat Club of the City of

New York. *Awards, honors:* Editorial achievement award from *Industrial Marketing,* 1957.

WRITINGS: (With Jacob Spolansky) *The Communist Trail in America,* Macmillan, 1950; *The Jewelry in Your Life,* Nelson Hall, 1979.

Unpublished scripts: "Invitation to Life" (documentary), first broadcast by ABC Radio Network, January, 1947; "The Mousetrap" (documentary), first broadcast by NBC-TV, November, 1954.

Author of radio scripts and short stories. Contributor to *American Oxford Encyclopedia, Grolier Encyclopedia,* and *New Book of Knowledge.* Contributor of articles and stories to magazines, including *Good Housekeeping* and *McCall's.* Editor of *National Jeweler,* 1954-60.

SIDELIGHTS: Sarett told *CA:* "While many careers are the result of accident or circumstance, writing is chosen with deliberation. If anyone were to ask me what special rewards writing brings, I should say they are the pleasures and excitement of exploring every facet of life and living without any limits. Nothing is beyond the imagination and reach of the writer and no other craft offers such a magic lifetime passport to countless adventures. In a sense, we are the sum total of all that writers have written.

"I have been particularly fortunate to have been able to develop other careers in addition to writing and to blend these with my work as a writer. They have enriched my ability to write for various media, diverse audiences, and on a wide range of subjects and interests. Knowledge is indivisible and the more versatile our talents the more versatile our writing endeavors."

*   *   *

SARGENT, David R(utledge) 1920-

PERSONAL: Born December 21, 1920, in Orange, N.J.; son of Dwight Swett (a corporation executive) and Margaret (Alling) Sargent; married Jane Oman, June 6, 1942; children: Karen Sargent Sirkin, Anne Sargent Walker, Dwight, Carl, David Rutledge, Jr., Thomas. *Education:* Dartmouth College, B.A., 1942; also attended Boston University, Northeastern University, and Harvard University. *Politics:* Independent. *Religion:* Unitarian-Universalist. *Home:* 15 Indian Springs Way, Wellesley Hills, Mass. 02181. *Office:* United Business Service Co., 210 Newbury St., Boston, Mass. 02116.

CAREER: United Business Service Co., Boston, Mass., junior counselor, 1946-48, investment consultant, 1948-51, assistant director of consultation, 1951, director of consultation, 1951-58, treasurer, 1958-61, president, 1961—. Member of investment advisory council for Massachusetts Department of the Treasury, 1976—. Member of board of selectmen of Wellesley, Mass., 1966-72, town moderator, 1974-80. Member of board of trustees of Boston Five Cents Savings Bank. *Military service:* Royal Air Force, 1943. U.S. Army Air Forces, pilot, 1943-45; became first lieutenant.

WRITINGS: Stock Market Profits and Higher Income for You, Simon & Schuster, 1975, revised edition, 1976; (contributor) Ronald K. Devine and Carolyn F. McIntyre, editors, *Successful Investing,* Simon & Schuster, 1979. Author of "Successful Investing," a daily syndicated column distributed by Los Angeles Times Syndicate to fifty newspapers, and "The Back Yard," a weekly column syndicated by United Business Service Co., 1960—.

WORK IN PROGRESS: A Vermont family-nature book.

SIDELIGHTS: Sargent told *CA:* "I have moved over the years from being a visceral bomber pilot to cerebral financial writer (in order to earn a living) to nature writer. I have paralleled all of this remunerative exercise with a twenty-year career in local politics, including the state level, and have loved every minute of it. I have discovered that just as one hand washes the other, public and private careers supplement one another to the benefit of the individual and I hope, society. Businessmen who rant against government, and politicians and bureaucrats who complain about business, to a great degree, simply need experience on the 'other side'. And for those too rushed to stop to listen to the fluted call of the white-throated sparrow, or watch the lethal stalk of the fisher, or the delicate and intricate pattern in a patch of reindeer moss, I feel pity. Only with the feet planted firmly in the earth can the spirit grow to the clouds."

*   *   *

SARSFIELD, C. P.
See MARSHNER, Connaught Coyne

*   *   *

SAUSER-HALL, Frederic 1887-1961
(Blaise Cendrars)

OBITUARY NOTICE: Born September 1, 1887, in Paris, France; died in 1961 in Paris. Novelist and poet. Cendrars traveled worldwide, from early childhood throughout his life, dabbling in such occupations as motion picture director, journalist, art critic, and businessman. His adventuresome and often autobiographical novels and poems featured resilient heroes who lived as colorfully as Cendrars himself did. His best known books are *L'Or (Sutter's Gold), Le Panama; ou, Les Aventures de mes sept oncles (Panama; or, The Adventures of My Seven Uncles),* and *L'Homme Foudroye.* Obituaries and other sources: *New York Times,* January 22, 1961; *Publishers Weekly,* February 13, 1961; *The Reader's Encyclopedia,* 2nd edition, Crowell, 1965; *The Oxford Companion to French Literature,* corrected edition, Oxford University Press, 1966; *Paris Review,* April, 1966; *Encyclopedia of World Literature in the Twentieth Century,* updated edition, Ungar, 1967; *Longman Companion to Twentieth Century Literature,* Longman, 1970; Jay Bochner, *Blaise Cendrars: Discovery and Re-Creation,* University of Toronto Press, 1978.

*   *   *

SAXTON, Mark 1914-

PERSONAL: Born November 28, 1914, in Mineola, N.Y.; son of Eugene Francis (an editor) and Martha (a teacher; maiden name Plaisted) Saxton; married Josephine Stocking, June 27, 1940 (deceased); children: Russell Steele, Martha Porter. *Education:* Harvard University, A.B., 1936. *Agent:* Harold Ober, 40 East 49th St., New York City, N.Y. 10017.

CAREER: Farrar & Rinehart, New York City, editor, 1938-43; Rinehart & Co., New York City, editor, 1946; William Sloane Associates, New York City, executive editor, 1946-50; McGraw-Hill, New York City, editor, 1950-52; Harvard University Press, Cambridge, Mass., promotion manager and editorial adviser, 1952-68; Gambit, Inc., Boston, Mass., editor-in-chief, 1968—. Faculty member of Breadloaf Writers Conference in Vermont, 1947-51 and 1961. Trustee and vice-president of Joseph Collins Foundation, 1952—. *Military service:* U.S. Naval Reserves, 1943-46; became lieutenant junior grade.

WRITINGS—All novels: Danger Road, Farrar & Rinehart, 1939; *The Broken Circle,* Farrar & Rinehart, 1941; *The Year of August,* Farrar & Rinehart, 1943; *Prepared for Rage,* William Sloane, 1947; *Paper Chase,* Bobbs-Merrill, 1964; *The Islar,* Houghton, 1969; *The Two Kingdoms,* Houghton, 1979.

Work represented in anthology, *The Best Short-Short Stories from Collier's,* edited by Barthold Fles, World Publishing, 1948. Contributor of numerous reviews to *New York Herald-Tribune Books.*

WORK IN PROGRESS: The Houghton Mifflin Story, publication by Houghton expected in 1982; a novel tentatively entitled *The League of Nobles.*

SIDELIGHTS: The Islar tells of an imaginary small country which has long been secure between its isolating yet protecting mountain borders. The king's assassination, foreign political intrigue, and citizen unrest cause a sudden upheaval in the formerly self-sufficient government. Saxton "has created enough suspension of disbelief to keep the reader interested until the very last page, no mean accomplishment in an era characterized by formless books with no clearcut beginnings, endings, etc.," declared a *Best Sellers* critic. "Any reader (with almost no difficulty) soon realizes that he is reading about what can happen to any small country." The same critic also noted that the book is somewhat unbelievable because the country has "so many *reasonable* men, most of them at the top level. Of one thing we *can* be sure; this is not the United States."

Saxton told *CA:* "I'm finding it increasingly difficult to write fiction about the current scene that satisfies me at all, and I gather I'm not alone. It's an odd time of the world in which, as Hannah Arendt said, people believe in nothing but will believe anything. The fashionable contemporary attitude of innocent selfishness isn't a happy one for the storyteller; he doesn't really like the people he has to write about and it shows. With little but behavior to work with, he can't find much in the inner or the outer world to give meaning to the other. So the storyteller feels banal, bores himself at least, and, if he's me, looks cross-eyed at the present, even while trying to imagine how to write about it once more."

BIOGRAPHICAL/CRITICAL SOURCES: Best Sellers, October 15, 1969.

*   *   *

SCARGALL, Jeanne Anna   1928-

PERSONAL: Born August 4, 1928, in Willowbunch, Saskatchewan, Canada; daughter of George Arthur (a banker) and Agnes (a secretary; maiden name, Campbell) Beatty; divorced; children: Brynne, Bettina, Paul. *Education:* University of Manitoba, B.Sc., 1949; University of Toronto, B.L.S., 1952. *Home:* 1 Talisman Cres., Markham, Ontario, Canada L3P 2C8. *Office:* Markham Public Library, 7755 Bayview Ave., Thornhill, Ontario, Canada L3T 4T1.

CAREER: Children's librarian in Thunder Bay, Ontario, 1952-54; London Public Library and Art Museum, London, Ontario, reference librarian, 1954-57; Scarborough Library, Scarborough, Ontario, librarian, 1964-70; Markham Public Library, Thornhill, Ontario, coordinator of community services, 1970—. Hostess and producer of "It's Your Library," a weekly program in Richmond Hill Cable Television.

WRITINGS: A Thousand and One Ways to Have Fun With Children, Scribner, 1973; (illustrator) Peter Sulman and David Terhune, *Sailing: From Armchair to Sea Legs,* Burns & MacEachern, 1973; *Pioneer Potpourri* (recipes and memoirs of her mother and grandmother), Methuen, 1974, re-

vised edition published as *Canadian Homestead Cookbook,* 1980; (with Sheila Clarke and Marilyn Linton) *Toronto Is for Kids,* Greey de Pencier, 1976.

WORK IN PROGRESS: A book for children on the history of holiday traditions, publication by Personal Library expected in 1981; an adaptation of a Russian folktale, a picture book, with illustrations by Kathleen Gabriel.

SIDELIGHTS: Scargall commented to *CA:* "My scrapbook of ideas for doing simple crafts to planning birthday parties, that helped me keep my sanity while raising my own children, became my first book. I was asked to write and illustrate it because of the interest shown in it by neighborhood children, who in turn told a publisher parent. As a librarian, I found the actual researching for this book fascinating—using ideas from friends, newspapers, books, and magazines. The overflow material gradually developed into the material for my new book on the reasons for holiday traditions that I hope to complete in 1981.

"I drafted the illustrations for *Sailing* to help a neighbor who is an Olympic sailor. This book on Canadian sailing regulations was needed prior to the 1974 Olympics. Being this kind of illustrator was an interesting, if not very lucrative, experience.

"*Pioneer Potpourri* is the result of my own family's memories of pioneering in Saskatchewan at the beginning of the century. My mother was developing cataracts and I was concerned that these treasures would be lost, so I recorded her thoughts on old recipes, remedies, and reminiscences to preserve her family life experiences in the isolation of the Canadian prairies.

"After my first book came out I wrote articles, appeared on television, and attended other child-oriented public events. Due to this exposure, I was asked in 1974 to write a book of things children could do within a one-hundred-mile radius of Toronto, Canada. This, combined with the findings of two other people, became *Toronto Is for Kids.*

"One of the great benefits of being an author is the opportunity of joining the Writer's Union of Canada and the Canadian Society of Children's Authors, Illustrators, and Performers. Not only does one meet others with similar problems and interests, but speaking tours are arranged which enable one to meet the readers who are using the books. It is said that writers are people who express themselves with the pen to enable them to communicate with an uncertain world. Perhaps my childhood as a banker's daughter, being one of constant change, and an adulthood of a similar variety, has given me the urge to share my experiences to help others to survive confusion in a way that I found made my life the interesting experience it has been."

*   *   *

SCARROTT, Michael
See FISHER, A(rthur) Stanley T(heodore)

*   *   *

SCHEIBER, Jane L(ang)   1937-

PERSONAL: Born in 1937, in New York, N.Y.; married Harry N. Scheiber (a professor of history), 1958; children: two. *Education:* Cornell University, A.B. (with high honors), 1958, graduate study, 1958-59; attended Columbia University, summer, 1958. *Residence:* La Jolla, Calif. *Office:* Courses by Newspaper, University of California at San Diego, X-002, La Jolla, Calif. 92093.

CAREER: Teacher of English and literature at girls' school in Columbus, Ohio, 1959-60; Dartmouth College, Hanover, N.H., library acquisitions assistant, 1960-61, research associate at Public Affairs Center, 1961-63, research assistant, 1964-68; research and editorial assistant, 1968-71; University of California at San Diego, La Jolla, writer for extension, 1971, continuing education specialist, editorial director, and assistant project director of Courses by Newspaper, 1972—. *Member:* Phi Beta Kappa, Phi Kappa Phi. *Awards, honors:* Woodrow Wilson fellowship, 1958-59.

WRITINGS: (Contributor) Milton Cantor, editor, *Black Labor in America*, Negro Universities Press, 1970; (editor) *America and the Future of Man: A Reader for the First Course by Newspaper*, CRM Books, 1973; (editor with Robert C. Elliott) *In Search of the American Dream: A Reader for the Second Course by Newspaper*, Publisher's, Inc., 1974; (editor with Daniel Aaron, Michael Parrish, and Allen Weinstein) *American Issues Forum*, Publisher's, Inc., Volume I: *American Society in the Making*, 1975, Volume II: *The Molding of American Values*, with study guide edited with Parrish and Helen Hawkins, 1976; (editor with H. William Menard) *Oceans: Our Continuing Frontier*, Publisher's, Inc., 1976; (editor with Jerome H. Skolnick and Martin L. Forst) *Crime and Justice in America*, Publisher's, Inc., 1977; (editor with Robert Fulton, Eric Markusen, and Greg Owen) *Death and Dying: Challenge and Change*, Addison-Wesley, 1978; (editor with Melvin Kranzberg and Timothy A. Hall) *Energy and the Way We Live*, Boyd & Fraser, 1979.

SIDELIGHTS: Scheiber told *CA:* "Courses by Newspaper is a nontraditional, adult education program, originated and administered by University Extension, University of California, San Diego, with funding primarily from the National Endowment for the Humanities. Since its inception in 1973, it has been preparing materials for college-level courses that are offered to the general public each September and January through the cooperation of hundreds of participating newspapers and educational institutions. Each course features a series of newspaper articles, a reader, and a study guide. The program enables millions of people to become better informed on issues of vital interest, as well as providing an opportunity for part-time students to obtain college credit."

*   *   *

SCHENKEN, Howard   1904(?)-1979

PERSONAL: Born c. 1904; died February 20, 1979, in Palm Springs, Calif.; married wife, Bea Gale; stepchildren: Susan Ruskin, Sandra Brandler. *Residence:* New York, N.Y.

CAREER: Championship contract bridge player; writer and authority on contract bridge. Member of four world team title groups, 1936, 1950, 1951, 1953. Author of syndicated bridge column for more than thirty years. *Awards, honors:* Winner of numerous titles and awards for bridge playing, including five victories in the Life Master Pair Championship and ten triumphs in each of the major knockout team events.

WRITINGS: Better Bidding in 15 Minutes, Expert Bidding in a Week, introduction by Albert H. Morehead, Simon & Schuster, 1963; *Howard Schenken's Big Club: A Revolutionary, Highly Competitive, and Accurate Way to Bid for Every Bridge Player,* Simon & Schuster, 1968; *The Education of a Bridge Player* (autobiography), Simon & Schuster, 1973. Also author of *Four Aces System of Contract Bridge*.

SIDELIGHTS: Howard Schenken, who played contract bridge for more than fifty years, was considered one of the world's leading players by many bridge authorities. During his lifetime he won nearly every possible honor for his exper-

tise in the game, and was a member of the Four Aces team that dominated American tournaments during the 1930's. After World War II, Schenken teamed up with such notable players as B. Jay Becker, John Crawford, George Rapee, and Sam Stayman, to once again control tournament play. In world team competition he represented the United States four times, and played against the preeminent Italian Blue Team twice. It was after his experiences with the Italian team that Schenken decided to develop his Big Club system, which gained popularity in later years. Regarded as an innovator in theoretical bridge ideas, Schenken initiated into play the forcing two-over-one response, the prepared opening bid, and the weak two-bid.

OBITUARIES: New York Times, February 21, 1979; *Chicago Tribune,* February 22, 1979; *Washington Post,* February 22, 1979.*

*   *   *

SCHLAMM, William S(iegmund)   1904-1978

PERSONAL: Born June 10, 1904, in Pramysl, Austria-Hungary (now in Poland); died of a heart attack, September 1, 1978, in Salzburg, Austria; married Stephanie Kohaut. *Education:* Attended University of Vienna.

CAREER: Editor of *Die Weltbuehne* until 1938; assistant to editor-in-chief of *Time, Life,* and *Fortune,* New York City, 1941-50; editor of *Freeman,* 1951-54; *National Review,* New York City, co-founder and editor, 1955-57; former columnist in *Der Stern; Zeitbuehne,* West Germany, founder and editor, 1972-78.

WRITINGS—In English: The Second War of Independence: A Call to Action, Dutton, c. 1940, chapter eight reprinted as *Hitler's Conquest of America* (booklet), Farrar & Rinehart, 1941; *Germany and the East-West Crisis: The Decisive Challenge to American Policy,* McKay, 1959.

Other works: *Diktatur der luege, eine abrechnung* (title means "Dictatorship of the Lie"), Der Aufbruch, 1937; *Die Grenzen des Wunders: ein Bericht ueber Deutschland,* Europa, 1959; *Wer is Jude?, eine Selbstgespraech,* Seewald, 1964; *Am Rande des Buergerkriegs,* Zeit, 1970; *Zorn und Gelaechter: Zeitgeschichte aus spitzer Feder,* Langen-Mueller, 1977. Contributor to magazines, including *New York Times, Life, America,* and *Mercury.*

SIDELIGHTS: In the *Chicago Sunday Tribune,* Francis Schwarzenberg critiqued Schlamm's book *Germany and the East-West Crisis* as being "a major contribution to the literature on the German problem. Its importance is not only in the novelty and incisiveness, but even more in the amount of contradictory emotions the book is bound to stir and the controversy it will evoke."

Through his journalistic efforts, first in Vienna, then in Prague, in the United States, and finally in Germany, Schlamm was "an indefatigable fighter for all the great values of our civilization," wrote Erik von Kuehnelt-Leddihn. With a penchant for extremes, Schlamm was a loyal Communist until, at age twenty-five, he made an about-face to become a right-wingconservative.

Schlamm edited the leftist monthly *Die Weltbuehne* in Prague until he was ousted from that post by the Nazis in the late 1930's. Subsequently, he traveled to New York City where he became, in William F. Buckley's words, "one of the most important influences in Time Inc., which was in those days about the only show in town." A maverick, Schlamm eventually found it necessary to move on. He joined the staff of the *Freeman* where he remained as editor until the journal folded.

Before returning to Germany in 1957, Schlamm was instrumental in launching the conservative *National Review,* which he edited for two years. Once back in Germany, he achieved success as a lecturer, a writer, and the pilot of his own journal, *Die Zeitbuehne.* He was, in von Kuehnelt-Leddihn's view, "one of the most remarkable men of our times."

BIOGRAPHICAL/CRITICAL SOURCES: Saturday Review, May 30, 1959; *Chicago Sunday Tribune,* May 31, 1959; *Nation,* June 13, 1959; *New York Times,* September 20, 1959; *National Review,* September 29, 1968, October 13, 1978.

OBITUARIES: Time, October 2, 1978.*

*   *   *

SCHLEE, Susan   1940-

PERSONAL: Born January 22, 1940, in New York, N.Y.; daughter of John I. H. (an art museum director) and Louisa (a teacher; maiden name, Chase) Baur; married John Schlee (a marine geologist), December, 1969; children: Scottland, Louisa. *Education:* Vassar College, A.B., 1961; graduate study at Florida Atlantic University, 1967, and Duke University, 1968. *Agent:* Russell & Volkening, Inc., 551 Fifth Ave., New York, N.Y. 10017. *Office:* Marine Biological Laboratory, Woods Hole, Mass. 02543.

CAREER: Binghamton Sun Bulletin, Binghamton, N.Y., journalist, 1963-65; *Palm Beach Post-Times,* Palm Beach, Fla., journalist, 1967; Sea Education Association, Woods Hole, Mass., lecturer, 1975-79; Marine Biological Laboratory, Woods Hole, guest investigator, 1969—. *Awards, honors:* Pfizer Award from History of Science Society, 1974, for *The Edge of an Unfamiliar World.*

WRITINGS: The Edge of an Unfamiliar World: A History of Oceanography, Dutton, 1973 (published in England as *A History of Oceanography: The Edge of an Unfinished World,* R. Hale, 1975); *On Almost Any Wind: The Saga of the Oceanographic Research Vessel "Atlantis,"* Cornell University Press, 1978. Contributor of several dozen articles to magazines, including *Natural History, Smithsonian, Oceans,* and *Sailing.*

WORK IN PROGRESS: Research on the history of medicine.

*   *   *

SCHMITT, Raymond L(ouis)   1936-

PERSONAL: Born July 11, 1936, in South Bend, Ind.; son of Edward Schmitt; married; wife's name, Margo; children: Laury, Bowan, Tiffani. *Education:* University of Notre Dame, B.A., 1958, M.A., 1959; University of Iowa, Ph.D., 1964. *Home:* 1204 Jersey Ave., Normal, Ill. 61761. *Office:* Department of Sociology, Illinois State University, Normal, Ill. 61761.

CAREER: Southern Illinois University, Carbondale, assistant professor of sociology, 1963-65; Eastern Michigan University, Ypsilanti, associate professor of sociology, 1965-68; Illinois State University, Normal, associate professor, 1968-73, professor of sociology, 1973—. Visiting associate professor at University of Michigan, summer, 1966.

WRITINGS: (Contributor) Thomas E. Lasswell, John H. Burma, and Sidney H. Arronson, editors, *Life in Society,* Scott, Foresman, 1970; *The Reference Other Orientation: An Extension of the Reference Group Concept,* Southern Illinois University Press, 1972; (contributor) Stanley E.

Grupp, editor, *The Marihuana Muddle,* Heath, 1973; (with Edward B. Jelks) *Trick Taking Potential: A Quantitative Analysis of Bridge,* JETT Publishing, 1974; (contributor) Norman K. Denzin, editor, *Studies in Symbolic Interaction,* JAI Press, Volume II, 1978, Volume III, 1980. Contributor of about twenty-five articles and reviews to journals in the social sciences.

*   *   *

SCHOLEY, Arthur   1932-

PERSONAL: Born June 17, 1932, in Sheffield, England; son of Edward and Lucy Scholey. *Home:* 1 Cranbourne Rd., London N10 2BT, England.

CAREER: Writer.

WRITINGS: Song of Caedmon (one-act cantata; first produced in London at Holy Trinity Church, 1971), Bodley Head, 1971, Galaxy, 1972; (with David Owen) *Christmas Plays and Ideas for Worship: Materials and Ideas for Teachers and Leaders in School or Church,* Denholm House, 1974; *The Discontented Dervishes and Other Persian Tales,* Deutsch, 1977; *Sallinka and the Golden Bird,* Evans Brothers, 1978, Prentice-Hall, 1979; *Wacky and His Fuddlejig* (one-act musical play; first produced in London at St. James Church, 1977), Alfred A. Kalmus, 1978; *Singalive!* (songs), Collins Liturgical, 1979; *The Dickens Christmas Carol Show* (two-act musical play; first produced in London, 1977), Anchorage Press, 1979; *Twelve Tales for a Christmas Night,* Rex Collings, 1979; *Herod and the Rooster* (one-act cantata; first produced in London, 1975), Grail Publications, 1979; *Baboushka* (one-act cantata; first produced in Guildford, England, at St. Joseph's R. C. Middle School, December, 1978), Collins Liturgical, 1980.

WORK IN PROGRESS: "The True History of Dick Whittington," a two-act Christmas play with music; "The Visitors," a two-act opera with music by Donald Swann; *O, And I Also Saw a Dragon,* a picture book for children; *The Caliph's Reward,* retold tales of Rumi for children; *Issunboshi and the Magic Mallet,* a picture book for children; "Jekyll and Hyde," a solo dramatic version of Robert Louis Stevenson's story.

SIDELIGHTS: Scholey told *CA:* "Most of my writing so far has stemmed from a deep interest in myth, legend, folk tale and fable, and indeed in tales of all kinds. Some of these stories I have retold (*The Discontented Dervishes* is a selection from the twelfth-century Persian poet Sa'di), others, like *Song of Caedmon,* have been re-cast into 'celebratory dramatic community events.' *The Dickens Christmas Carol Show* expands the one-acts into a full-length stage medium, while still retaining the celebratory community aspect. In fiction, *Twelve Tales for a Christmas Night* combines old tales with some new ones of my own; *Sallinka* is completely new but so imbued with a sense of folk tale that most people are sure they have 'read it somewhere before.' (I dread, one day, being presented with evidence!) In *Singalive!* all these interests emerge as songs, composed by Donald Swann, with whom I have worked a lot. Mainly I think of myself as a storyteller, though using today's media (radio, television, stage, picture books, song, music drama, etc.) to carry out the once-upon-a-time profession."

*   *   *

SCHRAFFENBERGER, Nancy   1933-

PERSONAL: Born October 20, 1933, in Gloversville, N.Y.; daughter of Robert Pierce and Ruth (Sponnoble) Spraker;

married David Schraffenberger (a writer), October 18, 1969; children: Rebecca. *Education:* Bennington College, B.A., 1954. *Home:* 500 Second Ave., New York, N.Y. 10016. *Agent:* Virginia Barber Literary Agency, Inc., 44 Greenwich Ave., New York, N.Y. 10011.

CAREER: Good Housekeeping, New York City, staff writer, 1954-60; worked as sales promotion writer for Macy's, Collier Books, and *House and Garden* magazine, New York City, 1960-63; *Woman's Day,* New York City, staff writer and editor, 1963-71; free-lance writer, 1971—.

WRITINGS: (With Mildred and Kenneth Cooper) *Aerobics for Women,* M. Evans, 1972; (with Joy Herrick) *Something's Got to Help—And Yoga Can,* M. Evans, 1974; *Woman's Day Celebrating Christmas,* Columbia House, 1979. Contributor to popular magazines, including/ *Cosmopolitan* and *Reader's Digest.*

WORK IN PROGRESS: "Researching needlework books for CBS Special Marketing Division."

SIDELIGHTS: Schraffenberger told *CA:* "I have had an ardent interest in reading—and thus in writing—since childhood. Although I did a lot of copywriting during my early career, I didn't do a by-lined piece until the mid-1960's, when Geraldine E. Rhoads, editor of *Woman's Day,* began to give me assignments that challenged my abilities. I have always written 'service' material, but in my heart of hearts I long to be able to write publishable essays and/or short fiction, and perhaps I will someday. When I was a child, writing was free and easy. Now it is costly and hard. No other work makes me demand more of myelf, and so, for me, it is the only work worth doing."

*   *   *

SCHRAMM, Sarah Slavin   1942-

PERSONAL: Born March 26, 1942, in Salt Lake City, Utah; daughter of Hale Burgher (a physician) and Ruth (Martin) Slavin; married William Lloyd Woofter, May 16, 1958 (divorced March, 1959); married Victor LeRoy Schramm, Jr. (a physician), October 16, 1962; children: (first marriage) Heidi Ruth, (second marriage) Beth, Victor Hale. *Education:* University of Iowa, B.A., 1962, graduate study, 1964-65; Webster College, M.A.T., 1972; George Washington University, Ph.D., 1979. *Politics:* "Considerable, mostly Democrat." *Religion:* "Member of St. Louis Ethical Society." *Home and office:* 1265 Beechwood Blvd., Pittsburgh, Pa. 15206.

CAREER: Editorial intern for *American Political Science Review,* 1976-78; founding editor of *Women and Politics: A Journal of Research and Policy Studies,* 1978—. Lecturer at Webster College, 1973; visiting professor at U.S. Department of Justice Law Enforcement Assistance Agency, 1974; lecturer at Mt. Vernon College, Washington, D.C., 1977, 1978.

MEMBER: American Political Science Association, Center for the Study of the Presidency, Policy Studies Organization, National Women's Studies Association (charter member), Coalition of Women in the Humanities and Social Sciences (steering committee member), Coordinating Committee on Women in the Historical Profession, Women's Caucus for Political Science (member of executive council, 1974—; president, 1979-80), Midwestern Political Science Association, Southern Political Science Association, Pi Sigma Alpha.

WRITINGS: (Editor) *Female Studies Series,* Volume VIII, Know, Inc., 1975; (contributor) Kathleen O'Connor Blum-

hagen and Walter D. Johnson, editors, *Readings in Women's Studies: Interdisciplinary Collection,* Greenwood Press, 1978; (contributor) Marian Lief Palley and Michael Preston, editors, *Minorities and Policy Problems,* Lexington Books, 1979; *Plow Women Rather Than Reapers: An Intellectual History of Feminism in the United States,* Scarecrow, 1979. Contributor to journals in the political and social sciences.

WORK IN PROGRESS: The Politics of Executive Orders; editing *The Study of Women and Politics: A Symposium Exploring Methodological Issues; Women in the Political System; For the Love of Women: An Allegory,* a novel.

SIDELIGHTS: Schramm told *CA:* "I have been writing all my life: letters, papers, speeches, poetry, articles, and now books. The intensity I bring to particular kinds of written expression varies with my personal circumstances and the situation in which I find myself.

"I am most interested in relationships among women and feminism, in a humanism which includes ecological considerations, and in social change and human behavior. I bring to these topics a lifetime of social and political activism. In many ways, writing is for me inextricably related to and intertwined with that activism. It is hard for me to say where one lays off and the other begins.

"I believe profoundly that it takes personal commitment to better human circumstances, and that those circumstances need to be and deserve to be changed. I am not so much committed to the creation of an individually perfect world, as for example Anais Nin was. I am more inclined toward Virginia Woolf's concern for translating the freedom of women's minds into the minds of others, and toward Lillian Hellman's emphasis on seeing old ways of thinking and then seeing them again through newer choices—which is only to say that I believe one person can accomplish a great deal in a complex and even determined world; but such accomplishment must be in tune with what is possible and with the tribulations and tendencies of important others.

"I realize that I am as limited in life chances as any other woman, as in fact any people who are status-deprived. For me at least, those limitations are as nothing in the end, when I consider the leeway I can seize and make use of. The need to express this credo is perhaps the greatest impetus to write that I experience."

BIOGRAPHICAL/CRITICAL SOURCES: Iowa City Press Citizen, January 28, 1965; *St. Louis Globe-Democrat,* March 28, 1973.

*   *   *

SCHROEDER, Andreas (Peter)   1946-

PERSONAL: Born November 26, 1946, in Hoheneggelsen, Germany; son of Ernst (a carpenter) and Ruth (an organist; maiden name, Bartel) Schroeder; married Sharon Elizabeth Brown (in business management); children: Sabrina Anne. *Education:* University of British Columbia, B.A., 1969, M.A., 1971. *Politics:* New Democrat. *Religion:* Mennonite. *Home address:* P.O. Box 3127, Mission, British Columbia, Canada V2V 4J3.

CAREER: Prism International, Vancouver, British Columbia, editorial assistant, 1968-69; *Contemporary Literature in Translation,* Vancouver, founding editor, 1969-79; free-lance writer, 1979—. Member of faculty at University of Victoria, 1975-77. Member of board of directors of British Columbia Film Co-Op, 1970-71. *Member:* International P.E.N., Writers Union of Canada (chair, 1976-77), League of Canadian Poets, Canadian Periodical Publishers Association, Periodical Writers Association. *Awards, honors:* Gordon Woodward Memorial Award from University of British Columbia, 1969, for short story, "The Past People"; script prize from National Film Board, 1971, for "The Late Man"; Canada Council grants, 1968, 1971, 1973, 1975, 1979.

WRITINGS: The Ozone Minotaur (poems), Sono Nis Press, 1969; *File of Uncertainties* (poems), Sono Nis Press, 1971; (with David Frith) *uniVerse* (concrete poems), MassAge Press, 1971; *The Late Man* (stories), Sono Nis Press, 1972; *Shaking It Rough: A Prison Memoir,* Doubleday, 1976; *The Illegal Smile* (novel), Doubleday, in press.

Screenplays: "The Plastic Mile," Ruvinsky Productions, 1969; "Immobile," MassAge Productions, 1969; "The Pub," MassAge Productions, 1970; "The Late Man," Odyssey Films, 1973.

Editor: (With Joel Michael Yates) *Contemporary Poetry of British Columbia,* Sono Nis Press, Volume I, 1970, Volume II, 1972; (with Rudy Wiebe) *Stories of the Pacific Northwest,* Macmillan, 1974; (with Wiebe) *Stories From Pacific and Arctic Canada,* Macmillan, 1975.

Translator: (With Michael Bullock) *The Stage and Creative Arts,* New York Graphic Society, 1969; *Collected Stories of Ilse Aichinger,* Sono Nis Press, 1974.

Author of a weekly column in *Vancouver Province,* 1968-73. Editor of *Poetry Canada,* 1970-71; literary critic for *Vancouver Province-Pacific Press,* 1970-73; member of editorial board of *Canadian Fiction,* 1971—.

SIDELIGHTS: In his book, *Shaking It Rough: A Prison Memoir,* Schroeder attempts to reveal the inadequacies and injustices of the penal system. Incarcerated for eight months, though sentenced to two years, he writes of the prison experience first-hand. Punishing a criminal by putting him in jail will not rehabilitate him, Schroeder insists; it will only help to reinforce the degradation, hopelessness, and rebellion that led the offender into a life of crime initially. The vicious cycle continues forever on.

Schroeder feels disillusioned with many governmental policies. Considering those in power too slow in dealing with important social issues, he related that he "occasionally [becomes] incensed enough about Canada's idiotic cultural politics to accept an official position which enables me to lock horns with the politicians who seem most at fault. Invariably, I rue the day. Meanwhile, writing seems to get harder the more I commit it. That seems a trifle unfair, somehow."

BIOGRAPHICAL/CRITICAL SOURCES: Saturday Night, October, 1976; *Best Sellers,* June, 1977.

*   *   *

SCHWARTZ, Betty   1927-
(Betty Black)

PERSONAL: Born July 17, 1927, in Philadelphia, Pa.; daughter of Frank (a teacher) and Jean (a store proprietor; maiden name, Snyder) Fisher; married Sol Schwartz (a jewelry store owner), September 7, 1947; children: Karen Schwartz Green. *Education:* Graduated from high school in Philadelphia, Pa. *Residence:* Beverly Hills, Calif. *Agent:* Jane Jordan Browne, Multimedia Product Development, Inc., 410 South Michigan Ave., Room 828, Chicago, Ill. 60605.

CAREER: Fashion model, 1948-50; Sol Schwartz Jewelry Co., Beverly Hills, Calif., vice-president and secretary, 1950—. Also worked as business manager for entertainers. *Member:* Writers Guild of America (West). *Awards, honors:*

First prize in fashion promotion competition sponsored by Philadelphia Fashion Group, 1958.

WRITINGS—All under pseudonym Betty Black: (With daughter, Karen Green) *How to Cook His Goose* (cookbook), Winchester Press, 1973; (with Casey Bishop) *The Sisterhood* (novel), W. H. Allen, 1977.

WORK IN PROGRESS: (Under pseudonym Betty Black) *I Want to Die With Dignity* (tentative title), an account of her sister's death from a rare disease.

SIDELIGHTS: Betty Schwartz wrote: "Whenever I am swept up by a subject—confronted with the challenge of preparing wild fowl, game, and fishermen's catch (*How to Cook His Goose*), enveloped by horror and anger (*The Sisterhood* is a novel about rape victims), or totally engulfed by love and desperation (my current work), I head for my typewriter. I am by nature an introvert and I find that expressing my feelings on paper to be a great catharsis that offers me emotional satisfaction."

*   *   *

SCHWEITZER, Albert   1875-1965

OBITUARY NOTICE: Born January 14, 1875, in Kaisersberg, Alsace, Germany; died September 4, 1965, in Lambarene, Gabon. Physician, clergyman, missionary, musician, theologian, author, and winner of the Nobel Peace Prize in 1952. At the age of thirty, after earning numerous degrees in music, theology, and medicine, Schweitzer decided to devote the rest of his life "to the direct service of humanity." In 1914 he journeyed to French Equatorial Africa where he established a hospital. The humanitarian supported the hospital himself by giving organ recitals and lectures around the world and by writing many books about theology, music, and his experiences in Africa. Schweitzer worked at the hospital until his death. His works include *The Quest of the Historical Jesus, Out of My Life and Thought,* and *On the Edge of the Primeval Forest.* Obituaries and other sources: *Current Biography,* Wilson, 1948, July, 1965, November, 1965; *New York Times,* September 6, 1965; *Publishers Weekly,* September 27, 1965; *The Reader's Encyclopedia,* 2nd edition, Crowell, 1965; *Twentieth Century Writing: A Reader's Guide to Contemporary Literature,* Transatlantic, 1969; *Longman Companion to Twentieth Century Literature,* Longman, 1970; *Biography News,* Volume I, Gale, 1974; *The Oxford Companion to German Literature,* Clarendon Press, 1976.

*   *   *

SCOTT, Dorothea Hayward

PERSONAL: Born in London, England; came to the United States in 1960; daughter of Edward (a land surveyor) and Margaret Denvil (Connelly) Hayward; married A. C. Scott (a professor of theatre, writer, and artist), 1936; children: Tim. *Education:* University of London, A.L.A., 1934. *Home:* 3201 Stevens St., #5, Madison, Wis. 53705. *Office:* Library School, University of Wisconsin, Madison, Wis. 53706.

CAREER: Victoria and Albert Museum, London, England, library cataloger, 1933-36; British Broadcasting Corp. (BBC), London, records monitor in European Intelligence Division, 1940-41; Surrey County Library, England, senior assistant, 1942-46; British Council librarian in Nanking, China, 1947-49; University of Hong Kong, Hong Kong, director of library, 1950-60; Columbia University, New York, N.Y., assistant to the director, 1960-62; Cornell University, Ithaca, N.Y., East Asian bibliographer, 1962-64;

University of Wisconsin—Madison, lecturer in library science, 1964—.

WRITINGS: Chinese Popular Literature and the CUILD: An Outline History, American Library Association, 1979. Contributor of articles and reviews to library journals. Editor of *Annual Bibliography of Asian Studies*, of *Journal of Asian Studies*, 1961.

WORK IN PROGRESS: Research on the history of book illustration and the history of books and printing.

SIDELIGHTS: Dorothea Scott has lived in France and Indonesia, as well as the Far East, and has traveled widely in Asia and Europe. Her special interest is Asian (especially Chinese) juvenile literature.

Scott told *CA:* "I regularly review books on East and Southeast Asia generally, China and Japan in particular, for *School Library Journal.* I am concerned above all with accuracy of information about these countries and with authenticity in illustration. My study of Chinese popular literature traces the origins of stories for Chinese children often culled from classical sources and forming a living tradition in the hands of storytellers, in puppet dramas, live plays and films. It is from these sources that re-tellings are drawn for Western children."

* * *

SEARCH-LIGHT
See FRANK, Waldo (David)

* * *

SEGAL, Elliot A(lan) 1938-

PERSONAL: Born June 26, 1938, in Boston, Mass.; son of Hyman and Lena (Wolfson) Segal; married Ann Shimkin, June 5, 1966; children: Daniel, Laura, Misha. *Education:* Brandeis University, B.A., 1960; Yale University, M.Ur.S. and M.P.H., both 1965. *Home:* 8105 Thoreau Dr., Bethesda, Md. 20034. *Office:* U.S. House of Representatives, Washington, D.C. 20515.

CAREER: Yale University, New Haven, Conn., faculty member and assistant dean, 1965-73; U.S. House of Representatives, Washington, D.C., director of health task force for oversight subcommittee, 1975-79, staff director of health and environment subcommittee, 1979—. *Military service:* U.S. Army Reserve, Medical Service Corps, 1960-65. *Member:* American Association for the Advancement of Science, American Public Health Association (fellow). *Awards, honors:* Congressional science fellow of American Association for the Advancement of Science, 1973-74.

WRITINGS: (With Warren G. Magnuson) *How Much for Health?*, Luce, 1974. Contributor to health journals.

* * *

SEGEL, Thomas D(onald) 1931-

PERSONAL: Born June 11, 1931, in Tacoma, Wash.; son of Nathan R. Segel and Vesta May (Stater) Segel Fisher; married Pattie Beatrice Hood, December 30, 1950; children: Jason Barry. *Education:* Attended San Diego State College (now University), 1952-53, and Washington State University; Arlington State University, B.A., 1961; also attended University of Tokyo, 1963-64. *Religion:* Presbyterian. *Home:* 1629 Clarke St., Harlingen, Tex. 78550. *Office:* Marine Military Academy, 320 Iwo Jima Blvd., Harlingen, Tex. 78550.

CAREER: U.S. Marine Corps, career officer, 1948-74, infantry unit leader, 1948-53, in public relations for Marine recruiting, Seattle, Wash., 1954-58, editor of *Flight Jacket*, El Toro, Calif., 1958-60, in public relations for Marine recruiting, Dallas, Tex., 1960-63, member of press team for Olympic Games, Tokyo, Japan, 1963-64, combat correspondent, Vietnam, 1965, station manager of Armed Forces Television in Okinawa, Japan, 1966-69, commander of American Forces Radio and Television in Tuy Hoa, Vietnam, 1970, operations director of American Forces Network in Saigon, Vietnam, 1971, station manager and network operations officer of Far East Network in Tokyo, 1971-74, retiring as master gunnery sergeant; Marine Military Academy, Harlingen, Tex., director of public affairs, 1974—. President of Rebel Days, Inc., 1974-77. Member of Republican town committee.

MEMBER: International Good Neighbor Council, American Legion, Disabled American Veterans, National Broadcasters Association, Writers Guild, Military Writers League, Christian Writers Association, Combat Correspondents Association (past president), Advertising Publishers Association, Fleet Reserve Association, Veterans of Foreign Wars, Marine Corps League, First Marine Division Association, Confederate Air Force Inc., Texas Association of Publishers, Elks, Lions, Rotary International, Arroyo Boat Club (commodore). *Awards, honors*—Military: Bronze Star, three Purple Hearts, Cross of Gallantry. Other: Named military writer of the year by Armed Forces Writers League, 1965, for photo-journalism coverage of Vietnam war; Silver Anchor Award from Armed Forces Writers League, 1967, for best feature story in a military publication for "Biggest Little Train in the World," 1968, for best news story for "Mount Out," and 1969, for best editorial for "Thanks Doc"; radio production award from Combat Correspondents Association, 1972, for world wide coverage of reversion of Okinawa; Thomas Jefferson Award for Journalistic Excellence from Army/Navy Times Foundation, 1974, for publication on the energy crisis.

WRITINGS: Dateline Vietnam, Gallant, 1966; *Men in Space*, Paladin Press, 1975; *In the Shadow of Honor*, Media Inc., 1979. Author of "Tell It Like It Is," a column in *Valley Citizen* and other newspapers, 1976—. Editor-in-chief of *Valley Citizen* and *MMA Journal* (of Marine Military Academy).

WORK IN PROGRESS: An examination of the cruel treatment of Mexican-Americans during the late 1800's, tentatively titled *Terror by Law*, publication expected in 1981.

SIDELIGHTS: Segel commented: "My writing has been centered around politics, defense, and education. I write as a strong Conservative.

"Half my adult life was spent in Asia. I speak Japanese, and have written, taught, and lived in Japan. I have also traveled to almost all the countries and islands of the Pacific. The self-pride and nationalism I saw in the people of Japan has created in me the desire to see these traits reborn in America. I write with the hope of aiding that idea.

"Many say I am an angry writer. I must admit to some degree of anger, but there is really more sad than mad in my work. I almost cry when I see my own countrymen selling their land, their history, their souls, for the fake promises of another 'free lunch' and a bigger government handout. These are the views I report on and they are seen by many as cries of anger."

SEIDEL, Michael Alan 1943-

PERSONAL: Born August 24, 1943, in New York, N.Y.; son of Jack (a businessman) and Ann (an X-ray technician; maiden name, Guthaim) Seidel; married Maria DiBattista (a professor), June 28, 1976. *Education:* University of California, Los Angeles, B.A., 1966, Ph.D., 1970. *Office:* Department of English, Columbia University, 409 Hamilton Hall, New York, N.Y. 10027.

CAREER: Yale University, New Haven, Conn., assistant professor, 1970-76, associate professor of English, 1976-77; Columbia University, New York, N.Y., associate professor, 1977-79, professor of English, 1980—. *Member:* Modern Language Association of America, American Society for Eighteenth Century Studies. *Awards, honors:* National Endowment for the Humanities junior fellowship, 1974-75.

WRITINGS: Epic Geography: James Joyce's Ulysses, Princeton University Press, 1976; (editor) *Homer to Brecht,* Yale University Press, 1977; (contributor) Edward Mendelson, editor, *Twentieth-Century Views,* Prentice-Hall, 1977; *Satiric Inheritance: Rabelais to Sterne,* Princeton University Press, 1979.

WORK IN PROGRESS: A book on the theory of the novel from the eighteenth to twentieth century; serving as associate editor of *The Works of Daniel Defoe.*

SIDELIGHTS: Seidel told *CA:* "I am a baseball fan at the expense of all other matters (serious or trivial)."

*   *   *

SEIGEL, Jules 1931-

PERSONAL: Born October 10, 1931, in Liberty, N.Y.; son of Samuel and Charlotte (Schutzman) Seigel; married Catharine Dolores Fressie, 1959; children: Julia Anne, Sean, Jessica. *Education:* State University of New York College at Cortland, B.A., 1959; University of Maryland, M.A., 1962, Ph.D., 1965. *Home address:* Saugatucket Rd., Peace Dale, R.I. 02879. *Office:* Department of English, University of Rhode Island, Kingston, R.I. 02881.

CAREER: University of Rhode Island, Kingston, assistant professor, 1965-71, associate professor, 1971-76, professor of literature, 1976—. *Military service:* U.S. Air Force, 1950-54.

WRITINGS: (Editor) *Carlyle: The Critical Heritage,* Routledge & Kegan Paul, 1971; (author of new introduction) *Diderot's Early Philosophical Works* (translated by Margaret Jourdain), AMS Press, 1973; (contributor) K. J. Fielding and Rodger L. Tarr, editor, *Carlyle Past and Present: A Collection of New Essays,* Vision Press, 1976; (contributor) Robert Rieber, editor, *Psychology of Language and Thought,* Plenum, 1980. Also contributor to *Realms of Gold: Essays in Honor of H. E. Robinson,* edited by Allan MacLaine and others, 1977.

Contributor to literature journals and literary magazines, including *New England Quarterly, Journal of the History of Ideas,* and *Studies in English Literature.*

WORK IN PROGRESS: Editing a critical edition of Carlyle's *Latter-Day Pamphlets* with Michael Goldberg; research on Carlyle in Ireland.

*   *   *

SELF, Carolyn Shealy 1931-

PERSONAL: Born December 3, 1931, in Ocala, Fla.; daughter of Edgar Clarence (a tax collector) and Elsie (a teacher; maiden name, Stubbs) Shealy; married William Lee Self (a minister), August 2, 1953; children: William Lee, Jr., Bryan Edgar. *Education:* Stetson University, A.B., 1953; attended Georgia Mental Health Institute for Pastoral Care and Counseling, 1975; also attended Tift College. *Religion:* Southern Baptist. *Home:* 609 Old Ivy Rd. N.E., Atlanta, Ga. 30342.

CAREER: Lecturer and workshop director; member of board of directors of Horizon House (halfway house for women prisoners), 1977-78. *Member:* Kappa Delta Pi.

WRITINGS: (With husband, William L. Self) *Survival Kit for the Stranded,* Broadman, 1975; *Confident Entertaining,* Thomas Nelson, 1976; (with W. L. Self) *Learning to Pray,* Word, Inc., 1978.

WORK IN PROGRESS: A study guide, *Till Death (or the Congregation) Do Us Part;* a novel based on alcohol-drug abusers and their families.

SIDELIGHTS: Carolyn Self commented: "I travel for the Foreign Mission Board of the Southern Baptist Convention, holding seminars for missionaries on the problems of living. I have also made trips for the governments of the United States, the Republic of China, and South Korea, including a diplomatic tour. I have traveled around the world several times and visited remote areas. I work with hurting people wherever they are."

*   *   *

SERPIERES
See GUILLEVIC, (Eugene)

*   *   *

SESSIONS, Roger Huntington 1896-

PERSONAL: Born December 28, 1896, in Brooklyn, N.Y.; son of Archibald Lowery and Ruth Gregson (Huntington) Sessions; married Barbara Foster, 1920 (marriage ended); married Elizabeth Franck, November 26, 1936; children: John Porter, Elizabeth Phelps. *Education:* Harvard University, A.B., 1915; Yale University, Mus.B., 1917; studied music and composition privately with Edward Burlingame Hill, Horatio Parker, and Ernest Bloch. *Home:* 63 Stanworth Lane, Princeton, N.J. 08540. *Office:* Department of Composition, Juilliard School of Music, New York, N.Y. 10023.

CAREER: Composer. Smith College, Northampton, Mass., teacher, 1917-19, instructor in music, 1919-21; Cleveland Institute of Music, Cleveland, Ohio, teacher in theory and assistant to director, 1921-25; "Copland-Sessions" concerts, New York City, co-director, 1928-31; teacher and lecturer at New School for Social Research, New York City, Malkin Conservatory and Boston University, Boston, Mass., and Dalcroze School of Music, 1933-35; Princeton University, Princeton, N.J., instructor, 1935-37, assistant professor, 1937-40, associate professor of music, 1940-45; University of California, Berkeley, professor of music, 1945; Academia Luigi Cherubini, Florence, Italy, lecturer in music, 1951-52; Princeton University, William Shubael Conant Professor of Music, 1953-65; University of California, Berkeley, Ernest Bloch Professor of Music, 1966-67; Harvard University, Cambridge, Mass., Charles Elliot Norton Professor of Music, 1966-69; Juilliard School of Music, New York City, member of faculty, 1966—. Co-director, Columbia-Princeton Electronic Music Center, 1961—.

MEMBER: International Society for Contemporary Music (president of U.S. section, 1934-42), National Institute of Arts and Letters, American Academy of Arts and Letters, American Academy of Arts and Sciences, American Composers Alliance (member of executive committee), Akademie der Kuenste, League of Composers, Broadcast Music. *Award, honors:* Steinert Prize for "Symphonic Prelude"; Guggenheim fellow, 1926-28; Walter Damrosch fellow, 1928-31; Carnagie Foundation fellow, 1931-33; New York Music Critic's Award, 1950, for "Symphony No. 2"; Creative Arts award from Brandeis University, 1958; elected Ausserordentliches Mitglied from Akademie der Kuenste, 1960; gold medal from National Institute of Arts and Sciences, 1961; Academico Corr from Academia Nacional de Bellas Artes, Argentina, 1965; medal from Edward MacDowell Association, 1968; charter member of Berkeley Fellows, 1968; Pulitzer Special Citation for Music, 1974; honorary degrees from more than ten colleges and universities in the United States.

WRITINGS: (Contributor) Augusto Centeno, editor, *The Intent of the Artist,* Princeton University Press, 1941; (translator with Alexander H. Krappe and Oliver Strunk) Alfred Einstein, *The Italian Madrigal,* Princeton University Press, 1949; *The Musical Experience of Composer, Performer, Listener,* Princeton University Press, 1950; *Harmonic Practice,* Harcourt, 1951; *Reflections on the Musical Life in the United States,* Merlin, 1956; *Questions About Music,* Harvard University Press, 1970; *Roger Sessions on Music: Collected Essays,* edited by Edward T. Cone, Princeton University Press, 1979. Also author of *The Reminiscences of Roger Sessions,* a transcript of interviews conducted by F. Rounds and Cone for Oral History Research Office of Columbia University, 1962.

Musical compositions: "Symphonic Prelude," 1916; "The Black Maskers," 1923; "Three Chorale Preludes for Organ," 1926; "Symphony No. 1," 1927; "Sonata for Piano," 1930; "Concerto for Violin," 1935; "Chorale for Organ," 1938; *String Quartet No. 1,* Arrow Music, 1938; "Three Dirges for Orchestra," 1938; "Duo for Violin and Piano," 1942; "The Trial of Lucullus" (one-act opera), first produced in Berkeley, California, April 18, 1947; *Sonata No. 2 for Piano,* E. B. Marks, 1948; *Symphony No. 2,* G. Schirmer, 1949; *String Quartet No. 2,* E. B. Marks, 1952; "Idyll of Theocritus," 1954; "Mass," 1956; "Symphony No. 3," 1957; "String Quintet," 1958; "Symphony No. 4," 1958.

"Divertimento for Orchestra," 1960; "Montezuma" (three-act opera), first produced at Deutsch Oper in West Berlin, April 19, 1964; "Psalm 140," 1963; "Six Pieces for Cello," 1966; "Six Pieces for Violin Solo," 1966; "Symphony No. 7," 1967; "Rhapsody for Orchestra," 1970; "Canons," 1971; *Symphony No. 5,* E. B. Marks, 1971; *Symphony No. 8,* E. B. Marks, 1973; *Concertino for Chamber Orchestra,* E. B. Marks, 1974; *When Lilacs Last in the Dooryard Bloom'd,* Merion Music, 1974; *Symphony No. 6,* Merion Music, 1975; *Three Choruses on Biblical Texts,* Merion Music, 1976.

SIDELIGHTS: Although Roger Sessions has written an impressive sum of music, few of his compositions get to the concert hall. One reason for this is the complexity of his scores. The "Concerto for Violin" (1935), for example, is considered one of the most difficult pieces ever composed for this instrument—even the violinist for whom it was written declared it "unplayable." A composition sharing a similar reputation and fate is the "Symphony No. 8" (1973). Condemned by one reviewer as "a brassy percussive jungle of fluctuating density and baleful garish colors," the piece was staunchly defended by Sessions. He conceded, though, that "Symphony No. 8" makes even more demands on its listeners than his other typically difficult works.

Sessions's apparent lack of concern for changing musical trends is yet another factor keeping his works from public acclaim. He has often stated that he does not write "American," or "modern," or any other *kind* of music, but composes only what is right for him, regardless of how difficult or ponderous it may seem to the general listener. "Musical communication is a two-way proposition in which the listener must be perceptive," he maintains. "All the contemporary composer demands is an open mind and a willing ear—and also a gracious ear."

When the twelve-tone system of composition (dodecaphony) came into being early in this century, Sessions employed it in several works, though never with drastic alterations in his regular mode of writing. As one reviewer suggested, his "twelve-tone music *sounded* hardly different from his pre-twelve-tone music. It retained the dense texture, the proliferation of contrapuntal filigree work, the lengthy, non-repetitive and usually non-sequential melodic line, and the Classic-Romantic traditional expressive gestures of his earlier music."

Sessions has long been considered one of the greatest twentieth-century composers in the United States. In 1961, a special concert featuring only Sessions's works was presented in New York City to commemorate his sixty-fifth birthday. Benjamin Boretz summarized the occasion in an article for *Musical Quarterly:* "This is certainly a profound tribute to the qualities of mind, determination, and native gift that Sessions has brought to bear on his work, which has now brought him to the status of an old master, who unburdoned by any necessity to struggle furiously to the head of the mainstream, is content simply to cast one masterwork after another into its midst."

BIOGRAPHICAL/CRITICAL SOURCES: Musical Quarterly, July, 1959, July, 1961; *New York Times,* February 15, 1960, April 14, 1968, May 3, 1968; *Time,* May 10, 1968; *Newsweek,* May 13, 1968; David Ewen, editor, *Composers Since 1900,* H. W. Wilson, 1969; *Nation,* April 19, 1975; *New Yorker,* April 19, 1976.*

*   *   *

SEWALL, Richard B(enson)   1908-

PERSONAL: Born February 11, 1908, in Albany, N.Y.; son of Charles Grenville (a minister) and Kate (Strong) Sewall; married Mathilde Parmelee, October 18, 1940 (deceased); children: Stephen Parmelee, Richard Strong, David. *Education:* Williams College, B.A., 1929; Yale University, Ph.D., 1933. *Politics:* Democrat. *Home:* 63 Downs Rd., Bethany, Conn. 06525. *Office:* Department of English, Yale University, New Haven, Conn. 06520.

CAREER: Clark University, Worcester, Mass., instructor in English, 1933-34; Yale University, New Haven, Conn., instructor, 1934-40, assistant professor, 1940-50, associate professor, 1950-59, professor, 1959-76, professor emeritus of English, 1976—, associate dean of freshmen, 1947-51, master of Ezra Stiles College, 1959-70. Visiting professor at Hebrew University, 1967, Williams College, 1976 and 1977, and Warren Wilson College, fall, 1979; teacher of English at Hopkins Day Prospect Hill School, 1977—; lecturer. Trustee of Choate School, 1954-59, and Putney School, 1967—. Member of Bethany Conservation Trust and New Haven Library Association. *Member:* American Academy of Arts and Sciences, Modern Language Association of America, College English Association, Elizabethan Club, Phi Beta Kappa. *Awards, honors:* Ford Foundation fellow, 1952-53; William C. DeVane medal from Yale University, 1966; Poetry Society of America award, 1974, and National Book

Award, 1975, both for *The Life of Emily Dickinson;* Litt.D. from Williams College, 1975; L.H.D. from Albertus Magnus College, 1975; Wilbur Lucius Cross medal from Yale University, 1979.

WRITINGS: (Editor with Raymond Wright Short) *Short Stories for Study: An Anthology,* Holt, 1941, 3rd edition, 1956; *The Vision of Tragedy,* Yale University Press, 1959, new edition, 1980; (editor) *Emily Dickinson: A Collection of Critical Essays,* Prentice-Hall, 1963; (editor with Laurence Anthony Michel) *Tragedy: Modern Essays in Criticism,* Prentice-Hall, 1963; *The Lyman Letters: New Light on Emily Dickinson and Her Family,* University of Massachusetts Press, 1965; (author of introduction) William Shakespeare, *Romeo and Juliet,* Houghton, 1966; *The Life of Emily Dickinson,* two volumes, Farrar, Straus, 1974. Contributor to literary journals.

WORK IN PROGRESS: "Several projects having to do with Emily Dickinson."

SIDELIGHTS: Richard Sewall considers himself first and foremost a teacher, and all of his books are related to his experience in the classroom. For instance, his classroom lectures on tragedy led to the writing of *The Vision of Tragedy,* a book that has become a standard in its field. For several years *The Vision of Tragedy* was called an "academic best-seller." Kenneth Millar wrote that this study "has a breadth and depth which qualify it to be placed among late entries on that shelf of critical works where Aristotle's 'Poetics' stands first." Eliseo Vivas was equally admiring. "Each chapter is a little jewel, a miracle of brevity and relevance, a compact expression of sensitive comment and of fresh insight," he observed.

Although Sewall has written on other topics, his interest since the work on tragedy has been Emily Dickinson. Again, his fascination with her work began in the classroom. In 1965 he published a slender volume of letters and papers by Joseph Bardwell Lyman, a distant relation of the Dickinsons, who had lived in the Dickinson household for several months in the 1840's. Because Lyman had kept in close contact with the family throughout his life, his observations on Emily are of particular significance. Unfortunately, the letters Lyman received from the poet have not survived, but in his own papers he quotes from seven of them. Since no one can be sure that Lyman quoted from the letters with absolute accuracy, at least one critic is dubious about admitting them to the canon; but they are now generally accepted as genuine. "Richard B. Sewall has bound together the fragmentary correspondence with sound and intelligent exposition, never permitting himself to run wild in the fields of fancy," Constance Wagner remarked. Calling *The Lyman Letters* "a model of unobtrusive scholarship," a critic for the *Yale Review* noted that "we now have in print a good record of great importance."

A much larger undertaking was *The Life of Emily Dickinson,* which took Sewall twenty years to research and write. In the introduction, Sewall states that because Dickinson was more concerned with private affairs than public matters, "the biographer must mediate between her and the world to which she refused so much, fill out the hints she dropped, be discursive where she was elliptical; give her a lineage, a background and a foreground; a believable family, home, and friends; an education, culture, and (above all) a vocation. This must be done, I'm convinced, *in the large,* in the richest possible profusion of detail." In order to achieve these ends, Sewall divided the work into two volumes. Volume I describes Dickinson's background: her family, her ancestors,

her acquaintances, and the town where she lived, Amherst. Volume II deals with her life, but it too is organized about her various relationships.

Sewall's decision to arrange his material in this way aroused much admiration. R.W.B. Lewis termed the structure of the work "original" and "daring." There is a problem inherent in this method, however. Richard Todd observed that the biography's organization makes it "difficult to keep in mind the complex of forces and events that were affecting her at any one moment, and you have to struggle for a sense of the sweep of her life." While acknowledging these difficulties, Charles R. Larson felt they faded to insignificance when the account of Dickinson's life was viewed as a whole: "If the organization of the work itself . . . leads to a few minor structural weaknesses, these are unimportant once the reader has completed a reading of the whole work."

Sewall's meticulous scholarship was also worthy of note. Among the new materials that he sets forth in the biography is the story of the affair between Austin Dickinson, Emily's brother, and Mabel Loomis Todd, Emily's first editor. He also includes such minutiae as Emily's schoolbooks, her daily schedule in college, and her favorite recipes. "A scrupulous, tactful, reticent scholar decently reluctant to transgress the bounds of the known, [Sewall] inundates us with everything remotely bearing on the life of his subject," Saul Maloff remarked, and Irvin Ehrenpreis applauded the "fullness and impartiality of his presentation." A few critics felt the treatment was too full. Dorothy Rabinowitz complained that the biography "is overdrawn and full of digressions which chop into the texture of the work to make it unwieldy, a fault that is the more regrettable because it is, in many ways, a stupendous work of research and analysis."

By presenting the material in such massive detail, Sewall hoped to banish many of the myths that had surrounded Dickinson for years. In the biography he eschews the psychological approach in favor of a careful examination of the facts. In the past Dickinson had often been portrayed as a neurotic recluse arrayed in white, pining over an unrequited love, or a woman deprived of suitors by a tyrannical father. The figure who emerges from Sewall's book is quite different from the legend. Dickinson did not turn to poetry as a solace for an unhappy life, he argues; rather, she deliberately chose poetry as her vocation early in life. It was for this reason (not heartbreak over a failed romance) that she elected to evade social intercourse—although she was far from being a hermit. She grew up in a house full of people and carried on a vast correspondence with many men and women of affairs. Sewall depicts her as a busy woman, dedicated to writing poetry, who cooked, baked, sewed, tended her flowers, and nursed (when she had to) her invalid mother. Furthermore, he suggests that many of the legends that arose about her were of her own making, for she was often willfully obscure. "Not the least of the virtues of Sewall's able and solid 'Life of Emily Dickinson' . . . is that it disposes of . . . [the] simplistic theories and the romantic claptrap that her own secretiveness and a gossipy posterity have foisted on us," Herbert Leibowitz declared.

While some reviewers were disappointed that Sewall had not been more psychoanalytical, critical reception of the book was overwhelmingly favorable. Todd held that *The Life of Emily Dickinson* "is by far the best and the most complete study of the poet's life yet to be written." Hailing the biography as a "major event in American letters," Lewis extolled its "ingenuity, stylistic pungency and common sense." A critic for *New Yorker* joined the chorus, calling the book "fair-minded, reliable, of fine literary quality, and utterly engrossing." A further tribute was paid to *The Life of Emily Dickinson* in 1975, when it won a National Book Award.

CA INTERVIEWS THE AUTHOR

Richard Sewall was interviewed by phone on July 6, 1979, just after his arrival in Christmas Cove, Maine, for the remainder of the summer.

CA: We read almost daily about the deteriorating quality of education. Is this reflected in the students you see?

SEWALL: I think the generalization is probably true of the country as a whole. I've been very lucky in teaching highly selective classes in Yale for forty-three years and as a visiting professor in Williams College; so I don't have a nation-wide experience to talk from. I think the most serious problem exists in the high schools in the large cities, where teachers have to teach thirty-five or forty students in classes that are restless and undisciplined. But the Yale students, I find, are more interesting than they were in the 1930's, when I first began teaching, and perhaps in the 1950's. The contemporary student is a lot more sophisticated, politically and sociologically, certainly, than they were in my day. I've looked back at some papers I wrote as an undergraduate—I went to Exeter and to Williams—and found that, though the spelling and punctuation were better than what I get now, there were hardly two ideas to rub together. These young people are much more thoughtful, original, and critical than I ever was. So, I'm a little skeptical of the people who sing songs of despair about American education, certainly at the level I'm involved with. The columnists and some of the educators are talking gloom a little too glibly, I think. Although let me say again: the problem of the inner cities must be awful, the blackboard jungle where teachers are sometimes even in fear of their lives. That's a problem I don't know anything of firsthand; I just read about it. But I'd say things are going well where I teach.

CA: Is there among Yale students now a greater interest in business education than in the more traditional courses of study?

SEWALL: At Yale the humanities are still on top. English, history, philosophy, and the history of art still get the greatest number of majors. This may not be true nationwide, but it is at Yale; and it's a great tribute, I think, to what we've been doing. I don't know how it is, say, at Harvard or Princeton; but I think the humanities are holding up well. I'm told that, nationally, there is a trend toward the so-called practical courses—business administration, economics, and so forth—and it may be that in the last three years, since I retired, there's been a similar swing at Yale. But the humanities are still very strong, I'm glad to say.

CA: There's some opinion that the traditional education is a luxury for today's society. How do you feel about that?

SEWALL: I think the opinion is wrong. The traditional education, with its emphasis on reading, writing, the basics of science, mathematics, the arts, philosophy, history, is essential. In the short-term view, there's something to be said for the practical way of looking at things. For instance, if there's a student who is working his way through college, has no outside support, and has to get a paying job to support himself—and maybe a new wife and a baby coming on—there's no argument. He's got to do something practical, and I have every sympathy for him. I've had plenty of students in that situation. All you can say is, "Take as much of the humanities as you can, but if you have to major in electronics, go to

it." But the majority of students at the Ivy League Colleges and such places as Williams and Wesleyan and Amherst are not in such a rush. The four years of absorption in the best our culture has produced are terribly important. Otherwise, we're going to become a race of unimaginative, hard-nosed, small-minded, "practical" people with no vision. And without vision, as you may have heard, the people perish.

One of the great scientists of our time, Dr. Lewis Thomas, head of Sloan-Kettering in New York, said his best advice to premedical students was to major in Greek. And one of the ablest doctors I know majored in music at Harvard. I believe in what Cardinal Newman said in *The Idea of the University* about the importance of those years between eighteen and twenty-two. I hope that America won't lose its senses and go all out for technological and vocational training. Recently, Yale instituted a graduate course in business administration. I'm a little dubious about it, just as I was dubious about the business school at Harvard and still am. I'm not sure they do well by us. I don't see them as the civilizing force they should be. Their concern is profits—how to make money, and they don't spend much time on the basic ethical and moral problems of our society. A few years ago the Yale law school did a fine thing. They engaged a philosophy professor to teach the ethics of the law. It was a great success. Lawyers, businessmen, bankers, executives of all sorts should be trained in these matters as carefully as preachers and teachers.

CA: What attracted you to Emily Dickinson?

SEWALL: I began teaching her poems to a small group in the middle 1930's. Then in the 1940's, *Bolts of Melody* (660 new poems by Emily Dickinson) was published, and I was asked to review it. The editor was Millicent Todd Bingham, the daughter of Mabel Loomis Todd, who was the original editor of Emily Dickinson in the 1890's. That started a series of meetings between Mrs. Bingham and me, culminating in her invitation to write the biography. She put at my disposal all the Dickinson material that had come down from her mother. Bit by bit she led me into the whole story of the Dickinson family and her mother's involvement with Emily's brother Austin. It took me twenty years to write the biography, what with the other things I had to do. But that's the way it came about, and I enjoyed every minute of it.

CA: You predicted in the early 1960's that critical opinion of Dickinson would become stronger and less sentimental. Do you see this happening now?

SEWALL: Yes. Critics are at last taking her seriously. For a while, Dickinson criticism and scholarship were simply uninformed. It wasn't until the mid-1950's that we had an adequate text to work on when Harvard finally published the three-volume edition of the poems, and then in 1958 came the three-volume edition of the letters. Then a few years later came Jay Leyda's factual two-volume *Years and Hours of Emily Dickinson* and Mrs. Bingham's *Emily Dickinson's Home,* with much new documentary material. Right now I know of at least three more studies on the way. There's work in progress on Emily Dickinson all over the world.

At first the great problem was personal—who was this extraordinary Amherst recluse? How could she know so much? How could she write about love and death and passion, and all the rest, from such limited experience? Many theories and legends sprang up—her frustrated love affair, her ogre father, and so. But now the focus more and more is on the poetry. She's emerging with Whitman as one of two great seminal poets that America has produced. She had a boundless imagination, a fertility of metaphor and image, a linguistic virtuosity that reminds one of Shakespeare. After all these years I'm as fascinated (and bewildered!) as I was when I began. That's not true of Robert Frost or Wallace Stevens or T. S. Eliot—they were public figures. They told us a lot about themselves. They gave lectures; they wrote letters; they wrote essays. But Emily Dickinson was a very private figure. She is still a mystery, and I think she always will be.

CA: In your introduction to Short Stories for Study, *published in 1941, you wrote, "A work of art is an ordered structure." In view of that, would you comment on some of the seemingly obscure stories and poems being written today?*

SEWALL: I'm not much in sympathy with the kind of writing I think you're referring to. When I was Master of Ezra Stiles College for ten years at Yale, we had, during the late 1960's, a series of poetry readings, about fourteen in the space of three months, such was student enthusiasm. As Master, I felt it incumbent upon me to attend them. They were all by published poets—from New York, Boston, Chicago. Some of the stuff was so bad you couldn't believe it—either so simple and childish that there was nothing to it at all, or so complicated and fragmented and disordered you couldn't understand it. I remember one particularly perplexing evening. The next day I met one of my colleagues in the courtyard, and he asked how I liked the poetry reading. I said, "Well, I liked what I understood." He looked at me with high irony and said, "Oh, *that's* what you're after, is it?" Oh, the generation gap! What the young people were fascinated by bored me to death. But to get back to the problem of obscurity. The trouble is that the obscurity doesn't seem to obscure much. I find much of this work too introspective, arch, mannered, and self-conscious. I'm not excited by it. I think our last great poets were Wallace Stevens and Frost, but I still will put Frost up with any of them. For a while I was under the spell of T. S. Eliot; I'm getting out of it more and more. Eliot excited us young people in the late 1920's and the 1930's. But now things have changed.

CA: Do you think the women's liberation movement is having much of an impact on literary criticism?

SEWALL: I don't think so, although there's a new book just out on Emily Dickinson in which I detect a bit of that spirit. It's by a woman, a fine and sensitive critic; but I find her reading things into Emily Dickinson—a kind of rage against the secondary position of women and a deep sexual frustration—that I wonder about. Emily Dickinson simply wasn't a women's libber. She accepted her life and gloried in it, even in her "renunciations." Rebecca Patterson wrote a book on Emily Dickinson that had a little of that spirit, making her out to be a lesbian who knew she was involved in an illicit passion, the central tragedy of her life. I doubt it. Emily Dickinson had a way of falling in love (if you want to call it that) with anybody who could fan an intellectual spark in her, male or female. But other than that, no.

As to women's lib in general, I don't know enough about current criticism to make any coherent comment. I don't suppose Anne Sexton and Sylvia Plath can be called women's lib; it just happened that they were very good poets during the period of the movement. As to literary criticism, it's true that more and more is being written by women—which means that the woman's point of view is being better represented all the time. But in the best of it, sexism doesn't seem to function much at all. A woman once told me that I, a man, had no business writing the life of Emily Dickinson. I was

undeterred!

Remember, I don't consider myself a writer; I'm a teacher. The Emily Dickinson biography really came out of the teaching, and I hope what the book will do is teach Emily Dickinson to a lot of people, because I think she's important. Though I'm supposed to be retired (I am, officially, from Yale), I'm still teaching my head off—high school students and adult seminars—and having a fine time. I suppose I'll do it till I drop.

BIOGRAPHICAL/CRITICAL SOURCES: Saturday Review, March 28, 1959, February 22, 1975; *Yale Review,* June, 1959, June, 1966, summer, 1975; *San Francisco Chronicle,* July 19, 1959; *Christian Science Monitor,* August 22, 1963, March 27, 1975; *New York Times Book Review,* November 17, 1963, December 22, 1974; *New England Quarterly,* December, 1963, December, 1966, June, 1975; *Books Abroad,* winter, 1967; *Atlantic Monthly,* January, 1975; *Newsweek,* January 6, 1975; *New Yorker,* January 20, 1975; *New York Review of Books,* January 23, 1975; *Washington Post Book World,* January 26, 1975; *New Republic,* February 8, 1975; *Commonweal,* May 9, 1975; *Commentary,* July, 1975; *American Scholar,* autumn, 1975; *Journal of English and Germanic Philology,* January, 1976; *Sewanee Review,* April, 1976; *Times Literary Supplement,* May 7, 1976.

—*Sketch by Ann F. Ponikvar*
—*Interview by Jean W. Ross*

*   *   *

SHACKLETON, Doris (Cavell) 1918-
(Doris French)

PERSONAL: Born February 15, 1918, in Regina, Saskatchewan, Canada; daughter of Harold E. (a druggist) and Myrtle M. Martin; married Robert J. French, October 20, 1941 (divorced, 1965); married Philip S. Shackleton (a writer), June 25, 1968; children: (first marriage) Jordan Lee French Brooks, Colin James. *Education:* Attended high school in Raymore, Saskatchewan. *Politics:* New Democrat. *Home and office address:* R.R.5, Box 429, Ottawa, Ontario, Canada K1G 3N3.

CAREER: Country schoolteacher in Outlook, Saskatchewan, 1939-41; political organizer and newspaper correspondent, 1945-60; commentator for Canadian Broadcasting Corp. (CBC), 1960-67; *Canadian Welfare,* Ottawa, Ontario, editor, 1967-69; writer and editorial consultant, 1970—. Member of Gloucester Township Municipal Council, 1976-79. *Member:* Writers' Union of Canada, Civil Liberties Union.

WRITINGS: (Under name Doris French; with Margaret Stewart) *Ask No Quarter: The Story of Agnes McPhail,* Longmans, Green, 1959; (under name Doris French) *Faith, Sweat, and Politics* (on early Canadian trade unions), McClelland & Stewart, 1962; (under name Doris French) *High Button Bootstraps,* Ryerson, 1968; *Tommy Douglas* (biography), McClelland & Stewart, 1975; *Powertown: Democracy Discarded,* McClelland & Stewart, 1977. Author of "Shackleton Speaking," a political gossip column in *Ottawa Journal,* 1972-74. Contributor to magazines.

WORK IN PROGRESS: A biography of Countess Ishbel, 1857-1939, a Canadian governor-general's wife, publication by McClelland & Stewart expected in 1981.

SIDELIGHTS: Doris Shackleton told *CA:* "Politics has been an important motivation. Associated with the New Democratic party and its predecessor since 1939, I ran as a candidate in federal elections in 1972 and 1974, and have held other party positions. Women in politics are embattled creatures and well worth writing about. Nobody knows how hard it is until they try. But there will be more of us.''

About her work in progress, Shackleton commented: ''What interests me about Countess Ishbel is that she was, most improperly, an ardent, partisan politician. I fill in great gaps in my education by intensive research on biography. It's a fine way to learn. This one involved two months in Scotland and England I might not have had otherwise.''

BIOGRAPHICAL/CRITICAL SOURCES: Toronto Globe & Mail, January 23, 1960; *Time* (Canadian edition), October 27, 1975.

* * *

SHANKMAN, Paul (Andrew) 1943-

PERSONAL: Born December 22, 1943, in Los Angeles, Calif.; son of Solomon (a chemist) and Elizabeth (a physician; maiden name, Stern) Shankman; married Sally N. Bates (a writer and editor), August 8, 1970. *Education:* Attended Occidental College, 1961-63; University of California, Santa Barbara, B.A., 1965; Harvard University, Ph.D., 1973. *Home:* 956 University, Boulder, Colo. 80302. *Office:* Department of Anthropology, University of Colorado, Boulder, Colo. 80309.

CAREER: California State University, Northridge, assistant professor of anthropology, 1970-71; University of Colorado, Boulder, visiting assistant professor, 1973-74, assistant professor, 1974-78, associate professor of anthropology, 1979—. Lecturer at California State University, Hayward, summer, 1973; research associate of Center for South Pacific Studies, University of California, Santa Cruz, 1978. Conducted field studies in Samoa, Tonga, and Fiji. Member of board of directors of Anthropology Resource Center.

MEMBER: American Anthropological Association, American Association for the Advancement of Science, Polynesian Society, Association for Social Anthropology in Oceania, Social Science History Association, Association for Political and Legal Anthropology, Anthropological Study Group on Agrarian Systems, Colorado-Wyoming Academy of Sciences (head of anthropology section, 1977). *Awards, honors:* U.S. Public Health Service grant, 1978.

WRITINGS: Migration and Underdevelopment: The Case of Western Samoa, Westview Press, 1976; (contributor) C. Macpherson, B. Shore, and R. Franco, editors, *New Neighbors: Islanders in Adaptation* (monograph), Center for South Pacific Studies, University of California, Santa Cruz, 1978; (contributor) Ahamed Idris-Soven, Elizabeth Idris-Soven, and Mark K. Vaughn, editors, *The World as a Company Town: Multinational Corporations and Social Change,* Mouton, 1978; (contributor) R. Grant and E. S. Wellhofer, editors, *Ethno-Nationalism, Multinational Corporations, and the Modern State,* Graduate School of International Studies, University of Denver, 1979; (contributor) D. Counts and W. Rodman, editors, *Political Middlemen and Brokers in Oceania,* University of Michigan Press, 1979. Contributor of about a dozen articles and reviews to anthropology journals.

WORK IN PROGRESS: An introductory anthropology textbook.

SIDELIGHTS: Shankman comments: ''I wrote *Migration and Underdevelopment* to call attention to processes that are occurring in the South Pacific, an area long considered to be out of the orbit of such processes.''

SHANNON, Robert L(eroy) 1926-

PERSONAL: Born May 15, 1926, in Fort Wayne, Ind.; son of Grover (a salesman) and Vera (Coleman) Shannon; married Donna Marie Klindt (a media specialist), July 23, 1976; children: Susan Shannon Long, Jennifer. *Education:* Wittenberg University, A.B., 1950, B.S., 1952; Ball State University, M.A., 1954; Florida State University, Ed.D., 1960. *Home:* 2506 Bordeaux Way, Lutz, Fla. 33549. *Office:* College of Education, University of South Florida, Tampa, Fla. 33620.

CAREER: Elementary and junior high school teacher of history, science, literature, physical education, and health in Fort Wayne, Ind., 1951-54; Ball State University, Muncie, Ind., assistant professor of education, 1954-56; Florida State University, Tallahassee, assistant professor of education, 1956-59; Wittenberg University, Springfield, Ohio, assistant professor of education, 1959-60; University of South Florida, Tampa, assistant professor, 1960-62, associate professor, 1962-65, professor of education, 1965—, distinguished university professor, 1973. Staff director of education committee of Florida House of Representatives, 1972-73; conducts workshops. *Military service:* U.S. Navy, 1944-46. *Member:* Association for Childhood Education International, National Education Association.

WRITINGS: (With J. A. Battle) *The New Idea in Education,* Harper, 1968, 2nd edition, 1973; *Where the Truth Comes Up,* C. E. Merrill, 1971. Contributor to education journals. Co-editor of *University of South Florida Educational Review,* 1962-65.

WORK IN PROGRESS: A book presenting ''a design of education for an America that accepts that education will be the primary activity for most people for a lifetime''; a novel about tennis, for teenagers.

SIDELIGHTS: Shannon has conducted academic programs in England, Guatemala, and Guam. His travels have taken him through Europe, Central America, and South America.

In an unpublished article, ''Clinical Professoring: One Solution for Teacher Education,'' Shannon wrote: ''Converting teacher education into a viable undertaking for the 1980's can happen if those involved in the endeavor will acknowledge that most of what goes on with both graduates and undergraduates in teacher education is essentially a waste of time. It doesn't do what it purports to do. From that point it is possible to fashion effective new styles for the teacher education business. One new style can be that of the Clinical Professor. . . .

''Fifty miles from the University there are two small towns. I was designated as Clinical Professor at three elementary schools in those rural towns. They are my clinics. The faculties are the clinic's clients. Responsibility of the Clinical Professor is to deal with teachers on a one-to-one basis and be of value to them as they try to do a better job with the education of children. The Clinical Professor is an on-site, problem-solving, facilitating, grass roots practitioner who responds to diverse needs of a diverse group of clients. . . .

''A necessary prerequisite is a willingness to become visible in situations where results (or lack of) will be conspicuous and immediate. Away from the congenial, protective environment of the college campus there is no place for the theoretician. Buck-passing is not possible. . . . Each situation requires a fresh solution. There is no model. Functioning as a Clinical Professor demands a totally personalized approach. . . .

''The Clinical Professor role is one that cannot be ignored. It works. Perhaps the idea of the Clinical Professor is but a first phase in the total re-shaping of teacher education in the United States. This much needed re-shaping will transform graduate and undergraduate programs, bringing significance to an aspect of higher education in desperate need of completely new forms.''

* * *

SHAPIRO, Norman R(ichard) 1930-

PERSONAL: Born November 1, 1930, in Boston, Mass.; son of Harry Alexander (a pharmacist) and Eva (a writer and poet; maiden name, Goldberg) Shapiro. *Education:* Harvard University, B.A., 1951, M.A., 1952, Ph.D., 1958; Universite d'Aix-Marseille, dipl. langue et lettres francaises, 1956. *Religion:* Jewish. *Home:* 8 Plympton St., Cambridge, Mass. 02138; and 214 High St., Middletown, Conn. 06457. *Agent:* Samuel French, Inc., 25 West 45th St., New York, N.Y. 10036. *Office:* Department of Romance Languages, Wesleyan University, Middletown, Conn. 06457.

CAREER: Amherst College, Amherst, Mass., instructor in French, 1958-60; Wesleyan University, Middletown, Conn., assistant professor, 1960-65, associate professor, 1965-71, professor of Romance languages and literatures, 1971—. *Member:* Esperanto League of North America, American Association of Teachers of French, African Studies Association, Judezmo Society, Universala Esperanto-Asocio, Delta Kappa Epsilon, Signet Society. *Awards, honors:* Fulbright fellowship for France, 1955-56; Ford Foundation grant, 1966; M.A. from Wesleyan University, Middletown, Conn., 1972; National Book Award nomination, 1971, for translation of *Four Farces.*

WRITINGS: (Editor) *Echoes,* Heath, 1965; (editor and translator) *Negritude: Black Poetry From Africa and the Caribbean,* October House, 1970; (editor, translator from French, and author of introduction) Georges Feydeau, *Four Farces,* University of Chicago Press, 1970; (translator) *The Comedy of Eros: Medieval Guides to the Art of Love,* University of Illinois Press, 1971; (editor) *Palabres,* Scott, Foresman, 1973; (translator) Anne Hebert, *Kamouraska,* Crown, 1973; (translator) Joseph Majault, *Virginie; or, The Dawning of the World,* Crown, 1974; (translator) Jean Raspail, *The Camp of the Saints,* Scribner, 1975; (translator) Feydeau, *Tooth and Consequences,* Samuel French, 1979. Composer of "Three Songs," 1961. Contributor of articles, translations, and reviews to scholarly journals.

WORK IN PROGRESS: A collection of translations of one-act plays by Georges Feydeau, publication by Cornell University Press expected in 1981; a collection of verse translations of Old French Aesopic fables; translating work of nineteenth-century comic authors and the poetry of Leon Laleau; research on French theatre.

SIDELIGHTS: Shapiro writes: "In addition to being a professor of Romance languages, I find time for the usual academic pursuits, concentrating mainly in the fields of French theatre, black francophone literature, and linguistics. This last has taken me, during the last few years, into the field of American Sign Language.

"As a writer, I have turned more and more to literary translation. It is an art form in itself, demanding and frustrating when conscientiously practiced, but artistically fulfilling and creative in its own special way. Sometimes I think it takes a kind of masochistic urge to be a translator, and to spend inordinate amounts of time searching for the perfect word, when critics seldom notice translations at all. That is, unless they are bad. A translation is like a pane of glass. No one

sees that it's there unless it has flaws. But the satisfactions can be great, and most of the time—happily—outweigh the frustrations.''

* * *

SHARP, Hal
See SHARP, Harold W(ilson)

* * *

SHARP, Harold W(ilson) 1914-
(Hal Sharp)

PERSONAL: Born January 29, 1914, in War Eagle, Ark.; son of James Berry (a laborer and salesperson) and Jewel (Ledbetter) Sharp; married Marie Peelman, 1940 (died, 1962); married Jane Renis, 1965 (divorced, 1967); married Thelma Arens, 1967 (divorced, 1968); married Alice Jane Campbell, August 23, 1978. *Education:* Attended Chouinard Art Institute, Los Angeles, Calif., 1936; further study at University of California, Los Angeles, 1970-72. *Religion:* Christian. *Residence:* Los Angeles, Calif. *Agent:* Toni Mendez, Toni Mendez, Inc., 140 E. 56th St., New York, N.Y. 10022. *Office:* Los Angeles Times Syndicate, Times Mirror Sq., Los Angeles, Calif. 90053.

CAREER: Worked in animation and special effects for various animated cartoon studios near Hollywood, Calif., 1936-38; free-lance advertising illustrator in New York City, 1938-39; comic book illustrator in New York City, 1939-42; Alma & Jonquires Railway Co. and Atchison, Topeka & Santa Fe Railway Co., Gallup, N.M., locomotive fireman, 1942-44; Willow Grove Naval Installation, Willow Grove, Pa., technical illustrator for "Installation Project Group," 1944-45; free-lance advertising illustrator in Philadelphia, Pa., 1945-50; author and illustrator of syndicated column "Sportsman's Digest" for General Features Corp., 1950-66, and Los Angeles Times Syndicate, 1966—. Photographer, with photographs chosen for exhibits by Professional Photographers West, 1974-75, and with photographs appearing in exhibit in Museum of Science and Industry, Los Angeles, 1975. *Wartime service:* Civilian technician for Philco Corp., Milwaukee, Wis., as illustrator of radar installation prototypes in navy aircraft, 1944-45. *Member:* Outdoor Writers Association of America, Professional Photographers West, American Artists of the West (member of board of directors, 1973), Professional Photographers of California. *Awards, honors:* "Most Outstanding Achievement" award from American Artists of the West, 1973.

WRITINGS—All under name Hal Sharp: *Sportsman's Digest of Hunting,* Sterling, 1952; *Sportman's Digest of Fishing,* Sterling, 1953; *Spin Fishing,* Sterling, 1954, published as *Sportsman's Guide of Spin-Fishing,* Barnes & Noble, 1954; (contributor) Norman Strung, editor, *Communicating the Outdoor Experience: Modern Media/Modern Method,* Outdoor Writers Association of America, 1975. Author and illustrator of syndicated column, "Sportsman's Digest," 1950—.

WORK IN PROGRESS: An autobiography.

SIDELIGHTS: Sharp writes: "In art school during the 1930's I never once thought of being anything but a magazine illustrator. Until the late 1940's I worked in various areas as an artist. All my life I had loved the outdoors and had fished and hunted whenever possible. Then, after World War II, it dawned on me that there was almost nothing published in newspapers or magazines of 'how-to-do-it' about hunting and fishing. Thus, I set out to work up a brief panel, titled 'Sportsman's Digest,' that contained tips for outdoor sportsmen and women. In 1950, I had revised it to the point where I showed it to General Features Corp. I signed a contract with them at once. In the twenty-nine years after that, my daily feature has appeared in hundreds of newspapers in North America, Italy, and Arabia. Since the beginning of my feature, the first of its kind, there have been imitators of this format. Despite competition, my 'Sportsman's Digest' format has survived twenty-nine years and perhaps been exposed to more readers than any similar feature for all time.''

Sharp had completed much of the work on his autobiography when he broke his leg in 1976. The "crippling" injury delayed his plans for publication.

AVOCATIONAL INTERESTS: Cinematography, oil painting.

* * *

SHARP, James
    See KINGHORN, A(lexander) M(anson)

* * *

SHARP, John Kean 1892-1979

OBITUARY NOTICE: Born in 1892 in New York, N.Y.; died November 27, 1979, in Long Island, N.Y. Clergyman, educator, and author. Sharp served as a pastor in Long Island for over thirty years. He also taught classes in theology and literature in parochial schools and at the Immaculate Conception Seminary. Sharp's work includes an autobiography, *An Old Priest Remembers.* Obituaries and other sources: *New York Times,* November 29, 1979.

* * *

SHARPE, Roger Carter 1948-

PERSONAL: Born August 1, 1948, in Chicago, Ill.; son of Jesse J. (a professor of economics) and Adrienne (Rosaire) Sharpe; married Ellen Steinberg Cammeyer (an artist), November 14, 1978. *Education:* University of Wisconsin—Madison, B.B.A., 1971. *Residence:* New York, N.Y. *Agent:* Bill Adler, 1230 Avenue of the Americas, New York, N.Y. 10021. *Office: Gentlemen's Quarterly,* 488 Madison Ave., New York, N.Y. 10022.

CAREER: Free-lance writer, 1965-71; advertising copywriter in New York City, 1971-75; *Gentlemen's Quarterly,* New York City, 1974—, began as associate editor, became managing editor. Pinball designer and consultant. *Awards, honors:* Award from International Television and Film Festival, 1972.

WRITINGS: Pinball!, Dutton, 1977; (with Robert Nideffer) *How to Put Anxiety Behind You,* Stein & Day, 1978; (with Nideffer) *A.C.T.: Attention Control Training,* Peter H. Wyden, 1978; *How to Get a Great Tan,* Bantam, 1979. Contributor to magazines and newspapers, including *Cashbox, Games, Youth Beat,* and *Family Weekly.* Contributing editor of *Play Meter.*

WORK IN PROGRESS: A novel, *Joshua's Story;* two books of poems, *Shadows* and *Forever;* a book on pinball machines and the pinball industry, *That's Pinball!* (tentative title).

SIDELIGHTS: Sharpe wrote: "I suppose that the biggest motivating force in my life has been my father and the fact that he passed away when I was very young. Above and beyond this, I would like to think that my work in general is serving a purpose of informing or entertaining people. Conveying ideas and feelings through the printed word is an incredible experience that I have always found deeply satisfy-

ing. Unfortunately, the publishing industry isn't one that can often be used as an open forum.

"A problem stems from the fact that everyone feels that he or she can write. It is a craft that looks far more simplistic than many other creative arts. However, anyone who has sat before a typewriter looking for the next idea, or worse, the next sentence, knows that the process is far more intricate and taxing than any writing course in college could ever teach."

* * *

SHEPARD, David W. 1922-

PERSONAL: Born January 10, 1922, in River Falls, Wis. *Education:* University of Minnesota, B.S., 1947, M.A., 1949, Ph.D., 1953. *Home:* 3800 West Gilbert, Muncie, Ind. 47304. *Office:* Ball State University, Muncie, Ind. 47306.

CAREER: University of Minnesota, Minneapolis, instructor, 1949-51; Hamline University, St. Paul, Minn., instructor, 1951-54; Ball State University, Muncie, Ind., professor, 1954—. *Military service:* U.S. Marine Corps, 1941-45; became technical sergeant. *Member:* Speech Communication Association of America, American Forensic Association, American Institute of Parliamentarians, American Association of University Professors, Central States Speech Association, Indiana Speech Association, Indiana Institute of Parliamentarians.

WRITINGS: (With Paul H. Cashman) *Handbook for Beginning Debaters,* Burgess, 1966; (with Edward S. Strother) *The Practical Guide to Parliamentary Procedure,* Kendall/Hunt, 1977. Editor of *Indiana Speech Journal.*

WORK IN PROGRESS: Comparing "Watson-Glaser" scores of current students at Ball State University with the scores of undergraduates of 1969; experimenting with a "rural myth" test.

* * *

SHERIDAN, Adora
    See HONG, Jane Fay

* * *

SHEV, Edward E(lmer) 1919-

PERSONAL: Born August 3, 1919, in Lincoln, Neb.; son of Isaac (a blacksmith) and Esther (Schuchman) Shev; married Eleanor Brown (a physician); children: Randall Herbert, Karen Barbara (Mrs. Matthew Dunn), Anne Elizabeth. *Education:* University of Nebraska, B.S., 1944, M.D., 1945. *Office:* 3838 California St., Suite 706, San Francisco, Calif. 94118.

CAREER: Mt. Sinai Hospital, Chicago, Ill., intern, 1945-46; Indiana University, Indianapolis, associate resident in psychiatry, 1946-48; University of California, San Francisco, assistant resident in neurology, 1948-49; Langley Porter Institute, San Francisco, resident in neuropathology, 1949-50; University of California, San Francisco, senior assistant resident in neurology, 1950-51; Mt. Zion Hospital, San Francisco, director of electroencephalography department and attending neurologist, 1951-57; Marin General Hospital, San Rafael, Calif., director of electroencephalography laboratory, 1955—, and electrodiagnostic laboratory, 1956—. Certified by American Board of Psychiatry and Neurology and American Board of Electroencephalography. Lecturer at University of California, San Francisco, 1948-66, clinical instructor, 1951-57. In charge of electromyography laboratory at San Francisco's Children's Hospital, 1959-71; vice-president of medical staff at Golden Gate Hospital, 1961-63; director of electroencephalography laboratories at Mary's Help Hospital, Daly City, Calif., 1963-65, Hahnemann Hospital, San Francisco (also member of staff), 1965—, and Callison Memorial Hospital, 1965-71; member of neurology staff at Garden Hospital's Jerd Sullivan Rehabilitation Center, 1970—. Independent medical examiner for Industrial Accident Commission, 1951—; psychiatric consultant to California and Michigan police departments. *Military service:* U.S. Navy, 1946-48; became lieutenant.

MEMBER: American Academy of Neurology (fellow), American Electroencephalography Society, American Federation of Clinical Research, American Medical Association, American Medical Electroencephalographic Association, American Association of Electromyography and Electrodiagnosis, Child Neurology Society, National Aid to the Visually Handicapped (chairperson of board of directors; past president), Western Electroencephalography Society (member of board of directors, 1963-70; president, 1969-70; archivist, 1970—; chairperson of ethics and professional relations committee, 1970—), California Medical Association, Marin County Medical Society, Marin County Epilepsy Foundation, Marin Academy (member of board of trustees), San Francisco Medical Association, Sausalito Foundation (member of board of directors; past president).

WRITINGS: (Contributor) *Cerebral Anoxia and the Electroencephalogram,* C. C Thomas, 1960; *Good Cops and Bad Cops: Memoirs of a Police Psychiatrist,* San Francisco Book Co., 1977. Contributor of about thirty articles to medical journals.

*   *   *

SHIPPEN, Katherine B(inney)   1892-1980

OBITUARY NOTICE—See index for *CA* sketch: Born April 1, 1892, in Hoboken, N.J.; died February 20, 1980, in Suffern, N.Y. Teacher and writer of books for young people. Before taking up her writing career, Shippen worked as a history teacher and as curator of social studies at the Brooklyn Children's Museum. Among her historical works are *New Found World, Passage to America,* and *Miracle in Motion.* She also produced several biographies, including *Leif Eriksson, Andrew Carnegie and the Age of Steel,* and *Milton S. Hershey.* Obituaries and other sources: *Current Biography,* Wilson, 1954; *Authors of Books for Young People,* 2nd edition, Scarecrow, 1971; *New York Times,* February 23, 1980.

*   *   *

SHURTLEFF, William   1941-

PERSONAL: Born April 28, 1941, in Oakland, Calif.; son of Lawton L. (in business) and Barbara (Reinhardt) Shurtleff; married Akiko Aoyagi (an illustrator), March 10, 1977. *Education:* Stanford University, B.Sc., 1962, B.A. (with honors), 1963, M.A., 1966; attended International Christian University, Tokyo, Japan, 1971-72. *Home and office address:* New-Age Foods Study Center, P.O. Box 234, Lafayette, Calif. 94549.

CAREER: U.S. Steel, Pittsburg, Calif., industrial engineer, 1963; U.S. Peace Corps, Washington, D.C., teacher of physics and mathematics in Nigeria, 1964-66; Stanford University, Stanford, Calif., director of Esalen Program in Human Awareness, 1967-68; Tassajara Zen Mountain Center, Carmel Valley, Calif., monk, 1968-71; writer and researcher in Japan, 1972-76; New-Age Foods Study Center, Lafayette, Calif., director, 1976—. Lecturer in the United States, Thai-

land, the Philippines, Singapore, and Japan; consultant to food and equipment companies.

WRITINGS—All with wife, Akiko Aoyagi: *The Book of Tofu,* Autumn, 1975, revised edition, Ballantine, 1979; *The Book of Miso,* Autumn, 1976; *The Book of Kudzu,* Autumn, 1977; *Miso Production,* New-Age Foods Study Center, 1977; *The Book of Tempeh,* Harper, 1979; *Tofu and Soymilk Production,* New-Age Foods Study Center, 1979; *Tempeh Production,* New-Age Foods Study Center, 1980.

WORK IN PROGRESS: Soyfoods, completion expected in 1982.

SIDELIGHTS: Shurtleff has done extensive field research on soy-protein foods. His present work, which includes more than one hundred programs, workshops, and media appearances worldwide, is aimed at disseminating the results of his research.

A monk, writer, and publisher, he aims to combine both ancient and futuristic knowledge in language for the lay person as well as the professional. Influenced by his practice of meditation and his commitment to the problem of human suffering, he attempts to link East and West, bringing together the spiritual way with the rational and scientific.

In *The Book of Tempeh,* Shurtleff and his wife wrote: "The present momentum of the world and all its forces, traveling on a course which many projections show will almost certainly lead to widespread suffering, is great indeed. A powerful and revolutionary force will be needed to swerve its course, to turn it around. We believe that force will come primarily from one source: *deeply committed individuals,* people who are not afraid to work hard and selflessly, to study deeply, to serve, and to persist. People who realize that global change does not begin on a global level, but begins with single individuals then expands to ever larger groups. People who know that 'All the forces in the world are not so powerful as an idea whose time has come.'" Shurtleff believes that voluntary simplicity, ecological awareness, and self-realization are three closely interrelated ethics "which promise to help accommodate human numbers, ways of living, and consumption to basic human needs and the earth's limited resources."

The Book of Tofu and *The Book of Miso* have been published in four foreign language editions.

BIOGRAPHICAL/CRITICAL SOURCES: East-West Journal, March, 1977; *Mother Earth News,* May, 1977; William Shurtleff and Akiko Aoyagi, *The Book of Tempeh,* Harper, 1979; *Soycraft,* summer, 1979.

*   *   *

SHUTE, Nevil
See NORWAY, Nevil Shute

*   *   *

SHUTTLE, Penelope (Diane)   1947-

PERSONAL: Born May 12, 1947, in Staines, Middlesex, England; daughter of Jack Frederick (a business executive) and Joan (Lipscombe) Shuttle; lives with Peter Redgrove (a poet and novelist); children: Zoe Teresa Redgrove. *Education:* Educated in England. *Politics:* "Feminist radical Social Democrat." *Agent:* David Highams Associates Ltd., 5-8 Lower John St., Golden Square, London W1R 4HA, England. *Office:* c/o Falmouth School of Art, Wood Lane, Falmouth, Cornwall, England.

CAREER: Writer. *Awards, honors:* Arts Council awards,

1969, 1972; Greenwood Prize for poetry, 1972, for poem sequence *Witchskin*.

WRITINGS: (Contributor) Carol Burns, editor, *Infatuation*, Calder & Boyars, 1967; *Nostalgia Neurosis and Other Poems*, S. Albert's Press, 1968; *All the Usual Hours of Sleeping* (novel), Calder & Boyars, 1969; *Branch* (poetry), Sceptre Press, 1971; *Jesusa* (novel), Granite Press, 1972; *Midwinter Mandala* (poetry), Headland Publications, 1973; *Wailing Monkey Embracing a Tree* (novel), Calder & Boyars, 1973; *Moon Meal* (poetry), Sceptre Press, 1973; *Autumn Piano, and Other Poems*, Rondo Publications, 1974; *Photographs of Persephone* (poetry), Quarto Press, 1974; *The Songbook of the Snow, and Other Poems*, Janus Press, 1974; *The Dream* (poetry), Sceptre Press, 1975; *Four American Sketches*, Sceptre Press, 1976; *Rainsplitter in the Zodiac Garden*, M. Boyars, 1977; *The Mirror of the Giant* (novel), M. Boyars, 1980; *The Orchard Upstairs* (poetry), Oxford University Press, 1980.

With Peter Redgrove: *The Hermaphrodite Album*, Fuller d'Arch Smith, Ltd., 1973; *The Terrors of Dr. Treviles: A Romance*, Routledge & Kegan Paul, 1974; *The Glass Cottage: A Nautical Romance*, Routledge & Kegan Paul, 1976; *The Wise Wound: Eve's Curse and Everyman* (nonfiction), R. Marek, 1978 (published in England as *The Wise Wound: Menstruation and Everywoman*, Gollancz, 1978).

Author of radio plays, including "The Girl Who Lost Her Glove," 1974, and "The Dauntless Girl," 1978.

WORK IN PROGRESS: Deepening (psychology and sociology).

SIDELIGHTS: One of Shuttle's best known books is *Wailing Monkey Embracing a Tree*. Robert Nye called it "a highly original piece of work." He added that "Shuttle's work is assuredly ambitious enough in scope, and sufficiently rich in detail." A reviewer for *Times Literary Supplement* referred to Shuttle as a "nervous and exciting talent" and deemed the novel one of "many beautiful, fresh and turbulent passages."

Shuttle's collaborations with Peter Redgrove have all been praised for their readability and insight. In a review of *The Terrors of Dr. Treviles*, Marie Peel noted, "There is . . . a good deal of acute satire of academics. More than once the authors deftly place themselves in their own work." However, Peel felt that Redgrove and Shuttle were capable of better work. "I think the revolution for them as novelists, though," she offered, "will occur when they do not want to do this."

Neil Hepburn wrote of *The Glass Cottage* that "whatever its true preoccupations, [it] is full of marvellous writing, especially where concrete if esoteric experience is described." Hepburn also observed that the "preoccupations" of the two authors can sometimes confuse readers. Hepburn contended that "there is a busy system of cross-references: blood, menstruation, a female christ, silk, horns, skin, trigger off echoes in and from the whole corpus of Redgrove-Shuttle work. This makes it difficult—even more difficult—to say what any single work is 'about.'"

Shuttle's most recent collaboration, *The Wise Wound*, deals with menstruation. Hermione Lee called it "an important book because it is the first to deal fully with 'the Curse' in order to persuade readers of both sexes, by invoking a great deal of suggestive information from many sources (anthropology, biology, history, sociology, and psychology), that the Curse is, in fact, a blessing." Rosemary Dinnage declared that *The Wise Wound* "is well organized, annotated,

and written in an engaging and lucid style." She also stated that "the book is exhilirating even where it soars off into fantasy." Margaret Drabble observed that the book "opens up new fields of thought."

Shuttle told *CA:* "For the past three years I have been mainly, though not exclusively, concerned with the care of my young daughter. Now she attends school in the morning, and I am once again (almost) a full-time writer. I give readings of my poetry whenever possible."

BIOGRAPHICAL/CRITICAL SOURCES: Listener, February 7, 1974, January 27, 1977, June 2, 1977, May 25, 1978; *Times Literary Supplement*, February 15, 1974, September 23, 1976, January 28, 1977, July 1, 1977, June 9, 1978, February 1, 1980; *London Magazine*, June/July, 1974; *Books and Bookmen*, November, 1974, February, 1975; *Guardian*, September 23, 1976; *Observer*, October 3, 1976; *Contemporary Literary Criticism*, Volume 7, Gale, 1977.

*   *   *

SIDER, Ronald J(ames)   1939-

PERSONAL: Born September 17, 1939, in Stevensville, Ontario, Canada; came to United States in 1962, naturalized citizen, 1974; son of James Peter (a minister) and Ida (Cline) Sider; married Arbutus Lichti, August 19, 1961; children: Theodore Ronald, Michael Jay, Sonya Maria. *Education:* Waterloo Lutheran University, B.A. (with honors), 1962; Yale University, M.A., 1963, B.D., 1967, Ph.D., 1969. *Religion:* Brethren in Christ. *Home:* 312 West Logan St., Philadelphia, Pa. 19144. *Office:* Department of Theology, Eastern Baptist Theological Seminary, Lancaster Ave. at City Line, Philadelphia, Pa. 19151.

CAREER: Messiah College, Philadelphia, Pa., instructor, 1968-70, assistant professor, 1970-74, associate professor of history and religion, 1974-78, dean, 1971-75; Eastern Baptist Theological Seminary, Philadelphia, Pa., associate professor of theology, 1978—. Co-chairperson of National Workshop on Race and Reconciliation, 1975; member of board of directors of Evangelicals for Social Action, 1973—, chairperson of board, 1973-75, president, 1978—; member of board of directors of Mennonite Central Committee and Bread for the World, 1978—. *Member:* American Society for Reformation Research, American Society of Church History, Conference on Faith and History, National Association of Evangelicals. *Awards, honors:* Fellow of Institute for Advanced Christian Studies, 1976.

WRITINGS: Andreas Bodenstein von Karlstadt, E. J. Brill, 1974; (editor and contributor) *The Chicago Declaration*, Creation House, 1974; *Rich Christians in an Age of Hunger: A Biblical Study*, Inter-Varsity Press, 1977; *Evangelism, Salvation, and Social Justice*, Grove, 1977; (editor) *Karlstadt's Battle With Luther: Documents in a Liberal-Radical Debate*, Fortress, 1978.

Contributor: Mary Evelyn Jegen and Bruno V. Manno, editors, *The Earth Is the Lord's: Essays on Stewardship*, Paulist/Newman, 1978; Donald E. Hoke, editor, *Evangelicals Face the Future*, William Carey Library, 1978; C. Norman Kraus, editor, *Evangelicalism and Anabaptism*, Herald Press, 1979; Kenneth S. Kantzer and Stanley N. Gundry, editors, *Perspectives on Evangelical Theology*, Baker Book, 1979. Contributor to *Baker's Dictionary of Christian Ethics*. Contributor of about twenty-five articles to theology journals. Member of editorial board of *Other Side*.

WORK IN PROGRESS: "Action and Faith: Discerning and Doing Justice," for inclusion in a volume to be published by

Seabury Press; general editor of a ten-volume series, *Christianity and Social Ethics: An International Perspective*.

SIDELIGHTS: Sider told *CA:* "I love tennis, jog to stay in shape, and try desperately to kindly decline most speaking invitations in order to stay home with my family. Discipleship begins at home. So does peace and reconciliation. It is a farce to write and speak about peace, love, and justice unless, by God's grace, it is becoming a reality in one's own home and church."

BIOGRAPHICAL/CRITICAL SOURCES: Eternity, April, 1979.

* * *

SIFTON, Claire 1897(?)-1980

OBITUARY NOTICE: Born c. 1897 in Sao Paulo, Brazil; died of a heart attack, February 9, 1980, in Oaxaca, Mexico. Educator, playwright, and author. Sifton taught journalism at the University of Missouri, becoming the first female instructor ever to teach in that field. She also worked with the U.S. Children's Bureau and wrote for many governmental publications on children's education and family living. Sifton wrote several plays with her husband Paul Sifton, including "The Belt," "Blood on the Moon," and "Midnight," in addition to a book she authored on child care called *The Perfect Baby.* Obituaries and other sources: *New York Times,* February 11, 1980; *Washington Post,* February 16, 1980.

* * *

SILET, Charles L(oring) P(rovine) 1942-

PERSONAL: Born April 25, 1942, in Chicago, Ill.; son of Charles Leonard (a mechanical engineer) and Elizabeth (an artist; maiden name, Provine) Silet; married Kay Zickefoose (an editor), February 21, 1976; children: Kristin, Scott, Karin, Emily. *Education:* Attended University of Illinois, 1960-62, and University of Vienna, 1963-64; Butler University, B.A., 1966; Indiana University, M.A., 1968, Ph.D., 1973; attended Jesus College, Cambridge, 1970-71. *Home:* 2400 Timberland Rd., Ames, Iowa 50010. *Office:* Department of English, Iowa State University, Ames, Iowa 50011.

CAREER: Indiana University, Bloomington, associate instructor in English, 1969-70, 1971-73; Iowa State University, Ames, instructor, 1973-74, assistant professor, 1974-79, associate professor of English, 1979—. *Member:* Modern Language Association of America, American Studies Association, Society for the Study of the Multi-Ethnic Literature of the United States, Midcontinent American Studies Association. *Awards, honors:* National Endowment for the Humanities fellowship, summer, 1978.

WRITINGS: (With Ronald Gottesmann) *Literary Manuscripts of Upton Sinclair,* Ohio State University Press, 1972; *Henry Blake Fuller and Hamlin Garland: A Reference Guide,* G. K. Hall, 1977; (with Gretchen Bataille and David Gradwohl) *The Worlds Between Two Rivers: Perspectives on American Indians in Iowa,* Iowa State University Press, 1978; (editor with David Cummings, Will C. Jumper, and Zora Devrnja Zimmerman) *The Arc From Now: Poems, 1959-1977, by Richard Gustafson,* Iowa State University Press, 1978; *Lindsay Anderson: A Guide to References and Resources,* G. K. Hall, 1979; *Transition: An Author Index,* Whitston Publishing, 1979; *The Writings of Paul Rosenfeld: An Annotated Bibliography,* Garland Publishing, 1979; (with Bataille) *The Pretend Indians: Images of the Native Americans in the Film,* Iowa State University Press, 1980. Contributing editor of *Poet and Critic.*

WORK IN PROGRESS: A biographical-critical study of arts critic Paul Rosenfeld, publication expected in 1981.

SIDELIGHTS: Silet writes: "My current research is an outgrowth of my continuing interest in the intellectual and artistic climate of the period surrounding the First World War. But my interests are wide-ranging, encompassing scholarship on little magazines, contemporary poetry, film, and photography. I am becoming increasingly fascinated by photography, especially at the turn of the century, and am contemplating some work on Alfred Stieglitz and his circle.

"The work I am now doing on Paul Rosenfeld and Alfred Stieglitz signals a return to an intellectual fascination which I have carried with me since undergraduate days, when I first became interested in the literature of the United States. These projects also mark the end of my academic apprenticeship with its emphasis on the more formal and technical side of literary scholarship, the bibliographies, indices, and reference guides which have formed much of my work.

"Rather than feeling that my life is taking a new direction, however, I feel that it is returning to my literary beginnings. After a brief and fruitful detour I am now back to exploring the period and writers who have attracted me the longest and with the greatest intensity. The attraction stems in part from the commitment that such cultural figures as Stieglitz and Rosenfeld had for their vocation as critics and appreciators of what Rosenfeld called 'the green American tradition,' and in part from my own search for a vocation as a student of American arts and letters."

* * *

SILLANPAA, Frans Emil 1888-1964

OBITUARY NOTICE: Born September 16, 1888, in Hameenkyro, Finland; died June 3, 1964, in Helsinki, Finland. Editor, author, and winner of the Nobel Prize for Literature in 1939. Sillanpaa was editor of *Panu,* a literary publication, and a writer of novels and short stories about Finnish life and history. His works include *The Life and the Sun, Meek Heritage,* and *Fallen Asleep While Young.* Obituaries and other sources: *Current Biography,* Wilson, 1940, July, 1964; *The Reader's Encyclopedia,* 2nd edition, Crowell, 1965; *Encyclopedia of World Literature in the Twentieth Century,* updated edition, Ungar, 1967; *Everyman's Dictionary of European Writers,* Dent & Sons, 1968; *The Penguin Companion to European Literature,* McGraw, 1969; *Cassell's Encyclopaedia of World Literature,* revised edition, Morrow, 1973.

* * *

SILVER, Marjorie A. 1948-

PERSONAL: Born April 11, 1948, in Brooklyn, N.Y.; daughter of Irving Lewis (an attorney) and Blanche Belle (Einnehmer) Schuh; married Jonathan L. F. Silver, June 15, 1969 (separated February, 1976); children: Joshua Jacob Seder. *Education:* Brandeis University, B.A. (summa cum laude), 1970; University of Pennsylvania, J.D. (magna cum laude), 1973. *Home:* 31 Dolphin Green, Port Washington, N.Y. 11050. *Office:* Office of the General Counsel, U.S. Department of Health, Education, and Welfare, 26 Federal Plaza, Room 3908, New York, N.Y. 10007.

CAREER: U.S. Department of Health, Education, and Welfare, New York City, assistant regional attorney, 1977-79, chief regional civil rights attorney, 1979—. Special assistant U.S. attorney in New York City, 1978-79.

WRITINGS: (With Bernard Wolfman and Jonathan L. F. Silver) *Dissent Without Opinion: The Behavior of Justice*

William O. Douglas in Federal Tax Cases, University of Pennsylvania Press, 1975.

* * *

SILVERS, Vicki 1941-

PERSONAL: Born January 22, 1941, in New York, N.Y.; daughter of Louis and Diane (Aronson) Meyers; divorced; children: Lisa Melanie, Juliette Joy. *Home:* 60 Noble St., Brentwood, N.Y. 11717.

CAREER: Writer. Worked as adult education teacher in Brentwood, N.Y. *Awards, honors:* Poetry awards.

WRITINGS: Sing a Song of Sound, Scroll Press, 1973. Author of columns. Contributor of poems to magazines and newspapers.

* * *

SIMIC, Andrei 1930-

PERSONAL: Born August 21, 1930, in San Francisco, Calif.; married; children: two. *Education:* University of California, Berkeley, B.A., 1954, M.A., 1968, Ph.D., 1970. *Religion:* Eastern Orthodox. *Office:* Department of Anthropology, University of Southern California, Los Angeles, Calif. 90007.

CAREER: Alameda County Welfare Department, Oakland, Calif., social worker, 1957-62; U.S. Information Service, Washington, D.C., foreign service officer in Lima, Peru, 1962-63; Alameda County Welfare Department, social worker, 1963-65; Contra Costa County Juvenile Hall, Martinez, Calif., group counselor, 1965-69; University of California, Berkeley, lecturer in anthropology, 1970-71; University of Southern California, Los Angeles, assistant professor, 1971-75, associate professor of anthropology, 1975—, research associate at Ethel Percy Andrus Gerontology Center, 1974-77, director of anthropology section, 1974-75. Technical translator at University of California, Berkeley, 1964-65, member of summer faculty, 1971-72, research associate in anthropology, 1977—; lecturer at Wright Institute, 1975—; member of summer faculty at California State University, Hayward, 1975. Consultant to American Council of Learned Societies: East Europe Committee. *Member:* American Anthropological Association, Popular Culture Association. *Awards, honors:* Grants for Yugoslavia from National Institutes of Health, 1966, 1968-69, Wenner-Gren Foundation for Anthropological Research and American Philosophical Society, 1970, and National Science Foundation, 1973-74.

WRITINGS: The Peasant Urbanites, Seminar Press, 1972; *The Ethnology of Traditional and Complex Societies,* American Association for the Advancement of Science, 1975; (editor with Barbara Myerhoff, and contributor) *Life's Career—Aging: Cultural Variations on Growing Old,* Sage Publications, 1978.

Contributor: Ante Kadic, editor, *Modern Yugoslav Literature,* University of California Press, 1956; George M. Foster and Robert Van Kemper, editors, *Anthropologists in Cities,* Little, Brown, 1973; Vern L. Bengtson, editor, *Gerontological Research and Community Concern: A Case Study of a Multidisciplinary Project,* Laboratory for Social Organization and Behavior, Andrus Gerontology Center, University of Southern California, 1974; Bernard L. Faber, editor, *The Social Structure of Eastern Europe,* Praeger, 1976; Robert F. Byrnes, editor, *Communal Families in the Balkans: The Zadruga,* University of Notre Dame Press, 1976. Contributor of articles and reviews to scholarly journals. Member of editorial board of *Sociology and Social Research: An International Journal,* 1971-77.

WORK IN PROGRESS: A survey of non-English-speaking ethnic groups in San Francisco and Los Angeles; a survey of Eastern European populations and related sources in the United States; a survey of the Portuguese community in Alameda County, Calif.; research on sex-role models and behavior in Yugoslavia, on ethnic boundaries and solidarity among American "white ethnics," and on problems of aging and seniority in Yugoslavia and among Yugoslavian-born Americans.

* * *

SIMMONS, Patricia A. 1930-

PERSONAL: Born November 16, 1930, in Lebanon, Mo.; daughter of William M. (a farmer) and Phoebe Anna (Berry) Murphy; married Donald L. Simmons (a chartered life underwriter), July 21, 1951; children: Brad Alan, Cathy Dawn. *Education:* Southwest Missouri State University, B.S.Ed., 1952. *Politics:* Republican. *Religion:* Methodist. *Home:* 2010 East Sunset Dr., Springfield, Mo. 65804.

CAREER: Springfield Public Schools, Springfield, Mo., substitute teacher, 1964, 1965; writer. *Member:* Missouri Writers Association.

WRITINGS: Between You and Me, God, Broadman, 1974; *Guess What, God,* Broadman, 1976.

WORK IN PROGRESS: A book of meditations for women, for Broadman.

* * *

SIMON, Marcia L. 1939-

PERSONAL: Born April 16, 1939, in Jersey City, N.J.; daughter of Ernest (a chemist and economist) and Rachael (Schecter) Solomon; married James F. Simon (a writer and professor of law), March 30, 1963; children: David Uriah, Lauren Ruth, Sara Richelle. *Education:* Brown University, B.A., 1961; Yale University, M.A., 1964; further graduate study at Harvard University, 1975-76; also attended Rhode Island School of Design. *Religion:* Jewish. *Home:* 135 Van Houten Fields, West Nyack, N.Y. 10994. *Agent:* Wendy Weil, Julian Bach Literary Agency, Inc., 747 Third Ave., New York, N.Y. 10017.

CAREER: Smithsonian Institution, Washington, D.C., research assistant at National Portrait Gallery, 1966; writer. Instructor at Rockland Community College, summer, 1970, and Truro Center for the Arts, summers, 1976-79. Member of Van Houten Fields Association and Rockland Center for the Arts. *Member:* Authors Guild of Authors League of America, Phi Beta Kappa.

WRITINGS: A Special Gift (juvenile), Harcourt, 1978.

WORK IN PROGRESS: A juvenile novel on the ballet; a book on image-making and the relation of verbal and visual images, for Prentice-Hall.

SIDELIGHTS: "A Special Gift" was aired as a film by ABC-TV in 1979.

Marcia Simon comments: "Several previously unrelated aspects of my life came together in the writing of my first piece of fiction. My interest in writing a non-sexist children's book about a boy who dances and his special problems grew from my experiences as a mother and teacher, and from my lifelong love of dance. *A Special Gift* is based specifically on my experience of watching a young friend dance with the New Jersey Ballet in their 1975 production of the 'Nutcracker.'

"I had only a few years of ballet lessons as a child, but have been taking classes regularly, and teaching occasionally, since 1971. I have also studied modern dance, and had daily lessons in classical Indian dance while living in India, 1964-65.

"Writing for children, while taking care of my own three, is my great joy and constant dilemma."

BIOGRAPHICAL/CRITICAL SOURCES: Rockland Journal-News, December 21, 1978.

*   *   *

SIMONDS, Roger (Tyrrell) 1929-

PERSONAL: Born August 10, 1929, in New Haven, Conn.; son of Bruce (a concert pianist and college professor) and Rosalind (a concert pianist and teacher; maiden name, Brown) Simonds; married Peggy Munoz (a professor of English), November 23, 1956; children: Robin Pinckney, Martha Munoz. *Education:* Yale University, B.A., 1951, M.A., 1954, Ph.D., 1957; postdoctoral study at Harvard University, 1964-65. *Home:* 5332 42nd St. N.W., Washington, D.C. 20015. *Office:* Department of Philosophy and Religion, American University, Washington, D.C. 20016.

CAREER: New Haven Symphony Orchestra, New Haven, Conn., cellist, 1950-53; University of Oklahoma, Norman, assistant professor of philosophy, 1955-58; American University, Washington, D.C., assistant professor, 1958-61, associate professor, 1961-71, professor of philosophy, 1971—. Church organist. *Member:* American Philosophical Association, Association for Symbolic Logic, American Association of University Professors.

WRITINGS: (Contributor) Henry Margenau, editor, *Integrative Concepts of Modern Thought,* Gordon & Breach, 1970; (contributor) Harold A. Durfee and others, editors, *Exploration: New Directions in Philosophy,* Nijhoff, 1973; *Beginning Philosophical Logic,* University Press of America, 1977. Contributor to law and philosophy journals.

WORK IN PROGRESS: Research on history and philosophy of law in the Western world, with a special interest in the relationships between the Roman-Continental and the Anglo-American traditions.

SIDELIGHTS: Simonds writes: "After twenty years of teaching logic out of various textbooks, none of which exactly suited my purposes, I wrote one of my own. The book is unconventional because it treats logic as part of philosophy and introduces various philosophical topics. I also have strong interests in aesthetics. In my opinion there is no adequate text or anthology in philosophy of the arts, and before long I may have to do something about it."

*   *   *

SINGER, Neil M(ichael) 1939-

PERSONAL: Born November 21, 1939, in New York, N.Y.; son of Maxwell (a bookseller) and Laura (a teacher; maiden name, Halpern) Singer; married Linda Rubin (an attorney), December 14, 1964; children: Elizabeth Anne, Daniel Mark. *Education:* Harvard University, A.B. (magna cum laude), 1960; Stanford University, M.A., 1961, Ph.D., 1965. *Home:* 3701 Upton St. N.W., Washington, D.C. 20016. *Office:* Special Projects Group, Office of the Assistant Secretary of Defense, Pentagon, Room 3E787, Washington, D.C. 20301.

CAREER: U.S. Bureau of the Census, Washington, D.C., statistician, 1962; Golden Gate College, San Francisco, Calif., acting instructor in principles of economics, 1963; Center for Naval Analyses, Arlington, Va., economist with Naval Warfare Analysis Group, 1964-65; Office of the Secretary of Defense, Washington, D.C., consultant, 1965-66; University of Maryland, College Park, assistant professor, 1966-72, associate professor of economics, 1972-79; Office of the Assistant Secretary of Defense, Washington, D.C., special assistant for economic planning, 1978-79, director of Special Projects Group, 1979—. Visiting associate professor at Stanford University, 1975. Member of advisory board of American Bar Association's Correctional Economics Center, 1974-77. *Member:* American Economic Association, National Tax Association, Southern Economic Association.

WRITINGS: (Contributor) Eugene McLoone, Gabrielle Lupo, and Selma Mushkin, editors, *Long-Range Revenue Estimation,* George Washington University Press, 1967; (contributor) *Revenue Sharing and Its Alternatives,* Volume II, U.S. Government Printing Office, 1967; (contributor) *The Economics and Financing of Higher Education in the United States,* U.S. Government Printing Office, 1969; *Public Microeconomics,* Little, Brown, 1972, 2nd edition published as *Public Microeconomics: An Introduction to Government Finance,* 1976; (with Henry Aaron and Frank Russek) *Tax Policy and Returns to Alternative Investments,* Fund for Public Research, 1972; (with Virginia B. Wright) *Cost Analysis of Correctional Standards: Institutional-Based Programs and Parole,* National Institute of Law Enforcement and Criminal Justice, U.S. Law Enforcement Assistance Administration, Volume I, 1975, Volume II, 1976; (contributor) Marc Reidel and Pedro A. Vales, editors, *Treating the Offender: Problems and Issues,* Praeger, 1977; (contributor) *The Evaluation of Patuxent Institution,* Contract Research Corp., 1977. Contributor of about twenty-five articles and reviews to professional journals and newspapers.

WORK IN PROGRESS: Research on the economic consequences of defense spending.

SIDELIGHTS: Singer told *CA* that the nature of his research on the economic consequences of defense spending "is a critique of some recent assessment of the economic damage done by defense spending. The critics allege that resources allocated to national defense (a) contribute to inflation, (b) increase unemployment, (c) diminish the productivity of American workers, and (d) adversely affect our balance of payments. My present view is that all of these assertions have received more attention than serious analysis would justify. It is too soon to predict whether my view will change as the result of further analysis, or whether my arguments will ever see the light of published day."

*   *   *

SINGH, Surendra Nihal
See NIHAL SINGH, Surendra

*   *   *

SITZFLEISCH, Vladimir
See SPIRER, Herbert F(rederick)

*   *   *

SLOAN, Thomas 1928-

PERSONAL: Born June 16, 1928, in Hamilton, Ontario, Canada; son of Thomas Reginald (a lawyer) and Sarah Mildred (Sheeper) Sloan; married Lorraine Derry, April 1, 1961 (divorced); children: Maureen. *Education:* University of Toronto, B.A., 1949, M.A., 1951; attended Sorbonne, University of Paris, 1949-50, 1951-52, and London School of Economics and Political Science, London, 1952-54. *Reli-*

gion: Unitarian-Universalist. *Home:* 4000 de Maisonneuve W., Montreal, Quebec, Canada H3Z 1J9.

CAREER: Bishop Ridley College, St. Catherines, Ontario, teacher in French and Spanish, 1956-57; *Toronto Globe & Mail,* Toronto, Ontario, news correspondent, 1957-64; associated with *Welland Evening Tribune,* Welland, Ontario, 1957-64, and *Montreal Star,* Montreal, Quebec, 1968-70; Laval University, Quebec City, Quebec, director of journalism and information program, 1968-70; Office of the Leader of the Opposition, Ottawa, Ontario, senior assistant, 1970-73; Carleton University, Ottawa, associate professor of journalism, 1973-75; Canadian Daily Newspaper Publishers Association, Toronto, supervisor of editorial services, 1975-76; Public Service Commission of Canada, Bureau of Executive Education, Ottawa, academic visitor, 1976-77; *Montreal Gazette,* Montreal, editor of editorial page, 1977-79; free-lance writer and broadcaster, 1978—. *Member:* National Press Club of Canada, Union des Artistes, Le Cercle Universitaire de Quebec. *Awards, honors:* Associate Nieman fellow at Harvard University, 1967-68.

WRITINGS: Quebec: The Not-So-Quiet Revolution, Ryerson, 1964; (contributor) Earl Toppings, editor, *Canada,* Follett, 1967; (contributor) R. St. John Macdonald and John P. Humphrey, editors, *The Practice of Freedom,* Butterworth, 1979.

WORK IN PROGRESS: Nationalism in Canada and Quebec: Can They Be Reconciled?

SIDELIGHTS: Sloan writes: "My basic goal has been to work out the implications of English and French Canadian co-existence over a two-hundred-year period. Can the two peoples continue to live in one country? The jury is still out."

* * *

SLOBIN, Mark 1943-

PERSONAL: Born March 15, 1943, in Detroit, Mich.; son of Norval (a teacher) and Judith (a teacher; maiden name, Liepah) Slobin; married Greta Nachtajler (a college teacher), June 11, 1966; children: Maya. *Education:* University of Michigan, B.A., 1964, M.A., 1966, Ph.D., 1969; attended Manhattan School of Music, 1962-64. *Office:* Department of Music, Wesleyan University, Middletown, Conn. 06457.

CAREER: Wesleyan University, Middletown, Conn., 1971—, began as assistant professor, became associate professor of music. Visiting member of faculty at Yiddish Scientific Institute's Institute for Jewish Research, 1979; research associate at University of Nebraska. Consultant to General Learning Corp. *Member:* Society for Ethnomusicology (member of executive board, 1972-74, 1976-78). *Awards, honors:* Grants from Wenner-Gren Foundation, 1970, 1971, National Endowment for the Arts, 1976, 1979, and International Research & Exchanges Board, for the Soviet Union, 1976.

WRITINGS: Kirgiz Instrumental Music, Asian Music Publications, 1969; *Central Asian Music,* Wesleyan University Press, 1975; *Music in the Culture of Northern Afghanistan,* University of Arizona Press, 1976. Contributor to *Encyclopaedia Britannica, Grove's New Dictionary of Music,* and *Oxford Companion to Music.* Contributor of articles and reviews to music, anthropology, and Asian studies journals. Editor of *Asian Music,* 1972—.

WORK IN PROGRESS: A critical edition of the works of M. Beregovskii on Yiddish folk music; a study of Jewish-American immigrant music, 1880-1925.

SIDELIGHTS: Slobin commented: "My continuing interest is in how music is part of people's (individual and collective) sense of who they are. To this end I have worked among people whose backgrounds are very different from mine (in Afghanistan and Central Asia) and on the music of my own background (Yiddish). This has involved considerable travel through Europe, the Soviet Union, Israel, and the Middle East and India, as well as work on the Lower East Side of New York. Since 1976 I have also been involved in producing and reproducing immigrant entertainment of the turn-of-the-century period, and find I truly enjoy the show-business side of the work as much as the scholarship."

* * *

SMETANA, Josette 1928-

PERSONAL: Born May 17, 1928, in Limoges, France; daughter of Andre and Camille (a teacher; maiden name, Beaubert) Laborde; married John W. Smetana (a high school administrator), June 30, 1952; children: Ann Smetana Kroell, Isabelle, Gilles. *Education:* Sorbonne, University of Paris, lic. es lettres, 1951, dipl. d'etudes superieures, 1952, Ph.D., 1964. *Religion:* Roman Catholic. *Home:* 617 Jefferson St., Westbury, N.Y. 11590. *Office:* Department of Languages and International Studies, Adelphi University, South Ave., Garden City, N.Y. 11530.

CAREER: Part-time teacher at schools in Paris, France, 1952, and Marrakesh, Morocco, 1953, full-time teacher in Marrakesh, 1954-60, and Loches, France, 1960-61; Queens College of the City University of New York, Flushing, N.Y., instructor in French, 1961-64; Adelphi University, Garden City, N.Y., assistant professor, 1964-68, associate professor, 1968-75, professor of French, 1975—, head of department, 1968-72, coordinator of Center of Foreign Languages, 1970-72. Guest lecturer at Hofstra University, 1972. *Member:* Modern Language Association of America, American Association of University Professors, Societe des Professeurs Francais en Amerique, Northeast Conference on the Teaching of Foreign Languages (member of advisory council, 1977, 1979). *Awards, honors:* Palmes Academiques from Government of France, 1976.

WRITINGS: La Philosophie de l'action chez Saint-Exupery and Hemingway, La Marjolaine J.A.M., 1965, 2nd edition, 1980; (with M. Myron) *Melange Litteraire,* Holt, 1970, 2nd edition, in press; (with Myron) *Plaisir de la lecture,* Appleton, 1972; (with Myron) *Perspectives,* Holt, 1974.

SIDELIGHTS: Josette Smetana commented: "I lived in Marrakesh for eight years. I was married there and our three children were born there. They were the best years of my life. I have also traveled in England, Italy, Greece, Spain, Haiti, and Martinique."

* * *

SMITH, David H. 1939-

PERSONAL: Born April 28, 1939; married Mary Louise Arnaud, 1961; children: Alexandra Marie-Louise, Zachary David, Jacob Arnaud. *Education:* Carleton College, B.A., 1961; Yale University, B.D., 1964; Princeton University, Ph.D., 1967. *Religion:* Episcopalian. *Office:* Department of Religion, Indiana University, Bloomington, Ind. 47401.

CAREER: Indiana University, Bloomington, assistant professor, 1967-70, associate professor, 1970-79, professor of religious studies, 1979—, head of department, 1976—. Senior research scholar at Joseph and Rose Kennedy Institute for Bioethics, 1973-74; member of Hastings Institute's National Commission on the Teaching of Biomedical Ethics, 1974-76; member of research group on death and dying, of Institute for Society, Ethics, and the Life Sciences, 1977—. President of advisory council of Southern Indiana Health Systems Agency, 1978-79. President of Elm Heights Neighborhood Association, 1972-73. *Awards, honors:* Grants from National Endowment for the Humanities, 1969, 1978, 1979, Danforth Foundation, 1971-72, Poynter Center on American Institutions, 1976, Lilly Endowment, 1977, 1977-79, 1978-80, and Indiana Committee for the Humanities, 1976, 1977; distinguished teaching award from Amoco, 1978.

WRITINGS: The Achievement of John C. Bennett, Herder & Herder, 1970; (editor with James T. Johnson, and contributor) *Love and Society: Essays in the Ethics of Paul Ramsey,* Scholars' Press, 1974; (editor and contributor) *No Rush to Judgment,* Poynter Center on American Institutions, Indiana University, 1977; (contributor) *Teaching Biomedical and Health Care Ethics to Liberal Arts Undergraduates,* Associated Colleges of the Midwest, 1977; (contributor) Ronald A. Carson, Richard C. Reynolds, and Harold Gene Moss, editors, *Patient Wishes and Physician Obligations,* University of Florida Press, 1978. Contributor to *Encyclopedia of Bioethics.* Contributor of about fifteen articles and reviews to scientific journals.

*   *   *

SMITH, Jackie M. 1930-

PERSONAL: Born August 28, 1930, in Arlington, Tex.; daughter of Virgil V. (in sales) and Frances (Eavenson) Smith. *Education:* Rice University, B.A., 1952, graduate study, 1952-53; Presbyterian School of Christian Education, M.A., 1956; also attended Virginia Commonwealth University, 1967, 1972. *Religion:* Presbyterian. *Home:* 1197 Hancock Dr. N.E., Atlanta, Ga. 30306.

CAREER: American Society of Medical Technologists, Houston, Tex., office worker, 1952-53; elementary school teacher in Houston, 1953-54, and Spotsylvania County, Va., 1956-57; Presbyterian Board of Christian Education, Richmond, Va., staff member and editor of "Special Studies for Children," 1965-68; high school teacher of Bible and ethics at religious school in Richmond, 1968-74; General Assembly Mission Board, Division of Corporate and Social Mission, Atlanta, Ga., staff associate for education through mission, 1974—. Worked with interracial groups for Fredericksburg Welfare Department. *Awards, honors:* Tower scholar at Union Theological Seminary, Richmond, Va., 1967.

WRITINGS: Is God Cruel? (juvenile study guide on the Book of Job), Covenant Life Curriculum Press, 1964; *My Church at Work in the World* (juvenile), Covenant Life Curriculum Press, 1965; *Face to Face,* John Knox, 1973; *Leading Groups in Personal Growth,* John Knox, 1973. Author of church school curriculum material. Contributor to religious magazines, including *Presbyterian Survey, They Will My Will,* and *Day by Day.*

WORK IN PROGRESS: Study-action guides on global justice issues.

SIDELIGHTS: Jackie Smith's writings have covered the future of church education in views of global crises, the new international economic order, lifestyles, and the Christian faith and economics. Her books have been distributed in Germany, New Zealand, and Australia.

She wrote: "My objectives are to help individuals and groups identify sources of oppression that limit their human growth and development and to use both external educa-

tional procedures and experiential (internal) learning processes to help persons make value judgments that issue in personal growth integrated with concerted action for reform of and liberation from oppressive structures."

*   *   *

SMITH, Joan K(aren) 1939-

PERSONAL: Born March 17, 1939, in Oak Park, Ill.; daughter of Raymond D. (a consulting engineer) and Mildred (Engman) Johnsos; married Robert Paul Zerwekh, August 3, 1963 (divorced, 1971); married Leonard Glenn Smith (a professor and writer), August 7, 1971; children: Jeffrey Robert. *Education:* University of Illinois, B.S., 1961; Iowa State University, M.S., 1970, Ph.D., 1976. *Home:* 9 Kenfield Circle, Bloomington, Ill. 61701. *Office:* Department of Educational Administration and Foundations, Illinois State University, 340-A DeGarmo Hall, Normal, Ill. 61761.

CAREER: Elementary school teacher in Ames, Iowa, 1964-65; Des Moines Area Community College, Ankeny, Iowa, classroom consultant, 1970, counselor, 1970-71; Iowa State University, Ames, instructor in education, 1976; Illinois State University, Normal, assistant professor of education, 1978—. *Member:* American Educational Studies Association, American Educational Research Association, Delta Kappa Gamma (president), Phi Kappa Phi. *Awards, honors:* Grant from Delta Kappa Gamma, 1979.

WRITINGS: Ella Flagg Young: Portrait of a Leader, Educational Studies Press, 1979.

Contributor: Michael Belok, editor, *Women: An International Perspective,* Anu, 1977; L. Glenn Smith and Charles R. Kniker, editors, *Myth and Reality,* Allyn & Bacon, 1972, revised edition, 1975. Contributor to education and philosophy journals. Managing editor of *Educational Studies,* 1977-79, editor, 1979-82.

WORK IN PROGRESS: A biography of Margaret Haley, teacher, union organizer, and feminist, publication expected in 1981; *Lives in Education* (tentative title), a textbook on foundations of education, with husband, L. Glenn Smith, publication expected in 1981.

SIDELIGHTS: Joan Smith comments: "My elementary teaching and college counseling experiences have given me a keen interest in people—both past and present. I am particularly interested in the past status of women and children. I think that historical research has sadly neglected these two minorities. Educational history has certainly neglected the contributions of women to the field and I hope to remedy that through my future research."

*   *   *

SMITH, L(eonard) Glenn 1939-

PERSONAL: Born May 20, 1939, in Runnels County, Tex.; son of Leonard Frank and Letha (Bowen) Smith; married Mona Jeanne Boles, May 31, 1960 (divorced, 1971); married Joan Karen Johnsos (a professor and writer), August 7, 1971; children: Jeffrey Robert. *Education:* Abilene Christian College, B.S., 1960; Trinity University, San Antonio, Tex., M.S., 1963; University of Oklahoma, Ph.D., 1967. *Home:* 9 Kenfield Circle, Bloomington, Ill. 61701. *Office:* Department of Secondary Education, Iowa State University, 17 Quadrangle, Ames, Iowa 50011.

CAREER: Junior high school history teacher in San Antonio, Tex., 1962-63; Oklahoma Christian College, Oklahoma City, instructor in history, 1963-64; University of Oklahoma, Norman, instructor in education, 1966-67; Iowa State University, Ames, assistant professor, 1967-70, associate professor, 1970-75, professor of education, 1975—. Founder of Educational Studies Press. *Member:* American Educational Studies Association, Educational Press Association, American Educational Research Association, Society of Educational Publishers, Kiwanis. *Awards, honors:* First prize in Phi Delta Kappa's bicentennial essay contest, 1976, for "American Education in Centennial Perspective."

WRITINGS: (Editor with Charles R. Kniker) *Myth and Reality: Readings in Education,* Allyn & Bacon, 1972, revised edition, 1975. Contributor to education journals and newspapers. Editor of *Educational Studies,* 1976-79, managing editor, 1979-82.

WORK IN PROGRESS: Lives in Education (tentative title), textbook on the history of American education, with wife, Joan K. Smith, publication expected in 1981.

SIDELIGHTS: Smith comments: "I have a strong interest in people and in what makes them tick. I think people make the world and its institutions what they are. I am also interested in teaching and learning, and in how we got the kinds of schools and educational agencies that we have. Combined with my own desire to know, is a wish to share with others—hence a natural curiosity about publishing and the communications processes.

"My wife and I are in the same field and work at two different universities in adjoining states. My interest in flying comes in handy, as I commute to work in my own plane. During the week, I live like a fourteenth-century monk at Iowa State University. On the weekend, it's more like Buck Rogers and the twenty-fifth century, as I fly over Iowa and Illinois. It keeps life fresh and interesting."

*   *   *

SMITH, Lena (Kennedy)   1914-
(Lena Kennedy)

PERSONAL: Born June 15, 1914, in London, England; daughter of Cornelius Erin (a stonemason) and Margaret Kennedy; married Frederick George Smith, 1935; children: Angela Smith Welford, Keith. *Education:* Attended secondary school in London, England. *Politics:* Conservative. *Religion:* Roman Catholic. *Residence:* London, England. *Address:* c/o Paddington Press, 21 Bentinck St., London W1M 5RL, England.

CAREER: Factory worker during World War II; writer.

*WRITINGS—*Novels; all under name Lena Kennedy: *Maggie,* Paddington Press, 1979; *Autumn Alley,* Paddington Press, 1980; *Nelly Kelly,* Paddington Press, 1981; *Owen Oliver,* Paddington Press, in press; *Tudor Rebel,* Paddington Press, in press; *Kate of Cline Shore,* Paddington Press, in press.

WORK IN PROGRESS: Journey to Orphanage; research on the Hoxton section of London; a work of historical fiction tracing the lives of fourteenth-century Irish kings.

SIDELIGHTS: Lena Smith told *CA:* "I am very interested in history. *Tudor Rebel* and *Kate of Cline Shore* are historical novels. *Tudor Rebel* is about Penelope Devereux, sister of the sixteenth-century Earl of Essex. I also enjoy visiting castles, old mansions, and haunted public houses.

"I find writing stories easy and I always have. I have never liked all the bother of sending them away to magazines, though. I found the business side of writing very difficult, and I believe that is why I wrote six novels before publishing anything. I write for the sheer enjoyment of creating people

and moving them around, especially if they do something courageous or exciting—you feel it's something you would love to do yourself. I escape in my writing and become very fond of the characters. Sometimes I find it difficult when they have to die, because they have become so real to me.

"I have no set routine with my writing, except that I often create when I'm tidying the house, and when I have it all clear in my mind, I pop upstairs to my typewriter and write it straight down."

BIOGRAPHICAL/CRITICAL SOURCES: Paperback and Popular Hardback Buyer, March, 1979; *Daily Express,* April 6, 1979; *Woman's Realm,* April 6, 1979; *Daily Mail,* April 12, 1979; Leyton *Guardian,* May 11, 1979.

*   *   *

SMITH, M. Weston
See WESTON-SMITH, M.

*   *   *

SMITH, Patti   1946-

PERSONAL: Born in 1946, in New Jersey; married Frederick Smith (a musician under stage name Fred Sonic), 1979—; children: one. *Residence:* Ann Arbor, Mich.

CAREER: Poet and performer. Worked in factory, c. 1964; clerk for Scribner's (bookstore), c. 1970; staff writer for *Rock,* c. 1971; reader of poetry and singer of songs in concerts; associated with Arista Records, 1975—. *Member:* Radio Ethiopia. *Awards, honors:* Numerous awards from publications, including *Creem,* for performances in concerts and on recordings.

WRITINGS: (Contributor) Sam Shepard, *Mad Dog Blues and Other Plays* (includes "Cowboy Mouth" by Shepard and Smith, first produced in New York City, c. 1972), Winter House, 1972; *Kodak* (verse), Middle Earth Bookshop, 1972; *Seventh Heaven* (verse), Telegraph Books, 1972; *Witt* (verse), Gotham Book Mart, 1973; (with Tom Verlaine) *The Night* (verse), Aloes Books, 1976; *Ha! Ha! Houdini,* Gotham Book Mart, 1977; *Babel* (verse), Putnam, 1978. Also author of *Early Morning Dream,* 1972.

Author of recordings for Arista Records, including "Horses," 1975, "Radio Ethiopia," 1976, "Easter," 1978, and "Wave," 1979.

Contributor to periodicals, including *Creem, Rolling Stone,* and *Rock.*

SIDELIGHTS: "I get into so many genders I couldn't even tell you," Smith declares. "I've written from the mouth of a dog, a horse, dead people, anything, I don't limit myself." Influenced by such diverse artists and performers as Antonin Artaud, Jimi Hendrix, Marlon Brando, Arthur Rimbaud, and Robert Bresson, Smith has distinguished herself as a playwright, a singer, a songwriter, and a poet. R. Meltzer compares her as a performer to Billie Holiday, and Tony Glover calls her "one of the greatest poets writing in English." Smith assesses herself in more mystical terms. "I am the seed of mystery," she sings in "Easter," "the veil, the thorn . . . , the Prince of Peace."

Smith's early interests were black performers, including James Brown, John Coltrane, and Little Richard. Recalling her high-school days, she notes that she was "really into jazz and poetry. . . . It was the best education I ever had." Her interests expanded into rock music after her father's enraged reaction to a televised performance of the Rolling Stones. Claiming that "for him to react so violently attracted me," she writes, "blind love for my father was the first thing I sacrificed to Mick Jagger."

Smith developed a similar interest in Bob Dylan after her mother presented her with two of his recordings following an argument. Confessing that she "really doesn't understand poetry," Smith contends that she was attracted to Dylan's "delivery, his phrasing, his physical image, his energy." Her adulation for Dylan led to one for Rimbaud. Spotting a copy of his poetry, Smith was taken by his resemblance to Dylan. "The first thing I got from Rimbaud was the power of the outer image: his face," she recalls. "He sorta looked like Dylan."

After high school, Smith worked in a factory. Her experiences there were later recounted in her first musical recording, "Piss Factory." She then enrolled in a junior college, but was forced to withdraw due to pregnancy. In a prose poem she writes: "bloated. pregnant. I crawl thru the sand. like a lame dog. like a crab. pull my fat baby belly to the sea." Smith asserts that giving birth gave her a new perspective on life. "It developed me as a person," she reveals, "made me start to value life, to value chance."

She traveled for the next three years: to New York City, where she met Robert Mapplethorpe, a photographer who urged her to pursue her artistic skills; to Paris, where she joined a street troupe and dreamed of guitarist Brian Jones's death; and back to New York City, where she joined the staff of *Rock* magazine, found a publisher for her poems, and co-wrote a play with Sam Shepard.

Smith published her first written works in 1972—two collections of poetry and "Cowboy Mouth," the play co-written with Shepard. "I love writing because there's acoustic-type typewriters and electric ones," Smith notes. She does have some reservations about playwriting, however, because "the word is still trapped on the stage."

She decided that her poems were better suited to being read aloud and so, accompanied by guitarist Lenny Kaye, she took to performing. "My push is to get beyond the word into something that's more fleshy," she explains, "that's why I like performing. The Word is just, for me, when I'm alone late at night and I'm ... pouring out streams of words. That's a very one-to-one process, but I'm interested in communication."

Performing with a guitarist, though, was not enough for Smith. "I don't wanna be no simp reading boring intellectual s—— to a YMCA," she charges. Smith added another guitarist, a rhythm section, and a pianist as musical background, and with a repertoire featuring songs by the Ronettes and Jimi Hendrix as well as her own material, she became a bona fide rock performer. After attending one of her concerts, Stephen Holden reported: "Onstage ..., she exudes an inimitable aura of tough street punk and mystic waif, in whose skinny, sexy person the spirits of Rimbaud and William Burroughs miraculously intersect with the mystic qualities of Jim Morrison, Jimi Hendrix.... She seems destined to be the queen of rock & roll for the Seventies."

In 1975, Smith recorded her first album, "Horses," which John Rockwell considers "a great record." It features such pop standards as "Gloria" and "Land of a Thousand Dances," as well as surreal recountings of a lesbian suicide and a homosexual rape. "Like all real poets," writes Rockwell, "Smith offers visions that embrace a multiplicity of meanings, all of them valid if they touch an emotional chord. Tony Hiss and David McLelland call "Horses" "the most literate magic in rock 'n' roll."

Other critics were unimpressed with the recording, dubbing it both pretentious and derivative. Paul Nelson claims that it sounds "like a morbid, pretentious rehash of Jim Morrison and Lou Reed.... Even *Land*, the best song on it ..., metamorphoses from the Velvet Underground into the Doors." Steve Lake bemoans Smith's coupling of rock 'n' roll nostalgia with her intellectual interests. He also regrets "that half assed critics with no musical sensibilities whatever will drag their volumes of Freud from dusty top shelves and begin to thunder about Oedipal tendencies and bore us all over again." Griel Marcus concedes that "Smith's posturing ultimately seems an end in itself," and adds that "if you're going to mess around with the kind of stuff Bunuel, Dali, and Rimbaud were putting out, you have to come up with a lot more than *homage*."

"Horses," however, fared better with several critics than its successor, "Radio Ethiopia," in which Smith chose to record only songs written within her group. "At least 'Horses' had the dubious privilege of a rabble-rousing version of Them's 'Gloria,'" claims Marianne Partridge, "but on 'Radio Ethiopia' all the cuts are by Patti and Band." She called the record "an inarticulate mess." Dave Marsh writes that "on 'Radio Ethiopia,' her group dominates," and sums them up as "another loud punk-rock gang of primitives, riff-based and redundant." He concludes that "the Patti Smith Group isn't much more than a distant evocation of psychedelic amateurs."

Following the release of "Radio Ethiopia," Smith embarked on a concert/promotion tour. Her schedule, though, was abbreviated in Florida when she pitched headfirst into the orchestra pit during a performance of "Aint It Strange" and broke her neck. "I was opting for communication with my Creator," she asserts, "and it led me down the most nondisciplined path I've ever taken. Disintegrating and going into a black tube, that's what I felt like. I was losing consciousness, and then I was in a tunnel of light, a classic Jungian dream space. I felt like I was being pulled and it was not at all unpleasurable."

While incapacitated, Smith revived talents in both writing poetry and drawing. Some of her poems from this period were published in the 1978 collection, *Babel*. Jonathan Cott describes it as "an alternately dazzling, uneven, arousing, annoying, imitative, original work." In the book, notes Cott, "she contacts ghosts, makes love with the dead and transforms herself into animals (a ... skunk dog in one poem)." Some of Smith's poems are fusions of her interests in surrealism, violence, and rock 'n' roll. In "Rape," for instance, the narrator issues an invitation to dance to a woman whom the speaker has just sexually violated. "Oh don't cry," Smith writes. "Come on get up. lets dance in the grass / lets cut a rug lets jitterbug. roll those tiny white / stockings down. bobby sock-o lets flow. come on this is a / dance contest. under the stars, lets alice in the grass. / lets swing betty boop hoop / lets birdland lets stroll / lets rock lets roll / lets whale-bone lets go / lets deodorize the night."

In 1978 Smith released "Easter," an album filled with religious imagery. Ken Tucker states that "Smith uses the New Testament in the same way she used 'Gloria' on *Horses*—as a hunk of raw myth for her and her boys to gnash and wail over." He adds: "What Smith admires about Jesus is not His teachings ... but His example, His ordeal and triumph—that He was a real little scrapper, just like Patti. Thus Christ gains admission to Smith's eccentric pantheon of 'Rock 'n' Roll Niggers.'"

Smith returned to the concert circuit that year, despite her previous accident. "My period of immobility gave me the time to reassess myself," she claims. "I've accepted certain responsibilities. We really care about kids, we care about rock & roll, we care about the future and we work as hard as we can." Recalling her mishap, Smith notes that "in pursuit of communicating with God, you can enter some very dangerous territory. I also have come to realize that total communication with God is physical death."

Some critics, though, remain unimpressed by Smith's religious and artistic postures and allusions. "Because she cultivates the look of a possessed poet," writes Charles M. Young, "she can say things like 'the word art must be redefined' and get away with it." He contends that "Smith believes her own line and has constructed an imposing edifice of egomania to protect her mediocre ideas from doubt." Robert Christgau writes: "She theorizes that rock and roll is 'the highest and most universal form of expression since the lost tongue. . . .' She believes that the 'neo-artist' is 'the nigger of the universe.' In short, she would appear to be full of s——.''

Smith, however, defends herself in "Rock and Roll Nigger" by singing, "I am an American artist and I have no guilt." She contends: "I stuck it out, you know, I stuck it out. And I'm determined to make us kids . . . , us ones who could never get a degree in college, whatever, have a family, or do regular stuff, social stuff, prove that there's a place for us." She also insists that she'd "rather be a housewife, and a *good* housewife, admired by all the other housewives in the area, than be a mediocre rock singer. The only crime in art is to do lousy art."

BIOGRAPHICAL/CRITICAL SOURCES: Creem, June, 1972, September, 1972, January, 1977; *Rolling Stone,* August 14, 1975, January 1, 1976, February 12, 1976, January 13, 1977, July 27, 1978; *Mademoiselle,* September, 1975; *Crawdaddy,* December, 1975; *Melody Maker,* December 13, 1975, October 23, 1976, May 5, 1979; *New York Times Magazine,* December 21, 1975; *Newsweek,* December 29, 1975; *Stereo Review,* February, 1976, April, 1976; *Village Voice,* January 17, 1977, May 1, 1978; *New York Times Book Review,* February 19, 1978; Patti Smith, *Babel,* Putnam, 1978; *Contemporary Literary Criticism,* Volume 12, Gale, 1980.*

—Sketch by Les Stone

* * *

SMITH, Tony

PERSONAL—Education: University of Texas, B.A., 1964; Harvard University, Ph.D., 1971. *Office:* Department of Political Science, Tufts University, Medford, Mass. 02155.

CAREER: Tufts University, Medford, Mass., professor of political science, 1970—.

WRITINGS: (Editor) *The End of European Empire,* Heath, 1975; *The French Stake in Algeria, 1945-62,* Cornell University Press, 1978.

WORK IN PROGRESS: Research on imperialism, past and present.

* * *

SNELLING, W(illiam) Rodman 1931-

PERSONAL: Born February 10, 1931, in Pittsfield, Mass.; son of Samuel William and Beatrice (Bamforth) Snelling; married Anne Kurtz (a company vice-president), January 24, 1953; children: Roxanne, Glenn. *Education:* Bowdoin College, A.B., 1953; Harvard University, A.B., 1953; College of William and Mary, M.Ed., 1956; University of Virginia,

D.Ed., 1957. *Home:* 1100 Pennsylvania Ave., Wilmington, Del. 19806. *Office:* Independent School Management, P.O. Box 3897, Wilmington, Del. 19807.

CAREER: High school mathematics teacher in Portsmouth, Va., 1953-54, and Schenectady, N.Y., 1957-59; mathematics teacher and department head at private school in Chicago, Ill., 1959-61; headmaster of private day school in Birmingham, Mich., 1961-67; Research Corp., New York, N.Y., education consultant, 1967-68; headmaster of private school in Wilmington, Del., 1968-79; Independent School Management (consulting firm), Wilmington, Del., president and author of newsletter, "Ideas and Perspectives," 1975—. Research assistant for New York State Department of Education, summers, 1957-58; teacher at private school in Andover, Mass., summers, 1959-60. *Military service:* U.S. Army, 1954-56. *Member:* National Association of Secondary School Administrators, Delaware Association of Independent Schools, Phi Delta Kappa.

WRITINGS: (With Robert F. Boruch) *Science in Liberal Arts Colleges: A Longitudinal Study of Forty-Nine Selective Colleges,* Columbia University Press, 1971. Contributor to mathematics and education journals.

* * *

SNYDER, Susan 1934-

PERSONAL: Born July 12, 1934, in Yonkers, N.Y.; daughter of John (an insurance executive) and Virginia (Hartung) Snyder. *Education:* Hunter College (now of the City University of New York), A.B., 1955; Columbia University, M.A., 1958, Ph.D., 1963. *Office:* Department of English, Swarthmore College, Swarthmore, Pa. 19081.

CAREER: Queens College of the City University of New York, Flushing, N.Y., lecturer in English, 1961-63; Swarthmore College, Swarthmore, Pa., instructor, 1963-66, assistant professor, 1966-70, associate professor, 1970-75, professor of English and head of department, 1975—. *Member:* Renaissance Society of America, Shakespeare Association of America, American Association of University Professors. *Awards, honors:* National Endowment for the Humanities fellowship, 1967-68; Folger Shakespeare Library senior fellowship, 1972-73.

WRITINGS: (Editor) *The Divine Weeks and Works of Guillaume de Saluste, Sieur du Bartas,* translated by Joshua Sylvester, two volumes, Oxford University Press, 1979; *The Comic Matrix of Shakespeare's Tragedies,* Princeton University Press, 1979. Contributor to literature journals. Member of editorial board of *Shakespeare Quarterly,* 1973—.

WORK IN PROGRESS: Research on Renaissance pastoral poetry.

* * *

SOGLOW, Otto 1900-1975

PERSONAL: Born December 23, 1900, in Yorkville, N.Y.; died April 3, 1975, in New York, N.Y.; married Anna Rosen (an artist), October 11, 1928; children: Tona. *Education:* Studied with John Sloan at Art Student's League. *Residence:* New York, N.Y.

CAREER: Cartoonist and illustrator for numerous publications, including *New Yorker, Life, Judge, Collier's, Harper's Bazaar,* and *New York World,* 1925-33; King Features Syndicate, New York, N.Y., cartoonist, 1934-75. *Member:* National Cartoonists Society (organizer and past president), Society of Illustrators. *Awards, honors:* Founders Medal from National Cartoonists Society, 1966; Reuben award from National Cartoonists Society, 1967, for outstanding cartoonist of the year; Elzie Segar award, 1972, for outstanding cartooning; recipient of Freedom Foundation award.

WRITINGS: Pretty Pictures, Farrar & Rinehart, 1931; *Everything's Rosy*, Farrar & Rinehart, 1932; *The Little King*, Farrar & Rinehart, 1933; *Wasn't the Depression Terrible?*, Covici, Friede, 1934; *Soglow's "Confidential" History of Modern England*, Frederick A. Stokes, 1939.

Illustrator: Richard Hyman, *It's the Law*, Doubleday, 1936; Richard Hyman, *Looney Laws*, Arpy, 1946; Hyman, *Of All Fool Things: A Book of Nonsensical Americana*, Duell, Sloan & Pearce, 1948; Hyman, *It's Against the Law!*, A & S Publishing, 1949; Dick Shaw, *Liberated Latin*, Doubleday, 1951; Hyman, *Nonsense, U.S.A.: A Collection of Nonsensical Americana*, Dutton, 1953; Hyman, *It's Still the Law*, McKay, 1961; (with Bob Dunn) *Now See Here, Judge!*, Hawthorn, 1967.

OBITUARIES: New York Times, April 4, 1975; *Current Biography*, May, 1975.*

* * *

SOLOMON, Shirl 1928-

PERSONAL: Born January 29, 1928, in Philadelphia, Pa.; daughter of William (a cantor) and Fannie (Lobel) Goldhirsh; married Jay Lewis Solomon, October, 1967 (divorced July 24, 1974); children: Cindy, Mark, Lori. *Education:* Attended Pennsylvania Academy of Fine Arts, University of Pennsylvania, Dallas Art Institute, and Instituto Allende. *Religion:* Jewish. *Home and office:* 200 Tamoshanter Dr., Palm Springs, Fla. 33460. *Agent:* Audrey Adler, Q St., Washington, D.C.

CAREER: Philadelphia Better Hearing Center, Philadelphia, Pa., hearing aid consultant, 1955-57; Pennsylvania Department of Welfare, Philadelphia, caseworker, 1959-63; youth group director of Jewish Federation of Palm Beach County, Palm Beach, Fla.; art teacher at schools in Florida, New York, Pennsylvania, and New Hampshire; teacher of Spanish in Florida; WPBR-Radio, Palm Beach, Fla., presented weekly program, "Very Truly Yours, Shirl," 1977-79; graphology lecturer, researcher, and consultant, 1979—. Conducted research in juvenile and criminal courts, as well as public and private schools.

WRITINGS: How to Really Know Yourself Through Your Handwriting, Taplinger, 1973; *Scryptics*, New American Library, 1977; *Knowing Your Child Through His Handwriting and Drawings*, Crown, 1978.

WORK IN PROGRESS: Evaluating and helping children with learning disabilities.

SIDELIGHTS: Shirl Solomon writes: "None of us had control over our childhood, not the circumstances nor the age it takes to see ourselves in perspective to those circumstances. If I could change one thing in my own childhood, it would be to have been given the assurance that I deserved to achieve something special and that I was capable of it. If my work with teachers and parents can help bring this about in the small child, the investment of my years will have received the greatest return I could imagine."

* * *

SORRELL, Alan 1904-1974

PERSONAL: Born February 11, 1904, in London, England; died December 21, 1974; son of Ernest and Edith Sorrell; married Elizabeth Tanner, 1947; children: Richard, Mark, Julie. *Education:* Royal College of Art, A.R.C.A., 1927; also studied at British School at Rome.

CAREER: Painter and designer, 1927-74, with work in permanent collections, including Tate Gallery, Imperial War Museum, Museum of London, and National Museum of Wales, as well as private collections; had exhibits at Royal Academy; and one-man shows. Senior assistant instructor at Royal College of Art, 1931-39, 1946-48. *Military service:* Royal Air Force, 1939-46. *Member:* Royal Society of Painters in Water-Colour.

WRITINGS: (With Aileen Fox) *Roman Britain*, Lutterworth Press, 1961; (with J.R.C. Hamilton) *Saxon England*, Lutterworth Press, 1964; *Living History*, Batsford, 1965; (with Henry Loyn) *Norman Britain*, Lutterworth Press, 1966; (with E. B. Green) *Prehistoric Britain*, Lutterworth Press, 1967; *Roman London*, Batsford, 1968; (with Margaret S. Drower) *Nubia: A Drowning Land*, Longmans, Green, 1970; (with Anthony Birley) *Imperial Rome*, Lutterworth Press, 1970; (illustrator) *The Bible*, Lutterworth Press, 1970; *British Castles*, Hastings, 1974; *Roman Towns in Britain*, Hippocrene Books, 1977; *Reconstructing the Past* (paintings), Batsford, 1980. Illustrator for television programs. contributor to journals.

SIDELIGHTS: Sorrell's son, Mark, writes that his father was an authority on Roman Britain, responsible for many important archaeological reconstructions for England's Ministry of Works.

[Sketch verified by son, Mark Sorrell]

* * *

SPANO, Charles 1948-

PERSONAL: Born May 21, 1948, in Scranton, Pa.; son of Charles (in watch repair) and Olga (Sabbatini) Spano; married JoAnn Sabatell, June 26, 1971; children: Steven, Amanda. *Education:* Wilkes College, B.A., 1970; University of Scranton, M.S., 1973. *Politics:* "Pragmatic liberal." *Religion:* None. *Home:* 539 Birch St., Scranton, Pa. 18505. *Office:* Scranton Schools, Elementary Plaza, Elm St., Scranton, Pa. 18505.

CAREER: Scranton Schools, Scranton, Pa., science specialist in elementary schools, 1970—. *Member:* Science Fiction Writers of America, National Science Teachers Association, Institute for Twenty-First Century Studies (fellow), Council of Elementary Science Instruction, Scranton Federation of Teachers.

WRITINGS: (With Theodore R. Cogswell) *Spock: Messiah!*, Bantam, 1976.

Work represented in anthologies, including *Microcosmic Dreams*, edited by J. Oleander, M. Greenberg, and Isaac Asimov, Taplinger, 1979; *A Spadeful of Spacetime*, edited by Fred Saberhagen, Ace Books, 1980. Book reviewer for *Voice of Youth Advocates*.

WORK IN PROGRESS: Chains of Corona, a science fiction novel for young people; short stories.

SIDELIGHTS: Spano writes: "What I hope will turn into a long and increasingly better career in writing is just beginning for me. I can always remember loving books and the strange places contained in them. I remember entertaining friends in school with crudely written action stories. My main reading interest is science fiction, though I have read many other fields and genres.

"In my case, critical mass came the day I bought a new typewriter. Here was this brand-new shiny machine throbbing with electric life and nowhere to go. I began exercising my fingers, its keys, and ideas. They went out. They came back. The longer I tried writing the more hooked I got, until no number of rejection slips mattered.

"I balance my writing time against my job of teaching science. Over the last few years I've introduced science fiction to every class I've had. With the impetus of 'Star Wars,' it's been much easier to discuss the science in science fiction with elementary children. I think I've exposed more than a thousand children to a deeper knowledge of science fiction with, I hope, benefit for the field.

"Education and science fiction are important to me because they are alike in several important ways. In both there is the need to approach children and concepts with an open mind and flexible attitude, to anticipate outcomes based on past performance, to deal with the human element, and to appreciate the wonders of children and the universe.

"*Spock: Messiah!* is the first in a series of science fiction books commissioned by Bantam. The series uses the hardware and personalities of the television show 'Star Trek' to continue those characters beyond time, space, and Nielsen ratings."

*   *   *

SPAULDING, William E(llsworth)   1898-1979

OBITUARY NOTICE: Born in 1898; died December 19, 1979, in Woburn, Mass. Publisher and president of Houghton Mifflin Co. Spaulding worked at Houghton for over fifty years, rising from salesman to president and chairman of the publishing firm. He was also president of the American Textbook Publishers Institute and the American Book Publishers Council. Obituaries and other sources: *Publishers Weekly*, May 6, 1957, December 12, 1960; *New York Times*, December 21, 1979, December 22, 1979; *Chicago Tribune*, December 22, 1979; *AB Bookman's Weekly*, January 1, 1980.

*   *   *

SPEER, Michael L.   1934-

PERSONAL: Born February 10, 1934, in Desloge, Mo.; son of Irvin O. (a lead miner) and Ruth (a postal employee; maiden name, Smith) Speer; married Mary Louise Donley (an accountant); children: Melinda Lou Speer Mahand, Maria Lee. *Education:* Oklahoma Baptist University, B.A., 1958; Southern Baptist Theological Seminary, M.R.E., 1960. *Home:* 2418 Moran Rd., Franklin, Tenn. 37064. *Office:* Stewardship Commission, 460 James Robertson Parkway, Nashville, Tenn. 37219.

CAREER: Carver Missions and Social Work, Louisville, Ky., director of administration, 1959-61; minister of education at Baptist church in Norfolk, Va., 1961-63; Kentucky Baptist Convention, Middletown, associate in church training department, 1963-64, director of promotion and stewardship development, 1964-67; currently associated with Stewardship Commission, Nashville, Tenn. *Military service:* U.S. Navy, Naval Aviation Cadet Choir, 1954-56.

WRITINGS: *A Complete Guide to the Christian's Budget*, Broadman, 1975; *Put Your Best Foot Forward*, Broadman, 1977. Contributor to Baptist periodicals.

SIDELIGHTS: Speer comments: "Money management is vital to all persons. However, it is of primary importance to the Christian who views all possessions as belonging to God, with man simply acting as a manager (steward). In time of runaway inflation this becomes even more important.

"Man should 'image' God even in his physical characteristics, including how he dresses and his basic social manners. *Put Your Best Foot Forward* is a book for men on dress and grooming."

AVOCATIONAL INTERESTS: Travel, yard work, swimming.

*   *   *

SPERONI, Charles   1911-

PERSONAL: Born November 2, 1911, in Santa Fiora, Italy; came to the United States in 1929, naturalized citizen, 1941; son of Edoardo and Aida (Falchi) Speroni; married Carmela Helen Corica (a volunteer worker), June 15, 1938. *Education:* University of California, Berkeley, A.B., 1933, Ph.D., 1938. *Religion:* Roman Catholic. *Home:* 376 Dalkeith Ave., Los Angeles, Calif. 90049. *Office:* College of Fine Arts, University of California, Los Angeles, Calif. 90024.

CAREER: University of California, Los Angeles, research associate, 1935-38, instructor, 1938-41, assistant professor, 1941-47, associate professor, 1947-53, professor of Italian, 1953—, head of department, 1949-56, dean of College of Fine Arts, 1968—. *Member:* Modern Language Association of America, American Association of Teachers of Italian (president, 1949), Philological Association of the Pacific Coast, Folklore Society of California, Phi Beta Kappa, University of California Club. *Awards, honors:* Star of Italian Solidarity, 1951; *cavaliere ufficiale* of Repubblica Italiana, 1965; *commendatore* of Ordine al Merito della Repubblica Italiana, 1973; chevalier of Ordre des Palmes Academiques, 1977.

WRITINGS: *Proverbs and Proverbial Phrases in Basile's "Pentameron"*, University of California Press, 1941; *Elementary Italian Conversation*, Heath, 1941; *Intermediate Italian Conversation*, Heath, 1942; *Advanced Italian Conversation*, Heath, 1943; (editor and author of notes) Charles Merbury, *Proverbi Vulgari*, University of California Press, 1946; *Spoken Italian for Students and Travelers*, Heath, 1946, 2nd edition, 1978; (with Charles Kary) *Italian Course*, with sound recordings, Decca Records, 1948; *The Italian Wellerism to the End of the Seventeenth Century*, University of California Press, 1953; (with C. L. Golino) *Basic Italian*, Holt, 1958, 4th edition, 1977; *Giulio Cesare Croce: "Il Tre,"* *Operetta dilettevole* (title means "Number Three: An Entertaining Little Work"), Olschki, 1959.

(With Golino) *Panorama italiano*, Holt, 1960, 3rd edition, 1974; (with Irving Stone) *Lettere di Michelangelo Buonarroti*, dall'Oglio, 1963; *Wit and Wisdom of the Italian Renaissance*, University of California Press, 1964; (with Golino) *Leggendo e ripassando* (title means "Reading and Reviewing"), Holt, 1968; *The Aphorisms of Orazio Rinaldi, Robert Greene, and Lucas Gracian Dantisco*, University of California Press, 1968; (with Maddalena Mauro and A. B. Seldis) *L'Italia Oggi* (title means "Italy Today"), Holt, 1976. Head of board of directors of "Modern Philology Series," University of California Press, 1949-54. Assistant editor of *Modern Language Forum*, 1947-49.

WORK IN PROGRESS: Revisions of *Panorama italiano* and *Basic Italian;* articles on Italian proverbs.

SIDELIGHTS: Speroni told *CA:* "Besides an interest of long-standing in the Italian-English exchange during the Renaissance, I am deeply committed to writing interesting, practical, and cultural textbooks, for they help a great deal in expanding the study of Italian language and culture."

SPIRER, Herbert F(rederick) 1925-
(Vladimir Sitzfleisch)

PERSONAL: Born October 8, 1925, in Philadelphia, Pa.; son of Irvin E. (an architect) and Rose (Rice) Spirer; married Louise Ziegler (a writer and public information director), February 3, 1950; children: Jeffrey David, Daniel Rice, Ellen Ruth. *Education:* Cornell University, B.Eng.Physics, 1952; New York University, M.S., 1965, Ph.D., 1970. *Home:* 71 Big Oak Rd., Stamford, Conn. 06903. *Office:* Department of Management and Administrative Sciences, University of Connecticut, Sofieldtown Rd., Stamford, Conn. 06903.

CAREER: TOR Education, Inc., Stamford, Conn., vice-president, 1960-62; American Machine & Foundry Corp., Stamford, Conn., section manager, 1962-64; General Time Corp., Stanford, Conn., group manager, 1964-69; University of Connecticut, Stamford, lecturer, 1966-70, associate professor, 1970-74, professor of management and administrative sciences, 1974—. Vice-president of Stamford Educational Program, Inc., 1963—. Conductor of seminars; speaker at professional meetings; consultant to business. *Military service:* U.S. Navy, 1944-46; became radio technician first class. *Member:* American Statistical Association (vice-president), American Institute of Decision Sciences, American Association of University Professors, American Society for Quality Control, American Society for Engineering Education, Association of Teachers of Quantitative Methods (member of board of directors).

WRITINGS: Foundations of Mathematical Analysis for Students of Business Administration, MGI Management Institute, 1970; (with wife, Louise Spirer) *Computers for Business,* MGI Management Institute, 1970; *Introductory Applied Statistics for Business and Administration,* privately printed, 1973; *The Engineering Manager Game Seminar,* MGI Management Institute, Volume I: *The Basic Skills of Engineering Management,* 1973, Volume II: *The Practice of Management in Engineering,* 1974, Volume III: *The Management of Engineering Departments,* 1974; (with wife, Louise Ziegler) *Financial Administration for Managers,* with manual, MGI Management Institute, 1974; *Business Statistics: A Problem-Solving Approach,* Irwin, 1975; *Study Guide* (to accompany *Introduction to Electronic Data Processing,* revised edition), Irwin, 1976; *Achieving Results With Statistical Methods,* three volumes, MGI Management Institute, 1977; (with H. M. Levine) *Information Systems for the Administrative Manager,* MGI Management Institute, 1977; *Personnel Management,* MGI Management Institute, 1980; *Management Science/Operations Research,* Wiley, 1981.

Books about dogs: (With wife, L. Spirer) *This Is the Miniature Schnauzer,* T.F.H. Publications, 1963; (with L. Spirer) *This Is the Pomeranian,* T.F.H. Publications, 1965; (with L. Spirer) *This Is the Pug,* T.F.H. Publications, 1968; (with L. Spirer) *This Is the German Pointer,* T.F.H. Publications, 1970.

Contributor to *System Designer's Handbook.* Contributor of more than thirty articles and reviews (sometimes under pseudonym Vladimir Sitzfleisch) to scientific journals. Editor of *Quantitative Methods;* contributing editor of *Digital Design.*

WORK IN PROGRESS: How to Assure Reliability, MGI Management Institute, 1982; *Project Management for the Eighties,* MGI Management Institute, 1983.

SIDELIGHTS: Spirer writes: "My concern in my activities is the use of mathematical techniques (which includes matrix models, schedules, and decision trees) and statistics to make better decisions and to carry out the productive work of the world.

"My gift is to be able to explain these tools to people of all types, whether in writing or seminar or classroom experiences. Within this field I believe I have pioneered some methods. For example, in the course/text on quality control the concepts of statistical quality control are given as part of a *novel:* a young person enters industry and experiences occur—all realistic because they come from actual experience—and in the process he learns how to handle these situations with increasingly more sophisticated methods, growing in personal maturity as well. So few writers (excepting Pynchon and Solzhenitsyn) seem to know what the world of work is really like. In both the course and my class work I rarely work with 'exercises' in the traditional sense, using dummied up problems of trivial interest; I send the students and readers out to get their own data and we work with that.

"I live to work and not vice versa; I am lucky enough to rarely have to do anything that has no meaning or that I don't like doing."

AVOCATIONAL INTERESTS: "I get most of my literary input from books recorded on tapes (how much time we spend traveling; usually lost). I ride a bike rather continuously and actively and have no taste for watching someone else do anything I can do. My only spectator sport is the ballet."

*   *   *

STAAF, Robert J(ames) 1939-

PERSONAL: Born March 2, 1939, in Pittsburgh, Pa.; son of Richard V. (in business) and Elsa (Dunmyer) Staaf; married Berdenz Shovey, 1961; children: three. *Education:* Duquesne University, A.B., 1964; University of Delaware, M.A., 1968; Temple University, Ph.D., 1971; postdoctoral study at Virginia Polytechnic Institute and State University, 1971-72; University of Miami, Coral Gables, Fla., J.D., 1980. *Home:* 611 Progress St., Blacksburg, Va. 24060. *Office:* Department of Economics, Virginia Polytechnic Institute and State University, Blacksburg, Va. 24061.

CAREER: U.S. Steel Corp., Pittsburgh, Pa., management trainee, 1964, division cost analyst, 1965-66; University of Delaware, Newark, instructor, 1967-69, assistant professor of economics, 1969-71, associate economist with Division of Urban Affairs, 1970-71; Virginia Polytechnic Institute and State University, Blacksburg, visiting lecturer, 1971-72, assistant professor of economics, beginning 1972, research associate at Center for the Study of Public Choice, 1972-73; National Center for Higher Education Management Systems, Western Interstate Commission for Higher Education, Boulder, Colo., senior staff associate, 1973-74; Virginia Polytechnic Institute and State University, director of Center for Economic Education, 1974-77, associate professor of economics, 1975—. *Military service:* U.S. Air Force, 1957-61. *Awards, honors:* Grants from National Institute of Education, 1972-74, Foundation for Economic Education, 1972, Ford Foundation, 1975-77, American Enterprise Institute for Public Policy Research, 1976, and National Right to Work Legal Defense Foundation, 1978-79.

WRITINGS: (Editor with Francis X. Tannian, and contributor) *Externalities: Theoretical Dimensions of Political Economy,* Dunellen, 1973; (with Richard B. McKenzie) *An Economic Theory of Learning: Student Sovereignty and Academic Freedom* (monograph), University Publications, Virginia Polytechnic Institute and State University, 1975.

Contributor: Robert J. Mackay and Arthur T. Denzau, editors, *Essays on Unorthodox Economic Strategies,* University Publications, Virginia Polytechnic Institute and State University, 1975; Thomas C. Fischer and Richard F. Zehnle, editors, *Introduction to Law and Legal Reasoning,* West Publishing, 1977; Thomas Borcherding, editor, *Budgets and Bureaucrats: The Origins of Government Growth,* Duke University Press, 1977; Donald Wentworth and Lee Hansen, editors, *Perspectives in Economic Education,* Joint Council of Economic Education, 1977; David Turer, editor, *The Political Economy of Advertising,* American Enterprise Institute for Public Policy Research, 1978. Contributor of about fifteen articles to law and economic journals, and *Annals of the American Academy of Political and Social Science.*

WORK IN PROGRESS: In Defense of Caveat Venditor; Individual Choice, Social Choice, and Common Law Efficiency, with W. Wares; *The Entanglement Consequences of Agency Shops,* with E. G. West.

* * *

STADT, Ronald W(ilmer) 1935-

PERSONAL: Born September 5, 1935, in Beecher, Ill.; son of Elmer (a barber) and Alma (Schmaedeke) Stadt; married Lorraine Reed (a teacher), August 25, 1957; children: Rory, Ronda. *Education:* Illinois State University, B.S., 1957; University of Illinois, M.Ed., 1958, Ed.D., 1962. *Home:* 609 Terrace, Carbondale, Ill. 62901. *Office:* College of Education, Southern Illinois University, Carbondale, Ill. 62901.

CAREER: University of Alberta, Edmonton, assistant professor, 1962-63, associate professor of education, 1963-64; American Institute of Baking, Chicago, Ill., director of education, 1964-67; Southern Illinois University, Carbondale, associate professor, 1967-69, professor of vocational education, 1969—, head of faculty of technical and industrial education, 1967-71, and occupational education, 1971-75, coordinator of development, 1975. Member of National Committee for Vocational Education and Manpower Training and Mississippi Valley Industrial Education Conference; member of Carbondale Community Education Advisory Committee, 1977—. Conductor of workshops. *Member:* American Industrial Arts Association (life member), American Council on Industrial Arts Teacher Education (life member), American Vocational Association (life member), American Vocational Education Research Association, National Association of Industrial and Technical Teacher Educators, Illinois Vocational Association, Illinois Industrial Education Association, Phi Delta Kappa (vice-president of Gamma Lambda chapter, 1970-71).

WRITINGS: (Contributor) Harry S. Broudy, editor, *Selected Readings in the Philosophy of Education,* Volume II: *Problems of Education,* Macmillan, 1967; (with Raymond E. Bittle, Larry J. Kenneke, and Dennis C. Nystrom) *Managing Career Education Programs,* Prentice-Hall, 1973; (with Kenneke and Nystrom) *Planning and Organizing Career Curricula: Articulated Education,* Sams, 1973; (with Larry J. Bailey) *Career Education: New Approaches to Human Development,* McKnight, 1973; (with Bill G. Gooch) *Cooperative Education: Vocational Occupational Career,* Sams, 1976. Contributor of more than sixty articles to education and baking trade journals. Assistant editor of *Journal of Industrial Teacher Education,* 1971-73, associate editor, 1973-74, editor, 1974-75.

WORK IN PROGRESS: Successful Family Finance: A Planning Book, with Michael Adams, publication by McGraw expected in 1981; a retirement book, *Planning Tomorrow Today,* with Adams and Irma Housdorff, publication by McGraw expected in 1981.

SIDELIGHTS: Stadt comments: "I am successful at onsight evaluation of educational programs. My motivation is to put unique books on the market and beat the competition. But this is subordinate to an abiding concern to promote human resource development, whether it be via vocational education for school and community college students or via continuing education and counseling for adults. My present concern is to make educators aware of what they might do for older persons and retirees—many of whom will be working at least part time. People are coming to have keen senses of agency about their careers. Formal education and employers must respond to this fact—which permeates my writings."

AVOCATIONAL INTERESTS: Trap shooting, quail hunting, collecting shotguns and shells.

* * *

STARENKO, Ronald C(harles) 1930-

PERSONAL: Born November 14, 1930, in Detroit, Mich.; son of Michael and Rose (Semrock) Starenko; married Catherine M. Wood (a registered nurse), June 6, 1953; children: Michael, Deborah, Stephen, Christopher, David. *Education:* Attended Concordia College, Milwaukee, Wis., 1948-50; Concordia Seminary, St. Louis, Mo., B.A., 1952, B.D., 1955; Lutheran School of Theology, Chicago, Ill., S.T.M., 1967; University of Bridgeport, M.S., 1977; attended Fairleigh Dickinson University. *Home:* 100 Iona Place, Paramus, N.J. 07652.

CAREER: Ordained Lutheran minister, 1955; Immanuel Lutheran Church, Charlottesville, Va., pastor, 1955-57; Zion Lutheran Church, Fort Wayne, Ind., pastor, 1958-61; pastor in Lutheran church in Livonia, Mich., 1961-69; Church of the Savior, Paramus, N.J., pastor, 1969—. Certified pastoral counselor and part-time psychotherapist. Counselor at Garden State Counseling Center. Chaplain of Paramus police and fire departments. *Military service:* U.S. Navy, chaplain, 1957-59. U.S. Naval Reserve, chaplain, 1959-68; became lieutenant commander. *Member:* American Association of Pastoral Counselors, Lutheran Education Association.

WRITINGS: It's Time to Live, Concordia, 1969; *Eat, Drink, and Be Merry!,* Concordia, 1971; *God, Grass, and Grace: A Theology of Death,* Concordia, 1975. Contributor of articles and reviews to theology journals.

SIDELIGHTS: Starenko writes: "As a professional in preaching and pastoral care I have concentrated throughout my ministry on developing skills by which I would become a more effective communicator. Most of my writing has been a revision of my preaching, and since my style of preaching lends itself to writing, I have found it easy to express myself in print. My most articulate moments have come when I was dealing with such subjects as life, death, resurrection, and celebration.

"In addition, I have received extensive training in psychotherapy, which has had a significant impact on my personal and professional life. With new insights, psychologically and theologically, I have become still more effective as a communicator of the love of God relative to the human predicament. Having been in therapy myself, I have a greater sensitivity and understanding of human need and the resources available for more powerful living.

"At present I have no plans for any specific book, as I am reluctant to put into print what is still a fermenting time in my life. The one growing edge that I am aware of is my ongoing interest in the relationship between psychology and theology. If I ever write a book on that issue, it will not take the form of revised sermons, but will be the outgrowth of a lot of thinking and feeling and living.''

AVOCATIONAL INTERESTS: Athletics, classical music, reading, home maintenance.

* * *

STEELE, Erskine
See HENDERSON, Archibald

* * *

STEELE, Timothy (Reid)   1948-

PERSONAL: Born January 22, 1948, in Burlington, Vt.; son of Edward William (a teacher) and Ruth (a nurse; maiden name, Reid) Steele; married Victoria Lee Erpelding (a librarian), January 14, 1979. *Education:* Stanford University, B.A., 1970; Brandeis University, Ph.D., 1977. *Home:* 2130½ Barry Ave., Los Angeles, Calif. 90025. *Office:* Department of English, University of California, Los Angeles, Calif. 90024.

CAREER: Stanford University, Stanford, Calif., Jones Lecturer in Poetry, 1975-77; University of California, Los Angeles, lecturer in English, 1977—.

WRITINGS: Uncertainties and Rest (poems), Louisiana State University Press, 1979. Contributor of poems and articles to literary magazines, including *Southern Review, Poetry,* and *PN Review.*

WORK IN PROGRESS: Another collection of poems; essays on aspects of modern aestheticism.

SIDELIGHTS: Steele commented: "I have several times seen my work referred to as 'classical.' I suspect this adjective is applied to my poems because they are written in meter. I don't object to the adjective, but it means more to me than simply an interest in structural matters; it means—or indicates—an attempt to strike a working balance between the need for normative procedure and technical rigor on the one hand, and the demands of individual talent and inspiration on the other. It is this balance which seems to me perhaps the most crucial element of consistently lively and distinctive art, and it is this balance, among other things, that I'm aiming for in my work.''

* * *

STEERE, Daniel C(onrad)   1938-

PERSONAL: Born October 2, 1938, in Memphis, Tenn.; son of Richard M. (a college professor) and Bennett (Sellers) Steere; married Norma Helmer (a teacher of the deaf). *Education:* Louisiana Tech University, B.A., 1961; Southern Methodist University, M.Th., 1964. *Home:* 3788 Westerman, Houston, Tex. 77005. *Office:* First United Methodist Church, 1320 Main St., Houston, Tex. 77002.

CAREER: Ordained Methodist minister, 1964; pastor of Methodist churches in Baton Rouge, La., 1966-68, and Houston, Tex., 1969-70; First United Methodist Church, Houston, Tex., staff minister, 1971—. Producer of "Turn On," a program for teenagers on KTRK-TV, 1971-76. Public speaker; member of state and national church boards and conferences. Member of Houston Symphony Society and Texas Sickle Cell Disease Research Foundation; member of board of directors of Wesley Community Center. *Member:* Omicron Delta Kappa. *Awards, honors:* Catholic Broadcast-

ers Association distinguished writing award for individual leadership in Christian broadcasting and Gabriel Award for "Who Will Answer?," both 1973; Golden Mike Award from National American Legion, 1974, for "Turn On."

WRITINGS: I Am—I Can, Revell, 1973; *Power for Living,* Revell, 1977; (editor and contributor) *Tarbell's Teacher's Guide,* Revell, 1977. Author of script for "Who Will Answer?," aired by KTRK-TV on June 6, 1970, and released as a film by United Methodist Church.

WORK IN PROGRESS: A book about building loving relationships that last, publication by Revell expected in 1980; a novel about a time-travel project of the National Aeronautics and Space Administration, 1981.

SIDELIGHTS: Steere comments: "The agony and struggle that go into the production of a book makes me wonder sometimes if there isn't an easier way to make money and advance ideas. It is times like a recent Sunday evening when, as I was watching the Mary Tyler Moore show and suddenly heard a guest comedian use the title of my book, *I Am—I Can,* to set up a comedy routine, that I say to myself, 'Yep, it's worth it.' "

* * *

STEFFEN, Albert   1884-1963

OBITUARY NOTICE: Born December 10, 1884, in Murgenthal, Switzerland; died July 13, 1963, in Dornach, Switzerland. Essayist, novelist, playwright, and philosopher. In 1925, Steffen inherited the leadership of Rudolf Steiner's anthroposophic cult after the latter's death. His Christian-mystic beliefs are revealed in many of his plays, including the trilogy of "Hieram und Salomo," "Barnabas," and "Das Toderserlebnis des Manes." Despite his reputation as an important Swiss author, Steffen's writings—more than seventy works—are largely unavailable in translation. Obituaries and other sources: *Modern World Drama: An Encyclopedia,* Dutton, 1972; *Cassell's Encyclopaedia of World Literature,* revised edition, Morrow, 1973; *The Oxford Companion to German Literature,* Clarendon Press, 1976.

* * *

STEINTRAGER, James A(lvin)   1936-

PERSONAL: Born May 22, 1936, in Detroit, Mich.; son of Harold R. and Clara (Jetke) Steintrager; married Marianne O'Niell, September 17, 1960; children: Kirsten, James Alvin, Jr., Rebecca, Megan. *Education:* University of Notre Dame, B.A. (magna cum laude), 1958; University of Chicago, M.A., 1960, Ph.D., 1963. *Politics:* Democrat. *Religion:* Roman Catholic. *Home:* 3391 Poteat Court, Winston-Salem, N.C. 27106. *Office:* Department of Politics, Wake Forest University, Winston-Salem, N.C. 27109.

CAREER: Louisiana State University, Baton Rouge, instructor in government, 1961-63; University of Texas, Austin, assistant professor of government, 1963-69; Wake Forest University, Winston-Salem, N.C., associate professor, 1969-76, professor of politics and head of department, 1977—. *Member:* North American Bentham Committee, American Political Science Association, American Society for Legal and Political Philosophy, American Association of University Professors, Conference for the Study of Political Thought, Southern Political Science Association. *Awards, honors:* H. B. Earhart fellowships and travel grants for study in England, 1966-67 and 1973-74; fellowship for study in England from Society for Religion in Higher Education, 1968-69; American Philosophical Society travel grant, 1968-69, and R. J. Reynolds travel grant, 1973-74, both for study in England.

WRITINGS: Bentham, Cornell University Press, 1977. Contributor of articles and reviews to scholarly journals.

WORK IN PROGRESS: Editing *Church Establishments* (two volumes) for *Collected Works of Jeremy Bentham,* publication by Oxford University Press expected in 1985; *Not Paul But Jesus,* publication expected in 1985; *Analysis of the Influence of Religion,* publication expected in 1987.

SIDELIGHTS: Steintrager writes: "My interest is in the crisis of Western liberal democracy, especially in the United States and Great Britain, focusing on the uneasy attempts to reconcile liberty, equality, and fraternity in theory and practice, and on the crisis of value-free social science (and its theoretical foundations in logical positivism) as it relates to the theory and practice of liberal democracy."

AVOCATIONAL INTERESTS: Indoor and outdoor gardening, soccer, travel.

*   *   *

STEVENS, David Harrison   1884-1980

OBITUARY NOTICE—See index for *CA* sketch: Born December 20, 1884, in Berlin, Wis.; died January 29, 1980, in La Jolla, Calif. Educator, administrator, and writer. From 1932 to 1950 Stevens was the director of humanities at the Rockefeller Foundation. Before holding that post, he had been an administrator and English professor at the University of Chicago. One of his books, *A Time for Humanities,* received a citation from the Wisconsin Academy of Sciences, Arts, and Letters in 1974. Among his other publications are *The Teaching of College Composition, Reference Guide to Milton,* and *Ten Talents in the American Theatre.* Obituaries and other sources: *Who's Who in America,* 40th edition, Marquis, 1978; *Chicago Tribune,* February 3, 1980; *New York Times,* February 4, 1980.

*   *   *

STEVENS, James (Richard)   1940-

PERSONAL: Born June 11, 1940, in Stratford, Ontario, Canada; son of David Richard (a farmer) and Madge (a teacher; maiden name, Newman) Stevens; married Catherine Arthur (an accountant), March 15, 1961 (divorced March 1, 1972); children: Clarence M., Jean Michal. *Education:* Cornell University, B.Sc., 1964, M.A., 1966. *Home address:* R.R. 13, Thunder Bay, Ontario, Canada P7B 5E4.

CAREER: High school counselor in Red Lake, Ontario, 1966-68, and Kenora, Ontario, 1968-69; Confederation College, Thunder Bay, Ontario, counselor, 1969—. *Member:* Academy of Canadian Writers. *Awards, honors:* Canada Council grants, 1971, 1973.

WRITINGS: A-too-soo-ka'-nan, Confederation College, 1970; (with Carl Ray) *Sacred Legends of the Sandy Lake Cree,* McClelland & Stewart, 1971; (editor) James Redsky, *Great Leader of the Ojibway,* McClelland & Stewart, 1973; (editor) Dan Kennedy, *Recollections of an Assinaboine Chief,* McClelland & Stewart, 1973; *Paddy Wilson's Gold Fever,* Upland Peddlers Press, 1976; (editor) Mae Carroll, *Phillip Neault, Pioneer,* Upland Peddlers Press, 1977.

WORK IN PROGRESS: The Forest Dynasty, a two hundred-year history of the Sucker Clan of Cree Indians, with Chief Thomas Fiddler.

SIDELIGHTS: Stevens commented: "My writing and editing is focused entirely on the vast boreal forests south of Hudson's Bay."

STEVENS, Peter   1927-

PERSONAL: Born November 17, 1927, in Manchester, England; son of Stanley Edgar (a railroad worker) and Elsie (Hill) Stevens; married June Sidebotham, April 13, 1957; children: Gillian, Kirsty, Martin. *Education:* University of Nottingham, B.A. (with honors), 1951; McMaster University, M.A., 1963; University of Saskatchewan, Ph.D., 1968. *Home:* 2055 Richmond St., Windsor, Ontario, Canada N8Y 1L3. *Office:* Department of English, University of Windsor, Windsor, Ontario, Canada.

CAREER: High school teacher of English and department head in Hamilton, Ontario, 1957-64; University of Saskatchewan, Saskatoon, lecturer in English, 1964-67; University of Windsor, Windsor, Ontario, assistant professor, 1967-69, associate professor, 1969-75, professor of English, 1975—. Director and editor of Sesame Press. Creator of jazz radio programs for national distribution by Canadian Broadcasting Corp. *Member:* League of Canadian Poets. *Awards, honors:* Fellow of Institute of Humanities, Calgary, Alberta, and Clifford E. Lee Playwriting Award finalist, both 1979.

WRITINGS—Poems: *Plain Geometry,* Ganglia Press, 1968; *Nothing But Spoons,* Delta, 1969; *A Few Myths,* Talonbooks, 1970; *Breadcrusts and Glass,* Fiddlehead, 1972; *Family Feelings,* Alive Press, 1974; *A Momentary Stay,* Killaly Press, 1974; *And the Dying Sky Like Glass,* Borealis Press, 1974; *The Bogman Pavese Tactics,* Fiddlehead, 1977; (contributor) *Modern English-Canadian Poetry,* Gage, 1978.

Editor: *The McGill Movement,* Ryerson, 1969; (with J. L. Granatstein) *Forum,* University of Toronto Press, 1972; *The First Day of Spring: The Prose of R. Knister,* University of Toronto Press, 1977; *Modern English Canadian Poetry: A Guide to Information Sources,* Gale, 1978. Author of "Jazz," a weekly jazz column in *Windsor Star.* Jazz reviewer for *Coda.*

WORK IN PROGRESS: Two books of poems; a novel; three plays.

SIDELIGHTS: Stevens told *CA:* "In recent years I have rediscovered an early interest in theatre. I find that increasingly my poems take an other personae, not only extensions of my own voice and life, but other speakers in the poetic shape of dramatic monologues. Looking back, I see now that much of my poetry has been dramatic either as narrative or in the speaking voices used, so in a sense, the work I am doing now is simply a development from my earlier work."

*   *   *

STEWART, Garrett (Fitzgerald)   1945-

PERSONAL: Born January 5, 1945, in Detroit, Mich.; son of Gordon Eldwin and Rosemary (Fitzgerald) Stewart; married Deborah Dentler (a lawyer), May 25, 1974. *Education:* University of Southern California, B.A., 1967; Yale University, Ph.M., 1970, Ph.D., 1971. *Office:* Department of English, University of California, Santa Barbara, Calif. 93106.

CAREER: Boston University, Boston, Mass., assistant professor of English, 1971-76; University of California, Santa Barbara, associate professor of English, 1976—. *Member:* Modern Language Association of America, Dickens Society. *Awards, honors:* Guggenheim fellowship, 1978-79.

WRITINGS: (With Virginia Tufte) *Grammar as Style: Exercises in Creativity,* Holt, 1971; *Dickens and the Trials of Imagination,* Harvard University Press, 1974. Contributor to academic journals.

WORK IN PROGRESS: Death Bequeathed: The Literary

Legacy of the Victorian Death Scene, publication expected in 1981; a study of self-reflexiveness in the cinema.

SIDELIGHTS: Stewart writes: "My interest in literary style as a vehicle of symbolism and value, has carried over into my work on film and the details of its imagery. My time is now actively divided, both as teacher and critic, between fiction and film." *Avocational interests:* Cooking, travel.

* * *

STEWART, Hilary 1924-

PERSONAL: Born November 3, 1924, on St. Lucia Island, British West Indies; daughter of Frank Lawson (a consulting engineer) and Dorothy (Smith) Stewart. *Education:* St. Martins School of Art, N.D.D., 1951. *Home and office:* 2986 Point Grey Rd., Vancouver, British Columbia, Canada V6K 1B1.

CAREER: Marion Cooper Interiors, Edmonton, Alberta, associate artist, 1952-56; costume designer for a Canadian Broadcasting Corp. television station in Vancouver, British Columbia, 1960-62; art director for television station in Burnaby, British Columbia, 1960-72; lecturer in Northwest Coast Indian arts and technologies at learning institutions in Alaska and British Columbia, 1973—. Commissioned by Art Gallery of Greater Victoria as researcher and photographer for "Images: Stone: BC" exhibition, 1975-76; commissioned by University of British Columbia to make archaeological drawings in Turkey, 1978. Adviser to Children of the Raven Gallery, Vancouver, 1977; guest curator for exhibitions at Centennial Museum, Vancouver, 1977, and University of British Columbia Museum of Anthropology, 1979; member of board of trustees of Centennial Museum, 1979—. *Military service:* Women's Royal Air Force, 1943-47. *Member:* Canadian Authors Association, Archaeological Society of British Columbia (member of executive board, 1969—). *Awards, honors:* Canada Council grant, 1974.

WRITINGS: (Self-illustrated) *Indian Artifacts of the Northwest Coast,* University of Washington Press, 1973 (published in Canada as *Artifacts of the Northwest Coast Indians,* Hancock House, 1973); (illustrator and photographer) Wilson Duff, *Images: Stone: BC,* University of Washington Press, 1975; (self-illustrated) *Indian Fishing: Early Methods on the Northwest Coast,* University of Washington Press, 1977; *Looking at Indian Art,* University of Washington Press, 1979; *Robert Davidson: Haida Printmaker,* University of Washington Press, 1979. Contributor to *The Midden.*

WORK IN PROGRESS: Continuing research on ethnobotany and technologies of Northwest Coast Indians; researching, writing, and illustrating a certain aspect of wild edible plants of western Canada; preliminary research on the native Indian's use of the cedar tree.

SIDELIGHTS: Hilary Stewart wrote: "There have been several forks in the road of my career. After art school I got into interior design, stage design, and television design; I did a lot of painting and exhibited. Then came writing and lecturing, all interwoven with my special interests: all things wild and natural, animals, reptiles, botany, wild edible plants and survival, marine biology, boating, photography, archaeology, anthropology, carving and other craftwork.

"Besides lecturing on Northwest Coast Indian cultures, I work with wilderness survival groups at an outdoor education centre. We go to the Pacific west coast, out to magnificent wilderness beaches where no one else ever goes, and we learn to live with the environment, to respect it. Out there, surrounded by the hugeness of mountain, forest, and ocean, I sometimes write poetry, but it's very private.

"Some day I may go back to painting—or perhaps branch off in yet another direction; I just flow with the river, a philosophy that came about while rafting the wild rivers of British Columbia. But right now the rich culture of the Northwest Coast Indians holds my fascination and unending curiosity. Their technology interests me most. I spend a lot of time recreating tools, implements, and other items, using original techniques and working with roots, barks, rushes, bone, and other natural materials which I gather from woods and beaches of the coast.

"The best part of writing a book is the research—the challenge of discovery and learning is the great motivation. I am lucky that I can do my own illustrations. The Indian artifacts book has over one thousand of my drawings and many of my photographs. It would be far too costly to pay someone to do all that, and I enjoy making the drawings as much as I enjoy the writing.

"I love the freedom to steer my life around what interests me most, whatever comes up that I find exciting or challenging. I feel very much in charge of my own life, but I also recognize the incredible hand of fate—so we work hand in hand."

BIOGRAPHICAL/CRITICAL SOURCES: Vanguard, May, 1975; *Scientific American,* June, 1978.

* * *

STITZEL, Thomas E(dward) 1936-

PERSONAL: Born March 1, 1936, in Walla Walla, Wash.; son of Walter Edward; and Ellen Louise (Anderson) Stitzel; married Bonnie Elaine Steward, 1955; children: Nancy, Matthew, Jeffrey, Peter, Lisa, Jennifer. *Education:* Washington State University, B.S., 1957; University of Oregon, M.B.A., 1964, Ph.D., 1966. *Home:* 1309 East Pennsylvania, Boise, Idaho 83706. *Office:* School of Business, Boise State University, Boise, Idaho 83725.

CAREER: Phillips Petroleum Co., chemical engineer, 1957-62; Oregon State University, Corvallis, assistant professor, 1966-69, associate professor of finance, 1969-75; Boise State University, Boise, Idaho, professor of finance, 1975—, dean of School of Business, 1977—. Consultant to Idaho Power Co. and Challenge Corp. of New Zealand. *Member:* Institute of Chartered Financial Analysts, American Finance Association, Financial Management Association, Western Finance Association (member of board of directors, 1978), Portland Society of Financial Analysts, Western Association of Collegiate Schools of Business (director, 1979-80), Boise Rotary Club. *Awards, honors:* NDEA fellowship from University of Oregon, 1963-66; fellowship from Lincoln College, Christchurch, New Zealand, 1973-74.

WRITINGS: (With Wilbur Widicus) *Today's Investments for Tomorrow's Security,* Dow Jones-Irwin, 1970; (with Widicus) *Personal Investing,* Irwin, 1970, 3rd edition, 1980; *Study Guide to Accompany Introduction to Financial Management,* McGraw, 1977, 2nd edition, 1980.

SIDELIGHTS: Stitzel told *CA:* "The underlying philosophy of *Personal Investing* is that individuals must know the risk-return characteristics of alternative investments and their personal abilities for exposure to risk and the likely return. The informed investor is best served by observing these two fundamentals."

* * *

STOKESBURY, James L(awton) 1934-

PERSONAL: Born December 27, 1934, in Derby, Conn.; son of James E. (a civil servant) and Estelle (Little) Stokesbury; married Elizabeth D'Orsay Dickinson, August 29, 1961; children: Kevin, Brianna, Michael. *Education:* Acadia University, B.A., 1960; University of Western Ontario, M.A., 1962; Duke University, Ph.D., 1968. *Politics:* None. *Religion:* Congregationalist. *Home address:* R.R.1, Wolfville, Nova Scotia, Canada B0P 1X0. *Agent:* Ann Elmo Agency, Inc., 60 East 42nd St., New York, N.Y. 10017. *Office:* Department of History, Acadia University, Wolfville, Nova Scotia, Canada B0P 1X0.

CAREER: Acadia University, Wolfville, Nova Scotia, lecturer in history, 1960-61; University of Western Ontario, London, lecturer in history, 1962; Acadia University, assistant professor, 1964-68, associate professor, 1968-73, professor of history, 1973—. Sessional lecturer at University of Waterloo, 1968. *Military service:* U.S. Navy, 1953-57; became quartermaster first class.

WRITINGS: (With Martin Blumenson) *Masters of the Art of Command,* Houghton, 1975; *A Short History of World War II,* Morrow, 1979. Contributor of about forty articles to history journals.

WORK IN PROGRESS: A Short History of World War I; Napoleon and Hitler.

SIDELIGHTS: Stokesbury told *CA:* "My interests have always been in military and naval history, and by choice I would write about the Napoleonic period. However, by the accidents of the publishing business, most of my publications have been either in colonial American military history or World Wars I and II; hence the development of the theme of *Masters of the Art of Command,* and the more recent development of a general survey of World War II, and now of World War I. The treatment of Napoleon and Hitler is an obvious combination of my first love and my current direction of interest, and there are surprising parallels between the two, some accidental, some historical, some geographical.

"I have always wanted to write. I think the particular area in which I like to write lies in the gap between the scholar who writes only for his peers, and does not reach any wider audience, and the popular writer who may reach the wider audience, but is not up on the latest scholarly advances. There are some real problems in this, and it's rather like being a 'philosophe' instead of a philosopher, but it seems to me a useful thing; I'd be quite happy to have someone think I was a philosophe. Mostly, it's a lot of fun."

*　　*　　*

STOOKEY, Richard 1938-

PERSONAL: Born March 2, 1938, in Rockford, Ill.; son of Dale Jeffreys and Dorotha Amy (Phelps) Stookey; married Martha Milton (a sculptress), March 24, 1962; children: Margaret Amy, Nathaniel Milton. *Education:* University of California, Davis, A.B., 1960; Stanford University, LL.B., 1963. *Home:* 361 Laidley St., San Francisco, Calif. 94131.

CAREER: Author. *Member:* Authors Guild. *Awards, honors:* Distinguished recognition award from Friends of American Writers, 1975, for *A Still and Woven Blue.*

WRITINGS: A Still and Woven Blue (novel), Houghton, 1974. Contributor to *Translation.*

WORK IN PROGRESS: A novel, publication expected in 1985; translations.

SIDELIGHTS: Stookey wrote: "My literary orientation could be termed religious, in the broadest sense of that word. There is in my opinion only one question worthy of the seri-

ous and sustained attention of man: the question of the nature of God. My books are no more than a meditation upon this question, carried on through the medium of fictional characters who, in conscious or unconscious tension with it, confront the events out of which each is doomed to define his own being."

*　　*　　*

STRACHEY, (Evelyn) John (St. Loe) 1901-1963

OBITUARY NOTICE: Born October 21, 1901, in Guildford, England; died July 15, 1963. Politician, economist, and author. A Marxist sympathizer, Strachey criticized capitalism in works including *The Coming Struggle for Power* and *The Nature of Capitalist Crisis.* He served as Minister of Food in 1946 and Secretary of State for War in 1950. Obituaries and other sources: *Current Biography,* Wilson, 1946, September, 1963; *New York Times,* July 16, 1963; *The Reader's Encyclopedia,* 2nd edition, Crowell, 1965; *Longman Companion to Twentieth Century Literature,* Longman, 1970.

*　　*　　*

STRAUSS, Joyce 1936-

PERSONAL: Born August 12, 1936, in Los Angeles, Calif.; daughter of Benjamin and Pearl Strauss; married Allan Shoff, August 5, 1956 (divorced August 4, 1977); children: Beverly, Karen, Dan. *Education:* Attended East Los Angeles College, 1955-56, and Santa Monica College, 1972-74. *Home:* 6050 Canterbury Dr., #E-119, Culver City, Calif. 90230.

CAREER: Counselor for Dr. Wayne Weber in Marina Del Rey, Calif., 1975-76; Family Planning Educator, Los Angeles, Calif., director, 1976-79; worker for Human Concern Foundation, Los Angeles.

WRITINGS: How Does It Feel?, Velvet Flute Books, 1979.

SIDELIGHTS: Joyce Strauss wrote: "My intention is to aid people of all ages, in a most gentle way, to reach out and touch, examine, and play with feelings, and risk exposing themselves to themselves, to each other, and to their children.

"Feelings come in all sizes and shapes, as well as combinations of them mixed together. Good and bad feelings can be felt simultaneously and can be recalled in the same instance.

"Sharing goes on constantly, especially between peers, but adults sometimes fail to realize the importance of *sharing feelings* with children. Children can grow up barely realizing that adults have, and have had, some of those same feelings that the children are currently experiencing. Sharing instances is one thing. Adding the feelings surrounding those instances is another, each equally important. Sharing feelings also adds a special quality to the closeness that a child and an adult are attempting to reach, and that is what my book is about. It is intended to increase greater awareness by stimulating more means of communication on levels that everyone can identify with."

*　　*　　*

STRONG, Tracy B(urr) 1943-

PERSONAL: Born August 6, 1943, in Weihsien, China; son of Robbins and Katherine (Stiven) Strong; married Helene Keyssar; children: David, Anise. *Education:* Oberlin College, B.A. (with honors), 1963; Harvard University, M.A., 1965, Ph.D., 1968. *Home:* 263 South Pleasant St., Amherst, Mass. 01002. *Office:* Department of Political Science, Amherst College, Amherst, Mass. 01002.

CAREER: Harvard University, Cambridge, Mass., instructor in social studies and government, 1968-69; University of Pittsburgh, Pittsburgh, Pa., assistant professor, 1969-74, associate professor of political science, 1974-76; Amherst College, Amherst, Mass., visiting associate professor of political science, 1976—. Oscar Jaszi Memorial Lecturer at Oberlin College, 1972 and 1979. *Awards, honors:* National Endowment for the Humanities younger humanist fellow, 1974-75.

WRITINGS: (Contributor) Philip Green and Sanford Levinson, editors, *Power and Community: Dissenting Essays in American Political Science,* Pantheon, 1971; (contributor) Robert Solomon, editor, *Nietzsche,* Doubleday, 1974; *Friedrich Nietzsche and the Politics of Transfiguration,* University of California Press, 1975; (contributor) Stan Lyman and Brown, editors, *Structure, Consciousness, and History: New Writings in the Sociology of the Absurd,* Cambridge University Press, 1977; (contributor) Jean Ehlstein, editor, *Political Theory and the Family,* Rutgers University Press, 1979; (contributor) M. McGrath, editor, *Artistic Vision and Public Policy,* Transaction, 1980. Contributor to history and political science journals. Corresponding editor of *Theory and Society.*

WORK IN PROGRESS: A biography of Anna Louise Strong, publication expected in 1982; *Political Values and Political Choices: An Introduction to the Experience of Politics,* with Austin Sarat; *The Stage and the Community: A Book of Essays in Political Thought and Drama,* with Helene Keyssar, completion expected in 1983; *Theory and Community: The Status of Theory in the Social Sciences,* completion expected in 1983.

SIDELIGHTS: Tracy Strong comments: "I have a general concern with the circumstances which surround and affect perception and understanding of the world with which one lives, and with the processes which affect a change in understanding."

*   *   *

STRUBLE, Mitch   1945-

PERSONAL: Born July 14, 1945, in Phillipsburg, N.J.; son of Fredrick S. and Catherine (Hann) Struble. *Education:* Montclair State College, A.B., 1967; University of Pennsylvania, M.S., 1970, Ph.D., 1978. *Residence:* Philadelphia, Pa. *Office:* Department of Astronomy and Astrophysics, University of Pennsylvania, Philadelphia, Pa. 19104.

CAREER: Franklin Institute, Philadelphia, Pa., lecturer, 1968-76; University of Pennsylvania, Philadelphia, lecturer in astronomy and astrophysics, 1978—. *Member:* American Astronomical Society, Sigma Xi.

WRITINGS: Stretching a Point, Westminster, 1971; *The Web of Space-Time,* Westminster, 1973. Contributor to astronomy and space science journals.

WORK IN PROGRESS: The Earth-Moon Double Planet; research on computer studies of N-body systems, small companions of large galaxies, and identification of X-ray sources with clusters of galaxies.

SIDELIGHTS: Struble writes: "I have an interest in the historical development of mathematics and science (astronomy in particular); I am also interested in debunking pseudo-science and pseudo-archaeology from historical, scientific, and logical-statistical viewpoints. I have appeared on local television and radio programs and given lectures on these subjects."

Struble feels that his early interest in science (especially as-

tronomy), math, and history, helped motivate his career. He read little fiction as a child; instead he devoted his reading to factual and scientific books. Now, he says, his objective in writing is "to present complete, coherent ideas of science and math, with ideas—both confirmed and competing—to stimulate the reader's thinking; I would hope a book to be memorable." Struble has been influenced by such writers as George Gamow, Jagit Singh, Martin Gardner, and Walter Sullivan.

Both *Stretching a Point* and *The Web of Space-Time* have been translated and published in Japanese.

AVOCATIONAL INTERESTS: Art, architecture, archaeology, painting, classical music (especially recorded music).

*   *   *

SUMMERSKILL, Edith   1901-1980

OBITUARY NOTICE: Born April 19, 1901, in London, England; died of a heart attack, February 4, 1980, in London, England. Politician and champion of women's causes. While serving in a number of bureaucratic positions, Summerskill proposed legislation resulting in property rights and financial equality for married women. She also made less painful childbearing procedures available to expectant mothers. Summerskill lobbied hard against oral contraception, though, on grounds that its harmful side effects were not thoroughly investigated. She also opposed boxing and unsuccessfully sought to have it banned from England. She later documented her anti-boxing position in *The Ignoble Sport.* Summerskill wrote three other books, including *A Woman's World.* During World War II, she originated the Women's Home Defense Movement. Obituaries and other sources: *Current Biography,* Wilson, 1943, July, 1963; *Washington Post,* February 5, 1980; *New York Times,* February 5, 1980.

*   *   *

SUNAGEL, Lois A(nn)   1926-

PERSONAL: Born January 9, 1926, in Cleveland, Ohio; daughter of Harry William (a machinist) and Leona (Vollman) Sunagel. *Education:* Attended Phoenix Junior College, 1959-60; also took correspondence courses in writing. *Religion:* Protestant. *Home:* 17835 North 21st St., Phoenix, Ariz. 85022.

CAREER: General assignment reporter for the *Painesville Telegraph,* and the *Cleveland News,* 1947-52; display advertiser for *Lewisburg Leader,* 1952-53; National Cash Register Co., Dayton, Ohio, did work on A1A bombing and navigational computer, 1953-56; Sperry Flight Systems, Phoenix, Ariz., precision mechanical assembler, 1958-63; worked on NASA tape/data recorder for Borg Warner, 1964-68; freelance writer, 1972—. *Member:* Mystery Writers of America.

WRITINGS: The Amethyst Quest, Bouregy, 1975; *The Shadow of the Needle,* Bouregy, 1976; *The Tangled Web,* Major Books, 1979; *The Last Member of the Family,* Manor Books, 1980.

WORK IN PROGRESS: Rest in Peace, a straight mystery with a female protagonist.

SIDELIGHTS: Sunagel told *CA:* "I have been writing for as long as I can remember, a line here, a paragraph there, a gem of philosophy here and half a story there, but never managing to complete a thing. Finally, I set myself a deadline to publish or give up the idea of being a writer.

"This seemed to do the trick. I began to finish what I started.

My short stories failed to impress any editors but, fortunately, my confessions did some what better. Then, in 1972, *Writer's Digest* and Lancer Books co-sponsored their first (and only) annual Gothic Mystery Contest. I had never thought of this being my field, but since everything else was sour, I decided to give it a try. And I've been at it ever since.

"Although reading and writing occupy most of my time, I love to work in my garden and take long walks in the desert surrounding my home. I've worked out many a plotting problem while doing either or both."

*   *   *

SUNSERI, Alvin R(aymond) 1925-

PERSONAL: Born February 11, 1925, in New Orleans, La.; son of Anthony F. (a gambler) and Elizabeth (a dancer for Ziegfield Follies; maiden name, Weiser) Sunseri; married Elaine T. Zerwas, 1952 (divorced August 3, 1978); married Linda Lou Petersen (a teacher), 1978; children: (first marriage) six. *Education:* Attended Montana State University; Southeastern Louisiana University, B.A., 1953; Louisiana State University, M.A., 1955, Ph.D., 1973; graduate study at Tulane University, 1957, 1959, and University of Washington, Seattle, 1958, 1962. *Politics:* Democrat. *Religion:* Roman Catholic. *Home:* 2058 Rainbow Dr., Waterloo, Iowa 50704. *Office:* Department of History, University of Northern Iowa, Cedar Falls, Iowa 50613.

CAREER: Teacher of history and government at private preparatory school, 1954-56; history teacher at military institute in New Mexico, 1956-59; College of Santa Fe, Santa Fe, N.M., assistant professor of history and head of department, 1959-61, public relations director, 1959-61, athletic director, 1960-61; New Mexico Highlands University, Las Vegas, assistant professor of history, 1961-63; Western State College of Colorado, Gunnison, assistant professor of history, 1965-67; University of Northern Iowa, Cedar Falls, assistant professor, 1967-73, associate professor, 1973-75, professor of history, 1975—. Member of summer faculty at University of New Hampshire, 1973, and University of Albuquerque, 1974-75; guest professor at Wartburg College, 1976-77, and University of Dubuque, 1977-78; guest lecturer at colleges, universities, and professional meetings. *Military service:* U.S. Army, 1943-46, 1949-53; served in European Theater, became first lieutenant. *Member:* American Historical Association, Organization of American Historians, Historical Association (England), Southern Historical Association, Phi Alpha Theta, Pi Gamma Mu. *Awards, honors:* Award from Colonial Dames of America, 1964.

WRITINGS: Seeds of Discord: New Mexico Following the Anglo-American Conquest, 1846-1861, Nelson-Hall, 1978.

Contributor: Robin Higham and Carol Brandt, editors, *The United States Army in Peacetime: Essays in Honor of the Bicentennial, 1775-1975,* Military Aff. Aero, 1975; George E. Carter and James R. Parker, editors, *Essays on Minority Cultures,* University of Wisconsin Press, 1976; B. F. Cooling, editor, *War, Business, and American Society,* Kennikat, 1977. Also contributor to *Identity and Awareness in the Minority Experience,* edited by Carter and Bruce L. Mouser, 1975. Contributor to *Catholic Youth Encyclopedia* and *Encyclopedia of Southern History.* Contributor of about ninety articles and reviews to history, military, and education journals. Associate editor of *Book Forum.*

WORK IN PROGRESS: From Medieval Madness to the M.I.T.L.A.M.P.: War and Society in the Modern World; Tonitza: The Myths and Realities of the Dixie Mafia.

SIDELIGHTS: Sunseri has traveled through every section of Europe, Central America, and North America.

*   *   *

SUTHERLAND, John (Anthony) 1933-

PERSONAL: Born October 3, 1933, in Glasgow, Scotland; son of James (a seaman) and Marjorie (Thom) Sutherland; married Patricia McDonald, October 3, 1964; children: Donald, Marjorie, John, James. *Education:* Attended technical secondary school in Greenock, Scotland. *Politics:* Labour. *Religion:* Roman Catholic. *Home:* 34 Eynort St., Glasgow G22 6PJ, Scotland.

CAREER: Wireless operator in British Merchant Navy, 1951-59; industrial engineer in Singer, Scotland, 1959—. *Member:* Scottish Society of Playwrights. *Awards, honors:* Keir-Pavilion Award from Pavilion Theatre Management, 1975, for "We Arra People."

WRITINGS—Plays: "We Arra People" (three-act), first produced in Glasgow, Scotland, at Glasgow Pavilion, August, 1975; "Danny Boy" (three-act), first produced in Dundee, Scotland, at Dundee Repertory Theatre, 1977; "Sundog Saturday" (three-act), first produced in Scotland at Pitlochry Festival Theatre, August, 1977.

Unproduced plays: "A Kind'a Welcome" (two-act), 1976; "Somewhere There's a Laughing Place" (three-act), 1976; "Patsy Girl" (three-act), 1979.

WORK IN PROGRESS—Plays: "Haw, Welder" (three-act), on the collapse of Upper Clyde shipbuilders, 1972-79; "Echoes" (two-act), a lathe operator's escape into a dream world while recalling his oppressed upbringing under his mother's tyrany.

SIDELIGHTS: Sutherland wrote: "I am very much influenced by playwrights Williams and O'Casey and authors Steinbeck and Trellis (the ragged-trousered philanthropists).

"If you have heard that I was born into the heritage and splendour of one of the country's oldest families; the son of a French convent-educated mother and a titled father whose wide business interests include banking and shipping; educated at Eton, Oxford, and Sandhurst, followed by a distinguished and meritorious military service in the Brigade of Guards; then on to Parliament where, at present, I get the name of being one of our more polished and forceful younger M.P.'s with a sense of wit, turn of phrase, devastating charm and dashing handsomeness; listing among his hobbies polo, motor racing, and a certain love of cricket . . . This then is *not* John. Definitely *not* John.

"My father was indeed in shipping—an Anchor Line steward, and my mother was educated by nuns, but left a local secondary school at age fourteen to work as a pawnbroker's assistant. There is no need to paint any further picture of industrial working class life in Britain today. Suffice it to say that, at present, the specter of starvation no longer haunts such people. I am grateful to my native city for the education I received which enabled me to attend a technical training college and later to write plays about the city, its character, and its people."

*   *   *

SUTTON, Max Keith 1937-

PERSONAL: Born June 3, 1937, in Huntsville, Ark.; son of Keith Clifford (a farmer and teacher) and Mary Doris (Long) Sutton; married Claire Hultsman (a proofreader), February 26, 1960; children: Stephen, Julia, Katie. *Education:* University of Arkansas, B.A., 1959; Duke University, M.A., 1960, Ph.D., 1964. *Religion:* Episcopalian. *Residence:* Lawrence, Kan. *Office:* Department of English, University of Kansas, Lawrence, Kan. 66045.

CAREER: Duke University, Durham, N.C., assistant instructor in English, 1962-64; University of Kansas, Lawrence, assistant professor, 1964-68, associate professor, 1968-76, professor of English, 1976—.

WRITINGS: W. S. Gilbert, Twayne, 1975; *R. D. Blackmore,* Twayne, 1979.

WORK IN PROGRESS: The Rural Community in Nineteenth-Century British and American Literature, publication expected in the mid 1980's.

SIDELIGHTS: Sutton writes: "In the last ten years I have moved from an attraction to comic fantasies and satire to a concern with images of rural community in literature. The latter is part of a bigger concern with the role of the church in creating and preserving a sense of community, with the failures as well as the successes in this difficult endeavor. Ideally, the church provides a center for people's loyalties and thus unifies them within the Body of Christ. In nineteenth-century fiction, however, the loyalties of the characters often have no ultimate center, and the church itself is fractured by class distinctions and denominationalism."

*   *   *

SWETNAM, Evelyn (Frances)   1919-

PERSONAL: Born August 23, 1919, in Wichita Falls, Tex.; daughter of Scott S. (in sales) and Josephine (Gorleski) Smith; married Vernon E. Swetnam (a plant operator), November 30, 1941; children: Scott Vernon, Tom Christopher. *Education:* Long Beach City College, A.A., 1939, certificate in nursery school education, 1969. *Religion:* Protestant. *Residence:* Long Beach, Calif.

CAREER: Long Beach Independent, Long Beach, Calif., reporter, author of column, "Campus Notes," and editor of women's page, 1939-42; California Naval Shipyard, Terminal Island, in material control, 1942-44; *Bellflower Herald Enterprise,* Bellflower, Calif., reporter and feature writer, 1944-46; Broadway Nursery Preschool, Anaheim, Calif., nature study and science teacher, 1967-70; free-lance writer, 1970—. Member of Docents of Rancho Los Cerritos. *Member:* Society of Children's Book Writers.

WRITINGS—For children: *Jean Ellen Learns to Swim,* Western Publishing, 1970; *The Day You Were Born,* Western Publishing, 1970, revised edition, 1975; *The Magic Next Door,* Western Publishing, 1971; *Look for a Rainbow,* Rand McNally, 1973; *Baby's First Book,* Western Publishing, 1973; *In Baby's House,* Western Publishing, 1974; *Outside With Baby,* Western Publishing, 1974; *Yes, My Darling Daughter,* Harvey House, 1978.

Work represented in anthologies, including *When Girls Meet Boys,* Random House, 1965. Contributor to magazines, including *American Girl* and *Parents' Magazine,* and to newspapers.

WORK IN PROGRESS: Research on early California ranches and early American coins, for a children's mystery book.

SIDELIGHTS: Swetnam told *CA:* "I think about a story for a long time before sitting down to the typewriter. But it may often change in the typing, to my surprise. When people ask how long it takes to write a book, I have to wonder: mentally or physically?

"When I am putting a story on paper I move around a lot and look out of windows. I may go out to water the garden when a sentence I have typed doesn't say what I want it to say. I wrote a children's book by a stream, for instance, under the pine trees in a campground in Oregon. Sometimes I plan a story in my mind while I am in our boat and the fishing is slow.

"*Yes, My Darling Daughter* was inspired by conversations with my sister about her experiences working with foster children, and also by a bulletin from a social service office asking if anyone knew of a good book about a foster child. My book has been taped as a radio series for blind children in Pittsburgh, Pa. It is a story of adjustment, hurt, love, trust, and the seashore.

"When asked what I hope to achieve through my books I must answer, 'an audience.' I would like to entertain readers, to make somebody laugh, to intrigue, and to make people want to do instead of watch.

"When children ask me how they can become writers, I tell them to do and learn many things so they will have something to write about before they sit down to a blank sheet of paper. I tell them to prepare for a career other than writing so that many paths remain open to them."

*   *   *

SWINNERTON, James Guilford   1875-1974

OBITUARY NOTICE: Born November 13, 1875, in Eureka, Calif.; died of complications from a broken leg, September 5, 1974, in Palm Springs, Calif. Originator of one of the country's earliest comic strips and cartoonist best known for his comic strips "Little Jimmy." Swinnerton was discovered by publisher William Randolph Hearst while still in art school. He remained a Hearst employee for seventy-five years until declining hand coordination forced his retirement. Obituaries and other sources: *New York Times,* September 7, 1974.

*   *   *

SYBERBERG, Hans-Juergen   1935-

PERSONAL: Born in 1935 in Pomerania, Prussia (now East Germany); came to West Germany, 1953; married wife, Helga (a secretary), c. 1963; children: Amelie. *Education:* Attended University of Munich, 1962. *Residence:* Munich, West Germany. *Office:* c/o Omni-Zoetrope, 916 Kearny St., San Francisco, Calif. 94133.

CAREER: Producer, writer, and director of motion pictures. Filmed stagings of Bertolt Brecht's Berliner Ensemble, 1951-53; worked as free-lance television director. *Awards, honors:* Recipient of numerous awards for documentaries and other films, 1965-70; best film award from British Film Institute, 1977, for "Hitler—A Film From Germany."

WRITINGS: Interpretationen zum Drama Friedrich Duerrenmatts: Zwei Modellinterpretationen zur Wesensdeutung des moderner Dramas (title means "An Interpretation of the Drama of Friedrich Duerrenmatts: Two Models of the Presentation of Reality in Modern Drama"), Verlag Uni-Druck, 1965; *Le Film musique de l'avenir* (title means "The Music Film of the Future"), Cinematheque Francaise Musee du Cinema, 1975; *Syberbergs Filmbuch* (title means "Syberberg's Film Book"), Nymphenburger, 1976; (screen-writer and director) *Hitler, ein Film aus Deutschland* (released by TMS Films/British Broadcasting Corp./WDR/INA, 1977; released in the U.S. as "Hitler: A Film From Germany"), Rowohlt Verlag, 1978, translation published as *Hitler: A Film From Germany,* Farrar, Straus, 1980.

Other screenplays; also director: "Scarabea," [West Germany], 1968; "San Domingo," [West Germany], 1970; "Ludwig—Requiem fuer einem jungfraeulich Konig" (biography; title means "Ludwig—Requiem for a Virgin King"), [West Germany], 1972; "Theodor Hierneis," [West Germany], 1972; "Karl May" (biography), [West Germany], 1974; "Die Gestaendnis Winifred Wagners" (documentary; released in the United States as "The Confessions of Winifred Wagner"), Bauer International, 1975.

Aiso writer and director of 185 short films, 1963-65, and five documentaries, 1965-70, including "Die Grafen Pocci."

WORK IN PROGRESS: Directing "Parsifal," a motion picture adapted from the opera by Richard Wagner.

SIDELIGHTS: Despite almost universal praise for the German *neue kino* ("new cinema"), Syberberg remained unknown to film-goers for most of the 1970's. He was unable to crack the monopoly held by R. W. Fassbinder, Werner Herzog, and Wim Wenders on American audiences, and was virtually ignored by West German reviewers, except for those branding him pro-Hitler, thus assuring his failure at the box office. In 1977, Syberberg refused to circulate "Our Hitler" in West Germany because of the "destructive attitude" held by critics. Comparing his classical German background, which includes a familiarity with the works of Goethe and Schiller, with the "Americanized" education of reviewers and peers such as Wenders, Syberberg stated: "I am an outsider, an irritant; an intellectual aesthete. . . . I am the antithesis of what life and values in Germany have become. My three sins are that I believe Hitler came out of us; that I am not interested in money, except to work with; and that I love Germany."

Syberberg's concern for the state of German intellectualism is rooted in his beginnings as a filmmaker. After two years of filming performances of Bertolt Brecht's Berliner Ensemble, Syberberg relocated in West Germany and began freelancing as a documentary filmmaker. Studying art and philology, he developed an intellectual background dissimilar to that of his peers. He noted that "when I look upon my colleagues and friends—or maybe enemies, they are all coming from this part of West Germany. I'm the only Prussian and that makes at the end some difference."

For Syberberg, the fragmentation of the German intellectual tradition has yet to be repaired. "Young German intellectuals know nothing of Wagner and Nietzsche." he observed. He also contended that "Germans today are a people without passion, without invention of their own. . . . Before Hitler, there was invention, even genius, in every aspect of life. . . . Today, Germans don't want to speak about honor of living, much less grandeur; only about the ugly things of life, like drugs taken to kill thinking. Today we live a debased life divorced from any vision. To imagine Germany without a vision is horrible! Today there is nothing. Without a vision, Germany is nothing."

Though Syberberg incurred critical wrath by attempting to analyze the lapse in Germany's "vision," he progressed into cinematic analysis slowly and with the critics' approval. Eckert Schmidt, a reviewer in West Germany, told *Saturday Review* that Syberberg "got prize after prize" for his documentaries in the late 1960's, adding that "the critics heaped praise . . . for his novel approach." Schmidt isolated "San Domingo" as the film that sparked the anti-Syberberg attitude. In "San Domingo," he noted, Syberberg "took issue with communes, the rock lifestyle, and even the first stirrings of terrorism, he began to touch the raw nerve of our German taboos and immediately lost his rapport with the critics. Their campaign against him intensified with each of his subsequent films, which were increasingly offensive to our special German sensibilities."

After "San Domingo," Syberberg alienated himself further from the West German critics with "Ludwig—Requiem for a Virgin King." He intended the film as a "joke" that equated the bizarre nineteenth-century ruler with rock 'n' roll fans and motorcyclers, but soon found himself immersed in a deeper theme: the mystical power of Richard Wagner. "King Ludwig had sold Bavaria to Bismark, led a life which resembled that of a contemporary drug addict, and was finally destroyed by his homosexuality," Syberberg related. "And yet . . . he *made* Richard Wagner. Without Ludwig, there would have been no Wagner."

"Ludwig" proved to be the source of inspiration for two of Syberberg's next films, "Karl May" and "Our Hitler." The three title characters appear together in "Ludwig" as avid Wagnerians pondering the future of Germany in one of the king's nightmares. "Here I had them all together," Syberberg commented. "Ludwig, Karl May, Hitler—three pathological egocentrics in 'recent' German history—and the link, Wagner." After the completion of "Our Hitler," Syberberg deemed the films a historical trilogy. He noted that "the whole thing really covers 100 years of German history. Ludwig was before the foundation of the German Reich. Karl May covers the time of Bismark and Wilhelm II—the German Kaiser era. And then, of course, 'Our Hitler.'"

But before Syberberg completed "Our Hitler," he made "The Confessions of Winifred Wagner," a five-hour interview with the daughter-in-law of Richard Wagner. Throughout the film, Winifred Wagner professes unabashed affection for Hitler who, in return, was both a personal friend to her and an ardent supporter of her father-in-law's works. "If Hitler walked through that door today," she claimed, "I would be just as pleased and happy to see him here as ever I was." Stanley Kauffmann found that the paradox posed by Syberberg in the film was one of "ethics, if not morality." As a patron of German music, literature, and philosophy, Kauffmann asks, "How can we neatly disconnect ourselves from German filth?" In "Our Hitler," Syberberg offers the possibility of understanding through acceptance, not disconnection.

Syberberg defined "Our Hitler" as a "trial" that presents Hitler as an artist. "He thought of himself as somebody like Richard Wagner," declared Syberberg, "whose task it was to put all of the arts together, including the film, the art of our century. So, in my film, I take Hitler by his word. If he wants to be an artist, OK, let him be that: A man who wants to make a political art of the masses."

Hitler is thus portrayed as an artist with ambitions beyond his capabilities who, through the desperation of the German people, was nevertheless given the opportunity to indulge himself. "I sometimes think that Hitler was a poor guy, much too small for what he wanted," Syberberg confessed. "He was not a devil who seduced the German people. No, *they* elected him and he was the poor guy to do their dirty work. A lot of people wanted him subconsciously. Of course, they couldn't imagine all of the war's worst, most horrible details. They were too simple; he was their genius."

Syberberg's radically different view of Hitler and the German public provoked a refusal from many West German reviewers to even acknowledge the film's existence. In response to the ostracism, he removed the film from circulation there and took it abroad—to Paris, where it enjoyed a successful commercial showing, and to Britain, where it was declared the finest film of 1977 by the British Film Institute.

Despite its seven-hour length, "Our Hitler" enthralled viewers with its unique cinematic, as well as historical, presentation of the fuehrer. Jack Kroll called it "a vast cinematic collage of documentary footage, puppets, mannequins, recorded speeches, Hitler's favorite music from Wagner to Lehar, and a brilliant cast that through a device called front projection is able seemingly to walk through, into and out of images of the Third Reich." He deemed Syberberg's screenplay "a daunting, unsettling masterwork, quite likely the most astonishing feat of pure writing in film history." A reviewer in the *New York Times* summed up Syberberg's achievement as "extraordinary."

Syberberg concedes that "Our Hitler" is not the sort of film most viewers are accustomed to seeing. He insists that "the aesthetic of my film is opposed to the easy moralizing of Hollywood with its cheap stories for the masses on celluloid." He expects viewers to "imagine the historical events. That means . . . to combine sound and picture, because very often it is not congruent."

But in the end, Syberberg sees his film as a medium through which the audience can understand both themselves and the past. "We have to go into the interior of ourselves," he insisted. "Film has the possibility to do that, as I do as a filmmaker now. I ask the audience to follow me. I play a lot with the mythology of our cultural background. I think Hitler got his power out of that. If I give him a chance to express himself, I have to defeat him with his own weapons. And so I say I want to win against Hitler . . . And I hope the audience does it. . . . I don't want to be the teacher of the audience."

BIOGRAPHICAL/CRITICAL SOURCES: New Republic, January 1, 1978; *Saturday Review,* April 28, 1979; *Literature/Film Quarterly,* Volume 7, number 3, 1979; *New York Times,* January 13, 1980, January 15, 1980; *Village Voice,* January 14, 1980; *Newsweek,* January 28, 1980; *New York Review of Books,* February 21, 1980; *Cahiers du Cinema,* March, 1980.

—Sketch by Les Stone

T

TALBOTT, Strobe 1946-

PERSONAL: Born April 25, 1946, in Dayton, Ohio; son of Nelson S. (a businessman) and Helen Josephine (Large) Talbott; married Brooke Lloyd Shearer (a journalist), November 17, 1971; children: Devin Lloyd. *Education:* Yale University, B.A. (summa cum laude), 1968; Oxford University, B.Litt. (now M.Litt.), 1971. *Home:* 2842 28th St. N.W., Washington, D.C. 20008. *Agent:* James Moore, Moore, Foster, and Oehmann, 1625 K St., Washington, D.C. 20006. *Office:* Time Magazine, 888 16th St. N.W., Washington, D.C. 20006.

CAREER: Time magazine, Washington, D.C., Eastern Europe correspondent, 1971-73, State Department correspondent, 1974-76, White House correspondent, 1976-77, diplomatic correspondent, 1977—. Notable assignments include coverage of the Iranian revolution, visits by Henry Kissinger and James Schlesinger to the People's Republic of China, the Presidential mission to Hanoi and Vientiane in search of Americans missing-in-action, and the Non-Aligned Movement Summit in Havana in 1979. Fellow of Yale Corp., 1976—. *Member:* Council on Foreign Relations, Phi Beta Kappa. *Awards, honors:* Rhodes scholar at Oxford University; honorary M.A. from Yale University, 1976.

WRITINGS: (Editor and translator; introduction and notes by Edward Crankshaw) Nikita Khrushchev, *Khrushchev Remembers,* Little, Brown, 1970; (editor and translator; introduction by Jerrold L. Schecter and foreword by Crankshaw) Khrushchev, *Khrushchev Remembers: The Last Testament,* Little, Brown, 1974; *Endgame: The Inside Story of SALT II,* Harper, 1979. Author of foreign affairs column for Time International, 1977-78. Contributor to *Foreign Affairs.*

SIDELIGHTS: "I decided on a career in journalism early in my college years at Yale," Talbott told *CA.* "Russian language and literature was my academic major, and it has been a continuing interest of mine; but I always saw that study primarily as a way of developing a tool that would be useful to me as a journalist. Thus, even as I was working on a senior thesis about the nineteenth-century poet Fyodor Tyutchev, I spent much of my time as chairman (editor-in-chief) of the *Yale Daily News.* At Oxford, where I continued my study of Russian literature, I worked as a stringer for *Time* and, between my second and third years at Oxford, as a substitute for the Moscow bureau chief of *Time,* who was then on leave. In that capacity I did some small translating projects for the magazine."

Those small translating projects led to bigger things. A year later *Time* acquired some tapes that contained the reminiscences of former Soviet premier Nikita Khrushchev. The editors asked the twenty-four-year-old Talbott to undertake the task of translating and editing Khrushchev's memoirs, a job that he accepted. When the first volume of these memoirs was published in 1970 as *Khrushchev Remembers,* it generated considerable publicity. Because no outside authority had been permitted to examine the tapes on which the text was based (a condition imposed by the Khrushchev family as long as the retired leader was alive), there was some question as to the book's authenticity. By and large, however, critics concluded that the majority of the material in the book had originated with Khrushchev. By the time that the second volume came out in 1974, after Khrushchev's death, there was no longer any doubt that the memoirs were genuine. After the memoirs were completed, the tapes and Russian transcripts were deposited in the Columbia University archives. An independent voice printing company had verified that the voice on the tapes was indeed Khrushchev's.

Describing his work on this massive project, Talbott told an interviewer for the *Cleveland Press* that he had worked from a direct Russian transcript of Khrushchev's tapes. "Much of it was rambling and sometimes confusing, so I had to do quite a bit of editing to make it into a readable book," he explained. "Some of the dates he [Khrushchev] refers to are faulty and should be checked against other sources. But although he was in his late 70's I was amazed at how he remembers events of 50 and 60 years ago. He was by no means senile."

In a review of the first volume of *Khrushchev Remembers,* H. E. Salisbury marveled that Talbott and his associates had been able to make a coherent book out of the jumble of tapes. He asserted that the "editor-specialists of Time, Inc., and Little, Brown, . . . have remarkably transformed this bundle into a fascinating document which . . . gives us a Hogarthian picture of Russian life at the top under Stalin, under Khrushchev, and as it is today." Other commentators felt that Khrushchev's memoirs could have benefited from tighter editing. After reading the second volume of memoirs, Walter Clemons remarked: "The collation and editing of the second volume of 'Khrushchev Remembers' is as puzzling as before. . . . In fact, both books skip back and forth a good deal, and one cannot avoid the suspicion that the new one contains leftover material from the earlier tapings. Subjects recur; whole paragraphs, worded slightly differently, are repeated.... As political history, Khrushchev's ruminations are simplistic and sketchy. But some of the man's irrepressibility comes through, and that makes this fat, often boring volume worth reading."

Talbott's background in Russian studies was also useful when he took on another major project for *Time,* the reconstruction of the two-and-a-half years of the Strategic Arms Limitations Treaty negotiations. Originally run as a *Time* cover story on May 21, 1979, the article expanded into a book, *Endgame: The Inside Story of SALT II.* "My purpose in writing both the article and the book was to give people a coherent, narrative explanation of what SALT II is and how it came about," Talbott pointed out. "I have decided not to editorialize but to concentrate on trying to make an extremely complex, technical, and secrecy-shrouded subject comprehensible to the layman. I'm most satisfied both with the result and with its reception."

It is not surprising that Talbott was pleased with the book's reception; most critics felt that he had accomplished the purpose stated above, and they were generous with their praise. A reviewer for *Foreign Affairs* declared: "Talbott seems to have had unusual access to the principal Washington policymakers and he describes their deliberation and struggles over two and a half years with skill, apparent accuracy and considerable detail.... This remarkable book does for SALT II what John Newhouse's *Cold Dawn* did for SALT I, but it is made even more comprehensive by outlining the policy preferences of a wider range of bureaucratic actors." Robert W. Sellen was equally admiring. "This book is not light reading; the subject prevents that," he noted. "But Talbott explains complex matters clearly and has written a model of explanation of how international agreements are made—the process inside the U.S. government and the problem of dealing with Russians so wary as to be almost intractable."

Washington Post reviewer Deborah Shapley had some reservations about *Endgame.* Although she termed it "a remarkably detailed and readable history of the horse-trading within the administration and with the Soviets," she faulted the book for not being analytical enough. She also complained that the story of SALT II was written largely from the perspective of Secretary of State Cyrus Vance, and that other viewpoints received short shrift in the book. In contrast, Leslie H. Gelb, one of the key figures in the SALT II negotiations, felt that the strongest point of *Endgame* was that it gave "full play to different versions of reality rather than insisting on finding a single truth to each event." Like Shapley, Gelb wished that *Endgame* had been more analytical, but he praised Talbott for cutting through to the heart of the negotiations: "In the SALT II negotiations—and here Mr. Talbott unravels their very essence—'the object of the game is a draw.' If either side attempted to checkmate the other's king, to threaten vital interests, the whole board would be overthrown. This is a very subtle and central insight into nuclear diplomacy."

Asked by *CA* for an account of his career, Talbott commented: "Since I've been at *Time,* I've concentrated on foreign affairs. The one exception: throughout most of 1976, I covered Gerald Ford's White House. Since that was an election year, I spent most of my time on the campaign, following Ford and, for a while, his Republican rival, Ronald Reagan.

"I first became deeply interested in SALT covering Kissin-ger. I followed him to Moscow as he sought to break the deadlock that had developed in the negotiations in 1975-76. I also covered a number of his Middle East shuttles.

"During the Carter administration, I've had an assignment from *Time* to embark on special projects in the foreign-policy and national-security area. In late 1978, for example, I set off for Iran, Pakistan, and Afghanistan and ended up, quite fortuitously, being in Tehran for an interview with the Shah the very day that he declared martial law. That turned out to be the beginning of the end for him. Part of the essence of journalism is being in the right place at the right time, and part of the essence of that is sheer luck.

"In general, I find journalism an almost sinfully satisfying profession. One of my heroes in that profession, I. F. Stone, once said that he has so much fun in it, there probably ought to be a law against it. (If some of the politicians and judges we cover had their way, there would be.) What attracted me to journalism in college was that it seemed like a good way to see the world, meet interesting people, have adventures, continue one's education—and get paid for it. That's what attracts me to the job today, too."

BIOGRAPHICAL/CRITICAL SOURCES: Washington Post, December 23, 1970; *Saturday Review,* December 26, 1970; *New York Times Book Review,* January 3, 1971, June 30, 1974, November 4, 1979; *Christian Science Monitor,* January 7, 1971, July 31, 1974; *Newsweek,* January 11, 1971, June 24, 1974; *Times Literary Supplement,* January 22, 1971; *Observer Review,* January 24, 1971; *Best Sellers,* February 15, 1971, August 1, 1974; *New York Review of Books,* February 25, 1971, August 8, 1974; *Washington Post Book World,* March 14, 1971, October 28, 1979; *Commentary,* June, 1971; *Cleveland Press,* March 7, 1974; *New Republic,* June 29, 1974; *New Yorker,* July 22, 1974; *Authors in the News,* Volume 1, Gale, 1976; *Kansas City Times,* November 9, 1979; *Foreign Affairs,* winter, 1979/1980.

* * *

TANAY, Emanuel 1928-

PERSONAL: Born March 5, 1928, in Wilno, Poland; married wife, Sandra J.; children: Elaine, Anita, David. *Education:* Attended United Nations Relief and Rehabilitation Administration University, 1945-46; University of Munich, M.D., 1952; postdoctoral study at University of Michigan, 1956-58. *Home:* 701 Westchester, Grosse Pointe Park, Mich. 48230. *Office:* 852 Fisher Building, Detroit, Mich. 48202.

CAREER: Michael Reese Hospital, Chicago, Ill., intern, 1952-53; Elgin State Hospital, Elgin, Ill., resident in psychiatry, 1953-56; Ypsilanti State Hospital, Ypsilanti, Mich., assistant chief of admission service, 1956-58; Detroit Receiving Hospital, Detroit, Mich., director of in-patient service in department of psychiatry, 1958-63; Detroit General Hospital, Detroit, director of community and social psychiatry, 1965-67; private practice of psychiatry in Detroit, 1967—. Diplomate of American Board of Psychiatry and Neurology (past associate examiner); head of psychiatric curriculum review committee at Sinai Hospital, 1974; affiliated with Detroit General Hospital, Sinai Hospital, William Beaumont Hospital, Harper-Grace Hospitals, and Cottage Hospital. Adjunct associate professor and clinical professor at Wayne State University; teacher at Detroit Police Academy; participant in professional seminars and workshops. Member of Detroit mayor's committee on law enforcement and administration of justice, 1966; consultant to Social Security Disability Determination Service and U.S. Veterans Administration.

MEMBER: American Medical Association, American Psychiatric Association (fellow; head of committee on psychiatry and the law, 1977), American Academy of Forensic Sciences, American Academy of Psychiatry and Law, American Society of Criminology, American Judicature Society, Michigan State Medical Society, Michigan Psychiatric Society (head of committee on law and psychiatry and committee on confidentiality, both 1978), Michigan Association for Law and Psychiatry (president, 1969), Michigan Inter-Professional Association on Marriage, Divorce, and the Family (vice-president), Wayne County Medical Society (head of committee on social perspectives in medicine, 1974), Cottage Hospital and Macomb Association for Continuing Medical Education. *Awards, honors:* Flag Award from Michigan State Medical Society, 1969; special award from Sinai Hospital, 1974; certificate from *Medical Economics,* 1976, for paper, "Society Is Getting the Doctors It Deserves."

WRITINGS: (Contributor) Henry Krystal, editor, *Massive Psychic Trauma,* International Universities Press, 1968; *The Murderers,* Bobbs-Merrill, 1976. Contributor of about twenty-five articles to medical and law journals. Member of editorial board of *Journal of Forensic Sciences,* 1979.

* * *

TANDON, Prakash 1911-

PERSONAL: Born June 11, 1911, in Bullokee, India; son of Ram Das (an engineer) and Somitra Devi (Vinayak) Tandon; married Gaerd Skoglar, 1939; children: Maya Tandon Malhotra, Manu, Gautam. *Education:* Punjab University, B.A., 1929; Victoria University of Manchester, B.A. (Com.), 1932. *Politics:* None. *Religion:* Hindu. *Home:* Dakshin Pali, D'Monte Park Rd., Bandra, Bombay 400 050, India. *Office:* National Council of Applied Economic Research, 11 Indraprastha Estate, New Delhi 110 002, India.

CAREER: Hindustan Lever, Bombay, India, marketing manager, 1937-51, director, 1951-61, chairperson, 1961-68; State Trading Corp. of India, New Delhi, chairperson, 1968-72; Punjab National Bank, New Delhi, chairperson, 1972-75; National Council of Applied Economic Research, New Delhi, director general, 1975—. Visiting professor at University of California, Los Angeles, 1967, University of California, Berkeley, 1970, Indian Institute of Management, 1975-77, Boston University, 1977, University of Delhi, and Punjab University; senator of Punjab University, University of Delhi, and Himachal Pradesh University. Chairperson, Indian Institute of Management, Ahmedabad, 1964-68, United Nations Asian and Pacific Development Institute, Bangkok, Thailand, 1976-78. *Member:* Institute of Chartered Accountants (India; fellow), Institute of Chartered Accountants (England and Wales; fellow). *Awards, honors:* Sir Jehangir Ghandi Medal for Industrial Peace from president of India, 1972.

WRITINGS: *Punjab Century, 1857-1947,* Harcourt, 1961; *Beyond Punjab: A Sequel to Punjabi Century,* University of California Press, 1971; *Return to Punjab,* University of California Press, in press. Contributor to journals all over the world.

SIDELIGHTS: Tandon writes: "The 'Punjab Trilogy' is a social history of the change in the country from 1857 to 1975. It narrates, through a family, the life of the people from the time the British arrived till they left, through the first quarter century of independence. It attempts to enshrine a life, its traditions and mores that have changed.

"Since the dawn of history, the Punjab—Land of the Five Rivers—has been the main invasion route into India, with invaders filing through the northwest passes from central Asia, Afghanistan, Iran, Turkey, and elsewhere. Some of them made India their home and founded dynasties; others laid waste to the land and departed, laden with bounty. The most recent were the British, who gained control of the Punjab in 1852 in a battle fought outside the city of Bullokee. On their departure a century later, the Punjab was divided between India and the new nation of Pakistan. Because the successive waves of invaders deposited incremental cultural layers, the Punjabi temperament was molded over millenia by civilizations as disparate as those of China and of Europe.

"Punjabi personal characteristics came to include depth of feeling, pragmatic adaptability, and an inclination to heterodoxy that appealed to the British, who valued the province for its military traditions, its numerous trained professionals, and its ample granary."

* * *

TANIGUCHI, Kazuko 1946-

PERSONAL: Born January 1, 1946, in Tokyo, Japan; came to the United States in 1973; daughter of Shinpei and Yaeko Goto; married Hiromu Taniguchi, September 12, 1969 (divorced July 20, 1973); married Robert Stone, March 20, 1974; children: (second marriage) Dorian G. *Education:* Tama Fine Art University, B.A., 1964, M.A., 1968. *Religion:* Shinto. *Home:* 28-30 East Fourth St., New York, N.Y. 10003.

CAREER: Photo Ziv (studio), Tokyo, Japan, photographer, 1969-71; Yamaha Co. Ltd., Tokyo, photographer and graphic designer, 1971-72; free-lance photographer, graphic designer, and writer, 1972—.

WRITINGS: *Monster Mary Mischief Maker* (self-illustrated children's book), McGraw, 1976.

WORK IN PROGRESS: Three children's books, all self-illustrated, *Flower Belly Button, Uncle Frisbee and the Space Patrol, 10 Colors.*

SIDELIGHTS: Kazuko Taniguchi commented: "I like to make books that give children beautiful images. Children should always see beautiful things, but especially when they are little. I want to make something that has not been seen before. My latest work is a combination of illustration, photography, and poetry."

BIOGRAPHICAL/CRITICAL SOURCES: *Baton Rouge Morning Advocate,* December 12, 1976; *Baton Rouge Sunday Advocate,* December 12, 1976.

* * *

TANIZAKI, Jun'ichiro 1886-1965

PERSONAL: Born July 24, 1886, in Tokyo, Japan; died July 30, 1965, in Yugawara, Tokyo, Japan; son of Sogoro Tanizaki (a rice merchant); married Chiyoko Ishikawa, 1915 (divorced, 1930); married Furukawa Tomiko, April, 1931 (divorced). *Education:* Attended Tokyo Imperial University, 1908-10. *Residence:* Tokyo, Japan.

CAREER: Novelist, playwright, and short story writer. *Member:* American Academy (honorary member), National Institute of Arts and Letters (honorary member). *Awards, honors:* Imperial Prize for Literature, 1949.

WRITINGS—In English: *A Spring-Time Case,* translation by Zenchi Iwado from the original "Otsuya koroshi," Japan Times, c. 1927; *Shunkin Sho,* [Japan], 1933, translation by Howard S. Hibbett published as *A Portrait of Shunkin* (text in English and Japanese), Hara Shobo, 1965; *Ashikari* [and] *Shunkin Sho*, Hokuseido Press, 1936, translation by Roy Humpherson and Hajime Okita published as *Ashikari* [and] *The Story of Shunkin: Two Japanese Novels*, Greenwood Press, 1970; *Tade kuu mushi*, [Japan], 1936, translation by Edward G. Seidensticker published as *Some Prefer Nettles*, Knopf, 1955; *Sasame yuki*, [Japan], 1949, translation by Seidensticker published as *The Makioka Sisters*, Knopf, 1957; *Kagi*, [Japan], 1957, translation by Hibbett published as *The Key*, Knopf, 1960; *Futen Rojin*, [Japan], 1962, translation by Hibbett published as *Diary of an Old Man*, Knopf, 1965; *Seven Japanese Tales*, translated by Hibbett, Knopf, 1963. Also author of *Inei Raisan*, translation by Thomas J. Harper and Seidensticker published as *In Praise of Shadows*, Leetes Island Books, 1977.

In Japanese; all published in Japan; fiction: *Kojin*, 1926; *Neko to Shozo to futari onna*, 1949; *Rangiku mongatari*, 1949; *Shoso Sigemoto no hahn*, 1950; *Shonen*, 1970; *Hagi no hana*, 1973.

Collections of short stories: *Hyofu*, 1950; *Yume no ukihashi*, 1960; *Kokumin no bungaku*, 1964; *Shisei*, 1973; *Shisei, Shonen*, 1974.

Collections of plays: *Alsureba koso*, 1923; *Shinzei*, 1949.

Omnibus volumes: *Tanizaki Jun'ichiro zenshu*, twelve volumes, 1931, thirty volumes, 1958-59, twenty-eight volumes, 1966-70; *Tanizaki Jun'ichiro shu*, volume from "Gendai bungo meisaku zenshu" series, 1953, volume of short stories, 1970, two volumes of fiction, 1975, two volumes of short stories, 1975-77, volume of fiction, 1977; *Tanizaki Jun'ichiro bunko*, twelve volumes, 1973.

Other: *Momoku mongatari*, 1932; *Banshu tokuhon*, 1936, reprinted, 1973; *Sasameyuki*, 1949; *Kyo no yume: Osaka no yume*, 1950; *Toshei shika modoki*, 1961; *Setsugoan yawa*, 1968; *Kasai Zenzo to Hirotsu Kazuo*, 1972; *Adachi*, 1974.

Also author with Jo Cem of film reproduction "Sumiko."

SIDELIGHTS: Jun'ichiro Tanizaki was destined to live a life of extremes. Although his family had come into a substantial sum of money from his mother's wealthy relation, his father grossly mismanaged the funds, sending his rice business swinging like a pendulum back and forth, from success to failure and back again. Subsequently, when it came time for young Jun'ichiro to enter middle school, his family lacked the necessary tuition. Upon recommendation of his teachers, however, he was allowed to continue his education.

By the time Tanizaki enrolled at Tokyo University, he was already displaying a talent for writing, and five years later began his literary career in earnest. As the Russo-Japanese war had recently ended, influences from the West slowly started to seep into the East, freeing Japanese literature from centuries of binding conventions. Tanizaki revelled in Western thought and practices and advocated them in his early writings.

The turning point in Tanizaki's career came in 1923, the year of the great earthquake. He moved to Okamoto and enjoyed a simpler life-style, becoming increasingly interested in the traditional Japanese life, and critical of Western values and the modern industrialization of his homeland.

"In Praise of Shadows," an essay written early in the thirties, reflects this change of loyalties. The author discusses the opposing factions of East and West, and the dubious benefits derived from the juxtaposition of the two. According to D. J. Enright, the work is "a graceful, nostalgic piece," adding that "fanaticism and cultural chauvinism are calmly subverted by the humour that tinges Tanizaki's 'aes-

thetic' and the strong hints of earthly appetite which escape from it." While Tanizaki expresses gratitude for Western conveniences such as modern lavatories, he summons back the "shadows" of the past for the realm of art and culture.

Tanizaki's later works continued this apparent dichotomy of co-existing values, but presented it in an extremely different fashion. Condemned as indecent and pornographic by many reviewers, his works are praised by others as "excellent studies." *Diary of an Old Man*, for example, depicts an impotent elderly gentleman who receives erotic pleasures from a beautiful and sensual young girl in return for expensive trinkets. The conflict of East and West, of old and new, is apparent also in *Some Prefer Nettles*. It is a story of a married couple, the wife very westernized and the husband firmly rooted in tradition, who have long since grown tired of one another, yet do not separate.

BIOGRAPHICAL/CRITICAL SOURCES: San Francisco Chronicle, November 17, 1957; *Atlantic*, December 14, 1957; *New Yorker*, December 14, 1957; *New Statesman*, August 18, 1961; *Time*, August 20, 1965; *Saturday Review*, August 21, 1965; *Nation*, May 22, 1972; *Times Literary Supplement*, December 16, 1977; *World Literature Today*, spring, 1978; *Contemporary Literary Criticism*, Volume 8, Gale, 1978.

OBITUARIES: New York Times, July 31, 1965; *Time*, August 6, 1965; *Publishers Weekly*, August 9, 1965; *Books Abroad*, spring, 1966.*

*   *   *

TARPY, Roger M(aynard)   1941-

PERSONAL: Born November 18, 1941, in Dayton, Ohio; son of Roger M. (in business) and Nellie M. (an administrative assistant; maiden name, Livingston) Tarpy; married Alicia Spinner (a teacher), February 11, 1967; children: Elizabeth, David. *Education:* Amherst College, A.B., 1963; College of William and Mary, M.A., 1965; Princeton University, M.A., 1966, Ph.D., 1967. *Office:* Department of Psychology, Bucknell University, Lewisburg, Pa. 17837.

CAREER: Williams College, Williamstown, Mass., assistant professor, 1967-73, associate professor of psychology, 1973-74; Bucknell University, Lewisburg, Pa., associate professor, 1974-79, professor of psychology, 1979—. Visiting scientist at Oxford University. *Member:* Society of Neuroscience, Psychonomic Society, Animal Behavior Society, Eastern Psychological Association. *Awards, honors:* Fellow at University of Durham, 1970-71.

WRITINGS: (Contributor) E. Zamis, editor, *NGF and Its Antiserum*, Athlone Press, 1972; *Basic Principles of Learning*, Scott, Foresman, 1975; *Emotion*, Brooks/Cole, 1977; (with R. A. Mayer) *Foundations of Learning and Memory*, Scott, Foresman, 1978; (with Mayer) *Readings in Learning and Memory*, Scott, Foresman, 1979. Contributor of more than twenty-five articles to psychology journals.

WORK IN PROGRESS: Principles of Animal Learning and Behavior, for Scott, Foresman.

*   *   *

TAVES, Ernest H(enry)   1916-

PERSONAL: Born February 1, 1916, in Aberdeen, Idaho; son of Henry C. (a merchant) and Louisa (Hardy) Taves; married Judith B. de Forest (a psychoanalyst), October 20, 1949; children: Henry V. *Education:* Columbia University, A.B., 1937, M.A., 1938, Ph.D., 1941; New York University, M.D., 1945; W. A. White Institute of Psychology, Psychiatry, and Psychoanalysis, graduated, 1954. *Home and office:* 12 Hubbard Park Rd., Cambridge, Mass. 02138.

CAREER: Bellevue Hospital, New York City, intern, 1945-46, resident and assistant director of Mental Hygiene Clinic, 1948-51; private practice of psychiatry and psychoanalysis in New York City, 1949-54, and Cambridge, Mass., 1954-72; Directions, Inc., Cambridge, co-founder and president, 1972—. Diplomate of National Board of Medical Examiners and American Board of Neurology and Psychiatry. Member of visitors' committee at Harvard University, 1976-79. Assistant director of National Geographic-Smithsonian Institution-Harvard University solar eclipse expedition to Mauritania, 1973; consultant to Committee for the Scientific Investigation of Claims of the Paranormal. *Military service:* U.S. Army, Medical Corps, chief of neuropsychiatric service, 1946-48; served in Japan; became captain. *Member:* American Psychological Association, American Psychiatric Association, Academy of Psychoanalysis, Science Fiction Writers of America, Sigma Delta Chi, St. Botolph Club, Dublin Lake Club, Port Royal Club.

WRITINGS: (With Donald H. Menzel) *The UFO Enigma,* Doubleday, 1977. Contributor of articles, stories, and reviews to parapsychology journals, science fiction magazines, *Playboy,* and newspapers.

WORK IN PROGRESS: A biography of Lafcadio Hearn; a science fiction novel dealing with cryogenics; a psychological study of Joseph Smith.

SIDELIGHTS: Taves's master's thesis was the basis for the first degree awarded by Columbia University for a parapsychological study. He has conducted additional parapsychological studies since, investigating mediums and psychics, and performing a three-week experiment on a national radio network program. He reports that all results have been negative.

Taves told *CA:* "I had always wanted to write, but other things kept getting in the way. After twenty years of psychoanalytic practice, I decided it was finally time to get down to it. *Playboy* bought my first short story, whereupon I phased out of psychoanalytic practice and have been writing, when other activities allow, ever since. Most of my short works have been science fiction. All of the time I now have available for writing is going into the Joseph Smith book."

*   *   *

TAWNEY, R(ichard) H(enry)   1880-1962

OBITUARY NOTICE: Born in 1880 in Calcutta, India; died in 1962. British economist and author of works in his field, including *The Acquisitive Society, Religion and the Rise of Capitalism,* and *Equality.* Tawney served on several economic boards, including the Consultative Committee of the London Board of Education and the Cotton Trade Conciliation Committee. His fields of specialization were British industry and agriculture and Chinese labor conditions. Obituaries and other sources: *The Reader's Encyclopedia,* 2nd edition, Crowell, 1965; *The New Century Handbook of English Literature,* revised edition, Appleton, 1967; *Longman Companion to Twentieth Century Literature,* Longman, 1970; *The Penguin Companion to English Literature,* Mc-Graw, 1971; *Cassell's Encyclopaedia of World Literature,* revised edition, Morrow, 1973.

*   *   *

TAYLOR, John   1916-
PERSONAL: Born November 5, 1916, in Dunmore, Pa.; son

of James F. and Helen (Nooney) Taylor; married Marcella Gilmore, May 10, 1947; children: Patricia Taylor Zimmerman, Evelyn, Kathleen, Michael. *Education:* East Stroudsburg State College, B.S., 1941; Pennsylvania State University, M.Ed., 1946, Ph.D., 1949. *Religion:* Roman Catholic. *Home:* 28 Barnard Dr., Newington, Conn. 06111. *Office:* Department of Psychology, Central Connecticut State College, New Britain, Conn. 06050.

CAREER: California State Teacher's College (now California State College), California, Pa., instructor in psychology, 1949-51; United Aircraft Corp., Pratt & Whitney Aircraft division, East Hartford, Conn., conference leader of personnel department, 1951-57; Central Connecticut State College, New Britain, assistant professor, 1957-60, associate professor, 1960-66, professor of psychology, 1966—. *Member:* American Psychological Association, New England Psychological Association, Connecticut Psychological Association.

WRITINGS: Introduction to Psychology, Kendall/Hunt, 1978.

*   *   *

TAYLOR, Ronald (Jack)   1924-
PERSONAL: Born May 19, 1924, in London, England; son of J. Arthur (a banker) and Mary (Biggar) Taylor; children: Mark, Diana. *Education:* Royal Academy of Music, L.R.A.M., 1942; King's College, London, B.A., 1949, M.A., 1951, Ph.D., 1956. *Office:* Arts Building, University of Sussex, Brighton, England.

CAREER: High school teacher of English language and culture in Germersheim, West Germany, 1947, 1948; University of Wales, University College of Swansea, assistant lecturer, 1950-52, lecturer, 1952-59, senior lecturer in German, 1959-62; Northwestern University, Evanston, Ill., visiting professor of German, 1963-64; University of Sussex, Brighton, England, professor of German, 1965—. Visiting professor at University of Chicago, 1960, and University of British Columbia, 1974, 1976. Member of management committee of Institute of Germanic Studies, London.

WRITINGS: (With Arthur T. Hatto) *The Songs of Neidhart von Reuental,* Manchester University Press, 1958; (editor) E.T.A. Hoffmann, *Das Fraeulein von Scuderi,* Thomas Nelson, 1959, 2nd edition, 1962; (with Walter Gottschalk) *A German-English Dictionary of Idioms,* Hueber Verlag, 1960, 5th edition, 1978; *Die Melodien der weltlichen Lieder des Mettelalters* (title means "The Melodies of the Secular Songs of the Middle Ages"), two volumes, Metzler Verlag, 1964; *E.T.A. Hoffmann,* Bowes, 1964; *The Art of the Minnesinger,* two volumes, University of Wales Press, 1968; *The Romantic Tradition in Germany,* Methuen, 1970; *The Intellectual Tradition of Modern Germany,* two volumes, Bell & Sons, 1973; (translation editor) *Aesthetics and Politics: Debates Between Ernst Bloch, Georg Lukacs, Berthold Brecht, Walter Benjamin, Theodor Adorno,* New Left Books, 1977; *Richard Wagner: His Life, Art, and Thought,* Taplinger, 1979; *Between Two Wars: Literature and Society in Germany, 1918-1945,* Harvester, 1980.

Translator: Hoffmann, *The Devil's Elixirs,* J. Calder, 1963; Gottfried Keller, *A Village Romeo and Juliet,* J. Calder, 1966; Theodor Storm, *Immensee,* J. Calder, 1966; Eichendorff, *Memoirs of a Good-for-Nothing,* J. Calder, 1966; Bruno Boesch, editor, *German Literature: A Critical Survey,* Methuen, 1971; Herbert von Einem, *Michelangelo,* Methuen, 1973; Konrad Lorenz, *Behind the Mirror: A Search for a Natural History of Human Knowledge,* Methuen, 1977.

Contributor: Raghavan Iyer, editor, *The Glass Curtain Between Europe and Asia,* Oxford University Press, 1965; Frederick Norman, editor, *Essays in German Literature,* Volume I, Institute of Germanic Studies, University of London, 1965; *Studies Presented to F. Norman,* Institute of Germanic Studies, University of London, 1965; Siegbert S. Prawer, editor, *The Romantic Period in German Literature,* Weidenfeld & Nicolson, 1970; J. Malcolm S. Pasley, editor, *Germany: A Companion to German Studies,* Methuen, 1972; Keith Bullivant, editor, *Society and Culture in the Weimar Republic,* Manchester University Press, 1977. Contributor to *Penguin Companion to European Literature* and *Encyclopaedia Britannica.* Contributor of more than twenty articles and reviews to language and literature journals.

WORK IN PROGRESS: The Philosophical and Political Thought of Richard Wagner; The Price of Romanticism: The Life and Work of Robert Schumann, publication by Granada expected in 1981.

SIDELIGHTS: Taylor writes: "I am by nature and by training as much a musician as a writer on literature, and I have pursued the relationship between the two areas in various historical periods. Further, I am concerned to study all art in its historical and social setting as a manifestation of human creativity.

"My earliest publications dealt with the medieval German lyric, especially the relationship between words and music. This is an analytical and highly specialized field of research in which the intellect is paramount, but the emotions barely touched. After a few years I felt my satisfaction in this work growing less and less. Hence I moved, still via the combination of literature and music, to the Romantic nineteenth century, to the philosophy of Romanticism, and to the problems of the relationship between art and life that it poses. This in turn led to my book, *The Intellectual Tradition of Modern Germany,* with its attempt to show, through the writings of leading German thinkers through the ages, the dominant strands in the German personality.

"My concern with present-day Germany, both as teacher and writer, has led me to spend a good deal of time in East Germany. Some of my conclusions on the East-West problem have found their way into newspapers, including the *London Daily Telegraph.*

"The generous reviews given to my recent book on Wagner led to a commission by the same publisher to do a new biography of Schumann, for which I have collected rare and new material in East Germany. When this is finished, I hope to return to my work on Wagner's philosophical and political thought.

"In all of this activity I am concerned above all with what might be called intellectual and cultural continuity as it shows itself in different periods of German and European history (my forthcoming book on literature and society in Germany between 1918 and 1945 is another part of this picture). Perhaps this is a natural interest for one whose activity centers on Germany, a country whose tortured history through the centuries seems to me to make it almost inevitable, if one is to seek a blend of mind and spirit, that one's net should be cast wide in the attempt to understand the subject more fully."

* * *

TERSTEGGE, Mabel Alice   1905-
   (Sister Georgiana)

PERSONAL: Born December 2, 1905, in Terre Haute, Ind.; daughter of Joseph Henry (a pharmacist) and Mary Philomena (Nacke) Terstegge. *Education:* St. Mary-of-the-Woods College, B.A., 1928; Indiana University, M.A., 1931; Catholic University of America, Ph.D., 1948. *Address:* Providence Convent, St. Mary-of-the-Woods, Ind. 47876.

CAREER: Entered Sisters of Providence (S.P.), 1924, became Roman Catholic nun, 1924, name in religion, Sister Georgiana; high school French teacher in Evanston, Ill., 1925-33, Malden, Mass., 1926-27, and Washington, D.C., 1929-30; St. Mary-of-the-Woods College, St. Mary-of-the-Woods, Ind., instructor, 1934-40, assistant professor, 1940-44, associate professor, 1947-49, professor of French, 1949-75, professor emeritus, 1975-77, head of department, 1970-76. Exchange teacher in Ruille-sur-Loir, France, 1967-68. Member of Terre Haute Architectural Commission. *Member:* American Translators Association (past president), Tree Club (founder, 1972). *Awards, honors:* Les Bois Award from St. Mary-of-the-Woods College, 1974, for translation course proposal; chevalier of L'Ordre des Palmes Academiques, 1977.

WRITINGS—Under name Sister Georgiana: *Successful Devices in Teaching French,* J. Weston Walch, 1957, revised edition published as *Teaching French Today,* 1977; *French Dramatizations,* J. Weston Walch, 1961; *Pattern Drills for French Dramatizations,* J. Weston Walch, 1963; *Project Proficiency,* J. Weston Walch, Volume I: *Grammar,* 1963, Volume II: *Reading and Writing French,* 1971; (translator from the French, with her students) A. M. Besnard, *Your Name Is Written in Heaven,* Dimension Publishing, 1975.

SIDELIGHTS: Sister Georgiana writes: "I have loved French since my first lesson in it in high school, and as I love people, I have always wanted to share this pleasure with them. Teaching is fun and teaching is forever! I am now 'emeritus,' but I can't keep my fingers out of the pie; I still teach French to little children every Saturday, and I still direct translation projects for postgraduate students. Besides that I have an evening course during the academic year for adults, and do translating from French to English for a Bishop's Pastoral Research Project."

AVOCATIONAL INTERESTS: Travel.

* * *

TERTIS, Lionel   1876-1975

PERSONAL: Born December 29, 1876, in West Hartlepool, England; died February 22, 1975, in London, England; married Ada Gawthorp (died, 1951); married Lillian Florence Margaret Warmington (a cellist), 1959. *Education:* Attended Royal Academy of Music, London; also studied in Leipzig, Germany (now East Germany). *Residence:* Wimbledon, England.

CAREER: Violist; designer of musical instruments. Author. *Member:* Sesame Club. *Awards, honors:* Commander of the Order of the British Empire and Kreisler Award of Merit, 1950; Gold Medal from the Royal Philharmonic Society, 1964; honorary fellow of Trinity College, London, 1966; Eugene Ysave Medal and Diploma of Honor, 1968, from the Ysave Foundation; fellow of the Royal Academy of Music.

WRITINGS: Beauty of Tone in String Playing, Oxford University Press, 1938; *Cinderella No More* (autobiography), Nevill, 1953; *My Viola and I: A Complete Autobiography* (includes "Beauty of Tone in String Playing" and other essays), Elek, 1974, Crescendo, 1975. Also author of numerous arrangements for viola.

SIDELIGHTS: In 1896 Lionel Tertis set out to lift the viola from its obscure status and establish it as a respected solo instrument. He succeeded: his own solo performances, many of which were written expressly for him by such composers as Cyril Scott and Ralph Vaughan Williams, made him the world's first internationally acclaimed violist. Tertis also performed alongside Pablo Casals (the two share the exact same birthdate) in chamber music sessions for more than forty years. One of their more legendary performances came during a London blackout when violinist Eugene Ysaye and pianist Arthur Rubinstein joined Tertis and Casals in playing the Brahms Piano Quartet in C minor.

Tertis's fame as a musician is matched by his success as designer of the Tertis Model Viola. Characterized by "its large dimensions and consequent C string sonority," it is used today by many of the world's premier violists. Later, Tertis used his viola as a model for designing the Tertis cello and violin. According to *Spectator,* "the Tertis Model Viola will remain the true monument to his genius."

My Viola and I is the autobiography of "the man who put the viola on the map and also . . . the man who mapped the viola," wrote the *Economist.* Published when he was ninety-nine, these memoirs include "a list of craftsmen who make the Tertis Model Viola; a list of works for viola solos written for the author or arranged and edited for the viola by the author; and an impressive discography of recordings by Mr. Tertis beginning in 1920."

BIOGRAPHICAL/CRITICAL SOURCES: Lionel Tertis, *Cinderella No More,* Nevill, 1953; *Spectator,* October 23, 1953; Tertis, *My Viola and I: A Complete Autobiography,* Elek, 1974, Crescendo, 1975; *Economist,* November 30, 1974.*

* * *

THAYER, Peter
    See WYLER, Rose

* * *

THIRKELL, Angela (Margaret)   1890-1961

OBITUARY NOTICE: Born January 30, 1890, in London, England; died January 30, 1961. Novelist whose subtle, easygoing humor in novels such as *Before Lunch* and *Cheerfulness Breaks In* made her a favorite of readers in both the United States and Britain. Obituaries and other sources: *The Reader's Encyclopedia,* 2nd edition, Crowell, 1965; *The New Century Handbook of English Literature,* revised edition, Appleton, 1967; *Twentieth Century Writing: A Reader's Guide to Contemporary Literature,* Transatlantic, 1969; *Longman Companion to Twentieth Century Literature,* Longman, 1970.

* * *

THOMAS, William G(ordan)   1931-

PERSONAL: Born June 5, 1931, in Los Angeles, Calif.; son of Ernest Leslie (a theater manager) and Marian (an actress; maiden name, Bowers) Thomas; married Diane Ruth McCulloch (a health educator), September 8, 1951; children: Gregory Scott, Mark William, Scott Jeffrey, Christopher Kent. *Education:* Attended Occidental College, 1949-50, and University of California, Berkeley, 1952-54; University of California, Los Angeles, B.A. (cum laude), 1956, M.A., 1957, Ed.D., 1965, postdoctoral study, 1975—. *Home:* 17187 Marilla St., Northridge, Calif. 91325. *Office:* Los Angeles Community Colleges, 400 West Washington Blvd., Los Angeles, Calif. 90016.

CAREER: Immaculate Heart College, Los Angeles, Calif., instructor in speech and drama, 1956-57; U.S. Army, civilian director of cultural programs in West Germany, 1957-59; William G. Thomas & Associates, Inc., Los Angeles, in public relations and theatrical management, 1959-61; University of California, Los Angeles, college and university placement adviser at Office of Educational Placement, 1961-62, associate dean of students in placement and manager of Student and Alumni Placement Center, 1962-67, dean of Educational Career Center, 1968-75, lecturer in education, 1971-75, and management, 1975, dean of experimental education programs, 1973-75; University of Redlands, Redlands, Calif., chancellor of Johnston College and fellow in behavioral science, 1975-76; Los Angeles Community Colleges, Los Angeles, dean and director, 1976—. Member of board of directors of Innoved. Instructor at Mount St. Mary's College, Los Angeles, 1956-57; director of public relations for Immaculate Heart College, 1959-61; dean of students at California State University, Northridge, 1967-68; visiting professor at California State University, Los Angeles, 1968-70, 1971-75; lecturer at Loyola University, Los Angeles, 1969-70, 1971-75; currently part-time professor of management at California State College, Dominguez Hills. Organizer and director of California Colloquia on Experiential Education, 1973-74; public speaker; private management consultant. *Military service:* U.S. Navy, instructor and flight observer, 1950-54.

MEMBER: European Council of International Schools, American Association of Higher Education, American Association of School Administrators, American Association of School, College, and University Staffing, American Association of Community and Junior Colleges, American College Personnel Association, American Personnel and Guidance Association, American College Public Relations Association, National Association of Student Personnel Administrators, College Placement Council, College Student Personnel Institute, Cooperative Assessment of Experiential Learning, Sierra Club, Western College Placement Association, California Guidance and Counseling Association, California Junior College Association, California Personnel and Guidance Association, Southern California College Federal Council (past chairperson), University of California Los Angeles Supervisors and Administrators Association.

WRITINGS: (Contributor) *Southern Placement Association Handbook,* Tulane University, 1964; (contributor) *Student Personnel Services in the United States,* McGraw, 1969; (with Donald Gerth, Edmond Hallberg, and Milo Milfs) *The Urban Grant College: A College Without Walls,* Ombudsman Foundation, 1970; (with Lorraine Mathies) *Overseas Opportunities for American Educators,* Macmillan Information, 1971, revised edition published as *Overseas Opportunities for American Educators and Students,* 1973; (with Jane Permaul) *Careers in College and University Student Affairs* (monograph), California College Personnel and Guidance Association, 1974; (with Hallberg) *When I Was Your Age: STOP,* Free Press, 1974; (editor) *American Education Abroad,* Macmillan Information, 1974. Contributor to education journals. Guest editor of *Educational Horizons,* summer, 1973.

WORK IN PROGRESS: A novel dealing with education in urban areas; research on international education.

SIDELIGHTS: Thomas has designed projects to better relate liberal arts curricula to current societal needs and courses in experiential education, which incorporate an individualized learning contract prior to field experience. His consulting experiences have involved relating organizational behavior, management by objectives, and the behavioral sciences to educational administration.

He wrote: "I am currently involved in the early organization of an educational research and program development association, Innoved. Innoved is engaged in literacy and numeracy programs, use of media in education, cross-cultural and outdoor education. It exists to pick up where schools and colleges end. This past year we have designed cultural seminars in England as well as a government education center and treks in the western United States."

AVOCATIONAL INTERESTS: Jogging, tennis, backpacking, camping, theatre, youth activities, community service.

* * *

THORNTON, Gene

PERSONAL—Home: 452 West 25th St., New York, N.Y. 10001.

CAREER: Writer and lecturer. Guest director for American Federation of Art exhibition, "Masters of the Camera," 1976; lecturer at Smithsonian Institution, New York University, Houston Museum of Art, International Center of Photography, Pratt Institute, National Geographic Society, and Canada's National Film Board; guest on television and radio programs, including "Today Show."

WRITINGS: Masters of the Camera: Stieglitz, Steichen, and Their Successors, Holt, 1976. Contributor to magazines, including *Saturday Review, Town and Country, Aperture, Zoom, U.S. News & World Report,* and *Camera.* Contributing editor of *Time,* 1969-70, and *Art News,* 1973—; photography critic for *New York Times,* 1970—.

WORK IN PROGRESS: An introductory history of photography, with publication by New American Library.

* * *

TIBBETTS, Arnold M(acLean)   1927-

PERSONAL: Born October 20, 1927, in San Antonio, Tex.; son of Martelle Arnold (a geologist) and Alice (MacLean) Tibbetts; married Charlene Hansen (a professor), 1951; children: Susan Tibbetts Ducey, Alice, John, Caroline. *Education:* University of Colorado, B.A., 1949; University of Iowa, M.A., 1957; Vanderbilt University, Ph.D., 1964. *Office:* 100 English Building, University of Illinois, Urbana, Ill. 61801.

CAREER: United Geophysical Co., Tulsa, Oklahoma, geophysicist, 1949-51; Pure Oil Co., Tulsa, geophysicist, 1951-54; University of Iowa, Iowa City, instructor in English, 1954-57; Western Illinois University, Macomb, assistant professor of English, 1957-59; Air University, Montgomery, Ala., assistant professor of communication skills, 1959-61; Vanderbilt University, Nashville, Tenn., instructor, 1961-64; University of Illinois at Urbana-Champaign, Urbana, assistant professor, 1964-70, associate professor of English, 1970—, director of rhetoric program, 1977—. Member of Council for Basic Education's National Commission on Writing, 1977—. *Member:* Modern Language Association of America, National Council of Teachers of English, American Association of University Professors, Conference on College Composition and Communication.

WRITINGS: (With wife, Charlene Tibbetts) *Strategies of Rhetoric,* Scott, Foresman, 1969, 3rd edition, 1979; (with C. Tibbetts) *Critical Man,* Scott, Foresman, 1972; (with C. Tibbetts) *What's Happening to American English?,* Scribner, 1978. Contributor of about forty articles to academic jour-

nals. Editor of *Journal* and *Bulletin* of the American Business Communication Association, 1979—; acting editor, *Bulletin* of the Illinois Association of Teachers of English, 1979—.

WORK IN PROGRESS: On Successful Compositions.

SIDELIGHTS: Arnold Tibbetts writes: "My interests include sensible changes in composition teaching and courses and practical adaptation of grammatical and rhetorical theory for the modern student.

"My wife and I recently spent five months traveling around the United States visiting high school English departments. Mainly, we looked into changes in curricula, methods of teaching and grading student papers, types of textbooks used, emphases in the teaching of grammar, usage, and composition, and the training and administration of English teachers. We tried to find causal relationships between these matters and test scores."

* * *

TIBBETTS, Charlene   1921-

PERSONAL: Born March 10, 1921, in Dunning, Neb.; daughter of Henry C. (a physician) and Nelle (a musician; maiden name, Dellinger) Hansen; married Arnold M. Tibbetts (a professor), 1951; children: Susan Tibbetts Ducey, Alice, John, Caroline. *Education:* Kearney State College, B.A., 1942; George Peabody College for Teachers, M.A., 1964. *Office:* Curriculum Laboratory, University of Illinois, 1212 West Springfield, Urbana, Ill. 61801.

CAREER: High school English teacher in Montgomery, Ala., 1960-61, and Nashville, Tenn., 1961-63; University of Illinois, University High School, Urbana, teacher of English and humanities, 1964—, head of department, 1966—. *Member:* Modern Language Association of America, National Council of Teachers of English, American Association of University Professors.

WRITINGS: (With husband, Arnold M. Tibbetts) *Strategies of Rhetoric,* Scott, Foresman, 1969, 3rd edition, 1979; (with A. M. Tibbetts) *Critical Man,* Scott, Foresman, 1972; (with Edward R. Levy) *Rhetic in Thought and Writing,* eight volumes, Holt, 1970, 2nd edition, 1972; (with A. M. Tibbetts) *What's Happening to American English?,* Scribner, 1978. Contributor to education journals.

SIDELIGHTS: Charlene Tibbetts writes: "My interests are high school teaching of grammar and composition, the interrelations between grammar, composition, and literature, and accountability, as well as relationships between English curricula and test scores."

* * *

TIFTON, Leo
See PAGE, Gerald W(ilburn)

* * *

TILLYARD, E(ustace) M(andeville) W(etenhall)   1889-1962

OBITUARY NOTICE: Born in 1889 in Cambridge, England; died in 1962. Literary scholar and author of works in his field. Tillyard specialized in the works of both John Milton and William Shakespeare. His books include *The Elizabethan World Picture* and *Studies in Milton.* Obituaries and other sources: *The Reader's Encyclopedia,* 2nd edition, Crowell, 1965; *The New Century Handbook of English Literature,* revised edition, Appleton, 1967; *Longman Companion to Twentieth Century Literature,* Longman, 1970.

TIOMKIN, Dimitri 1899-1979

OBITUARY NOTICE: Born May 10, 1899, in Russia (now U.S.S.R.); died November 11, 1979, in London, England. Scorer of motion picture soundtracks and author of his autobiography, *Please Don't Hate Me.* Tiomkin received Academy Awards for his musical contribution to "The Alamo," "The Old Man and the Sea," and "The High and the Mighty." Obituaries and other sources: *Celebrity Register,* 3rd edition, Simon & Schuster, 1973; *International Motion Picture Almanac,* Quigley, 1979; *The International Who's Who,* 43rd edition, Europa, 1979; *Who's Who in America,* 40th edition, Marquis, 1979; *AB Bookman's Weekly,* December 24, 1979.

* * *

TOBIAS, Sheila 1935-

PERSONAL: Born April 26, 1935, in Brooklyn, N.Y.; daughter of Paul Jay and Rose (Steinberger) Tobias; married Carlos Stern (an environmentalist), 1970. *Education:* Radcliffe College, A.B., 1957; Columbia University, A.M., 1961, M. Phil. History, 1974. *Politics:* Independent. *Religion:* Jewish. *Home:* 4845 W St. N.W., Washington, D.C. 20007. *Agent:* Gloria Stern, Gloria Stern Literary Agency, 1230 Park Ave., New York, N.Y. 10028. *Office:* Suite 203, 1302 18th St. N.W., Washington, D.C. 20036.

CAREER: American Weekend, Frankfurt, West Germany, journalist and salesperson, 1958-60; journalist in New York, N.Y., for American Broadcasting Co. (ABC), National Educational Television (NET), and Columbia Broadcasting System (CBS), 1963-67; Cornell University, Ithaca, N.Y., assistant to vice-president of academic affairs, 1967-70; Wesleyan University, Middletown, Conn., associate provost, 1970-78; educational consultant, 1978—. Lecturer in history, City College of the City University of New York, 1965-67; American specialist for U.S. Department of State to Eastern Europe, 1976; visiting professor of women's studies, Vanderbilt University, 1977-80; member of board of curators, Stephens College. *Member:* National Organization of Women (NOW; founding member; member of board of Legal, Defense, and Education Fund), Phi Beta Kappa. *Awards, honors:* Woodrow Wilson fellow.

WRITINGS: Overcoming Math Anxiety, Norton, 1978. Editor, *Cornell Conference on Women,* 1969, *Female Studies I,* 1970. Contributor of more than one hundred articles on math anxiety, women's studies, and the status of women to popular and scholarly journals.

SIDELIGHTS: Sheila Tobias is best known for her work in women's studies and for her efforts in achieving educational and occupational equity for women and minorities. While an associate provost at Wesleyan University, she observed the continuing occupational segregation of women due to the unwillingness of most female students to choose math or math-based fields of study. From her observations, Tobias developed a theory that certain members of our society are systematically discouraged from quantitative areas because of popular mythology and ideological prejudices. To correct this, Tobias, herself a "mathematics avoider," co-founded a "Math Clinic" at Wesleyan University to help students overcome their irrational fears. She is presently continuing her work on math anxiety.

BIOGRAPHICAL/CRITICAL SOURCES: Washington Post, October 23, 1978.

TOLISCHUS, Otto D(avid) 1890-1967

OBITUARY NOTICE: Born November 20, 1890, in Russ, Germany; died February 24, 1967. Journalist and author. Tolischus was a foreign correspondent in Berlin, Germany, for the *New York Times* during the 1930's. After predicting the Nazi-Soviet pact and uncovering the German economic plight, he was denied permission by the German government to remain in Germany. His efforts were recognized by the Pulitzer committee, though, who awarded him their 1939 prize for journalism. Tolischus later documented his years in Berlin in *They Wanted War.* Obituaries and other sources: *Current Biography,* Wilson, 1940, April, 1967; *New York Times,* February 2, 1967.

* * *

TOLLEY, William Pearson 1900-

PERSONAL: Born September 13, 1900, in Honesdale, Pa.; son of Adolphus Charles (a merchant) and Emma Grace (Sumner) Tolley; married Ruth Marian Canfield, July 3, 1925; children: Nelda Ruth (Mrs. Richard Preston Price), William Pearson, Jr., Kathryn (Mrs. Arthur Fritz, Jr.). *Education:* Syracuse University, A.B., 1922, M.A., 1924; Drew Theological Seminary, B.D., 1925; Columbia University, M.A., 1927, Ph.D., 1930. *Politics:* Republican. *Home:* 107 Windsor Place, Syracuse, N.Y. 13210.

CAREER: Ordained Methodist Episcopal minister, 1923; Drew Theological Seminary, Madison, N.J., alumni secretary, 1925-27, instructor in systematic theology, 1926-28, and philosophy, 1928-29, professor of philosophy, 1930-31, dean of Brothers College, 1929-31; Allegheny College, Meadville, Pa., president, 1931-42; Syracuse University, Syracuse, N.Y., chancellor, 1942-69, chancellor emeritus, 1969—. Mansbridge Memorial Lecturer at University of Leeds, 1967. Head of board of directors of Mohawk Airlines, 1970-71, chairperson and president, 1971-72; member of board of directors of schools, banks, and businesses, including New York Telephone Co., 1943-71, and Allegheny Airlines, 1971-75. Vice-president of Japan International Christian University Foundation; president of University Senate of the Methodist Church, 1960-70, and National Methodist Foundation for Christian Higher Education, 1969-73. *Military service:* U.S. Army, 1918.

MEMBER: Association of American Colleges (president and member of board of directors, 1942-43), Association of Colleges and Universities of the State of New York (past president), Newcomen Society, Phi Beta Kappa, Beta Gamma Sigma, Delta Sigma Rho, Phi Kappa Phi, Pi Delta Epsilon, Pi Kappa Alpha (president of memorial foundation), Omicron Delta Kappa, Phi Delta Kappa, Cosmos Club, Iron City Fishing Club, Century Association, Grolier Club, University Club, Century Club (Syracuse), Oswelewgois Club, Wolf Hollow Racket Club, First String Tennis Club. *Awards, honors:* Chevalier of French Legion of Honor; George Arents Alumni Medal and Salzberg Medal from Syracuse University, thirty-six honorary degrees, including D.D. from Mt. Union College, Alliance, Ohio, 1931, and LL.D. from Boston University, 1950, Columbia University, 1955, and Syracuse University, 1969.

WRITINGS: (Editor) *Alumni Record of Drew Theological Seminary, Madison, New Jersey, 1867-1925,* Drew Theological Seminary, 1929; *The Idea of God in the Philosophy of St. Augustine,* R. R. Smith, 1930; (editor) *Preface to Philosophy,* Macmillan, 1944; *The Transcendent Aim: Selected Addresses* (edited by Frank P. Piskor), Syracuse University Press, 1969; *The Meaning of Freedom,* Syracuse University

Press, 1969; *The Adventure of Learning,* Syracuse University Press, 1978.

WORK IN PROGRESS: The Survival of Hellenistic Culture in the Latin West.

AVOCATIONAL INTERESTS: Fishing, tennis, collecting rare books.

*   *   *

TOMKINSON, Michael 1940-

PERSONAL: Born March 10, 1940, in London, England; son of Albert William and Florence (Wells) Tomkinson; married Sheryl Ann Schaeffer, September 8, 1973; children: Luke Douglas. *Education:* Queen's College, Oxford, B.A. (with honors), 1963, M.A., 1967; attended Sorbonne, University of Paris, 1961-62, and Middle East Centre for Arab Studies, 1963-64. *Home:* Residence Jennet, Hammamet, Tunisia. *Office:* Michael Tomkinson Publishing, 36 Oakdale, London N14 5RE, England.

CAREER: British Diplomatic Service, London, England, vice-consul in Kuwait, 1964, court registrar in Qatar, 1964-66, press attache in Baghdad, Iraq, 1966-67, and Jedda, Saudi Arabia, 1967-68; private traveling and exploration, 1968-70; Michael Tomkinson Publishing, London, England, owner, 1973—; writer. *Member:* Institute of Linguists (fellow), Translators' Guild.

WRITINGS: Tunisia: A Holiday Guide, Scribner, 1970, 8th edition, 1980; *Kenya: A Holiday Guide,* Scribner, 1973, 5th edition, 1980; *Jamaica: A Holiday Guide,* Tomkinson Publishing, in press; *The Gambia: A Holiday Guide,* Tomkinson Publishing, in press. Also author of *The United Arab Emirates,* 1975. Contributor to *Punch, Guardian,* and *Geographical.*

SIDELIGHTS: Tomkinson's books have been published in French, Dutch, German, Italian, and Swedish. He has studied and speaks several languages, including French, German, and Arabic, and combines that with writing and photography by producing books in several languages on the regions he knows best—North and East Africa and the Middle East. He lives and writes in Tunisia, in a villa on the beach in Hammamet.

*   *   *

TOMPKINS, Kathleen Burns 1934-

PERSONAL: Born May 12, 1934, in St. Cloud, Minn.; daughter of Harry E. (a lawyer) and Mathilda (Ohmann) Burns; married Alan D. Tompkins (a systems engineer), January, 1961; children: Deborah, Nancy, Edward, Charles. *Education:* College of St. Benedict, B.A., 1956; Southern Connecticut State College, M.S., 1974. *Home:* 122-C Rolston Rd., Waitsfield, Vt. 05673.

CAREER: Special Services Club, Hevzogenaurach, West Germany, director, 1958-61; Yale University, Responsive Environments Laboratory, New Haven, Conn., teacher in reading, 1961-64; Foster School for Exceptional Children, New Haven, head teacher, 1964-72; reading teacher at private day school and academy in Hamden and Cheshire, Conn., 1974-76; Stowe Public Schools, Stowe, Vt., learning disabilities coordinator, 1976—, special education coordinator, 1978.

WRITINGS: The Alphabet Kids (juvenile), Vermont Crossroads Press, 1978.

WORK IN PROGRESS: The Alphabet Kids Reading Readiness Program, publication expected in 1980 or 1981.

SIDELIGHTS: Tompkins told *CA:* "Children with specific learning disabilities make up approximately 8 percent of our school population. For these children, learning the mechanics of reading and writing is a painful task often accompanied by criticism from teachers, parents, and peers who do not understand their hidden handicaps. I designed the *Alphabet Kids* and the forthcoming *Alphabet Kids Reading Readiness Program* after working for many years with beginning disabled readers. Its primary objective is to require active participation on the part of the beginning reader. This act of discovery enhances its educational value."

*   *   *

TOPOL, Allan 1941-

PERSONAL: Born June 16, 1941, in Pittsburgh, Pa.; son of Morry (a restaurateur) and Selma (Wiseman) Topol; married Barbara Rubenstein (a teacher and book reviewer), July 27, 1962; children: David, Rebecca, Deborah, Daniella. *Education:* Carnegie-Mellon University, B.S., 1962; Yale University, LL.B., 1965. *Office:* 888 16th St. N.W., Washington, D.C. 20006.

CAREER: Covington & Burling (law firm), Washington, D.C., partner, 1965—. Admitted to the District of Columbia Bar, 1966. *Member:* District of Columbia Bar Association. *Awards, honors:* Order of the Coif, 1962; ODK, Hamilton award from Carnegie-Mellon University, 1962.

WRITINGS: The Fourth of July War, Morrow, 1978; *A Woman of Valor,* Morrow, 1980. Contributor of articles to the *New York Times, Washington Post,* and *Saturday Review.*

SIDELIGHTS: Topol told *CA:* "In my first novel, *The Fourth of July War,* I set out to address one of our country's major economic and political problems: the continuing dependence on vast imports of foreign oil.

"Being a Washington lawyer, I understand how indecisively and how slowly our governmental bureaucracy operates. Yet after the oil embargo of 1973, and the long gas lines, I expected to see some great national plan that would protect us in the future from the complete and utter chaos that came with a shortage of oil. Gradually, I began to realize that there would be no great plan.

"My mind then jumped to 1983, when America's dependence on foreign oil will even be greater. Now I was asking myself what will happen then if the OPEC countries sharply raise the price of oil or turn off the spigot? And, what if in the midst of our crew of indecisive and buck-passing politicians, there is appointed a Director of Energy who is a dynamic, hard-driving businessman, a self-made multi-millionaire, who refuses to do things the Washington way? And, what if there is a top-ranking military man unhappy about our nation's foreign policy in the post-Vietnam era? And, what if. . . .

"As these questions gestated in my mind, I began writing *The Fourth of July War.* My objective became to shake Americans out of complacency with a novel that was a fantasy thriller and at the same time a futuristic story sufficiently realistic that it might very well occur in the next decade.

"I chose the novel form because of its potential for making an impact upon a large and diverse audience. By permitting readers to become involved with fictional and yet realistic characters, the novel presents a unique medium for providing exposure to a complex societal problem. At the same time the novel can provide the entertainment that is so widely sought in America today."

BIOGRAPHICAL/CRITICAL SOURCES: Washington Post, January 15, 1979; *Los Angeles Times,* January 21, 1979; *New York Post,* January 27, 1979; *Houston Chronicle,* February 18, 1979, March 25, 1979; *San Francisco Examiner,* March 14, 1979; *Chicago Tribune,* April 12, 1979.

* * *

TOULIATOS, John 1944-

PERSONAL: Born March 17, 1944, in Houston, Tex.; son of Constantine I. and Ann (Michalinos) Touliatos; married Paula Creedon (an accountant), May 5, 1963; children: Kara. *Education:* University of Houston, B.A. (magna cum laude), 1967, M.Ed., 1968, Ed.D., 1971. *Home:* 4221 Capilla, Fort Worth, Tex. 76133. *Office:* Department of Home Economics, Texas Christian University, Fort Worth, Tex. 76129.

CAREER: Auburn University, Auburn, Ala., assistant professor, 1971-75, associate professor of family and child development, 1975-78, head of department, 1972-78, director of Child Study and Family Life Center, 1975-78; Texas Christian University, Fort Worth, associate professor of home economics, 1978—. *Member:* American Psychological Association, Society for Research in Child Development, American Home Economics Association, Council for Exceptional Children, Southeastern Council on Family Relations, Texas Council on Family Relations, Alabama Council on Family Relations (president, 1976-78), Sigma Xi, Phi Kappa Phi, Psi Chi, Omicron Nu, Phi Delta Kappa, Sigma Delta Pi, Kappa Delta Pi.

WRITINGS: (Editor) *Family and Human Development,* MSS Information Corp., 1972; (editor with B. W. Lindholm) *The Family and Child Mental Health,* MSS Information Corp., 1973; (editor with Lindholm) *Introduction to Human Development and Family Studies,* College and Universities Press, 1975; (with N. C. Compton) *Approaches to Child Study,* Burgess, 1980. Author of tests. Contributor to psychology and education journals.

SIDELIGHTS: Touliatos told *CA:* "Most of my research and writing has been guided by a firm belief that the family exerts the single greatest influence on the behavior and development of a child. This is closely related to the parents' important position among the child's interpersonal relationships and to the extent of parental contact with the youngster especially during his early, formative years. Over the past nine years, I have engaged in several dozen studies to explore the relationships of family structure, parental attitudes and characteristics, and childrearing practices to children's personality development, mental health, and achievement. I have also devoted portions of my previous books to a description of family influences on behavior and development. My forthcoming textbook, *Approaches to Child Study,* will include an entire chapter on family assessment. Since the home has such a strong impact on the child, it is imperative that we carefully investigate as many dimensions of family life as possible in order to arrive at an adequate understanding of the child's current functioning."

* * *

TRENSKY, Paul I. 1929-

PERSONAL: Born March 29, 1929, in Ostrava, Czechoslovakia; came to the United States in 1957, naturalized citizen, 1963; son of Karl (a businessman) and Jane (Vrana) Trensky; married Ann Tropp (divorced December, 1976); children: Michael. *Education:* Attended Comenius University, 1950-54, and University of Vienna, 1956-57; Harvard University, Ph.D., 1963. *Politics:* None. *Religion:* None. *Home:* 2080

Grand Concourse, #22, Bronx, N.Y. 10457. *Office:* Department of Modern Languages, Fordham University, Rosehill, Bronx, N.Y. 10458.

CAREER: University of Illinois, Urbana-Champaign, assistant professor of Russian studies, 1962-64; Fordham University, Bronx, N.Y., assistant professor, 1964-69, associate professor, 1969-79, professor of Russian literature and comparative literature, 1979—. Vice-president of Masaryk Institute. *Member:* American Association for the Advancement of Slavic Studies, American Association of Teachers of Slavic and East European Languages, American Association of University Professors.

WRITINGS: Czech Drama Since World War II, M. E. Sharpe, 1978.

WORK IN PROGRESS: Co-editing *Czech Literature: A Symposium* (tentative title), with William E. Harkins, for Columbia Slavic Studies.

SIDELIGHTS: Trensky's scholarly interests include Slavic literatures and comparative literature, especially theatre and drama history.

* * *

TRUDEAU, Margaret (Joan) 1948-

PERSONAL: Born September 10, 1948, in Vancouver, British Columbia, Canada; daughter of James (a former Canadian minister of fisheries) and Kathleen (Bernard) Sinclair; married Pierre Elliot Trudeau (a prime minister of Canada), March 4, 1971 (separated); children: Justin Pierre, Alexandre Emmanuel, Michel Charles-Emile. *Education:* Graduate of Simon Fraser University. *Residence:* Ottawa, Canada.

CAREER: Junior sociologist with Department of Manpower and Immigration, Ottawa, Ontario; free-lance photojournalist; actress appearing in "The Guardian Angel" and "Kings and Desperate Men."

WRITINGS: (With Caroline Moorehead) *Beyond Reason* (autobiography), Paddington Press, 1979.

SIDELIGHTS: Margaret Trudeau, "the most scandalous first lady in history," is a woman few people feel indifference toward. She receives either hateful and malicious criticism or vigorous and enduring support; her advocates praise her free spirit and spontaneity, while her detractors denounce her selfishness and "child-like" behavior. *Beyond Reason,* the story of this controversial lady, is her own attempt to set the record straight and reveal the true Margaret Joan Sinclair Trudeau. "I don't, I realize, come out of this story very well," she admits in the epilogue of her book. "I have tried at least to be honest."

Margaret Trudeau's life has often been referred to as a fantastic fairy-tale. She was Cinderella, swept off her pretty feet by the handsome Prince Charming. "Margaret went and shattered that make-believe and that is her real crime," insisted Coates Redmon, "one for which she will not too soon be pardoned."

The love story began late in the turbulent 1960's. While vacationing with her family on the isle paradise of Tahiti, Margaret met an interesting but older man by the name of Pierre Trudeau, prime minister of Canada. Although a pleasant enough encounter, it was to be eighteen months before their paths again crossed. At the suggestion of Pierre, Margaret moved east to Ottawa to assume the post of junior sociologist with a governmental agency. They began seeing more and more of each other, and although never linked romantically by the press, their relationship deepened. The news of their secret wedding in 1971 rocked the nation.

"If there was one thing that I learned faster than anything else," wrote Margaret in *Beyond Reason*, "it was that a prime minister's wife has an extraordinarily varied life. One minute I was firing a cook, the next discussing icefloes with strange, non-English-speaking geologists; one day sitting at home watching television, the next, in full regalia, waltzing with a head of state. There was no studying for the part, no understudy to take over when confidence fails. In the first year I had a taste of almost everything that would come my way during my marriage to Pierre: a state visit abroad, a number of receptions at home, a household to reorganize, official and formal clothes to buy, a style of life to master, even a pregnancy." In addition to this, Mrs. Pierre Trudeau was soon to learn that a hungry press must also be reckoned with.

Although she shunned public exposure in the first years of marriage, Margaret joined actively in her husband's 1974 bid for the seat of prime minister. During a campaign visit to Vancouver, she was unexpectedly called upon to say a few words. Totally unprepared, but wishing to convey the warmth and charm of the man behind the public image, the nervous young woman stammered: "Pierre has taught me everything I know about loving." The audience was aghast; even Margaret was taken aback by her words, for she had not meant them the way they sounded. It was to be but the first of many embarrassments.

"If it were within my power to wave a magic wand and have things today, right now, as I really want them," Margaret wrote, "I'd be happily married with lots of little children at my feet, baking bread, canning preserves, making jam. To hell with suitcases and airplanes. Basically, I'm a home-body." Many people, including Margaret herself, believed she was not cut out for the high-pressured world of politics: "a life of appendageness, relentless, boring rituals, constant public scrutiny and an almost intolerable lack of personal freedom and privacy ... it is no wonder to me that such a young woman floundered and could not discover the essential truth about herself," observed Redmon.

In the end, the pressures and demands of "life in a goldfish bowl" caught up with her and she rebelled. "I suppose every person asks themselves just how much can they take," reflected Margaret to Carole Taylor in an interview broadcast over Canadian television. "I certainly am no exception." At first it was innocent "freedom trips," as she referred to them, a chance to get away on her own and enjoy a bit of privacy. But as time went on, the freedom trips came with increased frequency and length, and both Pierre and Margaret knew things could no longer go on as before. In 1977, an official statement was issued from the office of the prime minister—the storybook romance had ended; they would "begin living separately and apart," it read.

The following years saw Margaret exploring the fields of photo-journalism and acting. Although neither has proven exceptionally lucrative as yet, she continues the struggle for "self-identity" and worth. She asks at the end of her book, "Is is beyond reason for me to hope for a peaceful life, or has my past put me beyond reach of such a dream?"

BIOGRAPHICAL/CRITICAL SOURCES: Look, March 19, 1971; *Time*, July 8, 1974; *Detroit News*, November 3, 1974; *Biography News*, Gale, December, 1974; *Spectator*, March 19, 1977; *New Republic*, May 7, 1977; *Ladies' Home Journal*, July, 1977, April, 1979; *People*, September 4, 1978, April 9, 1979; Margaret Trudeau and Caroline Moorehead, *Beyond Reason*, Paddington Press, 1979; *Washington Post*, March 18, 1979; *Chicago Tribune*, April 3, 1979, April 5,

1979, April 6, 1979; *Nation*, May 5, 1979; *Esquire*, May 8, 1979; *Washington Post Book World*, May 20, 1979; *New York Times Book Review*, June 3, 1979.*

—*Sketch by Kathleen Ceton Newman*

* * *

TUAN, Yi-Fu 1930-

PERSONAL: Born December 5, 1930, in Tientsin, China; came to the United States in 1951, naturalized citizen, 1973; son of Mao-Lan (a diplomat) and Lui Kung (Tao) Tuan. *Education:* Oxford University, B.A., 1951, M.A., 1955; University of California, Berkeley, Ph.D., 1957. *Office:* Department of Geography, University of Minnesota, Minneapolis, Minn. 55455.

CAREER: Indiana University, Bloomington, instructor in geography, 1956-58; University of Chicago, Chicago, Ill., research fellow in statistics, 1958-59; University of New Mexico, Albuquerque, 1959-65, began as assistant professor, became associate professor of geography; University of Toronto, Toronto, Ontario, associate professor of geography, 1966-68; University of Minnesota, Minneapolis, professor of geography, 1968—. Visiting instructor at Oxford University, 1966, and University of Hawaii, 1973; Morrison Lecturer at Australian National University, 1975; distinguished visiting professor at University of California, Davis, 1975-76; guest lecturer at colleges and universities. *Member:* American Association for the Advancement of Science, Association of American Geographers, Association for Asian Studies, American Geographical Society, Association for the Study of Man-Environment Relations. *Awards, honors:* Guggenheim fellowship, 1967-68; meritorious contribution to geography award from Association of American Geographers, 1973; Fulbright-Hays senior scholarship, 1975.

WRITINGS: Pediments in Southeastern Arizona, University of California Press, 1959; *The Hydrologic Cycle and the Wisdom of God*, University of Toronto Press, 1968; *China*, Aldine, 1970; *Man and Nature*, Association of American Geographers, 1971; *Topophilia*, Prentice-Hall, 1974; *Space and Place: The Perspective of Experience*, University of Minnesota Press, 1977; *Landscapes of Fear*, Pantheon, 1980. Contributor to geography journals.

WORK IN PROGRESS: Research into spacial segmentation and self.

BIOGRAPHICAL/CRITICAL SOURCES: Washington Post Book World, February 10, 1980.

* * *

TYL, Noel 1936-

PERSONAL: Born December 31, 1936, in West Chester, Pa.; divorced; children: Kimberly. *Education:* Harvard University, B.A., 1958. *Home and office address:* P.O. Box 927, McLean, Va. 22101.

CAREER: Writer, 1970—; lecturer and counselor. Has worked as business manager of the Houston Opera Company, and as account executive with Ruder & Finn. Opera singer. Director of astrology library and editor of *Sourceworld* for Telecomputing Corp. of America, McLean, Va.

WRITINGS: The Horoscope as Identity, Llewellyn, 1974; *The Principles and Practice of Astrology*, twelve volumes, with teaching and study guides, Llewellyn, 1974-76; *The Missing Moon*, Llewellyn, 1979; *Holistic Astrology: The Analysis of Inner and Outer Environments*, TAI Books, 1980. Editor of *Astrology Now*.

SIDELIGHTS: Tyl told *CA:* "I am an opera singer specializing in dramatic baritone roles of Wagner and Strauss, and I am a private counselor and therapist, using astrology, as well as a busy lecturer.

"I group all my activities under the concept of 'communication.' Specialization in astrological studies emerged from psychology and theology courses at Harvard (Paul Tillich was one principal inspiration). My interest in music began early and matured through private study, emerged in winning American opera auditions in 1964, and bloomed in performances throughout the United States and Europe.

"My life seems dedicated to helping others to feel, and in turn to help still others, through the life wisdom symbolized within astrology and through the sounds and meanings of drama orchestrated in opera."

U

UGBOAJAH, (Francis) Okwu 1945-

PERSONAL: Born July 28, 1945, in Arochukwa, Imostate, Nigeria; son of Martin Umeoha (a civil servant) and Helen (Ugojii) Ugboajah; married Sabina Uche, August 22, 1964 (divorced September 1, 1971); married Clitheroe C. D. Ugboajah (a public health educator), August 30, 1972; children: (first marriage) Pele Onyeoruru. Education: University of Minnesota, B.A., 1970, M.A., 1971, Ph.D., 1975. Religion: Christian. Home: Block 5, Ransome-Kuti Rd., University of Lagos, Lagos, Nigeria. Office: Department of Mass Communication, University of Lagos, Lagos, Nigeria.

CAREER: University of Lagos, Lagos, Nigeria, senior lecturer in mass communication, 1971—. Member: International Association of Mass Communication Research (coordinator for Africa), Nigerian Union of Journalists, Nigerian Institute of Public Relations, Association for Education in Journalism, Public Relations Society of America. Awards, honors: UNESCO fellow in Paris, 1973-75, and at Salzburg Seminar, 1979.

WRITINGS: Mass Media Perspectives and the Uses of Communication in Nigeria, University of Lagos, 1977; (contributor) George Gerbner, editor, Mass Media Policies in Changing Cultures, Wiley, 1977; Communications Policies in Nigeria, UNESCO, 1979. Editor of "Mass Communication, Culture, and Society in West Africa" series, Routledge & Kegan Paul, 1980—. Contributor to professional journals in the United States and Nigeria and to Nigerian newspapers. Editor of Unilag Communication Review; contributing editor of Journal of Communication and Zeszyty (Krakow, Poland).

WORK IN PROGRESS: Broadcasting in Nigeria, a book commissioned by the International Institute of Communications in London, completion expected in 1980; "a study of the images of foreign countries, an analytical evaluation of how national news media treated news on other countries within a selected time period," sponsored by UNESCO in collaboration with the Centre for Mass Communication, University of Leicester, England; television message analysis (a cultural indicator's project) with George Gerbner; Group Interaction and Village Development: A Sociometric Study of Communication Networks in Rural Nigeria, sponsored by the Central Research Committee, University of Lagos.

SIDELIGHTS: Ugboajah comments: "I direct my perspectives to the problems of mass communication in the African continent in general and Nigeria in particular. I am against sweeping statements about mass communication phenomena, and advocate its contextual cultural specificity in all my writings. I have traveled to intellectual seminars in England, Italy, Yugoslavia, Mexico, Kenya, the Philippines, Thailand, U.S.S.R., Austria, and Germany.

"My books focus attention on some of the factors that inhibited efficient communication planning when Nigeria attained its independence. I direct attention to the need for involving indigenous systems for modernizational planning because of the psychological advantage it gives those for whom planning is meant to benefit. I welcome technology transfer in so much as it does not limit or discourage inborn know-how. It is therefore wise to support mass mediated information by activating native mass media systems which are oral, small, and relevant. This approach is very important in planning for rural development."

*   *   *

UROFF, Margaret Dickie 1935-

PERSONAL: Born September 13, 1935, in Bennington, Vt.; daughter of Henry Hodgeson (an athletic director) and Dorothy Isabelle (a librarian; maiden name, Sweet) Dickie; married Benjamin Uroff, February 11, 1961 (divorced, 1978); children: Elizabeth, Catherine. Education: Middlebury College, A.B., 1956; Brown University, Ph.D., 1965. Home: 305 West Michigan, Urbana, Ill. 61801. Office: Department of English, University of Illinois, 100 English Building, Urbana, Ill. 61801.

CAREER: University of Illinois, Urbana-Champaign, assistant professor, 1966-74, associate professor of English, 1974—.

WRITINGS: Becoming a City (nonfiction), Harcourt, 1966; Hart Crane: The Patterns of His Poetry, University of Illinois Press, 1974; Sylvia Plath and Ted Hughes, University of Illinois Press, 1979. Editor of New England Review, 1961-63.

WORK IN PROGRESS: The Waste Land and Modern American Poetry (tentative title), a study of six modernist poets.

BIOGRAPHICAL/CRITICAL SOURCES: New York Times Book Review, September 30, 1979.

UZZELL, J(ohn) Douglas 1937-

PERSONAL: Born December 11, 1937, in Houston, Tex.; son of Douglas Drew and Barbara (Collier) Uzzell; married Melanie Myers, December 6, 1959 (divorced); married Linda M. Whiteford (an anthropologist), June 13, 1976; children: Shawn Lynn, Gwendolyn Rachel. *Education:* University of Houston, B.A., 1963, M.A., 1964; University of Texas, Ph.D., 1972. *Office:* Department of Anthropology, Southern Methodist University, Dallas, Tex. 75275.

CAREER: Tarleton State University, Stephenville, Tex., instructor in English, 1964-66; Rice University, Houston, Tex., assistant professor of anthropology, 1972-79; Southern Methodist University, Dallas, Tex., assistant professor of anthropology, 1979—. Adjunct assistant professor at University of Texas, 1975-79. Family Connection (home for runaway children), member of board of directors, 1973-77, chairman of board, 1977. *Military service:* U.S. Army, 1956-58. *Member:* American Anthropological Association, Southern Anthropological Society, Sigma Xi.

WRITINGS: (With Ronald Provencher) *Urban Anthropology,* W. C. Brown, 1976; (editor with David Guillet) *New Approaches to the Study of Migration,* Rice University Press, 1976. Also author of unpublished book, *Pueblo Joven: An Emerging Population in Lima, Peru.* Contributor to anthropology and sociology journals.

WORK IN PROGRESS: Anthropology, Ecology, and Systemics: An Expanded View of Ecological Anthropology; research on Mexican migrants to the southwestern United States.

SIDELIGHTS: Uzzell writes: "I became an anthropologist because I wasn't a good enough writer of fiction to make a living at it. I do not see very much difference between what I write as an anthropologist and what I wrote as a fiction writer. I regard anthropology as a language, a way of looking at the world based on a few fundamental concepts, which I find to be superior to the undergirding concepts of the other social sciences. In my research I am primarily interested in the economic decision-making of individuals, and the flow of power, wealth, and information through socio-economic systems.

"At the moment, I am particularly concerned with the social systems that generate urban wealth and poverty, and with Mexican migration to the United States. It seems to me that the latter phenomenon is grossly distorted by politicians, the press, and others who are acting either in ignorance or who benefit from creating misinformation."

V

VAGO, Bela Adalbert 1922-

PERSONAL: Born June 6, 1922, in Sighet, Romania; son of Avraham and Frieda (Fuchs) Vago; married Lidia Rosenfeld, 1945; children: Raphael, Ariel. *Education:* University of Cluj, M.A., 1947, Ph.D., 1949. *Home:* 4 Morad Hazamir, Haifa, Israel. *Office:* Department of History, Haifa University, Mount Carmel, Haifa, Israel.

CAREER: Bolyai University, Cluj, Romania, lecturer in history, 1949-57; Hebrew University of Jerusalem, Givat-Ram, Israel, research fellow at Institute of Research of the Holocaust, 1957-64, teaching fellow, 1964-75; Haifa University, Haifa, Israel, 1964—, began as lecturer, became senior lecturer, associate professor, professor of history, member of board of governors, head of department, 1970-72, head of Research Institute of the Holocaust Period, 1974—. Yad Vashem Institute, Jerusalem, Israel, research fellow, 1958-64, member of scientific advisory committee and board of governors. Head of Ghetto Fighters House. *Awards, honors:* Nordau Prize from the Hungarian-Jewish Organization, 1967, for historical works on Hungarian Jewry.

WRITINGS: The Szekler Society in the Eighteenth Century, Editura Stiintifica (Bucharest, Hungary), 1957; (editor with George L. Mosse) *Jews and Non-Jews in Eastern Europe, 1918-1945,* John Wiley, 1974; *The Shadow of the Swastika: The Rise of Fascism and Anti-Semitism in the Danube Basin, 1936-1939,* Saxon House, 1975; *Romanian Jewry During the Holocaust,* two volumes, Yad Vashem Institute, 1981; *Transylvania in World Politics,* Macmillan, 1981. Contributor of more than sixty articles and essays to scholarly journals. Member of editorial board of four scholarly journals.

WORK IN PROGRESS: Editing *The Comprehensive History of the Holocaust.*

SIDELIGHTS: Vago told *CA:* "My book about Transylvania will be the first which deals with the fate of this important area in the context of the great power rivalry in Europe. My two volumes about Jews in Romania will constitute the first comprehensive work about the once one-million-strong Jewish community. Romanian Jewry was one of the most heterogeneous Jewish communities of Europe, subject to more territorial and political changes than any other Jewish minority in Europe. The emphasis in this work is laid on the World War II period, when a high percentage of the Jews in Romania survived the Holocaust."

VALLEN, Jerome J(ay) 1928-

PERSONAL: Born October 2, 1928, in Philadelphia, Pa.; son of Harry and Frances Vallen; married Florence R. Levinson, 1950; children: Marc, Gary, Randy, Rebecca. *Education:* Cornell University, B.S., 1950, Ph.D., 1978; St. Lawrence University, M.Ed., 1959. *Office:* College of Hotel Administration, University of Nevada, Las Vegas, Nev. 89154.

CAREER: Commodore Hotel, Miami Beach, Fla., assistant manager, 1950; Adelphia Hotel, Philadelphia, Pa., beverage manager, 1953; State University of New York, Canton, professor and chairman of Department of Hotel and Food Service Administration, 1954-67; University of Nevada, Las Vegas, professor and dean of College of Hotel Administration, 1967—. Vice-president of University Associates, Inc. (consultants), 1972—. Resident auditor and assistant manager of Forest Hills Hotel, Franconia, N.H., summers, 1954-55; food service manager of Noyes Lodge, Cornell University, Ithaca, N.Y., 1959-60; general manager of Pine Tree Point Club, Alexandria Bay, N.Y., summer, 1964. Member of board of directors of Nevada World Trade and International Tourism Association and Grandissimo Hotel. *Member:* Council on Hotel, Restaurant, and Institutional Education (president, 1974-76; chairman of board, 1976-77).

WRITINGS: (With James R. Abbey and Dunnovan L. Sapienza) *The Art and Science of Modern Innkeeping,* Hayden, 1968, reprinted as *The Art and Science of Managing Hotels/Restaurants/Institutions,* 1978; *Organization and Administration in Innkeeping,* American Hotel and Motel Association, 1969; *Check In—Check Out: Principles of Effective Front Office Management,* W. C. Brown, 1974, revised edition, 1980; (with Abbey and Sapienza) *Readings in Hotel, Restaurant, and Institutional Management,* Ahrens, 1977; (contributor) Lester Bittel, editor, *Encyclopedia of Professional Management,* McGraw, 1978. Editorial consultant to William C. Brown Co.

* * *

VILDRAC, Charles
See MESSAGER, Charles

* * *

VILLERS, Robert 1921-1980

OBITUARY NOTICE: Born June 23, 1921, in Paris, France;

died January 18, 1980, in Paris, France. Journalist. Villers was editor of *France-Soir* from 1960 to 1972. He was also a contributor to newspapers in the United States and Switzerland. Obituaries and other sources: *Who's Who in the World,* 2nd edition, Marquis, 1973; *New York Times,* January 19, 1980.

* * *

VINGE, Joan D(ennison) 1948-

PERSONAL: Surname is pronounced *Vin*-jee; born April 2, 1948, in Baltimore, Md.; daughter of Seymour W. (an engineer) and Carol (an executive secretary; maiden name, Erwin) Dennison; married Vernor S. Vinge, January 17, 1972 (divorced December, 1979). *Education:* San Diego State University, B.A. (with highest honors), 1971. *Home:* 26 Douglas Rd., Chappaqua, N.Y. 10514. *Agent:* Frances Collin, Marie Rodell-Frances Collin Literary Agency, 156 East 52nd St., New York, N.Y. 10022.

CAREER: San Diego County, San Diego, Calif., salvage archaeologist, 1971; writer, 1974—. *Member:* Science Fiction Writers of America, Phi Kappa Phi, Alpha Mu Gamma. *Awards, honors:* Hugo Award for best novelette from 36th World Science Fiction Convention, 1977, for "Eyes of Amber."

WRITINGS—Science fiction: *Fireship* (collection), Signet, 1978; *The Outcasts of Heaven Belt* (novel), Signet, 1978; *Eyes of Amber and Other Stories,* Signet, 1979; *The Snow Queen* (novel), Dial, 1980.

Work represented in anthologies, including *Orbit 14,* 1974, and *Millennial Women.* Contributor to science fiction magazines, including *Analog, Galileo,* and *Isaac Asimov's Science Fiction Magazine.*

WORK IN PROGRESS: Psion, a novel about telepathy, for young adults, publication by Delacorte expected in 1981; research for a science fiction novel based on Hopi mythology, *The Origem Loop,* completion expected in 1982.

SIDELIGHTS: Joan Vinge writes: "I've been a science fiction reader since junior high school, although I've only been writing it for a few years. I write full time, but do most of my best writing after midnight, when there are no interruptions. I have written some poetry, although now I concentrate on prose.

"Originally I had planned to be an artist, but I wound up getting a degree in anthropology, and have worked as a salvage archaeologist. Anthropology is very similar to science fiction: they both give you fresh viewpoints for looking at 'human' behavior. Archaeology is the anthropology of the past, and science fiction is the anthropology of the future.

"I am very interested in mythology and mythological archetypes. *The Snow Queen* contains many elements inspired by Robert Graves's *The White Goddess.''*

AVOCATIONAL INTERESTS: Horseback riding, needlework, aerobic dance.

* * *

VINZ, Mark 1942-

PERSONAL: Born September 27, 1942, in Rugby, N.D.; son of George and Bernadine Vinz; married Elizabeth Casler, January 30, 1965; children: Katie, Sarah. *Education:* University of Kansas, B.A., 1964, M.A., 1966; further graduate study at University of New Mexico, 1966-68. *Home:* 510 Fifth Ave. S., Moorhead, Minn. 56560. *Office:* Department of English, Moorhead State University, Moorhead, Minn. 56560.

CAREER: Moorhead State University, Moorhead, Minn., assistant professor, 1968-77, associate professor of English, 1977—. President of Plains Distribution Service, Inc. (distributors of "little" magazines). Producer of "Poetry on the Prairie," on KCCM-FM Radio. Member of Library of Congress Conference on Publishing, 1975; member of individual artist panel of Minnesota State Arts Board; gives readings and workshops; works in the Poets in the Schools programs of Minnesota and North Dakota. *Awards, honors:* National Endowment for the Arts fellow, 1974-75.

WRITINGS—Books of poems: *Winter Poems,* Bookmark, 1975; *Letters to the Poetry Editor,* Capra, 1975; *Red River Blues,* Poetry Texas, 1977; *Songs for a Hometown Boy,* Solo Press, 1977; *Contingency Plans,* Ohio Review, 1978; *Deep Water, Dakota,* Juniper Press, 1979.

Work represented in anthologies, including *Heartland II: Poets of the Midwest,* Northern Illinois University Press; *A Geography of Poets,* Bantam. Contributor of poems to more than eighty magazines, including *Paris Review, Poetry Now, Poetry Northwest,* and *Nation.* Founding editor of *Dacotah Territory,* 1971—, and *Dakota Arts Quarterly,* 1977—.

WORK IN PROGRESS: Two books of poems.

SIDELIGHTS: Vinz comments: "I'm especially interested in the relationship between poetry and *place,* poetry and dream, poetry and the photographic image. For the past few years I've been very much involved with noncommercial publishing (small presses and little magazines), with the groundswell of activity that is taking place all across the country and is a sign that there is still both health and vitality in American publishing."

* * *

VISOCCHI, Mark 1938-

PERSONAL: Surname is pronounced Vee-*saw*-kee; born January 8, 1938, in Blairgowrie, Scotland; son of Serafino Fortunato and Jolanda (Forte) Visocchi; married Fiona Lynette Blair, July 20, 1967; children: Marisa Fiona, Nicola Anne. *Education:* Royal Scottish Academy of Music, diploma in music education (with honors), 1960. *Home:* 2 Coronation Way, Bearsden, Glasgow, Scotland. *Office:* Department of Music, Notre Dame College of Education, Bearsden, Glasgow, Scotland.

CAREER: Elementary and high school teacher of music in Perthshire, Scotland, 1961-63; principal teacher of music at grammar school in Argyllshire, Scotland, 1963-64; Callendar Park College of Education, Falkirk, Scotland, lecturer in music, 1964-78; Notre Dame College of Education, Glasgow, Scotland, head of music department, 1978—. *Member:* Society of Authors.

WRITINGS—All with David Jenkins: *Mix'n'Match* (juvenile), Universal Editions, 1977; *Children's Overture* (for children), Oxford University Press, 1978; *Mendelssohn in Scotland,* Chappell, 1978; *Portraits in Music* (young adult), Oxford University Press, Volume I, 1979, Volume II, 1980; *More Mix'n'Match,* Universal Editions, 1979. Author of "Mendelssohn in Scotland," aired by Scottish Television, July, 1979.

SIDELIGHTS: Visocchi writes: "My partnership with David Jenkins is based on our mutual interest in music education and began when we were both appointed to the staff of the music department at Callendar Park College.

"With the exception of *Mendelssohn in Scotland,* all Jenkins/Visocchi publications are intended for use in schools: *Children's Overture* is an introduction to songs and music activities for children at nursery and infant stages; *Mix'n'Match,* for use in elementary schools and junior division of high schools, is an approach to singing based on folk, traditional and 'pop' song combinations; and *Portraits in Music,* for high school students, is a collection of background material to be used in conjunction with pieces of music (including works by Ives, Gershwin, Copland, and Bernstein) for listening.''

*   *   *

VOIGT, Robert J(oseph) 1916-

PERSONAL: Born March 27, 1916, in Sauk Rapids, Minn.; son of Henry and Clara (Walz) Voigt. *Education:* Pontifical College Josephinum, B.A., 1938; Ohio State University, M.A. (Latin and Greek), 1948; St. Cloud State University, M.A. (English), 1970; St. John's University, Collegeville, Minn., M.Div., 1972. *Home and office:* 316 North Seventh Ave., St. Cloud, Minn. 56301.

CAREER: Ordained Roman Catholic priest, 1942; pastor of Roman Catholic churches in St. Cloud, Minn., 1942-45; Josephinum College, Worthington, Ohio, instructor in Latin and Greek, 1945-50; pastor of Roman Catholic churches in St. Cloud, Minn., 1950—; part-time instructor in English, at St. Cloud State University, 1969-78. Member of Maneage Tribunal, 1953—. Dean of St. Cloud Catholic Clergy, 1974-79. *Member:* Knights of Columbus.

WRITINGS: Symbols in Stained Glass, North Central Publishing, 1957; (translator) Ottile Mosshamer, *The Priest and Womanhood,* Newman Press, 1964; *Pierzana: A History of Pierz, Minnesota,* Mills Publishing, 1965; *Thomas Merton: A Different Drummer,* Liguori Publications, 1972; *The Arban Way: A History of Arban, Minnesota,* Volkmuth Printers, 1973; *Go to the Mountain: An Insight Into the Charismatic Renewal,* Abbey Press, 1975.

WORK IN PROGRESS: A History of the Holy Angels Parish, St. Cloud, Minnesota, publication expected by 1983.

SIDELIGHTS: Voigt writes: "I have been delighted that St. Cloud State University allowed me, a priest, to be on the faculty in the English department. This helped keep me young.

"I try to make a Holy Hour every day, spend one hour a day with God. I like to counsel people, help them have better lives by getting rid of guilt feelings and starting anew. I would like to build myself a little cabin near a lake with primitive facilties to spend a day per week there, away from everything, so that I can be a better person when back in the maelstrom. I am now sixty-three years old and thank God for every extra day I have.''

AVOCATIONAL INTERESTS: International travel (especially Europe).

*   *   *

von DREELE, W(illiam) H(enry) 1924-

PERSONAL: Born August 6, 1924, in New York, N.Y.; son of William H. (an engineer) and Helen M. (a registered nurse; maiden name, Wilhelmsen) von Dreele. *Education:* Middlebury College, B.A., 1949; New York University, M.A., 1950. *Politics:* Conservative. *Religion:* Presbyterian. *Home:* 255 West 84th St., New York, N.Y. 10024.

CAREER: International Business Machines World Trade Corp., White Plains, N.Y., staff writer, 1954-79; free-lance writer, 1979—. *Military service:* U.S. Army, 1943-46; became technical sergeant.

WRITINGS: If Liberals Had Feathers . . . (poems), Devin-Adair, 1967; *There's Something About a Liberal* (poems), Arlington House, 1970. Contributing editor of *National Review,* 1960—.

SIDELIGHTS: Von Dreele writes: ''My first verse, submitted to William F. Buckley's *National Review* in 1960, had Marya Mannes as an ideal. Through the sixties (and earlier) Miss Mannes contributed stylish, witty lines to *Reporter.* Although my first efforts were turned down, I was persistent—some say aggressive.

"In any event, first one, then two 'von Dreeles' began appearing in *National Review* until one wonderful day I received a note from the editor-in-chief asking if I could be listed as a contributor. But of course! Of course!

"Writing verse for a fortnightly requires, besides the amusement value of the material, a constant reading of the daily press. When one works for IBM, as I did, this means a great deal of covert, secret reading. If an election takes place on the Tuesday before closing, Mr. Buckley likes to have comments on said election; this denies the verse writer the luxury of preparing material the weekend before. It must be current. If not current, it must have wit and bite.

"Writing verse for a national audience means correspondence with readers. The readers of *National Review* are a most literate group, and the first to spot any slight faltering in utterly precise rhyme and meter. One of my most prized possessions is a reputation for sanitation in rhyme and utter orthodoxy in meter. I have yet to lose a battle in the letters column on this subject. And woe to the correspondent who implies that 'doggerel' is to be used interchangeably with verse. No and no and no.

"Is verse then on the way up? Not really. Verse is still used as filler by the slicks. (Verse in this sense is NOT used interchangeably with that much more demanding discipline, poetry.) And when it comes to political verse—my specialty—one must go back to the eighteenth-century Augustans to find the genre. Most people today expect verse to describe kitchen comics (as in the *Wall Street Journal*) or bland, 'nature' observations (as in *Good Housekeeping*). Only in Mr. Buckley's *National Review* is a verse writer rewarded for wit, bite, nastiness, throw-weight, and an ability to get under the skin.''

*   *   *

von HIPPEL, Frank 1937-

PERSONAL: Born December 26, 1937, in Cambridge, Mass.; son of Arthur R. (a physicist) and Dagmar (Franck) von Hippel; divorced; children: Paul. *Education:* Massachusetts Institute of Technology, B.S., 1959; Oxford University, D.Phil., 1962. *Office:* Center for Energy and Environmental Studies, Princeton University, Princeton, N.J. 08540.

CAREER: University of Chicago, Chicago, Ill., research associate at Enrico Fermi Institute for Nuclear Studies, 1962-64; Cornell University, Ithaca, N.Y., research associate at Newman Laboratory for Nuclear Studies, 1964-66; Stanford University, Stanford, Calif., assistant professor of physics, 1966-69; Lawrence Berkeley Laboratory, Berkeley, Calif., research fellow, 1969-70; Argonne National Laboratory, Argone, Ill., associate physicist in High Energy Physics Division, 1970-73; National Academy of Sciences, Washington, D.C., resident fellow, 1973-74; Princeton University, Princeton, N.J., research physicist, 1974-78, senior research physicist at Center for Energy and Environmental Studies, 1978—. Member of National Research Council panel on breeder reactor safety, 1976-77, steering committee of Breeder Reactor Program Review, 1977, risk assessment review group of Nuclear Regulatory Commission, 1977-78, U.S. delegation to International Fuel Cycle Evaluation, 1977-78, subcommittee on science for citizens, of National Science Foundation, 1977—, and New York City public health advisory committee on radiation, 1978. Testified before U.S. Senate and House of Representatives.

MEMBER: American Physical Society, American Association for the Advancement of Science (member of council, 1974-76), Federation of American Scientists (member of council, 1975—; chairman, 1979—). *Awards, honors:* Rhodes scholar, 1959-62; A. P. Sloan Foundation fellow, 1969-70; shared American Physical Society Forum Award for Promoting the Understanding of the Relationship of Physics and Society, 1977.

WRITINGS: (With Joel Primack) *Advice and Dissent: Scientists in the Political Arena,* Basic Books, 1974. Contributor of about forty articles to scientific journals and newspapers. Member of editorial advisory board of *Bulletin of the Atomic Scientists,* 1975—.

WORK IN PROGRESS: Policy analysis in the areas of automotive fuel economy and solar energy.

SIDELIGHTS: Von Hippel told *CA:* "My writings concern the necessity to protect dissenters within organizations from retaliation if they object to decisions by their organizations which may endanger the public health and welfare."

*   *   *

von KASCHNITZ-WEINBERG, Marie Luise 1901-1974

(Marie Luise Kaschnitz)

OBITUARY NOTICE: Born January 31, 1901, in Karlsruhe, Baden, Germany; died in 1974. Poet, essayist, novelist, and playwright. Kaschnitz married archaeologist Guido Kaschnitz-Weinberg in 1925 and published her first novel, *Liebe beginnt,* in 1933. After World War II, she began writing poetry using traditional forms that called for a return to classicism. She also wrote numerous essays and radio plays,

and her 1960 book, *Lange Schatten,* was translated into English and published in 1973 as *Long Shadows.* Her other writings included *Neue Gedichte, Dein Schweigen meine Stimme,* and *Ein Wort weiter,* all poetry, and such prose works as *Wohin denn ich, Gustave Courbet,* and *Tage, Tage, Jahre.* Obituaries and other sources: *Encyclopedia of World Literature in the Twentieth Century,* updated edition, Ungar, 1967; *The Penguin Companion to European Literature,* McGraw, 1969; *Cassell's Encyclopaedia of World Literature,* revised edition, Morrow, 1973; *The International Who's Who,* Europa, 1974; *The Oxford Companion to German Literature,* Clarendon Press, 1976.

*   *   *

VORZIMMER, Peter J. 1937-

PERSONAL: Born May 7, 1937, in New York, N.Y.; son of Jefferson J. and Florence E. Vorzimmer; children: Jefferson, Mark, Jennifer, Jessica. *Education:* University of California, Santa Barbara, B.A., 1958; St. Catharine's College, Cambridge, Ph.D., 1963; law studies at University of Pennsylvania, 1978—. *Home:* 2245 Wallace St., Philadelphia, Pa. 19130. *Office:* Department of History, Temple University, Philadelphia, Pa. 19122.

CAREER: NSA, Washington, D.C., consultant, 1958-69; Time, Inc., London, England, stringer for *Time* and *Life,* 1960-63; historian of "Gemini" project for National Aeronautics and Space Administration, Manned Spacecraft Center; SITA, Inc. (travel company), Philadelphia, Pa., president, 1969-72; currently associated with Temple University, Philadelphia. *Member:* Mensa, Cult (science fiction group; founder).

WRITINGS: Project Gemini: A Chronological History, U.S. Government Printing Office, 1970; *Charles Darwin: The Years of Controversy,* Temple University Press, 1971. Contributor to magazines, including *Playboy.*

SIDELIGHTS: Vorzimmer writes: "I have run with the bulls in Pamplona every year since 1965."

AVOCATIONAL INTERESTS: Flying.

W

WADSWORTH, Michael E(dwin) J(ohn) 1942-

PERSONAL: Born January 20, 1942, in High Wycombe, England; son of Cecil (a probation officer) and Amelia (a teacher; maiden name, Gray) Wadsworth; married Jane Arnott (a statistician), December 17, 1966; children: Emma, Harry. *Education:* University of Leeds, B.A., 1963, M.Phil., 1969; London School of Economics and Political Science, London, Ph.D., 1977. *Home:* 57 Pembroke Rd., Bristol 8, England. *Office:* Medical Research Council Survey of Health and Development, Department of Community Medicine, University of Bristol, Canynge Hall, Whiteladies Rd., Bristol 8, England.

CAREER: University of London, London, England, research assistant in social science at Guy's Hospital Medical School, 1963-66; University of Edinburgh, Medical School, Edinburgh, Scotland, research fellow in social science, 1966-68; London School of Economics and Political Science, London, member of scientific staff of the Medical Research Council unit for the study of environmental factors in mental and physical illness, 1968-79; University of Bristol, Bristol, England, member of scientific staff of Medical Research Council's National Survey of Health and Development, 1979—. *Member:* British Society for Social Medicine, Association of Child Psychology and Psychiatry.

WRITINGS: (With W.J.H. Butterfield and R. Blaney) *Health and Sickness: The Choice of Treatment,* Tavistock Publications, 1971; (editor with D. Robinson) *Studies in Everyday Medical Life,* Martin Robertson, 1976; *Roots of Delinquency, Infancy, Adolescence, and Crime,* Barnes & Noble, 1979.

Contributor: G. McLachlan, editor, *Problems and Progress in Medical Care,* Oxford University Press, 1966; S. B. Burman and H. G. Genn, editors, *Accidents in the Home,* Croom Helm, 1977; S. B. Sells, M. Roff, J. S. Strauss, and W. Pollin, editors, *Human Functioning in Longitudinal Perspective,* Williams & Wilkins, 1980; M. J. Christie and P. G. Mellett, editors, *Psychosomatic Approaches to Medicine: Behavioral Science Foundations,* Wiley, 1980; F. A. Boddy, F. M. Martin, and M. Jeffreys, editors, *The Behavioral Sciences in General Practice,* Tavistock Publications, 1980. Contributor to medical and social science journals.

WORK IN PROGRESS: Continuing studies of child-rearing methods and offspring of more than five thousand people observed since their birth in 1946.

SIDELIGHTS: In a Medical Research Council pamphlet, Michael Wadsworth explained the National Survey of Health and Development: "The National Survey of Health and Development is a longitudinal study of a wide range of social, psychological and medical characteristics and experiences in the lives of 5362 individuals living in England, Wales and Scotland. It was begun at the time of their birth in March 1946 and has continued, with only very small losses, to the present day. Two other large, national longitudinal studies have since been started by other investigators, one in 1958 and the most recent in 1970. There is a particular advantage to be gained from the existence of three studies of this nature, since the present work began before the inception of the National Health Service and when education was almost wholly selective, and the others began after the National Health Service and when education had become almost entirely nonselective. Comparisons between the studies to look for the effects of policy change are already being carried out."

* * *

WAGEMAKER, Herbert, Jr. 1929-

PERSONAL: Born December 17, 1929, in East Grand Rapids, Mich.; son of Herbert (a grocery store owner) and Maude (Meyers) Wagemaker; married Mary Ann Lomel, June 16, 1956; children: Robyn, Roberta, Lori. *Education:* Wheaton College, Wheaton, Ill., B.A., 1952; University of Michigan, M.S., 1957; Hahnemann Medical School, M.D., 1961. *Home:* 6612 Falls Creek Rd., Louisville, Ky. 40222. *Office:* Louisville General Hospital, 323 East Chestnut St., Louisville, Ky. 40202.

CAREER: Detroit Receiving Hospital, Detroit, Mich., intern, 1961-62; Duval Medical Center, Jacksonville, Fla., resident in surgery, 1962-63; University of Florida, Gainesville, resident in surgery and gastric physiology, 1963-65; practiced general medicine in Gainesville, 1965-67; University of Florida, physician in infirmary, 1967-69, resident in psychiatry, 1969-72; Community Mental Health, Gainesville, psychiatrist and director of inpatient psychiatric unit, 1972-75; Louisville General Hospital, Louisville, Ky., director of inpatient psychiatry, 1975-78, and outpatient psychiatry, 1978, director of section on renal dialysis research in schizophrenia, 1978—. Member of faculty at Young Life Graduate Training Institute, 1972-73; assistant professor at University of Louisville, 1975—. Founder, organizer, and director of

Gainesville's young life program, 1965-71. *Military service:* U.S. Army, 1953-55; served in Korea. *Member:* American Psychiatric Association, Society for Biological Psychiatry. *Awards, honors:* National Institute of Mental Health grant, 1978.

WRITINGS: Why Can't I Understand My Kids?, Zondervan, 1973; *A Special Kind of Belonging,* Word, Inc., 1978. Contributor of about fifteen articles to medical journals.

WORK IN PROGRESS: Continuing research on schizophrenia.

SIDELIGHTS: Wagemaker writes: "My basic interest revolves around psychiatric treatment of people in the inner city and people who are poor. Along with this, I'm also involved in research that deals with the use of hemodialysis in the treatment of schizophrenia. I'm very interested in the biological aspects of mental illness. I believe that the major psychiatric illnesses are biological and that they include schizophrenia, manic depressive illness, psychotic depression and schizo-affective illness. We will be finding in the next decade or two the causative agents and ways to inhibit these agents in the treatment of these illnesses."

Wagemaker added a word about his books: "*Why Can't I Understand My Kids?* is about the relationships between adolescents and their parents. *A Special Kind of Belonging* talks about Christian community and the ramifications of that in a person's life."

* * *

WAGMAN, Robert John 1942-

PERSONAL: Born November 11, 1942, in Chicago, Ill.; married Carol Ann Mueller; children: Jennifer, Robert, Patricia, Marilyn. *Education:* St. Louis University, B.A., 1965, M.A., 1968, J.D., 1971. *Home:* 8806 First Ave., Silver Spring, Md. 20910. *Office:* North American Newspaper Alliance, 890 National Press Building, Washington, D.C. 20045.

CAREER: Dun & Bradstreet, Inc., St. Louis, Mo., began as reporter trainee, became reporter, special reporter, and supervisor, 1963-66; Columbia Broadcasting System News, with News Election Unit, 1966-68, regional manager of News Election Service in Atlanta, Ga., 1968-69; St. Louis University, St. Louis, Mo., assistant to dean of School of Law and director of Student Medical/Legal Institute and continuing legal education program, 1969-73; Columbia Broadcasting System News, producer for Midwest Bureau in Chicago, Ill., 1973-75, Evening News Investigative Unit in New York City, 1975-76, and "Sixty Minutes" in New York City, 1976-77; North American Newspaper Alliance, Washington, D.C., bureau chief, 1977—, and chief political correspondent. Producer and consultant for KMOX-TV, 1969-70; chief investigative reporter for North American Newspaper Alliance, 1973-76. *Awards, honors:* Thomas Stokes Award from Washington Journalism Center, 1976, for reporting on environmental issues.

WRITINGS: (With Sheldon Engelmayer) *Hubert Humphrey: The Man and His Dream,* Methuen, 1978; (with Engelmayer) *Guide to the Tax Revolt,* Dale Books, 1978, revised edition, Arlington House, 1980. Contributor to magazines, including *Nation's Business.*

WORK IN PROGRESS: Two nonfiction works, a novel, and a screenplay, all with Sheldon Engelmayer.

SIDELIGHTS: Wagman's investigative reporting concentrates on the American political scene, but assignments for "Sixty Minutes" and Walter Cronkite's news program include reports on strip mining, nuclear power, and automo-

bile fuel tank construction. He covered the Wounded Knee Indian occupation for North American Newspaper Alliance, as well as the Rockefeller family, federal bank examinations, and the activities of Richard Nixon and his entourage during the Watergate proceedings.

* * *

WAHLBERG, Rachel Conrad 1922-

PERSONAL: Born December 23, 1922, in High Point, N.C.; daughter of Flavius (a minister) and Mary (a teacher; maiden name, Huffman) Conrad; married Philip L. Wahlberg (a church executive), June 1, 1946; children: David, Christopher, Pauli, Sharon. *Education:* Lenoir Rhyne College, B.A. (summa cum laude), 1944; University of Virginia, M.A., 1945; attended University of Texas, 1974-76. *Religion:* Lutheran. *Home:* 5804 Cary Dr., Austin, Tex. 78757. *Office:* Department of Industrial Education, University of Texas, Austin, Tex. 78701.

CAREER: English teacher at private academy in Winston-Salem, N.C., 1945-46; Armstrong Junior College, Savannah, Ga., instructor in English and German, 1946-47; University of Texas, Austin, instructor in management, 1976—. Member of faculty at Texas Lutheran College, 1974, 1976. Member of church governing committees and advisory groups. Conducted lecture tour in 1972; speaker at conventions and retreats in the United States, Korea, and Japan. *Member:* National Organization for Women, Common Cause, Women in Communication. *Awards, honors:* LL.D. from Bethany College, Lindsborg, Kan., 1972.

WRITINGS: Leave a Little Dust, Fortress, 1971; *Jesus According to a Woman,* Paulist/Newman, 1975; (with John C. Cooper) *Your Exciting Middle Years,* Word Books, 1976; *Jesus and the Freed Woman,* Paulist/Newman, 1978. Contributor of more than one hundred-fifty articles to religious magazines, including *Lutheran, New Catholic World, Theology Today,* and *Lutheran Women.* Author and publisher of *Women's Network News* (Christian feminist newsletter).

SIDELIGHTS: Rachel Wahlberg wrote: "My two books on Jesus and women have brought me the most popularity because apparently I touched on a sore spot with thousands of women—the inability of the Christian churches to see them as other than an Eve or a relational human being. Christianity has reflected and reinforced the sexist institutions not only of our society but of the first-century and later societies in which it grew. I began to re-interpret some scriptural stories and images according to a woman's feelings and perceptions. This coincided with the women's movement which was already opening women's eyes to their potentials and to the way patriarchal institutions had treated them. Now many women theologians, and some men, are also doing this sort of re-interpretation. Even radical conservative groups such as Roman Catholics and Missouri Lutherans are being forced to consider why women are not permitted to be priests and ministers."

* * *

WALDO, Myra

PERSONAL: Born in New York, N.Y.; daughter of Mortimer (a manufacturer) and Dora (Rogoff) Waldo; married Robert J. Schwartz (an attorney and writer). *Education:* Attended Columbia University. *Home:* 900 Fifth Ave., New York, N.Y. 10021.

CAREER: Macmillan Publishing Co., New York City, special projects director, 1965-70; WCBS, New York City, food and travel editor, 1968-72; free-lance writer, 1972—. Consultant to airlines and hotels. *Member:* Overseas Press Club of America (member of board of governors), American Women in Radio and Television, Society of Magazine Writers, Society of American Travel Writers (vice-president), New York Society of Travel Writers.

WRITINGS—All cookbooks; except as noted: (Editor) *The Complete Round-the-World Cookbook: Recipes Gathered by Pan American World Airways From the 84 Countries They Serve, With Food and Travel Comments by Myra Waldo,* Doubleday, 1954, revised edition, 1973; *Serve at Once: The Souffle Cookbook,* Crowell, 1954, revised edition published as *The Souffle Cookbook,* Collier, 1961; (with Gertrude Berg) *The Molly Goldberg Cookbook,* Doubleday, 1955; (contributor) *Little & Ives Family Health Encyclopedia* (popular medicine), Little & Ives, 1956; *Dining Out in Any Language,* Bantam, 1956, revised edition, 1962; *The Slenderella Cook Book,* Putnam, 1957; *Beer and Good Food,* Doubleday, 1958; *1001 Ways to Please a Husband,* Van Nostrand, 1958; *The Diners' Club Cookbook: Great Recipes From Great Restaurants,* Farrar, Straus, 1959, revised edition published as *Great Recipes From Great Restaurants,* Collier, 1966.

The Complete Book of Gourmet Cooking for the American Kitchen, Putnam, 1960; *The Complete Book of Oriental Cooking,* McKay, 1960; *Cooking for the Freezer,* Doubleday, 1960; *The Slenderella Cook Book: The Complete Reducing Cook Book for the Whole Family,* 1960; *The Art of South American Cookery,* Doubleday, 1961; *Cooking for Your Heart and Health,* Putnam, 1961; *Cook as the Romans Do: Recipies [sic] of Rome and Northern Italy,* Collier, 1961; *Cooking From the Pantry Shelf,* Collier, 1962; *The Complete Book of Vegetable Cookery; or, How to Cook Vegetables so Your Family and Friends Will Rave About Them and You,* Bantam, 1962; *Cakes, Cookies, and Pastries,* Collier, 1962; *The Hamburger Cookbook,* Collier, 1962; *The Casserole Cookbook,* Collier, 1963; *The Pleasures of Wine: A Guide to the Wines of the World,* Crowell-Collier, 1963; *The Home Book of Barbecue Cooking,* Fawcett, 1963; *The Pancake Cookbook,* Bantam, 1963; *The Art of Spaghetti Cookery,* Doubleday, 1964; *The Complete Round-the-World Hors D'Oeuvre Book,* Doubleday, 1964; *Complete Meals in One Dish,* Doubleday, 1965; *The Complete Book of Wine Cookery,* Bantam, 1965; *The Flavor of Spain: A Basic Spanish Cookbook,* Macmillan, 1965.

Inter-continental Gourmet Cookbook, Macmillan, 1967; *The International Encyclopedia of Cooking,* two volumes, Macmillan, 1967, Volume II published separately as *Dictionary of International Food and Cooking Terms,* Macmillan, 1967; *The Complete Round-the-World Meat Cookbook,* Doubleday, 1967; *Round-the-World Diet Cookbook,* Macmillan, 1968; *Chinese Cookbook,* Macmillan, 1968; *Restaurant Guide to New York City and Vicinity,* Collier, 1971, 3rd revised edition published as *Myra Waldo's Restaurant Guide to New York City and Vicinity,* 1978; *The Diet Delight Cookbook,* Macmillan, 1971; *Seven Wonders of the Cooking World,* Dodd, 1971; *The Low Salt, Low Cholesterol Cookbook,* Putnam, 1972; *Myra Waldo's Dessert Cookbook,* Macmillan, 1973; *Lose Pounds the Low-Carbohydrate Way,* New American Library, 1973; *The Great International Barbeque Book,* McGraw, 1979.

Travel books: *Travel Guide to Europe,* Farrar, Straus, 1960, revised edition, Macmillan, 1966; *Travel Guide to Europe: The Mediterranean and Northern Europe,* Bantam, 1960; *Travel Guide to Europe: The British Isles and Western Europe,* Bantam, 1960; *Myra Waldo's Travel and Motoring Guide to Europe,* Macmillan, 1964, 7th edition, 1979; *Myra Waldo's Travel Guide to the Orient and the Pacific,* Macmillan, 1964, 7th edition, 1978; *Myra Waldo's Travel Guide to South America,* Macmillan, 1968, 3rd edition, 1976; *Japan Expo '70 Guide,* Collier, 1970.

*   *   *

WALES, Robert   1923-

PERSONAL: Born July 12, 1923, in Greenock, Scotland; son of Robert (a provision merchant) and Agnes (McKenzie) Wales; married Joan Austin, 1947 (divorced, 1970); married Susan Claire Richardson, May 15, 1970; children: (first marriage) Angela, Katrina Wales Blomfield, Philomena Wales O'Neill, Aidan, Robert; (second marriage) Duncan-John. *Education:* Received certificate in agriculture, 1952, and certificate in navigation, 1978. *Politics:* "Apolitical." *Religion:* None. *Home and office:* 2 Thorne St., London S.W.13, England. *Agent:* Fraser & Dunlop Ltd., 91 Regent St., London W.1, England.

CAREER: Worked as analytical chemist, 1941; textile machine parts manufacturer, 1947-49; company director in textiles in Australia, 1949-53; sheep and cattle farmer in Australia, 1953-62; gold prospector in Australia, 1962-63; television presentation assistant for Australian Broadcasting Commission, 1963-66; television director for American Broadcasting Corp. (ABC), 1966-69; Visnews, London, England, film producer, 1972-73; writer, 1973—. Also worked as landscape painter and artist. *Military service:* Royal Navy, Fleet Air Arm, 1939-46; served in Pacific theater; became lieutenant (A).

MEMBER: Authors Lending and Copyright Society, British Academy of Film and Television Arts, Society of Authors (chairperson of broadcasting committee and radio awards), Writers Guild of Great Britain. *Awards, honors:* First prize from University of New England play competition, 1960; FNQATA drama competition award, 1961; winner of Coff's Harbour National Play Competition, 1961; British Academy of Film and Television Arts award, 1976.

WRITINGS: The Cell, Evans Brothers, 1971.

Stage plays: 'Wings on the Morning," "White Bird Passing," "The Hobby Horse," "The Grotto."

Television plays: "The Swallow's Nest." Writer for television series, including "Ten Who Dared," "The Crossroads of Civilization," and "Luke's Kingdom." Author of radio plays. Contributor of articles and stories to magazines.

WORK IN PROGRESS: A book of Australian short stories; a biographical novel on international gold smuggling.

SIDELIGHTS: Wales told *CA:* "Suffering from cultural withdrawal symptoms after nine years in the Australian bush, I believe I turned to writing as a survival therapy and got stuck with it. The main attraction continues to be the examination of man's condition and a study of conflicts. Tragedy of the classical Greek variety has such magnetism for me that I often have to pull back from it deliberately. But I also like to inject most things with humor. The greatest writing influences in my life have been Tolstoy and Haldor Laxness in the novel, and Sophocles and Eugene O'Neill in drama, while Conrad still holds my first prize when writing about the sea."

*   *   *

WALKER, Danton (MacIntyre)   1899-1960

OBITUARY NOTICE: Born July 26, 1899, in Marietta, Ga.;

died August 8, 1960. Journalist and author. Walker was the author of a popular syndicated column for the *New York Daily News*. He also wrote *Spooks Deluxe* and *Guide to New York Night Life*, as well as an autobiography, *Danton's Inferno: The Story of a Columnist*. Obituaries and other sources: *Who Was Who in America*, 4th edition, Marquis, 1968; *American Authors and Books, 1640 to the Present Day*, Crown, 1972.

* * *

WALKER, Geoffrey James 1936-

PERSONAL: Born May 29, 1936, in Liverpool, England; son of Frank (a banker) and Hilda (Pass) Walker; married Ana Carmen Maria Antonia Espinosa (a researcher), December 28, 1958. *Education:* Cambridge University, B.A., 1958, M.A., 1961, and Ph.D., 1963. *Politics:* "Moderate Centre." *Religion:* Christian. *Home:* 35 Thornton Rd., Cambridge CB3 0NP, England. *Office:* Faculty of Modern and Medieval Languages, Cambridge University, Cambridge CB3 0DG, England.

CAREER: Cambridge University, Cambridge, England, lecturer in Spanish and fellow of Fitzwilliam College, 1967—, director of studies in modern and medieval languages, 1974—. Academic adviser to University of Guyana. *Member:* Associacio Internacional Llengua i Literatura Catalanes (founding secretary), Asociacion Internacional de Hispanistas, Association of Hispanists of Great Britain and Ireland, Anglo-Catalan Society (treasurer).

WRITINGS: Politica Espanola y Comercio Colonial, 1700-1789, Ariel, 1979, translation published as *Spanish Politics and Imperial Trade, 1700-1789*, Indiana University Press, 1979. Contributor to *Year's Work in Modern Language Studies*.

WORK IN PROGRESS: The British Government of the Island of Minorca in the Eighteenth Century.

SIDELIGHTS: Walker writes: "I am interested in the Hispanic world in general, and within that world, regional and national questions in which group empathies and antipathies may be observed. My particular interests are Catalan studies and the history of Latin America (especially the colonial period), and recently I have also been developing an interest in eighteenth-century Anglo-Spanish relations in the fields of cultural and economic history.

"I take an active interest in modern-language teaching in schools. I believe there should be a maximum of cooperation and understanding between university and school teachers in the preparation of students, and I work to promote a fruitful relationship. I also believe in international cooperation at all levels. I am a strong supporter of the European Economic Community."

Walker's languages are Castilian, Catalan, French, Portuguese, and Italian. He has traveled widely throughout Europe and Latin America.

* * *

WALKER, Hill M(ontague) 1939-

PERSONAL: Born June 21, 1939, in Front Royal, Va.; son of Deward Edgar (in insurance sales) and Matilda (a teacher; maiden name, Clark) Walker; married Janet Eaton (a reading teacher), August 22, 1964; children: Seth Clark. *Education:* Eastern Oregon College, B.A. (cum laude), 1962; University of Oregon, M.A., 1964, Ph.D. (with honors), 1967. *Home:* 3230 Fillmore St., Eugene, Ore. 97405. *Office:* College of Education, Division of Special Education, University of Oregon, Room 206, Eugene, Ore. 97403.

CAREER: Junior high school teacher of English and social studies in Eugene, Ore., 1962-63; University of Oregon, Eugene, assistant professor, 1967-70, associate professor, 1970-75, professor of special education, 1975—, director of Center at Oregon for Research in the Behavioral Education of the Handicapped, 1971-79. Member of professional advisory board of Regional Child Study Center, 1973—; member of boards of directors and task forces on mental health; conducts workshops on classroom behavior management. *Military service:* Oregon National Guard, 1958-64. *Awards, honors:* Grants from Early Childhood Education Center, 1969-71, Center at Oregon for Research in the Behavioral Education of the Handicapped, 1971-79, U.S. Bureau of Education for the Handicapped, 1974-77 and 1974-76, and U.S. Office of Education, 1979-82.

WRITINGS: (With N. K. Buckley) *Modifying Classroom Behavior*, Research Press, 1970; (contributor) W. C. Becker, editor, *An Empirical Basis for Change in Education*, Science Research Associates, 1971; (contributor) L. A. Hamerlynck, L. C. Handy, and E. F. Mash, editors, *Behavior Change: Methodology, Concepts, and Practice*, Research Press, 1973; (with Buckley) *Token Reinforcement Techniques*, E-B Press, 1974; *The Acting Out Child: Coping With Disruptive Classroom Behavior*, Allyn & Bacon, 1979. Author of tests and behavior management packages. Guest reviewer for *Journal of Applied Behavior Analysis*, 1968-71, member of board of editors, 1972-74.

WORK IN PROGRESS: A book on behavior disorders in children, for graduate students, with Hyman Hops and Charles R. Greenwood, publication by Allyn & Bacon expected in 1982; a book on behavior disorders in children, for professional educators, Allyn & Bacon, 1984; research on mainstreaming of handicapped children in school and on a model program for inservice training of teachers.

SIDELIGHTS: Walker's work is with the negatively aggressive/disruptive child in the classroom, and most of his research and teaching is aimed at correcting this kind of disruptive behavior. But he has also developed a program for increasing the social interaction of the shy withdrawn child with poor social skills, suggesting that his more general concern is the integration of all children into a functional and productive classroom situation.

Walker wrote: "I am generally an active, intense person who must always be occupied with something. I have been strongly achievement-oriented all my life.

"Since 1966 I have been totally involved in conducting federally-funded research and development activities on behavior disorders in children.

"I am considered an expert on classroom management, but conducting research on behavior disorders is what I do best. I enjoy the entire process, from the initial concept to writing the results. The feedback from published material is another source of motivation to continue producing."

AVOCATIONAL INTERESTS: Foreign travel, horseback riding, golf, tennis, basketball, chess, bridge.

* * *

WALKER, Robert W(ayne) 1948-

PERSONAL: Born November 17, 1948, in Corinth, Miss.; son of Richard Herman (a truck driver) and Janie (McEachern) Walker; married Cheryl Ann Ernst (an accountant), September 8, 1967; children: Stephen Robert. *Education:* Northwestern University, B.S., 1971, M.S., 1972. *Politics:* "Nonpartisan." *Home:* 1062 Hecker Dr., Elgin, Ill.

60120. *Agent:* Jane Jordan Browne, 410 South Michigan, Chicago, Ill. 60605. *Office:* American Dietetic Association, 430 North Michigan, Chicago, Ill. 60611.

CAREER: Elementary school teacher in La Grange Park, Ill., 1971-72; Northwestern University, Evanston, Ill., associate registrar, 1972-76; American Dietetic Association, Chicago, Ill., assistant coordinator of records, 1976—. Substitute teacher.

WRITINGS: Sub-Zero! (suspense novel), Belmont-Tower, 1979. Contributor of articles, stories, and reviews to magazines.

WORK IN PROGRESS: Brain Games, a murder mystery and science fiction; *Hell Stirred,* a novel about John Brown's followers at Harper's Ferry; *Satan Transformed,* a novel set in Salem, Mass., in 1692, publication expected in 1982; *The Adventures of Daniel Webster Jackson,* a historical novel for young adults, publication expected in 1983.

SIDELIGHTS: Walker writes: "I begin a murder mystery with a chapter which raises untold questions, for which no one knows the answers, not even me. All my books require an evolutionary period in which plot and character percolate, grow, ripen, and answer the questions created in the first chapter. I combine the murder mystery with science fiction/science fact in a 'what if' plot. All of my science fiction is careful to build on science fact. A 'what if' plot is the basic tool of the science fiction and mystery writer. What if the sun doesn't come up tomorrow? What if it starts to rain and never stops? What if all the plants begin to die? What happens to people?

"My purpose in writing at all is to fulfill a need in myself. I feel empty when I'm not writing in the same way a star athlete feels when he's warming the bench. Behind *Sub-Zero* there lurks a purpose that is less personal, that being to popularize a body of knowledge, a science—meterology—for people. My next book is a murder mystery with just as much science fiction in the area of brain research. *Brain Games,* I hope, makes brain research fascinating and understandable for the general public. Shakespeare wrote about Queen Elizabeth's court in much the same way, to popularize a mysterious arena.

"I have returned to the historical novels I began before I published *Sub-Zero,* turning them into 'mystery histories'. In effect, the principles used in writing a winning murder mystery can and should be applied to writing historical fiction to culminate in a fast-paced historical novel that enhances and retains the integrity of historic fact. Salem witchcraft in 1692 is the subject of *Satan Transformed.* The subject matter is complex, the stories manifold and fragmented, the documents white with dust. How does one pull it all together? Dramatic plot development and dramatic dialogue mouthed by knowledgeable, real characters, that's how. The Salem experience has always been relegated to an unimportant place in American history, made into a parable for McCarthyism or a fable to frighten children with. Only the novel form, embracing the mystery of all time—Satan's transformations—can do the complex story justice.

"I began writing in the mystery genre late, having completed two-and-one-half historical novels, my first in high school. I wish I had begun my first novel as a mystery. Writing the mystery teaches you to plot and plot tightly, shoring up a sagging middle and tying up loose ends. Most importantly, it teaches you to write in a compelling manner, so that any 'dull' science or 'history' can be made exciting if someone's become a 'victim' of the science or the history.

"Every novel I've written has taught me the truth of doing: writing is an activity. Learning to write is not theoretical classroom stuff. It's a professional activity. No class can teach the craft. You become a craftsman at writing by doing it—picking up pen, pencil, typewriter, and going after the words. 'Write' is active, so if you're going to write, do it actively. Write your novel and don't look back. If the draft you complete is a terrible novel, you rewrite it or you go on to another, but in the original writing (and rewriting) you learn more than anyone can teach. It's here you learn your limitations, strengths, likes, dislikes, and style.

"Publishers are turning to the manuscripts that come to them in polished, final form. They have the upper hand in that they are daily supplied with much more than they *can* publish, so why not simply dispose of the immature and messy manuscript immediately?"

BIOGRAPHICAL/CRITICAL SOURCES: Esprit, July, 1979; *Elgin Herald,* July 2, 1979.

*   *   *

WALKER, Ronald G(ary) 1945-

PERSONAL: Born September 12, 1945, in South Gate, Calif.; son of Ty C. (a life insurance agent) and Edna (Trammell) Walker; married Leslie Tucker (a La Leche League leader), November 24, 1967; children: Matthew Gregory, Ryan Geoffrey. *Education:* University of Redlands, B.A., 1967; University of California, Los Angeles, M.A., 1968; University of Maryland, Ph.D., 1974; postdoctoral study at University of California, Irvine, 1977. *Home:* 2305 Terrace St., Victoria, Tex. 77901. *Office:* Division of Arts and Sciences, University of Houston, Victoria Campus, 2302-C Red River St., Victoria, Tex. 77901.

CAREER: Barber-Scotia College, Concord, N.C., instructor in English, 1968-69; University of Maryland, College Park, part-time instructor in English, 1969-72; University of Houston, Victoria Campus, Victoria, Tex., instructor, 1973-74, assistant professor, 1974-78, associate professor of English, 1978—. Visiting professor at Instituto Allende, summer, 1978. *Member:* Modern Language Association of America, College English Association, South Central Modern Language Association. *Awards, honors:* University of Houston faculty research initiation grant, summer, 1976; National Endowment for the Humanities summer seminar stipend, 1979.

WRITINGS: Infernal Paradise: Mexico and the Modern English Novel, University of California Press, 1978; (contributor) Hans-Bernhard Moeller, editor, *European Exiles in Latin America,* University of Texas Press, 1979. Contributor of articles and poems to language and humanities journals.

WORK IN PROGRESS: Narrative Poetics: Time and Space in the Novels of Graham Greene (tentative title), completion expected in 1981; a collection of poems, completion expected in 1981; research on theory of narrative, the phenomenology of reading, and fictional setting.

SIDELIGHTS: Walker writes: "The main impulse behind *Infernal Paradise* was an effort to sound a complex and compelling mystery; the double-edged fascination that Mexico has exerted on the imaginations of Anglo-American visitors through the years. In the works of D. H. Lawrence, Katherine Anne Porter, Graham Greene, Malcolm Lowry, and others, I found echoes of my own less articulate response to Mexico—to its history, landscape, myths, art—in short, to the Mexican 'mystique.' Written with the intention of invoking as well as elucidating that fascination, the book as I see it is an exercise of the sympathizing imagination as much as of the analytical intellect.''

Infernal Paradise has been published in Spanish.

*   *   *

WALKER, Stanley   1898-1962

OBITUARY NOTICE: Born October 21, 1898, in Lampasas, Tex.; died November 25, 1962. Journalist and author. Walker worked as city editor of the *New York Herald Tribune* from 1928 to 1935. He spent the remainder of the 1930's in brief stints at *New Yorker, New York Woman,* and *Philadelphia Evening Public Ledger.* Walker also contributed to numerous periodicals and documented his experiences in journalism in a pair of works, *City Editor* and *Mrs. Astor's Horse.* Perhaps his most controversial book, though, was his 1944 biography, *Dewey: An American of This Century,* in which he lashed out at the literati—both authors and journalists—who opposed his subject. Obituaries and other sources: *Current Biography,* Wilson, 1944, January, 1963; *New York Times,* November 26, 1962.

*   *   *

WALL, Elizabeth S(pooner)   1924-

PERSONAL: Born January 22, 1924, in New York, N.Y.; daughter of Frank H. (a civil engineer) and Martha (Mogk) Spooner; married David B. Bolton (a banker; divorced); married Alexander C. Wall (an engineer); children: (first marriage) Barbara E., Peter S. *Education:* State Teachers College (now State University of New York College at New Paltz), B.A., 1945; Columbia University, M.A., 1965; University of Bridgeport, M.A., 1972. *Home and office:* 705 Bayshore Rd., Nokomis, Fla. 33555.

CAREER: Elementary school teacher in Armonk, N.Y., 1945-47; Yale University Library, New Haven, Conn., library aide, 1947-48; Nokoton Presbyterian Nursery School, Darien, Conn., director, 1955-62; elementary school teacher in Darien, 1962-68; media specialist for public schools of Stamford, Conn., 1971-77; teacher in Sarasota County Public Schools, Sarasota, Fla., 1977—. Co-founder of Bayshore Books, 1978.

WRITINGS: The Computer Alphabet Book (juvenile), Bayshore Books, 1979. Author of scripts for audio tape sound series on social studies, for 3M Co.

WORK IN PROGRESS: Two books for the ''Beginning Computer Literacy'' series, *Computer Sign Book* and *Easy Computer Dictionary.*

SIDELIGHTS: Wall told *CA:* ''The *Computer Alphabet Book* is a book for computer readiness. It brings some of the basic computer terms to the young child via the alphabet. I wanted to write a book which would be a first step to computer literacy for elementary school students in a computerless school. The familiar alphabet was used to introduce the unfamiliar computer words, and each definition was then related to a familiar experience for the young child. This first computer reference book is intended to lead the reader through simple explanations of basic computer terms which tell about computers without the need for expensive hardware.

''I was sensitized to the need for computer awareness library books when I worked as a media specialist in an elementary school which had a computer terminal installed in the office. A search through *Books in Print* revealed that for the K-6 age group there was a dearth of titles dealing with computers. My husband and I are computer hobbyists and have a micro-

computer at home. As a hobbyist, former teacher, and media specialist, I felt that I should be equipped to write a series of books which would demystify the computer and show young readers that the computer was not only a complex machine to send space ships off to galaxies or a blinking cash register to tally groceries at the supermarket, but could be a small, personal machine, a microcomputer, with the ability to be a patient tutor, an accurate scorekeeper, and a lightning calculator which they could learn to use at home or in school.

''Be assured, computers are coming to the elementary school. They have become much smaller and much cheaper in the past five years and the end is not in sight. All educators are going to be responsible for the education of a computer literate population. Computer literacy must be taught not only to develop the students who will become technological experts, but also taught to all students who must have some general knowledge of what a computer is and what it is not. A computer literate society needs to know about the wide and diversified uses of a machine upon which we are becoming more and more dependent for information.''

BIOGRAPHICAL/CRITICAL SOURCES: Business Week, April 16, 1979; *Sun Coast Gondolier,* June 16, 1979.

*   *   *

WALLACE, Philip (Adrian) Hope
See HOPE-WALLACE, Philip (Adrian)

*   *   *

WALLACE, Tom   1874-1961

OBITUARY NOTICE: Born November 26, 1874, in Hurricane, Ky.; died June 5, 1961. Journalist best known as the editor of the *Louisville Times* during the 1930's and 1940's. Wallace was also a conservationist. Obituaries and other sources: *Who Was Who in America,* 4th edition, Marquis, 1968.

*   *   *

WALLEN, Carl J(oseph)   1931-

PERSONAL: Born December 12, 1931, in Glendale, Calif.; son of Carl Joseph (a veterinarian) and Winifred (a teacher; maiden name, Batten) Wallen; married LaDonna Leigh Stanley (an educational consultant), November 29, 1959; children: Eric, Todd, Michael. *Education:* University of California, Santa Barbara, B.A., 1956; San Francisco State College (now California State University, San Francisco), M.A., 1960; Stanford University, Ed.D., 1962. *Home:* 525 East Alameda Dr., Tempe, Ariz. 85282. *Office:* Department of Elementary Education, Arizona State University, 406-H Farmer, Tempe, Ariz. 85281.

CAREER: Elementary school teacher in Mount Eden, Calif., 1956-58, and Laguna Salada, Calif., 1958-60; Oregon State University, Corvallis, assistant professor of elementary education, 1962-65; Oregon State System of Higher Education, Teaching Research Division, Monmouth, associate professor of education, 1965-67; University of Oregon, Eugene, associate professor of education, 1967-73; Arizona State University, Tempe, professor of elementary education, 1973—, head of department, 1973-78. Arizona State Right-to-Read Advisory Council, member, 1975—, chairman, 1976-78. *Military service:* U.S. Army, 1952-54. *Member:* International Reading Association, American Educational Research Association, National Council of Teachers of English, Arizona Education Association, Phi Delta Kappa.

WRITINGS: (Editor and contributor) *Developing Inquiry*

Process in Four Subject Areas, Oregon Council for Curriculum Improvement, 1965; (with Bert Kersh) *Low Cost Instructional Simulation Materials for Teacher Education,* with multi-media package and workbooks, Teaching Research Division, Oregon State System of Higher Education, 1967; (with Paul Twelker and Jack Crawford) *Of Men and Machines,* with multi-media package, Teaching Research Division, Oregon State System of Higher Education, 1967; *Word Attack Skills in Reading,* C. E. Merrill, 1969.

(Contributor) Barbara Bateman, editor, *Learning Disorders,* Special Child Publications, 1971; (with Sam L. Sebesta) *The First R: Readings on Teaching Reading,* Science Research Associates, 1972; *Competency in Teaching Reading,* Science Research Associates, 1972, revised edition, 1980; (contributor) Michael Labuda, editor, *Creative Reading for Gifted Learners,* International Reading Association, 1971; (with wife, LaDonna Wallen) *Effective Classroom Management,* Allyn & Bacon, 1978. Author of over thirty pamphlets and journal articles.

WORK IN PROGRESS: Second edition of *Competency in Teaching Reading.*

SIDELIGHTS: Wallen told *CA:* "I believe that the central problem in institutionalized education, preschool through university, is that teachers do not use a theoretical body of knowledge to guide their practice. Lacking this knowledge, teachers tend to operate on the basis of conscious and unconscious routinized procedures, much like the common sense procedures followed by people not trained as teachers. The challenge in the preparation of teachers is twofold: to identify a theoretical body of knowledge that is both operationally useful and supported by research on learning, and to organize and carry out training programs that will enable people to make active use of the body of knowledge in their regular teaching. Most of the books I have written have been attempts to accomplish these two challenges."

* * *

WALSH, W(alter) Bruce 1936-

PERSONAL: Born November 6, 1936, in Buffalo, N.Y.; son of Mason (a broker) and Elizabeth (a counselor and educator; maiden name, Brenneman) Walsh; married Jane Chilcote (a manager), June 13, 1975. *Education:* Pennsylvania State University, B.S., 1959; Kent State University, M.A., 1961; University of Iowa, Ph.D., 1965. *Office:* Department of Psychology, Ohio State University, 1945 North High St., Columbus, Ohio 43210.

CAREER: Ohio State University, Columbus, assistant professor, 1965-69, associate professor, 1969-73, professor of psychology, 1973—, counselor, 1967. Member of board of trustees of Central Ohio Rehabilitation Center, 1978. *Member:* American Psychological Association (fellow), American Personnel and Guidance Association, American College Personnel Association. *Awards, honors:* Grant from American College Testing Program, 1970.

WRITINGS: (With L. E. Tyler) *Tests and Measurements,* Prentice-Hall, 1963, 3rd edition, 1979; (with S. H. Osipow) *Strategies in Counseling for Behavior Change,* Appleton, 1970; (with Osipow) *Behavior Change in Counseling: Readings and Cases,* Appleton, 1970; *Theories of Person-Environment Interaction,* American College Testing Program, 1973; (contributor) J. H. Banning, editor, *Campus Ecology: History, Perspective, and Application* (monograph), National Association of Student Personnel Administrators, 1978; (with Osipow and D. J. Tosi) *A Survey of Counseling Methods,* Dorsey, 1980. Contributor of more

than fifty articles and reviews to psychology journals. Member of editorial board of *Journal of College Student Personnel,* 1970-74, *Journal of Vocational Behavior* (acting editor, 1972-73), and *Journal of Counseling Psychology.*

SIDELIGHTS: Walsh's research interests include behavior as a function of the individual and environment, the relationship between self-reported behavior and actual behavior, and personality and career choice.

* * *

WALTERS, Roy W(ashington) 1918-

PERSONAL: Born October 22, 1918, in Chattanooga, Tenn.; son of Roy W. (an oral surgeon) and Ruth (Gokey) Walters; married Mary Campbell, August 23, 1941; children: Roy W. III, Christine Walters Crowther, Carolyn Walters Fox, Ruth S. *Education:* University of Pittsburgh, B.S., 1940. *Home:* 344 Grandview Circle, Ridgewood, N.J. 07450. *Office:* Whitney Industrial Park, Mahwah, N.J. 07430.

CAREER: Bell Telephone Co. of Pennsylvania, Philadelphia, 1940-60, began as cable splicer, became director of employment and development; American Telephone & Telegraph (AT&T), New York, N.Y., director of employment and development, 1960-67; Roy W. Walters & Associates, Inc., Mahwah, N.J., president, 1967—. *Military service:* U.S. Army Air Forces, 1942-46; became major. *Member:* American Society for Training and Development, American Society for Personnel Administration, Sales Executives Club.

WRITINGS: Job Enrichment for Results, Addison-Wesley, 1975. Contributor to business and management journals.

WORK IN PROGRESS: A book on developing managers in a systematic approach: "from manpower planning to recruiting to initial development to performance evaluation."

SIDELIGHTS: Walters told *CA:* "Our nation's only way to beat inflation and improve productivity is to redesign work and work systems to permit better utilization of our human resources."

* * *

WANDEL, Joseph 1918-

PERSONAL: Born January 4, 1918, in Duisburg, Germany (now West Germany); came to the United States, 1952, naturalized citizen, 1957; son of Wilhelm (a postal clerk) and Bertha (Kotthoff) Wandel; married Maria E. Riesenkonig, February 1, 1952; children: William, John, Gerda, Bernie. *Education:* Attended University of Cologne, 1946-50; Marquette University, M.A., 1958; Northwestern University, Ph.D., 1965. *Home:* 1913 West Dobson, Evanston, Ill. 60202. *Office:* Department of Modern Languages, Loyola University, 820 North Michigan Ave., Chicago, Ill. 60611.

CAREER: Loyola University, Chicago, Ill., instructor, 1958-65, assistant professor, 1965-79, associate professor of German, 1979—. *Member:* Modern Language Association of America, American Association of Teachers of German, German American National Congress, Chicago Literary Society.

WRITINGS: The German Dimension of American History, Nelson-Hall, 1979. Contributor to academic journals.

WORK IN PROGRESS: Rainer Maria Rilke and the Painters.

SIDELIGHTS: Wandel told *CA:* "*The German Dimension* is a readable and informative book of special interest to German-Americans. Rilke is the greatest lyric poet in

CONTEMPORARY AUTHORS • *Volumes 93-96*

twentieth-century German literature. His personal relationship to contemporary painters and his study of famous painters of the past helped him to become the great lyric poet he was.''

* * *

WARD-PERKINS, John Bryan 1912-

PERSONAL: Born February 3, 1912, in Bromley, England; son of Bryan (in Indian civil service) and Winifred (Hickman) Ward-Perkins; married Margaret Sheilah Long, 1943; children: Catherine, David, Bryan, Hugh. *Education:* New College, Oxford, B.A., 1934; Magdalen College, Oxford, M.A., 1939. *Politics:* Liberal. *Religion:* Church of England. *Home:* Old Barn, Stratton, Cirencester, Gloucestershire GL7 2LF, England.

CAREER: London Museum, London, England, assistant, 1936-38; Royal University of Malta, professor of archaeology, 1939; British School at Rome, Rome, Italy, director, 1946-74; writer and researcher, 1974—. Director of archaeological excavations and field studies in England, Turkey, and Italy. Visiting professor at New York University, 1957, and University of Sydney, 1977; Carl Newell Jackson Lecturer at Harvard University, 1957; Rhind Lecturer at Society of Antiquaries of Scotland, 1960; Myres Memorial Lecturer at Oxford University, 1963; M. V. Taylor Memorial Lecturer at the Society for Roman Studies, 1968; Jerome Lecturer at University of Michigan, 1969; Mortimer Wheeler Lecturer at the British Academy, 1971; Shuffrey Lecturer at Lincoln College, Oxford, 1976; Semple Lecturer at University of Cincinnati, 1979-80. Visiting member of Institute for Advanced Study, Princeton, N.J., 1974-75. Head of international committee for the map of the Roman world, 1971—; president of Eleventh International Congress of Classical Archaeology, 1978. *Military service:* British Army, Royal Artillery, 1939-45; served in Italy and Africa; became lieutenant colonel; mentioned in dispatches.

MEMBER: International Union of Institutes (founding member; president, 1953, 1964, 1976), International Association for Classical Archaeology (founding member; president, 1974-78), Society of Antiquaries (fellow), British Academy (fellow), Society for Libyan Studies (president, 1978—), Pontifical Academy of Archaeology (fellow), German Archaeological Institute (fellow), Royal Academy of History, Antiquity, and Letters (Sweden; corresponding member), Academy of Archaeology, Letters, and Fine Arts, Naples, Italy, (corresponding member). *Awards, honors:* Craven traveling fellowship from Oxford University, 1934-36; commander of Order of the British Empire, 1955; gold medal from Government of Italy, 1958; Serena Medal from British Academy, 1962; D.Litt. from University of Birmingham, 1968; LL.D. from University of Alberta, 1969; companion of Order of St. Michael and St. George, 1975; gold medal from city of Rome, Italy, 1979.

WRITINGS: Medieval Catalogue, London Museum, 1942; (with J. M. Reynolds) *Inscriptions of Roman Tripolitania,* British School at Rome, 1952; (with J.M.C. Toynbee) *The Shrine of St. Peter,* Longmans, Green, 1955; (with David Talbot-Rice) *The Great Palace of the Byzantine Emperors,* University of St. Andrews, 1955; *The Historical Topography of Veii,* British School at Rome, 1961; *The North-Eastern Ager Veientanus,* British School at Rome, 1969; (with Axel Boethius) *Etruscan and Roman Architecture,* Penguin, 1970, revised edition of Ward-Perkins's contribution published as *Roman Imperial Architecture,* 1981; *Cities of Ancient Greece and Italy: Planning in Classical Antiquity,* Braziller,

1974; *Architettura Romana,* Electa, 1975, translation published as *Roman Architecture,* Abrams, 1977; (with Amanda Claridge) *Pompeii, A.D. 79,* Westerham, 1976, revised edition, Boston Museum of Fine Arts, 1978; (with Elisabeth Alfoeldi) *The Christian Mosaics of Cyrenaica,* L'Erma di Bretschneider, 1980. Editor of ''Papers of the British School at Rome,'' 1946-74. Contributor to learned journals.

WORK IN PROGRESS: The Christian Architecture of Cyrenaica, completion expected in 1981; *Three Early Medieval Sites in South Etruria,* publication by the British School at Rome expected in 1983; *The Severan Monuments of Leptis Magna,* 1984; editing and writing contribution for *Excavations at Sabratha, Tripolitania, 1948-51,* 1985; research for a book on the commerce and uses of marble in the ancient world.

SIDELIGHTS: Ward-Perkins writes: ''A great deal of my basic work is specialized and technical, appearing in professional publications, but even at that level clear, simple writing is a valuable asset. Moreover, although one hears much about the obligation of scholars to communicate their results, it is less widely recognized that there is often a valuable feedback from such communication, clarifying and refining the results of scholarly research. I give a great deal of time and effort to furthering international scholarship, which I find a very satisfying activity.''

* * *

WASHBURN, Jan(ice) 1926-

PERSONAL: Born October 13, 1926, in Brockton, Mass.; daughter of Thomas W. (an attorney) and Louise (a legal secretary; maiden name, Attwood) Prince; married Roy Butrum, March 8, 1950 (divorced May 21, 1953); married John Washburn (a teacher), August 28, 1954; children: Linda Butrum Washburn Becker, Heather J., John D. *Education:* Bates College, A.B., 1947; also attended George Washington University, 1950-51, Barry College, 1963-64, and University of Miami, 1964. *Politics:* Republican. *Religion:* Congregational. *Home:* 4693 Southwest 19th St., Fort Lauderdale, Fla. 33317. *Office:* Southeast Bank of Broward, 1710 South Andrews Ave., Fort Lauderdale, Fla. 33316.

CAREER: Teacher of Latin, English, and physical education at girls' school in Alexandria, Va., 1948-49; U.S. Immigration Service, Washington, D.C., training clerk, 1949-52; substitute teacher at secondary schools in Fort Lauderdale, Fla., 1957-58, teacher of English and German, 1958-61, substitute teacher, 1961-63, teacher of English, 1963-65, substitute teacher, 1965-73; Southeast Bank of Broward, Fort Lauderdale, personnel officer, 1973—. *Member:* American Society for Personnel Administration, Personnel Association of Broward County, Broadview Park Civic Association. *Awards, honors:* Community service award from *Broward Times,* 1971.

WRITINGS: The Family Name (novel for teenagers), Western Publishing, 1971; *Secret of the Spanish Treasure* (novel for teenagers), David Cook, 1979.

Work represented in anthologies, including *The Special Type and Other Stories.* Author of ''Silver Beach,'' a column in *Brockton Enterprise,* 1942. Contributor of stories, poems, and articles to magazines and newspapers, including *Catholic Miss, Retirement Living, Reader's Digest, Swimming World,* and *Ladies' Home Journal.* Editor of newspapers of Broadview Park Civic Association, 1956-63, and Fort Lauderdale Swimming Association, 1968.

WORK IN PROGRESS: A teen-age novel set at a private school in Washington, D.C.

SIDELIGHTS: Jan Washburn's articles and stories have covered a wide range of subjects for all ages. She has written about confidence games aimed at older women, teaching toddlers to swim, and the attempts of a concentration camp victim to receive monetary compensation for her years of incarceration. In addition, she has written historical fiction for young people and light verse.

Washburn wrote: "Through my many years of teaching junior and senior high school and working with young people in sports and scouting, I relate well to teenagers. My favorite field of writing is fiction for young teens. I have found my personal experiences (family, jobs) to be a never-ending source of material. My primary purpose is always to tell an entertaining story, but if I can simultaneously teach a lesson or pass on some useful or unusual information, I feel I have truly succeeded as a writer."

BIOGRAPHICAL/CRITICAL SOURCES: Fort Lauderdale News, February 28, 1960; *Hollywood Sun Tattler,* November 22, 1963; *Bank Account,* May, 1976; *Fort Lauderdale,* November, 1976.

*   *   *

WATERS, Brian Power
See POWER-WATERS, Brian

*   *   *

WATSON, Janet Lynch
See LYNCH-WATSON, Janet

*   *   *

WAXMAN, Ruth B(ilgray)   1916-

PERSONAL: Born February 22, 1916, in Jaffa, Palestine (now Israel); came to the United States in 1920, naturalized citizen, 1926; daughter of Chaim S. (in business) and Bertha (Waldman) Bilgray; married Mordecai Waxman (a rabbi), December 27, 1942; children: Jonathan, David, Hillel. *Education:* University of Chicago, B.A., 1937, Ph.D., 1941. *Politics:* Democrat. *Home:* 85 Bayview Ave., Great Neck, N.Y. 11021. *Office:* 15 East 84th St., New York, N.Y. 10028.

CAREER: Wilson College, Chicago, Ill., instructor, 1946-47; Adelphi University, Garden City, N.Y., instructor in English, 1947-59; Long Island University, C. W. Post College, Greenvale, N.Y., assistant professor of English, 1958-69; *Judaism,* New York, N.Y., managing editor, 1970—. Lecturer at University of Judaism, 1970, State University of New York at Stony Brook, 1973, and Hofstra University, 1974. Plenum member of Synagogue Council of America.

WRITINGS: (Editor with Robert Gordis) *Faith and Reason,* Ktav, 1973.

SIDELIGHTS: Ruth Waxman writes that she travels extensively, lecturing on current books and the role of women in literature, American life, and Jewish life.

AVOCATIONAL INTERESTS: Cooking, baking, crafts.

*   *   *

WAY, Irene   1924-

PERSONAL: Born May 18, 1924, in East London, England; daughter of Christopher (a driver) and Rose (Broomfield) Stothard; married Norman Way (a piano teacher), August 8, 1959; children: Peter, Eleanor (adopted children). *Education:* Attended South Devon Technical College, 1940-41. *Politics:* Conservative. *Religion:* Seventh-Day Adventist. *Home:* 49 Spring Gardens, Garston, Watford, Hertfordshire WD2 6JJ, England.

CAREER: Bank clerk in Ilford, England, 1941-45; export clerk in London, England, 1945-48; secretary in London, 1948-61; typist in England, 1961-76; A. B. Engineering Co., Woburn, England, sales office administrator, 1976—.

WRITINGS: Armada Quest (juvenile), Pickering & Inglis, 1976. Also author of *Amazon Adventure* (juvenile), Pickering & Inglis. Contributor of juvenile stories to *Peoples Friend.*

WORK IN PROGRESS: Little Miss Pied Piper, a children's adventure; *Sword of Gemellen.*

SIDELIGHTS: Irene Way told *CA:* "All my life I have written poetry, purely for my own amusement and satisfaction. I never thought seriously of writing until I had left work and my children were small. Now I write a lot of religious poetry, some set to music by my father-in-law." *Avocational interests:* Reading (especially history), listening to classical music (Chopin, Bach, Rachmaninov).

*   *   *

WAYMACK, W(illiam) W(esley)   1888-1960

OBITUARY NOTICE: Born October 18, 1888, in Savanna, Ill.; died November 5, 1960. Journalist. Waymack, editor of both the *Des Moines Register* and the *Des Moines Tribune* for more than twenty years, received the Pulitzer Prize for distinguished editorial writing in 1937. He was one of the first members of the Atomic Energy Commission. Obituaries and other sources: *Current Biography,* Wilson, 1947, January, 1961; *New York Times,* November 6, 1960.

*   *   *

WEDDING, Dan   1949-

PERSONAL: Born April 30, 1949, in Rising Star, Tex.; son of Vincent D. and Gerry (Herring) Wedding; married Cynthia Townsend (a social worker), August 4, 1979. *Education:* Illinois State University, B.A., 1973, M.S., 1974; University of Hawaii at Manoa, M.A., 1976, Ph.D., 1979. *Politics:* Democrat. *Religion:* Unitarian-Universalist. *Home:* 1355 North Jefferson, #S-14, Jackson, Miss. 39202. *Office:* Department of Psychiatry, Medical Center, University of Mississippi, Jackson, Miss. 39216.

CAREER: University of Mississippi, Medical Center, Jackson, resident in psychology, 1979—. Co-founder of Social Research Consultants Group, Honolulu, Hawaii. *Military service:* U.S. Air Force, 1968-72. U.S. Naval Reserve, 1975—; present rank, lieutenant. *Member:* American Psychological Association, Association for the Advancement of Psychology, Association for the Advancement of Behavior Therapy, Mississippi Psychological Association.

WRITINGS: (Editor with Raymond J. Corsini) *Great Cases in Psychotherapy,* Peacock Publishers, 1979. Contributor to scholarly journals.

WORK IN PROGRESS: A Primer of Clinical Neuropsychology, publication expected in 1981.

SIDELIGHTS: Wedding comments: "My primary interests are neuropsychology, behavior therapy, and Adlerian psychotherapy. I am concerned because clinical practice is so often divorced from theoretical considerations. Practicing clinical psychologists often lack firm theoretical underpinnings for their practice while academicians—who teach students how to be clinicians—are frequently completely out of touch with clinical realities. In addition, I am very excited about the tremendous strides which are being made today in the neurosciences. It is clear that we are on the verge of major breakthroughs in our understanding of the brain and its relationship to both normal and abnormal behavior. I find it an incredibly exciting time to be a clinical psychologist and I cannot imagine myself doing anything else.''

AVOCATIONAL INTERESTS: Travel (Europe and Asia), skiing, modern American poetry, Delta blues.

* * *

WEIHS, Erika   1917-

PERSONAL: Surname pronounced wise; born November 4, 1917, in Vienna, Austria; daughter of Arthur S. (a woodworker and businessman) and Vilma (a milliner; maiden name, Friedman) Foster; married Kurt Weihs (an artist and art director), June 6, 1942; children: Tom, John. *Education:* Attended Graphische Lehr und Versuchsanstalt, Vienna, Austria, 1934-37, and Leonardo da Vince Art School. *Home:* 113 West 11th St., New York, N.Y. 10011. *Agent:* Nettie King, 330 Woodland Pl., Leonia, N.J. 07605. *Office:* 24 East 21st St., New York, N.Y. 10010.

CAREER: Herbert Dubler, Inc., New York, N.Y., designer of greeting cards, 1940-42; free-lance painter and illustrator, 1942—. Has held numerous exhibitions, including shows at Roko Gallery, New York City, 1950, 1961, 1963, 1967, 1970, 1974, and 1976, New York University, Loeb Student Center, New York City, 1972 and 1975, Marist College, Poughkeepsie, N.Y., 1975, and Jefferson Market Public Library, New York City, 1977. *Member:* National Association of Woman Artists (oil jury chairperson, 1976, 1977), Audubon Artists, Artists Equity Association of N.Y., Inc. *Awards, honors:* Lillian Cotton Memorial Prize, 1971, from National Association of Women Artists; Dr. Samuel Gelband Memorial Prize, 1978, from National Association of Women Artists.

WRITINGS—Self-illustrated: *Count the Cats* (juvenile), Doubleday, 1976.

* * *

WEIK, Mary Hays   1898(?)-1979

OBITUARY NOTICE—See index for *CA* sketch: Born c. 1898 in Greencastle, Ind.; died December 25, 1979, in Manhattan, N.Y. Journalist and writer of books, poetry, short stories, and radio scripts. Weik began her career as a newspaper reporter in Chicago and Indianapolis; later she moved to New York City to work as a staff writer for Street & Smith Publications. Among her books are *The Jazz Man,* which was a runner-up for the Caldecott Medal, and *A House on Liberty Street.* A political activist, Weik established the Fellowship of World Citizens after World War II. Her opposition to nuclear power led her to found the Committee to End Radiological Hazards and to edit an anti-nuclear newsletter, *Window on the World.* Obituaries and other sources: *Who's Who in America,* 39th edition, Marquis, 1976; *New York Times,* December 29, 1979.

* * *

WEIL, Dorothy   1929-

PERSONAL: Born October 29, 1929, in Clinton, Ill.; daughter of James H. (a riverboat captain and in business) and Mildred (in business; maiden name, Beamer) Coomer; married Sidney Weil (an attorney), September 9, 1950; children: Rex, Bruce. *Education:* University of Chicago, A.B., 1949; University of Cincinnati, M.A., 1969, Ph.D., 1974. *Home:* 8 Belsaw Place, Cincinnati, Ohio 45220. *Agent:* Frances Collin, Marie Rodell-Frances Collin Literary Agency, 156 East 52nd St., New York, N.Y. 10022.

CAREER: University of Cincinnati, Cincinnati, Ohio, in-

structor in English, 1971-74; Edgecliff College, Cincinnati, professor of English, black studies, and women's studies, 1973-77. Currently writer-in-residence at Edgecliff College. Member of board of trustees of Cincinnati Art Museum, 1975—. Co-founder of Cincinnati Women's Press.

WRITINGS: In Defense of Women: Susanna Rowson, 1762-1824, Pennsylvania State University Press, 1976; *Continuing Education,* Rawson Wade, 1979. Contributor to magazines and newspapers, including *Atlantic Monthly, New York Times,* and *Cincinnati Enquirer Magazine.*

WORK IN PROGRESS: Kate Chopin: A Biography, publication by Harper expected in 1980 or 1981.

SIDELIGHTS: Weil told *CA:* ''Although my writing includes a variety of genres, I am (it appears) developing a central theme: the life of the woman artist. The book on Susanna Rowson, *In Defense of Women,* was my Ph.D. dissertation and is a scholarly study of the most popular of early American women writers; it examines the feminist theme in Rowson's work and brings out what a strong woman she was in spite of the sentimental touches in her writing for which she is usually remembered. Her vast canon, written while Rowson engaged in careers as actress, song lyricist, educator, and editor, demonstrates her energy and dedication to her profession.

''*Continuing Education,* a comic novel written in a very light vein, is on the surface a wild departure from *In Defense of Women.* Still, the protagonist is a woman artist. Unlike Susanna Rowson, she does not have to work to survive, but wants to paint professionally. The story consists of her good-natured struggle against conflicting desires for family happiness and a successful career. Like Rowson, she is basically a strong character, and although a 'Candide,' even a bit of a 'patsy,' she manages to confront her own attitudes and those of others that would keep her from realizing her complicated and often conflicting goals.

''The upcoming biography of Kate Chopin continues the theme of the woman artist. Chopin was born before the Civil War, and she was subjected to a terrible series of personal blows before adolescence: the death of her father, her favorite brother, her only sister, and her beloved great-grandmother. Yet, with the strong figure of her mother guiding her, Chopin also survived the death of her husband, raised six children alone, and produced not only two volumes of short stories, but the novel *The Awakening,* considered by many eminent critics to be one of American literature's few masterpieces. The story of how Chopin accomplished all this, what went into the making of her character, is what interests me. The biography will attempt to recreate her, her social and literary milieu.

''I had not realized the relationship between these seemingly very different books until recently when it suddenly struck me that I was not so versatile—nor so all over the place—as might appear. My other efforts, humor pieces on such subjects as gun control and the E.R.A., are written for fun, and for butter and egg money, and are satiric comments on the contemporary scene. The features, on subjects from church architecture to horse-napping, reflect permanent and passing interests. Surely they have no connection whatsoever to the books. . . .''

* * *

WEIL, James L(ehman)   1929-

PERSONAL: Born June 15, 1929, in New York, N.Y.; son of Morris (a financier) and Charlotte (a painter; maiden name, Ullman) Weil; married Gloria Rosenbaum (a teacher), January 3, 1953; children: Anthony, Peter, Jennifer. *Education:* University of Chicago, A.B., 1950; Oxford University, certificate, 1954. *Religion:* Jewish. *Home:* 103 Van Etten Blvd., New Rochelle, N.Y. 10804. *Office:* Liz Pub Ltd., P.O. Box 285, Wykagyl Station, New Rochelle, N.Y. 10804.

CAREER: Dialight Corp. (manufacturer of electronic components), New York, N.Y., aide to the president, 1954-56, secretary, 1956-58, vice-president, 1958-61, senior vice president, 1961-68; Elizabeth Press, New Rochelle, N.Y., editor and publisher, 1961—. President of Liz Pub Ltd., 1977—. Member of advisory board and writer-in-residence of Wesleyan Writers Conference. *Awards, honors:* Chapbook award from *American Weave,* 1958, for *Quarrel With the Rose;* award from National Endowment for the Arts, 1967.

WRITINGS—All books of poems: *Quarrel With the Rose,* American Weave Press, 1958; *A Fool Turns Clockwise,* American Weave Press, 1960; *The Oboe Player,* Golden Quill, 1961; *Sorrow's Spy,* American Weave Press, 1963; *The Thing Said,* American Weave Press, 1965; (editor) *Of Poem,* Elizabeth Press, 1966; *The Correspondences,* American Weave Press, 1968; *Your Father,* Elizabeth Press, 1973; *Saying So,* Sceptre Press, 1973; (editor) *My Music Bent,* Elizabeth Press, 1973; *Perfectly Yours,* Elizabeth Press, 1974; *Uses,* Elizabeth Press, 1974; *Three,* Sceptre Press, 1976; *Portrait of the Artist Painting Her Son,* Sparrow Press, 1976; *After All,* Elizabeth Press, 1977; *Uses,* Elizabeth Press, 1977; *Quarrel With the Rose,* Elizabeth Press, 1978.

WORK IN PROGRESS: Selected Poems for Sparrow Press.

SIDELIGHTS: Weil writes: "My central interest is poetry—study, writing, editing, and publishing. A related avocation is the study of printing, printing papers, and book binding. I have traveled in England, France, Mexico, Russia, Spain, and Switzerland, and make regular excursions to Italy, where our books are printed and bound."

BIOGRAPHICAL/CRITICAL SOURCES: Poetry, February, 1964; *New York Times,* July 3, 1977.

*   *   *

WEIN, Jacqueline 1938-

PERSONAL: Born April 28, 1938, in New York, N.Y.; daughter of Sol (a printer and retailer) and Jeannette Wein. *Home:* 150 East 49th St., New York, N.Y. 10018. *Office:* Sussman & Sugar, Inc., 24 West 40th St., New York, N.Y. 10018.

CAREER: Sussman & Sugar, Inc. (advertising firm), New York, N.Y., secretary to the president, 1963—.

WRITINGS: Roommate (novel), Crown, 1979.

WORK IN PROGRESS: Another novel.

SIDELIGHTS: Jacqueline Wein comments: "I traveled around the world on a limited budget for a year before settling down to work. *Roommate* is my first attempt at a novel, and I wrote it in six consecutive Sundays."

*   *   *

WEINER, Annette B. 1933-

PERSONAL: Born February 14, 1933, in Philadelphia, Pa.; daughter of Archibald W. (in business) and Phyllis (in business; maiden name, Stein) Cohen; married Martin Weiner, September 27, 1953 (divorced, May, 1973); married Robert Monroe Palter (a professor of philosophy), May 22, 1979; children: (first marriage) Linda, Jonathan. *Education:* University of Pennsylvania, B.A., 1968; Bryn Mawr College,

Ph.D., 1974. *Residence:* Austin, Tex. *Office:* Department of Anthropology, University of Texas, Austin, Tex. 78712.

CAREER: Murette Publishing Co., Chester, Pa., vice-president, 1960-64; M & N Publishing Co., New York, N.Y., co-founder and co-publisher of *Lady's Circle,* 1963-64; Franklin and Marshall College, Lancaster, Pa., visiting assistant professor of anthropology, 1973-74; University of Texas, Austin, assistant professor of anthropology, 1974—. Conducted field studies in Guatemala, the Trobriand Islands, northwest Pakistan, and research in England and France. Speaker at international conferences; consultant to British Broadcasting Corp. (BBC) and Maryland Center for Public Broadcasting.

MEMBER: American Anthropological Association (fellow), American Ethnological Society, American Association for the Advancement of Science, Association for Social Anthropology in Oceania (fellow), Society for the Anthropology of Visual Communication, Royal Anthropological Institute (fellow), Cibola Anthropological Association (co-founder; president, 1977-79), Sigma Xi. *Awards, honors:* Ford Foundation fellow in Guatemala, 1970; Fanny Bullock Workman traveling fellow of Bryn Mawr College in the Trobriand Islands, 1971-72; research grant from National Institute of Mental Health, 1972-73; National Endowment for the Humanities fellow, 1976; American Council of Learned Societies fellow, 1976-77; associate of Clare Hall, Cambridge, 1976; Guggenheim fellow, 1979.

WRITINGS: Women of Value, Men of Renown: New Perspectives in Trobriand Exchange, University of Texas Press, 1976. Also author of *Let's Color in French, Let's Color in Spanish, Let's Color in German,* and *Let's Color in Hebrew,* all published by Morette Publishing.

Contributor: Eleanor Leacock and Mona Etienne, editors, *Women in History: Studies in the Colonization of Precapitalist Societies,* J. F. Bergin, 1979; Jerry W. Leach and Edmund R. Leach, editors, *New Perspectives on the Kula,* Cambridge University Press, 1980. Contributor of articles and reviews to anthropology journals.

WORK IN PROGRESS: Contributing to *Sexual Meaning,* edited by Sherry Ortner and Harriet Whitehead; editing *Reality and the Camera: Essays in Ethnographic Film Theory; A Comparative Model of Reproduction in the Pacific;* ethnographic field research on women and exchange in the Trobriand Islands, Papua New Guinea, and Western Samoa; ethnographic research on kinship and family in central Texas.

SIDELIGHTS: Annette Weiner writes: "During my first summers in graduate school I co-directed archaeological excavations in Antigua, Guatemala. My later work in cultural anthropology was very much influenced by this archaeological experience.

"My original proposal for field work was to study the styles of traditional and contemporary woodcarving as a projection of Trobriand world view adapting to new ideas and influences. I spent ten months in Kiriwina, but my original plans to study art suddenly shifted.

"The first day that I moved into a village in northern Kiriwina, I was taken by some village women to another village where, for five hours, I watched hundreds of women distribute and control their own wealth objects—bundles of dried banana leaves and fibrous skirts. Although Malinowski had mentioned the general importance of Trobriand women, he never wrote about their wealth or the specifics of women's economic interaction with Trobriand men. From that first day, I not only studied women, I also began seriously to re-evaluate what had been written previously about Trobriand men.

"My doctoral dissertation was a study of Trobriand kinship and exchange through the perspective of both women and men. The following year I completed a book manuscript in which I emphasized that power must be understood within a framework that incorporates both a cosmic and social ordering of time and space. Therefore, regardless of whether or not women have political power in any society, the domains women *do* control must be analyzed in complementarity to the domains that men control."

BIOGRAPHICAL/CRITICAL SOURCES: Times Literary Supplement, October 14, 1977; *American Ethnologist,* November, 1977; *Man,* March, 1978.

*   *   *

WEINGARTNER, James J(oseph) 1940-

PERSONAL: Born August 21, 1940, in Bethlehem, Pa.; son of James Joseph and Catherine (Grim) Weingartner; married Jane Vahle, August 20, 1966; children: Kirsten Ann, Mary Catherine. *Education:* Muhlenberg College, B.A., 1962; University of Wisconsin (now University of Wisconsin—Madison), M.S., 1963, Ph.D., 1967. *Office:* Department of History, Southern Illinois University, Edwardsville, Ill. 62025.

CAREER: University of New Hampshire, Durham, assistant professor of history, 1967-69; Southern Illinois University, Edwardsville, assistant professor, 1969-71, associate professor, 1971-77, professor of history, 1977—. *Member:* American Historical Association, American Committee on the History of the Second World War, Conference Group for Central European History.

WRITINGS: Hitler's Guard: The Story of the Leibstandarte S.S. Adolf Hitler, 1933-1945, Southern Illinois University Press, 1974; *Crossroads of Death: The Story of the Malmedy Massacre and Trial,* University of California Press, 1979. Contributor to history journals.

WORK IN PROGRESS: Research on war crimes trials in postwar Germany.

*   *   *

WEINSTEIN, Warren 1941-

PERSONAL: Born July 3, 1941, in Brooklyn, N.Y.; son of Sidney (a transport specialist) and Fannie (Silverstein) Weinstein; married Elaine L. Katz (a teacher and consultant), June 23, 1968; children: Jennifer Lynn, Alisa Michelle. *Education:* Brooklyn College of the City University of New York, B.A., 1963; Columbia University, M.A., 1966, Ph.D., 1970. *Home:* 14305 Brad Dr., Rockville, Md. 20853. *Office:* Coordinating Council for International Issues, 14305 Brad Dr., Rockville, Md. 20853.

CAREER: Foreign Research Development Corp., New York City, senior analyst, 1963-65; City College of the City University of New York, New York City, instructor in political science, 1967 and 1969; State University of New York College at Oswego, assistant professor, 1970-73, associate professor of political science, 1973-76; Institute for International Law and Economic Development, Washington, D.C., director for international research and policy planning, 1976-78; Council for Policy and Social Research, Washington, D.C., director, 1978-79; Coordinating Council for International Issues, Washington, D.C., vice-president and director, 1979—. Instructor for Mission of the People's Republic of

Mongolia to the United Nations, 1963-65; adjunct professor at American University, 1978; guest lecturer at University of California, Los Angeles, George Washington University, and schools all over the world; participant and director of professional meetings and conferences. Project director for Carnegie Endowment for International Peace, 1974-75; coordinator for international research and policy planning for Pacific Consultants, 1978-79; scholar-diplomat for U.S. State Department's Africa and European programs, 1973-74. Member of board of directors of Human Rights Internet, 1977—; consultant to International Communications Agency, African American Labor Center, Department of State, and Agency for International Development.

MEMBER: American Society of International Law, American Political Science Association, African Studies Association, New York State African Studies Association (president, 1975). *Awards, honors:* Fulbright grant for Free University of Brussels, 1967-69; Lady Jackson grant from Columbia University, 1968, for University of Bujumbura.

WRITINGS: (With John Grotpeter) *The Pattern of African Decolonization: A New Interpretation,* Eastern African Studies Program, Syracuse University, 1973; (contributor) R. Ned Lebow and other editors, *Divided Nations in a Divided World,* McKay, 1974; (contributor) Morris Davis, editor, *Humanitarian Aid in Civil Wars,* Praeger, 1975; *Chinese and Soviet Aid to Africa,* Praeger, 1975; (with Robert Schrire) *Political Conflict and Ethnic Strategies: A Case Study of Burundi,* Eastern African Studies Program, Syracuse University, 1976; *Historical Dictionary of Burundi,* Scarecrow, 1976; (with Tom Henriksen) *Africa's Alternative: Soviet and Chinese Aid to African Nations?,* Praeger, 1979; *African Perspectives on Human Rights,* Council for Policy and Social Research, 1979; *Rwanda and Burundi,* Cornell University Press, in press; *Historical Dictionary of Rwanda,* Scarecrow, in press. Author of columns on international affairs and human rights.

Contributor of more than twenty articles and reviews to political science and sociology journals. Associate editor of *Panafrican Journal,* 1973—; member of editorial board of *African Studies Review,* 1975—; editorial writer for *Palladium Times,* 1976.

WORK IN PROGRESS: The Economics of Human Rights.

SIDELIGHTS: Weinstein's research interests include international law and relations, transcultural communications, economic development in the Third World, human rights, and the military and politics in Africa.

*   *   *

WEIR, Robert M(cColloch) 1933-

PERSONAL: Born in 1933, in Philadelphia, Pa.; son of Horace (a chemist) and Helen (a chemist; maiden name, Gillette) Weir; married Anne Highstrete (a teacher), 1955; children: Carol, Suzanne. *Education:* Pennsylvania State University, B.A., 1958; Case Western Reserve University, M.A., 1961, Ph.D., 1966. *Residence:* Columbia, S.C. *Office:* Department of History, University of South Carolina, Columbia, S.C. 29208.

CAREER: University of Houston, Houston, Tex., instructor, 1965-66, assistant professor of history, 1966-67; University of South Carolina, Columbia, assistant professor, 1967-70, associate professor, 1970-78, professor of history, 1978—. *Member:* Southern Historical Association, South Carolina Historical Association (member of executive committee, 1972—; vice-president, 1974-75; president, 1975-76),

Phi Beta Kappa, Phi Kappa Phi, Phi Alpha Theta. *Awards, honors:* Fellow of National Endowment for the Humanities, 1967-68; grant from American Philosophical Society and American Council of Learned Societies, 1972.

WRITINGS: "*A Most Important Epocha*": *The Coming of the Revolution in South Carolina,* University of South Carolina Press, 1970; (editor and author of introduction) William Henry Drayton and others, *The Letters of Freeman, Etc.,* University of South Carolina Press, 1977; (contributor) Jeffrey J. Crow and Larry E. Tise, editors, *The Southern Experience in the American Revolution,* University of North Carolina Press, 1978; (contributor) Bernard Bailyn and J. Russell Wiggins, editors, *The Press and the American Revolution,* American Antiquarian Society, 1980. Contributor to *Encyclopedia of Southern History.* Contributor of about thirty-five articles and reviews to history journals and regional magazines, including *American Heritage* and *Sandlapper.*

WORK IN PROGRESS: A history of colonial South Carolina, publication by Kraus-Thomson Organization expected in 1982.

SIDELIGHTS: Weir told *CA:* "Historical paradox and anomaly have long fascinated me—which, I suppose, explains why my work has dealt mainly with the South and especially South Carolina, for the history of the area is replete with puzzles." *Avocational interests:* Travel, canoeing, camping, photography, jogging.

*   *   *

WEISS, Jonathan A(rthur)   1939-

PERSONAL: Born May 1, 1939, in Bryn Mawr, Pa.; son of Paul and Victoria (Brodkin) Weiss. *Education:* Yale University, B.A. (cum laude), 1960, LL.B., 1963; also attended University of Chicago, 1960-61. *Home:* 142 West 87th Street, #B2, New York, N.Y. 10024. *Office:* 2095 Broadway, New York, N.Y. 10023.

CAREER: Admitted to the Bar of District of Columbia, 1964, New York State, 1967, and U.S. Supreme Court, 1967; Department of Labor, Solicitor General's Office, Washington, D.C., attorney, 1963-65; Neighborhood Legal Services Project, Washington, D.C., managing attorney, 1965-66; Columbia University School of Law, Center on Social Welfare Policy and Law, New York City, attorney, 1967; Mobilization for Youth Legal Services, Inc., New York City, managing attorney, 1967-69; Legal Services for the Elderly Poor, New York City, director, 1969—. Guest lecturer at Hebrew University, Jerusalem, Israel, 1966; visiting professor of law at Texas Southern University, 1971. Member of board of directors of Asian-American Legal Defense and Education Fund and due process committee of American Civil Liberties Union. Consultant to various government and business organizations, including President's Commission on Civil Disorder, National Institute for Mental Health on Children, Office of Economic Opportunity, Senate Committee on Aging, and Moreland Act Commission on Nursing Home Reform. *Member:* District of Columbia Bar Association, Yale Law Journal. *Awards, honors:* Distinguished scholar medal from Hofstra University, 1973.

WRITINGS: (With Paul Weiss) *Right and Wrong: A Philosophical Dialogue Between Father and Son,* Basic Books, 1968; (editor and contributor) *The Law and the Elderly,* Practising Law Institute, 1976. Contributor of over thirty articles to professional journals.

WORK IN PROGRESS: Two novels, *A Moment of Tenderness* and *Waiting on Death;* a play, "Three's Company."

WELLES, (George) Orson   1915-

PERSONAL: Born May 6, 1915, in Kenosha, Wis.; son of Richard Head (an inventor and manufacturer) and Beatrice (a pianist; maiden name, Ives) Welles; married Virginia Nicholson (an actress), December 20, 1934 (divorced, 1940); married Rita Hayworth (an actress), September 7, 1942 (divorced, 1948); married Paolo Mori (an actress), May 8, 1955; children: Christopher, Rebecca, Beatrice. *Education:* Graduated from Todd High School in Woodstock, Ill., 1930. *Residence:* Laurel Canyon, Calif.

CAREER: Actor, director, producer, and writer of productions for radio, stage, television, and motion pictures. Actor in stage productions, including "The Jew Suss," 1931, "Romeo and Juliet," 1933, "Macbeth," 1936, "Doctor Faustus," 1937, "Julius Caesar," 1937, "Five Kings," 1939, "The Unthinking Lobster," 1950, "King Lear," 1956, and "Chimes at Midnight," 1960; actor in radio productions, including "The Shadow," 1935, and in motion pictures, including "Citizen Kane," 1941, "Jane Eyre," 1944, "The Third Man," 1949, "Othello," 1952, and "Falstaff," 1966; actor in television productions, including "King Lear," 1953, and "The Immortal Story," 1968. Director of stage productions, including "Horse Eats Hat," 1936, "The Cradle Will Rock," 1937, "Moby Dick," 1955, and "Rhinoceros," 1960, radio productions, including "Dracula," 1938, and "Invasion From Mars," 1938, and motion pictures, including "Citizen Kane," 1941, "The Magnificent Ambersons," 1942, "Othello," 1952, "The Trial," 1962, and "Falstaff," 1966. Narrator of numerous productions for radio, stage, television, and motion pictures. Co-director with John Houseman of Federal Theatre Project's Negro People's Theatre, 1936-37; co-founder with Houseman of Mercury Productions, 1937. Announcer for radio program "Hello, Americans," 1942; toured in "The Mercury Wonder Show," 1943.

AWARDS, HONORS: Claire M. Senie Plaque from Drama Study Club, 1938; co-winner with Herman Mankiewicz of Academy Award for best screenplay from Academy of Motion Picture Arts and Sciences and nominations for best actor and best director, all 1941, all for "Citizen Kane"; Golden Palm award for best film from Cannes Film Festival, 1956, for "Othello"; Grand Prize from Brussels Film Festival, 1958, for "Touch of Evil"; co-winner of best actor award from Cannes Film Festival, 1959, for "Compulsion"; "Citizen Kane" was selected as "best film in motion picture history" by international film critics in polls taken in 1962 and 1972; Twentieth Anniversary Special Prize from Cannes Film Festival, 1966, for "Chimes at Midnight"; Special Academy Award from Academy of Motion Picture Arts and Sciences, 1971; Life Achievement Award from American Film Institute, 1974; and numerous other film awards.

WRITINGS: The Free Company Presents . . . His Honor, the Mayor (radio play; first broadcast by Columbia Broadcasting System, April 6, 1941), [New York], 1941; (compiler) *Invasion From Mars, Interplanetary Stories: Thrilling Adventures in Space,* Dell, 1949; (with others) *The Lives of Harry Lime,* News of the World, 1952; *Mr. Arkadin* (novel), Crowell, 1956; (and director) *Moby Dick—Rehearsed* (two-act play; produced in London at Duke of York's Theatre, June 16, 1955; adapted from the novel by Herman Melville), Samuel French, 1965; (and director) *The Trial* (screenplay; produced by Paris Europa Productions/FI-C-IT/Hisa-Films, 1962; adapted from the novel by Franz Kafka), translated by Nicholas Fry, Simon & Schuster, 1970; (with Herman Mankiewicz) *The Citizen Kane Book* (contains shooting script and screenplay by Welles and Mankiewicz for "Citizen Kane," Mercury, 1941), introduction by Pauline Kael, Little, Brown, 1971. Also co-editor with R. Hill of *Everybody's Shakespeare*, 1934, and *The Mercury Shakespeare*, 1939.

Other screenplays; all as director, except as noted: "The Magnificent Ambersons" (adapted from the novel by Booth Tarkington), Mercury, 1942; (screen story only) Charles Chaplin, "Monsieur Verdoux," United Artists, 1947; "The Lady From Shanghai" (adapted from the novel by Sherwood King, *If I Die Before I Wake*), Mercury, 1946; "Macbeth" (adapted from the play by William Shakespeare), Mercury, 1948; "Othello" (adapted from the play by Shakespeare), Mercury, 1952; "Mr. Arkadin" (released in England as "Confidential Report"; adapted from own novel), Cervantes Film Organization/Sevilla Studios, 1955; "Touch of Evil" (adapted from the novel by Whit Masterson, *Badge of Evil*), Universal, 1958; "Falstaff" (released in England as "Chimes at Midnight"; adapted from various plays by Shakespeare), International Films Espanola/Alpine, 1966; "The Immortal Story" (adapted for French television from the novel by Isak Dinesen), ORTF/Albina Films, 1968; "F for Fake" (documentary), Specialty Films, 1975; "Filming Othello" (documentary), 1979. Also author and director of unreleased motion picture "Too Much Johnson," Mercury, 1938, and unfinished films including "It's All True," with Norman Foster and John Fante, Mercury, 1942, and "The Deep," adapted from the novel by Charles Williams, *Dead Calm*, 1967-69. Author of numerous unproduced screenplays, including "Operation Cinderella."

Other: Author of libretto for ballet "The Lady in Ice," 1953. Co-author and narrator of adaptations of novels for radio and for recordings. Author of column, "Orson Welles' Almanac," for *New York Post*, 1945.

WORK IN PROGRESS: Re-editing "Don Quixote," a film adapted from the novel by Cervantes, begun in 1955; "The Other Side of the Wind," a film about Hollywood's movie industry, begun in 1972.

SIDELIGHTS: Although Welles is probably best known for his film "Citizen Kane" and his 1938 radio broadcast of the Martian "invasion," he first received recognition for his work in the theatre. As a youth Welles exhibited precocity as an actor, artist, and magician (he studied under Houdini); at ten he had already read Nietzsche and all of Shakespeare. Upon graduation from high school at fifteen he decided to tour Ireland and sketch his impressions. There he attended a performance by the Gate Players, after which he convinced the troupe's director to cast him in "The Jew Suss." Welles toured briefly with the players before arriving in London, where his roles were assumed by British actors.

He returned to America and then abruptly departed for Morocco, where he lived in a tent writing plays and stories. After returning to the United States, he submitted his writings to publishers and magazines but with little success. Then he attended a party and met Thornton Wilder, who had heard of Welles's accomplishments as an actor in Ireland. With Wilder's assistance, Welles managed to land the roles of Tybalt and Mercutio in "Romeo and Juliet."

After "Romeo and Juliet," Welles distinguished himself in productions of "Candida" and "Panic," the latter produced by John Houseman. Welles then directed and acted at the Woodstock Dramatic Festival, and afterwards teamed with Houseman to establish an independent theatre. Welles's parents were both wealthy but his father, alarmed by his son's financial nonchalance, had stipulated that young Orson turn twenty-five before collecting his inheritance. Undaunt-

ed, Welles, who possessed an impressive voice, began working for radio programs to obtain funds for the theatre. Among his best-known roles for the radio shows was that of The Shadow in the program of the same title.

In 1935, Welles and Houseman accepted a position with the Federal Theatre Project as co-directors of the Negro People's Theatre. Some of Welles's most impressive innovations derived from this association. "Macbeth," his initial production as director with the company, was marked by daring use of an all black cast in Haitian setting. Welles also replaced the witches with voodoo doctors. The play was an enormous critical success, and Welles followed it with an even greater one, "Doctor Faustus." Directing himself in the title role, Welles astonished audiences by replacing conventional props and backgrounds with huge, wandering columns of light and exaggerated shadows. Critics began hailing Welles as the theatre's "boy genius."

But critical success was not enough to perpetuate the project. Welles had to fund much of "Doctor Faustus" himself, and his association with the project closed in grandiose fashion when the company was left without a theatre for the first performance of "The Cradle Will Rock." Since the audience had already arrived, Welles led them through New York City with cast in tow and eventually performed the play in another theatre.

With the Negro People's Theatre defunct, Welles and Houseman created their own company, Mercury Theatre. They chose "Julius Caesar" as their first effort, in which Welles played Brutus and directed. By now the public was expecting radical interpretations from Welles and Houseman, and "Julius Caesar" was no disappointment. Caesar appeared in Fascist uniform while other characters wore modern dress (Welles wore "intellectual"'s garb). The background was the brick wall surrounding the stage.

"Julius Caesar" was produced in 1938 when Welles was twenty-six. The same year Mercury Theatre began presenting a radio program, "Mercury Theatre of the Air," which Welles edited, directed, broadcast, and co-wrote. The show is remembered for its adaptation of the H. G. Wells novel, *The War of the Worlds*. By presenting the program as a series of newscasts covering an invasion of Earth by Martians, the Mercury Theatre unintentionally created a minor panic: listeners actually believed that Martians were attacking! People fled their homes and caused traffic jams while armed citizens patrolled the streets for signs of alien life. The public swamped Welles with complaints and threats. The Mercury Theatre survived the incident, though, only to fold the following year.

The telling blow for the Mercury Theatre was the play "Five Kings," an amalgam of five historical plays by Shakespeare. Welles had worked intermittently on it since childhood but was overwhelmed by its demands. The production proved disastrous and in 1940 he left New York City for Hollywood and movies, taking the Mercury Theatre ensemble with him.

Welles was greeted less than enthusiastically upon arrival in the film capital. Members of the movie industry, infuriated by Welles's arrogance, hoped he would fail in his filmmaking debut; some columnists suggested in print that film moguls were overestimating his talents, and they lambasted RKO Pictures for signing Welles to a contract that granted him total control of his films.

At first it seemed as if Welles's critics were correct. His first two proposals, including an adaptation of Joseph Conrad's *Heart of Darkness* in which Welles planned to substitute the narrator with subjective camera, were both rejected by

RKO. The studio finally agreed on the third offer, "Citizen Kane," for which Welles would write, produce, direct, and act.

Welles began writing a version of the screenplay in Hollywood while his collaborator, Herman Mankiewicz, was miles away doing the same under Houseman's guidance. Explaining why the two writers worked separately, Welles told Peter Bogdanovich: "I left him on his own finally, because we'd started to waste too much time haggling. So, after mutual agreements on storyline and character, Mank went off with Houseman and did his version, while I stayed in Hollywood and wrote mine." Years later, Pauline Kael accused Welles of underplaying Mankiewicz's contribution to the script. But Welles informed Bogdanovich, "At the end, naturally, I was the one making the picture, after all—who had to make the decisions. I used what I wanted of Mank's and, rightly or wrongly, kept what I liked of my own."

Filming "Citizen Kane" took ten weeks. The pace was a hectic one for Welles who, aside from his acting and directing duties, was constantly revising the script. "Orson was always writing and rewriting," recalled his secretary, Katherine Trosper. "I saw scenes written during production. Even while he was being made up, he'd be dictating dialogue."

Welles received assistance throughout the filming from his cinematographer, Gregg Toland, whom Welles later called "the *fastest* cameraman who ever lived." He revealed that Toland had volunteered to film "Citizen Kane." "He asked me who did the lighting," Welles said. "I told him in the theater most directors have a lot to do with it . . . and he said, 'Well, fine. I want to work with somebody who never made a movie.' Now partly because of that, I somehow assumed that movie lighting was supervised by movie *directors*. And, like a damned fool, for the first few days of *Kane* I 'supervised' like crazy. Behind me . . . Gregg was balancing lights and telling everybody to shut their faces. . . . He was quietly fixing it so as many of my notions as possible would work. Later he told me, 'That's the only way to learn anything—from somebody who doesn't know anything.'" Although Kael also accused Welles of taking credit from Toland, Welles acknowledged, "It's impossible to say how much I owe to Gregg. He was superb."

"Citizen Kane" was hailed as a masterpiece when first shown in 1941. It concerns newspaper tycoon Charles Foster Kane who, as a child, is sent to live with a banker. Upon reaching adulthood, Kane inherits a newspaper business and enormous wealth. For all his wealth, though, Kane never really finds what he wants most: "Love on my own terms." The story unfolds in flashback fashion, with a dying Kane speaking the word "rosebud." Then the film cuts sharply to "News on the March," a parody of the popular "March of Time" newsreels, which delivers a capsule biography of the millionaire. The story centers around a reporter's efforts to discover why Kane said "rosebud" as his dying words by interviewing Kane's friends and associates. The interviews present a composite portrait of the tycoon. In the final scene, "rosebud" is revealed to be the name of Kane's childhood sled.

Although it was virtually ignored at the Academy Awards, "Citizen Kane" is now hailed as one of the greatest films ever made. Andrew Sarris called it "the work that influenced the cinema more profoundly than any American film since *Birth of a Nation.*"

Welles's good fortune began to turn after his highly regarded first film. "The Magnificent Ambersons," adapted from the novel by Booth Tarkington, traces the lives of two prestigious families at the turn of the century. The changing values of that time are reflected in George Minaver, a brash young man who scorns the coming of the automobile and plans to devote his life to yachting. Eventually, his family's fortunes depleted, George must work on a dangerous job. After his injury in an explosives accident, George realizes that times have changed and surrenders his affections to the daughter of Eugene Morgan. George has despised Mr. Morgan through most of the film because Morgan signifies the changing times (he favors use of the automobile) and because he was once romantically involved with George's mother.

Welles's misfortune regarding "The Magnificent Ambersons" occurred while he was filming a documentary in Latin America. When he returned to the United States he discovered that RKO had ended his contract and had confiscated the film. Dissatisfied with its tone (Welles had intended a less "all's well" ending than George falling in love), and displeased with its length, the studio made its own ending and inserted it into the film after cutting out more than forty minutes.

The revised version of "The Magnificent Ambersons" altered Welles's intentions with the film. However, he bore little grudge against the studio and, except for the ending, he believes "The Magnificent Ambersons" to be superior to "Citizen Kane." In the early 1960's, Welles entertained the notion of gathering the film's cast and remaking the end. Unfortunately, while he was occupied with other business, one of the film's actors died.

During World War II, Welles involved himself in a number of projects. He was the announcer for the radio program "Hello, Americans," and an entertainer in "The Mercury Wonder Show." He also distinguished himself as an actor in such films as "Journey Into Fear" and "Jane Eyre." His next directing effort, "The Stranger," was released in 1946. It details the uncovering of a fugitive Nazi posing as a professor in a New England town. After the professor, played by Welles, resorts to murder to preserve his identity, he is discovered by an FBI agent. In an exciting climax, the Nazi is spotted atop the town clock, whereupon he tries to escape only to become impaled on a rotating statue.

Because "The Stranger" was more to the audience's liking than "Citizen Kane" and "The Magnificent Ambersons," Welles found himself in good standing with the Hollywood moguls. He was hired by Columbia as writer, producer, director, and star of "The Lady From Shanghai." The release of that film signified Welles's final days in "movieland." When the Columbia upper-echelon viewed Welles's concoction of double-crosses and deceptions, they confessed that they couldn't follow the story. Upon seeing it, even Welles admitted having the same problem. The studio added footage, but it didn't matter: nothing, it seemed, could reduce its incoherence. Defined by James Naremore as "essentially a dark, grotesquely stylized comedy, a film that takes us beyond expressionism toward absurdity," the film contains at least one memorable scene: a bizarre shoot-out in an abandoned funhouse involving Welles (who plays an Irish sailor duped into a fake-murder, fraud, and blackmail scheme), the woman who involved him in the scheme, and her crippled husband, a famous criminal lawyer. "For all its imperfections," noted Naremore, "it manages to retain many of the qualities of Welles's best work."

But Welles was now financially strapped. In 1946 he had sunk much of his own money into an elaborate staging of

"Around the World in Eighty Days" that managed to last only seventy-five performances. Welles lost $350,000. And the poorly received "Lady From Shanghai" had left him *persona non grata* in Hollywood. Welles decided to work in Europe, where he could seek independent financing and thus control his own films.

Before Welles left America he made a low-budget film of "Macbeth" for Republic Pictures. Welles made the whole film in three weeks using sets from westerns. In order to save time and money, he performed the play from beginning to end and recorded the dialogue. Then, during filming, he played the recording over the loudspeakers and had the actors mouth the dialogue they were hearing. As a result, some of the dialogue seems to come from characters who aren't moving their mouths. Also, Welles omitted more than one-third of the play and introduced an entirely new character, the "Holy Father." Some critics suggested that the film be called "Welles's Macbeth," claiming that Shakespeare would scarcely have recognized his play. But Welles defended his actions by contending, "I use Shakespeare's words and characters to make motion pictures." Welles called these motion pictures "variations on [Shakespeare's] themes."

The critical standing of "Macbeth" has improved through recognition of its virtues as a character study. "It is not surprising that Welles' experiment did not wholly succeed," wrote Michael Mullin. "Nonetheless, his treatment of the play is true to the major concerns of his art, in both style and substance: his simplifications—or clarifications—of moral complexities, his obsession with a single, superhuman character . . . , and, ultimately, his need to break with the conventional in everything he did. In his *Macbeth* Welles suggests an expressionistic alternative to the realism that makes many Shakespeare films . . . seem bad mixtures of intense poetry and prosaic filming. At its best moments, Welles' *Macbeth* leads us deep into the nightmare realms where Macbeth lives, where nothing is but what is not, where fair is foul and foul is fair."

After arriving in Europe, Welles appeared in a number of British films, including "Prince of Foxes" and "Trouble in the Glen." At the same time, he was directing and starring in his own production of Shakespeare's "Othello." This film proved extremely troublesome in production. Welles began making "Othello" in 1949 but quickly ran into funding difficulties. When financial stipulations forced a change in locations, Welles then had to recast certain roles. Throughout the next three years he traveled from locations in Morocco and Rome and back to Britain to fulfill acting obligations.

Welles's most noteworthy achievement as an actor during this turbulent time was as Harry Lime in Carol Reed's film, "The Third Man." Lime lives in the sewers of Vienna while bootlegging watered-down penicillin. Believed to be dead, Lime is eventually discovered by a friend who is then faced with a moral dilemma: should he protect Lime or turn him over to the police? After visiting a hospital ward full of children crippled by Lime's diluted penicillin, the friend cooperates with the police. Lime is finally shot by him after a furious chase through the sewers. Although Welles only had one scene with dialogue, he carried it off with such aplomb that many critics consider it one of his most memorable film appearances.

In 1954, Welles finished "Othello" and rushed it to the Cannes Film Festival, where it won the Grand Prize. As with "Macbeth," Welles took many liberties with the text of "Othello." He eliminated some scenes, condensed others,

and placed most of the action outdoors. Because he was forced to substitute so many actors, Welles shot much of the film from a distance to make the replacements less noticeable. The dialogue is once again a source of irritation, however, since much of it was postsynchronized. Welles used his own voice for many of the characters.

The film is now considered to be one of the finest Shakespearean adaptations. "Full of flamboyant cinematography, composed and edited in what has been called the 'bravura style,' *Othello* transcends categories," wrote Jack J. Jorgens, "blending the deep focus 'realistic' photography hailed by Bazin with the expressionist montage of Eisenstein. What the film lacks in acting—subtle characterization and emotional range—it makes up in rich, thematically significant compositions."

Upon completion of "Othello," Welles turned to British television to produce a pair of shows and star in a special performance of "King Lear." He also presented his adaptation of *Moby Dick* at this time. All three projects were enormously successful, but Welles's good fortune did not last long. In 1956, while starring in another production of "King Lear," Welles injured his leg and was forced to deliver the first several performances from a wheelchair. The critics denounced the show vehemently.

Shortly after "Othello," Welles made "Mr. Arkadin," a film about a wealthy European, Gregory Arkadin, who hires another man, Van Stratten, to investigate his past. Whenever Van Stratten discovers anyone who has knowledge about how Arkadin acquired his wealth, Arkadin has them killed. Eventually Van Stratten falls in love with Arkadin's daughter. Arkadin, thinking Van Stratten has told his daughter about his unscrupulous actions, jumps from an airplane. The film has enjoyed cult status in Europe for many years, especially among the French critics. Francois Truffaut observed: "In this gorgeous film, once again we find Welles's inspiration behind every image, that touch of madness and of genius, his power, his brilliant heartiness, his gnarled poetry. There isn't a single scene which isn't based on a new or unusual idea."

In 1957 Welles agreed to direct "Touch of Evil" for Universal, provided he be allowed to write the screenplay. The film details a confrontation between a corrupt American cop named Quinlan, played by Welles, and a Mexican officer, Vargas. Thinking that Quinlan has planted evidence on a bombing suspect, Vargas sets a trap for him using bugging devices. Quinlan discovers the device taped to an associate whom he then kills. Before dying though, the associate also kills Quinlan. Ironically, Vargas learns at films's end that Quinlan's suspect has confessed.

Following the release of "Touch of Evil," a film virtually ignored by American distributors and critics, Welles was unable to find financiers for his own film projects. But he was approached by foreign producers anxious to have him direct one of their projects. As Welles related: "A man came to see me and told me he believed he could find money so that I could make a film in France. He gave me a list of films and asked that I choose. And from that list of fifteen films I chose the one that, I believe, was the best: *The Trial*. Since I couldn't do a film written by myself, I chose Kafka."

"The Trial" proved to be another of Welles's controversial films. He altered the mood from the novel so that the film resembled a dream and he exaggerated the death-by-stabbing climax of the novel by having his protagonist destroyed by dynamite. Critics were sharply divided on the possible merits of the film. Andrew Sarris called it "the most hateful, the most repellent, and the most perverted film Welles ever made.'' Peter Cowie, however, called it ''Welles' finest film since *Kane* and, far from being a travesty of Kafka's work, achieves an effect through cinematic means that conveys perfectly the terrifying vision of the modern world that marks every page of the original book.'' Welles justified the changes by stating: ''When I make a film . . . , the critics habitually say, 'This work is not as good as the one of three years ago.' And if I look for a criticism of that one, three years back, I find an unfavourable review that says that that isn't as good as what I did three years earlier. And so it goes. I admit that experiences can be false but I believe that it is also false to want to be fashionable. If one is fashionable for the greatest part of one's career, one will produce second-class work. Perhaps by chance one will arrive at being a success but this means that one is a follower and not an innovator. An artist should lead, blaze trails.''

Welles returned to Shakespeare for his next film, ''Falstaff'' (released in England as ''Chimes at Midnight''), an adaptation of his play ''Chimes at Midnight'' which was, in turn, culled from various plays by Shakespeare that featured the portly character. The filming circumstances were similar to ''Othello'': with Welles shooting scenes from afar to mask stand-in actors, substituting own voice for several characters, and enduring countless delays due to sporadic funding and short-term contracts for some of the actors.

When the film was finally released in 1966, it received the most praise of any Welles film since ''Citizen Kane'' and ''The Magnificent Ambersons.'' Joseph McBride hailed it as ''Welles' masterpiece, the fullest, most completely realized expression of everything he had been working toward since *Citizen Kane*.'' Kael referred to it as ''Welles's finest Shakespearean production to date—another near masterpiece.'' Welles himself deemed it one of his most successful film ventures. ''*The Ambersons* and *Chimes at Midnight* [''Falstaff''] represent more than anything else what I would like to do in films,'' he said.

''Falstaff'' also marked a high point for Welles as an actor. In earlier films, critics often accused him of being ''wooden'' and ''unemotional.'' He especially failed to impress critics with his characterizations in ''Macbeth'' and ''Othello.'' In a review of Welles's acting in the latter, Jorgens cited Eric Bentley's observation that Welles ''never acts, he is photographed.'' And his ''King Lear'' performed from a wheelchair drew jeers from many New York City critics. Other performances, however, drew raves. His portrayal in ''Doctor Faustus'' during the mid-1930's was considered a classic, as was his ''King Lear'' done in England prior to the wheelchair fiasco. He was nominated for an Academy Award for his performance in ''Citizen Kane.'' Perhaps his most noteworthy role, though, aside from Harry Lime in ''The Third Man,'' is that of Falstaff. As Kael noted, ''Welles as an actor has always been betrayed by his voice. It was too much and it was inexpressive; there was no warmth in it, no sense of a life lived. It was just an instrument that he played, and it seemed to be the key to something shallow and unfelt even in his best performances, and most fraudulent when he tried to make it tender.'' She added, ''In *Falstaff*, Welles seems to have grown into his voice; he's not too young for it anymore, and he's certainly big enough. And his emotions don't seem fake anymore; he's grown into them, too.''

Welles's themes are closely related to the roles he chooses. His characters are almost always victims—men doomed by their own actions and those of others—and their actions usually lead to death. Kane, Macbeth, Othello, Arkadin, Quinlan, and Falstaff all die in their films' ends and, except

for Falstaff, they are all great men who have brought about their own undoing. Even in ''The Magnificent Ambersons,'' in which Welles does not appear, there is a concern for the once-great. Stephen Farber, in an article on that film, inquired, ''But how does one explain this obsession with rot and decay in a man of 26, who seemed to the world to be the most youthful and vigorous of artists, the 'boy genius?' The scenes of death in *The Magnificent Ambersons* seem to transfix the young Welles. Is this the famous 'self-destructiveness' of the Welles legend evidence of a morbid, irresistible attraction to decadence?'' And in a review of ''Falstaff,'' a film made more than twenty years after ''The Magnificent Ambersons,'' McBride noted, ''Death hangs over the entire film, and the gaity seems forced.'' After ''Falstaff,'' Welles expressed his fear of decadence. He told McBride that he was becoming more interested in forms: ''That's what I'm reaching for, what I hope is true. If it is, then I'm reaching maturity as an artist. If it isn't true, then I'm in decadence, you know?''

In 1968 Welles made ''The Immortal Story,'' a film for French television. This story of an aging man who ''directs'' a film in which his wife and a young sailor make love was dismissed by most critics as a disappointment. The lighting, sound, and sets were all inferior, even when compared to those of Welles's previous low-budget films. But Charles Silver felt that the film was important as ''one of the most poignantly personal works in all cinema.'' He explained that ''most of what is important about *The Immortal Story* . . . is the extent to which the director makes the film an expression of self. . . . In no previous film . . . has Welles' conception of himself been so crucial to the essence of the work.''

Welles's most recent films, ''F for Fake'' and ''Filming Othello,'' are both documentaries. The former deals with forgeries in the art world and includes an interview with expert Clifford Irving, ironic since Irving was later revealed as a forger himself in a fraudulent ''collaboration'' with Howard Hughes. Another irony of ''F for Fake'' is that Welles actually directed little of the film—most of it was culled from a documentary by Francois Reichenbach! ''Filming Othello'' is much less complex, dealing instead with the chaotic period in which Welles made his second Shakespearean film.

Throughout the 1970's, Welles managed to sustain interest in his incomplete films, ''Don Quixote'' and ''The Other Side of the Wind,'' by screening clips from each at retrospectives honoring his accomplishments. According to Todd McCarthy, ''Don Quixote'' can be edited into ''an allegorical tale about fascism in Spain'' or a ''moon trip.'' In fact, Welles's original ending to his adaptation of Cervantes's classic featured Quixote and Sancho Panza on the moon. Welles insisted that he scrapped that ending, though, after moon landings became reality. He also publicized his intentions to make the film into an ''essay about the pollution of the old Spain.'' But when queried about the film's eventual shape, Welles responded: ''That's really my business. . . . I am making it for myself, with my own money. I keep changing my approach, the subject takes hold of me and I grow dissatisfied with the old footage.''

''The Other Side of the Wind,'' Welles's study of decadence in the filmmaking industry, has been plagued by financial difficulties. Prevented by the Internal Revenue Service from funding the film himself, Welles accepted payments from Iranian investors. However, that country became embroiled in a revolution towards the end of the decade, leaving knowledge concerning the lone print of the film (which Welles contended was 96 percent finished) considerably vague.

Welles has been most visible in the 1970's as an actor in other filmmakers' works, including "It Happened One Christmas" and "The Muppet Movie." He has also appeared on numerous talk shows, where he entertains with humorous anecdotes and magic tricks. Many critics have speculated on whether Welles will ever make another film. "At fifty-one," wrote Kael in 1967, "Welles seems already the grand old master of film." Indeed, few filmmakers have suffered the same hardships as Welles, including the confiscation and remaking of "The Magnificent Ambersons" and "The Lady From Shanghai" and financial difficulties with numerous others. But Welles is reluctant to complain. Referring to his first years as a filmmaker, he commented, "I had luck as no one had; afterwards I had the worst bad luck in the history of the cinema, but that is the order of things: I had to pay for having had the best luck in the history of the cinema." He also told McBride, "I'd like to think I wouldn't have made all bad films if I could have stayed in Hollywood. But of course you don't know." Perhaps Kael put Welles's career in proper perspective when she wrote that he "might have done for American talkies what D. W. Griffith did for the silent film. But when he lost his sound and his original, verbal wit, he seemed to lose his brashness, his youth, and some of his vitality.... An *enfant terrible* defeated ages very fast."

AVOCATIONAL INTERESTS: Gourmet food, magic.

BIOGRAPHICAL/CRITICAL SOURCES—Books: Andre Bazin, *Orson Welles,* Editions Chavane, 1950, translation by Jonathan Rosenbaum published as *Orson Welles: A Critical View,* Harper, 1978; Michael MacLiammoir, *Put Money in Thy Purse,* preface by Orson Welles, Methuen, 1952; Peter Noble, *The Fabulous Orson Welles,* Hutchinson, 1956; Andrew Sarris, editor, *Hollywood Voices: Interviews With Film Directors,* Bobbs-Merrill, 1967; Sarris, *The American Cinema: Directors and Direction: 1929-1968,* Dutton, 1968.

Charles Higham, *The Films of Orson Welles,* University of California Press, 1970; Welles and Herman Mankiewicz, *The Citizen Kane Book,* introduction by Pauline Kael, Little, Brown, 1971; Ronald Gottesman, editor, *Focus on "Citizen Kane,"* Prentice-Hall, 1971; Joseph McBride, *Orson Welles,* Viking, 1972; John Houseman, *Run-Through: A Memoir,* Simon & Schuster, 1972; Peter Cowie, *A Ribbon of Dreams: The Cinema of Orson Welles,* A. S. Barnes, 1973; Francois Truffaut, *Les Films de ma vie,* Flammarion, 1975, translation by Leonard Mayhew published as *The Films of My Life,* Simon & Schuster, 1978; Gottesman, editor, *Focus on Orson Welles,* Prentice-Hall, 1976; Kael, *Kiss Kiss Bang Bang,* Little, Brown, 1976; Richard France, *The Theatre of Orson Welles,* Bucknell University Press, 1977; McBride, *Orson Welles: Actor and Director,* Harcourt, 1978; James Naremore, *The Magic World of Orson Welles,* Oxford University Press, 1978.

Periodicals: *Collier's,* January 29, 1938; *New Yorker,* October 8, 1938; *Newsweek,* January 20, 1941; *Sight and Sound,* autumn, 1961; *Show,* October/November, 1961; *New York Times,* September 13, 1969, August 30, 1970; *Film Quarterly,* spring, 1970; *Film Comment,* summer, 1971, November, December, 1978, March/April, 1979.*

—*Sketch by Les Stone*

*   *   *

WENAR, Charles 1922-

PERSONAL: Born October 27, 1922, in New Orleans, La.; son of Clarence H. (a designer) and Irma (Schoen) Wenar; married Solveig Cederloo (a psychologist), September 27, 1958; children: Johnerik, Leif. *Education:* Swarthmore College, B.A., 1943; Iowa State University, Ph.D., 1951. *Residence:* Worthington, Ohio. *Office:* Department of Psychology, Ohio State University, Columbus, Ohio 43210.

CAREER: Illinois Neuropsychiatric Institute, Chicago, member of staff, 1951-57; University of Pennsylvania, Philadelphia, assistant professor of psychiatry, 1957-65; Ohio State University, Columbus, associate professor, 1966-67; professor of psychology, 1967—. Diplomate of American Board of Examiners in Professional Psychology. *Member:* American Psychological Association, Society for Research in Child Development.

WRITINGS: (With Ann M. Garner) *The Mother-Child Interaction in Psychosomatic Disorders,* University of Illinois Press, 1959; (with Garner and Marion W. Handlon) *Origins of Psychosomatic and Emotional Disturbances,* Hoeber, 1962; *Personality Development From Infancy to Adulthood,* Houghton, 1971. Contributor to psychology journals.

WORK IN PROGRESS: Developmental Psychopathology, publication by Random House expected in 1982.

SIDELIGHTS: Wenar's current research is on negativism in preschoolers and autism. He told *CA:* "I am a writer at heart because some of my happiest moments come when I have something to say and say it well. By the same token, I am in despair when I can only summarize what others have said. My first love is literature and my second love is ideas. When my own ideas run dry in writing a book, what excites me is the discovery of new ideas in other people's writings. In my present book I am trying to reconceptualize the entire field of childhood psychopathology. At times the magic works, at times I catch fire from others, at times I slog through the dismal swamp. In short—I suspect I'm little different from most writers."

*   *   *

WENDERS, Wim 1945-

PERSONAL: Born in 1945 in Dusseldorf, Germany (now West Germany); married Ronee Blakely (an actress, singer, and songwriter), 1979. *Education:* Attended Munich Film Academy, 1967-70. *Office:* c/o Omni-Zoetrope, 916 Kearney St., San Francisco, Calif. 94133.

CAREER: Writer, director, and producer of motion pictures; film critic.

WRITINGS—Screenplays; all as director: (With Peter Handke) "Die Angst des Tormanns beim Elfmeter" (released in the U.S. as "The Goalie's Anxiety at the Penalty Kick"; adapted from the novel by Handke), [West Germany], 1971; "Alice in Den Staedten" (released in the U.S. as "Alice in the Cities"), Filmverlag der Autorens, 1974; "Im Lauf der Zweit" (title means "As Time Goes By"; released in the U.S. as "Kings of the Road"), Wim Wenders/Filmverlag der Autorens, 1976; "Der Amerikanische Freund" (released in the U.S. as "The American Friend"; adapted from the novel by Patricia Highsmith, *Ripley's Game*), Road Movies/Les Films du Losange/Wim Wenders/Westdeutschen Rundfunk, 1977.

Writer and director of short films, including "Schauplatze"; an experimental film released in the U.S. as "Summer in the City," 1970; and an adaptation of Nathaniel Hawthorne's novel *The Scarlet Letter,* for West German television.

Contributor to *Filmkritic* and *Sueddeutsche Zeitung.*

WORK IN PROGRESS: Directing "Hammett," a motion picture based on the life of mystery writer Dashiell Hammett.

SIDELIGHTS: Wenders is considered by a number of critics to be one of the most unconventional and philosophic German filmmakers in a field that includes the more prolific R. W. Fassbinder and the more popular Werner Herzog. Scorning the melodrama and conventional plotting of Fassbinder and the obscure personal vision of Herzog, Wenders uses film as a medium for exploring his obsessions with *angst* and rootlessness, two characteristics of German society that he attributes to the imposition of American culture on one eager to reject its past.

Wenders calls his attitude "schizophrenic" and blames it on the lack of culture in post-World War II Germany. "The most dominant effect was the tendency to stick to other histories or to become involved in other countries," Wenders insisted. "In the early '50s or even the '60s, it was American culture."

Yet he harbors no resentment towards America's influence. "It is incredible to me," he confessed, "how Americans disparage their culture, as if it were cheap or inferior. I don't know if you can understand what American culture meant to me. I was born in '45, in Dusseldorf, two months after the war ended. Everything about German culture was suspect. There was great insecurity about our culture, about any national feeling." For Wenders, American culture offered an alternative to Germany's Nazi past. "When I listened to rock and roll over the Armed Forces Radio Network," he revealed, "it was a culture which was not approved of by my father's generation."

This preoccupation with American culture is evident in Wenders's early films: one entitled "3 American LPs," another named after a song "Summer in the City," popularized by the Lovin' Spoonful, and a third adapted from Nathaniel Hawthorne's *Scarlet Letter*, one of the first classic American novels. The latter film was deemed "a minor work" by Michael Covino, "partly because it does embrace subject matter so apparently foreign to Wenders." However, Covino observed that "The Scarlet Letter" was more than adequate in its depiction of the isolation that is a consistent force in Wenders's films. "The lucidly cool color compositions and the simple strains of mournful music," noted Covino, "add to the sense of strangeness that seeps into us, to the feeling that none of the characters are quite in touch with one another, to that haunting atmosphere of foreigners lost in a strange country that really permeates all of Wenders's films."

Covino's description of "The Scarlet Letter" could also be applied to "The Goalie's Anxiety at the Penalty Kick," the German film that Stanley Kauffmann deemed his personal favorite in 1977. The film is essentially a study in *angst:* shot primarily at dusk, it depicts the anxieties of a soccer goalie deserting his team in mid-game, murdering a woman, and fleeing to Austria. Kauffmann described the goalie as "a man barren of the irrationality that leads to and away from morality, a man who can still make contact with society . . . , but whose vacancy is, paradoxically, like a volcano that can boil at any time."

The goalie is haunted by the memory of his actions: a television clip features him failing to stop a goal; newspapers detail the maneuvering of his pursuers. But although the film contains these "thriller" conventions, Wenders never lets the film actually become one. The film ends with the goalie attending another soccer game. He sits in the bleachers, explaining the mental agony that a goalie endures while awaiting the charge of the penalty kicker. "We are left not with a criminal," wrote Covino, "but a man quietly going mad."

Wenders's next film, "Alice in the Cities," is the first of three films that he collectively refers to as "road movies." As Shelly Frisch stated, the films all share "a common theme, seemingly aimless movement." "Alice in the Cities" deals with the relationship between a German photojournalist in New York City and an abandoned German girl. Together, they return to Germany with only a photograph to assist them in tracking down the girl's relatives.

Some reviewers have paired "Alice in the Cities" with "The Scarlet Letter" as films exemplifying Wenders's inability to accurately portray American life. Covino contended that "all the vignettes with Americans . . . seem stilted, as if Wenders were trying too hard to get these Americans to be . . . Americans."

Peter Handke wrote the screenplay for Wenders's second road film, "The Wrong Movement," an adaptation of Goethe's novel, *Whilhelm Meister's Apprenticeship.* The wanderer of "The Wrong Movement" is Meister, a prospective writer unable to accept modern art's failure, as John L. Fell noted, "either to sustain or to reflect a modern sensibility." Meister's journey involves him with a variety of characters, including an actress infatuated with him, a former Nazi, and an industrialist. The film culminates with a disastrous meeting of all the characters at the industrialist's home: the host commits suicide, forcing the others to flee to the actress's apartment, whereupon she rejects Meister for his sexual incapacity; he, in turn, tries unsuccessfully to murder the ex-Nazi. This last effort by Meister is, according to Fell, one to "sever his tie with Germany's history."

In their adaptation of Goethe's novel, Wenders and Handke reversed both the theme and the character of Meister: Goethe's protagonist celebrates the creative process and the arts, whereas Wenders's Meister laments its shortcomings; he sees German art in limbo, the victim of confusion bred from Germany's reaction to its Nazi past. For Wenders, Germany can only escape its creative impotence by exploring its past. Summing up the road films, Frisch wrote, "Each character gradually comes to realize that his struggle for self-definition must involve an identification with the recent German past. Wenders's characters are haunted by ex-Nazis and the atrocities of an era that remains all-too-alive, and they are forced to see themselves as struggling with both a personal and a national crisis."

Wenders insists, however, that any search for self-identity be done outside a society that still prefers blustering courage to painful analysis. Frisch wrote: "The modern Wilhelm Meister must fail in what Goethe's Meister had achieved so effortlessly: to effect a successful synthesis of individual goals and societal realities. The society in which Wenders's Wilhelm Meister must function only serves to paralyze him."

Wenders's contention that he "never wanted to show things that are shown in general" is evident in "Kings of the Road," the final film in his road trilogy. The film is concerned with two men who tour the Northern border of West Germany while one repairs film projectors. Although the audience learns much about the characters during the film's three-hour length, there is actually little action. Wenders chose to avoid conventional plot techniques by developing his characters in a lateral manner. This process serves to reteach audiences how to view films, for preconceived notions inevitably prove useless while watching Wenders's work. "The film is always teaming with possibilities—possibilities that are always allowed to fade out," wrote Covino. He asserted that mid-way in a scene's development, "it's over; we see that our own expectations were artificial, founded upon previous films rather than any real experience.''

Yet by the film's end, the audience realizes that Wenders has not merely flirted with *avant-garde* techniques. ''Slowly,'' wrote Covino, ''imperceptibly, the film pulls together before our eyes and emerges as a coherent whole that progresses not along the usual dramatic story line but by cautiously circling around certain . . . areas of experience, drawing closer and closer to the elusive heart of the matter.''

This concept of circling ''the elusive heart of the matter'' may also serve as an apt summation of the characters' learning process in ''Kings of the Road.'' They meet when Robert, a linguist who has abandoned his wife, drives his Volkswagon into the ocean. He escapes his sinking auto and befriends Bruno, a projector repairman who lives in his van and happened to be parked along the beach. The two travel together for a brief time, during which each person learns a bit more about himself.

The focal point occurs when Robert and Bruno spend the night in a deserted army bunker decorated with American graffiti. During the night, they each confess certain secrets they've kept, as well as revealing to each other what they've observed and suspected about the other. The two eventually come to blows, after which Robert decides to return to his wife.

A critic for *Nation* was disturbed by the ''metaphysical'' lives depicted in ''Kings of the Road.'' ''One does not live metaphysically,'' the writer insisted. The same reviewer also accused Wenders of deriving his work ''from an abstract disillusionment, an *a priori* negativism.'' Wenders confessed that ''even the first film I made at film school had the sense of a missing story,'' and Covino argued that to analyze Wenders's films from a conventional perspective is to misinterpret them, for meaning is secondary to feeling. ''And so it seems almost accidental that what Wenders's films leave us with finally is simply a mood,'' Covino asserted, ''a chilling and exacting mood . . . that somehow corresponds to what our nerves tell us about the world.''

Wender's preference for mood over plot failed to impress some reviewers of ''The American Friend.'' Terry Curtis-Fox dubbed it ''a hard, anti-classical movie very critical of the conventions upon which it plays *and* a convincing thriller.'' But he also regretted that it ''is not a perfect film.'' Pauline Kael noted that in Wenders's efforts to enrich the mood, he ends up ''losing more in clarity than he gains in depth.''

The plot of ''The American Friend'' revolves around two characters: Ripley, an American working in Europe as a distributor of paintings by an artist who has faked his own death to escalate the price of his paintings; and Jonathan, a framemaker with a blood disease, who suspects that Ripley's dealings are not entirely legitimate. When Jonathan snubs him at an art auction, Ripley returns the favor by setting up Jonathan to fulfill an underworld murder contract by convincing him that his blood disease is fatal. If Jonathan carries out the murder, Ripley reassures him, then his wife and child will be financially provided for after he dies. Jonathan completes the agreement by murdering an enemy of some pornographic filmmaking friends of Ripley's, but during a second murder, he errs, and Ripley comes to his aid. The two begin an uneasy friendship that becomes stronger when they realize that a victim they have thrown off a train has not died but is coming back to kill them. The two manage to escape, though, and drive out to a beach where, accompanied by his wife, Jonathan deserts Ripley only to die moments afterwards.

In this already confusing film, Wenders's decision to emphasize mood proved extremely detrimental. The multiplicity of languages, together with the use of jump-cutting between Paris, New York City, and Hamburg, and the omission of key scenes, tends to leave the audience baffled. Fox noted that ''Wenders jettisoned scenes that explained crucial points in the plot. When a body turns up in an ambulance near the end of the film . . . , there is no longer any indication that the man beneath the bandages is the bodyguard who was earlier thrown off of a train and is now about to finger his killers. Asked by a puzzled viewer how he felt about the cut, Wenders . . . answered, 'I feel guilty.' ''

Despite the ambivalent responses to ''The American Friend,'' Wenders is revered in the film community as one of the few German filmmakers dealing with the implications of life in Germany following World War II. Frisch declared that ''all five of Wenders' major films continue to explore precisely those themes that the earlier generation of German writers had found so compelling, centering on the question: what does it mean to be German in the aftermath of World War II. . . . Wenders is the first film director to focus the consciousness of his young post-war characters on Germany's catastrophic past.''

AVOCATIONAL INTERESTS: Collecting Americana.

BIOGRAPHICAL/CRITICAL SOURCES: Nation, October 23, 1976, October 15, 1977; Jan Dawson, *Wim Wenders,* translated by Carla Watenberg, New York Zoetrope, 1976; *New Republic,* January 29, 1977; *Village Voice,* October 3, 1977; *New Yorker,* October 17, 1977; *Film Quarterly,* winter, 1977-78, winter, 1978-79; *Time,* March 20, 1978; *Literature/Film Quarterly,* Volume 7, number 3, 1979.*

—*Sketch by Les Stone*

*   *   *

WERNER, Victor (Emile) 1894-1980

OBITUARY NOTICE—See index for *CA* sketch: Born September 22, 1894, in Brooklyn, N.Y.; died January 16, 1980, in Washington, D.C. Businessman, management analyst, civil servant, and writer. Werner was employed by various U.S. government agencies as a management analyst. A specialist on memory improvement and the occult, he was the author of *Short Cut Memory.* Obituaries and other sources: *The Writers Directory, 1980-82,* St. Martin's, 1979; *Washington Post,* January 17, 1980.

*   *   *

WESCHE, L(ilburn) E(dgar) 1929-

PERSONAL: Born November 21, 1929, in Taming, China; son of Kenneth (a professor) and Agnes (a nurse; maiden name, Taylor) Wesche; married Esther Rinker (an elementary school teacher), August 21, 1953; children: Kenneth, Cheryl, Barbara. *Education:* Northwest Nazarene College, A.B., 1951; Trinity University, San Antonio, Tex., M.Ed., 1954; University of Northern Colorado, Ed.D., 1961; also attended San Jose State University and University of Cincinnati. *Politics:* Democrat. *Religion:* Protestant. *Home:* 8425 Wyndham Lane, Boise, Idaho 83604. *Office:* Department of Education, Northwest Nazarene College, Nampa, Idaho 83651.

CAREER: Junior high school principal in Meridian, Idaho, 1957-61; Northwest Nazarene College, Nampa, Idaho, professor of education and director of teacher education, 1961—, director of graduate studies, 1974—. *Member:* National Education Association, Idaho Education Association (member of board of directors; head of professional development committee), Phi Delta Kappa.

WRITINGS: *Advising the Student Newspaper,* Pageant, 1967; (with Mel Schroeder) *Audiovisual Tools in the Church,* Beacon Press, 1971, revised edition published as *Media in the Church,* Beacon Hill, 1980. Contributor to education journals.

WORK IN PROGRESS: *Unit Construction.*

SIDELIGHTS: Wesche writes: "My primary interest is in teaching procedures, strategies, and instructional organization.

"The science of teaching has advanced considerably in the past decade or so. Instructional theory has moved from the conceptual stage to the implementation stage and the classroom teacher is the one responsible for that implementation. Equipping the classroom teacher with the skills and knowledge recently identified through research is the task of teacher education and related elements in higher education. This makes particularly important, strong inservice programs for practicing teachers, and well organized, vital preservice programs for incoming teachers. New knowledge about the teaching/learning process also underscores the need for the public to limit the function of the schools to that of education. Schools should not be 'containment institutions' for children for two thirds of the year. Rather, the educational program should be designed to encourage learning; with youngsters present at the school site some of the time but with provisions for them to learn in other places or to be elsewhere during the so-called 'school day' when the instructional program dictates."

* * *

WEST, V(ictoria Mary) Sackville
See SACKVILLE-WEST, V(ictoria Mary)

* * *

WESTERINK, Leendert Gerrit 1913-

PERSONAL: Born November 2, 1913, in Velp, Netherlands; came to United States in 1965; son of Reinier Marinus Westerink (a minister) and Neeltje Petronella Johanna Vuyk; married Barbara Wilhelmina Schmidz, August 28, 1945; children: Reinier Marinus, Anna Martina, Maria Anna Julia, Joannes Jacobus Aloysius. *Education:* Catholic University of Nijmegen, Drs. Classical Languages & Literature, 1939, Drs. English Language & Literature, 1945, Litt.D., 1948. *Home:* 61 Little Robin Rd., Amherst, N.Y. 14228. *Office:* Department of Classics, State University of New York at Buffalo, Amherst Campus, Buffalo, N.Y. 14260.

CAREER: Teacher of English, Greek, and Latin at secondary school in Emmen, Netherlands, 1945-65; State University of New York at Buffalo, professor of classics, 1965—, distinguished professor, 1974, Andrew V. Raymond Professor, 1975. Visiting professor at College de France, 1970-71; visiting scholar at Dumbarton Oaks, 1971; research associate of Centre National de la Recherche Scientifique, 1973-74. *Member:* International Society for Neoplatonic Studies (member of advisory committee, 1973), Royal Netherlands Academy of Sciences (corresponding member).

WRITINGS: (Editor) Proclus Diadochus, *Commentary on the First Alcibiades of Plato,* North-Holland Publishing, 1954; (editor) Olympiodorus, *Commentary on the First Alcibiades of Plato,* North-Holland Publishing, 1956; (editor and translator) Damascius, *Lectures on the Philebus,* North-Holland Publishing, 1959.

(Editor and translator) *Anonymous Prolegomena to Platonic Philosophy,* North-Holland Publishing, 1962; (editor) Pseudo-Elias, *Lectures on Porphyry's Isagoge,* North-Holland Publishing, 1966; (editor) Arethae archiepiscopi Caesariensis, *Scripta minora* (title means "Minor Writings"), Teubner, Volume I, 1968, Volume II, 1972; (editor and translator with H. D. Saffrey) Proclus, *Theologie Platonicienne* (title means "Platonic Theology"), Bude, Volume I, 1968, Volume II, 1974, Volume III, 1978, Volume IV, 1979.

(Editor) Olympiodorus, *In Platonis Gorgiam commentaria* (title means "Commentary on Plato's Gorgias"), Teubner, 1970; (editor) Nicetas Magistros, *Lettres d'un exile, 928-946* (title means "Letters of an Exile"), Centre National de la Recherche Scientifique, 1973; (editor and translator with Romilly J. H. Jenkins) Nicholas I, *Letters,* Dumbarton Oaks, 1973; *The Greek Commentaries on Plato's Phaedo,* North-Holland Publishing, Volume I, 1976, Volume II, 1977; (editor and translator with Charles Garton) Theophylactus Simocates, *On Predestined Terms of Life* (monograph), Department of Classics, State University of New York at Buffalo, 1978; (editor and translator with Jean Darrouzes) Theodore Daphnopates, *Correspondance,* Centre National de la Recherche Scientifique, 1978; (editor and translator with Garton) Germanos, *On Terms of Life* (monograph), Department of Classics, State University of New York at Buffalo, 1979; *Texts and Studies in Neoplatonism and Byzantine Literature,* A. M. Hakkert, 1979; (editor and translator) Nicholas I, *Miscellaneous Writings,* Dumbarton Oaks, 1980; (editor with Basil Laourdas) *Photii patriarchae Constantinopolitani,* three volumes, Bibliotheca Teubneriana, 1981. Editor of "Arethusa Monographs," published by Department of Classics, State University of New York at Buffalo. Contributor of more than sixty articles and reviews to scholarly journal.

WORK IN PROGRESS—Editing: *Theologie Platonicienne* (title means "Platonic Theology"), by Proclus, with H. D. Saffrey, publication of Volume V expected by Bude; *Commentary on the Aphorisms of Hippocrates,* by Stephanus, three volumes, Corpus Medicorum Graecorum; *The Catalogues of Greek Manuscripts of the Library of San Antonio, Venice,* with Saffrey and Aubrey Diller; Photii, *Amphilochia* (title means "Questions and Answers to Amphilochins"), two volumes, Bibliotheca Teubneriana; (and translator) *Traite des Principes* (title means "Treatise on the First Principles"), by Damascius, with Joseph Combes, three volumes.

SIDELIGHTS: Westerink comments: "In spite of an innate aversion to travel, motion, or change of any kind, I moved to the United States to escape a teaching schedule of from twenty-five to thirty hours a week. In spite of the same aversion, I made trips to Paris, Turin, Moscow, the Escorial, Rome, Venice, Patmos, Mt. Athos, Athens, because some of the most attractive places in the world happen to be those where Greek manuscripts are to be found."

* * *

WESTMAN, Jack C(onrad) 1927-

PERSONAL: Born October 28, 1927, in Cadillac, Mich.; son of Conrad A. and Alice (Pedersen) Westman; married Nancy K. Baehre, July 17, 1953; children: Daniel P., John C., Eric C. *Education:* University of Michigan, B.S., 1949, M.D., 1952, M.S., 1959. *Home:* 1234 Dartmouth St., Madison, Wis. 53705. *Office:* Department of Psychiatry, University of Wisconsin—Madison, 600 Highland Ave., Madison, Wis. 53792.

CAREER: University of Michigan Medical School, Ann Arbor, Mich., assistant professor, 1959-60, associate professor, 1961-64; University of Wisconsin—Madison, professor of psychiatry, 1965—, director of Child Psychiatry Division, 1965-73. Director of Outpatient Services, Children's Hospital, Ann Arbor, Mich., 1961-65. Vice-president of Big Brothers of Dane County, 1970-73; co-chairman of Project Understanding, 1968-76. Consultant to Madison public schools, 1965-74, and Dane County Mental Health Center, 1965-68. *Military service:* U.S. Navy, 1953-55; served as a psychiatrist in Jacksonville, Fla., and with U.S. Marine Corps in Japan; became lieutenant. *Member:* American Association of Psychiatric Services for Children (president, 1978-80), American Orthopsychiatric Association (director, 1973-76), American Psychiatric Association, American Academy of Child Psychiatry, Wisconsin Association for Mental Health (vice-president, 1968-72), Wisconsin Council of Child and Adolescent Psychiatry (president, 1977—), Sigma Xi. *Awards, honors:* Wisconsin Association for Mental Health award for service to children, 1974, and citizen of the year award, 1976.

WRITINGS: Individual Differences in Children, Wiley-Interscience, 1973; *Child Advocacy,* Free Press, 1979. Editor of proceedings of the University of Wisconsin Conference on Child Advocacy, 1976. Author of more than fifty articles on child psychiatry, learning disabilities, child advocacy, divorce and children, and noise pollution.

WORK IN PROGRESS: A book on learning disabilities; developing criteria for evaluating the interests of children in custody cases.

*   *   *

WESTON-SMITH, M. 1956-

PERSONAL: Born June 1, 1956, in London, England; daughter of John H. and Margaret (Milne) Weston Smith. *Education:* Attended girls' school in London, England. *Home and office:* 10 Green St., Cambridge, England. *Agent:* Eric Glass, 28 Berkeley Sq., London W.1, England.

CAREER: Editor and writer, 1977—.

WRITINGS: (Editor with Ronald Duncan) *Encyclopedia of Ignorance,* Pergamon, 1977; (editor with Duncan) *Lying Truths,* Pergamon, 1979.

WORK IN PROGRESS: Editing the third volume of *Encyclopedia of Ignorance,* essays on Marxism, with Ronald Duncan, publication expected in 1981.

*   *   *

WEXLEY, Kenneth N.

EDUCATION: University of Tennessee, Ph.D., 1969. *Office:* Department of Psychology, University of Akron, Akron, Ohio 44325.

CAREER: University of Akron, Akron, Ohio, professor of psychology, 1969—. Visiting professor at University of California, Berkeley, 1974-75, and University of Sheffield, 1977. *Member:* American Psychological Association (fellow), American Society for Training and Development, American Society for Personnel Administration, Academy of Management.

WRITINGS: (With Gary A. Yukl) *Readings in Organizational and Industrial Psychology,* Oxford University Press, 1971; (editor with Yukl) *Organizational Behavior and Industrial Psychology,* Oxford University Press, 1975; (with Yukl) *Organizational Behavior and Personnel Psychology,*

Irwin, 1977; (with Gary P. Latham) *Motivating Subordinates Through Performance Appraisal,* Addison-Wesley, 1979; *Management Development and Employee Training in Organizations,* Goodyear Publishing, 1979. Past editor of *Journal of Applied Psychology, Academy of Management Journal,* and *Journal of Business Research.*

*   *   *

WHARTON, William [a pseudonym]

PERSONAL: Born in Philadelphia, Pa.; married; children: four. *Education:* Attended University of California, Los Angeles; also studied psychology. *Residence:* Paris, France.

CAREER: Painter and novelist. Has also worked as a teacher. *Awards, honors:* American Book Award for first novel and nomination for Pulitzer Prize in fiction, both 1980, both for *Birdy.*

WRITINGS: Birdy (novel; Book-of-the-Month Club selection), Knopf, 1978.

SIDELIGHTS: William Wharton's first novel has enjoyed a success imagined by neither its publisher nor its author. After submitting the manuscript for *Birdy* to a New York literary agent, Wharton heard no response, so he allowed a friend's friend to circulate his work among some publishers. It first came to Alfred Knopf Inc., which seemed impressed by Wharton's novel but suggested the author make some needed revisions. Wharton complied, and Knopf accepted the book. Still, the publisher considered it a gamble when it ran a first printing of ten thousand. The gamble obviously paid off: Knopf soon increased the printing to twenty-five thousand and then sold the paperback rights to Avon.

The *Birdy* story is as unique as the success of the novel itself. It begins in an Army insane asylum where a young man, known to the reader only as Birdy, is seen squatting, flapping his arms, and hunching over like a bird. In fact, it is later revealed, he is actually trying to be one. To help himself understand his patient, a baffled Army psychiatrist summons Al, a childhood friend of Birdy and also a victim of World War II—his shrapnel-torn face has been repaired by plastic surgery. In a series of alternating monologues, through Al's words and Birdy's thoughts, the two explain the present by revealing the events of the past.

Implausible as this tale might seem, critics have agreed that, in the hands of Wharton, it has succeeded wonderfully. "This first novel is a stunning achievement," wrote George Hill of the *New Leader.* "All the more so given the improbability of its plot and the skill required to bring it to life." Even as the novel progresses and the events become increasingly singular, when Birdy's erotic fantasies with his canaries are revealed, Wharton maintains his grip on the reader. "What might have seemed ridiculous, even disgusting, is believable," commented Merryl Maleska of the *Chicago Tribune. Newsweek* reviewer Peter S. Prescott also praised *Birdy.* "Only the most rigorous imagination can make a story of this sort work for a reader who is generally indifferent to birds," he declared. "Wharton has just such an imagination." Wharton's detailed study of birds has been compared to Melville's treatment of cetology in *Moby Dick.*

Birdy's obsession with birds grows from a childhood interest in pigeons both he and Al shared. But whereas Al graduates to the more typical adolescent interests of girls and cars, Birdy submerges himself even more deeply into his private world. When he survives a fall after attempting to fly from a one hundred-foot gas tower, his parents have his pigeon loft destroyed and award him a canary as a consolation. His canary collection grows and he spends his time observing their mating habits, their movements, their motions in flight; his fascination turns into an obsession. Every night he dreams of mating with his beloved bird, Perta, and raising their family. The awareness that military service awaits him after high school only increases his preoccupation with his aviary. But Birdy is drafted, torn away from his world, and eventually injured in the Okinawa invasion. The combination of circumstances leads him to the condition he's in at the story's beginning, behaving like a bird in his Army asylum cell.

The novel, however, is not only Birdy's story. Al, as he recalls the events of his and Birdy's past, becomes an increasingly important figure, one with his own share of problems. The muscular veteran has been affected by a war which has disfigured his face and proved him a coward in battle. And though he does not always understand Birdy, he is sympathetic to his condition and continues to try to reach his friend. At last he succeeds—Birdy does speak—but their resolution forecasts little promise. Robert R. Harris summarized the conclusion: "Al is eventually successful at reaching the catatonic Birdy, and the book ends with a surreal scene . . . from which Birdy and Al emerge wiser, ready to go on with life, their rites of passage complete. Their childhoods, which didn't prepare them (but should have) for the world and the war that showed them how insane they are because they 'can't accept the idea that things happen for no reason at all and that it doesn't mean anything,' are behind them."

Wharton's treatment of Al and the book's conclusion have been cited among the faults in *Birdy*. "The fact that Wharton relies so heavily upon Al as a symbolic foil to Birdy weakens the ending of the novel, making it seem too schematic and preachy," commented Robert Towers of the *New York Review of Books*. Maleska also had reservations about the ending, saying, "But when Birdy leaves his birdstance, straightens up, and comes forward to greet Al with his own engaging definition of craziness, it is all too facile. . . . Ironically, it was easier to believe that Birdy could fly." Other critics objected to Wharton's laboriously detailed descriptions of canaries and their world. But John Leonard of the *New York Times* contended that "this immersion in birdness is necessary if we are to believe that Birdy can become a bird; that he can in his dreams fly and fall in love."

Wharton has succeeded in making his readers believe—both in his story and in his talents as a writer. "Like his afflicted hero," wrote *Time*'s Paul Gray, "Wharton tries the impossible, and the result, though linked to earth, mysteriously soars." Critics acknowledge that the book does have its faults, but the overall strength of this first novel attests to Wharton's promise as a writer. They, like Robert Towers, seem to agree that "the talent and energy displayed in *Birdy* sufficiently outweigh its crudities to make one wish for another book from the same pseudonymous source."

CA INTERVIEWS THE AUTHOR

CA interviewed William Wharton on September 20, 1979, by phone in Ocean Grove, N.J., just before his return to France, where he lives with his family.

CA: You've just written a very successful first novel. How do you feel about it?

WHARTON: I'm glad I wrote it. The success was a fine surprise to everybody, including my publisher. My editor at Knopf showed me in their records how most first novels are money-losers. Typically they do a five thousand first print-

ing, but rarely sell it out. So *Birdy* was a pleasant surprise for us all. Knopf thought they were taking a literary shot in the dark, and *Birdy* happened to have some commercial value. My editor tries to sample just about everything that comes in to her, solicited and unsolicited, looking for that needle in the haystack. I think it's a commendable effort on the part of Knopf to keep up their reputation as a literary publisher.

CA: Was Knopf the first publisher you approached with the book?

WHARTON: Yes.

CA: Did you anticipate the reviews with any sort of uneasiness, or did it really matter to you at that point?

WHARTON: I don't think it mattered too much. I didn't know enough to be nervous. I'm glad they were so generally favorable. That helped to sell the book. I had hoped to get more direction for my own writing from reviews, but have been generally disappointed. Reviewers have been extremely diverse in what they like and what they don't like; what are the strong points and the weak points of *Birdy*. Also, I don't think anyone has really talked about what I consider the subject of my book. This is a disappointment. The best reviews so far have come out of campus publications. Stanford, UCLA, and several others have done a beautiful job.

CA: You feel the reviewers for the more accessible magazines failed to fathom the book's depth?

WHARTON: I think so. Such an emphasis was put on the idea of a poor, *crazy* kid. I didn't, and still don't, consider Birdy crazy, or even poor. He had a personal reality he tried to live with, and his illusion failed him, as most people's do sooner or later. I feel one of the book's main themes is that neither fight nor flight is adequate, that fantasy is necessary as a coping system. No one has mentioned this. In fact, Birdy's fantasy did pull him through a trauma few could have survived.

CA: Didn't many reviewers fail to understand the ending's meaning? One referred to it as the "false resolution at the end."

WHARTON: The ending has been enthusiastically approved and enormously condemned in different reviews. My idea is there are no endings. I tried to say this within the context of *Birdy*, that there's only one vast, unending middle; no beginnings, no endings. We tend to hook beginnings and endings onto things, constructing stories, something we can grab hold of. This is what Al and Birdy were trying to say. That it's not so simple. It's very difficult to understand if there's meaning to life, and if there is, *what* it is. The last line of the book is "But it's worth trying." It's something else no one picked up. All of the book was printed either in roman or oblique, but that last line is printed in italic. Also, it is not in quotes, *on purpose*. It's the one time in the book where the author speaks directly. It's not spoken by either of the narrative voices. I consider Birdy and Al to be two aspects of a single person: on one side, the husbanding, loving, protective; on the other, the aggressive, dominant, fear ridden. There is continual interaction between the two. The question of which will be manifest in the course of a young male's growth is important. I've read over forty reviews, and not one mentions this. It's a bit discouraging.

CA: You're a painter. When did you decide to be a writer also?

WHARTON: I've always been both. But I've supported my family and had a public image as painter over the last twenty-five years. I think it's because the writing has been so personal and private; I didn't try for publication. I'd mostly only show what I'd written to friends and talk about it.

I deeply resist the pragmatic McLuhan viewpoint that the medium is the message. I object to it strenuously. I've been writing as long as I've been painting. I got into the world of painting in terms of life survival and stayed with it, and I still am primarily a painter. People ask, "Are you going to paint now that you're a writer?" Obviously I can't change at this time of life; I'm too far gone to start switching my identity that easily. I don't want to, either.

CA: So it didn't mean a great change in your life, then, or even in your routine?

WHARTON: No, I'm working about the same, but with a little more flexibility. So far, writing for me has provided more economic mobility than painting. Painting's a tougher world. There are fewer people who look at paintings than read, so the market is much more limited. Over a long period of time, it's a harder way to live than writing.

CA: Do you develop an idea the same way in painting and writing?

WHARTON: I think so. I take my percepts, which grow into concepts, then become something I can share. Two-thirds of the work is done by the time I get to the point of concept. The actual manipulation of material, the arrangement into presentable form, varies. There are some things that are not paintable. For example, the concepts I was dealing with in *Birdy,* the male problem and the fight-flight-fantasy concept, were not paintable, but they were writable. When I have something bubbling around in my mind, whatever it might be, I decide early which direction it's going, whether it's something I'm going to paint or something I'm going to write about. At this point I would say there's one big difference. Writing has a time element and is much more stretched out. Your view of yourself and your reader has a time-elapsing quality. It might take two or three years to write a book, then seven or eight hours to read it. But painting explodes on the viewer. Later it breaks down into parts as the viewer grazes over the surface. Writing is exposed a bit at a time. Then, one hopes, in the end the reader may put it back together. You approach the same problem from two different time directions; that's the real difference, as I see it.

Incidentally, I think it's one fault of our schools that the musician, the writer, and the painter are too early specialized. They don't get enough mutual interacting experience. I think all writers, painters, and musicians—those are the three I think of particularly—would profit greatly by a broader position, by being trained to think as creative people and not necessarily tied exclusively to their medium. It has to be done early on; by high school most people already think in a particular discipline, and much is lost.

CA: Why did you choose to write under a pseudonym?

WHARTON: For personal privacy, first of all. That's the main reason. I have a right to the name in that it's my mother's maiden name and my middle name. It's also the name of my godfather, so the name is appropriate. I have as much right to it as Frank O'Connor has to his writing name. (O'Connor is his mother's name and Frank his middle name.) The tradition is there. I also chose it because the writer in me comes from the feminine side of my parenthood, not from my father.

CA: Were you interested in birds before you began work on the book?

WHARTON: Yes. I was raising birds as a child, much as Birdy did. I still have birds; I raised a dozen canaries last year. It's been a lifetime interest with me. I didn't have to do any research. I wanted to bring people into an almost unbelievable fantasy—the idea of Birdy being married to a bird, fathering birds, living as a bird, and most of all, flying. So I used the birds *as birds* intermediate to moving people from the mundane foreground to a middle ground of bird observer, then, through that, to the fantasy-dream state. That was the reason I chose birds; I know them.

CA: Was it difficult to sustain the tones of the two dissimilar narrative voices?

WHARTON: I didn't have to think about it. In fact, most of what I write is written in the running present, first person, multiple voices. I prefer it to the third person and find limiting my position to a single narrator too confining. So, for me, this is the most comfortable position. It's somewhere, in a sense, between the novel and play form. Without using capital names for each individual, I can have dialogue going back and forth. For example, when you are in the voice of Al, there are times you are hearing someone else's dialogue. You are in the passive mode. As a writer, I find this extremely attractive, being able to get the reader into a quietly participant mood. The recent book I've written and the one I'm projecting now have multiple voices.

This way you can internalize the identity of your characters, as opposed to having someone out there saying, "He had red hair, large ears, etc." You become that person, and external description is not so necessary. It gives the writer a sense of involvement. In a way it's like oil painting as opposed to watercolor. You're working from inside the forms instead of cutting them out of white. I feel the third-person book resembles watercolor painting. You stand back outside things, seeing events as objects, seeing your characters as objects. Then you've got that old business of "he said," "they said," "Harry said," "Mary said."

CA: When you are writing children characters, do you fall back into your own childhood?

WHARTON: Kafka said writing is a way of keeping open the tiny keyhole back to your past, your memories. There's no question about it. Especially in *Birdy,* when I went to the format of my childhood and used people I knew—my closest friends—as models for the roles, I went back. I found myself becoming more and more aware of things that happened, emotions, all the way down to smells. I don't think I can write any other way. I feel the difference between ordinary fiction and literature in novels is the element of personal memoir. Not only in the strict sense of biographical material, but the way you feel things happened at that time. One dimension of a novel must be based on personal memoir; otherwise it's only fiction.

CA: One reviewer speculated that Birdy *might "become a cult book for the disaffected young." Is that happening?*

WHARTON: I'm getting letters. I just wrote to my editor saying I've figured out what the word cult means. A cult is something someone else believes in that you don't believe yourself. Most people who talk about a book being a cult book are saying some other group is going to become seriously involved with and believe in this book. So I object to the term. Right now, Avon, who bought the paperback rights, is going for the eighteen-to thirty-five-year-old market. They're putting a tremendous emphasis on schools, campuses: film advertising, buttons, bookmarks, T-shirts, whatever. Their conviction is this is where the market will be.

Most of the major reviewers are over thirty-five, so therefore they mean the young are going to like the book. And I think this is true. In writing *Birdy,* one of the things I wanted to say was basically a pacifist message: "Don't get caught." I tried to present this not in a didactic mode but in a demonstrative way, showing how sensitive, feeling, young people are desensitized by their environment and then finally used. As Al says, "We have no control over our own lives. It doesn't matter what we think about ourselves, they will use us as interchangeable parts. When they're finished with us, if we're dead they'll bury us. If we're hurt, they'll give us money." I think the young are going to relate to this theme. Also, I think many older people are questioning viewpoints they've held most of their lives. I have several friends my age who share these feelings and want to see them stated. Even though we deal with young people in *Birdy,* it's stated within the context of the time when people now fifty were young. Birdy and Al are Depression kids.

One of the problems I had was dealing with anachronisms; getting rid of rhythms and expressions that are part of our speech today but weren't then, and still maintaining the flavor of young people talking. It meant a tremendous paring out. I needed to keep the spirit of the time I was writing, and at the same time transcend it somewhat.

CA: Where do you live in France?

WHARTON: We live in three places. We have an apartment in Paris and a houseboat about fifteen kilometers outside of Paris. We're usually at the boat during the week; weekends in Paris. We spend the three summer months in an old water mill between Paris and Geneva.

CA: Was your water mill hard to find?

WHARTON: It kind of fell on us. It was an absolute ruin, and we bought it for practically nothing. We've had it now for eleven years. We've been piling up stones, cementing them together, fixing roofs, putting in plumbing. Now it's reasonably comfortable, except we don't have heating or hot water.

CA: Why did you choose to live in France rather than the United States?

WHARTON: We have four children. When our oldest got into the beginning of the television age, we decided we didn't want our children growing up like that. We felt a strong desire to get out of the pressure from the American competitive-comparative-consumer society. Since as a painter I could live anywhere, and at that time it was cheaper to live in Europe than America (now reversed), we left and moved to Europe. At first we lived around—Spain, Germany, Italy, France—but as the kids got older, the school problem became serious. We had to select one place for the school year, so we chose France. For the last thirteen years we've lived almost exclusively there. It's by choice. I like being a foreigner; so does my wife. There's something about not having everybody's expectations—your neighbors', your relatives'—hanging over you. Its releasing. Also, you can sit on a bus or a metro and not understand what everybody's saying; that helps.

CA: What trends do you see in painting?

WHARTON: I have remained a figurative painter over all

these years through thick and thin—more thin than thick. I was trained as an abstract painter at UCLA. It took me five years to wipe that off my mind, because I'm really not an abstract person. I worked hard getting to the point where I could use what I had learned concerning color and form, then apply it to my observations of the so-called real world. Later, there was my gradual recognition that there is no reality out there, but that my personal reality has validity if I can learn to present it. That is my background, my battleground. I think there are some movements—this whole gradual slide through op and pop into superrealism—that have begun to tickle the edges of what has to happen. I think in the end painters will come to the realization that the plastic, or material, nature of painting is not necessarily in conflict with the representation of a three-dimensional world on two dimensions.

One can present in form what one seems to see, *knowing* it's not actually what one sees, and still be true. *Truth* and *true* are different, neither one more honest than the other. At the turn of the century, with the advent of photography, many painters felt their raison d'être had been usurped. In this big seventy-five-year scramble to find a new place for artists, all kinds of insane things were tried. However, in the end, the reintegration of the decorative, expressive, and descriptive elements of painting has got to happen; it is happening. I know several good, young painters who are putting it together. I feel we've gone through a long, necessary dark age of painting, but it's coming back. I can wait.

CA: Do you think we've been through a similar period of experimentation in fiction?

WHARTON: I don't think it's been as extreme as in painting. There has been, compared to painting, relatively little experimentation in the twentieth century. When you're locked into words, you are already removed from the capacity for anything truly innovative. All you can do is push it around. You can start putting words together without sequence, or you can try all kinds of time anomalies, but in the end you're storytelling. No one's going to read totally meaningless material. People are more demanding of books. They aren't willing to have a book that doesn't say anything, whereas they might hang something on the wall they don't understand because it can be a decorative piece of furniture. A book doesn't make good furniture.

Some of the things that happened in the early part of the twentieth century were new—the big push of Fitzgerald, Hemingway, Stein, Anderson, all the rest, sure—but since then not much. I feel American writing has been on a thirty-year plateau. The New York school of writing has dominated so thoroughly (as the New York school of painting dominated painting until 1965) that no one can move. It's time for a breakout in American writing, a really big one. If I had to guess at directions, I think it would be a movement toward an oral, lyrical tradition as opposed to the verbal, literary tradition. Also a subject matter move away from Freudian prurience toward fantasy—supported, sustained fantasy.

BIOGRAPHICAL/CRITICAL SOURCES: Chicago Tribune Book World, January 7, 1979; *New York Times,* January 8, 1979; *Newsweek,* January 8, 1979; *Washington Post Book World,* January 14, 1979; *Time,* January 15, 1979; *New York Times Book Review,* January 21, 1979, February 11, 1979; *Saturday Review,* February 3, 1979; *New Republic,* February 10, 1979; *New York Review of Books,* March 8, 1979; *Christian Science Monitor,* March 12, 1979; *America,* April 7, 1979; *Nation,* April 7, 1979; *New Leader,* April 9, 1979.

—Sketch by David Versical
—Interview by Jean W. Ross

WHEELER, Thomas H(utchin)   1947-
(Tom Wheeler)

PERSONAL: Born December 15, 1947, in West Point, N.Y.; son of Lester Lewes (an army officer) and Dorothy (Hutchin) Wheeler. *Education:* University of California, Los Angeles, B.A., 1969; Loyola University, Juris Doctor, 1975. *Politics:* Democrat. *Residence:* Palo Alto, Calif. *Office:* GPI Publications, Box 615, Saratoga, Calif. 95070.

CAREER: Worked as musician and guitar instructor in Los Angeles, Calif., 1971-76; *Guitar Player,* Saratoga, Calif., assistant editor, 1978, associate editor, 1979—. *Member:* National Association of Music Merchants.

WRITINGS—Under name Tom Wheeler: *The Guitar Book* (foreword by B. B. King), Harper, 1974, revised edition (with photographs by Wheeler), Harper, 1978. Author of column in *Crawdaddy,* 1977. Contributor to periodicals, including *Loyola Law Review, Rolling Stone,* and *Player* (Japan).

WORK IN PROGRESS: American Guitar: An Illustrated History.

SIDELIGHTS: Wheeler told *CA:* "I began to teach myself—slowly and inefficiently—to play guitar at age thirteen when I lived in Alaska. I had been enchanted with Chuck Berry, and I adopted his style as best I could. I discovered soul music in Atlanta during my high school years, and at the same time was swept up in the British musical invasion. In college my delusions of being Chuck Berry matured into delusions of being Eric Clapton. I embraced electric blues and performed in various bands, one of which lucked into a job following Duke Ellington every night. I majored in political science at UCLA for no particular reason, and attended Loyola School of Law in Los Angeles on a teaching fellowship, with a vague notion of doing one of the 'so many things you can do with a law degree.' After nine months of monastic research, an article of mine, 'Drug Lyrics, the FCC, and the First Amendment,' appeared in Loyola's *Law Review.* The first draft, which had taken six months, was hacked to ribbons by editors and cite-checkers, and (while contemplating nonlegal careers) I learned good lessons about writing and research.

"In the early 1970's I played guitar, wrote songs, and recorded elaborate demo tapes as part of some nebulous scheme to become a record producer. Before graduating from law school and while teaching music in a West Los Angeles studio, I began to write a brief guitar method book. It was to have a four-page appendix. I began work on the appendix, found that I loved to write prose, couldn't stop, and eventually wound up with an encyclopedia on guitars.

"*The Guitar Book*'s topics include history, resonance and acoustics, types of guitars, guitar construction, parts and adjustments, mechanical and electronic accessories, amplifiers, speakers, special effects, guitar synthesizers, systems and methods of tuning, dealers, trade-ins, retailing, collector's items, photo tours through several factories, plus a general attempt throughout to make sense of American guitar, a phenomenon shot through with fable and rumor."

The Guitar Book has been translated into Japanese and Dutch.

AVOCATIONAL INTERESTS: Photography, backpacking, working on educational films, playing guitar, "trying to read the books I should have read in college."

WHEELER, Tom
See WHEELER, Thomas H(utchin)

*   *   *

WHITE, Anne S(hanklin)

PERSONAL: Born in Ensenada, Puerto Rico; came to the United States in 1931; daughter of William (a civil engineer) and Anna C. (a teacher; maiden name, Lancaster) Shanklin; married Richard Daniel White (a naval officer), August 29, 1936 (deceased); children: Maryanna S. White Kay, Richard Terrill. *Education:* Wellesley College, B.A., 1935. *Religion:* Episcopalian. *Home:* 120 Trismen Ter., Winter Park, Fla. 32789. *Office:* Victorious Ministry Through Christ, P.O. Box 1804, Winter Park, Fla. 32790.

CAREER: In business, 1935-c. 1940; Victorious Ministry Through Christ, Winter Park, Fla., president, Christian teacher, and counselor, 1971—. Member of faculty at Japan Women's University, 1953-54. Leads retreats and training missions; speaks at Christian conferences all over the world.

WRITINGS: God Can Transform the World, Christopher, 1957, 4th edition published as *The Transforming Power of God,* Victorious Ministry Through Christ, 1975; *Healing Adventure,* Logos International, 1969; *Dayspring,* Logos International, 1972; *Trial by Fire,* Victorious Ministry Through Christ, 1974; *Healing Devotions,* Morehouse, 1974. Contributor to Christian periodicals.

SIDELIGHTS: Anne White told *CA:* "In 1953 I had a deep conversion experience, when our son was healed instantly of a serious ailment. I began writing and teaching in an effort to help other Christians find God's healing love and power.

"As a naval officer's wife I traveled extensively and lived in Japan and England. Now I hardly unpack my suitcase before it is time to repack and leave. This traveling ministry is authorized by my rector and bishop."

*   *   *

WHITE, Glenn M.   1918(?)-1978

PERSONAL: Born c. 1918 in Indiana; died November 27, 1978, in San Francisco, Calif.; married Irene Parker; children: John, Jay. *Education:* Received undergraduate degree from Ball State University and graduate degree from University of Iowa School of Journalism. *Residence:* Bethesda, Md.

CAREER: Writer and editor. *Ladies' Home Journal,* 1947-63, began as member of editorial staff, became senior associate editor; lecturer at Annenberg School of Communications, University of Pennsylvania; medical writer for *Psychiatric Reporter;* information officer, Department of Agriculture; writer, Environmental Protection Agency. *Military service:* With U.S. Navy during World War II. *Member:* Washington Press Club.

WRITINGS: The Ball State Story: From Normal Institute to University, Ball State University, 1967; *Connecticut Handbook,* Connecticut Council of Teachers of English, 1976. Contributor of articles to *Good Housekeeping, Woman's Day,* and *Cosmopolitan.* Contributing editor, *Dynamic Maturity.*

OBITUARIES: Washington Post, December 2, 1978.*

*   *   *

WHITE, Kenneth Steele   1922-

PERSONAL: Born November 19, 1922, in State College, Pa.; son of William Marsh (a professor) and Stella M.

(Steele) White; married Marie-Juliette Anta Montet (a professor), May 16, 1957; children: Alan Montet, Valerie Miriam. *Education:* Pennsylvania State University, B.A., 1944; Johns Hopkins University, M.A., 1948; Stanford University, Ph.D., 1958; attended Middlebury College, summers, 1947-49, 1951. *Politics:* Democrat. *Religion:* Presbyterian. *Home:* 2819 Harvard St., Lawrence, Kan. 66044. *Office:* Department of French and Italian, University of Kansas, Lawrence, Kan. 66045.

CAREER: University of Michigan, Ann Arbor, instructor, 1957-60, assistant professor of French, 1960-65; University of Kansas, Lawrence, associate professor, 1965-70, professor of French, 1970—, director of International Theatre Study Center, 1968—. Visiting lecturer at Institute for American Universities, Aix-en-Provence, France, 1961-62, summer, 1969. *Military service:* U.S. Army, 1943-46; served in European theater; received Purple Heart. *Member:* Modern Language Association of America, American Association of Teachers of French, Phi Beta Kappa, Phi Kappa Phi, Phi Sigma Iota, Blue Key. *Awards, honors:* Rackham Award from University of Michigan, 1960, for advanced research on French drama centers.

WRITINGS: (Translator and editor) Ghelderode, *School for Buffoons,* Chandler Publishing, 1958; (contributor) Roger Johnson, Jr., Edith S. Neumann, and Guy T. Trail, editors, *Moliere and the Commonwealth of Letters,* University of Southern Mississippi, 1973; *Savage Comedy Since "King Ubu": A Tangent to "the Absurd",* University Press of America, 1977; (editor) *Savage Comedy: Structures of Humor,* Rodopi, 1978; *Centers of a Universe* (poems), Lawton Press, 1978; *Man's New Shapes: French Avant-Garde Drama's Metamorphoses,* University Press of America, 1979; *Les Centres Dramatiques Nationaux de Province, 1945-1965* (title means "The National Drama Centers in the Provinces, 1945-1965"), Peter Lang, 1979. Contributor of poems to literary magazines. Book review editor of *Modern Language Journal,* 1970—.

WORK IN PROGRESS: Einstein's Relativity and Modern French Drama; Animals as Reflections of Human Beings in Modern French Drama; The Gentle Generation, on the current generation of university students; *The Tigress and the Innocent,* a novel.

SIDELIGHTS: White writes: "Twenty-four sojourns in France have led to discoveries of art, classical music, sculpture, ballet, the dance, French ways of life, cuisine, and wine. Greece, classical antiquity, *paysages* and seascapes, French poets and writing poetry, Martinique, and Mexico are other interests.

"I believe peace will eventually come. The younger generation will do much. I am optimistic."

AVOCATIONAL INTERESTS: Golf, tennis, swimming, skiing, dancing.

* * *

WHITE, Ronald C(edric), Jr.   1939-

PERSONAL: Born May 22, 1939, in Minneapolis, Minn.; son of Ronald Cedric (a produce shipper) and Evelyn (a secretary; maiden name, Pearson) White; married Sherrie Rosalind Derrick, May 18, 1943; children: Melissa Gale, Bradley Derrick. *Education:* Attended Northwestern University, 1957; University of California, Los Angeles, B.A., 1961; Princeton Theological Seminary, M.Div., 1964; attended Lincoln Theological College, 1966-67; Princeton University, M.A., 1970, Ph.D., 1972. *Home:* North 10105 Ivanhoe Rd.,

Spokane, Wash. 99218. *Office:* Whitworth College, Spokane, Wash. 99251.

CAREER: Ordained Presbyterian minister; associate pastor of Presbyterian church in Colorado Springs, Colo., 1964-68; Rider College, Trenton, N.J., assistant professor of American studies and chaplain, 1972-74; Whitworth College, Spokane, Wash., assistant professor, 1974-78, associate professor of religion, 1978—, chaplain, 1974—, founding dean of Institute of Ministry. Lecturer at Colorado College, 1965-66; adjunct professor at Fuller Theological Seminary, San Francisco Theological Seminary, New College, Berkeley, Calif., and Karlshohe College; visiting professor at San Francisco Theological Seminary and Graduate Theological Union, 1979. Member of church governing committees; delegate to church conferences in the United States and abroad. Founding president of Martin Luther King Memorial Education Fund, 1968; member of board of directors of Spokane Peace and Justice Center and Martin Luther King Center. *Member:* American Historical Association, Organization of American Historians, American Society of Church History, American Academy of Religion, National Association of College and University Chaplains.

WRITINGS: (With C. Howard Hopkins) *The Social Gospel: Religion and Reform in Changing America,* Temple University Press, 1976; (contributor) Julio de Santa Ana, editor, *Separation Without Hope: Essays on the Relation Between the Church and the Poor During the Industrial Revolution and the Western Colonial Expansion,* World Council of Churches, 1978. Editor of social gospel reprint series, Hyperion Press (Westport, Conn.), 1979. Contributor of articles and reviews to theology journals.

WORK IN PROGRESS: Neither Slave Nor Free: The Social Gospel and Racial Reform; Bittersweet; Piety and Politics; The Reformed Tradition: The Enigma of Social Concern.

SIDELIGHTS: White told *CA:* "My writings on various aspects of social justice come out of my own grappling with these issues as one involved in the college chaplaincy. I am interested in writing for an academic audience, but also want to reach others who struggle with putting personal and social faith together."

* * *

WHITE, Stephen D(aniel)   1945-

PERSONAL: Born April 16, 1945, in New York, N.Y.; son of Morton G. (a professor) and Lucia (a writer; maiden name, Perry) White; married Katharine Murray Gilbert (a writer), June 10, 1979. *Education:* Harvard University, A.B. (summa cum laude), 1965, Ph.D., 1972. *Home:* 80 Chestnut St., New Haven, Conn. 06511. *Office:* Department of History, Wesleyan University, Middletown, Conn. 06511.

CAREER: Harvard University, Cambridge, Mass., junior fellow, 1971-74, research associate in law, 1974-75, lecturer in history, 1974-75; Wesleyan University, Middletown, Conn., assistant professor of history, 1975—. *Member:* Selden Society, Phi Beta Kappa. *Awards, honors:* Grants from American Council of Learned Societies, National Endowment for the Humanities, and American Bar Foundation, all 1978-79.

WRITINGS: Sir Edward Coke and "The Grievances of the Commonwealth," 1621-1628: Studies in Legal History, University of North Carolina Press, 1979 (published in England as *Sir Edward Coke and the Grievances of the Commonwealth,* Manchester University Press, 1979); (editor with Morris S. Arnold, Thomas H. Green, and Sally Scully) *On the Laws and Customs of England: Essays in Honor of Samuel E. Thorne,* University of North Carolina Press, in press. Contributor of articles and reviews to history and law journals.

WORK IN PROGRESS: A monograph, tentatively entitled *Disputes and Dispute-Settlement in Eleventh-Century Western France.*

* * *

WHITNAH, Dorothy L.   1926-

PERSONAL: Born December 16, 1926, in Portland, Ore.; daughter of David Warren (a reporter) and Irma (in real estate sales; maiden name, Wullenwaber) Lupher; married Kerwin Whitnah, 1962 (divorced, 1965). *Education:* University of California, Berkeley, B.A., 1948, B.L.S., 1952. *Politics:* "Cynical Democrat." *Address:* c/o Wilderness Press, 2440 Bancroft Way, Berkeley, Calif. 94704.

CAREER: University of California, Berkeley, librarian for Bureau of International Relations, 1952-57; Book Club of California, San Francisco, executive secretary, 1962-70; Book Club of California, member of board of directors, 1977—. *Member:* Mensa, Sierra Club, Audubon Society, California Native Plant Society, Gleeson Library Associates (president, 1979—).

WRITINGS: An Outdoor Guide to the San Francisco Bay Area: Exploring With Boots, Backpacks, Bikes, Boats, Books, and BART, Wilderness Press, 1976; *Guide to the Golden Gate Recreation Area,* Wilderness Press, 1978.

WORK IN PROGRESS: Guides to the outdoors, encouraging use of transportation other than the private automobile.

* * *

WHITNEY, George D(ana)   1918-

PERSONAL: Born December 19, 1918, in Hadley, Mass.; son of Leon Fradley (a veterinarian and writer) and Katharine Carrol (Sackett) Whitney; married Nancy Dines (divorced); married Dorothy Lindsay, December 31, 1963; children: (first marriage) Carolyn Whitney Sabol, Charles D., Kate Whitney Consiglio, Lee E. *Education:* Auburn University, D.V.M., 1943. *Religion:* "Humanist." *Home and office address:* Oakwood Rd., Orange, Conn. 06477. *Agent:* Blassingame, McCauley & Wood, 60 East 42nd St., New York, N.Y. 10017.

CAREER: Practice of veterinary medicine, 1945—. Past president of Orange Land Trust; member of Orange Energy Committee and Democratic Town Committee. *Military service:* U.S. Army, Veterinary Corps, 1943-45; became captain. *Member:* International Society to Study Pain, National Audubon Society, Veterinary Heartworm Society, Veterinary Cancer Society, Sierra Club, Connecticut Veterinary Medical Association (past president), Connecticut Herpetological Society, Naugatuck Valley Audubon Society, New Haven County Veterinary Medical Association (past president), Paugusset Club (past president), Rotary International (past local president). *Awards, honors:* Paul Harris fellow of Rotary International.

WRITINGS: (With father, Leon F. Whitney) *Disease of the Distemper Complex,* Popular Science Publishing Co., 1953; *This Is the Beagle,* Practical Science Publishing, 1955; (with L. F. Whitney) *Animal Doctor,* David McKay, 1972; *The Health and Happiness of Your Old Dog,* William Morrill, 1977; (author of revision) L. F. Whitney, *The Complete Book of Cat Care,* Doubleday, 1980; (author of revision) L. F. Whitney, *The Complete Book of Dog Care,* Doubleday, 1980. Contributor to scientific journals.

WORK IN PROGRESS: A book on reptile husbandry, publication expected in 1981; research for a book on the effects of pets on people, completion expected in 1981.

SIDELIGHTS: Whitney writes: "An incident early in life influenced my thinking, in that I have been a doubter who wants to find answers. Clarence Darrow was a frequent house guest, and after my father said a blessing over food, Mr. Darrow said, 'Leon, why do you carry on with that nonsense?' My father never said another blessing and I became a doubter about more than organized sects.

"I like to set goals for myself and work steadily toward their completion. One goal was the establishment of a central hospital for veterinary medicine in New Haven, offering twenty-four-hour service and equipment too costly for a small practice to provide.

"I was raised as a hunter with hounds, but some time ago decided I do not choose to kill wild animals unless I have good cause. Some expertise was also developed by active involvement in man trailing with bloodhounds, rattlesnake hunting, bee hunting, raising skunks and raccoons, beagle field trials, maple sugaring, and butter scoring.

"Research has been part of my life. Until recently my late father and I maintained a kennel of about two hundred dogs and a cattery of thirty-six cats. The nutrition and genetic studies were rewarding.

"My interest in conservation and utilization of energy sources resulted in a solar installation in my veterinary office which saves fifty percent of previous oil purchases. I am also involved with a group trying to utilize forms of energy other than fossil fuels.

"There was a time when the quotation, 'If you would be remembered, do things worth writing about or write things worth reading about,' seemed to be important to me. However, I am inclined to think my one motivation in life is to leave this place a little better than I found it. I do not consider I write well but I would like to think that I have things about which to write which will be meaningful to some people. In younger days I was a Cub Scout Master for six years, and I have carried on my association with youngsters by lecturing to them at the young grade school level on one of my hobbies, herpetology, and particularly snakes, emphasizing to them that if they can learn to tolerate a creature which so many detest, such as a snake, they may learn one day to tolerate their fellow man."

AVOCATIONAL INTERESTS: Fruit and vegetable gardening.

* * *

WHITTLESEY, E(unice) S.   1907-

PERSONAL: Born September 7, 1907, in New York, N.Y.; daughter of Clarence B. (a lawyer) and Catharine (a writer; maiden name, Cook) Smith; married Julian H. Whittlesey (an archaeologist); children: Peregrine Whittlesey Freund. *Education:* Studied ballet in Paris, France, 1924-25; attended Laboratory Theatre School, 1926-27. *Politics:* Democrat. *Religion:* Protestant. *Home:* 29 Chicken St., Wilton, Conn. 06897. *Agent:* Paul R. Reynolds, Inc., 12 East 41st St., New York, N.Y. 10017.

CAREER: Actress, 1928-40; New School for Social Research, New York, N.Y., lecture moderator, 1946-50; archaeological photographer. Presented "This Woman's Word" on WMCA-Radio, 1946-47. Member of board of directors of New York City's Citizen's Housing Council, 1949-54.

WRITINGS: Symbols and Legends in Western Art: A Museum Guide, Scribner, 1972. Also author of a cookbook, some plays, and articles for bulletins.

SIDELIGHTS: Eunice Whittlesey writes: "I now work with my husband, doing specialized photography from galleons, and surveying with electronic distance measuring instruments.

"*Symbols and Legends* was written because I felt there was a great need for a handbook for tourists who were quite lost in galleries. It was written as a paperback, but its purpose was aborted. The hardback publication is too cumbersome and expensive for tourists' use."

*   *   *

WIEGNER, Kathleen K(napp)   1938-

PERSONAL: Surname is pronounced *Weeg*-ner; born April 12, 1938, in Milwaukee, Wis.; daughter of Russell D. (an educator) and Angelyn (an educator; maiden name, Spicuzza) Knapp; married Edward A. Wiegner, December 16, 1960 (divorced August 17, 1970); children: Christine Elizabeth. *Education:* University of Wisconsin—Madison, B.A., 1960, M.A., 1962, Ph.D., 1967. *Home:* 2444 Cloverfield Blvd., Santa Monica, Calif. 90405. *Office: Forbes,* 1900 Avenue of the Stars, #660, Los Angeles, Calif. 90067.

CAREER: University of Wisconsin—Milwaukee, assistant professor of English, 1964-73; *Forbes,* West Coast Bureau, Los Angeles, Calif., associate editor, 1974—. *Awards, honors:* Poetry prize from Wisconsin Writers Council, 1974, for *Country Western Breakdown.*

WRITINGS: Encounters, Membrane Press, 1973; *Country Western Breakdown* (poems), Crossing Press, 1974; *Freeway Driving* (poems), Hanging Loose Press, 1980.

Work represented in anthologies, including *Mountain Moving Day,* Crossing Press, and *Brewing: Twenty Milwaukee Poets,* Gilagia Press. Contributor to literary journals, including *Minnesota Review, Beloit Poetry Journal,* and *Hanging Loose.* Poetry reviewer for *American Poetry Review,* 1975-77.

WORK IN PROGRESS: Battle Stations, a book of short stories.

SIDELIGHTS: Kathleen Wiegner wrote: "I have been writing poems since I was eight or nine and poetry is my favorite kind of writing. I think my work is easily grasped, at least on some level, by almost anyone and I work for that. I do not believe in being 'difficult' in my work.

"I like poems that are raspy, give the sense of an immediate presence, and I must confess, tug at the old heartstrings a bit. I like to think that, at their best, my poems are wry, sometimes even comedic, contain a bit of the dramatic, tough it out, but we all know they have a heart of gold underneath that act. My secret ambition would be to live in a world where poems were performed in Las Vegas, where the poet sat on a piano like Ruth Etting and 'sang' poems to an audience that clapped and wept. I like a strong emotional response, as you can see.

"On the other hand, these are not dumb poems. Unless you believe that only the intellect is 'smart.' I like to think that my poems are *world*-wise. They've traveled, read books, have thoughts about their experiences, but they are not out to put anyone down by their education."

AVOCATIONAL INTERESTS: Travel in search of archaeological ruins (including Mexico), reading "everything from cereal boxes to novels."

WILCOXON, George Dent, Jr.   1913-

PERSONAL: Born October 6, 1913, in Grant's Pass, Ore.; son of George Dent (a physician) and Cora M. (a teacher; maiden name, Stewart) Wilcoxon. *Education:* University of California, Los Angeles, A.B., 1936, A.M., 1938, Ph.D., 1941. *Home:* 325 North 17th St., Manhattan, Kan. 66502. *Office:* Department of History, Kansas State University, Manhattan, Kan. 66502.

CAREER: Lewis and Clark College, Portland, Ore., associate professor of history, 1941-43; Hastings College, Hastings, Neb., professor of history, 1944-46; Kansas State University, Manhattan, associate professor, 1946-48, professor of history, 1948—. *Member:* American Historical Association, Association of American Historians.

WRITINGS: Athens Ascendant, Iowa State University Press, 1979.

*   *   *

WILDE, Jennifer
   See HUFF, T(om) E.

*   *   *

WILKINS, Ronald J(ohn)   1916-

PERSONAL: Born January 6, 1916, in Chicago, Ill.; son of Albert W. and Mary Catherine (Chisholm) Wilkins; married Nancy Lyle Browne, April 22, 1967. *Education:* St. Mary's College, Winona, Minn., B.A., 1939, M.A., 1967. *Religion:* Roman Catholic. *Home and office:* 3208 West Golfview Ter., McHenry, Ill. 60050.

CAREER: High school teacher of English and religion in Memphis, Tenn., 1936-39, in St. Paul, Minn., and Minneapolis, Minn., 1939-48, and in Evanston, Ill. and Chicago, Ill., 1938-62; writer, 1962—. Director of teacher training for Confraternity of Christian Doctrine, Archdiocese of Chicago, 1956-65. Head of McHenry Zoning Board of Appeals.

WRITINGS: (With Joseph Pluth and Mark LaMont) *Living With Christ,* four volumes, St. Mary's College Press, 1939-42; (with Joseph Hoffman) *English Language Arts Handbook,* St. Mary's College Press, 1952; (with others) *English Arts and Skills,* Macmillan, 1962; (with others) *The Pageant of Literature,* Macmillan, 1963; *Teaching in the C.C.D. High School,* Regnery, 1964; (with William J. Kalt) *To Live Is Christ,* two volumes, Regnery, 1965.

All published by W. C. Brown: *Challenge!,* 1973, revised edition, 1977; *The Jesus Book,* with teacher's manual, 1973, revised edition, 1978; *Focus on Faith,* 1974, revised edition, 1975; *Focus on Growth,* 1974, revised edition, 1975; *The Religions of Man,* with teacher's manual, 1974, revised edition, 1976; *The Emerging Church,* 1975, revised edition, 1978; *Focus on Life,* 1975, revised edition, 1975; *Man and Woman,* 1975, revised edition, with teacher's manual, 1980; *Opinionnaires: Duplicating Masters for Use With the Man and Woman Text,* 1975; *Achieving Social Justice: A Christian Perspective,* 1976; *Understanding Christian Morality,* 1977, abridged edition, 1977; *Understanding Christian Worship,* 1977, abridged edition, 1977; *Understanding the Bible,* 1977, abridged edition, 1977; *Reading the New Testament,* with teacher's manual, 1978, abridged edition, 1978; *Religions of the World,* 1979; *Religion in North America,* 1979; *Focus on Faith in Jesus,* 1980; *Focus on Growth in the Church,* 1980.

Co-author of "DeLaSalle, Founder of Modern Education" (radio play), first aired by numerous radio stations throughout the United States, 1949. Author of "Awareness of God: A Layman's Guide to the Bible" (filmstrip series), three volumes, Roa's Films, 1972. Contributor to magazines.

SIDELIGHTS: Wilkins writes: "I started out as a high school teacher. My writing career developed, I think, from my frustrations with materials students were subjected to in school. Most textbooks were content-structured, responding to the question: 'What does the subject matter demand?' rather than being structured to the needs of the students at their own stage of educational/psychological development. So, rather than 'teach by the book,' I began to write my own materials.

"My first national audience came when I wrote an article about the thrill of flying at night from New York to Chicago. I forget the name of the now-defunct magazine the piece appeared in, but it brought me immense satisfaction and some small attention.

"Even though my writing at the moment is directed at filling a specific need in religious schools, I feel that my materials would fill a larger need if the political/religious climate in the United States were different. Religion as a field of study is important. It is important in itself as a branch of human knowledge; it is a fact of life in every society in the world; it plays an important role in the lives of nearly ninety per cent of all people; and it has shaped the development of civilization and culture for over ten thousand years. I think people in general, and students in particular, would benefit from a better knowledge of religion (most don't know what it is, really!) for, among other things, it would help them understand other people, which is the first step in accepting others and relating to them in a peaceful way.

"The most important travel I do is not to explore the places I write about, but to interview students and teachers concerning a book I am preparing to write. Because I am writing for students and teachers (not for critics and theologians) I try to find out what the students' interests are and the teachers' needs might be. In this way, I can direct my materials to them."

* * *

WILKINSON, David

PERSONAL—Education: Harvard University, A.B., 1960; Columbia University, M.A., 1962, Ph.D., 1965. *Office:* Department of Political Science, University of California, Los Angeles, Calif. 90024.

CAREER: University of California, Los Angeles, associate professor of political science, 1965—.

WRITINGS: Malraux: An Essay in Political Criticism, Harvard University Press, 1967; (co-author) *International Law and Political Crisis,* Little, Brown, 1968; *Comparative Foreign Relations,* Dickenson, 1969; *Revolutionary Civil War,* Page-Ficklin, 1975. Also author of *Deadly Quarrels,* University of California Press.

* * *

WILLEM, John M.   1909-1979

OBITUARY NOTICE—See index for *CA* sketch: Born November 1, 1909, in Milwaukee, Wis.; died December 15, 1979, in Port Washington, N.Y. Business executive, numismatist, and writer. After Willem retired from his position as senior vice-president of the J. Walter Thompson advertising agency, he held posts with the Bureau of Foreign Commerce and the West Indies and Caribbean Development Ltd. A contributor to numismatic and economic journals, Willem wrote one book, *The United States Trade Dollar: America's Only Unwanted, Unhonored Coin.* Obituaries and other sources: *New York Times,* December 18, 1979.

WILLIAMS, Denis Joseph Ivan   1923-

PERSONAL: Born February 1, 1923, in Georgetown, Guyana; son of Joseph Alexander (a merchant) and Isabel (Adonis) Williams; married Catherine Hughes, 1949 (divorced, 1974); married Toni Dixon (a poultry farmer), August 21, 1975; children (first marriage) Janice, Evelyn, Isabel, Charlotte, Beatrice; (second marriage) Miles, Morag, Everard, Rachael, Denis. *Education:* Attended Camberwell School of Art, 1946-48; University of Guyana, M.A., 1979. *Politics:* None. *Religion:* Christian. *Home:* 18-D Thorn's Dr., D'Urban Backlands, Botanic Gardens, Georgetown, Guyana. *Agent:* John Wolfers, 42 Russel Sq., London W.C.1, England. *Office:* Department of Culture, Ministry of Education, 15 Carifesta Ave., Georgetown, Guyana.

CAREER: Central School of Art, London, England, lecturer in art, 1950-57; Khartoum School of Art, Khartoum, Sudan, lecturer in art, 1957-62; University of Ife, Ife, Nigeria, lecturer in African studies, 1962-66; University of Lagos, Lagos, Nigeria, lecturer in African studies, 1966-68; National History and Arts Council, Georgetown, Guyana, art consultant, 1968-74; Ministry of Education, Georgetown, director of art and department of culture, 1974—. Visiting tutor at Slade School of Fine Art, London, 1950-52; visiting professor at Makerere University, 1966. Chairman of National Trust, Georgetown, 1978—.

Member: National Commission for the Acquisition, Preservation, and Republication of Research Materials on Guyana. *Awards, honors:* Second prize from *London Daily Express* "Artists Under Thirty-five" competition, 1955; national honor from government of Guyana, 1973, for "The Golden Arrow of Achievement"; first prize in National Theatre's mural competition, 1976.

WRITINGS: Other Leopards (novel), Hutchinson, 1963; *The Third Temptation* (novel), Calder & Boyars, 1968; *Giglioli in Guyana, 1922-1972* (biography), National History and Arts Council (Georgetown, Guyana), 1970; *Image and Idea in the Arts of the Caribbean,* National History and Arts Council (Georgetown, Guyana), 1970; *Icon and Image: A Study of Sacred and Secular Forms of African Classical Art,* New York University Press, 1974.

Contributor: Joseph C. Anene and Godfrey N. Brown, editors, *Africa in the Nineteenth and Twentieth Centuries,* Thomas Nelson, 1966; John Ferguson and L. A. Thompson, editors, *Africa in Classical Antiquity,* Ibadan University Press, 1969; S. O. Biobaku, editor, *Sources of Yoruba History,* Clarendon Press, 1973.

Work represented in anthologies, including *Island Voices,* Liveright, 1970; *New Writing in the Caribbean,* National History and Arts Council (Georgetown, Guyana), 1972. Contributor of about twelve articles to African studies and anthropology journals. Editor of *Odu,* 1964, *Lagos Notes and Records,* 1967, and *Archaeology and Anthropology,* 1978.

WORK IN PROGRESS: Prehistoric Guyana, based on studies of petroglyphs indicating contrasting patterns of environmental adaptation, completion expected in 1983.

SIDELIGHTS: Williams writes: "A Colonial artist or writer who has received his professional education in Britain and made his first home there is not likely easily to forget that experience. I find that in my own case the experience has proven not only formative, but to a degree even determinative. It seems to have shaped the entire course of my subsequent development. Thus, to me, it is impossible to imagine a career built other than upon the solid foundation of early recognition and acceptance which was accorded to me during the first half of the fifties in London. Paradoxically, however, as Fanon has so perceptively shown, given the circumstances and the day, acceptance on this level was in fact far the most unacceptable, indeed probably the most humiliating, of choices open to the Colonial artist.

"This may explain the rapid and apparently permanent darkness which followed the explosion of Caribbean writing in Britain during the time I was there. Colonial territories were all becoming independent, which was quickly to render the Colonial artist or writer obsolete; for just as national independence seems to have pulled the rug from under the feet of the Colonial writer, new national writers were arising in English- and French-speaking West Africa and in the Caribbean.

"By this time I was myself in Africa writing *Other Leopards,* or trying to resolve some of the problems of identity which provided the theme for that novel. By the time of its completion it was becoming evident that even though the new African literature was being written all around me, and by familiar hands, Africa did not represent the uttermost swing of the pendulum in my reaction from an unwilling acceptance in Europe. Indeed, the African experience tended to reveal to me deeply ingrained attitudes to various aspects of European art, life, and literature that had remained so far undetected. Odd as it may seem, it was very easy for me to write *The Third Temptation* (in an experimental French idiom) simultaneously with my study of African classical art, which in itself represented an intellectual search for African roots.

"I have since returned to Guyana, and see clearly that such a thing could never take place against my rediscovered background. However, if this means that the pendulum has at last reached its ultimate distance of travel, it is no comfort to realize that my first true Caribbean novel, *The Sperm of God,* has remained unfinished now for thirteen years."

BIOGRAPHICAL/CRITICAL SOURCES: Listener, July 14, 1949, December 14, 1950; *Time,* December, 1950; *Daily Express,* April 28, 1955; *Times British Colonies Review,* spring, 1955; Walter Michel and C. J. Fox, editors, *Wyndham Lewis on Art: Collected Writings, 1913-1956,* Thames & Hudson, 1969; Gerald Moore, *The Chosen Tongue,* Longman, 1969; O. R. Dathorne, *The Black Mind: A History of African Literature,* University of Minnesota Press, 1974; Kenneth Ramchand, *The West Indian Novel and Its Background,* Faber, 1974.

*   *   *

WILLIAMS, (George) Emlyn   1905-1974

OBITUARY NOTICE: Born November 26, 1905, in Mostyn, Wales; died in 1974. Actor and playwright best known for "Night Must Fall" and "The Corn Is Green." Williams played the lead character in "Night Must Fall" in New York City in 1936. He also appeared in the film "The Girl in the News," which he wrote. Obituaries and other sources: *The Author's and Writer's Who's Who,* 6th edition, Burke's Peerage, 1971; *Crowell's Handbook of Contemporary Drama,* Crowell, 1971; *McGraw-Hill Encyclopedia of World Drama,* McGraw, 1972; *Cassell's Encyclopaedia of World Literature,* revised edition, Morrow, 1973; *Contemporary Dramatists,* St. Martin's, 1973; *Encyclopedia of Mystery and Detection,* McGraw, 1976.

*   *   *

WILLIAMS, Henry
See MANVILLE, W(illiam) H(enry)

WILLIAMS, John B.   1919-

PERSONAL: Born August 4, 1919, in New York, N.Y.; son of Elmer Reed (in advertising) and Stella (Brindley) Williams; married Jean Elizabeth Humphrey, August 24, 1951; children: Marilyn, Evelyn Williams Sherven, Heather Williams Stauble, Laura. *Education:* Long Beach City College, A.A., 1942; University of Southern California, B.A., 1948, Ph.D., 1965. *Politics:* "Moderate." *Religion:* Presbyterian. *Home:* 9791 El Tulipan Circle, Fountain Valley, Calif. 92708. *Office:* Department of English, California State University, Long Beach, Calif. 90840.

CAREER: San Pedro News Pilot, San Pedro, Calif., reporter, suburban editor, feature writer, 1948-53; Glendale College, Glendale, Calif., instructor in English, 1955-56, 1958-66; California State University, Long Beach, 1966—, became professor of English, 1974—. *Military service:* U.S. Army, 1943-45; served in European theater. *Member:* Modern Language Association of America, National Council of Teachers of English, National Education Association, Conference on College Composition and Communication, Melville Society, California Association of Teachers of English. *Awards, honors:* Phi Beta Kappa University Scholar at California State University, Long Beach, 1978.

WRITINGS: Style and Grammar: A Writer's Handbook of Transformations, Dodd, 1973.

WORK IN PROGRESS: White Fire: Emerson, Melville, and the Creative Community (tentative title), publication expected in 1980.

SIDELIGHTS: Williams comments: "The controlling idea of *Style and Grammar* is that a writer's meaning depends at last on what he knows how to say. The more grammatical options a writer has the better he will be able to say what he means. Clear and effective writing depends not only on the ability to think clearly, but also on the writer's control of language."

*   *   *

WILLIAMS, John Edwin   1928-

PERSONAL: Born June 12, 1928, in Bluefield, W.Va.; son of Marvin G. (a professor) and Kathleen (a musician; maiden name, Stinson) Williams; married Jeanne Crawford, July 15, 1948 (divorced, 1971); married Kathryn Bond (a psychologist), June 19, 1971; children: Kathleen Williams Kater, James, Thomas, Kimberly, Jeannette, Brock. *Education:* Attended Bluefield College, Bluefield, Va., 1945-46, 1948-49; University of Richmond, B.A., 1951; University of Iowa, M.A., 1953, Ph.D., 1954. *Home:* 1230 Polo Rd., Winston-Salem, N.C. 27106. *Office:* Department of Psychology, Wake Forest University, Winston-Salem, N.C. 27109.

CAREER: Yale University, New Haven, Conn., instructor in psychology, 1954-55; University of Richmond, Richmond, Va., assistant professor, 1955-57, associate professor of psychology, 1957-59; Wake Forest University, Winston-Salem, N.C., professor of psychology, 1959—, head of department, 1960—. Instructor for Western Electric Co., 1960—. Director of Spectrum Psychological Services, 1977—. *Military service:* U.S. Army, 1946-48; became sergeant. *Member:* International Association for Cross Cultural Psychology, American Psychological Association (fellow), American Association of University Professors, Society for Research in Child Development, Southeastern Psychological Association, North Carolina Psychological Association (fellow; president, 1964-65), Phi Beta Kappa, Sigma Xi, Psi Chi.

WRITINGS: (With J. K. Morland) *Race, Color, and the*

Young Child, University of North Carolina Press, 1976. Contributor of more than sixty articles to professional journals.

WORK IN PROGRESS: Research for a book on sex-trait stereotypes, with emphasis on a cross-national study comparing such stereotypes among children and young adults in about twenty-five countries, publication expected in 1981.

SIDELIGHTS: Williams writes: "Having spent several years studying race bias, which led to the publication of my book, my interest has now shifted to sex bias. An interesting fringe benefit associated with the cross-national study has been the opportunity to travel. I have been to Europe, South America, and the Far East, and look forward to visiting other places where research is being conducted."

*   *   *

WILLIAMS, Paul (Revere)   1894-1980

OBITUARY NOTICE: Born February 18, 1894, in Los Angeles, Calif.; died January 23, 1980, in Los Angeles. Architect and author of *Small Homes for Tomorrow* and *New Homes for Today.* Williams was best known for his designs for buildings for corporate and public use, including the Los Angeles County Courthouse and the United Nations Building in Paris. He also designed the Grave of the Unknown Soldier at Pearl Harbor. Obituaries and other sources: *Current Biography,* Wilson, 1941, March, 1980; *Who's Who in America,* 39th edition, Marquis, 1976; *International Who's Who,* 43rd edition, Europa, 1979; *New York Times,* January 26, 1980.

*   *   *

WILNER, Eleanor   1937-

PERSONAL: Born July 29, 1937, in Cleveland, Ohio; daughter of Bernard Everett (a lawyer) and Gertrude (Sherby) Rand; married Robert Weinberg (a professor of physics); children: Trudy Wilner. *Education:* Goucher College, B.A., 1959; Johns Hopkins University, M.A., 1964, Ph.D., 1973. *Home:* 324 South 12th St., Philadelphia, Pa. 19107. *Office:* Department of English, Goucher College, Towson, Md. 21204.

CAREER: Baltimore News American, Baltimore, Md., reporter, 1959-60; WFBR Radio, Baltimore, feature writer, 1961-62; Morgan State University, Baltimore, instructor in English, 1964-69; Goucher College, Towson, Md., instructor in English, 1971-73; *American Poetry Review,* Philadelphia, Pa., editor, 1975-77; Goucher College, assistant professor of English, 1977-78, lecturer in English, 1978—. Consultant to Maryland State Commission on the Aging, 1962-63. *Member:* Phi Beta Kappa. *Awards, honors:* Manuscript award from Writers Conference at University of Colorado, 1970, for poetry; creative writing grant from National Endowment for the Arts, 1976-77; Juniper Prize from University of Massachusetts Press, 1979, for *Maya.*

WRITINGS: Gathering the Winds: Visionary Imagination and Radical Transformation of Self and Society, Johns Hopkins Press, 1975; *Maya* (poems), University of Massachusetts Press, 1979.

Work represented in anthologies, including *Best Poems of 1976; Borestone Mountain Poetry Awards, 1977,* Pacific Books. Contributor of poems and reviews to literary journals.

WORK IN PROGRESS: Another book of poems.

WILSON, Clifford (Allan)   1923-

PERSONAL: Born May 10, 1923, in Sydney, Australia; son of William Lucas (a printer) and Isabelle (a teacher; maiden name, Peacock) Wilson; married Avis Williams, July 4, 1942; children: Bruce, Elaine Wilson Reeves, David, Lynette Wilson Hallihan. *Education:* University of Sydney, B.A., 1950, M.A., 1958; Melbourne College of Divinity, B.Div., 1968; University of South Carolina, Ph.D., 1972. *Religion:* Baptist. *Residence:* Mount Waverley, Victoria, Australia. *Office:* Monash University, Clayton, Victoria, Australia.

CAREER: Australian Institute of Archaeology, Melbourne, lecturer, 1951-53; associated with Melbourne Bible Institute, Melbourne, 1961-67; Australian Institute of Archaeology, director, 1967-70; associated with Columbia Bible College, Columbia, S.C., 1970-72, and Monash University, Clayton, Australia, 1974—. Director of Word of Truth Productions. Radio speaker in the United States. *Military service:* Royal Australian Navy, 1942-46. *Member:* Commercial Education Society of Australia (fellow), Australian Psychological Society, American Psychological Association. *Awards, honors:* D.D. from Toronto Baptist Seminary, 1970.

WRITINGS: (With Warner Hutchinson) *Let the People Rejoice,* Crusader Bookroom, 1959; *Exploring the Old Testament,* Word of Truth Productions, 1970; *Exploring Bible Backgrounds,* Word of Truth Productions, 1970; *Crash Go the Chariots: An Alternative to Chariots of the Gods,* Lancer Books, 1972, revised edition, Master Books, 1977; *The Search* (historical novel), Collins, 1973; *Jesus the Teacher,* Baker Book, 1975; *That Incredible Book, the Bible,* Pyramid Publications, 1975; *New Light on the Gospels,* Baker Book, 1975; *New Light on New Testament Letters,* Baker Book, 1975; *Language Abilities Guide,* Word of Truth Productions, 1975; *In the Beginning God,* Baker Book, 1976; *East Meets West in the Occult Explosion,* Master Books, 1976; *Ebla Tablets: Secrets of a Forgotten City,* Master Books, 1977; *Rocks, Relics, and Biblical Reality,* Zondervan, 1977; *War of the Chariots,* Master Books, 1978; *Monkeys Will Never Talk—Or Will They?,* Master Books, 1978; (with John Weldon) *Close Encounters: A Better Explanation, Involving Trauma, Terror, and Tragedy,* Master Books, 1978; (with Weldon) *Approaching the Decade of Shock,* Master Books, 1978; *The Joseph Scroll* (historical novel), Master Books, 1979.

Also author of *Crash Goes the Exorcist,* 1974; *Gods in Chariots and Other Fantasies,* 1975, and *The Passover Plot—Exposed,* 1977. Author of more than twenty audiovisual tapes on biblical subjects, archaeology, and unidentified flying objects. Contributor to *Bible and Spade.*

WORK IN PROGRESS: Continuing research on psycholinguistics, biblical archaeology, and biblical apologetics.

*   *   *

WILSON, David   1942-

PERSONAL: Born August 15, 1942, in Liverpool, England; son of Ronald (a works manager) and Gladys (Griffiths) Wilson. *Education:* Hertford College, Oxford, B.A. (with honors), 1965. *Home:* 4 St. Michaels Gardens, Flat 1, London W.10, England. *Office:* British Film Institute, 81 Dean St., London W.1, England.

CAREER: British Film Institute (BFI), London, England, editor of *Monthly Film Bulletin,* 1966-70, associate editor of *Sight and Sound,* 1970-80, editorial director of BFI Publishing, 1980—.

WRITINGS: (Translator with Gertrud Mander) Erwin Leiser, *Nazi Cinema,* Secker & Warburg, 1974.

Editor—All published by British Film Institute: *Fassbinder,* 1976; *Structural Film Anthology,* 1977; *Cable and Community Television in Britain,* 1978.

General editor of "Cinema One," a book series, British Film Institute. Contributor to magazines and newspapers, including *New Statesman* and *Guardian.*

SIDELIGHTS: Wilson told *CA:* "I have written frequently about television, especially the way television 'constructs' a view of the world. Are we creating a visual culture whose version of the world is more 'real' than reality? A consensus society in which individuality is drowned by the incessant noise from the screen in the corner? In which people have stopped talking for fear that they will interrupt the talk show?

"Another particular interest is the history and politics of modern Greece: the way in which the Hellenistic and Byzantine strains in the Greek character have combined to create a 'dualism'—a precarious balance between Western clarity and Eastern mysticism which has echoes far beyond Greece itself."

*   *   *

WILSON, Everett K(eith) 1913-

PERSONAL: Born in 1913; children: two. *Education:* Antioch College, A.B.; University of Chicago, M.A. and Ph.D. *Office:* Department of Sociology, University of North Carolina, Chapel Hill, N.C. 27514.

CAREER: Manchester College, North Manchester, Ind., 1946-48, began as assistant professor, became associate professor of sociology; Antioch College, Yellow Springs, Ohio, 1948-66, began as assistant professor, became professor of sociology, also head of department of sociology and anthropology, associate dean of faculty; American Sociological Association, Washington, D.C., sociologist-in-chief for curriculum project, 1966-68; University of North Carolina, Chapel Hill, professor of sociology, 1968—. Visiting associate professor at University of Michigan, 1957-58, 1959. *Military service:* U.S. Army Air Forces, Chinese Detachment, 1942-45. *Member:* American Sociological Association, Southern Sociological Society, North Carolina Sociological Society (president, 1974). *Awards, honors:* Ford Foundation fellow, 1952-53; American Council of Learned Societies fellow; Social Science Research Council fellow; Fulbright scholar in Paris, France, 1960-61.

WRITINGS: (Editor and translator) Emile Durkheim, *Moral Education,* Free Press, 1961, 2nd edition, 1973; *Sociology: Rules, Roles, and Relationships,* Dorsey, 1966, revised edition, 1971; (editor with Theodore M. Newcomb, and contributor) *The Study of College Peer Groups: Problems and Prospects for Research* (monograph), Aldine, 1966; (contributor) Morris Keeton and Conrad Hilberry, editors, *Struggle and Promise: A Future for Colleges,* McGraw, 1969; (contributor) Mark M. Krug, William B. Gillies III, and John B. Poster, editors, *The New Social Studies: Analysis of Materials and Theory,* F. E. Peacock, 1970.

Co-author of high school instruction units; all published by Allyn & Bacon: *Analyzing Views on Civil Liberties; Family Roles; Delinquency; Social Change: The Case of Rural China; Religion in the United States; Social Mobility in the United States; Testing for Truth: A Study of Hypothesis Evaluation; The Incidence and Effects of Poverty in the United States; Images of People; Social Basis for Democracy.*

Contributor of more than thirty articles and reviews to journals in the social sciences. Editor of *Social Forces;* member of editorial board of *Issues and Trends,* 1974-76.

*   *   *

WILSON, John Dover 1881-1969

OBITUARY NOTICE: Born July 13, 1881, in London, England; died January 15, 1969. Educator and literary scholar known for his expertise in the works of William Shakespeare. His writings include *The Essential Shakespeare, What Happens in Hamlet, Shakespeare's Happy Comedies,* and an autobiography, *Milestones on the Dover Road.* Obituaries and other sources: *The Reader's Encyclopedia,* 2nd edition, Crowell, 1965; *The New Century Handbook of English Literature,* revised edition, Appleton, 1967; *Longman Companion to Twentieth Century Literature,* Longman, 1970.

*   *   *

WILSON, Louis D(oull) 1917-

PERSONAL: Born December 17, 1917, in Philadelphia, Pa.; son of Jacob A. (an insurance broker) and Fannie (Doull) Wilson; married Eleanor Dorfman, December 21, 1941 (died May 24, 1978); children: Gerald Alan, Joyce Diane Wilson Scott. *Education:* Temple University, B.A., 1941, M.A., 1942; doctoral study at University of Pennsylvania, 1941, and Massachusetts Institute of Technology, 1942-46. *Religion:* Jewish. *Home and office:* Louis D. Wilson Associates, Inc., 7908 Glen Oak Rd., Elkins Park, Pa. 19117.

CAREER: Massachusetts Institute of Technology, Cambridge, instructor in electrical communications, 1945-47, senior engineer on Whirlwind computer project, 1947-49; Univac, Blue Bell, Pa., senior development engineer, 1949-51, engineering project manager, 1951, national sales manager in scientific systems, corporate manager in technical publications; Auerbach Corp., Philadelphia, Pa., manager of European operations, 1963-64, program manager, 1965-68, director of technical staff, 1968-70; Analytics, Inc., Willow Grove, Pa., vice-president in commercial systems, 1970-76; Cara Corp., Philadelphia, Pa., program manager, 1976-77; Louis D. Wilson Associates, Inc., Elkins Park, Pa., president, 1977—. Vice-president and member of board of directors of Symmetrics, Inc. Adjunct member of faculty at Pennsylvania State University, Ogontz Campus. Fundraiser for United Jewish Appeal. Computer designer; engineering management consultant.

MEMBER: Institute of Electrical and Electronics Engineers, American Association for the Advancement of Science, National Association of Watch and Clock Collectors, Pennsylvania Academy of Fine Arts, Philadelphia Orchestra Association, Sigma Pi Sigma.

WRITINGS: Use of Secondhand Computers in the Developing Countries, Center for Industrial Development, United Nations Department of Economic and Social Affairs, 1965; (with Stephen W. Leibholz) *A User's Guide to Computer Crime,* Chilton, 1974. Contributor to scientific journals.

SIDELIGHTS: Wilson has lived in Switzerland and the Netherlands, and traveled in Europe, the Far East, and Israel.

*   *   *

WILSON, Louis Round 1876-1980

OBITUARY NOTICE: Born December 27, 1876; died December 10, 1980. American librarian and author of works in his field. Wilson worked in North Carolina and neighboring regions for thirty years before accepting a position at the University of Chicago in 1932. The previous year, he founded the School of Library Science in North Carolina. Among his books is *Libraries of the Southeast.* Obituaries and other sources: *AB Bookman's Weekly,* January 28, 1980.

* * *

WILSON, Richard Guy   1940-

PERSONAL: Born May 16, 1940, in Los Angeles, Calif.; son of Guy C. (in business) and Elizabeth (an interior designer; maiden name, Jacobsen) Wilson; married Eleanor Vernon (a teacher), August 15, 1964; children: Kristina F., Abigail Elizabeth Victoria. *Education:* University of Colorado, B.A., 1963; University of Michigan, M.A., 1968, Ph.D., 1972. *Politics:* Democrat. *Religion:* Episcopalian. *Home:* 1860 Field Rd., Charlottesville, Va. 22903. *Office:* School of Architecture, Division of Architectural History, University of Virginia, Charlottesville, Va. 22903.

CAREER: Iowa State University, Ames, assistant professor, 1972-76, associate professor of architecture, 1976; University of Virginia, Charlottesville, associate professor of architectural history, 1976—, chair of architectural history and historic preservation, 1979—. Guest curator at Brooklyn Museum, 1977—; coordinator of summer school for Victorian Society in America, 1978-80. Member of Ames Community Development Committee, 1975-76, and state review board for National Register nominations, of Virginia Landmarks Commission, 1979—. *Military service:* U.S. Navy, 1964-67; became lieutenant junior grade. *Member:* College Art Association of America, American Studies Association, National Trust for Historic Preservation, Society of Architectural Historians, Classical America, Prairie School Society, Phi Beta Phi, Beta Phi Mu. *Awards, honors:* National Science Foundation grant, 1974; grants from National Endowment for the Arts and Iowa Arts Council, 1975-76.

WRITINGS: (With Sidney K. Robinson) *The Prairie School in Iowa,* Iowa State University Press, 1977; (with Dianne Pilgrim and Richard Murray) *The American Renaissance, 1876-1917,* Pantheon, 1979; *McKim, Mead, and White and American Architecture,* Academy Editions, 1980. Contributor to architecture and history journals. Assistant editor of newsletter of Society of Architectural Historians, 1975-78.

WORK IN PROGRESS: American Architecture and Design Between the Wars, 1918-1941, publication by Pantheon expected in 1982.

SIDELIGHTS: Wilson writes: "Born in a house designed by a notable 'modern' architect, Rudolph Schindler, I was perhaps doomed to be concerned with architecture and design. However, my father was an amateur historian and led me in another direction. The twin influences ultimately were reconciled in the profession of architectural history. While the 'modern' style is still of interest, most of my work has been concerned with discovering what we lost when we abandoned history, image, and ornament in architecture—hence The American Renaissance. My principal interest is in communicating, whether through books, articles, or museum shows."

* * *

WINCH, Terence   1945-

PERSONAL: Born November 1, 1945, in New York, N.Y.; son of Patrick and Bridie (Flynn) Winch. *Education:* Iona College, B.A. (summa cum laude), 1967; Fordham Univer-

sity, M.A., 1969, doctoral study, 1969-71. *Home:* 1920 S St. N.W., Washington, D.C. 20009.

CAREER: Dover Publications, Inc., New York, N.Y., copywriter, 1971; Discount Book Shop, Washington, D.C., poetry buyer, 1971-75; Corcoran School of Art, Washington, D.C., instructor and artist-in-residence, 1975-76; Titanic Books, Washington, D.C., founder and editor, 1976—. Founder and editor of Some of Us Press, 1971-74; director of poetry and music programs for WGTB-FM and WAMU-FM Radio, 1972-75; gives readings at colleges and poetry centers all over the United States; has organized poetry exhibitions and readings series. Composer and performer with "The Fast Flying Vestibule," 1972-77, and "Celtic Thunder," 1977—. *Awards, honors:* Guest at Yaddo, 1975.

WRITINGS: Boning Up (poetry), Some of Us Press, 1973; *Irish Musicians* (poetry), O Press, 1974; *The Beautiful Indifference* (poetry), O Press, 1975; *Luncheonette Jealousy* (prose and poetry), Washington Writers Publishing House, 1975; *Nuns* (poetry), Wyrd Press, 1976; *The Attachment Sonnets,* Jawbone, 1978; *Irish Musicians/American Friends* (poetry), Blue Wind Press, in press; *Total Strangers* (fiction), Toothpaste Press, in press.

Work represented in anthologies, including *None of the Above,* edited by Michael Lally, Crossing Press, 1976; *Self-Portrait: Book People Picture Themselves,* edited by Burt Britton, Random House, 1976; *City Celebration 1976,* District of Columbia Bicentennial Commission, 1977.

Contributor to *Dictionary of Irish Literature.* Contributor of poems, articles, stories, songs, and reviews to magazines, including *Washington Post Book World, Poetry Northwest, Granite, Greenfield Review, West Coast Poetry Review,* and *Unicorn Times.* Founding editor of *Mass Transit,* 1972-74; associate editor (and member of board of trustees) of *Washington Review,* 1976—.

WORK IN PROGRESS: A novel; short stories.

SIDELIGHTS: Winch made a record album, "Union Station," released by Rolling Donut Records in 1976. Currently he is making a record album of traditional Irish music with his band, Celtic Thunder, to be released by Green Linnet in 1980.

BIOGRAPHICAL/CRITICAL SOURCES: Daily Rag, April, 1973; *Washington Post,* June 27, 1973, July 27, 1975, December 26, 1976; *Washington Star,* August 27, 1973; *Washington,* December, 1974; *Margins,* May, 1975.

* * *

WINDER, Alvin E.   1923-

PERSONAL: Born February 17, 1923, in New York, N.Y.; son of Martin (an attorney) and Frances (Erdrick) Winder; married Barbara Dietz (a professor), June 17, 1950; children: Mark, Joshua, Sarah, Susan. *Education:* Brooklyn College (now of City University of New York), B.A. (cum laude), 1947; University of Illinois, M.S., 1948; University of Chicago, Ph.D., 1952. *Home:* 85 Juggler Meadow Rd., Amherst, Mass. 01002. *Office:* Department of Psychology, University of Massachusetts, Amherst, Mass. 01003.

CAREER: Roosevelt University, Chicago, Ill., instructor in psychology and counselor, 1948-52; Downey Veterans Administration Hospital, Downey, Ill., staff psychologist, 1952-53; Veterans Administration Mental Hygiene Clinic, Miami, Fla., chief psychologist, 1953-56; Clark University, Worcester, Mass., assistant professor of psychology and research associate, 1956-58; Veterans Administration Clinic, Springfield, Mass., chief psychologist, 1958-61; Springfield College, Springfield, associate professor of psychology and director of Counseling Center, 1961-63; Westfield State College, Westfield, Mass., head of department of psychology, 1963-65; University of Massachusetts—Amherst, associate professor, 1965-69, professor of counselor education, 1969-78, psychology, 1973—, and public health, 1978—.

MEMBER: American Psychological Association, American Group Psychotherapy Association, New England Psychotherapy Association, New England Educational Research Organization, Massachusetts Psychological Association, Western Massachusetts Personnel and Guidance Association. *Awards, honors:* Grants from U.S. Office of Economic Opportunity, 1965-66, 1966-67, Massachusetts Division of Child Guardianship, 1965-66, 1966-67, Dexter Foundation, 1968-69, and National Institute of Mental Health, 1969-74.

WRITINGS: (Contributor) John F. McGowan and Lyle Schmidt, editors, *Counseling: Readings in Theory and Practice,* Holt, 1962; (editor with David Angus, and contributor) *Adolescence: Contemporary Studies,* American Book Co., 1968, 2nd edition, Van Nostrand, 1974; (contributor) Alfred Kadushin, editor, *Child Welfare Services: A Source Book,* Macmillan, 1970; (contributor) R. F. Dickie, editor, *Counseling Parents of Exceptional Children,* Simon & Schuster, 1970; (with Dee Appley) *Groups in a Changing Society: Introduction to T-Groups and Group Psychotherapy,* Jossey-Bass, 1973. Contributor of about forty articles to academic journals and popular magazines, including *Nation, New Leader,* and *Trend.*

WORK IN PROGRESS: Collaboration: An Instrumental Value–Effects on Work, Health, and Education.

SIDELIGHTS: Winder writes: "A major reason for my writing is to provide professionals and the lay public with the opportunity to think of alternatives to the disorganizing and alienating qualities of contempopary life. With this motivation in mind, my edition of the thirtieth anniversary issue of the *Journal of Applied Behavioral Science* presents collaboration as an alternative value upon which to base the world of work. The presentation of several case studies in which industrial organizations have developed a collaborative work structure strikes an optimistic note. I believe that alternatives to the competitive approach to work represent, at the present stage of our industrial development, a practical solution to human survival. *Groups in a Changing Society* is devoted to the skills involved both in managing the collaborative group and in the educational technology necessary to reeducate and socialize people to work together in this manner.

"Many of my other writings have looked at the mental health effects of the current system. 'Family Therapy: A Necessary Part of the Cancer Patient's Care' begins: 'An all-important, but unrecognized, part of the overall treatment plan for the cancer patient—and indeed all patients with a terminal illness—is professional attention to the pervasive pain, anguish, and distress experienced by the entire immediate family.' While this paper presents case studies of treatment it is basically a plea to professionals to understand and seriously consider the effects of the illness of one member on the entire family system. This is an attempt to challenge the current concept of the individual in our health treatment system. Finally, my most recent paper, 'Collaboration: An Alternative Value and Its Implications for Health Education,' presents a human ecological viewpoint. This perspective asks health educators to help people challenge health-damaging conditions in their environment and to aid them further by providing opportunities that make it possible for them to work toward the promotion of good health."

"The current literature in the field of what I would like to call collaborative effort remains sparse. It is, however, impressive to observe that this idea of an alternative approach to living is beginning to appear in several fields. My wish is that somehow through my writing, as well as my teaching, I can join my voice with others who would also like to make the world a little happier place for all humanity to live in."

*   *   *

WINE, Sherwin T.   1928-

PERSONAL: Born January 25, 1928, in Detroit, Mich.; son of William and Tillie (Israel) Wine. *Education:* University of Michigan, B.A., 1950, M.A., 1952; Hebrew Union College—Jewish Institute of Religion, B.H.L. and M.H.L., 1956. *Home:* 555 South Woodward, Birmingham, Mich. 48011. *Office:* Birmingham Temple, 28611 West Twelve Mile Rd., Farmington Hills, Mich. 48018.

CAREER: Temple Beth El, Detroit, Mich., rabbi, 1956-60; Temple Beth El, Windsor, Ontario, rabbi, 1960-64; Birmingham Temple, Birmingham, Mich., rabbi, 1964—; Center for New Thinking, Birmingham, director, 1977—. Speaker. *Military service:* U.S. Army, 1957-58; became first lieutenant. *Member:* Central Conference of American Rabbis, Society for Humanistic Judaism (founder), Michigan Foundation for the Arts (member of board of directors).

WRITINGS: A Philosophy of Humanistic Judaism, Birmingham Temple, 1965; *Meditation Services for Humanistic Judaism,* Society for Humanistic Judaism, 1977; *Humanistic Judaism,* Prometheus Books, 1977; *Humanist Haggadah,* Society for Humanistic Judaism, 1979; *High Holidays for Humanists,* Society for Humanistic Judaism, 1979. Contributor of articles to journals, including *Humanist, Religious Humanism,* and *American Rationalist.*

WORK IN PROGRESS: A Real History of the Jews; New Thinking.

SIDELIGHTS: Rabbi Sherwin Wine, who emphasizes the potential of the human person in religion rather than an omnipresent God, is a controversial figure in local Jewish communities. The founder of humanistic Judaism, Wine was recently censured by the Detroit Rabbinic Commission for inviting Jewish liberal I. F. Stone to speak to his congregation. Wine is considered by many to be a pioneer in both humanistic and futuristic thinking. As director of the Center for New Thinking, he teaches numerous classes that are designed to help Americans cope with the problems of a growing urban society and the single life, often zeroing in on specific writers, such as Margaret Mead and Isaac Asimov, as prophets of American culture.

Wine commented: "I am interested in philosophy, ethics, and religion in so far as they guide human behavior. I believe that contemporary urban society requires an ethical system that goes beyond the primacy of the individual or the family. I am also interested in developing a humanistic religion that accommodates modern science and avoids theology."

*   *   *

WINK, Richard L(ee)   1930-

PERSONAL: Born August, 1930, in Fairbury, Ill.; son of Edward C. and Elizabeth (Darnall) Wink; married Jayma Thompson, 1954; children: Deborah Ann, Dazna Lynn. *Education:* Findlay College, A.B., 1952; Ohio State University, M.A., 1959, Ph.D., 1967; doctoral study at Indiana University, summers, 1960-62. *Office:* School of Music, Ohio State University, Mansfield Campus, 1680 University Dr., Mansfield, Ohio 44906.

CAREER: Music teacher at public schools in Wyandot County, Arcadia, Van Wert, and Worthington, Ohio, 1954-63; Ohio State University, Mansfield Campus, Mansfield, instructor, 1966-68, assistant professor, 1968-73, associate professor, 1973-78, professor of music, 1978—, associate dean of Mansfield Campus, 1978—. Church choir director and voice teacher; guest conductor at concerts and festivals; tenor performer in opera and oratorio; public speaker. *Member:* Music Educators National Conference.

WRITINGS: (With L. G. Williams) *Invitation to Listening: An Introduction to Music,* Houghton, 1972, 2nd edition, 1976; *Fundamentals of Music,* Houghton, 1977.

Composer: "Turn Thee to Me," World Library of Sacred Music; (editor) "Domine ad Adiuvandum," Lawson-Gould Music Publishers. Contributor to music and music education journals.

WORK IN PROGRESS: "A book on how to look at a painting—utilizing the same principles as those to listen to music."

*   *   *

WINSTON, Richard 1917-1979

OBITUARY NOTICE—See index for *CA* sketch: Born July 21, 1917, in New York, N.Y.; died of cancer, December 22, 1979, in Brattleboro, Vt. Translator and biographer. Working together, Winston and his wife, Clara, translated more than one-hundred fifty books from German into English. By translating the works of such well-known writers as Carl Jung, Albert Speer, Thomas Mann, and Herman Hesse, they gained a reputation as the foremost German translators in the United States. Among the awards that Winston received were the P.E.N. Translation Prize and a National Book Award for translation. He was also the author of two biographies, *Charlemagne: From the Hammer to the Cross* and *Thomas Becket.* At the time of his death he was writing a biography of Thomas Mann. Obituaries and other sources: *New York Times,* January 5, 1980.

*   *   *

WIRT, Winola Wells
(Sarah Frazier)

PERSONAL: Born in Towanda, Pa.; daughter of John Eppes (a pharmacist and singer) and Faith (an artist and musician; maiden name, McCain) Wells; married Sherwood Eliot Wirt (a minister and writer), July 2, 1940; children: Alexander Wells. *Education:* Attended Ithaca College, Mansfield State College, Pennsylvania State University, and University of Arizona. *Politics:* Republican. *Religion:* Presbyterian. *Residence:* Poway, Calif.

CAREER: Elementary school teacher in Pennsylvania, 1927-28, and Englewood, N.J., 1929-30; teacher at private boys' school in Englewood, N.J., 1930-31; worked as fashion coordinator and buyer; currently writer and lecturer. *Member:* National League of American Penwomen, United Federation of Doll Clubs, South Wind Doll Club.

WRITINGS: Interludes in a Woman's Day, Moody, 1964; *Of All Places: Interludes in a Woman's Travels,* Zondervan, 1969; (under pseudonym Sarah Frazier) *Living With Depression and Winning,* Tyndale House, 1975. Author of a monthly prayer letter. Contributor to Christian periodicals, including *Decision, Light and Life,* and *Moody Monthly.*

SIDELIGHTS: Winola Wirt comments: "My husband and I have traveled and lectured on all continents. My motivation is that my writings and lectures have proven helpful to peo-

ple, especially *Living With Depression and Winning.* One college student wrote that it prevented his suicide. I am concerned with people and their problems and how my own surmounted difficulties can help, especially by providing humor and laughter."

AVOCATIONAL INTERESTS: Foster orphans in Europe, Asia, Guatemala, and Appalachia, art, antiques, symphony and ballet, animals, collecting dolls from around the world.

BIOGRAPHICAL/CRITICAL SOURCES: Christian Times, March 26, 1967.

*   *   *

WISE, Gene 1936-

PERSONAL: Born April 15, 1936, in Spartanburg, Ind.; son of Merrill C. (a tool engineer) and Grace M. (Stuckey) Wise; married wife, Margaret, June 14, 1959 (divorced, 1973). *Education:* Hanover College, B.A. (magna cum laude), 1958; Syracuse University, Ph.D., 1963. *Home:* 6000 Breezewood Dr., #302, Greenbelt, Md. 20770. *Office:* American Studies Program, University of Maryland, 2140 Taliaferro Hall, College Park, Md. 20742.

CAREER: University of the Pacific, Raymond College, Stockton, Calif., 1963-69, began as assistant professor, became associate professor of social studies and American civilization; Case Western Reserve University, Cleveland, Ohio, associate professor of American studies, 1969-77; University of Maryland, College Park, professor of American studies and director of program, 1977—. Visiting associate professor at University of New Mexico, summer, 1974; visiting distinguished professor at San Diego State University, spring, 1975; visiting Mellon Foundation lecturer at Trinity College, Hartford, Conn., 1977; lecturer at Hobart and William Smith Colleges, University of California, Davis, University of Minnesota, Cleveland State University, University of Iowa, University of Michigan, Dickinson College, and University of North Carolina. Member of Maryland Committee for Humanities and Public Policy. *Member:* Organization of American Historians, American Studies Association. *Awards, honors:* Annual award from *American Quarterly,* 1967, for "Political 'Reality' in Recent American Scholarship: Progressives Versus 'Symbolists.'"

WRITINGS: American Historical Explanations: A Strategy for Grounded Inquiry, Dorsey, 1973, revised edition, University of Minnesota Press, 1980; (contributor) Ronald Hyman, editor, *Approaches to Curriculum,* Prentice-Hall, 1973. Contributor to history journals. Guest editor of *American Quarterly,* summer, 1979.

WORK IN PROGRESS: From the "Modell of Christian Clarity" to the Declaration of Independence: A Study of Changing "Social Rhetorics" in Colonial America, 1630-1776; American Historical Explanations: From Intellectual History to Cultural History; Critics of American Culture: From Tocqueville to the New Journalism; Experience and Explanation in American Culture Studies: An Interdisciplinary Model for Inquiry.

*   *   *

WITTE, John 1948-

PERSONAL: Surname is pronounced Witt-*ee*; born December 28, 1948, in Albany, N.Y.; son of Michael (a chemist) and Louise (a librarian; maiden name, Wujek) Witte. *Education:* Colby College, B.A., 1971; University of Oregon, M.F.A., 1977. *Home:* 75 West 24th Place, Eugene, Ore. 97405. *Office:* 369 PLC, Department of English, University of Oregon, Eugene, Ore. 97403.

CAREER: Brentano's Book Store, Short Hills, N.J., assistant manager, 1971-72; Selecto-Flash, Inc., East Orange, N.J., silk screen designer and printer, 1972-73; adult education creative writing teacher in Waterville, Me., 1973-75, school librarian, 1974-75; University of Oregon, Eugene, instructor of creative writing workshops, 1976-77, editor of *Northwest Review*, 1979—. Also worked as logger, manager of Vermont ski area, and in wood and steel construction. *Awards, honors:* Fellowship from Fine Arts Work Center, Provincetown, Mass., 1977-78.

WRITINGS: *Loving the Days* (poems), Wesleyan University Press, 1978. Contributor of poems, articles, and reviews to literary journals, including *Ohio Review, American Poetry Review, Iowa Review, Kayak, New Yorker, Paris Review, Antioch Review,* and *Poetry Northwest.*

WORK IN PROGRESS: Another book of poems, publication expected in 1980.

SIDELIGHTS: Witte writes: "Although I am influenced by my experience in universities, I recall with greatest clarity and warmth my experiences outside the academy. These have been, for me, the greater source of understanding, if not of learning. I think my writing is improved by my contact with people whose lives are not boring to them, who have neither the time nor the inclination to indulge in the luxury of self-pity."

*   *   *

WITTERS, Weldon L. 1929-

PERSONAL: Born December 13, 1929, in Dayton, Ohio; son of Samuel (a plumber) and Olive (Armstrong) Witters; married Patricia Jones (a professor of zoology), August 15, 1967; children: Sean Jones. *Education:* Ball State University, B.S., 1952, M.S., 1956; Indiana University, M.S., 1958; Purdue University, M.S., 1964, Ph.D., 1967. *Politics:* Independent. *Religion:* Protestant. *Home:* 47 Avon, Athens, Ohio 45701. *Office:* Department of Zoology, Ohio University, Athens, Ohio 45701.

CAREER: High school biology teacher in Muncie, Ind., 1956-60, and West Lafayette, Ind., 1960-67; Ohio University, Athens, assistant professor, 1967-69, associate professor, 1969-75, professor of zoology, 1975—. Consultant on drug abuse to State of Ohio. *Military service:* U.S. Air Force Reserve, 1952—; present rank, lieutenant colonel. *Member:* National Association of Biology Teachers, National Education Association, Society for the Study of Reproduction, Ohio Education Association, Kiwanis. *Awards, honors:* Grants from National Science Foundation, 1969-70, 1970-71, and 1975-76; National Science Foundation faculty fellow, 1975-76.

WRITINGS: (Contributor) T. R. Porter, editor, *The Best of The Science Teacher*, National Education Association, 1967; *Overhead Visuals in Biology: Twenty-Five Overlays*, Houghton, 1969; *Investigations in General Zoology*, Kendall/Hunt, 1969; *Investigations Into General Biology*, Kendall/Hunt, 1970, 2nd edition, 1973; *Heavy Biology: Drugs and Sex*, Dee Publishing, 1972, 2nd edition, 1973; *Heavy Biology: Ecostudies*, Dee Publishing, 1973; *Drugs and Sex*, Macmillan, 1975; *Environmental Biology: The Human Factor*, Kendall/Hunt, 1976, 2nd edition, 1978; *An Audio-Tutorial Course in Introductory Biology*, Ohio University Press, 1977; *Human Sexuality: A Biological Perspective*, Van Nostrand, 1980; *Human Sexuality: Drugs and Their Influence on Human Sexuality*, Dee Publishing, 1980. Contributor of about fifty articles to scientific journals.

WORK IN PROGRESS: Research on hallucinogens and their influence on fetal development.

SIDELIGHTS: Witters writes: "Flying and scuba diving are hobbies used in my research. I take one or two groups of students each year to the Bahamas or Jamaica to study marine biology intensively for about two weeks. I have spent three summers excavating old ships. One of these expeditions, on an old galleon, circa A.D. 1650, was mentioned in *National Geographic*.

"During the last nine years I have also run an analytical street laboratory to test abused drugs. I have a state and federal drug license to do this, in order to warn about dangerous drugs and adulterants. I have traveled through more than forty countries on all continents (except Antarctica) looking at ecological problems and at drug cultures."

*   *   *

WOLFE, James H(astings) 1934-

PERSONAL: Born October 3, 1934, in Newport News, Va.; son of Walter John (in U.S. Army) and Grace (a teacher; maiden name, Hastings) Wolfe; married Irgard Hedwig Pfender (a librarian), June 10, 1965; children: Christine Maria, Karin Jean. *Education:* Harvard University, B.A., 1955; University of Connecticut, M.A., 1958; University of Maryland, Ph.D., 1962. *Home:* 2600 Sunset Dr., Hattiesburg, Miss. 39401. *Office:* Department of Political Science, University of Southern Mississippi, P.O. Box 8261, Southern Station, Hattiesburg, Miss. 39401.

CAREER: University of South Carolina, Columbia, assistant professor of political science, 1962-65; University of Maryland, College Park, associate professor of political science, 1965-75; University of Southern Mississippi, Hattiesburg, professor of political science, 1975—. *Military service:* U.S. Army, 1955-57. *Member:* International Political Science Association, International Studies Association, Conference Group on German Politics, Southern Political Science Association.

WRITINGS: *Indivisible Germany: Illusion or Reality?*, Nijhoff, 1963; (with Theodore A. Couloumbis) *Introduction to International Relations: Power and Justice*, Prentice-Hall, 1978, 2nd edition, in press; *Cyprus, A Study in International Relations: Power and Justice*, Institute for Nationality Rights and Regionalism, in press.

SIDELIGHTS: Wolfe comments: "My motivation is a humanistic concern over conflict in world affairs and the belief that political scientists should employ their training to contribute toward a peaceful resolution of international disputes."

*   *   *

WOLFE, Thomas W. 1914-

PERSONAL: Born January 1, 1914, in San Francisco, Calif.; son of Thomas A. (an entrepreneur) and Marguerite (Kimberly) Wolfe; married Elizabeth Bobbit (a psychotherapist), May 20, 1939; children: Stephen A., Timothy B., Ellen M. *Education:* Hiram College, B.A., 1935; Columbia University, M.A., 1950; attended Naval War College, 1954-55; Georgetown University, Ph.D., 1955. *Politics:* Independent. *Religion:* Protestant. *Home:* 6379 Dockser Ter., Falls Church, Va. 22041. *Office:* RAND Corp., 2100 M St. N.W., Washington, D.C.

CAREER: Associated with *Cleveland Plain Dealer*, Cleveland, Ohio, 1936-41; U.S. Air Force, career officer, 1942-62, squadron intelligence officer, 1942-43, group intelligence officer and assistant glider operations officer in Europe, 1944-45, on air staff at headquarters and in schools, 1946-55, U.S. Air attache at American Embassy in Moscow, U.S.S.R., 1956-58, chief of special advisory group, 1959, staff officer with Joint Chiefs of Staff, 1959-60, member of Coolidge Committee for Disarmament Policy Review, member of U.S. delegations to disarmament conference in Geneva, Switzerland, and summit conference in Paris, France, all 1960, adviser to McCloy-Zorin talks in Moscow, 1961, director of Sino-Soviet region of office of the assistant secretary of defense, 1960-62, retiring as colonel; RAND Corp., Washington, D.C., senior member of staff. Member of faculty at George Washington University; lecturer at military schools and other institutions, including Harvard University, Columbia University, and Ohio State University. Member of natural science expedition to Panama and the Amazon Valley.

MEMBER: International Institute for Strategic Studies, American Political Science Association, American Association for the Advancement of Slavic Studies, Council on Foreign Relations, Cosmos Club, Annapolis Yacht Club. *Awards, honors*—Military: Legion of Merit with oak leaf cluster; commendation medal with oak leaf cluster.

WRITINGS: (Co-editor and translator) V. C. Sokolovskii, *Soviet Military Strategy*, Prentice-Hall, 1963; *Soviet Strategy at the Crossroads*, Harvard University Press, 1964; *Soviet Power and Europe, 1945-1970*, Johns Hopkins Press, 1970; *The SALT Experience*, Ballinger, 1979.

Contributor: *American Strategy for the Nuclear Age*, Doubleday, 1960; *Soviet Nuclear Strategy*, Center for Strategic Studies, Georgetown University, 1963; *Detente: Cold War Strategies in Transition*, Praeger, 1965; *The Military Technical Revolution*, Praeger, 1966; *Sino-Soviet Rivalry*, Praeger, 1966; *Eastern Europe in Transition*, Johns Hopkins Press, 1966; *Prospects for Soviet Society*, Council on Foreign Relations, 1968; *Soviet Sea Power*, Center for Strategic Studies, Georgetown University, 1969; *Soviet Naval Development*, Praeger, 1973; *The Soviet Impact on World Politics*, Praeger, 1973; *SALT: Implications for Arms Control in the 1970's*, University of Pittsburgh Press, 1973; *Comparative Defense Policy*, Johns Hopkins Press, 1974; *The Soviet Empire: Expansion and Detente*, Heath, 1976. Contributor of articles and reviews to history, military, and Slavic studies journals, and *Saturday Review*.

WORK IN PROGRESS: Soviet Policy in the Third World.

AVOCATIONAL INTERESTS: Sailing ("I have yachts in the Caribbean and Chesapeake Bay, and use them for charter, sailing, and celestial navigation instruction").

*   *   *

WOLFE, (William) Willard 1936-

PERSONAL: Born July 29, 1936, in Benzonia, Mich.; son of Herbert Snow (a professor) and Mary (Willard) Wolfe. *Education:* Davidson College, A.B. (cum laude), 1958; attended University of North Carolina, 1958-59, and London School of Economics and Political Science, London, 1961-62; Yale University, Ph.D., 1967. *Home:* 234 Maine St., Brunswick, Me. 04011. *Office:* Department of History, Bowdoin College, Brunswick, Me. 04011.

CAREER: University of California, Riverside, instructor in history, 1964-67; Roosevelt University, Chicago, Ill., assistant professor of history, 1967-74; Montclair State College, Upper Montclair, N.J., visiting assistant professor of history, 1974-75; American University, Washington, D.C., visiting associate professor of history, 1975-76; Bowdoin College, Brunswick, Me., assistant professor of history, 1976—. *Military service:* U.S. Naval Reserve, 1955-61. *Member:* American Historical Association, Conference on British Studies. *Awards, honors:* Woodrow Wilson fellow, 1958-59; annual award from Pacific Coast Branch of American Historical Association, 1968, for manuscript of *From Radicalism to Socialism;* National Endowment for the Humanities fellow, 1970, summer seminar grant, 1978.

WRITINGS: From Radicalism to Socialism: Men and Ideas in the Formation of Fabian Socialist Doctrines, Yale University Press, 1975. Contributor of articles and reviews to history journals. Assistant editor of *British Studies Monitor,* 1976—.

WORK IN PROGRESS: The Playwright as Propagandist, on the political and social thought of Bernard Shaw; *Socialism and Empire,* a monograph on the work of Fabian imperial administrator, Sydney Oliver; research on Fabian socialist thought and activities, 1870-1919.

*   *   *

WOLFSON, Robert J(oseph) 1925-

PERSONAL: Born February 9, 1925, in Buffalo, N.Y.; son of Jacob (a chemist) and Rose (Ladinsky) Wolfson; married Betty Bunes, October, 1954; children: Paul Jacob, Anne Rose, Laura Esther. *Education:* University of Chicago, B.S., 1947, M.A., 1950, Ph.D., 1956. *Home:* 111 Circle Rd., Syracuse, N.Y. 13210. *Office:* Syracuse University, 712 Ostrom Ave., Syracuse, N.Y. 13210.

CAREER: University of Chicago, Chicago, Ill., lecturer in economics, 1949-50; University of Michigan, Ann Arbor, assistant study director at Survey Research Center, 1951-53; University of Chicago, instructor in social sciences, 1953-56; Michigan State University, East Lansing, assistant professor of economics, 1956-60; University of California, Los Angeles, assistant professor of business economics and project director, 1960-61; Corp. for Economics and Industrial Research, Beverly Hills, Calif., senior project director, 1961-63; RAND Corp., Santa Monica, Calif., staff economist, 1963-65; System Development Corp., Santa Monica, principal scientist in long-range corporate and social planning, 1965-66; Syracuse University, Syracuse, N.Y., professor of economics at Maxwell Graduate School of Citizenship and Public Affairs, 1966-76, professor of social science, 1974—, co-founder and associate director of Educational Policy Research Center, 1967-70. Visiting professor at Washington University, St. Louis, Mo., 1976-77; summer lecturer at Roosevelt College (now University), 1951, and Vanderbilt University, 1956. Participant in conferences and workshops; consultant to government and business. *Military service:* U.S. Navy, Construction Battalion (Seabees), 1943-46.

MEMBER: American Economic Association, American Association for the Advancement of Science, American Association of University Professors (past local president, vice-president, and member of executive committee; member of Committee Z on economic circumstances of the profession, 1970-76; member of national council, 1971-74, 1978-81; head of council committee on long-range planning), Econometric Society, Philosophy of Science Association. *Awards, honors:* Ford Foundation fellowship, 1959-60.

WRITINGS: (With E. M. Hoover, Raymond Vernon, and others) *The Anatomy of a Metropolis,* Harvard University Press, 1959; (contributor) N. F. Washburne, editor, *Decisions, Values, and Groups,* Volume II, Pergamon, 1962; (contributor) K. E. Boulding, editor, *Penn and the War Industry,* second edition, Transaction Books, 1973; (contributor) H. I. Safa and G. Levitas, editors, *Social Problems in Corporate America*, Harper, 1975. Contributor to *Encyclopaedia Britannica*. Contributor of about twenty-five articles and reviews to scholarly journals. Acting co-editor of *Economic Development and Cultural Change*, 1954-55.

WORK IN PROGRESS: With R. B. Barett, Jr., and R. S. Rudner, development and application of a constructional system of definitions for the social sciences.

* * *

WONG, Molly 1920-

PERSONAL: Born March 21, 1920, in Shanghai, China. *Education:* University of Shanghai, B.A., 1951; Hong Kong Baptist Theological Seminary, M.R.E., 1960; Southwestern Baptist Theological Seminary, G.S.R.E., 1969. *Home:* 797-D Don Chueng, Sai Kung, Kowloon N.T., Hong Kong. *Office:* Hong Kong Baptist Press, 322 Prince Edward Rd., Kowloon N.T., Hong Kong.

CAREER: Hong Kong Baptist Press, Hong Kong, church curriculum editor, 1973—.

WRITINGS: They Changed My China, Broadman, 1970. Author of church school curriculum material in Chinese. Translator into Chinese and editor of *Adult Bible Teacher*, 1970—.

SIDELIGHTS: Molly Wong comments: "My goal is to help readers to know, trust, and love God steadily."

* * *

WOOD, David (Bowne) 1945-

PERSONAL: Born June 18, 1945, in New York, N.Y.; son of Moyer (an interior designer) and Elizabeth (a librarian; maiden name, Smedley) Wood; married Barbara Jeanne Brooks (an educator), August 22, 1970; children: Seth, Peter. *Education:* Attended Allegheny College, 1963-66; Temple University, B.S., 1970. *Office address: Washington Star*, Washington, D.C.

CAREER/WRITINGS: Pioneer Press, Evanston, Ill., reporter, 1970-72; *Time*, New York, N.Y., correspondent, 1972-76, Nairobi bureau chief, 1976-79; *Washington Star*, Washington, D.C., national correspondent, 1979—. Notable assignments include coverage of coups in Uganda and Equatorial Guinea, political developments in the Sudan, Nigeria, and Ghana, wars in Rhodesia and Ethiopia, and the presidential campaign of Senator Edward Kennedy. *Member:* Foreign Correspondents Association of East Africa.

* * *

WOOD, Derek Harold 1930-

PERSONAL: Born March 19, 1930, in Thornton Heath, England; son of Henry Alfred and Ellen (Ford) Wood; married Belinda Valerie Squire, July 23, 1955; children: Nicola Jane, Jonathan Squire. *Education:* Attended high school in Chichester, England. *Home:* Stroods, Whiteman's Green, Cuckfield, Sussex, England. *Agent:* Curtis Brown Ltd., 1 Craven Hill, London W2 3EP, England. *Office:* 149 Fleet St., London E.C.4, England.

CAREER: Aerosphere, Bognos Regis, Sussex, England, editor, 1948-49; free-lance writer, 1949-53; *Interavia*, London, England, editor, 1953—, managing director of Interavia Ltd., 1956—. *Member:* Institute of Journalists, London Press Club. *Awards, honors:* C. P. Robertson Memorial Trophy from Air Public Relations Association, 1961, for *The Narrow Margin*; companion of Royal Aeronautical Society, 1969.

WRITINGS: (With Derek Dempster) *The Narrow Margin: The Battle of Britain and the Rise of Air Power, 1930-40*, McGraw, 1961, revised edition, Paperback Library, 1969; *Project Cancelled: British Aircraft That Never Flew*, Bobbs-Merrill, 1975; *Attack Warning Red: History of the R.O.C.*, Macdonald & Jane's, 1976; *Jane's World Aircraft Recognition Handbook*, Macdonald & Jane's, 1979. Air correspondent for *Liverpool Daily Post*, 1952-60, Westminster Press Provincial Newspapers, 1954-60, and *Sunday Telegraph*, 1961—. Member of editorial staff of *British Trade Journal* and *Electrical Journal*, both 1950-53.

WORK IN PROGRESS: A pictorial history of Britain in 1940 and the Battle of Britain, publication by Macdonald & Jane's expected in 1980.

BIOGRAPHICAL/CRITICAL SOURCES: Sunday Telegraph Magazine, December 9, 1979.

* * *

WOOD, Esther
See BRADY, Esther Wood

* * *

WOOD, Peter 1930-

PERSONAL: Born November 13, 1930, in New York, N.Y.; son of Richard C. (an architect) and Alice (Farny) Wood; married Shirley Estabrook Butler (an editor); children: Lesley, Heather. *Education:* Hamilton College, B.A., 1952. *Home and office:* 25 Bridge St., Newport, R.I. 02840. *Agent:* Virginia Barber Literary Agency, Inc., 44 Greenwich Ave., New York, N.Y. 10011.

CAREER: New Yorker, New York City, checker, 1956-65; Time-Life Books, New York City, staff writer, 1965-75; free-lance writer, 1975—. *Military service:* U.S. Navy, 1952-55; became lieutenant junior grade. *Member:* University Club of New York.

WRITINGS: The Book of Squash, Van Nostrand, 1972; *The Caribbean Isles*, Time-Life, 1975; (with David Dale Jackson) *Sierra Madre*, Time-Life, 1976; *Running the Rivers of North America*, C. N. Potter, 1978; *The Spanish Main*, Time-Life, 1980. Contributor to magazines, including *New Yorker*, *Smithsonian*, and *New York Times Magazine*.

WORK IN PROGRESS: A book on picture frames, with Barbara Kulicke, publication by Pantheon expected in 1980.

SIDELIGHTS: Wood comments: "Sports and the outdoors are my particular interests. However, for hire, I will write on any subject."

* * *

WOODS, Stuart 1938-

PERSONAL: Original surname Lee, legally changed to stepfather's surname in 1955; born January 9, 1938, in Manchester, Ga.; son of Stuart Franklin (in business) and Dorothy (in business; maiden name, Callaway) Lee. *Education:* University of Georgia, B.A., 1959. *Politics:* Democrat. *Home and office:* 4340 Tree Haven Dr. N.E., Atlanta, Ga. 30342. *Agent:* Peter Shepherd, Harold Ober Associates, Inc., 40 East 49th St., New York, N.Y. 10017.

CAREER: Advertising writer and creative director with firms in New York, N.Y., 1960-69, including Batten, Barton, Durstine & Osborne, Paper, Koenig & Lois, Young & Rubicam, and J. Walter Thompson; creative director and consultant with firms in London, England, 1970-73, including Grey Advertising and Dorland; consultant to Irish International

Advertising and Hunter Advertising, both in Dublin, both 1973-74; free-lance writer, 1973—. Past member of board of directors of Denham's, Inc. *Military service:* Air National Guard, 1960-68, active duty, 1961; served in Germany. *Member:* Authors Guild, Georgia Conservancy, New York Yacht Club, Royal Oak Yacht Club, Royal Ocean Racing Club, Galway Bay Sailing Club (honorary member). *Awards, honors:* Advertising awards from numerous organizations in New York, including Clio award for television writing and Gold Key award for print writing.

WRITINGS: Blue Water, Green Skipper (Dolphin Book Club selection), Norton, 1977; *A Romantic's Guide to the Country Inns of Britain and Ireland,* Norton, 1979; *Chiefs* (novel), Norton, 1980; *A Romantic's Guide to London,* Norton, 1980; *A Romantic's Guide to Paris,* Norton, 1981; *A Romantic's Guide to the Country Inns of France,* Norton, 1981. Contributor to magazines, including *Yachting.* Contributing editor and restaurant critic for *Atlanta.*

SIDELIGHTS: Woods writes: "Although it is my earnest intention to concentrate on fiction after the publication of *Chiefs,* writing fiction is terribly hard work, and I intend to alleviate this oppression by continuing to write about yachting, travel, food and wine, and whatever else takes my fancy. I have found the secret to happiness: finding a way to make a living doing all the things you like best, or, to put it another way, finding a way to make all the things you like to do best tax-deductible.

"*Blue Water, Green Skipper* is a memoir deriving from my decision to sail in the 1976 *Observer* Single-Handed Transatlantic Race (OSTAR), though I had only eighteen months to build a boat and learn to sail it. I also sailed in the 1979 Fastnet race, in which many lives were lost, and I expect to continue ocean racing and cruising, including a transatlantic crossing from England to Antigua."

In reviewing *Blue Water, Green Skipper,* Holger Lundbergh of *Yachting* declared, "The step-by-step account of how this green skipper in a remarkably short time became a seasoned blue-water sailor is beautifully told by a young American from Georgia, a brilliant stylist, a man of humor, courage, and patience," adding that the book is "dramatic and inspiring reading of rare quality."

BIOGRAPHICAL/CRITICAL SOURCES: Atlanta Journal/Constitution Magazine, February 8, 1977; *Yachting,* September, 1977, September, 1978.

* * *

WOODY, Robert H(enley) 1936-

PERSONAL: Born October 4, 1936, in Bridgeport, Ala; son of Robert Henley (a factory worker) and Wilma (a bookkeeper; maiden name, Loving) Woody; married Phyllis Jane Divita, January 7, 1965; children: Jennifer, Robert III, Matthew. *Education:* Western Michigan University, B.Mus., 1958, S.Ed., 1962; Michigan State University, M.A., 1960, Ph.D., 1964; Washington School of Psychiatry, postdoctoral certificate in group psychotherapy, 1969; University of Pittsburgh, Sc.D., 1975. *Office:* Office of the Dean for Graduate Studies and Research, University of Nebraska, Omaha, Neb. 68182.

CAREER: Teacher at public schools in Mattawan, Mich., 1958-60; school psychologist in Oceana County, Mich., 1960-62; school administrator in St. Joseph County, Mich., 1962-63; State University of New York at Buffalo, assistant professor of rehabilitation counseling, 1964-66; University of Maryland, College Park, associate professor of psychology

and director of psychological services in the schools training program, 1967-69; Grand Valley State Colleges, Allendale, Mich., dean of student development and director of counseling and mental health services, 1970-72; Ohio University, Athens, professor of education and psychology, 1972-75; University of Nebraska, Omaha, professor of psychology, 1975—, dean for graduate studies and research, 1975-79. Fellow of Maudsley Hospital Institute of Psychiatry, London, 1966-67. Diplomate in clinical psychology of American Board of Professional Psychology and diplomate in psychological hypnosis of American Board of Examiners in Psychological Hypnosis.

MEMBER: American Psychological Association (fellow), American Academy of Psychotherapists, American Association for Marriage and Family Therapy (fellow and life member), American Personnel and Guidance Association (life member), American Rehabilitation Counselors Association, American Public Health Association, American Society of Clinical Hypnosis (fellow), American Psychology-Law Society, American Association of Sex Educators, Counselors, and Therapists (life member), National Vocational Guidance Association, Association of Counselor Education and Supervision, Society for Personality Assessment (fellow), Nebraska Psychological Association.

WRITINGS: A Psychosocial Behavioral Science Curriculum Model for Counselor Education (monograph), College of Education, University of Maryland, 1969; (editor) *Counseling Techniques Monograph,* College of Education, University of Maryland, 1969; *Behavioral Problem Children in the Schools: Recognition, Diagnosis, and Behavioral Modification,* Appleton, 1969; *Psychobehavioral Counseling and Therapy: Integrating Behavioral and Insight Techniques,* Appleton, 1971; (editor with Jane D. Woody, and contributor) *Clinical Assessment in Counseling and Psychotherapy,* Appleton, 1972; (with J. D. Woody) *Sexual, Marital, and Familial Relations: Therapeutic Interventions for Professional Helping,* C. C Thomas, 1973; *Legal Aspects of Mental Retardation: A Search for Reliability,* C. C Thomas, 1974; *Getting Custody: Winning the Last Battle of a Marital War,* Macmillan, 1978; *Using Massage to Facilitate Holistic Health,* C. C Thomas, 1979; *Encyclopedia of Clinical Assessment,* Volumes I and II, Jossey-Bass, 1980; *Bodymind Liberation,* C. C Thomas, 1980; *More Than a Job,* Simon & Schuster, 1980.

Contributor: E. J. Lieberman, editor, *Mental Health: The Public Health Challenge,* American Public Health Association, 1975; B. D. Sales, editor, *Psychology in the Legal Process,* Spectrum, 1977. Contributor of about two hundred articles, poems, and reviews to psychology, medicine, law, music, and education journals.

SIDELIGHTS: Woody told *CA* about his most recent book, *More Than a Job:* "Many people feel trapped in their jobs. They find little or no personal fulfillment from their particular work and consider themselves destined to a life of drudgery. The outcome may be stress from work causing physical and mental health problems, frustration from not getting ahead leading to tortured marriages and family relations, dissatisfaction breeding attitudes that result in poor social encounters and limited friendships, and self-depreciation draining energy needed to enjoy life. This introduces a vicious cycle: negative feelings about work bring on personal and interpersonal problems and they, in turn, create barriers to work satisfactions, promotions, and improved job opportunities. Deprived of rewards, the person continues in this cycle of defeat and negativism. But the cycle can be broken. It is possible to achieve a frame of reference for work that will counteract negativism and make both the job and life in general more gratifying.''

* * *

WRIGHT, A(mos) J(asper) 1952-

PERSONAL: Born March 3, 1952, in Gadsden, Ala.; son of Amos Jasper (a computer systems manager) and Carolyn (an artist; maiden name, Shores) Wright. Education: Auburn University, B.A., 1973. Politics: "Anarchist." Religion: "Neo-mystic." Home address: P.O. Box 1043, Auburn, Ala. 36830.

CAREER: Auburn University, Auburn, Ala., library assistant, 1973—. Announcer on WEGL-FM Radio, 1975-78, music director, 1976-77, producer of jazz, rock, and classical programs, including "Jazz Primer," 1975-78; announcer on WAUD-AM Radio, 1978. Editor of Doctor Jazz Press. Member of Alabama Writers Council and Free for All (national skills exchange). Member: Amnesty International.

WRITINGS: Frozen Fruit (poems), du Bois Zone Press, 1978; Right Now I Feel Like Robert Johnson (poems), du Bois Zone Press, 1980.

Work represented in anthologies, including Text-Sound Texts, Morrow, 1980. Contributor of nearly two hundred fifty articles, poems, and reviews to literary magazines and music journals, including Kansas Quarterly, Poem, Red Cedar Review, Mississippi Review, Southern Exposure, Apalachee Quarterly, and Alabama Life, and local newspapers.

WORK IN PROGRESS: Anecdotal History of the Diving Bell, poems, completion expected in 1980; Lost and Found, poems, publication expected in 1981; Manhole Papers, poems, completion expected in 1981; Postcards From the Hotel Melancholy, a poem cycle, completion expected in 1982.

SIDELIGHTS: Wright comments: "I am striving for a poetic language somewhere between the hermetic (Ezra Pound) and the moronic (Rod McKuen). Inside the true poem (as opposed to verse) is a vortex around which the words are spinning. The poet has set the words in motion, and the reader must catch up to the pace. No intensity, no poetry. No spinning vortex of words in the reader's face, no poetry. Period. Anything else is an inter-office memorandum.

"Thus Whitman, Dickinson, Baudelaire, and Rimbaud set the twentieth century's pace. Everything since has embellished, strengthened, decorated, or retreated from their passions, but nothing has surpassed them. The poetry of the world still awaits those who must call the pace in the century to come.

"On the landscape ahead more missile silos will be hidden in the wheat. The blue whales and the whooping cranes will be gone. Huge sections of the land will speak only to geiger counters. Meanwhile, in the freshman English class students will read the poetry of the blind Homer, who has been dead a long time.

"Also up ahead is the mystical vortex beyond which no questions are asked because no answers are needed.''

* * *

WRIGHT, Dare 1926(?)-

PERSONAL: Born c. 1926, in Ontario, Canada. Education: Attended American Academy of Dramatic Arts and Art Students League. Home: 11 East 80th St., New York, N.Y. 10021.

CAREER: Writer, illustrator, and photographer. Worked as fashion model and in advertising; free-lance photographer for periodicals, including Harper's Bazaar and Vogue.

WRITINGS—Juvenile: (Self-illustrated) The Lonely Doll (Junior Literary Guild selection), Doubleday, 1957; (self-illustrated) Holiday for Edith and the Bears, Doubleday, 1958; (self-illustrated) The Little One, Doubleday, 1959; (self-illustrated) The Doll and the Kitten, Doubleday, 1960; The Lonely Doll Learns a Lesson, Random House, 1961; Lona: A Fairy Tale, Random House, 1963; Edith and Mr. Bear, Random House, 1964; A Gift From the Lonely Doll, Random House, 1966; Look at a Gull, Random House, 1967; Edith and Big Bad Bill, Random House, 1968; Look at a Colt, Random House, 1969; The Kitten's Little Boy, Four Winds, 1971; Edith and Little Bear Lend a Hand, Random House, 1972; Look at a Calf, Random House, 1974; Look at a Kitten, Random House, 1975; Edith and Midnight, Doubleday, 1978.

Other: Date With London, Random House, 1962; Take Me Home, Random House, 1965.

SIDELIGHTS: The Christian Science Monitor praised Wright's Holiday for Edith: "Those who love islands, those who value skillful photographs, and little girls who cherish dolls will revel in Holiday for Edith and the Bears.... The toys have a wonderfully animated look and the island background is a delight, with real horses, a lighthouse and a wobbling baby gull.''

BIOGRAPHICAL/CRITICAL SOURCES: Christian Science Monitor, November 6, 1958; Booklist, November 1, 1975.*

* * *

WRIGHT, Lawrence 1947-

PERSONAL: Born August 2, 1947, in Oklahoma City, Okla.; son of John Donald (a banker) and Dorothy Ann (Peacock) Wright; married Roberta Gordon Murphy, January 22, 1970; children: John Gordon. Education: Tulane University, B.A., 1969; American University of Cairo, M.A., 1971. Agent: Patricia Berens, Sterling Lord Agency, Inc., 660 Madison Ave., New York, N.Y. 10021.

CAREER: American University of Cairo, Cairo, Egypt, member of faculty, 1969-71; Race Relations Reporter, Nashville, Tenn., staff writer, 1971-72. Writer-in-residence at University of Georgia, 1976.

WRITINGS: City Children, Country Summer, Scribner, 1979.

WORK IN PROGRESS: "Cracker Jack," a play.

* * *

WRIGHT, Leigh Richard 1925-

PERSONAL: Born April 20, 1925, in Brookfield, Vt.; son of Carroll Amos and Julia Alberta (Luce) Wright; married Charlene Beverly Smith (a publisher), February 14, 1959 (divorced). Education: Middlebury College, A.B., 1950; University of New Hampshire, M.A., 1953; School of Oriental and African Studies, London, Ph.D., 1963. Home: 2 Hatton Rd. (Midlevels), Hong Kong. Office: Department of History, Faculty of Arts, University of Hong Kong, Hong Kong.

CAREER: High school social studies teacher in North Bennington, Vt., 1950-51; U.S. Government, Washington, D.C., political analyst, 1953-59; Center for International Economic Growth, Washington, D.C., staff writer, 1961; high school history teacher in Harrow, Middlesex, England, 1962-63;

University of Hong Kong, Hong Kong, lecturer in history, 1963-65; Russell Sage College, Troy, N.Y., assistant professor of history, 1965-66; University of Hong Kong, senior lecturer, 1966-71, reader in history, 1971—. Visiting professor at University of Vermont and visiting lecturer at Northern Illinois University, both summer, 1969; visiting professor at University of New Mexico, 1975, and University of New Hampshire, 1978. *Military service:* U.S. Navy, Medical Service Corps, 1943-46. *Member:* Royal Asiatic Society (Hong Kong; member of council), Royal Asiatic Society (England), American Historical Association, Association of Asian Studies. *Awards, honors:* Fellow of Borneo Research Council, 1969—.

WRITINGS: (Contributor) K. K. Sinha, editor, *Problems of Defence of South and Southeast Asia,* Institute of Political and Social Studies (Calcutta, India), 1969; *The Origins of British Borneo,* Oxford University Press, 1970; *Vanishing World: The Ibans of Borneo,* Weatherhill, 1972; *Potash and Pine: The Formative Years in Randolph History,* Randolph Historical Society, 1977; (with J. deV. Allen and A. J. Stockwell) *Malaysia Treaties: A Collection of Agreements and Other Documents Affecting the States of Malaysia, 1761-1763,* two volumes, Oceana, 1979; (with G. N. Appell) *The Status of Social Science Research in Borneo,* Cornell University Press, 1978. Contributor to history and Asian studies journals.

WORK IN PROGRESS: The Pirate States of Borneo (tentative title), on the influence of piracy upon politics and relations of the powers in Southeast Asia, 1700-1900.

SIDELIGHTS: Wright commented: "I have a general interest in American foreign relations, particularly in Asia, and a knowledgable (not specialist) interest in American-Vietnamese affairs."

*   *   *

WYLER, Rose 1909-
(Peter Thayer)

PERSONAL: Born October 29, 1909, in New York, N.Y.; daughter of Otto Samuel and Kati (Bach) Wyler; married second husband, Gerald Ames (a writer), September 8, 1948; children: (first marriage) Joseph, Karl; (stepchildren) Eva-Lee Baird. *Education:* Barnard College, B.A., 1929; Columbia University, M.A., 1931. *Home:* 45 Fairview Ave., New York, N.Y. 10040.

CAREER: Glen Falls public schools, Glen Falls, N.Y., supervisor of elementary science programs, 1931-34; Columbia University, New York City, instructor in science education, 1934-41; Columbia Broadcasting System (CBS), New York City, science script writer and adviser for Encyclopaedia Britannica Films, 1945-50; free-lance writer, 1948—. Science editor, Scholastic Publications, 1956-61; elementary science consultant, Basic Books, 1961-63. *Member:* Authors Guild.

WRITINGS: Tuffy, the Truck, Avon Publishing, 1952; *Planet Earth,* Schuman, 1952; *The First Book of Science Experiments,* F. Watts, 1952, revised edition, 1971; (under pseudonym Peter Thayer) *The Hungriest Robin,* Messner, 1953, published as *The Flyingest Robin,* Melmont, 1965; *My*

Little Golden Book About the Sky, Simon & Schuster, 1956; *The First Book of Weather,* F. Watts, 1956, revised edition, 1966; *The Golden Picture Book of Science,* Simon & Schuster, 1957, new edition published as *Science: Animals, Plants, Rocks, Gravity, Day and Night, Rain and Snow, the Sky and the Ocean, With 45 Experiments and Activities,* Golden Press, 1965; *Exploring Space: A True Story About the Rockets of Today and a Glimpse of the Rockets That Are to Come,* Simon & Schuster, 1958; (with stepdaughter, Eva-Lee Baird) *Science Teasers,* Harper, 1966; *Arrow Book of Science Riddles,* Scholastic Book Services, 1969; *Real Science Riddles,* Hastings House, 1972; *Professor Egghead's Best Riddles,* Simon & Schuster, 1973; *What Happens If . . .?,* Walker, 1974; (with Baird) *Nutty Number Riddles,* Doubleday, 1977; (with Mary Elting) *The New Answer Book,* Grosset, 1977; *Going Metric the Fun Way,* Doubleday, 1980; *The Answer Book About You,* Grosset, 1980.

With husband, Gerald Ames: *Life on the Earth* (with illustrations by Ames), Schuman, 1953; *Restless Earth,* Abelard, 1954; *The Golden Book of Astronomy,* Simon & Schuster, 1955, revised edition published as *The New Golden Book of Astronomy: An Introduction to the Wonders of Space,* Golden Press, 1965; *The Story of the Ice Age,* Harper, 1956; *The Earth's Story,* Creative Educational Society, 1957; *The First People in the World,* Harper, 1958; *First Days of the World,* Harper, 1958; *What Makes It Go?,* Whittles House, 1958; *The Giant Golden Book of Biology,* Golden Press, 1961, revised edition published as *The Golden Book of Biology: An Introduction to the Wonders of Life,* 1967; *Planet Earth,* Golden Press, 1963; *Prove It!,* Harper, 1963; *Food and Life,* Creative Educational Society, 1966; *Magic Secrets,* Harper, 1967; *Spooky Tricks,* Harper, 1968; *Secrets in Stones* (photographs by Ames), Four Winds Press, 1970; *Funny Magic: Easy Tricks for Young Magicians,* Parents' Magazine Press, 1972; *Funny Number Tricks: Easy Magic With Arithmetic,* Parents' Magazine Press, 1976; *It's All Done With Numbers: Astounding and Confounding Feats of Mathematical Magic,* Doubleday, 1979.

WORK IN PROGRESS: Super Riddles for Super Kids, with Gerald Ames, for Doubleday.

SIDELIGHTS: Wyler commented: "My favorite pastime these days is an outgrowth of hiking and camping experiences that I had with my older sister and brother. After we made camp, I was given nature guides (such as they were over sixty years ago), and told to find everything I could. I guess I've been doing that ever since, not only in familiar woodlands, but in the jungles of the Amazon, the tundra of the Andes, among Mayan ruins, and in colorful coral reefs. As well as seeking animals, I like to attract them. In Maine, where our family summers, I have lured generations of raccoons and skunks to our home, baiting them with marshmallows. My ambition—still unfulfilled—is to get chummy with that most intelligent of invertebrates, the octopus."

BIOGRAPHICAL/CRITICAL SOURCES: Chicago Sunday Tribune, November 13, 1955; *New York Herald Tribune Book Review,* August 12, 1956; *Kirkus Reviews,* April 15, 1958; *Christian Science Monitor,* May 8, 1958; *Natural History,* November, 1964.

Y

YAMANOUCHI, Hisaaki 1934-

PERSONAL: Born July 10, 1934, in Hiroshima, Japan; son of Tsuneo and Chieko Yamanouchi; married Reiko Nagano, April 4, 1965; children: Fumiaki. *Education:* University of Tokyo, B.A., 1958, M.A., 1960; Columbia University, M.A., 1964; Cambridge University, Ph.D., 1975. *Home:* Todoroki 7-14-6, Setagaya-ku, Tokyo 158, Japan. *Office:* Department of English, College of General Education, University of Tokyo, Komaba 3-8-1, Meguro-ku, Tokyo 153, Japan.

CAREER: Tsuda College, Tokyo, Japan, lecturer in English, 1964-67; Cambridge University, Cambridge, England, lector in Japanese, 1968-73; Tokyo Institute of Technology, Tokyo, associate professor of English, 1976-79; University of Tokyo, Tokyo, associate professor of English, 1979—.

WRITINGS: The Search for Authenticity in Modern Japanese Literature, Cambridge University Press, 1978.

WORK IN PROGRESS: Research on English literature of the late eighteenth and early nineteenth century.

SIDELIGHTS: Yamanouchi told *CA:* "*The Search for Authenticity in Modern Japanese Literature* traces the development of Japanese literature since 1868 with reference to some twelve representative writers. The tension they felt between the impact of the West and the claims of a native tradition led to feelings of estrangement which find expression in their work. The book attempts to analyze the inner psychological conflicts of the writers concerned and to explain why the careers of so many of them ended in mental breakdown or suicide."

* * *

YODER, Paton 1912-

PERSONAL: Born March 9, 1912, in Goshen, Ind.; son of Silvanus S. (a farmer) and Susanna (Troyer) Yoder; married Hazel Smucker, June 14, 1936; children: Devon, James, Kenneth, Susan Yoder Stempel, Katharine Yoder Martin. *Education:* Goshen College, A.B., 1935; Indiana University, M.A., 1936, Ph.D., 1941. *Politics:* Democrat. *Religion:* Mennonite. *Home:* 1608 South 14th St., Goshen, Ind. 46526.

CAREER: Westmont College, Santa Barbara, Calif., professor of history, 1940-50, dean, 1946-50; Taylor University, Upland, Ind., professor of history and chair of Division of Social Sciences, 1950-61; Hesston College, Hesston, Kan.,

professor of history and dean, 1961-70; Malone College, Canton, Ohio, professor of history and chair of Division of Social Sciences, 1971-77; writer, 1977—. *Member:* Organization of American Historians, Conference on Faith and History, Mennonite Historical Society.

WRITINGS: Taverns and Travelers: Inns of the Early Midwest, Indiana University Press, 1969; *Eine Wuerzel: Tennessee John Stoltzfus,* Sutter House, 1979. Contributor to history journals.

* * *

YOGIJI, Harbhajan Singh Khalsa 1929-
(Yogi Bhajan)

PERSONAL: Born August 26, 1929, in Kot Harkan, Tehsil Wazirabad, India (now in Pakistan), came to the United States in 1968; son of Kartar Singh (a physician) and Leela Wanti (Kaur) Puri; married Inderjit Kaur (a lecturer and counselor); children: Ranbir Singh, Kulbir Singh, Kamaljit Kaur. *Education:* Punjab University, B.A., 1954. *Office:* 3HO Foundation, 1620 Preuss Rd., Los Angeles, Calif. 90035.

CAREER: Customs officer, 1954-69; 3HO Foundation, Los Angeles, Calif., director of spiritual education, 1969—. Chief religious and administrative authority for the Sikh Dharma in the western hemisphere, Japan, and Asia Minor, 1971—, also Siri Singh Sahib, head of the ministry in the West. Co-president of World Parliament of Religions; co-chairperson of World Fellowship of Religions; director of Unity of Man Conference. Member of Los Angeles World Affairs Council and Interreligious Council of Southern California. *Member:* American Council of Executives in Religion (member of board of directors). *Awards, honors:* Named Bhai Sahib by the Sikh Dharma, 1974.

WRITINGS—All under name Yogi Bhajan: *Women in Training,* 3HO Foundation, Volume I, 1976, Volume II, 1977, Volume III, 1979; *The Teachings of Yogi Bhajan,* Hawthorn, 1977; *Man to Man,* three volumes, KRI Publications, Volume I, 1978, Volume II, 1978, Volume III, 1979; *The Golden Temple Vegetarian Cookbook,* Hawthorn, 1979.

WORK IN PROGRESS: A poetry book defining the various aspects of Sikh Dharma, in Gurmuki script with English translation and commentary.

SIDELIGHTS: Yogiji commented: "The law of the teacher is a law of feeling, a law of living. The teacher is a source of life. The process of achieving and more achieving and more achieving towards the positive goodness is a never-ending process.

"One day you have to rest, my friend. You sleep, and the teacher sleeps: you sleep for yourself, the teacher sleeps for others. Once you conquer the inner conflict you become a first rate servant to all who look upon you. That is the requirement of the teacher. Saints, sages, holy men, swamis and yogis, all set an example which you can follow. The teacher doesn't set an example, he or she makes an example out of you. Try to understand the difference. A teacher doesn't set an example. He or she is like dye. Anything you put in the dye will change. A teacher is not a saint, he is the maker of the saint. A teacher is not a yogi, he is the maker of a yogi. A teacher is not a swami, he is the maker of a swami. A teacher is not beautiful, he creates beauty. Try to understand the difference between a teacher and a saint. One is at peace with his inner duality, the other has conquered his inner duality."

BIOGRAPHICAL/CRITICAL SOURCES: Sardani Premka Kaur Khalsa and Sat Kirpal Kaur Khalsa, editors, *The Man Called the Siri Singh Sahib,* Sikh Dharma (Los Angeles), 1979.

* * *

YOUCHA, Geraldine   1925-

PERSONAL: Born September 24, 1925, in Suffern, N.Y.; daughter of Joseph (a storekeeper) and Hilda Shavelson; married Isaac Z. Youcha (a psychoanalyst), August 31, 1950; children: Victoria Youcha Rab, Sharon, Joseph. *Education:* Northwestern University, B.S., 1946. *Residence:* New City, N.Y. *Agent:* Fox Chase Agency, Inc., 419 East 57th St., New York, N.Y. 10022.

CAREER: Coronet, New York, N.Y., member of editorial staff, 1946-52; writer, 1952—. Member of board of directors of Family Service Association of Rockland County, 1972-73, and Rockland County Center for the Arts.

WRITINGS: A Dangerous Pleasure: Alcohol From the Woman's Perspective, Hawthorn Books, 1978. Author of "As I Was Saying," a weekly column in *Rockland County Journal News.* Contributor of articles to newspapers and magazines, including *Good Housekeeping, Redbook,* and *New York Daily News.*

WORK IN PROGRESS: A social history of the breast.

SIDELIGHTS: Geraldine Youcha told *CA:* "In writing, my aim has been to say simply what seems complicated, whether I am dealing with the effects of alcohol on women or the juvenile justice system. Free-lance writing is also the perfect occupation for a dilettante, which is how I see myself." *Avocational interests:* Travel, potting, reading, sailing.

* * *

YOUNG, Bob
See YOUNG, James Robert

* * *

YOUNG, Charles M(atthew)   1951-

PERSONAL: Born February 6, 1951, in Waukesha, Wis.; son of George Aubrey (a minister) and Alice (a teacher; maiden name, Auld) Young. *Education:* Macalester College, B.A., 1973; Columbia University, M.S., 1975. *Residence:* New York, N.Y. *Office: Rolling Stone,* 745 Fifth Ave., New York, N.Y. 10022.

CAREER: Free-lance writer, 1975-76; *Rolling Stone,* New York, N.Y., associate editor, 1976—, author of column, "Random Notes," 1976-77. *Awards, honors:* College journalism award from *Rolling Stone,* 1976.

WRITINGS: (Contributor) Maryanne Partridge and Timothy White, editors, *Rolling Stone Visits "Saturday Night Live,"* Doubleday, 1979. Contributor to magazines, including *Crawdaddy,* and newspapers.

WORK IN PROGRESS: A novel about college life, publication by Summit Books expected in 1981.

SIDELIGHTS: Young comments: "I try to write from a rock and roll sensibility, which at its best finds humor in the absurdity of life. A friend once accused me of liking punk rock because I never outgrew being fourteen. This is true, and there is nothing more absurd than being an adolescent in America. I aspire to play my typewriter as well as Charlie Watts plays the drums."

* * *

YOUNG, James J(oseph)   1940-

PERSONAL: Born August 3, 1940, in Philadelphia, Pa.; son of John J. and Nora A. (Hogan) Young. *Education:* St. Paul's College, Washington, D.C., A.B., 1963, A.M., 1967. *Politics:* Democrat. *Home and office:* St. Paul's College, 3015 Fourth St. N.W., Washington, D.C. 20017.

CAREER: Entered Congregatio Sancti Pauli (Paulists; C.S.P.), 1958, ordained Roman Catholic priest, 1967; Old St. Mary's Church, Chicago, Ill., priest, 1967-71; Paulist Center, Boston, Mass., co-director, 1971-75; Weston School of Theology, Cambridge, Mass., director of ministerial studies, 1975-78; St. Paul's College, Washington, D.C., rector, 1978—. Member of board of directors of Catholic Committee on Urban Ministry; workshop director.

WRITINGS: (Editor) *Living Room Dialogues,* Paulist/ Newman, 1965; (editor) *Bring Us Together: Third Living Room Dialogues,* Friendship, 1970; (with Edward A. Peters) *Large Type Prayerbook,* Paulist/Newman, 1972; (editor) *Ministering to the Divorced Catholic,* Paulist/Newman, 1978; *Facing Divorce,* Paulist/Newman, 1980. Contributor of more than a dozen articles to religious magazines, and to *Commonweal.*

* * *

YOUNG, James Robert   1921-
(Bob Young)

PERSONAL: Born March 16, 1921, in St. Louis, Mo.; son of Lyman W. (a cartoonist) and Marguerite I. (Sturgess) Young; married Ethel Spilly (a teacher and registered nurse), August 27, 1955; children: Lyman, Bruce, Matthew. *Education:* Georgetown University, B.S., 1943. *Residence:* Sequim, Wash. *Office:* King Features Syndicate, 235 East 45th St., New York, N.Y. 10017.

CAREER/WRITINGS: King Features Syndicate, New York, N.Y., artist and writer under name Bob Young for adventure comic strip, "Tim Tyler's Luck," 1946—. *Military service:* U.S. Army, Signal Corps, in intelligence as Japanese cryptanalyst, 1943-45. *Member:* Northern California Cartoon and Humor Association.

SIDELIGHTS: Young told *CA:* "'Tim Tyler' was created by my father as a flying feature in 1928, shortly after Lindbergh's famous flight. In the early thirties the scene switched to Africa because of broad readership interest in animals. Today Tim and Spud roam the world aboard a large research vessel. A helicopter on the flight deck takes the boys anywhere inland to new animal adventures; however, having a ship as home-base assures that many stories are marine-oriented as well. Generally, continuities have a light environmental touch, and are researched in the hope that adventure entertainment can also provide the reader with a learning experience.''

AVOCATIONAL INTERESTS: Amateur radio, photography.

*   *   *

YUAN, Lei Chen
  See De JAEGHER, Raymond-Joseph

*   *   *

YUDEWITZ, Hyman   1906-

PERSONAL: Born May 4, 1906, in New York, N.Y.; son of Samuel (in the theatre) and Esther Molly (Goldberg) Yudewitz. *Education:* Cornell University, B.A., 1933; City College of the City University of New York, M.A., 1963. *Politics:* Socialist. *Religion:* Jewish. *Home:* 224 Sullivan St., #D-52, New York, N.Y. 10012.

CAREER: Cornell University, Ithaca, N.Y., assistant instructor in French literature, 1927-28, 1933-34; Meriden Junior College, Meriden, Conn., teacher of French, 1934-35; free-lance multi-lingual proof reader, 1935-58; Institute for Special Education, Far Rockaway, N.Y., teacher of exceptional children, 1958-59; teacher of exceptional children, 1959-63; Trenton Central High School, Trenton, N.J., teacher of Spanish, French, and English, 1963-77. Member of local Council on Economic Priorities and Metropolitan Council on Housing. Member of social action committees of Sirovich Senior Center and Greenwich House Senior Center. *Member:* National Council of Senior Citizens, United Senior Citizens, Gray Panthers.

WRITINGS: Passacaglia, Pilgrim House, 1934; *Tourist Carrousel* (travelogue), Celeste & Co., 1976.

Author of "Farce of Master Trouble-Tete" (one-act play; first produced at Cornell Theatre, 1928), published in *Cornell Plays,* edited by Alec M. Drummond, Samuel French, c. 1936.

WORK IN PROGRESS: Research on the *Romance of Tristan and Iseult.*

SIDELIGHTS: Yudewitz writes: "Like Thompson, all my life I have been fleeing a heavenly hound: writing. Charles Dickens taught me how to write; and Thoreau, how to think and write. And because Cornell's departments of Romance Languages and English had, neither of them, seen fit to continue me at a teaching post, the sequestration from the exciting environment of college life alienated my scriptural abilities to a point where I began hopping about the business world, in a futile attempt to validate Shaw's preposterous notion that 'Those who can, do; and those who can't, teach.' When my eyes were opened to the truth (that the most inefficient people in the world are doing the doing, and ruining the world thereby; and that the world of ideas houses the world's greatest doers), I began slowly to return to teaching and to the world of ideas—with John Dewey's assurances (instead of Shaw's) that *teaching is the highest of the arts,* and with feelings of satisfaction, and even of happiness, almost as great as writing had afforded me. I am convinced—and have so reminded my students, often—that God dwells more in a schoolroom than in a church, inasmuch as it is dreaming and thinking that are continually creating the world.''

Z

ZANUCK, Daryl F(rancis) 1902-1979

OBITUARY NOTICE: Born September 5, 1902, in Wahoo, Neb.; died of complications from pneumonia, December 22, 1979, in Palm Springs, Calif. Screenwriter and producer of motion pictures. Zanuck was considered one of the most influential and colorful film producers. He broke into the film industry at the age of twenty-two by peddling his published collection of scenarios, *Habit: A Thrilling Yarn That Starts Where Fiction Ends and Life Begins,* to each of the major studios. Three of the four stories in the collection were purchased and Zanuck was hired by Mack Sennett to write gags. That job led to one at Warner Brothers writing episodes in the "Rin Tin Tin" series. Jack Warner was so impressed with Zanuck's prolificity that in 1927 he named him production supervisor. At Warner Brothers, Zanuck was involved in the production of such classics as "The Jazz Singer" and "The Public Enemy." Despite phenomenal success, Zanuck left Warner Brothers in 1933 to help form Twentieth Century Films (now Twentieth Century-Fox). There he helped bring films like "Gentleman's Agreement" and "The Grapes of Wrath" to the public. In 1963, after a brief stint as an independent producer, Zanuck reassumed leadership at Fox to help the studio recoup losses incurred making "Cleopatra." Among the films he produced during the mid-1960's are "The Sound of Music" and "The Longest Day." He retired in 1971. Obituaries and other sources: *Current Biography,* Wilson, 1941, 1954; Mel Gussow, *Don't Say Yes Until I Finish Talking,* Doubleday, 1971; *Celebrity Register,* 3rd edition, Simon & Schuster, 1973; *Who's Who in the World,* 4th edition, Marquis, 1978; *International Motion Picture Almanac,* Quigley, 1979; *Who's Who,* 131st edition, St. Martin's, 1979; *Washington Post,* December 23, 1979, December 24, 1979; *Chicago Tribune,* December 24, 1979.

*   *   *

ZEVIN, Jack 1940-

PERSONAL: Born December 22, 1940, in Chicago, Ill.; son of Solomon S. (a chemist) and Celia (in sales; maiden name, Bavnick) Zevin; married Iris Lynne Becker (a teacher), August 25, 1969; children: Sarah, Micah. *Education:* University of Chicago, B.A., 1962, M.A.T., 1964; University of Michigan, Ph.D., 1969. *Home:* 63-212 Alderton St., Rego Park, N.Y. 11374. *Office:* Department of Secondary Education, Queens College of the City University of New York, Flushing, N.Y. 11367.

CAREER: High school social studies teacher in Chicago, Ill., 1963-66, and Ann Arbor, Mich., 1966-69; Queens College of the City University of New York, Flushing, N.Y., assistant professor, 1969-73, associate professor of secondary education, 1973-79, professor of education, 1980—, director of Center for Economic Education, 1978—, member of board of directors of ethnic studies program, 1979—. Guest lecturer at Hebrew Union College, winters, 1974-75; consultant to Law in American Society Foundation and Union of American Hebrew Congregations. *Member:* American Educational Research Association, American Historical Association, American Sociological Association, National Council for the Social Studies, Association for Supervision and Curriculum Development, National Council of Temple Educators, Association of Teachers of Social Studies of New York, New York State Council of Temple Educators. *Awards, honors:* Fellow at Purdue University, 1976-77; grants from National Science Foundation, 1971-80, and National Endowment for the Humanities, 1977-79; City University of New York faculty research award, 1979-80.

WRITINGS: (With Byron G. Massialas) *Creative Encounters in the Classroom: Teaching and Learning Through Discovery,* Wiley, 1967; (with Massialas) *World History Through Inquiry,* nine volumes, Rand McNally, 1969; (with Massialas) *Man and His Environment,* Rand McNally, 1969; (with Massialas) *Economic Organization,* Rand McNally, 1969.

(With Massialas) *Two Societies in Perspective,* Rand McNally, 1970; (with Richard Groll) *Law and the City,* Houghton, 1970; (with Edmund Parker, Isidore Starr, and others) *Vital Issues of the Constitution,* Houghton, 1971; *Violence in America: What Is the Alternative?,* Prentice-Hall, 1973, revised edition, 1976; (contributor) *Human Sciences Program Modules,* Biological Science Curriculum Study (Boulder, Colo.), Volume I: *Change,* 1975, Volume II: *Invention,* 1976, Volume III: *Surroundings,* 1976; (with Martin A. Cohen) *Adventures in Living Judaism,* Union of American Hebrew Congregations, Volume I: *Identity,* 1977, Volume II: *Survival,* 1979, Volume III: *Values,* 1980, Volume IV: *K'lal Yisrael* (title means "All the People of Israel"), 1980; *Law and Urban Government,* C. E. Merrill, 1978; (with Alvin Wolf) *Participation, Protest, and Apathy: A Question of Involvement?,* Allyn & Bacon, 1979. Contributor to journals in the social studies. Contributing editor of *Social Studies,* 1976—.

WORK IN PROGRESS: A History of the Jewish People, with Cohen, publication by Union of Hebrew Congregations expected in 1983; *Teaching the Gifted*, with Lawrence Castiglione.

SIDELIGHTS: Zevin told *CA*: "My major interest is in an approach to teaching usually termed a problem-solving or inquiry methodology. Within this approach, the burden of thinking and activity falls upon the students rather than the teacher, while topics such as law, apathy, and participation are critically examined from several points of view. It is my very strong belief, grounded in research and experience, that deep understanding and involvement grow out of experiences, generally, or especially those where propaganda and polemics are absent and people are faced with problems they must solve themselves. An interesting consequence of this teaching theory is that a critical teacher who questions views and weighs evidence, while considering both popular and unusual theories, produces more true commitment and involvement than those engaged in forceful inculcation of values."

*   *   *

ZIETLOW, Paul Nathan 1935-

PERSONAL: Born February 14, 1935, in Neenah, Wis.; son of Carl F. (a minister) and Ruth (a teacher; maiden name, Paulia) Zietlow; married Charlotte Thiele (a merchant), August 28, 1957; children: Rebecca, Nathan. *Education:* Yale University, B.A., 1956; University of Michigan, M.A., 1957, Ph.D., 1965. *Office:* Department of English, Indiana University, Bloomington, Ind. 47401.

CAREER: University of Michigan, Ann Arbor, instructor in English, 1962-64; Indiana University, Bloomington, lecturer, 1964-65, assistant professor, 1965-68, associate professor, 1968-73, professor of English, 1973—, director of graduate studies, 1975-79. Exchange teacher in Germany, 1961-62, and Czechoslovakia, 1969-70. *Member:* Modern Language Association of America. *Awards, honors:* Jule and Avery Hopwood Awards in Drama and Fiction from University of Michigan, 1957, for "Stories" and "Three Short Plays."

WRITINGS: Moments of Vision: The Poetry of Thomas Hardy, Harvard University Press, 1974. Contributor to language and literature journals. Book review editor of *Victorian Studies*, 1965-69, now member of advisory board.

*   *   *

ZIMRING, Franklin E(ster) 1942-

PERSONAL: Born December 2, 1942, in Los Angeles, Calif.; son of Maurice (a writer) and Molly (an attorney; maiden name, Dilman) Zimring; married Susan Hilty, February 18, 1967; children: Carl, Daniel. *Education:* Wayne State University, B.A. (with distinction), 1963; University of Chicago, J.D. (cum laude), 1967. *Religion:* Jewish. *Office:* Law School, University of Chicago, 1111 East 60th St., Chicago, Ill. 60637.

CAREER: University of Chicago, Chicago, Ill., assistant professor and research associate at Center for Studies in Criminal Justice, 1967-69, associate professor, 1969-72, professor of law, 1972—, associate director of center, 1971-73, co-director, 1973-75, director, 1975—. Member of National Science Foundation and National Academy of Sciences panels and committees; chairperson of advisory committee of Vera Institute of Justice Project, 1976—, and Assessment Center for Alternatives to Juvenile Courts, 1977.

MEMBER: National Pre-Trial Services Association (mem-

ber of advisory committee, 1975—), American Civil Liberties Union, Illinois Academy of Criminology (member of executive committee, 1968-71, 1977—), Illinois Youth Services Association (honorary member of board of directors, 1977—), Phi Beta Kappa, Coif. *Awards, honors:* Gavel Award from American Bar Association, 1973; civilian award of merit from Chicago Crime Commission, 1975.

WRITINGS: (With George N. Newton) *Firearms and Violence in American Life*, U.S. Government Printing Office, 1969; *Perspectives on Deterrence* (monograph), National Institute of Mental Health, 1971; (with Gordon Hawkins) *Deterrence: The Legal Threat in Crime Control*, University of Chicago Press, 1973; *Confronting Youth Crime: Report of the Twentieth Century Fund Task Force on Sentencing Policy Toward Young Offenders*, Holmes & Meier, 1978; (with Richard Frase) *The Criminal Justice System*, Little, Brown, 1980.

Contributor: Rainwater, editor, *Deviance and Liberty*, Aldine, 1974; Boesen and Grupp, editors, *Community Based Corrections: Theory, Practice, and Research*, Davis Publishing, 1976; (author of foreward) Richard Block, *Violent Crime*, Heath, 1977; Greenborg, editor, *Punishment and Corrections*, Sage Publications, 1977; *The Serious Juvenile Offender*, U.S. Government Printing Office, 1978.

Contributor of about thirty-five articles to scholarly journals, popular magazines, and newspapers, including *Annals of the American Academy of Political and Social Science*, *Nation*, and *Trial*. Member of editorial board of *Evaluation Quarterly*, *Law and Behavior*, *Crime and Delinquency*, and *Journal of Criminal Justice*, all 1976—.

WORK IN PROGRESS: The Changing Legal World of Adolescence.

SIDELIGHTS: Zimring commented: "My father never wanted me to write for a living, but books are the only way to think with permanent effect. To undertake research is to commit oneself to report it—I am thus an involuntary writer."

*   *   *

ZIMROTH, Evan 1943-

PERSONAL: Born February 24, 1943, in Philadelphia, Pa.; daughter of Lester (an international lawyer and banker) and Janet (in child development) Nurick; married Peter Zimroth (marriage ended); married Henry Wollman (an architect), October 29, 1977; children: (second marriage) Lilly Sophia, Else Kathryn. *Education:* Barnard College, B.A., 1965; Columbia University, Ph.D., 1972. *Religion:* Jewish. *Home:* 600 West 115th St., New York, N.Y. 10025. *Office:* Department of English, Queens College of the City University of New York, Flushing, N.Y. 11367.

CAREER: Washington Ballet, Washington, D.C., professional dancer, 1957-61; Queens College of the City University of New York, Flushing, N.Y., 1969—, currently associate professor of English. Visiting professor at University of Paris—Vincennes, 1975. *Member:* Poets and Writers.

WRITINGS: Giselle Considers Her Future (poetry), Ohio State University Press, 1978. Co-founder of *Poesie Vincennes*, 1975; member of editorial staff of *Little Magazine*.

WORK IN PROGRESS: Adapting the work of German-Jewish poet Else Lasker-Schueler, for a collection of poems.

*   *   *

ZIMROTH, Peter L. 1943-

PERSONAL: Born January 11, 1943. *Education:* Columbia

University, B.A., 1963; Yale University, LL.B., 1966. *Home:* 505 West End Ave., New York, N.Y. 10024. *Office:* Office of the District Attorney of New York County, 155 Leonard St., New York, N.Y. 10013.

CAREER: U.S. Supreme Court, Washington, D.C., law clerk, 1967-68; Office of the U.S. Attorney of the Southern District of New York, New York City, assistant U.S. attorney, 1968-70; associated with New York University, School of Law, New York City, 1970; Office of the District Attorney of New York County, New York City, legal counsel, 1975-77, chief assistant district attorney, 1977—. Member of New York governor's task force on law enforcement, 1974-76. *Member:* American Civil Liberties Union, New York State Bar Association, New York State District Attorneys Association, Association of the Bar of the City of New York.

WRITINGS: Perversions of Justice, Viking, 1974. Contributor to law journals and newspapers.

The cumulative index that would have appeared in this volume under the usual schedule will appear instead in the next volume, 97-100, which is scheduled to be published late in 1980.